ST/ESA/STAT/SER.R/44

Department of Economic and Social Affairs
Département des affaires économiques et sociales

2014
Demographic Yearbook
Annuaire démographique
Sixty-fifth issue/Soixante-cinquième édition

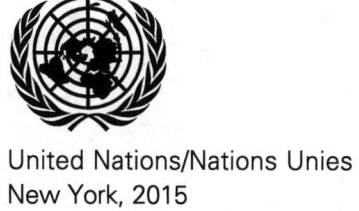

United Nations/Nations Unies
New York, 2015

The Department of Economic and Social Affairs of the United Nations Secretariat is a vital interface between global policies in the economic, social and environmental spheres and national action. The Department works in three main interlinked areas: (i) it compiles, generates and analyses a wide range of economic, social and environmental data and information on which States Members of the United Nations draw to review common problems and to take stock of policy options; (ii) it facilitates the negotiations of Member States in many intergovernmental bodies on joint courses of action to address ongoing or emerging global challenges; and (iii) it advises interested Governments on the ways and means of translating policy frameworks developed in United Nations conferences and summits into programmes at the country level and, through technical assistance, helps build national capacities.

Le Département des affaires économiques et sociales du Secrétariat de l'Organisation des Nations Unies sert de relais entre les orientations arrêtées au niveau international dans les domaines économiques, sociaux et environnementaux et les politiques exécutées à l'échelon national. Il intervient dans trois grands domaines liés les uns aux autres : i) il compile, produit et analyse une vaste gamme de données et d'éléments d'information sur des questions économiques, sociales et environnementales dont les États Membres de l'Organisation se servent pour examiner des problèmes communs et évaluer les options qui s'offrent à eux; ii) il facilite les négociations entre les États Membres dans de nombreux organes intergouvernementaux sur les orientations à suivre de façon collective afin de faire face aux problèmes mondiaux existants ou en voie d'apparition; iii) il conseille les gouvernements intéressés sur la façon de transposer les orientations politiques arrêtées à l'occasion des conférences et sommets des Nations Unies en programmes exécutables au niveau national et aide à renforcer les capacités nationales au moyen de programmes d'assistance technique.

NOTE

Symbols of United Nations documents are composed of capital letters combined with figures. Mention of such a symbol indicates reference to a United Nations document.

The designations employed and the presentation of material in this publication do not imply the expression of any opinion whatsoever on the part of the Secretariat of the United Nations concerning the legal status of any country, territory, city or area, or of its authorities, or concerning the delimitation of its frontiers or boundaries.

Where the designation "country or area" appears in the headings of tables, it covers countries, territories, or areas.

NOTE

Les cotes des documents de l'Organisation des Nations Unies se composent de lettres majuscules et de chiffres. La simple mention d'une cote dans un texte signifie qu'il s'agit d'un document de l'Organisation.

Les appellations employées dans cette publication et la présentation des données qui y figurent n'impliquent de la part du Secrétariat de l'Organisation des Nations Unies aucune prise de position quant au statut juridique des pays, territoires, villes ou zones, ou de leurs autorités, ni quant au tracé de leurs frontières ou limites.

L'appellation "pays ou zone" figurant dans les titres des rubriques des tableaux désigne des pays, des territoires, ou des zones.

ST/ESA/STAT/SER.R/44

UNITED NATIONS PUBLICATION
Sales number: B.16.XIII.1 H

PUBLICATION DES NATIONS UNIES
Numéro de vente: B.16.XIII.1 H

ISBN 978-92-1-051108-7
eISBN 978-92-1-057559-1
ISSN 0082-8041

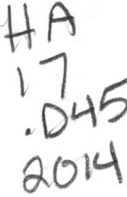
Topics of the Demographic Yearbook series: 1948 - 2014

Sujets des diverses éditions de l'Annuaire démographique : 1948 - 2014

Year Année	Sales No. - Numéro de vente	Issue - Edition	Special topic - Sujet spécial
1948	49.XIII.1	First-Première	General demography-Démographie générale
1949-50	51.XIII.1	Second-Deuxième	Natality statistics-Statistiques de la natalité
1951	52.XIII.1	Third-Trosième	Mortality statistics-Statistiques de la mortalité
1952	53.XIII.1	Fourth-Quatrième	Population distribution-Répartition de la population
1953	54.XIII.1	Fifth-Cinquième	General demography-Démographie générale
1954	55.XIII.1	Sixth-Sixième	Natality statistics -Statistiques de la natalité
1955	56.XIII.1	Seventh-Septième	Population censuses-Recensement de population
1956	57.XIII.1	Eighth-Huitième	Ethnic and economic characteristics of population-Caractéristiques ethniques et économiques de la population
1957	58.XIII.1	Ninth-Neuvième	Mortality statistics- Statistiques de la mortalité
1958	59.XIII.1	Tenth-Dixième	Marriage and divorce statistics- Statistiques de la nuptialité et de la divortialité
1959	60.XIII.1	Eleventh-Onzième	Natality statistics- Statistiques de la natalité
1960	61.XIII.1	Twelfth-Douzième	Population trends- l' évolution de la population
1961	62.XIII.1	Thirteenth-Treizième	Mortality Statistics- Statistiques de la mortalité
1962	63.XIII.1	Fourteenth-Quatorzième	Population census statistics I- Statistiques des recensements de population I
1963	64.XIII.1	Fifteenth-Quinzième	Population census statistics II- Statistiques des recensements de population II
1964	65.XIII.1	Sixteenth-Seizième	Population census statistics III- Statistiques des recensements de population III
1965	66.XIII.1	Seventeenth-Dix-septième	Natality statistics- Statistiques de la natalité
1966	67.XIII.1	Eighteenth-Dix-huitième	Mortality statistics I- Statistiques de la mortalité I
1967	E/F.68.XIII.1	Nineteenth-Dix-neuvième	Mortality statistics II - Statistiques de la mortalité II
1968	E/F.69.XIII.1	Twentieth-Vingtième	Marriage and divorce statistics-Statistiques de la nuptialité et de la divortialité
1969	E/F.70.XIII.1	Twenty-first-Vingt et unième	Natality statistics-Statistiques de la natalité
1970	E/F.71.XIII.1	Twenty-second-Vingt-deuxième	Population trends-l' évolution de la population
1971	E/F.72.XIII.1	Twenty-third-Vingt-troisième	Population census statistics I- Statistiques de recensements de population I
1972	E/F.73.XIII.1	Twenty-fourth-Vingt-quatrième	Population census statistics II- Statistiques des recensements de population II
1973	E/F.74.XIII.1	Twenty-fifth-Vingt-cinquième	Population census statistics III- Statistiques des recensements de population III
1974	E/F.75.XIII.1	Twenty-sixth-Vingt-sixième	Mortality statistics - Statistiques de la mortalité
1975	E/F.76.XIII.1	Twenty-seventh-Vingt-septième	Natality statistics- Statistiques de la natalité
1976	E/F.77.XIII.1	Twenty-eighth-Vingt-huitième	Marriage and divorce statistics- Statistiques de la nuptialité et de la divortialité
1977	E/F.78.XIII.1	Twenty-ninth-Vingt-neuvième	International Migration Statistics- internationales
1978	E/F.79.XIII.1	Thirtieth-Trentième	General tables- Tableaux de caractère général
1978	E/F.79.XIII.8	Special issue-Edition spéciale	Historical supplement-Supplément rétrospectif
1979	E/F.80.XIII.1	Thirty-first-Trente et unième	Population census statistics-Statistiques des recensements de population
1980	E/F.81.XIII.1	Thirty-second-Trente-deuxième	Mortality statistics- Statistiques de la mortalité
1981	E/F.82.XIII.1	Thirty-third-Trente-troisième	Natality statistics-Statistiques de la natalité
1982	E/F.83.XIII.1	Thirty-fourth-Trente-quatrième	Marriage and divorce statistics-Statistiques de la nuptialité et de la divortialité
1983	E/F.84.XIII.1	Thirty fifth-Trente-cinquième	Population census statistics I-Statistiques des recensements de population I

Year Année	Sales No. - Numéro de vente	Issue - Edition	Special topic - Sujet spécial
1984	E/F.85.XIII.1	Thirty-sixth- Trente-sixième	Population census statistics II- Statistiques des recensements de population II
1985	E/F.86.XIII.1	Thirty-seventh- Trente-septième	Mortality statistics- Statistiques de la mortalité
1986	E/F.87.XIII.1	Thirty-eighth- Trente-huitième	Natality statistics- Statistiques de la natalité
1987	E/F.88.XIII.1	Thirty-ninth- Trente-neuvième	Household composition- Les éléments du ménage
1988	E/F.89.XIII.1	Fortieth- Quarantième	Population census statistics- Statistiques des recensements de population
1989	E/F.90.XIII.1	Forty-first- Quarante-et-unième	International Migration Statistics- Statistiques des migration internationales
1990	E/F.91.XIII.1	Forty-second- Quarante-deuxième	Marriage and divorce statistics- Statistiques de la nuptialité et de la divortialité
1991	E/F.92.XIII.1	Forty-third- Quarante-troisième	General tables- Tableaux de caractère général
1991	E/F.92.XIII.9	Special Issue	Population Ageing and the Situation of Elderly Persons Vieillissement de la population et situation des personnes âgées
1992	E/F.94.XIII.1	Forty-fourth- Quarante-quatrième	Fertility and mortality statistics- Statistiques de la fecondité et de la mortalité
1993	E/F.95.XIII.1	Forty-fifth- Quarante-cinquième	Population census statistics I- Statistiques des recensements de population I
1994	E/F.96.XIII.1	Forty-sixth- Quarante-sixième	Population census statistics II- Statistiques des recensements de population II
1995	E/F.97.XIII.1	Forty-seventh- Quarante-septième	Household composition-Les éléments du ménage
1996	E/F.98.XIII.1	Forty-eighth- Quarante-huitième	Mortality statistics- Statistiques de la mortalité
1997	E/F.99.XIII.1	Forty-ninth- Quarante-neuvième	General tables- Tableaux de caractère général
1997	E/F.99.XIII.12	Special issue- Edition spéciale (CD)	Historical supplement- Supplément rétrospectif
1998	E/F.00.XIII.1	Fiftieth- Cinquantième	General tables- Tableaux de caractère général
1999	E/F.01.XIII.1	Fifty-first- Cinquante-et-unième	General tables- Tableaux de caractère général
1999	E/F.02.XIII.6	Special issue- Edition spéciale (CD)	Natality Statistics- Statistiques de la natalité
2000	E/F.02.XIII.1	Fifty-second- Cinquante-deuxième	General tables- Tableaux de caractère général
2001	E/F.03.XIII.1	Fifty-third- Cinquante- troisième	General tables- Tableaux de caractère général
2002	E/F.05.XIII.1	Fifty-fourth- Cinquante-quatrième	General tables- Tableaux de caractère général
2003	E/F.06.XIII.1	Fifty-fifth- Cinquante-cinquième	General tables- Tableaux de caractère général
2004	E/F.07.XIII.1	Fifty-sixth- Cinquante-sixième	General tables- Tableaux de caractère général
2005	E/F.08.XIII.1	Fifty-seventh- Cinquante-septième	General tables- Tableaux de caractère général
2006	E/F.09.XIII.1	Fifty-eighth- Cinquante-huitième	General tables- Tableaux de caractère général
2007	E/F.10.XIII.1	Fifty-ninth- Cinquante-neuvième	General tables- Tableaux de caractère général
2008	E/F.11.XIII.1	Sixtieth- Soixantième	General tables- Tableaux de caractère général
2009 - 2010	B.12.XIII.1 H	Sixty-first Soixante-et-unième	General tables- Tableaux de caractère général
2011	B.13.XIII.1 H	Sixty-second Soixante- deuxième	General tables- Tableaux de caractère général

Topics of the Demographic Yearbook series: 1948 - 2014

Sujets des diverses éditions de l'Annuaire démographique : 1948 - 2014

Year Année	Sales No. - Numéro de vente	Issue - Edition	Special topic - Sujet spécial
2012	B.14.XIII.1 H	Sixty-third Soixante- troisième	General tables- Tableaux de caractère général
2013	B.15.XIII.1 H	Sixty-fourth Soixante- quatrième	General tables- Tableaux de caractère général
2014	B.16.XIII.1 H	Sixty-fifth Soixante- cinquième	General tables and Whipple's Index, censuses,1985-2014 - Tableaux de caractère général et l'indice de Whipple, recensements, 1985-2014

CONTENTS - TABLE DES MATIERES

EXPLANATIONS OF SYMBOLS

Category not applicable	..
Data not available	...
Magnitude zero or less than half of unit employed	-
Provisional	*
Data tabulated by year of registration rather than occurrence	+
Based on less than specified minimum	◆
Relatively reliable data	Roman type
Data of lesser reliability	*Italics*

EXPLICATION DES SIGNES

Sans objet	..
Données non disponibles	...
Néant ou chiffre inférieur à la moitié de l'unité employée	-
Données provisoires	*
Donnée exploitées selon l'année de l'enregistrement et non l'année de l'événement	+
Rapport fondé sur un nombre inférieur à celui spécifié	◆
Données relativement sûres	Caractères romains
Données dont l'exactitude est moindre	*Italiques*

INTRODUCTION

The *Demographic Yearbook* is an international compendium of national demographic statistics provided by national statistical authorities to the Statistics Division of the United Nations Department of Economic and Social Affairs. The *Demographic Yearbook* is part of the set of coordinated and interrelated publications issued by the United Nations and its specialized agencies, designed to supply statistical data for such users as demographers, economists, public-health workers and sociologists. Through the co-operation of national statistical services, available official demographic statistics are compiled in the *Demographic Yearbook* for more than 230 countries or areas throughout the world.

The *Demographic Yearbook 2014* is the sixty-fifth issue in a series published by the United Nations since 1948. It contains tables on a wide range of demographic statistics, including a world summary of selected demographic statistics, statistics on the size, distribution and trends in national populations, fertility, foetal mortality, infant and maternal mortality, general mortality, nuptiality and divorce. Data are shown by urban/rural residence, as available. The volume provides Technical Notes, a synoptic table, a historical index and a listing of the issues of the *Demographic Yearbook* published to date. This issue of *Demographic Yearbook* contains data as available including reference year 2014.

This edition of the *Demographic Yearbook* features a special tabulation (table 3a) with Whipple's index by sex and urban/rural residence for the past three rounds of population censuses, namely the population censuses conducted worldwide since 1985. Whipple's index is an index of age preference in age reporting and can therefore serve to highlight some of the problems related to age distribution.

The Technical Notes on the Statistical Tables are provided to assist the reader in using the tables. Table A, the synoptic table, provides an overview of the completeness of data coverage of the current *Demographic Yearbook*. The cumulative historical index is a guide on content and coverage of all sixty-five issues, and indicates, for each of the topics that have been published, the issues in which they are presented and the years covered. A list of the *Demographic Yearbook* issues, with their corresponding sales numbers and the special topics featured in each issue are shown on pages iii and iv.

Until the 48th issue (1996), each issue consisted of two parts, the general tables and special topic tables, published in the same volume[1]. Beginning with the 49th issue (1997), the special topic tables were being disseminated in digital format as supplements to the regular issues. Two CD-ROMs have been issued: the *Demographic Yearbook Historical Supplement*, which presents a wide panorama of basic demographic statistics for the period 1948 to 1997, and the *Demographic Yearbook: Natality Statistics*, which contains a series of detailed tables dedicated to natality and covering the period from 1980 to 1998. Later on, three volumes of *Demographic Yearbook* Special Census Topics for the 2000 round of censuses, covering the period from 1995 to 2004, were published on-line at http://unstats.un.org/unsd/demographic/products/dyb/dybcens.htm. Current *Demographic Yearbook* population and housing censuses data for the 2000 and 2010 rounds (1995 to the present) are presented at http://unstats.un.org/unsd/demographic/products/dyb/dybcensusdata.htm. These datasets cover basic population characteristics, educational, household, ethnocultural and economic characteristics, and also foreign-born and foreign population. Special tabulations on household and economic characteristics with data based on population censuses since 1995 are available respectively at http://unstats.un.org/unsd/demographic/products/dyb/dyb_Household/dyb_household.htm and http://unstats.un.org/unsd/demographic/products/dyb/dyb_Eco/dyb_eco.htm.

Population statistics are not available for all countries or areas, for a variety of reasons. In an effort to provide estimates of mid-year population and of selected vital statistics for all countries and areas, two annexes are presented. Annex I presents United Nations population estimates for the period 2005-2014 and Annex II presents the medium variant estimates of crude birth and death rates, infant mortality and total fertility rates, as well as life expectancy at birth over the period 2010-2015. These data were produced by the United Nations Population Division and are published in the *2015 Revision of World Population Prospects*[2].

Demographic statistics shown in this issue of the *Demographic Yearbook* are available online at the *Demographic Yearbook* website http://unstats.un.org/unsd/demographic/products/dyb/dyb2014.htm. Information about the Statistics Division's data collection and dissemination programme is also available on the same website. Additional information can be made available by contacting the Statistics Division of the United Nations Department of Economic and Social Affairs at demostat@un.org.

TECHNICAL NOTES ON THE STATISTICAL TABLES

1. GENERAL REMARKS

1.1 Arrangement of Technical Notes

These Technical Notes are designed to provide the reader with relevant information related to the statistical tables. Information pertaining to the *Demographic Yearbook* in general is presented in the sections dealing with geographical aspects, population and vital statistics. In addition, preceding each table are notes describing the variables, remarks on the reliability and limitation of the data, countries and areas covered, and information on the presentation of earlier data. When appropriate, details on computation of rates, ratios or percentages are presented.

1.2 Arrangement of tables

The numbering of tables from one issue of *Demographic Yearbook* to the next is preserved to the extent possible. However, since for some of the tables the numbering may not correspond exactly to those in previous issues, the reader is advised to use the historical index that appears at the end of this book to find the reference to data in earlier issues.

1.3 Source of data

The statistics presented in the *Demographic Yearbook* are national data provided by official statistical authorities unless otherwise indicated. The primary source of data for the *Demographic Yearbook* is a set of questionnaires sent annually by the United Nations Statistics Division to over 230 national statistical services. Data reported on these questionnaires are supplemented, to the extent possible, with data taken from official national publications, official websites and through correspondence with national statistical services. In the interest of comparability, rates, ratios and percentages have been calculated by the Statistics Division of the United Nations, except for the life table functions, the total fertility rate, and also crude birth rate and crude death rate for some countries or areas as appropriately noted. The methods used by the Statistics Division to calculate these rates and ratios are described in the Technical Notes for each table. The population figures used for these computations are those pertaining to the corresponding years published in this or previous issues of the *Demographic Yearbook*.

In cases when data in this issue of the *Demographic Yearbook* differ from those published in earlier issues or related publications, statistics in this issue may be assumed to reflect revisions to the data received by June 2015.

2. GEOGRAPHICAL ASPECTS

2.1 Coverage

Data are shown for all individual countries or areas that provided information. Table 3 is the most comprehensive in geographical coverage, presenting data on population and surface area for all countries or areas with a population of at least 50 persons. Not all of these countries or areas appear in subsequent tables. In many cases the data required for a particular table are not available. In general, the more detailed the data required for a table, the fewer the number of countries or areas that can provide them.

In addition, rates and ratios are presented only for countries or areas reporting at least a minimum number of relevant events. The minimums are stated in the Technical Notes to individual tables.

Except for summary data shown for the world and by major areas and regions in tables 1 and 2 and data shown for capital cities and cities with a population of 100 000 or more in table 8, all data are presented at the national level. The number of countries shown in each table is provided in table A, the synoptic table.

2.2 Territorial composition

To the extent possible, all data, including time series data, relate to the territory within 2014 boundaries. Exceptions are footnoted in individual tables. Relevant clarifications are specified below.

Data relating to **Denmark** exclude Faeroe Islands and Greenland, which are shown separately.

Data relating to **Finland** include Åland Islands, unless otherwise indicated by a footnote.

Data relating to **France** exclude Overseas Departments, namely, French Guiana, Guadeloupe, Martinique and Réunion, which are shown separately, unless otherwise indicated by a footnote.

Data relating to **United Kingdom of Great Britain and Northern Ireland** exclude Guernsey, Isle of Man and Jersey which are shown separately.

Data relating to **Western Sahara** comprise the Northern Region (former Saguia el Hamra) and Southern Region (former Rio de Oro).

2.3 Nomenclature

Because of space limitations, the country or area names listed in the tables are generally the commonly employed short titles currently in use[3] in the United Nations, the full titles being used only when a short form is not available. The latest version of the *Standard Country or Area Codes for Statistics Use* can be accessed at http://unstats.un.org/unsd/methods/m49/m49alpha.htm.

2.3.1 Order of presentation

Countries or areas are listed in English alphabetical order within the following continents: Africa, North America, South America, Asia, Europe and Oceania.

The designations and presentation of the material in this publication were adopted solely for the purpose of providing a convenient geographical basis for the accompanying statistical series. The same qualification applies to all notes and explanations concerning the geographical units for which data are presented.

2.4 Surface area data

Surface area data, shown in tables 1 and 3, represent the total surface area, comprising land area and inland waters (assumed to consist of major rivers and lakes) and excluding only Polar Regions and uninhabited islands. The surface area given is the most recent estimate available. They are presented in square kilometres, a conversion factor of 2.589988 having been applied to surface areas originally reported in square miles.

2.4.1 Comparability over time

Comparability over time in surface area estimates for any given country or area may be affected by changes in the surface area estimation procedures, increases in actual land surface by reclamation, boundary changes, changes in the concept of "land surface area" used or a change in the unit of measurement used. In most cases it was possible to ascertain the reason for a revision; otherwise, the latest figures have generally been accepted as correct and substituted those previously on file.

2.4.2 International comparability

Lack of international comparability between surface area estimates arises primarily from differences in definition. In particular, there is considerable variation in the treatment of coastal bays, inlets and gulfs, rivers and lakes. International comparability is also impaired by the variation in methods employed to estimate surface area. These range from surveys based on modern scientific methods to conjectures based on diverse types of information. Some estimates are recent while others may not be. Since neither the exact method of determining the surface area nor the precise definition of its composition and time reference is known for all countries or areas, the estimates in table 3 should not be considered strictly comparable from one country or area to another.

3. POPULATION

Population statistics, that is, those pertaining to the size, geographical distribution and demographic characteristics of the population, are presented in a number of tables of the *Demographic Yearbook*.

Summary estimates of the mid-year population of the world, major areas and regions for selected years and of its age and sex distribution in 2014 are set forth in tables 1 and 2, respectively.

Data for countries or areas include population census figures, estimates based on results of sample surveys (in the absence of a census), postcensal or intercensal estimates and those derived from continuous population registers. In the present issue of the *Demographic Yearbook*, the latest available census figure of the total population of each country or area and mid-year estimates for 2010 and 2014 are presented in table 3. Mid-year estimates of total population for ten years (2005-2014) are shown in table 5 and mid-year estimates of urban and total population by sex for ten years (2005-2014) are shown in table 6. The latest available data on population by age, sex and urban/rural residence are given in table 7. The latest available figures on the population of capital cities and of cities or urban agglomerations of 100 000 or more inhabitants are presented in table 8.

The statistics on total population, population by age, sex, or urban/rural distribution are used for the calculation of rates in the *Demographic Yearbook*. Vital rates by residence (urban/rural), age or sex were calculated using data presented in tables 6 or 7 in this issue or the corresponding tables of previous issues of the *Demographic Yearbook*.

3.1 Sources of variation of data

The comparability of data is affected by several factors, including (1) the definition of total population; (2) the definition used to classify the population into its urban/rural components; (3) the accuracy of age reporting; (4) the extent of over-enumeration or under-enumeration in the most recent census or other source of benchmark population statistics; and (5) the quality of population estimates. These five factors will be discussed in some detail in sections 3.1.1 to 3.2 below. Other relevant problems are discussed in the technical notes to the individual tables. Readers interested in more detail, relating in particular to the basic concepts of population size, distribution and characteristics as elaborated by the United Nations, should consult the *Principles and Recommendations for Population and Housing Censuses, Revision 2*[4].

3.1.1 Total population

The most important impediment to comparability of total populations is the difference between the concept of a *de facto* and *de jure* population. A *de facto* population includes all persons physically present in the country or area at the reference date. The *de jure* population, by contrast, includes all usual residents of the given country or area, whether or not they were physically present in the area at the reference date. By definition, therefore, a *de facto* total and a *de jure* total are not entirely comparable.

Comparability of even two *de facto* or *de jure* totals is often affected by the fact that strict conformity to either of these concepts is rare. For example, some so-called *de facto* counts do not include foreign military, naval and diplomatic personnel present in the country or area on official duty, and their accompanying family and household members; some do not include foreign visitors in transit through the country or area or transients on ships in harbours. On the other hand, they may include such persons as merchant seamen and fishermen who are temporarily out of the country or area working at their trade.

The *de jure* population figure presents even greater variations in comparability, in part because it depends in the first place on the concept of "usual residence", which varies from one country or area to another and is difficult to apply consistently in a census or survey enumeration. For example, non-national civilians temporarily in a country or area as short-term workers may officially be considered residents after a stay of a specified period of time or they may be considered as non-residents throughout the duration of their stay; at the same time, these individuals may be officially considered as residents or non-residents of the country or area from which they came, depending on the duration and/or purpose of their absence. Furthermore, regardless of the official treatment, individual respondents may apply their own interpretation of residence in responding to the inquiry. In addition, there may be considerable differences in the accuracy with which countries or areas are informed about the number of their residents temporarily out of the country or area.

The population statistics presented in the tables of the *Demographic Yearbook* refer to the *de facto* population or to the *de jure* population. In an effort to overcome, to the extent possible, the effect of the lack of strict conformity to either the *de facto* or the *de jure* concept given above, significant exceptions with respect to inclusions and exclusions of specific population groups, are footnoted when they are known.

A possible source of variation within the statistics of a single country or area may arise from the fact that some countries or areas collect information on both the *de facto* and the *de jure* population in, for example, a census, but prepare detailed tabulations for only the *de jure* population. Hence, even though the total population shown in table 3 is de facto, the figures shown in the tables presenting various characteristics of the population, for example, urban/rural distribution, age and sex distribution, may be on the *de jure* concept.

3.1.2 Urban/rural classification

International comparability of urban/rural distributions is seriously impaired by the wide variation among national definitions of the concept of "urban". The definitions used by individual countries or areas and their implications are shown at the end of technical notes for table 6.

3.1.3 Age distribution

The classification of population by age is a core element of most analyses, estimation and projection of population statistics. Unfortunately, age data are subject to a number of sources of error and non-comparability. Accordingly, the reliability of age data should be of concern to users of these statistics.

3.1.3.1 Collection and compilation of age data

Age is the estimated or calculated interval of time between the date of birth and the date of the census or survey, expressed in completed solar years[5]. There are two methods of collecting information on age. The first is to obtain the date of birth for each member of the population in a census or survey and then to calculate the completed age of the individual by subtracting the date of birth from the date of enumeration[6]. The second method is to record the individual's completed age at the time of the census or survey, that is to say, age at last birthday.

The recommended method is to calculate age at last birthday by subtracting the exact date of birth from the date of the census. Some practices, however, do not use this method but instead calculate the difference between the year of birth and the year of the census. Classifications of this type are footnoted whenever possible. They can be identified to a certain extent by a smaller than expected population under one year of age. However, an irregular number of births from one year to the next or age selective omission of infants may also obscure the expected population under one year of age.

3.1.3.2 Errors in age data

Errors in age data may be due to a variety of causes, including ignorance of the correct age; reporting years of age in terms of a calendar concept other than completed solar years since birth[7]; carelessness in reporting and recording age; a general tendency to state age in figures ending in certain digits (such as zero, two, five and eight); a tendency to exaggerate length of life at advanced ages; a subconscious aversion to certain numbers; and wilful misrepresentations.

These reasons for errors in reported age data are common to most investigations of age and to most countries or areas, and they may significantly impair comparability of the data.

As a result of the above-mentioned difficulties, the age-sex distribution of population in many countries or areas shows irregularities which may be summarized as follows: (1) a deficiency in the number of infants and young children; (2) a concentration at ages ending with zero and five (that is, 5, 10, 15, 20, ...); (3) heaping at even ages (for example, 10, 12, 14, ...) relative to odd ages (for example, 11, 13, 15, ...); (4) unexpectedly large differences between the frequency of males and females at certain ages; and (5) unaccountably large differences between the frequencies in adjacent age groups. Comparing of identical age-sex cohorts from successive censuses, as well as studying the age-sex composition of each census, may reveal these and other inconsistencies, some of which in varying degree are characteristic of even the most modern censuses.

This edition of the *Demographic Yearbook* features a special tabulation (table 3a) with Whipple's index by sex and urban/ rural residence for the past three rounds of population censuses, namely the population censuses conducted worldwide since 1985. Whipple's index is an index of age preference in age reporting and can therefore serve to highlight some of the problems related to age distribution.

4. VITAL STATISTICS

For purposes of the *Demographic Yearbook*, vital statistics of concern are those of live birth, death, foetal death, marriage and divorce.

This volume of the *Demographic Yearbook* presents tables on fertility, nuptiality and divorce as well as tables on mortality referring to foetal mortality, infant and maternal mortality and general mortality.

4.1 Sources of variation of data

Most of the vital statistics data published in this *Demographic Yearbook* come from national civil registration systems. The completeness and the accuracy of the data that these systems produce vary from one country or area to another.

The provision for a national civil registration system is not universal, and in some cases, the registration system covers only certain vital events. For example, in some countries or areas only births and deaths are registered. There are also differences in the effectiveness with which national laws pertaining to civil registration operate in the various countries or areas. The manner in which the law is implemented and the degree to which the public complies with the legislation determine the reliability of vital statistics obtained from the civil registers.

It should be noted that some statistics on marriage and divorce are obtained from sources other than civil registers. For example, in some countries or areas, the only source for data on marriages is church registers. Divorce statistics, on the other hand, are obtained from court records and/or civil registers according to national practice. The actual compilation of these statistics may be the responsibility of the civil registrar, the national statistical office or other government offices.

Other factors affecting international comparability of vital statistics are much the same as those that must be considered in evaluating the variations in other population statistics. Differences in statistical definitions of vital events, differences in geographical and ethnic coverage of the data and diverse tabulation procedures may also influence comparability.

In addition to vital statistics from civil registers, some vital statistics published in the *Demographic Yearbook* are official estimates. These estimates are frequently from population censuses and sample surveys. As such, their comparability may be affected by the national completeness of reporting in population censuses and household surveys, whether a *de facto* or *de jure* based census, non-sampling and sampling errors and other sources of bias.

Readers interested in more detailed information on standards for vital statistics should consult the *Principles and Recommendations for a Vital Statistics System Revision 3*[8]; *Handbook on Civil Registration and Vital Statistics Systems: Preparation of a Legal Framework*[9]; *Handbook on Civil Registration and Vital Statistics Systems: Management, Operation and Maintenance*[10]; *Handbook on Civil Registration and Vital Statistics Systems: Developing Information, Education and Communication*[11]; *Handbook on Civil Registration and Vital Statistics Systems: Policies and Protocols for the Release and Archiving of Individual Records*[12]; and *Handbook on Civil Registration and Vital Statistics Systems: Computerization*[13]. The *Handbook on the Collection of Fertility and Mortality Data*[14] provides information in collection and evaluation of data on fertility and mortality collected in population censuses and household surveys. These publications are also available on the website at http://unstats.un.org/unsd/demographic/standmeth/handbooks/default.htm.

4.1.1 Statistical definition of events

An important source of variation lies in the statistical definition of each vital event. The *Demographic Yearbook* attempts to collect data on vital events, using the standard definitions put forth in Chapter I of *Principles and Recommendations for a Vital Statistics System Revision 3*[8]. These definitions are as follows:

LIVE BIRTH is the complete expulsion or extraction from its mother of a product of conception, irrespective of the duration of pregnancy, which after such separation breathes or shows any other evidence of life such as beating of the heart, pulsation of the umbilical cord, or definite movement of voluntary muscles, whether or not the umbilical cord has been cut or the placenta is attached; each product of such a birth is considered live-born.

DEATH is the permanent disappearance of all evidence of life at any time after the occurrence of live birth, i.e., the postnatal cessation of vital functions without capability of resuscitation. This definition excludes foetal deaths.

FOETAL DEATH is death prior to the complete expulsion or extraction from its mother of a product of conception, irrespective of the duration of the period of gestation. Death is indicated by the fact that after such separation, the foetus does not breathe or show any other evidence of life, such as beating of the heart, pulsation of the umbilical cord, or definite movement of voluntary muscles.

MARRIAGE is an act, ceremony or process by which the legal relationship of spouses is constituted. The legality of the union may be established by civil, religious or other means as recognized by the laws of each country. Countries may wish to expand the definition to cover civil unions if they are registered. In that case, registered partnership usually refers to a legal construct, entailing registration with the public authorities according to the laws of each country, that becomes the basis for legal conjugal obligations between two persons.

DIVORCE is a final legal dissolution of a marriage, that is, the separation of spouses that confers on the parties the right to remarriage under civil, religious and/or other provisions, according to the laws of each country. In the case where a country recognizes registered partnerships, a legal dissolution of a registered partnership constitutes the legal final dissolution of such a partnership, according to national laws, which confers on the parties the right to enter into another partnership or marriage.

In addition to these internationally recommended definitions, the *Demographic Yearbook* collects and presents data on abortions, defined as:

ABORTION is defined, with reference to the woman, as any interruption of pregnancy before 28 weeks of gestation with a dead foetus. There are two major categories of abortion: spontaneous and induced. Induced abortions are those initiated by deliberate action undertaken with the intention of terminating pregnancy; all other abortions are considered spontaneous.

4.1.2 Problems relating to standard definitions

A basic problem affecting international comparability of vital statistics is deviations from the standard definitions of vital events. An example of this can be seen in the cases of live births and foetal deaths. In some countries or areas, an infant must survive for at least 24 hours, to be inscribed in the live-birth register. Infants who die before the expiration of the 24-hour period are classified as late foetal deaths and, barring special tabulation procedures, they would not be counted either as live births or as deaths. Similarly, in several other countries or areas, those infants who are born alive but die before registration of their birth, are also considered late foetal deaths.

Unless special tabulation procedures are adopted in such cases, the live-birth and death statistics will both be deficient by the number of these infants, while the incidence of late foetal deaths will be increased by the same amount. Hence the infant mortality rate is underestimated. Although both components (infant deaths and live births) are deficient by the same absolute amount, the deficiency is proportionately greater in relation to the infant deaths, causing greater errors in the infant mortality rate than in the birth rate.

Moreover, the practice exaggerates the late foetal death ratios. Some countries or areas make provision for correcting this deficiency (at least in the total frequencies) at the tabulation stage. Data for which the correction has not been made are indicated by a footnote whenever possible.

The definitions used for marriage and divorce also present problems for international comparability. Unlike birth and death, which are biological events, marriage and divorce are defined only in terms of law and custom and as such are less amenable to universally applicable statistical definitions. They have therefore been defined for statistical purposes in general terms referring to the laws of individual countries or areas. Laws pertaining to marriage and particularly to divorce, vary from one country or area to another. With respect to marriage, the most widespread requirement relates to the minimum age at which persons may marry but frequently other requirements are specified.

When known the minimum legal age of men and women at which marriage can occur with or without parental consent is presented in table 23-1. Laws and regulations relating to the dissolution of marriage by divorce range from total prohibition, through a wide range of grounds upon which divorces may be granted, to the granting of divorce in response to a simple statement of desire or intention by spouses.

4.1.3 Fragmentary geographical or ethnic coverage

Ideally, vital statistics for any given country or area should cover the entire geographical area and include all ethnic groups. Fragmentary coverage is, however, not uncommon. In some countries or areas, registration is compulsory for only a small part of the population, limited to certain ethnic groups, for example. In other places there is no national provision for compulsory registration, but only municipal or state ordinances that do not cover the entire geographical area. Still others have developed a registration area that comprises only a part of the country or area, the remainder being excluded because of inaccessibility or for economic and cultural considerations that make regular registration practically impossible.

4.1.4 Tabulation procedures

4.1.4.1 By place of occurrence

Vital statistics presented at the national level relate to the de facto, that is, the present-in-area population. Thus, unless otherwise noted, vital statistics for a given country or area cover all the events that occur within its present boundaries and among all segments of the population therein. They may be presumed to include events among nomadic tribes and indigenous peoples, and among nationals and foreigners. When known, deviations from the *de facto* concept are footnoted.

Urban/rural differentials in vital rates for some countries may vary considerably depending on whether the relevant vital events were tabulated on the basis of place of occurrence or place of usual residence. For example, if a substantial number of women residing in rural areas near major urban centres travel to hospitals or maternity homes located in a city to give birth, urban fertility and neo-natal and infant mortality rates will usually be higher (and the corresponding rural rates will usually be lower) if the events are tabulated on the basis of place of occurrence rather than on the basis of place of usual residence. A similar process will affect general mortality differentials if substantial numbers of persons residing in rural areas use urban health facilities when seriously ill.

4.1.4.2 By date of occurrence versus by date of registration

To the extent possible, the vital statistics presented in the *Demographic Yearbook* refer to events that occurred during the specified year, rather than to those that were registered during that period. However, a considerable number of countries or areas tabulate their vital statistics not by date of occurrence, but by date of registration. Because such statistics can be misleading, the countries or areas known to tabulate vital statistics by date of registration are identified in the tables by a plus sign "+". Since information on the method of tabulating vital statistics is not available for all countries and areas, tabulation by date of registration may be more prevalent than the symbols on the vital statistics tables would indicate.

Because quality of data is inextricably related to the timeliness of registration, this must always be considered in conjunction with the quality code description in section 4.2.1 below. If registration of births is complete and timely (code "C"), the ill effects of tabulating by date of registration, are, for all practical purposes, nullified. Similarly, with respect to death statistics, the effect of tabulating events by date of registration may be minimized in many countries or areas in which the sanitary code requires that a death must be registered before a burial permit can be issued, and this regulation tends to make registration prompt. With respect to foetal death, registration is usually done right away or not at all. Therefore, if registration is prompt, the difference between statistics tabulated by date of occurrence and those tabulated by date of registration may be negligible. In many cases, the length of the statutory time period allowed for registering various vital events plays an important part in determining the effects of tabulation by date of registration on comparability of data.

With respect to marriage and divorce, the practice of tabulating data by date of registration does not generally pose serious problems. In many countries or areas marriage is a civil legal contract which, to establish its legality, must be celebrated before a civil officer. It follows that for these countries or areas registration would tend to be almost automatic at the time of, or immediately following, the marriage ceremony. Because the registration of a divorce in many countries or areas is the responsibility solely of the court or the authority which granted it, and since the registration record in such cases is part of the records of the court proceedings, it follows that divorces are likely to be registered soon after the decree is granted.

On the other hand, if registration is not prompt, vital statistics by date of registration will not produce internationally comparable data. Under the best circumstances, statistics by date of registration will include primarily events that occurred in the immediately preceding year; in countries or areas with less developed systems, tabulations will include some events that occurred many years in the past. Examination of available information reveals that delays of many years are not uncommon for birth registration, though the majority is recorded between two to four years after birth.

As long as registration is not prompt, statistics by date of registration will not be internationally comparable either among themselves or with statistics by date of occurrence.

It should also be mentioned that lack of international comparability is not the only limitation introduced by date-of-registration tabulation. Even within the same country or area, comparability over time may be lost by the practice of counting registrations rather than occurrences. If the number of events registered from year to year fluctuates because of *ad hoc* incentives to stimulate registration, or to the sudden need, for example, for proof of (unregistered) birth or death to meet certain requirements, vital statistics tabulated by date of registration are not useful in measuring and analyzing demographic levels and trends. All they can give is an indication of the fluctuations in the need for a birth, death or marriage certificate and the work-load of the registrars. Therefore, statistics tabulated by date of registration may be of very limited use for either national or international studies.

4.2 Methods used to indicate quality of published vital statistics

The quality of vital statistics can be assessed in terms of a number of factors. Most fundamental is the completeness of the civil registration system on which these statistics are based. In some cases, the incompleteness of the data obtained from civil registration systems is revealed when these events are used to compute rates. However, this technique applies only where the data are markedly deficient, where they are tabulated by date of occurrence and where the population base is correctly estimated. Tabulation by date of registration will often produce rates which appear correct, simply because the numerator is artificially inflated by the inclusion of delayed registration and, conversely, rates may be of credible magnitude because the population at risk has been underestimated. Moreover, it should be remembered that knowledge of what is credible in regard to levels of fertility, mortality and nuptiality is extremely scant for many parts of the world, and borderline cases, which are the most difficult to appraise, are frequent.

4.2.1   Quality code for vital statistics from registers.

In the *Demographic Yearbook* annual "Questionnaire on Vital Statistics" national statistical offices are asked to provide their own estimates of the completeness of the births, deaths, late foetal deaths, marriages and divorces recorded in their civil registers.

On the basis of information from the questionnaires, from direct correspondence and from relevant official publications, it has been possible to classify current national statistics from civil registers of birth, death, infant death, late foetal death, marriage and divorce into three broad quality categories, as follows:

C: Data estimated to be virtually complete, that is, representing at least 90 per cent of the events occurring each year.

U: Data estimated to be incomplete, that is representing less than 90 per cent of the events occurring each year.

|: Data not derived from civil registration systems but considered reliable, such as estimates derived from projections, other estimation techniques or population and housing censuses.

...: Data for which no specific information is available regarding completeness.

These quality codes appear in the first column of the tables which show total frequencies and crude rates (or ratios) over a period of years for all tables on live births, late foetal deaths, infant deaths, deaths, marriages, and divorces.   Reliability of maternal mortality statistics is provided by the World Health Organisation.

The classification of countries and areas in terms of these quality codes may not be uniform. Nevertheless, it was felt that national statistical offices were in the best position to judge the quality of their data. It was considered that even the very broad categories that could be established on the basis of the available information would provide useful indicators of the quality of the vital statistics presented in this *Demographic Yearbook*.

Among the countries or areas indicating that the registration of live births was estimated to be 90 per cent or more complete (and hence classified as "C" or "+C" in table 9), the following countries or areas provided information on the method used to evaluate the completeness estimate:

(a) Demographic analysis -- Argentina, Austria, Bulgaria, Chile, China - Hong Kong SAR, Croatia, Egypt, Estonia, Italy, Latvia, Lithuania, Malaysia, Malta, Mauritius, Mexico, New Zealand, Republic of Korea, Republic of Moldova, Romania, Seychelles, South Africa and Sweden.

(b) Dual record check -- Austria, Cuba, Cyprus, Estonia, Hungary, Israel, Italy, Malaysia, Montserrat, New Zealand, Norway, Qatar, Republic of Korea, Switzerland and Uruguay.

(c) Other specified methods -- Aruba, Australia, Austria, Bahrain, Curaçao, Denmark, Dominican Republic, France, Guatemala, Ireland, Kyrgyzstan, Liechtenstein, Luxembourg, Malaysia, Panama, Poland, Puerto Rico, Singapore, Slovenia, Spain, State of Palestine and Sweden.

Among the countries or areas indicating that the registration of late foetal-deaths was estimated to be 90 per cent or more complete (and hence classified as "C" or "+C" in table 12), the following countries or areas provided information on the method used to evaluate the completeness estimate:

(a) Demographic analysis -- Argentina, Austria, Bulgaria, Croatia, Egypt, Estonia, Italy, Latvia, Lithuania, Malta, Mauritius, Mexico, Romania and Sweden.

(b) Dual record check -- Austria, Cuba, Estonia, Hungary, Israel, Italy, Lithuania, Montserrat, New Zealand, Norway, Qatar, Switzerland and Venezuela (Bolivarian Republic of).

(c) Other specified methods – Austria, Bahrain, Denmark, Kyrgyzstan, Luxembourg, Poland, Puerto Rico, Slovenia, Spain and Sweden.

Among the countries or areas indicating that the registration of infant deaths was estimated to be 90 per cent or more complete (and hence classified as "C" or "+C" in table 15), the following countries or areas provided information on the method used to evaluate the completeness estimate:

(a) Demographic analysis -- Argentina, Australia, Austria, Bulgaria, Chile, China - Hong Kong SAR, Croatia, Egypt, Estonia, Israel, Italy, Latvia, Lithuania, Malta, Mauritius, Mexico, New Zealand, Republic of Korea, Republic of Moldova, Romania, Seychelles and Sweden.

(b) Dual record check -- Austria, Cuba, Cyprus, Estonia, Hungary, Ireland, Israel, Italy, Lithuania, Montserrat, New Zealand, Norway, Qatar, Republic of Korea, Switzerland and Venezuela (Bolivarian Republic of).

(c) Other specified methods -- Austria, Bahrain, Curaçao, Cayman Islands, Denmark, Kyrgyzstan, Liechtenstein, Luxembourg, Poland, Puerto Rico, Singapore, Slovenia, Spain and Sweden.

Among the countries or areas indicating that the registration of deaths was estimated to be 90 per cent or more complete (and hence classified as "C" or "+C" in table 18), the following countries or areas provided information on the method used to evaluate the completeness estimate:

(a) Demographic analysis -- Argentina, Australia, Austria, Bulgaria, Chile, China - Hong Kong SAR, Croatia, Egypt, Estonia, Israel, Italy, Latvia, Lithuania, Malta, Mauritius, Mexico, New Zealand, Republic of Korea, Republic of Moldova, Romania, Seychelles, South Africa and Sweden.

(b) Dual record check -- Austria, Cuba, Cyprus, Estonia, Hungary, Israel, Italy, Lithuania, Montserrat, New Zealand, Norway, Qatar, Republic of Korea, Switzerland and Venezuela (Bolivarian Republic of).

(c) Other specified methods -- Aruba, Austria, Bahrain, Curaçao, Denmark, Dominican Republic, France, Kyrgyzstan, Liechtenstein, Luxembourg, Malaysia, Poland, Puerto Rico, Singapore, Slovenia, Spain and Sweden.

Among the countries or areas indicating that the registration of marriages was estimated to be 90 per cent or more complete (and hence classified as "C" or "+C" in table 23), the following countries or areas provided information on the method used to evaluate the completeness estimate:

(a) Demographic analysis -- Argentina, Australia, Austria, Bulgaria, Chile, China - Hong Kong SAR, Croatia, Egypt, Estonia, Italy, Latvia, Lithuania, Malta, Mauritius, Mexico, Republic of Korea, Republic of Moldova, Romania, Seychelles and Sweden.

(b) Dual record check -- Cuba, Estonia, Hungary, Israel, Italy, New Zealand, Norway, Qatar, Republic of Korea, State of Palestine, Switzerland and Venezuela (Bolivarian Republic of).

(c) Other specified methods -- Aruba, Austria, Curaçao, Denmark, Dominican Republic, France, Kyrgyzstan, Liechtenstein, Luxembourg, Poland, Puerto Rico, Slovenia, Spain, Sweden and Tajikistan.

Among the countries or areas indicating that the registration of divorces was estimated to be 90 per cent or more complete (and hence classified as "C" or "+C" in table 24), the following countries or areas provided information on the method used to evaluate the completeness estimate:

(a) Demographic analysis – Australia, Austria, Bulgaria, Croatia, Egypt, Estonia, Italy, Latvia, Lithuania, Mexico, Republic of Korea, Republic of Moldova, Romania, Seychelles and Sweden.

(b) Dual record check -- Cuba, Estonia, Hungary, Israel, Italy, New Zealand, Norway, Qatar, Republic of Korea, State of Palestine and Switzerland.

(c) Other specified methods -- Aruba, Austria, Curaçao, Cyprus, Denmark, Dominican Republic, Kyrgyzstan, Liechtenstein, Luxembourg, Mauritius, Poland, Puerto Rico, Slovenia, Sweden and Tajikistan.

4.2.2 Treatment of vital statistics from registers

On the basis of the quality code described above, the vital statistics shown in all tables of the *Demographic Yearbook* are treated as either reliable or unreliable. Data coded "C" are considered reliable and appear in roman type. Data coded "U" or "..." are considered unreliable and appear in *italics*. Although the quality code itself appears only in certain tables, the indication of reliability (that is, the use of *italics* to indicate unreliable data) is shown in all tables presenting vital statistics data.

It should be noted that the indications of reliability used for infant mortality rates, maternal mortality ratios and late foetal death ratios (all of which are calculated using the number of live births in the denominator) are determined on the basis of the quality codes for infant deaths, deaths and late foetal deaths respectively. To evaluate these rates and ratios more precisely, one would have to take into account the quality of the live-birth data used in the denominator of these rates and ratios. The quality codes for live births are shown in table 9 and described more fully in the text of the technical notes for that table.

4.2.3 Treatment of time series of vital statistics from registers

The quality of a time series of vital statistics is more difficult to determine than the quality of data for a single year. Since a time series of vital statistics is usually generated only by a system of continuous civil registration, it was assumed that the quality of the entire series was the same as that for the latest year's data obtained from the civil register. The entire series is treated as described in section 4.2.2 above. That is, if the quality code for the latest registered data is "C", the frequencies and rates for earlier years are also considered reliable and appear in roman type. Conversely, if the latest registered data are coded as "U" or "..." then data for earlier years are considered unreliable and appear in *italics*. It is recognized that this method is not entirely satisfactory because it is known that data from earlier years in many of the series were considerably less reliable than the current code implies. Efforts are being made to gradually move away from this method and code the registered data of each year or range of years separately.

4.2.4 Treatment of estimated vital statistics

In addition to data from vital registration systems, estimated frequencies and rates of the events, usually *ad hoc* official estimates that have been derived either from the results of a population census or sample survey or by demographic analyses, also appear in the *Demographic Yearbook*. Estimated frequencies and rates have been included in the tables because it is assumed that they provide information that is more accurate than that from existing civil registration systems. By implication, they are assumed to be reliable and as such they are set in roman type.

In tables showing the quality code, the code applies only to data from civil registers. Estimated data are denoted by the symbol "|".

4.3 Cause of death

World Health Organization (WHO) Member States are bound by the International Nomenclature Regulations to provide the Organization with cause of death data coded in accordance with the current revision of the International Statistical Classification of Diseases and Related Health Problems (ICD). In order to promote international comparability of cause of death statistics, the World Health Organization organizes and conducts an international conference for the revision of the ICD on a regular basis in order to ensure that the Classification is kept current with the most recent clinical and statistical concepts. The data are now usually submitted to WHO at the full four-character level of detail provided by the ICD and are compiled and stored in the WHO Mortality Database at the level of detail as provided by the country. Data from the WHO Mortality Database are available in electronic format at http://www3.who.int/whosis/menu.cfm.

Although revisions provide an up-to-date version of the ICD, such revisions create several problems related to the comparability of cause of death statistics. The first is the lack of comparability over time that inevitably accompanies the use of a new classification. The second problem affects comparability between countries and areas because they may adopt a new classification at different times. The more refined the classification becomes the greater is the need for expert clinical diagnosis of cause of death. In many countries or areas, few of the deaths occur in the presence of an attendant, who is medically trained, i.e., most deaths are certified by a lay attendant. Because the ICD contains many diagnoses that cannot be identified by a non-medical person, the ICD is not always accurately or precisely used, which affects international comparability particularly between countries and areas where the level of medical services differ widely.

The chapters of the tenth revision[15], consist of an alphanumeric coding scheme of one letter followed by three numbers at the four-character level. Chapter one contains infectious and parasitic diseases, chapter two refers to all neoplasms, chapter three to disorders of the immune mechanism including diseases of the blood and blood-forming organs; and chapter four to endocrine, nutritional and metabolic diseases. The remaining chapters group diseases according to the anatomical site affected, except for chapters that refer to mental disorders; complications of pregnancy, childbirth and the puerperium; congenital malformations; and conditions originating in the perinatal period. Finally, an entire chapter is devoted to symptoms, signs, and abnormal findings.

4.3.1 Maternal mortality

According to the tenth revision of the ICD, "Maternal death" is defined as the death of a woman while pregnant or within 42 days of termination of pregnancy, irrespective of the duration and the site of the pregnancy, from any cause related to or aggravated by the pregnancy or its management but not from accidental or incidental causes.

"Maternal deaths" should be subdivided into direct and indirect obstetric deaths. Direct obstetric deaths are those resulting from obstetric complications of the pregnant state (pregnancy, labour and puerperium), from interventions, omissions, incorrect treatment, or from a chain of events resulting from any of the above. Indirect obstetric deaths are those resulting from previous existing disease or disease that developed during pregnancy and which was not due to direct obstetric causes, but which was aggravated by physiologic effects of pregnancy.

While the denominator for the maternal mortality ratio theoretically should be the number of pregnant women, it is impossible to determine the number of pregnant women. A further recommendation by the tenth revision is therefore that maternal mortality ratios be expressed per 100,000 live births or per 100,000 total births (live births and foetal deaths). The maternal mortality ratio calculated here is expressed per 100,000 live births. Although live births do not represent an unbiased estimate of pregnant women, this figure is more reliable than other estimates, in particular, live births are more accurately registered than live births plus foetal deaths.

---

[1] There are two exceptions – the 1978 and 1991 issues, which were disseminated in separate volumes from the respective regular issues.

[2] United Nations, Department of Economic and Social Affairs, Population Division (2015). *2015 Revision of World Population Prospects* (http://esa.un.org/unpd/wpp/).

[3] ST/ESA/STAT/SER.M/49/Rev.4/WWW ; http://unstats.un.org/unsd/methods/m49/m49.htm; see also Standard Country or Area Codes for Statistical Use, Sales No. M.98.XVII.9, United Nations, New York, 1999.

[4] Sales No. E.07.XVII.8, United Nations, New York, 2007.

[5] Ibid, para. 2.135.

[6] Alternatively, if a population register is used, completed ages are calculated by subtracting the date of birth of individuals listed in the register from a reference date to which the age data pertain.

[7] A source of non-comparability may result from differences in the method of reckoning age, for example, the Western versus the Eastern or, as it is usually known, the English versus the Chinese system. By the latter, a child is considered one year old at birth and advances an additional year at each Chinese New Year. The effect of this system is most obvious at the beginning of the age span, where the frequencies in the under-one-year category are markedly understated. The effect on higher age groups is not so apparent. Distributions constructed on this basis are often adjusted before publication, but the possibility of such aberrations should not be excluded when census data by age are compared.

[8] Sales No. E.13.XVII.10, United Nations, New York, 2014.

[9]   Sales No. E.98.XVII.7, United Nations, New York, 1998.

[10] Sales No. E.98.XVII.11, United Nations, New York, 1998.

[11] Sales No. E.98.XVII.4, United Nations, New York, 1998.

[12] Sales No. E.98.XVII.6, United Nations, New York, 1998.

[13] Sales No. E.98.XVII.10, United Nations, New York, 1998.

[14] Sales No. E.03.XVII.11, United Nations, New York, 2004.

[15] *International Statistical Classification of Diseases and Related Health Problems*, Tenth Revision, Volume 2, World Health Organization, Geneva, 1992.

INTRODUCTION

L'Annuaire démographique est un recueil de statistiques démographiques internationales qui est établi par la Division de statistique du Département des affaires économiques et sociales de l'Organisation des Nations Unies. Il fait partie d'un ensemble de publications complémentaires publiées par l'Organisation des Nations Unies et les institutions spécialisées, qui ont pour objet de fournir des statistiques aux démographes, aux économistes, aux spécialistes de la santé publique et aux sociologues. Grâce à la coopération des services nationaux de statistique, il a été possible de faire figurer dans la présente édition de *l'Annuaire démographique* les statistiques officielles disponibles pour plus de 230 pays ou zones du monde entier.

L'Annuaire démographique 2014 est la soixante-cinquième édition d'une série que publie l'ONU depuis 1948. Le présent volume comprend un aperçu mondial des statistiques démographiques de base et des tableaux qui regroupent des statistiques sur la dimension, la répartition et les tendances de la population, la natalité, la mortalité fœtale, la mortalité infantile et la mortalité liée à la maternité, la mortalité générale, la nuptialité et la divortialité. Des données classées selon le lieu de résidence (zone urbaine ou rurale) sont présentées dans un grand nombre de tableaux. *L'Annuaire démographique* contient des notes techniques, un tableau synoptique, un index historique et une liste des éditions de *l'Annuaire démographique* publiées jusqu'à présent. Cette édition de *l'Annuaire démographique* contient les données disponibles couvrant les années de référence jusqu'à 2014.

La présente édition de *l'Annuaire démographique* comprend comme un sujet spécial le tableau 3a avec l'indice de Whipple selon le sexe et la résidence urbaine/rurale pour les trois derniers cycles de recensements de la population, à savoir les recensements de la population effectués dans le monde entier depuis 1985. L'indice de Whipple est un indice de préférence pour certains âges dans la déclaration de l'âge et peut donc servir à mettre en évidence certaines des difficultés liées à la répartition par âge.

Les notes techniques sur les tableaux statistiques sont destinées à aider le lecteur. Le tableau A, qui correspond au tableau synoptique, donne un aperçu de l''exhaustivité des données publiées dans la présente édition de *l'Annuaire démographique*. Un index cumulatif donne des renseignements sur les matières traitées dans chacune des 64 éditions et sur les années sur lesquelles portent les données. Les numéros de vente des éditions antérieures et une liste des sujets spéciaux traités dans les différentes éditions sont indiqués aux pages iii et iv.

Jusqu'à la 48e édition (1996), chaque édition se composait de deux parties : les tableaux de caractère général et ceux sur des sujets spéciaux, publiés dans le même volume[1]. À partir de 49e édition (1997), les tableaux sur les sujets spéciaux ont été publiés dans un format numérique en tant que suppléments à *l'Annuaire démographique*. Deux CD-ROM ont été produits : *l'Annuaire démographique : Supplément historique*, qui présente un grand nombre de statistiques démographiques pour la période allant de 1948 à 1997, et *l'Annuaire démographique : Statistiques de la natalité*, qui contient des tableaux détaillés sur la natalité pour la période allant de 1980 à 1998. Par la suite, trois volumes concernant *l'Annuaire démographique* consacrés à des thèmes de recensement spéciaux pour le cycle de recensements de 2000 ont été publiés en ligne à l'adresse suivante : http://unstats.un.org/unsd/demographic/products/dyb/dybcens.htm. Les données actuelles sur les thèmes du recensement de *l'Annuaire démographique* pour les années de référence entre 1995 et aujourd'hui, lorsqu'elles sont disponibles, sont présentées sur http://unstats.un.org/unsd/demographic/products/dyb/dybcensusdata.htm. Ils comprennent des données sur la population selon les principales caractéristiques démographiques, scolaires, ethnoculturelles et économiques, les caractéristiques des ménages ainsi que des données sur les étrangers dans le pays ou les personnes nées à l'étranger. Particulièrement, on a présenté sous forme de table aux adresses suivantes, les données des recensements pour les années de référence entre 1995 et aujourd'hui, qui portent sur les thèmes des caractéristiques des ménages et des caractéristiques économiques : http://unstats.un.org/unsd/demographic/products/dyb/dyb_Household/dyb_household.htm et http://unstats.un.org/unsd/demographic/products/dyb/dyb_Eco/dyb_eco.htm

Les statistiques sur la population ne sont pas disponibles pour tous les pays et zones pour plusieurs raisons. Deux annexes sont présentées afin d'offrir des estimations sur la population en milieu d'année et un aperçu des statistiques de l'état civil pour chaque pays ou zone. La première porte sur des estimations concernant la population pour la période 2005-2014. La seconde présente les estimations des variantes moyennes concernant les taux bruts de natalité et de mortalité, la mortalité infantile, les indicateurs synthétiques de fécondité et l'espérance de vie à la naissance pour la période 2010-2015. Ces données ont été établies par la Division de la population de l'ONU et publiées dans les *Perspectives de la population mondiale : La révision de 2015*[2].

Les statistiques démographiques figurant dans la présente édition de l'*Annuaire démographique* sont disponibles en ligne sur les pages Web consacrées à *l'Annuaire démographique* :

. On trouvera également des renseignements sur le programme de collecte et de diffusion des données de la Division de statistique sur le même site. Il est possible de se procurer d'autres données en contactant la Division de statistique du Département des affaires économiques et sociales de l'Organisation des Nations Unies à l'adresse suivante : demostat@un.org.

NOTES TECHNIQUES SUR LES TABLEAUX STATISTIQUES

1. REMARQUES D'ORDRE GÉNÉRAL

1.1 Notes techniques

Les notes techniques ont pour but de donner au lecteur des informations pertinentes en lien avec les tableaux statistiques. Les renseignements qui concernent l'*Annuaire démographique* en général sont présentés dans des sections portant sur diverses considérations géographiques, sur la population et sur les statistiques de natalité et de mortalité. Les tableaux sont ensuite commentés séparément et l'on trouvera pour chacun une description des variables et des observations sur la fiabilité et les lacunes des données ainsi que sur les pays et zones visés et sur les données publiées antérieurement. Des détails sont également donnés, le cas échéant, sur le mode de calcul des taux, quotients et pourcentages.

1.2 Tableaux

Dans la mesure du possible, la numérotation des tableaux dans les éditions successives de *l'Annuaire démographique* est préservée. Comme la numérotation des tableaux ne correspond pas exactement à celle des éditions précédentes, il est recommandé de se reporter à l'index qui figure à la fin du présent ouvrage pour trouver les données publiées dans les précédentes éditions.

1.3 Origine des données

Sauf indication contraire, les statistiques présentées dans *l'Annuaire démographique* sont des données nationales fournies par les organismes de statistique officiels. Elles sont recueillies essentiellement au moyen de questionnaires qui sont envoyés tous les ans à plus de 230 services nationaux de statistique. Les données communiquées en réponse à ces questionnaires sont complétées, dans toute la mesure possible, par des données tirées de publications nationales officielles et des sites web d'organismes officiels et des renseignements communiqués par les services nationaux de statistique à la demande de l'ONU. Pour que les données soient comparables, les taux, rapports et pourcentages ont été calculés par la Division de statistique de l'ONU, à l'exception des paramètres des tables de mortalité et des indicateurs synthétiques de fécondité ainsi que des taux bruts de natalité et de mortalité pour certains pays et zones, qui ont été dûment signalés en note. Les méthodes suivies par la Division pour le calcul des taux et rapports sont décrites dans les notes techniques relatives à chaque tableau. Les chiffres de population utilisés pour ces calculs sont ceux qui figurent dans la présente édition de *l'Annuaire démographique* ou qui ont paru dans des éditions antérieures.

Chaque fois que l'on constatera des différences entre les données du présent volume et celles des éditions antérieures de *l'Annuaire démographique*, ou de certaines publications apparentées, on pourra en conclure que les statistiques publiées cette année sont des chiffres révisés communiqués à la Division de statistique avant juin 2015.

2. CONSIDÉRATIONS GÉOGRAPHIQUES

2.1 Portée

Des données sont présentées sur tous les pays ou zones qui en ont communiquées. Le tableau 3, le plus complet, contient des données sur la population et la superficie de chaque pays ou zone ayant une population d'au moins 50 habitants. Ces pays ou zones ne figurent pas tous dans les tableaux qui suivent. Dans bien des cas, les données requises pour un tableau particulier n'étaient pas disponibles. En général, les pays ou zones qui peuvent fournir des données sont d'autant moins nombreux que les données demandées sont plus détaillées.

De plus les taux et rapports ne sont présentés que pour les pays ou zones ayant communiqué des chiffres correspondant à un nombre minimal de faits considérés. Les minimums sont indiqués dans les notes techniques relatives à chacun des tableaux.

À l'exception des données récapitulatives présentées dans les tableaux 1 et 2 pour l'ensemble du monde et les grandes zones et régions et des données relatives aux capitales et aux villes de 100 000 habitants ou plus dans le tableau 8, toutes les données se rapportent aux pays. Le nombre de pays sur lequel porte chacun des tableaux est indiqué dans le tableau A.

2.2 Composition territoriale

Autant que possible, toutes les données, y compris les séries chronologiques, se rapportent au territoire de 2014. Les exceptions à cette règle sont signalées en note à la fin des tableaux. Des clarifications importantes sont présentées ci-dessous.

Les données relatives au **Danemark** ne comprennent pas les Iles Féroé et le Groenland, qui font l'objet de rubriques distinctes.

Les données relatives à la **Finlande** comprennent les Îles d'Åland, sauf indication contraire en note de bas de page.

Les données relatives à la **France** ne comprennent pas les départements d'outre-mer, à savoir, la Guyane française, Guadeloupe, la Martinique et La Réunion, qui font l'objet de rubriques distinctes, sauf indication contraire en note de bas de page.

Les données relatives au **Royaume-Uni de Grande-Bretagne et d'Irlande du Nord** ne comprennent pas la Guernesey, l'île de Man et Jersey, qui font l'objet de rubriques distinctes.

Les données relatives au **Sahara Occidental** comprennent la région septentrionale (ancien Saguia-el-Hamra) et la région méridionale (ancien Rio de Oro).

2.3 Nomenclature

En règle générale, pour gagner de la place, on a jugé commode de désigner dans les tableaux les pays ou zones par les noms abrégés couramment utilisés par l'Organisation des Nations Unies[3], les désignations complètes n'étant utilisées que lorsqu'il n'existait pas de forme abrégée. La liste des désignations des pays ou zones est disponible à l'adresse suivante : http://unstats.un.org/unsd/methods/m49/m49alphaf.htm.

2.3.1 Ordre de présentation

Les pays ou zones sont classés dans l'ordre alphabétique anglais et regroupés par continent comme ci-après : Afrique, Amérique du Nord, Amérique du Sud, Asie, Europe et Océanie.

Les appellations employées dans la présente édition et la présentation des données qui y figurent n'ont d'autre objet que de donner un cadre géographique commode aux séries statistiques. La même observation vaut pour toutes les notes et précisions concernant les unités géographiques pour lesquelles des données sont présentées.

2.4 Superficie

Les données relatives à la superficie qui figurent dans les tableaux 1 et 3 représentent la superficie totale, c'est-à-dire qu'elles englobent les terres émergées et les eaux intérieures (qui sont censées comprendre les principaux lacs et cours d'eau), mais excluent les régions polaires et les îles inhabitées. Les données relatives à la superficie correspondent aux chiffres estimatifs les plus récents. Les superficies sont toutes exprimées en kilomètres carrés ; les chiffres qui avaient été communiqués en miles carrés ont été convertis au moyen d'un coefficient de 2,589988.

2.4.1 Comparabilité dans le temps

La révision des estimations antérieures de la superficie, des augmentations effectives de la superficie terrestre due par exemple à des travaux d'assèchement, à des rectifications de frontières, à des changements d'interprétation du concept de « terres émergées » ou à l'utilisation de nouvelles unités de mesure peut avoir des incidences sur la comparabilité dans le temps des estimations relatives à la superficie d'un pays ou d'une zone donnés. Dans la plupart des cas, il a été possible de déterminer la raison de ces révisions; toutefois, même lorsque la raison n'était pas connue, on a remplacé les anciens chiffres par les nouveaux et on a généralement admis que ce sont ces derniers qui sont exacts.

2.4.2 Comparabilité internationale

Le manque de comparabilité internationale entre les données relatives à la superficie est dû principalement à des différences de définition. En particulier, la définition des golfes, baies et criques, lacs et cours d'eau varie sensiblement d'un pays à l'autre. La diversité des méthodes employées pour estimer les superficies nuit elle aussi à la comparabilité internationale. Certaines données proviennent de levés effectués selon des méthodes scientifiques modernes ; d'autres ne représentent que des conjectures reposant sur diverses catégories de renseignements. Certains chiffres sont récents, d'autres pas. Étant donné que ni la méthode de calcul de la superficie ni la composition du territoire et la date à laquelle se rapportent les données ne sont connues avec précision pour tous les pays ou zones, les estimations figurant dans le tableau 3 ne doivent pas être considérées comme rigoureusement comparables d'un pays ou d'une zone à une autre.

3. POPULATION

Les statistiques de la population, c'est-à-dire celles qui se rapportent à la dimension, à la répartition géographique et aux caractéristiques démographiques de la population, sont présentées dans un certain nombre de tableaux de l'Annuaire démographique.

Les tableaux 1 et 2 présentent respectivement des estimations récapitulatives de milieu d'année de la population du monde, des grandes zones et régions, pour certaines années présélectionnées, ainsi que de sa répartition selon l'âge et le sexe pour l'année 2014.

Les données concernant les pays ou les zones représentent les résultats de recensements de population, des estimations fondées sur les résultats d'enquêtes par sondage (s'il n'y a pas eu recensement), des estimations postcensitaires ou intercensitaires, ou des estimations établies à partir de données provenant des registres permanents de population. Dans la présente édition, le tableau 3 indique pour chaque pays ou zone le chiffre le plus récent de la population totale issu du dernier recensement et des estimations établies au milieu de l'année 2010 et de l'année 2014. Le tableau 5 contient des estimations de la population totale au milieu de chaque année pendant 10 ans (2005-2014), et le tableau 6 des estimations de la population urbaine et de la population totale, par sexe, au milieu de chaque année pendant 10 ans (2005-2014). Les dernières données disponibles sur la répartition de la population selon l'âge, le sexe et le lieu de résidence (zone urbaine ou rurale) sont présentées dans le tableau 7. Les derniers chiffres disponibles sur la population des capitales et des villes de 100 000 habitants ou plus sont regroupés dans le tableau 8.

On a utilisé pour le calcul des taux les statistiques de la population totale et de la population répartie selon l'âge, le sexe ou le lieu de résidence (zone urbaine ou rurale). Les taux démographiques selon la résidence (urbaine/rurale), l'âge ou le sexe ont été calculés à partir des données présentées dans les tableaux 6 ou 7 de la présente édition ou dans les tableaux correspondants d'éditions précédentes de l'Annuaire démographique.

3.1 Sources de variation des données

Plusieurs facteurs influent sur la comparabilité des données : 1) la définition de la population totale ; 2) les définitions utilisées pour faire la distinction entre population urbaine et population rurale ; 3) les difficultés liées aux déclarations d'âge ; 4) l'étendue du surdénombrement ou du sous-dénombrement dans le recensement le plus récent ou dans une autre source de statistiques de référence sur la population ; 5) la qualité des estimations relatives à la population. Ces cinq facteurs sont analysés en détail aux sections 3.1.1 à 3.2 ci-après. D'autres questions seront traitées dans les notes techniques relatives à chaque tableau. Pour plus de précisions concernant, notamment, les notions fondamentales de dimension, de répartition et de caractéristiques de la population qui ont été élaborées par l'Organisation des Nations Unies, le lecteur est invité à se reporter aux Principes et recommandations concernant les recensements de la population et de l'habitat, Révision 2[4].

3.1.1 Population totale

Le principal obstacle à la comparabilité des données relatives à la population totale est la différence qui existe entre population de fait et population de droit. La population de fait comprend toutes les personnes présentes dans le pays ou la zone à la date de référence, tandis que la population de droit comprend toutes celles qui résident habituellement dans le pays ou la zone, qu'elles y aient été ou non présentes à la date de référence. Par définition, la population totale de fait et la population totale de droit ne sont donc pas rigoureusement comparables entre elles.

Même lorsque l'on veut comparer deux totaux qui se rapportent à des populations de fait ou deux totaux qui se rapportent à des populations de droit, on risque souvent de faire des erreurs pour cette raison qu'il est rare que l'une et l'autre notions soient appliquées strictement. Pour citer quelques exemples, certains chiffres qui sont censés porter sur la population de fait ne tiennent pas compte du personnel militaire, naval et diplomatique étranger en fonction dans le pays ou la zone, ni des membres de leurs familles et de leurs ménages; d'autres ne comprennent pas les visiteurs étrangers de passage dans le pays ou la zone ni les personnes à bord de navires ancrés dans des ports. En revanche, il arrive que l'on compte des personnes, inscrits maritimes et marins pêcheurs par exemple, qui, en raison de leur activité professionnelle, se trouvent hors du pays ou de la zone de recensement.

Les risques de disparités sont encore plus grands quand il s'agit de comparer des populations de droit, car les comparaisons dépendent au premier chef de la définition que l'on donne à l'expression « lieu de résidence habituel », qui varie d'un pays ou d'une zone à l'autre et qu'il est, de toute façon, difficile d'appliquer uniformément pour le dénombrement lors d'un recensement ou d'une enquête. Par exemple, les civils étrangers qui se trouvent temporairement dans un pays ou une zone comme travailleurs à court terme peuvent officiellement être considérés comme résidents après un séjour d'une durée déterminée, mais ils peuvent aussi être considérés comme non-résidents pendant toute la durée de leur séjour ; ailleurs, ces mêmes personnes peuvent être considérées officiellement comme résidents ou comme non-résidents du pays ou de la zone d'où elles viennent, selon la durée et, éventuellement, la raison de leur absence. Qui plus est, quel que soit son statut officiel, chacun des recensés peut, au moment de l'enquête, interpréter à sa façon la notion de résidence. De plus, les autorités nationales ou les entités responsables des zones ne savent pas toutes avec la même précision combien de leurs résidents se trouvent temporairement à l'étranger.

Les chiffres de population présentés dans les tableaux de l'*Annuaire démographique* représentent la population de fait ou la population de droit. Lorsque l'on savait que les données avaient été recueillies selon une définition de la population de fait ou de la population de droit qui s'écartait sensiblement de celle exposée plus haut, on l'a signalé en note, de manière à compenser dans toute la mesure possible les conséquences des divergences.

Il peut y avoir hétérogénéité dans les statistiques d'un même pays ou d'une même zone dans le cas des pays ou zones qui ne font une exploitation statistique détaillée des données que pour la population de droit alors qu'ils recueillent des données sur la population de droit et sur la population de fait à l'occasion d'un recensement, par exemple. Ainsi, tandis que les chiffres relatifs à la population totale qui figurent au tableau 3 se rapportent à la population de fait, ceux des tableaux qui présentent des données sur diverses caractéristiques de la population, par exemple le lieu de résidence (zone urbaine ou rurale), l'âge et le sexe, peuvent être basés sur le concept de la population de droit.

3.1.2 Lieu de résidence (zone urbaine ou rurale)

L'hétérogénéité des définitions nationales du terme « urbain » nuit considérablement à la comparabilité internationale des données concernant la répartition selon le lieu de résidence. Les définitions utilisées par les différents pays ou zones et leurs implications sont exposées à la fin des notes techniques correspondant au tableau 6.

3.1.3 Répartition par âge

La répartition de la population selon l'âge est un paramètre fondamental de la plupart des analyses, estimations et projections relatives aux statistiques de la population. Malheureusement, ces données sont sujettes à un certain nombre d'erreurs et difficilement comparables. C'est pourquoi pratiquement tous les utilisateurs de ces statistiques doivent considérer ces répartitions avec la plus grande circonspection.

3.1.3.1 Collecte et exploitation des données sur l'âge

L'âge est l'intervalle de temps déterminé par calcul ou par estimation qui sépare la date de naissance de la date du recensement et qui est exprimé en années solaires révolues[5]. Les données sur l'âge peuvent être recueillies selon deux méthodes : la première consiste à obtenir la date de naissance de chaque personne à l'occasion d'un recensement ou d'un sondage, puis à calculer l'âge en années révolues en soustrayant la date de naissance de celle du dénombrement[6]. La seconde consiste à enregistrer l'âge en années révolues au moment du recensement, c'est-à-dire l'âge au dernier anniversaire.

La méthode recommandée consiste à calculer l'âge au dernier anniversaire en soustrayant la date exacte de la naissance de la date du recensement. Toutefois, on n'a pas toujours recours à cette méthode ; certains pays ou zones calculent l'âge en faisant la différence entre l'année du recensement et l'année de la naissance. Lorsque les données sur l'âge ont été établies de cette façon, on l'a signalé chaque fois que possible par une note. On peut d'ailleurs s'en rendre compte dans une certaine mesure, car les chiffres dans la catégorie des moins d'un an sont plus faibles qu'ils ne devraient l'être. Cependant, un nombre irrégulier de naissances d'une année à l'autre ou l'omission de certains âges parmi les moins d'un an peut aussi fausser les chiffres de la population de moins d'un an.

Les causes d'erreurs dans les données sur l'âge sont diverses : on peut citer notamment l'ignorance de l'âge exact, la déclaration d'années d'âge correspondant à un calendrier différent de celui des années solaires révolues depuis la naissance[7], la négligence dans les déclarations et dans la façon dont elles sont consignées, la tendance générale à déclarer des âges se terminant par certains chiffres tels que 0, 2, 5 ou 8, la tendance pour les personnes âgées à exagérer leur âge, une aversion subconsciente pour certains nombres, et les fausses déclarations faites délibérément.

Les causes d'erreurs mentionnées ci-dessus, communes à la plupart des enquêtes sur l'âge et à la plupart des pays ou zones, peuvent nuire sensiblement à la comparabilité.

À cause des difficultés indiquées ci-dessus, les répartitions par âge et par sexe de la population d'un grand nombre de pays ou de zones font apparaître les irrégularités suivantes : 1) sous-estimation des groupes d'âge correspondant aux enfants de moins d'un an et aux jeunes enfants ; 2) polarisation des déclarations sur les âges se terminant par les chiffres 0 ou 5 (c'est-à-dire 5, 10, 15, 20...) ; 3) prépondérance des âges pairs (par exemple 10, 12, 14...) au détriment des âges impairs (par exemple 11, 13, 15...) ; 4) écart considérable et surprenant entre le rapport masculin/féminin à certains âges ; 5) différences importantes et difficilement explicables entre les données concernant des groupes d'âge voisins. En comparant les statistiques provenant de recensements successifs pour des cohortes identiques sur le plan de l'âge et de la répartition par sexe et en étudiant la répartition par âge et par sexe de la population à chaque recensement, on peut déceler l'existence de ces incohérences et de quelques autres, un certain nombre d'entre elles se retrouvant à des degrés divers même dans les recensements les plus modernes.

La présente édition de l'*Annuaire démographique* comprend comme un sujet spécial le tableau 3a avec l'indice de Whipple selon le sexe et la résidence urbaine/rurale pour les trois derniers cycles de recensements de la population, à savoir les recensements de la population effectués dans le monde entier depuis 1985. L'indice de Whipple est un indice de préférence pour certains âges dans la déclaration de l'âge et peut donc servir à mettre en évidence certaines des difficultés liées à la répartition par âge.

4. STATISTIQUES DE L'ÉTAT CIVIL

Aux fins de l'*Annuaire démographique*, on entend par statistiques de l'état civil les statistiques des naissances vivantes, des décès, des morts fœtales, des mariages et des divorces.

Dans le présent volume de l'*Annuaire démographique*, on a présenté des tableaux sur la natalité, la mortalité, la nuptialité et la divortialité. Les tableaux consacrés à la mortalité sont groupés sous les rubriques suivantes : mortalité fœtale, mortalité infantile, mortalité liée à la maternité et mortalité générale.

4.1 Sources de variations des données

La plupart des statistiques de l'état civil publiées dans le présent volume de l'*Annuaire démographique* émanent des systèmes nationaux d'enregistrement des faits d'état civil. Le degré d'exhaustivité et d'exactitude de ces données varie d'un pays ou d'une zone à l'autre.

Il n'existe pas partout de système national d'enregistrement des faits d'état civil et, dans quelques cas, seuls certains faits sont enregistrés. Par exemple, dans certains pays ou zones, seuls les naissances et les décès sont enregistrés. Il existe également des différences quant au degré d'efficacité avec lequel les lois relatives à l'enregistrement des faits d'état civil sont appliquées dans les divers pays ou zones. La fiabilité des statistiques provenant des registres d'état civil dépend des modalités d'application de la loi et de la mesure dans laquelle le public s'y soumet.

Il est à signaler que dans certains cas les statistiques de la nuptialité et de la divortialité sont tirées d'autres sources que les registres d'état civil. Dans certains pays ou zones, par exemple, les seules données disponibles sur la nuptialité proviennent des registres des églises. Selon la pratique suivie par chaque pays, les statistiques de la divortialité sont tirées des actes des tribunaux et/ou des registres d'état civil. L'officier de l'état civil, le service national de statistique ou d'autres services administratifs peuvent être chargés d'établir ces statistiques.

Les autres facteurs qui influent sur la comparabilité internationale des statistiques de l'état civil sont à peu près les mêmes que ceux qu'il convient de prendre en considération pour interpréter les variations observées dans les statistiques de la population. La définition des faits d'état civil aux fins de statistique, la portée des données du point de vue géographique et ethnique ainsi que les méthodes d'exploitation des données sont autant d'éléments qui peuvent influer sur la comparabilité.

En plus des statistiques tirées des registres d'état civil, l'*Annuaire démographique* présente des statistiques de l'état civil qui sont des estimations officielles nationales, fondées souvent sur les résultats de sondages ou des recensements de la population. Aussi leur comparabilité varie-t-elle en fonction du degré d'exhaustivité des déclarations recueillies lors des recensements de la population ou d'enquêtes sur les ménages, des erreurs d'échantillonnage ou autres, et des distorsions d'origines diverses.

Pour plus de détails sur les normes d'établissement des statistiques d'état civil, le lecteur pourra se reporter aux : *Principes et recommandations pour un système de statistiques de l'état civil, troisième révision*[8] ; *Manuel des systèmes d'enregistrement des faits d'état civil et de statistiques de l'état civil : Élaboration d'un cadre juridique*[9] ; *Manuel des systèmes d'enregistrement des faits d'état civil et de statistiques de l'état civil : Gestion, fonctionnement et tenue*[10] ; *Manuel des systèmes d'enregistrement des faits d'état civil et de statistiques de l'état civil : Élaboration de programmes d'information, d'éducation et de communication*[11] ; *Manuel des systèmes d'enregistrement des faits d'état civil et de statistiques de l'état civil : Principes et protocoles concernant la communication et l'archivage des documents individuels*[12]; *Manuel des systèmes d'enregistrement des faits d'état civil et de statistiques de l'état civil : Informatisation*[13]. Le *Manuel de collecte de données sur la fécondité et la mortalité*[14] fournit des informations ayant trait à la collecte et à l'évaluation des données sur la fécondité, sur la mortalité et sur d'autres faits d'état civil, qui ont été recueillies au cours des enquêtes sur les ménages. Ces publications sont également disponibles sur le Web à partir de l'adresse suivante : http://unstats.un.org/unsd/demographic/standmeth/handbooks/default.htm.

4.1.1 Définition des faits d'état civil aux fins de la statistique

Une cause importante d'hétérogénéité dans les données est le manque d'uniformité des définitions des différents faits d'état civil. Aux fins de *l'Annuaire démographique*, il est recommandé de recueillir les données relatives aux faits d'état civil en utilisant les définitions établies au Chapitre I des *Principes et recommandations pour un système de statistiques de l'état civil, troisième révision*[8]. Ces définitions sont les suivantes :

La NAISSANCE VIVANTE est l'expulsion ou l'extraction complète du corps de la mère, indépendamment de la durée de la gestation, d'un produit de la conception qui, après cette séparation, respire ou manifeste tout autre signe de vie, tel que battement de cœur, pulsation du cordon ombilical ou contraction effective d'un muscle soumis à l'action de la volonté, que le cordon ombilical ait été coupé ou non et que le placenta soit ou non demeuré attaché ; tout produit d'une telle naissance est considéré comme « enfant né vivant ».

Le DÉCÈS est la disparition permanente de tout signe de vie à un moment quelconque postérieur à la naissance vivante (cessation des fonctions vitales après la naissance sans possibilité de réanimation). Cette définition ne comprend pas les morts fœtales.

La MORT FŒTALE est le décès d'un produit de la conception lorsque ce décès est survenu avant l'expulsion ou l'extraction complète du corps de la mère, indépendamment de la durée de la gestation. Le décès est indiqué par le fait qu'après cette séparation le fœtus ne respire ni ne manifeste aucun signe de vie, tel que battement de cœur, pulsation du cordon ombilical ou contraction effective d'un muscle soumis à l'action de la volonté.

Le MARIAGE est l'acte, la cérémonie ou la procédure qui établit un rapport légal entre les époux. L'union peut être rendue légale par une procédure civile ou religieuse, ou par toute autre procédure, conformément à la législation du pays.

Le DIVORCE est la dissolution légale et définitive des liens du mariage, c'est-à-dire la séparation des époux qui confère aux parties le droit de se remarier civilement ou religieusement, ou selon toute autre procédure, conformément à la législation du pays.

En plus de ces notions définies internationalement, l'*Annuaire démographique* recueille et met à disposition ces données sur les avortements :

Par référence à la femme, l'AVORTEMENT se définit comme toute interruption de grossesse qui est survenue avant 28 semaines de gestation et dont le produit est un fœtus mort. Il existe deux grandes catégories d'avortement : l'avortement spontané et l'avortement provoqué. L'avortement provoqué a pour origine une action délibérée entreprise en vue d'interrompre une grossesse. Tout autre avortement est considéré comme spontané.

4.1.2 Problèmes posés par les définitions établies

Les variations par rapport aux définitions établies des faits d'état civil sont le principal obstacle à la comparabilité internationale des statistiques de l'état civil. Un exemple en est fourni par le cas des naissances vivantes et celui des morts fœtales. Dans certains pays ou zones, il faut que le nouveau-né ait vécu 24 heures pour pouvoir être inscrit sur le registre des naissances vivantes. Les décès d'enfants qui surviennent avant l'expiration du délai de 24 heures sont classés parmi les morts fœtales tardives et, en l'absence de méthodes spéciales d'exploitation des données, ne sont comptés ni dans les naissances vivantes ni dans les décès. De même, dans plusieurs autres pays ou zones, les décès d'enfants nés vivants et décédés avant l'enregistrement de leur naissance sont également comptés parmi les morts fœtales tardives.

À moins que des méthodes spéciales n'aient été adoptées pour l'exploitation de ces données, les statistiques des naissances vivantes et des décès ne tiendront pas compte de ces cas, qui viendront en revanche accroître d'autant le nombre des morts fœtales tardives. Le taux de mortalité infantile sera donc sous-estimé. Bien que les éléments constitutifs du taux (décès d'enfants de moins d'un an et naissances vivantes) accusent exactement la même insuffisance en valeur absolue, les lacunes sont proportionnellement plus fortes pour les décès de moins d'un an, ce qui cause des erreurs plus importantes dans les taux de mortalité infantile.

De plus, cette pratique augmente les rapports de mortinatalité. Quelques pays ou zones effectuent les ajustements nécessaires pour corriger cette anomalie (du moins dans les fréquences totales) au moment de l'établissement des tableaux. Si aucun ajustement n'a été effectué, cela est indiqué dans les notes chaque fois que possible.

Les définitions du mariage et du divorce posent aussi un problème du point de vue de la comparabilité internationale. Contrairement à la naissance et au décès, qui sont des faits biologiques, le mariage et le divorce sont uniquement déterminés par la législation et la coutume et, de ce fait, il est moins facile d'en donner une définition statistique qui ait une application universelle. À des fins statistiques, ces notions ont donc été définies de manière générale par référence à la législation de chaque pays ou zone. La législation relative au mariage et plus particulièrement au divorce varie d'un pays ou d'une zone à l'autre. En ce qui concerne le mariage, l'âge de nubilité est la condition la plus fréquemment requise, mais il arrive souvent que d'autres conditions soient exigées.

Lorsqu'il est connu, l'âge minimum auquel le mariage peut avoir lieu avec le consentement des parents (et dans certains cas sans le consentement des parents) est indiqué au tableau 23-1. Les lois et règlements relatifs à la dissolution du mariage par le divorce vont de l'interdiction absolue, en passant par diverses conditions requises pour l'obtention du divorce, jusqu'à la simple déclaration, par l'épouse, de son désir ou de son intention de divorcer.

4.1.3 Couverture géographique ou ethnique fragmentaire

En principe, les statistiques de l'état civil devraient s'étendre à l'ensemble du pays ou de la zone auxquels elles se rapportent et englober tous les groupes ethniques. En fait, il n'est pas rare que les données soient fragmentaires. Dans certains pays ou zones, l'enregistrement n'est obligatoire que pour une petite partie de la population, par exemple pour certains groupes ethniques. Dans d'autres, il n'existe pas de disposition qui prescrive l'enregistrement obligatoire sur le plan national, mais seulement des règlements ou décrets des municipalités ou des États, qui ne s'appliquent pas à l'ensemble du territoire. Il en est encore autrement dans d'autres pays ou zones où les autorités ont institué une zone d'enregistrement comprenant seulement une partie du territoire, le reste étant exclu en raison des difficultés d'accès ou parce qu'il est pratiquement impossible, pour des raisons d'ordre économique ou culturel, d'y procéder à un enregistrement régulier.

4.1.4 Méthodes de présentation des données

4.1.4.1 Selon le lieu de l'événement

Les statistiques de l'état civil qui sont présentées pour l'ensemble du territoire national se rapportent à la population de fait ou population présente. En conséquence, sauf indication contraire, les statistiques de l'état civil relatives à une zone ou à un pays donné portent sur tous les faits survenus dans l'ensemble de la population, à l'intérieur des frontières actuelles de la zone ou du pays considéré. On peut donc estimer qu'elles englobent les faits d'état civil survenus dans les tribus nomades et parmi les populations autochtones ainsi que parmi les ressortissants du pays et les étrangers. Des notes signalent les exceptions lorsque celles-ci sont connues.

Pour certains pays, les écarts entre les taux démographiques pour les zones urbaines et pour les zones rurales peuvent varier notablement selon que les faits d'état civil ont été exploités sur la base du lieu de l'événement ou du lieu de résidence habituel. Par exemple, si un nombre appréciable de femmes résidant dans des zones rurales proches de grands centres urbains accouchent dans les hôpitaux ou maternités d'une ville, les taux de fécondité ainsi que les taux de mortalité néo-natale et infantile seront généralement plus élevés dans les zones urbaines (et par conséquent plus faibles dans les zones rurales) si les faits sont exploités en se fondant sur le lieu de l'événement et non sur le lieu de résidence habituel. Le phénomène sera le même dans le cas de la mortalité générale si un bon nombre de personnes résidant dans des zones rurales font appel aux services de santé des villes lorsqu'elles sont gravement malades.

4.1.4.2 Selon la date de l'événement ou la date de l'enregistrement

Autant que possible, les statistiques de l'état civil figurant dans *l'Annuaire démographique* se rapportent aux faits survenus pendant l'année considérée et non aux faits enregistrés au cours de ladite année. Bon nombre de pays ou zones, toutefois, exploitent leurs statistiques de l'état civil selon la date de l'enregistrement et non selon la date de l'événement. Comme ces statistiques risquent d'induire en erreur, les pays ou zones dont on sait qu'ils établissent leurs statistiques d'après la date de l'enregistrement sont signalés dans les tableaux par un signe plus « + ». On ne dispose toutefois pas pour tous les pays ou zones de renseignements complets sur la méthode d'exploitation des statistiques de l'état civil et les données sont peut-être exploitées selon la date de l'enregistrement plus souvent que ne le laisserait supposer l'emploi des signes.

Étant donné que la qualité des données est inextricablement liée aux retards dans l'enregistrement, il faudra toujours considérer en même temps le code de qualité qui est décrit à la section 4.2.1 ci-après. Évidemment, si l'enregistrement des naissances est complet et effectué en temps voulu (code « C »), les effets perturbateurs de la méthode consistant à exploiter les données selon la date de l'enregistrement seront pratiquement annulés. De même, s'agissant des statistiques des décès, les effets pourront bien souvent être réduits au minimum dans les pays ou zones où le code sanitaire subordonne la délivrance du permis d'inhumer à l'enregistrement du décès, ce qui tend à hâter l'enregistrement. Quant aux morts fœtales, elles sont généralement déclarées immédiatement ou ne sont pas déclarées du tout. En conséquence, si l'enregistrement se fait dans un délai très court, la différence entre les statistiques établies selon la date de l'événement et celles qui sont établies selon la date de l'enregistrement peut être négligeable. Dans bien des cas, la durée des délais légaux accordés pour l'enregistrement des faits d'état civil est un facteur dont dépend dans une large mesure l'incidence sur la comparabilité de l'exploitation des données selon la date de l'enregistrement.

En ce qui concerne le mariage et le divorce, la pratique consistant à exploiter les statistiques selon la date de l'enregistrement ne pose généralement pas de graves problèmes. Le mariage étant, dans de nombreux pays ou zones, un contrat juridique civil qui, pour être légal, doit être conclu devant un officier de l'état civil, il s'ensuit dans ces pays ou zones l'enregistrement a lieu presque systématiquement au moment de la cérémonie ou immédiatement après. De même, dans de nombreux pays ou zones, le tribunal ou l'autorité qui a prononcé le divorce est seul habilité à enregistrer cet acte, et comme l'acte d'enregistrement figure alors sur les registres du tribunal l'enregistrement suit généralement de peu le jugement.

En revanche, si l'enregistrement n'a lieu qu'avec un certain retard, les statistiques de l'état civil établies selon la date de l'enregistrement ne sont pas comparables sur le plan international. Au mieux, les statistiques par date de l'enregistrement prendront surtout en considération des faits survenus au cours de l'année précédente ; dans les pays ou zones où le système d'enregistrement n'est pas très développé, il y entrera des faits datant de plusieurs années. Il ressort des documents dont on dispose que des retards de plusieurs années dans l'enregistrement des naissances ne sont pas rares, encore que, dans la majorité des cas, les retards ne dépassent pas deux à quatre ans.

Tant que l'enregistrement se fera avec retard, les statistiques fondées sur la date d'enregistrement ne seront comparables sur le plan international ni entre elles ni avec les statistiques établies selon la date de fait d'état civil.

Il convient également de noter que l'exploitation des données selon la date de l'enregistrement ne nuit pas seulement à la comparabilité internationale des statistiques. Même à l'intérieur d'un pays ou d'une zone, le procédé qui consiste à compter les enregistrements et non les faits peut compromettre la comparabilité des chiffres sur une longue période. Si le nombre des faits d'état civil enregistrés varie d'une année à l'autre (par suite de l'application de mesures visant tout particulièrement à encourager l'enregistrement ou parce qu'il est subitement devenu nécessaire de produire le certificat d'une naissance ou d'un décès non enregistré pour l'accomplissement de certaines formalités), les statistiques de l'état civil établies d'après la date de l'enregistrement ne permettent pas de quantifier ni d'analyser l'état et l'évolution de la population. Tout au plus peuvent-elles révéler l'évolution des conditions d'exigibilité de l'acte de naissance, de décès ou de mariage et les fluctuations du volume de travail des bureaux d'état civil. Les statistiques établies selon la date de l'enregistrement peuvent donc ne présenter qu'une utilité très réduite pour des études nationales ou internationales.

4.2 Méthodes utilisées pour indiquer la qualité des statistiques de l'état civil qui sont publiées

La qualité des statistiques de l'état civil peut être évaluée en se fondant sur plusieurs facteurs. Le facteur essentiel est la complétude du système d'enregistrement des faits d'état civil d'après lequel ces statistiques sont établies. Dans certains cas, on constate que les données tirées de l'enregistrement ne sont pas complètes lorsque l'on les utilise pour le calcul des taux. Toutefois, cette observation est valable uniquement lorsque les statistiques présentent des lacunes évidentes, qu'elles sont exploitées d'après la date de l'événement et que l'estimation du chiffre de population pris pour base est exacte. L'exploitation des données d'après la date de l'enregistrement donne souvent des taux qui paraissent exacts, tout simplement parce que le numérateur est artificiellement gonflé par suite de l'inclusion d'enregistrements tardifs ; inversement, il arrive que des taux paraissent vraisemblables parce que l'on a sous-évalué la population étudiée. Il ne faut pas non plus oublier que les renseignements dont on dispose sur les taux de fécondité, de mortalité et de nuptialité considérés comme normaux sont extrêmement sommaires dans un grand nombre de régions du monde et que les cas limites, qui sont les plus difficiles à évaluer, sont fréquents.

4.2.1 Codage qualitatif des statistiques provenant des registres de l'état civil

Dans le questionnaire relatif au mouvement de la population qui leur est envoyé chaque année dans le cadre de l'établissement de *l'Annuaire démographique*, les services nationaux de statistique sont invités à donner leur propre évaluation du degré de complétude des données sur les naissances, les décès, les décès d'enfants de moins d'un an, les morts fœtales tardives, les mariages et les divorces figurant dans leurs registres d'état civil.

D'après les renseignements directement communiqués par les gouvernements ou extraits des questionnaires ou de publications officielles pertinentes, il a été possible de classer les statistiques de l'enregistrement des faits d'état civil (naissances, décès, décès d'enfants de moins d'un an, morts fœtales tardives, mariages et divorces) en trois grandes catégories, selon leur qualité :

C : Données jugées pratiquement complètes, c'est-à-dire représentant au moins 90 % des faits d'état civil survenant chaque année.

U : Données jugées incomplètes, c'est-à-dire représentant moins de 90 % des faits survenant chaque année.

| : Données ne provenant pas des systèmes nationaux d'enregistrement des faits d'état civil, mais jugées fiables, telles que les estimations dérivées des projections, d'autres techniques d'estimation ou recensements de population ou du logement.

... : Données dont le degré de complétude ne fait pas l'objet de renseignements précis.

Ces codes de qualité figurent dans la première colonne des tableaux qui présentent, pour un nombre d'années déterminé les chiffres absolus et les taux (ou rapports) bruts concernant les naissances vivantes, les morts fœtales tardives, les décès d'enfants de moins d'un an, les décès, les mariages et les divorces. Les niveaux de fiabilité des statistiques de mortalité maternelle sont transmis par l'Organisation mondiale de la santé.

La classification des pays ou zones selon ces codes de qualité peut ne pas être uniforme. On a estimé néanmoins que les services nationaux de statistique étaient les mieux placés pour juger de la qualité de leurs données. On a pensé que les catégories que l'on pouvait distinguer sur la base des renseignements disponibles, bien que très larges, permettaient cependant de se faire une idée de la qualité des statistiques de l'état civil publiées dans *l'Annuaire démographique*.

Sur les pays ou zones qui ont estimé à 90 % ou plus le degré d'exhaustivité de leur enregistrement des naissances vivantes (classé « C » ou « +C » dans le tableau 9), les pays ou zones suivants ont communiqué des renseignements concernant les bases sur lesquelles leur estimation reposait :

a) Analyse démographique : Afrique du Sud, Argentine, Autriche, Bulgarie, Chili, Chine - Hong Kong RAS, Croatie, Égypte, Estonie, Italie, Lettonie, Lituanie, Malaisie, Malte, Maurice, Mexique, Nouvelle-Zélande, République de Corée, République de Moldova, Roumanie, Seychelles et Suède.

b) Double contrôle des registres : Autriche, Chypre, Cuba, Estonie, Hongrie, Israël, Italie, Malaisie, Montserrat, Norvège, Nouvelle-Zélande, Qatar, République de Corée, Roumanie, Suisse et Uruguay.

c) Autre méthode : Aruba, Australie, Autriche, Bahreïn, Curaçao, Danemark, Espagne, État de Palestine, France, Guatemala, Irlande, Kirghizstan, Liechtenstein, Luxembourg, Malaisie, Mexique, Panama, Pologne, Porto Rico, République dominicaine, Singapour, Slovénie et Suède.

Sur les pays ou zones qui ont estimé à 90 % ou plus le degré d'exhaustivité de leur enregistrement des morts fœtales tardives (classé « C » ou « +C » dans le tableau 12), les pays ou zones suivants ont communiqué des renseignements concernant les bases sur lesquelles leur estimation reposait :

a) Analyse démographique : Argentine, Autriche, Bulgarie, Croatie, Égypte, Estonie, Italie, Lettonie, Lituanie, Malte, Maurice, Mexique, Roumanie et Suède.

b) Double contrôle des registres : Autriche, Cuba, Estonie, Hongrie, Israël, Italie, Lituanie, Montserrat, Norvège, Nouvelle-Zélande, Qatar, Suisse et Venezuela (République bolivarienne du).

c) Autre méthode : Autriche, Bahreïn, Danemark, Espagne, Kirghizstan, Luxembourg, Pologne, Porto Rico, Slovénie et Suède.

Sur les pays ou zones qui ont estimé à 90 % ou plus le degré d'exhaustivité de leur enregistrement des décès à moins d'un an (classé « C » ou « +C » dans le tableau 15), les pays ou zones suivants ont donné des indications touchant la base de cette estimation :

a) Analyse démographique : Argentine, Australie, Autriche, Bulgarie, Chili, Chine - Hong Kong RAS, Croatie, Égypte, Estonie, Israël, Italie, Lettonie, Lituanie, Malte, Maurice, Mexique, Nouvelle-Zélande, République de Corée, République de Moldova, Roumanie, Seychelles et Suède.

b) Double contrôle des registres : Autriche, Cuba, Chypre, Estonie, Hongrie, Irlande, Israël, Italie, Lituanie, Montserrat, Norvège, Nouvelle-Zélande, Qatar, République de Corée, Suisse et Venezuela (République bolivarienne du).

c) Autre méthode : Autriche, Bahreïn, Curaçao, Danemark, Espagne, Îles Caïmans, Kirghizstan, Liechtenstein, Luxembourg, Pologne, Porto Rico, Singapour, Slovénie et Suède.

Sur les pays ou zones qui ont estimé à 90 % ou plus le degré d'exhaustivité de leur enregistrement des décès (classé « C » ou « +C » dans le tableau 18), les pays ou zones suivants ont donné des indications touchant la base de cette estimation :

a) Analyse démographique : Afrique du Sud, Argentine, Australie, Autriche, Bulgarie, Chili, Chine - Hong Kong RAS, Croatie, Égypte, Estonie, Israël, Italie, Lettonie, Lituanie, Malte, Maurice, Mexique, Nouvelle-Zélande, République de Corée, République de Moldova, Roumanie, Seychelles et Suède.

b) Double contrôle des registres : Autriche, Cuba, Chypre, Estonie, Hongrie, Israël, Italie, Lituanie, Montserrat, Norvège, Nouvelle-Zélande, Qatar, République de Corée, Suisse et Venezuela (République bolivarienne du).

c) Autre méthode : Aruba, Autriche, Bahreïn, Curaçao, Danemark, Espagne, France, Kirghizstan, Liechtenstein, Luxembourg, Malaisie, Pologne, Porto Rico, République dominicaine, Singapour, Slovénie et Suède.

Sur les pays ou zones qui ont estimé à 90 % ou plus le degré d'exhaustivité de leur enregistrement des mariages (classé « C » ou « +C «» dans le tableau 23), les pays ou zones suivants ont communiqué des renseignements concernant les bases sur lesquelles leur estimation reposait :

a) Analyse démographique : Argentine, Australie, Autriche, Bulgarie, Chili, Chine - Hong Kong RAS, Croatie, Égypte, Estonie, Italie, Lettonie, Lituanie, Malte, Maurice, Mexique, République de Corée, République de Moldova, Roumanie, Seychelles et Suède.

b) Double contrôle des registres : Cuba, Estonie, État de Palestine, Hongrie, Israël, Italie, Norvège, Nouvelle-Zélande, Qatar, République de Corée, Suisse et Venezuela (République bolivarienne du).

c) Autre méthode : Aruba, Autriche, Curaçao, Danemark, Espagne, France, Kirghizstan, Liechtenstein, Luxembourg, Pologne, Porto Rico, République dominicaine, Slovénie, Suède et Tadjikistan.

Sur les pays ou zones qui ont estimé à 90 % ou plus le degré d'exhaustivité de leur enregistrement des divorces (classé « C » ou « +C » dans le tableau 24), les pays ou zones suivants ont communiqué des renseignements concernant les bases sur lesquelles leur estimation reposait :

a) Analyse démographique : Australie, Autriche, Bulgarie, Croatie, Égypte, Estonie, Italie, Lettonie, Lituanie, Mexique, République de Corée, République de Moldova, Roumanie, Seychelles et Suède.

b) Double contrôle des registres : Cuba, Estonie, État de Palestine, Hongrie, Israël, Italie, Norvège, Nouvelle-Zélande, Qatar, République de Corée et Suisse.

c) Autre méthode : Aruba, Autriche, Chypre, Curaçao, Danemark, Kirghizstan, Liechtenstein, Luxembourg, Maurice, Pologne, Porto Rico, République dominicaine, Slovénie, Suède et Tadjikistan.

4.2.2 Traitement des statistiques tirées des registres d'état civil

Dans tous les tableaux de l'*Annuaire démographique*, on a indiqué le degré de fiabilité des statistiques de l'état civil en se fondant sur le codage qualitatif décrit ci-dessus. Les statistiques codées « C », jugées sûres, sont imprimées en caractères romains. Celles qui sont codées « U » ou « ... », jugées douteuses, sont reproduites en *italique*. Bien que le codage qualitatif proprement dit n'apparaisse que dans certains tableaux, l'indication du degré de fiabilité (c'est-à-dire l'emploi des caractères italiques pour désigner les données douteuses) se retrouve dans tous les tableaux présentant des statistiques de l'état civil.

Il convient de noter que, pour les taux de mortalité infantile, les taux de mortalité maternelle et les rapports de morts fœtales tardives (calculées en utilisant au dénominateur le nombre de naissances vivantes), les indications relatives à la fiabilité sont déterminées sur la base des codes de qualité utilisés pour les décès d'enfants de moins d'un an, les décès totaux et les morts fœtales tardives, respectivement. Pour évaluer ces taux et rapports de façon plus précise, il faudrait tenir compte de la qualité des données relatives aux naissances vivantes, utilisées au dénominateur dans leur calcul. Les codes de qualité pour les naissances vivantes figurent au tableau 9 et sont décrits plus en détail dans les notes techniques se rapportant à ce tableau.

4.2.3 Traitement des séries chronologiques de statistiques tirées des registres d'état civil

Il est plus difficile de déterminer la qualité des séries chronologiques de statistiques de l'état civil que celle des données pour une seule année. Étant donné qu'une série chronologique de statistiques de l'état civil ne peut généralement avoir pour source qu'un système permanent d'enregistrement des faits d'état civil, on a arbitrairement supposé que le degré d'exactitude de la série tout entière était le même que celui de la dernière tranche annuelle de données tirées du registre d'état civil. La série tout entière est traitée de la manière décrite à la section 4.2.2 ci-dessus : lorsque le code de qualité relatif aux données d'enregistrement les plus récentes est « C », les fréquences et les taux relatifs aux années antérieures sont eux aussi considérés comme sûrs et figurent en caractères romains. Inversement, si les données d'enregistrement les plus récentes sont codées « U » ou «...», les données des années antérieures sont jugées douteuses et figurent en italique. Cette méthode n'est certes pas entièrement satisfaisante, car les données des premières années de la série sont souvent beaucoup moins sûres que le code actuel ne le laisse supposer. On s'efforce d'abandonner progressivement cette méthode et de coder les données enregistrées pour chaque année séparément.

4.2.4 Traitement des estimations fondées sur les statistiques de l'état civil

En plus des données provenant des systèmes d'enregistrement des faits d'état civil, l'Annuaire démographique contient aussi des estimations relatives aux fréquences et aux taux. Il s'agit d'estimations officielles, généralement calculées à partir des résultats d'un recensement de la population ou d'un sondage ou par analyse démographique. Si des estimations concernant les fréquences et les taux figurent dans les tableaux, c'est parce que l'on considère qu'elles fournissent des renseignements plus exacts que les systèmes existants d'enregistrement des faits d'état civil. En conséquence, elles sont également jugées sûres et sont donc imprimées en caractères romains.

Dans les tableaux qui indiquent le code de qualité, ce code ne s'applique qu'aux données tirées des registres d'état civil. Les données estimatives sont dénotées par le «|».

4.3 Causes de décès

Les États membres de l'Organisation mondiale de la santé (OMS) sont tenus de communiquer à celle-ci les données sur les causes de décès codifiées selon la révision en vigueur de la Classification internationale des maladies et des problèmes de santé connexes (CIM). Pour assurer la comparabilité internationale des statistiques des causes de décès, l'OMS organise régulièrement des conférences internationales de révision de la Classification internationale des maladies afin de suivre, au fur et à mesure, les progrès les plus récents de la médecine clinique et de la statistique. Les données sont généralement présentées à l'OMS selon le degré de détail à tous les quatre caractères requis par la CIM et sont compilées et archivées dans la Base de données sur la mortalité de l'OMS au degré de détail présenté par le pays. Les données de la Base de données sur la mortalité de l'OMS sont disponibles sur le site Internet suivant : http://www3.who.int/whosis/menu.cfm.

Les révisions de la CIM permettent certes de disposer d'une version actualisée, mais elles posent plusieurs problèmes de comparabilité des statistiques des causes de décès. Le premier tient au manque de comparabilité dans le temps, qui accompagne inévitablement la mise en œuvre d'une classification nouvelle. Le deuxième est celui de la comparabilité entre pays ou zones, car les différents pays peuvent adopter la nouvelle classification à des époques différentes. Établir la cause des décès exige des compétences de plus en plus poussées à mesure que la classification devient plus précise. Or, dans beaucoup de pays ou zones, il est rare que les décès se produisent en présence d'un témoin possédant une formation médicale et le certificat de décès est le plus souvent établi par quelqu'un qui n'est pas qualifié sur le plan médical. Étant donné que la CIM répertorie de nombreux diagnostics qu'il est impossible d'établir si l'on n'a pas de formation en médecine, la CIM n'est pas toujours exactement ou précisément utilisée ce qui affecte la comparabilité internationale, notamment entre pays ou zones où la qualité des services médicaux est très disparate.

Les chapitres de la dixième révision[15] se fondent sur un système de codification alphanumérique à une lettre suivie de trois chiffres pour les catégories à quatre caractères. Le chapitre 1 concerne les maladies infectieuses et parasitaires et le chapitre 2 l'ensemble des néoplasmes. Le chapitre 3 a trait aux troubles du système immunitaire, aux maladies du sang et aux organes hématopoïétiques. Le chapitre 4 porte sur les maladies du système endocrinien, de la nutrition et du métabolisme. Les autres chapitres groupent les maladies selon leur site anatomique, à l'exception de ceux qui concernent les affections mentales, les complications de la grossesse, de l'accouchement et des suites de couches, les malformations congénitales et les affections de la période périnatale. Enfin, un chapitre entier est consacré aux symptômes, manifestations et résultats anormaux.

4.3.1 Mortalité liée à la maternité

D'après la dixième révision de la CIM, la « mortalité liée à la maternité » est définie comme le décès d'une femme survenu au cours de la grossesse ou dans un délai de 42 jours après sa terminaison, quelle qu'en soit la durée et la localisation, pour une cause quelconque déterminée ou aggravée par la grossesse ou les soins qu'elle a motivés, mais ni accidentelle ni fortuite.

Les « décès liés à la maternité » doivent se répartir en décès par cause obstétricale directe et indirecte. Les décès par cause obstétricale directe sont ceux qui résultent de complications obstétricales de l'état de grossesse (grossesse, travail et suites de couches), d'interventions, d'omissions, d'un traitement incorrect ou d'un enchaînement d'événements de l'un quelconque des facteurs ci-dessus. Les décès par cause obstétricale indirecte sont ceux qui résultent d'une maladie préexistante ou d'une affection apparue au cours de la grossesse, sans qu'elle soit due à des causes obstétricales directes, mais qui a été aggravée par les effets physiologiques de la grossesse.

En théorie, le nombre de femmes enceintes aurait dû être pris comme dénominateur pour le taux de mortalité maternelle, mais il est impossible de déterminer ce nombre. En conséquence, il est en outre recommandé dans la dixième révision d'exprimer les taux de mortalité maternelle sur la base de 100 000 naissances vivantes ou 100 000 naissances totales (naissances vivantes et morts fœtales). Le taux de mortalité maternelle est ici calculé par 100 000 naissances vivantes. Bien que les naissances vivantes ne permettent pas d'évaluer sans distorsion le nombre des femmes enceintes, leur nombre est plus fiable que d'autres estimations car le nombre des naissances vivantes est plus exactement enregistré que celui des naissances vivantes et des morts fœtales.

---

[1] Les éditions de 1978 et de 1991 font exception à la règle, puisque les tableaux sur des sujets spéciaux ont été publiés séparément.

[2] Organisation des Nations Unies, Département des affaires économiques et sociales, Division de la population (2015). *Perspectives de la population mondiale : La révision de 2015* (http://esa.un.org/unpd/wpp/).

[3] ST/ESA/STAT/SER.M/49/Rev.4/WWW ; http://unstats.un.org/unsd/methods/m49/m49frnch.htm; voir également *Code standard des pays et des zones à usage statistique*, numéro de vente : M.98.XVII.9, Nations Unies, New York, 1999.

[4] Numéro de vente : F.07.XVII.8, Nations Unies, New York, 2007.

[5] Ibid., par. 2.135.

[6] Lorsque l'on utilise un registre de la population, on peut également calculer l'âge en années révolues en soustrayant la date de naissance de chaque personne inscrite sur le registre de la date de référence à laquelle se rapportent les données sur l'âge.

[7] L'emploi de méthodes différentes de calcul de l'âge, par exemple la méthode occidentale et la méthode orientale, ou, comme on les désigne plus communément, la méthode anglaise et la méthode chinoise, représente une cause de non-comparabilité. Selon la méthode chinoise, on considère que l'enfant est âgé d'un an à sa naissance et qu'il avance d'un an à chaque nouvelle année chinoise. Les répercussions de cette méthode sont particulièrement apparentes dans les données pour le premier âge : les données concernant les enfants de moins d'un an sont nettement inférieures à la réalité. Les effets sur les chiffres relatifs aux groupes d'âge suivants sont moins visibles. Les séries ainsi établies sont souvent ajustées avant d'être publiées, mais il ne faut pas exclure la possibilité d'aberrations de ce genre lorsque l'on compare des données censitaires sur l'âge.

[8] Numéro de vente : E.13.XVII.10, publication des Nations Unies, New York, 2014.

[9] Numéro de vente : F. 98.XVII.7, publication des Nations Unies, New York, 1998.

[10] Numéro de vente : F.98.XVII.11, publication des Nations Unies, New York, 1998.

[11] Numéro de vente : F.98.XVII.4, publication des Nations Unies, New York, 1998.

[12] Numéro de vente : F.98.XVII.6, publication des Nations Unies, New York, 1998.

[13] Numéro de vente : F.98.XVII.10, publication des Nations Unies, New York, 1998.

[14] Numéro de vente : F.03.XVII.11, United Nations, New York, 2004.

[15] Organisation mondiale de la santé, *Classification statistique internationale des maladies et problèmes de santé connexes,* dixième révision, vol. 2, Genève, 1992.

Table A. Demographic Yearbook 2014 synoptic table: Availability of data by country/area, table and sex, where applicable
Tableau A. Tableau synoptique de l'Annuaire démographique 2014 : Disponibilité des données par pays ou zone, tableau et le sexe, si disponible

General topic and table number - Sujet général et numéro de tableau

Continent and country or area / Continent et pays ou zone	Table totals	Summary - Apercu 3 Total	3 M/F	4	5	Population 6 Total[1]	6 M/F	7 Total	7 M/F	8 Total	8 M/F	Fertility - Natalité 9	10 Total	10 M/F	11	Foetal mortality - Mortalité foetale 12	13	14
Total number of countries or areas - Total des pays ou zones	..	240	229	183	220	224	224	209	207	201	160	171	150	130	87	86	67	48

AFRICA - AFRIQUE

Continent and country or area	Table totals	3 Total	3 M/F	4	5	6 Total[1]	6 M/F	7 Total	7 M/F	8 Total	8 M/F	9	10 Total	10 M/F	11	12	13	14
Algeria - Algérie	17	•	•	•	•	•	•	•	•	•	...	•	...	...	...	•	...	...
Angola	4	•	•	...	...	•	•	...	...	•	...	•	...	...	...	•	...	...
Benin - Bénin	13	•	•	•	•	•	•	•	•	•	•	•	...	...	...	•	...	...
Botswana	19	•	•	•	•	•	•	•	•	•	•	•	•	•	•	•	...	...
Burkina Faso	10	•	•	...	•	•	•	•	•	•	•	...	•	...	...	•	...	...
Burundi	14	•	•	•	•	•	•	•	•	•	•	•	...	...	•	•	•	...
Cabo Verde	14	•	•	•	•	•	•	•	•	•	•	•	...	...	...	•	...	...
Cameroon - Cameroun	8	•	•	...	•	•	•	•	•	...	...	...	...	...	...	•	...	...
Central African Republic - République centrafricaine	2	•	•	...	...	...	...	...	...	...	...	...	...	...	...	...	...	...
Chad - Tchad	4	•	•	...	•	•	•	...	...	...	...	...	...	...	...	•	...	...
Comoros - Comores	2	•	•	...	•	•	•	...	...	...	...	...	...	...	...	...	...	...
Congo	8	•	•	•	•	•	•	•	•	...	...	...	...	...	...	•	...	...
Côte d'Ivoire	6	•	•	...	•	•	•	•	•	...	...	...	...	...	...	...	...	...
Democratic Republic of the Congo - République démocratique du Congo	2	•	•	...	...	...	...	...	...	...	...	...	...	...	...	...	...	...
Djibouti	10	•	•	•	•	•	•	•	•	•	•	...	...	...	...	•	...	...
Egypt - Égypte	27	•	•	•	•	•	•	•	•	•	•	•	•	•	•	•	•	...
Equatorial Guinea - Guinée équatoriale	4	•	•	...	...	...	...	...	...	•	...	•	...	...	...	•	...	...
Eritrea - Érythrée	2	•	•	...	...	...	...	...	...	...	...	...	...	...	...	...	...	...
Ethiopia - Éthiopie	9	•	•	...	•	•	•	•	•	•	...	•	...	...	...	•	...	...
Gabon	4	•	...	...	•	•	•	...	...	•	...	•	...	...	...	...	...	...
Gambia - Gambie	5	•	•	•	•	•	•	...	...	•	...	...	...	...	...	...	...	...
Ghana	17	•	•	•	•	•	•	•	•	•	•	•	•	•	•	...	...	...
Guinea - Guinée	10	•	•	•	•	•	•	•	•	•	...	•	...	...	...	•	...	...
Guinea-Bissau - Guinée-Bissau	9	•	•	...	•	•	•	•	•	•	...	•	...	...	...	•	...	...
Kenya	18	•	•	•	•	•	•	•	•	•	•	•	•	•	•	•	...	...
Lesotho	20	•	•	•	•	•	•	•	•	•	•	•	•	•	•	•	...	...
Liberia - Libéria	10	•	•	•	•	•	•	•	•	•	...	•	•	•	...	•	...	...
Libya - Libye	8	•	•	...	•	•	•	•	•	...	...	•	...	...	...	•	...	...
Madagascar	5	•	•	...	•	•	•	...	...	•	...	•	...	...	...	•	...	...
Malawi	13	•	•	•	•	•	•	•	•	•	...	•	•	•	...	•	...	...
Mali	11	•	•	•	•	•	•	•	•	•	...	•	•	•	...	...	...	...
Mauritania - Mauritanie	8	•	...	•	•	•	•	•	•	•	...	...	...	...	...	...	...	...
Mauritius - Maurice	27	•	•	•	•	•	•	•	•	•	•	•	•	•	•	•	...	...
Mayotte	7	•	•	...	...	•	•	•	•	...	...	•	...	...	...	•	...	...
Morocco - Maroc	13	•	•	•	•	•	•	•	•	•	...	•	•	•	...	...	...	...
Mozambique	12	•	•	•	•	•	•	•	•	•	...	•	•	•	...	...	...	...
Namibia - Namibie	17	•	•	•	•	•	•	•	•	•	•	•	•	•	•	•	...	...
Niger	15	•	•	•	•	•	•	•	•	•	•	•	•	•	...	•	...	...
Nigeria - Nigéria	8	•	•	...	•	•	•	•	•	...	...	...	...	•	...	...	...	...
Republic of South Sudan - République de Soudan du Sud	14	•	•	•	•	•	•	•	•	•	•	...	...	...	...	...	...	...
Reunion - Réunion	23	•	•	•	•	•	•	•	•	•	•	•	•	•	•	•	•	...
Rwanda	14	•	•	•	•	•	•	•	•	•	...	•	•	•	...	...	...	...
Saint Helena ex. dep. - Sainte-Hélène sans dép.	23	•	•	•	•	•	•	•	•	•	•	•	•	•	•	•	•	•
Saint Helena: Ascension - Sainte-Hélène: Ascension	7	•	•	•	•	•	•	•	•	...	...	...	...	...	...	...	...	...
Saint Helena: Tristan da Cunha - Sainte-Hélène: Tristan da Cunha	5	•	•	...	•	•	•	...	...	...	...	...	...	...	...	...	...	...
Sao Tome and Principe - Sao Tomé-et-Principe	15	•	•	•	•	•	•	•	•	•	...	•	•	•	...	•	...	...
Senegal - Sénégal	14	•	•	•	•	•	•	•	•	•	...	•	•	•	...	...	...	...
Seychelles	25	•	•	•	•	•	•	•	•	•	...	•	•	•	•	•	•	...
Sierra Leone	15	•	•	•	•	•	•	•	•	•	...	•	•	•	...	•	...	...
Somalia - Somalie	3	•	•	...	...	...	...	•	...	...	...	...	...	...	...	...	...	...
South Africa - Afrique du Sud	26	•	•	•	•	•	•	•	•	•	•	•	•	•	•	•	...	...
Sudan - Soudan	5	•	•	...	•	•	•	•	•	...	...	...	...	...	...	...	...	...
Swaziland	13	•	•	•	•	•	•	•	•	•	...	•	•	•	...	•	...	...
Togo	9	•	•	...	•	•	•	•	•	...	...	•	...	...	...	•	...	...
Tunisia - Tunisie	17	•	•	•	•	•	•	•	•	•	...	•	•	•	...	•	...	...

Table A. Demographic Yearbook 2014 synoptic table: Availability of data by country/area, table and sex, where applicable
Tableau A. Tableau synoptique de l'Annuaire démographique 2014 : Disponibilité des données par pays ou zone, tableau et le sexe, si disponible

General topic and table number - Sujet général et numéro de tableau

Continent and country or area / Continent et pays ou zone	15	16 Total	16 M/F	17	18	19 Total	19 M/F	20	21	22	23	24	25
Total number of countries or areas - Total des pays ou zones	122	109	105	123	167	155	152	70	178	130	109	107	84

AFRICA - AFRIQUE

Continent and country or area / Continent et pays ou zone	15	16 Total	16 M/F	17	18	19 Total	19 M/F	20	21	22	23	24	25
Algeria - Algérie	•	...	...	...	•	•	...	•	•	...	...	...	...
Angola	...	...	...	...	...	...	...	...	•	...	...	...	...
Benin - Bénin	...	...	...	...	•	...	...	...	•	...	...	...	...
Botswana	...	...	...	•	•	...	...	...	•	•	•	...	...
Burkina Faso	...	...	...	...	...	...	...	...	•	...	...	...	...
Burundi	...	...	...	...	...	...	...	...	•	...	...	...	...
Cabo Verde	...	•	...	...	...	...	...	...	...	•	...	...	...
Cameroon - Cameroun	...	...	...	...	...	...	...	...	...	...	...	...	...
Central African Republic - République centrafricaine	...	...	...	...	...	...	...	...	...	...	...	...	...
Chad - Tchad	...	...	...	...	...	...	...	...	...	...	...	...	...
Comoros - Comores	...	...	...	...	...	...	...	...	...	...	...	...	...
Congo	...	...	...	...	•	...	...	...	...	...	...	...	...
Côte d'Ivoire	...	...	...	...	...	...	...	...	•	...	...	...	...
Democratic Republic of the Congo - République démocratique du Congo	...	...	...	...	...	...	...	...	...	...	...	...	...
Djibouti	...	...	...	•	...	...	...	...	•	...	...	...	...
Egypt - Égypte	•	•	•	•	•	•	...	•	•	•	•	•	•
Equatorial Guinea - Guinée équatoriale	...	...	...	...	...	...	...	...	...	...	...	...	...
Eritrea - Érythrée	...	...	...	...	...	...	...	...	...	...	...	...	...
Ethiopia - Éthiopie	...	...	...	...	...	...	...	...	...	...	...	...	...
Gabon	...	...	...	...	...	...	...	...	...	...	...	...	...
Gambia - Gambie	...	...	...	...	...	...	...	...	...	...	...	...	...
Ghana	...	...	...	...	•	•	•	...	•	...	...	...	...
Guinea - Guinée	...	...	...	...	...	...	...	...	•	...	...	...	...
Guinea-Bissau - Guinée-Bissau	...	...	...	...	...	...	...	...	•	...	...	...	...
Kenya	•	...	...	...	•	•	•	...	•	...	...	...	...
Lesotho	...	...	...	...	•	•	•	...	•	•	•	•	•
Liberia - Libéria	...	...	...	...	...	...	...	...	•	...	...	...	...
Libya - Libye	...	...	...	...	•	...	...	...	...	...	...	...	...
Madagascar	...	...	...	...	...	...	...	...	...	...	...	...	...
Malawi	...	...	...	...	...	...	...	...	...	...	...	...	...
Mali	...	...	...	...	...	...	...	...	...	...	...	...	...
Mauritania - Mauritanie	...	...	...	...	...	...	...	...	...	...	...	...	...
Mauritius - Maurice	•	•	•	•	•	•	•	...	•	•	•	•	•
Mayotte	...	...	...	•	...	...	...	...	...	...	...	...	...
Morocco - Maroc	...	...	...	•	•	...	...	...	...	...	...	•	...
Mozambique	...	...	...	...	...	...	...	...	...	...	...	•	...
Namibia - Namibie	...	...	...	...	•	•	...	...	•	...	...	...	...
Niger	...	...	...	...	•	•	...	...	...	•	...	...	...
Nigeria - Nigéria	...	...	...	...	...	...	...	...	...	...	...	...	...
Republic of South Sudan - République de Soudan du Sud	...	...	...	...	...	•	...	•	•	...	...	...	...
Reunion - Réunion	...	•	•	•	•	•	•	...	•	...	•	...	...
Rwanda	•	...	...	...	•	...	...	...	•	...	...	...	...
Saint Helena ex. dep. - Sainte-Hélène sans dép.	•	•	•	...	•	...	...	...	•	...	...	...	...
Saint Helena: Ascension - Sainte-Hélène: Ascension	...	...	...	...	...	...	...	...	...	...	...	...	...
Saint Helena: Tristan da Cunha - Sainte-Hélène: Tristan da Cunha	...	...	...	...	...	...	...	...	...	...	...	...	...
Sao Tome and Principe - Sao Tomé-et-Principe	...	...	...	...	•	...	...	...	•	...	...	...	...
Senegal - Sénégal	•	...	...	...	•	...	...	...	•	...	...	...	...
Seychelles	•	•	•	•	•	...	...	...	•	•	•	•	•
Sierra Leone	•	...	...	...	•	...	...	...	•	...	...	...	...
Somalia - Somalie	...	...	...	...	...	...	...	...	...	...	...	...	...
South Africa - Afrique du Sud	•	•	•	•	•	•	•	...	•	•	•	•	•
Sudan - Soudan	...	...	...	...	...	...	...	...	...	...	...	...	...
Swaziland	...	...	...	...	...	...	...	...	...	...	...	...	...
Togo	...	...	...	...	...	...	...	...	...	...	...	...	...
Tunisia - Tunisie	...	...	...	...	•	...	...	•	•	•	•	...	...

Table A. Demographic Yearbook 2014 synoptic table: Availability of data by country/area, table and sex, where applicable
Tableau A. Tableau synoptique de l'Annuaire démographique 2014 : Disponibilité des données par pays ou zone, tableau et le sexe, si disponible (continued - suite)

General topic and table number - Sujet général et numéro de tableau

Continent and country or area / Continent et pays ou zone	Table totals	Summary - Apercu 3 Total	3 M/F	4	5	Population 6 Total¹	6 M/F	7 Total	7 M/F	8 Total	8 M/F	9	Fertility - Natalité 10 Total	10 M/F	11	Foetal mortality - Mortalité foetale 12	13	14
AFRICA - AFRIQUE																		
Uganda - Ouganda	9	•	•	•	•	•	•	•	...	•	...	...	...	...	...	...	...	...
United Republic of Tanzania - République Unie de Tanzanie	10	•	•	•	•	•	•	•	...	...	•	...	...	•	...	...	...	...
Western Sahara - Sahara occidental	3	•	•	...	•	...	...	...	...	•	...	...	...	...	...	...	...	...
Zambia - Zambie	16	•	•	•	•	•	•	•	•	•	•	•	•	•	•	...	...	...
Zimbabwe	11	•	•	...	•	•	•	•	•	•	...	...	...	...	...	...	...	...
AMERICA, NORTH - AMÉRIQUE DU NORD																		
Anguilla	17	•	...	•	•	•	•	...	...	•	...	•	•	...	•	...	•	...
Antigua and Barbuda - Antigua-et-Barbuda	12	•	...	•	•	•	•	...	...	•	...	•	•	...	•	...	...	...
Aruba	25	•	•	•	•	•	•	•	•	•	•	•	•	•	•	•	...	...
Bahamas	26	•	•	•	•	•	•	•	•	•	•	•	•	•	•	•	...	...
Barbados - Barbade	15	•	•	...	•	•	•	•	•	•	•	•	•	•	•	...	...	...
Belize	10	•	•	•	•	•	•	•	•	•	•	•	•	•	•	...	...	...
Bermuda - Bermudes	28	•	•	•	•	•	•	•	•	•	•	•	•	•	•	•	...	...
British Virgin Islands - Îles Vierges britanniques	7	•	•	...	•	•	•	•	•	•	•	•	•	•	•	•	•	•
Canada	25	•	•	•	•	•	•	•	•	•	•	•	•	•	•	•	•	•
Cayman Islands - Îles Caïmanes	20	•	•	•	•	•	•	•	•	•	•	•	•	•	...	•	...	...
Costa Rica	29	•	•	•	•	•	•	•	•	•	•	•	•	•	•	•	•	...
Cuba	29	•	•	•	•	•	•	•	•	•	...	•	•	•	•	•	•	...
Curaçao	22	•	•	•	•	•	•	•	•	•	...	•	•	•	•	...	...	...
Dominica - Dominique	16	•	•	•	•	•	•	•	•	•	•	•	•	•	•	...	...	...
Dominican Republic - République dominicaine	28	•	•	•	•	•	•	•	•	•	•	•	•	•	•	•	•	...
El Salvador	26	•	•	•	•	•	•	•	•	•	•	•	•	•	•	...	...	...
Greenland - Groenland	23	•	•	•	•	•	•	•	•	•	•	•	•	•	•	•	•	...
Grenada - Grenade	6	•	•	•	•	•	...	•	•	•	...	•	•	•	•	...	...	...
Guadeloupe	17	•	•	•	•	•	•	•	•	•	•	•	•	•	•	•	•	...
Guatemala	25	•	•	•	•	•	•	•	•	•	•	•	•	•	•	•	•	...
Haiti - Haïti	10	•	•	...	•	•	•	•	•	•	•	•	•	•	•	•	•	...
Honduras	12	•	•	•	•	•	•	•	•	•	•	•	•	•	•	...	...	...
Jamaica - Jamaïque	23	•	•	•	•	•	•	•	•	•	•	•	•	•	•	•	•	...
Martinique	25	•	•	•	•	•	•	•	•	•	•	•	•	•	•	•	•	...
Mexico - Mexique	30	•	•	•	•	•	•	•	•	•	•	•	•	•	•	•	•	•
Montserrat	21	•	•	•	•	•	•	•	•	•	...	•	•	•	•	•	•	...
Nicaragua	19	•	•	•	•	•	•	•	•	•	•	•	•	•	•	•	...	...
Panama	28	•	•	•	•	•	•	•	•	•	•	•	•	•	•	•	•	...
Puerto Rico - Porto Rico	28	•	•	•	•	•	•	•	•	•	•	•	•	•	•	•	•	•
Saint Kitts and Nevis - Saint-Kitts-et-Nevis	5	•	•	...	•	...	...	•	•	•	...	...	...	...	...	...	...	...
Saint Lucia - Sainte-Lucie	14	•	•	...	•	•	•	•	•	•	•	...	...	...	...	...	...	...
Saint Pierre and Miquelon - Saint Pierre-et-Miquelon	8	•	...	•	•	•	•	•	•	•	...	...	...	...	...	...	...	...
Saint Vincent and the Grenadines - Saint-Vincent-et-les Grenadines	19	•	•	•	•	•	•	•	•	•	...	•	•	•	•	...	...	...
Saint-Barthélemy	1	•	...	...	...	...	...	...	...	...	...	...	...	...	...	...	...	...
Saint-Martin (French part) - Saint-Martin (partie française)	1	•	...	...	...	...	...	...	...	...	...	...	...	...	...	...	...	...
Sint Maarten (Dutch part) - Saint-Martin (partie néerlandaise)	13	•	•	•	•	•	•	•	•	•	...	•	•	•	•	...	...	...
Trinidad and Tobago - Trinité-et-Tobago	16	•	...	•	•	•	•	•	•	•	•	•	•	•	•	•	...	...
Turks and Caicos Islands - Îles Turques et Caïques	17	•	•	•	•	•	•	•	•	•	•	•	•	•	•	•	•	...
United States of America - États-Unis d'Amérique	26	•	•	•	•	•	•	•	•	•	•	•	•	•	•	•	•	...
United States Virgin Islands - Îles Vierges américaines	14	•	•	•	•	•	•	•	•	•	•	...	•	•	...	...	...	...

Table A. Demographic Yearbook 2014 synoptic table: Availability of data by country/area, table and sex, where applicable
Tableau A. Tableau synoptique de l'Annuaire démographique 2014 : Disponibilité des données par pays ou zone, tableau et le sexe, si disponible (continued - suite)

Continent and country or area / Continent et pays ou zone	General topic and table number - Sujet général et numéro de tableau												
	Infant and maternal mortality - Mortalité infantile et mortalité liée à la maternité				General mortality - Mortalité générale					Nuptiality and divorces - Nuptialité et divortialité			
	15	16 Total	16 M/F	17	18	19 Total	19 M/F	20	21	22	23	24	25
AFRICA - AFRIQUE													
Uganda - Ouganda	...	...	...	...	...	...	...	...	•	...	...	...	...
United Republic of Tanzania - République Unie de Tanzanie	...	...	...	...	•	...	...	...	...	...	...	...	...
Western Sahara - Sahara occidental	...	...	...	...	...	...	...	...	...	...	...	...	...
Zambia - Zambie	...	...	...	...	•	•	•	...	...	...	...	...	...
Zimbabwe	...	...	...	...	...	...	...	•	•	...	...	...	...
AMERICA, NORTH - AMÉRIQUE DU NORD													
Anguilla	•	...	...	•	•	•	...	•	...	•	•	...	...
Antigua and Barbuda - Antigua-et-Barbuda	•	...	...	•	•	...	...	•	•	•	•	...	...
Aruba	•	•	•	•	•	•	...	•	•	•	•	•	...
Bahamas	•	•	•	•	•	•	•	•	•	•	•	•	...
Barbados - Barbade	...	•	•	•	•	...	...	•	•	•	•	•	...
Belize	•	...	...	•	•	...	...	•	•	•	•	•	...
Bermuda - Bermudes	•	•	•	•	•	•	•	•	•	•	•	•	...
British Virgin Islands - Îles Vierges britanniques	...	...	...	•	•	•	...	•	...	•	•	...	...
Canada	...	•	•	•	•	•	•	•	...	•	•	...	...
Cayman Islands - Îles Caïmanes	•	•	•	•	•	•	•	•	...	•	•	•	...
Costa Rica	•	•	•	•	•	•	•	•	•	•	•	•	...
Cuba	•	•	•	•	•	•	•	•	•	•	•	•	•
Curaçao	•	•	•	...	•	•	•	•	•	•	•	•	•
Dominica - Dominique	...	...	...	•	•	•	...	•	•	•	•	...	...
Dominican Republic - République dominicaine	•	•	•	•	•	•	•	•	•	•	•	•	...
El Salvador	•	•	•	•	•	•	•	•	•	•	•	•	...
Greenland - Groenland	•	•	•	...	•	•	•	•	•	•	•	•	...
Grenada - Grenade	...	...	...	•	•	...	...	•	•	•	•	...	...
Guadeloupe	•	•	•	•	•	...	...	•	•	•	•	...	...
Guatemala	•	•	•	•	•	•	•	•	•	•	•	•	...
Haiti - Haïti	•	•	•	•	...	...	...	•	...	•	...	...	...
Honduras	•	•	•	•	•	...	...	•	...	•	...	...	...
Jamaica - Jamaïque	•	•	•	•	•	•	...	•	•	•	•	...	...
Martinique	•	•	•	•	•	•	...	•	•	•	•	...	...
Mexico - Mexique	•	•	•	•	•	•	•	•	•	•	•	•	...
Montserrat	•	•	•	•	•	•	•	•	•	•	•	...	...
Nicaragua	...	•	•	•	•	•	•	•	•	•	•	•	...
Panama	•	•	•	•	•	•	•	•	•	•	•	•	•
Puerto Rico - Porto Rico	•	•	•	•	•	•	•	...	•	•	•	•	...
Saint Kitts and Nevis - Saint-Kitts-et-Nevis	...	...	...	•	...	...	...	•	...	...	...	...	...
Saint Lucia - Sainte-Lucie	...	...	...	•	...	...	...	•	...	...	...	...	...
Saint Pierre and Miquelon - Saint Pierre-et-Miquelon	...	...	...	•	...	...	...	...	...	...	...	...	...
Saint Vincent and the Grenadines - Saint-Vincent-et-les Grenadines	...	•	•	•	•	•	...	...	•	•	•	...	...
Saint-Barthélemy	...	...	...	...	...	...	...	...	...	...	...	...	...
Saint-Martin (French part) - Saint-Martin (partie française)	...	...	...	...	...	...	...	...	...	...	...	...	...
Sint Maarten (Dutch part) - Saint-Martin (partie néerlandaise)	...	...	...	...	•	...	...	•	•	...	•	...	...
Trinidad and Tobago - Trinité-et-Tobago	...	...	...	•	...	•	...	...	•	•	...	•	...
Turks and Caicos Islands - Îles Turques et Caïques	...	...	...	•	•	•	...	•	•	...	...	...	•
United States of America - États-Unis d'Amérique	•	•	•	•	•	•	•	•	•	•	...	•	...
United States Virgin Islands - Îles Vierges américaines	...	...	...	•	...	•	...	...	...	...	...	...	...

Table A. Demographic Yearbook 2014 synoptic table: Availability of data by country/area, table and sex, where applicable
Tableau A. Tableau synoptique de l'Annuaire démographique 2014 : Disponibilité des données par pays ou zone, tableau et le sexe, si disponible (continued - suite)

General topic and table number - Sujet général et numéro de tableau

Continent and country or area / Continent et pays ou zone	Table totals	Summary - Aperçu 3 Total	3 M/F	4	5	Population 6 Total[1]	6 M/F	7 Total	7 M/F	8 Total	8 M/F	Fertility - Natalité 9	10 Total	10 M/F	11	Foetal mortality - Mortalité foetale 12	13	14
AMERICA, SOUTH - AMÉRIQUE DU SUD																		
Argentina - Argentine	22	•	•	•	•	•	•	•	•	•	...	•	•	...	•	...	...	
Bolivia (Plurinational State of) - Bolivie (État plurinational de)	18	•	•	•	•	•	•	•	•	•	•	...	...	...	•	...	...	
Brazil - Brésil	27	•	•	•	•	•	•	•	•	•	•	•	•	•	...	...	...	
Chile - Chili	29	•	•	•	•	•	•	•	•	•	•	•	•	•	•	•	•	
Colombia - Colombie	23	•	•	•	•	•	•	•	•	•	•	•	•	•	•	...	...	
Ecuador - Équateur	28	•	•	•	•	•	•	•	•	•	•	•	•	•	•	...	...	
Falkland Islands (Malvinas) - Îles Falkland (Malvinas)	7	•	•	...	...	•	•	•	•	•	...	...	...	•	•	...	...	
French Guiana - Guyane française	25	•	•	•	•	•	•	•	•	•	•	•	•	•	•	•	...	
Guyana	13	•	•	•	•	•	•	•	•	•	...	...	•	•	•	...	...	
Paraguay	23	•	•	•	•	•	•	•	•	•	•	•	•	•	•	•	...	
Peru - Pérou	24	•	•	•	•	•	•	•	•	•	•	•	•	•	...	...	...	
Suriname	23	•	•	•	•	•	•	•	•	•	•	•	•	•	•	...	...	
Uruguay	23	•	•	•	•	•	•	•	•	•	•	•	•	•	•	...	...	
Venezuela (Bolivarian Republic of) - Venezuela (République bolivarienne du)	27	•	•	•	•	•	•	•	•	•	•	•	•	•	•	...	...	
ASIA - ASIE																		
Afghanistan	10	•	•	...	•	•	•	•	•	•	•	...	...	...	...	...	...	
Armenia - Arménie	28	•	•	•	•	•	•	•	•	•	•	•	•	...	•	•	•	•
Azerbaijan - Azerbaïdjan	30	•	•	•	•	•	•	•	•	•	•	•	•	•	•	•	•	•
Bahrain - Bahreïn	28	•	•	•	•	•	•	•	•	•	•	•	•	•	•	•	•	•
Bangladesh	20	•	•	•	•	•	•	•	•	•	•	•	•	•	•	...	...	
Bhutan - Bhoutan	14	•	•	...	•	•	•	•	•	•	•	...	...	...	...	...	...	
Brunei Darussalam - Brunéi Darussalam	25	•	•	•	•	•	•	•	•	•	•	•	•	•	•	•	•	
Cambodia - Cambodge	9	•	•	...	•	•	•	•	•	•	•	...	...	...	...	...	...	
China - Chine[2]	17	•	•	•	•	•	•	•	•	•	•	...	...	•	•	...	...	
China, Hong Kong SAR - Chine, Hong Kong RAS	29	•	•	•	•	•	•	•	•	•	•	•	•	•	•	•	•	
China, Macao SAR - Chine, Macao RAS	27	•	•	•	•	•	•	•	•	•	•	•	•	•	•	•	•	
Cyprus - Chypre	25	•	•	•	•	•	•	•	•	•	...	•	•	•	•	•	•	
Democratic People's Republic of Korea - République populaire démocratique de Corée	13	•	•	...	...	•	•	•	•	•	•	...	•	•	•	...	...	
Georgia - Géorgie	27	•	•	•	•	•	•	•	•	...	•	•	•	•	...	•	•	•
India - Inde[3]	14	•	•	•	•	•	•	•	•	•	•	...	...	...	•	...	...	
Indonesia - Indonésie	13	•	•	•	•	•	•	•	•	•	•	...	...	...	•	...	...	
Iran (Islamic Republic of) - Iran (République islamique d')	22	•	•	•	•	•	•	•	•	•	•	•	•	•	...	...	...	
Iraq	12	•	•	•	•	•	•	•	•	...	•	•	•	•	...	...	...	
Israel - Israël[4]	30	•	•	•	•	•	•	•	•	•	•	•	•	•	•	•	•	•
Japan - Japon	30	•	•	•	•	•	•	•	•	•	•	•	•	•	•	•	•	•
Jordan - Jordanie	17	•	•	•	•	•	•	•	•	•	•	•	...	...	...	•	...	
Kazakhstan	29	•	•	•	•	•	•	•	•	•	•	•	•	•	•	•	•	...
Kuwait - Koweït	26	•	•	•	•	•	•	•	•	•	•	•	•	•	•	•	...	
Kyrgyzstan - Kirghizstan	30	•	•	•	•	•	•	•	•	•	•	•	•	•	•	•	•	•
Lao People's Democratic Republic - République démocratique populaire lao	11	•	•	•	•	•	•	•	•	•	•	...	...	...	...	...	...	...
Lebanon - Liban	13	•	•	•	...	•	•	•	•	•	•	...	...	...	...	...	...	
Malaysia - Malaisie	20	•	•	•	•	•	•	•	•	...	•	•	•	•	•	...	...	
Maldives	23	•	•	•	•	•	•	•	•	•	•	•	•	•	•	...	...	
Mongolia - Mongolie	23	•	•	•	•	•	•	•	•	•	•	•	•	•	•	•	...	
Myanmar	21	•	•	•	•	•	•	•	•	•	•	•	•	•	•	...	...	
Nepal - Népal	14	•	•	•	•	•	•	•	•	•	•	...	...	...	•	...	...	
Oman	25	•	•	•	•	•	•	•	•	•	•	•	•	•	•	•	...	
Pakistan[5]	16	•	•	...	•	•	•	•	•	•	•	...	...	...	•	...	...	
Philippines	24	•	•	•	•	•	•	•	•	•	•	•	•	•	•	...	...	
Qatar	29	•	•	•	•	•	•	•	•	•	•	•	•	•	•	•	•	...
Republic of Korea - République de Corée	28	•	•	•	•	•	•	•	•	•	•	•	•	•	•	•	•	
Saudi Arabia - Arabie saoudite	19	•	•	•	•	•	•	•	•	•	•	•	•	•	...	...	...	
Singapore - Singapour	29	•	•	•	•	•	•	•	•	•	•	...	•	•	•	•	•	

Table A. Demographic Yearbook 2014 synoptic table: Availability of data by country/area, table and sex, where applicable
Tableau A. Tableau synoptique de l'Annuaire démographique 2014 : Disponibilité des données par pays ou zone, tableau et le sexe, si disponible (continued - suite)

Continent and country or area / Continent et pays ou zone	General topic and table number - Sujet général et numéro de tableau											
	Infant and maternal mortality - Mortalité infantile et mortalité liée à la maternité				General mortality - Mortalité générale				Nuptiality and divorces - Nuptialité et divortialité			
	15	16 Total	16 M/F	17	18	19 Total	19 M/F	20	21	22	23	24	25

AMERICA, SOUTH - AMÉRIQUE DU SUD

	15	16T	16MF	17	18	19T	19MF	20	21	22	23	24	25
Argentina - Argentine	•	•	•	•	•	•	•	•	•	•	...	...	...
Bolivia (Plurinational State of) - Bolivie (État plurinational de)	...	...	...	...	•	•	•	•	•	•	•	•	...
Brazil - Brésil	•	•	•	•	•	•	•	•	•	•	•	•	•
Chile - Chili	•	•	•	•	•	•	•	•	•	•	•	•	•
Colombia - Colombie	•	•	•	•	•	•	•	•	•	...	•	•	•
Ecuador - Équateur	•	•	•	•	•	•	•	•	•	•	•	•	•
Falkland Islands (Malvinas) - Îles Falkland (Malvinas)	...	...	...	...	...	...	...	•	...	...	...	...	...
French Guiana - Guyane française	...	•	•	•	•	•	•	...	•	•	•	•	•
Guyana	...	...	...	•	•	•	...	...	•	•	•	•	...
Paraguay	•	...	...	•	•	•	•	•	•	•	•	•	...
Peru - Pérou	•	•	•	•	•	•	•	•	•	•	•	•	...
Suriname	•	...	...	•	•	•	•	...	•	•	•	•	•
Uruguay	•	...	...	•	•	•	•	•	•	•	...	...	...
Venezuela (Bolivarian Republic of) - Venezuela (République bolivarienne du)	•	•	•	•	•	•	•	...	•	•	•	•	•

ASIA - ASIE

	15	16T	16MF	17	18	19T	19MF	20	21	22	23	24	25
Afghanistan	...	...	...	...	...	...	...	...	•	...	...	...	...
Armenia - Arménie	•	•	•	•	•	•	•	•	•	•	•	•	•
Azerbaijan - Azerbaïdjan	•	•	•	•	•	•	•	•	•	•	•	•	•
Bahrain - Bahreïn	•	•	•	•	•	•	•	•	•	•	•	•	•
Bangladesh	•	...	...	•	•	•	...	•	•	•	...	•	...
Bhutan - Bhoutan	...	...	...	...	•	•	...	•	•	•	•	...	...
Brunei Darussalam - Brunéi Darussalam	•	...	...	•	•	•	•	•	•	•	•	•	...
Cambodia - Cambodge	...	...	...	...	•	•	...	•	•	•	•	•	...
China - Chine[2]	...	...	...	...	•	•	•	•	•	•	...	•	...
China, Hong Kong SAR - Chine, Hong Kong RAS	•	•	•	•	•	•	•	•	•	•	...	•	...
China, Macao SAR - Chine, Macao RAS	•	•	•	•	•	•	•	•	•	•	•	•	•
Cyprus - Chypre	•	•	•	•	•	•	•	•	•	•	•	•	•
Democratic People's Republic of Korea - République populaire démocratique de Corée	...	...	...	...	...	...	...	•	...	...	...	...	...
Georgia - Géorgie	•	•	•	•	•	•	•	•	•	•	•	•	•
India - Inde[3]	•	...	...	...	•	•	...	•	•	...	...	•	...
Indonesia - Indonésie	...	...	...	...	...	...	...	...	•	...	...	...	...
Iran (Islamic Republic of) - Iran (République islamique d')	•	...	...	...	•	•	•	•	•	•	•	•	•
Iraq	...	...	...	...	•	•	...	...	•	•	•	•	•
Israel - Israël[4]	•	•	•	•	•	•	•	•	•	•	•	•	•
Japan - Japon	•	•	•	•	•	•	•	•	•	•	•	•	•
Jordan - Jordanie	•	•	•	•	•	•	...	...	•	•	•	•	...
Kazakhstan	•	•	•	•	•	•	•	•	•	•	•	•	•
Kuwait - Koweït	•	•	•	•	•	•	...	•	•	•	•	•	•
Kyrgyzstan - Kirghizstan	•	•	•	•	•	•	•	•	•	•	•	•	•
Lao People's Democratic Republic - République démocratique populaire lao	...	...	...	...	...	...	...	...	•	...	...	...	...
Lebanon - Liban	...	...	...	...	...	...	...	•	...	•	...	•	...
Malaysia - Malaisie	•	...	...	•	•	•	...	•	•	•	•	•	•
Maldives	•	•	•	•	•	•	•	•	•	•	...	•	...
Mongolia - Mongolie	•	•	•	•	•	•	•	•	•	•	•	•	...
Myanmar	•	...	...	•	•	•	...	...	•	•	•	•	...
Nepal - Népal	•	•	•	•	•	•	...	...	•	•	•	•	...
Oman	•	•	•	•	•	•	•	•	•	•	...	•	...
Pakistan[5]	...	...	...	...	•	•	...	...	•	...	...	...	...
Philippines	•	•	•	•	•	•	•	•	•	•	...	•	...
Qatar	•	•	•	•	•	•	•	•	•	•	•	•	•
Republic of Korea - République de Corée	•	•	•	•	•	•	•	•	•	•	•	•	•
Saudi Arabia - Arabie saoudite	•	...	...	•	•	•	•	•	•	•	•	...	...
Singapore - Singapour	•	•	•	•	•	•	•	•	•	•	•	•	•

Table A. Demographic Yearbook 2014 synoptic table: Availability of data by country/area, table and sex, where applicable
Tableau A. Tableau synoptique de l'Annuaire démographique 2014 : Disponibilité des données par pays ou zone, tableau et le sexe, si disponible (continued - suite)

General topic and table number - Sujet général et numéro de tableau

Continent and country or area / Continent et pays ou zone	Table totals	Summary - Apercu 3 Total	3 M/F	4	5	Population 6 Total[1]	6 M/F	7 Total	7 M/F	8 Total	8 M/F	9	Fertility - Natalité 10 Total	10 M/F	11	Foetal mortality - Mortalité foetale 12	13	14
ASIA - ASIE																		
Sri Lanka	20	•	•	•	•	•	•	•	•	•	•	•	•	•	...	•	...	...
State of Palestine - État de Palestine	23	•	•	•	•	•	•	•	•	•	...	•	•	•	...	...	...	...
Syrian Arab Republic - République arabe syrienne	14	•	•	•	•	•	•	•	•	...	...	•	...	...	...	...	...	...
Tajikistan - Tadjikistan	26	•	•	•	•	•	•	•	•	•	•	•	...	...	...	•	...	•
Thailand - Thaïlande	21	•	•	•	•	•	•	•	•	•	•	•	•	•	...	...	...	...
Timor-Leste	9	•	•	...	•	•	•	•	•	•	•	...	...	...	...	...	...	...
Turkey - Turquie	27	•	•	•	•	•	•	•	•	•	•	•	•	•	...	•	...	...
Turkmenistan - Turkménistan	2	•	...	...	...	...	...	...	...	...	...	...	...	...	...	...	...	...
United Arab Emirates - Émirats arabes unis	14	•	•	•	•	...	•	•	•	•	•	•	...	...	...	...	...	...
Uzbekistan - Ouzbékistan	11	•	•	•	•	...	•	...	•	•	•	•	...	...	...	...	...	...
Viet Nam	9	•	•	•	•	•	•	•	•	...	...	•	...	...	...	...	...	...
Yemen - Yémen	12	•	•	•	•	•	•	•	•	...	...	•	...	...	...	...	...	...
EUROPE																		
Åland Islands - Îles d'Åland	27	•	•	•	•	•	•	•	•	•	•	•	•	•	•	•	•	•
Albania - Albanie	26	•	•	•	•	•	•	•	•	•	•	•	•	•	•	•	•	...
Andorra - Andorre	20	•	•	•	•	•	•	•	•	•	•	•	•	•	...	•	...	...
Austria - Autriche	28	•	•	•	•	•	•	•	•	•	•	•	•	•	•	•	•	...
Belarus - Bélarus	30	•	•	•	•	•	•	•	•	•	•	•	•	•	•	•	•	•
Belgium - Belgique	30	•	•	•	•	•	•	•	•	•	•	•	•	•	•	•	•	•
Bosnia and Herzegovina - Bosnie-Herzégovine	23	•	...	•	•	•	•	•	...	...	•	•	•	•	...	•	...	...
Bulgaria - Bulgarie	30	•	•	•	•	•	•	•	•	•	•	•	•	•	•	•	•	•
Croatia - Croatie	28	•	•	•	•	•	•	•	•	•	•	•	•	•	•	•	•	•
Czech Republic - République tchèque	30	•	•	•	•	•	•	•	•	•	•	•	•	•	•	•	•	•
Denmark - Danemark	30	•	•	•	•	•	•	•	•	•	•	•	•	•	•	•	•	•
Estonia - Estonie	30	•	•	•	•	•	•	•	•	•	•	•	•	•	•	•	•	•
Faeroe Islands - Îles Féroé	22	•	•	•	•	•	•	•	•	•	•	•	•	•	•	...	...	•
Finland - Finlande	30	•	•	•	•	•	•	•	•	•	•	•	•	•	•	•	•	•
France	30	•	•	•	•	•	•	•	•	•	•	•	•	•	•	•	•	•
Germany - Allemagne	30	•	•	•	•	•	•	•	•	•	•	•	•	•	•	•	•	•
Gibraltar	20	•	•	•	•	•	•	•	•	•	•	•	•	•	•	•	...	...
Greece - Grèce	29	•	•	•	•	•	•	•	•	•	•	•	•	•	•	•	•	...
Guernsey - Guernesey	12	•	•	•	•	•	•	•	•	...	•	...	...	...	...	...	...	...
Holy See - Saint-Siège	6	•	•	...	•	•	...	...	•	...	...	...	...	...	...	...	...	...
Hungary - Hongrie	30	•	•	•	•	•	•	•	•	•	•	•	•	•	•	•	•	•
Iceland - Islande	30	•	•	•	•	•	•	•	•	•	•	•	•	•	•	•	•	•
Ireland - Irlande	27	•	•	•	•	•	•	•	•	•	•	•	•	•	•	...	•	...
Isle of Man - Île de Man	14	•	•	•	•	•	•	•	•	•	•	...	•	•	...	...	...	...
Italy - Italie	30	•	•	•	•	•	•	•	•	•	•	•	•	•	•	•	•	•
Jersey	15	•	•	•	•	•	•	•	•	•	•	•	•	•	...	...	...	...
Latvia - Lettonie	30	•	•	•	•	•	•	•	•	•	•	•	•	•	•	•	•	•
Liechtenstein	23	•	•	•	•	•	•	•	•	•	•	•	•	•	...	...	...	...
Lithuania - Lituanie	30	•	•	•	•	•	•	•	•	•	•	•	•	•	•	•	•	•
Luxembourg	28	•	•	•	•	•	•	•	•	•	•	•	•	•	•	•	...	...
Malta - Malte	28	•	•	•	•	•	•	•	•	•	•	•	•	•	•	•	...	...
Monaco	12	•	•	•	•	•	•	•	•	...	...	•	...	...	...	•	...	...
Montenegro - Monténégro	27	•	•	•	•	•	•	•	•	•	•	•	•	•	•	...	•	...
Netherlands - Pays-Bas	27	•	•	•	•	•	•	•	•	•	•	•	•	•	•	•	...	...
Norway - Norvège	30	•	•	•	•	•	•	•	•	•	•	•	•	•	•	•	•	•
Poland - Pologne	30	•	•	•	•	•	•	•	•	•	•	•	•	•	•	•	•	•
Portugal	29	•	•	•	•	•	•	•	•	•	•	•	•	•	•	•	•	•
Republic of Moldova - République de Moldova	29	•	•	•	•	•	•	•	•	•	•	•	•	•	•	...	•	...
Romania - Roumanie	30	•	•	•	•	•	•	•	•	•	•	•	•	•	•	•	•	•
Russian Federation - Fédération de Russie	30	•	•	•	•	•	•	•	•	•	•	•	•	•	•	•	•	•
San Marino - Saint-Marin	25	•	•	•	•	•	•	•	•	•	•	•	•	•	•	...	...	...
Serbia - Serbie	30	•	•	•	•	•	•	•	•	•	•	•	•	•	•	•	•	•
Slovakia - Slovaquie	30	•	•	•	•	•	•	•	•	•	•	•	•	•	•	•	•	•
Slovenia - Slovénie	30	•	•	•	•	•	•	•	•	•	•	•	•	•	•	•	•	•
Spain - Espagne	30	•	•	•	•	•	•	•	•	•	•	•	•	•	•	•	•	•

Table A. Demographic Yearbook 2014 synoptic table: Availability of data by country/area, table and sex, where applicable
Tableau A. Tableau synoptique de l'Annuaire démographique 2014 : Disponibilité des données par pays ou zone, tableau et le sexe, si disponible (continued - suite)

Continent and country or area / Continent et pays ou zone	General topic and table number - Sujet général et numéro de tableau												
	Infant and maternal mortality - Mortalité infantile et mortalité liée à la maternité				General mortality - Mortalité générale					Nuptiality and divorces - Nuptialité et divortialité			
	15	16 Total	16 M/F	17	18	19 Total	19 M/F	20	21	22	23	24	25
ASIA - ASIE													
Sri Lanka	...	...	...	•	•	•	•	...		•	•	...	...
State of Palestine - État de Palestine	•	•	•	...	•	•	•	...		•	•	•	•
Syrian Arab Republic - République arabe syrienne	...	...	...	...	•	...	•	...		•	...	•	...
Tajikistan - Tadjikistan	•	•	•	•	•	•	•	•		•	•	•	•
Thailand - Thaïlande	•	•	•	•	•	•	•	•	...	...	...	...	
Timor-Leste	...	...	...	...	•	...	...	...		...	...	...	...
Turkey - Turquie	•	•	•	•	•	•	•	•	•	•	•	•	•
Turkmenistan - Turkménistan	...	...	...	...	•	...	...	...		...	...	...	...
United Arab Emirates - Émirats arabes unis	...	...	...	•	•	...	•	...		•	...	•	...
Uzbekistan - Ouzbékistan	...	...	...	•	•	...	...	...		•	•	...	...
Viet Nam	...	...	...	...	•	...	...	...		...	...	...	...
Yemen - Yémen	...	...	...	...	•	...	...	•		...	...	...	...
EUROPE													
Åland Islands - Îles d'Åland	•	•	•	...	•	•	•	•		•	•	•	...
Albania - Albanie	•	•	•	•	•	•	•	•	•	•	•	•	...
Andorra - Andorre	•	•	•	...	•	•	•	...		•	•	...	...
Austria - Autriche	•	•	•	•	•	•	•	•	•	•	•	•	•
Belarus - Bélarus	•	•	•	•	•	•	•	•	•	•	•	•	•
Belgium - Belgique	•	•	•	•	•	•	•	•	•	•	•	•	•
Bosnia and Herzegovina - Bosnie-Herzégovine	•	•	•	•	•	•	•	•	...	•	•	•	•
Bulgaria - Bulgarie	•	•	•	•	•	•	•	•	•	•	•	•	•
Croatia - Croatie	•	•	•	•	•	•	•	...	...	•	•	•	•
Czech Republic - République tchèque	•	•	•	•	•	•	•	•	•	•	•	•	•
Denmark - Danemark	•	•	•	•	•	•	•	•	•	•	•	•	•
Estonia - Estonie	•	•	•	•	•	•	•	•	•	•	•	•	•
Faeroe Islands - Îles Féroé	•	...	...	...	•	•	•	•		•	...	...	...
Finland - Finlande	•	•	•	•	•	•	•	•	•	•	•	•	•
France	•	•	•	•	•	•	•	•	•	•	•	•	•
Germany - Allemagne	•	•	•	•	•	•	•	•	•	•	•	•	•
Gibraltar	•	•	•	...	•	...	•	•		•	•	•	•
Greece - Grèce	•	•	•	•	•	•	•	•	•	•	•	•	•
Guernsey - Guernesey	...	...	...	...	•	...	...	...		•	...	...	...
Holy See - Saint-Siège	...	...	...	...	...	...	...	...		...	...	...	...
Hungary - Hongrie	•	•	•	•	•	•	•	•	•	•	•	•	•
Iceland - Islande	•	•	•	•	•	•	•	•	•	•	•	•	•
Ireland - Irlande	•	•	•	•	•	•	•	•	•	•	•	•	...
Isle of Man - Île de Man	...	...	...	...	•	...	...	...		...	...	...	...
Italy - Italie	•	•	•	•	•	•	•	•	•	•	•	•	•
Jersey	...	...	...	...	•	...	...	...		•	...	...	...
Latvia - Lettonie	•	•	•	•	•	•	•	•	•	•	•	•	•
Liechtenstein	•	•	•	...	•	•	•	...	...	•	•	•	•
Lithuania - Lituanie	•	•	•	•	•	•	•	•	•	•	•	•	•
Luxembourg	•	•	•	•	•	•	•	•	•	•	•	•	•
Malta - Malte	•	•	•	•	•	•	•	•	•	•	•	•	•
Monaco	•				•					•	•	•	•
Montenegro - Monténégro	•	•	•	•	•	•	•	...	...	•	•	•	•
Netherlands - Pays-Bas	•	•	...	•	•	•	•	•		•	•	•	•
Norway - Norvège	•	•	•	•	•	•	•	•	•	•	•	•	•
Poland - Pologne	•	•	•	•	•	•	•	•	•	•	•	•	•
Portugal	•	•	•	•	•	•	•	•	•	•	•	•	•
Republic of Moldova - République de Moldova	•	•	•	•	•	•	•	•	•	•	•	•	•
Romania - Roumanie	•	•	•	•	•	•	•	•	•	•	•	•	•
Russian Federation - Fédération de Russie	•	•	•	•	•	•	•	•	•	•	•	•	•
San Marino - Saint-Marin	•	•	...	•	•	•	•	•		•	•	•	•
Serbia - Serbie	•	•	•	•	•	•	•	•	•	•	•	•	•
Slovakia - Slovaquie	•	•	•	•	•	•	•	•	•	•	•	•	•
Slovenia - Slovénie	•	•	•	•	•	•	•	•	•	•	•	•	•
Spain - Espagne	•	•	•	•	•	•	•	•	•	•	•	•	•

Continent and country or area / Continent et pays ou zone	Table totals	Summary - Apercu 3 Total	3 M/F	4	5	Population 6 Total¹	6 M/F	7 Total	7 M/F	8 Total	8 M/F	9	Fertility - Natalité 10 Total	10 M/F	11	Foetal mortality - Mortalité foetale 12	13	14
EUROPE																		
Svalbard and Jan Mayen Islands - Îles Svalbard et Jan Mayen	3	•	•	...	•	...	...	...	...	...	...	...	...	...	...	...	...	...
Sweden - Suède	30	•	•	•	•	•	•	•	•	•	•	•	•	•	•	•	•	•
Switzerland - Suisse	30	•	•	•	•	•	•	•	•	•	•	•	•	•	•	•	•	•
TFYR of Macedonia - L'ex-R. y. de Macédoine	28	•	•	•	•	•	•	•	•	•	•	•	•	•	•	•	...	...
Ukraine	29	•	•	•	•	•	•	•	•	•	•	•	•	...	•	•	•	•
United Kingdom of Great Britain and Northern Ireland - Royaume-Uni de Grande-Bretagne et d'Irlande du Nord	30	•	•	•	•	•	•	•	•	•	•	•	•	•	•	•	...	•
OCEANIA - OCÉANIE																		
American Samoa - Samoas américaines	17	•	•	•	•	•	•	•	•	•	...	•	•	...	...	...	...	...
Australia - Australie	27	•	•	•	•	•	•	•	•	•	•	•	•	•	•	...	...	...
Cook Islands - Îles Cook	17	•	•	•	•	•	•	•	•	•	...	•	•	...	...	...	...	...
Fiji - Fidji	18	•	•	•	•	•	•	•	•	•	•	•	•	...	...	...	...	...
French Polynesia - Polynésie française	16	•	•	•	•	•	•	•	•	•	...	•	...	...	...	...	...	...
Guam	17	•	•	•	•	•	•	•	•	•	...	•	...	...	...	•	•	...
Kiribati	13	•	•	•	•	•	•	•	•	...	...	...	•	...	...	...	...	...
Marshall Islands - Îles Marshall	12	•	•	...	•	•	•	•	•	•	...	...	•	...	...	...	...	...
Micronesia (Federated States of) - Micronésie (États fédérés de)	10	•	•	•	•	•	•	•	•	...	...	...	•	...	...	...	...	...
Nauru	12	•	•	•	...	•	...	...	...	•	•	•	•	•	...	...	...	...
New Caledonia - Nouvelle-Calédonie	22	•	...	•	•	•	•	•	•	•	...	...	•	...	•	...	...	...
New Zealand - Nouvelle-Zélande	30	•	•	•	•	•	•	•	•	•	•	•	•	•	•	•	•	•
Niue - Nioué	17	•	•	•	•	•	•	•	•	•	...	•	•	...	...	...	...	...
Norfolk Island - Île Norfolk	12	•	•	•	•	•	•	•	•	•	...	•	•	...	...	...	...	...
Northern Mariana Islands - Îles Mariannes septentrionales	15	•	•	•	•	•	•	•	•	•	...	•	•	...	...	...	...	...
Palau - Palaos	16	•	•	•	•	•	•	•	•	•	...	•	•	...	...	...	...	...
Papua New Guinea - Papouasie-Nouvelle-Guinée	7	•	•	...	...	•	•	•	•	•	...	...	...	...	...	...	...	...
Pitcairn	12	•	•	•	•	•	•	•	•	•	...	•	•	...	...	...	...	...
Samoa	18	•	•	•	•	•	•	•	•	•	•	•	•	•	•	...	...	...
Solomon Islands - Îles Salomon	9	•	•	...	•	•	•	•	•	•	...	•	•	...	...	...	...	...
Tokelau - Tokélaou	10	•	•	•	•	•	•	•	•	...	...	•	•	...	...	...	...	...
Tonga	12	•	•	...	•	•	•	•	•	•	...	...	•	...	...	...	...	...
Tuvalu	10	•	•	...	•	•	•	...	...	•	...	...	•	...	...	...	...	...
Vanuatu	9	•	•	...	•	•	•	•	•	•	...	...	•	...	...	...	...	...
Wallis and Futuna Islands - Îles Wallis et Futuna	9	•	...	...	...	•	•	...	...	•	...	...	•	...	...	...	...	...

Table A. Demographic Yearbook 2014 synoptic table: Availability of data by country/area, table and sex, where applicable
Tableau A. Tableau synoptique de l'Annuaire démographique 2014 : Disponibilité des données par pays ou zone, tableau et le sexe, si disponible (continued - suite)

Continent and country or area / Continent et pays ou zone	Infant and maternal mortality - Mortalité infantile et mortalité liée à la maternité				General mortality - Mortalité générale					Nuptiality and divorces - Nuptialité et divortialité			
	15	16 Total	16 M/F	17	18	19 Total	19 M/F	20	21	22	23	24	25
EUROPE													
Svalbard and Jan Mayen Islands - Îles Svalbard et Jan Mayen	...	...	...	...	...	...	...	...	...	...	...	...	...
Sweden - Suède	•	•	•	•	•	•	•	•	•	•	•	•	•
Switzerland - Suisse	•	•	•	•	•	•	•	•	•	•	•	•	•
TFYR of Macedonia - L'ex-R. y. de Macédoine	•	•	•	•	•	•	•	•	•	•	•	•	•
Ukraine	•	•	•	•	•	•	•	•	•	•	•	•	•
United Kingdom of Great Britain and Northern Ireland - Royaume-Uni de Grande-Bretagne et d'Irlande du Nord	•	•	•	•	•	•	•	•	•	•	•	•	•
OCEANIA - OCÉANIE													
American Samoa - Samoas américaines	•	...	...	...	•	...	...	...	•	•	•	...	...
Australia - Australie	•	•	•	...	•	•	•	...	•	•	•	•	•
Cook Islands - Îles Cook	•	...	...	...	•	...	...	...	•	...	•	...	•
Fiji - Fidji	...	...	...	•	•	...	...	...	•	...	•	...	...
French Polynesia - Polynésie française	•	•	...	...	•	...	...	...	•	•	•	...	...
Guam	•	...	...	...	•	...	...	...	•	•	...	•	...
Kiribati	...	...	...	...	•	...	...	...	•	...	...	...	...
Marshall Islands - Îles Marshall	...	...	...	...	...	•	...	...	•	...	...	...	...
Micronesia (Federated States of) - Micronésie (États fédérés de)	...	...	...	...	...	...	...	...	•	...	...	...	...
Nauru	...	...	...	...	•	...	...	...	•	...	...	...	...
New Caledonia - Nouvelle-Calédonie	•	...	•	...	•	...	...	...	•	•	•	...	...
New Zealand - Nouvelle-Zélande	•	•	•	...	•	•	•	...	•	•	•	•	•
Niue - Nioué	...	...	...	...	•	...	...	...	•	...	•	...	...
Norfolk Island - Île Norfolk	...	...	...	...	•	...	...	...	...	•	...	...	...
Northern Mariana Islands - Îles Mariannes septentrionales	...	...	...	...	•	...	...	...	•	...	...	...	•
Palau - Palaos	...	...	...	...	•	...	...	...	•	...	...	...	...
Papua New Guinea - Papouasie-Nouvelle-Guinée	...	...	...	...	...	...	...	...	•	...	...	...	...
Pitcairn	...	...	...	...	•	...	...	...	...	...	...	...	...
Samoa	...	...	...	...	•	...	...	...	•	...	•	...	...
Solomon Islands - Îles Salomon	...	...	...	...	•	...	...	...	•	...	...	...	...
Tokelau - Tokélaou	...	...	...	...	...	...	...	...	•	...	...	...	...
Tonga	...	...	...	...	•	•	...	...	•	...	•	...	...
Tuvalu	...	...	...	...	•	•	...	...	•	...	...	...	...
Vanuatu	...	...	...	...	•	...	...	...	•	...	...	...	...
Wallis and Futuna Islands - Îles Wallis et Futuna	...	...	...	...	•	...	...	...	•	...	•	...	...

FOOTNOTES - NOTES

*   Data presented in the table. - Les données présentées dans le tableau.

···   Data not available. - Données non disponibles.

1   Including countries with data on total population only and without data on urban population. - Y compris les pays avec des données sur la population totale mais pas sur la population urbaine.

2   For statistical purposes, the data for China do not include those for the Hong Kong Special Administrative Region (Hong Kong SAR), Macao special Administrative Region (Macao SAR) and Taiwan province of China. - Pour la présentation des statistiques, les données pour Chine ne comprennent pas la Région Administrative Spéciale de Hong Kong (Hong Kong RAS), la Région Administrative Spéciale de Macao (Macao RAS) et Taïwan province de Chine.

3   Including data for the Indian-held part of Jammu and Kashmir, the final status of which has not yet been determined. - Y compris les données pour la partie du Jammu et du Cachemire occupée par l'Inde dont le statut définitif n'a pas encore été déterminé.

4   Including data for East Jerusalem and Israeli residents in certain other territories under occupation by Israeli military forces since June 1967. - Y compris les données pour Jérusalem-Est et les résidents israéliens dans certains autres territoires occupés depuis 1967 par les forces armées israéliennes.

5   Excluding data for the Pakistan-held part of Jammu and Kashmir, the final status of which has not yet been determined. - Non compris les données concernant la partie du Jammu et Cachemire occupée par le Pakistan dont le statut définitif n'a pas été déterminé.

Table 1 – *Demographic Yearbook 2014*

Table 1 presents for the world and major areas and regions estimates of the order of magnitude of population size, rates of population increase, crude birth and death rates, surface area as well as population density.

Description of variables: Estimates of world population by major areas and by regions are presented for 1960, 1970, 1980, 1990, 2000, 2010 and 2014. Average annual percentage rates of population growth, crude birth and crude death rates are shown for the period from 2010 to 2015. Surface area in square kilometers and population density estimates relate to 2014.

All population estimates and rates presented in this table were prepared by the Population Division of the United Nations Department of Economic and Social Affairs, and have been published in the *2015 Revision of World Population Prospects*[1].

The scheme of regionalization used for these estimates is described below. Although some continental totals are given, and all can be derived, this table presents six major areas that are so drawn as to obtain greater homogeneity in sizes of population, types of demographic circumstances and accuracy of demographic statistics. Five of the major areas are subdivided into a total of 20 regions, which are arranged within the major areas; these regions together with Northern America, which is not subdivided, make a total of 21 regions.

The major areas of Northern America and Latin America and the Caribbean are distinguished, rather than the conventional continents of North America and South America, because population trends in the middle American mainland and the Caribbean region more closely resemble those of South America than those of America north of Mexico. Data for the traditional continents of North and South America can be obtained by adding Central America and Caribbean region to Northern America and deducting from Latin America. Latin America, as defined here, has somewhat wider limits than it would be if defined only to include the Spanish-speaking, French-speaking and Portuguese-speaking countries.

The average annual percentage rates of population growth are calculated by the Population Division of the United Nations using an exponential rate of increase.

Crude birth and crude death rates are expressed in terms of the average annual number of births and deaths, respectively, per 1 000 mid-year population. These rates are estimated.

Surface area totals are estimated by the Population Division of the United Nations.

Computation: Density, calculated by the Statistics Division of the United Nations, is the number of persons in the total population of 2014 per square kilometer of total surface area.

Reliability of data: With the exception of surface area, all data are set in *italic* type to indicate their conjectural quality.

Limitations: The estimated orders of magnitude of population and surface area are subject to all the basic limitations set forth in connection with table 3, and to the same qualifications set forth for population and surface area statistics in sections 3 and 2.4 of the Technical Notes, respectively.

Likewise, rates of population increase and density index are affected by the limitations of the original figures. However, it may be noted that, in compiling data for regional and major areas totals, errors in the components may tend to compensate each other and the resulting aggregates may be more reliable than the quality of the individual components would imply.

Because of their estimated character, many of the birth and death rates shown should also be considered only as orders of magnitude, and not as measures of the true level of fertility or mortality.

In interpreting the population densities, one should consider that some of the regions include large segments of land that are uninhabitable or barely habitable, and density values calculated as described make no allowance for this, nor for differences in patterns of land settlement.

Composition of major areas and regions

AFRICA

Eastern Africa
Burundi
Comoros
Djibouti
Eritrea
Ethiopia
Kenya
Madagascar
Malawi
Mauritius
Mayotte
Mozambique
Réunion
Rwanda
Seychelles
Somalia
South Sudan
Uganda
United Republic of Tanzania
Zambia
Zimbabwe

Middle Africa
Angola
Cameroon
Central African Republic
Chad
Congo
Democratic Republic of the
  Congo
Equatorial Guinea
Gabon
Sao Tome and Principe

Northern Africa
Algeria
Egypt
Libyan Arab Jamahiriya
Morocco
Sudan
Tunisia
Western Sahara

Southern Africa
Botswana
Lesotho
Namibia
South Africa
Swaziland

Western Africa
Benin
Burkina Faso
Cabo Verde
Côte d'Ivoire
Gambia

Ghana
Guinea
Guinea-Bissau
Liberia
Mali
Mauritania
Niger
Nigeria
Saint Helena
Senegal
Sierra Leone
Togo

ASIA

Eastern Asia
China
China, Hong Kong SAR
China, Macao SAR
Democratic People's
  Republic of Korea
Japan
Mongolia
Republic of Korea

South-Central Asia
Afghanistan
Bangladesh
Bhutan
India
Iran (Islamic Republic of)
Kazakhstan
Kyrgyzstan
Maldives
Nepal
Pakistan
Sri Lanka
Tajikistan
Turkmenistan
Uzbekistan

South-Eastern Asia
Brunei Darussalam
Cambodia
Indonesia
Lao People's Democratic
  Republic
Malaysia
Myanmar
Philippines
Singapore
Thailand
Timor Leste
Viet Nam

Western Asia
Armenia
Azerbaijan

Bahrain
Cyprus
Georgia
Iraq
Israel
Jordan
Kuwait
Lebanon
Oman
Qatar
Saudi Arabia
State of Palestine
Syrian Arab Republic
Turkey
United Arab Emirates
Yemen

EUROPE

Eastern Europe
Belarus
Bulgaria
Czech Republic
Hungary
Poland
Republic of Moldova
Romania
Russian Federation
Slovakia
Ukraine

Northern Europe
Åland Islands
Denmark
Estonia
Faeroe Islands
Finland
Guernsey
Iceland
Ireland
Isle of Man
Jersey
Latvia
Lithuania
Norway
Sweden
United Kingdom of Great Britain
  and Northern Ireland

Southern Europe
Albania
Andorra
Bosnia and Herzegovina
Croatia
Gibraltar
Greece
Holy See

Italy
Malta
Montenegro
Portugal
San Marino
Serbia
Slovenia
Spain
TFYR of Macedonia

Western Europe
Austria
Belgium
France
Germany
Liechtenstein
Luxembourg
Monaco
Netherlands
Switzerland

**LATIN AMERICA
and the CARIBBEAN**

Caribbean
Anguilla
Antigua and Barbuda
Aruba
Bahamas
Barbados
Bonaire, Saba and Sint Eustatius
British Virgin Islands
Cayman Islands
Cuba
Curaçao
Dominica
Dominican Republic
Grenada
Guadaloupe
Haiti
Jamaica
Martinique

Montserrat
Puerto Rico
Saint Kitts and Nevis
Saint Lucia
Saint Vincent and the
 Grenadines
Sint Maarten (Dutch part)
Trinidad and Tobago
Turks and Caicos Islands
United States Virgin
 Islands

Central America
Belize
Costa Rica
El Salvador
Guatemala
Honduras
Mexico
Nicaragua
Panama

South America
Argentina
Bolivia (Plurinational State of)
Brazil
Chile
Colombia
Ecuador
Falkland Islands (Malvinas)
French Guiana
Guyana
Paraguay
Peru
Suriname
Uruguay
Venezuela (Bolivarian Republic of)

NORTHERN AMERICA

Bermuda

Canada
Greenland
Saint Pierre and Miquelon
United States of America

OCEANIA

Australia and New Zealand
Australia
New Zealand
Norfolk Island

Melanesia
Fiji
New Caledonia
Papua New Guinea
Solomon Islands
Vanuatu

Micronesia
Guam
Kiribati
Marshall Islands
Micronesia (Federated States of)
Nauru
Northern Mariana Islands
Palau

Polynesia
American Samoa
Cook Islands
French Polynesia
Niue
Pitcairn
Samoa
Tokelau
Tonga
Tuvalu
Wallis and Futuna Islands

---

[1] United Nations, Department of Economic and Social Affairs, Population Division (2015). *2015 Revision of World Population Prospects* (http://esa.un.org/unpd/wpp/).

Tableau 1 – *Annuaire démographique 2014*

Le tableau 1 présente, pour l'ensemble du monde et les grandes zones et régions, des estimations concernant l'ordre de grandeur de la population, les taux d'accroissement démographique, les taux bruts de natalité et de mortalité, la superficie et la densité de peuplement.

Description des variables : des estimations de la population mondiale par grandes zones et régions sont présentées pour 1960, 1970, 1980, 1990, 2000 et 2010 ainsi que pour 2014. Les taux annuels moyens d'accroissement de la population et les taux bruts de natalité et de mortalité portent sur la période allant de 2010 à 2015. Les indications concernant la superficie exprimée en kilomètres carrés et les estimations de la densité de population se rapportent à 2014.

Toutes les estimations de population et les taux de natalité, taux de mortalité et taux annuels d'accroissement de la population qui sont présentés dans le tableau 1 ont été établis par la Division de la population du Département des affaires économiques et sociales de l'Organisation des Nations Unies, et ont été publiés dans les *Perspectives de la population mondiale : La révision de 2015*[1].

Bien que l'on ait donné certains totaux pour les continents (tous les autres pouvant être calculés), on a réparti le monde en six grandes zones qui ont été découpées de manière à obtenir une plus grande homogénéité du point de vue des dimensions de population, des types de situations démographiques et de l'exactitude des statistiques démographiques.

Cinq de ces six grandes zones ont été subdivisées en 20 régions. Avec l'Amérique septentrionale, qui n'est pas subdivisée, on arrive à un total de 21 régions.

Au lieu de faire la distinction classique entre l'Amérique du Nord et l'Amérique du Sud, on a choisi d'opérer une comparaison entre l'Amérique septentrionale et l'Amérique latine et Caraïbes, parce que les tendances démographiques dans la partie continentale de l'Amérique centrale et dans la région des Caraïbes se rapprochent davantage de celles de l'Amérique du Sud que de celles de l'Amérique au nord du Mexique. On obtient les données pour les continents traditionnels de l'Amérique du Nord et de l'Amérique du Sud en extrayant les données concernant l'Amérique centrale et les Caraïbes de celles relatives à l'Amérique latine et en les regroupant avec celles relatives à l'Amérique septentrionale. L'Amérique latine ainsi définie a par conséquent des limites plus larges que celles des pays ou zones de langues espagnole, portugaise et française qui constituent l'Amérique latine au sens le plus strict du terme.

Les taux annuels moyens d'accroissement de la population sont calculés par la Division de la population de l'Organisation des Nations Unies en appliquant un taux d'accroissement exponentiel.

Les taux bruts de natalité et de mortalité représentent respectivement le nombre annuel moyen de naissances et de décès par millier d'habitants en milieu d'année. Ces taux sont estimatifs.

La superficie totale a été estimée par la Division de la population de l'Organisation des Nations Unies.

Calculs : la densité, calculée par la Division de statistique de l'Organisation des Nations Unies, est égale au rapport entre l'effectif total de la population en 2014 et la superficie totale exprimée en kilomètres carrés.

Fiabilité des données : á l'exception des données concernant la superficie, toutes les données sont reproduites en *italique* pour en faire ressortir le caractère conjectural.

Insuffisance des données : les estimations concernant l'ordre de grandeur de la population et la superficie reposent en partie sur les données du tableau 3 ; elles appellent donc toutes les réserves fondamentales formulées à propos de ce tableau, et celles qui ont été respectivement formulées aux sections 3 et 2.4 des Notes techniques en ce qui concerne les statistiques relatives à la population et à la superficie.

Les taux d'accroissement et les indices de densité de la population se ressentent eux aussi des insuffisances inhérentes aux données de base. Toutefois, il est à noter que, lorsque l'on additionne des données par territoire pour obtenir des totaux régionaux et par grandes zones, les erreurs qu'elles comportent arrivent parfois à s'équilibrer, de sorte que les agrégats obtenus peuvent être un peu plus exacts que chacun des éléments dont on est parti.

Vu leur caractère estimatif, nombre des taux de natalité et de mortalité du tableau 1 doivent être considérés uniquement comme des ordres de grandeur et ne sont pas censés mesurer exactement le niveau de la natalité ou de la mortalité.

Pour interpréter les valeurs de la densité de population, on se souviendra qu'il existe dans certaines des régions de vastes étendues de terres inhabitables ou à peine habitables et que les chiffres calculés selon la méthode indiquée ne tiennent compte ni de ce fait ni des différences de dispersion de la population selon le mode d'habitat.

Composition des grandes zones et régions

AFRIQUE

Afrique orientale
Burundi
Comores
Djibouti
Érythrée
Éthiopie
Kenya
Madagascar
Malawi
Maurice
Mayotte
Mozambique
Ouganda
République-Unie de Tanzanie
Réunion
Rwanda
Seychelles
Somalie
Soudan du Sud
Zambie
Zimbabwe

Afrique centrale
Angola
Cameroun
Congo
Gabon
Guinée équatoriale
République centrafricaine
République démocratique du Congo
Sao Tomé-et-Principe
Tchad

Afrique septentrionale
Algérie
Égypte
Jamahiriya arabe libyenne
Maroc
Sahara occidental
Soudan
Tunisie

Afrique australe
Afrique du Sud
Botswana
Lesotho
Namibie
Swaziland

Afrique occidentale
Bénin
Burkina Faso
Cabo Verde
Côte d'Ivoire
Gambie
Ghana
Guinée
Guinée-Bissau
Libéria
Mali
Mauritanie
Niger
Nigéria
Sainte-Hélène
Sénégal
Sierra Leone
Togo

AMÉRIQUE LATINE ET CARAÏBES

Caraïbes
Anguilla
Antigua-et-Barbuda
Aruba
Bahamas
Barbade
Bonaire, Saint-Eustache et Saba
Cuba
Curaçao
Dominique
Grenade
Guadeloupe
Haïti
Îles Caïmanes
Îles Turques et Caïques
Îles Vierges américaines
Îles Vierges britanniques
Jamaïque
Martinique
Montserrat
Porto Rico
République dominicaine
Saint-Kitts-et-Nevis
Sainte-Lucie
Saint-Martin
(partie néerlandaise)
Saint-Vincent-et-les
Grenadines
Trinité-et-Tobago

Amérique centrale
Belize
Costa Rica
El Salvador
Guatemala
Honduras
Mexique
Nicaragua
Panama

Amérique du Sud
Argentine
Bolivie (État plurinational de)
Brésil
Chili
Colombie
Équateur
Guyana
Guyane française
Îles Falkland (Malvinas)
Paraguay
Pérou
Suriname
Uruguay
Venezuela (République bolivarienne du)

AMÉRIQUE SEPTENTRIONALE

Bermudes
Canada
États-Unis d'Amérique
Groenland
Saint-Pierre-et-Miquelon

ASIE

Asie orientale
Chine
Chine, Région administrative spéciale de Hong Kong
Chine, Région administrative spéciale de Macao
Japon
Mongolie
République de Corée
République populaire démocratique de Corée

Asie centrale et Asie du Sud
Afghanistan
Bangladesh
Bhoutan
Inde
Iran (République Islamique d')
Kazakhstan
Kirghizistan

Maldives
Népal
Ouzbékistan
Pakistan
Sri Lanka
Tadjikistan
Turkménistan

Asie du Sud-Est
Brunéi Darussalam
Cambodge
Indonésie
Malaisie
Myanmar
Philippines
République démocratique populaire
lao
Singapour
Thaïlande
Timor-Leste
Viet Nam

Asie occidentale
Arabie saoudite
Arménie
Azerbaïdjan
Bahreïn
Chypre
Émirats arabes unis
État de Palestine
Géorgie
Iraq
Israël
Jordanie
Koweït
Liban
Oman
Qatar
République arabe syrienne
Turquie
Yémen

EUROPE

Europe orientale
Bélarus
Bulgarie

Fédération de Russie
Hongrie
Pologne
République de Moldova
République tchèque
Roumanie
Slovaquie
Ukraine

Europe septentrionale
Danemark
Estonie
Finlande
Guernesey
Île de Man
Îles d'Åland
Îles Féroé
Îles Svalbard et Jan Mayen
Irlande
Islande
Jersey
Lettonie
Lituanie
Norvège
Royaume-Uni de Grande-
  Bretagne et d'Irlande du
  Nord
Suède

Europe méridionale
Albanie
Andorre
Bosnie-Herzégovine
Croatie
Espagne
Gibraltar
Grèce
Italie
L'ex-R. y. de Macédoine
Malte
Monténégro
Portugal
Saint-Marin
Saint-Siège
Serbie
Slovénie

Europe occidentale
Allemagne
Autriche
Belgique
France
Liechtenstein
Luxembourg
Monaco
Pays-Bas
Suisse

OCÉANIE

Australie et Nouvelle-Zélande
Australie
Île Norfolk
Nouvelle-Zélande

Mélanésie
Fidji
Îles Salomon
Nouvelle-Calédonie
Papouasie-Nouvelle-Guinée
Vanuatu

Micronésie
Guam
Îles Mariannes septentrionales
Îles Marshall
Kiribati
Micronésie (États fédérés de)
Nauru
Palaos

Polynésie
Îles Cook
Îles Wallis et Futuna
Nioué
Pitcairn
Polynésie française
Samoa
Samoa américaines
Tokélaou
Tonga
Tuvalu

NOTE

[1] Organisation des Nations Unies, Département des affaires économiques et sociales, Division de la population (2015). *Perspectives de la population mondiale : La révision de 2015* (http://esa.un.org/unpd/wpp/).

1. Population, rate of increase, birth and death rates, surface area and density for the world, major areas and regions: selected years
Population, taux d'accroissement, taux de natalité et taux de mortalité, superficie et densité pour l'ensemble du monde, les régions macro géographiques et les composantes géographiques : diverses années

Major areas and regions / Régions macro géographiques et composantes	Mid-year population estimates - Estimations de population au milieu de l'année (millions)							Annual rate of increase - Taux d'accroissement annuel (%)	Crude birth rate - Taux bruts de natalité	Crude death rate - Taux bruts de mortalité	Surface area (km2) - Superficie (km2) (000s)	Density - Densité[1]
	1960	1970	1980	1990	2000	2010	2014	2010-2015	2010-2015	2010-2015	2014	2014
WORLD TOTAL - ENSEMBLE DU MONDE	3 018.3	3 682.5	4 439.6	5 309.7	6 126.6	6 929.7	7 265.8	1.2	20	8	136 162	53
AFRICA - AFRIQUE	284.9	365.6	478.0	631.6	814.1	1 044.1	1 156.6	2.6	36	10	30 311	38
Eastern Africa - Afrique orientale	84.3	110.4	147.5	198.2	259.4	342.7	383.7	2.8	37	9	7 005	55
Middle Africa - Afrique centrale	32.2	40.8	53.1	70.9	96.1	130.6	147.5	3.0	42	12	6 613	22
Northern Africa - Afrique septentrionale	63.7	82.9	106.9	140.1	171.9	203.7	219.7	1.9	27	6	7 880	28
Southern Africa - Afrique méridionale	19.7	25.5	33.0	42.0	51.5	59.1	62.0	1.2	22	12	2 675	23
Western Africa - Afrique occidentale	84.9	106.0	137.4	180.3	235.2	308.0	343.8	2.7	40	12	6 138	56
LATIN AMERICA AND CARIBBEAN - AMÉRIQUE LATIN ET CARAÏBES	221.2	288.5	365.0	446.9	526.9	599.8	627.6	1.1	18	6	20 546	31
Caribbean - Caraïbes	20.7	25.3	29.7	34.2	38.3	41.6	42.9	0.7	18	8	234	183
Central America - Amérique centrale	51.4	69.7	92.4	114.8	138.8	161.1	170.5	1.4	20	5	2 480	69
South America - Amérique méridionale	149.1	193.5	242.9	297.9	349.8	397.1	414.3	1.0	17	6	17 832	23
NORTHERN AMERICA - AMÉRIQUE SEPTENTRIONALE	204.2	231.0	254.2	280.6	313.7	344.1	355.2	0.8	12	8	21 776	16
ASIA - ASIE	1 686.7	2 120.4	2 625.6	3 202.5	3 714.5	4 169.9	4 349.6	1.0	18	7	31 915	136
Eastern Asia - Asie orientale	788.1	978.1	1 173.4	1 368.6	1 496.3	1 575.3	1 605.4	0.5	12	7	11 799	136
South Central Asia - Asie centrale méridionale	618.6	774.8	980.3	1 239.7	1 507.1	1 765.1	1 865.4	1.4	22	7	10 791	173
South Eastern Asia - Asie méridionale orientale	213.8	281.5	358.1	445.7	526.2	596.7	626.2	1.2	19	7	4 495	139
Western Asia - Asie occidentale	66.2	86.0	113.8	148.6	185.0	232.7	252.6	2.0	23	5	4 831	52
EUROPE	605.6	657.2	693.9	721.1	726.4	735.4	738.0	0.1	11	11	23 049	32
Eastern Europe - Europe orientale	253.6	276.4	295.0	310.0	303.8	294.6	293.3	-0.1	12	13	18 814	16
Northern Europe - Europe septentrionale	81.8	87.3	89.8	92.0	94.4	99.7	101.8	0.5	12	9	1 810	56
Southern Europe - Europe méridionale	117.9	127.6	138.5	143.4	145.1	153.4	152.6	-0.1	9	10	1 317	116
Western Europe - Europe occidentale	152.3	165.9	170.5	175.6	183.2	187.8	190.2	0.3	10	10	1 108	172
OCEANIA - OCÉANIA	15.8	19.7	23.0	27.0	31.1	36.4	38.8	1.5	17	7	8 564	5
Australia and New Zealand - Australie et Nouvelle Zélande	12.7	15.7	17.9	20.5	23.0	26.5	28.1	1.4	14	7	8 012	4
Melanesia - Melanésie	2.6	3.3	4.3	5.5	7.0	8.7	9.4	2.0	28	7	541	17
Micronesia	0.2	0.2	0.3	0.4	0.5	0.5	0.5	0.9	21	6	3	174
Polynesia - Polynésie	0.3	0.4	0.5	0.5	0.6	0.7	0.7	0.7	21	6	8	85

FOOTNOTES - NOTES

[1] Population per square kilometre of surface area. Figures are estimates of population divided by surface area and are not to be considered as either reflecting density in the urban sense or as indicating the supporting power of a territory's land and resources. - Habitants par kilomètre carré. Il s'agit simplement du quotient calculé en divisant la population par la superficie et n'est par considéré comme indiquant la densité au sens urbain du terme ni l'effectif de population que les terres et les ressources du territoire sont capables de nourrir.

Table 2 - *Demographic Yearbook 2014*

Table 2 presents estimates of population and the percentage distribution by age and sex as well as the sex ratio for all ages; data are presented for the world, the six major areas and the twenty regions for 2014.

Description of variables: All population estimates presented in this table are prepared by the Population Division of the United Nations Department of Economic and Social Affairs. These estimates are published (using more detailed age groups) in the *2015 Revision of World Population Prospects*[1].

The scheme of regionalization used for these estimates is discussed in detail in the technical notes for table 1. Age groups presented in this table are: 0-14 years, 15-64 years, and 65 years or over. Sex ratio refers to the number of males per 100 females of all ages.

The percentage distributions and the sex ratios that appear in this table were calculated by the Statistics Division of the United Nations Department of Economic and Social Affairs using the estimates prepared by the Population Division of the United Nations Department of Economic and Social Affairs.

Reliability of data: All data are set in *italic* type to indicate their conjectural quality.

Limitations: The data presented in this table are from the same series of estimates, prepared by the Population Division of the United Nations, presented in table 1. The estimated orders of magnitude of population are subject to all the basic limitations set forth for population statistics in section 3 of the Technical Notes. In brief, because they are estimates, these distributions by broad age groups and sex should be considered only as orders of magnitude. However, in compiling data for regional and major areas' totals, errors in the components tend to compensate each other and the resulting aggregates may be somewhat more reliable than the quality of the individual components would imply.

In addition, data in this table are limited by factors affecting data by age. These factors are described in the technical notes for table 7. Because the age groups presented in this table are broad, these problems are minimized.

NOTES

[1] United Nations, Department of Economic and Social Affairs, Population Division (2015). *2015 Revision of World Population Prospects* (http://esa.un.org/unpd/wpp/).

Tableau 2 – *Annuaire démographique 2014*

Le tableau 2 présente, pour l'ensemble du monde, les six grandes zones et les vingt régions, des estimations concernant la population en 2014 ainsi que sa répartition en pourcentage selon l'âge et le sexe, et le rapport de masculinité pour tous les âges.

Description des variables : toutes les données figurant dans le tableau 2 ont été établies par la Division de la population du Département des affaires économiques et sociales de l'Organisation des Nations Unies, et ont été publiés dans les *Perspectives de la population mondiale : La révision de 2015*[1].

La classification géographique utilisée pour établir ces estimations est exposée en détail dans les notes techniques relatives au tableau 1. Les groupes d'âge présentés dans ce tableau sont définis comme suit : de 0 à 14 ans, de 15 à 64 ans et 65 ans ou plus. Le rapport de masculinité correspond au nombre d'individus de sexe masculin pour 100 individus de sexe féminin sans considération d'âge.

Les pourcentages et les rapports de masculinité qui sont présentés dans le tableau 2 ont été calculés par la Division de statistique du Département des affaires économiques et sociales de l'Organisation des Nations Unies à partir des estimations établies par la Division de la population de l'Organisation des Nations Unies.

Fiabilité des données : toutes les données figurant dans ce tableau sont reproduites en *italique* pour en faire ressortir le caractère conjectural.

Insuffisance des données : les données de ce tableau appartiennent à la même série d'estimations, établie par la Division de la population de l'Organisation des Nations Unies, que celles qui figurent au tableau 1. Les estimations concernant l'ordre de grandeur de la population appellent donc toutes les réserves fondamentales qui ont été formulées à la section 3 des Notes techniques à propos des statistiques relatives à la population. Sans entrer dans le détail, il convient de préciser que les données relatives à la répartition par grand groupe d'âge et par sexe doivent être considérées uniquement comme des ordres de grandeur en raison de leur caractère estimatif. Toutefois, il est à noter que, lorsque l'on additionne des données par territoire pour obtenir des totaux régionaux et par grandes zones, les erreurs qu'elles comportent arrivent parfois à s'équilibrer, de sorte que les agrégats obtenus peuvent être un peu plus exacts que chacun des éléments dont on est parti.

En outre, les donnés figurant dans le tableau 2 comportent certaines imprécisions en raison des facteurs influant sur les données par âge (voir à ce propos les notes techniques relatives au tableau 7). Ces imprécisions sont cependant atténuées du fait de l'étendue des groupes d'âge présentés dans le tableau 2.

NOTE

[1] Organisation des Nations Unies, Département des affaires économiques et sociales, Division de la population (2015). *Perspectives de la population mondiale : La révision de 2015* (http://esa.un.org/unpd/wpp/).

2. Estimates of population and its percentage distribution, by age and sex and sex ratio for all ages for the world, major areas and regions: 2014

Estimations de la population et pourcentage de répartition selon l'âge et le sexe et rapport de masculinité pour l'ensemble du monde, les grandes régions et les régions géographiques : 2014

Major areas and regions / Grandes régions et régions	Both sexes - Les deux sexes				Male - Masculin				Female - Féminin				Sex ratio - Rapport de masculinité[1]
	All ages - Tous âges	0-14	15-64	65+	All ages - Tous âges	0-14	15-64	65+	All ages - Tous âges	0-14	15-64	65+	
WORLD TOTAL - ENSEMBLE DU MONDE													
Number - Nombre	7 266	1 902	4 774	589	3 665	983	2 418	264	3 601	919	2 357	325	
Percent - Pourcentage	100.0	26.2	65.7	8.1	100.0	26.8	66.0	7.2	100.0	25.5	65.4	9.0	101.8
AFRICA - AFRIQUE													
Number - Nombre	1 157	475	641	40	579	241	320	18	578	234	321	22	
Percent - Pourcentage	100.0	41.1	55.4	3.5	100.0	41.6	55.2	3.1	100.0	40.5	55.6	3.8	100.1
Eastern Africa - Afrique orientale													
Number - Nombre	384	168	204	12	191	84	101	5	193	83	103	7	
Percent - Pourcentage	100.0	43.7	53.2	3.1	100.0	44.3	52.9	2.8	100.0	43.1	53.5	3.4	98.9
Middle Africa - Afrique centrale													
Number - Nombre	147	67	76	4	74	34	38	2	74	33	38	2	
Percent - Pourcentage	100.0	45.6	51.5	2.9	100.0	46.1	51.3	2.6	100.0	45.2	51.6	3.2	99.4
Northern Africa - Afrique septentrionale													
Number - Nombre	220	70	138	11	110	36	69	5	109	34	69	6	
Percent - Pourcentage	100.0	32.1	62.8	5.2	100.0	32.7	62.6	4.7	100.0	31.4	62.9	5.7	100.8
Southern Africa - Afrique méridionale													
Number - Nombre	62	19	40	3	30	10	20	1	31	9	20	2	
Percent - Pourcentage	100.0	30.3	64.8	4.9	100.0	31.2	65.4	3.4	100.0	29.4	64.3	6.3	96.7
Western Africa - Afrique occidentale													
Number - Nombre	344	151	183	10	174	77	92	5	170	74	91	5	
Percent - Pourcentage	100.0	43.9	53.2	2.8	100.0	44.4	53.0	2.6	100.0	43.5	53.5	3.0	101.9
LATIN AMERICA AND CARIBBEAN - AMÉRIQUE LATIN ET CARAÏBES													
Number - Nombre	628	164	417	46	310	84	206	20	317	80	211	26	
Percent - Pourcentage	100.0	26.1	66.5	7.4	100.0	27.0	66.5	6.6	100.0	25.3	66.5	8.2	97.7
Caribbean - Caraïbes													
Number - Nombre	43	11	28	4	21	6	14	2	22	5	14	2	
Percent - Pourcentage	100.0	25.4	65.5	9.2	100.0	26.1	65.5	8.4	100.0	24.6	65.5	9.9	98.3
Central America - Amérique centrale													
Number - Nombre	170	50	110	11	85	25	54	5	86	24	56	6	
Percent - Pourcentage	100.0	29.0	64.8	6.2	100.0	29.9	64.4	5.7	100.0	28.2	65.1	6.6	98.3
South America - Amérique méridionale													
Number - Nombre	414	104	279	32	204	53	138	14	210	51	141	18	
Percent - Pourcentage	100.0	25.0	67.3	7.7	100.0	25.8	67.4	6.7	100.0	24.2	67.1	8.7	97.4
NORTHERN AMERICA - AMÉRIQUE SEPTENTRIONALE													
Number - Nombre	355	67	237	52	176	34	119	23	179	33	118	29	
Percent - Pourcentage	100.0	18.8	66.7	14.5	100.0	19.3	67.7	13.0	100.0	18.2	65.8	16.0	98.2
ASIA - ASIE													
Number - Nombre	4 350	1 072	2 959	319	2 225	561	1 515	149	2 125	511	1 444	170	
Percent - Pourcentage	100.0	24.6	68.0	7.3	100.0	25.2	68.1	6.7	100.0	24.0	68.0	8.0	104.7
Eastern Asia - Asie orientale													
Number - Nombre	1 605	270	1 165	171	821	144	597	80	784	126	568	91	
Percent - Pourcentage	100.0	16.8	72.6	10.7	100.0	17.5	72.7	9.7	100.0	16.0	72.4	11.6	104.7
South Central Asia - Asie centrale méridionale													
Number - Nombre	1 865	558	1 209	99	959	292	620	47	906	266	589	51	
Percent - Pourcentage	100.0	29.9	64.8	5.3	100.0	30.4	64.7	4.9	100.0	29.4	65.0	5.7	105.9
South Eastern Asia - Asie méridionale orientale													
Number - Nombre	626	168	422	36	313	86	211	16	314	82	211	21	
Percent - Pourcentage	100.0	26.8	67.4	5.8	100.0	27.5	67.4	5.0	100.0	26.1	67.3	6.6	99.7
Western Asia - Asie occidentale													
Number - Nombre	253	76	163	13	132	39	87	6	121	37	77	7	
Percent - Pourcentage	100.0	30.2	64.7	5.1	100.0	29.7	66.0	4.3	100.0	30.8	63.3	5.9	109.1
EUROPE													
Number - Nombre	738	116	495	128	356	59	245	52	382	56	250	76	
Percent - Pourcentage	100.0	15.7	67.1	17.3	100.0	16.6	68.8	14.6	100.0	14.7	65.5	19.8	93.1
Eastern Europe - Europe orientale													
Number - Nombre	293	46	205	42	138	24	100	15	155	22	105	28	
Percent - Pourcentage	100.0	15.6	69.9	14.5	100.0	17.0	72.2	10.8	100.0	14.4	67.9	17.8	88.9
Northern Europe - Europe septentrionale													
Number - Nombre	102	18	66	18	50	9	33	8	52	9	33	10	
Percent - Pourcentage	100.0	17.6	64.8	17.7	100.0	18.3	65.8	15.9	100.0	16.9	63.8	19.4	97.0
Southern Europe - Europe méridionale													
Number - Nombre	153	22	100	30	74	11	50	13	78	11	50	17	
Percent - Pourcentage	100.0	14.6	65.7	19.7	100.0	15.4	67.3	17.3	100.0	13.8	64.2	22.0	95.2

2. Estimates of population and its percentage distribution, by age and sex and sex ratio for all ages for the world, major areas and regions: 2014
Estimations de la population et pourcentage de répartition selon l'âge et le sexe et rapport de masculinité pour l'ensemble du monde, les grandes régions et les régions géographiques : 2014 (continued - suite)

| Major areas and regions | Population (millions) | | | | | | | | | | | | Sex ratio - Rapport de masculinité[1] |
| | Both sexes - Les deux sexes | | | | Male - Masculin | | | | Female - Féminin | | | | |
Grandes régions et régions	All ages - Tous âges	0-14	15-64	65+	All ages - Tous âges	0-14	15-64	65+	All ages - Tous âges	0-14	15-64	65+	
Western Europe - Europe occidentale													
Number - Nombre	190	30	124	37	93	15	62	16	97	14	62	21	
Percent - Pourcentage	100.0	15.5	64.9	19.5	100.0	16.2	66.4	17.3	100.0	14.9	63.5	21.6	96.2
OCEANIA - OCÉANIA													
Number - Nombre	38.76	9.13	25.10	4.53	19.43	4.70	12.61	2.11	19.33	4.43	12.49	2.42	
Percent - Pourcentage	100.0	23.6	64.8	11.7	100.0	24.2	64.9	10.9	100.0	22.9	64.6	12.5	100.5
Australia and New Zealand - Australie et Nouvelle Zélande													
Number - Nombre	28.12	5.33	18.66	4.13	14.00	2.74	9.34	1.93	14.11	2.59	9.32	2.20	
Percent - Pourcentage	100.0	19.0	66.4	14.7	100.0	19.5	66.7	13.8	100.0	18.4	66.0	15.6	99.2
Melanesia - Melanésie													
Number - Nombre	9.44	3.44	5.68	0.33	4.81	1.78	2.89	0.14	4.63	1.66	2.79	0.18	
Percent - Pourcentage	100.0	36.4	60.1	3.5	100.0	37.0	60.0	3.0	100.0	35.8	60.3	3.9	103.9
Micronesia													
Number - Nombre	0.52	0.16	0.33	0.03	0.26	0.08	0.17	0.01	0.26	0.08	0.17	0.02	
Percent - Pourcentage	100.0	30.0	64.2	5.8	100.0	30.5	64.2	5.2	100.0	29.4	64.2	6.4	102.3
Polynesia - Polynésie													
Number - Nombre	0.68	0.20	0.43	0.04	0.35	0.11	0.22	0.02	0.33	0.10	0.21	0.02	
Percent - Pourcentage	100.0	30.1	63.5	6.4	100.0	30.5	63.8	5.8	100.0	29.7	63.3	7.0	103.7

FOOTNOTES - NOTES

[1] Males per 100 females of all ages - Hommes pour 100 femmes de tous âges

Table 3 - *Demographic Yearbook 2014*

Table 3 presents for each country or area of the world the total, male and female population enumerated at the latest population census, estimates of the mid-year total population for 2010 and 2014, the average annual exponential rate of population increase (or decrease) for the period 2010 to 2014, the surface area and the population density for 2014.

Description of variables: The total, male and female population is the population enumerated at the most recent census for which data are available. The date of this census is given. Population census data are usually the results of a nation-wide gathering of individual information through full field enumeration. Alternatively other approaches for generating reliable statistics on population and housing can be used by countries, such as the use of population registers. Data that are the result of such an alternative approach are also coded as census and are footnoted accordingly. Also, the results of sample surveys, essentially national in character, may be presented showing the appropriate code.

Mid-year population estimates refer to the population on 1 July. Otherwise, a footnote is appended. Mid-year estimates of the total population are those provided by national statistical offices.

Surface area, expressed in square kilometres, refers to the total surface area, comprising land area and inland waters (assumed to consist of major rivers and lakes) and excluding polar regions as well as uninhabited islands. Exceptions to this are noted. Surface areas, originally reported in square miles by the country or area, have been converted to square kilometres using a conversion factor of 2.589988.

Computation: The annual rate of population increase is the average annual exponential rate of population growth between 2010 and 2014, computed by the Statistics Division of the United Nations Department of Economic and Social Affairs using the unrounded mid-year estimates of 2010 and 2014. This rate is expressed as percentage.

Density is the number of persons in the 2014 total population per square kilometre of total surface area.

Reliability of data: Reliable mid-year population estimates are those that are based on a complete census (or a sample survey) and have been adjusted by a continuous population register or on the basis of the calculated balance of births, deaths and migration. Mid-year estimates of this type are considered reliable and appear in roman type. Mid-year estimates not calculated on this basis are considered less reliable and are shown in italics.

Census data and sample survey results are considered reliable and, therefore, appear in roman type.

Rates of population increase that were calculated using population estimates considered less reliable, as described above, are set in italics rather than roman type.

All surface area data are assumed to be reliable and therefore appear in roman type.

Population density data, however, are considered reliable or less reliable on the basis of the reliability of the 2014 population estimates used as the numerator.

Limitations: Statistics on the total population enumerated at the time of the census, estimates of the mid-year total population and surface area data are subject to the same qualifications as have been set forth for population and surface area statistics in sections 3 and 2.4 of the Technical Notes, respectively.

Regarding the limitations of census data, it should be noted that although census data are considered reliable, and therefore appear in roman type, the actual quality of census data varies widely from one country or area to another. When known, an estimate of the extent of over-enumeration or under-enumeration is given in footnotes.

Rates of population increase are subject to all the qualifications of the population estimates mentioned above. In some cases, they simply reflect the rate calculated or assumed in constructing the estimates themselves when adequate measures of natural increase and net migration were not available. Despite their shortcomings, these rates provide a useful index for studying population change and can be also useful in evaluating the accuracy of vital and migration statistics.

Population density data as shown in this table give only an indication of actual population density as they do not take account of the dispersion or concentration of population within countries or areas nor the proportion of habitable land. They should not be interpreted as reflecting density in the urban sense or as indicating the supporting power of a territory's land and resources.

Tableau 3 – *Annuaire démographique 2014*

Le tableau 3 indique pour chaque pays ou zone du monde la population totale selon le sexe d'après les derniers recensements effectués, les estimations concernant la population totale au milieu de l'année 2010 et de l'année 2014, le taux moyen d'accroissement annuel exponentiel positif ou négatif de la population pour la période allant de 2010 à 2014, ainsi que la superficie et la densité de population en 2014.

Description des variables : la population masculine et féminine totale est, la population enregistrée lors du recensement le plus récent sur lequel on dispose de données. La date de ce recensement est indiquée. Les données des recensements de la population sont habituellement le résultat d'un collecte à l'échelle nationale des données individuelles obtenues au moyen d'un dénombrement complet. Les pays peuvent recourir à d'autres moyens pour établir des statistiques fiables sur la population et le logement, tels que des registres de la population. Les données obtenues par ce moyen sont présentées comme celles d'un recensement et sont annotées en conséquence. Par ailleurs, les résultats des enquêtes par sondage, réalisées habituellement à l'échelle nationale, peuvent être présentés à l'aide du code correspondant.

Les estimations de la population en milieu d'année sont celles de la population au 1er juillet. Lorsque la date est différente, cela est signalé par une note. Les estimations de la population totale en milieu d'année sont celles qui ont été communiquées par les services nationaux de statistique.

La superficie - exprimée en kilomètres carrés - représente la superficie totale, c'est-à-dire qu'elle englobe les terres émergées et les eaux intérieures (qui sont censées comprendre les principaux lacs et cours d'eau) mais exclut les régions polaires et certaines îles inhabitées. Les exceptions à cette règle sont signalées en note. Les superficies initialement exprimées en miles carrés par les pays ou les zones ont été transformées en kilomètres carrés au moyen d'un coefficient de conversion de 2,589988.

Calculs : le taux d'accroissement annuel est le taux exponentiel annuel moyen de variation (en pourcentage) de la population entre 2010 et 2014, calculé par la Division de statistique du Département des affaires économiques et sociales de l'Organisation des Nations Unies à partir des estimations en milieu d'année non arrondies pour les années 2010 et 2014.

La densité est égale au rapport de l'effectif total de la population en 2014 à la superficie totale, exprimée en kilomètres carrés.

Fiabilité des données : les estimations en milieu d'année qui sont considérées sûres sont fondées sur un recensement complet (ou sur une enquête par sondage) et ont été ajustées en fonction des données provenant d'un registre permanent de population ou en fonction de la balance établie par le calcul des naissances, des décès et des migrations. Les estimations de ce type sont considérées comme sûres et apparaissent en caractères romains. Les estimations en milieu d'année dont le calcul n'a pas été effectué sur cette base sont considérées comme moins sûres et apparaissent en italique.

Les données de recensements ou les résultats d'enquêtes par sondage sont considérés comme sûrs et apparaissent par conséquent en caractères romains.

Les taux d'accroissement de la population, calculés à partir d'estimations jugées moins sûres d'après les normes décrites ci-dessus, sont indiqués en italique plutôt qu'en caractères romains.

Toutes les données de superficie sont présumées sûres et apparaissent par conséquent en caractères romains. En revanche, les données relatives à la densité de la population sont considérées plus ou moins sûres en fonction de la fiabilité des estimations de la population en 2014 ayant servi de numérateur.

Insuffisance des données : les statistiques portant sur la population totale dénombrée lors d'un recensement, les estimations de la population totale en milieu d'année et les données de superficie appellent les mêmes réserves que celles formulées aux sections 3 et 2.4 des Notes techniques à propos des statistiques relatives à la population et à la superficie.

S'agissant de l'insuffisance des données obtenues par recensement, il convient d'indiquer que, bien que ces données soient considérées comme sûres et apparaissent par conséquent en caractères romains, leur qualité réelle varie considérablement d'un pays ou d'une région à l'autre. Lorsque l'on possédait les renseignements voulus, on a donné une estimation du degré de sur-dénombrement ou de sous-dénombrement.

Les taux d'accroissement appellent toutes les réserves formulées plus haut à propos des estimations concernant la population. Dans certains cas, ils représentent seulement le taux calculé ou que l'on a pris pour base pour établir les estimations elles-mêmes lorsque l'on ne disposait pas de mesures appropriées de l'accroissement naturel et des migrations nettes. Malgré leurs imperfections, ces taux fournissent des indications intéressantes pour l'étude du mouvement de la population et, utilisés avec les précautions nécessaires, ils peuvent également servir à évaluer l'exactitude des statistiques de l'état civil et des migrations.

Les données relatives à la densité de population figurant dans le tableau 3 n'ont qu'une valeur indicative en ce qui concerne la densité de population effective, car elles ne tiennent compte ni de la dispersion ou de la concentration de la population à l'intérieur des pays ou zones, ni de la proportion du territoire qui est habitable. Il ne faut donc y voir d'indication ni de la densité au sens urbain du terme ni du nombre d'habitants qui pourraient vivre sur les terres et avec les ressources naturelles du territoire considéré.

3. Population by sex, annual rate of population increase, surface area and density
Population selon le sexe, taux d'accroissement annuel de la population, superficie et densité

Continent, country or area and census date — Continent, pays ou zone et date du recensement	Census type[a]	Population at the latest available census — Population d'après le dernier recensement disponible (in units — en unités)			Estimate type[a]	Mid-year estimates — Estimations au milieu de l'année (in thousands — en milliers)		Annual rate of increase Taux d' accrois sement annuel 2010-14	Surface area Superficie (km²) 2014	Density Densité 2014[b]
		Both sexes Les deux sexes	Male Masculin	Female Feminin		2010	2014			

AFRICA - AFRIQUE

Algeria - Algérie										
16 IV 2008 .... DF		34 452 759[1]	17 428 500[1]	17 024 259[1]	DJ	35 978	39 114	2.1	2 381 741	16
Angola										
16 V 2014 .... DF		*24 383 301	*11 803 488	*12 579 813		...	...	...	1 246 700	...
Benin - Bénin										
11 V 2013 .... DJ		*9 983 884	*4 868 180	*5 115 704	DF	8 779[2]	...	...	114 763	...
Botswana										
9 VIII 2011 .... DF		2 024 904	988 957	1 035 947	DJ	1 823	...	...	582 000	...
Burkina Faso										
9 XII 2006 .... DF		14 196 259	6 842 560	7 353 699	DJ	15 731[2]	...	...	272 967	...
Burundi										
16 VIII 2008 .... DF		7 877 728	3 838 045	4 039 683	DF	8 488[3]	9 530[3]	2.9	27 834	342
Cabo Verde										
16 VI 2010 .... DJ		491 683	243 401	248 282	DF	518	...	...	4 033	...
Cameroon - Cameroun										
11 XI 2005 .... DF		17 052 134	8 408 495	8 643 639	DJ	19 406[4]	...	...	475 650	...
Central African Republic - République centrafricaine										
8 XII 2003 .... DF		3 151 072	1 569 446	1 581 626		...	...	...	622 984	...
Chad - Tchad										
20 V 2009 .... DJ		11 175 915	5 509 522	5 666 393		...	...	...	1 284 000	...
Comoros - Comores										
1 IX 2003 .... DF		575 660[5]	285 590[5]	290 070[5]		...	...	...	2 235	...
Congo										
28 IV 2007 .... DF		3 697 490	1 821 357	1 876 133		...	...	...	342 000	...
Côte d'Ivoire										
15 V 2014 .... DF		22 671 331	11 708 244	10 963 087		...	...	...	322 463	...
Democratic Republic of the Congo - République démocratique du Congo										
1 VII 1984 .... DF		29 916 800	14 543 800	15 373 000		...	...	...	2 344 858	...
Djibouti										
29 V 2009 .... DF		818 159	440 067	378 092	DF	841[6]	...	...	23 200	...
Egypt - Égypte										
21 XI 2006 .... DF		72 798 031	37 219 056	35 578 975	DF	78 685	86 814	2.5	1 002 000	87
Equatorial Guinea - Guinée équatoriale										
1 II 2002 .... DF		1 014 999	501 387	513 612		...	...	...	28 051	...
Eritrea - Érythrée										
9 V 1984 .... DF		2 748 304	1 374 452	1 373 852		...	...	...	117 600	...
Ethiopia - Éthiopie										
29 V 2007 .... DF		73 750 932	37 217 130	36 533 802		...	...	...	1 104 300	...
Gabon										
1 XII 2003 .... DF		1 269 732	...	...		...	...	...	267 668	...
Gambia - Gambie										
15 IV 2013 .... DF		*1 882 450	*930 699	*951 751		...	...	...	11 295	...
Ghana										
26 IX 2010 .... DF		24 658 823	12 024 845	12 633 978	DF	...	27 043[2]	...	238 537	113
Guinea - Guinée										
1 III 2014 .... DF		*10 628 972	*5 142 088	*5 486 884	DF	10 537[2]	...	...	245 857	...
Guinea-Bissau - Guinée-Bissau										
15 III 2009 .... DF		1 520 830	737 634	783 196	DF	1 558[2]	...	...	36 125	...
Kenya										
24 VIII 2009 .... DF		38 610 097	19 192 458	19 417 639	DF	38 910[7]	42 961[7]	2.5	591 958	73
Lesotho										
13 IV 2006 .... DF		1 741 406	818 379	923 027	DF	1 892[2]	...	...	30 355	...
Liberia - Libéria										
21 III 2008 .... DF		3 476 608	1 739 945	1 736 663	DF	3 627	3 946	2.1	111 369	35
Libya - Libye										
15 IV 2006 .... DF		*5 298 152	*2 687 513	*2 610 639	DF	5 689	6 096	1.7	1 676 198	4
Madagascar										
1 VIII 1993 .... DF		12 238 914	6 088 116	6 150 798	DF	20 142	...	...	587 295	...

3. Population by sex, annual rate of population increase, surface area and density
Population selon le sexe, taux d'accroissement annuel de la population, superficie et densité (continued - suite)

Continent, country or area and census date / Continent, pays ou zone et date du recensement	Census type[a]	Population at the latest available census / Population d'après le dernier recensement disponible (in units — en unités)			Estimate type[a]	Mid-year estimates Estimations au milieu de l'année (in thousands — en milliers)		Annual rate of increase Taux d' accrois sement annuel 2010-14	Surface area Superficie (km²) 2014	Density Densité 2014[b]
		Both sexes Les deux sexes	Male Masculin	Female Feminin		2010	2014			
AFRICA - AFRIQUE										
Malawi										
8 VI 2008 .... DF	DF	13 077 160	6 358 933	6 718 227	DF	13 949[8]	...	...	118 484	...
Mali										
1 IV 2009 .... DF	DF	14 528 662	7 204 990	7 323 672		...	...	...	1 240 192	...
Mauritania - Mauritanie										
24 III 2013 .... DF	DF	3 460 388[9]	...	...	DF	3 341[2]	...	...	1 030 700	...
Mauritius - Maurice[10]										
4 VII 2011 .... DF	DF	1 237 000	611 053	625 947	DJ	1 281[11]	1 261[12]	-0.4	1 969	640
Mayotte										
21 VIII 2012 .... DJ	DJ	212 645	103 164	109 481		...	...	...	...	...
Morocco - Maroc										
1 IX 2004 .... DF	DF	29 680 069	14 640 662	15 039 407	DF	31 894[13]	33 774[13]	1.4	446 550	76
Mozambique										
1 VIII 2007 .... DF	DF	20 252 223	9 746 690	10 505 533	DF	22 417[2]	25 042[2]	2.8	799 380	31
Namibia - Namibie										
28 VIII 2011 .... DF	DF	2 113 077	1 021 912	1 091 165	DF	2 143[2]	2 238[14]	1.1	824 268	3
Niger										
10 XII 2012 .... DJ	DJ	17 138 707	8 518 818	8 619 889	DJ	15 204[2]	...	...	1 267 000	...
Nigeria - Nigéria										
21 III 2006 .... DF	DF	140 431 790	71 345 488	69 086 302		...	...	...	923 768	...
Republic of South Sudan - République de Soudan du Sud										
21 IV 2008 .... DF	DF	8 260 490	4 287 300	3 973 190	DF	9 497[15]	11 071[15]	3.8	658 841	17
Reunion - Réunion										
1 I 2010 .... DJ	DJ	821 136	398 006	423 130	DJ	*828[16]	...	...	2 513	...
Rwanda										
15 VIII 2012 .... DJ	DJ	*10 537 222	*5 074 942	*5 462 280	DF	10 413[2]	...	...	26 338	...
Saint Helena ex. dep. - Sainte-Hélène sans dép.										
10 II 2008 .... DF	DF	4 257	2 165	2 092	DF	4	4	0.9	122	36
Saint Helena: Ascension - Sainte-Hélène: Ascension										
8 III 1998 .... DJ	DJ	712	458	254		...	...	...	88	...
Saint Helena: Tristan da Cunha - Sainte-Hélène: Tristan da Cunha										
31 XII 1988 .... DF	DF	296	139	157		...	...	...	98	...
Sao Tome and Principe - Sao Tomé-et-Principe										
13 V 2012 .... DF	DF	178 739	88 867	89 872	DF	164	...	...	964	...
Senegal - Sénégal										
19 XI 2013 .... DF	DF	*12 873 601	*6 428 189	*6 445 412	DJ	12 509[17]	...	...	196 712[18]	...
Seychelles										
26 VIII 2010 .... DF	DF	90 945	46 912	44 033	DF	90	91	0.4	457	200
Sierra Leone										
4 XII 2004 .... DF	DF	4 976 871	2 420 218	2 556 653	DF	5 747	...	...	72 300	...
Somalia - Somalie										
15 II 1987 .... DF	DF	7 114 431	3 741 664	3 372 767		...	...	...	637 657	...
South Africa - Afrique du Sud										
10 X 2011 .... DF	DF	51 770 560	25 188 791	26 581 769	DF	50 896	54 002	1.5	1 221 037	44
Sudan - Soudan										
21 IV 2008 .... DF	DF	30 894 000	15 786 677	15 107 323	DF	32 962	37 292	3.1	...	...
Swaziland										
11 III 2007 .... DF	DF	844 223	405 868	438 355	DF	1 056	1 106	1.2	17 363	64
Togo										
6 XI 2010 .... DJ	DJ	6 191 155	3 009 095	3 182 060		...	...	...	56 785	...
Tunisia - Tunisie										
23 IV 2014 .... DF	DF	10 982 754	5 472 338	5 510 416	DF	10 547	...	...	163 610	...
Uganda - Ouganda										
27 VIII 2014 .... DF	DF	*34 856 813	*16 935 456	*17 921 357	DF	31 785	...	...	241 550	...

3. Population by sex, annual rate of population increase, surface area and density
Population selon le sexe, taux d'accroissement annuel de la population, superficie et densité (continued - suite)

Continent, country or area and census date / Continent, pays ou zone et date du recensement	Census type[a]	Population at the latest available census / Population d'après le dernier recensement disponible (in units — en unités)			Estimate type[a]	Mid-year estimates Estimations au milieu de l'année (in thousands — en milliers)		Annual rate of increase Taux d' accrois sement annuel 2010-14	Surface area Superficie (km²) 2014	Density Densité 2014[b]
		Both sexes Les deux sexes	Male Masculin	Female Feminin		2010	2014			
AFRICA - AFRIQUE										
United Republic of Tanzania - République Unie de Tanzanie										
26 VIII 2012 .... DF		44 928 923[19]	21 869 990[19]	23 058 933[19]	DF	43 188[20]	...	...	947 303	...
Western Sahara - Sahara occidental[21]										
31 XII 1970 .... DF		76 425	43 981	32 444		...	...	...	266 000	...
Zambia - Zambie										
16 X 2010 .... DF		12 526 314	6 117 253	6 409 061	DF	...	15 023[2]	...	752 612	20
Zimbabwe										
17 VIII 2012 .... DF		13 061 239	6 280 539	6 780 700		...	...	...	390 757	...
AMERICA, NORTH - AMÉRIQUE DU NORD										
Anguilla										
11 V 2011 .... DF		*13 550	...	...	DF	16	...	...	91	...
Antigua and Barbuda - Antigua-et-Barbuda										
27 V 2011 .... DF		88 566	...	...	DF	91	...	...	442	...
Aruba										
29 IX 2010 .... DJ		101 484	48 241	53 243	DJ	102	108	1.4	180	599
Bahamas										
3 V 2010 .... DJ		351 461	170 257	181 204	DF	335[2]	372[2]	2.6	13 940	27
Barbados - Barbade										
1 V 2010 .... DJ		277 821	133 018	144 803	DF	276[22]	...	...	430	...
Belize										
12 V 2010 .... DJ		322 453	161 227	161 226	DF	324	359	2.6	22 966	16
Bermuda - Bermudes										
20 V 2010 .... DJ		64 237[23]	30 858[23]	33 379[23]	DJ	64[24]	62[24]	-0.9	53	1 166
British Virgin Islands - Îles Vierges britanniques										
21 V 2001 .... DF		20 647	10 627	10 020	DF	28	...	...	151	...
Canada										
2 V 2011 .... DJ		33 476 690	16 414 225	17 062 455	DJ	34 005[25]	*35 540[26]	1.1	9 984 670	4
Cayman Islands - Îles Caïmanes										
10 X 2010 .... DJ		55 036[27]	27 218[27]	27 818[27]	DJ	55	58[22]	1.5	264	221
Costa Rica										
30 V 2011 .... DJ		4 301 712	2 106 063	2 195 649	DJ	4 538[28]	4 772[28]	1.3	51 100	93
Cuba										
14 IX 2012 .... DF		11 167 325	5 570 825	5 596 500	DJ	11 171	11 224	0.1	109 884	102
Curaçao										
26 III 2011 .... DF		150 563	68 848	81 715	DJ	149[29]	156[30]	1.2	444	351
Dominica - Dominique										
14 V 2011 .... DF		*71 293	*36 411	*34 882		...	...	...	750	...
Dominican Republic - République dominicaine										
1 XII 2010 .... DJ		9 445 281	4 739 038	4 706 243	DF	9 479[2]	9 883[2]	1.0	48 231	205
El Salvador										
12 V 2007 .... DJ		5 744 113	2 719 371	3 024 742	DF	6 183[31]	6 328[31]	0.6	21 041[32]	301
Greenland - Groenland										
1 I 2008 .... DJ		56 462[33]	29 885[33]	26 577[33]	DJ	57[33]	56[33]	-0.1	2 166 086	0
Grenada - Grenade										
25 V 2001 .... DF		102 632	50 481	52 151	DF	105	...	...	345	...
Guadeloupe										
1 I 2010 .... DJ		403 355[34]	187 932[34]	215 423[34]	DJ	403[35]	404[35]	0.0	1 705	237
Guatemala										
24 XI 2002 .... DJ		11 237 196	5 496 839	5 740 357	DF	14 362[20]	...	...	108 889	...
Haiti - Haïti										
11 I 2003 .... DJ		8 373 750	4 039 272	4 334 478	DJ	10 085[36]	...	...	27 750	...
Honduras										
28 VII 2001 .... DF		6 071 200	3 000 530	3 070 670	DF	8 046[37]	...	...	112 492	...

3. Population by sex, annual rate of population increase, surface area and density
Population selon le sexe, taux d'accroissement annuel de la population, superficie et densité (continued - suite)

Continent, country or area and census date / Continent, pays ou zone et date du recensement	Census type[a]	Population at the latest available census / Population d'après le dernier recensement disponible (in units — en unités)			Estimate type[a]	Mid-year estimates / Estimations au milieu de l'année (in thousands — en milliers)		Annual rate of increase / Taux d' accrois sement annuel 2010-14	Surface area / Superficie (km²) 2014	Density / Densité 2014[b]
		Both sexes / Les deux sexes	Male / Masculin	Female / Feminin		2010	2014			
AMERICA, NORTH - AMÉRIQUE DU NORD										
Jamaica - Jamaïque 4 IV 2011	DJ	2 697 983	1 334 533	1 363 450	DJ	2 702	...	...	10 991	...
Martinique 1 I 2010	DJ	394 173	182 073	212 100	DJ	*396[16]	...	...	1 128	...
Mexico - Mexique 12 VI 2010	DF	112 336 538[38]	54 855 231[38]	57 481 307[38]	DJ	114 256[2]	119 713[2]	1.2	1 964 375	61
Montserrat 12 V 2011	DJ	4 922	2 546	2 376	DF	5	5	-0.2	103	48
Nicaragua 4 VI 2005	DJ	5 142 098	2 534 491	2 607 607	DJ	5 816	6 198	1.6	130 373	48
Panama 16 V 2010	DF	3 405 813	1 712 584	1 693 229	DF	3 662[24]	3 913[24]	1.7	75 320	52
Puerto Rico - Porto Rico 1 IV 2010	DJ	3 725 789[39]	1 785 171[39]	1 940 618[39]	DJ	3 721[40]	3 548[40]	-1.2	8 868	400
Saint Kitts and Nevis - Saint-Kitts-et-Nevis 14 V 2001	DF	45 841	22 784	23 057	...	...	...	...	261	...
Saint Lucia - Sainte-Lucie 10 V 2010	DF	*173 720	*86 595	*87 125	...	...	...	...	539[41]	...
Saint Pierre and Miquelon - Saint Pierre-et-Miquelon 1 I 2010	DJ	6 312	...	...	...	...	...	...	242	...
Saint Vincent and the Grenadines - Saint-Vincent-et-les Grenadines 12 VI 2012	DF	*109 991	*56 419	*53 572	DF	110	110	0.1	389	283
Saint-Barthélemy 1 I 2010	DJ	9 072	...	...	...	...	...	...	...	...
Saint-Martin (French part) - Saint-Martin (partie française) 1 I 2010	DJ	37 630	...	...	...	...	...	...	...	...
Sint Maarten (Dutch part) - Saint-Martin (partie néerlandaise) 9 IV 2011	DF	33 609	15 868	17 741	DJ	36	37[16]	1.1	34	1 092
Trinidad and Tobago - Trinité-et-Tobago 9 I 2011	DF	1 332 901	...	...	DF	1 318[11]	1 345[12]	0.5	5 130	262
Turks and Caicos Islands - Îles Turques et Caïques 25 I 2012	DF	31 458	16 037	15 421	DJ	40	...	...	948[42]	...
United States of America - États-Unis d'Amérique 1 IV 2010	DJ	308 745 538	151 781 326	156 964 212	DJ	309 326[43]	...	...	9 833 517	...
United States Virgin Islands - Îles Vierges américaines 1 IV 2010	DJ	106 405[39]	50 854[39]	55 551[39]	DJ	*110[39]	...	...	347	...
AMERICA, SOUTH - AMÉRIQUE DU SUD										
Argentina - Argentine 27 X 2010	DF	40 117 096	19 523 766	20 593 330	DF	40 788[44]	42 674[44]	1.1	2 780 400	15
Bolivia (Plurinational State of) - Bolivie (État plurinational de) 21 XI 2012	DF	10 059 856	5 019 447	5 040 409	DF	10 023	10 681	1.6	1 098 581[45]	10
Brazil - Brésil 31 VII 2010	DJ	190 755 799	93 406 990	97 348 809	...	193 253[46]	202 769[47]	...	8 514 877	24

3. Population by sex, annual rate of population increase, surface area and density
Population selon le sexe, taux d'accroissement annuel de la population, superficie et densité (continued - suite)

Continent, country or area and census date / Continent, pays ou zone et date du recensement	Census type[a]	Population at the latest available census / Population d'après le dernier recensement disponible (in units — en unités)			Estimate type[a]	Mid-year estimates Estimations au milieu de l'année (in thousands — en milliers)		Annual rate of increase Taux d' accrois sement annuel 2010-14	Surface area Superficie (km²) 2014	Density Densité 2014[b]
		Both sexes Les deux sexes	Male Masculin	Female Feminin		2010	2014			
AMERICA, SOUTH - AMÉRIQUE DU SUD										
Chile - Chili										
24 IV 2002 .... DF	DF	15 116 435	7 447 695	7 668 740	DF	17 094	17 819	1.0	756 102	24
Colombia - Colombie										
22 V 2005 .... DF	DF	41 468 384	20 336 117	21 132 267	DJ	45 510[48]	47 662[48]	1.2	1 141 748	42
Ecuador - Équateur										
28 XI 2010 .... DF	DF	14 483 499	7 177 683	7 305 816	DF	15 012[49]	16 027[49]	1.6	257 217	62
Falkland Islands (Malvinas) - Îles Falkland (Malvinas)[50]										
8 X 2006 .... DF	DF	2 955	1 569	1 386		...	...	...	12 173	...
French Guiana - Guyane française										
1 I 2010 .... DJ	DJ	229 040	113 599	115 441	DJ	*230[16]	...	...	83 534	...
Guyana										
15 IX 2012 .... DF	DF	*747 884	*372 547	*375 337	DF	752	...	...	214 969	...
Paraguay										
28 VIII 2002 .... DF	DF	5 163 198	2 603 242	2 559 956	DF	6 451[20]	6 894[20]	1.7	406 752	17
Peru - Pérou										
21 X 2007 .... DF	DF	27 412 157	13 622 640	13 789 517	DF	29 462[51]	30 814[51]	1.1	1 285 216	24
Suriname										
13 VIII 2012 .... DJ	DJ	541 638	270 629	271 009	DJ	531	...	...	163 820	...
Uruguay										
4 X 2011 .... DJ	DJ	3 286 314	1 577 725[52]	1 708 481[52]	DF	3 397	3 454[2]	0.4	173 626	20
Venezuela (Bolivarian Republic of) - Venezuela (République bolivarienne du)										
1 IX 2011 .... DF	DF	27 227 930	13 549 752	13 678 178	DF	28 524	30 206	1.4	912 050	33
ASIA - ASIE										
Afghanistan										
23 VI 1979 .... DF	DF	13 051 358[53]	6 712 377[53]	6 338 981[53]	DF	24 486[54]	26 557[54]	2.0	652 864	41
Armenia - Arménie										
12 X 2011 .... DF	DF	2 871 771	1 346 729	1 525 042	DJ	3 256	...	...	29 743	...
Azerbaijan - Azerbaïdjan										
13 IV 2009 .... DJ	DJ	8 922 447	4 414 398	4 508 049	DF	9 054	9 529	1.3	86 600	110
Bahrain - Bahreïn										
27 IV 2010 .... DJ	DJ	1 234 571	768 414	466 157	DJ	1 229	1 315	1.7	771	1 705
Bangladesh										
15 III 2011 .... DF	DF	144 043 697	72 109 796	71 933 901	DF	148 620	156 880	1.4	147 570	1 063
Bhutan - Bhoutan										
30 V 2005 .... DF	DF	634 982	333 595	301 387	DF	696[55]	745[55]	1.7	38 394	19
Brunei Darussalam - Brunéi Darussalam										
20 VI 2011 .... DJ	DJ	393 372	203 144	190 228	DF	387[12]	...	...	5 765	...
Cambodia - Cambodge										
3 III 2008 .... DF	DF	13 395 682[56]	6 516 054[56]	6 879 628[56]	DF	14 303[57]	15 184[57]	1.5	181 035	84
China - Chine										
1 XI 2010 .... DJ	DJ	1 339 724 852[58]	686 852 572[58]	652 872 280[58]	DF	1 337 700[59]	1 364 270[59]	0.5	9 596 961	142
China, Hong Kong SAR - Chine, Hong Kong RAS										
30 VI 2011 .... DJ	DJ	7 071 576[60]	3 303 015[60]	3 768 561[60]	DJ	7 024	7 242	0.8	1 106	6 550
China, Macao SAR - Chine, Macao RAS										
12 VIII 2011 .... DF	DF	625 674	305 398	320 276	DJ	537	622	3.7	30	20 723
Cyprus - Chypre										
1 X 2011 .... DJ	DJ	840 407[61]	408 780[61]	431 627[61]	DJ	829[62]	*858[63]	0.8	9 251	93
Democratic People's Republic of Korea - République populaire démocratique de Corée										
1 X 2008 .... DJ	DJ	24 052 231	11 721 838	12 330 393		...	...	...	120 538	...

3. Population by sex, annual rate of population increase, surface area and density
Population selon le sexe, taux d'accroissement annuel de la population, superficie et densité (continued - suite)

Continent, country or area and census date / Continent, pays ou zone et date du recensement	Census type[a]	Population at the latest available census / Population d'après le dernier recensement disponible (in units — en unités)			Estimate type[a]	Mid-year estimates / Estimations au milieu de l'année (in thousands — en milliers)		Annual rate of increase Taux d'accroissement annuel 2010-14	Surface area Superficie (km²) 2014	Density Densité 2014[b]
		Both sexes Les deux sexes	Male Masculin	Female Feminin		2010	2014			
ASIA - ASIE										
Georgia - Géorgie										
17 I 2002	DF	4 355 673	2 049 786	2 305 887	DF	4 453	4 490[16]	0.2	69 700	64
India - Inde										
9 II 2011	DF	1 210 854 977[64]	623 270 258[64]	587 584 719[64]	DF	1 182 105[65]	...	...	3 287 263	...
Indonesia - Indonésie										
1 V 2010	DJ	237 641 326	119 630 913	118 010 413	DJ	238 519[66]	252 165[66]	1.4	1 910 931	132
Iran (Islamic Republic of) - Iran (République islamique d')										
24 X 2011	DJ	75 149 669	37 905 669	37 244 000	DJ	74 340[67]	77 856[67]	1.2	1 628 750[68]	48
Iraq										
16 X 1997	DF	19 184 543[69]	9 536 570[69]	9 647 973[69]	DF	32 211	35 695	2.6	435 052	82
Israel - Israël										
27 XII 2008	DF	7 412 180[70]	3 663 910[70]	3 748 270[70]	DJ	7 624[71]	*8 216[71]	1.9	22 072	372
Japan - Japon										
1 X 2010	DJ	128 057 352[72]	62 327 737[72]	65 729 615[72]	DJ	128 070[73]	127 132[73]	-0.2	377 930[74]	336
Jordan - Jordanie										
1 X 2004	DF	5 103 639[75]	2 626 287[75]	2 477 352[75]	DF	6 113[76]	6 675[76]	2.2	89 318	75
Kazakhstan										
25 II 2009	DF	16 009 597	7 712 224	8 297 373	DF	16 322	17 161[16]	1.3	2 724 902	6
Kuwait - Koweït										
20 IV 2011	DF	*3 065 850	*1 738 372	*1 327 478	DF	2 933	...	...	17 818	...
Kyrgyzstan - Kirghizstan										
24 III 2009	DJ	5 362 793	2 645 921	2 716 872	...	5 193[6]	5 836	...	199 949	29
Lao People's Democratic Republic - République démocratique populaire lao										
1 III 2005	DJ	5 621 982	2 800 551	2 821 431	DF	6 289[77]	6 809[77]	2.0	236 800	29
Lebanon - Liban										
1 X 2011	SDF	3 779 859[78]	1 840 940[78]	1 938 919[78]		...	...	...	10 452	...
Malaysia - Malaisie										
6 VII 2010	DJ	28 334 135[79]	14 562 638[79]	13 771 497[79]	DJ	28 589[80]	30 262[80]	1.4	330 396	92
Maldives										
20 IX 2014	DF	*341 256	*173 172	*168 084	DF	320	...	...	300	...
Mongolia - Mongolie										
11 XI 2010	DF	2 647 199	1 314 246	1 332 953	DF	2 739	2 963	2.0	1 564 116	2
Myanmar										
29 III 2014	DF	50 279 900[81]	24 228 714[81]	26 051 186[81]	DF	59 780[82]	51 486[83]	-3.7	676 577	76
Nepal - Népal										
22 VI 2011	DJ	26 494 504	12 849 041	13 645 463	DJ	28 044	27 646[14]	-0.4	147 181	188
Oman										
12 XII 2010	DF	2 773 479	1 612 408	1 161 071	DF	...	3 993[84]	...	309 500	13
Pakistan										
2 III 1998	DF	130 579 571[85]	67 840 137[85]	62 739 434[85]	DF	173 510[85]	...	...	796 095	...
Philippines										
1 V 2010	DJ	92 335 113[86]	46 634 257[86]	45 700 856[86]	DJ	93 135[24]	99 880[24]	1.7	300 000	333
Qatar										
21 IV 2010	DF	1 699 435	1 284 739	414 696	DF	1 715	2 216	6.4	11 607	191
Republic of Korea - République de Corée										
1 XI 2010	DJ	48 580 293[87]	24 167 098[87]	24 413 195[87]	DJ	49 410	50 424[2]	0.5	100 266	503
Saudi Arabia - Arabie saoudite										
28 IV 2010	DF	*27 136 977	*15 306 793	*11 830 184	DF	*27 563[88]	...	...	2 206 714	...
Singapore - Singapour										
30 VI 2010	DJ	3 771 721[89]	1 861 133[89]	1 910 588[89]	DJ	5 077[90]	5 470[90]	1.9	718[91]	7 618
Sri Lanka										
27 II 2012	DJ	20 263 723	9 832 401	10 431 322	DF	20 653	20 675	0.0	65 610	315
State of Palestine - État de Palestine										
1 XII 2007	DF	3 669 244[92]	1 862 027[92]	1 807 217[92]	DF	4 048	4 550	2.9	6 020	756
Syrian Arab Republic - République arabe syrienne										
22 IX 2004	DF	*17 921 000[93]	*9 161 000[93]	*8 760 000[93]	DF	20 619[93]	...	...	185 180	...

3. Population by sex, annual rate of population increase, surface area and density
Population selon le sexe, taux d'accroissement annuel de la population, superficie et densité (continued - suite)

Continent, country or area and census date / Continent, pays ou zone et date du recensement	Census type[a]	Population at the latest available census Population d'après le dernier recensement disponible (in units — en unités)			Estimate type[a]	Mid-year estimates Estimations au milieu de l'année (in thousands — en milliers)		Annual rate of increase Taux d' accrois sement annuel 2010-14	Surface area Superficie (km²) 2014	Density Densité 2014[b]
		Both sexes Les deux sexes	Male Masculin	Female Feminin		2010	2014			
ASIA - ASIE										
Tajikistan - Tadjikistan										
21 IX 2010 .... DF	DF	7 564 502	3 817 004	3 747 498	DF	7 519	*8 200	2.2	142 600	58
Thailand - Thaïlande										
1 IX 2010 .... DJ	DJ	65 981 659	32 355 032	33 626 627	DJ	67 312[2]	68 610[2]	0.5	513 120	134
Timor-Leste										
11 VII 2010 .... DF	DF	1 066 409	544 198	522 211		...	...	...	14 919	...
Turkey - Turquie										
3 X 2011 .... DJ	DJ	*74 526 000[94]	*37 431 000[94]	*37 095 000[94]	...	73 142	76 903[95]	...	783 562	98
Turkmenistan - Turkménistan										
10 I 1995 .... DF	DF	4 483 251	2 225 331	2 257 920		...	...	...	488 100	...
United Arab Emirates - Émirats arabes unis										
5 XII 2005 .... DF	DF	4 106 427[96]	2 806 141[96]	1 300 286[96]	DF	8 264[96]	...	...	83 600	...
Uzbekistan - Ouzbékistan										
12 I 1989 .... DJ	DJ	19 810 077	9 784 156	10 025 921	DJ	28 001[16]	30 493[16]	2.1	447 400	68
Viet Nam										
1 IV 2009 .... DJ	DJ	85 846 997	42 413 143	43 433 854	DF	86 933	90 729	1.1	330 967	274
Yemen - Yémen										
16 XII 2004 .... DF	DF	19 685 161	10 036 953	9 648 208	DJ	23 154[2]	25 956[2]	2.9	527 968	49
EUROPE										
Åland Islands - Îles d'Åland										
31 XII 2000 .... DJ	DJ	25 776[97]	12 700[97]	13 076[97]	DJ	28[33]	29[33]	0.8	1 581	18
Albania - Albanie										
1 X 2011 .... DJ	DJ	2 800 138	1 403 059	1 397 079	DF	2 913	2 896[16]	-0.1	28 748	101
Andorra - Andorre										
31 XII 2000 .... DJ	DJ	65 844[33]	34 268[33]	31 576[33]	DJ	85[33]	...	...	468	...
Austria - Autriche										
31 X 2011 .... DJ	DJ	8 401 940	4 093 938	4 308 002	DJ	8 361	8 507[16]	0.4	83 871	101
Belarus - Bélarus										
14 X 2009 .... DJ	DJ	9 503 807	4 420 039	5 083 768	...	9 491	9 468[16]	...	207 600	46
Belgium - Belgique										
1 I 2011 .... DJ	DJ	11 000 638	5 401 718	5 598 920	DJ	10 896	11 204[16]	0.7	30 528	367
Bosnia and Herzegovina - Bosnie-Herzégovine										
30 IX 2013 .... DJ	DJ	*3 791 622	...	...	DF	3 843	*3 831[16]	-0.1	51 209	75
Bulgaria - Bulgarie										
1 II 2011 .... DJ	DJ	7 364 570	3 586 571	3 777 999	DJ	7 534	7 246[16]	-1.0	111 002	65
Croatia - Croatie										
1 IV 2011 .... DJ	DJ	4 284 889	2 066 335	2 218 554	DJ	4 295	4 247[16]	-0.3	56 594	75
Czech Republic - République tchèque										
25 III 2011 .... DJ	DJ	10 436 560	5 109 766	5 326 794	DJ	10 474	10 512[16]	0.1	78 867	133
Denmark - Danemark[98]										
1 I 2011 .... DJ	DJ	5 560 628[33]	2 756 582[33]	2 804 046[33]	DJ	5 545[33]	5 640[33]	0.4	42 921	131
Estonia - Estonie										
31 XII 2011 .... DJ	DJ	1 294 455	600 526	693 929	DJ	1 331	1 316[16]	-0.3	45 227	29
Faeroe Islands - Îles Féroé										
11 XI 2011 .... DJ	DJ	48 346	25 125	23 221	DJ	49	48	-0.2	1 393	35
Finland - Finlande										
31 XII 2010 .... DJ	DJ	5 375 276	2 638 416	2 736 860	DJ	5 335[99]	5 451[100]	0.5	336 855[101]	16
France										
1 I 2006 .... DJ	DJ	61 399 541[102]	29 714 539[102]	31 685 002[102]	DJ	62 918[102]	*64 062[102]	0.5	551 500	116
Germany - Allemagne										
9 V 2011 .... DJ	DJ	80 219 695	39 145 941	41 073 754	DJ	81 757	80 767[16]	-0.3	357 340	226
Gibraltar										
12 XI 2012 .... DJ	DJ	32 194[103]	16 061[103]	16 133[103]	DF	31[104]	...	...	6	...
Greece - Grèce										
9 V 2011 .... DF	DF	10 816 286	5 303 223	5 513 063	DF	11 153[105]	10 904[106]	-0.6	131 957	83

Continent, country or area and census date — Continent, pays ou zone et date du recensement	Census type[a]	Population at the latest available census — Population d'après le dernier recensement disponible (in units — en unités)			Estimate type[a]	Mid-year estimates — Estimations au milieu de l'année (in thousands — en milliers)		Annual rate of increase — Taux d' accrois sement annuel 2010-14	Surface area — Superficie (km²) 2014	Density — Densité 2014[b]
		Both sexes — Les deux sexes	Male — Masculin	Female — Feminin		2010	2014			

EUROPE

Guernsey - Guernesey										
29 IV 2001 .... DJ	DJ	59 807	29 138	30 669	DF	62[107]	63[107]	0.1	64	986
Holy See - Saint-Siège[108]										
1 VII 2000 .... DF	DF	798[109]	529[109]	269[109]	DF	0[110]	...	...	0[111]	...
Hungary - Hongrie										
1 X 2011 .... DF	DF	9 937 628	4 718 479	5 219 149	DJ	10 000	9 877[106]	-0.3	93 024	106
Iceland - Islande										
1 VII 2000 .... DJ	DJ	281 154[112]	140 718[112]	140 436[112]	DJ	318[112]	326[113]	0.6	103 000	3
Ireland - Irlande										
10 IV 2011 .... DF	DF	4 588 252	2 272 699	2 315 553	DF	4 560	4 606[106]	0.2	69 797	66
Isle of Man - Île de Man										
27 III 2011 .... DJ	DJ	84 497	41 971	42 526	DJ	83[114]	86[114]	1.1	572	151
Italy - Italie										
9 X 2011 .... DJ	DJ	59 433 744	28 745 507	30 688 237	DJ	59 277	60 783[106]	0.6	302 073	201
Jersey										
27 III 2011 .... DF	DF	97 857	48 296	49 561	DJ	97	...	...	116	...
Latvia - Lettonie										
1 III 2011 .... DJ	DJ	2 070 371	946 102	1 124 269	DJ	2 098	2 001[16]	-1.2	64 573	31
Liechtenstein										
31 XII 2010 .... DF	DF	36 149	17 886	18 263	DJ	36	37[115]	0.8	160	232
Lithuania - Lituanie										
1 III 2011 .... DJ	DJ	3 043 429	1 402 604	1 640 825	DJ	3 097	2 943[106]	-1.3	65 300	45
Luxembourg										
1 II 2011 .... DJ	DJ	512 353	254 967	257 386	DJ	507	550[16]	2.0	2 586	213
Malta - Malte										
20 XI 2011 .... DF	DF	417 432	207 625	209 807	DJ	415[116]	425[117]	0.6	316	1 346
Monaco										
9 VI 2008 .... DJ	DJ	31 109	15 076[118]	15 914[118]	DJ	36	...	...	2	...
Montenegro - Monténégro										
1 IV 2011 .... DJ	DJ	620 029	306 236	313 793	DJ	617	622[106]	0.2	13 812	45
Netherlands - Pays-Bas										
1 I 2002 .... DJ	DJ	16 105 285[119]	7 971 967[119]	8 133 318[119]	DJ	16 615	16 829[113]	0.3	37 354	451
Norway - Norvège										
19 XI 2011 .... DJ	DJ	4 979 955[120]	2 495 777[120]	2 484 178[120]	DJ	4 889[121]	5 108[122]	1.1	323 787	16
Poland - Pologne										
31 III 2011 .... DJ	DJ	38 044 565[123]	18 420 389[123]	19 624 176[123]	DJ	38 517[123]	38 018[124]	-0.3	311 888	122
Portugal										
21 III 2011 .... DF	DF	10 282 306	4 868 755	5 413 551	DJ	10 573	10 427[106]	-0.3	92 225	113
Republic of Moldova - République de Moldova										
5 X 2004 .... DF	DF	3 386 673[125]	1 629 689[125]	1 756 984[125]	DJ	3 562[125]	3 559[126]	0.0	33 846	105
Romania - Roumanie										
20 X 2011 .... DF	DF	20 039 141	9 736 342	10 302 799	DJ	20 247	19 947[106]	-0.4	238 391	84
Russian Federation - Fédération de Russie										
14 X 2010 .... DF	DF	143 436 145	66 457 074	76 979 071	DJ	142 849	...	...	17 098 246	...
San Marino - Saint-Marin										
7 XI 2010 .... DF	DF	*30 652	*14 791[127]	*15 818[127]	DF	33[33]	34[33]	0.3	61	556
Serbia - Serbie										
1 X 2011 .... DJ	DJ	7 186 862[128]	3 499 176[128]	3 687 686[128]	DJ	7 291[128]	7 147[129]	-0.5	88 361	81
Slovakia - Slovaquie										
21 V 2011 .... DJ	DJ	5 397 036	2 627 772	2 769 264	DJ	5 391	5 416[106]	0.1	49 035[130]	110
Slovenia - Slovénie										
1 I 2011 .... DF	DF	2 058 051	1 019 826	1 038 225	DJ	2 049	2 061[131]	0.1	20 273	102
Spain - Espagne										
1 XI 2011 .... DJ	DJ	46 815 915	23 104 350	23 711 560	DJ	46 562	46 512[113]	0.0	505 970	92
Svalbard and Jan Mayen Islands - Îles Svalbard et Jan Mayen										
1 XI 1960 .... DF	DF	3 431[132]	2 545[132]	886[132]		...	...	...	62 422	...
Sweden - Suède										
31 XII 2011 .... DJ	DJ	9 482 855[33]	4 726 834[33]	4 756 021[33]	DJ	9 378[33]	9 645[113]	0.7	450 295	21

3. Population by sex, annual rate of population increase, surface area and density
Population selon le sexe, taux d'accroissement annuel de la population, superficie et densité (continued - suite)

Continent, country or area and census date Continent, pays ou zone et date du recensement	Census type[a] type[a]	Population at the latest available census Population d'après le dernier recensement disponible (in units — en unités)			Estimate type[a] type[a]	Mid-year estimates Estimations au milieu de l'année (in thousands — en milliers)		Annual rate of increase Taux d'accrois sement annuel 2010-14	Surface area Superficie (km²) 2014	Density Densité 2014[b]
		Both sexes Les deux sexes	Male Masculin	Female Feminin		2010	2014			
EUROPE										
Switzerland - Suisse										
31 XII 2011 ...... DF	DF	8 035 391	3 973 280	4 062 111	DJ	7 825	8 140[115]	1.0	41 285	197
TFYR of Macedonia - L'ex-R. y. de Macédoine										
31 X 2002 ...... DJ	DJ	2 022 547	1 015 377	1 007 170	DF	2 055	2 066[16]	0.1	25 713	80
Ukraine										
5 XII 2001 ...... DF	DF	48 240 902	22 316 317	25 924 585	DF	45 871	*42 988[133]	-1.6	603 500	71
United Kingdom of Great Britain and Northern Ireland - Royaume-Uni de Grande-Bretagne et d'Irlande du Nord[134]										
27 III 2011 ...... DF	DF	63 379 787	31 126 054	32 253 733	DJ	62 759	64 308[106]	0.6	242 495	265
OCEANIA - OCÉANIE										
American Samoa - Samoas américaines										
1 IV 2010 ...... DJ	DJ	55 519[39]	28 164[39]	27 355[39]	DJ	67[39]	...	...	199	...
Australia - Australie										
9 VIII 2011 ...... DF	DF	21 727 158[135]	10 737 148[135]	10 990 010[135]	DJ	22 032	*23 491	1.6	7 692 024	3
Cook Islands - Îles Cook[136]										
1 XII 2011 ...... DF	DF	17 794	8 815	8 979	DF	24	*19	-6.1	236	79
Fiji - Fidji										
16 IX 2007 ...... DF	DF	837 271	427 176	410 095	DF	857	...	...	18 272	...
French Polynesia - Polynésie française										
22 VIII 2012 ...... DJ	DJ	268 207	136 996	131 211	DF	269	...	...	4 000	...
Guam										
1 IV 2010 ...... DJ	DJ	159 358	81 552	77 806	DJ	...	161[137]	...	549	293
Kiribati										
10 X 2010 ...... DF	DF	103 058	50 796	52 262		...	...	...	726[138]	...
Marshall Islands - Îles Marshall										
3 IV 2011 ...... DF	DF	53 158	27 243	25 915	DF	54[139]	...	...	181	...
Micronesia (Federated States of) - Micronésie (États fédérés de)										
1 IV 2010 ...... DJ	DJ	102 843	52 193	50 650	DJ	108[2]	106[2]	-0.3	702	152
Nauru										
31 X 2011 ...... DF	DF	*10 086	*5 105	*4 979		...	...	...	21	...
New Caledonia - Nouvelle-Calédonie										
26 VIII 2014 ...... DF	DF	268 767	...	...	DF	250	...	...	18 575	...
New Zealand - Nouvelle-Zélande										
7 III 2006 ...... DF	DF	4 143 282[140]	2 021 277[140]	2 122 005[140]	DJ	4 351[141]	4 510[141]	0.9	268 107	17
Niue - Nioué										
11 IX 2011 ...... DF	DF	1 611	802	809	DJ	1	...	...	260	...
Norfolk Island - Île Norfolk										
9 VIII 2011 ...... DF	DF	2 302	1 082	1 220		...	...	...	36	...
Northern Mariana Islands - Îles Mariannes septentrionales										
1 IV 2010 ...... DF	DF	53 883	27 746	26 137	DF	48	...	...	457	...
Palau - Palaos										
1 IV 2005 ...... DJ	DJ	19 907	10 699	9 208	DF	21	...	...	459	...
Papua New Guinea - Papouasie-Nouvelle-Guinée										
10 VII 2011 ...... DF	DF	*7 059 653	*3 663 249	*3 396 404		...	...	...	462 840	...
Pitcairn										
31 XII 2013 ...... DJ	DJ	49	23	26		...	...	...	5	...

3. Population by sex, annual rate of population increase, surface area and density
Population selon le sexe, taux d'accroissement annuel de la population, superficie et densité (continued - suite)

Continent, country or area and census date / Continent, pays ou zone et date du recensement	Census type[a]	Population at the latest available census Population d'après le dernier recensement disponible (in units — en unités)			Estimate type[a]	Mid-year estimates Estimations au milieu de l'année (in thousands — en milliers)		Annual rate of increase Taux d' accrois sement annuel 2010-14	Surface area Superficie (km²) 2014	Density Densité 2014[b]
		Both sexes Les deux sexes	Male Masculin	Female Feminin		2010	2014			
OCEANIA - OCÉANIE										
Samoa										
7 XI 2011 .... DF	DF	187 820	96 990	90 830	DF	*184*	...	...	2 842	...
Solomon Islands - Îles Salomon										
22 XI 2009 .... DF	DF	515 870	264 455	251 415	DF	*531*[2]	...	...	28 896	...
Tokelau - Tokélaou										
18 X 2011 .... DF	DF	1 205	600	605		...	...	...	12	...
Tonga										
30 XI 2011 .... DJ	DJ	103 252	51 979	51 273		...	...	...	747	...
Tuvalu										
1 XI 2002 .... DF	DF	9 561	4 729	4 832		...	...	...	26	...
Vanuatu										
16 XI 2009 .... DJ	DJ	234 023	119 091	114 932	DF	*239*	...	...	12 189	...
Wallis and Futuna Islands - Îles Wallis et Futuna										
22 VII 2013 .... DF	DF	12 197	...	...		...	...	...	142	...

FOOTNOTES - NOTES

Italics: estimates which are less reliable. - Italiques : estimations moins sûres.

* Provisional. - Données provisoires.

[a] 'Code' indicates the source of data, as follows:
DF - De facto
DJ - De jure
SDF - Sample survey, de facto
SDJ - Sample survey, de jure

Le 'Code' indique la source des données, comme suit :
DF - Population de fait
DJ - Population de droit
SDF - Enquête par sondage, population de fait
SDJ - Enquête par sondage, Population de droit

[b] Population per square kilometre of surface area. Figures are estimates of population divided by surface area and are not to be considered either as reflecting density in the urban sense or as indicating the supporting power of a territory's land and resources. - Nombre d'habitants au kilomètre carré. Il s'agit simplement d'éstimations de la population divisé par celui de la superficie: il ne faut pas y voir d'indication de la densité au sens urbain du terme ni de l'effectif de population que les terres et les ressources du territoire sont capables de nourrir.

[1] Total resident population including common and collective households of nomadic population, and population counted separately. - Population résidente totale y compris les ménages ordinaires et collectifs de la population nomade, et la population comptée à part.
[2] Data refer to national projections. - Les données se réfèrent aux projections nationales.
[3] Data based on the 2008 Population Census. - Données fondées sur le recensement de population de 2008.
[4] Data refer to national projections. Data refer to 1 January. - Les données se réfèrent aux projections nationales. Données se raportent au 1 janvier.
[5] Excluding Mayotte. - Non compris Mayotte.
[6] Data are calculated from the results of the Population and Housing Census of 2009. - Les données sont calculées à partir des résultats du recensement de la population et de l'habitat de 2009.
[7] Post-censal estimates based on the 2009 Population Census. - Les estimations post-censitaire fondées sur le recensement de la population de 2009.
[8] Data refer to national projections. Revised data. - Les données se réfèrent aux projections nationales. Données révisées.
[9] Including nomadic population. - Y compris la population nomade.

[10] Excludes the islands of St. Brandon and Agalega. - Non compris les îles St. Brandon et Agalega.
[11] Based on the results of the 2000 Population Census. - Basé sur les résultats du recensement de la population de 2000.
[12] Based on the results of the 2011 Population Census. - Basé sur les résultats du recensement de la population de 2011.
[13] Based on the results of the 2004 Population Census. - D'après des résultats du recensement de la population de 2004.
[14] Data refer to projections based on the 2011 Population Census. - Les données se réfèrent aux projections basées sur le recensement de la population de 2011.
[15] Data are projections based on the 2008 Population and Housing Census. - Projection basée sur le recensement 2008 de la population et des logements.
[16] Data refer to 1 January. - Données se raportent au 1 janvier.
[17] Data refer to 31 December. Projections based on the 2002 Population Census. - Données se raportent au 31 décembre. Projections fondées sur le recensement de la population de 2002.
[18] Surface area is based on the 2002 population and housing census. - La superficie est fondée sur les données provenant du recensement de la population et du logement de 2002.
[19] Data have not been adjusted for underenumeration, estimated at 7 per cent. - Les données n'ont pas été ajustées pour compenser les lacunes du dénombrement, estimées à 7 p. 100.
[20] Projections based on the 2002 Population Census. - Projections fondées sur le recensement de la population de 2002.
[21] Comprising the Northern Region (former Saguia el Hamra) and Southern Region (former Rio de Oro). - Comprend la région septentrionale (ancien Saguia-el-Hamra) et la région méridionale (ancien Rio de Oro).
[22] Data refer to 31 December. - Données se raportent au 31 décembre.
[23] Bermuda is 100 per cent urban. - 100 pour cent de la population des Bermudes est urbaine.
[24] Data refer to projections based on the 2010 Population Census. - Les données se réfèrent aux projections basées sur le recensement de la population de 2010.
[25] Final intercensal estimates. - Estimations inter-censitaires definitives.
[26] Preliminary postcensal estimates. - Estimations post censitaires préliminaires.
[27] Excluding the institutional population. - Non compris la population dans les institutions.
[28] Based on the national household surveys 2010-2014 and the 2011 population census. - D'après les données de l'enquête nationale des ménages 2010-2014 et les résultats du recensement de la population de 2011.
[29] Intercensal estimates. - Estimations inter-censitaires.
[30] Postcensal estimates. - Estimations post censitaires.
[31] Estimates based on the 2007 Population Census. - Estimations fondées sur le recensement de la population de 2007.

[32] The total surface is 21040.79 square kilometers, without taking into account the last ruling of The Hague. - La superficie totale est égale à 21040.79 km2, sans tenir compte de la dernière décision de la Haye.

[33] Population statistics are compiled from registers. - Les statistiques de la population sont compilées à partir des registres.

[34] Excluding data for Saint Barthélémy and Saint Martin. - Non compris les données pour Saint Barthélémy et Saint Martin.

[35] Excluding data for Saint Barthélémy and Saint Martin. Data refer to 1 January. - Non compris les données pour Saint Barthélémy et Saint Martin. Données se raportent au 1 janvier.

[36] Projections produced by l'Institut Haïtien de Statistique et d'Informatique (IHSI) and the Latin American and Caribbean Demographic Centre (CELADE) - Population Division of ECLAC. - Les données sont projections produits par l'Institut Haïtien de Statistique et d'Informatique (IHSI) et le centre démographique de l'Amérique latine et les Caraïbes - Division de la population de la CEPALC.

[37] Data refer to projections based on the 2001 Population Census. - Les données se réfèrent aux projections basées sur le recensement de la population de 2001.

[38] Including an estimation of 1 334 585 persons corresponding to 448 195 housing units without information of the occupants. - Y compris une estimation de 1 334 585 personnes correspondant aux 448 195 unités d'habitation sans information sur les occupants.

[39] Including armed forces stationed in the area. - Y compris les militaires en garnison sur le territoire.

[40] Including armed forces stationed in the area. Based on the results of the 2010 Population Census. - Y compris les militaires en garnison sur le territoire. D'après le résultats du recensement de la population de 2010.

[41] Refers to habitable area. Excludes St. Lucia's Forest Reserve. - S'applique à la zone habitable. Exclut la réserve forestière de Sainte-Lucie.

[42] Including low water level for all islands (area to shoreline). - Incluent le niveau de basses eaux pour toutes les îles.

[43] Excluding U.S. Armed Forces overseas and civilian U.S. citizens whose usual place of residence is outside the United States. Postcensal estimates. - Non compris les militaires américains à l'étranger et les civils américains dont le lieu de résidence habituel est en dehors des États-Unis. Estimations post censitaires.

[44] Data refer to projections based on the 2010 Population and Housing Census. - Les données se réfèrent aux projections basées sur le recensement 2010 de la population et des logements.

[45] Data updated according to "Superintendencia Agraria". Interior waters correspond to natural or artificial bodies of water or snow. - Données actualisées d'après la « Superintendencia Agraria ». Les eaux intérieures correspondent aux étendues d'eau naturelles ou artificielles et aux étendues neigeuses.

[46] Data include persons in remote areas, military personnel outside the country, merchant seamen at sea, civilian seasonal workers outside the country, and other civilians outside the country, and exclude nomads, foreign military, civilian aliens temporarily in the country, transients on ships and Indian jungle population. - Y compris les personnes vivant dans des régions éloignées, le personel militaire en dehors du pays, les marins marchands, les ouvriers saisonniers en dehors du pays, et autres civils en dehors du pays, et non compris les nomades, les militaires étrangers, les étrangers civils temporairement dans le pays, les transiteurs sur des bateaux et les Indiens de la jungle.

[47] Data include persons in remote areas, military personnel outside the country, merchant seamen at sea, civilian seasonal workers outside the country, and other civilians outside the country, and exclude nomads, foreign military, civilian aliens temporarily in the country, transients on ships and Indian jungle population. Data refer to national projections. - Y compris les personnes vivant dans des régions éloignées, le personel militaire en dehors du pays, les marins marchands, les ouvriers saisonniers en dehors du pays, et autres civils en dehors du pays, et non compris les nomades, les militaires étrangers, les étrangers civils temporairement dans le pays, les transiteurs sur des bateaux et les Indiens de la jungle. Les données se réfèrent aux projections nationales.

[48] Data are revised projections taking into consideration also the results of the 2005 census. - Les données sont des projections révisées tenant compte également des résultats du recensement de 2005.

[49] Data refer to projections based on the 2010 Population Census. Excludes nomadic Indian tribes. - Les données se réfèrent aux projections basées sur le recensement de la population de 2010. Non compris les tribus d'Indiens nomades.

[50] A dispute exists between the governments of Argentina and the United Kingdom of Great Britain and Northern Ireland concerning sovereignty over the Falkland Islands (Malvinas). - La souveraineté sur les îles Falkland (Malvinas) fait l'objet d'un différend entre le Gouvernement argentin et le Gouvernement du Royaume-Uni de Grande-Bretagne et d'Irlande du Nord.

[51] Data refer to 30 June. Estimates based on the 2007 Population Census. - Données se raportent au 30 juin. Estimations fondées sur le recensement de la population de 2007.

[52] Figures for male and female population do not add up to the figure for total population, because they exclude 108 homeless people of unknown sex. - Les chiffres relatifs à la population masculine et féminine ne correspondent pas au chiffre de la population totale, parce que l'on en a exclu 108 personnes sans toit dont le sexe n'est pas connu.

[53] Data refer to the settled population based on the 1979 Population Census and the latest household prelisting. The refugees of Afghanistan in Iran, Pakistan, and an estimated 1.5 million nomads, are not included. Excluding nomad population. - Les données se rapportent à la population stationnaire sur la base du recensement de 1979 et du recensement préliminaire des logements le plus récent. Sont exclus les réfugiés d'Afghanistan en Iran et au Pakistan et les nomades estimés à 1,5 million. Non compris les nomades.

[54] Data refer to the settled population based on the 1979 Population Census and the latest household prelisting. The refugees of Afghanistan in Iran, Pakistan, and an estimated 1.5 million nomads, are not included. - Les données se rapportent à la population stationnaire sur la base du recensement de 1979 et du recensement préliminaire des logements le plus récent. Sont exclus les réfugiés d'Afghanistan en Iran et au Pakistan et les nomades estimés à 1,5 million.

[55] Data refer to projected figures based on the Population and Housing Census 2005 (district projection). - Les données se réfèrent aux projections basées sur le recensement de la population et de l'habitat de 2005 (projections locales).

[56] Excluding foreign diplomatic personnel and their dependants. - Non compris le personnel diplomatique étranger et les membres de leur famille les accompagnant.

[57] Excluding foreign diplomatic personnel and their dependants. Data based on the 2008 Population Census. - Non compris le personnel diplomatique étranger et les membres de leur famille les accompagnant. Données fondées sur le recensement de population de 2008.

[58] For statistical purposes, the data for China do not include those for the Hong Kong Special Administrative Region (Hong Kong SAR), Macao Special Administrative Region (Macao SAR) and Taiwan province of China. Data are from Communique of the National Bureau of Statistics of the People's Republic of China on Major Figures of the 2010 Population Census (No.1). - Pour la présentation des statistiques, les données pour la Chine ne comprennent pas la Région Administrative Spéciale de Hong Kong (Hong Kong RAS), la Région Administrative Spéciale de Macao (Macao RAS) et Taïwan province de Chine. Données issues du communiqué du Bureau national de la statistique de la République populaire de Chine sur les chiffres importants du recensement de 2010 (n° 1).

[59] For statistical purposes, the data for China do not include those for the Hong Kong Special Administrative Region (Hong Kong SAR), Macao Special Administrative Region (Macao SAR) and Taiwan province of China. Data have been estimated on the basis of the annual National Sample Survey on Population Changes. - Pour la présentation des statistiques, les données pour la Chine ne comprennent pas la Région Administrative Spéciale de Hong Kong (Hong Kong RAS), la Région Administrative Spéciale de Macao (Macao RAS) et Taïwan province de Chine. Les données ont été estimées sur la base de l'enquête annuelle "National Sample Survey on Population Changes".

[60] Data refer to Hong Kong resident population at the census moment, which covers usual residents and mobile residents. Usual residents refer to two categories of people: (1) Hong Kong permanent residents who had stayed in Hong Kong for at least three months during the six months before or for at least three months during the six months after the census moment, regardless of whether they were in Hong Kong or not at the census moment; and (2) Hong Kong non-permanent residents who were in Hong Kong at the census moment. Mobile Residents, they are Hong Kong permanent residents who had stayed in Hong Kong for at least one month but less than three months during the six months before or for at least one month but less than three months during the six months after the census moment, regardless of whether they were in Hong Kong or not at the census moment. - Les données se rapportent à la population résidente à Hong Kong au moment du recensement. Cette population est composée des résidants habituels et des résidants mobiles. La population résidente est partagée en deux catégories: (1) les résidents permanents qui ont habité à Hong Kong au moins trois mois pendant les six mois précédents ou les six mois suivants le recensement; (2) les habitants non-permanents de Hong Kong qui étaient à Hong Kong au moment du recensement. La population mobile se rapporte aux résidents permanents de Hong Kong qui ont habité à Hong Kong pendant les six mois après le recensement pour une période comprise entre un mois et trois mois, indépendamment du fait qu'ils étaient à Hong Kong au moment du recensement au pays.

[61] Data refer to government controlled areas. - Les données se rapportent aux zones contrôlées par le Gouvernement.

62 Data refer to government controlled areas. Data refer to annual average population. - Les données se rapportent aux zones contrôlées par le Gouvernement. Les données correspondent à la population annuelle moyenne.

63 Data refer to government controlled areas. Data refer to 1 January. - Les données se rapportent aux zones contrôlées par le Gouvernement. Données se raportent au 1 janvier.

64 Includes data for the Indian-held part of Jammu and Kashmir, the final status of which has not yet been determined. - Y compris les données pour la partie du Jammu et du Cachemire occupée par l'Inde dont le statut définitif n'a pas encore été déterminé.

65 Includes data for the Indian-held part of Jammu and Kashmir, the final status of which has not yet been determined. Data refer to projections based on the 2001 Population Census. - Y compris les données pour la partie du Jammu et du Cachemire occupée par l'Inde dont le statut définitif n'a pas encore été déterminé. Les données se réfèrent aux projections basées sur le recensement de la population de 2001.

66 Data are based on the publication: "Indonesia Population Projection 2010-2035" - Les données sont basées sur la publication : << Indonesia Population Projection 2010-2035 >>

67 Data refer to the Iranian Year which begins on 21 March and ends on 20 March of the following year. - Les données concernent l'année iranienne, qui commence le 21 mars et se termine le 20 mars de l'année suivante.

68 Land area only. - La superficie des terres seulement.

69 Excluding the population in three autonomous provinces in the north of the country. - La population des trois provinces autonomes dans le nord du pays est exclue.

70 Data are rounded for confidentiality reasons. Includes data for East Jerusalem and Israeli residents in certain other territories under occupation by Israeli military forces since June 1967. - Chiffres arrondis pour des raisons de confidentialité. Y compris les données pour Jérusalem-Est et les résidents israéliens dans certains autres territoires occupés depuis 1967 par les forces armées israéliennes.

71 Includes data for East Jerusalem and Israeli residents in certain other territories under occupation by Israeli military forces since June 1967. - Y compris les données pour Jérusalem-Est et les résidents israéliens dans certains autres territoires occupés depuis 1967 par les forces armées israéliennes.

72 Excluding diplomatic personnel outside the country and foreign military and civilian personnel and their dependants stationed in the area. - Non compris le personnel diplomatique hors du pays ni les militaires et agents civils étrangers en poste sur le territoire et les membres de leur famille les accompagnant.

73 Excluding diplomatic personnel outside the country and foreign military and civilian personnel and their dependants stationed in the area. Estimates based on the complete counts of the 2010 Population Census. - Non compris le personnel diplomatique hors du pays ni les militaires et agents civils étrangers en poste sur le territoire et les membres de leur famille les accompagnant. Estimations basées sur le dénombrement complet du recensement de la population de 2010.

74 Data refer to 1 October 2007. - Les données se réfèrent au 1er octobre 2007.

75 Excluding data for Jordanian territory under occupation since June 1967 by Israeli military forces. Including registered Palestinian refugees and Jordanians abroad. - Non compris les données pour le territoire jordanien occupé depuis juin 1967 par les forces armées israéliennes. Y compris les réfugiés palestiniens enregistrés et les Jordaniens à l'étranger.

76 Data refer to 31 December. Excluding data for Jordanian territory under occupation since June 1967 by Israeli military forces. Excluding foreigners, including registered Palestinian refugees. - Données se raportent au 31 décembre. Non compris les données pour le territoire jordanien occupé depuis juin 1967 par les forces armées israéliennes. Non compris les étrangers, mais y compris les réfugiés de Palestine enregistrés.

77 Based on the results of the 2005 Population and Housing Census. - Données fondées sur les résultats du recensement de la population et de l'habitat de 2005.

78 Source: Living conditions of household survey, October 2011 to September 2012. - Source: Enquête sur les conditions de vie des ménages, octobre 2011 à septembre 2012.

79 Data have been adjusted for underenumeration. - Les données ont été ajustées pour compenser les lacunes du dénombrement.

80 Estimates based on the adjusted Population and Housing Census of 2010. - Les estimations sont fondée sur les résultats ajustées du recensement de la population et de l'habitat de 2010.

81 Data refer to enumerated population. - Les données se rapportent à la population dénombrée.

82 Data refer to 1 October. - Données se raportent au 1 octobre.

83 Data refer to 1 October. Based on the results of the 2014 Population Census. - Données se raportent au 1 octobre. D'après les résultats du recensement de la population de 2014.

84 Data refer to registered population data from Royal Oman Police. - Les données portent sur la population enregistrée par la police royale de l'Oman.

85 Excluding data for the Pakistan-held part of Jammu and Kashmir, the final status of which has not yet been determined. - Non compris les données concernant la partie du Jammu et Cachemire occupée par le Pakistan dont le statut définitif n'a pas été déterminé.

86 Excluding 2739 Filipinos in Philippine Embassies, Consulates and Missions Abroad. - Excepté 2739 Philippins travaillant dans les ambassies, les consulats et les missions des Philippines à l'étranger.

87 Excluding usual residents not in the country at the time of census. - À l'exclusion des résidents habituels qui ne sont pas dans le pays au moment du recensement.

88 Data based on the preliminary results of the 2010 Population and Housing Census. - D'après les résultats préliminaires du recensement de la population et des logements de 2010.

89 Data are based on the latest register-based population estimates for 2010. Data refer to resident population which comprises Singapore citizens and permanent residents. Urban and rural breakdown not applicable as Singapore is a city-state. - Données basées sur les estimations démographiques les plus récentes fondées sur les registres de 2010. Les données se rapportent à la population résidente composé des citoyens de Singapour et des résidents permanents. La ventilation entre zones urbaines et zones rurales ne s'applique pas à Singapour, puisqu'il s'agit d'une ville État.

90 Data refer to 30 June. Data exclude residents who have been away from Singapore for a continuous period of 12 months or longer as at the reference date. - Données se raportent au 30 juin. Non compris les résidents hors de Singapour pour une période ininterrompue de 12 mois ou plus avant de la date de référence.

91 The land area of Singapore comprises the mainland and other islands. - La superficie terrestre de Singapour comprend l'île principale et les autres îles.

92 Data have not been adjusted for underenumeration. - Les données n'ont pas été ajustées pour compenser les lacunes du dénombrement.

93 Including Palestinian refugees. - Y compris les réfugiés de Palestine.

94 Based on a sample taken at the time of census. Because of rounding, totals are not in all cases the sum of the respective components. - D'après un échantillon obtenu au moment du recensement. Les chiffres étant arrondis, les totaux ne correspondent pas toujours rigoureusement à la somme des composants respectifs.

95 Data based on address-based population registration system. - Les données sont basées sur le registre national de la population basé sur l'adresse.

96 Data include non-national population. - Les données comprennent les non-nationaux.

97 Statistics are compiled from registers. - Les statistiques sont compilées à partir des registres.

98 Excluding Faeroe Islands and Greenland shown separately, if available. - Non compris les Iles Féroé et le Groenland, qui font l'objet de rubriques distinctes, si disponible.

99 Excluding Åland Islands. Population statistics are compiled from registers. - Non compris les Îles d'Åland. Les statistiques de la population sont compilées à partir des registres.

100 Population statistics are compiled from registers. Data refer to 1 January. - Les statistiques de la population sont compilées à partir des registres. Données se raportent au 1 janvier.

101 Excluding Åland Islands. - Non compris les Îles d'Åland.

102 Excluding diplomatic personnel outside the country and including members of alien armed forces not living in military camps and foreign diplomatic personnel not living in embassies or consulates. - Non compris le personnel diplomatique hors du pays et y compris les militaires étrangers ne vivant pas dans des camps militaires et le personnel diplomatique étranger ne vivant pas dans les ambassades ou les consulats.

103 Excluding military personnel, visitors and transients. - Non compris les militaires, ni les visiteurs et transients.

104 Excluding military personnel, visitors and transients. Data refer to 31 December. - Non compris les militaires, ni les visiteurs et transients. Données se raportent au 31 décembre.

105 Excluding armed forces stationed outside the country, but including alien armed forces stationed in the area. - Non compris les militaires en garnison hors du pays, mais y compris les militaires étrangers en garnison sur le territoire.

106 Data refer to 1 January. Data refer to usually resident population. - Données se raportent au 1 janvier. Les données concernent la population habituellement résidente.

107 Data refer to 31 March. - Données se raportent au 31 mars.

108 Data refer to the Vatican City State. - Les données se rapportent à l'Etat de la Cité du Vatican.

109 Including nationals outside the country. Population statistics are compiled from registers. - Y compris les nationaux hors du pays. Les statistiques de la population sont compilées à partir des registres.

110 Data refer to 6 December. The population figure is 466 persons. - Données se raportent au 6 décembre. La population est égale à 466 personnes.

111 Surface area is 0.44 km². - Superficie: 0,44 km².

112 Data refer to registered resident population. - Les données concernent la population enregistrée résidente.

113 Data refer to registered resident population. Data refer to 1 January. - Les données concernent la population enregistrée résidente. Données se raportent au 1 janvier.

114 Data refer to 30 April. - Données se raportent au 30 avril.

115 Data refer to 1 January. Data refer to legal resident population. - Données se raportent au 1 janvier. Les données concernent la population légalement résidente.

116 Including civilian nationals temporarily outside the country. - Y compris les civils nationaux temporairement hors du pays.

117 Including civilian nationals temporarily outside the country. Data refer to 1 January. - Y compris les civils nationaux temporairement hors du pays. Données se raportent au 1 janvier.

118 Figures for male and female population do not add up to the figure for total population, because they exclude 119 persons of unknown sex. - Les chiffres relatifs à la population masculine et féminine ne correspondent pas au chiffre de la population totale, parce que l'on en a exclu 119 personnes de sexe inconnu.

119 Census results based on compilation of continuous accounting and sample surveys. - Les résultat du recensement, d'après les résultats des dénombrements et enquêtes par sondage continue.

120 Including residents temporarily outside the country. Population statistics are compiled from registers. - Y compris les résidents se trouvant temporairement hors du pays. Les statistiques de la population sont compilées à partir des registres.

121 Including residents temporarily outside the country. - Y compris les résidents se trouvant temporairement hors du pays.

122 Including residents temporarily outside the country. Data refer to 1 January. Data refer to usually resident population. - Y compris les résidents se trouvant temporairement hors du pays. Données se raportent au 1 janvier. Les données concernent la population habituellement résidente.

123 Excluding civilian aliens within the country, but including civilian nationals temporarily outside the country. - Non compris les civils étrangers dans le pays, mais y compris les civils nationaux temporairement hors du pays.

124 Excluding civilian aliens within the country, but including civilian nationals temporarily outside the country. Data refer to 1 January. Data refer to usually resident population. - Non compris les civils étrangers dans le pays, mais y compris les civils nationaux temporairement hors du pays. Données se raportent au 1 janvier. Les données concernent la population habituellement résidente.

125 Excluding Transnistria and the municipality of Bender. - Les données ne tiennent pas compte de l'information sur la Transnistria et la municipalité de Bender.

126 Excluding Transnistria and the municipality of Bender. Data refer to 1 January. - Les données ne tiennent pas compte de l'information sur la Transnistria et la municipalité de Bender. Données se raportent au 1 janvier.

127 Figures for male and female may not add up to the total, since they do not include the category "Unknown". - La somme des chiffres indiqués pour les sexes masculin et féminin peut n'être pas égale au total parce qu'elle n'inclut pas la catégorie " inconnue ".

128 Excludes data for Kosovo and Metohia. - Sans les données pour le Kosovo et Metohie.

129 Excludes data for Kosovo and Metohia. Data refer to 1 January. Data refer to usually resident population. - Sans les données pour le Kosovo et Metohie. Données se raportent au 1 janvier. Les données concernent la population habituellement résidente.

130 Excluding inland water. - Exception faite des eaux intérieures.

131 The data for urban and rural exclude the nationals temporarily outside the country. Data refer to 1 January. Data refer to usually resident population. - Les données relatives à la population urbaine et rurale n'englobent pas les nationaux se trouvant provisoirement à l'étranger. Données se raportent au 1 janvier. Les données concernent la population habituellement résidente.

132 Inhabited only during the winter season. The Norwegian population of these islands is included also in the de jure population of Norway. - N'est habitée que pendant la saison d'hiver. La population norvégienne de ces îles est comprise également dans la population de droit de la Norvège.

133 The Government of Ukraine has informed the United Nations that it is not in a position to provide statistical data concerning the Autonomous Republic of Crimea and the city of Sevastopol. - Le gouvernement Ukrainien a informé l'ONU qu'il n'est pas en mesure de fournir des données statistiques concernant la République autonome de Crimée et la ville de Sébastopol.

134 Excluding Channel Islands (Guernsey and Jersey) and Isle of Man, shown separately, if available. - Non compris les îles Anglo-Normandes (Guernesey et Jersey) et l'île de Man, qui font l'objet de rubriques distinctes, si disponible.

135 This data has been randomly rounded to protect confidentiality. Individual figures may not add up to totals, and values for the same data may vary in different tables. Including population in off-shore, migratory and shipping. - Ces données ont été arrondies de façon aléatoire afin d'en préserver la confidentialité. La somme de certains chiffres peut ne pas correspondre aux totaux indiqués et les valeurs des mêmes données peuvent varier d'un tableau à un autre. Y compris les populations extraterritoriales, les populations nomades et les populations maritimes.

136 Excluding Niue, shown separately, which is part of Cook Islands, but because of remoteness is administered separately. - Non compris Nioué, qui fait l'objet d'une rubrique distincte et qui fait partie des îles Cook, mais qui, en raison de son éloignement, est administrée séparément.

137 Including armed forces stationed in the area. Data refer to projections based on the 2010 Population Census. - Y compris les militaires en garnison sur le territoire. Les données se réfèrent aux projections basées sur le recensement de la population de 2010.

138 Land area only. Excluding 84 square km of uninhabited islands. - La superficie des terres seulement. Exclut des îles inhabitées d'une superficie de 84 kilomètres carrés.

139 Projections are prepared by the Secretariat of the Pacific Community based on 1999 census of population and housing. - Les projections sont preparées par le Secrétariat de la Communauté du Pacifique à partir des résultats du recensement de la population et de l'habitat de 1999.

140 This data has been randomly rounded to protect confidentiality. Individual figures may not add up to totals, and values for the same data may vary in different tables. - Ces données ont été arrondies de façon aléatoire afin d'en préserver la confidentialité. La somme de certains chiffres peut ne pas correspondre aux totaux indiqués et les valeurs des mêmes données peuvent varier d'un tableau à un autre.

141 Because of rounding, totals are not in all cases the sum of the respective components. - Les chiffres étant arrondis, les totaux ne correspondent pas toujours rigoureusement à la somme des composants respectifs.

Table 3a presents the values of the Whipple's index by sex, urban or rural residence, for total area and both sexes combined, according to the availability of the underlying data in the *Demographic Yearbook* database.

The data used to compile these indices are the datasets of population by single years of age, sex, and urban or rural residence, for the past three rounds of population censuses, namely the population censuses conducted worldwide since 1985. These datasets have been reported by the National Statistical Offices to the United Nations Statistics Division via the *Demographic Yearbook* questionnaires.

The footnotes that appear at the end of this table are notes that refer to the respective dataset of population by single years of age, sex, and urban or rural residence.

Whipple's index is an index of age preference in age reporting. The way it is calculated for this table, it is meant to indicate preference or avoidance of ages ending in digits "0" (zero) or "5" (five) during age reporting for a population census.

The formula used to calculate the values of the Whipple's index for this table is:

$$\frac{P25+P30+P35+P40+P45+P50+P55+P60}{\frac{1}{5}(P23+P24+P25+\cdots+P58+P59+P60+P61+P62)} *100$$

where Px refers to the number of persons of age x in completed years. The sum in brackets in the denominator is the sum of the number of persons of every single age from 23 to 62.

The values of the Whipple's index generally vary between 100, indicating no preference for "0" or "5" (in other words no heaping in ages ending in "0" or "5"), and 500, indicating that age reporting was entirely concentrated in ages ending in digits "0" or "5". The higher than 100 the value of the index, the higher is the heaping of age reporting in ages ending in "0" or "5".

For more information about the measurement of age and digit preference, please refer to *The Methods and Materials of Demography, Second Edition* (2004), Edited by Jacob S. Siegel and David A. Swanson.

Tableau 3a – *Annuaire démographique 2014*

Le tableau 3a présente les valeurs de l'indice de Whipple par sexe, résidence urbaine ou rurale, pour la superficie totale et les sexes combinés, selon la disponibilité des données sous-jacentes dans la base de données de l'*Annuaire démographique*.

Les données utilisées pour établir ces indices sont les séries de données de la population par âge simple, sexe et résidence urbaine ou rurale, pour les trois derniers cycles de recensements de la population, à savoir les recensements de la population effectués dans le monde entier depuis 1985. Ces séries de données sont communiquées par les services nationaux de statistique à la Division de statistique de l'Organisation des Nations Unies par le biais des questionnaires de l'*Annuaire démographique*.

Les notes qui figurent à la fin de ce tableau sont des notes renvoyant aux différentes séries de données de la population par âge simple, sexe et résidence urbaine ou rurale.

L'indice de Whipple est un indice de préférence de certains âges dans les déclarations de l'âge. La manière dont il est calculé pour ce tableau permet d'indiquer l'attraction ou la répulsion pour des âges se terminant par les chiffres « 0 » (zéro) ou « 5 » (cinq) lors de la déclaration de l'âge effectuée dans le cadre d'un recensement de population.

La formule utilisée pour calculer les valeurs de l'indice de Whipple pour ce tableau est la suivante:

$$\frac{P25+P30+P35+P40+P45+P50+P55+P60}{\frac{1}{5}(P23+P24+P25+\cdots+P58+P59+P60+P61+P62)}*100$$

Px étant le nombre de personnes d'âge x en années révolues. La somme entre parenthèses en dénominateur est la somme du nombre de personnes selon l'âge simple de 23 à 62 ans.

Les valeurs de l'indice de Whipple varient généralement entre 100, indication d'absence de préférence pour « 0 » ou « 5 »(en d'autres termes pas de prépondérance des âges se terminant par « 0 » ou « 5 »), et 500, indiquant que les déclarations de l'âge étaient entièrement polarisées sur les âges se terminant par les chiffres « 0 » ou « 5 ». Plus la valeur de l'indice est supérieure à 100, plus les déclarations de l'âge sont polarisées sur les âges se terminant par « 0 » ou « 5 ».

Pour en savoir plus sur la mesure de l'âge et la préférence pour les chiffres, prière de consulter l'ouvrage intitulé *The Methods and Materials of Demography, Second Edition (2004)*, publié sous la direction de Jacob S. Siegel et David A. Swanson.

3a. Whipple's Index by sex and urban/rural residence, 1985 - 2014
L'indice de Whipple par le sexe et la résidence urbaine/rurale, 1985 - 2014

Continent, country or area, date and code[a] / Continent, pays ou zone, date et code[a]	Total			Urban - Urbaine			Rural - Rurale		
	Both sexes Les deux sexes	Male Masculin	Female Féminin	Both sexes Les deux sexes	Male Masculin	Female Féminin	Both sexes Les deux sexes	Male Masculin	Female Féminin
AFRICA - AFRIQUE									
Algeria - Algérie[1]									
16 IV 2008 (CDJC)	100.7	100.5	100.9	100.7	100.5	100.9	100.7	100.6	100.8
Benin - Bénin									
15 II 1992 (CDFC)	216.1	205.6	224.6	185.4	171.6	197.9	234.6	228	239.6
11 II 2002 (CDJC)	229.1	218.9	237.8	190.4	180.1	200	257.5	250	263.5
Botswana									
21 VIII 1991 (CDFC)	104.8	106.6	103.3	102.4	103.6	101.4	107.7	110.8	105.3
17 VIII 2001 (CDFC)	100.9	101.8	100.2	...	...	...	...	...	...
9 VIII 2011 (CDFC)	100.8	101.3	100.3	101.7	101.8	101.6	99	100.5	97.5
Burkina Faso									
10 XII 1985 (CDJC)	193	173.8	208.4	153.1	140.9	166.7	198.6	179.4	213.2
10 XII 1996 (CDJC)	162.6[2]	144[2]	177.5[2]	99.5[3]	99.6[3]	99.5[3]	99.6[3]	99.7[3]	99.5[3]
9 XII 2006 (CDJC)	145.1	133.8	154.5	131.1	130.5	131.8	150.2	135.3	161.5
Burundi									
16 VIII 1990 (CDJC)	152.9	141.7	163	...	...	...	...	...	...
16 VIII 2008 (CDJC)	156.8	149.4	164.4	137.2	136.5	138.3	159.4	151.5	167.1
Cabo Verde									
23 VI 1990 (CDFC)	111.9	110.7	112.8	108	107.7	108.3	115.3	113.7	116.4
Cameroon - Cameroun									
11 XI 2005 (CDJC)	173.5	165.1	181.4	...	...	...	...	...	...
Central African Republic - République centrafricaine									
8 XII 1988 (CDFC)	139.4	132	146.1	129.9	125.2	134.3	144.5	135.8	152.3
Congo									
1 I 1985 (CDJC)	107.3	107.5	107.1	...	...	...	...	...	...
28 IV 2007 (CDFC)	103.5	103.1	103.8	...	...	...	...	...	...
Côte d'Ivoire									
1 III 1988 (CDFC)	126.3	117.3	136.2	116.4	112.7	121	132.7	120.5	145
Egypt - Égypte									
21 XI 2006 (CDFC)	196.5	175.3	218.2	177.1	162.7	191.9	213.5	186.4	241.4
Ethiopia - Éthiopie									
11 X 1994 (CDFC)	272.3	258.9	285	248.7	232.6	264	276.5	263.7	288.7
29 V 2007 (CDFC)	252.1	241	262.9	232.3	222.5	242.4	256.7	245.4	267.5
Gabon									
31 VII 1993 (CDFC)	116.6	115.9	117.4	...	...	...	...	...	...
Gambia - Gambie									
15 IV 1993 (CDFC)	229.8	215.2	244.5	191.2	183.2	201.2	256.2	241.6	268.9
Ghana									
26 III 2000 (CDFC)	184	175.8	191.6	159.7	154.7	164.5	205.6	195.2	215.3
26 IX 2010 (CDFC)	159.1	155.2	162.5	138.3	136.6	139.8	184.7	178.2	190.6
Guinea-Bissau - Guinée-Bissau									
15 III 2009 (CDJC)	137.8	128.9	145.7	...	...	...	...	...	...
Kenya									
24 VIII 1989 (CDJC)	147.8	142.6	152.8	144.1	140.8	149.4	148.9	143.3	153.5
24 VIII 1999 (CDJC)	148.3	143.2	153.2	...	...	...	...	...	...
24 VIII 2009 (CDJC)	146.4	144.6	148.2	141.1	141.1	141.2	149.8	147.1	152.2
Lesotho									
13 IV 2006 (CDJC)	105.3	105.8	104.9	...	...	...	...	...	...
Liberia - Libéria									
21 III 2008 (CDFC)	142.2	136.3	148.1	...	...	...	...	...	...
Malawi									
1 IX 1987 (CDFC)	138.5	137.9	139.1	...	...	...	...	...	...
1 IX 1998 (CDFC)	147.7	149.2	146.4	142.6	146.5	137.3	148.7	149.7	147.7
8 VI 2008 (CDFC)	120.6	121	120.2	113	114.7	111	122.2	122.5	121.9
Mali									
1 IV 1987 (CDJC)	184.5	171.4	195.9	163.7	154.1	173	190.4	176.7	202
1 IV 1998 (CDFC)	180.1	166.8	192.3	166.5	158	175.2	185.6	170.7	198.6
1 IV 2009 (CDFC)	156.5	145.7	166.6	142.7	139.1	146.8	161.1	148.2	172.5
Mauritius - Maurice[4]									
1 VII 1990 (CDFC)	103.4	102.4	104.3	...	...	...	...	...	...
2 VII 2000 (CDJC)	102.4	102.1	102.7	102.3	102	102.7	102.5	102.2	102.7
4 VII 2011 (CDJC)	100.6	101	100.3	100.8	101.2	100.3	100.5	100.9	100.2
Mayotte									
31 VII 2007 (CDJC)	124.4	126.9	122.3	...	...	...	...	...	...
Morocco - Maroc									
1 IX 2004 (CDFC)	113.4	108.4	118	110.1	107.5	112.5	118.2	109.8	126.2

Continent, country or area, date and code[a] Continent, pays ou zone, date et code[a]	Total			Urban - Urbaine			Rural - Rurale		
	Both sexes Les deux sexes	Male Masculin	Female Féminin	Both sexes Les deux sexes	Male Masculin	Female Féminin	Both sexes Les deux sexes	Male Masculin	Female Féminin
AFRICA - AFRIQUE									
Mozambique									
1 VIII 1997 (CDJC)	118.6	117.9	119.3	111.7	110.9	112.4	121.5	121	121.9
1 VIII 2007 (CDFC)	126	126.2	125.9	...	...	...	...	...	...
Namibia - Namibie									
21 X 1991 (CDFC)	105.8	104.9	106.5	103.5	102.9	104.2	107.1	106.4	107.6
27 VIII 2001 (CDFC)	103.9	103.2	104.5	103.6	102.9	104.4	104.1	103.5	104.6
28 VIII 2011 (CDFC)	103.9	103.8	104	104.3	103.6	105	103.4	104.1	102.9
Niger									
20 V 2001 (CDJC)	270.1	254.7	285.2	...	...	...	...	...	...
10 XII 2012 (CDJC)	105.1	104.7	105.4	...	...	...	...	...	...
Nigeria - Nigéria									
26 XI 1991 (CDFC)	293.5	279.8	307.1	...	...	...	...	...	...
Republic of South Sudan - République de Soudan du Sud									
21 IV 2008 (CDFC)	183.1	178.4	187.9	...	...	...	...	...	...
Reunion - Réunion									
15 III 1990 (CDFC)	99.9	99.8	100.1	...	...	...	...	...	...
8 III 1999 (CDJC)	100	100.3	99.7	...	...	...	...	...	...
Rwanda									
16 VIII 2002 (CDJC)	106.3	106.6	106.1	107.4	108.3	106.2	106	106	106.1
Saint Helena ex. dep. - Sainte-Hélène sans dép.									
8 III 1998 (CDJC)	101	98.8	103.3	...	...	...	...	...	...
10 II 2008 (CDJC)[5]	98.8	99.9	97.8	...	...	...	...	...	...
Saint Helena: Ascension - Sainte-Hélène: Ascension									
8 III 1998 (CDJC)	117.5	111	130.7	...	...	...	...	...	...
Saint Helena: Tristan da Cunha - Sainte-Hélène: Tristan da Cunha									
22 II 1987 (CDFC)	55.2	48.6	61	...	...	...	...	...	...
Sao Tome and Principe - Sao Tomé-et-Principe									
4 VIII 1991 (CDFC)	102.7	101.5	103.8	...	...	...	...	...	...
25 VIII 2001 (CDJC)	105.7	106.2	105.3	...	...	...	...	...	...
Seychelles									
17 VIII 1987 (CDFC)	100.9	102.8	99	...	...	...	...	...	...
26 VIII 1994 (CDFC)	100.9	99.9	102	...	...	...	...	...	...
29 VIII 1997 (CDFC)	101.6	100.8	102.5	...	...	...	...	...	...
26 VIII 2002 (CDJC)	100.8	99.2	102.5	...	...	...	...	...	...
26 VIII 2010 (CDFC)	101.3	101.7	101	...	...	...	...	...	...
South Africa - Afrique du Sud									
5 III 1985 (CDFC)	124.3	120.9	127.7	...	...	...	...	...	...
7 III 1991 (CDFC)	113.1	111.5	114.7	...	...	...	...	...	...
10 X 1996 (CDFC)[6]	100.5	100.3	100.7	99.3	99.5	99.1	102.5	101.7	103.1
Swaziland									
25 VIII 1986 (CDFC)	125.9	125.4	126.3	118.3	118.2	118.5	129.3	130.1	128.8
11 V 1997 (CDFC)	120.6	121.5	119.7	116.9	117.9	115.8	122.3	123.7	121.2
11 V 2007 (CDJC)	99.8	101.2	98.6	99	100.7	97.4	100.1	101.5	99.1
Tunisia - Tunisie									
20 IV 1994 (CDFC)	102.4	102.4	102.4	102.4	102.4	102.4	102.4	102.3	102.4
Uganda - Ouganda									
12 I 1991 (CDFC)	168	154.8	180.5	158.6	150.8	167.3	169.4	155.5	182.2
12 IX 2002 (CDFC)	134.2	129.6	138.4	128.2	128.5	128	135.2	129.7	140
United Republic of Tanzania - République Unie de Tanzanie									
28 VIII 1988 (CDFC)	189.2	175.1	201.8	173.7	167.3	180.7	193.3	177.4	206.7
26 VIII 2012 (CDFC)	154.4	152.6	156.1	139.5	141.5	137.7	162.3	158.8	165.5
Zambia - Zambie									
20 VIII 1990 (CDFC)	120.7	121.9	119.6	117.2	119.8	114.2	123.1	123.5	122.7
25 X 2000 (CDFC)	127.6	128.9	126.3	123.9	125.3	122.4	129.9	131.4	128.5
16 X 2010 (CDJC)	123.8	126.8	120.7	122.3	125.2	119.3	124.9	128.2	121.8
Zimbabwe									
18 VIII 1992 (CDFC)	120.6	122.2	119.2	115.9	119.5	111.4	123.7	124.6	123
17 VIII 2002 (CDFC)	115.1	115.2	115	109.7	110.9	108.4	119	119	119.1
17 VIII 2012 (CDFC)	110.8	110.8	110.8	...	...	...	...	...	...

3a. Whipple's Index by sex and urban/rural residence, 1985 - 2014
L'indice de Whipple par le sexe et la résidence urbaine/rurale, 1985 - 2014 (continued - suite)

Continent, country or area, date and code[a] / Continent, pays ou zone, date et code[a]	Total			Urban - Urbaine			Rural - Rurale		
	Both sexes Les deux sexes	Male Masculin	Female Féminin	Both sexes Les deux sexes	Male Masculin	Female Féminin	Both sexes Les deux sexes	Male Masculin	Female Féminin
AMERICA, NORTH - AMÉRIQUE DU NORD									
Anguilla									
13 IV 1992 (CDFC)	104.8	109	100.4	...	...	...	...	...	...
9 V 2001 (CDFC)	104.4	105.8	103.1	...	...	...	...	...	...
Antigua and Barbuda - Antigua-et-Barbuda									
28 V 2001 (CDFC)	104.3	103.1	105.4	...	...	...	...	...	...
Aruba									
6 X 1991 (CDJC)	99.3	99.4	99.3	...	...	...	...	...	...
14 X 2000 (CDJC)	103.9[7]	103.3	104.5	...	...	...	...	...	...
29 IX 2010 (CDJC)[7]	103.4	103.6	103.3	...	...	...	...	...	...
Bahamas									
1 V 1990 (CDFC)	103.4	102.3	104.5	...	...	...	...	...	...
1 V 2000 (CDFC)	101.5	100.4	102.5	...	...	...	...	...	...
3 V 2010 (CDJC)	101.3	101.6	101.1	...	...	...	...	...	...
Barbados - Barbade									
1 V 2000 (CDFC)	103.8	104.4	103.3	...	...	...	...	...	...
Belize									
12 V 1991 (CDFC)	103.5	103.2	103.8	...	...	...	...	...	...
12 V 2010 (CDJC)	104.2	103.9	104.5	...	...	...	...	...	...
Bermuda - Bermudes									
20 V 1991 (CDJC)	99	97.9	100	...	...	...	...	...	...
20 V 2000 (CDJC)[8]	100.2	100	100.3	...	...	...	...	...	...
20 V 2010 (CDJC)[9]	100.9	101.1	100.8	100.9	101.1	100.8	...	...	...
British Virgin Islands - Îles Vierges britanniques									
12 V 1991 (CDJC)	102.6	104.5	100.5	...	...	...	...	...	...
Canada									
4 VI 1991 (CDJC)	99.6	99.6	99.6	99.6	99.6	99.7	99.6	99.6	99.5
14 V 1996 (CDJC)	99.7	99.7	99.7	...	...	...	...	...	...
15 V 2001 (CDJC)	99.7	99.7	99.8	99.8	99.8	99.8	99.6	99.5	99.8
16 V 2006 (CDJC)[7]	99.9	100	99.9	100	100	100	99.6	99.6	99.7
2 V 2011 (CDJC)	100.8	101	100.7	100.9	101.1	100.8	100.4	100.6	100.3
Cayman Islands - Îles Caïmanes									
15 X 1989 (CDFC)	104.1	102.7	105.5	...	...	...	...	...	...
10 X 2010 (CDJC)[10]	102.3	102.8	101.8	102.3	102.8	101.8	...	...	...
Costa Rica									
26 VI 2000 (CDJC)	109.1	109.8	108.4	108.6	108.9	108.3	109.9	111.1	108.6
30 V 2011 (CDJC)	104	104.2	103.9	103.8	103.8	103.9	104.6	105.2	103.9
Cuba									
7 IX 2002 (CDJC)	102.2	102.5	101.9	102.5	102.7	102.2	101.5	102	100.9
14 IX 2012 (CDFC)	101.5	101.6	101.3	...	...	...	...	...	...
Dominican Republic - République dominicaine									
24 IX 1993 (CDJC)	116.5	114.9	118	111.5	109.9	113	123.5	121.4	125.5
18 X 2002 (CDJC)	108	108.9	107.1	105.8	106.3	105.4	112.1	113.5	110.7
1 XII 2010 (CDJC)	111.5	113.8	109.2	109.9	111.9	108.1	116.5	119.3	113.1
El Salvador									
27 IX 1992 (CDFC)	126	127.5	124.6	119.9	119.7	120	133.5	136.6	130.7
12 V 2007 (CDJC)	105.9	107.1	105	105.3	106.3	104.5	107.3	108.7	106.2
Guadeloupe									
8 III 1999 (CDJC)	100.5	100.5	100.4	...	...	...	...	...	...
Honduras									
11 V 1988 (CDFC)	104.1	104.5	103.6	102.4	102.5	102.3	105.3	105.9	104.8
28 VII 2001 (CDJC)	121.8	123.3	120.4	118.5	118.8	118.3	125.1	127.5	122.7
Jamaica - Jamaïque									
7 IV 1991 (CDJC)	107.6	108.8	106.5	...	...	...	...	...	...
10 IX 2001 (CDJC)[11]	107.4	108.7	106.1	106.9	107.5	106.4	107.9	110	105.7
4 IV 2011 (CDJC)	103.3	103.4	103.1	103.6	103.6	103.6	102.8	103.2	102.5
Martinique									
15 III 1990 (CDJC)	104.4	104.1	104.6	...	...	...	...	...	...
Mexico - Mexique									
12 III 1990 (CDJC)	125.2	123.5	126.8	...	...	...	...	...	...
14 II 2000 (CDJC)	116.7	116.5	116.9	114.8	114.3	115.3	123.4	124.3	122.7
17 X 2005 (CDJC)	118.8	118.7	118.9	117.5	117	117.9	123.8	124.8	122.8
12 VI 2010 (CDFC)[12]	114	114.1	113.9	113.7	113.6	113.9	115.1	116.2	114.1

Continent, country or area, date and code[a] Continent, pays ou zone, date et code[a]	Total			Urban - Urbaine			Rural - Rurale		
	Both sexes Les deux sexes	Male Masculin	Female Féminin	Both sexes Les deux sexes	Male Masculin	Female Féminin	Both sexes Les deux sexes	Male Masculin	Female Féminin
AMERICA, NORTH - AMÉRIQUE DU NORD									
Montserrat									
12 V 2011 (CDJC)	101.9	95.9	108.4	...	...	...	...	...	...
Nicaragua									
4 VI 2005 (CDJC)	111.6	112.8	110.5	108.5	109.2	107.8	116.4	117.8	115.1
Panama									
13 V 1990 (CDFC)	109.3	109.2	109.3	104.6	104.5	104.8	115.6	115	116.3
14 V 2000 (CDFC)	103.2	103.3	103.2	...	...	...	...	...	...
Puerto Rico - Porto Rico									
1 IV 1990 (CDJC)	105.6	106.1	105.1	...	...	...	...	...	...
1 IV 2000 (CDJC)	101.7	102	101.6	...	...	...	...	...	...
1 IV 2010 (CDJC)[13]	102	102	102	...	...	...	...	...	...
Saint Lucia - Sainte-Lucie									
12 V 1991 (CDFC)	110.5	110.5	110.4	...	...	...	...	...	...
22 V 2001 (CDFC)	105.5	105.8	105.2	104	100.5	107.3	106.2	108	104.4
Saint Pierre and Miquelon - Saint Pierre-et-Miquelon									
8 III 1999 (CDFC)	100.5	104.6	96.1	...	...	...	...	...	...
Saint Vincent and the Grenadines - Saint-Vincent-et-les Grenadines									
12 V 1991 (CDFC)	106.6	105.2	107.9	...	...	...	...	...	...
Sint Maarten (Dutch part) - Saint-Martin (partie néerlandaise)									
9 IV 2011 (CDFC)	100.7	100.2	101.2	...	...	...	...	...	...
Trinidad and Tobago - Trinité-et-Tobago									
9 I 2011 (CDJC)	106.6	107.2	105.9	...	...	...	...	...	...
Turks and Caicos Islands - Îles Turques et Caïques									
10 IX 2001 (CDFC)	104.2	100.1	108.6	...	...	...	...	...	...
United States of America - États-Unis d'Amérique									
1 IV 1990 (CDJC)	104.5	104.8	104.2	...	...	...	...	...	...
1 IV 2000 (CDJC)[14]	101.8	102.1	101.5	102.1	102.4	101.7	100.8	101	100.5
1 IV 2010 (CDJC)	102.2	102.5	102	102.4	102.7	102.2	101.5	101.7	101.2
AMERICA, SOUTH - AMÉRIQUE DU SUD									
Argentina - Argentine									
15 V 1991 (CDFC)	104.2	103.3	105.2	...	...	...	...	...	...
18 XI 2001 (CDFC)	102.4	101.8	103	...	...	...	...	...	...
27 X 2010 (CDFC)	102.6	102.5	102.7	102.6	102.5	102.7	102.5	102.9	102
Bolivia (Plurinational State of) - Bolivie (État plurinational de)									
3 VI 1992 (CDFC)	125.4	121.1	129.5	111.4	108	114.4	146.1	139.4	152.7
5 IX 2001 (CDFC)	114.6	113.1	116	109.1	108	110.2	124.6	121.9	127.6
21 XI 2012 (CDFC)	110.4	110.5	110.3	108	108.1	108	115.7	115.4	116.1
Brazil - Brésil									
1 IX 1991 (CDJC)	103.3	103.3	103.3	102.3	102.3	102.2	107.2	106.9	107.4
1 VIII 2000 (CDJC)[15]	104.2	104.3	104	103.6	103.7	103.5	107.1	107.3	107
31 VII 2010 (CDJC)	104.8	105.6	104.1	104.7	105.4	104	105.6	106.6	104.4
Chile - Chili									
22 IV 1992 (CDFC)	100.3	98.9	101.7	100.2	98.6	101.7	101	100.2	101.9
24 IV 2002 (CDFC)	99.5	98.5	100.5	99.4	98.2	100.5	100.2	100	100.4
Colombia - Colombie									
15 X 1985 (CDFC)	147.9	146.5	149.2	139.8	136.8	142.4	166.9	166.5	167.3
24 X 1993 (CDFC)	118.9	117.7	120	111.7	108.9	114.1	139.6	139.9	139.4
22 V 2005 (CDFC)	103.5	104.2	102.9	102.1	102.4	101.8	108.6	109.8	107.3
22 V 2005 (CDJC)	103.5	104.2	102.9	102.1	102.4	101.8	108.7	109.9	107.3
Ecuador - Équateur									
25 XI 1990 (CDFC)[16]	132.5	131.2	133.8	122.9	121	124.7	146.6	145.4	147.9
25 XI 2001 (CDFC)[16]	112.1	111.8	112.4	107.9	107	108.7	119.9	120.4	119.4
28 XI 2010 (CDFC)	103.7	104.1	103.3	103	103.4	102.7	104.9	105.4	104.4
French Guiana - Guyane française									
15 III 1990 (CDJC)	106.2	105.7	106.7	...	...	...	...	...	...

Continent, country or area, date and code[a] Continent, pays ou zone, date et code[a]	Total			Urban - Urbaine			Rural - Rurale		
	Both sexes Les deux sexes	Male Masculin	Female Féminin	Both sexes Les deux sexes	Male Masculin	Female Féminin	Both sexes Les deux sexes	Male Masculin	Female Féminin
AMERICA, SOUTH - AMÉRIQUE DU SUD									
8 III 1999 (CDJC)	101.1	100.9	101.3	...	...	...	...	...	...
Paraguay									
26 VIII 1992 (CDFC)	108.6	107.9	109.3	105.7	104.3	107	112	111.8	112.3
28 VIII 2002 (CDFC)	104.8	104.3	105.2	103.2	102.6	103.7	107.1	106.5	107.8
Peru - Pérou									
21 X 2007 (CDFC)	109.4	109.1	109.6	106.9	106.5	107.3	118.8	118.5	119.1
Suriname									
2 VIII 2004 (CDJC)	101.1	100.4	102	102.4[17]	101.4[17]	103.5[17]	98.3[17]	98.2[17]	98.4[17]
13 VIII 2012 (CDJC)	101.7	101.8	101.7	...	...	...	...	...	...
Uruguay									
23 X 1985 (CDFC)	106.2	104.9	107.4	106.2	104.7	107.5	106.3	106.1	106.5
22 V 1996 (CDFC)[18]	103.3	102.8	103.8	103.2	102.5	103.8	104	104.5	103.3
1 VI 2004 (CDFC)[19]	106	105.9	106.2	106.1	105.9	106.3	105.4	105.7	105
4 X 2011 (CDJC)	101.8	101.9	101.7	101.8	101.9	101.7	101.8	101.6	102
Venezuela (Bolivarian Republic of) - Venezuela (République bolivarienne du)[20]									
20 X 1990 (CDFC)	106.4	106.5	106.3	105	104.8	105.3	114.9	116.1	113.4
ASIA - ASIE									
Armenia - Arménie									
10 X 2001 (CDJC)	103	102.8	103.3	103.7	103.7	103.8	101.6	101.1	102.1
12 X 2011 (CDJC)	101.8	101.5	102	102.4	102.3	102.6	100.6	100.2	101
Azerbaijan - Azerbaïdjan									
27 I 1999 (CDJC)	100.4	99.8	101	100.3	99.8	100.8	100.5	99.7	101.2
13 IV 2009 (CDJC)	100.4	100.1	100.7	100.8	100.3	101.3	99.9	99.7	100.1
Bahrain - Bahreïn									
16 XI 1991 (CDFC)	96.6	98.3	93.6	...	...	...	...	...	...
7 IV 2001 (CDJC)	100.2	99.9	100.9	...	...	...	...	...	...
27 IV 2010 (CDJC)	100.2	99.3	101.9	...	...	...	...	...	...
Bangladesh[21]									
22 I 2001 (CDFC)	299.5	295.8	303.4	283.1	277.9	289.8	305	302.6	307.4
Bhutan - Bhoutan									
30 V 2005 (CDFC)	116.4	117.7	114.9	118.7	119.6	117.4	115.4	116.8	113.9
Brunei Darussalam - Brunéi Darussalam									
7 VIII 1991 (CDFC)	98.8	98.7	98.8	...	...	...	...	...	...
20 VI 2011 (CDJC)	100.9	101.6	100.2	100.6	101.3	99.8	102	102.3	101.6
Cambodia - Cambodge									
3 III 1998 (CDFC)	118.1	116.2	119.6	119.8	117.6	121.8	117.6	115.9	119.1
3 III 2008 (CDFC)[22]	109.9	108.2	111.3	109.7	108.5	110.8	109.9	108.1	111.5
China - Chine									
1 VII 1990 (CDFC)	101	101.1	100.9	101.9	102	101.8	100.6	100.7	100.5
1 XI 2000 (CDFC)	101.7	101.7	101.6	101.6	101.8	101.4	101.7	101.7	101.7
1 XI 2010 (CDJC)[23]	98.8	98.9	98.8	98.7	98.9	98.6	98.9	98.9	99
China, Hong Kong SAR - Chine, Hong Kong RAS									
11 III 1986 (CDFC)	101.7	101.4	102.1	101.7	101.3	102.1	102.1	102.5	101.7
15 III 1996 (CDFC)	99.7	99.8	99.7	...	...	...	...	...	...
14 III 2001 (CDJC)[24]	100.2	100.3	100.1	...	...	...	...	...	...
14 VII 2006 (CDJC)[25]	98.3	98.4	98.3	...	...	...	...	...	...
30 VI 2011 (CDJC)[24]	99.4	100	98.9	...	...	...	...	...	...
China, Macao SAR - Chine, Macao RAS									
30 VIII 1991 (CDJC)	100.8	101.4	100.3	...	...	...	...	...	...
23 VIII 2001 (CDJC)	95.5	94.7	96.2	...	...	...	...	...	...
12 VIII 2011 (CDJC)	98.9	97.6	100	...	...	...	...	...	...
Cyprus - Chypre									
1 X 1992 (CDJC)	98.7	98.3	99	98.8	98.4	99.3	98.4	98.3	98.5
1 X 2001 (CDJC)[26]	100.7	100.7	100.6	100.9	101.4	100.4	100.1	99.1	101.1
1 X 2011 (CDJC)[26]	105.4	106.6	104.4	...	...	...	...	...	...

Continent, country or area, date and code[a] Continent, pays ou zone, date et code[a]	Total			Urban - Urbaine			Rural - Rurale		
	Both sexes Les deux sexes	Male Masculin	Female Féminin	Both sexes Les deux sexes	Male Masculin	Female Féminin	Both sexes Les deux sexes	Male Masculin	Female Féminin
ASIA - ASIE									
Democratic People's Republic of Korea - République populaire démocratique de Corée									
31 XII 1993 (CDJC)	105	105.2	104.7	104.4	104.6	104.2	105.8	106.2	105.5
1 X 2008 (CDJC)	101	100.6	101.3	...	...	...	...	...	...
Georgia - Géorgie									
17 I 2002 (CDJC)	101.4	101.7	101.1	101.6	102	101.3	101.1	101.4	100.8
India - Inde									
1 III 1991 (CDFC)[27]	290.3	292.6	287.9	258.7	253.8	264.3	302.1	307.7	296.2
1 III 2001 (CDFC)[28]	230	241	218.4	217.2	216.8	217.8	235.5	252	218.7
9 II 2011 (CDFC)[29]	171	174.6	167.4	152.9	151	154.9	180.5	187.1	173.8
Indonesia - Indonésie									
31 X 1990 (CDFC)	163.3	160.2	166.3	139.7	135.8	143.7	174.2	171.7	176.5
30 VI 2000 (CDJC)[30]	152.2	151.3	153.1	136.8	136.4	137.2	164.2	163.1	165.2
1 V 2010 (CDJC)	114.5	114.2	114.9	...	...	...	...	...	...
Iran (Islamic Republic of) - Iran (République islamique d')									
22 IX 1986 (CDFC)	122.6	121.1	124.1	114.4	113.4	115.5	133.1	131.3	134.8
11 IX 1991 (CDJC)	128.7	127	130.4	122.5	121.3	123.9	138.5	136.4	140.6
11 IX 1994 (CDJC)	107.4	106.8	108.1	107.1	108	106.2	107.8	104.5	111.2
23 X 1996 (CDJC)	108.8	108.6	109	105.7	105.6	105.8	114.1	114	114.3
28 X 2006 (CDJC)[31]	111.6	110.4	112.8	109.3	108.5	110.1	117.2	115.2	119.2
24 X 2011 (CDJC)	103.7	103.8	103.5	103.6	103.8	103.5	103.7[32]	103.8[32]	103.6[32]
Iraq									
16 X 1997 (CDFC)	106.2	105.6	106.8	105.5	104.9	106.1	108	107.6	108.5
Israel - Israël									
4 XI 1995 (CDFC)[33]	101.4	101.8	101	101.3	101.8	100.9	101.9	101.5	102.3
4 XI 1995 (CDJC)	101.1	101.1	101.1	101	101	101	101.5	101.6	101.4
27 XII 2008 (CDFC)[34]	98.9	99	98.9	99	99.1	98.9	98.6	98.3	99
Japan - Japon									
1 X 1985 (CDFC)	98.4	98.4	98.3	98.3	98.4	98.2	98.7	98.5	98.8
1 X 1990 (CDFC)	98.9	98.9	98.9	98.9	99	98.8	98.8	98.6	99
1 X 1995 (CDFC)	99	99	99	99	99.1	99	98.8	98.6	98.9
1 X 2000 (CDJC)	99.1	99.1	99	99.1	99.2	99	99	98.8	99.2
1 X 2005 (CDJC)[35]	99.1	99.2	99.1	99.2	99.2	99.1	99	98.8	99.1
1 X 2010 (CDJC)[35]	100.9	100.9	100.9	100.9	100.9	100.8	101	100.9	101.1
Jordan - Jordanie[36]									
1 X 2004 (CDFC)	100.8	100.4	101.3	...	...	...	...	...	...
Kazakhstan									
12 I 1989 (CDFC)	98.9	98.8	99	98.7	98.6	98.8	99.2	99	99.4
26 II 1999 (CDJC)[18]	99.9	99.8	99.9	100.1	100	100.2	99.5	99.5	99.4
Kuwait - Koweït									
20 IV 1985 (CDFC)	139.5	142.6	133.9	...	...	...	...	...	...
Kyrgyzstan - Kirghizstan									
12 I 1989 (CDJC)	99.3	99.1	99.5	98.4	98	98.8	99.9	99.8	100.1
24 III 1999 (CDJC)	99.4	99.2	99.6	99.2	98.9	99.5	99.5	99.3	99.7
24 III 2009 (CDJC)	100.6	100.5	100.8	...	...	...	...	...	...
Lao People's Democratic Republic - République démocratique populaire lao									
1 III 2005 (CDJC)	138.3	136.4	140.2	120.8[37]	120.9[37]	120.6[37]	146[37]	143.3[37]	148.5[37]
Malaysia - Malaisie									
14 VIII 1991 (CDFC)	114.2	113.8	114.6	110.3	110.2	110.3	118.8	117.9	119.7
6 VII 2010 (CDJC)	120.4	120.7	120	120.6	120.7	120.5	119.7	120.6	118.7
6 VII 2010 (CDJC)[38]	120.7	121.1	120.3	...	...	...	...	...	...
Maldives									
25 III 1985 (CDFC)	176.7	175.3	178.4	166.3	170.9	159.4	180.7	177.2	184.2
8 III 1990 (CDFC)	156.4	159.9	152.7	149.3	154.5	142.6	159.2	162.4	156.1
25 III 1995 (CDFC)	143.1	144.5	141.7	137.3	137.9	136.7	145.5	147.5	143.5
31 III 2000 (CDFC)	106.9	109.5	104.3	...	...	...	...	...	...
21 III 2006 (CDFC)[39]	103.8	104.9	102.8	104	105.5	102.5	103.7	104.5	102.9
Mongolia - Mongolie									
5 I 2000 (CDFC)	99.9	99.6	100.2	99.9	99.7	100.1	99.9	99.5	100.2
11 XI 2010 (CDJC)	101.6	101.3	101.9	101.7	101.4	102	101.5	101.3	101.7
Myanmar[40]									
29 III 2014 (CDFC)	123.3	124	122.6	...	...	...	...	...	...

Continent, country or area, date and code[a] / Continent, pays ou zone, date et code[a]	Total			Urban - Urbaine			Rural - Rurale		
	Both sexes Les deux sexes	Male Masculin	Female Féminin	Both sexes Les deux sexes	Male Masculin	Female Féminin	Both sexes Les deux sexes	Male Masculin	Female Féminin
ASIA - ASIE									
Nepal - Népal									
22 VI 1991 (CDJC)	202.4	195.6	209	186.2	179.2	193.9	204.2	197.6	210.5
22 VI 2001 (CDJC)	206.1	205.7	206.6	...	...	...	...	...	...
22 VI 2011 (CDJC)	188.6	191.3	186.2	169.9	167.8	172	193.1	197.5	189.3
Oman									
7 XII 2003 (CDFC)	158.5	165.6	146.9	154.9	163.1	141.1	170.2	174.1	164.4
Philippines									
1 IX 1995 (CDJC)	115.7	116.5	114.9	...	...	...	...	...	...
1 V 2000 (CDJC)[41]	110.8	111.6	110	...	...	...	...	...	...
1 VIII 2007 (CDJC)	104.8	104.9	104.7	...	...	...	...	...	...
1 V 2010 (CDJC)[42]	108.5	109.1	107.9	...	...	...	...	...	...
Qatar									
16 III 1986 (CDFC)	149.1	151.9	140.2	...	...	...	...	...	...
Republic of Korea - République de Corée									
1 XI 1985 (CDFC)	99.4	98.9	99.8	99.6	99.4	99.8	98.8	97.9	99.6
1 XI 1990 (CDFC)	99.5	99.2	99.8	99.6	99.4	99.8	99.1	98.5	99.7
1 XI 1995 (CDJC)	99.9	99.7	100.1	100	99.8	100.2	99.4	99.2	99.6
1 XI 2000 (CDJC)[43]	100	99.8	100.2	100.2	100	100.4	99.2	98.9	99.4
1 XI 2005 (CDJC)[43]	100.4	100.2	100.6	100.6	100.4	100.8	99.4	99.2	99.7
Singapore - Singapour									
30 VI 2000 (CDJC)	98.2	98.1	98.3	...	...	...	...	...	...
30 VI 2010 (CDJC)[44]	99.7	99.7	99.7	...	...	...	...	...	...
Sri Lanka[45]									
17 VII 2001 (CDFC)	97	97.5	96.4	98.2	98.5	97.8	96.8[46]	97.3[46]	96.2[46]
State of Palestine - État de Palestine									
9 XII 1997 (CDFC)[47]	109.1	103	115.3	...	...	...	...	...	...
1 XII 2007 (CDFC)[30]	103.8	102.6	104.9	104.4[48]	103.2[48]	105.7[48]	100.8	100	101.6
Syrian Arab Republic - République arabe syrienne[49]									
3 IX 1994 (CDFC)	111.8	109.9	113.8	111.9	110.4	113.5	111.7	109.2	114.1
Tajikistan - Tadjikistan									
12 I 1989 (CDJC)	99	98.9	99.1	97.6	97.1	98	99.9	100	99.9
20 I 2000 (CDFC)	99.3	99.2	99.4	100.1	100	100.1	99	98.9	99.1
21 IX 2010 (CDFC)	103.6	103.9	103.4	105.8	106.6	105	102.8	102.9	102.7
Thailand - Thaïlande									
1 IV 2000 (CDJC)[50]	104.7	104.7	104.8	108.1	108.1	108.1	103	103	103
1 IX 2010 (CDJC)	110.6	111.1	110.1	115.6	116.2	115	106.3	106.8	105.8
Timor-Leste									
11 VII 2010 (CDFC)	130.3	128.9	131.7	126	125.6	126.5	132.3	130.6	134
Turkey - Turquie									
20 X 1985 (CDFC)	149.4	133.8	165.3	...	...	...	...	...	...
21 X 1990 (CDFC)	139.7	128.9	150.8	...	...	...	...	...	...
22 X 2000 (CDFC)	125.7	123.2	128.3	122.7	121.3	124.2	131.7	127.2	136.4
Viet Nam									
1 IV 1989 (CDJC)	98.5	98.1	98.8	98.3	97.8	98.8	98.4	98	98.7
1 IV 1999 (CDJC)	99.2	98.8	99.6	99.1	98.6	99.6	99.3	98.8	99.7
1 IV 2009 (CDJC)	100.4	99.8	100.9	100.6	100	101.1	100.3	99.8	100.8
Yemen - Yémen									
16 XII 1994 (CDFC)	293.9	282.6	304.9	245	229.6	265	311.7	305.8	316.8
EUROPE									
Åland Islands - Îles d'Åland[51]									
31 XII 2000 (CDJC)	100.7	101.5	99.8	102.9	101.9	103.8	99	101.2	96.7
Austria - Autriche									
15 V 1991 (CDJC)	97.9	97.9	97.9	97.8	97.9	97.7	98.2	98.1	98.2
15 V 2001 (CDJC)	97.4	97.5	97.3	97.3	97.5	97.2	97.5	97.3	97.6
31 X 2011 (CDJC)	100	100.1	100	100.2	100.2	100.2	99.7	99.8	99.7
Belarus - Bélarus									
12 I 1989 (CDJC)	99.4	99.3	99.5	98.9	98.8	99.1	100.3	100.3	100.2
16 II 1999 (CDJC)	99.6	99.4	99.8	99.7	99.6	99.9	99.2	98.9	99.5
14 X 2009 (CDJC)	101.5	101.6	101.5	101.7	101.6	101.7	101	101.3	100.7
Belgium - Belgique									
1 X 2001 (CDJC)	99.5	99.4	99.7	99.5	99.4	99.7	99.2	98.9	99.4
1 I 2011 (CDJC)	100	99.9	100.1	100	99.9	100.1	100.3	99.1	101.6

3a. Whipple's Index by sex and urban/rural residence, 1985 - 2014
L'indice de Whipple par le sexe et la résidence urbaine/rurale, 1985 - 2014 (continued - suite)

Continent, country or area, date and code[a] Continent, pays ou zone, date et code[a]	Total			Urban - Urbaine			Rural - Rurale		
	Both sexes Les deux sexes	Male Masculin	Female Féminin	Both sexes Les deux sexes	Male Masculin	Female Féminin	Both sexes Les deux sexes	Male Masculin	Female Féminin
EUROPE									
Bosnia and Herzegovina - Bosnie-Herzégovine									
31 III 1991 (CDJC)	100.4	100.5	100.2	...	...	...	...	...	...
Bulgaria - Bulgarie									
1 II 2011 (CDJC)	101.2	101	101.4	101.1	100.9	101.3	101.4	101.4	101.4
Croatia - Croatie									
31 III 1991 (CDFC)	99.1	99.2	99.1	99	99.3	98.8	99.2	99.1	99.4
31 III 2001 (CDJC)	98.2	98.4	98.1	98.3	98.6	98.1	98.1	98.1	98.2
1 IV 2011 (CDJC)	100.3	100.5	100.2	100.3	100.4	100.2	100.4	100.5	100.2
Czech Republic - République tchèque									
3 III 1991 (CDJC)	99	98.8	99.1	...	...	...	...	...	...
1 III 2001 (CDJC)	99.2	99.1	99.3	99	98.9	99.1	99.8	99.8	99.9
25 III 2011 (CDJC)	99.6	99.6	99.7	95.5	99.4	99.6	99.9	100.1	99.8
Denmark - Danemark[52]									
1 I 1991 (CDJC)	100.5	100.6	100.5	...	...	...	...	...	...
Estonia - Estonie									
31 III 2000 (CDJC)	100	99.7	100.3	100.2	100	100.4	99.7	99.1	100.2
31 XII 2011 (CDJC)	100	100	100.1	100.1	100	100.1	100	99.9	100.2
Finland - Finlande									
17 XI 1985 (CDJC)	99.8	99.9	99.6	...	...	...	...	...	...
31 XII 1990 (CDJC)	99.5	99.6	99.5	...	...	...	...	...	...
31 XII 2000 (CDJC)	99.5	99.6	99.4	99.9	100.1	99.7	98.9	98.9	98.8
31 XII 2010 (CDJC)	100.1	100.1	100	100	100.1	99.8	100.3	100	100.5
France									
5 III 1990 (CDJC)	99.2	99	99.3	99.5	99.4	99.6	98.2	98.1	98.4
8 III 1999 (CDJC)[53]	100.5	100.5	100.5	100.5	100.5	100.5	100.8	100.7	100.8
Germany - Allemagne									
9 V 2011 (CDJC)	100	100	100.1	100	100	100.1	100.1	100.1	100.1
Gibraltar									
14 X 1991 (CDFC)	105.7	104.9	106.6	...	...	...	...	...	...
12 XI 2001 (CDFC)[54]	98	98.6	97.5	...	...	...	...	...	...
12 XI 2012 (CDJC)[55]	99.5	100.3	98.7	...	...	...	...	...	...
Greece - Grèce									
17 III 1991 (CDFC)	108.8	107.4	110.1	108.5	107.3	109.7	109.1	107.6	110.7
18 III 2001 (CDJC)[56]	105	104.9	105.1	104.8	104.6	104.9	105.8	105.7	106
9 V 2011 (CDFC)	101.4	101.8	101.1	101.3	101.6	101.1	101.8	102.3	101.2
Guernsey - Guernesey									
23 III 1986 (CDJC)	96.1	96.1	96	...	...	...	...	...	...
13 III 1996 (CDJC)	97.5	98.5	96.6	...	...	...	...	...	...
29 IV 2001 (CDJC)	97.2	97.4	96.9	...	...	...	...	...	...
Hungary - Hongrie									
1 I 1990 (CDFC)	102.1	102.5	101.8	102.4	102.8	102	101.7	101.9	101.5
1 II 2001 (CDFC)	101.6	101.8	101.5	101.9	102.2	101.6	101.2	101.2	101.2
1 X 2011 (CDFC)	100.2	100.2	100.2	100.1	100.2	100.1	100.4	100.3	100.5
Ireland - Irlande									
21 IV 1991 (CDFC)	100.5	100.5	100.4	...	...	...	...	...	...
28 IV 1996 (CDFC)	100.2	100.2	100.1	100.3	100.5	100.2	99.9	99.7	100
28 IV 2002 (CDFC)	99.5	99.8	99.2	99.7	99.9	99.4	99.3	99.5	99
23 IV 2006 (CDFC)	100.9	101	100.8	101	101.2	100.8	100.8	100.7	100.8
10 IV 2011 (CDFC)[57]	100.7	101	100.5	100.9	101.2	100.5	100.5	100.5	100.4
Isle of Man - Île de Man									
6 IV 1986 (CDJC)	99.2	98.6	99.8	...	...	...	...	...	...
14 IV 1991 (CDJC)	97.7	98.1	97.3	...	...	...	...	...	...
14 IV 1996 (CDJC)	97.9	98.9	97	...	...	...	...	...	...
29 IV 2001 (CDJC)	97.8	98	97.5	...	...	...	...	...	...
23 IV 2006 (CDJC)	98.3	98.4	98.3	...	...	...	...	...	...
27 III 2011 (CDJC)	99.3	100.4	98.2	...	...	...	...	...	...
Italy - Italie									
21 X 2001 (CDJC)	101.1	101	101.1	...	...	...	...	...	...
9 X 2011 (CDJC)	99.8	99.8	99.8	...	...	...	...	...	...
Jersey									
23 III 1986 (CDFC)	98	98	98	...	...	...	...	...	...
10 III 1991 (CDJC)	99.2	100.6	97.8	...	...	...	...	...	...
10 III 1996 (CDJC)	99.4	100.7	98.1	...	...	...	...	...	...
11 III 2001 (CDJC)	98.9	99.6	98.3	...	...	...	...	...	...
27 III 2011 (CDFC)	100	100.7	99.3	...	...	...	...	...	...

3a. Whipple's Index by sex and urban/rural residence, 1985 - 2014
L'indice de Whipple par le sexe et la résidence urbaine/rurale, 1985 - 2014 (continued - suite)

Continent, country or area, date and code[a] / Continent, pays ou zone, date et code[a]	Total			Urban - Urbaine			Rural - Rurale		
	Both sexes Les deux sexes	Male Masculin	Female Féminin	Both sexes Les deux sexes	Male Masculin	Female Féminin	Both sexes Les deux sexes	Male Masculin	Female Féminin
EUROPE									
Latvia - Lettonie									
31 III 2000 (CDJC)[58]	100.5	100.2	100.7	100.4	100.4	100.4	100.6	99.8	101.5
1 III 2011 (CDJC)	99.4	99.6	99.3	99.5	99.7	99.3	99.3	99.3	99.4
Liechtenstein									
31 XII 2010 (CDFC)	100.5	102.1	99	...	...	...	...	...	...
Lithuania - Lituanie									
12 I 1989 (CDJC)	100.6	100.5	100.7	100.7	100.6	100.8	100.3	100.2	100.4
6 IV 2001 (CDJC)	99.8	99.7	99.9	99.4	99	99.7	100.8	101.1	100.5
1 III 2011 (CDJC)	100	100.1	99.9	100	100.2	99.8	100	99.9	100
Luxembourg									
15 II 2001 (CDJC)	99.2	98.9	99.6	...	...	...	...	...	...
1 II 2011 (CDJC)	99.7	99	100.4	...	...	...	...	...	...
Malta - Malte									
26 XI 1995 (CDJC)	101.2	101.2	101.2	101.2	101.2	101.2	125.7	107.6	138.4
27 XI 2005 (CDJC)	101.3	101.9	100.6	101.2	102	100.5	114.3	100	127.3
20 XI 2011 (CDFC)	99.4	100	98.9	99.4	99.9	98.9	100.3	102.3	98.1
Monaco									
21 VI 2000 (CDJC)	100.9	99.9	101.9	...	...	...	...	...	...
Montenegro - Monténégro									
31 X 2003 (CDJC)	100.2	99.9	100.5	100.2	99.6	100.8	100.2	100.3	100
1 IV 2011 (CDJC)	100	99.7	100.3	99.9	99.3	100.5	100.1	100.2	99.9
Netherlands - Pays-Bas									
1 I 2002 (CDJC)	101.2	101.3	101	101.3	101.5	101.1	101	101.1	101
Norway - Norvège									
3 XI 1990 (CDJC)	99.9	99.9	99.9	99.9	99.9	100	99.9	100	99.8
3 XI 2001 (CDJC)[59]	100.1	100.1	100.1	100.1	100.1	100.2	99.7	99.9	99.6
19 XI 2011 (CDJC)[59]	99.8	99.8	99.7	99.7[60]	99.6[60]	99.7[60]	100.1[60]	100.4[60]	99.8[60]
Poland - Pologne									
6 XII 1988 (CDFC)	100.5	100.6	100.4	100.5	100.6	100.4	100.5	100.6	100.5
20 V 2002 (CDJC)[61]	100.7	100.7	100.7	100.9	100.8	100.9	100.4	100.5	100.2
31 III 2011 (CDJC)	100.1	100.1	100.1	100.1	100.1	100.1	100.1	100.1	100
Portugal									
15 IV 1991 (CDFC)	101.4	101.7	101.1	101.4	101.7	101.2	101.3	101.6	101.1
21 III 2011 (CDJC)	100.7	100.8	100.5	100.8	101	100.7	100.4	100.4	100.3
Republic of Moldova - République de Moldova									
12 I 1989 (CDJC)	100.5	100.4	100.5	100.2	99.9	100.4	100.7	100.8	100.6
5 X 2004 (CDFC)[62]	103.2	103.3	103.2	102.9	102.9	102.9	103.5	103.5	103.5
Romania - Roumanie									
7 I 1992 (CDJC)	96.2	96.2	96.2	95.6	95.8	95.4	97.1	96.8	97.4
18 III 2002 (CDJC)	95.8	95.9	95.8	95.3	95.5	95.2	96.5	96.3	96.7
20 X 2011 (CDJC)	96.6	96.6	96.6	96.4	96.5	96.3	96.8	96.7	96.9
Russian Federation - Fédération de Russie									
12 I 1989 (CDJC)	97.8	97.7	97.9	97.7	97.6	97.7	98.3	98.2	98.4
14 X 2010 (CDJC)	103	103	103	103.5	103.5	103.5	101.7	101.6	101.7
Serbia - Serbie[63]									
31 III 2002 (CDJC)	99.9	99.9	100	100.4	100.4	100.5	99.2	99.3	99.2
1 X 2011 (CDJC)	99.4	99.2	99.5	99.7	99.3	100	98.9	99.1	98.7
Slovakia - Slovaquie									
3 III 1991 (CDJC)	100	99.8	100.2	...	...	...	...	...	...
25 V 2001 (CDJC)	99.5	99.5	99.6	99.7	99.6	99.8	99.3	99.3	99.3
21 V 2011 (CDJC)	100.2	100.2	100.3	100.3	100.2	100.4	100.2	100.2	100.1
Slovenia - Slovénie									
31 III 1991 (CDJC)	99	99.1	98.9	99.7	99.7	99.6	98.4	98.6	98.1
31 III 2002 (CDJC)	101.9	102.1	101.8	102.2	102.3	102.2	101.6	101.9	101.3
1 I 2011 (CDJC)	100.6	100.1	101.3	100.7	100.1	101.3	100.6	100	101.3
Spain - Espagne									
1 III 1991 (CDJC)	102.4	102.4	102.3	...	...	...	...	...	...
1 XI 2001 (CDFC)[64]	99	99	99	99	99	98.9	99.1	99	99.1
1 XI 2011 (CDJC)	98.3	98.6	98.1	...	...	...	...	...	...
Sweden - Suède									
1 XI 1990 (CDJC)	99.7	99.8	99.6	...	...	...	...	...	...
31 XII 2003 (CDJC)	100	100	100.1	...	...	...	...	...	...
31 XII 2011 (CDJC)	99.7	99.8	99.6	...	...	...	...	...	...
Switzerland - Suisse									
4 XII 1990 (CDJC)	100.6	100.9	100.2	100.7	100.9	100.5	100.2	100.7	99.7

3a. Whipple's Index by sex and urban/rural residence, 1985 - 2014
L'indice de Whipple par le sexe et la résidence urbaine/rurale, 1985 - 2014 (continued - suite)

Continent, country or area, date and code[a] / Continent, pays ou zone, date et code[a]	Total			Urban - Urbaine			Rural - Rurale		
	Both sexes Les deux sexes	Male Masculin	Female Féminin	Both sexes Les deux sexes	Male Masculin	Female Féminin	Both sexes Les deux sexes	Male Masculin	Female Féminin
EUROPE									
5 XII 2000 (CDFC)............................	99.7	99.9	99.5	99.7	99.9	99.6	99.5	99.9	99.1
31 XII 2011 (CDJC)	99.9	99.9	99.9	99.9	99.9	99.8	100	99.9	100.1
TFYR of Macedonia - L'ex-R. y. de Macédoine									
20 VI 1994 (CDJC)........................	100.2	100.2	100.2	100	100.1	99.8	100.6	100.5	100.8
31 X 2002 (CDJC)........................	100.3	100.3	100.3	...	...	...	...	...	...
Ukraine									
5 XII 2001 (CDFC)........................	102.7	102.7	102.7	103.1	103.1	103.2	101.7	101.8	101.5
United Kingdom of Great Britain and Northern Ireland - Royaume-Uni de Grande-Bretagne et d'Irlande du Nord[65]									
21 IV 1991 (CDFC)[66]	98	98	98	...	...	...	...	...	...
29 IV 2001 (CDFC)[67]	98.1	98	98.1	98.2	98.2	98.2	97.6	97.5	97.7
27 III 2011 (CDJC)........................	100.2	100.3	100.2	100.3	100.3	100.3	99.8	99.8	99.8
OCEANIA - OCÉANIE									
Australia - Australie									
30 VI 1986 (CDFC)........................	101.6	101.7	101.5	101.6	101.6	101.5	101.8	102	101.6
6 VIII 1991 (CDFC)........................	101.7	101.4	102.1	...	...	...	...	...	...
9 VIII 1996 (CDFC)........................	101.6	101.5	101.7	...	...	...	...	...	...
7 VIII 2001 (CDJC)........................	101.4	101.3	101.5	101.4	101.3	101.5	101.3	101.4	101.3
8 VIII 2006 (CDJC)[68]	100.2[69]	100.3[69]	100.2[69]	100.2	100.2	100.1	100.4	100.5	100.3
9 VIII 2011 (CDJC)[68]	100.8[69]	100.8[69]	100.7[69]	100.7	100.7	100.7	101.3	101.3	101.3
Cook Islands - Îles Cook[70]									
1 XII 1996 (CDJC)........................	99.1	97.2	101.1	...	...	...	...	...	...
Fiji - Fidji									
31 VIII 1986 (CDFC)........................	105.4	105	105.7	...	...	...	...	...	...
25 VIII 1996 (CDFC)........................	100.2	100.6	99.8	99.8	99.9	99.7	100.6	101.3	99.9
French Polynesia - Polynésie française									
3 IX 1996 (CDFC)........................	98.6	97.8	99.5	...	...	...	...	...	...
20 VIII 2007 (CDJC)........................	102.8	103.2	102.4	...	...	...	...	...	...
Guam									
1 IV 1990 (CDJC)........................	107.1	106.2	108.2	107	105.5	108.7	107.2	106.6	107.8
1 IV 2000 (CDJC)[13]	100.3	100.4	100.3	...	...	...	...	...	...
Kiribati									
10 X 2010 (CDFC)........................	104.7	103.3	105.9	106	106	106.1	103.3	100.7	105.7
Marshall Islands - Îles Marshall									
13 XI 1988 (CDFC)........................	101.2	103.3	98.9	...	...	...	...	...	...
1 VI 1999 (CDFC)........................	104	106.2	101.7	...	...	...	...	...	...
New Caledonia - Nouvelle-Calédonie									
4 IV 1989 (CDFC)........................	99.5	99.4	99.6	...	...	...	...	...	...
New Zealand - Nouvelle-Zélande									
4 III 1986 (CDJC)........................	100.7[71]	100.6[71]	100.7[71]	100.7[71]	100.7[71]	100.8[71]	100.2[71]	99.9[71]	100.6[71]
5 III 1991 (CDFC)........................	100.3	100.4	100.3	100.5	100.6	100.4	99.7	99.3	100
5 III 1996 (CDJC)[72]	100	100	100	100.1	100.1	100.1	99.5	99.5	99.5
6 III 2001 (CDJC)[68]	100	99.9	100	100.2	100.1	100.2	99	99	99.1
7 III 2006 (CDFC)[68]	99.7	...	...	...	...	...	...	...	...
7 III 2006 (CDJC)[68]	99.6	99.7	99.6	99.7	99.8	99.7	99.1	99.3	98.9
Niue - Nioué									
29 IX 1986 (CDFC)........................	105.8	106	105.6	...	...	...	...	...	...
7 IX 2001 (CDFC)........................	98.5	93.8	103.4	...	...	...	...	...	...
Northern Mariana Islands - Îles Mariannes septentrionales									
1 IV 1990 (CDFC)........................	108	108.4	107.4	111.7	111.2	112.1	106.6	107.5	105.3
Palau - Palaos									
15 IV 2000 (CDFC)........................	103.4	105.5	100.5	...	...	...	...	...	...
Papua New Guinea - Papouasie-Nouvelle-Guinée									
11 VII 1990 (CDFC)........................	139	140.1	137.7	...	...	...	...	...	...
9 VII 2000 (CDFC)........................	134	134.2	133.8	131	133.4	128	134.5	134.4	134.7
Pitcairn									
31 XII 1991 (CDFC)........................	96.2	90.9	100	...	...	...	...	...	...

3a. Whipple's Index by sex and urban/rural residence, 1985 - 2014
L'indice de Whipple par le sexe et la résidence urbaine/rurale, 1985 - 2014 (continued - suite)

Continent, country or area, date and code[a] Continent, pays ou zone, date et code[a]	Total			Urban - Urbaine			Rural - Rurale		
	Both sexes Les deux sexes	Male Masculin	Female Féminin	Both sexes Les deux sexes	Male Masculin	Female Féminin	Both sexes Les deux sexes	Male Masculin	Female Féminin
OCEANIA - OCÉANIE									
Samoa									
5 XI 2001 (CDFC)............................	96.4	95.9	97	...	...	...	...	...	...
Tokelau - Tokélaou[73]									
18 X 2011 (CDJC)	105.7	109.6	102	...	...	...	...	...	...
Tonga									
28 XI 1986 (CDJC)	98.2	99	97.4	...	...	...	...	...	...
30 XI 1996 (CDFC)[74]	100.7	101.7	99.6	...	...	...	...	...	...
30 XI 2006 (CDJC)........................	98.6	97.8	99.4	95.2	93.3	97.2	99.7	99.3	100.1
Tuvalu									
1 XI 2002 (CDFC)...........................	98.5	100.8	96.4	...	...	...	...	...	...
Vanuatu									
16 V 1989 (CDJC)	106.9	104.8	109	102.4	98.1	107.8	108.1	106.8	109.3
16 XI 2009 (CDJC)	110.5	111.3	109.7	...	...	...	...	...	...
Wallis and Futuna Islands - Îles Wallis et Futuna									
3 X 1996 (CDFC)............................	96	97.8	94.3	...	...	...	...	...	...

FOOTNOTES - NOTES

Italics: estimates which are less reliable. - Italiques : estimations moins sûres.

* Provisional. - Données provisoires.

[a] 'Code' indicates the source of data, as follows:
CDFC - Census, de facto, complete tabulation
CDFS - Census, de facto, sample tabulation
CDJC - Census, de jure, complete tabulation
CDJS - Census, de jure, sample tabulation
SSDF - Sample survey, de facto
SSDJ - Sample survey, de jure
ESDF - Estimates, de facto
ESDJ - Estimates, de jure

Le 'Code' indique la source des données, comme suit :
CDFC - Recensement, population de fait, tabulation complète
CDFS - Recensement, population de fait, tabulation par sondage
CDJC - Recensement, population de droit, tabulation complète
CDJS - Recensement, population de droit, tabulation par sondage
SSDF - Enquête par sondage, population de fait
SSDJ - Enquête par sondage, population de droit
ESDF - Estimations, population de fait
ESDJ - Estimations, population de droit

[1] Data refer to population in housing units and collective living quarters only. - Correspond aux personnes qui vivent dans des unités d'habitation et dans des logements collectifs seulement.

[2] Data for urban and rural do not add up to the total; reason for discrepancy not ascertained. - La somme des données pour la résidence urbaine et rurale n'est pas égale au total; on ne sait pas comment s'explique la divergence.

[3] Urban and rural data were reported in different years and do not add up to the total. - Les données concernant la population urbaine et la population rurale portent sur des années différentes et leur somme ne correspond pas au total cité.

[4] Excludes the islands of St. Brandon and Agalega. - Non compris les îles St. Brandon et Agalega.

[5] Data refer to Saint Helenian resident population. - Pour la population résidante de Sainte-Hélène.

[6] Data have been adjusted for underenumeration, estimated at 6.8 per cent. - Les données ont été ajustées pour compenser les lacunes du dénombrement estimées à 6,8 p. 100.

[7] Because of rounding, totals are not in all cases the sum of the respective components. - Les chiffres étant arrondis, les totaux ne correspondent pas toujours rigoureusement à la somme des composants respectifs.

[8] Excluding the institutional population. - Non compris la population dans les institutions.

[9] Bermuda is 100 per cent urban. - 100 pour cent de la population des Bermudes est urbaine.

[10] Because of rounding, totals are not in all cases the sum of the respective components. Excluding the institutional population. - Les chiffres étant arrondis, les totaux ne correspondent pas toujours rigoureusement à la somme des composants respectifs. Non compris la population dans les institutions.

[11] Total represents population in private dwellings, the non-institutional population and persons found on the streets between the hours of 5am and 7am on September 26, 2001; the figures represent the census counts adjusted for under-coverage. - Le total représente la population des logements privés et les personnes trouvées dans la rue entre 5 et 7 heures du matin le 26 septembre 2001, mais ne tient pas compte des personnes vivant dans des établissements; les chiffres sont ceux du recensement corrigés pour tenir compte du sous-dénombrement.

[12] Including an estimation of 1 334 585 persons corresponding to 448 195 housing units without information of the occupants. - Y compris une estimation de 1 334 585 personnes correspondant aux 448 195 unités d'habitation sans information sur les occupants.

[13] Including armed forces stationed in the area. - Y compris les militaires en garnison sur le territoire.

[14] Excluding U.S. Armed Forces overseas and civilian U.S. citizens whose usual place of residence is outside the United States. - Non compris les militaires américains à l'étranger et les civils américains dont le lieu de résidence habituel est en dehors des États-Unis.

[15] Data include persons in remote areas, military personnel outside the country, merchant seamen at sea, civilian seasonal workers outside the country, and other civilians outside the country, and exclude nomads, foreign military, civilian aliens temporarily in the country, transients on ships and Indian jungle population. - Y compris les personnes vivant dans des régions éloignées, le personel militaire en dehors du pays, les marins marchands, les ouvriers saisonniers en dehors du pays, et autres civils en dehors du pays, et non compris les nomades, les militaires étrangers, les étrangers civils temporairement dans le pays, les transiteurs sur des bateaux et les Indiens de la jungle.

[16] Excludes nomadic Indian tribes. - Non compris les tribus d'Indiens nomades.

[17] The districts of Paramaribo and Wanica are considered urban areas, whereas all other districts are considered more or less rural areas. - Les districts de Paramaribo et de Wanica sont considérés comme des zones urbaines, les autres districts étant considérés comme des zones rurales à divers degrés.

[18] Unrevised data. - Les données n'ont pas été révisées.

[19] Unrevised data. Data refer to resident population in Uruguay according to Census Phase 1, carried out between the months of June and July 2004. - Les données n'ont pas été révisées. Les données se rapportent à la population résidente en Uruguay d'après la phase 1 du recensement, qui a eu lieu entre juin et juillet 2004.

[20] Excluding Indian jungle population. - Non compris les Indiens de la jungle.

[21] Data have not been adjusted for underenumeration, estimated at 4.96 per cent. - Les données n'ont pas été ajustées pour compenser les lacunes du dénombrement, estimées à 4,96 p.100.

[22] Excluding foreign diplomatic personnel and their dependants. - Non compris le personnel diplomatique étranger et les membres de leur famille les accompagnant.

[23] For statistical purposes, the data for China do not include those for the Hong Kong Special Administrative Region (Hong Kong SAR), Macao Special Administrative Region (Macao SAR) and Taiwan province of China. Data exclude 2.3 million servicemen, 4.65 million persons with permanent resident status difficult to define, and 0.12 per cent undercount based on the post enumeration survey. - Pour la présentation des statistiques, les données pour la Chine ne comprennent pas la Région Administrative Spéciale de Hong Kong (Hong Kong RAS), la Région Administrative Spéciale de Macao (Macao RAS) et Taïwan province de Chine. Les données ne comprennent pas 2,3 millions de militaires, 4,65 millions de personnes ayant le statut de résident permanent mais difficiles à définir, et des lacunes estimées à 0,12 pour cent sur la base de l'enquête de vérification du recensement.

[24] Data refer to Hong Kong resident population at the census moment, which covers usual residents and mobile residents. Usual residents refer to two categories of people: (1) Hong Kong permanent residents who had stayed in Hong Kong for at least three months during the six months before or for at least three months during the six months after the census moment, regardless of whether they were in Hong Kong or not at the census moment; and (2) Hong Kong non-permanent residents who were in Hong Kong at the census moment. Mobile Residents, they are Hong Kong permanent residents who had stayed in Hong Kong for at least one month but less than three months during the six months before or for at least one month but less than three months during the six months after the census moment, regardless of whether they were in Hong Kong or not at the census moment. - Les données se rapportent à la population résidente à Hong Kong au moment du recensement. Cette population est composée des résidants habituels et des résidants mobiles. La population résidente est partagée en deux catégories: (1) les résidents permanents qui ont habité à Hong Kong au moins trois mois pendant les six mois précédents ou les six mois suivants le recensement; (2) les habitants non-permanents de Hong Kong qui étaient à Hong Kong au moment du recensement. La population mobile se rapporte aux résidents permanents de Hong Kong qui ont habité à Hong Kong pendant les six mois après le recensement pour une période comprise entre un mois et trois mois, indépendamment du fait qu'ils étaient à Hong Kong au moment du recensement au pays.

[25] Data refer to Hong Kong resident population at the census moment, which covers usual residents and mobile residents. Usual residents refer to two categories of people: (1) Hong Kong permanent residents who had stayed in Hong Kong for at least three months during the six months before or for at least three months during the six months after the census moment, regardless of whether they were in Hong Kong or not at the census moment; and (2) Hong Kong non-permanent residents who were in Hong Kong at the census moment. Mobile Residents, they are Hong Kong permanent residents who had stayed in Hong Kong for at least one month but less than three months during the six months before or for at least one month but less than three months during the six months after the census moment, regardless of whether they were in Hong Kong or not at the census moment. Data are estimates from sample enquiry. - Les données se rapportent à la population résidente à Hong Kong au moment du recensement. Cette population est composée des résidants habituels et des résidants mobiles. La population résidente est partagée en deux catégories: (1) les résidents permanents qui ont habité à Hong Kong au moins trois mois pendant les six mois précédents ou les six mois suivants le recensement; (2) les habitants non-permanents de Hong Kong qui étaient à Hong Kong au moment du recensement. La population mobile se rapporte aux résidents permanents de Hong Kong qui ont habité à Hong Kong pendant les six mois après le recensement pour une période comprise entre un mois et trois mois, indépendamment du fait qu'ils étaient à Hong Kong au moment du recensement au pays. Les données sont des chiffres estimatifs dérivés d'une enquête par sondage.

[26] Data refer to government controlled areas. - Les données se rapportent aux zones contrôlées par le Gouvernement.

[27] Excluding Jammu and Kashmir. - Non compris les données concernant la partie du Jammu et Cachemire.

[28] Includes data for the Indian-held part of Jammu and Kashmir, the final status of which has not yet been determined. Excluding Mao-Maram, Paomata and Purul sub-divisions of Senapati district of Manipur. The population of Manipur including the estimated population of the three sub-divisions of Senapati district is 2,291,125 (Males 1,161,173 and females 1,129,952). - Y compris les données pour la partie du Jammu et du Cachemire occupée par l'Inde dont le statut définitif n'a pas encore été déterminé. Non compris les subdivisions Mao-Maram Paomata et Purul du district de Senapati dans l'État du Manipur. Cet État compte 2 291 125 habitants (1 161 173 hommes et 1 129 952 femmes), y compris la population estimative des trois subdivisions du district de Senapati.

[29] Includes data for the Indian-held part of Jammu and Kashmir, the final status of which has not yet been determined. - Y compris les données pour la partie du Jammu et du Cachemire occupée par l'Inde dont le statut définitif n'a pas encore été déterminé.

[30] Data have not been adjusted for underenumeration. - Les données n'ont pas été ajustées pour compenser les lacunes du dénombrement.

[31] Differences between the total country figures and sum of urban and rural areas are due to the inclusion of unsettled population. - Les différences entre les chiffres pour l'ensemble du pays et la somme des zones urbaines et rurales s'expliquent par l'inclusion de la population non sédentaire.

[32] Including unsettled population. - Y compris la population non sédentaire.

[33] The data is from the census sample. - Données extraites de l'échantillon de recensement.

[34] Because of rounding, totals are not in all cases the sum of the respective components. Includes data for East Jerusalem and Israeli residents in certain other territories under occupation by Israeli military forces since June 1967. Data are rounded for confidentiality reasons. - Les chiffres étant arrondis, les totaux ne correspondent pas toujours rigoureusement à la somme des composants respectifs. Y compris les données pour Jérusalem-Est et les résidents israéliens dans certains autres territoires occupés depuis 1967 par les forces armées israéliennes. Chiffres arrondis pour des raisons de confidentialité.

[35] Excluding diplomatic personnel outside the country and foreign military and civilian personnel and their dependants stationed in the area. - Non compris le personnel diplomatique hors du pays ni les militaires et agents civils étrangers en poste sur le territoire et les membres de leur famille les accompagnant.

[36] Excluding data for Jordanian territory under occupation since June 1967 by Israeli military forces. Including registered Palestinian refugees and Jordanians abroad. - Non compris les données pour le territoire jordanien occupé depuis juin 1967 par les forces armées israéliennes. Y compris les réfugiés palestiniens enregistrés et les Jordaniens à l'étranger.

[37] Excluding usual residents not in the country at the time of census. - À l'exclusion des résidents habituels qui ne sont pas dans le pays au moment du recensement.

[38] Data have been adjusted for underenumeration. - Les données ont été ajustées pour compenser les lacunes du dénombrement.

[39] Total population is taken as de facto and de jure together. - Population totale considérée comme de fait et de droit.

[40] Data refer to enumerated population. - Les données se rapportent à la population dénombrée.

[41] Data refer to projections based on the 1995 Population Census. - Correspond à des projections fondées sur le recensement de population de 1995.

[42] Excluding 2739 Filipinos in Philippine Embassies, Consulates and Missions Abroad. - Excepté 2739 Philippins travaillant dans les ambassades, les consulats et les missions des Philippines à l'étranger.

[43] Excluding foreigners. - Non compris étrangers.

[44] Data are based on the latest register-based population estimates for 2010. Data refer to resident population which comprises Singapore citizens and permanent residents. - Données basées sur les estimations démographiques les plus récentes fondées sur les registres de 2010. Les données se rapportent à la population résidente composé des citoyens de Singapour et des résidents permanents.

[45] The Population and Housing Census 2001 did not cover the whole area of the country due to the security problems; data refer to the 18 districts for which the census was completed only (in three districts it was not possible to conduct the census at all and in four districts it was partially conducted). Unrevised data. - Le recensement de la population et du logement de 2001 n'a pas été réalisé sur la superficie totale du pays à cause de problèmes de sécurité; les données ne concernent que les 18 districts entièrement recensés (3 districts n'ont pas été recensés du tout, et 4 ont été recensés en partie). Les données n'ont pas été révisées.

[46] Data for rural areas include data of estate sectors consist of all plantations which are 20 acres or more in extent and with ten or more resident labourers. - Les données pour les zones rurales comprennent celles pour les domaines, dont l'ensemble des plantations de plus de 10 hectares comptant au moins 10 travailleurs résidents.

[47] Total population does not include Palestinian population living in those parts of Jerusalem governorate which were annexed by Israel in 1967, amounting to 210 209 persons. Likewise, the results does not include the estimates of not enumerated population based on the findings of the post enumeration study, i.e 83 805 persons. - Les données relatives à la population totale ne comprennent pas la population palestinienne -équivalent à 210 209 personnes - habitant dans les territoires du gouvernorat de Jérusalem qui ont été annexés par Israël en 1967. Egalement, les données ne tiennent pas compte des estimations de la population calculée sur la base des résultats de l'enquête postcensitaire, équivalent à 83 805 personnes.

[48] Data for urban include population in refugee camps. - Les données pour la population urbaine comprennent la population dans les camps réfugiés.

[49] Including Palestinian refugees. - Y compris les réfugiés de Palestine.

[50] All persons falling within the scope of the census were enumerated on a de jure basis, except students who were enumerated on a de facto basis. - Toutes les personnes englobées dans le recensement ont été dénombrées comme population de droit, à l'exception des étudiants qui ont été dénombrés comme population de fait.

[51] Statistics are compiled from registers. - Les statistiques sont compilées à partir des registres.

[52] Excluding Faeroe Islands and Greenland shown separately, if available. - Non compris les Iles Féroé et le Groenland, qui font l'objet de rubriques distinctes, si disponible.

[53] Data include Overseas Departments. - Y compris les données des départements d'outre-mer.

[54] Excluding families of military personnel, visitors and transients. - Non compris les familles des militaires, ni les visiteurs et transients.

[55] Excluding military personnel, visitors and transients. - Non compris les militaires, ni les visiteurs et transients.

[56] Including armed forces stationed outside the country and alien armed forces in the area. - Y compris les militaires nationaux hors du pays et les militaires étrangers en garnison sur le territoire.

[57] The figures refer to usual residents in private households and persons present in communal establishments during the 2011 census. - Données se rapportant aux résidents habituels membres de ménages privés et aux personnes recensées dans des établissements collectifs au recensement de 2011.

[58] Age classification based on year of birth rather than on completed years of age. - La classification par âge est fondée sur l'année de naissance et non sur l'âge en années révolues.

[59] Including residents temporarily outside the country. Population statistics are compiled from registers. - Y compris les résidents se trouvant temporairement hors du pays. Les statistiques de la population sont compilées à partir des registres.

[60] The total number may include 'Unknown residence', but the categories urban and rural do not. - Le nombre total peut inclure les personnes dont la résidence n'est pas connue, à l'inverse des catégories de population urbaine et rurale.

[61] Excluding civilian aliens within the country, but including civilian nationals temporarily outside the country. - Non compris les civils étrangers dans le pays, mais y compris les civils nationaux temporairement hors du pays.

[62] Excluding Transnistria and the municipality of Bender. Excluding non-residents present in country at time of census. - Les données ne tiennent pas compte de l'information sur la Transnistria et la municipalité de Bender. Non compris les non-résidents présents dans le pays au moment du recensement.

[63] Excludes data for Kosovo and Metohia. - Sans les données pour le Kosovo et Metohie.

[64] Excluding transients visitors. - Non compris les visiteurs en transit.

[65] Excluding Channel Islands (Guernsey and Jersey) and Isle of Man, shown separately, if available. - Non compris les îles Anglo-Normandes (Guernesey et Jersey) et l'île de Man, qui font l'objet de rubriques distinctes, si disponible.

[66] Counts for the 1991 Census are taken from 'Key Statistics for Urban and Rural Areas: Great Britain 1991' published volume basen on the usually resident population. - Les chiffres du recensement de 1991 sont extraits de l'ouvrage « Key Statistics for Urban Areas: Great Britain 1991 » et sont fondés sur la notion de résidence habituelle

[67] Counts for the 2001 Census are taken from 'Key Statistics table 1 for the Urban/Rural classification: England and Wales' available on CD based on the usually resident population. - Les chiffres du recensement de 2001 proviennent du tableau intitulé « Key Statistics table 1 for the Urban/Rural classification: England and Wales » disponible sur CD-ROM et sont fondés sur la notion de résidence habituelle.

[68] This data has been randomly rounded to protect confidentiality. Individual figures may not add up to totals, and values for the same data may vary in different tables. - Ces données ont été arrondies de façon aléatoire afin d'en préserver la confidentialité. La somme de certains chiffres peut ne pas correspondre aux totaux indiqués et les valeurs des mêmes données peuvent varier d'un tableau à un autre.

[69] Including population in off-shore, migratory and shipping. - Y compris les populations extraterritoriales, les populations nomades et les populations maritimes.

[70] Excluding Niue, shown separately, which is part of Cook Islands, but because of remoteness is administered separately. - Non compris Nioué, qui fait l'objet d'une rubrique distincte et qui fait partie des îles Cook, mais qui, en raison de son éloignement, est administrée séparément.

[71] Excluding diplomatic personnel and armed forces stationed outside country; also excluding alien armed forces within the country. Data refer to usual residents in country at time of census. - Non compris le personnel diplomatique et les militaires hors du pays; non compris également les militaires étrangers en garnison dans le pays. Pour les personnes qui résident habituellement dans le pays au moment du recensement.

[72] Summation of frequencies for age groups gives a different total; reason for discrepancy not ascertained. - La somme des fréquences par groupes d'âges donne un total différent; on ne sait pas comment s'explique la divergence.

[73] Data includes Tokelaun Public Service employees and their immediate families based in Apia but excludes non-residents present at the time of the census. - Les données comprennent les agents de la fonction publique des Tokélaou et leur famille directe basés à Apia mais excluent les non-résidents présents au moment du recensement.

[74] Data refer to Tongans and part-Tongans only. - Les données ne concernent que la population tongane et partie-Tongans seulement.

Table 4 - *Demographic Yearbook 2014*

Table 4 presents, for each country or area of the world, basic vital statistics for the period 2010 - 2014: live births, crude birth rate, deaths, crude death rate, rate of natural increase, infant deaths, infant death rate, life expectancy at birth by sex and total fertility rate.

Description of variables: The vital events and rates shown in this table are defined as follows[1]:

Live birth is the complete expulsion or extraction from its mother of a product of conception, irrespective of the duration of pregnancy, which after such separation breathes or shows any other evidence of life such as beating of the heart, pulsation of the umbilical cord, definite movement of voluntary muscles, whether or not the umbilical cord has been cut or the placenta is attached; each product of such a birth is considered live born.

Death is the permanent disappearance of all evidence of life at any time after live birth has taken place (post-natal cessation of vital functions without capability of resuscitation).

Infant deaths are deaths of live born infants under one year of age.

Life expectancy at birth is defined as the average number of years of life for males and females if they continued to be subject to the same mortality experienced in the year(s) to which these life expectancies refer.

The total fertility rate is the average number of children that would be born alive to a hypothetical cohort of women if, throughout their reproductive years, the age-specific fertility rates remained unchanged. The standard method of calculating the total fertility rate is the sum of the age-specific fertility rates.

Crude birth rates and crude death rates presented in this table are calculated using the number of live births and the number of deaths obtained from civil registers. These civil registration data are used only if they are considered reliable (estimated completeness of 90 per cent or more).

Similarly, infant mortality rates presented in this table are calculated using the number of live births and the number of infant deaths obtained from civil registers. If, however, the registration of births or infant deaths for any given country or area is estimated to be less than 90 per cent complete, the rates are not calculated.

For some countries, the data and rates presented in this table are based on vital statistics data sourced from censuses or demographic surveys.

Rate computation: The crude birth and death rates are the annual number of each of these vital events per 1 000 mid-year population. Infant mortality rate is the annual number of deaths of infants under one year of age per 1 000 live births in the same year.

Rates of natural increase are the difference between the crude birth rate and the crude death rate. It should be noted that the rates of natural increase presented here may differ from the population growth rates presented in table 3 as rates of natural increase do not take net international migration into account while the population growth rates do.

Crude birth rates, crude death rates and infant mortality rates that appear in this table have been calculated by the United Nations Statistics Division, unless otherwise noted. Exceptions include official estimated rates for India, which were based on the sample registration system. Rates calculated by the United Nations Statistics Division presented in this table have been limited to those countries or areas having a minimum number of 30 events (for live births, deaths or infant deaths) in a given year.

Reliability of data: Rates calculated on the basis of registered vital statistics which are considered unreliable (estimated to be less than 90 per cent complete) are not calculated. Estimated rates, prepared by individual countries or areas, are presented whenever applicable.

The designation of vital statistics as being either reliable or unreliable is discussed in general in section 4.2 of the Technical Notes. The technical notes for tables 9, 15 and 18 provide specific information on reliability of statistics on live births, infant deaths and deaths, respectively.

The values shown for life expectancy in this table come from official life tables. It is assumed that, if necessary, the basic data (population and deaths classified by age and sex) have been adjusted for deficiencies before their use in constructing the life tables.

Limitations: Statistics on births, deaths and infant deaths are subject to the same qualifications as have been set forth for vital statistics, in general, in section 4 of the Technical Notes and in the technical notes for individual tables presenting detailed data on these events (table 9, live births; table 15, infant deaths; table 18, deaths).

In assessing comparability it is important to take into account the reliability of the data used to calculate the rates, as discussed above.

The problem of obtaining precise correspondence between numerator (births and deaths) and denominator (population for crude birth and death rates) as regards the inclusion or exclusion of armed forces, refugees, displaced persons and other special groups is particularly difficult where vital rates are concerned.

It should also be noted that crude rates are particularly affected by the age-sex structure of the population. Infant mortality rates, and to a much lesser extent crude birth rates and crude death rates, are affected by the variation in the definition of a live birth and tabulation procedures.

NOTES

[1] *Principles and Recommendations for a Vital Statistics System Revision 3,* Sales No. E.13.XVII.10, United Nations, New York, 2014.

Tableau 4 – *Annuaire démographique 2014*

Le tableau 4 présente, pour chaque pays ou zone du monde, des statistiques de base de l'état civil pour les années 2010 – 2014 : les naissances vivantes, le taux brut de natalité, les décès, le taux brut de mortalité et le taux d'accroissement naturel de la population, les décès d'enfants de moins d'un an et le taux de mortalité infantile, l'espérance de vie à la naissance par sexe et l'indice synthétique de fécondité.

Description des variables : les faits d'état civil utilisés aux fins du calcul des taux présentés dans le tableau 4 sont définis comme suit[1] :

La naissance vivante est l'expulsion ou l'extraction complète du corps de la mère, indépendamment de la duré de la gestation, d'un produit de la conception qui après cette séparation, respire ou manifeste tout autre signe de vie, tel que battement de cœur, pulsation du cordon ombilical ou contraction effective d'un muscle soumis à l'action de la volonté, que le cordon ombilical ait été coupé ou non et que le placenta soit ou non demeuré attaché ; tout produit d'une telle naissance est considéré comme « enfant né vivant ».

Le décès est la disparition permanente de tout signe de vie à un moment quelconque postérieur à la naissance vivante (cessation des fonctions vitales après la naissance sans possibilité de réanimation).

Il convient de préciser que les chiffres relatifs aux décès d'enfants de moins d'un an se rapportent aux naissances vivantes.

L'espérance de vie à la naissance est le nombre moyen d'années que vivraient les individus de sexe masculin et de sexe féminin s'ils continuaient d'être soumis aux mêmes conditions de mortalité que celles qui existaient pendant les années auxquelles se rapportent les valeurs indiquées.

L'indice synthétique de fécondité représente le nombre moyen d'enfants que mettrait au monde une cohorte hypothétique de femmes qui seraient soumises, tout au long de leur vie, aux mêmes conditions de fécondité par âge que celles auxquelles sont soumises les femmes, dans chaque groupe d'âge, au cours d'une année ou d'une période donnée. La méthode standard pour calculer l'indice synthétique de fécondité consiste à additionner les taux de fécondité par âge simple.

Les taux bruts de natalité et de mortalité ont été établis sur la base du nombre de naissances vivantes et du nombre de décès inscrits sur les registres de l'état civil. Ces données n'ont été utilisées que lorsqu'elles étaient considérées comme sûres (degré estimatif de complétude égal ou supérieur à 90 p. 100).

De même, les taux de mortalité infantile présentés dans le tableau 4 ont été établis à partir du nombre de naissances vivantes et du nombre de décès d'enfants de moins d'un an inscrits sur les registres de l'état civil. Toutefois, lorsque les données relatives aux naissances ou aux décès d'enfants de moins d'un an pour un pays ou zone quelconque n'étaient pas considérées complètes à 90 p. 100 au moins, les indices n'ont pas été calculés.

Pour quelques pays, les données et les taux présentés dans ce tableau ont été extraites des recensements de la population ou des enquêtes démographiques.

Calcul des taux : les taux bruts de natalité et de mortalité, représentent le nombre annuel de chacun de ces faits d'état civil pour 1 000 habitants au milieu de l'année considérée. Les taux de mortalité infantile correspondent au nombre annuel de décès d'enfants de moins d'un an pour 1 000 naissances vivantes survenues pendant la même année.

Le taux d'accroissement naturel est égal à la différence entre le taux brut de natalité et le taux brut de mortalité. Il y a lieu de noter que les taux d'accroissement naturel indiqués dans le tableau 4 peuvent différer des taux d'accroissement de la population figurant dans le tableau 3, les taux d'accroissement naturel ne tenant pas compte des taux nets de migration internationale, alors que ceux-ci sont inclus dans les taux d'accroissement de la population.

Sauf indication contraire, les taux bruts de natalité et de mortalité, et les taux de mortalité infantile figurant dans le tableau 4, ont été calculés par la Division des statistiques de l'Organisation des Nations Unies. Les exceptions comprennent l'Inde, pour laquelle les taux estimatifs officiels ont été fournis sur la base d'un système d'enregistrement par échantillonnage. Les taux calculés par la Division des statistiques de l'Organisation des Nations Unies qui sont présentés dans le tableau 4 se rapportent aux pays ou zones où l'on a enregistré au moins 30 événements (pour les naissances vivantes, les décès ou pour les décès d'enfants de moins d'un an) au cours d'une année donnée.

Fiabilité des données : les taux n'ont pas été calculés lorsque les statistiques de l'état civil issues de systèmes d'enregistrement d'état civil étaient jugées douteuses (degré estimatif de complétude inférieur à 90 p.100) et des taux estimatifs, calculés par les pays ou zones, ont été présentés lorsqu'ils étaient disponibles.

On trouve à la section 4.2 des Notes techniques des explications générales concernant la façon dont les statistiques de l'état civil ont été classées selon leur degré de fiabilité. Les notes techniques relatives aux tableaux 9, 15 et 18 ont trait respectivement à la fiabilité des statistiques des naissances vivantes, des décès d'enfants de moins d'un an et des décès.

Les valeurs relatives à l'espérance de vie figurant dans le tableau 4 proviennent de tables officielles de mortalité. On présume que les données de base (la population et les décès par sexe et âge) ont été rectifiées d'éventuelles insuffisances avant d'être utilisées pour construire les tables de mortalité.

Insuffisance des données : les statistiques des naissances, décès et décès d'enfants de moins d'un an appellent toutes les réserves qui ont été formulées à propos des statistiques de l'état civil en général à la section 4 des Notes techniques et dans les notes techniques relatives aux différents tableaux présentant des données détaillées sur ces événements [tableau 9 (naissances vivantes), tableau 15 (décès d'enfants de moins d'un an) et tableau 18 (décès)].

Pour évaluer la comparabilité des divers taux, il importe de tenir compte de la fiabilité des données utilisées pour calculer ces taux, comme il a été indiqué précédemment.

Le calcul des taux est particulièrement affecté par la difficulté à obtenir une correspondance parfaite entre le numérateur (naissances et décès) et le dénominateur (population, pour les taux bruts de natalité et de mortalité) en raison de l'inclusion ou non dans la population des forces armées, des réfugiés, des personnes déplacées ou d'autres groupes sociaux.

Il y a lieu de noter que la structure par âge et par sexe de la population influe de façon particulière sur les taux bruts. Le manque d'uniformité dans la définition des naissances vivantes et dans les procédures de mise en tableaux a une incidence sur les taux de mortalité infantile et, à un moindre degré, sur les taux bruts de natalité et les taux bruts de mortalité.

NOTE

[1] *Principles and Recommendations for a Vital Statistics System Revision 3,* Sales No. E.13.XVII.10, United Nations, New York, 2014

Continent, country or area and year / Continent, pays ou zone et année	Live births / Naissances vivantes			Deaths / Décès			Rate of natural increase / Taux d'accroissement naturel	Infant deaths / Décès d'enfants de moins d'un an			Life expectancy at birth / Espérance de vie à la naissance		Total fertility rate / L'indice synthétique de fécondité
	Code[a]	Number / Nombre	Crude birth rate / Taux brut de natalité	Code[a]	Number / Nombre	Crude death rate / Taux brut de mortalité		Code[a]	Number / Nombre	Rate (per 1000 births) / Taux (par 1000 naissances)	Male[b] / Masculin[b]	Female[b] / Féminin[b]	
AFRICA - AFRIQUE													
Algeria - Algérie													
2010	C	888 029[1]	24.7	U	157 193[1]	...	...	U	21 046[1]	...	75.6[2]	77.0[2]	2.870
2011	C	909 787[1]	24.8	U	161 862[1]	...	...	U	21 055[1]	...	75.6[2]	77.4[2]	2.870
2012	C	978 233[1]	26.1	U	169 815[1]	...	...	U	22 088[1]	...	75.8[2]	77.1[2]	3.020
2013	C	962 722[1]	25.1	U	168 136[1]	...	...	U	21 586[1]	...	76.5[2]	77.6[2]	2.930
2014	C	1 014 248[1]	25.9	U	173 781[1]	...	...	U	22 282[1]	...	76.6[2]	77.8[2]	3.030
Benin - Bénin[3]													
2010	I	358 830	40.9	I	78 248	8.9	32.0		...	...	...	...	...
2011	I	366 889	40.5	I	78 670	8.7	31.8		...	...	...	...	...
2012	I	376 439	40.2	I	79 116	8.4	31.7		...	...	...	...	...
Botswana													
2010		...	...		...	...	...		...	...	...	...	2.791[4]
2011	U	39 368[5]	...		...	...	...		...	...	...	...	2.689[4]
2012	U	40 856[5]	...	U	12 270[5]	...	...		...	...	...	...	...
Burundi													
2010	+U	240 684[6]	...		...	...	...		...	...	...	...	6.060
2011	+U	216 398[6]	...		...	...	...		...	...	...	...	5.990
2012	+U	221 289[6]	...		...	...	...		...	...	...	...	5.910
2013	+U	248 395[6]	...		...	...	...		...	...	...	...	5.840
2014		...	...		...	...	...		...	...	...	...	5.770
Cabo Verde													
2010	C	13 415	25.9	C	2 917	5.6	20.3		...	...	...	...	...
Djibouti													
2010	U	10 538	...	U	1 051	...	...		...	...	...	...	...
2011	U	10 871	...	U	1 011	...	...		...	...	...	...	...
Egypt - Égypte													
2010	+C	2 261 409	28.7	C	483 385	6.1	22.6	C	31 698	14.0	68.2	70.9	3.000
2011	+C	2 442 094	30.3	C	493 086	6.1	24.2	C	35 997	14.7	68.6	71.4	3.000
2012	+C	2 629 769	31.9	C	529 512	6.4	25.4	C	39 942	15.2	...	...	3.000
2013	+C	2 621 902	31.0	C	511 183	6.0	24.9	C	38 753	14.8	...	...	3.000
2014		...	...		...	...	...		...	...	...	...	3.500
Ghana[7]													
2010	I	623 700	25.3	I	163 534	6.6	18.7		...	...	...	...	...
Guinea - Guinée													
2013	+U	205 658	...		...	...	...		...	...	...	...	...
Kenya													
2010	U	798 016	...	U	185 100	...	...		...	...	...	...	...
2011	U	771 150	...	U	182 652	...	...	U	23 167	...	...	...	...
2012	U	801 815	...	U	187 811	...	...	U	21 209	...	...	...	...
2013	U	870 599	...	U	194 332	...	...	U	20 888	...	...	...	...
2014	U	954 254	...	U	198 611	...	...	U	18 672	...	...	...	...
Lesotho													
2010	+U	6 369	...	+U	7 864	...	...		...	...	...	...	...
2011	+U	3 931	...	+U	5 314	...	...		...	...	39.4	45.3	3.350
2012	+U	1 718	...	+U	7 751	...	...		...	...	...	...	...
Liberia - Libéria													
2010		...	...		...	...	...		...	...	...	...	4.900
2011		...	...		...	...	...		...	...	...	...	4.900
2012		...	...		...	...	...		...	...	...	...	4.800
2013		...	...		...	...	...		...	...	...	...	4.700
2014		...	...		...	...	...		...	...	...	...	4.600
Mauritius - Maurice[8]													
2010	+C	15 005	11.7	+C	9 131	7.1	4.6	+C	187	12.5	III69.5	76.7	1.466
2011	+C	14 701	11.7	+C	9 170	7.3	4.4	+C	189	12.9	III69.7	77.0	1.446
2012	+C	14 494	11.5	+C	9 343	7.4	4.1	+C	199	13.7	III70.2	77.1	1.544
2013	+C	13 488	10.7	+C	9 440	7.5	3.2	+C	165	12.2	...	...	1.438
2014	+C	13 283	10.5	+C	9 682	7.7	2.9	+C	194	14.6	III71.0	77.6	1.424

4. Vital statistics summary and life expectancy at birth: 2010 - 2014
Aperçu des statistiques de l'état civil et de l'espérance de vie à la naissance : 2010 - 2014 (continued - suite)

Continent, country or area and year / Continent, pays ou zone et année	Live births Naissances vivantes			Deaths Décès			Rate of natural increase Taux d'accrois-sement naturel	Infant deaths Décès d'enfants de moins d'un an			Life expectancy at birth Espérance de vie à la naissance		Total fertility rate L'indice synthétique de fécondité
	Code[a]	Number Nombre	Crude birth rate Taux brut de natalité	Code[a]	Number Nombre	Crude death rate Taux brut de mortalité		Code[a]	Number Nombre	Rate (per 1000 births) Taux (par 1000 naiss-ances)	Male[b] Masculin[b]	Female[b] Féminin[b]	
AFRICA - AFRIQUE													
Morocco - Maroc													
2013		...	...		...	...	...		...	...	72.4	75.1	...
Mozambique													
2010		...	...		...	...	...		...	...	...	...	5.600
2011		...	...		...	...	...		...	...	...	...	5.600
2012		...	...		...	...	...		...	...	...	...	5.500
2013		...	...		...	...	...		...	...	...	...	5.400
2014		...	...		...	...	...		...	...	50.2	55.4	...
Namibia - Namibie													
2011	I	61 523[9]	29.1	I	22 668[9]	10.7	18.4		...	...	53.3	60.5	...
Niger													
2010	+U	181 195	...	+U	1 023	...	...		...	...	...	...	...
2011	+U	198 499	...	+U	6 761	...	...		...	...	...	...	...
Republic of South Sudan - République de Soudan du Sud													
2010		...	...		...	...	...		...	...	54.4	54.5	7.500
Reunion - Réunion													
2010	C	14 146[10]	17.1	C	4 221	5.1	12.0		...	...	...	...	...
Rwanda													
2010	U	408 267	...	U	141 256	...	...	U	27	...	...	...	5.380
2011	U	406 838	...	U	140 519	...	...		...	...	...	...	5.340
2012	U	404 067	...	U	139 499	...	...		...	...	...	...	5.300
Saint Helena ex. dep. - Sainte-Hélène sans dép.													
2010	C	34	8.0	C	53	12.5	-4.5	C	-	...	...	...	...
2011	C	34	8.0	C	49	11.5	-3.5	C	-	...	...	...	...
2012	C	32	7.8	C	62	15.0	-7.3	C	1	...	X72.0	79.7	...
2013	C	35	8.3	C	55	13.1	-4.7	C	-	...	...	...	...
2014	C	48	10.9	C	61	13.8	-2.9	C	1	...	...	...	...
Sao Tome and Principe - Sao Tomé-et-Principe													
2010	C	4 890	29.9		...	...	...		...	...	...	...	...
2011	C	5 232	31.4		...	...	...		...	...	...	...	...
2012	C	5 173	27.6	I	1 287[11]	6.9	20.7		...	...	II62.1	68.7	...
Senegal - Sénégal													
2010	I	456 212[12]	36.5	I	132 218[12]	10.6	25.9	I	32 314[12]	70.8	...	...	4.860[4]
2011	I	464 464[12]	36.2	I	134 450[12]	10.5	25.7		...	...	56.9[4]	59.8[4]	...
2012	I	471 629[12]	35.7	I	135 468[12]	10.3	25.5		...	...	...	...	...
2013	I	478 898[12]	35.3	I	136 460[12]	10.1	25.2		...	...	...	...	...
Seychelles													
2010	+C	1 504	16.8	+C	664	7.4	9.4	+C	21	...	...	...	2.170
2011	+C	1 625	18.6	+C	691	7.9	10.7	+C	16	...	67.7	78.1	2.380
2012	+C	1 645	18.6	+C	651	7.4	11.3		...	...	...	...	2.420
2013	+C	1 566	17.4	+C	717	8.0	9.4	+C	29	...	69.9	76.5	2.370
2014	+C	1 557	17.0	+C	725	7.9	9.1	+C	17	...	68.4	78.3	2.340
Sierra Leone													
2010	...	101 185	...	...	10 847	...	...	...	1 935	...	...	...	5.820
2011	...	117 207	...	...	13 674	...	...	...	1 289	...	...	...	5.820
2012	...	147 958	...	...	12 767	...	...	...	2 135	...	...	...	5.820
South Africa - Afrique du Sud													
2010	U	1 163 629	...	U	578 953	...	...		34 656	...	...	...	...
2011	U	1 173 164	...	U	580 460	...	...		27 981	...	...	...	...
2012	U	1 184 867	...	U	575 546	...	...		...	...	...	...	...
2013	U	1 196 395	...	U	565 310	...	...		...	...	...	...	...
2014	U	1 207 711	...	U	551 389	...	...		...	...	...	...	...
Swaziland													
2010		...	...		...	...	...		...	...	...	...	3.800
2011		...	...		...	...	...		...	...	...	...	3.700

Continent, country or area and year / Continent, pays ou zone et année	Live births / Naissances vivantes			Deaths / Décès			Rate of natural increase / Taux d'accrois-sement naturel	Infant deaths / Décès d'enfants de moins d'un an			Life expectancy at birth / Espérance de vie à la naissance		Total fertility rate / L'indice synthétique de fécondité
	Code[a]	Number Nombre	Crude birth rate Taux brut de natalité	Code[a]	Number Nombre	Crude death rate Taux brut de mortalité		Code[a]	Number Nombre	Rate (per 1000 births) Taux (par 1000 naiss-ances)	Male[b] Masculin[b]	Female[b] Féminin[b]	
AFRICA - AFRIQUE													
Swaziland													
2012		...	...		...	...	...		...	...	...	...	3.600
2013		...	...		...	...	...		...	...	...	...	3.600
Tunisia - Tunisie													
2010	C	196 039	18.6	U	60 438	...	...		...	...	72.7	76.6	2.130
2011	C	201 120	18.8	U	63 258	...	...		...	...	72.9	76.9	2.150
2012	C	214 909	19.9	U	62 224	...	...		...	...	...	...	...
2013	C*	221 147	20.3	U	60 386	...	...		...	...	...	...	...
Uganda - Ouganda[13]													
2011		...			...	...	...		...	...	...	...	6.200
United Republic of Tanzania - République Unie de Tanzanie													
2010	...	1 678 325	...	...	573 213	...	...		...	...	...	...	5.100
2011	...	1 687 203	...	...	565 099	...	...		...	...	...	...	5.000
2012	...	1 694 943	...	...	555 975	...	...		...	...	...	...	3.685[14]
Zambia - Zambie[15]													
2010	I	442 998	35.4	I	164 385	13.1	22.2		...	...	...	...	...
AMERICA, NORTH - AMÉRIQUE DU NORD													
Anguilla													
2010	+C	182	11.1	+C	66[16]	4.0	7.1	+C	2	...	...	...	...
2011	+C	185	13.7	+C	55[16]	4.1	9.6	+C	1	...	...	...	...
2012	+C	192	14.3	+C	38[16]	2.8	11.5	+C	-	...	...	...	...
2013	+C	165	12.2	+C	72[16]	5.3	6.9	+C	3	...	...	...	...
2014	+C	149	...		...	...	...		...	...	...	...	...
Antigua and Barbuda - Antigua-et-Barbuda													
2010	+C	1 255	13.8	+C	491	5.4	8.4	+C	11	...	74.0	79.7	...
Aruba													
2010	C	1 223	12.0	C	619	6.1	5.9	+U	4	...	...	...	1.920
2011	C	1 236	12.0	C	633	6.2	5.9	+U	7	...	II73.9	79.8	1.918
2012	C	1 288	12.3	C	595	5.7	6.6	+U	3	...	...	...	1.973
2013	C	1 346	12.7	C	560	5.3	7.4	+U	5	...	...	...	2.032
2014	C	1 376	12.8	C	643	6.0	6.8	+U	5	...	...	...	2.041
Bahamas													
2010	+U	4 915	...	+C	2 023	6.0	...	+C	67	...	...	...	1.825
2011	+U	4 747	...	+C	2 117	5.9	...	+C	48	...	...	...	1.798
2012	+U	4 469	...	+C	1 995	5.5	...	+C	57	...	...	...	1.740
2013	+U*	4 322	...	+C*	2 062	5.6	...	+U*	48	...	...	...	1.725
2014	+U*	4 196	...		...	...	...		...	...	...	...	1.475*
Bermuda - Bermudes													
2010	C	769[17]	12.0	C	475[17]	7.4	4.6	C	1	...	76.9	82.3	1.751
2011	C	670[17]	10.6	C	429[17]	6.8	3.8	C	-	...	76.6	82.1	1.587
2012	C	648[17]	10.4	C	422[17]	6.8	3.6	C	1	...	77.2	82.4	1.590
2013	C	648[17]	10.5	C	471[17]	7.6	2.9	C	1	...	76.9	84.5	1.633
2014		...			...	...	...		...	...	77.1	84.7	1.625
British Virgin Islands - Îles Vierges britanniques													
2012	C*	288	10.2		...	...	...		...	...	...	...	...
Canada[18]													
2010	C	376 951	11.1	C	244 968	7.2	3.9		...	...	...	...	...
2011	C	377 897	11.0	C	243 651	7.1	3.9		...	...	...	...	...
2012	C	382 980	11.0	C	252 309	7.3	3.8		...	...	...	...	...
2013	C	386 044	11.0	C	256 982	7.3	3.7		...	...	...	...	...
2014	C*	388 729	10.9	C*	268 056	7.5	3.4		...	...	...	...	...

Continent, country or area and year / Continent, pays ou zone et année	Code[a]	Live births — Naissances vivantes — Number Nombre	Crude birth rate Taux brut de natalité	Code[a]	Deaths — Décès — Number Nombre	Crude death rate Taux brut de mortalité	Rate of natural increase Taux d'accroissement naturel	Code[a]	Infant deaths — Décès d'enfants de moins d'un an — Number Nombre	Rate (per 1000 births) Taux (par 1000 naissances)	Life expectancy at birth — Espérance de vie à la naissance — Male[b] Masculin[b]	Female[b] Féminin[b]	Total fertility rate L'indice synthétique de fécondité
AMERICA, NORTH - AMÉRIQUE DU NORD													
Cayman Islands - Îles Caïmanes													
2010	C	821	15.0	C	152	2.8	12.2	C	2	...	...	...	...
2011	C	800	14.5	C	176	3.2	11.3		...	...	...	...	...
2012	C*	759	13.4	C*	172	3.0	10.3		...	...	...	...	...
2013	C*	697	12.4	C*	170	3.0	9.4		...	...	...	...	...
2014	C	710[19]	12.2	C	153	2.6	9.6		...	...	...	...	...
Costa Rica													
2010	C	70 922	15.6	C	19 077	4.2	11.4	C	671	9.5	76.8	81.8	1.810
2011	C	73 459	16.0	C	18 801	4.1	11.9	C	666	9.1	...	...	1.870
2012	C	73 326	15.8	C	19 200	4.1	11.6	C	624	8.5	...	...	1.880
2013	C	70 550	15.0	C	19 647	4.2	10.8	C	612	8.7	...	...	1.760
2014	C*	71 793	15.0	C*	20 553	4.3	10.7	C*	575	8.0	77.2	82.3	1.860
Cuba													
2010	C	127 746	11.4	C	91 065	8.2	3.3	C	581	4.5	...	...	1.687
2011	C	133 067	11.9	C	87 044	7.8	4.1	C	653	4.9	...	...	1.771
2012	C	125 674	11.2	C	89 372	8.0	3.2	C	581	4.6	...	...	1.690
2013	C	125 880	11.2	C	92 273	8.2	3.0	C	525	4.2	[III]76.5	80.4	1.714
2014	C	122 643	10.9	C	96 312	8.6	2.3	C	514	4.2	...	...	...
Curaçao													
2010	C	2 032	13.7	C	1 246	8.4	5.3	C	26	...	[III]72.0[20]	78.8[20]	2.199
2011	C	1 974	13.1	C	1 276	8.5	4.6	C	15	...	...	...	2.076
2012	C	2 039	13.4	C	1 246	8.2	5.2	C	23	...	[II]74.4	80.7	2.168
2013	C	1 962	12.8	C	1 250	8.1	4.6	C	15	...	...	...	2.052
2014	C	1 963	12.6	C	1 370	8.8	3.8	C	24	...	[IV]74.8	81.0	2.009
Dominica - Dominique													
2010	+C	933	...	+C	588	...	...		...	...	...	...	...
Dominican Republic - République dominicaine													
2010	U	150 473	...	U	35 735	...	...	U	492	...	[VI]69.2	75.5	2.463
2011	U	153 035	...	U	35 301	...	...	U	679	...	...	...	2.440
2012	U	144 100	...	U	35 392	...	...	U	468	...	...	...	2.418
2013	U	130 402	...	U	34 375	...	...	U	643	...	...	...	2.391
2014		...	...		...	...	...		...	...	...	...	2.364
El Salvador													
2010	C	104 939[21]	17.0	C	32 586	5.3	11.7	C	749[22]	7.1	...	...	...
2011	C	109 384[21]	17.6	C	33 211	5.3	12.3	C	826[22]	7.6	...	...	...
2012	C	110 843[21]	17.7	C	32 148	5.1	12.6	C	795[22]	7.2	...	...	2.300
2013		...	...		...	...	...		...	...	...	...	2.200
Greenland - Groenland													
2010	C	869	15.4	C	504	8.9	6.5	C	6	...	[V]67.8	72.8	2.259
2011	C	821	14.5	C	476	8.4	6.1	C	9	...	[V]68.2	72.9	2.104
2012	C	786	13.8	C	459	8.1	5.8	C	7	...	[V]68.7	73.5	1.987
2013	C	820	14.5	C	444	7.9	6.7	C	7	...	[V]68.5	73.7	2.051
2014	C	805	14.3	C	461	8.2	6.1	C	6	...	...	...	1.999
Grenada - Grenade													
2010		...	...	+C	828	7.9	...		...	...	...	...	...
2011		...	...	+C	803	7.5	...		...	...	...	...	...
2012		...	...	+C	856	8.0	...		...	...	...	...	...
Guadeloupe[10]													
2010	C	5 341	13.2	C	2 963	7.3	5.9		...	...	...	...	...
2011	C	5 384	13.3	C	2 835	7.0	6.3		...	...	...	...	...
2012	C	5 233	13.0	C	2 873	7.1	5.9		...	...	...	...	...
2013	C	5 069	12.6	C	2 951	7.3	5.2		...	...	...	...	...
Guatemala													
2010	C	361 906	25.2	C	72 748	5.1	20.1	C	7 562	20.9	...	...	...
2011	C	373 692	25.4	C	72 354	4.9	20.5	C	7 413	19.8	...	...	...
2012	C	388 440	25.8	C	71 980	4.8	21.0		...	...	...	...	...

Continent, country or area and year / Continent, pays ou zone et année	Live births / Naissances vivantes			Deaths / Décès			Rate of natural increase / Taux d'accrois-sement naturel	Infant deaths / Décès d'enfants de moins d'un an			Life expectancy at birth / Espérance de vie à la naissance		Total fertility rate / L'indice synthétique de fécondité
	Code[a]	Number Nombre	Crude birth rate Taux brut de natalité	Code[a]	Number Nombre	Crude death rate Taux brut de mortalité		Code[a]	Number Nombre	Rate (per 1000 births) Taux (par 1000 naiss-ances)	Male[b] Masculin[b]	Female[b] Féminin[b]	
AMERICA, NORTH - AMÉRIQUE DU NORD													
Honduras													
2010	+U	223 345	...	+U	36 812	...	...		...	...	...	...	...
2011	+U	224 409	...	+U	37 211	...	...		...	...	...	...	...
Jamaica - Jamaïque													
2010	C	40 508[23]	15.0	U	21 503[24]	...	...		...	...	...	...	...
2011	C	39 673[23]	14.7	U	16 926[24]	...	...		...	...	...	...	...
2012	C	39 348[23]	14.5	U	16 998[24]	...	...		...	...	...	...	...
2013	C*	36 745[23]	...	U	15 427[24]	...	...		...	...	...	...	...
Martinique[10]													
2010	C	4 889	12.3	C	2 844	7.2	5.2		...	...	...	...	...
Mexico - Mexique													
2010	+U	2 168 952[25]	...	+C	590 886[26]	5.2	...	+U	28 861[26]	...	...	...	...
2011	C	2 262 024[25]	19.6	+C	589 646[26]	5.1	14.5	+U	29 037[26]	...	...	...	...
2012	C	2 190 159[25]	18.7	+C	601 259[26]	5.1	13.6	+U	28 946[26]	...	73.4	78.1	...
2013	C	2 169 810[25]	18.3	+C	610 730[26]	5.2	13.2	+C	27 760[26]	12.8	71.7	77.4	...
2014		...	...		...	...	...		...	...	72.1	77.6	...
Montserrat													
2010	+C	62	12.4	+C	40	8.0	4.4	+C	1	...	...	...	...
2011	+C	46	9.3	+C	55	11.2	-1.8	+C	-	...	...	...	...
2012	+C	53	10.7	+C	44	8.9	1.8	+C	-	...	...	...	...
2013	+C	41	8.3	+C	45	9.1	-0.8	+C	-	...	...	...	...
2014	+C	50	10.0	+C	32	6.4	3.6	+C	-	...	...	...	...
Nicaragua													
2010	+U	132 165	...	+U	19 944	...	...		...	...	VI63.4	68.9	...
Panama													
2010	C	67 955	18.6	U	16 542	...	...	U	910	...	73.4[27]	78.7[27]	2.400
2011	C	73 292	19.7	U	16 367	...	...	U	971	...	...	...	2.500
2012	C	75 486	19.9	U	17 350	...	...	U	1 083	...	74.1[27]	80.4[27]	2.500
2013	C	73 804	19.2	U	17 767	...	...	U	1 106	...	74.4[27]	80.5[27]	2.400
2014	C*	72 490	18.5	U	16 913	...	...		...	...	...	...	...
Puerto Rico - Porto Rico													
2010	C	42 248	11.4	C	29 526	7.9	3.4	C	358	8.5	III74.9	82.6	1.622
2011	C	41 133	11.2	C	30 146	8.2	3.0	C	364	8.8	...	...	1.604
2012	C	38 975	10.7	C	30 053	8.2	2.4	C	374	9.6	...	...	1.543
2013	C	36 578	10.1	C	29 368	8.1	2.0	C	270	7.4	...	...	1.470
2014	C	34 485	9.7	C	30 224	8.5	1.2	C	242	7.0	...	...	...
Saint Vincent and the Grenadines - Saint-Vincent-et-les Grenadines													
2010	+C	1 784	16.2	+C	827	7.5	8.7		...	...	...	...	...
2011	+C	1 725	15.7	+C	882	8.0	7.7		...	...	...	...	...
2012	+C	1 840	16.7	+C	858	7.8	8.9		...	...	...	...	...
2013	+C	1 738	15.8		...	...	...		...	...	...	...	...
Sint Maarten (Dutch part) - Saint-Martin (partie néerlandaise)													
2010	+C	496[28]	14.0	+C	160[28]	4.5	9.5		...	...	...	...	...
2011	+C	432[28]	12.9	+C	173[28]	5.2	7.7		...	...	...	...	...
2012	+C	414[28]	11.9	+C	180[28]	5.2	6.7		...	...	II69.2	77.1	...
2013	+C	511[28]	14.0	+C	171[28]	4.7	9.3		...	...	...	...	...
United States of America - États-Unis d'Amérique													
2010	C	3 999 386	12.9	C	2 468 435	8.0	4.9	C	24 586	6.1	76.2	81.0	1.931
2011	C	3 953 590	12.7	C	2 515 458	8.1	4.6	C	23 985	6.1	76.3	81.1	1.895
2012	C	3 952 841	12.6	C	2 543 279	8.1	4.5	C	23 629	6.0	76.4	81.2	1.880
2013	C	3 932 181	12.4	C	2 596 993	8.2	4.2	C	23 440	6.0	76.4	81.2	1.857

Continent, country or area and year / Continent, pays ou zone et année	Live births / Naissances vivantes			Deaths / Décès			Rate of natural increase / Taux d'accrois-sement naturel	Infant deaths / Décès d'enfants de moins d'un an			Life expectancy at birth / Espérance de vie à la naissance		Total fertility rate / L'indice synthétique de fécondité
	Code[a]	Number Nombre	Crude birth rate Taux brut de natalité	Code[a]	Number Nombre	Crude death rate Taux brut de mortalité		Code[a]	Number Nombre	Rate (per 1000 births) Taux (par 1000 naiss-ances)	Male[b] Masculin[b]	Female[b] Féminin[b]	
AMERICA, NORTH - AMÉRIQUE DU NORD													
United States Virgin Islands - Îles Vierges américaines													
2010	C	1 600	14.5		...	...	...		...	...	...	...	...
AMERICA, SOUTH - AMÉRIQUE DU SUD													
Argentina - Argentine													
2010	C	756 176	18.5	C	318 602	7.8	10.7	C	8 961	11.9	VI71.6[4]	79.1[4]	2.392
2011	C	758 042	18.4	C	319 059	7.7	10.6	C	8 878	11.7	...	...	2.379
2012	C	738 318	17.7	C	319 539	7.7	10.0	C	8 227	11.1	...	...	...
2013	C	754 603	17.9	C	326 197	7.7	10.2	C	8 174	10.8	...	...	...
Bolivia (Plurinational State of) - Bolivie (État plurinational de)													
2010	+U	159 098	...		...	...	...		...	...	...	...	3.287
2011	+U	160 499	...		...	...	...		...	...	64.6	68.9	3.207
2012	+U	128 738	...	I	127 050[29]	12.3			...	...	...	...	...
Brazil - Brésil													
2010	U	2 760 961[30]	...	U	1 117 675[31]	...	...	U	31 733[32]	...	...	...	1.869[33]
2011	U	2 824 776[30]	...	U	1 148 165[31]	...	...	U	32 184[32]	...	...	...	1.833[33]
2012	U	2 830 458[30]	...	U	1 157 214[31]	...	...	U	31 596[32]	...	70.9[27]	78.2[27]	1.801[33]
2013	U	2 832 590[30]	...	U	1 180 796[31]	...	...	U	31 944[32]	...	71.3[27]	78.5[27]	1.770[33]
Chile - Chili													
2010	C	250 643	14.7	C	97 930	5.7	8.9	C	1 862	7.4	VI75.5	81.5	1.910
2011	C	247 358	14.3	C	94 985	5.5	8.8	C	1 908	7.7	75.7	81.0	1.890
2012	C	243 635	14.0	C	98 711	5.7	8.3	C	1 812	7.4	76.1	81.3	1.840
2013	C*	242 862	13.8	C*	99 770	5.7	8.2						
Colombia - Colombie													
2010	U	654 627	...	U	200 524	...	...	U	8 355	...	VI70.7[34]	77.5[34]	...
2011	U	665 499	...	U	195 823	...	...	U	8 152	...	...	...	...
2012	U	676 835	...	U	199 756	...	...	U	8 220	...	...	...	2.350[35]
Ecuador - Équateur													
2010	+U	219 162	...	U	61 681[36]	...	...	U	3 204[36]	...	VI72.1[37]	78.0[37]	2.794
2011	+U	229 780	...	U	62 304[36]	...	...	U	3 046[36]	...	...	...	2.737
2012	+U	235 237	...	U	63 511[36]	...	...	U	3 002[36]	...	...	...	2.684
2013	+U	220 896	...	U	63 104[36]	...	...	U	2 928[36]	...	...	...	2.634
2014		...			...	...	...		...	...	73.2[37]	78.6[37]	2.587
French Guiana - Guyane française[10]													
2010	C	6 083	26.4	C	773	3.4	23.0		...	...	...	...	...
Guyana													
2010		...	...	+C	4 651	6.2	...		...	...	...	...	...
2011		...	...	+C	4 527	6.0	...		...	...	...	...	...
Paraguay													
2010		...	...		...	...	...			...	VI69.7	73.9	...
2012	+U	118 549	...	+U	22 807	...	...	+U	465	...	...	...	...
Peru - Pérou													
2010	+U	402 493[38]	...	+U	99 334[38]	...	...	+U	5 287[38]	...	...	...	2.489
2011	+U	396 839[38]	...	+U	96 852[38]	...	...	+U	4 569[38]	...	...	...	2.445
2012	+U	414 081[38]	...	+U	97 989[38]	...	...	+U	4 523[38]	...	...	...	2.403
2013	+U	475 349[38]	...	+U	94 394[38]	...	...	+U	4 390[38]	...	...	...	2.364
2014	+U*	581 450			...	...	...		...	...	...	...	...
Suriname													
2010	C	9 712	18.3	C	3 484	6.6	11.7	C	178	18.3	...	...	2.300
2011	C	9 703	18.0	C	3 441	6.4	11.6	C	153	15.8	...	...	2.268

Continent, country or area and year / Continent, pays ou zone et année	Live births / Naissances vivantes Code[a]	Number Nombre	Crude birth rate Taux brut de natalité	Deaths / Décès Code[a]	Number Nombre	Crude death rate Taux brut de mortalité	Rate of natural increase Taux d'accroissement naturel	Infant deaths / Décès d'enfants de moins d'un an Code[a]	Number Nombre	Rate (per 1000 births) Taux (par 1000 naissances)	Life expectancy at birth / Espérance de vie à la naissance Male[b] Masculin[b]	Female[b] Féminin[b]	Total fertility rate L'indice synthétique de fécondité
AMERICA, SOUTH - AMÉRIQUE DU SUD													
Suriname													
2012	C	10 217	18.9	C	3 687	6.8	12.1	C	162	15.9	...	...	2.406
2013	C	10 012	18.2	C	3 557	6.5	11.7	C	168	16.8	[III]69.3	75.1	2.323
Uruguay													
2010	C	47 420	14.0	C	33 157	9.8	4.2	C	366	7.7	72.8	80.0	1.918
2011	C	46 712	13.7	C	32 807	9.6	4.1	C	417	8.9	...	...	1.896
2012	C	48 059	14.0	C	33 354	9.7	4.3	C	448	9.3	...	...	1.943
2013	C	48 681	14.2	C	32 795	9.5	4.6		...	...	...	...	1.957
2014		...	...		...	...	...		...	...	...	...	1.936
Venezuela (Bolivarian Republic of) - Venezuela (République bolivarienne du)													
2010	C	591 303	20.7	C	130 597	4.6	16.2	C	7 025	11.9	...	...	...
2011	C	615 132	21.3	C	136 803	4.7	16.5	C	7 121	11.6	...	...	...
2012	C	619 530	21.1	C	142 988	4.9	16.2	C	7 331	11.8	...	...	...
2013	C	597 902	20.1	C	147 901	5.0	15.1	C	7 630	12.8	...	...	...
ASIA - ASIE													
Armenia - Arménie													
2010	C	44 825	13.8	C	27 921[39]	8.6	5.2	C	512[39]	11.4	...	...	...
2011	C	43 340	13.3	C	27 963[39]	8.6	4.7	C	507[39]	11.7	...	...	...
2012	C*	42 333	13.4	C*	27 514[39]	8.7	4.7		...	...	...	...	...
2013	C*	41 790	13.8	C*	27 196[39]	9.0	4.8		...	...	...	...	...
2014	C*	43 183	...	C*	27 872[39]	...	...		...	...	...	...	...
Azerbaijan - Azerbaïdjan													
2010	+C	165 643[39]	18.3	+C	53 580[39]	5.9	12.4	+C	1 843[39]	11.1	70.9	76.1	2.266
2011	+C	176 072[39]	19.2	+C	53 762[39]	5.9	13.3	+C	1 903[39]	10.8	...	...	...
2012	+C	174 469[39]	18.8	+C	55 017[39]	5.9	12.9	+C	1 884[39]	10.8	71.4	76.3	2.336
2013	+C	172 671[39]	18.3	+C	54 383[39]	5.8	12.6	+C	1 862[39]	10.8	71.4	76.5	...
2014	+C	170 503[39]	17.9		...	...	...		...	...	...	...	...
Bahrain - Bahreïn													
2010	C	18 150	14.8	C	2 401	2.0	12.8	C	140[40]	7.7	...	...	1.877
2011	C	17 573	14.7	C	2 528	2.1	12.6	C	139[40]	7.9	...	...	1.967
2012	C	19 119	15.8	C	2 613	2.2	13.7	C	149[40]	7.8	...	...	2.134
2013	C	19 995	16.0	C	2 588	2.1	13.9	C	141[40]	7.1	...	...	2.157
2014	C	20 931	15.9		...	...	...		...	...	...	...	2.173
Bangladesh													
2010	U	2 868 494	...	U	842 095	...	...	U	104 591	...	66.7	68.8	2.120
2011	U	2 891 000	...	U	828 000	...	...	U	100 751	...	67.9	70.3	2.110
2012	U	2 933 000	...	U	826 000	...	...	U	96 254	...	...	...	2.120
2013		...	...		...	...	...		...	...	68.8	71.4	2.110
Brunei Darussalam - Brunéi Darussalam													
2010	+C	6 412	16.6		...	...	...		...	...	...	...	1.800
2011	+C	6 724	17.1	+C	1 235	3.1	14.0	+C	56	8.3	...	...	1.900
2012	+C	6 909	...	+C	1 216	...	...	+C	64	9.3	...	...	1.900
2013	+C	6 680	...	+C	1 398	...	...	+C	51	7.6	...	...	1.900
China - Chine[41]													
2010	I	15 920 000[42]	11.9	I	9 510 000[42]	7.1	4.8		...	...	66.8	70.5	...
2011	I	16 040 000[42]	11.9	I	9 600 000[42]	7.1	4.8		...	...	...	...	...
2012	I	16 350 000[42]	12.1	I	9 660 000[42]	7.2	5.0		...	...	...	...	...
2013	I	16 400 000[42]	12.1	I	9 720 000[42]	7.2	4.9		...	...	...	...	...
2014	I	16 870 000[42]	12.4	I	9 770 000[42]	7.2	5.2		...	...	...	...	...

4. Vital statistics summary and life expectancy at birth: 2010 - 2014
Aperçu des statistiques de l'état civil et de l'espérance de vie à la naissance : 2010 - 2014 (continued - suite)

Continent, country or area and year / Continent, pays ou zone et année	Live births / Naissances vivantes Code[a]	Number Nombre	Crude birth rate Taux brut de natalité	Deaths / Décès Code[a]	Number Nombre	Crude death rate Taux brut de mortalité	Rate of natural increase Taux d'accrois-sement naturel	Infant deaths / Décès d'enfants de moins d'un an Code[a]	Number Nombre	Rate (per 1000 births) Taux (par 1000 naiss-ances)	Life expectancy at birth / Espérance de vie à la naissance Male[b] Masculin[b]	Female[b] Féminin[b]	Total fertility rate L'indice synthétique de fécondité
ASIA - ASIE													
China, Hong Kong SAR - Chine, Hong Kong RAS													
2010	C	88 584	12.6	C	42 194	6.0	6.6	C	149	1.7	...	...	1.127[43]
2011	C	95 451	13.5	C	42 346	6.0	7.5	C	127	1.3	80.3	86.7	1.204[43]
2012	C	91 558	12.8	C	43 917	6.1	6.7	C	137	1.5	...	...	1.285[43]
2013	C	57 084	7.9	C	43 397	6.0	1.9	C	100	1.8	81.1	86.7	1.124[43]
2014	C*	62 300	8.6	C*	45 100	6.2	2.4		...	...	...	...	...
China, Macao SAR - Chine, Macao RAS													
2010	C	5 114	9.5	C	1 774	3.3	6.2	C	15	...	IV79.5	85.4	1.070
2011	C	5 852	10.6	C	1 845	3.4	7.3	C	17	...	...	...	1.150
2012	C	7 315	12.9	C	1 841	3.2	9.6	C	18	...	IV79.1	85.7	1.357
2013	C	6 571	11.1	C	1 920	3.2	7.9	C	13	...	...	...	1.150
2014	C	7 360	11.8	C	1 939	3.1	8.7	C	15	...	IV79.6	86.0	1.224
Cyprus - Chypre[44]													
2010	C	9 801	11.8	C	5 103	6.2	5.7	C	31	3.2	...	...	1.437
2011	C	9 622	11.3	C	5 504	6.5	4.8	C	30	3.1	II79.0	82.9	1.349
2012	C	10 161	11.8	C	5 665	6.6	5.2	C	36	3.5	...	...	...
2013	C	9 341	10.8	C	5 141[45]	6.0	4.9	C	15	...	80.0	84.8	...
2014	C*	9 258	10.8		...	...	...		...	...	...	...	...
Georgia - Géorgie													
2010	C	62 585	14.1	C	47 864[39]	10.7	3.3	C	701[39]	11.2	70.2	78.6	1.830
2011	C	58 014	12.9	C	49 818[39]	11.1	1.8	C	703[39]	12.1	...	...	1.690
2012	C	57 031	12.7	C	49 348[39]	11.0	1.7	C	715[39]	12.5	...	...	...
2013	C	57 878	...	C	48 553[39]	...	...	C	640[39]	11.1	...	...	...
India - Inde[46]													
2010	I	...	22.1[47]	I	...	7.2[47]	...	I	...	47.0[47]	...	...	2.500
2011	I	...	21.1[47]	I	...	7.1[47]	...	I	...	44.0[47]	...	...	2.400
2012	I	...	21.6[47]	I	...	7.0[47]	...	I	...	42.0[47]	...	...	2.400
2013	I	...	21.4[47]	I	...	7.0[47]	...	I	...	40.0[47]	...	...	2.300
Indonesia - Indonésie													
2010		...	...		...	...	...		...	...	68.7	72.6	2.410[48]
2012		...	...		...	...	...		...	...	67.7	71.7	2.600[48]
Iran (Islamic Republic of) - Iran (République islamique d')													
2010	C	1 363 542[49]	18.3	C	441 042[49]	5.9	12.4	C	11 677[49]	8.6	...	...	...
2011	C	1 382 229[49]	18.4	C	383 504[49]	5.1	13.3	C	11 021[49]	8.0	71.5	74.0	1.790
2012	C	1 421 689[49]	18.7	C	367 539[49]	4.8	13.9	C	10 401[49]	7.3	...	...	...
2013	C	1 471 834[49]	19.1	C	372 279[49]	4.8	14.3	C	8 015[49]	5.4	...	...	...
Iraq													
2013	U*	1 077 645	...	U*	189 118	...	...		...	...	...	...	...
Israel - Israël[50]													
2010	C	166 255	21.8	C	39 613[51]	5.2	16.6	C	618[51]	3.7	79.7	83.6	3.029
2011	C	166 296	21.4	C	40 889[51]	5.3	16.1	C	588[51]	3.5	79.9	83.6	3.004
2012	C	170 940	21.6	C	42 100[51]	5.3	16.3	C	611[51]	3.6	79.9	83.6	3.052
2013	C	171 444	21.3	C	41 643[51]	5.2	16.1	C	537[51]	3.1	80.3	83.9	3.030
2014	C*	176 221	21.4	C	42 085[51]	5.1	16.3	C	529[51]	3.0	...	...	...
Japan - Japon[52]													
2010	C	1 071 304	8.4	C	1 197 012	9.3	-1.0	C	2 450	2.3	79.6	86.4	1.387
2011	C	1 050 806	8.2	C	1 253 066	9.8	-1.6	C	2 463	2.3	79.4	85.9	1.393
2012	C	1 037 231	8.1	C	1 256 359	9.8	-1.7	C	2 299	2.2	79.9	86.4	1.405
2013	C	1 029 816	8.1	C	1 268 436	10.0	-1.9	C	2 185	2.1	80.2	86.6	1.427
Jordan - Jordanie[53]													
2010	C	183 948	30.1	U	21 550	...	...		...	...	...	...	3.800
2011	C	178 435	28.6	U	21 730	...	...		...	...	71.6	74.4	3.800
2012	C	177 695	27.8	U	22 785	...	...		...	...	72.7	76.7	3.500
2013	C	178 143	27.3	U	23 898	...	...		...	...	...	...	3.500
2014		...	...		...	...	...		...	...	...	...	3.500

4. Vital statistics summary and life expectancy at birth: 2010 - 2014
Aperçu des statistiques de l'état civil et de l'espérance de vie à la naissance : 2010 - 2014 (continued - suite)

Continent, country or area and year / Continent, pays ou zone et année	Code[a] / Co-de[a]	Live births — Naissances vivantes — Number Nombre	Crude birth rate Taux brut de natalité	Code[a] / Co-de[a]	Deaths — Décès — Number Nombre	Crude death rate Taux brut de mortalité	Rate of natural increase Taux d'accrois-sement naturel	Code[a] / Co-de[a]	Infant deaths — Décès d'enfants de moins d'un an — Number Nombre	Rate (per 1000 births) Taux (par 1000 naiss-ances)	Life expectancy at birth — Espérance de vie à la naissance — Male[b] Masculin[b]	Female[b] Féminin[b]	Total fertility rate L'indice synthétique de fécondité
ASIA - ASIE													
Kazakhstan													
2010	C	367 942[39]	22.5	C	146 370[39]	9.0	13.6	C	6 078[39]	16.5	...	...	2.600
2011	C	372 801[39]	22.5	C	144 944[39]	8.8	13.8	C	5 556[39]	14.9	...	...	2.590
2012	C	381 005[39]	22.7	C	142 880[39]	8.5	14.2	C	5 121[39]	13.4	64.8	74.3	2.620
2013	C	387 227[39]	22.7	C	135 950[39]	8.0	14.8	C	4 367[39]	11.3	...	...	2.640
Kuwait - Koweït													
2010	C	57 533	19.6	C	5 448	1.9	17.8	C	496	8.6	...	...	...
2011	C	58 198	18.8	C	5 339	1.7	17.1	C	484	8.3	...	...	...
2012	C	59 753	18.3	C	5 950	1.8	16.5	C	459	7.7	...	...	...
2013	C	59 426	17.2	C	5 909	1.7	15.5	C	453	7.6	...	...	...
Kyrgyzstan - Kirghizstan													
2010	C	146 123	28.1	C	36 174	7.0	21.2	C	3 337	22.8	65.3	73.5	3.062
2011	C	149 612	28.4	C	35 941	6.8	21.6	C	3 150	21.1	65.7	73.7	3.085
2012	C	154 918	28.9	C	36 186	6.8	22.2	C	3 091	20.0	66.1	74.1	3.148
2013	C	155 520	27.2	C	34 880	6.1	21.1	C	3 093	19.9	66.3	74.3	3.109
2014	C*	161 813	27.7	C*	35 564	6.1	21.6		...	...	...	...	...
Lao People's Democratic Republic - République démocratique populaire lao[54]													
2010		...	...		...	...	...		...	...	...	...	3.200
Lebanon - Liban													
2010	C	95 218	...	C	22 926	...	...		...	...	...	...	...
2011	C	98 569	26.1	C	26 070	6.9	19.2		...	...	...	...	...
2012	C	94 842	...	C	23 452	...	...		...	...	...	...	...
2013	C	95 246	...	C	24 013	...	...		...	...	...	...	...
2014	C	104 872	...	C	27 020	...	...		...	...	...	...	...
Malaysia - Malaisie													
2010	C	491 239	17.2	C	130 978	4.6	12.6	C	3 295	6.7	71.9	76.6	2.136
2011	C	511 594	17.6	C	135 463	4.7	12.9	C	3 330	6.5	...	...	2.174
2012	C*	508 774	17.2	C*	136 836	4.6	12.6	C*	3 204	6.3	...	...	2.118*
Maldives													
2010	C	7 115	22.3	C	1 105	3.5	18.8	C	78	11.0	72.6	74.4	...
2011	C	7 180	22.1	C	1 137	3.5	18.6	C	65	9.1	72.8	74.8	...
2012	C	7 431	22.5	C	1 135	3.4	19.0	C	66	8.9	...	...	...
2013	C	7 153	21.3	C	1 120	3.3	17.9	C	46	6.4	...	...	...
Mongolia - Mongolie													
2010	+C	63 270	23.1	+C	18 293	6.7	16.4	+C	1 275	20.2	64.9	72.3	2.400
2011	+C	69 853	25.1	+C	19 155	6.9	18.2	+C	1 152	16.5	...	...	2.600
2012	+C	73 839	26.0	+C	17 761	6.3	19.7	+C	1 143	15.5	...	...	2.700
2013	+C	79 780	27.5	+C	17 247	5.9	21.6	+C	1 166	14.6	65.4	75.0	3.000
2014	+C	82 839	28.0	+C	16 521	5.6	22.4	+C	1 251	15.1	65.9	75.5	3.100
Myanmar													
2010	+U	965 937	...	+U	346 205	...	...	+U	26 206	...	64.6[55]	68.6[55]	2.030[55]
2011	+U	1 007 039	...	+U	342 420	...	...	+U	27 184	...	65.9[55]	70.9[55]	2.010[55]
2012	+U*	856 279	...	+U*	250 874	...	...	+U*	11 406	...	...	...	2.010[55]
2013	+U*	835 595	...	+U*	257 216	...	...	+U*	11 516	...	...	...	2.290[56]
Nepal - Népal													
2011	I	326 725[57]	11.4	I	129 978[57]	4.5	6.9	I	10 132[57]	31.0	65.4	67.9	2.520
Oman													
2010	U	64 730[58]	...	U	7 414[58]	...	...	U	581[58]	...	73.6	78.7	3.000
2011	U	67 922[58]	...	U	7 667[58]	...	...	U	640[58]	...	73.1	77.7	2.900
2012	U	72 867[58]	...	U	7 884[58]	...	...	U	676[58]	...	74.5	78.0	2.800
2013	U	79 417[58]	...	U	7 669[58]	...	...	U	772[58]	...	74.8	78.5	2.900
2014	U*	80 163[58]	...		...	...	...		...	...	...	...	...
Philippines													
2010	C	1 782 981	19.1	C	488 265	5.2	13.9	C	22 476	12.6	...	...	...
2011	C	1 746 685	18.4	C	498 486	5.3	13.2	C	22 283	12.8	...	...	...
2012	C	1 790 367	18.6	C	514 745	5.3	13.2	C	22 254	12.4	...	...	...

Continent, country or area and year / Continent, pays ou zone et année	Live births — Naissances vivantes			Deaths — Décès			Rate of natural increase — Taux d'accroissement naturel	Infant deaths — Décès d'enfants de moins d'un an			Life expectancy at birth — Espérance de vie à la naissance		Total fertility rate — L'indice synthétique de fécondité
	Code[a]	Number / Nombre	Crude birth rate / Taux brut de natalité	Code[a]	Number / Nombre	Crude death rate / Taux brut de mortalité		Code[a]	Number / Nombre	Rate (per 1000 births) / Taux (par 1000 naissances)	Male[b] / Masculin[b]	Female[b] / Féminin[b]	
ASIA - ASIE													
Qatar													
2010	C	19 504	11.4	C	1 970	1.1	10.2	C	132	6.8	78.0	78.8	2.076
2011	C	20 802	12.0	C	1 949	1.1	10.9	C	156	7.5	76.5	81.0	2.118
2012	C	21 423	11.7	C	2 031	1.1	10.6	C	148	6.9	...	...	3.400
2013	C	23 708	11.8	C	2 133	1.1	10.8	C	157	6.6	...	...	...
2014	C*	25 443	11.5	C*	2 366	1.1	10.4		...	...	...	...	...
Republic of Korea - République de Corée													
2010	C	470 171[59]	9.4	C	255 405[60]	5.1	4.3	C	1 508[60]	3.2	77.2	84.1	1.226[60]
2011	C	471 265[59]	9.4	C	257 396[60]	5.1	4.3	C	1 435[60]	3.0	77.7	84.5	1.244[60]
2012	C	484 550[59]	9.6	C	267 221[60]	5.3	4.3	C	1 405[60]	2.9	77.9	84.6	1.297[60]
2013	C	436 455[59]	8.6	C	266 257[60]	5.3	3.4	C	1 305[60]	3.0	78.5	85.1	1.187[60]
Saudi Arabia - Arabie saoudite													
2010		...	...	...	100 073[61]	...	...	...	10 219[61]	...	...	...	2.980[61]
2011		...	...	...	102 066[61]	...	...	...	10 023[61]	...	...	...	2.930[61]
2012		...	...	...	104 195[61]	...	...	...	9 843[61]	...	72.8[61]	75.2[61]	2.870[61]
2013	...	607 806	...	...	106 521[61]	...	...		...	...	...	...	...
Singapore - Singapour													
2010	C	37 967	10.1	+C	17 610	4.7	5.4	+C	100	2.6	79.2[62]	84.0[62]	1.150[63]
2011	C	39 654	10.5	+C	18 027	4.8	5.7	+C	97	2.4	79.5[62]	84.1[62]	1.200[63]
2012	C	42 663	11.2	+C	18 481	4.8	6.3	+C	98	2.3	79.8[62]	84.3[62]	1.290[63]
2013	C	39 720	10.3	+C	18 938	4.9	5.4	+C	94	2.4	80.1[62]	84.5[62]	1.190[63]
2014	C	42 232	10.9	+C	19 393	5.0	5.9	+C	83	2.0	80.5[64]	84.9[64]	1.250[63]
Sri Lanka													
2010	+C*	364 565	17.7	+C*	128 603	6.2	11.4		...	...	...	...	...
2011	+C*	363 415	17.4	+C*	123 261	5.9	11.5		...	...	...	...	...
2012	+C*	355 900	17.5	+C*	122 063	6.0	11.5		...	...	...	...	...
2013	+C*	365 792	17.9	+C*	127 124	6.2	11.7		...	...	...	...	...
State of Palestine - État de Palestine													
2010	U	137 085[65]	...	U	10 764[65]	...	...	U	956[65]	...	...	...	4.400[66]
2011	U	131 430[65]	...	U	11 333[65]	...	...	U	1 051[65]	...	71.0	73.9	...
2012	U	129 826[65]	...	U	11 676[65]	...	...	U	1 050[65]	...	71.3	74.1	...
2013	U	126 912[65]	...	U	11 013[65]	...	...	U	827[65]	...	71.5	74.4	4.100[67]
2014		...	...		...	...	...		...	...	71.8	74.7	...
Syrian Arab Republic - République arabe syrienne[68]													
2010	+U	870 100	...	+U	91 981	...	...		...	...	...	...	...
Tajikistan - Tadjikistan													
2010	U	239 805[69]	...	U	31 937[39]	...	...	U	3 092[39]	...	...	...	2.905
2011	U	224 178[69]	...	U	32 909[39]	Taux	...	U	3 131[39]	...	70.9	74.1	2.766
2012	U	219 281[69]	...	U	32 828[39]	...	...	U	2 884[39]	...	...	...	...
2013	U	209 417[69]	...	U	31 706[39]	...	...	U	3 622[39]	...	...	...	...
Thailand - Thaïlande													
2010	+U	761 689	...	+U	411 331	...	...	+U	5 357	...	...	...	...
2011	+U	795 031	...	+U	414 670	...	...	+U	5 275	...	...	...	...
2012	+U	801 737	...	+U	415 141	...	...		...	...	...	...	...
2013	+U	748 081	...	+U	426 065	...	...		...	...	...	...	...
2014	+U	711 081	...	+U	435 624	...	...		...	...	...	...	...
Turkey - Turquie													
2010	C	1 258 252	17.2	C	366 187	5.0	12.2	C	15 137	12.0	...	...	2.110
2011	C	1 244 673	16.8	C	375 923	5.1	11.7	C	14 548	11.7	72.0	77.1	2.020
2012	C	1 286 828	17.1	C	376 000	5.0	12.1	C	14 931	11.6	72.0	77.2	2.080
2013	C	1 283 062	16.8	C	372 094	4.9	12.0	C	13 900	10.8	73.7	79.4	...
2014	C	1 337 504	17.4	C*	390 121	5.1	12.3		...	...	...	...	...

4. Vital statistics summary and life expectancy at birth: 2010 - 2014
Aperçu des statistiques de l'état civil et de l'espérance de vie à la naissance : 2010 - 2014 (continued - suite)

Continent, country or area and year / Continent, pays ou zone et année	Live births Naissances vivantes			Deaths Décès			Rate of natural increase Taux d'accrois-sement naturel	Infant deaths Décès d'enfants de moins d'un an			Life expectancy at birth Espérance de vie à la naissance		Total fertility rate L'indice synthétique de fécondité
	Co-de[a]	Number Nombre	Crude birth rate Taux brut de natalité	Co-de[a]	Number Nombre	Crude death rate Taux brut de mortalité		Co-de[a]	Number Nombre	Rate (per 1000 births) Taux (par 1000 naiss-ances)	Male[b] Masculin[b]	Female[b] Féminin[b]	
ASIA - ASIE													
United Arab Emirates - Émirats arabes unis[70]													
2010	...	79 625	...	...	7 414	...	...	...	...	...	...	...	...
2011	...	83 950	...	...	7 350	...	...	...	...	...	...	...	...
Uzbekistan - Ouzbékistan													
2010	C	634 810	22.7	C	138 411[39]	4.9	17.7	...	...	...	...	...	...
2011	C	622 835	21.4	C	143 253[39]	4.9	16.5	...	...	...	...	...	...
2012	C	625 106	21.2	C	145 988[39]	4.9	16.2	...	...	...	...	...	...
2013	C	679 519	22.7	C	145 672[39]	4.9	17.8	...	...	...	...	...	...
Viet Nam													
2010		...	...		...	...	...	...	...	...	...	...	2.000
2011		...	...		...	...	...	...	...	...	70.4	75.8	1.990
2012		...	...		...	...	...	...	...	...	70.4	75.8	2.050
2013		...	...		...	...	...	...	...	...	70.5	75.8	2.100
2014		...	...		...	...	...	...	...	...	70.6	76.0	2.090
Yemen - Yémen													
2010	U	318 936	...	U	28 494	...	...	...	...	...	...	...	...
2011	U	239 980	...	U	23 662	...	...	...	...	...	...	...	...
2012	U	279 719	...	U	28 596	...	...	...	...	...	...	...	...
2013	U	425 165[71]	...	U	35 066[72]	...	...	...	...	...	...	...	...
EUROPE													
Åland Islands - Îles d'Åland													
2010	C	286	10.3	C	233	8.4	1.9	C	1	...	81.2	84.2	1.834
2011	C	285	10.1	C	277	9.8	0.3	C	-	...	79.5	84.8	1.801
2012	C	292	10.3	C	323	11.4	-1.1	C	-	...	...	...	1.847
2013	C	287	10.0	C	269	9.4	0.6	C	-	...	79.0	85.9	1.800
2014	C*	282	9.8	C*	246	8.5	1.3				...	...	...
Albania - Albanie													
2010	C	34 061	11.7	C	20 107	6.9	4.8	C	328	9.6	...	...	...
2011	C	34 285	11.8	C	20 012	6.9	4.9	C	299	8.7	...	...	...
2012	C	35 473	12.2	C	20 870	7.2	5.0	C	312	8.8	...	...	...
2013	C	35 750	12.3	C	20 442	7.1	5.3	C	282	7.9	76.0	80.3	...
2014	C	35 760	12.3		...	...	...		...	...	...	...	...
Andorra - Andorre													
2010	C	828	9.8	C	239	2.8	7.0	C	-	...	...	...	1.246
2011	C	793	10.0	C	275	3.5	6.5	C	...	...	...	...	1.260
2012	C	737	9.5	C	303	3.9	5.6	C	4	...	...	...	1.151
Austria - Autriche													
2010	C	78 742	9.4	C	77 199[73]	9.2	0.2	C	307	3.9	77.7	83.2	1.440
2011	C	78 109	9.3	C	76 479[73]	9.1	0.2	C	281	3.6	78.1	83.4	1.430
2012	C	78 952	9.4	C	79 436[73]	9.4	-0.1	C	252	3.2	78.3	83.3	1.441
2013	C	79 330	9.4	C	79 526[73]	9.4	0.0	C	245	3.1	78.5	83.6	...
2014	C	81 722	9.6	C*	77 667	9.1	0.5		...	...	...	...	...
Belarus - Bélarus													
2010	C	108 050	11.4	C	137 132	14.4	-3.1	C	429	4.0	64.6	76.5	...
2011	C	109 147	11.5	C	135 090	14.3	-2.7	C	420	3.8	64.7	76.7	1.515
2012	C	115 893	12.2	C	126 531	13.4	-1.1	C	386	3.3	66.6	77.6	1.620
2013	C	117 997	12.5	C	125 326	13.2	-0.8	C	407	3.4	67.3	77.9	...
2014	C	118 534	12.5		...	...	...		...	...	...	...	...
Belgium - Belgique													
2010	C	130 100[74]	11.9	C	105 152[74]	9.7	2.3	C	465[74]	3.6	...	...	1.845
2011	C	128 705[74]	11.7	C	104 292[74]	9.4	2.2	C	434[74]	3.4	...	...	1.810
2012	C	128 051[74]	11.5	C	109 076[74]	9.8	1.7	C	483[74]	3.8	...	...	...
2013	C	125 606[74]	11.2	C	109 334[74]	9.8	1.5	C	436[74]	3.5	...	...	...
2014	C	125 014[74]	11.2	C*	104 755	9.3	1.8		...	...	...	...	...

4. Vital statistics summary and life expectancy at birth: 2010 - 2014
Aperçu des statistiques de l'état civil et de l'espérance de vie à la naissance : 2010 - 2014 (continued - suite)

Continent, country or area and year / Continent, pays ou zone et année	Code[a]	Live births Naissances vivantes — Number Nombre	Crude birth rate Taux brut de natalité	Code[a]	Deaths Décès — Number Nombre	Crude death rate Taux brut de mortalité	Rate of natural increase Taux d'accroissement naturel	Code[a]	Infant deaths Décès d'enfants de moins d'un an — Number Nombre	Rate (per 1000 births) Taux (par 1000 naissances)	Life expectancy at birth Espérance de vie à la naissance — Male[b] Masculin[b]	Female[b] Féminin[b]	Total fertility rate L'indice synthétique de fécondité
EUROPE													
Bosnia and Herzegovina - Bosnie-Herzégovine													
2010	C	33 528	8.7	C	35 118	9.1	-0.4	C	216	6.4	...	...	1.266
2011	C	31 875	8.3	C	35 522	9.2	-0.9		...	...	...	...	...
2012	C	32 072	8.4	C	35 692	9.3	-0.9	C	161	5.0	...	...	...
2013	C	31 103	8.1	C	35 837	9.3	-1.2	C	161	5.2	...	...	...
2014	C	29 247	7.6	C	34 824	9.1	-1.5	C	140	4.8	...	...	...
Bulgaria - Bulgarie													
2010	C	75 513	10.0	C	110 165	14.6	-4.6	C	708	9.4	[III]70.0	77.2	1.486
2011	C	70 846	9.6	C	108 258	14.7	-5.1	C	601	8.5	[III]70.4	77.4	1.508
2012	C	69 121	9.5	C	109 281	15.0	-5.5	C	536	7.8	[III]70.6	77.5	1.501
2013	C	66 578	9.2	C	104 345	14.4	-5.2	C	489	7.3	...	...	...
2014	C	67 585	9.3	C*	108 952	15.0	-5.7		...	...	...	...	...
Croatia - Croatie													
2010	C	43 361	10.1	C	52 096	12.1	-2.0	C	192	4.4	...	...	1.460
2011	C	41 197	9.6	C	51 019	11.9	-2.3	C	192	4.7	...	...	1.407
2012	C	41 771	9.8	C	51 710	12.1	-2.3	C	150	3.6	...	...	1.517
2013	C	39 939	9.4	C	50 386	11.8	-2.5	C	162	4.1	...	...	...
2014	C	39 566	9.3	C*	50 839	12.0	-2.7		...	...	...	...	...
Czech Republic - République tchèque													
2010	C	117 153[75]	11.2	C	106 844	10.2	1.0	C	313	2.7	74.4	80.6	1.493
2011	C	108 673[75]	10.4	C	106 848	10.2	0.2	C	298	2.7	74.7	80.7	1.426
2012	C	108 576	10.3	C	108 189	10.3	0.0	C	285	2.6	75.0	80.9	1.452
2013	C	106 751	10.2	C	109 160	10.4	-0.2	C	265	2.5	75.2	81.1	...
2014	C	109 860	10.4	C*	105 665	10.0	0.4		...	...	...	...	...
Denmark - Danemark[76]													
2010	C	63 411	11.4	C	54 368	9.8	1.6	C	216	3.4	[II]77.1	81.2	1.875
2011	C	58 998	10.6	C	52 516	9.4	1.2	C	208	3.5	[II]77.3	81.6	1.756
2012	C	57 916	10.4	C	52 325	9.4	1.0	C	197	3.4	[II]77.9	81.9	1.733
2013	C	55 873	10.0	C	52 470	9.4	0.6	C	194	3.5	[II]78.0	81.9	...
2014	C	56 870	10.1		...	...	...		...	...	...	...	...
Estonia - Estonie													
2010	C	15 825	11.9	C	15 790	11.9	0.0	C	53	3.3	70.6	80.7	1.636
2011	C	14 679	11.1	C	15 244	11.5	-0.4	C	36	2.5	71.2	81.3	1.524
2012	C	14 056	10.6	C	15 450	11.7	-1.1	C	50	3.6	71.5	81.5	1.547
2013	C	13 531	10.3	C	15 244	11.6	-1.3	C	28	...	72.7	81.4	...
2014	C	13 551	10.3		...	...	...		...	...	...	...	...
Faeroe Islands - Îles Féroé													
2010	C	639	13.1	C	348	7.2	6.0	C	2	...	...	...	2.440
2011	C	576	11.9	C	371	7.6	4.2	C	3	...	...	...	2.269
2012	C	618	12.8	C	406	8.4	4.4	C	9	...	...	...	2.527
2013	C	624	13.0	C	364	7.6	5.4	C	-	...	...	...	2.490
Finland - Finlande													
2010	C	60 694[77]	11.4	C	50 654[77]	9.5	1.9	C	139[77]	2.3	76.7[77]	83.2[77]	1.870
2011	C	59 676[77]	11.1	C	50 308[77]	9.4	1.7	C	143[77]	2.4	...	...	1.827
2012	C	59 201[77]	11.0	C	51 384[77]	9.5	1.5	C	141[77]	2.4	77.5[77]	83.4[77]	1.801
2013	C	58 134	10.7	C	51 472	9.5	1.2	C	102[77]	1.8	...	...	...
2014	C	57 232	10.5	C	51 595	9.5	1.0		...	...	...	...	...
France													
2010	C	802 224[78]	12.8	C	540 469[78]	8.6	4.2	C	2 785[78]	3.5	[III]77.8	84.5	2.016
2011	C	792 996[78]	12.5	C	534 795[78]	8.5	4.1	C	2 604[78]	3.3	[III]78.1	84.7	1.997
2012	C	790 290[78]	12.4	C	559 227[78]	8.8	3.6	C	2 643[78]	3.3	[III]78.3[79]	84.8[79]	1.995
2013	C	781 621[78]	12.3	C	558 408[78]	8.8	3.5	C	2 710[78]	3.5	...	...	...
2014	C*	766 400[78]	12.0	C*	542 800[78]	8.5	3.5		...	...	...	...	...
Germany - Allemagne													
2010	C	677 947	8.3	C	858 768	10.5	-2.2	C	2 322	3.4	[III]77.5	82.6	1.393
2011	C	662 685	8.3	C	852 328	10.6	-2.4	C	2 408	3.6	[III]77.7	82.7	1.364
2012	C	673 544	8.4	C	869 582	10.8	-2.4	C	2 202	3.3	...	...	...

98

Continent, country or area and year / Continent, pays ou zone et année	Code[a]	Live births Naissances vivantes — Number Nombre	Crude birth rate Taux brut de natalité	Code[a]	Deaths Décès — Number Nombre	Crude death rate Taux brut de mortalité	Rate of natural increase Taux d'accrois-sement naturel	Code[a]	Infant deaths Décès d'enfants de moins d'un an — Number Nombre	Rate (per 1000 births) Taux (par 1000 naiss-ances)	Life expectancy at birth Espérance de vie à la naissance — Male[b] Masculin[b]	Female[b] Féminin[b]	Total fertility rate L'indice synthétique de fécondité
EUROPE													
Germany - Allemagne													
2013	C	682 069	8.5	C	893 825	11.1	-2.6	C	2 250	3.3	...	...	...
2014	C*	700 000	8.7	C*	868 373	10.8	-2.1		...	...	...	...	...
Gibraltar													
2010	+C	493[80]	15.7	+C	231[81]	7.3	8.3		...	...	...	...	...
2011	+C	442[80]	13.8	+C	241[81]	7.5	6.3		...	...	...	...	...
2012	+C	461[80]	14.2	+C	264[81]	8.1	6.0		...	...	...	...	...
2013	+C	426[80]	13.0	+C	230[81]	7.0	6.0	+C	-	...	...	...	...
Greece - Grèce													
2010	C	114 766	10.3	C	109 084	9.8	0.5	C	436	3.8	...	...	1.500
2011	C	106 428	9.6	C	111 099	10.0	-0.4	C	357	3.4	78.3	83.1	1.390
2012	C	100 371	9.0	C	116 668	10.5	-1.5	C	293	2.9	77.9	83.0	1.340
2013	C	94 134	8.5	C	111 794	10.1	-1.6	C	347	3.7	...	...	...
2014	C*	92 094	8.4	C*	113 877	10.4	-2.0		...	...	...	...	...
Guernsey - Guernesey													
2010	C	613	9.8	C	497	8.0	1.9		...	...	...	...	...
2011	C	650	10.3	C	535	8.5	1.8		...	...	...	...	...
2012	C	674	10.7	C	547	8.7	2.0		...	...	...	...	...
2013	C	667	10.6	C	556	8.9	1.8		...	...	...	...	...
2014	C	627	10.0	C	526	8.4	1.6		...	...	...	...	...
Hungary - Hongrie													
2010	C	90 335	9.0	C	130 456	13.0	-4.0	C	481	5.3	70.5	78.1	1.256
2011	C	88 049	8.8	C	128 795	12.9	-4.1	C	433	4.9	70.9	78.2	1.238
2012	C	90 269	9.1	C	129 440	13.0	-3.9	C	438	4.9	71.5	78.4	1.337
2013	C	89 524	9.0	C	126 677	12.8	-3.8	C	448[82]	5.0	72.0	78.7	...
2014	C*	93 300	9.4	C*	121 489	12.3	-2.9		...	...	...	...	...
Iceland - Islande													
2010	C	4 907	15.4	C	2 020	6.4	9.1	C	11	...	‖79.5	83.5	2.197
2011	C	4 492[83]	14.1	C	1 986[83]	6.2	7.9	C	4[83]	...	‖79.9	82.8	2.017
2012	C	4 533	14.1	C	1 955	6.1	8.0	C	5	...	‖80.8	83.9	2.037
2013	C	4 326	13.4	C	2 154	6.7	6.7	C	8	...	‖80.8	83.7	...
2014	C	4 375	13.4		...	...	...		...	...	...	...	...
Ireland - Irlande													
2010	C	75 174[84]	16.5[84]	C	27 961[84]	6.1[84]	10.4	+C	271	3.6	...	...	2.060
2011	C	74 033[84]	16.2[84]	C	28 456[84]	6.2[84]	10.0	+C	262	3.5	...	...	2.020
2012	+C	72 225	15.7	C	29 186[84]	6.4[84]	9.4	+C	250	3.5	...	...	2.010
2013	+C	68 930	15.0	+C	30 018	6.5	8.5	+C	243	3.5	...	...	...
2014	+C	67 462	14.6	+C	29 095	6.3	8.3	+C	249	3.7	...	...	...
Isle of Man - Île de Man													
2010	+C	1 023	12.4	+C	809	9.8	2.6		...	...	...	...	...
2011	+C	938	11.1	+C	816	9.7	1.4		...	...	...	...	...
2012	+C	890	10.5	+C	799	9.4	1.1		...	...	...	...	...
2013	+C	859	10.0	+C	792	9.2	0.8		...	...	...	...	...
2014	+C	805	9.3	+C	787	9.1	0.2		...	...	...	...	...
Italy - Italie													
2010	+C	561 944	9.5	C	587 488	9.9	-0.4	C	1 773	3.2	...	...	1.410
2011	+C	546 585	9.2	C	593 402	10.0	-0.8	C	1 595	2.9	...	...	1.390
2012	+C	534 186	9.0	C	612 883	10.3	-1.3	C	1 532	2.9	...	...	1.390
2013	+C	514 308	8.5	C	600 744	10.0	-1.4	C	1 493	2.9	79.8	84.6	...
2014	+C	502 596	8.3		...	...	...		...	...	...	...	...
Jersey													
2010	+C	1 066[25]	11.0	+C	801	8.3	2.7		...	...	...	...	...
2011	+C	1 100[25]	11.3	+C	727	7.4	3.8		...	...	...	...	...
2012	+C	1 120[25]	11.4	+C	774	7.9	3.5		...	...	...	...	...
2013		...	...	+C	717	...	...		...	...	...	...	...
Latvia - Lettonie													
2010	C	19 781	9.4	C	30 040	14.3	-4.9	C	110	5.6	68.8	78.4	1.363
2011	C	18 828	9.1	C	28 540	13.9	-4.7	C	124	6.6	...	...	...
2012	C	19 897	9.8	C	29 025	14.3	-4.5	C	125	6.3	69.1	78.9	1.444

Continent, country or area and year / Continent, pays ou zone et année	Live births Naissances vivantes			Deaths Décès			Rate of natural increase Taux d'accrois-sement naturel	Infant deaths Décès d'enfants de moins d'un an			Life expectancy at birth Espérance de vie à la naissance		Total fertility rate L'indice synthétique de fécondité
	Code[a]	Number Nombre	Crude birth rate Taux brut de natalité	Code[a]	Number Nombre	Crude death rate Taux brut de mortalité		Code[a]	Number Nombre	Rate (per 1000 births) Taux (par 1000 naiss-ances)	Male[b] Masculin[b]	Female[b] Féminin[b]	
EUROPE													
Latvia - Lettonie													
2013	C	20 596	10.2	C	28 691	14.3	-4.0	C	91	4.4	69.5	79.0	...
2014	C	21 746	10.8	C*	28 438	14.2	-3.3		...	...	...	...	...
Liechtenstein													
2010	C	329	9.1	C	238	6.6	2.5	C	1	...	...	...	1.402
2011	C	395	10.9	C	248	6.8	4.1	C	1	...	...	...	1.688
2012	C	357	9.7	C	224	6.1	3.6	C	3	...	...	...	1.507
2013	C	339	9.2	C	246	6.7	2.5	C	2	...	...	...	...
2014	C*	370	10.0		...	...	...		...	...	...	...	...
Lithuania - Lituanie													
2010	C	30 676	9.9	C	42 120	13.6	-3.7	C	153	5.0	68.0	78.8	1.499
2011	C	30 268	10.0	C	41 037	13.6	-3.6	C	144	4.8	68.1	79.1	1.551
2012	C	30 459	10.2	C	40 938	13.7	-3.5	C	118	3.9	68.4	79.4	1.595
2013	C	29 885	10.1	C	41 511	14.0	-3.9	C	110	3.7	68.5	79.4	...
2014	C	30 369	10.4	C*	40 210	13.7	-3.4		...	...	...	...	...
Luxembourg													
2010	C	5 874	11.6	C	3 760	7.4	4.2	C	20	...	...	...	1.625
2011	C	5 639	10.9	C	3 819	7.4	3.5	C	24	...	...	...	1.513
2012	C	6 026	11.3	C	3 876	7.3	4.0	C	25	...	III79.5	84.3	1.570
2013	C	6 115	11.3	C	3 822	7.0	4.2	C	24	...	III79.9	84.3	...
2014	C	6 070	11.0		...	...	...		...	...	...	...	...
Malta - Malte													
2010	C	3 898	9.4	C	3 010	7.3	2.1	C	22	...	78.9	83.1	1.362
2011	C	4 165	10.0	C	3 267	7.8	2.2	C	27	...	78.4	82.7	1.448
2012	C	4 130	9.8	C	3 418	8.1	1.7	C	22	...	78.0	82.2	1.435
2013	C	4 032	9.5	C	3 236	7.6	1.9	C	27	...	79.6	84.0	...
2014	C	4 191	9.9		...	...	...		...	...	...	...	...
Monaco[85]													
2010	C	961	26.9	C	535	15.0	11.9		...	...	...	...	...
2011	C	1 028	28.5	C	499	13.8	14.6		...	...	...	...	...
2012	C	979	27.2	C	429	11.9	15.3		...	...	...	...	...
2013	C	992	26.8	C	567[86]	15.3	11.5		...	...	...	...	...
2014	C	974	...	C	524[86]	...	...		...	...	...	...	...
Montenegro - Monténégro													
2010	C	7 418	12.0	C	5 633	9.1	2.9	C	50	6.7	...	...	...
2011	C	7 215	11.6	C	5 847	9.4	2.2	C	32	4.4	...	...	1.652
2012	C	7 459	12.0	C	5 922	9.5	2.5	C	33	4.4	...	...	1.709
2013	C	7 475	12.0	C	5 917	9.5	2.5	C	33	4.4	...	...	...
2014	C	7 529	12.1	C	6 014	9.7	2.4		...	...	...	...	...
Netherlands - Pays-Bas													
2010	C	184 397[87]	11.1	C	136 058[87]	8.2	2.9	C	695[87]	3.8	78.8	82.7	1.800
2011	C	180 060[87]	10.8	C	135 741[87]	8.1	2.7	C	654[87]	3.6	79.2	82.8	1.760
2012	C	175 959[87]	10.5	C	140 813[87]	8.4	2.1		...	...	...	...	1.720
2013	C	171 341[87]	10.2	C	141 245[87]	8.4	1.8		...	...	...	...	...
2014	C*	175 182[87]	10.4		...	...	...		...	...	...	...	...
Norway - Norvège													
2010	C	61 442	12.6	C	41 499[88]	8.5	4.1	C	171[88]	2.8	78.9	83.2	1.950
2011	C	60 220	12.2	C	41 393[88]	8.4	3.8	C	142[88]	2.4	79.0	83.5	1.880
2012	C	60 255	12.0	C	41 992[88]	8.4	3.6	C	150[88]	2.5	79.4	83.4	1.851
2013	C	58 878	11.6	C	41 131[88]	8.1	3.5	C	140[88]	2.4	...	...	...
2014	C	59 084	11.6	C*	40 435[88]	7.9	3.7		...	...	...	...	...
Poland - Pologne													
2010	C	413 300	10.7	C	378 478	9.8	0.9	C	2 057	5.0	72.1	80.6	1.382
2011	C	388 416	10.1	C	375 501	9.7	0.3	C	1 836	4.7	72.4	80.9	1.301
2012	C	386 257	10.0	C	384 788	10.0	0.0	C	1 791	4.6	72.7	81.0	1.299
2013	C	369 576	9.7	C	387 312	10.1	-0.5	C	1 684	4.6	...	...	...
2014	C	375 160	9.7		...	...	...		...	...	...	...	...
Portugal													
2010	C	101 381[25]	9.6	C	105 954[26]	10.0	-0.4	C	256[26]	2.5	III76.1	82.1	1.393
2011	C	96 856[25]	9.2	C	102 848[26]	9.7	-0.6	C	302[26]	3.1	III76.4	82.3	1.351

4. Vital statistics summary and life expectancy at birth: 2010 - 2014
Aperçu des statistiques de l'état civil et de l'espérance de vie à la naissance : 2010 - 2014 (continued - suite)

Continent, country or area and year / Continent, pays ou zone et année	Code[a]	Live births / Naissances vivantes — Number Nombre	Crude birth rate Taux brut de natalité	Code[a]	Deaths / Décès — Number Nombre	Crude death rate Taux brut de mortalité	Rate of natural increase Taux d'accroissement naturel	Code[a]	Infant deaths / Décès d'enfants de moins d'un an — Number Nombre	Rate (per 1000 births) Taux (par 1000 naissances)	Male[b] Masculin[b]	Female[b] Féminin[b]	Total fertility rate L'indice synthétique de fécondité
EUROPE													
Portugal													
2012	C	89 841[25]	8.5	C	107 612[26]	10.2	-1.7	C	303[26]	3.4	III76.7	82.6	1.284
2013	C	82 787[25]	7.9	C	106 543[26]	10.2	-2.3	C	244[26]	2.9	III76.9	82.8	...
2014	C	82 367[25]	7.9	C*	104 782[26]	10.0	-2.1	...	...	...	...	...	...
Republic of Moldova - République de Moldova[89]													
2010	C	40 474	11.4	C	43 631	12.2	-0.9	C	476	11.8	65.0	73.4	1.309
2011	C	39 182	11.0	C	39 249	11.0	0.0	C	431	11.0	...	...	1.266
2012	C	39 435	11.1	C	39 560	11.1	0.0	C	387	9.8	67.2	75.0	1.279
2013	C	37 871	10.6	C	38 060	10.7	-0.1	C	359	9.5	...	...	...
2014	C	38 616	10.9	C*	39 489	11.1	-0.2	...	...	...	...	...	...
Romania - Roumanie													
2010	C	212 199	10.5	C	259 723	12.8	-2.3	C	2 078	9.8	III69.8	77.3	1.327
2011	C	196 242	9.7	C	251 439	12.5	-2.7	C	1 850	9.4	III70.1	77.5	1.251
2012	C	201 104	10.0	C	255 539	12.7	-2.7	C	1 812	9.0	III70.7	77.9	1.302
2013	C	182 313	9.1	C	246 967	12.4	-3.2	C	1 677	9.2	III71.2	78.3	...
2014	C*	183 785	9.2	...	...	...	...	...	...	...	...	...	...
Russian Federation - Fédération de Russie													
2010	C	1 788 948[39]	12.5	C	2 028 516[39]	14.2	-1.7	C	13 405[39]	7.5	...	...	...
2011	C	1 796 629[39]	12.6	C	1 925 720[39]	13.5	-0.9	C	13 168[39]	7.3	64.0	75.6	...
2012	C	1 902 084[39]	13.3	C	1 906 335[39]	13.3	0.0	C	16 306[39]	8.6	64.6	75.9	...
2013	C*	1 901 182[39]	13.2	C*	1 878 269[39]	13.1	0.2	...	...	...	...	...	...
2014	C	1 942 683[39]	...	C*	1 913 613[39]	...	...	...	...	...	...	...	...
San Marino - Saint-Marin													
2010	+C	334	10.0	+C	222	6.7	3.4	+C	1	...	...	...	...
2011	+C	325	9.7	+C	222	6.6	3.1	+C	1	...	...	...	...
2012	+C	292	8.7	+C	237	7.1	1.6	+C	-	...	81.5	86.1	...
2013	+C	320	9.6	+C	247	7.4	2.2	+C	1	...	81.7	86.4	...
2014	+C	296	8.8	...	...	...	...	...	...	...	...	...	...
Serbia - Serbie[90]													
2010	+C	68 304	9.4	+C	103 211	14.2	-4.8	+C	460	6.7	71.4	76.6	1.410
2011	+C	65 598	9.1	+C	102 935	14.2	-5.2	+C	414	6.3	71.6	76.8	1.360
2012	+C	67 257	9.3	+C	102 400	14.2	-4.9	+C	415	6.2	72.2	77.3	1.449
2013	+C	65 554	9.2	+C	100 300	14.0	-4.8	+C	413	6.3	72.5	77.7	...
2014	+C	66 461	9.3	+C*	102 197	14.3	-5.0	...	...	...	...	...	...
Slovakia - Slovaquie													
2010	C	60 410	11.2	C	53 445	9.9	1.3	C	344	5.7	71.6	78.8	1.398
2011	C	60 647	11.2	C	53 594	9.9	1.3	C	300	4.9	72.2	79.4	1.447
2012	C	55 535	10.3	C	52 437	9.7	0.6	C	321	5.8	72.5	79.5	1.339
2013	C	54 823	10.1	C	52 089	9.6	0.5	C	301	5.5	72.9	79.6	...
2014	C	55 033	10.2	...	...	...	...	...	...	...	...	...	...
Slovenia - Slovénie													
2010	C	22 343	10.9	C	18 609	9.1	1.8	C	56	2.5	76.3	82.7	1.574
2011	C	21 947	10.7	C	18 699	9.1	1.6	C	64	2.9	76.6	82.9	1.562
2012	C	21 938	10.7	C	19 257	9.4	1.3	C	36	1.6	77.0	82.9	1.581
2013	C	21 111	10.3	C	19 334	9.4	0.9	C	62	2.9	77.0	83.2	...
2014	C	21 165	10.3	C*	18 886	9.2	1.1	...	...	...	...	...	...
Spain - Espagne													
2010	C	485 252	10.4	C	380 234	8.2	2.3	C	1 531	3.2	78.9	84.9	1.369
2011	C	470 553	10.1	C	386 017	8.3	1.8	C	1 477	3.1	79.2	85.0	1.342
2012	C	453 348	9.7	C	401 122	8.6	1.1	C	1 389	3.1	79.4	85.1	1.320
2013	C	424 440	9.1	C	388 600	8.3	0.8	C	1 149	2.7	80.0	85.6	...
2014	C*	426 042	9.2	...	...	...	...	...	...	...	...	...	...
Sweden - Suède													
2010	C	115 641	12.3	C	90 487	9.6	2.7	C	294	2.5	79.5	83.5	1.985
2011	C	111 770	11.8	C	89 938	9.5	2.3	C	235	2.1	79.8	83.7	1.900
2012	C	113 177	11.9	C	91 938	9.7	2.2	C	293	2.6	79.9	83.5	1.910
2013	C	113 593	11.8	C	90 402	9.4	2.4	C	306	2.7	...	...	...
2014	C	114 907	11.8	C*	88 781	9.1	2.7	...	...	...	...	...	...

4. Vital statistics summary and life expectancy at birth: 2010 - 2014
Aperçu des statistiques de l'état civil et de l'espérance de vie à la naissance : 2010 - 2014 (continued - suite)

Continent, country or area and year — Continent, pays ou zone et année	Live births — Naissances vivantes			Deaths — Décès			Rate of natural increase — Taux d'accroissement naturel	Infant deaths — Décès d'enfants de moins d'un an			Life expectancy at birth — Espérance de vie à la naissance		Total fertility rate — L'indice synthétique de fécondité
	Code[a]	Number Nombre	Crude birth rate Taux brut de natalité	Code[a]	Number Nombre	Crude death rate Taux brut de mortalité		Code[a]	Number Nombre	Rate (per 1000 births) Taux (par 1000 naissances)	Male[b] Masculin[b]	Female[b] Féminin[b]	
EUROPE													
Switzerland - Suisse													
2010	C	80 290	10.3	C	62 649	8.0	2.3	C	307	3.8	II79.9	84.4	1.540
2011	C	80 808	10.2	C	62 091	7.8	2.4	C	305	3.8	II80.2	84.5	...
2012	C	82 164	10.3	C	64 173	8.0	2.2	C	296	3.6	II80.4	84.6	1.526
2013	C	82 731	10.2	C	64 961	8.0	2.2	...	...	...	...	...	...
2014	C	83 753	10.3	C*	62 800	7.7	2.6	...	...	...	...	...	...
TFYR of Macedonia - L'ex-R. y. de Macédoine													
2010	C	24 296	11.8	C	19 113	9.3	2.5	C	185	7.6	...	...	1.553
2011	C	22 770	11.1	C	19 465	9.5	1.6	C	172	7.6	73.0	77.0	1.458
2012	C	23 568	11.4	C	20 134	9.8	1.7	C	230	9.8	...	...	1.507
2013	C	23 138	11.2	C	19 208	9.3	1.9	C	237	10.2	...	...	...
2014	C	23 596	11.4	C*	19 682	9.5	1.9	...	...	...	...	...	...
Ukraine													
2010	+C	497 689[91]	10.8	+C	698 235[92]	15.2	-4.4	+C	4 564[92]	9.2	II65.3	75.5	1.430
2011	+C	502 595[91]	11.0	+C	664 588[92]	14.5	-3.5	+C	4 511[92]	9.0	66.0	75.9	1.459
2012	+C	520 705[91]	11.4	+C	663 139[92]	14.5	-3.1	+C	4 371[92]	8.4	66.1	76.0	1.531
2013	+C	503 657[91]	11.1	+C	662 368[92]	14.6	-3.5	+C	4 030[92]	8.0	66.3	76.2	...
United Kingdom of Great Britain and Northern Ireland - Royaume-Uni de Grande-Bretagne et d'Irlande du Nord[93]													
2010	C	807 271[94]	12.9	+C	561 666	8.9	3.9	+C	3 504	4.3	...	...	...
2011	C	807 776[94]	12.8	+C	552 232	8.7	4.0	+C	3 502	4.3	...	...	1.913
2012	C	812 970[94]	12.8	+C	569 024	8.9	3.8	+C	3 347	4.1	79.0	82.7	1.920
2013	C	778 358[94]	12.1	+C	574 945	9.0	3.2	...	...	...	...	...	...
2014	C*	776 351[94]	12.1	...	...	...	...	...	...	...	...	...	...
OCEANIA - OCÉANIE													
American Samoa - Samoas américaines													
2010	C	1 279	19.0	C	247	3.7	15.3	C	19	...	...	...	...
2011	C	1 287	...	C	283	...	...	C	9	...	...	...	...
Australia - Australie													
2010	+C	303 318	13.8	+C	143 473	6.5	7.3	+C	1 229	4.1	III79.5	84.0	1.954
2011	+C	301 617	13.5	+C	146 932	6.6	6.9	+C	1 140	3.8	III79.8	84.2	1.917
2012	+C	309 582	13.6	+C	147 098	6.5	7.1	+C	1 031	3.3	III79.9	84.3	1.930
2013	+C	308 065	13.3	+C	147 678	6.4	6.9	+C	1 094	3.6	III80.1	84.3	1.882
Cook Islands - Îles Cook[95]													
2010	+C	286	12.1	+C	92	3.9	8.2	+C	2	...	...	...	...
2011	+C	262	13.6	+C	72	3.7	9.8	+C	2	...	...	...	...
2012	+C	259	13.3	+C	104	5.3	7.9	+C	1	...	...	...	...
2013	+C	256	13.8	+C	115	6.2	7.6	+C	-	...	...	...	...
2014	+C*	204	11.0	+C*	113	6.1	4.9	...	...	...	...	...	...
Fiji - Fidji													
2012	+C	20 178	23.5	+C	6 724	7.8	15.7	...	...	...	...	...	...
French Polynesia - Polynésie française													
2010	C	4 578	17.1	C	1 261	4.7	12.4	C	25	...	73.2	78.3	2.130
2011	C	4 375	16.2	C	1 242	4.6	11.6	C	22	...	...	...	...
2012	C	4 295	16.0	C	1 359	5.1	10.9	C	32	7.5	73.3	78.2	...
Guam													
2010	C	3 419[96]	21.5	C	872[96]	5.5	16.0	C	51[96]	14.9	75.1	81.4	2.520
2011	C	3 298[96]	20.7	C	842[96]	5.3	15.4	C	42[96]	12.7	75.3	81.6	2.480
2012	C	3 604[96]	22.5	C	894[96]	5.6	16.9	C	42[96]	11.7	75.5	81.7	2.450

4. Vital statistics summary and life expectancy at birth: 2010 - 2014
Aperçu des statistiques de l'état civil et de l'espérance de vie à la naissance : 2010 - 2014 (continued - suite)

Continent, country or area and year / Continent, pays ou zone et année	Code[a]	Live births Number	Live births Crude birth rate	Code[a]	Deaths Number	Deaths Crude death rate	Rate of natural increase	Code[a]	Infant deaths Number	Infant deaths Rate (per 1000 births)	Male[b]	Female[b]	Total fertility rate
OCEANIA - OCÉANIE													
Guam													
2013	C	3 329[96]	20.8	C	904[96]	5.6	15.1	C	21[96]	...	75.6	81.9	2.410
2014	C	3 396[96]	21.1	C	952[96]	5.9	15.2	C	28[96]	...	75.8	82.1	2.380
Kiribati													
2010		...	...	U	599	...	...		...	...	...	...	...
2011		...	...	U	494	...	...		...	...	...	...	...
Nauru													
2010	C	322	...	C	69	...	...		...	...	...	...	...
2011	C	370	36.7	C	75	7.4	29.2		...	...	...	...	...
2012	C	319	...		...	...	...		...	...	...	...	...
2013	C	366	...		...	...	...		...	...	...	...	...
New Caledonia - Nouvelle-Calédonie													
2010	C	4 178	16.7	C	1 191	4.8	11.9	C	19	...	74.4	80.7	...
2011	C	4 119	16.2	C	1 320	5.2	11.0	C	20	...	...	...	...
2012	C	4 389	17.0	C	1 322	5.1	11.9	C	17	...	...	...	...
New Zealand - Nouvelle-Zélande													
2010	+C	63 897	14.7	+C	28 438[26]	6.5	8.2	+C	325[26]	5.1	...	...	2.174
2011	+C	61 403	14.0	+C	30 082[26]	6.9	7.1	+C	290[26]	4.7	III79.1	82.8	2.095
2012	+C	61 178	13.9	+C	30 099[26]	6.8	7.1	+C	256[26]	4.2	III79.3	83.0	2.097
2013	+C	58 717	13.2	+C	29 568[26]	6.7	6.6	+C	260[26]	4.4	III79.7	83.2	2.007
2014	+C	57 242	12.7	+C	31 063[26]	6.9	5.8	+C	326[26]	5.7	III79.6	83.3	1.924
Niue - Nioué													
2010	C	25[97]	...	C	15[98]	...	...		...	...	...	...	...
2011	C	22[97]	...	C	9[98]	...	...		...	...	...	...	...
Norfolk Island - Île Norfolk[99]													
2010	+C	21	...	+C	16	...	...		...	...	...	...	...
2011	+C	13	...	+C	18	...	...		...	...	...	...	...
2012	+C	4	...	+C	20	...	...		...	...	...	...	...
2013		...	...	+C	11	...	...		...	...	...	...	...
2014		...	...	+C	13	...	...		...	...	...	...	...
Northern Mariana Islands - Îles Mariannes septentrionales													
2010	U	1 072[100]	...		...	...	...		...	...	...	...	2.200
Palau - Palaos													
2010	C	247	11.9	C	168	8.1	3.8	C	3	...	...	...	...
2011	C	247	11.8	C	173	8.3	3.5	C	1	...	...	...	...
2012	C	268	12.7	C	164	7.8	4.9	C	2	...	...	...	...
2013	C	229	...	C	192	...	...	C	4	...	...	...	...
Pitcairn													
2011	C	-	...		...	...	...		...	...	...	...	...
2012	C	-	...		...	...	...		...	...	...	...	...
2013	C	-	...		...	...	...		...	...	...	...	...
Samoa													
2010	+U	1 381[101]	...	+U	127[101]	...	...		...	...	...	...	...
2011	+U	2 354[101]	...	+U	591[101]	...	...		...	...	...	...	4.700
Tokelau - Tokélaou[102]													
2011	I	16	...		...	...	...		...	...	...	...	...

FOOTNOTES - NOTES

Italics: data from civil registers which are incomplete or of unknown completeness. - Italiques : données incomplètes ou dont le degré d'exactitude n'est pas connu, provenant des registres de l'état civil.

* Provisional. - Données provisoires.

[a] 'Code' indicates the source of data, as follows:
C - Civil registration, estimated over 90% complete
U - Civil registration, estimated less than 90% complete
| - Other source, estimated reliable
+ - Data tabulated by date of registration rather than occurence
... - Information not available

Le 'Code' indique la source des données, comme suit :

C - Registres de l'état civil considérés complets à 90 p. 100 au moins

U - Registres de l'état civil qui ne sont pas considérés complets à 90 p. 100 au moins

| - Autre source, considérée fiable

+ - Données exploitées selon la date de l'enregistrement et non la date de l'événement

... - Information non disponible

[b] A Roman number in front of the data for males specifies the range of the reference period of life expectancy for males and females presented on the row. For example, a reference year of 2005 and a range of V years means that the reference period for the life expectancy is 2001 - 2005. The absence of a Roman number means the reference period is one year and the reference period therefore coincides with the reference year. - Un chiffre romain devant la donnée relative aux hommes indique l'étendue de la période de référence concernant l'espérance de vie des hommes et des femmes présentée dans la ligne. Par exemple, une année de référence 2005 et une étendue de V signifie que la période de référence pour l'espérance de vie est 2001-2005. L'absence de chiffre romain signifie que la période de référence est d'un an et donc coïncide avec l'année de référence.

[1] Excluding live-born infants who died before their birth was registered. Data refer to Algerian population only. - Non compris les enfants nés vivants décédés avant l'enregistrement de leur naissance. Les données ne concernent que la population algérienne.

[2] Data refer to Algerian population only. - Les données ne concernent que la population algérienne.

[3] Data are projections presented in Annuaire Statistique 2010. - Les données sont des projections présentées dans l'Annuaire Statistique 2010.

[4] Data refer to national projections. - Les données se réfèrent aux projections nationales.

[5] Source: Vital Statistics Report 2012. - Source: Vital Statistics Report 2012.

[6] Data refer to the recorded events in Ministry of Health hospitals and health centres only. - Les données se rapportent aux faits d'état civil enregistrés dans les hôpitaux et les dispensaires du Ministère de la santé seulement.

[7] Data refer to the 12 months preceding the census in September. - Les données se rapportent aux 12 mois précédant le recensement de septembre.

[8] Excludes the islands of St. Brandon and Agalega. - Non compris les îles St. Brandon et Agalega.

[9] Data refer to the 12 months preceding the census in August. - Les données se rapportent aux 12 mois précédant le recensement d'août.

[10] Excluding live-born infants who died before their birth was registered. - Non compris les enfants nés vivants décédés avant l'enregistrement de leur naissance.

[11] Data refer to the 12 months preceding the census in May. - Les données se rapportent aux 12 mois précédant le recensement de mai.

[12] Based on estimates and projections from 'Agence Nationale de la Statistique et de la Démographie'. - Données fondées sur des estimations et des projections provenant de l'Agence Nationale de la Statistique et de la Démographie.

[13] Based on preliminary findings of 2011 Uganda Demographic and Health Survey. - D'après les résultats préliminaires de l'enquête de 2011 sur la démographie et la santé en Ouganda.

[14] Based on the results of the 2012 Population and Housing Census. - D'après les résultats du recensement de la population et des logements de 2012.

[15] Data refer to the 12 months preceding the census in October. - Les données se rapportent aux 12 mois précédant le recensement d'octobre.

[16] Excluding visitors. - Ne comprend pas les visiteurs.

[17] Excluding non-residents and foreign service personnel and their dependants. - À l'exclusion des non-résidents et du personnel diplomatique et de leurs charges de famille.

[18] Including Canadian residents temporarily in the United States, but excluding United States residents temporarily in Canada. Data refer to the twelve months from 1 July of the current year to 30 June of the following year. - Y compris les résidents canadiens se trouvant temporairement aux Etats-Unis, mais ne comprenant pas les résidents des Etats-Unis se trouvant temporairement au Canada. Les données font référence aux douze mois de 1 juillet de l'année actuelle à 30 juin de l'année suivante.

[19] Including unknown sex. - Y compris le sexe inconnu.

[20] Because of the small population and the resulting small numbers of deaths, the data for the calendar years 2008-2010 have been aggregated to construct a more reliable life table. - La population étant peu élevée et, par conséquent, le nombre de décès aussi, les données des années civiles 2008, 2009 et 2010 ont été agrégées afin d'améliorer la fiabilité de la table de mortalité.

[21] Excluding children born in the country of non-resident mothers. - Exceptés les enfants nés dans le pays des mères non-résidentes.

[22] Excluding infant deaths to mothers living abroad. - Exception faite des décès d'enfants en bas âge survenus lorsque la mère résidait à l'étranger.

[23] Data have been adjusted for underenumeration. - Les données ont été ajustées pour compenser les lacunes du dénombrement.

[24] Data have been adjusted for undercoverage of infant deaths and sudden and violent deaths. - Ajusté pour la sous-estimation de la mortalité infantile, du nombre de morts soudaines et de morts violentes.

[25] Data refer to births to resident mothers. - Ces données concernent les enfants nés de mères résidentes.

[26] Data refer to resident population only. - Pour la population résidante seulement.

[27] Excluding Indian jungle population. - Non compris les Indiens de la jungle.

[28] Source: Population Registry and STAT/CBS estimates. - Source: Estimations du registre de la population/STAT/CBS.

[29] Data refer to the 12 months preceding the census in November. - Données se rapportant aux 12 mois précédant le recensement de novembre.

[30] Including births abroad and births of unknown residence of mother. - Y compris les naissances à l'étranger et les naissances pour lesquelles le lieu de résidence de la mère est inconnu.

[31] Including deaths abroad and deaths of unknown place of residence. - Y compris décès à l'étranger et décès dont le lieu de résidence n'est pas connu.

[32] Including deaths abroad and deaths of unknown residence of mother. - Y compris décès à l'étranger et décès de nourrissons nés de mères dont le lieu de résidence n'est pas connu.

[33] Projected value based on the results of 2000 and 2010 censuses, statistics from civil registration and reporting of live births in the ministry of health system. - Projection basée sur les résultats des recensements de 2000 et 2010, des statistiques d'état civil et les registres des naissances vivantes du Ministère de la santé.

[34] Data refer to projections based on the 2005 Population Census. - Les données se réfèrent aux projections basées sur le recensement de la population de 2005.

[35] Estimate for 2010 – 2015. - Estimation pour la période 2010-2015.

[36] Excludes nomadic Indian tribes. - Non compris les tribus d'Indiens nomades.

[37] Excludes nomadic Indian tribes. Data refer to national projections. - Non compris les tribus d'Indiens nomades. Les données se réfèrent aux projections nationales.

[38] Source: Reports of the Ministry of Health. - Source : Rapports du Ministère de la Santé.

[39] Excluding infants born alive of less than 28 weeks' gestation, of less than 1 000 grams in weight and 35 centimeters in length, who die within seven days of birth. - Non compris les enfants nés vivants après moins de 28 semaines de gestation, pesant moins de 1 000 grammes, mesurant moins de 35 centimètres et décédés dans les sept jours qui ont suivi leur naissance.

[40] Deaths include deaths among some visitors. Sources: Births and Deaths National Registration System database, and Salmaniya Medical Complex Discharges System database. - Les décès comprennent des décès parmi certains visiteurs. Les sources: Les bases de données des << Births and Deaths National Registration System >> et << Salmaniya Medical Complex Discharges System >>.

[41] For statistical purposes, the data for China do not include those for the Hong Kong Special Administrative Region (Hong Kong SAR), Macao Special Administrative Region (Macao SAR) and Taiwan province of China. - Pour la présentation des statistiques, les données pour la Chine ne comprennent pas la Région Administrative Spéciale de Hong Kong (Hong Kong RAS), la Région Administrative Spéciale de Macao (Macao RAS) et Taïwan province de Chine.

[42] Data have been estimated on the basis of the annual National Sample Survey on Population Changes. - Les données ont été estimées sur la base de l'enquête annuelle "National Sample Survey on Population Changes".

[43] The fertility rates have been compiled using a population denominator which has excluded female foreign domestic helpers. - Les taux de fécondité ont été compilés pour une population (en dénominateur) ne comprenant pas les domestiques étrangères.

[44] Data refer to government controlled areas. - Les données se rapportent aux zones contrôlées par le Gouvernement.

[45] Data refer to deaths of residents only. - Les données renvoient aux décès de résidents uniquement.

[46] Includes data for the Indian-held part of Jammu and Kashmir, the final status of which has not yet been determined. - Y compris les données pour la partie du Jammu et du Cachemire occupée par l'Inde dont le statut définitif n'a pas encore été déterminé.

[47] Rates were obtained by the Sample Registration System of India, which is a large demographic survey. - Les taux ont été obtenus par le Système de l'enregistrement par échantillon de l'Inde qui est une large enquête démographique.

[48] Data are based on the publication: "Welfare Indicators", table "Health and Nutrition Indicators, Infant Mortality Rates" - Les données sont basées sur la publication : << Welfare Indicators >>, le tableau << Health and Nutrition Indicators, Infant Mortality Rates >>

[49] Data refer to the Iranian Year which begins on 21 March and ends on 20 March of the following year. - Les données concernent l'année iranienne, qui commence le 21 mars et se termine le 20 mars de l'année suivante.

[50] Includes data for East Jerusalem and Israeli residents in certain other territories under occupation by Israeli military forces since June 1967. - Y compris les données pour Jérusalem-Est et les résidents israéliens dans certains autres territoires occupés depuis 1967 par les forces armées israéliennes.

[51] Including deaths abroad of Israeli residents who were out of the country for less than a year. - Y compris les décès à l'étranger de résidents israéliens qui ont quitté le pays depuis moins d'un an.

[52] Data refer to Japanese nationals in Japan only. - Les données se raportent aux nationaux japonais au Japon seulement.

[53] Excluding data for Jordanian territory under occupation since June 1967 by Israeli military forces. Excluding foreigners, including registered Palestinian refugees. - Non compris les données pour le territoire jordanien occupé depuis juin 1967 par les forces armées israéliennes. Non compris les étrangers, mais y compris les réfugiés de Palestine enregistrés.

[54] Based on the results of the 2005 Population and Housing Census. - Données fondées sur les résultats du recensement de la population et de l'habitat de 2005.

[55] Data refer to urban areas only. - Données ne concernant que les zones urbaines.

[56] Based on the results of the 2014 Population Census. - D'après les résultats du recensement de la population de 2014.

[57] Data refer to the 12 months preceding the census in June. - Les données se rapportent aux 12 mois précédant le recensement de juin.

[58] Data from Births and Deaths Notification System (Ministry of Health and all health care providers). Data for all population, citizens and foreigners. - Les données proviennent du système de notification des naissances et des décès (Ministère de la santé et tous prestataires de soins de santé). Les données portent sur la population entière, les citoyens et les étrangers.

[59] Data refer to residence of child. Excluding alien armed forces, civilian aliens employed by armed forces, and foreign diplomatic personnel and their dependants. - Les données correspondent à la résidence de l'enfant. Non compris les militaires étrangers, les civils étrangers employés par les forces armées ni le personnel diplomatique étranger et les membres de leur famille les accompagnant.

[60] Excluding alien armed forces, civilian aliens employed by armed forces, and foreign diplomatic personnel and their dependants. - Non compris les militaires étrangers, les civils étrangers employés par les forces armées ni le personnel diplomatique étranger et les membres de leur famille les accompagnant.

[61] Projections based on the final results of the 2004 Population and Housing Census. - Projections basées sur les résultats définitifs du recensement de la population et de l'habitat de 2004.

[62] Data refer to resident population which comprises Singapore citizens and permanent residents. - Les données se rapportent à la population résidente composé des citoyens de Singapour et des résidents permanents.

[63] Data refer to resident total fertility rate. - Les données se rapportent aux indices synthétique de fécondité de la population résidante.

[64] Provisional data. Data refer to resident population which comprises Singapore citizens and permanent residents. - Données provisoires. Les données se rapportent à la population résidente composé des citoyens de Singapour et des résidents permanents.

[65] Source: Palestinian Central Bureau of Statistics, Population Register, updated version 05/01/2015. - Source: Bureau central de statistique palestinien, registre de la population, version actualisée jusqu'au 05/01/2015.

[66] Source: Palestinian Family Health Survey, 2010. - Source: Enquête palestinienne sur la santé familiale, 2010.

[67] Source: Palestinian Multiple Indicator Cluster Survey 2014. - Source: Enquête palestinienne par grappes à indicateurs multiples, 2014.

[68] Excluding live-born infants who died before their birth was registered. Excluding nomad population and Palestinian refugees. - Non compris les enfants nés vivants décédés avant l'enregistrement de leur naissance. Non compris la population nomade et les réfugiés de Palestine.

[69] Data have been adjusted for under-registration. Excluding infants born alive of less than 28 weeks' gestation, of less than 1 000 grams in weight and 35 centimeters in length, who die within seven days of birth. - Y compris un ajustement pour sous-enregistrement. Non compris les enfants nés vivants après moins de 28 semaines de gestations, pesant moins de 1 000 grammes, mesurant moins de 35 centimètres et décédés dans les sept jours qui ont suivi leur naissance.

[70] The registration of births and deaths is conducted by the Ministry of Health. An estimate of completeness is not provided. - L'enregistrement des naissances et des décès est mené par le Ministère de la Santé. Le degré estimatif de complétude n'est pas fourni.

[71] Including Non-Yemeni births. - Y compris les naissances non-yéménites.

[72] Including Non-Yemeni deaths. - Y compris les décès non-yéménites.

[73] Including deaths of nationals abroad. - Y compris les décès des nationaux survenus à l'étranger.

[74] Including armed forces stationed outside the country, but excluding alien armed forces stationed in the area. - Y compris les militaires nationaux hors du pays, mais non compris les militaires étrangers en garnison sur le territoire.

[75] A live-born child is a child fully expelled or removed out of the mother's body, who gives a sign of life and whose birth weight is (a) 500 g or more, or (b) lower than 500 g, if it survives 24 hours after delivery. - Un enfant né vivant est un enfant qui a été entièrement expulsé ou retiré du corps de la mère, qui présente des signes de vie et dont le poids à la naissance est : a) soit égal ou supérieur à 500 grammes; b) soit inférieur à 500 grammes s'il survit plus de 24 heures après l'accouchement.

[76] Excluding Faeroe Islands and Greenland shown separately, if available. - Non compris les Iles Féroé et le Groenland, qui font l'objet de rubriques distinctes, si disponible.

[77] Excluding Åland Islands. - Non compris les Îles d'Åland.

[78] Including armed forces stationed outside the country. - Y compris les militaires nationaux hors du pays.

[79] Provisional data. - Données provisoires.

[80] Including live births by military personnel and their dependants. - Y compris les naissances vivantes parmi les membres du personnel militaire et leurs personnes à charge.

[81] Excluding armed forces. - Non compris les militaires en garnison.

[82] Starting from 2013 data refer only to infant deaths among usual residents regardless whether it occurred in the country or abroad. - A partir de 2013, les données se rapportent seulement aux décès d'enfants de moins d'un an parmi les résidents habituels, survenus dans le pays ou hors du pays.

[83] Definition of localities was revised in 2011 causing a break with the previous series. - La rupture par rapport aux séries précédentes s'explique par le fait que la définition des localités a été révisée depuis 2011.

[84] Data refer to events registered within one year of occurrence. - Les données portent sur des événements enregistrés dans l'année pendant laquelle ils sont survenus.

[85] Including residents outside the country. - Y compris les résidents hors du pays.

[86] Including still births. - Les données comprennent les mortinaissances.

[87] Including residents outside the country if listed in a Netherlands population register. - Englobe les résidents se trouvant à l'étranger à condition qu'ils soient inscrits sur le registre de population des Pays-Bas.

[88] Including residents temporarily outside the country. - Y compris les résidents se trouvant temporairement hors du pays.

[89] Excluding Transnistria and the municipality of Bender. - Les données ne tiennent pas compte de l'information sur la Transnistria et la municipalité de Bender.

[90] Excludes data for Kosovo and Metohia. - Sans les données pour le Kosovo et Metohie.

[91] Data refer to births with weight 500g and more (if weight is unknown - with length 25 centimeters and more, or with gestation during 22 weeks or more). - Données concernant les nouveau-nés de 500 grammes ou plus (si le poids est inconnu – de 25 centimètres de long ou plus, ou après une grossesse de 22 semaines ou plus).

[92] Data includes deaths resulting from births with weight 500g and more (if weight is unknown - with length 25 centimeters and more, or with gestation during 22 weeks or more). - Y compris les décès de nouveau-nés de 500 grammes ou plus (si le poids est inconnu – de 25 centimètres de long ou plus, ou après une grossesse de 22 semaines ou plus).

[93] Excluding Channel Islands (Guernsey and Jersey) and Isle of Man, shown separately, if available. - Non compris les îles Anglo-Normandes (Guernesey et Jersey) et l'île de Man, qui font l'objet de rubriques distinctes, si disponible.

[94] Data tabulated by date of occurrence for England and Wales, and by date of registration for Northern Ireland and Scotland. - Données exploitées selon la date de l'événement pour l'Angleterre et le pays de Galles, et selon la date de l'enregistrement pour l'Irlande du Nord et l'Ecosse.

[95] Excluding Niue, shown separately, which is part of Cook Islands, but because of remoteness is administered separately. - Non compris Nioué, qui fait l'objet d'une rubrique distincte et qui fait partie des îles Cook, mais qui, en raison de son éloignement, est administrée séparément.

[96] Including United States military personnel, their dependants and contract employees. - Y compris les militaires des Etats-Unis, les membres de leur famille les accompagnant et les agents contractuels des Etats-Unis.

[97] Includes children born in New Zealand to women resident in Niue who chose to travel to New Zealand to give birth. - Y compris les enfants nés en Nouvelle-Zélande de femmes résidant à Nioué qui ont choisi de se rendre en Nouvelle-Zélande pour accoucher.

[98] Includes deaths occurred in New Zealand but buried in Niue and deaths occurred in Niue but buried elsewhere. - Y compris les personnes décédées en Nouvelle-Zélande qui sont enterrées à Nioué et les personnes décédées à Nioué qui sont enterrées ailleurs.

[99] Data cover the period from 1 July of the previous year to 30 June of the present year. - Pour la période allant du 1er juillet de l'année précédente au 30 juin de l'année en cours.

[100] Source: U.S. National Center for Health Statistics, National Vital Statistics Reports (NVSR). - Source : US National Center for Health Statistics, National Vital Statistics Reports (NVSR).

[101] The coverage of registration is estimated at 70 per cent. - Le degré de complétude de l'enregistrement est évalué à 70 pour cent.

[102] Data refer to usually resident population present on census night. Data refer to the 12 months preceding the census in October. - Les données concernent la population habituellement résidente présente la nuit du recensement. Les données se rapportent aux 12 mois précédant le recensement de octobre.

Table 5 - *Demographic Yearbook 2014*

Table 5 presents national estimates of mid-year population for all available years between 2005 and 2014.

Description of variables: Mid-year estimates of the total population are those provided by national statistical offices. They refer to the *de facto* or *de jure* population on 1 July of the reference year. Exceptions to this are footnoted accordingly. The data are presented in thousands, rounded by the Statistics Division of the United Nations Department of Economic and Social Affairs.

For some countries or areas the figures presented in this table and the figures used to calculate rates in subsequent tables are not the same, as these countries have provided a reference population for vital events that is different than the total population.

Unless otherwise indicated, all estimates relate to the population within present geographical boundaries. Major exceptions to this principle are explained in footnotes.

Reliability of data: Reliable mid-year population estimates are those that are based on a complete census (or on a sample survey) and have been adjusted on a basis of a continuous population register or on the balance of births, deaths and migration. Reliable mid-year estimates appear in roman type. Mid-year estimates that are not calculated on this basis are considered less reliable and are shown in *italics*.

Limitations: Statistics on estimates of the mid-year total population are subject to the same qualifications as have been set forth for population statistics in general in section 3 of the Technical Notes.

International comparability of mid-year population estimates is also affected by the fact that some of these estimates refer to the *de jure*, and not the *de facto*, population. These are indicated in the column titled "Code". The difference between the *de facto* and the *de jure* population is discussed in section 3.1.1 of the Technical Notes.

Earlier data: Estimates of mid-year population have been shown in previous issues of the *Demographic Yearbook*. Information on the years and specific topics covered is presented in the Historical Index.

Tableau 5 – *Annuaire démographique 2014*

Le tableau 5 présente des estimations nationales de la population en milieu d'année pour le plus grand nombre possible d'années entre 2005 et 2014.

Description des variables : les estimations de la population totale en milieu d'année sont celles qui ont été communiquées par les services nationaux de statistique. Elles correspondent à la population de fait ou se réfèrent à la population de droit, au 1er juillet de l'année de référence. Lorsque la date est différente, cela est signalé par une note. Sauf indication contraire, tous les chiffres sont exprimés en milliers. Les données ont été arrondies par la Division de statistique du Département des affaires économiques et sociales de l'Organisation des Nations Unies.

Pour certains pays ou territoires, les données présentées dans ce tableau sont différentes des données utilisées pour calculer les taux dans les tableaux suivants, parce que ces pays ont fourni une population de référence pour les événements démographiques différente de la population totale.

Sauf indication contraire, toutes les estimations se rapportent à la population présente sur le territoire actuel des pays ou zones considérés. Les principales exceptions à cette règle sont expliquées en note.

Fiabilité des données : les estimations de la population en milieu d'année sont considérées sûres quand elles sont fondées sur un recensement complet (ou sur une enquête par sondage) et ont été ajustées en fonction des données provenant d'un registre permanent de population ou en fonction des naissances, décès et mouvements migratoires qui ont eu lieu pendant la période. Les estimations considérées comme sûres apparaissent en caractères romains. Les estimations dont le calcul n'a pas été effectué sur cette base sont considérées comme moins sûres et apparaissent en italique.

Insuffisance des données : les statistiques concernant les estimations de la population totale en milieu d'année appellent toutes les réserves qui ont été formulées à la section 3 des Notes techniques à propos des statistiques de la population en général.

Le fait que certaines des estimations concernant la population en milieu d'année se réfèrent à la population de droit et non à la population de fait influe sur la comparabilité internationale. Ces cas ont été signalés dans la colonne « Code ». La différence entre la population de fait et la population de droit est expliquée à la section 3.1.1 des Notes techniques.

Données publiées antérieurement : des estimations de la population en milieu d'année ont été publiées dans des éditions antérieures de l'*Annuaire démographique*. Pour plus de précisions concernant les années et les sujets pour lesquels des données ont été publiées, se reporter à l'index.

5. Estimates of mid-year population: 2005 - 2014
Estimations de la population au milieu de l'année : 2005 - 2014

Continent and country or area / Continent et pays ou zone	Code[a]	Population estimates (in thousands) - Estimations (en milliers)									
		2005	2006	2007	2008	2009	2010	2011	2012	2013	2014
AFRICA - AFRIQUE											
Algeria - Algérie	DJ	32 906	33 481	34 096	34 591	35 268	35 978	36 717	37 495	38 297	39 114
Benin - Bénin[1]	DF	7 447	7 700	7 959	8 225	8 498	8 779	9 067	9 365	...	...
Botswana	DJ	1 708	1 720	1 736	1 755	1 776	1 823	1 850	...	...	...
Burkina Faso	DJ	13 374	...	14 252[1]	14 731[1]	15 225[1]	15 731[1]	...	...	...	...
Burundi[2]	DF	...	...	...	...	8 263	8 488	8 727	8 981	9 249	9 530
Cabo Verde	DF	475	483	491	500	509	518	527	...	...	...
Cameroon - Cameroun[3]	DJ	...	...	...	...	18 928	19 406	19 865	20 387	21 143	...
Congo	DF	3 488[1]	3 589[1]	3 616[1]	3 741	3 838	...	...	...	4 278	...
Côte d'Ivoire[1]	DF	19 097	19 658	20 228	20 807	21 395	...	...	...	...	...
Djibouti[4]	DF	...	754	775	797	...	841	865	...	...	...
Egypt - Égypte	DF	70 653	72 009	73 644	75 194	76 925	78 685	80 530	82 550	84 629	86 814
Ethiopia - Éthiopie[5]	DF	73 044	75 067	77 127	79 221	...	...	...	...	...	...
Gabon[6]	DF	1 313	...	...	...	...	...	...	...	...	...
Gambia - Gambie	DF	1 436	1 510	...	...	...	...	...	...	...	...
Ghana[1]	DF	21 367	21 876	22 388	22 901	23 417	...	25 235	25 825	26 428	27 043
Guinea - Guinée[1]	DF	9 064	...	...	10 183	10 218	10 537	10 864	...	...	...
Guinea-Bissau - Guinée-Bissau[1]	DF	1 326	1 357	1 389	...	...	1 558	...	...	...	...
Kenya	DF	35 267[7]	36 433[7]	37 184[7]	38 300[7]	...	38 910[8]	39 545[8]	40 652[8]	41 793[8]	42 961[8]
Lesotho[1]	DF	...	1 866	1 880	1 884	1 887	1 892	1 897	...	...	...
Liberia - Libéria	DF	...	3 332	3 404	...	3 551	3 627	3 705	3 784	3 865	3 946
Libya - Libye	DF	5 209	...	5 393	5 490	5 589	5 689	5 791	5 892	5 994	6 096
Madagascar	DF	17 550	18 048	18 556	19 072	19 601	20 142	20 696	...	...	...
Malawi[1]	DF	12 341	12 758	13 188	13 630	14 085	13 949[9]	14 389[9]	14 845[9]	...	...
Mali[10]	DF	11 732	12 051	12 378	12 706	...	...	...	...	...	...
Mauritania - Mauritanie[1]	DF	2 906	2 990	3 075	3 162	3 251	3 341	3 297	...	...	...
Mauritius - Maurice[11]	DJ	1 243[12]	1 253[12]	1 260[12]	1 269[12]	1 275[12]	1 281[12]	1 252[13]	1 256[13]	1 259[13]	1 261[13]
Morocco - Maroc[14]	DF	30 172	30 509	30 850	31 195	31 543	31 894	32 245	32 597	32 950	33 774
Mozambique[1]	DF	19 420	19 889	20 632	21 208	21 803	22 417	23 050	23 701	24 366	25 042
Namibia - Namibie	DF	1 957[1]	1 992[1]	2 028[1]	2 065[1]	2 104[1]	2 143[1]	2 116[15]	2 155[15]	2 196[15]	2 238[15]
Niger[1]	DJ	12 628	13 045	13 716	14 198	14 693	15 204	15 731	16 275	17 807[16]	...
Nigeria - Nigéria	DF	133 767[1]	*140 004[17]	...	...	...	...	...	...	...	...
Republic of South Sudan - République de Soudan du Sud[18]	DF	...	...	...	8 491	8 988	9 497	10 018	10 552	10 809	11 071
Reunion - Réunion	DJ	777	786	794[10]	806[10]	816[10]	*828[10]	*839[10]	...	...	...
Rwanda[1]	DF	9 225	9 468	9 557	9 832	10 117	10 413	10 718	11 033	11 356	...
Saint Helena ex. dep. - Sainte-Hélène sans dép.	DF	...	...	4	4	4	4	4	4	4[19]	4
Saint Helena: Ascension - Sainte-Hélène: Ascension	DJ	...	...	...	1	...	...	...	...	...	...
Saint Helena: Tristan da Cunha - Sainte-Hélène: Tristan da Cunha[20]	DF	...	...	0	0	0	...	...	...	...	...
Sao Tome and Principe - Sao Tomé-et-Principe	DF	149	152	155	158	161	164	167	*187	*194	...
Senegal - Sénégal[21]	DJ	10 901[19]	11 206[19]	11 519[19]	11 841[19]	12 171[19]	12 509[19]	12 842[19]	13 208	13 567	...
Seychelles	DF	83	85	85	87	87	90	87	88	90	91
Sierra Leone	DF	5 095	5 217	5 343	5 474	5 608	5 747	5 890	6 038	...	...
South Africa - Afrique du Sud	DF	47 640	48 270	48 910	49 561	50 223	50 896	51 580	52 275	52 982	54 002
Sudan - Soudan	DF	...	...	...	30 979	31 957	32 962	33 998	35 064	36 163	37 292
Swaziland	DF	1 126	1 146	1 018	1 032	1 044	1 056	1 068	1 080	1 093	1 106
Togo	DF	5 212	5 337	5 465	5 596	5 731	...	...	...	...	...
Tunisia - Tunisie	DF	10 029	10 128	10 225	10 329	10 440	10 547	10 674	10 778	10 887	...
Uganda - Ouganda	DF	26 741	27 629	28 581	29 593	30 661	31 785	32 940	34 131	...	...
United Republic of Tanzania - République Unie de Tanzanie[21]	DF	37 083	38 251	39 446	40 668	41 916	43 188	44 485	45 798	47 133	...
Zambia - Zambie[1]	DF	11 441	11 799	12 161	12 526	12 897	...	13 719	14 145	14 580	15 023
Zimbabwe[21]	DF	11 830	11 930	12 040	12 150	13 668	...	...	...	...	...
AMERICA, NORTH - AMÉRIQUE DU NORD											
Anguilla	DF	14	14	15	16	16	16	...	13	14	...
Antigua and Barbuda - Antigua-et-Barbuda	DF	83	84	86	88	89	91	...	...	...	...
Aruba	DJ	98	99	100	101	102	102	103	105	106	108

5. Estimates of mid-year population: 2005 - 2014
Estimations de la population au milieu de l'année : 2005 - 2014 (continued - suite)

Continent and country or area / Continent et pays ou zone	Code[a]	Population estimates (in thousands) - Estimations (en milliers)									
		2005	2006	2007	2008	2009	2010	2011	2012	2013	2014
AMERICA, NORTH - AMÉRIQUE DU NORD											
Bahamas[1]	DF	325	330	334	338	342	335	358	363	368	372
Barbados - Barbade	DF	273	273	274	275	...	276[19]	278	278	...	...
Belize	DF	292	301	311	307	315	324	332	341	350	359
Bermuda - Bermudes	DJ	64[22]	64[22]	64[22]	64[22]	64[22]	64[23]	63[23]	62[23]	62[23]	62[23]
British Virgin Islands - Îles Vierges britanniques	DF	25	26	27	28	28	28	28	28	29	...
Canada	DJ	32 242[24]	32 571[24]	32 888[24]	33 246[24]	33 629[24]	34 005[24]	34 343[25]	34 752[26]	35 154[26]	*35 540[27]
Cayman Islands - Îles Caïmanes	DJ	48	52	54	56	53	55	56[19]	57[19]	56[19]	58[19]
Costa Rica	DJ	4 266	4 354	4 443	4 533[28]	4 620[28]	4 538[29]	4 592[29]	4 651[29]	4 712[29]	4 772[29]
Cuba	DJ	11 218	11 211	11 195	11 181	11 174	11 171	11 172	11 174	11 192	11 224
Curaçao	DJ	138[30]	141[30]	144[30]	146[30]	147[30]	149[30]	151[30]	152[31]	154[31]	156[31]
Dominica - Dominique	DF	71	71	71	71	72	...	69	70	...	...
Dominican Republic - République dominicaine[1]	DF	8 968	9 071	9 174	9 280	9 380	9 479	9 580	9 681	9 785	9 883
El Salvador[32]	DF	6 049	6 074	6 099	6 125	6 153	6 183	6 216	6 251	6 289	6 328
Greenland - Groenland[33]	DJ	57	57	57	56	56	57	57	57	56	56
Grenada - Grenade	DF	104	105	105	105	105	105	107	108	109	...
Guadeloupe	DJ	446	458	401[34]	402[34]	402[34]	403[34]	405[34]	403[34]	404[34]	404[34]
Guatemala	DF	12 700	13 019[21]	13 345[21]	13 678[21]	14 017[21]	14 362[21]	14 714[21]	15 073[21]	...	...
Haiti - Haïti[35]	DJ	9 292	9 445	9 602	9 762	9 923	10 085	10 248	10 413	...	...
Honduras[36]	DF	7 197	7 367	7 537	7 707	7 877	8 046	8 215	...	...	...
Jamaica - Jamaïque	DJ	2 650	2 663	2 676	2 687	2 696	2 702	2 700	*2 708	...	...
Martinique[10]	DJ	396	398	398	398	396	*396	*396			
Mexico - Mexique	DJ	107 151	108 409	109 787	111 299	112 853	114 256[1]	115 683[1]	117 054[1]	118 395[1]	119 713[1]
Montserrat	DF	5	5	5	5	5	5	5	5	5	5
Nicaragua	DJ	5 450	5 523	5 596	5 669	5 742	5 816	5 889	6 071	6 134	6 198
Panama[23]	DF	3 351	3 413	3 476	3 538	3 600	3 662	3 724	3 788	3 851	3 913
Puerto Rico - Porto Rico[37]	DJ	3 821	3 805	3 783	3 761	3 740	3 721[38]	3 687[38]	3 652[38]	3 615[38]	3 548[38]
Saint Kitts and Nevis - Saint-Kitts-et-Nevis	DF	*49	*50	*51	*51	*52	...	...	...	...	...
Saint Lucia - Sainte-Lucie	DF	164	166	168	170	172	...	...	...	...	...
Saint Vincent and the Grenadines - Saint-Vincent-et-les Grenadines	DF	109	109	110	110	110	110	110	...	110	110
Sint Maarten (Dutch part) - Saint-Martin (partie néerlandaise)	DJ	37	38	39	40	39	36	33	35	37	37[10]
Trinidad and Tobago - Trinité-et-Tobago	DF	1 294[12]	1 298[12]	1 303[12]	1 309[12]	1 310[12]	1 318[12]	...	1 335[13]	1 341[13]	1 345[13]
Turks and Caicos Islands - Îles Turques et Caïques	DJ	31	33	35	*37	38	40	...	...	...	...
United States of America - États-Unis d'Amérique[39]	DJ	295 517[30]	298 380[30]	301 231[30]	304 094[30]	306 772[30]	309 326[31]	311 588[31]	313 914[31]	316 129[31]	...
United States Virgin Islands - Îles Vierges américaines[37]	DJ	110	110	110	110	*110	*110	...	...	...	...
AMERICA, SOUTH - AMÉRIQUE DU SUD											
Argentina - Argentine	DF	38 592	38 971	39 356	39 746	40 134	40 788[40]	41 262[40]	41 735[40]	42 206[40]	42 674[40]
Bolivia (Plurinational State of) - Bolivie (État plurinational de)	DF	9 211	9 373	9 535	9 697	9 859	10 023	10 187	10 351	10 516	10 681
Brazil - Brésil[41]	DF	183 383	185 564	187 642	189 613	191 481	193 253	192 376	193 947	...	...
	DJ	...	...	...	...	...	...	...	...	201 033[1]	202 769[1]
Chile - Chili	DF	16 267	16 433	16 598	16 763	16 929	17 094	17 248	17 403	17 557	17 819
Colombia - Colombie[42]	DJ	42 889	43 406	43 927	44 451	44 979	45 510	46 045	46 582	47 121	47 662
Ecuador - Équateur[43]	DF	13 721	13 965	14 215	14 473	14 738	15 012	15 266	15 521	15 775	16 027
French Guiana - Guyane française[10]	DJ	199	206	213	219	224	*230	...	...	...	...
Guyana	DF	758	768	771	774	753	752	751	749	747	...
Paraguay[21]	DF	5 899	6 009	6 120	6 230	6 341	6 451	6 562	6 673	6 783	6 894
Peru - Pérou[44]	DF	27 811	28 151	28 482[32]	28 807[32]	29 132[32]	29 462[32]	29 798[32]	30 136[32]	30 475[32]	30 814[32]
Suriname	DJ	499	506	510	517	524	531	540	...	550	...

5. Estimates of mid-year population: 2005 - 2014
Estimations de la population au milieu de l'année : 2005 - 2014 (continued - suite)

Continent and country or area / Continent et pays ou zone	Code[a]	Population estimates (in thousands) - Estimations (en milliers)									
		2005	2006	2007	2008	2009	2010	2011	2012	2013	2014
AMERICA, SOUTH - AMÉRIQUE DU SUD											
Uruguay	DF	3 352	3 358	3 359	3 363	3 378	3 397	3 413	3 426[1]	3 440[1]	3 454[1]
Venezuela (Bolivarian Republic of) - Venezuela (République bolivarienne du)	DF	26 445	26 858	27 273	27 689	28 106	28 524	28 944	29 365	29 786	30 206
ASIA - ASIE											
Afghanistan[45]	DF	22 098	22 576	23 039	23 511	23 994	24 486	24 988	25 500	26 023	26 557
Armenia - Arménie	DJ	3 218	3 221	3 227	3 234	3 244	3 256	3 268	3 151	3 022	...
Azerbaijan - Azerbaïdjan	DF	8 500[30]	8 610[30]	8 723[30]	8 839[30]	8 947	9 054	9 173	9 296	9 417	9 529
Bahrain - Bahreïn	DJ	889	960	1 039	1 103	1 178	1 229	1 195	1 209	1 253	1 315
Bangladesh	DF	138 600	140 600	142 600	144 500	146 600	148 620	150 611	152 700	154 790	156 880
Bhutan - Bhoutan[46]	DF	...	647	659	671	683	696	708	721	733	745
Brunei Darussalam - Brunéi Darussalam[13]	DF	359	365	370	375	380	387	...	...	...	...
Cambodia - Cambodge[47]	DF	13 807[48]	14 081[48]	14 364[48]	13 868[2]	14 085[2]	14 303[2]	14 521[2]	14 741[2]	14 963[2]	15 184[2]
China - Chine[49]	DF	1 307 560[50]	1 314 480[50]	1 317 900[50]	1 324 700[50]	1 331 300[50]	1 337 700[50]	1 344 100[51]	1 350 695[51]	1 357 380[50]	1 364 270[50]
China, Hong Kong SAR - Chine, Hong Kong RAS	DJ	6 813	6 857	6 916	6 958	6 973	7 024	7 072	7 155	7 188	7 242
China, Macao SAR - Chine, Macao RAS	DJ	473	499	521	541	535	537	550	568	592	622
Cyprus - Chypre[52]	DJ	739[53]	751[53]	767[53]	787[53]	808[53]	829[53]	851[53]	864[53]	862[53]	*858[10]
Georgia - Géorgie	DF	4 361	4 398	4 388	4 384	4 411	4 453	4 483	4 491	...	4 490[10]
India - Inde[54]	DF	1 101 318	1 117 734	1 134 023	1 150 196	1 166 228	1 182 105	1 197 813	1 213 370	...	...
Indonesia - Indonésie	DJ	219 852[55]	222 747[55]	225 642[55]	228 523[55]	231 370[55]	238 519[56]	241 991[56]	245 425[56]	248 818[56]	252 165[56]
Iran (Islamic Republic of) - Iran (République islamique d')[57]	DJ	69 390	70 603	71 279	72 182	73 202	74 340	...	76 038	76 942	77 856
Iraq	DF	27 723	28 562	29 427	30 315	31 393	32 211	33 052	33 913	34 794	35 695
Israel - Israël[58]	DJ	6 930	7 054	7 180	7 309	7 486	7 624	7 766	7 911	8 059	*8 216
Japan - Japon[59]	DJ	127 773	127 854[60]	128 001[60]	128 063[60]	128 047[60]	128 070[60]	127 817[60]	127 561[60]	127 339[60]	127 132[60]
Jordan - Jordanie[61]	DF	5 473	5 600	5 723	5 850	5 980	6 113	6 249	6 388	6 530	6 675
Kazakhstan	DF	15 147	15 308	15 484	15 674	16 093	16 322	16 557	16 791	17 035	17 161[10]
Kuwait - Koweït	DF	2 245	2 328	2 411	2 496	2 778	2 933	3 099[62]	3 268	3 448	...
Kyrgyzstan - Kirghizstan	DF	5 007[4]	5 034[4]	5 056[4]	5 078[4]	5 128[4]	5 193[4]	5 260[4]	5 352[4]	...	...
	DJ	...	...	...	...	...	...	...	...	5 720	5 836
Lao People's Democratic Republic - République démocratique populaire lao[63]	DF	5 651	5 778	5 904	6 032	6 160	6 289	6 419	6 549	6 679	6 809
Malaysia - Malaisie	DJ	26 046[64]	26 550[64]	27 058[64]	27 568[64]	28 081[64]	28 589[65]	29 062[65]	29 510[65]	29 915[65]	30 262[65]
Maldives	DF	294	...	305	310	315	320	325	331	336	...
Mongolia - Mongolie	DF	2 551	2 583	2 602	2 643	2 691	2 739	2 786	2 840	2 899	2 963
Myanmar[66]	DF	55 396	56 515	57 504	58 377	59 130	59 780	50 149[67]	50 667[67]	51 184[67]	51 486[67]
Nepal - Népal	DJ	25 343	25 887	26 427	26 967	27 504	28 044	28 585	26 873[15]	27 257[15]	27 646[15]
Oman	DF	2 509	2 577	2 743	2 867	3 174	...	3 295[68]	3 623[68]	3 855[68]	3 993[68]
Pakistan[69]	DF	...	...	...	166 410	169 940	173 510	177 100	...	184 350	...
	DJ	144 367[70]	147 100	149 860[71]	...	...	...	...	...	...	...
Philippines	DJ	85 261[22]	86 973[22]	88 706[22]	90 457[22]	92 227[22]	93 135[23]	94 824[23]	96 511[23]	98 197[23]	99 880[23]
Qatar	DF	906	1 043	1 218	1 448	1 639	1 715	1 733	1 833	2 004	2 216
Republic of Korea - République de Corée	DJ	48 138	48 372	48 598	48 949	49 182	49 410	49 779[1]	50 004[1]	50 220[1]	50 424[1]
Saudi Arabia - Arabie saoudite[72]	DF	*23 330	*24 122	*24 941	*25 787	*26 661	*27 563	*28 376	*29 196	*29 994	...
Singapore - Singapour[73]	DJ	4 266	4 401	4 589	4 839	4 988	5 077	5 184	5 312	5 399	5 470
Sri Lanka	DF	19 644	19 858	20 039	20 216	20 450	20 653	20 869	20 328	20 483	20 675
State of Palestine - État de Palestine	DF	3 508	3 612	3 719	3 826	3 935	4 048	4 169	4 293	4 421	4 550
Syrian Arab Republic - République arabe syrienne[74]	DF	18 138	18 717	19 172	19 644	20 125	20 619	21 124	...	...	...
Tajikistan - Tadjikistan	DF	6 850	6 992	7 140	7 295	7 334	7 519	7 714	7 897	8 074	*8 200
Thailand - Thaïlande[1]	DJ	64 839	65 306	66 042	66 480	66 903	67 312	67 599	67 912	...	68 610
Timor-Leste[1]	DF	983	1 015	1 048	1 081	1 115	...	...	...	...	...
Turkey - Turquie	DF	72 065	72 971	70 138	71 052	72 039	73 142	74 224	75 176	76 148	...
	DJ	...	...	...	...	...	...	...	...	...	76 903[75]
United Arab Emirates - Émirats arabes unis[76]	DF	4 041	5 012[19]	6 219[19]	8 074[19]	8 200[19]	8 264	...	...	...	...

5. Estimates of mid-year population: 2005 - 2014
Estimations de la population au milieu de l'année : 2005 - 2014 (continued - suite)

Continent and country or area / Continent et pays ou zone	Code[a]	Population estimates (in thousands) - Estimations (en milliers)									
		2005	2006	2007	2008	2009	2010	2011	2012	2013	2014
ASIA - ASIE											
Uzbekistan - Ouzbékistan[10]	DJ	26 021	26 313	26 664	27 072	27 533	28 001	29 123	29 555	29 994	30 493
Viet Nam	DF	82 394[77]	83 313[77]	84 221[77]	85 122[77]	86 025	86 933	87 840	88 773	89 709	90 729
Yemen - Yémen	DF	20 283[19]	20 901[19]	21 539[19]	22 198[19]	...	...	...	...	...	...
	DJ	...	...	...	...	22 492[1]	23 154[1]	23 833[1]	24 527[1]	25 235[1]	25 956[1]
EUROPE											
Åland Islands - Îles d'Åland[33]	DJ	27	27	27	27	28	28	28	28	29	29
Albania - Albanie	DF	3 011	2 993	2 970	2 947	2 928	2 913	2 905	2 900	2 897	2 896[10]
Andorra - Andorre[33]	DJ	79	80	82	84	85	85	79[78]	77	76[10]	
Austria - Autriche	DJ	8 225	8 268	8 295	8 322	8 341	8 361	8 389	8 426	8 477	8 507[10]
Belarus - Bélarus	DF	9 664	9 605	9 561	9 528	9 507	...	...	...	...	9 468[10]
	DJ	...	...	...	...	...	9 491	9 473	9 464	9 466	...
Belgium - Belgique	DJ	10 473	10 542	10 623	10 710	10 796	10 896	11 044	11 128	11 162[10]	11 204[10]
Bosnia and Herzegovina - Bosnie-Herzégovine	DF	3 843	3 843	3 843	3 842	3 843	3 843	3 841	*3 837	*3 833	*3 831[10]
Bulgaria - Bulgarie	DJ	7 740	7 699	7 660	7 623	7 585	7 534	7 348	7 306	7 265	7 246[10]
Croatia - Croatie	DJ	4 310	4 311	4 310	4 310	4 305	4 295	4 281	4 268	4 256	4 247[10]
Czech Republic - République tchèque	DJ	10 211	10 239	10 299	10 385	10 444	10 474	10 496	10 511	10 511	10 512[10]
Denmark - Danemark[79]	DJ	5 416	5 435	5 457	5 489	5 519	5 545	5 567	5 587	5 609	5 640
Estonia - Estonie	DJ	1 355	1 347	1 341	1 337	1 335	1 331	1 327	1 323	1 318	1 316[10]
Faeroe Islands - Îles Féroé	DJ	48	48	48	48	49	49	49	48	48	48
Finland - Finlande[33]	DJ	5 219[80]	5 239[80]	5 262[80]	5 286[80]	5 311[80]	5 335[80]	5 360[80]	5 386[80]	5 410[80]	5 451[10]
France[81]	DJ	61 181	61 597	61 965	62 300	62 615	62 918	63 223	63 519	63 794	*64 062
Germany - Allemagne	DJ	82 464	82 366	82 263	82 120	81 875	81 757	80 210	80 426	80 646	80 767[10]
Gibraltar[82]	DF	29	30	30	30	31	31	31	32	33	33
Greece - Grèce	DF	11 093[83]	11 128[83]	11 163[83]	11 186[83]	11 187[83]	11 153[83]	11 123[83]	11 093[83]	11 028[83]	10 904[84]
Guernsey - Guernesey[85]	DF	...	61	61	62	62	62	63	63	63	63
Holy See - Saint-Siège[86]	DF	...	...	...	...	0[87]	0[88]	...	0[89]	...	...
Hungary - Hongrie	DJ	10 087	10 071	10 056	10 038	10 023	10 000	9 972	9 920	9 894	9 877[84]
Iceland - Islande[90]	DJ	296	304	311	319	319	318	319[91]	321	324	326[10]
Ireland - Irlande	DF	4 160	4 260	4 357	4 426	4 459	4 560	4 577	4 587	4 598	4 606[84]
Isle of Man - Île de Man[92]	DJ	79	...	81	82	82	83	...	85	86	86
Italy - Italie	DJ	57 969	58 144	58 438	58 827	59 095	59 277	59 379	59 540	60 234	60 783[84]
Jersey	DJ	91	92	93	95	96	97	98	99	...	...
Latvia - Lettonie	DJ	2 239	2 218	2 200	2 177	2 142	2 098	2 060	2 034	2 013	2 001[10]
Liechtenstein	DJ	35	35	35	35	36	36	36	37	37	37[93]
Lithuania - Lituanie	DJ	3 323	3 270	3 231	3 198	3 163	3 097	3 028	2 988	2 958	2 943[84]
Luxembourg	DJ	465	473	480	489	498	507	518	531	543	550[10]
Malta - Malte[94]	DJ	404	405	407	409	413	415	416	420	423	425[10]
Monaco	DJ	...	...	...	...	35	36	36	36	37	...
Montenegro - Monténégro	DJ	623	624	626	629	632	617	621	622	624	622[84]
Netherlands - Pays-Bas	DJ	16 320	16 346	16 382	16 446	16 530	16 615	16 693	16 755	16 804	16 829[95]
Norway - Norvège[96]	DJ	4 623	4 661	4 709	4 768	4 829	4 889	4 953	5 019	5 080[97]	5 108[84]
Poland - Pologne[98]	DJ	38 161	38 132	38 116	38 116	38 153	38 517	38 526	38 534	38 276[97]	38 018[84]
Portugal	DJ	10 503	10 522	10 543	10 558	10 568	10 573	10 558	10 515	10 457	10 427[84]
Republic of Moldova - République de Moldova[99]	DJ	3 595	3 585	3 577	3 570	3 566	3 562	3 560	3 560	3 559	3 559[10]
Romania - Roumanie	DJ	21 320	21 194	20 883	20 538	20 367	20 247	20 148	20 060	19 986	19 947[84]
Russian Federation - Fédération de Russie	DJ	143 519	143 050	142 805	142 742	142 785	142 849	142 961	143 202	*143 507	...
San Marino - Saint-Marin[33]	DF	30	30	31	32	33	33	33	34	33	34
Serbia - Serbie[100]	DJ	7 441	7 412	7 382	7 350	7 321	7 291	7 234[13]	7 199[13]	7 164[13]	7 147[84]
Slovakia - Slovaquie	DJ	5 373	5 373	5 375	5 379	5 386	5 391	5 398	5 408	5 413	5 416[84]
Slovenia - Slovénie	DJ	2 001	2 009	2 019	2 023	2 042	2 049	2 052	2 056	2 059	2 061[101]
Spain - Espagne	DJ	43 663	44 361	45 236	45 983	46 368	46 562	46 736	46 766	46 593	46 512[95]
Svalbard and Jan Mayen Islands - Îles Svalbard et Jan Mayen[102]	DF	2	...	...	2	...	...	...	...	...	...
Sweden - Suède	DJ	9 030[33]	9 081[33]	9 148[33]	9 220[33]	9 299[33]	9 378[33]	9 449[33]	9 519[33]	9 600[90]	9 645[95]
Switzerland - Suisse	DJ	7 437	7 484	7 551	7 648	7 744	7 825	7 912	7 997	8 089[103]	8 140[93]
TFYR of Macedonia - L'ex-R. y. de Macédoine	DF	2 037	2 040	2 044	2 047	2 051	2 055	2 059	2 061	2 064	2 066[10]
Ukraine	DF	47 105	46 788	46 509	46 258	46 053	45 871	45 706	45 593	45 553[10]	*42 988[104]

5. Estimates of mid-year population: 2005 - 2014
Estimations de la population au milieu de l'année : 2005 - 2014 (continued - suite)

Continent and country or area / Continent et pays ou zone	Code[a]	Population estimates (in thousands) - Estimations (en milliers)									
		2005	2006	2007	2008	2009	2010	2011	2012	2013	2014
EUROPE											
United Kingdom of Great Britain and Northern Ireland - Royaume-Uni de Grande-Bretagne et d'Irlande du Nord[105]	DJ	60 413	60 827	61 319	61 824	62 260	62 759	63 285	63 705	64 102[97]	64 308[84]
OCEANIA - OCÉANIE											
American Samoa - Samoas américaines[37]	DJ	66	67	68	69	70	67	...	...	...	...
Australia - Australie	DJ	20 177	20 451	20 828	21 249	21 692	22 032	22 340	22 728	23 135	*23 491
Cook Islands - Îles Cook[106]	DF	22	24	21	22	23	24	19	20	*19	*19
Fiji - Fidji	DF	825	830	834	841	843	857	...	858[19]	859[107]	...
French Polynesia - Polynésie française	DF	253	256	259	262	265	269	270[10]	...	...	...
Guam[108]	DJ	158	159	159	159	159	...	160	160	160	161
Kiribati[107]	DF	...	...	...	...	...	...	...	...	109	...
Marshall Islands - Îles Marshall	DF	...	52[109]	53[109]	53[109]	54[109]	54[109]	...	...	54[107]	...
Micronesia (Federated States of) - Micronésie (États fédérés de)[1]	DJ	108	108	108	108	108	108	108	107	107	106
New Caledonia - Nouvelle-Calédonie	DF	234	238	240[10]	242	...	250	254	258	260[10]	...
New Zealand - Nouvelle-Zélande[110]	DJ	4 134	4 185	4 224	4 260	4 303	4 351	4 384	4 408	4 442	4 510
Niue - Nioué	DJ	2	2	2	...	2	1	1	...	...	...
Norfolk Island - Île Norfolk	DF	2	2	...	...	...	...	...	...	...	...
Northern Mariana Islands - Îles Mariannes septentrionales	DF	71	61	59	55	51	48	46	...	...	...
Palau - Palaos	DF	...	22	20	20	21	21	21	21	...	...
Pitcairn[111]	DF	...	...	0	0	...	...	...	...	...	...
Samoa	DF	183	185	182	182	183	184	185	189	191	...
Solomon Islands - Îles Salomon	DF	471[1]	483[1]	495[1]	507[1]	518[1]	531[1]	542[1]	554[1]	611[107]	...
Tokelau - Tokélaou[112]	DF	...	...	...	...	...	...	...	...	1	...
Tonga[113]	DF	102	103	103	104	...	...	...	...	...	...
Tuvalu	DF	10	11	11	...	...	...	...	11	...	11	...
Vanuatu	DF	...	221[1]	...	...	...	239	245	245	265	...

FOOTNOTES - NOTES

Italics: estimates which are less reliable. - Italiques : estimations moins sûres.

* Provisional. - Données provisoires.

[a] 'Code' indicates source of data, as follows: - Le 'Code' indique la source des données, comme suit :
DF: Population de facto - Population de fait
DJ : Population de jure - Population de droit

[1] Data refer to national projections. - Les données se réfèrent aux projections nationales.
[2] Data based on the 2008 Population Census. - Données fondées sur le recensement de population de 2008.
[3] Data refer to 1 January. Data refer to national projections. - Données se raportent au 1 janvier. Les données se réfèrent aux projections nationales.
[4] Data are calculated from the results of the Population and Housing Census of 2009. - Les données sont calculées à partir des résultats du recensement de la population et de l'habitat de 2009.
[5] Projections based on the 1994 Population Census. - Projections fondées sur le recensement de la population de 1994.
[6] Based on the results of the Gabonese Survey for the Evaluation and Tracking of Poverty. - Sur base des résultats de l'enquête gabonaise sur l'évaluation et le suivi de la pauvreté.
[7] Post-censal estimates based on the 1999 Population Census. - Les estimations post-censitaire fondées sur le recensement de la population de 1999.

[8] Post-censal estimates based on the 2009 Population Census. - Les estimations post-censitaire fondées sur le recensement de la population de 2009.
[9] Revised data. - Données révisées.
[10] Data refer to 1 January. - Données se raportent au 1 janvier.
[11] Excludes the islands of St. Brandon and Agalega. - Non compris les îles St. Brandon et Agalega.
[12] Based on the results of the 2000 Population Census. - Basé sur les résultats du recencement de la population de 2000.
[13] Based on the results of the 2011 Population Census. - Basé sur les résultats du recencement de la population de 2011.
[14] Based on the results of the 2004 Population Census. - D'après des résultats du recencement de la population de 2004.
[15] Data refer to projections based on the 2011 Population Census. - Les données se réfèrent aux projections basées sur le recensement de la population de 2011.
[16] Based on the results of the 2012 Population and Housing Census. - D'après les résultats du recensement de la population et des logements de 2012.
[17] Based on the results of the 2006 Population Census. - D'après des résultats du recensement de la population de 2006.
[18] Data are projections based on the 2008 Population and Housing Census. - Projection basée sur le recensement 2008 de la population et des logements.
[19] Data refer to 31 December. - Données se raportent au 31 décembre.
[20] Data refer to 31 December. Based on the results of a population count. The population figures are 264, 263 and 262 persons for 2007, 2008 and 2009 respectively. - Données se raportent au 31 décembre. D'après les rêsultats d'un comptage de la population. La population est respectivement égale à 264, 263 et 262 personnes pour les années 2007, 2008 et 2009.

[21] Projections based on the 2002 Population Census. - Projections fondées sur le recensement de la population de 2002.

[22] Data refer to projections based on the 2000 Population Census. - Les données se réfèrent aux projections basées sur le recensement de la population de 2000.

[23] Data refer to projections based on the 2010 Population Census. - Les données se réfèrent aux projections basées sur le recensement de la population de 2010.

[24] Final intercensal estimates. - Estimations inter-censitaires definitives.

[25] Final postcensal estimates. - Estimations postcensitaires definitives.

[26] Updated postcensal estimates. - Estimations post censitaires mises à jour.

[27] Preliminary postcensal estimates. - Estimations post censitaires préliminaires.

[28] The source of data is the national household survey. - La source des données est l'enquête nationale des ménages.

[29] Based on the national household surveys 2010-2014 and the 2011 population census. - D'après les données de l'enquête nationale des ménages 2010-2014 et les résultats du recensement de la population de 2011.

[30] Intercensal estimates. - Estimations inter-censitaires.

[31] Postcensal estimates. - Estimations post censitaires.

[32] Estimates based on the 2007 Population Census. - Estimations fondées sur le recensement de la population de 2007.

[33] Population statistics are compiled from registers. - Les statistiques de la population sont compilées à partir des registres.

[34] Data refer to 1 January. Excluding data for Saint Barthélémy and Saint Martin. - Données se rapportent au 1 janvier. Non compris les données pour Saint Barthélémy et Saint Martin.

[35] Projections produced by l'Institut Haïtien de Statistique et d'Informatique (IHSI) and the Latin American and Caribbean Demographic Centre (CELADE) - Population Division of ECLAC. - Les données sont projections produits par l'Institut Haïtien de Statistique et d'Informatique (IHSI) et le centre démographique de l'Amérique latine et les Caraïbes - Division de la population de la CEPALC.

[36] Data refer to projections based on the 2001 Population Census. - Les données se réfèrent aux projections basées sur le recensement de la population de 2001.

[37] Including armed forces stationed in the area. - Y compris les militaires en garnison sur le territoire.

[38] Based on the results of the 2010 Population Census. - D'après le résultats du recensement de la population de 2010.

[39] Excluding U.S. Armed Forces overseas and civilian U.S. citizens whose usual place of residence is outside the United States. - Non compris les militaires américains à l'étranger et les civils américains dont le lieu de résidence habituel est en dehors des États-Unis.

[40] Data refer to projections based on the 2010 Population and Housing Census. - Les données se réfèrent aux projections basées sur le recensement 2010 de la population et des logements.

[41] Data include persons in remote areas, military personnel outside the country, merchant seamen at sea, civilian seasonal workers outside the country, and other civilians outside the country, and exclude nomads, foreign military, civilian aliens temporarily in the country, transients on ships and Indian jungle population. - Y compris les personnes vivant dans des régions éloignées, le personel militaire en dehors du pays, les marins marchands, les ouvriers saisonniers en dehors du pays, et autres civils en dehors du pays, et non compris les nomades, les militaires étrangers, les étrangers civils temporairement dans le pays, les transiteurs sur des bateaux et les Indiens de la jungle.

[42] Data are revised projections taking into consideration also the results of the 2005 census. - Les données sont des projections révisées tenant compte également des résultats du recensement de 2005.

[43] Excludes nomadic Indian tribes. Data refer to projections based on the 2010 Population Census. - Non compris les tribus d'Indiens nomades. Les données se réfèrent aux projections basées sur le recensement de la population de 2010.

[44] Data refer to 30 June. - Données se raportent au 30 juin.

[45] Data refer to the settled population based on the 1979 Population Census and the latest household prelisting. The refugees of Afghanistan in Iran, Pakistan, and an estimated 1.5 million nomads, are not included. - Les données se rapportent à la population stationnaire sur la base du recensement de 1979 et du recensement préliminaire des logements le plus récent. Sont exclus les réfugiés d'Afghanistan en Iran et au Pakistan et les nomades estimés à 1,5 million.

[46] Data refer to projected figures based on the Population and Housing Census 2005 (district projection). - Les données se réfèrent aux projections basées sur le recensement de la population et de l'habitat de 2005 (projections locales).

[47] Excluding foreign diplomatic personnel and their dependants. - Non compris le personnel diplomatique étranger et les membres de leur famille les accompagnant.

[48] Based on the results of 1998 census. - A partir des résultats de recensement de l'année 1998.

[49] For statistical purposes, the data for China do not include those for the Hong Kong Special Administrative Region (Hong Kong SAR), Macao Special Administrative Region (Macao SAR) and Taiwan province of China. - Pour la présentation des statistiques, les données pour la Chine ne comprennent pas la Région Administrative Spéciale de Hong Kong (Hong Kong RAS), la Région Administrative Spéciale de Macao (Macao RAS) et Taïwan province de Chine.

[50] Data have been estimated on the basis of the annual National Sample Survey on Population Changes. - Les données ont été estimées sur la base de l'enquête annuelle "National Sample Survey on Population Changes".

[51] Data have been adjusted on the basis of the Population Census of 2010. - Les données ont été ajustées à partir des résultats du recensement de la population de 2010.

[52] Data refer to government controlled areas. - Les données se rapportent aux zones contrôlées par le Gouvernement.

[53] Data refer to annual average population. - Les données correspondent à la population annuelle moyenne.

[54] Includes data for the Indian-held part of Jammu and Kashmir, the final status of which has not yet been determined. Data refer to projections based on the 2001 Population Census. - Y compris les données pour le Jammu et du Cachemire occupée par l'Inde dont le statut définitif n'a pas encore été déterminé. Les données se réfèrent aux projections basées sur le recensement de la population de 2001.

[55] Data are based on the publication: "Indonesia Population Projection 2005-2015" - Les données sont basées sur la publication : << Indonesia Population Projection 2005-2015 >>

[56] Data are based on the publication: "Indonesia Population Projection 2010-2035" - Les données sont basées sur la publication : << Indonesia Population Projection 2010-2035 >>

[57] Data refer to the Iranian Year which begins on 21 March and ends on 20 March of the following year. - Les données concernent l'année iranienne, qui commence le 21 mars et se termine le 20 mars de l'année suivante.

[58] Includes data for East Jerusalem and Israeli residents in certain other territories under occupation by Israeli military forces since June 1967. - Y compris les données pour Jérusalem-Est et les résidents israéliens dans certains autres territoires occupés depuis 1967 par les forces armées israéliennes.

[59] Excluding diplomatic personnel outside the country and foreign military and civilian personnel and their dependants stationed in the area. - Non compris le personnel diplomatique hors du pays ni les militaires et agents civils étrangers en poste sur le territoire et les membres de leur famille les accompagnant.

[60] Estimates based on the complete counts of the 2010 Population Census. - Estimations basées sur le dénombrement complet du recensement de la population de 2010.

[61] Data refer to 31 December. Excluding data for Jordanian territory under occupation since June 1967 by Israeli military forces. Excluding foreigners, including registered Palestinian refugees. - Données se raportent au 31 décembre. Non compris les données pour le territoire jordanien occupé depuis juin 1967 par les forces armées israéliennes. Non compris les étrangers, mais y compris les réfugiés de Palestine enregistrés.

[62] Estimates based on the population census data of 2005 and 2011. - Estimations basées sur les données des recensements de la population de 2005 et 2011.

[63] Based on the results of the 2005 Population and Housing Census. - Données fondées sur les résultats du recensement de la population et de l'habitat de 2005.

[64] Intercensal Mid-Year Population Estimates based on the adjusted Population and Housing Census of 2000 and 2010. - Les estimations inter-censitaires au millieu de l'année sont fondée sur les résultats ajustées des recensements de la population et de l'habitat de 2000 et 2010.

[65] Estimates based on the adjusted Population and Housing Census of 2010. - Les estimations sont fondée sur les résultats ajustées du recensement de la population et de l'habitat de 2010.

[66] Data refer to 1 October. - Données se raportent au 1 octobre.

[67] Based on the results of the 2014 Population Census. - D'après les résultats du recensement de la population de 2014.

[68] Data refer to registered population data from Royal Oman Police. - Les données portent sur la population enregistrée par la police royale de l'Oman.

[69] Excluding data for the Pakistan-held part of Jammu and Kashmir, the final status of which has not yet been determined. - Non compris les données concernant la partie du Jammu et Cachemire occupée par le Pakistan dont le statut définitif n'a pas été déterminé.

[70] Based on the results of the Pakistan Demographic Survey (PDS 2005). These estimates do not reflect completely accurately the actual population and vital events of the country. - D'après les résultats de l'enquête démographique effectuée par le Pakistan en 2005. Ces estimations ne dénotent pas d'une manière complètement ponctuelle la population actuelle et les statistiques de l'état civil du pays.

114

[71] Based on the results of the Pakistan Demographic Survey (PDS 2007). - D'après les résultats de l'enquête démographique effectuée par le Pakistan en 2007.

[72] Data based on the preliminary results of the 2010 Population and Housing Census. - D'après les résultats préliminaires du recensement de la population et des logements de 2010.

[73] Data refer to 30 June. Data exclude residents who have been away from Singapore for a continuous period of 12 months or longer as at the reference date. - Données se raportent au 30 juin. Non compris les résidents hors de Singapour pour une période ininterrompue de 12 mois ou plus avant de la date de référence.

[74] Including Palestinian refugees. - Y compris les réfugiés de Palestine.

[75] Data based on address-based population registration system. - Les données sont basées sur le registre national de la population basé sur l'adresse.

[76] Data include non-national population. - Les données comprennent les non-nationaux.

[77] Data are adjusted according to the results of the 1999 and 2009 censuses. - Les données ont été ajustées à partir des résultats des recensements de la population de 1999 et 2009.

[78] Decrease in population due to revision in administrative registers. - Diminution de la population due à la révision des registres administratifs.

[79] Excluding Faeroe Islands and Greenland shown separately, if available. Population statistics are compiled from registers. - Non compris les Iles Féroé et le Groenland, qui font l'objet de rubriques distinctes, si disponible. Les statistiques de la population sont compilées à partir des registres.

[80] Excluding Åland Islands. - Non compris les Îles d'Åland.

[81] Excluding diplomatic personnel outside the country and including members of alien armed forces not living in military camps and foreign diplomatic personnel not living in embassies or consulates. - Non compris le personnel diplomatique hors du pays et y compris les militaires étrangers ne vivant pas dans des camps militaires et le personnel diplomatique étranger ne vivant pas dans les ambassades ou les consulats.

[82] Data refer to 31 December. Excluding military personnel, visitors and transients. - Données se raportent au 31 décembre. Non compris les militaires, ni les visiteurs et transients.

[83] Excluding armed forces stationed outside the country, but including alien armed forces stationed in the area. - Non compris les militaires en garnison hors du pays, mais y compris les militaires étrangers en garnison sur le territoire.

[84] Data refer to 1 January. Data refer to usually resident population. - Données se raportent au 1 janvier. Les données concernent la population habituellement résidente.

[85] Data refer to 31 March. - Données se raportent au 31 mars.

[86] Data refer to the Vatican City State. - Les données se rapportent à l'Etat de la Cité du Vatican.

[87] The population figure is 466 persons. - La population est égale à 466 personnes.

[88] Data refer to 26 February. The population figure is 460 persons. - Données se raportent au 26 février. La population est égale à 460 personnes.

[89] Data refer to 21 June. The population figure is 451 persons. - Données se raportent au 21 juin. La population est égale à 451 personnes.

[90] Data refer to registered resident population. - Les données concernent la population enregistrée résidente.

[91] Definition of localities was revised in 2011 causing a break with the previous series. - La rupture par rapport aux séries précédentes s'explique par le fait que la définition des localités a été révisée depuis 2011.

[92] Data refer to 30 April. - Données se raportent au 30 avril.

[93] Data refer to 1 January. Data refer to legal resident population. - Données se raportent au 1 janvier. Les données concernent la population légalement résidente.

[94] Including civilian nationals temporarily outside the country. - Y compris les civils nationaux temporairement hors du pays.

[95] Data refer to 1 January. Data refer to registered resident population. - Données se raportent au 1 janvier. Les données concernent la population enregistrée résidente.

[96] Including residents temporarily outside the country. - Y compris les résidents se trouvant temporairement hors du pays.

[97] Data refer to usually resident population. - Les données concernent la population habituellement résidente.

[98] Excluding civilian aliens within the country, but including civilian nationals temporarily outside the country. - Non compris les civils étrangers dans le pays, mais y compris les civils nationaux temporairement hors du pays.

[99] Excluding Transnistria and the municipality of Bender. - Les données ne tiennent pas compte de l'information sur la Transnistria et la municipalité de Bender.

[100] Excludes data for Kosovo and Metohia. - Sans les données pour le Kosovo et Metohie.

[101] Data refer to 1 January. The data for urban and rural exclude the nationals temporarily outside the country. Data refer to usually resident population. - Données se raportent au 1 janvier. Les données relatives à la population urbaine et rurale n'englobent pas les nationaux se trouvant provisoirement à l'étranger. Les données concernent la population habituellement résidente.

[102] Data refer to 1 January. Data refer to Svalbard only. - Données se raportent au 1 janvier. Données ne concernant que le Svalbard.

[103] Data refer to legal resident population. - Les données concernent la population légalement résidente.

[104] The Government of Ukraine has informed the United Nations that it is not in a position to provide statistical data concerning the Autonomous Republic of Crimea and the city of Sevastopol. - Le gouvernement Ukrainien a informé l'ONU qu'il n'est pas en mesure de fournir des données statistiques concernant la République autonome de Crimée et la ville de Sébastopol.

[105] Excluding Channel Islands (Guernsey and Jersey) and Isle of Man, shown separately, if available. - Non compris les îles Anglo-Normandes (Guernesey et Jersey) et l'île de Man, qui font l'objet de rubriques distinctes, si disponible.

[106] Excluding Niue, shown separately, which is part of Cook Islands, but because of remoteness is administered separately. - Non compris Nioué, qui fait l'objet d'une rubrique distincte et qui fait partie des îles Cook, mais qui, en raison de son éloignement, est administrée séparément.

[107] Projections are prepared by the Secretariat of the Pacific Community based on the last population and housing census. - Les projections sont preparées par le Secrétariat de la Communauté du Pacifique à partir des résultats du dernier recensement de la population et de l'habitat.

[108] Including armed forces stationed in the area. Data refer to projections based on the 2010 Population Census. - Y compris les militaires en garnison sur le territoire. Les données se réfèrent aux projections basées sur le recensement de la population de 2010.

[109] Projections are prepared by the Secretariat of the Pacific Community based on 1999 census of population and housing. - Les projections sont preparées par le Secrétariat de la Communauté du Pacifique à partir des résultats du recensement de la population et de l'habitat de 1999.

[110] Because of rounding, totals are not in all cases the sum of the respective components. - Les chiffres étant arrondis, les totaux ne correspondent pas toujours rigoureusement à la somme des composants respectifs.

[111] Data refer to 31 December. The population figures are 64 and 58 persons for 2007 and 2008 respectively. - Données se raportent au 31 décembre. La population est respectivement égale à 64 et 58 personnes pour les années 2007 et 2008.

[112] Data refer to 1 December. - Données se raportent au 1 décembre.

[113] Data refer to national projections. Based on the results of the 1996 population census. - Les données se réfèrent aux projections nationales. À partir des résultats du recensement de la population de 1996.

Table 6 - *Demographic Yearbook 2014*

Table 6 presents total population by sex for as many years as possible between 2005 and 2014, as well as urban population as available.

Description of variables: Data are from nation-wide population censuses or are estimates, some of which are based on sample surveys of population carried out among all segments of the population. This characteristic of the data is indicated in the column "Code". The codes used are explained at the end of the table.

Urban is defined according to the national census definition. The definition for each country is set forth at the end of the technical notes to this table.

Percentage computation: Urban percentages are the number of persons residing in an area defined as "urban" per 100 total population. They are calculated by the Statistics Division of the United Nations Department of Economic and Social Affairs. In very few cases the data for total population have been revised but the data for the urban and rural population have not been. These data are footnoted accordingly. In these cases, particular caution should be used in interpreting the figures for percentage urban.

Reliability of data: Estimates that are believed to be less reliable are set in *italics* rather than in roman type. Classification in terms of reliability is based on the method of construction of the total population estimate discussed in the technical notes for table 3.

Limitations: Statistics on urban population by sex are subject to the same qualifications as have been set forth for population statistics in general, as discussed in section 3 of the Technical Notes.

The basic limitations imposed by variations in the definition of the total population and in the degree of under-enumeration are perhaps more important in relation to urban/rural than to any other distributions. The classification by urban and rural is affected by variations in defining usual residence for purposes of sub-national tabulations. Likewise, the geographical differentials in the degree of under-enumeration in censuses affect the comparability of these categories throughout the table. The distinction between *de facto* and *de jure* population is also very important with respect to urban/rural distributions. The difference between the *de facto* and the *de jure* population is discussed at length in section 3.1.1 of the Technical Notes.

A most important and specific limitation, however, lies in the national differences in the definition of urban. Because the distinction between urban and rural areas is made in so many different ways, the definitions have been included at the end of this table. The definitions are necessarily brief and, where the classification of urban involves administrative civil divisions, they are often given in the terminology of the particular country or area. As a result of variations in terminology, it may appear that differences between countries or areas are greater than they actually are. On the other hand, similar or identical terms (for example, town, village, district) as used in different countries or areas may have quite different meanings.

It will be seen from an examination of the definitions that they fall roughly into three major types: (1) classification of localities as urban based on size; (2) classification of administrative centres of minor civil divisions as urban and the remainder of the division as rural; and (3) classification of minor civil divisions on a set of criteria, which may include type of local government, number of inhabitants or proportion of population engaged in agriculture.

The designation of areas as urban or rural is so closely bound to historical, political, cultural, and administrative considerations that the process of developing uniform definitions and procedures moves very slowly. Not only do the definitions differ from one country or area to the other, but, they may also no longer reflect the original intention for distinguishing urban from rural. The criteria once established on the basis of administrative subdivisions (as most of these are) become fixed and resistant to change. For this reason, comparisons of time-series data may be severely affected because the definitions used become outdated. Special care must be taken in comparing data from censuses with those from sample surveys because the definitions of urban used may differ.

Despite their shortcomings, however, statistics on urban and rural population are useful in describing the diversity of population distribution within a country or area.

The definition of urban/rural areas is based on both qualitative and quantitative criteria that may include any combination of the following: size of population, population density, distance between built-up areas, predominant type of economic activity, conformity to legal or administrative status and urban characteristics such as specific services and facilities[1]. Although statistics classified by urban/rural areas are widely available, no international standard definition appears to be possible at this time since the meaning differs from one country or area to another. The urban/rural classification of population used here is reported according to the national definition.

Earlier data: Urban and total population by sex have been shown in previous issues of the Demographic Yearbook. For information on specific years covered, readers should consult the Historical Index.

DEFINITION OF "URBAN"

AFRICA

Algeria: The urban/rural delimitation is performed after the census operation based on the classification of built-up areas. Groupings of 100 or more constructions, distant less than 200 metres from one another are considered urban.
Botswana: Agglomeration of 5 000 or more inhabitants where 75 per cent of the economic activity is non-agricultural.
Burundi: Commune of Bujumbura.
Burkina Faso: All administrative centres of provinces (total of 45) plus 4 medium-sized towns are considered as urban areas.
Comoros: Every locality or administrative centre of an island, region or prefecture that has the following facilities: asphalted roads, electricity, a medical centre, telephone services, etc.
Egypt: Governorates of Cairo, Alexandria, Port Said, Ismailia, Suez, frontier governorates and capitals of other governorates, as well as district capitals (Markaz). The definition of urban areas for the 2006 Census is "shiakha", a part of a district.
Equatorial Guinea: District centres and localities with 300 dwellings and/or 1 500 inhabitants or more.
Ethiopia: Localities of 2 000 or more inhabitants.
Kenya: Areas having a population of 2 000 or more inhabitants that have transport systems, build-up areas, industrial/manufacturing structures and other developed structures.
Lesotho: All administrative headquarters and settlements of rapid growth.
Liberia: Localities of 2 000 or more inhabitants.
Malawi: All townships and town planning areas and all district centres.
Mauritius: The five Municipal Council Areas which are subdivided into twenty Municipal Wards defined according to proclaimed boundaries.
Namibia: Proclaimed urban areas for which cadastral data is available and other unplanned squatter areas.
Niger: Capital city, capitals of the departments and districts.
Rwanda: All administrative areas recognized as urban by the law. These are all administrative centres of provinces, and the cities of Kigali, Nyanza, Ruhango and Rwamagana.
Senegal: Agglomerations of 10 000 or more inhabitants.
South Africa: Places with some form of local authority.
Sudan: Localities of administrative and/or commercial importance or with population of 5 000 or more inhabitants.
Swaziland: A geographical area constituting of a city or town, characterized by higher population density and vast human features in comparison to areas surrounding it.
Tunisia: Population living in communes.
Uganda: Gazettes, cities, municipalities and towns.
United Republic of Tanzania: 16 gazetted townships.
Zambia: Localities of 5 000 or more inhabitants, the majority of whom all depend on non-agricultural activities.

AMERICA, NORTH

Canada: Places of 1 000 or more inhabitants, having a population density of 400 or more per square kilometre.
Costa Rica: Administrative centres of cantons.
Cuba: Towns that fulfil a political or administrative function, or that have a population of 2 000 or more and definite urban characteristics.
Dominican Republic: Administrative centres of municipalities and municipal districts, some of which include suburban zones of rural character.
El Salvador: Administrative centres of municipalities.
Greenland: Localities of 200 or more inhabitants.
Guatemala: Municipality of Guatemala Department and officially recognized centres of other departments and municipalities.
Haiti: Administrative centres of communes.
Honduras: Localities of 2 000 or more inhabitants, having essentially urban characteristics.
Jamaica: Localities of 2 000 or more inhabitants, having urban characteristics.
Mexico: Localities of 2 500 or more inhabitants.

Nicaragua: Administrative centres of municipalities and localities of 1 000 or more inhabitants or with more than 150 dwellings, with streets, electric light, water service, school and health centre.

Panama: Localities of 1 500 or more inhabitants having essentially urban characteristics. Beginning 1970, localities of 1 500 or more inhabitants with such urban characteristics as streets, water supply systems, sewerage systems and electric light.

Puerto Rico: Agglomerations of 2 500 or more inhabitants, generally having population densities of 1 000 persons per square mile or more. Two types of urban areas: urbanized areas of 50 000 or more inhabitants and urban clusters of at least 2 500 and less than 50 000 inhabitants.

United States of America: Agglomerations of 2 500 or more inhabitants, generally having population densities of 1 000 persons per square mile or more. Two types of urban areas: urbanized areas of 50 000 or more inhabitants and urban clusters of at least 2 500 and less than 50 000 inhabitants.

United States Virgin Islands: Agglomerations of 2 500 or more inhabitants, generally having population densities of 1 000 persons per square mile or more. Two types of urban areas: urbanized areas of 50 000 or more inhabitants and urban clusters of at least 2 500 and less than 50 000 inhabitants. (As of the 2000 Census, no urbanized areas are identified in the United States Virgin Islands.)

AMERICA, SOUTH

Argentina: Populated centres with 2 000 or more inhabitants.
Bolivia: Localities of 2 000 or more inhabitants.
Brazil: Area inside the urban perimeter of a city or town, defined by municipal law.
Chile: Areas of concentrated housing units with more than 2 000 inhabitants, or between 1 001 and 2 000 inhabitants having 50 per cent or more of its economically active population doing secondary or tertiary activities. As an exception, centres of tourism and recreation with more than 250 housing units that do not satisfy the population requirement are nevertheless considered urban.
Colombia: Areas with a city hall, defined by an urban perimeter established by municipal agreements.
Ecuador: Capitals of provinces and cantons.
Falkland Islands (Malvinas): Town of Stanley.
Paraguay: Cities, towns and administrative centres of departments and districts.
Peru: Populated centres with 100 or more dwellings.
Suriname: The districts of Paramaribo and Wanica.
Uruguay: Cities, villages, towns and other populated areas as defined by the Law of Population Centers.
Venezuela (Bolivarian Republic of): Centres with a population of 2 500 or more inhabitants.

ASIA

Armenia: Cities and urban-type localities, officially designated as such, usually according to the criteria of number of inhabitants and predominance of agricultural, or number of non-agricultural workers and their families.
Azerbaijan: An administrative division which covers more than 15 000 population, engaging mainly in industrial and other economic and social activities and which include administrative and cultural centers.
Bahrain: Communes or villages of 2 500 or more inhabitants.
Cambodia: Areas at the commune level satisfying the following three conditions: (1) Population Density exceeding 200 per square Km, (2) Percentage of male employed in agriculture below 50 per cent, (3) Total population of the commune exceeds 2 000 inhabitants.
China: According to the Regulation on the Classification of Urban/Rural Residence for Statistical Purposes.
Cyprus: As determined by the Department of Town Planning and Housing of the Ministry of Interior.
Georgia: Cities and urban-type localities, officially designated as such, usually according to the criteria of number of inhabitants and predominance of agricultural, or number of non-agricultural workers and their families.
India: Towns (places with municipal corporation, municipal area committee, town committee, notified area committee or cantonment board); also, all places having 5 000 or more inhabitants, a density of not less than 1 000 persons per square mile or 400 per square kilometre, pronounced urban characteristics and at least three fourths of the adult male population employed in pursuits other than agriculture.
Indonesia: Area which satisfies certain criteria in terms of population density, percentage of agricultural households, and a number of urban facilities such as roads, formal education facilities, public health services, etc.
Iran (Islamic Republic of): Every district with a municipality.
Israel: Localities with 2 000 or more residents.
Japan: City (shi) having 50 000 or more inhabitants with 60 per cent or more of the houses located in the main built-up areas and 60 per cent or more of the population (including their dependants) engaged in manufacturing, trade or other urban type of business.
Jordan: Localities of 5 000 or more inhabitants.
Kazakhstan: Cities and urban-type localities, officially designated as such, usually according to the criteria of number of inhabitants and predominance of agricultural, or number of non-agricultural workers and their families.

Kyrgyzstan: Cities and urban-type localities, officially designated as such, usually according to the criteria of number of inhabitants and predominance of agricultural, or number of non-agricultural workers and their families.

Lao People's Democratic Republic: Areas or villages that satisfy at least three of the following five conditions: located in metropolitan areas of district or province, there is access to road in dry and rainy seasons, about 70 per cent or 2/3 of the population has access to piped water, about 70 per cent or 2/3 of the population has access to public electricity, there is a market operating every day.

Malaysia: Gazetted areas with their adjoining built-up areas which have a combined population of 10 000 or more. Built-up areas are defined as areas contiguous to a gazetted area and have at least 60 per cent of their population (aged 15 years and over) engaged in non-agricultural activities. The definition of urban areas also takes into account the special development area which is not gazetted and can be indentified and separated from the gazetted area or built-up area of more than 5km and a population of at least 10 000 with 60 per cent of the population (aged 15 years and over) engaged in non-agricultural activities.

Maldives: Malé, the capital.

Mongolia: Capital and district centres.

Nepal: As declared by the government municipalities.

Pakistan: Places with municipal corporation, town committee or cantonment.

Philippines: Cities and municipalities and their central districts with a population density of at least 500 persons per square km. Urban areas are considered other districts regardless of population size that have streets, at least six establishments (commercial, manufacturing, recreational and/or personal services), and at least three public structures such as town hall, church, public park, school, hospital, library, etc.

Republic of Korea: For estimates: Places with 50 000 or more inhabitants. For census: the figures are composed in the basis of the minor administrative divisions such as Dongs (mostly urban areas) and Eups or Myeons (rural areas).

Sri Lanka: All areas administered by municipal and urban councils.

State of Palestine: Any locality where the population amounts to 10 000 persons or more. This applies to all governorates/districts regardless of their size, and to all localities whose populations vary from 4 000 to 9 999 persons provided they have at least four of the following elements: public electricity network, public water network, post office, health center with a full time physician and a school offering a general secondary education certificate.

Syrian Arab Republic: Cities, Mohafaza centres and Mantika centres, and communities with 20 000 or more inhabitants.

Tajikistan: Cities and urban-type localities, officially designated as such, usually according to the criteria of number of inhabitants and predominance of agricultural, or number of non-agricultural workers and their families.

Thailand: Municipal areas.

Turkey: Localities with 20 000 inhabitants or more.

Turkmenistan: Cities and urban-type localities, officially designated as such, usually according to the criteria of number of inhabitants and predominance of agricultural, or number of non-agricultural workers and their families.

Uzbekistan: Cities and urban-type localities, officially designated as such, usually according to the criteria of number of inhabitants and predominance of agricultural, or number of non-agricultural workers and their families.

Viet Nam: Urban areas include inside urban districts of cities, urban quarters and towns. All other local administrative units (communes) belong to rural areas.

EUROPE

Albania: Towns and other industrial centres of more than 400 inhabitants.

Austria: Urban areas are localities with 2 000 or more inhabitants. The delineation of localities goes back to 1991.

Belarus: Urban settlements are settlements authorized under the law as towns, urban-type settlements, workers settlements and health resort areas.

Bulgaria: All towns and cities according to the Territorial and Administrative-Territorial Division of the country.

Czech Republic: Localities with 2 000 or more inhabitants.

Estonia: Urban settlements include cities, cities without municipal status and towns.

Finland: Urban communes including those municipalities in which at least 90 per cent of the population lives in urban settlements or in which the population of the largest urban settlement is at least 15 000.

France: Communes containing an agglomeration of more than 2 000 inhabitants living in contiguous houses or with not more than 200 metres between houses, also communes of which the major portion of the population is part of a multi-communal agglomeration of this nature.

Greece: Urban is considered every municipal or communal department of which the largest locality has 2 000 inhabitants and over.

Hungary: Localities recognized by the President of the Republic with the title of town, on the basis of specific (economic, commercial, institutional, cultural etc.) criteria.

Iceland: Localities of 200 or more inhabitants.

Ireland: Cities and towns including suburbs of 1 500 or more inhabitants.

Latvia: Cities and urban-type localities, officially designated as such, usually according to the criteria of number of inhabitants and predominance of agricultural, or number of non-agricultural workers and their families.

Liechtenstein: Communes with 10 000 inhabitants or more.

Lithuania: Urban population refers to persons who live in cities and towns, i.e., the population areas with closely built permanent dwellings and with the resident population of more than 3 000 of which 2/3 of employees work in industry, social infrastructure and business. In a number of towns the population may be less than 3 000 since these areas had already the status of "town" before the law was enforced (July 1994)

Malta: Grid cells of 1 square km with a density of at least 300 inhabitants per square km and a minimum population of 5 000; and densely populated areas (i.e. areas with a density superior to 500 inhabitants per square km).

Montenegro: According to the current law of territorial division of Montenegro. This means that each local community has the obligation to decide which settlements are urban and which are rural.

Netherlands: Urban: Municipalities with a population of 2 000 and more inhabitants. Semi-urban: Municipalities with a population of less than 2 000 but with not more than 20 per cent of their economically active male population engaged in agriculture, and specific residential municipalities of commuters.

Norway: A hub of buildings inhabited by at least 200 people and where the distance between the buildings does not exceed 50 metres. The boundaries are dynamic and may be changed due to developments and population changes.

Poland : All areas which have town rights or the status of a town with provisions of separate laws.

Portugal: Localities with 2 000 or more inhabitants.

Republic of Moldova: Cities and urban-type localities, officially designated as such, usually according to the criteria of number of inhabitants and predominance of agricultural, or number of non-agricultural workers and their families.

Romania : Localities in which the majority of the work resources are employed in non-agricultural activities with a diversified level of endowment, having a constant and significant socio-economic influence on the whole area.

Russian Federation: Cities and urban-type localities, officially designated as such, usually according to the criteria of number of inhabitants and predominance of agricultural, or number of non-agricultural workers and their families.

Serbia: Municipalities, cities and the city of Belgrade.

Slovakia: Municipalities with the status of towns, according to the following criteria: 1) it is an economic, administrative, cultural or tourism centre, 2) provides services for other municipalities, 3) has urban character (at least partly) and 4) has 5 000 inhabitants or more.

Slovenia: Settlements of 3 000 or more inhabitants, settlements that serve as seats of municipalities with at least 1 400 inhabitants, and sub-urban areas that are being gradually integrated with an urban settlement of 5 000 or more inhabitants.

Spain: For the purposes of publishing comparable results at the European level, Eurostat proposes to consider as urban, intermediate and rural, areas formed by municipalities with respectively a population over 10 000 inhabitants, 2 001 to 10 000 inhabitants, and 2 000 or less inhabitants.

Switzerland: Agglomerations and isolated towns (towns not attached to a cluster and with at least 10,000 inhabitants) are the urban space.

Ukraine: Cities and urban-type localities officially designated as such, usually according to the criteria of number of inhabitants and predominance of agricultural, or number of non-agricultural workers and their families.

United Kingdom of Great Britain and Northern Ireland: For England and Wales, the built-up areas of 10 000 or more inhabitants; for Scotland, the settlements of 3 000 or more inhabitants; and for Northern Ireland, the settlements of 5 000 or more inhabitants.

OCEANIA

Australia: An urban centre is generally defined as a population cluster of 1 000 or more people.

American Samoa: Agglomerations of 2 500 or more inhabitants, generally having population densities of 1 000 persons per square mile or more. Two types of urban areas: urbanized areas of 50 000 or more inhabitants and urban clusters of at least 2 500 and less than 50 000 inhabitants. (As of Census 2000, no urbanized areas are identified in American Samoa.)

Cook Islands: Raratonga, the most populous island.

Guam: Agglomerations of 2 500 or more inhabitants, generally having population densities of 1 000 persons per square mile or more, referred to as "urban clusters".

New Caledonia: Nouméa and communes of Païta, Nouvel Dumbéa and Mont-Dore.

New Zealand: All cities, plus boroughs, town districts, townships and country towns with a population of 1 000 or more usual residents.

Northern Mariana Islands: Agglomerations of 2 500 or more inhabitants, generally having population densities of 1 000 persons per square mile or more. Two types of urban areas: urbanized areas of 50 000 or more inhabitants and urban clusters of at least 2 500 and less than 50 000 inhabitants.

Palau: States with 2 500 inhabitants or more (the only state which satisfies this condition is Koror state).

Tokelau: All of Tokelau's population is considered to be rural.

Tonga: Nuku'alofa.

Vanuatu: Luganville centre and Vila urban.

NOTES

[1] For further information, see *Social and Demographic Statistics: Classifications of Size and Type of Locality and Urban/Rural Areas.* E/CN.3/551, United Nations, New York, 1980.

Tableau 6 – *Annuaire démographique 2014*

Le tableau 6 présente des données sur la population totale selon le sexe pour le plus grand nombre possible d'années entre 2005 et 2014, ainsi que la population urbaine si disponible.

Description des variables : les données proviennent de recensements de la population ou sont des estimations fondées, dans certains cas, sur des enquêtes par sondage portant sur toute la population. Le code qui figure dans la colonne « Code » du tableau indique comment les données ont été obtenues. Les codes utilisés sont expliqués à la fin du tableau.

Le sens donné au terme « urbain » est conforme aux définitions utilisées dans les recensements nationaux. La définition pour chaque pays figure à la fin des présentes notes technique.

Calcul des pourcentages : les pourcentages de la population urbaine sont calculés par la Division de statistique du Département des affaires économiques et sociales de l'Organisation des Nations Unies et représentent le nombre de personnes qui vivent dans des régions considérées comme urbaines pour 100 personnes de la population totale. Dans de très rares cas, les données pour la population totale ont été révisées mais les données pour la population urbaine et la population rurale ne l'ont pas été. Ces données sont indiquées en note. Dans ces cas, les proportions de population urbaine ou rurale sont à interpréter avec précaution.

Fiabilité des données : les estimations considérées comme moins sûres sont indiquées en italique plutôt qu'en caractères romains. Le classement du point de vue de la fiabilité est fondé sur la méthode utilisée pour établir l'estimation de la population totale qui figure au tableau 3 (voir les explications dans les notes techniques relatives à ce même tableau).

Insuffisance des données : les statistiques de la population urbaine selon le sexe appellent toutes les réserves qui ont été formulées à la section 3 des Notes techniques à propos des statistiques de la population en général.

Les limitations fondamentales imposées par les variations de la définition de la population totale et par les lacunes du recensement se font peut-être sentir davantage dans la répartition de la population en population urbaine et population rurale que dans sa répartition suivant toute autre caractéristique. De fait, des différences dans la définition du lieu de résidence habituel utilisée pour l'exploitation des données à l'échelon sous-national influent sur la classification en population urbaine et en population rurale. De même, les différences de degré de sous-dénombrement suivant la zone, à l'occasion des recensements, ont une incidence sur la comparabilité de ces deux catégories dans l'ensemble du tableau. La distinction entre population de fait et population de droit est également très importante du point de vue de la répartition de la population en population urbaine et en population rurale. Cette distinction est expliquée en détail à la section 3.1.1 des Notes techniques.

Toutefois, la difficulté la plus importante tient aux différences de définition du terme « urbain » selon le pays. Les distinctions faites entre « zone urbaine » et « zone rurale » varient tellement que les définitions utilisées ont été reproduites à la fin des notes techniques du tableau 6. Les définitions sont forcément brèves et, lorsque le classement en « zone urbaine » repose sur des divisions administratives, on a souvent désigné celles-ci par le nom qu'elles portent dans la zone ou le pays considéré. Par suite des variations dans la terminologie, les différences entre pays ou zones peuvent sembler plus grandes qu'elles ne le sont réellement. Il se peut aussi que des termes similaires ou identiques, tels que ville, village ou district, aient des significations très différentes selon les pays ou zones.

On constatera, en examinant les définitions adoptées par les différents pays ou zones, qu'elles peuvent être ramenées à trois types principaux : 1) les localités dépassant certaines dimensions sont classées parmi les zones urbaines ; 2) les centres administratifs de petites circonscriptions administratives sont classées parmi les zones urbaines, le reste de la circonscription étant considéré comme zone rurale ; 3) les petites divisions administratives sont classées parmi les zones urbaines selon un critère déterminé, qui peut être soit le type d'administration locale, soit le nombre d'habitants, soit le pourcentage de la population exerçant une activité agricole.

La distinction entre régions urbaines et régions rurales est si étroitement liée à des considérations d'ordre historique, politique, culturel et administratif que l'on ne peut progresser que très lentement vers des définitions et des méthodes uniformes. Non seulement les définitions sont différentes d'une zone ou d'un pays à un autre, mais on n'y retrouve parfois même plus l'intention originale de distinguer les régions rurales des régions urbaines. Lorsque la classification est fondée, en particulier, sur le critère des circonscriptions administratives (comme la plupart le sont), elle a tendance à devenir rigide avec le temps et à décourager toute modification. Pour cette raison, la comparaison des données appartenant à des séries chronologiques risque d'être gravement faussée du fait que les définitions employées sont désormais périmées. Il faut être particulièrement prudent lorsque l'on compare des données issues de recensements avec des données provenant d'enquêtes par sondage, car il se peut que les définitions du terme « urbain » auxquelles ces données se réfèrent respectivement soient différentes.

Malgré leurs insuffisances, les statistiques sur la population urbaine et rurale permettent de mettre en évidence la diversité de la répartition de la population au sein d'un pays ou d'une zone.

La distinction entre « zone urbaine » et « zone rurale » repose sur une série de critères qualitatifs aussi bien que quantitatifs, notamment l'effectif de la population, la densité de peuplement, la distance entre îlots d'habitations, le type prédominant d'activité économique, le statut juridique ou administratif, et les caractéristiques d'une agglomération urbaine, c'est-à-dire l'existence de services publics et d'équipements collectifs[1]. Bien que les statistiques différenciant les zones urbaines des zones rurales soient très répandues, il ne paraît pas possible pour le moment d'adopter une classification internationale type de ces zones, vu la diversité des interprétations nationales. La classification de la population en population urbaine et population rurale retenue ici est celle qui correspond aux définitions nationales.

Données publiées antérieurement : des statistiques concernant la population urbaine et la population totale selon le sexe ont été publiées dans des éditions antérieures de l'*Annuaire démographique*. Pour plus de précisions concernant les années pour lesquelles ces données ont été publiées, se reporter à l'index historique.

DÉFINITIONS DU TERME « URBAIN »

AFRIQUE

Algérie : La délimitation des zones urbaines et rurales se font après l'opération du recensement sur la base de la classification des agglomérations. Regroupement de 100 constructions ou plus distantes l'une à l'autre de moins de 200m ont été considérées comme zones urbaines.
Afrique du Sud : Zones dotées d'une administration locale.
Botswana : Agglomération de 5 000 habitants ou plus dont 75 p. 100 de l'activité économique n'est pas de type agricole.
Burkina Faso : Tous les chefs-lieux de province (45 au total) plus 4 villes moyennes ont été considérées comme zones urbaines.
Burundi : Commune de Bujumbura.
Comores : Toute localité ou chef-lieu d'une île, région/préfecture disposant des infrastructures suivantes : route bitumée, électricité, centre hospitalier, téléphone, etc.
Égypte : Chefs-lieux des gouvernorats du Caire, d'Alexandrie, de Port Saïd, d'Ismaïlia, de Suez ; chefs-lieux des gouvernorats frontaliers, autres chefs-lieux de gouvernorat et chefs-lieux de district (Markaz). La définition des zones urbaines pour le recensement de 2006 est celle de « shiakha », une partie d'un district.
Éthiopie : Localités de 2 000 habitants ou plus.
Guinée équatoriale : Chefs-lieux de district et localités comprenant 300 habitations et/ou 1 500 habitants ou plus.
Kenya : Zone ayant une population de 2 000 habitants ou plus qui dispose de réseaux de transport, comporte des zones bâties, des structures industrielles ou manufacturières et d'autres équipements modernes.
Lesotho : Tous les chefs-lieux administratifs et établissements urbains en forte croissance.
Libéria : Localités de 2 000 habitants ou plus.
Malawi : Toutes les villes et zones urbanisées et tous les chefs-lieux de district.
Maurice : Les cinq circonscriptions municipales, divisées en vingt arrondissements municipaux dont les limites ont été officiellement définies.
Namibie : Zones urbaines déclarées pour lesquelles il existe des données cadastrales et autres zones d'habitat non planifié.
Niger: Ville capital, villes capitales de départements ou de districts.
Ouganda : «Gazettes», villes, municipalités et bourgs.
République-Unie de Tanzanie : 16 townships érigées en communes.

Rwanda : Toutes les zones administratives reconnues comme urbaines par la loi. Il s'agit de tous les chefs-lieux des provinces, de la ville de Kigali ainsi que des villes de Nyanza, Ruhango et Rwamagana.

Sénégal : Agglomérations de 10 000 habitants ou plus.

Soudan : Centres administratifs et/ou commerciaux ou localités ayant une population de 5 000 habitants ou plus.

Swaziland : Zone géographique qui constitue une ville et se caractérise par une densité de population et de constructions humaines plus élevée que dans les zones qui l'entourent.

Tunisie : Population vivant dans les communes.

Zambie : Localités de 5 000 habitants ou plus dont l'activité économique prédominante n'est pas de type agricole.

AMÉRIQUE DU NORD

Canada : Agglomérations de 1 000 habitants ou plus ayant une densité de population d'au moins 400 habitants au kilomètre carré.

Costa Rica : Chefs-lieux de canton.

Cuba : Villes ayant une fonction politique ou administrative, ou une population supérieure à 2 000 habitants et présentant des traits urbains.

El Salvador : Chefs-lieux de municipios.

États-Unis d'Amérique : Agglomérations de 2 500 habitants ou plus ayant généralement une densité de population d'au moins 1 000 habitants au mile carré. Deux types de zones urbaines : zones urbanisées de 50 000 habitants ou plus et groupements urbains comptant au moins 2 500 habitants mais moins de 50 000.

Groenland : Localités d'au moins 200 habitants.

Guatemala : Municipio du département de Guatemala et centres administratifs officiels d'autres départements et municipios.

Haïti : Chefs-lieux de communes.

Honduras : Localités d'au moins 2 000 habitants ayant des caractéristiques essentiellement urbaines.

Îles Vierges américaines : Agglomérations de 2 500 habitants ou plus ayant généralement une densité de population d'au moins 1 000 habitants au mile carré. Deux types de zones urbaines : zones urbanisées de 50 000 habitants ou plus et groupements urbains comptant au moins 2 500 habitants mais moins de 50 000. (D'après les résultats du recensement de 2 000, les Îles Vierges américaines ne comptent aucune zone urbanisée.)

Jamaïque : Localités de 2 000 habitants ou plus présentant des traits urbains.

Mexique : Localités d'au moins 2 500 habitants.

Nicaragua : Centres administratifs des municipalités et localités d'au moins 1 000 habitants ou d'au moins 150 logements, possédant des rues, un éclairage électrique, un réseau de distribution d'eau, une école et un dispensaire.

Panama : Localités d'au moins 1 500 habitants ayant des caractéristiques essentiellement urbaines. À partir de 1970, localités de 1 500 habitants ou plus présentant des caractéristiques urbaines, telles que rues, éclairage électrique, systèmes d'approvisionnement en eau et réseaux d'égouts.

Porto Rico : Agglomérations de 2 500 habitants ou plus ayant généralement une densité de population d'au moins 1 000 habitants au mile carré. Deux types de zones urbaines : zones urbanisées de 50 000 habitants ou plus et groupements urbains comptant au moins 2 500 habitants mais moins de 50 000.

République dominicaine : Chefs-lieux de municipios et districts municipaux, dont certains comprennent des zones suburbaines ayant des caractéristiques rurales.

AMÉRIQUE DU SUD

Argentine : Centres comptant au moins 2 000 habitants.

Bolivie : Localités de 2 000 habitants ou plus.

Brésil : Zone à l'intérieur du périmètre urbain d'une ville, définie par la législation municipale.

Chili : Zones d'habitat concentré comptant 2 000 habitants ou plus, ou comptant entre 1 001 et 2 000 habitants dont 50 pour cent au moins de la population active a une activité secondaire ou tertiaire. Par dérogation, les centres qui ont une fonction touristique ou récréative et plus de 250 unités de logement mais n'atteignent pas le critère de population sont néanmoins considérés comme zones urbaines.

Colombie : Zone avec une mairie, définie par un périmètre urbain qui est établie par des accords municipaux.

Équateur : Capitales des provinces et chefs-lieux de canton.

Îles Falkland (Malvinas) : Ville de Stanley.

Paraguay : Grandes villes, villes et chefs-lieux des départements et des districts.

Pérou : Centres de peuplement comptant plus de 100 logements.

Suriname : Les districts de Paramaribo et de Wanica.

Uruguay : Les villes, villages et autres zones habitées répondant aux définitions de la loi sur les agglomérations.

Venezuela (République bolivarienne du) : Centres de 2 500 habitants ou plus.

ASIE

Arménie : Grandes villes et localités de type urbain, officiellement désignées comme telles, généralement sur la base du nombre d'habitants et de la prédominance des travailleurs agricoles ou non agricoles avec leur famille.

Azerbaïdjan : Division administrative regroupant plus de 15 000 habitants se livrant principalement à des activités industrielles et autres activités économiques et sociales et comprennant des centres administratifs et culturels.

Bahreïn : Communes ou villages comptant au moins 2 500 habitants.

Cambodge : Zones au niveau de la commune répondant aux trois conditions suivantes: 1) Densité démographique supérieure à 200 habitants au km carré, 2) pourcentage d'hommes travaillant dans l'agriculture inférieur à 50 pour cent, 3) population totale de la commune supérieure à 2 000 habitants.

Chine : Suivant la Réglementation sur la classification de la résidence urbaine/rurale à des fins de statistiques.

Chypre : Selon la définition du Département de l'urbanisme et du logement du Ministère de l'intérieur.

État de Palestine : Localités peuplées de plus de 10 000 personnes. L'expression désigne tous les gouvernorats (districts), quelle qu'en soit la taille, ainsi que toutes les villes dont la population est comprise entre 4 000 et 9 999 personnes qui disposent d'au moins quatre des éléments suivants : réseau public de distribution d'électricité, réseau public de distribution d'eau, bureau de poste, centre médical doté d'un médecin à temps plein et école préparant les élèves au certificat général de l'enseignement secondaire.

Géorgie : Grandes villes et localités de type urbain, officiellement désignées comme telles, généralement sur la base du nombre d'habitants et de la prédominance des travailleurs agricoles ou non agricoles avec leur famille.

Inde : Villes [localités dotées d'une charte municipale, d'un comité de zone municipale, d'un comité de zone déclarée urbaine ou d'un comité de zone de regroupement (cantonnement)] ; également toutes les localités qui ont une population de 5 000 habitants au moins, une densité de population d'au moins 1 000 habitants au mile carré ou 400 au kilomètre carré, des caractéristiques urbaines prononcées et où les trois quarts au moins des adultes de sexe masculin ont une occupation non agricole.

Indonésie : Zones qui répondent à certains critères de densité démographique et de pourcentage des ménages agricoles et possèdent un certain nombre d'équipements urbains tels que routes, écoles, services de santé publique, etc.

Iran (République islamique d') : Tous les districts comptant une municipalité.

Israël : Tous les lieux comptant au moins 2 000 résidents.

Japon : Villes (shi), comptant au moins 50 000 habitants, où 60 p. 100 au moins des logements sont situés dans les principales zones bâties, et dont 60 p. 100 au moins de population (y compris les personnes à charge) exercent un métier dans l'industrie, le commerce et d'autres branches d'activités essentiellement urbaines.

Jordanie : Localités comptant 5 000 habitants ou plus.

Kazakhstan : Grandes villes et localités de type urbain, officiellement désignées comme telles, généralement sur la base du nombre d'habitants et de la prédominance des travailleurs agricoles ou non agricoles avec leur famille.

Kirghizistan : Grandes villes et localités de type urbain, officiellement désignées comme telles, généralement sur la base du nombre d'habitants et de la prédominance des travailleurs agricoles ou non agricoles avec leur famille.

Malaisie : Zone ayant le statut de centre urbain et dont la population totale dépasse 10 000 habitants. On nomme périphérie toute zone contiguë à un centre urbain dont au moins 60 % de la population (âgée de 15 ans et plus) a une activité non agricole. La définition des zones urbaines couvre également les zones spéciales de développement qui n'ont pas officiellement le statut de centre urbain, se trouvent à 5 kilomètres ou plus d'un tel centre ou de sa périphérie et comptent au moins 10 000 habitants dont 60 % (parmi les plus de 15 ans) ont une activité non agricole.

Maldives : Malé (capitale).

Mongolie : Capitale et chefs-lieux de district.

Népal : Zones déclarées telles par les municipalités.

Ouzbékistan : Grandes villes et localités de type urbain, officiellement désignées comme telles, généralement sur la base du nombre d'habitants et de la prédominance des travailleurs agricoles ou non agricoles avec leur famille.

Pakistan : Localités dotées d'une charte municipale ou d'un comité municipal et regroupements (cantonments).

Philippines : Villes et municipalités et leurs quartiers centraux dont la densité démographique est d'au moins 500 habitants au km carré. Sont considérés comme zones urbaines les autres quartiers quelle que soit leur population qui sont équipés de routes et possèdent au moins six établissements (commerce, industrie manufacturière, équipements récréatifs ou services aux personnes), et au moins trois équipements publics tels que hôtel de ville, église, parc public, école, hôpital, bibliothèque, etc.

République arabe syrienne : Villes, chefs-lieux de district (Mohafaza) et chefs-lieux de sous district (Mantika), et communes d'au moins 20 000 habitants.

République de Corée : Pour les estimations : localités de 50 000 habitants ou plus. Pour recensements, les données sont établies sont la base des divisions administratives mineures comme les Dongs (principalement en zone urbaines) et des Eups ou Myeons (en zones rurales).

République démocratique populaire lao : Zones ou villages répondant à au moins trois des cinq conditions suivantes: situés dans l'aire métropolitaine du district ou de la province, accessibles par la route en toute saison, quelque 70 pour cent ou deux tiers de la population ayant accès à de l'eau distribuée par canalisation, quelque 70 pour cent ou deux tiers de la population ayant accès au réseau d'électricité et existence d'un marché ouvert tous les jours.

Sri Lanka : Toutes les zones administrées par les conseils municipaux et urbains.

Tadjikistan : Grandes villes et localités de type urbain, officiellement désignées comme telles, généralement sur la base du nombre d'habitants et de la prédominance des travailleurs agricoles ou non agricoles avec leur famille.

Thaïlande : Zones municipales.

Turkménistan : Grandes villes et localités de type urbain, officiellement désignées comme telles, généralement sur la base du nombre d'habitants et de la prédominance des travailleurs agricoles ou non agricoles avec leur famille.

Turquie : Localités comptant 20 000 habitants ou plus.

Viet Nam : Zones urbaines comprises à l'intérieur des districts urbains des villes ainsi que des quartiers urbains et des localités. Toutes les autres unités administratives locales (communes) sont considérées comme zones rurales.

EUROPE

Albanie : Villes et autres centres industriels de plus de 400 habitants.

Autriche : Les zones urbaines sont les localités comptant 2 000 habitants ou plus. Leur délimitation remonte à 1991.

Bélarus : Les établissements urbains sont des établissements autorisés en vertu de la loi comme les villes, les agglomérations de type urbain, les cités ouvrières et les zones de villégiature de santé.

Bulgarie : Toutes les zones considérées comme villes et bourgs selon la Division territoriale et administrative du pays.

Espagne : Aux fins de la publication de résultats qui soient comparables au niveau européen, Eurostat propose de considérer comme zones urbaines, intermédiaires et rurales les communes comptant respectivement plus de 10 000 habitants, de 2 001 à 10 000 habitants et moins de 2 000 habitants.

Estonie : Les établissements urbains comprennent les villes et les agglomérations n'ayant pas de statut municipal.

Fédération de Russie : Grandes villes et localités de type urbain, officiellement désignées comme telles, généralement sur la base du nombre d'habitants et de la prédominance des travailleurs agricoles ou non agricoles avec leur famille.

Finlande : Communes urbaines (communes où au moins 90 % de la population vit en milieu urbain ou dont le plus grand centre urbain compte au moins 15 000 habitants).

France : Communes comprenant une agglomération de plus de 2 000 habitants vivant dans des habitations contiguës ou qui ne sont pas distantes les unes des autres de plus de 200 mètres et communes où la majeure partie de la population vit dans une agglomération regroupant plusieurs communes de cette nature.

Grèce : Est considérée comme zone urbaine toute municipalité ou commune dont la plus grande localité compte 2 000 habitants ou plus.

Hongrie : Localités dont le statut de ville a été reconnu par le Président de la République compte tenu de critères spécifiques (économiques, commerciaux, institutionnels, culturels, etc.).

Irlande : Localités, y compris leur banlieues, comptant 1 500 habitants ou plus.

Islande : Localités de 200 habitants ou plus.

Lettonie : Grandes villes et localités de type urbain, officiellement désignées comme telles, généralement sur la base du nombre d'habitants et de la prédominance des travailleurs agricoles ou non agricoles avec leur famille.

Liechtenstein : Communes comptant 10 000 habitants ou plus.

Lituanie : Par population urbaine, on entend les personnes qui vivent dans des villes ou des localités, à savoir les zones habitées comportant des logements permanents proches les uns des autres et dont la population est d'au moins 3 000 habitants, les deux tiers desquels étant employés dans le secteur industriel, l'infrastructure sociale ou le commerce. Un certain nombre de villes peuvent compter moins de 3 000 habitants dans la mesure où elles avaient acquis le statut de ville avant l'entrée en vigueur de la nouvelle loi en juillet 1994.

Malte : Zones de 1 kilomètre carré avec une densité minimum de 300 et un minimum de 5 000 habitants au kilomètre carré; et zones à forte densité de population (supérieure à 500 habitants au kilomètre carré).

Monténégro : D'après la législation actuelle relative à l'organisation territoriale du Monténégro, qui oblige chaque collectivité à déterminer quelles sont ses zones urbaines et rurales.

Norvège : Ensemble construit habité par au moins 200 personnes, où les bâtiments ne sont pas éloignés de plus de 50 mètres les uns des autres. Les limites en sont évolutives et peuvent être redéfinies pour tenir compte de l'urbanisation et de l'évolution de la population.

Pays Bas : Zones urbaines : municipalités comptant au moins 2 000 habitants. Zones semi-urbaines : municipalités comptant moins de 2 000 habitants, mais où 20 p. 100 au maximum de la population active de sexe masculin pratiquent l'agriculture, et certaines municipalités de caractère résidentiel dont les habitants travaillent ailleurs.

Pologne : Toutes les zones qui ont les droits d'une ville ou le statut d'une ville avec dispositions de lois distinctes.

Portugal : Localités comptant 2 000 habitants ou davantage.

République de Moldova : Grandes villes et localités de type urbain, officiellement désignées comme telles, généralement sur la base du nombre d'habitants et de la prédominance des travailleurs agricoles ou non agricoles avec leur famille.

République tchèque : Localités d'au moins 2 000 habitants.

Roumanie : Localités où la majorité des ressources en main-d'œuvre est employée dans des activités non agricoles avec un niveau diversifié de ressources, exerçant une influence socioéconomique constante et importante sur l'ensemble de la zone.

Royaume-Uni de Grande-Bretagne et d'Irlande du Nord : Pour l'Angleterre et le Pays de Galles, les zones bâties comptant 10 000 habitants ou plus; pour l'Écosse, les établissements humains comptant 3 000 habitants ou davantage et pour l'Irlande du Nord, les établissements comptant 5 000 habitants.

Serbie : Municipalités, villes et Belgrade.

Slovaquie : Municipalités avec statut de ville, suivant les critères ci-après: 1) est un centre économique, administratif, culturel ou touristique, 2) fournit des services pour d'autres municipalités, 3) a un caractère urbain, au moins en partie, et 4) compte 5 000 habitants ou plus.

Slovénie : Établissements de 3 000 habitants ou plus, chefs-lieux de municipalités comptant au moins 1 400 habitants, et quartiers suburbains qui s'intègrent progressivement dans une ville de 5 000 habitants ou plus.

Suisse : L'espace urbain comprend les agglomérations et les villes isolées (n'appartenant pas à une agglomération et ayant au moins 10 000 habitants à elles seules).

Ukraine : Grandes villes et localités de type urbain, officiellement désignées comme telles, généralement sur la base du nombre d'habitants et de la prédominance des travailleurs agricoles ou non agricoles avec leur famille.

OCÉANIE

Australie : Un regroupement de population de 1 000 personnes ou plus est généralement considéré comme un centre urbain.

Guam : Agglomérations de 2 500 habitants ou plus ayant généralement une densité de population d'au moins 1 000 habitants au mile carré et considérées comme étant des groupements urbains.

Îles Cook : Rarotonga, île la plus peuplée.

Îles Mariannes septentrionales : Agglomérations de 2 500 habitants ou plus ayant généralement une densité de population d'au moins 1 000 habitants au mile carré. Deux types de zones urbaines : zones urbanisées de 50 000 habitants ou plus et groupements urbains comptant au moins 2 500 habitants mais moins de 50 000.

Nouvelle-Calédonie : Nouméa et communes de Païta, Dumbéa et Mont-Dore.

Nouvelle-Zélande : Toutes les villes et les quartiers, districts et bourgs ayant 1 000 habitants permanents ou plus.

Palaos : États comptant 2 500 habitants ou plus (le seul État qui remplit cette condition est l'État de Koror).

Samoa américaines : Agglomérations de 2 500 habitants ou plus ayant généralement une densité de population d'au moins 1 000 habitants au mile carré. Deux types de zones urbaines : zones urbanisées de 50 000 habitants ou plus et groupements urbains comptant au moins 2 500 habitants mais moins de 50 000. (D'après les résultats du recensement de 2000, les Samoa américaines ne comptent aucune zone urbanisée.)

Tokélaou : L'ensemble de la population est considéré comme vivant en milieu rural.

Tonga : Nuku'alofa.

Vanuatu : Centre de Luganville et Port-Vila.

NOTES

[1] Pour plus de précisions, voir *Social and Demographic Statistics: Classifications of Size and Type of Locality and Urban/Rural Areas*, E/CN.3/551, publication des Nations Unies, New York, 1980.

Continent, country or area, and date / Continent, pays ou zone et date	Code[a]	Both sexes - Les deux sexes Total	Urban - Urbaine Number Nombre	Urban - Urbaine Percent P.100	Male - Masculin Total	Urban - Urbaine Number Nombre	Urban - Urbaine Percent P.100	Female - Féminin Total	Urban - Urbaine Number Nombre	Urban - Urbaine Percent P.100
AFRICA - AFRIQUE										
Algeria - Algérie										
1 VII 2005	ESDJ	32 906 000	...	...	16 624 000	...	...	16 282 000	...	...
1 VII 2006	ESDJ	33 481 000	...	...	16 915 000	...	...	16 566 000	...	...
1 VII 2007	ESDJ	34 096 000	...	...	17 225 000	...	...	16 871 000	...	...
16 IV 2008[1]	CDFC	34 452 759	...	...	17 428 500	...	...	17 024 259	...	...
1 VII 2008	ESDJ	34 591 000	22 808 000	65.9	17 493 000	...	...	17 098 000	...	...
1 VII 2009	ESDJ	35 268 000	...	...	17 846 000	...	...	17 422 000	...	...
1 VII 2010	ESDJ	35 978 000	...	...	18 205 000	...	...	17 773 000	...	...
1 VII 2011	ESDJ	36 717 000	...	...	18 579 000	...	...	18 138 000	...	...
1 VII 2012	ESDJ	37 495 000	...	...	18 976 000	...	...	18 519 000	...	...
1 VII 2013	ESDJ	38 297 000	...	...	19 383 000	...	...	18 914 000	...	...
1 VII 2014	ESDJ	39 114 275	...	...	19 801 163	...	...	19 313 112	...	...
Angola										
16 V 2014*	CDFC	24 383 301	15 182 898	62.3	11 803 488	7 373 503	62.5	12 579 813	7 809 395	62.1
Benin - Bénin										
1 VII 2005[2]	ESDF	7 447 454	3 002 229	40.3	3 627 613	1 467 342	40.4	3 819 841	1 534 887	40.2
1 VII 2006[2]	ESDF	7 699 697	3 156 172	41.0	3 755 408	1 544 515	41.1	3 944 289	1 611 657	40.9
1 VII 2007[2]	ESDF	7 958 813	3 324 220	41.8	3 886 596	1 628 650	41.9	4 072 217	1 695 570	41.6
1 VII 2008[2]	ESDF	8 224 642	3 499 506	42.5	4 021 094	1 716 411	42.7	4 203 548	1 783 095	42.4
1 VII 2009[2]	ESDF	8 497 827	3 682 496	43.3	4 159 291	1 808 057	43.5	4 338 536	1 874 439	43.2
1 VII 2010[2]	ESDF	8 778 648	3 873 462	44.1	4 301 224	1 903 683	44.3	4 477 424	1 969 779	44.0
1 VII 2011[2]	ESDF	9 067 076	4 072 574	44.9	4 446 877	2 003 366	45.1	4 620 199	2 069 208	44.8
1 VII 2012[2]	ESDF	9 364 619	4 280 693	45.7	4 597 122	...	...	4 767 497	...	...
11 V 2013*	CDJC	9 983 884	...	...	4 868 180	...	...	5 115 704	...	...
Botswana										
1 VII 2005	ESDJ	1 708 327	...	...	829 850	...	...	878 477	...	...
1 VII 2006	ESDJ	1 719 996	...	...	837 114	...	...	882 882	...	...
1 VIII 2006[3]	SSDJ	1 773 240	1 000 443	56.4	851 670	473 136	55.6	921 570	527 307	57.2
1 VII 2007	ESDJ	1 736 396	...	...	847 539	...	...	888 857	...	...
1 VII 2008	ESDJ	1 755 246	...	...	859 167	...	...	896 079	...	...
1 VII 2009	ESDJ	1 776 494	...	...	871 964	...	...	904 530	...	...
1 VII 2010	ESDJ	1 822 859	...	...	895 007	...	...	927 852	...	...
1 VII 2011	ESDJ	1 849 692	...	...	910 404	...	...	939 288	...	...
9 VIII 2011	CDFC	2 024 904	1 297 287	64.1	988 957	619 472	62.6	1 035 947	677 815	65.4
Burkina Faso										
1 VII 2005	ESDJ	13 373 670	...	...	6 456 103	...	...	6 917 567	...	...
9 XII 2006	CDFC	14 196 259	3 230 504	22.8	6 842 560	1 609 349	23.5	7 353 699	1 621 155	22.0
1 VII 2007[2]	ESDJ	14 252 012	3 322 360	23.3	6 880 824	1 629 956	23.7	7 371 188	1 692 404	23.0
1 VII 2008[2]	ESDJ	14 731 167	...	...	7 110 097	...	...	7 621 070	...	...
1 VII 2009[2]	ESDJ	15 224 780	...	...	7 346 835	...	...	7 877 945	...	...
1 VII 2010[2]	ESDJ	15 730 977	...	...	7 590 133	...	...	8 140 844	...	...
Burundi										
16 VIII 2008	CDFC	7 877 728	799 802	10.2	3 838 045	432 442	11.3	4 039 683	367 360	9.1
1 VII 2009[4]	ESDF	8 262 912	892 394	10.8	4 065 512	439 075	10.8	4 197 400	453 319	10.8
1 VII 2010[4]	ESDF	8 487 650	976 080	11.5	4 173 862	479 994	11.5	4 313 788	496 086	11.5
1 VII 2011[4]	ESDF	8 727 180	1 064 716	12.2	4 289 661	523 339	12.2	4 437 519	541 377	12.2
1 VII 2012[4]	ESDF	8 981 318	1 158 590	12.9	4 412 830	569 255	12.9	4 568 488	589 335	12.9
1 VII 2013[4]	ESDF	9 249 336	1 257 910	13.6	4 543 008	617 849	13.6	4 706 328	640 061	13.6
1 VII 2014[4]	ESDF	9 530 434	1 362 852	14.3	4 679 790	669 210	14.3	4 850 644	693 642	14.3
Cabo Verde										
1 VII 2005	ESDF	475 465	278 947	58.7	230 063	...	...	245 402	...	...
1 VII 2006	ESDF	483 090	286 687	59.3	233 729	...	...	249 361	...	...
1 VII 2007	ESDF	491 419	295 046	60.0	237 842	...	...	253 577	...	...
1 VII 2008	ESDF	499 796	303 512	60.7	241 914	...	...	257 882	...	...
1 VII 2009	ESDF	508 633	310 958	61.1	246 219	...	...	262 414	...	...
16 VI 2010	CDJC	491 683	303 673	61.8	243 401	151 217	62.1	248 282	152 456	61.4
1 VII 2010	ESDF	517 831	320 111	61.8	250 710	...	...	267 121	...	...
1 VII 2011	ESDF	527 269	328 177	62.2	255 327	...	...	271 942	...	...
Cameroon - Cameroun										
11 XI 2005	CDFC	17 052 134	...	...	8 408 495	...	...	8 643 639	...	...
1 I 2010[2]	ESDJ	19 406 100	10 091 172	52.0	9 599 224	5 029 993	52.4	9 806 876	5 061 179	51.6

6. Total and urban population by sex: 2005 - 2014
Population totale et population urbaine selon le sexe : 2005 - 2014 (continued - suite)

Continent, country or area, and date / Continent, pays ou zone et date	Code[a]	Both sexes - Les deux sexes			Male - Masculin			Female - Féminin		
		Total	Urban - Urbaine		Total	Urban - Urbaine		Total	Urban - Urbaine	
			Number Nombre	Percent P.100		Number Nombre	Percent P.100		Number Nombre	Percent P.100
AFRICA - AFRIQUE										
Chad - Tchad										
20 V 2009 ....CDJC		11 175 915	...	...	5 509 522	...	...	5 666 393	...	...
Congo										
28 IV 2007 ....CDFC		3 697 490	2 285 551	61.8	1 821 357	1 132 510	62.2	1 876 133	1 153 041	61.5
1 VII 2008 ....ESDF		3 740 851	...	...	1 841 589	...	...	1 899 262	...	...
1 VII 2009 ....ESDF		3 838 238	...	...	1 891 558	...	...	1 946 680	...	...
Côte d'Ivoire										
1 VII 2005[2]..................ESDF		19 096 988	...	...	9 740 427	...	...	9 356 561	...	...
1 VII 2006[2]..................ESDF		19 657 738	...	...	10 023 964	...	...	9 633 774	...	...
1 VII 2007[2]..................ESDF		20 227 876	...	...	10 312 061	...	...	9 915 815	...	...
1 VII 2008[2]..................ESDF		20 807 216	...	...	10 604 596	...	...	10 202 620	...	...
1 VII 2009[2]..................ESDF		21 395 198	...	...	10 901 322	...	...	10 493 876	...	...
15 V 2014 ....CDFC		22 671 331	...	...	11 708 244	...	...	10 963 087	...	...
Djibouti										
29 V 2009 ....CDFC		818 159	577 933	70.6	440 067	322 796	73.4	378 092	255 137	67.5
Egypt - Égypte										
1 VII 2005 ....ESDF		70 653 326	30 187 331	42.7	36 037 030	...	...	34 616 296	...	...
1 VII 2006 ....ESDF		72 008 900	30 699 375	42.6	36 725 501	...	...	35 283 399	...	...
21 XI 2006 ....CDFC		72 798 031	31 370 925	43.1	37 219 056	16 013 864	43.0	35 578 975	15 357 061	43.2
1 VII 2007 ....ESDF		73 643 587	31 719 927	43.1	37 643 353	16 186 484	43.0	36 000 234	15 533 443	43.1
1 VII 2008 ....ESDF		75 193 567	32 248 476	42.9	38 413 404	16 437 464	42.8	36 780 163	15 811 012	43.0
1 VII 2009 ....ESDF		76 925 139	33 082 770	43.0	39 327 098	16 887 176	42.9	37 598 041	16 195 594	43.1
1 VII 2010 ....ESDF		78 684 622	33 804 181	43.0	40 228 119	17 255 735	42.9	38 456 503	16 548 446	43.0
1 VII 2011 ....ESDF		80 529 566	34 495 468	42.8	41 152 525	17 596 284	42.8	39 377 041	16 899 184	42.9
1 VII 2012 ....ESDF		82 549 976	35 372 982	42.9	42 167 660	18 031 407	42.8	40 382 316	17 341 575	42.9
1 VII 2013 ....ESDF		84 628 982	36 213 473	42.8	43 217 105	18 470 748	42.7	41 411 877	17 742 725	42.8
1 VII 2014 ....ESDF		86 813 723	37 094 960	42.7	44 304 619	18 904 449	42.7	42 509 104	18 190 511	42.8
Ethiopia - Éthiopie										
1 VII 2005[5]..................ESDF		73 043 510	11 674 521	16.0	36 604 591	5 802 931	15.9	36 438 919	5 871 590	16.1
1 VII 2006[5]..................ESDF		75 067 000	12 172 000	16.2	37 615 000	6 050 000	16.1	37 452 000	6 122 000	16.3
29 V 2007 ....CDFC		73 750 932	11 862 821	16.1	37 217 130	5 895 916	15.8	36 533 802	5 966 905	16.3
1 VII 2007[5]..................ESDF		77 127 000	12 689 000	16.5	38 644 000	6 307 000	16.3	38 483 000	6 382 000	16.6
1 VII 2008[5]..................ESDF		79 221 000	13 225 000	16.7	39 691 000	6 575 000	16.6	39 530 000	6 650 000	16.8
Gabon[6]										
1 VII 2005 ....ESDF		1 312 500	...	...	645 700	...	...	666 700	...	...
Gambia - Gambie										
15 IV 2013* ....CDFC		1 882 450	...	...	930 699	...	...	951 751	...	...
Ghana										
1 VII 2005[2]..................ESDF		21 367 006	...	...	10 579 368	...	...	10 787 638	...	...
1 VII 2006[2]..................ESDF		21 876 031	...	...	10 833 033	...	...	11 042 998	...	...
1 VII 2007[2]..................ESDF		22 387 911	...	...	11 088 060	...	...	11 299 851	...	...
1 VII 2008[2]..................ESDF		22 900 927	...	...	11 343 581	...	...	11 557 346	...	...
1 VII 2009[2]..................ESDF		23 416 518	10 243 312	43.7	11 600 326	5 006 198	43.2	11 816 192	5 237 114	44.3
26 IX 2010 ....CDFC		24 658 823	12 545 229	50.9	12 024 845	6 016 059	50.0	12 633 978	6 529 170	51.7
1 VII 2011[2]..................ESDF		25 235 268	12 844 745	50.9	12 319 770	6 270 758	50.9	12 915 498	6 573 987	50.9
1 VII 2012[2]..................ESDF		25 824 920	13 144 879	50.9	12 621 125	6 424 150	50.9	13 203 795	6 720 729	50.9
1 VII 2013[2]..................ESDF		26 427 760	13 451 714	50.9	12 928 916	6 580 808	50.9	13 498 844	6 870 906	50.9
1 VII 2014[2]..................ESDF		27 043 093	13 764 931	50.9	13 242 709	6 740 539	50.9	13 800 384	7 024 392	50.9
Guinea - Guinée										
1 VII 2008[2]..................ESDF		10 182 926	2 851 219	28.0	...	...	...	...	...	...
1 VII 2009[2]..................ESDF		10 217 591	...	...	5 038 823	...	...	5 178 768	...	...
1 VII 2010[2]..................ESDF		10 537 234	...	...	5 200 608	...	...	5 336 626	...	...
1 VII 2011[2]..................ESDF		10 863 888	...	...	5 309 110	...	...	5 554 778	...	...
1 III 2014* ....CDFC		10 628 972	...	...	5 142 088	...	...	5 486 884	...	...
Guinea-Bissau - Guinée-Bissau										
15 III 2009 ....CDFC		1 520 830	...	...	737 634	...	...	783 196	...	...
1 VII 2010[2]..................ESDF		1 558 090	...	...	802 384	...	...	755 706	...	...
Kenya										
1 VII 2005[7]..................ESDF		35 267 222	6 213 505	17.6	17 457 906	3 688 113	21.1	17 809 316	2 525 392	14.2
1 VII 2006[7]..................ESDF		36 432 866	...	...	18 052 944	...	...	18 379 922	...	...
1 VII 2007[7]..................ESDF		37 183 923	...	...	18 440 822	...	...	18 743 102	...	...
24 VIII 2009 ....CDFC		38 610 097	12 487 375	32.3	19 192 458	6 278 811	32.7	19 417 639	6 208 564	32.0
1 VII 2010[8]..................ESDF		38 910 323	...	...	19 342 322[9]	...	...	19 571 892[9]	...	...
1 VII 2011[8]..................ESDF		39 545 118	...	...	19 657 878[9]	...	...	19 891 194[9]	...	...

6. Total and urban population by sex: 2005 - 2014
Population totale et population urbaine selon le sexe : 2005 - 2014 (continued - suite)

Continent, country or area, and date / Continent, pays ou zone et date	Code[a]	Both sexes - Les deux sexes — Total	Urban - Urbaine Number Nombre	Urban - Urbaine Percent P.100	Male - Masculin — Total	Urban - Urbaine Number Nombre	Urban - Urbaine Percent P.100	Female - Féminin — Total	Urban - Urbaine Number Nombre	Urban - Urbaine Percent P.100
AFRICA - AFRIQUE										
Kenya										
1 VII 2012[8]	ESDF	40 651 744	...	...	20 207 982[9]	...	...	20 447 827[9]	...	...
1 VII 2013[8]	ESDF	41 792 563	...	...	20 775 083[9]	...	...	21 021 659[9]	...	...
1 VII 2014[8]	ESDF	42 961 187	...	...	21 289 752	...	...	21 671 435	...	...
Lesotho										
13 IV 2006	CDFC	1 741 406	403 104	23.1	818 379	181 351	22.2	923 027	221 753	24.0
1 VII 2006[2]	ESDF	1 866 471	421 655	22.6	...	...	...	...	...	...
Liberia - Libéria										
1 VII 2006	ESDF	3 332 320	1 540 608	46.2	1 669 253	760 049	45.5	1 663 067	780 559	46.9
1 VII 2007	ESDF	3 403 700	1 586 481	46.6	1 704 232	780 788	45.8	1 699 468	805 693	47.4
21 III 2008	CDFC	3 476 608	1 633 719	47.0	1 739 945	802 092	46.1	1 736 663	831 627	47.9
1 VII 2009	ESDF	3 551 078	1 682 364	47.4	1 776 406	823 978	46.4	1 774 672	858 386	48.4
1 VII 2010	ESDF	3 627 144	1 732 457	47.8	1 813 631	846 461	46.7	1 813 513	885 996	48.9
1 VII 2011	ESDF	3 704 838	1 784 042	48.2	1 851 636	869 557	47.0	1 853 202	914 485	49.3
1 VII 2012	ESDF	3 784 197	1 837 163	48.5	1 890 438	893 283	47.3	1 893 759	943 880	49.8
1 VII 2013	ESDF	3 865 256	1 891 865	48.9	1 930 053	917 657	47.5	1 935 203	974 208	50.3
1 VII 2014	ESDF	3 946 311	1 946 567	49.3	1 969 668	942 031	47.8	1 976 643	1 004 536	50.8
Libya - Libye										
1 VII 2005	ESDF	5 209 360	...	...	2 642 899	...	...	2 566 461	...	...
15 IV 2006*	CDFC	5 298 152	4 670 858	88.2	2 687 513	2 372 379	88.3	2 610 639	2 298 479	88.0
1 VII 2007	ESDF	5 393 325	4 754 540	88.2	2 735 343	2 414 477	88.3	2 657 982	2 340 064	88.0
1 VII 2008	ESDF	5 490 478	4 839 715	88.1	2 784 122	2 457 272	88.3	2 706 356	2 382 443	88.0
1 VII 2009	ESDF	5 589 289	4 926 097	88.1	2 833 691	2 500 626	88.2	2 755 598	2 425 471	88.0
1 VII 2010	ESDF	5 689 419	5 013 386	88.1	2 883 880	2 544 388	88.2	2 805 538	2 468 998	88.0
1 VII 2011	ESDF	5 790 518	5 101 275	88.1	2 934 512	2 588 402	88.2	2 856 006	2 512 874	88.0
1 VII 2012	ESDF	5 892 239	5 189 460	88.1	2 985 408	2 632 510	88.2	2 906 831	2 556 950	88.0
1 VII 2013	ESDF	5 994 241	5 277 638	88.0	3 036 393	2 676 558	88.1	2 957 849	2 601 081	87.9
1 VII 2014	ESDF	6 096 208	5 365 529	88.0	3 087 301	2 720 398	88.1	3 008 907	2 645 131	87.9
Malawi										
1 VII 2005[2]	ESDF	12 341 170	1 616 169[10]	13.1	6 067 563	833 812[10]	13.7	6 273 607	782 357[10]	12.5
1 VII 2006[2]	ESDF	12 757 883	1 700 379	13.3	6 275 533	875 943	14.0	6 482 350	824 436	12.7
1 VII 2007[2]	ESDF	13 187 632	1 786 434	13.5	6 490 146	918 991	14.2	6 697 486	867 443	13.0
8 VI 2008	CDFC	13 077 160	2 003 309	15.3	6 358 933	1 014 477	16.0	6 718 227	988 832	14.7
1 VII 2008[2]	ESDF	13 630 164	1 874 199[10]	13.8	6 711 263	962 887[10]	14.3	6 918 901	911 312[10]	13.2
1 VII 2010[11]	ESDF	13 948 594	...	...	6 804 310	...	...	7 143 284	...	...
1 VII 2011[11]	ESDF	14 388 551	...	...	7 029 149	...	...	7 359 401	...	...
1 VII 2012[11]	ESDF	14 844 822	...	...	7 261 499	...	...	7 583 323	...	...
Mali										
1 I 2005	ESDF	11 732 416	3 707 315	31.6	5 808 166	1 856 224	32.0	5 924 252	1 851 091	31.2
1 I 2006	ESDF	12 051 021	3 900 404	32.4	5 966 339	1 952 802	32.7	6 084 681	1 947 601	32.0
1 I 2007	ESDF	12 377 542	4 102 223	33.1	6 128 544	2 053 767	33.5	6 248 999	2 048 456	32.8
1 IV 2009	CDFC	14 528 662	3 274 727	22.5	7 204 990	1 643 671	22.8	7 323 672	1 631 056	22.3
Mauritania - Mauritanie										
1 VII 2005[2]	ESDF	2 905 727	...	...	1 450 418	...	...	1 455 309	...	...
1 VII 2008[2]	ESDF	3 162 338	...	...	1 584 913	...	...	1 577 425	...	...
1 VII 2010[2]	ESDF	3 340 627	...	...	1 678 324	...	...	1 662 303	...	...
1 VII 2011[2]	ESDF	3 296 958	...	...	1 644 572	...	...	1 652 386	...	...
24 III 2013	CDFC	3 460 388[12]	1 697 792	49.1	...	...	...	...	...	...
Mauritius - Maurice[13]										
1 VII 2005[14]	ESDJ	1 243 253	524 318	42.2	614 786	257 785	41.9	628 467	266 533	42.4
1 VII 2006[14]	ESDJ	1 252 698	527 138	42.1	619 243	259 028	41.8	633 455	268 110	42.3
1 VII 2007[14]	ESDJ	1 260 403	528 961	42.0	622 926	259 800	41.7	637 477	269 161	42.2
1 VII 2008[14]	ESDJ	1 268 565	531 097	41.9	626 556	260 675	41.6	642 009	270 422	42.1
1 VII 2009[14]	ESDJ	1 275 032	532 591	41.8	629 157	261 041	41.5	645 875	271 550	42.0
1 VII 2010[14]	ESDJ	1 280 924	533 771	41.7	631 692	261 489	41.4	649 232	272 282	41.9
1 VII 2011[15]	ESDJ	1 252 404	509 229	40.7	619 591	249 439	40.3	632 813	259 790	41.1
4 VII 2011	CDFC	1 237 000	496 841	40.2	611 053	243 629	39.9	625 947	253 212	40.5
1 VII 2012[15]	ESDJ	1 255 882	509 177	40.5	621 297	249 422	40.1	634 585	259 755	40.9
1 VII 2013[15]	ESDJ	1 258 653	519 306	41.3	622 861	254 605	40.9	635 792	264 701	41.6
1 VII 2014[15]	ESDJ	1 260 934	518 370	41.1	624 002	254 204	40.7	636 932	264 166	41.5
Mayotte										
31 VII 2007	CDJC	186 387	...	...	91 405	...	...	94 982	...	...
21 VIII 2012	CDJC	212 645	...	...	103 164	...	...	109 481	...	...

Continent, country or area, and date / Continent, pays ou zone et date	Code[a]	Both sexes - Les deux sexes			Male - Masculin			Female - Féminin		
		Total	Urban - Urbaine		Total	Urban - Urbaine		Total	Urban - Urbaine	
			Number Nombre	Percent P.100		Number Nombre	Percent P.100		Number Nombre	Percent P.100
AFRICA - AFRIQUE										
Morocco - Maroc[16]										
1 VII 2005	ESDF	30 172 000	16 755 000	55.5	14 981 000	8 275 000	55.2	15 190 000	8 480 000	55.8
1 VII 2006	ESDF	30 509 000	17 082 000	56.0	15 146 000	8 426 000	55.6	15 363 000	8 656 000	56.3
1 VII 2007	ESDF	30 850 000	17 415 000	56.5	15 314 000	8 579 000	56.0	15 536 000	8 836 000	56.9
1 VII 2008	ESDF	31 195 000	17 753 000	56.9	15 484 000	8 734 000	56.4	15 711 000	9 019 000	57.4
1 VII 2009	ESDF	31 543 000	18 097 000	57.4	15 657 000	8 891 000	56.8	15 886 000	9 205 000	57.9
1 VII 2010	ESDF	31 894 046	18 446 241	57.8	15 831 463	9 051 145	57.2	16 062 583	9 395 096	58.5
1 VII 2011	ESDF	32 245 120	18 802 208	58.3	16 010 979	9 212 763	57.5	16 234 141	9 589 444	59.1
1 VII 2012	ESDF	32 596 997	19 157 539	58.8	16 190 815	9 373 546	57.9	16 406 182	9 783 993	59.6
1 VII 2013	ESDF	32 950 445	19 512 904	59.2	16 371 475	9 533 742	58.2	16 578 971	9 979 162	60.2
1 VII 2014	ESDF	33 773 630	20 357 619	60.3	...	...	...	...	...	...
Mozambique										
1 VII 2005[2]	ESDF	19 420 036	6 022 319	31.0	9 368 425	3 009 531	32.1	10 051 611	3 012 788	30.0
1 VII 2006[2]	ESDF	19 888 701	...	...	9 603 031	...	...	10 285 670	...	...
1 VII 2007[2]	ESDF	20 632 434	6 269 621	30.4	9 930 196	3 079 809	31.0	10 702 238	3 189 812	29.8
1 VIII 2007	CDFC	20 252 223	6 151 974	30.4	9 746 690	3 021 756	31.0	10 505 533	3 130 218	29.8
1 VII 2008[2]	ESDF	21 207 929	6 472 214	30.5	10 210 267	3 176 209	31.1	10 997 662	3 296 005	30.0
1 VII 2009[2]	ESDF	21 802 866	6 685 108	30.7	10 499 954	3 277 805	31.2	11 302 912	3 407 303	30.1
1 VII 2010[2]	ESDF	22 416 881	6 908 291	30.8	10 799 284	3 384 605	31.3	11 617 597	3 523 686	30.3
1 VII 2011[2]	ESDF	23 049 621	7 141 715	31.0	11 108 128	3 496 582	31.5	11 941 493	3 645 133	30.5
1 VII 2012[2]	ESDF	23 700 715	7 385 294	31.2	11 426 321	3 613 684	31.6	12 274 394	3 771 610	30.7
1 VII 2013[2]	ESDF	24 366 112	7 639 557	31.4	11 751 849	3 736 166	31.8	12 614 263	3 903 391	30.9
1 VII 2014[2]	ESDF	25 041 922	7 905 004	31.6	12 082 782	3 864 267	32.0	12 959 140	4 040 737	31.2
Namibia - Namibie										
1 VII 2005[2]	ESDF	1 956 900	...	...	952 788	...	...	1 004 112	...	...
1 VII 2006[2]	ESDF	1 991 747	...	...	970 617	...	...	1 021 130	...	...
1 VII 2007[2]	ESDF	2 027 871	...	...	989 067	...	...	1 038 804	...	...
1 VII 2008[2]	ESDF	2 065 226	...	...	1 008 115	...	...	1 057 111	...	...
1 VII 2009[2]	ESDF	2 103 761	...	...	1 027 736	...	...	1 076 025	...	...
1 VII 2010[2]	ESDF	2 143 410	...	...	1 047 900	...	...	1 095 510	...	...
1 VII 2011[17]	ESDF	2 116 077	900 163	42.5	1 026 911	439 993	42.8	1 089 166	460 170	42.2
28 VIII 2011	CDFC	2 113 077	903 434	42.8	1 021 912	440 334	43.1	1 091 165	463 100	42.4
1 VII 2012[17]	ESDF	2 155 440	940 825	43.6	1 046 434	459 668	43.9	1 109 006	481 157	43.4
1 VII 2013[17]	ESDF	2 196 086	982 519	44.7	1 066 541	479 844	45.0	1 129 545	502 675	44.5
1 VII 2014[17]	ESDF	2 237 894	1 025 147	45.8	1 087 178	500 469	46.0	1 150 716	524 678	45.6
Niger										
1 VII 2005[2]	ESDJ	12 628 241	2 054 453	16.3	6 298 641	1 027 814	16.3	6 329 600	1 026 640	16.2
1 VII 2006[2]	ESDJ	13 044 973	2 184 605	16.7	6 506 496	1 092 927	16.8	6 538 477	1 091 678	16.7
1 VII 2007[2]	ESDJ	13 716 233	2 556 499	18.6	6 851 314	1 280 155	18.7	6 864 919	1 276 344	18.6
1 VII 2008[2]	ESDJ	14 197 601	2 728 541	19.2	7 088 858	1 366 304	19.3	7 108 743	1 362 237	19.2
1 VII 2009[2]	ESDJ	14 693 112	2 911 006	19.8	7 339 392	1 458 250	19.9	7 353 720	1 452 756	19.8
1 VII 2010[2]	ESDJ	15 203 822	3 104 574	20.4	7 594 565	1 555 187	20.5	7 609 257	1 549 387	20.4
1 VII 2011[2]	ESDJ	15 730 754	...	...	7 857 845	...	...	7 872 909	...	...
1 VII 2012[2]	ESDJ	16 274 738	3 527 852	21.7	8 129 650	1 767 255	21.7	8 145 088	1 760 597	21.6
10 XII 2012	CDJC	17 138 707	2 778 337	16.2	8 518 818	1 397 695	16.4	8 619 889	1 380 642	16.0
1 VII 2013[18]	ESDJ	17 807 117	...	...	8 850 137	...	...	8 956 980	...	...
Nigeria - Nigéria										
1 VII 2005[2]	ESDF	133 767 000	...	...	67 111 000	...	...	66 656 000	...	...
21 III 2006	CDFC	140 431 790	...	...	71 345 488	...	...	69 086 302	...	...
Republic of South Sudan - République de Soudan du Sud										
21 IV 2008	CDFC	8 260 490	1 405 186	17.0	4 287 300	754 086	17.6	3 973 190	651 100	16.4
1 VII 2008[19]	ESDF	8 490 767	1 443 430	17.0	4 406 708	749 140	17.0	4 084 059	694 290	17.0
1 VII 2009[19]	ESDF	8 987 784	1 527 923	17.0	4 323 124	734 931	17.0	4 664 660	792 992	17.0
1 VII 2010[19]	ESDF	9 496 844	1 614 463	17.0	4 567 982	776 557	17.0	4 928 862	837 907	17.0
1 VII 2011[19]	ESDF	10 018 240	1 703 101	17.0	4 818 773	819 191	17.0	5 199 467	883 909	17.0
1 VII 2012[19]	ESDF	10 552 270	1 793 886	17.0	5 075 642	862 859	17.0	5 476 628	931 027	17.0
1 VII 2013[19]	ESDF	10 808 588	1 837 460	17.0	5 198 931	883 818	17.0	5 609 657	953 642	17.0
1 VII 2014[19]	ESDF	11 071 132	1 882 093	17.0	5 325 215	905 286	17.0	5 745 917	976 806	17.0
Reunion - Réunion										
1 VII 2005	ESDJ	777 435	...	...	377 593	...	...	399 842	...	...
1 I 2006	CDJC	781 962	...	...	379 176	...	...	402 786	...	...
1 VII 2006	ESDJ	786 231	...	...	381 030	...	...	405 202	...	...
1 I 2007	ESDJ	794 107	...	...	385 335	...	...	408 772	...	...

Continent, country or area, and date / Continent, pays ou zone et date	Code[a]	Both sexes - Les deux sexes			Male - Masculin			Female - Féminin		
		Total	Urban - Urbaine		Total	Urban - Urbaine		Total	Urban - Urbaine	
			Number Nombre	Percent P.100		Number Nombre	Percent P.100		Number Nombre	Percent P.100
AFRICA - AFRIQUE										
Reunion - Réunion										
1 I 2008	ESDJ	805 500	...	...	390 645	...	...	414 855	...	...
1 I 2009	ESDJ	816 364	...	...	395 688	...	...	420 676	...	...
1 I 2010	CDJC	821 136	808 540	98.5	398 006	391 623	98.4	423 130	416 917	98.5
1 I 2010*	ESDJ	828 054	...	...	399 728	...	...	428 326	...	...
Rwanda										
1 VII 2005[2]	ESDF	*9 225 000*	*1 476 000*	*16.0*	*4 372 650*	...	...	*4 852 350*	...	...
1 VII 2006[2]	ESDF	*9 468 000*	*1 514 880*	*16.0*	*4 487 832*	...	...	*4 980 168*	...	...
1 VII 2007[2]	ESDF	*9 556 669*	*1 726 613*	*18.1*	*4 597 277*	*812 148*	*17.7*	*4 959 393*	*914 465*	*18.4*
1 VII 2008[2]	ESDF	*9 831 501*	...	...	*4 736 104*	...	...	*5 095 397*	...	...
1 VII 2009[2]	ESDF	*10 117 029*	...	...	*4 880 233*	...	...	*5 236 796*	...	...
1 VII 2010[2]	ESDF	*10 412 820*	*1 541 097*	*14.8*	*5 029 450*	...	...	*5 383 371*	...	...
1 VII 2011[2]	ESDF	*10 718 379*	*1 564 883*	*14.6*	*5 183 505*	...	...	*5 534 874*	...	...
1 VII 2012[2]	ESDF	*11 033 141*	...	...	*5 342 112*	...	...	*5 691 029*	...	...
15 VIII 2012*	CDJC	10 537 222	...	...	5 074 942	...	...	5 462 280	...	...
1 VII 2013[2]	ESDF	*11 355 940*	...	...	*5 504 823*	...	...	*5 851 118*	...	...
Saint Helena ex. dep. - Sainte-Hélène sans dép.										
10 II 2008	CDFC	4 257	...	...	2 165	...	...	2 092	...	...
1 VII 2008	ESDF	3 981	...	...	2 022	...	...	1 959	...	...
1 VII 2012	ESDF	4 123	...	...	2 094	...	...	2 029	...	...
31 XII 2013	ESDF	4 211	...	...	2 139	...	...	2 072	...	...
Saint Helena: Ascension - Sainte-Hélène: Ascension										
1 VII 2008	ESDJ	702	...	...	397	...	...	305	...	...
Saint Helena: Tristan da Cunha - Sainte-Hélène: Tristan da Cunha[20]										
31 XII 2009	ESDF	262[21]	...	...	123	...	...	139	...	...
Sao Tome and Principe - Sao Tomé-et-Principe										
1 VII 2005	ESDF	*148 968*	...	...	*73 506*	...	...	*75 462*	...	...
1 VII 2006	ESDF	*151 912*	...	...	*74 876*	...	...	*77 036*	...	...
1 VII 2007	ESDF	*154 875*	...	...	*76 256*	...	...	*78 619*	...	...
1 VII 2008	ESDF	*157 847*	...	...	*77 641*	...	...	*80 206*	...	...
1 VII 2009	ESDF	*160 820*	...	...	*79 027*	...	...	*81 794*	...	...
1 VII 2010	ESDF	*163 783*	...	...	*80 409*	...	...	*83 375*	...	...
1 VII 2011	ESDF	*166 728*	...	...	*81 783*	...	...	*84 945*	...	...
13 V 2012	CDFC	178 739	...	...	88 867	...	...	89 872	...	...
Senegal - Sénégal										
31 XII 2005[22]	ESDJ	10 901 006	4 432 909	40.7	5 365 938	2 197 676	41.0	5 535 068	2 235 233	40.4
31 XII 2006[22]	ESDJ	11 205 774	4 556 843	40.7	5 515 959	2 259 118	41.0	5 689 815	2 297 725	40.4
31 XII 2007[22]	ESDJ	11 519 242	4 684 315	40.7	5 670 261	2 322 314	41.0	5 848 981	2 362 001	40.4
31 XII 2008[22]	ESDJ	11 841 137	4 815 214	40.7	5 828 711	2 387 209	41.0	6 012 426	2 428 005	40.4
31 XII 2009[22]	ESDJ	12 171 264	4 949 461	40.7	5 991 214	2 453 764	41.0	6 180 050	2 495 697	40.4
31 XII 2010[22]	ESDJ	12 509 434	5 086 978	40.7	6 157 675	2 521 940	41.0	6 351 759	2 565 038	40.4
31 XII 2011[22]	ESDJ	12 841 702	6 086 966	47.4	6 350 673	3 010 218	47.4	6 491 029	3 076 748	47.4
19 XI 2013*	CDFC	12 873 601	5 824 977	45.2	6 428 189	...	...	6 445 412	...	...
Seychelles										
1 VII 2005	ESDF	82 852	...	...	41 233	...	...	41 619	...	...
1 VII 2006	ESDF	84 600	...	...	42 875	...	...	41 725	...	...
1 VII 2007	ESDF	85 032	...	...	43 160	...	...	41 872	...	...
1 VII 2008	ESDF	86 956	...	...	44 999	...	...	41 957	...	...
1 VII 2009	ESDF	87 298	...	...	45 022	...	...	42 276	...	...
1 VII 2010	ESDF	89 770	...	...	45 907	...	...	43 863	...	...
26 VIII 2010	CDFC	90 945	...	...	46 912	...	...	44 033	...	...
1 VII 2011	ESDF	87 441	...	...	43 127	...	...	44 314	...	...
1 VII 2012	ESDF	88 303	...	...	43 313	...	...	44 990	...	...
1 VII 2013	ESDF	89 949	...	...	44 735	...	...	45 214	...	...
1 VII 2014	ESDF	91 359	...	...	45 278	...	...	46 081	...	...
Sierra Leone										
1 VII 2005	ESDF	*5 094 500*	*1 934 235*	*38.0*	*2 468 832*	*955 441*	*38.7*	*2 625 668*	*978 794*	*37.3*
1 VII 2006	ESDF	*5 216 890*	*1 999 707*	*38.3*	*2 528 430*	*987 782*	*39.1*	*2 688 460*	*1 011 925*	*37.6*

Continent, country or area, and date / Continent, pays ou zone et date	Code[a]	Both sexes - Les deux sexes Total	Urban - Urbaine Number Nombre	Urban - Urbaine Percent P.100	Male - Masculin Total	Urban - Urbaine Number Nombre	Urban - Urbaine Percent P.100	Female - Féminin Total	Urban - Urbaine Number Nombre	Urban - Urbaine Percent P.100
AFRICA - AFRIQUE										
Sierra Leone										
1 VII 2007 ....ESDF	5 343 200	2 069 160	38.7	2 589 965	1 022 089	39.5	2 753 235	1 047 071	38.0
1 VII 2008 ....ESDF	5 473 530	2 142 918	39.2	2 653 490	1 058 523	39.9	2 820 040	1 084 395	38.5
1 VII 2009 ....ESDF	5 607 930	2 221 331	39.6	2 719 034	1 097 256	40.4	2 888 896	1 124 075	38.9
1 VII 2010 ....ESDF	5 746 800	2 304 955	40.1	2 786 797	1 138 563	40.9	2 960 003	1 166 392	39.4
1 VII 2011 ....ESDF	5 890 080	2 394 041	40.6	2 856 755	1 182 568	41.4	3 033 325	1 211 473	39.9
1 VII 2012 ....ESDF	6 037 660	2 489 123	41.2	2 928 862	1 229 535	42.0	3 108 798	1 259 588	40.5
South Africa - Afrique du Sud										
1 VII 2005 ....ESDF	47 639 556	...	...	23 034 778	...	...	24 604 777	...	...
1 VII 2006 ....ESDF	48 269 753	...	...	23 362 669	...	...	24 907 084	...	...
1 VII 2007 ....ESDF	48 910 248	...	...	23 696 203	...	...	25 214 046	...	...
1 VII 2008 ....ESDF	49 561 256	...	...	24 035 505	...	...	25 525 751	...	...
1 VII 2009 ....ESDF	50 222 996	...	...	24 380 706	...	...	25 842 290	...	...
1 VII 2010 ....ESDF	50 895 698	...	...	24 731 940	...	...	26 163 758	...	...
1 VII 2011 ....ESDF	51 579 599	...	...	25 089 348	...	...	26 490 251	...	...
10 X 2011 ....CDFC	51 770 560	32 559 331	62.9	25 188 791	...	...	26 581 769	...	...
1 VII 2012 ....ESDF	52 274 945	...	...	25 453 074	...	...	26 821 871	...	...
1 VII 2013 ....ESDF	52 981 991	...	...	25 823 270	...	...	27 158 721	...	...
1 VII 2014 ....ESDF	54 001 953	...	...	26 366 008	...	...	27 635 944	...	...
Sudan - Soudan										
21 IV 2008 ....CDFC	30 894 000	...	...	15 786 677	...	...	15 107 323	...	...
1 VII 2008 ....ESDF	30 978 758	10 314 730	33.3	15 790 134	5 350 451	33.9	15 188 624	4 964 279	32.7
1 VII 2009 ....ESDF	31 956 791	10 860 950	34.0	16 275 239	5 531 361	34.0	15 681 552	5 329 589	34.0
1 VII 2010 ....ESDF	32 961 966	11 296 966	34.3	16 774 288	5 749 007	34.3	16 187 678	5 547 959	34.3
1 VII 2011 ....ESDF	33 997 538	11 749 240	34.6	17 289 105	5 974 957	34.6	16 708 434	5 774 283	34.6
1 VII 2012 ....ESDF	35 064 299	12 218 313	34.8	17 820 009	6 209 462	34.8	17 244 290	6 008 851	34.8
1 VII 2013 ....ESDF	36 162 516	12 704 550	35.1	18 367 086	6 452 691	35.1	17 795 430	6 251 858	35.1
1 VII 2014 ....ESDF	37 292 376	13 208 281	35.4	18 930 385	6 704 798	35.4	18 361 991	6 503 483	35.4
Swaziland										
11 III 2007 ....CDFC	844 223	186 890	22.1	405 868	93 918	23.1	438 355	92 972	21.2
1 VII 2007 ....ESDF	1 018 449	225 293	22.1	481 428	108 071	22.4	537 021	117 222	21.8
1 VII 2008 ....ESDF	1 031 747	229 516	22.2	488 132	109 937	22.5	543 615	119 579	22.0
1 VII 2009 ....ESDF	1 043 509	233 504	22.4	494 061	111 704	22.6	549 448	121 800	22.2
1 VII 2010 ....ESDF	1 055 506	237 641	22.5	500 070	113 554	22.7	555 436	124 087	22.3
1 VII 2011 ....ESDF	1 067 773	241 947	22.7	506 186	115 493	22.8	561 587	126 454	22.5
1 VII 2012 ....ESDF	1 080 337	246 441	22.8	512 432	117 528	22.9	567 905	128 913	22.7
1 VII 2013 ....ESDF	1 093 158	251 122	23.0	518 788	119 658	23.1	574 370	131 464	22.9
1 VII 2014 ....ESDF	1 106 189	255 986	23.1	525 232	121 881	23.2	580 957	134 105	23.1
Togo										
6 XI 2010 ....CDJC	6 191 155	2 334 495	37.7	3 009 095	1 131 533	37.6	3 182 060	1 202 962	37.8
Tunisia - Tunisie										
1 VII 2005 ....ESDF	10 029 000	...	...	5 020 000	...	...	5 009 000	...	...
1 VII 2006 ....ESDF	10 127 900	...	...	5 062 100	...	...	5 065 800	...	...
1 VII 2007 ....ESDF	10 225 100	...	...	5 105 100	...	...	5 120 000	...	...
1 VII 2008 ....ESDF	10 328 900	...	...	5 156 300	...	...	5 172 600	...	...
1 VII 2009 ....ESDF	10 439 600	...	...	5 207 200	...	...	5 232 400	...	...
1 VII 2010 ....ESDF	10 547 100	...	...	5 261 700	...	...	5 285 400	...	...
1 VII 2011 ....ESDF	10 673 800	...	...	5 316 900	...	...	5 356 800	...	...
23 IV 2014 ....CDFC	10 982 754	7 437 671	67.7	5 472 338	3 713 527	67.9	5 510 416	3 724 144	67.6
Uganda - Ouganda										
1 VII 2005 ....ESDF	26 741 300	3 953 200	14.8	12 944 800	1 889 800	14.6	13 796 500	2 063 400	15.0
1 VII 2006 ....ESDF	27 629 300	4 084 700	14.8	13 386 100	1 953 300	14.6	14 243 200	2 131 400	15.0
1 VII 2007 ....ESDF	28 581 300	4 223 800	14.8	13 866 700	2 022 200	14.6	14 714 600	2 201 600	15.0
1 VII 2008 ....ESDF	29 592 600	4 372 000	14.8	14 383 200	2 095 700	14.6	15 209 400	2 276 300	15.0
1 VII 2009 ....ESDF	30 661 300	4 524 900	14.8	14 933 900	2 171 400	14.5	15 727 400	2 353 500	15.0
1 VII 2010 ....ESDF	31 784 600	...	...	15 516 600	...	...	16 268 000	...	...
1 VII 2011 ....ESDF	32 939 800	...	...	16 118 600	...	...	16 821 200	...	...
1 VII 2012 ....ESDF	34 131 400	...	...	16 741 400	...	...	17 390 000	...	...
27 VIII 2014* ....CDFC	34 856 813	6 426 013	18.4	16 935 456	...	...	17 921 357	...	...
United Republic of Tanzania - République Unie de Tanzanie										
1 VII 2005[22] ....ESDF	37 083 346	9 090 703	24.5	18 161 261	4 478 982	24.7	18 922 085	4 611 721	24.4
1 VII 2006[22] ....ESDF	38 250 927	9 518 688	24.9	18 748 743	4 691 158	25.0	19 502 184	4 827 530	24.8
1 VII 2007[22] ....ESDF	39 446 061	9 962 731	25.3	19 352 480	4 911 847	25.4	20 093 581	5 050 884	25.1

Continent, country or area, and date / Continent, pays ou zone et date	Code[a]	Both sexes - Les deux sexes			Male - Masculin			Female - Féminin		
		Total	Urban - Urbaine		Total	Urban - Urbaine		Total	Urban - Urbaine	
			Number Nombre	Percent P.100		Number Nombre	Percent P.100		Number Nombre	Percent P.100
AFRICA - AFRIQUE										
United Republic of Tanzania - République Unie de Tanzanie										
1 VII 2008[22] ....ESDF		40 667 794	10 419 287	25.6	19 970 944	5 139 187	25.7	20 696 850	5 280 100	25.5
1 VII 2009[22] ....ESDF		41 915 880	10 892 350	26.0	20 604 730	5 375 260	26.1	21 311 150	5 517 090	25.9
1 VII 2010[22] ....ESDF		43 187 823	11 378 015	26.3	21 252 423	5 618 133	26.4	21 935 400	5 759 882	26.3
1 VII 2011[22] ....ESDF		44 484 857	11 875 395	26.7	21 914 229	5 867 287	26.8	22 570 628	6 008 108	26.6
1 VII 2012[22] ....ESDF		45 798 475	12 386 841	27.0	22 585 634	6 123 839	27.1	23 212 841	6 263 002	27.0
26 VIII 2012[23] ....CDFC		44 928 923	13 305 004	29.6	21 869 990	6 407 396	29.3	23 058 933	6 897 608	29.9
1 VII 2013[22] ....ESDF		47 132 580	12 909 536	27.4	23 267 957	6 386 303	27.4	23 864 623	6 523 233	27.3
Zambia - Zambie										
16 X 2010 ....CDFC		12 526 314	5 021 022	40.1	6 117 253	2 452 904	40.1	6 409 061	2 568 118	40.1
Zimbabwe										
1 VII 2005[22] ....ESDF		11 830 000	4 098 422	34.6	5 730 183	2 022 053	35.3	6 099 817	2 076 367	34.0
1 VII 2006[22] ....ESDF		11 930 000	4 133 066	34.6	5 778 621	2 039 146	35.3	6 151 379	2 093 919	34.0
1 VII 2007[22] ....ESDF		12 040 000	4 171 175	34.6	5 831 902	2 057 948	35.3	6 208 098	2 113 226	34.0
1 VII 2008[22] ....ESDF		12 150 000	3 495 205	28.8	5 885 184	1 691 434	28.7	6 264 816	1 803 752	28.8
1 VII 2009[22] ....ESDF		13 667 894	...	...	6 642 551	...	...	7 025 344	...	...
17 VIII 2012 ....CDFC		13 061 239	4 284 145	32.8	6 280 539	2 039 224	32.5	6 780 700	2 244 921	33.1
AMERICA, NORTH - AMÉRIQUE DU NORD										
Anguilla										
11 V 2011* ....CDJC		13 037	...	...	6 469	...	...	6 568	...	...
Antigua and Barbuda - Antigua-et-Barbuda										
1 VII 2005 ....ESDF		82 786	...	...	38 878	...	...	43 908	...	...
1 VII 2006 ....ESDF		84 330	...	...	39 603	...	...	44 727	...	...
1 VII 2007 ....ESDF		85 903	...	...	40 342	...	...	45 561	...	...
27 V 2011 ....CDJC		85 567	...	...	40 986	...	...	44 581	...	...
Aruba										
1 VII 2005 ....ESDJ		97 635	...	...	46 397	...	...	51 238	...	...
1 VII 2006 ....ESDJ		99 405	...	...	47 189	...	...	52 216	...	...
1 VII 2007 ....ESDJ		100 150	...	...	47 490	...	...	52 660	...	...
1 VII 2008 ....ESDJ		100 917	...	...	47 890	...	...	53 027	...	...
1 VII 2009 ....ESDJ		101 604	...	...	48 291	...	...	53 312	...	...
1 VII 2010 ....ESDJ		101 873	...	...	48 419	...	...	53 454	...	...
29 IX 2010 ....CDJC		101 484	...	...	48 241	...	...	53 243	...	...
1 VII 2011 ....ESDJ		102 809	...	...	48 801	...	...	54 008	...	...
1 VII 2012 ....ESDJ		104 574	...	...	49 558	...	...	55 016	...	...
1 VII 2013 ....ESDJ		106 390	...	...	50 334	...	...	56 056	...	...
1 VII 2014 ....ESDJ		107 839	...	...	50 999	...	...	56 840	...	...
Bahamas										
1 VII 2005[2] ....ESDF		325 200	...	...	158 000	...	...	167 200	...	...
1 VII 2006[2] ....ESDF		329 500	...	...	160 100	...	...	169 400	...	...
1 VII 2007[2] ....ESDF		334 000	...	...	162 300	...	...	171 700	...	...
1 VII 2008[2] ....ESDF		338 300	...	...	164 800	...	...	173 500	...	...
1 VII 2009[2] ....ESDF		342 400	...	...	166 800	...	...	175 600	...	...
3 V 2010 ....CDJC		351 461	...	...	170 257	...	...	181 204	...	...
1 VII 2010[2] ....ESDF		334 642	...	...	162 730	...	...	171 911	...	...
1 VII 2011[2] ....ESDF		357 750	...	...	175 029	...	...	182 721	...	...
1 VII 2012[2] ....ESDF		362 590	...	...	177 440	...	...	185 150	...	...
1 VII 2013[2] ....ESDF		368 390	...	...	179 850	...	...	188 540	...	...
1 VII 2014[2] ....ESDF		372 000	...	...	182 000	...	...	190 000	...	...
Barbados - Barbade										
1 VII 2005 ....ESDF		273 018	...	...	131 721	...	...	141 297	...	...
1 VII 2006 ....ESDF		273 428	...	...	131 916	...	...	141 512	...	...
1 VII 2007 ....ESDF		274 197	...	...	132 413	...	...	141 784	...	...
1 VII 2008 ....ESDF		274 937	...	...	132 839	...	...	142 098	...	...
1 V 2010 ....CDJC		277 821	...	...	133 018	...	...	144 803	...	...
Belize										
1 VII 2005 ....ESDF		291 800	146 600	50.2	147 400	72 200	49.0	144 400	74 400	51.5
1 VII 2006 ....ESDF		301 386	152 583	50.6	149 676	73 495	49.1	151 710	79 089	52.1

Continent, country or area, and date / Continent, pays ou zone et date	Code[a]	Both sexes - Les deux sexes			Male - Masculin			Female - Féminin		
		Total	Urban - Urbaine		Total	Urban - Urbaine		Total	Urban - Urbaine	
			Number Nombre	Percent P.100		Number Nombre	Percent P.100		Number Nombre	Percent P.100
AMERICA, NORTH - AMÉRIQUE DU NORD										
Belize										
1 VII 2008	ESDF	306 809	138 716	45.2	153 570	67 647	44.0	153 239	71 069	46.4
1 VII 2009	ESDF	315 082	142 447	45.2	157 622	69 450	44.1	157 460	72 997	46.4
12 V 2010	CDJC	322 453	145 832	45.2	161 227	71 087	44.1	161 226	74 745	46.4
1 VII 2010	ESDF	323 598	146 322	45.2	161 800	71 328	44.1	161 798	74 995	46.4
1 VII 2011	ESDF	332 084	149 955	45.2	166 043	73 110	44.0	166 041	76 845	46.3
1 VII 2012	ESDF	340 792	153 683	45.1	170 397	74 938	44.0	170 395	78 745	46.2
1 VII 2013	ESDF	349 728	157 508	45.0	174 865	76 815	43.9	174 863	80 693	46.1
1 VII 2014	ESDF	358 899	161 434	45.0	179 451	78 741	43.9	179 448	82 693	46.1
Bermuda - Bermudes										
1 VII 2005[24]	ESDJ	63 571	...	...	30 424	...	...	33 147	...	...
1 VII 2006[24]	ESDJ	63 797	...	...	30 504	...	...	33 293	...	...
1 VII 2007[24]	ESDJ	64 009	...	...	30 577	...	...	33 432	...	...
1 VII 2008[24]	ESDJ	64 209	...	...	30 644	...	...	33 565	...	...
1 VII 2009[24]	ESDJ	64 395	...	...	30 704	...	...	33 691	...	...
20 V 2010[25]	CDJC	64 237	64 237	100.0	30 858	30 858	100.0	33 379	33 379	100.0
1 VII 2010[26]	ESDJ	64 129	...	...	30 792	...	...	33 337	...	...
1 VII 2011[26]	ESDJ	63 193	...	...	30 218	...	...	32 975	...	...
1 VII 2012[26]	ESDJ	62 408	...	...	29 819	...	...	32 589	...	...
1 VII 2013[26]	ESDJ	61 954	...	...	29 587	...	...	32 367	...	...
1 VII 2014[26]	ESDJ	61 777	...	...	29 499	...	...	32 278	...	...
Canada										
1 VII 2005[27]	ESDJ	32 242 364	...	...	15 978 534	...	...	16 263 830	...	...
16 V 2006[28]	CDJC	31 612 895	25 350 585	80.2	15 475 970	12 289 025	79.4	16 136 930	13 061 560	80.9
1 VII 2006[27]	ESDJ	32 570 505	...	...	16 144 446	...	...	16 426 059	...	...
1 VII 2007[27]	ESDJ	32 887 928	...	...	16 298 320	...	...	16 589 608	...	...
1 VII 2008[27]	ESDJ	33 245 773	...	...	16 473 545	...	...	16 772 228	...	...
1 VII 2009[27]	ESDJ	33 628 571	...	...	16 663 222	...	...	16 965 349	...	...
1 VII 2010[27]	ESDJ	34 005 274	...	...	16 847 961	...	...	17 157 313	...	...
2 V 2011	CDJC	33 476 690	27 147 190	81.1	16 414 225	13 190 225	80.4	17 062 455	13 956 960	81.8
1 VII 2011[29]	ESDJ	34 342 780	...	...	17 015 959	...	...	17 326 821	...	...
1 VII 2012[30]	ESDJ	34 752 128	...	...	17 225 435	...	...	17 526 693	...	...
1 VII 2013[30]	ESDJ	35 154 279	...	...	17 430 227	...	...	17 724 052	...	...
1 VII 2014*[31]	ESDJ	35 540 419	...	...	17 624 990	...	...	17 915 429	...	...
Cayman Islands - Îles Caïmanes										
31 XII 2009	ESDJ	52 830	...	...	26 255	...	...	26 575	...	...
10 X 2010[32]	CDJC	55 036	55 036	100.0	27 218	27 218	100.0	27 818	27 818	100.0
31 XII 2010	ESDJ	55 036	...	...	27 219	...	...	27 817	...	...
31 XII 2011	ESDJ	55 517	...	...	27 454	...	...	28 063	...	...
31 XII 2012	ESDJ	56 732	...	...	27 753	...	...	28 979	...	...
31 XII 2013	ESDJ	55 691	...	...	27 106	...	...	28 585	...	...
31 XII 2014	ESDJ	58 238	...	...	28 322	...	...	29 916	...	...
Costa Rica										
1 VII 2005	ESDJ	4 266 185	2 516 602	59.0	2 116 648	1 231 912	58.2	2 149 537	1 284 690	59.8
1 VII 2006	ESDJ	4 353 843	2 567 797	59.0	2 146 610	1 243 202	57.9	2 207 233	1 324 595	60.0
1 VII 2007	ESDJ	4 443 100	2 619 591	59.0	2 195 652	1 273 998	58.0	2 247 448	1 345 593	59.9
1 VII 2008[33]	ESDJ	4 533 162	2 671 667	58.9	2 246 474	1 299 940	57.9	2 286 688	1 371 727	60.0
1 VII 2009[33]	ESDJ	4 620 482	2 722 273	58.9	2 291 886	1 325 468	57.8	2 328 596	1 396 805	60.0
1 VII 2010[34]	ESDJ	4 538 307	3 304 248	72.8	2 206 526	1 579 816	71.6	2 331 781	1 724 432	74.0
30 V 2011	CDJC	4 301 712	3 130 871	72.8	2 106 063	1 509 161	71.7	2 195 649	1 621 710	73.9
1 VII 2011[34]	ESDJ	4 592 346	3 343 241	72.8	2 238 615	1 603 354	71.6	2 353 731	1 739 887	73.9
1 VII 2012[34]	ESDJ	4 651 166	3 384 925	72.8	2 266 220	1 621 617	71.6	2 384 946	1 763 308	73.9
1 VII 2013[34]	ESDJ	4 711 986	3 427 548	72.7	2 276 708	1 624 941	71.4	2 435 278	1 802 607	74.0
1 VII 2014[34]	ESDJ	4 772 098	3 469 802	72.7	2 325 438	1 662 288	71.5	2 446 660	1 807 514	73.9
Cuba										
1 VII 2005	ESDJ	11 218 107	8 479 433	75.6	5 614 981	4 171 219	74.3	5 603 125	4 308 214	76.9
1 VII 2006	ESDJ	11 210 628	8 466 895	75.5	5 613 921	4 165 162	74.2	5 596 706	4 301 733	76.9
1 VII 2007	ESDJ	11 195 330	8 446 381	75.4	5 605 756	4 155 581	74.1	5 589 574	4 290 800	76.8
1 VII 2008	ESDJ	11 181 012	8 426 393	75.4	5 597 673	4 146 862	74.1	5 583 339	4 279 531	76.6
1 VII 2009	ESDJ	11 174 474	8 420 630	75.4	5 594 504	4 145 111	74.1	5 579 971	4 275 519	76.6
1 VII 2010	ESDJ	11 171 443	8 416 524	75.3	5 592 729	4 143 388	74.1	5 578 714	4 273 136	76.6
1 VII 2011	ESDJ	11 171 679	8 409 543	75.3	5 592 332	4 140 377	74.0	5 579 347	4 269 166	76.5
1 VII 2012	ESDJ	11 174 287	8 494 128	76.0	5 583 306	4 159 342	74.5	5 590 981	4 334 786	77.5

6. Total and urban population by sex: 2005 - 2014
Population totale et population urbaine selon le sexe : 2005 - 2014 (continued - suite)

Continent, country or area, and date / Continent, pays ou zone et date — Code[a]	Both sexes - Les deux sexes			Male - Masculin			Female - Féminin		
	Total	Urban - Urbaine Number Nombre	Percent P.100	Total	Urban - Urbaine Number Nombre	Percent P.100	Total	Urban - Urbaine Number Nombre	Percent P.100
AMERICA, NORTH - AMÉRIQUE DU NORD									
Cuba									
14 IX 2012 .... CDFC	11 167 325	8 575 189	76.8	5 570 825	4 177 485	75.0	5 596 500	4 397 704	78.6
1 VII 2013 .... ESDJ	11 191 608	8 596 991	76.8	5 580 810	4 186 436	75.0	5 610 798	4 410 555	78.6
1 VII 2014 .... ESDJ	11 224 190	8 625 144	76.8	5 595 379	4 199 578	75.1	5 628 811	4 425 566	78.6
Curaçao									
1 VII 2005[35] .... ESDJ	137 672	...	...	63 062	...	...	74 610	...	...
1 VII 2006[35] .... ESDJ	141 249	...	...	64 679	...	...	76 570	...	...
1 VII 2007[35] .... ESDJ	144 061	...	...	65 952	...	...	78 109	...	...
1 VII 2008[35] .... ESDJ	145 882	...	...	66 746	...	...	79 136	...	...
1 VII 2009[35] .... ESDJ	146 833	...	...	67 237	...	...	79 596	...	...
1 VII 2010[35] .... ESDJ	148 703	...	...	68 065	...	...	80 639	...	...
26 III 2011 .... CDFC	150 563	...	...	68 848	...	...	81 715	...	...
1 VII 2011[35] .... ESDJ	150 831	...	...	68 910	...	...	81 921	...	...
1 VII 2012[36] .... ESDJ	152 088	...	...	69 490	...	...	82 598	...	...
1 VII 2013[36] .... ESDJ	153 821	...	...	70 342	...	...	83 479	...	...
1 VII 2014[36] .... ESDJ	155 909	...	...	71 269	...	...	84 640	...	...
Dominica - Dominique									
1 VII 2005 .... ESDF	70 665	...	...	35 991	...	...	34 675	...	...
1 VII 2006 .... ESDF	71 008	...	...	36 169	...	...	34 839	...	...
14 V 2011* .... CDFC	71 293	...	...	36 411	...	...	34 882	...	...
Dominican Republic - République dominicaine									
1 VII 2005[2] .... ESDF	8 968 144	6 020 856	67.1	4 497 384	2 951 819	65.6	4 470 760	3 069 037	68.6
1 VII 2006[2] .... ESDF	9 071 458	6 209 005	68.4	4 547 998	3 044 805	66.9	4 523 460	3 164 200	70.0
1 VII 2007[2] .... ESDF	9 174 058	6 399 362	69.8	4 598 212	3 138 848	68.3	4 575 846	3 260 514	71.3
1 VII 2008[2] .... ESDF	9 279 602	6 594 497	71.1	4 649 902	3 235 238	69.6	4 629 700	3 359 259	72.6
1 VII 2009[2] .... ESDF	9 380 152	6 788 782	72.4	4 699 042	3 331 179	70.9	4 681 110	3 457 603	73.9
1 VII 2010[2] .... ESDF	9 478 612	6 992 189	73.8	4 747 103	3 431 480	72.3	4 731 509	3 560 709	75.3
1 XII 2010 .... CDJC	9 445 281	7 013 575	74.3	4 739 038	3 449 122	72.8	4 706 243	3 564 453	75.7
1 VII 2011[2] .... ESDF	9 580 139	7 172 502	74.9	4 796 628	3 520 702	73.4	4 783 511	3 651 800	76.3
1 VII 2012[2] .... ESDF	9 680 963	7 348 975	75.9	4 845 755	3 608 025	74.5	4 835 208	3 740 950	77.4
1 VII 2013[2] .... ESDF	9 784 680	7 524 149	76.9	4 896 319	3 694 713	75.5	4 888 361	3 829 436	78.3
1 VII 2014[2] .... ESDF	9 883 486	7 691 885	77.8	4 944 386	3 777 718	76.4	4 939 100	3 914 167	79.2
El Salvador									
1 VII 2005[37] .... ESDF	6 049 412	3 646 537	60.3	2 874 929	1 701 356	59.2	3 174 483	1 945 181	61.3
1 VII 2006[37] .... ESDF	6 073 859	3 706 525	61.0	2 881 162	1 726 983	59.9	3 192 697	1 979 542	62.0
12 V 2007 .... CDJC	5 744 113	3 598 836	62.7	2 719 371	1 676 313	61.6	3 024 742	1 922 523	63.6
1 VII 2007[37] .... ESDF	6 098 714	3 766 800	61.8	2 887 804	1 752 851	60.7	3 210 910	2 013 949	62.7
1 VII 2008[37] .... ESDF	6 124 705	3 828 004	62.5	2 895 210	1 779 210	61.5	3 229 495	2 048 794	63.4
1 VII 2009[37] .... ESDF	6 152 558	3 890 523	63.2	2 903 737	1 806 310	62.2	3 248 821	2 084 213	64.2
1 VII 2010[37] .... ESDF	6 183 002	3 954 803	64.0	2 913 743	1 834 400	63.0	3 269 259	2 120 404	64.9
1 VII 2011[37] .... ESDF	6 216 143	4 019 742	64.7	2 925 284	1 862 924	63.7	3 290 858	2 156 818	65.5
1 VII 2012[37] .... ESDF	6 251 495	4 086 880	65.4	2 938 123	1 892 642	64.4	3 313 372	2 194 238	66.2
1 VII 2013[37] .... ESDF	6 288 899	4 156 007	66.1	2 952 174	1 923 447	65.2	3 336 726	2 232 560	66.9
1 VII 2014[37] .... ESDF	6 328 196	...	...	2 967 351	...	...	3 360 845	...	...
Greenland - Groenland[38]									
1 VII 2005 .... ESDJ	56 935	47 080	82.7	30 251	24 837	82.1	26 685	22 243	83.4
1 VII 2006 .... ESDJ	56 775	47 037	82.8	30 094	24 763	82.3	26 681	22 274	83.5
1 VII 2007 .... ESDJ	56 555	47 056	83.2	29 945	24 746	82.6	26 610	22 310	83.8
1 I 2008 .... CDJC	56 462	...	...	29 885	...	...	26 577	...	...
1 VII 2008 .... ESDJ	56 328	47 103	83.6	29 847	24 790	83.1	26 481	22 313	84.3
1 VII 2009 .... ESDJ	56 323	47 230	83.9	29 873	24 865	83.2	26 451	22 366	84.6
1 VII 2010 .... ESDJ	56 534	47 646	84.3	29 939	25 045	83.7	26 595	22 601	85.0
1 VII 2011 .... ESDJ	56 682	48 045	84.8	29 992	25 233	84.1	26 690	22 812	85.5
1 VII 2012 .... ESDJ	56 810	48 224	84.9	30 105	25 331	84.1	26 705	22 893	85.7
1 VII 2013 .... ESDJ	56 483	48 221	85.4	29 867	25 333	84.8	26 616	22 888	86.0
1 VII 2014 .... ESDJ	56 295	48 232	85.7	29 742	25 320	85.1	26 553	22 912	86.3
Guadeloupe[39]									
1 I 2005 .... ESDJ	399 178	...	...	188 158	...	...	211 020	...	...
1 I 2006 .... CDJC	400 736	...	...	188 720	...	...	212 016	...	...
1 I 2007 .... ESDJ	400 584	...	...	188 325	...	...	212 259	...	...
1 I 2008 .... ESDJ	401 784	...	...	188 385	...	...	213 399	...	...
1 I 2009 .... ESDJ	401 554	...	...	187 867	...	...	213 687	...	...

137

Continent, country or area, and date / Continent, pays ou zone et date	Code[a]	Both sexes - Les deux sexes			Male - Masculin			Female - Féminin		
		Total	Urban - Urbaine		Total	Urban - Urbaine		Total	Urban - Urbaine	
			Number Nombre	Percent P.100		Number Nombre	Percent P.100		Number Nombre	Percent P.100
AMERICA, NORTH - AMÉRIQUE DU NORD										
Guadeloupe[39]										
1 I 2010	CDJC	403 355	397 070	98.4	187 932	184 752	98.3	215 423	212 318	98.6
1 I 2010	ESDJ	403 355	...	...	187 912	...	...	215 443	...	...
1 I 2011	ESDJ	404 635	...	...	187 782	...	...	216 853	...	...
1 I 2012	ESDJ	403 314	...	...	187 038	...	...	216 276	...	...
1 I 2013	ESDJ	403 645	...	...	186 725	...	...	216 920	...	...
1 I 2014	ESDJ	403 750	...	...	186 235	...	...	217 515	...	...
Guatemala										
1 VII 2005	ESDF	12 699 780	6 345 918	50.0	6 197 399	3 059 570	49.4	6 502 381	3 286 348	50.5
1 VII 2008[22]	ESDF	13 677 815	...	...	6 673 533	...	...	7 004 282	...	...
1 VII 2009[22]	ESDF	14 017 057	...	...	6 836 849	...	...	7 180 208	...	...
1 VII 2010[22]	ESDF	14 361 666	...	...	7 003 337	...	...	7 358 328	...	...
Haiti - Haïti[40]										
1 VII 2005	ESDJ	9 292 282	...	...	4 596 593	...	...	4 695 689	...	...
1 VII 2006	ESDJ	9 445 410	...	...	4 673 089	...	...	4 772 321	...	...
1 VII 2007	ESDJ	9 602 304	...	...	4 751 622	...	...	4 850 682	...	...
1 VII 2008	ESDJ	9 761 927	...	...	4 831 621	...	...	4 930 306	...	...
1 VII 2009	ESDJ	9 923 243	...	...	4 912 515	...	...	5 010 728	...	...
1 VII 2010	ESDJ	10 085 214	4 817 666	47.8	4 993 731	2 321 608	46.5	5 091 483	2 496 059	49.0
1 VII 2011	ESDJ	10 248 306	...	...	5 075 517	...	...	5 172 789	...	...
1 VII 2012	ESDJ	10 413 211	5 154 940	49.5	5 158 254	2 495 108	48.4	5 254 957	2 659 832	50.6
Honduras[41]										
1 VII 2005	ESDF	7 197 303	3 504 730	48.7	3 552 360	1 673 434	47.1	3 644 943	1 831 296	50.2
1 VII 2006	ESDF	7 367 021	3 628 228	49.2	3 634 900	1 733 290	47.7	3 732 121	1 894 938	50.8
1 VII 2007	ESDF	7 536 952	3 752 579	49.8	3 717 577	1 793 588	48.2	3 819 375	1 958 991	51.3
1 VII 2008	ESDF	7 706 907	...	...	3 800 300	...	...	3 906 607	...	...
1 VII 2009	ESDF	7 876 662	...	...	3 882 957	...	...	3 993 705	...	...
1 VII 2010	ESDF	8 045 990	...	...	3 965 430	...	...	4 080 560	...	...
Jamaica - Jamaïque										
1 VII 2005	ESDJ	2 650 402	1 377 546	52.0	1 305 639	657 546	50.4	1 344 763	720 000	53.5
1 VII 2006	ESDJ	2 663 106	1 384 145	52.0	1 312 025	660 763	50.4	1 351 081	723 383	53.5
1 VII 2007	ESDJ	2 675 831	1 390 754	52.0	1 318 444	663 995	50.4	1 357 387	726 759	53.5
1 VII 2008	ESDJ	2 687 241	1 396 470	52.0	1 324 277	666 761	50.3	1 362 964	729 709	53.5
1 VII 2009	ESDJ	2 695 583	...	...	1 328 124	...	...	1 367 460	...	...
1 VII 2010	ESDJ	2 702 314	...	...	1 324 134	...	...	1 378 180	...	...
4 IV 2011	CDJC	2 697 983	1 454 153	53.9	1 334 533	700 957	52.5	1 363 450	753 196	55.2
1 VII 2011	ESDJ	2 699 838	...	...	1 335 466	...	...	1 364 372	...	...
1 VII 2012*	ESDJ	2 707 805	...	...	1 339 740	...	...	1 368 065	...	...
Martinique										
1 I 2005	ESDJ	395 982	...	...	184 841	...	...	211 141	...	...
1 I 2006	CDJC	397 732	355 189	89.3	185 604	165 012	88.9	212 128	190 177	89.7
1 I 2007	ESDJ	397 730	...	...	184 970	...	...	212 760	...	...
1 I 2008	ESDJ	397 693	...	...	184 404	...	...	213 289	...	...
1 I 2009	ESDJ	396 404	...	...	183 655	...	...	212 749	...	...
1 I 2010	CDJC	394 173	380 973	96.7	182 073	175 573	96.4	212 100	205 400	96.8
1 I 2010*	ESDJ	396 308	...	...	182 644	...	...	213 664	...	...
Mexico - Mexique										
1 VII 2005	ESDJ	107 151 011	...	...	52 449 843	...	...	54 701 168	...	...
17 X 2005	CDJC	103 263 388	78 986 852	76.5	50 249 955	38 300 417	76.2	53 013 433	40 686 435	76.7
1 VII 2006	ESDJ	108 408 827	...	...	53 011 285	...	...	55 397 542	...	...
1 VII 2007	ESDJ	109 787 388	...	...	53 646 464	...	...	56 140 924	...	...
1 VII 2008	ESDJ	111 299 015	...	...	54 373 653	...	...	56 925 362	...	...
1 VII 2009	ESDJ	112 852 594	...	...	55 144 845	...	...	57 707 749	...	...
12 VI 2010[42]	CDFC	112 336 538	86 287 410	76.8	54 855 231	41 946 540	76.5	57 481 307	44 340 870	77.1
1 VII 2010[2]	ESDJ	114 255 555	82 629 456	72.3	55 801 919	...	...	58 453 636	...	...
1 VII 2011[2]	ESDJ	115 682 868	83 726 767	72.4	56 519 798	...	...	59 163 070	...	...
1 VII 2012[2]	ESDJ	117 053 750	84 776 446	72.4	57 174 268	...	...	59 879 482	...	...
1 VII 2013[2]	ESDJ	118 395 054	85 792 843	72.5	57 810 955	...	...	60 584 099	...	...
1 VII 2014[2]	ESDJ	119 713 203	86 782 031	72.5	58 435 900	...	...	61 277 304	...	...
Montserrat										
12 V 2011	CDJC	4 922	...	...	2 546	...	...	2 376	...	...
Nicaragua										
4 VI 2005	CDJC	5 142 098	2 875 550	55.9	2 534 491	1 368 622	54.0	2 607 607	1 506 928	57.8
1 VII 2005	ESDJ	5 450 387	3 047 740	55.9	2 707 309	1 462 218	54.0	2 743 078	1 585 522	57.8

6. Total and urban population by sex: 2005 - 2014
Population totale et population urbaine selon le sexe : 2005 - 2014 (continued - suite)

Continent, country or area, and date / Continent, pays ou zone et date	Code[a]	Both sexes - Les deux sexes Total	Urban - Urbaine Number Nombre	Urban - Urbaine Percent P.100	Male - Masculin Total	Urban - Urbaine Number Nombre	Urban - Urbaine Percent P.100	Female - Féminin Total	Urban - Urbaine Number Nombre	Urban - Urbaine Percent P.100
AMERICA, NORTH - AMÉRIQUE DU NORD										
Nicaragua										
1 VII 2006 .... ESDJ		5 522 606	3 099 918	56.1	2 741 414	1 488 694	54.3	2 781 192	1 611 224	57.9
1 VII 2007 .... ESDJ		5 595 541	3 152 807	56.3	2 775 638	1 515 432	54.6	2 819 903	1 637 375	58.1
1 VII 2008 .... ESDJ		5 668 866	3 206 205	56.6	2 809 918	1 542 386	54.9	2 858 948	1 663 819	58.2
1 VII 2009 .... ESDJ		5 742 316	3 259 955	56.8	2 844 244	1 569 555	55.2	2 898 072	1 690 400	58.3
Panama										
1 VII 2005[26] .... ESDF		3 351 007	...	...	1 687 105	...	...	1 663 902	...	...
1 VII 2006[26] .... ESDF		3 413 399	...	...	1 718 193	...	...	1 695 206	...	...
1 VII 2007[26] .... ESDF		3 475 741	...	...	1 749 211	...	...	1 726 530	...	...
1 VII 2008[26] .... ESDF		3 537 986	...	...	1 780 140	...	...	1 757 846	...	...
1 VII 2009[26] .... ESDF		3 600 000	...	...	1 810 794	...	...	1 789 206	...	...
16 V 2010 .... CDFC		3 405 813	...	...	1 712 584	...	...	1 693 229	...	...
1 VII 2010[26] .... ESDF		3 661 835	2 385 445	65.1	1 841 305	1 171 489	63.6	1 820 530	1 213 956	66.7
1 VII 2011[26] .... ESDF		3 723 821	2 449 917	65.8	1 871 749	1 203 430	64.3	1 852 072	1 246 487	67.3
1 VII 2012[26] .... ESDF		3 787 511	2 514 402	66.4	1 903 085	1 235 377	64.9	1 884 426	1 279 025	67.9
1 VII 2013[26] .... ESDF		3 850 735	2 578 868	67.0	1 934 264	1 267 319	65.5	1 916 471	1 311 549	68.4
1 VII 2014[26] .... ESDF		3 913 275	2 643 353	67.5	1 965 087	1 299 262	66.1	1 948 188	1 344 091	69.0
Puerto Rico - Porto Rico[43]										
1 VII 2005 .... ESDJ		3 821 362	...	...	1 834 718	...	...	1 986 644	...	...
1 VII 2006 .... ESDJ		3 805 214	...	...	1 825 958	...	...	1 979 256	...	...
1 VII 2007 .... ESDJ		3 782 995	...	...	1 814 288	...	...	1 968 707	...	...
1 VII 2008 .... ESDJ		3 760 866	...	...	1 803 341	...	...	1 957 525	...	...
1 VII 2009 .... ESDJ		3 740 410	...	...	1 793 049	...	...	1 947 361	...	...
1 IV 2010 .... CDJC		3 725 789	3 493 256	93.8	1 785 171	...	...	1 940 618	...	...
1 VII 2010[44] .... ESDJ		3 721 208	...	...	1 782 619	...	...	1 938 589	...	...
1 VII 2011[44] .... ESDJ		3 686 580	...	...	1 764 715	...	...	1 921 865	...	...
1 VII 2012[44] .... ESDJ		3 651 545	...	...	1 746 970	...	...	1 904 575	...	...
1 VII 2013[44] .... ESDJ		3 615 086	...	...	1 728 634	...	...	1 886 452	...	...
Saint Lucia - Sainte-Lucie										
1 VII 2005 .... ESDF		164 330	...	...	80 440	...	...	83 890	...	...
1 VII 2006 .... ESDF		166 387	...	...	81 558	...	...	84 829	...	...
1 VII 2007 .... ESDF		168 338	...	...	82 426	...	...	85 912	...	...
1 VII 2008 .... ESDF		170 331	...	...	83 478	...	...	86 853	...	...
1 VII 2009 .... ESDF		172 370	...	...	84 465	...	...	87 905	...	...
10 V 2010* .... CDFC		173 720	...	...	86 595	...	...	87 125	...	...
Saint Pierre and Miquelon - Saint Pierre-et-Miquelon										
19 I 2006 .... CDFC		6 125	...	...	3 034	...	...	3 091	...	...
Saint Vincent and the Grenadines - Saint-Vincent-et-les Grenadines										
1 VII 2005 .... ESDF		109 374	...	...	55 635	...	...	53 739	...	...
1 VII 2006 .... ESDF		109 462	...	...	55 680	...	...	53 782	...	...
1 VII 2007 .... ESDF		109 551	...	...	55 725	...	...	53 826	...	...
1 VII 2008 .... ESDF		109 639	...	...	55 770	...	...	53 869	...	...
1 VII 2009 .... ESDF		109 727	...	...	55 814	...	...	53 912	...	...
1 VII 2010 .... ESDF		109 815	...	...	55 859	...	...	53 956	...	...
1 VII 2011 .... ESDF		109 903	...	...	55 904	...	...	53 999	...	...
12 VI 2012* .... CDFC		109 991	...	...	56 419	...	...	53 572	...	...
1 VII 2013 .... ESDF		110 079	...	...	56 464	...	...	53 615	...	...
1 VII 2014 .... ESDF		110 167	...	...	56 509	...	...	53 658	...	...
Sint Maarten (Dutch part) - Saint-Martin (partie néerlandaise)										
1 VII 2005 .... ESDJ		36 941	...	...	17 885	...	...	19 056	...	...
1 VII 2006 .... ESDJ		38 276	...	...	18 510	...	...	19 766	...	...
1 VII 2007 .... ESDJ		39 466	...	...	19 106	...	...	20 361	...	...
1 VII 2008 .... ESDJ		40 461	...	...	19 632	...	...	20 829	...	...
1 VII 2009 .... ESDJ		39 172	...	...	18 918	...	...	20 254	...	...
1 VII 2010 .... ESDJ		35 526	...	...	16 927	...	...	18 600	...	...

6. Total and urban population by sex: 2005 - 2014
Population totale et population urbaine selon le sexe : 2005 - 2014 (continued - suite)

Continent, country or area, and date / Continent, pays ou zone et date	Code[a]	Both sexes - Les deux sexes			Male - Masculin			Female - Féminin		
		Total	Urban - Urbaine		Total	Urban - Urbaine		Total	Urban - Urbaine	
			Number Nombre	Percent P.100		Number Nombre	Percent P.100		Number Nombre	Percent P.100
AMERICA, NORTH - AMÉRIQUE DU NORD										
Sint Maarten (Dutch part) - Saint-Martin (partie néerlandaise)										
9 IV 2011 ....CDFC		33 609	...	...	15 868	...	...	17 741	...	...
1 VII 2011 ....ESDJ		33 436	...	...	15 772	...	...	17 656	...	...
1 VII 2012 ....ESDJ		34 670	...	...	16 656	...	...	18 005	...	...
1 VII 2013 ....ESDJ		36 611	...	...	17 910	...	...	18 701	...	...
1 I 2014 ....ESDJ		37 132	...	...	18 159	...	...	18 973	...	...
Trinidad and Tobago - Trinité-et-Tobago										
1 VII 2005[14] ....ESDF		1 294 494	...	...	649 189	...	...	645 305	...	...
1 VII 2006[14] ....ESDF		1 297 944	...	...	650 919	...	...	647 025	...	...
1 VII 2007[14] ....ESDF		1 303 188	...	...	653 549	...	...	649 639	...	...
1 VII 2008[14] ....ESDF		1 308 587	...	...	656 257	...	...	652 330	...	...
1 VII 2010[14] ....ESDF		1 317 714	...	...	656 892	...	...	660 822	...	...
9 I 2011 ....CDJC		1 328 019	...	...	666 305	...	...	661 714	...	...
Turks and Caicos Islands - Îles Turques et Caïques										
1 VII 2005 ....ESDJ		*30 602*	...	...	*15 230*	...	...	*15 372*	...	...
1 VII 2006 ....ESDJ		*33 202*	...	...	*16 524*	...	...	*16 678*	...	...
1 VII 2007 ....ESDJ		*34 862*	...	...	*18 023*	...	...	*16 839*	...	...
25 I 2012 ....CDFC		31 458	...	...	16 037	...	...	15 421	...	...
United States of America - États-Unis d'Amérique										
1 VII 2005[45] ....ESDJ		295 516 599	...	...	145 197 078	...	...	150 319 521	...	...
1 VII 2006[45] ....ESDJ		298 379 912	...	...	146 647 265	...	...	151 732 647	...	...
1 VII 2007[45] ....ESDJ		301 231 207	...	...	148 064 854	...	...	153 166 353	...	...
1 VII 2008[45] ....ESDJ		304 093 966	...	...	149 489 951	...	...	154 604 015	...	...
1 VII 2009[45] ....ESDJ		306 771 529	...	...	150 807 454	...	...	155 964 075	...	...
1 IV 2010 ....CDJC		308 745 538	249 253 271	80.7	151 781 326	121 698 595	80.2	156 964 212	127 554 676	81.3
1 VII 2010[46] ....ESDJ		309 326 225	...	...	152 088 297	...	...	157 237 928	...	...
1 VII 2011[46] ....ESDJ		311 587 816	...	...	153 261 429	...	...	158 326 387	...	...
1 VII 2012[46] ....ESDJ		313 914 040	...	...	154 492 067	...	...	159 421 973	...	...
1 VII 2013[46] ....ESDJ		316 128 839	...	...	155 651 602	...	...	160 477 237	...	...
United States Virgin Islands - Îles Vierges américaines[43]										
1 VII 2005 ....ESDJ		109 600	...	...	52 081	...	...	57 519	...	...
1 VII 2006 ....ESDJ		109 764	...	...	52 113	...	...	57 651	...	...
1 VII 2007 ....ESDJ		109 821	...	...	52 089	...	...	57 732	...	...
1 VII 2008 ....ESDJ		109 840	...	...	52 045	...	...	57 795	...	...
1 IV 2010 ....CDJC		106 405	...	...	50 854	...	...	55 551	...	...
AMERICA, SOUTH - AMÉRIQUE DU SUD										
Argentina - Argentine										
1 VII 2005 ....ESDF		38 592 150	34 894 057	90.4	18 898 472	16 961 698	89.8	19 693 678	17 932 359	91.1
1 VII 2006 ....ESDF		38 970 611	35 304 205	90.6	19 083 828	17 170 659	90.0	19 886 783	18 133 546	91.2
1 VII 2007 ....ESDF		39 356 383	35 719 891	90.8	19 273 494	17 383 239	90.2	20 082 889	18 336 652	91.3
1 VII 2008 ....ESDF		39 745 613	36 137 648	90.9	19 465 305	17 597 280	90.4	20 280 308	18 540 368	91.4
1 VII 2009 ....ESDF		40 134 425	36 553 965	91.1	19 657 086	17 810 843	90.6	20 477 339	18 743 122	91.5
1 VII 2010[47] ....ESDF		40 788 453	37 126 653	91.0	19 940 704	17 996 224	90.2	20 847 749	19 130 429	91.8
27 X 2010 ....CDFC		40 117 096	36 467 245	90.9	19 523 766	17 596 022	90.1	20 593 330	18 871 223	91.6
1 VII 2011[47] ....ESDF		41 262 408	37 603 614	91.1	20 181 263	18 238 292	90.4	21 081 145	19 365 322	91.9
1 VII 2012[47] ....ESDF		41 735 190	38 079 552	91.2	20 421 377	18 479 951	90.5	21 313 813	19 599 601	92.0
1 VII 2013[47] ....ESDF		42 205 936	38 553 619	91.3	20 660 580	18 720 747	90.6	21 545 356	19 832 872	92.1
1 VII 2014[47] ....ESDF		42 673 657	39 024 881	91.4	20 898 342	18 960 180	90.7	21 775 315	20 064 701	92.1

6. Total and urban population by sex: 2005 - 2014
Population totale et population urbaine selon le sexe : 2005 - 2014 (continued - suite)

Continent, country or area, and date / Continent, pays ou zone et date	Codea	Both sexes - Les deux sexes			Male - Masculin			Female - Féminin		
		Total	Urban - Urbaine		Total	Urban - Urbaine		Total	Urban - Urbaine	
			Number Nombre	Percent P.100		Number Nombre	Percent P.100		Number Nombre	Percent P.100

AMERICA, SOUTH - AMÉRIQUE DU SUD

Bolivia (Plurinational State of) - Bolivie (État plurinational de)

1 VII 2005 .... ESDF		9 210 782	5 906 986	64.1	4 649 808	2 917 362	62.7	4 560 974	2 989 624	65.5
1 VII 2006 .... ESDF		9 372 643	6 053 113	64.6	4 731 015	2 989 418	63.2	4 641 628	3 063 695	66.0
1 VII 2007 .... ESDF		9 534 639	6 200 789	65.0	4 812 179	3 062 167	63.6	4 722 460	3 138 622	66.5
1 VII 2008 .... ESDF		9 696 806	6 350 052	65.5	4 893 275	3 135 600	64.1	4 803 531	3 214 452	66.9
1 VII 2009 .... ESDF		9 859 417	6 501 067	65.9	4 974 432	3 209 796	64.5	4 884 985	3 291 271	67.4
1 VII 2010 .... ESDF		10 022 682	6 653 996	66.4	5 055 762	3 284 825	65.0	4 966 920	3 369 171	67.8
1 VII 2011 .... ESDF		10 186 660	6 808 877	66.8	5 137 330	3 360 738	65.4	5 049 330	3 448 139	68.3
1 VII 2012 .... ESDF		10 351 118	6 965 568	67.3	5 219 006	3 437 451	65.9	5 132 112	3 528 117	68.7
21 XI 2012 .... CDFC		10 059 856	6 788 962	67.5	5 019 447	3 314 824	66.0	5 040 409	3 474 138	68.9
1 VII 2013 .... ESDF		10 516 073	7 111 771	67.6	5 300 912	3 509 212	66.2	5 215 161	3 602 559	69.1
1 VII 2014 .... ESDF		10 681 367	7 268 748	68.1	5 382 966	3 586 253	66.6	5 298 401	3 682 495	69.5

Brazil - Brésil

1 VII 2005[48] .... ESDF		183 383 216	...	...	90 135 967	...	...	93 247 249	...	...
1 VII 2006[48] .... ESDF		185 564 212	...	...	91 171 295	...	...	94 392 917	...	...
1 VII 2007[48] .... ESDF		187 641 714	...	...	92 154 636	...	...	95 487 078	...	...
1 VII 2008[48] .... ESDF		189 612 814	...	...	93 084 588	...	...	96 528 226	...	...
1 VII 2009[48] .... ESDF		191 480 630	...	...	93 962 767	...	...	97 517 863	...	...
1 VII 2010[48] .... ESDF		193 252 604	...	...	94 792 952	...	...	98 459 652	...	...
31 VII 2010 .... CDJC		190 755 799	160 925 804	84.4	93 406 990	77 710 179	83.2	97 348 809	83 215 625	85.5
1 VII 2011[49] .... ESDJ		197 397 018	...	...	97 610 297	...	...	99 786 721	...	...
1 VII 2012[49] .... ESDJ		199 242 462	...	...	98 487 258	...	...	100 755 204	...	...
1 VII 2013[49] .... ESDJ		201 032 714	...	...	99 336 858	...	...	101 695 856	...	...
1 VII 2014[49] .... ESDJ		202 768 562	...	...	100 159 507	...	...	102 609 055	...	...

Chile - Chili

1 VII 2005 .... ESDF		16 267 278	14 123 527	86.8	8 052 564	6 910 230	85.8	8 214 714	7 213 297	87.8
1 VII 2006 .... ESDF		16 432 674	14 272 454	86.9	8 134 314	6 983 850	85.9	8 298 360	7 288 604	87.8
1 VII 2007 .... ESDF		16 598 074	14 421 386	86.9	8 216 068	7 057 476	85.9	8 382 006	7 363 910	87.9
1 VII 2008 .... ESDF		16 763 470	14 570 311	86.9	8 297 819	7 131 097	85.9	8 465 651	7 439 214	87.9
1 VII 2009 .... ESDF		16 928 873	14 719 246	86.9	8 379 571	7 204 720	86.0	8 549 302	7 514 526	87.9
1 VII 2010 .... ESDF		17 094 275	14 868 172	87.0	8 461 327	7 278 342	86.0	8 632 948	7 589 830	87.9
1 VII 2011 .... ESDF		17 248 450	15 006 226	87.0	8 536 904	7 346 185	86.1	8 711 546	7 660 041	87.9
1 VII 2012 .... ESDF		17 402 630	15 144 277	87.0	8 612 483	7 414 026	86.1	8 790 147	7 730 251	87.9
1 VII 2013 .... ESDF		17 556 815	15 282 334	87.0	8 688 067	7 481 874	86.1	8 868 748	7 800 460	88.0
1 VII 2014 .... ESDF		17 819 054	...	...	8 819 725	...	...	8 999 329	...	...

Colombia - Colombie

22 V 2005 .... CDFC		41 468 384	31 510 379	76.0	20 336 117	15 086 536	74.2	21 132 267	16 423 843	77.7
1 VII 2005[50] .... ESDJ		42 888 592	31 889 299	74.4	21 169 835	15 356 383	72.5	21 718 757	16 532 916	76.1
1 VII 2006[50] .... ESDJ		43 405 956	32 386 530	74.6	21 426 954	15 605 323	72.8	21 979 002	16 781 207	76.4
1 VII 2007[50] .... ESDJ		43 926 929	32 888 860	74.9	21 683 071	15 850 700	73.1	22 243 858	17 038 160	76.6
1 VII 2008[50] .... ESDJ		44 451 147	33 396 380	75.1	21 942 355	16 100 320	73.4	22 508 792	17 296 060	76.8
1 VII 2009[50] .... ESDJ		44 978 832	33 892 634	75.4	22 203 708	16 343 820	73.6	22 775 124	17 548 814	77.1
1 VII 2010[50] .... ESDJ		45 509 584	34 388 013	75.6	22 466 660	16 587 100	73.8	23 042 924	17 800 913	77.3
1 VII 2011[50] .... ESDJ		46 044 601	34 883 399	75.8	22 731 299	16 830 795	74.0	23 313 302	18 052 604	77.4
1 VII 2012[50] .... ESDJ		46 581 823	35 377 138	75.9	22 997 087	17 073 806	74.2	23 584 736	18 303 332	77.6
1 VII 2013[50] .... ESDJ		47 121 089	35 869 246	76.1	23 264 039	17 315 981	74.4	23 857 050	18 553 265	77.8
1 VII 2014[50] .... ESDJ		47 661 787	36 359 268	76.3	23 531 670	17 556 826	74.6	24 130 117	18 802 442	77.9

Ecuador - Équateur

1 VII 2005[51] .... ESDF		13 721 297	8 575 069	62.5	6 842 019	4 221 757	61.7	6 879 278	4 353 312	63.3
1 VII 2006[51] .... ESDF		13 964 606	8 733 912	62.5	6 955 272	4 295 578	61.8	7 009 334	4 438 334	63.3
1 VII 2007[51] .... ESDF		14 214 982	8 896 925	62.6	7 071 884	4 371 337	61.8	7 143 098	4 525 588	63.4
1 VII 2008[51] .... ESDF		14 472 881	9 064 267	62.6	7 192 128	4 449 107	61.9	7 280 753	4 615 160	63.4
1 VII 2009[51] .... ESDF		14 738 472	9 236 112	62.7	7 316 020	4 528 987	61.9	7 422 452	4 707 125	63.4
1 VII 2010[51] .... ESDF		15 012 228	9 412 612	62.7	7 443 875	4 611 039	61.9	7 568 353	4 801 573	63.4
28 XI 2010 .... CDFC		14 483 499	9 090 786	62.8	7 177 683	4 451 434	62.0	7 305 816	4 639 352	63.5
1 VII 2011[51] .... ESDF		15 266 431	9 596 628	62.9	7 567 676	4 700 620	62.1	7 698 755	4 896 008	63.6
1 VII 2012[51] .... ESDF		15 520 973	9 780 650	63.0	7 691 912	4 790 437	62.3	7 829 061	4 990 213	63.7
1 VII 2013[51] .... ESDF		15 774 749	9 963 884	63.2	7 815 935	4 880 045	62.4	7 958 814	5 083 839	63.9
1 VII 2014[51] .... ESDF		16 027 466	10 145 875	63.3	7 939 552	4 969 197	62.6	8 087 914	5 176 678	64.0

Continent, country or area, and date	Code[a]	Both sexes - Les deux sexes			Male - Masculin			Female - Féminin		
			Urban - Urbaine			Urban - Urbaine			Urban - Urbaine	
Continent, pays ou zone et date		Total	Number Nombre	Percent P.100	Total	Number Nombre	Percent P.100	Total	Number Nombre	Percent P.100
AMERICA, SOUTH - AMÉRIQUE DU SUD										
Falkland Islands (Malvinas) - Îles Falkland (Malvinas)[52]										
8 X 2006 .... CDFC		2 955	...	...	1 569	...	...	1 386	...	...
French Guiana - Guyane française										
1 I 2005 .... ESDJ		199 206	...	...	99 223	...	...	99 983	...	...
1 I 2006 .... CDJC		205 954	167 454	81.3	101 930	81 888	80.3	104 023	85 565	82.3
1 I 2006 .... ESDJ		205 954	...	...	102 032	...	...	103 922	...	...
1 I 2007 .... ESDJ		213 031	...	...	105 546	...	...	107 485	...	...
1 I 2008 .... ESDJ		219 266	...	...	108 662	...	...	110 604	...	...
1 I 2009 .... ESDJ		224 469	...	...	111 201	...	...	113 268	...	...
1 I 2010 .... CDJC		229 040	201 042	87.8	113 599	98 933	87.1	115 441	102 109	88.5
1 I 2010* .... ESDJ		230 441	...	...	113 824	...	...	116 617	...	...
Guyana										
1 VII 2005 .... ESDF		758 183	...	...	379 515	...	...	378 668	...	...
1 VII 2006 .... ESDF		768 339	...	...	384 539	...	...	383 800	...	...
1 VII 2007 .... ESDF		770 992	...	...	385 882	...	...	385 110	...	...
1 VII 2008 .... ESDF		774 443	...	...	387 649	...	...	386 794	...	...
1 VII 2009 .... ESDF		753 227	...	...	377 759	...	...	375 468	...	...
1 VII 2010 .... ESDF		752 113	...	...	377 267	...	...	374 846	...	...
1 VII 2011 .... ESDF		750 663	...	...	376 596	...	...	374 067	...	...
1 VII 2012 .... ESDF		748 917	...	...	375 767	...	...	373 150	...	...
15 IX 2012* .... CDFC		747 884	...	...	372 547	...	...	375 337	...	...
1 VII 2013 .... ESDF		746 880	...	...	374 782	...	...	372 098	...	...
Paraguay[22]										
1 VII 2005 .... ESDF		5 898 651	3 347 793	56.8	2 983 123	1 634 869	54.8	2 915 528	1 712 924	58.8
1 VII 2006 .... ESDF		6 009 143	3 430 619	57.1	3 038 590	1 675 752	55.1	2 970 553	1 754 868	59.1
1 VII 2007 .... ESDF		6 119 642	3 513 944	57.4	3 094 044	1 716 874	55.5	3 025 598	1 797 070	59.4
1 VII 2008 .... ESDF		6 230 143	3 597 588	57.7	3 149 475	1 758 138	55.8	3 080 668	1 839 450	59.7
1 VII 2009 .... ESDF		6 340 639	3 681 375	58.1	3 204 871	1 799 444	56.1	3 135 767	1 881 931	60.0
1 VII 2010 .... ESDF		6 451 122	3 765 127	58.4	3 260 223	1 840 694	56.5	3 190 899	1 924 433	60.3
1 VII 2011 .... ESDF		6 561 785	3 848 934	58.7	3 315 636	1 881 940	56.8	3 246 149	1 966 994	60.6
1 VII 2012 .... ESDF		6 672 631	3 932 915	58.9	3 371 117	1 923 249	57.1	3 301 514	2 009 666	60.9
1 VII 2013 .... ESDF		6 783 374	4 016 934	59.2	3 426 508	1 964 541	57.3	3 356 867	2 052 393	61.1
1 VII 2014 .... ESDF		6 893 727	4 100 854	59.5	3 481 648	2 005 735	57.6	3 412 079	2 095 119	61.4
Peru - Pérou										
30 VI 2005 .... ESDF		27 810 540	19 782 408	71.1	13 948 639	9 791 272	70.2	13 861 901	9 991 136	72.1
18 VII 2005*[53] .... CDFC		26 152 265	...	...	13 061 026	...	...	13 091 239	...	...
30 VI 2006 .... ESDF		28 151 443	20 191 318	71.7	14 118 112	9 991 965	70.8	14 033 331	10 199 353	72.7
30 VI 2007[37] .... ESDF		28 481 901	20 594 600	72.3	14 282 346	10 189 918	71.3	14 199 555	10 404 682	73.3
21 X 2007 .... CDFC		27 412 157	20 810 288	75.9	13 622 640	10 226 205	75.1	13 789 517	10 584 083	76.8
30 VI 2008[37] .... ESDF		28 807 034	20 995 699	72.9	14 443 858	10 386 799	71.9	14 363 176	10 608 900	73.9
30 VI 2009[37] .... ESDF		29 132 013	21 398 222	73.5	14 605 206	10 584 348	72.5	14 526 807	10 813 874	74.4
30 VI 2010[37] .... ESDF		29 461 933	21 805 837	74.0	14 768 901	10 784 345	73.0	14 693 032	11 021 492	75.0
30 VI 2011[37] .... ESDF		29 797 694	22 219 201	74.6	14 935 396	10 987 090	73.6	14 862 298	11 232 111	75.6
30 VI 2012[37] .... ESDF		30 135 875	22 635 742	75.1	15 103 003	11 191 332	74.1	15 032 872	11 444 410	76.1
30 VI 2013[37] .... ESDF		30 475 144	23 054 394	75.6	15 271 062	11 396 589	74.6	15 204 082	11 657 805	76.7
30 VI 2014[37] .... ESDF		30 814 175	23 474 069	76.2	15 438 887	11 602 321	75.1	15 375 288	11 871 748	77.2
Suriname										
1 VII 2007 .... ESDJ		509 970	...	...	257 181	...	...	252 789	...	...
1 VII 2008 .... ESDJ		517 052	...	...	260 898	...	...	256 154	...	...
13 VIII 2012 .... CDJC		541 638	359 146	66.3	270 629	177 215	65.5	271 009	181 931	67.1
1 VII 2013 .... ESDJ		550 222	...	...	274 859	...	...	275 363	...	...
Uruguay										
1 VII 2005 .... ESDF		3 352 355	...	...	1 621 184	...	...	1 731 170	...	...
1 VII 2006 .... ESDF		3 358 005	...	...	1 623 413	...	...	1 734 592	...	...
1 VII 2007 .... ESDF		3 358 794	...	...	1 623 189	...	...	1 735 604	...	...
1 VII 2008 .... ESDF		3 363 060	...	...	1 624 932	...	...	1 738 128	...	...
1 VII 2009 .... ESDF		3 378 083	...	...	1 632 052	...	...	1 746 031	...	...
1 VII 2010 .... ESDF		3 396 706	...	...	1 640 886	...	...	1 755 820	...	...
1 VII 2011 .... ESDF		3 412 636	...	...	1 648 466	...	...	1 764 170	...	...
4 X 2011 .... CDJC		3 286 314	3 110 701	94.7	1 577 725[54]	1 478 967[54]	93.7	1 708 481[54]	1 631 626[54]	95.5
1 VII 2012[2] .... ESDF		3 426 466	...	...	1 655 693	...	...	1 770 774	...	...

Continent, country or area, and date / Continent, pays ou zone et date	Code[a]	Both sexes - Les deux sexes			Male - Masculin			Female - Féminin		
		Total	Urban - Urbaine		Total	Urban - Urbaine		Total	Urban - Urbaine	
			Number Nombre	Percent P.100		Number Nombre	Percent P.100		Number Nombre	Percent P.100
AMERICA, SOUTH - AMÉRIQUE DU SUD										
Uruguay										
1 VII 2013[2] .... ESDF		3 440 157	...	...	1 662 884	...	...	1 777 273	...	...
1 VII 2014[2] .... ESDF		3 453 691	...	...	1 670 026	...	...	1 783 665	...	...
Venezuela (Bolivarian Republic of) - Venezuela (République bolivarienne du)										
1 VII 2005 .... ESDF		26 444 921	23 268 442	88.0	13 272 966	...	...	13 171 955	...	...
1 VII 2006 .... ESDF		26 858 165	23 639 927	88.0	13 477 276	...	...	13 380 889	...	...
1 VII 2007 .... ESDF		27 272 712	24 012 062	88.0	13 682 677	...	...	13 590 035	...	...
1 VII 2008 .... ESDF		27 688 638	24 384 883	88.1	13 889 561	...	...	13 799 077	...	...
1 VII 2009 .... ESDF		28 105 913	24 758 144	88.1	14 097 305	...	...	14 008 608	...	...
1 VII 2010 .... ESDF		28 524 411	25 131 837	88.1	14 305 797	...	...	14 218 614	...	...
1 VII 2011 .... ESDF		28 944 070	25 504 003	88.1	14 514 965	...	...	14 429 105	...	...
1 IX 2011 .... CDFC		27 227 930	...	...	13 549 752	...	...	13 678 178	...	...
1 VII 2012 .... ESDF		29 365 451	25 881 582	88.1	14 725 042	...	...	14 640 409	...	...
1 VII 2013 .... ESDF		29 786 263	26 255 358	88.1	14 935 119	...	...	14 851 144	...	...
1 VII 2014 .... ESDF		30 206 307	26 628 251	88.2	15 144 744	13 228 428	87.3	15 061 563	13 399 823	89.0
ASIA - ASIE										
Afghanistan[55]										
1 VII 2005 .... ESDF		22 097 900	4 759 200	21.5	11 301 300	2 450 100	21.7	10 796 600	2 309 100	21.4
1 VII 2006 .... ESDF		22 575 900	4 862 100	21.5	11 545 800	2 503 100	21.7	11 030 100	2 359 000	21.4
1 VII 2007 .... ESDF		23 038 900	5 159 200	22.4	11 783 600	2 656 200	22.5	11 255 300	2 503 000	22.2
1 VII 2008 .... ESDF		23 511 400	5 330 200	22.7	12 025 700	2 744 400	22.8	11 485 700	2 585 800	22.5
1 VII 2009 .... ESDF		23 993 500	5 507 300	23.0	12 272 900	2 835 900	23.1	11 720 600	2 671 400	22.8
1 VII 2010 .... ESDF		24 485 600	5 690 300	23.2	12 524 700	2 929 900	23.4	11 960 900	2 760 400	23.1
1 VII 2011 .... ESDF		24 987 700	5 879 200	23.5	12 782 000	3 027 400	23.7	12 205 700	2 851 800	23.4
1 VII 2012 .... ESDF		25 500 100	6 074 200	23.8	13 044 400	3 127 700	24.0	12 455 700	2 946 500	23.7
1 VII 2013 .... ESDF		26 023 100	6 275 600	24.1	13 312 400	3 231 600	24.3	12 710 700	3 044 000	23.9
1 VII 2014 .... ESDF		26 556 754	6 483 434	24.4	13 585 933	3 338 764	24.6	12 970 821	3 144 670	24.2
Armenia - Arménie										
1 VII 2005 .... ESDJ		3 217 535	2 062 472	64.1	1 552 382	978 396	63.0	1 665 153	1 084 076	65.1
1 VII 2006 .... ESDJ		3 221 094	2 064 268	64.1	1 555 755	980 272	63.0	1 665 339	1 083 996	65.1
1 VII 2007 .... ESDJ		3 226 520	2 067 650	64.1	1 559 978	982 632	63.0	1 666 542	1 085 018	65.1
1 VII 2008 .... ESDJ		3 234 031	2 071 942	64.1	1 565 411	985 913	63.0	1 668 620	1 086 029	65.1
1 VII 2009 .... ESDJ		3 243 729	2 077 181	64.0	1 572 046	989 609	63.0	1 671 683	1 087 572	65.1
1 VII 2010 .... ESDJ		3 256 066	...	...	1 579 705	...	...	1 676 361	...	...
1 VII 2011 .... ESDJ		3 268 468	...	...	1 586 935	...	...	1 681 533	...	...
12 X 2011 .... CDFC		2 871 771	1 847 124	64.3	1 346 729	851 475	63.2	1 525 042	995 649	65.3
1 I 2012 .... ESDJ		3 274 285	...	...	1 590 285	...	...	1 684 000	...	...
Azerbaijan - Azerbaïdjan										
1 VII 2005[35] .... ESDF		8 500 300	4 462 900	52.5	4 184 900	2 186 100	52.2	4 315 400	2 276 800	52.8
1 VII 2006[35] .... ESDF		8 609 600	4 533 300	52.7	4 244 200	2 223 100	52.4	4 365 400	2 310 200	52.9
1 VII 2007[35] .... ESDF		8 723 000	4 608 200	52.8	4 305 800	2 262 400	52.5	4 417 200	2 345 800	53.1
1 VII 2008[35] .... ESDF		8 838 500	4 690 000	53.1	4 368 600	2 304 800	52.8	4 469 900	2 385 200	53.4
13 IV 2009 .... CDJC		8 922 447	4 739 123	53.1	4 414 398	2 330 527	52.8	4 508 049	2 408 596	53.4
1 VII 2009 .... ESDF		8 947 300	4 751 400	53.1	4 427 900	2 337 100	52.8	4 519 400	2 414 300	53.4
1 VII 2010 .... ESDF		9 054 300	4 802 200	53.0	4 486 300	2 364 400	52.7	4 568 000	2 437 800	53.4
1 VII 2011 .... ESDF		9 173 100	4 859 100	53.0	4 550 300	2 394 700	52.6	4 622 800	2 464 400	53.3
1 VII 2012 .... ESDF		9 295 784	4 936 922	53.1	4 616 139	2 435 213	52.8	4 679 646	2 501 709	53.5
1 VII 2013 .... ESDF		9 416 800	5 016 000	53.3	4 681 200	2 476 300	52.9	4 735 600	2 539 700	53.6
1 VII 2014 .... ESDF		9 528 900	5 075 700	53.3	4 736 900	2 505 700	52.9	4 792 000	2 570 000	53.6
Bahrain - Bahreïn										
1 VII 2005 .... ESDJ		888 824	...	...	533 501	...	...	355 323	...	...
1 VII 2006 .... ESDJ		960 425	...	...	580 285	...	...	380 141	...	...
1 VII 2007 .... ESDJ		1 039 297	...	...	632 074	...	...	407 223	...	...
1 VII 2008 .... ESDJ		1 103 496	...	...	676 590	...	...	426 906	...	...
1 VII 2009 .... ESDJ		1 178 415	...	...	731 997	...	...	446 418	...	...
27 IV 2010 .... CDJC		1 234 571	1 234 571	100.0	768 414	768 414	100.0	466 157	466 157	100.0
1 VII 2010 .... ESDJ		1 228 543	...	...	764 357	...	...	464 186	...	...
1 VII 2011 .... ESDJ		1 195 020	...	...	741 483	...	...	453 537	...	...

6. Total and urban population by sex: 2005 - 2014
Population totale et population urbaine selon le sexe : 2005 - 2014 (continued - suite)

Continent, country or area, and date / Continent, pays ou zone et date	Code[a]	Both sexes - Les deux sexes Total	Urban - Urbaine Number Nombre	Urban - Urbaine Percent P.100	Male - Masculin Total	Urban - Urbaine Number Nombre	Urban - Urbaine Percent P.100	Female - Féminin Total	Urban - Urbaine Number Nombre	Urban - Urbaine Percent P.100
ASIA - ASIE										
Bahrain - Bahreïn										
1 VII 2012	ESDJ	1 208 964	...	...	760 449	...	...	448 515	...	...
1 VII 2013	ESDJ	1 253 191	...	...	788 381	...	...	464 810	...	...
1 VII 2014	ESDJ	1 314 562	...	...	806 487	...	...	508 075	...	...
Bangladesh										
1 VII 2005	ESDF	138 600 000	33 600 000	24.2	71 000 000	...	...	67 600 000	...	...
1 VII 2006	ESDF	140 600 000	34 600 000	24.6	72 000 000	...	...	68 600 000	...	...
1 VII 2007	ESDF	142 600 000	35 700 000	25.0	73 100 000	...	...	69 500 000	...	...
1 VII 2008	ESDF	144 500 000	36 700 000	25.4	74 000 000	...	...	70 500 000	...	...
1 VII 2010	ESDF	148 620 000	38 540 000	25.9	76 120 000	20 427 000	26.8	72 500 000	18 113 000	25.0
15 III 2011[56]	CDFC	149 772 364	...	...	74 980 386			74 791 978	...	...
1 VII 2011	ESDF	150 611 000	39 000 000	25.9	77 101 062	20 560 587	26.7	73 509 938	18 439 413	25.1
1 VII 2012	ESDF	152 700 000	41 100 000	26.9	78 200 000	...	...	74 500 000	...	...
1 VII 2013	ESDF	154 790 000	42 580 000	27.5	77 510 000	...	...	77 280 000	...	...
1 VII 2014	ESDF	156 880 000	44 110 000	28.1	78 560 000	...	...	78 320 000	...	...
Bhutan - Bhoutan										
30 V 2005	CDFC	634 982	196 111	30.9	333 595	105 559	31.6	301 387	90 552	30.0
1 VII 2006[57]	ESDF	646 851	204 691	31.6	339 403	109 920	32.4	307 448	94 771	30.8
1 VII 2007[57]	ESDF	658 888	213 571	32.4	345 298	114 593	33.2	313 590	98 978	31.6
1 VII 2008[57]	ESDF	671 083	222 753	33.2	351 269	119 342	34.0	319 814	103 411	32.3
1 VII 2009[57]	ESDF	683 407	232 232	34.0	357 305	124 246	34.8	326 102	107 986	33.1
1 VII 2010[57]	ESDF	695 823	242 001	34.8	363 384	129 298	35.6	332 439	112 703	33.9
1 VII 2011[57]	ESDF	708 265	252 038	35.6	369 476	134 484	36.4	338 789	117 554	34.7
1 VII 2012[57]	ESDF	720 679	262 325	36.4	375 554	139 798	37.2	345 125	122 530	35.5
1 VII 2013[57]	ESDF	733 004	272 839	37.2	381 582	145 219	38.1	351 421	127 619	36.3
1 VII 2014[57]	ESDF	745 153	283 543	38.1	387 520	150 737	38.9	357 633	132 806	37.1
Brunei Darussalam - Brunéi Darussalam										
1 VII 2005[15]	ESDF	358 500	...	...	185 100	...	...	173 400	...	...
1 VII 2006[15]	ESDF	364 500	...	...	188 200	...	...	176 300	...	...
1 VII 2007[15]	ESDF	370 000	...	...	191 100	...	...	178 900	...	...
1 VII 2008[15]	ESDF	375 000	...	...	193 700	...	...	181 300	...	...
1 VII 2009[15]	ESDF	380 100	...	...	196 300	...	...	183 800	...	...
1 VII 2010[15]	ESDF	386 800	...	...	199 800	...	...	187 000	...	...
20 VI 2011	CDJC	393 372	296 257	75.3	203 144	151 663	74.7	190 228	144 594	76.0
Cambodia - Cambodge										
1 VII 2005[58]	ESDF	13 806 923	...	...	6 698 783	...	...	7 108 140	...	...
1 VII 2006[58]	ESDF	14 080 653	...	...	6 836 759	...	...	7 243 894	...	...
1 VII 2007[58]	ESDF	14 363 519	...	...	6 979 452	...	...	7 384 067	...	...
3 III 2008[59]	CDFC	13 395 682	2 614 027	19.5	6 516 054	1 255 570	19.3	6 879 628	1 358 457	19.7
1 VII 2008[60]	ESDF	13 868 227	2 707 240	19.5	6 745 592	1 299 799	19.3	7 122 635	1 407 441	19.8
1 VII 2009[60]	ESDF	14 085 324	2 814 943	20.0	6 859 756	1 351 939	19.7	7 225 568	1 463 004	20.2
1 VII 2010[60]	ESDF	14 302 779	2 926 810	20.5	6 973 994	1 406 183	20.2	7 328 785	1 520 627	20.7
1 VII 2011[60]	ESDF	14 521 275	3 042 794	21.0	7 088 691	1 462 518	20.6	7 432 584	1 580 276	21.3
1 VII 2012[60]	ESDF	14 741 414	3 165 683	21.5	7 204 166	1 520 722	21.1	7 537 248	1 644 961	21.8
3 III 2013[61]	SSDF	14 676 591	3 146 212	21.4	7 121 508	1 527 479	21.4	7 555 083	1 618 734	21.4
1 VII 2013[60]	ESDF	14 962 591	3 285 951	22.0	7 320 112	1 580 866	21.6	7 642 479	1 705 085	22.3
1 VII 2014[60]	ESDF	15 184 116	3 412 183	22.5	7 436 178	1 642 397	22.1	7 747 938	1 769 786	22.8
China - Chine[62]										
1 VII 2005[63]	ESDF	1 307 560 000	562 120 000[64]	43.0	673 750 000	...	...	633 810 000	...	...
1 VII 2006[63]	ESDF	1 314 480 000	577 060 000[64]	43.9	677 280 000	...	...	637 200 000	...	...
1 VII 2007[63]	ESDF	1 317 900 000	606 330 000[65]	46.0	680 480 000[28]	...	...	640 810 000[28]	...	...
1 VII 2008[63]	ESDF	1 324 700 000	624 030 000[65]	47.1	683 570 000[28]	...	...	644 450 000[28]	...	...
1 VII 2009[63]	ESDF	1 331 300 000	645 120 000[65]	48.5	686 470 000[28]	...	...	648 030 000[28]	...	...
1 VII 2010[63]	ESDF	1 337 700 000	669 780 000[65]	50.1	687 480 000[28]	...	...	653 430 000[28]	...	...
1 XI 2010[66]	CDJC	1 339 724 852	665 575 306	49.7	686 852 572	...	...	652 872 280	...	...
1 VII 2011[67]	ESDF	1 344 100 000	691 000 000[65]	51.4	691 000 000[28]	...	...	657 000 000[28]	...	...
1 VII 2012[67]	ESDF	1 350 695 000	701 305 000[64]	51.9	692 315 000	...	...	658 380 000	...	...
1 VII 2013[63]	ESDF	1 357 380 000	721 465 000[64]	53.2	695 615 000	...	...	661 765 000	...	...
1 VII 2014[63]	ESDF	1 364 270 000	740 135 000[64]	54.3	699 035 000	...	...	665 235 000	...	...
China, Hong Kong SAR - Chine, Hong Kong RAS										
1 VII 2005	ESDJ	6 813 200	...	...	3 264 000	...	...	3 549 200	...	...
1 VII 2006	ESDJ	6 857 100	...	...	3 270 100	...	...	3 587 000	...	...

Continent, country or area, and date / Continent, pays ou zone et date	Code[a]	Both sexes - Les deux sexes			Male - Masculin			Female - Féminin		
		Total	Urban - Urbaine		Total	Urban - Urbaine		Total	Urban - Urbaine	
			Number Nombre	Percent P.100		Number Nombre	Percent P.100		Number Nombre	Percent P.100
ASIA - ASIE										
China, Hong Kong SAR - Chine, Hong Kong RAS										
14 VII 2006[68]	CDJC	6 864 346	...	...	3 272 956	...	...	3 591 390	...	...
1 VII 2007	ESDJ	6 916 300	...	...	3 283 900	...	...	3 632 400	...	...
1 VII 2008	ESDJ	6 957 800	...	...	3 290 200	...	...	3 667 600	...	...
1 VII 2009	ESDJ	6 972 800	...	...	3 284 800	...	...	3 688 000	...	...
1 VII 2010	ESDJ	7 024 200	...	...	3 294 300	...	...	3 729 900	...	...
30 VI 2011[69]	CDJC	7 071 576	...	...	3 303 015	...	...	3 768 561	...	...
1 VII 2011	ESDJ	7 071 600	...	...	3 303 000	...	...	3 768 600	...	...
1 VII 2012	ESDJ	7 154 600	...	...	3 327 300	...	...	3 827 300	...	...
1 VII 2013	ESDJ	7 187 500	...	...	3 330 700	...	...	3 856 800	...	...
1 VII 2014	ESDJ	7 241 700	...	...	3 345 100	...	...	3 896 600	...	...
China, Macao SAR - Chine, Macao RAS										
1 VII 2005	ESDJ	473 457	...	...	227 600	...	...	245 857	...	...
1 VII 2006	ESDJ	498 852	...	...	243 009	...	...	255 843	...	...
19 VIII 2006	CDJC	502 113	...	...	245 167	...	...	256 946	...	...
1 VII 2007	ESDJ	520 900	...	...	256 500	...	...	264 400	...	...
1 VII 2008	ESDJ	540 700	...	...	264 900	...	...	275 800	...	...
1 VII 2009	ESDJ	535 000	...	...	257 900[28]	...	...	277 200[28]	...	...
1 VII 2010	ESDJ	537 000	...	...	257 200[28]	...	...	279 700[28]	...	...
1 VII 2011	ESDJ	549 600	...	...	263 500	...	...	286 100	...	...
12 VIII 2011	CDFC	625 674	...	...	305 398	...	...	320 276	...	...
1 VII 2012	ESDJ	567 900	...	...	274 300	...	...	293 600	...	...
1 VII 2013	ESDJ	591 900	...	...	285 700	...	...	306 200	...	...
1 VII 2014	ESDJ	621 700	...	...	305 500	...	...	316 200	...	...
Cyprus - Chypre[70]										
1 VII 2005[71]	ESDJ	738 540	...	...	361 952	...	...	376 589	...	...
1 VII 2006[71]	ESDJ	750 965	...	...	368 048	...	...	382 917	...	...
1 VII 2007[71]	ESDJ	767 125	...	...	375 986	...	...	391 139	...	...
1 VII 2008[71]	ESDJ	786 632	...	...	385 192	...	...	401 440	...	...
1 VII 2009[71]	ESDJ	808 035	...	...	394 766	...	...	413 270	...	...
1 VII 2010[71]	ESDJ	829 446	...	...	404 182	...	...	425 264	...	...
1 VII 2011[71]	ESDJ	850 881	...	...	413 876	...	...	437 006	...	...
1 X 2011	CDJC	840 407	566 191	67.4	408 780	273 065	66.8	431 627	293 126	67.9
1 VII 2012[71]	ESDJ	863 945	...	...	420 015	...	...	443 930	...	...
1 VII 2013[71]	ESDJ	861 930	...	...	419 183	...	...	442 747	...	...
Democratic People's Republic of Korea - République populaire démocratique de Corée										
1 X 2008	CDJC	24 052 231	...	...	11 721 838	...	...	12 330 393	...	...
Georgia - Géorgie										
1 VII 2005	ESDF	4 361 400	2 284 000	52.4	2 060 300	...	...	2 301 100	...	...
1 VII 2006	ESDF	4 398 000	2 309 700	52.5	2 081 700	...	...	2 316 300	...	...
1 VII 2007	ESDF	4 388 400	2 306 400	52.6	2 079 000	...	...	2 309 400	...	...
1 VII 2008	ESDF	4 383 800	2 306 500	52.6	2 079 600	...	...	2 304 200	...	...
1 VII 2009	ESDF	4 410 900	2 332 700	52.9	2 094 800	...	...	2 316 100	...	...
1 VII 2010	ESDF	4 452 800	2 360 900	53.0	2 118 100	...	...	2 334 700	...	...
1 VII 2011	ESDF	4 483 400	2 381 500	53.1	2 135 600	...	...	2 347 800	...	...
1 VII 2012	ESDF	4 490 700	...	...	2 141 300	...	...	2 349 400	...	...
1 I 2014	ESDF	4 490 498	...	...	2 141 372	...	...	2 349 126	...	...
India - Inde[72]										
1 VII 2005[73]	ESDF	1 101 317 709	316 648 000	28.8	569 882 367	166 604 533	29.2	531 435 342	150 043 467	28.2
1 VII 2006[73]	ESDF	1 117 733 826	323 827 490	29.0	578 411 677	170 384 885	29.5	539 322 149	153 442 605	28.5
1 VII 2007[73]	ESDF	1 134 023 232	331 060 644	29.2	586 879 523	174 195 527	29.7	547 143 709	156 865 117	28.7
1 VII 2008[73]	ESDF	1 150 196 000	338 356 000	29.4	595 291 000	178 041 000	29.9	554 905 000	160 315 000	28.9
9 II 2011	CDFC	1 210 854 977	377 106 125	31.1	623 270 258	195 489 200	31.4	587 584 719	181 616 925	30.9
1 VII 2011*[73]	ESDF	1 192 503 000	...	...	617 315 000	...	...	575 188 000	...	...
Indonesia - Indonésie										
1 VII 2005[74]	ESDJ	219 852 000	...	...	110 092 400	...	...	109 759 600	...	...
31 X 2005[75]	SSDF	213 375 287	92 005 069	43.1	107 274 528	46 055 993	42.9	106 100 759	45 949 076	43.3
1 VII 2006[74]	ESDJ	222 746 900	...	...	111 528 600	...	...	111 218 300	...	...
1 VII 2007[74]	ESDJ	225 642 000	...	...	112 966 900	...	...	112 675 100	...	...
1 VII 2008[74]	ESDJ	228 523 300	...	...	114 399 200	...	...	114 124 100	...	...

Continent, country or area, and date / Continent, pays ou zone et date	Code[a]	Both sexes - Les deux sexes Total	Urban - Urbaine Number Nombre	Urban - Urbaine Percent P.100	Male - Masculin Total	Urban - Urbaine Number Nombre	Urban - Urbaine Percent P.100	Female - Féminin Total	Urban - Urbaine Number Nombre	Urban - Urbaine Percent P.100
ASIA - ASIE										
Indonesia - Indonésie										
1 VII 2009[74]	ESDJ	231 369 500	...	...	115 817 900	...	...	115 551 600	...	...
1 V 2010	CDJC	237 641 326	118 320 256	49.8	119 630 913	59 559 622	49.8	118 010 413	58 760 634	49.8
1 VII 2010[76]	ESDJ	238 518 800	...	...	119 852 700	...	...	118 666 100	...	...
1 VII 2011[76]	ESDJ	241 990 700	...	...	121 602 400	...	...	120 388 300	...	...
1 VII 2012[76]	ESDJ	245 425 200	...	...	123 331 000	...	...	122 094 200	...	...
1 VII 2013[76]	ESDJ	248 818 100	...	...	125 036 000	...	...	123 782 100	...	...
1 VII 2014[76]	ESDJ	252 164 800	...	...	126 715 200	...	...	125 449 600	...	...
Iran (Islamic Republic of) - Iran (République islamique d')										
1 VII 2005[77]	ESDJ	69 390 405	47 095 882	67.9	35 298 812	23 989 204	68.0	34 091 593	23 106 678	67.8
28 X 2006	CDJC	70 495 782	48 259 964[78]	68.5	35 866 362	24 576 442[78]	68.5	34 629 420	23 683 522[78]	68.4
1 VII 2007[77]	ESDJ	71 278 952	48 874 656	68.6	36 247 296	24 891 876	68.7	35 031 392	23 982 780	68.5
1 VII 2008[77]	ESDJ	72 181 632	49 576 146	68.7	36 691 780	25 253 132	68.8	35 489 488	24 323 014	68.5
1 VII 2009[77]	ESDJ	73 202 096	50 365 184	68.8	37 198 776	25 660 500	69.0	36 003 320	24 704 684	68.6
1 VII 2010[77]	ESDJ	74 339 576	51 242 546	68.9	37 767 220	26 114 342	69.1	36 572 356	25 128 204	68.7
24 X 2011	CDJC	75 149 669	53 646 661	71.4	37 905 669	27 023 638	71.3	37 244 000	26 623 023	71.5
1 VII 2012[77]	ESDJ	76 037 535	54 611 776[79]	71.8	38 336 983	27 547 622[79]	71.9	37 700 552	27 064 154[79]	71.8
1 VII 2013[77]	ESDJ	76 942 276	55 506 192[79]	72.1	38 777 566	27 988 342[79]	72.2	38 164 710	27 517 850[79]	72.1
1 VII 2014[77]	ESDJ	77 856 411	56 412 837	72.5	39 224 036	28 435 933	72.5	38 632 375	27 976 904	72.4
Iraq										
1 VII 2005	ESDF	27 722 714	...	...	13 934 225	...	...	13 788 488	...	...
1 VII 2006	ESDF	28 562 436	...	...	14 368 462	...	...	14 193 974	...	...
1 VII 2007	ESDF	29 426 942	...	...	14 814 595	...	...	14 612 348	...	...
1 VII 2008	ESDF	30 315 243	...	...	15 261 719	...	...	15 053 524	...	...
1 VII 2009	ESDF	31 392 903	...	...	16 010 232	...	...	15 382 671	...	...
1 VII 2010	ESDF	32 210 813	...	...	16 418 691	...	...	15 792 122	...	...
1 VII 2011	ESDF	33 051 526	...	...	16 839 048	...	...	16 212 479	...	...
1 VII 2012	ESDF	33 913 305	23 475 543	69.2	17 270 036	11 954 703	69.2	16 643 269	11 520 840	69.2
1 VII 2013	ESDF	34 794 194	24 162 634	69.4	17 710 750	12 299 131	69.4	17 083 444	11 863 502	69.4
Israel - Israël[80]										
1 VII 2005	ESDJ	6 930 128	6 359 940[28]	91.8	3 423 132	3 131 229[28]	91.5	3 506 996	3 228 711[28]	92.1
1 VII 2006	ESDJ	7 053 707	6 475 600[81]	91.8	3 485 501	3 189 511[81]	91.5	3 568 206	3 286 089[81]	92.1
1 VII 2007	ESDJ	7 180 115	6 589 632[81]	91.8	3 549 216	3 247 280[81]	91.5	3 630 899	3 342 352[81]	92.1
1 VII 2008	ESDJ	7 308 795	6 701 217[82]	91.7	3 614 125	3 303 732[82]	91.4	3 694 671	3 397 485[82]	92.0
27 XII 2008[83]	CDFC	7 412 180	6 799 340[28]	91.7	3 663 910	3 350 610[28]	91.4	3 748 270	3 448 730[28]	92.0
1 VII 2009	ESDJ	7 485 565	6 864 957[28]	91.7	3 701 159	3 384 295[28]	91.4	3 784 406	3 480 662[28]	92.0
1 VII 2010	ESDJ	7 623 561	6 987 615[28]	91.7	3 771 020	3 446 730[28]	91.4	3 852 541	3 540 885[28]	91.9
1 VII 2011	ESDJ	7 765 832	7 111 015[28]	91.6	3 843 068	3 509 308[28]	91.3	3 922 764	3 601 706[28]	91.8
1 VII 2012	ESDJ	7 910 525	7 235 231[28]	91.5	3 916 125	3 572 531[28]	91.2	3 994 400	3 662 700[28]	91.7
1 VII 2013	ESDJ	8 059 456	7 369 053[28]	91.4	3 991 347	3 640 471[28]	91.2	4 068 109	3 728 581[28]	91.7
Japan - Japon[84]										
1 VII 2005	ESDJ	127 773 000	...	...	62 332 000	...	...	65 441 000	...	...
1 X 2005	CDJC	127 767 994	110 264 324	86.3	62 348 977	53 886 000	86.4	65 419 017	56 378 324	86.2
1 VII 2006[85]	ESDJ	127 854 000	...	...	62 357 000	...	...	65 497 000	...	...
1 VII 2007[85]	ESDJ	128 001 000	...	...	62 401 000[28]	...	...	65 599 000[28]	...	...
1 VII 2008[85]	ESDJ	128 063 000	...	...	62 409 000	...	...	65 654 000	...	...
1 VII 2009[85]	ESDJ	128 047 000	...	...	62 354 000	...	...	65 693 000	...	...
1 VII 2010[85]	ESDJ	128 070 000	...	...	62 330 000	...	...	65 740 000	...	...
1 X 2010	CDJC	128 057 352	116 156 631	90.7	62 327 737	56 569 051	90.8	65 729 615	59 587 580	90.7
1 VII 2011[85]	ESDJ	127 817 000	...	...	62 189 000	...	...	65 628 000	...	...
1 VII 2012[85]	ESDJ	127 561 000	...	...	62 041 000	...	...	65 520 000	...	...
1 VII 2013[85]	ESDJ	127 339 000	...	...	61 918 000[28]	...	...	65 420 000[28]	...	...
1 VII 2014[85]	ESDJ	127 132 000	...	...	61 812 000	...	...	65 320 000	...	...
Jordan - Jordanie[86]										
31 XII 2005	ESDF	5 473 000	4 520 600	82.6	2 821 100	...	...	2 651 900	...	...
31 XII 2006	ESDF	5 600 000	4 625 600	82.6	2 886 600	...	...	2 713 400	...	...
31 XII 2007	ESDF	5 723 000	4 727 100	82.6	2 950 000	...	...	2 773 000	...	...
31 XII 2008	ESDF	5 850 000	4 832 100	82.6	3 015 000	...	...	2 835 000	...	...
31 XII 2009	ESDF	5 980 000	4 939 400	82.6	3 082 000	...	...	2 898 000	...	...
31 XII 2010	ESDF	6 113 000	5 049 300	82.6	3 151 000	...	...	2 962 000	...	...
31 XII 2011	ESDF	6 249 000	5 161 600	82.6	3 221 100	...	...	3 027 900	...	...
31 XII 2012	ESDF	6 388 000	5 276 400	82.6	3 293 000	...	...	3 095 000	...	...

Continent, country or area, and date / Continent, pays ou zone et date	Code[a]	Both sexes - Les deux sexes			Male - Masculin			Female - Féminin		
			Urban - Urbaine			Urban - Urbaine			Urban - Urbaine	
		Total	Number Nombre	Percent P.100	Total	Number Nombre	Percent P.100	Total	Number Nombre	Percent P.100
ASIA - ASIE										
Jordan - Jordanie[86]										
31 XII 2013 ....ESDF		6 530 000	5 393 700	82.6	3 366 000	...	...	3 164 000	...	...
31 XII 2014 ....ESDF		6 675 000	5 513 400	82.6	3 441 000	...	...	3 234 000	...	...
Kazakhstan										
1 VII 2005 ....ESDF		15 147 029	8 655 586	57.1	7 290 852	4 044 092	55.5	7 856 177	4 611 494	58.7
1 VII 2006 ....ESDF		15 308 084	8 764 884	57.3	7 367 032	4 094 572	55.6	7 941 052	4 670 312	58.8
1 VII 2007 ....ESDF		15 484 192	8 195 389	52.9	7 450 418	3 815 422	51.2	8 033 774	4 379 967	54.5
1 VII 2008 ....ESDF		15 674 000	8 331 030	53.2	7 541 053	3 877 559	51.4	8 132 947	4 453 471	54.8
25 II 2009 ....CDFC		16 009 597	8 662 432	54.1	7 712 224	4 055 341	52.6	8 297 373	4 607 091	55.5
1 VII 2009 ....ESDF		16 092 701	8 741 149	54.3	7 753 360	4 092 724	52.8	8 339 341	4 648 425	55.7
1 VII 2010 ....ESDF		16 321 581	8 896 402	54.5	7 866 332	4 165 526	53.0	8 455 249	4 730 876	56.0
1 VII 2011 ....ESDF		16 556 601	9 050 267	54.7	7 983 081	4 237 719	53.1	8 573 520	4 812 548	56.1
1 VII 2012 ....ESDF		16 791 427	9 202 381	54.8	8 100 113	4 309 859	53.2	8 691 314	4 892 522	56.3
1 VII 2013 ....ESDF		17 035 275	9 348 738	54.9	8 221 848	4 380 550	53.3	8 813 427	4 968 188	56.4
1 I 2014 ....ESDF		17 160 774	9 433 482	55.0	8 284 815	4 421 972	53.4	8 875 959	5 011 510	56.5
Kuwait - Koweït										
20 IV 2005 ....CDFC		2 193 651	2 193 651	100.0	1 300 347	1 300 347	100.0	893 304	893 304	100.0
1 VII 2005 ....ESDF		2 244 995	...	...	1 326 871	...	...	918 124	...	...
1 VII 2006 ....ESDF		2 328 116	...	...	1 378 341	...	...	949 775	...	...
1 VII 2007 ....ESDF		2 410 829	...	...	1 430 584	...	...	980 245	...	...
1 VII 2008 ....ESDF		2 495 851	...	...	1 484 422	...	...	1 011 429	...	...
1 VII 2009 ....ESDF		2 777 861	...	...	1 597 843	...	...	1 180 018	...	...
1 VII 2010* ....ESDF		2 933 268	...	...	1 674 156	...	...	1 259 112	...	...
20 IV 2011* ....CDFC		3 065 850	3 065 850	100.0	1 738 372	1 738 372	100.0	1 327 478	1 327 478	100.0
1 VII 2011[87] ....ESDF		3 098 892	...	...	1 754 248	...	...	1 344 644	...	...
1 VII 2012 ....ESDF		3 268 431	...	...	1 834 776	...	...	1 433 655	...	...
1 VII 2013 ....ESDF		3 448 139	...	...	1 918 959	...	...	1 529 180	...	...
Kyrgyzstan - Kirghizstan										
1 VII 2005[88] ....ESDF		5 006 514	1 788 181	35.7	2 450 975	841 960	34.4	2 555 539	946 221	37.0
1 VII 2006[88] ....ESDF		5 033 953	1 790 295	35.6	2 460 578	841 414	34.2	2 573 375	948 881	36.9
1 VII 2007[88] ....ESDF		5 055 671	1 791 267	35.4	2 467 458	839 913	34.0	2 588 213	951 354	36.8
1 VII 2008[88] ....ESDF		5 077 722	1 794 620	35.3	2 475 331	839 873	33.9	2 602 391	954 747	36.7
24 III 2009 ....CDJC		5 362 793	1 827 136	34.1	2 645 921	863 002	32.6	2 716 872	964 134	35.5
1 VII 2009[88] ....ESDF		5 128 124	1 809 738	35.3	2 499 977	846 861	33.9	2 628 147	962 877	36.6
1 VII 2010[88] ....ESDF		5 192 806	1 828 955	35.2	2 532 547	856 262	33.8	2 660 259	972 693	36.6
1 VII 2011[88] ....ESDF		5 259 601	1 847 757	35.1	2 566 031	865 260	33.7	2 693 570	982 497	36.5
1 VII 2012[88] ....ESDF		5 352 358	1 856 305	34.7	2 613 586	869 564	33.3	2 738 772	986 741	36.0
1 VII 2013 ....ESDJ		5 719 852	1 921 936	33.6	2 827 672	909 216	32.2	2 892 180	1 012 720	35.0
1 VII 2014 ....ESDJ		5 835 816	1 965 159	33.7	2 886 758	930 751	32.2	2 949 058	1 034 408	35.1
Lao People's Democratic Republic - République démocratique populaire lao										
1 III 2005 ....CDJC		5 621 982	1 522 137[89]	27.1	2 800 551	763 043[89]	27.2	2 821 431	759 094[89]	26.9
1 VII 2005[90] ....ESDF		5 651 497	...	...	2 815 254	...	...	2 836 244	...	...
1 VII 2006[90] ....ESDF		5 777 797	...	...	2 879 511	...	...	2 898 285	...	...
1 VII 2007[90] ....ESDF		5 904 453	...	...	2 943 941	...	...	2 960 512	...	...
1 VII 2008[90] ....ESDF		6 031 881	...	...	3 008 754	...	...	3 023 128	...	...
1 VII 2009[90] ....ESDF		6 160 083	...	...	3 073 951	...	...	3 086 131	...	...
1 VII 2010[90] ....ESDF		6 289 042	...	...	3 139 533	...	...	3 149 508	...	...
1 VII 2011[90] ....ESDF		6 418 577	...	...	3 205 405	...	...	3 213 173	...	...
1 VII 2012[90] ....ESDF		6 548 633	...	...	3 271 538	...	...	3 277 095	...	...
1 VII 2013[90] ....ESDF		6 678 899	...	...	3 337 780	...	...	3 341 118	...	...
1 VII 2014[90] ....ESDF		6 809 054	...	...	3 403 964	...	...	3 405 090	...	...
Lebanon - Liban										
3 III 2007[91] ....SSDF		3 759 134	...	...	1 857 659	...	...	1 901 475	...	...
1 X 2011[92] ....SSDF		3 779 859	...	...	1 840 940	...	...	1 938 919	...	...
Malaysia - Malaisie										
1 VII 2005[93] ....ESDJ		26 045 529	17 321 266	66.5	13 353 253	8 847 217	66.3	12 692 276	8 474 049	66.8
1 VII 2006[93] ....ESDJ		26 549 855	17 892 686	67.4	13 627 408	9 148 357	67.1	12 922 447	8 744 329	67.7
1 VII 2007[93] ....ESDJ		27 058 428	18 475 499	68.3	13 903 701	9 455 573	68.0	13 154 727	9 019 926	68.6
1 VII 2008[93] ....ESDJ		27 567 636	19 068 738	69.2	14 179 117	9 767 066	68.9	13 388 519	9 301 672	69.5
1 VII 2009[93] ....ESDJ		28 081 497	19 675 873	70.1	14 456 940	10 085 460	69.8	13 624 557	9 590 413	70.4
1 VII 2010[94] ....ESDJ		28 588 637	20 290 864	71.0	14 730 542	10 404 757	70.6	13 858 095	9 886 107	71.3
6 VII 2010[56] ....CDJC		28 334 135	20 124 970	71.0	14 562 638	10 298 698	70.7	13 771 497	9 826 272	71.4

Continent, country or area, and date / Continent, pays ou zone et date	Code[a]	Both sexes - Les deux sexes Total	Urban - Urbaine Number Nombre	Urban - Urbaine Percent P.100	Male - Masculin Total	Urban - Urbaine Number Nombre	Urban - Urbaine Percent P.100	Female - Féminin Total	Urban - Urbaine Number Nombre	Urban - Urbaine Percent P.100
ASIA - ASIE										
Malaysia - Malaisie										
1 VII 2011[94]	ESDJ	29 062 036	20 606 546	70.9	14 980 010	10 568 602	70.6	14 082 026	10 037 944	71.3
1 VII 2012[94]	ESDJ	29 510 022	21 355 255	72.4	15 215 309	10 965 006	72.1	14 294 713	10 390 249	72.7
1 VII 2013[94]	ESDJ	29 915 286	21 833 403	73.0	15 427 305	11 210 108	72.7	14 487 981	10 623 295	73.3
1 VII 2014[94]	ESDJ	30 261 700	22 275 575	73.6	15 594 295	11 430 681	73.3	14 667 405	10 844 894	73.9
Maldives										
1 VII 2005	ESDF	293 746	...	...	148 929	...	...	144 817	...	...
21 III 2006[95]	CDFC	298 968	103 693	34.7	151 459	51 992	34.3	147 509	51 701	35.0
1 VII 2007	ESDF	304 869	...	...	154 391	...	...	150 478	...	...
1 VII 2008	ESDF	309 575	...	...	156 714	...	...	152 861	...	...
1 VII 2009	ESDF	314 542	...	...	159 159	...	...	155 383	...	...
1 VII 2010	ESDF	319 738	...	...	161 708	...	...	158 030	...	...
1 VII 2011	ESDF	325 135	...	...	164 349	...	...	160 786	...	...
1 VII 2012	ESDF	330 655	...	...	167 058	...	...	163 597	...	...
1 VII 2013	ESDF	336 224	...	...	169 800	...	...	166 424	...	...
20 IX 2014*	CDFC	341 256	133 019	39.0	173 172	66 155	38.2	168 084	66 864	39.8
Mongolia - Mongolie										
1 VII 2005	ESDF	2 551 081	1 579 385	61.9	1 265 614	...	...	1 285 467	...	...
1 VII 2006	ESDF	2 583 254	1 621 686	62.8	1 259 653	780 791	62.0	1 323 601	840 895	63.5
1 VII 2007	ESDF	2 601 850	1 638 567	63.0	1 268 447	788 695	62.2	1 333 403	849 872	63.7
1 VII 2008	ESDF	2 643 201	1 684 282	63.7	1 289 282	811 224	62.9	1 353 919	873 058	64.5
1 VII 2009	ESDF	2 691 115	1 743 008	64.8	1 314 729	840 520	63.9	1 376 386	902 488	65.6
1 VII 2010	ESDF	2 738 622	1 799 648	65.7	1 335 111	863 536	64.7	1 403 511	936 112	66.7
11 XI 2010	CDFC	2 647 199	1 797 338	67.9	1 314 246	869 827	66.2	1 332 953	927 511	69.6
1 VII 2011	ESDF	2 786 322	1 856 224	66.6	1 354 472	886 139	65.4	1 431 850	970 085	67.8
1 VII 2012	ESDF	2 839 711	1 911 462	67.3	1 379 091	910 746	66.0	1 460 620	1 000 716	68.5
1 VII 2013	ESDF	2 899 011	1 961 169	67.6	1 409 648	936 682	66.4	1 489 363	1 024 487	68.8
1 VII 2014	ESDF	2 963 113	1 993 017	67.3	1 446 149	955 833	66.1	1 516 964	1 037 184	68.4
Myanmar										
1 X 2005	ESDF	55 396 343	16 828 570	30.4	27 539 748	8 195 258	29.8	27 856 595	8 633 312	31.0
1 X 2006	ESDF	56 515 349	17 239 318	30.5	28 096 895	8 425 026	30.0	28 418 454	8 814 292	31.0
1 X 2007	ESDF	57 504 368	17 567 506	30.5	28 585 910	8 582 809	30.0	28 918 458	8 984 697	31.1
1 X 2008	ESDF	58 376 839	17 894 194	30.7	29 025 480	8 798 657	30.3	29 351 359	9 095 537	31.0
1 X 2009	ESDF	59 129 900	18 133 654	30.7	29 399 744	8 888 838	30.2	29 730 156	9 244 816	31.1
1 X 2010	ESDF	59 780 329	18 342 824	30.7	29 723 184	8 992 226	30.3	30 057 145	9 350 598	31.1
1 X 2011[96]	ESDF	50 149 496	14 650 579	29.2	24 185 705	7 009 280	29.0	25 963 791	7 641 299	29.4
1 X 2012[96]	ESDF	50 666 887	14 824 883	29.3	24 435 871	7 092 798	29.0	26 231 016	7 732 085	29.5
1 X 2013[96]	ESDF	51 184 273	14 999 184	29.3	24 686 034	7 176 313	29.1	26 498 239	7 822 871	29.5
29 III 2014[97]	CDFC	50 279 900	14 877 943	29.6	24 228 714	7 114 224	29.4	26 051 186	7 763 719	29.8
1 X 2014[96]	ESDF	51 486 253	...	...	24 824 586	...	...	26 661 667	...	...
Nepal - Népal										
1 VII 2005	ESDJ	25 342 638		...	12 685 375		...	12 657 263		...
1 VII 2006	ESDJ	25 886 736		...	12 963 722		...	12 923 014		...
1 VII 2007	ESDJ	26 427 399		...	13 240 233		...	13 187 166		...
1 VII 2008	ESDJ	26 966 581		...	13 515 938		...	13 450 643		...
1 VII 2009	ESDJ	27 504 280		...	13 790 836		...	13 713 444		...
1 VII 2010	ESDJ	28 043 744		...	14 066 638		...	13 977 106		...
22 VI 2011	CDJC	26 494 504	4 523 820	17.1	12 849 041	2 306 049	17.9	13 645 463	2 217 771	16.3
1 VII 2011	ESDJ	28 584 975	...	...	14 343 343	...	...	14 241 632	...	...
1 VII 2012[17]	ESDJ	26 873 066	...	...	13 030 795	...	...	13 842 271	...	...
1 VII 2013[17]	ESDJ	27 257 347	...	...	13 215 791	...	...	14 041 556	...	...
1 VII 2014[17]	ESDJ	27 646 053	...	...	13 403 432	...	...	14 242 621	...	...
Oman										
1 VII 2005	ESDF	2 508 837	1 804 995	71.9	1 458 845	1 063 202	72.9	1 049 992	741 793	70.6
1 VII 2006	ESDF	2 577 062	1 857 263	72.1	1 498 143	1 093 546	73.0	1 078 919	763 717	70.8
1 VII 2007	ESDF	2 743 499	1 984 158	72.3	1 622 119	1 188 537	73.3	1 121 380	795 621	71.0
1 VII 2008	ESDF	2 867 428	2 077 862	72.5	1 687 414	1 238 527	73.4	1 180 014	839 335	71.1
1 VII 2009	ESDF	3 173 917	2 314 865	72.9	1 971 115	1 457 197	73.9	1 202 802	857 668	71.3
12 XII 2010	CDFC	2 773 479	2 079 831	75.0	1 612 408	1 220 557	75.7	1 161 071	859 274	74.0
1 VII 2011[98]	ESDF	3 295 298	...	...	2 090 883	...	...	1 204 415	...	...
1 VII 2012[98]	ESDF	3 623 001	...	...	2 332 687	...	...	1 290 314	...	...
1 VII 2013[98]	ESDF	3 855 206	...	...	2 502 235	...	...	1 352 971	...	...
1 VII 2014[98]	ESDF	3 992 893	...	...	2 579 811	...	...	1 413 082	...	...

6. Total and urban population by sex: 2005 - 2014
Population totale et population urbaine selon le sexe : 2005 - 2014 (continued - suite)

Continent, country or area, and date / Continent, pays ou zone et date	Code[a]	Both sexes - Les deux sexes			Male - Masculin			Female - Féminin		
		Total	Urban - Urbaine		Total	Urban - Urbaine		Total	Urban - Urbaine	
			Number Nombre	Percent P.100		Number Nombre	Percent P.100		Number Nombre	Percent P.100

ASIA - ASIE

Pakistan[99]										
1 VII 2005[100] .... ESDJ		144 367 293	51 408 193	35.6	74 247 400	26 556 848	35.8	70 119 893	24 851 345	35.4
1 VII 2006 .... ESDJ		147 099 534	...	...	75 582 494	...	...	71 517 040	...	...
1 VII 2007[101] .... ESDJ		149 860 388	52 807 585	35.2	76 857 737	27 178 203	35.4	73 002 651	25 629 382	35.1
1 VII 2008 .... ESDF		166 410 000	...	...	86 130 000	...	...	80 280 000	...	...
1 VII 2009 .... ESDF		169 940 000	...	...	87 940 000	...	...	82 010 000	...	...
1 VII 2010 .... ESDF		173 510 000	...	...	89 760 000	...	...	83 750 000	...	...
1 VII 2011 .... ESDF		177 100 000	...	...	91 590 000	...	...	85 510 000	...	...
Philippines										
1 VII 2005[24] .... ESDJ		85 261 000	...	...	42 887 300	...	...	42 373 700	...	...
1 VII 2006[24] .... ESDJ		86 972 500	...	...	43 742 100	...	...	43 230 400	...	...
1 VII 2007[24] .... ESDJ		88 706 300	...	...	44 608 300	...	...	44 098 000	...	...
1 VII 2008[24] .... ESDJ		90 457 200	...	...	45 483 100	...	...	44 974 100	...	...
1 VII 2009[24] .... ESDJ		92 226 600	...	...	46 368 900	...	...	45 857 700	...	...
1 V 2010[102] .... CDJC		92 335 113	41 855 571	45.3	46 634 257	20 840 798	44.7	45 700 856	21 014 773	46.0
1 VII 2010[26] .... ESDJ		93 135 100	...	...	46 980 200	...	...	46 154 900	...	...
1 VII 2011[26] .... ESDJ		94 823 800	...	...	47 832 400	...	...	46 991 400	...	...
1 VII 2012[26] .... ESDJ		96 510 900	...	...	48 684 200	...	...	47 826 700	...	...
1 VII 2013[26] .... ESDJ		98 196 500	...	...	49 535 100	...	...	48 661 400	...	...
1 VII 2014[26] .... ESDJ		99 880 300	...	...	50 385 100	...	...	49 495 200	...	...
Qatar										
1 VII 2005 .... ESDF		906 123	...	...	637 070	...	...	269 053	...	...
1 VII 2006 .... ESDF		1 042 947	...	...	754 298	...	...	288 649	...	...
1 VII 2007 .... ESDF		1 218 250	...	...	905 747	...	...	312 503	...	...
1 VII 2008 .... ESDF		1 448 479	...	...	1 111 176	...	...	337 303	...	...
1 VII 2009 .... ESDF		1 638 626	...	...	1 265 146	...	...	373 480	...	...
21 IV 2010 .... CDFC		1 699 435	...	...	1 284 739	...	...	414 696	...	...
1 VII 2010 .... ESDF		1 715 010	...	...	1 296 107	...	...	418 903	...	...
1 VII 2011 .... ESDF		1 732 717	...	...	1 288 590	...	...	444 127	...	...
1 VII 2012 .... ESDF		1 832 903	...	...	1 355 199	...	...	477 704	...	...
1 VII 2013 .... ESDF		2 003 700	...	...	1 477 632	...	...	526 068	...	...
Republic of Korea - République de Corée										
1 VII 2005 .... ESDJ		48 138 077	...	...	24 190 906	...	...	23 947 171	...	...
1 XI 2005[89] .... CDJC		47 278 951	38 514 753	81.5	23 623 954	19 258 840	81.5	23 654 997	19 255 913	81.4
1 VII 2006 .... ESDJ		48 371 946	...	...	24 302 796	...	...	24 069 150	...	...
1 VII 2007 .... ESDJ		48 597 652	...	...	24 410 110	...	...	24 187 542	...	...
1 VII 2008 .... ESDJ		48 948 698	...	...	24 576 155	...	...	24 372 543	...	...
1 VII 2009 .... ESDJ		49 182 038	...	...	24 664 502	...	...	24 517 536	...	...
1 VII 2010 .... ESDJ		49 410 366	...	...	24 757 776	...	...	24 652 590	...	...
1 XI 2010[89] .... CDJC		48 580 293	39 822 647	82.0	24 167 098	19 798 739	81.9	24 413 195	20 023 908	82.0
1 VII 2011[2] .... ESDJ		49 779 440	...	...	24 942 339	...	...	24 837 101	...	...
1 VII 2012[2] .... ESDJ		50 004 441	...	...	25 039 557	...	...	24 964 884	...	...
1 VII 2013[2] .... ESDJ		50 219 669	...	...	25 132 612	...	...	25 087 057	...	...
1 VII 2014[2] .... ESDJ		50 423 955	...	...	25 219 810	...	...	25 204 145	...	...
Saudi Arabia - Arabie saoudite										
1 VII 2005*[103] .... ESDF		23 329 584	...	...	12 959 625	...	...	10 369 959	...	...
1 VII 2006*[103] .... ESDF		24 121 890	...	...	13 444 010	...	...	10 677 880	...	...
1 VII 2007*[103] .... ESDF		24 941 298	...	...	13 947 610	...	...	10 993 688	...	...
1 VII 2008*[103] .... ESDF		25 787 025	...	...	14 470 381	...	...	11 316 644	...	...
1 VII 2009*[103] .... ESDF		26 660 857	...	...	15 013 600	...	...	11 647 257	...	...
28 IV 2010* .... CDFC		27 136 977	...	...	15 306 793	...	...	11 830 184	...	...
1 VII 2010*[103] .... ESDF		27 563 432	...	...	15 578 015	...	...	11 985 417	...	...
1 VII 2011*[103] .... ESDF		28 376 355	...	...	16 041 361	...	...	12 334 994	...	...
1 VII 2012*[103] .... ESDF		29 195 895	...	...	16 543 836	...	...	12 652 059	...	...
Singapore - Singapour[104]										
30 VI 2005[105] .... ESDJ		3 467 814	...	...	1 721 139	...	...	1 746 675	...	...
30 VI 2006[105] .... ESDJ		3 525 894	...	...	1 748 242	...	...	1 777 652	...	...
30 VI 2007[105] .... ESDJ		3 583 082	...	...	1 775 477	...	...	1 807 605	...	...
30 VI 2008[105] .... ESDJ		3 642 659	...	...	1 802 992	...	...	1 839 667	...	...
30 VI 2009[105] .... ESDJ		3 733 876	...	...	1 844 732	...	...	1 889 144	...	...
30 VI 2010[106] .... CDJC		3 771 721	...	...	1 861 133	...	...	1 910 588	...	...
30 VI 2010[105] .... ESDJ		3 771 721	...	...	1 861 133	...	...	1 910 588	...	...
30 VI 2011[105] .... ESDJ		3 789 251	...	...	1 868 170	...	...	1 921 081	...	...

Continent, country or area, and date / Continent, pays ou zone et date	Code[a]	Both sexes - Les deux sexes			Male - Masculin			Female - Féminin		
		Total	Urban - Urbaine		Total	Urban - Urbaine		Total	Urban - Urbaine	
			Number Nombre	Percent P.100		Number Nombre	Percent P.100		Number Nombre	Percent P.100
ASIA - ASIE										
Singapore - Singapour[104]										
30 VI 2012[105]	ESDJ	3 818 205	...	...	1 880 046	...	...	1 938 159	...	...
30 VI 2013[105]	ESDJ	3 844 751	...	...	1 891 504	...	...	1 953 247	...	...
30 VI 2014[105]	ESDJ	3 870 739	...	...	1 902 410	...	...	1 968 329	...	...
Sri Lanka										
1 VII 2005	ESDF	19 644 000	...	...	9 782 000	...	...	9 862 000	...	...
1 VII 2006	ESDF	19 858 000	...	...	9 889 000	...	...	9 969 000	...	...
1 VII 2007	ESDF	20 039 000	...	...	9 956 000	...	...	10 083 000	...	...
1 VII 2008	ESDF	20 216 000	...	...	9 980 000	...	...	10 236 000	...	...
1 VII 2009	ESDF	20 450 000	...	...	10 148 000	...	...	10 302 000	...	...
1 VII 2010	ESDF	20 653 000	...	...	10 249 000	...	...	10 404 000	...	...
1 VII 2011	ESDF	20 869 000	...	...	10 357 000	...	...	10 512 000	...	...
27 II 2012	CDJC	20 263 723	...	...	9 832 401	...	...	10 431 322	...	...
1 VII 2012	ESDF	20 328 000	...	...	9 864 000	...	...	10 464 000	...	...
1 VII 2013	ESDF	20 483 000	...	...	9 940 000	...	...	10 544 000	...	...
1 VII 2014	ESDF	20 675 000	...	...	10 033 000	...	...	10 642 000	...	...
State of Palestine - État de Palestine										
1 VII 2005	ESDF	3 508 126	2 508 310[107]	71.5	1 780 506	...	...	1 727 620	...	...
1 VII 2006	ESDF	3 611 998	2 582 579[107]	71.5	1 833 225	...	...	1 778 773	...	...
1 VII 2007	ESDF	3 719 189	3 086 102[107]	83.0	1 887 628	...	...	1 831 561	...	...
1 XII 2007[108]	CDFC	3 669 244	3 040 039[107]	82.9	1 862 027	1 542 604[107]	82.8	1 807 217	1 497 435[107]	82.9
1 VII 2008	ESDF	3 825 512	3 175 546[107]	83.0	1 941 742	...	...	1 883 770	...	...
1 VII 2009	ESDF	3 935 249	3 267 977[107]	83.0	1 997 625	...	...	1 937 624	...	...
1 VII 2010	ESDF	4 048 403	3 363 385[107]	83.1	2 055 211	...	...	1 993 192	...	...
1 VII 2011	ESDF	4 168 860	3 465 483[107]	83.1	2 116 782	...	...	2 052 078	...	...
1 VII 2012	ESDF	4 293 313	3 571 037[107]	83.2	2 180 386	...	...	2 112 927	...	...
1 VII 2013	ESDF	4 420 549	3 679 034[107]	83.2	2 245 400	...	...	2 175 149	...	...
1 VII 2014	ESDF	4 550 368	3 789 308[107]	83.3	2 311 721	...	...	2 238 647	...	...
Syrian Arab Republic - République arabe syrienne[109]										
1 VII 2005	ESDF	18 138 000	9 705 000	53.5	9 268 000	4 977 000	53.7	8 870 000	4 728 000	53.3
1 VII 2006	ESDF	18 717 000	10 013 000	53.5	9 563 000	5 139 000	53.7	9 154 000	4 874 000	53.2
1 VII 2007	ESDF	19 172 000	10 257 000	53.5	9 798 000	5 265 000	53.7	9 374 000	4 992 000	53.3
1 VII 2008	ESDF	19 644 000	10 511 000	53.5	10 042 000	5 394 000	53.7	9 602 000	5 117 000	53.3
1 VII 2009	ESDF	20 125 000	10 769 000	53.5	10 287 000	5 526 000	53.7	9 838 000	5 243 000	53.3
1 VII 2010	ESDF	20 619 000	11 033 000	53.5	10 539 000	5 661 000	53.7	10 080 000	5 372 000	53.3
1 VII 2011	ESDF	21 124 000	11 297 000	53.5	10 794 000	5 795 000	53.7	10 330 000	5 502 000	53.3
Tajikistan - Tadjikistan										
1 VII 2005	ESDF	6 850 324	1 808 339	26.4	3 436 922	906 229	26.4	3 413 402	902 110	26.4
1 VII 2006	ESDF	6 992 066	1 841 258	26.3	3 508 345	923 963	26.3	3 483 721	917 295	26.3
1 VII 2007	ESDF	7 139 772	1 877 203	26.3	3 581 930	943 032	26.3	3 557 842	934 171	26.3
1 VII 2008	ESDF	7 294 747	1 918 996	26.3	3 659 238	965 220	26.4	3 635 510	953 776	26.2
1 VII 2009	ESDF	7 334 083	1 944 038	26.5	3 699 641	979 510	26.5	3 634 442	964 528	26.5
1 VII 2010	ESDF	7 519 280	1 996 961	26.6	3 794 467	1 007 796	26.6	3 724 813	989 165	26.6
21 IX 2010	CDFC	7 564 502	2 006 605	26.5	3 817 004	1 012 642	26.5	3 747 498	993 963	26.5
1 VII 2011	ESDF	7 714 198	2 042 660	26.5	3 893 798	1 032 106	26.5	3 820 401	1 010 554	26.5
1 VII 2012	ESDF	7 897 313	2 085 698	26.4	3 987 517	1 054 904	26.5	3 909 796	1 030 794	26.4
1 VII 2013	ESDF	8 074 266	2 138 737	26.5	4 078 857	1 083 119	26.6	3 995 409	1 055 618	26.4
Thailand - Thaïlande										
1 VII 2005[2]	ESDJ	64 838 628	19 538 420	30.1	31 848 905	9 360 642	29.4	32 989 723	10 177 778	30.9
1 VII 2006[2]	ESDJ	65 305 736	19 792 296	30.3	32 060 034	9 474 510	29.6	33 245 702	10 317 786	31.0
1 VII 2007[2]	ESDJ	66 041 512	20 117 497	30.5	32 467 223	9 733 251	30.0	33 574 289	10 384 246	30.9
1 VII 2008[2]	ESDJ	66 480 004	20 471 816	30.8	32 671 831	9 802 741	30.0	33 808 173	10 669 075	31.6
1 VII 2009[2]	ESDJ	66 903 277	21 133 663	31.6	32 872 931	10 112 852	30.8	34 030 346	11 020 811	32.4
1 VII 2010[2]	ESDJ	67 311 917	23 096 811	34.3	33 067 359	11 070 161	33.5	34 244 558	12 026 650	35.1
1 IX 2010	CDJC	65 981 659	29 133 829	44.2	32 355 032	14 120 842	43.6	33 626 627	15 012 987	44.6
1 VII 2011[2]	ESDJ	67 598 735	23 309 100	34.5	33 190 193	11 167 094	33.6	34 408 542	12 142 006	35.3
1 VII 2012[2]	ESDJ	67 911 720	23 430 180	34.5	33 328 645	11 219 175	33.7	34 583 075	12 211 005	35.3
Timor-Leste										
1 VII 2005[2]	ESDF	983 000	...	...	500 000[28]	...	...	484 000[28]	...	...
1 VII 2006[2]	ESDF	1 015 000	...	...	515 000	...	...	500 000	...	...
1 VII 2007[2]	ESDF	1 048 000	...	...	532 000	...	...	516 000	...	...

Continent, country or area, and date / Continent, pays ou zone et date	Code[a]	Both sexes - Les deux sexes			Male - Masculin			Female - Féminin		
		Total	Urban - Urbaine		Total	Urban - Urbaine		Total	Urban - Urbaine	
			Number Nombre	Percent P.100		Number Nombre	Percent P.100		Number Nombre	Percent P.100
ASIA - ASIE										
Timor-Leste										
1 VII 2008[2]............ESDF		1 080 742	...	...	549 000[28]	...	...	532 000[28]	...	...
11 VII 2010 ....CDFC		1 066 409	316 086	29.6	544 198	166 163	30.5	522 211	149 923	28.7
Turkey - Turquie										
1 VII 2005 ....ESDF		72 064 992	...	...	36 349 233	...	...	35 715 759	...	...
1 VII 2006 ....ESDF		72 971 474	...	...	36 796 216	...	...	36 175 258	...	...
1 VII 2007 ....ESDF		70 137 756	...	...	35 158 437	...	...	34 979 319	...	...
1 VII 2008 ....ESDF		71 051 678	...	...	35 638 843	...	...	35 412 835	...	...
31 XII 2008[110]...........CDJC		71 517 100	...	...	35 901 154	...	...	35 615 946	...	...
1 VII 2009 ....ESDF		72 039 206	...	...	36 181 812	...	...	35 857 394	...	...
1 VII 2010 ....ESDF		73 142 150	...	...	36 752 826	...	...	36 389 324	...	...
1 VII 2011 ....ESDF		74 223 629	...	...	37 288 068	...	...	36 935 561	...	...
3 X 2011*[111]..............CDJC		74 526 000	53 321 000	71.5	37 431 000	26 777 000	71.5	37 095 000	26 544 000	71.6
1 VII 2012 ....ESDF		75 175 827	54 168 017	72.1	37 744 561	27 195 122	72.1	37 431 266	26 972 895	72.1
31 XII 2013[110]...........ESDJ		76 667 864	66 488 105	86.7	38 473 360	33 344 846	86.7	38 194 504	33 143 259	86.8
United Arab Emirates - Émirats arabes unis[112]										
5 XII 2005 ....CDFC		4 106 427	3 384 839	82.4	2 806 141	...	...	1 300 286	...	...
31 XII 2006 ....ESDF		5 012 384	...	...	3 533 564	...	...	1 478 820	...	...
31 XII 2007 ....ESDF		6 219 006	...	...	4 533 281	...	...	1 685 725	...	...
31 XII 2008 ....ESDF		8 073 626	...	...	6 039 971	...	...	2 033 655	...	...
31 XII 2009 ....ESDF		8 199 996	...	...	6 120 885	...	...	2 079 111	...	...
1 VII 2010 ....ESDF		8 264 070	...	...	6 161 820	...	...	2 102 250	...	...
Viet Nam										
1 VII 2005[113].............ESDF		82 393 519	22 332 173	27.1	40 522 211	...	...	41 871 308	...	...
1 VII 2006[113].............ESDF		83 312 993	23 046 110	27.7	40 999 887	...	...	42 313 106	...	...
1 VII 2007[113].............ESDF		84 221 105	23 746 705	28.2	41 448 572	...	...	42 772 533	...	...
1 VII 2008[113].............ESDF		85 122 271	24 673 681	29.0	41 957 844	...	...	43 164 427	...	...
1 IV 2009 ....CDJC		85 846 997	25 436 896	29.6	42 413 143	12 349 995	29.1	43 433 854	13 086 901	30.1
1 VII 2009 ....ESDF		86 024 979	25 584 740	29.7	42 523 416	...	...	43 501 563	...	...
1 VII 2010 ....ESDF		86 932 527	26 515 940	30.5	42 986 075	...	...	43 946 452	...	...
1 VII 2011 ....ESDF		87 840 038	27 888 152	31.7	43 444 777	...	...	44 395 261	...	...
1 VII 2012 ....ESDF		88 772 884	28 356 363	31.9	43 907 154	...	...	44 865 730	...	...
1 VII 2013 ....ESDF		89 708 892	28 874 850	32.2	44 454 271	...	...	45 254 621	...	...
1 VII 2014 ....ESDF		90 728 941	30 035 405	33.1	44 758 132	...	...	45 970 809	...	...
Yemen - Yémen										
31 XII 2005 ....ESDF		20 282 944	5 849 749	28.8		...			...	
31 XII 2006 ....ESDF		20 900 532	6 070 613	29.0		...			...	
31 XII 2007 ....ESDF		21 538 995	6 256 462	29.0		...			...	
1 VII 2008[2]................ESDJ		21 843 554	6 281 475	28.8	11 127 218	...	...	10 716 336	...	...
1 VII 2009[2]................ESDJ		22 492 035	6 475 802	28.8	11 454 963	...	...	11 037 072	...	...
1 VII 2010[2]................ESDJ		23 153 982	6 673 916	28.8	11 789 814	...	...	11 364 168	...	...
1 VII 2011[2]................ESDJ		23 832 569	6 875 789	28.9	12 133 362	...	...	11 699 207	...	...
1 VII 2012[2]................ESDJ		24 526 703	7 075 639	28.8	12 485 039	...	...	12 041 664	...	...
1 VII 2013[2]................ESDJ		25 235 079	7 280 367	28.9	12 844 169	...	...	12 390 910	...	...
EUROPE										
Åland Islands - Îles d'Åland[38]										
1 VII 2005 ....ESDJ		26 648	10 746	40.3	13 174	5 087	38.6	13 475	5 660	42.0
1 VII 2006 ....ESDJ		26 845	10 802	40.2	13 299	5 123	38.5	13 546	5 680	41.9
1 VII 2007 ....ESDJ		27 038	10 863	40.2	13 407	5 151	38.4	13 631	5 712	41.9
1 VII 2008 ....ESDJ		27 305	10 954	40.1	13 552	5 189	38.3	13 753	5 765	41.9
1 VII 2009 ....ESDJ		27 595	11 064	40.1	13 724	5 264	38.4	13 871	5 800	41.8
1 VII 2010 ....ESDJ		27 871	11 157	40.0	13 880	5 327	38.4	13 991	5 830	41.7
1 VII 2011 ....ESDJ		28 181	11 227	39.8	14 045	5 364	38.2	14 137	5 863	41.5
1 VII 2012 ....ESDJ		28 429	11 305	39.8	14 172	5 408	38.2	14 257	5 897	41.4
1 VII 2013 ....ESDJ		28 585	11 370	39.8	14 255	5 445	38.2	14 330	5 925	41.3
1 VII 2014 ....ESDJ		28 792	11 437	39.7	14 375	5 490	38.2	14 417	5 947	41.2
Albania - Albanie										
1 VII 2005 ....ESDF		3 011 487	1 423 739	47.3	1 503 127	704 398	46.9	1 508 360	719 341	47.7
1 VII 2006 ....ESDF		2 992 547	1 448 706	48.4	1 494 341	717 077	48.0	1 498 206	731 629	48.8
1 VII 2007 ....ESDF		2 970 017	1 472 486	49.6	1 483 616	729 192	49.1	1 486 401	743 294	50.0

Continent, country or area, and date / Continent, pays ou zone et date	Code[a]	Both sexes - Les deux sexes			Male - Masculin			Female - Féminin		
		Total	Urban - Urbaine		Total	Urban - Urbaine		Total	Urban - Urbaine	
			Number Nombre	Percent P.100		Number Nombre	Percent P.100		Number Nombre	Percent P.100
EUROPE										
Albania - Albanie										
1 VII 2008 ....ESDF		2 947 314	1 495 552	50.7	1 472 660	740 747	50.3	1 474 654	754 805	51.2
1 VII 2009 ....ESDF		2 927 519	1 518 397	51.9	1 463 537	752 178	51.4	1 463 982	766 219	52.3
1 VII 2010 ....ESDF		2 913 021	1 541 310	52.9	1 457 661	763 780	52.4	1 455 360	777 530	53.4
1 VII 2011 ....ESDF		2 904 780	1 564 139	53.8	1 455 074	775 313	53.3	1 449 706	788 826	54.4
1 X 2011 ....CDJC		2 800 138	1 498 508	53.5	1 403 059	742 671	52.9	1 397 079	755 837	54.1
1 VII 2012 ....ESDF		2 900 489	1 595 701	55.0	1 455 904	787 167	54.1	1 444 585	808 534	56.0
1 VII 2013 ....ESDF		2 897 364	1 633 617	56.4	1 458 648	798 615	54.8	1 438 716	835 002	58.0
1 I 2014 ....ESDF		2 895 947	...	...	1 459 963	...	...	1 435 984	...	...
Andorra - Andorre[38]										
1 VII 2005 ....ESDJ		78 607	...	...	41 097	...	...	37 510	...	...
1 VII 2006 ....ESDJ		80 104	...	...	41 876	...	...	38 228	...	...
1 VII 2007 ....ESDJ		82 392	...	...	43 100	...	...	39 292	...	...
1 VII 2008 ....ESDJ		83 884	...	...	43 911	...	...	39 973	...	...
1 VII 2009 ....ESDJ		85 116	...	...	44 444	...	...	40 672	...	...
1 VII 2010 ....ESDJ		84 549	...	...	43 992	...	...	40 557	...	...
1 VII 2011[114] ....ESDJ		79 280	...	...	40 529	...	...	38 751	...	...
1 VII 2012 ....ESDJ		77 181	...	...	39 351	...	...	37 830	...	...
1 I 2013 ....ESDJ		76 246	...	...	38 838			37 408		
Austria - Autriche										
1 VII 2005 ....ESDJ		8 225 278	...	...	3 998 952	...	...	4 226 326	...	...
1 VII 2006 ....ESDJ		8 267 948	...	...	4 022 516	...	...	4 245 432	...	...
1 VII 2007 ....ESDJ		8 295 189	...	...	4 036 548	...	...	4 258 641	...	...
1 VII 2008 ....ESDJ		8 321 541	...	...	4 050 215	...	...	4 271 326	...	...
1 VII 2009 ....ESDJ		8 341 483	...	...	4 061 195	...	...	4 280 288	...	...
1 VII 2010 ....ESDJ		8 361 069	...	...	4 071 773	...	...	4 289 296	...	...
1 VII 2011 ....ESDJ		8 388 534	...	...	4 087 188	...	...	4 301 346	...	...
31 X 2011 ....CDJC		8 401 940	5 643 239	67.2	4 093 938	2 713 930	66.3	4 308 002	2 929 309	68.0
1 VII 2012 ....ESDJ		8 426 311	...	...	4 109 431	...	...	4 316 880	...	...
1 VII 2013 ....ESDJ		8 477 230	...	...	4 138 693	...	...	4 338 537	...	...
1 I 2014 ....ESDJ		8 506 889	...	...	4 155 636	...	...	4 351 253	...	...
Belarus - Bélarus										
1 VII 2005 ....ESDF		9 663 915	6 961 016	72.0	4 507 843	3 241 302	71.9	5 156 072	3 719 714	72.1
1 VII 2006 ....ESDF		9 604 924	6 960 276	72.5	4 475 094	3 235 250	72.3	5 129 830	3 725 026	72.6
1 VII 2007 ....ESDF		9 560 953	6 976 543	73.0	4 450 877	3 238 281	72.8	5 110 076	3 738 262	73.2
1 VII 2008 ....ESDF		9 527 985	7 008 135	73.6	4 433 031	3 249 263	73.3	5 094 954	3 758 872	73.8
1 VII 2009 ....ESDF		9 506 765	7 052 045	74.2	4 421 789	3 266 240	73.9	5 084 976	3 785 805	74.5
14 X 2009 ....CDJC		9 503 807	7 064 529	74.3	4 420 039	3 271 014	74.0	5 083 768	3 793 515	74.6
1 VII 2010 ....ESDJ		9 490 583	7 100 147	74.8	4 413 225	3 285 104	74.4	5 077 358	3 815 043	75.1
1 VII 2011 ....ESDJ		9 473 172	7 148 636	75.5	4 403 227	3 303 932	75.0	5 069 945	3 844 704	75.8
1 VII 2012 ....ESDJ		9 464 495	7 198 575	76.1	4 397 910	3 324 299	75.6	5 066 585	3 874 276	76.5
1 VII 2013 ....ESDJ		9 465 997	7 247 854	76.6	4 399 369	3 345 878	76.1	5 066 628	3 901 976	77.0
1 I 2014 ....ESDF		9 468 154	7 274 775	76.8	4 401 211	3 357 966	76.3	5 066 943	3 916 809	77.3
Belgium - Belgique										
1 VII 2005 ....ESDJ		10 472 842	10 322 099	98.6	5 125 387	5 049 822	98.5	5 347 455	5 272 277	98.6
1 VII 2006 ....ESDJ		10 541 893	10 389 801	98.6	5 159 947	5 083 829	98.5	5 381 946	5 305 972	98.6
1 VII 2007 ....ESDJ		10 622 604	10 469 341	98.6	5 201 670	5 125 007	98.5	5 420 934	5 344 334	98.6
1 VII 2008 ....ESDJ		10 709 973	10 555 681	98.6	5 246 480	5 169 223	98.5	5 463 493	5 386 458	98.6
1 VII 2009 ....ESDJ		10 796 493	10 641 089	98.6	5 290 436	5 212 557	98.5	5 506 057	5 428 532	98.6
1 VII 2010 ....ESDJ		10 895 638	10 739 291	98.6	5 341 252	5 262 796	98.5	5 554 386	5 476 495	98.6
1 I 2011 ....CDJC		11 000 638	10 842 520	98.6	5 401 718	5 322 172	98.5	5 598 920	5 520 348	98.6
1 VII 2011 ....ESDJ		11 043 788	10 884 939	98.6	5 425 814	5 345 964	98.5	5 617 974	5 538 975	98.6
1 VII 2012 ....ESDJ		11 128 246	...	...	5 469 608	...	...	5 658 638	...	...
1 I 2013 ....ESDJ		11 161 642	...	...	5 487 436	...	...	5 674 206	...	...
1 I 2014 ....ESDJ		11 203 992	...	...	5 508 069	...	...	5 695 923	...	...
Bosnia and Herzegovina - Bosnie-Herzégovine										
1 VII 2005 ....ESDF		3 842 537	...	...	1 882 843	...	...	1 959 694	...	...
1 VII 2006 ....ESDF		3 842 762	...	...	1 882 953	...	...	1 959 809	...	...
1 VII 2007 ....ESDF		3 842 562	...	...	1 877 309	...	...	1 965 253	...	...
1 VII 2008 ....ESDF		3 842 265	...	...	1 877 165	...	...	1 965 100	...	...
1 VII 2009 ....ESDF		3 842 566	...	...	1 877 312	...	...	1 965 254	...	...
1 VII 2010 ....ESDF		3 843 126	...	...	1 877 587	...	...	1 965 539	...	...
1 VII 2011 ....ESDF		3 841 224	...	...	1 876 546	...	...	1 964 678	...	...
1 VII 2012* ....ESDF		3 837 455	...	...	1 874 608	...	...	1 962 848	...	...
1 I 2013* ....ESDF		3 835 645	...	...	1 873 605	...	...	1 962 040	...	...

Continent, country or area, and date / Continent, pays ou zone et date	Code[a]	Both sexes - Les deux sexes			Male - Masculin			Female - Féminin		
		Total	Urban - Urbaine		Total	Urban - Urbaine		Total	Urban - Urbaine	
			Number Nombre	Percent P.100		Number Nombre	Percent P.100		Number Nombre	Percent P.100
EUROPE										
Bulgaria - Bulgarie										
1 VII 2005	ESDJ	7 739 900	5 424 661	70.1	3 755 469	2 613 346	69.6	3 984 431	2 811 315	70.6
1 VII 2006	ESDJ	7 699 020	5 428 388	70.5	3 732 130	2 613 030	70.0	3 966 890	2 815 358	71.0
1 VII 2007	ESDJ	7 659 764	5 414 260	70.7	3 710 315	2 604 175	70.2	3 949 449	2 810 085	71.2
1 VII 2008	ESDJ	7 623 395	5 405 147	70.9	3 690 485	2 597 929	70.4	3 932 910	2 807 218	71.4
1 VII 2009	ESDJ	7 585 131	5 408 330	71.3	3 670 296	2 598 442	70.8	3 914 835	2 809 888	71.8
1 VII 2010	ESDJ	7 534 289	5 388 142	71.5	3 644 560	2 587 844	71.0	3 889 729	2 800 298	72.0
1 II 2011	CDJC	7 364 570	5 338 261	72.5	3 586 571	2 580 734	72.0	3 777 999	2 757 527	73.0
1 VII 2011	ESDJ	7 348 328	5 336 366	72.6	3 577 847	2 579 205	72.1	3 770 481	2 757 161	73.1
1 VII 2012	ESDJ	7 305 888	5 316 384	72.8	3 555 920	2 568 535	72.2	3 749 968	2 747 849	73.3
1 I 2013	ESDJ	7 282 041	...	...	3 543 606	...	...	3 738 435	...	...
1 I 2014	ESDJ	7 245 677	...	...	3 524 945	...	...	3 720 732	...	...
Croatia - Croatie										
1 VII 2005	ESDJ	4 310 145	...	...	2 072 293	...	...	2 237 852	...	...
1 VII 2006	ESDJ	4 311 159	...	...	2 074 504	...	...	2 236 655	...	...
1 VII 2007	ESDJ	4 310 217	...	...	2 075 547	...	...	2 234 670	...	...
1 VII 2008	ESDJ	4 309 705	...	...	2 076 517	...	...	2 233 188	...	...
1 VII 2009	ESDJ	4 305 181	...	...	2 075 321	...	...	2 229 860	...	...
1 VII 2010	ESDJ	4 295 427	...	...	2 071 195	...	...	2 224 232	...	...
1 IV 2011	CDJC	4 284 889	2 368 506	55.3	2 066 335	1 121 328	54.3	2 218 554	1 247 178	56.2
1 VII 2011	ESDJ	4 280 622	...	...	2 064 314	...	...	2 216 308	...	...
1 VII 2012	ESDJ	4 267 558	...	...	2 058 701	...	...	2 208 857	...	...
1 VII 2013	ESDJ	4 255 689	...	...	2 053 788	...	...	2 201 901	...	...
1 I 2014	ESDJ	4 246 809	...	...	2 049 748	...	...	2 197 061	...	...
Czech Republic - République tchèque										
1 VII 2005	ESDJ	10 211 216	...	...	4 980 154	...	...	5 231 062	...	...
1 VII 2006	ESDJ	10 238 905	...	...	5 000 124	...	...	5 238 781	...	...
1 VII 2007	ESDJ	10 298 828	...	...	5 037 856	...	...	5 260 972	...	...
1 VII 2008	ESDJ	10 384 603	...	...	5 090 898	...	...	5 293 705	...	...
1 VII 2009	ESDJ	10 443 936	...	...	5 126 422	...	...	5 317 514	...	...
1 VII 2010	ESDJ	10 474 410	...	...	5 141 699	...	...	5 332 711	...	...
25 III 2011	CDJC	10 436 560	7 650 450	73.3	5 109 766	3 712 348	72.7	5 326 794	3 938 102	73.9
1 VII 2011	ESDJ	10 496 088	...	...	5 152 721	...	...	5 343 368	...	...
1 VII 2012	ESDJ	10 510 786	...	...	5 161 280	...	...	5 349 506	...	...
1 VII 2013	ESDJ	10 510 719	7 683 793	73.1	5 161 617	3 740 790	72.5	5 349 102	3 943 003	73.7
1 I 2014	ESDJ	10 512 419	7 679 501	73.1	5 162 380	3 738 054	72.4	5 350 039	3 941 447	73.7
Denmark - Danemark[115]										
1 VII 2005	ESDJ	5 415 978	...	...	2 679 857	...	...	2 736 121	...	...
1 VII 2006	ESDJ	5 434 567	...	...	2 690 179	...	...	2 744 388	...	...
1 VII 2007	ESDJ	5 457 415	...	...	2 702 894	...	...	2 754 521	...	...
1 VII 2008	ESDJ	5 489 022	...	...	2 720 016	...	...	2 769 006	...	...
1 VII 2009	ESDJ	5 519 441	...	...	2 735 983	...	...	2 783 458	...	...
1 VII 2010	ESDJ	5 545 039	...	...	2 748 439	...	...	2 796 600	...	...
1 I 2011	CDJC	5 560 628	...	...	2 756 582	...	...	2 804 046	...	...
1 VII 2011	ESDJ	5 566 856	...	...	2 760 140	...	...	2 806 716	...	...
1 VII 2012	ESDJ	5 587 085	...	...	2 771 208	...	...	2 815 877	...	...
1 VII 2013	ESDJ	5 608 784	...	...	2 782 661	...	...	2 826 123	...	...
1 VII 2014	ESDJ	5 639 719	...	...	2 799 895	...	...	2 839 824	...	...
Estonia - Estonie										
1 VII 2005	ESDJ	1 354 775	930 700	68.7	629 820	421 145	66.9	724 955	509 555	70.3
1 VII 2006	ESDJ	1 346 810	922 625	68.5	626 095	416 985	66.6	720 715	505 640	70.2
1 VII 2007	ESDJ	1 340 680	916 015	68.3	623 155	413 710	66.4	717 525	502 305	70.0
1 VII 2008	ESDJ	1 337 090	911 285	68.2	621 685	411 555	66.2	715 405	499 730	69.9
1 VII 2009	ESDJ	1 334 515	907 675	68.0	621 060	410 130	66.0	713 455	497 545	69.7
1 VII 2010	ESDJ	1 331 475	904 365	67.9	620 250	408 720	65.9	711 225	495 645	69.7
1 VII 2011	ESDJ	1 327 439	903 066	68.0	618 919	408 988	66.1	708 520	494 078	69.7
31 XII 2011	CDJC	1 294 455	879 157	67.9	600 526	396 719	66.1	693 929	482 438	69.5
1 VII 2012	ESDJ	1 322 696	902 743	68.3	617 153	409 784	66.4	705 543	492 959	69.9
1 VII 2013	ESDJ	1 317 997	900 071	68.3	615 543	408 564	66.4	702 454	491 507	70.0
1 I 2014	ESDJ	1 315 819	898 476	68.3	614 919	407 836	66.3	700 900	490 640	70.0
Faeroe Islands - Îles Féroé										
1 VII 2005	ESDJ	48 258	17 464	36.2	25 070	8 822	35.2	23 188	8 642	37.3
1 VII 2006	ESDJ	48 254	17 518	36.3	25 071	8 843	35.3	23 183	8 676	37.4
1 VII 2007	ESDJ	48 249	17 513	36.3	25 074	8 841	35.3	23 175	8 672	37.4

6. Total and urban population by sex: 2005 - 2014
Population totale et population urbaine selon le sexe : 2005 - 2014 (continued - suite)

Continent, country or area, and date / Continent, pays ou zone et date	Code[a]	Both sexes - Les deux sexes			Male - Masculin			Female - Féminin		
		Total	Urban - Urbaine		Total	Urban - Urbaine		Total	Urban - Urbaine	
			Number Nombre	Percent P.100		Number Nombre	Percent P.100		Number Nombre	Percent P.100
EUROPE										
Faeroe Islands - Îles Féroé										
1 I 2008[38]	CDJC	48 433	...	...	25 174	...	...	23 259	...	...
1 VII 2008	ESDJ	48 344	17 558	36.3	25 125	8 868	35.3	23 219	8 690	37.4
1 VII 2009	ESDJ	48 531	17 713	36.5	25 223	8 973	35.6	23 309	8 740	37.5
1 VII 2010	ESDJ	48 635	17 931	36.9	25 283	9 098	36.0	23 353	8 833	37.8
1 VII 2011	ESDJ	48 542	18 059	37.2	25 216	9 129	36.2	23 326	8 930	38.3
11 XI 2011	CDJC	48 346	...	...	25 125	...	...	23 221	...	...
1 VII 2012	ESDJ	48 363	18 032	37.3	25 111	9 088	36.2	23 253	8 944	38.5
1 VII 2013	ESDJ	48 152	18 009	37.4	24 993	9 068	36.3	23 159	8 942	38.6
1 VII 2014	ESDJ	48 160	18 151	37.7	24 943	9 118	36.6	23 217	9 033	38.9
Finland - Finlande										
1 VII 2005[116]	ESDJ	5 219 448	3 506 347	67.2	2 554 040	1 693 841	66.3	2 665 408	1 812 507	68.0
1 VII 2006[116]	ESDJ	5 239 423	3 528 484	67.3	2 564 748	1 705 689	66.5	2 674 676	1 822 796	68.2
1 VII 2007[116]	ESDJ	5 261 682	3 552 580	67.5	2 576 858	1 718 698	66.7	2 684 824	1 833 883	68.3
1 VII 2008[116]	ESDJ	5 286 095	3 580 776	67.7	2 590 669	1 734 274	66.9	2 695 426	1 846 503	68.5
1 VII 2009[116]	ESDJ	5 311 276	3 609 998	68.0	2 604 636	1 750 168	67.2	2 706 640	1 859 830	68.7
1 VII 2010[116]	ESDJ	5 335 481	3 637 292	68.2	2 617 862	1 764 878	67.4	2 717 620	1 872 414	68.9
31 XII 2010	CDJC	5 375 276	3 662 915	68.1	2 638 416	1 777 697	67.4	2 736 860	1 885 218	68.9
1 VII 2011[116]	ESDJ	5 360 091	3 665 970	68.4	2 631 431	1 780 112	67.6	2 728 660	1 885 858	69.1
1 VII 2012[116]	ESDJ	5 385 543	3 696 159	68.6	2 645 408	1 796 105	67.9	2 740 136	1 900 054	69.3
1 VII 2013[116]	ESDJ	5 410 389	3 727 221	68.9	2 659 239	1 812 926	68.2	2 751 150	1 914 295	69.6
1 I 2014[38]	ESDJ	5 451 270	...	...	2 680 364	...	...	2 770 906	...	...
France[117]										
1 VII 2005	ESDJ	61 181 499	...	...	29 616 894	...	...	31 564 605	...	...
1 I 2006	CDJC	61 399 541	...	...	29 714 539	...	...	31 685 002	...	...
1 VII 2006	ESDJ	61 597 486	...	...	29 815 995	...	...	31 781 491	...	...
1 VII 2007	ESDJ	61 965 052	...	...	30 001 162	...	...	31 963 890	...	...
1 VII 2008	ESDJ	62 300 288	...	...	30 166 091	...	...	32 134 197	...	...
1 VII 2009	ESDJ	62 615 472	...	...	30 322 692	...	...	32 292 780	...	...
1 I 2010	CDJS	62 765 235	48 387 303	77.1	30 393 079	23 208 841	76.4	32 372 156	25 178 462	77.8
1 VII 2010	ESDJ	62 917 790	...	...	30 475 789	...	...	32 442 001	...	...
1 VII 2011	ESDJ	63 223 158	...	...	30 626 399	...	...	32 596 759	...	...
1 VII 2012	ESDJ	63 519 077	...	...	30 780 362	...	...	32 738 715	...	...
1 I 2013	ESDJ	63 659 608	...	...	30 852 796	...	...	32 806 812	...	...
1 VII 2014*	ESDJ	64 062 247	...	...	31 047 688	...	...	33 014 559	...	...
Germany - Allemagne										
1 VII 2005	ESDJ	82 464 344	...	...	40 348 986	...	...	42 115 358	...	...
1 VII 2006	ESDJ	82 365 810	...	...	40 317 807	...	...	42 048 003	...	...
1 VII 2007	ESDJ	82 262 642	...	...	40 287 823	...	...	41 974 819	...	...
1 VII 2008	ESDJ	82 119 776	...	...	40 238 595	...	...	41 881 181	...	...
1 VII 2009	ESDJ	81 874 770	...	...	40 133 270	...	...	41 741 500	...	...
1 VII 2010	ESDJ	81 757 471	...	...	40 099 871	...	...	41 657 600	...	...
9 V 2011	CDJC	80 219 695	64 444 232	80.3	39 145 941	31 227 832	79.8	41 073 754	33 216 400	80.9
1 VII 2011	ESDJ	80 209 997	...	...	39 140 044	...	...	41 069 953	...	...
1 VII 2012	ESDJ	80 425 823	...	...	39 305 616	...	...	41 120 207	...	...
1 VII 2013	ESDJ	80 645 605	...	...	39 469 105	...	...	41 176 500	...	...
1 I 2014	ESDJ	80 767 463	...	...	39 557 079	...	...	41 210 384	...	...
Gibraltar[118]										
31 XII 2005	ESDF	29 313	...	...	14 454	...	...	14 859	...	...
31 XII 2006	ESDF	29 672	...	...	14 651	...	...	15 021	...	...
31 XII 2007	ESDF	30 066	...	...	14 871	...	...	15 195	...	...
31 XII 2008	ESDF	30 496	...	...	15 113	...	...	15 383	...	...
31 XII 2009	ESDF	30 963	...	...	15 378	...	...	15 585	...	...
31 XII 2010	ESDF	31 465	...	...	15 666	...	...	15 799	...	...
31 XII 2011	ESDF	32 003	...	...	15 977	...	...	16 026	...	...
12 XI 2012	CDJC	32 194	...	...	16 061	...	...	16 133	...	...
31 XII 2012	ESDF	32 577	...	...	16 311	...	...	16 266	...	...
31 XII 2013	ESDF	32 734	...	...	16 460	...	...	16 274	...	...
Greece - Grèce										
1 VII 2005[119]	ESDF	11 092 913	...	...	5 461 732	...	...	5 631 182	...	...
1 VII 2006[119]	ESDF	11 127 947	...	...	5 475 805	...	...	5 652 142	...	...
1 VII 2007[119]	ESDF	11 163 002	...	...	5 490 485	...	...	5 672 517	...	...
1 VII 2008[119]	ESDF	11 186 439	...	...	5 499 189	...	...	5 687 250	...	...
1 VII 2009[119]	ESDF	11 187 085	...	...	5 494 098	...	...	5 692 987	...	...

Continent, country or area, and date / Continent, pays ou zone et date	Code[a]	Both sexes - Les deux sexes			Male - Masculin			Female - Féminin		
		Total	Urban - Urbaine		Total	Urban - Urbaine		Total	Urban - Urbaine	
			Number Nombre	Percent P.100		Number Nombre	Percent P.100		Number Nombre	Percent P.100
EUROPE										
Greece - Grèce										
1 VII 2010[119]	ESDF	11 153 454	...	...	5 471 122	...	...	5 682 332	...	...
9 V 2011	CDFC	10 816 286	8 285 259	76.6	5 303 223	4 022 889	75.9	5 513 063	4 262 370	77.3
1 VII 2011[119]	ESDF	11 123 213	...	...	5 451 624	...	...	5 671 590	...	...
1 VII 2012[119]	ESDF	11 092 771	...	...	5 431 547	...	...	5 661 225	...	...
1 I 2013[119]	ESDF	11 062 508	...	...	5 413 290	...	...	5 649 218	...	...
1 I 2014[120]	ESDF	10 903 704	...	...	5 301 430	...	...	5 602 274	...	...
Guernsey - Guernesey										
31 III 2006	ESDF	61 029	...	...	30 034	...	...	30 995	...	...
31 III 2007	ESDF	61 175	...	...	30 022	...	...	31 153	...	...
31 III 2008	ESDF	61 726	...	...	30 405	...	...	31 321	...	...
31 III 2009	ESDF	62 274	...	...	30 777	...	...	31 497	...	...
31 III 2010	ESDF	62 431	...	...	30 695	...	...	31 736	...	...
31 III 2011	ESDF	62 915	...	...	31 025	...	...	31 890	...	...
31 III 2012	ESDF	63 085	...	...	31 147	...	...	31 938	...	...
31 III 2013	ESDF	62 732	...	...	31 081	...	...	31 651	...	...
31 III 2014	ESDF	62 711	...	...	30 994	...	...	31 717	...	...
Holy See - Saint-Siège[121]										
1 VII 2009	ESDF	466[122]	...	...	320	...	...	146	...	...
Hungary - Hongrie										
1 VII 2005	ESDJ	10 087 065	6 670 187	66.1	4 788 847	3 125 833	65.3	5 298 218	3 544 354	66.9
1 VII 2006	ESDJ	10 071 370	6 749 388	67.0	4 781 829	3 163 716	66.2	5 289 541	3 585 673	67.8
1 VII 2007	ESDJ	10 055 780	6 737 792	67.0	4 774 320	3 156 954	66.1	5 281 460	3 580 839	67.8
1 VII 2008	ESDJ	10 038 188	6 810 173	67.8	4 766 306	3 191 030	66.9	5 271 882	3 619 143	68.6
1 VII 2009	ESDJ	10 022 650	6 861 432	68.5	4 759 975	3 215 749	67.6	5 262 675	3 645 683	69.3
1 VII 2010	ESDJ	10 000 023	6 953 071	69.5	4 750 401	3 260 344	68.6	5 249 623	3 692 727	70.3
1 VII 2011	ESDJ	9 971 727	6 945 873	69.7	4 737 813	3 256 796	68.7	5 233 914	3 689 077	70.5
1 X 2011	CDFC	9 937 628	6 903 858	69.5	4 718 479	3 241 911	68.7	5 219 149	3 661 947	70.2
1 VII 2012	ESDJ	9 920 362	6 877 231	69.3	4 720 310	3 234 447	68.5	5 200 052	3 642 785	70.1
1 I 2013	ESDJ	9 908 798	...	...	4 715 953	...	...	5 192 845	...	...
1 I 2014[120]	ESDJ	9 877 365	...	...	4 703 391	...	...	5 173 974	...	...
Iceland - Islande[123]										
1 VII 2005	ESDJ	295 864	275 017	93.0	148 449	137 003	92.3	147 415	138 014	93.6
1 VII 2006	ESDJ	304 334	281 961	92.6	154 287	141 673	91.8	150 047	140 288	93.5
1 VII 2007	ESDJ	311 396	289 119	92.8	158 866	146 168	92.0	152 530	142 951	93.7
1 VII 2008	ESDJ	319 355	298 024	93.3	163 176	151 378	92.8	156 179	146 646	93.9
1 VII 2009	ESDJ	319 246	298 890	93.6	161 548	150 604	93.2	157 698	148 286	94.0
1 VII 2010	ESDJ	318 006	297 432	93.5	159 838	148 901	93.2	158 168	148 531	93.9
1 VII 2011[124]	ESDJ	319 014	314 413	98.6	160 185	157 797	98.5	158 829	156 616	98.6
1 VII 2012	ESDJ	320 716	300 237	93.6	160 901	150 074	93.3	159 815	150 163	94.0
1 VII 2013	ESDJ	323 764	303 136	93.6	162 378	151 471	93.3	161 386	151 665	94.0
1 I 2014	ESDJ	325 671	...	...	163 318	...	...	162 353	...	...
Ireland - Irlande										
1 VII 2005	ESDF	4 159 914	...	...	2 076 400	...	...	2 083 515	...	...
23 IV 2006	CDFC	4 239 848	2 574 313	60.7	2 121 171	1 267 960	59.8	2 118 677	1 306 353	61.7
1 VII 2006	ESDF	4 260 341	...	...	2 130 565	...	...	2 129 776	...	...
1 VII 2007	ESDF	4 356 931	...	...	2 177 582	...	...	2 179 349	...	...
1 VII 2008	ESDF	4 425 683	...	...	2 206 165	...	...	2 219 518	...	...
1 VII 2009	ESDF	4 458 942	...	...	2 215 646	...	...	2 243 297	...	...
1 VII 2010	ESDF	4 560 155	...	...	2 265 200	...	...	2 294 955	...	...
10 IV 2011	CDFC	4 588 252	2 846 882	62.0	2 272 699	1 389 160	61.1	2 315 553	1 457 722	63.0
1 VII 2011	ESDF	4 576 794	...	...	2 269 608	...	...	2 307 186	...	...
1 VII 2012	ESDF	4 586 897	...	...	2 271 290	...	...	2 315 607	...	...
1 I 2013	ESDF	4 591 087	...	...	2 272 790	...	...	2 318 297	...	...
1 I 2014[120]	ESDF	4 605 501	...	...	2 278 225	...	...	2 327 276	...	...
Isle of Man - Île de Man										
30 IV 2005	ESDJ	78 800	...	...	38 775	...	...	40 025	...	...
23 IV 2006	CDJC	80 058	...	...	39 523	...	...	40 535	...	...
30 IV 2007	ESDJ	80 885	...	...	39 995	...	...	40 889	...	...
30 IV 2008	ESDJ	81 722	...	...	40 472	...	...	41 250	...	...
30 IV 2009	ESDJ	82 371	...	...	40 849	...	...	41 522	...	...
30 IV 2010	ESDJ	82 691	...	...	41 053	...	...	41 638	...	...
27 III 2011	CDJC	84 497	...	...	41 971	...	...	42 526	...	...
30 IV 2012	ESDJ	85 047	...	...	42 273	...	...	42 775	...	...

Continent, country or area, and date / Continent, pays ou zone et date	Code[a]	Both sexes - Les deux sexes			Male - Masculin			Female - Féminin		
		Total	Urban - Urbaine		Total	Urban - Urbaine		Total	Urban - Urbaine	
			Number Nombre	Percent P.100		Number Nombre	Percent P.100		Number Nombre	Percent P.100
EUROPE										
Isle of Man - Île de Man										
30 IV 2013	ESDJ	85 682	...	...	42 622	...	...	43 060	...	...
30 IV 2014	ESDJ	86 322	...	...	42 971	...	...	43 352	...	...
Italy - Italie										
1 VII 2005	ESDJ	57 969 484	...	...	28 091 394	...	...	29 878 090	...	...
1 VII 2006	ESDJ	58 143 979	...	...	28 175 406	...	...	29 968 574	...	...
1 VII 2007	ESDJ	58 438 310	...	...	28 311 738	...	...	30 126 572	...	...
1 VII 2008	ESDJ	58 826 731	...	...	28 490 625	...	...	30 336 106	...	...
1 VII 2009	ESDJ	59 095 365	...	...	28 609 696	...	...	30 485 669	...	...
1 VII 2010	ESDJ	59 277 417	...	...	28 682 321	...	...	30 595 096	...	...
1 VII 2011	ESDJ	59 379 449	...	...	28 720 928	...	...	30 658 521	...	...
9 X 2011	CDJC	59 433 744	...	...	28 745 507	...	...	30 688 237	...	...
1 VII 2012	ESDJ	59 539 717	...	...	28 808 098	...	...	30 731 619	...	...
1 VII 2013	ESDJ	60 233 948	...	...	29 187 081	...	...	31 046 867	...	...
1 I 2014[120]	ESDJ	60 782 668	...	...	29 484 564	...	...	31 298 104	...	...
Jersey										
27 III 2011	CDFC	97 857	...	...	48 296	...	...	49 561	...	...
Latvia - Lettonie										
1 VII 2005	ESDJ	2 238 799	1 518 410	67.8	1 027 084	682 091	66.4	1 211 715	836 319	69.0
1 VII 2006	ESDJ	2 218 357	1 505 865	67.9	1 017 925	676 209	66.4	1 200 432	829 656	69.1
1 VII 2007	ESDJ	2 200 325	1 494 615	67.9	1 010 416	671 274	66.4	1 189 909	823 341	69.2
1 VII 2008	ESDJ	2 177 322	1 478 831	67.9	999 845	663 658	66.4	1 177 477	815 173	69.2
1 VII 2009	ESDJ	2 141 669	1 453 570	67.9	981 789	650 486	66.3	1 159 880	803 084	69.2
1 VII 2010	ESDJ	2 097 555	1 422 675	67.8	959 435	634 393	66.1	1 138 120	788 282	69.3
1 III 2011	CDJC	2 070 371	1 404 251	67.8	946 102	625 150	66.1	1 124 269	779 101	69.3
1 VII 2011	ESDJ	2 059 709	1 394 429	67.7	941 375	620 484	65.9	1 118 334	773 945	69.2
1 VII 2012	ESDJ	2 034 319	1 374 215	67.6	930 696	611 604	65.7	1 103 623	762 611	69.1
1 VII 2013	ESDJ	2 012 647	1 362 004	67.7	921 813	606 624	65.8	1 090 834	755 380	69.2
1 I 2014	ESDJ	2 001 468	1 357 682	67.8	...	...	...	...	...	...
Liechtenstein										
1 VII 2005	ESDJ	34 734	...	...	17 100	...	...	17 634	...	...
1 VII 2006	ESDJ	35 010	...	...	17 256	...	...	17 754	...	...
1 VII 2007	ESDJ	35 322	...	...	17 426	...	...	17 896	...	...
1 VII 2008	ESDJ	35 446	...	...	17 508	...	...	17 938	...	...
1 VII 2009	ESDJ	35 789	...	...	17 716	...	...	18 073	...	...
1 VII 2010	ESDJ	36 010	...	...	17 817	...	...	18 193	...	...
31 XII 2010	CDFC	36 149	...	...	17 886	...	...	18 263	...	...
1 VII 2011	ESDJ	36 281	...	...	17 950	...	...	18 331	...	...
1 VII 2012	ESDJ	36 657	...	...	18 145	...	...	18 512	...	...
1 I 2013	ESDJ	36 838	...	...	18 247	...	...	18 591	...	...
1 I 2014[125]	ESDJ	37 129	...	...	18 400	...	...	18 729	...	...
Lithuania - Lituanie										
1 VII 2005	ESDJ	3 322 528	2 212 089	66.6	1 545 364	1 008 471	65.3	1 777 164	1 203 618	67.7
1 VII 2006	ESDJ	3 269 909	2 179 007	66.6	1 517 629	990 840	65.3	1 752 280	1 188 167	67.8
1 VII 2007	ESDJ	3 231 294	2 155 871	66.7	1 497 107	977 988	65.3	1 734 187	1 177 883	67.9
1 VII 2008	ESDJ	3 198 231	2 134 908	66.8	1 480 386	966 638	65.3	1 717 845	1 168 270	68.0
1 VII 2009	ESDJ	3 162 916	2 112 248	66.8	1 461 776	953 885	65.3	1 701 140	1 158 363	68.1
1 VII 2010	ESDJ	3 097 282	2 068 095	66.8	1 428 711	931 128	65.2	1 668 571	1 136 967	68.1
1 III 2011	CDJC	3 043 429	2 031 211	66.7	1 402 604	912 943	65.1	1 640 825	1 118 268	68.2
1 VII 2011	ESDJ	3 028 115	2 021 365	66.8	1 395 367	907 995	65.1	1 632 748	1 113 370	68.2
1 VII 2012	ESDJ	2 987 773	1 997 436	66.9	1 376 201	896 102	65.1	1 611 572	1 101 334	68.3
1 VII 2013	ESDJ	2 957 689	1 981 924	67.0	1 362 443	888 578	65.2	1 595 246	1 093 346	68.5
1 I 2014[120]	ESDJ	2 943 472	...	...	1 355 995	...	...	1 587 477	...	...
Luxembourg										
1 VII 2005	ESDJ	465 158	...	...	230 128	...	...	235 030	...	...
1 VII 2006	ESDJ	472 637	...	...	233 946	...	...	238 691	...	...
1 VII 2007	ESDJ	479 993	...	...	237 700	...	...	242 294	...	...
1 VII 2008	ESDJ	488 650	...	...	242 221	...	...	246 429	...	...
1 VII 2009	ESDJ	497 782	...	...	247 120	...	...	250 662	...	...
1 VII 2010	ESDJ	506 953	...	...	252 013	...	...	254 941	...	...
1 II 2011	CDJC	512 353	...	...	254 967	...	...	257 386	...	...
1 VII 2011	ESDJ	518 347	...	...	258 220	...	...	260 127	...	...
1 VII 2012	ESDJ	530 946	...	...	265 116	...	...	265 830	...	...
1 VII 2013	ESDJ	543 360	...	...	271 765	...	...	271 595	...	...
1 I 2014	ESDJ	549 680	...	...	275 117	...	...	274 563	...	...

Continent, country or area, and date / Continent, pays ou zone et date	Code[a]	Both sexes - Les deux sexes Total	Urban - Urbaine Number Nombre	Urban - Urbaine Percent P.100	Male - Masculin Total	Urban - Urbaine Number Nombre	Urban - Urbaine Percent P.100	Female - Féminin Total	Urban - Urbaine Number Nombre	Urban - Urbaine Percent P.100
EUROPE										
Malta - Malte										
1 VII 2005[126]	ESDJ	403 879	...	...	200 232	...	...	203 647	...	...
27 XI 2005	CDJC	404 962	404 544	99.9	200 819	200 611	99.9	204 143	203 933	99.9
1 VII 2006[126]	ESDJ	405 355	...	...	201 201	...	...	204 154	...	...
1 VII 2007[126]	ESDJ	406 778	...	...	202 150	...	...	204 628	...	...
1 VII 2008[126]	ESDJ	409 429	...	...	203 696	...	...	205 733	...	...
1 VII 2009[126]	ESDJ	412 530	...	...	205 432	...	...	207 098	...	...
1 VII 2010[126]	ESDJ	414 562	...	...	206 333	...	...	208 229	...	...
1 VII 2011[126]	ESDJ	416 318	...	...	207 072	...	...	209 246	...	...
20 XI 2011	CDFC	417 432	400 557	96.0	207 625	199 151	95.9	209 807	201 406	96.0
1 VII 2012[126]	ESDJ	419 507	...	...	208 811	...	...	210 696	...	...
1 VII 2013[126]	ESDJ	423 431	...	...	211 182	...	...	212 249	...	...
1 I 2014[126]	ESDJ	425 384	...	...	212 424	...	...	212 960	...	...
Monaco										
9 VI 2008	CDJC	31 109	...	...	15 076[127]	...	...	15 914[127]	...	...
Montenegro - Monténégro										
1 VII 2005	ESDJ	623 277	389 678	62.5	306 839	189 222	61.7	316 439	200 456	63.3
1 VII 2006	ESDJ	624 241	391 884	62.8	307 271	190 286	61.9	316 970	201 598	63.6
1 VII 2007	ESDJ	626 104	394 653	63.0	308 267	191 692	62.2	317 836	202 961	63.9
1 VII 2008	ESDJ	628 804	397 747	63.3	309 787	193 393	62.4	319 018	204 354	64.1
1 VII 2009	ESDJ	631 536	400 928	63.5	311 258	195 088	62.7	320 278	205 840	64.3
1 VII 2010	ESDJ	617 304	...	...	304 861	...	...	312 443	...	...
1 IV 2011	CDJC	620 029	399 264	64.4	306 236	193 691	63.2	313 793	205 573	65.5
1 VII 2011	ESDJ	620 556	...	...	306 472	...	...	314 084	...	...
1 VII 2012	ESDJ	622 009	...	...	307 252	...	...	314 757	...	...
1 I 2013	ESDJ	622 777	...	...	307 700	...	...	315 077	...	...
1 I 2014[120]	ESDJ	621 521	...	...	307 155	...	...	314 366	...	...
Netherlands - Pays-Bas										
1 VII 2005	ESDJ	16 319 868	10 764 171	66.0	8 071 693	5 292 532	65.6	8 248 175	5 471 640	66.3
1 VII 2006	ESDJ	16 346 101	10 803 902	66.1	8 082 961	5 311 812	65.7	8 263 141	5 492 090	66.5
1 VII 2007	ESDJ	16 381 696	10 825 307	66.1	8 100 294	5 322 596	65.7	8 281 402	5 502 712	66.4
1 VII 2008	ESDJ	16 445 593	10 877 858	66.1	8 134 235	5 350 572	65.8	8 311 359	5 527 286	66.5
1 VII 2009	ESDJ	16 530 388	10 938 780	66.2	8 179 936	5 383 776	65.8	8 350 452	5 555 004	66.5
1 VII 2010	ESDJ	16 615 394	11 096 288	66.8	8 223 479	5 464 083	66.4	8 391 915	5 632 205	67.1
1 VII 2011	ESDJ	16 693 074	...	...	8 263 177	...	...	8 429 897	...	...
1 VII 2012	ESDJ	16 754 962	...	...	8 295 105	...	...	8 459 857	...	...
1 I 2013	ESDJ	16 779 575	...	...	8 307 339	...	...	8 472 236	...	...
1 I 2014[123]	ESDJ	16 829 289	...	...	8 334 385	...	...	8 494 904	...	...
Norway - Norvège[128]										
1 VII 2005	ESDJ	4 623 291	...	...	2 293 026	...	...	2 330 266	...	...
1 VII 2006	ESDJ	4 660 677	...	...	2 313 885	...	...	2 346 792	...	...
1 VII 2007	ESDJ	4 709 153	...	...	2 342 739	...	...	2 366 414	...	...
1 VII 2008	ESDJ	4 768 212	...	...	2 377 372	...	...	2 390 840	...	...
1 VII 2009	ESDJ	4 828 726	...	...	2 410 903	...	...	2 417 823	...	...
1 VII 2010	ESDJ	4 889 252	...	...	2 443 801	...	...	2 445 452	...	...
1 VII 2011	ESDJ	4 953 088	...	...	2 479 860	...	...	2 473 228	...	...
19 XI 2011[38]	CDJC	4 979 955	3 951 427[79]	79.3	2 495 777	1 959 424[79]	78.5	2 484 178	1 992 003[79]	80.2
1 VII 2012	ESDJ	5 018 573	...	...	2 517 390	...	...	2 501 183	...	...
1 VII 2013[120]	ESDJ	5 079 623	...	...	2 551 458	...	...	2 528 165	...	...
1 I 2014[120]	ESDJ	5 107 970	...	...	2 567 007	...	...	2 540 963	...	...
Poland - Pologne[129]										
1 VII 2005	ESDJ	38 161 313	23 450 597	61.5	18 460 730	11 135 706	60.3	19 700 583	12 314 891	62.5
1 VII 2006	ESDJ	38 132 177	23 400 565	61.4	18 436 101	11 103 869	60.2	19 696 176	12 296 696	62.4
1 VII 2007	ESDJ	38 115 967	23 350 920	61.3	18 417 074	11 070 886	60.1	19 698 893	12 280 034	62.3
1 VII 2008	ESDJ	38 115 909	23 305 018	61.1	18 408 405	11 041 359	60.0	19 707 504	12 263 659	62.2
1 VII 2009	ESDJ	38 153 389	23 293 906	61.1	18 423 343	11 032 562	59.9	19 730 046	12 261 344	62.1
1 VII 2010	ESDJ	38 516 689	23 448 497	60.9	18 647 604	11 136 164	59.7	19 869 085	12 312 333	62.0
31 III 2011	CDJC	38 044 565	23 116 673	60.8	18 420 389	10 977 424	59.6	19 624 176	12 139 249	61.9
1 VII 2011	ESDJ	38 525 670	23 404 926	60.8	18 650 105	11 111 443	59.6	19 875 565	12 293 483	61.9
1 VII 2012	ESDJ	38 533 789	23 360 022	60.6	18 651 441	11 086 177	59.4	19 882 348	12 273 845	61.7
1 VII 2013[120]	ESDJ	38 275 578	...	...	18 526 649	...	...	19 748 929	...	...
1 I 2014[120]	ESDJ	38 017 856	...	...	18 403 964	...	...	19 613 892	...	...

Continent, country or area, and date / Continent, pays ou zone et date	Code[a]	Both sexes - Les deux sexes			Male - Masculin			Female - Féminin		
		Total	Urban - Urbaine		Total	Urban - Urbaine		Total	Urban - Urbaine	
			Number Nombre	Percent P.100		Number Nombre	Percent P.100		Number Nombre	Percent P.100
EUROPE										
Portugal										
1 VII 2005	ESDJ	10 503 330	...	...	5 056 268	...	...	5 447 063	...	...
1 VII 2006	ESDJ	10 522 288	...	...	5 061 604	...	...	5 460 684	...	...
1 VII 2007	ESDJ	10 542 964	...	...	5 067 071	...	...	5 475 893	...	...
1 VII 2008	ESDJ	10 558 177	...	...	5 067 993	...	...	5 490 184	...	...
1 VII 2009	ESDJ	10 568 247	...	...	5 064 992	...	...	5 503 255	...	...
1 VII 2010	ESDJ	10 573 100	...	...	5 058 644	...	...	5 514 456	...	...
21 III 2011	CDFC	10 282 306	6 286 712	61.1	4 868 755	2 949 862	60.6	5 413 551	3 336 850	61.6
1 VII 2011	ESDJ	10 557 560	...	...	5 041 990	...	...	5 515 570	...	...
1 VII 2012	ESDJ	10 514 844	...	...	5 013 067	...	...	5 501 777	...	...
1 VII 2013	ESDJ	10 457 295	...	...	4 976 859	...	...	5 480 437	...	...
1 I 2014[120]	ESDJ	10 427 301	...	...	4 958 020	...	...	5 469 281	...	...
Republic of Moldova - République de Moldova[130]										
1 VII 2005	ESDJ	3 595 187	1 472 929	41.0	1 722 105	710 796	41.3	1 873 082	762 133	40.7
1 VII 2006	ESDJ	3 585 209	1 481 398	41.3	1 720 139	706 649	41.1	1 865 070	774 749	41.5
1 VII 2007	ESDJ	3 576 910	1 477 062	41.3	1 719 246	694 308	40.4	1 857 664	782 754	42.1
1 VII 2008	ESDJ	3 570 108	1 475 609	41.3	1 716 195	693 550	40.4	1 853 913	782 059	42.2
1 VII 2009	ESDJ	3 565 604	1 476 390	41.4	1 714 209	694 134	40.5	1 851 395	782 257	42.3
1 VII 2010	ESDJ	3 562 045	1 479 196	41.5	1 712 783	695 603	40.6	1 849 262	783 593	42.4
1 VII 2011	ESDJ	3 559 986	1 483 731	41.7	1 711 916	697 492	40.7	1 848 070	786 239	42.5
1 VII 2012	ESDJ	3 559 520	1 488 966	41.8	1 712 036	699 880	40.9	1 847 484	789 086	42.7
1 I 2014	ESDJ	3 559 497	...	...	1 712 346	...	...	1 847 151	...	...
Romania - Roumanie										
1 VII 2005	ESDJ	21 319 673	11 732 958	55.0	10 384 483	5 629 594	54.2	10 935 190	6 103 364	55.8
1 VII 2006	ESDJ	21 193 749	11 748 344	55.4	10 320 907	5 630 452	54.6	10 872 842	6 117 892	56.3
1 VII 2007	ESDJ	20 882 980	11 455 494	54.9	10 169 596	5 489 050	54.0	10 713 384	5 966 444	55.7
1 VII 2008	ESDJ	20 537 848	11 102 802	54.1	10 000 515	5 314 752	53.1	10 537 333	5 788 050	54.9
1 VII 2009	ESDJ	20 367 437	10 976 558	53.9	9 916 107	5 249 975	52.9	10 451 330	5 726 583	54.8
1 VII 2010	ESDJ	20 246 798	10 922 169	53.9	9 856 669	5 223 471	53.0	10 390 129	5 698 698	54.8
1 VII 2011	ESDJ	20 147 657	10 878 099	54.0	9 805 108	5 198 460	53.0	10 342 549	5 679 639	54.9
20 X 2011	CDFC	20 039 141	10 858 790	54.2	9 736 342	5 185 636	53.3	10 302 799	5 673 154	55.1
1 VII 2012	ESDJ	20 060 182	10 823 218	54.0	9 770 353	5 170 875	52.9	10 289 829	5 652 343	54.9
1 VII 2013	ESDJ	19 985 814	10 770 879	53.9	9 754 851	5 152 718	52.8	10 230 963	5 618 161	54.9
1 I 2014[120]	ESDJ	19 947 311	...	...	9 746 052	...	...	10 201 259	...	...
Russian Federation - Fédération de Russie										
1 VII 2005	ESDJ	143 518 814	105 000 366	73.2	66 498 963	48 169 679	72.4	77 019 851	56 830 687	73.8
1 VII 2006	ESDJ	143 049 637	104 775 157	73.2	66 176 725	47 967 026	72.5	76 872 912	56 808 131	73.9
1 VII 2007	ESDJ	142 805 114	104 798 401	73.4	66 013 796	47 923 326	72.6	76 791 318	56 875 075	74.1
1 VII 2008	ESDJ	142 742 366	104 890 297	73.5	65 968 338	47 938 815	72.7	76 774 028	56 951 482	74.2
1 VII 2009	ESDJ	142 785 349	104 988 448	73.5	65 988 356	47 969 474	72.7	76 796 993	57 018 974	74.2
1 VII 2010	ESDJ	142 849 468	105 241 319	73.7	66 033 070	48 081 267	72.8	76 816 398	57 160 052	74.4
14 X 2010	CDFC	143 436 145	...	...	66 457 074	...	...	76 979 071	...	...
1 VII 2011	ESDJ	142 960 908	105 581 615	73.9	66 113 269	48 243 019	73.0	76 847 639	57 338 596	74.6
1 VII 2012	ESDJ	143 201 730	105 930 122	74.0	66 264 910	48 419 208	73.1	76 936 820	57 510 914	74.8
San Marino - Saint-Marin										
1 VII 2005[38]	ESDF	29 836	...	...	14 625	...	...	15 212	...	...
1 VII 2006[38]	ESDF	30 184	...	...	14 814	...	...	15 370	...	...
1 VII 2007[38]	ESDF	31 211	...	...	15 664	...	...	15 547	...	...
1 VII 2008[38]	ESDF	31 662	...	...	15 874	...	...	15 788	...	...
1 VII 2009[38]	ESDF	33 066	...	...	16 088	...	...	16 978	...	...
1 VII 2010[38]	ESDF	33 270	...	...	16 171	...	...	17 099	...	...
7 XI 2010*	CDFC	30 652	...	...	14 791[9]	...	...	15 818[9]	...	...
1 VII 2011[38]	ESDF	33 389	...	...	16 221	...	...	17 169	...	...
1 VII 2012[38]	ESDF	33 518	...	...	16 296	...	...	17 222	...	...
1 VII 2013[38]	ESDF	33 469	...	...	16 280	...	...	17 189	...	...
1 VII 2014[38]	ESDF	33 648	...	...	16 396	...	...	17 252	...	...
Serbia - Serbie[131]										
1 VII 2005	ESDJ	7 440 769	4 257 880	57.2	3 618 040	2 033 179	56.2	3 822 729	2 224 701	58.2
1 VII 2006	ESDJ	7 411 569	4 263 386	57.5	3 603 698	2 034 616	56.5	3 807 871	2 228 770	58.5
1 VII 2007	ESDJ	7 381 579	4 270 400	57.9	3 588 957	2 037 012	56.8	3 792 622	2 233 388	58.9
1 VII 2008	ESDJ	7 350 222	4 275 245	58.2	3 573 814	2 038 642	57.0	3 776 408	2 236 603	59.2
1 VII 2009	ESDJ	7 320 807	4 279 035	58.5	3 560 048	2 039 934	57.3	3 760 759	2 239 101	59.5

Continent, country or area, and date / Continent, pays ou zone et date	Code[a]	Both sexes - Les deux sexes			Male - Masculin			Female - Féminin		
		Total	Urban - Urbaine		Total	Urban - Urbaine		Total	Urban - Urbaine	
			Number Nombre	Percent P.100		Number Nombre	Percent P.100		Number Nombre	Percent P.100
EUROPE										
Serbia - Serbie[131]										
1 VII 2010 .... ESDJ		7 291 436	4 283 985	58.8	3 546 374	2 041 975	57.6	3 745 062	2 242 010	59.9
1 VII 2011[15] .... ESDJ		7 234 099	4 284 218	59.2	3 522 690	2 045 719	58.1	3 711 409	2 238 499	60.3
1 X 2011 .... CDJC		7 186 862	4 271 872	59.4	3 499 176	2 039 105	58.3	3 687 686	2 232 767	60.5
1 VII 2012[15] .... ESDJ		7 199 077	4 271 615	59.3	3 505 713	2 040 826	58.2	3 693 364	2 230 789	60.4
1 VII 2013[15] .... ESDJ		7 164 132	4 272 059	59.6	3 488 466	2 037 550	58.4	3 675 666	2 234 509	60.8
1 I 2014[120] .... ESDJ		7 146 759	...	...	3 479 863	...	...	3 666 896	...	...
Slovakia - Slovaquie										
1 VII 2005 .... ESDJ		5 372 807	...	...	2 609 440	...	...	2 763 367	...	...
1 VII 2006 .... ESDJ		5 373 054	...	...	2 610 255	...	...	2 762 799	...	...
1 VII 2007 .... ESDJ		5 374 622	...	...	2 612 172	...	...	2 762 451	...	...
1 VII 2008 .... ESDJ		5 379 233	...	...	2 616 013	...	...	2 763 220	...	...
1 VII 2009 .... ESDJ		5 386 406	...	...	2 620 942	...	...	2 765 464	...	...
1 VII 2010 .... ESDJ		5 391 428	...	...	2 624 360	...	...	2 767 069	...	...
21 V 2011 .... CDJC		5 397 036	2 937 735	54.4	2 627 772	1 412 818	53.8	2 769 264	1 524 917	55.1
1 VII 2011 .... ESDJ		5 398 384	2 938 053	54.4	2 628 463	1 412 966	53.8	2 769 922	1 525 087	55.1
1 VII 2012 .... ESDJ		5 407 579	2 935 710	54.3	2 633 866	1 411 738	53.6	2 773 714	1 523 972	54.9
1 VII 2013 .... ESDJ		5 413 393	2 931 444	54.2	2 637 520	1 409 503	53.4	2 775 873	1 521 941	54.8
1 I 2014[120] .... ESDJ		5 415 949	...	...	2 639 060	...	...	2 776 889	...	...
Slovenia - Slovénie										
1 VII 2005 .... ESDJ		2 001 114	965 538[132]	48.3	980 070[132]	457 869[132]	46.7	1 021 044[132]	507 669[132]	49.7
1 VII 2006 .... ESDJ		2 008 516	962 740[132]	47.9	985 876[132]	456 764[132]	46.3	1 022 640[132]	505 976[132]	49.5
1 VII 2007 .... ESDJ		2 019 406	1 006 767	49.9	995 125	490 610	49.3	1 024 281	516 157	50.4
1 VII 2008 .... ESDJ		2 022 629	1 012 477	50.1	996 969	491 605	49.3	1 025 660	520 872	50.8
1 VII 2009 .... ESDJ		2 042 335	1 024 087	50.1	1 011 767	500 253	49.4	1 030 568	523 834	50.8
1 VII 2010 .... ESDJ		2 049 261	1 024 812	50.0	1 014 716	500 063	49.3	1 034 545	524 749	50.7
1 I 2011 .... CDFC		2 058 051	1 030 172	50.1	1 019 826	503 083	49.3	1 038 225	527 089	50.8
1 VII 2011 .... ESDJ		2 052 496	1 023 650	49.9	1 015 430	498 490	49.1	1 037 066	525 160	50.6
1 VII 2012 .... ESDJ		2 056 262	1 023 236	49.8	1 017 414	498 297	49.0	1 038 848	524 939	50.5
1 VII 2013 .... ESDJ		2 059 114	1 047 560	50.9	1 019 658	513 084	50.3	1 039 456	534 476	51.4
1 I 2014[133] .... ESDJ		2 061 085	...	...	1 020 874	...	...	1 040 211	...	...
Spain - Espagne										
1 VII 2005 .... ESDJ		43 662 617	...	...	21 541 969	...	...	22 120 648	...	...
1 VII 2006 .... ESDJ		44 360 525	...	...	21 900 707	...	...	22 459 818	...	...
1 VII 2007 .... ESDJ		45 236 002	...	...	22 362 075	...	...	22 873 927	...	...
1 VII 2008 .... ESDJ		45 983 167	...	...	22 756 861	...	...	23 226 306	...	...
1 VII 2009 .... ESDJ		46 367 545	...	...	22 934 497	...	...	23 433 048	...	...
1 VII 2010 .... ESDJ		46 562 486	...	...	23 008 587	...	...	23 553 899	...	...
1 VII 2011 .... ESDJ		46 736 255	...	...	23 073 274	...	...	23 662 981	...	...
1 XI 2011 .... CDJC		46 815 915	...	...	23 104 350	...	...	23 711 560	...	...
1 VII 2012 .... ESDJ		46 766 399	...	...	23 055 715	...	...	23 710 684	...	...
1 VII 2013 .... ESDJ		46 593 236	...	...	22 933 751	...	...	23 659 485	...	...
1 I 2014[123] .... ESDJ		46 512 199	...	...	22 877 461	...	...	23 634 738	...	...
Sweden - Suède										
1 VII 2005[38] .... ESDJ		9 029 572	...	...	4 476 431	...	...	4 553 142	...	...
1 VII 2006[38] .... ESDJ		9 080 505	...	...	4 505 037	...	...	4 575 468	...	...
1 VII 2007[38] .... ESDJ		9 148 092	...	...	4 543 722	...	...	4 604 370	...	...
1 VII 2008[38] .... ESDJ		9 219 637	...	...	4 583 816	...	...	4 635 822	...	...
1 VII 2009[38] .... ESDJ		9 298 515	...	...	4 626 362	...	...	4 672 153	...	...
1 VII 2010[38] .... ESDJ		9 378 126	...	...	4 669 629	...	...	4 708 497	...	...
1 VII 2011[38] .... ESDJ		9 449 213	...	...	4 708 539	...	...	4 740 674	...	...
31 XII 2011[38] .... CDJC		9 482 855	...	...	4 726 834	...	...	4 756 021	...	...
1 VII 2012[38] .... ESDJ		9 519 375	...	...	4 746 370	...	...	4 773 005	...	...
1 VII 2013[123] .... ESDJ		9 600 379	...	...	4 790 131	...	...	4 810 248	...	...
1 I 2014[123] .... ESDJ		9 644 864	...	...	4 814 357	...	...	4 830 507	...	...
Switzerland - Suisse										
1 VII 2005 .... ESDJ		7 437 116	5 452 361	73.3	3 640 600	2 650 983	72.8	3 796 516	2 801 378	73.8
1 VII 2006 .... ESDJ		7 483 935	5 489 614	73.4	3 665 931	2 671 318	72.9	3 818 004	2 818 296	73.8
1 VII 2007 .... ESDJ		7 551 117	5 543 848	73.4	3 703 187	2 701 296	72.9	3 847 930	2 842 552	73.9
1 VII 2008 .... ESDJ		7 647 675	5 622 042	73.5	3 756 845	2 744 671	73.1	3 890 831	2 877 371	74.0
1 VII 2009 .... ESDJ		7 743 832	5 699 003	73.6	3 808 621	2 786 186	73.2	3 935 211	2 912 817	74.0
1 VII 2010 .... ESDJ		7 824 909	...	...	3 851 027	...	...	3 973 882	...	...
1 VII 2011 .... ESDJ		7 912 398	5 831 864	73.7	3 899 840	2 857 476	73.3	4 012 559	2 974 388	74.1
31 XII 2011 .... CDFC		8 035 391	5 920 706	73.7	3 973 280	2 909 793	73.2	4 062 111	3 010 913	74.1
1 VII 2012 .... ESDJ		7 996 861	5 896 568	73.7	3 945 389	2 892 243	73.3	4 051 473	3 004 325	74.2

Continent, country or area, and date / Continent, pays ou zone et date	Code[a]	Both sexes - Les deux sexes			Male - Masculin			Female - Féminin		
		Total	Urban - Urbaine		Total	Urban - Urbaine		Total	Urban - Urbaine	
			Number Nombre	Percent P.100		Number Nombre	Percent P.100		Number Nombre	Percent P.100
EUROPE										
Switzerland - Suisse										
1 VII 2013[125]	ESDJ	8 089 346	...	...	3 995 308	...	...	4 094 038	...	...
1 I 2014[125]	ESDJ	8 139 631	...	...	4 022 091	...	...	4 117 540	...	...
TFYR of Macedonia - L'ex-R. y. de Macédoine										
1 VII 2005	ESDF	2 036 855	...	...	1 021 772	...	...	1 015 083	...	...
1 VII 2006	ESDF	2 040 228	...	...	1 023 069	...	...	1 017 159	...	...
1 VII 2007	ESDF	2 043 559	...	...	1 024 489	...	...	1 019 070	...	...
1 VII 2008	ESDF	2 046 898	...	...	1 026 022	...	...	1 020 876	...	...
1 VII 2009	ESDF	2 050 671	...	...	1 027 810	...	...	1 022 861	...	...
1 VII 2010	ESDF	2 055 004	...	...	1 029 848	...	...	1 025 156	...	...
1 VII 2011	ESDF	2 058 539	...	...	1 031 403	...	...	1 027 136	...	...
1 VII 2012	ESDF	2 061 044	...	...	1 032 532	...	...	1 028 512	...	...
1 VII 2013	ESDF	2 064 032	...	...	1 033 990	...	...	1 030 042	...	...
1 I 2014	ESDF	2 065 769	...	...	1 034 841	...	...	1 030 928	...	...
Ukraine										
1 VII 2005	ESDF	47 105 171	31 943 515	67.8	21 770 304	14 698 072	67.5	25 334 867	17 245 443	68.1
1 VII 2006	ESDF	46 787 786	31 827 539	68.0	21 610 648	14 628 495	67.7	25 177 138	17 199 044	68.3
1 VII 2007	ESDF	46 509 355	31 723 062	68.2	21 472 153	14 567 851	67.8	25 037 202	17 155 212	68.5
1 VII 2008	ESDF	46 258 189	31 627 980	68.4	21 347 279	14 512 344	68.0	24 910 910	17 115 637	68.7
1 VII 2009	ESDF	46 053 307	31 556 002	68.5	...	...	...	...	...	...
1 VII 2010	ESDF	45 870 741	31 483 222	68.6	21 175 816	14 436 554	68.2	24 694 925	17 046 668	69.0
1 VII 2011	ESDF	45 706 086	31 411 262	68.7	21 110 638	14 401 999	68.2	24 595 448	17 009 263	69.2
1 VII 2012	ESDF	45 593 342	31 379 757	68.8	21 075 702	14 392 490	68.3	24 517 640	16 987 267	69.3
1 I 2013	ESDF	45 553 047	31 378 639	68.9	21 068 718	14 397 904	68.3	24 484 329	16 980 735	69.4
United Kingdom of Great Britain and Northern Ireland - Royaume-Uni de Grande-Bretagne et d'Irlande du Nord[134]										
1 VII 2005	ESDJ	60 413 276	...	...	29 540 981	...	...	30 872 295	...	...
1 VII 2006	ESDJ	60 827 067	...	...	29 761 579	...	...	31 065 488	...	...
1 VII 2007	ESDJ	61 319 075	...	...	30 027 882	...	...	31 291 193	...	...
1 VII 2008	ESDJ	61 823 772	...	...	30 300 623	...	...	31 523 149	...	...
1 VII 2009	ESDJ	62 260 486	...	...	30 532 212	...	...	31 728 274	...	...
1 VII 2010	ESDJ	62 759 456	...	...	30 805 493	...	...	31 953 963	...	...
27 III 2011	CDFC	63 379 787	51 399 714	81.1	31 126 054	25 214 631	81.0	32 253 733	26 185 083	81.2
1 VII 2011	ESDJ	63 285 145	...	...	31 097 259	...	...	32 187 886	...	...
1 VII 2012	ESDJ	63 705 030	...	...	31 315 072	...	...	32 389 958	...	...
1 VII 2013[120]	ESDJ	64 102 166	...	...	31 535 963	...	...	32 566 204	...	...
1 I 2014[120]	ESDJ	64 308 261	...	...	31 648 586	...	...	32 659 675	...	...
OCEANIA - OCÉANIE										
American Samoa - Samoas américaines[43]										
1 IV 2010	CDJC	55 519	...	...	28 164	...	...	27 355	...	...
Australia - Australie										
1 VII 2005	ESDJ	20 176 844	17 062 242	84.6	10 019 633	8 425 486	84.1	10 157 211	8 636 756	85.0
1 VII 2006	ESDJ	20 450 966	17 316 174	84.7	10 159 424	8 555 046	84.2	10 291 542	8 761 128	85.1
8 VIII 2006[135]	CDFC	20 061 646[136]	17 670 009	88.1	9 896 500[136]	8 651 811	87.4	10 165 146[136]	9 018 198	88.7
1 VII 2007	ESDJ	20 827 622	17 666 467	84.8	10 353 636	8 734 627	84.4	10 473 986	8 931 840	85.3
1 VII 2008	ESDJ	21 249 199	18 052 915	85.0	10 572 045	8 934 070	84.5	10 677 154	9 118 845	85.4
1 VII 2009	ESDJ	21 691 653	18 453 978	85.1	10 800 797	9 141 216	84.6	10 890 856	9 312 762	85.5
1 VII 2010	ESDJ	22 031 750	18 762 982	85.2	10 967 831	9 292 721	84.7	11 063 919	9 470 261	85.6
1 VII 2011	ESDJ	22 340 024	19 046 939	85.3	11 118 234	9 431 506	84.8	11 221 790	9 615 433	85.7
9 VIII 2011[135]	CDFC	21 727 158[136]	19 312 642	88.9	10 737 148[136]	9 471 918	88.2	10 990 010[136]	9 840 724	89.5
1 VII 2012	ESDJ	22 728 254	19 402 437	85.4	11 312 823	9 608 375	84.9	11 415 431	9 794 062	85.8
1 VII 2013	ESDJ	23 135 281	19 778 495	85.5	11 518 199	9 796 858	85.1	11 617 082	9 981 637	85.9
1 VII 2014*	ESDJ	23 490 736	...	...	11 692 500	...	...	11 798 236	...	...

Continent, country or area, and date / Continent, pays ou zone et date	Code[a]	Both sexes - Les deux sexes			Male - Masculin			Female - Féminin		
		Total	Urban - Urbaine		Total	Urban - Urbaine		Total	Urban - Urbaine	
			Number Nombre	Percent P.100		Number Nombre	Percent P.100		Number Nombre	Percent P.100
OCEANIA - OCÉANIE										
Cook Islands - Îles Cook[137]										
1 XII 2006 ....CDFC		19 342	...	...	9 816	...	...	9 526	...	...
1 XII 2011 ....CDFC		17 794	...	...	8 815	...	...	8 979	...	...
Fiji - Fidji										
16 IX 2007 ....CDFC		837 271	424 846	50.7	427 176	212 454	49.7	410 095	212 392	51.8
1 VII 2008 ....ESDF		841 351	426 931	50.7	...	...	...	...	...	...
1 VII 2010 ....ESDF		857 000	446 000	52.0	...	...	...	...	...	...
French Polynesia - Polynésie française										
20 VIII 2007 ....CDJC		259 706	...	...	133 109	...	...	126 597	...	...
1 I 2009 ....ESDF		264 000	...	...	135 200	...	...	128 800	...	...
1 I 2011.....................ESDF		269 989	...	...	138 127	...	...	131 862	...	...
22 VIII 2012 ....CDJC		268 207	...	...	136 996	...	...	131 211	...	...
Guam										
1 VII 2005[138]..............ESDJ		158 398	...	...	80 744	...	...	77 654	...	...
1 VII 2006[138]..............ESDJ		158 711	...	...	80 851	...	...	77 860	...	...
1 VII 2007[138]..............ESDJ		158 967	...	...	80 930	...	...	78 037	...	...
1 VII 2008[138]..............ESDJ		159 169	...	...	80 982	...	...	78 187	...	...
1 VII 2009[138]..............ESDJ		159 323	...	...	81 010	...	...	78 313	...	...
1 IV 2010 ....CDJC		159 358	149 918	94.1	81 552	...	...	77 806	...	...
1 VII 2011[138]..............ESDJ		159 600	...	...	81 053	...	...	78 547	...	...
1 VII 2012[138]..............ESDJ		159 914	...	...	81 165	...	...	78 749	...	...
1 VII 2013[138]..............ESDJ		160 378	...	...	81 354	...	...	79 024	...	...
1 VII 2014[138]..............ESDJ		161 001	...	...	81 625	...	...	79 376	...	...
Kiribati										
7 XII 2005 ....CDFC		92 533	40 311	43.6	45 612	19 435	42.6	46 921	20 876	44.5
10 X 2010 ....CDFC		103 058	...	...	50 796	...	...	52 262	...	...
Marshall Islands - Îles Marshall										
1 VII 2006[139]..............ESDF		52 163	...	...	26 746	...	...	25 417	...	...
1 VII 2007[139]..............ESDF		52 701	...	...	27 022	...	...	25 679	...	...
1 VII 2008[139]..............ESDF		53 236	...	...	27 297	...	...	25 939	...	...
1 VII 2009[139]..............ESDF		53 763	...	...	27 567	...	...	26 196	...	...
1 VII 2010[139]..............ESDF		54 305	...	...	27 843	...	...	26 462	...	...
3 IV 2011 ....CDFC		53 158	...	...	27 243	...	...	25 915	...	...
Micronesia (Federated States of) - Micronésie (États fédérés de)										
1 VII 2005[2]..................ESDJ		107 885	...	...	54 419	...	...	53 466	...	...
1 VII 2006[2]..................ESDJ		107 965	...	...	54 411	...	...	53 554	...	...
1 VII 2007[2]..................ESDJ		108 031	...	...	54 403	...	...	53 628	...	...
1 VII 2008[2]..................ESDJ		108 026	...	...	54 350	...	...	53 676	...	...
1 VII 2009[2]..................ESDJ		107 973	...	...	54 275	...	...	53 698	...	...
1 IV 2010 ....CDJC		102 843	22 924	22.3	52 193	...	...	50 650	...	...
1 VII 2010[2]..................ESDJ		107 839	...	...	54 158	...	...	53 681	...	...
1 VII 2011[2]..................ESDJ		107 581	...	...	53 975	...	...	53 606	...	...
1 VII 2012[2]..................ESDJ		107 249	...	...	53 749	...	...	53 500	...	...
1 VII 2013[2]..................ESDJ		106 841	...	...	53 488	...	...	53 353	...	...
1 VII 2014[2]..................ESDJ		106 374	...	...	53 200	...	...	53 174	...	...
Nauru										
31 X 2011* ....CDFC		10 086	...	...	5 105	...	...	4 979	...	...
New Caledonia - Nouvelle-Calédonie										
1 I 2005 ....ESDF		232 258	...	...	117 221	...	...	115 037	...	...
1 I 2006 ....ESDF		236 528	...	...	119 415	...	...	117 113	...	...
1 I 2007 ....ESDF		240 390	150 831	62.7	121 299	...	...	119 091	...	...
1 VII 2008 ....ESDF		242 400	...	...	122 261	...	...	120 139	...	...
27 VII 2009 ....CDFC		245 580	...	...	124 524	...	...	121 056	...	...
1 VII 2010 ....ESDF		250 040	...	...	126 771	...	...	123 269	...	...
1 I 2013 ....ESDF		260 000	...	...	131 481	...	...	128 519	...	...
New Zealand - Nouvelle-Zélande										
1 VII 2005[28] ....ESDJ		4 133 900	3 562 300[140]	86.2	2 025 200	1 731 100[140]	85.5	2 108 700	1 831 200[140]	86.8
7 III 2006[135] ....CDFC		4 143 282	...	...	2 021 277	...	...	2 122 005	...	...

Continent, country or area, and date / Continent, pays ou zone et date	Code[a]	Both sexes - Les deux sexes			Male - Masculin			Female - Féminin		
		Total	Urban - Urbaine		Total	Urban - Urbaine		Total	Urban - Urbaine	
			Number Nombre	Percent P.100		Number Nombre	Percent P.100		Number Nombre	Percent P.100
OCEANIA - OCÉANIE										
New Zealand - Nouvelle-Zélande										
1 VII 2006[28] ....ESDJ		4 184 600	3 606 700[140]	86.2	2 048 300	1 751 400[140]	85.5	2 136 200	1 855 300[140]	86.9
1 VII 2007[28] ....ESDJ		4 223 800	3 640 200[141]	86.2	2 066 400	1 766 900[141]	85.5	2 157 300	1 873 300[141]	86.8
1 VII 2008[28] ....ESDJ		4 259 800	3 669 100[141]	86.1	2 083 400	1 780 600[141]	85.5	2 176 300	1 888 600[141]	86.8
1 VII 2009[28] ....ESDJ		4 302 600	3 703 800[141]	86.1	2 104 700	1 797 800[141]	85.4	2 197 900	1 906 000[141]	86.7
1 VII 2010[28] ....ESDJ		4 350 700	3 743 300[141]	86.0	2 127 700	1 816 700[141]	85.4	2 222 900	1 926 600[141]	86.7
1 VII 2011[28] ....ESDJ		4 384 000	3 765 400[141]	85.9	2 143 600	1 826 900[141]	85.2	2 240 400	1 938 500[141]	86.5
1 VII 2012[28] ....ESDJ		4 408 100	3 784 600[141]	85.9	2 155 000	1 836 200[141]	85.2	2 253 100	1 948 500[141]	86.5
1 VII 2013[28] ....ESDJ		4 442 100	3 818 300[141]	86.0	2 172 200	1 853 100[141]	85.3	2 269 900	1 965 200[141]	86.6
1 VII 2014[28] ....ESDJ		4 509 700	3 884 000[141]	86.1	2 209 600	1 889 100[141]	85.5	2 300 200	1 995 000[141]	86.7
Niue - Nioué										
1 VII 2005 ....ESDJ		1 746	...	...	849	...	...	896	...	...
1 VII 2006 ....ESDJ		1 679	...	...	815	...	...	864	...	...
9 IX 2006 ....CDFC		1 625	...	...	802	...	...	823	...	...
1 VII 2010 ....ESDJ		1 496	...	...	754	...	...	740	...	...
11 IX 2011 ....CDFC		1 611	...	...	802	...	...	809	...	...
Norfolk Island - Île Norfolk										
8 VIII 2006 ....CDFC		2 523	...	...	1 218	...	...	1 305	...	...
9 VIII 2011 ....CDFC		2 302	...	...	1 082	...	...	1 220	...	...
Northern Mariana Islands - Îles Mariannes septentrionales										
1 VII 2005 ....ESDF		*70 636*	...	...	*32 093*	...	...	*38 543*	...	...
1 VII 2006 ....ESDF		*60 662*	...	...	*29 071*	...	...	*31 591*	...	...
1 VII 2007 ....ESDF		*58 629*	...	...	*28 124*	...	...	*30 505*	...	...
1 VII 2008 ....ESDF		*55 244*	...	...	*26 524*	...	...	*28 720*	...	...
1 VII 2009 ....ESDF		*51 484*	...	...	*24 738*	...	...	*26 746*	...	...
1 IV 2010 ....CDFC		53 883	...	...	27 746	...	...	26 137	...	...
1 VII 2010 ....ESDF		*48 317*	...	...	*23 231*	...	...	*25 086*	...	...
1 VII 2011 ....ESDF		*46 050*	...	...	*22 153*	...	...	*23 897*	...	...
Palau - Palaos										
1 IV 2005 ....CDJC		19 907	15 399	77.4	10 699	...	...	9 208		
Papua New Guinea - Papouasie-Nouvelle-Guinée										
10 VII 2011* ....CDFC		7 059 653	...	...	3 663 249	...	...	3 396 404		
Pitcairn										
31 XII 2007 ....ESDF		64[142]	...	...	37	...	...	27	...	...
31 XII 2008 ....ESDF		58[142]	...	...	30	...	...	28	...	...
10 VIII 2012 ....CDJC		48	...	...	22	...	...	26	...	...
31 XII 2013 ....CDJC		49	...	...	23	...	...	26	...	...
Samoa										
1 VII 2005 ....ESDF		*183 275*	*40 279*	*22.0*	*95 470*	*20 574*	*21.6*	*87 805*	*19 705*	*22.4*
1 VII 2006 ....ESDF		*184 955*	*40 648*	*22.0*	*96 345*	*20 763*	*21.6*	*88 610*	*19 885*	*22.4*
5 XI 2006 ....CDFC		180 741	37 708	20.9	93 677	19 120	20.4	87 064	18 588	21.3
1 VII 2007 ....ESDF		*181 588*	*37 878*	*20.9*	*94 101*	*19 206*	*20.4*	*87 458*	*18 672*	*21.3*
1 VII 2008 ....ESDF		*182 379*	*38 050*	*20.9*	*94 526*	*19 293*	*20.4*	*87 853*	*18 756*	*21.3*
1 VII 2009 ....ESDF		*183 204*	*38 222*	*20.9*	*94 953*	*19 381*	*20.4*	*88 250*	*18 841*	*21.3*
1 VII 2010 ....ESDF		*184 032*	*38 395*	*20.9*	*95 383*	*19 468*	*20.4*	*88 649*	*18 926*	*21.3*
1 VII 2011 ....ESDF		*184 864*	*38 568*	*20.9*	*95 814*	*19 556*	*20.4*	*89 050*	*19 012*	*21.3*
7 XI 2011 ....CDFC		187 820	36 735	19.6	96 990	18 485	19.1	90 830	18 250	20.1
1 VII 2012 ....ESDF		*189 236*	*36 540*	*19.3*	...	...	...	...	...	...
1 VII 2013 ....ESDF		*190 652*	*36 346*	*19.1*	...	...	...	...	...	...
Solomon Islands - Îles Salomon										
1 VII 2005[2] ....ESDF		*471 266*	...	...	*242 927*	...	...	*228 339*	...	...
1 VII 2006[2] ....ESDF		*483 083*	...	...	*248 944*	...	...	*234 139*	...	...
1 VII 2007[2] ....ESDF		*495 026*	...	...	*255 063*	...	...	*239 963*	...	...
1 VII 2008[2] ....ESDF		*506 992*	...	...	*261 214*	...	...	*245 778*	...	...
1 VII 2009[2] ....ESDF		*518 321*	...	...	*267 704*	...	...	*250 617*	...	...
22 XI 2009 ....CDFC		515 870	102 030	19.8	264 455	53 596	20.3	251 415	48 434	19.3
1 VII 2013[143] ....ESDF		*610 800*	...	...	*311 300*	...	...	*299 500*	...	...

6. Total and urban population by sex: 2005 - 2014
Population totale et population urbaine selon le sexe : 2005 - 2014 (continued - suite)

Continent, country or area, and date / Continent, pays ou zone et date	Code[a]	Both sexes - Les deux sexes			Male - Masculin			Female - Féminin		
		Total	Urban - Urbaine		Total	Urban - Urbaine		Total	Urban - Urbaine	
			Number Nombre	Percent P.100		Number Nombre	Percent P.100		Number Nombre	Percent P.100
OCEANIA - OCÉANIE										
Tokelau - Tokélaou										
19 X 2006 ....CDFC		1 151	...	...	583	...	...	568	...	...
18 X 2011 ....CDFC		1 205	...	...	600	...	...	605	...	...
1 XII 2013 ....ESDF		*1 383*	...	...	*683*	...	...	*700*	...	...
Tonga										
1 VII 2005[144] ....ESDF		*102 371*	...	...	*52 261*	...	...	*50 109*	...	...
1 VII 2006[144] ....ESDF		*102 907*	...	...	*52 561*	...	...	*50 346*	...	...
30 XI 2006 ....CDJC		101 991	23 658	23.2	51 772	11 860	22.9	50 219	11 798	23.5
1 VII 2007[144] ....ESDF		*103 289*	...	...	*52 771*	...	...	*50 518*	...	...
1 VII 2008[144] ....ESDF		*103 647*	...	...	*52 972*	...	...	*50 673*	...	...
30 XI 2011 ....CDJC		103 252	24 229	23.5	51 979	12 156	23.4	51 273	12 073	23.5
Tuvalu										
1 VII 2011 ....ESDF		*11 206*	...	...	*5 582*	...	...	*5 625*	...	...
1 VII 2013 ....ESDF		*10 900*	...	...	*5 600*	...	...	*5 400*	...	...
Vanuatu										
1 VII 2006[2] ....ESDF		*221 417*	...	...	*113 034*	...	...	*108 383*	...	...
16 XI 2009 ....CDJC		234 023	57 195	24.4	119 091	29 618	24.9	114 932	27 577	24.0
1 VII 2010 ....ESDF		*239 374*	...	...	*121 726*	...	...	*117 648*	...	...
1 VII 2011 ....ESDF		*244 847*	...	...	*124 420*	...	...	*120 427*	...	...
1 VII 2012 ....ESDF		*244 847*	...	...	*127 173*	...	...	*123 273*	...	...
1 VII 2013 ....ESDF		*264 652*	...	...	*135 170*	...	...	*129 483*	...	...
Wallis and Futuna Islands - Îles Wallis et Futuna										
21 VII 2008 ....CDFC		13 445	...	...	6 669	...	...	6 776	...	...

FOOTNOTES - NOTES

Italics: estimates which are less reliable. - Italiques : estimations moins sûres.

* Provisional. - Données provisoires.

[a] 'Code' indicates the source of data, as follows:
CDFC - Census, de facto, complete tabulation
CDFS - Census, de facto, sample tabulation
CDJC - Census, de jure, complete tabulation
CDJS - Census, de jure, sample tabulation
SSDF - Sample survey, de facto
SSDJ - Sample survey, de jure
ESDF - Estimates, de facto
ESDJ - Estimates, de jure

Le 'Code' indique la source des données, comme suit :
CDFC - Recensement, population de fait, tabulation complète
CDFS - Recensement, population de fait, tabulation par sondage
CDJC - Recensement, population de droit, tabulation complète
CDJS - Recensement, population de droit, tabulation par sondage
SSDF - Enquête par sondage, population de fait
SSDJ - Enquête par sondage, population de droit
ESDF - Estimations, population de fait
ESDJ - Estimations, population de droit

[1] Total resident population including common and collective households of nomadic population, and population counted separately. - Population résidente totale y compris les ménages ordinaires et collectifs de la population nomade, et la population comptée à part.
[2] Data refer to national projections. - Les données se réfèrent aux projections nationales.
[3] Based on the results of the 2006 Demographic Survey. - D'après les résultats de l'enquête Démographique par Sondage de 2006.
[4] Data based on the 2008 Population Census. - Données fondées sur le recensement de population de 2008.
[5] Projections based on the 1994 Population Census. - Projections fondées sur le recensement de la population de 1994.

[6] Based on the results of the Gabonese Survey for the Evaluation and Tracking of Poverty. - Sur base des résultats de l'enquête gabonaise sur l'évaluation et le suivi de la pauvreté.
[7] Post-censal estimates based on the 1999 Population Census. - Les estimations post-censitaire fondées sur le recensement de la population de 1999.
[8] Post-censal estimates based on the 2009 Population Census. - Les estimations post-censitaire fondées sur le recensement de la population de 2009.
[9] Figures for male and female may not add up to the total, since they do not include the category "Unknown". - La somme des chiffres indiqués pour les sexes masculin et féminin peut n'être pas égale au total parce qu'elle n'inclut pas la catégorie " inconnue ".
[10] Reason for discrepancy between these figures and corresponding figures shown elsewhere not ascertained. - On ne sait pas comment s'explique la divergence entre ces chiffres et les chiffres correspondants indiqués ailleurs.
[11] Data refer to national projections. Revised data. - Les données se réfèrent aux projections nationales. Données révisées.
[12] Including nomadic population. - Y compris la population nomade.
[13] Excludes the islands of St. Brandon and Agalega. - Non compris les îles St. Brandon et Agalega.
[14] Based on the results of the 2000 Population Census. - Basé sur les résultats du recencement de la population de 2000.
[15] Based on the results of the 2011 Population Census. - Basé sur les résultats du recencement de la population de 2011.
[16] Based on the results of the 2004 Population Census. - D'après des résultats du recensement de la population de 2004.
[17] Data refer to projections based on the 2011 Population Census. - Les données se réfèrent aux projections basées sur le recensement de la population de 2011.
[18] Based on the results of the 2012 Population and Housing Census. Data refer to national projections. - D'après les résultats du recensement de la population et des logements de 2012. Les données se réfèrent aux projections nationales.
[19] Data are projections based on the 2008 Population and Housing Census. - Projection basée sur le recensement 2008 de la population et des logements.
[20] Based on the results of a population count. - D'après les résultats d'un comptage de la population.

[21] The population figures are 264, 263 and 262 persons for 2007, 2008 and 2009 respectively. - La population est respectivement égale à 264, 263 et 262 personnes pour les années 2007, 2008 et 2009.

[22] Projections based on the 2002 Population Census. - Projections fondées sur le recensement de la population de 2002.

[23] Data have not been adjusted for underenumeration, estimated at 7 per cent. - Les données n'ont pas été ajustées pour compenser les lacunes du dénombrement, estimées à 7 p. 100.

[24] Data refer to projections based on the 2000 Population Census. - Les données se réfèrent aux projections basées sur le recensement de la population de 2000.

[25] Bermuda is 100 per cent urban. - 100 pour cent de la population des Bermudes est urbaine.

[26] Data refer to projections based on the 2010 Population Census. - Les données se réfèrent aux projections basées sur le recensement de la population de 2010.

[27] Final intercensal estimates. - Estimations inter-censitaires definitives.

[28] Because of rounding, totals are not in all cases the sum of the respective components. - Les chiffres étant arrondis, les totaux ne correspondent pas toujours rigoureusement à la somme des composants respectifs.

[29] Final postcensal estimates. - Estimations postcensitaires definitives.

[30] Updated postcensal estimates. - Estimations post censitaires mises à jour.

[31] Preliminary postcensal estimates. - Estimations post censitaires préliminaires.

[32] Excluding the institutional population. - Non compris la population dans les institutions.

[33] The source of data is the national household survey. - La source des données est l'enquête nationale des ménages.

[34] Based on the national household surveys 2010-2014 and the 2011 population census. - D'après les données de l'enquête nationale des ménages 2010-2014 et les résultats du recensement de la population de 2011.

[35] Intercensal estimates. - Estimations inter-censitaires.

[36] Postcensal estimates. - Estimations post censitaires.

[37] Estimates based on the 2007 Population Census. - Estimations fondées sur le recensement de la population de 2007.

[38] Population statistics are compiled from registers. - Les statistiques de la population sont compilées à partir des registres.

[39] Excluding data for Saint Barthélémy and Saint Martin. - Non compris les données pour Saint Barthélémy et Saint Martin.

[40] Projections produced by l'Institut Haïtien de Statistique et d'Informatique (IHSI) and the Latin American and Caribbean Demographic Centre (CELADE) - Population Division of ECLAC. - Les données sont projections produits par l'Institut Haïtien de Statistique et d'Informatique (IHSI) et le centre démographique de l'Amérique latine et les Caraïbes - Division de la population de la CEPALC.

[41] Data refer to projections based on the 2001 Population Census. - Les données se réfèrent aux projections basées sur le recensement de la population de 2001.

[42] Including an estimation of 1 334 585 persons corresponding to 448 195 housing units without information of the occupants. - Y compris une estimation de 1 334 585 personnes correspondant aux 448 195 unités d'habitation sans information sur les occupants.

[43] Including armed forces stationed in the area. - Y compris les militaires en garnison sur le territoire.

[44] Based on the results of the 2010 Population Census. - D'après le résultats du recensement de la population de 2010.

[45] Intercensal estimates. Excluding U.S. Armed Forces overseas and civilian U.S. citizens whose usual place of residence is outside the United States. - Estimations inter-censitaires. Non compris les militaires américains à l'étranger et les civils américains dont le lieu de résidence habituel est en dehors des États-Unis.

[46] Excluding U.S. Armed Forces overseas and civilian U.S. citizens whose usual place of residence is outside the United States. Postcensal estimates. - Non compris les militaires américains à l'étranger et les civils américains dont le lieu de résidence habituel est en dehors des États-Unis. Estimations post censitaires.

[47] Data refer to projections based on the 2010 Population and Housing Census. - Les données se réfèrent aux projections basées sur le recensement 2010 de la population et des logements.

[48] Data include persons in remote areas, military personnel outside the country, merchant seamen at sea, civilian seasonal workers outside the country, and other civilians outside the country, and exclude nomads, foreign military, civilian aliens temporarily in the country, transients on ships and Indian jungle population. - Y compris les personnes vivant dans des régions éloignées, le personel militaire en dehors du pays, les marins marchands, les ouvriers saisonniers en dehors du pays, et autres civils en dehors du pays, et non compris les nomades, les militaires étrangers, les étrangers civils temporairement dans le pays, les transiteurs sur des bateaux et les Indiens de la jungle.

[49] Data include persons in remote areas, military personnel outside the country, merchant seamen at sea, civilian seasonal workers outside the country, and other civilians outside the country, and exclude nomads, foreign military, civilian aliens temporarily in the country, transients on ships and Indian jungle population. Data refer to national projections. - Y compris les personnes vivant dans des régions éloignées, le personel militaire en dehors du pays, les marins marchands, les ouvriers saisonniers en dehors du pays, et autres civils en dehors du pays, et non compris les nomades, les militaires étrangers, les étrangers civils temporairement dans le pays, les transiteurs sur des bateaux et les Indiens de la jungle. Les données se réfèrent aux projections nationales.

[50] Data are revised projections taking into consideration also the results of the 2005 census. - Les données sont des projections révisées tenant compte également des résultats du recensement de 2005.

[51] Data refer to projections based on the 2010 Population Census. Excludes nomadic Indian tribes. - Les données se réfèrent aux projections basées sur le recensement de la population de 2010. Non compris les tribus d'Indiens nomades.

[52] A dispute exists between the governments of Argentina and the United Kingdom of Great Britain and Northern Ireland concerning sovereignty over the Falkland Islands (Malvinas). - La souveraineté sur les îles Falkland (Malvinas) fait l'objet d'un différend entre le Gouvernement argentin et le Gouvernement du Royaume-Uni de Grande-Bretagne et d'Irlande du Nord.

[53] The population for the year 2005 corresponds to the population actually enumerated in the census conducted between 18 July and 20 August 2005. The total (adjusted) population is 27 219 264 inhabitants. - La population pour 2005 correspond à la population effectivement dénombrée lors du recensement réalisé entre le 18 juillet et le 20 août 2005. La population totale (après ajustement) compte 27 219 264 habitants.

[54] Figures for male and female population do not add up to the figure for total population, because they exclude 108 homeless people of unknown sex. - Les chiffres relatifs à la population masculine et féminine ne correspondent pas au chiffre de la population totale, parce que l'on en a exclu 108 personnes sans toit dont le sexe n'est pas connu.

[55] Data refer to the settled population based on the 1979 Population Census and the latest household prelisting. The refugees of Afghanistan in Iran, Pakistan, and an estimated 1.5 million nomads, are not included. - Les données se rapportent à la population stationnaire sur la base du recensement de 1979 et du recensement préliminaire des logements le plus récent. Sont exclus les réfugiés d'Afghanistan en Iran et au Pakistan et les nomades estimés à 1,5 million.

[56] Data have been adjusted for underenumeration. - Les données ont été ajustées pour compenser les lacunes du dénombrement.

[57] Data refer to projected figures based on the Population and Housing Census 2005 (district projection). - Les données se réfèrent aux projections basées sur le recensement de la population et de l'habitat de 2005 (projections locales).

[58] Excluding foreign diplomatic personnel and their dependants. Based on the results of 1998 census. - Non compris le personnel diplomatique étranger et les membres de leur famille les accompagnant. A partir des résultats de recensement de l'année 1998.

[59] Excluding foreign diplomatic personnel and their dependants. - Non compris le personnel diplomatique étranger et les membres de leur famille les accompagnant.

[60] Excluding foreign diplomatic personnel and their dependants. Data based on the 2008 Population Census. - Non compris le personnel diplomatique étranger et les membres de leur famille les accompagnant. Données fondées sur le recensement de population de 2008.

[61] Based on the results of the Cambodia Intercensal Population Survey. Data exclude foreign diplomatic personnel and their dependants. - Sur la base de l'enquête intercensitaire de la population de Cambodge. Non compris le personnel diplomatique étranger et les membres de leur famille les accompagnant.

[62] For statistical purposes, the data for China do not include those for the Hong Kong Special Administrative Region (Hong Kong SAR), Macao Special Administrative Region (Macao SAR) and Taiwan province of China. - Pour la présentation des statistiques, les données pour la Chine ne comprennent pas la Région Administrative Spéciale de Hong Kong (Hong Kong RAS), la Région Administrative Spéciale de Macao (Macao RAS) et Taïwan province de Chine.

[63] Data have been estimated on the basis of the annual National Sample Survey on Population Changes. - Les données ont été estimées sur la base de l'enquête annuelle "National Sample Survey on Population Changes".

[64] The military personnel are classified as urban population. - Le personnel militaire est classé dans la population urbaine.

[65] The military personnel are classified as urban population. Because of rounding, totals are not in all cases the sum of the respective components. - Le personnel militaire est classé dans la population urbaine. Les chiffres étant

arrondis, les totaux ne correspondent pas toujours rigoureusement à la somme des composants respectifs.

[66] Data are from Communique of the National Bureau of Statistics of the People's Republic of China on Major Figures of the 2010 Population Census (No.1). - Données issues du communiqué du Bureau national de la statistique de la République populaire de Chine sur les chiffres importants du recensement de 2010 (n° 1).

[67] Data have been adjusted on the basis of the Population Census of 2010. - Les données ont été ajustées à partir des résultats du recensement de la population de 2010.

[68] Data are estimates from sample enquiry. Data refer to Hong Kong resident population at the census moment, which covers usual residents and mobile residents. Usual residents refer to two categories of people: (1) Hong Kong permanent residents who had stayed in Hong Kong for at least three months during the six months before or for at least three months during the six months after the census moment, regardless of whether they were in Hong Kong or not at the census moment; and (2) Hong Kong non-permanent residents who were in Hong Kong at the census moment. Mobile Residents, they are Hong Kong permanent residents who had stayed in Hong Kong for at least one month but less than three months during the six months before or for at least one month but less than three months during the six months after the census moment, regardless of whether they were in Hong Kong or not at the census moment. - Les données sont des chiffres estimatifs dérivés d'une enquête par sondage. Les données se rapportent à la population résidente à Hong Kong au moment du recensement. Cette population est composée des résidants habituels et des résidants mobiles. La population résidente est partagée en deux catégories: (1) les résidents permanents qui ont habité à Hong Kong au moins trois mois pendant les six mois précédents ou les six mois suivants le recensement; (2) les habitants non-permanents de Hong Kong qui étaient à Hong Kong au moment du recensement. La population mobile se rapporte aux résidents permanents de Hong Kong qui ont habité à Hong Kong pendant les six mois après le recensement pour une période comprise entre un mois et trois mois, indépendamment du fait qu'ils étaient à Hong Kong au moment du recensement au pays.

[69] Data refer to Hong Kong resident population at the census moment, which covers usual residents and mobile residents. Usual residents refer to two categories of people: (1) Hong Kong permanent residents who had stayed in Hong Kong for at least three months during the six months before or for at least three months during the six months after the census moment, regardless of whether they were in Hong Kong or not at the census moment; and (2) Hong Kong non-permanent residents who were in Hong Kong at the census moment. Mobile Residents, they are Hong Kong permanent residents who had stayed in Hong Kong for at least one month but less than three months during the six months before or for at least one month but less than three months during the six months after the census moment, regardless of whether they were in Hong Kong or not at the census moment. - Les données se rapportent à la population résidente à Hong Kong au moment du recensement. Cette population est composée des résidants habituels et des résidants mobiles. La population résidente est partagée en deux catégories: (1) les résidents permanents qui ont habité à Hong Kong au moins trois mois pendant les six mois précédents ou les six mois suivants le recensement; (2) les habitants non-permanents de Hong Kong qui étaient à Hong Kong au moment du recensement. La population mobile se rapporte aux résidents permanents de Hong Kong qui ont habité à Hong Kong pendant les six mois après le recensement pour une période comprise entre un mois et trois mois, indépendamment du fait qu'ils étaient à Hong Kong au moment du recensement au pays.

[70] Data refer to government controlled areas. - Les données se rapportent aux zones contrôlées par le Gouvernement.

[71] Data refer to annual average population. - Les données correspondent à la population annuelle moyenne.

[72] Includes data for the Indian-held part of Jammu and Kashmir, the final status of which has not yet been determined. - Y compris les données pour la partie du Jammu et du Cachemire occupée par l'Inde dont le statut définitif n'a pas encore été déterminé.

[73] Data refer to projections based on the 2001 Population Census. - Les données se réfèrent aux projections basées sur le recensement de la population de 2001.

[74] Data are based on the publication: "Indonesia Population Projection 2005-2015" - Les données sont basées sur la publication : << Indonesia Population Projection 2005-2015 >>

[75] Excluding Province Nanggroe Aceh Darussalam, Regency Nias & Nias Selatan, Regency Boven Digul & Teluk Wondama. Data refer to the "Intercensal Population Survey". - En excluant les provinces de Nanggroe Aceh Darussalam, Regency Nias & Nias Selatan, Regency Boven Digul & Teluk Wondama. Les données concernent l'enquête intercensitaire sur la population.

[76] Data are based on the publication: "Indonesia Population Projection 2010-2035" - Les données sont basées sur la publication : << Indonesia Population Projection 2010-2035 >>

[77] Data refer to the Iranian Year which begins on 21 March and ends on 20 March of the following year. - Les données concernent l'année iranienne, qui commence le 21 mars et se termine le 20 mars de l'année suivante.

[78] Differences between the total country figures and sum of urban and rural areas are due to the inclusion of unsettled population. - Les différences entre les chiffres pour l'ensemble du pays et la somme des zones urbaines et rurales s'expliquent par l'inclusion de la population non sédentaire.

[79] The total number may include 'Unknown residence', but the categories urban and rural do not. - Le nombre total peut inclure les personnes dont la résidence n'est pas connue, à l'inverse des catégories de population urbaine et rurale.

[80] Includes data for East Jerusalem and Israeli residents in certain other territories under occupation by Israeli military forces since June 1967. - Y compris les données pour Jérusalem-Est et les résidents israéliens dans certains autres territoires occupés depuis 1967 par les forces armées israéliennes.

[81] Because of rounding, totals are not in all cases the sum of the respective components. Excluding residents who had been registered in the Israeli localities (the Jewish localities) in the Gaza Area and northern Samaria, which were evacuated in August 2005, but did not notify the Ministry of Interior of their new address. These residents are included in total. - Les chiffres étant arrondis, les totaux ne correspondent pas toujours rigoureusement à la somme des composants respectifs. Hors résidents enregistrés dans les localités d'Israel (localités juives) de la Bande de Gaza (verfify) et du nord de la Samarie, qui ont été évacués en Août 2005, mais qui n'ont pas notifié leur nouvelle adresse au ministère de l'intérieur. Ces résidents sont inclus dans le total.

[82] Excluding residents who had been registered in the Israeli localities (the Jewish localities) in the Gaza Area and northern Samaria, which were evacuated in August 2005, but did not notify the Ministry of Interior of their new address. These residents are included in total. - Hors résidents enregistrés dans les localités d'Israel (localités juives) de la Bande de Gaza (verfify) et du nord de la Samarie, qui ont été évacués en Août 2005, mais qui n'ont pas notifié leur nouvelle adresse au ministère de l'intérieur. Ces résidents sont inclus dans le total.

[83] Data are rounded for confidentiality reasons. - Chiffres arrondis pour des raisons de confidentialité.

[84] Excluding diplomatic personnel outside the country and foreign military and civilian personnel and their dependants stationed in the area. - Non compris le personnel diplomatique hors du pays ni les militaires et agents civils étrangers en poste sur le territoire et les membres de leur famille les accompagnant.

[85] Estimates based on the complete counts of the 2010 Population Census. - Estimations basées sur le dénombrement complet du recensement de la population de 2010.

[86] Excluding data for Jordanian territory under occupation since June 1967 by Israeli military forces. Excluding foreigners, including registered Palestinian refugees. - Non compris les données pour le territoire jordanien occupé depuis juin 1967 par les forces armées israéliennes. Non compris les étrangers, mais y compris les réfugiés de Palestine enregistrés.

[87] Estimates based on the population census data of 2005 and 2011. - Estimations basées sur les données des recensements de la population de 2005 et 2011.

[88] Data are calculated from the results of the Population and Housing Census of 2009. - Les données sont calculées à partir des résultats du recensement de la population et de l'habitat de 2009.

[89] Excluding usual residents not in the country at the time of census. - À l'exclusion des résidents habituels qui ne sont pas dans le pays au moment du recensement.

[90] Based on the results of the 2005 Population and Housing Census. - Données fondées sur les résultats du recensement de la population et de l'habitat de 2005.

[91] Based on the results of a household survey. - D'après les résultats d'une enquête des ménages.

[92] Source: Living conditions of household survey, October 2011 to September 2012. - Source: Enquête sur les conditions de vie des ménages, octobre 2011 à septembre 2012.

[93] Intercensal Mid-Year Population Estimates based on the adjusted Population and Housing Census of 2000 and 2010. - Les estimations inter-censitaires au milieu de l'année sont fondée sur les résultats ajustées des recensements de la population et de l'habitat de 2000 et 2010.

[94] Estimates based on the adjusted Population and Housing Census of 2010. - Les estimations sont fondée sur les résultats ajustées du recensement de la population et de l'habitat de 2010.

[95] Total population is taken as de facto and de jure together. - Population totale considérée comme de fait et de droit.

[96] Based on the results of the 2014 Population Census. - D'après les résultats du recensement de la population de 2014.

[97] Data refer to enumerated population. - Les données se rapportent à la population dénombrée.

[98] Data refer to registered population data from Royal Oman Police. - Les données portent sur la population enregistrée par la police royale de l'Oman.

[99] Excluding data for the Pakistan-held part of Jammu and Kashmir, the final status of which has not yet been determined. - Non compris les données concernant la partie du Jammu et Cachemire occupée par le Pakistan dont le statut définitif n'a pas été déterminé.

[100] Based on the results of the Pakistan Demographic Survey (PDS 2005). These estimates do not reflect completely accurately the actual population and vital events of the country. - D'après les résultats de l'enquête démographique effectuée par le Pakistan en 2005. Ces estimations ne dénotent pas d'une manière complètement ponctuelle la population actuelle et les statistiques de l'état civil du pays.

[101] Based on the results of the Pakistan Demographic Survey (PDS 2007). - D'après les résultats de l'enquête démographique effectuée par le Pakistan en 2007.

[102] Excluding 2739 Filipinos in Philippine Embassies, Consulates and Missions Abroad. - Excepté 2739 Philippins travaillant dans les ambassades, les consulats et les missions des Philippines à l'étranger.

[103] Data based on the preliminary results of the 2010 Population and Housing Census. - D'après les résultats préliminaires du recensement de la population et des logements de 2010.

[104] Data refer to resident population which comprises Singapore citizens and permanent residents. - Les données se rapportent à la population résidente composé des citoyens de Singapour et des résidents permanents.

[105] Data exclude residents who have been away from Singapore for a continuous period of 12 months or longer as at the reference date. - Non compris les résidents hors de Singapour pour une période ininterrompue de 12 mois ou plus avant de la date de référence.

[106] Data are based on the latest register-based population estimates for 2010. Urban and rural breakdown not applicable as Singapore is a city-state. - Données basées sur les estimations démographiques les plus récentes fondées sur les registres de 2010. La ventilation entre zones urbaines et zones rurales ne s'applique pas à Singapour, puisqu'il s'agit d'une ville État.

[107] Data for urban include population in refugee camps. - Les données pour la population urbaine comprennent la population dans les camps réfugiés.

[108] Data have not been adjusted for underenumeration. - Les données n'ont pas été ajustées pour compenser les lacunes du dénombrement.

[109] Including Palestinian refugees. - Y compris les réfugiés de Palestine.

[110] Data based on address-based population registration system. - Les données sont basées sur le registre national de la population basé sur l'adresse.

[111] Based on a sample taken at the time of census. Because of rounding, totals are not in all cases the sum of the respective components. - D'après un échantillon obtenu au moment du recensement. Les chiffres étant arrondis, les totaux ne correspondent pas toujours rigoureusement à la somme des composants respectifs.

[112] Data include non-national population. - Les données comprennent les non-nationaux.

[113] Data are adjusted according to the results of the 1999 and 2009 censuses. - Les données ont été ajustées à partir des résultats des recensements de la population de 1999 et 2009.

[114] Decrease in population due to revision in administrative registers. - Diminution de la population due à la révision des registres administratifs.

[115] Excluding Faeroe Islands and Greenland shown separately, if available. Population statistics are compiled from registers. - Non compris les Îles Féroé et le Groenland, qui font l'objet de rubriques distinctes, si disponible. Les statistiques de la population sont compilées à partir des registres.

[116] Population statistics are compiled from registers. Excluding Åland Islands. - Les statistiques de la population sont compilées à partir des registres. Non compris les Îles d'Åland.

[117] Excluding diplomatic personnel outside the country and including members of alien armed forces not living in military camps and foreign diplomatic personnel not living in embassies or consulates. - Non compris le personnel diplomatique hors du pays et y compris les militaires étrangers ne vivant pas dans des camps militaires et le personnel diplomatique étranger ne vivant pas dans les ambassades ou les consulats.

[118] Excluding military personnel, visitors and transients. - Non compris les militaires, ni les visiteurs et transients.

[119] Excluding armed forces stationed outside the country, but including alien armed forces stationed in the area. - Non compris les militaires en garnison hors du pays, mais y compris les militaires étrangers en garnison sur le territoire.

[120] Data refer to usually resident population. - Les données concernent la population habituellement résidente.

[121] Data refer to the Vatican City State. - Les données se rapportent à l'Etat de la Cité du Vatican.

[122] The population figure is 466 persons. - La population est égale à 466 personnes.

[123] Data refer to registered resident population. - Les données concernent la population enregistrée résidente.

[124] Definition of localities was revised in 2011 causing a break with the previous series. - La rupture par rapport aux séries précédentes s'explique par le fait que la définition des localités a été révisée depuis 2011.

[125] Data refer to legal resident population. - Les données concernent la population légalement résidente.

[126] Including civilian nationals temporarily outside the country. - Y compris les civils nationaux temporairement hors du pays.

[127] Figures for male and female population do not add up to the figure for total population, because they exclude 119 persons of unknown sex. - Les chiffres relatifs à la population masculine et féminine ne correspondent pas au chiffre de la population totale, parce que l'on en a exclu 119 personnes de sexe inconnu.

[128] Including residents temporarily outside the country. - Y compris les résidents se trouvant temporairement hors du pays.

[129] Excluding civilian aliens within the country, but including civilian nationals temporarily outside the country. - Non compris les civils étrangers dans le pays, mais y compris les civils nationaux temporairement hors du pays.

[130] Excluding Transnistria and the municipality of Bender. - Les données ne tiennent pas compte de l'information sur la Transnistria et la municipalité de Bender.

[131] Excludes data for Kosovo and Metohia. - Sans les données pour le Kosovo et Metohie.

[132] The data for urban and rural exclude the nationals temporarily outside the country. - Les données relatives à la population urbaine et rurale n'englobent pas les nationaux se trouvant provisoirement à l'étranger.

[133] The data for urban and rural exclude the nationals temporarily outside the country. Data refer to usually resident population. - Les données relatives à la population urbaine et rurale n'englobent pas les nationaux se trouvant provisoirement à l'étranger. Les données concernent la population habituellement résidente.

[134] Excluding Channel Islands (Guernsey and Jersey) and Isle of Man, shown separately, if available. - Non compris les îles Anglo-Normandes (Guernesey et Jersey) et l'île de Man, qui font l'objet de rubriques distinctes, si disponible.

[135] This data has been randomly rounded to protect confidentiality. Individual figures may not add up to totals, and values for the same data may vary in different tables. - Ces données ont été arrondies de façon aléatoire afin d'en préserver la confidentialité. La somme de certains chiffres peut ne pas correspondre aux totaux indiqués et les valeurs des mêmes données peuvent varier d'un tableau à un autre.

[136] Including population in off-shore, migratory and shipping. - Y compris les populations extraterritoriales, les populations nomades et les populations maritimes.

[137] Excluding Niue, shown separately, which is part of Cook Islands, but because of remoteness is administered separately. - Non compris Nioué, qui fait l'objet d'une rubrique distincte et qui fait partie des îles Cook, mais qui, en raison de son éloignement, est administrée séparément.

[138] Including armed forces stationed in the area. Data refer to projections based on the 2010 Population Census. - Y compris les militaires en garnison sur le territoire. Les données se réfèrent aux projections basées sur le recensement de la population de 2010.

[139] Projections are prepared by the Secretariat of the Pacific Community based on 1999 census of population and housing. - Les projections sont préparées par le Secrétariat de la Communauté du Pacifique à partir des résultats du recensement de la population et de l'habitat de 1999.

[140] Based on the census, updated for residents missed or counted more than once by the census (net census undercount); residents temporarily overseas on census night, and births, deaths and net migration between the census night and the date of the estimate. Population estimates by urban/rural residence exclude inland waters and oceanic areas. - D'après le recensement, mise à jour pour les résidents omis ou dénombrés plus d'une fois par le recensement (sous-dénombrement net); résidents temporairement à l'étranger la nuit du recensement, et naissances, décès et migration nette entre la nuit du recensement et la date de l'estimation. Les estimations de la population par lieu de résidence urbaine ou rurale excluent les eaux intérieures et les zones océaniques.

[141] Population estimates by urban/rural residence exclude inland waters and oceanic areas. - Les estimations de la population par lieu de résidence urbaine ou rurale excluent les eaux intérieures et les zones océaniques.

[142] The population figures are 64 and 58 persons for 2007 and 2008 respectively. - La population est respectivement égale à 64 et 58 personnes pour les années 2007 et 2008.

[143] Projections are prepared by the Secretariat of the Pacific Community based on the last population and housing census. - Les projections sont préparées par

le Secrétariat de la Communauté du Pacifique à partir des résultats du dernier recensement de la population et de l'habitat.
[144] Data refer to national projections. Based on the results of the 1996 population census. - Les données se réfèrent aux projections nationales. À partir des résultats du recensement de la population de 1996.

Table 7 - *Demographic Yearbook 2014*

Table 7 presents population by age, sex and urban/rural residence for the latest available year between 2005 and 2014.

Description of variables: Data in this table are either population census figures or estimates, some of which are based on sample surveys. The source of data is indicated by the 'code' explained at the end of the table.

The reference date of the census or estimate appears in the left-most column of the table. In general, the estimates refer to mid-year, i.e. 1 July.

Age is defined as age at last birthday, that is, the difference between the date of birth and the reference date of the age distribution expressed in completed solar years. The age classification used in this table is the following: under 1 year, 1-4 years, 5-year groups through 95-99 years, and 100 years or over.

Statistics are presented for one year, the most recent available. However, if more complete disaggregation is available for an earlier year, both are displayed.

The urban/rural classification of population is that provided by each country or area; it is presumed to be based on the national census definitions of urban population that have been set forth at the end of the technical notes to table 6.

Reliability of data: Estimates which are believed to be less reliable are set in *italics* rather than in roman type.

Limitations: Statistics on population by age and sex are subject to the same qualifications as have been set forth for population statistics in general and age distributions in particular, as discussed in sections 3 and 3.1.3, respectively, of the Technical Notes.

Comparability of population data classified by age and sex is limited by variations in the definition of total population, discussed in detail in section 3 of the Technical Notes, and by the accuracy of the original enumeration. Both factors are more important in relation to certain age groups than to others. For example, under-enumeration is known to be more prevalent among infants and young children than among older persons. Similarly, the exclusion from the total population of certain groups that tend to be of selected ages (such as the armed forces) can markedly affect the age structure and its comparability with that for other countries or areas. Consideration should be given to the implications of these basic limitations in using the data.

In addition to these general qualifications are the special problems of comparability that arise in relation to age statistics in particular. Age distributions of population are known to suffer from certain deficiencies that have their origin in irregularities in age reporting. Although some of the irregularities tend to be obscured or eliminated when data are tabulated in five-year age groups rather than by single years, precision still continues to be affected, though the degree of distortion is not always readily seen.

Another factor limiting comparability is the age classification employed by the various countries or areas. Age may be based on the year of birth rather than the age at last birthday, in other words, calculated using the day, month and year of birth. Distributions based only on the year of birth are footnoted when known.

The absence of data in the unknown age group does not necessarily indicate completely accurate reporting and tabulation of the age item. The unknowns may have been eliminated by assigning ages to them before tabulation, or by proportionately distributing the unknown category across the age groups after tabulation.

As noted in connection with table 5, intercensal estimates of total population are usually revised to accord with the results of a census of population if inexplicable discontinuities appear to exist. Postcensal age-sex distributions, however, are less likely to be revised in this way.   When it is known that a total population estimate for a given year has been revised and the corresponding age distribution has not been, the age distribution is shown as provisional. Distributions of this type should be used with caution when studying trends over a period of years, though their utility for studying age structure for the specified year is probably unimpaired.

The comparability of data by urban/rural residence is affected by the national definitions of urban and rural used in tabulating these data. When known, the definitions of urban used in national population censuses are presented at the end of the technical notes for table 6. As discussed in detail in the technical notes for table 6, these definitions vary considerably from one country or area to another.

Earlier data: Population by age, sex and urban/rural residence has been shown in previous issues of the *Demographic Yearbook*. For more information on specific topics, and years for which data are reported, readers should consult the Historical Index. In addition, population data by single years of age, sex and urban/rural residence, for censuses conducted since 1995, are shown in the *Demographic Yearbook* webpage http://unstats.un.org/unsd/demographic/products/dyb/dybcensusdata.htm.

Tableau 7 – *Annuaire démographique 2014*

Le tableau 7 présente les données les plus récentes disponibles pour la période 2005-2014 sur la population selon l'âge, le sexe et le lieu de résidence (zone urbaine ou rurale).

Description des variables : les données de ce tableau proviennent de recensements de la population ou correspondent à des estimations, fondées dans certains cas, sur des enquêtes par sondage. Le 'code' indique comment les données ont été obtenues. Les codes utilisés sont expliqués à la fin du tableau.

La date du recensement ou de l'estimation figure dans la colonne de gauche du tableau. En général, les estimations se rapportent au milieu de l'année (1er juillet).

L'âge désigne l'âge au dernier anniversaire, c'est-à-dire la différence entre la date de naissance et la date de référence de la répartition par âge exprimée en années solaires révolues. La classification par âge utilisée dans ce tableau est la suivante : moins d'un an, 1 à 4 ans, groupes quinquennaux jusqu'à 95-99 ans et 100 ans ou plus.

Les statistiques portent sur une année, qui correspond à celle pour laquelle on dispose des statistiques les plus récentes. Toutefois, si l'on dispose de répartitions plus complètes pour des années antérieures, les statistiques sont alors présentées pour les deux années.

La classification par zones urbaines et rurales de la population est celle qui est communiquée par chaque pays ou zone ; on part du principe qu'elle repose sur les définitions de la population urbaine utilisées pour les recensements de la population nationaux telles qu'elles sont reproduites à la fin des notes techniques du tableau 6.

Fiabilité des données : les estimations considérées comme moins sûres sont indiquées en italique plutôt qu'en caractères romains.

Insuffisance des données : les statistiques de la population selon l'âge et le sexe appellent les mêmes réserves que celles qui ont été formulées aux sections 3 et 3.1.3 des Notes techniques à propos des statistiques de la population en général et des répartitions par âge en particulier.

La comparabilité des statistiques de la population selon l'âge et le sexe pâtit du manque d'uniformité dans la définition de la population totale (voir la section 3 des Notes techniques) et des lacunes des dénombrements. L'influence de ces deux facteurs varie selon les groupes d'âge. Ainsi, le dénombrement des enfants de moins d'un an et des jeunes enfants comporte souvent plus de lacunes que celui des personnes plus âgées. De même, le fait que certains groupes de personnes appartenant souvent à des groupes d'âge déterminés, par exemple les militaires, ne soient pas pris en compte dans la population totale peut influer sensiblement sur la structure par âge et sur la comparabilité des données avec celles d'autres pays ou zones. Il conviendra de tenir compte de ces facteurs fondamentaux lorsque l'on utilisera les données du tableau.

Outre ces difficultés d'ordre général, la comparabilité pose des problèmes particuliers lorsqu'il s'agit des données par âge. On sait que les répartitions de la population selon l'âge présentent certaines imperfections dues à l'inexactitude des déclarations d'âge. Certaines de ces anomalies ont tendance à s'estomper ou à disparaître lorsque l'on classe les données par groupes d'âge quinquennaux et non par années d'âge, mais une certaine imprécision subsiste, même s'il n'est pas toujours facile de voir à quel point il y a distorsion.

Le degré de comparabilité dépend également de la classification par âge employée dans les divers pays ou zones. L'âge retenu peut être défini par date exacte (jour, mois et année) de naissance ou par celle du dernier anniversaire. Lorsqu'elles étaient connues, les répartitions établies seulement d'après l'année de la naissance ont été signalées en note à la fin du tableau.

Si aucun nombre ne figure dans la rangée réservée aux âges inconnus, cela ne signifie pas nécessairement que les déclarations d'âge et l'exploitation des données par âge aient été tout à fait exactes. C'est souvent une indication que l'on a attribué un âge aux personnes d'âge inconnu avant l'exploitation des données ou qu'elles ont été réparties proportionnellement entre les différents groupes après cette opération.

Comme on l'a indiqué à propos du tableau 5, les estimations intercensitaires de la population totale sont d'ordinaire rectifiées d'après les résultats des recensements de population si l'on constate des discontinuités inexplicables. Les données postcensitaires concernant la répartition de la population par âge et par sexe ont toutefois moins de chance d'être rectifiées de cette manière. Lorsque l'on savait qu'une estimation de la population totale pour une année donnée avait été rectifiée sans qu'il en soit de même pour la répartition par âge correspondante, cette dernière a été indiquée comme ayant un caractère provisoire. Les répartitions de ce type doivent être utilisées avec prudence lorsque l'on étudie les tendances sur un certain nombre d'années, quoique leur utilité pour l'étude de la structure par âge de la population pour l'année visée reste probablement entière.

La comparabilité des données selon le lieu de résidence (zone urbaine ou rurale) peut être limitée par les définitions nationales des termes « urbain » et « rural » utilisées pour la mise en tableaux de ces données. Les définitions du terme « urbain » utilisées pour les recensements nationaux de population ont été présentées à la fin des notes techniques du tableau 6 lorsqu'elles étaient connues. Comme on l'a précisé dans les notes techniques relatives au tableau 6, ces définitions varient considérablement d'un pays ou d'une zone à l'autre.

Données publiées antérieurement : des statistiques concernant la population selon l'âge, le sexe et le lieu de résidence (zone urbaine ou rurale) ont été présentées dans des éditions antérieures de l'*Annuaire démographique*. Pour plus de précisions concernant les années et les sujets pour lesquels des données ont été publiées, se reporter à l'index historique. En plus, des statistiques disponibles concernant la « Population selon chaque année d'âge, le sexe et la résidence urbaine/rurale », pour les recensements depuis 1995, ont été présentées dans la page internet suivante de l'*Annuaire démographique* http://unstats.un.org/unsd/demographic/products/dyb/dybcensusdata.htm.

7. Population by age, sex and urban/rural residence: latest available year, 2005 - 2014
Population selon l'âge, le sexe et la résidence, urbaine/rurale : dernière année disponible, 2005 - 2014

Continent, country or area, date, code[a] and age (in years) / Continent, pays ou zone, date, code[a] et âge (en années)	Total			Urban - Urbaine			Rural - Rurale		
	Both sexes Les deux sexes	Male Masculin	Female Féminin	Both sexes Les deux sexes	Male Masculin	Female Féminin	Both sexes Les deux sexes	Male Masculin	Female Féminin

AFRICA - AFRIQUE

Algeria - Algérie
16 IV 2008 (CDJC)[1]

Total	34 080 030	17 232 753	16 847 277	22 413 189	11 288 724	11 124 466	11 666 841	5 944 029	5 722 812
0 - 4	3 404 918	1 750 097	1 654 821	2 242 705	1 151 239	1 091 466	1 162 213	598 858	563 355
5 - 9	2 888 376	1 475 674	1 412 702	1 888 091	963 262	924 829	1 000 285	512 412	487 873
10 - 14	3 258 773	1 662 262	1 596 511	2 096 819	1 067 727	1 029 092	1 161 954	594 535	567 419
15 - 19	3 635 171	1 847 312	1 787 859	2 309 568	1 169 541	1 140 028	1 325 603	677 772	647 831
20 - 24	3 763 504	1 895 703	1 867 801	2 378 019	1 188 465	1 189 553	1 385 485	707 238	678 247
25 - 29	3 422 377	1 730 411	1 691 966	2 186 560	1 096 016	1 090 545	1 235 816	634 395	601 421
30 - 34	2 740 996	1 379 085	1 361 910	1 802 265	901 021	901 245	938 730	478 064	460 666
35 - 39	2 342 779	1 167 250	1 175 529	1 601 928	793 133	808 795	740 852	374 118	366 734
40 - 44	2 018 327	1 007 683	1 010 644	1 414 371	705 266	709 105	603 956	302 417	301 539
45 - 49	1 629 436	817 005	812 432	1 132 297	570 706	561 591	497 140	246 299	250 841
50 - 54	1 346 695	682 358	664 336	927 655	474 005	453 650	419 040	208 353	210 687
55 - 59	1 062 578	547 180	515 398	720 761	371 528	349 233	341 817	175 652	166 165
60 - 64	711 482	354 694	356 788	479 760	236 949	242 811	231 722	117 745	113 977
65 - 69	631 303	314 958	316 345	420 685	207 760	212 925	210 618	107 198	103 420
70 - 74	504 926	248 672	256 254	336 819	164 109	172 710	168 107	84 563	83 544
75 - 79	363 843	181 478	182 364	240 563	118 362	122 201	123 280	63 116	60 164
80 - 84	187 130	93 472	93 657	121 942	59 267	62 675	65 187	34 205	30 982
85 - 89	89 722	43 307	46 416	58 550	27 171	31 379	31 172	16 136	15 037
90 - 94	29 672	13 575	16 097	19 375	8 488	10 887	10 297	5 087	5 210
95 - 99	10 028	4 178	5 851	6 647	2 638	4 009	3 382	1 540	1 842
100 +	650	252	398	445	170	274	205	82	123
Unknown - Inconnu	37 347	16 146	21 200	27 365	11 901	15 464	9 981	4 245	5 736

1 VII 2014 (ESDJ)

Total	39 114 275	19 801 163	19 313 112	...	...	...	...	...	...
0	964 206	495 156	469 050	...	...	...	...	...	...
1 - 4	3 565 708	1 831 593	1 734 115	...	...	...	...	...	...
5 - 9	3 628 326	1 868 022	1 760 304	...	...	...	...	...	...
10 - 14	2 952 021	1 510 337	1 441 684	...	...	...	...	...	...
15 - 19	3 212 275	1 639 433	1 572 842	...	...	...	...	...	...
20 - 24	3 620 614	1 841 565	1 779 049	...	...	...	...	...	...
25 - 29	3 812 614	1 920 537	1 892 077	...	...	...	...	...	...
30 - 34	3 559 343	1 796 722	1 762 621	...	...	...	...	...	...
35 - 39	2 884 259	1 452 308	1 431 951	...	...	...	...	...	...
40 - 44	2 419 220	1 205 776	1 213 444	...	...	...	...	...	...
45 - 49	2 088 552	1 040 225	1 048 328	...	...	...	...	...	...
50 - 54	1 694 340	846 528	847 812	...	...	...	...	...	...
55 - 59	1 378 988	693 870	685 118	...	...	...	...	...	...
60 - 64	1 094 525	559 232	535 293	...	...	...	...	...	...
65 - 69	722 904	359 208	363 695	...	...	...	...	...	...
70 - 74	582 289	285 688	296 601	...	...	...	...	...	...
75 - 79	449 007	217 044	231 963	...	...	...	...	...	...
80 - 84	295 388	143 881	151 507	...	...	...	...	...	...
85 +	189 696	94 038	95 658	...	...	...	...	...	...

Benin - Bénin[2]
1 VII 2011 (ESDF)

Total	9 067 076	4 446 877	4 620 199	4 072 574	2 003 366	2 069 208	4 994 502	2 443 511	2 550 991
0 - 4	1 629 512	828 064	801 448	633 629	321 667	311 962	995 883	506 397	489 486
0	350 292	178 565	171 727	...	...	...	...	...	...
1 - 4	1 279 220	649 499	629 721	...	...	...	...	...	...
5 - 9	1 335 166	675 912	659 254	511 822	251 283	260 539	823 344	424 629	398 715
10 - 14	1 137 068	572 756	564 312	517 373	244 437	272 936	619 695	328 319	291 376
15 - 19	1 081 199	553 241	527 958	550 694	279 420	271 274	530 505	273 821	256 684
20 - 24	767 946	398 920	369 026	406 496	224 092	182 404	361 450	174 828	186 622
25 - 29	609 489	291 598	317 891	303 896	153 731	150 165	305 593	137 867	167 726
30 - 34	537 893	227 400	310 493	264 521	117 596	146 925	273 372	109 804	163 568
35 - 39	494 619	213 385	281 234	236 804	106 800	130 004	257 815	106 585	151 230
40 - 44	378 111	175 956	202 155	178 115	86 225	91 890	199 996	89 731	110 265
45 - 49	308 866	142 056	166 810	145 334	68 351	76 983	163 532	73 705	89 827
50 - 54	232 650	110 074	122 576	101 866	48 831	53 035	130 784	61 243	69 541
55 - 59	171 970	82 190	89 780	77 819	37 319	40 500	94 151	44 871	49 280
60 - 64	135 768	64 968	70 800	52 261	24 642	27 619	83 507	40 326	43 181
65 - 69	75 534	35 915	39 619	31 238	14 546	16 692	44 296	21 369	22 927

Continent, country or area, date, code[a] and age (in years) Continent, pays ou zone, date, code[a] et âge (en annèes)	Total			Urban - Urbaine			Rural - Rurale		
	Both sexes Les deux sexes	Male Masculin	Female Féminin	Both sexes Les deux sexes	Male Masculin	Female Féminin	Both sexes Les deux sexes	Male Masculin	Female Féminin
AFRICA - AFRIQUE									
Benin - Bénin[2]									
1 VII 2011 (ESDF)									
70 - 74	82 740	36 511	46 229	30 032	12 558	17 474	52 708	23 953	28 755
75 - 79	36 453	15 591	20 862	14 064	5 573	8 491	22 389	10 018	12 371
80 +	52 092	22 340	29 752	16 610	6 295	10 315	35 482	16 045	19 437
1 VII 2012 (ESDF)									
Total	9 364 619	4 597 122	4 767 497	...	...	...	...	...	...
0 - 4	1 669 537	848 381	821 156	...	...	...	...	...	...
5 - 9	1 409 820	714 423	695 397	...	...	...	...	...	...
10 - 14	1 121 609	564 146	557 463	...	...	...	...	...	...
15 - 19	1 128 426	574 540	553 886	...	...	...	...	...	...
20 - 24	817 057	425 448	391 609	...	...	...	...	...	...
25 - 29	631 847	309 616	322 231	...	...	...	...	...	...
30 - 34	542 868	232 752	310 116	...	...	...	...	...	...
35 - 39	510 224	217 217	293 007	...	...	...	...	...	...
40 - 44	394 530	182 127	212 403	...	...	...	...	...	...
45 - 49	321 261	147 450	173 811	...	...	...	...	...	...
50 - 54	245 694	115 563	130 131	...	...	...	...	...	...
55 - 59	177 199	84 453	92 746	...	...	...	...	...	...
60 - 64	146 276	69 667	76 609	...	...	...	...	...	...
65 - 69	75 643	36 370	39 273	...	...	...	...	...	...
70 - 74	84 454	37 398	47 056	...	...	...	...	...	...
75 - 79	37 723	16 114	21 609	...	...	...	...	...	...
80 +	50 451	21 457	28 994	...	...	...	...	...	...
Botswana									
9 VIII 2011 (CDFC)									
Total	2 024 904	988 957	1 035 947	1 297 287	619 472	677 815	727 617	369 485	358 132
0 - 4	237 314	119 999	117 315	137 134	69 359	67 775	100 180	50 640	49 540
5 - 9	215 162	108 544	106 618	126 224	63 146	63 078	88 938	45 398	43 540
10 - 14	207 294	104 419	102 875	125 427	62 520	62 907	81 867	41 899	39 968
15 - 19	210 746	104 818	105 928	144 299	68 841	75 458	66 447	35 977	30 470
20 - 24	200 350	97 249	103 101	141 377	66 208	75 169	58 973	31 041	27 932
25 - 29	207 852	101 194	106 658	147 689	69 567	78 122	60 163	31 627	28 536
30 - 34	170 542	84 515	86 027	121 956	58 698	63 258	48 586	25 817	22 769
35 - 39	135 219	68 435	66 784	94 329	46 341	47 988	40 890	22 094	18 796
40 - 44	99 297	48 767	50 530	67 345	32 518	34 827	31 952	16 249	15 703
45 - 49	82 261	37 881	44 380	52 842	24 123	28 719	29 419	13 758	15 661
50 - 54	66 362	29 742	36 620	40 264	18 087	22 177	26 098	11 655	14 443
55 - 59	54 049	24 368	29 681	30 470	13 592	16 878	23 579	10 776	12 803
60 - 64	37 584	17 344	20 240	19 235	8 310	10 925	18 349	9 034	9 315
65 - 69	27 747	12 243	15 504	13 597	5 530	8 067	14 150	6 713	7 437
70 - 74	22 261	9 464	12 797	10 696	4 006	6 690	11 565	5 458	6 107
75 - 79	17 892	6 968	10 924	8 578	2 914	5 664	9 314	4 054	5 260
80 - 84	13 219	4 875	8 344	6 112	1 939	4 173	7 107	2 936	4 171
85 - 89	8 247	2 825	5 422	3 946	1 217	2 729	4 301	1 608	2 693
90 - 94	3 921	1 377	2 544	1 842	598	1 244	2 079	779	1 300
95 +	7 585	3 930	3 655	3 925	1 958	1 967	3 660	1 972	1 688
Burkina Faso									
9 XII 2006 (CDJC)									
Total	14 017 262	6 768 739	7 248 523	3 181 967	1 588 895	1 593 072	10 835 295	5 179 844	5 655 451
0	466 516	235 090	231 426	87 021	44 072	42 949	379 495	191 018	188 477
1 - 4	1 970 397	995 520	974 877	333 623	169 737	163 886	1 636 774	825 783	810 991
5 - 9	2 315 710	1 176 473	1 139 237	401 898	200 004	201 894	1 913 812	976 469	937 343
10 - 14	1 746 588	900 103	846 485	369 532	178 639	190 893	1 377 056	721 464	655 592
15 - 19	1 475 285	710 323	764 962	411 383	192 566	218 817	1 063 902	517 757	546 145
20 - 24	1 185 378	530 425	654 953	366 029	178 980	187 049	819 349	351 445	467 904
25 - 29	1 009 285	448 431	560 854	296 420	150 350	146 070	712 865	298 081	414 784
30 - 34	794 820	363 408	431 412	228 658	122 850	105 808	566 162	240 558	325 604
35 - 39	656 824	298 236	358 588	172 705	92 889	79 816	484 119	205 347	278 772
40 - 44	549 287	250 143	299 144	136 961	71 800	65 161	412 326	178 343	233 983
45 - 49	427 739	195 016	232 723	99 671	52 052	47 619	328 068	142 964	185 104
50 - 54	358 810	166 281	192 529	78 866	41 122	37 744	279 944	125 159	154 785
55 - 59	273 563	132 254	141 309	56 234	29 228	27 006	217 329	103 026	114 303
60 - 64	238 962	111 176	127 786	45 740	21 983	23 757	193 222	89 193	104 029
65 - 69	163 609	80 542	83 067	29 765	14 189	15 576	133 844	66 353	67 491

Continent, country or area, date, code[a] and age (in years) / Continent, pays ou zone, date, code[a] et âge (en annèes)	Total			Urban - Urbaine			Rural - Rurale		
	Both sexes Les deux sexes	Male Masculin	Female Féminin	Both sexes Les deux sexes	Male Masculin	Female Féminin	Both sexes Les deux sexes	Male Masculin	Female Féminin
AFRICA - AFRIQUE									
Burkina Faso									
9 XII 2006 (CDJC)									
70 - 74	136 282	63 727	72 555	23 129	10 103	13 026	113 153	53 624	59 529
75 - 79	77 113	37 186	39 927	12 366	5 449	6 917	64 747	31 737	33 010
80 - 84	50 317	21 791	28 526	8 171	2 957	5 214	42 146	18 834	23 312
85 - 89	21 694	9 645	12 049	3 512	1 230	2 282	18 182	8 415	9 767
90 - 94	11 529	4 480	7 049	1 898	619	1 279	9 631	3 861	5 770
95 +	13 067	4 727	8 340	1 956	467	1 489	11 111	4 260	6 851
Unknown - Inconnu	74 487	33 762	40 725	16 429	7 609	8 820	58 058	26 153	31 905
1 VII 2009 (ESDJ)[2]									
Total	15 224 780	7 346 835	7 877 945	...	...	...	...	...	...
0	652 074	332 861	319 213	...	...	...	...	...	...
1 - 4	2 262 278	1 166 932	1 095 346	...	...	...	...	...	...
5 - 9	2 416 407	1 236 776	1 179 631	...	...	...	...	...	...
10 - 14	1 973 815	988 126	985 689	...	...	...	...	...	...
15 - 19	1 577 324	774 081	803 243	...	...	...	...	...	...
20 - 24	1 309 638	579 080	730 558	...	...	...	...	...	...
25 - 29	1 045 616	455 063	590 553	...	...	...	...	...	...
30 - 34	878 095	389 101	488 994	...	...	...	...	...	...
35 - 39	679 903	308 106	371 797	...	...	...	...	...	...
40 - 44	589 777	263 840	325 937	...	...	...	...	...	...
45 - 49	453 094	206 387	246 707	...	...	...	...	...	...
50 - 54	382 895	172 330	210 565	...	...	...	...	...	...
55 - 59	280 518	133 841	146 677	...	...	...	...	...	...
60 - 64	254 972	118 221	136 751	...	...	...	...	...	...
65 - 69	167 320	81 902	85 418	...	...	...	...	...	...
70 - 74	138 614	64 975	73 639	...	...	...	...	...	...
75 - 79	75 664	37 101	38 563	...	...	...	...	...	...
80 +	86 776	38 112	48 664	...	...	...	...	...	...
Burundi									
16 VIII 2008 (CDJC)									
Total	8 053 574	3 964 906	4 088 668	811 866	442 596	369 270	7 241 708	3 522 310	3 719 398
0 - 4	1 424 016	701 119	722 897	121 181	60 098	61 083	1 302 835	641 021	661 814
5 - 9	1 133 011	554 819	578 192	93 103	46 020	47 083	1 039 908	508 799	531 109
10 - 14	992 125	479 874	512 251	81 559	39 261	42 298	910 566	440 613	469 953
15 - 19	967 635	462 251	505 384	102 274	51 816	50 458	865 361	410 435	454 926
20 - 24	771 686	364 574	407 112	95 104	52 641	42 463	676 582	311 933	364 649
25 - 29	607 541	304 842	302 699	87 743	52 567	35 176	519 798	252 275	267 523
30 - 34	414 453	209 982	204 471	61 717	38 063	23 654	352 736	171 919	180 817
35 - 39	371 931	186 018	185 913	45 180	27 712	17 468	326 751	158 306	168 445
40 - 44	303 720	153 694	150 026	32 626	20 899	11 727	271 094	132 795	138 299
45 - 49	280 890	146 870	134 020	25 095	15 625	9 470	255 795	131 245	124 550
50 - 54	228 246	116 798	111 448	17 525	10 673	6 852	210 721	106 125	104 596
55 - 59	141 758	76 723	65 035	10 835	6 528	4 307	130 923	70 195	60 728
60 - 64	107 403	52 602	54 801	7 274	3 910	3 364	100 129	48 692	51 437
65 - 69	67 434	34 477	32 957	4 369	2 260	2 109	63 065	32 217	30 848
70 - 74	63 458	28 759	34 699	3 656	1 646	2 010	59 802	27 113	32 689
75 - 79	35 140	18 344	16 796	2 120	973	1 147	33 020	17 371	15 649
80 - 84	28 212	12 675	15 537	1 403	556	847	26 809	12 119	14 690
85 - 89	11 836	6 328	5 508	639	298	341	11 197	6 030	5 167
90 - 94	8 545	4 074	4 471	417	156	261	8 128	3 918	4 210
95 +	7 300	3 585	3 715	493	295	198	6 807	3 290	3 517
Unknown - Inconnu	87 234	46 498	40 736	17 553	10 599	6 954	69 681	35 899	33 782
Cabo Verde									
1 VII 2011 (ESDF)									
Total	527 269	255 327	271 942	...	...	...	...	...	...
0	13 460	6 778	6 682	...	...	...	...	...	...
1 - 4	50 678	25 438	25 240	...	...	...	...	...	...
5 - 9	57 789	28 923	28 866	...	...	...	...	...	...
10 - 14	57 177	28 773	28 404	...	...	...	...	...	...
15 - 19	60 912	30 486	30 426	...	...	...	...	...	...
20 - 24	61 465	30 479	30 986	...	...	...	...	...	...
25 - 29	48 416	23 782	24 634	...	...	...	...	...	...
30 - 34	35 452	17 379	18 073	...	...	...	...	...	...
35 - 39	27 130	13 085	14 045	...	...	...	...	...	...

7. Population by age, sex and urban/rural residence: latest available year, 2005 - 2014
Population selon l'âge, le sexe et la résidence, urbaine/rurale : dernière année disponible, 2005 - 2014 (continued - suite)

Continent, country or area, date, code[a] and age (in years) / Continent, pays ou zone, date, code[a] et âge (en années)	Total			Urban - Urbaine			Rural - Rurale		
	Both sexes Les deux sexes	Male Masculin	Female Féminin	Both sexes Les deux sexes	Male Masculin	Female Féminin	Both sexes Les deux sexes	Male Masculin	Female Féminin
AFRICA - AFRIQUE									
Cabo Verde									
1 VII 2011 (ESDF)									
40 - 44	26 081	12 350	13 731	...	...	...	...	...	...
45 - 49	24 501	11 490	13 011	...	...	...	...	...	...
50 - 54	19 163	8 591	10 572	...	...	...	...	...	...
55 - 59	13 045	5 240	7 805	...	...	...	...	...	...
60 - 64	6 603	2 691	3 912	...	...	...	...	...	...
65 - 69	5 293	2 140	3 153	...	...	...	...	...	...
70 - 74	7 492	2 838	4 654	...	...	...	...	...	...
75 - 79	6 261	2 425	3 836	...	...	...	...	...	...
80 +	6 351	2 439	3 912	...	...	...	...	...	...
Cameroon - Cameroun									
11 XI 2005 (CDJC)									
Total	17 463 836	8 632 036	8 831 800	8 514 938	4 276 130	4 238 808	8 948 898	4 355 906	4 592 992
0 - 4	2 951 848	1 492 147	1 459 701	1 266 753	641 744	625 009	1 685 095	850 403	834 692
5 - 9	2 504 901	1 270 842	1 234 059	1 059 035	533 904	525 131	1 445 866	736 938	708 928
10 - 14	2 161 608	1 107 718	1 053 890	1 013 456	510 450	503 006	1 148 152	597 268	550 884
15 - 19	1 956 647	963 639	993 008	1 096 260	548 763	547 497	860 387	414 876	445 511
20 - 24	1 650 049	767 928	882 121	971 812	469 728	502 084	678 237	298 200	380 037
25 - 29	1 368 560	638 765	729 795	773 656	377 621	396 035	594 904	261 144	333 760
30 - 34	1 086 007	527 529	558 478	588 336	300 465	287 871	497 671	227 064	270 607
35 - 39	847 768	413 432	434 336	455 295	231 267	224 028	392 473	182 165	210 308
40 - 44	713 376	348 534	364 842	364 581	189 090	175 491	348 795	159 444	189 351
45 - 49	576 662	290 515	286 147	291 912	154 100	137 812	284 750	136 415	148 335
50 - 54	470 027	235 024	235 003	214 603	114 218	100 385	255 424	120 806	134 618
55 - 59	305 741	161 120	144 621	127 992	69 483	58 509	177 749	91 637	86 112
60 - 64	285 354	139 764	145 590	101 852	51 216	50 636	183 502	88 548	94 954
65 - 69	206 489	100 090	106 399	71 860	34 018	37 842	134 629	66 072	68 557
70 - 74	171 498	80 293	91 205	54 095	23 767	30 328	117 403	56 526	60 877
75 - 79	89 291	42 836	46 455	28 893	12 990	15 903	60 398	29 846	30 552
80 - 84	64 668	28 500	36 168	19 127	7 545	11 582	45 541	20 955	24 586
85 - 89	24 177	11 007	13 170	7 426	3 009	4 417	16 751	7 998	8 753
90 - 94	14 122	6 228	7 894	4 095	1 461	2 634	10 027	4 767	5 260
95 +	15 043	6 125	8 918	3 899	1 291	2 608	11 144	4 834	6 310
1 VII 2010* (ESDJ)[2]									
Total	19 406 100	9 599 224	9 806 876	...	...	...	...	...	...
0 - 4	3 287 234	1 662 298	1 624 936	...	...	...	...	...	...
5 - 9	2 783 459	1 412 467	1 370 992	...	...	...	...	...	...
10 - 14	2 394 671	1 227 470	1 167 201	...	...	...	...	...	...
15 - 19	2 170 035	1 068 509	1 101 526	...	...	...	...	...	...
20 - 24	1 837 289	855 334	981 955	...	...	...	...	...	...
25 - 29	1 525 816	712 550	813 266	...	...	...	...	...	...
30 - 34	1 209 607	588 210	621 397	...	...	...	...	...	...
35 - 39	942 713	460 394	482 319	...	...	...	...	...	...
40 - 44	793 846	388 539	405 307	...	...	...	...	...	...
45 - 49	640 247	323 507	316 740	...	...	...	...	...	...
50 - 54	521 910	261 626	260 284	...	...	...	...	...	...
55 - 59	337 988	178 876	159 112	...	...	...	...	...	...
60 - 64	315 879	155 208	160 671	...	...	...	...	...	...
65 - 69	227 290	110 645	116 645	...	...	...	...	...	...
70 - 74	189 571	88 969	100 602	...	...	...	...	...	...
75 - 79	98 078	47 173	50 905	...	...	...	...	...	...
80 - 84	71 585	31 609	39 976	...	...	...	...	...	...
85 - 89	26 564	12 109	14 455	...	...	...	...	...	...
90 - 94	15 715	6 942	8 773	...	...	...	...	...	...
95 +	16 603	6 789	9 814	...	...	...	...	...	...
Congo									
1 VII 2009 (ESDF)									
Total	3 838 238	1 891 558	1 946 680	...	...	...	...	...	...
0 - 4	586 578	294 305	292 273	...	...	...	...	...	...
5 - 9	475 864	238 682	237 182	...	...	...	...	...	...
10 - 14	417 074	208 162	208 912	...	...	...	...	...	...
15 - 19	382 673	186 405	196 268	...	...	...	...	...	...
20 - 24	358 745	167 519	191 226	...	...	...	...	...	...
25 - 29	339 133	160 897	178 236	...	...	...	...	...	...

7. Population by age, sex and urban/rural residence: latest available year, 2005 - 2014
Population selon l'âge, le sexe et la résidence, urbaine/rurale : dernière année disponible, 2005 - 2014 (continued - suite)

Continent, country or area, date, code[a] and age (in years) Continent, pays ou zone, date, code[a] et âge (en années)	Total			Urban - Urbaine			Rural - Rurale		
	Both sexes Les deux sexes	Male Masculin	Female Féminin	Both sexes Les deux sexes	Male Masculin	Female Féminin	Both sexes Les deux sexes	Male Masculin	Female Féminin
AFRICA - AFRIQUE									
Congo									
1 VII 2009 (ESDF)									
30 - 34	304 009	152 642	151 367	...	...	...	...	...	...
35 - 39	254 997	131 794	123 203	...	...	...	...	...	...
40 - 44	198 594	103 248	95 346	...	...	...	...	...	...
45 - 49	148 798	76 921	71 877	...	...	...	...	...	...
50 - 54	111 812	54 925	56 887	...	...	...	...	...	...
55 - 59	80 842	38 051	42 791	...	...	...	...	...	...
60 - 64	59 601	27 592	32 009	...	...	...	...	...	...
65 - 69	46 706	20 879	25 827	...	...	...	...	...	...
70 - 74	34 961	14 954	20 007	...	...	...	...	...	...
75 - 79	21 868	8 820	13 048	...	...	...	...	...	...
80 +	15 983	5 762	10 221	...	...	...	...	...	...
Egypt - Égypte									
1 VII 2014 (ESDF)									
Total	86 813 723	44 304 619	42 509 104	37 094 960	18 904 449	18 190 511	49 718 763	25 400 170	24 318 593
0 - 4	9 829 921	5 101 944	4 727 977	4 200 159	2 176 962	2 023 197	5 629 762	2 924 982	2 704 780
5 - 9	9 126 024	4 728 899	4 397 125	3 899 406	2 017 786	1 881 620	5 226 618	2 711 113	2 515 505
10 - 14	8 183 738	4 224 190	3 959 548	3 496 802	1 802 431	1 694 371	4 686 936	2 421 759	2 265 177
15 - 19	8 388 912	4 311 966	4 076 946	3 584 492	1 839 884	1 744 608	4 804 420	2 472 082	2 332 338
20 - 24	8 929 427	4 564 320	4 365 107	3 815 480	1 947 562	1 867 918	5 113 947	2 616 758	2 497 189
25 - 29	8 398 687	4 279 050	4 119 637	3 588 716	1 825 839	1 762 877	4 809 971	2 453 211	2 356 760
30 - 34	6 731 457	3 412 268	3 319 189	2 876 338	1 455 990	1 420 348	3 855 119	1 956 278	1 898 841
35 - 39	5 281 272	2 677 149	2 604 123	2 256 677	1 142 319	1 114 358	3 024 595	1 534 830	1 489 765
40 - 44	4 739 858	2 391 878	2 347 980	2 025 344	1 020 596	1 004 748	2 714 514	1 371 282	1 343 232
45 - 49	4 350 256	2 194 384	2 155 872	1 858 868	936 327	922 541	2 491 388	1 258 057	1 233 331
50 - 54	3 776 526	1 898 142	1 878 384	1 613 721	809 922	803 799	2 162 805	1 088 220	1 074 585
55 - 59	3 083 900	1 547 040	1 536 860	1 317 764	660 110	657 654	1 766 136	886 930	879 206
60 - 64	2 261 407	1 130 107	1 131 300	966 314	482 208	484 106	1 295 093	647 899	647 194
65 - 69	1 590 425	789 978	800 447	679 605	337 077	342 528	910 820	452 901	457 919
70 - 74	1 049 312	515 680	533 632	448 388	220 036	228 352	600 924	295 644	305 280
75 +	1 092 601	537 624	554 977	466 886	229 400	237 486	625 715	308 224	317 491
Ethiopia - Éthiopie[3]									
1 VII 2008 (ESDF)									
Total	79 221 000	39 691 000	39 530 000	13 225 000	6 575 000	6 650 000	65 996 000	33 116 000	32 880 000
0 - 4	12 634 128	6 381 651	6 252 477	1 608 103	837 115	770 988	11 027 607	5 545 365	5 482 242
5 - 9	11 375 406	5 742 553	5 632 853	1 572 449	796 842	775 606	9 804 015	4 946 304	4 857 711
10 - 14	9 860 705	4 983 414	4 877 291	1 510 467	746 491	763 976	8 350 671	4 237 207	4 113 464
15 - 19	8 178 673	4 146 348	4 032 325	1 390 318	679 466	710 851	6 788 253	3 466 879	3 321 374
20 - 24	7 442 221	3 777 710	3 664 510	1 433 539	700 859	732 680	6 008 054	3 076 545	2 931 509
25 - 29	6 446 813	3 269 384	3 177 429	1 326 898	654 980	671 918	5 119 126	2 613 980	2 505 146
30 - 34	5 337 998	2 677 364	2 660 634	1 100 820	556 544	544 276	4 236 510	2 120 406	2 116 104
35 - 39	4 293 830	2 112 022	2 181 807	871 216	440 672	430 544	3 422 119	1 671 022	1 751 097
40 - 44	3 447 552	1 663 907	1 783 644	658 160	328 837	329 322	2 789 134	1 334 886	1 454 248
45 - 49	2 727 580	1 292 456	1 435 124	491 450	241 120	250 330	2 236 012	1 051 240	1 184 772
50 - 54	2 194 347	1 045 893	1 148 454	378 827	183 526	195 301	1 815 478	862 329	953 149
55 - 59	1 740 176	844 895	895 281	291 867	142 040	149 828	1 448 305	702 849	745 456
60 - 64	1 322 620	649 306	673 314	220 967	103 852	117 115	1 101 659	545 471	556 189
65 - 69	951 626	471 805	479 820	159 064	72 250	86 814	792 569	399 578	392 991
70 - 74	639 657	318 537	321 119	106 400	46 747	59 653	533 265	271 814	261 451
75 +	627 670	313 753	313 917	104 457	43 659	60 798	523 224	270 126	253 098
Ghana									
26 IX 2010 (CDFC)									
Total	24 658 823	12 024 845	12 633 978	12 545 229	6 016 059	6 529 170	12 113 594	6 008 786	6 104 808
0 - 4	3 405 406	1 731 787	1 673 619	1 541 391	783 017	758 374	1 864 015	948 770	915 245
5 - 9	3 128 952	1 589 632	1 539 320	1 389 660	697 031	692 629	1 739 292	892 601	846 691
10 - 14	2 916 040	1 477 525	1 438 515	1 391 229	672 906	718 323	1 524 811	804 619	720 192
15 - 19	2 609 989	1 311 112	1 298 877	1 364 124	651 829	712 295	1 245 865	659 283	586 582
20 - 24	2 323 491	1 100 727	1 222 764	1 356 838	642 140	714 698	966 653	458 587	508 066
25 - 29	2 050 111	943 213	1 106 898	1 194 867	553 927	640 940	855 244	389 286	465 958
30 - 34	1 678 809	790 301	888 508	955 698	455 204	500 494	723 111	335 097	388 014
35 - 39	1 421 403	676 768	744 635	781 852	373 678	408 174	639 551	303 090	336 461
40 - 44	1 186 350	572 620	613 730	632 049	304 875	327 174	554 301	267 745	286 556
45 - 49	938 098	452 975	485 123	487 192	231 146	256 046	450 906	221 829	229 077
50 - 54	833 098	394 600	438 498	421 478	195 556	225 922	411 620	199 044	212 576

7. Population by age, sex and urban/rural residence: latest available year, 2005 - 2014
Population selon l'âge, le sexe et la résidence, urbaine/rurale : dernière année disponible, 2005 - 2014 (continued - suite)

Continent, country or area, date, code[a] and age (in years) / Continent, pays ou zone, date, code[a] et âge (en années)	Total			Urban - Urbaine			Rural - Rurale		
	Both sexes Les deux sexes	Male Masculin	Female Féminin	Both sexes Les deux sexes	Male Masculin	Female Féminin	Both sexes Les deux sexes	Male Masculin	Female Féminin
AFRICA - AFRIQUE									
Ghana									
26 IX 2010 (CDFC)									
55 - 59	523 695	258 582	265 113	275 958	132 984	142 974	247 737	125 598	122 139
60 - 64	475 849	227 050	248 799	225 385	105 738	119 647	250 464	121 312	129 152
65 - 69	293 871	136 244	157 627	143 114	64 588	78 526	150 757	71 656	79 101
70 - 74	351 330	149 512	201 818	153 951	63 786	90 165	197 379	85 726	111 653
75 - 79	205 953	89 149	116 804	93 297	38 300	54 997	112 656	50 849	61 807
80 - 84	159 084	62 357	96 727	67 888	25 271	42 617	91 196	37 086	54 110
85 - 89	83 070	32 937	50 133	37 719	13 683	24 036	45 351	19 254	26 097
90 - 94	51 081	19 004	32 077	21 270	6 985	14 285	29 811	12 019	17 792
95 +	23 143	8 750	14 393	10 269	3 415	6 854	12 874	5 335	7 539
Guinea - Guinée[2]									
1 VII 2009 (ESDF)									
Total	10 217 591	5 038 823	5 178 768	...	...	...	...	...	...
0 - 4	1 708 508	866 996	841 512	...	...	...	...	...	...
5 - 9	1 355 253	686 211	669 042	...	...	...	...	...	...
10 - 14	1 155 226	581 127	574 099	...	...	...	...	...	...
15 - 19	1 225 991	621 661	604 330	...	...	...	...	...	...
20 - 24	996 391	517 007	479 384	...	...	...	...	...	...
25 - 29	668 191	344 997	323 194	...	...	...	...	...	...
30 - 34	565 801	260 720	305 081	...	...	...	...	...	...
35 - 39	494 352	216 535	277 817	...	...	...	...	...	...
40 - 44	478 364	204 559	273 805	...	...	...	...	...	...
45 - 49	366 578	163 816	202 762	...	...	...	...	...	...
50 - 54	315 033	147 915	167 118	...	...	...	...	...	...
55 - 59	240 705	118 129	122 576	...	...	...	...	...	...
60 - 64	182 506	87 782	94 724	...	...	...	...	...	...
65 - 69	139 166	66 929	72 237	...	...	...	...	...	...
70 - 74	111 293	54 579	56 714	...	...	...	...	...	...
75 +	214 233	99 860	114 373	...	...	...	...	...	...
Guinea-Bissau - Guinée-Bissau									
15 III 2009 (CDJC)									
Total	1 449 230	702 826	746 404	573 533	284 347	289 186	875 697	418 479	457 218
0 - 4	228 997	115 009	113 988	74 456	37 205	37 251	154 541	77 804	76 737
5 - 9	208 007	104 650	103 357	70 667	34 189	36 478	137 340	70 461	66 879
10 - 14	178 596	89 814	88 782	71 326	33 988	37 338	107 270	55 826	51 444
15 - 19	171 120	83 844	87 276	77 861	38 149	39 712	93 259	45 695	47 564
20 - 24	145 375	68 624	76 751	70 533	35 491	35 042	74 842	33 133	41 709
25 - 29	127 128	58 472	68 656	57 989	29 161	28 828	69 139	29 311	39 828
30 - 34	84 741	39 733	45 008	38 524	19 667	18 857	46 217	20 066	26 151
35 - 39	73 721	34 109	39 612	30 438	15 322	15 116	43 283	18 787	24 496
40 - 44	52 372	24 647	27 725	22 103	11 390	10 713	30 269	13 257	17 012
45 - 49	48 121	22 654	25 467	19 093	9 802	9 291	29 028	12 852	16 176
50 - 54	33 678	15 685	17 993	12 759	6 628	6 131	20 919	9 057	11 862
55 - 59	26 397	13 105	13 292	9 140	4 794	4 346	17 257	8 311	8 946
60 - 64	21 649	9 984	11 665	6 366	3 103	3 263	15 283	6 881	8 402
65 - 69	15 829	7 348	8 481	4 304	1 982	2 322	11 525	5 366	6 159
70 - 74	11 016	5 001	6 015	2 673	1 167	1 506	8 343	3 834	4 509
75 - 79	7 948	3 504	4 444	1 679	637	1 042	6 269	2 867	3 402
80 +	11 252	4 715	6 537	1 981	647	1 334	9 271	4 068	5 203
Unknown - Inconnu	3 283	1 928	1 355	1 641	1 025	616	1 642	903	739
Kenya									
24 VIII 2009 (CDFC)									
Total	38 610 097	19 192 458	19 417 639	12 487 375	6 278 811	6 208 564	26 122 722	12 913 647	13 209 075
0 - 4	5 939 306	3 000 439	2 938 867	1 739 251	875 830	863 421	4 200 055	2 124 609	2 075 446
5 - 9	5 597 716	2 832 669	2 765 047	1 484 285	742 473	741 812	4 113 431	2 090 196	2 023 235
10 - 14	5 034 855	2 565 313	2 469 542	1 312 671	650 438	662 233	3 722 184	1 914 875	1 807 309
15 - 19	4 169 543	2 123 653	2 045 890	1 244 054	587 384	656 670	2 925 489	1 536 269	1 389 220
20 - 24	3 775 103	1 754 105	2 020 998	1 572 026	708 458	863 568	2 203 077	1 045 647	1 157 430
25 - 29	3 201 226	1 529 116	1 672 110	1 442 798	715 957	726 841	1 758 428	813 159	945 269
30 - 34	2 519 506	1 257 035	1 262 471	1 056 483	568 615	487 868	1 463 023	688 420	774 603
35 - 39	2 008 632	1 004 361	1 004 271	785 390	431 054	354 336	1 223 242	573 307	649 935
40 - 44	1 476 169	743 594	732 575	533 174	297 202	235 972	942 995	446 392	496 603
45 - 49	1 272 745	635 276	637 469	422 941	235 467	187 474	849 804	399 809	449 995

Continent, country or area, date, code[a] and age (in years) / Continent, pays ou zone, date, code[a] et âge (en années)	Total			Urban - Urbaine			Rural - Rurale		
	Both sexes Les deux sexes	Male Masculin	Female Féminin	Both sexes Les deux sexes	Male Masculin	Female Féminin	Both sexes Les deux sexes	Male Masculin	Female Féminin
AFRICA - AFRIQUE									
Kenya									
24 VIII 2009 (CDFC)									
50 - 54	956 206	478 346	477 860	286 074	159 814	126 260	670 132	318 532	351 600
55 - 59	711 953	359 466	352 487	187 793	103 563	84 230	524 160	255 903	268 257
60 - 64	593 778	295 197	298 581	139 271	73 800	65 471	454 507	221 397	233 110
65 - 69	390 763	183 151	207 612	83 728	41 299	42 429	307 035	141 852	165 183
70 - 74	339 301	160 301	179 000	68 868	32 691	36 177	270 433	127 610	142 823
75 - 79	218 508	99 833	118 675	42 247	19 276	22 971	176 261	80 557	95 704
80 +	383 701	159 125	224 576	77 003	30 335	46 668	306 698	128 790	177 908
Unknown - Inconnu	21 086	11 478	9 608	9 318	5 155	4 163	11 768	6 323	5 445
1 VII 2014 (ESDF)[4]									
Total	*42 961 187*	*21 289 752*	*21 671 435*	...	...	...	...	...	...
0 - 4	*6 739 755*	*3 385 952*	*3 353 803*	...	...	...	...	...	...
5 - 9	*5 842 961*	*2 941 123*	*2 901 838*	...	...	...	...	...	...
10 - 14	*5 248 304*	*2 661 057*	*2 587 247*	...	...	...	...	...	...
15 - 19	*4 618 997*	*2 345 347*	*2 273 650*	...	...	...	...	...	...
20 - 24	*4 109 175*	*2 031 402*	*2 077 773*	...	...	...	...	...	...
25 - 29	*3 668 881*	*1 713 590*	*1 955 291*	...	...	...	...	...	...
30 - 34	*3 051 156*	*1 437 408*	*1 613 748*	...	...	...	...	...	...
35 - 39	*2 378 371*	*1 189 195*	*1 189 176*	...	...	...	...	...	...
40 - 44	*1 871 645*	*942 826*	*928 819*	...	...	...	...	...	...
45 - 49	*1 425 254*	*709 802*	*715 452*	...	...	...	...	...	...
50 - 54	*1 101 693*	*547 327*	*554 366*	...	...	...	...	...	...
55 - 59	*860 917*	*426 415*	*434 502*	...	...	...	...	...	...
60 - 64	*652 824*	*320 360*	*332 464*	...	...	...	...	...	...
65 - 69	*486 113*	*232 506*	*253 607*	...	...	...	...	...	...
70 - 74	*345 646*	*161 703*	*183 943*	...	...	...	...	...	...
75 - 79	*237 838*	*108 599*	*129 239*	...	...	...	...	...	...
80 +	*321 657*	*135 140*	*186 517*	...	...	...	...	...	...
Lesotho									
13 IV 2006 (CDJC)									
Total	1 862 860	904 392	958 468	421 105	194 097	227 008	1 441 755	710 295	731 460
0 - 4	201 995	101 397	100 598	39 245	19 604	19 641	162 750	81 793	80 957
5 - 9	211 947	106 695	105 252	40 208	20 051	20 157	171 739	86 644	85 095
10 - 14	220 938	110 778	110 160	42 546	20 751	21 795	178 392	90 027	88 365
15 - 19	229 389	114 800	114 589	48 783	21 971	26 812	180 606	92 829	87 777
20 - 24	207 062	101 385	105 677	52 026	21 394	30 632	155 036	79 991	75 045
25 - 29	164 867	82 202	82 665	49 796	21 948	27 848	115 071	60 254	54 817
30 - 34	119 530	60 107	59 423	36 708	17 327	19 381	82 822	42 780	40 042
35 - 39	93 490	45 645	47 845	28 605	13 639	14 966	64 885	32 006	32 879
40 - 44	83 299	39 596	43 703	22 742	10 805	11 937	60 557	28 791	31 766
45 - 49	72 621	34 102	38 519	17 782	8 461	9 321	54 839	25 641	29 198
50 - 54	63 084	28 723	34 361	13 153	6 037	7 116	49 931	22 686	27 245
55 - 59	50 148	23 225	26 923	9 367	4 266	5 101	40 781	18 959	21 822
60 - 64	37 699	16 724	20 975	6 325	2 851	3 474	31 374	13 873	17 501
65 - 69	32 028	13 369	18 659	4 794	1 977	2 817	27 234	11 392	15 842
70 - 74	35 609	13 380	22 229	4 158	1 569	2 589	31 451	11 811	19 640
75 - 79	18 141	6 327	11 814	2 281	742	1 539	15 860	5 585	10 275
80 - 84	10 498	3 251	7 247	1 336	380	956	9 162	2 871	6 291
85 +	10 515	2 686	7 829	1 250	324	926	9 265	2 362	6 903
Liberia - Libéria									
21 III 2008 (CDFC)									
Total	3 476 608	1 739 945	1 736 663	...	...	...	...	...	...
0 - 4	534 475	270 564	263 911	...	...	...	...	...	...
5 - 9	501 931	251 411	250 520	...	...	...	...	...	...
10 - 14	421 666	214 859	206 807	...	...	...	...	...	...
15 - 19	375 695	189 407	186 288	...	...	...	...	...	...
20 - 24	342 930	161 951	180 979	...	...	...	...	...	...
25 - 29	291 858	141 006	150 852	...	...	...	...	...	...
30 - 34	219 632	107 326	112 306	...	...	...	...	...	...
35 - 39	203 536	99 136	104 400	...	...	...	...	...	...
40 - 44	155 737	81 670	74 067	...	...	...	...	...	...
45 - 49	118 807	63 827	54 980	...	...	...	...	...	...
50 - 54	82 940	44 870	38 070	...	...	...	...	...	...
55 - 59	56 460	30 975	25 485	...	...	...	...	...	...

7. Population by age, sex and urban/rural residence: latest available year, 2005 - 2014
Population selon l'âge, le sexe et la résidence, urbaine/rurale : dernière année disponible, 2005 - 2014 (continued - suite)

Continent, country or area, date, code[a] and age (in years) / Continent, pays ou zone, date, code[a] et âge (en années)	Total			Urban - Urbaine			Rural - Rurale		
	Both sexes Les deux sexes	Male Masculin	Female Féminin	Both sexes Les deux sexes	Male Masculin	Female Féminin	Both sexes Les deux sexes	Male Masculin	Female Féminin
AFRICA - AFRIQUE									
Liberia - Libéria									
21 III 2008 (CDFC)									
60 - 64	52 830	25 473	27 357	...	...	...	...	...	...
65 - 69	39 807	19 250	20 557	...	...	...	...	...	...
70 - 74	25 746	12 343	13 403	...	...	...	...	...	...
75 - 79	22 913	11 580	11 333	...	...	...	...	...	...
80 - 84	12 007	5 408	6 599	...	...	...	...	...	...
85 +	17 638	8 889	8 749	...	...	...	...	...	...
Libya - Libye									
15 IV 2006* (CDFC)									
Total	5 298 152	2 687 513	2 610 639	4 670 858	2 372 379	2 298 479	627 294	315 134	312 160
0	117 479	60 167	57 312	103 670	53 129	50 541	13 809	7 038	6 771
1 - 4	457 866	234 512	223 354	403 509	206 639	196 870	54 357	27 873	26 484
5 - 9	527 595	269 079	258 516	465 506	237 468	228 038	62 089	31 611	30 478
10 - 14	542 893	277 270	265 623	476 896	243 693	233 203	65 997	33 577	32 420
15 - 19	573 026	290 568	282 458	501 444	254 266	247 178	71 582	36 302	35 280
20 - 24	573 287	289 663	283 624	502 229	253 539	248 690	71 058	36 124	34 934
25 - 29	566 458	287 101	279 357	497 522	252 364	245 158	68 936	34 737	34 199
30 - 34	492 828	248 875	243 953	434 821	220 019	214 802	58 007	28 856	29 151
35 - 39	390 800	195 328	195 472	347 316	174 078	173 238	43 484	21 250	22 234
40 - 44	281 849	140 872	140 977	251 876	126 302	125 574	29 973	14 570	15 403
45 - 49	199 142	100 653	98 489	178 471	90 336	88 135	20 671	10 317	10 354
50 - 54	132 619	64 677	67 942	119 463	58 576	60 887	13 156	6 101	7 055
55 - 59	122 277	61 439	60 838	109 004	55 174	53 830	13 273	6 265	7 008
60 - 64	95 127	51 295	43 832	84 339	45 822	38 517	10 788	5 473	5 315
65 - 69	80 018	42 724	37 294	70 241	37 786	32 455	9 777	4 938	4 839
70 - 74	57 851	30 325	27 526	50 282	26 511	23 771	7 569	3 814	3 755
75 - 79	45 675	23 125	22 550	39 337	19 978	19 359	6 338	3 147	3 191
80 - 84	24 576	12 158	12 418	20 930	10 332	10 598	3 646	1 826	1 820
85 +	16 786	7 682	9 104	14 002	6 367	7 635	2 784	1 315	1 469
Malawi									
8 VI 2008 (CDFC)									
Total	13 077 160	6 358 933	6 718 227	2 003 309	1 014 477	988 832	11 073 851	5 344 456	5 729 395
0	503 385	247 809	255 576	67 264	33 375	33 889	436 121	214 434	221 687
1 - 4	1 866 626	922 138	944 488	248 703	122 976	125 727	1 617 923	799 162	818 761
5 - 9	1 968 299	972 307	995 992	261 838	127 930	133 908	1 706 461	844 377	862 084
10 - 14	1 670 391	826 076	844 315	232 203	110 545	121 658	1 438 188	715 531	722 657
15 - 19	1 276 692	625 664	651 028	218 307	105 746	112 561	1 058 385	519 918	538 467
20 - 24	1 240 329	554 799	685 530	248 790	117 648	131 142	991 539	437 151	554 388
25 - 29	1 102 976	530 103	572 873	236 512	122 761	113 751	866 464	407 342	459 122
30 - 34	827 547	417 599	409 948	162 061	91 637	70 424	665 486	325 962	339 524
35 - 39	623 330	323 643	299 687	105 572	61 564	44 008	517 758	262 079	255 679
40 - 44	441 231	218 546	222 685	67 267	37 061	30 206	373 964	181 485	192 479
45 - 49	343 190	167 285	175 905	47 706	25 811	21 895	295 484	141 474	154 010
50 - 54	269 634	126 778	142 856	33 849	18 400	15 449	235 785	108 378	127 407
55 - 59	258 214	122 616	135 598	26 253	14 525	11 728	231 961	108 091	123 870
60 - 64	184 679	87 008	97 671	16 622	9 256	7 366	168 057	77 752	90 305
65 - 69	153 829	72 038	81 791	11 298	6 217	5 081	142 531	65 821	76 710
70 - 74	106 020	46 481	59 539	6 992	3 573	3 419	99 028	42 908	56 120
75 - 79	106 769	46 003	60 766	5 629	2 769	2 860	101 140	43 234	57 906
80 - 84	55 970	21 945	34 025	2 926	1 262	1 664	53 044	20 683	32 361
85 - 89	40 784	16 680	24 104	1 895	818	1 077	38 889	15 862	23 027
90 - 94	18 739	6 967	11 772	780	323	457	17 959	6 644	11 315
95 +	18 526	6 448	12 078	842	280	562	17 684	6 168	11 516
Mali									
1 IV 2009 (CDFC)									
Total	14 528 662	7 204 990	7 323 672	3 274 727	1 643 671	1 631 056	11 253 935	5 561 319	5 692 616
0 - 4	2 623 385	1 328 871	1 294 514	501 628	253 735	247 893	2 121 757	1 075 136	1 046 621
5 - 9	2 357 823	1 202 875	1 154 948	438 784	220 467	218 317	1 919 039	982 408	936 631
10 - 14	1 784 004	918 866	865 138	382 494	183 203	199 291	1 401 510	735 663	665 847
15 - 19	1 516 146	732 526	783 620	427 554	194 158	233 396	1 088 592	538 368	550 224
20 - 24	1 141 903	529 535	612 368	341 272	171 703	169 569	800 631	357 832	442 799
25 - 29	995 702	449 099	546 603	267 899	132 127	135 772	727 803	316 972	410 831
30 - 34	812 798	385 003	427 795	206 544	109 060	97 484	606 254	275 943	330 311
35 - 39	651 949	325 055	326 894	164 783	89 830	74 953	487 166	235 225	251 941

Continent, country or area, date, code[a] and age (in years) Continent, pays ou zone, date, code[a] et âge (en années)	Total			Urban - Urbaine			Rural - Rurale		
	Both sexes Les deux sexes	Male Masculin	Female Féminin	Both sexes Les deux sexes	Male Masculin	Female Féminin	Both sexes Les deux sexes	Male Masculin	Female Féminin
AFRICA - AFRIQUE									
Mali									
1 IV 2009 (CDFC)									
40 - 44	546 603	271 239	275 364	128 845	70 127	58 718	417 758	201 112	216 646
45 - 49	445 887	228 626	217 261	103 042	56 502	46 540	342 845	172 124	170 721
50 - 54	381 806	189 424	192 382	82 013	44 826	37 187	299 793	144 598	155 195
55 - 59	282 677	148 594	134 083	57 960	31 957	26 003	224 717	116 637	108 080
60 - 64	251 018	127 557	123 461	46 442	23 790	22 652	204 576	103 767	100 809
65 - 69	165 374	88 292	77 082	30 159	15 641	14 518	135 215	72 651	62 564
70 - 74	133 382	67 319	66 063	23 729	11 518	12 211	109 653	55 801	53 852
75 - 79	77 101	40 904	36 197	12 871	6 306	6 565	64 230	34 598	29 632
80 +	85 594	41 992	43 602	14 246	6 009	8 237	71 348	35 983	35 365
Unknown - Inconnu	275 510	129 213	146 297	44 462	22 712	21 750	231 048	106 501	124 547
Mauritania - Mauritanie[5]									
24 III 2013 (CDJC)									
Total	3 537 368	1 743 074	1 794 294	...	...	...	...	...	...
0 - 4	614 692	316 217	298 475	...	...	...	...	...	...
5 - 9	520 102	263 263	256 839	...	...	...	...	...	...
10 - 14	429 505	212 838	216 667	...	...	...	...	...	...
15 - 19	361 404	176 116	185 288	...	...	...	...	...	...
20 - 24	302 440	144 478	157 962	...	...	...	...	...	...
25 - 29	257 353	121 586	135 767	...	...	...	...	...	...
30 - 34	213 525	99 834	113 691	...	...	...	...	...	...
35 - 39	178 957	83 578	95 379	...	...	...	...	...	...
40 - 44	151 336	72 108	79 228	...	...	...	...	...	...
45 - 49	124 813	60 297	64 516	...	...	...	...	...	...
50 - 54	102 490	50 739	51 751	...	...	...	...	...	...
55 - 59	81 720	41 075	40 645	...	...	...	...	...	...
60 - 64	62 119	31 660	30 459	...	...	...	...	...	...
65 - 69	47 175	24 120	23 055	...	...	...	...	...	...
70 - 74	35 296	18 167	17 129	...	...	...	...	...	...
75 - 79	24 901	12 670	12 231	...	...	...	...	...	...
80 - 84	16 664	8 080	8 584	...	...	...	...	...	...
85 +	12 876	6 248	6 628	...	...	...	...	...	...
Mauritius - Maurice[6]									
4 VII 2011 (CDJC)									
Total	1 236 817	610 848	625 969	499 349	244 688	254 661	737 468	366 160	371 308
0 - 4	73 078	36 702	36 376	26 297	13 220	13 077	46 781	23 482	23 299
5 - 9	89 015	44 947	44 068	32 036	16 177	15 859	56 979	28 770	28 209
10 - 14	93 639	47 302	46 337	35 028	17 523	17 505	58 611	29 779	28 832
15 - 19	101 008	50 715	50 293	39 403	19 725	19 678	61 605	30 990	30 615
20 - 24	92 671	46 871	45 800	37 224	18 836	18 388	55 447	28 035	27 412
25 - 29	90 937	45 589	45 348	35 908	17 899	18 009	55 029	27 690	27 339
30 - 34	103 429	52 182	51 247	39 099	19 805	19 294	64 330	32 377	31 953
35 - 39	87 797	44 241	43 556	32 781	16 142	16 639	55 016	28 099	26 917
40 - 44	89 386	45 150	44 236	34 449	17 010	17 439	54 937	28 140	26 797
45 - 49	99 341	49 800	49 541	41 705	20 637	21 068	57 636	29 163	28 473
50 - 54	86 337	42 996	43 341	37 429	18 627	18 802	48 908	24 369	24 539
55 - 59	73 054	35 713	37 341	32 421	15 983	16 438	40 633	19 730	20 903
60 - 64	57 342	27 143	30 199	25 449	12 058	13 391	31 893	15 085	16 808
65 - 69	35 439	15 846	19 593	16 700	7 527	9 173	18 739	8 319	10 420
70 - 74	25 375	10 986	14 389	12 872	5 661	7 211	12 503	5 325	7 178
75 - 79	18 044	7 349	10 695	9 320	3 851	5 469	8 724	3 498	5 226
80 - 84	11 369	4 176	7 193	6 028	2 253	3 775	5 341	1 923	3 418
85 - 89	6 368	2 135	4 233	3 427	1 179	2 248	2 941	956	1 985
90 - 94	1 982	512	1 470	1 046	275	771	936	237	699
95 - 99	491	107	384	297	60	237	194	47	147
100 +	96	13	83	55	7	48	41	6	35
Unknown - Inconnu	619	373	246	375	233	142	244	140	104
1 VII 2014 (ESDJ)[7]									
Total	1 260 934	624 002	636 932	...	...	...	...	...	...
0	13 522	6 852	6 670	...	...	...	...	...	...
1 - 4	57 817	29 322	28 495	...	...	...	...	...	...
5 - 9	85 499	43 388	42 111	...	...	...	...	...	...
10 - 14	97 540	49 594	47 946	...	...	...	...	...	...
15 - 19	97 782	49 383	48 399	...	...	...	...	...	...

Continent, country or area, date, code[a] and age (in years) / Continent, pays ou zone, date, code[a] et âge (en années)	Total			Urban - Urbaine			Rural - Rurale		
	Both sexes Les deux sexes	Male Masculin	Female Féminin	Both sexes Les deux sexes	Male Masculin	Female Féminin	Both sexes Les deux sexes	Male Masculin	Female Féminin
AFRICA - AFRIQUE									
Mauritius - Maurice[6]									
1 VII 2014 (ESDJ)[7]									
20 - 24	99 667	50 354	49 313	...	...	...	...	...	...
25 - 29	86 670	43 717	42 953	...	...	...	...	...	...
30 - 34	98 040	49 338	48 702	...	...	...	...	...	...
35 - 39	95 786	48 602	47 184	...	...	...	...	...	...
40 - 44	84 385	42 695	41 690	...	...	...	...	...	...
45 - 49	93 154	46 823	46 331	...	...	...	...	...	...
50 - 54	92 577	46 093	46 484	...	...	...	...	...	...
55 - 59	79 271	38 866	40 405	...	...	...	...	...	...
60 - 64	66 941	31 971	34 970	...	...	...	...	...	...
65 - 69	43 332	19 630	23 702	...	...	...	...	...	...
70 - 74	27 625	11 903	15 722	...	...	...	...	...	...
75 - 79	19 724	8 011	11 713	...	...	...	...	...	...
80 - 84	11 704	4 344	7 360	...	...	...	...	...	...
85 +	9 898	3 116	6 782	...	...	...	...	...	...
Mayotte									
31 VII 2007 (CDJC)									
Total	186 387	91 405	94 982	...	...	...	...	...	...
0	6 424	3 255	3 169	...	...	...	...	...	...
1 - 4	25 429	12 948	12 481	...	...	...	...	...	...
5 - 9	27 239	13 739	13 500	...	...	...	...	...	...
10 - 14	23 403	11 483	11 920	...	...	...	...	...	...
15 - 19	18 724	9 144	9 580	...	...	...	...	...	...
20 - 24	13 660	5 789	7 871	...	...	...	...	...	...
25 - 29	14 987	6 262	8 725	...	...	...	...	...	...
30 - 34	14 376	6 651	7 725	...	...	...	...	...	...
35 - 39	12 390	6 468	5 922	...	...	...	...	...	...
40 - 44	8 375	4 385	3 990	...	...	...	...	...	...
45 - 49	6 133	3 261	2 872	...	...	...	...	...	...
50 - 54	4 763	2 508	2 255	...	...	...	...	...	...
55 - 59	3 566	1 948	1 618	...	...	...	...	...	...
60 - 64	2 522	1 329	1 193	...	...	...	...	...	...
65 - 69	1 621	833	788	...	...	...	...	...	...
70 - 74	1 266	671	595	...	...	...	...	...	...
75 - 79	689	348	341	...	...	...	...	...	...
80 - 84	459	234	225	...	...	...	...	...	...
85 - 89	199	89	110	...	...	...	...	...	...
90 - 94	101	35	66	...	...	...	...	...	...
95 +	61	25	36	...	...	...	...	...	...
Morocco - Maroc[8]									
1 VII 2013 (ESDF)									
Total	32 950 445	16 371 475	16 578 971	19 512 904	9 533 742	9 979 162	13 437 541	6 837 733	6 599 809
0 - 4	2 903 919	1 482 899	1 421 020	1 538 623	784 659	753 964	1 365 296	698 240	667 056
5 - 9	2 845 161	1 453 315	1 391 847	1 534 498	777 963	756 534	1 310 664	675 351	635 312
10 - 14	2 894 204	1 473 231	1 420 973	1 568 834	789 667	779 167	1 325 370	683 564	641 806
15 - 19	3 043 535	1 547 292	1 496 243	1 648 978	814 055	834 924	1 394 557	733 237	661 319
20 - 24	3 178 851	1 614 483	1 564 368	1 789 076	862 131	926 945	1 389 775	752 352	637 423
25 - 29	2 972 219	1 477 952	1 494 267	1 776 381	851 252	925 128	1 195 838	626 699	569 139
30 - 34	2 747 687	1 338 558	1 409 129	1 722 868	829 862	893 006	1 024 819	508 696	516 123
35 - 39	2 306 566	1 106 764	1 199 802	1 486 948	704 701	782 247	819 618	402 063	417 556
40 - 44	2 045 869	975 428	1 070 441	1 349 956	644 385	705 571	695 913	331 043	364 871
45 - 49	1 809 846	862 688	947 158	1 210 448	575 188	635 260	599 398	287 500	311 898
50 - 54	1 762 347	859 927	902 421	1 147 448	562 942	584 506	614 899	296 985	317 914
55 - 59	1 375 290	704 367	670 923	895 355	464 283	431 072	479 935	240 084	239 851
60 - 64	1 073 646	543 733	529 913	667 089	343 552	323 537	406 556	200 181	206 375
65 - 69	662 674	314 577	348 098	400 434	188 734	211 700	262 241	125 843	136 398
70 - 74	609 636	276 251	333 385	358 211	157 374	200 837	251 425	118 877	132 548
75 +	718 996	340 012	378 983	417 758	182 994	234 764	301 238	157 018	144 220
Mozambique[2]									
1 VII 2014 (ESDF)									
Total	25 041 922	12 082 782	12 959 140	7 905 004	3 864 267	4 040 737	17 136 918	8 218 515	8 918 403
0 - 4	4 325 645	2 161 487	2 164 158	1 087 331	542 740	544 591	3 238 314	1 618 747	1 619 567
5 - 9	3 723 981	1 847 870	1 876 111	1 037 587	515 378	522 209	2 686 394	1 332 492	1 353 902
10 - 14	3 225 408	1 612 325	1 613 083	999 709	492 977	506 732	2 225 699	1 119 348	1 106 351

181

Continent, country or area, date, code[a] and age (in years) / Continent, pays ou zone, date, code[a] et âge (en annèes)	Total			Urban - Urbaine			Rural - Rurale		
	Both sexes Les deux sexes	Male Masculin	Female Féminin	Both sexes Les deux sexes	Male Masculin	Female Féminin	Both sexes Les deux sexes	Male Masculin	Female Féminin
AFRICA - AFRIQUE									
Mozambique[2]									
1 VII 2014 (ESDF)									
15 - 19	2 696 713	1 333 286	1 363 427	948 906	466 982	481 924	1 747 807	866 304	881 503
20 - 24	2 222 255	1 038 698	1 183 557	848 745	416 316	432 429	1 373 510	622 382	751 128
25 - 29	1 875 376	830 329	1 045 047	710 209	336 257	373 952	1 165 167	494 072	671 095
30 - 34	1 541 357	702 043	839 314	562 115	264 656	297 459	979 242	437 387	541 855
35 - 39	1 252 907	588 607	664 300	443 022	212 706	230 316	809 885	375 901	433 984
40 - 44	1 051 581	490 084	561 497	358 734	173 410	185 324	692 847	316 674	376 173
45 - 49	818 753	396 621	422 132	266 566	133 412	133 154	552 187	263 209	288 978
50 - 54	634 400	314 623	319 777	197 245	100 661	96 584	437 155	213 962	223 193
55 - 59	515 314	239 045	276 269	150 253	73 940	76 313	365 061	165 105	199 956
60 - 64	392 488	179 458	213 030	107 915	52 317	55 598	284 573	127 141	157 432
65 - 69	295 271	135 995	159 276	76 135	35 753	40 382	219 136	100 242	118 894
70 - 74	208 293	95 295	112 998	50 032	22 276	27 756	158 261	73 019	85 242
75 - 79	134 944	61 341	73 603	31 534	13 438	18 096	103 410	47 903	55 507
80 +	127 236	55 675	71 561	28 966	11 048	17 918	98 270	44 627	53 643
Namibia - Namibie[9]									
1 VII 2014 (ESDF)									
Total	2 237 894	1 087 178	1 150 716	1 025 147	500 469	524 678	1 212 747	586 709	626 038
0 - 4	313 007	158 229	154 778	135 778	68 604	67 174	177 229	89 625	87 604
5 - 9	263 264	132 713	130 551	90 226	45 189	45 037	173 038	87 524	85 514
10 - 14	239 023	119 477	119 546	83 409	40 489	42 920	155 614	78 988	76 626
15 - 19	243 203	119 995	123 208	90 294	41 602	48 692	152 909	78 393	74 516
20 - 24	228 320	112 074	116 246	112 641	52 586	60 055	115 679	59 488	56 191
25 - 29	196 214	96 205	100 009	125 044	61 032	64 012	71 170	35 173	35 997
30 - 34	159 244	77 560	81 684	101 087	50 183	50 904	58 157	27 377	30 780
35 - 39	133 989	65 263	68 726	79 749	39 953	39 796	54 240	25 310	28 930
40 - 44	108 850	52 124	56 726	61 067	30 481	30 586	47 783	21 643	26 140
45 - 49	86 084	40 171	45 913	45 627	22 976	22 651	40 457	17 195	23 262
50 - 54	69 283	31 124	38 159	34 250	17 242	17 008	35 033	13 882	21 151
55 - 59	51 965	22 549	29 416	23 814	11 704	12 110	28 151	10 845	17 306
60 - 64	41 488	18 291	23 197	15 660	7 548	8 112	25 828	10 743	15 085
65 - 69	33 735	14 572	19 163	9 915	4 380	5 535	23 820	10 192	13 628
70 - 74	24 388	9 982	14 406	6 415	2 680	3 735	17 973	7 302	10 671
75 - 79	17 037	6 934	10 103	4 451	1 790	2 661	12 586	5 144	7 442
80 +	28 800	9 915	18 885	5 720	2 030	3 690	23 080	7 885	15 195
Niger									
10 XII 2012 (CDJC)									
Total	17 138 707	8 518 818	8 619 889	2 778 337	1 397 695	1 380 642	14 360 370	7 121 123	7 239 247
0 - 4	3 696 791	1 891 826	1 804 965	472 139	240 745	231 394	3 224 652	1 651 081	1 573 571
5 - 9	2 995 004	1 524 504	1 470 500	412 567	206 414	206 153	2 582 437	1 318 090	1 264 347
10 - 14	2 163 813	1 088 679	1 075 134	363 784	176 755	187 029	1 800 029	911 924	888 105
15 - 19	1 727 779	834 345	893 434	314 251	161 949	152 302	1 413 528	672 396	741 132
20 - 24	1 320 316	631 280	689 036	292 612	150 135	142 477	1 027 704	481 145	546 559
25 - 29	1 070 992	521 141	549 851	194 852	96 249	98 603	876 140	424 892	451 248
30 - 34	897 561	430 506	467 055	163 519	81 175	82 344	734 042	349 331	384 711
35 - 39	729 784	349 963	379 821	134 412	66 061	68 351	595 372	283 902	311 470
40 - 44	582 219	285 869	296 350	105 367	55 554	49 813	476 852	230 315	246 537
45 - 49	499 732	243 368	256 364	92 198	46 654	45 544	407 534	196 714	210 820
50 - 54	392 556	195 591	196 965	69 374	35 559	33 815	323 182	160 032	163 150
55 - 59	304 324	151 019	153 305	52 925	26 577	26 348	251 399	124 442	126 957
60 - 64	229 406	114 428	114 978	36 394	18 711	17 683	193 012	95 717	97 295
65 - 69	184 733	90 566	94 167	28 230	13 837	14 393	156 503	76 729	79 774
70 - 74	141 279	69 752	71 527	20 105	9 897	10 208	121 174	59 855	61 319
75 - 79	103 206	50 476	52 730	13 277	6 184	7 093	89 929	44 292	45 637
80 - 84	66 273	31 506	34 767	8 054	3 456	4 598	58 219	28 050	30 169
85 +	32 939	13 999	18 940	4 277	1 783	2 494	28 662	12 216	16 446
1 VII 2013 (ESDJ)[10]									
Total	17 807 117	8 850 137	8 956 980	...	...	...	...	...	...
0 - 4	3 781 472	1 904 227	1 877 245	...	...	...	...	...	...
5 - 9	3 165 490	1 614 326	1 551 164	...	...	...	...	...	...
10 - 14	2 235 375	1 154 040	1 081 334	...	...	...	...	...	...
15 - 19	1 711 861	837 649	874 212	...	...	...	...	...	...
20 - 24	1 370 731	652 981	717 750	...	...	...	...	...	...
25 - 29	1 172 608	536 594	636 014	...	...	...	...	...	...

7. Population by age, sex and urban/rural residence: latest available year, 2005 - 2014
Population selon l'âge, le sexe et la résidence, urbaine/rurale : dernière année disponible, 2005 - 2014 (continued - suite)

Continent, country or area, date, code[a] and age (in years) / Continent, pays ou zone, date, code[a] et âge (en annèes)	Total			Urban - Urbaine			Rural - Rurale		
	Both sexes Les deux sexes	Male Masculin	Female Féminin	Both sexes Les deux sexes	Male Masculin	Female Féminin	Both sexes Les deux sexes	Male Masculin	Female Féminin
AFRICA - AFRIQUE									
Niger									
1 VII 2013 (ESDJ)[10]									
30 - 34	952 133	444 623	507 510	...	...	...	...	...	...
35 - 39	757 826	359 694	398 132	...	...	...	...	...	...
40 - 44	611 657	293 008	318 649	...	...	...	...	...	...
45 - 49	491 201	241 779	249 422	...	...	...	...	...	...
50 - 54	389 280	200 490	188 790	...	...	...	...	...	...
55 - 59	305 221	162 469	142 751	...	...	...	...	...	...
60 - 64	231 274	121 809	109 465	...	...	...	...	...	...
65 - 69	182 463	99 315	83 148	...	...	...	...	...	...
70 - 74	142 126	74 923	67 203	...	...	...	...	...	...
75 - 79	101 410	53 489	47 920	...	...	...	...	...	...
80 - 84	66 555	31 949	34 606	...	...	...	...	...	...
85 +	76 446	30 686	45 760	...	...	...	...	...	...
Unknown - Inconnu	61 987	36 085	25 902	...	...	...	...	...	...
Nigeria - Nigéria									
21 III 2006 (CDFC)									
Total	140 431 790	71 345 488	69 086 302	...	...	...	...	...	...
0 - 4	22 594 967	11 569 218	11 025 749	...	...	...	...	...	...
5 - 9	20 005 380	10 388 611	9 616 769	...	...	...	...	...	...
10 - 14	16 135 950	8 504 319	7 631 631	...	...	...	...	...	...
15 - 19	14 899 419	7 536 532	7 362 887	...	...	...	...	...	...
20 - 24	13 435 079	6 237 549	7 197 530	...	...	...	...	...	...
25 - 29	12 211 426	5 534 458	6 676 968	...	...	...	...	...	...
30 - 34	9 467 538	4 505 186	4 962 352	...	...	...	...	...	...
35 - 39	7 331 755	3 661 133	3 670 622	...	...	...	...	...	...
40 - 44	6 456 470	3 395 489	3 060 981	...	...	...	...	...	...
45 - 49	4 591 293	2 561 526	2 029 767	...	...	...	...	...	...
50 - 54	4 249 219	2 363 937	1 885 282	...	...	...	...	...	...
55 - 59	2 066 247	1 189 770	876 477	...	...	...	...	...	...
60 - 64	2 450 286	1 363 219	1 087 067	...	...	...	...	...	...
65 - 69	1 151 048	628 436	522 612	...	...	...	...	...	...
70 - 74	1 330 597	765 988	564 609	...	...	...	...	...	...
75 - 79	579 838	327 416	252 422	...	...	...	...	...	...
80 - 84	760 053	408 680	351 373	...	...	...	...	...	...
85 +	715 225	404 021	311 204	...	...	...	...	...	...
Republic of South Sudan - République de Soudan du Sud									
21 IV 2008 (CDFC)									
Total	8 260 490	4 287 300	3 973 190	1 405 186	754 086	651 100	6 855 304	3 533 214	3 322 090
0	231 146	121 882	109 264	43 300	22 617	20 683	187 846	99 265	88 581
1 - 4	1 072 985	567 545	505 440	174 976	91 509	83 467	898 009	476 036	421 973
5 - 9	1 297 816	688 385	609 431	196 136	101 760	94 376	1 101 680	586 625	515 055
10 - 14	1 057 390	569 537	487 853	160 054	84 981	75 073	897 336	484 556	412 780
15 - 19	889 829	462 902	426 927	153 683	81 602	72 081	736 146	381 300	354 846
20 - 24	739 006	360 788	378 218	148 237	78 336	69 901	590 769	282 452	308 317
25 - 29	698 011	335 398	362 613	141 623	76 445	65 178	556 388	258 953	297 435
30 - 34	536 915	258 531	278 384	101 597	56 705	44 892	435 318	201 826	233 492
35 - 39	475 813	238 985	236 828	87 844	49 346	38 498	387 969	189 639	198 330
40 - 44	339 704	173 493	166 211	58 645	33 444	25 201	281 059	140 049	141 010
45 - 49	276 100	149 941	126 159	45 605	26 316	19 289	230 495	123 625	106 870
50 - 54	197 265	104 812	92 453	31 870	17 548	14 322	165 395	87 264	78 131
55 - 59	121 795	67 845	53 950	18 520	10 557	7 963	103 275	57 288	45 987
60 - 64	115 631	64 236	51 395	16 523	8 849	7 674	99 108	55 387	43 721
65 - 69	73 155	41 455	31 700	9 750	5 239	4 511	63 405	36 216	27 189
70 - 74	59 287	34 785	24 502	7 756	4 087	3 669	51 531	30 698	20 833
75 - 79	28 919	17 424	11 495	3 522	1 898	1 624	25 397	15 526	9 871
80 - 84	24 514	14 314	10 200	2 867	1 497	1 370	21 647	12 817	8 830
85 - 89	10 982	6 731	4 251	1 121	550	571	9 861	6 181	3 680
90 - 94	7 361	4 477	2 884	873	472	401	6 488	4 005	2 483
95 +	6 866	3 834	3 032	684	328	356	6 182	3 506	2 676

Continent, country or area, date, code[a] and age (in years) / Continent, pays ou zone, date, code[a] et âge (en années)	Total			Urban - Urbaine			Rural - Rurale		
	Both sexes Les deux sexes	Male Masculin	Female Féminin	Both sexes Les deux sexes	Male Masculin	Female Féminin	Both sexes Les deux sexes	Male Masculin	Female Féminin
AFRICA - AFRIQUE									
Reunion - Réunion									
1 I 2010* (ESDJ)									
Total	828 054	399 728	428 326	...	...	...	...	...	...
0 - 4	68 137	35 044	33 093	...	...	...	...	...	...
5 - 9	71 223	36 404	34 819	...	...	...	...	...	...
10 - 14	70 827	36 292	34 535	...	...	...	...	...	...
15 - 19	71 254	35 775	35 479	...	...	...	...	...	...
20 - 24	56 332	28 067	28 265	...	...	...	...	...	...
25 - 29	50 540	22 922	27 618	...	...	...	...	...	...
30 - 34	55 239	24 936	30 303	...	...	...	...	...	...
35 - 39	60 586	28 029	32 557	...	...	...	...	...	...
40 - 44	67 780	32 311	35 469	...	...	...	...	...	...
45 - 49	62 291	30 352	31 939	...	...	...	...	...	...
50 - 54	49 960	24 261	25 699	...	...	...	...	...	...
55 - 59	42 397	20 577	21 820	...	...	...	...	...	...
60 - 64	31 315	15 588	15 727	...	...	...	...	...	...
65 - 69	24 247	11 380	12 867	...	...	...	...	...	...
70 - 74	18 441	7 912	10 529	...	...	...	...	...	...
75 - 79	12 549	5 036	7 513	...	...	...	...	...	...
80 - 84	8 243	2 948	5 295	...	...	...	...	...	...
85 - 89	4 641	1 438	3 203	...	...	...	...	...	...
90 - 94	1 523	350	1 173	...	...	...	...	...	...
95 +	529	106	423	...	...	...	...	...	...
Rwanda[2]									
1 VII 2012 (ESDF)									
Total	11 033 141	5 342 112	5 691 029	...	...	...	...	...	...
0	430 920	218 488	212 432	...	...	...	...	...	...
1 - 4	1 499 630	754 959	744 672	...	...	...	...	...	...
5 - 9	1 534 001	770 292	763 709	...	...	...	...	...	...
10 - 14	1 230 213	608 836	621 378	...	...	...	...	...	...
15 - 19	1 120 730	552 629	568 101	...	...	...	...	...	...
20 - 24	1 075 971	525 485	550 486	...	...	...	...	...	...
25 - 29	1 049 712	508 839	540 872	...	...	...	...	...	...
30 - 34	782 772	366 700	416 072	...	...	...	...	...	...
35 - 39	532 702	241 362	291 340	...	...	...	...	...	...
40 - 44	425 733	197 005	228 728	...	...	...	...	...	...
45 - 49	358 499	165 096	193 402	...	...	...	...	...	...
50 - 54	333 839	153 080	180 759	...	...	...	...	...	...
55 - 59	239 433	107 200	132 234	...	...	...	...	...	...
60 - 64	164 223	71 924	92 299	...	...	...	...	...	...
65 - 69	96 710	38 125	58 585	...	...	...	...	...	...
70 - 74	75 521	29 285	46 236	...	...	...	...	...	...
75 - 79	45 293	17 736	27 557	...	...	...	...	...	...
80 +	37 239	15 071	22 168	...	...	...	...	...	...
Saint Helena ex. dep. - Sainte-Hélène sans dép.									
31 XII 2013 (ESDF)									
Total	4 211	2 139	2 072	...	...	...	...	...	...
0 - 4	176	89	87	...	...	...	...	...	...
5 - 9	209	115	94	...	...	...	...	...	...
10 - 14	249	131	118	...	...	...	...	...	...
15 - 19	301	157	144	...	...	...	...	...	...
20 - 24	164	84	80	...	...	...	...	...	...
25 - 29	171	77	94	...	...	...	...	...	...
30 - 34	196	88	108	...	...	...	...	...	...
35 - 39	297	138	159	...	...	...	...	...	...
40 - 44	341	178	163	...	...	...	...	...	...
45 - 49	362	179	183	...	...	...	...	...	...
50 - 54	305	166	139	...	...	...	...	...	...
55 - 59	345	182	163	...	...	...	...	...	...
60 - 64	350	208	142	...	...	...	...	...	...
65 - 69	256	138	118	...	...	...	...	...	...
70 - 74	194	111	83	...	...	...	...	...	...
75 - 79	135	57	78	...	...	...	...	...	...
80 - 84	88	28	60	...	...	...	...	...	...

Continent, country or area, date, code[a] and age (in years) / Continent, pays ou zone, date, code[a] et âge (en annèes)	Total			Urban - Urbaine			Rural - Rurale		
	Both sexes Les deux sexes	Male Masculin	Female Féminin	Both sexes Les deux sexes	Male Masculin	Female Féminin	Both sexes Les deux sexes	Male Masculin	Female Féminin
AFRICA - AFRIQUE									
Saint Helena ex. dep. - Sainte-Hélène sans dép.									
31 XII 2013 (ESDF)									
85 - 89	48	10	38	...	...	...	...	...	...
90 - 94	19	2	17	...	...	...	...	...	...
95 - 99	4	-	4	...	...	...	...	...	...
100 +	-	-	-	...	...	...	...	...	...
Unknown - Inconnu	1	1	-	...	...	...	...	...	...
Saint Helena: Ascension - Sainte-Hélène: Ascension									
1 VII 2008 (ESDJ)									
Total	702	397	305	...	...	...	...	...	...
0 - 4	32	16	16	...	...	...	...	...	...
5 - 9	19	9	10	...	...	...	...	...	...
10 - 14	41	20	21	...	...	...	...	...	...
15 - 19	30	19	11	...	...	...	...	...	...
20 - 24	63	29	34	...	...	...	...	...	...
25 - 29	73	42	31	...	...	...	...	...	...
30 - 34	76	41	35	...	...	...	...	...	...
35 - 39	92	58	34	...	...	...	...	...	...
40 - 44	85	42	43	...	...	...	...	...	...
45 - 49	65	36	29	...	...	...	...	...	...
50 - 54	51	32	19	...	...	...	...	...	...
55 - 59	43	29	14	...	...	...	...	...	...
60 - 64	21	15	6	...	...	...	...	...	...
65 - 69	10	9	1	...	...	...	...	...	...
70 - 74	-	-	-	...	...	...	...	...	...
75 - 79	-	-	-	...	...	...	...	...	...
80 +	1	-	1	...	...	...	...	...	...
Sao Tome and Principe - Sao Tomé-et-Principe									
13 V 2012 (CDFC)									
Total	178 739	88 867	89 872	...	...	...	...	...	...
0 - 4	27 720	13 962	13 758	...	...	...	...	...	...
5 - 9	25 472	12 730	12 742	...	...	...	...	...	...
10 - 14	21 427	10 726	10 701	...	...	...	...	...	...
15 - 19	18 457	9 353	9 104	...	...	...	...	...	...
20 - 24	15 974	7 978	7 996	...	...	...	...	...	...
25 - 29	14 815	7 366	7 449	...	...	...	...	...	...
30 - 34	12 522	6 203	6 319	...	...	...	...	...	...
35 - 39	9 731	4 875	4 856	...	...	...	...	...	...
40 - 44	7 879	3 971	3 908	...	...	...	...	...	...
45 - 49	6 311	3 050	3 261	...	...	...	...	...	...
50 - 54	5 364	2 606	2 758	...	...	...	...	...	...
55 - 59	3 816	1 807	2 009	...	...	...	...	...	...
60 - 64	2 661	1 338	1 323	...	...	...	...	...	...
65 - 69	1 925	918	1 007	...	...	...	...	...	...
70 - 74	1 878	850	1 028	...	...	...	...	...	...
75 - 79	1 411	609	802	...	...	...	...	...	...
80 +	1 376	525	851	...	...	...	...	...	...
Senegal - Sénégal									
19 XI 2013* (CDFC)									
Total	12 873 601	6 428 189	6 445 412	...	...	...	...	...	...
0 - 4	1 896 808	969 976	926 832	...	...	...	...	...	...
5 - 9	1 922 412	998 659	923 753	...	...	...	...	...	...
10 - 14	1 597 064	834 583	762 481	...	...	...	...	...	...
15 - 19	1 364 899	689 282	675 617	...	...	...	...	...	...
20 - 24	1 163 869	567 280	596 589	...	...	...	...	...	...
25 - 29	1 033 035	489 390	543 645	...	...	...	...	...	...
30 - 34	841 899	406 808	435 091	...	...	...	...	...	...
35 - 39	666 643	322 291	344 352	...	...	...	...	...	...
40 - 44	555 359	263 253	292 106	...	...	...	...	...	...
45 - 49	425 881	201 038	224 843	...	...	...	...	...	...
50 - 54	405 797	194 098	211 699	...	...	...	...	...	...
55 - 59	288 564	145 668	142 896	...	...	...	...	...	...

Continent, country or area, date, codeᵃ and age (in years) / Continent, pays ou zone, date, codeᵃ et âge (en années)	Total			Urban - Urbaine			Rural - Rurale		
	Both sexes Les deux sexes	Male Masculin	Female Féminin	Both sexes Les deux sexes	Male Masculin	Female Féminin	Both sexes Les deux sexes	Male Masculin	Female Féminin
AFRICA - AFRIQUE									
Senegal - Sénégal									
19 XI 2013* (CDFC)									
60 - 64	257 942	126 634	131 308	...	...	...	...	...	...
65 - 69	146 034	73 175	72 859	...	...	...	...	...	...
70 - 74	135 935	64 071	71 864	...	...	...	...	...	...
75 - 79	72 820	36 558	36 262	...	...	...	...	...	...
80 - 84	55 005	25 272	29 733	...	...	...	...	...	...
85 - 89	23 026	11 591	11 435	...	...	...	...	...	...
90 - 94	11 933	5 150	6 783	...	...	...	...	...	...
95 - 99	5 413	2 288	3 125	...	...	...	...	...	...
100 +	3 253	1 119	2 134	...	...	...	...	...	...
Unknown - Inconnu	10	5	5	...	...	...	...	...	...
Seychelles									
1 VII 2014 (ESDF)									
Total	91 359	45 278	46 081	...	...	...	...	...	...
0	1 522	784	738	...	...	...	...	...	...
1 - 4	5 992	3 070	2 922	...	...	...	...	...	...
5 - 9	6 405	3 191	3 214	...	...	...	...	...	...
10 - 14	5 947	2 932	3 015	...	...	...	...	...	...
15 - 19	5 746	3 012	2 734	...	...	...	...	...	...
20 - 24	6 458	3 379	3 079	...	...	...	...	...	...
25 - 29	7 068	3 740	3 328	...	...	...	...	...	...
30 - 34	7 981	3 964	4 017	...	...	...	...	...	...
35 - 39	7 133	3 456	3 677	...	...	...	...	...	...
40 - 44	7 495	3 989	3 506	...	...	...	...	...	...
45 - 49	6 611	3 049	3 562	...	...	...	...	...	...
50 - 54	7 193	3 507	3 686	...	...	...	...	...	...
55 - 59	4 865	2 505	2 360	...	...	...	...	...	...
60 - 64	3 570	1 719	1 851	...	...	...	...	...	...
65 - 69	2 505	1 209	1 296	...	...	...	...	...	...
70 - 74	1 812	812	1 000	...	...	...	...	...	...
75 - 79	1 356	493	863	...	...	...	...	...	...
80 - 84	972	296	676	...	...	...	...	...	...
85 - 89	487	124	363	...	...	...	...	...	...
90 - 94	183	41	142	...	...	...	...	...	...
95 - 99	50	5	45	...	...	...	...	...	...
100 +	8	1	7	...	...	...	...	...	...
Sierra Leone									
1 VII 2010 (ESDF)									
Total	5 746 800	2 786 797	2 960 003	2 304 955	1 138 563	1 166 392	3 441 845	1 648 234	1 793 611
0 - 4	878 231	437 908	440 323	297 865	147 565	150 300	580 366	290 343	290 023
5 - 9	856 605	424 222	432 383	307 007	145 641	161 366	549 598	278 581	271 017
10 - 14	662 651	338 453	324 198	303 094	148 401	154 693	359 557	190 052	169 505
15 - 19	637 914	308 982	328 932	287 597	141 564	146 033	350 317	167 418	182 899
20 - 24	488 054	221 932	266 122	241 599	119 622	121 977	246 455	102 310	144 145
25 - 29	473 952	210 004	263 948	205 137	102 492	102 645	268 815	107 512	161 303
30 - 34	356 727	160 822	195 905	149 414	73 308	76 106	207 313	87 514	119 799
35 - 39	341 470	160 326	181 144	133 461	66 104	67 357	208 009	94 222	113 787
40 - 44	247 978	123 279	124 699	97 102	51 623	45 479	150 876	71 656	79 220
45 - 49	201 708	107 932	93 776	76 536	41 832	34 704	125 172	66 100	59 072
50 - 54	149 167	77 236	71 931	55 139	30 564	24 575	94 028	46 672	47 356
55 - 59	96 801	51 344	45 457	37 477	21 157	16 320	59 324	30 187	29 137
60 - 64	99 394	44 873	54 521	31 058	14 915	16 143	68 336	29 958	38 378
65 - 69	71 174	34 054	37 120	24 423	11 420	13 003	46 751	22 634	24 117
70 - 74	61 847	28 198	33 649	18 941	8 268	10 673	42 906	19 930	22 976
75 - 79	41 728	21 586	20 142	12 876	6 356	6 520	28 852	15 230	13 622
80 +	81 399	35 646	45 753	26 229	7 731	18 498	55 170	27 915	27 255
South Africa - Afrique du Sud									
1 VII 2014 (ESDF)									
Total	54 001 953	26 366 008	27 635 944	...	...	...	...	...	...
0 - 4	5 719 329	2 892 219	2 827 110	...	...	...	...	...	...
5 - 9	5 336 710	2 692 433	2 644 277	...	...	...	...	...	...
10 - 14	5 123 726	2 580 229	2 543 497	...	...	...	...	...	...
15 - 19	5 217 561	2 624 166	2 593 395	...	...	...	...	...	...
20 - 24	5 267 117	2 662 829	2 604 288	...	...	...	...	...	...

Continent, country or area, date, code[a] and age (in years) / Continent, pays ou zone, date, code[a] et âge (en années)	Total			Urban - Urbaine			Rural - Rurale		
	Both sexes Les deux sexes	Male Masculin	Female Féminin	Both sexes Les deux sexes	Male Masculin	Female Féminin	Both sexes Les deux sexes	Male Masculin	Female Féminin
AFRICA - AFRIQUE									
South Africa - Afrique du Sud									
1 VII 2014 (ESDF)									
25 - 29	4 954 532	2 515 096	2 439 436	...	...	...	...	...	...
30 - 34	4 090 283	2 034 229	2 056 054	...	...	...	...	...	...
35 - 39	3 503 217	1 739 688	1 763 529	...	...	...	...	...	...
40 - 44	3 121 822	1 482 086	1 639 736	...	...	...	...	...	...
45 - 49	2 753 470	1 270 867	1 482 603	...	...	...	...	...	...
50 - 54	2 377 730	1 089 941	1 287 789	...	...	...	...	...	...
55 - 59	1 994 390	907 807	1 086 583	...	...	...	...	...	...
60 - 64	1 570 178	703 921	866 257	...	...	...	...	...	...
65 - 69	1 176 466	492 791	683 675	...	...	...	...	...	...
70 - 74	831 263	327 812	503 451	...	...	...	...	...	...
75 - 79	530 877	202 623	328 254	...	...	...	...	...	...
80 +	433 281	147 270	286 011	...	...	...	...	...	...
Swaziland									
1 VII 2014 (ESDF)									
Total	1 106 189	525 232	580 957	255 986	121 881	134 105	850 203	403 351	446 852
0	31 983	16 210	15 773	...	...	...	...	...	...
1 - 4	116 154	59 235	56 919	19 941	10 151	9 790	96 213	49 084	47 129
5 - 9	129 126	65 793	63 333	21 838	11 109	10 729	107 288	54 684	52 604
10 - 14	130 434	65 175	65 259	20 711	9 885	10 826	109 723	55 290	54 433
15 - 19	127 817	62 535	65 282	22 326	9 798	12 528	105 491	52 737	52 754
20 - 24	117 696	56 700	60 996	28 127	12 308	15 819	89 569	44 392	45 177
25 - 29	100 827	46 692	54 135	33 613	15 496	18 117	67 214	31 196	36 018
30 - 34	83 531	36 738	46 793	30 495	14 735	15 760	53 036	22 003	31 033
35 - 39	65 153	27 681	37 472	22 707	11 159	11 548	42 446	16 522	25 924
40 - 44	50 644	21 160	29 484	17 072	8 345	8 727	33 572	12 815	20 757
45 - 49	39 779	16 819	22 960	12 171	6 023	6 148	27 608	10 796	16 812
50 - 54	31 154	13 499	17 655	8 292	4 178	4 114	22 862	9 321	13 541
55 - 59	24 526	10 761	13 765	5 622	2 746	2 876	18 904	8 015	10 889
60 - 64	19 049	8 526	10 523	3 462	1 595	1 867	15 587	6 931	8 656
65 - 69	14 610	6 675	7 935	1 870	769	1 101	12 740	5 906	6 834
70 - 74	10 542	4 950	5 592	1 090	414	676	9 452	4 536	4 916
75 - 79	6 626	3 152	3 474	614	228	386	6 012	2 924	3 088
80 +	6 538	2 931	3 607	455	109	346	6 083	2 822	3 261
Togo									
6 XI 2010 (CDJC)									
Total	6 191 155	3 009 095	3 182 060	...	...	...	...	...	...
0	190 136	96 043	94 093	...	...	...	...	...	...
1 - 4	711 135	360 481	350 654	...	...	...	...	...	...
5 - 9	951 700	482 501	469 199	...	...	...	...	...	...
10 - 14	747 726	390 477	357 249	...	...	...	...	...	...
15 - 19	606 401	313 257	293 144	...	...	...	...	...	...
20 - 24	545 245	252 807	292 438	...	...	...	...	...	...
25 - 29	496 822	214 803	282 019	...	...	...	...	...	...
30 - 34	424 380	199 636	224 744	...	...	...	...	...	...
35 - 39	352 008	166 528	185 480	...	...	...	...	...	...
40 - 44	291 584	139 731	151 853	...	...	...	...	...	...
45 - 49	228 446	112 191	116 255	...	...	...	...	...	...
50 - 54	178 233	82 969	95 264	...	...	...	...	...	...
55 - 59	115 950	54 936	61 014	...	...	...	...	...	...
60 - 64	102 694	44 431	58 263	...	...	...	...	...	...
65 - 69	66 324	26 700	39 624	...	...	...	...	...	...
70 - 74	61 756	24 127	37 629	...	...	...	...	...	...
75 - 79	33 574	13 250	20 324	...	...	...	...	...	...
80 +	73 591	27 960	45 631	...	...	...	...	...	...
Unknown - Inconnu	13 450	6 267	7 183	...	...	...	...	...	...
Tunisia - Tunisie									
23 IV 2014 (CDFC)									
Total	10 982 753	5 472 333	5 510 420	...	...	...	...	...	...
0 - 4	972 171	505 509	466 662	...	...	...	...	...	...
5 - 9	849 006	440 644	408 362	...	...	...	...	...	...
10 - 14	789 622	407 938	381 684	...	...	...	...	...	...
15 - 19	827 508	421 716	405 792	...	...	...	...	...	...
20 - 24	925 409	459 814	465 595	...	...	...	...	...	...

7. Population by age, sex and urban/rural residence: latest available year, 2005 - 2014
Population selon l'âge, le sexe et la résidence, urbaine/rurale : dernière année disponible, 2005 - 2014 (continued - suite)

Continent, country or area, date, code[a] and age (in years) / Continent, pays ou zone, date, code[a] et âge (en années)	Total			Urban - Urbaine			Rural - Rurale		
	Both sexes Les deux sexes	Male Masculin	Female Féminin	Both sexes Les deux sexes	Male Masculin	Female Féminin	Both sexes Les deux sexes	Male Masculin	Female Féminin
AFRICA - AFRIQUE									
Tunisia - Tunisie									
23 IV 2014 (CDFC)									
25 - 29	934 617	449 932	484 685	...	...	...	...	...	...
30 - 34	983 781	477 322	506 459	...	...	...	...	...	...
35 - 39	816 986	397 594	419 392	...	...	...	...	...	...
40 - 44	727 848	357 353	370 495	...	...	...	...	...	...
45 - 49	682 956	331 283	351 673	...	...	...	...	...	...
50 - 54	650 608	324 423	326 185	...	...	...	...	...	...
55 - 59	535 168	268 380	266 788	...	...	...	...	...	...
60 - 64	425 424	212 900	212 524	...	...	...	...	...	...
65 - 69	262 303	127 168	135 135	...	...	...	...	...	...
70 - 74	220 681	107 097	113 584	...	...	...	...	...	...
75 - 79	166 896	81 732	85 164	...	...	...	...	...	...
80 +	211 769	101 528	110 241	...	...	...	...	...	...
Uganda - Ouganda									
1 VII 2012 (ESDF)									
Total	34 131 400	...	...	...	...	...	...	...	...
0 - 4	7 220 700	...	...	...	...	...	...	...	...
5 - 9	5 930 300	...	...	...	...	...	...	...	...
10 - 14	4 160 000	...	...	...	...	...	...	...	...
15 - 19	3 661 100	...	...	...	...	...	...	...	...
20 - 24	3 033 800	...	...	...	...	...	...	...	...
25 - 29	2 468 500	...	...	...	...	...	...	...	...
30 - 34	1 969 300	...	...	...	...	...	...	...	...
35 - 39	1 549 200	...	...	...	...	...	...	...	...
40 - 44	1 206 400	...	...	...	...	...	...	...	...
45 - 49	927 600	...	...	...	...	...	...	...	...
50 - 54	695 700	...	...	...	...	...	...	...	...
55 - 59	501 900	...	...	...	...	...	...	...	...
60 - 64	344 400	...	...	...	...	...	...	...	...
65 - 69	221 300	...	...	...	...	...	...	...	...
70 - 74	130 300	...	...	...	...	...	...	...	...
75 - 79	67 800	...	...	...	...	...	...	...	...
80 +	43 100	...	...	...	...	...	...	...	...
United Republic of Tanzania - République Unie de Tanzanie[11]									
1 VII 2013 (ESDF)									
Total	47 132 580	23 267 957	23 864 623	12 909 536	6 386 303	6 523 233	34 223 044	16 881 654	17 341 390
0	1 776 107	895 971	880 136	403 952	203 710	200 242	1 372 155	692 261	679 894
1 - 4	6 536 000	3 295 033	3 240 967	1 521 372	766 466	754 906	5 014 628	2 528 567	2 486 061
5 - 9	7 160 846	3 608 891	3 551 955	1 723 220	857 109	866 111	5 437 626	2 751 782	2 685 844
10 - 14	5 464 181	2 735 494	2 728 687	1 364 854	661 195	703 659	4 099 327	2 074 299	2 025 028
15 - 19	4 985 943	2 494 983	2 490 960	1 427 786	682 734	745 052	3 558 157	1 812 249	1 745 908
20 - 24	4 340 143	2 179 173	2 160 970	1 333 476	672 789	660 687	3 006 667	1 506 384	1 500 283
25 - 29	3 484 607	1 730 600	1 754 007	1 134 814	563 796	571 018	2 349 793	1 166 804	1 182 989
30 - 34	2 852 197	1 289 114	1 563 083	974 580	450 823	523 757	1 877 617	838 291	1 039 326
35 - 39	2 601 610	1 207 182	1 394 428	867 422	418 436	448 986	1 734 188	788 746	945 442
40 - 44	2 121 302	1 032 605	1 088 697	672 984	346 836	326 148	1 448 318	685 769	762 549
45 - 49	1 568 017	770 149	797 868	469 417	248 681	220 736	1 098 600	521 468	577 132
50 - 54	1 234 201	604 621	629 580	339 138	180 385	158 753	895 063	424 236	470 827
55 - 59	881 484	422 141	459 343	223 562	117 172	106 390	657 922	304 969	352 953
60 - 64	734 938	347 604	387 334	172 297	88 004	84 293	562 641	259 600	303 041
65 - 69	466 882	223 365	243 517	100 337	50 363	49 974	366 545	173 002	193 543
70 - 74	387 755	179 960	207 795	78 544	35 541	43 003	309 211	144 419	164 792
75 - 79	245 872	115 076	130 796	46 843	20 380	26 463	199 029	94 696	104 333
80 +	290 495	135 995	154 500	54 938	21 883	33 055	235 557	114 112	121 445
Zambia - Zambie									
16 X 2010 (CDJC)									
Total	13 092 666	6 454 647	6 638 019	5 173 450	2 548 011	2 625 439	7 919 216	3 906 636	4 012 580
0 - 4	2 252 748	1 121 468	1 131 280	764 592	380 464	384 128	1 488 156	741 004	747 152
5 - 9	1 916 287	954 332	961 955	656 170	322 268	333 902	1 260 117	632 064	628 053
10 - 14	1 774 134	878 572	895 562	672 089	320 423	351 666	1 102 045	558 149	543 896
15 - 19	1 531 115	748 616	782 499	656 061	311 922	344 139	875 054	436 694	438 360
20 - 24	1 194 642	553 267	641 375	544 640	251 543	293 097	650 002	301 724	348 278

Continent, country or area, date, code[a] and age (in years) Continent, pays ou zone, date, code[a] et âge (en annèes)	Total			Urban - Urbaine			Rural - Rurale		
	Both sexes Les deux sexes	Male Masculin	Female Féminin	Both sexes Les deux sexes	Male Masculin	Female Féminin	Both sexes Les deux sexes	Male Masculin	Female Féminin
AFRICA - AFRIQUE									
Zambia - Zambie									
16 X 2010 (CDJC)									
25 - 29	1 057 077	497 774	559 303	492 713	233 826	258 887	564 364	263 948	300 416
30 - 34	840 308	425 227	415 081	393 374	202 930	190 444	446 934	222 297	224 637
35 - 39	682 921	357 097	325 824	307 182	167 113	140 069	375 739	189 984	185 755
40 - 44	473 238	250 415	222 823	200 717	111 062	89 655	272 521	139 353	133 168
45 - 49	376 164	189 047	187 117	151 364	78 278	73 086	224 800	110 769	114 031
50 - 54	284 864	138 764	146 100	111 791	55 850	55 941	173 073	82 914	90 159
55 - 59	194 162	96 718	97 444	75 456	39 790	35 666	118 706	56 928	61 778
60 - 64	168 563	78 301	90 262	55 664	28 866	26 798	112 899	49 435	63 464
65 - 69	122 931	56 814	66 117	35 552	17 637	17 915	87 379	39 177	48 202
70 - 74	93 348	43 945	49 403	24 207	11 599	12 608	69 141	32 346	36 795
75 - 79	63 063	31 929	31 134	15 591	7 323	8 268	47 472	24 606	22 866
80 - 84	33 598	16 569	17 029	8 349	3 788	4 561	25 249	12 781	12 468
85 - 89	19 118	9 651	9 467	4 762	2 118	2 644	14 356	7 533	6 823
90 - 94	6 450	3 245	3 205	1 477	652	825	4 973	2 593	2 380
95 +	7 935	2 896	5 039	1 699	559	1 140	6 236	2 337	3 899
Zimbabwe									
17 VIII 2012 (CDFC)									
Total	13 061 239	6 280 539	6 780 700	4 284 145	2 039 224	2 244 921	8 777 094	4 241 315	4 535 779
0 - 4	1 978 474	986 596	991 878	598 256	297 469	300 787	1 380 218	689 127	691 091
5 - 9	1 698 160	845 062	853 098	444 636	216 870	227 766	1 253 524	628 192	625 332
10 - 14	1 695 647	849 473	846 174	436 641	206 681	229 960	1 259 006	642 792	616 214
15 - 19	1 412 033	699 230	712 803	465 606	199 010	266 596	946 427	500 220	446 207
20 - 24	1 195 664	543 466	652 198	491 795	214 391	277 404	703 869	329 075	374 794
25 - 29	1 131 691	519 834	611 857	487 413	224 788	262 625	644 278	295 046	349 232
30 - 34	920 747	443 539	477 208	387 867	192 046	195 821	532 880	251 493	281 387
35 - 39	736 741	362 497	374 244	293 412	152 117	141 295	443 329	210 380	232 949
40 - 44	524 786	268 460	256 326	208 628	113 140	95 488	316 158	155 320	160 838
45 - 49	348 014	161 257	186 757	128 657	64 099	64 558	219 357	97 158	122 199
50 - 54	350 855	139 101	211 754	105 536	49 123	56 413	245 319	89 978	155 341
55 - 59	282 344	120 776	161 568	79 861	39 203	40 658	202 483	81 573	120 910
60 - 64	226 716	96 779	129 937	52 275	24 852	27 423	174 441	71 927	102 514
65 - 69	167 113	73 055	94 058	34 232	15 508	18 724	132 881	57 547	75 334
70 - 74	137 697	62 230	75 467	24 860	10 889	13 971	112 837	51 341	61 496
75 +	226 894	96 640	130 254	34 907	14 342	20 565	191 987	82 298	109 689
Unknown - Inconnu	27 663	12 544	15 119	9 563	4 696	4 867	18 100	7 848	10 252
AMERICA, NORTH - **AMÉRIQUE DU NORD**									
Antigua and Barbuda - Antigua-et-Barbuda									
27 V 2011 (CDJC)									
Total	85 567	40 986	44 581	...	...	...	...	...	...
0 - 4	6 623	3 361	3 262	...	...	...	...	...	...
5 - 9	6 460	3 272	3 188	...	...	...	...	...	...
10 - 14	7 329	3 690	3 638	...	...	...	...	...	...
15 - 19	7 073	3 554	3 519	...	...	...	...	...	...
20 - 24	6 624	3 206	3 418	...	...	...	...	...	...
25 - 29	6 647	3 135	3 512	...	...	...	...	...	...
30 - 34	6 617	3 101	3 516	...	...	...	...	...	...
35 - 39	6 748	3 049	3 699	...	...	...	...	...	...
40 - 44	6 712	3 124	3 588	...	...	...	...	...	...
45 - 49	6 241	2 893	3 348	...	...	...	...	...	...
50 - 54	5 110	2 416	2 694	...	...	...	...	...	...
55 - 59	3 721	1 763	1 957	...	...	...	...	...	...
60 - 64	2 968	1 398	1 569	...	...	...	...	...	...
65 - 69	2 238	1 066	1 172	...	...	...	...	...	...
70 - 74	1 500	690	810	...	...	...	...	...	...
75 - 79	1 181	527	654	...	...	...	...	...	...
80 - 84	850	331	520	...	...	...	...	...	...
85 - 89	512	214	298	...	...	...	...	...	...
90 - 94	193	72	122	...	...	...	...	...	...

Continent, country or area, date, code[a] and age (in years) Continent, pays ou zone, date, code[a] et âge (en annèes)	Total			Urban - Urbaine			Rural - Rurale		
	Both sexes Les deux sexes	Male Masculin	Female Féminin	Both sexes Les deux sexes	Male Masculin	Female Féminin	Both sexes Les deux sexes	Male Masculin	Female Féminin
AMERICA, NORTH - AMÉRIQUE DU NORD									
Antigua and Barbuda - Antigua-et-Barbuda									
27 V 2011 (CDJC)									
95 + ...	84	27	57	...	...	...	...	...	...
Unknown - Inconnu	136	96	40	...	...	...	...	...	...
Aruba									
1 VII 2014 (ESDJ)									
Total..................................	107 839	50 999	56 840	...	...	...	...	...	...
0	1 372	704	669	...	...	...	...	...	...
1 - 4	5 241	2 644	2 597	...	...	...	...	...	...
5 - 9	6 985	3 602	3 383	...	...	...	...	...	...
10 - 14	7 295	3 693	3 602	...	...	...	...	...	...
15 - 19	7 538	3 822	3 716	...	...	...	...	...	...
20 - 24	6 339	3 271	3 068	...	...	...	...	...	...
25 - 29	5 940	2 879	3 061	...	...	...	...	...	...
30 - 34	6 606	3 033	3 573	...	...	...	...	...	...
35 - 39	7 157	3 243	3 913	...	...	...	...	...	...
40 - 44	8 299	3 840	4 459	...	...	...	...	...	...
45 - 49	8 714	3 995	4 718	...	...	...	...	...	...
50 - 54	9 327	4 340	4 987	...	...	...	...	...	...
55 - 59	8 022	3 675	4 347	...	...	...	...	...	...
60 - 64	6 348	2 949	3 399	...	...	...	...	...	...
65 - 69	4 629	2 048	2 581	...	...	...	...	...	...
70 - 74	3 240	1 440	1 800	...	...	...	...	...	...
75 - 79	2 368	955	1 413	...	...	...	...	...	...
80 - 84	1 449	556	892	...	...	...	...	...	...
85 - 89	647	224	424	...	...	...	...	...	...
90 - 94	236	69	167	...	...	...	...	...	...
95 - 99	67	14	54	...	...	...	...	...	...
100 + ...	21	4	16	...	...	...	...	...	...
Bahamas									
1 VII 2014* (ESDF)									
Total..................................	364 000	177 800	186 200	...	...	...	...	...	...
0	6 540	3 300	3 240	...	...	...	...	...	...
1 - 4	26 000	13 440	12 570	...	...	...	...	...	...
5 - 9	31 590	16 400	15 090	...	...	...	...	...	...
10 - 14	30 390	15 420	14 950	...	...	...	...	...	...
15 - 19	29 770	14 780	15 010	...	...	...	...	...	...
20 - 24	30 600	15 140	15 470	...	...	...	...	...	...
25 - 29	27 310	13 220	14 080	...	...	...	...	...	...
30 - 34	26 120	12 960	13 150	...	...	...	...	...	...
35 - 39	26 300	12 860	13 440	...	...	...	...	...	...
40 - 44	28 190	13 630	14 560	...	...	...	...	...	...
45 - 49	26 770	12 890	13 940	...	...	...	...	...	...
50 - 54	25 250	12 220	13 030	...	...	...	...	...	...
55 - 59	19 260	9 160	10 120	...	...	...	...	...	...
60 - 64	13 640	6 400	7 240	...	...	...	...	...	...
65 - 69	9 640	4 400	5 230	...	...	...	...	...	...
70 - 74	7 130	3 130	4 000	...	...	...	...	...	...
75 - 79	4 470	1 880	2 600	...	...	...	...	...	...
80 + ...	3 410	1 030	2 380	...	...	...	...	...	...
Barbados - Barbade									
1 V 2010 (CDJC)									
Total..................................	277 821	133 018	144 803	...	...	...	...	...	...
0 - 4	17 352	8 873	8 479	...	...	...	...	...	...
5 - 9	18 838	9 683	9 155	...	...	...	...	...	...
10 - 14	18 567	9 445	9 122	...	...	...	...	...	...
15 - 19	18 870	9 452	9 418	...	...	...	...	...	...
20 - 24	18 169	9 061	9 108	...	...	...	...	...	...
25 - 29	19 088	9 313	9 775	...	...	...	...	...	...
30 - 34	18 785	9 150	9 635	...	...	...	...	...	...
35 - 39	20 516	9 884	10 632	...	...	...	...	...	...
40 - 44	20 113	9 663	10 450	...	...	...	...	...	...
45 - 49	21 365	10 062	11 303	...	...	...	...	...	...

Continent, country or area, date, code[a] and age (in years) Continent, pays ou zone, date, code[a] et âge (en années)	Total			Urban - Urbaine			Rural - Rurale		
	Both sexes Les deux sexes	Male Masculin	Female Féminin	Both sexes Les deux sexes	Male Masculin	Female Féminin	Both sexes Les deux sexes	Male Masculin	Female Féminin
AMERICA, NORTH - **AMÉRIQUE DU NORD**									
Barbados - Barbade									
1 V 2010 (CDJC)									
50 - 54	20 050	9 411	10 639	...	...	...	...	...	...
55 - 59	16 653	7 871	8 782	...	...	...	...	...	...
60 - 64	13 486	6 326	7 160	...	...	...	...	...	...
65 - 69	10 151	4 511	5 640	...	...	...	...	...	...
70 - 74	8 680	3 804	4 876	...	...	...	...	...	...
75 - 79	6 937	2 863	4 074	...	...	...	...	...	...
80 - 84	5 153	1 986	3 167	...	...	...	...	...	...
85 +	5 048	1 660	3 388	...	...	...	...	...	...
Belize									
1 VII 2006 (ESDF)[12]									
Total	301 298	149 598	151 700	151 994	73 576	78 418	149 394	76 101	73 293
0 - 4	36 761	18 145	18 616	17 720	8 446	9 274	19 808	10 070	9 738
5 - 9	40 974	20 850	20 124	19 294	9 792	9 502	21 574	11 011	10 563
10 - 14	40 474	20 611	19 862	19 185	9 790	9 395	21 185	10 775	10 410
15 - 19	33 960	17 192	16 769	16 629	8 785	7 844	17 246	8 369	8 877
20 - 24	24 423	11 939	12 484	12 728	5 973	6 755	11 631	5 939	5 692
25 - 29	20 990	9 733	11 256	11 262	5 018	6 244	9 673	4 693	4 980
30 - 34	20 405	9 522	10 883	11 277	5 183	6 094	9 075	4 318	4 757
35 - 39	18 464	8 747	9 718	9 745	4 294	5 451	8 672	4 433	4 239
40 - 44	15 793	7 735	8 058	8 174	3 931	4 243	7 579	3 787	3 792
45 - 49	12 378	6 295	6 065	6 555	3 305	3 250	5 791	2 976	2 815
50 - 54	9 686	4 983	4 703	5 176	2 385	2 791	4 485	2 586	1 899
55 - 59	6 637	3 363	3 264	3 385	1 636	1 749	3 235	1 720	1 515
60 - 64	5 692	2 913	2 778	2 838	1 376	1 462	2 839	1 531	1 308
65 - 69	4 877	2 547	2 330	2 584	1 201	1 383	2 281	1 341	940
70 - 74	3 867	2 073	1 794	2 203	999	1 204	1 654	1 069	585
75 - 79	2 708	1 374	1 330	1 511	716	795	1 191	656	535
80 - 84	1 578	782	798	794	327	467	784	453	331
85 +	1 629	794	835	934	419	515	691	374	317
1 VII 2014 (ESDF)									
Total	358 899	179 451	179 448	...	...	...	...	...	...
0	8 247	4 201	4 046	...	...	...	...	...	...
1 - 4	33 857	17 278	16 579	...	...	...	...	...	...
5 - 9	43 669	21 994	21 675	...	...	...	...	...	...
10 - 14	41 964	20 998	20 966	...	...	...	...	...	...
15 - 19	38 568	19 293	19 275	...	...	...	...	...	...
20 - 24	33 995	16 698	17 297	...	...	...	...	...	...
25 - 29	29 502	14 273	15 229	...	...	...	...	...	...
30 - 34	25 420	12 339	13 081	...	...	...	...	...	...
35 - 39	23 018	11 237	11 781	...	...	...	...	...	...
40 - 44	19 303	9 593	9 710	...	...	...	...	...	...
45 - 49	16 645	8 500	8 145	...	...	...	...	...	...
50 - 54	13 046	6 617	6 429	...	...	...	...	...	...
55 - 59	9 616	5 012	4 604	...	...	...	...	...	...
60 - 64	6 926	3 662	3 264	...	...	...	...	...	...
65 - 69	4 894	2 604	2 290	...	...	...	...	...	...
70 - 74	3 889	2 062	1 827	...	...	...	...	...	...
75 - 79	2 853	1 448	1 405	...	...	...	...	...	...
80 +	3 487	1 642	1 845	...	...	...	...	...	...
Bermuda - Bermudes									
20 V 2010 (CDJC)[13]									
Total	64 237	30 858	33 379	64 237	30 858	33 379	-	-	-
0	709	372	337	709	372	337	-	-	-
1 - 4	2 858	1 479	1 379	2 858	1 479	1 379	-	-	-
5 - 9	3 456	1 759	1 697	3 456	1 759	1 697	-	-	-
10 - 14	3 481	1 706	1 775	3 481	1 706	1 775	-	-	-
15 - 19	3 431	1 682	1 749	3 431	1 682	1 749	-	-	-
20 - 24	3 342	1 608	1 734	3 342	1 608	1 734	-	-	-
25 - 29	4 076	1 947	2 129	4 076	1 947	2 129	-	-	-
30 - 34	4 645	2 259	2 386	4 645	2 259	2 386	-	-	-
35 - 39	5 050	2 572	2 478	5 050	2 572	2 478	-	-	-
40 - 44	5 158	2 588	2 570	5 158	2 588	2 570	-	-	-

7. Population by age, sex and urban/rural residence: latest available year, 2005 - 2014
Population selon l'âge, le sexe et la résidence, urbaine/rurale : dernière année disponible, 2005 - 2014 (continued - suite)

Continent, country or area, date, code[a] and age (in years) Continent, pays ou zone, date, code[a] et âge (en annèes)	Total			Urban - Urbaine			Rural - Rurale		
	Both sexes Les deux sexes	Male Masculin	Female Féminin	Both sexes Les deux sexes	Male Masculin	Female Féminin	Both sexes Les deux sexes	Male Masculin	Female Féminin
AMERICA, NORTH - AMÉRIQUE DU NORD									
Bermuda - Bermudes									
20 V 2010 (CDJC)[13]									
45 - 49	5 731	2 811	2 920	5 731	2 811	2 920	-	-	-
50 - 54	5 427	2 531	2 896	5 427	2 531	2 896	-	-	-
55 - 59	4 498	2 146	2 352	4 498	2 146	2 352	-	-	-
60 - 64	3 692	1 733	1 959	3 692	1 733	1 959	-	-	-
65 - 69	2 807	1 290	1 517	2 807	1 290	1 517	-	-	-
70 - 74	2 163	961	1 202	2 163	961	1 202	-	-	-
75 - 79	1 768	747	1 021	1 768	747	1 021	-	-	-
80 - 84	1 120	432	688	1 120	432	688	-	-	-
85 - 89	584	185	399	584	185	399	-	-	-
90 - 94	187	41	146	187	41	146	-	-	-
95 - 99	48	8	40	48	8	40	-	-	-
100 +	6	1	5	6	1	5	-	-	-
1 VII 2014 (ESDJ)[14]									
Total	61 777	29 499	32 278	...	...	...	...	...	...
0	641	321	320	...	...	...	...	...	...
1 - 4	2 607	1 289	1 318	...	...	...	...	...	...
5 - 9	3 219	1 654	1 565	...	...	...	...	...	...
10 - 14	3 104	1 581	1 523	...	...	...	...	...	...
15 - 19	2 992	1 462	1 530	...	...	...	...	...	...
20 - 24	3 034	1 438	1 596	...	...	...	...	...	...
25 - 29	3 385	1 572	1 813	...	...	...	...	...	...
30 - 34	4 271	2 063	2 208	...	...	...	...	...	...
35 - 39	4 299	2 158	2 141	...	...	...	...	...	...
40 - 44	4 752	2 406	2 346	...	...	...	...	...	...
45 - 49	4 949	2 450	2 499	...	...	...	...	...	...
50 - 54	5 551	2 678	2 873	...	...	...	...	...	...
55 - 59	5 023	2 285	2 738	...	...	...	...	...	...
60 - 64	3 996	1 907	2 089	...	...	...	...	...	...
65 - 69	3 314	1 539	1 775	...	...	...	...	...	...
70 - 74	2 459	1 092	1 367	...	...	...	...	...	...
75 - 79	1 828	776	1 052	...	...	...	...	...	...
80 - 84	1 349	525	824	...	...	...	...	...	...
85 +	1 004	303	701	...	...	...	...	...	...
Canada									
2 V 2011 (CDJC)									
Total	33 476 685	16 414 230	17 062 460	27 147 190	13 190 225	13 956 965	6 329 495	3 224 005	3 105 500
0 - 4	1 877 095	961 150	915 945	1 531 620	784 165	747 460	345 480	176 985	168 490
5 - 9	1 809 895	925 960	883 935	1 455 570	743 510	712 060	354 325	182 450	171 875
10 - 14	1 920 355	983 990	936 365	1 526 165	781 760	744 410	394 185	202 230	191 955
15 - 19	2 178 135	1 115 845	1 062 290	1 745 370	890 940	854 430	432 765	224 900	207 860
20 - 24	2 187 450	1 108 780	1 078 670	1 858 035	935 265	922 765	329 415	173 510	155 900
25 - 29	2 169 585	1 077 275	1 092 310	1 879 840	930 835	949 005	289 745	146 445	143 305
30 - 34	2 162 900	1 058 810	1 104 095	1 838 125	897 275	940 855	324 775	161 535	163 235
35 - 39	2 173 930	1 064 195	1 109 735	1 814 025	884 235	929 785	359 910	179 965	179 945
40 - 44	2 324 875	1 141 715	1 183 155	1 908 095	933 115	974 980	416 780	208 605	208 175
45 - 49	2 675 130	1 318 715	1 356 420	2 142 125	1 050 625	1 091 500	533 005	268 085	264 915
50 - 54	2 658 965	1 309 025	1 349 940	2 091 050	1 021 340	1 069 700	567 920	287 680	280 235
55 - 59	2 340 635	1 147 300	1 193 335	1 809 810	876 210	933 600	530 825	271 090	259 735
60 - 64	2 052 670	1 002 685	1 049 980	1 573 340	754 910	818 430	479 330	247 780	231 550
65 - 69	1 521 715	738 010	783 700	1 163 785	549 495	614 290	357 930	188 515	169 415
70 - 74	1 153 065	543 435	609 630	906 035	413 260	492 775	247 025	130 175	116 850
75 - 79	922 695	417 945	504 755	751 575	329 760	421 815	171 125	88 185	82 940
80 - 84	702 070	291 085	410 985	591 015	237 310	353 705	111 055	53 775	57 280
85 - 89	427 015	149 415	277 600	369 925	125 615	244 310	57 090	23 800	33 290
90 - 94	170 285	48 470	121 815	148 965	41 530	107 435	21 315	6 940	14 380
95 - 99	42 390	9 455	32 935	37 515	8 225	29 285	4 875	1 230	3 645
100 +	5 825	955	4 870	5 195	840	4 355	630	115	510
1 VII 2014* (ESDJ)[15]									
Total	35 540 419	17 624 990	17 915 429	...	...	...	...	...	...
0	384 566	197 178	187 388	...	...	...	...	...	...
1 - 4	1 540 384	789 136	751 248	...	...	...	...	...	...
5 - 9	1 918 244	982 928	935 316	...	...	...	...	...	...

7. Population by age, sex and urban/rural residence: latest available year, 2005 - 2014
Population selon l'âge, le sexe et la résidence, urbaine/rurale : dernière année disponible, 2005 - 2014 (continued - suite)

Continent, country or area, date, code[a] and age (in years) / Continent, pays ou zone, date, code[a] et âge (en années)	Total			Urban - Urbaine			Rural - Rurale		
	Both sexes Les deux sexes	Male Masculin	Female Féminin	Both sexes Les deux sexes	Male Masculin	Female Féminin	Both sexes Les deux sexes	Male Masculin	Female Féminin
AMERICA, NORTH - AMÉRIQUE DU NORD									
Canada									
1 VII 2014* (ESDJ)[15]									
10 - 14	1 865 473	958 809	906 664	...	...	...	...	...	...
15 - 19	2 138 700	1 099 561	1 039 139	...	...	...	...	...	...
20 - 24	2 472 109	1 263 092	1 209 017	...	...	...	...	...	...
25 - 29	2 437 776	1 225 436	1 212 340	...	...	...	...	...	...
30 - 34	2 479 864	1 237 253	1 242 611	...	...	...	...	...	...
35 - 39	2 367 133	1 179 781	1 187 352	...	...	...	...	...	...
40 - 44	2 358 693	1 179 503	1 179 190	...	...	...	...	...	...
45 - 49	2 492 147	1 250 319	1 241 828	...	...	...	...	...	...
50 - 54	2 774 627	1 393 217	1 381 410	...	...	...	...	...	...
55 - 59	2 557 316	1 276 205	1 281 111	...	...	...	...	...	...
60 - 64	2 168 130	1 071 261	1 096 869	...	...	...	...	...	...
65 - 69	1 830 877	893 066	937 811	...	...	...	...	...	...
70 - 74	1 314 681	623 234	691 447	...	...	...	...	...	...
75 - 79	972 182	443 596	528 586	...	...	...	...	...	...
80 - 84	736 617	314 275	422 342	...	...	...	...	...	...
85 - 89	465 319	172 779	292 540	...	...	...	...	...	...
90 - 94	213 949	64 773	149 176	...	...	...	...	...	...
95 - 99	44 025	8 644	35 381	...	...	...	...	...	...
100 +	7 607	944	6 663	...	...	...	...	...	...
Cayman Islands - Îles Caïmanes									
31 XII 2014 (ESDJ)									
Total	58 238	28 322	29 916	...	...	...	...	...	...
0 - 14	10 342	5 689	4 654	...	...	...	...	...	...
15 - 24	5 386	2 550	2 836	...	...	...	...	...	...
25 - 34	10 298	4 949	5 349	...	...	...	...	...	...
35 - 44	11 147	5 165	5 981	...	...	...	...	...	...
45 - 54	10 786	5 317	5 469	...	...	...	...	...	...
55 - 64	6 486	2 887	3 599	...	...	...	...	...	...
65 +	3 793	1 766	2 027	...	...	...	...	...	...
Costa Rica[16]									
1 VII 2014 (ESDJ)									
Total	4 772 098	2 325 438	2 446 660	3 469 802	1 662 288	1 807 514	1 302 296	663 150	639 146
0 - 4	292 294	148 214	144 080	197 264	100 623	96 641	95 030	47 591	47 439
5 - 9	331 942	173 543	158 399	226 831	118 700	108 131	105 111	54 843	50 268
10 - 14	371 352	188 100	183 252	250 947	126 252	124 695	120 405	61 848	58 557
15 - 19	439 724	226 139	213 585	307 139	154 844	152 295	132 585	71 295	61 290
20 - 24	433 236	223 852	209 384	319 183	162 730	156 453	114 053	61 122	52 931
25 - 29	409 809	203 705	206 104	309 745	154 208	155 537	100 064	49 497	50 567
30 - 34	349 745	170 556	179 189	260 015	127 376	132 639	89 730	43 180	46 550
35 - 39	322 418	154 998	167 420	238 066	114 401	123 665	84 352	40 597	43 755
40 - 44	309 910	146 293	163 617	223 228	104 355	118 873	86 682	41 938	44 744
45 - 49	293 278	142 257	151 021	209 843	100 363	109 480	83 435	41 894	41 541
50 - 54	316 110	140 138	175 972	237 387	101 978	135 409	78 723	38 160	40 563
55 - 59	261 310	123 481	137 829	199 620	92 155	107 465	61 690	31 326	30 364
60 - 64	195 394	89 714	105 680	150 121	65 564	84 557	45 273	24 150	21 123
65 - 69	150 012	66 315	83 697	112 204	47 573	64 631	37 808	18 742	19 066
70 - 74	98 405	44 377	54 028	72 524	29 835	42 689	25 881	14 542	11 339
75 - 79	83 287	36 726	46 561	64 941	27 018	37 923	18 346	9 708	8 638
80 - 84	60 426	26 109	34 317	48 835	19 274	29 561	11 591	6 835	4 756
85 - 89	33 125	11 309	21 816	26 142	7 861	18 281	6 983	3 448	3 535
90 - 94	12 386	4 304	8 082	9 901	3 134	6 767	2 485	1 170	1 315
95 - 99	3 767	1 684	2 083	2 947	1 428	1 519	820	256	564
Unknown - Inconnu	4 168	3 624	544	2 919	2 616	303	1 249	1 008	241
Cuba									
1 VII 2014 (ESDJ)									
Total	11 224 190	5 595 379	5 628 811	8 625 144	4 199 578	4 425 566	2 599 046	1 395 801	1 203 245
0 - 4	628 319	323 420	304 899	475 142	244 591	230 551	153 176	78 829	74 347
5 - 9	578 371	297 949	280 422	430 273	221 263	209 010	148 097	76 685	71 412
10 - 14	683 771	352 046	331 724	517 102	265 327	251 775	166 669	86 719	79 949
15 - 19	703 940	363 281	340 658	537 195	275 332	261 863	166 744	87 949	78 795
20 - 24	791 198	408 818	382 380	603 748	306 835	296 913	187 450	101 983	85 467

7. Population by age, sex and urban/rural residence: latest available year, 2005 - 2014
Population selon l'âge, le sexe et la résidence, urbaine/rurale : dernière année disponible, 2005 - 2014 (continued - suite)

Continent, country or area, date, code[a] and age (in years) Continent, pays ou zone, date, code[a] et âge (en années)	Total			Urban - Urbaine			Rural - Rurale		
	Both sexes Les deux sexes	Male Masculin	Female Féminin	Both sexes Les deux sexes	Male Masculin	Female Féminin	Both sexes Les deux sexes	Male Masculin	Female Féminin
AMERICA, NORTH - AMÉRIQUE DU NORD									
Cuba									
1 VII 2014 (ESDJ)									
25 - 29	790 218	407 303	382 915	607 228	306 496	300 732	182 990	100 807	82 183
30 - 34	652 415	333 841	318 574	494 655	247 759	246 896	157 760	86 082	71 678
35 - 39	742 717	374 123	368 593	552 773	271 666	281 107	189 943	102 457	87 486
40 - 44	999 136	498 436	500 700	750 892	364 397	386 495	248 244	134 039	114 205
45 - 49	1 027 382	505 357	522 025	789 945	377 286	412 659	237 437	128 071	109 366
50 - 54	884 384	432 524	451 860	697 037	331 818	365 219	187 346	100 705	86 641
55 - 59	624 077	301 436	322 641	487 942	228 608	259 334	136 134	72 827	63 307
60 - 64	584 835	283 081	301 753	463 635	217 148	246 487	121 200	65 933	55 266
65 - 69	498 785	237 855	260 929	396 657	183 254	213 403	102 127	54 601	47 526
70 - 74	401 259	191 354	209 905	318 987	146 130	172 857	82 272	45 223	37 048
75 - 79	278 319	129 654	148 665	220 755	97 606	123 149	57 563	32 047	25 516
80 - 84	184 536	83 307	101 228	146 067	61 725	84 342	38 468	21 582	16 886
85 +	170 526	71 590	98 936	135 105	52 333	82 772	35 421	19 257	16 164
Curaçao[17]									
1 VII 2014 (ESDJ)									
Total	155 909	71 269	84 640	...	...	...	...	...	...
0	1 947	986	962	...	...	...	...	...	...
1 - 4	7 847	4 036	3 811	...	...	...	...	...	...
5 - 9	9 467	4 843	4 624	...	...	...	...	...	...
10 - 14	10 360	5 323	5 037	...	...	...	...	...	...
15 - 19	10 616	5 380	5 236	...	...	...	...	...	...
20 - 24	8 991	4 417	4 574	...	...	...	...	...	...
25 - 29	8 367	3 818	4 549	...	...	...	...	...	...
30 - 34	8 614	3 681	4 934	...	...	...	...	...	...
35 - 39	8 983	3 863	5 120	...	...	...	...	...	...
40 - 44	11 165	4 957	6 208	...	...	...	...	...	...
45 - 49	11 931	5 269	6 662	...	...	...	...	...	...
50 - 54	12 930	5 617	7 314	...	...	...	...	...	...
55 - 59	11 251	4 917	6 334	...	...	...	...	...	...
60 - 64	9 872	4 349	5 523	...	...	...	...	...	...
65 - 69	8 237	3 641	4 597	...	...	...	...	...	...
70 - 74	5 850	2 475	3 375	...	...	...	...	...	...
75 - 79	4 427	1 863	2 565	...	...	...	...	...	...
80 - 84	2 777	1 113	1 664	...	...	...	...	...	...
85 - 89	1 438	497	941	...	...	...	...	...	...
90 - 94	633	185	449	...	...	...	...	...	...
95 - 99	211	44	167	...	...	...	...	...	...
100 +	40	9	31	...	...	...	...	...	...
Dominica - Dominique									
31 XII 2006 (ESDF)									
Total	71 180	36 238	34 942	...	...	...	...	...	...
0 - 4	6 317	3 250	3 067	...	...	...	...	...	...
5 - 9	7 554	3 951	3 603	...	...	...	...	...	...
10 - 14	7 105	3 558	3 547	...	...	...	...	...	...
15 - 19	6 818	3 452	3 366	...	...	...	...	...	...
20 - 24	4 578	2 438	2 140	...	...	...	...	...	...
25 - 29	5 121	2 601	2 520	...	...	...	...	...	...
30 - 34	5 663	2 886	2 777	...	...	...	...	...	...
35 - 39	5 296	2 841	2 455	...	...	...	...	...	...
40 - 44	4 476	2 417	2 059	...	...	...	...	...	...
45 - 49	3 561	1 947	1 614	...	...	...	...	...	...
50 - 54	2 820	1 467	1 353	...	...	...	...	...	...
55 - 59	2 391	1 209	1 182	...	...	...	...	...	...
60 - 64	2 255	1 022	1 233	...	...	...	...	...	...
65 - 69	2 324	1 091	1 233	...	...	...	...	...	...
70 - 74	1 844	871	973	...	...	...	...	...	...
75 - 79	1 332	596	736	...	...	...	...	...	...
80 - 84	901	354	547	...	...	...	...	...	...
85 +	825	288	537	...	...	...	...	...	...

7. Population by age, sex and urban/rural residence: latest available year, 2005 - 2014
Population selon l'âge, le sexe et la résidence, urbaine/rurale : dernière année disponible, 2005 - 2014 (continued - suite)

Continent, country or area, date, code[a] and age (in years) Continent, pays ou zone, date, code[a] et âge (en annèes)	Total			Urban - Urbaine			Rural - Rurale		
	Both sexes Les deux sexes	Male Masculin	Female Féminin	Both sexes Les deux sexes	Male Masculin	Female Féminin	Both sexes Les deux sexes	Male Masculin	Female Féminin
AMERICA, NORTH - **AMÉRIQUE DU NORD**									
Dominican Republic - **République dominicaine[2]** 1 VII 2014 (ESDF)									
Total	9 883 486	4 944 386	4 939 100	7 691 885	3 777 718	3 914 167	2 191 601	1 166 668	1 024 933
0 - 4	974 068	496 964	477 104	754 581	383 604	370 977	219 487	113 360	106 127
5 - 9	973 480	495 799	477 681	748 020	378 642	369 378	225 460	117 157	108 303
10 - 14	980 784	497 591	483 193	753 651	378 205	375 446	227 133	119 386	107 747
15 - 19	949 556	478 833	470 723	737 154	365 566	371 588	212 402	113 267	99 135
20 - 24	901 704	451 539	450 165	709 316	348 118	361 198	192 388	103 421	88 967
25 - 29	820 461	407 933	412 528	650 955	317 235	333 720	169 506	90 698	78 808
30 - 34	736 655	363 614	373 041	584 386	283 142	301 244	152 269	80 472	71 797
35 - 39	660 829	325 366	335 463	522 383	252 315	270 068	138 446	73 051	65 395
40 - 44	592 702	292 546	300 156	467 084	225 808	241 276	125 618	66 738	58 880
45 - 49	530 821	263 245	267 576	416 890	201 795	215 095	113 931	61 450	52 481
50 - 54	463 355	230 771	232 584	362 378	175 745	186 633	100 977	55 026	45 951
55 - 59	377 736	187 733	190 003	292 151	140 856	151 295	85 585	46 877	38 708
60 - 64	296 061	146 190	149 871	226 205	107 978	118 227	69 856	38 212	31 644
65 - 69	220 103	109 135	110 968	165 543	79 006	86 537	54 560	30 129	24 431
70 - 74	162 310	79 833	82 477	121 138	57 085	64 053	41 172	22 748	18 424
75 - 79	119 582	58 345	61 237	88 646	41 175	47 471	30 936	17 170	13 766
80 +	123 279	58 949	64 330	91 404	41 443	49 961	31 875	17 506	14 369
El Salvador 12 V 2007 (CDJC)									
Total	5 744 113	2 719 371	3 024 742	3 598 836	1 676 313	1 922 523	2 145 277	1 043 058	1 102 219
0 - 4	555 893	283 272	272 621	324 299	165 397	158 902	231 594	117 875	113 719
5 - 9	684 727	349 150	335 577	390 873	199 184	191 689	293 854	149 966	143 888
10 - 14	706 347	359 523	346 824	404 755	205 222	199 533	301 592	154 301	147 291
15 - 19	600 565	298 384	302 181	355 376	174 488	180 888	245 189	123 896	121 293
20 - 24	486 542	228 001	258 541	309 107	143 779	165 328	177 435	84 222	93 213
25 - 29	457 890	206 963	250 927	306 456	138 320	168 136	151 434	68 643	82 791
30 - 34	402 249	178 400	223 849	274 037	121 278	152 759	128 212	57 122	71 090
35 - 39	353 147	156 514	196 633	242 566	106 882	135 684	110 581	49 632	60 949
40 - 44	303 631	132 218	171 413	209 958	90 559	119 399	93 673	41 659	52 014
45 - 49	252 122	109 957	142 165	170 464	73 027	97 437	81 658	36 930	44 728
50 - 54	215 734	95 275	120 459	143 882	62 014	81 868	71 852	33 261	38 591
55 - 59	183 075	81 718	101 357	119 193	51 574	67 619	63 882	30 144	33 738
60 - 64	151 864	68 207	83 657	97 101	41 821	55 280	54 763	26 386	28 377
65 - 69	125 157	55 781	69 376	79 690	33 492	46 198	45 467	22 289	23 178
70 - 74	97 457	43 449	54 008	62 075	25 726	36 349	35 382	17 723	17 659
75 - 79	75 984	33 658	42 326	48 760	20 096	28 664	27 224	13 562	13 662
80 - 84	46 870	20 401	26 469	30 578	12 261	18 317	16 292	8 140	8 152
85 +	44 859	18 500	26 359	29 666	11 193	18 473	15 193	7 307	7 886
1 VII 2014 (ESDF)[18]									
Total	6 328 196	2 967 351	3 360 845	...	...	...	...	...	...
0	125 001	63 863	61 139	...	...	...	...	...	...
1 - 4	487 875	249 348	238 527	...	...	...	...	...	...
5 - 9	591 525	302 344	289 181	...	...	...	...	...	...
10 - 14	622 838	317 944	304 894	...	...	...	...	...	...
15 - 19	701 789	351 798	349 991	...	...	...	...	...	...
20 - 24	636 728	308 246	328 482	...	...	...	...	...	...
25 - 29	506 397	228 281	278 115	...	...	...	...	...	...
30 - 34	423 811	182 371	241 441	...	...	...	...	...	...
35 - 39	389 426	167 000	222 425	...	...	...	...	...	...
40 - 44	360 527	155 410	205 117	...	...	...	...	...	...
45 - 49	314 188	135 028	179 160	...	...	...	...	...	...
50 - 54	266 940	114 542	152 398	...	...	...	...	...	...
55 - 59	224 280	97 091	127 189	...	...	...	...	...	...
60 - 64	190 126	82 699	107 427	...	...	...	...	...	...
65 - 69	156 282	68 433	87 850	...	...	...	...	...	...
70 - 74	125 726	55 315	70 411	...	...	...	...	...	...
75 - 79	95 552	41 525	54 027	...	...	...	...	...	...
80 +	109 183	46 112	63 071	...	...	...	...	...	...

7. Population by age, sex and urban/rural residence: latest available year, 2005 - 2014
Population selon l'âge, le sexe et la résidence, urbaine/rurale : dernière année disponible, 2005 - 2014 (continued - suite)

Continent, country or area, date, code[a] and age (in years) Continent, pays ou zone, date, code[a] et âge (en années)	Total			Urban - Urbaine			Rural - Rurale		
	Both sexes Les deux sexes	Male Masculin	Female Féminin	Both sexes Les deux sexes	Male Masculin	Female Féminin	Both sexes Les deux sexes	Male Masculin	Female Féminin
AMERICA, NORTH - AMÉRIQUE DU NORD									
Greenland - Groenland[19]									
1 VII 2014 (ESDJ)									
Total	56 295	29 742	26 553	48 232	25 320	22 912	8 063	4 422	3 641
0 - 4	3 957	2 086	1 871	3 370	1 779	1 591	587	307	280
5 - 9	3 962	2 021	1 941	3 355	1 725	1 630	607	296	311
10 - 14	4 038	2 061	1 977	3 368	1 733	1 635	670	328	342
15 - 19	4 127	2 056	2 071	3 510	1 752	1 758	617	304	313
20 - 24	4 566	2 334	2 232	3 915	1 993	1 922	651	341	310
25 - 29	4 345	2 180	2 165	3 767	1 851	1 916	578	329	249
30 - 34	3 964	2 018	1 946	3 447	1 727	1 720	517	291	226
35 - 39	3 171	1 723	1 448	2 765	1 502	1 263	406	221	185
40 - 44	3 351	1 850	1 501	2 899	1 593	1 306	452	257	195
45 - 49	5 235	2 833	2 402	4 513	2 423	2 090	722	410	312
50 - 54	4 936	2 700	2 236	4 259	2 299	1 960	677	401	276
55 - 59	3 737	2 112	1 625	3 166	1 765	1 401	571	347	224
60 - 64	2 651	1 508	1 143	2 263	1 269	994	388	239	149
65 - 69	1 767	1 050	717	1 522	896	626	245	154	91
70 - 74	1 312	697	615	1 110	587	523	202	110	92
75 - 79	653	309	344	542	252	290	111	57	54
80 - 84	376	149	227	330	125	205	46	24	22
85 - 89	124	45	79	110	40	70	14	5	9
90 - 94	19	8	11	18	7	11	1	1	-
95 - 99	4	2	2	3	2	1	1	1	-	1
Guadeloupe[20]									
1 I 2014 (ESDJ)									
Total	403 750	186 235	217 515	...	...	...	...	...	...
0 - 4	23 367	11 590	11 777	...	...	...	...	...	...
5 - 9	28 232	14 262	13 970	...	...	...	...	...	...
10 - 14	30 645	15 590	15 055	...	...	...	...	...	...
15 - 19	28 850	14 806	14 044	...	...	...	...	...	...
20 - 24	20 665	10 493	10 172	...	...	...	...	...	...
25 - 29	18 064	8 261	9 803	...	...	...	...	...	...
30 - 34	19 934	8 192	11 742	...	...	...	...	...	...
35 - 39	23 703	9 648	14 055	...	...	...	...	...	...
40 - 44	29 979	12 865	17 114	...	...	...	...	...	...
45 - 49	32 253	14 357	17 896	...	...	...	...	...	...
50 - 54	32 060	14 879	17 181	...	...	...	...	...	...
55 - 59	27 740	12 853	14 887	...	...	...	...	...	...
60 - 64	23 982	10 792	13 190	...	...	...	...	...	...
65 - 69	19 967	9 311	10 656	...	...	...	...	...	...
70 - 74	15 030	6 739	8 291	...	...	...	...	...	...
75 - 79	11 932	5 254	6 678	...	...	...	...	...	...
80 - 84	8 115	3 222	4 893	...	...	...	...	...	...
85 - 89	5 432	1 920	3 512	...	...	...	...	...	...
90 - 94	2 785	916	1 869	...	...	...	...	...	...
95 +	1 015	285	730	...	...	...	...	...	...
Guatemala									
1 VII 2005 (ESDF)									
Total	12 699 780	6 197 399	6 502 381	6 345 918	3 059 570	3 286 348	6 353 862	3 137 829	3 216 033
0 - 4	2 036 312	1 035 549	1 000 763	866 844	447 724	419 120	1 169 468	587 825	581 643
5 - 9	1 823 642	921 924	901 718	790 225	405 750	384 475	1 033 417	516 174	517 243
10 - 14	1 624 119	815 791	808 328	755 292	378 704	376 587	868 827	437 087	431 741
15 - 19	1 379 574	685 359	694 215	715 501	351 554	363 947	664 073	333 805	330 268
20 - 24	1 180 264	571 385	608 879	636 046	306 874	329 172	544 218	264 511	279 707
25 - 29	952 695	446 309	506 386	523 699	243 461	280 237	428 996	202 848	226 149
30 - 34	753 145	340 378	412 767	416 357	184 973	231 384	336 788	155 405	181 383
35 - 39	600 160	270 907	329 253	326 576	144 824	181 752	273 584	126 083	147 501
40 - 44	492 747	225 243	267 504	270 162	120 913	149 248	222 585	104 330	118 256
45 - 49	409 688	191 635	218 053	221 123	100 439	120 685	188 565	91 196	97 368
50 - 54	367 062	175 311	191 751	201 790	92 775	109 014	165 272	82 536	82 737
55 - 59	310 913	149 593	161 320	171 480	79 044	92 436	139 433	70 549	68 884
60 - 64	233 643	113 686	119 957	128 803	58 925	69 878	104 840	54 761	50 079
65 - 69	192 992	94 128	98 864	111 865	51 579	60 285	81 127	42 549	38 579
70 - 74	156 267	74 463	81 804	93 750	42 080	51 669	62 517	32 383	30 135

Continent, country or area, date, code[a] and age (in years) / Continent, pays ou zone, date, code[a] et âge (en années)	Total			Urban - Urbaine			Rural - Rurale		
	Both sexes Les deux sexes	Male Masculin	Female Féminin	Both sexes Les deux sexes	Male Masculin	Female Féminin	Both sexes Les deux sexes	Male Masculin	Female Féminin
AMERICA, NORTH - AMÉRIQUE DU NORD									
Guatemala									
1 VII 2005 (ESDF)									
75 - 79	107 429	50 340	57 089	66 759	29 241	37 519	40 670	21 099	19 570
80 +	79 128	35 398	43 730	49 648	20 709	28 939	29 480	14 689	14 791
1 VII 2010 (ESDF)[11]									
Total	14 361 666	7 003 337	7 358 328	...	...	...	...	...	...
0 - 4	2 165 745	1 103 521	1 062 224	...	...	...	...	...	...
5 - 9	2 004 670	1 017 180	987 490	...	...	...	...	...	...
10 - 14	1 798 262	906 603	891 659	...	...	...	...	...	...
15 - 19	1 590 147	794 459	795 688	...	...	...	...	...	...
20 - 24	1 322 125	646 911	675 214	...	...	...	...	...	...
25 - 29	1 128 960	538 214	590 746	...	...	...	...	...	...
30 - 34	913 192	418 535	494 657	...	...	...	...	...	...
35 - 39	725 691	323 010	402 681	...	...	...	...	...	...
40 - 44	580 303	258 454	321 849	...	...	...	...	...	...
45 - 49	475 449	215 304	260 145	...	...	...	...	...	...
50 - 54	393 702	182 662	211 040	...	...	...	...	...	...
55 - 59	350 124	165 910	184 214	...	...	...	...	...	...
60 - 64	292 331	139 395	152 936	...	...	...	...	...	...
65 - 69	214 491	103 433	111 058	...	...	...	...	...	...
70 - 74	170 028	81 809	88 219	...	...	...	...	...	...
75 - 79	128 990	60 257	68 733	...	...	...	...	...	...
80 +	107 456	47 678	59 778	...	...	...	...	...	...
Haiti - Haïti[21]									
1 VII 2010 (ESDJ)									
Total	10 085 214	4 993 731	5 091 483	4 817 666	2 321 608	2 496 059	5 267 548	2 672 123	2 595 424
0 - 4	1 263 322	644 550	618 772	532 352	274 597	257 755	730 970	369 953	361 017
5 - 9	1 195 479	608 495	586 984	493 368	249 982	243 386	702 111	358 513	343 598
10 - 14	1 158 478	588 618	569 860	532 573	255 002	277 571	625 905	333 616	292 289
15 - 19	1 092 364	551 467	540 897	583 183	276 258	306 925	509 181	275 209	233 972
20 - 24	1 019 589	509 042	510 547	600 175	296 233	303 943	419 414	212 809	206 604
25 - 29	919 636	454 123	465 513	537 063	267 198	269 865	382 573	186 925	195 648
30 - 34	702 596	340 518	362 078	390 054	189 432	200 622	312 542	151 086	161 456
35 - 39	548 004	261 157	286 847	272 855	128 575	144 280	275 149	132 582	142 567
40 - 44	488 482	235 182	253 300	225 057	106 072	118 985	263 425	129 110	134 315
45 - 49	423 377	204 077	219 300	179 712	81 240	98 472	243 665	122 837	120 828
50 - 54	342 913	166 418	176 495	138 580	61 854	76 726	204 333	104 564	99 769
55 - 59	284 731	136 034	148 697	107 391	46 062	61 329	177 340	89 972	87 368
60 - 64	206 835	95 939	110 896	73 562	29 974	43 588	133 273	65 965	67 308
65 - 69	175 898	81 854	94 044	61 671	24 975	36 696	114 227	56 879	57 348
70 - 74	129 436	58 181	71 255	44 448	17 100	27 347	84 988	41 081	43 908
75 - 79	80 898	35 538	45 360	27 630	10 473	17 158	53 268	25 065	28 202
80 +	53 176	22 538	30 638	17 992	6 581	11 412	35 184	15 957	19 226
1 VII 2011 (ESDJ)									
Total	10 248 306	5 075 517	5 172 789	...	...	...	...	...	...
0 - 4	1 268 897	647 465	621 432	...	...	...	...	...	...
5 - 9	1 201 161	611 472	589 690	...	...	...	...	...	...
10 - 14	1 163 085	591 018	572 066	...	...	...	...	...	...
15 - 19	1 100 883	556 085	544 798	...	...	...	...	...	...
20 - 24	1 029 132	514 235	514 898	...	...	...	...	...	...
25 - 29	940 847	465 396	475 451	...	...	...	...	...	...
30 - 34	737 993	358 927	379 066	...	...	...	...	...	...
35 - 39	566 936	270 574	296 362	...	...	...	...	...	...
40 - 44	495 026	237 754	257 273	...	...	...	...	...	...
45 - 49	433 416	208 671	224 746	...	...	...	...	...	...
50 - 54	353 800	171 468	182 332	...	...	...	...	...	...
55 - 59	293 134	140 392	152 742	...	...	...	...	...	...
60 - 64	214 819	99 846	114 973	...	...	...	...	...	...
65 - 69	177 069	82 201	94 868	...	...	...	...	...	...
70 - 74	132 790	59 833	72 957	...	...	...	...	...	...
75 - 79	83 834	36 751	47 083	...	...	...	...	...	...
80 +	55 484	23 431	32 053	...	...	...	...	...	...

7. Population by age, sex and urban/rural residence: latest available year, 2005 - 2014
Population selon l'âge, le sexe et la résidence, urbaine/rurale : dernière année disponible, 2005 - 2014 (continued - suite)

Continent, country or area, date, code[a] and age (in years) / Continent, pays ou zone, date, code[a] et âge (en années)	Total			Urban - Urbaine			Rural - Rurale		
	Both sexes Les deux sexes	Male Masculin	Female Féminin	Both sexes Les deux sexes	Male Masculin	Female Féminin	Both sexes Les deux sexes	Male Masculin	Female Féminin
AMERICA, NORTH - AMÉRIQUE DU NORD									
Honduras[22]									
1 VII 2007 (ESDF)									
Total	7 536 952	3 717 577	3 819 375	3 752 579	1 793 588	1 958 991	3 784 373	1 923 989	1 860 384
0 - 4	1 063 247	541 070	522 177	478 059	243 771	234 288	585 188	297 299	287 889
5 - 9	1 009 399	511 733	497 666	432 422	221 023	211 399	576 977	290 710	286 267
10 - 14	920 850	464 403	456 447	414 394	208 459	205 935	506 456	255 944	250 512
15 - 19	802 793	402 792	400 001	398 138	192 053	206 085	404 655	210 739	193 916
20 - 24	710 751	353 317	357 434	390 899	179 723	211 176	319 852	173 594	146 258
25 - 29	626 413	308 283	318 130	352 025	165 114	186 911	274 388	143 169	131 219
30 - 34	522 679	255 818	266 861	286 860	136 186	150 674	235 819	119 632	116 187
35 - 39	425 045	205 171	219 874	235 598	109 749	125 849	189 447	95 422	94 025
40 - 44	334 632	157 492	177 140	184 004	84 081	99 923	150 628	73 411	77 217
45 - 49	276 277	128 813	147 464	149 861	67 682	82 179	126 416	61 131	65 285
50 - 54	227 421	105 428	121 993	118 577	52 986	65 591	108 844	52 442	56 402
55 - 59	180 676	83 643	97 033	92 810	40 714	52 096	87 866	42 929	44 937
60 - 64	137 652	63 863	73 789	67 361	29 245	38 116	70 291	34 618	35 673
65 - 69	107 540	49 404	58 136	52 443	22 197	30 246	55 097	27 207	27 890
70 - 74	82 118	37 134	44 984	41 131	17 107	24 024	40 987	20 027	20 960
75 - 79	54 593	24 368	30 225	28 183	11 568	16 615	26 410	12 800	13 610
80 +	54 866	24 845	30 021	29 814	11 930	17 884	25 052	12 915	12 137
1 VII 2010 (ESDF)									
Total	8 045 990	3 965 430	4 080 560	...	...	...	...	...	...
0 - 4	1 079 289	549 179	530 110	...	...	...	...	...	...
5 - 9	1 035 077	525 938	509 139	...	...	...	...	...	...
10 - 14	973 613	492 090	481 523	...	...	...	...	...	...
15 - 19	866 193	434 856	431 337	...	...	...	...	...	...
20 - 24	747 514	371 818	375 696	...	...	...	...	...	...
25 - 29	663 903	326 377	337 526	...	...	...	...	...	...
30 - 34	577 561	282 042	295 519	...	...	...	...	...	...
35 - 39	474 884	230 506	244 378	...	...	...	...	...	...
40 - 44	381 715	181 554	200 161	...	...	...	...	...	...
45 - 49	301 565	140 031	161 534	...	...	...	...	...	...
50 - 54	251 618	116 240	135 378	...	...	...	...	...	...
55 - 59	203 187	93 205	109 982	...	...	...	...	...	...
60 - 64	157 317	72 071	85 246	...	...	...	...	...	...
65 - 69	117 790	53 835	63 955	...	...	...	...	...	...
70 - 74	90 125	40 470	49 655	...	...	...	...	...	...
75 - 79	62 138	27 381	34 757	...	...	...	...	...	...
80 +	62 501	27 837	34 664	...	...	...	...	...	...
Jamaica - Jamaïque									
4 IV 2011 (CDJC)									
Total	2 697 983	1 334 533	1 363 450	1 454 151	700 957	753 194	1 243 832	633 576	610 256
0 - 4	209 871	106 107	103 764	109 121	55 157	53 965	100 750	50 950	49 799
5 - 9	226 378	114 792	111 586	114 520	57 817	56 703	111 858	56 975	54 883
10 - 14	266 586	136 183	130 403	138 596	70 428	68 168	127 990	65 755	62 235
15 - 19	274 658	139 777	134 881	143 644	72 173	71 471	131 014	67 604	63 410
20 - 24	250 711	125 243	125 468	140 770	68 692	72 078	109 941	56 551	53 390
25 - 29	226 120	109 919	116 201	129 961	61 980	67 981	96 159	47 939	48 220
30 - 34	185 495	87 810	97 685	106 228	49 452	56 776	79 267	38 358	40 909
35 - 39	183 756	86 647	97 109	103 560	47 408	56 152	80 196	39 239	40 957
40 - 44	173 924	85 656	88 268	97 069	46 377	50 693	76 855	39 279	37 575
45 - 49	155 389	79 201	76 188	88 044	41 385	46 658	67 345	37 816	29 530
50 - 54	137 895	67 297	70 598	74 271	34 341	39 930	63 624	32 956	30 668
55 - 59	100 798	50 717	50 081	54 090	26 020	28 070	46 708	24 697	22 011
60 - 64	88 057	44 407	43 650	46 868	22 549	24 319	41 189	21 858	19 331
65 - 69	65 164	32 543	32 621	33 182	15 691	17 491	31 982	16 852	15 130
70 - 74	51 276	24 627	26 649	25 354	11 785	13 569	25 922	12 842	13 080
75 - 79	42 762	19 847	22 915	20 542	9 085	11 458	22 220	10 762	11 457
80 - 84	30 738	13 258	17 480	14 941	6 132	8 809	15 797	7 126	8 671
85 - 89	18 457	7 267	11 190	8 789	3 151	5 638	9 668	4 116	5 552
90 - 94	6 921	2 303	4 618	3 238	957	2 281	3 683	1 346	2 337
95 - 99	2 503	808	1 695	1 119	326	793	1 384	482	902
100 +	524	124	400	243	53	190	281	71	210

Continent, country or area, date, code[a] and age (in years) Continent, pays ou zone, date, code[a] et âge (en années)	Total			Urban - Urbaine			Rural - Rurale		
	Both sexes Les deux sexes	Male Masculin	Female Féminin	Both sexes Les deux sexes	Male Masculin	Female Féminin	Both sexes Les deux sexes	Male Masculin	Female Féminin
AMERICA, NORTH - AMÉRIQUE DU NORD									
Martinique									
1 I 2010* (ESDJ)									
Total	396 308	182 644	213 664	...	...	...	...	...	...
0 - 4	23 686	12 113	11 573	...	...	...	...	...	...
5 - 9	26 410	13 174	13 236	...	...	...	...	...	...
10 - 14	27 636	14 074	13 562	...	...	...	...	...	...
15 - 19	29 421	14 763	14 658	...	...	...	...	...	...
20 - 24	22 587	11 099	11 488	...	...	...	...	...	...
25 - 29	18 188	7 989	10 199	...	...	...	...	...	...
30 - 34	19 910	8 326	11 584	...	...	...	...	...	...
35 - 39	27 580	11 585	15 995	...	...	...	...	...	...
40 - 44	32 091	14 036	18 055	...	...	...	...	...	...
45 - 49	33 120	15 044	18 076	...	...	...	...	...	...
50 - 54	28 690	13 186	15 504	...	...	...	...	...	...
55 - 59	24 930	11 376	13 554	...	...	...	...	...	...
60 - 64	21 653	10 057	11 596	...	...	...	...	...	...
65 - 69	16 961	7 816	9 145	...	...	...	...	...	...
70 - 74	15 415	7 038	8 377	...	...	...	...	...	...
75 - 79	11 423	4 898	6 525	...	...	...	...	...	...
80 - 84	8 464	3 461	5 003	...	...	...	...	...	...
85 - 89	5 093	1 785	3 308	...	...	...	...	...	...
90 - 94	2 125	593	1 532	...	...	...	...	...	...
95 +	925	231	694	...	...	...	...	...	...
Mexico - Mexique									
12 VI 2010 (CDFC)[23]									
Total	112 336 538	54 855 231	57 481 307	86 287 410	41 946 540	44 340 870	26 049 128	12 908 691	13 140 437
0 - 4	10 528 322	5 346 943	5 181 379	7 766 149	3 945 636	3 820 513	2 762 173	1 401 307	1 360 866
5 - 9	11 047 537	5 604 175	5 443 362	8 124 337	4 124 524	3 999 813	2 923 200	1 479 651	1 443 549
10 - 14	10 939 937	5 547 613	5 392 324	7 974 649	4 041 649	3 933 000	2 965 288	1 505 964	1 459 324
15 - 19	11 026 112	5 520 121	5 505 991	8 191 229	4 097 876	4 093 353	2 834 883	1 422 245	1 412 638
20 - 24	9 892 271	4 813 204	5 079 067	7 725 598	3 775 245	3 950 353	2 166 673	1 037 959	1 128 714
25 - 29	8 788 177	4 205 975	4 582 202	6 985 279	3 354 569	3 630 710	1 802 898	851 406	951 492
30 - 34	8 470 798	4 026 031	4 444 767	6 719 047	3 188 789	3 530 258	1 751 751	837 242	914 509
35 - 39	8 292 987	3 964 738	4 328 249	6 642 253	3 160 713	3 481 540	1 650 734	804 025	846 709
40 - 44	7 009 226	3 350 322	3 658 904	5 633 205	2 676 230	2 956 975	1 376 021	674 092	701 929
45 - 49	5 928 730	2 824 364	3 104 366	4 739 911	2 241 753	2 498 158	1 188 819	582 611	606 208
50 - 54	5 064 291	2 402 451	2 661 840	4 051 487	1 904 317	2 147 170	1 012 804	498 134	514 670
55 - 59	3 895 365	1 869 537	2 025 828	3 043 924	1 443 868	1 600 056	851 441	425 669	425 772
60 - 64	3 116 466	1 476 667	1 639 799	2 403 645	1 119 077	1 284 568	712 821	357 590	355 231
65 - 69	2 317 265	1 095 273	1 221 992	1 719 078	794 137	924 941	598 187	301 136	297 051
70 - 74	1 873 934	873 893	1 000 041	1 338 906	603 945	734 961	535 028	269 948	265 080
75 - 79	1 245 483	579 689	665 794	892 237	399 026	493 211	353 246	180 663	172 583
80 - 84	798 936	355 277	443 659	576 855	244 082	332 773	222 081	111 195	110 886
85 - 89	454 164	197 461	256 703	322 844	132 826	190 018	131 320	64 635	66 685
90 - 94	164 924	68 130	96 794	116 950	45 123	71 827	47 974	23 007	24 967
95 - 99	65 732	25 920	39 812	44 084	16 122	27 962	21 648	9 798	11 850
100 +	18 475	7 228	11 247	10 451	3 753	6 698	8 024	3 475	4 549
Unknown - Inconnu	1 397 406	700 219	697 187	1 265 292	633 280	632 012	132 114	66 939	65 175
1 VII 2014 (ESDJ)[2]									
Total	119 713 203	58 435 900	61 277 304	...	...	...	...	...	...
0	2 216 136	1 133 750	1 082 385	...	...	...	...	...	...
1 - 4	8 847 471	4 527 847	4 319 623	...	...	...	...	...	...
5 - 9	11 210 963	5 732 886	5 478 077	...	...	...	...	...	...
10 - 14	11 249 994	5 734 709	5 515 284	...	...	...	...	...	...
15 - 19	11 172 570	5 634 049	5 538 521	...	...	...	...	...	...
20 - 24	10 596 614	5 220 903	5 375 712	...	...	...	...	...	...
25 - 29	9 661 742	4 651 468	5 010 274	...	...	...	...	...	...
30 - 34	9 062 203	4 295 116	4 767 086	...	...	...	...	...	...
35 - 39	8 626 500	4 073 288	4 553 212	...	...	...	...	...	...
40 - 44	7 958 359	3 770 800	4 187 559	...	...	...	...	...	...
45 - 49	6 932 815	3 289 014	3 643 801	...	...	...	...	...	...
50 - 54	5 777 019	2 733 252	3 043 768	...	...	...	...	...	...
55 - 59	4 731 387	2 237 077	2 494 309	...	...	...	...	...	...
60 - 64	3 677 039	1 738 832	1 938 207	...	...	...	...	...	...

7. Population by age, sex and urban/rural residence: latest available year, 2005 - 2014
Population selon l'âge, le sexe et la résidence, urbaine/rurale : dernière année disponible, 2005 - 2014 (continued - suite)

Continent, country or area, date, code[a] and age (in years) / Continent, pays ou zone, date, code[a] et âge (en années)	Total			Urban - Urbaine			Rural - Rurale		
	Both sexes Les deux sexes	Male Masculin	Female Féminin	Both sexes Les deux sexes	Male Masculin	Female Féminin	Both sexes Les deux sexes	Male Masculin	Female Féminin
AMERICA, NORTH - AMÉRIQUE DU NORD									
Mexico - Mexique									
1 VII 2014 (ESDJ)[2]									
65 - 69	2 758 041	1 295 373	1 462 669	...	...	...	...	...	...
70 - 74	2 038 901	945 340	1 093 562	...	...	...	...	...	...
75 - 79	1 435 054	655 637	779 417	...	...	...	...	...	...
80 - 84	933 354	417 624	515 730	...	...	...	...	...	...
85 - 89	512 148	221 182	290 966	...	...	...	...	...	...
90 - 94	224 623	92 733	131 891	...	...	...	...	...	...
95 - 99	71 547	28 111	43 436	...	...	...	...	...	...
100 +	18 724	6 908	11 816	...	...	...	...	...	...
Montserrat									
12 V 2011 (CDJC)									
Total	4 922	2 546	2 376	...	...	...	...	...	...
0 - 4	301	157	144	...	...	...	...	...	...
5 - 9	311	146	165	...	...	...	...	...	...
10 - 14	359	187	172	...	...	...	...	...	...
15 - 19	319	179	140	...	...	...	...	...	...
20 - 24	269	152	117	...	...	...	...	...	...
25 - 29	299	154	145	...	...	...	...	...	...
30 - 34	298	138	160	...	...	...	...	...	...
35 - 39	368	172	196	...	...	...	...	...	...
40 - 44	406	189	217	...	...	...	...	...	...
45 - 49	381	196	185	...	...	...	...	...	...
50 - 54	331	183	148	...	...	...	...	...	...
55 - 59	314	181	133	...	...	...	...	...	...
60 - 64	275	165	110	...	...	...	...	...	...
65 - 69	231	130	101	...	...	...	...	...	...
70 - 74	145	75	70	...	...	...	...	...	...
75 - 79	116	61	55	...	...	...	...	...	...
80 - 84	94	44	50	...	...	...	...	...	...
85 +	105	37	68	...	...	...	...	...	...
Nicaragua									
1 VII 2009 (ESDJ)									
Total	5 742 316	2 844 244	2 898 072	3 259 955	1 569 555	1 690 400	2 482 361	1 274 689	1 207 672
0 - 4	680 125	347 205	332 920	335 635	172 875	162 760	344 490	174 330	170 160
5 - 9	660 096	336 817	323 279	332 694	169 358	163 336	327 402	167 459	159 943
10 - 14	677 756	344 831	332 925	359 316	180 457	178 859	318 440	164 374	154 066
15 - 19	660 608	331 536	329 072	363 427	178 690	184 737	297 181	152 846	144 335
20 - 24	576 923	286 484	290 439	332 187	160 315	171 872	244 736	126 169	118 567
25 - 29	511 402	250 672	260 730	306 186	145 137	161 049	205 216	105 535	99 681
30 - 34	412 087	197 120	214 967	251 145	115 523	135 622	160 942	81 597	79 345
35 - 39	337 317	162 472	174 845	208 505	96 540	111 965	128 812	65 932	62 880
40 - 44	279 795	136 223	143 572	177 594	83 709	93 885	102 201	52 514	49 687
45 - 49	239 942	115 914	124 028	154 027	71 955	82 072	85 915	43 959	41 956
50 - 54	206 088	98 355	107 733	130 198	59 417	70 781	75 890	38 938	36 952
55 - 59	154 329	74 173	80 156	95 879	43 653	52 226	58 450	30 520	27 930
60 - 64	93 681	45 221	48 460	57 189	25 734	31 455	36 492	19 487	17 005
65 - 69	89 351	43 121	46 230	54 102	24 079	30 023	35 249	19 042	16 207
70 - 74	67 861	32 418	35 443	41 515	18 145	23 370	26 346	14 273	12 073
75 - 79	48 205	22 249	25 956	30 640	12 935	17 705	17 565	9 314	8 251
80 +	46 750	19 433	27 317	29 716	11 033	18 683	17 034	8 400	8 634
Panama[14]									
1 VII 2014 (ESDF)									
Total	3 913 275	1 965 087	1 948 188	2 643 353	1 299 262	1 344 091	1 269 922	665 825	604 097
0	74 474	38 060	36 414	45 899	23 497	22 402	28 575	14 563	14 012
1 - 4	294 378	150 376	144 002	179 117	91 574	87 543	115 261	58 802	56 459
5 - 9	362 185	184 905	177 280	218 106	111 311	106 795	144 079	73 594	70 485
10 - 14	356 620	181 951	174 669	215 416	109 400	106 016	141 204	72 551	68 653
15 - 19	340 482	173 448	167 034	212 762	106 574	106 188	127 720	66 874	60 846
20 - 24	319 489	162 049	157 440	210 390	105 223	105 167	109 099	56 826	52 273
25 - 29	308 315	155 836	152 479	211 309	104 381	106 928	97 006	51 455	45 551
30 - 34	295 172	149 100	146 072	214 435	106 327	108 108	80 737	42 773	37 964
35 - 39	282 963	142 546	140 417	210 319	104 718	105 601	72 644	37 828	34 816
40 - 44	265 976	133 385	132 591	198 487	97 873	100 614	67 489	35 512	31 977

Continent, country or area, date, code[a] and age (in years)	Total			Urban - Urbaine			Rural - Rurale		
Continent, pays ou zone, date, code[a] et âge (en années)	Both sexes Les deux sexes	Male Masculin	Female Féminin	Both sexes Les deux sexes	Male Masculin	Female Féminin	Both sexes Les deux sexes	Male Masculin	Female Féminin

AMERICA, NORTH -
AMÉRIQUE DU NORD

Panama[14]
 1 VII 2014 (ESDF)

45 - 49	234 420	117 065	117 355	176 197	85 517	90 680	58 223	31 548	26 675
50 - 54	201 040	99 772	101 268	149 671	71 997	77 674	51 369	27 775	23 594
55 - 59	161 328	79 352	81 976	118 222	56 015	62 207	43 106	23 337	19 769
60 - 64	126 080	61 372	64 708	89 272	41 224	48 048	36 808	20 148	16 660
65 - 69	97 487	46 962	50 525	65 776	29 666	36 110	31 711	17 296	14 415
70 - 74	73 838	35 066	38 772	47 681	20 996	26 685	26 157	14 070	12 087
75 - 79	52 682	24 536	28 146	33 770	14 368	19 402	18 912	10 168	8 744
80 - 84	34 304	15 559	18 745	23 278	9 523	13 755	11 026	6 036	4 990
85 +	...	...	...	23 246	9 078	14 168	8 796	4 669	4 127
85 - 89	19 517	8 557	10 960	...	...	...	...	...	...
90 - 94	8 992	3 779	5 213	...	...	...	...	...	...
95 - 99	3 005	1 207	1 798	...	...	...	...	...	...
100 +	528	204	324	...	...	...	...	...	...

Puerto Rico - Porto Rico[24]
 1 VII 2013 (ESDJ)

Total	3 615 086	1 728 634	1 886 452	...	...	...	...	...	...
0 - 4	199 345	101 983	97 362	...	...	...	...	...	...
5 - 9	217 721	112 020	105 701	...	...	...	...	...	...
10 - 14	241 227	124 824	116 403	...	...	...	...	...	...
15 - 19	262 747	134 701	128 046	...	...	...	...	...	...
20 - 24	264 689	133 456	131 233	...	...	...	...	...	...
25 - 29	226 616	110 589	116 027	...	...	...	...	...	...
30 - 34	232 729	110 904	121 825	...	...	...	...	...	...
35 - 39	230 829	109 987	120 842	...	...	...	...	...	...
40 - 44	231 953	111 438	120 515	...	...	...	...	...	...
45 - 49	237 119	111 739	125 380	...	...	...	...	...	...
50 - 54	235 517	109 190	126 327	...	...	...	...	...	...
55 - 59	225 630	103 219	122 411	...	...	...	...	...	...
60 - 64	209 297	94 698	114 599	...	...	...	...	...	...
65 - 69	196 201	88 834	107 367	...	...	...	...	...	...
70 - 74	149 141	66 614	82 527	...	...	...	...	...	...
75 - 79	109 997	47 907	62 090	...	...	...	...	...	...
80 - 84	73 221	30 089	43 132	...	...	...	...	...	...
85 +	71 107	26 442	44 665	...	...	...	...	...	...

Saint Lucia - Sainte-Lucie
 1 VII 2009 (ESDF)

Total	172 370	84 465	87 905	...	...	...	...	...	...
0 - 4	15 344	7 808	7 536	...	...	...	...	...	...
5 - 9	13 188	6 514	6 674	...	...	...	...	...	...
10 - 14	16 105	8 047	8 058	...	...	...	...	...	...
15 - 19	17 386	8 735	8 651	...	...	...	...	...	...
20 - 24	17 430	8 553	8 877	...	...	...	...	...	...
25 - 29	15 114	7 422	7 692	...	...	...	...	...	...
30 - 34	13 317	6 469	6 848	...	...	...	...	...	...
35 - 39	12 240	5 895	6 345	...	...	...	...	...	...
40 - 44	11 709	5 644	6 065	...	...	...	...	...	...
45 - 49	10 541	5 107	5 434	...	...	...	...	...	...
50 - 54	7 978	3 988	3 990	...	...	...	...	...	...
55 - 59	5 957	2 977	2 980	...	...	...	...	...	...
60 - 64	4 559	2 142	2 417	...	...	...	...	...	...
65 - 69	3 647	1 662	1 985	...	...	...	...	...	...
70 - 74	3 077	1 410	1 667	...	...	...	...	...	...
75 - 79	2 276	1 034	1 242	...	...	...	...	...	...
80 +	2 502	1 058	1 444	...	...	...	...	...	...

Saint Pierre and Miquelon -
Saint Pierre-et-Miquelon
 19 I 2006 (CDFC)

Total	6 125	3 034	3 091	...	...	...	...	...	...
0 - 4	289	143	146	...	...	...	...	...	...
5 - 9	417	211	206	...	...	...	...	...	...
10 - 14	461	237	224	...	...	...	...	...	...
15 - 19	366	188	178	...	...	...	...	...	...

7. Population by age, sex and urban/rural residence: latest available year, 2005 - 2014
Population selon l'âge, le sexe et la résidence, urbaine/rurale : dernière année disponible, 2005 - 2014 (continued - suite)

Continent, country or area, date, code[a] and age (in years) / Continent, pays ou zone, date, code[a] et âge (en années)	Total			Urban - Urbaine			Rural - Rurale		
	Both sexes Les deux sexes	Male Masculin	Female Féminin	Both sexes Les deux sexes	Male Masculin	Female Féminin	Both sexes Les deux sexes	Male Masculin	Female Féminin
AMERICA, NORTH - AMÉRIQUE DU NORD									
Saint Pierre and Miquelon - Saint Pierre-et-Miquelon									
19 I 2006 (CDFC)									
20 - 24	258	136	122	...	...	...	...	...	...
25 - 29	333	166	167	...	...	...	...	...	...
30 - 34	431	202	229	...	...	...	...	...	...
35 - 39	568	294	274	...	...	...	...	...	...
40 - 44	575	293	282	...	...	...	...	...	...
45 - 49	471	246	225	...	...	...	...	...	...
50 - 54	435	238	197	...	...	...	...	...	...
55 - 59	432	231	201	...	...	...	...	...	...
60 - 64	280	143	137	...	...	...	...	...	...
65 - 69	243	115	128	...	...	...	...	...	...
70 - 74	208	83	125	...	...	...	...	...	...
75 - 79	128	42	86	...	...	...	...	...	...
80 - 84	114	35	79	...	...	...	...	...	...
85 - 89	75	19	56	...	...	...	...	...	...
90 - 94	30	12	18	...	...	...	...	...	...
95 +	11	-	11	...	...	...	...	...	...
Saint Vincent and the Grenadines - Saint-Vincent-et-les Grenadines[25]									
1 VII 2008 (ESDF)									
Total	99 086	50 009	49 077	...	...	...	...	...	...
0 - 4	9 302	4 782	4 520	...	...	...	...	...	...
5 - 9	10 684	5 352	5 332	...	...	...	...	...	...
10 - 14	10 391	5 269	5 122	...	...	...	...	...	...
15 - 19	10 531	5 293	5 238	...	...	...	...	...	...
20 - 24	9 060	4 639	4 420	...	...	...	...	...	...
25 - 29	7 941	4 057	3 884	...	...	...	...	...	...
30 - 34	7 155	3 747	3 408	...	...	...	...	...	...
35 - 39	7 525	3 911	3 614	...	...	...	...	...	...
40 - 44	6 243	3 214	3 029	...	...	...	...	...	...
45 - 49	4 410	2 252	2 158	...	...	...	...	...	...
50 - 54	3 481	1 807	1 674	...	...	...	...	...	...
55 - 59	2 595	1 299	1 296	...	...	...	...	...	...
60 - 64	2 550	1 222	1 328	...	...	...	...	...	...
65 - 69	2 379	1 143	1 236	...	...	...	...	...	...
70 - 74	1 819	831	989	...	...	...	...	...	...
75 - 79	1 412	591	821	...	...	...	...	...	...
80 - 84	879	359	520	...	...	...	...	...	...
85 +	729	241	488	...	...	...	...	...	...
Sint Maarten (Dutch part) - Saint-Martin (partie néerlandaise)									
1 I 2013 (ESDJ)									
Total	36 090	17 661	18 429	...	...	...	...	...	...
0 - 4	2 352	1 235	1 117	...	...	...	...	...	...
5 - 9	2 531	1 289	1 242	...	...	...	...	...	...
10 - 14	2 692	1 348	1 344	...	...	...	...	...	...
15 - 19	2 469	1 302	1 167	...	...	...	...	...	...
20 - 24	2 161	1 047	1 114	...	...	...	...	...	...
25 - 29	2 462	1 161	1 300	...	...	...	...	...	...
30 - 34	2 816	1 290	1 526	...	...	...	...	...	...
35 - 39	3 142	1 452	1 689	...	...	...	...	...	...
40 - 44	3 259	1 556	1 703	...	...	...	...	...	...
45 - 49	3 360	1 693	1 667	...	...	...	...	...	...
50 - 54	2 790	1 345	1 445	...	...	...	...	...	...
55 - 59	2 295	1 127	1 167	...	...	...	...	...	...
60 - 64	1 690	835	854	...	...	...	...	...	...
65 - 69	990	490	500	...	...	...	...	...	...
70 - 74	516	258	258	...	...	...	...	...	...
75 - 79	289	143	147	...	...	...	...	...	...

Continent, country or area, date, code[a] and age (in years) / Continent, pays ou zone, date, code[a] et âge (en années)	Total			Urban - Urbaine			Rural - Rurale		
	Both sexes Les deux sexes	Male Masculin	Female Féminin	Both sexes Les deux sexes	Male Masculin	Female Féminin	Both sexes Les deux sexes	Male Masculin	Female Féminin
AMERICA, NORTH - AMÉRIQUE DU NORD									
Sint Maarten (Dutch part) - Saint-Martin (partie néerlandaise)									
1 I 2013 (ESDJ)									
80 - 84	146	51	95	...	...	...	...	...	...
85 +	130	37	93	...	...	...	...	...	...
Trinidad and Tobago - Trinité-et-Tobago[7]									
1 VII 2014 (ESDF)									
Total	1 345 343	...	...	...	...	...	...	...	...
0 - 14	276 982	...	...	...	...	...	...	...	...
15 - 19	99 662	...	...	...	...	...	...	...	...
20 - 24	115 730	...	...	...	...	...	...	...	...
25 - 29	125 129	...	...	...	...	...	...	...	...
30 - 34	106 957	...	...	...	...	...	...	...	...
35 - 39	93 746	...	...	...	...	...	...	...	...
40 - 44	87 287	...	...	...	...	...	...	...	...
45 - 49	97 368	...	...	...	...	...	...	...	...
50 - 54	88 321	...	...	...	...	...	...	...	...
55 - 59	74 170	...	...	...	...	...	...	...	...
60 - 64	59 412	...	...	...	...	...	...	...	...
65 +	120 578	...	...	...	...	...	...	...	...
United States of America - États-Unis d'Amérique									
1 IV 2010 (CDJC)									
Total	308 745 538	151 781 326	156 964 212	249 253 271	121 698 595	127 554 676	59 492 267	30 082 731	29 409 536
0 - 4	20 201 362	10 319 427	9 881 935	16 838 001	8 597 234	8 240 767	3 363 361	1 722 193	1 641 168
5 - 9	20 348 657	10 389 638	9 959 019	16 597 127	8 464 939	8 132 188	3 751 530	1 924 699	1 826 831
10 - 14	20 677 194	10 579 862	10 097 332	16 576 171	8 466 809	8 109 362	4 101 023	2 113 053	1 987 970
15 - 19	22 040 343	11 303 666	10 736 677	17 946 265	9 149 187	8 797 078	4 094 078	2 154 479	1 939 599
20 - 24	21 585 999	11 014 176	10 571 823	18 653 468	9 450 066	9 203 402	2 932 531	1 564 110	1 368 421
25 - 29	21 101 849	10 635 591	10 466 258	18 163 244	9 110 029	9 053 215	2 938 605	1 525 562	1 413 043
30 - 34	19 962 099	9 996 500	9 965 599	16 857 801	8 409 694	8 448 107	3 104 298	1 586 806	1 517 492
35 - 39	20 179 642	10 042 022	10 137 620	16 629 937	8 249 301	8 380 636	3 549 705	1 792 721	1 756 984
40 - 44	20 890 964	10 393 977	10 496 987	16 837 761	8 347 894	8 489 867	4 053 203	2 046 083	2 007 120
45 - 49	22 708 591	11 209 085	11 499 506	17 847 074	8 760 812	9 086 262	4 861 517	2 448 273	2 413 244
50 - 54	22 298 125	10 933 274	11 364 851	17 279 058	8 401 091	8 877 967	5 019 067	2 532 183	2 486 884
55 - 59	19 664 805	9 523 648	10 141 157	15 060 179	7 204 444	7 855 735	4 604 626	2 319 204	2 285 422
60 - 64	16 817 924	8 077 500	8 740 424	12 750 365	6 020 393	6 729 972	4 067 559	2 057 107	2 010 452
65 - 69	12 435 263	5 852 547	6 582 716	9 299 030	4 275 616	5 023 414	3 136 233	1 576 931	1 559 302
70 - 74	9 278 166	4 243 972	5 034 194	7 011 129	3 115 814	3 895 315	2 267 037	1 128 158	1 138 879
75 - 79	7 317 795	3 182 388	4 135 407	5 693 807	2 409 946	3 283 861	1 623 988	772 442	851 546
80 - 84	5 743 327	2 294 374	3 448 953	4 629 581	1 800 531	2 829 050	1 113 746	493 843	619 903
85 - 89	3 620 459	1 273 867	2 346 592	3 005 285	1 036 583	1 968 702	615 174	237 284	377 890
90 - 94	1 448 366	424 387	1 023 979	1 216 647	351 491	865 156	231 719	72 896	158 823
95 - 99	371 244	82 263	288 981	315 589	69 008	246 581	55 655	13 255	42 400
100 +	53 364	9 162	44 202	45 752	7 713	38 039	7 612	1 449	6 163
1 VII 2012 (ESDJ)[26]									
Total	313 914 040	154 492 067	159 421 973	...	...	...	...	...	...
0	3 943 077	2 016 738	1 926 339	...	...	...	...	...	...
1 - 4	16 056 267	8 199 397	7 856 870	...	...	...	...	...	...
5 - 9	20 475 536	10 459 193	10 016 343	...	...	...	...	...	...
10 - 14	20 669 218	10 567 214	10 102 004	...	...	...	...	...	...
15 - 19	21 360 702	10 962 861	10 397 841	...	...	...	...	...	...
20 - 24	22 583 203	11 549 456	11 033 747	...	...	...	...	...	...
25 - 29	21 398 326	10 844 886	10 553 440	...	...	...	...	...	...
30 - 34	20 910 995	10 493 906	10 417 089	...	...	...	...	...	...
35 - 39	19 488 199	9 714 613	9 773 586	...	...	...	...	...	...
40 - 44	21 028 221	10 458 994	10 569 227	...	...	...	...	...	...
45 - 49	21 689 479	10 726 625	10 962 854	...	...	...	...	...	...
50 - 54	22 579 259	11 080 245	11 499 014	...	...	...	...	...	...
55 - 59	20 772 517	10 068 409	10 704 108	...	...	...	...	...	...
60 - 64	17 813 685	8 534 485	9 279 200	...	...	...	...	...	...
65 - 69	13 977 353	6 606 856	7 370 497	...	...	...	...	...	...

Continent, country or area, date, code[a] and age (in years) Continent, pays ou zone, date, code[a] et âge (en années)	Total			Urban - Urbaine			Rural - Rurale		
	Both sexes Les deux sexes	Male Masculin	Female Féminin	Both sexes Les deux sexes	Male Masculin	Female Féminin	Both sexes Les deux sexes	Male Masculin	Female Féminin
AMERICA, NORTH - AMÉRIQUE DU NORD									
United States of America - États-Unis d'Amérique 1 VII 2012 (ESDJ)[26]									
70 - 74	10 008 039	4 596 006	5 412 033	...	...	...	...	...	...
75 - 79	7 489 583	3 291 452	4 198 131	...	...	...	...	...	...
80 - 84	5 783 051	2 356 698	3 426 353	...	...	...	...	...	...
85 - 89	3 754 853	1 351 142	2 403 711	...	...	...	...	...	...
90 - 94	1 654 635	504 187	1 150 448	...	...	...	...	...	...
95 - 99	415 857	97 725	318 132	...	...	...	...	...	...
100 +	61 985	10 979	51 006	...	...	...	...	...	...
United States Virgin Islands - Îles Vierges américaines[27] 1 IV 2010 (CDJC)									
Total	106 405	50 854	55 551	...	...	...	...	...	...
0 - 4	7 500	3 736	3 764	...	...	...	...	...	...
5 - 9	7 150	3 694	3 456	...	...	...	...	...	...
10 - 14	7 484	3 849	3 635	...	...	...	...	...	...
15 - 19	7 560	3 765	3 795	...	...	...	...	...	...
20 - 24	5 894	2 707	3 187	...	...	...	...	...	...
25 - 29	5 969	2 695	3 274	...	...	...	...	...	...
30 - 34	6 137	2 825	3 312	...	...	...	...	...	...
35 - 39	6 675	3 133	3 542	...	...	...	...	...	...
40 - 44	7 450	3 506	3 944	...	...	...	...	...	...
45 - 49	7 743	3 680	4 063	...	...	...	...	...	...
50 - 54	7 900	3 800	4 100	...	...	...	...	...	...
55 - 59	7 192	3 341	3 851	...	...	...	...	...	...
60 - 64	7 367	3 510	3 857	...	...	...	...	...	...
65 - 69	5 853	2 883	2 970	...	...	...	...	...	...
70 - 74	3 717	1 739	1 978	...	...	...	...	...	...
75 - 79	2 328	1 043	1 285	...	...	...	...	...	...
80 - 84	1 332	568	764	...	...	...	...	...	...
85 +	1 154	380	774	...	...	...	...	...	...
AMERICA, SOUTH - AMÉRIQUE DU SUD									
Argentina - Argentine[28] 1 VII 2014 (ESDF)									
Total	42 673 657	20 898 342	21 775 315	39 024 881	18 960 180	20 064 701	3 648 776	1 938 162	1 710 614
0 - 4	3 749 454	1 930 065	1 819 389	3 358 753	1 727 615	1 631 138	390 701	202 450	188 251
5 - 9	3 541 277	1 820 696	1 720 581	3 197 720	1 642 189	1 555 531	343 557	178 507	165 050
10 - 14	3 510 972	1 794 187	1 716 785	3 176 947	1 620 991	1 555 956	334 025	173 196	160 829
15 - 19	3 553 323	1 803 727	1 749 596	3 184 254	1 609 635	1 574 619	369 069	194 092	174 977
20 - 24	3 527 756	1 774 922	1 752 834	3 207 935	1 602 988	1 604 947	319 821	171 934	147 887
25 - 29	3 294 752	1 643 565	1 651 187	3 039 609	1 506 301	1 533 308	255 143	137 264	117 879
30 - 34	3 153 557	1 565 005	1 588 552	2 908 686	1 436 705	1 471 981	244 871	128 300	116 571
35 - 39	3 047 084	1 504 228	1 542 856	2 819 965	1 384 760	1 435 205	227 119	119 468	107 651
40 - 44	2 607 886	1 279 832	1 328 054	2 414 402	1 176 058	1 238 344	193 484	103 774	89 710
45 - 49	2 284 141	1 113 958	1 170 183	2 108 202	1 016 585	1 091 617	175 939	97 373	78 566
50 - 54	2 150 006	1 040 061	1 109 945	1 983 824	947 386	1 036 438	166 182	92 675	73 507
55 - 59	1 972 273	943 466	1 028 807	1 818 451	857 232	961 219	153 822	86 234	67 588
60 - 64	1 755 623	825 113	930 510	1 617 051	747 137	869 914	138 572	77 976	60 596
65 - 69	1 466 752	669 445	797 307	1 352 193	605 760	746 433	114 559	63 685	50 874
70 - 74	1 125 320	489 754	635 566	1 037 674	442 150	595 524	87 646	47 604	40 042
75 - 79	840 330	338 695	501 635	777 065	305 854	471 211	63 265	32 841	30 424
80 - 84	585 187	212 435	372 752	545 134	193 499	351 635	40 053	18 936	21 117
85 - 89	335 445	104 823	230 622	314 221	96 206	218 015	21 224	8 617	12 607
90 - 94	135 283	36 397	98 886	127 597	33 708	93 889	7 686	2 689	4 997
95 - 99	31 507	6 898	24 609	29 803	6 419	23 384	1 704	479	1 225
100 +	5 729	1 070	4 659	5 395	1 002	4 393	334	68	266

Continent, country or area, date, codeᵃ and age (in years) Continent, pays ou zone, date, codeᵃ et âge (en années)	Total			Urban - Urbaine			Rural - Rurale		
	Both sexes Les deux sexes	Male Masculin	Female Féminin	Both sexes Les deux sexes	Male Masculin	Female Féminin	Both sexes Les deux sexes	Male Masculin	Female Féminin
AMERICA, SOUTH -									
AMÉRIQUE DU SUD									
Bolivia (Plurinational State of) - Bolivie (État plurinational de)									
1 VII 2014 (ESDF)									
Total	10 681 367	5 382 966	5 298 401	7 268 748	3 586 253	3 682 495	3 412 619	1 796 713	1 615 906
0 - 4	1 208 187	617 248	590 939	803 644	409 995	393 649	404 543	207 253	197 290
0	244 220	124 866	119 354	...	...	...	...	...	...
1 - 4	963 967	492 382	471 585	...	...	...	...	...	...
5 - 9	1 188 676	606 371	582 305	784 982	398 976	386 006	403 694	207 395	196 299
10 - 14	1 154 358	588 489	565 869	773 173	389 368	383 805	381 185	199 121	182 064
15 - 19	1 104 661	562 423	542 238	770 234	383 726	386 508	334 427	178 697	155 730
20 - 24	1 016 011	515 703	500 308	732 545	361 136	371 409	283 466	154 567	128 899
25 - 29	903 561	456 980	446 581	662 309	324 673	337 636	241 252	132 307	108 945
30 - 34	789 134	397 863	391 271	571 001	278 635	292 366	218 133	119 228	98 905
35 - 39	669 739	336 800	332 939	476 158	231 481	244 677	193 581	105 319	88 262
40 - 44	558 013	279 659	278 354	384 481	186 097	198 384	173 532	93 562	79 970
45 - 49	465 036	232 729	232 307	311 991	151 057	160 934	153 045	81 672	71 373
50 - 54	392 616	196 166	196 450	255 134	123 516	131 618	137 482	72 650	64 832
55 - 59	328 053	163 168	164 885	206 494	99 667	106 827	121 559	63 501	58 058
60 - 64	274 904	135 603	139 301	168 171	80 607	87 564	106 733	54 996	51 737
65 - 69	215 731	105 677	110 054	128 182	60 974	67 208	87 549	44 703	42 846
70 - 74	164 072	78 782	85 290	95 491	44 561	50 930	68 581	34 221	34 360
75 - 79	114 669	52 959	61 710	66 896	29 973	36 923	47 773	22 986	24 787
80 - 84	75 936	33 578	42 358	44 354	19 022	25 332	31 582	14 556	17 026
85 - 89	40 248	16 674	23 574	23 240	9 359	13 881	17 008	7 315	9 693
90 - 94	14 315	5 144	9 171	8 306	2 903	5 403	6 009	2 241	3 768
95 +	3 447	950	2 497	1 962	527	1 435	1 485	423	1 062
Brazil - Brésil									
31 VII 2010 (CDJC)									
Total	190 755 799	93 406 990	97 348 809	160 925 804	77 710 179	83 215 625	29 829 995	15 696 811	14 133 184
0	2 713 244	1 378 532	1 334 712	2 246 034	1 141 784	1 104 250	467 210	236 748	230 462
1 - 4	11 082 914	5 638 455	5 444 459	9 055 114	4 603 340	4 451 774	2 027 800	1 035 115	992 685
5 - 9	14 969 375	7 624 144	7 345 231	12 135 285	6 169 531	5 965 754	2 834 090	1 454 613	1 379 477
10 - 14	17 166 761	8 725 413	8 441 348	13 956 987	7 062 057	6 894 930	3 209 774	1 663 356	1 546 418
15 - 19	16 990 872	8 558 868	8 432 004	14 039 001	6 998 102	7 040 899	2 951 871	1 560 766	1 391 105
20 - 24	17 245 192	8 630 229	8 614 963	14 706 068	7 276 963	7 429 105	2 539 124	1 353 266	1 185 858
25 - 29	17 104 414	8 460 995	8 643 419	14 772 957	7 225 732	7 547 225	2 331 457	1 235 263	1 096 194
30 - 34	15 744 512	7 717 658	8 026 854	13 611 921	6 586 877	7 025 044	2 132 591	1 130 781	1 001 810
35 - 39	13 888 579	6 766 664	7 121 915	11 975 407	5 750 498	6 224 909	1 913 172	1 016 166	897 006
40 - 44	13 009 364	6 320 568	6 688 796	11 187 429	5 344 982	5 842 447	1 821 935	975 586	846 349
45 - 49	11 833 352	5 692 014	6 141 338	10 181 394	4 806 322	5 375 072	1 651 958	885 692	766 266
50 - 54	10 140 402	4 834 995	5 305 407	8 708 339	4 074 679	4 633 660	1 432 063	760 316	671 747
55 - 59	8 276 221	3 902 344	4 373 877	7 025 474	3 238 531	3 786 943	1 250 747	663 813	586 934
60 - 64	6 509 120	3 041 035	3 468 085	5 474 944	2 479 882	2 995 062	1 034 176	561 153	473 023
65 - 69	4 840 810	2 224 065	2 616 745	4 040 016	1 792 798	2 247 218	800 794	431 267	369 527
70 - 74	3 741 636	1 667 372	2 074 264	3 142 173	1 349 329	1 792 844	599 463	318 043	281 420
75 - 79	2 563 447	1 090 517	1 472 930	2 174 038	889 908	1 284 130	389 409	200 609	188 800
80 - 84	1 666 972	668 623	998 349	1 423 603	546 865	876 738	243 369	121 758	121 611
85 - 89	819 483	310 759	508 724	695 385	251 112	444 273	124 098	59 647	64 451
90 - 94	326 558	114 964	211 594	273 348	90 960	182 388	53 210	24 004	29 206
95 - 99	98 335	31 529	66 806	81 121	24 365	56 756	17 214	7 164	10 050
100 +	24 236	7 247	16 989	19 766	5 562	14 204	4 470	1 685	2 785
1 VII 2014 (ESDJ)[29]									
Total	202 768 562	100 159 507	102 609 055	...	...	...	...	...	...
0	2 915 415	1 491 806	1 423 609	...	...	...	...	...	...
1 - 4	12 022 718	6 148 030	5 874 688	...	...	...	...	...	...
5 - 9	16 009 509	8 178 587	7 830 922	...	...	...	...	...	...
10 - 14	17 036 612	8 685 434	8 351 178	...	...	...	...	...	...
15 - 19	17 144 248	8 710 088	8 434 160	...	...	...	...	...	...
20 - 24	17 079 105	8 631 969	8 447 136	...	...	...	...	...	...
25 - 29	17 325 091	8 706 325	8 618 766	...	...	...	...	...	...
30 - 34	17 483 642	8 737 916	8 745 726	...	...	...	...	...	...
35 - 39	15 473 785	7 687 579	7 786 206	...	...	...	...	...	...
40 - 44	13 700 143	6 758 883	6 941 260	...	...	...	...	...	...

Continent, country or area, date, code[a] and age (in years) / Continent, pays ou zone, date, code[a] et âge (en années)	Total			Urban - Urbaine			Rural - Rurale		
	Both sexes Les deux sexes	Male Masculin	Female Féminin	Both sexes Les deux sexes	Male Masculin	Female Féminin	Both sexes Les deux sexes	Male Masculin	Female Féminin
AMERICA, SOUTH - AMÉRIQUE DU SUD									
Brazil - Brésil									
1 VII 2014 (ESDJ)[29]									
45 - 49	12 662 331	6 194 845	6 467 486	...	...	...	...	...	...
50 - 54	11 442 231	5 538 560	5 903 671	...	...	...	...	...	...
55 - 59	9 485 114	4 526 467	4 958 647	...	...	...	...	...	...
60 - 64	7 499 452	3 513 756	3 985 696	...	...	...	...	...	...
65 - 69	5 575 432	2 545 918	3 029 514	...	...	...	...	...	...
70 - 74	3 925 728	1 724 737	2 200 991	...	...	...	...	...	...
75 - 79	2 818 329	1 182 129	1 636 200	...	...	...	...	...	...
80 - 84	1 733 123	686 155	1 046 968	...	...	...	...	...	...
85 - 89	931 944	347 268	584 676	...	...	...	...	...	...
90 +	504 610	163 055	341 555	...	...	...	...	...	...
Chile - Chili									
1 VII 2013 (ESDF)									
Total	17 556 815	8 688 067	8 868 748	15 282 334	7 481 874	7 800 460	2 274 481	1 206 193	1 068 288
0	252 089	128 432	123 657	219 140	111 627	107 513	32 949	16 805	16 144
1 - 4	1 002 945	510 838	492 107	874 300	445 110	429 190	128 645	65 728	62 917
5 - 9	1 243 745	633 287	610 458	1 089 439	554 130	535 309	154 306	79 157	75 149
10 - 14	1 274 249	648 484	625 765	1 114 159	566 092	548 067	160 090	82 392	77 698
15 - 19	1 392 383	707 959	684 424	1 205 990	611 526	594 464	186 393	96 433	89 960
20 - 24	1 476 990	749 460	727 530	1 275 807	644 063	631 744	201 183	105 397	95 786
25 - 29	1 404 077	710 354	693 723	1 220 766	611 575	609 191	183 311	98 779	84 532
30 - 34	1 258 431	634 056	624 375	1 109 101	551 513	557 588	149 330	82 543	66 787
35 - 39	1 193 842	598 029	595 813	1 055 443	523 414	532 029	138 399	74 615	63 784
40 - 44	1 230 157	612 898	617 259	1 078 655	532 283	546 372	151 502	80 615	70 887
45 - 49	1 231 666	610 366	621 300	1 070 989	523 991	546 998	160 677	86 375	74 302
50 - 54	1 166 669	574 320	592 349	1 013 989	490 389	523 600	152 680	83 931	68 749
55 - 59	961 200	468 437	492 763	837 617	399 907	437 710	123 583	68 530	55 053
60 - 64	749 746	359 065	390 681	651 793	305 292	346 501	97 953	53 773	44 180
65 - 69	593 617	276 510	317 107	511 723	232 429	279 294	81 894	44 081	37 813
70 - 74	448 283	200 585	247 698	381 557	165 385	216 172	66 726	35 200	31 526
75 - 79	317 614	133 715	183 899	267 239	107 873	159 366	50 375	25 842	24 533
80 +	359 112	131 272	227 840	304 627	105 275	199 352	54 485	25 997	28 488
1 VII 2014 (ESDF)									
Total	17 819 054	8 819 725	8 999 329	...	...	...	...	...	...
0	246 478	125 450	121 028	...	...	...	...	...	...
1 - 4	991 619	505 316	486 303	...	...	...	...	...	...
5 - 9	1 201 816	613 382	588 434	...	...	...	...	...	...
10 - 14	1 225 673	625 023	600 650	...	...	...	...	...	...
15 - 19	1 346 539	688 256	658 283	...	...	...	...	...	...
20 - 24	1 480 522	752 828	727 694	...	...	...	...	...	...
25 - 29	1 472 719	744 576	728 143	...	...	...	...	...	...
30 - 34	1 319 539	664 141	655 398	...	...	...	...	...	...
35 - 39	1 239 763	620 725	619 038	...	...	...	...	...	...
40 - 44	1 244 802	620 014	624 788	...	...	...	...	...	...
45 - 49	1 261 612	625 244	636 368	...	...	...	...	...	...
50 - 54	1 201 108	591 677	609 431	...	...	...	...	...	...
55 - 59	1 008 041	492 681	515 360	...	...	...	...	...	...
60 - 64	789 354	380 422	408 932	...	...	...	...	...	...
65 - 69	621 043	291 060	329 983	...	...	...	...	...	...
70 - 74	467 091	210 245	256 846	...	...	...	...	...	...
75 - 79	331 705	139 687	192 018	...	...	...	...	...	...
80 +	369 630	128 998	240 632	...	...	...	...	...	...
Colombia - Colombie[30]									
1 VII 2014 (ESDJ)									
Total	47 661 787	23 531 670	24 130 117	36 359 268	17 556 826	18 802 442	11 302 519	5 974 844	5 327 675
0 - 4	4 310 123	2 205 140	2 104 983	3 060 852	1 563 993	1 496 859	1 249 271	641 147	608 124
0	870 130	445 282	424 848	...	...	...	...	...	...
1 - 4	3 439 993	1 759 858	1 680 135	...	...	...	...	...	...
5 - 9	4 260 992	2 178 087	2 082 905	3 078 424	1 569 059	1 509 365	1 182 568	609 028	573 540
10 - 14	4 301 474	2 196 672	2 104 802	3 155 635	1 598 177	1 557 458	1 145 839	598 495	547 344
15 - 19	4 367 653	2 231 913	2 135 740	3 263 490	1 638 156	1 625 334	1 104 163	593 757	510 406
20 - 24	4 264 257	2 182 627	2 081 630	3 248 090	1 633 301	1 614 789	1 016 167	549 326	466 841
25 - 29	3 889 676	1 961 986	1 927 690	3 023 889	1 497 899	1 525 990	865 787	464 087	401 700

Continent, country or area, date, code[a] and age (in years) / Continent, pays ou zone, date, code[a] et âge (en années)	Total			Urban - Urbaine			Rural - Rurale		
	Both sexes Les deux sexes	Male Masculin	Female Féminin	Both sexes Les deux sexes	Male Masculin	Female Féminin	Both sexes Les deux sexes	Male Masculin	Female Féminin
AMERICA, SOUTH - AMÉRIQUE DU SUD									
Colombia - Colombie[30]									
1 VII 2014 (ESDJ)									
30 - 34	3 478 846	1 700 271	1 778 575	2 755 719	1 318 166	1 437 553	723 127	382 105	341 022
35 - 39	3 141 854	1 525 194	1 616 660	2 482 295	1 177 013	1 305 282	659 559	348 181	311 378
40 - 44	2 869 549	1 378 539	1 491 010	2 268 001	1 060 511	1 207 490	601 548	318 028	283 520
45 - 49	2 879 512	1 373 706	1 505 806	2 285 266	1 057 191	1 228 075	594 246	316 515	277 731
50 - 54	2 617 116	1 245 714	1 371 402	2 093 215	963 102	1 130 113	523 901	282 612	241 289
55 - 59	2 134 484	1 008 294	1 126 190	1 684 804	765 350	919 454	449 680	242 944	206 736
60 - 64	1 659 236	782 667	876 569	1 294 830	584 342	710 488	364 406	198 325	166 081
65 - 69	1 250 825	583 881	666 944	962 622	428 769	533 853	288 203	155 112	133 091
70 - 74	891 781	406 288	485 493	676 687	293 210	383 477	215 094	113 078	102 016
75 - 79	674 766	293 335	381 431	509 413	207 678	301 735	165 353	85 657	79 696
80 +	669 643	277 356	392 287	516 036	200 909	315 127	153 607	76 447	77 160
Ecuador - Équateur[31]									
1 VII 2014 (ESDF)									
Total	16 027 466	7 939 552	8 087 914	10 145 875	4 969 197	5 176 678	5 881 591	2 970 355	2 911 236
0	336 328	171 911	164 417	199 491	102 402	97 089	136 837	69 509	67 328
1 - 4	1 350 471	690 246	660 225	802 677	410 702	391 975	547 794	279 544	268 250
5 - 9	1 679 973	859 265	820 708	999 586	511 012	488 574	680 387	348 253	332 134
10 - 14	1 615 610	824 704	790 883	972 573	494 645	477 928	643 014	330 059	312 955
15 - 19	1 514 164	768 031	746 133	945 054	475 342	469 712	569 110	292 689	276 421
20 - 24	1 390 316	697 957	692 359	903 529	449 132	454 397	486 787	248 825	237 962
25 - 29	1 275 550	631 695	643 855	847 917	416 404	431 513	427 633	215 291	212 342
30 - 34	1 172 832	570 725	602 107	783 088	377 669	405 419	389 744	193 056	196 688
35 - 39	1 057 356	507 231	550 125	705 428	334 135	371 293	351 928	173 096	178 832
40 - 44	935 873	447 786	488 087	627 199	295 084	332 115	308 674	152 702	155 972
45 - 49	825 984	396 328	429 656	555 745	261 985	293 760	270 239	134 343	135 896
50 - 54	717 270	345 188	372 082	478 947	226 732	252 215	238 323	118 456	119 867
55 - 59	598 561	288 760	309 801	390 597	185 081	205 516	207 964	103 679	104 285
60 - 64	479 614	231 040	248 574	300 834	141 675	159 159	178 780	89 365	89 415
65 - 69	373 082	178 285	194 797	223 437	103 571	119 866	149 645	74 714	74 931
70 - 74	279 507	131 761	147 746	162 075	73 322	88 753	117 432	58 439	58 993
75 - 79	196 452	91 696	104 756	112 841	50 189	62 652	83 611	41 507	42 104
80 - 84	124 167	58 008	66 159	72 008	32 061	39 947	52 159	25 947	26 212
85 - 89	66 298	31 077	35 221	39 336	17 589	21 747	26 962	13 488	13 474
90 - 94	28 347	13 223	15 124	17 376	7 695	9 681	10 971	5 528	5 443
95 - 99	9 267	4 395	4 872	5 840	2 622	3 218	3 427	1 773	1 654
100 +	467	240	227	297	148	149	170	92	78
Falkland Islands (Malvinas) - Îles Falkland (Malvinas)[32]									
8 X 2006 (CDFC)									
Total	2 955	1 569	1 386	...	...	...	...	...	...
0 - 4	156	79	77	...	...	...	...	...	...
5 - 9	161	75	86	...	...	...	...	...	...
10 - 14	154	71	83	...	...	...	...	...	...
15 - 19	155	90	65	...	...	...	...	...	...
20 - 24	207	89	118	...	...	...	...	...	...
25 - 29	232	126	106	...	...	...	...	...	...
30 - 34	266	131	135	...	...	...	...	...	...
35 - 39	291	165	126	...	...	...	...	...	...
40 - 44	261	156	105	...	...	...	...	...	...
45 - 49	249	128	121	...	...	...	...	...	...
50 - 54	215	123	92	...	...	...	...	...	...
55 - 59	194	113	81	...	...	...	...	...	...
60 - 64	148	87	61	...	...	...	...	...	...
65 - 69	98	57	41	...	...	...	...	...	...
70 - 74	68	36	32	...	...	...	...	...	...
75 - 79	48	18	30	...	...	...	...	...	...
80 +	52	25	27	...	...	...	...	...	...
French Guiana - Guyane française									
1 I 2010* (ESDJ)									
Total	230 441	113 824	116 617	...	...	...	...	...	...
0 - 4	28 440	14 591	13 849	...	...	...	...	...	...

Continent, country or area, date, code[a] and age (in years) / Continent, pays ou zone, date, code[a] et âge (en annèes)	Total			Urban - Urbaine			Rural - Rurale		
	Both sexes Les deux sexes	Male Masculin	Female Féminin	Both sexes Les deux sexes	Male Masculin	Female Féminin	Both sexes Les deux sexes	Male Masculin	Female Féminin
AMERICA, SOUTH - AMÉRIQUE DU SUD									
French Guiana - Guyane française									
1 I 2010* (ESDJ)									
5 - 9	27 708	14 090	13 618	...	...	...	...	...	...
10 - 14	24 867	12 843	12 024	...	...	...	...	...	...
15 - 19	21 401	10 729	10 672	...	...	...	...	...	...
20 - 24	16 206	7 728	8 478	...	...	...	...	...	...
25 - 29	16 390	7 281	9 109	...	...	...	...	...	...
30 - 34	16 368	7 692	8 676	...	...	...	...	...	...
35 - 39	16 742	7 877	8 865	...	...	...	...	...	...
40 - 44	15 065	7 415	7 650	...	...	...	...	...	...
45 - 49	13 280	6 698	6 582	...	...	...	...	...	...
50 - 54	10 545	5 397	5 148	...	...	...	...	...	...
55 - 59	8 314	4 207	4 107	...	...	...	...	...	...
60 - 64	5 615	2 931	2 684	...	...	...	...	...	...
65 - 69	3 433	1 740	1 693	...	...	...	...	...	...
70 - 74	2 343	1 083	1 260	...	...	...	...	...	...
75 - 79	1 726	752	974	...	...	...	...	...	...
80 - 84	1 052	433	619	...	...	...	...	...	...
85 - 89	627	225	402	...	...	...	...	...	...
90 - 94	221	77	144	...	...	...	...	...	...
95 +	98	35	63	...	...	...	...	...	...
Guyana[33]									
1 VII 2010 (ESDF)									
Total	784 894	393 059	391 835	...	...	...	...	...	...
0 - 4	67 701	34 029	33 673	...	...	...	...	...	...
5 - 9	65 201	32 778	32 423	...	...	...	...	...	...
10 - 14	77 921	39 978	37 943	...	...	...	...	...	...
15 - 19	85 004	43 487	41 518	...	...	...	...	...	...
20 - 24	69 423	34 877	34 545	...	...	...	...	...	...
25 - 29	55 510	26 816	28 694	...	...	...	...	...	...
30 - 34	54 824	27 189	27 635	...	...	...	...	...	...
35 - 39	53 454	27 764	25 690	...	...	...	...	...	...
40 - 44	52 434	27 112	25 322	...	...	...	...	...	...
45 - 49	50 689	25 775	24 914	...	...	...	...	...	...
50 - 54	45 438	22 163	23 275	...	...	...	...	...	...
55 - 59	35 160	17 672	17 488	...	...	...	...	...	...
60 - 64	27 873	13 995	13 878	...	...	...	...	...	...
65 - 69	17 455	7 988	9 467	...	...	...	...	...	...
70 - 74	12 451	5 440	7 012	...	...	...	...	...	...
75 - 79	8 114	3 529	4 585	...	...	...	...	...	...
80 +	6 242	2 469	3 773	...	...	...	...	...	...
Paraguay[11]									
1 VII 2014 (ESDF)									
Total	6 893 727	3 481 648	3 412 079	4 100 854	2 005 735	2 095 119	2 792 873	1 475 913	1 316 960
0	149 497	76 292	73 205	82 190	41 921	40 269	67 307	34 371	32 936
1 - 4	592 752	302 081	290 671	329 110	167 318	161 792	263 642	134 763	128 879
5 - 9	732 572	373 032	359 540	414 266	209 925	204 341	318 306	163 107	155 199
10 - 14	718 808	365 801	353 007	409 801	206 133	203 668	309 007	159 668	149 339
15 - 19	695 129	353 337	341 792	396 365	196 907	199 458	298 764	156 430	142 334
20 - 24	660 768	335 017	325 751	374 262	184 053	190 209	286 505	150 963	135 542
25 - 29	609 697	307 963	301 734	350 726	168 983	181 742	258 972	138 979	119 992
30 - 34	531 175	267 895	263 280	335 966	157 173	178 792	195 210	110 722	84 488
35 - 39	420 493	211 739	208 753	290 071	137 473	152 598	130 421	74 266	56 155
40 - 44	351 991	176 306	175 685	237 125	114 658	122 467	114 866	61 649	53 218
45 - 49	324 401	162 786	161 614	209 177	101 643	107 535	115 223	61 144	54 080
50 - 54	285 223	143 859	141 364	178 037	86 922	91 115	107 186	56 937	50 249
55 - 59	243 012	123 235	119 777	148 982	72 588	76 394	94 030	50 647	43 383
60 - 64	196 794	99 963	96 832	119 147	58 279	60 868	77 647	41 684	35 963
65 - 69	141 649	70 841	70 808	84 013	40 163	43 851	57 636	30 679	26 957
70 - 74	101 558	49 351	52 206	60 302	27 893	32 409	41 255	21 458	19 797
75 - 79	71 414	33 466	37 948	41 666	18 111	23 555	29 748	15 356	14 392
80 +	66 795	28 682	38 112	39 648	15 593	24 055	27 146	13 089	14 057

Continent, country or area, date, code[a] and age (in years) / Continent, pays ou zone, date, code[a] et âge (en annèes)	Total			Urban - Urbaine			Rural - Rurale		
	Both sexes Les deux sexes	Male Masculin	Female Féminin	Both sexes Les deux sexes	Male Masculin	Female Féminin	Both sexes Les deux sexes	Male Masculin	Female Féminin
AMERICA, SOUTH - AMÉRIQUE DU SUD									
Peru - Pérou[18]									
30 VI 2014 (ESDF)									
Total	30 814 175	15 438 887	15 375 288	23 474 069	11 602 321	11 871 748	7 340 106	3 836 566	3 503 540
0 - 4	2 880 686	1 470 162	1 410 524	1 994 738	1 021 859	972 879	885 948	448 303	437 645
5 - 9	2 930 450	1 493 358	1 437 092	2 066 874	1 051 752	1 015 122	863 576	441 606	421 970
10 - 14	2 916 314	1 483 692	1 432 622	2 101 592	1 062 220	1 039 372	814 722	421 472	393 250
15 - 19	2 889 781	1 466 502	1 423 279	2 163 276	1 083 829	1 079 447	726 505	382 673	343 832
20 - 24	2 815 952	1 425 476	1 390 476	2 205 123	1 098 544	1 106 579	610 829	326 932	283 897
25 - 29	2 628 320	1 326 218	1 302 102	2 050 609	1 015 249	1 035 360	577 711	310 969	266 742
30 - 34	2 389 602	1 202 936	1 186 666	1 886 699	928 649	958 050	502 903	274 287	228 616
35 - 39	2 221 569	1 116 238	1 105 331	1 763 609	865 080	898 529	457 960	251 158	206 802
40 - 44	1 936 256	969 304	966 952	1 535 295	750 729	784 566	400 961	218 575	182 386
45 - 49	1 688 346	841 434	846 912	1 356 401	663 005	693 396	331 945	178 429	153 516
50 - 54	1 443 077	714 437	728 640	1 167 893	569 960	597 933	275 184	144 477	130 707
55 - 59	1 166 684	572 076	594 608	933 518	451 402	482 116	233 166	120 674	112 492
60 - 64	933 698	452 965	480 733	729 123	350 368	378 755	204 575	102 597	101 978
65 - 69	710 008	339 335	370 673	545 797	259 173	286 624	164 211	80 162	84 049
70 - 74	530 116	247 189	282 927	404 346	187 110	217 236	125 770	60 079	65 691
75 - 79	382 689	171 765	210 924	292 300	129 212	163 088	90 389	42 553	47 836
80 +	350 627	145 800	204 827	276 876	114 180	162 696	73 751	31 620	42 131
Suriname									
13 VIII 2012 (CDJC)									
Total	541 638	270 629	271 009	359 146	177 215	181 931	182 492	93 414	89 078
0 - 4	50 548	25 968	24 580	30 755	15 787	14 968	19 793	10 181	9 612
5 - 9	47 735	24 549	23 186	28 390	14 549	13 841	19 345	10 000	9 345
10 - 14	50 484	26 166	24 318	31 147	16 037	15 110	19 338	10 130	9 208
15 - 19	45 108	22 772	22 336	30 010	15 040	14 970	15 097	7 731	7 366
20 - 24	43 762	21 656	22 106	31 096	15 201	15 895	12 666	6 455	6 211
25 - 29	43 946	21 761	22 185	30 679	15 107	15 572	13 267	6 654	6 613
30 - 34	39 051	19 355	19 696	26 819	13 234	13 585	12 232	6 121	6 111
35 - 39	36 429	18 316	18 113	24 050	11 860	12 190	12 379	6 456	5 923
40 - 44	37 383	18 763	18 620	24 796	12 167	12 629	12 587	6 596	5 991
45 - 49	36 031	18 083	17 948	24 438	12 032	12 406	11 593	6 051	5 542
50 - 54	30 651	15 313	15 338	21 072	10 258	10 814	9 579	5 055	4 525
55 - 59	22 588	10 929	11 659	15 699	7 417	8 282	6 889	3 512	3 377
60 - 64	16 497	7 734	8 763	11 475	5 304	6 171	5 022	2 430	2 592
65 - 69	13 008	5 951	7 057	9 134	4 166	4 968	3 874	1 785	2 089
70 - 74	10 133	4 619	5 514	6 983	3 211	3 772	3 150	1 408	1 742
75 - 79	7 556	3 393	4 163	5 149	2 296	2 853	2 407	1 097	1 310
80 - 84	4 433	1 934	2 499	3 019	1 308	1 711	1 414	626	788
85 +	2 900	1 081	1 819	2 088	758	1 330	812	323	489
85 - 89	1 978	743	1 235	...	...	...	...	...	...
90 - 94	712	274	438	...	...	...	...	...	...
95 +	210	64	146	...	...	...	...	...	...
Unknown - Inconnu	3 395	2 286	1 109	2 347	1 483	864	1 048	803	245
1 VII 2013 (ESDJ)									
Total	550 222	274 859	275 363	...	...	...	...	...	...
0 - 4	50 469	25 987	24 482	...	...	...	...	...	...
5 - 9	49 356	25 385	23 971	...	...	...	...	...	...
10 - 14	48 746	24 941	23 805	...	...	...	...	...	...
15 - 19	47 243	24 016	23 227	...	...	...	...	...	...
20 - 24	45 355	22 822	22 533	...	...	...	...	...	...
25 - 29	43 306	21 677	21 629	...	...	...	...	...	...
30 - 34	41 172	20 572	20 600	...	...	...	...	...	...
35 - 39	38 842	19 391	19 451	...	...	...	...	...	...
40 - 44	37 145	18 598	18 547	...	...	...	...	...	...
45 - 49	33 945	16 957	16 988	...	...	...	...	...	...
50 - 54	29 687	14 702	14 985	...	...	...	...	...	...
55 - 59	25 008	12 249	12 759	...	...	...	...	...	...
60 - 64	19 325	9 254	10 071	...	...	...	...	...	...
65 - 69	14 817	6 945	7 872	...	...	...	...	...	...
70 - 74	10 890	4 982	5 908	...	...	...	...	...	...
75 - 79	7 433	3 300	4 135	...	...	...	...	...	...
80 +	7 483	3 081	4 402	...	...	...	...	...	...

Continent, country or area, date, code[a] and age (in years) / Continent, pays ou zone, date, code[a] et âge (en années)	Total			Urban - Urbaine			Rural - Rurale		
	Both sexes Les deux sexes	Male Masculin	Female Féminin	Both sexes Les deux sexes	Male Masculin	Female Féminin	Both sexes Les deux sexes	Male Masculin	Female Féminin
AMERICA, SOUTH - AMÉRIQUE DU SUD									
Uruguay									
4 X 2011 (CDJC)									
Total	3 285 877[34]	1 577 416	1 708 461	3 110 264	1 478 658	1 631 606	175 613	98 758	76 855
0 - 4	220 345	112 704	107 641	209 663	107 163	102 500	10 682	5 541	5 141
5 - 9	238 068	121 820	116 248	225 974	115 560	110 414	12 094	6 260	5 834
10 - 14	256 552	131 022	125 530	243 701	124 289	119 412	12 851	6 733	6 118
15 - 19	261 691	133 042	128 649	248 573	125 655	122 918	13 118	7 387	5 731
20 - 24	241 006	119 928	121 078	229 054	112 626	116 428	11 952	7 302	4 650
25 - 29	228 385	112 852	115 533	216 541	105 936	110 605	11 844	6 916	4 928
30 - 34	233 365	113 884	119 481	220 934	106 771	114 163	12 431	7 113	5 318
35 - 39	222 521	108 704	113 817	210 125	101 642	108 483	12 396	7 062	5 334
40 - 44	203 098	98 612	104 486	191 369	92 030	99 339	11 729	6 582	5 147
45 - 49	198 773	95 812	102 961	187 356	89 304	98 052	11 417	6 508	4 909
50 - 54	194 565	93 175	101 390	183 306	86 750	96 556	11 259	6 425	4 834
55 - 59	173 007	81 828	91 179	162 340	75 635	86 705	10 667	6 193	4 474
60 - 64	150 775	69 864	80 911	141 192	64 288	76 904	9 583	5 576	4 007
65 - 69	131 563	58 769	72 794	123 640	54 149	69 491	7 923	4 620	3 303
70 - 74	112 395	47 705	64 690	106 246	44 102	62 144	6 149	3 603	2 546
75 - 79	93 659	36 806	56 853	89 142	34 280	54 862	4 517	2 526	1 991
80 - 84	70 505	24 912	45 593	67 588	23 393	44 195	2 917	1 519	1 398
85 - 89	37 426	11 535	25 891	35 994	10 888	25 106	1 432	647	785
90 - 94	14 113	3 636	10 477	13 599	3 432	10 167	514	204	310
95 - 99	3 546	733	2 813	3 421	694	2 727	125	39	86
100 +	519	73	446	506	71	435	13	2	11
1 VII 2014 (ESDF)[2]									
Total	3 453 691	1 670 026	1 783 665	...	...	...	...	...	...
0	46 065	23 576	22 489	...	...	...	...	...	...
1 - 4	186 074	95 107	90 967	...	...	...	...	...	...
5 - 9	239 815	122 629	117 186	...	...	...	...	...	...
10 - 14	257 459	131 565	125 893	...	...	...	...	...	...
15 - 19	272 540	138 758	133 782	...	...	...	...	...	...
20 - 24	258 936	130 976	127 961	...	...	...	...	...	...
25 - 29	247 007	124 276	122 731	...	...	...	...	...	...
30 - 34	238 405	118 507	119 898	...	...	...	...	...	...
35 - 39	243 098	120 026	123 072	...	...	...	...	...	...
40 - 44	221 657	108 678	112 979	...	...	...	...	...	...
45 - 49	205 304	99 379	105 925	...	...	...	...	...	...
50 - 54	206 572	99 446	107 126	...	...	...	...	...	...
55 - 59	189 936	90 331	99 605	...	...	...	...	...	...
60 - 64	160 747	74 742	86 006	...	...	...	...	...	...
65 - 69	138 393	62 219	76 174	...	...	...	...	...	...
70 - 74	115 526	49 469	66 057	...	...	...	...	...	...
75 - 79	92 892	36 615	56 277	...	...	...	...	...	...
80 - 84	71 235	25 350	45 885	...	...	...	...	...	...
85 - 89	41 096	12 956	28 140	...	...	...	...	...	...
90 +	20 931	5 420	15 511	...	...	...	...	...	...
Venezuela (Bolivarian Republic of) - Venezuela (République bolivarienne du)									
1 VII 2014 (ESDF)									
Total	30 206 307	15 144 744	15 061 563	26 628 251	13 228 428	13 399 823	3 578 056	1 916 316	1 661 740
0 - 4	2 744 697	1 412 806	1 331 891	2 319 332	1 200 556	1 118 776	425 365	212 250	213 115
0	545 507	280 976	264 531	...	...	...	...	...	...
1 - 4	2 199 190	1 131 830	1 067 360	...	...	...	...	...	...
5 - 9	2 787 268	1 433 260	1 354 008	2 382 642	1 230 193	1 152 449	404 626	203 067	201 559
10 - 14	2 779 169	1 428 687	1 350 482	2 413 385	1 240 551	1 172 834	365 784	188 136	177 648
15 - 19	2 706 025	1 388 519	1 317 506	2 381 375	1 212 698	1 168 677	324 650	175 821	148 829
20 - 24	2 637 084	1 344 052	1 293 032	2 336 822	1 178 789	1 158 033	300 262	165 263	134 999
25 - 29	2 598 270	1 312 023	1 286 247	2 305 604	1 151 178	1 154 426	292 666	160 845	131 821
30 - 34	2 382 055	1 194 042	1 188 013	2 133 722	1 056 890	1 076 832	248 333	137 152	111 181
35 - 39	2 117 336	1 055 685	1 061 651	1 907 507	939 760	967 747	209 829	115 925	93 904
40 - 44	1 939 452	963 415	976 037	1 753 003	860 892	892 111	186 449	102 523	83 926
45 - 49	1 820 360	901 864	918 496	1 643 462	805 586	837 876	176 898	96 278	80 620
50 - 54	1 582 657	780 406	802 251	1 418 351	691 226	727 125	164 306	89 180	75 126

Continent, country or area, date, code[a] and age (in years) Continent, pays ou zone, date, code[a] et âge (en annèes)	Total			Urban - Urbaine			Rural - Rurale		
	Both sexes Les deux sexes	Male Masculin	Female Féminin	Both sexes Les deux sexes	Male Masculin	Female Féminin	Both sexes Les deux sexes	Male Masculin	Female Féminin
AMERICA, SOUTH - **AMÉRIQUE DU SUD**									
Venezuela (Bolivarian Republic of) - Venezuela (République bolivarienne du) 1 VII 2014 (ESDF)									
55 - 59	1 255 629	614 779	640 850	1 116 220	536 843	579 377	139 409	77 936	61 473
60 - 64	938 518	454 848	483 670	827 514	391 408	436 106	111 004	63 440	47 564
65 - 69	698 384	331 482	366 902	613 760	282 860	330 900	84 624	48 622	36 002
70 - 74	496 243	231 202	265 041	436 553	198 103	238 450	59 690	33 099	26 591
75 - 79	330 759	149 422	181 337	291 751	127 902	163 849	39 008	21 520	17 488
80 +	392 401	148 252	244 149	347 248	122 993	224 255	45 153	25 259	19 894
80 - 84	201 684	85 347	116 337	...	...	...	...	...	...
85 - 89	111 733	41 201	70 532	...	...	...	...	...	...
90 - 94	53 384	15 948	37 436	...	...	...	...	...	...
95 - 99	20 808	4 737	16 071	...	...	...	...	...	...
100 +	4 792	1 019	3 773	...	...	...	...	...	...
ASIA - ASIE									
Afghanistan[35] 1 VII 2014 (ESDF)									
Total	26 556 756	13 585 933	12 970 823	6 483 434	3 338 764	3 144 670	20 073 322	10 247 169	9 826 153
0 - 4	5 183 389	2 522 393	2 660 997	1 220 264	607 176	613 088	3 963 126	1 915 217	2 047 909
5 - 9	3 980 764	2 022 226	1 958 537	991 520	505 319	486 201	2 989 244	1 516 908	1 472 336
10 - 14	3 082 101	1 621 326	1 460 775	804 765	415 948	388 817	2 277 336	1 205 378	1 071 958
15 - 19	2 519 131	1 329 985	1 189 146	664 427	340 034	324 393	1 854 703	989 951	864 752
20 - 24	2 156 300	1 104 060	1 052 240	550 976	274 956	276 020	1 605 324	829 104	776 220
25 - 29	1 779 776	879 132	900 644	442 875	220 003	222 872	1 336 902	659 129	677 773
30 - 34	1 483 076	706 978	776 098	360 667	180 894	179 773	1 122 409	526 084	596 324
35 - 39	1 301 751	622 947	678 803	304 345	155 395	148 950	997 405	467 552	529 853
40 - 44	1 123 853	568 646	555 206	258 490	135 786	122 703	865 363	432 860	432 503
45 - 49	974 149	515 488	458 661	218 672	118 635	100 038	755 477	396 854	358 623
50 - 54	821 885	452 884	369 001	181 411	101 273	80 137	640 475	351 611	288 864
55 - 59	661 715	375 088	286 627	146 085	83 868	62 218	515 630	291 220	224 410
60 - 64	510 789	293 152	217 637	114 518	66 890	47 628	396 271	226 262	170 009
65 - 69	369 018	212 765	156 253	84 257	49 316	34 941	284 761	163 449	121 312
70 - 74	253 765	147 550	106 215	58 422	34 348	24 074	195 343	113 202	82 141
75 - 79	162 203	94 910	67 293	37 253	22 148	15 106	124 950	72 762	52 187
80 - 84	98 003	57 726	40 278	22 558	13 499	9 060	75 445	44 227	31 218
85 +	95 088	58 677	36 411	21 928	13 276	8 651	73 160	45 400	27 760
Armenia - Arménie 12 X 2011 (CDJC)									
Total	3 018 854	1 448 052	1 570 802	1 911 287	895 372	1 015 915	1 107 567	552 680	554 887
0 - 4	207 572	110 565	97 007	127 653	67 466	60 187	79 919	43 099	36 820
5 - 9	179 929	96 429	83 500	110 826	58 712	52 114	69 103	37 717	31 386
10 - 14	178 637	95 458	83 179	105 685	56 068	49 617	72 952	39 390	33 562
15 - 19	233 075	117 938	115 137	134 853	67 252	67 601	98 222	50 686	47 536
20 - 24	292 234	143 897	148 337	175 999	83 968	92 031	116 235	59 929	56 306
25 - 29	271 929	132 109	139 820	173 093	81 320	91 773	98 836	50 789	48 047
30 - 34	223 005	108 114	114 891	148 671	71 158	77 513	74 334	36 956	37 378
35 - 39	187 421	89 073	98 348	123 792	58 479	65 313	63 629	30 594	33 035
40 - 44	176 964	82 502	94 462	109 718	49 721	59 997	67 246	32 781	34 465
45 - 49	211 060	98 064	112 996	126 779	55 920	70 859	84 281	42 144	42 137
50 - 54	234 532	109 294	125 238	150 258	66 623	83 635	84 274	42 671	41 603
55 - 59	177 758	80 989	96 769	122 931	54 136	68 795	54 827	26 853	27 974
60 - 64	127 599	56 189	71 410	93 673	40 621	53 052	33 926	15 568	18 358
65 - 69	65 373	28 020	37 353	47 797	20 459	27 338	17 576	7 561	10 015
70 - 74	107 678	44 041	63 637	71 461	29 585	41 876	36 217	14 456	21 761
75 - 79	75 377	30 734	44 643	47 483	19 373	28 110	27 894	11 361	16 533
80 - 84	48 906	18 662	30 244	28 738	10 892	17 846	20 168	7 770	12 398
85 +	19 805	5 974	13 831	11 877	3 619	8 258	7 928	2 355	5 573

Continent, country or area, date, code[a] and age (in years) / Continent, pays ou zone, date, code[a] et âge (en années)	Total			Urban - Urbaine			Rural - Rurale		
	Both sexes Les deux sexes	Male Masculin	Female Féminin	Both sexes Les deux sexes	Male Masculin	Female Féminin	Both sexes Les deux sexes	Male Masculin	Female Féminin
ASIA - ASIE									
Azerbaijan - Azerbaïdjan									
1 VII 2013 (ESDF)									
Total	9 416 801	4 681 171	4 735 630	5 016 014	2 476 345	2 539 669	4 400 787	2 204 826	2 195 961
0	173 570	93 081	80 489	86 660	46 218	40 442	86 910	46 863	40 047
1 - 4	649 116	349 320	299 796	319 660	171 385	148 275	329 456	177 935	151 521
5 - 9	629 478	336 045	293 433	320 693	170 668	150 025	308 785	165 377	143 408
10 - 14	650 650	345 814	304 836	323 728	172 960	150 768	326 922	172 854	154 068
15 - 19	782 374	408 097	374 277	387 662	203 534	184 128	394 712	204 563	190 149
20 - 24	928 770	468 670	460 100	480 394	240 898	239 496	448 376	227 772	220 604
25 - 29	910 905	449 630	461 275	497 908	242 870	255 038	412 997	206 760	206 237
30 - 34	779 354	387 167	392 187	436 312	215 317	220 995	343 042	171 850	171 192
35 - 39	644 717	317 319	327 398	351 258	171 062	180 196	293 459	146 257	147 202
40 - 44	637 984	307 020	330 964	340 244	160 105	180 139	297 740	146 915	150 825
45 - 49	661 348	314 928	346 420	352 678	164 324	188 354	308 670	150 604	158 066
50 - 54	658 917	316 576	342 341	371 405	178 076	193 329	287 512	138 500	149 012
55 - 59	467 876	222 515	245 361	273 059	130 088	142 971	194 817	92 427	102 390
60 - 64	295 787	137 089	158 698	181 006	84 563	96 443	114 781	52 526	62 255
65 - 69	149 923	66 426	83 497	93 078	41 587	51 491	56 845	24 839	32 006
70 - 74	150 419	63 557	86 862	83 410	35 613	47 797	67 009	27 944	39 065
75 - 79	141 182	57 707	83 475	69 273	28 434	40 839	71 909	29 273	42 636
80 - 84	71 159	28 991	42 168	33 005	13 332	19 673	38 154	15 659	22 495
85 - 89	24 448	8 859	15 589	11 179	4 133	7 046	13 269	4 726	8 543
90 - 94	6 756	2 018	4 738	2 879	1 034	1 845	3 877	984	2 893
95 - 99	1 315	313	1 002	381	140	241	934	173	761
100 +	753	29	724	142	4	138	611	25	586
Bahrain - Bahreïn									
1 VII 2014 (ESDJ)									
Total	1 314 562	806 487	508 075	...	...	...	...	...	...
0	21 379	11 043	10 336	...	...	...	...	...	...
1 - 4	79 217	40 357	38 860	...	...	...	...	...	...
5 - 9	89 812	45 836	43 976	...	...	...	...	...	...
10 - 14	79 179	40 703	38 476	...	...	...	...	...	...
15 - 19	73 589	38 148	35 441	...	...	...	...	...	...
20 - 24	105 972	62 487	43 485	...	...	...	...	...	...
25 - 29	177 999	121 005	56 994	...	...	...	...	...	...
30 - 34	170 791	116 947	53 844	...	...	...	...	...	...
35 - 39	135 098	89 221	45 877	...	...	...	...	...	...
40 - 44	106 200	71 325	34 875	...	...	...	...	...	...
45 - 49	87 287	55 580	31 707	...	...	...	...	...	...
50 - 54	69 440	42 796	26 644	...	...	...	...	...	...
55 - 59	51 854	32 566	19 288	...	...	...	...	...	...
60 - 64	29 136	17 917	11 219	...	...	...	...	...	...
65 - 69	14 889	8 583	6 306	...	...	...	...	...	...
70 - 74	9 878	5 285	4 593	...	...	...	...	...	...
75 - 79	6 366	3 303	3 063	...	...	...	...	...	...
80 - 84	3 757	1 969	1 788	...	...	...	...	...	...
85 +	2 719	1 416	1 303	...	...	...	...	...	...
Bangladesh									
15 III 2011 (CDFC)									
Total	144 043 697	72 109 796	71 933 901	33 563 183[36]	17 529 792[36]	16 033 391[36]	110 480 514	54 580 004	55 900 510
0 - 4	15 061 970	7 638 523	7 423 447	3 015 500[36]	1 534 508[36]	1 480 992[36]	12 046 470	6 104 015	5 942 455
5 - 9	18 173 229	9 322 514	8 850 715	3 520 080[36]	1 810 786[36]	1 709 294[36]	14 653 149	7 511 728	7 141 421
10 - 14	16 646 615	8 614 889	8 031 726	3 609 866[36]	1 868 428[36]	1 741 438[36]	13 036 749	6 746 461	6 290 288
15 - 19	12 861 890	6 509 492	6 352 398	3 417 088[36]	1 735 931[36]	1 681 157[36]	9 444 802	4 773 561	4 671 241
20 - 24	13 299 789	5 777 370	7 522 419	3 750 754[36]	1 803 092[36]	1 947 662[36]	9 549 035	3 974 278	5 574 757
25 - 29	13 479 508	6 225 252	7 254 256	3 638 634[36]	1 846 338[36]	1 792 296[36]	9 840 874	4 378 914	5 461 960
30 - 34	10 499 765	5 079 106	5 420 659	2 757 615[36]	1 460 253[36]	1 297 362[36]	7 742 150	3 618 853	4 123 297
35 - 39	9 556 428	4 697 349	4 859 079	2 424 331[36]	1 291 114[36]	1 133 217[36]	7 132 097	3 406 235	3 725 862
40 - 44	8 261 662	4 280 923	3 980 739	2 014 793[36]	1 124 193[36]	890 545[36]	6 246 924	3 156 730	3 090 194
45 - 49	6 380 073	3 363 273	3 016 800	1 504 983[36]	849 659[36]	655 324[36]	4 875 090	2 513 614	2 361 476
50 - 54	5 552 271	2 952 596	2 599 675	1 225 174[36]	703 282[36]	521 892[36]	4 327 097	2 249 314	2 077 783
55 - 59	3 500 997	1 923 534	1 577 463	758 757[36]	448 673[36]	310 084[36]	2 742 240	1 474 861	1 267 379
60 - 64	3 934 014	2 081 306	1 852 708	759 025[36]	425 996[36]	333 029[36]	3 174 989	1 655 310	1 519 679
65 - 69	2 113 490	1 149 569	963 921	386 330[36]	217 634[36]	168 696[36]	1 727 160	931 935	795 225

Continent, country or area, date, code[a] and age (in years) / Continent, pays ou zone, date, code[a] et âge (en annèes)	Total			Urban - Urbaine			Rural - Rurale		
	Both sexes Les deux sexes	Male Masculin	Female Féminin	Both sexes Les deux sexes	Male Masculin	Female Féminin	Both sexes Les deux sexes	Male Masculin	Female Féminin
ASIA - ASIE									
Bangladesh									
15 III 2011 (CDFC)									
70 - 74	2 231 712	1 206 398	1 025 314	379 459[36]	207 611[36]	171 848[36]	1 852 253	998 787	853 466
75 - 79	874 727	488 338	386 389	146 831[36]	80 832[36]	65 999[36]	727 896	407 506	320 390
80 - 84	880 079	443 239	436 840	138 128[36]	68 117[36]	70 011[36]	741 951	375 122	366 829
85 - 89	262 611	138 268	124 343	42 824[36]	21 933[36]	20 891[36]	219 787	116 335	103 452
90 - 94	250 189	116 916	133 273	38 679[36]	16 945[36]	21 734[36]	211 510	99 971	111 539
95 +	222 678	100 941	121 737	34 387[36]	14 467[36]	19 920[36]	188 291	86 474	101 817
Bhutan - Bhoutan[37]									
1 VII 2014 (ESDF)									
Total	745 153	387 520	357 633	283 544	150 737	132 806	461 610	236 783	224 827
0 - 4	83 772	42 244	41 527	28 568	14 291	14 277	55 204	27 954	27 250
5 - 9	80 682	40 722	39 960	30 524	15 268	15 255	50 158	25 454	24 704
10 - 14	62 800	31 653	31 147	25 673	12 824	12 848	37 127	18 829	18 299
15 - 19	68 801	34 860	33 941	29 545	14 960	14 586	39 255	19 900	19 355
20 - 24	71 548	36 568	34 980	32 733	16 935	15 799	38 814	19 633	19 181
25 - 29	68 251	35 589	32 662	31 419	16 736	14 683	36 832	18 853	17 979
30 - 34	63 034	33 855	29 179	28 369	15 824	12 545	34 665	18 031	16 634
35 - 39	54 788	29 760	25 028	23 300	13 327	9 973	31 488	16 433	15 055
40 - 44	44 773	24 554	20 219	16 553	9 764	6 789	28 220	14 790	13 430
45 - 49	37 054	20 236	16 818	12 117	7 206	4 910	24 938	13 030	11 908
50 - 54	29 453	15 804	13 649	8 127	4 792	3 335	21 326	11 011	10 314
55 - 59	23 835	12 671	11 164	5 737	3 331	2 406	18 099	9 340	8 759
60 - 64	18 810	9 899	8 911	3 932	2 166	1 766	14 878	7 734	7 145
65 - 69	14 412	7 475	6 936	2 728	1 418	1 310	11 684	6 057	5 626
70 - 74	10 402	5 304	5 098	1 822	870	953	8 580	4 435	4 145
75 - 79	6 821	3 418	3 403	1 211	514	697	5 611	2 905	2 706
80 +	5 918	2 905	3 012	1 187	511	676	4 731	2 394	2 337
Brunei Darussalam - Brunéi Darussalam									
20 VI 2011 (CDJC)									
Total	393 372	203 144	190 228	296 257	151 663	144 594	97 115	51 481	45 634
0 - 4	30 323	15 690	14 633	23 250	11 966	11 284	7 073	3 724	3 349
5 - 9	33 659	17 271	16 388	25 840	13 253	12 587	7 819	4 018	3 801
10 - 14	35 453	18 424	17 029	26 734	13 946	12 788	8 719	4 478	4 241
15 - 19	34 967	17 954	17 013	25 706	13 158	12 548	9 261	4 796	4 465
20 - 24	38 150	19 916	18 234	28 301	14 585	13 716	9 849	5 331	4 518
25 - 29	39 185	20 756	18 429	29 567	15 337	14 230	9 618	5 419	4 199
30 - 34	36 896	19 324	17 572	28 516	14 629	13 887	8 380	4 695	3 685
35 - 39	33 796	17 331	16 465	25 962	13 022	12 940	7 834	4 309	3 525
40 - 44	30 122	15 289	14 833	22 900	11 487	11 413	7 222	3 802	3 420
45 - 49	24 610	12 840	11 770	18 737	9 714	9 023	5 873	3 126	2 747
50 - 54	19 781	10 333	9 448	14 978	7 841	7 137	4 803	2 492	2 311
55 - 59	14 044	7 158	6 886	10 214	5 270	4 944	3 830	1 888	1 942
60 - 64	8 518	4 164	4 354	6 112	3 008	3 104	2 406	1 156	1 250
65 - 69	5 088	2 584	2 504	3 522	1 770	1 752	1 566	814	752
70 - 74	3 901	1 827	2 074	2 680	1 208	1 472	1 221	619	602
75 - 79	2 601	1 193	1 408	1 713	764	949	888	429	459
80 - 84	1 405	702	703	943	452	491	462	250	212
85 +	873	388	485	582	253	329	291	135	156
Cambodia - Cambodge[38]									
1 VII 2014 (ESDF)									
Total	15 184 116	7 436 178	7 747 938	3 412 183	1 642 397	1 769 786	11 771 933	5 793 781	5 978 152
0	350 142	178 409	171 733	84 792	43 600	41 191	265 350	134 808	130 542
1 - 4	1 242 660	632 562	610 098	271 835	138 462	133 374	970 825	494 101	476 724
5 - 9	1 443 536	735 088	708 448	243 958	124 438	119 520	1 199 578	610 650	588 928
10 - 14	1 461 984	746 374	715 610	223 866	114 602	109 264	1 238 118	631 772	606 346
15 - 19	1 678 877	861 481	817 396	281 268	139 760	141 508	1 397 609	721 721	675 888
20 - 24	1 678 918	866 690	812 228	418 665	192 262	226 403	1 260 253	674 428	585 825
25 - 29	1 429 146	703 748	725 398	471 354	218 088	253 266	957 792	485 660	472 132
30 - 34	1 307 903	639 761	668 142	398 425	192 636	205 789	909 478	447 125	462 353
35 - 39	768 572	372 230	396 342	196 442	97 722	98 720	572 130	274 508	297 622
40 - 44	817 786	394 829	422 957	186 882	93 714	93 168	630 904	301 115	329 789
45 - 49	763 452	357 780	405 672	164 466	82 027	82 439	598 986	275 753	323 233
50 - 54	665 614	306 359	359 255	140 953	67 945	73 008	524 661	238 414	286 247

Continent, country or area, date, code[a] and age (in years) / Continent, pays ou zone, date, code[a] et âge (en années)	Total			Urban - Urbaine			Rural - Rurale		
	Both sexes Les deux sexes	Male Masculin	Female Féminin	Both sexes Les deux sexes	Male Masculin	Female Féminin	Both sexes Les deux sexes	Male Masculin	Female Féminin
ASIA - ASIE									
Cambodia - Cambodge[38]									
1 VII 2014 (ESDF)									
55 - 59	504 322	205 337	298 985	113 432	49 140	64 292	390 890	156 197	234 693
60 - 64	386 642	157 137	229 505	84 230	35 908	48 322	302 412	121 229	181 183
65 - 69	266 243	110 939	155 304	54 269	22 789	31 480	211 974	88 150	123 824
70 - 74	187 739	77 653	110 086	34 615	13 929	20 686	153 124	63 724	89 400
75 - 79	122 884	48 943	73 941	22 144	8 402	13 742	100 740	40 541	60 199
80 +	107 696	40 858	66 838	20 587	6 973	13 614	87 109	33 885	53 224
China - Chine[39]									
1 XI 2010 (CDJC)[40]									
Total	1332810869	682 329 104	650 481 765	670 005 546	343 040 783	326 964 763	662 805 323	339 288 321	323 517 002
0 - 4	75 532 610	41 062 566	34 470 044	30 936 470	16 749 729	14 186 741	44 596 140	24 312 837	20 283 303
5 - 9	70 881 549	38 464 665	32 416 884	30 565 659	16 580 910	13 984 749	40 315 890	21 883 755	18 432 135
10 - 14	74 908 462	40 267 277	34 641 185	32 807 526	17 664 790	15 142 736	42 100 936	22 602 487	19 498 449
15 - 19	99 889 114	51 904 830	47 984 284	53 589 992	27 603 777	25 986 215	46 299 122	24 301 053	21 998 069
20 - 24	127 412 518	64 008 573	63 403 945	71 058 518	36 041 784	35 016 734	56 354 000	27 966 789	28 387 211
25 - 29	101 013 852	50 837 038	50 176 814	57 679 956	28 973 516	28 706 440	43 333 896	21 863 522	21 470 374
30 - 34	97 138 203	49 521 822	47 616 381	56 010 957	28 432 073	27 578 884	41 127 246	21 089 749	20 037 497
35 - 39	118 025 959	60 391 104	57 634 855	65 025 365	33 349 280	31 676 085	53 000 594	27 041 824	25 958 770
40 - 44	124 753 964	63 608 678	61 145 286	63 786 496	32 845 769	30 940 727	60 967 468	30 762 909	30 204 559
45 - 49	105 594 553	53 776 418	51 818 135	53 629 541	27 723 132	25 906 409	51 965 012	26 053 286	25 911 726
50 - 54	78 753 171	40 363 234	38 389 937	39 186 388	20 130 395	19 055 993	39 566 783	20 232 839	19 333 944
55 - 59	81 312 474	41 082 938	40 229 536	37 437 535	18 762 887	18 674 648	43 874 939	22 320 051	21 554 888
60 - 64	58 667 282	29 834 426	28 832 856	26 036 917	13 067 045	12 969 872	32 630 365	16 767 381	15 862 984
65 - 69	41 113 282	20 748 471	20 364 811	17 910 329	8 866 594	9 043 735	23 202 953	11 881 877	11 321 076
70 - 74	32 972 397	16 403 453	16 568 944	14 777 260	7 241 891	7 535 369	18 195 137	9 161 562	9 033 575
75 - 79	23 852 133	11 278 859	12 573 274	10 531 503	5 048 471	5 483 032	13 320 630	6 230 388	7 090 242
80 - 84	13 373 198	5 917 502	7 455 696	5 762 828	2 665 218	3 097 610	7 610 370	3 252 284	4 358 086
85 - 89	5 631 928	2 199 810	3 432 118	2 392 190	982 284	1 409 906	3 239 738	1 217 526	2 022 212
90 - 94	1 578 307	530 872	1 047 435	687 763	246 031	441 732	890 544	284 841	605 703
95 - 99	369 979	117 716	252 263	176 542	60 991	115 551	193 437	56 725	136 712
100 +	35 934	8 852	27 082	15 811	4 216	11 595	20 123	4 636	15 487
31 XII 2011 (ESDF)[41]									
Total	1347304706	690 634 118	656 670 588	...	...	...	...	...	...
0 - 4	76 270 588	41 467 059	34 803 529	...	...	...	...	...	...
5 - 9	72 092 941	39 108 235	32 984 706	...	...	...	...	...	...
10 - 14	73 507 059	39 657 647	33 849 412	...	...	...	...	...	...
15 - 19	94 574 118	49 489 412	45 084 706	...	...	...	...	...	...
20 - 24	127 725 882	64 991 765	62 732 941	...	...	...	...	...	...
25 - 29	105 010 588	52 912 941	52 096 471	...	...	...	...	...	...
30 - 34	96 644 706	49 303 529	47 341 176	...	...	...	...	...	...
35 - 39	113 994 118	58 317 647	55 676 471	...	...	...	...	...	...
40 - 44	126 342 353	64 477 647	61 864 706	...	...	...	...	...	...
45 - 49	118 650 588	60 510 588	58 140 000	...	...	...	...	...	...
50 - 54	73 181 176	37 436 471	35 744 706	...	...	...	...	...	...
55 - 59	84 314 118	42 603 529	41 709 412	...	...	...	...	...	...
60 - 64	62 009 412	31 397 647	30 611 765	...	...	...	...	...	...
65 - 69	42 416 471	21 251 765	21 164 706	...	...	...	...	...	...
70 - 74	33 912 941	16 934 118	16 978 824	...	...	...	...	...	...
75 - 79	24 910 588	11 716 471	13 195 294	...	...	...	...	...	...
80 - 84	14 075 294	6 263 529	7 811 765	...	...	...	...	...	...
85 - 89	5 642 353	2 182 353	3 460 000	...	...	...	...	...	...
90 - 94	1 690 588	524 706	1 165 882	...	...	...	...	...	...
95 +	341 176	85 882	254 118	...	...	...	...	...	...
China, Hong Kong SAR - Chine, Hong Kong RAS									
1 VII 2014 (ESDJ)									
Total	7 241 700	3 345 100	3 896 600	...	...	...	...	...	...
0	50 000	25 900	24 100	...	...	...	...	...	...
1 - 4	216 200	111 800	104 400	...	...	...	...	...	...
5 - 9	262 800	136 000	126 800	...	...	...	...	...	...
10 - 14	275 400	141 500	133 900	...	...	...	...	...	...
15 - 19	384 500	197 700	186 800	...	...	...	...	...	...
20 - 24	450 700	223 700	227 000	...	...	...	...	...	...
25 - 29	515 900	224 200	291 700	...	...	...	...	...	...

Continent, country or area, date, code[a] and age (in years)	Total			Urban - Urbaine			Rural - Rurale		
Continent, pays ou zone, date, code[a] et âge (en années)	Both sexes Les deux sexes	Male Masculin	Female Féminin	Both sexes Les deux sexes	Male Masculin	Female Féminin	Both sexes Les deux sexes	Male Masculin	Female Féminin

ASIA - ASIE

China, Hong Kong SAR - Chine, Hong Kong RAS
1 VII 2014 (ESDJ)

30 - 34	581 100	233 000	348 100	...	...	...	...	...	...
35 - 39	560 000	226 900	333 100	...	...	...	...	...	...
40 - 44	579 500	239 600	339 900	...	...	...	...	...	...
45 - 49	589 100	258 300	330 800	...	...	...	...	...	...
50 - 54	659 000	310 200	348 800	...	...	...	...	...	...
55 - 59	590 900	291 600	299 300	...	...	...	...	...	...
60 - 64	460 700	227 700	233 000	...	...	...	...	...	...
65 - 69	326 500	163 100	163 400	...	...	...	...	...	...
70 - 74	211 800	109 800	102 000	...	...	...	...	...	...
75 - 79	209 500	100 100	109 400	...	...	...	...	...	...
80 - 84	165 100	73 500	91 600	...	...	...	...	...	...
85 +	153 000	50 500	102 500	...	...	...	...	...	...

China, Macao SAR - Chine, Macao RAS
1 VII 2014 (ESDJ)

Total	621 700	305 500	316 200	...	...	...	...	...	...
0	6 500	3 400	3 100	...	...	...	...	...	...
1 - 4	22 800	12 000	10 800	...	...	...	...	...	...
5 - 9	20 400	10 700	9 700	...	...	...	...	...	...
10 - 14	20 400	10 700	9 700	...	...	...	...	...	...
15 - 19	31 600	16 200	15 400	...	...	...	...	...	...
20 - 24	50 000	25 100	24 900	...	...	...	...	...	...
25 - 29	71 200	34 700	36 500	...	...	...	...	...	...
30 - 34	59 100	29 600	29 500	...	...	...	...	...	...
35 - 39	48 100	24 000	24 100	...	...	...	...	...	...
40 - 44	52 900	24 700	28 200	...	...	...	...	...	...
45 - 49	51 800	23 000	28 800	...	...	...	...	...	...
50 - 54	56 600	27 200	29 400	...	...	...	...	...	...
55 - 59	47 900	24 400	23 500	...	...	...	...	...	...
60 - 64	32 300	16 200	16 100	...	...	...	...	...	...
65 - 69	20 300	10 800	9 500	...	...	...	...	...	...
70 - 74	9 700	5 000	4 700	...	...	...	...	...	...
75 - 79	8 100	3 700	4 400	...	...	...	...	...	...
80 - 84	6 000	2 300	3 700	...	...	...	...	...	...
85 +	6 000	1 800	4 200	...	...	...	...	...	...

Cyprus - Chypre[42]
1 X 2011 (CDJC)

Total	840 407	408 780	431 627	566 191	273 065	293 126	274 216	135 715	138 501
0 - 4	45 015	23 061	21 954	29 726	15 202	14 524	15 289	7 859	7 430
5 - 9	42 635	21 921	20 714	28 050	14 386	13 664	14 585	7 535	7 050
10 - 14	47 298	24 179	23 119	30 926	15 730	15 196	16 372	8 449	7 923
15 - 19	55 818	28 683	27 135	36 345	18 593	17 752	19 473	10 090	9 383
20 - 24	66 073	33 891	32 182	44 948	22 847	22 101	21 125	11 044	10 081
25 - 29	74 114	36 992	37 122	51 855	25 842	26 013	22 259	11 150	11 109
30 - 34	69 834	33 149	36 685	48 938	23 133	25 805	20 896	10 016	10 880
35 - 39	61 862	27 754	34 108	43 232	19 204	24 028	18 630	8 550	10 080
40 - 44	59 728	27 031	32 697	41 295	18 416	22 879	18 433	8 615	9 818
45 - 49	57 240	27 059	30 181	39 233	18 225	21 008	18 007	8 834	9 173
50 - 54	56 128	27 517	28 611	38 287	18 499	19 788	17 841	9 018	8 823
55 - 59	47 762	23 771	23 991	31 716	15 541	16 175	16 046	8 230	7 816
60 - 64	45 034	22 057	22 977	29 704	14 438	15 266	15 330	7 619	7 711
65 - 69	36 328	17 656	18 672	23 459	11 295	12 164	12 869	6 361	6 508
70 - 74	29 433	14 044	15 389	18 991	9 048	9 943	10 442	4 996	5 446
75 - 79	21 058	9 647	11 411	13 545	6 239	7 306	7 513	3 408	4 105
80 +	24 948	10 342	14 606	15 853	6 408	9 445	9 095	3 934	5 161
Unknown - Inconnu	99	26	73	88	19	69	11	7	4

1 VII 2013 (ESDJ)

Total	861 930	419 183	442 747	...	...	...	...	...	...
0	9 278	4 700	4 578	...	...	...	...	...	...
1 - 4	39 636	20 310	19 326	...	...	...	...	...	...
5 - 9	46 073	23 714	22 359	...	...	...	...	...	...
10 - 14	45 248	23 200	22 048	...	...	...	...	...	...

7. Population by age, sex and urban/rural residence: latest available year, 2005 - 2014
Population selon l'âge, le sexe et la résidence, urbaine/rurale : dernière année disponible, 2005 - 2014 (continued - suite)

Continent, country or area, date, code[a] and age (in years) / Continent, pays ou zone, date, code[a] et âge (en années)	Total			Urban - Urbaine			Rural - Rurale		
	Both sexes Les deux sexes	Male Masculin	Female Féminin	Both sexes Les deux sexes	Male Masculin	Female Féminin	Both sexes Les deux sexes	Male Masculin	Female Féminin
ASIA - ASIE									
Cyprus - Chypre[42]									
1 VII 2013 (ESDJ)									
15 - 19	55 102	28 283	26 819	...	...	...	...	...	...
20 - 24	67 760	34 610	33 150	...	...	...	...	...	...
25 - 29	72 978	36 273	36 705	...	...	...	...	...	...
30 - 34	71 392	34 248	37 144	...	...	...	...	...	...
35 - 39	61 898	28 491	33 407	...	...	...	...	...	...
40 - 44	59 861	27 323	32 538	...	...	...	...	...	...
45 - 49	56 950	26 745	30 205	...	...	...	...	...	...
50 - 54	57 730	28 034	29 696	...	...	...	...	...	...
55 - 59	51 276	25 252	26 024	...	...	...	...	...	...
60 - 64	47 197	23 231	23 966	...	...	...	...	...	...
65 - 69	39 423	18 990	20 433	...	...	...	...	...	...
70 - 74	30 459	14 430	16 029	...	...	...	...	...	...
75 - 79	23 012	10 454	12 558	...	...	...	...	...	...
80 - 84	15 287	6 415	8 872	...	...	...	...	...	...
85 - 89	7 955	3 149	4 806	...	...	...	...	...	...
90 - 94	2 811	1 104	1 707	...	...	...	...	...	...
95 +	604	227	377	...	...	...	...	...	...
Democratic People's Republic of Korea - République populaire démocratique de Corée									
1 X 2008 (CDJC)									
Total	24 052 231	11 721 838	12 330 393	...	...	...	...	...	...
0 - 4	1 710 039	872 173	837 866	...	...	...	...	...	...
5 - 9	1 846 785	943 048	903 737	...	...	...	...	...	...
10 - 14	2 021 350	1 035 282	986 068	...	...	...	...	...	...
15 - 19	2 052 342	1 050 113	1 002 229	...	...	...	...	...	...
20 - 24	1 841 400	941 017	900 383	...	...	...	...	...	...
25 - 29	1 737 185	887 573	849 612	...	...	...	...	...	...
30 - 34	1 680 272	853 276	826 996	...	...	...	...	...	...
35 - 39	2 214 929	1 118 391	1 096 538	...	...	...	...	...	...
40 - 44	2 015 514	1 005 140	1 010 374	...	...	...	...	...	...
45 - 49	1 559 527	766 054	793 473	...	...	...	...	...	...
50 - 54	1 315 101	637 737	677 364	...	...	...	...	...	...
55 - 59	902 876	423 625	479 251	...	...	...	...	...	...
60 - 64	1 058 263	476 727	581 536	...	...	...	...	...	...
65 - 69	913 304	379 456	533 848	...	...	...	...	...	...
70 - 74	662 627	228 286	434 341	...	...	...	...	...	...
75 - 79	335 467	79 231	256 236	...	...	...	...	...	...
80 - 84	132 149	18 884	113 265	...	...	...	...	...	...
85 - 89	42 760	4 930	37 830	...	...	...	...	...	...
90 - 94	8 634	809	7 825	...	...	...	...	...	...
95 - 99	1 643	86	1 557	...	...	...	...	...	...
100 +	64	-	64	...	...	...	...	...	...
Georgia - Géorgie									
1 VII 2012 (ESDF)									
Total	4 490 700	2 141 300	2 349 400	...	...	...	...	...	...
0	56 900	29 700	27 200	...	...	...	...	...	...
1 - 4	232 900	122 950	109 950	...	...	...	...	...	...
5 - 9	233 350	123 200	110 150	...	...	...	...	...	...
10 - 14	238 850	125 850	113 000	...	...	...	...	...	...
15 - 19	293 600	151 600	142 000	...	...	...	...	...	...
20 - 24	368 200	186 250	181 950	...	...	...	...	...	...
25 - 29	359 550	181 250	178 300	...	...	...	...	...	...
30 - 34	330 750	164 650	166 100	...	...	...	...	...	...
35 - 39	313 700	153 900	159 800	...	...	...	...	...	...
40 - 44	302 100	145 300	156 800	...	...	...	...	...	...
45 - 49	312 250	145 550	166 700	...	...	...	...	...	...
50 - 54	327 550	151 550	176 000	...	...	...	...	...	...
55 - 59	272 400	123 800	148 600	...	...	...	...	...	...
60 - 64	230 300	101 950	128 350	...	...	...	...	...	...
65 - 69	129 900	54 950	74 950	...	...	...	...	...	...
70 - 74	191 950	74 350	117 600	...	...	...	...	...	...

Continent, country or area, date, code[a] and age (in years) / Continent, pays ou zone, date, code[a] et âge (en années)	Total			Urban - Urbaine			Rural - Rurale		
	Both sexes Les deux sexes	Male Masculin	Female Féminin	Both sexes Les deux sexes	Male Masculin	Female Féminin	Both sexes Les deux sexes	Male Masculin	Female Féminin
ASIA - ASIE									
Georgia - Géorgie									
1 VII 2012 (ESDF)									
75 - 79	139 450	53 750	85 700	...	...	...	...	...	...
80 - 84	93 500	33 600	59 900	...	...	...	...	...	...
85 +	63 500	17 150	46 350	...	...	...	...	...	...
India - Inde[43]									
9 II 2011 (CDFC)									
Total	1210854977	623 270 258	587 584 719	377 106 125	195 489 200	181 616 925	833 748 852	427 781 058	405 967 794
0 - 4	112 806 778	58 632 074	54 174 704	29 820 118	15 595 697	14 224 421	82 986 660	43 036 377	39 950 283
5 - 9	126 928 126	66 300 466	60 627 660	33 120 514	17 475 207	15 645 307	93 807 612	48 825 259	44 982 353
10 - 14	132 709 212	69 418 835	63 290 377	35 904 718	18 930 677	16 974 041	96 804 494	50 488 158	46 316 336
15 - 19	120 526 449	63 982 396	56 544 053	36 623 977	19 411 839	17 212 138	83 902 472	44 570 557	39 331 915
20 - 24	111 424 222	57 584 693	53 839 529	37 589 176	19 446 031	18 143 145	73 835 046	38 138 662	35 696 384
25 - 29	101 413 965	51 344 208	50 069 757	35 345 695	17 968 219	17 377 476	66 068 270	33 375 989	32 692 281
30 - 34	88 594 951	44 660 674	43 934 277	30 683 172	15 726 482	14 956 690	57 911 779	28 934 192	28 977 587
35 - 39	85 140 684	42 919 381	42 221 303	29 077 977	14 793 820	14 284 157	56 062 707	28 125 561	27 937 146
40 - 44	72 438 112	37 545 386	34 892 726	24 857 104	12 980 151	11 876 953	47 581 008	24 565 235	23 015 773
45 - 49	62 318 327	32 138 114	30 180 213	21 630 099	11 273 844	10 356 255	40 688 228	20 864 270	19 823 958
50 - 54	49 069 254	25 843 266	23 225 988	17 037 466	9 053 719	7 983 747	32 031 788	16 789 547	15 242 241
55 - 59	39 146 055	19 456 012	19 690 043	13 284 541	6 919 483	6 365 058	25 861 514	12 536 529	13 324 985
60 - 64	37 663 707	18 701 749	18 961 958	11 372 462	5 770 157	5 602 305	26 291 245	12 931 592	13 359 653
65 - 69	26 454 983	12 944 326	13 510 657	7 538 713	3 736 015	3 802 698	18 916 270	9 208 311	9 707 959
70 - 74	19 208 842	9 651 499	9 557 343	5 401 242	2 673 320	2 727 922	13 807 600	6 978 179	6 829 421
75 - 79	9 232 503	4 490 603	4 741 900	2 848 786	1 377 179	1 471 607	6 383 717	3 113 424	3 270 293
80 - 84	6 220 229	2 927 040	3 293 189	1 800 347	807 610	992 737	4 419 882	2 119 430	2 300 452
85 - 89	2 383 167	1 120 106	1 263 061	785 179	349 809	435 370	1 597 988	770 297	827 691
90 - 94	1 446 534	652 465	794 069	422 547	180 500	242 047	1 023 987	471 965	552 022
95 - 99	633 297	294 759	338 538	187 628	84 120	103 508	445 669	210 639	235 030
100 +	605 778	289 325	316 453	198 314	95 860	102 454	407 464	193 465	213 999
Unknown - Inconnu	4 489 802	2 372 881	2 116 921	1 576 350	839 461	736 889	2 913 452	1 533 420	1 380 032
Indonesia - Indonésie									
1 V 2010 (CDJC)									
Total	237 641 326	119 630 913	118 010 413	118 320 256	59 559 622	58 760 634	119 321 070	60 071 291	59 249 779
0 - 4	22 678 702	11 662 369	11 016 333	11 025 060	5 679 790	5 345 270	11 653 642	5 982 579	5 671 063
0	4 397 046	2 259 245	2 137 801	...	...	...	...	...	...
1 - 4	18 275 014	9 399 611	8 875 403	...	...	...	...	...	...
5 - 9	23 253 480	11 974 094	11 279 386	11 016 095	5 674 648	5 341 447	12 237 385	6 299 446	5 937 939
10 - 14	22 671 081	11 662 417	11 008 664	10 542 167	5 399 311	5 142 856	12 128 914	6 263 106	5 865 808
15 - 19	20 880 734	10 614 306	10 266 428	10 755 586	5 343 102	5 412 484	10 125 148	5 271 204	4 853 944
20 - 24	19 891 633	9 887 713	10 003 920	10 903 811	5 416 588	5 487 223	8 987 822	4 471 125	4 516 697
25 - 29	21 310 443	10 631 311	10 679 132	11 447 502	5 752 629	5 694 873	9 862 941	4 878 682	4 984 259
30 - 34	19 830 685	9 949 357	9 881 328	10 476 109	5 286 436	5 189 673	9 354 576	4 662 921	4 691 655
35 - 39	18 505 131	9 337 517	9 167 614	9 517 824	4 816 398	4 701 426	8 987 307	4 521 119	4 466 188
40 - 44	16 524 852	8 322 712	8 202 140	8 400 678	4 249 643	4 151 035	8 124 174	4 073 069	4 051 105
45 - 49	14 040 982	7 032 740	7 008 242	6 936 515	3 481 077	3 455 438	7 104 467	3 551 663	3 552 804
50 - 54	11 561 321	5 865 997	5 695 324	5 599 670	2 858 242	2 741 428	5 961 651	3 007 755	2 953 896
55 - 59	8 448 570	4 400 316	4 048 254	4 010 840	2 091 487	1 919 353	4 437 730	2 308 829	2 128 901
60 - 64	6 058 761	2 927 191	3 131 570	2 664 404	1 290 725	1 373 679	3 394 357	1 636 466	1 757 891
65 - 69	4 694 031	2 225 133	2 468 898	2 030 370	960 508	1 069 862	2 663 661	1 264 625	1 399 036
70 - 74	3 456 331	1 531 459	1 924 872	1 435 408	630 505	804 903	2 020 923	900 954	1 119 969
75 - 79	1 977 905	842 344	1 135 561	815 975	336 277	479 698	1 161 930	506 067	655 863
80 - 84	1 143 170	481 462	661 708	459 569	186 943	272 626	683 601	294 519	389 082
85 - 89	437 961	182 432	255 529	177 571	69 631	107 940	260 390	112 801	147 589
90 - 94	170 899	63 948	106 951	66 489	23 159	43 330	104 410	40 789	63 621
95 +	104 654	36 095	68 559	38 613	12 523	26 090	66 041	23 572	42 469
1 VII 2014 (ESDJ)[44]									
Total	252 164 800	126 715 200	125 449 600	...	...	...	...	...	...
0 - 4	24 086 800	12 301 400	11 785 400	...	...	...	...	...	...
5 - 9	23 109 500	11 857 300	11 252 200	...	...	...	...	...	...
10 - 14	22 360 200	11 448 300	10 911 900	...	...	...	...	...	...
15 - 19	22 024 700	11 237 800	10 786 900	...	...	...	...	...	...
20 - 24	21 352 400	10 768 500	10 583 900	...	...	...	...	...	...
25 - 29	20 716 300	10 398 200	10 318 100	...	...	...	...	...	...
30 - 34	20 430 900	10 150 200	10 280 700	...	...	...	...	...	...
35 - 39	19 587 100	9 802 600	9 784 500	...	...	...	...	...	...

7. Population by age, sex and urban/rural residence: latest available year, 2005 - 2014
Population selon l'âge, le sexe et la résidence, urbaine/rurale : dernière année disponible, 2005 - 2014 (continued - suite)

Continent, country or area, date, code[a] and age (in years) / Continent, pays ou zone, date, code[a] et âge (en années)	Total			Urban - Urbaine			Rural - Rurale		
	Both sexes Les deux sexes	Male Masculin	Female Féminin	Both sexes Les deux sexes	Male Masculin	Female Féminin	Both sexes Les deux sexes	Male Masculin	Female Féminin
ASIA - ASIE									
Indonesia - Indonésie									
1 VII 2014 (ESDJ)[44]									
40 - 44	18 004 700	9 054 200	8 950 500	...	...	...	...	...	...
45 - 49	15 867 400	7 949 200	7 918 200	...	...	...	...	...	...
50 - 54	13 313 700	6 650 600	6 663 100	...	...	...	...	...	...
55 - 59	10 518 100	5 319 600	5 198 500	...	...	...	...	...	...
60 - 64	7 518 800	3 804 700	3 714 100	...	...	...	...	...	...
65 - 69	5 253 400	2 500 200	2 753 200	...	...	...	...	...	...
70 - 74	3 757 000	1 715 000	2 042 000	...	...	...	...	...	...
75 +	4 263 800	1 757 400	2 506 400	...	...	...	...	...	...
Iran (Islamic Republic of) - Iran (République islamique d')[45]									
1 VII 2014 (ESDJ)									
Total	77 856 411	39 224 036	38 632 375	56 412 837	28 435 933	27 976 904	21 443 574	10 788 103	10 655 471
0 - 4	6 620 164	3 385 257	3 234 907	4 523 717	2 315 639	2 208 078	2 096 447	1 069 618	1 026 829
5 - 9	6 029 807	3 089 150	2 940 657	4 143 220	2 124 661	2 018 559	1 886 587	964 489	922 098
10 - 14	5 567 992	2 846 405	2 721 587	3 898 375	1 992 042	1 906 333	1 669 617	854 363	815 254
15 - 19	5 902 925	3 001 612	2 901 313	4 084 294	2 069 334	2 014 960	1 818 631	932 278	886 353
20 - 24	7 322 968	3 680 184	3 642 784	5 218 125	2 590 346	2 627 779	2 104 843	1 089 838	1 015 005
25 - 29	8 747 685	4 367 596	4 380 089	6 489 370	3 217 346	3 272 024	2 258 315	1 150 250	1 108 065
30 - 34	8 095 434	4 068 757	4 026 677	6 051 338	3 037 322	3 014 016	2 044 096	1 031 435	1 012 661
35 - 39	6 289 546	3 189 621	3 099 925	4 674 432	2 371 468	2 302 964	1 615 114	818 153	796 961
40 - 44	5 234 915	2 673 543	2 561 372	3 982 769	2 045 740	1 937 029	1 252 146	627 803	624 343
45 - 49	4 517 512	2 278 946	2 238 566	3 485 632	1 773 184	1 712 448	1 031 880	505 762	526 118
50 - 54	3 759 702	1 883 333	1 876 369	2 858 879	1 449 820	1 409 059	900 823	433 513	467 310
55 - 59	3 144 854	1 563 730	1 581 124	2 351 716	1 196 158	1 155 558	793 138	367 572	425 566
60 - 64	2 239 366	1 082 810	1 156 556	1 629 818	809 184	820 634	609 548	273 626	335 922
65 - 69	1 510 325	702 758	807 567	1 080 203	510 778	569 425	430 122	191 980	238 142
70 - 74	1 102 572	528 918	573 654	764 294	365 314	398 980	338 278	163 604	174 674
75 - 79	856 281	430 369	425 912	571 410	281 976	289 434	284 871	148 393	136 478
80 +	914 363	451 047	463 316	605 245	285 621	319 624	309 118	165 426	143 692
Iraq									
1 VII 2013 (ESDF)									
Total	34 794 194	17 710 750	17 083 444	24 162 634	12 299 131	11 863 502	10 631 560	5 411 619	5 219 941
0	1 034 224	524 904	509 319	679 205	341 245	337 960	355 019	183 659	171 360
1 - 4	3 866 770	1 970 227	1 896 543	2 539 317	1 280 864	1 258 452	1 327 453	689 363	638 090
5 - 9	4 566 714	2 374 908	2 191 807	2 962 730	1 543 007	1 419 723	1 603 984	831 901	772 084
10 - 14	4 281 603	2 232 712	2 048 891	2 815 272	1 463 192	1 352 080	1 466 332	769 520	696 811
15 - 19	3 763 677	1 937 714	1 825 963	2 574 623	1 327 325	1 247 298	1 189 054	610 388	578 665
20 - 24	3 295 563	1 701 884	1 593 679	2 378 531	1 217 609	1 160 922	917 032	484 275	432 757
25 - 29	2 741 201	1 424 739	1 316 462	1 971 618	1 033 676	937 942	769 583	391 063	378 519
30 - 34	2 311 316	1 176 433	1 134 882	1 647 004	850 318	796 686	664 312	326 115	338 197
35 - 39	2 027 895	983 570	1 044 325	1 436 709	698 508	738 202	591 186	285 062	306 124
40 - 44	1 831 722	933 785	897 936	1 328 332	666 390	661 942	503 390	267 395	235 995
45 - 49	1 510 195	746 884	763 311	1 122 133	561 328	560 805	388 062	185 557	202 506
50 - 54	1 070 772	508 498	562 274	852 339	410 452	441 887	218 433	98 045	120 388
55 - 59	750 093	356 581	393 511	556 088	268 246	287 842	194 004	88 335	105 669
60 - 64	724 285	345 830	378 456	544 535	259 360	285 175	179 750	86 470	93 280
65 - 69	406 617	187 626	218 991	304 591	144 702	159 889	102 026	42 924	59 102
70 - 74	271 651	133 277	138 375	209 694	106 825	102 869	61 957	26 452	35 505
75 - 79	172 373	81 742	90 630	128 194	61 305	66 889	44 179	20 438	23 741
80 +	167 523	89 436	78 087	111 719	64 780	46 939	55 804	24 656	31 148
Israel - Israël[46]									
1 VII 2013 (ESDJ)									
Total	8 059 456	3 991 347	4 068 109	7 369 053	3 640 471	3 728 581	690 404	350 876	339 528
0	170 651	87 512	83 139	155 258	79 630	75 628	15 393	7 882	7 511
1 - 4	662 797	339 469	323 328	599 207	306 744	292 463	63 590	32 726	30 865
5 - 9	748 381	383 698	364 684	674 587	345 667	328 920	73 794	38 031	35 764
10 - 14	691 510	354 177	337 333	626 573	320 704	305 869	64 937	33 473	31 464
15 - 19	624 637	319 859	304 777	564 455	287 948	276 507	60 182	31 911	28 271
20 - 24	596 779	303 892	292 887	547 471	277 938	269 534	49 308	25 955	23 353
25 - 29	582 110	293 046	289 064	538 297	270 510	267 787	43 813	22 536	21 277
30 - 34	562 959	281 023	281 935	518 881	259 323	259 557	44 078	21 700	22 378
35 - 39	546 615	271 920	274 696	497 388	248 037	249 352	49 227	23 883	25 344

Continent, country or area, date, code[a] and age (in years) / Continent, pays ou zone, date, code[a] et âge (en années)	Total			Urban - Urbaine			Rural - Rurale		
	Both sexes Les deux sexes	Male Masculin	Female Féminin	Both sexes Les deux sexes	Male Masculin	Female Féminin	Both sexes Les deux sexes	Male Masculin	Female Féminin
ASIA - ASIE									
Israel - Israël[46]									
1 VII 2013 (ESDJ)									
40 - 44	486 588	240 899	245 689	441 620	218 455	223 165	44 968	22 444	22 524
45 - 49	414 324	204 607	209 717	378 119	186 080	192 040	36 205	18 528	17 677
50 - 54	393 200	190 538	202 662	361 446	174 427	187 019	31 753	16 111	15 642
55 - 59	375 038	179 758	195 280	345 507	164 644	180 863	29 531	15 115	14 417
60 - 64	354 615	168 581	186 034	327 645	154 650	172 995	26 970	13 931	13 039
65 - 69	275 618	129 548	146 070	255 867	119 589	136 278	19 752	9 960	9 792
70 - 74	182 866	82 744	100 122	170 753	76 688	94 065	12 113	6 056	6 057
75 - 79	163 888	71 213	92 675	153 860	66 481	87 380	10 028	4 732	5 295
80 - 84	115 003	47 006	67 997	107 783	43 965	63 818	7 220	3 041	4 179
85 - 89	72 981	27 067	45 914	68 234	25 241	42 993	4 747	1 826	2 921
90 - 94	29 730	11 271	18 459	27 638	10 459	17 178	2 093	812	1 281
95 - 99	6 549	2 387	4 162	6 024	2 213	3 811	525	174	351
100 +	2 616	1 130	1 487	2 439	1 079	1 360	177	51	126
Japan - Japon[47]									
1 X 2010 (CDJC)									
Total	128 057 352	62 327 737	65 729 615	116 156 631	56 569 051	59 587 580	11 900 721	5 758 686	6 142 035
0 - 4	5 296 748	2 710 581	2 586 167	4 831 346	2 472 475	2 358 871	465 402	238 106	227 296
5 - 9	5 585 661	2 859 805	2 725 856	5 061 966	2 591 629	2 470 337	523 695	268 176	255 519
10 - 14	5 921 035	3 031 943	2 889 092	5 348 569	2 737 977	2 610 592	572 466	293 966	278 500
15 - 19	6 063 357	3 109 229	2 954 128	5 506 483	2 823 085	2 683 398	556 874	286 144	270 730
20 - 24	6 426 433	3 266 240	3 160 193	5 925 984	3 012 027	2 913 957	500 449	254 213	246 236
25 - 29	7 293 701	3 691 723	3 601 978	6 720 343	3 397 748	3 322 595	573 358	293 975	279 383
30 - 34	8 341 497	4 221 011	4 120 486	7 675 385	3 879 081	3 796 304	666 112	341 930	324 182
35 - 39	9 786 349	4 950 122	4 836 227	9 015 173	4 556 572	4 458 601	771 176	393 550	377 626
40 - 44	8 741 865	4 400 375	4 341 490	8 046 407	4 051 948	3 994 459	695 458	348 427	347 031
45 - 49	8 033 116	4 027 969	4 005 147	7 328 789	3 675 150	3 653 639	704 327	352 819	351 508
50 - 54	7 644 499	3 809 576	3 834 923	6 878 402	3 425 836	3 452 566	766 097	383 740	382 357
55 - 59	8 663 734	4 287 489	4 376 245	7 753 645	3 830 707	3 922 938	910 089	456 782	453 307
60 - 64	10 037 249	4 920 468	5 116 781	9 046 242	4 424 879	4 621 363	991 007	495 589	495 418
65 - 69	8 210 173	3 921 774	4 288 399	7 424 237	3 543 535	3 880 702	785 936	378 239	407 697
70 - 74	6 963 302	3 225 503	3 737 799	6 249 910	2 895 658	3 354 252	713 392	329 845	383 547
75 - 79	5 941 013	2 582 940	3 358 073	5 276 323	2 294 753	2 981 570	664 690	288 187	376 503
80 - 84	4 336 264	1 692 584	2 643 680	3 804 707	1 485 631	2 319 076	531 557	206 953	324 604
85 - 89	2 432 588	744 222	1 688 366	2 121 067	649 324	1 471 743	311 521	94 898	216 623
90 - 94	1 021 707	241 799	779 908	889 810	210 257	679 553	131 897	31 542	100 355
95 - 99	296 756	55 739	241 017	258 266	48 545	209 721	38 490	7 194	31 296
100 +	43 882	5 851	38 031	38 068	5 060	33 008	5 814	791	5 023
Unknown - Inconnu	976 423	570 794	405 629	955 509	557 174	398 335	20 914	13 620	7 294
1 VII 2014 (ESDJ)[48]									
Total	127 132 000	61 812 000	65 320 000	...	...	...	...	...	...
0 - 4	5 216 000	2 674 000	2 541 000	...	...	...	...	...	...
5 - 9	5 330 000	2 727 000	2 602 000	...	...	...	...	...	...
10 - 14	5 739 000	2 940 000	2 799 000	...	...	...	...	...	...
15 - 19	6 033 000	3 089 000	2 944 000	...	...	...	...	...	...
20 - 24	6 199 000	3 185 000	3 014 000	...	...	...	...	...	...
25 - 29	6 743 000	3 445 000	3 298 000	...	...	...	...	...	...
30 - 34	7 500 000	3 804 000	3 696 000	...	...	...	...	...	...
35 - 39	8 775 000	4 445 000	4 329 000	...	...	...	...	...	...
40 - 44	9 738 000	4 924 000	4 814 000	...	...	...	...	...	...
45 - 49	8 565 000	4 305 000	4 260 000	...	...	...	...	...	...
50 - 54	7 742 000	3 876 000	3 866 000	...	...	...	...	...	...
55 - 59	7 689 000	3 818 000	3 871 000	...	...	...	...	...	...
60 - 64	9 141 000	4 485 000	4 657 000	...	...	...	...	...	...
65 - 69	9 004 000	4 339 000	4 665 000	...	...	...	...	...	...
70 - 74	7 879 000	3 667 000	4 212 000	...	...	...	...	...	...
75 - 79	6 262 000	2 762 000	3 499 000	...	...	...	...	...	...
80 - 84	4 841 000	1 929 000	2 911 000	...	...	...	...	...	...
85 - 89	3 037 000	1 019 000	2 019 000	...	...	...	...	...	...
90 - 94	1 285 000	306 000	978 000	...	...	...	...	...	...
95 - 99	355 000	63 000	291 000	...	...	...	...	...	...
100 +	60 000	8 000	52 000	...	...	...	...	...	...

Continent, country or area, date, code[a] and age (in years) / Continent, pays ou zone, date, code[a] et âge (en annèes)	Total			Urban - Urbaine			Rural - Rurale		
	Both sexes Les deux sexes	Male Masculin	Female Féminin	Both sexes Les deux sexes	Male Masculin	Female Féminin	Both sexes Les deux sexes	Male Masculin	Female Féminin
ASIA - ASIE									
Jordan - Jordanie[49]									
31 XII 2014 (ESDF)									
Total	6 675 000	3 441 000	3 234 000	...	...	...	...	...	...
0	160 687	82 156	78 531	...	...	...	...	...	...
1 - 4	690 583	354 854	335 729	...	...	...	...	...	...
5 - 9	841 250	431 500	409 750	...	...	...	...	...	...
10 - 14	798 940	410 860	388 080	...	...	...	...	...	...
15 - 19	732 550	377 130	355 420	...	...	...	...	...	...
20 - 24	707 020	366 470	340 550	...	...	...	...	...	...
25 - 29	597 480	314 510	282 970	...	...	...	...	...	...
30 - 34	522 790	271 840	250 950	...	...	...	...	...	...
35 - 39	423 640	220 220	203 420	...	...	...	...	...	...
40 - 44	315 710	162 420	153 290	...	...	...	...	...	...
45 - 49	223 230	114 240	108 990	...	...	...	...	...	...
50 - 54	167 770	84 650	83 120	...	...	...	...	...	...
55 - 59	148 630	72 950	75 680	...	...	...	...	...	...
60 - 64	129 250	68 130	61 120	...	...	...	...	...	...
65 - 69	93 810	48 540	45 270	...	...	...	...	...	...
70 - 74	61 150	30 710	30 440	...	...	...	...	...	...
75 - 79	31 695	16 555	15 140	...	...	...	...	...	...
80 - 84	17 745	8 040	9 705	...	...	...	...	...	...
85 - 89	6 575	3 200	3 375	...	...	...	...	...	...
90 - 94	3 025	1 325	1 700	...	...	...	...	...	...
95 +	1 470	700	770	...	...	...	...	...	...
Kazakhstan									
1 I 2014 (ESDF)									
Total	17 160 774	8 284 815	8 875 959	9 433 482	4 421 972	5 011 510	7 727 292	3 862 843	3 864 449
0	383 507	197 722	185 785	206 925	106 746	100 179	176 582	90 976	85 606
1 - 4	1 453 960	747 077	706 883	774 383	398 197	376 186	679 577	348 880	330 697
5 - 9	1 478 444	759 906	718 538	727 159	374 068	353 091	751 285	385 838	365 447
10 - 14	1 142 469	584 661	557 808	541 266	278 151	263 115	601 203	306 510	294 693
15 - 19	1 229 114	627 497	601 617	589 482	299 106	290 376	639 632	328 391	311 241
20 - 24	1 549 891	776 520	773 371	899 705	431 037	468 668	650 186	345 483	304 703
25 - 29	1 593 969	789 257	804 712	941 249	451 323	489 926	652 720	337 934	314 786
30 - 34	1 323 571	655 904	667 667	766 862	370 961	395 901	556 709	284 943	271 766
35 - 39	1 195 873	583 523	612 350	677 270	319 428	357 842	518 603	264 095	254 508
40 - 44	1 112 543	537 147	575 396	628 467	291 881	336 586	484 076	245 266	238 810
45 - 49	1 041 284	495 478	545 806	579 844	264 313	315 531	461 440	231 165	230 275
50 - 54	1 055 814	491 529	564 285	594 574	266 110	328 464	461 240	225 419	235 821
55 - 59	825 252	369 231	456 021	467 435	200 179	267 256	357 817	169 052	188 765
60 - 64	626 713	263 189	363 524	363 041	145 102	217 939	263 672	118 087	145 585
65 - 69	358 005	142 912	215 093	212 061	80 423	131 638	145 944	62 489	83 455
70 - 74	328 827	118 456	210 371	187 797	63 704	124 093	141 030	54 752	86 278
75 - 79	268 284	91 291	176 993	158 629	50 542	108 087	109 655	40 749	68 906
80 - 84	114 520	33 815	80 705	70 087	19 640	50 447	44 433	14 175	30 258
85 - 89	62 266	15 583	46 683	38 006	8 850	29 156	24 260	6 733	17 527
90 - 94	13 270	3 142	10 128	7 688	1 730	5 958	5 582	1 412	4 170
95 - 99	2 224	628	1 596	1 091	305	786	1 133	323	810
100 +	974	347	627	461	176	285	513	171	342
Kuwait - Koweït									
1 VII 2013 (ESDF)									
Total	3 448 139	1 918 959	1 529 180	...	...	...	...	...	...
0 - 4	296 270	151 288	144 982	...	...	...	...	...	...
5 - 9	249 998	126 558	123 440	...	...	...	...	...	...
10 - 14	222 883	113 001	109 882	...	...	...	...	...	...
15 - 19	201 679	104 366	97 313	...	...	...	...	...	...
20 - 24	293 522	145 773	147 749	...	...	...	...	...	...
25 - 29	447 631	243 663	203 968	...	...	...	...	...	...
30 - 34	466 380	278 320	188 060	...	...	...	...	...	...
35 - 39	381 133	224 155	156 978	...	...	...	...	...	...
40 - 44	316 461	189 903	126 558	...	...	...	...	...	...
45 - 49	224 245	135 007	89 238	...	...	...	...	...	...
50 - 54	147 779	92 094	55 685	...	...	...	...	...	...
55 - 59	89 345	55 118	34 227	...	...	...	...	...	...
60 - 64	48 782	27 843	20 939	...	...	...	...	...	...

Continent, country or area, date, code[a] and age (in years) / Continent, pays ou zone, date, code[a] et âge (en années)	Total			Urban - Urbaine			Rural - Rurale		
	Both sexes Les deux sexes	Male Masculin	Female Féminin	Both sexes Les deux sexes	Male Masculin	Female Féminin	Both sexes Les deux sexes	Male Masculin	Female Féminin
ASIA - ASIE									
Kuwait - Koweït									
1 VII 2013 (ESDF)									
65 - 69	27 099	14 095	13 004	...	...	...	...	...	...
70 - 74	17 349	9 073	8 276	...	...	...	...	...	...
75 - 79	9 490	4 717	4 773	...	...	...	...	...	...
80 +	8 093	3 985	4 108	...	...	...	...	...	...
Kyrgyzstan - Kirghizstan									
1 VII 2014 (ESDJ)									
Total	5 835 816	2 886 758	2 949 058	1 965 159	930 751	1 034 408	3 870 657	1 956 007	1 914 650
0	155 997	80 183	75 814	52 815	27 154	25 661	103 182	53 029	50 153
1 - 4	583 389	298 752	284 637	194 942	99 907	95 035	388 447	198 845	189 602
5 - 9	579 678	295 590	284 088	172 482	87 591	84 891	407 196	207 999	199 197
10 - 14	500 632	255 114	245 518	140 614	71 310	69 304	360 018	183 804	176 214
15 - 19	535 845	272 857	262 988	149 333	75 358	73 975	386 512	197 499	189 013
20 - 24	580 227	294 269	285 958	197 766	95 395	102 371	382 461	198 874	183 587
25 - 29	556 342	278 274	278 068	216 469	100 914	115 555	339 873	177 360	162 513
30 - 34	430 206	216 829	213 377	153 547	73 371	80 176	276 659	143 458	133 201
35 - 39	361 035	179 577	181 458	128 572	60 253	68 319	232 463	119 324	113 139
40 - 44	331 065	161 835	169 230	119 854	54 012	65 842	211 211	107 823	103 388
45 - 49	305 798	147 525	158 273	110 313	50 160	60 153	195 485	97 365	98 120
50 - 54	291 962	138 294	153 668	103 205	46 420	56 785	188 757	91 874	96 883
55 - 59	222 698	102 805	119 893	78 895	34 244	44 651	143 803	68 561	75 242
60 - 64	149 617	66 114	83 503	54 386	22 359	32 027	95 231	43 755	51 476
65 - 69	83 882	35 177	48 705	33 233	12 784	20 449	50 649	22 393	28 256
70 - 74	56 005	22 903	33 102	20 542	7 389	13 153	35 463	15 514	19 949
75 - 79	57 839	21 805	36 034	21 282	7 173	14 109	36 557	14 632	21 925
80 - 84	30 506	10 751	19 755	9 611	2 864	6 747	20 895	7 887	13 008
85 - 89	17 357	6 269	11 088	5 598	1 617	3 981	11 759	4 652	7 107
90 - 94	4 500	1 499	3 001	1 359	396	963	3 141	1 103	2 038
95 - 99	945	259	686	256	66	190	689	193	496
100 +	291	77	214	85	14	71	206	63	143
Lao People's Democratic Republic - République démocratique populaire lao									
1 III 2005 (CDJC)									
Total	5 621 982	2 800 551	2 821 431	1 522 137[50]	763 043[50]	759 094[50]	4 093 248[50]	2 033 289[50]	2 059 959[50]
0 - 4	700 915	351 559	349 356	135 758[50]	68 543[50]	67 215[50]	565 003[50]	282 939[50]	282 064[50]
5 - 9	749 208	379 137	370 071	155 490[50]	78 713[50]	76 777[50]	593 565[50]	300 341[50]	293 224[50]
10 - 14	767 156	391 785	375 371	188 311[50]	95 769[50]	92 542[50]	578 719[50]	295 944[50]	282 775[50]
15 - 19	647 269	323 729	323 540	202 877[50]	101 383[50]	101 494[50]	443 763[50]	221 962[50]	221 801[50]
20 - 24	515 297	253 926	261 371	180 777[50]	91 079[50]	89 698[50]	332 618[50]	161 532[50]	171 086[50]
25 - 29	429 609	211 279	218 330	132 858[50]	66 079[50]	66 779[50]	295 521[50]	144 368[50]	151 153[50]
30 - 34	359 995	176 515	183 480	110 035[50]	53 414[50]	56 621[50]	249 181[50]	122 647[50]	126 534[50]
35 - 39	329 777	164 415	165 362	99 816[50]	49 495[50]	50 321[50]	229 447[50]	114 592[50]	114 855[50]
40 - 44	265 867	132 335	133 532	80 714[50]	40 532[50]	40 182[50]	184 777[50]	91 575[50]	93 202[50]
45 - 49	227 167	113 869	113 298	65 746[50]	34 044[50]	31 702[50]	161 139[50]	79 640[50]	81 499[50]
50 - 54	177 980	86 770	91 210	47 891[50]	24 815[50]	23 076[50]	129 913[50]	61 854[50]	68 059[50]
55 - 59	128 331	62 691	65 640	34 546[50]	17 693[50]	16 853[50]	93 669[50]	44 925[50]	48 744[50]
60 - 64	105 014	50 006	55 008	26 734[50]	13 110[50]	13 624[50]	78 226[50]	36 864[50]	41 362[50]
65 - 69	79 540	38 289	41 251	21 869[50]	10 664[50]	11 205[50]	57 637[50]	27 609[50]	30 028[50]
70 - 74	59 579	27 652	31 927	16 214[50]	7 614[50]	8 600[50]	43 343[50]	20 020[50]	23 323[50]
75 - 79	37 172	17 964	19 208	10 859[50]	5 142[50]	5 717[50]	26 293[50]	12 813[50]	13 480[50]
80 - 84	22 582	10 402	12 180	6 248[50]	2 842[50]	3 406[50]	16 320[50]	7 553[50]	8 767[50]
85 - 89	10 328	4 631	5 697	3 070[50]	1 256[50]	1 814[50]	7 254[50]	3 371[50]	3 883[50]
90 - 94	4 745	1 964	2 781	1 216[50]	479[50]	737[50]	3 526[50]	1 484[50]	2 042[50]
95 - 99	2 375	982	1 393	665[50]	252[50]	413[50]	1 710[50]	730[50]	980[50]
100 +	1 416	480	936	252[50]	76[50]	176[50]	1 164[50]	404[50]	760[50]
Unknown - Inconnu	660	171	489	191[50]	49[50]	142[50]	460[50]	122[50]	338[50]
1 VII 2014 (ESDF)[51]									
Total	6 809 054	3 403 964	3 405 090	...	...	...	...	...	...
0 - 4	957 556	488 292	469 266	...	...	...	...	...	...
5 - 9	856 858	435 237	421 620	...	...	...	...	...	...
10 - 14	699 873	351 957	347 917	...	...	...	...	...	...
15 - 19	736 046	373 176	362 869	...	...	...	...	...	...

7. Population by age, sex and urban/rural residence: latest available year, 2005 - 2014
Population selon l'âge, le sexe et la résidence, urbaine/rurale : dernière année disponible, 2005 - 2014 (continued - suite)

Continent, country or area, date, code[a] and age (in years) / Continent, pays ou zone, date, code[a] et âge (en années)	Total			Urban - Urbaine			Rural - Rurale		
	Both sexes Les deux sexes	Male Masculin	Female Féminin	Both sexes Les deux sexes	Male Masculin	Female Féminin	Both sexes Les deux sexes	Male Masculin	Female Féminin
ASIA - ASIE									
Lao People's Democratic Republic - République démocratique populaire lao									
1 VII 2014 (ESDF)[51]									
20 - 24	712 861	363 105	349 756	...	...	...	...	...	...
25 - 29	570 196	283 469	286 727	...	...	...	...	...	...
30 - 34	448 768	220 333	228 436	...	...	...	...	...	...
35 - 39	374 526	183 557	190 967	...	...	...	...	...	...
40 - 44	326 261	159 725	166 538	...	...	...	...	...	...
45 - 49	300 963	149 307	151 659	...	...	...	...	...	...
50 - 54	237 923	117 317	120 605	...	...	...	...	...	...
55 - 59	195 544	96 115	99 428	...	...	...	...	...	...
60 - 64	141 761	67 257	74 507	...	...	...	...	...	...
65 - 69	94 845	44 685	50 159	...	...	...	...	...	...
70 - 74	68 480	31 300	37 181	...	...	...	...	...	...
75 +	86 589	39 132	47 454	...	...	...	...	...	...
Lebanon - Liban[52]									
3 III 2007 (SSDF)									
Total	3 759 134	1 857 659	1 901 475	...	...	...	...	...	...
0 - 4	261 021	136 514	124 507	...	...	...	...	...	...
5 - 9	312 902	160 577	152 325	...	...	...	...	...	...
10 - 14	354 049	183 613	170 436	...	...	...	...	...	...
15 - 19	363 626	195 984	167 642	...	...	...	...	...	...
20 - 24	367 778	191 471	176 307	...	...	...	...	...	...
25 - 29	305 933	148 321	157 612	...	...	...	...	...	...
30 - 34	276 775	132 105	144 670	...	...	...	...	...	...
35 - 39	249 550	111 833	137 717	...	...	...	...	...	...
40 - 44	233 003	102 405	130 598	...	...	...	...	...	...
45 - 49	208 752	95 595	113 157	...	...	...	...	...	...
50 - 54	179 899	84 091	95 808	...	...	...	...	...	...
55 - 59	143 376	66 993	76 383	...	...	...	...	...	...
60 - 64	140 030	65 701	74 329	...	...	...	...	...	...
65 - 69	122 014	59 900	62 114	...	...	...	...	...	...
70 - 74	105 259	53 267	51 992	...	...	...	...	...	...
75 - 79	71 315	38 353	32 962	...	...	...	...	...	...
80 - 84	45 481	21 083	24 398	...	...	...	...	...	...
85 +	18 371	9 853	8 518	...	...	...	...	...	...
Malaysia - Malaisie[53]									
1.VII 2014 (ESDJ)									
Total	30 261 700	15 594 295	14 667 405	22 275 575	11 430 681	10 844 894	7 986 125	4 163 614	3 822 511
0	502 586	260 530	242 056	355 810	184 984	170 826	146 776	75 546	71 230
1 - 4	2 045 036	1 056 314	988 722	1 454 928	753 101	701 827	590 108	303 213	286 895
5 - 9	2 526 499	1 296 982	1 229 517	1 824 918	935 625	889 293	701 581	361 357	340 224
10 - 14	2 664 224	1 367 292	1 296 932	1 902 973	975 788	927 185	761 251	391 504	369 747
15 - 19	2 822 192	1 452 417	1 369 775	1 972 611	1 013 869	958 742	849 581	438 548	411 033
20 - 24	3 085 933	1 607 719	1 478 214	2 240 948	1 151 329	1 089 619	844 985	456 390	388 595
25 - 29	2 979 154	1 574 585	1 404 569	2 268 326	1 175 562	1 092 764	710 828	399 023	311 805
30 - 34	2 564 042	1 351 988	1 212 054	1 998 510	1 034 436	964 074	565 532	317 552	247 980
35 - 39	2 047 014	1 073 105	973 909	1 592 560	825 267	767 293	454 454	247 838	206 616
40 - 44	1 853 137	945 106	908 031	1 417 510	717 718	699 792	435 627	227 388	208 239
45 - 49	1 699 481	857 189	842 292	1 289 026	648 115	640 911	410 455	209 074	201 381
50 - 54	1 521 768	786 693	735 075	1 145 613	598 867	546 746	376 155	187 826	188 329
55 - 59	1 257 065	639 464	617 601	927 094	477 615	449 479	329 971	161 849	168 122
60 - 64	960 123	485 660	474 463	696 623	355 770	340 853	263 500	129 890	133 610
65 - 69	708 488	351 219	357 269	500 444	249 650	250 794	208 044	101 569	106 475
70 - 74	439 736	215 199	224 537	299 188	148 848	150 340	140 548	66 351	74 197
75 - 79	308 398	146 354	162 044	205 278	99 207	106 071	103 120	47 147	55 973
80 - 84	148 278	68 182	80 096	97 439	45 525	51 914	50 839	22 657	28 182
85 - 89	84 251	37 061	47 190	55 593	24 730	30 863	28 658	12 331	16 327
90 +	44 295	21 236	23 059	30 183	14 675	15 508	14 112	6 561	7 551
Maldives									
21 III 2006 (CDFC)[54]									
Total	298 968	151 459	147 509	103 693	51 992	51 701	195 275	99 467	95 808
0	5 462	2 777	2 685	1 601	832	769	3 861	1 945	1 916
1 - 4	20 709	10 585	10 124	5 743	2 912	2 831	14 966	7 673	7 293

Continent, country or area, date, code[a] and age (in years) / Continent, pays ou zone, date, code[a] et âge (en années)	Total			Urban - Urbaine			Rural - Rurale		
	Both sexes Les deux sexes	Male Masculin	Female Féminin	Both sexes Les deux sexes	Male Masculin	Female Féminin	Both sexes Les deux sexes	Male Masculin	Female Féminin
ASIA - ASIE									
Maldives									
21 III 2006 (CDFC)[54]									
5 - 9	29 867	15 352	14 515	7 538	3 829	3 709	22 329	11 523	10 806
10 - 14	36 999	19 111	17 888	10 082	5 171	4 911	26 917	13 940	12 977
15 - 19	39 904	20 155	19 749	15 656	7 457	8 199	24 248	12 698	11 550
20 - 24	34 809	16 933	17 876	15 535	7 401	8 134	19 274	9 532	9 742
25 - 29	24 581	11 915	12 666	10 176	5 054	5 122	14 405	6 861	7 544
30 - 34	20 635	10 022	10 613	8 137	4 089	4 048	12 498	5 933	6 565
35 - 39	18 174	8 780	9 394	6 616	3 381	3 235	11 558	5 399	6 159
40 - 44	15 871	7 828	8 043	5 529	2 731	2 798	10 342	5 097	5 245
45 - 49	13 569	6 872	6 697	4 394	2 207	2 187	9 175	4 665	4 510
50 - 54	7 936	4 147	3 789	2 601	1 415	1 186	5 335	2 732	2 603
55 - 59	5 859	3 046	2 813	1 863	987	876	3 996	2 059	1 937
60 - 64	5 566	2 852	2 714	1 520	752	768	4 046	2 100	1 946
65 - 69	5 678	3 014	2 664	1 265	619	646	4 413	2 395	2 018
70 - 74	4 186	2 333	1 853	765	363	402	3 421	1 970	1 451
75 - 79	2 377	1 444	933	409	217	192	1 968	1 227	741
80 - 84	1 064	617	447	204	92	112	860	525	335
85 - 89	396	241	155	94	48	46	302	193	109
90 - 94	159	89	70	34	14	20	125	75	50
95 +	84	52	32	19	8	11	65	44	21
Unknown - Inconnu	5 083	3 294	1 789	3 912	2 413	1 499	1 171	881	290
1 VII 2013 (ESDF)									
Total	336 224	169 800	166 424	...	...	...	...	...	...
0	7 021	3 545	3 476	...	...	...	...	...	...
1 - 4	26 122	13 169	12 953	...	...	...	...	...	...
5 - 9	27 144	13 826	13 318	...	...	...	...	...	...
10 - 14	28 169	14 498	13 671	...	...	...	...	...	...
15 - 19	34 948	18 153	16 795	...	...	...	...	...	...
20 - 24	40 383	20 743	19 640	...	...	...	...	...	...
25 - 29	38 492	19 091	19 401	...	...	...	...	...	...
30 - 34	28 882	14 054	14 828	...	...	...	...	...	...
35 - 39	22 024	10 761	11 263	...	...	...	...	...	...
40 - 44	19 344	9 409	9 935	...	...	...	...	...	...
45 - 49	16 857	8 270	8 587	...	...	...	...	...	...
50 - 54	14 761	7 421	7 340	...	...	...	...	...	...
55 - 59	9 904	5 105	4 799	...	...	...	...	...	...
60 - 64	6 002	3 118	2 884	...	...	...	...	...	...
65 - 69	5 037	2 542	2 495	...	...	...	...	...	...
70 - 74	4 768	2 430	2 338	...	...	...	...	...	...
75 - 79	3 619	1 971	1 648	...	...	...	...	...	...
80 +	2 747	1 693	1 054	...	...	...	...	...	...
Mongolia - Mongolie									
11 XI 2010 (CDJC)									
Total	2 647 545	1 313 968	1 333 577	1 798 147	872 989	925 158	849 398	440 979	408 419
0 - 4	288 497	146 516	141 981	188 882	95 671	93 211	99 615	50 845	48 770
5 - 9	216 214	110 117	106 097	133 740	68 119	65 621	82 474	41 998	40 476
10 - 14	236 865	120 064	116 801	143 846	72 244	71 602	93 019	47 820	45 199
15 - 19	257 645	130 560	127 085	188 334	92 124	96 210	69 311	38 436	30 875
20 - 24	292 183	147 472	144 711	221 784	107 751	114 033	70 399	39 721	30 678
25 - 29	247 983	124 490	123 493	171 685	83 922	87 763	76 298	40 568	35 730
30 - 34	222 522	111 976	110 546	149 461	73 525	75 936	73 061	38 451	34 610
35 - 39	202 383	100 819	101 564	136 034	66 149	69 885	66 349	34 670	31 679
40 - 44	179 267	88 273	90 994	120 105	57 388	62 717	59 162	30 885	28 277
45 - 49	158 756	77 475	81 281	108 736	51 528	57 208	50 020	25 947	24 073
50 - 54	122 082	58 009	64 073	83 084	38 547	44 537	38 998	19 462	19 536
55 - 59	71 989	33 384	38 605	49 342	22 373	26 969	22 647	11 011	11 636
60 - 64	49 453	22 106	27 347	34 724	15 234	19 490	14 729	6 872	7 857
65 - 69	38 232	17 262	20 970	26 004	11 578	14 426	12 228	5 684	6 544
70 - 74	29 332	13 081	16 251	19 556	8 594	10 962	9 776	4 487	5 289
75 - 79	18 617	7 252	11 365	12 384	4 742	7 642	6 233	2 510	3 723
80 - 84	9 166	3 258	5 908	6 234	2 225	4 009	2 932	1 033	1 899
85 - 89	4 415	1 378	3 037	2 948	945	2 003	1 467	433	1 034
90 - 94	1 459	383	1 076	962	274	688	497	109	388

Continent, country or area, date, code[a] and age (in years) Continent, pays ou zone, date, code[a] et âge (en annèes)	Total			Urban - Urbaine			Rural - Rurale		
	Both sexes Les deux sexes	Male Masculin	Female Féminin	Both sexes Les deux sexes	Male Masculin	Female Féminin	Both sexes Les deux sexes	Male Masculin	Female Féminin
ASIA - ASIE									
Mongolia - Mongolie 11 XI 2010 (CDJC)									
95 - 99	402	80	322	251	47	204	151	33	118
100 +	83	13	70	51	9	42	32	4	28
1 VII 2014 (ESDF)									
Total	2 963 113	1 446 149	1 516 964	...	...	...	...	...	...
0	72 486	37 024	35 463	...	...	...	...	...	...
1 - 4	260 209	132 460	127 750	...	...	...	...	...	...
5 - 9	260 010	131 601	128 409	...	...	...	...	...	...
10 - 14	229 174	115 765	113 410	...	...	...	...	...	...
15 - 19	248 888	124 133	124 755	...	...	...	...	...	...
20 - 24	288 299	142 736	145 563	...	...	...	...	...	...
25 - 29	301 991	148 218	153 773	...	...	...	...	...	...
30 - 34	256 510	125 179	131 331	...	...	...	...	...	...
35 - 39	233 392	113 490	119 902	...	...	...	...	...	...
40 - 44	204 932	98 794	106 138	...	...	...	...	...	...
45 - 49	177 247	83 941	93 306	...	...	...	...	...	...
50 - 54	149 707	70 181	79 526	...	...	...	...	...	...
55 - 59	102 507	46 941	55 566	...	...	...	...	...	...
60 - 64	62 720	27 847	34 873	...	...	...	...	...	...
65 - 69	41 340	17 819	23 522	...	...	...	...	...	...
70 - 74	34 083	15 046	19 037	...	...	...	...	...	...
75 - 79	20 223	8 390	11 834	...	...	...	...	...	...
80 - 84	12 412	4 452	7 960	...	...	...	...	...	...
85 - 89	4 614	1 534	3 080	...	...	...	...	...	...
90 - 94	1 890	505	1 385	...	...	...	...	...	...
95 - 99	387	83	304	...	...	...	...	...	...
100 +	97	16	82	...	...	...	...	...	...
Myanmar[55] 29 III 2014 (CDFC)									
Total	50 279 900	24 228 714	26 051 186	14 877 943	7 114 224	7 763 719	35 401 957	17 114 490	18 287 467
0	823 378	416 645	406 733	208 571	105 968	102 603	614 807	310 677	304 130
1 - 4	3 648 752	1 846 138	1 802 614	872 557	443 616	428 941	2 776 195	1 402 522	1 373 673
5 - 9	4 819 077	2 438 372	2 380 705	1 146 876	583 310	563 566	3 672 201	1 855 062	1 817 139
10 - 14	5 108 362	2 595 749	2 512 613	1 355 792	703 305	652 487	3 752 570	1 892 444	1 860 126
15 - 19	4 625 989	2 290 998	2 334 991	1 467 120	740 956	726 164	3 158 869	1 550 042	1 608 827
20 - 24	4 331 069	2 091 525	2 239 544	1 460 572	711 405	749 167	2 870 497	1 380 120	1 490 377
25 - 29	4 146 134	1 995 465	2 150 669	1 320 591	638 841	681 750	2 825 543	1 356 624	1 468 919
30 - 34	3 898 861	1 884 549	2 014 312	1 229 010	595 549	633 461	2 669 851	1 289 000	1 380 851
35 - 39	3 563 480	1 705 630	1 857 850	1 092 916	518 880	574 036	2 470 564	1 186 750	1 283 814
40 - 44	3 283 073	1 548 942	1 734 131	1 025 669	474 286	551 383	2 257 404	1 074 656	1 182 748
45 - 49	2 946 148	1 375 041	1 571 107	918 610	414 377	504 233	2 027 538	960 664	1 066 874
50 - 54	2 559 232	1 182 341	1 376 891	783 327	346 474	436 853	1 775 905	835 867	940 038
55 - 59	2 051 937	935 979	1 115 958	631 743	275 176	356 567	1 420 194	660 803	759 391
60 - 64	1 576 845	712 040	864 805	477 041	206 172	270 869	1 099 804	505 868	593 936
65 - 69	1 064 493	466 618	597 875	333 747	140 316	193 431	730 746	326 302	404 444
70 - 74	713 170	301 679	411 491	212 747	87 697	125 050	500 423	213 982	286 441
75 - 79	553 298	228 315	324 983	165 732	65 960	99 772	387 566	162 355	225 211
80 - 84	335 576	130 875	204 701	99 573	36 945	62 628	236 003	93 930	142 073
85 - 89	158 069	56 979	101 090	51 127	17 118	34 009	106 942	39 861	67 081
90 - 94	51 382	17 695	33 687	17 705	5 770	11 935	33 677	11 925	21 752
95 +	21 575	7 139	14 436	6 917	2 103	4 814	14 658	5 036	9 622
Nepal - Népal 22 VI 2011 (CDJC)									
Total	26 494 504	12 849 041	13 645 463	4 523 820	2 306 049	2 217 771	21 970 684	10 542 992	11 427 692
0 - 4	2 567 963	1 314 957	1 253 006	327 100	172 598	154 502	2 240 863	1 142 359	1 098 504
5 - 9	3 204 859	1 635 176	1 569 683	431 121	227 618	203 503	2 773 738	1 407 558	1 366 180
10 - 14	3 475 424	1 764 630	1 710 794	507 618	266 722	240 896	2 967 806	1 497 908	1 469 898
15 - 19	2 931 980	1 443 191	1 488 789	520 714	273 601	247 113	2 411 266	1 169 590	1 241 676
20 - 24	2 358 071	1 043 981	1 314 090	520 546	260 529	260 017	1 837 525	783 452	1 054 073
25 - 29	2 079 354	917 243	1 162 111	452 256	220 230	232 026	1 627 098	697 013	930 085
30 - 34	1 735 305	770 577	964 728	372 219	181 542	190 677	1 363 086	589 035	774 051
35 - 39	1 604 319	740 200	864 119	324 965	161 347	163 618	1 279 354	578 853	700 501
40 - 44	1 386 121	660 290	725 831	263 008	136 600	126 408	1 123 113	523 690	599 423
45 - 49	1 172 959	575 101	597 858	205 833	106 627	99 206	967 126	468 474	498 652

Continent, country or area, date, code[a] and age (in years) / Continent, pays ou zone, date, code[a] et âge (en années)	Total			Urban - Urbaine			Rural - Rurale		
	Both sexes Les deux sexes	Male Masculin	Female Féminin	Both sexes Les deux sexes	Male Masculin	Female Féminin	Both sexes Les deux sexes	Male Masculin	Female Féminin
ASIA - ASIE									
Nepal - Népal									
22 VI 2011 (CDJC)									
50 - 54	1 005 476	505 864	499 612	165 685	86 471	79 214	839 791	419 393	420 398
55 - 59	818 263	412 892	405 371	123 667	63 841	59 826	694 596	349 051	345 545
60 - 64	756 827	368 451	388 376	105 862	52 258	53 604	650 965	316 193	334 772
65 - 69	554 449	277 782	276 667	76 074	37 256	38 818	478 375	240 526	237 849
70 - 74	395 153	199 610	195 543	55 001	26 400	28 601	340 152	173 210	166 942
75 - 79	235 135	117 358	117 777	35 764	16 538	19 226	199 371	100 820	98 551
80 - 84	128 777	62 787	65 990	21 053	9 435	11 618	107 724	53 352	54 372
85 - 89	52 526	25 810	26 716	9 857	4 350	5 507	42 669	21 460	21 209
90 - 94	20 335	8 940	11 395	3 788	1 474	2 314	16 547	7 466	9 081
95 +	11 208	4 201	7 007	1 689	612	1 077	9 519	3 589	5 930
Oman									
1 VII 2009 (ESDF)									
Total	3 173 917	1 971 115	1 202 802	2 314 865	1 457 197	857 668	859 049	513 917	345 132
0 - 4	272 144	139 614	132 530	184 595	94 803	89 792	87 549	44 811	42 738
5 - 9	245 026	124 776	120 250	162 307	82 954	79 353	82 718	41 821	40 897
10 - 14	254 610	129 964	124 646	168 924	86 326	82 598	85 685	43 638	42 047
15 - 19	284 826	145 215	139 611	194 123	99 854	94 269	90 703	45 361	45 342
20 - 24	387 448	238 483	148 965	285 594	176 341	109 253	101 854	62 142	39 712
25 - 29	475 403	327 686	147 717	362 531	249 782	112 749	112 871	77 904	34 967
30 - 34	367 536	247 107	120 429	288 055	192 969	95 086	79 481	54 138	25 343
35 - 39	272 100	192 483	79 617	212 145	150 865	61 280	59 955	41 618	18 337
40 - 44	207 202	149 090	58 112	161 282	117 670	43 612	45 920	31 420	14 500
45 - 49	145 430	103 908	41 522	111 077	81 065	30 012	34 353	22 843	11 510
50 - 54	113 587	83 057	30 530	84 975	63 752	21 223	28 612	19 305	9 307
55 - 59	59 890	40 488	19 402	42 674	29 489	13 185	17 216	10 999	6 217
60 - 64	39 730	23 538	16 192	26 050	15 494	10 556	13 680	8 044	5 636
65 - 69	20 811	11 811	9 000	13 363	7 537	5 826	7 448	4 274	3 174
70 - 74	14 933	7 721	7 212	9 224	4 703	4 521	5 709	3 018	2 691
75 - 79	6 817	3 303	3 514	4 201	1 981	2 220	2 616	1 322	1 294
80 +	6 424	2 871	3 553	3 745	1 612	2 133	2 679	1 259	1 420
1 VII 2014 (ESDF)[56]									
Total	3 992 893	2 579 811	1 413 082	...	...	...	...	...	...
0	71 009	36 496	34 513	...	...	...	...	...	...
1 - 4	290 786	147 911	142 875	...	...	...	...	...	...
5 - 9	288 291	146 997	141 294	...	...	...	...	...	...
10 - 14	234 597	119 741	114 856	...	...	...	...	...	...
15 - 19	239 220	122 675	116 545	...	...	...	...	...	...
20 - 24	391 869	244 236	147 633	...	...	...	...	...	...
25 - 29	691 916	506 642	185 274	...	...	...	...	...	...
30 - 34	552 009	404 263	147 746	...	...	...	...	...	...
35 - 39	386 620	273 648	112 972	...	...	...	...	...	...
40 - 44	269 982	197 869	72 113	...	...	...	...	...	...
45 - 49	186 618	135 911	50 707	...	...	...	...	...	...
50 - 54	136 173	93 478	42 695	...	...	...	...	...	...
55 - 59	98 169	66 267	31 902	...	...	...	...	...	...
60 - 64	54 409	31 028	23 381	...	...	...	...	...	...
65 - 69	33 770	17 657	16 113	...	...	...	...	...	...
70 - 74	28 164	14 059	14 105	...	...	...	...	...	...
75 - 79	17 338	9 572	7 766	...	...	...	...	...	...
80 - 84	11 835	6 125	5 710	...	...	...	...	...	...
85 - 89	5 225	2 714	2 511	...	...	...	...	...	...
90 - 94	3 279	1 651	1 628	...	...	...	...	...	...
95 +	1 614	871	743	...	...	...	...	...	...
Pakistan[57]									
1 VII 2007 (ESDJ)									
Total	149 860 388	76 857 737	73 002 651	52 807 585	27 178 203	25 629 382	97 052 803	49 679 534	47 373 269
0 - 4	19 540 467	9 783 859	9 756 608	5 761 626	2 854 601	2 907 026	13 778 841	6 929 259	6 849 582
5 - 9	22 554 631	11 710 324	10 844 307	6 759 356	3 414 295	3 345 061	15 795 276	8 296 029	7 499 246
10 - 14	20 255 889	10 636 015	9 619 874	6 854 564	3 572 029	3 282 536	13 401 325	7 063 987	6 337 339
15 - 19	17 275 679	9 063 876	8 211 804	6 630 532	3 454 683	3 175 849	10 645 147	5 609 193	5 035 954
20 - 24	13 558 584	6 824 723	6 733 861	5 604 996	2 913 936	2 691 060	7 953 588	3 910 786	4 042 801
25 - 29	10 833 092	5 268 436	5 564 656	4 174 036	2 128 117	2 045 919	6 659 055	3 140 318	3 518 737
30 - 34	8 432 325	3 957 414	4 474 911	3 112 553	1 539 219	1 573 334	5 319 772	2 418 195	2 901 576

Continent, country or area, date, code[a] and age (in years) / Continent, pays ou zone, date, code[a] et âge (en annèes)	Total			Urban - Urbaine			Rural - Rurale		
	Both sexes Les deux sexes	Male Masculin	Female Féminin	Both sexes Les deux sexes	Male Masculin	Female Féminin	Both sexes Les deux sexes	Male Masculin	Female Féminin
ASIA - ASIE									
Pakistan[57]									
1 VII 2007 (ESDJ)									
35 - 39	8 352 417	4 132 910	4 219 507	3 081 885	1 522 176	1 559 709	5 270 532	2 610 734	2 659 798
40 - 44	6 777 652	3 496 263	3 281 389	2 564 848	1 348 144	1 216 704	4 212 804	2 148 119	2 064 685
45 - 49	6 276 492	3 277 150	2 999 342	2 458 241	1 271 498	1 186 743	3 818 252	2 005 652	1 812 599
50 - 54	4 586 117	2 429 295	2 156 822	1 772 219	967 032	805 188	2 813 897	1 462 263	1 351 634
55 - 59	3 544 175	1 864 568	1 679 608	1 325 845	693 075	632 770	2 218 330	1 171 493	1 046 838
60 - 64	2 933 669	1 637 251	1 296 418	1 003 276	574 578	428 698	1 930 393	1 062 673	867 720
65 - 69	2 038 506	1 106 476	932 030	713 604	371 079	342 526	1 324 901	735 397	589 504
70 - 74	1 464 156	857 310	606 846	499 821	282 013	217 808	964 335	575 297	389 039
75 - 79	654 088	358 255	295 833	244 044	125 467	118 577	410 044	232 788	177 256
80 - 84	428 280	250 734	177 547	129 604	84 073	45 531	298 676	166 661	132 015
85 +	354 168	202 880	151 288	116 534	62 189	54 345	237 634	140 691	96 943
Philippines									
1 V 2010 (CDJC)[58]									
Total	92 335 113	46 634 257	45 700 856	41 855 571	20 840 798	21 014 773	50 479 542	25 793 459	24 686 083
0	1 968 131	1 018 386	949 745	873 792	453 065	420 727	1 094 339	565 321	529 018
1 - 4	8 265 653	4 274 825	3 990 828	3 571 743	1 850 296	1 721 447	4 693 910	2 424 529	2 269 381
5 - 9	10 321 543	5 332 287	4 989 256	4 384 024	2 267 726	2 116 298	5 937 519	3 064 561	2 872 958
10 - 14	10 179 610	5 237 006	4 942 604	4 286 862	2 195 115	2 091 747	5 892 748	3 041 891	2 850 857
15 - 19	9 705 354	4 931 506	4 773 848	4 301 712	2 120 800	2 180 912	5 403 642	2 810 706	2 592 936
20 - 24	8 408 656	4 256 999	4 151 657	4 050 916	1 989 031	2 061 885	4 357 740	2 267 968	2 089 772
25 - 29	7 423 723	3 746 311	3 677 412	3 693 442	1 821 972	1 871 470	3 730 281	1 924 339	1 805 942
30 - 34	6 772 929	3 443 582	3 329 347	3 353 327	1 676 968	1 676 359	3 419 602	1 766 614	1 652 988
35 - 39	6 013 953	3 057 323	2 956 630	2 886 723	1 448 968	1 437 755	3 127 230	1 608 355	1 518 875
40 - 44	5 471 588	2 778 661	2 692 927	2 588 569	1 292 882	1 295 687	2 883 019	1 485 779	1 397 240
45 - 49	4 680 649	2 367 809	2 312 840	2 180 936	1 082 303	1 098 633	2 499 713	1 285 506	1 214 207
50 - 54	3 894 850	1 953 952	1 940 898	1 808 298	890 919	917 379	2 086 552	1 063 033	1 023 519
55 - 59	2 987 148	1 475 861	1 511 287	1 358 685	660 616	698 069	1 628 463	815 245	813 218
60 - 64	2 228 399	1 064 116	1 164 283	979 510	461 508	518 002	1 248 889	602 608	646 281
65 - 69	1 497 557	680 227	817 330	593 219	263 603	329 616	904 338	416 624	487 714
70 - 74	1 142 562	492 152	650 410	437 280	181 972	255 308	705 282	310 180	395 102
75 - 79	707 115	286 079	421 036	265 280	102 308	162 972	441 835	183 771	258 064
80 - 84	394 188	145 937	248 251	145 081	50 979	94 102	249 107	94 958	154 149
85 - 89	188 511	64 125	124 386	67 310	21 250	46 060	121 201	42 875	78 326
90 - 94	60 102	19 598	40 504	21 070	6 202	14 868	39 032	13 396	25 636
95 - 99	18 099	5 684	12 415	6 223	1 753	4 470	11 876	3 931	7 945
100 +	4 793	1 831	2 962	1 569	562	1 007	3 224	1 269	1 955
1 VII 2014 (ESDJ)[14]									
Total	99 880 300	50 385 100	49 495 200	...	...	...	...	...	...
0 - 4	11 221 300	5 761 200	5 460 100	...	...	...	...	...	...
5 - 9	10 616 400	5 437 800	5 178 600	...	...	...	...	...	...
10 - 14	10 281 300	5 304 900	4 976 400	...	...	...	...	...	...
15 - 19	10 063 600	5 161 800	4 901 800	...	...	...	...	...	...
20 - 24	9 396 400	4 774 300	4 622 100	...	...	...	...	...	...
25 - 29	8 153 000	4 128 800	4 024 200	...	...	...	...	...	...
30 - 34	7 233 700	3 653 800	3 579 900	...	...	...	...	...	...
35 - 39	6 553 800	3 326 000	3 227 800	...	...	...	...	...	...
40 - 44	5 832 100	2 955 800	2 876 300	...	...	...	...	...	...
45 - 49	5 217 200	2 636 000	2 581 200	...	...	...	...	...	...
50 - 54	4 402 000	2 207 400	2 194 600	...	...	...	...	...	...
55 - 59	3 556 200	1 758 000	1 798 200	...	...	...	...	...	...
60 - 64	2 655 200	1 279 900	1 375 300	...	...	...	...	...	...
65 - 69	1 878 800	863 900	1 014 900	...	...	...	...	...	...
70 - 74	1 228 700	529 600	699 100	...	...	...	...	...	...
75 - 79	836 800	336 500	500 300	...	...	...	...	...	...
80 +	753 800	269 400	484 400	...	...	...	...	...	...
Qatar									
1 VII 2013 (ESDF)									
Total	2 003 700	1 477 632	526 068	...	...	...	...	...	...
0	22 441	11 195	11 246	...	...	...	...	...	...
1 - 4	90 700	46 539	44 161	...	...	...	...	...	...
5 - 9	101 189	51 840	49 349	...	...	...	...	...	...
10 - 14	81 233	41 546	39 687	...	...	...	...	...	...
15 - 19	75 897	45 092	30 805	...	...	...	...	...	...

Continent, country or area, date, code[a] and age (in years) / Continent, pays ou zone, date, code[a] et âge (en années)	Total			Urban - Urbaine			Rural - Rurale		
	Both sexes Les deux sexes	Male Masculin	Female Féminin	Both sexes Les deux sexes	Male Masculin	Female Féminin	Both sexes Les deux sexes	Male Masculin	Female Féminin
ASIA - ASIE									
Qatar									
1 VII 2013 (ESDF)									
20 - 24	218 475	179 820	38 655	...	...	...	...	...	...
25 - 29	354 242	281 045	73 197	...	...	...	...	...	...
30 - 34	326 348	253 924	72 424	...	...	...	...	...	...
35 - 39	244 013	187 192	56 821	...	...	...	...	...	...
40 - 44	188 078	148 262	39 816	...	...	...	...	...	...
45 - 49	124 089	97 259	26 830	...	...	...	...	...	...
50 - 54	82 169	64 303	17 866	...	...	...	...	...	...
55 - 59	50 050	39 133	10 917	...	...	...	...	...	...
60 - 64	22 108	16 407	5 701	...	...	...	...	...	...
65 - 69	9 925	6 668	3 257	...	...	...	...	...	...
70 - 74	5 375	3 215	2 160	...	...	...	...	...	...
75 - 79	3 574	2 166	1 408	...	...	...	...	...	...
80 +	3 794	2 026	1 768	...	...	...	...	...	...
Republic of Korea - République de Corée									
1 XI 2010 (CDJC)[59]									
Total	47 990 761	23 840 896	24 149 865	39 363 373	19 558 869	19 804 504	8 627 388	4 282 027	4 345 361
0 - 4	2 219 084	1 142 220	1 076 864	1 837 552	945 626	891 926	381 532	196 594	184 938
5 - 9	2 394 663	1 243 294	1 151 369	1 993 280	1 034 401	958 879	401 383	208 893	192 490
10 - 14	3 173 226	1 654 964	1 518 262	2 669 649	1 393 007	1 276 642	503 577	261 957	241 620
15 - 19	3 438 414	1 826 179	1 612 235	2 922 281	1 548 832	1 373 449	516 133	277 347	238 786
20 - 24	3 055 420	1 625 371	1 430 049	2 640 489	1 383 435	1 257 054	414 931	241 936	172 995
25 - 29	3 538 949	1 802 805	1 736 144	3 080 113	1 549 579	1 530 534	458 836	253 226	205 610
30 - 34	3 695 348	1 866 397	1 828 951	3 167 638	1 589 121	1 578 517	527 710	277 276	250 434
35 - 39	4 099 147	2 060 233	2 038 914	3 483 148	1 732 781	1 750 367	615 999	327 452	288 547
40 - 44	4 131 423	2 071 431	2 059 992	3 508 366	1 735 872	1 772 494	623 057	335 559	287 498
45 - 49	4 073 358	2 044 641	2 028 717	3 426 557	1 703 858	1 722 699	646 801	340 783	306 018
50 - 54	3 798 131	1 887 973	1 910 158	3 131 150	1 548 965	1 582 185	666 981	339 008	327 973
55 - 59	2 766 695	1 360 747	1 405 948	2 209 244	1 087 271	1 121 973	557 451	273 476	283 975
60 - 64	2 182 236	1 057 035	1 125 201	1 675 619	813 834	861 785	506 617	243 201	263 416
65 - 69	1 812 168	833 242	978 926	1 307 441	612 023	695 418	504 727	221 219	283 508
70 - 74	1 566 014	672 894	893 120	1 035 369	451 635	583 734	530 645	221 259	309 386
75 - 79	1 084 367	410 726	673 641	676 567	257 200	419 367	407 800	153 526	254 274
80 - 84	595 509	186 008	409 501	370 966	113 906	257 060	224 543	72 102	152 441
85 - 89	271 167	74 118	197 049	168 707	44 883	123 824	102 460	29 235	73 225
90 - 94	78 329	17 770	60 559	48 720	10 873	37 847	29 609	6 897	22 712
95 - 99	15 278	2 593	12 685	9 424	1 619	7 805	5 854	974	4 880
100 +	1 835	255	1 580	1 093	148	945	742	107	635
1 VII 2014 (ESDJ)[2]									
Total	50 423 955	25 219 810	25 204 145	...	...	...	...	...	...
0	455 129	234 578	220 551	...	...	...	...	...	...
1 - 4	1 835 462	947 091	888 371	...	...	...	...	...	...
5 - 9	2 266 044	1 168 930	1 097 114	...	...	...	...	...	...
10 - 14	2 642 349	1 375 660	1 266 689	...	...	...	...	...	...
15 - 19	3 264 482	1 715 370	1 549 112	...	...	...	...	...	...
20 - 24	3 489 975	1 868 977	1 620 998	...	...	...	...	...	...
25 - 29	3 284 644	1 723 162	1 561 482	...	...	...	...	...	...
30 - 34	3 949 186	2 034 127	1 915 059	...	...	...	...	...	...
35 - 39	3 829 465	1 952 708	1 876 757	...	...	...	...	...	...
40 - 44	4 337 823	2 205 892	2 131 931	...	...	...	...	...	...
45 - 49	4 176 603	2 113 773	2 062 830	...	...	...	...	...	...
50 - 54	4 274 677	2 147 620	2 127 057	...	...	...	...	...	...
55 - 59	3 674 546	1 832 311	1 842 235	...	...	...	...	...	...
60 - 64	2 558 011	1 241 553	1 316 458	...	...	...	...	...	...
65 - 69	2 026 187	961 301	1 064 886	...	...	...	...	...	...
70 - 74	1 729 106	761 353	967 753	...	...	...	...	...	...
75 - 79	1 314 319	531 700	782 619	...	...	...	...	...	...
80 - 84	805 837	273 135	532 702	...	...	...	...	...	...
85 - 89	359 164	98 573	260 591	...	...	...	...	...	...
90 - 94	124 041	27 514	96 527	...	...	...	...	...	...
95 - 99	23 887	4 092	19 795	...	...	...	...	...	...
100 +	3 018	390	2 628	...	...	...	...	...	...

7. Population by age, sex and urban/rural residence: latest available year, 2005 - 2014
Population selon l'âge, le sexe et la résidence, urbaine/rurale : dernière année disponible, 2005 - 2014 (continued - suite)

Continent, country or area, date, code[a] and age (in years) / Continent, pays ou zone, date, code[a] et âge (en annèes)	Total			Urban - Urbaine			Rural - Rurale		
	Both sexes Les deux sexes	Male Masculin	Female Féminin	Both sexes Les deux sexes	Male Masculin	Female Féminin	Both sexes Les deux sexes	Male Masculin	Female Féminin
ASIA - ASIE									
Saudi Arabia - Arabie saoudite[60]									
1 VII 2012* (ESDF)									
Total	29 195 895	16 543 836	12 652 059	...	...	...	...	...	...
0 - 4	3 167 691	1 633 572	1 534 119	...	...	...	...	...	...
5 - 9	2 952 321	1 513 790	1 438 531	...	...	...	...	...	...
10 - 14	2 747 749	1 400 265	1 347 484	...	...	...	...	...	...
15 - 19	2 522 817	1 272 690	1 250 127	...	...	...	...	...	...
20 - 24	2 367 651	1 205 747	1 161 904	...	...	...	...	...	...
25 - 29	2 531 191	1 407 320	1 123 871	...	...	...	...	...	...
30 - 34	2 977 277	1 829 598	1 147 679	...	...	...	...	...	...
35 - 39	2 869 678	1 806 034	1 063 644	...	...	...	...	...	...
40 - 44	2 242 581	1 456 742	785 839	...	...	...	...	...	...
45 - 49	1 616 863	1 091 008	525 855	...	...	...	...	...	...
50 - 54	1 142 848	750 777	392 071	...	...	...	...	...	...
55 - 59	774 226	483 991	290 235	...	...	...	...	...	...
60 - 64	486 001	281 396	204 605	...	...	...	...	...	...
65 - 69	314 687	166 489	148 198	...	...	...	...	...	...
70 - 74	206 964	104 259	102 705	...	...	...	...	...	...
75 - 79	130 712	65 183	65 529	...	...	...	...	...	...
80 +	144 638	74 975	69 663	...	...	...	...	...	...
Singapore - Singapour[61]									
30 VI 2014 (ESDJ)									
Total	3 870 739	1 902 410	1 968 329	...	...	...	...	...	...
0 - 4	181 369	92 528	88 841	...	...	...	...	...	...
5 - 9	205 790	104 588	101 202	...	...	...	...	...	...
10 - 14	220 796	112 959	107 837	...	...	...	...	...	...
15 - 19	247 337	126 514	120 823	...	...	...	...	...	...
20 - 24	263 918	132 902	131 016	...	...	...	...	...	...
25 - 29	265 659	129 304	136 355	...	...	...	...	...	...
30 - 34	292 287	138 954	153 333	...	...	...	...	...	...
35 - 39	302 029	144 959	157 070	...	...	...	...	...	...
40 - 44	316 023	154 320	161 703	...	...	...	...	...	...
45 - 49	308 533	153 194	155 339	...	...	...	...	...	...
50 - 54	315 503	158 734	156 769	...	...	...	...	...	...
55 - 59	288 392	144 316	144 076	...	...	...	...	...	...
60 - 64	231 502	115 217	116 285	...	...	...	...	...	...
65 - 69	161 198	78 285	82 913	...	...	...	...	...	...
70 - 74	106 815	49 438	57 377	...	...	...	...	...	...
75 - 79	76 294	33 753	42 541	...	...	...	...	...	...
80 - 84	48 418	19 515	28 903	...	...	...	...	...	...
85 +	38 876	12 930	25 946	...	...	...	...	...	...
Sri Lanka									
1 VII 2014 (ESDF)									
Total	20 675 000	10 033 000	10 642 000	...	...	...	...	...	...
0 - 4	1 780 000	900 000	880 000	...	...	...	...	...	...
5 - 9	1 781 000	903 000	878 000	...	...	...	...	...	...
10 - 14	1 661 000	843 000	818 000	...	...	...	...	...	...
15 - 19	1 674 000	827 000	847 000	...	...	...	...	...	...
20 - 24	1 544 000	760 000	784 000	...	...	...	...	...	...
25 - 29	1 571 000	758 000	813 000	...	...	...	...	...	...
30 - 34	1 664 000	807 000	857 000	...	...	...	...	...	...
35 - 39	1 434 000	695 000	739 000	...	...	...	...	...	...
40 - 44	1 397 000	679 000	718 000	...	...	...	...	...	...
45 - 49	1 303 000	630 000	673 000	...	...	...	...	...	...
50 - 54	1 239 000	591 000	648 000	...	...	...	...	...	...
55 - 59	1 076 000	510 000	566 000	...	...	...	...	...	...
60 - 64	932 000	432 000	500 000	...	...	...	...	...	...
65 - 69	641 000	289 000	352 000	...	...	...	...	...	...
70 - 74	416 000	183 000	233 000	...	...	...	...	...	...
75 - 79	289 000	118 000	171 000	...	...	...	...	...	...
80 +	273 000	108 000	165 000	...	...	...	...	...	...

7. Population by age, sex and urban/rural residence: latest available year, 2005 - 2014
Population selon l'âge, le sexe et la résidence, urbaine/rurale : dernière année disponible, 2005 - 2014 (continued - suite)

Continent, country or area, date, code[a] and age (in years) / Continent, pays ou zone, date, code[a] et âge (en années)	Total			Urban - Urbaine			Rural - Rurale		
	Both sexes Les deux sexes	Male Masculin	Female Féminin	Both sexes Les deux sexes	Male Masculin	Female Féminin	Both sexes Les deux sexes	Male Masculin	Female Féminin
ASIA - ASIE									
State of Palestine - État de Palestine									
1 XII 2007 (CDFC)[62]									
Total	3 443 828	1 747 284	1 696 544	2 814 623[63]	1 427 861[63]	1 386 762[63]	629 205	319 423	309 782
0	107 187	54 782	52 405	88 830[63]	45 359[63]	43 471[63]	18 357	9 423	8 934
1 - 4	412 748	211 270	201 478	340 784[63]	174 537[63]	166 247[63]	71 964	36 733	35 231
5 - 9	466 880	239 156	227 724	381 348[63]	195 338[63]	186 010[63]	85 532	43 818	41 714
10 - 14	466 273	238 306	227 967	381 583[63]	194 860[63]	186 723[63]	84 690	43 446	41 244
15 - 19	414 439	211 464	202 975	339 534[63]	173 038[63]	166 496[63]	74 905	38 426	36 479
20 - 24	309 935	158 374	151 561	253 464[63]	128 975[63]	124 489[63]	56 471	29 399	27 072
25 - 29	252 227	128 068	124 159	206 038[63]	104 199[63]	101 839[63]	46 189	23 869	22 320
30 - 34	215 288	108 945	106 343	174 749[63]	88 330[63]	86 419[63]	40 539	20 615	19 924
35 - 39	177 060	90 155	86 905	142 888[63]	72 771[63]	70 117[63]	34 172	17 384	16 788
40 - 44	156 514	81 186	75 328	127 937[63]	66 510[63]	61 427[63]	28 577	14 676	13 901
45 - 49	117 580	60 832	56 748	95 564[63]	49 594[63]	45 970[63]	22 016	11 238	10 778
50 - 54	83 301	41 606	41 695	67 461[63]	33 829[63]	33 632[63]	15 840	7 777	8 063
55 - 59	63 010	32 011	30 999	51 678[63]	26 340[63]	25 338[63]	11 332	5 671	5 661
60 - 64	47 829	22 060	25 769	38 987[63]	18 162[63]	20 825[63]	8 842	3 898	4 944
65 - 69	33 697	13 853	19 844	27 124[63]	11 192[63]	15 932[63]	6 573	2 661	3 912
70 - 74	29 316	12 689	16 627	23 300[63]	10 221[63]	13 079[63]	6 016	2 468	3 548
75 - 79	21 135	8 599	12 536	16 540[63]	6 744[63]	9 796[63]	4 595	1 855	2 740
80 - 84	11 749	4 861	6 888	8 940[63]	3 705[63]	5 235[63]	2 809	1 156	1 653
85 - 89	5 344	2 318	3 026	3 984[63]	1 721[63]	2 263[63]	1 360	597	763
90 - 94	2 004	871	1 133	1 512[63]	646[63]	866[63]	492	225	267
95 +	1 061	464	597	744[63]	331[63]	413[63]	317	133	184
Unknown - Inconnu	49 251	25 414	23 837	41 634[63]	21 459[63]	20 175[63]	7 617	3 955	3 662
1 VII 2014 (ESDF)									
Total	4 550 368	2 311 721	2 238 647	...	...	...	...	...	...
0	144 278	73 777	70 501	...	...	...	...	...	...
1 - 4	532 758	272 203	260 555	...	...	...	...	...	...
5 - 9	587 705	299 675	288 030	...	...	...	...	...	...
10 - 14	543 257	277 570	265 687	...	...	...	...	...	...
15 - 19	520 310	265 524	254 786	...	...	...	...	...	...
20 - 24	468 998	239 158	229 840	...	...	...	...	...	...
25 - 29	376 268	192 080	184 188	...	...	...	...	...	...
30 - 34	293 395	149 930	143 465	...	...	...	...	...	...
35 - 39	250 160	127 098	123 062	...	...	...	...	...	...
40 - 44	210 316	106 467	103 849	...	...	...	...	...	...
45 - 49	176 152	90 493	85 659	...	...	...	...	...	...
50 - 54	142 816	74 222	68 594	...	...	...	...	...	...
55 - 59	102 683	52 558	50 125	...	...	...	...	...	...
60 - 64	69 333	34 300	35 033	...	...	...	...	...	...
65 - 69	50 541	23 304	27 237	...	...	...	...	...	...
70 - 74	35 080	14 720	20 360	...	...	...	...	...	...
75 - 79	23 406	9 461	13 945	...	...	...	...	...	...
80 +	22 912	9 181	13 731	...	...	...	...	...	...
Syrian Arab Republic - République arabe syrienne[64]									
1 VII 2011 (ESDF)									
Total	21 124 000	10 794 000	10 330 000	11 297 000	5 795 000	5 502 000	9 827 000	4 999 000	4 828 000
0 - 4	2 775 000	1 428 000	1 347 000	1 384 000	713 000	671 000	1 391 000	715 000	676 000
5 - 9	2 654 000	1 384 000	1 270 000	1 357 000	719 000	638 000	1 297 000	665 000	632 000
10 - 14	2 430 000	1 232 000	1 198 000	1 270 000	637 000	633 000	1 160 000	595 000	565 000
15 - 19	2 279 000	1 191 000	1 088 000	1 193 000	626 000	567 000	1 086 000	565 000	521 000
20 - 24	1 979 000	1 035 000	944 000	1 045 000	545 000	500 000	934 000	490 000	444 000
25 - 29	1 737 000	864 000	873 000	937 000	475 000	462 000	800 000	389 000	411 000
30 - 34	1 371 000	674 000	697 000	733 000	359 000	374 000	638 000	315 000	323 000
35 - 39	1 229 000	601 000	628 000	694 000	336 000	358 000	535 000	265 000	270 000
40 - 44	1 096 000	545 000	551 000	644 000	325 000	319 000	452 000	220 000	232 000
45 - 49	870 000	437 000	433 000	536 000	272 000	264 000	334 000	165 000	169 000
50 - 54	792 000	387 000	405 000	458 000	232 000	226 000	334 000	155 000	179 000
55 - 59	573 000	293 000	280 000	322 000	168 000	154 000	251 000	125 000	126 000
60 - 64	481 000	254 000	227 000	260 000	139 000	121 000	221 000	115 000	106 000
65 +	858 000	469 000	389 000	464 000	249 000	215 000	394 000	220 000	174 000

Continent, country or area, date, codeª and age (in years) Continent, pays ou zone, date, codeª et âge (en années)	Total			Urban - Urbaine			Rural - Rurale		
	Both sexes Les deux sexes	Male Masculin	Female Féminin	Both sexes Les deux sexes	Male Masculin	Female Féminin	Both sexes Les deux sexes	Male Masculin	Female Féminin
ASIA - ASIE									
Tajikistan - Tadjikistan									
1 VII 2013 (ESDF)									
Total	8 074 266	4 078 857	3 995 409	2 138 737	1 083 119	1 055 618	5 935 529	2 995 738	2 939 791
0	210 926	109 642	101 285	50 728	26 334	24 395	160 198	83 308	76 890
1 - 4	882 260	455 094	427 166	207 541	106 809	100 732	674 719	348 285	326 434
5 - 9	881 978	453 224	428 754	214 799	110 511	104 288	667 179	342 713	324 466
10 - 14	852 725	437 293	415 432	218 100	112 425	105 676	634 625	324 868	309 757
15 - 19	862 909	440 389	422 520	226 205	117 951	108 255	636 704	322 439	314 265
20 - 24	850 284	428 230	422 055	251 306	138 872	112 435	598 978	289 358	309 620
25 - 29	761 416	382 376	379 040	191 922	97 453	94 469	569 494	284 923	284 571
30 - 34	566 356	286 675	279 681	147 677	72 814	74 864	418 679	213 861	204 818
35 - 39	461 983	230 478	231 505	129 567	61 304	68 264	332 416	169 175	163 241
40 - 44	418 139	206 328	211 812	125 177	59 477	65 701	292 962	146 851	146 111
45 - 49	376 222	184 234	191 988	110 875	53 255	57 620	265 347	130 979	134 368
50 - 54	332 487	163 910	168 577	96 416	46 531	49 885	236 072	117 380	118 692
55 - 59	221 879	108 532	113 347	63 490	30 403	33 087	158 389	78 129	80 261
60 - 64	144 133	69 788	74 346	41 494	19 527	21 967	102 640	50 261	52 379
65 - 69	74 589	37 799	36 790	21 393	10 287	11 106	53 197	27 512	25 685
70 - 74	73 883	37 495	36 388	19 466	9 345	10 121	54 417	28 150	26 268
75 - 79	53 256	25 173	28 084	12 570	5 653	6 918	40 686	19 520	21 166
80 - 84	31 319	14 482	16 838	6 559	2 813	3 746	24 760	11 669	13 092
85 - 89	13 136	6 091	7 046	2 617	1 026	1 592	10 519	5 065	5 454
90 - 94	3 408	1 301	2 108	655	247	408	2 754	1 054	1 700
95 - 99	696	262	434	121	62	59	575	200	375
100 +	287	69	218	63	27	37	224	42	182
Thailand - Thaïlande²									
1 VII 2012 (ESDJ)									
Total	67 911 720	33 328 645	34 583 075	23 430 180	11 219 175	12 211 005	44 481 540	22 109 470	22 372 070
0 - 4	3 979 864	2 041 071	1 938 793	1 303 276	660 378	642 898	2 676 588	1 380 693	1 295 895
5 - 9	4 624 088	2 353 198	2 270 890	1 653 192	829 716	823 476	2 970 896	1 523 482	1 447 414
10 - 14	4 766 188	2 438 774	2 327 414	1 567 479	790 354	777 125	3 198 709	1 648 420	1 550 289
15 - 19	5 067 031	2 593 629	2 473 402	1 561 571	784 752	776 819	3 505 460	1 808 877	1 696 583
20 - 24	5 237 205	2 673 846	2 563 359	1 615 627	803 045	812 582	3 621 578	1 870 801	1 750 777
25 - 29	5 262 148	2 673 201	2 588 947	1 709 395	839 146	870 249	3 552 753	1 834 055	1 718 698
30 - 34	5 320 960	2 683 015	2 637 945	1 966 999	953 695	1 013 304	3 353 961	1 729 320	1 624 641
35 - 39	5 432 820	2 673 404	2 759 416	2 079 909	992 437	1 087 472	3 352 911	1 680 967	1 671 944
40 - 44	5 543 422	2 672 891	2 870 531	2 045 686	963 854	1 081 832	3 497 736	1 709 037	1 788 699
45 - 49	5 344 099	2 574 423	2 769 676	1 923 474	905 363	1 018 111	3 420 625	1 669 060	1 751 565
50 - 54	4 818 743	2 315 177	2 503 566	1 713 371	804 718	908 653	3 105 372	1 510 459	1 594 913
55 - 59	3 906 749	1 854 719	2 052 030	1 372 422	637 639	734 783	2 534 327	1 217 080	1 317 247
60 - 64	2 881 942	1 347 251	1 534 691	995 295	456 060	539 235	1 886 647	891 191	995 456
65 - 69	2 118 712	963 728	1 154 984	711 804	317 607	394 197	1 406 908	646 121	760 787
70 - 74	1 603 467	695 434	908 033	533 040	226 340	306 700	1 070 427	469 094	601 333
75 - 79	1 111 421	451 737	659 684	375 550	149 055	226 495	735 871	302 682	433 189
80 +	892 861	323 147	569 714	302 090	105 016	197 074	590 771	218 131	372 640
Timor-Leste									
11 VII 2010 (CDFC)									
Total	1 066 409	544 198	522 211	316 086	166 163	149 923	750 323	378 035	372 288
0 - 4	153 334	79 169	74 165	40 622	20 978	19 644	112 712	58 191	54 521
5 - 9	153 108	78 980	74 128	39 668	20 480	19 188	113 440	58 500	54 940
10 - 14	135 464	70 513	64 951	33 309	17 369	15 940	102 155	53 144	49 011
15 - 19	116 535	58 754	57 781	42 791	21 249	21 542	73 744	37 505	36 239
20 - 24	94 427	47 336	47 091	41 612	22 175	19 437	52 815	25 161	27 654
25 - 29	76 836	38 269	38 567	31 190	16 578	14 612	45 646	21 691	23 955
30 - 34	51 911	25 805	26 106	19 454	10 623	8 831	32 457	15 182	17 275
35 - 39	57 508	29 961	27 547	18 377	10 284	8 093	39 131	19 677	19 454
40 - 44	48 372	25 407	22 965	13 599	7 748	5 851	34 773	17 659	17 114
45 - 49	38 917	20 430	18 487	9 971	5 692	4 279	28 946	14 738	14 208
50 - 54	30 084	15 539	14 545	7 205	3 954	3 251	22 879	11 585	11 294
55 - 59	22 346	11 796	10 550	5 007	2 725	2 282	17 339	9 071	8 268
60 - 64	37 333	17 419	19 914	5 419	2 596	2 823	31 914	14 823	17 091
65 - 69	23 106	11 573	11 533	3 407	1 638	1 769	19 699	9 935	9 764
70 - 74	12 705	6 285	6 420	2 079	991	1 088	10 626	5 294	5 332
75 - 79	7 125	3 404	3 721	1 127	508	619	5 998	2 896	3 102

Continent, country or area, date, code[a] and age (in years) / Continent, pays ou zone, date, code[a] et âge (en annèes)	Total			Urban - Urbaine			Rural - Rurale		
	Both sexes Les deux sexes	Male Masculin	Female Féminin	Both sexes Les deux sexes	Male Masculin	Female Féminin	Both sexes Les deux sexes	Male Masculin	Female Féminin
ASIA - ASIE									
Timor-Leste									
11 VII 2010 (CDFC)									
80 - 84	3 755	1 818	1 937	614	275	339	3 141	1 543	1 598
85 +	3 543	1 740	1 803	635	300	335	2 908	1 440	1 468
Turkey - Turquie[65]									
31 XII 2013 (ESDJ)									
Total	76 667 864	38 473 360	38 194 504	66 488 105	33 344 846	33 143 259	10 179 759	5 128 514	5 051 245
0	1 229 012	631 750	597 262	1 086 651	558 669	527 982	142 361	73 081	69 280
1 - 4	4 977 403	2 555 509	2 421 894	4 382 576	2 250 735	2 131 841	594 827	304 774	290 053
5 - 9	6 271 234	3 218 411	3 052 823	5 491 135	2 818 697	2 672 438	780 099	399 714	380 385
10 - 14	6 372 165	3 269 578	3 102 587	5 502 371	2 824 822	2 677 549	869 794	444 756	425 038
15 - 19	6 477 722	3 327 238	3 150 484	5 585 535	2 867 301	2 718 234	892 187	459 937	432 250
20 - 24	6 214 024	3 166 104	3 047 920	5 418 279	2 728 759	2 689 520	795 745	437 345	358 400
25 - 29	6 286 332	3 189 167	3 097 165	5 607 728	2 823 328	2 784 400	678 604	365 839	312 765
30 - 34	6 543 669	3 305 734	3 237 935	5 882 890	2 962 410	2 920 480	660 779	343 324	317 455
35 - 39	5 826 149	2 946 289	2 879 860	5 224 257	2 638 903	2 585 354	601 892	307 386	294 506
40 - 44	5 308 260	2 673 800	2 634 460	4 702 969	2 367 817	2 335 152	605 291	305 983	299 308
45 - 49	4 721 763	2 389 852	2 331 911	4 130 494	2 090 304	2 040 190	591 269	299 548	291 721
50 - 54	4 232 792	2 123 029	2 109 763	3 639 746	1 827 279	1 812 467	593 046	295 750	297 296
55 - 59	3 555 185	1 769 399	1 785 786	2 990 618	1 493 076	1 497 542	564 567	276 323	288 244
60 - 64	2 760 460	1 346 426	1 414 034	2 263 921	1 108 868	1 155 053	496 539	237 558	258 981
65 - 69	2 045 398	950 337	1 095 061	1 632 320	762 039	870 281	413 078	188 298	224 780
70 - 74	1 507 728	674 943	832 785	1 167 519	523 111	644 408	340 209	151 832	188 377
75 - 79	1 077 295	461 225	616 070	826 256	349 410	476 846	251 039	111 815	139 224
80 - 84	820 606	335 943	484 663	613 354	245 012	368 342	207 252	90 931	116 321
85 - 89	341 662	112 700	228 962	261 469	84 220	177 249	80 193	28 480	51 713
90 +	99 005	25 926	73 079	78 017	20 086	57 931	20 988	5 840	15 148
United Arab Emirates - Émirats arabes unis									
5 XII 2005 (CDFC)									
Total	4 106 427	2 806 141	1 300 286	3 384 839[66]	2 328 906[66]	1 055 933[66]	721 588[66]	477 235[66]	244 353[66]
0 - 4	282 139	145 601	136 538	224 169[66]	115 800[66]	108 369[66]	57 970[66]	29 801[66]	28 169[66]
5 - 9	269 382	139 929	129 453	213 815[66]	111 645[66]	102 170[66]	55 567[66]	28 284[66]	27 283[66]
10 - 14	249 057	130 778	118 279	192 350[66]	101 461[66]	90 889[66]	56 707[66]	29 317[66]	27 390[66]
15 - 19	232 226	121 388	110 838	173 192[66]	91 065[66]	82 127[66]	59 034[66]	30 323[66]	28 711[66]
20 - 24	433 566	272 036	161 530	349 079[66]	222 387[66]	126 692[66]	84 487[66]	49 649[66]	34 838[66]
25 - 29	661 794	483 657	178 137	558 690[66]	410 228[66]	148 462[66]	103 104[66]	73 429[66]	29 675[66]
30 - 34	640 361	489 879	150 482	548 499[66]	417 909[66]	130 590[66]	91 862[66]	71 970[66]	19 892[66]
35 - 39	500 606	386 762	113 844	427 468[66]	329 059[66]	98 409[66]	73 138[66]	57 703[66]	15 435[66]
40 - 44	341 261	262 718	78 543	288 792[66]	220 959[66]	67 833[66]	52 469[66]	41 759[66]	10 710[66]
45 - 49	225 770	174 459	51 311	188 732[66]	145 298[66]	43 434[66]	37 038[66]	29 161[66]	7 877[66]
50 - 54	138 878	107 339	31 539	116 519[66]	89 983[66]	26 536[66]	22 359[66]	17 356[66]	5 003[66]
55 - 59	67 107	51 303	15 804	55 810[66]	42 788[66]	13 022[66]	11 297[66]	8 515[66]	2 782[66]
60 - 64	27 347	18 820	8 527	22 157[66]	15 510[66]	6 647[66]	5 190[66]	3 310[66]	1 880[66]
65 - 69	14 457	9 172	5 285	10 515[66]	6 623[66]	3 892[66]	3 942[66]	2 549[66]	1 393[66]
70 - 74	9 404	5 391	4 013	6 421[66]	3 659[66]	2 762[66]	2 983[66]	1 732[66]	1 251[66]
75 +[66]	...	...	...	8 631	4 532	4 099	4 441	2 377	2 064
75 - 79	4 277	2 440	1 837	...	...	...	...	...	...
80 - 84	2 976	1 537	1 439	...	...	...	...	...	...
85 +	2 415	1 250	1 165	...	...	...	...	...	...
Unknown - Inconnu	3 404	1 682	1 722	...	...	...	...	...	...
Viet Nam									
1 IV 2009 (CDJC)									
Total	85 846 997	42 413 143	43 433 854	25 436 896	12 349 995	13 086 901	60 410 101	30 063 148	30 346 953
0 - 4	7 034 144	3 662 889	3 371 255	1 949 105	1 019 547	929 558	5 085 039	2 643 342	2 441 697
5 - 9	6 710 737	3 458 159	3 252 578	1 757 679	910 339	847 340	4 953 058	2 547 820	2 405 238
10 - 14	7 248 378	3 725 369	3 523 009	1 761 650	904 731	856 919	5 486 728	2 820 638	2 666 090
15 - 17	5 236 771	2 681 653	2 555 118	1 311 350	662 369	648 981	3 925 421	2 019 284	1 906 137
18 - 19	3 727 131	1 896 261	1 830 870	1 188 578	562 169	626 409	2 538 553	1 334 092	1 204 461
20 - 24	8 432 867	4 253 618	4 179 249	2 759 456	1 305 436	1 454 020	5 673 411	2 948 182	2 725 229
25 - 29	7 790 003	3 904 730	3 885 273	2 519 920	1 205 518	1 314 402	5 270 083	2 699 212	2 570 871
30 - 34	6 868 158	3 462 905	3 405 253	2 164 824	1 062 838	1 101 986	4 703 334	2 400 067	2 303 267
35 - 39	6 531 607	3 298 266	3 233 341	2 059 356	1 027 075	1 032 281	4 472 251	2 271 191	2 201 060
40 - 44	5 966 856	2 967 934	2 998 922	1 818 188	896 290	921 898	4 148 668	2 071 644	2 077 024

7. Population by age, sex and urban/rural residence: latest available year, 2005 - 2014
Population selon l'âge, le sexe et la résidence, urbaine/rurale : dernière année disponible, 2005 - 2014 (continued - suite)

Continent, country or area, date, code[a] and age (in years) Continent, pays ou zone, date, code[a] et âge (en annèes)	Total			Urban - Urbaine			Rural - Rurale		
	Both sexes Les deux sexes	Male Masculin	Female Féminin	Both sexes Les deux sexes	Male Masculin	Female Féminin	Both sexes Les deux sexes	Male Masculin	Female Féminin
ASIA - ASIE									
Viet Nam									
1 IV 2009 (CDJC)									
45 - 49	5 450 928	2 642 466	2 808 462	1 728 008	840 047	887 961	3 722 920	1 802 419	1 920 501
50 - 54	4 412 051	2 082 098	2 329 953	1 435 970	683 749	752 221	2 976 081	1 398 349	1 577 732
55 - 59	2 984 619	1 364 319	1 620 300	931 382	421 296	510 086	2 053 237	943 023	1 110 214
60 - 64	1 937 948	861 897	1 076 051	590 161	259 193	330 968	1 347 787	602 704	745 083
65 - 69	1 554 678	653 287	901 391	453 756	195 857	257 899	1 100 922	457 430	643 492
70 - 74	1 412 538	568 312	844 226	378 105	155 224	222 881	1 034 433	413 088	621 345
75 - 79	1 198 893	480 088	718 805	306 226	125 948	180 278	892 667	354 140	538 527
80 - 84	725 985	264 997	460 988	182 550	69 573	112 977	543 435	195 424	348 011
85 +	622 705	183 895	438 810	140 632	42 796	97 836	482 073	141 099	340 974
1 VII 2014 (ESDF)									
Total	90 728 941	44 758 132	45 970 809	30 035 405	...	...	60 693 536	...	...
0 - 4	7 229 575	3 806 055	3 423 520	2 277 662	...	...	4 951 913	...	...
5 - 9	7 162 460	3 730 617	3 431 843	2 242 988	...	...	4 919 472	...	...
10 - 14	6 900 099	3 555 440	3 344 659	2 037 720	...	...	4 862 379	...	...
15 - 17	4 110 225	2 116 797	1 993 428	1 145 205	...	...	2 965 020	...	...
18 - 19	2 883 280	1 463 525	1 419 755	925 185	...	...	1 958 095	...	...
20 - 24	8 018 270	4 058 691	3 959 579	2 657 695	...	...	5 360 575	...	...
25 - 29	7 839 917	3 951 220	3 888 697	2 707 694	...	...	5 132 223	...	...
30 - 34	7 458 996	3 689 395	3 769 601	2 685 662	...	...	4 773 334	...	...
35 - 39	6 830 249	3 390 462	3 439 787	2 385 570	...	...	4 444 679	...	...
40 - 44	6 587 945	3 292 933	3 295 012	2 290 504	...	...	4 297 441	...	...
45 - 49	6 048 831	2 980 442	3 068 389	2 040 158	...	...	4 008 673	...	...
50 - 54	5 670 624	2 699 165	2 971 459	1 974 928	...	...	3 695 696	...	...
55 - 59	4 501 600	2 096 032	2 405 568	1 619 754	...	...	2 881 846	...	...
60 - 64	3 048 482	1 376 861	1 671 621	1 043 564	...	...	2 004 918	...	...
65 - 69	1 916 960	832 090	1 084 870	654 526	...	...	1 262 434	...	...
70 - 74	1 462 836	600 732	862 104	479 489	...	...	983 347	...	...
75 - 79	1 234 535	477 293	757 242	373 313	...	...	861 222	...	...
80 +	1 824 057	640 382	1 183 675	493 788	...	...	1 330 269	...	...
Yemen - Yémen[2]									
1 VII 2013 (ESDJ)									
Total	25 235 079	12 844 169	12 390 910	...	...	...	...	...	...
0	867 766	442 297	425 470	...	...	...	...	...	...
1 - 4	3 183 851	1 627 558	1 556 293	...	...	...	...	...	...
5 - 9	3 377 146	1 723 755	1 653 391	...	...	...	...	...	...
10 - 14	3 007 245	1 539 447	1 467 798	...	...	...	...	...	...
15 - 19	2 954 657	1 530 854	1 423 803	...	...	...	...	...	...
20 - 24	2 738 574	1 426 490	1 312 083	...	...	...	...	...	...
25 - 29	2 226 915	1 146 775	1 080 140	...	...	...	...	...	...
30 - 34	1 688 248	851 154	837 094	...	...	...	...	...	...
35 - 39	1 276 748	635 492	641 256	...	...	...	...	...	...
40 - 44	916 385	448 186	468 200	...	...	...	...	...	...
45 - 49	758 743	366 733	392 010	...	...	...	...	...	...
50 - 54	644 689	310 025	334 665	...	...	...	...	...	...
55 - 59	488 859	238 877	249 982	...	...	...	...	...	...
60 - 64	352 671	178 041	174 631	...	...	...	...	...	...
65 - 69	266 902	135 090	131 812	...	...	...	...	...	...
70 - 74	195 287	98 257	97 029	...	...	...	...	...	...
75 - 79	133 347	66 656	66 691	...	...	...	...	...	...
80 +	157 047	78 482	78 565	...	...	...	...	...	...
EUROPE									
Åland Islands - Îles d'Åland[19]									
1 VII 2014 (ESDJ)									
Total	28 792	14 375	14 417	11 437	5 490	5 947	17 355	8 885	8 470
0	286	150	137	96	52	44	190	97	93
1 - 4	1 221	614	607	418	215	203	803	399	404
5 - 9	1 618	848	771	539	263	276	1 079	584	495
10 - 14	1 553	823	730	536	274	262	1 017	548	469
15 - 19	1 688	856	833	697	341	356	991	514	477
20 - 24	1 538	842	696	760	405	355	778	436	342

Continent, country or area, date, code[a] and age (in years) / Continent, pays ou zone, date, code[a] et âge (en annèes)	Total			Urban - Urbaine			Rural - Rurale		
	Both sexes Les deux sexes	Male Masculin	Female Féminin	Both sexes Les deux sexes	Male Masculin	Female Féminin	Both sexes Les deux sexes	Male Masculin	Female Féminin
EUROPE									
Åland Islands - Îles d'Åland[19]									
1 VII 2014 (ESDJ)									
25 - 29	1 585	841	744	784	434	350	801	407	394
30 - 34	1 741	902	839	737	389	348	1 004	513	491
35 - 39	1 779	919	860	680	341	339	1 099	578	521
40 - 44	1 878	940	939	703	338	365	1 175	601	574
45 - 49	2 164	1 064	1 100	812	383	429	1 352	681	671
50 - 54	1 954	957	997	733	323	410	1 221	634	587
55 - 59	1 945	921	1 024	750	332	418	1 195	590	605
60 - 64	2 043	975	1 069	814	361	453	1 229	614	615
65 - 69	1 991	1 007	985	807	383	424	1 184	623	561
70 - 74	1 353	706	647	548	262	286	805	444	361
75 - 79	978	443	535	415	177	238	563	266	297
80 - 84	708	314	394	290	126	164	418	188	230
85 - 89	513	190	324	203	65	138	310	125	185
90 - 94	209	60	150	97	24	73	112	36	76
95 - 99	48	9	39	21	3	18	27	6	21
100 +	4	1	3	2	-	2	2	1	1
Albania - Albanie									
1 VII 2013 (ESDF)									
Total	2 897 364	1 458 648	1 438 716	1 633 617	798 615	835 002	1 263 747	660 033	603 714
0 - 4	173 349	90 068	83 281	75 341	39 381	35 960	98 008	50 687	47 321
0	35 445	18 414	17 031	...	...	...	...	...	...
1 - 4	137 903	71 653	66 250	...	...	...	...	...	...
5 - 9	171 833	90 701	81 132	100 478	52 421	48 057	71 355	38 280	33 075
10 - 14	220 582	114 164	106 418	117 500	60 576	56 924	103 082	53 587	49 494
15 - 19	261 669	132 810	128 859	134 718	67 303	67 414	126 952	65 507	61 445
20 - 24	235 615	126 936	108 680	153 986	75 706	78 280	81 630	51 230	30 400
25 - 29	209 075	112 236	96 839	136 959	65 999	70 960	72 116	46 237	25 879
30 - 34	187 077	92 149	94 928	95 098	44 074	51 024	91 979	48 075	43 904
35 - 39	173 587	82 445	91 142	89 169	40 432	48 737	84 418	42 013	42 405
40 - 44	189 099	89 772	99 327	106 471	50 381	56 091	82 627	39 391	43 236
45 - 49	197 020	95 657	101 363	113 719	55 342	58 377	83 301	40 315	42 986
50 - 54	209 575	104 084	105 490	121 293	60 655	60 638	88 282	43 430	44 852
55 - 59	184 593	92 037	92 556	105 093	51 906	53 188	79 500	40 131	39 369
60 - 64	141 532	71 276	70 256	83 065	40 768	42 296	58 467	30 508	27 960
65 - 69	106 945	54 278	52 666	60 973	29 333	31 640	45 971	24 945	21 026
70 - 74	102 875	49 827	53 048	55 109	26 020	29 089	47 766	23 807	23 959
75 - 79	71 589	35 241	36 348	41 911	19 956	21 955	29 678	15 285	14 393
80 - 84	38 203	16 977	21 226	25 030	11 374	13 656	13 174	5 603	7 570
85 +	23 147	7 992	15 155	17 705	6 988	10 717	5 443	1 004	4 438
1 I 2014 (ESDF)									
Total	2 895 947	1 459 963	1 435 984	...	...	...	...	...	...
0	35 196	18 328	16 868	...	...	...	...	...	...
1 - 4	137 321	71 092	66 229	...	...	...	...	...	...
5 - 9	166 011	87 690	78 321	...	...	...	...	...	...
10 - 14	216 490	112 159	104 331	...	...	...	...	...	...
15 - 19	256 553	130 580	125 973	...	...	...	...	...	...
20 - 24	229 529	124 337	105 192	...	...	...	...	...	...
25 - 29	210 829	114 197	96 632	...	...	...	...	...	...
30 - 34	191 900	94 950	96 950	...	...	...	...	...	...
35 - 39	176 491	84 004	92 487	...	...	...	...	...	...
40 - 44	186 144	88 592	97 552	...	...	...	...	...	...
45 - 49	197 531	95 598	101 933	...	...	...	...	...	...
50 - 54	210 687	104 617	106 070	...	...	...	...	...	...
55 - 59	189 265	94 245	95 020	...	...	...	...	...	...
60 - 64	143 754	72 519	71 235	...	...	...	...	...	...
65 - 69	108 400	54 945	53 455	...	...	...	...	...	...
70 - 74	104 308	50 427	53 881	...	...	...	...	...	...
75 - 79	73 204	36 096	37 108	...	...	...	...	...	...
80 - 84	39 002	17 349	21 653	...	...	...	...	...	...
85 +	23 332	8 238	15 094	...	...	...	...	...	...

Continent, country or area, date, code[a] and age (in years) / Continent, pays ou zone, date, code[a] et âge (en années)	Total			Urban - Urbaine			Rural - Rurale		
	Both sexes Les deux sexes	Male Masculin	Female Féminin	Both sexes Les deux sexes	Male Masculin	Female Féminin	Both sexes Les deux sexes	Male Masculin	Female Féminin
EUROPE									
Andorra - Andorre[19]									
1 VII 2012 (ESDJ)									
Total	77 181	39 351	37 830	...	...	...	...	...	...
0	581	288	293	...	...	...	...	...	...
1 - 4	3 126	1 573	1 553	...	...	...	...	...	...
5 - 9	4 016	2 112	1 904	...	...	...	...	...	...
10 - 14	4 246	2 194	2 052	...	...	...	...	...	...
15 - 19	3 794	2 035	1 759	...	...	...	...	...	...
20 - 24	3 834	1 952	1 882	...	...	...	...	...	...
25 - 29	5 039	2 497	2 542	...	...	...	...	...	...
30 - 34	6 768	3 394	3 375	...	...	...	...	...	...
35 - 39	7 536	3 794	3 742	...	...	...	...	...	...
40 - 44	7 281	3 712	3 570	...	...	...	...	...	...
45 - 49	7 002	3 615	3 387	...	...	...	...	...	...
50 - 54	5 884	3 069	2 816	...	...	...	...	...	...
55 - 59	4 646	2 469	2 177	...	...	...	...	...	...
60 - 64	3 699	1 959	1 741	...	...	...	...	...	...
65 - 69	2 912	1 543	1 369	...	...	...	...	...	...
70 - 74	2 009	973	1 036	...	...	...	...	...	...
75 - 79	1 712	838	874	...	...	...	...	...	...
80 - 84	1 477	664	813	...	...	...	...	...	...
85 - 89	929	389	540	...	...	...	...	...	...
90 - 94	448	180	268	...	...	...	...	...	...
95 - 99	174	70	104	...	...	...	...	...	...
100 +	71	36	36	...	...	...	...	...	...
Austria - Autriche									
31 X 2011 (CDJC)									
Total	8 401 940	4 093 938	4 308 002	5 643 239	2 713 930	2 929 309	2 758 701	1 380 008	1 378 693
0 - 4	394 706	202 637	192 069	267 743	137 645	130 098	126 963	64 992	61 971
5 - 9	406 027	207 779	198 248	268 770	137 636	131 134	137 257	70 143	67 114
10 - 14	426 957	218 499	208 458	276 347	141 429	134 918	150 610	77 070	73 540
15 - 19	488 818	251 251	237 567	313 792	160 620	153 172	175 026	90 631	84 395
20 - 24	527 675	267 651	260 024	364 267	181 574	182 693	163 408	86 077	77 331
25 - 29	552 783	277 236	275 547	390 454	193 719	196 735	162 329	83 517	78 812
30 - 34	538 307	270 267	268 040	375 886	187 248	188 638	162 421	83 019	79 402
35 - 39	564 817	280 207	284 610	383 183	187 902	195 281	181 634	92 305	89 329
40 - 44	675 242	338 455	336 787	453 188	224 449	228 739	222 054	114 006	108 048
45 - 49	710 388	358 163	352 225	470 749	234 757	235 992	239 639	123 406	116 233
50 - 54	626 162	312 890	313 272	409 191	200 993	208 198	216 971	111 897	105 074
55 - 59	517 280	253 019	264 261	339 245	161 747	177 498	178 035	91 272	86 763
60 - 64	480 665	231 598	249 067	322 367	151 726	170 641	158 298	79 872	78 426
65 - 69	402 829	189 221	213 608	283 946	130 760	153 186	118 883	58 461	60 422
70 - 74	410 314	187 956	222 358	273 352	123 395	149 957	136 962	64 561	72 401
75 - 79	262 203	110 870	151 333	165 864	68 812	97 052	96 339	42 058	54 281
80 - 84	218 133	83 066	135 067	142 903	52 895	90 008	75 230	30 171	45 059
85 - 89	141 772	40 153	101 619	99 777	27 332	72 445	41 995	12 821	29 174
90 - 94	46 362	10 997	35 365	34 057	7 767	26 290	12 305	3 230	9 075
95 - 99	9 388	1 836	7 552	7 274	1 377	5 897	2 114	459	1 655
100 +	1 112	187	925	884	147	737	228	40	188
1 I 2014 (ESDJ)									
Total	8 506 889	4 155 636	4 351 253	...	...	...	...	...	...
0	78 311	40 427	37 884	...	...	...	...	...	...
1 - 4	321 127	165 176	155 951	...	...	...	...	...	...
5 - 9	404 598	207 182	197 416	...	...	...	...	...	...
10 - 14	414 806	212 692	202 114	...	...	...	...	...	...
15 - 19	469 778	241 161	228 617	...	...	...	...	...	...
20 - 24	542 518	276 255	266 263	...	...	...	...	...	...
25 - 29	559 820	282 640	277 180	...	...	...	...	...	...
30 - 34	571 000	287 038	283 962	...	...	...	...	...	...
35 - 39	545 202	272 193	273 009	...	...	...	...	...	...
40 - 44	629 534	312 709	316 825	...	...	...	...	...	...
45 - 49	711 805	358 842	352 963	...	...	...	...	...	...
50 - 54	673 359	337 818	335 541	...	...	...	...	...	...
55 - 59	558 162	274 205	283 957	...	...	...	...	...	...
60 - 64	470 136	226 776	243 360	...	...	...	...	...	...

7. Population by age, sex and urban/rural residence: latest available year, 2005 - 2014
Population selon l'âge, le sexe et la résidence, urbaine/rurale : dernière année disponible, 2005 - 2014 (continued - suite)

Continent, country or area, date, code[a] and age (in years) / Continent, pays ou zone, date, code[a] et âge (en années)	Total			Urban - Urbaine			Rural - Rurale		
	Both sexes Les deux sexes	Male Masculin	Female Féminin	Both sexes Les deux sexes	Male Masculin	Female Féminin	Both sexes Les deux sexes	Male Masculin	Female Féminin
EUROPE									
Austria - Autriche									
1 I 2014 (ESDJ)									
65 - 69	420 468	197 990	222 478	...	...	...	...	...	...
70 - 74	443 428	202 881	240 547	...	...	...	...	...	...
75 - 79	266 664	115 089	151 575	...	...	...	...	...	...
80 - 84	217 202	84 658	132 544	...	...	...	...	...	...
85 - 89	140 708	44 380	96 328	...	...	...	...	...	...
90 - 94	59 257	13 823	45 434	...	...	...	...	...	...
95 - 99	7 634	1 478	6 156	...	...	...	...	...	...
100 +	1 372	223	1 149	...	...	...	...	...	...
Belarus - Bélarus									
1 I 2014 (ESDF)									
Total	9 468 154	4 401 211	5 066 943	7 274 775	3 357 966	3 916 809	2 193 379	1 043 245	1 150 134
0	118 029	60 773	57 256	91 009	46 880	44 129	27 020	13 893	13 127
1 - 4	444 026	228 597	215 429	346 276	178 225	168 051	97 750	50 372	47 378
5 - 9	479 639	246 370	233 269	373 901	192 245	181 656	105 738	54 125	51 613
10 - 14	447 088	229 555	217 533	336 924	173 072	163 852	110 164	56 483	53 681
15 - 19	482 256	248 418	233 838	387 454	196 404	191 050	94 802	52 014	42 788
20 - 24	671 668	344 808	326 860	582 340	291 203	291 137	89 328	53 605	35 723
25 - 29	781 505	399 208	382 297	649 073	325 264	323 809	132 432	73 944	58 488
30 - 34	727 041	366 062	360 979	603 873	300 562	303 311	123 168	65 500	57 668
35 - 39	667 409	328 482	338 927	533 917	259 919	273 998	133 492	68 563	64 929
40 - 44	649 993	313 157	336 836	496 333	234 179	262 154	153 660	78 978	74 682
45 - 49	659 294	312 426	346 868	491 728	225 158	266 570	167 566	87 268	80 298
50 - 54	763 327	356 227	407 100	574 417	256 895	317 522	188 910	99 332	89 578
55 - 59	696 903	311 780	385 123	528 789	226 859	301 930	168 114	84 921	83 193
60 - 64	562 068	235 845	326 223	428 543	174 181	254 362	133 525	61 664	71 861
65 - 69	359 109	140 810	218 299	264 016	102 942	161 074	95 093	37 868	57 225
70 - 74	317 522	107 773	209 749	208 902	71 856	137 046	108 620	35 917	72 703
75 - 79	309 685	92 407	217 278	187 906	57 157	130 749	121 779	35 250	86 529
80 - 84	197 626	50 828	146 798	107 794	27 573	80 221	89 832	23 255	66 577
85 - 89	104 646	22 549	82 097	61 656	13 854	47 802	42 990	8 695	34 295
90 - 94	25 276	4 504	20 772	16 687	2 999	13 688	8 589	1 505	7 084
95 - 99	3 475	545	2 930	2 726	460	2 266	749	85	664
100 +	569	87	482	511	79	432	58	8	50
Belgium - Belgique									
1 I 2011 (CDJC)									
Total	11 000 638	5 401 718	5 598 920	10 842 520	5 322 172	5 520 348	158 118	79 546	78 572
0 - 4	645 512	330 184	315 328	636 217	325 336	310 881	9 295	4 848	4 447
5 - 9	607 325	310 560	296 765	597 723	305 654	292 069	9 602	4 906	4 696
10 - 14	614 460	313 738	300 722	604 574	308 723	295 851	9 886	5 015	4 871
15 - 19	649 018	331 790	317 228	638 725	326 452	312 273	10 293	5 338	4 955
20 - 24	684 093	344 647	339 446	674 173	339 520	334 653	9 920	5 127	4 793
25 - 29	700 373	351 045	349 328	691 593	346 539	345 054	8 780	4 506	4 274
30 - 34	722 936	364 728	358 208	713 667	360 044	353 623	9 269	4 684	4 585
35 - 39	741 204	375 815	365 389	730 809	370 490	360 319	10 395	5 325	5 070
40 - 44	789 895	401 530	388 365	778 159	395 446	382 713	11 736	6 084	5 652
45 - 49	828 167	418 827	409 340	816 018	412 531	403 487	12 149	6 296	5 853
50 - 54	781 240	391 809	389 431	770 016	385 999	384 017	11 224	5 810	5 414
55 - 59	702 331	349 489	352 842	692 496	344 347	348 149	9 835	5 142	4 693
60 - 64	650 904	320 714	330 190	641 771	316 010	325 761	9 133	4 704	4 429
65 - 69	480 199	230 217	249 982	473 668	226 987	246 681	6 531	3 230	3 301
70 - 74	448 374	205 382	242 992	441 884	202 344	239 540	6 490	3 038	3 452
75 - 79	401 594	171 538	230 056	395 900	168 962	226 938	5 694	2 576	3 118
80 - 84	304 788	115 591	189 197	300 342	113 821	186 521	4 446	1 770	2 676
85 - 89	180 495	57 963	122 532	177 932	57 048	120 884	2 563	915	1 648
90 - 94	52 708	13 541	39 167	52 007	13 341	38 666	701	200	501
95 - 99	13 392	2 412	10 980	13 233	2 381	10 852	159	31	128
100 +	1 630	198	1 432	1 613	197	1 416	17	1	16
1 I 2014 (ESDJ)									
Total	11 203 992	5 508 069	5 695 923	...	...	...	...	...	...
0	125 375	64 224	61 151	...	...	...	...	...	...
1 - 4	524 860	268 290	256 570	...	...	...	...	...	...
5 - 9	643 167	329 207	313 960	...	...	...	...	...	...
10 - 14	612 711	312 915	299 796	...	...	...	...	...	...

7. Population by age, sex and urban/rural residence: latest available year, 2005 - 2014
Population selon l'âge, le sexe et la résidence, urbaine/rurale : dernière année disponible, 2005 - 2014 (continued - suite)

Continent, country or area, date, code[a] and age (in years) Continent, pays ou zone, date, code[a] et âge (en années)	Total			Urban - Urbaine			Rural - Rurale		
	Both sexes Les deux sexes	Male Masculin	Female Féminin	Both sexes Les deux sexes	Male Masculin	Female Féminin	Both sexes Les deux sexes	Male Masculin	Female Féminin
EUROPE									
Belgium - Belgique 1 I 2014 (ESDJ)									
15 - 19	631 171	322 780	308 391	...	...	...	...	...	...
20 - 24	704 113	355 410	348 703	...	...	...	...	...	...
25 - 29	712 515	356 406	356 109	...	...	...	...	...	...
30 - 34	739 456	372 182	367 274	...	...	...	...	...	...
35 - 39	724 289	365 975	358 314	...	...	...	...	...	...
40 - 44	777 650	394 316	383 334	...	...	...	...	...	...
45 - 49	810 543	411 217	399 326	...	...	...	...	...	...
50 - 54	808 781	406 525	402 256	...	...	...	...	...	...
55 - 59	739 760	367 873	371 887	...	...	...	...	...	...
60 - 64	655 234	323 076	332 158	...	...	...	...	...	...
65 - 69	578 277	278 831	299 446	...	...	...	...	...	...
70 - 74	422 267	195 334	226 933	...	...	...	...	...	...
75 - 79	395 900	172 571	223 329	...	...	...	...	...	...
80 - 84	320 768	125 602	195 166	...	...	...	...	...	...
85 - 89	188 670	62 725	125 945	...	...	...	...	...	...
90 - 94	75 812	20 320	55 492	...	...	...	...	...	...
95 - 99	10 783	2 051	8 732	...	...	...	...	...	...
100 +	1 890	239	1 651	...	...	...	...	...	...
Bosnia and Herzegovina - Bosnie-Herzégovine 1 VII 2010 (ESDF)									
Total	3 843 126	1 877 587	1 965 539	...	...	...	...	...	...
0	33 314	17 123	16 191	...	...	...	...	...	...
1 - 4	133 257	68 494	64 763	...	...	...	...	...	...
5 - 9	229 608	117 330	112 278	...	...	...	...	...	...
10 - 14	274 779	139 862	134 917	...	...	...	...	...	...
15 - 19	279 370	146 390	132 980	...	...	...	...	...	...
20 - 24	284 994	144 777	140 217	...	...	...	...	...	...
25 - 29	268 273	131 991	136 282	...	...	...	...	...	...
30 - 34	240 986	120 975	120 011	...	...	...	...	...	...
35 - 39	246 721	121 633	125 088	...	...	...	...	...	...
40 - 44	283 887	141 943	141 944	...	...	...	...	...	...
45 - 49	306 958	150 410	156 548	...	...	...	...	...	...
50 - 54	266 575	135 687	130 888	...	...	...	...	...	...
55 - 59	231 595	105 145	126 450	...	...	...	...	...	...
60 - 64	182 787	86 092	96 695	...	...	...	...	...	...
65 - 69	202 274	90 012	112 262	...	...	...	...	...	...
70 - 74	184 389	82 422	101 967	...	...	...	...	...	...
75 - 79	120 364	50 553	69 811	...	...	...	...	...	...
80 - 84	47 932	19 605	28 327	...	...	...	...	...	...
85 +	25 063	7 143	17 920	...	...	...	...	...	...
Bulgaria - Bulgarie 1 VII 2012 (ESDJ)									
Total	7 305 888	3 555 920	3 749 968	5 316 384	2 568 535	2 747 849	1 989 504	987 385	1 002 119
0	66 072	34 082	31 990	49 710	25 724	23 986	16 362	8 358	8 004
1 - 4	280 165	143 865	136 300	208 103	106 901	101 202	72 062	36 964	35 098
5 - 9	324 559	167 057	157 502	235 618	121 101	114 517	88 941	45 956	42 985
10 - 14	314 174	161 486	152 688	226 483	116 269	110 214	87 691	45 217	42 474
15 - 19	346 622	178 574	168 352	250 855	128 646	122 209	96 071	49 928	46 143
20 - 24	466 758	240 138	226 620	360 989	182 904	178 085	105 769	57 234	48 535
25 - 29	489 520	253 779	235 741	380 805	194 743	186 062	108 715	59 036	49 679
30 - 34	514 109	266 962	247 147	402 004	206 433	195 571	112 105	60 529	51 576
35 - 39	553 955	285 447	268 508	434 249	221 237	213 012	119 706	64 210	55 496
40 - 44	525 895	270 703	255 192	401 223	203 117	198 106	124 672	67 586	57 086
45 - 49	480 082	243 855	236 227	358 986	178 351	180 635	121 096	65 504	55 592
50 - 54	506 689	252 294	254 395	376 212	182 697	193 515	130 477	69 597	60 880
55 - 59	521 824	251 394	270 430	382 836	180 438	202 398	138 988	70 956	68 032
60 - 64	526 885	242 476	284 409	373 390	169 637	203 753	153 495	72 839	80 656
65 - 69	439 615	193 281	246 334	291 001	127 275	163 726	148 614	66 006	82 608
70 - 74	341 305	141 732	199 573	211 176	86 328	124 848	130 129	55 404	74 725
75 - 79	299 387	117 689	181 698	181 312	69 060	112 252	118 075	48 629	69 446
80 - 84	192 907	72 021	120 886	119 850	43 583	76 267	73 057	28 438	44 619
85 - 89	90 647	31 255	59 392	56 432	19 218	37 214	34 215	12 037	22 178

Continent, country or area, date, code[a] and age (in years) Continent, pays ou zone, date, code[a] et âge (en années)	Total			Urban - Urbaine			Rural - Rurale		
	Both sexes Les deux sexes	Male Masculin	Female Féminin	Both sexes Les deux sexes	Male Masculin	Female Féminin	Both sexes Les deux sexes	Male Masculin	Female Féminin
EUROPE									
Bulgaria - Bulgarie									
1 VII 2012 (ESDJ)									
90 - 94	21 736	7 020	14 716	13 463	4 363	9 100	8 273	2 657	5 616
95 - 99	2 366	699	1 667	1 486	437	1 049	880	262	618
100 +	312	111	201	201	73	128	111	38	73
1 I 2014 (ESDJ)									
Total	7 245 677	3 524 945	3 720 732	...	...	...	...	...	...
0	64 755	33 054	31 701	...	...	...	...	...	...
1 - 4	277 725	142 685	135 040	...	...	...	...	...	...
5 - 9	334 783	172 308	162 475	...	...	...	...	...	...
10 - 14	318 881	163 878	155 003	...	...	...	...	...	...
15 - 19	318 714	164 105	154 609	...	...	...	...	...	...
20 - 24	433 186	223 177	210 009	...	...	...	...	...	...
25 - 29	488 936	253 073	235 863	...	...	...	...	...	...
30 - 34	498 179	259 290	238 889	...	...	...	...	...	...
35 - 39	553 603	285 514	268 089	...	...	...	...	...	...
40 - 44	529 290	272 767	256 523	...	...	...	...	...	...
45 - 49	482 688	245 513	237 175	...	...	...	...	...	...
50 - 54	498 188	249 183	249 005	...	...	...	...	...	...
55 - 59	511 031	246 883	264 148	...	...	...	...	...	...
60 - 64	518 051	239 372	278 679	...	...	...	...	...	...
65 - 69	460 811	202 315	258 496	...	...	...	...	...	...
70 - 74	346 837	143 806	203 031	...	...	...	...	...	...
75 - 79	288 002	112 278	175 724	...	...	...	...	...	...
80 - 84	200 282	74 580	125 702	...	...	...	...	...	...
85 - 89	93 765	32 147	61 618	...	...	...	...	...	...
90 - 94	25 479	8 239	17 240	...	...	...	...	...	...
95 - 99	2 185	679	1 506	...	...	...	...	...	...
100 +	306	99	207	...	...	...	...	...	...
Croatia - Croatie									
1 IV 2011 (CDJC)									
Total	4 284 889	2 066 335	2 218 554	2 368 506	1 121 328	1 247 178	1 916 383	945 007	971 376
0 - 4	212 709	109 251	103 458	116 367	59 768	56 599	96 342	49 483	46 859
5 - 9	204 317	104 841	99 476	108 481	55 715	52 766	95 836	49 126	46 710
10 - 14	235 402	120 633	114 769	124 241	63 763	60 478	111 161	56 870	54 291
15 - 19	244 177	124 918	119 259	130 369	66 506	63 863	113 808	58 412	55 396
20 - 24	261 658	133 455	128 203	142 681	72 037	70 644	118 977	61 418	57 559
25 - 29	289 066	147 416	141 650	164 754	82 466	82 288	124 312	64 950	59 362
30 - 34	294 619	149 998	144 621	173 166	86 363	86 803	121 453	63 635	57 818
35 - 39	284 754	143 984	140 770	165 450	81 745	83 705	119 304	62 239	57 065
40 - 44	286 933	143 603	143 330	161 295	78 845	82 450	125 638	64 758	60 880
45 - 49	307 561	152 446	155 115	167 593	80 182	87 411	139 968	72 264	67 704
50 - 54	320 502	157 981	162 521	174 963	81 945	93 018	145 539	76 036	69 503
55 - 59	311 818	153 750	158 068	174 376	81 746	92 630	137 442	72 004	65 438
60 - 64	272 740	127 851	144 889	154 706	69 577	85 129	118 034	58 274	59 760
65 - 69	202 002	89 364	112 638	114 109	49 018	65 091	87 893	40 346	47 547
70 - 74	212 401	88 912	123 489	113 737	47 978	65 759	98 664	40 934	57 730
75 - 79	175 526	66 456	109 070	91 966	35 801	56 165	83 560	30 655	52 905
80 - 84	108 104	35 999	72 105	56 658	19 022	37 636	51 446	16 977	34 469
85 - 89	47 641	12 415	35 226	26 213	7 045	19 168	21 428	5 370	16 058
90 - 94	10 758	2 580	8 178	6 081	1 517	4 564	4 677	1 063	3 614
95 - 99	2 003	446	1 557	1 181	270	911	822	176	646
100 +	198	36	162	119	19	100	79	17	62
1 I 2014 (ESDJ)									
Total	4 246 809	2 049 748	2 197 061	...	...	...	...	...	...
0	39 786	20 649	19 137	...	...	...	...	...	...
1 - 4	170 033	87 426	82 607	...	...	...	...	...	...
5 - 9	207 846	106 904	100 942	...	...	...	...	...	...
10 - 14	209 973	107 655	102 318	...	...	...	...	...	...
15 - 19	245 481	125 465	120 016	...	...	...	...	...	...
20 - 24	249 756	127 746	122 010	...	...	...	...	...	...
25 - 29	275 367	140 028	135 339	...	...	...	...	...	...
30 - 34	294 016	150 009	144 007	...	...	...	...	...	...
35 - 39	286 813	145 527	141 286	...	...	...	...	...	...
40 - 44	277 716	139 667	138 049	...	...	...	...	...	...

Continent, country or area, date, code[a] and age (in years) / Continent, pays ou zone, date, code[a] et âge (en années)	Total			Urban - Urbaine			Rural - Rurale		
	Both sexes Les deux sexes	Male Masculin	Female Féminin	Both sexes Les deux sexes	Male Masculin	Female Féminin	Both sexes Les deux sexes	Male Masculin	Female Féminin
EUROPE									
Croatia - Croatie									
1 I 2014 (ESDJ)									
45 - 49	297 619	147 844	149 775	...	...	...	...	...	...
50 - 54	309 449	152 117	157 332	...	...	...	...	...	...
55 - 59	315 155	154 402	160 753	...	...	...	...	...	...
60 - 64	285 115	136 104	149 011	...	...	...	...	...	...
65 - 69	213 740	95 491	118 249	...	...	...	...	...	...
70 - 74	201 716	84 908	116 808	...	...	...	...	...	...
75 - 79	177 305	68 436	108 869	...	...	...	...	...	...
80 - 84	119 868	40 556	79 312	...	...	...	...	...	...
85 - 89	52 603	14 816	37 787	...	...	...	...	...	...
90 - 94	15 804	3 634	12 170	...	...	...	...	...	...
95 - 99	1 359	296	1 063	...	...	...	...	...	...
100 +	289	68	221	...	...	...	...	...	...
Czech Republic - République tchèque									
1 I 2014 (ESDJ)									
Total	10 512 419	5 162 380	5 350 039	7 679 501	3 738 054	3 941 447	2 832 918	1 424 326	1 408 592
0	106 829	54 722	52 107	78 263	40 069	38 194	28 566	14 653	13 913
1 - 4	459 433	235 181	224 252	333 799	170 869	162 930	125 634	64 312	61 322
5 - 9	551 324	282 780	268 544	394 941	202 519	192 422	156 383	80 261	76 122
10 - 14	459 869	236 534	223 335	324 861	166 730	158 131	135 008	69 804	65 204
15 - 19	479 874	245 993	233 881	337 160	172 259	164 901	142 714	73 734	68 980
20 - 24	645 014	329 504	315 510	465 410	236 495	228 915	179 604	93 009	86 595
25 - 29	704 759	361 884	342 875	524 770	269 333	255 437	179 989	92 551	87 438
30 - 34	776 816	399 991	376 825	574 273	295 114	279 159	202 543	104 877	97 666
35 - 39	934 397	479 441	454 956	679 694	346 655	333 039	254 703	132 786	121 917
40 - 44	788 383	405 320	383 063	571 294	290 380	280 914	217 089	114 940	102 149
45 - 49	699 388	357 628	341 760	512 356	258 230	254 126	187 032	99 398	87 634
50 - 54	642 764	324 766	317 998	469 839	234 336	235 503	172 925	90 430	82 495
55 - 59	709 023	348 560	360 463	515 945	249 477	266 468	193 078	99 083	93 995
60 - 64	729 002	348 147	380 855	532 322	250 097	282 225	196 680	98 050	98 630
65 - 69	657 256	301 181	356 075	487 061	218 828	268 233	170 195	82 353	87 842
70 - 74	452 772	196 196	256 576	340 895	145 981	194 914	111 877	50 215	61 662
75 - 79	303 467	120 319	183 148	226 717	89 540	137 177	76 750	30 779	45 971
80 - 84	237 196	84 423	152 773	177 459	63 171	114 288	59 737	21 252	38 485
85 - 89	128 160	38 404	89 756	96 670	29 155	67 515	31 490	9 249	22 241
90 - 94	42 044	10 445	31 599	32 214	8 082	24 132	9 830	2 363	7 467
95 - 99	3 894	787	3 107	2 993	601	2 392	901	186	715
100 +	755	174	581	565	133	432	190	41	149
Denmark - Danemark[67]									
1 VII 2014 (ESDJ)									
Total	5 639 719	2 799 895	2 839 824	...	...	...	...	...	...
0	56 032	28 747	27 285	...	...	...	...	...	...
1 - 4	244 521	125 350	119 171	...	...	...	...	...	...
5 - 9	331 139	169 888	161 251	...	...	...	...	...	...
10 - 14	332 675	170 177	162 498	...	...	...	...	...	...
15 - 19	354 261	181 683	172 578	...	...	...	...	...	...
20 - 24	370 408	188 887	181 521	...	...	...	...	...	...
25 - 29	339 464	172 467	166 997	...	...	...	...	...	...
30 - 34	320 114	161 245	158 869	...	...	...	...	...	...
35 - 39	362 787	181 723	181 064	...	...	...	...	...	...
40 - 44	388 216	194 996	193 220	...	...	...	...	...	...
45 - 49	418 666	211 720	206 946	...	...	...	...	...	...
50 - 54	389 010	195 861	193 149	...	...	...	...	...	...
55 - 59	354 671	177 189	177 482	...	...	...	...	...	...
60 - 64	337 073	166 716	170 357	...	...	...	...	...	...
65 - 69	354 997	174 391	180 606	...	...	...	...	...	...
70 - 74	264 646	126 705	137 941	...	...	...	...	...	...
75 - 79	183 441	83 509	99 932	...	...	...	...	...	...
80 - 84	120 511	50 483	70 028	...	...	...	...	...	...
85 - 89	74 703	27 036	47 667	...	...	...	...	...	...
90 - 94	33 569	9 375	24 194	...	...	...	...	...	...
95 - 99	7 771	1 589	6 182	...	...	...	...	...	...
100 +	1 044	158	886	...	...	...	...	...	...

Continent, country or area, date, code[a] and age (in years) Continent, pays ou zone, date, code[a] et âge (en annèes)	Total			Urban - Urbaine			Rural - Rurale		
	Both sexes Les deux sexes	Male Masculin	Female Féminin	Both sexes Les deux sexes	Male Masculin	Female Féminin	Both sexes Les deux sexes	Male Masculin	Female Féminin
EUROPE									
Estonia - Estonie									
1 I 2014 (ESDJ)									
Total	1 315 819	614 919	700 900	898 476	407 836	490 640	417 343	207 083	210 260
0	13 581	6 922	6 659	9 272	4 737	4 535	4 309	2 185	2 124
1 - 4	60 092	30 854	29 238	39 801	20 354	19 447	20 291	10 500	9 791
5 - 9	73 072	37 680	35 392	47 650	24 425	23 225	25 422	13 255	12 167
10 - 14	61 283	31 460	29 823	39 115	20 061	19 054	22 168	11 399	10 769
15 - 19	61 311	31 459	29 852	38 335	19 459	18 876	22 976	12 000	10 976
20 - 24	85 651	44 345	41 306	60 029	29 810	30 219	25 622	14 535	11 087
25 - 29	97 499	50 299	47 200	73 338	37 034	36 304	24 161	13 265	10 896
30 - 34	91 694	47 114	44 580	65 506	33 320	32 186	26 188	13 794	12 394
35 - 39	90 268	46 040	44 228	61 611	30 892	30 719	28 657	15 148	13 509
40 - 44	91 851	46 267	45 584	60 956	29 864	31 092	30 895	16 403	14 492
45 - 49	84 690	41 553	43 137	55 742	26 397	29 345	28 948	15 156	13 792
50 - 54	91 948	43 966	47 982	61 948	28 338	33 610	30 000	15 628	14 372
55 - 59	88 964	40 624	48 340	60 896	26 335	34 561	28 068	14 289	13 779
60 - 64	82 132	35 311	46 821	57 020	23 229	33 791	25 112	12 082	13 030
65 - 69	64 621	26 084	38 537	43 756	16 763	26 993	20 865	9 321	11 544
70 - 74	60 720	22 243	38 477	41 112	14 241	26 871	19 608	8 002	11 606
75 - 79	52 273	16 775	35 498	36 824	11 416	25 408	15 449	5 359	10 090
80 - 84	36 746	10 251	26 495	26 021	7 076	18 945	10 725	3 175	7 550
85 - 89	20 230	4 478	15 752	14 588	3 236	11 352	5 642	1 242	4 400
90 - 94	6 040	1 027	5 013	4 193	723	3 470	1 847	304	1 543
95 - 99	1 013	155	858	667	116	551	346	39	307
100 +	140	12	128	96	10	86	44	2	42
Faeroe Islands - Îles Féroé									
1 I 2013 (ESDJ)									
Total	48 092	24 949	23 143	18 038	9 076	8 962	30 054	15 873	14 181
0	608	320	288	242	123	119	366	197	169
1 - 4	2 509	1 319	1 190	979	501	478	1 530	818	712
5 - 9	3 547	1 805	1 742	1 327	654	673	2 220	1 151	1 069
10 - 14	3 579	1 856	1 723	1 373	694	679	2 206	1 162	1 044
15 - 19	3 546	1 836	1 710	1 407	717	690	2 139	1 119	1 020
20 - 24	3 021	1 700	1 321	1 097	594	503	1 924	1 106	818
25 - 29	2 246	1 299	947	795	442	353	1 451	857	594
30 - 34	2 663	1 348	1 315	986	494	492	1 677	854	823
35 - 39	3 072	1 645	1 427	1 167	592	575	1 905	1 053	852
40 - 44	3 173	1 647	1 526	1 237	619	618	1 936	1 028	908
45 - 49	3 517	1 891	1 626	1 527	796	731	1 990	1 095	895
50 - 54	3 169	1 604	1 565	1 220	627	593	1 949	977	972
55 - 59	2 923	1 526	1 397	1 097	540	557	1 826	986	840
60 - 64	2 887	1 485	1 402	1 072	539	533	1 815	946	869
65 - 69	2 398	1 288	1 110	822	424	398	1 576	864	712
70 - 74	1 808	926	882	604	283	321	1 204	643	561
75 - 79	1 326	663	663	414	204	210	912	459	453
80 - 84	1 085	460	625	351	136	215	734	324	410
85 - 89	654	222	432	206	71	135	448	151	297
90 - 94	283	89	194	84	22	62	199	67	132
95 +	78	20	58	31	4	27	47	16	31
1 I 2014 (ESDJ)									
Total	48 228	24 937	23 291	...	...	...	...	...	...
0	629	325	304	...	...	...	...	...	...
1 - 4	2 487	1 290	1 197	...	...	...	...	...	...
5 - 9	3 540	1 801	1 739	...	...	...	...	...	...
10 - 14	3 579	1 839	1 740	...	...	...	...	...	...
15 - 19	3 523	1 854	1 669	...	...	...	...	...	...
20 - 24	2 948	1 648	1 300	...	...	...	...	...	...
25 - 29	2 356	1 292	1 064	...	...	...	...	...	...
30 - 34	2 616	1 368	1 248	...	...	...	...	...	...
35 - 39	2 985	1 562	1 423	...	...	...	...	...	...
40 - 44	3 121	1 621	1 500	...	...	...	...	...	...
45 - 49	3 501	1 876	1 625	...	...	...	...	...	...
50 - 54	3 208	1 648	1 560	...	...	...	...	...	...
55 - 59	2 965	1 535	1 430	...	...	...	...	...	...
60 - 64	2 890	1 483	1 407	...	...	...	...	...	...

Continent, country or area, date, code[a] and age (in years) Continent, pays ou zone, date, code[a] et âge (en années)	Total			Urban - Urbaine			Rural - Rurale		
	Both sexes Les deux sexes	Male Masculin	Female Féminin	Both sexes Les deux sexes	Male Masculin	Female Féminin	Both sexes Les deux sexes	Male Masculin	Female Féminin
EUROPE									
Faeroe Islands - Îles Féroé									
1 I 2014 (ESDJ)									
65 - 69	2 452	1 335	1 117	...	...	...	...	...	...
70 - 74	1 933	990	943	...	...	...	...	...	...
75 - 79	1 366	663	703	...	...	...	...	...	...
80 - 84	1 067	464	603	...	...	...	...	...	...
85 - 89	672	231	441	...	...	...	...	...	...
90 - 94	303	84	219	...	...	...	...	...	...
95 +	87	28	59	...	...	...	...	...	...
Finland - Finlande[19]									
1 VII 2013 (ESDJ)[68]									
Total	5 410 389	2 659 239	2 751 150	3 727 221	1 812 926	1 914 295	1 683 168	846 314	836 855
0	58 730	30 042	28 689	41 733	21 341	20 392	16 998	8 701	8 297
1 - 4	243 321	124 288	119 033	169 093	86 337	82 756	74 228	37 951	36 277
5 - 9	297 323	151 924	145 399	200 620	102 566	98 054	96 703	49 358	47 345
10 - 14	289 172	147 891	141 281	190 047	97 109	92 938	99 126	50 782	48 344
15 - 19	315 448	160 823	154 626	214 705	107 773	106 933	100 743	53 050	47 693
20 - 24	338 751	173 164	165 587	268 614	134 090	134 524	70 137	39 074	31 063
25 - 29	339 075	173 997	165 079	267 086	136 237	130 849	71 990	37 760	34 230
30 - 34	346 041	178 123	167 918	261 497	134 737	126 760	84 545	43 387	41 158
35 - 39	333 188	171 215	161 973	242 378	124 586	117 792	90 810	46 629	44 181
40 - 44	319 767	162 987	156 781	224 597	114 346	110 252	95 170	48 641	46 529
45 - 49	368 631	186 375	182 256	253 130	126 585	126 545	115 501	59 790	55 712
50 - 54	371 106	185 940	185 166	247 636	122 024	125 612	123 470	63 916	59 554
55 - 59	374 727	185 283	189 444	244 009	117 396	126 613	130 719	67 887	62 832
60 - 64	383 357	188 112	195 245	247 426	117 342	130 084	135 931	70 770	65 161
65 - 69	341 965	163 976	177 989	223 365	103 788	119 577	118 601	60 188	58 413
70 - 74	233 577	106 608	126 970	149 973	66 448	83 526	83 604	40 160	43 444
75 - 79	186 862	79 627	107 236	116 497	48 025	68 472	70 365	31 602	38 764
80 - 84	143 790	53 744	90 046	88 487	31 856	56 632	55 303	21 889	33 415
85 - 89	86 057	26 447	59 610	52 095	15 298	36 797	33 962	11 150	22 813
90 - 94	32 260	7 427	24 834	19 614	4 325	15 289	12 646	3 102	9 545
95 - 99	6 541	1 162	5 379	4 187	674	3 513	2 355	488	1 867
100 +	703	89	615	437	47	390	267	42	225
1 I 2014 (ESDJ)									
Total	5 451 270	2 680 364	2 770 906	...	...	...	...	...	...
0	58 409	29 982	28 427	...	...	...	...	...	...
1 - 4	244 597	124 919	119 678	...	...	...	...	...	...
5 - 9	300 873	153 815	147 058	...	...	...	...	...	...
10 - 14	291 142	148 863	142 279	...	...	...	...	...	...
15 - 19	313 546	159 903	153 643	...	...	...	...	...	...
20 - 24	340 871	174 276	166 595	...	...	...	...	...	...
25 - 29	339 934	174 367	165 567	...	...	...	...	...	...
30 - 34	350 780	180 608	170 172	...	...	...	...	...	...
35 - 39	340 126	174 775	165 351	...	...	...	...	...	...
40 - 44	315 840	161 204	154 636	...	...	...	...	...	...
45 - 49	368 266	186 147	182 119	...	...	...	...	...	...
50 - 54	374 932	187 930	187 002	...	...	...	...	...	...
55 - 59	374 239	184 987	189 252	...	...	...	...	...	...
60 - 64	381 168	186 942	194 226	...	...	...	...	...	...
65 - 69	356 236	170 935	185 301	...	...	...	...	...	...
70 - 74	235 915	107 976	127 939	...	...	...	...	...	...
75 - 79	191 561	81 987	109 574	...	...	...	...	...	...
80 - 84	143 760	54 199	89 561	...	...	...	...	...	...
85 - 89	88 085	27 473	60 612	...	...	...	...	...	...
90 - 94	33 563	7 773	25 790	...	...	...	...	...	...
95 - 99	6 721	1 214	5 507	...	...	...	...	...	...
100 +	706	89	617	...	...	...	...	...	...
France[69]									
1 I 2014* (ESDJ)									
Total	63 928 608	30 991 282	32 937 326	...	...	...	...	...	...
0	754 794	387 085	367 709	...	...	...	...	...	...
1 - 4	3 114 728	1 594 263	1 520 465	...	...	...	...	...	...
5 - 9	3 936 994	2 015 118	1 921 876	...	...	...	...	...	...
10 - 14	3 944 857	2 015 151	1 929 706	...	...	...	...	...	...

Continent, country or area, date, code[a] and age (in years) / Continent, pays ou zone, date, code[a] et âge (en années)	Total			Urban - Urbaine			Rural - Rurale		
	Both sexes Les deux sexes	Male Masculin	Female Féminin	Both sexes Les deux sexes	Male Masculin	Female Féminin	Both sexes Les deux sexes	Male Masculin	Female Féminin
EUROPE									
France[69]									
1 I 2014* (ESDJ)									
15 - 19	3 855 034	1 974 054	1 880 980	...	...	...	...	...	...
20 - 24	3 784 032	1 909 144	1 874 888	...	...	...	...	...	...
25 - 29	3 837 223	1 896 824	1 940 399	...	...	...	...	...	...
30 - 34	4 000 041	1 973 623	2 026 418	...	...	...	...	...	...
35 - 39	3 944 996	1 963 145	1 981 851	...	...	...	...	...	...
40 - 44	4 439 242	2 208 765	2 230 477	...	...	...	...	...	...
45 - 49	4 373 956	2 161 092	2 212 864	...	...	...	...	...	...
50 - 54	4 273 735	2 096 407	2 177 328	...	...	...	...	...	...
55 - 59	4 075 366	1 975 028	2 100 338	...	...	...	...	...	...
60 - 64	3 974 649	1 908 161	2 066 488	...	...	...	...	...	...
65 - 69	3 387 089	1 612 047	1 775 042	...	...	...	...	...	...
70 - 74	2 340 534	1 077 680	1 262 854	...	...	...	...	...	...
75 - 79	2 179 627	936 644	1 242 983	...	...	...	...	...	...
80 - 84	1 844 125	716 347	1 127 778	...	...	...	...	...	...
85 - 89	1 202 429	399 748	802 681	...	...	...	...	...	...
90 - 94	553 936	149 917	404 019	...	...	...	...	...	...
95 - 99	90 769	18 189	72 580	...	...	...	...	...	...
100 +	20 452	2 850	17 602	...	...	...	...	...	...
Germany - Allemagne									
9 V 2011 (CDJC)									
Total	80 219 695	39 145 941	41 073 754	64 444 232	31 227 832	33 216 400	15 775 463	7 918 109	7 857 354
0 - 4	3 338 895	1 714 872	1 624 023	2 712 601	1 393 763	1 318 838	626 294	321 109	305 185
5 - 9	3 525 830	1 809 024	1 716 806	2 798 622	1 435 745	1 362 877	727 208	373 279	353 929
10 - 14	3 940 566	2 021 305	1 919 261	3 074 610	1 575 684	1 498 926	865 956	445 621	420 335
15 - 19	4 013 880	2 057 155	1 956 725	3 144 832	1 606 068	1 538 764	869 048	451 087	417 961
20 - 24	4 835 639	2 463 932	2 371 707	3 993 247	2 003 582	1 989 665	842 392	460 350	382 042
25 - 29	4 872 533	2 455 885	2 416 648	4 113 697	2 057 507	2 056 190	758 836	398 378	360 458
30 - 34	4 751 911	2 385 305	2 366 606	3 942 747	1 977 628	1 965 119	809 164	407 677	401 487
35 - 39	4 742 893	2 378 055	2 364 838	3 833 417	1 920 448	1 912 969	909 476	457 607	451 869
40 - 44	6 351 189	3 209 481	3 141 708	5 029 918	2 540 433	2 489 485	1 321 271	669 048	652 223
45 - 49	6 999 679	3 547 254	3 452 425	5 488 622	2 771 239	2 717 383	1 511 057	776 015	735 042
50 - 54	6 206 294	3 113 463	3 092 831	4 845 747	2 413 038	2 432 709	1 360 547	700 425	660 122
55 - 59	5 419 450	2 668 976	2 750 474	4 252 008	2 066 178	2 185 830	1 167 442	602 798	564 644
60 - 64	4 702 815	2 298 903	2 403 912	3 753 504	1 808 314	1 945 190	949 311	490 589	458 722
65 - 69	4 173 351	1 999 287	2 174 064	3 423 376	1 624 839	1 798 537	749 975	374 448	375 527
70 - 74	4 861 239	2 247 196	2 614 043	3 931 373	1 801 914	2 129 459	929 866	445 282	484 584
75 - 79	3 270 283	1 413 881	1 856 402	2 633 648	1 128 379	1 505 269	636 635	285 502	351 133
80 - 84	2 328 083	878 797	1 449 286	1 890 025	704 565	1 185 460	438 058	174 232	263 826
85 - 89	1 335 076	369 029	966 047	1 108 944	302 059	806 885	226 132	66 970	159 162
90 - 94	430 600	95 074	335 526	368 116	79 884	288 232	62 484	15 190	47 294
95 - 99	106 044	17 388	88 656	93 152	15 094	78 058	12 892	2 294	10 598
100 +	13 445	1 679	11 766	12 026	1 471	10 555	1 419	208	1 211
1 I 2014 (ESDJ)									
Total	80 767 463	39 557 079	41 210 384	...	...	...	...	...	...
0	682 569	350 029	332 540	...	...	...	...	...	...
1 - 4	2 704 837	1 388 109	1 316 728	...	...	...	...	...	...
5 - 9	3 463 263	1 778 442	1 684 821	...	...	...	...	...	...
10 - 14	3 756 160	1 928 033	1 828 127	...	...	...	...	...	...
15 - 19	4 029 611	2 070 324	1 959 287	...	...	...	...	...	...
20 - 24	4 662 330	2 385 991	2 276 339	...	...	...	...	...	...
25 - 29	5 045 335	2 572 257	2 473 078	...	...	...	...	...	...
30 - 34	5 042 559	2 547 050	2 495 509	...	...	...	...	...	...
35 - 39	4 676 493	2 354 890	2 321 603	...	...	...	...	...	...
40 - 44	5 493 441	2 769 036	2 724 405	...	...	...	...	...	...
45 - 49	6 899 690	3 497 629	3 402 061	...	...	...	...	...	...
50 - 54	6 717 785	3 380 900	3 336 885	...	...	...	...	...	...
55 - 59	5 690 453	2 824 024	2 866 429	...	...	...	...	...	...
60 - 64	5 078 700	2 467 842	2 610 858	...	...	...	...	...	...
65 - 69	3 908 954	1 876 575	2 032 379	...	...	...	...	...	...
70 - 74	4 658 479	2 165 257	2 493 222	...	...	...	...	...	...
75 - 79	3 897 223	1 711 398	2 185 825	...	...	...	...	...	...
80 - 84	2 297 441	902 933	1 394 508	...	...	...	...	...	...
85 - 89	1 410 061	444 528	965 533	...	...	...	...	...	...

Continent, country or area, date, code[a] and age (in years) Continent, pays ou zone, date, code[a] et âge (en annèes)	Total			Urban - Urbaine			Rural - Rurale		
	Both sexes Les deux sexes	Male Masculin	Female Féminin	Both sexes Les deux sexes	Male Masculin	Female Féminin	Both sexes Les deux sexes	Male Masculin	Female Féminin
EUROPE									
Germany - Allemagne									
1 I 2014 (ESDJ)									
90 - 94	559 570	126 419	433 151	...	...	...	...	...	...
95 - 99	76 616	13 177	63 439	...	...	...	...	...	...
100 +	15 893	2 236	13 657	...	...	...	...	...	...
Gibraltar[70]									
12 XI 2012 (CDJC)									
Total	32 194	16 061	16 133	...	...	...	...	...	...
0 - 4	1 952	982	970	...	...	...	...	...	...
5 - 9	1 894	967	927	...	...	...	...	...	...
10 - 14	1 987	1 050	937	...	...	...	...	...	...
15 - 19	1 997	1 038	959	...	...	...	...	...	...
20 - 24	2 028	1 042	986	...	...	...	...	...	...
25 - 29	1 985	999	986	...	...	...	...	...	...
30 - 34	2 154	1 107	1 047	...	...	...	...	...	...
35 - 39	2 217	1 080	1 137	...	...	...	...	...	...
40 - 44	2 198	1 076	1 122	...	...	...	...	...	...
45 - 49	2 384	1 203	1 181	...	...	...	...	...	...
50 - 54	2 158	1 072	1 086	...	...	...	...	...	...
55 - 59	2 041	1 054	987	...	...	...	...	...	...
60 - 64	1 954	1 034	920	...	...	...	...	...	...
65 - 69	1 655	853	802	...	...	...	...	...	...
70 - 74	1 176	563	613	...	...	...	...	...	...
75 - 79	1 021	456	565	...	...	...	...	...	...
80 - 84	732	297	435	...	...	...	...	...	...
85 - 89	437	141	296	...	...	...	...	...	...
90 - 94	180	37	143	...	...	...	...	...	...
95 - 99	39	10	29	...	...	...	...	...	...
100 +	5	-	5	...	...	...	...	...	...
Greece - Grèce									
9 V 2011 (CDFC)									
Total	10 816 286	5 303 223	5 513 063	8 285 259	4 022 889	4 262 370	2 531 027	1 280 334	1 250 693
0 - 4	537 243	274 788	262 455	431 611	220 917	210 694	105 632	53 871	51 761
5 - 9	512 596	262 432	250 164	405 436	207 479	197 957	107 160	54 953	52 207
10 - 14	519 429	265 787	253 642	406 962	208 070	198 892	112 467	57 717	54 750
15 - 19	553 276	286 386	266 890	440 869	226 682	214 187	112 407	59 704	52 703
20 - 24	627 097	325 127	301 970	510 067	259 795	250 272	117 030	65 332	51 698
25 - 29	723 771	371 617	352 154	583 506	295 880	287 626	140 265	75 737	64 528
30 - 34	822 475	417 861	404 614	666 145	334 794	331 351	156 330	83 067	73 263
35 - 39	812 829	409 681	403 148	651 826	323 821	328 005	161 003	85 860	75 143
40 - 44	832 666	414 026	418 640	663 331	323 632	339 699	169 335	90 394	78 941
45 - 49	748 429	367 086	381 343	590 034	283 391	306 643	158 395	83 695	74 700
50 - 54	731 486	355 552	375 934	565 986	268 882	297 104	165 500	86 670	78 830
55 - 59	660 368	321 466	338 902	501 507	240 725	260 782	158 861	80 741	78 120
60 - 64	625 769	301 589	324 180	459 249	219 165	240 084	166 520	82 424	84 096
65 - 69	508 276	241 832	266 444	356 701	167 557	189 144	151 575	74 275	77 300
70 - 74	542 165	246 264	295 901	363 133	162 560	200 573	179 032	83 704	95 328
75 - 79	475 077	209 983	265 094	309 622	134 691	174 931	165 455	75 292	90 163
80 - 84	352 373	146 455	205 918	229 214	91 916	137 298	123 159	54 539	68 620
85 - 89	159 841	60 933	98 908	104 058	37 922	66 136	55 783	23 011	32 772
90 - 94	53 445	18 760	34 685	34 608	11 513	23 095	18 837	7 247	11 590
95 - 99	15 187	4 948	10 239	9 822	3 081	6 741	5 365	1 867	3 498
100 +	2 488	650	1 838	1 572	416	1 156	916	234	682
1 VII 2012 (ESDF)[71]									
Total	11 092 771	5 431 547	5 661 225	...	...	...	...	...	...
0	102 821	52 951	49 870	...	...	...	...	...	...
1 - 4	450 132	230 152	219 980	...	...	...	...	...	...
5 - 9	536 643	274 642	262 001	...	...	...	...	...	...
10 - 14	536 275	274 108	262 168	...	...	...	...	...	...
15 - 19	551 863	281 887	269 976	...	...	...	...	...	...
20 - 24	630 307	323 374	306 934	...	...	...	...	...	...
25 - 29	707 690	366 203	341 487	...	...	...	...	...	...
30 - 34	828 923	424 293	404 631	...	...	...	...	...	...
35 - 39	831 089	419 858	411 231	...	...	...	...	...	...
40 - 44	852 546	423 993	428 553	...	...	...	...	...	...

Continent, country or area, date, code[a] and age (in years) / Continent, pays ou zone, date, code[a] et âge (en années)	Total			Urban - Urbaine			Rural - Rurale		
	Both sexes Les deux sexes	Male Masculin	Female Féminin	Both sexes Les deux sexes	Male Masculin	Female Féminin	Both sexes Les deux sexes	Male Masculin	Female Féminin
EUROPE									
Greece - Grèce									
1 VII 2012 (ESDF)[71]									
45 - 49	786 496	386 014	400 483	...	...	...	...	...	...
50 - 54	747 208	360 934	386 274	...	...	...	...	...	...
55 - 59	682 382	329 174	353 209	...	...	...	...	...	...
60 - 64	639 744	305 485	334 259	...	...	...	...	...	...
65 - 69	570 164	270 102	300 063	...	...	...	...	...	...
70 - 74	525 827	241 078	284 749	...	...	...	...	...	...
75 - 79	495 333	217 269	278 064	...	...	...	...	...	...
80 - 84	360 031	152 585	207 447	...	...	...	...	...	...
85 - 89	180 505	69 875	110 630	...	...	...	...	...	...
90 - 94	58 098	21 475	36 624	...	...	...	...	...	...
95 - 99	15 325	5 044	10 281	...	...	...	...	...	...
100 +	3 372	1 054	2 318	...	...	...	...	...	...
Guernsey - Guernesey									
31 III 2014 (ESDF)									
Total	62 711	30 994	31 717	...	...	...	...	...	...
0 - 4	3 253	1 667	1 586	...	...	...	...	...	...
5 - 9	3 134	1 654	1 480	...	...	...	...	...	...
10 - 14	3 131	1 586	1 545	...	...	...	...	...	...
15 - 19	3 454	1 772	1 682	...	...	...	...	...	...
20 - 24	4 103	2 085	2 018	...	...	...	...	...	...
25 - 29	3 948	2 022	1 926	...	...	...	...	...	...
30 - 34	3 953	2 017	1 936	...	...	...	...	...	...
35 - 39	3 757	1 858	1 899	...	...	...	...	...	...
40 - 44	4 642	2 310	2 332	...	...	...	...	...	...
45 - 49	4 963	2 418	2 545	...	...	...	...	...	...
50 - 54	4 849	2 390	2 459	...	...	...	...	...	...
55 - 59	4 213	2 154	2 059	...	...	...	...	...	...
60 - 64	3 827	1 883	1 944	...	...	...	...	...	...
65 - 69	3 639	1 787	1 852	...	...	...	...	...	...
70 - 74	2 416	1 170	1 246	...	...	...	...	...	...
75 - 79	2 211	1 040	1 171	...	...	...	...	...	...
80 - 84	1 598	659	939	...	...	...	...	...	...
85 - 89	1 026	354	672	...	...	...	...	...	...
90 - 94	480	146	334	...	...	...	...	...	...
95 +	114	22	92	...	...	...	...	...	...
Hungary - Hongrie									
1 VII 2013* (ESDJ)									
Total	9 893 082	4 709 672	5 183 410	6 864 757	3 229 480	3 635 277	3 028 325	1 480 192	1 548 133
0	89 178	45 950	43 229	62 273	32 156	30 118	26 905	13 794	13 111
1 - 4	370 067	189 855	180 212	259 233	132 913	126 321	110 834	56 942	53 892
5 - 9	488 099	250 560	237 539	331 012	169 920	161 092	157 087	80 640	76 447
10 - 14	480 998	247 080	233 918	314 242	161 142	153 100	166 756	85 939	80 818
15 - 19	555 877	285 243	270 634	374 237	190 727	183 511	181 640	94 517	87 124
20 - 24	628 710	323 010	305 700	427 686	218 010	209 677	201 024	105 000	96 024
25 - 29	609 964	311 954	298 010	429 173	216 318	212 855	180 791	95 636	85 155
30 - 34	697 824	352 922	344 903	504 039	251 251	252 788	193 786	101 671	92 115
35 - 39	851 186	431 214	419 972	611 076	305 799	305 278	240 110	125 416	114 694
40 - 44	723 465	364 755	358 710	504 114	250 989	253 126	219 351	113 767	105 584
45 - 49	638 349	317 543	320 806	434 161	212 233	221 928	204 188	105 310	98 879
50 - 54	613 510	296 286	317 224	410 280	193 192	217 089	203 230	103 095	100 136
55 - 59	757 934	354 570	403 364	521 452	236 922	284 530	236 482	117 649	118 834
60 - 64	671 182	301 154	370 028	470 438	206 300	264 139	200 744	94 854	105 890
65 - 69	536 772	229 384	307 388	384 666	162 429	222 237	152 106	66 956	85 151
70 - 74	442 105	173 413	268 693	310 771	122 473	188 298	131 334	50 940	80 395
75 - 79	329 068	114 342	214 727	227 557	80 274	147 284	101 511	34 068	67 443
80 - 84	236 602	75 042	161 561	164 946	53 568	111 378	71 657	21 474	50 183
85 - 89	122 561	33 230	89 331	87 015	23 899	63 116	35 546	9 331	26 215
90 - 94	43 105	10 495	32 610	31 409	7 686	23 723	11 697	2 809	8 888
95 - 99	5 258	1 233	4 025	4 003	964	3 039	1 255	269	987
100 +	1 274	442	832	978	322	656	296	120	176

Continent, country or area, date, code[a] and age (in years) / Continent, pays ou zone, date, code[a] et âge (en années)	Total			Urban - Urbaine			Rural - Rurale		
	Both sexes Les deux sexes	Male Masculin	Female Féminin	Both sexes Les deux sexes	Male Masculin	Female Féminin	Both sexes Les deux sexes	Male Masculin	Female Féminin
EUROPE									
Iceland - Islande[72]									
1 VII 2013 (ESDJ)									
Total	323 764	162 378	161 386	303 136	151 471	151 665	20 629	10 907	9 722
0	4 436	2 228	2 209	4 227	2 129	2 098	209	99	111
1 - 4	18 876	9 692	9 185	18 023	9 249	8 775	853	443	410
5 - 9	22 156	11 371	10 785	20 961	10 744	10 217	1 195	628	568
10 - 14	21 170	10 680	10 490	19 867	10 003	9 865	1 303	678	626
15 - 19	22 624	11 604	11 020	21 087	10 834	10 254	1 537	771	767
20 - 24	24 561	12 611	11 950	22 893	11 713	11 180	1 668	898	770
25 - 29	22 506	11 396	11 110	21 327	10 760	10 568	1 179	637	542
30 - 34	23 257	11 922	11 335	22 194	11 380	10 815	1 063	542	521
35 - 39	21 238	10 739	10 499	20 193	10 203	9 991	1 045	537	509
40 - 44	20 786	10 470	10 316	19 590	9 856	9 734	1 196	614	582
45 - 49	21 523	10 591	10 933	20 070	9 840	10 231	1 453	751	702
50 - 54	21 512	10 736	10 776	19 865	9 856	10 009	1 647	880	768
55 - 59	19 857	9 991	9 866	18 320	9 141	9 179	1 537	850	687
60 - 64	16 905	8 562	8 344	15 572	7 841	7 731	1 333	721	613
65 - 69	13 535	6 848	6 687	12 407	6 212	6 196	1 128	637	492
70 - 74	9 508	4 573	4 935	8 718	4 139	4 579	790	434	356
75 - 79	7 586	3 546	4 040	6 967	3 208	3 759	619	339	281
80 - 84	6 266	2 786	3 480	5 771	2 515	3 257	495	272	224
85 - 89	3 698	1 462	2 236	3 449	1 336	2 113	249	127	123
90 - 94	1 441	484	957	1 339	434	905	102	50	53
95 - 99	289	84	205	262	79	183	28	5	23
100 +	39	6	33	37	6	32	2	1	1
Ireland - Irlande									
10 IV 2011 (CDFC)[73]									
Total	4 588 252	2 272 699	2 315 553	2 846 882	1 389 160	1 457 722	1 741 370	883 539	857 831
0 - 4	356 329	182 076	174 253	224 004	114 284	109 720	132 325	67 792	64 533
5 - 9	320 770	164 037	156 733	188 818	96 160	92 658	131 952	67 877	64 075
10 - 14	302 491	155 076	147 415	172 930	88 433	84 497	129 561	66 643	62 918
15 - 19	283 019	144 262	138 757	170 523	86 129	84 394	112 496	58 133	54 363
20 - 24	297 231	146 636	150 595	208 146	100 226	107 920	89 085	46 410	42 675
25 - 29	361 122	173 714	187 408	266 457	126 362	140 095	94 665	47 352	47 313
30 - 34	393 945	194 774	199 171	278 935	137 689	141 246	115 010	57 085	57 925
35 - 39	364 261	182 237	182 024	233 417	116 912	116 505	130 844	65 325	65 519
40 - 44	330 812	166 330	164 482	198 432	99 162	99 270	132 380	67 168	65 212
45 - 49	305 185	151 516	153 669	178 630	87 087	91 543	126 555	64 429	62 126
50 - 54	274 386	136 737	137 649	158 031	77 106	80 925	116 355	59 631	56 724
55 - 59	244 522	122 121	122 401	137 973	66 919	71 054	106 549	55 202	51 347
60 - 64	218 786	109 869	108 917	122 606	59 521	63 085	96 180	50 348	45 832
65 - 69	173 638	86 298	87 340	97 999	46 741	51 258	75 639	39 557	36 082
70 - 74	131 190	63 476	67 714	76 683	35 378	41 305	54 507	28 098	26 409
75 - 79	102 036	46 631	55 405	59 519	25 708	33 811	42 517	20 923	21 594
80 - 84	70 113	28 423	41 690	40 585	15 449	25 136	29 528	12 974	16 554
85 - 89	39 887	13 591	26 296	22 742	7 303	15 439	17 145	6 288	10 857
90 - 94	14 877	4 155	10 722	8 363	2 200	6 163	6 514	1 955	4 559
95 - 99	3 263	682	2 581	1 884	360	1 524	1 379	322	1 057
100 +	389	58	331	205	31	174	184	27	157
15 IV 2013 (ESDJ)									
Total	4 593 125	2 273 846	2 319 279	...	...	...	...	...	...
0	71 201	36 394	34 807	...	...	...	...	...	...
1 - 4	294 546	149 922	144 624	...	...	...	...	...	...
5 - 9	333 083	169 866	163 217	...	...	...	...	...	...
10 - 14	308 853	157 737	151 116	...	...	...	...	...	...
15 - 19	274 539	141 315	133 224	...	...	...	...	...	...
20 - 24	258 766	131 863	126 903	...	...	...	...	...	...
25 - 29	319 966	154 101	165 865	...	...	...	...	...	...
30 - 34	387 466	187 070	200 396	...	...	...	...	...	...
35 - 39	363 818	180 418	183 400	...	...	...	...	...	...
40 - 44	342 791	171 649	171 142	...	...	...	...	...	...
45 - 49	312 123	155 548	156 575	...	...	...	...	...	...
50 - 54	283 081	140 550	142 531	...	...	...	...	...	...
55 - 59	251 148	124 836	126 312	...	...	...	...	...	...
60 - 64	223 641	111 307	112 334	...	...	...	...	...	...

Continent, country or area, date, code[a] and age (in years) Continent, pays ou zone, date, code[a] et âge (en années)	Total			Urban - Urbaine			Rural - Rurale		
	Both sexes Les deux sexes	Male Masculin	Female Féminin	Both sexes Les deux sexes	Male Masculin	Female Féminin	Both sexes Les deux sexes	Male Masculin	Female Féminin
EUROPE									
Ireland - Irlande									
15 IV 2013 (ESDJ)									
65 - 69	189 433	94 559	94 874	...	...	...	...	...	...
70 - 74	138 156	67 173	70 983	...	...	...	...	...	...
75 - 79	105 829	48 789	57 040	...	...	...	...	...	...
80 - 84	72 619	30 632	41 987	...	...	...	...	...	...
85 - 89	41 087	14 365	26 722	...	...	...	...	...	...
90 - 94	16 790	4 822	11 968	...	...	...	...	...	...
95 +	4 189	930	3 259	...	...	...	...	...	...
Isle of Man - Île de Man									
27 III 2011 (CDJC)									
Total	84 497	41 971	42 526	...	...	...	...	...	...
0 - 4	4 634	2 386	2 248	...	...	...	...	...	...
5 - 9	4 517	2 373	2 144	...	...	...	...	...	...
10 - 14	4 885	2 543	2 342	...	...	...	...	...	...
15 - 19	5 108	2 627	2 481	...	...	...	...	...	...
20 - 24	4 719	2 441	2 278	...	...	...	...	...	...
25 - 29	4 569	2 228	2 341	...	...	...	...	...	...
30 - 34	4 935	2 423	2 512	...	...	...	...	...	...
35 - 39	5 675	2 754	2 921	...	...	...	...	...	...
40 - 44	6 517	3 297	3 220	...	...	...	...	...	...
45 - 49	6 748	3 430	3 318	...	...	...	...	...	...
50 - 54	6 055	3 017	3 038	...	...	...	...	...	...
55 - 59	5 335	2 707	2 628	...	...	...	...	...	...
60 - 64	5 814	2 953	2 861	...	...	...	...	...	...
65 - 69	4 512	2 239	2 273	...	...	...	...	...	...
70 - 74	3 581	1 748	1 833	...	...	...	...	...	...
75 - 79	2 723	1 280	1 443	...	...	...	...	...	...
80 - 84	2 122	850	1 272	...	...	...	...	...	...
85 +	2 048	675	1 373	...	...	...	...	...	...
Italy - Italie									
1 VII 2013 (ESDJ)									
Total	60 233 948	29 187 081	31 046 867	...	...	...	...	...	...
0	516 537	265 453	251 085	...	...	...	...	...	...
1 - 4	2 214 087	1 138 014	1 076 073	...	...	...	...	...	...
5 - 9	2 840 402	1 461 214	1 379 188	...	...	...	...	...	...
10 - 14	2 827 211	1 454 355	1 372 856	...	...	...	...	...	...
15 - 19	2 843 494	1 466 169	1 377 325	...	...	...	...	...	...
20 - 24	3 100 775	1 585 749	1 515 026	...	...	...	...	...	...
25 - 29	3 277 373	1 651 658	1 625 715	...	...	...	...	...	...
30 - 34	3 692 727	1 849 162	1 843 565	...	...	...	...	...	...
35 - 39	4 450 917	2 223 945	2 226 972	...	...	...	...	...	...
40 - 44	4 824 441	2 400 965	2 423 476	...	...	...	...	...	...
45 - 49	4 920 788	2 436 721	2 484 067	...	...	...	...	...	...
50 - 54	4 383 390	2 145 440	2 237 950	...	...	...	...	...	...
55 - 59	3 875 306	1 879 051	1 996 255	...	...	...	...	...	...
60 - 64	3 639 118	1 753 485	1 885 633	...	...	...	...	...	...
65 - 69	3 357 271	1 598 426	1 758 845	...	...	...	...	...	...
70 - 74	3 055 735	1 406 019	1 649 716	...	...	...	...	...	...
75 - 79	2 597 219	1 129 831	1 467 388	...	...	...	...	...	...
80 - 84	1 990 660	780 087	1 210 573	...	...	...	...	...	...
85 - 89	1 220 384	404 279	816 105	...	...	...	...	...	...
90 - 94	492 604	133 628	358 977	...	...	...	...	...	...
95 - 99	96 377	20 559	75 819	...	...	...	...	...	...
100 +	17 137	2 876	14 261	...	...	...	...	...	...
Jersey									
27 III 2011 (CDFC)									
Total	97 857	48 296	49 561	...	...	...	...	...	...
0 - 4	5 015	2 466	2 549	...	...	...	...	...	...
5 - 9	4 852	2 470	2 382	...	...	...	...	...	...
10 - 14	5 302	2 729	2 573	...	...	...	...	...	...
15 - 19	5 495	2 863	2 632	...	...	...	...	...	...
20 - 24	5 944	3 006	2 938	...	...	...	...	...	...
25 - 29	6 705	3 351	3 354	...	...	...	...	...	...
30 - 34	7 236	3 670	3 566	...	...	...	...	...	...

7. Population by age, sex and urban/rural residence: latest available year, 2005 - 2014
Population selon l'âge, le sexe et la résidence, urbaine/rurale : dernière année disponible, 2005 - 2014 (continued - suite)

Continent, country or area, date, code[a] and age (in years) / Continent, pays ou zone, date, code[a] et âge (en annèes)	Total			Urban - Urbaine			Rural - Rurale		
	Both sexes Les deux sexes	Male Masculin	Female Féminin	Both sexes Les deux sexes	Male Masculin	Female Féminin	Both sexes Les deux sexes	Male Masculin	Female Féminin
EUROPE									
Jersey									
27 III 2011 (CDFC)									
35 - 39	7 225	3 615	3 610	...	...	...	...	...	...
40 - 44	8 363	4 183	4 180	...	...	...	...	...	...
45 - 49	8 357	4 187	4 170	...	...	...	...	...	...
50 - 54	7 198	3 536	3 662	...	...	...	...	...	...
55 - 59	6 042	2 955	3 087	...	...	...	...	...	...
60 - 64	5 650	2 832	2 818	...	...	...	...	...	...
65 - 69	4 048	1 938	2 110	...	...	...	...	...	...
70 - 74	3 632	1 732	1 900	...	...	...	...	...	...
75 - 79	2 893	1 343	1 550	...	...	...	...	...	...
80 - 84	2 005	822	1 183	...	...	...	...	...	...
85 - 89	1 225	446	779	...	...	...	...	...	...
90 - 94	483	115	368	...	...	...	...	...	...
95 +	187	37	150	...	...	...	...	...	...
Latvia - Lettonie									
1 VII 2013 (ESDJ)									
Total	2 012 647	921 813	1 090 834	1 362 004	606 624	755 380	650 643	315 189	335 454
0	20 063	10 287	9 776	13 779	7 107	6 672	6 284	3 180	3 104
1 - 4	80 120	41 216	38 904	54 901	28 300	26 601	25 219	12 916	12 303
5 - 9	102 485	52 512	49 973	68 569	35 084	33 485	33 916	17 428	16 488
10 - 14	90 682	46 355	44 327	58 101	29 528	28 573	32 581	16 827	15 754
15 - 19	95 734	49 259	46 475	58 700	30 041	28 659	37 034	19 218	17 816
20 - 24	138 919	71 439	67 480	88 580	44 491	44 089	50 339	26 948	23 391
25 - 29	148 194	75 864	72 330	103 545	51 512	52 033	44 649	24 352	20 297
30 - 34	133 225	67 633	65 592	94 640	47 005	47 635	38 585	20 628	17 957
35 - 39	133 714	66 492	67 222	92 897	45 197	47 700	40 817	21 295	19 522
40 - 44	139 351	68 016	71 335	94 134	44 683	49 451	45 217	23 333	21 884
45 - 49	137 671	65 924	71 747	91 158	42 016	49 142	46 513	23 908	22 605
50 - 54	151 495	70 412	81 083	101 107	44 819	56 288	50 388	25 593	24 795
55 - 59	137 583	61 586	75 997	94 385	40 183	54 202	43 198	21 403	21 795
60 - 64	122 711	51 315	71 396	85 445	33 851	51 594	37 266	17 464	19 802
65 - 69	98 532	38 239	60 293	67 951	25 290	42 661	30 581	12 949	17 632
70 - 74	105 929	37 234	68 695	71 694	24 394	47 300	34 235	12 840	21 395
75 - 79	81 268	25 319	55 949	55 775	17 048	38 727	25 493	8 271	17 222
80 - 84	56 157	15 159	40 998	39 030	10 537	28 493	17 127	4 622	12 505
85 - 89	29 476	5 972	23 504	21 085	4 421	16 664	8 391	1 551	6 840
90 - 94	8 007	1 359	6 648	5 629	960	4 669	2 378	399	1 979
95 - 99	1 165	202	963	787	144	643	378	58	320
100 +	166	19	147	112	13	99	54	6	48
Liechtenstein									
1 VII 2013* (ESDJ)									
Total	36 947	18 316	18 631	...	...	...	...	...	...
0	362	199	163	...	...	...	...	...	...
1 - 4	1 493	796	697	...	...	...	...	...	...
5 - 9	1 864	950	914	...	...	...	...	...	...
10 - 14	1 941	978	963	...	...	...	...	...	...
15 - 19	2 189	1 106	1 083	...	...	...	...	...	...
20 - 24	2 250	1 160	1 090	...	...	...	...	...	...
25 - 29	2 240	1 116	1 124	...	...	...	...	...	...
30 - 34	2 338	1 194	1 144	...	...	...	...	...	...
35 - 39	2 494	1 250	1 244	...	...	...	...	...	...
40 - 44	2 988	1 504	1 484	...	...	...	...	...	...
45 - 49	3 204	1 556	1 648	...	...	...	...	...	...
50 - 54	3 013	1 500	1 513	...	...	...	...	...	...
55 - 59	2 647	1 320	1 327	...	...	...	...	...	...
60 - 64	2 311	1 160	1 151	...	...	...	...	...	...
65 - 69	1 991	998	993	...	...	...	...	...	...
70 - 74	1 462	702	760	...	...	...	...	...	...
75 - 79	960	412	548	...	...	...	...	...	...
80 - 84	620	247	373	...	...	...	...	...	...
85 - 89	391	113	278	...	...	...	...	...	...
90 - 94	159	43	116	...	...	...	...	...	...
95 - 99	25	10	15	...	...	...	...	...	...
100 +	5	2	3	...	...	...	...	...	...

7. Population by age, sex and urban/rural residence: latest available year, 2005 - 2014
Population selon l'âge, le sexe et la résidence, urbaine/rurale : dernière année disponible, 2005 - 2014 (continued - suite)

Continent, country or area, date, code[a] and age (in years) / Continent, pays ou zone, date, code[a] et âge (en annèes)	Total			Urban - Urbaine			Rural - Rurale		
	Both sexes Les deux sexes	Male Masculin	Female Féminin	Both sexes Les deux sexes	Male Masculin	Female Féminin	Both sexes Les deux sexes	Male Masculin	Female Féminin
EUROPE									
Lithuania - Lituanie									
1 VII 2013 (ESDJ)									
Total	2 957 689	1 362 443	1 595 246	1 981 924	888 578	1 093 346	975 765	473 865	501 900
0	30 162	15 378	14 784	20 837	10 622	10 215	9 325	4 756	4 569
1 - 4	120 900	62 072	58 828	85 478	43 825	41 653	35 422	18 247	17 175
5 - 9	134 978	69 004	65 974	90 149	46 194	43 955	44 829	22 810	22 019
10 - 14	147 293	75 796	71 497	92 220	47 212	45 008	55 073	28 584	26 489
15 - 19	182 450	93 604	88 846	113 899	58 261	55 638	68 551	35 343	33 208
20 - 24	213 969	110 043	103 926	140 408	69 754	70 654	73 561	40 289	33 272
25 - 29	194 552	99 495	95 057	141 096	69 237	71 859	53 456	30 258	23 198
30 - 34	175 902	88 515	87 387	127 817	62 668	65 149	48 085	25 847	22 238
35 - 39	186 569	91 233	95 336	129 097	61 620	67 477	57 472	29 613	27 859
40 - 44	209 529	101 097	108 432	138 789	64 946	73 843	70 740	36 151	34 589
45 - 49	214 707	102 448	112 259	139 765	63 535	76 230	74 942	38 913	36 029
50 - 54	236 526	110 413	126 113	158 579	70 162	88 417	77 947	40 251	37 696
55 - 59	196 253	88 386	107 867	133 636	57 108	76 528	62 617	31 278	31 339
60 - 64	171 431	72 515	98 916	116 603	46 583	70 020	54 828	25 932	28 896
65 - 69	136 915	53 668	83 247	91 771	34 339	57 432	45 144	19 329	25 815
70 - 74	141 332	51 266	90 066	92 665	32 841	59 824	48 667	18 425	30 242
75 - 79	119 539	39 045	80 494	76 837	24 734	52 103	42 702	14 311	28 391
80 - 84	85 851	25 056	60 795	54 416	16 196	38 220	31 435	8 860	22 575
85 - 89	43 989	10 387	33 602	28 264	6 782	21 482	15 725	3 605	12 120
90 - 94	12 596	2 535	10 061	8 088	1 637	6 451	4 508	898	3 610
95 - 99	1 872	398	1 474	1 243	264	979	629	134	495
100 +	374	89	285	267	58	209	107	31	76
Luxembourg									
1 I 2014 (ESDJ)									
Total	549 680	275 117	274 563	...	...	...	...	...	...
0	6 114	3 129	2 985	...	...	...	...	...	...
1 - 4	24 960	12 829	12 131	...	...	...	...	...	...
5 - 9	30 394	15 578	14 816	...	...	...	...	...	...
10 - 14	31 086	15 961	15 125	...	...	...	...	...	...
15 - 19	32 451	16 635	15 816	...	...	...	...	...	...
20 - 24	33 715	17 325	16 390	...	...	...	...	...	...
25 - 29	38 940	19 769	19 171	...	...	...	...	...	...
30 - 34	42 118	21 016	21 102	...	...	...	...	...	...
35 - 39	41 945	21 056	20 889	...	...	...	...	...	...
40 - 44	43 324	22 148	21 176	...	...	...	...	...	...
45 - 49	44 711	23 219	21 492	...	...	...	...	...	...
50 - 54	40 512	20 887	19 625	...	...	...	...	...	...
55 - 59	34 130	17 419	16 711	...	...	...	...	...	...
60 - 64	27 906	14 167	13 739	...	...	...	...	...	...
65 - 69	22 449	11 153	11 296	...	...	...	...	...	...
70 - 74	18 303	8 546	9 757	...	...	...	...	...	...
75 - 79	14 935	6 517	8 418	...	...	...	...	...	...
80 - 84	12 037	4 872	7 165	...	...	...	...	...	...
85 - 89	6 778	2 203	4 575	...	...	...	...	...	...
90 - 94	2 393	591	1 802	...	...	...	...	...	...
95 - 99	417	84	333	...	...	...	...	...	...
100 +	62	13	49	...	...	...	...	...	...
Unknown - Inconnu	-	-	-	...	...	...	...	...	...
Malta - Malte									
20 XI 2011 (CDFC)									
Total	417 432	207 625	209 807	400 557	199 151	201 406	16 875	8 474	8 401
0 - 4	20 061	10 347	9 714	19 247	9 926	9 321	814	421	393
5 - 9	19 419	9 971	9 448	18 602	9 562	9 040	817	409	408
10 - 14	22 248	11 355	10 893	21 218	10 854	10 364	1 030	501	529
15 - 19	26 182	13 509	12 673	25 026	12 907	12 119	1 156	602	554
20 - 24	29 450	15 062	14 388	28 269	14 475	13 794	1 181	587	594
25 - 29	30 320	15 722	14 598	29 154	15 110	14 044	1 166	612	554
30 - 34	30 194	15 641	14 553	29 141	15 074	14 067	1 053	567	486
35 - 39	28 799	14 757	14 042	27 712	14 202	13 510	1 087	555	532
40 - 44	25 236	12 840	12 396	24 151	12 293	11 858	1 085	547	538
45 - 49	26 895	13 574	13 321	25 716	12 972	12 744	1 179	602	577
50 - 54	30 596	15 292	15 304	29 293	14 628	14 665	1 303	664	639

7. Population by age, sex and urban/rural residence: latest available year, 2005 - 2014
Population selon l'âge, le sexe et la résidence, urbaine/rurale : dernière année disponible, 2005 - 2014 (continued - suite)

Continent, country or area, date, code[a] and age (in years) / Continent, pays ou zone, date, code[a] et âge (en annèes)	Total			Urban - Urbaine			Rural - Rurale		
	Both sexes Les deux sexes	Male Masculin	Female Féminin	Both sexes Les deux sexes	Male Masculin	Female Féminin	Both sexes Les deux sexes	Male Masculin	Female Féminin
EUROPE									
Malta - Malte									
20 XI 2011 (CDFC)									
55 - 59	29 246	14 655	14 591	28 127	14 052	14 075	1 119	603	516
60 - 64	30 595	15 130	15 465	29 452	14 551	14 901	1 143	579	564
65 - 69	23 728	11 429	12 299	22 791	10 986	11 805	937	443	494
70 - 74	16 205	7 389	8 816	15 572	7 106	8 466	633	283	350
75 - 79	13 287	5 579	7 708	12 749	5 332	7 417	538	247	291
80 - 84	8 494	3 181	5 313	8 121	3 036	5 085	373	145	228
85 - 89	4 567	1 622	2 945	4 371	1 546	2 825	196	76	120
90 - 94	1 583	480	1 103	1 532	455	1 077	51	25	26
95 - 99	296	82	214	284	77	207	12	5	7
100 +	31	8	23	29	7	22	2	1	1
1 VII 2013 (ESDJ)[74]									
Total	423 431	211 182	212 249	...	...	...	...	...	...
0	4 118	2 146	1 972	...	...	...	...	...	...
1 - 4	16 585	8 499	8 086	...	...	...	...	...	...
5 - 9	19 551	10 125	9 426	...	...	...	...	...	...
10 - 14	21 018	10 679	10 339	...	...	...	...	...	...
15 - 19	25 209	13 099	12 110	...	...	...	...	...	...
20 - 24	30 144	15 556	14 588	...	...	...	...	...	...
25 - 29	30 641	16 019	14 622	...	...	...	...	...	...
30 - 34	31 064	16 029	15 035	...	...	...	...	...	...
35 - 39	29 843	15 434	14 409	...	...	...	...	...	...
40 - 44	26 123	13 348	12 775	...	...	...	...	...	...
45 - 49	25 669	12 942	12 727	...	...	...	...	...	...
50 - 54	29 924	14 981	14 943	...	...	...	...	...	...
55 - 59	29 968	15 061	14 907	...	...	...	...	...	...
60 - 64	29 400	14 575	14 825	...	...	...	...	...	...
65 - 69	28 501	13 767	14 734	...	...	...	...	...	...
70 - 74	15 608	7 171	8 437	...	...	...	...	...	...
75 - 79	13 996	6 032	7 964	...	...	...	...	...	...
80 - 84	9 114	3 397	5 717	...	...	...	...	...	...
85 - 89	4 901	1 723	3 178	...	...	...	...	...	...
90 - 94	1 691	511	1 180	...	...	...	...	...	...
95 - 99	315	73	242	...	...	...	...	...	...
100 +	48	15	33	...	...	...	...	...	...
Unknown - Inconnu	-	-	-	...	...	...	...	...	...
Monaco									
9 VI 2008 (CDJC)									
Total	31 109[75]	15 076	15 914	...	...	...	...	...	...
0 - 4	1 134	577	557	...	...	...	...	...	...
5 - 9	1 430	706	724	...	...	...	...	...	...
10 - 14	1 401	727	674	...	...	...	...	...	...
15 - 19	1 398	724	674	...	...	...	...	...	...
20 - 24	1 248	647	601	...	...	...	...	...	...
25 - 29	1 305	638	667	...	...	...	...	...	...
30 - 34	1 514	751	766	...	...	...	...	...	...
35 - 39	2 122	1 003	1 119	...	...	...	...	...	...
40 - 44	2 342	1 163	1 179	...	...	...	...	...	...
45 - 64	2 359	1 194	1 165	...	...	...	...	...	...
50 - 54	2 218	1 128	1 090	...	...	...	...	...	...
55 - 59	2 217	1 120	1 097	...	...	...	...	...	...
60 - 64	2 337	1 134	1 203	...	...	...	...	...	...
65 - 69	1 960	945	1 015	...	...	...	...	...	...
70 - 74	1 648	801	847	...	...	...	...	...	...
75 +	3 758	1 530	2 228	...	...	...	...	...	...
Unknown - Inconnu	715[75]	288	308	...	...	...	...	...	...
Montenegro - Monténégro									
1 IV 2011 (CDJC)									
Total	620 029	306 236	313 793	399 264	193 691	205 573	220 765	112 545	108 220
0 - 4	38 950	20 361	18 589	25 277	13 247	12 030	13 673	7 114	6 559
5 - 9	38 430	20 016	18 414	24 781	12 973	11 808	13 649	7 043	6 606
10 - 14	41 371	21 389	19 982	26 526	13 698	12 828	14 845	7 691	7 154
15 - 19	44 093	22 815	21 278	28 376	14 654	13 722	15 717	8 161	7 556
20 - 24	42 816	22 084	20 732	28 218	14 347	13 871	14 598	7 737	6 861

Continent, country or area, date, code[a] and age (in years) / Continent, pays ou zone, date, code[a] et âge (en années)	Total			Urban - Urbaine			Rural - Rurale		
	Both sexes Les deux sexes	Male Masculin	Female Féminin	Both sexes Les deux sexes	Male Masculin	Female Féminin	Both sexes Les deux sexes	Male Masculin	Female Féminin
EUROPE									
Montenegro - Monténégro									
1 IV 2011 (CDJC)									
25 - 29	45 793	23 299	22 494	31 083	15 290	15 793	14 710	8 009	6 701
30 - 34	44 495	22 188	22 307	30 133	14 495	15 638	14 362	7 693	6 669
35 - 39	41 879	20 523	21 356	27 869	13 311	14 558	14 010	7 212	6 798
40 - 44	40 496	20 136	20 360	26 265	12 539	13 726	14 231	7 597	6 634
45 - 49	43 089	21 401	21 688	28 332	13 444	14 888	14 757	7 957	6 800
50 - 54	43 613	21 817	21 796	28 705	13 851	14 854	14 908	7 966	6 942
55 - 59	41 223	20 509	20 714	27 021	13 143	13 878	14 202	7 366	6 836
60 - 64	34 196	15 941	18 255	21 738	9 981	11 757	12 458	5 960	6 498
65 - 69	22 121	9 774	12 347	12 692	5 522	7 170	9 429	4 252	5 177
70 - 74	25 141	10 909	14 232	14 441	6 116	8 325	10 700	4 793	5 907
75 - 79	17 184	7 251	9 933	9 665	4 041	5 624	7 519	3 210	4 309
80 - 84	10 021	4 050	5 971	5 375	2 112	3 263	4 646	1 938	2 708
85 - 89	3 739	1 324	2 415	2 038	699	1 339	1 701	625	1 076
90 - 94	885	283	602	453	130	323	432	153	279
95 - 99	202	61	141	103	30	73	99	31	68
100 +	44	13	31	23	7	16	21	6	15
Unknown - Inconnu	248	92	156	150	61	89	98	31	67
Netherlands - Pays-Bas									
1 I 2011 (ESDJ)									
Total	16 655 799	8 243 482	8 412 317	11 124 721	5 478 213	5 646 508	5 531 078	2 765 269	2 765 809
0 - 4	923 106	472 308	450 798	633 381	323 854	309 527	289 725	148 454	141 271
0	184 007	93 892	90 115	...	...	...	...	...	...
1 - 4	739 099	378 416	360 683	...	...	...	...	...	...
5 - 9	985 229	503 882	481 347	640 541	327 757	312 784	344 688	176 125	168 563
10 - 14	998 740	510 974	487 766	633 115	323 581	309 534	365 625	187 393	178 232
15 - 19	1 006 744	514 830	491 914	658 458	333 676	324 782	348 286	181 154	167 132
20 - 24	1 034 729	522 667	512 062	757 280	373 366	383 914	277 449	149 301	128 148
25 - 29	1 001 538	504 117	497 421	749 880	373 340	376 540	251 658	130 777	120 881
30 - 34	1 004 764	503 323	501 441	736 350	368 630	367 720	268 414	134 693	133 721
35 - 39	1 121 568	560 289	561 279	779 994	391 390	388 604	341 574	168 899	172 675
40 - 44	1 295 925	653 664	642 261	861 292	436 235	425 057	434 633	217 429	217 204
45 - 49	1 298 292	655 302	642 990	850 566	428 796	421 770	447 726	226 506	221 220
50 - 54	1 196 319	601 040	595 279	776 285	388 221	388 064	420 034	212 819	207 215
55 - 59	1 090 247	546 952	543 295	700 036	348 502	351 534	390 211	198 450	191 761
60 - 64	1 103 652	553 446	550 206	700 926	349 188	351 738	402 726	204 258	198 468
65 - 69	790 560	390 725	399 835	488 433	238 792	249 641	302 127	151 933	150 194
70 - 74	637 518	302 542	334 976	401 165	187 850	213 315	236 353	114 692	121 661
75 - 79	499 321	219 108	280 213	316 949	136 949	180 000	182 372	82 159	100 213
80 - 84	360 828	139 348	221 480	234 884	89 412	145 472	125 944	49 936	76 008
85 - 89	212 056	66 949	145 107	141 532	44 184	97 348	70 524	22 765	47 759
90 - 94	76 191	18 812	57 379	51 102	12 438	38 664	25 089	6 374	18 715
95 +	18 472	3 204	15 268	12 552	2 052	10 500	5 920	1 152	4 768
Norway - Norvège[76]									
19 XI 2011 (CDJC)[19]									
Total	4 979 955	2 495 777	2 484 178	3 951 427[77]	1 959 424[77]	1 992 003[77]	1 011 071[77]	524 519[77]	486 552[77]
0 - 4	310 523	159 582	150 941	252 348[77]	129 655[77]	122 693[77]	57 552[77]	29 590[77]	27 962[77]
5 - 9	300 625	153 598	147 027	239 702[77]	122 174[77]	117 528[77]	60 262[77]	31 070[77]	29 192[77]
10 - 14	312 618	160 122	152 496	245 562[77]	125 764[77]	119 798[77]	66 422[77]	34 008[77]	32 414[77]
15 - 19	324 682	167 701	156 981	254 774[77]	131 385[77]	123 389[77]	69 376[77]	36 049[77]	33 327[77]
20 - 24	329 537	167 828	161 709	268 150[77]	135 424[77]	132 726[77]	60 351[77]	31 776[77]	28 575[77]
25 - 29	321 171	163 754	157 417	268 356[77]	135 940[77]	132 416[77]	51 166[77]	26 654[77]	24 512[77]
30 - 34	325 241	166 578	158 663	269 924[77]	137 478[77]	132 446[77]	53 565[77]	27 843[77]	25 722[77]
35 - 39	352 008	180 904	171 104	286 185[77]	146 143[77]	140 042[77]	64 091[77]	33 501[77]	30 590[77]
40 - 44	373 191	191 483	181 708	297 629[77]	151 231[77]	146 398[77]	73 666[77]	38 863[77]	34 803[77]
45 - 49	350 537	180 834	169 703	275 817[77]	140 624[77]	135 193[77]	73 001[77]	38 909[77]	34 092[77]
50 - 54	322 729	165 233	157 496	250 381[77]	126 209[77]	124 172[77]	70 881[77]	37 897[77]	32 984[77]
55 - 59	304 335	154 029	150 306	233 724[77]	116 035[77]	117 689[77]	69 504[77]	37 194[77]	32 310[77]
60 - 64	286 319	144 699	141 620	218 480[77]	108 289[77]	110 191[77]	67 016[77]	35 823[77]	31 193[77]
65 - 69	247 451	122 740	124 711	188 932[77]	91 896[77]	97 036[77]	57 895[77]	30 414[77]	27 481[77]
70 - 74	166 680	78 850	87 830	126 640[77]	58 122[77]	68 518[77]	39 687[77]	20 517[77]	19 170[77]
75 - 79	130 209	58 013	72 196	99 673[77]	42 842[77]	56 831[77]	30 271[77]	15 028[77]	15 243[77]
80 - 84	108 243	44 024	64 219	84 440[77]	32 980[77]	51 460[77]	23 582[77]	10 955[77]	12 627[77]

Continent, country or area, date, code[a] and age (in years) / Continent, pays ou zone, date, code[a] et âge (en années)	Total			Urban - Urbaine			Rural - Rurale		
	Both sexes Les deux sexes	Male Masculin	Female Féminin	Both sexes Les deux sexes	Male Masculin	Female Féminin	Both sexes Les deux sexes	Male Masculin	Female Féminin
EUROPE									
Norway - Norvège[76]									
19 XI 2011 (CDJC)[19]									
85 - 89	74 057	25 608	48 449	58 579[77]	19 436[77]	39 143[77]	15 272[77]	6 085[77]	9 187[77]
90 - 94	32 243	8 769	23 474	25 938[77]	6 706[77]	19 232[77]	6 185[77]	2 017[77]	4 168[77]
95 - 99	6 825	1 310	5 515	5 593[77]	1 001[77]	4 592[77]	1 199[77]	300[77]	899[77]
100 +	731	118	613	600[77]	90[77]	510[77]	127[77]	26[77]	101[77]
1 VII 2012 (ESDJ)									
Total	5 018 573	2 517 390	2 501 183	...	...	...	...	...	...
0	60 498	31 081	29 417	...	...	...	...	...	...
1 - 4	251 493	129 180	122 313	...	...	...	...	...	...
5 - 9	303 386	155 013	148 373	...	...	...	...	...	...
10 - 14	310 103	158 725	151 378	...	...	...	...	...	...
15 - 19	325 530	167 933	157 597	...	...	...	...	...	...
20 - 24	334 821	170 921	163 901	...	...	...	...	...	...
25 - 29	326 813	166 615	160 198	...	...	...	...	...	...
30 - 34	330 404	169 553	160 851	...	...	...	...	...	...
35 - 39	348 451	179 203	169 249	...	...	...	...	...	...
40 - 44	375 351	192 847	182 504	...	...	...	...	...	...
45 - 49	355 288	183 290	171 998	...	...	...	...	...	...
50 - 54	324 796	166 544	158 252	...	...	...	...	...	...
55 - 59	306 930	155 297	151 634	...	...	...	...	...	...
60 - 64	285 397	144 349	141 048	...	...	...	...	...	...
65 - 69	256 539	127 371	129 169	...	...	...	...	...	...
70 - 74	170 764	81 081	89 683	...	...	...	...	...	...
75 - 79	130 427	58 306	72 121	...	...	...	...	...	...
80 - 84	107 993	44 095	63 898	...	...	...	...	...	...
85 - 89	73 090	25 531	47 559	...	...	...	...	...	...
90 - 94	32 802	8 947	23 855	...	...	...	...	...	...
95 - 99	6 932	1 380	5 552	...	...	...	...	...	...
100 +	768	131	637	...	...	...	...	...	...
Poland - Pologne[78]									
1 VII 2012 (ESDJ)									
Total	38 533 789	18 651 441	19 882 348	23 360 022	11 086 177	12 273 845	15 173 767	7 565 264	7 608 503
0	384 280	197 871	186 409	222 352	114 616	107 736	161 928	83 255	78 673
1 - 4	1 680 663	862 003	818 660	972 484	498 615	473 869	708 179	363 388	344 791
5 - 9	1 843 366	945 643	897 723	1 031 194	528 940	502 254	812 172	416 703	395 469
10 - 14	1 900 015	974 509	925 506	1 012 558	519 440	493 118	887 457	455 069	432 388
15 - 19	2 266 634	1 158 367	1 108 267	1 212 063	617 725	594 338	1 054 571	540 642	513 929
20 - 24	2 736 154	1 394 761	1 341 393	1 573 579	793 273	780 306	1 162 575	601 488	561 087
25 - 29	3 198 618	1 623 072	1 575 546	1 969 888	988 292	981 596	1 228 730	634 780	593 950
30 - 34	3 161 358	1 602 736	1 558 622	1 992 477	998 627	993 850	1 168 881	604 109	564 772
35 - 39	2 903 573	1 470 751	1 432 822	1 782 067	891 666	890 401	1 121 506	579 085	542 421
40 - 44	2 440 834	1 231 083	1 209 751	1 438 923	712 685	726 238	1 001 911	518 398	483 513
45 - 49	2 389 500	1 196 548	1 192 952	1 406 626	681 323	725 303	982 874	515 225	467 649
50 - 54	2 784 254	1 369 258	1 414 996	1 717 873	808 906	908 967	1 066 381	560 352	506 029
55 - 59	2 926 281	1 404 141	1 522 140	1 914 912	880 046	1 034 866	1 011 369	524 095	487 274
60 - 64	2 514 619	1 163 935	1 350 684	1 678 077	751 679	926 398	836 542	412 256	424 286
65 - 69	1 537 157	675 573	861 584	1 022 506	441 278	581 228	514 651	234 295	280 356
70 - 74	1 306 461	529 739	776 722	839 597	334 563	505 034	466 864	195 176	271 688
75 - 79	1 144 656	424 407	720 249	719 337	264 687	454 650	425 319	159 720	265 599
80 - 84	844 554	278 428	566 126	511 821	170 799	341 022	332 733	107 629	225 104
85 - 89	426 601	115 213	311 388	255 282	69 341	185 941	171 319	45 872	125 447
90 - 94	119 788	28 565	91 223	70 696	16 676	54 020	49 092	11 889	37 203
95 - 99	22 879	4 614	18 265	14 423	2 793	11 630	8 456	1 821	6 635
100 +	1 544	224	1 320	1 287	207	1 080	257	17	240
Portugal									
21 III 2011 (CDJC)									
Total	10 562 178	5 046 600	5 515 578	6 438 593	3 047 968	3 390 625	4 123 585	1 998 632	2 124 953
0 - 4	482 647	246 396	236 251	316 068	161 365	154 703	166 579	85 031	81 548
5 - 9	525 087	268 965	256 122	329 692	168 925	160 767	195 395	100 040	95 355
10 - 14	564 595	288 638	275 957	344 809	176 287	168 522	219 786	112 351	107 435
15 - 19	565 250	288 525	276 725	342 328	174 252	168 076	222 922	114 273	108 649
20 - 24	582 065	293 023	289 042	358 412	178 982	179 430	223 653	114 041	109 612
25 - 29	656 076	324 848	331 228	425 629	208 104	217 525	230 447	116 744	113 703
30 - 34	773 567	378 734	394 833	508 225	247 125	261 100	265 342	131 609	133 733

Continent, country or area, date, code[a] and age (in years) / Continent, pays ou zone, date, code[a] et âge (en années)	Total			Urban - Urbaine			Rural - Rurale		
	Both sexes Les deux sexes	Male Masculin	Female Féminin	Both sexes Les deux sexes	Male Masculin	Female Féminin	Both sexes Les deux sexes	Male Masculin	Female Féminin
EUROPE									
Portugal									
21 III 2011 (CDJC)									
35 - 39	824 683	402 307	422 376	529 287	255 858	273 429	295 396	146 449	148 947
40 - 44	773 098	374 962	398 136	478 840	228 255	250 585	294 258	146 707	147 551
45 - 49	770 294	370 989	399 305	466 564	219 783	246 781	303 730	151 206	152 524
50 - 54	722 360	346 248	376 112	435 982	203 867	232 115	286 378	142 381	143 997
55 - 59	677 651	322 095	355 556	410 020	190 860	219 160	267 631	131 235	136 396
60 - 64	634 741	298 546	336 195	382 547	177 485	205 062	252 194	121 061	131 133
65 - 69	551 701	253 004	298 697	319 398	146 189	173 209	232 303	106 815	125 488
70 - 74	496 438	220 461	275 977	273 513	119 844	153 669	222 925	100 617	122 308
75 - 79	429 706	180 131	249 575	231 208	94 394	136 814	198 498	85 737	112 761
80 - 84	297 888	113 325	184 563	159 578	57 948	101 630	138 310	55 377	82 933
85 - 89	164 356	55 635	108 721	88 444	28 423	60 021	75 912	27 212	48 700
90 - 94	53 847	15 679	38 168	29 038	7 847	21 191	24 809	7 832	16 977
95 - 99	14 602	3 816	10 786	8 158	2 029	6 129	6 444	1 787	4 657
100 +	1 526	273	1 253	853	146	707	673	127	546
1 VII 2013 (ESDJ)									
Total	10 457 295	4 976 859	5 480 437	...	...	...	...	...	...
0	86 132	44 121	42 012	...	...	...	...	...	...
1 - 4	386 092	197 111	188 981	...	...	...	...	...	...
5 - 9	510 652	261 549	249 103	...	...	...	...	...	...
10 - 14	553 152	283 658	269 494	...	...	...	...	...	...
15 - 19	549 338	280 574	268 765	...	...	...	...	...	...
20 - 24	567 644	286 012	281 633	...	...	...	...	...	...
25 - 29	596 320	296 604	299 716	...	...	...	...	...	...
30 - 34	703 522	342 164	361 358	...	...	...	...	...	...
35 - 39	819 639	396 906	422 733	...	...	...	...	...	...
40 - 44	787 201	381 615	405 586	...	...	...	...	...	...
45 - 49	770 090	370 605	399 485	...	...	...	...	...	...
50 - 54	745 922	357 876	388 047	...	...	...	...	...	...
55 - 59	684 891	325 304	359 587	...	...	...	...	...	...
60 - 64	645 478	303 334	342 144	...	...	...	...	...	...
65 - 69	567 469	256 732	310 737	...	...	...	...	...	...
70 - 74	479 850	210 896	268 954	...	...	...	...	...	...
75 - 79	435 549	180 861	254 689	...	...	...	...	...	...
80 - 84	319 547	122 062	197 485	...	...	...	...	...	...
85 - 89	170 947	56 604	114 343	...	...	...	...	...	...
90 - 94	60 632	17 640	42 992	...	...	...	...	...	...
95 - 99	14 231	3 812	10 419	...	...	...	...	...	...
100 +	3 002	824	2 178	...	...	...	...	...	...
Republic of Moldova - République de Moldova[79]									
1 VII 2012 (ESDJ)									
Total	3 559 519	1 712 036	1 847 484	1 488 966	699 880	789 086	2 070 554	1 012 156	1 058 398
0	38 856	20 015	18 842	14 501	7 501	7 000	24 356	12 514	11 842
1 - 4	155 545	80 386	75 159	57 044	29 740	27 305	98 501	50 646	47 855
5 - 9	185 646	95 525	90 121	67 697	35 209	32 489	117 949	60 317	57 632
10 - 14	194 993	100 101	94 893	66 615	34 473	32 142	128 379	65 628	62 751
15 - 19	257 790	131 414	126 376	88 575	45 309	43 267	169 215	86 106	83 110
20 - 24	333 714	169 543	164 171	138 548	69 044	69 505	195 166	100 499	94 667
25 - 29	343 489	174 869	168 620	174 571	84 151	90 420	168 918	90 718	78 200
30 - 34	289 604	146 740	142 864	133 836	65 353	68 483	155 769	81 387	74 382
35 - 39	251 655	124 669	126 986	111 448	54 088	57 360	140 207	70 581	69 627
40 - 44	225 706	109 887	115 819	97 757	46 129	51 629	127 949	63 758	64 191
45 - 49	237 350	112 506	124 844	102 616	46 409	56 207	134 735	66 097	68 638
50 - 54	274 163	127 681	146 482	119 669	52 882	66 787	154 495	74 799	79 696
55 - 59	235 036	106 431	128 605	104 053	44 876	59 177	130 983	61 555	69 428
60 - 64	182 091	79 587	102 504	79 353	34 316	45 038	102 738	45 272	57 467
65 - 69	105 809	44 763	61 046	43 360	18 966	24 394	62 449	25 797	36 652
70 - 74	100 565	38 142	62 423	39 059	15 111	23 948	61 506	23 031	38 475
75 - 79	72 497	25 841	46 656	24 995	8 598	16 397	47 502	17 243	30 259
80 - 84	47 586	15 881	31 706	15 963	5 051	10 912	31 624	10 830	20 794
85 - 89	20 400	5 920	14 480	6 963	1 957	5 006	13 437	3 963	9 474
90 - 94	5 438	1 597	3 841	1 780	526	1 254	3 658	1 071	2 588

Continent, country or area, date, code[a] and age (in years) Continent, pays ou zone, date, code[a] et âge (en années)	Total			Urban - Urbaine			Rural - Rurale		
	Both sexes Les deux sexes	Male Masculin	Female Féminin	Both sexes Les deux sexes	Male Masculin	Female Féminin	Both sexes Les deux sexes	Male Masculin	Female Féminin
EUROPE									
Republic of Moldova - **République de Moldova[79]** 1 VII 2012 (ESDJ)									
95 - 99	1 163	395	768	391	150	241	772	245	527
100 +	429	148	282	177	45	132	253	103	150
Romania - Roumanie 1 VII 2013 (ESDJ)									
Total	19 985 814	9 754 851	10 230 963	10 770 879	5 152 718	5 618 161	9 214 935	4 602 133	4 612 802
0	179 855	92 507	87 348	96 383	49 670	46 713	83 472	42 837	40 635
1 - 4	802 350	412 325	390 025	418 243	215 555	202 688	384 107	196 770	187 337
5 - 9	1 062 299	545 767	516 532	527 273	270 752	256 521	535 026	275 015	260 011
10 - 14	1 072 925	550 824	522 101	487 460	249 522	237 938	585 465	301 302	284 163
15 - 19	1 089 493	557 984	531 509	514 120	260 466	253 654	575 373	297 518	277 855
20 - 24	1 233 468	640 632	592 836	703 659	352 894	350 765	529 809	287 738	242 071
25 - 29	1 368 581	709 453	659 128	821 598	416 257	405 341	546 983	293 196	253 787
30 - 34	1 424 680	728 787	695 893	844 425	424 802	419 623	580 255	303 985	276 270
35 - 39	1 576 764	804 774	771 990	886 910	441 595	445 315	689 854	363 179	326 675
40 - 44	1 605 228	821 469	783 759	883 753	430 611	453 142	721 475	390 858	330 617
45 - 49	1 323 017	675 103	647 914	768 202	367 328	400 874	554 815	307 775	247 040
50 - 54	1 208 770	601 134	607 636	718 467	336 671	381 796	490 303	264 463	225 840
55 - 59	1 443 030	689 332	753 698	873 286	405 926	467 360	569 744	283 406	286 338
60 - 64	1 317 171	606 534	710 637	733 827	338 070	395 757	583 344	268 464	314 880
65 - 69	929 552	411 784	517 768	457 337	201 246	256 091	472 215	210 538	261 677
70 - 74	834 539	344 824	489 715	381 712	156 263	225 449	452 827	188 561	264 266
75 - 79	737 421	285 509	451 912	320 030	121 596	198 434	417 391	163 913	253 478
80 - 84	482 377	177 541	304 836	205 195	72 578	132 617	277 182	104 963	172 219
85 - 89	224 431	77 135	147 296	97 234	31 872	65 362	127 197	45 263	81 934
90 - 94	62 109	19 170	42 939	27 862	7 952	19 910	34 247	11 218	23 029
95 - 99	6 575	1 900	4 675	3 300	915	2 385	3 275	985	2 290
100 +	1 179	363	816	603	177	426	576	186	390
Russian Federation - **Fédération de Russie** 1 VII 2012 (ESDJ)									
Total	143 201 730	66 264 910	76 936 820	105 930 122	48 419 208	57 510 914	37 271 608	17 845 702	19 425 906
0	1 837 406	944 299	893 107	1 299 253	668 312	630 941	538 153	275 987	262 166
1 - 4	6 695 802	3 433 227	3 262 575	4 714 200	2 419 141	2 295 059	1 981 602	1 014 086	967 516
5 - 9	7 350 838	3 762 806	3 588 032	5 189 787	2 657 166	2 532 621	2 161 051	1 105 640	1 055 411
10 - 14	6 628 125	3 396 364	3 231 761	4 584 611	2 348 219	2 236 392	2 043 514	1 048 145	995 369
15 - 19	7 391 866	3 776 026	3 615 840	5 367 803	2 718 897	2 648 906	2 024 063	1 057 129	966 934
20 - 24	11 223 730	5 708 187	5 515 543	8 636 085	4 330 536	4 305 549	2 587 645	1 377 651	1 209 994
25 - 29	12 442 007	6 262 379	6 179 628	9 541 009	4 744 648	4 796 361	2 900 998	1 517 731	1 383 267
30 - 34	11 231 149	5 583 513	5 647 636	8 675 785	4 272 864	4 402 921	2 555 364	1 310 649	1 244 715
35 - 39	10 419 383	5 087 565	5 331 818	7 966 185	3 854 320	4 111 865	2 453 198	1 233 245	1 219 953
40 - 44	9 451 487	4 589 504	4 861 983	7 068 002	3 394 309	3 673 693	2 383 485	1 195 195	1 188 290
45 - 49	9 784 092	4 632 279	5 151 813	7 108 256	3 298 718	3 809 538	2 675 836	1 333 561	1 342 275
50 - 54	11 498 441	5 279 364	6 219 077	8 339 186	3 721 713	4 617 473	3 159 255	1 557 651	1 601 604
55 - 59	10 298 414	4 480 855	5 817 559	7 573 444	3 197 844	4 375 600	2 724 970	1 283 011	1 441 959
60 - 64	8 534 857	3 523 990	5 010 867	6 428 296	2 585 856	3 842 440	2 106 561	938 134	1 168 427
65 - 69	4 174 510	1 602 839	2 571 671	3 204 644	1 214 486	1 990 158	969 866	388 353	581 513
70 - 74	5 965 072	1 989 724	3 975 348	4 331 090	1 428 165	2 902 925	1 633 982	561 559	1 072 423
75 - 79	3 888 860	1 179 476	2 709 384	2 762 682	822 673	1 940 009	1 126 178	356 803	769 375
80 - 84	2 795 954	722 151	2 073 803	1 965 242	501 515	1 463 727	830 712	220 636	610 076
85 - 89	1 261 655	253 028	1 008 627	927 939	193 530	734 409	333 716	59 498	274 218
90 - 94	266 163	46 736	219 427	200 155	37 401	162 754	66 008	9 335	56 673
95 - 99	52 622	8 634	43 988	39 307	7 154	32 153	13 315	1 480	11 835
100 +	9 297	1 964	7 333	7 161	1 741	5 420	2 136	223	1 913
San Marino - Saint-Marin[19] 1 VII 2014 (ESDF)									
Total	33 648	16 396	17 252	...	...	...	...	...	...
0	318	179	139	...	...	...	...	...	...
1 - 4	1 358	698	660	...	...	...	...	...	...
5 - 9	1 695	881	814	...	...	...	...	...	...
10 - 14	1 717	900	817	...	...	...	...	...	...
15 - 19	1 606	845	761	...	...	...	...	...	...
20 - 24	1 469	746	723	...	...	...	...	...	...

7. Population by age, sex and urban/rural residence: latest available year, 2005 - 2014
Population selon l'âge, le sexe et la résidence, urbaine/rurale : dernière année disponible, 2005 - 2014 (continued - suite)

Continent, country or area, date, code[a] and age (in years) Continent, pays ou zone, date, code[a] et âge (en années)	Total			Urban - Urbaine			Rural - Rurale		
	Both sexes Les deux sexes	Male Masculin	Female Féminin	Both sexes Les deux sexes	Male Masculin	Female Féminin	Both sexes Les deux sexes	Male Masculin	Female Féminin
EUROPE									
San Marino - Saint-Marin[19]									
1 VII 2014 (ESDF)									
25 - 29	1 593	795	798	...	...	...	...	...	...
30 - 34	2 029	986	1 043	...	...	...	...	...	...
35 - 39	2 651	1 270	1 381	...	...	...	...	...	...
40 - 44	2 983	1 456	1 527	...	...	...	...	...	...
45 - 49	3 174	1 523	1 651	...	...	...	...	...	...
50 - 54	2 835	1 389	1 446	...	...	...	...	...	...
55 - 59	2 193	1 068	1 125	...	...	...	...	...	...
60 - 64	1 922	937	985	...	...	...	...	...	...
65 - 69	1 698	816	882	...	...	...	...	...	...
70 - 74	1 427	686	741	...	...	...	...	...	...
75 - 79	1 174	552	622	...	...	...	...	...	...
80 - 84	927	390	537	...	...	...	...	...	...
85 - 89	532	186	346	...	...	...	...	...	...
90 - 94	281	81	200	...	...	...	...	...	...
95 - 99	57	11	46	...	...	...	...	...	...
100 +	9	1	8	...	...	...	...	...	...
Serbia - Serbie[80]									
1 VII 2013 (ESDJ)									
Total	7 164 132	3 488 466	3 675 666	4 272 059	2 037 550	2 234 509	2 892 073	1 450 916	1 441 157
0	65 994	33 888	32 106	45 361	23 285	22 076	20 633	10 603	10 030
1 - 4	265 298	136 817	128 481	171 910	88 711	83 199	93 388	48 106	45 282
5 - 9	344 878	177 318	167 560	207 356	106 461	100 895	137 522	70 857	66 665
10 - 14	351 277	180 704	170 573	206 626	106 374	100 252	144 651	74 330	70 321
15 - 19	388 223	200 046	188 177	225 131	115 527	109 604	163 092	84 519	78 573
20 - 24	428 407	219 361	209 046	255 401	128 758	126 643	173 006	90 603	82 403
25 - 29	473 867	242 073	231 794	299 451	148 402	151 049	174 416	93 671	80 745
30 - 34	493 156	250 940	242 216	322 675	159 838	162 837	170 481	91 102	79 379
35 - 39	502 933	254 226	248 707	320 510	157 798	162 712	182 423	96 428	85 995
40 - 44	475 829	237 771	238 058	291 543	142 003	149 540	184 286	95 768	88 518
45 - 49	474 449	233 992	240 457	282 440	134 617	147 823	192 009	99 375	92 634
50 - 54	508 900	248 480	260 420	301 084	140 707	160 377	207 816	107 773	100 043
55 - 59	559 372	270 809	288 563	327 794	152 130	175 664	231 578	118 679	112 899
60 - 64	555 353	263 055	292 298	324 890	147 775	177 115	230 463	115 280	115 183
65 - 69	375 710	171 334	204 376	214 726	94 850	119 876	160 984	76 484	84 500
70 - 74	332 379	144 654	187 725	179 733	76 041	103 692	152 646	68 613	84 033
75 - 79	291 278	119 874	171 404	155 033	63 388	91 645	136 245	56 486	79 759
80 - 84	184 812	71 340	113 472	92 039	34 389	57 650	92 773	36 951	55 822
85 - 89	73 180	25 709	47 471	38 201	13 264	24 937	34 979	12 445	22 534
90 - 94	17 184	5 524	11 660	9 237	2 952	6 285	7 947	2 572	5 375
95 - 99	1 390	465	925	778	244	534	612	221	391
100 +	263	86	177	140	36	104	123	50	73
Slovakia - Slovaquie									
1 VII 2013 (ESDJ)									
Total	5 413 393	2 637 520	2 775 873	2 931 444	1 409 503	1 521 941	2 481 949	1 228 017	1 253 932
0	55 502	28 517	26 985	29 099	14 939	14 160	26 403	13 577	12 826
1 - 4	235 711	120 722	114 989	121 489	62 173	59 316	114 222	58 549	55 673
5 - 9	271 394	139 473	131 921	134 590	69 302	65 288	136 805	70 172	66 633
10 - 14	267 645	137 274	130 371	128 376	65 824	62 552	139 269	71 450	67 819
15 - 19	309 450	158 649	150 801	150 483	77 130	73 354	158 967	81 520	77 448
20 - 24	383 885	195 827	188 059	200 127	101 864	98 263	183 758	93 963	89 796
25 - 29	424 790	216 660	208 130	236 412	119 786	116 626	188 378	96 874	91 504
30 - 34	449 441	230 868	218 573	254 998	130 529	124 470	194 443	100 340	94 104
35 - 39	453 353	232 685	220 668	250 963	127 649	123 314	202 390	105 036	97 354
40 - 44	378 212	191 854	186 359	203 357	100 600	102 757	174 855	91 254	83 602
45 - 49	363 236	181 893	181 343	198 351	95 160	103 191	164 885	86 734	78 152
50 - 54	370 183	183 452	186 731	209 720	99 555	110 165	160 463	83 897	76 566
55 - 59	387 076	186 522	200 554	226 150	105 266	120 884	160 926	81 256	79 670
60 - 64	341 839	158 710	183 129	198 407	90 059	108 348	143 433	68 651	74 782
65 - 69	240 720	104 157	136 563	136 147	58 230	77 917	104 574	45 928	58 646
70 - 74	183 706	72 794	110 912	98 541	39 241	59 300	85 165	33 553	51 612
75 - 79	134 167	48 035	86 133	70 142	25 654	44 488	64 025	22 381	41 645
80 - 84	96 919	31 041	65 879	49 947	16 635	33 312	46 973	14 406	32 567
85 - 89	48 119	13 566	34 553	24 764	7 314	17 451	23 355	6 252	17 103

Continent, country or area, date, code[a] and age (in years) / Continent, pays ou zone, date, code[a] et âge (en années)	Total			Urban - Urbaine			Rural - Rurale		
	Both sexes Les deux sexes	Male Masculin	Female Féminin	Both sexes Les deux sexes	Male Masculin	Female Féminin	Both sexes Les deux sexes	Male Masculin	Female Féminin
EUROPE									
Slovakia - Slovaquie									
1 VII 2013 (ESDJ)									
90 - 94	15 616	4 122	11 494	7 977	2 187	5 790	7 639	1 935	5 704
95 - 99	1 946	546	1 401	1 110	308	802	836	238	599
100 +	488	159	329	297	101	196	191	58	133
Slovenia - Slovénie									
1 VII 2013 (ESDJ)									
Total	2 059 114	1 019 658	1 039 456	1 047 560	513 084	534 476	1 011 554	506 574	504 980
0	21 471	11 082	10 389	10 957	5 598	5 359	10 514	5 484	5 030
1 - 4	89 367	45 955	43 412	45 660	23 566	22 094	43 707	22 389	21 318
5 - 9	97 105	49 723	47 382	48 615	24 960	23 655	48 490	24 763	23 727
10 - 14	91 345	47 233	44 112	43 823	22 836	20 987	47 522	24 397	23 125
15 - 19	97 464	50 095	47 369	47 532	24 225	23 307	49 932	25 870	24 062
20 - 24	114 245	58 843	55 402	61 859	30 965	30 894	52 386	27 878	24 508
25 - 29	138 064	71 977	66 087	70 669	36 892	33 777	67 395	35 085	32 310
30 - 34	154 728	81 193	73 535	79 730	41 576	38 154	74 998	39 617	35 381
35 - 39	154 587	80 990	73 597	79 085	41 294	37 791	75 502	39 696	35 806
40 - 44	146 358	75 942	70 416	73 387	37 569	35 818	72 971	38 373	34 598
45 - 49	156 067	79 335	76 732	78 194	39 274	38 920	77 873	40 061	37 812
50 - 54	152 979	77 831	75 148	76 477	38 151	38 326	76 502	39 680	36 822
55 - 59	152 262	77 131	75 131	76 777	37 980	38 797	75 485	39 151	36 334
60 - 64	137 213	68 436	68 777	70 357	34 151	36 206	66 856	34 285	32 571
65 - 69	97 548	46 057	51 491	50 956	23 388	27 568	46 592	22 669	23 923
70 - 74	90 611	40 235	50 376	46 891	20 432	26 459	43 720	19 803	23 917
75 - 79	73 234	29 374	43 860	37 693	15 310	22 383	35 541	14 064	21 477
80 - 84	54 704	18 537	36 167	28 062	9 625	18 437	26 642	8 912	17 730
85 - 89	28 919	7 475	21 444	15 043	4 071	10 972	13 876	3 404	10 472
90 - 94	9 426	1 994	7 432	4 980	1 081	3 899	4 446	913	3 533
95 - 99	1 191	183	1 008	682	116	566	509	67	442
100 +	226	37	189	131	24	107	95	13	82
Spain - Espagne									
1 VII 2014* (ESDJ)									
Total	46 464 056	22 843 721	23 620 335	...	...	...	...	...	...
0	421 748	217 446	204 302	...	...	...	...	...	...
1 - 4	1 861 772	959 871	901 901	...	...	...	...	...	...
5 - 9	2 480 495	1 279 343	1 201 152	...	...	...	...	...	...
10 - 14	2 286 699	1 175 982	1 110 717	...	...	...	...	...	...
15 - 19	2 145 971	1 104 576	1 041 395	...	...	...	...	...	...
20 - 24	2 344 967	1 193 644	1 151 323	...	...	...	...	...	...
25 - 29	2 693 339	1 348 427	1 344 912	...	...	...	...	...	...
30 - 34	3 361 932	1 692 839	1 669 093	...	...	...	...	...	...
35 - 39	3 991 809	2 037 042	1 954 767	...	...	...	...	...	...
40 - 44	3 874 208	1 975 504	1 898 704	...	...	...	...	...	...
45 - 49	3 690 425	1 860 703	1 829 722	...	...	...	...	...	...
50 - 54	3 371 835	1 680 389	1 691 446	...	...	...	...	...	...
55 - 59	2 928 773	1 442 156	1 486 617	...	...	...	...	...	...
60 - 64	2 500 558	1 215 892	1 284 666	...	...	...	...	...	...
65 - 69	2 342 807	1 113 678	1 229 129	...	...	...	...	...	...
70 - 74	1 879 653	869 616	1 010 037	...	...	...	...	...	...
75 - 79	1 600 742	694 044	906 698	...	...	...	...	...	...
80 - 84	1 411 739	565 897	845 842	...	...	...	...	...	...
85 - 89	838 092	293 789	544 303	...	...	...	...	...	...
90 - 94	344 801	101 631	243 170	...	...	...	...	...	...
95 - 99	77 081	18 048	59 033	...	...	...	...	...	...
100 +	14 610	3 204	11 406	...	...	...	...	...	...
Sweden - Suède[19]									
1 VII 2012 (ESDJ)									
Total	9 519 375	4 746 370	4 773 005	...	...	...	...	...	...
0	112 801	57 834	54 967	...	...	...	...	...	...
1 - 4	457 676	235 340	222 336	...	...	...	...	...	...
5 - 9	537 465	275 778	261 688	...	...	...	...	...	...
10 - 14	490 124	251 936	238 188	...	...	...	...	...	...
15 - 19	578 502	297 779	280 723	...	...	...	...	...	...
20 - 24	659 008	337 232	321 776	...	...	...	...	...	...
25 - 29	602 098	308 888	293 210	...	...	...	...	...	...

Continent, country or area, date, code[a] and age (in years) / Continent, pays ou zone, date, code[a] et âge (en années)	Total			Urban - Urbaine			Rural - Rurale		
	Both sexes Les deux sexes	Male Masculin	Female Féminin	Both sexes Les deux sexes	Male Masculin	Female Féminin	Both sexes Les deux sexes	Male Masculin	Female Féminin
EUROPE									
Sweden - Suède[19]									
1 VII 2012 (ESDJ)									
30 - 34	588 299	300 639	287 661	...	...	...	...	...	...
35 - 39	621 363	315 902	305 461	...	...	...	...	...	...
40 - 44	643 205	326 046	317 159	...	...	...	...	...	...
45 - 49	669 951	341 137	328 814	...	...	...	...	...	...
50 - 54	586 605	296 548	290 057	...	...	...	...	...	...
55 - 59	575 312	289 128	286 184	...	...	...	...	...	...
60 - 64	590 494	293 993	296 502	...	...	...	...	...	...
65 - 69	587 197	291 654	295 544	...	...	...	...	...	...
70 - 74	412 013	199 492	212 521	...	...	...	...	...	...
75 - 79	309 083	140 668	168 416	...	...	...	...	...	...
80 - 84	245 036	101 305	143 731	...	...	...	...	...	...
85 - 89	162 527	59 159	103 368	...	...	...	...	...	...
90 - 94	73 217	22 134	51 083	...	...	...	...	...	...
95 - 99	15 602	3 509	12 093	...	...	...	...	...	...
100 +	1 803	276	1 528	...	...	...	...	...	...
Switzerland - Suisse									
1 VII 2012 (ESDJ)									
Total	7 996 861	3 945 389	4 051 473	5 896 568	2 892 243	3 004 325	2 100 294	1 053 146	1 047 148
0	39 811	20 566	19 245	29 573	15 243	14 331	10 237	5 323	4 914
1 - 4	322 318	165 728	156 590	237 492	122 148	115 344	84 826	43 580	41 246
5 - 9	388 479	199 156	189 323	280 730	144 027	136 703	107 749	55 129	52 620
10 - 14	404 586	207 845	196 741	287 183	147 496	139 687	117 404	60 350	57 054
15 - 19	440 226	225 697	214 529	309 288	158 284	151 004	130 938	67 413	63 526
20 - 24	492 827	250 663	242 164	356 915	180 107	176 808	135 912	70 556	65 356
25 - 29	524 665	265 316	259 349	402 495	201 788	200 707	122 170	63 528	58 642
30 - 34	553 719	279 059	274 660	430 733	216 846	213 888	122 986	62 214	60 772
35 - 39	550 448	276 169	274 280	419 984	211 097	208 887	130 465	65 072	65 393
40 - 44	612 978	307 573	305 406	453 037	227 500	225 538	159 941	80 073	79 868
45 - 49	666 356	337 300	329 056	487 259	246 112	241 148	179 097	91 189	87 909
50 - 54	599 986	303 276	296 710	434 694	218 784	215 911	165 292	84 493	80 799
55 - 59	513 174	258 365	254 810	371 196	184 749	186 448	141 978	73 616	68 362
60 - 64	460 468	227 441	233 028	334 845	162 506	172 340	125 623	64 935	60 688
65 - 69	422 792	205 247	217 545	311 017	148 635	162 382	111 775	56 612	55 163
70 - 74	328 900	153 072	175 828	245 330	112 620	132 710	83 570	40 452	43 118
75 - 79	264 878	116 177	148 701	197 693	85 827	111 866	67 185	30 350	36 835
80 - 84	206 625	81 952	124 673	154 033	60 373	93 660	52 592	21 580	31 013
85 - 89	131 471	44 897	86 574	98 393	33 242	65 151	33 078	11 655	21 423
90 - 94	56 946	16 478	40 468	42 975	12 253	30 722	13 972	4 225	9 747
95 - 99	13 344	3 090	10 254	10 245	2 365	7 880	3 099	726	2 374
100 +	1 871	327	1 544	1 462	247	1 215	409	80	329
TFYR of Macedonia - L'ex-R. y. de Macédoine									
1 VII 2012 (ESDF)									
Total	2 061 044	1 032 532	1 028 512	...	...	...	...	...	...
0	22 969	11 891	11 078	...	...	...	...	...	...
1 - 4	92 609	47 962	44 647	...	...	...	...	...	...
5 - 9	113 143	58 282	54 861	...	...	...	...	...	...
10 - 14	123 721	63 848	59 873	...	...	...	...	...	...
15 - 19	144 319	74 287	70 032	...	...	...	...	...	...
20 - 24	160 127	82 371	77 756	...	...	...	...	...	...
25 - 29	164 376	84 126	80 250	...	...	...	...	...	...
30 - 34	159 617	82 120	77 497	...	...	...	...	...	...
35 - 39	152 030	77 259	74 771	...	...	...	...	...	...
40 - 44	146 266	73 897	72 369	...	...	...	...	...	...
45 - 49	146 799	74 382	72 417	...	...	...	...	...	...
50 - 54	141 691	71 581	70 110	...	...	...	...	...	...
55 - 59	133 751	67 034	66 717	...	...	...	...	...	...
60 - 64	114 019	54 483	59 536	...	...	...	...	...	...
65 - 69	81 682	37 971	43 711	...	...	...	...	...	...
70 - 74	68 459	31 008	37 451	...	...	...	...	...	...
75 - 79	54 228	23 687	30 541	...	...	...	...	...	...
80 - 84	27 699	11 260	16 439	...	...	...	...	...	...
85 - 89	10 066	3 948	6 118	...	...	...	...	...	...

7. Population by age, sex and urban/rural residence: latest available year, 2005 - 2014
Population selon l'âge, le sexe et la résidence, urbaine/rurale : dernière année disponible, 2005 - 2014 (continued - suite)

Continent, country or area, date, code[a] and age (in years) / Continent, pays ou zone, date, code[a] et âge (en années)	Total			Urban - Urbaine			Rural - Rurale		
	Both sexes Les deux sexes	Male Masculin	Female Féminin	Both sexes Les deux sexes	Male Masculin	Female Féminin	Both sexes Les deux sexes	Male Masculin	Female Féminin
EUROPE									
TFYR of Macedonia - L'ex-R. y. de Macédoine									
1 VII 2012 (ESDF)									
90 - 94	2 282	803	1 479	...	...	...	...	...	...
95 +	779	245	534	...	...	...	...	...	...
Unknown - Inconnu	412	87	325	...	...	...	...	...	...
Ukraine									
1 I 2013 (ESDJ)									
Total	45 372 692	20 962 744	24 409 948	31 123 007	14 259 600	16 863 407	14 249 685	6 703 144	7 546 541
0	517 301	266 820	250 481	339 538	175 547	163 991	177 763	91 273	86 490
1 - 4	2 004 486	1 033 711	970 775	1 327 019	684 897	642 122	677 467	348 814	328 653
5 - 9	2 168 158	1 113 505	1 054 653	1 449 410	745 034	704 376	718 748	368 471	350 277
10 - 14	1 930 653	991 443	939 210	1 203 306	618 657	584 649	727 347	372 786	354 561
15 - 19	2 405 136	1 233 934	1 171 202	1 579 769	804 869	774 900	825 367	429 065	396 302
20 - 24	3 232 157	1 657 101	1 575 056	2 195 942	1 118 307	1 077 635	1 036 215	538 794	497 421
25 - 29	3 868 992	1 969 672	1 899 320	2 801 899	1 408 147	1 393 752	1 067 093	561 525	505 568
30 - 34	3 476 598	1 750 016	1 726 582	2 553 790	1 276 839	1 276 951	922 808	473 177	449 631
35 - 39	3 270 101	1 609 508	1 660 593	2 323 493	1 130 939	1 192 554	946 608	478 569	468 039
40 - 44	3 113 544	1 507 589	1 605 955	2 153 127	1 021 499	1 131 628	960 417	486 090	474 327
45 - 49	3 085 767	1 450 559	1 635 208	2 123 186	966 883	1 156 303	962 581	483 676	478 905
50 - 54	3 500 369	1 594 318	1 906 051	2 461 151	1 084 460	1 376 691	1 039 218	509 858	529 360
55 - 59	3 097 369	1 347 030	1 750 339	2 209 140	931 767	1 277 373	888 229	415 263	472 966
60 - 64	2 796 743	1 157 385	1 639 358	2 006 621	812 407	1 194 214	790 122	344 978	445 144
65 - 69	1 656 868	629 382	1 027 486	1 139 209	432 839	706 370	517 659	196 543	321 116
70 - 74	2 153 251	742 717	1 410 534	1 391 669	483 905	907 764	761 582	258 812	502 770
75 - 79	1 492 884	489 204	1 003 680	927 376	307 461	619 915	565 508	181 743	383 765
80 - 84	974 774	274 742	700 032	568 852	164 927	403 925	405 922	109 815	296 107
85 - 89	492 650	114 882	377 768	289 117	71 285	217 832	203 533	43 597	159 936
90 - 94	114 583	24 566	90 017	65 707	15 513	50 194	48 876	9 053	39 823
95 - 99	14 543	3 307	11 236	9 446	2 362	7 084	5 097	945	4 152
100 +	5 765	1 353	4 412	4 240	1 056	3 184	1 525	297	1 228
United Kingdom of Great Britain and Northern Ireland - Royaume-Uni de Grande-Bretagne et d'Irlande du Nord[81]									
27 III 2011 (CDJC)									
Total	63 182 178	31 028 143	32 154 035	51 217 521	25 124 237	26 093 284	11 964 657	5 903 906	6 060 751
0 - 4	3 913 953	2 002 494	1 911 459	3 302 119	1 689 719	1 612 400	611 834	312 775	299 059
5 - 9	3 516 615	1 799 999	1 716 616	2 878 114	1 472 489	1 405 625	638 501	327 510	310 991
10 - 14	3 669 326	1 878 838	1 790 488	2 951 079	1 509 796	1 441 283	718 247	369 042	349 205
15 - 19	3 996 452	2 040 725	1 955 727	3 277 414	1 667 480	1 609 934	719 038	373 245	345 793
20 - 24	4 297 198	2 164 141	2 133 057	3 737 543	1 863 922	1 873 621	559 655	300 219	259 436
25 - 29	4 306 340	2 145 054	2 161 286	3 781 906	1 876 471	1 905 435	524 434	268 583	255 851
30 - 34	4 125 449	2 059 312	2 066 137	3 573 410	1 789 511	1 783 899	552 039	269 801	282 238
35 - 39	4 194 477	2 082 310	2 112 167	3 495 390	1 745 563	1 749 827	699 087	336 747	362 340
40 - 44	4 625 635	2 283 902	2 341 733	3 734 709	1 851 446	1 883 263	890 926	432 456	458 470
45 - 49	4 643 100	2 293 572	2 349 528	3 683 527	1 821 257	1 862 270	959 573	472 315	487 258
50 - 54	4 094 454	2 028 748	2 065 706	3 216 769	1 593 822	1 622 947	877 685	434 926	442 759
55 - 59	3 614 078	1 785 598	1 828 480	2 790 096	1 378 906	1 411 190	823 982	406 692	417 290
60 - 64	3 807 974	1 868 912	1 939 062	2 869 025	1 404 882	1 464 143	938 949	464 030	474 919
65 - 69	3 017 480	1 463 355	1 554 125	2 248 845	1 082 105	1 166 740	768 635	381 250	387 385
70 - 74	2 462 745	1 162 621	1 300 124	1 874 997	873 593	1 001 404	587 748	289 028	298 720
75 - 79	2 006 019	903 433	1 102 586	1 549 014	686 269	862 745	457 005	217 164	239 841
80 - 84	1 498 896	615 163	883 733	1 166 619	470 552	696 067	332 277	144 611	187 666
85 - 89	918 343	324 063	594 280	717 808	249 645	468 163	200 535	74 418	126 117
90 - 94	368 425	104 072	264 353	287 454	80 165	207 289	80 971	23 907	57 064
95 - 99	92 951	19 756	73 195	72 117	15 038	57 079	20 834	4 718	16 116
100 +	12 268	2 075	10 193	9 566	1 606	7 960	2 702	469	2 233
1 VII 2012 (ESDJ)									
Total	63 705 030	31 315 072	32 389 958	...	...	...	...	...	...
0	815 994	418 090	397 904	...	...	...	...	...	...
1 - 4	3 180 406	1 627 157	1 553 249	...	...	...	...	...	...
5 - 9	3 640 999	1 864 230	1 776 769	...	...	...	...	...	...
10 - 14	3 576 365	1 831 322	1 745 043	...	...	...	...	...	...

7. Population by age, sex and urban/rural residence: latest available year, 2005 - 2014
Population selon l'âge, le sexe et la résidence, urbaine/rurale : dernière année disponible, 2005 - 2014 (continued - suite)

Continent, country or area, date, code[a] and age (in years) / Continent, pays ou zone, date, code[a] et âge (en années)	Total			Urban - Urbaine			Rural - Rurale		
	Both sexes Les deux sexes	Male Masculin	Female Féminin	Both sexes Les deux sexes	Male Masculin	Female Féminin	Both sexes Les deux sexes	Male Masculin	Female Féminin
EUROPE									
United Kingdom of Great Britain and Northern Ireland - Royaume-Uni de Grande-Bretagne et d'Irlande du Nord[81]									
1 VII 2012 (ESDJ)									
15 - 19	3 926 550	2 013 226	1 913 324	...	...	...	...	...	...
20 - 24	4 332 232	2 191 539	2 140 693	...	...	...	...	...	...
25 - 29	4 317 845	2 152 085	2 165 760	...	...	...	...	...	...
30 - 34	4 239 908	2 109 169	2 130 739	...	...	...	...	...	...
35 - 39	4 036 354	2 008 678	2 027 676	...	...	...	...	...	...
40 - 44	4 567 284	2 253 651	2 313 633	...	...	...	...	...	...
45 - 49	4 685 698	2 312 799	2 372 899	...	...	...	...	...	...
50 - 54	4 235 821	2 097 878	2 137 943	...	...	...	...	...	...
55 - 59	3 684 198	1 819 823	1 864 375	...	...	...	...	...	...
60 - 64	3 624 420	1 776 207	1 848 213	...	...	...	...	...	...
65 - 69	3 345 053	1 626 032	1 719 021	...	...	...	...	...	...
70 - 74	2 475 948	1 170 152	1 305 796	...	...	...	...	...	...
75 - 79	2 046 899	928 768	1 118 131	...	...	...	...	...	...
80 - 84	1 533 663	637 528	896 135	...	...	...	...	...	...
85 - 89	925 944	335 580	590 364	...	...	...	...	...	...
90 +	513 449	141 158	372 291	...	...	...	...	...	...
OCEANIA - OCÉANIE									
American Samoa - Samoas américaines[27]									
1 IV 2010 (CDJC)									
Total	55 519	28 164	27 355	...	...	...	...	...	...
0 - 4	6 611	3 417	3 194	...	...	...	...	...	...
5 - 9	6 535	3 470	3 065	...	...	...	...	...	...
10 - 14	6 279	3 214	3 065	...	...	...	...	...	...
15 - 19	6 296	3 218	3 078	...	...	...	...	...	...
20 - 24	3 891	1 944	1 947	...	...	...	...	...	...
25 - 29	3 324	1 670	1 654	...	...	...	...	...	...
30 - 34	3 510	1 726	1 784	...	...	...	...	...	...
35 - 39	3 609	1 845	1 764	...	...	...	...	...	...
40 - 44	3 600	1 793	1 807	...	...	...	...	...	...
45 - 49	3 389	1 673	1 716	...	...	...	...	...	...
50 - 54	2 679	1 335	1 344	...	...	...	...	...	...
55 - 59	2 049	1 011	1 038	...	...	...	...	...	...
60 - 64	1 480	755	725	...	...	...	...	...	...
65 - 69	960	500	460	...	...	...	...	...	...
70 - 74	654	321	333	...	...	...	...	...	...
75 - 79	337	155	182	...	...	...	...	...	...
80 - 84	206	76	130	...	...	...	...	...	...
85 +	110	41	69	...	...	...	...	...	...
Australia - Australie									
1 VII 2013 (ESDJ)									
Total	23 135 281	11 518 199	11 617 082	19 778 495	9 796 858	9 981 637	3 356 786	1 721 341	1 635 445
0 - 4	1 517 808	779 797	738 011	1 309 022	672 060	636 962	208 786	107 737	101 049
5 - 9	1 455 775	747 953	707 822	1 230 631	632 010	598 621	225 144	115 943	109 201
10 - 14	1 398 497	716 436	682 061	1 171 926	599 964	571 962	226 571	116 472	110 099
15 - 19	1 466 622	753 963	712 659	1 255 803	643 732	612 071	210 819	110 231	100 588
20 - 24	1 642 229	838 246	803 983	1 475 779	749 044	726 735	166 450	89 202	77 248
25 - 29	1 729 391	874 356	855 035	1 556 114	784 279	771 835	173 277	90 077	83 200
30 - 34	1 657 894	833 060	824 834	1 478 451	742 040	736 411	179 443	91 020	88 423
35 - 39	1 552 086	773 867	778 219	1 359 179	677 129	682 050	192 907	96 738	96 169
40 - 44	1 664 010	824 943	839 067	1 431 015	707 532	723 483	232 995	117 411	115 584
45 - 49	1 529 107	758 315	770 792	1 297 804	640 315	657 489	231 303	118 000	113 303
50 - 54	1 549 283	766 491	782 792	1 293 578	635 451	658 127	255 705	131 040	124 665
55 - 59	1 393 587	688 311	705 276	1 149 011	561 686	587 325	244 576	126 625	117 951
60 - 64	1 240 824	614 472	626 352	1 012 795	495 066	517 729	228 029	119 406	108 623
65 - 69	1 081 958	537 242	544 716	878 612	430 279	448 333	203 346	106 963	96 383

Continent, country or area, date, code[a] and age (in years) / Continent, pays ou zone, date, code[a] et âge (en années)	Total			Urban - Urbaine			Rural - Rurale		
	Both sexes Les deux sexes	Male Masculin	Female Féminin	Both sexes Les deux sexes	Male Masculin	Female Féminin	Both sexes Les deux sexes	Male Masculin	Female Féminin
OCEANIA - OCÉANIE									
Australia - Australie									
1 VII 2013 (ESDJ)									
70 - 74	781 304	383 269	398 035	636 671	307 425	329 246	144 633	75 844	68 789
75 - 79	589 482	277 129	312 353	488 939	225 645	263 294	100 543	51 484	49 059
80 - 84	445 829	193 859	251 970	376 225	160 977	215 248	69 604	32 882	36 722
85 - 89	288 213	110 612	177 601	246 756	93 393	153 363	41 457	17 219	24 238
90 - 94	120 948	38 561	82 387	104 515	32 685	71 830	16 433	5 876	10 557
95 - 99	26 680	6 531	20 149	22 536	5 478	17 058	4 144	1 053	3 091
100 +	3 754	786	2 968	3 133	668	2 465	621	118	503
1 VII 2014* (ESDJ)									
Total	23 490 736	11 692 500	11 798 236	...	...	...	...	...	...
0 - 4	1 527 538	784 542	742 996	...	...	...	...	...	...
5 - 9	1 488 170	764 441	723 729	...	...	...	...	...	...
10 - 14	1 407 178	721 502	685 676	...	...	...	...	...	...
15 - 19	1 475 143	758 254	716 889	...	...	...	...	...	...
20 - 24	1 652 227	845 407	806 820	...	...	...	...	...	...
25 - 29	1 751 348	883 361	867 987	...	...	...	...	...	...
30 - 34	1 712 093	859 800	852 293	...	...	...	...	...	...
35 - 39	1 560 317	778 307	782 010	...	...	...	...	...	...
40 - 44	1 667 775	826 914	840 861	...	...	...	...	...	...
45 - 49	1 541 519	763 678	777 841	...	...	...	...	...	...
50 - 54	1 561 451	771 725	789 726	...	...	...	...	...	...
55 - 59	1 425 771	703 484	722 287	...	...	...	...	...	...
60 - 64	1 264 018	623 689	640 329	...	...	...	...	...	...
65 - 69	1 120 081	555 407	564 674	...	...	...	...	...	...
70 - 74	819 234	401 418	417 816	...	...	...	...	...	...
75 - 79	612 042	289 632	322 410	...	...	...	...	...	...
80 - 84	448 298	196 036	252 262	...	...	...	...	...	...
85 - 89	295 510	115 261	180 249	...	...	...	...	...	...
90 - 94	129 440	41 784	87 656	...	...	...	...	...	...
95 - 99	27 537	6 975	20 562	...	...	...	...	...	...
100 +	4 046	883	3 163	...	...	...	...	...	...
Cook Islands - Îles Cook[82]									
1 XII 2011 (CDFC)									
Total	17 794	8 815	8 979	...	...	...	...	...	...
0 - 4	1 584	806	778	...	...	...	...	...	...
5 - 9	1 539	768	771	...	...	...	...	...	...
10 - 14	1 504	794	710	...	...	...	...	...	...
15 - 19	1 495	768	727	...	...	...	...	...	...
20 - 24	1 273	611	662	...	...	...	...	...	...
25 - 29	1 263	590	673	...	...	...	...	...	...
30 - 34	1 122	534	588	...	...	...	...	...	...
35 - 39	1 179	543	636	...	...	...	...	...	...
40 - 44	1 252	605	647	...	...	...	...	...	...
45 - 49	1 282	636	646	...	...	...	...	...	...
50 - 54	1 059	534	525	...	...	...	...	...	...
55 - 59	863	430	433	...	...	...	...	...	...
60 - 64	749	394	355	...	...	...	...	...	...
65 - 69	649	333	316	...	...	...	...	...	...
70 - 74	496	251	245	...	...	...	...	...	...
75 - 79	285	130	155	...	...	...	...	...	...
80 +	200	88	112	...	...	...	...	...	...
Fiji - Fidji									
16 IX 2007 (CDFC)									
Total	837 271	427 176	410 095	424 846	212 454	212 392	412 425	214 722	197 703
0 - 4	82 718	42 835	39 883	39 209	20 264	18 945	43 509	22 571	20 938
5 - 9	78 019	40 441	37 578	35 981	18 528	17 453	42 038	21 913	20 125
10 - 14	82 384	42 369	40 015	38 916	19 790	19 126	43 468	22 579	20 889
15 - 19	79 518	40 818	38 700	42 458	21 051	21 407	37 060	19 767	17 293
20 - 24	80 352	41 325	39 027	45 837	22 896	22 941	34 515	18 429	16 086
25 - 29	73 487	37 390	36 097	40 669	20 260	20 409	32 818	17 130	15 688
30 - 34	63 535	32 825	30 710	33 612	17 017	16 595	29 923	15 808	14 115
35 - 39	56 552	28 778	27 774	29 288	14 674	14 614	27 264	14 104	13 160
40 - 44	56 274	28 598	27 676	28 147	14 058	14 089	28 127	14 540	13 587
45 - 49	50 322	25 835	24 487	25 556	12 780	12 776	24 766	13 055	11 711

Continent, country or area, date, code[a] and age (in years) Continent, pays ou zone, date, code[a] et âge (en années)	Total			Urban - Urbaine			Rural - Rurale		
	Both sexes Les deux sexes	Male Masculin	Female Féminin	Both sexes Les deux sexes	Male Masculin	Female Féminin	Both sexes Les deux sexes	Male Masculin	Female Féminin
OCEANIA - OCÉANIE									
Fiji - Fidji									
16 IX 2007 (CDFC)									
50 - 54	40 009	20 215	19 794	20 581	10 118	10 463	19 428	10 097	9 331
55 - 59	31 161	15 735	15 426	15 667	7 715	7 952	15 494	8 020	7 474
60 - 64	24 120	11 956	12 164	11 655	5 647	6 008	12 465	6 309	6 156
65 - 69	16 808	8 098	8 710	7 597	3 509	4 088	9 211	4 589	4 622
70 - 74	10 110	4 716	5 394	4 360	1 887	2 473	5 750	2 829	2 921
75 +	11 902	5 242	6 660	5 313	2 260	3 053	6 589	2 982	3 607
75 - 79	6 138	2 811	3 327	...	...	...	...	...	...
80 - 84	3 236	1 376	1 860	...	...	...	...	...	...
85 - 89	1 638	702	936	...	...	...	...	...	...
90 - 94	572	212	360	...	...	...	...	...	...
95 +	318	141	177	...	...	...	...	...	...
31 XII 2008 (ESDF)									
Total	842 621	430 418	412 203	...	...	...	...	...	...
0	16 852	8 808	8 044	...	...	...	...	...	...
1 - 4	67 137	34 726	32 411	...	...	...	...	...	...
5 - 9	77 959	40 425	37 534	...	...	...	...	...	...
10 - 14	80 218	41 292	38 926	...	...	...	...	...	...
15 - 19	79 267	40 768	38 499	...	...	...	...	...	...
20 - 24	78 985	40 668	38 317	...	...	...	...	...	...
25 - 29	73 799	37 723	36 076	...	...	...	...	...	...
30 - 34	64 585	33 343	31 242	...	...	...	...	...	...
35 - 39	57 517	29 413	28 104	...	...	...	...	...	...
40 - 44	55 676	28 341	27 335	...	...	...	...	...	...
45 - 49	50 813	25 955	24 858	...	...	...	...	...	...
50 - 54	41 579	21 095	20 484	...	...	...	...	...	...
55 - 59	32 329	16 348	15 981	...	...	...	...	...	...
60 - 64	24 662	12 199	12 463	...	...	...	...	...	...
65 - 69	17 754	8 588	9 166	...	...	...	...	...	...
70 - 74	10 865	5 131	5 734	...	...	...	...	...	...
75 +	12 624	5 595	7 029	...	...	...	...	...	...
French Polynesia - Polynésie française									
1 I 2011 (ESDF)									
Total	269 989	138 127	131 862	...	...	...	...	...	...
0 - 4	22 060	11 344	10 716	...	...	...	...	...	...
5 - 9	21 893	11 036	10 857	...	...	...	...	...	...
10 - 14	23 567	12 115	11 452	...	...	...	...	...	...
15 - 19	24 936	12 766	12 170	...	...	...	...	...	...
20 - 24	24 430	12 544	11 886	...	...	...	...	...	...
25 - 29	21 135	10 662	10 473	...	...	...	...	...	...
30 - 34	19 951	10 154	9 797	...	...	...	...	...	...
35 - 39	20 911	10 655	10 256	...	...	...	...	...	...
40 - 44	20 715	10 780	9 935	...	...	...	...	...	...
45 - 49	18 232	9 441	8 791	...	...	...	...	...	...
50 - 54	14 919	7 867	7 052	...	...	...	...	...	...
55 - 59	11 744	6 115	5 629	...	...	...	...	...	...
60 - 64	8 646	4 416	4 230	...	...	...	...	...	...
65 - 69	6 564	3 381	3 183	...	...	...	...	...	...
70 - 74	4 722	2 349	2 373	...	...	...	...	...	...
75 - 79	3 158	1 463	1 695	...	...	...	...	...	...
80 +	2 406	1 039	1 367	...	...	...	...	...	...
Guam[83]									
1 VII 2014 (ESDJ)									
Total	161 001	81 625	79 376	...	...	...	...	...	...
0 - 4	13 656	7 023	6 633	...	...	...	...	...	...
5 - 9	13 631	7 009	6 622	...	...	...	...	...	...
10 - 14	14 512	7 488	7 024	...	...	...	...	...	...
15 - 19	13 958	7 285	6 673	...	...	...	...	...	...
20 - 24	13 315	6 824	6 491	...	...	...	...	...	...
25 - 29	11 660	5 868	5 792	...	...	...	...	...	...
30 - 34	10 200	5 109	5 091	...	...	...	...	...	...
35 - 39	9 925	5 076	4 849	...	...	...	...	...	...
40 - 44	10 811	5 449	5 362	...	...	...	...	...	...

Continent, country or area, date, code[a] and age (in years) / Continent, pays ou zone, date, code[a] et âge (en années)	Total			Urban - Urbaine			Rural - Rurale		
	Both sexes Les deux sexes	Male Masculin	Female Féminin	Both sexes Les deux sexes	Male Masculin	Female Féminin	Both sexes Les deux sexes	Male Masculin	Female Féminin
OCEANIA - OCÉANIE									
Guam[83]									
1 VII 2014 (ESDJ)									
45 - 49	10 616	5 525	5 091	...	...	...	...	...	...
50 - 54	10 131	5 258	4 873	...	...	...	...	...	...
55 - 59	8 062	4 096	3 966	...	...	...	...	...	...
60 - 64	6 832	3 387	3 445	...	...	...	...	...	...
65 - 69	5 092	2 479	2 613	...	...	...	...	...	...
70 - 74	3 367	1 604	1 763	...	...	...	...	...	...
75 - 79	2 626	1 141	1 485	...	...	...	...	...	...
80 - 84	1 592	639	953	...	...	...	...	...	...
85 +	1 015	365	650	...	...	...	...	...	...
Kiribati									
10 X 2010 (CDFC)									
Total	103 058	50 796	52 262	50 182	24 233	25 949	52 876	26 563	26 313
0 - 4	13 992	7 126	6 866	6 934	3 563	3 371	7 058	3 563	3 495
5 - 9	11 026	5 739	5 287	4 822	2 504	2 318	6 204	3 235	2 969
10 - 14	12 166	6 198	5 968	5 363	2 693	2 670	6 803	3 505	3 298
15 - 19	10 926	5 582	5 344	5 713	2 846	2 867	5 213	2 736	2 477
20 - 24	10 366	5 242	5 124	5 658	2 763	2 895	4 708	2 479	2 229
25 - 29	8 416	4 070	4 346	4 413	2 035	2 378	4 003	2 035	1 968
30 - 34	6 721	3 223	3 498	3 389	1 624	1 765	3 332	1 599	1 733
35 - 39	5 625	2 682	2 943	2 767	1 304	1 463	2 858	1 378	1 480
40 - 44	6 116	2 908	3 208	2 803	1 302	1 501	3 313	1 606	1 707
45 - 49	5 234	2 519	2 715	2 479	1 137	1 342	2 755	1 382	1 373
50 - 54	3 892	1 813	2 079	1 897	855	1 042	1 995	958	1 037
55 - 59	2 927	1 349	1 578	1 437	627	810	1 490	722	768
60 - 64	1 985	919	1 066	922	396	526	1 063	523	540
65 - 69	1 520	642	878	700	278	422	820	364	456
70 - 74	1 108	428	680	438	161	277	670	267	403
75 - 79	637	223	414	264	89	175	373	134	239
80 - 84	272	97	175	119	41	78	153	56	97
85 - 89	89	25	64	48	11	37	41	14	27
90 - 94	29	9	20	15	4	11	14	5	9
95 +	11	2	9	1	-	1	10	2	8
Marshall Islands - Îles Marshall[84]									
1 VII 2010 (ESDF)									
Total	54 305	27 843	26 462	...	...	...	...	...	...
0 - 4	7 899	4 053	3 846	...	...	...	...	...	...
5 - 9	7 131	3 660	3 470	...	...	...	...	...	...
10 - 14	7 207	3 732	3 475	...	...	...	...	...	...
15 - 19	6 120	3 126	2 993	...	...	...	...	...	...
20 - 24	6 347	3 310	3 038	...	...	...	...	...	...
25 - 29	4 808	2 478	2 330	...	...	...	...	...	...
30 - 34	2 761	1 389	1 372	...	...	...	...	...	...
35 - 39	2 128	1 071	1 058	...	...	...	...	...	...
40 - 44	2 039	1 043	996	...	...	...	...	...	...
45 - 49	2 023	1 025	998	...	...	...	...	...	...
50 - 54	1 814	878	936	...	...	...	...	...	...
55 - 59	1 592	854	737	...	...	...	...	...	...
60 - 64	1 089	573	516	...	...	...	...	...	...
65 - 69	572	299	273	...	...	...	...	...	...
70 - 74	361	165	196	...	...	...	...	...	...
75 +	412	184	228	...	...	...	...	...	...
Micronesia (Federated States of) - Micronésie (États fédérés de)[2]									
1 VII 2014 (ESDJ)									
Total	106 374	53 200	53 174	...	...	...	...	...	...
0 - 4	12 062	6 178	5 884	...	...	...	...	...	...
5 - 9	12 617	6 453	6 164	...	...	...	...	...	...
10 - 14	12 204	6 226	5 978	...	...	...	...	...	...
15 - 19	10 693	5 428	5 265	...	...	...	...	...	...
20 - 24	8 613	4 365	4 248	...	...	...	...	...	...
25 - 29	7 316	3 758	3 558	...	...	...	...	...	...

Continent, country or area, date, code[a] and age (in years) / Continent, pays ou zone, date, code[a] et âge (en années)	Total			Urban - Urbaine			Rural - Rurale		
	Both sexes Les deux sexes	Male Masculin	Female Féminin	Both sexes Les deux sexes	Male Masculin	Female Féminin	Both sexes Les deux sexes	Male Masculin	Female Féminin
OCEANIA - OCÉANIE									
Micronesia (Federated States of) - Micronésie (États fédérés de)[2]									
1 VII 2014 (ESDJ)									
30 - 34	6 780	3 309	3 471	...	...	...	...	...	...
35 - 39	5 785	2 857	2 928	...	...	...	...	...	...
40 - 44	5 952	2 760	3 192	...	...	...	...	...	...
45 - 49	5 479	2 575	2 904	...	...	...	...	...	...
50 - 54	5 249	2 598	2 651	...	...	...	...	...	...
55 - 59	4 750	2 389	2 361	...	...	...	...	...	...
60 - 64	3 708	1 894	1 814	...	...	...	...	...	...
65 - 69	2 288	1 142	1 146	...	...	...	...	...	...
70 - 74	1 217	539	678	...	...	...	...	...	...
75 +	1 661	729	932	...	...	...	...	...	...
New Caledonia - Nouvelle-Calédonie									
1 I 2013 (ESDF)									
Total	260 000	131 481	128 519	...	...	...	...	...	...
0 - 4	20 127	10 368	9 759	...	...	...	...	...	...
5 - 9	20 576	10 626	9 950	...	...	...	...	...	...
10 - 14	22 365	11 403	10 962	...	...	...	...	...	...
15 - 19	21 998	11 335	10 663	...	...	...	...	...	...
20 - 24	18 654	9 516	9 138	...	...	...	...	...	...
25 - 29	19 636	9 907	9 729	...	...	...	...	...	...
30 - 34	19 598	9 756	9 842	...	...	...	...	...	...
35 - 39	19 744	9 830	9 914	...	...	...	...	...	...
40 - 44	20 071	10 103	9 968	...	...	...	...	...	...
45 - 49	17 926	9 111	8 815	...	...	...	...	...	...
50 - 54	14 975	7 562	7 413	...	...	...	...	...	...
55 - 59	12 082	6 147	5 935	...	...	...	...	...	...
60 - 64	10 143	5 267	4 876	...	...	...	...	...	...
65 - 69	8 172	4 197	3 975	...	...	...	...	...	...
70 - 74	5 932	2 834	3 098	...	...	...	...	...	...
75 - 79	3 830	1 812	2 018	...	...	...	...	...	...
80 - 84	2 403	1 028	1 375	...	...	...	...	...	...
85 - 89	1 205	471	734	...	...	...	...	...	...
90 - 94	402	153	249	...	...	...	...	...	...
95 +	161	55	106	...	...	...	...	...	...
New Zealand - Nouvelle-Zélande[85]									
1 VII 2014 (ESDJ)									
Total	4 509 700	2 209 600	2 300 200	3 884 000[86]	1 889 100[86]	1 995 000[86]	625 000[86]	320 100[86]	304 900[86]
0	58 880	30 330	28 560	51 650[86]	26 640[86]	25 010[86]	7 240[86]	3 690[86]	3 540[86]
1 - 4	249 930	128 030	121 890	216 540[86]	110 940[86]	105 600[86]	33 370[86]	17 080[86]	16 290[86]
5 - 9	306 460	157 230	149 220	260 110[86]	133 420[86]	126 690[86]	46 340[86]	23 810[86]	22 530[86]
10 - 14	295 830	151 460	144 370	249 870[86]	127 730[86]	122 150[86]	45 940[86]	23 720[86]	22 210[86]
15 - 19	313 580	161 440	152 140	273 260[86]	139 810[86]	133 450[86]	40 300[86]	21 620[86]	18 680[86]
20 - 24	325 650	166 320	159 330	295 250[86]	149 630[86]	145 620[86]	30 380[86]	16 680[86]	13 700[86]
25 - 29	291 250	143 380	147 870	263 610[86]	129 140[86]	134 470[86]	27 620[86]	14 230[86]	13 390[86]
30 - 34	277 630	133 470	144 170	248 400[86]	119 050[86]	129 350[86]	29 200[86]	14 400[86]	14 790[86]
35 - 39	273 020	129 980	143 040	238 500[86]	113 250[86]	125 250[86]	34 490[86]	16 720[86]	17 770[86]
40 - 44	313 640	148 830	164 810	267 950[86]	126 500[86]	141 460[86]	45 660[86]	22 310[86]	23 350[86]
45 - 49	311 290	149 510	161 780	261 950[86]	125 080[86]	136 880[86]	49 270[86]	24 400[86]	24 880[86]
50 - 54	317 410	153 370	164 040	263 820[86]	126 420[86]	137 400[86]	53 500[86]	26 890[86]	26 610[86]
55 - 59	279 540	135 850	143 680	229 810[86]	110 480[86]	119 340[86]	49 620[86]	25 310[86]	24 310[86]
60 - 64	245 230	119 500	125 730	201 700[86]	97 010[86]	104 700[86]	43 410[86]	22 410[86]	21 000[86]
65 - 69	216 280	105 690	110 590	179 170[86]	86 080[86]	93 090[86]	37 020[86]	19 560[86]	17 460[86]
70 - 74	160 150	77 250	82 900	135 490[86]	63 980[86]	71 510[86]	24 610[86]	13 240[86]	11 380[86]
75 - 79	113 540	52 980	60 560	99 410[86]	45 350[86]	54 060[86]	14 120[86]	7 620[86]	6 500[86]
80 - 84	82 750	36 510	46 250	74 960[86]	32 430[86]	42 530[86]	7 780[86]	4 070[86]	3 710[86]
85 +	77 690	28 470	49 220	72 540[86]	26 140[86]	46 400[86]	5 140[86]	2 320[86]	2 820[86]

Continent, country or area, date, code[a] and age (in years) Continent, pays ou zone, date, code[a] et âge (en annèes)	Total			Urban - Urbaine			Rural - Rurale		
	Both sexes Les deux sexes	Male Masculin	Female Féminin	Both sexes Les deux sexes	Male Masculin	Female Féminin	Both sexes Les deux sexes	Male Masculin	Female Féminin
OCEANIA - OCÉANIE									
Niue - Nioué									
1 VII 2010 (ESDJ)									
Total	1 496[87]	754	740	...	...	...	...	...	...
0 - 4	135[87]	69	64	...	...	...	...	...	...
5 - 9	134	58	76	...	...	...	...	...	...
10 - 14	116	60	56	...	...	...	...	...	...
15 - 19	124	79	45	...	...	...	...	...	...
20 - 24	100	50	50	...	...	...	...	...	...
25 - 29	90	38	52	...	...	...	...	...	...
30 - 34	71	39	32	...	...	...	...	...	...
35 - 39	85	45	40	...	...	...	...	...	...
40 - 44	101	55	46	...	...	...	...	...	...
45 - 49	92	42	50	...	...	...	...	...	...
50 - 54	107	58	49	...	...	...	...	...	...
55 - 59	89	42	47	...	...	...	...	...	...
60 - 64	70	34	36	...	...	...	...	...	...
65 - 69	75	37	38	...	...	...	...	...	...
70 - 74	53	23	30	...	...	...	...	...	...
75 +	54	25	29	...	...	...	...	...	...
Norfolk Island - Île Norfolk									
9 VIII 2011 (CDFC)									
Total	2 302	1 082	1 220	...	...	...	...	...	...
0 - 4	106	53	53	...	...	...	...	...	...
5 - 9	123	63	60	...	...	...	...	...	...
10 - 14	132	69	63	...	...	...	...	...	...
15 - 19	73	35	38	...	...	...	...	...	...
20 - 24	41	20	21	...	...	...	...	...	...
25 - 29	60	19	41	...	...	...	...	...	...
30 - 34	100	48	52	...	...	...	...	...	...
35 - 39	127	56	71	...	...	...	...	...	...
40 - 44	146	64	82	...	...	...	...	...	...
45 - 49	167	81	86	...	...	...	...	...	...
50 - 54	180	86	94	...	...	...	...	...	...
55 - 59	232	103	129	...	...	...	...	...	...
60 - 64	262	120	142	...	...	...	...	...	...
65 - 69	205	99	106	...	...	...	...	...	...
70 - 74	142	70	72	...	...	...	...	...	...
75 - 79	96	49	47	...	...	...	...	...	...
80 - 84	58	24	34	...	...	...	...	...	...
85 +	52	23	29	...	...	...	...	...	...
Northern Mariana Islands - Îles Mariannes septentrionales									
1 VII 2011 (ESDF)									
Total	46 050	22 153	23 897	...	...	...	...	...	...
0 - 4	4 852	2 495	2 357	...	...	...	...	...	...
5 - 9	3 622	1 883	1 739	...	...	...	...	...	...
10 - 14	3 500	1 971	1 529	...	...	...	...	...	...
15 - 19	3 802	2 121	1 681	...	...	...	...	...	...
20 - 24	3 398	1 607	1 791	...	...	...	...	...	...
25 - 29	3 831	1 050	2 781	...	...	...	...	...	...
30 - 34	3 696	1 008	2 688	...	...	...	...	...	...
35 - 39	3 211	1 550	1 661	...	...	...	...	...	...
40 - 44	3 584	1 858	1 726	...	...	...	...	...	...
45 - 49	3 738	1 967	1 771	...	...	...	...	...	...
50 - 54	3 441	1 824	1 617	...	...	...	...	...	...
55 - 59	2 270	1 260	1 010	...	...	...	...	...	...
60 - 64	1 440	769	671	...	...	...	...	...	...
65 - 69	794	366	428	...	...	...	...	...	...
70 - 74	416	248	168	...	...	...	...	...	...
75 - 79	239	101	138	...	...	...	...	...	...
80 - 84	147	54	93	...	...	...	...	...	...
85 - 89	53	17	36	...	...	...	...	...	...
90 - 94	14	3	11	...	...	...	...	...	...

Continent, country or area, date, code[a] and age (in years) / Continent, pays ou zone, date, code[a] et âge (en annèes)	Total			Urban - Urbaine			Rural - Rurale		
	Both sexes Les deux sexes	Male Masculin	Female Féminin	Both sexes Les deux sexes	Male Masculin	Female Féminin	Both sexes Les deux sexes	Male Masculin	Female Féminin
OCEANIA - OCÉANIE									
Northern Mariana Islands - Îles Mariannes septentrionales									
1 VII 2011 (ESDF)									
95 - 99	*1*	*1*	-	...	...	...	...	...	...
100 + ...	*1*	-	*1*	...	...	...	...	...	...
Palau - Palaos									
1 IV 2005 (CDJC)									
Total.............................	19 907	10 699	9 208	...	...	...	...	...	...
0 - 4	1 363	685	678	...	...	...	...	...	...
5 - 9	1 521	805	716	...	...	...	...	...	...
10 - 14	1 914	964	950	...	...	...	...	...	...
15 - 19	1 462	715	747	...	...	...	...	...	...
20 - 24	1 266	712	554	...	...	...	...	...	...
25 - 29	1 583	942	641	...	...	...	...	...	...
30 - 34	1 856	1 072	784	...	...	...	...	...	...
35 - 39	1 965	1 132	833	...	...	...	...	...	...
40 - 44	1 887	1 096	791	...	...	...	...	...	...
45 - 49	1 534	842	692	...	...	...	...	...	...
50 - 54	1 182	624	558	...	...	...	...	...	...
55 - 59	732	393	339	...	...	...	...	...	...
60 - 64	506	254	252	...	...	...	...	...	...
65 - 69	373	170	203	...	...	...	...	...	...
70 - 74	257	119	138	...	...	...	...	...	...
75 - 79	214	71	143	...	...	...	...	...	...
80 - 84	151	56	95	...	...	...	...	...	...
85 + ...	141	47	94	...	...	...	...	...	...
Pitcairn									
31 XII 2013 (CDJC)									
Total.............................	49	23	26	...	...	...	...	...	...
0 - 17	8	3	5	...	...	...	...	...	...
18 - 40	7	4	3	...	...	...	...	...	...
41 - 64	24	13	11	...	...	...	...	...	...
65 + ...	10	3	7	...	...	...	...	...	...
Samoa									
7 XI 2011 (CDFC)									
Total.............................	187 820	96 990	90 830	...	...	...	...	...	...
0 - 4	26 829	13 953	12 876	...	...	...	...	...	...
5 - 9	23 044	11 899	11 145	...	...	...	...	...	...
10 - 14	22 017	11 497	10 520	...	...	...	...	...	...
15 - 19	19 814	10 391	9 423	...	...	...	...	...	...
20 - 24	14 833	7 700	7 133	...	...	...	...	...	...
25 - 29	12 767	6 601	6 166	...	...	...	...	...	...
30 - 34	11 543	5 945	5 598	...	...	...	...	...	...
35 - 39	10 877	5 735	5 142	...	...	...	...	...	...
40 - 44	10 436	5 602	4 834	...	...	...	...	...	...
45 - 49	8 887	4 574	4 313	...	...	...	...	...	...
50 - 54	7 576	3 966	3 610	...	...	...	...	...	...
55 - 59	5 904	3 007	2 897	...	...	...	...	...	...
60 - 64	3 978	2 002	1 976	...	...	...	...	...	...
65 - 69	3 374	1 605	1 769	...	...	...	...	...	...
70 - 74	2 557	1 187	1 370	...	...	...	...	...	...
75 + ...	3 354	1 302	2 052	...	...	...	...	...	...
Unknown - Inconnu	30	24	6	...	...	...	...	...	...
Solomon Islands - Îles Salomon									
22 XI 2009 (CDFC)									
Total.............................	515 870	264 455	251 415	102 030	53 596	48 434	413 840	210 859	202 981
0 - 4	76 227	39 728	36 499	12 500	6 573	5 927	63 727	33 155	30 572
5 - 9	71 126	36 974	34 152	11 328	5 853	5 475	59 798	31 121	28 677
10 - 14	61 931	32 562	29 369	10 354	5 382	4 972	51 577	27 180	24 397
15 - 19	51 212	26 189	25 023	10 995	5 525	5 470	40 217	20 664	19 553
20 - 24	45 419	22 399	23 020	12 344	6 360	5 984	33 075	16 039	17 036
25 - 29	42 674	20 794	21 880	11 160	5 696	5 464	31 514	15 098	16 416
30 - 34	37 592	18 807	18 785	8 817	4 568	4 249	28 775	14 239	14 536

7. Population by age, sex and urban/rural residence: latest available year, 2005 - 2014
Population selon l'âge, le sexe et la résidence, urbaine/rurale : dernière année disponible, 2005 - 2014 (continued - suite)

Continent, country or area, date, code[a] and age (in years) / Continent, pays ou zone, date, code[a] et âge (en années)	Total			Urban - Urbaine			Rural - Rurale		
	Both sexes Les deux sexes	Male Masculin	Female Féminin	Both sexes Les deux sexes	Male Masculin	Female Féminin	Both sexes Les deux sexes	Male Masculin	Female Féminin
OCEANIA - OCÉANIE									
Solomon Islands - Îles Salomon									
22 XI 2009 (CDFC)									
35 - 39	33 151	17 010	16 141	7 447	4 000	3 447	25 704	13 010	12 694
40 - 44	23 638	12 070	11 568	5 161	2 808	2 353	18 477	9 262	9 215
45 - 49	19 713	10 189	9 524	4 064	2 265	1 799	15 649	7 924	7 725
50 - 54	14 339	7 498	6 841	2 818	1 650	1 168	11 521	5 848	5 673
55 - 59	11 787	6 111	5 676	2 011	1 198	813	9 776	4 913	4 863
60 - 64	8 916	4 535	4 381	1 272	726	546	7 644	3 809	3 835
65 - 69	7 021	3 693	3 328	822	466	356	6 199	3 227	2 972
70 - 74	4 698	2 402	2 296	478	259	219	4 220	2 143	2 077
75 - 79	3 374	1 784	1 590	279	160	119	3 095	1 624	1 471
80 - 84	1 525	800	725	102	58	44	1 423	742	681
85 - 89	894	512	382	58	34	24	836	478	358
90 - 94	301	170	131	8	4	4	293	166	127
95 - 99	332	228	104	12	11	1	320	217	103
Tokelau - Tokélaou									
1 XII 2013 (ESDF)									
Total	1 383	683	700	...	...	...	...	...	...
0	25	12	13	...	...	...	...	...	...
1 - 4	115	62	53	...	...	...	...	...	...
5 - 9	139	75	64	...	...	...	...	...	...
10 - 14	134	64	70	...	...	...	...	...	...
15 - 19	142	76	66	...	...	...	...	...	...
20 - 24	130	57	73	...	...	...	...	...	...
25 - 29	93	40	53	...	...	...	...	...	...
30 - 34	78	43	35	...	...	...	...	...	...
35 - 39	59	28	31	...	...	...	...	...	...
40 - 44	75	39	36	...	...	...	...	...	...
45 - 49	84	41	43	...	...	...	...	...	...
50 - 54	66	32	34	...	...	...	...	...	...
55 - 59	63	28	35	...	...	...	...	...	...
60 - 64	62	29	33	...	...	...	...	...	...
65 - 69	34	18	16	...	...	...	...	...	...
70 - 74	32	14	18	...	...	...	...	...	...
75 +	31	13	18	...	...	...	...	...	...
Unknown - Inconnu	21	12	9	...	...	...	...	...	...
Tonga									
30 XI 2006 (CDJC)									
Total	101 991	51 772	50 219	23 658	11 860	11 798	78 333	39 912	38 421
0 - 4	13 782	7 174	6 608	3 015	1 514	1 501	10 767	5 660	5 107
5 - 9	12 804	6 745	6 059	2 721	1 447	1 274	10 083	5 298	4 785
10 - 14	12 320	6 412	5 908	2 631	1 357	1 274	9 689	5 055	4 634
15 - 19	10 280	5 383	4 897	2 362	1 196	1 166	7 918	4 187	3 731
20 - 24	9 191	4 648	4 543	2 503	1 276	1 227	6 688	3 372	3 316
25 - 29	7 304	3 639	3 665	1 872	913	959	5 432	2 726	2 706
30 - 34	6 337	3 146	3 191	1 551	787	764	4 786	2 359	2 427
35 - 39	6 229	3 112	3 117	1 448	711	737	4 781	2 401	2 380
40 - 44	5 014	2 578	2 436	1 240	647	593	3 774	1 931	1 843
45 - 49	3 982	1 923	2 059	982	458	524	3 000	1 465	1 535
50 - 54	3 465	1 634	1 831	844	406	438	2 621	1 228	1 393
55 - 59	2 849	1 359	1 490	639	323	316	2 210	1 036	1 174
60 - 64	2 470	1 169	1 301	556	260	296	1 914	909	1 005
65 - 69	2 174	1 092	1 082	466	211	255	1 708	881	827
70 - 74	1 586	777	809	340	152	188	1 246	625	621
75 - 79	1 099	510	589	253	107	146	846	403	443
80 - 84	625	260	365	144	48	96	481	212	269
85 - 89	246	96	150	45	21	24	201	75	126
90 - 94	86	22	64	15	5	10	71	17	54
95 - 99	20	6	14	5	2	3	15	4	11
100 +	6	-	6	-	-	-	6	-	6
Unknown - Inconnu	122	87	35	26	19	7	96	68	28
1 VII 2008 (ESDF)[88]									
Total	103 647	52 972	50 673	...	...	...	...	...	...
0 - 4	11 970	6 164	5 806	...	...	...	...	...	...

7. Population by age, sex and urban/rural residence: latest available year, 2005 - 2014
Population selon l'âge, le sexe et la résidence, urbaine/rurale : dernière année disponible, 2005 - 2014 (continued - suite)

Continent, country or area, date, code[a] and age (in years) / Continent, pays ou zone, date, code[a] et âge (en années)	Total			Urban - Urbaine			Rural - Rurale		
	Both sexes Les deux sexes	Male Masculin	Female Féminin	Both sexes Les deux sexes	Male Masculin	Female Féminin	Both sexes Les deux sexes	Male Masculin	Female Féminin
OCEANIA - OCÉANIE									
Tonga									
1 VII 2008 (ESDF)[88]									
5 - 9	*11 419*	*5 910*	*5 508*	...	...	...	...	...	...
10 - 14	*11 968*	*6 212*	*5 756*	...	...	...	...	...	...
15 - 19	*11 383*	*6 060*	*5 323*	...	...	...	...	...	...
20 - 24	*10 612*	*5 573*	*5 040*	...	...	...	...	...	...
25 - 29	*8 609*	*4 406*	*4 204*	...	...	...	...	...	...
30 - 34	*5 874*	*2 955*	*2 919*	...	...	...	...	...	...
35 - 39	*5 397*	*2 718*	*2 680*	...	...	...	...	...	...
40 - 44	*5 250*	*2 661*	*2 590*	...	...	...	...	...	...
45 - 49	*4 471*	*2 186*	*2 285*	...	...	...	...	...	...
50 - 54	*3 914*	*1 867*	*2 047*	...	...	...	...	...	...
55 - 59	*3 294*	*1 556*	*1 737*	...	...	...	...	...	...
60 - 64	*2 844*	*1 355*	*1 489*	...	...	...	...	...	...
65 - 69	*2 482*	*1 243*	*1 239*	...	...	...	...	...	...
70 - 74	*1 896*	*981*	*915*	...	...	...	...	...	...
75 +	*2 263*	*1 127*	*1 136*	...	...	...	...	...	...
Vanuatu									
16 XI 2009 (CDJC)									
Total	234 023	119 091	114 932	57 195	29 618	27 577	176 828	89 473	87 355
0 - 4	33 367	17 310	16 057	7 224	3 828	3 396	26 143	13 482	12 661
5 - 9	29 685	15 455	14 230	5 591	2 850	2 741	24 094	12 605	11 489
10 - 14	27 921	14 762	13 159	5 250	2 755	2 495	22 671	12 007	10 664
15 - 19	23 882	12 027	11 855	6 460	3 122	3 338	17 422	8 905	8 517
20 - 24	21 541	10 415	11 126	7 186	3 606	3 580	14 355	6 809	7 546
25 - 29	18 415	9 124	9 291	5 542	2 937	2 605	12 873	6 187	6 686
30 - 34	15 693	7 790	7 903	4 517	2 300	2 217	11 176	5 490	5 686
35 - 39	14 171	7 076	7 095	3 844	1 965	1 879	10 327	5 111	5 216
40 - 44	11 523	5 814	5 709	3 242	1 710	1 532	8 281	4 104	4 177
45 - 49	10 241	5 066	5 175	2 817	1 474	1 343	7 424	3 592	3 832
50 - 54	7 415	3 789	3 626	1 923	1 036	887	5 492	2 753	2 739
55 - 59	6 363	3 261	3 102	1 495	845	650	4 868	2 416	2 452
60 - 64	4 319	2 192	2 127	826	455	371	3 493	1 737	1 756
65 - 69	3 826	2 054	1 772	590	355	235	3 236	1 699	1 537
70 +	5 661	2 956	2 705	688	380	308	4 973	2 576	2 397

FOOTNOTES - NOTES

Italics: estimates which are less reliable. - Italiques : estimations moins sûres.

* Provisional. - Données provisoires.

[a] 'Code' indicates the source of data, as follows:
CDFC - Census, de facto, complete tabulation
CDFS - Census, de facto, sample tabulation
CDJC - Census, de jure, complete tabulation
CDJS - Census, de jure, sample tabulation
SSDF - Sample survey, de facto
SSDJ - Sample survey, de jure
ESDF - Estimates, de facto
ESDJ - Estimates, de jure

Le 'Code' indique la source des données, comme suit :
CDFC - Recensement, population de fait, tabulation complète
CDFS - Recensement, population de fait, tabulation par sondage
CDJC - Recensement, population de droit, tabulation complète
CDJS - Recensement, population de droit, tabulation par sondage
SSDF - Enquête par sondage, population de fait
SSDJ - Enquête par sondage, population de droit
ESDF - Estimations, population de fait
ESDJ - Estimations, population de droit

[1] Data refer to population in housing units and collective living quarters only. - Correspond aux personnes qui vivent dans des unités d'habitation et dans des logements collectifs seulement.

[2] Data refer to national projections. - Les données se réfèrent aux projections nationales.

[3] Data refer to national projections. Data as reported by national statistical authorities. Figures for urban and rural do not add up to the total. - Les données se réfèrent aux projections nationales. Les données comme elles ont été déclarées par l'institut national de la statistique. La somme des données pour la residence urbaine et rurale n'est pas égale au total.

[4] Post-censal estimates based on the 2009 Population Census. - Les estimations post-censitaire fondées sur le recensement de la population de 2009.

[5] Including nomadic population. - Y compris la population nomade.

[6] Excludes the islands of St. Brandon and Agalega. - Non compris les îles St. Brandon et Agalega.

[7] Based on the results of the 2011 Population Census. - Basé sur les résultats du rencencement de la population de 2011.

[8] Based on the results of the 2004 Population Census. - D'après les résultats du recensement de la population de 2004.

[9] Data refer to projections based on the 2011 Population Census. - Les données se réfèrent aux projections basées sur le recensement de la population de 2011.

[10] Data refer to national projections. Based on the results of the 2012 Population and Housing Census. - Les données se réfèrent aux projections nationales. D'après les résultats du recensement de la population et des logements de 2012.

[11] Projections based on the 2002 Population Census. - Projections fondées sur le recensement de la population de 2002.

[12] Data as reported by national statistical authorities. Summation of frequencies gives a different total; reason for discrepancy not ascertained. - Les données comme elles ont été déclarées par l'institut national de la statistique. La somme des fréquences un total différent; on ne sait pas comment s'explique la divergence.

[13] Bermuda is 100 per cent urban. - 100 pour cent de la population des Bermudes est urbaine.

[14] Data refer to projections based on the 2010 Population Census. - Les données se réfèrent aux projections basées sur le recensement de la population de 2010.

[15] Preliminary postcensal estimates. - Estimations post censitaires préliminaires.

[16] Based on the national household surveys 2010-2014 and the 2011 population census. - D'après les données de l'enquête nationale des ménages 2010-2014 et les résultats du recensement de la population de 2011.

[17] Postcensal estimates. - Estimations post censitaires.

[18] Estimates based on the 2007 Population Census. - Estimations fondées sur le recensement de la population de 2007.

[19] Population statistics are compiled from registers. - Les statistiques de la population sont compilées à partir des registres.

[20] Excluding data for Saint Barthélémy and Saint Martin. - Non compris les données pour Saint Barthélémy et Saint Martin.

[21] Projections produced by l'Institut Haïtien de Statistique et d'Informatique (IHSI) and the Latin American and Caribbean Demographic Centre (CELADE) - Population Division of ECLAC. - Les données sont projections produits par l'Institut Haïtien de Statistique et d'Informatique (IHSI) et le centre démographique de l'Amérique latine et les Caraïbes - Division de la population de la CEPALC.

[22] Data refer to projections based on the 2001 Population Census. - Les données se réfèrent aux projections basées sur le recensement de la population de 2001.

[23] Including an estimation of 1 334 585 persons corresponding to 448 195 housing units without information of the occupants. - Y compris une estimation de 1 334 585 personnes correspondant aux 448 195 unités d'habitation sans information sur les occupants.

[24] Including armed forces stationed in the area. Based on the results of the 2010 Population Census. - Y compris les militaires en garnison sur le territoire. D'après le résultats du recensement de la population de 2010.

[25] Because of rounding, totals are not in all cases the sum of the respective components. Unrevised data. - Les chiffres étant arrondis, les totaux ne correspondent pas toujours rigoureusement à la somme des composants respectifs. Les données n'ont pas été révisées.

[26] Excluding U.S. Armed Forces overseas and civilian U.S. citizens whose usual place of residence is outside the United States. Postcensal estimates. - Non compris les militaires américains à l'étranger et les civils américains dont le lieu de résidence habituel est en dehors des États-Unis. Estimations post censitaires.

[27] Including armed forces stationed in the area. - Y compris les militaires en garnison sur le territoire.

[28] Data refer to projections based on the 2010 Population and Housing Census. - Les données se réfèrent aux projections basées sur le recensement 2010 de la population et des logements.

[29] Data include persons in remote areas, military personnel outside the country, merchant seamen at sea, civilian seasonal workers outside the country, and other civilians outside the country, and exclude nomads, foreign military, civilian aliens temporarily in the country, transients on ships and Indian jungle population. Data refer to national projections. - Y compris les personnes vivant dans des régions éloignées, le personel militaire en dehors du pays, les marins marchands, les ouvriers saisonniers en dehors du pays, et autres civils en dehors du pays, et non compris les nomades, les militaires étrangers, les étrangers civils temporairement dans le pays, les transiteurs sur des bateaux et les Indiens de la jungle. Les données se réfèrent aux projections nationales.

[30] Data are revised projections taking into consideration also the results of the 2005 census. - Les données sont des projections révisées tenant compte également des résultats du recensement de 2005.

[31] Excludes nomadic Indian tribes. Data refer to projections based on the 2010 Population Census. - Non compris les tribus d'Indiens nomades. Les données se réfèrent aux projections basées sur le recensement de la population de 2010.

[32] A dispute exists between the governments of Argentina and the United Kingdom of Great Britain and Northern Ireland concerning sovereignty over the Falkland Islands (Malvinas). - La souveraineté sur les îles Falkland (Malvinas) fait l'objet d'un différend entre le Gouvernement argentin et le Gouvernement du Royaume-Uni de Grande-Bretagne et d'Irlande du Nord.

[33] Unrevised data. - Les données n'ont pas été révisées.

[34] Excluding 437 homeless persons. - On n'a pas pris en compte 437 personnes sans abri.

[35] Data refer to the settled population based on the 1979 Population Census and the latest household prelisting. The refugees of Afghanistan in Iran, Pakistan, and an estimated 1.5 million nomads, are not included. - Les données se rapportent à la population stationnaire sur la base du recensement de 1979 et du recensement préliminaire des logements le plus récent. Sont exclus les réfugiés d'Afghanistan en Iran et au Pakistan et les nomades estimés à 1,5 million.

[36] Including "Other Urban" (Total of Both Sexes-6094394, Male-3127003, Female-29673941). - Y compris "Autres citadins" (total des deux sexes 6 094 394; hommes : 3 127 003; femmes: 2 967 391).

[37] Data refer to projected figures based on the Population and Housing Census 2005 (district projection). - Les données se réfèrent aux projections basées sur le recensement de la population et de l'habitat de 2005 (projections locales).

[38] Excluding foreign diplomatic personnel and their dependants. Data based on the 2008 Population Census. - Non compris le personnel diplomatique étranger et les membres de leur famille les accompagnant. Données fondées sur le recensement de population de 2008.

[39] For statistical purposes, the data for China do not include those for the Hong Kong Special Administrative Region (Hong Kong SAR), Macao Special Administrative Region (Macao SAR) and Taiwan province of China. - Pour la présentation des statistiques, les données pour la Chine ne comprennent pas la Région Administrative Spéciale de Hong Kong (Hong Kong RAS), la Région Administrative Spéciale de Macao (Macao RAS) et Taïwan province de Chine.

[40] Data exclude 2.3 million servicemen, 4.65 million persons with permanent resident status difficult to define, and 0.12 per cent undercount based on the post enumeration survey. - Les données ne comprennent pas 2,3 millions de militaires, 4,65 millions de personnes ayant le statut de résident permanent mais difficiles à définir, et des lacunes estimées à 0,12 pour cent sur la base de l'enquête de vérification du recensement.

[41] Because of rounding, totals are not in all cases the sum of the respective components. Data have been adjusted on the basis of the Population Census of 2010. - Les chiffres étant arrondis, les totaux ne correspondent pas toujours rigoureusement à la somme des composants respectifs. Les données ont été ajustées à partir des résultats du recensement de la population de 2010.

[42] Data refer to government controlled areas. - Les données se rapportent aux zones contrôlées par le Gouvernement.

[43] Includes data for the Indian-held part of Jammu and Kashmir, the final status of which has not yet been determined. - Y compris les données pour la partie du Jammu et du Cachemire occupée par l'Inde dont le statut définitif n'a pas encore été déterminé.

[44] Data are based on the publication: "Indonesia Population Projection 2010-2035" - Les données sont basées sur la publication : << Indonesia Population Projection 2010-2035 >>

[45] Data refer to the Iranian Year which begins on 21 March and ends on 20 March of the following year. - Les données concernent l'année iranienne, qui commence le 21 mars et se termine le 20 mars de l'année suivante.

[46] Includes data for East Jerusalem and Israeli residents in certain other territories under occupation by Israeli military forces since June 1967. - Y compris les données pour Jérusalem-Est et les résidents israéliens dans certains autres territoires occupés depuis 1967 par les forces armées israéliennes.

[47] Excluding diplomatic personnel outside the country and foreign military and civilian personnel and their dependants stationed in the area. - Non compris le personnel diplomatique hors du pays ni les militaires et agents civils étrangers en poste sur le territoire et les membres de leur famille les accompagnant.

[48] Because of rounding, totals are not in all cases the sum of the respective components. Estimates based on the complete counts of the 2010 Population Census. - Les chiffres étant arrondis, les totaux ne correspondent pas toujours rigoureusement à la somme des composants respectifs. Estimations basées sur le dénombrement complet du recensement de la population de 2010.

[49] Because of rounding, totals are not in all cases the sum of the respective components. Excluding data for Jordanian territory under occupation since June 1967 by Israeli military forces. Excluding foreigners, including registered Palestinian refugees. - Les chiffres étant arrondis, les totaux ne correspondent pas toujours rigoureusement à la somme des composants respectifs. Non compris les données pour le territoire jordanien occupé depuis juin 1967 par les forces armées israéliennes. Non compris les étrangers, mais y compris les réfugiés de Palestine enregistrés.

[50] Excluding usual residents not in the country at the time of census. - À l'exclusion des résidents habituels qui ne sont pas dans le pays au moment du recensement.

[51] Based on the results of the 2005 Population and Housing Census. - Données fondées sur les résultats du recensement de la population et de l'habitat de 2005.

[52] Based on the results of a household survey. - D'après les résultats d'une enquête des ménages.

53 Estimates based on the adjusted Population and Housing Census of 2010. - Les estimations sont fondée sur les résultats ajustées du recensement de la population et de l'habitat de 2010.

54 Total population is taken as de facto and de jure together. - Population totale considérée comme de fait et de droit.

55 Data refer to enumerated population. - Les données se rapportent à la population dénombrée.

56 Data refer to registered population data from Royal Oman Police. - Les données portent sur la population enregistrée par la police royale de l'Oman.

57 Excluding data for the Pakistan-held part of Jammu and Kashmir, the final status of which has not yet been determined. Based on the results of the Pakistan Demographic Survey (PDS 2007). - Non compris les données concernant la partie du Jammu et Cachemire occupée par le Pakistan dont le statut définitif n'a pas été déterminé. D'après les résultats de l'enquête démographique effectuée par le Pakistan en 2007.

58 Excluding 2739 Filipinos in Philippine Embassies, Consulates and Missions Abroad. - Excepté 2739 Philippins travaillant dans les ambassades, les consulats et les missions des Philippines à l'étranger.

59 Data refer to Korean population only. - les données ne concernent que la population coréenne.

60 Data based on the preliminary results of the 2010 Population and Housing Census. - D'après les résultats préliminaires du recensement de la population et des logements de 2010.

61 Data refer to resident population which comprises Singapore citizens and permanent residents. Data exclude residents who have been away from Singapore for a continuous period of 12 months or longer as at the reference date. - Les données se rapportent à la population résidente composé des citoyens de Singapour et des résidents permanents. Non compris les résidents hors de Singapour pour une période ininterrompue de 12 mois ou plus avant de la date de référence.

62 Data have not been adjusted for underenumeration. Excluding data from the parts of Jerusalem which were annexed by Israel in 1967. - Les données n'ont pas été ajustées pour compenser les lacunes du dénombrement. Non compris les données provenant des parties de Jérusalem qui ont été annexées par Israël en 1967.

63 Data for urban include population in refugee camps. - Les données pour la population urbaine comprennent la population dans les camps réfugiés.

64 Including Palestinian refugees. - Y compris les réfugiés de Palestine.

65 Data based on address-based population registration system. - Les données sont basées sur le registre national de la population basé sur l'adresse.

66 As published by the United Nations Economic and Social Commission for Western Asia. - Publié par la Commission économique et sociale des Nations Unies pour l'Asie occidentale.

67 Excluding Faeroe Islands and Greenland shown separately, if available. Population statistics are compiled from registers. - Non compris les Iles Féroé et le Groenland, qui font l'objet de rubriques distinctes, si disponible. Les statistiques de la population sont compilées à partir des registres.

68 Excluding Åland Islands. - Non compris les Îles d'Åland.

69 Excluding diplomatic personnel outside the country and including members of alien armed forces not living in military camps and foreign diplomatic personnel not living in embassies or consulates. - Non compris le personnel diplomatique hors du pays et y compris les militaires étrangers ne vivant pas dans des camps militaires et le personnel diplomatique étranger ne vivant pas dans les ambassades ou les consulats.

70 Excluding military personnel, visitors and transients. - Non compris les militaires, ni les visiteurs et transients.

71 Excluding armed forces stationed outside the country, but including alien armed forces stationed in the area. - Non compris les militaires en garnison hors du pays, mais y compris les militaires étrangers en garnison sur le territoire.

72 Definition of localities was revised in 2011 causing a break with the previous series. Data refer to registered resident population. - La rupture par rapport aux séries précédentes s'explique par le fait que la définition des localités a été révisée depuis 2011. Les données concernent la population enregistrée résidente.

73 The figures refer to usual residents in private households and persons present in communal establishments during the 2011 census. - Données se rapportant aux résidents habituels membres de ménages privés et aux personnes recensées dans des établissements collectifs au recensement de 2011.

74 Including civilian nationals temporarily outside the country. - Y compris les civils nationaux temporairement hors du pays.

75 Figures for male and female population do not add up to the figure for total population, because they exclude 119 persons of unknown sex. - Les chiffres relatifs à la population masculine et féminine ne correspondent pas au chiffre de la population totale, parce que l'on en a exclu 119 personnes de sexe inconnu.

76 Including residents temporarily outside the country. - Y compris les résidents se trouvant temporairement hors du pays.

77 The total number may include 'Unknown residence', but the categories urban and rural do not. - Le nombre total peut inclure les personnes dont la résidence n'est pas connue, à l'inverse des catégories de population urbaine et rurale.

78 Excluding civilian aliens within the country, but including civilian nationals temporarily outside the country. - Non compris les civils étrangers dans le pays, mais y compris les civils nationaux temporairement hors du pays.

79 Excluding Transnistria and the municipality of Bender. - Les données ne tiennent pas compte de l'information sur la Transnistria et la municipalité de Bender.

80 Excludes data for Kosovo and Metohia. Based on the results of the 2011 Population Census. - Sans les données pour le Kosovo et Metohie. Basé sur les résultats du recencement de la population de 2011.

81 Excluding Channel Islands (Guernsey and Jersey) and Isle of Man, shown separately, if available. - Non compris les îles Anglo-Normandes (Guernesey et Jersey) et l'île de Man, qui font l'objet de rubriques distinctes, si disponible.

82 Excluding Niue, shown separately, which is part of Cook Islands, but because of remoteness is administered separately. - Non compris Nioué, qui fait l'objet d'une rubrique distincte et qui fait partie des îles Cook, mais qui, en raison de son éloignement, est administrée séparément.

83 Including armed forces stationed in the area. Data refer to projections based on the 2010 Population Census. - Y compris les militaires en garnison sur le territoire. Les données se réfèrent aux projections basées sur le recensement de la population de 2010.

84 Projections are prepared by the Secretariat of the Pacific Community based on 1999 census of population and housing. - Les projections sont preparées par le Secrétariat de la Communauté du Pacifique à partir des résultats du recensement de la population et de l'habitat de 1999.

85 Because of rounding, totals are not in all cases the sum of the respective components. - Les chiffres étant arrondis, les totaux ne correspondent pas toujours rigoureusement à la somme des composants respectifs.

86 Population estimates by urban/rural residence exclude inland waters and oceanic areas. - Les estimations de la population par lieu de résidence urbaine ou rurale excluent les eaux intérieures et les zones océaniques.

87 Including unknown sex. - Y compris le sexe inconnu.

88 Because of rounding, totals are not in all cases the sum of the respective components. Data refer to national projections. Based on the results of the 1996 population census. - Les chiffres étant arrondis, les totaux ne correspondent pas toujours rigoureusement à la somme des composants respectifs. Les données se réfèrent aux projections nationales. À partir des résultats du recensement de la population de 1996.

Table 8 - *Demographic Yearbook 2014*

Table 8 presents population of capital cities and cities of 100 000 or more inhabitants for the latest available year between 1995 and 2014.

Description of variables: Since the way in which cities are delimited differs from one country or area to another, the table not only presents data for the so-called city proper, but also for the urban agglomeration, if available.

City proper is defined as a locality with legally fixed boundaries and an administratively recognized urban status, usually characterized by some form of local government.

Urban agglomeration has been defined as comprising the city or town proper and also the suburban fringe or densely settled territory lying outside of, but adjacent to, the city boundaries.

For some countries or areas, however, the data relate to entire administrative divisions known, for example, as shi or municipalities (municipios) which are composed of a populated centre and adjoining territory, some of which may contain other, often separate urban localities or may be distinctively rural in character. For this group of countries or areas the type of civil division is given in a footnote.

The surface area of the city or urban agglomeration is presented, when available.

City names are presented in the original language of the country or area in which the cities are located. In cases where the original names are not in the Roman alphabet, they have been romanized. Cities are listed in English alphabetical order.

Capital cities are shown in the table regardless of their population size. The names of the capital cities are printed in capital letters. The designation of any specific city as a capital city is as reported by the country or area.

The table also covers cities whose urban agglomeration's population exceeds 100 000; that is, while the urban agglomeration should have a population of 100 000 or more to be included in the table, the city proper may be of a smaller population size.

The reference date of each population figure appears in the left-most column of the table. Estimates based on results of sample surveys and city censuses or from other sources are explained by the 'code' also appearing in the left-most column of the table. The codes are explained at the end of the table.

Reliability of data: Specific information is generally not available on the reliability of the estimates of the population of cities or urban agglomerations presented in this table.

In the absence of such quality assessment, data from population censuses, sample surveys and city censuses are considered to be reliable and, therefore, set in Roman type. Other estimates are considered to be reliable if they are based on a complete census (or a sample survey), and have been adjusted by a continuous population register or adjusted on the basis of the calculated balance of births, deaths, and migration.

Limitations: Statistics on the population of capital cities and cities of 100 000 or more inhabitants are subject to the same qualifications as have been set forth for population statistics in general as discussed in section 3 of the Technical Notes.

International comparability of data on city population is limited to a great extent by variations in national concepts and definitions. Although an effort is made to reduce the sources of non-comparability somewhat by presenting the data for both city proper and urban agglomeration, many serious problems of comparability remain.

Data presented in the "city proper" column for some countries represent an urban administrative area legally distinguished from surrounding rural territory, while for other countries these data represent a commune or an equally small administrative unit. In still other countries, the administrative units may be relatively extensive and thereby include considerable territories beyond the urban centre itself.

City data are also especially affected by whether the data refer to *de facto* or *de jure* population, as well as variations among countries in how each of these concepts is applied. With reference to the total population, the difference between the *de facto* and *de jure* population is discussed at length in section 3.1.1 of the Technical Notes.

Data on city populations based on intercensal estimates present additional problems: comparability is impaired by the different methods used in making the estimates, and by the loss of precision in applying to selected segments of the population methods best suited for the whole population. For example, it is far more difficult to apply the component method of estimating population growth to cities than it is to the entire country.

Births and deaths occurring in the cities do not all originate in the population present in or resident of that area. Therefore, the use of natural increase to estimate the probable size of the city population is a potential source of error. Internal migration is another component of population change that cannot be measured with accuracy in many areas. Because of these factors, estimates in this table may be less valuable in general and in particular limited for purposes of international comparison.

City data, even when set in Roman type, are often not as reliable as estimates for the total population of the country or area. Furthermore, because the sources of these data include censuses (national or city), surveys and estimates, the years to which they refer vary widely. In addition, because city boundaries may alter over time, comparisons covering different years should be carried out with caution.

Earlier data: Population of capital cities and cities with a population of 100 000 or more have been shown in previous issues of the *Demographic Yearbook*. For more information on specific topics and years for which data are reported, readers should consult the Historical Index.

Tableau 8 – *Annuaire démographique 2014*

Le tableau 8 présente les données les plus récentes disponibles pour la période 1995 – 2014 sur la population des capitales et des villes de 100 000 habitants ou plus.

Description des variables : étant donné que les villes ne sont pas délimitées de la même manière dans tous les pays ou zones, on s'est efforcé de donner, dans ce tableau, des chiffres correspondant non seulement aux villes proprement dites, mais aussi, le cas échéant, aux agglomérations urbaines.

On entend par villes proprement dites les localités qui ont des limites juridiquement définies et sont administrativement considérées comme villes, ce qui se caractérise généralement par l'existence d'une autorité locale.

L'agglomération urbaine comprend, par définition, la ville proprement dite ainsi que la proche banlieue, c'est-à-dire la zone fortement peuplée qui est extérieure, mais contiguë aux limites de la ville.

En outre, dans certains pays ou zones, les données se rapportent à des divisions administratives entières, connues par exemple sous le nom de shi ou de municipios, qui comportent une agglomération et le territoire avoisinant, lequel peut englober d'autres agglomérations urbaines tout à fait distinctes ou être à caractère essentiellement rural. Pour ce groupe de pays ou zones, le type de division administrative est indiqué en note.

On trouvera à la fin du tableau la superficie de la ville ou agglomération urbaine chaque fois que possible.

Les noms des villes sont indiqués dans la langue du pays ou zone où ces villes sont situées. Les noms de villes qui ne sont pas à l'origine libellés en caractères latins ont été romanisés. Les villes sont énumérées dans l'ordre alphabétique anglais.

Les capitales figurent dans le tableau quel que soit le chiffre de leur population et leur nom a été imprimé en lettres majuscules. Ne sont indiquées comme capitales que les villes ainsi désignées par le pays ou zone intéressé.

En ce qui concerne les autres villes, le tableau indique celles dont la population est égale ou supérieure à 100 000 habitants. Ce chiffre limite s'applique à l'agglomération urbaine et non à la ville proprement dite, dont la population peut être moindre.

La date à laquelle se réfère le chiffre correspondant, figure dans la colonne de gauche du tableau. Le 'code' aussi figurant dans la colonne de gauche du tableau, permet de savoir si les estimations sont fondées sur les résultats d'enquêtes par sondage ou de recensements municipaux ou sont tirées d'autres sources. Les codes utilisés sont expliqués à la fin du tableau.

Fiabilité des données : on ne possède généralement pas de renseignements précis sur la fiabilité des estimations de la population des villes ou agglomérations urbaines présentées dans ce tableau.

Les données provenant de recensements de la population, d'enquêtes par sondage ou de recensements municipaux sont jugées sûres et figurent par conséquent en caractères romains. D'autres estimations sont considérées comme sûres si elles sont fondées sur un recensement complet (ou une enquête par sondage) et ont été ajustées en fonction des données provenant d'un registre permanent de population ou en fonction de la balance, établie par le calcul des naissances, des décès et des migrations.

Insuffisance des données : les statistiques portant sur la population des capitales et des villes de 100 000 habitants ou plus appellent toutes les réserves qui ont été formulées à la section 3 des Notes techniques à propos des statistiques de la population en général.

La comparabilité internationale des données portant sur la population des villes est compromise dans une large mesure par la diversité des définitions nationales. Bien que l'on se soit efforcé de réduire les facteurs de non-comparabilité en présentant à la fois dans le tableau les données relatives aux villes proprement dites et celles concernant les agglomérations urbaines, de graves problèmes de comparabilité n'en subsistent pas moins.

Pour certains pays, les données figurant dans la colonne intitulée « Ville proprement dite » correspondent à une zone administrative urbaine juridiquement distincte du territoire rural environnant, tandis que pour d'autres pays ces données correspondent à une commune ou petite unité administrative analogue. Pour d'autres encore, les unités administratives en cause peuvent être relativement étendues et englober par conséquent un vaste territoire au-delà du centre urbain lui-même.

L'emploi de données se rapportant tantôt à la population de fait, tantôt à la population de droit, ainsi que les différences de traitement de ces deux notions d'un pays à l'autre influent particulièrement sur les statistiques urbaines. En ce qui concerne la population totale, la différence entre population de fait et population de droit est expliquée en détail à la section 3.1.1 des Notes techniques.

Les statistiques relatives à la population urbaine qui sont fondées sur des estimations intercensitaires posent encore plus de problèmes que les données issues de recensement. Leur comparabilité est compromise par la diversité des méthodes employées pour établir les estimations, et par l'imprécision qui résulte de l'application de certaines méthodes qui sont conçues pour être appliquées à l'ensemble de la population. La méthode des composantes, par exemple, est beaucoup plus difficile à appliquer en vue de l'estimation de l'accroissement de la population lorsqu'il s'agit de villes que lorsqu'il s'agit d'un pays tout entier.

Les naissances et décès qui surviennent dans les villes ne correspondent pas tous à la population présente ou résidente. En conséquence, des erreurs peuvent se produire si l'on établit pour les villes des estimations fondées sur l'accroissement naturel de la population. Les migrations intérieures constituent un second élément d'estimation que, dans bien des régions, on ne peut pas toujours mesurer avec exactitude. Pour ces raisons, les estimations présentées dans ce tableau risquent dans l'ensemble d'être peu fiables et leur valeur est particulièrement limitée du point de vue des comparaisons internationales.

Même lorsqu'elles figurent en caractères romains, il arrive souvent que les statistiques urbaines ne soient pas aussi fiables que les estimations concernant la population totale de la zone ou du pays considéré. De surcroît, comme ces statistiques proviennent aussi bien de recensements (nationaux ou municipaux) que d'enquêtes ou d'estimations, les années auxquelles elles se rapportent sont extrêmement variables. Enfin, comme les limites urbaines varient parfois d'une époque à une autre, il y a lieu d'être prudent lorsque l'on compare des données se rapportant à des années différentes.

Données publiées antérieurement : des statistiques concernant la population des capitales et des villes de 100 000 habitants ou plus ont été présentées dans des éditions antérieures de l'*Annuaire démographique*. Pour plus de précisions concernant les années et les sujets pour lesquels des données ont été publiées, se reporter à l'index historique.

8. Population of capital cities and cities of 100 000 or more inhabitants: latest available year, 1995 - 2014
Population des capitales et des villes de 100 000 habitants ou plus : dernière année disponible, 1995 - 2014

Continent, country or area, date, code[a] and city / Continent, pays ou zone, date, code[a] et ville	City proper - Ville proprement dite				Urban agglomeration - Agglomération urbaine			
	Population			Surface area - Superficie (km²)	Population			Surface area - Superficie (km²)
	Both sexes - Les deux sexes	Male - Masculin	Female - Féminin		Both sexes - Les deux sexes	Male - Masculin	Female - Féminin	
AFRICA - AFRIQUE								
Algeria - Algérie								
25 VI 1998 (CDJC)								
ALGIERS (EL DJAZAIR)	1 569 897	...	...	...	...	...	...	...
Annaba	352 523	...	...	...	...	...	...	...
Batna	246 800	...	...	...	...	...	...	...
Béchar	134 523	...	...	...	...	...	...	...
Bejaïa	144 405	...	...	...	...	...	...	...
Beskra	177 060	...	...	...	...	...	...	...
Bordj Bou Arreridj	129 004	...	...	...	...	...	...	...
Bordj el Kiffan	103 690	...	...	...	...	...	...	...
Ech Cheliff (El Asnam)	174 314	...	...	...	...	...	...	...
El Boulaïda (Blida)	229 788	...	...	...	...	...	...	...
El Djelfa	158 679	...	...	...	...	...	...	...
El Eulma	104 758	...	...	...	...	...	...	...
El Wad	105 151	...	...	...	...	...	...	...
Ghardaïa	127 959	...	...	...	...	...	...	...
Ghilizane	104 644	...	...	...	...	...	...	...
Guelma	108 682	...	...	...	...	...	...	...
Jijel	106 306	...	...	...	...	...	...	...
Lemdiyya (Medea)	128 427	...	...	...	...	...	...	...
Mestghanem (Mostaganem)	125 911	...	...	...	...	...	...	...
M'Sila	102 151	...	...	...	...	...	...	...
Qacentina (Constantine)	465 021	...	...	...	...	...	...	...
Saïda	113 533	...	...	...	...	...	...	...
Sidi-bel-Abbès	183 931	...	...	...	...	...	...	...
Skikda	153 531	...	...	...	...	...	...	...
Souq Ahras	114 512	...	...	...	...	...	...	...
Stif (Sétif)	214 842	...	...	...	...	...	...	...
Tbessa	154 335	...	...	...	...	...	...	...
Tihert	148 850	...	...	...	...	...	...	...
Tilimsen (Tlemcen)	156 258	...	...	...	...	...	...	...
Touggourt	114 183	...	...	...	...	...	...	...
Wahran (Oran)	705 335	...	...	...	...	...	...	...
Wargla	139 381	...	...	...	...	...	...	...
Benin - Bénin								
1 VII 2010* (ESDF)								
Cotonou	862 445[1]	426 247[1]	436 198[1]	79	...	...	...	...
Parakou	194 247[1]	98 756[1]	95 490[1]	441	...	...	...	...
PORTO-NOVO	289 880[1]	139 960[1]	149 920[1]	50	...	...	...	...
Botswana								
9 VIII 2011 (CDFC)								
GABORONE	231 592	113 580	118 012	169	...	...	...	...
Burkina Faso								
9 XII 2006 (CDFC)								
Banfora	75 917	38 399	37 518	...	109 824	54 581	55 243	...
Bobo Dioulasso	489 967	244 136	245 831	...	554 042	275 703	278 339	...
Dori	21 078	10 431	10 647	...	106 808	52 992	53 816	...
Fada N'gourma	41 785	21 220	20 565	...	124 577	62 193	62 384	...
Gorom-Gorom	8 882	4 509	4 373	...	106 346	53 129	53 217	...
Kaya	54 365	26 989	27 376	...	117 122	56 209	60 913	...
Koudougou	88 184	42 803	45 381	...	138 209	64 362	73 847	...
OUAGADOUGOU	1 475 223	745 289	729 934	...	1 475 223	745 289	729 934	...
Ouahigouya	73 153	36 370	36 783	...	125 030	61 002	64 028	...
Solenzo	16 850	8 557	8 293	...	121 819	59 892	61 927	...
Tenkodogo	44 491	21 476	23 015	...	124 985	58 003	66 982	...
Burundi								
16 VIII 2008 (CDJC)								
BUJUMBURA	497 169	274 979	222 190	...	...	...	...	...
Cabo Verde								
1 VII 2011 (ESDF)								
PRAIA	...	...	...	...	133 863	65 412	68 451	...
Cameroon - Cameroun								
11 XI 2005 (CDJC)								
Bafoussam	239 287	...	...	...	...	...	...	...
Bamenda	269 530	...	...	...	...	...	...	...

8. Population of capital cities and cities of 100 000 or more inhabitants: latest available year, 1995 - 2014
Population des capitales et des villes de 100 000 habitants ou plus : dernière année disponible, 1995 - 2014 (continued - suite)

Continent, country or area, date, code[a] and city Continent, pays ou zone, date, code[a] et ville	City proper - Ville proprement dite				Urban agglomeration - Agglomération urbaine			
	Population			Surface area - Superficie (km²)	Population			Surface area - Superficie (km²)
	Both sexes - Les deux sexes	Male - Masculin	Female - Féminin		Both sexes - Les deux sexes	Male - Masculin	Female - Féminin	
AFRICA - AFRIQUE								
Cameroon - Cameroun								
11 XI 2005 (CDJC)								
Douala	1 907 479	...	...	...	...	...	...	...
Garoua	235 996	...	...	...	...	...	...	...
Kumba	144 268	...	...	...	...	...	...	...
Maroua	201 371	...	...	...	...	...	...	...
Ngaoundéré	152 698	...	...	...	...	...	...	...
Nkongsamba	104 050	...	...	...	...	...	...	...
YAOUNDE	1 817 524	...	...	...	...	...	...	...
Djibouti								
1 VII 1995 (ESDF)								
DJIBOUTI	383 000	...	...	...	...	...	...	...
Egypt - Égypte								
1 VII 2010* (ESDF)								
6th of October City	802 306	420 009	382 297	...	...	...	...	...
Alexandria	4 358 439	2 225 558	2 132 881	...	...	...	...	...
Assyût	991 929	508 403	483 526	...	...	...	...	...
Aswan	543 396	277 732	265 664	...	...	...	...	...
Behera	985 850	500 999	484 851	...	...	...	...	...
Beni-Suef	582 396	293 887	288 509	...	...	...	...	...
CAIRO	7 248 671	3 682 152	3 566 519	...	...	...	...	...
Dakahlia	1 503 395	758 471	744 924	...	...	...	...	...
Damietta	462 154	236 522	225 632	...	...	...	...	...
Faiyûm	621 268	318 679	302 589	...	...	...	...	...
Gharbia	1 285 492	645 533	639 959	...	...	...	...	...
Giza	3 122 041	1 592 292	1 529 749	...	...	...	...	...
Helwan	1 295 854	660 776	635 078	...	...	...	...	...
Ismailia	472 655	237 174	235 481	...	...	...	...	...
Kafr-Elsheikh	655 002	327 445	327 557	...	...	...	...	...
Kalyoubia	2 053 859	1 051 232	1 002 627	...	...	...	...	...
Luxer	391 460	200 250	191 210	...	...	...	...	...
Matrouh	258 699	136 995	121 704	...	...	...	...	...
Menia	859 719	434 498	425 221	...	...	...	...	...
Menoufia	724 352	368 333	356 019	...	...	...	...	...
North Sinai	229 462	120 302	109 160	...	...	...	...	...
Port Said	610 468	310 881	299 587	...	...	...	...	...
Qena	534 766	270 422	264 344	...	...	...	...	...
Red Sea	295 993	180 622	115 371	...	...	...	...	...
Sharkia	1 340 060	682 941	657 119	...	...	...	...	...
Sohag	870 362	443 082	427 280	...	...	...	...	...
Suez	556 665	283 571	273 094	...	...	...	...	...
Equatorial Guinea - Guinée équatoriale								
1 VII 2001 (ESDF)								
MALABO	...	...	...	...	211 276	106 923	104 353	...
Ethiopia - Éthiopie								
1 VII 2002 (ESDF)								
ADDIS ABABA	2 646 000	1 273 000	1 373 000	...	...	...	...	...
Awassa	103 725	52 308	51 417	...	...	...	...	...
Bahir Dar	140 084	72 736	67 348	28	...	...	...	...
Debre Zeit	108 632	53 648	54 984	...	...	...	...	...
Dessie	141 616	72 578	69 038	15	...	...	...	...
Dire Dawa	237 012	118 880	118 132	18	...	...	...	...
Gondar	163 097	82 229	80 868	40	...	...	...	...
Harar	105 000	53 000	52 000	...	...	...	...	...
Jimma	131 708	67 138	64 570	...	...	...	...	...
Mekele	141 433	71 990	69 443	24	...	...	...	...
Nazareth	189 362	94 822	94 540	...	...	...	...	...
Ghana								
26 IX 2010 (CDFC)								
ACCRA	1 594 419	763 870	830 549	...	...	...	...	...
Ashiaman	190 972	93 727	97 245	...	...	...	...	...
Koforidua	122 300	59 056	63 244	...	...	...	...	...
Kumasi	1 730 249	826 479	903 770	...	...	...	...	...
Madina	111 926	54 271	57 655	...	...	...	...	...
Obuasi	168 641	81 015	87 626	...	...	...	...	...

8. Population of capital cities and cities of 100 000 or more inhabitants: latest available year, 1995 - 2014
Population des capitales et des villes de 100 000 habitants ou plus : dernière année disponible, 1995 - 2014 (continued - suite)

Continent, country or area, date, code[a] and city / Continent, pays ou zone, date, code[a] et ville	City proper - Ville proprement dite				Urban agglomeration - Agglomération urbaine			
	Population			Surface area - Superficie (km²)	Population			Surface area - Superficie (km²)
	Both sexes - Les deux sexes	Male - Masculin	Female - Féminin		Both sexes - Les deux sexes	Male - Masculin	Female - Féminin	
AFRICA - AFRIQUE								
Ghana								
26 IX 2010 (CDFC)								
Tamale	223 252	111 109	112 143	...	...	...	...	...
Tema	292 773	139 958	152 815	...	...	...	...	...
Guinea - Guinée								
1 XII 1996 (CDFC)								
CONAKRY	1 091 500	...	...	...	...	...	...	...
Kankan	...	...	...	...	261 341	...	...	...
Kindia	...	...	...	...	287 607	...	...	...
Labé	...	...	...	...	249 515	...	...	...
Nzérékoré	...	...	...	...	282 772	...	...	...
Guinea-Bissau - Guinée-Bissau								
15 III 2009 (CDFC)								
BISSAU	387 909	...	...	...	...	...	...	...
Kenya								
24 VIII 2009 (CDFC)								
Eldoret	252 061	127 808	124 253	311	...	...	...	...
Garissa	110 383	56 893	53 490	...	...	...	...	...
Kikuyu	190 208	93 036	97 172	...	...	...	...	...
Kisumu	259 258	131 062	128 196	275	...	...	...	...
Mavoko/AthiRiver	110 396	59 393	51 003	...	...	...	...	...
Mombasa	915 101	473 433	441 668	126	...	...	...	...
NAIROBI	3 133 518	1 602 104	1 531 414	695	...	...	...	...
Nakuru	286 411	145 038	141 373	344	...	...	...	...
Ngong	104 073	52 453	51 620	...	...	...	...	...
Ruiru	236 961	118 143	118 818	...	...	...	...	...
Thika	136 576	68 254	68 322	...	...	...	...	...
Lesotho								
13 IV 2006 (CDJC)								
MASERU	431 998	205 702	226 296	4 279	...	...	...	...
Madagascar								
1 VII 2005 (ESDF)								
ANTANANARIVO[2]	1 015 140	495 393	519 747	...	...	...	...	...
Antsirabe	...	...	...	...	180 180	87 691	92 489	...
Fianarantsoa	...	...	...	...	165 220	80 410	84 810	...
Mahajanga	...	...	...	...	152 785	74 359	78 426	...
Toamasina	...	...	...	...	203 469	99 026	104 443	...
Toliara	...	...	...	...	113 993	55 479	58 514	...
Malawi								
8 VI 2008 (CDFC)								
Blantyre City	661 444	...	...	220	...	...	...	...
LILONGWE	669 021	...	...	328	...	...	...	...
Mauritania - Mauritanie[1]								
1 VII 2008 (ESDF)								
NOUAKCHOTT	846 871	471 243	375 628	...	...	...	...	...
Mauritius - Maurice[3]								
1 VII 2014 (ESDJ)								
Beau Bassin - Rose Hill	104 865	51 995	52 870	21	...	...	...	...
PORT LOUIS	150 353	75 003	75 350	61	...	...	...	...
Vacoas - Phoenix	106 444	51 389	55 055	106	...	...	...	...
Morocco - Maroc								
1 VII 2014 (ESDF)								
Agadir	505 765	...	...	...	598 484	...	...	...
Al Hoceima	137 024	...	...	...	399 586	...	...	...
Azilal	100 327	...	...	...	553 121	...	...	...
Béni-Mellal	325 405	...	...	...	549 559	...	...	...
Benslimane	113 341	...	...	...	232 509	...	...	...
Berkane	182 203	...	...	...	288 807	...	...	...
Berrechid	272 356	...	...	...	482 119	...	...	...
Casablanca (Dar-el-Beida)	3 352 399	...	...	...	3 352 399	...	...	...
Chtouka-Ait Baha	111 522	...	...	...	369 706	...	...	...
El Hajeb	121 226	...	...	...	246 461	...	...	...
El Kelâa des Sraghna	152 900	...	...	...	536 191	...	...	...
El-Jadida	311 038	...	...	...	784 432	...	...	...
Errachidia	193 748	...	...	...	418 069	...	...	...

8. Population of capital cities and cities of 100 000 or more inhabitants: latest available year, 1995 - 2014
Population des capitales et des villes de 100 000 habitants ou plus : dernière année disponible, 1995 - 2014 (continued - suite)

Continent, country or area, date, code[a] and city / Continent, pays ou zone, date, code[a] et ville	City proper - Ville proprement dite				Urban agglomeration - Agglomération urbaine			
	Population			Surface area - Superficie (km²)	Population			Surface area - Superficie (km²)
	Both sexes - Les deux sexes	Male - Masculin	Female - Féminin		Both sexes - Les deux sexes	Male - Masculin	Female - Féminin	
AFRICA - AFRIQUE								
Morocco - Maroc								
1 VII 2014 (ESDF)								
Essaouira	106 319	...	...	...	450 569	...	...	...
Fès	1 126 551	...	...	...	1 146 967	...	...	...
Fquih Ben Salah	204 732	...	...	...	502 021	...	...	...
Guelmim	138 788	...	...	...	187 428	...	...	...
Inezgane ait Melloul	511 209	...	...	...	538 786	...	...	...
Kénitra	604 206	...	...	...	1 058 359	...	...	...
Khemisset	279 890	...	...	...	541 868	...	...	...
Khénifra	228 509	...	...	...	370 952	...	...	...
Khouribga	376 829	...	...	...	541 365	...	...	...
Laayoune	234 870	...	...	...	237 384	...	...	...
Larache	264 802	...	...	...	496 264	...	...	...
Marrakech	978 045	...	...	...	1 325 571	...	...	...
M'Diq-Fnideq	196 586	...	...	...	208 337	...	...	...
Médiouna	119 054	...	...	...	171 684	...	...	...
Meknès	685 408	...	...	...	833 456	...	...	...
Midelt	124 684	...	...	...	288 757	...	...	...
Mohammedia	288 131	...	...	...	403 087	...	...	...
Nador	390 913	...	...	...	564 354	...	...	...
Nouaceur	271 052	...	...	...	331 651	...	...	...
Ouarzazate	113 230	...	...	...	297 018	...	...	...
Oued Ed-Dahab	105 193	...	...	...	125 747	...	...	...
Oujda	504 480	...	...	...	550 406	...	...	...
RABAT	578 644	...	...	...	578 644	...	...	...
Rehamna	102 715	...	...	...	314 605	...	...	...
Safi	345 595	...	...	...	691 128	...	...	...
Salé	912 957	...	...	...	979 228	...	...	...
Sefrou	154 973	...	...	...	286 009	...	...	...
Settat	215 665	...	...	...	633 500	...	...	...
Sidi Kacem	168 302	...	...	...	521 694	...	...	...
Sidi Slimane	130 576	...	...	...	319 528	...	...	...
Skhirate-Témara	512 867	...	...	...	570 855	...	...	...
Tanger	998 972	...	...	...	1 059 562	...	...	...
Taourirt	149 604	...	...	...	232 712	...	...	...
Taroudannt	247 428	...	...	...	837 797	...	...	...
Taza	207 719	...	...	...	528 917	...	...	...
Tétouan	396 806	...	...	...	549 062	...	...	...
Youssoufia	100 617	...	...	...	251 692	...	...	...
Mozambique								
1 VII 2014 (ESDF)								
Beira	459 430	231 165	228 264	...	...	...	...	...
Chimoio	304 871	153 715	151 156	...	...	...	...	...
Lichinga	204 860	103 217	101 643	...	...	...	...	...
MAPUTO	1 225 868	590 224	635 644	...	...	...	...	...
Matola	892 963	430 795	462 168	...	...	...	...	...
Maxixe	125 208	56 164	69 044	...	...	...	...	...
Nacala	238 064	116 972	121 092	...	...	...	...	...
Nampula	605 760	305 386	300 374	...	...	...	...	...
Pemba	190 741	95 216	95 525	...	...	...	...	...
Quelimane	235 910	119 169	116 741	...	...	...	...	...
Tete	205 630	103 116	102 514	...	...	...	...	...
Xai-Xai	116 530	54 194	62 336	...	...	...	...	...
Namibia - Namibie								
28 VIII 2011 (CDFC)								
WINDHOEK	325 858	160 730	165 128	...	...	...	...	...
Niger								
20 V 2001 (CDJC)								
Maradi	148 017	...	...	...	...	...	...	...
NIAMEY	707 951	358 500	349 451	...	...	...	...	...
Zinder	170 575	...	...	...	...	...	...	...

8. Population of capital cities and cities of 100 000 or more inhabitants: latest available year, 1995 - 2014
Population des capitales et des villes de 100 000 habitants ou plus : dernière année disponible, 1995 - 2014 (continued - suite)

Continent, country or area, date, code[a] and city / Continent, pays ou zone, date, code[a] et ville	City proper - Ville proprement dite				Urban agglomeration - Agglomération urbaine			
	Population			Surface area - Superficie (km²)	Population			Surface area - Superficie (km²)
	Both sexes - Les deux sexes	Male - Masculin	Female - Féminin		Both sexes - Les deux sexes	Male - Masculin	Female - Féminin	
AFRICA - AFRIQUE								
Republic of South Sudan - République de Soudan du Sud								
21 IV 2008 (CDFC)								
JUBA	230 195	129 427	100 768	56	...	...	...	...
Malakal	114 528	60 440	54 088	25	...	...	...	...
Wau	118 331	63 777	54 554	75	...	...	...	...
Reunion - Réunion								
1 I 2010 (CDJC)								
SAINT-DENIS	145 022	68 075	76 947	143	174 973	82 815	92 158	...
Saint-Paul	103 346	51 327	52 019	...	172 137	84 793	87 344	...
Rwanda								
16 VIII 2002 (CDJC)								
Butare	137 334	...	...	...	...	...	...	...
Gitarama	137 995	...	...	...	...	...	...	...
KIGALI	603 049	325 778	277 271	...	...	...	...	...
Saint Helena ex. dep. - Sainte-Hélène sans dép.								
10 II 2008 (CDFC)								
JAMESTOWN	714	354	360	4	...	...	...	...
Sao Tome and Principe - Sao Tomé-et-Principe								
25 VIII 2001 (CDJC)								
SAO TOME	...	...	...	...	49 957	24 003	25 954	...
Senegal - Sénégal								
31 XII 2011 (ESDJ)								
DAKAR	1 056 009[4]	526 299[4]	529 710[4]	500	...	...	...	...
Diourbel[4]	279 667	136 961	142 706	...	...	...	...	...
Guediawaye[4]	317 464	157 992	159 472	...	...	...	...	...
Kaolack[4]	410 577	199 057	211 520	...	...	...	...	...
Mbour[4]	605 346	307 461	297 885	...	...	...	...	...
Pikine[4]	941 245	472 868	468 377	...	...	...	...	...
Rufisque[4]	333 032	167 942	165 090	...	...	...	...	...
Saint Louis[4]	277 245	136 957	140 289	...	...	...	...	...
Thiès[4]	618 436	304 087	314 349	...	...	...	...	...
Ziguinchor[4]	337 295	167 048	170 247	...	...	...	...	...
Seychelles								
29 VIII 1997 (CDFC)								
VICTORIA	...	...	...	...	24 701	...	...	...
Sierra Leone								
1 VII 2010 (ESDF)								
Bo	*231 494*	*111 731*	*119 763*	...	...	...	...	...
FREETOWN	*945 423*	*479 526*	*465 897*	...	...	...	...	...
Kenema	*195 498*	*95 988*	*99 510*	...	...	...	...	...
Makeni	*114 960*	*55 388*	*59 572*	...	...	...	...	...
Somalia - Somalie								
1 VII 2001 (ESDF)								
MOGADISHU	*1 212 000*	...	...	...	...	...	...	...
South Africa - Afrique du Sud								
10 X 1996 (CDFC)								
Alexandra	171 284	...	...	...	...	...	...	...
Benoni	366 343	...	...	...	...	...	...	...
BLOEMFONTEIN[5]	350 504	...	...	...	...	...	...	...
Boksburg	263 179	...	...	...	...	...	...	...
Botshabelo	177 971	...	...	...	...	...	...	...
CAPE TOWN[5]	987 007	...	...	...	...	...	...	...
Durban	669 242	...	...	...	...	...	...	...
Germiston	164 252	...	...	...	...	...	...	...
Johannesburg	752 349	...	...	...	...	...	...	...
Kathlehong	344 803	...	...	...	...	...	...	...
Kempton Park	344 426	...	...	...	...	...	...	...
Khayelitsa	314 239	...	...	...	...	...	...	...
Kimberley	206 070	...	...	...	...	...	...	...
Mangaung	176 525	...	...	...	...	...	...	...
Pietermaritzburg	405 385	...	...	...	...	...	...	...
Port Elizabeth	775 255	...	...	...	...	...	...	...
PRETORIA[5]	692 348	340 363	351 985	...	...	...	...	...
Roodepoort	279 340	...	...	...	...	...	...	...

8. Population of capital cities and cities of 100 000 or more inhabitants: latest available year, 1995 - 2014
Population des capitales et des villes de 100 000 habitants ou plus : dernière année disponible, 1995 - 2014 (continued - suite)

Continent, country or area, date, code[a] and city Continent, pays ou zone, date, code[a] et ville	City proper - Ville proprement dite				Urban agglomeration - Agglomération urbaine			
	Population			Surface area - Superficie (km²)	Population			Surface area - Superficie (km²)
	Both sexes - Les deux sexes	Male - Masculin	Female - Féminin		Both sexes - Les deux sexes	Male - Masculin	Female - Féminin	
AFRICA - AFRIQUE								
South Africa - Afrique du Sud								
10 X 1996 (CDFC)								
Soweto	904 165	...	...	...	...	...	...	...
Springs	163 304	...	...	...	...	...	...	...
Tembisa	237 676	...	...	...	...	...	...	...
Umlazi	339 715	...	...	...	...	...	...	...
Vereeniging	379 638	...	...	...	...	...	...	...
Togo								
6 XI 2010 (CDJC)								
LOME	839 566	402 172	437 394	...	...	...	...	...
Tunisia - Tunisie								
1 VII 1998 (ESDF)								
Bizerte	*105 520*	...	...	...	...	...	...	...
Gabes	*104 950*	...	...	...	...	...	...	...
Kairouan	*110 280*	...	...	...	...	...	...	...
Sfax	*248 800*	...	...	...	...	...	...	...
TUNIS	*702 330*	...	...	...	...	...	...	...
Uganda - Ouganda								
27 VIII 2014* (CDFC)								
KAMPALA	1 516 210	...	...	...	...	...	...	...
Western Sahara - Sahara occidental[6]								
1 VII 1999 (ESDF)								
EL AAIUN	*169 000*	...	...	...	...	...	...	...
Zambia - Zambie								
16 X 2010 (CDJC)								
Chingola	216 626	108 464	108 162	1 678	...	...	...	...
Chipata	455 783	224 934	230 849	...	...	...	...	...
Kabwe	202 360	98 781	103 579	1 572	...	...	...	...
Kasama	231 824	114 208	117 616	...	...	...	...	...
Kitwe	517 543	256 740	260 803	777	...	...	...	...
Livingstone	139 509	68 763	70 746	...	...	...	...	...
Luanshya	156 059	77 368	78 691	811	...	...	...	...
LUSAKA	1 747 152	860 424	886 728	360	...	...	...	...
Mufulira	162 889	81 355	81 534	1 637	...	...	...	...
Ndola	451 246	223 020	228 226	1 103	...	...	...	...
Zimbabwe								
17 VIII 2012 (CDFC)								
Bulawayo	653 337	303 346	349 991	479	...	...	...	...
Chitungwiza	356 840	168 600	188 240	...	...	...	...	...
HARARE	1 485 231	716 595	768 636	872	...	...	...	...
Mutare	262 124	125 850	136 274	...	...	...	...	...
AMERICA, NORTH - AMÉRIQUE DU NORD								
Anguilla								
1 VII 2001 (ESDF)								
THE VALLEY	4 904	...	...	...	...	...	...	...
Aruba								
29 IX 2010 (CDJC)								
ORANJESTAD	28 295	13 139	15 156	...	...	...	...	...
Bahamas								
1 VII 2009 (ESDF)								
NASSAU	244 400	119 700	124 700	...	...	...	...	...
Belize								
1 VII 2000 (ESDF)								
BELMOPAN	*8 305*	*4 050*	*4 255*	...	...	...	...	...
Bermuda - Bermudes								
1 VII 2010 (ESDJ)								
HAMILTON	3 686	1 986	1 700	1	...	...	...	...
Canada								
1 VII 2014* (ESDJ)								
Abbotsford-Mission	...	...	...	...	178 967[7]	89 970[7]	88 997[7]	605
Barrie	145 544[7]	71 090[7]	74 454[7]	77	200 416[7]	99 194[7]	101 222[7]	898
Brampton	570 290[7]	283 214[7]	287 076[7]	266	...	...	...	...

8. Population of capital cities and cities of 100 000 or more inhabitants: latest available year, 1995 - 2014
Population des capitales et des villes de 100 000 habitants ou plus : dernière année disponible, 1995 - 2014 (continued - suite)

Continent, country or area, date, code[a] and city / Continent, pays ou zone, date, code[a] et ville	City proper - Ville proprement dite				Urban agglomeration - Agglomération urbaine			
	Population			Surface area - Superficie (km²)	Population			Surface area - Superficie (km²)
	Both sexes - Les deux sexes	Male - Masculin	Female - Féminin		Both sexes - Les deux sexes	Male - Masculin	Female - Féminin	
AMERICA, NORTH - AMÉRIQUE DU NORD								
Canada								
1 VII 2014* (ESDJ)								
Brantford	98 874[7]	48 123[7]	50 751[7]	72	143 074[7]	70 204[7]	72 870[7]	1 073
Burlington	193 871[7]	93 946[7]	99 925[7]	186	...	...	...	...
Burnaby	239 059[7]	118 601[7]	120 458[7]	91	...	...	...	...
Calgary	1 265 531[7]	640 832[7]	624 699[7]	825	1 406 721[7]	712 991[7]	693 730[7]	5 108
Cambridge	134 284[7]	66 384[7]	67 900[7]	113	...	...	...	...
Chatham-Kent	105 260[7]	51 470[7]	53 790[7]	2 458	...	...	...	...
Coquitlam	134 962[7]	67 170[7]	67 792[7]	122	...	...	...	...
Edmonton	928 182[7]	470 582[7]	457 600[7]	684	1 328 290[7]	674 022[7]	654 268[7]	9 427
Gatineau	276 338[7]	135 309[7]	141 029[7]	343	328 144[7]	162 186[7]	165 958[7]	...
Greater Sudbury / Grand Sudbury	165 175[7]	81 351[7]	83 824[7]	3 227	165 690[7]	81 555[7]	84 135[7]	3 411
Guelph	129 079[7]	62 950[7]	66 129[7]	87	150 946[7]	74 075[7]	76 871[7]	594
Halifax	414 129[7]	203 584[7]	210 545[7]	5 490	414 398[7]	203 742[7]	210 656[7]	5 496
Hamilton	551 751[7]	271 584[7]	280 167[7]	1 117	765 228[7]	375 015[7]	390 213[7]	1 372
Kelowna	124 951[7]	60 644[7]	64 307[7]	212	191 237[7]	93 711[7]	97 526[7]	2 905
Kingston	129 653[7]	63 289[7]	66 364[7]	451	168 353[7]	82 960[7]	85 393[7]	1 939
Kitchener-Cambridge-Waterloo	...	...	...	...	506 858[7]	251 171[7]	255 687[7]	827
Laval	420 870[7]	206 695[7]	214 175[7]	247	...	...	...	...
Lévis V	142 887[7]	70 546[7]	72 341[7]	449	...	...	...	...
London	388 615[7]	188 802[7]	199 813[7]	421	502 360[7]	245 221[7]	257 139[7]	2 666
Longueuil	241 606[7]	118 475[7]	123 131[7]	116	...	...	...	...
Markham	329 204[7]	161 707[7]	167 497[7]	213	...	...	...	...
Mississauga	781 057[7]	384 469[7]	396 588[7]	292	...	...	...	...
Moncton	72 321[7]	35 488[7]	36 833[7]	141	146 073[7]	72 516[7]	73 557[7]	2 406
Montréal	1 741 296[7]	857 007[7]	884 289[7]	365	4 027 121[7]	1 985 787[7]	2 041 334[7]	4 258
Oakville	200 534[7]	97 718[7]	102 816[7]	139	...	...	...	...
Oshawa	162 005[7]	79 344[7]	82 661[7]	146	384 143[7]	189 080[7]	195 063[7]	904
OTTAWA	947 031[7]	462 927[7]	484 104[7]	2 790	989 978[7]	484 176[7]	505 802[7]	...
Ottawa - Gatineau	...	...	...	...	1 318 122[7]	646 362[7]	671 760[7]	6 287
Peterborough	81 779[7]	38 592[7]	43 187[7]	64	123 270[7]	59 259[7]	64 011[7]	1 507
Québec	538 238[7]	263 187[7]	275 051[7]	454	799 632[7]	394 197[7]	405 435[7]	3 349
Regina	216 528[7]	107 981[7]	108 547[7]	145	237 758[7]	119 077[7]	118 681[7]	3 408
Richmond	203 178[7]	98 739[7]	104 439[7]	129	...	...	...	...
Richmond Hill	201 125[7]	98 524[7]	102 601[7]	101	...	...	...	...
Saanich	113 624[7]	55 780[7]	57 844[7]	104	...	...	...	...
Saguenay	146 849[7]	73 196[7]	73 653[7]	1 126	160 138[7]	80 150[7]	79 988[7]	2 564
Saint John	69 734[7]	33 404[7]	36 330[7]	316	127 314[7]	62 090[7]	65 224[7]	3 363
Saskatoon	254 569[7]	127 157[7]	127 412[7]	210	300 634[7]	150 884[7]	149 750[7]	5 215
Sherbrooke	162 638[7]	79 879[7]	82 759[7]	353	212 061[7]	104 592[7]	107 469[7]	1 460
St Catharines-Niagara	...	...	...	...	405 906[7]	197 616[7]	208 290[7]	1 398
St. John's	111 796[7]	54 199[7]	57 597[7]	446	211 724[7]	103 926[7]	107 798[7]	805
Surrey	498 720[7]	249 620[7]	249 100[7]	316	...	...	...	...
Thunder Bay	110 984[7]	54 165[7]	56 819[7]	328	125 112[7]	61 506[7]	63 606[7]	2 556
Toronto	2 808 503[7]	1 360 717[7]	1 447 786[7]	630	6 055 724[7]	2 960 331[7]	3 095 393[7]	5 906
Trois-Rivières	134 846[7]	65 812[7]	69 034[7]	289	155 813[7]	76 557[7]	79 256[7]	1 041
Vancouver	647 540[7]	320 582[7]	326 958[7]	115	2 470 289[7]	1 222 694[7]	1 247 595[7]	2 883
Vaughan	312 176[7]	153 443[7]	158 733[7]	274	...	...	...	...
Victoria	84 289[7]	40 321[7]	43 968[7]	19	358 685[7]	175 242[7]	183 443[7]	696
Whitby	130 341[7]	63 920[7]	66 421[7]	147	...	...	...	...
Windsor	218 270[7]	106 712[7]	111 558[7]	146	333 937[7]	164 367[7]	169 570[7]	1 022
Winnipeg	709 253[7]	348 660[7]	360 593[7]	464	782 640[7]	386 292[7]	396 348[7]	5 303
Cayman Islands - Îles Caïmanes								
1 IV 2007 (SSDJ)								
GEORGE TOWN	28 836	...	...	...	...	...	...	...
Costa Rica								
30 V 2011 (CDJC)								
Alajuela	254 886	125 773	129 113	388	...	...	...	...
Cartago	147 898	72 491	75 407	288	...	...	...	...
Desamparados	208 411	99 974	108 437	188	...	...	...	...
Goicoechea	115 084	54 269	60 815	32	...	...	...	...
Heredia	123 616	58 667	64 949	283	...	...	...	...

8. Population of capital cities and cities of 100 000 or more inhabitants: latest available year, 1995 - 2014
Population des capitales et des villes de 100 000 habitants ou plus : dernière année disponible, 1995 - 2014 (continued - suite)

Continent, country or area, date, code[a] and city / Continent, pays ou zone, date, code[a] et ville	City proper - Ville proprement dite				Urban agglomeration - Agglomération urbaine			
	Population			Surface area - Superficie (km²)	Population			Surface area - Superficie (km²)
	Both sexes - Les deux sexes	Male - Masculin	Female - Féminin		Both sexes - Les deux sexes	Male - Masculin	Female - Féminin	
AMERICA, NORTH - AMÉRIQUE DU NORD								
Costa Rica								
30 V 2011 (CDJC)								
Pérez Zeledón	134 534	65 389	69 145	1 906	...	...	...	...
Pococí	125 962	63 273	62 689	2 403	...	...	...	...
Puntarenas	115 019	57 246	57 773	1 842	...	...	...	...
San Carlos	163 745	82 048	81 697	3 348	...	...	...	...
SAN JOSÉ	288 054	136 371	151 683	45	...	...	...	...
Cuba								
1 VII 2014 (ESDJ)								
Bayamo	158 973	...	...	27[8]	...	...	...	...
Camagüey	304 027	...	...	82[8]	...	...	...	...
Ciego de Ávila	117 308	...	...	21[8]	...	...	...	...
Cienfuegos	149 129	...	...	46[8]	...	...	...	...
Guantánamo	217 978	...	...	34[8]	...	...	...	...
Holguín	291 560	...	...	58[8]	...	...	...	...
LA HABANA	2 121 871	...	...	721[8]	...	...	...	...
Las Tunas	166 231	...	...	31[8]	...	...	...	...
Matanzas	136 486	...	...	44[8]	...	...	...	...
Pinar del Río	142 397	...	...	32[8]	...	...	...	...
Sancti Spíritus	107 026	...	...	23[8]	...	...	...	...
Santa Clara	214 370	...	...	44[8]	...	...	...	...
Santiago de Cuba	434 268	...	...	70[8]	...	...	...	...
Dominican Republic - République dominicaine								
1 VII 2011 (ESDF)								
Azua	102 339[1]	51 620[1]	50 719[1]	155	...	...	...	...
Bajos de Haina	143 807[1]	71 130[1]	72 677[1]	40	...	...	...	...
Baní	177 588[1]	88 818[1]	88 770[1]	740	...	...	...	...
Boca Chica	122 216[1]	61 317[1]	60 899[1]	142	...	...	...	...
Bonao	148 857[1]	73 877[1]	74 980[1]	674	...	...	...	...
Higüey	211 453[1]	106 575[1]	104 878[1]	2 026	...	...	...	...
La Romana	152 454[1]	73 291[1]	79 163[1]	263	...	...	...	...
La Vega	273 547[1]	137 511[1]	136 036[1]	641	...	...	...	...
Los Alcarrizos	249 595[1]	126 001[1]	123 594[1]	46	...	...	...	...
Moca	182 767[1]	91 506[1]	91 261[1]	337	...	...	...	...
Puerto Plata	156 123[1]	76 741[1]	79 382[1]	496	...	...	...	...
San Cristóbal	278 767[1]	138 614[1]	140 153[1]	214	...	...	...	...
San Francisco de Macorís	185 925[1]	92 282[1]	93 643[1]	760	...	...	...	...
San Juan de la Maguana	137 881[1]	70 406[1]	67 475[1]	1 722	...	...	...	...
San Pedro de Macorís	233 255[1]	113 249[1]	120 006[1]	146	...	...	...	...
Santiago de los Caballeros	757 933[1]	372 332[1]	385 601[1]	529	...	...	...	...
SANTO DOMINGO	1 126 306[1]	537 506[1]	588 800[1]	91	1 126 306[1]	537 506[1]	588 800[1]	91
Santo Domingo East - Santo Domingo Este	966 393[1]	468 484[1]	497 909[1]	169	...	...	...	...
Santo Domingo North - Santo Domingo Norte	453 046[1]	228 840[1]	224 206[1]	388	...	...	...	...
Santo Domingo West - Santo Domingo Oeste	349 175[1]	170 849[1]	178 326[1]	54	...	...	...	...
El Salvador[9]								
1 IV 2014 (ESDF)								
Ahuachapán	118 164	55 953	62 212	245	...	...	...	...
Apopa	165 897	74 664	91 232	52	...	...	...	...
Ciudad Delgado	128 635	59 916	68 719	33	...	...	...	...
Ilopango	124 522	55 110	69 413	35	...	...	...	...
Mejicanos	146 915	67 462	79 452	22	...	...	...	...
San Miguel	249 638	114 939	134 700	594	...	...	...	...
SAN SALVADOR	281 870	133 352	148 518	72	...	...	...	...
Santa Ana	265 518	126 100	139 418	400	...	...	...	...
Santa Tecla	135 483	61 289	74 194	112	...	...	...	...
Soyapango	275 868	123 363	152 505	30	...	...	...	...
Greenland - Groenland[10]								
1 VII 2014 (ESDJ)								
NUUK (GODTHAB)	16 786	8 812	7 974	...	...	...	...	...
Guadeloupe								
8 III 1999 (CDJC)								
BASSE-TERRE	12 377	5 687	6 690	...	44 747	21 252	23 495	...
Pointe-à-Pitre	...	...	...	...	171 773	...	...	...

8. Population of capital cities and cities of 100 000 or more inhabitants: latest available year, 1995 - 2014
Population des capitales et des villes de 100 000 habitants ou plus : dernière année disponible, 1995 - 2014 (continued - suite)

Continent, country or area, date, code[a] and city / Continent, pays ou zone, date, code[a] et ville	City proper - Ville proprement dite				Urban agglomeration - Agglomération urbaine			
	Population			Surface area - Superficie (km²)	Population			Surface area - Superficie (km²)
	Both sexes - Les deux sexes	Male - Masculin	Female - Féminin		Both sexes - Les deux sexes	Male - Masculin	Female - Féminin	

AMERICA, NORTH - AMÉRIQUE DU NORD

Guatemala								
1 VII 2001 (ESDF)								
CUIDAD DE GUATEMALA	1 022 001	491 891	530 110	228	...	...	...	...
Escuintla	114 626	57 893	56 733	332	...	...	...	...
Mixco	452 134	221 928	230 206	99	...	...	...	...
Quetzaltenango	152 223	76 272	75 951	120	...	...	...	...
Villa Nueva	390 329	192 238	198 091	114	...	...	...	...
Haiti - Haïti								
1 VII 1999 (ESDJ)								
Cap-Haitien	113 555	50 064	63 491	10	...	...	...	...
Carrefour	336 222	146 838	189 384	23	...	...	...	...
Delmas	284 079	124 774	159 305	26	...	...	...	...
PORT-AU-PRINCE	990 558	436 170	554 388	21	...	...	...	...
Honduras								
1 VII 2003 (ESDF)								
La Ceiba	137 815	67 691	70 124	...	...	...	...	...
San Pedro Sula	518 736	251 514	267 222	...	...	...	...	...
TEGUCIGALPA	858 437	411 687	446 749	...	...	...	...	...
Jamaica - Jamaïque								
4 IV 2011 (CDJC)								
KINGSTON[11]	...	...	...	...	592 291	285 509	306 782	149
Montego Bay	...	...	...	...	111 037	53 601	57 436	77
Portmore	...	...	...	...	182 800	85 380	97 420	182
Spanish Town	...	...	...	...	149 479	72 885	76 594	65
Martinique								
1 I 2006 (CDJC)								
FORT-DE-FRANCE	90 347	40 128	50 219	...	133 281	59 945	73 336	...
Mexico - Mexique[1]								
1 VII 2014 (ESDJ)								
Acapulco	...	...	...	...	913 406	441 690	471 717	...
Acayucan	...	...	...	...	118 374	57 021	61 354	...
Aguascalientes	...	...	...	...	1 002 449	487 905	514 544	...
Apizaco-Tlaxcala	...	...	...	...	538 798	259 159	279 639	...
Campeche	...	...	...	...	247 362	...	...	...
Cancún	...	...	...	...	779 315	394 093	385 222	...
Celaya	...	...	...	...	634 920	304 025	330 894	...
Chetumal	...	...	...	...	176 027	...	...	...
Chihuahua	...	...	...	...	938 237	455 355	482 882	...
Chilpacingo de los Bravo	...	...	...	...	211 751	...	...	...
Ciudad Acuña	...	...	...	...	141 265	...	...	...
Ciudad Del Carmen	...	...	...	...	184 337	...	...	...
Ciudad Lázaro Cárdenas	...	...	...	...	142 796	...	...	...
Ciudad Obregón	...	...	...	...	329 263	...	...	...
Ciudad Valles	...	...	...	...	131 584	...	...	...
Ciudad Victoria	...	...	...	...	328 940	...	...	...
Coatzacoalcos	...	...	...	...	367 116	178 198	188 918	...
Córdoba	...	...	...	...	331 090	156 596	174 495	...
Cuauhtemoc	...	...	...	...	127 627	...	...	...
Cuautla	...	...	...	...	467 904	225 950	241 954	...
Cuernavaca	...	...	...	...	986 027	474 092	511 936	...
Delicias	...	...	...	...	129 471	...	...	...
Ensenada	...	...	...	...	304 768	...	...	...
Fresnillo	...	...	...	...	131 998	...	...	...
Guadalajara	...	...	...	...	4 737 096	2 318 362	2 418 734	...
Guanajuato	...	...	...	...	113 824	...	...	...
Hermosillo	...	...	...	...	777 954	...	...	...
Heroica Nogales	...	...	...	...	232 082	...	...	...
Hidalgo del Parral	...	...	...	...	112 437	...	...	...
Iguala de la Independencia	...	...	...	...	122 672	...	...	...
Irapuato	...	...	...	...	412 641	...	...	...
Juárez	...	...	...	...	1 411 179	698 392	712 787	...
La Paz	...	...	...	...	238 810	...	...	...
La Piedad-Pénjamo	...	...	...	...	260 011	123 436	136 575	...
León	...	...	...	...	1 698 890	826 837	872 053	...
Los Mochis	...	...	...	...	280 260	...	...	...

8. Population of capital cities and cities of 100 000 or more inhabitants: latest available year, 1995 - 2014
Population des capitales et des villes de 100 000 habitants ou plus : dernière année disponible, 1995 - 2014 (continued - suite)

Continent, country or area, date, code[a] and city Continent, pays ou zone, date, code[a] et ville	City proper - Ville proprement dite				Urban agglomeration - Agglomération urbaine			
	Population			Surface area - Superficie (km²)	Population			Surface area - Superficie (km²)
	Both sexes - Les deux sexes	Male - Masculin	Female - Féminin		Both sexes - Les deux sexes	Male - Masculin	Female - Féminin	
AMERICA, NORTH - AMÉRIQUE DU NORD								
Mexico - Mexique[1]								
1 VII 2014 (ESDJ)								
Manzanillo	...	...	...	...	154 596	...	...	...
Matamoros	...	...	...	...	519 226	256 777	262 449	...
Mazatlán	...	...	...	...	412 815	...	...	...
Mérida	...	...	...	...	1 049 433	510 529	538 904	...
Mexicali	...	...	...	...	1 012 099	509 694	502 405	...
MEXICO, CIUDAD DE	8 874 724	...	...	...	...	...	...	...
Minatitlán	...	...	...	...	374 712	181 207	193 505	...
Monclova-Frontera	...	...	...	...	334 963	166 300	168 664	...
Monterrey	...	...	...	...	4 414 800	2 193 805	2 220 995	...
Morelia	...	...	...	...	879 774	420 891	458 883	...
Moroleón Uriangato - Moroleón-Uriangato	...	...	...	...	113 148	53 749	59 399	...
Navojoa	...	...	...	...	123 445	...	...	...
Nuevo Laredo	...	...	...	...	409 688	202 831	206 858	...
Oaxaca	...	...	...	...	648 813	305 572	343 242	...
Ocotlán	...	...	...	...	148 127	72 496	75 630	...
Orizaba	...	...	...	...	447 240	212 343	234 897	...
Pachuca	...	...	...	...	561 141	268 209	292 933	...
Piedras Negras	...	...	...	...	189 085	94 786	94 299	...
Playa del Carmen	...	...	...	...	186 678	...	...	...
Poza Rica	...	...	...	...	534 710	258 160	276 551	...
Puebla-Tlaxcala	...	...	...	...	2 921 157	1 401 701	1 519 456	...
Puerto Vallarta	...	...	...	...	434 264	218 241	216 023	...
Querétaro	...	...	...	...	1 194 218	580 563	613 655	...
Reynosa-Río Bravo	...	...	...	...	797 411	396 395	401 017	...
Rioverde-Ciudad Fernández	...	...	...	...	142 396	69 570	72 826	...
Salamanca	...	...	...	...	168 920	...	...	...
Saltillo	...	...	...	...	888 386	440 541	447 845	...
San Cristóbal de las Casas	...	...	...	...	171 355	...	...	...
San Francisco del Rincón	...	...	...	...	193 260	94 375	98 886	...
San Juan Bautista Tuxtepec	...	...	...	...	110 894	...	...	...
San Juan del Río	...	...	...	...	149 691	...	...	...
San Luis Potosí-Soledad de Graciano Sánchez	...	...	...	...	1 112 995	536 846	576 149	...
San Luis Rio Colorado	...	...	...	...	172 447	...	...	...
Tampico	...	...	...	...	918 555	446 152	472 403	...
Tecomán	...	...	...	...	154 055	77 338	76 717	...
Tehuacán	...	...	...	...	315 264	149 061	166 203	...
Tepic	...	...	...	...	475 754	231 091	244 663	...
Tijuana	...	...	...	...	1 909 074	958 327	950 746	...
Toluca	...	...	...	...	2 152 552	1 050 032	1 102 520	...
Tula	...	...	...	...	217 612	106 056	111 557	...
Tulancingo	...	...	...	...	258 235	122 370	135 865	...
Túxpan de Rodríguez Cano	...	...	...	...	114 512	...	...	...
Tuxtla Gutiérrez	...	...	...	...	751 879	360 871	391 008	...
Uruapan	...	...	...	...	293 502	...	...	...
Veracruz	...	...	...	...	856 367	406 759	449 607	...
Villahermosa	...	...	...	...	814 165	396 888	417 277	...
Xalapa	...	...	...	...	711 963	336 687	375 276	...
Zacatecas-Guadalupe	...	...	...	...	334 034	160 551	173 483	...
Zamora-Jacona	...	...	...	...	260 391	125 573	134 818	...
Nicaragua								
1 VII 2009 (ESDJ)								
Chinandega	...	...	...	...	106 635	...	...	...
León	...	...	...	...	156 049	...	...	...
MANAGUA	...	...	...	...	985 143	...	...	...
Masaya	...	...	...	...	110 491	...	...	...
Tipitapa	...	...	...	...	105 773	...	...	...
Panama								
1 VII 2014 (ESDF)								
CIUDAD DE PANAMÁ	465 179[12]	221 267[12]	243 912[12]	98	1 025 425[12]	501 693[12]	523 732[12]	268
San Miguelito	350 949[12]	171 512[12]	179 437[12]	50	...	...	...	...

8. Population of capital cities and cities of 100 000 or more inhabitants: latest available year, 1995 - 2014
Population des capitales et des villes de 100 000 habitants ou plus : dernière année disponible, 1995 - 2014 (continued - suite)

Continent, country or area, date, code[a] and city / Continent, pays ou zone, date, code[a] et ville	City proper - Ville proprement dite				Urban agglomeration - Agglomération urbaine			
	Population			Surface area - Superficie (km²)	Population			Surface area - Superficie (km²)
	Both sexes - Les deux sexes	Male - Masculin	Female - Féminin		Both sexes - Les deux sexes	Male - Masculin	Female - Féminin	

AMERICA, NORTH - AMÉRIQUE DU NORD

Puerto Rico - Porto Rico
1 VII 2013 (ESDJ)

Bayamón	198 958[13]	94 517[13]	104 441[13]	71	...	...	...	...
Caguas	139 559[13]	65 375[13]	74 184[13]	94	...	...	...	...
Carolina	169 597[13]	78 173[13]	91 424[13]	73	...	...	...	...
Ponce	157 118[13]	75 574[13]	81 544[13]	184	...	...	...	...
SAN JUAN	374 682[13]	172 035[13]	202 647[13]	77	...	...	...	...

Saint Lucia - Sainte-Lucie
22 V 2001 (CDFC)

CASTRIES	11 092	5 238	5 854	...	...	...	...	...

Saint Pierre and Miquelon - Saint Pierre-et-Miquelon
8 III 1999 (CDFC)

SAINT-PIERRE	5 618	2 781	2 837	...	...	...	...	...

Trinidad and Tobago - Trinité-et-Tobago
1 VII 1996 (ESDF)

PORT-OF-SPAIN	43 396	20 739	22 657	12	...	...	...	...

Turks and Caicos Islands - Îles Turques et Caïques
1 VII 2006 (ESDJ)

GRAND TURK	5 718	2 846	2 872	17	...	...	...	...

United States of America - États-Unis d'Amérique[14]
1 VII 2012 (ESDJ)

Abilene (TX)	118 887[15]	...	...	276[16]	...	...	...	...
Akron (OH)	198 549[15]	...	...	161[16]	...	...	...	...
Albuquerque (NM)	555 417[15]	...	...	487[16]	...	...	...	...
Alexandria (VA)	146 294[15]	...	...	39[16]	...	...	...	...
Allentown (PA)	118 974[15]	...	...	45[16]	...	...	...	...
Amarillo (TX)	195 250[15]	...	...	258[16]	...	...	...	...
Anaheim (CA)	343 248[15]	...	...	129[16]	...	...	...	...
Anchorage (AK)	298 610[15]	...	...	4 415[16]	...	...	...	...
Ann Arbor (MI)	116 121[15]	...	...	72[16]	...	...	...	...
Antioch (CA)	105 508[15]	...	...	73[16]	...	...	...	...
Arlington (TX)	375 600[15]	...	...	248[16]	...	...	...	...
Arvada (CO)	109 745[15]	...	...	97[16]	...	...	...	...
Athens (GA)	118 999[15]	...	...	301[16]	...	...	...	...
Atlanta (GA)	443 775[15]	...	...	345[16]	...	...	...	...
Augusta (GA)	197 872[15]	...	...	783[16]	...	...	...	...
Aurora (CO)	339 030[15]	...	...	399[16]	...	...	...	...
Aurora (IL)	199 932[15]	...	...	116[16]	...	...	...	...
Austin (TX)	842 592[15]	...	...	772[16]	...	...	...	...
Bakersfield (CA)	358 597[15]	...	...	385[16]	...	...	...	...
Baltimore (MD)	621 342[15]	...	...	210[16]	...	...	...	...
Baton Rouge (LA)	230 058[15]	...	...	201[16]	...	...	...	...
Beaumont (TX)	118 228[15]	...	...	213[16]	...	...	...	...
Bellevue (WA)	126 439[15]	...	...	83[16]	...	...	...	...
Berkeley (CA)	115 403[15]	...	...	27[16]	...	...	...	...
Billings (MT)	106 954[15]	...	...	112[16]	...	...	...	...
Birmingham (AL)	212 038[15]	...	...	378[16]	...	...	...	...
Boise City (ID)	212 303[15]	...	...	208[16]	...	...	...	...
Boston (MA)	636 479[15]	...	...	125[16]	...	...	...	...
Boulder (CO)	101 808[15]	...	...	64[16]	...	...	...	...
Bridgeport (CT)	146 425[15]	...	...	42[16]	...	...	...	...
Brownsville (TX)	180 097[15]	...	...	343[16]	...	...	...	...
Buffalo (NY)	259 384[15]	...	...	105[16]	...	...	...	...
Burbank (CA)	104 391[15]	...	...	45[16]	...	...	...	...
Cambridge (MA)	106 471[15]	...	...	17[16]	...	...	...	...
Cape Coral (FL)	161 248[15]	...	...	274[16]	...	...	...	...
Carlsbad (CA)	109 318[15]	...	...	98[16]	...	...	...	...
Carrollton (TX)	125 409[15]	...	...	94[16]	...	...	...	...
Cary (NC)	145 693[15]	...	...	142[16]	...	...	...	...
Cedar Rapids (IA)	128 119[15]	...	...	183[16]	...	...	...	...
Centennial (CO)	103 743[15]	...	...	75[16]	...	...	...	...

8. Population of capital cities and cities of 100 000 or more inhabitants: latest available year, 1995 - 2014
Population des capitales et des villes de 100 000 habitants ou plus : dernière année disponible, 1995 - 2014 (continued - suite)

Continent, country or area, date, code[a] and city / Continent, pays ou zone, date, code[a] et ville	City proper - Ville proprement dite				Urban agglomeration - Agglomération urbaine			
	Population			Surface area - Superficie (km²)	Population			Surface area - Superficie (km²)
	Both sexes - Les deux sexes	Male - Masculin	Female - Féminin		Both sexes - Les deux sexes	Male - Masculin	Female - Féminin	

AMERICA, NORTH - AMÉRIQUE DU NORD

United States of America - États-Unis d'Amérique[14]
1 VII 2012 (ESDJ)

City	Both sexes	Male	Female	Surface area	Both sexes	Male	Female	Surface area
Chandler (AZ)	245 628[15]	...	...	167[16]	...	...	...	...
Charleston (SC)	125 583[15]	...	...	283[16]	...	...	...	...
Charlotte (NC)	775 202[15]	...	...	781[16]	...	...	...	...
Chattanooga (TN)	171 279[15]	...	...	365[16]	...	...	...	...
Chesapeake (VA)	228 417[15]	...	...	883[16]	...	...	...	...
Chicago (IL)	2 714 856[15]	...	...	590[16]	...	...	...	...
Chula Vista (CA)	252 422[15]	...	...	129[16]	...	...	...	...
Cincinnati (OH)	296 550[15]	...	...	202[16]	...	...	...	...
Clarksville (TN)	142 519[15]	...	...	255[16]	...	...	...	...
Clearwater (FL)	108 732[15]	...	...	66[16]	...	...	...	...
Cleveland (OH)	390 928[15]	...	...	201[16]	...	...	...	...
Colorado Springs (CO)	431 834[15]	...	...	505[16]	...	...	...	...
Columbia (MO)	113 225[15]	...	...	165[16]	...	...	...	...
Columbia (SC)	131 686[15]	...	...	344[16]	...	...	...	...
Columbus (GA)	198 413[15]	...	...	561[16]	...	...	...	...
Columbus (OH)	809 798[15]	...	...	563[16]	...	...	...	...
Concord (CA)	124 711[15]	...	...	79[16]	...	...	...	...
Coral Springs (FL)	125 287[15]	...	...	62[16]	...	...	...	...
Corona (CA)	158 391[15]	...	...	101[16]	...	...	...	...
Corpus Christi (TX)	312 195[15]	...	...	416[16]	...	...	...	...
Costa Mesa (CA)	111 918[15]	...	...	41[16]	...	...	...	...
Dallas (TX)	1 241 162[15]	...	...	882[16]	...	...	...	...
Daly City (CA)	103 690[15]	...	...	20[16]	...	...	...	...
Davenport (IA)	101 363[15]	...	...	163[16]	...	...	...	...
Dayton (OH)	141 359[15]	...	...	144[16]	...	...	...	...
Denton (TX)	121 123[15]	...	...	238[16]	...	...	...	...
Denver (CO)	634 265[15]	...	...	396[16]	...	...	...	...
Des Moines (IA)	206 688[15]	...	...	230[16]	...	...	...	...
Detroit (MI)	701 475[15]	...	...	359[16]	...	...	...	...
Downey (CA)	112 873[15]	...	...	32[16]	...	...	...	...
Durham (NC)	239 358[15]	...	...	281[16]	...	...	...	...
El Monte (CA)	115 111[15]	...	...	25[16]	...	...	...	...
El Paso (TX)	672 538[15]	...	...	661[16]	...	...	...	...
Elgin (IL)	109 927[15]	...	...	97[16]	...	...	...	...
Elizabeth (NJ)	126 458[15]	...	...	32[16]	...	...	...	...
Elk Grove (CA)	159 038[15]	...	...	109[16]	...	...	...	...
Erie (PA)	101 047[15]	...	...	50[16]	...	...	...	...
Escondido (CA)	147 575[15]	...	...	95[16]	...	...	...	...
Eugene (OR)	157 986[15]	...	...	113[16]	...	...	...	...
Evansville (IN)	120 235[15]	...	...	123[16]	...	...	...	...
Everett (WA)	104 655[15]	...	...	86[16]	...	...	...	...
Fairfield (CA)	107 684[15]	...	...	97[16]	...	...	...	...
Fargo (ND)	109 779[15]	...	...	126[16]	...	...	...	...
Fayetteville (NC)	202 103[15]	...	...	379[16]	...	...	...	...
Flint (MI)	100 515[15]	...	...	87[16]	...	...	...	...
Fontana (CA)	201 812[15]	...	...	110[16]	...	...	...	...
Fort Collins (CO)	148 612[15]	...	...	141[16]	...	...	...	...
Fort Lauderdale (FL)	170 747[15]	...	...	90[16]	...	...	...	...
Fort Wayne (IN)	254 555[15]	...	...	287[16]	...	...	...	...
Fort Worth (TX)	777 992[15]	...	...	882[16]	...	...	...	...
Fremont (CA)	221 986[15]	...	...	201[16]	...	...	...	...
Fresno (CA)	505 882[15]	...	...	291[16]	...	...	...	...
Frisco (TX)	128 176[15]	...	...	160[16]	...	...	...	...
Fullerton (CA)	138 574[15]	...	...	58[16]	...	...	...	...
Gainesville (FL)	126 047[15]	...	...	159[16]	...	...	...	...
Garden Grove (CA)	174 389[15]	...	...	46[16]	...	...	...	...
Garland (TX)	233 564[15]	...	...	148[16]	...	...	...	...
Gilbert (AZ)	221 140[15]	...	...	176[16]	...	...	...	...
Glendale (AZ)	232 143[15]	...	...	152[16]	...	...	...	...

8. Population of capital cities and cities of 100 000 or more inhabitants: latest available year, 1995 - 2014
Population des capitales et des villes de 100 000 habitants ou plus : dernière année disponible, 1995 - 2014 (continued - suite)

Continent, country or area, date, code[a] and city / Continent, pays ou zone, date, code[a] et ville	City proper - Ville proprement dite				Urban agglomeration - Agglomération urbaine			
	Population			Surface area - Superficie (km²)	Population			Surface area - Superficie (km²)
	Both sexes - Les deux sexes	Male - Masculin	Female - Féminin		Both sexes - Les deux sexes	Male - Masculin	Female - Féminin	
AMERICA, NORTH - AMÉRIQUE DU NORD								
United States of America - États-Unis d'Amérique[14]								
1 VII 2012 (ESDJ)								
Glendale (CA)	194 478[15]	...	...	79[16]	...	...	...	...
Grand Prairie (TX)	181 824[15]	...	...	187[16]	...	...	...	...
Grand Rapids (MI)	190 411[15]	...	...	115[16]	...	...	...	...
Green Bay (WI)	104 868[15]	...	...	118[16]	...	...	...	...
Greensboro (NC)	277 080[15]	...	...	329[16]	...	...	...	...
Gresham (OR)	108 956[15]	...	...	60[16]	...	...	...	...
Hampton (VA)	136 836[15]	...	...	133[16]	...	...	...	...
Hartford (CT)	124 893[15]	...	...	45[16]	...	...	...	...
Hayward (CA)	149 392[15]	...	...	118[16]	...	...	...	...
Henderson (NV)	265 679[15]	...	...	279[16]	...	...	...	...
Hialeah (FL)	231 941[15]	...	...	56[16]	...	...	...	...
High Point City (NC)	106 586[15]	...	...	140[16]	...	...	...	...
Hollywood (FL)	145 236[15]	...	...	71[16]	...	...	...	...
Houston (TX)	2 160 821[15]	...	...	1 553[16]	...	...	...	...
Huntington Beach (CA)	194 708[15]	...	...	70[16]	...	...	...	...
Huntsville (AL)	183 739[15]	...	...	551[16]	...	...	...	...
Independence (MO)	117 270[15]	...	...	201[16]	...	...	...	...
Indianapolis (IN)	834 852[15]	...	...	936[16]	...	...	...	...
Inglewood (CA)	111 182[15]	...	...	23[16]	...	...	...	...
Irvine (CA)	229 985[15]	...	...	170[16]	...	...	...	...
Irving (TX)	225 427[15]	...	...	174[16]	...	...	...	...
Jackson (MS)	175 437[15]	...	...	288[16]	...	...	...	...
Jacksonville (FL)	836 507[15]	...	...	1 935[16]	...	...	...	...
Jersey City (NJ)	254 441[15]	...	...	38[16]	...	...	...	...
Joliet (IL)	148 268[15]	...	...	162[16]	...	...	...	...
Kansas City (KS)	147 268[15]	...	...	323[16]	...	...	...	...
Kansas City (MO)	464 310[15]	...	...	816[16]	...	...	...	...
Killeen (TX)	134 654[15]	...	...	139[16]	...	...	...	...
Knoxville (TN)	182 200[15]	...	...	255[16]	...	...	...	...
Lafayette (LA)	122 761[15]	...	...	133[16]	...	...	...	...
Lakewood (CO)	145 516[15]	...	...	111[16]	...	...	...	...
Lancaster (CA)	159 055[15]	...	...	244[16]	...	...	...	...
Lansing (MI)	113 996[15]	...	...	93[16]	...	...	...	...
Laredo (TX)	244 731[15]	...	...	237[16]	...	...	...	...
Las Vegas (NV)	596 424[15]	...	...	352[16]	...	...	...	...
Lexington-Fayette (KY)	305 489[15]	...	...	735[16]	...	...	...	...
Lincoln (NE)	265 404[15]	...	...	232[16]	...	...	...	...
Little Rock (AR)	196 537[15]	...	...	309[16]	...	...	...	...
Long Beach (CA)	467 892[15]	...	...	130[16]	...	...	...	...
Los Angeles (CA)	3 857 799[15]	...	...	1 214[16]	...	...	...	...
Louisville (KY)	605 110[15]	...	...	842[16]	...	...	...	...
Lowell (MA)	108 522[15]	...	...	35[16]	...	...	...	...
Lubbock (TX)	236 065[15]	...	...	317[16]	...	...	...	...
Madison (WI)	240 323[15]	...	...	198[16]	...	...	...	...
Manchester (NH)	110 209[15]	...	...	86[16]	...	...	...	...
McAllen (TX)	134 719[15]	...	...	125[16]	...	...	...	...
McKinney City (TX)	143 223[15]	...	...	161[16]	...	...	...	...
Memphis (TN)	655 155[15]	...	...	816[16]	...	...	...	...
Mesa (AZ)	452 084[15]	...	...	354[16]	...	...	...	...
Mesquite (TX)	143 195[15]	...	...	122[16]	...	...	...	...
Miami (FL)	413 892[15]	...	...	93[16]	...	...	...	...
Miami Gardens (FL)	110 754[15]	...	...	47[16]	...	...	...	...
Midland City (TX)	119 385[15]	...	...	188[16]	...	...	...	...
Milwaukee (WI)	598 916[15]	...	...	249[16]	...	...	...	...
Minneapolis (MN)	392 880[15]	...	...	140[16]	...	...	...	...
Miramar (FL)	128 729[15]	...	...	76[16]	...	...	...	...
Mobile (AL)	194 822[15]	...	...	360[16]	...	...	...	...
Modesto (CA)	203 547[15]	...	...	115[16]	...	...	...	...
Montgomery (AL)	205 293[15]	...	...	414[16]	...	...	...	...

8. Population of capital cities and cities of 100 000 or more inhabitants: latest available year, 1995 - 2014
Population des capitales et des villes de 100 000 habitants ou plus : dernière année disponible, 1995 - 2014 (continued - suite)

Continent, country or area, date, code[a] and city / Continent, pays ou zone, date, code[a] et ville	City proper - Ville proprement dite				Urban agglomeration - Agglomération urbaine			
	Population			Surface area - Superficie (km²)	Population			Surface area - Superficie (km²)
	Both sexes - Les deux sexes	Male - Masculin	Female - Féminin		Both sexes - Les deux sexes	Male - Masculin	Female - Féminin	

AMERICA, NORTH - AMÉRIQUE DU NORD

United States of America - États-Unis d'Amérique[14]
  1 VII 2012 (ESDJ)

City	Both sexes	Male	Female	Surface	Both sexes	Male	Female	Surface
Moreno Valley (CA)	199 552[15]	...	...	133[16]	...	...	...	...
Murfreesboro (TN)	114 038[15]	...	...	145[16]	...	...	...	...
Murrieta (CA)	106 810[15]	...	...	87[16]	...	...	...	...
Naperville (IL)	143 684[15]	...	...	101[16]	...	...	...	...
Nashville-Davidson (TN)	624 496[15]	...	...	1 233[16]	...	...	...	...
New Haven (CT)	130 741[15]	...	...	48[16]	...	...	...	...
New Orleans (LA)	369 250[15]	...	...	439[16]	...	...	...	...
New York (NY)	8 336 697[15]	...	...	784[16]	...	...	...	...
Newark (NJ)	277 727[15]	...	...	63[16]	...	...	...	...
Newport News (VA)	180 726[15]	...	...	178[16]	...	...	...	...
Norfolk (VA)	245 782[15]	...	...	140[16]	...	...	...	...
Norman (OK)	115 562[15]	...	...	463[16]	...	...	...	...
North Charleston (SC)	101 989[15]	...	...	190[16]	...	...	...	...
North Las Vegas (NV)	223 491[15]	...	...	264[16]	...	...	...	...
Norwalk (CA)	106 278[15]	...	...	25[16]	...	...	...	...
Oakland (CA)	400 740[15]	...	...	145[16]	...	...	...	...
Oceanside (CA)	171 293[15]	...	...	107[16]	...	...	...	...
Odessa (TX)	106 102[15]	...	...	109[16]	...	...	...	...
Oklahoma City (OK)	599 199[15]	...	...	1 571[16]	...	...	...	...
Olathe (KS)	130 045[15]	...	...	155[16]	...	...	...	...
Omaha (NE)	421 570[15]	...	...	330[16]	...	...	...	...
Ontario (CA)	167 211[15]	...	...	129[16]	...	...	...	...
Orange (CA)	139 419[15]	...	...	64[16]	...	...	...	...
Orlando (FL)	249 562[15]	...	...	267[16]	...	...	...	...
Overland Park (KS)	178 919[15]	...	...	194[16]	...	...	...	...
Oxnard (CA)	201 555[15]	...	...	70[16]	...	...	...	...
Palm Bay City (FL)	104 124[15]	...	...	170[16]	...	...	...	...
Palmdale (CA)	155 650[15]	...	...	274[16]	...	...	...	...
Pasadena (CA)	138 547[15]	...	...	60[16]	...	...	...	...
Pasadena (TX)	152 272[15]	...	...	111[16]	...	...	...	...
Paterson (NJ)	145 219[15]	...	...	22[16]	...	...	...	...
Pembroke Pines (FL)	160 306[15]	...	...	85[16]	...	...	...	...
Peoria (AZ)	159 789[15]	...	...	454[16]	...	...	...	...
Peoria (IL)	115 687[15]	...	...	124[16]	...	...	...	...
Philadelphia (PA)	1 547 607[15]	...	...	347[16]	...	...	...	...
Phoenix (AZ)	1 488 750[15]	...	...	1 339[16]	...	...	...	...
Pittsburgh (PA)	306 211[15]	...	...	143[16]	...	...	...	...
Plano (TX)	272 068[15]	...	...	185[16]	...	...	...	...
Pomona (CA)	150 812[15]	...	...	59[16]	...	...	...	...
Pompano Beach (FL)	102 984[15]	...	...	62[16]	...	...	...	...
Port St. Lucie (FL)	168 716[15]	...	...	295[16]	...	...	...	...
Portland (OR)	603 106[15]	...	...	346[16]	...	...	...	...
Providence (RI)	178 432[15]	...	...	48[16]	...	...	...	...
Provo (UT)	115 919[15]	...	...	108[16]	...	...	...	...
Pueblo (CO)	107 772[15]	...	...	138[16]	...	...	...	...
Raleigh (NC)	423 179[15]	...	...	373[16]	...	...	...	...
Rancho Cucamonga (CA)	170 746[15]	...	...	103[16]	...	...	...	...
Reno (NV)	231 027[15]	...	...	278[16]	...	...	...	...
Rialto (CA)	101 740[15]	...	...	58[16]	...	...	...	...
Richardson (TX)	103 297[15]	...	...	74[16]	...	...	...	...
Richmond (CA)	106 516[15]	...	...	78[16]	...	...	...	...
Richmond (VA)	210 309[15]	...	...	155[16]	...	...	...	...
Riverside (CA)	313 673[15]	...	...	210[16]	...	...	...	...
Rochester (MN)	108 992[15]	...	...	141[16]	...	...	...	...
Rochester (NY)	210 532[15]	...	...	93[16]	...	...	...	...
Rockford (IL)	150 843[15]	...	...	164[16]	...	...	...	...
Roseville (CA)	124 519[15]	...	...	94[16]	...	...	...	...
Round Rock (TX)	106 573[15]	...	...	88[16]	...	...	...	...
Sacramento (CA)	475 516[15]	...	...	254[16]	...	...	...	...

8. Population of capital cities and cities of 100 000 or more inhabitants: latest available year, 1995 - 2014
Population des capitales et des villes de 100 000 habitants ou plus : dernière année disponible, 1995 - 2014 (continued - suite)

Continent, country or area, date, code[a] and city / Continent, pays ou zone, date, code[a] et ville	City proper - Ville proprement dite				Urban agglomeration - Agglomération urbaine			
	Population			Surface area - Superficie (km²)	Population			Surface area - Superficie (km²)
	Both sexes - Les deux sexes	Male - Masculin	Female - Féminin		Both sexes - Les deux sexes	Male - Masculin	Female - Féminin	

AMERICA, NORTH - AMÉRIQUE DU NORD

United States of America - États-Unis d'Amérique[14]
1 VII 2012 (ESDJ)

Salem (OR)	157 429[15]	...	...	124[16]	...	...	...	...
Salinas (CA)	154 484[15]	...	...	61[16]	...	...	...	...
Salt Lake City (UT)	189 314[15]	...	...	288[16]	...	...	...	...
San Antonio (TX)	1 382 951[15]	...	...	1 194[16]	...	...	...	...
San Bernardino (CA)	213 295[15]	...	...	159[16]	...	...	...	...
San Buenaventura (CA)	107 734[15]	...	...	56[16]	...	...	...	...
San Diego (CA)	1 338 348[15]	...	...	842[16]	...	...	...	...
San Francisco (CA)	825 863[15]	...	...	121[16]	...	...	...	...
San Jose (CA)	982 765[15]	...	...	459[16]	...	...	...	...
Santa Ana (CA)	330 920[15]	...	...	71[16]	...	...	...	...
Santa Clara (CA)	119 311[15]	...	...	48[16]	...	...	...	...
Santa Clarita (CA)	179 013[15]	...	...	137[16]	...	...	...	...
Santa Maria (CA)	101 459[15]	...	...	59[16]	...	...	...	...
Santa Rosa (CA)	170 685[15]	...	...	107[16]	...	...	...	...
Savannah (GA)	142 022[15]	...	...	267[16]	...	...	...	...
Scottsdale (AZ)	223 514[15]	...	...	476[16]	...	...	...	...
Seattle (WA)	634 535[15]	...	...	217[16]	...	...	...	...
Shreveport (LA)	201 867[15]	...	...	278[16]	...	...	...	...
Simi Valley (CA)	125 793[15]	...	...	107[16]	...	...	...	...
Sioux Falls (SD)	159 908[15]	...	...	189[16]	...	...	...	...
South Bend (IN)	100 800[15]	...	...	107[16]	...	...	...	...
Spokane (WA)	209 525[15]	...	...	178[16]	...	...	...	...
Springfield (IL)	117 126[15]	...	...	154[16]	...	...	...	...
Springfield (MA)	153 552[15]	...	...	83[16]	...	...	...	...
Springfield (MO)	162 191[15]	...	...	212[16]	...	...	...	...
St. Louis (MO)	318 172[15]	...	...	160[16]	...	...	...	...
St. Paul (MN)	290 770[15]	...	...	135[16]	...	...	...	...
St. Petersburg (FL)	246 541[15]	...	...	160[16]	...	...	...	...
Stamford (CT)	125 109[15]	...	...	97[16]	...	...	...	...
Sterling Heights (MI)	130 410[15]	...	...	95[16]	...	...	...	...
Stockton (CA)	297 984[15]	...	...	160[16]	...	...	...	...
Sunnyvale (CA)	146 197[15]	...	...	57[16]	...	...	...	...
Surprise (AZ)	121 287[15]	...	...	279[16]	...	...	...	...
Syracuse (NY)	144 170[15]	...	...	65[16]	...	...	...	...
Tacoma (WA)	202 010[15]	...	...	129[16]	...	...	...	...
Tallahassee (FL)	186 971[15]	...	...	260[16]	...	...	...	...
Tampa (FL)	347 645[15]	...	...	294[16]	...	...	...	...
Temecula (CA)	105 208[15]	...	...	96[16]	...	...	...	...
Tempe (AZ)	166 842[15]	...	...	104[16]	...	...	...	...
Thornton (CO)	124 140[15]	...	...	90[16]	...	...	...	...
Thousand Oaks (CA)	128 412[15]	...	...	144[16]	...	...	...	...
Toledo (OH)	284 012[15]	...	...	209[16]	...	...	...	...
Topeka (KS)	127 939[15]	...	...	156[16]	...	...	...	...
Torrance (CA)	147 027[15]	...	...	53[16]	...	...	...	...
Tucson (AZ)	524 295[15]	...	...	587[16]	...	...	...	...
Tulsa (OK)	393 987[15]	...	...	510[16]	...	...	...	...
Urban Honolulu (HI)	345 610[15]	...	...	157[16]	...	...	...	...
Vallejo (CA)	117 796[15]	...	...	79[16]	...	...	...	...
Vancouver (WA)	165 489[15]	...	...	121[16]	...	...	...	...
Victorville City (CA)	120 336[15]	...	...	190[16]	...	...	...	...
Virginia Beach (VA)	447 021[15]	...	...	645[16]	...	...	...	...
Visalia (CA)	127 081[15]	...	...	96[16]	...	...	...	...
Waco (TX)	127 018[15]	...	...	230[16]	...	...	...	...
Warren (MI)	134 141[15]	...	...	89[16]	...	...	...	...
WASHINGTON (DC)	632 323[15]	...	...	158[16]	...	...	...	...
Waterbury (CT)	109 915[15]	...	...	74[16]	...	...	...	...
West Covina (CA)	107 440[15]	...	...	42[16]	...	...	...	...
West Jordan (UT)	108 383[15]	...	...	84[16]	...	...	...	...
West Palm Beach (FL)	101 903[15]	...	...	143[16]	...	...	...	...

8. Population of capital cities and cities of 100 000 or more inhabitants: latest available year, 1995 - 2014
Population des capitales et des villes de 100 000 habitants ou plus : dernière année disponible, 1995 - 2014 (continued - suite)

Continent, country or area, date, code[a] and city / Continent, pays ou zone, date, code[a] et ville	City proper - Ville proprement dite				Urban agglomeration - Agglomération urbaine			
	Population			Surface area - Superficie (km²)	Population			Surface area - Superficie (km²)
	Both sexes - Les deux sexes	Male - Masculin	Female - Féminin		Both sexes - Les deux sexes	Male - Masculin	Female - Féminin	
AMERICA, NORTH - AMÉRIQUE DU NORD								
United States of America - États-Unis d'Amérique[14]								
1 VII 2012 (ESDJ)								
West Valley City (UT)	132 434[15]	...	...	92[16]	...	...	...	...
Westminster (CO)	109 169[15]	...	...	82[16]	...	...	...	...
Wichita (KS)	385 577[15]	...	...	414[16]	...	...	...	...
Wichita Falls (TX)	104 552[15]	...	...	187[16]	...	...	...	...
Wilmington (NC)	109 922[15]	...	...	133[16]	...	...	...	...
Winston-Salem (NC)	234 349[15]	...	...	343[16]	...	...	...	...
Worcester (MA)	182 669[15]	...	...	97[16]	...	...	...	...
Yonkers (NY)	198 449[15]	...	...	47[16]	...	...	...	...
United States Virgin Islands - Îles Vierges américaines[17]								
1 IV 2010 (CDJC)								
CHARLOTTE AMALIE	10 354	...	...	...	...	...	...	...
AMERICA, SOUTH - AMÉRIQUE DU SUD								
Argentina - Argentine[18]								
1 VII 2013 (ESDF)								
Bahía Blanca-Cerri	...	...	...	...	317 326	...	...	...
BUENOS AIRES[19]	...	...	...	...	13 339 002	...	...	...
Catamarca	...	...	...	...	215 795	...	...	...
Comodoro Rivadavia-Rada Tilly	...	...	...	...	146 557	...	...	...
Concordia	...	...	...	...	157 706	...	...	...
Córdoba	...	...	...	...	1 442 001	...	...	...
Corrientes	...	...	...	...	373 981	...	...	...
Formosa	...	...	...	...	253 508	...	...	...
La Plata	...	...	...	...	764 469	...	...	...
La Rioja	...	...	...	...	193 764	...	...	...
Mar del Plata-Batán	...	...	...	...	633 906	...	...	...
Mendoza	...	...	...	...	923 203	...	...	...
Neuquén-Plottier	...	...	...	...	277 610	...	...	...
Paraná	...	...	...	...	286 659	...	...	...
Posadas	...	...	...	...	312 163	...	...	...
Resistencia	...	...	...	...	406 284	...	...	...
Río Cuarto	...	...	...	...	168 401	...	...	...
Rosario	...	...	...	...	1 284 951	...	...	...
Salta	...	...	...	...	562 807	...	...	...
San Juan	...	...	...	...	486 313	...	...	...
San Luis - El Chorrillo	...	...	...	...	216 610	...	...	...
San Salvador de Jujuy-Palpalá	...	...	...	...	322 873	...	...	...
Santa Fé	...	...	...	...	521 233	...	...	...
Santa Rosa-Toay	...	...	...	...	127 399	...	...	...
Santiago del Estero-La Banda	...	...	...	...	387 320	...	...	...
Tucumán-Tafí Viejo[20]	...	...	...	...	836 412	...	...	...
Ushuaia-Río Grande	...	...	...	...	130 617	...	...	...
Bolivia (Plurinational State of) - Bolivie (État plurinational de)								
1 VII 2010 (ESDF)								
Cochabamba	618 376	294 711	323 666	...	...	...	...	...
El Alto	953 253	463 069	490 184	...	...	...	...	...
LA PAZ	835 361	397 608	437 753	...	...	...	...	...
Oruro	216 724	104 294	112 430	...	...	...	...	...
Potosí	154 693	74 591	80 103	...	...	...	...	...
Sacaba	155 668	75 113	80 555	...	...	...	...	...
Santa Cruz	1 616 063	785 941	830 122	...	...	...	...	...
SUCRE	284 032	137 943	146 090	...	...	...	...	...
Tarija	194 313	94 231	100 082	...	...	...	...	...
Yacuiba	112 096	55 346	56 750	...	...	...	...	...
Brazil - Brésil								
31 VII 2010 (CDJC)								
Aguas Lindas de Goiás	159 138	79 587	79 551	...	159 138	79 587	79 551	154
Alagoinhas	122 324	57 341	64 983	...	124 042	58 132	65 910	55

8. Population of capital cities and cities of 100 000 or more inhabitants: latest available year, 1995 - 2014
Population des capitales et des villes de 100 000 habitants ou plus : dernière année disponible, 1995 - 2014 (continued - suite)

Continent, country or area, date, code[a] and city / Continent, pays ou zone, date, code[a] et ville	City proper - Ville proprement dite				Urban agglomeration - Agglomération urbaine			
	Population			Surface area - Superficie (km²)	Population			Surface area - Superficie (km²)
	Both sexes - Les deux sexes	Male - Masculin	Female - Féminin		Both sexes - Les deux sexes	Male - Masculin	Female - Féminin	
AMERICA, SOUTH - AMÉRIQUE DU SUD								
Brazil - Brésil								
31 VII 2010 (CDJC)								
Alvorada	175 575	85 010	90 565	...	195 673	95 080	100 593	71
Americana	209 654	102 644	107 010	...	209 654	102 644	107 010	99
Ananindeua	470 819	226 022	244 797	...	470 819	226 022	244 797	81
Anápolis	325 163	158 366	166 798	...	328 755	160 123	168 632	191
Angra dos Reis	65 364	32 348	33 016	...	163 199	81 424	81 775	220
Aparecida de Goiania	157 296	79 581	77 715	...	455 193	224 602	230 591	227
Apucarana	108 887	52 548	56 339	...	114 104	55 070	59 034	121
Aracaju	571 149	265 484	305 665	...	571 149	265 484	305 665	182
Araçatuba	178 077	85 466	92 611	...	178 077	85 466	92 611	69
Araguaina	142 925	69 468	73 457	...	142 925	69 468	73 457	133
Araguario	100 753	49 272	51 480	...	102 583	50 186	52 397	75
Arapiraca	181 481	85 682	95 799	...	181 481	85 682	95 799	68
Arapongas	101 851	49 820	52 031	...	101 851	49 820	52 031	123
Araraquara	143 071	68 476	74 594	...	202 739	97 512	105 227	81
Araras	112 444	55 341	57 103	...	112 444	55 341	57 103	33
Araruama	76 872	36 937	39 935	...	106 486	51 488	54 998	219
Araucária	109 484	54 663	54 820	...	110 205	55 026	55 179	91
Atibaia	115 229	56 235	58 994	...	115 229	56 235	58 994	170
Balneário Camboriú	108 089	51 393	56 696	...	108 089	51 393	56 696	46
Barbacena	107 207	50 395	56 812	...	115 568	54 566	61 002	48
Barra Mansa	171 125	82 488	88 637	...	176 230	84 915	91 315	96
Barreiras	123 741	60 645	63 096	...	123 741	60 645	63 096	112
Barretos	108 306	52 145	56 161	...	108 686	52 342	56 344	58
Barueri	112 726	54 658	58 068	...	240 749	117 051	123 698	66
Bauru	337 094	161 473	175 621	...	338 186	162 058	176 128	188
Belém	143 474	63 156	80 318	...	1 381 475	652 860	728 615	285
Belford Roxo	469 332	226 757	242 575	...	469 332	226 757	242 575	78
Belo Horizonte	1 433 244	663 016	770 227	...	2 375 151	1 113 513	1 261 638	331
Betim	375 331	184 905	190 426	...	375 331	184 905	190 426	225
Birigui	105 487	51 249	54 238	...	105 487	51 249	54 238	51
Blumenou	248 655	122 039	126 616	...	294 821	144 384	150 437	207
Boa Vista	277 799	136 877	140 922	...	277 799	136 877	140 922	508
Botucatu	115 606	55 535	60 071	...	122 744	59 384	63 360	141
Bragança Paulista	142 255	69 700	72 555	...	142 255	69 700	72 555	311
BRASILIA	2 481 272	1 180 060	1 301 212	...	2 481 272	1 180 060	1 301 212	1 190
Brusque	102 025	50 586	51 439	...	102 025	50 586	51 439	139
Cabo de Santo Agostinho	95 979	46 752	49 227	...	167 783	81 917	85 866	108
Cabo Frio	140 269	67 889	72 380	...	140 486	68 010	72 476	113
Cachoeirinha	118 278	57 173	61 105	...	118 278	57 173	61 105	44
Cachoeiro de Itapemirim	162 947	78 891	84 056	...	173 589	84 201	89 388	146
Camacari	161 226	79 499	81 726	...	231 973	114 874	117 099	299
Camaragibe	144 466	69 212	75 254	...	144 466	69 212	75 254	51
Campina Grande	355 014	167 240	187 774	...	367 209	173 191	194 018	99
Campinas	952 659	458 571	494 087	...	1 061 540	511 483	550 057	384
Campo Grande	774 202	374 202	400 000	...	776 242	375 248	400 994	359
Campos dos Goytacazes	356 608	169 535	187 073	...	418 725	200 256	218 469	364
Canoas	323 827	155 936	167 891	...	323 827	155 936	167 891	131
Carapicuíba	230 355	110 869	119 486	...	369 584	179 284	190 300	34
Cariacica	115 513	56 889	58 625	...	337 643	164 374	173 269	106
Caruaru	277 982	130 512	147 470	...	279 589	131 317	148 272	113
Cascavel	266 835	129 171	137 664	...	270 049	130 813	139 236	112
Castanhal	149 918	72 577	77 341	...	153 378	74 176	79 202	75
Catanduva	111 914	54 307	57 607	...	111 914	54 307	57 607	96
Caucaia	149 896	73 475	76 421	...	290 220	141 210	149 010	221
Caxias	118 534	55 811	62 723	...	118 534	55 811	62 723	124
Caxias do Sul	415 822	203 357	212 466	...	419 406	205 081	214 325	255
Chapecó	166 040	81 182	84 858	...	168 113	82 179	85 934	55
Colombo	203 203	100 016	103 187	...	203 203	100 016	103 187	77
Conselheiro Lafaiete	110 588	53 478	57 110	...	111 266	53 751	57 515	88
Contagem	379 044	185 545	193 499	...	601 400	291 709	309 691	148
Coronel Fabriciano	47 625	22 800	24 825	...	102 395	49 378	53 017	73
Cotia	170 507	83 280	87 227	...	201 150	98 455	102 695	323
Crato	93 469	43 665	49 804	...	100 916	47 285	53 631	76

8. Population of capital cities and cities of 100 000 or more inhabitants: latest available year, 1995 - 2014
Population des capitales et des villes de 100 000 habitants ou plus : dernière année disponible, 1995 - 2014 (continued - suite)

Continent, country or area, date, code[a] and city / Continent, pays ou zone, date, code[a] et ville	City proper - Ville proprement dite				Urban agglomeration - Agglomération urbaine			
	Population			Surface area - Superficie (km²)	Population			Surface area - Superficie (km²)
	Both sexes - Les deux sexes	Male - Masculin	Female - Féminin		Both sexes - Les deux sexes	Male - Masculin	Female - Féminin	

AMERICA, SOUTH - AMÉRIQUE DU SUD

Brazil - Brésil
31 VII 2010 (CDJC)

City	Both sexes	Male	Female	Surface	Both sexes	Male	Female	Surface
Criciúma	133 031	65 077	67 954	...	189 630	93 047	96 583	168
Cubatao	118 720	59 229	59 491	...	118 720	59 229	59 491	142
Cuiabá	220 859	105 753	115 106	...	540 814	263 510	277 304	270
Curitiba	1 751 907	835 115	916 792	...	1 751 907	835 115	916 792	435
Diadema	386 089	186 803	199 286	...	386 089	186 803	199 286	31
Divinópolis	202 220	98 046	104 174	...	207 516	100 880	106 636	212
Dourados	173 647	84 344	89 303	...	181 005	88 555	92 450	118
Duque de Caxias	341 304	161 359	179 945	...	852 138	409 537	442 601	267
Embu	240 230	116 728	123 502	...	240 230	116 728	123 502	70
Feira de Santana	495 516	234 015	261 501	...	510 635	241 310	269 325	172
Ferraz de Vasconcelos	111 727	54 485	57 242	...	160 754	78 255	82 499	17
Florianópolis	249 477	118 470	131 007	...	405 189	194 916	210 273	258
Fortaleza	862 750	394 154	468 596	...	2 452 185	1 147 918	1 304 267	314
Foz do Iguaçu	253 962	123 104	130 858	...	253 962	123 104	130 858	161
Franca	313 046	152 402	160 644	...	313 046	152 402	160 644	80
Francisco Morato	154 207	76 459	77 748	...	154 207	76 459	77 748	43
Franco da Rocha	121 244	59 594	61 650	...	121 244	59 594	61 650	53
Garanhuns	112 462	52 448	60 014	...	115 356	53 825	61 531	62
Goiânia	1 296 324	617 923	678 401	...	1 297 154	618 292	678 862	424
Governador Valadares	245 125	115 658	129 467	...	253 300	119 609	133 691	172
Gravatai	228 093	110 712	117 381	...	243 497	118 532	124 965	158
Guarapari	100 528	48 985	51 543	...	100 528	48 985	51 543	259
Guarapuava	142 163	68 934	73 230	...	152 993	74 273	78 720	92
Guaratinguetá	106 762	51 197	55 565	...	106 762	51 197	55 565	69
Guarujá	138 753	67 812	70 941	...	290 696	141 682	149 014	132
Guarulhos	784 971	380 278	404 693	...	1 221 979	595 043	626 936	317
Hortolandia	192 692	97 439	95 253	...	192 692	97 439	95 253	61
Ibirité	83 765	41 054	42 712	...	158 590	77 644	80 946	50
Ilhéus	148 437	70 579	77 858	...	155 281	74 049	81 232	113
Imperatriz	234 547	112 566	121 981	...	234 547	112 566	121 981	90
Indaiatuba	199 592	99 101	100 491	...	199 592	99 101	100 491	203
Ipatinga	148 687	72 081	76 606	...	236 968	114 954	122 014	75
Itabiraí	100 300	47 822	52 478	...	102 316	48 931	53 385	64
Itaboraí	107 527	52 098	55 429	...	215 327	104 856	110 471	216
Itabuna	199 749	94 271	105 478	...	199 749	94 271	105 478	47
Itaguaí	104 195	51 776	52 419	...	104 209	51 783	52 426	81
Itajaí	173 452	85 030	88 422	...	173 452	85 030	88 422	100
Itapecerica da Serra	151 349	75 626	75 723	...	151 349	75 626	75 723	134
Itapetininga	123 439	59 980	63 460	...	131 050	63 919	67 131	87
Itapevi	200 769	98 746	102 023	...	200 769	98 746	102 023	83
Itaquaquecetuba	321 770	158 542	163 228	...	321 770	158 542	163 228	83
Itu	144 269	71 002	73 267	...	144 269	71 002	73 267	115
Jaboatao dos Guarapes	335 371	157 757	177 614	...	630 595	297 903	332 692	154
Jacareí	187 144	91 007	96 138	...	208 297	101 489	106 808	196
Jandira	108 344	53 063	55 281	...	108 344	53 063	55 281	18
Jaraguá do Sul	132 800	66 511	66 289	...	132 800	66 511	66 289	123
Jaú	118 895	57 902	60 993	...	126 943	62 004	64 939	65
Jequié	136 518	65 445	71 074	...	139 426	66 855	72 571	71
Ji-Paraná	103 256	50 786	52 470	...	104 858	51 589	53 269	116
Joao Pessoa	720 954	336 616	384 338	...	720 954	336 616	384 338	165
Joinville	486 803	241 130	245 673	...	497 850	246 707	251 143	218
Juazeiro	151 336	73 035	78 301	...	160 775	77 799	82 976	73
Juàzeiro do Norte	238 889	112 789	126 099	...	240 128	113 404	126 724	79
Juiz de Fora	489 801	230 511	259 290	...	510 378	240 877	269 501	412
Jundiaí	354 204	171 931	182 273	...	354 204	171 931	182 273	176
Lages	153 676	74 329	79 347	...	153 937	74 458	79 479	213
Lauro de Freitas	163 449	79 276	84 173	...	163 449	79 276	84 173	58
Limeira	267 804	131 372	136 432	...	267 804	131 372	136 432	168
Linhares	109 653	53 923	55 729	...	121 567	59 882	61 685	101
Londrina	485 822	231 869	253 953	...	493 520	235 638	257 882	249
Luziânia	98 752	48 951	49 801	...	162 807	80 684	82 123	127
Macae	194 652	96 205	98 447	...	202 859	100 337	102 522	228
Macapá	369 287	180 649	188 638	...	381 091	186 588	194 503	319

8. Population of capital cities and cities of 100 000 or more inhabitants: latest available year, 1995 - 2014
Population des capitales et des villes de 100 000 habitants ou plus : dernière année disponible, 1995 - 2014 (continued - suite)

Continent, country or area, date, code[a] and city / Continent, pays ou zone, date, code[a] et ville	City proper - Ville proprement dite				Urban agglomeration - Agglomération urbaine			
	Population			Surface area - Superficie (km²)	Population			Surface area - Superficie (km²)
	Both sexes - Les deux sexes	Male - Masculin	Female - Féminin		Both sexes - Les deux sexes	Male - Masculin	Female - Féminin	
AMERICA, SOUTH - AMÉRIQUE DU SUD								
Brazil - Brésil								
31 VII 2010 (CDJC)								
Maceió	932 078	436 139	495 938	...	932 078	436 139	495 938	221
Magé	54 633	26 750	27 883	...	215 236	104 479	110 757	160
Manaus	1 792 881	874 749	918 132	...	1 792 881	874 749	918 132	860
Maraba	186 270	92 780	93 490	...	186 270	92 780	93 490	111
Maracanau	163 853	79 680	84 173	...	207 635	101 359	106 276	81
Maricá	40 074	18 993	21 082	...	125 401	61 585	63 816	244
Marília	197 342	93 820	103 523	...	207 021	99 682	107 339	101
Maringá	342 310	164 162	178 148	...	350 653	168 417	182 236	135
Marituba	107 123	53 327	53 796	...	107 123	53 327	53 796	42
Mauá	417 064	204 093	212 971	...	417 064	204 093	212 971	61
Mesquita	168 376	79 790	88 586	...	168 376	79 790	88 586	39
Moji das Cruzes	163 259	78 240	85 019	...	357 313	173 193	184 120	233
Moji-Guaçu	127 452	63 013	64 439	...	130 295	64 407	65 888	43
Montes Claros	338 381	161 936	176 445	...	344 427	164 985	179 442	108
Mossoró	237 241	113 580	123 661	...	237 241	113 580	123 661	114
Natal	803 739	377 947	425 792	...	803 739	377 947	425 792	166
Nilópolis	102 161	47 772	54 389	...	157 425	73 674	83 751	19
Niterói	487 562	225 838	261 724	...	487 562	225 838	261 724	134
Nossa Senhora do Socorro	155 823	75 707	80 116	...	155 823	75 707	80 116	71
Nova Friburgo	113 217	53 310	59 906	...	159 372	75 599	83 773	152
Nova Iguaçu	787 563	377 336	410 227	...	787 563	377 336	410 227	399
Nôvo Hamburgo	234 798	113 628	121 170	...	234 798	113 628	121 170	103
Olinda	370 332	171 066	199 266	...	370 332	171 066	199 266	35
Osasco	666 740	320 436	346 304	...	666 740	320 436	346 304	64
Ourinhos	100 374	48 586	51 788	...	100 374	48 586	51 788	63
Palhoça	119 360	59 293	60 067	...	135 311	67 385	67 926	194
Palmas	217 056	106 742	110 314	...	221 742	109 092	112 650	290
Paranaguá	133 761	65 667	68 094	...	135 421	66 562	68 859	91
Parauapebas	138 690	70 054	68 636	...	138 690	70 054	68 636	49
Parnaíba	137 485	65 418	72 067	...	137 485	65 418	72 067	96
Parnamirim	202 456	96 995	105 461	...	202 456	96 995	105 461	124
Passo Fundo	179 630	85 396	94 235	...	180 120	85 646	94 474	73
Passos	100 859	49 518	51 341	...	100 859	49 518	51 341	40
Patos de Minas	124 349	60 210	64 139	...	127 724	61 949	65 775	58
Paulista	300 466	141 630	158 836	...	300 466	141 630	158 836	97
Pelotas	306 193	142 848	163 345	...	306 193	142 848	163 345	197
Petrolina	217 093	103 808,	113 285	...	219 172	104 817	114 355	132
Petrópolis	185 876	87 599	98 277	...	281 286	133 694	147 592	371
Pindamonhangaba	103 395	50 374	53 021	...	141 708	69 505	72 203	150
Pinhais	117 008	56 809	60 199	...	117 008	56 809	60 199	61
Piracicaba	297 767	144 689	153 079	...	356 743	174 190	182 553	206
Poà	99 116	47 857	51 259	...	104 338	50 443	53 895	16
Poços de Caldas	148 722	71 676	77 046	...	148 722	71 676	77 046	87
Ponta Grossa	303 399	147 034	156 366	...	304 717	147 714	157 003	204
Porto Alegre	1 409 351	653 787	755 564	...	1 409 351	653 787	755 564	497
Porto Seguro	80 240	39 610	40 630	...	104 078	51 512	52 566	132
Porto Velho	369 259	182 618	186 641	...	392 475	195 229	197 246	180
Pouso Alegre	118 847	58 159	60 687	...	119 590	58 566	61 024	41
Praia Grande	201 259	96 557	104 702	...	262 051	125 926	136 125	148
Presidente Prudente	200 042	95 432	104 609	...	203 382	97 105	106 277	124
Queimados	137 962	66 585	71 377	...	137 962	66 585	71 377	76
Recife	1 537 704	709 819	827 885	...	1 537 704	709 819	827 885	218
Resende	77 848	37 498	40 350	...	112 331	54 405	57 926	60
Ribeirao das Neves	134 449	67 974	66 475	...	294 158	145 902	148 256	140
Ribeirao Pires	77 660	37 507	40 153	...	113 068	55 318	57 750	99
Ribeirao Prêto	590 593	283 287	307 306	...	603 186	289 446	313 741	352
Rio Branco	308 545	148 437	160 108	...	308 545	148 437	160 108	145
Rio Claro	178 613	86 652	91 961	...	181 720	88 224	93 496	81
Rio de Janeiro	6 320 446	2 959 817	3 360 629	...	6 320 446	2 959 817	3 360 629	1 198
Rio Grande	178 454	84 991	93 463	...	189 429	90 514	98 915	160
Rio Verde	160 661	81 404	79 257	...	163 540	82 870	80 670	61
Rondonópolis	144 049	71 561	72 488	...	188 028	93 785	94 243	313
Sabára	44 206	21 375	22 830	...	123 084	59 080	64 004	45

8. Population of capital cities and cities of 100 000 or more inhabitants: latest available year, 1995 - 2014
Population des capitales et des villes de 100 000 habitants ou plus : dernière année disponible, 1995 - 2014 (continued - suite)

Continent, country or area, date, code[a] and city / Continent, pays ou zone, date, code[a] et ville	City proper - Ville proprement dite				Urban agglomeration - Agglomération urbaine			
	Population			Surface area - Superficie (km²)	Population			Surface area - Superficie (km²)
	Both sexes - Les deux sexes	Male - Masculin	Female - Féminin		Both sexes - Les deux sexes	Male - Masculin	Female - Féminin	
AMERICA, SOUTH - AMÉRIQUE DU SUD								
Brazil - Brésil								
31 VII 2010 (CDJC)								
Salto	104 688	51 738	52 950	...	104 688	51 738	52 950	90
Salvador	2 674 923	1 248 513	1 426 410	...	2 674 923	1 248 513	1 426 410	348
Santa Bárbara D'Oeste	178 596	88 478	90 118	...	178 596	88 478	90 118	82
Santa Cruz do Sul	102 891	48 988	53 903	...	105 190	50 142	55 048	154
Santa Luzia (Minas Gerais)	72 187	35 327	36 860	...	202 378	98 202	104 176	194
Santa Maria	246 544	116 243	130 300	...	248 347	117 104	131 243	136
Santa Rita	101 319	48 482	52 838	...	103 717	49 703	54 014	24
Santana de Parnaíba	108 813	53 671	55 142	...	108 813	53 671	55 142	179
Santarém	205 711	98 921	106 790	...	215 790	104 001	111 789	99
Santo André	568 538	271 994	296 544	...	676 407	324 458	351 949	175
Santos	419 086	191 754	227 332	...	419 086	191 754	227 332	80
Sao Bernardo do Campo	736 466	355 313	381 154	...	752 658	363 148	389 510	148
Sao Caetano do Sul	149 263	68 853	80 410	...	149 263	68 853	80 410	15
Sao Carlo	116 765	56 422	60 342	...	213 061	104 241	108 820	80
Sao Gonçalo	337 273	159 766	177 507	...	998 999	474 894	524 105	210
Sao Joao de Meriti	234 340	111 799	122 540	...	458 673	218 104	240 569	35
Sao José	25 993	11 699	14 294	...	207 312	100 118	107 194	94
Sao José do Rio Prêto	372 492	177 603	194 889	...	383 490	182 947	200 543	115
Sao José dos Campos	533 501	260 627	272 874	...	617 119	301 893	315 226	362
Sao José dos Pinhais	200 521	98 276	102 244	...	236 895	116 457	120 438	101
Sao Leopoldo	213 238	103 790	109 448	...	213 238	103 790	109 448	72
Sao Luís	958 545	447 020	511 525	...	958 545	447 020	511 525	322
Sao Paulo	105 269	49 119	56 150	...	11 152 968	5 278 434	5 874 534	991
Sao Vicente	331 817	159 303	172 514	...	331 817	159 303	172 514	71
Sapucaia do Sul	130 469	63 500	66 969	...	130 469	63 500	66 969	46
Serra	112 555	55 292	57 263	...	406 411	199 645	206 766	227
Sertaozinho	101 784	50 254	51 530	...	108 772	54 013	54 759	71
Sete Lagoas	208 847	101 205	107 642	...	208 956	101 263	107 693	92
Simoes Filho	105 811	51 624	54 187	...	105 811	51 624	54 187	57
Sobral	147 353	70 898	76 455	...	166 310	80 213	86 097	80
Sorocaba	580 621	283 854	296 767	...	580 621	283 854	296 767	229
Sumaré	97 696	48 435	49 261	...	238 470	118 381	120 089	73
Susano	152 003	74 026	77 977	...	253 240	123 883	129 357	103
Taboao da Serra	244 528	116 895	127 633	...	244 528	116 895	127 633	20
Tatuí	102 256	50 323	51 933	...	102 256	50 323	51 933	137
Taubaté	232 049	113 563	118 486	...	272 673	133 530	139 143	138
Teixeira de Freitas	128 407	62 801	65 605	...	129 263	63 334	65 929	45
Teófilo Otoni	105 621	49 404	56 217	...	110 076	51 536	58 540	29
Teresina	767 559	356 608	410 951	...	767 559	356 608	410 951	251
Teresópolis	134 156	63 517	70 640	...	146 231	69 454	76 777	223
Timon	134 827	64 855	69 972	...	135 133	65 025	70 108	100
Toledo	103 644	50 409	53 235	...	108 259	52 625	55 634	71
Trindade	100 106	49 070	51 036	...	100 106	49 070	51 036	47
Uberaba	289 376	140 640	148 736	...	289 376	140 640	148 736	411
Uberlândia	584 102	283 948	300 154	...	587 266	285 611	301 655	224
Uruguaiana	116 276	55 938	60 339	...	117 415	56 486	60 929	52
Valinhos	101 626	49 974	51 652	...	101 626	49 974	51 652	62
Valparaíso de Goiás	132 982	64 624	68 358	...	132 982	64 624	68 358	61
Varginha	119 061	57 831	61 230	...	119 061	57 831	61 230	61
Varzea Grande	184 069	91 183	92 886	...	248 704	123 112	125 592	167
Varzea Paulista	107 089	53 415	53 674	...	107 089	53 415	53 674	34
Vespasiano	104 527	51 006	53 521	...	104 527	51 006	53 521	71
Viamao	87 753	42 460	45 293	...	224 943	109 013	115 930	175
Vila Velha	171 772	81 290	90 482	...	412 575	197 926	214 649	120
Vitória	211 529	100 014	111 515	...	327 801	153 948	173 853	88
Vitória da Conquista	260 260	123 976	136 284	...	274 739	131 262	143 477	286
Vitória de Santo Antao	111 541	52 913	58 629	...	113 429	53 820	59 609	31
Volta Redonda	257 686	122 859	134 827	...	257 686	122 859	134 827	140
Votorantim	104 659	51 858	52 801	...	104 659	51 858	52 801	28
Chile - Chili								
1 VII 2014 (ESDF)								
Alto Hospicio	107 935[21]	52 513[21]	55 422[21]	17[22]	...	...	...	...
Antofagasta	390 832[21]	203 227[21]	187 605[21]	44[22]	...	...	...	...

8. Population of capital cities and cities of 100 000 or more inhabitants: latest available year, 1995 - 2014
Population des capitales et des villes de 100 000 habitants ou plus : dernière année disponible, 1995 - 2014 (continued - suite)

Continent, country or area, date, code[a] and city / Continent, pays ou zone, date, code[a] et ville	City proper - Ville proprement dite				Urban agglomeration - Agglomération urbaine			
	Population			Surface area - Superficie (km²)	Population			Surface area - Superficie (km²)
	Both sexes - Les deux sexes	Male - Masculin	Female - Féminin		Both sexes - Les deux sexes	Male - Masculin	Female - Féminin	

AMERICA, SOUTH - AMÉRIQUE DU SUD

Chile - Chili
1 VII 2014 (ESDF)

Arica	157 568[21]	73 219[21]	84 349[21]	42[22]	...	...	...	...
Calama	147 666[21]	74 895[21]	72 771[21]	18[22]	...	...	...	...
Chiguallante	137 070[21]	63 554[21]	73 516[21]	34[22]	...	...	...	...
Chillán	163 560[21]	77 425[21]	86 135[21]	33[22]	...	...	...	...
Concepción	223 798[21]	107 833[21]	115 965[21]	56[22]	...	...	...	...
Copiapó	202 749[21]	99 814[21]	102 935[21]	48[22]	...	...	...	...
Coquimbo	106 492[21]	51 348[21]	55 144[21]	42[22]	...	...	...	...
Coronel	166 929[21]	83 727[21]	83 202[21]	25[22]	...	...	...	...
Curicó	102 029[21]	50 060[21]	51 969[21]	21[22]	...	...	...	...
Iquique	181 773[21]	86 919[21]	94 854[21]	22[22]	...	...	...	...
La Serena	209 651[21]	101 595[21]	108 056[21]	66[22]	...	...	...	...
Los Ángeles	145 631[21]	70 798[21]	74 833[21]	27[22]	...	...	...	...
Osorno	148 350[21]	73 204[21]	75 146[21]	32[22]	...	...	...	...
Puente Alto	802 109[21]	393 192[21]	408 917[21]	64[22]	...	...	...	...
Puerto Montt	220 800[21]	110 622[21]	110 178[21]	40[22]	...	...	...	...
Punta Arenas	123 401[21]	61 750[21]	61 651[21]	39[22]	...	...	...	...
Quilpué	167 938[21]	81 991[21]	85 947[21]	38[22]	...	...	...	...
Rancagua	243 983[21]	121 736[21]	122 247[21]	50[22]	...	...	...	...
San Bernardo	316 094[21]	155 056[21]	161 038[21]	52[22]	...	...	...	...
San Pedro de la Paz	101 345[21]	48 233[21]	53 112[21]	49[22]	...	...	...	...
SANTIAGO	5 128 041[23]	2 486 468[23]	2 641 573[23]	843[22]	...	...	...	...
Talca	222 039[21]	108 184[21]	113 855[21]	46[22]	...	...	...	...
Talcahuano	113 181[21]	50 295[21]	62 886[21]	51[22]	...	...	...	...
Temuco	264 642[21]	127 223[21]	137 419[21]	46[22]	...	...	...	...
Valdivia	138 970[21]	67 923[21]	71 047[21]	42[22]	...	...	...	...
Valparaíso	249 897[21]	124 940[21]	124 957[21]	47[22]	...	...	...	...
Villa Alemana	140 401[21]	68 801[21]	71 600[21]	31[22]	...	...	...	...
Viña del Mar	288 329[21]	138 419[21]	149 910[21]	87[22]	...	...	...	...

Colombia - Colombie[24]
1 VII 2014 (ESDJ)

Apartadó	...	...	...	...	173 008	87 491	85 517	607[8]
Armenia	...	...	...	...	295 143	142 397	152 746	115[8]
Barrancabermeja	...	...	...	...	191 784	94 572	97 212	1 274[8]
Barranquilla	...	...	...	...	1 212 943	588 218	624 725	166[8]
Bello	...	...	...	...	447 185	216 246	230 939	151[8]
BOGOTÁ, D.C.	...	...	...	...	7 776 845	3 758 224	4 018 621	1 605[8]
Bucaramanga	...	...	...	...	527 451	253 298	274 153	154[8]
Buenaventura	...	...	...	...	392 054	190 683	201 371	6 785[8]
Cali	...	...	...	...	2 344 734	1 120 994	1 223 740	552[8]
Cartagena	...	...	...	...	990 179	478 281	511 898	559[8]
Cartago	...	...	...	...	131 545	63 213	68 332	260[8]
Caucasia	...	...	...	...	109 511	52 994	56 517	1 058[8]
Chía	...	...	...	...	123 673	59 433	64 240	76[8]
Ciénaga	...	...	...	...	104 060	51 959	52 101	1 366[8]
Cúcuta	...	...	...	...	643 666	311 354	332 312	1 098[8]
Dosquebradas	...	...	...	...	196 926	95 518	101 408	80[8]
Duitama	...	...	...	...	112 243	52 065	60 178	229[8]
Envigado	...	...	...	...	217 343	104 685	112 658	51[8]
Facatativá	...	...	...	...	129 671	64 670	65 001	160[8]
Florencia	...	...	...	...	169 336	83 208	86 128	2 292[8]
Floridablanca	...	...	...	...	264 695	125 785	138 910	101[8]
Fusagasugá	...	...	...	...	131 914	65 099	66 815	206[8]
Girardot	...	...	...	...	104 476	49 390	55 086	130[8]
Girón	...	...	...	...	175 528	87 399	88 129	681[8]
Gudalajara de Buga	...	...	...	...	115 432	56 559	58 873	873[8]
Ibagué	...	...	...	...	548 209	266 329	281 880	1 439[8]
Ipiales	...	...	...	...	135 542	66 707	68 835	1 707[8]
Itagüí	...	...	...	...	264 775	128 929	135 846	17[8]
Jamundí	...	...	...	...	117 117	56 986	60 131	603[8]

8. Population of capital cities and cities of 100 000 or more inhabitants: latest available year, 1995 - 2014
Population des capitales et des villes de 100 000 habitants ou plus : dernière année disponible, 1995 - 2014 (continued - suite)

Continent, country or area, date, code[a] and city / Continent, pays ou zone, date, code[a] et ville	City proper - Ville proprement dite				Urban agglomeration - Agglomération urbaine			
	Population			Surface area - Superficie (km²)	Population			Surface area - Superficie (km²)
	Both sexes - Les deux sexes	Male - Masculin	Female - Féminin		Both sexes - Les deux sexes	Male - Masculin	Female - Féminin	
AMERICA, SOUTH - AMÉRIQUE DU SUD								
Colombia - Colombie[24]								
1 VII 2014 (ESDJ)								
Lorica	...	...	...	...	117 439	58 814	58 625	890[8]
Magangué	...	...	...	...	123 618	62 501	61 117	1 102[8]
Maicao	...	...	...	...	154 343	75 870	78 473	1 789[8]
Malambo	...	...	...	...	119 286	60 612	58 674	108[8]
Manizales	...	...	...	...	394 627	187 977	206 650	477[8]
Medellín	...	...	...	...	2 441 123	1 148 961	1 292 162	387[8]
Montería	...	...	...	...	434 950	211 074	223 876	3 043[8]
Neiva	...	...	...	...	340 046	162 697	177 349	1 468[8]
Palmira	...	...	...	...	302 727	146 364	156 363	1 044[8]
Pasto	...	...	...	...	434 486	209 538	224 948	1 131[8]
Pereira	...	...	...	...	467 185	221 893	245 292	702[8]
Piedecuesta	...	...	...	...	145 848	70 949	74 899	481[8]
Pitalito	...	...	...	...	123 430	61 292	62 138	653[8]
Popayán	...	...	...	...	275 129	133 231	141 898	464[8]
Quibdo	...	...	...	...	115 517	57 657	57 860	3 075[8]
Riohacha	...	...	...	...	250 236	123 064	127 172	3 171[8]
Rionegro	...	...	...	...	118 264	58 771	59 493	198[8]
San Andrés de Tumaco	...	...	...	...	195 419	97 784	97 635	3 778[8]
Santa Marta	...	...	...	...	476 385	232 287	244 098	2 369[8]
Sincelejo	...	...	...	...	271 375	133 144	138 231	292[8]
Soacha	...	...	...	...	500 097	246 772	253 325	187[8]
Sogamoso	...	...	...	...	113 758	54 015	59 743	214[8]
Soledad	...	...	...	...	599 012	296 374	302 638	67[8]
Tuluá	...	...	...	...	209 086	100 522	108 564	818[8]
Tunja	...	...	...	...	184 864	88 347	96 517	118[8]
Turbo	...	...	...	...	155 173	78 544	76 629	3 090[8]
Uribia	...	...	...	...	168 286	82 512	85 774	7 904[8]
Valledupar	...	...	...	...	443 210	215 969	227 241	4 225[8]
Villavicencio	...	...	...	...	473 766	229 792	243 974	1 328[8]
Yopal	...	...	...	...	136 484	68 368	68 116	2 532[8]
Yumbo	...	...	...	...	114 427	57 398	57 029	243[8]
Zipaquirá	...	...	...	...	120 312	59 138	61 174	194[8]
Ecuador - Équateur								
28 XI 2010 (CDFC)								
Ambato	178 538	86 299	92 239	31	...	...	...	...
Calderon (Carapungo)	152 242	74 682	77 560	...	...	...	...	...
Cuenca	331 888	158 365	173 523	56	...	...	...	...
Durán	235 769	116 401	119 368	40	...	...	...	...
Esmeraldas	161 868	77 505	84 363	8	...	...	...	...
Guayaquil	2 291 158	1 127 137	1 164 021	369	...	...	...	...
Ibarra	139 721	67 165	72 556	36	...	...	...	...
Loja	180 617	86 631	93 986	25	...	...	...	...
Machala	241 606	120 643	120 963	34	...	...	...	...
Manta	221 122	108 677	112 445	45	...	...	...	...
Milagro	145 025	72 031	72 994	19	...	...	...	...
Portoviejo	223 086	108 878	114 208	50	...	...	...	...
Quevedo	158 694	79 218	79 476	20	...	...	...	...
QUITO	1 619 146	783 616	835 530	181	...	...	...	...
Riobamba	156 723	74 634	82 089	29	...	...	...	...
Santa Elena	305 632	150 428	155 204	36	...	...	...	...
Falkland Islands (Malvinas) - Îles Falkland (Malvinas)								
8 X 2006 (CDFC)								
STANLEY	2 115	...	...	...	...	...	...	...
French Guiana - Guyane française								
1 I 2006 (CDJC)								
CAYENNE	58 004	27 412	30 591	24	75 740	36 484	39 256	70
Guyana								
15 IX 2002 (CDFC)								
GEORGETOWN	134 497	63 973	70 524	...	...	...	...	...

Continent, country or area, date, code[a] and city / Continent, pays ou zone, date, code[a] et ville	City proper - Ville proprement dite				Urban agglomeration - Agglomération urbaine			
	Population			Surface area - Superficie (km²)	Population			Surface area - Superficie (km²)
	Both sexes - Les deux sexes	Male - Masculin	Female - Féminin		Both sexes - Les deux sexes	Male - Masculin	Female - Féminin	
AMERICA, SOUTH - AMÉRIQUE DU SUD								
Paraguay								
1 VII 2014 (ESDF)								
ASUNCIÓN[25]	512 919	236 790	276 129	117	2 887 087	1 402 891	1 484 196	2 582
Capiatá	257 116	127 676	129 440	88	...	...	...	...
Ciudad del Este	317 525	159 726	157 799	149	...	...	...	...
Fernando de la Mora	200 112	95 174	104 937	21	...	...	...	...
Lambaré	210 725	101 019	109 706	27	...	...	...	...
Luque	358 265	175 663	182 602	153	...	...	...	...
San Lorenzo	354 283	171 242	183 042	54	...	...	...	...
Peru - Pérou[26]								
30 VI 2014 (ESDF)								
Arequipa	861 145	415 111	446 034	...	...	...	...	...
Ayacucho	177 420	87 778	89 642	...	...	...	...	...
Cajamarca	218 775	107 412	111 363	...	...	...	...	...
Chiclayo	594 759	283 529	311 230	...	...	...	...	...
Chimbote	367 850	184 988	182 862	...	...	...	...	...
Chincha Alta	174 575	87 130	87 445	...	...	...	...	...
Cuzco	420 137	204 920	215 217	...	...	...	...	...
Huancayo	361 014	172 259	188 755	...	...	...	...	...
Huánuco	172 924	82 780	90 144	...	...	...	...	...
Huaraz	123 915	60 934	62 981	...	...	...	...	...
Ica	241 903	118 942	122 961	...	...	...	...	...
Iquitos	432 476	217 785	214 691	...	...	...	...	...
Juliaca	267 174	130 498	136 676	...	...	...	...	...
LIMA[27]	9 735 587	4 737 206	4 998 381	...	...	...	...	...
Pisco	104 349	53 166	51 183	...	...	...	...	...
Piura	430 319	208 681	221 638	...	...	...	...	...
Pucallpa	211 631	108 923	102 708	...	...	...	...	...
Puno	138 723	67 549	71 174	...	...	...	...	...
Sullana	199 606	97 531	102 075	...	...	...	...	...
Tacna	288 698	147 029	141 669	...	...	...	...	...
Tarapoto	141 053	73 205	67 848	...	...	...	...	...
Trujillo	788 236	382 376	405 860	...	...	...	...	...
Tumbes	110 279	59 783	50 496	...	...	...	...	...
Suriname								
13 VIII 2012 (CDJC)								
PARAMARIBO	240 924	119 439	121 485	182	...	...	...	...
Wanica	118 222	57 776	60 446	443	...	...	...	...
Uruguay								
4 X 2011 (CDJC)								
MONTEVIDEO	1 305 082	604 965[28]	700 013[28]	530	...	...	...	...
Salto	104 028	50 147	53 881	...	...	...	...	...
Venezuela (Bolivarian Republic of) - Venezuela (République bolivarienne du)								
1 VII 2011 (ESDF)								
Acarigua-Araure	290 146[18]	142 812[18]	147 334[18]	1 065	...	...	...	...
Anaco(F) (Capital)[18]	149 380	81 172	68 208	...	...	...	...	...
Barcelona	326 460[18]	163 915[18]	162 545[18]	463	...	...	...	...
Barcelona-Puerto La Cruz	435 940[18]	221 667[18]	214 273[18]	707	...	...	...	...
Barinas	307 364[18]	150 145[18]	157 219[18]	848	...	...	...	...
Barquisimeto	1 000 632[18]	489 530[18]	511 102[18]	2 645	...	...	...	...
Baruta[18]	266 261	124 876	141 385	...	...	...	...	...
Cabimas	240 765[18]	119 731[18]	121 034[18]	175	...	...	...	...
Cagua[18]	130 763	64 202	66 561	...	...	...	...	...
CARACAS	2 104 423[18]	1 019 207[18]	1 085 216[18]	433	...	...	...	...
Carora[18]	112 626	55 773	56 853	...	...	...	...	...
Carúpano	135 969[18]	66 660[18]	69 309[18]	203	...	...	...	...
Ciudad Bolívar	371 566[18]	182 183[18]	189 383[18]	5 851	...	...	...	...
Ciudad Guayana	850 262[18]	426 168[18]	424 094[18]	1 612	...	...	...	...
Ciudad Ojeda[18]	146 509	73 463	73 046	...	...	...	...	...
Coro	199 603[18]	97 900[18]	101 703[18]	438	...	...	...	...
Cua[18]	138 784	67 821	70 963	...	...	...	...	...
Cumaná	341 441[18]	168 253[18]	173 188[18]	405	...	...	...	...
El Silencio[18]	125 014	73 463	51 551	...	...	...	...	...

8. Population of capital cities and cities of 100 000 or more inhabitants: latest available year, 1995 - 2014
Population des capitales et des villes de 100 000 habitants ou plus : dernière année disponible, 1995 - 2014 (continued - suite)

Continent, country or area, date, code[a] and city / Continent, pays ou zone, date, code[a] et ville	City proper - Ville proprement dite				Urban agglomeration - Agglomération urbaine			
	Population			Surface area - Superficie (km²)	Population			Surface area - Superficie (km²)
	Both sexes - Les deux sexes	Male - Masculin	Female - Féminin		Both sexes - Les deux sexes	Male - Masculin	Female - Féminin	
AMERICA, SOUTH - AMÉRIQUE DU SUD								
Venezuela (Bolivarian Republic of) - Venezuela (République bolivarienne du)								
1 VII 2011 (ESDF)								
El Tigre[18]	224 887	122 795	102 092	...	...	...	...	...
Guacara[18]	147 733	74 070	73 663	...	...	...	...	...
Guanare[18]	151 170	73 851	77 319	...	...	...	...	...
Guarenas[18]	285 561[18]	139 992[18]	145 569[18]	180	...	...	...	...
Guatire[18]	184 375	88 570	95 805	...	...	...	...	...
Los Guayos[18]	166 116	83 614	82 502	...	...	...	...	...
Los Teques	272 301[18]	132 277[18]	140 024[18]	98	...	...	...	...
Maracaibo	1 339 019[18]	660 297[18]	678 722[18]	604	...	...	...	...
Maracay	446 271[18]	218 426[18]	227 845[18]	169	...	...	...	...
Maturín[18]	445 444	241 844	203 600	...	...	...	...	...
Mérida	231 861[18]	107 125[18]	124 736[18]	482	...	...	...	...
Naguanagua[18]	162 281	77 380	84 901	...	...	...	...	...
Ocumare Del Tuy[18]	134 451	66 675	67 776	...	...	...	...	...
Petare[18]	116 159	57 865	58 294	...	...	...	...	...
Pozuelos (F) (Capital)[18]	165 563	91 154	74 409	...	...	...	...	...
Puerto Cabello	203 859[18]	103 228[18]	100 631[18]	309	...	...	...	...
Puerto La Cruz[18]	109 480	57 752	51 728	...	...	...	...	...
Punto Fijo	150 496[18]	74 119[18]	76 377[18]	31	...	...	...	...
San Cristóbal	271 424[18]	130 059[18]	141 365[18]	248	...	...	...	...
San Fernando de Apure[18]	133 487	60 585	72 902	...	...	...	...	...
San Francisco[18]	128 509	63 495	65 014	...	...	...	...	...
Santa Lucía[18]	112 227	57 961	54 266	...	...	...	...	...
Táriba[18]	102 009	51 718	50 291	...	...	...	...	...
Tocuyito[18]	186 743	94 425	92 318	...	...	...	...	...
Valencia	917 999[18]	451 421[18]	466 578[18]	1 212	...	...	...	...
Valera	125 590[18]	60 672[18]	64 918[18]	55	...	...	...	...
ASIA - ASIE								
Afghanistan								
1 VII 2012 (ESDF)								
Baghalan Center (Puli Khumry)	*203 600*	*104 500*	*99 100*	...	...	...	...	...
Balkh Center (Mazar- Sharif)	*368 100*	*188 800*	*179 300*	...	...	...	...	...
Herat Center	*436 300*	*221 600*	*214 700*	...	...	...	...	...
KABUL CENTER	*3 289 000*	*1 702 300*	*1 586 700*	...	...	...	...	...
Kandhar Center (Kndhar)	*491 500*	*252 900*	*238 600*	...	...	...	...	...
Kunduz Center	*304 600*	*155 500*	*149 100*	...	...	...	...	...
Nngarhar Center (Jlal Abad)	*206 500*	*106 300*	*100 200*	...	...	...	...	...
Armenia - Arménie								
12 X 2011 (CDJC)								
Gyumri (Leninakan)	121 976	57 132	64 844	44	...	...	...	...
YEREVAN	1 060 138	490 362	569 776	223	...	...	...	...
Azerbaijan - Azerbaïdjan								
1 VII 2013 (ESDF)								
BAKU	2 166 355	1 074 374	1 091 981	2 150	...	...	...	...
Ganja	323 860	157 319	166 541	110	...	...	...	...
Sumgayit	327 291	160 791	166 500	80	...	...	...	...
Bahrain - Bahreïn								
1 VII 2006 (ESDF)								
MANAMA	*176 909*	*113 503*	*63 406*	30	...	...	...	...
Bangladesh								
22 I 2001 (CDFC)								
Barisal	...	...	...	...	192 810	103 785	89 025	20
Bogra	...	...	...	...	154 807	82 368	72 439	11
Brahmanbaria	...	...	...	...	129 278	66 890	62 388	18
Chittagong	...	...	...	...	2 023 489	1 127 516	895 973	168
Comilla	...	...	...	...	166 519	88 927	77 592	11
DHAKA	...	...	...	...	5 333 571	3 025 395	2 308 176	154
Dinajpur	...	...	...	...	157 914	82 068	75 846	19
Gazipur	...	...	...	...	122 801	65 522	57 279	49

8. Population of capital cities and cities of 100 000 or more inhabitants: latest available year, 1995 - 2014
Population des capitales et des villes de 100 000 habitants ou plus : dernière année disponible, 1995 - 2014 (continued - suite)

Continent, country or area, date, code[a] and city Continent, pays ou zone, date, code[a] et ville	City proper - Ville proprement dite				Urban agglomeration - Agglomération urbaine			
	Population			Surface area - Superficie (km²)	Population			Surface area - Superficie (km²)
	Both sexes - Les deux sexes	Male - Masculin	Female - Féminin		Both sexes - Les deux sexes	Male - Masculin	Female - Féminin	
ASIA - ASIE								
Bangladesh								
22 I 2001 (CDFC)								
Jamalpur	...	...	...	...	120 955	62 059	58 896	53
Jessore	...	...	...	...	176 655	94 203	82 452	15
Kadamrasul	...	...	...	...	128 561	66 799	61 762	6
Khulna	...	...	...	...	770 498	412 661	357 837	60
Mymensingh	...	...	...	...	227 204	119 172	108 032	22
Naogaon	...	...	...	...	124 046	65 406	58 640	37
Narayanganj	...	...	...	...	241 393	131 168	110 225	13
Narsingdi	...	...	...	...	124 204	67 575	56 629	9
Nawabganj	...	...	...	...	152 223	75 375	76 848	34
Pabna	...	...	...	...	116 305	60 666	55 639	27
Rajshahi	...	...	...	...	388 811	208 525	180 286	97
Rangpur	...	...	...	...	241 310	124 296	117 014	51
Saidpur	...	...	...	...	112 609	58 289	54 320	34
Sirajganj	...	...	...	...	128 144	66 673	61 471	28
Tangail	...	...	...	...	128 785	66 856	61 929	29
Tongi	...	...	...	...	283 099	156 335	126 764	30
Bhutan - Bhoutan								
30 V 2005 (CDFC)								
THIMPHU	...	...	...	...	79 185	42 465	36 720	...
Brunei Darussalam - Brunéi Darussalam								
21 VIII 2001 (CDFC)								
BANDAR SERI BEGAWAN	27 285	13 639	13 646	100	...	...	...	...
Cambodia - Cambodge								
1 VII 2011 (ESDF)								
Bat Dambang	*1 126 345*[29]	*558 945*[29]	*567 400*[29]	114	...	...	...	...
PHNOM PENH	*1 570 791*[29]	*738 159*[29]	*832 631*[29]	21	...	...	...	...
Seam Reab	*999 703*[29]	*493 184*[29]	*506 519*[29]	292	...	...	...	...
China - Chine								
1 VII 2010 (ESDF)								
BEIJING (PEKING)	*19 610 000*[30]	*10 130 000*[30]	*9 490 000*[30]	16 410	...	...	...	...
China, Hong Kong SAR - Chine, Hong Kong RAS								
1 VII 2014 (ESDJ)								
HONG KONG SAR	7 241 700	3 345 100	3 896 600	1 106	...	...	...	...
China, Macao SAR - Chine, Macao RAS								
1 VII 2014 (ESDJ)								
MACAO	621 700	305 500	316 200	30	...	...	...	...
Cyprus - Chypre								
1 I 2006 (ESDJ)								
LEFKOSIA[31]	...	...	...	...	*224 500*	...	...	...
Lemesos[32]	...	...	...	...	*176 900*	...	...	...
Democratic People's Republic of Korea - République populaire démocratique de Corée								
1 X 2008 (CDJC)								
Anju	167 646	79 187	88 459	...	...	...	...	...
Chongjin	614 892	292 741	322 151	...	...	...	...	...
Haeju	241 599	116 594	125 005	...	...	...	...	...
Hamhung	614 198	292 058	322 140	...	...	...	...	...
Huichon	136 093	64 547	71 546	...	...	...	...	...
Hyesan	174 015	82 604	91 411	...	...	...	...	...
Jongju	102 659	48 423	54 236	...	...	...	...	...
Kaechon	262 389	124 222	138 167	...	...	...	...	...
Kaesong	192 578	90 653	101 925	...	...	...	...	...
Kanggye	251 971	120 305	131 666	...	...	...	...	...
Kim Chaek	155 284	73 133	82 151	...	...	...	...	...
Kusong	155 181	73 677	81 504	...	...	...	...	...
Nampho	310 864	150 091	160 773	...	...	...	...	...
Phyongsong	236 583	115 817	120 766	...	...	...	...	...
PYONGYANG	2 581 076	1 233 765	1 347 311	...	...	...	...	...
Rason	158 337	74 777	83 560	...	...	...	...	...
Sariwon	271 434	130 181	141 253	...	...	...	...	...
Sinpho	130 951	63 207	67 744	...	...	...	...	...
Sinuiju	334 031	158 139	175 892	...	...	...	...	...
Sunchon	250 738	119 727	131 011	...	...	...	...	...

Continent, country or area, date, code[a] and city — Continent, pays ou zone, date, code[a] et ville	City proper - Ville proprement dite				Urban agglomeration - Agglomération urbaine			
	Population			Surface area - Superficie (km²)	Population			Surface area - Superficie (km²)
	Both sexes - Les deux sexes	Male - Masculin	Female - Féminin		Both sexes - Les deux sexes	Male - Masculin	Female - Féminin	
ASIA - ASIE								
Democratic People's Republic of Korea - République populaire démocratique de Corée								
1 X 2008 (CDJC)								
Tanchon	240 873	113 221	127 652	...	...	...	...	...
Tokchon	210 571	99 655	110 916	...	...	...	...	...
Wonsan	328 467	155 903	172 564	...	...	...	...	...
Georgia - Géorgie								
1 VII 2011 (ESDF)								
Batumi	125 800	...	...	...	...	...	...	...
Kutaisi	196 800	...	...	...	...	...	...	...
Rustavi	122 500	...	...	...	...	...	...	...
TBILISI	1 172 700	...	...	...	...	...	...	...
India - Inde[33]								
1 III 2001 (CDFC)								
Abohar	124 339	66 445	57 894	23	...	...	...	...
Achalpur	107 316	55 687	51 629	17	...	...	...	...
Adilabad	109 529	55 641	53 888	16	129 403	65 501	63 902	21
Adityapur	119 233	63 837	55 396	50	...	...	...	...
Adoni	157 305	79 639	77 666	30	162 458	82 345	80 113	...
Agartala	189 998	94 742	95 256	16	...	...	...	...
Agra	1 275 134	690 599	584 535	121	1 331 339	720 707	610 632	141
Ahmedabad	3 520 085	1 867 249	1 652 836	191	4 525 013	2 401 422	2 123 591	438
Ahmednagar	307 615	159 564	148 051	18	347 549	184 765	162 784	30
Aizawl	228 280	115 986	112 294	110	...	...	...	...
Ajmer	485 575	254 164	231 411	218	490 520	256 695	233 825	223
Akola	400 520	206 649	193 871	23	...	...	...	...
Alandur	146 287	74 836	71 451	20	...	...	...	...
Alappuzha	177 029	85 725	91 304	70	282 675	137 244	145 431	84
Aligarh	669 087	356 725	312 362	40	...	...	...	...
Alipurduar	...	...	...	...	114 035	58 503	55 532	26
Allahabad	975 393	539 772	435 621	63	1 042 229	576 122	466 107	86
Alwar	260 593	139 585	121 008	...	266 203	143 699	122 504	58
Ambala	139 279	74 016	65 263	17	168 316	92 977	75 339	38
Ambala Sadar	106 568	55 750	50 818	...	...	...	...	...
Ambarnath	203 804	107 325	96 479	36	...	...	...	...
Ambattur	310 967	160 282	150 685	40	...	...	...	...
Amravati	549 510	284 247	265 263	122	...	...	...	...
Amritsar	966 862	518 388	448 474	136	1 003 917	538 744	465 173	...
Amroha	165 129	86 943	78 186	6	...	...	...	...
Anand	130 685	68 074	62 611	21	218 486	115 295	103 191	60
Anantapur	218 808	110 979	107 829	...	243 143	123 713	119 430	...
Anklesvar	...	...	...	...	112 643	60 249	52 394	...
Arcot	...	...	...	...	126 671	62 787	63 884	19
Arrah	203 380	109 867	93 513	31	...	...	...	...
Asansol	475 439	250 886	224 553	128	1 067 369	564 837	502 532	352
Ashoknagar Kalyangarh	111 607	56 490	55 117	...	...	...	...	...
Aurangabad	873 311	459 295	414 016	139	892 483	469 237	423 246	148
Avadi	229 403	117 991	111 412	65	...	...	...	...
Bahadurgarh	119 846	65 859	53 987	21	131 925	72 873	59 052	30
Baharampur	160 143	81 737	78 406	17	170 322	86 969	83 353	19
Bahraich	168 323	89 581	78 742	13	...	...	...	...
Baidyabati	108 229	56 394	51 835	8	...	...	...	...
Baleshwar	106 082	55 691	50 391	...	156 430	82 106	74 324	42
Ballia	101 465	54 496	46 969	16	...	...	...	...
Bally	260 906	149 603	111 303	12	...	...	...	...
Balurghat	135 737	68 871	66 866	10	143 321	72 764	70 557	12
Banda	134 839	72 632	62 207	16	139 436	75 174	64 262	28
Bangalore	4 301 326	2 242 835	2 058 491	...	5 701 446	2 988 561	2 712 885	540
Bangaon	102 163	52 537	49 626	25	...	...	...	...
Bankura	128 781	66 429	62 352	19	...	...	...	...
Bansberia	104 412	55 389	49 023	9	...	...	...	...
Baranagar	250 768	132 559	118 209	7	...	...	...	...
Barasat	231 521	118 374	113 147	31	...	...	...	...
Barddhaman	285 602	148 562	137 040	23	...	...	...	...
Bareilly	718 395	378 848	339 547	106	748 353	397 304	351 049	125

8. Population of capital cities and cities of 100 000 or more inhabitants: latest available year, 1995 - 2014
Population des capitales et des villes de 100 000 habitants ou plus : dernière année disponible, 1995 - 2014 (continued - suite)

Continent, country or area, date, code[a] and city / Continent, pays ou zone, date, code[a] et ville	City proper - Ville proprement dite				Urban agglomeration - Agglomération urbaine			
	Population			Surface area - Superficie (km²)	Population			Surface area - Superficie (km²)
	Both sexes - Les deux sexes	Male - Masculin	Female - Féminin		Both sexes - Les deux sexes	Male - Masculin	Female - Féminin	
ASIA - ASIE								
India - Inde[33]								
1 III 2001 (CDFC)								
Baripada	...	...	...	...	100 651	53 606	47 045	38
Barrackpur	144 391	76 299	68 092	11	...	...	...	...
Barshi	104 785	53 848	50 937	36	...	...	...	...
Basirhat	113 159	57 965	55 194	22	...	...	...	...
Basti	107 601	57 053	50 548	19	...	...	...	...
Batala	125 677	66 508	59 169	9	147 872	78 393	69 479	...
Bathinda	217 256	116 946	100 310	110	...	...	...	...
Beawar	123 759	64 417	59 342	18	125 981	65 586	60 395	24
Begusarai	...	...	...	...	107 623	57 541	50 082	12
Belgaum	399 653	204 598	195 055	100	506 480	261 639	244 841	173
Bellary	316 766	162 699	154 067	66	...	...	...	...
Bettiah	116 670	61 753	54 917	8	...	...	...	...
Bhadravati	160 662	81 351	79 311	...	...	...	...	...
Bhadreswar	106 071	58 040	48 031	6	...	...	...	...
Bhagalpur	340 767	182 806	157 961	30	350 133	187 723	162 410	31
Bhalswa Jahangir Pur	152 339	83 802	68 537	7	...	...	...	...
Bharatpur	204 587	110 057	94 530	41	205 235	110 397	94 838	51
Bharuch	148 140	76 506	71 634	18	176 364	91 281	85 083	20
Bhatpara	442 385	243 157	199 228	30	...	...	...	...
Bhavani	...	...	...	...	104 646	52 998	51 648	10
Bhavnagar	511 085	266 838	244 247	90	517 708	270 278	247 430	91
Bheemavaram	137 409	69 473	67 936	26	142 064	71 929	70 135	26
Bhilai Nagar	556 366	291 070	265 296	141	...	...	...	...
Bhilwara	280 128	148 794	131 334	118	...	...	...	...
Bhind	153 752	82 945	70 807	17	...	...	...	...
Bhiwandi	598 741	367 565	231 176	26	621 427	382 184	239 243	28
Bhiwani	169 531	91 697	77 834	28	...	...	...	...
Bhopal	1 437 354	757 408	679 946	285	1 458 416	768 391	690 025	298
Bhubaneswar	648 032	360 739	287 293	135	658 220	366 134	292 086	148
Bhuj	...	...	...	...	136 429	71 056	65 373	...
Bhusawal	172 372	89 208	83 164	13	187 564	97 243	90 321	25
Bid	138 196	71 827	66 369	8	...	...	...	...
Bidar	172 877	89 934	82 943	...	174 257	90 662	83 595	47
Bidhan Nagar	164 221	83 220	81 001	34	...	...	...	...
Bihar	232 071	122 019	110 052	24	...	...	...	...
Bijapur	228 175	117 375	110 800	...	253 891	130 416	123 475	75
Bikaner	529 690	283 067	246 623	166	...	...	...	...
Bilaspur	275 694	143 518	132 176	36	335 293	174 351	160 942	46
Birnagar	...	...	...	...	115 127	59 232	55 895	40
Bokaro Steel City	393 805	213 231	180 574	163	497 780	268 969	228 811	188
Bommanahalli	201 652	108 108	93 544	36	...	...	...	...
Botad	100 194	52 752	47 442	10	...	...	...	...
Brahmapur	307 792	160 354	147 438	80	...	...	...	...
Budaun	148 029	78 141	69 888	4	...	...	...	...
Bulandshahr	176 425	93 531	82 894	12	...	...	...	...
Burhanpur	193 725	99 751	93 974	13	...	...	...	...
Byatarayanapura	181 744	95 508	86 236	45	...	...	...	...
Chakdaha	...	...	...	...	101 320	51 485	49 835	...
Champdani	103 246	57 842	45 404	6	...	...	...	...
Chandan Nagar	162 187	84 181	78 006	22	...	...	...	...
Chandausi	103 749	55 127	48 622	9	...	...	...	...
Chandigarh	808 515	450 122	358 393	79	...	...	...	...
Chandrapur	289 450	151 202	138 248	56	...	...	...	...
Chapra	179 190	95 494	83 696	17	...	...	...	...
Chennai (Madras)	4 343 645	2 219 539	2 124 106	174	6 560 242	3 355 524	3 204 718	702
Cherthala	...	...	...	...	141 558	68 756	72 802	92
Chhatarpur	...	...	...	...	109 078	58 421	50 657	17
Chhindwara	122 247	63 584	58 663	11	153 552	79 889	73 663	22
Chikmagalur	101 251	51 694	49 557	33	...	...	...	...
Chirala	...	...	...	...	166 294	82 954	83 340	48
Chirkunda	...	...	...	...	106 227	56 536	49 691	26
Chitradurga	122 702	62 845	59 857	24	125 170	64 112	61 058	26
Chittoor	152 654	76 879	75 775	33	...	...	...	...

8. Population of capital cities and cities of 100 000 or more inhabitants: latest available year, 1995 - 2014
Population des capitales et des villes de 100 000 habitants ou plus : dernière année disponible, 1995 - 2014 (continued - suite)

Continent, country or area, date, code[a] and city / Continent, pays ou zone, date, code[a] et ville	City proper - Ville proprement dite				Urban agglomeration - Agglomération urbaine			
	Population			Surface area - Superficie (km²)	Population			Surface area - Superficie (km²)
	Both sexes - Les deux sexes	Male - Masculin	Female - Féminin		Both sexes - Les deux sexes	Male - Masculin	Female - Féminin	

ASIA - ASIE

India - Inde[33]
1 III 2001 (CDFC)

Churu	...	...	...	...	101 874	53 079	48 795	30
Coimbatore	930 882	477 937	452 945	106	1 461 139	748 376	712 763	379
Coonoor	...	...	...	...	101 490	51 208	50 282	44
Cuddalore	158 634	80 012	78 622	28	...	...	...	...
Cuddapah	126 505	63 669	62 836	42	262 506	133 224	129 282	78
Cuttack	534 654	285 838	248 816	149	587 182	314 101	273 081	195
Dallo Pura	132 621	71 362	61 259	2	...	...	...	...
Damoh	112 185	58 962	53 223	16	127 967	67 321	60 646	36
Darbhanga	267 348	142 377	124 971	19	...	...	...	...
Darjiling	107 197	55 963	51 234	11	108 830	56 769	52 061	13
Dasarahalli	264 940	143 909	121 031	23	...	...	...	...
Davangere	364 523	187 987	176 536	...	...	...	...	...
Dehradun	426 674	224 546	202 128	52	530 263	283 064	247 199	103
Dehri	119 057	63 540	55 517	21	...	...	...	...
Delhi	9 879 172	5 412 497	4 466 675	554	12 877 470[34]	7 069 371[34]	5 808 099[34]	889[34]
Delhi Cantonment	124 917	75 827	49 090	43	...	...	...	...
Deoghar	...	...	...	...	112 525	61 442	51 083	22
Deoli	119 468	66 594	52 874	10	...	...	...	...
Deoria	104 227	54 681	49 546	16	...	...	...	...
Dewas	231 672	121 075	110 597	100	...	...	...	...
Dhanbad	199 258	108 512	90 746	23	1 065 327	579 150	486 177	223
Dharmavaram	103 357	52 785	50 572	40	...	...	...	...
Dhule	341 755	177 772	163 983	46	...	...	...	...
Dibrugarh	121 893	65 118	56 775	25	137 661	73 307	64 354	26
Dinapur Nizamat	131 176	69 419	61 757	12	...	...	...	...
Dindigul	196 955	99 124	97 831	14	...	...	...	...
Dohad	...	...	...	...	112 026	57 642	54 384	26
Dumdum	101 296	52 890	48 406	9	...	...	...	...
Durg	232 517	119 315	113 202	66	...	...	...	...
Durgapur	493 405	263 721	229 684	154	...	...	...	...
Durg-Bhilai Nagar	...	...	...	...	927 864	482 304	445 560	341
Eluru	190 062	92 790	97 272	15	215 804	105 476	110 328	...
English Bazar	161 456	82 845	78 611	...	224 415	115 356	109 059	19
Erode	150 541	76 462	74 079	8	389 906	198 842	191 064	132
Etah	107 110	56 763	50 347	13	...	...	...	...
Etawah	210 453	111 749	98 704	9	...	...	...	...
Faizabad	144 705	75 935	68 770	33	208 162	114 330	93 832	63
Faridabad	1 055 938	581 069	474 869	199	...	...	...	...
Farrukhabad-cum-Fategarh	228 333	120 829	107 504	17	242 997	129 643	113 354	21
Fatehpur	152 078	80 011	72 067	57	...	...	...	...
Firozabad	279 102	148 263	130 839	9	432 866	230 802	202 064	12
Gadag-Betgeri	154 982	78 713	76 269	35	...	...	...	...
Gajuwaka	259 180	133 469	125 711	128	...	...	...	...
Gandhidham	151 693	79 379	72 314	30	...	...	...	...
Gandhinagar	195 985	103 876	92 109	57	...	...	...	...
Ganganagar	210 713	115 321	95 392	21	222 858	121 865	100 993	...
Gangapur City	...	...	...	...	105 396	56 009	49 387	12
Gangawati	...	...	...	...	101 392	51 211	50 181	16
Gaya	385 432	204 483	180 949	29	394 945	210 410	184 535	32
Ghatlodiya	106 684	56 219	50 465	4	...	...	...	...
Ghaziabad	968 256	521 026	447 230	145	...	...	...	...
Ghazipur	...	...	...	...	103 298	54 371	48 927	20
Giridih	...	...	...	...	105 634	55 490	50 144	11
Godhra	121 879	63 176	58 703	20	131 172	67 969	63 203	23
Gonda	120 301	66 207	54 094	15	...	...	...	...
Gondiya	120 902	61 418	59 484	18	...	...	...	...
Gorakhpur	622 701	329 807	292 894	141	...	...	...	...
Gudivada	113 054	55 867	57 187	13	...	...	...	...
Gudiyatham	...	...	...	...	100 115	49 794	50 321	14
Gulbarga	422 569	219 409	203 160	...	430 265	223 594	206 671	43
Guna	137 175	72 538	64 637	46	...	...	...	...
Guntakul	117 103	59 211	57 892	41	...	...	...	...
Guntur	514 461	257 775	256 686	46	...	...	...	...

Continent, country or area, date, code[a] and city / Continent, pays ou zone, date, code[a] et ville	City proper - Ville proprement dite				Urban agglomeration - Agglomération urbaine			
	Population			Surface area - Superficie (km²)	Population			Surface area - Superficie (km²)
	Both sexes - Les deux sexes	Male - Masculin	Female - Féminin		Both sexes - Les deux sexes	Male - Masculin	Female - Féminin	
ASIA - ASIE								
India - Inde[33]								
1 III 2001 (CDFC)								
Gurgaon	172 955	92 934	80 021	15	228 820	123 377	105 443	24
Guruvayur	...	...	...	...	138 681	64 554	74 127	57
Guwahati	809 895	440 288	369 607	217	818 809	446 311	372 498	217
Gwalior	827 026	442 343	384 683	167	865 548	465 057	400 491	180
Habra	127 602	65 141	62 461	18	239 209	121 631	117 578	37
Hajipur	119 412	63 838	55 574	20	...	...	...	...
Haldia	170 673	89 893	80 780	69	...	...	...	...
Haldwani-cum-Kathgodam	129 015	68 755	60 260	11	158 896	84 541	74 355	...
Halisahar	124 510	67 151	57 359	8	...	...	...	...
Hanumangarh	129 556	69 532	60 024	13	...	...	...	...
Haora (Howrah)	1 007 532	547 068	460 464	52	...	...	...	...
Hapur	211 983	113 175	98 808	14	...	...	...	...
Hardoi	112 486	59 876	52 610	6	...	...	...	...
Hardwar	175 340	94 736	80 604	15	220 767	119 234	101 533	42
Hassan	116 574	59 743	56 831	27	133 262	68 242	65 020	30
Hathras	123 244	65 778	57 466	8	126 355	67 436	58 919	8
Hazaribag	127 269	67 900	59 369	26	135 473	72 288	63 185	27
Hindupur	125 074	64 132	60 942	38	...	...	...	...
Hisar	256 689	140 083	116 606	45	263 186	143 795	119 391	49
Hoshiarpur	149 668	79 454	70 214	35	...	...	...	...
Hospet	164 240	83 767	80 473	28	...	...	...	...
Hubli-Dharwad	786 195	403 085	383 110	213	...	...	...	...
Hugli-Chinsurah	170 206	86 788	83 418	17	...	...	...	...
Hyderabad	3 637 483	1 883 064	1 754 419	173	5 742 036	2 973 472	2 768 564	822
Ichalakaranji	257 610	136 063	121 547	30	285 860	150 977	134 883	38
Imphal	221 492	109 815	111 677	33	250 234	123 859	126 375	37
Indore	1 474 968	774 540	700 428	130	1 516 918	796 673	720 245	165
Itarsi	...	...	...	...	107 831	56 347	51 484	24
Jabalpur	932 484	488 479	444 005	119	1 098 000	580 038	517 962	205
Jagadhri	101 290	55 844	45 446	...	...	...	...	...
Jagdalpur	...	...	...	...	103 123	52 909	50 214	26
Jaipur	2 322 575	1 237 765	1 084 810	485	...	...	...	...
Jalandhar	706 043	379 439	326 604	102	714 077	383 624	330 453	...
Jalgaon	368 618	193 496	175 122	62	...	...	...	...
Jalna	235 795	121 922	113 873	82	...	...	...	...
Jalpaiguri	100 348	50 629	49 719	13	...	...	...	...
Jammu	369 959	198 956	171 003	40	612 163	334 452	277 711	202
Jamnagar	443 518	232 845	210 673	26	556 956	292 168	264 788	...
Jamshedpur	573 096	301 433	271 663	60	1 104 713	581 829	522 884	160
Jamuria	129 484	68 695	60 789	73	...	...	...	...
Jaunpur	160 055	84 203	75 852	25	...	...	...	...
Jetpur Navagadh	104 312	54 768	49 544	36	...	...	...	...
Jhansi	383 644	202 745	180 899	58	460 278	244 169	216 109	84
Jhunjhunun	100 485	52 781	47 704	37	...	...	...	...
Jind	135 855	73 407	62 448	15	...	...	...	...
Jodhpur	851 051	454 075	396 976	79	860 818	459 198	401 620	90
Jorhat	...	...	...	...	137 814	73 213	64 601	69
Junagadh	168 515	86 980	81 535	13	252 108	130 461	121 647	...
Kaithal	117 285	63 098	54 187	44	...	...	...	...
Kakinada	296 329	146 476	149 853	39	376 861	187 064	189 797	58
Kalol	100 008	53 110	46 898	17	112 013	59 539	52 474	30
Kalyan	1 193 512	633 508	560 004	105	...	...	...	...
Kamarhati	314 507	168 555	145 952	11	...	...	...	...
Kamptee	...	...	...	...	136 491	71 270	65 221	37
Kancheepuram	153 140	77 069	76 071	12	188 733	95 068	93 665	40
Kanchrapara	126 191	65 264	60 927	9	...	...	...	...
Kanhangad	65 503	31 627	33 876	40	129 367	62 002	67 365	84
Kannur	...	...	...	...	498 207	237 108	261 099	154
Kanpur	2 551 337	1 374 121	1 177 216	267	2 715 555	1 465 142	1 250 413	301
Kapra	159 002	82 579	76 423	65	...	...	...	...
Karaikkudi	...	...	...	...	125 717	62 479	63 238	43
Karawal Nagar	148 624	80 495	68 129	5	...	...	...	...
Karimnagar	205 653	105 336	100 317	24	218 302	111 875	106 427	...

Continent, country or area, date, code[a] and city / Continent, pays ou zone, date, code[a] et ville	City proper - Ville proprement dite				Urban agglomeration - Agglomération urbaine			
	Population			Surface area - Superficie (km²)	Population			Surface area - Superficie (km²)
	Both sexes - Les deux sexes	Male - Masculin	Female - Féminin		Both sexes - Les deux sexes	Male - Masculin	Female - Féminin	
ASIA - ASIE								
India - Inde[33]								
1 III 2001 (CDFC)								
Karnal	207 640	110 595	97 045	22	221 236	117 875	103 361	24
Karur	...	...	...	...	153 365	77 207	76 158	33
Katihar	175 199	93 617	81 582	25	190 873	102 161	88 712	...
Khammam	159 544	80 574	78 970	...	198 620	100 930	97 690	26
Khandwa	172 242	88 950	83 292	36	...	...	...	...
Khanna	103 099	55 276	47 823	25	...	...	...	...
Kharagpur	188 761	97 721	91 040	91	272 865	140 730	132 135	125
Khardaha	116 470	61 214	55 256	7	...	...	...	...
Khargone	...	...	...	...	103 448	53 921	49 527	33
Kirari Suleman Nagar	154 633	85 362	69 271	5	...	...	...	...
Kishangarh	116 222	61 075	55 147	25	...	...	...	...
Koch Bihar	...	...	...	...	103 008	52 275	50 733	17
Kochi	595 575	294 756	300 819	95	1 355 972	670 340	685 632	453
Kolar	113 907	58 060	55 847	18	...	...	...	...
Kolhapur	493 167	255 778	237 389	67	505 541	262 258	243 283	67
Kolkata (Calcutta)	4 572 876	2 500 040	2 072 836	185	13 205 697[35]	7 064 138[35]	6 141 559[35]	1 034[35]
Kollam	361 560	177 677	183 883	41	380 091	186 924	193 167	68
Korba	315 690	164 768	150 922	35	...	...	...	...
Kota	694 316	368 451	325 865	221	703 150	373 094	330 056	226
Kothagudem	...	...	...	...	105 266	52 318	52 948	25
Kottayam	...	...	...	...	172 878	84 960	87 918	64
Kozhikode	436 556	211 888	224 668	84	880 247	429 163	451 084	235
Krishnanagar	139 110	70 576	68 534	16	148 709	75 495	73 214	18
Krishnarajapura	186 210	97 412	88 798	25	...	...	...	...
Kukatpalle	292 289	153 331	138 958	72	...	...	...	...
Kulti	289 903	152 821	137 082	100	...	...	...	...
Kumbakonam	139 954	69 785	70 169	13	160 767	80 188	80 579	15
Kurnool	269 122	136 619	132 503	15	342 973	174 190	168 783	46
Lakhimpur	121 486	65 236	56 250	7	...	...	...	...
Lal Bahadur Nagar	268 689	138 667	130 022	85	...	...	...	...
Lalitpur	111 892	58 993	52 899	...	...	...	...	...
Latur	299 985	156 547	143 438	21	...	...	...	...
Loni	120 945	65 278	55 667	7	...	...	...	...
Lucknow	2 185 927	1 156 151	1 029 776	310	2 245 509	1 189 466	1 056 043	338
Ludhiana	1 398 467	793 142	605 325	159	...	...	...	...
Machilipatnam	179 353	89 100	90 253	27	...	...	...	...
Madanapalle	...	...	...	...	107 449	54 497	52 952	13
Madhyamgram	155 451	79 728	75 723	21	...	...	...	...
Madurai	928 869	469 396	459 473	52	1 203 095	608 531	594 564	141
Mahadevapura	135 794	72 882	62 912	53	...	...	...	...
Mahbubnagar	130 986	67 007	63 979	14	139 662	71 516	68 146	14
Mahesana	...	...	...	...	141 453	74 866	66 587	...
Maheshtala	385 266	202 304	182 962	44	...	...	...	...
Mainpuri	...	...	...	...	104 851	55 462	49 389	17
Malappuram	...	...	...	...	170 409	83 709	86 700	111
Malegaon	409 403	208 864	200 539	13	...	...	...	...
Malerkotla	107 009	56 767	50 242	21	...	...	...	...
Malkajgiri	193 863	98 972	94 891	18	...	...	...	...
Mancherial	...	...	...	...	118 195	60 371	57 824	62
Mandsaur	116 505	60 269	56 236	...	117 555	60 859	56 696	...
Mandya	131 179	66 551	64 628	17	...	...	...	...
Mangalore	399 565	200 630	198 935	118	539 387	269 562	269 825	201
Mango	166 125	87 375	78 750	19	...	...	...	...
Mathura	302 770	162 021	140 749	9	323 315	174 335	148 980	22
Maunath Bhanjan	212 657	109 958	102 699	9	...	...	...	...
Medinipur	149 769	76 503	73 266	15	...	...	...	...
Meerut	1 068 772	568 081	500 691	142	1 161 716	621 481	540 235	178
Mira-Bhayandar	520 388	286 391	233 997	79	...	...	...	...
Mirzapur-cum-Vindhyachal	205 053	109 647	95 406	39	...	...	...	...
Modinagar	113 218	60 468	52 750	16	139 929	74 788	65 141	23
Moga	125 573	66 888	58 685	16	135 279	72 043	63 236	...
Moradabad	641 583	340 314	301 269	89	...	...	...	...
Morena	150 959	82 305	68 654	12	...	...	...	...

8. Population of capital cities and cities of 100 000 or more inhabitants: latest available year, 1995 - 2014
Population des capitales et des villes de 100 000 habitants ou plus : dernière année disponible, 1995 - 2014 (continued - suite)

Continent, country or area, date, code[a] and city / Continent, pays ou zone, date, code[a] et ville	City proper - Ville proprement dite				Urban agglomeration - Agglomération urbaine			
	Population			Surface area - Superficie (km²)	Population			Surface area - Superficie (km²)
	Both sexes - Les deux sexes	Male - Masculin	Female - Féminin		Both sexes - Les deux sexes	Male - Masculin	Female - Féminin	
ASIA - ASIE								
India - Inde[33]								
1 III 2001 (CDFC)								
Mormugoa	...	...	...	...	104 758	55 954	48 804	40
Morvi	145 719	75 745	69 974	25	178 055	92 639	85 416	...
Motihari	100 683	54 261	46 422	14	108 428	59 148	49 280	16
Mughalsarai	...	...	...	...	116 308	61 579	54 729	29
Mumbai (Bombay)	11 978 450	6 619 966	5 358 484	603	16 434 386	9 021 789	7 412 597	1 133
Munger	188 050	101 264	86 786	18	...	...	...	...
Murwara (Katni)	187 029	97 843	89 186	107	...	...	...	...
Muzaffarnagar	316 729	167 397	149 332	...	331 668	175 283	156 385	12
Muzaffarpur	305 525	164 000	141 525	26	...	...	...	...
Mysore	755 379	383 480	371 899	89	799 228	406 363	392 865	132
Nabadwip	115 016	58 287	56 729	12	125 341	63 574	61 767	13
Nadiad	192 913	100 322	92 591	28	196 793	102 336	94 457	30
Nagaon	107 667	56 815	50 852	...	123 265	64 895	58 370	16
Nagercoil	208 179	102 907	105 272	24	...	...	...	...
Nagpur	2 052 066	1 059 765	992 301	218	2 129 500	1 102 009	1 027 491	229
Naihati	215 303	113 777	101 526	12	...	...	...	...
Nala Sopara	184 538	98 870	85 668	...	...	...	...	...
Nalgonda	110 286	56 299	53 987	12	111 380	56 848	54 532	51
Nanded	430 733	224 843	205 890	21	...	...	...	...
Nandyal	152 676	77 273	75 403	15	157 120	79 500	77 620	...
Nangloi Jat	150 948	82 687	68 261	7	...	...	...	...
Nashik	1 077 236	575 737	501 499	259	1 152 326	616 088	536 238	322
Navghar-Manikpur	116 723	61 757	54 966	...	...	...	...	...
Navi Mumbai (New Bombay)	704 002	395 705	308 297	133	...	...	...	...
Navsari	134 017	69 794	64 223	...	232 411	122 282	110 129	...
Neemuch	107 663	56 588	51 075	13	112 852	59 320	53 532	13
Nellore	378 428	190 522	187 906	48	404 775	203 823	200 952	...
NEW DELHI[36]	302 363	165 723	136 640	43	...	...	...	...
Neyveli	127 552	65 348	62 204	97	138 035	70 746	67 289	116
Nizamabad	288 722	146 198	142 524	37	...	...	...	...
Noida	305 058	168 958	136 100	90	...	...	...	...
North Barrackpur	123 668	63 796	59 872	9	...	...	...	...
North Dumdum	220 042	113 034	107 008	26	...	...	...	...
Ongole	150 471	76 511	73 960	27	153 829	78 242	75 587	27
Orai	139 318	74 703	64 615	20	...	...	...	...
Ozhukarai	217 707	110 042	107 665	35	...	...	...	...
Palakkad	130 767	64 379	66 388	30	197 369	96 928	100 441	59
Palanpur	110 419	58 055	52 364	20	122 300	64 365	57 935	40
Pali	187 641	99 267	88 374	84	...	...	...	...
Pallavaram	144 623	73 385	71 238	18	...	...	...	...
Palwal	100 722	53 648	47 074	8	...	...	...	...
Panchkula Urban Estate	140 925	75 897	65 028	26	...	...	...	...
Panihati	348 438	180 307	168 131	19	...	...	...	...
Panipat	261 740	143 644	118 096	21	354 148	194 850	159 298	...
Panvel	104 058	54 963	49 095	12	...	...	...	...
Parbhani	259 329	133 959	125 370	58	...	...	...	...
Patan	112 219	59 097	53 122	14	113 749	59 955	53 794	...
Pathankot	157 925	86 520	71 405	22	168 485	92 003	76 482	...
Patiala	303 151	162 573	140 578	65	323 884	173 682	150 202	...
Patna	1 366 444	746 344	620 100	99	1 697 976	922 971	775 005	135
Phagwara	...	...	...	...	102 253	55 335	46 918	...
Phusro	...	...	...	...	174 402	93 700	80 702	84
Pilibhit	124 245	65 853	58 392	10	...	...	...	...
Pimpri Chinchwad	1 012 472	547 050	465 422	171	...	...	...	...
Pollachi	...	...	...	...	128 458	64 657	63 801	29
Pondicherry	220 865	109 389	111 476	20	505 959	253 375	252 584	72
Porbandar	133 051	68 201	64 850	12	197 382	101 824	95 558	...
Proddatur	150 309	75 372	74 937	7	...	...	...	...
Pudukkottai	109 217	54 614	54 603	13	...	...	...	...
Pune	2 538 473	1 321 338	1 217 135	430	3 760 636	1 980 621	1 780 015	669
Puri	157 837	82 269	75 568	17	...	...	...	...
Purnia	171 687	92 826	78 861	45	197 211	106 313	90 898	60
Puruliya	113 806	59 092	54 714	14	...	...	...	...

8. Population of capital cities and cities of 100 000 or more inhabitants: latest available year, 1995 - 2014
Population des capitales et des villes de 100 000 habitants ou plus : dernière année disponible, 1995 - 2014 (continued - suite)

Continent, country or area, date, code[a] and city / Continent, pays ou zone, date, code[a] et ville	City proper - Ville proprement dite				Urban agglomeration - Agglomération urbaine			
	Population			Surface area - Superficie (km²)	Population			Surface area - Superficie (km²)
	Both sexes - Les deux sexes	Male - Masculin	Female - Féminin		Both sexes - Les deux sexes	Male - Masculin	Female - Féminin	
ASIA - ASIE								
India - Inde[33]								
1 III 2001 (CDFC)								
Quthbullapur	231 108	120 690	110 418	47	...	...	...	...
Rae Bareli	169 333	88 911	80 422	50	...	...	...	...
Raichur	207 421	105 763	101 658	...	...	...	...	...
Raiganj	165 212	87 458	77 754	11	175 047	92 703	82 344	15
Raigarh	111 154	57 650	53 504	18	115 908	60 101	55 807	21
Raipur	605 747	314 584	291 163	56	700 113	364 436	335 677	116
Rajahmundry	315 251	158 454	156 797	52	413 616	207 869	205 747	64
Rajapalayam	122 307	61 221	61 086	10	...	...	...	...
Rajarhat Gopalpur	271 811	140 218	131 593	35	...	...	...	...
Rajendranagar	143 240	74 889	68 351	52	...	...	...	...
Rajkot	967 476	506 993	460 483	105	1 003 015	525 898	477 117	163
Rajnandgaon	143 770	72 949	70 821	78	...	...	...	...
Rajpur Sonarpur	336 707	174 140	162 567	55	...	...	...	...
Ramagundam	236 600	120 687	115 913	28	237 686	121 250	116 436	...
Ramgarh	...	...	...	...	110 496	61 591	48 905	50
Rampur	281 494	146 652	134 842	20	...	...	...	...
Ranaghat	...	...	...	...	145 285	73 933	71 352	25
Ranchi	847 093	450 727	396 366	177	863 495	459 462	404 033	182
Raniganj	111 116	59 270	51 846	23	...	...	...	...
Ratlam	222 202	114 370	107 832	39	234 419	120 874	113 545	41
Raurkela	224 987	121 240	103 747	133	484 874	258 731	226 143	157
Raurkela Industrialship	206 693	109 394	97 299	122	...	...	...	...
Rewa	183 274	98 793	84 481	55	...	...	...	...
Rewari	100 684	53 935	46 749	12	...	...	...	...
Rishra	113 305	62 585	50 720	6	...	...	...	...
Robertson Pet	141 424	70 619	70 805	...	157 084	78 578	78 506	...
Rohtak	286 807	154 148	132 659	28	294 577	158 287	136 290	...
Roorkee	...	...	...	...	115 278	64 240	51 038	17
S.A.S. Nagar (Mohali)	123 484	65 642	57 842	24	...	...	...	...
Sagar	232 133	122 385	109 748	36	308 922	162 919	146 003	52
Saharanpur	455 754	241 508	214 246	26	...	...	...	...
Saharasa	125 167	67 718	57 449	21	...	...	...	...
Salem	696 760	353 933	342 827	91	751 438	382 211	369 227	108
Sambalpur	153 643	79 683	73 960	50	226 469	117 745	108 724	90
Sambhal	182 478	97 011	85 467	16	...	...	...	...
Sangli-Miraj-Kupwad	436 781	224 300	212 481	118	447 774	229 958	217 816	121
Santipur	138 235	70 089	68 146	25	...	...	...	...
Sasaram	131 172	69 682	61 490	11	...	...	...	...
Satara	108 048	55 938	52 110	...	...	...	...	...
Satna	225 464	120 277	105 187	...	229 307	122 401	106 906	...
Sawai Madhopur	...	...	...	...	101 997	53 903	48 094	60
Secunderabad	206 102	104 335	101 767	40	...	...	...	...
Serampore	197 857	105 415	92 442	15	...	...	...	...
Serilingampalle	153 364	79 225	74 139	98	...	...	...	...
Shahjahanpur	296 662	160 178	136 484	13	321 885	174 276	147 609	23
Shillong	132 867	66 106	66 761	10	267 662	134 497	133 165	25
Shimla	142 555	81 186	61 369	29	144 975	82 840	62 135	30
Shimoga	274 352	140 224	134 128	...	...	...	...	...
Shivapuri	146 892	78 433	68 459	81	...	...	...	...
Sikar	185 323	96 379	88 944	23	185 925	96 697	89 228	...
Silchar	142 199	72 679	69 520	16	184 105	94 306	89 799	...
Siliguri	472 374	250 645	221 729	42	...	...	...	...
Singrauli	185 190	100 149	85 041	...	...	...	...	...
Sirsa	160 735	85 993	74 742	19	...	...	...	...
Sitapur	151 908	79 767	72 141	26	...	...	...	...
Sivakasi	...	...	...	...	121 358	60 841	60 517	27
Siwan	109 919	58 262	51 657	13	...	...	...	...
Solapur	872 478	444 734	427 744	179	...	...	...	...
Sonipat	214 974	117 020	97 954	28	225 074	122 480	102 594	...
South Dum Dum	392 444	200 298	192 146	14	...	...	...	...
Srikakulam	109 905	54 926	54 979	12	117 320	58 753	58 567	14
Srinagar	898 440	484 627	413 813	184	988 210	537 512	450 698	243
Sultan Pur Majra	164 426	88 729	75 697	3	...	...	...	...

8. Population of capital cities and cities of 100 000 or more inhabitants: latest available year, 1995 - 2014
Population des capitales et des villes de 100 000 habitants ou plus : dernière année disponible, 1995 - 2014 (continued - suite)

Continent, country or area, date, code[a] and city Continent, pays ou zone, date, code[a] et ville	City proper - Ville proprement dite				Urban agglomeration - Agglomération urbaine			
	Population			Surface area - Superficie (km²)	Population			Surface area - Superficie (km²)
	Both sexes - Les deux sexes	Male - Masculin	Female - Féminin		Both sexes - Les deux sexes	Male - Masculin	Female - Féminin	
ASIA - ASIE								
India - Inde[33]								
1 III 2001 (CDFC)								
Sultanpur	100 065	53 189	46 876	12	...	...	...	...
Surat	2 433 835	1 372 415	1 061 420	112	2 811 614	1 597 156	1 214 458	237
Surendranagar Dudhrej	156 161	81 377	74 784	39	...	...	...	...
Tadepalligudem	102 622	50 925	51 697	21	...	...	...	...
Tambaram	137 933	70 419	67 514	21	...	...	...	...
Tenali	153 756	77 404	76 352	15	...	...	...	...
Tezpur	...	...	...	...	105 377	59 869	45 508	23
Thane	1 262 551	675 147	587 404	128	...	...	...	...
Thanesar	119 687	65 525	54 162	33	122 319	66 978	55 341	36
Thanjavur	215 314	106 625	108 689	15	...	...	...	...
Thiruvananthapuram	744 983	366 235	378 748	142	889 635	437 407	452 228	178
Thoothukkudi (Tuticorin)	216 054	107 758	108 296	13	243 415	121 428	121 987	140
Thrissur	317 526	154 248	163 278	...	330 122	160 443	169 679	88
Tinsukia	...	...	...	...	108 123	59 561	48 562	26
Tiruchchirappalli	752 066	376 125	375 941	147	866 354	434 321	432 033	196
Tirunelveli	411 831	203 232	208 599	109	433 352	214 133	219 219	135
Tirupati	228 202	118 187	110 015	16	303 521	155 468	148 053	20
Tiruppur	344 543	179 930	164 613	27	550 826	286 862	263 964	147
Tiruvannamalai	130 567	66 125	64 442	14	...	...	...	...
Tiruvottiyur	212 281	108 720	103 561	21	...	...	...	...
Titagarh	124 213	70 705	53 508	3	...	...	...	...
Tonk	135 689	70 255	65 434	61	...	...	...	...
Tumkur	248 929	129 273	119 656	...	...	...	...	...
Udaipur	389 438	205 335	184 103	64	...	...	...	...
Udupi	113 112	55 893	57 219	64	127 124	62 596	64 528	73
Ujjain	430 427	223 998	206 429	...	431 162	224 475	206 687	92
Ulhasnagar	473 731	251 888	221 843	13	...	...	...	...
Uluberia	202 135	105 843	96 292	34	...	...	...	...
Unnao	144 662	76 254	68 408	21	...	...	...	...
Uppal Kalan	117 217	60 857	56 360	20	...	...	...	...
Uttarpara Kotrung	150 363	78 808	71 555	16	...	...	...	...
Vadakara	...	...	...	...	124 083	59 803	64 280	51
Vadodara	1 306 227	684 013	622 214	108	1 491 045	782 251	708 794	214
Valsad	...	...	...	...	145 592	75 216	70 376	...
Vaniyambadi	...	...	...	...	103 950	51 886	52 064	16
Varanasi	1 091 918	582 096	509 822	92	1 203 961	643 043	560 918	111
Vasai	...	...	...	...	174 396	91 030	83 366	...
Vejalpur	113 445	58 878	54 567	7	...	...	...	...
Vellore	177 230	87 977	89 253	12	386 746	193 176	193 570	62
Veraval	141 357	72 148	69 209	38	158 032	80 889	77 143	41
Vidisha	125 453	66 572	58 881	6	...	...	...	...
Vijayawada	851 282	431 243	420 039	60	1 039 518	527 307	512 211	101
Virar	118 928	63 704	55 224	20	...	...	...	...
Visakhapatnam	982 904	501 406	481 498	112	1 345 938	687 985	657 953	326
Vizianagarm	174 651	86 375	88 276	21	195 801	97 032	98 769	30
Wadhwan	...	...	...	...	219 585	114 175	105 410	59
Warangal	530 636	268 954	261 682	68	579 216	293 709	285 507	97
Wardha	111 118	57 499	53 619	8	...	...	...	...
Yamunanagar	189 696	101 782	87 914	16	306 740	166 137	140 603	42
Yavatmal	120 676	61 780	58 896	10	139 835	71 908	67 927	13
Indonesia - Indonésie								
1 V 2010 (CDJC)								
Ambon	331 254	165 926	165 328	359	...	...	...	...
Balikpapan	557 579	288 847	268 732	503	...	...	...	...
Banda Aceh	223 446	115 097	108 349	61	...	...	...	...
Bandar Lampung	881 801	445 959	435 842	193	...	...	...	...
Bandjarmasin	625 481	312 740	312 741	72	...	...	...	...
Bandung	2 394 873	1 215 348	1 179 525	1 670	...	...	...	...
Batam	944 285	484 867	459 418	969	...	...	...	...
Bengkulu	308 544	155 288	153 256	145	...	...	...	...
Binjai	246 154	122 997	123 157	9	...	...	...	...
Bitung	187 652	96 001	91 651	304	...	...	...	...
Blitar	131 968	65 441	66 527	33	...	...	...	...

Continent, country or area, date, code[a] and city / Continent, pays ou zone, date, code[a] et ville	City proper - Ville proprement dite				Urban agglomeration - Agglomération urbaine			
	Population			Surface area - Superficie (km²)	Population			Surface area - Superficie (km²)
	Both sexes - Les deux sexes	Male - Masculin	Female - Féminin		Both sexes - Les deux sexes	Male - Masculin	Female - Féminin	
ASIA - ASIE								
Indonesia - Indonésie								
1 V 2010 (CDJC)								
Bogor	950 334	484 791	465 543	119	...	...	...	...
Cirebon (Tjirebon)	296 389	148 600	147 789	37	...	...	...	...
Denpasar	788 589	403 293	385 296	124	...	...	...	...
Gorontalo	180 127	88 283	91 844	65	...	...	...	...
JAKARTA	9 607 787	4 870 938	4 736 849	740	...	...	...	...
Jambi	531 857	268 102	263 755	205	...	...	...	...
Jayapura	256 705	136 587	120 118	740	...	...	...	...
Kediri	268 507	133 884	134 623	63	...	...	...	...
Madiun	170 964	82 738	88 226	34	...	...	...	...
Magelang	118 227	58 311	59 916	18	...	...	...	...
Makasar (Ujung Pandang)	1 338 663	662 009	676 654	199	...	...	...	...
Malang	820 243	404 553	415 690	145	...	...	...	...
Manado	410 481	206 292	204 189	157	...	...	...	...
Mataram	402 843	199 332	203 511	61	...	...	...	...
Medan	2 097 610	1 036 926	1 060 684	265	...	...	...	...
Mojokerto	120 196	59 127	61 069	16	...	...	...	...
Padang	833 562	415 315	418 247	694	...	...	...	...
Pakalongan	281 434	140 983	140 451	45	...	...	...	...
Pakanbaru	897 767	456 385	441 382	632	...	...	...	...
Palangkaraya	220 962	113 005	107 957	2 400	...	...	...	...
Palembang	1 455 284	728 296	726 988	369	...	...	...	...
Pangkal Pinang	174 758	89 500	85 258	89	...	...	...	...
Pare Pare	129 262	63 481	65 781	99	...	...	...	...
Pasuruan	186 262	92 370	93 892	35	...	...	...	...
Pematang Siantar	234 698	114 561	120 137	80	...	...	...	...
Pontianak	234 021	118 980	115 041	108	...	...	...	...
Probolinggo	217 062	106 915	110 147	57	...	...	...	...
Salatiga	170 332	83 479	86 853	57	...	...	...	...
Samarinda	727 500	377 283	350 217	781	...	...	...	...
Semarang	1 555 984	764 487	791 497	374	...	...	...	...
Sukabumi	298 681	152 080	146 601	48	...	...	...	...
Surabaya	2 765 487	1 367 841	1 397 646	351	...	...	...	...
Surakarta	499 337	243 296	256 041	44	...	...	...	...
Tangerang	1 798 601	921 043	877 558	187	...	...	...	...
Tanjung Balai	154 445	77 933	76 512	68	...	...	...	...
Tebing Tinggi	145 248	71 892	73 356	32	...	...	...	...
Tegal	239 599	118 872	120 727	35	...	...	...	...
Yogyakarta	388 627	189 137	199 490	33	...	...	...	...
Iran (Islamic Republic of) - Iran (République islamique d')								
24 X 2011 (CDJC)								
Abadan	212 744	106 181	106 563	...	...	...	...	...
Ahwaz	1 112 021	558 346	553 675	...	...	...	...	...
Amol	219 915	110 331	109 584	...	...	...	...	...
Andimeshk	126 811	63 990	62 821	...	...	...	...	...
Arak	484 212	244 614	239 598	...	...	...	...	...
Ardabil	482 632	245 335	237 297	...	...	...	...	...
Babol	219 467	109 407	110 060	...	...	...	...	...
Bam	107 131	53 492	53 639	...	...	...	...	...
Bandar-e-Abbas	435 751	222 798	212 953	...	...	...	...	...
Bandar-e-Anzali	116 664	57 675	58 989	...	...	...	...	...
Bandar-e-Mahshahr	153 778	77 487	76 291	...	...	...	...	...
Behbahan	107 412	54 163	53 249	...	...	...	...	...
Birjand	178 020	90 092	87 928	...	...	...	...	...
Bojnurd	199 791	100 605	99 186	...	...	...	...	...
Borujerd	240 654	118 508	122 146	...	...	...	...	...
Bukand	170 600	85 835	84 765	...	...	...	...	...
Bushehr	195 222	101 362	93 860	...	...	...	...	...
Dezful	248 380	128 430	119 950	...	...	...	...	...
Esfahan	1 756 126	884 018	872 108	...	...	...	...	...
Fasa	104 809	51 907	52 902	...	...	...	...	...
Golestan (Soltanabad)	259 480	133 531	125 949	...	...	...	...	...
Gonbad-e-Kavus	144 546	71 986	72 560	...	...	...	...	...

8. Population of capital cities and cities of 100 000 or more inhabitants: latest available year, 1995 - 2014
Population des capitales et des villes de 100 000 hahitants ou plus : dernière année disponible, 1995 - 2014 (continued - suite)

Continent, country or area, date, code[a] and city / Continent, pays ou zone, date, code[a] et ville	City proper - Ville proprement dite				Urban agglomeration - Agglomération urbaine			
	Population			Surface area - Superficie (km²)	Population			Surface area - Superficie (km²)
	Both sexes - Les deux sexes	Male - Masculin	Female - Féminin		Both sexes - Les deux sexes	Male - Masculin	Female - Féminin	

ASIA - ASIE

Iran (Islamic Republic of) - Iran (République islamique d')
24 X 2011 (CDJC)

Gorgan	329 536	165 001	164 535	...	...	...	...	...
Hamadan	525 794	261 577	264 217	...	...	...	...	...
Ilam	172 213	87 221	84 992	...	...	...	...	...
Islam Shahr (Qasemabad)	389 102	198 080	191 022	...	...	...	...	...
Izeh	117 093	58 080	59 013	...	...	...	...	...
Jahrom	114 108	57 865	56 243	...	...	...	...	...
Jiroft	111 034	57 168	53 866	...	...	...	...	...
Kamal Shahr	109 943	56 265	53 678	...	...	...	...	...
Karaj	1 614 626	813 551	801 075	...	...	...	...	...
Kashan	275 325	139 866	135 459	...	...	...	...	...
Kerman	534 441	269 661	264 780	...	...	...	...	...
Kermanshah	851 405	426 129	425 276	...	...	...	...	...
Khomeini shahr	244 696	126 326	118 370	...	...	...	...	...
Khoramabad	348 216	173 264	174 952	...	...	...	...	...
Khoramshahr	129 418	63 804	65 614	...	...	...	...	...
Khoy	200 958	100 593	100 365	...	...	...	...	...
Mahabad	147 268	73 626	73 642	...	...	...	...	...
Malard	290 817	147 954	142 863	...	...	...	...	...
Malayer	159 848	79 477	80 371	...	...	...	...	...
Marand	124 323	62 848	61 475	...	...	...	...	...
Maraqeh	162 275	81 229	81 046	...	...	...	...	...
Marivan	110 464	56 129	54 335	...	...	...	...	...
Marvadsht	138 649	70 221	68 428	...	...	...	...	...
Mashhad	2 766 258	1 384 599	1 381 659	...	...	...	...	...
Masjed Soleyman	103 369	51 852	51 517	...	...	...	...	...
Miandoab	123 081	62 883	60 198	...	...	...	...	...
Mohammad Shahr	100 519	51 359	49 160	...	...	...	...	...
Najafabad	221 814	111 915	109 899	...	...	...	...	...
Nasim Shahr	157 474	80 947	76 527	...	...	...	...	...
Nazar Abad	107 806	54 806	53 000	...	...	...	...	...
Neyshabur	239 185	119 845	119 340	...	...	...	...	...
Orumiyeh	667 499	334 136	333 363	...	...	...	...	...
Pakdasht	206 490	105 814	100 676	...	...	...	...	...
Qaem shahr	196 050	97 358	98 692	...	...	...	...	...
Qarchak	191 588	97 678	93 910	...	...	...	...	...
Qazvin	381 598	192 960	188 638	...	...	...	...	...
Qods	283 517	144 911	138 606	...	...	...	...	...
Qom	1 074 036	545 704	528 332	...	...	...	...	...
Quchan	103 760	52 240	51 520	...	...	...	...	...
Rafsanjan	151 420	75 643	75 777	...	...	...	...	...
Rasht	639 951	316 833	323 118	...	...	...	...	...
Sabzewar	231 557	115 158	116 399	...	...	...	...	...
Sanandaj	373 987	189 047	184 940	...	...	...	...	...
Saqez	139 738	69 856	69 882	...	...	...	...	...
Sari	296 417	147 875	148 542	...	...	...	...	...
Saveh	200 481	102 578	97 903	...	...	...	...	...
Semnan	153 680	77 575	76 105	...	...	...	...	...
Shahinshahr	143 308	71 357	71 951	...	...	...	...	...
Shahr-e-Kord	159 775	79 681	80 094	...	...	...	...	...
Shahreza	123 767	62 314	61 453	...	...	...	...	...
Shahriar	249 473	126 246	123 227	...	...	...	...	...
Shahrud	140 474	70 616	69 858	...	...	...	...	...
Shiraz	1 460 665	732 380	728 285	...	...	...	...	...
Shoosh	106 815	53 747	53 068	...	...	...	...	...
Sirjan	185 623	94 943	90 680	...	...	...	...	...
Tabriz	1 494 998	755 553	739 445	...	...	...	...	...
TEHRAN	8 154 051	4 059 301	4 094 750	...	...	...	...	...
Torbat-e-heydariyeh	131 150	66 310	64 840	...	...	...	...	...
Varamin	218 991	111 074	107 917	...	...	...	...	...
Yasooj	108 505	54 825	53 680	...	...	...	...	...
Yazd	486 152	246 985	239 167	...	...	...	...	...
Zabol	137 722	69 726	67 996	...	...	...	...	...

8. Population of capital cities and cities of 100 000 or more inhabitants: latest available year, 1995 - 2014
Population des capitales et des villes de 100 000 habitants ou plus : dernière année disponible, 1995 - 2014 (continued - suite)

Continent, country or area, date, code[a] and city Continent, pays ou zone, date, code[a] et ville	City proper - Ville proprement dite				Urban agglomeration - Agglomération urbaine			
	Population			Surface area - Superficie (km²)	Population			Surface area - Superficie (km²)
	Both sexes - Les deux sexes	Male - Masculin	Female - Féminin		Both sexes - Les deux sexes	Male - Masculin	Female - Féminin	

ASIA - ASIE

Iran (Islamic Republic of) - Iran (République islamique d')
24 X 2011 (CDJC)

Zahedan	560 725	283 680	277 045	...	...	...	...	...
Zanjan	386 851	195 382	191 469	...	...	...	...	...

Israel - Israël
1 VII 2013 (ESDJ)

Ashdod	215 699	105 351	110 348	51	...	...	...	...
Ashqelon	121 758	59 208	62 550	51	...	...	...	...
Bat Yam	129 154	61 475	67 679	8	...	...	...	...
Be'er Sheva	198 301	96 497	101 805	117	...	...	...	...
Bene Beraq	170 627	86 543	84 084	7	...	...	...	...
Haifa	272 679	130 957	141 722	73	...	...	...	...
Holon	185 852	89 727	96 126	19	...	...	...	...
JERUSALEM[37]	822 586	408 828	413 758	125	...	...	...	...
Netanya	194 568	94 841	99 728	35	...	...	...	...
Petah Tiqwa	216 601	105 742	110 859	36	...	...	...	...
Ramat Gan	148 995	70 974	78 021	16	...	...	...	...
Rehovot	122 959	60 202	62 758	24	...	...	...	...
Rishon Leziyyon	236 380	115 708	120 671	59	...	...	...	...
Tel Aviv-Yafo	416 577	205 244	211 333	54	...	...	...	...

Japan - Japon
1 X 2010 (CDJC)

Abiko	134 017[38]	65 732[38]	68 285[38]	43[39]	...	...	...	...
Ageo	223 926[38]	111 784[38]	112 142[38]	46[39]	...	...	...	...
Aizuwakamatsu	126 220[38]	59 854[38]	66 366[38]	383[39]	...	...	...	...
Akashi	290 959[38]	141 344[38]	149 615[38]	49[39]	...	...	...	...
Akishima	112 297[38]	56 320[38]	55 977[38]	17[39]	...	...	...	...
Akita	323 600[38]	152 456[38]	171 144[38]	906[39]	...	...	...	...
Amagasaki	453 748[38]	221 216[38]	232 532[38]	50[39]	...	...	...	...
Anjo	178 691[38]	91 424[38]	87 267[38]	86[39]	...	...	...	...
Aomori	299 520[38]	139 084[38]	160 436[38]	825[39]	...	...	...	...
Asahikawa	347 095[38]	160 094[38]	187 001[38]	748[39]	...	...	...	...
Asaka	129 691[38]	65 503[38]	64 188[38]	18[39]	...	...	...	...
Ashikaga	154 530[38]	75 382[38]	79 148[38]	178[39]	...	...	...	...
Atsugi	224 420[38]	116 927[38]	107 493[38]	94[39]	...	...	...	...
Beppu	125 385[38]	56 868[38]	68 517[38]	125[39]	...	...	...	...
Chiba	961 749[38]	480 194[38]	481 555[38]	272[39]	...	...	...	...
Chigasaki	235 081[38]	115 245[38]	119 836[38]	36[39]	...	...	...	...
Chikusei	108 527[38]	53 680[38]	54 847[38]	205[39]	...	...	...	...
Chikushino	100 172[38]	47 750[38]	52 422[38]	88[39]	...	...	...	...
Chofu	223 593[38]	110 805[38]	112 788[38]	22[39]	...	...	...	...
Daito	127 534[38]	63 810[38]	63 724[38]	18[39]	...	...	...	...
Ebetsu	123 722[38]	59 320[38]	64 402[38]	188[39]	...	...	...	...
Ebina	127 707[38]	64 483[38]	63 224[38]	26[39]	...	...	...	...
Fuchu	255 506[38]	131 558[38]	123 948[38]	29[39]	...	...	...	...
Fuji	254 027[38]	125 240[38]	128 787[38]	245[39]	...	...	...	...
Fujieda	142 151[38]	69 484[38]	72 667[38]	194[39]	...	...	...	...
Fujimi	106 736[38]	53 134[38]	53 602[38]	20[39]	...	...	...	...
Fujimino	105 695[38]	52 640[38]	53 055[38]	15[39]	...	...	...	...
Fujinomiya	132 001[38]	64 909[38]	67 092[38]	389[39]	...	...	...	...
Fujisawa	409 657[38]	203 778[38]	205 879[38]	70[39]	...	...	...	...
Fukaya	144 618[38]	72 146[38]	72 472[38]	138[39]	...	...	...	...
Fukui	266 796[38]	128 692[38]	138 104[38]	536[39]	...	...	...	...
Fukuoka	1 463 743[38]	692 648[38]	771 095[38]	341[39]	...	...	...	...
Fukushima	292 590[38]	140 723[38]	151 867[38]	768[39]	...	...	...	...
Fukuyama	461 357[38]	222 729[38]	238 628[38]	518[39]	...	...	...	...
Funabashi	609 040[38]	306 399[38]	302 641[38]	86[39]	...	...	...	...
Gifu	413 136[38]	196 525[38]	216 611[38]	203[39]	...	...	...	...
Habikino	117 681[38]	55 737[38]	61 944[38]	26[39]	...	...	...	...
Hachinohe	237 615[38]	113 340[38]	124 275[38]	305[39]	...	...	...	...
Hachioji	580 053[38]	293 462[38]	286 591[38]	186[39]	...	...	...	...
Hadano	170 145[38]	87 291[38]	82 854[38]	104[39]	...	...	...	...

Continent, country or area, date, code[a] and city / Continent, pays ou zone, date, code[a] et ville	City proper - Ville proprement dite				Urban agglomeration - Agglomération urbaine			
	Population			Surface area - Superficie (km²)	Population			Surface area - Superficie (km²)
	Both sexes - Les deux sexes	Male - Masculin	Female - Féminin		Both sexes - Les deux sexes	Male - Masculin	Female - Féminin	
ASIA - ASIE								
Japan - Japon								
1 X 2010 (CDJC)								
Hakodate	279 127[38]	127 046[38]	152 081[38]	678[39]	...	...	...	...
Hakusan	110 459[38]	53 563[38]	56 896[38]	755[39]	...	...	...	...
Hamamatsu	800 866[38]	397 146[38]	403 720[38]	1 558[39]	...	...	...	...
Hanamaki	101 438[38]	48 076[38]	53 362[38]	908[39]	...	...	...	...
Handa	118 828[38]	59 291[38]	59 537[38]	47[39]	...	...	...	...
Hatsukaichi	114 038[38]	54 101[38]	59 937[38]	489[39]	...	...	...	...
Higashihiroshima	190 135[38]	96 952[38]	93 183[38]	635[39]	...	...	...	...
Higashikurume	116 546[38]	57 613[38]	58 933[38]	13[39]	...	...	...	...
Higashimurayama	153 557[38]	75 461[38]	78 096[38]	17[39]	...	...	...	...
Higashiomi	115 479[38]	56 872[38]	58 607[38]	389[39]	...	...	...	...
Higashiosaka	509 533[38]	249 964[38]	259 569[38]	62[39]	...	...	...	...
Hikone	112 156[38]	55 173[38]	56 983[38]	197[39]	...	...	...	...
Himeji	536 270[38]	259 320[38]	276 950[38]	534[39]	...	...	...	...
Hino	180 052[38]	91 236[38]	88 816[38]	28[39]	...	...	...	...
Hirakata	407 978[38]	195 570[38]	212 408[38]	65[39]	...	...	...	...
Hiratsuka	260 780[38]	132 048[38]	128 732[38]	68[39]	...	...	...	...
Hirosaki	183 473[38]	84 064[38]	99 409[38]	524[39]	...	...	...	...
Hiroshima	1 173 843[38]	565 482[38]	608 361[38]	905[39]	...	...	...	...
Hitachi	193 129[38]	96 747[38]	96 382[38]	226[39]	...	...	...	...
Hitachinaka	157 060[38]	79 046[38]	78 014[38]	99[39]	...	...	...	...
Hofu	116 611[38]	56 191[38]	60 420[38]	189[39]	...	...	...	...
Ibaraki	274 822[38]	133 621[38]	141 201[38]	77[39]	...	...	...	...
Ichihara	280 416[38]	143 338[38]	137 078[38]	368[39]	...	...	...	...
Ichikawa	473 919[38]	239 222[38]	234 697[38]	57[39]	...	...	...	...
Ichinomiya	378 566[38]	184 221[38]	194 345[38]	114[39]	...	...	...	...
Ichinoseki	118 578[38]	56 885[38]	61 693[38]	1 133[39]	...	...	...	...
Iida	105 335[38]	50 105[38]	55 230[38]	659[39]	...	...	...	...
Iizuka	131 492[38]	62 166[38]	69 326[38]	214[39]	...	...	...	...
Ikeda	104 229[38]	50 721[38]	53 508[38]	22[39]	...	...	...	...
Ikoma	118 113[38]	56 311[38]	61 802[38]	53[39]	...	...	...	...
Imabari	166 532[38]	77 893[38]	88 639[38]	420[39]	...	...	...	...
Inazawa	136 442[38]	67 394[38]	69 048[38]	79[39]	...	...	...	...
Iruma	149 872[38]	74 107[38]	75 765[38]	45[39]	...	...	...	...
Isahaya	140 752[38]	66 192[38]	74 560[38]	321[39]	...	...	...	...
Ise	130 271[38]	61 482[38]	68 789[38]	209[39]	...	...	...	...
Isehara	101 039[38]	51 601[38]	49 438[38]	56[39]	...	...	...	...
Isesaki	207 221[38]	103 210[38]	104 011[38]	139[39]	...	...	...	...
Ishinomaki	160 826[38]	77 143[38]	83 683[38]	556[39]	...	...	...	...
Itami	196 127[38]	95 665[38]	100 462[38]	25[39]	...	...	...	...
Iwaki	342 249[38]	165 339[38]	176 910[38]	1 231[39]	...	...	...	...
Iwakuni	143 857[38]	67 597[38]	76 260[38]	874[39]	...	...	...	...
Iwata	168 625[38]	84 716[38]	83 909[38]	164[39]	...	...	...	...
Izumi (Osaka)	184 988[38]	89 613[38]	95 375[38]	85[39]	...	...	...	...
Izumisano	100 801[38]	48 161[38]	52 640[38]	55[39]	...	...	...	...
Izumo	143 796[38]	68 563[38]	75 233[38]	543[39]	...	...	...	...
Joetsu	203 899[38]	99 115[38]	104 784[38]	974[39]	...	...	...	...
Kadoma	130 282[38]	64 423[38]	65 859[38]	12[39]	...	...	...	...
Kagoshima	605 846[38]	281 133[38]	324 713[38]	547[39]	...	...	...	...
Kakamigahara	145 604[38]	71 516[38]	74 088[38]	88[39]	...	...	...	...
Kakegawa	116 363[38]	57 921[38]	58 442[38]	266[39]	...	...	...	...
Kakogawa	266 937[38]	130 931[38]	136 006[38]	139[39]	...	...	...	...
Kamagaya	107 853[38]	53 178[38]	54 675[38]	21[39]	...	...	...	...
Kamakura	174 314[38]	82 235[38]	92 079[38]	40[39]	...	...	...	...
Kanazawa	462 361[38]	224 087[38]	238 274[38]	468[39]	...	...	...	...
Kanoya	105 070[38]	49 808[38]	55 262[38]	448[39]	...	...	...	...
Kanuma	102 348[38]	50 452[38]	51 896[38]	491[39]	...	...	...	...
Karatsu	126 926[38]	59 221[38]	67 705[38]	487[39]	...	...	...	...
Kariya	145 781[38]	76 598[38]	69 183[38]	50[39]	...	...	...	...
Kashihara	125 605[38]	59 879[38]	65 726[38]	40[39]	...	...	...	...

8. Population of capital cities and cities of 100 000 or more inhabitants: latest available year, 1995 - 2014
Population des capitales et des villes de 100 000 habitants ou plus : dernière année disponible, 1995 - 2014 (continued - suite)

Continent, country or area, date, code[a] and city / Continent, pays ou zone, date, code[a] et ville	City proper - Ville proprement dite				Urban agglomeration - Agglomération urbaine			
	Population			Surface area - Superficie (km²)	Population			Surface area - Superficie (km²)
	Both sexes - Les deux sexes	Male - Masculin	Female - Féminin		Both sexes - Les deux sexes	Male - Masculin	Female - Féminin	
ASIA - ASIE								
Japan - Japon								
1 X 2010 (CDJC)								
Kashiwa	404 012[38]	201 045[38]	202 967[38]	115[39]	...	...	...	...
Kasuga	106 780[38]	51 445[38]	55 335[38]	14[39]	...	...	...	...
Kasugai	305 569[38]	152 765[38]	152 804[38]	93[39]	...	...	...	...
Kasukabe	237 171[38]	117 798[38]	119 373[38]	66[39]	...	...	...	...
Kawachinagano	112 490[38]	52 964[38]	59 526[38]	110[39]	...	...	...	...
Kawagoe	342 670[38]	171 590[38]	171 080[38]	109[39]	...	...	...	...
Kawaguchi	500 598[38]	255 780[38]	244 818[38]	56[39]	...	...	...	...
Kawanishi	156 423[38]	73 930[38]	82 493[38]	53[39]	...	...	...	...
Kawasaki	1 425 512[38]	728 525[38]	696 987[38]	143[39]	...	...	...	...
Kazo	115 002[38]	57 241[38]	57 761[38]	133[39]	...	...	...	...
Kirishima	127 487[38]	61 135[38]	66 352[38]	604[39]	...	...	...	...
Kiryu	121 704[38]	58 765[38]	62 939[38]	275[39]	...	...	...	...
Kisarazu	129 312[38]	65 242[38]	64 070[38]	139[39]	...	...	...	...
Kishiwada	199 234[38]	95 730[38]	103 504[38]	72[39]	...	...	...	...
Kitakyushu	976 846[38]	459 305[38]	517 541[38]	488[39]	...	...	...	...
Kitami	125 689[38]	60 171[38]	65 518[38]	1 428[39]	...	...	...	...
Kobe	1 544 200[38]	731 114[38]	813 086[38]	553[39]	...	...	...	...
Kochi	343 393[38]	159 644[38]	183 749[38]	309[39]	...	...	...	...
Kodaira	187 035[38]	92 886[38]	94 149[38]	20[39]	...	...	...	...
Kofu	198 992[38]	97 754[38]	101 238[38]	212[39]	...	...	...	...
Koga	142 995[38]	71 450[38]	71 545[38]	124[39]	...	...	...	...
Koganei	118 852[38]	59 515[38]	59 337[38]	11[39]	...	...	...	...
Kokubunji	120 650[38]	59 967[38]	60 683[38]	11[39]	...	...	...	...
Komaki	147 132[38]	74 161[38]	72 971[38]	63[39]	...	...	...	...
Komatsu	108 433[38]	52 465[38]	55 968[38]	371[39]	...	...	...	...
Konosu	119 639[38]	59 152[38]	60 487[38]	67[39]	...	...	...	...
Koriyama	338 712[38]	166 336[38]	172 376[38]	757[39]	...	...	...	...
Koshigaya	326 313[38]	162 374[38]	163 939[38]	60[39]	...	...	...	...
Kuki	154 310[38]	77 175[38]	77 135[38]	82[39]	...	...	...	...
Kumagaya	203 180[38]	101 430[38]	101 750[38]	160[39]	...	...	...	...
Kumamoto	734 474[38]	344 291[38]	390 183[38]	390[39]	...	...	...	...
Kurashiki	475 513[38]	230 061[38]	245 452[38]	355[39]	...	...	...	...
Kure	239 973[38]	115 432[38]	124 541[38]	354[39]	...	...	...	...
Kurume	302 402[38]	143 885[38]	158 517[38]	230[39]	...	...	...	...
Kusatsu	130 874[38]	67 819[38]	63 055[38]	68[39]	...	...	...	...
Kushiro	181 169[38]	85 474[38]	95 695[38]	1 363[39]	...	...	...	...
Kuwana	140 290[38]	68 914[38]	71 376[38]	137[39]	...	...	...	...
Kyoto	1 474 015[38]	701 088[38]	772 927[38]	828[39]	...	...	...	...
Machida	426 987[38]	209 580[38]	217 407[38]	72[39]	...	...	...	...
Maebashi	340 291[38]	166 043[38]	174 248[38]	312[39]	...	...	...	...
Marugame	110 473[38]	53 633[38]	56 840[38]	112[39]	...	...	...	...
Matsubara	124 594[38]	60 017[38]	64 577[38]	17[39]	...	...	...	...
Matsudo	484 457[38]	240 674[38]	243 783[38]	61[39]	...	...	...	...
Matsue	194 258[38]	93 736[38]	100 522[38]	530[39]	...	...	...	...
Matsumoto	243 037[38]	119 271[38]	123 766[38]	979[39]	...	...	...	...
Matsusaka	168 017[38]	80 960[38]	87 057[38]	624[39]	...	...	...	...
Matsuyama	517 231[38]	241 586[38]	275 645[38]	429[39]	...	...	...	...
Mihara	100 509[38]	47 865[38]	52 644[38]	471[39]	...	...	...	...
Minoh	129 895[38]	62 468[38]	67 427[38]	48[39]	...	...	...	...
Misato	131 415[38]	66 747[38]	64 668[38]	30[39]	...	...	...	...
Mishima	111 838[38]	54 911[38]	56 927[38]	62[39]	...	...	...	...
Mitaka	186 083[38]	91 997[38]	94 086[38]	17[39]	...	...	...	...
Mito	268 750[38]	130 918[38]	137 832[38]	217[39]	...	...	...	...
Miyakonojo	169 602[38]	79 553[38]	90 049[38]	653[39]	...	...	...	...
Miyazaki	400 583[38]	187 619[38]	212 964[38]	645[39]	...	...	...	...
Moriguchi	146 697[38]	71 272[38]	75 425[38]	13[39]	...	...	...	...
Morioka	298 348[38]	141 566[38]	156 782[38]	886[39]	...	...	...	...
Musashino	138 734[38]	66 406[38]	72 328[38]	11[39]	...	...	...	...
Nagahama	124 131[38]	60 973[38]	63 158[38]	681[39]	...	...	...	...

| Continent, country or area, date, code[a] and city
Continent, pays ou zone, date, code[a] et ville | City proper - Ville proprement dite | | | | Urban agglomeration - Agglomération urbaine | | | |
| | Population | | | Surface area - Superficie (km²) | Population | | | Surface area - Superficie (km²) |
	Both sexes - Les deux sexes	Male - Masculin	Female - Féminin		Both sexes - Les deux sexes	Male - Masculin	Female - Féminin	
ASIA - ASIE								
Japan - Japon								
1 X 2010 (CDJC)								
Nagano	381 511[38]	184 128[38]	197 383[38]	835[39]	...	...	...	...
Nagaoka	282 674[38]	137 780[38]	144 894[38]	891[39]	...	...	...	...
Nagareyama	163 984[38]	81 721[38]	82 263[38]	35[39]	...	...	...	...
Nagasaki	443 766[38]	203 574[38]	240 192[38]	406[39]	...	...	...	...
Nagoya	2 263 894[38]	1 116 211[38]	1 147 683[38]	326[39]	...	...	...	...
Naha	315 954[38]	151 848[38]	164 106[38]	39[39]	...	...	...	...
Nara	366 591[38]	171 410[38]	195 181[38]	277[39]	...	...	...	...
Narashino	164 530[38]	83 184[38]	81 346[38]	21[39]	...	...	...	...
Narita	128 933[38]	64 852[38]	64 081[38]	214[39]	...	...	...	...
Nasushiobara	117 812[38]	58 402[38]	59 410[38]	593[39]	...	...	...	...
Neyagawa	238 204[38]	116 132[38]	122 072[38]	25[39]	...	...	...	...
Niigata	811 901[38]	390 406[38]	421 495[38]	726[39]	...	...	...	...
Niihama	121 735[38]	58 219[38]	63 516[38]	234[39]	...	...	...	...
Niiza	158 777[38]	79 416[38]	79 361[38]	23[39]	...	...	...	...
Nishinomiya	482 640[38]	227 660[38]	254 980[38]	99[39]	...	...	...	...
Nishio	106 823[38]	54 066[38]	52 757[38]	76[39]	...	...	...	...
Nishitokyo	196 511[38]	96 437[38]	100 074[38]	16[39]	...	...	...	...
Nobeoka	131 182[38]	61 457[38]	69 725[38]	868[39]	...	...	...	...
Noda	155 491[38]	77 963[38]	77 528[38]	104[39]	...	...	...	...
Numazu	202 304[38]	99 184[38]	103 120[38]	187[39]	...	...	...	...
Obihiro	168 057[38]	80 584[38]	87 473[38]	619[39]	...	...	...	...
Odawara	198 327[38]	96 839[38]	101 488[38]	114[39]	...	...	...	...
Ogaki	161 160[38]	78 282[38]	82 878[38]	207[39]	...	...	...	...
Oita	474 094[38]	227 608[38]	246 486[38]	501[39]	...	...	...	...
Okayama	709 584[38]	341 158[38]	368 426[38]	790[39]	...	...	...	...
Okazaki	372 357[38]	187 649[38]	184 708[38]	387[39]	...	...	...	...
Okinawa	130 249[38]	63 195[38]	67 054[38]	49[39]	...	...	...	...
Ome	139 339[38]	69 742[38]	69 597[38]	103[39]	...	...	...	...
Omuta	123 638[38]	56 215[38]	67 423[38]	82[39]	...	...	...	...
Onomichi	145 202[38]	69 283[38]	75 919[38]	285[39]	...	...	...	...
Osaka	2 665 314[38]	1 293 798[38]	1 371 516[38]	222[39]	...	...	...	...
Osaki	135 147[38]	65 624[38]	69 523[38]	797[39]	...	...	...	...
Oshu	124 746[38]	59 935[38]	64 811[38]	993[39]	...	...	...	...
Ota	216 465[38]	109 204[38]	107 261[38]	176[39]	...	...	...	...
Otaru	131 928[38]	59 514[38]	72 414[38]	243[39]	...	...	...	...
Otsu	337 634[38]	163 250[38]	174 384[38]	464[39]	...	...	...	...
Oyama	164 454[38]	82 825[38]	81 629[38]	172[39]	...	...	...	...
Saga	237 506[38]	112 173[38]	125 333[38]	431[39]	...	...	...	...
Sagamihara	717 544[38]	361 394[38]	356 150[38]	329[39]	...	...	...	...
Saijo	112 091[38]	53 757[38]	58 334[38]	509[39]	...	...	...	...
Saitama	1 222 434[38]	611 236[38]	611 198[38]	217[39]	...	...	...	...
Sakado	101 700[38]	51 155[38]	50 545[38]	41[39]	...	...	...	...
Sakai	841 966[38]	404 756[38]	437 210[38]	150[39]	...	...	...	...
Sakata	111 151[38]	52 610[38]	58 541[38]	603[39]	...	...	...	...
Saku	100 552[38]	49 090[38]	51 462[38]	424[39]	...	...	...	...
Sakura	172 183[38]	84 246[38]	87 937[38]	104[39]	...	...	...	...
Sanda	114 216[38]	55 175[38]	59 041[38]	210[39]	...	...	...	...
Sanjo	102 292[38]	49 368[38]	52 924[38]	432[39]	...	...	...	...
Sano	121 249[38]	59 499[38]	61 750[38]	356[39]	...	...	...	...
Sapporo	1 913 545[38]	896 850[38]	1 016 695[38]	1 121[39]	...	...	...	...
Sasebo	261 101[38]	122 430[38]	138 671[38]	426[39]	...	...	...	...
Sayama	155 727[38]	78 637[38]	77 090[38]	49[39]	...	...	...	...
Sendai	1 045 986[38]	507 833[38]	538 153[38]	784[39]	...	...	...	...
Seto	132 224[38]	65 123[38]	67 101[38]	112[39]	...	...	...	...
Shibata	101 202[38]	48 606[38]	52 596[38]	533[39]	...	...	...	...
Shimada	100 276[38]	48 876[38]	51 400[38]	316[39]	...	...	...	...
Shimonoseki	280 947[38]	130 105[38]	150 842[38]	716[39]	...	...	...	...
Shizuoka	716 197[38]	348 609[38]	367 588[38]	1 412[39]	...	...	...	...
Shunan	149 487[38]	72 150[38]	77 337[38]	656[39]	...	...	...	...

8. Population of capital cities and cities of 100 000 or more inhabitants: latest available year, 1995 - 2014
Population des capitales et des villes de 100 000 habitants ou plus : dernière année disponible, 1995 - 2014 (continued - suite)

Continent, country or area, date, code[a] and city Continent, pays ou zone, date, code[a] et ville	City proper - Ville proprement dite				Urban agglomeration - Agglomération urbaine			
	Population			Surface area - Superficie (km²)	Population			Surface area - Superficie (km²)
	Both sexes - Les deux sexes	Male - Masculin	Female - Féminin		Both sexes - Les deux sexes	Male - Masculin	Female - Féminin	
ASIA - ASIE								
Japan - Japon 1 X 2010 (CDJC)								
Soka	243 855[38]	124 553[38]	119 302[38]	27[39]	...	...	...	...
Suita	355 798[38]	171 769[38]	184 029[38]	36[39]	...	...	...	...
Suzuka	199 293[38]	99 925[38]	99 368[38]	195[39]	...	...	...	...
Tachikawa	179 668[38]	89 470[38]	90 198[38]	24[39]	...	...	...	...
Tajimi	112 595[38]	54 342[38]	58 253[38]	91[39]	...	...	...	...
Takamatsu	419 429[38]	203 312[38]	216 117[38]	375[39]	...	...	...	...
Takaoka	176 061[38]	84 292[38]	91 769[38]	209[39]	...	...	...	...
Takarazuka	225 700[38]	105 289[38]	120 411[38]	102[39]	...	...	...	...
Takasaki	371 302[38]	181 667[38]	189 635[38]	459[39]	...	...	...	...
Takatsuki	357 359[38]	171 927[38]	185 432[38]	105[39]	...	...	...	...
Tama	147 648[38]	73 083[38]	74 565[38]	21[39]	...	...	...	...
Tochigi	139 262[38]	67 859[38]	71 403[38]	253[39]	...	...	...	...
Toda	123 079[38]	64 080[38]	58 999[38]	18[39]	...	...	...	...
Tokai	107 690[38]	56 305[38]	51 385[38]	43[39]	...	...	...	...
Tokorozawa	341 924[38]	170 598[38]	171 326[38]	72[39]	...	...	...	...
Tokushima	264 548[38]	125 619[38]	138 929[38]	192[39]	...	...	...	...
TOKYO	8 945 695[40]	4 412 050[40]	4 533 645[40]	622[39]	...	...	...	...
Tomakomai	173 320[38]	84 687[38]	88 633[38]	561[39]	...	...	...	...
Tondabayashi	119 576[38]	56 778[38]	62 798[38]	40[39]	...	...	...	...
Toride	109 651[38]	54 054[38]	55 597[38]	70[39]	...	...	...	...
Tottori	197 449[38]	95 959[38]	101 490[38]	766[39]	...	...	...	...
Toyama	421 953[38]	204 515[38]	217 438[38]	1 242[39]	...	...	...	...
Toyohashi	376 665[38]	188 200[38]	188 465[38]	261[39]	...	...	...	...
Toyokawa	181 928[38]	90 328[38]	91 600[38]	161[39]	...	...	...	...
Toyonaka	389 341[38]	185 103[38]	204 238[38]	36[39]	...	...	...	...
Toyota	421 487[38]	221 198[38]	200 289[38]	918[39]	...	...	...	...
Tsu	285 746[38]	138 643[38]	147 103[38]	711[39]	...	...	...	...
Tsuchiura	143 839[38]	71 600[38]	72 239[38]	123[39]	...	...	...	...
Tsukuba	214 590[38]	110 230[38]	104 360[38]	284[39]	...	...	...	...
Tsuruoka	136 623[38]	64 846[38]	71 777[38]	1 312[39]	...	...	...	...
Tsuyama	106 788[38]	50 787[38]	56 001[38]	506[39]	...	...	...	...
Ube	173 772[38]	83 000[38]	90 772[38]	288[39]	...	...	...	...
Ueda	159 597[38]	77 589[38]	82 008[38]	552[39]	...	...	...	...
Uji	189 609[38]	91 971[38]	97 638[38]	68[39]	...	...	...	...
Urasoe	110 351[38]	53 948[38]	56 403[38]	19[39]	...	...	...	...
Urayasu	164 877[38]	82 177[38]	82 700[38]	17[39]	...	...	...	...
Uruma	116 979[38]	58 198[38]	58 781[38]	86[39]	...	...	...	...
Utsunomiya	511 739[38]	254 605[38]	257 134[38]	417[39]	...	...	...	...
Wakayama	370 364[38]	174 104[38]	196 260[38]	209[39]	...	...	...	...
Yachiyo	189 781[38]	93 688[38]	96 093[38]	51[39]	...	...	...	...
Yaizu	143 249[38]	69 901[38]	73 348[38]	71[39]	...	...	...	...
Yamagata	254 244[38]	121 433[38]	132 811[38]	381[39]	...	...	...	...
Yamaguchi	196 628[38]	92 997[38]	103 631[38]	1 023[39]	...	...	...	...
Yamato	228 186[38]	114 700[38]	113 486[38]	27[39]	...	...	...	...
Yao	271 460[38]	131 121[38]	140 339[38]	42[39]	...	...	...	...
Yatsushiro	132 266[38]	61 446[38]	70 820[38]	681[39]	...	...	...	...
Yokkaichi	307 766[38]	152 580[38]	155 186[38]	206[39]	...	...	...	...
Yokohama	3 688 773[38]	1 849 767[38]	1 839 006[38]	437[39]	...	...	...	...
Yokosuka	418 325[38]	208 966[38]	209 359[38]	101[39]	...	...	...	...
Yonago	148 271[38]	70 133[38]	78 138[38]	132[39]	...	...	...	...
Zama	129 436[38]	65 448[38]	63 988[38]	18[39]	...	...	...	...
Jordan - Jordanie 31 XII 2014 (ESDF)								
AMMAN	2 376 022	1 220 932	1 155 090	...	...	...	...	...
Aqaba	114 088	64 010	50 078	...	...	...	...	...
Irbid	320 794	164 680	156 114	...	...	...	...	...
Russiefa	296 192	154 058	142 134	...	...	...	...	...
Zarqa	514 026	265 597	248 429	...	...	...	...	...

8. Population of capital cities and cities of 100 000 or more inhabitants: latest available year, 1995 - 2014
Population des capitales et des villes de 100 000 habitants ou plus : dernière année disponible, 1995 - 2014 (continued - suite)

Continent, country or area, date, code[a] and city / Continent, pays ou zone, date, code[a] et ville	City proper - Ville proprement dite				Urban agglomeration - Agglomération urbaine			
	Population			Surface area - Superficie (km²)	Population			Surface area - Superficie (km²)
	Both sexes - Les deux sexes	Male - Masculin	Female - Féminin		Both sexes - Les deux sexes	Male - Masculin	Female - Féminin	
ASIA - ASIE								
Kazakhstan								
1 I 2013 (ESDF)								
Aktau	181 541	87 636	93 905	29	184 175	89 043	95 132	...
Aktobe	377 752	176 438	201 314	234	428 024	201 192	226 832	...
Almaty	1 507 509	687 027	820 482	319	...	...	...	...
ASTANA	814 435	393 158	421 277	710	...	...	...	...
Atirau	209 699	99 168	110 531	347	280 634	134 498	146 136	...
Ekibastuz	139 778	66 234	73 544	31	149 132	71 017	78 115	...
Karaganda	484 510	221 248	263 262	50	484 768	221 388	263 380	...
Koktshetau	143 267	66 077	77 190	43	154 000	71 225	82 775	...
Kustanai	221 943	99 341	122 602	21	221 943	99 341	122 602	...
Kyzylorda	238 840	116 031	122 809	236	260 524	127 119	133 405	...
Pavlodar	339 153	153 922	185 231	56	352 693	160 532	192 161	...
Petropavlovsk (Severo- Kazakhstanskaya oblast)	207 399	93 015	114 384	22	208 362	93 491	114 871	...
Rudni	127 712	59 700	68 012	19	128 234	59 947	68 287	...
Semipalatinsk	315 750	146 133	169 617	9	337 633	156 958	180 675	...
Shimkent	682 565	323 899	358 666	36	682 565	323 899	358 666	...
Taldykorgan	135 184	62 277	72 907	39	158 984	74 068	84 916	...
Taraz	351 353	164 440	186 913	13	351 353	164 440	186 913	...
Temirtau	182 551	84 577	97 974	30	182 551	84 577	97 974	...
Turkestan	155 552	77 393	78 159	...	248 773	124 719	124 054	...
Uralsk	273 359	125 951	147 408	71	278 086	128 276	149 810	...
Ust-Kamenogorsk	314 069	141 596	172 473	54	325 803	147 288	178 515	...
Zhanaozen	106 220	52 515	53 705	...	130 652	64 533	66 119	...
Kuwait - Koweït								
1 VII 2010 (ESDF)								
Farwanyiah	101 867	68 326	33 541	...	...	...	...	...
Hawalli	127 982	84 506	43 477	...	...	...	...	...
Jaleeb Al-Shuykh	219 629	180 786	38 843	...	...	...	...	...
Salmiya	177 009	103 119	73 890	...	...	...	...	...
South Kheetan	113 426	104 655	8 770	...	...	...	...	...
Kyrgyzstan - Kirghizstan								
1 VII 2014 (ESDJ)								
BISHKEK	912 454[41]	424 792[41]	487 662[41]	...	926 512[41]	431 743[41]	494 769[41]	127
Osh	240 891[41]	115 094[41]	125 797[41]	...	267 748[41]	128 881[41]	138 867[41]	182
Lao People's Democratic Republic - République démocratique populaire lao[42]								
1 VII 2014 (ESDF)								
VIENTIANE	...	...	...	...	828 494	414 217	414 277	...
Lebanon - Liban[43]								
1 X 2011 (SSDF)								
BEIRUT	...	...	...	...	363 033	179 737	183 296	...
Malaysia - Malaisie[44]								
1 VII 2014 (ESDJ)								
Alor Setar	123 994	...	...	...	...	...	...	...
Bintulu Townland	122 329	...	...	...	...	...	...	...
Georgetown	206 970	...	...	...	...	...	...	...
Klang	259 151	...	...	...	...	...	...	...
Kota Kinabalu	217 711	...	...	...	...	...	...	...
KUALA LUMPUR	1 698 250	...	...	...	...	...	...	...
Kuala Terengganu	210 903	...	...	...	...	...	...	...
Kuantan	395 725	...	...	...	...	...	...	...
Kuching "Bandaraya Kuching Utara dan Selatan"	149 424	...	...	...	...	...	...	...
Majlis Perbandaran Ipoh	465 166	...	...	...	...	...	...	...
MB Johor Bahru (Johor Bahru)	469 239	...	...	...	...	...	...	...
Miri Townland	139 765	...	...	...	...	...	...	...
MP Kota Bharu	300 984	...	...	...	...	...	...	...
Petaling Jaya	195 797	...	...	...	...	...	...	...
Sandakan	172 062	...	...	...	...	...	...	...
Selayang Baru	159 184	...	...	...	...	...	...	...
Seremban	349 933	...	...	...	...	...	...	...
Shah Alam	174 764	...	...	...	...	...	...	...
Sibu "Majlis Perbandaran Sibu"	169 229	...	...	...	...	...	...	...

8. Population of capital cities and cities of 100 000 or more inhabitants: latest available year, 1995 - 2014
Population des capitales et des villes de 100 000 habitants ou plus : dernière année disponible, 1995 - 2014 (continued - suite)

Continent, country or area, date, code[a] and city / Continent, pays ou zone, date, code[a] et ville	City proper - Ville proprement dite				Urban agglomeration - Agglomération urbaine			
	Population			Surface area - Superficie (km²)	Population			Surface area - Superficie (km²)
	Both sexes - Les deux sexes	Male - Masculin	Female - Féminin		Both sexes - Les deux sexes	Male - Masculin	Female - Féminin	
ASIA - ASIE								
Malaysia - Malaisie[44]								
1 VII 2014 (ESDJ)								
Subang Jaya	*189 535*	...	...	...	...	...	...	...
Sungai Petani	*189 038*	...	...	...	...	...	...	...
Taiping	*231 812*	...	...	...	...	...	...	...
Tawau	*123 444*	...	...	...	...	...	...	...
Maldives								
20 IX 2014* (CDFC)								
MALÉ	133 019	66 155	66 864	2	...	...	...	...
Mongolia - Mongolie								
1 VII 2014 (ESDF)								
Hovsgol	122 361	60 854	61 508	101	...	...	...	...
Ovorhangay	107 307	53 908	53 399	63	...	...	...	...
Selenge	104 702	52 869	51 833	41	...	...	...	...
ULAANBAATAR	1 367 508	646 184	721 325	5	...	...	...	...
Myanmar								
29 III 2014* (CDFC)								
Bago	491 130	235 612	255 518	...	...	...	...	...
Dawei	125 239	59 941	65 298	...	...	...	...	...
Hpa-an	421 415	203 933	217 482	...	...	...	...	...
Loikaw	128 837	63 404	65 433	...	...	...	...	...
Magway	288 883	134 957	153 926	...	...	...	...	...
Mandalay	1 225 133	597 747	627 386	...	...	...	...	...
Mawlamyine	288 120	138 625	149 495	...	...	...	...	...
Monywa	371 963	172 303	199 660	...	...	...	...	...
Myitkyina	305 347	147 711	157 636	...	...	...	...	...
NAY PYI TAW[45]	...	...	...	...	1 158 367	565 181	593 186	...
Pathein	286 684	137 723	148 961	...	...	...	...	...
Sittway	149 348	71 628	77 720	...	...	...	...	...
Taunggyi	380 665	185 694	194 971	...	...	...	...	...
Yangon	5 209 541	2 468 725	2 740 816	...	...	...	...	...
Nepal - Népal								
22 VI 2011 (CDJC)								
Bharatpur	147 777	74 205	73 572	...	...	...	...	...
Bhimdutta	106 666	53 098	53 568	...	...	...	...	...
Biratnagar	204 949	104 935	100 014	58	...	...	...	...
Birgunj	139 068	75 382	63 686	21	...	...	...	...
Butwal	120 982	60 870	60 112	...	...	...	...	...
Dhangadhi	104 047	53 237	50 810	...	...	...	...	...
Dharan	119 915	57 562	62 353	...	...	...	...	...
KATHMANDU	1 003 285	533 127	470 158	49	...	...	...	...
Lalitpur	226 728	117 932	108 796	15	...	...	...	...
Pokhara	264 991	133 318	131 673	55	...	...	...	...
Oman								
7 XII 2003 (CDFC)								
As Seeb	223 449	128 068	95 381	...	...	...	...	...
As Suwayq	101 122	54 997	46 125	...	...	...	...	...
Bawshar	150 420	91 687	58 733	...	...	...	...	...
MUSCAT	24 893	13 695	11 198	...	...	...	...	...
Mutrah	153 526	96 878	56 648	...	...	...	...	...
Salalah	156 530	92 489	64 041	...	...	...	...	...
Sohar	104 312	57 695	46 617	...	...	...	...	...
Pakistan[46]								
2 III 1998 (CDFC)								
Abbotabad	106 101	61 698	44 403	...	...	...	...	...
Bahawalnagar	111 313	57 779	53 534	...	...	...	...	...
Bahawalpur	408 395	222 228	186 167	...	...	...	...	...
Burewala	152 097	78 726	73 371	...	...	...	...	...
Chiniot	172 522	90 474	82 048	...	...	...	...	...
Chishtian	102 287	52 427	49 860	...	...	...	...	...
Dadu	102 550	53 508	49 042	...	...	...	...	...
Daska	102 883	52 359	50 524	...	...	...	...	...
Dera Ghazi Khan	190 542	98 738	91 804	...	...	...	...	...
Faisalabad (Lyallpur)	2 008 861	1 053 085	955 776	...	...	...	...	...
Gojra	117 872	60 598	57 274	...	...	...	...	...

Continent, country or area, date, code[a] and city / Continent, pays ou zone, date, code[a] et ville	City proper - Ville proprement dite				Urban agglomeration - Agglomération urbaine			
	Population			Surface area - Superficie (km²)	Population			Surface area - Superficie (km²)
	Both sexes - Les deux sexes	Male - Masculin	Female - Féminin		Both sexes - Les deux sexes	Male - Masculin	Female - Féminin	
ASIA - ASIE								
Pakistan[46]								
2 III 1998 (CDFC)								
Gujranwala	1 132 509	588 512	543 997	...	...	...	...	...
Gujrat	251 792	128 524	123 268	...	...	...	...	...
Hafizabad	133 678	69 231	64 447	...	...	...	...	...
Hyderabad	1 166 894	612 283	554 611	...	...	...	...	...
ISLAMABAD	529 180	290 717	238 463	...	...	...	...	...
Jacobabad	138 780	71 854	66 926	...	...	...	...	...
Jaranwala	106 785	55 619	51 166	...	...	...	...	...
Jhang	293 366	153 123	140 243	...	...	...	...	...
Jhelum	147 392	79 169	68 223	...	...	...	...	...
Kamoke	152 288	78 848	73 440	...	...	...	...	...
Karachi	9 339 023	5 029 900	4 309 123	...	...	...	...	...
Kasur	245 321	129 553	115 768	...	...	...	...	...
Khairpur	105 637	55 358	50 279	...	...	...	...	...
Khanewal	133 986	69 145	64 841	...	...	...	...	...
Khanpur	120 382	62 371	58 011	...	...	...	...	...
Kohat	126 627	71 505	55 122	...	...	...	...	...
Lahore	5 143 495	2 707 220	2 436 275	...	...	...	...	...
Larkana	270 283	140 622	129 661	...	...	...	...	...
Mangora	173 868	91 742	82 126	...	...	...	...	...
Mardan	245 926	129 247	116 679	...	...	...	...	...
Mirpur Khas	189 671	97 940	91 731	...	...	...	...	...
Multan	1 197 384	637 911	559 473	...	...	...	...	...
Muridke	111 951	58 210	53 741	...	...	...	...	...
Muzaffargharh	123 404	66 556	56 848	...	...	...	...	...
Nawabshah	189 244	98 116	91 128	...	...	...	...	...
Okara	201 815	104 245	97 570	...	...	...	...	...
Pakpattan	109 033	56 676	52 357	...	...	...	...	...
Peshawar	982 816	521 901	460 915	...	...	...	...	...
Quetta	565 137	307 759	257 378	...	...	...	...	...
Rahimyar Khan	233 537	121 446	112 091	...	...	...	...	...
Rawalpindi	1 409 768	750 530	659 238	...	...	...	...	...
Sadiqabad	144 391	75 217	69 174	...	...	...	...	...
Sahiwal	208 778	108 992	99 786	...	...	...	...	...
Sargodha	458 440	239 837	218 603	...	...	...	...	...
Shakkarpur	134 883	69 713	65 170	...	...	...	...	...
Sheikhu Pura	280 263	146 739	133 524	...	...	...	...	...
Sialkote	421 502	227 398	194 104	...	...	...	...	...
Sukkur	335 551	175 679	159 872	...	...	...	...	...
Tandoadam	104 907	54 670	50 237	...	...	...	...	...
Wah Cantonment	198 891	104 230	94 661	...	...	...	...	...
Philippines								
1 V 2010 (CDJC)								
Angeles	326 336	161 791	164 545	60	...	...	...	...
Angono	102 407	50 859	51 548	26	...	...	...	...
Antipolo	677 741	338 392	339 349	306	...	...	...	...
Apalit	101 537	51 788	49 749	61	...	...	...	...
Arayat	121 348	61 593	59 755	134	...	...	...	...
Bacolod	511 820	251 910	259 910	163	...	...	...	...
Bacoor City	520 216	255 375	264 841	46	...	...	...	...
Bago	163 045	84 114	78 931	401	...	...	...	...
Baguio	318 676	156 259	162 417	58	...	...	...	...
Baliuag	143 565	71 947	71 618	45	...	...	...	...
Batangas	305 607	152 499	153 108	283	...	...	...	...
Bayambang	111 521	56 423	55 098	144	...	...	...	...
Bayawan (Tulong)	114 074	59 336	54 738	699	...	...	...	...
Baybay	102 841	52 935	49 906	459	...	...	...	...
Biñan	283 396	140 351	143 045	44	...	...	...	...
Binangonan	249 872	125 027	124 845	66	...	...	...	...
Bocaue	106 407	53 248	53 159	32	...	...	...	...
Butuan	309 709	157 204	152 505	817	...	...	...	...
Cabanatuan	272 676	136 432	136 244	283	...	...	...	...
Cabuyao	248 436	123 110	125 326	43	...	...	...	...
Cadiz	151 500	78 049	73 451	525	...	...	...	...

Continent, country or area, date, code[a] and city / Continent, pays ou zone, date, code[a] et ville	City proper - Ville proprement dite				Urban agglomeration - Agglomération urbaine			
	Population			Surface area - Superficie (km²)	Population			Surface area - Superficie (km²)
	Both sexes - Les deux sexes	Male - Masculin	Female - Féminin		Both sexes - Les deux sexes	Male - Masculin	Female - Féminin	
ASIA - ASIE								
Philippines								
1 V 2010 (CDJC)								
Cagayan de Oro	602 088	300 853	301 235	413	...	...	...	...
Cainta	311 845	152 400	159 445	43	...	...	...	...
Calamba	389 377	191 773	197 604	150	...	...	...	...
Calapan	124 173	62 588	61 585	250	...	...	...	...
Calbayog	172 778	88 540	84 238	881	...	...	...	...
Calumpit	101 068	50 840	50 228	56	...	...	...	...
Candaba	102 399	51 815	50 584	176	...	...	...	...
Candelaria	110 570	55 137	55 433	129	...	...	...	...
Capas	125 852	64 479	61 373	376	...	...	...	...
Carcar	107 323	54 718	52 605	117	...	...	...	...
Cauayan	122 335	62 362	59 973	336	...	...	...	...
Cavite City	101 120	49 710	51 410	11	...	...	...	...
Cebu	866 171	426 738	439 433	315	...	...	...	...
Concepcion	139 832	71 709	68 123	243	...	...	...	...
Consolacion	106 649	53 204	53 445	147	...	...	...	...
Cotabato	271 786	133 457	138 329	176	...	...	...	...
Dagupan	163 676	81 788	81 888	37	...	...	...	...
Danao City	119 252	60 251	59 001	107	...	...	...	...
Daraga (Locsin)	115 804	58 060	57 744	119	...	...	...	...
Dasmariñas	575 817	283 823	291 994	90	...	...	...	...
Davao	1 449 296	724 565	724 731	2 444	...	...	...	...
Digos	149 891	75 664	74 227	287	...	...	...	...
Dipolog	120 460	60 243	60 217	241	...	...	...	...
Dumaguete	120 883	58 711	62 172	34	...	...	...	...
Floridablanca	110 846	56 249	54 597	175	...	...	...	...
Gapan	101 488	51 331	50 157	164	...	...	...	...
Gen. Mariano Alvarez	138 540	69 226	69 314	9	...	...	...	...
General Santos	538 086	272 216	265 870	493	...	...	...	...
General Trias	243 322	118 771	124 551	90	...	...	...	...
Gingoog	117 908	60 628	57 280	568	...	...	...	...
Glan	106 518	54 919	51 599	534	...	...	...	...
Guagua	111 199	56 191	55 008	49	...	...	...	...
Guimba	104 894	53 633	51 261	245	...	...	...	...
Hagonoy	125 689	63 231	62 458	103	...	...	...	...
Himamaylan	103 006	53 254	49 752	367	...	...	...	...
Ilagan	135 174	69 256	65 918	1 166	...	...	...	...
Iligan	322 821	161 924	160 897	813	...	...	...	...
Iloilo	424 619	207 301	217 318	78	...	...	...	...
Imus City	301 624	145 358	156 266	172	...	...	...	...
Iriga	105 919	53 452	52 467	137	...	...	...	...
Jolo	118 307	58 271	60 036	126	...	...	...	...
Kabankalan	167 666	86 721	80 945	697	...	...	...	...
Kalookan (Caloocan)	1 489 040	742 113	746 927	56	...	...	...	...
Kidapawan	125 447	63 842	61 605	358	...	...	...	...
Koronadal	158 273	79 987	78 286	277	...	...	...	...
La Trinidad	107 188	52 999	54 189	70	...	...	...	...
Laoag	104 904	51 581	53 323	116	...	...	...	...
Lapu-Lapu	350 467	172 839	177 628	58	...	...	...	...
Las Piñas	552 573	268 114	284 459	33	...	...	...	...
Legazpi	182 201	91 174	91 027	154	...	...	...	...
Libmanan	100 002	51 549	48 453	343	...	...	...	...
Liloan	100 500	50 317	50 183	46	...	...	...	...
Lipa	283 468	141 822	141 646	209	...	...	...	...
Los Baños	101 884	50 245	51 639	54	...	...	...	...
Lubao	150 843	76 467	74 376	156	...	...	...	...
Lucena City	246 392	122 774	123 618	80	...	...	...	...
Mabalacat	215 610	107 996	107 614	83	...	...	...	...
Magalang	103 597	52 858	50 739	97	...	...	...	...
Makati	529 039	249 509	279 530	22	...	...	...	...
Malabalay	153 085	79 366	73 719	969	...	...	...	...
Malabon	353 337	176 450	176 887	16	...	...	...	...
Malasiqui	123 566	62 599	60 967	131	...	...	...	...
Malita	109 568	56 155	53 413	883	...	...	...	...

8. Population of capital cities and cities of 100 000 or more inhabitants: latest available year, 1995 - 2014
Population des capitales et des villes de 100 000 habitants ou plus : dernière année disponible, 1995 - 2014 (continued - suite)

Continent, country or area, date, code[a] and city Continent, pays ou zone, date, code[a] et ville	City proper - Ville proprement dite				Urban agglomeration - Agglomération urbaine			
	Population			Surface area - Superficie (km²)	Population			Surface area - Superficie (km²)
	Both sexes - Les deux sexes	Male - Masculin	Female - Féminin		Both sexes - Les deux sexes	Male - Masculin	Female - Féminin	

ASIA - ASIE

Philippines
1 V 2010 (CDJC)

Malolos	234 945	117 260	117 685	67	...	...	...	...
Mandaluyong	328 699	162 235	166 464	9	...	...	...	...
Mandaue	331 320	164 513	166 807	25	...	...	...	...
MANILA	1 652 171	811 788	840 383	25	...	...	...	...
Marawi	187 106	91 003	96 103	88	...	...	...	...
Marikina	424 150	206 821	217 329	22	...	...	...	...
Marilao	185 624	92 323	93 301	34	...	...	...	...
Mariveles	112 707	56 448	56 259	154	...	...	...	...
Mati	126 143	64 742	61 401	589	...	...	...	...
Mexico	146 851	74 426	72 425	117	...	...	...	...
Meycauayan	199 154	99 517	99 637	32	...	...	...	...
Midsayap	134 170	68 475	65 695	290	...	...	...	...
Minglanilla	113 178	57 598	55 580	66	...	...	...	...
Muntinlupa	459 941	233 606	226 335	40	...	...	...	...
Naga (Camarines Sur)	174 931	86 055	88 876	84	...	...	...	...
Naga (Cebu)	101 571	51 551	50 020	102	...	...	...	...
Nasugbu	122 483	61 972	60 511	279	...	...	...	...
Navotas	249 131	125 924	123 207	9	...	...	...	...
Norzagaray	103 095	52 419	50 676	310	...	...	...	...
Olongapo	221 178	109 316	111 862	185	...	...	...	...
Ormoc	191 200	97 722	93 478	614	...	...	...	...
Ozamis	131 527	65 963	65 564	170	...	...	...	...
Pagadian	186 852	93 264	93 588	379	...	...	...	...
Panabo	174 364	88 643	85 721	251	...	...	...	...
Paranaque	588 126	286 371	301 755	47	...	...	...	...
Pasay	392 869	192 097	200 772	14	...	...	...	...
Pasig	669 773	326 875	342 898	48	...	...	...	...
Philippines: Ligao	104 914	53 510	51 404	247	...	...	...	...
Pikit	113 014	56 762	56 252	605	...	...	...	...
Plaridel	101 441	50 554	50 887	32	...	...	...	...
Polomolok	138 273	70 501	67 772	340	...	...	...	...
Porac	111 441	56 693	54 748	314	...	...	...	...
Puerto Princesa	222 673	114 837	107 836	2 381	...	...	...	...
Quezon City	2 761 720	1 349 016	1 412 704	172	...	...	...	...
Rodriguez (Montalban)	280 904	141 127	139 777	173	...	...	...	...
Rosario	105 561	53 192	52 369	227	...	...	...	...
Roxas	156 197	77 693	78 504	95	...	...	...	...
Sagay City	140 740	72 410	68 330	330	...	...	...	...
San Carlos (Negros Occidental)	129 981	66 600	63 381	452	...	...	...	...
San Carlos (Pangasinan)	175 103	88 715	86 388	169	...	...	...	...
San Fernando (La Union)	114 963	57 002	57 961	103	...	...	...	...
San Fernando (Pampanga)	285 912	143 738	142 174	68	...	...	...	...
San Jose (Occidental Mindoro)	131 188	66 824	64 364	447	...	...	...	...
San Jose City (Nueva Ecija)	129 424	65 867	63 557	186	...	...	...	...
San Jose Del Monte	454 553	227 047	227 506	106	...	...	...	...
San Juan	121 430	54 796	66 634	6	...	...	...	...
San Mateo	205 255	101 991	103 264	55	...	...	...	...
San Miguel	142 854	72 199	70 655	231	...	...	...	...
San Pablo	248 890	123 210	125 680	198	...	...	...	...
San Pedro	294 310	144 967	149 343	24	...	...	...	...
Santa Cruz	110 943	55 794	55 149	39	...	...	...	...
Santa Maria	218 351	109 718	108 633	91	...	...	...	...
Santa Rosa	284 670	137 821	146 849	55	...	...	...	...
Santiago	132 804	67 134	65 670	256	...	...	...	...
Santo Tomas (Davao Del Norte)	109 269	56 703	52 566	222	...	...	...	...
Santo Tomas (Batangas)	124 740	61 500	63 240	95	...	...	...	...
Sariaya	138 894	70 418	68 476	212	...	...	...	...
Silang	213 490	105 117	108 373	209	...	...	...	...
Silay	120 999	61 335	59 664	215	...	...	...	...
Sorsogon	155 144	78 175	76 969	276	...	...	...	...
Surigao	140 540	70 424	70 116	245	...	...	...	...
Tabaco	125 083	63 437	61 646	117	...	...	...	...
Tabuk	103 912	52 894	51 018	700	...	...	...	...

8. Population of capital cities and cities of 100 000 or more inhabitants: latest available year, 1995 - 2014
Population des capitales et des villes de 100 000 habitants ou plus : dernière année disponible, 1995 - 2014 (continued - suite)

Continent, country or area, date, code[a] and city / Continent, pays ou zone, date, code[a] et ville	City proper - Ville proprement dite				Urban agglomeration - Agglomération urbaine			
	Population			Surface area - Superficie (km²)	Population			Surface area - Superficie (km²)
	Both sexes - Les deux sexes	Male - Masculin	Female - Féminin		Both sexes - Les deux sexes	Male - Masculin	Female - Féminin	
ASIA - ASIE								
Philippines								
1 V 2010 (CDJC)								
Tacloban	221 174	110 568	110 606	202	...	...	...	...
Taguig	644 473	319 916	324 557	45	...	...	...	...
Tagum	242 801	121 863	120 938	196	...	...	...	...
Talavera	112 515	56 975	55 540	141	...	...	...	...
Talisay	200 772	99 951	100 821	40	...	...	...	...
Tanauan	152 393	75 642	76 751	107	...	...	...	...
Tanza	188 755	93 634	95 121	96	...	...	...	...
Tarlac	318 332	161 365	156 967	275	...	...	...	...
Taytay	288 956	144 538	144 418	39	...	...	...	...
Toledo	157 078	80 619	76 459	216	...	...	...	...
Trece Martires	104 559	52 291	52 268	39	...	...	...	...
Tuguegarao	138 865	68 807	70 058	145	...	...	...	...
Urdaneta	125 451	63 025	62 426	100	...	...	...	...
Valencia	181 556	93 417	88 139	587	...	...	...	...
Valenzuela	575 356	288 659	286 697	47	...	...	...	...
Zamboanga	807 129	405 435	401 694	1 415	...	...	...	...
Qatar								
21 IV 2010 (CDFC)								
Al-Khoor	193 983	181 005	12 978	...	...	...	...	...
Al-Rayyan	455 623	301 842	153 781	...	...	...	...	...
Al-Wakrah	141 222	114 698	26 524	...	...	...	...	...
DOHA	796 947	610 817	186 130	...	...	...	...	...
Republic of Korea - République de Corée								
1 VII 2014 (ESDJ)								
Busan (Pusan)	3 416 651[1]	1 680 718[1]	1 735 933[1]	768	...	...	...	...
Daegu (Taegu)	2 467 158[1]	1 224 614[1]	1 242 544[1]	884	...	...	...	...
Daejeon (Taejon)	1 552 153[1]	778 936[1]	773 217[1]	540	...	...	...	...
Gwangju (Kwangchu)	1 521 704[1]	756 014[1]	765 690[1]	501	...	...	...	...
Incheon[1]	2 837 935	1 430 873	1 407 062	...	...	...	...	...
SEOUL	10 007 651[1]	4 919 002[1]	5 088 649[1]	605	...	...	...	...
Ulsan	1 124 112[1]	583 811[1]	540 301[1]	1 060	...	...	...	...
Saudi Arabia - Arabie saoudite								
15 IX 2004 (CDFC)								
Abha	201 912	113 102	88 810	...	...	...	...	...
Ad-Dammam	744 321	450 494	293 827	...	...	...	...	...
Al-Hawiyah	132 078	69 481	62 597	...	...	...	...	...
Al-Hufuf	287 841	155 924	131 917	...	...	...	...	...
Al-Jubayl	222 544	135 659	86 885	...	...	...	...	...
Al-Kharj	200 958	109 112	91 846	...	...	...	...	...
Al-Khubar	165 799	101 818	63 981	...	...	...	...	...
Al-Madinah	918 889	493 929	424 960	...	...	...	...	...
Al-Mubarraz	285 067	150 449	134 618	...	...	...	...	...
Al-Qurrayat	100 436	52 869	47 567	...	...	...	...	...
Ar'ar	145 237	77 744	67 493	...	...	...	...	...
Ath-Thuqbah	191 826	117 165	74 661	...	...	...	...	...
At-Ta'if	521 273	274 531	246 742	...	...	...	...	...
Buraydah	378 422	211 317	167 105	...	...	...	...	...
Hafar al-Batin	231 978	122 781	109 197	...	...	...	...	...
Ha'il	267 005	142 015	124 990	...	...	...	...	...
Jiddah	2 801 481	1 619 932	1 181 549	...	...	...	...	...
Jizan	100 694	57 988	42 706	...	...	...	...	...
Khamis Mushayt	372 695	208 397	164 298	...	...	...	...	...
Makkah	1 294 168	704 672	589 496	...	...	...	...	...
Najran (Aba as-Suud)	246 880	133 405	113 475	...	...	...	...	...
RIYADH	4 087 152	2 354 246	1 732 906	...	...	...	...	...
Sekaka	122 686	66 672	56 014	...	...	...	...	...
Tabuk	441 351	241 913	199 438	...	...	...	...	...
Unayzah	128 930	71 841	57 089	...	...	...	...	...
Yanbu al-Bahr	188 430	105 966	82 464	...	...	...	...	...
Singapore - Singapour								
30 VI 2014 (ESDJ)								
SINGAPORE	5 469 724[47]	...	...	718[48]	...	...	...	...

8. Population of capital cities and cities of 100 000 or more inhabitants: latest available year, 1995 - 2014
Population des capitales et des villes de 100 000 habitants ou plus : dernière année disponible, 1995 - 2014 (continued - suite)

Continent, country or area, date, code[a] and city / Continent, pays ou zone, date, code[a] et ville	City proper - Ville proprement dite				Urban agglomeration - Agglomération urbaine			
	Population			Surface area - Superficie (km²)	Population			Surface area - Superficie (km²)
	Both sexes - Les deux sexes	Male - Masculin	Female - Féminin		Both sexes - Les deux sexes	Male - Masculin	Female - Féminin	
ASIA - ASIE								
Sri Lanka[49]								
17 VII 2001 (CDFC)								
COLOMBO	647 100	346 366	300 734	...	...	...	...	...
Dehiwala-Mount Lavinia	210 546	105 522	105 024	...	...	...	...	...
Kandy	109 343	54 288	55 055	...	...	...	...	...
Moratuwa	177 563	87 313	90 250	...	...	...	...	...
Negombo	121 701	60 947	60 754	...	...	...	...	...
Sri Jayawardanapura Kotte	116 366	59 993	56 373	...	...	...	...	...
State of Palestine - État de Palestine								
1 VII 2014 (ESDF)								
EAST JERUSALEM - JÉRUSALEM-EST[50]	*255 686*	...	...	...	...	...	...	...
Gaza	*549 070*	...	...	38	...	...	...	...
Hebron	*202 172*	...	...	49	...	...	...	...
Jabalya	*158 754*	...	...	...	...	...	...	...
Khan Yunis	*174 240*	...	...	...	...	...	...	...
Nablus	*146 493*	...	...	26	...	...	...	...
Rafah	*152 950*	...	...	...	...	...	...	...
Syrian Arab Republic - République arabe syrienne								
1 VII 2008 (ESDF)								
Aleppo	*4 450 000*	*2 292 000*	*2 158 000*	...	...	...	...	...
Al-Hasakeh	*1 392 000*	*701 000*	*691 000*	...	...	...	...	...
Al-Raqqah	*865 000*	*456 000*	*409 000*	...	...	...	...	...
Al-Sweida	*349 000*	*171 000*	*178 000*	...	...	...	...	...
DAMASCUS	*1 680 000*	*857 000*	*823 000*	...	...	...	...	...
Damasus rural	*2 529 000*	*1 302 000*	*1 227 000*	...	...	...	...	...
Deir El-Zor	*1 111 000*	*563 000*	*548 000*	...	...	...	...	...
Dra'a	*930 000*	*472 000*	*458 000*	...	...	...	...	...
Hama	*1 508 000*	*768 000*	*740 000*	...	...	...	...	...
Homs	*1 667 000*	*852 000*	*815 000*	...	...	...	...	...
Idleb	*1 376 000*	*704 000*	*672 000*	...	...	...	...	...
Lattakia	*951 000*	*480 000*	*471 000*	...	...	...	...	...
Tartous	*756 000*	*383 000*	*373 000*	...	...	...	...	...
Tajikistan - Tadjikistan								
1 VII 2013 (ESDF)								
DUSHANBE	770 027	399 728	370 299	...	...	...	...	...
Thailand - Thaïlande								
1 IX 2010 (CDJC)								
Ang Thong	...	...	...	...	109 207	51 540	57 667	...
BANGKOK	...	...	...	...	8 305 218	4 032 586	4 272 632	1 569
Buri Ram	...	...	...	...	375 999	181 546	194 453	...
Chachoengsao	...	...	...	...	206 250	101 475	104 775	...
Chai Nat	...	...	...	...	205 456	97 373	108 083	...
Chaiyaphum	...	...	...	...	205 112	99 280	105 832	...
Chanthaburi	...	...	...	...	243 126	118 221	124 905	...
Chiang Mai	...	...	...	...	967 020	466 145	500 875	...
Chiang Rai	...	...	...	...	455 732	220 391	235 341	...
Chon Buri	...	...	...	...	1 158 989	575 208	583 781	...
Chumphon	...	...	...	...	147 912	75 339	72 573	...
Kalasin	...	...	...	...	428 940	208 863	220 077	...
Kamphaeng Phet	...	...	...	...	211 774	101 456	110 318	...
Kanchanaburi	...	...	...	...	292 521	143 986	148 535	...
Khon Kaen	...	...	...	...	703 123	339 011	364 112	...
Lampang	...	...	...	...	372 463	180 360	192 103	...
Lamphun	...	...	...	...	262 832	126 662	136 170	...
Loei	...	...	...	...	164 180	81 302	82 878	...
Lop Buri	...	...	...	...	235 827	118 964	116 863	...
Maha Sarakham	...	...	...	...	153 740	72 143	81 597	...
Mukdahan	...	...	...	...	180 600	89 190	91 410	...
Nakhon Pathom	...	...	...	...	339 736	166 150	173 586	...
Nakhon Phanom	...	...	...	...	123 720	59 683	64 037	...
Nakhon Ratchasima	...	...	...	...	653 075	316 329	336 746	...
Nakhon Sawan	...	...	...	...	225 903	107 298	118 605	...
Nakhon Si Thammarat	...	...	...	...	265 606	127 460	138 146	...
Narathiwat	...	...	...	...	133 718	64 616	69 102	...
Nong Bua Lam Phu	...	...	...	...	203 142	98 164	104 978	...

Continent, country or area, date, code[a] and city / Continent, pays ou zone, date, code[a] et ville	City proper - Ville proprement dite				Urban agglomeration - Agglomération urbaine			
	Population			Surface area - Superficie (km²)	Population			Surface area - Superficie (km²)
	Both sexes - Les deux sexes	Male - Masculin	Female - Féminin		Both sexes - Les deux sexes	Male - Masculin	Female - Féminin	
ASIA - ASIE								
Thailand - Thaïlande								
1 IX 2010 (CDJC)								
Nong Khai	...	...	...	...	232 798	113 989	118 809	...
Nonthaburi	...	...	...	...	797 739	383 826	413 913	...
Pathum Thani	...	...	...	...	757 175	358 679	398 496	...
Pattani	...	...	...	...	104 617	51 305	53 312	...
Phatthalung	...	...	...	...	244 783	117 039	127 744	...
Phayao	...	...	...	...	221 062	106 657	114 405	...
Phetchabun	...	...	...	...	172 275	82 257	90 018	...
Phetchaburi	...	...	...	...	175 675	83 735	91 940	...
Phichit	...	...	...	...	131 283	62 446	68 837	...
Phitsanulok	...	...	...	...	201 466	93 098	108 368	...
Phra Nakhon Si Ayutthaya	...	...	...	...	365 736	173 280	192 456	...
Phrae	...	...	...	...	156 099	75 175	80 924	...
Phuket	...	...	...	...	358 159	175 144	183 015	...
Prachuap Khiri Khan	...	...	...	...	177 011	87 525	89 486	...
Ranong	...	...	...	...	123 596	62 090	61 506	...
Ratchaburi	...	...	...	...	317 886	149 460	168 426	...
Rayong	...	...	...	...	445 939	224 068	221 871	...
Roi Et	...	...	...	...	365 113	176 648	188 465	...
Sa Kaeo	...	...	...	...	135 536	66 447	69 089	...
Sakon Nakhon	...	...	...	...	315 788	153 785	162 003	...
Samut Prakan	...	...	...	...	1 082 993	527 487	555 506	...
Samut Sakhon	...	...	...	...	479 186	237 778	241 408	...
Saraburi	...	...	...	...	239 281	114 885	124 396	...
Si Sa Ket	...	...	...	...	160 508	77 363	83 145	...
Songkhla	...	...	...	...	800 970	382 828	418 142	...
Sukhothai	...	...	...	...	166 782	79 139	87 643	...
Suphan Buri	...	...	...	...	228 496	108 666	119 830	...
Surat Thani	...	...	...	...	410 984	198 909	212 075	...
Surin	...	...	...	...	153 159	73 082	80 077	...
Tak	...	...	...	...	146 769	70 754	76 015	...
Trat	...	...	...	...	110 398	52 309	58 089	...
Ubon Ratchathani	...	...	...	...	411 954	198 655	213 299	...
Udon Thani	...	...	...	...	483 057	232 326	250 731	...
Uttaradit	...	...	...	...	151 047	72 244	78 803	...
Yala	...	...	...	...	119 744	58 041	61 703	...
Yasothon	...	...	...	...	127 173	63 885	63 288	...
Timor-Leste								
11 VII 2010 (CDFC)								
DILI	192 652	102 900	89 752	...	...	...	...	...
Turkey - Turquie[51]								
31 XII 2013 (ESDJ)								
Adana	...	...	...	...	2 149 260	1 074 778	1 074 482	...
Adıyaman	224 215	112 619	111 596	...	...	...	...	...
Afyonkarahisar	203 443	100 985	102 458	...	...	...	...	...
Ağrı	110 199	57 554	52 645	...	...	...	...	...
Aksaray	189 977	94 615	95 362	...	...	...	...	...
ANKARA	...	...	...	...	5 045 083	2 507 525	2 537 558	...
Antalya	...	...	...	...	2 158 265	1 090 843	1 067 422	...
Aydın	...	...	...	...	1 020 957	510 512	510 445	...
Balıkesir	...	...	...	...	1 162 761	581 403	581 358	...
Batman	369 478	185 576	183 902	...	...	...	...	...
Bolu	140 131	69 813	70 318	...	...	...	...	...
Bursa	...	...	...	...	2 740 970	1 371 914	1 369 056	...
Çanakkale	116 078	58 802	57 276	...	...	...	...	...
Cizre	110 166	55 901	54 265	...	...	...	...	...
Çorum	236 738	117 533	119 205	...	...	...	...	...
Denizli	...	...	...	...	963 464	480 224	483 240	...
Diyarbakir	...	...	...	...	1 607 437	809 791	797 646	...
Düzce	143 018	71 146	71 872	...	...	...	...	...
Edirne	150 260	74 779	75 481	...	...	...	...	...
Elazığ	332 810	164 933	167 877	...	...	...	...	...
Ereğli	111 449	55 430	56 019	...	...	...	...	...
Erzurum	...	...	...	...	766 729	384 015	382 714	...

8. Population of capital cities and cities of 100 000 or more inhabitants: latest available year, 1995 - 2014
Population des capitales et des villes de 100 000 habitants ou plus : dernière année disponible, 1995 - 2014 (continued - suite)

Continent, country or area, date, code[a] and city / Continent, pays ou zone, date, code[a] et ville	City proper - Ville proprement dite				Urban agglomeration - Agglomération urbaine			
	Population			Surface area - Superficie (km²)	Population			Surface area - Superficie (km²)
	Both sexes - Les deux sexes	Male - Masculin	Female - Féminin		Both sexes - Les deux sexes	Male - Masculin	Female - Féminin	
ASIA - ASIE								
Turkey - Turquie[51]								
31 XII 2013 (ESDJ)								
Eskişehir	...	...	...	...	799 724	399 189	400 535	...
Gaziantep	...	...	...	...	1 844 438	930 972	913 466	...
Giresun	102 307	50 638	51 669	...	...	...	...	...
Hatay	...	...	...	...	1 503 066	756 248	746 818	...
Isparta	201 873	100 729	101 144	...	...	...	...	...
İstanbul	...	...	...	...	14 160 467	7 115 721	7 044 746	...
İzmir	...	...	...	...	4 061 074	2 027 334	2 033 740	...
Kahramanmaraş	...	...	...	...	1 075 706	546 943	528 763	...
Karabük	110 338	56 357	53 981	...	...	...	...	...
Karaman	144 178	71 246	72 932	...	...	...	...	...
Kayseri	...	...	...	...	1 295 355	649 851	645 504	...
Kırıkkale	187 480	93 128	94 352	...	...	...	...	...
Kırşehir	117 730	58 887	58 843	...	...	...	...	...
Kocaeli	...	...	...	...	1 676 202	849 465	826 737	...
Konya	...	...	...	...	2 079 225	1 031 563	1 047 662	...
Kütahya	227 775	114 158	113 617	...	...	...	...	...
Lüleburgaz	106 545	54 180	52 365	...	...	...	...	...
Malatya	...	...	...	...	762 538	380 704	381 834	...
Manisa	...	...	...	...	1 359 463	682 097	677 366	...
Mardin	...	...	...	...	779 738	391 422	388 316	...
Mersin	...	...	...	...	1 705 774	849 548	856 226	...
Muğla	...	...	...	...	866 665	441 531	425 134	...
Niğde	124 774	62 310	62 464	...	...	...	...	...
Ordu	...	...	...	...	731 452	366 011	365 441	...
Osmaniye	213 045	106 854	106 191	...	...	...	...	...
Rize	104 991	51 971	53 020	...	...	...	...	...
Sakarya	...	...	...	...	917 373	458 987	458 386	...
Samsun	...	...	...	...	1 261 810	623 435	638 375	...
Şanlıurfa	...	...	...	...	1 801 980	901 868	900 112	...
Siirt	136 203	70 132	66 071	...	...	...	...	...
Sivas	315 107	156 549	158 558	...	...	...	...	...
Tekirdağ	...	...	...	...	874 475	450 149	424 326	...
Tokat	133 777	66 931	66 846	...	...	...	...	...
Trabzon	...	...	...	...	758 237	374 562	383 675	...
Uşak	192 144	95 856	96 288	...	...	...	...	...
Van	...	...	...	...	1 070 113	545 479	524 634	...
Yalova	104 737	51 772	52 965	...	...	...	...	...
Zonguldak	107 783	52 933	54 850	...	...	...	...	...
United Arab Emirates - Émirats arabes unis								
1 VII 2002 (ESDF)								
ABU DHABI	527 000	359 000	168 000	...	...	...	...	...
Ajman	205 000	122 000	83 000	...	...	...	...	...
Al-Ayn	328 000	215 000	113 000	...	...	...	...	...
Al-Sharjah	488 000	317 000	171 000	...	...	...	...	...
Dubai	1 089 000	759 000	330 000	...	...	...	...	...
Uzbekistan - Ouzbékistan								
1 VII 2001 (ESDF)								
Almalyk	113 114	56 317	56 797	...	...	...	...	...
Andizhan	338 366	165 159	173 207	...	...	...	...	...
Angren	128 757	64 060	64 697	...	...	...	...	...
Banjzak	131 512	68 441	63 071	...	...	...	...	...
Bukhara	237 361	118 613	118 748	...	...	...	...	...
Chirchik	141 742	70 203	71 539	...	...	...	...	...
Fergana	183 037	87 142	95 895	...	...	...	...	...
Karshi	204 690	104 159	100 531	...	...	...	...	...
Kokand	197 450	95 872	101 578	...	...	...	...	...
Margilan	149 646	73 899	75 747	...	...	...	...	...
Namangan	391 297	197 962	193 335	...	...	...	...	...
Navoi	138 082	70 577	67 505	...	...	...	...	...
Nukus	212 012	103 918	108 094	...	...	...	...	...
Samarkand	361 339	178 608	182 731	...	...	...	...	...
TASHKENT	2 137 218	1 043 213	1 094 005	...	...	...	...	...

8. Population of capital cities and cities of 100 000 or more inhabitants: latest available year, 1995 - 2014
Population des capitales et des villes de 100 000 habitants ou plus : dernière année disponible, 1995 - 2014 (continued - suite)

Continent, country or area, date, code[a] and city / Continent, pays ou zone, date, code[a] et ville	City proper - Ville proprement dite				Urban agglomeration - Agglomération urbaine			
	Population			Surface area - Superficie (km²)	Population			Surface area - Superficie (km²)
	Both sexes - Les deux sexes	Male - Masculin	Female - Féminin		Both sexes - Les deux sexes	Male - Masculin	Female - Féminin	
ASIA - ASIE								
Uzbekistan - Ouzbékistan								
1 VII 2001 (ESDF)								
Termez	116 467	60 031	56 436	...	...	...	...	...
Urgentch	138 609	67 667	70 942	...	...	...	...	...
Yemen - Yémen								
1 VII 2009* (ESDF)								
Adan	*684 322*	...	...	...	*684 322*	...	...	...
SANA'A	*1 976 286*	...	...	...	*2 022 867*	...	...	...
EUROPE								
Åland Islands - Îles d'Åland								
1 VII 2014 (ESDJ)								
MARIEHAMN	11 437[10]	5 490[10]	5 947[10]	12	...	...	...	...
Albania - Albanie								
1 X 2011 (CDJC)								
Durrës	113 249	56 511	56 738	...	...	...	...	...
TIRANA	418 495	203 239	215 256	31	...	...	...	...
Andorra - Andorre[10]								
1 VII 2011 (ESDJ)								
ANDORRA LA VELLA	...	...	...	...	22 205	11 056	11 149	...
Austria - Autriche								
1 I 2014 (ESDJ)								
Graz	269 997	131 145	138 852	128	...	...	...	...
Innsbruck	124 579	59 726	64 853	105	...	...	...	...
Linz	193 814	92 693	101 121	96	...	...	...	...
Salzburg	146 631	69 279	77 352	66	...	...	...	...
WIEN	1 766 746	850 596	916 150	415	...	...	...	...
Belarus - Bélarus								
1 VII 2013 (ESDJ)								
Baranovichi	173 932	78 644	95 288	85	...	...	...	...
Bobruisk	217 394	101 562	115 832	90	...	...	...	...
Borisov	145 441	68 300	77 141	46	...	...	...	...
Brest	328 681	151 285	177 396	146	...	...	...	...
Gomel	508 839	231 874	276 965	135	...	...	...	...
Grodno	354 521	161 200	193 321	142	...	...	...	...
MINSK	1 911 433	872 393	1 039 040	348	...	...	...	...
Mogilev	368 765	169 579	199 186	119	...	...	...	...
Mozir	111 755	53 086	58 669	44	...	...	...	...
Novopolotsk	101 583	48 342	53 241	48	...	...	...	...
Orsha	116 604	53 942	62 662	39	...	...	...	...
Pinsk	135 858	62 826	73 032	47	...	...	...	...
Soligorsk	105 060	49 326	55 734	15	...	...	...	...
Vitebsk	362 466	160 459	202 007	125	...	...	...	...
Belgium - Belgique								
1 I 2011 (CDJC)								
Anderlecht	108 940	53 707	55 233	18	...	...	...	...
Antwerpen (Anvers)	498 473	247 192	251 281	205	718 730	354 576	364 154	394
Brugge	117 260	56 952	60 308	138	117 260	56 952	60 308	138
BRUXELLES (BRUSSEL)	174 383	90 317	84 066	33	1 550 299[52]	754 208[52]	796 091[52]	573[52]
Charleroi	204 150	99 221	104 929	102	291 806	141 106	150 700	199
Gent (Gand)	248 358	122 457	125 901	156	280 151	137 980	142 171	207
Liège (Luik)	195 965	96 509	99 456	69	491 767	238 134	253 633	367
Namur	110 175	53 019	57 156	176	110 175	53 019	57 156	176
Schaerbeek	127 525	63 020	64 505	8	...	...	...	...
Bulgaria - Bulgarie								
1 VII 2012 (ESDJ)								
Burgas	199 284	96 462	102 822	...	...	...	...	...
Pleven	105 045	50 720	54 325	...	...	...	...	...
Plovdiv	338 657	161 523	177 134	...	...	...	...	...
Ruse	148 742	71 960	76 782	...	...	...	...	...
SOFIA	1 210 820	576 142	634 678	...	...	...	...	...
Stara Zagora	137 649	66 670	70 979	...	...	...	...	...
Varna	334 763	162 594	172 169	...	...	...	...	...

8. Population of capital cities and cities of 100 000 or more inhabitants: latest available year, 1995 - 2014
Population des capitales et des villes de 100 000 habitants ou plus : dernière année disponible, 1995 - 2014 (continued - suite)

Continent, country or area, date, code[a] and city / Continent, pays ou zone, date, code[a] et ville	City proper - Ville proprement dite				Urban agglomeration - Agglomération urbaine			
	Population			Surface area - Superficie (km²)	Population			Surface area - Superficie (km²)
	Both sexes - Les deux sexes	Male - Masculin	Female - Féminin		Both sexes - Les deux sexes	Male - Masculin	Female - Féminin	
EUROPE								
Croatia - Croatie								
1 IV 2011 (CDJC)								
Osijek	108 048	50 357	57 691	174	...	...	...	...
Rijeka	128 624	60 951	67 673	43	...	...	...	...
Split	178 102	84 477	93 625	79	...	...	...	...
ZAGREB	790 017	369 339	420 678	641	...	...	...	...
Czech Republic - République tchèque								
1 I 2014 (ESDJ)								
Brno	377 508	181 963	195 545	226	...	...	...	...
Liberec	102 301	49 368	52 933	105	...	...	...	...
Ostrava	295 653	143 044	152 609	205	...	...	...	...
Plzen	168 034	81 624	86 410	133	...	...	...	...
PRAHA	1 244 762	604 041	640 721	485	...	...	...	...
Denmark - Danemark[53]								
1 VII 2014 (ESDJ)								
Ålborg	205 630[10]	103 242[10]	102 388[10]	1 137	...	...	...	...
Århus	323 477[10]	159 051[10]	164 426[10]	468	...	...	...	...
Esbjerg	115 272[10]	57 696[10]	57 576[10]	795	...	...	...	...
Frederiksberg	102 658[10]	48 297[10]	54 361[10]	9	...	...	...	...
KOBENHAVN	572 287[10]	283 097[10]	289 190[10]	86	...	...	...	...
Odense	195 908[10]	96 516[10]	99 392[10]	306	...	...	...	...
Vejle	110 057[10]	54 855[10]	55 202[10]	1 058	...	...	...	...
Estonia - Estonie								
1 I 2014 (ESDJ)								
TALLINN	411 063	185 717	225 346	158	...	...	...	...
Faeroe Islands - Îles Féroé								
1 VII 2013 (ESDJ)								
TÓRSHAVN	12 292	6 121	6 171	6[54]	18 149[55]	9 117[55]	9 032[55]	15[56]
Finland - Finlande								
1 VII 2013 (ESDJ)								
Espoo	258 789[10]	127 897[10]	130 892[10]	312	...	...	...	...
HELSINKI	608 316[10]	286 760[10]	321 557[10]	214	...	...	...	...
Jyvaskyla	134 070[10]	65 458[10]	68 613[10]	1 171	...	...	...	...
Kuopio	105 739[10]	51 100[10]	54 640[10]	2 309	...	...	...	...
Lahti	103 190[10]	49 056[10]	54 135[10]	135	...	...	...	...
Oulu	192 323[10]	95 540[10]	96 783[10]	3 031	...	...	...	...
Tampere	218 934[10]	105 924[10]	113 010[10]	525	...	...	...	...
Turku	181 149[10]	85 880[10]	95 269[10]	246	...	...	...	...
Vantaa	206 705[10]	101 593[10]	105 113[10]	238	...	...	...	...
France								
1 I 2010 (CDJS)								
Aix-en-Provence	141 438[57]	65 940[57]	75 498[57]	186	...	...	...	...
Amiens	133 448[57]	63 030[57]	70 418[57]	49	162 718	77 241	85 477	137
Angers	147 571[57]	67 521[57]	80 050[57]	43	215 887	100 353	115 534	189
Argenteuil	103 125[57]	50 356[57]	52 769[57]	17	...	...	...	...
Besançon	116 914[57]	54 937[57]	61 977[57]	65	135 050	63 788	71 262	122
Bordeaux	239 157[57]	111 452[57]	127 705[57]	49	843 425	400 423	443 002	1 173
Boulogne-Billancourt	114 205[57]	53 038[57]	61 167[57]	6	...	...	...	...
Brest	141 303[57]	68 083[57]	73 220[57]	50	199 852	96 845	103 007	199
Caen	108 954[57]	50 828[57]	58 126[57]	26	196 743	93 132	103 611	142
Clermont-Ferrand	139 860[57]	65 886[57]	73 974[57]	43	260 681	123 262	137 419	181
Dijon	151 212[57]	71 041[57]	80 171[57]	40	237 117	112 013	125 104	166
Grenoble	155 637[57]	75 558[57]	80 079[57]	18	496 951	241 872	255 079	512
Le Havre	175 497[57]	82 703[57]	92 794[57]	47	241 037	114 634	126 403	195
Le Mans	142 626[57]	66 979[57]	75 647[57]	35	207 658	98 772	108 886	294
Lille	227 560[57]	108 257[57]	119 303[57]	78	1 018 356	486 736	531 620	443
Limoges	139 150[57]	64 643[57]	74 507[57]	48	186 499	87 294	99 205	236
Lyon	484 344[57]	226 203[57]	258 141[57]	53	1 551 108	741 745	809 363	1 178
Marseille	850 726[57]	400 977[57]	449 749[57]	241	1 559 789[58]	741 799[58]	817 990[58]	1 732
Metz	120 738[57]	58 537[57]	62 201[57]	42	288 940	140 573	148 367	307
Montpellier	257 351[57]	119 967[57]	137 384[57]	57	390 962	184 812	206 150	310
Montreuil	102 770[57]	51 166[57]	51 604[57]	9	...	...	...	...
Mulhouse	109 588[57]	52 989[57]	56 599[57]	22	242 353	117 380	124 973	239

Continent, country or area, date, code[a] and city / Continent, pays ou zone, date, code[a] et ville	City proper - Ville proprement dite				Urban agglomeration - Agglomération urbaine			
	Population			Surface area - Superficie (km²)	Population			Surface area - Superficie (km²)
	Both sexes - Les deux sexes	Male - Masculin	Female - Féminin		Both sexes - Les deux sexes	Male - Masculin	Female - Féminin	
EUROPE								
France								
1 I 2010 (CDJS)								
Nancy	105 421[57]	49 278[57]	56 143[57]	15	286 215	135 585	150 630	246
Nantes	284 970[57]	134 873[57]	150 097[57]	65	591 461	282 368	309 093	538
Nice	343 304[57]	159 260[57]	184 044[57]	72	941 777	443 854	497 923	744
Nîmes	142 205[57]	66 302[57]	75 903[57]	162	175 503	82 457	93 046	266
Orléans	114 167[57]	54 609[57]	59 558[57]	27	269 724	130 085	139 639	290
PARIS	2 243 833[57]	1 057 233[57]	1 186 600[57]	105	10 460 118[59]	5 037 278[59]	5 422 840[59]	2 845
Perpignan	117 419[57]	54 431[57]	62 988[57]	68	190 668	89 358	101 310	218
Reims	179 992[57]	84 862[57]	95 130[57]	47	208 639	98 645	109 994	94
Rennes	207 178[57]	97 794[57]	109 384[57]	50	310 672	148 841	161 831	284
Rouen	110 933[57]	52 383[57]	58 550[57]	21	463 748	219 416	244 332	453
Saint-Denis	106 785[57]	53 787[57]	52 998[57]	12	...	...	...	...
Saint-Étienne	171 260[57]	80 545[57]	90 715[57]	80	371 281	176 464	194 817	419
Strasbourg	271 782[57]	128 478[57]	143 304[57]	78	449 931	214 580	235 351	240
Toulon	164 532[57]	77 464[57]	87 068[57]	43	557 802	264 944	292 858	764
Toulouse	441 802[57]	213 198[57]	228 604[57]	118	879 683	427 944	451 739	812
Tours	134 817[57]	61 897[57]	72 920[57]	35	346 105	163 682	182 423	664
Villeurbanne	145 150[57]	70 377[57]	74 773[57]	15	...	...	...	...
Germany - Allemagne								
1 I 2014 (ESDJ)								
Aachen	241 683	124 192	117 491	161	...	...	...	...
Augsburg	276 542	134 549	141 993	147	...	...	...	...
Bergisch Gladbach	109 425	52 355	57 070	83	...	...	...	...
BERLIN	3 421 829	1 669 853	1 751 976	892	...	...	...	...
Bielefeld	328 864	158 461	170 403	259	...	...	...	...
Bochum	361 734	174 396	187 338	146	...	...	...	...
Bonn	311 287	147 304	163 983	141	...	...	...	...
Bottrop	116 055	56 061	59 994	101	...	...	...	...
Braunschweig	247 227	121 376	125 851	192	...	...	...	...
Bremen	548 547	267 621	280 926	325	...	...	...	...
Bremerhaven	108 844	53 611	55 233	94	...	...	...	...
Chemnitz	242 022	117 495	124 527	221	...	...	...	...
Darmstadt	149 743	75 275	74 468	122	...	...	...	...
Dortmund	575 944	281 116	294 828	281	...	...	...	...
Dresden	530 754	261 664	269 090	328	...	...	...	...
Duisburg	486 855	237 743	249 112	233	...	...	...	...
Düsseldorf	598 686	288 114	310 572	217	...	...	...	...
Erfurt	204 880	98 751	106 129	269	...	...	...	...
Erlangen	105 624	51 877	53 747	77	...	...	...	...
Essen	569 884	273 982	295 902	210	...	...	...	...
Frankfurt am Main	701 350	344 952	356 398	248	...	...	...	...
Freiburg im Breisgau	220 286	103 982	116 304	153	...	...	...	...
Fürth	119 808	58 052	61 756	63	...	...	...	...
Gelsenkirchen	257 850	126 979	130 871	105	...	...	...	...
Göttingen	116 891	56 414	60 477	117	...	...	...	...
Hagen	185 996	89 907	96 089	160	...	...	...	...
Halle	231 565	110 632	120 933	135	...	...	...	...
Hamburg	1 746 342	847 783	898 559	755	...	...	...	...
Hamm	176 048	85 813	90 235	226	...	...	...	...
Hannover	518 386	250 415	267 971	204	...	...	...	...
Heidelberg	152 113	72 422	79 691	109	...	...	...	...
Heilbronn	118 122	58 440	59 682	100	...	...	...	...
Herne	154 417	74 675	79 742	51	...	...	...	...
Ingolstadt	129 136	64 731	64 405	133	...	...	...	...
Jena	107 679	53 190	54 489	114	...	...	...	...
Karlsruhe	299 103	150 451	148 652	173	...	...	...	...
Kassel	194 087	93 967	100 120	107	...	...	...	...
Kiel	241 533	116 951	124 582	119	...	...	...	...
Koblenz	110 643	53 188	57 455	105	...	...	...	...
Köln	1 034 175	501 577	532 598	405	...	...	...	...
Krefeld	222 058	107 084	114 974	138	...	...	...	...
Leipzig	531 562	257 414	274 148	297	...	...	...	...
Leverkusen	160 819	77 865	82 954	79	...	...	...	...

Continent, country or area, date, code[a] and city / Continent, pays ou zone, date, code[a] et ville	City proper - Ville proprement dite				Urban agglomeration - Agglomération urbaine			
	Population			Surface area - Superficie (km²)	Population			Surface area - Superficie (km²)
	Both sexes - Les deux sexes	Male - Masculin	Female - Féminin		Both sexes - Les deux sexes	Male - Masculin	Female - Féminin	
EUROPE								
Germany - Allemagne								
1 I 2014 (ESDJ)								
Lübeck	212 958	101 734	111 224	214	...	...	...	...
Ludwigshafen am Rhein	161 518	79 764	81 754	78	...	...	...	...
Magdeburg	231 021	112 495	118 526	201	...	...	...	...
Mainz	204 268	98 529	105 739	98	...	...	...	...
Mannheim	296 690	146 345	150 345	145	...	...	...	...
Moers	103 108	49 785	53 323	68	...	...	...	...
Mönchengladbach	255 430	124 452	130 978	170	...	...	...	...
Mülheim an der Ruhr	166 640	79 425	87 215	91	...	...	...	...
München	1 407 836	683 126	724 710	311	...	...	...	...
Münster (Westf.)	299 708	143 029	156 679	303	...	...	...	...
Neuss	152 252	73 512	78 740	100	...	...	...	...
Nürnberg	498 876	240 640	258 236	186	...	...	...	...
Oberhausen	209 097	101 827	107 270	77	...	...	...	...
Offenbach am Main	119 203	58 963	60 240	45	...	...	...	...
Oldenburg	159 610	75 754	83 856	103	...	...	...	...
Osnabrück	156 315	74 822	81 493	120	...	...	...	...
Paderborn	143 659	70 685	72 974	180	...	...	...	...
Pforzheim	117 754	57 147	60 607	98	...	...	...	...
Potsdam	161 468	77 383	84 085	188	...	...	...	...
Recklinghausen	115 320	55 874	59 446	66	...	...	...	...
Regensburg	140 276	67 035	73 241	81	...	...	...	...
Remscheid	108 955	53 172	55 783	75	...	...	...	...
Reutlingen	111 357	54 265	57 092	87	...	...	...	...
Rostock	203 431	99 559	103 872	181	...	...	...	...
Saarbrücken	177 201	86 706	90 495	167	...	...	...	...
Solingen	155 768	74 822	80 946	90	...	...	...	...
Stuttgart	604 297	298 413	305 884	207	...	...	...	...
Trier	107 233	51 782	55 451	117	...	...	...	...
Ulm	119 218	58 341	60 877	119	...	...	...	...
Wiesbaden	273 871	130 760	143 111	204	...	...	...	...
Wolfsburg	122 457	60 349	62 108	204	...	...	...	...
Wuppertal	343 488	166 113	177 375	168	...	...	...	...
Würzburg	124 698	58 690	66 008	88	...	...	...	...
Gibraltar								
31 XII 2013 (ESDF)								
GIBRALTAR	32 734[60]	16 460[60]	16 274[60]	6	...	...	...	...
Greece - Grèce								
9 V 2011 (CDFC)								
ATHINAI	664 046	315 210	348 836	39	...	...	...	...
Calithèa	100 641	46 782	53 859	5	...	...	...	...
Iraclion	140 730	68 024	72 706	52	...	...	...	...
Larissa	144 651	70 797	73 854	88	...	...	...	...
Patrai	167 446	81 114	86 332	57	...	...	...	...
Pésterion	139 981	68 563	71 418	10	...	...	...	...
Pireas	163 688	78 200	85 488	...	...	...	...	...
Thessaloniki	315 196	143 813	171 383					
Guernsey - Guernesey								
29 IV 2001 (CDJC)								
ST. PETER PORT	16 488	...	...	...	...	...	...	...
Holy See - Saint-Siège[61]								
21 VI 2012 (ESDF)								
VATICAN CITY	451	...	...	0[62]	...	...	...	...
Hungary - Hongrie								
1 VII 2013* (ESDJ)								
BUDAPEST	1 740 188	804 480	935 708	525	2 548 428	1 194 493	1 353 936	2 538
Debrecen	204 124	95 033	109 091	462	239 587	112 650	126 937	805
Györ	128 735	60 671	68 064	175	187 363	89 572	97 791	783
Kecskemét	111 967	52 458	59 510	323	144 239	68 372	75 867	840
Miskolc	162 085	75 067	87 019	237	200 655	93 795	106 860	460
Nyiregyhaza	118 175	54 855	63 320	275	134 485	62 833	71 652	405
Pécs	147 150	67 233	79 918	163	171 999	79 514	92 485	430
Szeged	161 879	74 111	87 769	281	199 765	92 812	106 954	713

8. Population of capital cities and cities of 100 000 or more inhabitants: latest available year, 1995 - 2014
Population des capitales et des villes de 100 000 habitants ou plus : dernière année disponible, 1995 - 2014 (continued - suite)

Continent, country or area, date, code[a] and city / Continent, pays ou zone, date, code[a] et ville	City proper - Ville proprement dite				Urban agglomeration - Agglomération urbaine			
	Population			Surface area - Superficie (km²)	Population			Surface area - Superficie (km²)
	Both sexes - Les deux sexes	Male - Masculin	Female - Féminin		Both sexes - Les deux sexes	Male - Masculin	Female - Féminin	
EUROPE								
Iceland - Islande[63]								
1 VII 2013 (ESDJ)								
REYKJAVIK	120 497[64]	59 715[64]	60 783[64]	274[65]	207 214[66]	102 828[66]	104 386[66]	1 044[65]
Ireland - Irlande								
10 IV 2011 (CDFC)								
Cork	119 230	58 812	60 418	40	198 582	97 463	101 119	...
DUBLIN	527 612	257 303	270 309	118	1 110 627	539 742	570 885	...
Isle of Man - Île de Man								
23 IV 2006 (CDJC)								
DOUGLAS	26 218	13 000	13 218	...	...	...	...	...
Italy - Italie								
1 VII 2013 (ESDJ)								
Ancona	101 043	47 904	53 139	125	...	...	...	...
Bari	317 982	151 823	166 160	117	...	...	...	...
Bergamo	116 895	54 381	62 514	40	...	...	...	...
Bologna	382 419	179 226	203 193	141	...	...	...	...
Bolzano	104 802	49 967	54 835	52	...	...	...	...
Brescia	191 060	89 602	101 458	90	...	...	...	...
Cagliari	151 797	70 064	81 734	85	...	...	...	...
Catania	303 127	144 287	158 841	183	...	...	...	...
Ferrara	132 633	61 897	70 736	405	...	...	...	...
Firenze	371 623	173 096	198 528	102	...	...	...	...
Foggia	150 858	72 335	78 523	509	...	...	...	...
Forli	117 194	56 294	60 901	228	...	...	...	...
Genova	589 639	275 855	313 784	240	...	...	...	...
Giugliano in Campania	115 315	56 648	58 667	95	...	...	...	...
Latina	122 401	58 984	63 417	278	...	...	...	...
Livorno	158 755	75 621	83 135	105	...	...	...	...
Messina	242 132	115 868	126 265	214	...	...	...	...
Milano	1 293 135	611 635	681 500	182	...	...	...	...
Modena	181 939	86 541	95 398	183	...	...	...	...
Monza	121 796	58 291	63 505	33	...	...	...	...
Napoli	974 082	463 023	511 059	119	...	...	...	...
Novara	103 335	49 320	54 015	103	...	...	...	...
Padova	208 462	97 571	110 891	93	...	...	...	...
Palermo	666 740	317 831	348 909	161	...	...	...	...
Parma	182 826	86 274	96 552	261	...	...	...	...
Perugia	164 508	78 033	86 475	450	...	...	...	...
Pescara	119 208	55 824	63 385	34	...	...	...	...
Piacenza	101 624	48 163	53 461	118	...	...	...	...
Prato	189 214	91 371	97 843	97	...	...	...	...
Ravenna	156 536	75 492	81 045	654	...	...	...	...
Reggio di Calabria	182 812	87 466	95 346	239	...	...	...	...
Reggio nell'Emilia	168 227	81 358	86 869	231	...	...	...	...
Rimini	145 294	69 351	75 943	136	...	...	...	...
ROMA	2 751 082	1 299 220	1 451 862	1 287	...	...	...	...
Salerno	132 905	62 041	70 864	60	...	...	...	...
Sassari	126 694	60 595	66 099	547	...	...	...	...
Siracusa	120 474	58 897	61 577	208	...	...	...	...
Taranto	200 993	95 751	105 242	250	...	...	...	...
Terni	110 805	52 028	58 777	212	...	...	...	...
Torino	887 114	420 855	466 260	130	...	...	...	...
Trento	116 413	55 616	60 797	158	...	...	...	...
Trieste	202 999	95 622	107 377	85	...	...	...	...
Venezia	261 899	123 077	138 822	416	...	...	...	...
Verona	256 688	121 087	135 601	199	...	...	...	...
Vicenza	113 647	53 783	59 865	81	...	...	...	...
Jersey								
11 III 2001 (CDJC)								
ST. HELIER	28 310	13 669	14 641	9	...	...	...	...
Latvia - Lettonie								
1 VII 2013 (ESDJ)								
RIGA	643 492	283 947	359 545	304	...	...	...	...

Continent, country or area, date, code[a] and city / Continent, pays ou zone, date, code[a] et ville	City proper - Ville proprement dite				Urban agglomeration - Agglomération urbaine			
	Population			Surface area - Superficie (km²)	Population			Surface area - Superficie (km²)
	Both sexes - Les deux sexes	Male - Masculin	Female - Féminin		Both sexes - Les deux sexes	Male - Masculin	Female - Féminin	
EUROPE								
Liechtenstein								
1 VII 2013* (ESDJ)								
VADUZ	5 270	2 552	2 718	17	...	...	...	...
Lithuania - Lituanie								
1 VII 2013 (ESDJ)								
Kaunas	305 450	134 470	170 980	157	...	...	...	...
Klaipeda	157 923	71 528	86 395	98	...	...	...	...
Shauliai	106 040	46 944	59 096	81	...	...	...	...
VILNIUS	538 430	241 197	297 233	401	...	...	...	...
Luxembourg								
1 I 2014 (ESDJ)								
LUXEMBOURG-VILLE	107 247	54 564	52 683	51				
Malta - Malte								
1 VII 2013 (ESDJ)								
VALLETTA	5 710	2 792	2 918	1	...	...	...	...
Monaco								
1 VII 2000 (ESDJ)								
MONACO	*32 020*	*15 544*	*16 476*	...	...	...	...	...
Montenegro - Monténégro								
1 IV 2011 (CDJC)								
PODGORICA	185 937	90 614	95 323	1 441	...	...	...	...
Netherlands - Pays-Bas								
1 I 2011 (ESDJ)								
Almere	190 655	94 639	96 016	130	...	...	...	...
Amersfoort	146 592	71 979	74 613	63	175 201	85 980	89 221	122
AMSTERDAM	779 808	383 802	396 006	166	1 068 724	524 640	544 084	337
Apeldoorn	...	...	...	...	156 199	77 088	79 111	340
Arnhem	148 070	73 507	74 563	98	149 582	74 260	75 322	126
Breda	174 599	85 006	89 593	127	...	...	...	...
Dordrecht	118 810	58 526	60 284	79	236 734	116 326	120 408	139
Ede	108 285	53 146	55 139	318	...	...	...	...
Eindhoven	216 036	109 977	106 059	88	330 152	166 592	163 560	199
Emmen	109 259	54 040	55 219	337	...	...	...	...
Enschede	157 838	80 122	77 716	141	...	...	...	...
Geleen-Sittard	...	...	...	...	137 071	67 445	69 626	121
Groningen	189 991	94 064	95 927	78	208 506	102 801	105 705	124
Haarlem	150 670	73 260	77 410	29	199 006	96 039	102 967	94
Haarlemmermeer	143 374	71 310	72 064	179	...	...	...	...
Heerlen-Kerkrade	...	...	...	...	204 182	100 807	103 375	109
Leiden	117 915	57 527	60 388	22	253 200	123 679	129 521	77
Maastricht	119 664	57 538	62 126	57	...	...	...	...
Nijmegen	164 223	78 582	85 641	54	...	...	...	...
Rotterdam	610 386	300 319	310 067	206	1 003 088	492 492	510 596	329
s-Gravenhage	...	...	...	...	639 652	312 813	326 839	180
s-Hertogenbosch	140 786	69 200	71 586	84	166 440	81 951	84 489	118
The Hague	495 083	244 040	251 043	82	...	...	...	...
Tilburg	206 240	102 366	103 874	117	229 047	113 670	115 377	159
Utrecht	311 367	150 571	160 796	95	469 712	228 404	241 308	167
Zaanstad	190 655	94 639	96 016	74	...	...	...	...
Zoetermeer	146 592	71 979	74 613	35	...	...	...	...
Zwolle	120 355	58 697	61 658	112	...	...	...	...
Norway - Norvège								
1 I 2014 (ESDJ)								
OSLO	634 293	316 114	318 179	426	...	...	...	...
Poland - Pologne[67]								
1 VII 2012 (ESDJ)								
Bialystok	294 675	138 477	156 198	102[8]	...	...	...	...
Bielsko-Biala	174 291	82 143	92 148	125[8]	...	...	...	...
Bydgoszcz	362 286	170 457	191 829	176[8]	...	...	...	...
Bytom	175 377	84 118	91 259	69[8]	...	...	...	...
Chorzów	111 314	53 051	58 263	33[8]	...	...	...	...
Czestochowa	235 156	110 506	124 650	160[8]	...	...	...	...
Dabrowa Górnicza	125 063	60 206	64 857	189[8]	...	...	...	...
Elblag	123 977	59 427	64 550	80[8]	...	...	...	...
Gdansk	460 354	218 273	242 081	262[8]	...	...	...	...

8. Population of capital cities and cities of 100 000 or more inhabitants: latest available year, 1995 - 2014
Population des capitales et des villes de 100 000 habitants ou plus : dernière année disponible, 1995 - 2014 (continued - suite)

Continent, country or area, date, code[a] and city / Continent, pays ou zone, date, code[a] et ville	City proper - Ville proprement dite				Urban agglomeration - Agglomération urbaine			
	Population			Surface area - Superficie (km²)	Population			Surface area - Superficie (km²)
	Both sexes - Les deux sexes	Male - Masculin	Female - Féminin		Both sexes - Les deux sexes	Male - Masculin	Female - Féminin	
EUROPE								
Poland - Pologne[67]								
1 VII 2012 (ESDJ)								
Gdynia	248 574	118 140	130 434	135[8]	...	...	...	...
Gliwice	186 347	89 801	96 546	134[8]	...	...	...	...
Gorzów Wielkopolski	124 470	59 306	65 164	86[8]	...	...	...	...
Kalisz	104 867	48 802	56 065	69[8]	...	...	...	...
Katowice	308 269	146 571	161 698	165[8]	...	...	...	...
Kielce	201 363	94 999	106 364	110[8]	...	...	...	...
Koszalin	109 183	51 635	57 548	98[8]	...	...	...	...
Kraków	759 131	354 200	404 931	327[8]	...	...	...	...
Legnica	102 708	48 647	54 061	56[8]	...	...	...	...
Lódz	722 022	328 440	393 582	293[8]	...	...	...	...
Lublin	348 120	160 158	187 962	147[8]	...	...	...	...
Olsztyn	175 482	81 778	93 704	88[8]	...	...	...	...
Opole	122 120	57 115	65 005	97[8]	...	...	...	...
Plock	124 048	58 753	65 295	88[8]	...	...	...	...
Poznan	552 393	257 418	294 975	262[8]	...	...	...	...
Radom	220 062	104 699	115 363	112[8]	...	...	...	...
Ruda Slaska	142 672	69 292	73 380	78[8]	...	...	...	...
Rybnik	140 863	68 798	72 065	148[8]	...	...	...	...
Rzeszów	180 776	85 342	95 434	117[8]	...	...	...	...
Sosnowiec	214 488	101 857	112 631	91[8]	...	...	...	...
Szczecin	409 211	194 601	214 610	301[8]	...	...	...	...
Tarnów	113 188	53 499	59 689	72[8]	...	...	...	...
Torun	204 847	95 219	109 628	116[8]	...	...	...	...
Tychy	129 087	62 377	66 710	82[8]	...	...	...	...
Walbrzych	119 216	56 285	62 931	85[8]	...	...	...	...
WARSZAWA	1 711 324	785 187	926 137	517[8]	...	...	...	...
Wloclawek	115 982	54 738	61 244	84[8]	...	...	...	...
Wroclaw	631 377	294 627	336 750	293[8]	...	...	...	...
Zabrze	179 861	86 939	92 922	80[8]	...	...	...	...
Zielona Góra	119 182	56 032	63 150	58[8]	...	...	...	...
Portugal								
1 VII 2013 (ESDJ)								
Amadora	175 493	82 158	93 335	24	...	...	...	...
LISBOA	517 975	236 457	281 518	100	...	...	...	...
Porto	224 894	101 823	123 071	41	...	...	...	...
Republic of Moldova - République de Moldova								
1 I 2012 (ESDJ)								
Balti (Beltsy)	144 507	66 243	78 264	41	...	...	...	...
CHIŞINĂU (KISHINEV)	669 694	311 575	358 119	123	726 075	339 321	386 755	572
Romania - Roumanie								
1 VII 2012* (ESDJ)								
Arad	162 984	75 926	87 058	234	...	...	...	...
Bacau	172 952	82 144	90 808	43	...	...	...	...
Baia Mare	136 480	64 868	71 612	233	...	...	...	...
Botosani	113 107	53 825	59 282	41	...	...	...	...
Braila	206 599	97 938	108 661	44	...	...	...	...
Brasov	275 514	130 305	145 209	267	...	...	...	...
BUCURESTI	1 912 515	891 615	1 020 900	238	...	...	...	...
Buzau	129 368	61 262	68 106	81	...	...	...	...
Cluj-Napoca	303 047	141 869	161 178	180	...	...	...	...
Constanta	297 503	138 977	158 526	125	...	...	...	...
Craiova	293 567	139 020	154 547	81	...	...	...	...
Drobeta Turnu-Severin	102 839	49 098	53 741	...	...	...	...	...
Galati	286 530	137 587	148 943	246	...	...	...	...
Iasi	318 871	150 077	168 794	101	...	...	...	...
Oradea	201 547	94 370	107 177	116	...	...	...	...
Piatra Neamt	104 605	49 167	55 438	...	...	...	...	...
Pitesti	164 687	77 729	86 958	41	...	...	...	...
Ploiesti	224 406	105 016	119 390	58	...	...	...	...
Rimnicu Vilcea	110 527	52 505	58 022	...	...	...	...	...
Satu-Mare	109 728	51 564	58 164	15 024	...	...	...	...

8. Population of capital cities and cities of 100 000 or more inhabitants: latest available year, 1995 - 2014
Population des capitales et des villes de 100 000 habitants ou plus : dernière année disponible, 1995 - 2014 (continued - suite)

Continent, country or area, date, code[a] and city / Continent, pays ou zone, date, code[a] et ville	City proper - Ville proprement dite				Urban agglomeration - Agglomération urbaine			
	Population			Surface area - Superficie (km²)	Population			Surface area - Superficie (km²)
	Both sexes - Les deux sexes	Male - Masculin	Female - Féminin		Both sexes - Les deux sexes	Male - Masculin	Female - Féminin	
EUROPE								
Romania - Roumanie								
1 VII 2012* (ESDJ)								
Sibiu	425 906	207 118	218 788	122	...	...	...	...
Suceava	105 624	50 282	55 342	...	...	...	...	...
Timisoara	306 462	142 471	163 991	129	...	...	...	...
Tirgu-Mures	142 327	67 016	75 311	49	...	...	...	...
Russian Federation - Fédération de Russie								
1 VII 2012 (ESDJ)								
Abakan	168 655	77 052	91 603	...	...	...	...	...
Achinsk	107 943	48 069	59 874	...	109 229	...	...	...
Almetievsk	148 384	69 433	78 951	...	...	...	...	...
Anapa	...	...	...	...	156 928	...	...	...
Angarsk	231 944	105 405	126 539	...	...	...	...	...
Arkhangelsk	350 258	156 523	193 735	...	357 264	...	...	...
Armavir	190 831	87 524	103 307	...	209 742	...	...	...
Artem (Primorskiy Krai)	102 605	49 147	53 458	...	112 102	...	...	...
Arzamas	105 506	47 208	58 298	...	...	...	...	...
Astrakhan	526 363	241 489	284 874	...	...	...	...	...
Balakovo	196 918	88 075	108 843	...	...	...	...	...
Balashikha	228 567	112 191	116 376	...	238 284	...	...	...
Barnaul	625 679	279 300	346 379	...	686 306	...	...	...
Bataisk	115 016	54 477	60 539	...	...	...	...	...
Belgorod	369 815	167 120	202 695	...	...	...	...	...
Belovo	...	...	...	...	132 144	...	...	...
Berezniki	153 806	68 365	85 441	...	...	...	...	...
Biisk	206 327	91 943	114 384	...	215 780	...	...	...
Blagoveshchensk (Amurskaya oblast)	216 691	97 135	119 556	...	222 065	...	...	...
Bor	...	...	...	...	122 201	...	...	...
Bratsk	242 604	109 596	133 008	...	...	...	...	...
Bryansk	411 798	183 540	228 258	...	430 987	...	...	...
Cheboksary	462 669	206 721	255 948	...	473 189	...	...	...
Chelyabinsk	1 149 829	514 456	635 373	...	...	...	...	...
Cherepovets	315 186	142 977	172 209	...	...	...	...	...
Cherkessk	126 884	55 588	71 296	...	...	...	...	...
Chita	329 391	152 092	177 299	...	329 868	...	...	...
Derbent	119 647	57 527	62 120	...	...	...	...	...
Dimitrovgrad	120 750	55 838	64 912	...	...	...	...	...
Domodedovo	...	...	...	...	142 743	...	...	...
Dzerzhinsk (Nizhegorodskaya oblast)	238 327	105 346	132 981	...	248 649	...	...	...
Ekaterinburg	1 386 909	621 499	765 410	...	1 420 285	...	...	...
Elektrostal	156 136	71 093	85 043	...	...	...	...	...
Elets	107 347	48 757	58 590	...	...	...	...	...
Elista	104 177	47 317	56 860	...	108 753	...	...	...
Engels	210 190	95 953	114 237	...	211 825	...	...	...
Esentuky	101 851	45 327	56 524	...	...	...	...	...
Groznyi	276 524	136 615	139 909	...	...	...	...	...
Hasaviurt	133 188	63 867	69 321	...	...	...	...	...
Irkutsk	601 993	269 003	332 990	...	...	...	...	...
Ivanovo	408 952	180 083	228 869	...	...	...	...	...
Izhevsk	631 182	281 708	349 474	...	...	...	...	...
Kaliningrad (Kaliningradskaya oblast)	437 456	200 849	236 607	...	...	...	...	...
Kaluga	328 871	146 008	182 863	...	344 766	...	...	...
Kamensk-Uralsky	172 639	77 327	95 312	...	174 493	...	...	...
Kamyshin	117 352	53 822	63 530	...	...	...	...	...
Kaspiysk	102 421	49 393	53 028	...	...	...	...	...
Kazan	1 168 745	520 694	648 051	...	...	...	...	...
Kemerovo	538 188	240 431	297 757	...	...	...	...	...
Khabarovsk	589 596	273 949	315 647	...	...	...	...	...
Khimki	218 275	99 122	119 153	...	...	...	...	...
Kirov	480 594	211 205	269 389	...	505 346	...	...	...
Kiselevsk	...	...	...	...	101 180	...	...	...
Kislovodsk	129 313	58 854	70 459	...	136 142	...	...	...
Kolomna	144 838	66 469	78 369	...	...	...	...	...
Komsomolsk-na-Amure	259 081	120 197	138 884	...	...	...	...	...
Kopeysk	139 161	66 142	73 019	...	141 291	...	...	...

Continent, country or area, date, code[a] and city / Continent, pays ou zone, date, code[a] et ville	City proper - Ville proprement dite				Urban agglomeration - Agglomération urbaine			
	Population			Surface area - Superficie (km²)	Population			Surface area - Superficie (km²)
	Both sexes - Les deux sexes	Male - Masculin	Female - Féminin		Both sexes - Les deux sexes	Male - Masculin	Female - Féminin	

EUROPE

Russian Federation - Fédération de Russie
  1 VII 2012 (ESDJ)

City	Both sexes	Male	Female	Surface	Both sexes	Male	Female	Surface
Korolev (Moskovskaya oblast)	186 460	84 232	102 228	...	...	...	...	...
Kostroma	270 366	120 622	149 744	...	...	...	...	...
Kovrov	...	...	...	...	346 922	154 144	192 778	...
Krasnodar	773 970	350 519	423 451	...	861 181	...	...	...
Krasnogorsk	125 198	56 432	68 766	...	125 787	...	...	...
Krasnoyarsk	1 006 856	456 171	550 685	...	1 007 654	...	...	...
Kurgan	326 729	146 140	180 589	...	...	...	...	...
Kursk	425 950	189 025	236 925	...	...	...	...	...
Kyzyl	112 659	52 137	60 522	...	...	...	...	...
Leninsk-Kuznetsky	100 073	45 651	54 422	...	102 285	...	...	...
Lipetsk	508 585	230 178	278 407	...	...	...	...	...
Lyubertsy	178 884	80 564	98 320	...	...	...	...	...
Magadan	95 263	45 084	50 179	...	101 933	...	...	...
Magnitogorsk	410 733	186 534	224 199	...	...	...	...	...
Maikop	144 579	64 512	80 067	...	167 281	...	...	...
Makhachkala	575 243	271 687	303 556	...	701 753	...	...	...
Mezhdurechensk	100 278	46 498	53 780	...	102 465	...	...	...
Miass	150 806	67 824	82 982	...	166 205	...	...	...
MOSKVA	11 918 057	5 495 477	6 422 580	...	...	...	...	...
Murmansk	303 754	139 944	163 810	...	...	...	...	...
Murom	113 330	50 293	63 037	...	122 545	...	...	...
Mytishchi	176 825	80 425	96 400	...	185 204	...	...	...
Naberezhnye Tchelny	517 831	237 620	280 211	...	...	...	...	...
Nakhodka	158 649	75 081	83 568	...	159 633	...	...	...
Naltchik	239 230	106 648	132 582	...	265 051	...	...	...
Nazran	100 574	44 126	56 448	...	...	...	...	...
Neftekamsk	123 202	57 271	65 931	...	135 013	...	...	...
Nefteyugansk	125 528	61 635	63 893	...	...	...	...	...
Nevinnomyssk	117 949	53 611	64 338	...	...	...	...	...
Nizhnekamsk	235 179	111 262	123 917	...	235 279	...	...	...
Nizhnevartovsk	261 011	125 937	135 074	...	...	...	...	...
Nizhny Novgorod	1 257 260	552 285	704 975	...	1 266 231	...	...	...
Nizhny Tagil	358 651	162 731	195 920	...	362 185	...	...	...
Noginsk	101 779	45 741	56 038	...	103 843	...	...	...
Norilsk	177 506	89 198	88 308	...	178 363	...	...	...
Novocheboksarsk	...	...	...	...	124 288	...	...	...
Novocherkassk	171 081	81 921	89 160	...	...	...	...	...
Novokuybishevsk	107 244	48 418	58 826	...	109 521	...	...	...
Novokuznetsk	549 383	247 386	301 997	...	...	...	...	...
Novomoskovsk (Tulskaya oblast)	129 555	57 961	71 594	...	141 893	...	...	...
Novorossiysk	248 857	117 707	131 150	...	305 421	...	...	...
Novoshakhtinsk	110 243	50 410	59 833	...	...	...	...	...
Novosibirsk	1 511 369	694 959	816 410	...	...	...	...	...
Novotroitsk	...	...	...	...	103 061	...	...	...
Novy Urengoy	114 332	59 841	54 491	...	...	...	...	...
Noyabrsk	108 662	53 237	55 425	...	...	...	...	...
Obninsk	105 722	48 323	57 399	...	...	...	...	...
Odintsovo	137 706	63 405	74 301	...	143 848	...	...	...
Oktyabrsky	111 109	51 956	59 153	...	...	...	...	...
Omsk	1 158 627	526 757	631 870	...	...	...	...	...
Orekhovo-Zuevo	121 341	53 443	67 898	...	...	...	...	...
Orel	318 642	139 662	178 980	...	...	...	...	...
Orenburg	555 420	252 906	302 514	...	571 041	...	...	...
Orsk	237 194	106 127	131 067	...	241 327	...	...	...
Penza	519 948	234 270	285 678	...	...	...	...	...
Perm	1 007 272	444 386	562 886	...	1 007 285	...	...	...
Pervouralsk	125 421	56 144	69 277	...	149 796	...	...	...
Petropavlovsk-Kamchatsky	180 702	88 743	91 959	...	...	...	...	...
Petrozavodsk	267 102	118 638	148 464	...	...	...	...	...
Podolsk	200 059	89 931	110 128	...	...	...	...	...
Prokopyevsk	206 023	91 944	114 079	...	...	...	...	...
Pskov	205 062	92 439	112 623	...	...	...	...	...
Pushkino	104 020	46 649	57 371	...	...	...	...	...

8. Population of capital cities and cities of 100 000 or more inhabitants: latest available year, 1995 - 2014
Population des capitales et des villes de 100 000 habitants ou plus : dernière année disponible, 1995 - 2014 (continued - suite)

Continent, country or area, date, code[a] and city / Continent, pays ou zone, date, code[a] et ville	City proper - Ville proprement dite				Urban agglomeration - Agglomération urbaine			
	Population			Surface area - Superficie (km²)	Population			Surface area - Superficie (km²)
	Both sexes - Les deux sexes	Male - Masculin	Female - Féminin		Both sexes - Les deux sexes	Male - Masculin	Female - Féminin	
EUROPE								
Russian Federation - Fédération de Russie								
1 VII 2012 (ESDJ)								
Pyatigorsk	144 603	64 578	80 025	...	212 968	...	...	...
Rostov-na-Donu	1 100 091	501 068	599 023	...	...	...	...	...
Rubtsovsk	146 075	69 084	76 991	...	...	...	...	...
Ryazan	526 919	237 791	289 128	...	...	...	...	...
Rybinsk	197 359	87 921	109 438	...	...	...	...	...
Salavat	155 174	72 449	82 725	...	...	...	...	...
Samara (Samarskaya oblast)	1 170 381	522 660	647 721	...	1 170 485	...	...	...
Saransk	298 103	132 543	165 560	...	326 473	...	...	...
Sarapyul	100 362	44 678	55 684	...	...	...	...	...
Saratov	838 321	373 676	464 645	...	...	...	...	...
Sergiev Posad	109 076	48 786	60 290	...	115 858	...	...	...
Serov	...	...	...	...	107 904	...	...	...
Serpukhov	126 729	57 494	69 235	...	...	...	...	...
Severodvinsk	189 313	87 781	101 532	...	190 513	...	...	...
Seversk	109 630	50 705	58 925	...	116 340	...	...	...
Shakhty	238 031	107 544	130 487	...	...	...	...	...
Shchelkovo	111 406	50 812	60 594	...	113 726	...	...	...
Smolensk	330 451	147 446	183 005	...	...	...	...	...
Sochi	364 171	164 632	199 539	...	441 407	...	...	...
St. Petersburg	4 990 602	2 247 375	2 743 227	...	...	...	...	...
Stary Oskol	220 719	100 902	119 817	...	256 790	...	...	...
Stavropol	408 361	187 593	220 768	...	408 560	...	...	...
Sterlitamak	275 087	125 443	149 644	...	...	...	...	...
Surgut	321 062	153 832	167 230	...	...	...	...	...
Syktivkar	239 341	107 945	131 396	...	255 283	...	...	...
Syzran	177 404	79 804	97 600	...	178 205	...	...	...
Taganrog	255 671	114 508	141 163	...	...	...	...	...
Tambov	281 348	126 427	154 921	...	...	...	...	...
Tobolsk	...	...	...	...	101 955	...	...	...
Tolyatti	719 363	331 248	388 115	...	...	...	...	...
Tomsk	543 596	252 173	291 423	...	565 000	...	...	...
Tula	496 656	220 675	275 981	...	...	...	...	...
Tver	407 896	180 459	227 437	...	...	...	...	...
Tyumen	621 918	288 291	333 627	...	644 799	...	...	...
Ufa	1 075 007	484 893	590 114	...	1 084 420	...	...	...
Uhta	99 680	47 563	52 117	...	121 479	...	...	...
Ulan-Ude	413 850	191 732	222 118	...	...	...	...	...
Ulyanovsk	614 878	278 103	336 775	...	637 637	...	...	...
Ussuriisk	163 465	79 562	83 903	...	189 502	...	...	...
Velikiy Novgorod	219 941	95 446	124 495	...	...	...	...	...
Vladikavkaz (Osetinskaya ASSR)	309 173	139 818	169 355	...	327 448	...	...	...
Vladimir	346 922	154 144	192 778	...	349 525	...	...	...
Vladivostok	598 927	282 260	316 667	...	624 281	...	...	...
Volgodonsk	170 189	78 251	91 938	...	...	...	...	...
Volgograd	1 018 762	460 095	558 667	...	...	...	...	...
Vologda	305 397	135 292	170 105	...	313 679	...	...	...
Volzhsky	320 761	148 339	172 422	...	327 460	...	...	...
Voronezh	997 447	447 484	549 963	...	...	...	...	...
Yakutsk	282 419	132 612	149 807	...	298 926	...	...	...
Yaroslavl	597 161	262 042	335 119	...	...	...	...	...
Yoshkar-Ola	254 987	114 331	140 656	...	265 626	...	...	...
Yuzhno-Sakhalinsk	188 242	89 200	99 042	...	195 104	...	...	...
Zheleznodorozhny	138 814	62 719	76 095	...	...	...	...	...
Zhukovsky	106 555	49 027	57 528	...	...	...	...	...
Zlatoust	172 972	78 071	94 901	...	175 178	...	...	...
San Marino - Saint-Marin								
1 I 2013 (ESDF)								
SAN MARINO	4 438	2 117	2 321	...	...	...	...	...
Serbia - Serbie[68]								
1 VII 2013 (ESDJ)								
BEOGRAD (BELGRADE)	1 357 005	633 425	723 580	389	1 669 552[69]	789 266[69]	880 286[69]	3 235[69]
Čačak	72 955	34 932	38 023	35	114 141[69]	55 444[69]	58 697[69]	636[69]
Kragujevac	150 773	72 860	77 913	83	179 030[69]	87 059[69]	91 971[69]	834[69]

8. Population of capital cities and cities of 100 000 or more inhabitants: latest available year, 1995 - 2014
Population des capitales et des villes de 100 000 habitants ou plus : dernière année disponible, 1995 - 2014 (continued - suite)

Continent, country or area, date, code[a] and city / Continent, pays ou zone, date, code[a] et ville	City proper - Ville proprement dite				Urban agglomeration - Agglomération urbaine			
	Population			Surface area - Superficie (km²)	Population			Surface area - Superficie (km²)
	Both sexes - Les deux sexes	Male - Masculin	Female - Féminin		Both sexes - Les deux sexes	Male - Masculin	Female - Féminin	
EUROPE								
Serbia - Serbie[68]								
1 VII 2013 (ESDJ)								
Kraljevo	68 198	32 908	35 290	24	123 724[69]	60 686[69]	63 038[69]	1 530[69]
Kruševac	58 557	27 840	30 717	11	126 900[69]	62 000[69]	64 900[69]	853[69]
Leskovac	64 603	31 295	33 308	25	141 719[69]	70 409[69]	71 310[69]	1 025[69]
Niš	186 955	89 553	97 402	43	259 125[69]	125 890[69]	133 235[69]	597[69]
Novi Sad	281 998	132 128	149 870	81	346 163[69]	163 992[69]	182 171[69]	701[69]
Pancevo	90 172	43 308	46 864	162	122 492[69]	59 576[69]	62 916[69]	756[69]
Šabac	53 700	25 225	28 475	31	114 548[69]	55 979[69]	58 569[69]	798[69]
Smederevo	63 803	30 889	32 914	42	107 048[69]	52 786[69]	54 262[69]	484[69]
Subotica	105 005	49 956	55 049	162	140 223[69]	67 401[69]	72 822[69]	1 007[69]
Zrenjanin	75 885	36 126	39 759	193	121 683[69]	59 111[69]	62 572[69]	1 326[69]
Slovakia - Slovaquie								
1 VII 2013 (ESDJ)								
BRATISLAVA	416 489	194 695	221 795	368[8]	...	...	...	...
Kosice	239 981	115 112	124 869	244[8]	...	...	...	...
Slovenia - Slovénie								
1 VII 2013 (ESDJ)								
LJUBLJANA	274 517	131 733	142 784	164	276 290	132 605	143 685	171
Maribor	94 601	46 146	48 455	41	108 441	52 989	55 452	99
Spain - Espagne								
1 VII 2013 (ESDJ)								
A Coruña	245 367	113 948	131 419	38	...	...	...	...
Albacete	172 590	84 551	88 039	1 141	...	...	...	...
Alcalá de Henares	202 796	100 688	102 108	88	...	...	...	...
Alcobendas	112 192	54 192	58 000	45	...	...	...	...
Alcorcón	170 055	82 959	87 096	34	...	...	...	...
Algeciras	116 126	57 386	58 740	86	...	...	...	...
Alicante	333 560	162 106	171 454	202	...	...	...	...
Almería	193 024	93 876	99 148	296	...	...	...	...
Badajoz	150 569	73 252	77 317	1 474	...	...	...	...
Badalona	235 633	115 631	120 002	21	...	...	...	...
Baracaldo	100 291	48 558	51 733	25	...	...	...	...
Barcelona	1 607 104	761 009	846 095	103	...	...	...	...
Bilbao	347 965	164 159	183 806	41	...	...	...	...
Burgos	178 437	85 343	93 094	107	...	...	...	...
Cádiz	122 365	57 916	64 449	12	...	...	...	...
Cartagena	217 046	108 889	108 157	558	...	...	...	...
Castellón de la Plana	177 013	86 568	90 445	109	...	...	...	...
Córdoba	328 373	157 837	170 536	1 263	...	...	...	...
Donostia - San Sebastián	186 313	87 456	98 857	62	...	...	...	...
Dos Hermanas	130 044	64 222	65 822	160	...	...	...	...
Elche	229 436	114 014	115 422	326	...	...	...	...
Fuenlabrada	196 692	98 082	98 610	39	...	...	...	...
Getafe	172 792	84 991	87 801	79	...	...	...	...
Gijón	275 505	130 094	145 411	181	...	...	...	...
Granada	237 679	110 578	127 101	88	...	...	...	...
Hospitalet de Llobregat	236 613	116 287	120 326	13	...	...	...	...
Huelva	147 657	71 077	76 580	152	...	...	...	...
Jaén	116 007	55 979	60 028	424	...	...	...	...
Jérez de la Frontera	211 948	103 825	108 123	1 189	...	...	...	...
Leganés	186 846	91 415	95 431	43	...	...	...	...
León	130 076	59 422	70 654	39	...	...	...	...
Lleida	139 493	69 103	70 390	212	...	...	...	...
Logroño	152 514	73 002	79 512	79	...	...	...	...
MADRID	3 186 241	1 483 791	1 702 450	604	...	...	...	...
Málaga	567 696	273 075	294 621	395	...	...	...	...
Marbella	140 349	68 239	72 110	117	...	...	...	...
Mataró	122 155	61 070	61 085	22	...	...	...	...
Móstoles	206 082	101 337	104 745	45	...	...	...	...
Murcia	438 979	215 065	223 914	886	...	...	...	...
Ourense	107 224	49 168	58 056	85	...	...	...	...
Oviedo	224 427	104 555	119 872	187	...	...	...	...
Palma de Mallorca	398 628	194 281	204 347	...	...	...	...	...

8. Population of capital cities and cities of 100 000 or more inhabitants: latest available year, 1995 - 2014
Population des capitales et des villes de 100 000 habitants ou plus : dernière année disponible, 1995 - 2014 (continued - suite)

Continent, country or area, date, code[a] and city / Continent, pays ou zone, date, code[a] et ville	City proper - Ville proprement dite				Urban agglomeration - Agglomération urbaine			
	Population			Surface area - Superficie (km²)	Population			Surface area - Superficie (km²)
	Both sexes - Les deux sexes	Male - Masculin	Female - Féminin		Both sexes - Les deux sexes	Male - Masculin	Female - Féminin	

EUROPE

Spain - Espagne
1 VII 2013 (ESDJ)

Palmas de Gran Canaria	382 667	186 014	196 653	106	...	...	...	...
Pamplona	196 561	93 706	102 855	25	...	...	...	...
Parla	125 479	63 246	62 233	25	...	...	...	...
Reus	105 876	51 646	54 230	53	...	...	...	...
Sabadell	207 547	101 040	106 507	38	...	...	...	...
Salamanca	148 785	68 236	80 549	40	...	...	...	...
San Cristóbal de La Laguna	152 364	74 229	78 135	107	...	...	...	...
Santa Coloma de Gramanet	166 897	82 879	84 018	7	...	...	...	...
Santa Cruz de Tenerife	205 936	98 529	107 407	156	...	...	...	...
Santander	176 430	81 610	94 820	35	...	...	...	...
Sevilla	698 423	331 916	366 507	141	...	...	...	...
Tarragona	132 872	65 033	67 839	56	...	...	...	...
Telde	102 123	50 607	51 516	104	...	...	...	...
Terrassa	169 808	84 157	85 651	70	...	...	...	...
Torrejón de Ardoz	125 320	62 388	62 932	32	...	...	...	...
Valencia	789 364	376 965	412 399	136	...	...	...	...
Valladolid	308 272	145 691	162 581	197	...	...	...	...
Vigo	295 738	140 843	154 895	105	...	...	...	...
Vitoria-Gasteiz	241 734	118 517	123 217	277	...	...	...	...
Zaragoza	674 031	324 966	349 065	972	...	...	...	...

Sweden - Suède
1 VII 2007 (ESDJ)

Göteborg	491 630	242 916	248 714	449	...	...	...	...
Helsingborg	124 188	60 672	63 516	346	...	...	...	...
Jönköping	122 952	60 462	62 490	1 485	...	...	...	...
Linköping	139 474	70 239	69 235	1 431	...	...	...	...
Malmö	278 523	135 997	142 526	154	...	...	...	...
Norrköping	126 072	62 323	63 749	1 491	...	...	...	...
Orebro	129 703	63 123	66 581	1 371	...	...	...	...
STOCKHOLM	789 024	384 243	404 781	187	...	...	...	...
Umeå	111 503	55 549	55 955	2 316	...	...	...	...
Uppsala	186 364	91 149	95 215	2 465	...	...	...	...
Västerås	133 324	66 056	67 269	956	...	...	...	...

Switzerland - Suisse
1 VII 2012 (ESDJ)

Baden-Brugg	28 931	14 583	14 349	20	119 698	59 719	59 979	124
Bâle	165 041	79 413	85 629	24	502 207	243 885	258 322	481
BERNE	126 598	60 459	66 139	52	358 076	172 832	185 244	488
Fribourg	36 157	17 764	18 393	9	108 497	53 873	54 624	212
Genève	188 634	90 325	98 309	16	532 129	257 696	274 433	457
Lausanne	129 902	62 145	67 758	41	343 728	166 946	176 782	314
Lugano	55 595	26 449	29 146	32	135 837	65 373	70 465	220
Luzern	78 786	37 598	41 188	29	213 037	104 248	108 789	198
Olten-Zofingen	27 965	13 661	14 305	23	112 603	56 008	56 596	183
St. Gallen	73 808	35 870	37 938	39	151 874	74 500	77 374	175
Winterthur	103 772	50 620	53 152	68	143 290	70 317	72 973	151
Zug	27 219	13 733	13 486	22	111 481	56 272	55 210	180
Zürich	378 884	187 316	191 568	88	1 210 875	600 924	609 951	1 086

TFYR of Macedonia - L'ex-R. y. de Macédoine
1 VII 2012 (ESDF)

SKOPJE	536 271	262 676	273 595	...	...	...	...	...

Ukraine
1 I 2013 (ESDJ)

Alchevsk	110 878	50 786	60 092	49	...	...	...	...
Belaya Tserkov (Bila Crkva)	206 990	95 422	111 568	34	...	...	...	...
Berdyansk	116 249	51 540	64 709	83	119 371	53 036	66 335	90
Cherkassy	283 130	129 279	153 851	67	283 924	129 696	154 228	78
Chernigov	290 269	133 477	156 792	78	...	...	...	...
Chernovtsy	255 084	117 029	138 055	153	...	...	...	...
Dneprodzerzhinsk	241 330	108 459	132 871	118	248 237	111 564	136 673	138
Dnepropetrovsk	987 629	448 496	539 133	387	990 025	449 659	540 366	405
Donetsk (Donestskaya oblast)	944 552	418 132	526 420	363	960 646	425 457	535 189	571
Enakievo (Yenakievo)	82 941	36 713	46 228	67	131 250	58 850	72 400	425

8. Population of capital cities and cities of 100 000 or more inhabitants: latest available year, 1995 - 2014
Population des capitales et des villes de 100 000 habitants ou plus : dernière année disponible, 1995 - 2014 (continued - suite)

Continent, country or area, date, code[a] and city / Continent, pays ou zone, date, code[a] et ville	City proper - Ville proprement dite				Urban agglomeration - Agglomération urbaine			
	Population			Surface area - Superficie (km²)	Population			Surface area - Superficie (km²)
	Both sexes - Les deux sexes	Male - Masculin	Female - Féminin		Both sexes - Les deux sexes	Male - Masculin	Female - Féminin	
EUROPE								
Ukraine								
1 I 2013 (ESDJ)								
Evpatoriya (Yevpatoriya)	104 289	46 505	57 784	43	120 473	53 898	66 575	66
Gorlovka	254 526	113 970	140 556	186	274 942	123 190	151 752	422
Ivano-Frankovsk	223 165	104 982	118 183	37	240 934	113 229	127 705	84
Kamyanetsk Podilsky	102 039	47 523	54 516	29	...	...	...	...
Kertch	146 559	66 067	80 492	108	...	...	...	...
Kharkov	1 431 461	659 700	771 761	350	...	...	...	...
Kherson	295 450	132 426	163 024	65	332 767	149 883	182 884	423
Khmelnitsky (Hmilnyk)	262 154	121 083	141 071	86	...	...	...	...
KIEV	2 803 716	1 295 137	1 508 579	836	...	...	...	...
Kirovograd	231 181	104 288	126 893	96	239 253	107 962	131 291	103
Kramatorsk	163 831	72 928	90 903	77	197 392	88 449	108 943	356
Krasny Lutch	82 719	38 155	44 564	58	124 003	57 497	66 506	154
Krementchug	224 912	102 180	122 732	96	...	...	...	...
Kryvy Rig	654 964	294 972	359 992	430	657 760	296 390	361 370	431
Lugansk	422 373	187 593	234 780	257	461 459	206 111	255 348	286
Lutsk	211 644	95 328	116 316	42	...	...	...	...
Lvov	723 605	338 326	385 279	149	751 225	351 409	399 816	171
Lysychansk	104 023	46 935	57 088	76	119 725	54 085	65 640	96
Makeyevka	352 227	158 789	193 438	185	390 700	176 633	214 067	426
Mariupol	458 415	208 218	250 197	150	480 263	218 497	261 766	244
Melitopol	156 831	70 894	85 937	43	...	...	...	...
Mykolaiv (Nikolaevskaya oblast)	491 693	222 669	269 024	260	...	...	...	...
Nikopol	120 774	53 710	67 064	50	...	...	...	...
Odessa	997 189	465 200	531 989	162	...	...	...	...
Pavlograd	111 013	50 995	60 018	59	...	...	...	...
Poltava	289 831	132 965	156 866	104	...	...	...	...
Rivne	246 911	113 057	133 854	58	...	...	...	...
Sevastopol	340 735	154 947	185 788	...	381 474	173 812	207 662	864
Severodonetsk	109 791	48 887	60 904	32	120 217	53 861	66 356	58
Simferopol	331 936	146 690	185 246	107	356 771	158 116	198 655	107
Slavyansk	115 333	50 262	65 071	61	134 218	58 891	75 327	74
Sumy	268 375	120 965	147 410	111	271 295	122 346	148 949	146
Ternopol	215 636	99 716	115 920	59	...	...	...	...
Uzhgorod	114 789	53 241	61 548	32	...	...	...	...
Vinnutsya	369 860	169 356	200 504	69	...	...	...	...
Yevpatoriya	104 289	46 505	57 784	43	120 473	53 898	66 575	66
Zaporozhye	766 736	346 450	420 286	278	...	...	...	...
Zhitomir	270 046	124 389	145 657	61	...	...	...	...
United Kingdom of Great Britain and Northern Ireland - Royaume-Uni de Grande-Bretagne et d'Irlande du Nord[70]								
29 IV 2001 (CDFC)								
Aberdeen	...	...	...	...	212 125	103 818	108 307	...
Aberdeenshire	...	...	...	...	226 871	112 470	114 401	...
Aldershot	...	...	...	...	243 344	121 127	122 217	...
Angus	...	...	...	...	108 400	52 458	55 942	...
Basildon/North Benfleet	...	...	...	...	101 492	48 649	52 843	...
Bedford/Kempston	...	...	...	...	101 928	50 341	51 587	...
Belfast[71]	...	...	...	...	276 459	129 321	147 138	...
Birkenhead	...	...	...	...	319 675	152 133	167 542	...
Blackburn/Darwen	...	...	...	...	136 655	66 834	69 821	...
Blackpool	...	...	...	...	261 088	124 698	136 390	...
Bournemouth	...	...	...	...	383 713	182 875	200 838	...
Brighton/Worthing/Littlehampton	...	...	...	...	461 181	220 275	240 906	...
Bristol	...	...	...	...	551 066	269 689	281 377	...
Burnley/Nelson	...	...	...	...	149 796	72 657	77 139	...
Cambridge	...	...	...	...	131 465	65 343	66 122	...
Cardiff[72]	...	...	...	...	327 706	156 272	171 434	...
Cheltenham/Charlton Kings	...	...	...	...	110 320	53 526	56 794	...
Chesterfield/Staveley	...	...	...	...	100 879	49 204	51 675	...
Colchester	...	...	...	...	104 390	51 652	52 738	...
Coventry/Bedworth	...	...	...	...	336 452	166 666	169 786	...
Crawley	...	...	...	...	180 177	88 404	91 773	...

8. Population of capital cities and cities of 100 000 or more inhabitants: latest available year, 1995 - 2014
Population des capitales et des villes de 100 000 habitants ou plus : dernière année disponible, 1995 - 2014 (continued - suite)

Continent, country or area, date, code[a] and city / Continent, pays ou zone, date, code[a] et ville	City proper - Ville proprement dite				Urban agglomeration - Agglomération urbaine			
	Population			Surface area - Superficie (km²)	Population			Surface area - Superficie (km²)
	Both sexes - Les deux sexes	Male - Masculin	Female - Féminin		Both sexes - Les deux sexes	Male - Masculin	Female - Féminin	

EUROPE

United Kingdom of Great Britain and Northern Ireland - Royaume-Uni de Grande-Bretagne et d'Irlande du Nord[70]
29 IV 2001 (CDFC)

Dearne Valley	...	...	...	...	207 726	100 992	106 734	...
Derby	...	...	...	...	236 738	115 644	121 094	...
Doncaster	...	...	...	...	127 851	62 127	65 724	...
Dumfries & Galloway	...	...	...	...	147 765	71 303	76 462	...
Dundee	...	...	...	...	145 663	69 140	76 523	...
East Ayrshire	...	...	...	...	120 235	57 842	62 393	...
East Dunbartonshire	...	...	...	...	108 243	52 014	56 229	...
Eastbourne	...	...	...	...	106 562	49 369	57 193	...
Edinburgh[73]	...	...	...	...	448 624	214 711	233 913	...
Exeter	...	...	...	...	106 772	52 045	54 727	...
Falkirk	...	...	...	...	145 191	70 016	75 175	...
Fife	...	...	...	...	349 429	167 628	181 801	...
Glasgow	...	...	...	...	577 869	272 309	305 560	...
Gloucester	...	...	...	...	136 203	66 669	69 534	...
Grimsby/Cleethorpes	...	...	...	...	138 842	67 360	71 482	...
Hastings/Bexhill	...	...	...	...	126 386	59 247	67 139	...
High Wycombe	...	...	...	...	118 229	57 857	60 372	...
Highland	...	...	...	...	208 914	102 297	106 617	...
Ipswich	...	...	...	...	141 658	69 468	72 190	...
Kingston-upon-Hull	...	...	...	...	301 416	146 926	154 490	...
Leicester	...	...	...	...	441 213	214 060	227 153	...
Lincoln	...	...	...	...	104 221	50 794	53 427	...
Liverpool	...	...	...	...	816 216	389 119	427 097	...
LONDON[74]	...	...	...	...	8 278 251	4 007 297	4 270 954	...
Luton/Dunstable	...	...	...	...	236 318	117 707	118 611	...
Manchester	...	...	...	...	2 244 931	1 090 898	1 154 033	...
Mansfield	...	...	...	...	158 114	76 884	81 230	...
Milton Keynes	...	...	...	...	184 506	91 441	93 065	...
Newport	...	...	...	...	139 298	66 884	72 414	...
North Ayrshire	...	...	...	...	135 817	64 238	71 579	...
North Lanarkshire	...	...	...	...	321 067	153 966	167 101	...
Northampton	...	...	...	...	197 199	96 670	100 529	...
Norwich	...	...	...	...	194 839	94 523	100 316	...
Nottingham	...	...	...	...	666 358	327 851	338 507	...
Nuneaton	...	...	...	...	132 236	64 837	67 399	...
Oxford	...	...	...	...	143 016	70 462	72 554	...
Perth & Kinross	...	...	...	...	134 949	65 172	69 777	...
Peterborough	...	...	...	...	136 292	66 139	70 153	...
Plymouth	...	...	...	...	243 795	119 076	124 719	...
Portsmouth	...	...	...	...	442 252	216 341	225 911	...
Preston	...	...	...	...	264 601	129 665	134 936	...
Reading/Wokingham	...	...	...	...	369 804	185 475	184 329	...
Renfrewshire	...	...	...	...	172 867	82 525	90 342	...
Scottish Borders	...	...	...	...	106 764	51 361	55 403	...
Sheffield	...	...	...	...	640 720	312 619	328 101	...
Slough	...	...	...	...	141 848	70 286	71 562	...
South Ayrshire	...	...	...	...	112 097	53 406	58 691	...
South Lanarkshire	...	...	...	...	302 216	144 206	158 010	...
Southampton	...	...	...	...	304 400	151 534	152 866	...
Southend	...	...	...	...	269 415	129 650	139 765	...
Southport/Formby	...	...	...	...	115 882	54 337	61 545	...
St. Albans/Hatfield	...	...	...	...	114 710	56 585	58 125	...
Sunderland	...	...	...	...	182 974	88 892	94 082	...
Swansea	...	...	...	...	270 506	130 648	139 858	...
Swindon	...	...	...	...	155 432	77 551	77 881	...
Teesside	...	...	...	...	365 323	176 475	188 848	...
Telford	...	...	...	...	138 241	67 770	70 471	...
Thanet	...	...	...	...	119 144	56 266	62 878	...
The Medway Towns	...	...	...	...	231 659	114 069	117 590	...
The Potteries	...	...	...	...	362 403	176 467	185 936	...
Torbay	...	...	...	...	110 366	52 551	57 815	...

8. Population of capital cities and cities of 100 000 or more inhabitants: latest available year, 1995 - 2014
Population des capitales et des villes de 100 000 habitants ou plus : dernière année disponible, 1995 - 2014 (continued - suite)

Continent, country or area, date, code[a] and city / Continent, pays ou zone, date, code[a] et ville	City proper - Ville proprement dite				Urban agglomeration - Agglomération urbaine			
	Population			Surface area - Superficie (km²)	Population			Surface area - Superficie (km²)
	Both sexes - Les deux sexes	Male - Masculin	Female - Féminin		Both sexes - Les deux sexes	Male - Masculin	Female - Féminin	
EUROPE								
United Kingdom of Great Britain and Northern Ireland - Royaume-Uni de Grande-Bretagne et d'Irlande du Nord[70]								
29 IV 2001 (CDFC)								
Tyneside	...	...	...	...	879 996	425 119	454 877	...
Warrington	...	...	...	...	158 195	77 334	80 861	...
West Lothian	...	...	...	...	158 714	76 701	82 013	...
West Midlands	...	...	...	...	2 284 093	1 109 397	1 174 696	...
West Yorkshire	...	...	...	...	1 499 465	724 818	774 647	...
Wigan	...	...	...	...	166 840	81 254	85 586	...
York	...	...	...	...	137 505	66 142	71 363	...
OCEANIA - OCÉANIE								
American Samoa - Samoas américaines[17]								
1 IV 2010 (CDJC)								
PAGO PAGO	3 656	...	...	...	...	...	...	...
Australia - Australie								
1 VII 2013 (ESDJ)								
Adelaide	1 263 888[75]	621 484[75]	642 404[75]	2 024	...	...	...	...
Brisbane	2 143 121[75]	1 065 009[75]	1 078 112[75]	5 065	...	...	...	...
Cairns	145 003[75]	71 717[75]	73 286[75]	254	...	...	...	...
Canberra-Queanbeyan	418 856[75]	208 683[75]	210 173[75]	482	...	...	...	...
Central Coast	320 266[75]	155 491[75]	164 775[75]	566	...	...	...	...
Darwin	119 597[75]	62 751[75]	56 846[75]	295	...	...	...	...
Geelong	181 853[75]	89 865[75]	91 988[75]	919	...	...	...	...
Gold Coast-Tweed Heads	605 134[75]	296 281[75]	308 853[75]	1 403	...	...	...	...
Greater Adelaide	1 291 666[75]	635 458[75]	656 208[75]	3 258	...	...	...	...
Greater Brisbane	2 238 394[75]	1 113 036[75]	1 125 358[75]	15 826	...	...	...	...
Greater Darwin	136 245[75]	71 434[75]	64 811[75]	3 164	...	...	...	...
Greater Hobart	217 973[75]	107 800[75]	110 173[75]	1 696	...	...	...	...
Greater Melbourne	4 347 955[75]	2 147 775[75]	2 200 180[75]	9 991	...	...	...	...
Greater Perth	1 972 358[75]	986 935[75]	985 423[75]	6 418	...	...	...	...
Greater Sydney	4 757 083[75]	2 359 054[75]	2 398 029[75]	12 368	...	...	...	...
Hobart	206 560[75]	101 961[75]	104 599[75]	1 213	...	...	...	...
Melbourne	4 181 021[75]	2 064 826[75]	2 116 195[75]	5 679	...	...	...	...
Newcastle-Maitland	425 895[75]	211 337[75]	214 558[75]	1 019	...	...	...	...
Perth	1 901 582[75]	950 959[75]	950 623[75]	3 367	...	...	...	...
Sunshine Coast	292 354[75]	141 994[75]	150 360[75]	1 633	...	...	...	...
Sydney	4 373 433[75]	2 171 480[75]	2 201 953[75]	4 064	...	...	...	...
Toowoomba	112 588[75]	54 504[75]	58 084[75]	498	...	...	...	...
Townsville	176 035[75]	87 949[75]	88 086[75]	696	...	...	...	...
Wollongong	286 581[75]	142 774[75]	143 807[75]	572	...	...	...	...
Cook Islands - Îles Cook[76]								
1 XII 2011 (CDFC)								
RAROTONGA	13 095	...	...	...	...	...	...	...
Fiji - Fidji								
16 IX 2007 (CDFC)								
SUVA	74 481	37 032	37 449	...	...	...	...	...
French Polynesia - Polynésie française								
22 VIII 2012 (CDJC)								
PAPEETE	25 763	12 971	12 792	...	...	...	...	...
Guam								
1 VII 2010 (ESDJ)								
AGANA	1 051	...	...	3	...	...	...	...
Kiribati								
7 XII 2005 (CDFC)								
TARAWA	...	...	...	...	40 311	...	...	...
Marshall Islands - Îles Marshall								
3 IV 2011 (CDFC)								
MAJURO	27 797	...	...	...	...	...	...	...

8. Population of capital cities and cities of 100 000 or more inhabitants: latest available year, 1995 - 2014
Population des capitales et des villes de 100 000 habitants ou plus : dernière année disponible, 1995 - 2014 (continued - suite)

Continent, country or area, date, code[a] and city / Continent, pays ou zone, date, code[a] et ville	City proper - Ville proprement dite				Urban agglomeration - Agglomération urbaine			
	Population			Surface area - Superficie (km²)	Population			Surface area - Superficie (km²)
	Both sexes - Les deux sexes	Male - Masculin	Female - Féminin		Both sexes - Les deux sexes	Male - Masculin	Female - Féminin	
OCEANIA - OCÉANIE								
Micronesia (Federated States of) - Micronésie (États fédérés de)								
1 IV 2000 (CDJC)								
PALIKIR	6 227	...	...	...	...	...	...	...
New Caledonia - Nouvelle-Calédonie								
27 VII 2009 (CDFC)								
NOUMEA	97 579	...	...	46	...	...	...	...
New Zealand - Nouvelle-Zélande								
1 VII 2014 (ESDJ)								
Auckland	1 526 900	747 400	779 600	4 938[77]	...	...	...	...
Christchurch	361 900	180 100	181 900	1 415[77]	...	...	...	...
Dunedin	124 600	60 000	64 500	3 287[77]	...	...	...	...
Hamilton	153 000	73 900	79 200	110[77]	...	...	...	...
Lower Hutt	101 700	49 500	52 200	376[77]	...	...	...	...
Napier-Hastings	...	...	...	...	128 800[78]	61 600[78]	67 200[78]	390[77]
Tauranga	121 800	58 000	63 800	134[77]	...	...	...	...
WELLINGTON	200 000	97 400	102 600	290[77]	...	...	...	...
Niue - Nioué								
11 IX 2011 (CDFC)								
ALOFI	639	311	328	...	...	...	...	...
Norfolk Island - Île Norfolk								
1 VII 1997 (ESDF)								
KINGSTON	*800*	...	...	...	...	...	...	...
Northern Mariana Islands - Îles Mariannes septentrionales								
1 IV 2010 (CDFC)								
GARAPAN	3 983	1 953	2 030	...	...	...	...	...
Palau - Palaos								
1 IV 2005 (CDJC)								
KOROR	...	...	...	...	12 676	...	...	...
Papua New Guinea - Papouasie-Nouvelle-Guinée								
9 VII 2000 (CDFC)								
PORT MORESBY	254 158	138 974	115 184	...	...	...	...	...
Pitcairn								
31 XII 2013 (CDJC)								
ADAMSTOWN	49	23	26	...	...	...	...	...
Samoa								
7 XI 2011 (CDFC)								
APIA	36 735	...	...	...	...	...	...	...
Solomon Islands - Îles Salomon								
22 XI 2009 (CDFC)								
HONIARA	64 609	...	...	...	80 082	...	...	...
Tonga								
30 XI 2011 (CDJC)								
NUKU'ALOFA	...	...	...	...	36 045	18 100	17 945	...
Tuvalu								
1 XI 2002 (CDFC)								
FUNAFUTI	4 492	2 281	2 211	...	...	...	...	...
Vanuatu								
16 XI 2009 (CDJC)								
PORT VILA	44 039	...	...	...	...	...	...	...
Wallis and Futuna Islands - Îles Wallis et Futuna								
21 VII 2008 (CDFC)								
META-UTU	1 126	...	...	...	...	...	...	...

FOOTNOTES - NOTES

The capital city of each country is shown in capital letters. Figures in italics are estimates of questionnable reliability. For definition of city proper and urban agglomeration, method of evaluation and limitations of data see Technical Notes for this table. - Le nom de la capitale de chaque pays est imprimé en majuscules. Les chiffres en italique sont des estimations dont la fiabilité n'est pas assurée. Pour la définition de la ville proprement dite et de l'agglomération urbaine, et pour les méthodes d'évaluation et les insuffisances de données,

voir les notes techniques pour ce tableau.

Italics: estimates which are less reliable. - Italiques : estimations moins sûres.

* Provisional. - Données provisoires.

[a] 'Code' indicates the source of data, as follows:
CDFC - Census, de facto, complete tabulation
CDFS - Census, de facto, sample tabulation

CDJC - Census, de jure, complete tabulation
CDJS - Census, de jure, sample tabulation
SSDF - Sample survey, de facto
SSDJ - Sample survey, de jure
ESDF - Estimates, de facto
ESDJ - Estimates, de jure

Le 'Code' indique la source des données, comme suit :
CDFC - Recensement, population de fait, tabulation complète
CDFS - Recensement, population de fait, tabulation par sondage
CDJC - Recensement, population de droit, tabulation complète
CDJS - Recensement, population de droit, tabulation par sondage
SSDF - Enquête par sondage, population de fait
SSDJ - Enquête par sondage, population de droit
ESDF - Estimations, population de fait
ESDJ - Estimations, population de droit

[1] Data refer to national projections. - Les données se réfèrent aux projections nationales.

[2] Data refer to the urban commune of Antananarivo. - Pour la commune urbaine de Antananarivo.

[3] Excludes the islands of St. Brandon and Agalega. - Non compris les îles St. Brandon et Agalega.

[4] Projections based on the 2002 Population Census. - Projections fondées sur le recensement de la population de 2002.

[5] Bloemfontein is the judicial capital, Cape Town is the legislative capital and Pretoria is the administrative capital. - Bloemfontein est la capitale judiciaire, Le Cap est la capitale législative et Pretoria est la capitale administrative.

[6] Comprising the Northern Region (former Saguia el Hamra) and Southern Region (former Rio de Oro). - Comprend la région septentrionale (ancien Saguia-el-Hamra) et la région méridionale (ancien Rio de Oro).

[7] Preliminary postcensal estimates. - Estimations post censitaires préliminaires.

[8] Surface area includes interior waters. - La superficie comprend les eaux intérieures.

[9] Data refer to municipalities, which may contain an urban centre as well as rural areas. - Pour municipios qui peuvent comprendre un centre urbain et aussi une zone rurale.

[10] Population statistics are compiled from registers. - Les statistiques de la population sont compilées à partir des registres.

[11] Data refer to Kingston Metropolitan Area. - Données pour la zone métropolitaine de Kingston.

[12] Data refer to projections based on the 2010 Population Census. - Les données se réfèrent aux projections basées sur le recensement de la population de 2010.

[13] Including armed forces stationed in the area. Based on the results of the 2010 Population Census. - Y compris les militaires en garnison sur le territoire. D'après le résultats du recensement de la population de 2010.

[14] City refers to a type of incorporated place in 49 states and the District of Columbia, that has an elected government and provides a range of government functions and services. Also included among the cities on this list is Urban Honolulu, Hawaii Census Designated Place (CDP), for which the Census Bureau reports data under agreement with the State of Hawaii (instead of the combined city and county of Honolulu). - Par ville, on entend un lieu doté de la personnalité morale dans 49 États et dans le district de Columbia, qui a un gouvernement élu et fournit tout un ensemble de fonctions et de services publics. Sont également inclus Honolulu, lieu chargé du recensement pour Hawaii, pour lequel le Census Bureau établit les données en accord avec l'État de Hawaii (au lieu de la ville et du comté d'Honolulu).

[15] Excluding U.S. Armed Forces overseas and civilian U.S. citizens whose usual place of residence is outside the United States. - Non compris les militaires américains à l'étranger et les civils américains dont le lieu de résidence habituel est en dehors des États-Unis.

[16] Excluding inland water. - Exception faite des eaux intérieures.

[17] Including armed forces stationed in the area. - Y compris les militaires en garnison sur le territoire.

[18] Data refer to projections based on the 2001 Population Census. - Les données se réfèrent aux projections basées sur le recensement de la population de 2001.

[19] The urban agglomeration of Buenos Aires includes the city of Buenos Aires, and the 24 parts of the Buenos Aires province; among them, General San Martín, La Matanza, Lanús, Lomas de Zamora, Morón, Quilmes, San Fernando, San Isidro y Vicente López. - L'agglomération urbaine de Buenos Aires englobe la ville de Buenos Aires et les 24 circonscriptions de la province de Buenos Aires, dont General San Martín, La Matanza, Lanús, Lomas de Zamora, Morón, Quilmes, San Fernando, San Isidro y Vicente López.

[20] The urban agglomeration of Tucumán-Tafí Viejo includes San Miguel de Tucumán. - L'agglomération urbaine de Tucumán-Tafí Viejo englobe San Miguel de Tucumán.

[21] Estimates based on the 2002 Population Census. - Estimations basées sur le recensement de la population de 2002.

[22] Excluding interior waters. - Eaux intérieures non comprises.

[23] Data exclude the population of the cities of Puente Alto and San Bernardo. Estimates based on the 2002 Population Census. - Les données ne comprennent pas la population des villes de Puente Alto et de San Bernardo. Estimations basées sur le recensement de la population de 2002.

[24] Data are revised projections taking into consideration also the results of the 2005 census. - Les données sont des projections révisées tenant compte également des résultats du recensement de 2005.

[25] The Metropolitan Area of Asunción is made up of Asunción and the 19 Central Department districts. - La zone métropolitaine d'Asunción est composée d'Asunción et de 19 districts du Département central.

[26] Estimates based on the 2007 Population Census. - Estimations fondées sur le recensement de la population de 2007.

[27] Data refer to the Province of Lima and the Constitutional Province of Callao. - Les données concernent la province de Lima et la province constitutionnelle de Callao.

[28] Figures for male and female may not add up to the total, since they do not include the category "Unknown". - La somme des chiffres indiqués pour les sexes masculin et féminin peut n'être pas égale au total parce qu'elle n'inclut pas la catégorie " inconnue ".

[29] Excluding foreign diplomatic personnel and their dependants. Data based on the 2008 Population Census. - Non compris le personnel diplomatique étranger et les membres de leur famille les accompagnant. Données fondées sur le recensement de population de 2008.

[30] Because of rounding, totals are not in all cases the sum of the respective components. - Les chiffres étant arrondis, les totaux ne correspondent pas toujours rigoureusement à la somme des composants respectifs.

[31] The urban agglomeration of Lefkosia is composed of Lefkosia municipality, Agios Dometios, Egkomi, Strovolos, Aglangia, Lakatameia, Anthoupoli, Latsia and Geri. - L'agglomération urbaine de Lefkosia est composée de la municipalité de Lefkosia et Agios Dometios, Egkomi, Strovolos, Aglangia, Lakatameia, Anthoupoli, Latsia et Geri.

[32] The urban agglomeration of Lemesos is composed of Lemesos municipality, Mesa Geitonia, Agios Athanasios, Germasogeia, Pano Polemidia, Ypsonas, Kato Polemidia, and parts of Mouttagiaka, Agios Tychon, Parekklisia, Monagrouli, Moni, Pyrgos and Tserkezoi. - L'agglomération urbaine de Lemesos est composée de la municipalité de Lemesos et Mesa Geitonia, Agios Athanasios, Germasogeia, Pano Polemidia, Ypsonas, Kato Polemidia, et certaines parties des Mouttagiaka, Agios Tychon, Parekklisia, Monagrouli, Moni, Pyrgos et Tserkezoi.

[33] Includes data for the Indian-held part of Jammu and Kashmir, the final status of which has not yet been determined. - Y compris les données pour la partie du Jammu et du Cachemire occupée par l'Inde dont le statut définitif n'a pas encore été déterminé.

[34] Data for urban agglomeration include New Delhi. - Les données pour l'agglomération urbaine y compris New Delhi.

[35] Data for urban agglomeration include Bally, Baranagar, Barrackpur, Bhatpara, Calcutta Municipal Corporation, Chandan Nagar, Garden Reach, Houghly-Chinsura, Howrah, Jadarpur, Kamarhati, Naihati, Panihati, Serampore, South Dum Dum, South Suburban, and Titagarh. - Les données pour l'agglomération urbaine y compris Bally, Baranagar, Barrackpur, Bhatpara, Calcutta Municipal Corporation, Chandan Nagar, Garden Reach, Houghly Chinsura, Howrah, Jadarpur, Kamarhati, Naihati, Panihati, Serampopre, South Dum Dum, South Suburban et Titagarh.

[36] Included in urban agglomeration of Delhi. Data refer to the New Delhi Municipal Council. - Comprise dans l'agglomération urbaine de Delhi. Les données se rapportent au New Delhi Municipal Council.

[37] Designation and data provided by Israel. The position of the United Nations on the question of Jerusalem is contained in General Assembly resolution 181 (II) and subsequent resolutions of the General Assembly and the Security Council concerning this question. Including East Jerusalem. - Appelation de données fournies par Israel. La position des Nations Unies concernant la question de Jérusalem est décrite dans la resolution 181 (II) de l'Assemblée générale et résolutions ultérieures de l'Assemblée générale et du Conseil de sécurité sur cette question. Y compris Jérusalem-Est.

[38] Excluding diplomatic personnel outside the country and foreign military and civilian personnel and their dependants stationed in the area. - Non compris le personnel diplomatique hors du pays ni les militaires et agents civils étrangers en poste sur le territoire et les membres de leur famille les accompagnant.

[39] Land areas are based on the "Municipalities Area Statistics of Japan, 2010" published by the Geospatial Information Authority of Japan, Ministry of Land, Infrastructure, Transport and Tourism. The areas with indefinable boundaries are estimated by the Statistics Bureau, Ministry of Internal Affairs and

Communications. - Les zones terrestres sont déterminées selon les statistiques relatives aux municipalités du Japon en 2010, publiées par l'Autorité japonaise d'information géospatiale du Ministère de l'aménagement foncier, des infrastructures, des transports et du tourisme. Les zones sans délimitations définissables font l'objet d'une estimation réalisée par le Bureau de la statistique du Ministère des affaires intérieures et des communications.

[40] Excluding diplomatic personnel outside the country and foreign military and civilian personnel and their dependants stationed in the area. Data for Tokyo refer to 23 ku (wards) of Tokyo. - Non compris le personnel diplomatique hors du pays ni les militaires et agents civils étrangers en poste sur le territoire et les membres de leur famille les accompagnant. Données relatives à Tokyo concernant 23 ku (arrondissements de la ville).

[41] Data refer to annual average population. - Les données correspondent à la population annuelle moyenne.

[42] Based on the results of the 2005 Population and Housing Census. - Données fondées sur les résultats du recensement de la population et de l'habitat de 2005.

[43] Source: Living conditions of household survey, October 2011 to September 2012. - Source: Enquête sur les conditions de vie des ménages, octobre 2011 à septembre 2012.

[44] Estimates based on the adjusted Population and Housing Census of 2010. - Les estimations sont fondée sur les résultats ajustées du recensement de la population et de l'habitat de 2010.

[45] Including population from all eight townships. - Y compris la population des huit municipalités.

[46] Excluding data for the Pakistan-held part of Jammu and Kashmir, the final status of which has not yet been determined, and for Junagardh, Manavadar, Gilgit and Baltistan. - Non compris les données pour la partie de Jammu-Cachemire occupée par le Pakistan dont le status definitif n'a pas encore été déterminé, et le Junagardh, le Manavadar, le Gilgit et le Baltistan.

[47] Data exclude residents who have been away from Singapore for a continuous period of 12 months or longer as at the reference date. - Non compris les résidents hors de Singapour pour une période ininterrompue de 12 mois ou plus avant de la date de référence.

[48] The land area of Singapore comprises the mainland and other islands. - La superficie terrestre de Singapour comprend l'île principale et les autres îles.

[49] The Population and Housing Census 2001 did not cover the whole area of the country due to the security problems; data refer to the 18 districts for which the census was completed only (in three districts it was not possible to conduct the census at all and in four districts it was partially conducted). - Le recensement de la population et du logement de 2001 n'a pas été réalisé sur la superficie totale du pays à cause de problèmes de sécurité; les données ne concernent que les 18 districts entièrement recensés (3 districts n'ont pas été recensés du tout, et 4 ont été recensés en partie).

[50] Designation and data provided by the State of Palestine. The position of the United Nations on the question of Jerusalem is contained in General Assembly resolution 181 (II) and subsequent resolutions of the General Assembly and the Security Council concerning this question. - Appellation de données fournies par l'État de Palestine. La position des Nations Unies concernant la question de Jérusalem est décrite dans la résolution 181 (II) de l'Assemblée générale et résolutions ultérieures de l'Assemblée générale et du Conseil de sécurité sur cette question.

[51] Data based on address-based population registration system. - Les données sont basées sur le registre national de la population basé sur l'adresse.

[52] Data include Anderlecht and Schaerbeek. - Les données comprennent Anderlecht et Schaerbeek.

[53] Excluding Faeroe Islands and Greenland shown separately, if available. - Non compris les Iles Féroé et le Groenland, qui font l'objet de rubriques distinctes, si disponible.

[54] Land area refers to built over area. - Partie du territoire désigne une zone bâtie.

[55] Urban Agglomeration refers to Tórshavn, Hoyvík, Argir and Hvítanes. - Agglomération urbaine fait référence à Tórshavn, Hoyvík, Argir et Hvítanes.

[56] Urban Agglomeration refers to Tórshavn, Hoyvík, Argir and Hvítanes. Land area refers to built over area. - Agglomération urbaine fait référence à Tórshavn, Hoyvík, Argir et Hvítanes. Partie du territoire désigne une zone bâtie.

[57] City proper refers to commune or municipality. - La ville proprement dite se rapporte à la commune ou à la municipalité.

[58] The city of Aix-en-Provence is part of the urban agglomeration of Marseille. - La ville d'Aix-en-Provence fait partie de l'agglomération urbaine de Marseille.

[59] The communes of Argenteuil, Boulogne-Billancourt and Montreuil are parts of the urban agglomeration of Paris. - Les communes de Argenteuil, Boulogne-Billancourt et Montreuil font partie de l'agglomération urbaine de Paris.

[60] Excluding military personnel, visitors and transients. - Non compris les militaires, ni les visiteurs et transients.

[61] Data refer to the Vatican City State. - Les données se rapportent à l'Etat de la Cité du Vatican.

[62] Surface area is 0.44 km². - Superficie: 0,44 km².

[63] The boundaries of the city are related to the boundaries of the respective commune. - Les limites de la ville correspondent aux limites de la commune respective.

[64] Data refer to registered resident population. - Les données concernent la population enregistrée résidente.

[65] Land area includes inland water. - La zone terrestre comprend les eaux intérieures.

[66] The urban agglomeration of the capital area includes the following communes: Bessastaðahreppur, Garðabær, Hafnarfjörður, Kjósarhreppur, Kópavogur, Mosfellsbær ,Reykjavík, Seltjarnarnes. Data refer to registered resident population. - L'agglomération urbaine de la capitale comprend les communes suivantes : Bessastaðahreppur, Garðabær, Hafnarfjörður, Kjósarhreppur, Kópavogur, Mosfellsbær ,Reykjavík, Seltjarnarnes. Les données concernent la population enregistrée résidente.

[67] City is defined as an administratively separated area entitled to civil (municipal) rights. - Une ville est définie comme une zone administrativement distincte dotée de droits municipaux.

[68] Excludes data for Kosovo and Metohia. - Sans les données pour le Kosovo et Metohie.

[69] Data for urban agglomeration refer to communes which are administrative divisions. - Les données pour l'agglomération urbaine se rapportent aux communes qui sont des divisions administrative.

[70] Excluding Channel Islands (Guernsey and Jersey) and Isle of Man, shown separately, if available. Data refer to urban areas with more than 100 000 residents. - Non compris les îles Anglo-Normandes (Guernesey et Jersey) et l'île de Man, qui font l'objet de rubriques distinctes, si disponible. Les données se rapportent aux zones urbaines avec plus de 100 000 résidents.

[71] Capital of Northern Ireland. - Capitale de l'Irlande du Nord.

[72] Capital of Wales for certain purposes. - Considérée à certains égards comme la capitale du pays de Galles.

[73] Capital of Scotland. - Capitale de l'Ecosse.

[74] 'Greater London' conurbation as reconstituted in 1965 and comprising 32 new Greater London Boroughs. - Ensemble urbain du 'Grand Londres', tel qu'il a été reconstitué en 1965, comprenant 32 nouveaux Greater London Boroughs.

[75] These estimates are based on the new Australian Statistical Geography Standard (ASGS) and are the first released estimates based on the ASGS (released 31 July 2012). Previously, population estimates were based on the Australian Standard Geographical Classification (ASGC). These estimates are preliminary rebased and based on the 2011 Census. The populations for Greater Sydney, Melbourne, Brisbane, Perth, Adelaide, Hobart and Darwin are based on the 'Greater Capital City Statistical Area (GCCSA)' statistical area level. All other cities are based on the 'Significant Urban Areas (SUA)' statistical area level. It is not possible to distinguish for all regions between 'city proper' and 'urban agglomeration' areas, therefore data has been included under 'city proper'. - Ces estimations, qui suivent la nouvelle norme (Australian Statistical Geography Standard, du 31 juillet 2012), sont les premières de la sorte. Auparavant, les estimations de population suivaient la norme Australian Standard Geographical Classification. Les présentes estimations, qui ont été préalablement mises à la nouvelle norme, sont fondées sur le recensement de 2011. Le nombre d'habitants des agglomérations de Sydney, Melbourne, Brisbane, Perth, Adelaide, Hobart et Darwin a été établi à l'échelon statistique « Greater Capital City Statistical Area » alors que le nombre d'habitants de toutes les autres villes a été établi à l'échelon statistique « Significant Urban Areas ». Comme il n'est pas possible de faire la distinction entre les villes à proprement parler et les agglomérations urbaines pour toutes les régions, les données ont été portées à la rubrique « Ville proprement dite ».

[76] Excluding Niue, shown separately, which is part of Cook Islands, but because of remoteness is administered separately. - Non compris Nioué, qui fait l'objet d'une rubrique distincte et qui fait partie des îles Cook, mais qui, en raison de son éloignement, est administrée séparément.

Table 9 - *Demographic Yearbook 2014*

Table 9 presents live births and crude birth rates by urban/rural residence for as many years as possible between 2010 and 2014.

Description of variables: Live birth is defined as the complete expulsion or extraction from its mother of a product of conception, irrespective of the duration of pregnancy, which after such separation, breathes or shows any other evidence of life such as beating of the heart, pulsation of the umbilical cord, or definite movements of voluntary muscles, whether or not the umbilical cord has been cut or the placenta is attached; each product of such a birth is considered live-born[1].

Statistics on the number of live births are obtained from civil registers unless otherwise noted. For those countries or areas where civil registration statistics on live births are considered reliable the birth rates shown have been calculated on the basis of registered live births.

For certain countries, there is a discrepancy between the total number of live births shown in this table and those shown in subsequent tables for the same year. Usually this discrepancy arises because the total number of live births occurring in a given year is revised but not the remaining tabulations.

Rate computation: Crude birth rates are the annual number of live births per 1 000 mid-year population.

Rates by urban/rural residence are the annual number of live births, in the appropriate urban or rural category, per 1 000 corresponding mid-year population. Rates are calculated only for data considered complete, that is, coded with a "C" and for estimates and live births statistics for the 12 month period prior to the census date, coded with a "|". These rates are calculated by the Statistics Division of the United Nations based on the appropriate reference population (for example: total population, nationals only, etc.) if known and available. If the reference population is not known or unavailable, the total population is used to calculate the rates. Therefore, if the population that is used to calculate the rates is different from the correct reference population, the rates presented might under- or overstate the true situation in a country or area.

Rates presented in this table are limited to those countries or areas having a minimum number of 30 live births in a given year.

Reliability of data: Each country or area has been asked to indicate the estimated completeness of the live births recorded in its civil register. These national assessments are indicated by the quality codes "C" and "U" that appear in the first column of this table.

"C" indicates that the data are estimated to be virtually complete, that is, representing at least 90 per cent of the live births occurring each year, whereas "U" indicates that data are estimated to be incomplete, that is, representing less than 90 per cent of the live births occurring each year. A third code "..." indicates that no information was provided regarding completeness.

Data from civil registers that are reported as incomplete or of unknown completeness (coded "U" or "...") are considered unreliable. They appear in italics in this table and rates are not calculated for these data.

These quality codes apply only to data from civil registers. If data from other sources are presented, the symbol "|" is shown instead of the quality code. For more information about the quality of vital statistics data in general, and the information available on the basis of the completeness estimates in particular, see section 4.2 of the Technical Notes.

Limitations: Statistics on live births are subject to the same qualifications as have been set forth for vital statistics in general and birth statistics in particular as discussed in section 4 of the Technical Notes.

The reliability of data, an indication of which is described above, is an important factor in considering the limitations. In addition, some live births are tabulated by date of registration and not by date of occurrence; these have been indicated by a plus sign "+". Whenever the lag between the date of occurrence and date of registration is prolonged and, therefore, a large proportion of the live birth registrations are delayed, birth statistics for any given year may be seriously affected.

Another factor that limits international comparability is the practice of some countries or areas not to include in live birth statistics infants who were born alive but died before the registration of the birth or within the first 24 hours of life, thus underestimating the total number of life births. Statistics of this type are footnoted.

In addition, it should be noted that rates are affected also by the quality and limitations of the population estimates that are used in their computation. The problems of under-enumeration or over-enumeration and, to some extent, the differences in definition of total population have been discussed in section 3 of the Technical Notes dealing with population data in general, and specific information pertaining to individual countries or areas is given in the footnotes to table 3.

The rates estimated from the results of sample surveys are subject to possibilities of considerable error as a result of omissions in reporting of births, or as a result of erroneous reporting of births that occurred outside the reference period. However, rates estimated from sample surveys have the advantage of the availability of a built-in and strictly corresponding population base.

It should be emphasized that crude birth rates - like crude death, marriage and divorce rates - may be seriously affected by the age-sex structure of the populations to which they relate. Nevertheless, they do provide a simple measure of the level of and changes in fertility.

The urban/rural classification of birth may refer to the residence of mother or the place of delivery, according to the national practice and it is provided by each country or area. In addition, the comparability of data by urban/rural residence is affected by the national definition of urban and rural used in tabulating these data. It is assumed, in the absence of specific information to the contrary, that the definitions of urban and rural used in connection with the national population census were also used in the compilation of the vital statistics for each country or area. However, it cannot be ruled out that, for a given country or area, different definitions of urban and rural are used for the vital statistics data and the population census data respectively. When known, the definitions of urban used in national population census are presented at the end of the technical notes to table 6. As discussed in detail in the technical notes to table 6, these definitions vary considerably from one area or country to another. Urban/rural differentials in vital rates may also be affected by whether the vital events have been tabulated in terms of place of occurrence or place of usual residence. This problem is discussed in more detail in section 4.1.4.1 of the Technical notes.

Earlier data: Live births have been shown in each issue of the *Demographic Yearbook*. Information on the years and specific topics covered is presented in the Historical Index.

NOTES

[1] *Principles and Recommendations for a Vital Statistics System Revision 3,* Sales No. E.13.XVII.10, United Nations, New York, 2014.

Tableau 9 – *Annuaire démographique 2014*

Le tableau 9 présente des données sur les naissances vivantes et les taux bruts de natalité selon le lieu de résidence (zone urbaine ou rurale) pour le plus grand nombre d'années possible entre 2010 et 2014.

Description des variables : La naissance vivante est l'expulsion ou l'extraction complète du corps de la mère, indépendamment de la durée de gestation, d'un produit de la conception qui, après cette séparation, respire ou manifeste tout autre signe de vie, tel que battement de cœur, pulsation du cordon ombilical ou contraction effective d'un muscle soumis à l'action de la volonté, que le cordon ombilical ait été coupé ou non et que le placenta soit ou non demeuré attaché ; tout produit d'une telle naissance est considéré comme « enfant né vivant »[1].

Sauf indication contraire, les statistiques relatives au nombre de naissances vivantes sont établies sur la base des registres de l'état civil. Pour les pays ou zones où les statistiques obtenues auprès des services de l'état civil sont jugées sûres, les taux de natalité indiqués ont été calculés par la Division de statistique de l'ONU d'après les naissances vivantes enregistrées.

Pour quelques pays il y a une discordance entre le nombre total des décès présenté dans ce tableau et ceux présentés après pour la même année. Habituellement ces différences apparaissent lorsque le nombre total des décès pour une certaine année a été révisé alors que les autres tabulations ne l'ont pas été.

Calcul des taux : Les taux bruts de natalité représentent le nombre annuel de naissances vivantes pour 1 000 habitants au milieu de l'année.

Les taux selon le lieu de résidence (zone urbaine ou rurale) représentent le nombre annuel de naissances vivantes, classées selon la catégorie urbaine ou rurale appropriée pour 1 000 habitants au milieu de l'année. Les taux ont été calculés seulement pour les données considérées complètes, c'est-à-dire celles associées au code « C », ainsi que pour les estimations et les statistiques des naissances vivantes dans la periode des douze mois précédante la date de recensement associées au code « | ». Ces taux sont calculés par la division de statistique des Nations Unies sur la base de la population de référence adéquate (par exemple : population totale, nationaux seulement, etc.) si connue et disponible. Si la population de référence n'est pas connue ou n'est pas disponible, la population totale est utilisée pour calculer les taux. Par conséquent, si la population utilisée pour calculer les taux est différente de la population de référence adéquate, les taux présentés sont susceptibles de sous ou sur estimer la situation réelle d'un pays ou d'un territoire.

Les taux présentés dans ce tableau se rapportent seulement aux pays ou zones où l'on a enregistré un nombre minimal de 30 naissances vivantes au cours d'une année donnée.

Fiabilité des données : Il a été demandé à chaque pays ou zone d'indiquer le degré estimatif de complétude des données sur les naissances vivantes figurant dans ses registres d'état civil. Ces évaluations nationales sont signalées par les codes de qualité "C" et "U" qui apparaissent dans la deuxième colonne du tableau.

La lettre "C" indique que les données sont jugées à peu près complètes, c'est-à-dire qu'elles représentent au moins 90 p. 100 des naissances vivantes survenues chaque année ; la lettre "U" signifie que les données sont jugées incomplètes, c'est-à-dire qu'elles représentent moins de 90 p. 100 des naissances vivantes survenues chaque année. Un troisième code, "...", indique qu'aucun renseignement n'a été communiqué quant à la complétude des données.

Les données provenant des registres de l'état civil qui sont déclarées incomplètes ou dont le degré de complétude n'est pas connu (code "U" ou "...") sont jugées douteuses. Elles apparaissent en italique dans le tableau. Les taux pour ces données ne sont pas calculés.

Les codes de qualité ne s'appliquent qu'aux données provenant des registres de l'état civil. Si l'on présente des données autres que celles de l'état civil, le signe "|" est utilisé à la place du code de qualité. Pour plus de précisions sur la qualité des données reposant sur les statistiques de l'état civil en général et les estimations de complétude en particulier, voir la section 4.2 des Notes techniques.

Insuffisance des données : Les statistiques concernant les naissances vivantes appellent toutes les réserves qui ont été formulées à propos des statistiques de l'état civil en général et des statistiques des naissances en particulier (voir la section 4 des Notes techniques).

La fiabilité des données, au sujet de laquelle des indications ont été fournies plus haut, est un facteur important. Il faut également tenir compte du fait que, dans certains cas, les données relatives aux naissances vivantes sont exploitées selon la date de l'enregistrement et non selon la date de l'événement ; ces cas ont été signalés par le signe '+'. Chaque fois que le décalage entre l'événement et son enregistrement est grand et qu'une forte proportion des naissances vivantes fait l'objet d'un enregistrement tardif, les statistiques des naissances vivantes pour une année donnée peuvent être considérablement faussées.

Un autre facteur qui nuit à la comparabilité internationale est la pratique de certains pays ou zones qui consiste à ne pas inclure dans les statistiques des naissances vivantes les enfants nés vivants mais décédés avant l'enregistrement de leur naissance ou dans les 24 heures qui ont suivi la naissance, pratique qui conduit à sous-estimer le nombre total de naissances vivantes. Lorsque ce facteur a joué, cela a été signalé en note à la fin du tableau.

La qualité et les limitations des estimations concernant la population ont également une incidence sur le calcul des taux. Les problèmes liés au sur-dénombrement ou au sous-dénombrement et, dans une certaine mesure, aux différences dans la définition de la population totale ont été abordés à la section 3 des Notes techniques relative aux données sur la population en général et des précisions sur certains pays ou zones sont données dans les notes se rapportant au tableau 3.

Les taux estimatifs fondés sur les résultats d'enquêtes par sondage comportent des possibilités d'erreurs considérables dues soit à des omissions dans les déclarations, soit au fait que l'on a déclaré à tort des naissances survenues en réalité hors de la période considérée. Toutefois, les taux estimatifs fondés sur les résultats d'enquêtes par sondage présentent un gros avantage : le chiffre de population utilisé comme base est, par définition, rigoureusement correspondant.

Il faut souligner que les taux bruts de natalité, de même que les taux bruts de mortalité, de nuptialité et de divortialité, peuvent varier très sensiblement selon la structure par âge et par sexe de la population à laquelle ils se rapportent. Ils offrent néanmoins un moyen simple de mesurer le niveau et l'évolution de la natalité.

La classification des naissances selon le lieu de résidence (zone urbaine ou rurale) peut se rapporter au lieu de résidence de la mère ou au lieu d'occurrence et correspond à celle indiquée par chaque pays ou zone. En outre, la comparabilité des données selon le lieu de résidence (zone urbaine ou rurale) peut être limitée par les définitions nationales des termes « urbain » et « rural » utilisées pour la mise en tableaux de ces données. En l'absence d'indications contraires, on a supposé que les mêmes définitions avaient servi pour le recensement national de la population et pour l'établissement des statistiques de l'état civil pour chaque pays ou zone. Toutefois, il n'est pas exclu que, pour une zone ou un pays donné, des définitions différentes aient été retenues. Les définitions du terme « urbain » utilisées pour les recensements nationaux de population ont été présentées à la fin des notes techniques du tableau 6 lorsqu'elles étaient connues. Comme on l'a précisé dans les notes techniques relatives au tableau 6, ces définitions varient considérablement d'un pays ou d'une zone à l'autre. La différence entre ces taux pour les zones urbaines et rurales pourra aussi être faussée selon que les faits d'état civil auront été classés d'après le lieu de l'événement ou le lieu de résidence habituel. Ce problème est examiné plus en détail à la section 4.1.4.1 des Notes techniques.

Données publiées antérieurement : Les différentes éditions de l'*Annuaire démographique* contiennent des données sur les naissances vivantes. Pour plus de précisions concernant les années et les sujets pour lesquels des données ont été publiées, se reporter à l'index historique.

NOTES

[1] *Principes et recommandations pour un système de statistique de l'état civil, troisième révision*, numéro de vente : E.13.XVII.10, publication des Nations Unies, New York, 2014.

9. Live births and crude birth rates, by urban/rural residence: 2010 - 2014
Naissances vivantes et taux bruts de natalité selon la résidence, urbaine/rurale : 2010 - 2014

Continent, country or area, and urban/rural residence / Continent, pays ou zone et résidence, urbaine/rurale	Code[a]	Number - Nombre					Rate - Taux				
		2010	2011	2012	2013	2014	2010	2011	2012	2013	2014
AFRICA - AFRIQUE											
Algeria - Algérie[1]											
Total	C	888 029	909 787	978 233	962 722	1 014 248	24.7	24.8	26.1	25.1	25.9
Benin - Bénin[2]											
Total	I	358 830	366 889	376 439	...	...	40.9	40.5	40.2	...	...
Botswana[3]											
Total	U	...	39 368	40 856	...	...	...	...	...	...	...
Burundi[4]											
Total	+U	240 684	216 398	221 289	248 395	...	...	...	...	...	...
Cabo Verde											
Total	C	13 415	...	...	...	...	25.9	...	...	...	...
Djibouti											
Total	U	10 538	10 871	...	...	...	...	...	...	...	...
Egypt - Égypte											
Total	+C	2 261 409	2 442 094	2 629 769	2 621 902	...	28.7	30.3	31.9	31.0	...
Urban - Urbaine	+C	900 085	942 639	1 009 952	1 186 887	...	26.6	27.3	28.6	32.8	...
Rural - Rurale	+C	1 361 324	1 499 455	1 619 817	1 435 015	...	30.3	32.6	34.3	29.6	...
Ghana[5]											
Total	I	623 700	...	...	...	...	25.3	...	...	...	...
Urban - Urbaine	I	293 566	...	...	...	...	23.4	...	...	...	...
Rural - Rurale	I	330 134	...	...	...	...	27.3	...	...	...	...
Guinea - Guinée											
Total	+U	...	...	...	205 658	...	...	...	...	...	...
Kenya											
Total	U	798 016	771 150	801 815	870 599	954 254	...	...	...	...	...
Lesotho											
Total	+U	6 369	3 931	1 718	...	...	...	...	...	...	...
Mauritius - Maurice[6]											
Total	+C	15 005	14 701	14 494	13 488	13 283	11.7	11.7	11.5	10.7	10.5
Urban - Urbaine	+C	5 731	5 586	5 416	5 059	5 158	10.7	11.0	10.6	9.7	10.0
Rural - Rurale	+C	9 274	9 115	9 078	8 429	8 125	12.4	12.3	12.2	11.4	10.9
Namibia - Namibie[7]											
Total	I	...	61 523	...	...	...	...	29.1	...	...	...
Urban - Urbaine	I	...	26 836	...	...	...	...	29.8	...	...	...
Rural - Rurale	I	...	34 687	...	...	...	...	28.5	...	...	...
Niger											
Total	+U	181 195	198 499	...	...	...	...	...	...	...	...
Reunion - Réunion[8]											
Total	C	14 146	...	...	...	...	17.1	...	...	...	...
Rwanda											
Total	U	408 267	406 838	404 067	...	...	...	...	...	...	...
Saint Helena ex. dep. - Sainte-Hélène sans dép.											
Total	C	34	34	32	35	48	8.0	8.0	7.8	8.3	10.9
Sao Tome and Principe - Sao Tomé-et-Principe											
Total	C	4 890	5 232	5 173	...	...	29.9	31.4	27.6	...	...
Senegal - Sénégal[9]											
Total	I	456 212	464 464	471 629	478 898	...	36.5	36.2	35.7	35.3	...
Seychelles											
Total	+C	1 504	1 625	1 645	1 566	1 557	16.8	18.6	18.6	17.4	17.0
Sierra Leone											
Total	...	101 185	117 207	147 958	...	...	...	...	...	...	...
Urban - Urbaine	...	15 421	16 270	18 392	...	...	...	...	...	...	...
Rural - Rurale	...	85 764	100 937	129 566	...	...	...	...	...	...	...
South Africa - Afrique du Sud											
Total	U	1 163 629	1 173 164	1 184 867	1 196 395	1 207 711	...	...	...	...	...
Tunisia - Tunisie											
Total	C	196 039	201 120	214 909	*221 147	...	18.6	18.8	19.9	*20.3	...
United Republic of Tanzania - République Unie de Tanzanie											
Total	...	1 678 325	1 687 203	1 694 943	...	...	...	...	...	...	...
Zambia - Zambie[10]											
Total	I	442 998	...	...	...	...	35.4	...	...	...	...
Urban - Urbaine	I	148 195	...	...	...	...	29.5	...	...	...	...
Rural - Rurale	I	294 803	...	...	...	...	39.3	...	...	...	...

Continent, country or area, and urban/rural residence / Continent, pays ou zone et résidence, urbaine/rurale	Code[a]	Number - Nombre					Rate - Taux				
		2010	2011	2012	2013	2014	2010	2011	2012	2013	2014

AMERICA, NORTH - AMÉRIQUE DU NORD

Anguilla											
Total	+C	182	185	192	165	149	11.1	13.7	14.3	12.2	...
Antigua and Barbuda - Antigua-et-Barbuda											
Total	+C	1 255	...	...	...	...	13.8	...	...	...	...
Aruba											
Total	C	1 223	1 236	1 288	1 346	1 376	12.0	12.0	12.3	12.7	12.8
Bahamas											
Total	+U	4 915	4 747	4 469	*4 322	*4 196	...	...	...	...	...
Bermuda - Bermudes[11]											
Total	C	769	670	648	648	...	12.0	10.6	10.4	10.5	...
British Virgin Islands - Îles Vierges britanniques											
Total	C	...	...	*288	...	...	...	...	*10.2	...	...
Canada[12]											
Total	C	376 951	377 897	382 980	386 044	*388 729	11.1	11.0	11.0	11.0	*10.9
Cayman Islands - Îles Caïmanes											
Total	C	821	800	*759	*697	710[13]	15.0	14.5	*13.4	*12.4	12.2
Costa Rica											
Total	C	70 922	73 459	73 326	70 550	*71 793	15.6	16.0	15.8	15.0	*15.0
Urban - Urbaine	C	26 047	25 863	25 472	24 883	*41 631	7.9	7.7	7.5	7.3	*12.0
Rural - Rurale	C	44 875	47 596	47 854	45 667	*30 162	36.4	38.1	37.8	35.6	*23.2
Cuba											
Total	C	127 746	133 067	125 674	125 880	122 643	11.4	11.9	11.2	11.2	10.9
Urban - Urbaine	C	99 099	102 342	98 301	98 894	...	11.8	12.2	11.6	11.5	...
Rural - Rurale	C	28 647	30 725	27 373	26 986	...	10.4	11.1	10.2	10.4	...
Curaçao											
Total	C	2 032	1 974	2 039	1 962	1 963	13.7	13.1	13.4	12.8	12.6
Dominica - Dominique											
Total	+C	933	...	...	...	...	...	...	...	...	...
Dominican Republic - République dominicaine											
Total	U	150 473	153 035	144 100	130 402	...	...	...	...	...	...
Urban - Urbaine[14]	U	122 976	124 267	117 191	108 329	...	...	...	...	...	...
Rural - Rurale[14]	U	27 026	26 939	25 181	20 960	...	...	...	...	...	...
El Salvador[15]											
Total	C	104 939	109 384	110 843	...	...	17.0	17.6	17.7	...	...
Urban - Urbaine	C	66 619	75 495	75 808	...	...	16.8	18.8	18.5	...	...
Rural - Rurale	C	38 320	33 889	35 035	...	...	17.2	15.4	16.2	...	...
Greenland - Groenland											
Total	C	869	821	786	820	805	15.4	14.5	13.8	14.5	14.3
Urban - Urbaine	C	737	705	654	697	703	15.5	14.7	13.6	14.5	14.6
Rural - Rurale	C	132	116	132	123	102	14.9	13.4	15.4	14.9	12.7
Guadeloupe[8]											
Total	C	5 341	5 384	5 233	5 069	...	13.2	13.3	13.0	12.6	...
Guatemala											
Total	C	361 906	373 692	388 440	...	...	25.2	25.4	25.8	...	...
Urban - Urbaine[14]	C	201 656	221 638	...	...	...	...	...	...	...	...
Rural - Rurale[14]	C	154 536	146 505	...	...	...	...	...	...	...	...
Honduras											
Total	+U	223 345	224 409	...	...	...	...	...	...	...	...
Jamaica - Jamaïque[16]											
Total	C	40 508	39 673	39 348	*36 745	...	15.0	14.7	14.5	...	...
Martinique[8]											
Total	C	4 889	...	...	...	...	12.3	...	...	...	...
Mexico - Mexique[17]											
Total	+U	2 168 952	...	...	...	...	...	...	...	...	...
Urban - Urbaine[14]	+U	1 579 307	...	...	...	...	...	...	...	...	...
Rural - Rurale[14]	+U	500 217	...	...	...	...	...	...	...	...	...
Total	C	...	2 262 024	2 190 159	2 169 810	...	...	19.6	18.7	18.3	...
Urban - Urbaine[14]	C	...	1 601 091	1 563 853	1 523 223	...	...	19.1	18.4	17.8	...
Rural - Rurale[14]	C	...	541 168	515 520	483 583	...	...	16.9	16.0	14.8	...
Montserrat											
Total	+C	62	46	53	41	50	12.4	9.3	10.7	8.3	10.0

9. Live births and crude birth rates, by urban/rural residence: 2010 - 2014
Naissances vivantes et taux bruts de natalité selon la résidence, urbaine/rurale : 2010 - 2014 (continued - suite)

Continent, country or area, and urban/rural residence / Continent, pays ou zone et résidence, urbaine/rurale	Co-de[a]	Number - Nombre					Rate - Taux				
		2010	2011	2012	2013	2014	2010	2011	2012	2013	2014
AMERICA, NORTH - AMÉRIQUE DU NORD											
Nicaragua											
Total	+U	132 165	...	...	...	...	...	...	...	...	...
Urban - Urbaine	+U	67 660	...	...	...	...	...	...	...	...	...
Rural - Rurale	+U	64 505	...	...	...	...	...	...	...	...	...
Panama											
Total	C	67 955	73 292	75 486	73 804	*72 490	18.6	19.7	19.9	19.2	*18.5
Urban - Urbaine	C	42 225	46 208	47 801	47 901	...	17.7	18.9	19.0	18.6	...
Rural - Rurale	C	25 730	27 084	27 685	25 903	...	20.2	21.3	21.7	20.4	...
Puerto Rico - Porto Rico											
Total	C	42 248	41 133	38 975	36 578	34 485	11.4	11.2	10.7	10.1	9.7
Saint Vincent and the Grenadines - Saint-Vincent-et-les Grenadines											
Total	+C	1 784	1 725	1 840	1 738	...	16.2	15.7	16.7	15.8	...
Sint Maarten (Dutch part) - Saint-Martin (partie néerlandaise)[18]											
Total	+C	496	432	414	511	...	14.0	12.9	11.9	14.0	...
United States of America - États-Unis d'Amérique											
Total	C	3 999 386	3 953 590	3 952 841	3 932 181	...	12.9	12.7	12.6	12.4	...
United States Virgin Islands - Îles Vierges américaines											
Total	C	1 600	...	...	...	...	14.5	...	...	...	...
AMERICA, SOUTH - AMÉRIQUE DU SUD											
Argentina - Argentine											
Total	C	756 176	758 042	738 318	754 603	...	18.5	18.4	17.7	17.9	...
Bolivia (Plurinational State of) - Bolivie (État plurinational de)											
Total	+U	159 098	160 499	128 738	...	...	...	...	...	...	...
Brazil - Brésil[19]											
Total	U	2 760 961	2 824 776	2 830 458	2 832 590	...	...	...	...	...	...
Chile - Chili											
Total	C	250 643	247 358	243 635	*242 862	...	14.7	14.3	14.0	*13.8	...
Urban - Urbaine	C	225 225	223 086	219 348	...	...	15.1	14.9	14.5	...	...
Rural - Rurale	C	25 418	24 272	24 287	...	...	11.4	10.8	10.8	...	...
Colombia - Colombie											
Total	U	654 627	665 499	676 835	...	...	...	...	...	...	...
Urban - Urbaine[14]	U	512 468	520 343	529 856	...	...	...	...	...	...	...
Rural - Rurale[14]	U	133 019	142 440	145 838	...	...	...	...	...	...	...
Ecuador - Équateur											
Total	+U	219 162	229 780	235 237	220 896	...	...	...	...	...	...
Urban - Urbaine	+U	176 364	190 385	196 473	181 225	...	...	...	...	...	...
Rural - Rurale	+U	42 798	39 395	38 764	39 671	...	...	...	...	...	...
French Guiana - Guyane française[8]											
Total	C	6 083	...	...	...	...	26.4	...	...	...	...
Paraguay											
Total	+U	...	...	118 549	...	...	...	...	...	...	...
Peru - Pérou											
Total	+U	402 493[20]	396 839[20]	414 081[20]	475 349[20]	*581 450	...	...	...	...	...
Suriname											
Total	C	9 712	9 703	10 217	10 012	...	18.3	18.0	18.9	18.2	...
Urban - Urbaine	C	6 385	6 425	6 852	6 792	...	...	...	19.1	...	...
Rural - Rurale	C	3 327	3 278	3 365	3 220	...	...	...	18.4	...	...
Uruguay											
Total	C	47 420	46 712	48 059	48 681	...	14.0	13.7	14.0	14.2	...
Venezuela (Bolivarian Republic of) - Venezuela (République bolivarienne du)											
Total	C	591 303	615 132	619 530	597 902	...	20.7	21.3	21.1	20.1	...

9. Live births and crude birth rates, by urban/rural residence: 2010 - 2014
Naissances vivantes et taux bruts de natalité selon la résidence, urbaine/rurale : 2010 - 2014 (continued - suite)

Continent, country or area, and urban/rural residence / Continent, pays ou zone et résidence, urbaine/rurale	Code[a]	Number - Nombre					Rate - Taux				
		2010	2011	2012	2013	2014	2010	2011	2012	2013	2014
ASIA - ASIE											
Armenia - Arménie											
Total	C	44 825	43 340	*42 333	*41 790	*43 183	13.8	13.3	*13.4	*13.8	...
Azerbaijan - Azerbaïdjan[21]											
Total	+C	165 643	176 072	174 469	172 671	170 503	18.3	19.2	18.8	18.3	17.9
Urban - Urbaine	+C	81 752	85 539	86 364	86 429	...	17.0	17.6	17.5	17.2	...
Rural - Rurale	+C	83 891	90 533	88 105	86 242	...	19.7	21.0	20.2	19.6	...
Bahrain - Bahreïn											
Total	C	18 150	17 573	19 119	19 995	20 931	14.8	14.7	15.8	16.0	15.9
Bangladesh											
Total	U	2 868 494	2 891 000	2 933 000	...	...	...	...	...	...	...
Urban - Urbaine	U	658 570	631 000	701 000	...	...	...	...	...	...	...
Rural - Rurale	U	2 209 924	2 260 000	2 232 000	...	...	...	...	...	...	...
Brunei Darussalam - Brunéi Darussalam											
Total	+C	6 412	6 724	6 909	6 680	...	16.6	17.1	...	...	...
China - Chine[22]											
Total	I	15 920 000	16 040 000	16 350 000	16 400 000	16 870 000	11.9	11.9	12.1	12.1	12.4
China, Hong Kong SAR - Chine, Hong Kong RAS											
Total	C	88 584	95 451	91 558	57 084	*62 300	12.6	13.5	12.8	7.9	*8.6
China, Macao SAR - Chine, Macao RAS											
Total	C	5 114	5 852	7 315	6 571	7 360	9.5	10.6	12.9	11.1	11.8
Cyprus - Chypre[23]											
Total	C	9 801	9 622	10 161	9 341	*9 258	11.8	11.3	11.8	10.8	*10.8
Urban - Urbaine[14]	C	6 563	6 461	...	...	...	...	...	...	...	...
Rural - Rurale[14]	C	3 119	3 074	...	...	...	...	...	...	...	...
Georgia - Géorgie											
Total	C	62 585	58 014	57 031	57 878	...	14.1	12.9	12.7	...	...
Urban - Urbaine	C	34 129	33 452	...	...	...	14.5	14.0	...	...	...
Rural - Rurale	C	28 456	24 562	...	...	...	13.6	11.7	...	...	...
India - Inde[24]											
Total	I	...	...	...	...	...	22.1	21.1	21.6	21.4	...
Urban - Urbaine	I	...	...	...	...	...	18.0	17.6	17.4	17.3	...
Rural - Rurale	I	...	...	...	...	...	23.7	23.3	23.1	22.9	...
Iran (Islamic Republic of) - Iran (République islamique d')[25]											
Total	C	1 363 542	1 382 229	1 421 689	1 471 834	...	18.3	18.4	18.7	19.1	...
Urban - Urbaine	C	1 074 089	1 087 988	1 129 477	1 131 566	...	21.0	20.3	20.7	20.4	...
Rural - Rurale	C	289 453	294 241	292 212	340 268	...	12.5	13.7	13.7	15.9	...
Iraq											
Total	U	...	...	...	*1 077 645	...	...	...	...	...	...
Israel - Israël[26]											
Total	C	166 255	166 296	170 940	171 444	*176 221	21.8	21.4	21.6	21.3	*21.4
Urban - Urbaine	C	150 839	150 895	155 178	155 127	...	21.6	21.2	21.4	21.1	...
Rural - Rurale	C	15 416	15 401	15 762	16 317	...	24.2	23.5	23.3	23.6	...
Japan - Japon[27]											
Total	C	1 071 304	1 050 806	1 037 231	1 029 816	...	8.4	8.2	8.1	8.1	...
Urban - Urbaine[28]	C	980 669	963 922	953 933	948 589	...	...	...	...	...	...
Rural - Rurale[28]	C	90 510	86 762	83 231	81 173	...	...	...	...	...	...
Jordan - Jordanie[29]											
Total	C	183 948	178 435	177 695	178 143	...	30.1	28.6	27.8	27.3	...
Kazakhstan[21]											
Total	C	367 942	372 801	381 005	387 227	...	22.5	22.5	22.7	22.7	...
Urban - Urbaine	C	192 906	197 516	206 198	209 004	...	21.7	21.8	22.4	22.4	...
Rural - Rurale	C	175 036	175 285	174 807	178 223	...	23.6	23.4	23.0	23.2	...
Kuwait - Koweït											
Total	C	57 533	58 198	59 753	59 426	...	19.6	18.8	18.3	17.2	...
Kyrgyzstan - Kirghizstan											
Total	C	146 123	149 612	154 918	155 520	*161 813	28.1	28.4	28.9	27.2	*27.7
Urban - Urbaine	C	49 905	48 906	53 770	53 855	...	27.3	26.5	29.0	28.0	...
Rural - Rurale	C	96 218	100 706	101 148	101 665	...	28.6	29.5	28.9	26.8	...
Lebanon - Liban											
Total	C	95 218	98 569	94 842	95 246	104 872	...	26.1	...	...	...
Malaysia - Malaisie											
Total	C	491 239	511 594	*508 774	...	...	17.2	17.6	*17.2	...	...

9. Live births and crude birth rates, by urban/rural residence: 2010 - 2014
Naissances vivantes et taux bruts de natalité selon la résidence, urbaine/rurale : 2010 - 2014 (continued - suite)

Continent, country or area, and urban/rural residence / Continent, pays ou zone et résidence, urbaine/rurale	Co-de[a]	Number - Nombre					Rate - Taux				
		2010	2011	2012	2013	2014	2010	2011	2012	2013	2014
ASIA - ASIE											
Maldives											
Total	C	7 115	7 180	7 431	7 153	...	22.3	22.1	22.5	21.3	...
Urban - Urbaine[30]	C	3 811	3 987	4 460	4 698	...	...	...	...	...	...
Rural - Rurale[30]	C	3 249	3 155	2 676	2 439	...	...	...	...	...	...
Mongolia - Mongolie											
Total	+C	63 270	69 853	73 839	79 780	82 839	23.1	25.1	26.0	27.5	28.0
Urban - Urbaine	+C	41 907	47 193	50 967	57 069	56 148	23.3	25.4	26.7	29.1	28.2
Rural - Rurale	+C	21 363	22 660	22 872	22 711	26 691	22.8	24.4	24.6	24.2	27.5
Myanmar											
Total	+U	*965 937*	*1 007 039*	*856 279*	*835 595*	...	...	...	...	...	...
Urban - Urbaine	+U	*282 176*	*293 011*	*319 696*	*333 075*	...	...	...	...	...	...
Rural - Rurale	+U	*683 761*	*714 028*	*536 583*	*502 520*	...	...	...	...	...	...
Nepal - Népal[31]											
Total	I	...	326 725	...	...	...	...	11.4	...	...	...
Urban - Urbaine	I	...	41 626	...	...	...	...	...	...	...	...
Rural - Rurale	I	...	285 099	...	...	...	...	...	...	...	...
Oman[32]											
Total	U	*64 730*	*67 922*	*72 867*	*79 417*	*80 163*	...	...	...	...	...
Philippines											
Total	C	1 782 981	1 746 685	1 790 367	...	...	19.1	18.4	18.6	...	...
Qatar											
Total	C	19 504	20 802	21 423	23 708	*25 443	11.4	12.0	11.7	11.8	*11.5
Republic of Korea - République de Corée[33]											
Total	C	470 171	471 265	484 550	436 455	...	9.4	9.4	9.6	8.6	...
Urban - Urbaine[14]	C	386 271	389 640	402 650	365 381	...	9.6	9.6	9.8	8.9	...
Rural - Rurale[14]	C	83 519	81 503	81 843	71 070	...	8.8	8.6	8.7	7.6	...
Saudi Arabia - Arabie saoudite											
Total	...	...	...	...	607 806	...	...	...	...	...	...
Singapore - Singapour											
Total	C	37 967	39 654	42 663	39 720	42 232	10.1	10.5	11.2	10.3	10.9
Sri Lanka											
Total	+C	*364 565	*363 415	*355 900	*365 792	...	*17.7	*17.4	*17.5	*17.9	...
State of Palestine - État de Palestine[34]											
Total	U	*137 085*	*131 430*	*129 826*	*126 912*	...	...	...	...	...	...
Syrian Arab Republic - République arabe syrienne[35]											
Total	+U	*870 100*	...	...	...	...	...	...	...	...	...
Tajikistan - Tadjikistan[36]											
Total	U	*239 805*	*224 178*	*219 281*	*209 417*	...	...	...	...	...	...
Urban - Urbaine	U	*54 563*	*55 081*	*53 371*	*50 508*	...	...	...	...	...	...
Rural - Rurale	U	*185 242*	*169 097*	*165 910*	*158 909*	...	...	...	...	...	...
Thailand - Thaïlande											
Total	+U	*761 689*	*795 031*	*801 737*	*748 081*	*711 081*	...	...	...	...	...
Turkey - Turquie											
Total	C	1 258 252	1 244 673	1 286 828	1 283 062	1 337 504	17.2	16.8	17.1	16.8	17.4
United Arab Emirates - Émirats arabes unis[37]											
Total	...	79 625	83 950	...	...	...	...	...	...	...	...
Uzbekistan - Ouzbékistan											
Total	C	634 810	622 835	625 106	679 519	...	22.7	21.4	21.2	22.7	...
Yemen - Yémen											
Total	U	*318 936*	*239 980*	*279 719*	*425 165*[38]	...	...	...	...	...	...
EUROPE											
Åland Islands - Îles d'Åland											
Total	C	286	285	292	287	*282	10.3	10.1	10.3	10.0	*9.8
Urban - Urbaine	C	108	110	95	104	*98	9.7	9.8	8.4	9.1	*8.6
Rural - Rurale	C	178	175	197	183	*184	10.6	10.3	11.5	10.6	*10.6
Albania - Albanie											
Total	C	34 061	34 285	35 473	35 750	35 760	11.7	11.8	12.2	12.3	12.3
Andorra - Andorre											
Total	C	828	793	737	...	...	9.8	10.0	9.5	...	...

9. Live births and crude birth rates, by urban/rural residence: 2010 - 2014
Naissances vivantes et taux bruts de natalité selon la résidence, urbaine/rurale : 2010 - 2014 (continued - suite)

Continent, country or area, and urban/rural residence — Continent, pays ou zone et résidence, urbaine/rurale	Code[a]	Number - Nombre					Rate - Taux				
		2010	2011	2012	2013	2014	2010	2011	2012	2013	2014
EUROPE											
Austria - Autriche											
Total	C	78 742	78 109	78 952	79 330	81 722	9.4	9.3	9.4	9.4	9.6
Belarus - Bélarus											
Total	C	108 050	109 147	115 893	117 997	118 534	11.4	11.5	12.2	12.5	12.5
Urban - Urbaine	C	82 306	83 445	89 129	90 436	...	11.6	11.7	12.4	12.5	...
Rural - Rurale	C	25 744	25 702	26 764	27 561	...	10.8	11.1	11.8	12.4	...
Belgium - Belgique[39]											
Total	C	130 100	128 705	128 051	125 606	125 014	11.9	11.7	11.5	11.2	11.2
Urban - Urbaine	C	128 270	126 865	...	...	...	11.9	11.7	...	...	...
Rural - Rurale	C	1 830	1 840	...	...	...	11.7	11.6	...	...	...
Bosnia and Herzegovina - Bosnie-Herzégovine											
Total	C	33 528	31 875	32 072	31 103	29 247	8.7	8.3	8.4	8.1	7.6
Bulgaria - Bulgarie											
Total	C	75 513	70 846	69 121	66 578	67 585	10.0	9.6	9.5	9.2	9.3
Urban - Urbaine	C	57 077	53 396	51 658	...	...	10.6	10.0	9.7	...	...
Rural - Rurale	C	18 436	17 450	17 463	...	...	8.6	8.7	8.8	...	...
Croatia - Croatie											
Total	C	43 361	41 197	41 771	39 939	39 566	10.1	9.6	9.8	9.4	9.3
Urban - Urbaine	C	24 583	23 366	23 839	22 796	...	...	...	...	...	...
Rural - Rurale	C	18 778	17 831	17 932	17 143	...	...	...	...	...	...
Czech Republic - République tchèque											
Total	C	117 153[40]	108 673[40]	108 576	106 751	109 860	11.2	10.4	10.3	10.2	10.4
Urban - Urbaine	C	86 078[40]	79 742[40]	79 812	78 469	...	...	...	...	10.2	...
Rural - Rurale	C	31 075[40]	28 931[40]	28 764	28 282	...	...	...	...	10.0	...
Denmark - Danemark[41]											
Total	C	63 411	58 998	57 916	55 873	56 870	11.4	10.6	10.4	10.0	10.1
Estonia - Estonie											
Total	C	15 825	14 679	14 056	13 531	13 551	11.9	11.1	10.6	10.3	10.3
Urban - Urbaine	C	10 645	10 057	9 653	9 286	...	11.8	11.1	10.7	10.3	...
Rural - Rurale	C	5 180	4 622	4 403	4 245	...	12.1	10.9	10.5	10.2	...
Faeroe Islands - Îles Féroé											
Total	C	639	576	618	624	...	13.1	11.9	12.8	13.0	...
Urban - Urbaine	C	236	219	249	237	...	13.2	12.1	13.8	13.2	...
Rural - Rurale	C	403	357	369	387	...	13.1	11.7	12.2	12.8	...
Finland - Finlande											
Total	C	60 694[42]	59 676[42]	59 201[42]	58 134	57 232	11.4	11.1	11.0	10.7	10.5
Urban - Urbaine[42]	C	43 543	42 637	42 274	...	...	12.0	11.6	11.4	...	...
Rural - Rurale[42]	C	17 151	17 039	16 927	...	...	10.1	10.1	10.0	...	...
France[43]											
Total	C	802 224	792 996	790 290	781 621	*766 400	12.8	12.5	12.4	12.3	*12.0
Urban - Urbaine[44]	C	635 898	629 283	628 694	623 522	...	...	...	...	...	...
Rural - Rurale[44]	C	164 776	162 102	159 929	156 358	...	...	...	...	...	...
Germany - Allemagne											
Total	C	677 947	662 685	673 544	682 069	*700 000	8.3	8.3	8.4	8.5	*8.7
Gibraltar[45]											
Total	+C	493	442	461	426	...	15.7	13.8	14.2	13.0	...
Greece - Grèce											
Total	C	114 766	106 428	100 371	94 134	*92 094	10.3	9.6	9.0	8.5	*8.4
Urban - Urbaine	C	78 756	75 224	71 232	...	...	...	...	...	...	...
Rural - Rurale	C	36 010	31 204	29 139	...	...	...	...	...	...	...
Guernsey - Guernesey											
Total	C	613	650	674	667	627	9.8	10.3	10.7	10.6	10.0
Hungary - Hongrie											
Total	C	90 335	88 049	90 269	89 524	*93 300	9.0	8.8	9.1	9.0	*9.4
Urban - Urbaine[46]	C	62 454	60 698	61 985	61 996	...	9.0	8.7	9.0	...	...
Rural - Rurale[46]	C	26 938	26 349	27 278	27 511	...	8.8	8.7	9.0	...	...
Iceland - Islande											
Total	C	4 907	4 492[47]	4 533	4 326	4 375	15.4	14.1	14.1	13.4	13.4
Urban - Urbaine	C	4 705	4 441[47]	4 316	4 131	...	15.8	14.1	14.4	13.6	...
Rural - Rurale	C	202	51[47]	217	195	...	9.8	11.1	10.6	9.5	...
Ireland - Irlande											
Total[48]	C	75 174	74 033	...	...	...	16.5	16.2	...	...	...
Total	+C	...	...	72 225	68 930	67 462	...	...	15.7	15.0	14.6
Isle of Man - Île de Man											
Total	+C	1 023	938	890	859	805	12.4	11.1	10.5	10.0	9.3

9. Live births and crude birth rates, by urban/rural residence: 2010 - 2014
Naissances vivantes et taux bruts de natalité selon la résidence, urbaine/rurale : 2010 - 2014 (continued - suite)

Continent, country or area, and urban/rural residence / Continent, pays ou zone et résidence, urbaine/rurale	Co-de[a]	Number - Nombre					Rate - Taux				
		2010	2011	2012	2013	2014	2010	2011	2012	2013	2014
EUROPE											
Italy - Italie											
Total	+C	561 944	546 585	534 186	514 308	502 596	9.5	9.2	9.0	8.5	8.3
Jersey[17]											
Total	+C	1 066	1 100	1 120	...	...	11.0	11.3	11.4	...	...
Latvia - Lettonie											
Total	C	19 781	18 828	19 897	20 596	21 746	9.4	9.1	9.8	10.2	10.8
Urban - Urbaine	C	13 593	12 726	13 582	14 184	...	9.6	9.1	9.9	10.4	...
Rural - Rurale	C	6 188	6 099	6 315	6 412	...	9.2	9.2	9.6	9.9	...
Liechtenstein											
Total	C	329	395	357	339	*370	9.1	10.9	9.7	9.2	*10.0
Lithuania - Lituanie											
Total	C	30 676	30 268	30 459	29 885	30 369	9.9	10.0	10.2	10.1	10.4
Urban - Urbaine	C	20 991	20 693	21 393	20 195	...	10.1	10.2	10.7	10.2	...
Rural - Rurale	C	9 685	9 575	9 066	9 690	...	9.4	9.5	9.2	9.9	...
Luxembourg											
Total	C	5 874	5 639	6 026	6 115	6 070	11.6	10.9	11.3	11.3	11.0
Malta - Malte											
Total	C	3 898	4 165	4 130	4 032	4 191	9.4	10.0	9.8	9.5	9.9
Monaco[49]											
Total	C	961	1 028	979	992	974	26.9	28.5	27.2	26.8	...
Montenegro - Monténégro											
Total	C	7 418	7 215	7 459	7 475	7 529	12.0	11.6	12.0	12.0	12.1
Netherlands - Pays-Bas[50]											
Total	C	184 397	180 060	175 959	171 341	*175 182	11.1	10.8	10.5	10.2	*10.4
Urban - Urbaine	C	129 450	...	...	...	...	11.7	...	...	...	...
Rural - Rurale	C	54 947	...	...	...	...	10.0	...	...	...	...
Norway - Norvège											
Total	C	61 442	60 220	60 255	58 878	59 084	12.6	12.2	12.0	11.6	11.6
Poland - Pologne											
Total	C	413 300	388 416	386 257	369 576	375 160	10.7	10.1	10.0	9.7	9.7
Urban - Urbaine	C	241 920	225 701	223 815	...	...	10.3	9.6	9.6	...	...
Rural - Rurale	C	171 380	162 715	162 442	...	...	11.4	10.8	10.7	...	...
Portugal[17]											
Total	C	101 381	96 856	89 841	82 787	82 367	9.6	9.2	8.5	7.9	7.9
Republic of Moldova - République de Moldova[51]											
Total	C	40 474	39 182	39 435	37 871	38 616	11.4	11.0	11.1	10.6	10.9
Urban - Urbaine	C	15 142	14 599	14 890	...	...	10.2	9.8	10.0	...	...
Rural - Rurale	C	25 332	24 583	24 545	...	...	12.2	11.8	11.9	...	...
Romania - Roumanie											
Total	C	212 199	196 242	201 104	182 313	*183 785	10.5	9.7	10.0	9.1	*9.2
Urban - Urbaine	C	117 851	106 667	108 425	98 351	...	10.8	9.8	10.0	9.1	...
Rural - Rurale	C	94 348	89 575	92 679	83 962	...	10.1	9.7	10.0	9.1	...
Russian Federation - Fédération de Russie[21]											
Total	C	1 788 948	1 796 629	1 902 084	*1 901 182	1 942 683	12.5	12.6	13.3	*13.2	...
Urban - Urbaine	C	1 263 893	1 270 047	1 355 674	...	...	12.0	12.0	12.8	...	...
Rural - Rurale	C	525 055	526 582	546 410	...	...	14.0	14.1	14.7	...	...
San Marino - Saint-Marin											
Total	+C	334	325	292	320	296	10.0	9.7	8.7	9.6	8.8
Serbia - Serbie[52]											
Total	+C	68 304	65 598	67 257	65 554	66 461	9.4	9.1	9.3	9.2	9.3
Urban - Urbaine	+C	46 684	45 430	45 869	45 657	...	10.9	10.6	10.7	10.7	...
Rural - Rurale	+C	21 620	20 168	21 388	19 897	...	7.2	6.8	7.3	6.9	...
Slovakia - Slovaquie											
Total	C	60 410	60 647	55 535	54 823	55 033	11.2	11.2	10.3	10.1	10.2
Urban - Urbaine	C	32 119	32 130	29 174	28 692	...	...	10.9	9.9	9.8	...
Rural - Rurale	C	28 291	28 517	26 361	26 131	...	...	11.6	10.7	10.5	...
Slovenia - Slovénie											
Total	C	22 343	21 947	21 938	21 111	21 165	10.9	10.7	10.7	10.3	10.3
Urban - Urbaine	C	10 893	10 651	10 675	10 698	...	10.6	10.4	10.4	10.2	...
Rural - Rurale	C	11 450	11 296	11 263	10 413	...	11.2	11.0	10.9	10.3	...
Spain - Espagne											
Total	C	485 252	470 553	453 348	424 440	*426 042	10.4	10.1	9.7	9.1	*9.2
Sweden - Suède											
Total	C	115 641	111 770	113 177	113 593	114 907	12.3	11.8	11.9	11.8	11.8

9. Live births and crude birth rates, by urban/rural residence: 2010 - 2014
Naissances vivantes et taux bruts de natalité selon la résidence, urbaine/rurale : 2010 - 2014 (continued - suite)

Continent, country or area, and urban/rural residence / Continent, pays ou zone et résidence, urbaine/rurale	Co-de[a]	Number - Nombre					Rate - Taux				
		2010	2011	2012	2013	2014	2010	2011	2012	2013	2014
EUROPE											
Switzerland - Suisse											
Total	C	80 290	80 808	82 164	82 731	83 753	10.3	10.2	10.3	10.2	10.3
Urban - Urbaine	C	60 131	60 544	61 490	...	...	...	10.4	10.4	...	...
Rural - Rurale	C	20 159	20 264	20 674	...	...	...	9.7	9.8	...	...
TFYR of Macedonia - L'ex-R. y. de Macédoine											
Total	C	24 296	22 770	23 568	23 138	23 596	11.8	11.1	11.4	11.2	11.4
Urban - Urbaine	C	13 904	13 008	13 379	...	...	...	...	...	...	...
Rural - Rurale	C	10 392	9 762	10 189	...	...	...	...	...	...	...
Ukraine[53]											
Total	+C	497 689	502 595	520 705	503 657	...	10.8	11.0	11.4	11.1	...
Urban - Urbaine	+C	326 587	328 934	341 599	330 284	...	10.4	10.5	10.9	...	...
Rural - Rurale	+C	171 102	173 661	179 106	173 373	...	11.9	12.1	12.6	...	...
United Kingdom of Great Britain and Northern Ireland - Royaume-Uni de Grande-Bretagne et d'Irlande du Nord[54]											
Total	C	807 271	807 776	812 970	778 358	*776 351	12.9	12.8	12.8	12.1	*12.1
OCEANIA - OCÉANIE											
American Samoa - Samoas américaines											
Total	C	1 279	1 287	...	...	...	19.0	...	...	...	...
Australia - Australie											
Total	+C	303 318	301 617	309 582	308 065	...	13.8	13.5	13.6	13.3	...
Urban - Urbaine[55]	+C	203 520	203 060	210 139	209 397	...	10.8	10.7	10.8	10.6	...
Rural - Rurale[55]	+C	99 009	97 829	98 569	97 514	...	30.3	29.7	29.6	29.0	...
Cook Islands - Îles Cook[56]											
Total	+C	286	262	259	256	*204	12.1	13.6	13.3	13.8	*11.0
Fiji - Fidji											
Total	+C	...	...	20 178	...	...	...	...	23.5	...	...
French Polynesia - Polynésie française											
Total	C	4 578	4 375	4 295	...	...	17.1	16.2	16.0	...	...
Guam[57]											
Total	C	3 419	3 298	3 604	3 329	3 396	21.5	20.7	22.5	20.8	21.1
Nauru											
Total	C	322	370	319	366	...	...	36.7	...	...	...
New Caledonia - Nouvelle-Calédonie											
Total	C	4 178	4 119	4 389	...	...	16.7	16.2	17.0	...	...
New Zealand - Nouvelle-Zélande											
Total	+C	63 897	61 403	61 178	58 717	57 242	14.7	14.0	13.9	13.2	12.7
Urban - Urbaine[14]	+C	55 879	53 967	53 917	51 480	50 355	14.9	14.3	14.2	13.5	13.0
Rural - Rurale[14]	+C	7 945	7 419	7 253	7 228	6 874	13.1	12.0	11.6	11.6	11.0
Niue - Nioué[58]											
Total	C	25	22	...	...	...	...	...	...	...	...
Norfolk Island - Île Norfolk[59]											
Total	+C	21	13	4	...	...	...	...	...	...	...
Northern Mariana Islands - Îles Mariannes septentrionales[60]											
Total	U	*1 072*	...	...	...	...	...	...	...	...	...
Palau - Palaos											
Total	C	247	247	268	229	...	11.9	11.8	12.7	...	...
Pitcairn											
Total	C	...	-	-	-	...	...	...	...	...	...
Samoa[61]											
Total	+U	*1 381*	*2 354*	...	...	...	...	...	...	...	...
Tokelau - Tokélaou[62]											
Total	I	...	16	...	...	...	...	...	...	...	...

FOOTNOTES - NOTES

Italics: data from civil registers which are incomplete or of unknown completeness. - Italiques : données incomplètes ou dont le degré d'exactitude n'est pas connu, provenant des registres de l'état civil.

* Provisional. - Données provisoires.

a 'Code' indicates the source of data, as follows:
C - Civil registration, estimated over 90% complete
U - Civil registration, estimated less than 90% complete
| - Other source, estimated reliable
+ - Data tabulated by date of registration rather than occurence
... - Information not available

Le 'Code' indique la source des données, comme suit :
C - Registres de l'état civil considérés complets à 90 p. 100 au moins
U - Registres de l'état civil qui ne sont pas considérés complets à 90 p. 100 au moins
| - Autre source, considérée pas douteuses
+ - Données exploitées selon la date de l'enregistrement et non la date de l'événement
... - Information pas disponible

1 Excluding live-born infants who died before their birth was registered. Data refer to Algerian population only. - Non compris les enfants nés vivants décédés avant l'enregistrement de leur naissance. Les données ne concernent que la population algérienne.

2 Data are projections presented in Annuaire Statistique 2010. - Les données sont des projections présentées dans l'Annuaire Statistique 2010.

3 Source: Vital Statistics Report 2012. - Source: Vital Statistics Report 2012.

4 Data refer to the recorded events in Ministry of Health hospitals and health centres only. - Les données se rapportent aux faits d'état civil enregistrés dans les hôpitaux et les dispensaires du Ministère de la santé seulement.

5 Data refer to the 12 months preceding the census in September. - Les données se rapportent aux 12 mois précédant le recensement de septembre.

6 Excludes the islands of St. Brandon and Agalega. - Non compris les îles St. Brandon et Agalega.

7 Data refer to the 12 months preceding the census in August. - Les données se rapportent aux 12 mois précédant le recensement d'août.

8 Excluding live-born infants who died before their birth was registered. - Non compris les enfants nés vivants décédés avant l'enregistrement de leur naissance.

9 Based on estimates and projections from 'Agence Nationale de la Statistique et de la Démographie'. - Données fondées sur des estimations et des projections provenant de l'Agence Nationale de la Statistique et de la Démographie.

10 Data refer to the 12 months preceding the census in October. - Les données se rapportent aux 12 mois précédant le recensement de octobre.

11 Excluding non-residents and foreign service personnel and their dependants. - À l'exclusion des non-résidents et du personnel diplomatique et de leurs charges de famille.

12 Data refer to the twelve months from 1 July of the current year to 30 June of the following year. Including Canadian residents temporarily in the United States, but excluding United States residents temporarily in Canada. - Les données font référence aux douze mois de 1 juillet de l'année actuelle à 30 juin de l'année suivante. Y compris les résidents canadiens se trouvant temporairement aux Etats-Unis, mais ne comprenant pas les résidents des Etats-Unis se trouvant temporairement au Canada.

13 Including unknown sex. - Y compris le sexe inconnu.

14 The total number may include 'Unknown residence', but the categories urban and rural do not. - Le nombre total peut inclure les personnes dont la résidence n'est pas connue, à l'inverse des catégories de population urbaine et rurale.

15 Excluding children born in the country of non-resident mothers. - Exceptés les enfants nés dans le pays des mères non-résidentes.

16 Data have been adjusted for underenumeration. - Les données ont été ajustées pour compenser les lacunes du dénombrement.

17 Data refer to births to resident mothers. - Ces données concernent les enfants nés de mères résidentes.

18 Source: Population Registry and STAT/CBS estimates. - Source: Estimations du registre de la population/STAT/CBS.

19 Including births abroad and births of unknown residence of mother. - Y compris les naissances à l'étranger et les naissances pour lesquelles le lieu de résidence de la mère est inconnu.

20 Source: Reports of the Ministry of Health. - Source : Rapports du Ministère de la Santé.

21 Excluding infants born alive of less than 28 weeks' gestation, of less than 1 000 grams in weight and 35 centimeters in length, who die within seven days of birth. - Non compris les enfants nés vivants après moins de 28 semaines de gestations, pesant moins de 1 000 grammes, mesurant moins de 35 centimètres et décédés dans les sept jours qui ont suivi leur naissance.

22 Data have been estimated on the basis of the annual National Sample Survey on Population Changes. For statistical purposes, the data for China do not include those for the Hong Kong Special Administrative Region (Hong Kong SAR), Macao Special Administrative Region (Macao SAR) and Taiwan province of China. - Les données ont été estimées sur la base de l'enquête annuelle "National Sample Survey on Population Changes". Pour la présentation des statistiques, les données pour la Chine ne comprennent pas la Région Administrative Spéciale de Hong Kong (Hong Kong RAS), la Région Administrative Spéciale de Macao (Macao RAS) et Taïwan province de Chine.

23 Data refer to government controlled areas. - Les données se rapportent aux zones contrôlées par le Gouvernement.

24 Rates were obtained by the Sample Registration System of India, which is a large demographic survey. Includes data for the Indian-held part of Jammu and Kashmir, the final status of which has not yet been determined. - Les taux ont été obtenus par le Système de l'enregistrement par échantillon de l'Inde qui est une large enquête démographique. Y compris les données pour la partie du Jammu et du Cachemire occupée par l'Inde dont le statut définitif n'a pas encore été déterminé.

25 Data refer to the Iranian Year which begins on 21 March and ends on 20 March of the following year. - Les données concernent l'année iranienne, qui commence le 21 mars et se termine le 20 mars de l'année suivante.

26 Includes data for East Jerusalem and Israeli residents in certain other territories under occupation by Israeli military forces since June 1967. - Y compris les données pour Jérusalem-Est et les résidents israéliens dans certains autres territoires occupés depuis 1967 par les forces armées israéliennes.

27 Data refer to Japanese nationals in Japan only. - Les données se raportent aux nationaux japonais au Japon seulement.

28 The total number may include 'Unknown residence', but the categories urban and rural do not. Urban and rural distribution refers to the residence of the child. - Le nombre total peut inclure les personnes dont la résidence n'est pas connue, à l'inverse des catégories de population urbaine et rurale. La répartition urbain/rural se réfère au domicile de l'enfant.

29 Excluding data for Jordanian territory under occupation since June 1967 by Israeli military forces. Excluding foreigners, including registered Palestinian refugees. - Non compris les données pour le territoire jordanien occupé depuis juin 1967 par les forces armées israéliennes. Non compris les étrangers, mais y compris les réfugiés de Palestine enregistrés.

30 Excluding births occurred abroad. - Hormis les naissances intervenues à l'étranger.

31 Data refer to the 12 months preceding the census in June. - Les données se rapportent aux 12 mois précédant le recensement de juin.

32 Data for all population, citizens and foreigners. Data from Births and Deaths Notification System (Ministry of Health and all health care providers). - Les données portent sur la population entière, les citoyens et les étrangers. Les données proviennent du système de notification des naissances et des décès (Ministère de la santé et tous prestataires de soins de santé).

33 Data refer to residence of child. Excluding alien armed forces, civilian aliens employed by armed forces, and foreign diplomatic personnel and their dependants. - Les données correspondent à la résidence de l'enfant. Non compris les militaires étrangers, les civils étrangers employés par les forces armées ni le personnel diplomatique étranger et les membres de leur famille les accompagnant.

34 Source: Palestinian Central Bureau of Statistics, Population Register, updated version 05/01/2015. - Source: Bureau central de statistique palestinien, registre de la population, version actualisée jusqu'au 05/01/2015.

35 Excluding nomad population and Palestinian refugees. Excluding live-born infants who died before their birth was registered. - Non compris la population nomade et les réfugiés de Palestine. Non compris les enfants nés vivants décédés avant l'enregistrement de leur naissance.

36 Excluding infants born alive of less than 28 weeks' gestation, of less than 1 000 grams in weight and 35 centimeters in length, who die within seven days of birth. Data have been adjusted for under-registration. - Non compris les enfants nés vivants après moins de 28 semaines de gestations, pesant moins de 1 000 grammes, mesurant moins de 35 centimètres et décédés dans les sept jours qui ont suivi leur naissance. Y compris un ajustement pour sous-enregistrement.

37 The registration of births and deaths is conducted by the Ministry of Health. An estimate of completeness is not provided. - L'enregistrement des naissances et des décès est mené par le Ministère de la Santé. Le degré estimatif de complétude n'est pas fourni.

38 Including Non-Yemeni births. - Y compris les naissances non-yéménites.

[39] Including armed forces stationed outside the country, but excluding alien armed forces stationed in the area. - Y compris les militaires nationaux hors du pays, mais non compris les militaires étrangers en garnison sur le territoire.

[40] A live-born child is a child fully expelled or removed out of the mother's body, who gives a sign of life and whose birth weight is (a) 500 g or more, or (b) lower than 500 g, if it survives 24 hours after delivery. - Un enfant né vivant est un enfant qui a été entièrement expulsé ou retiré du corps de la mère, qui présente des signes de vie et dont le poids à la naissance est : a) soit égal ou supérieur à 500 grammes; b) soit inférieur à 500 grammes s'il survit plus de 24 heures après l'accouchement.

[41] Excluding Faeroe Islands and Greenland shown separately, if available. - Non compris les Iles Féroé et le Groenland, qui font l'objet de rubriques distinctes, si disponible.

[42] Excluding Åland Islands. - Non compris les Îles d'Åland.

[43] Including armed forces stationed outside the country. - Y compris les militaires nationaux hors du pays.

[44] The data for urban and rural exclude the nationals outside the country. - Les données relatives à la population urbaine et rurale n'englobent pas les nationaux se trouvant à l'étranger.

[45] Including live births by military personnel and their dependants. - Y compris les naissances vivantes parmi les membres du personnel militaire et leurs personnes à charge.

[46] The urban and rural categories do not include the data of foreigners, persons of unknown residence and the homeless, whereas the total category includes them. - Les chiffres portant sur la population urbaine et rurale n' incluent pas les données relatives aux étrangers, aux personnes dont la résidence n'est pas connue et aux personnes sans domicile fixe, à l'inverse, le total les inclut.

[47] Definition of localities was revised in 2011 causing a break with the previous series. - La rupture par rapport aux séries précédentes s'explique par le fait que la définition des localités a été révisée depuis 2011.

[48] Data refer to events registered within one year of occurrence. - Les données portent sur des événements enregistrés dans l'année pendant laquelle ils sont survenus.

[49] Including residents outside the country. - Y compris les résidents hors du pays.

[50] Including residents outside the country if listed in a Netherlands population register. - Englobe les résidents se trouvant à l'étranger à condition qu'ils soient inscrits sur le registre de population des Pays-Bas.

[51] Excluding Transnistria and the municipality of Bender. - Les données ne tiennent pas compte de l'information sur la Transnistria et la municipalité de Bender.

[52] Excludes data for Kosovo and Metohia. - Sans les données pour le Kosovo et Metohie.

[53] Data refer to births with weight 500g and more (if weight is unknown - with length 25 centimeters and more, or with gestation during 22 weeks or more). - Données concernant les nouveau-nés de 500 grammes ou plus (si le poids est inconnu – de 25 centimètres de long ou plus, ou après une grossesse de 22 semaines ou plus).

[54] Excluding Channel Islands (Guernsey and Jersey) and Isle of Man, shown separately, if available. Data tabulated by date of occurrence for England and Wales, and by date of registration for Northern Ireland and Scotland. - Non compris les îles Anglo-Normandes (Guernesey et Jersey) et l'île de Man, qui font l'objet de rubriques distinctes, si disponible. Données exploitées selon la date de l'événement pour l'Angleterre et le pays de Galles, et selon la date de l'enregistrement pour l'Irlande du Nord et l'Ecosse.

[55] Urban refers to Greater Capital City Statistical Areas, and rural refers to other areas within the state or territory. - Urbain renvoie aux zones statistiques de la capitale métropolitaine, et rural aux autres zones de l'État ou territoire.

[56] Excluding Niue, shown separately, which is part of Cook Islands, but because of remoteness is administered separately. - Non compris Nioué, qui fait l'objet d'une rubrique distincte et qui fait partie des îles Cook, mais qui, en raison de son éloignement, est administrée séparément.

[57] Including United States military personnel, their dependants and contract employees. - Y compris les militaires des Etats-Unis, les membres de leur famille les accompagnant et les agents contractuels des Etats-Unis.

[58] Includes children born in New Zealand to women resident in Niue who chose to travel to New Zealand to give birth. - Y compris les enfants nés en Nouvelle-Zélande de femmes résidant à Nioué qui ont choisi de se rendre en Nouvelle-Zélande pour accoucher.

[59] Data cover the period from 1 July of the previous year to 30 June of the present year. - Pour la période allant du 1er juillet de l'année précédente au 30 juin de l'année en cours.

[60] Source: U.S. National Center for Health Statistics, National Vital Statistics Reports (NVSR). - Source : US National Center for Health Statistics, National Vital Statistics Reports (NVSR).

[61] The coverage of registration is estimated at 70 per cent. - Le degré de complétude de l'enregistrement est évalué à 70 pour cent.

[62] Data refer to usually resident population present on census night. Data refer to the 12 months preceding the census in October. - Les données concernent la population habituellement résidente présente la nuit du recensement. Les données se rapportent aux 12 mois précédant le recensement de octobre.

Table 10 - *Demographic Yearbook 2014*

Table 10 presents live births by age of mother and sex of the child, general fertility rate, and age-specific fertility rates for the latest available year between 2005 and 2014.

Description of variables: Age is defined as age at last birthday, that is, the difference between the date of birth and the date of the occurrence of the event, expressed in completed solar years. The age classification used in this table is the following: under 15 years, 5-year age groups through 45-49 years, and 50 years and over. A different classification may appear as provided by the reporting country or area.

Rate computation: Age-specific fertility rates are the annual number of births to women in each age group per 1 000 female population in the same age group. These rates are calculated by the Statistics Division of the United Nations.

Since relatively few births occur to women below 15 or above 50 years of age, age-specific fertility rates for women under 20 years of age and for those 45 years of age or over are computed on the female population aged 15-19 and 45-49, respectively. Similarly, the rate for women of "All ages" is based on all live births irrespective of age of mother, and is computed on the female population aged 15-49 years. This rate for "All ages" is known as the general fertility rate. The age-specific fertility rates for age groups of women below 15 or 50 and above years of age are not calculated.

Births to mothers of unknown age are distributed proportionately across the age groups, by the Statistics Division of the United Nations, in accordance with the distribution of births by age of mother prior to the calculation of the rates.

The population used in computing the rates is the estimated or enumerated distribution of females by age. First priority was given to the estimated population and second priority to the enumerated population, i.e. to census returns of the year to which the births referred.

Rates presented in this table are limited to those for countries or areas having at least a total of 100 live births in a given year.

Reliability of data: Data from civil registers of live births which are reported as incomplete (less than 90 per cent completeness) or of unknown completeness are considered unreliable and are set in *italics* rather than in roman type. Rates are not computed if the data on live births from civil registers are reported as incomplete (less than 90 per cent completeness) or of unknown completeness. Table 9 and the technical notes for that table provide more detailed information on the completeness of live-birth registration. For more information about the quality of vital statistics data in general, see section 4.2 of the Technical Notes.

Limitations: Statistics on live births by age of mother are subject to the same qualifications as have been set forth for vital statistics in general and birth statistics in particular as discussed in section 4 of the Technical Notes. These include differences in the completeness of registration, the method used to determine age of mother and the quality of the reported information relating to age of mother.

The reliability of the data described above, is an important factor in considering the limitations. In addition, some live births are tabulated by date of registration and not by date of occurrence; these are indicated in the table by a plus sign "+". Whenever the lag between the date of occurrence and date of registration is prolonged and, therefore, a large proportion of the live birth registrations are delayed, birth statistics for any given year may be seriously affected. For example, the age of the mother will almost always refer to the date of registration rather than to the date of birth of the child. Hence, in those countries or areas where registration of births is delayed, possibly for years, statistics on births by age of mother should be used with caution.

Another factor which limits international comparability is the practice of some countries or areas of not including in live birth statistics infants who were born alive but died before the registration of the birth or within the first 24 hours of life, thus underestimating the total number of live births. Statistics of this type are footnoted.

Because these statistics are classified according to age, they are subject to the limitations with respect to accuracy of age reporting similar to those already discussed in connection with section 3.1.3 of the Technical Notes. The factors influencing the accuracy of reporting may be somewhat dissimilar in vital statistics (because of the differences in the method of taking a census and registering a birth) but, in general, the same errors can be observed. The absence of frequencies in the unknown age group does not necessarily indicate completely accurate reporting and tabulation of the age item. It is often an indication that the unknowns have been eliminated by assigning ages to them before tabulation, or by proportionate distribution after tabulation.

On the other hand, large frequencies in the unknown age category may indicate that a large proportion of the births are born outside of wedlock, the records for which tend to be incomplete so far as characteristics of the parents are concerned.

Another limitation of age reporting may result from calculating age of mother at birth of child (or at time of registration) from year of birth rather than from day, month and year of birth. Information on this factor is given in footnotes when known.

In few countries, data by age refer to deliveries rather than to live births causing under-enumeration in the event of a multiple birth. This practice leads to lack of strict comparability, both among countries or areas relying on this practice and between data shown in this table and table 9.

Rates shown in this table are subject to the same limitations that affect the corresponding statistics on live births. In cases of rates based on births tabulated by date of registration and not by date of occurrence; the effect of including delayed registration on the distribution of births by age of mother may be noted in the age-specific fertility rates for women at older ages. In some cases, high age-specific rates for women aged 45 years and over may reflect age of mother at registration of birth and not fertility at these older ages.

Earlier data: Live births and live-birth rates by age of mother (i.e. age-specific fertility rates), have been shown for the latest available year in each issue of the Yearbook. Information on the years and specific topics covered is presented in the Historical Index.

Tableau 10 – *Annuaire démographique 2014*

Le tableau 10 présente les données les plus récentes disponibles pour la période 2005 - 2014 sur les naissances vivantes selon l'âge de la mère et le sexe de l'enfant, le taux de fécondité et les taux de fécondité par âge.

Description des variables : l'âge désigne l'âge au dernier anniversaire, c'est-à-dire la différence entre la date de naissance et la date de l'événement exprimée en années solaires révolues. La classification par âge utilisée dans ce tableau comprend les catégories suivantes : moins de 15 ans, groupes quinquennaux jusqu'à 45-49 ans, 50 ans et plus, et âge inconnu. Des groupes d'âge différents sont parfois utilisés lorsque les pays ou territoires ont fourni les données dans une autre classification.

Les taux de fécondité par âge représentent le nombre annuel de naissances vivantes intervenues dans un groupe d'âge donné pour 1 000 femmes du groupe d'âge. Ces taux ont été calculés par la Division de statistique de l'ONU.

Étant donné que le nombre de naissances parmi les femmes de moins de 15 ans ou de plus de 50 ans est relativement peu élevé, les taux de fécondité par âge parmi les femmes âgées de moins de 20 ans et celles de 45 ans et plus ont été calculés sur la base des populations féminines âgées de 15 à 19 ans et de 45 à 49 ans, respectivement. De même, le taux pour les femmes de « tous âges » est fondé sur la totalité des naissances vivantes, indépendamment de l'âge de la mère et ce chiffre est rapporté à l'effectif de la population féminine âgée de 15 à 49 ans. Ce taux « tous âges » est le taux global de fécondité ou simplement taux de fécondité. Les taux de fécondité parmi les femmes âgées de moins de 15 ans ou celles de 50 ans et plus n'ont pas été calculés.

Les naissances pour lesquelles l'âge de la mère était inconnu ont été réparties par la Division de statistique de l'ONU, avant le calcul des taux, suivant les proportions observées pour celles où l'âge de la mère était connu.

Les chiffres de population utilisés pour le calcul des taux proviennent de dénombrements ou de répartitions estimatives de la population féminine selon l'âge. On a utilisé de préférence les estimations de la population; à défaut, on s'est contenté des données censitaires se rapportant à l'année des naissances.

Les taux présentés dans ce tableau ne concernent que les pays ou zones où l'on a enregistré un total d'au moins 100 naissances vivantes dans une année donnée.

Fiabilité des données : les données sur les naissances vivantes provenant des registres de l'état civil qui sont déclarées incomplètes (degré de complétude inférieur à 90 p. 100) ou dont le degré de complétude n'est pas connu, sont jugées douteuses et apparaissent en italique et non en caractères romains. On a choisi de ne pas faire figurer des taux calculés à partir de données sur les naissances vivantes issues de registres de l'état civil qui sont déclarées incomplètes (degré de complétude inférieur à 90 p. 100) ou dont le degré de complétude n'est pas connu. Le tableau 9 et les notes techniques qui s'y rapportent présentent des renseignements plus détaillés sur le degré de complétude de l'enregistrement des naissances vivantes. Pour plus de précisions sur la qualité des statistiques de l'état civil en général, voir la section 4.2 des Notes techniques.

Insuffisance des données : les statistiques relatives aux naissances vivantes selon l'âge de la mère appellent toutes les réserves qui ont été formulées à propos des statistiques de l'état civil en général et des statistiques de naissances en particulier (voir la section 4 des Notes techniques). Ceci inclut les différences de complétude d'enregistrement des faits d'état civil, de méthode pour déterminer l'âge de la mère et de qualité d'information concernant l'âge de la mère.

La fiabilité des données, au sujet de laquelle des indications ont été données plus haut, est un facteur important. Il faut également tenir compte du fait que, dans certains cas, les données relatives aux naissances vivantes sont exploitées selon la date de l'enregistrement et non la date de l'événement ; ces cas ont été signalés dans le tableau par le signe '+'. Chaque fois que le décalage entre l'événement et son enregistrement est grand et qu'une forte proportion des naissances vivantes fait l'objet d'un enregistrement tardif, les statistiques des naissances vivantes pour une année donnée peuvent être considérablement faussées. Par exemple, l'âge de la mère représente presque toujours son âge à la date de l'enregistrement et non à la date de la naissance de l'enfant. Ainsi, dans les pays ou zones où l'enregistrement des naissances est tardif, le retard atteignant parfois plusieurs années, il faut utiliser avec prudence les statistiques concernant les naissances selon l'âge de la mère.

Un autre facteur qui nuit à la comparabilité internationale est la pratique de certains pays ou zones qui consiste à ne pas inclure dans les statistiques des naissances vivantes les enfants nés vivants mais décédés avant l'enregistrement de leur naissance ou dans les 24 heures qui ont suivi la naissance, pratique qui conduit à sous-estimer le nombre total de naissances vivantes. Quand pareil facteur a joué, cela a été signalé en note à la fin du tableau.

Étant donné que les statistiques du tableau 10 sont classées selon l'âge, elles appellent les mêmes réserves concernant l'exactitude des déclarations d'âge que celles formulées à la section 3.1.3 des Notes techniques. Dans le cas des statistiques de l'état civil, les facteurs qui interviennent à cet égard sont parfois différents, étant donné que le recensement de la population et l'enregistrement des naissances se font par des méthodes différentes, mais, d'une manière générale, les erreurs observées seront les mêmes. Si aucun nombre ne figure dans la rangée réservée aux âges inconnus, cela ne signifie pas nécessairement que les déclarations d'âge et l'exploitation des données par âge ont été tout à fait exactes. C'est souvent une indication que l'on a attribué un âge aux personnes d'âge inconnu avant l'exploitation des données ou qu'elles ont été réparties proportionnellement entre les différents groupes après cette opération.

À l'inverse, lorsque le nombre des personnes d'âge inconnu est important, cela peut signifier que la proportion de naissances parmi les mères célibataires est élevée, étant donné qu'en pareil cas l'acte de naissance ne contient pas tous les renseignements concernant les parents.

Les déclarations par âge peuvent comporter des distorsions, du fait que l'âge de la mère au moment de la naissance d'un enfant (ou de la déclaration de naissance) est donné par année de naissance et non par date exacte (jour, mois et année).

Dans quelques pays, la classification par âges se réfère aux accouchements, et non aux naissances vivantes, ce qui conduit à un sous-dénombrement en cas de naissances gémellaires. Cette pratique nuit à la comparabilité des données, à la fois entre pays ou zones qui recourent à cette méthode et entre les données présentées dans le tableau 10 et celles du tableau 9.

Les taux présentés dans ce tableau sont sujets aux mêmes limitations qui affectent les statistiques correspondantes de naissances vivantes. Dans le cas des taux basés sur des naissances par date d'enregistrement et non par date d'occurrence, l'effet peut être visible sur les taux de fécondité par âge des femmes aux âges plus élevés. Dans certains cas, les taux de fécondité des femmes de plus de 45 ans peuvent refléter l'âge de la mère à l'enregistrement plus que la fécondité à ces âges.

Données publiées antérieurement : les différentes éditions de l'*Annuaire démographique* regroupent les dernières statistiques dont on disposait à l'époque sur les naissances vivantes selon l'âge de la mère et les taux des naissances vivantes selon l'âge de la mère (taux de fécondité par âge). Pour plus de précisions concernant les années pour lesquels des données ont été publiées, se reporter à l'index historique.

10. Live births by age of mother and sex of child, general and age-specific fertility rates: latest available year, 2005 - 2014
Naissances vivantes selon l'âge de la mère et le sexe de l'enfant, taux de fécondité et taux de fécondité par âge : dernière année disponible, 2005 - 2014

Continent, country or area, year, code[a] and age of mother (in years) / Continent, pays ou zone, année, code[a] et âge de la mère (en années)	Number - Nombre			Rate Taux
	Total	Male Masculin	Female Féminin	

AFRICA - AFRIQUE

Botswana				
2011 (|)[1]				
Total	51 447	26 283	25 164	104.3
0 - 14	42	20	22	..
15 - 19	4 111	2 069	2 042	40.6
20 - 24	14 104	7 223	6 881	141.0
25 - 29	14 471	7 312	7 159	163.6
30 - 34	9 934	5 112	4 822	134.4
35 - 39	5 933	3 101	2 832	105.9
40 - 44	2 224	1 154	1 070	54.9
45 - 49	628	292	336	19.1
50 +	-	-	-	..
2012 (U)[2]				
Total	40 856	...	...	...
10 - 14	44	...	...	..
15 - 19	4 073	...	...	..
20 - 24	11 236	...	...	..
25 - 29	11 051	...	...	..
30 - 34	8 157	...	...	..
35 - 39	4 434	...	...	..
40 - 44	1 286	...	...	...
45 - 49	137	...	...	..
50 +	17	...	...	..
Unknown - Inconnu	421	...	...	..
Egypt - Égypte				
2012 (+C)				
Total	2 629 769	1 343 402	1 286 367	121.1
0 - 19	71 275	36 022	35 253	23.8
20 - 24	1 298 851	665 452	633 399	403.8
25 - 29	399 915	201 967	197 948	127.5
30 - 34	223 307	111 754	111 553	86.0
35 - 39	83 362	41 121	42 241	41.3
40 - 44	21 510	11 229	10 281	12.2
45 +	3 802	2 233	1 569	2.3
Unknown - Inconnu	527 747	273 624	254 123	..
Ghana[3]				
2010 (|)				
Total	623 700	306 159	317 541	98.1
0 - 14	917	381	536	..
15 - 19	40 307	19 067	21 240	31.0
20 - 24	126 417	61 277	65 140	103.4
25 - 29	167 306	82 741	84 565	151.1
30 - 34	130 724	64 600	66 124	147.1
35 - 39	92 751	46 285	46 466	124.6
40 - 44	41 898	20 783	21 115	68.3
45 - 49	14 742	7 071	7 671	30.4
50 +	8 638	3 954	4 684	..
Kenya				
2009 (U)				
Total	691 312	354 154	337 158	...
0 - 14	3 877	2 019	1 858	...
15 - 19	89 664	45 562	44 102	...
20 - 24	221 828	113 572	108 256	...
25 - 29	174 571	89 674	84 897	...
30 - 34	103 940	53 395	50 545	...
35 - 39	49 527	25 424	24 103	...
40 - 44	13 231	6 713	6 518	...
45 - 49	2 165	1 097	1 068	...
50 +	823	423	400	..
Unknown - Inconnu	31 686	16 275	15 411	..
2012 (U)[4]				
Total	754 429	...	...	...
0 - 14	3 047	...	...	...
15 - 19	90 928	...	...	...
20 - 24	234 290	...	...	...

AFRICA - AFRIQUE

Kenya				
2012 (U)[4]				
25 - 29	204 221	...	...	...
30 - 34	122 883	...	...	...
35 - 39	64 386	...	...	...
40 - 44	16 674	...	...	...
45 - 49	2 975	...	...	...
50 +	560	...	...	..
Unknown - Inconnu	14 462	...	...	..
Lesotho				
2012 (+U)				
Total	1 718	...	...	...
10 - 14	97	...	...	..
15 - 19	96	...	...	..
20 - 24	378	...	...	..
25 - 29	506	...	...	..
30 - 34	409	...	...	..
35 - 39	183	...	...	..
40 - 44	42	...	...	..
45 +	7	...	...	..
Liberia - Libéria[5]				
2008 (|)				
Total	63 171	33 511	29 660	73.1
12 - 14	304	157	147	..
15 - 19	6 973	3 668	3 305	37.4
20 - 24	16 181	8 486	7 695	89.4
25 - 29	14 915	8 017	6 898	98.9
30 - 34	10 277	5 433	4 844	91.5
35 - 39	8 336	4 374	3 962	79.8
40 - 44	3 961	2 138	1 823	53.5
45 - 49	2 224	1 238	986	40.5
Libya - Libye[6]				
2009 (+U)				
Total	134 682	...	...	...
0 - 19	733	...	...	...
20 - 24	7 067	...	...	...
25 - 29	17 792	...	...	...
30 - 34	18 491	...	...	...
35 - 39	9 801	...	...	...
40 - 44	3 334	...	...	...
45 +	409	...	...	...
Unknown - Inconnu	77 055	...	...	...
Malawi[7]				
2008 (|)				
Total	516 629	247 753	268 876	160.1
12 - 14	1 621	751	870	..
15 - 19	70 737	34 137	36 600	101.2
20 - 24	169 406	81 379	88 027	284.1
25 - 29	130 331	62 810	67 521	241.6
30 - 34	79 232	37 758	41 474	153.2
35 - 39	43 747	20 776	22 971	116.8
40 - 44	15 956	7 553	8 403	57.8
45 - 49	5 599	2 589	3 010	25.0
Mali[8]				
2009 (|)				
Total	666 216	324 862	341 354	208.9
12 - 14	34 953	17 432	17 521	..
15 - 19	97 788	47 793	49 995	124.8
20 - 24	138 189	67 575	70 614	225.7
25 - 29	140 359	68 914	71 445	256.8
30 - 34	108 467	52 837	55 630	253.5
35 - 39	74 059	35 667	38 392	226.6
40 - 44	45 402	21 748	23 654	164.9
45 +	26 999	12 896	14 103	124.3

10. Live births by age of mother and sex of child, general and age-specific fertility rates: latest available year, 2005 - 2014
Naissances vivantes selon l'âge de la mère et le sexe de l'enfant, taux de fécondité et taux de fécondité par âge : dernière année disponible, 2005 - 2014 (continued - suite)

Continent, country or area, year, code[a] and age of mother (in years) / Continent, pays ou zone, année, code[a] et âge de la mère (en années)	Total	Male Masculin	Female Féminin	Rate Taux
AFRICA - AFRIQUE				
Mauritius - Maurice[9]				
2014 (+C)				
Total	13 283	6 722	6 561	40.9
0 - 14	29	11	18	..
15 - 19	1 163	596	567	24.2
20 - 24	3 201	1 583	1 618	65.3
25 - 29	3 850	1 939	1 911	90.1
30 - 34	3 210	1 676	1 534	66.3
35 - 39	1 438	712	726	30.7
40 - 44	296	149	147	7.1
45 - 49	18	11	7	♦0.4
50 +	2	1	1	..
Unknown - Inconnu	76	44	32	..
Namibia - Namibie[1]				
2011 (|)				
Total	61 523	30 560	30 963	110.8
0 - 14	873	443	430	..
15 - 19	7 593	3 723	3 870	62.5
20 - 24	16 655	8 235	8 420	152.3
25 - 29	14 296	7 109	7 187	157.7
30 - 34	11 017	5 632	5 385	145.3
35 - 39	7 237	3 531	3 706	113.0
40 - 44	2 982	1 451	1 531	58.4
45 +	870	436	434	20.2
Nigeria - Nigéria				
2007 (...)				
Total	1 807 025	...	...	...
0 - 14	2 528	...	...	...
15 - 19	129 716	...	...	...
20 - 24	471 036	...	...	...
25 - 29	588 454	...	...	...
30 - 34	377 593	...	...	...
35 - 39	172 081	...	...	...
40 - 44	49 519	...	...	...
45 - 49	13 411	...	...	...
50 +	2 687	...	...	..
Reunion - Réunion[10]				
2007 (C)				
Total	14 808	7 711	7 097	69.2
0 - 14	23	11	12	..
15 - 19	1 517	769	748	44.1
20 - 24	3 348	1 752	1 596	117.2
25 - 29	3 968	2 075	1 893	144.2
30 - 34	3 429	1 779	1 650	116.2
35 - 39	1 931	1 009	922	58.6
40 - 44	572	307	265	16.8
45 +	20	9	11	♦0.7
Saint Helena ex. dep. - Sainte-Hélène sans dép.				
2014 (C)				
Total	48	25	23	...
0 - 14	-	-	-	..
15 - 19	8	6	2	...
20 - 24	6	2	4	...
25 - 29	8	5	3	...
30 - 34	19	8	11	...
35 - 39	5	3	2	...
40 - 44	2	1	1	...
45 - 49	-	-	-	...
50 +	-	-	-	..
Unknown - Inconnu	-	-	-	..
Seychelles				
2014 (+C)				
Total	1 557	795	762	65.1
0 - 14	5	2	3	..

Continent, country or area, year, code[a] and age of mother (in years) / Continent, pays ou zone, année, code[a] et âge de la mère (en années)	Total	Male Masculin	Female Féminin	Rate Taux
AFRICA - AFRIQUE				
Seychelles				
2014 (+C)				
15 - 19	183	106	77	66.9
20 - 24	403	200	203	130.9
25 - 29	424	211	213	127.4
30 - 34	297	139	158	73.9
35 - 39	190	99	91	51.7
40 - 44	52	35	17	14.8
45 - 49	2	2	-	♦0.6
50 +	1	1	-	..
South Africa - Afrique du Sud[4]				
2012 (U)				
Total	926 726	467 058	459 668	...
0 - 14	822	415	407	..
15 - 19	112 605	56 816	55 789	...
20 - 24	253 843	128 346	125 497	...
25 - 29	244 006	122 994	121 012	...
30 - 34	178 694	89 924	88 770	...
35 - 39	101 654	51 081	50 573	...
40 - 44	32 046	15 961	16 085	...
45 - 49	2 584	1 289	1 295	...
50 +	237	111	126	..
Unknown - Inconnu	235	121	114	..
Swaziland[11]				
2007 (|)				
Total	33 084	18 905	14 179	152.2
0 - 14	67	33	34	..
15 - 19	3 581	1 775	1 806	71.0
20 - 24	8 303	4 449	3 854	184.4
25 - 29	6 839	3 830	3 009	187.1
30 - 34	5 039	2 969	2 070	188.5
35 - 39	3 839	2 324	1 515	166.8
40 - 44	2 008	1 340	668	104.7
45 - 49	1 246	892	354	75.8
50 +	2 155	1 288	867	..
Unknown - Inconnu	7	5	2	..
Tunisia - Tunisie				
2011 (C)				
Total	201 120	...	...	...
15 - 19	2 550	...	...	...
20 - 24	23 594	...	...	...
25 - 29	52 266	...	...	...
30 - 34	51 003	...	...	...
35 - 39	28 565	...	...	...
40 - 44	7 282	...	...	...
45 - 49	596	...	...	...
Unknown - Inconnu	35 265	...	...	...
Zambia - Zambie[12]				
2010 (|)				
Total	442 998	224 756	218 242	141.4
12 - 14	921	470	451	..
15 - 19	58 999	29 701	29 298	75.4
20 - 24	128 270	65 048	63 222	200.0
25 - 29	114 701	58 366	56 335	205.1
30 - 34	74 066	37 666	36 400	178.4
35 - 39	45 452	23 072	22 380	139.5
40 - 44	16 150	8 181	7 969	72.5
45 - 49	4 439	2 252	2 187	23.7

10. Live births by age of mother and sex of child, general and age-specific fertility rates: latest available year, 2005 - 2014
Naissances vivantes selon l'âge de la mère et le sexe de l'enfant, taux de fécondité et taux de fécondité par âge : dernière année disponible, 2005 - 2014 (continued - suite)

Continent, country or area, year, code[a] and age of mother (in years) / Continent, pays ou zone, année, code[a] et âge de la mère (en années)	Total	Male Masculin	Female Féminin	Rate Taux
AMERICA, NORTH - AMÉRIQUE DU NORD				
Anguilla				
2006 (+C)				
Total	183	...	...	...
0 - 14	2	...	...	..
15 - 19	26	...	...	...
20 - 24	56	...	...	...
25 - 29	42	...	...	...
30 - 34	26	...	...	...
35 - 39	27	...	...	...
40 +	4	...	...	...
Aruba				
2014 (C)				
Total	1 376	725	651	51.9
0 - 14	2	1	1	..
15 - 19	131	77	54	35.3
20 - 24	343	166	177	111.8
25 - 29	334	181	153	109.1
30 - 34	350	198	152	97.9
35 - 39	166	82	84	42.4
40 - 44	48	20	28	10.8
45 - 49	2	-	2	♦0.4
50 +	-	-	-	..
Bahamas				
2012 (+U)				
Total	4 469[13]	2 279	2 187	...
0 - 14	4	2	2	...
15 - 19	497	261	236	...
20 - 24	1 028	524	504	...
25 - 29	1 123	580	543	...
30 - 34	972	496	476	...
35 - 39	632	318	314	...
40 - 44	193	91	102	...
45 - 49	15	5	10	...
50 +	1	1	-	..
Unknown - Inconnu	1	1	-	..
Barbados - Barbade				
2007 (+C)				
Total	3 537	1 850	1 687	...
0 - 14	10	7	3	..
15 - 19	462	226	236	...
20 - 24	894	487	407	...
25 - 29	805	420	385	...
30 - 34	730	387	343	...
35 - 39	463	235	228	...
40 - 44	164	84	80	...
45 - 49	7	3	4	...
Unknown - Inconnu	2	1	1	..
Bermuda - Bermudes[14]				
2013 (C)				
Total	648	320	328	44.9
0 - 14	-	-	-	..
15 - 19	23	9	14	♦15.0
20 - 24	69	36	33	42.7
25 - 29	124	62	62	67.7
30 - 34	219	105	114	99.4
35 - 39	158	79	79	71.3
40 - 44	53	27	26	22.1
45 - 49	2	2	-	♦0.8
50 +	-	-	-	..
Canada[15]				
2009 (C)				
Total	380 863	195 445	185 418	46.0
0 - 14	104	52	52	..
15 - 19	15 534	7 997	7 537	14.1
20 - 24	57 778	29 564	28 214	51.2

Continent, country or area, year, code[a] and age of mother (in years) / Continent, pays ou zone, année, code[a] et âge de la mère (en années)	Total	Male Masculin	Female Féminin	Rate Taux
AMERICA, NORTH - AMÉRIQUE DU NORD				
Canada[15]				
2009 (C)				
25 - 29	116 878	60 099	56 779	100.7
30 - 34	120 734	62 132	58 602	107.0
35 - 39	57 733	29 493	28 240	50.6
40 - 44	11 364	5 720	5 644	9.2
45 - 49	605	316	289	0.4
Unknown - Inconnu[16]	133	72	61	
Cayman Islands - Îles Caïmanes				
2014 (C)				
Total	710	...	...	...
15 - 19	35	...	...	...
20 - 24	129	...	...	...
25 - 29	140	...	...	...
30 - 34	210	...	...	...
35 - 39	142	...	...	...
40 - 44	51	...	...	...
45 - 49	3	...	...	...
Costa Rica				
2014* (C)				
Total	71 793	36 719	35 074	55.6
0 - 14	509	277	232	..
15 - 19	11 997	6 089	5 908	56.4
20 - 24	19 674	10 224	9 450	94.3
25 - 29	18 634	9 492	9 142	90.8
30 - 34	13 301	6 776	6 525	74.5
35 - 39	5 960	2 974	2 986	35.7
40 - 44	1 351	695	656	8.3
45 - 49	81	43	38	0.5
Unknown - Inconnu	280	148	132	..
Cuba				
2013 (C)				
Total	125 880	65 293	60 587	44.1
0 - 14	439	252	187	..
15 - 19	17 977	9 317	8 660	52.9
20 - 24	41 100	21 310	19 790	104.0
25 - 29	35 440	18 370	17 070	95.2
30 - 34	18 555	9 635	8 920	60.0
35 - 39	9 663	4 976	4 687	24.1
40 - 44	2 545	1 356	1 189	5.0
45 - 49	100	45	55	0.2
50 +	32	18	14	..
Unknown - Inconnu	29	14	15	..
Curaçao				
2014 (C)				
Total	1 963	1 001	962	52.7
0 - 14	5	5	-	..
15 - 19	162	84	78	31.2
20 - 24	444	220	224	98.0
25 - 29	508	277	231	112.8
30 - 34	481	236	245	98.4
35 - 39	257	133	124	50.7
40 - 44	86	36	50	14.0
45 - 49	1	-	1	♦0.2
50 +	-	-	-	..
Unknown - Inconnu	19	10	9	..
Dominica - Dominique				
2006 (+C)				
Total	1 056	505	551	62.4
0 - 14	3	-	3	..
15 - 19	154	80	74	45.8
20 - 24	250	115	135	116.8
25 - 29	197	91	106	78.2
30 - 34	207	99	108	74.5

Continent, country or area, year, code[a] and age of mother (in years) / Continent, pays ou zone, année, code[a] et âge de la mère (en années)	Number - Nombre			Rate Taux
	Total	Male Masculin	Female Féminin	
AMERICA, NORTH - AMÉRIQUE DU NORD				
Dominica - Dominique				
2006 (+C)				
35 - 39	179	86	93	72.9
40 - 44	59	29	30	28.7
45 - 49	5	3	2	♦3.1
Dominican Republic - République dominicaine				
2013 (U)				
Total	130 402	67 063	63 339	...
0 - 14	416	219	197	..
15 - 19	19 894	10 159	9 735	...
20 - 24	42 765	21 970	20 795	...
25 - 29	33 366	17 105	16 261	...
30 - 34	21 803	11 217	10 586	...
35 - 39	8 764	4 594	4 170	...
40 - 44	1 864	975	889	...
45 - 49	143	66	77	...
50 +	54	28	26	..
Unknown - Inconnu	1 333	730	603	..
El Salvador[17]				
2012 (C)				
Total	110 843	57 480	53 363	...
0 - 14	1 033	520	513	...
15 - 19	23 410	12 093	11 317	...
20 - 24	32 655	16 988	15 667	...
25 - 29	24 285	12 567	11 718	...
30 - 34	17 595	9 189	8 406	...
35 - 39	8 687	4 473	4 214	...
40 - 44	2 262	1 193	1 069	...
45 - 49	177	86	91	...
50 +	16	5	11	..
Unknown - Inconnu	739	371	368	..
Greenland - Groenland				
2014 (C)				
Total	805	407	398	58.5
0 - 14	1	1	-	..
15 - 19	83	34	49	40.1
20 - 24	214	100	114	95.9
25 - 29	272	154	118	125.6
30 - 34	170	89	81	87.4
35 - 39	52	23	29	35.9
40 - 44	13	6	7	♦8.7
45 - 49	-	-	-	-
Guatemala				
2011 (C)				
Total	373 692	189 724	183 968	...
0 - 14	2 841	1 426	1 415	...
15 - 19	75 175	38 415	36 760	...
20 - 24	108 949	55 558	53 391	...
25 - 29	85 914	43 599	42 315	...
30 - 34	58 050	29 264	28 786	...
35 - 39	30 892	15 540	15 352	...
40 - 44	10 220	5 136	5 084	...
45 - 49	1 176	573	603	...
50 +	290	127	163	..
Unknown - Inconnu	185	86	99	...
Jamaica - Jamaïque[18]				
2011 (|)				
Total	49 676	23 949[19]	23 339[19]	66.0
15 - 19	6 167	3 034[19]	2 884[19]	50.5
20 - 24	13 977	6 852[19]	6 451[19]	129.9
25 - 29	12 348	5 923[19]	5 900[19]	108.7
30 - 34	8 746	4 182[19]	4 145[19]	73.9
35 - 39	6 001	2 816[19]	2 875[19]	48.9
AMERICA, NORTH - AMÉRIQUE DU NORD				
Jamaica - Jamaïque[18]				
2011 (|)				
40 - 44	2 109	1 014[19]	956[19]	21.2
45 - 49	328	128[19]	128[19]	4.8
Martinique[10]				
2007 (C)				
Total	5 317	2 676	2 641	51.0
0 - 14	2	1	1	..
15 - 19	305	165	140	19.8
20 - 24	911	447	464	77.6
25 - 29	1 202	617	585	117.2
30 - 34	1 376	678	698	98.2
35 - 39	1 105	560	545	64.1
40 - 44	393	194	199	20.9
45 +	23	14	9	♦1.4
Mexico - Mexique[20]				
2011 (C)				
Total	2 262 024	1 151 425[19]	1 110 491[19]	...
0 - 14	7 681	3 966[19]	3 715[19]	..
15 - 19	418 189	213 621[19]	204 548[19]	...
20 - 24	669 685	341 781[19]	327 871[19]	...
25 - 29	554 846	281 706[19]	273 113[19]	...
30 - 34	371 381	188 582[19]	182 788[19]	...
35 - 39	185 635	94 199[19]	91 430[19]	...
40 - 44	40 638	20 407[19]	20 229[19]	...
45 - 49	3 054	1 536[19]	1 518[19]	...
50 +	799	417[19]	381[19]	..
Unknown - Inconnu	10 116	5 210[19]	4 898[19]	..
Montserrat				
2014 (+C)				
Total	50	22	28	...
0 - 14	-	-	-	..
15 - 19	9	3	6	...
20 - 24	12	5	7	...
25 - 29	12	6	6	...
30 - 34	7	3	4	...
35 - 39	6	3	3	...
40 - 44	4	2	2	...
45 - 49	-	-	-	..
50 +	-	-	-	..
Nicaragua				
2010 (+U)				
Total	132 165	68 726	63 439	...
0 - 14	1 539	793	746	..
15 - 19	33 963	17 752	16 211	...
20 - 24	38 897	20 181	18 716	...
25 - 29	30 273	15 790	14 483	...
30 - 34	17 301	8 942	8 359	...
35 - 39	8 010	4 156	3 854	...
40 - 44	1 943	992	951	...
45 - 49	209	105	104	..
50 +	30	15	15	..
Panama				
2013 (C)				
Total	73 804	37 995	35 809	73.9
0 - 14	666	358	308	..
15 - 19	14 315	7 360	6 955	87.0
20 - 24	20 724	10 700	10 024	133.1
25 - 29	17 421	8 923	8 498	115.5
30 - 34	12 563	6 484	6 079	87.0
35 - 39	6 260	3 172	3 088	45.1
40 - 44	1 646	893	753	12.7
45 - 49	110	58	52	1.0
50 +	14	5	9	..
Unknown - Inconnu	85	42	43	..

10. Live births by age of mother and sex of child, general and age-specific fertility rates: latest available year, 2005 - 2014
Naissances vivantes selon l'âge de la mère et le sexe de l'enfant, taux de fécondité et taux de fécondité par âge : dernière année disponible, 2005 - 2014 (continued - suite)

Continent, country or area, year, code[a] and age of mother (in years) — Continent, pays ou zone, année, code[a] et âge de la mère (en années)	Number - Nombre			Rate Taux
	Total	Male Masculin	Female Féminin	

AMERICA, NORTH - AMÉRIQUE DU NORD

Puerto Rico - Porto Rico
2014 (C)

	Total	Male	Female	Rate
Total	34 485	17 740	16 745	...
0 - 14	51	27	24	..
15 - 19	4 901	2 557	2 344	...
20 - 24	11 552	5 927	5 625	...
25 - 29	8 774	4 507	4 267	...
30 - 34	5 890	3 049	2 841	...
35 - 39	2 701	1 358	1 343	...
40 - 44	577	297	280	...
45 - 49	31	15	16	...
50 +	-	-	-	...
Unknown - Inconnu	8	3	5	..

Saint Lucia - Sainte-Lucie
2005* (C)

	Total	Male	Female	Rate
Total	2 215	...	...	47.6
0 - 14	6	...	...	..
15 - 19	374	...	...	42.1
20 - 24	624	...	...	77.6
25 - 29	526	...	...	75.7
30 - 34	378	...	...	58.4
35 - 39	236	...	...	38.7
40 - 44	62	...	...	10.9
45 +	10	...	...	♦2.3

Saint Vincent and the Grenadines - Saint-Vincent-et-les Grenadines
2009 (+C)

	Total	Male	Female	Rate
Total	1 905	949	956	...
0 - 14	9	3	6	..
15 - 19	365	164	201	...
20 - 24	511	269	242	...
25 - 29	446	226	220	...
30 - 34	332	162	170	...
35 - 39	172	95	77	...
40 - 44	64	28	36	...
45 +	5	2	3	...
Unknown - Inconnu	1	-	1	..

Trinidad and Tobago - Trinité-et-Tobago
2006 (C)

	Total	Male	Female	Rate
Total	18 090	9 330	8 760	...
0 - 14	27	7	20	..
15 - 19	2 115	1 114	1 001	...
20 - 24	5 640	2 912	2 728	...
25 - 29	4 938	2 523	2 415	...
30 - 34	3 268	1 710	1 558	...
35 - 39	1 578	805	773	...
40 - 44	462	228	234	...
45 - 49	28	16	12	...
50 +	1	-	1	...
Unknown - Inconnu	33	15	18	..

Turks and Caicos Islands - Îles Turques et Caïques
2005 (C)

	Total	Male	Female	Rate
Total	318	158	160	...
0 - 14	1	-	1	..
15 - 19	28	13	15	...
20 - 24	65	29	36	...
25 - 29	83	40	43	...
30 - 34	76	47	29	...
35 - 39	52	23	29	...
40 - 44	11	5	6	...
45 +	2	1	1	...

AMERICA, NORTH - AMÉRIQUE DU NORD

United States of America - États-Unis d'Amérique
2013 (C)

	Total	Male	Female	Rate
Total	3 932 181	2 012 954	1 919 227	...
0 - 14	3 098	1 592	1 506	..
15 - 19	273 105	140 110	132 995	...
20 - 24	896 745	458 528	438 217	...
25 - 29	1 120 777	574 266	546 511	...
30 - 34	1 036 927	530 707	506 220	...
35 - 39	483 873	247 753	236 120	...
40 - 44	109 484	55 858	53 626	...
45 - 49	7 495	3 813	3 682	...
50 - 54	677	327	350	..

United States Virgin Islands - Îles Vierges américaines
2007 (C)

	Total	Male	Female	Rate
Total	1 771	...	...	65.9
0 - 14	2	...	...	..
15 - 19	226	...	...	53.1
20 - 24	550	...	...	146.6
25 - 29	424	...	...	146.1
30 - 34	319	...	...	93.9
35 - 39	196	...	...	48.6
40 +	46	...	...	5.5
Unknown - Inconnu	8	...	...	

AMERICA, SOUTH - AMÉRIQUE DU SUD

Argentina - Argentine
2013 (C)

	Total	Male	Female	Rate
Total	754 603	...	...	71.5
0 - 14	3 261	...	...	
15 - 19	114 125	...	...	68.2
20 - 24	185 621	...	...	111.3
25 - 29	170 655	...	...	106.2
30 - 34	158 021	...	...	99.3
35 - 39	91 091	...	...	60.2
40 - 44	23 124	...	...	18.3
45 +	1 520	...	...	1.3
Unknown - Inconnu	7 185	...	...	

Brazil - Brésil
2013 (U)

	Total	Male	Female	Rate
Total	2 832 590[21]	1 451 889[19]	1 380 396[19]	...
0 - 14	22 967[21]	11 659[19]	11 300[19]	..
15 - 19	502 255[21]	258 610[19]	243 601[19]	...
20 - 24	716 103[21]	367 568[19]	348 471[19]	...
25 - 29	685 617[21]	350 876[19]	334 691[19]	...
30 - 34	550 031[21]	281 304[19]	268 682[19]	...
35 - 39	262 344[21]	134 080[19]	128 243[19]	...
40 - 44	63 092[21]	32 243[19]	30 843[19]	...
45 - 49	4 055[21]	2 063[19]	1 991[19]	...
50 +	344[21]	199[19]	145[19]	...
Unknown - Inconnu	25 782[21]	13 287[19]	12 429[19]	...

Chile - Chili
2012 (C)

	Total	Male	Female	Rate
Total	243 635	124 083	119 552	53.4
0 - 14	879	456	423	..
15 - 19	34 305	17 442	16 863	49.0
20 - 24	58 146	29 694	28 452	80.2
25 - 29	57 491	29 199	28 292	84.5
30 - 34	52 386	26 651	25 735	85.9
35 - 39	31 475	16 035	15 440	52.2
40 - 44	8 449	4 357	4 092	13.7
45 - 49	466	230	236	0.7

10. Live births by age of mother and sex of child, general and age-specific fertility rates: latest available year, 2005 - 2014
Naissances vivantes selon l'âge de la mère et le sexe de l'enfant, taux de fécondité et taux de fécondité par âge : dernière année disponible, 2005 - 2014 (continued - suite)

Continent, country or area, year, code[a] and age of mother (in years) — Continent, pays ou zone, année, code[a] et âge de la mère (en années)	Number - Nombre			Rate Taux
	Total	Male Masculin	Female Féminin	
AMERICA, SOUTH - AMÉRIQUE DU SUD				
Chile - Chili				
2012 (C)				
50 +	8	4	4	..
Unknown - Inconnu	30	15	15	..
Colombia - Colombie				
2012 (U)				
Total	676 835	347 070	329 765	...
0 - 14	6 547	3 359	3 188	...
15 - 19	155 890	80 443	75 447	...
20 - 24	197 195	101 107	96 088	...
25 - 29	148 483	76 045	72 438	...
30 - 34	103 230	52 846	50 384	...
35 - 39	49 285	25 037	24 248	...
40 - 44	13 902	7 069	6 833	...
45 - 49	1 124	570	554	...
50 +	158	78	80	..
Unknown - Inconnu	1 021	516	505	..
Ecuador - Équateur				
2013 (+U)				
Total	220 896	112 711	108 185	...
0 - 14	1 692	895	797	..
15 - 19	43 036	21 913	21 123	...
20 - 24	59 920	30 551	29 369	...
25 - 29	51 091	26 175	24 916	...
30 - 34	37 871	19 407	18 464	...
35 - 39	18 781	9 519	9 262	...
40 - 44	5 424	2 663	2 761	...
45 - 49	476	236	240	...
50 +	-	-	-	..
Unknown - Inconnu	2 605	1 352	1 253	..
French Guiana - Guyane française[10]				
2007 (C)				
Total	6 386	3 269	3 117	114.5
0 - 14	23	12	11	..
15 - 19	828	428	400	83.3
20 - 24	1 477	726	751	182.2
25 - 29	1 590	821	769	195.5
30 - 34	1 312	707	605	154.0
35 - 39	844	414	430	102.2
40 - 44	289	152	137	40.9
45 - 49	22	8	14	♦3.8
50 +	1	1	-	..
Paraguay				
2008 (+U)				
Total	99 674	51 066	48 608	...
0 - 14	538	269	269	..
15 - 19	20 188	10 404	9 784	...
20 - 24	28 246	14 396	13 850	...
25 - 29	23 863	12 261	11 602	...
30 - 34	14 721	7 480	7 241	...
35 - 39	8 899	4 600	4 299	...
40 - 44	2 819	1 440	1 379	...
45 - 49	250	134	116	...
50 +	2	2	-	..
Unknown - Inconnu	148	80	68	..
Peru - Pérou[22]				
2013 (+U)				
Total	475 349	243 586	231 763	...
0 - 14	1 114	569	545	..
15 - 19	55 676	28 655	27 021	...
20 - 24	120 915	62 426	58 489	...
25 - 29	115 226	58 955	56 271	...
30 - 34	95 592	48 776	46 816	...
35 - 39	62 036	31 601	30 435	...
AMERICA, SOUTH - AMÉRIQUE DU SUD				
Peru - Pérou[22]				
2013 (+U)				
40 - 44	22 648	11 522	11 126	...
45 - 49	2 039	1 035	1 004	...
50 +	103	47	56	..
Suriname				
2013 (C)				
Total	10 012	5 119	4 893	70.0
0 - 14	46	...	...	..
15 - 19	1 359	...	...	58.7
20 - 24	2 640	...	...	117.6
25 - 29	2 656	...	...	123.2
30 - 34	1 976	...	...	96.3
35 - 39	971	...	...	50.1
40 - 44	309	...	...	16.7
45 +	19	...	...	♦1.1
Unknown - Inconnu	36	...	...	..
Uruguay				
2013 (C)				
Total	48 681	24 862[19]	23 790[19]	...
0 - 14	190	104[19]	86[19]	..
15 - 19	8 172	4 225[19]	3 943[19]	..
20 - 24	11 602	5 915[19]	5 680[19]	..
25 - 29	10 824	5 461[19]	5 358[19]	..
30 - 34	10 148	5 167[19]	4 974[19]	..
35 - 39	6 135	3 173[19]	2 958[19]	..
40 - 44	1 466	744[19]	721[19]	...
45 - 49	82	38[19]	44[19]	...
50 +	1	-[19]	1[19]	..
Unknown - Inconnu	61	35[19]	25[19]	..
Venezuela (Bolivarian Republic of) - Venezuela (République bolivarienne du)				
2013 (C)				
Total	597 902	306 566	291 336	75.3
0 - 14	7 146	3 685	3 461	..
15 - 19	130 791	67 454	63 337	98.7
20 - 24	170 549	87 322	83 227	129.8
25 - 29	136 722	70 220	66 502	108.0
30 - 34	92 500	47 194	45 306	79.9
35 - 39	43 229	21 996	21 233	41.9
40 - 44	11 232	5 744	5 488	12.2
45 - 49	1 114	552	562	1.3
50 +	343	171	172	..
Unknown - Inconnu	4 276	2 228	2 048	..
ASIA - ASIE				
Armenia - Arménie				
2009 (C)				
Total	44 413	23 652	20 761	48.4
15 - 19	4 035	2 055	1 980	27.6
20 - 24	19 686	10 292	9 394	125.8
25 - 29	13 628	7 422	6 206	95.4
30 - 34	5 156	2 859	2 297	43.1
35 - 39	1 590	866	724	15.3
40 - 44	287	141	146	2.6
45 - 49	27	14	13	♦0.2
50 +	4	3	1	..
Azerbaijan - Azerbaïdjan[23]				
2012 (+C)				
Total	174 469	93 587	80 882	64.6
12 - 14	4	2	2	..
15 - 19	20 333	10 491	9 842	51.4

10. Live births by age of mother and sex of child, general and age-specific fertility rates: latest available year, 2005 - 2014
Naissances vivantes selon l'âge de la mère et le sexe de l'enfant, taux de fécondité et taux de fécondité par âge : dernière année disponible, 2005 - 2014 (continued - suite)

Continent, country or area, year, code[a] and age of mother (in years) / Continent, pays ou zone, année, code[a] et âge de la mère (en années)	Total	Number - Nombre Male Masculin	Female Féminin	Rate Taux
ASIA - ASIE				
Azerbaijan - Azerbaïdjan[23]				
2012 (+C)				
20 - 24	73 642	38 739	34 903	157.0
25 - 29	50 476	27 675	22 801	112.3
30 - 34	20 677	11 452	9 225	54.8
35 - 39	7 396	4 143	3 253	23.0
40 - 44	1 731	979	752	5.1
45 - 49	168	85	83	0.5
50 +	42	21	21	..
Bahrain - Bahreïn				
2013 (C)				
Total	19 995	10 248	9 747	70.4
0 - 14	1	1	-	..
15 - 19	562	296	266	16.7
20 - 24	4 184	2 117	2 067	102.8
25 - 29	6 449	3 365	3 084	122.3
30 - 34	5 261	2 694	2 567	104.7
35 - 39	2 763	1 388	1 375	64.4
40 - 44	673	326	347	20.1
45 - 49	91	53	38	3.0
50 +	7	4	3	..
Unknown - Inconnu	4	4	-	..
Bangladesh				
2010 (U)				
Total	*2 868 494*	*1 451 664*	*1 416 831*	...
15 - 19	*404 570*	*209 615*	*194 955*	...
20 - 24	*1 055 194*	*527 993*	*527 201*	...
25 - 29	*762 338*	*383 627*	*378 710*	...
30 - 34	*389 547*	*199 767*	*189 780*	...
35 - 39	*192 438*	*97 826*	*94 613*	...
40 - 44	*49 380*	*25 206*	*24 174*	...
45 +	*15 027*	*7 630*	*7 397*	...
Bhutan - Bhoutan[11]				
2005 (I)				
Total	12 538	6 306	6 232	79.4
15 - 19	1 376	711	665	36.5
20 - 24	4 211	2 156	2 055	138.9
25 - 29	3 677	1 814	1 863	141.6
30 - 34	1 753	880	873	89.4
35 - 39	960	463	497	54.5
40 - 44	434	207	227	31.3
45 - 49	127	75	52	9.9
Brunei Darussalam - Brunéi Darussalam				
2008 (+C)				
Total	6 424	3 332	3 092	...
0 - 14	4	-	4	...
15 - 19	279	159	120	...
20 - 24	1 206	654	552	...
25 - 29	2 113	1 092	1 021	...
30 - 34	1 697	866	831	...
35 - 39	913	453	460	...
40 - 44	198	99	99	...
45 - 49	12	7	5	...
50 +	-	-	-	..
Unknown - Inconnu	2	2	-	..
2013 (+C)				
Total	6 680	...	...	..
0 - 14	7	...	...	..
15 - 19	221	...	...	...
20 - 24	1 097	...	...	...
25 - 29	2 124	...	...	...
30 - 34	1 886	...	...	...
35 - 39	1 044	...	...	...
40 - 44	279	...	...	...

Continent, country or area, year, code[a] and age of mother (in years) / Continent, pays ou zone, année, code[a] et âge de la mère (en années)	Total	Number - Nombre Male Masculin	Female Féminin	Rate Taux
ASIA - ASIE				
Brunei Darussalam - Brunéi Darussalam				
2013 (+C)				
45 - 49	20	...	...	...
50 +	1	...	...	..
Unknown - Inconnu	1	...	...	...
China, Hong Kong SAR - Chine, Hong Kong RAS				
2013 (C)				
Total	57 084	29 806	27 278	27.5
0 - 14	8	6	2	..
15 - 19	518	276	242	2.6
20 - 24	4 013	2 087	1 926	17.4
25 - 29	13 262	6 883	6 379	44.9
30 - 34	22 381	11 745	10 636	65.3
35 - 39	13 652	7 072	6 580	41.3
40 - 44	3 049	1 633	1 416	9.0
45 - 49	151	77	74	0.4
50 +	10	7	3	..
Unknown - Inconnu	40	20	20	..
China, Macao SAR - Chine, Macao RAS				
2014 (C)				
Total	7 360	3 850	3 510	39.3
0 - 24	947	493	454	23.5
25 - 29	3 013	1 586	1 427	82.5
30 - 34	2 190	1 126	1 064	74.2
35 - 39	971	511	460	40.3
40 +	239	134	105	4.2
Cyprus - Chypre[24]				
2011 (C)				
Total	9 622	4 891	4 731	41.4
12 - 14	2	-	2	..
15 - 19	171	87	84	5.7
20 - 24	1 187	598	589	34.1
25 - 29	3 277	1 660	1 617	87.0
30 - 34	3 325	1 696	1 629	92.1
35 - 39	1 333	690	643	39.9
40 - 44	287	144	143	9.3
45 - 49	29	11	18	♦1.0
Unknown - Inconnu	9	5	4	..
Democratic People's Republic of Korea - République populaire démocratique de Corée[12]				
2008 (I)				
Total	345 630	176 399	169 231	53.3
15 - 19	633	330	303	0.6
20 - 24	52 214	26 657	25 557	58.0
25 - 29	178 032	90 850	87 182	209.5
30 - 34	90 973	46 224	44 749	110.0
35 - 39	20 275	10 505	9 770	18.5
40 - 44	3 202	1 673	1 529	3.2
45 - 49	301	160	141	0.4
Georgia - Géorgie				
2012 (C)				
Total	57 031	29 801	27 230	49.5
0 - 14	26	15	11	..
15 - 19	5 636	2 956	2 680	39.7
20 - 24	19 571	10 238	9 333	107.6
25 - 29	16 833	8 851	7 982	94.4
30 - 34	9 734	5 070	4 664	58.6
35 - 39	4 131	2 116	2 015	25.9
40 - 44	980	500	480	6.3
45 - 49	91	38	53	0.5

10. Live births by age of mother and sex of child, general and age-specific fertility rates: latest available year, 2005 - 2014
Naissances vivantes selon l'âge de la mère et le sexe de l'enfant, taux de fécondité et taux de fécondité par âge : dernière année disponible, 2005 - 2014 (continued - suite)

Continent, country or area, year, code[a] and age of mother (in years) / Continent, pays ou zone, année, code[a] et âge de la mère (en années)	Total	Male Masculin	Female Féminin	Rate Taux
ASIA - ASIE				
Georgia - Géorgie				
2012 (C)				
50 +	16	8	8	..
Unknown - Inconnu	13	9	4	..
Iran (Islamic Republic of) - Iran (République islamique d')[25]				
2013 (+C)				
Total	1 430 678	735 393	695 285	...
0 - 14	1 727	873	854	..
15 - 19	107 585	55 111	52 474	...
20 - 24	357 480	183 767	173 713	...
25 - 29	460 586	236 762	223 824	...
30 - 34	325 359	167 011	158 348	...
35 - 39	137 551	70 722	66 829	...
40 - 44	29 822	15 467	14 355	...
45 - 49	2 110	1 082	1 028	...
50 +	386	198	188	..
Unknown - Inconnu	8 072	4 400	3 672	..
Israel - Israël[26]				
2013 (C)				
Total	171 444	88 195	83 249	90.3
0 - 14	1	1	-	..
15 - 19	3 165	1 686	1 479	10.4
20 - 24	31 086	16 073	15 013	106.4
25 - 29	50 350	25 901	24 449	174.6
30 - 34	49 840	25 628	24 212	177.2
35 - 39	28 848	14 789	14 059	105.2
40 - 44	7 141	3 636	3 505	29.1
45 - 49	573	270	303	2.7
50 +	73	35	38	..
Unknown - Inconnu	367	176	191	..
Japan - Japon[27]				
2013 (C)				
Total	1 029 816	527 657	502 159	38.8
0 - 14	51	28	23	..
15 - 19	12 913	6 624	6 289	4.4
20 - 24	91 250	46 782	44 468	30.0
25 - 29	282 794	145 026	137 768	83.5
30 - 34	365 404	187 117	178 287	96.6
35 - 39	229 741	117 699	112 042	50.9
40 - 44	46 546	23 772	22 774	9.8
45 - 49	1 069	583	486	0.3
50 +	47	26	21	..
Unknown - Inconnu	1	-	1	..
Kazakhstan[23]				
2013 (C)				
Total	387 227	199 880	187 347	84.3
0 - 14	20	12	8	..
15 - 19	20 727	10 653	10 074	32.8
20 - 24	124 737	64 434	60 303	155.1
25 - 29	124 145	63 987	60 158	160.1
30 - 34	71 453	36 850	34 603	109.3
35 - 39	37 140	19 237	17 903	61.4
40 - 44	8 560	4 458	4 102	15.1
45 - 49	387	217	170	0.7
50 +	33	20	13	..
Unknown - Inconnu	25	12	13	..
Kuwait - Koweït				
2013 (C)				
Total	59 426	30 555	28 871	58.8
15 - 19	685	359	326	7.7
20 - 24	9 181	4 778	4 403	68.0
25 - 29	18 244	9 347	8 897	97.8
30 - 34	15 398	7 962	7 436	89.6
ASIA - ASIE				
Kuwait - Koweït				
2013 (C)				
35 - 39	8 208	4 171	4 037	57.2
40 - 44	2 359	1 186	1 173	20.4
45 +	253	137	116	3.1
Unknown - Inconnu	5 098	2 615	2 483	..
Kyrgyzstan - Kirghizstan				
2013 (C)				
Total	155 520	79 924	75 596	...
0 - 14	6	3	3	..
15 - 19	11 313	5 821	5 492	...
20 - 24	55 661	28 677	26 984	...
25 - 29	46 323	23 788	22 535	...
30 - 34	25 546	13 089	12 457	...
35 - 39	12 467	6 405	6 062	...
40 - 44	3 647	1 850	1 797	...
45 - 49	383	199	184	...
50 +	7	5	2	..
Unknown - Inconnu	167	87	80	..
Malaysia - Malaisie				
2012* (C)				
Total	508 774	263 163	245 611	64.0
0 - 14	214	124	90	..
15 - 19	18 317	9 522	8 795	13.5
20 - 24	76 998	39 927	37 071	54.3
25 - 29	173 139	89 427	83 712	126.4
30 - 34	146 601	75 983	70 618	130.7
35 - 39	71 858	36 893	34 965	75.6
40 - 44	19 263	10 015	9 248	21.3
45 - 49	1 526	826	700	1.9
50 +	130	74	56	..
Unknown - Inconnu	728	372	356	..
Maldives				
2013 (C)				
Total	7 153	3 720	3 433	71.2
0 - 14	1	1	-	..
15 - 19	203	105	98	12.1
20 - 24	2 134	1 122	1 012	108.7
25 - 29	2 466	1 279	1 187	127.1
30 - 34	1 503	786	717	101.4
35 - 39	659	329	330	58.5
40 - 44	180	96	84	18.1
45 - 49	8	3	5	♦0.9
50 +	-	-	-	..
Unknown - Inconnu	1	-	1	..
Mongolia - Mongolie				
2014 (+C)				
Total	82 839	42 653	40 186	94.7
0 - 14	26	11	15	..
15 - 19	3 233	1 661	1 572	25.9
20 - 24	21 426	11 015	10 411	147.2
25 - 29	25 767	13 287	12 480	167.6
30 - 34	18 053	9 394	8 659	137.5
35 - 39	10 677	5 407	5 270	89.0
40 - 44	3 243	1 670	1 573	30.6
45 - 49	395	200	195	4.2
50 +	19	8	11	..
Myanmar				
2012* (+U)				
Total	856 279	443 008	413 271	...
0 - 14	-	-	-	...
15 - 19	45 738	23 484	22 254	...
20 - 24	203 633	105 461	98 173	...
25 - 29	256 990	132 810	124 181	...
30 - 34	191 032	98 799	92 233	...

10. Live births by age of mother and sex of child, general and age-specific fertility rates: latest available year, 2005 - 2014
Naissances vivantes selon l'âge de la mère et le sexe de l'enfant, taux de fécondité et taux de fécondité par âge : dernière année disponible, 2005 - 2014 (continued - suite)

Continent, country or area, year, code[a] and age of mother (in years) / Continent, pays ou zone, année, code[a] et âge de la mère (en années)	Number - Nombre			Rate Taux
	Total	Male Masculin	Female Féminin	

ASIA - ASIE

Myanmar
2012* (+U)
35 - 39	115 714	60 237	55 477	...
40 - 44	39 032	20 114	18 918	...
45 - 49	4 139	2 104	2 035	...
50 +	-	-	-	..

Oman[28]
2013 (U)
Total	79 417	40 560	38 857	...
0 - 14	10	8	2	..
15 - 19	1 751	864	887	...
20 - 24	15 960	8 117	7 843	...
25 - 29	26 602	13 548	13 054	...
30 - 34	20 928	10 713	10 215	...
35 - 39	10 904	5 578	5 326	...
40 - 44	2 858	1 504	1 354	...
45 - 49	365	206	159	...
50 +	39	22	17	..

Pakistan[29]
2005 (|)
Total	3 772 494	1 993 492	1 779 002	110.6
15 - 19	161 490	90 049	71 441	20.3
20 - 24	1 050 830	556 310	494 520	157.6
25 - 29	1 166 365	611 186	555 179	225.5
30 - 34	754 513	395 425	359 088	179.9
35 - 39	425 352	222 186	203 166	106.6
40 - 44	161 914	86 273	75 641	50.1
45 +	52 030	32 063	19 967	18.1

Philippines
2009 (C)
Total	1 745 585	907 221	838 364	...
0 - 14	1 113	568	545	..
15 - 19	194 549	101 139	93 410	...
20 - 24	495 958	258 047	237 911	...
25 - 29	461 020	240 170	220 850	...
30 - 34	328 063	170 311	157 752	...
35 - 39	187 578	97 061	90 517	...
40 - 44	66 064	34 216	31 848	...
45 - 49	7 712	3 885	3 827	...
50 +	528	282	246	..
Unknown - Inconnu	3 000	1 542	1 458	..

2012 (C)
Total	1 790 367	...	...	71.9
0 - 14	1 613	...	...	..
15 - 19	207 661	...	...	42.9
20 - 24	511 937	...	...	116.8
25 - 29	447 637	...	...	116.3
30 - 34	346 001	...	...	100.2
35 - 39	194 723	...	...	63.0
40 - 44	69 116	...	...	24.8
45 - 49	7 416	...	...	3.0
50 +	472	...	...	..
Unknown - Inconnu	3 791	...	...	..

Qatar
2013 (C)
Total	23 708	12 119	11 589	70.0
0 - 19	352	162	190	11.4
20 - 24	3 791	1 955	1 836	98.1
25 - 29	7 687	3 986	3 701	105.0
30 - 34	7 117	3 642	3 475	98.3
35 - 39	3 711	1 865	1 846	65.3
40 - 44	957	459	498	24.0
45 - 49	83	44	39	3.1
50 +	10	6	4	..

ASIA - ASIE

Republic of Korea - République de Corée[30]
2013 (C)
Total	436 455	223 883	212 572	34.0
0 - 14	20	7	13	..
15 - 19	2 813	1 493	1 320	1.8
20 - 24	22 051	11 227	10 824	13.8
25 - 29	102 801	52 618	50 183	64.3
30 - 34	220 346	113 071	107 275	112.8
35 - 39	77 183	39 646	37 537	40.6
40 - 44	10 714	5 554	5 160	5.0
45 - 49	284	137	147	0.1
50 +	28	11	17	..
Unknown - Inconnu	215	119	96	..

Saudi Arabia - Arabie saoudite[31]
2005 (...)
Total	582 582	298 396	284 186	...
15 - 19	25 652	13 139	12 513	...
20 - 24	153 901	78 827	75 074	...
25 - 29	194 252	99 495	94 757	...
30 - 34	135 325	69 313	66 012	...
35 - 39	57 941	29 677	28 264	...
40 - 44	14 373	7 362	7 011	...
45 - 49	1 137	583	555	...

Singapore - Singapour
2014 (C)
Total	42 232	21 679[19]	20 552[19]	41.6
0 - 14	4	2	2	..
15 - 19	402	212	190	3.3
20 - 24	2 671	1 402	1 269	20.4
25 - 29	11 004	5 790[19]	5 213[19]	80.7
30 - 34	17 732	8 973	8 759	115.6
35 - 39	8 799	4 470	4 329	56.0
40 - 44	1 566	806	760	9.7
45 - 49	52	23	29	0.3
50 +	2	1	1	..
Unknown - Inconnu	-	-	-	..

Sri Lanka
2006 (+C)
Total	373 538	191 263	182 275	67.9
0 - 14	113	57	56	..
15 - 19	20 040	10 335	9 705	21.2
20 - 24	81 003	41 508	39 495	87.5
25 - 29	121 968	62 480	59 488	151.5
30 - 34	90 483	46 346	44 137	118.4
35 - 39	46 534	23 759	22 775	61.6
40 - 44	12 104	6 149	5 955	17.4
45 - 49	1 275	622	653	2.1
50 +	18	7	11	..

State of Palestine - État de Palestine[32]
2007 (|)
Total	106 209	54 540	51 671	121.5
0 - 14	2	2	-	..
15 - 19	7 759	4 029	3 731	36.1
20 - 24	31 097	15 970	15 128	189.3
25 - 29	30 535	15 688	14 847	224.1
30 - 34	20 980	10 682	10 298	180.3
35 - 39	11 544	5 974	5 570	118.4
40 - 44	3 821	1 913	1 908	47.5
45 - 49	342	198	144	5.4
50 +	94	66	28	..
Unknown - Inconnu	35	18	17	

10. Live births by age of mother and sex of child, general and age-specific fertility rates: latest available year, 2005 - 2014
Naissances vivantes selon l'âge de la mère et le sexe de l'enfant, taux de fécondité et taux de fécondité par âge : dernière année disponible, 2005 - 2014 (continued - suite)

Continent, country or area, year, code[a] and age of mother (in years) / Continent, pays ou zone, année, code[a] et âge de la mère (en années)	Number - Nombre Total	Male Masculin	Female Féminin	Rate Taux
ASIA - ASIE				
Thailand - Thaïlande				
2011 (+U)				
Total	795 031	409 699	385 332	...
0 - 14	3 415	1 793	1 622	..
15 - 19	129 321	66 645	62 676	...
20 - 24	186 942	96 371	90 571	...
25 - 29	204 684	105 355	99 329	...
30 - 34	167 671	86 515	81 156	...
35 - 39	80 348	41 311	39 037	...
40 - 44	20 089	10 251	9 838	...
45 - 49	1 293	653	640	...
50 +	73	30	43	..
Unknown - Inconnu	1 195	775	420	
Turkey - Turquie				
2013 (C)				
Total	1 283 062	659 740	623 322	63.0
0 - 14	326	176	150	..
15 - 19	87 226	44 924	42 302	27.9
20 - 24	319 517	164 907	154 610	105.6
25 - 29	396 157	203 652	192 505	128.9
30 - 34	306 524	157 260	149 264	95.4
35 - 39	131 925	67 552	64 373	46.2
40 - 44	28 593	14 707	13 886	10.9
45 - 49	2 852	1 502	1 350	1.2
50 +	377	205	172	..
Unknown - Inconnu	9 565	4 855	4 710	..
EUROPE				
Åland Islands - Îles d'Åland				
2013 (C)				
Total	287	149	138	47.6
0 - 14	-	-	-	..
15 - 19	4	3	1	♦4.8
20 - 24	32	19	13	45.6
25 - 29	87	44	43	117.6
30 - 34	99	51	48	120.7
35 - 39	53	27	26	60.7
40 - 44	10	5	5	♦10.5
45 - 49	2	-	2	♦1.8
50 +	-	-	-	..
Albania - Albanie				
2013 (C)				
Total	35 750	18 661	17 089	49.6
0 - 14	22	16	6	..
15 - 19	2 613	1 337	1 276	20.3
20 - 24	11 737	6 083	5 654	108.2
25 - 29	11 990	6 255	5 735	124.0
30 - 34	6 559	3 482	3 077	69.2
35 - 39	2 298	1 216	1 082	25.3
40 - 44	429	223	206	4.3
45 - 49	33	19	14	0.3
50 +	13	7	6	..
Unknown - Inconnu	56	23	33	..
Andorra - Andorre				
2012 (C)				
Total	737	364	373	36.4
12 - 14	-	-	-	..
15 - 19	5	2	3	♦2.8
20 - 24	43	21	22	22.8
25 - 29	162	86	76	63.7
30 - 34	284	143	141	84.2
35 - 39	197	87	110	52.6
40 - 44	39	19	20	10.9

Continent, country or area, year, code[a] and age of mother (in years) / Continent, pays ou zone, année, code[a] et âge de la mère (en années)	Number - Nombre Total	Male Masculin	Female Féminin	Rate Taux
EUROPE				
Andorra - Andorre				
2012 (C)				
45 - 49	6	5	1	♦1.8
50 +	1	1	-	
Austria - Autriche				
2013 (C)				
Total	79 330	40 953	38 377	39.5
0 - 14	10	4	6	
15 - 19	1 872	953	919	8.0
20 - 24	11 374	5 845	5 529	43.0
25 - 29	23 699	12 296	11 403	86.3
30 - 34	26 113	13 496	12 617	94.2
35 - 39	13 033	6 678	6 355	47.2
40 - 44	3 028	1 586	1 442	9.2
45 - 49	178	85	93	0.5
50 +	23	10	13	..
Belarus - Bélarus				
2006 (C)				
Total	96 721	49 849	46 872	36.6
0 - 14	10	5	5	..
15 - 19	8 238	4 234	4 004	21.9
20 - 24	36 120	18 613	17 507	88.9
25 - 29	29 846	15 372	14 474	83.0
30 - 34	15 950	8 229	7 721	46.3
35 - 39	5 488	2 846	2 642	16.1
40 - 44	935	488	447	2.4
45 - 49	47	23	24	0.1
50 +	-	-	-	..
Unknown - Inconnu	87	39	48	..
2013 (C)				
Total	117 997	...	...	50.0
0 - 14	21	...	...	..
15 - 19	5 273	...	...	21.4
20 - 24	30 844	...	...	89.2
25 - 29	43 186	...	...	112.4
30 - 34	26 729	...	...	76.0
35 - 39	10 163	...	...	30.1
40 - 44	1 688	...	...	5.0
45 - 49	47	...	...	0.1
50 +	3	...	...	..
Unknown - Inconnu	43	...	...	..
Belgium - Belgique[33]				
2013 (C)				
Total	125 606	64 371	61 235	49.6
0 - 14	20	12	8	..
15 - 19	2 231	1 145	1 086	7.2
20 - 24	16 036	8 294	7 742	46.4
25 - 29	42 452	21 676	20 776	121.5
30 - 34	42 035	21 507	20 528	115.5
35 - 39	17 711	9 065	8 646	50.0
40 - 44	3 705	1 949	1 756	9.7
45 - 49	182	79	103	0.5
50 +	8	5	3	..
Unknown - Inconnu	1 226	639	587	..
Bosnia and Herzegovina - Bosnie-Herzégovine				
2010 (C)				
Total	33 528	17 277	16 251	35.2
12 - 14	8	6	2	..
15 - 19	1 792	950	842	13.5
20 - 24	8 293	4 282	4 011	59.4
25 - 29	11 690	5 949	5 741	86.2
30 - 34	7 985	4 144	3 841	66.8
35 - 39	3 027	1 560	1 467	24.3
40 - 44	557	287	270	3.9

10. Live births by age of mother and sex of child, general and age-specific fertility rates: latest available year, 2005 - 2014
Naissances vivantes selon l'âge de la mère et le sexe de l'enfant, taux de fécondité et taux de fécondité par âge : dernière année disponible, 2005 - 2014 (continued - suite)

Continent, country or area, year, code[a] and age of mother (in years) / Continent, pays ou zone, année, code[a] et âge de la mère (en années)	Number - Nombre			Rate Taux
	Total	Male Masculin	Female Féminin	
EUROPE				
Bosnia and Herzegovina - Bosnie-Herzégovine				
2010 (C)				
45 - 49	30	14	16	0.2
50 +	1	-	1	..
Unknown - Inconnu	145	85	60	..
Bulgaria - Bulgarie				
2013 (C)				
Total	66 578	34 044	32 534	41.0
0 - 14	298	159	139	..
15 - 19	6 670	3 461	3 209	41.0
20 - 24	15 002	7 733	7 269	67.6
25 - 29	20 433	10 323	10 110	86.7
30 - 34	15 591	7 985	7 606	64.0
35 - 39	7 305	3 742	3 563	27.0
40 - 44	1 202	602	600	4.7
45 - 49	69	34	35	0.3
50 +	5	2	3	..
Unknown - Inconnu	3	3	-	..
Croatia - Croatie				
2013 (C)				
Total	39 939	20 731	19 208	41.8
0 - 14	6	3	3	..
15 - 19	1 270	672	598	10.6
20 - 24	6 073	3 135	2 938	49.4
25 - 29	12 875	6 627	6 248	94.2
30 - 34	12 938	6 758	6 180	89.6
35 - 39	5 659	2 943	2 716	40.1
40 - 44	1 034	551	483	7.5
45 - 49	73	38	35	0.5
50 +	3	1	2	..
Unknown - Inconnu	8	3	5	..
Czech Republic - République tchèque				
2013 (C)				
Total	106 751	54 702	52 049	43.1
0 - 14	9	4	5	..
15 - 19	2 816	1 425	1 391	11.3
20 - 24	13 372	6 837	6 535	41.4
25 - 29	31 764	16 272	15 492	92.0
30 - 34	37 841	19 424	18 417	95.9
35 - 39	18 180	9 329	8 851	39.9
40 - 44	2 656	1 348	1 308	7.3
45 - 49	111	62	49	0.3
50 +	2	1	1	..
Denmark - Danemark[34]				
2013 (C)				
Total	55 873	28 590	27 283	44.3
0 - 14	-	-	-	..
15 - 19	738	362	376	4.3
20 - 24	6 140	3 101	3 039	34.6
25 - 29	17 229	8 792	8 437	106.6
30 - 34	19 623	10 065	9 558	121.8
35 - 39	10 005	5 187	4 818	54.3
40 - 44	2 006	1 020	986	10.4
45 - 49	120	55	65	0.6
50 +	12	8	4	..
Estonia - Estonie				
2013 (C)				
Total	13 531	6 901	6 630	45.0
0 - 14	1	-	1	..
15 - 19	497	272	225	16.0
20 - 24	2 365	1 216	1 149	53.1
25 - 29	4 415	2 283	2 132	94.1
30 - 34	3 659	1 813	1 846	82.8

Continent, country or area, year, code[a] and age of mother (in years) / Continent, pays ou zone, année, code[a] et âge de la mère (en années)	Number - Nombre			Rate Taux
	Total	Male Masculin	Female Féminin	
EUROPE				
Estonia - Estonie				
2013 (C)				
35 - 39	2 125	1 073	1 052	47.7
40 - 44	450	233	217	9.8
45 - 49	19	11	8	♦0.4
50 +	-	-	-	..
Faeroe Islands - Îles Féroé				
2007 (C)				
Total	674	318	356	64.7
15 - 19	20	11	9	♦10.5
20 - 24	104	47	57	83.5
25 - 29	187	93	94	160.9
30 - 34	211	102	109	154.4
35 - 39	129	56	73	83.0
40 - 44	23	9	14	♦13.9
45 +	-	-	-	..
Finland - Finlande				
2013 (C)				
Total	58 134	29 858	28 276	50.4
0 - 14	3	2	1	..
15 - 19	1 137	569	568	7.4
20 - 24	8 439	4 343	4 096	51.0
25 - 29	17 537	8 915	8 622	106.2
30 - 34	19 319	10 008	9 311	115.1
35 - 39	9 623	4 958	4 665	59.4
40 - 44	1 964	1 002	962	12.5
45 - 49	108	59	49	0.6
50 +	4	2	2	..
France[35]				
2012 (C)				
Total	790 290	404 774	385 516	55.6
12 - 14	147	73	74	..
15 - 19	17 512	8 954	8 558	9.4
20 - 24	111 364	57 130	54 234	58.2
25 - 29	253 800	130 005	123 795	131.0
30 - 34	255 606	130 913	124 693	127.2
35 - 39	121 563	62 225	59 338	59.1
40 - 44	28 620	14 598	14 022	12.9
45 - 49	1 557	818	739	0.7
50 +	121	58	63	..
Germany - Allemagne				
2013 (C)				
Total	682 069	349 820	332 249	38.5
0 - 14	105	52	53	..
15 - 19	15 247	7 951	7 296	7.8
20 - 24	82 504	42 345	40 159	35.8
25 - 29	192 962	98 655	94 307	78.7
30 - 34	238 521	122 361	116 160	96.4
35 - 39	124 065	63 665	60 400	53.8
40 - 44	26 641	13 798	12 843	9.5
45 - 49	1 417	696	721	0.4
50 +	87	46	41	..
Unknown - Inconnu	520	251	269	..
Gibraltar[36]				
2013 (+C)				
Total	419	217	202	...
0 - 19	13	3	10	...
20 - 24	66	36	30	...
25 - 29	113	69	44	...
30 - 34	141	66	75	...
35 - 39	71	38	33	...
40 +	15	5	10	...

10. Live births by age of mother and sex of child, general and age-specific fertility rates: latest available year, 2005 - 2014
Naissances vivantes selon l'âge de la mère et le sexe de l'enfant, taux de fécondité et taux de fécondité par âge : dernière année disponible, 2005 - 2014 (continued - suite)

Continent, country or area, year, code[a] and age of mother (in years) / Continent, pays ou zone, année, code[a] et âge de la mère (en années)	Number - Nombre			Rate Taux
	Total	Male Masculin	Female Féminin	

EUROPE

Greece - Grèce				
2013 (C)				
Total	94 134	48 430	45 704	37.1
0 - 14	93	42	51	..
15 - 19	2 172	1 119	1 053	8.1
20 - 24	8 544	4 379	4 165	28.1
25 - 29	23 160	11 855	11 305	69.8
30 - 34	35 433	18 169	17 264	88.5
35 - 39	19 697	10 296	9 401	48.3
40 - 44	4 307	2 202	2 105	10.1
45 - 49	639	321	318	1.6
50 +	89	47	42	..
Hungary - Hongrie				
2013 (C)				
Total	89 524	45 995	43 529	38.6
0 - 14	90	58	32	..
15 - 19	5 701	2 920	2 781	21.1
20 - 24	12 736	6 574	6 162	41.7
25 - 29	22 769	11 742	11 027	76.4
30 - 34	28 061	14 349	13 712	81.4
35 - 39	17 091	8 756	8 335	40.7
40 - 44	2 933	1 521	1 412	8.2
45 - 49	108	59	49	0.3
50 +	4	2	2	..
Unknown - Inconnu	31	14	17	..
Iceland - Islande				
2013 (C)				
Total	4 326	2 129	2 197	56.1
0 - 14	-	-	-	..
15 - 19	81	29	52	7.4
20 - 24	743	378	365	62.2
25 - 29	1 307	655	652	117.6
30 - 34	1 326	655	671	117.0
35 - 39	691	331	360	65.8
40 - 44	158	74	84	15.3
45 - 49	19	6	13	♦1.7
50 +	1	1	-	..
Ireland - Irlande				
2013 (+C)				
Total	68 949	35 346	33 603	60.3
0 - 14	8	7	1	..
15 - 19	1 375	695	680	10.3
20 - 24	6 391	3 294	3 097	49.2
25 - 29	13 898	7 163	6 735	81.5
30 - 34	25 383	12 926	12 457	126.8
35 - 39	17 889	9 198	8 691	97.6
40 - 44	3 779	1 949	1 830	22.2
45 - 49	218	107	111	1.4
50 +	8	7	1	..
Italy - Italie				
2013 (+C)				
Total	514 308	264 260	250 048	38.1
0 - 14	14	11	3	..
15 - 19	8 071	4 133	3 938	5.9
20 - 24	47 669	24 463	23 206	31.5
25 - 29	114 955	59 117	55 838	70.7
30 - 34	171 151	88 155	82 996	92.8
35 - 39	132 613	68 262	64 351	59.5
40 - 44	36 852	18 683	18 169	15.2
45 - 49	2 703	1 307	1 396	1.1
50 +	280	129	151	..
Jersey[20]				
2007 (+C)				
Total	1 031	515	516	...
0 - 14	-	-	-	..

EUROPE

Jersey[20]				
2007 (+C)				
15 - 19	29	14	15	...
20 - 24	114	56	58	...
25 - 29	228	114	114	...
30 - 34	325	170	155	...
35 - 39	273	134	139	...
40 - 44	61	27	34	...
45 - 49	1	-	1	...
50 +	-	-	-	..
Latvia - Lettonie				
2012 (C)				
Total	19 897	10 257	9 640	41.8
12 - 14	5	2	3	..
15 - 19	1 038	531	507	20.3
20 - 24	4 181	2 144	2 037	58.7
25 - 29	6 721	3 460	3 261	92.4
30 - 34	4 800	2 445	2 355	73.3
35 - 39	2 567	1 368	1 199	37.2
40 - 44	550	291	259	7.6
45 - 49	22	11	11	♦0.3
50 +	-	-	-	..
Unknown - Inconnu	13	5	8	..
Liechtenstein				
2013 (C)				
Total	339	179	160	38.4
0 - 14	-	-	-	..
15 - 19	-	-	-	..
20 - 24	19	10	9	♦17.4
25 - 29	102	51	51	90.7
30 - 34	128	76	52	111.9
35 - 39	68	28	40	54.7
40 - 44	19	12	7	♦12.8
45 - 49	3	2	1	♦1.8
50 +	-	-	-	..
Lithuania - Lituanie				
2012 (C)				
Total	30 459	15 560	14 899	43.0
12 - 14	3	2	1	..
15 - 19	1 380	728	652	14.5
20 - 24	5 844	2 970	2 874	55.9
25 - 29	11 104	5 698	5 406	117.0
30 - 34	7 872	3 985	3 887	88.6
35 - 39	3 494	1 784	1 710	35.4
40 - 44	738	384	354	6.7
45 - 49	19	8	11	♦0.2
50 +	-	-	-	..
Unknown - Inconnu	5	1	4	..
2013 (C)				
Total	29 885	...	...	43.2
0 - 14	6	...	...	..
15 - 19	1 262	...	...	14.2
20 - 24	5 566	...	...	53.6
25 - 29	10 929	...	...	115.0
30 - 34	7 825	...	...	89.6
35 - 39	3 493	...	...	36.7
40 - 44	766	...	...	7.1
45 - 49	27	...	...	♦0.2
50 +	1	...	...	..
Unknown - Inconnu	10	...	...	..
Luxembourg				
2013 (C)				
Total	6 115	3 129	2 986	45.8
0 - 14	2	2	-	..
15 - 19	82	44	38	5.2

10. Live births by age of mother and sex of child, general and age-specific fertility rates: latest available year, 2005 - 2014
Naissances vivantes selon l'âge de la mère et le sexe de l'enfant, taux de fécondité et taux de fécondité par âge : dernière année disponible, 2005 - 2014 (continued - suite)

Continent, country or area, year, code[a] and age of mother (in years) / Continent, pays ou zone, année, code[a] et âge de la mère (en années)	Total	Male Masculin	Female Féminin	Rate Taux
EUROPE				
Luxembourg				
2013 (C)				
20 - 24	555	277	278	34.3
25 - 29	1 602	833	769	86.7
30 - 34	2 245	1 150	1 095	109.0
35 - 39	1 311	666	645	64.8
40 - 44	297	148	149	14.0
45 - 49	15	5	10	♦0.7
50 +	-	-	-	..
Unknown - Inconnu	6	4	2	..
Malta - Malte				
2013 (C)				
Total	4 032	2 109	1 923	41.9
0 - 14	3	3	-	..
15 - 19	159	79	80	13.1
20 - 24	519	261	258	35.6
25 - 29	1 224	659	565	83.7
30 - 34	1 432	749	683	95.2
35 - 39	608	312	296	42.2
40 - 44	84	46	38	6.6
45 - 49	3	3	-	♦0.2
50 +	-	-	-	..
Montenegro - Monténégro				
2013 (C)				
Total	7 475	3 877	3 598	49.9
0 - 14	3	1	2	..
15 - 19	248	137	111	11.9
20 - 24	1 437	724	713	70.3
25 - 29	2 519	1 322	1 197	114.5
30 - 34	2 050	1 065	985	91.5
35 - 39	944	478	466	43.7
40 - 44	202	114	88	9.9
45 - 49	18	7	11	♦0.9
50 +	5	3	2	..
Unknown - Inconnu	49	26	23	..
Netherlands - Pays-Bas[37]				
2013 (C)				
Total	171 341	87 957	83 384	45.0
0 - 14	-	-	-	..
15 - 19	1 901	961	940	3.9
20 - 24	17 029	8 653	8 376	32.6
25 - 29	52 894	27 274	25 620	104.2
30 - 34	64 331	32 929	31 402	127.6
35 - 39	29 518	15 283	14 235	57.1
40 - 44	5 412	2 734	2 678	8.5
45 - 49	244	119	125	0.4
50 +	12	4	8	..
Norway - Norvège				
2013 (C)				
Total	58 878	30 084	28 794	49.9
0 - 14	2	1	1	..
15 - 19	892	462	430	5.6
20 - 24	8 040	4 114	3 926	48.4
25 - 29	18 728	9 561	9 167	113.2
30 - 34	19 708	10 087	9 621	120.2
35 - 39	9 479	4 865	4 614	56.8
40 - 44	1 947	948	999	10.7
45 - 49	79	43	36	0.4
50 +	3	3	-	..
Unknown - Inconnu	-	-	-	..
Poland - Pologne				
2013 (C)				
Total	369 576	189 917	179 659	39.9
0 - 14	48	30	18	..
15 - 19	14 444	7 436	7 008	13.7

Continent, country or area, year, code[a] and age of mother (in years) / Continent, pays ou zone, année, code[a] et âge de la mère (en années)	Total	Male Masculin	Female Féminin	Rate Taux
EUROPE				
Poland - Pologne				
2013 (C)				
20 - 24	62 949	32 272	30 677	48.6
25 - 29	130 958	67 300	63 658	86.9
30 - 34	109 789	56 586	53 203	70.6
35 - 39	43 343	22 201	21 142	29.9
40 - 44	7 714	3 924	3 790	6.3
45 - 49	328	166	162	0.3
50 +	3	2	1	..
Portugal[20]				
2013 (C)				
Total	82 787	42 220	40 567	33.9
0 - 14	53	27	26	..
15 - 19	2 808	1 428	1 380	10.4
20 - 24	9 254	4 758	4 496	32.9
25 - 29	20 050	10 214	9 836	66.9
30 - 34	28 833	14 836	13 997	79.8
35 - 39	17 908	9 050	8 858	42.4
40 - 44	3 680	1 804	1 876	9.1
45 - 49	193	100	93	0.5
50 +	8	3	5	..
Republic of Moldova - République de Moldova[38]				
2012 (C)				
Total	39 435	20 380	19 055	40.7
20 - 24	13 022	6 706	6 316	79.3
25 - 29	13 443	6 967	6 476	79.7
30 - 34	6 746	3 411	3 335	47.2
35 - 39	2 591	1 370	1 221	20.4
40 - 44	447	231	216	3.9
45 - 49	8	3	5	♦0.1
50 +	3	3	-	..
Unknown - Inconnu	3	1	2	..
Romania - Roumanie				
2013 (C)				
Total	182 313	93 986	88 327	38.9
0 - 14	691	340	351	..
15 - 19	17 944	9 359	8 585	33.8
20 - 24	39 562	20 383	19 179	66.7
25 - 29	56 116	28 821	27 295	85.1
30 - 34	43 619	22 451	21 168	62.7
35 - 39	20 473	10 625	9 848	26.5
40 - 44	3 701	1 918	1 783	4.7
45 - 49	199	89	110	0.3
50 +	8	-	8	..
Russian Federation - Fédération de Russie[23]				
2011 (C)				
Total	1 796 629	923 804	872 825	48.3
12 - 14	351	174	177	..
15 - 19	103 533	53 162	50 371	25.2
20 - 24	510 184	262 085	248 099	85.1
25 - 29	603 791	311 250	292 541	101.2
30 - 34	379 884	195 518	184 366	68.6
35 - 39	165 364	84 832	80 532	31.8
40 - 44	30 221	15 168	15 053	6.3
45 - 49	1 481	680	801	0.3
50 +	138	65	73	..
Unknown - Inconnu	1 682	870	812	..
San Marino - Saint-Marin				
2012 (+C)				
Total	292	146	146	36.0
12 - 14	-	-	-	..
15 - 19	-	-	-	-
20 - 24	13	6	7	♦19.2

10. Live births by age of mother and sex of child, general and age-specific fertility rates: latest available year, 2005 - 2014
Naissances vivantes selon l'âge de la mère et le sexe de l'enfant, taux de fécondité et taux de fécondité par âge : dernière année disponible, 2005 - 2014 (continued - suite)

Continent, country or area, year, code[a] and age of mother (in years) / Continent, pays ou zone, année, code[a] et âge de la mère (en années)	Total	Male Masculin	Female Féminin	Rate Taux
EUROPE				
San Marino - Saint-Marin				
2012 (+C)				
25 - 29	52	28	24	64.2
30 - 34	96	44	52	88.6
35 - 39	94	52	42	66.3
40 - 44	21	10	11	♦14.0
45 - 49	1	1	-	♦0.7
Unknown - Inconnu	14	5	9	..
Serbia - Serbie[39]				
2013 (+C)				
Total	65 554	33 710	31 844	41.0
0 - 14	43	15	28	..
15 - 19	3 389	1 703	1 686	18.1
20 - 24	12 614	6 433	6 181	60.5
25 - 29	20 905	10 723	10 182	90.4
30 - 34	18 632	9 737	8 895	77.1
35 - 39	8 200	4 235	3 965	33.1
40 - 44	1 449	709	740	6.1
45 - 49	118	50	68	0.5
50 +	15	6	9	..
Unknown - Inconnu	189	99	90	..
Slovakia - Slovaquie				
2013 (C)				
Total	54 823	28 068	26 755	40.5
0 - 14	38	21	17	..
15 - 19	3 325	1 705	1 620	22.0
20 - 24	9 265	4 762	4 503	49.3
25 - 29	17 033	8 750	8 283	81.8
30 - 34	16 609	8 517	8 092	76.0
35 - 39	7 444	3 791	3 653	33.7
40 - 44	1 076	509	567	5.8
45 - 49	33	13	20	0.2
50 +	-	-	-	..
Slovenia - Slovénie				
2013 (C)				
Total	21 111	10 804	10 307	45.6
0 - 14	3	1	2	..
15 - 19	221	124	97	4.7
20 - 24	2 449	1 256	1 193	44.2
25 - 29	7 158	3 655	3 503	108.3
30 - 34	7 621	3 924	3 697	103.6
35 - 39	3 113	1 567	1 546	42.3
40 - 44	520	257	263	7.4
45 - 49	26	20	6	♦0.3
50 +	-	-	-	..
Spain - Espagne				
2013 (C)				
Total	424 440	218 375	206 065	38.3
0 - 14	139	70	69	..
15 - 19	8 753	4 483	4 270	8.4
20 - 24	32 024	16 595	15 429	27.1
25 - 29	78 612	40 613	37 999	55.9
30 - 34	155 443	80 126	75 317	88.2
35 - 39	120 493	61 650	58 843	60.9
40 - 44	27 240	13 952	13 288	14.4
45 - 49	1 654	852	802	0.9
50 +	82	34	48	..
Sweden - Suède				
2013 (C)				
Total	113 593	58 472	55 121	53.1
0 - 14	4	1	3	..
15 - 19	1 424	724	700	5.3
20 - 24	14 936	7 676	7 260	45.7
25 - 29	33 608	17 336	16 272	111.0
30 - 34	38 665	19 946	18 719	132.8
EUROPE				
Sweden - Suède				
2013 (C)				
35 - 39	20 249	10 412	9 837	67.3
40 - 44	4 427	2 241	2 186	14.0
45 - 49	257	123	134	0.8
50 +	23	13	10	..
Switzerland - Suisse				
2013 (C)				
Total	82 731	42 595	40 136	43.2
0 - 14	4	1	3	..
15 - 19	652	337	315	3.0
20 - 24	7 330	3 800	3 530	29.9
25 - 29	21 489	11 093	10 396	80.8
30 - 34	30 972	16 076	14 896	110.7
35 - 39	18 185	9 232	8 953	65.6
40 - 44	3 827	1 910	1 917	12.6
45 - 49	247	131	116	0.7
50 +	25	15	10	..
TFYR of Macedonia - L'ex-R. y. de Macédoine				
2013 (C)				
Total	23 138	12 093	11 045	44.2
0 - 14	25	12	13	..
15 - 19	1 155	602	553	17.1
20 - 24	5 138	2 737	2 401	67.2
25 - 29	8 209	4 225	3 984	102.3
30 - 34	6 005	3 181	2 824	76.5
35 - 39	2 238	1 136	1 102	29.9
40 - 44	350	190	160	4.8
45 - 49	11	5	6	♦0.2
50 +	1	-	1	..
Unknown - Inconnu	6	5	1	..
Ukraine[40]				
2011 (+C)				
Total	502 595	...	...	43.6
12 - 14	141	...	...	..
15 - 19	35 559	...	...	27.9
20 - 24	152 369	...	...	89.8
25 - 29	166 675	...	...	89.2
30 - 34	98 457	...	...	58.0
35 - 39	40 918	...	...	24.6
40 - 44	7 294	...	...	4.6
45 - 49	350	...	...	0.2
50 +	40	...	...	..
Unknown - Inconnu	792	...	...	..
United Kingdom of Great Britain and Northern Ireland - Royaume-Uni de Grande-Bretagne et d'Irlande du Nord[41]				
2013 (C)				
Total	778 358	399 358	379 000	51.8
0 - 14	146	83	63	..
15 - 19	32 675	16 881	15 794	17.3
20 - 24	132 985	68 330	64 655	62.3
25 - 29	218 607	112 157	106 450	100.3
30 - 34	237 205	121 550	115 655	109.4
35 - 39	124 449	63 863	60 586	62.2
40 - 44	30 092	15 403	14 689	13.3
45 - 49	2 003	1 005	998	0.8
50 +	179	78	101	..
Unknown - Inconnu	17	8	9	..

10. Live births by age of mother and sex of child, general and age-specific fertility rates: latest available year, 2005 - 2014
Naissances vivantes selon l'âge de la mère et le sexe de l'enfant, taux de fécondité et taux de fécondité par âge : dernière année disponible, 2005 - 2014 (continued - suite)

Continent, country or area, year, code[a] and age of mother (in years) / Continent, pays ou zone, année, code[a] et âge de la mère (en années)	Number - Nombre			Rate Taux
	Total	Male Masculin	Female Féminin	

OCEANIA - OCÉANIE

American Samoa - Samoas américaines				
2011 (C)				
Total	1 287	...	...	...
0 - 14	1	...	...	..
15 - 19	138	...	...	...
20 - 24	368	...	...	...
25 - 29	313	...	...	...
30 - 34	260	...	...	...
35 - 39	168	...	...	...
40 - 44	35	...	...	...
45 - 49	4	...	...	...
Australia - Australie				
2013 (+C)				
Total	308 065	158 706	149 359	55.2
0 - 14	93	43	50	..
15 - 19	10 314	5 472	4 842	14.5
20 - 24	41 351	21 354	19 997	51.4
25 - 29	84 951	43 731	41 220	99.4
30 - 34	102 577	52 753	49 824	124.4
35 - 39	55 119	28 364	26 755	70.8
40 - 44	12 931	6 636	6 295	15.4
45 - 49	629	302	327	0.8
50 +	41	21	20	..
Unknown - Inconnu	59	30	29	..
Cook Islands - Îles Cook[42]				
2013 (+C)				
Total	256	...	...	...
0 - 19	34	...	...	...
20 - 24	80	...	...	...
25 - 29	56	...	...	...
30 - 34	38	...	...	...
35 - 39	35	...	...	...
40 +	13	...	...	...
Fiji - Fidji				
2008 (+C)				
Total	17 199	...	...	76.6
0 - 14	3	...	...	..
15 - 19	1 057	...	...	27.5
20 - 24	5 180	...	...	135.3
25 - 29	5 688	...	...	157.8
30 - 34	3 227	...	...	103.4
35 - 39	1 488	...	...	53.0
40 - 44	509	...	...	18.6
45 - 49	34	...	...	1.4
50 +	-	...	...	..
Unknown - Inconnu	13	...	...	..
Marshall Islands - Îles Marshall[43]				
2006 (+U)				
Total	*1 576*	...	...	..
0 - 14	*2*	...	...	..
15 - 19	*268*	...	...	...
20 - 24	*551*	...	...	...
25 - 29	*431*	...	...	...
30 - 34	*211*	...	...	...
35 - 39	*91*	...	...	...
40 - 44	*19*	...	...	...
45 - 49	*3*	...	...	...
Micronesia (Federated States of) - Micronésie (États fédérés de)				
2006 (+U)				
Total	*2 148*	...	...	..
10 - 14	*8*	...	...	..

OCEANIA - OCÉANIE				
Micronesia (Federated States of) - Micronésie (États fédérés de)				
2006 (+U)				
15 - 17	*89*	...	...	...
18 - 19	*155*	...	...	...
20 - 24	*619*	...	...	...
25 - 29	*514*	...	...	...
30 - 34	*379*	...	...	...
35 - 39	*259*	...	...	...
40 - 44	*43*	...	...	...
45 +	*9*	...	...	...
Unknown - Inconnu	*73*	...	...	...
Nauru				
2011 (C)				
Total	370	190	180	...
15 - 19	40	22	18	...
20 - 24	126	69	57	...
25 - 29	111	57	54	...
30 - 34	55	22	33	...
35 - 39	33	17	16	...
40 - 44	5	3	2	...
45 - 49	-	-	-	...
New Caledonia - Nouvelle-Calédonie				
2012 (C)				
Total	4 389	...	...	...
0 - 19	237	...	...	...
20 - 24	942	...	...	...
25 - 29	1 179	...	...	...
30 - 34	1 169	...	...	...
35 - 39	656	...	...	...
40 - 44	193	...	...	...
45 - 49	11	...	...	...
50 +	2	...	...	...
New Zealand - Nouvelle-Zélande				
2014 (+C)				
Total	57 242	29 595	27 647	53.3
0 - 14	27	13	14	..
15 - 19	2 895	1 464	1 431	19.0
20 - 24	9 915	5 179	4 736	62.2
25 - 29	15 211	7 853	7 358	102.9
30 - 34	17 201	8 810	8 391	119.3
35 - 39	9 535	4 990	4 545	66.7
40 - 44	2 341	1 225	1 116	14.2
45 - 49	112	60	52	0.7
50 +	5	1	4	..
Niue - Nioué[44]				
2009 (C)				
Total	31	...	...	...
0 - 14	-	...	...	...
15 - 19	1	...	...	...
20 - 24	9	...	...	...
25 - 29	12	...	...	...
30 - 34	6	...	...	...
35 - 39	1	...	...	...
40 - 44	1	...	...	...
45 +	1	...	...	...
Palau - Palaos				
2005 (C)				
Total	279	...	...	55.3
0 - 14	-	...	...	..
15 - 19	23	...	...	♦30.8
20 - 24	65	...	...	117.3

Continent, country or area, year, code[a] and age of mother (in years) / Continent, pays ou zone, année, code[a] et âge de la mère (en années)	Number - Nombre			Rate Taux
	Total	Male Masculin	Female Féminin	

OCEANIA - OCÉANIE

Palau - Palaos
2005 (C)

	Total	Male Masculin	Female Féminin	Rate Taux
25 - 29	56	...	...	87.4
30 - 34	73	...	...	93.1
35 - 39	40	...	...	48.0
40 - 44	20	...	...	♦25.3
45 - 49	2	...	...	♦2.9

Samoa[45]
2011 (|)

	Total	Male Masculin	Female Féminin	Rate Taux
Total	5 703	3 055	2 648	133.8
15 - 19	369	209	160	39.2
20 - 24	1 557	831	726	218.3
25 - 29	1 471	793	678	238.6
30 - 34	1 154	603	551	206.1
35 - 39	741	398	343	144.1
40 - 44	338	180	158	69.9
45 - 49	73	41	32	16.9

OCEANIA - OCÉANIE

Tokelau - Tokélaou[46]
2011 (|)

	Total	Male Masculin	Female Féminin	Rate Taux
Total	16	...	...	...
0 - 14	-	...	...	..
15 - 19	1	...	...	...
20 - 24	6	...	...	...
25 - 29	4	...	...	...
30 - 34	4	...	...	...
35 - 39	1	...	...	...

Wallis and Futuna Islands - Îles Wallis et Futuna
2008 (C)

	Total	Male Masculin	Female Féminin	Rate Taux
Total	185	...	...	...
0 - 14	-	...	...	..
15 - 19	9	...	...	...
20 - 24	38	...	...	...
25 - 29	53	...	...	...
30 - 34	51	...	...	...
35 - 39	29	...	...	...
40 - 44	5	...	...	...
45 +	-	...	...	...

FOOTNOTES - NOTES

♦ Rates based on 30 or fewer births. - Taux basés sur 30 naissances ou moins.

˙ Provisional. - Données provisoires.

[a] 'Code' indicates the source of data, as follows:
C - Civil registration, estimated over 90% complete
U - Civil registration, estimated less than 90% complete
| - Other source, estimated reliable
+ - Data tabulated by date of registration rather than occurrence
... Information not available

Le 'Code' indique la source des données, comme suit :
C - Registres de l'état civil considérés complets à 90 p. 100 au moins
U - Registres de l'état civil qui ne sont pas considérés complets à 90 p. 100 au moins
| - Autre source, considérée fiable
+ - Données exploitées selon la date de l'enregistrement et non la date de l'événement
... Information non disponible

[1] Data refer to the 12 months preceding the census in August. - Les données se rapportent aux 12 mois précédant le recensement d'août.
[2] Source: Vital Statistics Report 2012. - Source: Vital Statistics Report 2012.
[3] Data refer to the 12 months preceding the census in September. - Les données se rapportent aux 12 mois précédant le recensement de septembre.
[4] Unrevised data. - Les données n'ont pas été révisées.
[5] Data refer to the 12 months preceding the census in March. - Les données se rapportent aux 12 mois précédant le recensement de mars.
[6] Data refer to Libyan nationals only. - Les données se raportent aux nationaux libyens seulement.
[7] Data refer to the 12 months preceding the census in June. - Les données se raportent aux 12 mois précédant le recensement de juin.
[8] Data refer to the 12 months preceding the census in April. - Les données se rapportent aux douze mois précédant le recensement d'avril.
[9] Excludes the islands of St. Brandon and Agalega. - Non compris les îles St. Brandon et Agalega.
[10] Excluding live-born infants who died before their birth was registered. - Non compris les enfants nés vivants décédés avant l'enregistrement de leur naissance.

[11] Data refer to the 12 months preceding the census in May. - Les données se rapportent aux 12 mois précédant le recensement de mai.
[12] Data refer to the 12 months preceding the census in October. - Les données se rapportent aux 12 mois précédant le recensement de octobre.
[13] Including unknown sex. - Y compris le sexe inconnu.
[14] Excluding non-residents and foreign service personnel and their dependants. - À l'exclusion des non-résidents et du personnel diplomatique et de leurs charges de famille.
[15] Including Canadian residents temporarily in the United States, but excluding United States residents temporarily in Canada. - Y compris les résidents canadiens se trouvant temporairement aux Etats-Unis, mais ne comprenant pas les résidents des Etats-Unis se trouvant temporairement au Canada.
[16] For confidentiality reasons, live births to mothers aged 50 and over and the adopted children with no information on their birth mother are included in 'age of mother Unknown'. - Pour des raisons de confidentialité, on a classé dans la catégorie « âge de la mère Inconnu» les naissances vivantes concernant des femmes âgées de plus de 50 ans et les enfants adoptés nés de mères sur lesquelles on ne dispose pas d'information.
[17] Excluding children born in the country of non-resident mothers. - Exceptés les enfants nés dans le pays des mères non-résidentes.
[18] Data refer to population in private households. Data refer to period from 1 January 2010 to 3 April 2011. - Les données portent sur la population des ménages privés. Les données concernent la période du 1 janvier 2010 au 3 avril 2011.
[19] Figures for male and female may not add up to the total, since they do not include the category "Unknown". - La somme des chiffres indiqués pour les sexes masculin et féminin peut n'être pas égale au total parce qu'elle n'inclut pas la catégorie " inconnue ".
[20] Data refer to births to resident mothers. - Ces données concernent les enfants nés de mères résidentes.
[21] Including births abroad and births of unknown residence of mother. - Y compris les naissances à l'étranger et les naissances pour lesquelles le lieu de résidence de la mère est inconnu.
[22] Source: Reports of the Ministry of Health. - Source : Rapports du Ministère de la Santé.
[23] Excluding infants born alive of less than 28 weeks' gestation, of less than 1 000 grams in weight and 35 centimeters in length, who die within seven days of birth. - Non compris les enfants nés vivants après moins de 28 semaines de gestation, pesant moins de 1 000 grammes, mesurant moins de 35 centimètres et décédés dans les sept jours qui ont suivi leur naissance.
[24] Data refer to government controlled areas. - Les données se rapportent aux zones contrôlées par le Gouvernement.

25 Data refer to the Iranian Year which begins on 21 March and ends on 20 March of the following year. - Les données concernent l'année iranienne, qui commence le 21 mars et se termine le 20 mars de l'année suivante.

26 Includes data for East Jerusalem and Israeli residents in certain other territories under occupation by Israeli military forces since June 1967. - Y compris les données pour Jérusalem-Est et les résidents israéliens dans certains autres territoires occupés depuis 1967 par les forces armées israéliennes.

27 Data refer to Japanese nationals in Japan only. - Les données se raportent aux nationaux japonais au Japon seulement.

28 Data from Births and Deaths Notification System (Ministry of Health and all health care providers). Data for all population, citizens and foreigners. - Les données proviennent du système de notification des naissances et des décès (Ministère de la santé et tous prestataires de soins de santé). Les données portent sur la population entière, les citoyens et les étrangers.

29 Based on the results of the Pakistan Demographic Survey. Excluding data for the Pakistan-held part of Jammu and Kashmir, the final status of which has not yet been determined. - Données extraites de l'enquête démographique effectuée par le Pakistan. Non compris les données concernant la partie du Jammu et Cachemire occupée par le Pakistan dont le statut définitif n'a pas été déterminé.

30 Excluding alien armed forces, civilian aliens employed by armed forces, and foreign diplomatic personnel and their dependants. - Non compris les militaires étrangers, les civils étrangers employés par les forces armées ni le personnel diplomatique étranger et les membres de leur famille les accompagnant.

31 The registration of births and deaths is conducted by the Ministry of Health. An estimate of completeness is not provided. - L'enregistrement des naissances et des décès est mené par le Ministère de la Santé. Le degré estimatif de complétude n'est pas fourni.

32 Excluding data from the parts of Jerusalem which were annexed by Israel in 1967. Data have not been adjusted for underenumeration. Data refer to the 12 months preceding the census in December. - Non compris les données provenant des parties de Jérusalem qui ont été annexées par Israël en 1967. Les données n'ont pas été ajustées pour compenser les lacunes du dénombrement. Les données se rapportent aux 12 mois précédant le recensement de décembre.

33 Including armed forces stationed outside the country, but excluding alien armed forces stationed in the area. - Y compris les militaires nationaux hors du pays, mais non compris les militaires étrangers en garnison sur le territoire.

34 Excluding Faeroe Islands and Greenland shown separately, if available. - Non compris les Iles Féroé et le Groenland, qui font l'objet de rubriques distinctes, si disponible.

35 Including armed forces stationed outside the country. - Y compris les militaires nationaux hors du pays.

36 Total in this table is different from data presented in other tables due to different data source. Including live births by military personnel and their dependants. - Le total figurant dans ce tableau ne correspond pas aux données présentées dans d'autres tableaux parce que les sources de données ne sont pas les mêmes. Y compris les naissances vivantes parmi les membres du personnel militaire et leurs personnes à charge.

37 Including residents outside the country if listed in a Netherlands population register. - Englobe les résidents se trouvant à l'étranger à condition qu'ils soient inscrits sur le registre de population des Pays-Bas.

38 Excluding infants born alive of less than 28 weeks' gestation, of less than 1 000 grams in weight and 35 centimeters in length, who die within seven days of birth. Excluding Transnistria and the municipality of Bender. - Non compris les enfants nés vivants après moins de 28 semaines de gestations, pesant moins de 1 000 grammes, mesurant moins de 35 centimètres et décédés dans les sept jours qui ont suivi leur naissance. Les données ne tiennent pas compte de l'information sur la Transnistria et la municipalité de Bender.

39 Excludes data for Kosovo and Metohia. - Sans les données pour le Kosovo et Metohie.

40 Data refer to births with weight 500g and more (if weight is unknown - with length 25 centimeters and more, or with gestation during 22 weeks or more). - Données concernant les nouveau-nés de 500 grammes ou plus (si le poids est inconnu – de 25 centimètres de long ou plus, ou après une grossesse de 22 semaines ou plus).

41 Excluding Channel Islands (Guernsey and Jersey) and Isle of Man, shown separately, if available. Data tabulated by date of occurrence for England and Wales, and by date of registration for Northern Ireland and Scotland. - Non compris les îles Anglo-Normandes (Guernesey et Jersey) et l'île de Man, qui font l'objet de rubriques distinctes, si disponible. Données exploitées selon la date de l'événement pour l'Angleterre et le pays de Galles, et selon la date de l'enregistrement pour l'Irlande du Nord et l'Ecosse.

42 Excluding Niue, shown separately, which is part of Cook Islands, but because of remoteness is administered separately. - Non compris Nioué, qui fait l'objet d'une rubrique distincte et qui fait partie des îles Cook, mais qui, en raison de son éloignement, est administrée séparément.

43 Excluding United States military personnel, their dependants and contract employees. - Non compris les militaires des Etats-Unis, les membres de leur famille les accompagnant et les agents contractuels des Etats-Unis.

44 Includes children born in New Zealand to women resident in Niue who chose to travel to New Zealand to give birth. - Y compris les enfants nés en Nouvelle-Zélande de femmes résidant à Nioué qui ont choisi de se rendre en Nouvelle-Zélande pour accoucher.

45 Data refer to the 12 months preceding the census in November. - Données se rapportant aux 12 mois précédant le recensement de novembre.

46 Data refer to usually resident population present on census night. Data refer to the 12 months preceding the census in October. - Les données concernent la population habituellement résidente présente la nuit du recensement. Les données se rapportent aux 12 mois précédant le recensement de octobre.

Table 11 - *Demographic Yearbook 2014*

Table 11 presents live births by age of father and live birth rates by age of father for the latest available year between 2005 and 2014.

Description of variables: Age is defined as age at last birthday, that is, the difference between the date of birth and the date of the occurrence of the event, expressed in completed solar years. The age classification used in this table is the following: under 20 years, 5-year age groups through 60-64 years, 65 years and over, and age unknown. A different classification may appear as provided by reporting country or area.

Rate computation: Live-birth rates specific to age of father are the annual number of births to a man in each age group per 1 000 male population in the same age group. These rates are calculated by the Statistics Division of the United Nations.

Since relatively few births occur to men below 15 or above 59 years of age, birth rates for men under 20 years of age and for those 55 years of age or over are computed on the male population aged 15-19 and 55-59, respectively. Similarly, the rate for men of "All ages" is based on all live births irrespective of age of father, and is computed on the male population aged 15-59 years.

Births to fathers of unknown age are distributed proportionately across the age groups, by the Statistics Division of the United Nations, in accordance with the distribution of births by age of father prior to the calculation of the rates.

The population used in computing the rates is the estimated or enumerated distribution of males by age. First priority is given to the estimated population and second priority to the enumerated population, i.e. to census returns of the year to which the births refer.

Rates presented in this table are limited to those for countries or areas having at least a total of 100 live births in a given year.

Reliability of data: Data from civil registers of live births which are reported as incomplete (less than 90 per cent completeness) or of unknown completeness are considered unreliable and are set in *italics* rather than in roman type. Rates are not computed if the data on live births from civil registers are reported as incomplete (less than 90 per cent completeness) or of unknown completeness. Table 9 and the technical notes for that table provide more detailed information on the completeness of birth registration. For more information about the quality of vital statistics data in general, see section 4.2 of the Technical Notes.

Limitations: Statistics on live births by age of father are subject to the same qualifications as have been set forth for vital statistics in general and birth statistics in particular as discussed in section 4 of the Technical Notes. These include differences in the completeness of registration, the method used to determine age of father and the quality of the reported information relating to age of father.

The reliability of the data described above, is an important factor in considering the limitations. In addition, some live births are tabulated by date of registration and not by date of occurrence; these are indicated in the table by a plus sign "+". Whenever the lag between the date of occurrence and date of registration is prolonged and, therefore, a large proportion of the live-birth registrations are delayed, birth statistics for any given year may be seriously affected. For example, the age of the father will almost always refer to the date of registration rather than to the date of birth of the child. Hence, in those countries or areas where registration of births is delayed, possibly for years, statistics on births by age of father should be used with caution.

Another factor which limits international comparability is the practice of some countries or areas of not including in live birth statistics infants who were born alive but died before the registration of the birth or within the first 24 hours of life, thus underestimating the total number of live births. Statistics of this type are footnoted.

Because these statistics are classified according to age, they are subject to the limitations with respect to accuracy of age reporting similar to those already discussed in connection with section 3.1.3 of the Technical Notes. The factors influencing the accuracy of reporting may be somewhat dissimilar in vital statistics (because of the differences in the method of taking a census and registering a birth) but, in general, the same errors can be observed. The absence of frequencies in the unknown age group does not necessarily indicate completely accurate reporting and tabulation of the age item. It is often an indication that the unknowns have been eliminated by assigning ages to them before tabulation, or by proportionate distribution after tabulation.

On the other hand, large frequencies in the unknown age category may indicate that a large proportion of the births are born outside of wedlock, the records for which tend to be incomplete so far as characteristics of the parents are concerned.

Another limitation of age reporting may result from calculating age of father at birth of child (or at time of registration) from year of birth rather than from day, month and year of birth. Information on this factor is given in footnotes when known.

In few countries, data by age refer to deliveries rather than to live births causing under-enumeration in the event of a multiple birth. This practice leads to lack of strict comparability, both among countries or areas relying on this practice and between data shown in this table and table 9.

Rates shown in this table are subject to the same limitations that affect the corresponding statistics on live births. In cases of rates based on births tabulated by date of registration and not by date of occurrence; the effect of including delayed registration on the distribution of births by age of father may be noted in the age-specific fertility rates for men at older ages. In some cases, high age-specific rates for men aged 55 years and over may reflect age of father at registration of birth and not fertility at these older ages.

Earlier data: Live births and live birth rates by age of father have been shown in previous issues of the *Demographic Yearbook*. Information on the specific years is presented in the Historical Index.

Tableau 11 – *Annuaire démographique 2014*

Le tableau 11 présente les données les plus récentes disponibles pour la période 2005 - 2014 sur les naissances vivantes selon l'âge du père et les taux des naissances vivantes selon l'âge du père.

Description des variables : l'âge désigne l'âge au dernier anniversaire, c'est-à-dire la différence entre la date de naissance et la date de l'événement exprimée en années solaires révolues. La classification par âge utilisée dans ce tableau comprend les catégories suivantes : moins de 20 ans, groupes quinquennaux jusqu'à 60-64 ans, 65 ans et plus, et âge inconnu. Des groupes d'âge différents sont parfois utilisés lorsque les pays ou territoires ont fourni les données dans une autre classification.

Les taux de natalité selon l'âge du père représentent le nombre annuel de naissances vivantes intervenues dans un groupe d'âge donné pour 1 000 hommes du groupe d'âge. Ces taux ont été calculés par la Division de statistique de l'ONU.

Étant donné que le nombre de naissances parmi les hommes de moins de 15 ans ou de plus de 59 ans est relativement peu élevé, les taux de natalité parmi les hommes âgées de moins de 20 ans et celles de 55 ans et plus ont été calculés sur la base des populations masculines âgées de 15 à 19 ans et de 55 à 59 ans, respectivement. De même, le taux pour les hommes de « tous âges » est fondé sur la totalité des naissances vivantes, indépendamment de l'âge du père et ce chiffre est rapporté à l'effectif de la population masculine âgée de 15 à 59 ans.

Les naissances pour lesquelles l'âge du père était inconnu ont été réparties par la Division de statistique de l'ONU, avant le calcul des taux, suivant les proportions observées pour celles où l'âge du père était connu.

Les chiffres de population utilisés pour le calcul des taux proviennent de dénombrements ou de répartitions estimatives de la population masculine selon l'âge. On a utilisé de préférence les estimations de la population; à défaut, on s'est contenté des données censitaires se rapportant à l'année des naissances.

Les taux présentés dans ce tableau ne concernent que les pays ou zones où l'on a enregistré un total d'au moins 100 naissances vivantes dans une année donnée.

Fiabilité des données : les données sur les naissances vivantes provenant des registres de l'état civil qui sont déclarées incomplètes (degré de complétude inférieur à 90 p. 100) ou dont le degré de complétude n'est pas connu sont jugées douteuses et apparaissent en italique et non en caractères romains. On a choisi de ne pas faire figurer dans le tableau 11 des taux calculés à partir de données sur les naissances vivantes issues de registres de l'état civil qui sont déclarées incomplètes (degré de complétude inférieur à 90 p. 100) ou dont le degré de complétude n'est pas connu. Le tableau 9 et les notes techniques qui s'y rapportent présentent des renseignements plus détaillés sur le degré de complétude de l'enregistrement des naissances vivantes. Pour plus de précisions sur la qualité des statistiques de l'état civil en général, voir la section 4.2 des Notes techniques.

Insuffisance des données : les statistiques relatives aux naissances vivantes selon l'âge du père appellent toutes les réserves qui ont été formulées à propos des statistiques de l'état civil en général et des statistiques de naissances en particulier (voir la section 4 des Notes techniques). Ceci inclut les différences de complétude d'enregistrement des faits d'état civil, de méthode pour déterminer l'âge du père et de qualité d'information concernant l'âge du père.

La fiabilité des données, au sujet de laquelle des indications ont été données plus haut, est un facteur important. Il faut également tenir compte du fait que, dans certains cas, les données relatives aux naissances vivantes sont exploitées selon la date de l'enregistrement et non la date de l'événement ; ces cas ont été signalés dans le tableau par le signe '+'. Chaque fois que le décalage entre l'événement et son enregistrement est grand et qu'une forte proportion des naissances vivantes fait l'objet d'un enregistrement tardif, les statistiques des naissances vivantes pour une année donnée peuvent être considérablement faussées. Par exemple, l'âge du père représente presque toujours son âge à la date de l'enregistrement et non à la date de la naissance de l'enfant. Ainsi, dans les pays ou zones où l'enregistrement des naissances est tardif, le retard atteignant parfois plusieurs années, il faut utiliser avec prudence les statistiques concernant les naissances selon l'âge du père.

Un autre facteur qui nuit à la comparabilité internationale est la pratique de certains pays ou zones qui consiste à ne pas inclure dans les statistiques des naissances vivantes les enfants nés vivants mais décédés avant l'enregistrement de leur naissance ou dans les 24 heures qui ont suivi la naissance, pratique qui conduit à sous-estimer le nombre total de naissances vivantes. Quand pareil facteur a joué, cela a été signalé en note à la fin du tableau.

Étant donné que les statistiques du tableau 11 sont classées selon l'âge, elles appellent les mêmes réserves concernant l'exactitude des déclarations d'âge que celles formulées à la section 3.1.3 des Notes techniques. Dans le cas des statistiques de l'état civil, les facteurs qui interviennent à cet égard sont parfois différents, étant donné que le recensement de la population et l'enregistrement des naissances se font par des méthodes différentes, mais, d'une manière générale, les erreurs observées seront les mêmes. Si aucun nombre ne figure dans la rangée réservée aux âges inconnus, cela ne signifie pas nécessairement que les déclarations d'âge et l'exploitation des données par âge ont été tout à fait exactes. C'est souvent une indication que l'on a attribué un âge aux personnes d'âge inconnu avant l'exploitation des données ou qu'elles ont été réparties proportionnellement entre les différents groupes après cette opération.

À l'inverse, lorsque le nombre des personnes d'âge inconnu est important, cela peut signifier que la proportion de naissances parmi les parents célibataires est élevée, étant donné qu'en pareil cas l'acte de naissance ne contient pas tous les renseignements concernant les parents.

Les déclarations par âge peuvent comporter des distorsions, du fait que l'âge du père au moment de la naissance d'un enfant (ou de la déclaration de naissance) est donné par année de naissance et non par date exacte (jour, mois et année).

Dans quelques pays, la classification par âges se réfère aux accouchements, et non aux naissances vivantes, ce qui conduit à un sous-dénombrement en cas de naissances gémellaires. Cette pratique nuit à la comparabilité des données, à la fois entre pays ou zones qui recourent à cette méthode et entre les données présentées dans le tableau 11 et celles du tableau 9.

Les taux présentés dans ce tableau, sont sujets aux mêmes limitations qui affectent les statistiques correspondantes de naissances vivantes. Dans le cas des taux basés sur des naissances par date d'enregistrement et non par date d'occurrence, l'effet peut être visible sur les taux de fécondité par âge des hommes aux âges plus élevés. Dans certains cas, les taux de fécondité des hommes de plus de 55 ans peuvent refléter l'âge du père à l'enregistrement plus que la fécondité à ces âges.

Données publiées antérieurement : Les données sur les naissances vivantes selon l'âge du père et les taux des naissances vivantes selon l'âge du père ont été publié antérieurement dans l'*Annuaire démographique*. Pour plus de précisions concernant les années pour lesquels des données ont été publiées, se reporter à l'index historique.

11. Live births and live birth rates by age of father: latest available year, 2005 - 2014
Naissances vivantes et taux de natalité selon l'âge du père : dernière année disponible, 2005 - 2014

Continent, country or area, year, code[a] and age of father (in years) / Continent, pays ou zone, année, code[a] et âge du père (en années)	Number - Nombre — Both sexes Les deux sexes	Rate Taux
AFRICA - AFRIQUE		
Egypt - Égypte		
2012 (+C)		
Total	2 629 769	101.6
0 - 19	4 700	1.2
20 - 24	119 826	28.3
25 - 29	1 489 063	364.7
30 - 34	502 329	150.1
35 - 39	288 404	111.4
40 - 44	134 381	59.4
45 - 49	60 206	29.0
50 - 54	19 391	10.6
55 - 59	6 333	4.2
60 +	5 136	..
Mauritius - Maurice[1]		
2014 (+C)		
Total	13 283	31.9
0 - 19	190	4.0
20 - 24	1 393	29.0
25 - 29	2 610	62.5
30 - 34	3 983	84.5
35 - 39	2 806	60.4
40 - 44	1 107	27.1
45 - 49	409	9.1
50 - 54	135	3.1
55 - 59	36	1.0
60 - 64	14	..
65 +	4	..
Unknown - Inconnu	596	..
Reunion - Réunion[2]		
2007 (C)		
Total	14 808	61.9
0 - 19	352	10.0
20 - 24	2 409	88.2
25 - 29	3 283	139.4
30 - 34	3 693	141.6
35 - 39	2 860	96.2
40 - 44	1 488	46.6
45 - 49	491	19.2
50 - 54	151	6.8
55 - 59	53	3.0
60 - 64	28	..
AMERICA, NORTH - AMÉRIQUE DU NORD		
Bahamas		
2014* (+U)		
Total	4 196	...
0 - 19	63	...
20 - 24	576	...
25 - 29	742	...
30 - 34	815	...
35 - 39	659	...
40 - 44	388	...
45 - 49	167	...
50 - 54	60	...
55 - 59	23	...
60 - 64	5	..
65 +	6	..
Unknown - Inconnu	692	...
Barbados - Barbade		
2007 (+C)		
Total	3 537	...
0 - 19	95	...
20 - 24	564	...
25 - 29	745	...
30 - 34	784	...

Continent, country or area, year, code[a] and age of father (in years) / Continent, pays ou zone, année, code[a] et âge du père (en années)	Number - Nombre — Both sexes Les deux sexes	Rate Taux
AMERICA, NORTH - AMÉRIQUE DU NORD		
Barbados - Barbade		
2007 (+C)		
35 - 39	605	...
40 - 44	381	...
45 - 49	163	...
50 - 54	53	...
55 - 59	17	...
60 - 64	8	..
65 +	3	..
Unknown - Inconnu	119	..
Canada[3]		
2009 (C)		
Total	380 863	35.1
0 - 19	4 918	4.5
20 - 24	29 959	26.5
25 - 29	84 206	75.0
30 - 34	117 201	109.5
35 - 39	79 126	72.1
40 - 44	31 813	26.9
45 - 49	9 913	7.5
50 - 54	2 642	2.2
55 - 59	683	0.7
60 - 64	200	..
65 +	77	..
Unknown - Inconnu	20 125	..
Costa Rica		
2014* (C)		
Total	71 793	46.9
0 - 19	1 609	10.2
20 - 24	8 250	53.1
25 - 29	11 400	80.6
30 - 34	10 494	88.6
35 - 39	6 681	62.0
40 - 44	3 191	31.4
45 - 49	1 386	14.0
50 - 54	604	6.2
55 - 59	222	2.6
60 - 64	69	..
65 +	5 967	..
Unknown - Inconnu	21 920	..
Cuba		
2013 (C)		
Total	125 880	34.8
0 - 19	2 807	8.7
20 - 24	22 500	59.7
25 - 29	31 090	88.3
30 - 34	21 906	76.0
35 - 39	16 173	44.8
40 - 44	10 954	24.4
45 - 49	4 779	10.5
50 - 54	1 399	4.0
55 - 59	356	1.3
60 - 64	168	..
65 +	80	..
Unknown - Inconnu	13 668	..
Dominican Republic - République dominicaine		
2013 (U)		
Total	130 402	...
0 - 19	2 535	...
20 - 24	21 826	...
25 - 29	29 445	...
30 - 34	27 052	...
35 - 39	16 410	...
40 - 44	8 669	...
45 - 49	4 250	...
50 - 54	1 986	...
55 - 59	917	...

11. Live births and live birth rates by age of father: latest available year, 2005 - 2014
Naissances vivantes et taux de natalité selon l'âge du père : dernière année disponible, 2005 - 2014 (continued - suite)

Continent, country or area, year, code[a] and age of father (in years) Continent, pays ou zone, année, code[a] et âge du père (en années)	Number - Nombre Both sexes Les deux sexes	Rate Taux
AMERICA, NORTH - AMÉRIQUE DU NORD		
Dominican Republic - République dominicaine		
2013 (U)		
60 - 64	*348*	..
65 +	*210*	..
Unknown - Inconnu	*16 754*	..
El Salvador		
2011 (C)		
Total	109 384	65.6
0 - 19	6 580	21.5
20 - 24	22 778	94.9
25 - 29	22 364	122.7
30 - 34	19 678	125.6
35 - 39	11 744	80.1
40 - 44	6 226	47.8
45 - 49	3 029	27.3
50 - 54	1 396	14.8
55 - 59	693	8.5
60 - 64	347	..
65 +	266	..
Unknown - Inconnu	14 283	..
Greenland - Groenland		
2008 (C)		
Total	834	...
0 - 19	25	...
20 - 24	109	...
25 - 29	169	...
30 - 34	150	...
35 - 39	112	...
40 - 44	91	...
45 - 49	35	...
50 - 54	9	...
55 - 59	1	...
60 +	-	..
Unknown - Inconnu	133	..
Guatemala		
2011 (C)		
Total	373 692	...
0 - 19	23 425	...
20 - 24	82 898	...
25 - 29	83 786	...
30 - 34	64 952	...
35 - 39	39 412	...
40 - 44	20 601	...
45 - 49	9 366	...
50 - 54	3 893	...
55 - 59	1 723	...
60 - 64	769	..
65 +	556	..
Unknown - Inconnu	42 311	..
Jamaica - Jamaïque[4]		
2006 (C)		
Total	42 399	...
0 - 19	496	...
20 - 24	3 756	...
25 - 29	5 341	...
30 - 34	5 069	...
35 - 39	3 635	...
40 - 44	2 166	...
45 - 49	986	...
50 - 54	373	...
55 - 59	131	...
60 - 64	53	..
65 +	37	..
Unknown - Inconnu	20 356	..

Continent, country or area, year, code[a] and age of father (in years) Continent, pays ou zone, année, code[a] et âge du père (en années)	Number - Nombre Both sexes Les deux sexes	Rate Taux
AMERICA, NORTH - AMÉRIQUE DU NORD		
Martinique[2]		
2007 (C)		
Total	5 317	47.3
0 - 19	98	6.2
20 - 24	710	60.7
25 - 29	1 043	119.9
30 - 34	1 173	111.7
35 - 39	1 293	95.6
40 - 44	702	46.1
45 - 49	235	16.2
50 - 54	42	3.5
55 - 59	16	♦1.5
60 +	3	..
Mexico - Mexique[5]		
2011 (C)		
Total	2 262 024	...
0 - 19	149 890	...
20 - 24	501 228	...
25 - 29	535 713	...
30 - 34	417 041	...
35 - 39	255 125	...
40 - 44	111 471	...
45 - 49	44 389	...
50 - 54	16 394	...
55 - 59	6 688	...
60 - 64	2 776	..
65 +	1 779	..
Unknown - Inconnu	219 530	..
Panama		
2013 (C)		
Total	73 804	61.9
0 - 19	3 002	23.7
20 - 24	11 723	98.5
25 - 29	13 348	116.4
30 - 34	11 540	105.3
35 - 39	7 698	73.6
40 - 44	4 386	45.2
45 - 49	1 776	21.0
50 - 54	769	10.7
55 - 59	291	5.2
60 - 64	148	..
65 +	94	..
Unknown - Inconnu	19 029	..
Puerto Rico - Porto Rico		
2014 (C)		
Total	34 485	...
0 - 19	1 913	...
20 - 24	8 802	...
25 - 29	8 776	...
30 - 34	6 838	...
35 - 39	3 912	...
40 - 44	1 782	...
45 - 49	627	...
50 - 54	211	...
55 - 59	75	...
60 - 64	35	...
65 +	16	...
Unknown - Inconnu	1 498	...
Trinidad and Tobago - Trinité-et-Tobago		
2006 (C)		
Total	18 090	...
0 - 19	400	...
20 - 24	3 291	...
25 - 29	4 889	...
30 - 34	4 079	...
35 - 39	2 713	...
40 - 44	1 491	...

Continent, country or area, year, code[a] and age of father (in years) / Continent, pays ou zone, année, code[a] et âge du père (en années)	Number - Nombre Both sexes Les deux sexes	Rate Taux
AMERICA, NORTH - AMÉRIQUE DU NORD		
Trinidad and Tobago - Trinité-et-Tobago		
2006 (C)		
45 - 49	616	...
50 - 54	248	...
55 - 59	87	...
60 +	45	..
Unknown - Inconnu	231	..
United States of America - États-Unis d'Amérique		
2013 (C)		
Total	3 932 181	...
0 - 19	93 205	...
20 - 24	509 846	...
25 - 29	860 750	...
30 - 34	990 827	...
35 - 39	601 402	...
40 - 44	256 761	...
45 - 49	84 250	...
50 - 54	27 339	...
55 +	11 578	...
Unknown - Inconnu	496 223	..
AMERICA, SOUTH - AMÉRIQUE DU SUD		
Chile - Chili		
2012 (C)		
Total	243 635	43.3
0 - 19	14 604	22.4
20 - 24	42 490	63.3
25 - 29	48 366	77.3
30 - 34	50 384	90.6
35 - 39	35 666	65.6
40 - 44	17 280	31.4
45 - 49	6 707	12.2
50 +	3 449	3.8
Unknown - Inconnu	24 689	..
Colombia - Colombie		
2012 (U)		
Total	676 835	...
0 - 19	45 480	...
20 - 24	160 092	...
25 - 29	166 947	...
30 - 34	135 349	...
35 - 39	78 149	...
40 - 44	41 088	...
45 - 49	17 051	...
50 - 54	7 251	...
55 - 59	2 367	...
60 - 64	970	..
65 +	428	..
Unknown - Inconnu	21 663	..
Ecuador - Équateur		
2011 (+U)		
Total	229 780	...
0 - 19	4 219	...
20 - 24	16 514	...
25 - 29	17 040	...
30 - 34	14 115	...
35 - 39	8 339	...
40 - 44	4 405	...
45 - 49	1 864	...
50 - 54	719	...
55 - 59	274	...
60 - 64	104	..
65 +	94	..
Unknown - Inconnu	162 093	..

Continent, country or area, year, code[a] and age of father (in years) / Continent, pays ou zone, année, code[a] et âge du père (en années)	Number - Nombre Both sexes Les deux sexes	Rate Taux
AMERICA, SOUTH - AMÉRIQUE DU SUD		
French Guiana - Guyane française[2]		
2007 (C)		
Total	6 386	104.6
0 - 19	323	32.6
20 - 24	1 263	164.2
25 - 29	1 401	203.5
30 - 34	1 334	175.5
35 - 39	1 043	138.4
40 - 44	622	90.0
45 - 49	230	38.8
50 - 54	94	19.2
55 - 59	59	16.1
60 - 64	17	..
65 +	-	..
Uruguay		
2013 (C)		
Total	48 681	...
0 - 19	1 457	...
20 - 24	5 101	...
25 - 29	6 715	...
30 - 34	7 736	...
35 - 39	5 969	...
40 - 44	2 713	...
45 - 49	1 024	...
50 - 54	444	...
55 - 59	143	...
60 - 64	46	..
65 +	22	..
Unknown - Inconnu	17 311	..
Venezuela (Bolivarian Republic of) - Venezuela (République bolivarienne du)		
2013 (C)		
Total	597 902	63.9
0 - 19	36 725	32.3
20 - 24	116 236	104.2
25 - 29	123 283	116.4
30 - 34	99 547	104.0
35 - 39	59 443	70.2
40 - 44	31 060	41.3
45 - 49	13 866	19.8
50 +	10 135	9.2
Unknown - Inconnu	107 607	..
ASIA - ASIE		
Azerbaijan - Azerbaïdjan[6]		
2013 (+C)		
Total	158 195	49.6
0 - 19	426	1.0
20 - 24	25 221	53.8
25 - 29	62 750	139.6
30 - 34	42 094	108.7
35 - 39	18 217	57.4
40 - 44	6 662	21.7
45 - 49	2 005	6.4
50 - 54	588	1.9
55 +	232	1.0
Bahrain - Bahreïn		
2013 (C)		
Total	19 995	31.4
0 - 19	28	♦0.8
20 - 24	1 310	20.4
25 - 29	4 630	36.4
30 - 34	5 690	45.5
35 - 39	4 454	48.6
40 - 44	2 391	33.1

11. Live births and live birth rates by age of father: latest available year, 2005 - 2014

Naissances vivantes et taux de natalité selon l'âge du père : dernière année disponible, 2005 - 2014 (continued - suite)

Continent, country or area, year, code[a] and age of father (in years) Continent, pays ou zone, année, code[a] et âge du père (en années)	Number - Nombre Both sexes Les deux sexes	Rate Taux	Continent, country or area, year, code[a] and age of father (in years) Continent, pays ou zone, année, code[a] et âge du père (en années)	Number - Nombre Both sexes Les deux sexes	Rate Taux
ASIA - ASIE			**ASIA - ASIE**		
Bahrain - Bahreïn			**Israel - Israël[8]**		
2013 (C)			2013 (C)		
45 - 49	949	17.7	45 - 49	4 242	21.8
50 - 54	347	8.9	50 - 54	1 096	6.0
55 - 59	137	5.2	55 - 59	342	2.0
60 - 64	37	..	60 - 64	127	..
65 +	17	..	65 +	81	..
Unknown - Inconnu	5	..	Unknown - Inconnu	8 438	..
Brunei Darussalam - Brunéi Darussalam			**Japan - Japon[9]**		
2008 (+C)			2013 (C)		
Total	6 424	...	Total	1 007 026	28.7
0 - 19	23	...	0 - 19	4 066	1.3
20 - 24	466	...	20 - 24	56 870	17.8
25 - 29	1 612	...	25 - 29	220 104	62.4
30 - 34	1 733	...	30 - 34	335 098	86.1
35 - 39	1 125	...	35 - 39	255 586	55.1
40 - 44	555	...	40 - 44	103 593	21.3
45 - 49	212	...	45 - 49	24 115	5.8
50 - 54	57	...	50 - 54	5 415	1.4
55 +	23	...	55 - 59	1 459	0.4
Unknown - Inconnu	618	...	60 - 64	555	..
China, Hong Kong SAR - Chine, Hong Kong RAS			65 +	165	..
2013 (C)			Unknown - Inconnu	-	..
Total	57 084	25.7	**Kazakhstan[10]**		
0 - 19	122	0.6	2006 (C)		
20 - 24	1 821	8.2	Total	301 756	61.4
25 - 29	7 898	36.3	0 - 19	2 897	4.2
30 - 34	17 835	78.4	20 - 24	46 772	73.1
35 - 39	15 816	70.2	25 - 29	82 596	152.2
40 - 44	7 742	32.9	30 - 34	66 344	134.3
45 - 49	2 923	11.0	35 - 39	41 180	90.8
50 - 54	1 219	4.0	40 - 44	17 594	38.6
55 - 59	421	1.5	45 - 49	4 336	10.0
60 - 64	157	..	50 - 54	873	2.7
65 +	70	..	55 - 59	296	1.2
Unknown - Inconnu	1 060	..	60 - 64	74	..
China, Macao SAR - Chine, Macao RAS			65 +	74	..
2014 (C)			Unknown - Inconnu	38 720	..
Total	7 360	32.2	**Kyrgyzstan - Kirghizstan**		
0 - 24	399	9.8	2013 (C)		
25 - 29	2 199	64.2	Total	155 520	...
30 - 34	2 220	76.0	0 - 19	596	...
35 - 39	1 330	56.1	20 - 24	21 340	...
40 - 44	663	27.2	25 - 29	48 049	...
45 +	453	6.2	30 - 34	33 609	...
Unknown - Inconnu	96	..	35 - 39	19 815	...
Cyprus - Chypre[7]			40 - 44	9 460	...
2013 (C)			45 - 49	2 708	...
Total	9 341	34.7	50 - 54	751	...
0 - 19	26	♦0.9	55 - 59	203	...
20 - 24	425	12.5	60 - 64	75	...
25 - 29	2 057	57.9	65 +	34	...
30 - 34	3 332	99.3	Unknown - Inconnu	18 880	..
35 - 39	2 094	75.0	**Malaysia - Malaisie**		
40 - 44	785	29.3	2011 (C)		
45 - 49	292	11.1	Total	511 594	53.8
50 +	143	2.7	0 - 19	3 042	2.3
Unknown - Inconnu	187	..	20 - 24	33 865	27.0
Israel - Israël[8]			25 - 29	128 787	109.6
2013 (C)			30 - 34	146 537	132.0
Total	171 444	75.0	35 - 39	99 237	95.4
0 - 19	373	1.2	40 - 44	50 669	51.7
20 - 24	13 695	47.4	45 - 49	19 635	22.2
25 - 29	37 664	135.2	50 - 54	6 241	8.3
30 - 34	51 366	192.2	55 - 59	1 959	3.3
35 - 39	38 129	147.5	60 - 64	516	..
40 - 44	15 891	69.4			

11. Live births and live birth rates by age of father: latest available year, 2005 - 2014

Naissances vivantes et taux de natalité selon l'âge du père : dernière année disponible, 2005 - 2014 (continued - suite)

Continent, country or area, year, code[a] and age of father (in years) Continent, pays ou zone, année, code[a] et âge du père (en années)	Number - Nombre Both sexes Les deux sexes	Rate Taux	Continent, country or area, year, code[a] and age of father (in years) Continent, pays ou zone, année, code[a] et âge du père (en années)	Number - Nombre Both sexes Les deux sexes	Rate Taux
ASIA - ASIE			**ASIA - ASIE**		
Malaysia - Malaisie			**Republic of Korea - République de Corée**[12]		
2011 (C)			2013 (C)		
65 +	241	..	30 - 34	193 995	95.2
Unknown - Inconnu	20 865	..	35 - 39	131 473	67.0
Maldives			40 - 44	40 043	18.2
2013 (C)			45 - 49	6 723	3.2
Total	7 153	63.3	50 - 54	1 334	0.6
0 - 19	7	♦0.4	55 - 59	257	0.2
20 - 24	721	35.3	60 - 64	38	..
25 - 29	2 347	124.8	65 +	17	..
30 - 34	1 804	130.3	Unknown - Inconnu	5 064	..
35 - 39	1 176	111.0	**Singapore - Singapour**		
40 - 44	628	67.8	2014 (C)		
45 - 49	255	31.3	Total	42 232	32.9
50 - 54	60	8.2	0 - 19	93	0.7
55 - 59	36	7.2	20 - 24	1 014	7.7
60 - 64	7	..	25 - 29	6 226	48.7
65 +	4	..	30 - 34	15 323	111.5
Unknown - Inconnu	108	..	35 - 39	12 121	84.6
Oman[11]			40 - 44	4 838	31.7
2011 (U)			45 - 49	1 497	9.9
Total	*67 922*	...	50 - 54	448	2.9
0 - 19	*46*	...	55 - 59	131	0.9
20 - 24	*3 572*	...	60 - 64	47	..
25 - 29	*17 681*	...	65 +	18	..
30 - 34	*19 930*	...	Unknown - Inconnu	476	..
35 - 39	*12 744*	...	**Turkey - Turquie**		
40 - 44	*6 637*	...	2013 (C)		
45 - 49	*3 190*	...	Total	1 283 062	51.5
50 - 54	*1 343*	...	0 - 19	8 340	2.5
55 - 59	*573*	...	20 - 24	114 765	36.6
60 - 64	*328*	..	25 - 29	379 333	120.2
65 +	*368*	..	30 - 34	411 193	125.7
Unknown - Inconnu	*1 510*	..	35 - 39	227 874	78.2
Philippines			40 - 44	91 753	34.7
2012 (C)			45 - 49	26 252	11.1
Total	1 790 367	61.0	50 - 54	6 475	3.1
0 - 19	50 942	10.8	55 - 59	2 045	1.2
20 - 24	336 210	80.0	60 - 64	775	..
25 - 29	434 400	118.5	65 +	467	..
30 - 34	386 932	117.0	Unknown - Inconnu	13 790	..
35 - 39	243 027	81.8			
40 - 44	132 535	49.6	**EUROPE**		
45 - 49	52 538	22.6			
50 - 54	17 850	9.2	**Åland Islands - Îles d'Åland**		
55 - 59	6 380	4.2	2012 (C)		
60 - 64	2 601	..	Total	292	35.4
65 +	1 521	..	0 - 19	-	-
Unknown - Inconnu	125 431	..	20 - 24	20	♦25.1
Qatar			25 - 29	57	76.1
2010 (C)			30 - 34	83	100.3
Total	19 504	16.9	35 - 39	77	87.8
0 - 19	17	♦0.5	40 - 44	25	♦27.3
20 - 24	1 050	6.8	45 - 49	10	♦10.2
25 - 29	3 770	17.0	50 - 54	2	♦2.2
30 - 34	5 727	26.3	55 - 59	1	♦1.1
35 - 39	4 537	23.2	60 - 64	-	..
40 - 44	2 584	17.2	65 +	-	..
45 - 49	1 179	12.2	Unknown - Inconnu	17	..
50 +	637	7.5	**Albania - Albanie**		
Unknown - Inconnu	3	..	2013 (C)		
Republic of Korea - République de Corée[12]			Total	35 750	38.5
2013 (C)			0 - 19	113	0.9
Total	436 455	24.8	20 - 24	2 620	21.0
0 - 19	726	0.4	25 - 29	10 354	94.0
20 - 24	6 306	3.5	30 - 34	11 683	129.2
25 - 29	50 479	29.2			

11. Live births and live birth rates by age of father: latest available year, 2005 - 2014
Naissances vivantes et taux de natalité selon l'âge du père : dernière année disponible, 2005 - 2014 (continued - suite)

Continent, country or area, year, code[a] and age of father (in years) Continent, pays ou zone, année, code[a] et âge du père (en années)	Number - Nombre Both sexes Les deux sexes	Rate Taux	Continent, country or area, year, code[a] and age of father (in years) Continent, pays ou zone, année, code[a] et âge du père (en années)	Number - Nombre Both sexes Les deux sexes	Rate Taux
EUROPE			EUROPE		
Albania - Albanie			Bulgaria - Bulgarie		
2013 (C)			2012 (C)		
35 - 39	6 619	81.8	Total	69 121	30.8
40 - 44	2 667	30.3	0 - 19	834	5.7
45 - 49	768	8.2	20 - 24	6 247	31.5
50 - 54	183	1.8	25 - 29	14 643	69.8
55 - 59	33	0.4	30 - 34	17 865	81.0
60 - 64	15	..	35 - 39	11 930	50.6
65 +	14	..	40 - 44	4 065	18.2
Unknown - Inconnu	681	..	45 - 49	1 071	5.3
Austria - Autriche[13]			50 - 54	325	1.6
2013 (C)			55 - 59	96	0.5
Total	46 477	17.7	60 - 64	34	..
0 - 19	66	0.3	65 +	12	..
20 - 24	2 285	8.3	Unknown - Inconnu	11 999	..
25 - 29	8 964	32.3	Croatia - Croatie		
30 - 34	15 393	55.0	2013 (C)		
35 - 39	11 440	41.9	Total	39 939	31.0
40 - 44	5 568	17.1	0 - 19	228	1.9
45 - 49	1 949	5.4	20 - 24	2 640	20.9
50 - 54	563	1.7	25 - 29	9 296	67.2
55 - 59	161	0.6	30 - 34	13 748	93.6
60 - 64	68	..	35 - 39	8 524	60.2
65 +	20	..	40 - 44	3 231	23.6
Belarus - Bélarus[13]			45 - 49	976	6.7
2013 (C)			50 - 54	298	2.0
Total	98 991	33.0	55 - 59	66	0.4
0 - 19	876	3.4	60 - 64	21	..
20 - 24	15 731	43.0	65 +	2	..
25 - 29	36 546	91.5	Unknown - Inconnu	909	..
30 - 34	27 117	76.5	Czech Republic - République tchèque		
35 - 39	12 807	39.4	2013 (C)		
40 - 44	4 312	13.8	Total	106 751	32.5
45 - 49	1 138	3.5	0 - 19	496	2.1
50 - 54	346	1.0	20 - 24	5 010	16.2
55 +	118	0.4	25 - 29	18 719	55.7
Belgium - Belgique			30 - 34	34 895	90.9
2010 (C)			35 - 39	26 436	59.9
Total	130 100	39.7	40 - 44	8 486	24.1
0 - 19	659	2.1	45 - 49	2 634	7.9
20 - 24	7 464	24.1	50 - 54	790	2.7
25 - 29	30 127	93.6	55 - 59	337	1.0
30 - 34	41 391	126.4	60 - 64	91	..
35 - 39	25 239	71.6	65 +	32	..
40 - 44	10 766	28.8	Unknown - Inconnu	8 825	..
45 - 49	3 930	10.2	Denmark - Danemark[14]		
50 - 54	1 222	3.4	2013 (C)		
55 - 59	377	1.2	Total	55 873	33.7
60 - 64	139	..	0 - 19	120	0.7
65 +	33	..	20 - 24	2 507	15.1
Unknown - Inconnu	8 753	..	25 - 29	11 135	74.8
Bosnia and Herzegovina - Bosnie-Herzégovine			30 - 34	17 733	121.3
2010 (C)			35 - 39	12 160	73.3
Total	33 528	28.0	40 - 44	4 576	26.1
0 - 19	99	0.7	45 - 49	1 462	7.5
20 - 24	3 174	23.3	50 - 54	386	2.3
25 - 29	9 300	75.0	55 - 59	98	0.6
30 - 34	10 238	90.1	60 - 64	45	..
35 - 39	5 624	49.2	65 +	16	..
40 - 44	2 203	16.5	Unknown - Inconnu	5 635	..
45 - 49	672	4.8	Estonia - Estonie		
50 - 54	150	1.2	2013 (C)		
55 - 59	29	0.3	Total	13 531	34.2
60 - 64	9	..	0 - 19	100	3.2
65 +	4	..	20 - 24	1 207	26.8
Unknown - Inconnu	2 026	..	25 - 29	3 366	71.4
			30 - 34	3 751	85.4

11. Live births and live birth rates by age of father: latest available year, 2005 - 2014

Naissances vivantes et taux de natalité selon l'âge du père : dernière année disponible, 2005 - 2014 (continued - suite)

Continent, country or area, year, code[a] and age of father (in years) / Continent, pays ou zone, année, code[a] et âge du père (en années)	Number - Nombre — Both sexes Les deux sexes	Rate Taux
EUROPE		
Estonia - Estonie		
2013 (C)		
35 - 39	2 625	59.8
40 - 44	1 197	27.5
45 - 49	381	9.7
50 - 54	126	3.0
55 - 59	26	♦0.7
60 - 64	9	..
65 +	4	..
Unknown - Inconnu	739	..
Finland - Finlande[15]		
2012 (C)		
Total	59 201	37.4
0 - 19	416	2.6
20 - 24	4 760	28.8
25 - 29	14 189	83.8
30 - 34	18 786	111.2
35 - 39	12 015	74.9
40 - 44	4 643	28.6
45 - 49	1 609	8.9
50 - 54	469	2.6
55 - 59	137	0.8
60 - 64	32	..
65 +	13	..
Unknown - Inconnu	2 132	..
France[16]		
2013 (C)		
Total	781 621	43.0
0 - 19	2 874	1.5
20 - 24	45 946	23.7
25 - 29	173 301	91.9
30 - 34	256 974	130.2
35 - 39	176 030	87.5
40 - 44	83 507	38.0
45 - 49	28 753	13.2
50 - 54	9 647	4.7
55 - 59	3 279	1.7
60 - 64	1 165	..
65 +	145	..
Germany - Allemagne		
2013 (C)		
Total	682 069	28.0
0 - 19	2 310	1.2
20 - 24	34 137	15.2
25 - 29	119 349	50.5
30 - 34	203 946	86.8
35 - 39	157 907	72.5
40 - 44	79 327	29.7
45 - 49	28 094	8.6
50 - 54	7 447	2.4
55 - 59	1 942	0.7
60 - 64	594	..
65 +	276	..
Unknown - Inconnu	46 740	..
Greece - Grèce		
2012 (C)		
Total	100 371	30.3
0 - 19	157	0.6
20 - 24	1 974	6.6
25 - 29	12 772	37.6
30 - 34	32 168	81.7
35 - 39	28 230	72.4
40 - 44	12 642	32.1
45 - 49	3 902	10.9
50 - 54	998	3.0
55 - 59	254	0.8
60 - 64	62	..

Continent, country or area, year, code[a] and age of father (in years) / Continent, pays ou zone, année, code[a] et âge du père (en années)	Number - Nombre — Both sexes Les deux sexes	Rate Taux
EUROPE		
Greece - Grèce		
2012 (C)		
65 +	18	..
Unknown - Inconnu	7 194	..
Hungary - Hongrie		
2013 (C)		
Total	89 524	29.5
0 - 19	1 097	4.4
20 - 24	5 354	19.1
25 - 29	12 891	47.6
30 - 34	24 762	80.9
35 - 39	22 123	59.1
40 - 44	7 985	25.2
45 - 49	2 382	8.6
50 - 54	699	2.7
55 - 59	245	0.8
60 - 64	95	..
65 +	30	..
Unknown - Inconnu	11 861	..
Iceland - Islande		
2013 (C)		
Total	4 326	43.2
0 - 19	31	2.7
20 - 24	412	33.2
25 - 29	1 015	90.6
30 - 34	1 387	118.3
35 - 39	837	79.3
40 - 44	396	38.5
45 - 49	116	11.1
50 - 54	42	4.0
55 - 59	10	♦1.0
60 - 64	5	..
65 +	2	..
Unknown - Inconnu	73	..
Ireland - Irlande		
2006 (+C)		
Total	64 237	46.8
0 - 19	714	5.1
20 - 24	4 382	26.9
25 - 29	10 351	57.1
30 - 34	19 695	121.1
35 - 39	16 702	111.2
40 - 44	6 268	45.2
45 - 49	1 585	12.4
50 - 54	374	3.2
55 - 59	119	1.1
60 - 64	27	..
65 +	6	..
Unknown - Inconnu	4 014	..
Italy - Italie		
2013 (+C)		
Total	514 308	29.2
0 - 19	1 588	1.2
20 - 24	16 076	11.1
25 - 29	59 852	39.6
30 - 34	133 899	79.0
35 - 39	147 179	72.2
40 - 44	79 236	36.0
45 - 49	24 840	11.1
50 - 54	6 247	3.2
55 - 59	1 633	0.9
60 - 64	453	..
65 +	160	..
Unknown - Inconnu	43 145	..

11. Live births and live birth rates by age of father: latest available year, 2005 - 2014
Naissances vivantes et taux de natalité selon l'âge du père : dernière année disponible, 2005 - 2014 (continued - suite)

Continent, country or area, year, code[a] and age of father (in years) Continent, pays ou zone, année, code[a] et âge du père (en années)	Number - Nombre Both sexes Les deux sexes	Rate Taux	Continent, country or area, year, code[a] and age of father (in years) Continent, pays ou zone, année, code[a] et âge du père (en années)	Number - Nombre Both sexes Les deux sexes	Rate Taux
EUROPE			**EUROPE**		
Latvia - Lettonie			**Montenegro - Monténégro**		
2013 (C)			2009 (C)		
Total	20 596	34.5	35 - 39	1 574	85.9
0 - 19	147	3.1	40 - 44	800	43.7
20 - 24	1 935	28.4	45 - 49	287	14.9
25 - 29	5 517	76.2	50 - 54	89	4.6
30 - 34	5 813	90.1	55 - 59	23	♦1.3
35 - 39	3 609	56.9	60 - 64	1	..
40 - 44	1 726	26.6	65 +	6	..
45 - 49	589	9.4	Unknown - Inconnu	935	..
50 - 54	215	3.2	**Netherlands - Pays-Bas[17]**		
55 - 59	67	1.1	2010 (C)		
60 - 64	23	..	Total	184 397	36.4
65 +	12	..	0 - 19	284	0.6
Unknown - Inconnu	943	..	20 - 24	5 721	11.6
Lithuania - Lituanie			25 - 29	29 787	62.2
2013 (C)			30 - 34	60 664	127.1
Total	29 885	33.8	35 - 39	49 829	91.0
0 - 19	226	2.5	40 - 44	21 179	34.0
20 - 24	2 836	27.2	45 - 49	5 812	9.4
25 - 29	8 823	93.5	50 - 54	1 479	2.6
30 - 34	8 873	105.7	55 - 59	379	0.7
35 - 39	4 823	55.8	60 - 64	116	..
40 - 44	1 915	20.0	65 +	37	..
45 - 49	565	5.8	Unknown - Inconnu	9 110	..
50 - 54	202	1.9	**Norway - Norvège**		
55 - 59	53	0.6	2012 (C)		
60 - 64	16	..	Total	60 255	38.8
65 +	-	..	0 - 19	271	1.7
Unknown - Inconnu	1 553	..	20 - 24	3 931	23.9
Luxembourg			25 - 29	13 332	83.2
2013 (C)			30 - 34	19 068	116.9
Total	6 115	34.9	35 - 39	13 188	76.5
0 - 19	21	♦1.3	40 - 44	5 590	30.1
20 - 24	251	15.2	45 - 49	1 822	10.3
25 - 29	1 027	55.4	50 - 54	524	3.3
30 - 34	1 985	99.6	55 - 59	176	1.2
35 - 39	1 544	77.5	60 - 64	47	..
40 - 44	748	34.8	65 +	9	..
45 - 49	261	11.7	Unknown - Inconnu	2 297	..
50 - 54	69	3.6	**Poland - Pologne**		
55 - 59	30	1.8	2012 (C)		
60 - 64	8	..	Total	386 257	31.0
65 +	4	..	0 - 19	2 231	2.0
Unknown - Inconnu	167	..	20 - 24	33 640	25.1
Malta - Malte			25 - 29	114 291	73.3
2013 (C)			30 - 34	126 439	82.1
Total	4 032	30.4	35 - 39	65 320	46.2
0 - 19	36	2.9	40 - 44	20 696	17.5
20 - 24	259	17.5	45 - 49	6 013	5.2
25 - 29	810	53.0	50 - 54	1 819	1.4
30 - 34	1 419	92.9	55 - 59	577	0.4
35 - 39	922	62.7	60 +	217	..
40 - 44	291	22.9	Unknown - Inconnu	15 014	..
45 - 49	66	5.3	**Portugal[5]**		
50 - 54	26	♦1.8	2013 (C)		
55 - 59	11	♦0.8	Total	82 787	27.3
60 - 64	4	..	0 - 19	922	3.4
65 +	-	..	20 - 24	5 624	20.0
Unknown - Inconnu	188	..	25 - 29	14 900	51.2
Montenegro - Monténégro			30 - 34	26 685	79.5
2009 (C)			35 - 39	21 548	55.3
Total	8 642	43.2	40 - 44	8 061	21.5
0 - 19	32	1.5	45 - 49	2 354	6.5
20 - 24	616	27.3	50 - 54	749	2.1
25 - 29	2 011	90.0	55 - 59	275	0.9
30 - 34	2 268	113.7	60 - 64	67	..

11. Live births and live birth rates by age of father: latest available year, 2005 - 2014
Naissances vivantes et taux de natalité selon l'âge du père : dernière année disponible, 2005 - 2014 (continued - suite)

Continent, country or area, year, code[a] and age of father (in years) / Continent, pays ou zone, année, code[a] et âge du père (en années)	Number - Nombre Both sexes Les deux sexes	Rate Taux	Continent, country or area, year, code[a] and age of father (in years) / Continent, pays ou zone, année, code[a] et âge du père (en années)	Number - Nombre Both sexes Les deux sexes	Rate Taux
EUROPE			**EUROPE**		
Portugal[5]			**Serbia - Serbie[19]**		
2013 (C)			2013 (+C)		
65 +	22	..	30 - 34	20 042	89.0
Unknown - Inconnu	1 580		35 - 39	12 658	55.5
Republic of Moldova - République de Moldova[18]			40 - 44	4 244	19.9
2012 (C)			45 - 49	1 235	5.9
Total	39 435	32.8	50 - 54	375	1.7
0 - 19	269	2.3	55 - 59	106	0.4
20 - 24	6 290	41.0	60 - 64	42	..
25 - 29	13 306	84.1	65 +	7	..
30 - 34	8 980	67.6	Unknown - Inconnu	6 756	..
35 - 39	4 561	40.4	**Slovakia - Slovaquie[13]**		
40 - 44	1 640	16.5	2013 (C)		
45 - 49	446	4.4	Total	34 547	19.4
50 - 54	142	1.2	0 - 19	272	1.7
55 - 59	31	0.3	20 - 24	1 943	9.9
60 - 64	14	..	25 - 29	7 374	34.0
65 +	3	..	30 - 34	12 990	56.3
Unknown - Inconnu	3 753	..	35 - 39	8 671	37.3
Romania - Roumanie			40 - 44	2 527	13.2
2013 (C)			45 - 49	566	3.1
Total	182 313	29.3	50 - 54	141	0.8
0 - 19	2 763	5.3	55 - 59	44	0.2
20 - 24	17 890	29.9	60 - 64	13	..
25 - 29	45 053	67.9	65 +	6	..
30 - 34	54 102	79.4	**Slovenia - Slovénie**		
35 - 39	34 032	45.2	2013 (C)		
40 - 44	11 901	15.5	Total	21 111	32.3
45 - 49	3 501	5.5	0 - 19	55	1.1
50 - 54	893	1.6	20 - 24	972	16.8
55 - 59	281	0.4	25 - 29	4 846	68.3
60 - 64	99	..	30 - 34	7 748	96.8
65 +	25	..	35 - 39	4 915	61.6
Unknown - Inconnu	11 773	..	40 - 44	1 621	21.7
Russian Federation - Fédération de Russie[10]			45 - 49	478	6.1
2012 (C)			50 - 54	130	1.7
Total	1 902 084	41.9	55 - 59	36	0.5
0 - 19	12 731	3.9	60 - 64	5	..
20 - 24	256 939	51.4	65 +	5	..
25 - 29	564 777	103.0	Unknown - Inconnu	300	..
30 - 34	431 851	88.4	**Spain - Espagne**		
35 - 39	245 613	55.2	2013 (C)		
40 - 44	102 880	25.6	Total	424 440	29.3
45 - 49	33 963	8.4	0 - 19	2 376	2.2
50 - 54	11 671	2.5	20 - 24	15 288	12.8
55 - 59	3 196	0.8	25 - 29	48 689	35.2
60 +	1 203	..	30 - 34	132 325	74.8
Unknown - Inconnu	237 260	..	35 - 39	139 743	68.7
San Marino - Saint-Marin			40 - 44	56 906	29.5
2013 (+C)			45 - 49	14 741	8.1
Total	320	31.8	50 - 54	3 910	2.4
0 - 19	-	-	55 - 59	1 056	0.8
20 - 24	3	♦4.1	60 - 64	291	..
25 - 29	26	♦32.4	65 +	106	..
30 - 34	78	78.8	Unknown - Inconnu	9 009	..
35 - 39	105	81.1	**Sweden - Suède**		
40 - 44	60	42.2	2012 (C)		
45 - 49	25	♦16.7	Total	113 177	40.2
50 - 54	14	♦11.0	0 - 19	443	1.5
55 +	-	-	20 - 24	7 043	21.2
Unknown - Inconnu	9	..	25 - 29	23 661	77.8
Serbia - Serbie[19]			30 - 34	36 139	122.1
2013 (+C)			35 - 39	26 932	86.6
Total	65 554	30.4	40 - 44	11 433	35.6
0 - 19	403	2.2	45 - 49	4 023	12.0
20 - 24	4 588	23.3	50 - 54	1 169	4.0
25 - 29	15 098	69.5	55 - 59	404	1.4

Continent, country or area, year, code[a] and age of father (in years) / Continent, pays ou zone, année, code[a] et âge du père (en années)	Number - Nombre — Both sexes Les deux sexes	Rate Taux
EUROPE		
Sweden - Suède		
2012 (C)		
60 - 64	116	..
65 +	52	..
Unknown - Inconnu	1 762	..
Switzerland - Suisse[13]		
2012 (C)		
Total	65 587	26.2
0 - 19	15	♦0.1
20 - 24	1 491	5.9
25 - 29	9 815	37.0
30 - 34	21 372	76.6
35 - 39	19 263	69.8
40 - 44	10 241	33.3
45 - 49	2 125	6.3
50 - 54	864	2.8
55 - 59	245	0.9
60 - 64	94	..
65 +	62	..
Unknown - Inconnu	-	..
TFYR of Macedonia - L'ex-R. y. de Macédoine		
2012 (C)		
Total	23 568	34.3
0 - 19	197	2.8
20 - 24	2 321	29.6
25 - 29	6 789	84.7
30 - 34	7 672	98.1
35 - 39	3 842	52.2
40 - 44	1 194	17.0
45 - 49	326	4.6
50 - 54	83	1.2
55 - 59	23	♦0.4
60 - 64	6	..
65 +	3	..
Unknown - Inconnu	1 112	..
Ukraine[20]		
2013 (+C)		
Total	503 657	35.8
0 - 19	4 125	3.9
20 - 24	67 513	48.1
25 - 29	149 940	88.2
30 - 34	116 549	75.0
35 - 39	64 684	45.9
40 - 44	25 378	19.2
45 - 49	7 518	6.0
50 - 54	2 464	1.8
55 +	983	0.8
Unknown - Inconnu	64 503	..
United Kingdom of Great Britain and Northern Ireland - Royaume-Uni de Grande-Bretagne et d'Irlande du Nord[21]		
2012 (C)		
Total	812 970	42.9
0 - 19	13 166	6.9
20 - 24	85 617	41.4
25 - 29	168 503	83.1
30 - 34	226 297	113.8
35 - 39	160 698	84.9
40 - 44	76 266	35.9
45 - 49	25 537	11.7

Continent, country or area, year, code[a] and age of father (in years) / Continent, pays ou zone, année, code[a] et âge du père (en années)	Number - Nombre — Both sexes Les deux sexes	Rate Taux
EUROPE		
United Kingdom of Great Britain and Northern Ireland - Royaume-Uni de Grande-Bretagne et d'Irlande du Nord[21]		
2012 (C)		
50 - 54	7 396	3.7
55 - 59	2 061	1.2
60 - 64	585	..
65 +	290	..
Unknown - Inconnu	46 554	..
OCEANIA - OCÉANIE		
Australia - Australie		
2013 (+C)		
Total	308 065	43.3
0 - 19	4 109	5.6
20 - 24	24 187	29.8
25 - 29	61 909	73.2
30 - 34	96 565	119.8
35 - 39	68 443	91.4
40 - 44	30 089	37.7
45 - 49	8 805	12.0
50 - 54	2 740	3.7
55 - 59	826	1.2
60 - 64	290	..
65 +	133	..
Unknown - Inconnu	9 969	..
New Caledonia - Nouvelle-Calédonie		
2012 (C)		
Total	4 389	...
0 - 19	46	...
20 - 24	447	...
25 - 29	826	...
30 - 34	1 008	...
35 - 39	786	...
40 - 44	394	...
45 - 49	158	...
50 - 54	39	...
55 - 59	19	...
60 +	1	...
Unknown - Inconnu	665	...
New Zealand - Nouvelle-Zélande		
2014 (+C)		
Total	57 242	43.3
0 - 19	1 535	9.9
20 - 24	6 660	41.9
25 - 29	11 648	85.0
30 - 34	16 094	126.1
35 - 39	11 145	89.7
40 - 44	5 170	36.3
45 - 49	1 738	12.2
50 - 54	515	3.5
55 - 59	153	1.2
60 - 64	40	..
65 +	18	..
Unknown - Inconnu	2 526	..

FOOTNOTES - NOTES

♦ Rates based on 30 or fewer births. - Taux basés sur 30 naissances ou moins.

* Provisional. - Données provisoires.

[a] 'Code' indicates the source of data, as follows:
 C - Civil registration, estimated over 90% complete
 U - Civil registration, estimated less than 90% complete
 | - Other source, estimated reliable
 + - Data tabulated by date of registration rather than occurrence
 ... Information not available

[1] Excludes the islands of St. Brandon and Agalega. - Non compris les îles St. Brandon et Agalega.

[2] Excluding live-born infants who died before their birth was registered. - Non compris les enfants nés vivants décédés avant l'enregistrement de leur naissance.

[3] Including Canadian residents temporarily in the United States, but excluding United States residents temporarily in Canada. - Y compris les résidents canadiens se trouvant temporairement aux Etats-Unis, mais ne comprenant pas les résidents des Etats-Unis se trouvant temporairement au Canada.

[4] Data have not been adjusted for underenumeration. - Les données n'ont pas été ajustées pour compenser les lacunes du dénombrement.

[5] Data refer to births to resident mothers. - Ces données concernent les enfants nés de mères résidentes.

[6] Excluding newborns registered by application of mothers. Excluding infants born alive of less than 28 weeks' gestation, of less than 1 000 grams in weight and 35 centimeters in length, who die within seven days of birth. - Exception faite des nouveau-nés qui ont été enregistrés à la demande des mères. Non compris les enfants nés vivants après moins de 28 semaines de gestations, pesant moins de 1 000 grammes, mesurant moins de 35 centimètres et décédés dans les sept jours qui ont suivi leur naissance.

[7] Data refer to government controlled areas. - Les données se rapportent aux zones contrôlées par le Gouvernement.

[8] Includes data for East Jerusalem and Israeli residents in certain other territories under occupation by Israeli military forces since June 1967. - Y compris les données pour Jérusalem-Est et les résidents israéliens dans certains autres territoires occupés depuis 1967 par les forces armées israéliennes.

[9] Data refer to Japanese nationals in Japan only. Data refer to live births in wedlock only. - Les données se raportent aux nationaux japonais au Japon seulement. Les données ne concernent que les naissances vivantes de parents mariés.

[10] Excluding infants born alive of less than 28 weeks' gestation, of less than 1 000 grams in weight and 35 centimeters in length, who die within seven days of birth. - Non compris les enfants nés vivants après moins de 28 semaines de gestations, pesant moins de 1 000 grammes, mesurant moins de 35 centimètres et décédés dans les sept jours qui ont suivi leur naissance.

[11] Data for all population, citizens and foreigners. Data from Births and Deaths Notification System (Ministry of Health and all health care providers). - Les données portent sur la population entière, les citoyens et les étrangers. Les données proviennent du système de notification des naissances et des décès (Ministère de la santé et tous prestataires de soins de santé).

[12] Excluding alien armed forces, civilian aliens employed by armed forces, and foreign diplomatic personnel and their dependants. - Non compris les militaires étrangers, les civils étrangers employés par les forces armées ni le personnel diplomatique étranger et les membres de leur famille les accompagnant.

[13] Data refer to live births in wedlock only. - Les données ne concernent que les naissances vivantes de parents mariés.

[14] Excluding Faeroe Islands and Greenland shown separately, if available. - Non compris les Iles Féroé et le Groenland, qui font l'objet de rubriques distinctes, si disponible.

[15] Excluding Åland Islands. - Non compris les Îles d'Åland.

[16] Including armed forces stationed outside the country. - Y compris les militaires nationaux hors du pays.

[17] Including residents outside the country if listed in a Netherlands population register. - Englobe les résidents se trouvant à l'étranger à condition qu'ils soient inscrits sur le registre de population des Pays-Bas.

[18] Excluding Transnistria and the municipality of Bender. - Les données ne tiennent pas compte de l'information sur la Transnistria et la municipalité de Bender.

[19] Excludes data for Kosovo and Metohia. - Sans les données pour le Kosovo et Metohie.

[20] Data refer to births with weight 500g and more (if weight is unknown - with length 25 centimeters and more, or with gestation during 22 weeks or more). - Données concernant les nouveau-nés de 500 grammes ou plus (si le poids est inconnu – de 25 centimètres de long ou plus, ou après une grossesse de 22 semaines ou plus).

[21] Excluding Channel Islands (Guernsey and Jersey) and Isle of Man, shown separately, if available. Data tabulated by date of occurrence for England and Wales, and by date of registration for Northern Ireland and Scotland. - Non compris les îles Anglo-Normandes (Guernesey et Jersey) et l'île de Man, qui font l'objet de rubriques distinctes, si disponible. Données exploitées selon la date de l'événement pour l'Angleterre et le pays de Galles, et selon la date de l'enregistrement pour l'Irlande du Nord et l'Ecosse.

Table 12 - *Demographic Yearbook 2014*

Table 12 presents late foetal deaths and late foetal-death ratios by urban/rural residence for as many years as possible between 2010 and 2014.

Description of variables: Late foetal deaths are foetal deaths[1] of 28 or more completed weeks of gestation. Foetal deaths of unknown gestational age are included with those 28 or more weeks.

Statistics on the number of late foetal deaths are obtained from civil registers unless otherwise noted.

The urban/rural classification of late foetal deaths is as provided by each country or area; it is presumed to be based on the national census definitions of urban population that have been set forth at the end of the technical notes for table 6.

Ratio computation: Late foetal-death ratios are the annual number of late foetal deaths per 1 000 live births (as shown in table 9) in the same year. The live-birth base was adopted because it is assumed to be more comparable from one country or area to another than the sum of live births and foetal deaths.

Ratios by urban/rural residence are the annual number of late foetal deaths, in the appropriate urban or rural category, per 1 000 corresponding live births (as shown in table 9). These ratios are calculated by the United Nations Statistics Division.

Ratios presented in this table are limited to those for countries or areas and urban/rural areas having at least a total of 30 late foetal deaths in a given year.

Reliability of data: Each country or area is asked to indicate the estimated completeness of the late foetal deaths recorded in its civil register. These national assessments are indicated by the quality codes "C", "U" and "..." that appear in the first column of this table.

"C" indicates that the data are estimated to be virtually complete, that is, representing at least 90 per cent of the late foetal deaths occurring each year, while "U" indicates that data are estimated to be incomplete, that is, representing less than 90 per cent of the late foetal deaths occurring each year. The code "..." indicates that no information was provided regarding completeness.

Data from civil registers which are reported as incomplete or of unknown completeness (coded "U" or "...") are considered unreliable. They appear in italics in this table. Ratios are not computed for data so coded.

For more information about the quality of vital statistics data in general, see section 4.2 of the Technical Notes.

Limitations: Statistics on late foetal deaths are subject to the same qualifications as have been set forth for vital statistics in general and foetal-death statistics in particular as discussed in section 4 of the Technical Notes.

The reliability of the data is a very important factor. Of all vital statistics, the registration of foetal deaths is probably the most incomplete.

Variation in the definition of foetal deaths, and in particular late foetal deaths, also limits international comparability. The criterion of 28 or more completed weeks of gestation to distinguish late foetal deaths is not universally used; some countries or areas use different durations of gestation or other criteria such as size of the foetus. In addition, the difficulty of accurately determining gestational age further reduces comparability. However, to promote comparability, late foetal deaths shown in this table are restricted to those of at least 28 or more completed weeks of gestation. Wherever this is not possible, a footnote is provided.

Late foetal-death ratios are subject to the limitations of the data on live births with which they have been calculated. These have been set forth in the technical notes for table 9.

It must be pointed out that when late foetal deaths and live births are both under registered, the resulting ratios may be of reasonable magnitude. For the countries or areas where live-birth registration is poorest, the late foetal-death ratios may be the largest, effectively masking the completeness of the base data. For this reason, possible variations in birth-registration completeness as well as the reported completeness of late foetal deaths must always be borne in mind in evaluating late foetal-death ratios.

Finally, it may be noted that the counting of live-born infants as late foetal deaths, because they died before the registration of the birth or within the first 24 hours of life, has the effect of inflating the late foetal-death ratios unduly by decreasing the birth denominator and increasing the foetal-death numerator. This factor should not be overlooked in using data from this table.

The comparability of data by urban/rural residence is affected by the national definitions of urban and rural used in tabulating these data. It is assumed, in the absence of specific information to the contrary, that the definitions of urban and rural used in connection with the national population census were also used in the compilation of the vital statistics for each country or area. However, it cannot be excluded that, for a given country or area, different definitions of urban and rural are used for the vital statistics data and the population census data respectively. When known, the definitions of urban used in national population censuses are presented at the end of the technical notes for table 6. As discussed in detail in the technical notes for table 6, these definitions vary considerably from one country or area to another.

Urban/rural differentials in late foetal death ratios may also be affected by whether the late foetal deaths and live births have been tabulated in terms of place of occurrence or place of usual residence. This problem is discussed in more detail in section 4.1.4.1 of the Introduction.

Earlier data: Late foetal deaths and late foetal-death ratios have been shown in each issue of the Demographic Yearbook beginning with the 1951 issue. A special topic CD on natality published in 2001 presents the data for all available years from 1990 to 1998. For more information on specific topics, and years for which data are reported, readers should consult the Historical Index.

NOTES

[1] For definition, see section 4.1.1 of the Introduction.

Tableau 12 – *Annuaire démographique 2014*

Le tableau 12 présente des données sur les morts fœtales tardives et les rapports de mortinatalité selon le lieu de résidence (zone urbaine ou rurale) pour le plus grand nombre d'années possible entre 2010 et 2014.

Description des variables : Par mort fœtale tardive, on entend le décès d'un fœtus[1] survenu après 28 semaines complètes de gestation au moins. Les morts fœtales pour lesquelles la durée de la période de gestation n'est pas connue sont comprises dans cette catégorie.

Sauf indication contraire, les statistiques du nombre de morts fœtales tardives sont établies sur la base des registres de l'état civil.

La classification des morts fœtales tardives selon le lieu de résidence (zone urbaine ou rurale) est celle qui a été communiquée par chaque pays ou zone ; on part du principe qu'elle repose sur les définitions de la population urbaine utilisées pour les recensements nationaux, telles qu'elles sont reproduites à la fin des notes techniques du tableau 6.

Calcul des rapports : les rapports de mortinatalité représentent le nombre annuel de morts fœtales tardives pour 1 000 naissances vivantes (telles qu'elles sont présentées au tableau 9) survenues pendant la même année. On a pris pour base de calcul les naissances vivantes parce que l'on pense qu'elles sont plus facilement comparables d'un pays ou d'une zone à l'autre que la somme des naissances vivantes et des morts fœtales.

Les rapports selon le lieu de résidence (zone urbaine ou rurale) représentent le nombre annuel de morts fœtales tardives, classées selon la catégorie urbaine ou rurale appropriée pour 1 000 naissances vivantes (telles qu'elles sont présentées au tableau 9) survenues parmi la population correspondante. Ces rapports ont été calculés par la Division des statistiques de l'Organisation des Nations Unies.

Les rapports présentés dans le tableau 12 ne concernent que les pays ou zones où l'on a enregistré un total d'au moins 30 morts fœtales tardives pendant une année donnée.

Fiabilité des données : il a été demandé à chaque pays ou zone d'indiquer le degré estimatif de complétude des données sur les morts fœtales tardives figurant dans ses registres d'état civil. Ces évaluations nationales sont signalées par les codes de qualité "C", "U" et "..." qui apparaissent dans la deuxième colonne du tableau.

La lettre "C" indique que les données sont jugées à peu près complètes, c'est-à-dire qu'elles représentent au moins 90 p. 100 des morts fœtales tardives survenues chaque année ; la lettre "U" signifie que les données sont jugées incomplètes, c'est-à-dire qu'elles représentent moins de 90 p.100 des morts fœtales tardives survenues chaque année. Le code "..." indique qu'aucun renseignement n'a été communiqué quant à la complétude des données.

Les données provenant des registres de l'état civil qui sont déclarées incomplètes ou dont le degré de complétude n'est pas connu (code "U" ou "...") sont jugées douteuses. Elles apparaissent en italique dans le tableau ; les rapports, dans ces cas, n'ont pas été calculés.

Pour plus de précisions sur la qualité des données reposant sur les statistiques de l'état civil en général, voir la section 4.2 des Notes techniques.

Insuffisance des données : les statistiques des morts fœtales tardives appellent toutes les réserves qui ont été formulées à propos des statistiques de l'état civil en général et des statistiques concernant les morts fœtales en particulier (voir la section 4 des Notes techniques).

La fiabilité des données est un facteur très important. Les statistiques concernant les morts fœtales sont probablement les moins complètes de toutes les statistiques de l'état civil.

L'hétérogénéité des définitions de la mort fœtale et, en particulier, de la mort fœtale tardive nuit aussi à la comparabilité internationale des données. Le critère des 28 semaines complètes de gestation au moins n'est pas universellement utilisé ; certains pays ou zones retiennent des critères différents pour la durée de la période de gestation ou d'autres critères tels que la taille du fœtus. De surcroît, la comparabilité est rendue malaisée par le fait qu'il est difficile d'établir avec précision l'âge gestationnel. Pour faciliter les comparaisons, les morts fœtales tardives considérées ici sont exclusivement celles qui sont survenues au terme de 28 semaines de gestation au moins. Les exceptions sont signalées en note.

Les rapports de mortinatalité appellent en outre toutes les réserves qui ont été formulées à propos des statistiques des naissances vivantes qui ont servi à leur calcul (voir à ce sujet les notes techniques relatives au tableau 9).

En ce qui concerne le calcul des rapports, il convient de noter que, si l'enregistrement des morts fœtales tardives et celui des naissances vivantes sont loin d'être exhaustifs, les rapports de mortinatalité peuvent être raisonnables. C'est parfois pour les pays ou zones où l'enregistrement des naissances vivantes laisse le plus à désirer que les rapports de mortinatalité sont les plus élevés, ce qui masque le caractère incomplet des données de base. Aussi, pour porter un jugement sur la qualité des rapports de mortinatalité, il ne faut jamais oublier que la complétude de l'enregistrement des naissances comme celle de l'enregistrement des morts fœtales tardives peuvent varier sensiblement.

Enfin, on notera que l'inclusion parmi les morts fœtales tardives des décès d'enfants nés vivants qui sont décédés avant l'enregistrement de leur naissance ou dans les 24 heures qui ont suivi la naissance conduit à des rapports de mortinatalité exagérés parce que le dénominateur (nombre de naissances) se trouve alors diminué et le numérateur (morts fœtales) augmenté. Il importe de ne pas négliger ce facteur lorsque l'on utilise les données du tableau 12.

La comparabilité des données selon le lieu de résidence (zone urbaine ou rurale) peut être limitée par les définitions nationales des termes « urbain » et « rural » utilisées pour la mise en tableaux de ces données. En l'absence d'indications contraires, on a supposé que les mêmes définitions avaient servi pour le recensement national de la population et pour l'établissement des statistiques de l'état civil pour chaque pays ou zone. Toutefois, il n'est pas exclu que, pour une zone ou un pays donné, des définitions différentes aient été retenues. Les définitions du terme « urbain » utilisées pour les recensements nationaux de population ont été présentées à la fin des notes techniques du tableau 6 lorsqu'elles étaient connues. Comme on l'a précisé dans les notes techniques relatives au tableau 6, ces définitions varient considérablement d'un pays ou d'une zone à l'autre.

La différence entre les rapports de mortinatalité pour les zones urbaines et rurales pourra aussi être faussée selon que les morts fœtales tardives et les naissances vivantes auront été classées d'après le lieu de l'événement ou le lieu de résidence habituel. Ce problème est examiné plus en détail à la section 4.1.4.1 des Notes techniques.

Données publiées antérieurement : les éditions de l'*Annuaire démographique* parues à partir de 1951 contiennent des statistiques concernant les morts fœtales tardives et les rapports de mortinatalité. Un CD-ROM sur la natalité paru en 2001 présente les données pour toutes les années disponibles de 1990 à 1998. Pour plus de précisions concernant les années et les sujets pour lesquels des données ont été publiées, se reporter à l'index.

NOTE

[1] Pour la définition, voir la section 4.1.1 de l'Introduction.

12. Late foetal deaths and late foetal death ratios, by urban/rural residence: 2010 - 2014
Morts foetales tardives et rapports de mortinatalité, selon la résidence, urbaine/rurale : 2010 - 2014

Continent, country or area, and urban/rural residence / Continent, pays ou zone et résidence, urbaine/rurale	Co-de[a]	Number - Nombre					Ratio - Rapport				
		2010	2011	2012	2013	2014	2010	2011	2012	2013	2014
AFRICA - AFRIQUE											
Algeria - Algérie											
Total	+U	16 444	15 480	15 795	15 009	15 077	...	...	...	...	...
Burundi[1]											
Total	+U	4 889	3 099	2 448	2 141	...	...	...	...	...	...
Egypt - Égypte											
Total	+C	4 031	2 465	1 334	...	...	1.8	1.0	0.5	...	...
Urban - Urbaine	+C	3 295	1 957	1 093	...	...	3.7	2.1	1.1	...	...
Rural - Rurale	+C	736	508	241	...	...	0.5	0.3	0.1	...	...
Mauritius - Maurice[2]											
Total	+C	103	139	140	117	138	6.9	9.5	9.7	8.7	10.4
Urban - Urbaine	+C	43	57	52	46	54	7.5	10.2	9.6	9.1	10.5
Rural - Rurale	+C	60	82	88	71	84	6.5	9.0	9.7	8.4	10.3
Sierra Leone											
Total	...	1 834	1 663	1 638	...	...	...	...	...	...	...
Urban - Urbaine	...	586	230	1 066	...	...	...	...	...	...	...
Rural - Rurale	...	1 248	1 433	572	...	...	...	...	...	...	...
South Africa - Afrique du Sud											
Total	...	14 986	13 852	...	...	...	...	...	...	...	...
Tunisia - Tunisie											
Total	U	1 995	2 074	...	...	...	...	...	...	...	...
AMERICA, NORTH - AMÉRIQUE DU NORD											
Bahamas											
Total	+C	61	73	59	...	...	12.4	15.4	13.2	...	...
Bermuda - Bermudes											
Total	C	4	2	4	4	1	...	...	...	...	...
Canada[3]											
Total	C	1 084	*1 115	...	...	...	2.9	*3.0	...	...	...
Costa Rica											
Total[4]	C	389	471	332	327	*319	5.5	6.4	4.5	4.6	*4.4
Urban - Urbaine	C	169	...	134	108	*176	6.5	...	5.3	4.3	*4.2
Rural - Rurale	C	220	...	198	219	*143	4.9	...	4.1	4.8	*4.7
Cuba[5]											
Total	C	1 344	1 365	1 262	1 273	1 134	10.5	10.3	10.0	10.1	9.2
Dominican Republic - République dominicaine											
Total	U	...	1 376	1 131	1 886	1 528	...	...	...	...	...
Mexico - Mexique[6]											
Total	+U	11 188	11 096	10 442	9 911	...	...	...	...	...	...
Urban - Urbaine[7]	+U	8 344	8 299	7 806	7 249	...	...	...	...	...	...
Rural - Rurale[7]	+U	2 701	2 631	2 469	2 472	...	...	...	...	...	...
Montserrat											
Total	+C	-	-	-	-	2	...	...	...	...	...
Panama											
Total	U	396	399	426	370	...	...	...	...	...	...
Puerto Rico - Porto Rico[8]											
Total	C	414	464	382	417	406	9.8	11.3	9.8	11.4	11.8
United States of America - États-Unis d'Amérique											
Total	C	11 870	11 857	11 739	11 721	...	3.0	3.0	3.0	3.0	...
AMERICA, SOUTH - AMÉRIQUE DU SUD											
Argentina - Argentine											
Total	C	4 692	4 712	3 731	3 809	...	6.2	6.2	5.1	5.0	...
Brazil - Brésil											
Total	U	22 874	24 083	24 823	25 744	...	...	...	...	...	...
Chile - Chili[9]											
Total	C	1 380	1 294	1 276	...	...	5.5	5.2	5.2	...	...
Urban - Urbaine	C	1 210	1 179	996[10]	...	...	5.4	5.3	4.5	...	...
Rural - Rurale	C	170	115	125[10]	...	...	6.7	4.7	5.1	...	...

12. Late foetal deaths and late foetal death ratios, by urban/rural residence: 2010 - 2014
Morts foetales tardives et rapports de mortinatalité, selon la résidence, urbaine/rurale : 2010 - 2014 (continued - suite)

Continent, country or area, and urban/rural residence / Continent, pays ou zone et résidence, urbaine/rurale	Code[a]	Number - Nombre					Ratio - Rapport				
		2010	2011	2012	2013	2014	2010	2011	2012	2013	2014
AMERICA, SOUTH - AMÉRIQUE DU SUD											
Colombia - Colombie[11]											
Total	...	12 660	14 391	...	...	...	...	...	...	...	...
Urban - Urbaine[7]	...	10 295	11 798	...	...	...	...	...	...	...	...
Rural - Rurale[7]	...	2 067	2 467	...	...	...	...	...	...	...	...
Total	U	...	...	12 450	...	...	...	...	...	...	...
Urban - Urbaine[7]	U	...	...	9 865	...	...	...	...	...	...	...
Rural - Rurale[7]	U	...	...	2 505	...	...	...	...	...	...	...
Ecuador - Équateur[12]											
Total	...	1 815	1 672	1 717	1 040	...	...	...	...	...	...
Urban - Urbaine	...	...	1 432	1 535	875	...	...	...	...	...	...
Rural - Rurale	...	...	240	182	165	...	...	...	...	...	...
Suriname											
Total	...	207	182	...	...	...	...	...	...	...	...
Uruguay											
Total	C	202	...	200	...	...	4.3	...	4.2	...	...
Venezuela (Bolivarian Republic of) - Venezuela (République bolivarienne du)											
Total	...	2 151	1 143	1 006	2 400	...	...	...	...	...	...
ASIA - ASIE											
Azerbaijan - Azerbaïdjan											
Total	+C	728	669	602	643	...	4.4	3.8	3.5	3.7	...
Bahrain - Bahreïn											
Total	...	104	140	125	106	...	...	...	...	...	...
Brunei Darussalam - Brunéi Darussalam											
Total	+C	40	40	43	44	...	6.2	5.9	6.2	6.6	...
China, Hong Kong SAR - Chine, Hong Kong RAS											
Total	...	152	184	148	119	...	...	...	...	...	...
China, Macao SAR - Chine, Macao RAS											
Total	C	9	12	14	10	12	...	...	...	...	...
Georgia - Géorgie											
Total	C	653	563	...	567	...	10.4	9.7	...	9.8	...
Urban - Urbaine	C	345	323	...	...	...	10.1	9.7	...	...	...
Rural - Rurale	C	308	240	...	...	...	10.8	9.8	...	...	...
Israel - Israël[13]											
Total	C	518	530	...	...	...	3.1	3.2	...	...	...
Urban - Urbaine[7]	C	463	480	...	...	...	3.1	3.2	...	...	...
Rural - Rurale[7]	C	52	47	...	...	...	3.4	3.1	...	...	...
Japan - Japon[14]											
Total	C	2 187	2 137	1 969	1 897	...	2.0	2.0	1.9	1.8	...
Urban - Urbaine[7]	C	2 009	1 946	1 809	1 747	...	2.0	2.0	1.9	1.8	...
Rural - Rurale[7]	C	175	191	158	149	...	1.9	2.2	1.9	1.8	...
Kazakhstan											
Total	C	3 403	3 285	3 453	3 206	...	9.2	8.8	9.1	8.3	...
Urban - Urbaine	C	1 793	1 817	1 900	1 673	...	9.3	9.2	9.2	8.0	...
Rural - Rurale	C	1 610	1 468	1 553	1 533	...	9.2	8.4	8.9	8.6	...
Kuwait - Koweït											
Total	C	346	313	355	352	...	6.0	5.4	5.9	5.9	...
Kyrgyzstan - Kirghizstan											
Total	C	1 624	1 675	1 575	1 549	...	11.1	11.2	10.2	10.0	...
Urban - Urbaine[15]	C	1 124	1 176	1 144	1 142	...	22.5	24.0	21.3	21.2	...
Rural - Rurale[15]	C	500	499	431	407	...	5.2	5.0	4.3	4.0	...
Malaysia - Malaisie											
Total	C	2 222	2 305	*2 213	...	...	4.5	4.5	*4.3	...	...
Maldives[8]											
Total	...	48	43	50	51	...	...	...	...	...	...
Urban - Urbaine	...	23	25	29[10]	31	...	...	...	...	...	...
Rural - Rurale	...	25	18	20[10]	20	...	...	...	...	...	...

12. Late foetal deaths and late foetal death ratios, by urban/rural residence: 2010 - 2014
Morts foetales tardives et rapports de mortinatalité, selon la résidence, urbaine/rurale : 2010 - 2014 (continued - suite)

Continent, country or area, and urban/rural residence / Continent, pays ou zone et résidence, urbaine/rurale	Co-de[a]	Number - Nombre					Ratio - Rapport				
		2010	2011	2012	2013	2014	2010	2011	2012	2013	2014
ASIA - ASIE											
Myanmar											
Total	+U	12 234	11 275	*12 234	*11 718	...	...	...	...	...	...
Urban - Urbaine	+U	3 131	2 642	*5 741	*4 898	...	...	...	...	...	...
Rural - Rurale	+U	9 103	8 633	*6 493	*6 820	...	...	...	...	...	...
Oman[16]											
Total	U	392	333	...	...	...	...	...	...	...	...
Philippines											
Total	...	4 284	4 299	4 219	...	...	...	...	...	...	...
Qatar											
Total	C	130	...	...	...	...	6.7	...	...	...	...
Republic of Korea - République de Corée[17]											
Total	C	950	924	963	931	...	2.0	2.0	2.0	2.1	...
Urban - Urbaine[7]	C	703	697	685	697	...	1.8	1.8	1.7	1.9	...
Rural - Rurale[7]	C	177	153	151	126	...	2.1	1.9	1.8	1.8	...
Singapore - Singapour											
Total	+C	99	106	111	80	86	2.6	2.7	2.6	2.0	2.0
Sri Lanka											
Total	+U	958	998	972	...	...	...	...	...	...	...
Tajikistan - Tadjikistan											
Total	U	2 122	1 966	2 037	1 999	...	...	...	...	...	...
Urban - Urbaine	U	1 349	1 283	1 296	1 323	...	...	...	...	...	...
Rural - Rurale	U	773	683	741	676	...	...	...	...	...	...
EUROPE											
Åland Islands - Îles d'Åland											
Total	C	-	1	1	-	...	...	...	...	...	...
Urban - Urbaine	C	-	1	-	-	...	...	...	...	...	...
Rural - Rurale	C	-	-	1	-	...	...	...	...	...	...
Austria - Autriche											
Total	C	296	294	260	272	...	3.8	3.8	3.3	3.4	...
Belarus - Bélarus											
Total	C	265	249	257	260	...	2.5	2.3	2.2	2.2	...
Urban - Urbaine	C	187	174	204	185	...	2.3	2.1	2.3	2.0	...
Rural - Rurale	C	78	75	53	75	...	3.0	2.9	2.0	2.7	...
Belgium - Belgique											
Total	C	646	...	...	...	...	5.0	...	...	...	...
Urban - Urbaine[7]	C	632	...	...	...	...	4.9	...	...	...	...
Rural - Rurale[7]	C	9	...	...	...	...	...	...	...	...	...
Bulgaria - Bulgarie											
Total	C	592	556	557	483	...	7.8	7.8	8.1	7.3	...
Urban - Urbaine	C	409	401	393	...	...	7.2	7.5	7.6	...	...
Rural - Rurale	C	183	155	164	...	...	9.9	8.9	9.4	...	...
Croatia - Croatie[18]											
Total	C	185	145	130	144	...	4.3	3.5	3.1	3.6	...
Urban - Urbaine	C	95	76	78	75	...	3.9	3.3	3.3	3.3	...
Rural - Rurale	C	90	69	52	69	...	4.8	3.9	2.9	4.0	...
Czech Republic - République tchèque											
Total	C	283[19]	303[19]	287[20]	264[20]	...	2.4	2.8	2.6	2.5	...
Urban - Urbaine	C	202[19]	228[19]	211[20]	198[20]	...	2.3	2.9	2.6	2.5	...
Rural - Rurale	C	81[19]	75[19]	76[20]	66[20]	...	2.6	2.6	2.6	2.3	...
Denmark - Danemark[21]											
Total	C	269	262	213	...	...	4.2	4.4	3.7	...	...
Estonia - Estonie											
Total	C	41	42	31	30	...	2.6	2.9	2.2	2.2	...
Urban - Urbaine	C	28	33	17	20	...	...	3.3	...	...	...
Rural - Rurale	C	13	9	14	10	...	...	...	...	...	...
Finland - Finlande											
Total	C	128[22]	111[22]	113[22]	106	...	2.1	1.9	1.9	1.8	...
Urban - Urbaine[22]	C	81	77	74	...	...	1.9	1.8	1.8	...	...
Rural - Rurale[22]	C	47	34	39	...	...	2.7	2.0	2.3	...	...
France[23]											
Total	C	8 206	...	...	...	...	10.2	...	...	...	...

12. Late foetal deaths and late foetal death ratios, by urban/rural residence: 2010 - 2014
Morts foetales tardives et rapports de mortinatalité, selon la résidence, urbaine/rurale : 2010 - 2014 (continued - suite)

Continent, country or area, and urban/rural residence — Continent, pays ou zone et résidence, urbaine/rurale	Code[a]	Number - Nombre					Ratio - Rapport				
		2010	2011	2012	2013	2014	2010	2011	2012	2013	2014
EUROPE											
Germany - Allemagne											
Total	C	2 466	2 387	2 400	2 556	...	3.6	3.6	3.6	3.7	...
Greece - Grèce											
Total	C	500[8]	431[8]	446[8]	298	...	4.4	4.0	4.4	3.2	...
Urban - Urbaine[8]	C	358	308	332	...	...	4.5	4.1	4.7	...	...
Rural - Rurale[8]	C	142	123	114	...	...	3.9	3.9	3.9	...	...
Hungary - Hongrie[24]											
Total	C	387	392	378	392	...	4.3	4.5	4.2	4.4	...
Urban - Urbaine[25]	C	231	237	234	229	...	3.7	3.9	3.8	3.7	...
Rural - Rurale[25]	C	150	153	140	158	...	5.6	5.8	5.1	5.7	...
Iceland - Islande											
Total	C	9	4[26]	10	4	...	...	...	...	...	...
Urban - Urbaine	C	8	4[26]	10	4	...	...	...	...	...	...
Rural - Rurale	C	1	-[26]	-	-	...	...	...	...	...	...
Ireland - Irlande[27]											
Total	C	273	211	...	...	...	3.6	2.9	...	...	...
Italy - Italie											
Total	C	1 532	1 422	1 439	*1 262	...	2.7	2.6	2.7	*2.5	...
Latvia - Lettonie											
Total	C	79	87	81	81	...	4.0	4.6	4.1	3.9	...
Lithuania - Lituanie[18]											
Total	C	147	148	117	143	...	4.8	4.9	3.8	4.8	...
Urban - Urbaine	C	97	89	77	87	...	4.6	4.3	3.6	4.3	...
Rural - Rurale	C	50	59	40	56	...	5.2	6.2	4.4	5.8	...
Luxembourg											
Total	C	18	22	28	33	...	...	...	...	5.4	...
Malta - Malte[18]											
Total	C	14	18	10	...	...	...	...	...	...	...
Netherlands - Pays-Bas[28]											
Total	C	648	620	594	510	...	3.5	3.4	3.4	3.0	...
Norway - Norvège											
Total	C	190	198	184	171	...	3.1	3.3	3.1	2.9	...
Poland - Pologne											
Total	C	1 226	1 182	1 174	1 016	...	3.0	3.0	3.0	2.7	...
Urban - Urbaine	C	682	644	638	...	...	2.8	2.9	2.9	...	...
Rural - Rurale	C	544	538	536	...	...	3.2	3.3	3.3	...	...
Portugal[6]											
Total	C	241	227	249	180	...	2.4	2.3	2.8	2.2	...
Romania - Roumanie											
Total	C	856	811	779	771	...	4.0	4.1	3.9	4.2	...
Urban - Urbaine	C	420	363	348	325	...	3.6	3.4	3.2	3.3	...
Rural - Rurale	C	436	448	431	446	...	4.6	5.0	4.7	5.3	...
Russian Federation - Fédération de Russie											
Total	C	8 300	8 109	12 142	...	...	4.6	4.5	6.4	...	...
Urban - Urbaine	C	5 795	5 590	8 441	...	...	4.6	4.4	6.2	...	...
Rural - Rurale	C	2 505	2 519	3 701	...	...	4.8	4.8	6.8	...	...
Serbia - Serbie[29]											
Total	+C	388	328	370	307	...	5.7	5.0	5.5	4.7	...
Urban - Urbaine	+C	257	224	252	170	...	5.5	4.9	5.5	3.7	...
Rural - Rurale	+C	131	104	118	137	...	6.1	5.2	5.5	6.9	...
Slovakia - Slovaquie[30]											
Total	C	189	190	180	163	...	3.1	3.1	3.2	3.0	...
Urban - Urbaine	C	86	78	80	72	...	2.7	2.4	2.7	2.5	...
Rural - Rurale	C	103	112	100	91	...	3.6	3.9	3.8	3.5	...
Slovenia - Slovénie											
Total	C	60	59	51	...	...	2.7	2.7	2.3	...	...
Spain - Espagne											
Total	C	1 046	1 067	1 050	981	...	2.2	2.3	2.3	2.3	...
Sweden - Suède											
Total	C	426	429	453	441	...	3.7	3.8	4.0	3.9	...
Switzerland - Suisse[8]											
Total	C	346	349	350	402	...	4.3	4.3	4.3	4.9	...
Urban - Urbaine	C	266	246	282	...	...	4.4	4.1	4.6	...	...
Rural - Rurale	C	80	103	68	...	...	4.0	5.1	3.3	...	...

12. Late foetal deaths and late foetal death ratios, by urban/rural residence: 2010 - 2014
Morts foetales tardives et rapports de mortinatalité, selon la résidence, urbaine/rurale : 2010 - 2014 (continued - suite)

Continent, country or area, and urban/rural residence / Continent, pays ou zone et résidence, urbaine/rurale	Co-de[a]	Number - Nombre					Ratio - Rapport				
		2010	2011	2012	2013	2014	2010	2011	2012	2013	2014
EUROPE											
TFYR of Macedonia - L'ex-R. y. de Macédoine											
Total	C	211	202	184	196	...	8.7	8.9	7.8	8.5	...
Urban - Urbaine	C	101	120	108	...	...	7.3	9.2	8.1	...	...
Rural - Rurale	C	110	82	76	...	...	10.6	8.4	7.5	...	...
Ukraine											
Total	+C	3 300	3 158	3 230	...	...	6.6	6.3	6.2	...	...
Urban - Urbaine	+C	2 075	2 006	2 120	...	...	6.4	6.1	6.2	...	...
Rural - Rurale	+C	1 225	1 152	1 110	...	...	7.2	6.6	6.2	...	...
United Kingdom of Great Britain and Northern Ireland - Royaume-Uni de Grande-Bretagne et d'Irlande du Nord[31]											
Total	C	4 110	4 201	3 938	...	...	5.1	5.2	4.8	...	...
OCEANIA - OCÉANIE											
Guam[8]											
Total	C	49	...	27	42	36	14.3	...	...	12.6	10.6
New Zealand - Nouvelle-Zélande[6]											
Total	+C	185	184	158	141	146[7]	2.9	3.0	2.6	2.4	2.6
Urban - Urbaine	+C	165	160	141	126	123[7]	3.0	3.0	2.6	2.4	2.4
Rural - Rurale	+C	19	24	17	15	23[7]	...	...	...	...	...
Palau - Palaos											
Total	C	4	1	3	2	...	...	...	...	...	...

FOOTNOTES - NOTES

Italics: data from civil registers which are incomplete or of unknown completeness. - Italiques : données incomplètes ou dont le degré d'exactitude n'est pas connu, provenant des registres de l'état civil.

[*] Provisional. - Données provisoires.

[a] 'Code' indicates the source of data, as follows:
C - Civil registration, estimated over 90% complete
U - Civil registration, estimated less than 90% complete
| - Other source, estimated reliable
+ - Data tabulated by date of registration rather than occurence
... - Information not available

Le 'Code' indique la source des données, comme suit :
C - Registres de l'état civil considérés complets à 90 p. 100 au moins
U - Registres de l'état civil qui ne sont pas considérés complets à 90 p. 100 au moins
| - Autre source, considérée pas douteuses
+ - Données exploitées selon la date de l'enregistrement et non la date de l'événement
... - Information pas disponible

[1] Data refer to the recorded events in Ministry of Health hospitals and health centres only. - Les données se rapportent aux faits d'état civil enregistrés dans les hôpitaux et les dispensaires du Ministère de la santé seulement.
[2] Excludes the islands of St. Brandon and Agalega. - Non compris les îles St. Brandon et Agalega.
[3] Including Canadian residents temporarily in the United States, but excluding United States residents temporarily in Canada. - Y compris les résidents canadiens se trouvant temporairement aux Etats-Unis, mais ne comprenant pas les résidents des Etats-Unis se trouvant temporairement au Canada.
[4] Including unknown sex. - Y compris le sexe inconnu.
[5] Late foetal death is indicated by the fact that the foetus is at least 500 grams or more in weight. - Les décès foetaux tardifs sont caractérisés par le fait que le foetus pèse au moins 500 grammes.

[6] Data refer to resident population only. - Pour la population résidante seulement.
[7] The total number may include 'Unknown residence', but the categories urban and rural do not. - Le nombre total peut inclure les personnes dont la résidence n'est pas connue, à l'inverse des catégories de population urbaine et rurale.
[8] Data refer to total foetal deaths. - Y compris toutes les morts foetales.
[9] Late foetal death is indicated by the fact that the foetus is at least 22 completed weeks of gestational age. - Les décès intra-utérins tardifs sont définis comme survenant après 22 semaines au moins de gestation.
[10] Excluding deaths of unknown sex. - Non compris les décès dont on ignore le sexe.
[11] Data include foetal deaths of unknown gestational weeks. - Les données comprennnent les morts foetales où le nombre de semaines de gestation n'est pas connu.
[12] Data refer to total foetal deaths. Excludes nomadic Indian tribes. - Y compris toutes les morts foetales. Non compris les tribus d'Indiens nomades.
[13] Includes data for East Jerusalem and Israeli residents in certain other territories under occupation by Israeli military forces since June 1967. - Y compris les données pour Jérusalem-Est et les résidents israéliens dans certains autres territoires occupés depuis 1967 par les forces armées israéliennes.
[14] Data refer to Japanese nationals in Japan only. Data exclude unknown duration of pregnancy. - Les données se raportent aux nationaux japonais au Japon seulement. Exception faite des grossesses dont la durée n'est pas connue.
[15] Urban and rural figures refer to the late foetal deaths collected based on the location of the medical facilities, regardless of the mothers' permanent residence location. - Les chiffres urbains et ruraux concernent les décès tardifs du foetus recueillis sur la base de l'emplacement des établissements médicaux, indépendamment du lieu de résidence permanente des mères.
[16] Data for all population, citizens and foreigners. Data from Births and Deaths Notification System (Ministry of Health and all health care providers). - Les données portent sur la population entière, les citoyens et les étrangers. Les données proviennent du système de notification des naissances et des décès (Ministère de la santé et tous prestataires de soins de santé).
[17] Excluding alien armed forces, civilian aliens employed by armed forces, and foreign diplomatic personnel and their dependants. - Non compris les militaires

étrangers, les civils étrangers employés par les forces armées ni le personnel diplomatique étranger et les membres de leur famille les accompagnant.

[18] Late foetal death is defined as an infant born without any signs of life, weighing at least 500 grams, after duration of pregnancy of at least 22 weeks. - On dit qu'il y a mort intra-utérine tardive lorsqu'un enfant pesant au minimum 500 grammes naît sans donner aucun signe de vie au terme d'une grossesse qui a duré au moins 22 semaines.

[19] Late foetal death is defined as an infant born without any signs of life, weighing at least 1000 grams. - La mortalité fœtale en fin de période de gestation s'entend de nourrissons mort-nés et pesant au moins 1 kilo.

[20] Since 1 April 2012, a stillborn child is defined in guidelines for filling in a death certificate as a child fully expelled or removed out of the mother's body, not showing any sign of life and whose birth weight is 500g or more. If the weight is not possible to determine then duration of pregnancy must be 22 weeks or more. If the duration of pregnancy is not possible to determine, the foetus length must be 25cm or more. - Depuis le 1er avril 2012, un enfant mort-né est défini dans les directives relatives à l'établissement du certificat de décès comme un enfant complètement expulsé par la mère ou retiré de son corps, ne montrant aucun signe de vie et ayant atteint un poids de 500 grammes. S'il est impossible d'en déterminer le poids, la durée de gestation doit être au moins de 22 semaines. S'il est impossible de déterminer la durée de gestation, la longueur du fœtus doit être au moins de 25 centimètres.

[21] Excluding Faeroe Islands and Greenland shown separately, if available. - Non compris les Îles Féroé et le Groenland, qui font l'objet de rubriques distinctes, si disponible.

[22] Excluding Åland Islands. - Non compris les Îles d'Åland.

[23] Foetal deaths after at least 180 days (6 calendar months or 26 weeks) of gestation. - Morts foetales survenues après 180 jours (6 mois civils ou 26 semaines) au moins de gestation.

[24] Late foetal death is indicated by the fact that the foetus is at least 24 (it has been 28 weeks until 1996) completed weeks of gestation and does not show any sign of life after the separation from its mother; the foetus has to be 30 cm or more in length or 500 grams or more in weight if its gestational age cannot be determined. - Pour qu'il y ait mort foetale tardive, il faut que le décès d'un foetus survienne après 24 semaines complètes de gestation au moins (28 semaines jusqu'en 1996), que le foetus n'ait pas donné signe de vie après avoir été séparé de la mère, qu'il mesure 30 centimètres au moins ou pèse 500 grammes si la durée de la période de gestation n'est pas connue.

[25] The urban and rural categories do not include the data of foreigners, persons of unknown residence and the homeless, whereas the total category includes them. - Les chiffres portant sur la population urbaine et rurale n' incluent pas les données relatives aux étrangers, aux personnes dont la résidence n'est pas connue et aux personnes sans domicile fixe, à l'inverse, le total les inclut.

[26] Definition of localities was revised in 2011 causing a break with the previous series. - La rupture par rapport aux séries précédentes s'explique par le fait que la définition des localités a été révisée depuis 2011.

[27] Data refer to events registered within one year of occurrence. - Les données portent sur des événements enregistrés dans l'année pendant laquelle ils sont survenus.

[28] Including residents outside the country if listed in a Netherlands population register. - Englobe les résidents se trouvant à l'étranger à condition qu'ils soient inscrits sur le registre de population des Pays-Bas.

[29] Data refer to total foetal deaths. Excludes data for Kosovo and Metohia. - Y compris toutes les morts foetales. Sans les données pour le Kosovo et Metohie.

[30] Including foetal deaths of at least 1 000 grams in weight or 28 weeks of gestation. - Y compris les morts de fœtus pesant au moins 1 000 grammes ou après 28 semaines de gestation.

[31] Excluding Channel Islands (Guernsey and Jersey) and Isle of Man, shown separately, if available. Including unknown sex. - Non compris les îles Anglo-Normandes (Guernesey et Jersey) et l'île de Man, qui font l'objet de rubriques distinctes, si disponible. Y compris le sexe inconnu.

Table 13 - *Demographic Yearbook 2014*

Table 13 presents legally induced abortions for as many years as available between 2005 and 2014.

Description of variables: There are two major categories of abortion: spontaneous and induced. Induced abortions are those initiated by deliberate action undertaken with the intention of terminating pregnancy; all other abortions are considered spontaneous.

The induction of abortion is subject to governmental regulation in most, if not all, countries or areas. This regulation varies from complete prohibition in some countries or areas to abortion on request, with services provided by governmental health authorities, in others. More generally, governments have attempted to define the conditions under which a pregnancy may lawfully be terminated and have established procedures for authorizing abortion in individual cases.

Information on abortion policies is collected by the United Nations Population Division and published in the *Abortion Policies and Reproductive Health around the World*[1].

Reliability of data: Unlike data on live births and foetal deaths, which are generally collected through systems of vital registration, data on abortion are collected from a variety of sources. Because of this, the quality specification on the completeness of civil registers, which is presented for other tables, does not appear here.

Limitations: With regard to the collection of information on abortions, a variety of sources are used, but hospital records are the most common source of information. This implies that most cases that have no contact with hospitals are missed. Data from other sources are probably also incomplete. The data in the present table are limited to legally induced abortions, which, by their nature, might be assumed to be more complete than data on all induced abortions.

Earlier data: Legally induced abortions have been shown previously in all issues of the *Demographic Yearbook* since the twenty-third issue. For more information on specific topics and years for which data are reported, readers should consult the Historical Index.

NOTES

[1] United Nations, Department of Economic and Social Affairs, Population Division (2014). *Abortion Policies and Reproductive Health around the World* (United Nations publication, Sales No. E.14.XIII.11).

Tableau 13 – *Annuaire démographique 2014*

Le tableau 13 présente les données disponibles, relatives aux avortements provoqués légalement, entre 2005 et 2014.

Description des variables : l'avortement peut être spontané ou provoqué. L'avortement provoqué est celui qui résulte de manœuvres délibérées, entreprises afin d'interrompre la grossesse ; tous les autres avortements sont considérés comme spontanés.

L'interruption délibérée de la grossesse fait l'objet d'une réglementation officielle dans la plupart des pays ou zones, sinon dans tous. Cette réglementation va de l'interdiction totale à l'autorisation de l'avortement sur demande, pratiqué par des services de santé publique. Le plus souvent, les gouvernements se sont efforcés de définir les circonstances dans lesquelles la grossesse peut être interrompue licitement et de fixer une procédure d'autorisation.

La Division de la population des Nations Unies collecte des informations sur les politiques en matière d'avortement et les publient dans *Abortion Policies and Reproductive Health around the World*[1].

Fiabilité des données : à la différence des données sur les naissances vivantes et les morts fœtales, qui proviennent généralement des registres d'état civil, les données sur l'avortement sont tirées de sources diverses. Aussi ne trouve-t-on pas ici une évaluation de la qualité des données semblable à celle qui indique, pour les autres tableaux, le degré d'exhaustivité des données de l'état civil.

Insuffisance des données : en ce qui concerne les renseignements sur l'avortement, un grand nombre de sources sont utilisées, les relevés hospitaliers restant cependant la source la plus commune. Il s'ensuit que la plupart des cas qui ne passent pas par les hôpitaux sont ignorés. Il faut aussi tenir compte du fait que les données provenant d'autres sources sont probablement incomplètes. Les données du tableau 13 se limitent aux avortements provoqués pour raisons légales dont on peut supposer, en raison de leur nature même, que les statistiques sont plus complètes que les données concernant l'ensemble des avortements provoqués.

Données publiées antérieurement : des statistiques concernant les avortements provoqués pour raisons légales sont publiées dans *l'Annuaire démographique* depuis la vingt-troisième édition. Pour plus de précisions concernant les années et les sujets pour lesquels des données ont été publiées, se reporter à l'index historique.

NOTES

[1] United Nations, Department of Economic and Social Affairs, Population Division (2014). *Abortion Policies and Reproductive Health around the World* (United Nations publication, Sales No. E.14.XIII.11).

13. Legally induced abortions: 2005 - 2014
Avortements provoqués légalement : 2005 - 2014

Continent and country or area Continent et pays ou zone	Number - Nombre									
	2005	**2006**	**2007**	**2008**	**2009**	**2010**	**2011**	**2012**	**2013**	**2014**
AFRICA - AFRIQUE										
Burundi[1]	...	...	...	...	6 329	6 272	3 547	3 088	3 152	...
Reunion - Réunion	4 421	4 523	...	...	...	...	...	...	...	...
Seychelles	413	443	446	453	471	556	579	533	515	549
AMERICA, NORTH - AMÉRIQUE DU NORD										
Anguilla	21	...	...	...	...	...	...	...	...	...
Bermuda - Bermudes	237	222	90	283	303	284	278	278	275	248
Canada[2]	96 815	91 310[3]	...	...	...	...	...	...	...	...
Costa Rica[4]	8 411	8 367	8 504	8 733[5]	7 848	7 697	7 882	7 405	7 283	*7 137
Cuba	62 530	67 903	66 008	74 905	84 724	71 398	83 943	83 682	84 373	...
Dominican Republic - République dominicaine	29 167	...	29 526	26 318	22 828	22 551	25 284	26 303	26 180	25 999
Greenland - Groenland	899	904	887	899	799	858	743	784	...	...
Martinique	2 304	2 392	...	...	...	...	...	...	...	...
Mexico - Mexique[6]	729	793	833	764	867	*986	1 041	294	271	...
Puerto Rico - Porto Rico[7]	6 904	5 538[8]	...	...	...	...	...	...	...	...
Turks and Caicos Islands - Îles Turques et Caïques[9]	32	...	...	...	...	...	...	...	...	...
United States of America - États-Unis d'Amérique[10]	820 151	852 385	827 609	825 564	...	...	...	...	...	...
AMERICA, SOUTH - AMÉRIQUE DU SUD										
Chile - Chili	1 841	...	...	...	...	...	...	...	...	...
French Guiana - Guyane française	1 612	1 661	...	...	...	...	...	...	...	...
Paraguay	...	...	...	...	...	...	...	4 353	...	...
ASIA - ASIE										
Armenia - Arménie	10 925	11 132	11 501	12 469	13 797	...	...	...	...	...
Azerbaijan - Azerbaïdjan	19 577	20 864	22 323	25 247	24 554	26 799	27 787	31 037	27 892	...
Bahrain - Bahreïn[11]	2 078	2 297	2 014	2 575	2 394	2 525	2 452	2 463	...	...
China, Hong Kong SAR - Chine, Hong Kong RAS	14 192	13 510	13 515	13 199	12 028	11 231	11 864	11 298	10 653	...
Georgia - Géorgie	19 681	21 204	20 644	22 062	24 311	25 585	30 590	...	38 018	...
Israel - Israël[12]	19 090	19 452	19 470	19 638	19 849	19 575	18 974	18 822	...	...
Japan - Japon	289 127	276 352	256 672	242 326	226 878	212 694[13]	202 106	196 639	186 253	...
Kazakhstan	125 654	130 599	125 654	130 599	113 320	106 074	95 288	95 654	84 265	...
Kyrgyzstan - Kirghizstan[14]	20 035	19 762	21 884	20 800	22 088	21 675	23 728	23 547	21 673	24 456
Mongolia - Mongolie	9 064	12 594	15 817	10 688	12 602	12 492	...	...	...	...
Qatar	169	...	...	...	...	...	...	...	...	...
Singapore - Singapour	11 482	12 032	11 933	12 222	12 318	12 082	11 940	10 624	9 282	8 515
Tajikistan - Tadjikistan	19 418	17 489	18 986	18 481	19 470	19 510	17 503	16 618	15 984	...
EUROPE										
Åland Islands - Îles d'Åland	68	53	73	67	68	70	73	60	70	...
Albania - Albanie	9 403	9 552	9 030	8 335	8 139	6 919	7 042	6 755	6 442	...
Belarus - Bélarus	64 655	58 516	46 285	42 197	35 967	33 262	32 031	28 628	31 206	...
Belgium - Belgique	16 696	17 640	18 033	18 595	18 870	19 095	19 578	...	...	...
Bulgaria - Bulgarie	41 795	37 272	37 594	36 593	33 733	31 548	31 716	29 992	29 505	...
Croatia - Croatie	4 563	4 733	4 573	4 497	4 450	4 043	4 347	3 571	3 161	...
Czech Republic - République tchèque	26 453	25 352	25 414	25 760	24 636	23 998	24 055	23 032	22 714	...
Denmark - Danemark[15]	15 295	15 202	15 660	16 355	16 736	16 709	15 974	15 608	15 073	...
Estonia - Estonie[2]	9 610	9 378	8 883	8 409	7 542	7 068	6 668	6 056	5 777	...
Faeroe Islands - Îles Féroé	29	41	46	37	51	33	33	34	23	...
Finland - Finlande	10 969	10 645	10 533	10 423	10 359[16]	10 172[16]	10 418[16]	10 001[16]	10 120	...
France[17]	205 392	214 360	212 285	208 242	208 939	210 813	206 722	204 511	...	...
Germany - Allemagne	124 023	119 710	116 871	114 484	110 694	110 431	108 867	106 815	102 802	...

Continent and country or area	Number - Nombre									
Continent et pays ou zone	2005	2006	2007	2008	2009	2010	2011	2012	2013	2014

EUROPE

Greece - Grèce	16 495	...	...	...	...	...	...	...	...	...
Hungary - Hongrie	48 689	46 324	43 870	44 089	43 181	40 449	38 443	36 118	34 891	...
Iceland - Islande	868	904	905	959	981	977	970	980	963	...
Italy - Italie	129 272[18]	125 782[19]	125 116[20]	118 891[21]	114 793[22]	112 463[23]	110 041[23]	103 191[24]	...	...
Latvia - Lettonie	12 785	11 825	11 814	10 425	8 881	7 443	7 089	6 197	5 557	...
Lithuania - Lituanie	9 972	9 536	9 596	9 031	8 024	6 989	6 205	6 033	5 353	...
Montenegro - Monténégro	1 952	...	...	...	...	...	...	...	...	...
Norway - Norvège	13 989	14 417	15 165	16 054	15 774	15 735	15 343	...	...	...
Poland - Pologne[25]	225	339	328	506	538	644	669	752	745	...
Portugal	798	1 215	4 325	13 541	17 932	17 261	17 351	...	...	...
Republic of Moldova - République de Moldova	16 642	15 742	15 843	15 900	14 634	14 785	15 710	14 838	...	...
Romania - Roumanie	163 359	150 246	137 226	127 907	116 060	101 915	103 386	87 975	86 432	...
Russian Federation - Fédération de Russie	1 675 693	1 582 398	1 479 010	1 385 600	1 292 389	1 186 108	1 124 880	1 063 982	...	...
Serbia - Serbie[26]	26 645	25 665	24 273	22 867	...	...	...	...	...	...
Slovakia - Slovaquie	14 427	14 243	13 424	13 394	13 240	12 582	11 789	11 214	11 105	...
Slovenia - Slovénie	5 851	5 632	5 176	4 946	4 653	4 328	4 263	4 106	...	...
Spain - Espagne	91 664	101 592	112 138	115 812	111 482	113 031	118 359	112 390	...	...
Sweden - Suède	34 978	36 045	37 205	38 049	37 524	37 693	37 696	...	...	...
Switzerland - Suisse	10 818	10 594	10 035[27]	10 310[27]	10 187[27]	10 650[27]	10 715[27]	10 477[27]	10 137[27]	...
Ukraine	263 590	229 618[28]	225 336	217 413	194 845	176 774	169 131	153 147	147 736	...
United Kingdom of Great Britain and Northern Ireland - Royaume-Uni de Grande-Bretagne et d'Irlande du Nord[29]	207 018	214 340	219 376	216 062	208 854	209 048	208 636	203 419[30]	...	...

OCEANIA - OCÉANIE

Guam	...	...	...	327	266	269	295	275	213	209
New Zealand - Nouvelle-Zélande	17 531	17 934	18 382	17 940	17 550	16 630	15 863	14 745	14 073	...

FOOTNOTES - NOTES

* Provisional. - Données provisoires.

[1] Data refer to the recorded events in Ministry of Health hospitals and health centres only. - Les données se rapportent aux faits d'état civil enregistrés dans les hôpitaux et les dispensaires du Ministère de la santé seulement.
[2] Data refer to resident population only. - Pour la population résidante seulement.
[3] Significant undercoverage of medically induced abortions in clinics in 2006 due to non response in some provinces. - Sous-dénombrement notable des interruptions volontaires de grossesse pratiquées dans les centres médicaux en 2006 faute de réponse dans certaines provinces.
[4] Excluding abortions performed in private hospitals. - Non comprises les interruptions volontaires de grossesse effectuées dans des hôpitaux privés.
[5] Number of women who report having had a previous abortion when registering a newborn. - Nombre des femmes qui ont signalé d'avoir eu un avortement avant la naissance de l'enfant enregistré.
[6] Data refer to 'Therapeutic Abortions'. According to Mexican law, only induced abortions, prescribed by medical reasons or induced because of pregnancy coming from sexual aggression, are considered as legal; data refer only to the former. Refers to residence of the mother. To calculate the total number of abortions, only foetal deaths of less than 20 weeks of gestation were considered. Excluding abortions in the country by women with usual residence outside of the country. - Les données se rapportent aux « interruptions volontaires de grossesse pour des motifs thérapeutiques ». D'après la loi mexicaine, seuls sont considérés légaux les avortements déclenchés pour des raisons médicales ou parce que la grossesse est le résultat d'une agression sexuelle; les données se réfèrent seulement à la première. Correspond à la résidence de la mère. Seuls les morts fœtales survenues à moins de 20 semaines de gestation ont été prises en compte aux fins du calcul du nombre total d'avortements. Hors avortements dans le pays par des femmes avec résidence habituelle en dehors du pays.
[7] Data refer to the fiscal year from 1 July to 30 June. - Les données se réfèrent à l'année budgétaire de 1 juillet à 30 juin.

[8] Excluding abortions performed in a clinic which closed operations without reporting the data. - Non comprises les avortements effectuées dans une clinique qui a fermé sans envoyer les données.
[9] Data refer to abortions performed in hospitals at Grand Turk and Providenciales. - Pour des avortements exécutés dans les hôpitaux dans Grand Turk et Providenciales.
[10] Includes areas that reported abortion counts every year during the period of analysis. Excludes states that did not report abortion numbers: Alaska(1998-2002), California (1997-2008), Louisiana (2005), Maryland (2006-2008), New Hampshire (1998-2008), Oklahoma (1998-1999), and West Virginia (2003-2004). - Sont couvertes les régions qui ont indiqué le nombre annuel d'avortements pour la période analysée. Ne sont pas couverts les États qui n'ont pas fourni de chiffres : l'Alaska (1998-2002), la Californie (1997-2008), la Louisiane (2005), le Maryland (2006-2008), le New Hampshire (1998-2008), l'Oklahoma (1998-1999) et la Virginie occidentale (2003-2004).
[11] Data refer to spontaneous abortions and miscarriages. - Données se rapportant aux avortements spontanés et fausses couches.
[12] Includes data for East Jerusalem and Israeli residents in certain other territories under occupation by Israeli military forces since June 1967. Data refer to applications to commissions for termination of pregnancy and not to authorizations. - Y compris les données pour Jérusalem-Est et les résidents israéliens dans certains autres territoires occupés depuis 1967 par les forces armées israéliennes. Les données relatives aux avortements provoqués légalement se rapportent aux demandes d'autorisation et non aux autorisations elles-mêmes.
[13] Excluding data of cities and towns in the jurisdiction of Sousou Public Health and Welfare Office of Fukushima Prefecture due to the impact of the Great East Japan Earthquake. - Ne sont pas incluses les données relatives aux agglomérations relevant du bureau de la santé publique et des services sociaux de Sousou dans la préfecture de Fukushima, en raison des conséquences du grand séisme dans l'est du Japon.
[14] Based on administrative reporting of the Ministry of Health. - Les données reposent sur les rapports administratifs du Ministère de la santé.

15 Excluding Faeroe Islands and Greenland shown separately, if available. - Non compris les Iles Féroé et le Groenland, qui font l'objet de rubriques distinctes, si disponible.

16 Excluding Åland Islands. - Non compris les Îles d'Åland.

17 Data refer to women between 15 and 49 years of age. - Le total se rapporte uniquement aux femmes dont l'âge est compris entre 15 et 49 ans.

18 Data are incomplete for Friuli-Venezia Giulia, Campania, Molise and Sicilia regions. - Les données sont incomplètes pour le Frioul-Vénétie julienne, la Campanie, la Molise et la Sicile.

19 Data are incomplete for Friuli-Venezia Giulia, Campania and Sicilia regions. - Les données sont incomplètes pour les régions Frioul-Vénétie julienne, la Campanie et la Sicile.

20 Data are incomplete for Campania and Sicilia regions. - Les données sont incomplètes pour les régions de la Campanie et de la Sicile.

21 Data are incomplete for Campania, Calabria, Sicilia and Sardegna regions. - Les données sont incomplètes pour les régions de Campanie, de Calabrie, de Sicile et de Sardaigne.

22 Data are incomplete for Abruzzo, Campania, Basilicata, Sicilia and Sardegna regions. - Données incomplètes pour les régions des Abruzzes, de Campanie, de Basilicate, de Sicile et de Sardaigne.

23 Data are incomplete for Umbria, Campania and Sicilia regions. - Les données sont incomplètes pour l'Ombrie, la Campanie et la Sicile.

24 Data are incomplete for Umbria, Abruzzo, Campania, Puglia and Sicilia regions. - Les données sont incomplètes pour les régions d'Ombrie, des Abruzzes, de Campanie, des Pouilles et de Sicile.

25 Based on hospital and polyclinic records. - D'après les registres des hôpitaux et des polycliniques.

26 Excludes data for Kosovo and Metohia. Data refer to institutions included in the Health Institutions Network Plan in the Republic of Serbia. - Sans les données pour le Kosovo et Metohie. Les données se rapportent aux institutions membres du "Health Institutions Network Plan" de la République de Serbie.

27 Data refer to termination of pregnancy for women who are Switzerland residents. - Les données portent sur les interruptions de grossesse pratiquées sur des femmes qui résident en Suisse.

28 Data refer to the recorded events in Ministry of Health institutions only. - Données ne concernant que les faits enregistrés dans les institutions du Ministère de la santé.

29 Excluding Northern Ireland. Excluding Channel Islands (Guernsey and Jersey) and Isle of Man, shown separately, if available. - Non compris l'Irlande du Nord. Non compris les îles Anglo-Normandes (Guernesey et Jersey) et l'île de Man, qui font l'objet de rubriques distinctes, si disponible.

30 Including provisional data for Scotland. - Y compris les données provisoires pour l'Écosse.

Table 14 - *Demographic Yearbook 2014*

Table 14 presents legally induced abortions by age and number of previous live births of women for the latest available year between 2005 and 2014.

Description of variables: Age is defined as age at last birthday, that is, the difference between the date of birth and the date of the occurrence of the event, expressed in complete solar years. The age classification used in this table is the following: under 15 years, 5-year age groups through 45-49 years and 50 years and over.

Except where otherwise indicated, eight categories are used in classifying the number of previous live births: 0 through 5, 6 or more live births, and, if required, number of live births unknown.

Information on abortion policies is collected by the United Nations Population Division and published in the *Abortion Policies and Reproductive Health around the World*[1].

Reliability of data: Unlike data on live births and foetal deaths, which are generally collected through systems of vital registration, data on abortion are collected from a variety of sources. Because of this, the quality specification on the completeness of civil registers, which is presented for other tables, does not appear here.

Limitations: With regard to the collection of information on abortions, a variety of sources are used, but hospital records are the most common source of information. This implies that most cases that have no contact with hospitals are missed. Data from other sources are probably also incomplete. The data in the present table are limited to legally induced abortions, which, by their nature, might be assumed to be more complete than data on all induced abortions.

In addition, deficiencies in the reporting of age and number of previous live births of the woman, differences in the method used for obtaining the age of the woman, and the proportion of abortions for which age or previous live births of the woman are unknown must all be taken into account in using these data.

Earlier data: Legally induced abortions by age and previous live births of women have been shown previously in most issues of the *Demographic Yearbook* since the twenty-third issue. For more information on specific topics and years for which data are reported, readers should consult the Historical Index.

NOTES

[1] United Nations, Department of Economic and Social Affairs, Population Division (2014). *Abortion Policies and Reproductive Health around the World* (United Nations publication, Sales No. E.14.XIII.11).

Tableau 14 – *Annuaire démographique 2014*

Le tableau 14 présente les données les plus récentes disponibles entre 2005 et 2014 sur les avortements provoqués pour des raisons légales, selon l'âge de la mère et le nombre de naissances vivantes précédentes.

Description des variables : L'âge considéré est l'âge au dernier anniversaire, c'est-à-dire la différence entre la date de naissance et la date de l'avortement, exprimée en années solaires révolues. La classification par âge utilisée dans le tableau 14 est la suivante : moins de 15 ans, groupes quinquennaux jusqu'à 45-49 ans, 50 ans et plus, et âge inconnu.

Sauf indication contraire, les naissances vivantes antérieures sont classées dans les huit catégories suivantes: 0 à 5 naissances vivantes, 6 naissances vivantes ou plus et, le cas échéant, nombre de naissances vivantes inconnu.

La Division de la population des Nations Unies collecte des informations sur les politiques en matière d'avortement et les publient dans *Abortion Policies and Reproductive Health around the World*[1].

Fiabilité des données : à la différence des données sur les naissances vivantes et les morts fœtales, qui proviennent généralement des registres d'état civil, les données sur l'avortement sont tirées de sources diverses. Aussi ne trouve-t-on pas ici une évaluation de la qualité des données semblable à celle qui indique, pour les autres tableaux, le degré d'exhaustivité des données de l'état civil.

Insuffisance des données : en ce qui concerne les renseignements sur l'avortement, un grand nombre de sources sont utilisées, les relevés hospitaliers restant cependant la source la plus commune. Il s'ensuit que la plupart des cas qui ne passent pas par les hôpitaux sont ignorés. Il faut aussi tenir compte du fait que les données provenant d'autres sources sont probablement incomplètes. Les données du tableau 14 se limitent aux avortements provoqués pour raisons légales dont on peut supposer, en raison de leur nature même, que les statistiques sont plus complètes que les données concernant l'ensemble des avortements provoqués.

En outre, on doit tenir compte, lorsque l'on utilise ces données, des erreurs de déclaration de l'âge de la mère et du nombre des naissances vivantes précédentes, de l'hétérogénéité des méthodes de calcul de l'âge de la mère et de la proportion d'avortements pour lesquels l'âge de la mère ou le nombre des naissances vivantes ne sont pas connus.

Données publiées antérieurement : Depuis la vingt-troisième édition, la plupart des éditions de l'*Annuaire démographique* contiennent des statistiques concernant les avortements provoqués pour raisons légales, selon l'âge de la mère et le nombre de naissances vivantes antérieures. Pour plus de précisions concernant les années et les sujets pour lesquels des données ont été publiées, se reporter à l'index historique.

NOTES

[1] United Nations, Department of Economic and Social Affairs, Population Division (2014). *Abortion Policies and Reproductive Health around the World* (United Nations publication, Sales No. E.14.XIII.11).

14. Legally induced abortions by age and number of previous live births of women: latest available year, 2005 - 2014
Avortments provoqués légalement selon l'âge de la femme et selon le nombre des naissances vivantes précédentes : dernière année disponible, 2005 - 2014

Continent, country or area, year and age Continent, pays ou zone, année et âge	Number of previous live births Nombre des naissances vivantes précédentes								
	Total	0	1	2	3	4	5	6+	Unknown - Inconnu
AMERICA, NORTH - AMÉRIQUE DU NORD									
Bermuda - Bermudes									
2014									
Total	248	...	...	...	...	...	...	...	...
0 - 14	-	...	...	...	...	...	...	...	...
15 - 19	17	...	...	...	...	...	...	...	...
20 - 24	54	...	...	...	...	...	...	...	...
25 - 29	78	...	...	...	...	...	...	...	...
30 - 34	57	...	...	...	...	...	...	...	...
35 - 39	33	...	...	...	...	...	...	...	...
40 - 44	9	...	...	...	...	...	...	...	...
45 - 49	-	...	...	...	...	...	...	...	...
50 +	-	...	...	...	...	...	...	...	...
Unknown - Inconnu	-	...	...	...	...	...	...	...	...
Canada[1]									
2006									
Total	91 310	...	...	...	...	...	...	...	...
0 - 14	267	...	...	...	...	...	...	...	...
15 - 19	15 217	...	...	...	...	...	...	...	...
20 - 24	28 358	...	...	...	...	...	...	...	...
25 - 29	20 315	...	...	...	...	...	...	...	...
30 - 34	13 615	...	...	...	...	...	...	...	...
35 - 39	9 444	...	...	...	...	...	...	...	...
40 +	3 938	...	...	...	...	...	...	...	...
Unknown - Inconnu	156	...	...	...	...	...	...	...	...
Costa Rica[2]									
2009									
Total	7 848	...	...	...	...	...	...	...	...
10 - 14	68	...	...	...	...	...	...	...	...
15 - 19	1 275	...	...	...	...	...	...	...	...
20 - 44	6 437	...	...	...	...	...	...	...	...
45 +	68	...	...	...	...	...	...	...	...
Cuba									
2011									
Total	83 943	...	...	...	...	...	...	...	...
0 - 14	1 295	...	...	...	...	...	...	...	...
15 - 19	20 878	...	...	...	...	...	...	...	...
20 - 34	50 951	...	...	...	...	...	...	...	...
35 - 39	10 819	...	...	...	...	...	...	...	...
Mexico - Mexique[3]									
2013									
Total	271	86	91	45	13	5	2	2	27
0 - 14	2	1	1	-	-	-	-	-	-
15 - 19	31	17	8	-	-	-	-	-	6
20 - 24	72	36	20	7	1	1	-	-	7
25 - 29	69	16	30	10	1	2	-	1	9
30 - 34	49	9	14	15	7	2	-	-	2
35 - 39	31	5	12	11	2	-	-	-	1
40 - 44	10	1	3	1	2	-	1	1	1
45 - 49	1	-	-	1	-	-	-	-	-
50 +	-	-	-	-	-	-	-	-	-
Unknown - Inconnu	6	1	3	-	-	-	1	-	1
Puerto Rico - Porto Rico[4]									
2006									
Total	5 538	1 991	1 639	1 013	588	229	46	32	-
0 - 14	21	...	...	...	...	...	...	...	...
15 - 19	968	...	...	...	...	...	...	...	...
20 - 24	1 868	...	...	...	...	...	...	...	...
25 - 29	1 413	...	...	...	...	...	...	...	...
30 - 34	767	...	...	...	...	...	...	...	...
35 - 39	351	...	...	...	...	...	...	...	...
40 - 44	129	...	...	...	...	...	...	...	...
45 +	21	...	...	...	...	...	...	...	...
Turks and Caicos Islands - Îles Turques et Caïques[5]									
2005									
Total	32	...	...	...	...	...	...	...	...
15 - 19	4	...	...	...	...	...	...	...	...
20 - 24	7	...	...	...	...	...	...	...	...

14. Legally induced abortions by age and number of previous live births of women: latest available year, 2005 - 2014
Avortments provoqués légalement selon l'âge de la femme et selon le nombre des naissances vivantes précédentes : dernière année disponible, 2005 - 2014 (continued - suite)

Continent, country or area, year and age / Continent, pays ou zone, année et âge	Total	Number of previous live births — Nombre des naissances vivantes précédentes							Unknown - Inconnu
		0	1	2	3	4	5	6+	
AMERICA, NORTH - AMÉRIQUE DU NORD									
Turks and Caicos Islands - Îles Turques et Caïques[5]									
2005									
25 - 29	9	...	...	...	...	...	...	...	...
30 - 34	6	...	...	...	...	...	...	...	...
35 - 39	4	...	...	...	...	...	...	...	...
40 - 44	1	...	...	...	...	...	...	...	...
45 +	1	...	...	...	...	...	...	...	...
ASIA - ASIE									
Armenia - Arménie									
2008									
Total	12 469	...	...	...	...	...	...	...	...
0 - 14	1	...	...	...	...	...	...	...	...
15 - 19	610	...	...	...	...	...	...	...	...
20 - 24	9 459	...	...	...	...	...	...	...	...
25 +	2 399	...	...	...	...	...	...	...	...
Azerbaijan - Azerbaïdjan									
2013									
Total	27 892	...	...	...	...	...	...	...	...
0 - 14	-	...	...	...	...	...	...	...	...
15 - 19	1 147	...	...	...	...	...	...	...	...
20 - 24	5 710	...	...	...	...	...	...	...	...
25 - 29	8 958	...	...	...	...	...	...	...	...
30 - 34	7 849	...	...	...	...	...	...	...	...
35 +	4 228	...	...	...	...	...	...	...	...
China, Hong Kong SAR - Chine, Hong Kong RAS									
2013									
Total	10 653	5 784	2 168	2 203	411	71	14	2	...
0 - 14	16	16	-	-	-	-	-	-	...
15 - 19	874	829	41	4	-	-	-	-	...
20 - 24	2 137	1 909	167	51	9	-	1	-	...
25 - 29	2 179	1 494	393	251	36	4	1	-	...
30 - 34	2 278	921	634	598	107	17	1	-	...
35 - 39	2 098	466	636	798	157	35	4	2	...
40 - 44	964	140	267	442	94	14	7	-	...
45 - 49	107	9	30	59	8	1	-	-	...
50 +	-	-	-	-	-	-	-	-	...
Georgia - Géorgie									
2013									
Total	38 018	...	...	...	...	...	...	...	...
0 - 14	34	...	...	...	...	...	...	...	...
15 - 19	1 849	...	...	...	...	...	...	...	...
20 - 29	17 475	...	...	...	...	...	...	...	...
30 - 34	10 007	...	...	...	...	...	...	...	...
35 - 39	6 412	...	...	...	...	...	...	...	...
40 - 44	1 966	...	...	...	...	...	...	...	...
45 - 49	258	...	...	...	...	...	...	...	...
50 +	17	...	...	...	...	...	...	...	...
Israel - Israël[6]									
2012									
Total	18 822	8 390	2 589	3 640	2 539	1 036	354	274	...
0 - 14	67	64	2	1	-	-	-	-	...
15 - 19	2 099	2 039	51	6	-	2	1	-	...
20 - 24	3 735	3 001	454	192	74	11	1	2	...
25 - 29	3 799	1 907	768	722	271	98	24	9	...
30 - 34	3 752	901	712	1 123	624	253	84	55	...
35 - 39	3 554	376	426	1 082	1 028	407	134	101	...
40 - 44	1 653	85	167	479	486	242	100	94	...
45 - 49	154	15	8	34	54	20	10	13	...
50 +	9	2	1	1	2	3	-	-	...
Japan - Japon									
2013									
Total	186 253	...	...	...	...	...	...	...	...
0 - 14	318	...	...	...	...	...	...	...	...

14. Legally induced abortions by age and number of previous live births of women: latest available year, 2005 - 2014
Avortments provoqués légalement selon l'âge de la femme et selon le nombre des naissances vivantes précédentes : dernière année disponible, 2005 - 2014 (continued - suite)

Continent, country or area, year and age Continent, pays ou zone, année et âge	Total	Number of previous live births Nombre des naissances vivantes précédentes							Unknown - Inconnu
		0	1	2	3	4	5	6+	
ASIA - ASIE									
Japan - Japon									
2013									
15 - 19	19 041	...	...	...	...	...	...	...	...
20 - 24	40 268	...	...	...	...	...	...	...	...
25 - 29	37 999	...	...	...	...	...	...	...	...
30 - 34	36 757	...	...	...	...	...	...	...	...
35 - 39	34 115	...	...	...	...	...	...	...	...
40 - 44	16 477	...	...	...	...	...	...	...	...
45 - 49	1 237	...	...	...	...	...	...	...	...
50 +	22	...	...	...	...	...	...	...	...
Unknown - Inconnu	19	...	...	...	...	...	...	...	...
Kyrgyzstan - Kirghizstan[7]									
2008									
Total	20 800	...	...	...	...	...	...	...	...
0 - 14	1	...	...	...	...	...	...	...	...
15 - 19	1 814	...	...	...	...	...	...	...	...
20 - 24	5 018	...	...	...	...	...	...	...	...
25 - 29	5 462	...	...	...	...	...	...	...	...
30 - 34	4 598	...	...	...	...	...	...	...	...
35 - 39	2 776	...	...	...	...	...	...	...	...
40 - 44	1 019	...	...	...	...	...	...	...	...
45 +	112	...	...	...	...	...	...	...	...
Singapore - Singapour									
2014									
Total	8 515	3 718	1 727	2 080	721	^269	...	...	-
0 - 14	11	10	-	1	-	^-	...	...	-
15 - 19	438	405	29	4	-	^-	...	...	-
20 - 24	1 694	1 326	223	102	34	^9	...	...	-
25 - 29	2 102	1 147	460	358	90	^47	...	...	-
30 - 34	2 119	562	551	705	220	^81	...	...	-
35 - 39	1 496	214	314	628	251	^89	...	...	-
40 - 44	623	52	140	268	121	^42	...	...	-
45 +	32	2	10	14	5	^1	...	...	-
Unknown - Inconnu	-	-	-	-	-	^-	...	...	-
Tajikistan - Tadjikistan									
2013									
Total	15 984	...	...	...	...	...	...	...	...
0 - 14	-	...	...	...	...	...	...	...	...
15 - 17	10	...	...	...	...	...	...	...	...
18 - 19	1 380	...	...	...	...	...	...	...	...
20 - 34	10 857	...	...	...	...	...	...	...	...
35 +	3 737	...	...	...	...	...	...	...	...
EUROPE									
Åland Islands - Îles d'Åland									
2012									
Total	60	31	12	10	5	-	2	-	...
0 - 14	-	-	-	-	-	-	-	-	...
15 - 19	9	9	-	-	-	-	-	-	...
20 - 24	15	11	3	1	-	-	-	-	...
25 - 29	17	6	4	4	1	-	2	-	...
30 - 34	7	2	1	3	1	-	-	-	...
35 - 39	7	1	3	1	2	-	-	-	...
40 - 44	5	2	1	1	1	-	-	-	...
45 - 49	-	-	-	-	-	-	-	-	...
50 +	-	-	-	-	-	-	-	-	...
2013									
Total	70	...	...	...	...	...	...	...	...
0 - 14	-	...	...	...	...	...	...	...	...
15 - 19	16	...	...	...	...	...	...	...	...
20 - 24	25	...	...	...	...	...	...	...	...
25 - 29	14	...	...	...	...	...	...	...	...
30 - 34	8	...	...	...	...	...	...	...	...
35 - 39	6	...	...	...	...	...	...	...	...
40 - 44	1	...	...	...	...	...	...	...	...

14. Legally induced abortions by age and number of previous live births of women: latest available year, 2005 - 2014
Avortments provoqués légalement selon l'âge de la femme et selon le nombre des naissances vivantes précédentes : dernière année disponible, 2005 - 2014 (continued - suite)

Continent, country or area, year and age / Continent, pays ou zone, année et âge	Number of previous live births / Nombre des naissances vivantes précédentes								
	Total	0	1	2	3	4	5	6+	Unknown - Inconnu
EUROPE									
Åland Islands - Îles d'Åland									
2013									
45 - 49	-	...	...	...	...	...	...	...	...
50 +	-	...	...	...	...	...	...	...	...
Belarus - Bélarus									
2013									
Total	31 206	4 784	...	...	...	...	...	...	26 422
0 - 14	27	...	...	...	...	...	...	...	...
15 - 19	1 830	...	...	...	...	...	...	...	...
20 - 24	6 024	...	...	...	...	...	...	...	...
25 - 29	8 410	...	...	...	...	...	...	...	...
30 - 34	7 885	...	...	...	...	...	...	...	...
35 - 39	4 771	...	...	...	...	...	...	...	...
40 - 44	2 055	...	...	...	...	...	...	...	...
45 - 49	204	...	...	...	...	...	...	...	...
50 +	-	...	...	...	...	...	...	...	...
Belgium - Belgique									
2011									
Total	19 578	9 145	4 266	3 698	1 636	581	174	78	...
0 - 14	87	86	1	-	-	-	-	-	...
15 - 19	2 575	2 339	207	28	1	-	-	-	...
20 - 24	5 027	3 430	1 070	425	87	12	3	-	...
25 - 29	4 688	1 992	1 249	983	332	104	20	8	...
30 - 34	3 745	863	997	1 131	512	176	46	20	...
35 - 39	2 454	349	538	796	483	184	70	34	...
40 - 44	923	78	188	308	207	99	30	13	...
45 - 49	78	7	16	27	14	6	5	3	...
50 +	1	1	-	-	-	-	-	-	...
Bulgaria - Bulgarie									
2013									
Total	29 505	...	...	...	...	...	...	...	...
0 - 14	137	...	...	...	...	...	...	...	...
15 - 19	2 453	...	...	...	...	...	...	...	...
20 - 24	5 977	...	...	...	...	...	...	...	...
25 - 29	7 234	...	...	...	...	...	...	...	...
30 - 34	6 760	...	...	...	...	...	...	...	...
35 - 39	5 275	...	...	...	...	...	...	...	...
40 - 44	1 531	...	...	...	...	...	...	...	...
45 - 49	134	...	...	...	...	...	...	...	...
50 +	4	...	...	...	...	...	...	...	...
Croatia - Croatie									
2013									
Total	3 161	868	559	932	344	92	36	49	281
0 - 14	1	-	-	-	-	-	-	-	1
15 - 19	220	177	13	2	1	-	-	-	27
20 - 24	500	295	98	49	16	3	2	1	36
25 - 29	658	171	142	185	66	16	8	6	64
30 - 34	736	112	151	275	90	24	9	15	60
35 - 39	685	80	109	291	101	32	5	19	48
40 - 44	309	26	43	118	63	16	11	6	26
45 - 49	25	5	1	11	3	1	1	2	1
50 +	-	-	-	-	-	-	-	-	-
Unknown - Inconnu	27	2	2	1	4	-	-	-	18
Czech Republic - République tchèque									
2013									
Total	22 714	6 536	5 957	7 247	2 152	563	150	109	...
0 - 14	38	38	-	-	-	-	-	-	...
15 - 19	1 696	1 449	217	29	1	-	-	-	...
20 - 24	4 111	2 374	1 157	460	87	27	5	1	...
25 - 29	4 642	1 522	1 532	1 140	314	95	26	13	...
30 - 34	5 023	761	1 497	2 044	494	159	40	28	...
35 - 39	5 122	326	1 166	2 505	849	185	52	39	...
40 - 44	1 917	57	358	988	374	89	24	27	...
45 - 49	162	9	28	80	33	8	3	1	...
50 +	3	-	2	1	-	-	-	-	...
Denmark - Danemark[8]									
2013									
Total	15 073	...	...	...	...	...	...	...	...
0 - 19	2 206	...	...	...	...	...	...	...	...

14. Legally induced abortions by age and number of previous live births of women: latest available year, 2005 - 2014
Avortments provoqués légalement selon l'âge de la femme et selon le nombre des naissances vivantes précédentes : dernière année disponible, 2005 - 2014 (continued - suite)

Continent, country or area, year and age / Continent, pays ou zone, année et âge	Number of previous live births / Nombre des naissances vivantes précédentes								
	Total	0	1	2	3	4	5	6+	Unknown - Inconnu
EUROPE									
Denmark - Danemark[8]									
2013									
20 - 24	4 105	...	...	...	...	...	...	...	...
25 - 29	3 018	...	...	...	...	...	...	...	...
30 - 34	2 541	...	...	...	...	...	...	...	...
35 - 39	2 162	...	...	...	...	...	...	...	...
40 - 44	954	...	...	...	...	...	...	...	...
45 +	87	...	...	...	...	...	...	...	...
Estonia - Estonie[9]									
2013									
Total	5 777	1 495	1 843	1 656	588	134	47	12	2
0 - 14	13	13	-	-	-	-	-	-	-
15 - 19	510	432	71	5	2	-	-	-	-
20 - 24	1 282	641	475	137	25	2	1	-	1
25 - 29	1 327	281	568	364	87	18	8	1	-
30 - 34	1 179	80	368	508	168	38	15	2	-
35 - 39	971	39	233	445	190	41	14	8	1
40 - 44	458	9	122	182	105	31	8	1	-
45 - 49	37	-	6	15	11	4	1	-	-
50 +	-	-	-	-	-	-	-	-	-
Faeroe Islands - Îles Féroé									
2005									
Total	29	...	...	...	...	...	...	...	...
0 - 14	-	...	...	...	...	...	...	...	...
15 - 19	6	...	...	...	...	...	...	...	...
20 - 24	2	...	...	...	...	...	...	...	...
25 - 29	5	...	...	...	...	...	...	...	...
30 - 34	8	...	...	...	...	...	...	...	...
35 - 39	5	...	...	...	...	...	...	...	...
40 - 44	3	...	...	...	...	...	...	...	...
45 - 49	-	...	...	...	...	...	...	...	...
50 +	-	...	...	...	...	...	...	...	...
Finland - Finlande									
2013									
Total	10 120	5 216	1 853	1 744	840	294	83	46	44
0 - 14	35	34	1	-	-	-	-	-	-
15 - 19	1 598	1 509	84	3	-	-	-	-	2
20 - 24	2 915	2 111	563	199	30	5	1	-	6
25 - 29	2 104	902	488	453	185	56	9	1	10
30 - 34	1 674	415	367	516	236	94	26	10	10
35 - 39	1 254	183	258	394	265	93	32	18	11
40 - 44	481	55	83	157	110	40	15	16	5
45 - 49	56	6	9	20	14	6	-	1	-
50 +	3	1	-	2	-	-	-	-	-
France[10]									
2009									
Total[11]	208 290	...	...	...	...	...	...	...	...
15 - 19	29 004	...	...	...	...	...	...	...	...
20 - 24	52 360	...	...	...	...	...	...	...	...
25 - 29	46 237	...	...	...	...	...	...	...	...
30 - 34	36 351	...	...	...	...	...	...	...	...
35 - 39	30 125	...	...	...	...	...	...	...	...
40 - 44	12 805	...	...	...	...	...	...	...	...
45 - 49	1 408	...	...	...	...	...	...	...	...
Germany - Allemagne									
2013									
Total	102 802	40 506	26 718	23 711	8 260	2 431	746	430	...
0 - 14	322	322	-	-	-	-	-	-	...
15 - 19	3 297	3 271	26	-	-	-	-	-	...
20 - 24	5 969	5 086	789	89	5	-	-	-	...
25 - 29	23 723	14 654	6 260	2 240	445	87	21	16	...
30 - 34	24 407	9 294	7 581	5 354	1 622	413	99	44	...
35 - 39	21 785	4 739	6 280	7 062	2 570	775	256	103	...
40 - 44	15 452	2 182	3 942	5 842	2 323	768	245	150	...
45 - 49	7 137	880	1 682	2 850	1 168	353	107	97	...
50 +	695	77	153	273	123	34	17	18	...
Unknown - Inconnu	15	1	5	1	4	1	1	2	...

14. Legally induced abortions by age and number of previous live births of women: latest available year, 2005 - 2014
Avortments provoqués légalement selon l'âge de la femme et selon le nombre des naissances vivantes précédentes : dernière année disponible, 2005 - 2014 (continued - suite)

Continent, country or area, year and age Continent, pays ou zone, année et âge	Number of previous live births Nombre des naissances vivantes précédentes								
	Total	0	1	2	3	4	5	6+	Unknown - Inconnu
EUROPE									
Hungary - Hongrie									
2013									
Total	34 891	9 707	8 781	8 536	4 632	1 821	808	606	-
0 - 14	168	165	3	-	-	-	-	-	-
15 - 19	4 423	3 395	869	132	25	2	-	-	-
20 - 24	7 335	3 135	2 182	1 309	542	134	28	5	-
25 - 29	6 935	1 622	1 902	1 692	1 007	450	173	89	-
30 - 34	6 839	837	1 737	2 032	1 229	520	277	207	-
35 - 39	6 624	451	1 528	2 331	1 325	521	240	228	-
40 - 44	2 406	94	526	976	470	184	86	70	-
45 - 49	160	8	34	63	34	10	4	7	-
50 +	1	-	-	1	-	-	-	-	-
Unknown - Inconnu	-	-	-	-	-	-	-	-	-
Iceland - Islande									
2011									
Total	969	415	249	186	83	29	5	2	-
0 - 14	2	2	-	-	-	-	-	-	-
15 - 19	174	155	16	3	-	-	-	-	-
20 - 24	289	182	84	21	2	-	-	-	-
25 - 29	187	46	73	52	10	6	-	-	-
30 - 34	169	25	40	56	36	11	1	-	-
35 - 39	109	5	29	45	20	9	1	-	-
40 - 44	35	-	7	8	12	3	3	2	-
45 - 49	4	-	-	1	3	-	-	-	-
50 +	-	-	-	-	-	-	-	-	-
Unknown - Inconnu	-	-	-	-	-	-	-	-	-
Italy - Italie[12]									
2009									
Total	114 793	45 152	26 909	29 348	8 647	1 918	494	192	2 133
0 - 14	236	222	1	-	-	-	-	-	13
15 - 19	9 603	8 227	753	108	7	2	-	-	506
20 - 24	20 950	13 921	4 461	1 589	242	46	14	6	671
25 - 29	23 302	10 106	6 503	4 865	1 113	206	37	21	451
30 - 34	25 699	6 750	6 895	8 555	2 543	523	109	41	283
35 - 39	22 916	4 038	5 541	9 189	2 994	716	205	74	159
40 - 44	10 228	1 390	2 341	4 405	1 530	369	108	42	43
45 - 49	955	131	192	409	155	40	17	8	3
50 +	25	8	1	13	1	2	-	-	-
Unknown - Inconnu	879	359	221	215	62	14	4	-	4
Latvia - Lettonie									
2011									
Total	7 089	...	...	...	...	...	...	...	...
0 - 14	7	...	...	...	...	...	...	...	...
15 - 19	511	...	...	...	...	...	...	...	...
20 - 24	1 693	...	...	...	...	...	...	...	...
25 - 29	1 732	...	...	...	...	...	...	...	...
30 - 34	1 384	...	...	...	...	...	...	...	...
35 - 39	1 238	...	...	...	...	...	...	...	...
40 - 44	485	...	...	...	...	...	...	...	...
45 - 49	38	...	...	...	...	...	...	...	...
50 +	1	...	...	...	...	...	...	...	...
Unknown - Inconnu	-	...	...	...	...	...	...	...	...
Lithuania - Lituanie[13]									
2013									
Total	5 353	...	...	...	...	...	...	...	5 353
0 - 14	2	...	...	...	...	...	...	...	2
15 - 19	401	...	...	...	...	...	...	...	401
20 - 24	1 053	...	...	...	...	...	...	...	1 053
25 - 29	1 205	...	...	...	...	...	...	...	1 205
30 - 34	1 142	...	...	...	...	...	...	...	1 142
35 - 39	985	...	...	...	...	...	...	...	985
40 - 44	501	...	...	...	...	...	...	...	501
45 - 49	64	...	...	...	...	...	...	...	64
Montenegro - Monténégro									
2005									
Total	1 952	307	283	677	473	139	45	26	2
0 - 14	3	-	2	1	-	-	-	-	-
15 - 16	5	5	-	-	-	-	-	-	-
17 - 19	46	31	7	4	2	1	-	-	1

14. Legally induced abortions by age and number of previous live births of women: latest available year, 2005 - 2014
Avortments provoqués légalement selon l'âge de la femme et selon le nombre des naissances vivantes précédentes :
dernière année disponible, 2005 - 2014 (continued - suite)

Continent, country or area, year and age Continent, pays ou zone, année et âge	Total	0	1	2	3	4	5	6+	Unknown - Inconnu
				Number of previous live births Nombre des naissances vivantes précédentes					
EUROPE									
Montenegro - Monténégro									
2005									
20 - 29	685	179	155	219	98	21	10	3	-
30 - 39	982	80	108	365	286	91	33	18	1
40 - 49	223	11	11	86	82	26	2	5	-
50 +	4	1	-	1	2	-	-	-	-
Unknown - Inconnu	4	-	-	1	3	-	-	-	-
Norway - Norvège[10]									
2006									
Total	14 132	...	...	...	...	...	...	...	...
0 - 14	37	...	...	...	...	...	...	...	...
15 - 19	2 307	...	...	...	...	...	...	...	...
20 - 24	3 740	...	...	...	...	...	...	...	...
25 - 29	2 904	...	...	...	...	...	...	...	...
30 - 34	2 495	...	...	...	...	...	...	...	...
35 - 39	1 877	...	...	...	...	...	...	...	...
40 - 44	694	...	...	...	...	...	...	...	...
45 - 49	55	...	...	...	...	...	...	...	...
50 +	-	...	...	...	...	...	...	...	...
Unknown - Inconnu	23	...	...	...	...	...	...	...	...
Poland - Pologne[14]									
2013									
Total	745	...	...	...	...	...	...	...	...
0 - 14	-	...	...	...	...	...	...	...	...
15 - 19	16	...	...	...	...	...	...	...	...
20 - 24	90	...	...	...	...	...	...	...	...
25 - 29	202	...	...	...	...	...	...	...	...
30 - 34	218	...	...	...	...	...	...	...	...
35 +	219	...	...	...	...	...	...	...	...
Republic of Moldova - République de Moldova									
2012									
Total	14 838	...	...	...	...	...	...	...	...
0 - 14	9	...	...	...	...	...	...	...	...
15 - 19	1 383	...	...	...	...	...	...	...	...
Unknown - Inconnu	13 446	...	...	...	...	...	...	...	...
Romania - Roumanie									
2012									
Total	87 975	-	-	-	-	-	-	-	87 975
0 - 14	476	-	-	-	-	-	-	-	476
15 - 19	7 547	-	-	-	-	-	-	-	7 547
20 - 24	18 990	-	-	-	-	-	-	-	18 990
25 - 29	20 210	-	-	-	-	-	-	-	20 210
30 - 34	19 635	-	-	-	-	-	-	-	19 635
35 - 39	14 751	-	-	-	-	-	-	-	14 751
40 - 44	5 880	-	-	-	-	-	-	-	5 880
45 - 49	464	-	-	-	-	-	-	-	464
50 +	22	-	-	-	-	-	-	-	22
Unknown - Inconnu	-	-	-	-	-	-	-	-	-
2013									
Total	86 432	...	...	...	...	...	...	...	...
0 - 14	664	...	...	...	...	...	...	...	...
15 - 19	7 611	...	...	...	...	...	...	...	...
20 - 24	17 392	...	...	...	...	...	...	...	...
25 - 29	20 523	...	...	...	...	...	...	...	...
30 - 34	18 584	...	...	...	...	...	...	...	...
35 - 39	15 089	...	...	...	...	...	...	...	...
40 - 44	5 968	...	...	...	...	...	...	...	...
45 - 49	575	...	...	...	...	...	...	...	...
50 +	26	...	...	...	...	...	...	...	...
Russian Federation - Fédération de Russie									
2011									
Total	1 124 880	...	...	...	...	...	...	...	...
0 - 14	585	...	...	...	...	...	...	...	...
15 - 19	66 275	...	...	...	...	...	...	...	...
20 - 24	264 346	...	...	...	...	...	...	...	...
25 - 29	309 875	...	...	...	...	...	...	...	...
30 - 34	248 494	...	...	...	...	...	...	...	...
35 - 39	168 461	...	...	...	...	...	...	...	...

14. Legally induced abortions by age and number of previous live births of women: latest available year, 2005 - 2014
Avortments provoqués légalement selon l'âge de la femme et selon le nombre des naissances vivantes précédentes :
dernière année disponible, 2005 - 2014 (continued - suite)

Continent, country or area, year and age / Continent, pays ou zone, année et âge	Number of previous live births / Nombre des naissances vivantes précédentes								
	Total	0	1	2	3	4	5	6+	Unknown - Inconnu
EUROPE									
Russian Federation - Fédération de Russie									
2011									
40 - 44	60 768	...	...	...	...	...	...	...	...
45 - 49	5 904	...	...	...	...	...	...	...	...
50 +	172	...	...	...	...	...	...	...	...
Unknown - Inconnu	-	...	...	...	...	...	...	...	...
Serbia - Serbie[15]									
2008									
Total	22 867	6 601	4 346	8 509	2 437	663	198	113	-
0 - 14	9	6	1	2	-	-	-	-	-
15 - 19	975	808	124	35	7	1	-	-	-
20 - 24	3 427	1 823	848	570	122	52	9	3	-
25 - 29	5 117	1 510	1 173	1 757	479	141	47	10	-
30 - 34	5 953	1 240	1 114	2 569	719	212	62	37	-
35 - 39	4 929	806	768	2 354	730	170	59	42	-
40 - 44	2 174	363	279	1 072	347	76	17	20	-
45 - 49	266	40	34	146	31	10	4	1	-
50 +	16	5	4	4	2	1	-	-	-
Unknown - Inconnu	1	-	1	-	-	-	-	-	-
Slovakia - Slovaquie									
2013									
Total	11 105	3 475	3 123	2 918	971	327	138	153	...
0 - 14	20	20	-	-	-	-	-	-	...
15 - 19	743	616	108	14	4	-	1	-	...
20 - 24	1 821	996	523	206	61	28	5	2	...
25 - 29	2 406	948	727	465	165	55	28	18	...
30 - 34	2 751	574	905	857	233	98	30	54	...
35 - 39	2 350	251	653	947	331	80	48	40	...
40 - 44	949	66	200	393	166	60	26	38	...
45 - 49	63	4	7	34	11	6	-	1	...
50 +	2	-	-	2	-	-	-	-	...
Slovenia - Slovénie									
2012									
Total	4 106	1 365	1 017	1 294	328	73	18	8	3
0 - 14	2	2	-	-	-	-	-	-	-
15 - 19	277	263	11	2	-	-	-	-	1
20 - 24	642	470	124	33	13	2	-	-	-
25 - 29	855	331	264	202	43	12	3	-	-
30 - 34	1 056	183	310	436	98	23	4	1	1
35 - 39	901	89	222	435	119	24	8	4	-
40 - 44	342	24	84	163	53	12	3	3	-
45 - 49	30	3	2	23	2	-	-	-	-
50 +	1	-	-	-	-	-	-	-	1
Unknown - Inconnu	-	-	-	-	-	-	-	-	-
Spain - Espagne									
2012									
Total	112 390	...	...	...	...	...	...	...	...
0 - 14	460	...	...	...	...	...	...	...	...
15 - 19	13 198	...	...	...	...	...	...	...	...
20 - 24	24 339	...	...	...	...	...	...	...	...
25 - 29	25 584	...	...	...	...	...	...	...	...
30 - 34	24 298	...	...	...	...	...	...	...	...
35 - 39	17 389	...	...	...	...	...	...	...	...
40 - 44	6 600	...	...	...	...	...	...	...	...
45 +	522	...	...	...	...	...	...	...	...
Sweden - Suède[16]									
2010									
Total	37 693	19 435	6 240	7 203	2 993	814	264	137	607
0 - 14	191	178	4	1	-	-	-	-	8
15 - 19	6 199	5 826	214	14	2	-	-	-	143
20 - 24	10 068	7 708	1 587	480	76	5	2	2	208
25 - 29	7 495	3 558	1 838	1 476	385	79	28	10	121
30 - 34	6 124	1 424	1 336	2 113	884	208	77	18	64
35 - 39	5 073	572	862	2 073	1 053	318	88	62	45
40 - 44	2 248	137	353	948	524	174	58	39	15
45 - 49	238	11	33	85	66	27	10	4	2
50 +	56	20	13	13	3	3	1	2	1
Unknown - Inconnu	1	1	-	-	-	-	-	-	-

14. Legally induced abortions by age and number of previous live births of women: latest available year, 2005 - 2014
Avortments provoqués légalement selon l'âge de la femme et selon le nombre des naissances vivantes précédentes :
dernière année disponible, 2005 - 2014 (continued - suite)

Continent, country or area, year and age / Continent, pays ou zone, année et âge	Number of previous live births / Nombre des naissances vivantes précédentes								
	Total	0	1	2	3	4	5	6+	Unknown - Inconnu
EUROPE									
Switzerland - Suisse[17]									
2013									
Total	10 137	2 054	874	786	279	^85	...	...	6 059
0 - 14	7	3	-	-	-	^-	...	...	4
15 - 19	851	352	8	2	-	^-	...	...	489
20 - 24	2 212	751	155	38	5	^1	...	...	1 262
25 - 29	2 275	474	228	136	24	^12	...	...	1 401
30 - 34	2 201	296	240	216	95	^15	...	...	1 339
35 - 39	1 726	129	154	269	103	^37	...	...	1 034
40 - 44	756	40	77	115	48	^15	...	...	461
45 - 49	97	7	10	8	1	^5	...	...	66
50 +	3	-	-	-	1	^-	...	...	2
Unknown - Inconnu	9	2	2	2	2	^-	...	...	1
Ukraine									
2012									
Total	153 147	...	...	...	...	...	...	...	...
0 - 14	76	...	...	...	...	...	...	...	...
15 - 19	9 770	...	...	...	...	...	...	...	...
20 - 34	113 045	...	...	...	...	...	...	...	...
35 +	30 256	...	...	...	...	...	...	...	...
United Kingdom of Great Britain and Northern Ireland - Royaume-Uni de Grande-Bretagne et d'Irlande du Nord[18]									
2012									
Total	197 569	...	...	...	...	...	...	...	...
0 - 14	910	...	...	...	...	...	...	...	...
15 - 19	32 967	...	...	...	...	...	...	...	...
20 - 24	58 367	...	...	...	...	...	...	...	...
25 - 29	44 612	...	...	...	...	...	...	...	...
30 - 34	32 139	...	...	...	...	...	...	...	...
35 - 39	19 651	...	...	...	...	...	...	...	...
40 - 44	8 199	...	...	...	...	...	...	...	...
45 - 49	697	...	...	...	...	...	...	...	...
50 +	27	...	...	...	...	...	...	...	...
Unknown - Inconnu	-	...	...	...	...	...	...	...	...
OCEANIA - OCÉANIE									
New Zealand - Nouvelle-Zélande									
2013									
Total	14 073	6 159	2 875	2 816	1 355	512	188	168	-
0 - 14	48	48	-	-	-	-	-	-	-
15 - 19	2 096	1 772	274	47	3	-	-	-	-
20 - 24	4 386	2 480	1 056	616	187	42	2	3	-
25 - 29	3 174	1 133	728	711	388	129	55	30	-
30 - 34	2 237	484	457	678	334	162	67	55	-
35 - 39	1 451	171	235	513	304	132	40	56	-
40 - 44	637	63	115	238	134	44	21	22	-
45 +	44	8	10	13	5	3	3	2	-

FOOTNOTES - NOTES

* Provisional. - Données provisoires.

^ Indicates an open-ended group, for example 4+. - indique un groupe d'âge ouvert, par exemple 4 ou plus.

[1] Data refer to resident population only. Significant undercoverage of medically induced abortions in clinics in 2006 due to non response in some provinces. - Pour la population résidante seulement. Sous-dénombrement notable des interruptions volontaires de grossesse pratiquées dans les centres médicaux en 2006 faute de réponse dans certaines provinces.

[2] Excluding abortions performed in private hospitals. - Non comprises les interruptions volontaires de grossesse effectuées dans des hôpitaux privés.

[3] Data refer to 'Therapeutic Abortions'. According to Mexican law, only induced abortions, prescribed by medical reasons or induced because of pregnancy coming from sexual aggression, are considered as legal; data refer only to the former. Refers to residence of the mother. To calculate the total number of abortions, only foetal deaths of less than 20 weeks of gestation were considered. Excluding abortions in the country by women with usual residence outside of the country. - Les données se rapportent aux « interruptions volontaires de grossesse pour des motifs thérapeutiques ». D'après la loi mexicaine, seuls sont considérés légaux les avortements déclenchés pour des raisons médicales ou parce que la grossesse est le résultat d'une agression sexuelle; les données se réfèrent seulement à la première. Correspond à la résidence de la mère. Seuls les morts fœtales survenues à moins de 20 semaines de gestation ont été prises en compte aux fins du calcul du nombre total d'avortements. Hors avortements dans le pays par des femmes avec résidence habituelle en dehors du pays.

[4] Data refer to the fiscal year from 1 July to 30 June. Excluding abortions performed in a clinic which closed operations without reporting the data. - Les données se réfèrent à l'année budgétaire de 1 juillet à 30 juin. Non comprises les avortements effectuées dans une clinique qui a fermé sans envoyer les données.

[5] Data refer to abortions performed in hospitals at Grand Turk and Providenciales. - Pour des avortements exécutés dans les hôpitaux dans Grand Turk et Providenciales.

[6] Includes data for East Jerusalem and Israeli residents in certain other territories under occupation by Israeli military forces since June 1967. - Y compris les données pour Jérusalem-Est et les résidents israéliens dans certains autres territoires occupés depuis 1967 par les forces armées israéliennes.

[7] Based on administrative reporting of the Ministry of Health. - Les données reposent sur les rapports administratifs du Ministère de la santé.

[8] Excluding Faeroe Islands and Greenland shown separately, if available. - Non compris les Iles Féroé et le Groenland, qui font l'objet de rubriques distinctes, si disponible.

[9] Data refer to resident population only. - Pour la population résidante seulement.

[10] Unrevised data. - Les données n'ont pas été révisées.

[11] Data refer to women between 15 and 49 years of age. - Le total se rapporte uniquement aux femmes dont l'âge est compris entre 15 et 49 ans.

[12] Data are incomplete for Abruzzo, Campania, Basilicata, Sicilia and Sardegna regions. - Données incomplètes pour les régions des Abruzzes, de Campanie, de Basilicate, de Sicile et de Sardaigne.

[13] Late foetal death is defined as an infant born without any signs of life, weighing at least 500 grams, after duration of pregnancy of at least 22 weeks. - On dit qu'il y a mort intra-utérine tardive lorsqu'un enfant pesant au minimum 500 grammes naît sans donner aucun signe de vie au terme d'une grossesse qui a duré au moins 22 semaines.

[14] Based on hospital and polyclinic records. - D'après les registres des hôpitaux et des policliniques.

[15] Excludes data for Kosovo and Metohia. Data refer to institutions included in the Health Institutions Network Plan in the Republic of Serbia. - Sans les données pour le Kosovo et Metohie. Les données se rapportent aux institutions membres du "Health Institutions Network Plan" de la République de Serbie.

[16] Data refer to abortions by previous deliveries of mother rather than previous live births of mother. - Avortements selon les accouchements précédents de la mère plutôt que selon les naissances vivantes de la mère.

[17] Data refer to termination of pregnancy for women who are Switzerland residents. - Les données portent sur les interruptions de grossesse pratiquées sur des femmes qui résident en Suisse.

[18] Excluding Channel Islands (Guernsey and Jersey) and Isle of Man, shown separately, if available. Excluding Northern Ireland. - Non compris les îles Anglo-Normandes (Guernesey et Jersey) et l'île de Man, qui font l'objet de rubriques distinctes, si disponible. Non compris l'Irlande du Nord.

Table 15 - *Demographic Yearbook 2014*

Table 15 presents infant deaths and infant mortality rates by urban/rural residence for as many years as possible between 2010 and 2014.

Description of variables: Infant deaths are deaths of live-born infants under one year of age.

Statistics on the number of infant deaths are obtained from civil registers unless otherwise noted. Infant mortality rates are, in most instances, calculated from data on registered infant deaths and registered live births for a country or area where civil registration is considered reliable (that is, with an estimated completeness of 90 per cent or more).

The urban/rural classification of infant deaths is that provided by each reporting country or area; it is presumed to be based on the national census definitions of urban population that have been set forth at the end of the technical notes of table 6.

Rate computation: Infant mortality rates are the annual number of deaths of infants under one year of age per 1 000 live births (as shown in table 9) in the same year.

Rates by urban/rural residence are the annual number of infant deaths, in the appropriate urban or rural category, per 1 000 corresponding live births (as shown in table 9). These rates have been calculated by the United Nations Statistics Division.

Rates presented in this table have been limited to those countries or areas having at least a total of 30 infant deaths in a given year and for which the quality code is represented by a "C" or a symbol "|".

Reliability of data: Each country or area has been asked to indicate the estimated completeness of the infant deaths recorded in its civil register. These national assessments are indicated by the quality codes "C", "U" and "|" that appear in the first column of this table.

"C" indicates that the data are estimated to be virtually complete, that is, representing at least 90 per cent of the infant deaths occurring each year, while "U" indicates that data are estimated to be incomplete that is, representing less than 90 per cent of the infant deaths occurring each year. The code "|" indicates that the source of data is not civil registration, but is still considered reliable. The code "..." indicates that no information was provided regarding completeness.

Data from civil registers that are reported as incomplete or of unknown completeness (coded "U" or "...") are considered unreliable. They appear in italics in this table; rates are not computed for data so coded.

Limitations: Statistics on infant deaths are subject to the same qualifications as have been set forth for vital statistics in general and death statistics in particular as discussed in section 4 of the Technical Notes.

The reliability of the data, an indication of which is described above, is an important factor in considering the limitations. In addition, some infant deaths are tabulated by date of registration and not by date of occurrence; these have been indicated by a plus sign "+". Whenever the lag between the date of occurrence and date of registration is prolonged and, therefore, a large proportion of the infant-death registrations are delayed, infant-death statistics for any given year may be seriously affected.

Another factor that limits international comparability is the practice of some countries or areas not to include in infant-death statistics infants who were born alive but died before the registration of the birth or within the first 24 hours of life, thus underestimating the total number of infant deaths. Statistics of this type are footnoted.

The method of reckoning age at death for infants may also introduce non-comparability. If year alone, rather than completed minutes, hours, days and months elapsed since birth, is used to calculate age at time of death, many of the infants who died during the eleventh month of life and some of those who died at younger ages will be classified as having completed one year of age and thus be excluded. The effect would be to underestimate the number of infant deaths. Information on this factor is given in footnotes when known. Reckoning of infant age is further discussed in the technical notes for table 16.

In addition, infant mortality rates are subject to the limitations of the data on live births that have been used as denominators for these rates. These have been set forth in the technical notes for table 9.

Because the two components of the infant mortality rate, infant deaths in the numerator and live births in the denominator, are both obtained from systems of civil registration, the limitations which affect live birth statistics are very similar to those which have been mentioned above in connection with the infant death statistics. It is important to consider the reliability of the data (the completeness of registration) and the method of tabulation (by date of occurrence or by date of registration) of live birth statistics as well as infant death statistics, both of which are used to calculate infant mortality rates. The quality code and use of italics to indicate unreliable data presented in this table refer only to infant deaths. Similarly, the indication of the basis of tabulation (the use of the symbol "+" to indicate data tabulated by date of registration) presented in this table also refers only to infant deaths. Table 9 provides the corresponding information for live births.

If the registration of infant deaths is more complete than the registration of live births, then infant mortality rates would be biased upwards. If, however, the registration of live births is more complete than registration of infant deaths, infant mortality rates would be biased downwards. If both infant deaths and live births are tabulated by registration, it should be noted that deaths tend to be more promptly reported than births.

Infant mortality rates may be seriously affected by the practice of some countries or areas of not considering infants that were born alive but died before the registration of the birth or within the first 24 hours of life as live birth and subsequently infant death. Although this practice results in both the number of infant deaths in the numerator and the number of live births in the denominator being underestimated, its impact is greater on the numerator of the infant mortality rate. As a result this practice causes infant mortality rates to be biased downwards.

Infant mortality rates will also be underestimated if the method of reckoning age at death results in an underestimation of the number of infant deaths. This point has been discussed above.

Because of all these factors care should be taken in comparing infant mortality rates.

With respect to the method of calculating infant mortality rates used in this table, it should be noted that no adjustment was made to take account of the fact that a proportion of the infant deaths that occur during a given year are deaths of infants that were born during the preceding year and hence are not taken from the universe of births used to compute the rates. However, unless the number of live births or infant deaths is changing rapidly, the error involved is insignificant.

The comparability of data by urban/rural residence is affected by the national definitions of urban and rural used in tabulating these data. It is assumed, in the absence of specific information to the contrary, that the definitions of urban and rural used in connection with the national population census were also used in the compilation of the vital statistics for each country or area. However, it cannot be denied that, for some countries or areas, different definitions of urban and rural may be used for the vital statistics data and the population census data respectively. When known, the definitions of urban used in national population censuses are presented at the end of the technical notes for table 6. As discussed in detail in the technical notes for table 6, these definitions vary considerably from one country or area to another.

Urban/rural differentials in infant mortality rates may also be affected by whether the infant deaths and live births have been tabulated in terms of place of occurrence or place of usual residence. This problem is discussed in more detail in section 4.1.4.1 of the Technical Notes.

Earlier data: Infant deaths and infant mortality rates have been shown in previous issues of the *Demographic Yearbook*. For more information on specific topics and years for which data are reported, readers should consult the Historical Index.

Tableau 15 – *Annuaire démographique 2014*

Le tableau 15 présente des données sur les décès d'enfants de moins d'un an et les taux de mortalité infantile selon le lieu de résidence (zone urbaine ou rurale) pour le plus grand nombre d'années possible entre 2010 et 2014.

Description des variables : les chiffres se rapportent aux décès d'enfants de moins d'un an.

Sauf indication contraire, les statistiques concernant le nombre de décès d'enfants de moins d'un an sont établies à partir des registres de l'état civil. Dans la plupart des cas, les taux de mortalité infantile sont calculés à partir des données relatives aux décès enregistrés d'enfants de moins d'un an et aux naissances vivantes enregistrées dans un pays ou une zone lorsque les registres de l'état civil sont jugés fiables (exhaustivité estimée à 90 p. 100 ou plus).

La classification des décès d'enfants de moins d'un an selon le lieu de résidence (zone urbaine ou rurale) est celle qui a été communiquée par chaque pays ou zone ; on part du principe qu'elle repose sur les définitions de la population urbaine utilisées pour les recensements nationaux, telles qu'elles sont reproduites à la fin des notes techniques du tableau 6.

Calcul des taux : Les taux de mortalité infantile représentent le nombre annuel de décès d'enfants de moins d'un an pour 1 000 naissances vivantes (présentées dans le tableau 9) survenues pendant la même année.

Les taux selon le lieu de résidence (zone urbaine ou rurale) représentent le nombre annuel de décès d'enfants de moins d'un an, classés selon la catégorie urbaine ou rurale appropriée pour 1 000 naissances vivantes survenues parmi la population correspondante (présentées dans le tableau 9). Ces taux ont été calculés par la Division des statistiques de l'Organisation des Nations Unies.

Les taux présentés dans ce tableau se rapportent seulement aux pays ou zones où l'on a enregistré au moins un total de 30 décès d'enfants de moins d'un an au cours d'une année donnée et pour lesquels le code de qualité est soit "C" ou "|".

Fiabilité des données : il a été demandé à chaque pays ou zone d'indiquer le degré estimatif de complétude des données sur les décès d'enfants de moins d'un an figurant dans ses registres d'état civil. Ces évaluations nationales sont signalées par les codes de qualité "C", "U" et "|" qui apparaissent dans la deuxième colonne du tableau.

La lettre "C" indique que les données sont jugées à peu près complètes, c'est-à-dire qu'elles représentent au moins 90 p. 100 des décès d'enfants de moins d'un an survenus chaque année ; la lettre "U" signifie que les données sont jugées incomplètes, c'est-à-dire qu'elles représentent moins de 90 p.100 des décès d'enfants de moins d'un an survenus chaque année. Le symbole 'I' indique que la source des données n'est pas un registre de l'état civil, mais est quand même considérée fiable. Le code "..." dénote qu'aucun renseignement n'a été communiqué quant à la complétude des données.

Les données provenant des registres de l'état civil qui sont déclarées incomplètes ou dont le degré de complétude n'est pas connu (code "U" ou "...") sont jugées douteuses. Elles apparaissent en italique dans le tableau ; les taux, dans ces cas là, n'ont pas été calculés.

Insuffisance des données : les statistiques des décès d'enfants de moins d'un an appellent toutes les réserves qui ont été formulées à propos des statistiques de l'état civil en général et des statistiques concernant les décès en particulier (voir la section 4 des notes techniques).

La fiabilité des données, au sujet de laquelle des indications ont été fournies plus haut, est un facteur important. Il faut également tenir compte du fait que, dans certains cas, les données relatives aux décès d'enfants de moins d'un an sont exploitées selon la date de l'enregistrement et non la date de l'événement ; ces cas ont été signalés par le signe "+". Chaque fois que le décalage entre l'événement et son enregistrement est grand et qu'une forte proportion des décès d'enfants de moins d'un an fait l'objet d'un enregistrement tardif, les statistiques des décès d'enfants de moins d'un an pour une année donnée peuvent être considérablement faussées.

Un autre facteur qui nuit à la comparabilité internationale est la pratique de certains pays ou zones qui consiste à ne pas inclure dans les statistiques des décès d'enfants de moins d'un an les enfants nés vivants mais décédés avant l'enregistrement de leur naissance ou dans les 24 heures qui ont suivi la naissance, pratique qui conduit à sous-estimer le nombre total de décès d'enfants de moins d'un an. Quand pareil facteur a joué, cela a été signalé en note.

Les méthodes appliquées pour calculer l'âge au moment du décès peuvent également nuire à la comparabilité des données. Si l'on utilise à cet effet l'année seulement, et non pas les minutes, heures, jours et mois qui se sont écoulés depuis la naissance, de nombreux enfants décédés au cours du onzième mois qui a suivi leur naissance et certains enfants décédés encore plus jeunes seront classés comme décédés à un an révolu et donc exclus des données. Cette pratique conduit à sous-estimer le nombre de décès d'enfants de moins d'un an. Les renseignements dont on dispose sur ce facteur apparaissent en note à la fin du tableau. La question du calcul de l'âge au moment du décès est examinée plus en détail dans les notes techniques se rapportant au tableau 16.

Les taux de mortalité infantile appellent en outre toutes les réserves qui ont été formulées à propos des statistiques des naissances vivantes qui ont servi à leur calcul (voir à ce sujet les notes techniques relatives au tableau 9).

Les deux composantes du taux de mortalité infantile - décès d'enfants de moins d'un an au numérateur et naissances vivantes au dénominateur - étant obtenues à partir des registres de l'état civil, les statistiques des naissances vivantes appellent des réserves presque identiques à celles qui ont été formulées plus haut à propos des statistiques des décès d'enfants de moins d'un an. Il importe de prendre en considération la fiabilité des données (complétude de l'enregistrement) et le mode d'exploitation (selon la date de l'événement ou selon la date de l'enregistrement) dans le cas des statistiques des naissances vivantes tout comme dans le cas de celles des décès d'enfants de moins d'un an, puisque les unes et les autres servent au calcul des taux de mortalité infantile. Dans le tableau 15, le code de qualité et l'emploi de caractères italiques pour signaler les données moins sûres ne concernent que les décès d'enfants de moins d'un an. L'indication du mode d'exploitation des données (emploi du signe "+" pour signaler les données exploitées selon la date de l'enregistrement) ne porte là aussi que sur les décès d'enfants de moins d'un an. Le tableau 9 contient les renseignements correspondants pour les naissances vivantes.

Si l'enregistrement des décès d'enfants de moins d'un an est plus complet que l'enregistrement des naissances vivantes, les taux de mortalité infantile seront entachés d'une erreur par excès. En revanche, si l'enregistrement des naissances vivantes est plus complet que l'enregistrement des décès d'enfants de moins d'un an, les taux de mortalité infantile seront entachés d'une erreur par défaut. Si les décès d'enfants de moins d'un an et les naissances vivantes sont exploitées selon la date de l'enregistrement, il convient de ne pas perdre de vue que les décès sont, en règle générale, déclarés plus rapidement que les naissances.

Les taux de mortalité infantile peuvent être gravement faussés par la pratique de certains pays ou zones qui consiste à ne pas classer dans les naissances vivantes et ensuite dans les décès d'enfants de moins d'un an les enfants nés vivants mais décédés soit avant l'enregistrement de leur naissance, soit dans les 24 heures qui ont suivi la naissance. Cette pratique conduit à sous-estimer aussi bien le nombre des décès d'enfants de moins d'un an, qui constitue le numérateur, que le nombre des naissances vivantes, qui constitue le dénominateur, mais c'est pour le numérateur du taux de mortalité infantile que la distorsion est la plus marquée. Ce système a pour effet d'introduire une erreur par défaut dans les taux de mortalité infantile.

Les taux de mortalité infantile seront également sous-estimés si la méthode utilisée pour calculer l'âge au moment du décès conduit à sous-estimer le nombre de décès d'enfants de moins d'un an. Cette question a été examinée plus haut.

Tous ces facteurs sont importants et il faut donc en tenir compte lorsque l'on compare les taux de mortalité infantile.

En ce qui concerne la méthode de calcul des taux de mortalité infantile utilisée dans le tableau, il convient de noter qu'il n'a pas été tenu compte du fait qu'une partie des décès survenus pendant une année donnée sont des décès d'enfants nés l'année précédente et ne correspondent donc pas à l'ensemble des naissances utilisé pour le calcul des taux. Toutefois, l'erreur n'est pas grave, à moins que le nombre des naissances vivantes ou des décès d'enfants de moins d'un an ne varie rapidement.

La comparabilité des données selon le lieu de résidence (zone urbaine ou rurale) peut être limitée par les définitions nationales des termes « urbain » et « rural » utilisées pour la mise en tableaux de ces données. En l'absence d'indications contraires, on a supposé que les mêmes définitions avaient servi pour le recensement national de la population et pour l'établissement des statistiques de l'état civil pour chaque pays ou zone. Toutefois, il n'est pas exclu que, pour une zone ou un pays donné, des définitions différentes aient été retenues. Les définitions du terme « urbain » utilisées pour les recensements nationaux de population ont été présentées à la fin des notes techniques du tableau 6 lorsqu'elles étaient connues. Comme on l'a précisé dans les notes techniques relatives au tableau 6, ces définitions varient considérablement d'un pays ou d'une zone à l'autre.

La différence entre les taux de mortalité infantile pour les zones urbaines et rurales pourra aussi être faussée selon que les décès d'enfants de moins d'un an et les naissances vivantes auront été classés d'après le lieu de l'événement ou le lieu de résidence habituel. Ce problème est examiné plus en détail à la section 4.1.4.1 des Notes techniques.

Données publiées antérieurement : des statistiques concernant les décès d'enfants de moins d'un an et les taux de mortalité infantile ont déjà été présentées dans des éditions antérieures de l'*Annuaire démographique*. Pour plus de précisions concernant les années et les sujets pour lesquels des données ont été publiées, se reporter à l'index historique.

15. Infant deaths and infant mortality rates, by urban/rural residence: 2010 - 2014
Décès d'enfants de moins d'un an et taux de mortalité infantile, selon la résidence, urbaine/rurale : 2010 - 2014

Continent, country or area, and urban/rural residence / Continent, pays ou zone et résidence, urbaine/rurale	Code[a]	Number - Nombre					Rate - Taux				
		2010	2011	2012	2013	2014	2010	2011	2012	2013	2014
AFRICA - AFRIQUE											
Algeria - Algérie[1]											
Total	U	21 046	21 055	22 088	21 586	22 282	...	...	...	...	...
Egypt - Égypte											
Total	C	31 698	35 997	39 942	38 753	...	14.0	14.7	15.2	14.8	...
Urban - Urbaine	C	15 001	17 601	19 830	22 605	...	16.7	18.7	19.6	19.0	...
Rural - Rurale	C	16 697	18 396	20 112	16 148	...	12.3	12.3	12.4	11.3	...
Kenya											
Total	U	...	23 167	21 209	20 888	18 672	...	...	...	...	...
Mauritius - Maurice[2]											
Total	+C	187	189	199	165	194	12.5	12.9	13.7	12.2	14.6
Urban - Urbaine	+C	67	64	65	67	72	11.7	11.5	12.0	13.2	14.0
Rural - Rurale	+C	120	125	134	98	122	12.9	13.7	14.8	11.6	15.0
Rwanda											
Total	U	27	...	...	...	...	...	...	...	...	...
Saint Helena ex. dep. - Sainte-Hélène sans dép.											
Total	C	-	-	1	-	1	...	...	...	...	...
Senegal - Sénégal[3]											
Total	I	32 314	...	...	...	...	70.8	...	...	...	...
Seychelles											
Total	+C	21	16	...	29	17	...	...	...	...	...
Sierra Leone											
Total	...	1 935	1 289	2 135	...	...	...	...	...	...	...
Urban - Urbaine	...	749	547	1 508	...	...	...	...	...	...	...
Rural - Rurale	...	1 186	742	627	...	...	...	...	...	...	...
South Africa - Afrique du Sud											
Total	...	34 656	27 981	...	...	...	...	...	...	...	...
AMERICA, NORTH - AMÉRIQUE DU NORD											
Anguilla											
Total	+C	2	1	-	3	...	...	...	...	...	...
Antigua and Barbuda - Antigua-et-Barbuda											
Total	+C	11	...	...	...	...	...	...	...	...	...
Aruba											
Total	+U	4	7	3	5	5	...	...	...	...	...
Bahamas											
Total	+C	67	48	57	...	...	13.6	10.1	12.8	...	...
Total	+U	...	...	...	*48	...	...	...	...	...	...
Bermuda - Bermudes											
Total	C	1	-	1	1	...	...	...	...	...	...
Cayman Islands - Îles Caïmanes											
Total	C	2	...	...	...	...	...	...	...	...	...
Costa Rica											
Total	C	671	666	624	612	*575	9.5	9.1	8.5	8.7	*8.0
Urban - Urbaine	C	323	303	272	291	*362	12.4	11.7	10.7	11.7	*8.7
Rural - Rurale	C	348	363	352	321	*213	7.8	7.6	7.4	7.0	*7.1
Cuba											
Total	C	581	653	581	525	514	4.5	4.9	4.6	4.2	4.2
Urban - Urbaine	C	417	485	462	440	...	4.2	4.7	4.7	4.4	...
Rural - Rurale	C	164	168	119	85	...	5.7	5.5	4.3	3.1	...
Curaçao											
Total	C	26	15	23	15	24	...	...	...	...	...
Dominican Republic - République dominicaine											
Total	U	492	679	468	643	...	...	...	...	...	...
Urban - Urbaine[4]	U	256	503	354	536	...	...	...	...	...	...
Rural - Rurale[4]	U	40	64	38	37	...	...	...	...	...	...
El Salvador[5]											
Total	C	749	826	795	...	...	7.1	7.6	7.2	...	...
Urban - Urbaine	C	554	563	527	...	...	8.3	7.5	7.0	...	...
Rural - Rurale	C	195	263	268	...	...	5.1	7.8	7.6	...	...

15. Infant deaths and infant mortality rates, by urban/rural residence: 2010 - 2014
Décès d'enfants de moins d'un an et taux de mortalité infantile, selon la résidence, urbaine/rurale : 2010 - 2014 (continued - suite)

Continent, country or area, and urban/rural residence / Continent, pays ou zone et résidence, urbaine/rurale	Co-de[a]	Number - Nombre					Rate - Taux				
		2010	2011	2012	2013	2014	2010	2011	2012	2013	2014
AMERICA, NORTH - AMÉRIQUE DU NORD											
Greenland - Groenland											
Total	C	6	9	7	7	6	...	...	...	...	...
Urban - Urbaine	C	-	7	4	7	5	...	...	...	...	...
Rural - Rurale	C	6	2	3	-	1	...	...	...	...	...
Guatemala											
Total	C	7 562	7 413	...	...	...	20.9	19.8	...	...	...
Mexico - Mexique[6]											
Total	+U	28 861	29 037	28 946	...	...	...	...	...	...	...
Urban - Urbaine[4]	+U	21 930	21 980	22 254	...	...	...	...	...	...	...
Rural - Rurale[4]	+U	6 415	6 574	6 132	...	...	...	...	...	...	...
Total	+C	...	...	...	27 760	...	...	...	...	12.8	...
Urban - Urbaine[4]	+C	...	...	...	21 041	...	...	...	...	13.8	...
Rural - Rurale[4]	+C	...	...	...	6 037	...	...	...	...	12.5	...
Montserrat											
Total	+C	1	-	-	-	-	...	...	...	...	...
Panama											
Total	U	910	971	1 083	1 106	...	...	...	...	...	...
Urban - Urbaine	U	474	509	632	682	...	...	...	...	...	...
Rural - Rurale	U	436	462	451	424	...	...	...	...	...	...
Puerto Rico - Porto Rico											
Total	C	358	364	374	270	242	8.5	8.8	9.6	7.4	7.0
United States of America - États-Unis d'Amérique											
Total	C	24 586	23 985	23 629	23 440	...	6.1	6.1	6.0	6.0	...
AMERICA, SOUTH - AMÉRIQUE DU SUD											
Argentina - Argentine											
Total	C	8 961	8 878	8 227	8 174	...	11.9	11.7	11.1	10.8	...
Brazil - Brésil[7]											
Total	U	31 733	32 184	31 596	31 944	...	...	...	...	...	...
Chile - Chili											
Total	C	1 862	1 908	1 812	...	...	7.4	7.7	7.4	...	...
Urban - Urbaine	C	1 602	1 668	1 644	...	...	7.1	7.5	7.5	...	...
Rural - Rurale	C	260	240	168	...	...	10.2	9.9	6.9	...	...
Colombia - Colombie											
Total	U	8 355	8 152	8 220	...	...	...	...	...	...	...
Urban - Urbaine[4]	U	6 108	6 117	6 043	...	...	...	...	...	...	...
Rural - Rurale[4]	U	1 983	1 966	2 104	...	...	...	...	...	...	...
Ecuador - Équateur[8]											
Total	U	3 204	3 046	3 002	2 928	...	...	...	...	...	...
Urban - Urbaine	U	2 573	2 468	2 499	2 455	...	...	...	...	...	...
Rural - Rurale	U	631	578	503	473	...	...	...	...	...	...
Paraguay											
Total	+U	...	...	465	...	...	...	...	...	...	...
Peru - Pérou[9]											
Total	+U	5 287	4 569	4 523	4 390	...	...	...	...	...	...
Suriname											
Total	C	178	153	162	168	...	18.3	15.8	15.9	16.8	...
Urban - Urbaine	C	119	101	110	118	...	18.6	15.7	16.1	17.4	...
Rural - Rurale	C	59	52	52	50	...	17.7	15.9	15.5	15.5	...
Uruguay											
Total	C	366	417	448	...	...	7.7	8.9	9.3	...	...
Venezuela (Bolivarian Republic of) - Venezuela (République bolivarienne du)											
Total	C	7 025	7 121	7 331	7 630	...	11.9	11.6	11.8	12.8	...
ASIA - ASIE											
Armenia - Arménie[10]											
Total	C	512	507	...	...	...	11.4	11.7	...	...	...

15. Infant deaths and infant mortality rates, by urban/rural residence: 2010 - 2014
Décès d'enfants de moins d'un an et taux de mortalité infantile, selon la résidence, urbaine/rurale : 2010 - 2014 (continued - suite)

Continent, country or area, and urban/rural residence / Continent, pays ou zone et résidence, urbaine/rurale	Co- de[a]	Number - Nombre					Rate - Taux				
		2010	2011	2012	2013	2014	2010	2011	2012	2013	2014
ASIA - ASIE											
Azerbaijan - Azerbaïdjan[10]											
Total	+C	1 843	1 903	1 884	1 862	...	11.1	10.8	10.8	10.8	...
Urban - Urbaine	+C	1 173	1 536	1 524	1 459	...	14.3	18.0	17.6	16.9	...
Rural - Rurale	+C	670	367	360	403	...	8.0	4.1	4.1	4.7	...
Bahrain - Bahreïn[11]											
Total	C	140	139	149	141	...	7.7	7.9	7.8	7.1	...
Bangladesh											
Total	U	*104 591*	*100 751*	*96 254*	...	...	...	...	...	...	...
Urban - Urbaine	U	*23 094*	*20 484*	*19 906*	...	...	...	...	...	...	...
Rural - Rurale	U	*81 497*	*80 267*	*76 348*	...	...	...	...	...	...	...
Brunei Darussalam - Brunéi Darussalam											
Total	+C	...	56	64	51	...	...	8.3	9.3	7.6	...
China, Hong Kong SAR - Chine, Hong Kong RAS											
Total	C	149	127	137	100	...	1.7	1.3	1.5	1.8	...
China, Macao SAR - Chine, Macao RAS											
Total	C	15	17	18	13	15	...	...	...	...	...
Cyprus - Chypre[12]											
Total	C	31	30	36	15	...	3.2	3.1	3.5	...	...
Georgia - Géorgie[10]											
Total	C	701	703	715	640	...	11.2	12.1	12.5	11.1	...
Urban - Urbaine	C	379	342	...	...	...	11.1	10.2	...	...	...
Rural - Rurale	C	322	361	...	...	...	11.3	14.7	...	...	...
India - Inde[13]											
Total	I	...	...	...	...	...	47.0	44.0	42.0	40.0	...
Urban - Urbaine	I	...	...	...	...	...	31.0	29.0	28.0	27.0	...
Rural - Rurale	I	...	...	...	...	...	51.0	48.0	46.0	44.0	...
Iran (Islamic Republic of) - Iran (République islamique d')[14]											
Total	C	11 677	11 021	10 401	8 015	...	8.6	8.0	7.3	5.4	...
Urban - Urbaine	C	8 518[4]	7 980[4]	8 173[4]	5 993	...	7.9	7.3	7.2	5.3	...
Rural - Rurale	C	2 404[4]	2 574[4]	2 226[4]	2 022	...	8.3	8.7	7.6	5.9	...
Israel - Israël[15]											
Total	C	618	588	611	537	529	3.7	3.5	3.6	3.1	3.0
Urban - Urbaine	C	545[4]	522[4]	545[4]	468[4]	476	3.6	3.5	3.5	3.0	...
Rural - Rurale	C	72[4]	65[4]	65[4]	68[4]	53	4.7	4.2	4.1	4.2	...
Japan - Japon[16]											
Total	C	2 450	2 463	2 299	2 185	...	2.3	2.3	2.2	2.1	...
Urban - Urbaine[4]	C	2 247	2 244	2 106	2 019	...	2.3	2.3	2.2	2.1	...
Rural - Rurale[4]	C	200	214	192	163	...	2.2	2.5	2.3	2.0	...
Kazakhstan[10]											
Total	C	6 078	5 556	5 121	4 367	...	16.5	14.9	13.4	11.3	...
Urban - Urbaine	C	3 226	3 049	2 781	2 383	...	16.7	15.4	13.5	11.4	...
Rural - Rurale	C	2 852	2 507	2 340	1 984	...	16.3	14.3	13.4	11.1	...
Kuwait - Koweït											
Total	C	496	484	459	453	...	8.6	8.3	7.7	7.6	...
Kyrgyzstan - Kirghizstan											
Total	C	3 337	3 150	3 091	3 093	...	22.8	21.1	20.0	19.9	...
Urban - Urbaine	C	1 888	1 767	1 807	1 886	...	37.8	36.1	33.6	35.0	...
Rural - Rurale	C	1 449	1 383	1 284	1 207	...	15.1	13.7	12.7	11.9	...
Malaysia - Malaisie											
Total	C	3 295	3 330	*3 204	...	...	6.7	6.5	*6.3	...	...
Maldives											
Total	C	78	65	66	46	...	11.0	9.1	8.9	6.4	...
Urban - Urbaine[17]	C	43	41	46	24	...	11.3	10.3	10.3	...	...
Rural - Rurale[17]	C	33	20	18	19	...	10.2	...	...	...	...
Mongolia - Mongolie											
Total	+C	1 275	1 152	1 143	1 166	1 251	20.2	16.5	15.5	14.6	15.1
Myanmar											
Total	+U	*26 206*	*27 184*	*11 406*	*11 516*	...	...	...	...	...	...
Urban - Urbaine	+U	*7 223*	*7 593*	*6 170*	*6 840*	...	...	...	...	...	...
Rural - Rurale	+U	*18 983*	*19 591*	*5 236*	*4 676*	...	...	...	...	...	...

15. Infant deaths and infant mortality rates, by urban/rural residence: 2010 - 2014
Décès d'enfants de moins d'un an et taux de mortalité infantile, selon la résidence, urbaine/rurale : 2010 - 2014 (continued - suite)

Continent, country or area, and urban/rural residence / Continent, pays ou zone et résidence, urbaine/rurale	Code[a]	Number - Nombre					Rate - Taux				
		2010	2011	2012	2013	2014	2010	2011	2012	2013	2014
ASIA - ASIE											
Nepal - Népal[18]											
Total	|	...	10 132	...	...	...	...	31.0	...	...	...
Urban - Urbaine	|	...	767	...	...	...	...	18.4	...	...	...
Rural - Rurale	|	...	9 365	...	...	...	...	32.8	...	...	...
Oman[19]											
Total	U	581	640	676	772	...	...	...	...	...	...
Philippines											
Total	C	22 476	22 283	22 254	...	...	12.6	12.8	12.4	...	...
Qatar											
Total	C	132	156	148	157	...	6.8	7.5	6.9	6.6	...
Republic of Korea - République de Corée[20]											
Total	C	1 508	1 435	1 405	1 305	...	3.2	3.0	2.9	3.0	...
Urban - Urbaine	C	1 187[4]	1 158[4]	1 135	998[4]	...	3.1	3.0	2.8	2.7	...
Rural - Rurale	C	296[4]	265[4]	270	203[4]	...	3.5	3.3	3.3	2.9	...
Saudi Arabia - Arabie saoudite[21]											
Total	...	10 219	10 023	9 843	...	...	...	...	...	...	...
Singapore - Singapour											
Total	+C	100	97	98	94	83	2.6	2.4	2.3	2.4	2.0
State of Palestine - État de Palestine[22]											
Total	U	956	1 051	1 050	827	...	...	...	...	...	...
Tajikistan - Tadjikistan[10]											
Total	U	3 092	3 131	2 884	3 622	...	...	...	...	...	...
Urban - Urbaine	U	1 350	1 281	1 241	1 817	...	...	...	...	...	...
Rural - Rurale	U	1 742	1 850	1 643	1 805	...	...	...	...	...	...
Thailand - Thaïlande											
Total	+U	5 357	5 275	...	...	...	...	...	...	...	...
Turkey - Turquie											
Total	C	15 137	14 548	14 931	13 900	...	12.0	11.7	11.6	10.8	...
EUROPE											
Åland Islands - Îles d'Åland											
Total	C	1	-	-	-	...	...	...	...	...	...
Urban - Urbaine	C	-	-	-	-	...	...	...	...	...	...
Rural - Rurale	C	1	-	-	-	...	...	...	...	...	...
Albania - Albanie											
Total	C	328	299	312	282	...	9.6	8.7	8.8	7.9	...
Andorra - Andorre											
Total	C	-	...	4	...	...	...	...	...	...	...
Austria - Autriche											
Total	C	307	281	252	245	...	3.9	3.6	3.2	3.1	...
Belarus - Bélarus											
Total	C	429	420	386	407	...	4.0	3.8	3.3	3.4	...
Urban - Urbaine	C	278	286	278	291	...	3.4	3.4	3.1	3.2	...
Rural - Rurale	C	151	134	108	116	...	5.9	5.2	4.0	4.2	...
Belgium - Belgique[23]											
Total	C	465	434	483	436	...	3.6	3.4	3.8	3.5	...
Urban - Urbaine	C	460	428	477	...	...	3.6	3.4	...	...	...
Rural - Rurale	C	5	6	6	...	...	...	...	...	...	...
Bosnia and Herzegovina - Bosnie-Herzégovine											
Total	C	216	...	161	161	140	6.4	...	5.0	5.2	4.8
Bulgaria - Bulgarie											
Total	C	708	601	536	489	...	9.4	8.5	7.8	7.3	...
Urban - Urbaine	C	461	412	368	...	...	8.1	7.7	7.1	...	...
Rural - Rurale	C	247	189	168	...	...	13.4	10.8	9.6	...	...
Croatia - Croatie											
Total	C	192	192	150	162	...	4.4	4.7	3.6	4.1	...
Urban - Urbaine	C	109	126	95	82	...	4.4	5.4	4.0	3.6	...
Rural - Rurale	C	83	66	55	80	...	4.4	3.7	3.1	4.7	...

15. Infant deaths and infant mortality rates, by urban/rural residence: 2010 - 2014
Décès d'enfants de moins d'un an et taux de mortalité infantile, selon la résidence, urbaine/rurale : 2010 - 2014 (continued - suite)

Continent, country or area, and urban/rural residence / Continent, pays ou zone et résidence, urbaine/rurale	Code[a]	Number - Nombre					Rate - Taux				
		2010	2011	2012	2013	2014	2010	2011	2012	2013	2014
EUROPE											
Czech Republic - République tchèque											
Total	C	313	298	285	265	...	2.7	2.7	2.6	2.5	...
Urban - Urbaine	C	235	231	208	193	...	2.7	2.9	2.6	2.5	...
Rural - Rurale	C	78	67	77	72	...	2.5	2.3	2.7	2.5	...
Denmark - Danemark[24]											
Total	C	216	208	197	194	...	3.4	3.5	3.4	3.5	...
Estonia - Estonie											
Total	C	53	36	50	28	...	3.3	2.5	3.6	...	...
Urban - Urbaine	C	37	25	36	18	...	3.5	...	3.7	...	...
Rural - Rurale	C	16	11	14	10	...	...	...	...	...	...
Faeroe Islands - Îles Féroé											
Total	C	2	3	9	-	...	...	...	...	...	...
Finland - Finlande[25]											
Total	C	139	143	141	102	...	2.3	2.4	2.4	1.8	...
Urban - Urbaine	C	96	...	93	...	...	2.2	...	2.2	...	...
Rural - Rurale	C	43	...	48	...	...	2.5	...	2.8	...	...
France[26]											
Total	C	2 785	2 604	2 643	2 710	...	3.5	3.3	3.3	3.5	...
Urban - Urbaine[27]	C	2 252	2 140	2 140	2 233	...	3.5	3.4	3.4	3.6	...
Rural - Rurale[27]	C	492	440	485	457	...	3.0	2.7	3.0	2.9	...
Germany - Allemagne											
Total	C	2 322	2 408	2 202	2 250	...	3.4	3.6	3.3	3.3	...
Gibraltar											
Total	+C	...	...	...	-	...	...	...	...	...	...
Greece - Grèce											
Total	C	436	357	293	347	...	3.8	3.4	2.9	3.7	...
Urban - Urbaine	C	312	250	197	...	...	4.0	3.3	2.8	...	...
Rural - Rurale	C	124	107	96	...	...	3.4	3.4	3.3	...	...
Hungary - Hongrie											
Total	C	481	433	438	448[29]	...	5.3	4.9	4.9	5.0	...
Urban - Urbaine	C	316[28]	268[28]	259[28]	273[29]	...	5.1	4.4	4.2	4.4	...
Rural - Rurale	C	156[28]	160[28]	176[28]	175[29]	...	5.8	6.1	6.5	6.4	...
Iceland - Islande											
Total	C	11	4[30]	5	8	...	...	...	...	...	...
Urban - Urbaine	C	10	4[30]	5	8	...	...	...	...	...	...
Rural - Rurale	C	1	-[30]	-	-	...	...	...	...	...	...
Ireland - Irlande											
Total	+C	271	262	250	243	249	3.6	3.5	3.5	3.5	3.7
Italy - Italie											
Total	C	1 773	1 595	1 532	1 493	...	3.2	2.9	2.9	2.9	...
Latvia - Lettonie											
Total	C	110	124	125	91	...	5.6	6.6	6.3	4.4	...
Urban - Urbaine	C	68	74	87	55	...	5.0	5.8	6.4	3.9	...
Rural - Rurale	C	42	50	38	36	...	6.8	8.2	6.0	5.6	...
Liechtenstein											
Total	C	1	1	3	2	...	...	...	...	...	...
Lithuania - Lituanie											
Total	C	153	144	118	110	...	5.0	4.8	3.9	3.7	...
Urban - Urbaine	C	114	87	77	63	...	5.4	4.2	3.6	3.1	...
Rural - Rurale	C	39	57	41	47	...	4.0	6.0	4.5	4.9	...
Luxembourg											
Total	C	20	24	25	24	...	...	...	...	...	...
Malta - Malte											
Total	C	22	27	22	27	...	...	...	...	...	...
Montenegro - Monténégro											
Total	C	50	32	33	33	...	6.7	4.4	4.4	4.4	...
Netherlands - Pays-Bas[31]											
Total	C	695	654	...	...	...	3.8	3.6	...	...	...
Urban - Urbaine	C	503	...	...	...	...	3.9	...	...	...	...
Rural - Rurale	C	192	...	...	...	...	3.5	...	...	...	...
Norway - Norvège[32]											
Total	C	171	142	150	140	...	2.8	2.4	2.5	2.4	...
Poland - Pologne											
Total	C	2 057	1 836	1 791	1 684	...	5.0	4.7	4.6	4.6	...
Urban - Urbaine	C	1 198	1 059	1 006	...	...	5.0	4.7	4.5	...	...
Rural - Rurale	C	859	777	785	...	...	5.0	4.8	4.8	...	...

15. Infant deaths and infant mortality rates, by urban/rural residence: 2010 - 2014
Décès d'enfants de moins d'un an et taux de mortalité infantile, selon la résidence, urbaine/rurale : 2010 - 2014 (continued - suite)

Continent, country or area, and urban/rural residence — Continent, pays ou zone et résidence, urbaine/rurale	Co-de[a]	Number - Nombre					Rate - Taux				
		2010	2011	2012	2013	2014	2010	2011	2012	2013	2014
EUROPE											
Portugal[6]											
Total	C	256	302	303	244	...	2.5	3.1	3.4	2.9	...
Republic of Moldova - République de Moldova[33]											
Total	C	476	431	387	359	...	11.8	11.0	9.8	9.5	...
Urban - Urbaine	C	153	136	122	...	...	10.1	9.3	8.2	...	...
Rural - Rurale	C	323	295	265	...	...	12.8	12.0	10.8	...	...
Romania - Roumanie											
Total	C	2 078	1 850	1 812	1 677	...	9.8	9.4	9.0	9.2	...
Urban - Urbaine	C	913	797	720	738	...	7.7	7.5	6.6	7.5	...
Rural - Rurale	C	1 165	1 053	1 092	939	...	12.3	11.8	11.8	11.2	...
Russian Federation - Fédération de Russie[10]											
Total	C	13 405	13 168	16 306	...	...	7.5	7.3	8.6	...	...
Urban - Urbaine	C	8 641	8 398	10 843	...	...	6.8	6.6	8.0	...	...
Rural - Rurale	C	4 764	4 770	5 463	...	...	9.1	9.1	10.0	...	...
San Marino - Saint-Marin											
Total	+C	1	1	-	1	...	...	...	...	...	...
Serbia - Serbie[34]											
Total	+C	460	414	415	413	...	6.7	6.3	6.2	6.3	...
Urban - Urbaine	+C	310	283	274	281	...	6.6	6.2	6.0	6.2	...
Rural - Rurale	+C	150	131	141	132	...	6.9	6.5	6.6	6.6	...
Slovakia - Slovaquie											
Total	C	344	300	321	301	...	5.7	4.9	5.8	5.5	...
Urban - Urbaine	C	172	130	151	138	...	5.4	4.0	5.2	4.8	...
Rural - Rurale	C	172	170	170	163	...	6.1	6.0	6.4	6.2	...
Slovenia - Slovénie											
Total	C	56	64	36	62	...	2.5	2.9	1.6	2.9	...
Urban - Urbaine	C	34	28	15	37	...	3.1	...	...	3.5	...
Rural - Rurale	C	22	36	21	25	...	...	3.2	...	...	...
Spain - Espagne											
Total	C	1 531	1 477	1 389	1 149	...	3.2	3.1	3.1	2.7	...
Sweden - Suède											
Total	C	294	235	293	306	...	2.5	2.1	2.6	2.7	...
Switzerland - Suisse											
Total	C	307	305	296	...	...	3.8	3.8	3.6	...	...
Urban - Urbaine	C	230	218	235	...	...	3.8	3.6	3.8	...	...
Rural - Rurale	C	77	87	61	...	...	3.8	4.3	3.0	...	...
TFYR of Macedonia - L'ex-R. y. de Macédoine											
Total	C	185	172	230	237	...	7.6	7.6	9.8	10.2	...
Urban - Urbaine	C	89	93	123	...	...	6.4	7.1	9.2	...	...
Rural - Rurale	C	96	79	107	...	...	9.2	8.1	10.5	...	...
Ukraine[35]											
Total	+C	4 564	4 511	4 371	4 030	...	9.2	9.0	8.4	8.0	...
Urban - Urbaine	+C	2 792	2 811	2 763	2 536	...	8.5	8.5	8.1	7.7	...
Rural - Rurale	+C	1 772	1 700	1 608	1 494	...	10.4	9.8	9.0	8.6	...
United Kingdom of Great Britain and Northern Ireland - Royaume-Uni de Grande-Bretagne et d'Irlande du Nord[36]											
Total	+C	3 504	3 502	3 347	...	...	4.3	4.3	4.1	...	...
OCEANIA - OCÉANIE											
American Samoa - Samoas américaines											
Total	C	19	9	...	...	...	...	...	...	...	...
Australia - Australie											
Total	+C	1 229	1 140	1 031	1 094	...	4.1	3.8	3.3	3.6	...
Urban - Urbaine[37]	+C	741	661	634	658	...	3.6	3.3	3.0	3.1	...
Rural - Rurale[37]	+C	457	443	362	411	...	4.6	4.5	3.7	4.2	...
Cook Islands - Îles Cook[38]											
Total	+C	2	2	1	-	...	...	...	...	...	...

15. Infant deaths and infant mortality rates, by urban/rural residence: 2010 - 2014
Décès d'enfants de moins d'un an et taux de mortalité infantile, selon la résidence, urbaine/rurale : 2010 - 2014 (continued - suite)

Continent, country or area, and urban/rural residence / Continent, pays ou zone et résidence, urbaine/rurale	Code[a]	Number - Nombre					Rate - Taux				
		2010	2011	2012	2013	2014	2010	2011	2012	2013	2014
OCEANIA - OCÉANIE											
French Polynesia - Polynésie française											
Total	C	25	22	32	...	...	...	...	7.5	...	...
Guam[39]											
Total	C	51	42	42	21	28	14.9	12.7	11.7	...	...
New Caledonia - Nouvelle-Calédonie											
Total	C	19	20	17	...	...	...	...	...	...	...
New Zealand - Nouvelle-Zélande[6]											
Total	+C	325	290	256	260	326	5.1	4.7	4.2	4.4	5.7
Urban - Urbaine[4]	+C	282	255	229	222	287	5.0	4.7	4.2	4.3	5.7
Rural - Rurale[4]	+C	35	31	24	33	24	4.4	4.2	...	4.6	...
Palau - Palaos											
Total	C	3	1	2	4						

FOOTNOTES - NOTES

Italics: data from civil registers which are incomplete or of unknown completeness. - Italiques : données incomplètes ou dont le degré d'exactitude n'est pas connu, provenant des registres de l'état civil.

* Provisional. - Données provisoires.

[a] 'Code' indicates the source of data, as follows:
C - Civil registration, estimated over 90% complete
U - Civil registration, estimated less than 90% complete
| - Other source, estimated reliable
+ - Data tabulated by date of registration rather than occurence
... - Information not available

Le 'Code' indique la source des données, comme suit :
C - Registres de l'état civil considérés complets à 90 p. 100 au moins
U - Registres de l'état civil qui ne sont pas considérés complets à 90 p. 100 au moins
| - Autre source, considérée pas douteuses
+ - Données exploitées selon la date de l'enregistrement et non la date de l'événement
... - Information pas disponible

[1] Excluding live-born infants who died before their birth was registered. Data refer to Algerian population only. - Non compris les enfants nés vivants décédés avant l'enregistrement de leur naissance. Les données ne concernent que la population algérienne.
[2] Excludes the islands of St. Brandon and Agalega. - Non compris les îles St. Brandon et Agalega.
[3] Based on estimates and projections from 'Agence Nationale de la Statistique et de la Démographie'. - Données fondées sur des estimations et des projections provenant de l'Agence Nationale de la Statistique et de la Démographie.
[4] The total number may include 'Unknown residence', but the categories urban and rural do not. - Le nombre total peut inclure les personnes dont la résidence n'est pas connue, à l'inverse des catégories de population urbaine et rurale.
[5] Excluding infant deaths to mothers living abroad. - Exception faite des décès d'enfants en bas âge survenus lorsque la mère résidait à l'étranger.
[6] Data refer to resident population only. - Pour la population résidante seulement.
[7] Including deaths abroad and deaths of unknown residence of mother. - Y compris décès à l'étranger et décès de nourrissons nés de mères dont le lieu de résidence n'est pas connu.
[8] Excludes nomadic Indian tribes. - Non compris les tribus d'Indiens nomades.
[9] Source: Reports of the Ministry of Health. - Source : Rapports du Ministère de la Santé.
[10] Excluding infants born alive of less than 28 weeks' gestation, of less than 1 000 grams in weight and 35 centimeters in length, who die within seven days of birth. - Non compris les enfants nés vivants après moins de 28 semaines de gestations, pesant moins de 1 000 grammes, mesurant moins de 35 centimètres et décédés dans les sept jours qui ont suivi leur naissance.
[11] Deaths include deaths among some visitors. Sources: Births and Deaths National Registration System database, and Salmaniya Medical Complex Discharges System database. - Les décès comprennent des décès parmi certains visiteurs. Les sources: Les bases de données de << Births and Deaths National Registration System >> et << Salmaniya Medical Complex Discharges System >>.
[12] Data refer to government controlled areas. - Les données se rapportent aux zones contrôlées par le Gouvernement.
[13] Includes data for the Indian-held part of Jammu and Kashmir, the final status of which has not yet been determined. Rates were obtained by the Sample Registration System of India, which is a large demographic survey. - Y compris les données pour la partie du Jammu et du Cachemire occupée par l'Inde dont le statut définitif n'a pas encore été déterminé. Les taux ont été obtenus par le Système de l'enregistrement par échantillon de l'Inde qui est une large enquête démographique.
[14] Data refer to the Iranian Year which begins on 21 March and ends on 20 March of the following year. - Les données concernent l'année iranienne, qui commence le 21 mars et se termine le 20 mars de l'année suivante.
[15] Including deaths abroad of Israeli residents who were out of the country for less than a year. Includes data for East Jerusalem and Israeli residents in certain other territories under occupation by Israeli military forces since June 1967. - Y compris les décès à l'étranger de résidents israéliens qui ont quitté le pays depuis moins d'un an. Y compris les données pour Jérusalem-Est et les résidents israéliens dans certains autres territoires occupés depuis 1967 par les forces armées israéliennes.
[16] Data refer to Japanese nationals in Japan only. - Les données se raportent aux nationaux japonais au Japon seulement.
[17] Excluding deaths occurred abroad. - Hormis les décès à l'étranger.
[18] Data refer to the 12 months preceding the census in June. - Les données se rapportent aux 12 mois précédant le recensement de juin.
[19] Data from Births and Deaths Notification System (Ministry of Health and all health care providers). Data for all population, citizens and foreigners. - Les données proviennent du système de notification des naissances et des décès (Ministère de la santé et tous prestataires de soins de santé). Les données portent sur la population entière, les citoyens et les étrangers.
[20] Excluding alien armed forces, civilian aliens employed by armed forces, and foreign diplomatic personnel and their dependants. - Non compris les militaires étrangers, les civils étrangers employés par les forces armées ni le personnel diplomatique étranger et les membres de leur famille les accompagnant.
[21] Projections based on the final results of the 2004 Population and Housing Census. - Projections basées sur les résultats définitifs du recensement de la population et de l'habitat de 2004.
[22] Source: Palestinian Central Bureau of Statistics, Population Register, updated version 05/01/2015. - Source: Bureau central de statistique palestinien, registre de la population, version actualisée jusqu'au 05/01/2015.
[23] Including armed forces stationed outside the country, but excluding alien armed forces stationed in the area. - Y compris les militaires nationaux hors du pays, mais non compris les militaires étrangers en garnison sur le territoire.

[24] Excluding Faeroe Islands and Greenland shown separately, if available. - Non compris les Iles Féroé et le Groenland, qui font l'objet de rubriques distinctes, si disponible.

[25] Excluding Åland Islands. - Non compris les Îles d'Åland.

[26] Including armed forces stationed outside the country. - Y compris les militaires nationaux hors du pays.

[27] The data for urban and rural exclude the nationals outside the country. - Les données relatives à la population urbaine et rurale n'englobent pas les nationaux se trouvant à l'étranger.

[28] The urban and rural categories do not include the data of foreigners, persons of unknown residence and the homeless, whereas the total category includes them. - Les chiffres portant sur la population urbaine et rurale n' incluent pas les données relatives aux étrangers, aux personnes dont la résidence n'est pas connue et aux personnes sans domicile fixe, à l'inverse, le total les inclut.

[29] Starting from 2013 data refer only to infant deaths among usual residents regardless whether it occurred in the country or abroad. - A partir de 2013, les données se rapportent seulement aux décès d'enfants de moins d'un an parmi les résidents habituels, survenus dans le pays ou hors du pays.

[30] Definition of localities was revised in 2011 causing a break with the previous series. - La rupture par rapport aux séries précédentes s'explique par le fait que la définition des localités a été révisée depuis 2011.

[31] Including residents outside the country if listed in a Netherlands population register. - Englobe les résidents se trouvant à l'étranger à condition qu'ils soient inscrits sur le registre de population des Pays-Bas.

[32] Including residents temporarily outside the country. - Y compris les résidents se trouvant temporairement hors du pays.

[33] Excluding Transnistria and the municipality of Bender. - Les données ne tiennent pas compte de l'information sur la Transnistria et la municipalité de Bender.

[34] Excludes data for Kosovo and Metohia. - Sans les données pour le Kosovo et Metohie.

[35] Data includes deaths resulting from births with weight 500g and more (if weight is unknown - with length 25 centimeters and more, or with gestation during 22 weeks or more). - Y compris les décès de nouveau-nés de 500 grammes ou plus (si le poids est inconnu – de 25 centimètres de long ou plus, ou après une grossesse de 22 semaines ou plus).

[36] Excluding Channel Islands (Guernsey and Jersey) and Isle of Man, shown separately, if available. - Non compris les îles Anglo-Normandes (Guernesey et Jersey) et l'île de Man, qui font l'objet de rubriques distinctes, si disponible.

[37] Urban refers to Greater Capital City Statistical Areas, and rural refers to other areas within the state or territory. - Urbain renvoie aux zones statistiques de la capitale métropolitaine, et rural aux autres zones de l'État ou territoire.

[38] Excluding Niue, shown separately, which is part of Cook Islands, but because of remoteness is administered separately. - Non compris Nioué, qui fait l'objet d'une rubrique distincte et qui fait partie des îles Cook, mais qui, en raison de son éloignement, est administrée séparément.

[39] Including United States military personnel, their dependants and contract employees. - Y compris les militaires des Etats-Unis, les membres de leur famille les accompagnant et les agents contractuels des Etats-Unis.

Table 16 - *Demographic Yearbook 2014*

Table 16 presents infant deaths and infant mortality rates by age and sex for latest available year between 2005 and 2014.

Description of variables: Age is defined as hours, days and months of life completed, based on the difference between the hour, day, month and year of birth and the hour, day, month and year of death. The age classification used in this table is as follows: Main categories are "under 1 day", "1-6 days", "7-27 days" and "28 days – 11 months". Additional subcategories are shown within "7-27 days" and "28 days to 11 months" wherever available.

Rate computation: Infant mortality rates by age and sex are the annual number of infant deaths that occurred in a specific age-sex group per 1 000 live births of the corresponding sex. These rates have been calculated by the Statistics Division of the United Nations Department of Economic and Social Affairs. The denominator for all these rates, regardless of age of infant at death, is the total number of live births by sex.

Infant deaths of unknown age are included only in the rate for under one year of age. Infant deaths of unknown sex are included in the rate for the total and, hence, these rates, should agree with the infant mortality rates shown in table 15. Discrepancies are explained in footnotes.

Rates presented in this table have been limited to those for countries or areas having at least a total of 100 deaths in a given year. Moreover, rates specific for individual sub-categories based on 30 or fewer infant deaths are identified by the symbol "♦".

Reliability of data: Data from civil registers of infant deaths which are reported as incomplete (less than 90 percent completeness) or of unknown completeness are considered unreliable and are set in italics rather than in roman type. Rates on these data are not computed. Table 15 and its technical notes provide more detailed information on the completeness of infant death registration. For more information about the quality of vital statistics, and the information available on the basis of the completeness of estimates in particular, see section 4.2 of the Technical Notes.

Limitations: Statistics on infant deaths by age and sex are subject to the same qualifications as have been set forth for vital statistics in general and death statistics in particular as discussed in section 4 of the Technical Notes.

The reliability of the data, an indication of which is described above, is an important factor in considering the limitations. In addition, some infant deaths are tabulated by date of registration and not by date of occurrence; these have been indicated by a plus sign "+". Whenever the lag between the date of occurrence and date of registration is prolonged and, therefore, a large proportion of the infant-death registrations are delayed, infant-death statistics for any given year may be seriously affected.

Another factor that limits international comparability is the practice of some countries or areas of not including in infant-death statistics infants who were born alive but died before the registration of the birth or within the first 24 hours of life, thus underestimating the total number of infant deaths. Statistics of this type are footnoted. In this table in particular, this practice may contribute to the lack of comparability among deaths under one year, under 28 days, under one week and under one day.

Variation in the method of reckoning age at the time of death may also introduce non-comparability. Although it is to some degree a limiting factor throughout the age span, it is an especially important consideration with respect to deaths at ages under one day and under one week (early neonatal deaths) and under 28 days (neonatal deaths). As noted above, the recommended method of reckoning infant age at death is to calculate duration of life in minutes, hours and days, as appropriate. This gives age in completed units of time. In some countries or areas, however, infant age is calculated to the nearest day only, that is, age at death for an infant is the difference between the day, month and year of birth and the day, month and year of death. The result of this procedure is to classify as deaths at age one day, many deaths of infants that occurred before the infants had completed 24 hours of life. The under-one-day class is thus understated while the frequency in the 1-6-day age group is inflated.

A special limitation on comparability of neonatal (under 28 days) deaths is the variation in the classification of infant age used. It is evident from the footnotes that some countries or areas continue to report infant age in calendar, rather than lunar month (4-week or 28-day) periods. This failure to tabulate infant deaths under 4 weeks of age in terms of completed days introduces another source of variation between countries or areas. Deaths classified as occurring under one month usually connote deaths within any one calendar month; these frequencies are not strictly comparable with those referring to deaths within 4 weeks or 27 completed days.

In addition, infant mortality rates by age and sex are subject to the limitations of the data on live births with which they have been calculated. These have been set forth in the technical notes for table 9. These limitations have also been discussed in the technical notes for table 15.

In addition, it should be noted that infant mortality rates by age are affected by the problems related to the practice of excluding infants who were born alive but died before the registration of the birth or within the first 24 hours of life from both infant-death and live-birth statistics and the problems related to the reckoning of infant age at death. These factors, which have been described above, may affect certain age groups more than others. In so far as the numbers of infant deaths for the various age groups are underestimated or overestimated, the corresponding rates for the various age groups will also be underestimated or overestimated. The youngest age groups are more likely to be underestimated than other age groups; the youngest age group (under one day) is likely to be the most seriously affected.

Earlier data: Infant deaths and infant mortality rates by age and sex have been shown in previous issues of the *Demographic Yearbook*. For information on specific years covered, readers should consult the Historical Index.

Tableau 16 – *Annuaire démographique 2014*

Le tableau 16 présente les données les plus récentes disponible, entre 2005 et 2014, sur les décès d'enfants de moins d'un an et les taux de mortalité infantile selon l'âge et le sexe.

Description des variables : l'âge est exprimé en heures, jours et mois révolus et est calculé en retranchant la date de la naissance (heure, jour, mois et année) de celle du décès (heure, jour, mois et année). Les tranches d'âge utilisées dans ce tableau se présentent comme suit : les catégories principales sont « moins d'un jour », « 1-6 jours », « 7-27 jours » et « 28 jours à 11 mois ». Des sous-catégories additionnelles pour « 7-27 jours » et « 28 jours à 11 mois » sont présentées lorsque disponibles.

Calcul des taux : les taux de mortalité infantile selon l'âge et le sexe représentent le nombre annuel de décès d'enfants de moins d'un an intervenu dans un groupe d'âge donné parmi la population de sexe masculin ou féminin pour 1 000 naissances vivantes survenues parmi la population du même sexe. Ces taux ont été calculés par la Division de statistique du Département des affaires économiques et sociales de l'Organisation des Nations Unies. Le dénominateur de tous ces taux, quel que soit l'âge de l'enfant au moment du décès, est le nombre total de naissances vivantes selon le sexe.

Il n'est tenu compte des décès d'enfants d'âge « inconnu » que pour le calcul du taux relatif à l'ensemble des décès de moins d'un an. Étant donné que les décès d'enfants de sexe inconnu sont compris dans le numérateur des taux concernant le total, les chiffres obtenus devraient concorder avec les taux de mortalité infantile du tableau 15. Les divergences sont expliquées en note.

Les taux présentés dans le tableau 16 ne concernent que les pays ou zones où l'on a enregistré un total d'au moins 100 décès au cours d'une année donnée. Les taux relatifs à des sous-catégories qui sont fondées sur un nombre égal ou inférieur à 30 décès d'enfants âgés de moins d'un an sont signalés par le signe "♦".

Fiabilité des données : les données relatives aux décès d'enfants de moins d'un an provenant de registres de l'état civil qui sont déclarées incomplètes (degré de complétude inférieur à 90 p.100) ou dont le degré de complétude n'est pas connu sont jugées douteuses et apparaissent en italique et non en caractères romains. Les taux à partir de ces données n'ont pas été calculés. Le tableau 15 et les notes techniques se rapportant à ce tableau comportent des renseignements plus détaillés sur le degré de complétude de l'enregistrement des décès d'enfants de moins d'un an. Pour plus de précisions sur la qualité des données reposant sur les statistiques de l'état civil en général et les estimations de complétude en particulier, voir la section 4.2 des Notes techniques.

Insuffisance des données : les statistiques des décès d'enfants de moins d'un an selon l'âge et le sexe appellent toutes les réserves qui ont été formulées à propos des statistiques de l'état civil en général et des statistiques concernant les décès en particulier (voir la section 4 des Notes techniques).

La fiabilité des données, au sujet de laquelle des indications ont été fournies plus haut, est un facteur important. Il faut également tenir compte du fait que, dans certains cas, les données relatives aux décès d'enfants de moins d'un an sont exploitées selon la date de l'enregistrement et non la date de l'événement ; ces cas ont été signalés par le signe "+". Chaque fois que le décalage entre l'événement et son enregistrement est grand et qu'une forte proportion des décès d'enfants de moins d'un an fait l'objet d'un enregistrement tardif, les statistiques des décès d'enfants de moins d'un an pour une année donnée peuvent être considérablement faussées.

Un autre facteur qui nuit à la comparabilité internationale est la pratique de certains pays ou zones qui consiste à ne pas inclure dans les statistiques des décès d'enfants de moins d'un an les enfants nés vivants mais décédés soit avant l'enregistrement de leur naissance, soit dans les 24 heures qui ont suivi la naissance, pratique qui conduit à sous-estimer le nombre total de décès d'enfants de moins d'un an. Quand pareil facteur a joué, cela a été signalé en note. Dans le tableau 16 en particulier, ce système peut limiter la comparabilité des données concernant les décès d'enfants de moins d'un an, de moins de 28 jours, de moins d'une semaine et de moins d'un jour.

Le manque d'uniformité des méthodes suivies pour calculer l'âge au moment du décès nuit également à la comparabilité des données. Ce facteur influe dans une certaine mesure sur les données relatives à la mortalité à tous les âges, mais il a des répercussions particulièrement marquées sur les statistiques des décès de moins d'un jour et de moins d'une semaine (mortalité néo-natale précoce) et de moins de 28 jours (mortalité néo-natale). Comme on l'a dit, l'âge d'un enfant de moins d'un an à son décès est calculé, selon la méthode recommandée, en évaluant la durée de vie en minutes, heures et jours, selon le cas. L'âge est ainsi exprimé en unités de temps révolues. Toutefois, dans certains pays ou zones, l'âge de ces enfants est ramené au jour le plus proche en retranchant la date de la naissance (jour, mois et année) de celle du décès (jour, mois et année). Il s'ensuit que de nombreux décès survenus dans les vingt-quatre heures qui suivent la naissance sont classés comme décès d'un jour. Dans ces conditions, les données concernant les décès de moins d'un jour sont entachées d'une erreur par défaut et celles qui se rapportent aux décès de 1 à 6 jours d'une erreur par excès.

La comparabilité des données relatives à la mortalité néo-natale (moins de 28 jours) est influencée par un facteur spécial : l'hétérogénéité de la classification par âge utilisée pour les enfants de moins d'un an. Les notes figurant à la fin des tableaux montrent que, dans un certain nombre de pays ou zones, on continue d'utiliser le mois civil au lieu du mois lunaire (4 semaines ou 28 jours).

Lorsque les données relatives aux décès de moins de 4 semaines ne sont pas exploitées sur la base de l'âge en jours révolus, il existe une nouvelle cause de non-comparabilité internationale. Les décès de moins d'un mois sont généralement ceux qui se produisent au cours d'un mois civil ; les taux calculés sur la base de ces données ne sont pas strictement comparables à ceux qui sont établis à partir des données concernant les décès survenus dans les 4 semaines ou 27 jours révolus qui suivent la naissance.

Les taux de mortalité infantile selon l'âge et le sexe appellent en outre toutes les réserves qui ont été formulées à propos des statistiques des naissances vivantes qui ont servi à leur calcul (voir à ce sujet les notes techniques relatives au tableau 9). Ces insuffisances ont également été examinées dans les notes techniques relatives au tableau 15.

Il convient de signaler aussi que les taux de mortalité infantile selon l'âge peuvent être gravement faussés par la pratique qui consiste à ne pas classer dans les naissances vivantes et ensuite dans les décès d'enfants de moins d'un an les enfants nés vivants mais décédés soit avant l'enregistrement de leur naissance, soit dans les 24 heures qui ont suivi la naissance, et par les problèmes que pose le calcul de l'âge de l'enfant au moment du décès. Ces facteurs, qui ont été décrits plus haut, peuvent fausser les statistiques concernant certains groupes d'âge plus que d'autres. Si le nombre des décès d'enfants de moins d'un an pour chaque groupe d'âge est sous-estimé ou surestimé, les taux correspondants pour chacun de ces groupes d'âge seront eux aussi sous-estimés ou surestimés. Les risques de sous-estimation sont plus grands pour les groupes les plus jeunes ; c'est pour le groupe d'âge le plus jeune de tous (moins d'un jour) que les données risquent de comporter les plus grosses erreurs.

Données publiées antérieurement : des statistiques des décès d'enfants de moins d'un an et des taux de mortalité infantile selon l'âge et le sexe ont déjà été présentées dans des éditions antérieures de l'*Annuaire démographique*. Pour plus de précisions concernant les années pour lesquelles ces données ont été publiées, se reporter à l'index historique.

Continent, country or area, year, code[a] and age / Continent, pays ou zone, année, code[a] et âge	Number - Nombre			Rate - Taux		
	Both sexes Les deux sexes	Male Masculin	Female Féminin	Both sexes Les deux sexes	Male Masculin	Female Féminin
AFRICA - AFRIQUE						
Cabo Verde						
2008 (C)						
Total	316	...	...	24.9	...	...
Less than 7 days - Moins de 7 jours	160	...	...	12.6	...	...
7 - 27 days - 7 - 27 jours	52	...	...	4.1	...	...
28 days - 11 months - 28 jours - 11 mois	104	...	...	8.2	...	...
Egypt - Égypte						
2013 (C)						
Total	38 753	20 791	17 962	14.8	15.5	14.0
1 - 6 days - 1 - 6 jours	6 789	4 058	2 731	2.6	3.0	2.1
7 - 27 days - 7 - 27 jours	9 755	5 367	4 388	3.7	4.0	3.4
28 days - less than 2 months - 28 jours - moins de 2 mois	22 209	11 366	10 843	8.5	8.5	8.4
Mauritius - Maurice[1]						
2014 (+C)						
Total	194	96	98	14.6	14.3	14.9
Less than 1 day - Moins de 1 jour	27	12	15	♦2.0	♦1.8	♦2.3
1 - 6 days - 1 - 6 jours	55	27	28	4.1	♦4.0	♦4.3
7 - 27 days - 7 - 27 jours	45	21	24	3.4	♦3.1	♦3.7
7 - 13 days - 7 - 13 jours	24	11	13	♦1.8	♦1.6	♦2.0
14 - 20 days - 14 - 20 jours	11	5	6	♦0.8	♦0.7	♦0.9
21 - 27 days - 21 - 27 jours	10	5	5	♦0.8	♦0.7	♦0.8
28 days - 11 months - 28 jours - 11 mois	67	36	31	5.0	5.4	4.7
28 days - less than 2 months - 28 jours - moins de 2 mois	26	13	13	♦2.0	♦1.9	♦2.0
2 months - 2 mois	10	5	5	♦0.8	♦0.7	♦0.8
3 months - 3 mois	8	3	5	♦0.6	♦0.4	♦0.8
4 months - 4 mois	8	5	3	♦0.6	♦0.7	♦0.5
5 months - 5 mois	4	2	2	♦0.3	♦0.3	♦0.3
6 months - 6 mois	1	1	-	♦0.1	♦0.1	-
7 months - 7 mois	4	2	2	♦0.3	♦0.3	♦0.3
8 months - 8 mois	1	1	-	♦0.1	♦0.1	-
9 months - 9 mois	1	-	1	♦0.1	-	♦0.2
10 months - 10 mois	3	3	-	♦0.2	♦0.4	-
11 months - 11 mois	1	1	-	♦0.1	♦0.1	-
Reunion - Réunion[2]						
2007 (C)						
Total	91	48	43	...	...	...
Less than 1 day - Moins de 1 jour	24	14	10	...	...	...
1 - 6 days - 1 - 6 jours	20	9	11	...	...	...
7 - 27 days - 7 - 27 jours	18	7	11	...	...	...
7 - 13 days - 7 - 13 jours	7	3	4	...	...	...
14 - 20 days - 14 - 20 jours	9	2	7	...	...	...
21 - 27 days - 21 - 27 jours	7	2	5	...	...	...
28 days - 11 months - 28 jours - 11 mois	30	18	12	...	...	...
Saint Helena ex. dep. - Sainte-Hélène sans dép.						
2014 (C)						
Total	1	-	1	...	...	...
Less than 1 day - Moins de 1 jour	-	-	-	...	...	...
1 - 6 days - 1 - 6 jours	1	-	1	...	...	...
7 - 27 days - 7 - 27 jours	-	-	-	...	...	...
7 - 13 days - 7 - 13 jours	-	-	-	...	...	...
14 - 20 days - 14 - 20 jours	-	-	-	...	...	...
21 - 27 days - 21 - 27 jours	-	-	-	...	...	...
28 days - 11 months - 28 jours - 11 mois	-	-	-	...	...	...
28 days - less than 2 months - 28 jours - moins de 2 mois	-	-	-	...	...	...
2 months - 2 mois	-	-	-	...	...	...
3 months - 3 mois	-	-	-	...	...	...
4 months - 4 mois	-	-	-	...	...	...
5 months - 5 mois	-	-	-	...	...	...
6 months - 6 mois	-	-	-	...	...	...
7 months - 7 mois	-	-	-	...	...	...
8 months - 8 mois	-	-	-	...	...	...
9 months - 9 mois	-	-	-	...	...	...
10 months - 10 mois	-	-	-	...	...	...
11 months - 11 mois	-	-	-	...	...	...
Seychelles						
2006 (+C)						
Total	14	5	9	...	...	...
Less than 1 day - Moins de 1 jour	5	1	4	...	...	...

16. Infant deaths and infant mortality rates by age and sex: latest available year, 2005 - 2014
Décès d'enfants de moins d'un an et taux de mortalité infantile selon l'âge et le sexe : dernière année disponible, 2005 - 2014 (continued - suite)

Continent, country or area, year, code[a] and age Continent, pays ou zone, année, code[a] et âge	Number - Nombre			Rate - Taux		
	Both sexes Les deux sexes	Male Masculin	Female Féminin	Both sexes Les deux sexes	Male Masculin	Female Féminin
AFRICA - AFRIQUE						
Seychelles						
2006 (+C)						
1 - 6 days - 1 - 6 jours	2	1	1	...	...	...
7 - 27 days - 7 - 27 jours	2	-	2	...	...	...
7 - 13 days - 7 - 13 jours	1	-	1	...	...	...
14 - 20 days - 14 - 20 jours	-	-	-	...	...	...
21 - 27 days - 21 - 27 jours	1	-	1	...	...	...
28 days - 11 months - 28 jours - 11 mois	5	3	2	...	...	...
28 days - less than 2 months - 28 jours - moins de 2 mois	1	1	-	...	...	...
2 months - 2 mois	-	-	-	...	...	...
3 months - 3 mois	-	-	-	...	...	...
4 months - 4 mois	1	-	1	...	...	...
5 months - 5 mois	2	2	-	...	...	...
6 months - 6 mois	1	-	1	...	...	...
7 months - 7 mois	-	-	-	...	...	...
8 months - 8 mois	-	-	-	...	...	...
9 months - 9 mois	-	-	-	...	...	...
10 months - 10 mois	-	-	-	...	...	...
11 months - 11 mois	-	-	-	...	...	...
South Africa - Afrique du Sud[3]						
2006 (...)						
Total	47 703	25 178[4]	21 810[4]	...	...	...
Less than 1 day - Moins de 1 jour	2 422	1 387[4]	969[4]	...	...	...
1 - 6 days - 1 - 6 jours	7 217	4 146[4]	2 892[4]	...	...	...
7 - 27 days - 7 - 27 jours	3 640	1 991[4]	1 568[4]	...	...	...
7 - 13 days - 7 - 13 jours	1 613	912[4]	667[4]	...	...	...
14 - 20 days - 14 - 20 jours	1 074	589[4]	460[4]	...	...	...
21 - 27 days - 21 - 27 jours	953	490[4]	441[4]	...	...	...
28 days - 11 months - 28 jours - 11 mois	34 424	17 654[4]	16 381[4]	...	...	...
28 days - less than 2 months - 28 jours - moins de 2 mois	4 770	2 509[4]	2 175[4]	...	...	...
2 months - 2 mois	5 786	2 784[4]	2 934[4]	...	...	...
3 months - 3 mois	5 472	2 783[4]	2 621[4]	...	...	...
4 months - 4 mois	3 711	1 958[4]	1 714[4]	...	...	...
5 months - 5 mois	3 041	1 548[4]	1 465[4]	...	...	...
6 months - 6 mois	2 704	1 393[4]	1 281[4]	...	...	...
7 months - 7 mois	2 258	1 181[4]	1 059[4]	...	...	...
8 months - 8 mois	1 948	1 020[4]	910[4]	...	...	...
9 months - 9 mois	1 811	954[4]	841[4]	...	...	...
10 months - 10 mois	1 544	803[4]	730[4]	...	...	...
11 months - 11 mois	1 379	721[4]	651[4]	...	...	...
AMERICA, NORTH - AMÉRIQUE DU NORD						
Aruba						
2014 (+U)						
Total	5	4	1	...	...	...
Less than 1 day - Moins de 1 jour	-	-	-	...	...	...
1 - 6 days - 1 - 6 jours	5	4	1	...	...	...
7 - 27 days - 7 - 27 jours	-	-	-	...	...	...
7 - 13 days - 7 - 13 jours	-	-	-	...	...	...
14 - 20 days - 14 - 20 jours	-	-	-	...	...	...
21 - 27 days - 21 - 27 jours	-	-	-	...	...	...
28 days - 11 months - 28 jours - 11 mois	-	-	-	...	...	...
28 days - less than 2 months - 28 jours - moins de 2 mois	-	-	-	...	...	...
2 months - 2 mois	-	-	-	...	...	...
3 months - 3 mois	-	-	-	...	...	...
4 months - 4 mois	-	-	-	...	...	...
5 months - 5 mois	-	-	-	...	...	...
6 months - 6 mois	-	-	-	...	...	...
7 months - 7 mois	-	-	-	...	...	...
8 months - 8 mois	-	-	-	...	...	...
9 months - 9 mois	-	-	-	...	...	...
10 months - 10 mois	-	-	-	...	...	...
11 months - 11 mois	-	-	-	...	...	...

16. Infant deaths and infant mortality rates by age and sex: latest available year, 2005 - 2014
Décès d'enfants de moins d'un an et taux de mortalité infantile selon l'âge et le sexe : dernière année disponible, 2005 - 2014 (continued - suite)

Continent, country or area, year, code[a] and age Continent, pays ou zone, année, code[a] et âge	Number - Nombre			Rate - Taux		
	Both sexes Les deux sexes	Male Masculin	Female Féminin	Both sexes Les deux sexes	Male Masculin	Female Féminin
AMERICA, NORTH - AMÉRIQUE DU NORD						
Bahamas						
2012 (+C)						
Total	57	26	31	...	...	...
Less than 1 day - Moins de 1 jour	-	-	-	...	...	...
1 - 6 days - 1 - 6 jours	18	10	8	...	...	...
7 - 27 days - 7 - 27 jours	19	8	11	...	...	...
7 - 13 days - 7 - 13 jours	16	6	10	...	...	...
14 - 20 days - 14 - 20 jours	2	1	1	...	...	...
21 - 27 days - 21 - 27 jours	1	1	-	...	...	...
28 days - 11 months - 28 jours - 11 mois	20	8	12	...	...	...
28 days - less than 2 months - 28 jours - moins de 2 mois	9	5	4	...	...	...
2 months - 2 mois	3	1	2	...	...	...
3 months - 3 mois	2	1	1	...	...	...
4 months - 4 mois	3	-	3	...	...	...
5 months - 5 mois	-	-	-	...	...	...
6 months - 6 mois	-	-	-	...	...	...
7 months - 7 mois	1	-	1	...	...	...
8 months - 8 mois	1	1	-	...	...	...
9 months - 9 mois	1	-	1	...	...	...
10 months - 10 mois	-	-	-	...	...	...
11 months - 11 mois	-	-	-	...	...	...
Barbados - Barbade						
2007 (+C)						
Total	31	18	13	...	...	...
Less than 1 day - Moins de 1 jour	-	1	1	...	...	...
1 - 6 days - 1 - 6 jours	10	8	18	...	...	...
7 - 27 days - 7 - 27 jours	6	4	2	...	...	...
7 - 20 days - 7 - 20 jours	6	4	2	...	...	...
21 - 27 days - 21 - 27 jours	-	-	-	...	...	...
28 days - 11 months - 28 jours - 11 mois	4	2	2	...	...	...
28 days - 2 months - 28 jours - 2 mois	3	2	1	...	...	...
3 - 4 months - 3 - 4 mois	1	-	1	...	...	...
5 - 11 months - 5 - 11 mois	-	-	-	...	...	...
Unknown - Inconnu	2	2	-	...	...	...
Bermuda - Bermudes						
2012 (C)						
Total	1	1	-	...	...	...
Less than 1 day - Moins de 1 jour	-	-	-	...	...	...
1 - 6 days - 1 - 6 jours	-	-	-	...	...	...
7 - 27 days - 7 - 27 jours	-	-	-	...	...	...
7 - 13 days - 7 - 13 jours	-	-	-	...	...	...
14 - 20 days - 14 - 20 jours	-	-	-	...	...	...
21 - 27 days - 21 - 27 jours	-	-	-	...	...	...
28 days - 11 months - 28 jours - 11 mois	-	-	-	...	...	...
28 days - less than 2 months - 28 jours - moins de 2 mois	-	-	-	...	...	...
2 months - 2 mois	-	-	-	...	...	...
3 months - 3 mois	-	-	-	...	...	...
4 months - 4 mois	-	-	-	...	...	...
5 months - 5 mois	-	-	-	...	...	...
6 months - 6 mois	-	-	-	...	...	...
7 months - 7 mois	-	-	-	...	...	...
8 months - 8 mois	-	-	-	...	...	...
9 months - 9 mois	-	-	-	...	...	...
10 months - 10 mois	-	-	-	...	...	...
11 months - 11 mois	-	-	-	...	...	...
Canada[5]						
2006 (C)						
Total	1 771	983	788	5.0	5.4	4.6
Less than 1 day - Moins de 1 jour	888	481	407	2.5	2.6	2.4
1 - 6 days - 1 - 6 jours	194	110	84	0.5	0.6	0.5
7 - 27 days - 7 - 27 jours	214	123	91	0.6	0.7	0.5
7 - 13 days - 7 - 13 jours	110	62	48	0.3	0.3	0.3
14 - 20 days - 14 - 20 jours	60	34	26	0.2	0.2	♦0.2
21 - 27 days - 21 - 27 jours	44	27	17	0.1	♦0.1	♦0.1
28 days - 11 months - 28 jours - 11 mois	475	269	206	1.3	1.5	1.2
28 days - less than 2 months - 28 jours - moins de 2 mois	141	80	61	0.4	0.4	0.4
2 months - 2 mois	78	42	36	0.2	0.2	0.2
3 months - 3 mois	60	37	23	0.2	0.2	♦0.1

Continent, country or area, year, code[a] and age / Continent, pays ou zone, année, code[a] et âge	Number - Nombre			Rate - Taux		
	Both sexes Les deux sexes	Male Masculin	Female Féminin	Both sexes Les deux sexes	Male Masculin	Female Féminin
AMERICA, NORTH - AMÉRIQUE DU NORD						
Canada[5]						
2006 (C)						
4 months - 4 mois	55	33	22	0.2	0.2	♦0.1
5 months - 5 mois	42	21	21	0.1	♦0.1	♦0.1
6 months - 6 mois	24	16	8	♦0.1	♦0.1	-
7 months - 7 mois	19	9	10	♦0.1	-	♦0.1
8 months - 8 mois	19	14	5	♦0.1	♦0.1	-
9 months - 9 mois	18	8	10	♦0.1	-	♦0.1
10 months - 10 mois	9	4	5	-	-	-
11 months - 11 mois	10	5	5	-	-	-
Cayman Islands - Îles Caïmanes						
2007 (C)						
Total	5	4	1	...	...	...
Less than 1 day - Moins de 1 jour	3	2	1	...	...	...
1 - 6 days - 1 - 6 jours	2	2	-	...	...	...
7 - 27 days - 7 - 27 jours	-	-	-	...	...	...
28 days - 11 months - 28 jours - 11 mois	-	-	-	...	...	...
Costa Rica						
2014* (C)						
Total	575	301	274	8.0	8.2	7.8
Less than 1 day - Moins de 1 jour	170	88	82	2.4	2.4	2.3
1 - 6 days - 1 - 6 jours	165	82	83	2.3	2.2	2.4
7 - 27 days - 7 - 27 jours	107	63	44	1.5	1.7	1.3
7 - 13 days - 7 - 13 jours	51	34	17	0.7	0.9	♦0.5
14 - 20 days - 14 - 20 jours	30	19	11	0.4	♦0.5	♦0.3
21 - 27 days - 21 - 27 jours	26	10	16	♦0.4	♦0.3	♦0.5
28 days - 11 months - 28 jours - 11 mois	133	68	65	1.9	1.9	1.9
28 days - less than 2 months - 28 jours - moins de 2 mois	37	19	18	0.5	♦0.5	♦0.5
2 months - 2 mois	26	15	11	♦0.4	♦0.4	♦0.3
3 months - 3 mois	10	6	4	♦0.1	♦0.2	♦0.1
4 months - 4 mois	13	5	8	♦0.2	♦0.1	♦0.2
5 months - 5 mois	5	3	2	♦0.1	♦0.1	♦0.1
6 months - 6 mois	6	3	3	♦0.1	♦0.1	♦0.1
7 months - 7 mois	7	1	6	♦0.1	-	♦0.2
8 months - 8 mois	10	3	7	♦0.1	♦0.1	♦0.2
9 months - 9 mois	12	9	3	♦0.2	♦0.2	♦0.1
10 months - 10 mois	4	2	2	♦0.1	♦0.1	♦0.1
11 months - 11 mois	3	2	1	-	♦0.1	-
Cuba						
2013 (C)						
Total	525	291	234	4.2	4.5	3.9
Less than 1 day - Moins de 1 jour	49	28	21	0.4	♦0.4	♦0.3
1 - 6 days - 1 - 6 jours	154	93	61	1.2	1.4	1.0
7 - 27 days - 7 - 27 jours	106	56	50	0.8	0.9	0.8
7 - 13 days - 7 - 13 jours	38	21	17	0.3	♦0.3	♦0.3
14 - 20 days - 14 - 20 jours	38	20	18	0.3	♦0.3	♦0.3
21 - 27 days - 21 - 27 jours	30	15	15	0.2	♦0.2	♦0.2
28 days - 11 months - 28 jours - 11 mois	216	114	102	1.7	1.7	1.7
28 days - less than 2 months - 28 jours - moins de 2 mois	76	41	35	0.6	0.6	0.6
2 months - 2 mois	34	19	15	0.3	♦0.3	♦0.2
3 months - 3 mois	31	15	16	0.2	♦0.2	♦0.3
4 months - 4 mois	21	16	5	♦0.2	♦0.2	♦0.1
5 months - 5 mois	16	6	10	♦0.1	♦0.1	♦0.2
6 months - 6 mois	12	6	6	♦0.1	♦0.1	♦0.1
7 months - 7 mois	9	5	4	♦0.1	♦0.1	♦0.1
8 months - 8 mois	2	1	1	-	-	-
9 months - 9 mois	1	1	-	-	-	-
10 months - 10 mois	11	4	7	♦0.1	♦0.1	♦0.1
11 months - 11 mois	3	-	3	-	-	-
Curaçao						
2011 (C)						
Total	15	6	9	...	...	...
Less than 1 day - Moins de 1 jour	3	2	1	...	...	...
1 - 6 days - 1 - 6 jours	5	1	4	...	...	...
7 - 27 days - 7 - 27 jours	2	2	-	...	...	...
7 - 13 days - 7 - 13 jours	1	1	-	...	...	...
14 - 20 days - 14 - 20 jours	1	1	-	...	...	...
21 - 27 days - 21 - 27 jours	-	-	-	...	...	...

16. Infant deaths and infant mortality rates by age and sex: latest available year, 2005 - 2014
Décès d'enfants de moins d'un an et taux de mortalité infantile selon l'âge et le sexe : dernière année disponible, 2005 - 2014 (continued - suite)

Continent, country or area, year, code[a] and age / Continent, pays ou zone, année, code[a] et âge	Number - Nombre			Rate - Taux		
	Both sexes Les deux sexes	Male Masculin	Female Féminin	Both sexes Les deux sexes	Male Masculin	Female Féminin
AMERICA, NORTH - AMÉRIQUE DU NORD						
Curaçao						
2011 (C)						
28 days - 11 months - 28 jours - 11 mois	5	1	4	...	...	...
28 days - less than 2 months - 28 jours - moins de 2 mois	2	-	2	...	...	...
2 months - 2 mois	-	-	-	...	...	...
3 months - 3 mois	1	-	1	...	...	...
4 months - 4 mois	2	1	1	...	...	...
5 months - 5 mois	-	-	-	...	...	...
6 months - 6 mois	-	-	-	...	...	...
7 months - 7 mois	-	-	-	...	...	...
8 months - 8 mois	-	-	-	...	...	...
9 months - 9 mois	-	-	-	...	...	...
10 months - 10 mois	-	-	-	...	...	...
11 months - 11 mois	-	-	-	...	...	...
Dominican Republic - République dominicaine						
2013 (U)						
Total	643	438	205	...	...	...
Less than 1 day - Moins de 1 jour	113	62	51	...	...	...
1 - 6 days - 1 - 6 jours	179	138	41	...	...	...
7 - 27 days - 7 - 27 jours	94	63	31	...	...	...
7 - 13 days - 7 - 13 jours	52	34	18	...	...	...
14 - 20 days - 14 - 20 jours	20	13	7	...	...	...
21 - 27 days - 21 - 27 jours	22	16	6	...	...	...
28 days - 11 months - 28 jours - 11 mois	216	138	78	...	...	...
28 days - less than 2 months - 28 jours - moins de 2 mois	51	37	14	...	...	...
2 months - 2 mois	31	20	11	...	...	...
3 months - 3 mois	22	12	10	...	...	...
4 months - 4 mois	23	14	9	...	...	...
5 months - 5 mois	13	8	5	...	...	...
6 months - 6 mois	16	8	8	...	...	...
7 months - 7 mois	13	9	4	...	...	...
8 months - 8 mois	14	9	5	...	...	...
9 months - 9 mois	12	7	5	...	...	...
10 months - 10 mois	10	6	4	...	...	...
11 months - 11 mois	11	8	3	...	...	...
Unknown - Inconnu	41	37	4	...	...	...
El Salvador[6]						
2012 (C)						
Total	795	446	349	7.2	7.8	6.5
Less than 1 day - Moins de 1 jour	102	50	52	0.9	0.9	1.0
1 - 6 days - 1 - 6 jours	144	78	66	1.3	1.4	1.2
7 - 27 days - 7 - 27 jours	129	81	48	1.2	1.4	0.9
7 - 13 days - 7 - 13 jours	56	34	22	0.5	0.6	♦0.4
14 - 20 days - 14 - 20 jours	38	28	10	0.3	♦0.5	♦0.2
21 - 27 days - 21 - 27 jours	35	19	16	0.3	♦0.3	♦0.3
28 days - 11 months - 28 jours - 11 mois	420	237	183	3.8	4.1	3.4
28 days - less than 2 months - 28 jours - moins de 2 mois	95	54	41	0.9	0.9	0.8
2 months - 2 mois	63	35	28	0.6	0.6	♦0.5
3 months - 3 mois	48	25	23	0.4	♦0.4	♦0.4
4 months - 4 mois	57	35	22	0.5	0.6	♦0.4
5 months - 5 mois	30	17	13	0.3	♦0.3	♦0.2
6 months - 6 mois	23	12	11	♦0.2	♦0.2	♦0.2
7 months - 7 mois	27	15	12	♦0.2	♦0.3	♦0.2
8 months - 8 mois	23	12	11	♦0.2	♦0.2	♦0.2
9 months - 9 mois	12	6	6	♦0.1	♦0.1	♦0.1
10 months - 10 mois	16	11	5	♦0.1	♦0.2	♦0.1
11 months - 11 mois	26	15	11	♦0.2	♦0.3	♦0.2
Greenland - Groenland[3]						
2006 (C)						
Total	13	7	6	...	...	...
Less than 1 day - Moins de 1 jour	8	5	3	...	...	...
1 - 6 days - 1 - 6 jours	-	-	-	...	...	...
7 - 27 days - 7 - 27 jours	-	-	-	...	...	...
28 days - 11 months - 28 jours - 11 mois	5	2	3	...	...	...
28 days - less than 2 months - 28 jours - moins de 2 mois	5	2	3	...	...	...
2 - 11 months - 2 - 11 mois	-	-	-	...	...	...

16. Infant deaths and infant mortality rates by age and sex: latest available year, 2005 - 2014
Décès d'enfants de moins d'un an et taux de mortalité infantile selon l'âge et le sexe : dernière année disponible, 2005 - 2014 (continued - suite)

Continent, country or area, year, code[a] and age Continent, pays ou zone, année, code[a] et âge	Number - Nombre			Rate - Taux		
	Both sexes Les deux sexes	Male Masculin	Female Féminin	Both sexes Les deux sexes	Male Masculin	Female Féminin
AMERICA, NORTH - AMÉRIQUE DU NORD						
Guatemala						
2011 (C)						
Total..	7 413	4 202	3 211	19.8	22.1	17.5
Less than 1 day - Moins de 1 jour	123	76	47	0.3	0.4	0.3
1 - 6 days - 1 - 6 jours	1 481	860	621	4.0	4.5	3.4
7 - 27 days - 7 - 27 jours	1 684	938	746	4.5	4.9	4.1
7 - 13 days - 7 - 13 jours	813	451	362	2.2	2.4	2.0
14 - 20 days - 14 - 20 jours	521	288	233	1.4	1.5	1.3
21 - 27 days - 21 - 27 jours	350	199	151	0.9	1.0	0.8
28 days - 11 months - 28 jours - 11 mois................	4 125	2 328	1 797	11.0	12.3	9.8
28 days - less than 2 months - 28 jours - moins de 2 mois	1 198	694	504	3.2	3.7	2.7
2 months - 2 mois..	685	396	289	1.8	2.1	1.6
3 months - 3 mois..	475	283	192	1.3	1.5	1.0
4 months - 4 mois..	345	196	149	0.9	1.0	0.8
5 months - 5 mois..	290	159	131	0.8	0.8	0.7
6 months - 6 mois..	265	146	119	0.7	0.8	0.6
7 months - 7 mois..	245	129	116	0.7	0.7	0.6
8 months - 8 mois..	200	102	98	0.5	0.5	0.5
9 months - 9 mois..	207	115	92	0.6	0.6	0.5
10 months - 10 mois...	209	107	102	0.6	0.6	0.6
11 months - 11 mois...	6	1	5	-	-	-
Martinique[7]						
2007 (C)						
Total..	43	26	17	...	...	...
Less than 1 day - Moins de 1 jour	18	10	8	...	...	...
1 - 6 days - 1 - 6 jours	8	7	1	...	...	...
7 - 27 days - 7 - 27 jours	9	3	6	...	...	...
7 - 13 days - 7 - 13 jours	5	1	4	...	...	...
14 - 20 days - 14 - 20 jours	3	2	1	...	...	...
21 - 27 days - 21 - 27 jours	1	-	1	...	...	...
28 days - 11 months - 28 jours - 11 mois................	8	6	2	...	...	...
28 days - less than 2 months - 28 jours - moins de 2 mois	-	-	-	...	...	...
2 months - 2 mois..	5	3	2	...	...	...
3 months - 3 mois..	-	-	-	...	...	...
4 months - 4 mois..	1	1	-	...	...	...
5 months - 5 mois..	-	-	-	...	...	...
6 months - 6 mois..	-	-	-	...	...	...
7 months - 7 mois..	1	1	-	...	...	...
8 months - 8 mois..	-	-	-	...	...	...
9 - 11 months - 9 - 11 mois...............................	1	1	-	...	...	...
Mexico - Mexique[8]						
2013 (+C)						
Total..	27 760	15 524[4]	12 137[4]	12.8	14.0	11.4
Less than 1 day - Moins de 1 jour	5 123	2 808[4]	2 275[4]	2.4	2.5	2.1
1 - 6 days - 1 - 6 jours	6 333	3 692[4]	2 601[4]	2.9	3.3	2.4
7 - 27 days - 7 - 27 jours	5 156	2 924[4]	2 220[4]	2.4	2.6	2.1
7 - 13 days - 7 - 13 jours	2 665	1 521[4]	1 138[4]	1.2	1.4	1.1
14 - 20 days - 14 - 20 jours	1 478	846[4]	628[4]	0.7	0.8	0.6
21 - 27 days - 21 - 27 jours	1 013	557[4]	454[4]	0.5	0.5	0.4
28 days - 11 months - 28 jours - 11 mois................	11 148	6 100[4]	5 041[4]	5.1	5.5	4.7
28 days - less than 2 months - 28 jours - moins de 2 mois	3 307	1 813[4]	1 488[4]	1.5	1.6	1.4
2 months - 2 mois..	1 990	1 129[4]	861[4]	0.9	1.0	0.8
3 months - 3 mois..	1 449	806[4]	643[4]	0.7	0.7	0.6
4 months - 4 mois..	1 037	574[4]	463[4]	0.5	0.5	0.4
5 months - 5 mois..	769	401[4]	368[4]	0.4	0.4	0.3
6 months - 6 mois..	608	330[4]	277[4]	0.3	0.3	0.3
7 months - 7 mois..	514	273[4]	241[4]	0.2	0.2	0.2
8 months - 8 mois..	437	239[4]	198[4]	0.2	0.2	0.2
9 months - 9 mois..	367	191[4]	176[4]	0.2	0.2	0.2
10 months - 10 mois...	335	173[4]	162[4]	0.2	0.2	0.2
11 months - 11 mois...	335	171[4]	164[4]	0.2	0.2	0.2
Montserrat						
2014 (+C)						
Total..	-	-	-	...	...	...
Less than 1 day - Moins de 1 jour	-	-	-	...	...	...
1 - 6 days - 1 - 6 jours	-	-	-	...	...	...

Continent, country or area, year, code[a] and age / Continent, pays ou zone, année, code[a] et âge	Number - Nombre			Rate - Taux		
	Both sexes Les deux sexes	Male Masculin	Female Féminin	Both sexes Les deux sexes	Male Masculin	Female Féminin
AMERICA, NORTH - AMÉRIQUE DU NORD						
Montserrat						
2014 (+C)						
7 - 27 days - 7 - 27 jours	-	-	-	...	...	...
7 - 13 days - 7 - 13 jours	-	-	-	...	...	...
14 - 20 days - 14 - 20 jours	-	-	-	...	...	...
21 - 27 days - 21 - 27 jours	-	-	-	...	...	...
28 days - 11 months - 28 jours - 11 mois	-	-	-	...	...	...
28 days - less than 2 months - 28 jours - moins de 2 mois	-	-	-	...	...	...
2 months - 2 mois	-	-	-	...	...	...
3 months - 3 mois	-	-	-	...	...	...
4 months - 4 mois	-	-	-	...	...	...
5 months - 5 mois	-	-	-	...	...	...
6 months - 6 mois	-	-	-	...	...	...
7 months - 7 mois	-	-	-	...	...	...
8 months - 8 mois	-	-	-	...	...	...
9 months - 9 mois	-	-	-	...	...	...
10 months - 10 mois	-	-	-	...	...	...
11 months - 11 mois	-	-	-	...	...	...
Nicaragua						
2008 (+U)						
Total	1 932	1 123	809	...	...	...
Less than 1 day - Moins de 1 jour	386	219	167	...	...	...
1 - 6 days - 1 - 6 jours	664	418	246	...	...	...
7 - 27 days - 7 - 27 jours	277	151	126	...	...	...
7 - 13 days - 7 - 13 jours	156	89	67	...	...	...
14 - 20 days - 14 - 20 jours	74	41	33	...	...	...
21 - 27 days - 21 - 27 jours	47	21	26	...	...	...
28 days - 11 months - 28 jours - 11 mois	591	326	265	...	...	...
28 days - less than 2 months - 28 jours - moins de 2 mois	169	86	83	...	...	...
2 months - 2 mois	116	74	42	...	...	...
3 months - 3 mois	66	38	28	...	...	...
4 months - 4 mois	49	29	20	...	...	...
5 months - 5 mois	45	22	23	...	...	...
6 months - 6 mois	27	13	14	...	...	...
7 months - 7 mois	36	18	18	...	...	...
8 months - 8 mois	27	17	10	...	...	...
9 months - 9 mois	18	8	10	...	...	...
10 months - 10 mois	21	9	12	...	...	...
11 months - 11 mois	17	12	5	...	...	...
Panama						
2013 (U)						
Total	1 106	627	479	...	...	...
Less than 1 day - Moins de 1 jour	158	73	85	...	...	...
1 - 6 days - 1 - 6 jours	302	188	114	...	...	...
7 - 27 days - 7 - 27 jours	170	102	68	...	...	...
7 - 13 days - 7 - 13 jours	96	55	41	...	...	...
14 - 20 days - 14 - 20 jours	37	27	10	...	...	...
21 - 27 days - 21 - 27 jours	37	20	17	...	...	...
28 days - 11 months - 28 jours - 11 mois	476	264	212	...	...	...
28 days - less than 2 months - 28 jours - moins de 2 mois	119	72	47	...	...	...
2 months - 2 mois	93	51	42	...	...	...
3 months - 3 mois	45	22	23	...	...	...
4 months - 4 mois	41	26	15	...	...	...
5 months - 5 mois	31	17	14	...	...	...
6 months - 6 mois	24	12	12	...	...	...
7 months - 7 mois	26	15	11	...	...	...
8 months - 8 mois	22	13	9	...	...	...
9 months - 9 mois	24	14	10	...	...	...
10 months - 10 mois	26	13	13	...	...	...
11 months - 11 mois	25	9	16	...	...	...
Puerto Rico - Porto Rico						
2014 (C)						
Total	242	144	98	7.0	8.1	5.9
Less than 1 day - Moins de 1 jour	59	37	22	1.7	2.1	♦1.3
1 - 6 days - 1 - 6 jours	67	41	26	1.9	2.3	♦1.6
7 - 27 days - 7 - 27 jours	43	20	23	1.2	♦1.1	♦1.4
7 - 13 days - 7 - 13 jours	22	11	11	♦0.6	♦0.6	♦0.7
14 - 20 days - 14 - 20 jours	15	7	8	♦0.4	♦0.4	♦0.5

16. Infant deaths and infant mortality rates by age and sex: latest available year, 2005 - 2014
Décès d'enfants de moins d'un an et taux de mortalité infantile selon l'âge et le sexe : dernière année disponible, 2005 - 2014 (continued - suite)

Continent, country or area, year, code[a] and age / Continent, pays ou zone, année, code[a] et âge	Number - Nombre			Rate - Taux		
	Both sexes Les deux sexes	Male Masculin	Female Féminin	Both sexes Les deux sexes	Male Masculin	Female Féminin
AMERICA, NORTH - AMÉRIQUE DU NORD						
Puerto Rico - Porto Rico						
2014 (C)						
21 - 27 days - 21 - 27 jours	6	2	4	♦0.2	♦0.1	♦0.2
28 days - 11 months - 28 jours - 11 mois.................	47	29	18	1.4	♦1.6	♦1.1
28 days - less than 2 months - 28 jours - moins de 2 mois	2	2	-	♦0.1	♦0.1	-
2 months - 2 mois.................	10	7	3	♦0.3	♦0.4	♦0.2
3 months - 3 mois.................	10	5	5	♦0.3	♦0.3	♦0.3
4 months - 4 mois.................	7	3	4	♦0.2	♦0.2	♦0.2
5 months - 5 mois.................	3	2	1	♦0.1	♦0.1	♦0.1
6 months - 6 mois.................	7	5	2	♦0.2	♦0.3	♦0.1
7 months - 7 mois.................	2	2	-	♦0.1	♦0.1	-
8 months - 8 mois.................	3	1	2	♦0.1	♦0.1	♦0.1
9 months - 9 mois.................	2	2	-	♦0.1	♦0.1	-
10 months - 10 mois.................	-	-	-	-	-	-
11 months - 11 mois	1	-	1	-	-	♦0.1
Unknown - Inconnu	26	17	9	♦0.8	♦1.0	♦0.5
Saint Vincent and the Grenadines - Saint-Vincent-et-les Grenadines						
2005 (+C)						
Total.................	29	17	12	...	...	...
Less than 1 day - Moins de 1 jour	6	3	3	...	...	...
1 - 6 days - 1 - 6 jours	11	6	5	...	...	...
7 - 27 days - 7 - 27 jours	3	2	1	...	...	...
28 days - 11 months - 28 jours - 11 mois.................	9	6	3	...	...	...
28 days - less than 2 months - 28 jours - moins de 2 mois	-	-	-	...	...	...
2 - 11 months - 2 - 11 mois.................	9	6	3	...	...	...
United States of America - États-Unis d'Amérique						
2013 (C)						
Total.................	23 440	13 119	10 321	6.0	6.5	5.4
Less than 1 day - Moins de 1 jour	9 852	5 446	4 406	2.5	2.7	2.3
1 - 6 days - 1 - 6 jours	3 023	1 710	1 313	0.8	0.8	0.7
7 - 27 days - 7 - 27 jours	2 992	1 644	1 348	0.8	0.8	0.7
28 days - 11 months - 28 jours - 11 mois.................	7 573	4 319	3 254	1.9	2.1	1.7
AMERICA, SOUTH - AMÉRIQUE DU SUD						
Argentina - Argentine						
2006 (C)						
Total.................	8 986	5 063[4]	3 911[4]	12.9	14.1	11.7
Less than 7 days - Moins de 7 jours.................	4 312	2 465[4]	1 838[4]	6.2	6.8	5.5
7 - 27 days - 7 - 27 jours	1 591	898[4]	691[4]	2.3	2.5	2.1
28 days - 11 months - 28 jours - 11 mois.................	3 083	1 700[4]	1 382[4]	4.4	4.7	4.1
Brazil - Brésil						
2013 (U)						
Total.................	31 944[9]	17 827	14 082	...	...	...
Less than 1 day - Moins de 1 jour	7 087[9]	4 039	3 026	...	...	...
1 - 6 days - 1 - 6 jours	16 053[9]	9 173	6 851	...	...	...
7 - 27 days - 7 - 27 jours	5 493[9]	2 999	2 490	...	...	...
7 - 13 days - 7 - 13 jours	2 850[9]	1 537	1 312	...	...	...
14 - 20 days - 14 - 20 jours	1 553[9]	858	693	...	...	...
21 - 27 days - 21 - 27 jours	1 090[9]	604	485	...	...	...
28 days - 11 months - 28 jours - 11 mois.................	10 398[9]	5 655	4 741	...	...	...
28 days - less than 2 months - 28 jours - moins de 2 mois	3 234[9]	1 767	1 465	...	...	...
2 months - 2 mois.................	1 691[9]	934	757	...	...	...
3 months - 3 mois.................	1 225[9]	643	582	...	...	...
4 months - 4 mois.................	945[9]	523	422	...	...	...
5 months - 5 mois.................	758[9]	447	311	...	...	...
6 months - 6 mois.................	586[9]	322	264	...	...	...
7 months - 7 mois.................	498[9]	250	248	...	...	...
8 months - 8 mois.................	427[9]	239	188	...	...	...
9 months - 9 mois.................	414[9]	212	202	...	...	...
10 months - 10 mois.................	339[9]	190	149	...	...	...
11 months - 11 mois.................	281[9]	128	153	...	...	...

16. Infant deaths and infant mortality rates by age and sex: latest available year, 2005 - 2014
Décès d'enfants de moins d'un an et taux de mortalité infantile selon l'âge et le sexe : dernière année disponible, 2005 - 2014 (continued - suite)

Continent, country or area, year, code[a] and age Continent, pays ou zone, année, code[a] et âge	Number - Nombre			Rate - Taux		
	Both sexes Les deux sexes	Male Masculin	Female Féminin	Both sexes Les deux sexes	Male Masculin	Female Féminin
AMERICA, SOUTH - AMÉRIQUE DU SUD						
Chile - Chili						
2012 (C)						
Total	1 812	978	834	7.4	7.9	7.0
Less than 1 day - Moins de 1 jour	692	383	309	2.8	3.1	2.6
1 - 6 days - 1 - 6 jours	342	194	148	1.4	1.6	1.2
7 - 27 days - 7 - 27 jours	273	151	122	1.1	1.2	1.0
7 - 13 days - 7 - 13 jours	138	78	60	0.6	0.6	0.5
14 - 20 days - 14 - 20 jours	79	42	37	0.3	0.3	0.3
21 - 27 days - 21 - 27 jours	56	31	25	0.2	0.2	♦0.2
28 days - 11 months - 28 jours - 11 mois	505	250	255	2.1	2.0	2.1
28 days - less than 2 months - 28 jours - moins de 2 mois	165	86	79	0.7	0.7	0.7
2 months - 2 mois	94	37	57	0.4	0.3	0.5
3 months - 3 mois	54	31	23	0.2	0.2	♦0.2
4 months - 4 mois	45	24	21	0.2	♦0.2	♦0.2
5 months - 5 mois	33	16	17	0.1	♦0.1	♦0.1
6 months - 6 mois	25	12	13	♦0.1	♦0.1	♦0.1
7 months - 7 mois	25	10	15	♦0.1	♦0.1	♦0.1
8 months - 8 mois	24	16	8	♦0.1	♦0.1	♦0.1
9 months - 9 mois	16	7	9	♦0.1	♦0.1	♦0.1
10 months - 10 mois	13	6	7	♦0.1	-	♦0.1
11 months - 11 mois	11	5	6	-	-	♦0.1
Colombia - Colombie						
2012 (U)						
Total	8 220	4 608[4]	3 602[4]	...	...	...
Less than 1 day - Moins de 1 jour	1 466	845[4]	615[4]	...	...	...
1 - 6 days - 1 - 6 jours	2 010	1 159[4]	850[4]	...	...	...
7 - 27 days - 7 - 27 jours	1 719	953[4]	763[4]	...	...	...
7 - 13 days - 7 - 13 jours	895	490[4]	404[4]	...	...	...
14 - 20 days - 14 - 20 jours	499	266[4]	231[4]	...	...	...
21 - 27 days - 21 - 27 jours	325	197[4]	128[4]	...	...	...
28 days - 11 months - 28 jours - 11 mois	2 988	1 631[4]	1 357[4]	...	...	...
28 days - less than 2 months - 28 jours - moins de 2 mois	817	444[4]	373[4]	...	...	...
2 months - 2 mois	519	279[4]	240[4]	...	...	...
3 months - 3 mois	321	185[4]	136[4]	...	...	...
4 months - 4 mois	282	150[4]	132[4]	...	...	...
5 months - 5 mois	227	127[4]	100[4]	...	...	...
6 months - 6 mois	183	95[4]	88[4]	...	...	...
7 months - 7 mois	142	80[4]	62[4]	...	...	...
8 months - 8 mois	148	84[4]	64[4]	...	...	...
9 months - 9 mois	149	76[4]	73[4]	...	...	...
10 months - 10 mois	98	51[4]	47[4]	...	...	...
11 months - 11 mois	102	60[4]	42[4]	...	...	...
Unknown - Inconnu	37	20[4]	17[4]	...	...	...
Ecuador - Équateur[10]						
2013 (U)						
Total	2 928	1 612	1 316	...	...	...
Less than 1 day - Moins de 1 jour	531	291	240	...	...	...
1 - 6 days - 1 - 6 jours	568	326	242	...	...	...
7 - 27 days - 7 - 27 jours	475	276	199	...	...	...
7 - 13 days - 7 - 13 jours	222	127	95	...	...	...
14 - 20 days - 14 - 20 jours	143	81	62	...	...	...
21 - 27 days - 21 - 27 jours	110	68	42	...	...	...
28 days - 11 months - 28 jours - 11 mois	1 354	719	635	...	...	...
28 days - less than 2 months - 28 jours - moins de 2 mois	400	202	198	...	...	...
2 months - 2 mois	193	116	77	...	...	...
3 months - 3 mois	148	75	73	...	...	...
4 months - 4 mois	108	63	45	...	...	...
5 months - 5 mois	93	41	52	...	...	...
6 months - 6 mois	83	48	35	...	...	...
7 months - 7 mois	78	44	34	...	...	...
8 months - 8 mois	75	42	33	...	...	...
9 months - 9 mois	74	41	33	...	...	...
10 months - 10 mois	50	24	26	...	...	...
11 months - 11 mois	52	23	29	...	...	...

16. Infant deaths and infant mortality rates by age and sex: latest available year, 2005 - 2014
Décès d'enfants de moins d'un an et taux de mortalité infantile selon l'âge et le sexe : dernière année disponible, 2005 - 2014 (continued - suite)

Continent, country or area, year, code[a] and age / Continent, pays ou zone, année, code[a] et âge	Number - Nombre			Rate - Taux		
	Both sexes Les deux sexes	Male Masculin	Female Féminin	Both sexes Les deux sexes	Male Masculin	Female Féminin
AMERICA, SOUTH - AMÉRIQUE DU SUD						
French Guiana - Guyane française						
2007 (C)						
Total	73	39	34	...	...	...
Less than 1 day - Moins de 1 jour	18	10	8	...	...	...
1 - 6 days - 1 - 6 jours	15	5	10	...	...	...
7 - 27 days - 7 - 27 jours	17	12	5	...	...	...
7 - 13 days - 7 - 13 jours	9	5	4	...	...	...
14 - 20 days - 14 - 20 jours	3	3	-	...	...	...
21 - 27 days - 21 - 27 jours	5	4	1	...	...	...
28 days - 11 months - 28 jours - 11 mois	23	12	11	...	...	...
28 days - less than 2 months - 28 jours - moins de 2 mois	1	-	1	...	...	...
2 months - 2 mois	7	4	3	...	...	...
3 months - 3 mois	4	1	3	...	...	...
4 months - 4 mois	2	1	1	...	...	...
5 months - 5 mois	2	2	-	...	...	...
6 months - 6 mois	2	1	1	...	...	...
7 months - 7 mois	1	1	-	...	...	...
8 months - 8 mois	1	1	-	...	...	...
9 months - 9 mois	2	1	1	...	...	...
10 months - 10 mois	-	-	-	...	...	...
11 months - 11 mois	1	-	1	...	...	...
Paraguay						
2006 (U)						
Total	549	...	...	...	...	...
Less than 28 days - Moins de 28 jours	270	...	...	...	...	...
28 days - 11 months - 28 jours - 11 mois[11]	279	...	...	...	...	...
Peru - Pérou[12]						
2013 (+U)						
Total	4 390	2 434	1 956	...	...	...
Less than 1 day - Moins de 1 jour	650	374	276	...	...	...
1 - 6 days - 1 - 6 jours	1 043	617	426	...	...	...
7 - 27 days - 7 - 27 jours	669	372	297	...	...	...
7 - 13 days - 7 - 13 jours	325	189	136	...	...	...
14 - 20 days - 14 - 20 jours	183	98	85	...	...	...
21 - 27 days - 21 - 27 jours	161	85	76	...	...	...
28 days - 11 months - 28 jours - 11 mois	2 028	1 071	957	...	...	...
28 days - less than 2 months - 28 jours - moins de 2 mois	564	308	256	...	...	...
2 months - 2 mois	390	203	187	...	...	...
3 months - 3 mois	224	118	106	...	...	...
4 months - 4 mois	181	91	90	...	...	...
5 months - 5 mois	135	75	60	...	...	...
6 months - 6 mois	119	55	64	...	...	...
7 months - 7 mois	102	61	41	...	...	...
8 months - 8 mois	83	43	40	...	...	...
9 months - 9 mois	93	42	51	...	...	...
10 months - 10 mois	80	42	38	...	...	...
11 months - 11 mois	57	33	24	...	...	...
Venezuela (Bolivarian Republic of) - Venezuela (République bolivarienne du)						
2007 (C)						
Total	6 340	3 715	2 625	10.3	11.7	8.8
Less than 28 days - Moins de 28 jours	4 379	2 599	1 780	7.1	8.2	6.0
28 days - 11 months - 28 jours - 11 mois	1 961	1 116	845	3.2	3.5	2.8
28 days - less than 2 months - 28 jours - moins de 2 mois	455	258	197	0.7	0.8	0.7
2 months - 2 mois	325	182	143	0.5	0.6	0.5
3 months - 3 mois	231	136	95	0.4	0.4	0.3
4 months - 4 mois	190	119	71	0.3	0.4	0.2
5 months - 5 mois	157	87	70	0.3	0.3	0.2
6 months - 6 mois	153	89	64	0.2	0.3	0.2
7 months - 7 mois	104	57	47	0.2	0.2	0.2
8 months - 8 mois	122	63	59	0.2	0.2	0.2
9 months - 9 mois	77	39	38	0.1	0.1	0.1
10 months - 10 mois	81	50	31	0.1	0.2	0.1
11 months - 11 mois	66	36	30	0.1	0.1	0.1

Continent, country or area, year, code[a] and age / Continent, pays ou zone, année, code[a] et âge	Number - Nombre			Rate - Taux		
	Both sexes Les deux sexes	Male Masculin	Female Féminin	Both sexes Les deux sexes	Male Masculin	Female Féminin

ASIA - ASIE

Armenia - Arménie[13]						
2009 (C)						
Total	454	258	196	10.2	10.9	9.4
Less than 1 day - Moins de 1 jour	82	47	35	1.8	2.0	1.7
1 - 6 days - 1 - 6 jours	165	93	72	3.7	3.9	3.5
7 - 27 days - 7 - 27 jours	72	37	35	1.6	1.6	1.7
7 - 13 days - 7 - 13 jours	28	16	12	♦0.6	♦0.7	♦0.6
14 - 20 days - 14 - 20 jours	24	12	12	♦0.5	♦0.5	♦0.6
21 - 27 days - 21 - 27 jours	20	9	11	♦0.5	♦0.4	♦0.5
28 days - 11 months - 28 jours - 11 mois	135	81	54	3.0	3.4	2.6
28 days - less than 2 months - 28 jours - moins de 2 mois	37	23	14	0.8	♦1.0	♦0.7
2 months - 2 mois	24	14	10	♦0.5	♦0.6	♦0.5
3 months - 3 mois	20	10	10	♦0.5	♦0.4	♦0.5
4 months - 4 mois	15	12	3	♦0.3	♦0.5	♦0.1
5 months - 5 mois	13	7	6	♦0.3	♦0.3	♦0.3
6 months - 6 mois	4	2	2	♦0.1	♦0.1	♦0.1
7 months - 7 mois	1	1	-	-	-	-
8 months - 8 mois	4	3	1	♦0.1	♦0.1	-
9 months - 9 mois	9	6	3	♦0.2	♦0.3	♦0.1
10 months - 10 mois	6	3	3	♦0.1	♦0.1	♦0.1
11 months - 11 mois	2	-	2	-	-	♦0.1
Azerbaijan - Azerbaïdjan[13]						
2013 (+C)						
Total	1 862	1 028	834	10.8	11.1	10.4
Less than 1 day - Moins de 1 jour	300	178	122	1.7	1.9	1.5
1 - 6 days - 1 - 6 jours	829	465	364	4.8	5.0	4.5
7 - 27 days - 7 - 27 jours	76	42	34	0.4	0.5	0.4
7 - 13 days - 7 - 13 jours	37	15	22	0.2	♦0.2	♦0.3
14 - 20 days - 14 - 20 jours	20	13	7	♦0.1	♦0.1	♦0.1
21 - 27 days - 21 - 27 jours	19	14	5	♦0.1	♦0.2	♦0.1
28 days - 11 months - 28 jours - 11 mois	657	343	314	3.8	3.7	3.9
28 days - less than 2 months - 28 jours - moins de 2 mois	103	57	46	0.6	0.6	0.6
2 months - 2 mois	81	42	39	0.5	0.5	0.5
3 months - 3 mois	69	26	43	0.4	♦0.3	0.5
4 months - 4 mois	62	31	31	0.4	0.3	0.4
5 months - 5 mois	89	46	43	0.5	0.5	0.5
6 months - 6 mois	59	35	24	0.3	0.4	♦0.3
7 months - 7 mois	39	29	10	0.2	♦0.3	♦0.1
8 months - 8 mois	52	26	26	0.3	♦0.3	♦0.3
9 months - 9 mois	39	15	24	0.2	♦0.2	♦0.3
10 months - 10 mois	32	18	14	0.2	♦0.2	♦0.2
11 months - 11 mois	32	18	14	0.2	♦0.2	♦0.2
Bahrain - Bahreïn[14]						
2012 (C)						
Total	140	73	67	7.3	7.5	7.2
Less than 1 day - Moins de 1 jour	23	15	8	♦1.2	♦1.5	♦0.9
1 - 6 days - 1 - 6 jours	24	15	9	♦1.3	♦1.5	♦1.0
7 - 27 days - 7 - 27 jours	29	13	16	♦1.5	♦1.3	♦1.7
7 - 13 days - 7 - 13 jours	13	5	8	♦0.7	♦0.5	♦0.9
14 - 20 days - 14 - 20 jours	9	4	5	♦0.5	♦0.4	♦0.5
21 - 27 days - 21 - 27 jours	7	4	3	♦0.4	♦0.4	♦0.3
28 days - 11 months - 28 jours - 11 mois	64	30	34	3.3	3.1	3.6
28 days - less than 2 months - 28 jours - moins de 2 mois	26	14	12	♦1.4	♦1.4	♦1.3
2 months - 2 mois	7	3	4	♦0.4	♦0.3	♦0.4
3 months - 3 mois	6	3	3	♦0.3	♦0.3	♦0.3
4 months - 4 mois	5	2	3	♦0.3	♦0.2	♦0.3
5 months - 5 mois	5	2	3	♦0.3	♦0.2	♦0.3
6 months - 6 mois	1	1	-	♦0.1	♦0.1	-
7 months - 7 mois	4	2	2	♦0.2	♦0.2	♦0.2
8 months - 8 mois	3	1	2	♦0.2	♦0.1	♦0.2
9 months - 9 mois	2	-	2	♦0.1	-	♦0.2
10 months - 10 mois	2	1	1	♦0.1	♦0.1	♦0.1
11 months - 11 mois	3	1	2	♦0.2	♦0.1	♦0.2
Bangladesh						
2010 (U)						
Total	104 591	55 178	49 413	...	...	...
1 - 6 days - 1 - 6 jours	56 108	30 276	25 832	...	...	...

16. Infant deaths and infant mortality rates by age and sex: latest available year, 2005 - 2014
Décès d'enfants de moins d'un an et taux de mortalité infantile selon l'âge et le sexe : dernière année disponible, 2005 - 2014 (continued - suite)

Continent, country or area, year, code[a] and age / Continent, pays ou zone, année, code[a] et âge	Number - Nombre			Rate - Taux		
	Both sexes Les deux sexes	Male Masculin	Female Féminin	Both sexes Les deux sexes	Male Masculin	Female Féminin
ASIA - ASIE						
Bangladesh						
2010 (U)						
7 - 27 days - 7 - 27 jours	17 576	9 234	8 342	...	...	...
7 - 13 days - 7 - 13 jours	8 488	4 491	3 997	...	...	...
14 - 20 days - 14 - 20 jours	4 845	2 546	2 299	...	...	...
21 - 27 days - 21 - 27 jours	4 243	2 197	2 046	...	...	...
28 days - 11 months - 28 jours - 11 mois	30 907	15 668	15 239	...	...	...
28 days - less than 2 months - 28 jours - moins de 2 mois	7 377	3 906	3 471	...	...	...
2 months - 2 mois	5 234	2 674	2 560	...	...	...
3 months - 3 mois	4 381	2 248	2 133	...	...	...
4 months - 4 mois	2 628	1 333	1 295	...	...	...
5 months - 5 mois	1 188	606	582	...	...	...
6 months - 6 mois	2 123	1 050	1 073	...	...	...
7 months - 7 mois	1 361	669	692	...	...	...
8 months - 8 mois	1 905	918	987	...	...	...
9 months - 9 mois	1 420	696	724	...	...	...
10 months - 10 mois	1 188	566	622	...	...	...
11 months - 11 mois	2 102	1 002	1 100	...	...	...
China, Hong Kong SAR - Chine, Hong Kong RAS						
2013 (C)						
Total	100	65	35	1.8	2.2	1.3
Less than 1 day - Moins de 1 jour	14	3	11	♦0.2	♦0.1	♦0.4
1 - 6 days - 1 - 6 jours	31	21	10	0.5	♦0.7	♦0.4
7 - 27 days - 7 - 27 jours	11	5	6	♦0.2	♦0.2	♦0.2
7 - 13 days - 7 - 13 jours	4	-	4	♦0.1	-	♦0.1
14 - 20 days - 14 - 20 jours	4	2	2	♦0.1	♦0.1	♦0.1
21 - 27 days - 21 - 27 jours	3	3	-	♦0.1	♦0.1	-
28 days - 11 months - 28 jours - 11 mois	44	36	8	0.8	1.2	♦0.3
28 days - less than 2 months - 28 jours - moins de 2 mois	6	5	1	♦0.1	♦0.2	-
2 months - 2 mois	9	9	-	♦0.2	♦0.3	-
3 months - 3 mois	5	3	2	♦0.1	♦0.1	♦0.1
4 months - 4 mois	4	4	-	♦0.1	♦0.1	-
5 months - 5 mois	1	-	1	-	-	-
6 months - 6 mois	5	4	1	♦0.1	♦0.1	-
7 months - 7 mois	3	3	-	♦0.1	♦0.1	-
8 months - 8 mois	4	3	1	♦0.1	♦0.1	-
9 months - 9 mois	4	4	-	♦0.1	♦0.1	-
10 months - 10 mois	2	-	2	-	-	♦0.1
11 months - 11 mois	1	1	-	-	-	-
China, Macao SAR - Chine, Macao RAS						
2010 (C)						
Total	15	7	8	...	...	...
Less than 1 day - Moins de 1 jour	7	3	4	...	...	...
1 - 6 days - 1 - 6 jours	4	2	2	...	...	...
7 - 27 days - 7 - 27 jours	2	1	1	...	...	...
7 - 13 days - 7 - 13 jours	-	-	-	...	...	...
14 - 20 days - 14 - 20 jours	1	-	1	...	...	...
21 - 27 days - 21 - 27 jours	1	1	-	...	...	...
28 days - 11 months - 28 jours - 11 mois	2	1	1	...	...	...
28 days - less than 2 months - 28 jours - moins de 2 mois	1	-	1	...	...	...
2 months - 2 mois	-	-	-	...	...	...
3 months - 3 mois	-	-	-	...	...	...
4 months - 4 mois	1	1	-	...	...	...
5 months - 5 mois	-	-	-	...	...	...
6 months - 6 mois	-	-	-	...	...	...
7 months - 7 mois	-	-	-	...	...	...
8 months - 8 mois	-	-	-	...	...	...
9 months - 9 mois	-	-	-	...	...	...
10 months - 10 mois	-	-	-	...	...	...
11 months - 11 mois	-	-	-	...	...	...
Cyprus - Chypre[15]						
2011 (C)						
Total	30	18	12	...	...	...
Less than 1 day - Moins de 1 jour	10	6	4	...	...	...
1 - 6 days - 1 - 6 jours	8	4	4	...	...	...
7 - 27 days - 7 - 27 jours	3	2	1	...	...	...
28 days - 11 months - 28 jours - 11 mois	9	6	3	...	...	...

16. Infant deaths and infant mortality rates by age and sex: latest available year, 2005 - 2014
Décès d'enfants de moins d'un an et taux de mortalité infantile selon l'âge et le sexe : dernière année disponible, 2005 - 2014 (continued - suite)

Continent, country or area, year, code[a] and age Continent, pays ou zone, année, code[a] et âge	Number - Nombre			Rate - Taux		
	Both sexes Les deux sexes	Male Masculin	Female Féminin	Both sexes Les deux sexes	Male Masculin	Female Féminin
ASIA - ASIE						
Georgia - Géorgie[13]						
2013 (C)						
Total	640	379	261	11.1	12.6	9.4
Less than 1 day - Moins de 1 jour	107	63	44	1.8	2.1	1.6
1 - 6 days - 1 - 6 jours	195	111	84	3.4	3.7	3.0
7 - 27 days - 7 - 27 jours	151	94	57	2.6	3.1	2.0
28 days - 11 months - 28 jours - 11 mois	187	111	76	3.2	3.7	2.7
Israel - Israël[16]						
2014 (C)						
Total	529	287	242	3.0	...	...
Less than 1 day - Moins de 1 jour	115	66	49	0.7	...	...
1 - 6 days - 1 - 6 jours	133	73	60	0.8	...	...
7 - 27 days - 7 - 27 jours	113	59	54	0.6	...	...
7 - 13 days - 7 - 13 jours	64	30	34	0.4	...	...
14 - 20 days - 14 - 20 jours	32	19	13	0.2	...	...
21 - 27 days - 21 - 27 jours	17	10	7	♦0.1	...	...
28 days - 11 months - 28 jours - 11 mois	168	89	79	1.0	...	...
28 days - less than 2 months - 28 jours - moins de 2 mois	47	25	22	0.3	...	...
2 months - 2 mois	23	13	10	♦0.1	...	...
3 months - 3 mois	26	14	12	♦0.1	...	...
4 months - 4 mois	20	11	9	♦0.1	...	...
5 months - 5 mois	9	4	5	♦0.1	...	...
6 months - 6 mois	14	6	8	♦0.1	...	...
7 months - 7 mois	7	3	4	-	...	...
8 months - 8 mois	12	8	4	♦0.1	...	...
9 months - 9 mois	5	2	3	-	...	...
10 months - 10 mois	4	2	2	-	...	...
11 months - 11 mois	1	1	-	-	...	...
Japan - Japon[17]						
2013 (C)						
Total	2 185	1 193	992	2.1	2.3	2.0
Less than 1 day - Moins de 1 jour	506	279	227	0.5	0.5	0.5
1 - 6 days - 1 - 6 jours	246	136	110	0.2	0.3	0.2
7 - 27 days - 7 - 27 jours	274	152	122	0.3	0.3	0.2
7 - 13 days - 7 - 13 jours	106	59	47	0.1	0.1	0.1
14 - 20 days - 14 - 20 jours	93	50	43	0.1	0.1	0.1
21 - 27 days - 21 - 27 jours	75	43	32	0.1	0.1	0.1
28 days - 11 months - 28 jours - 11 mois	1 159	626	533	1.1	1.2	1.1
28 days - less than 2 months - 28 jours - moins de 2 mois	253	143	110	0.2	0.3	0.2
2 months - 2 mois	159	84	75	0.2	0.2	0.1
3 months - 3 mois	165	90	75	0.2	0.2	0.1
4 months - 4 mois	118	60	58	0.1	0.1	0.1
5 months - 5 mois	96	49	47	0.1	0.1	0.1
6 months - 6 mois	78	41	37	0.1	0.1	0.1
7 months - 7 mois	78	44	34	0.1	0.1	0.1
8 months - 8 mois	73	40	33	0.1	0.1	0.1
9 months - 9 mois	55	31	24	0.1	0.1	-
10 months - 10 mois	51	26	25	-	-	-
11 months - 11 mois	33	18	15	-	-	-
Kazakhstan[13]						
2013 (C)						
Total	4 367	2 502	1 865	11.3	12.5	10.0
Less than 1 day - Moins de 1 jour	381	209	172	1.0	1.0	0.9
1 - 6 days - 1 - 6 jours	1 439	869	570	3.7	4.3	3.0
7 - 27 days - 7 - 27 jours	927	529	398	2.4	2.6	2.1
7 - 13 days - 7 - 13 jours	534	325	209	1.4	1.6	1.1
14 - 20 days - 14 - 20 jours	233	127	106	0.6	0.6	0.6
21 - 27 days - 21 - 27 jours	160	77	83	0.4	0.4	0.4
28 days - 11 months - 28 jours - 11 mois	1 620	895	725	4.2	4.5	3.9
28 days - less than 2 months - 28 jours - moins de 2 mois	568	330	238	1.5	1.7	1.3
2 months - 2 mois	228	136	92	0.6	0.7	0.5
3 months - 3 mois	161	97	64	0.4	0.5	0.3
4 months - 4 mois	131	63	68	0.3	0.3	0.4
5 months - 5 mois	117	53	64	0.3	0.3	0.3
6 months - 6 mois	118	62	56	0.3	0.3	0.3
7 months - 7 mois	88	47	41	0.2	0.2	0.2
8 months - 8 mois	65	34	31	0.2	0.2	0.2
9 months - 9 mois	61	26	35	0.2	♦0.1	0.2

Continent, country or area, year, code[a] and age / Continent, pays ou zone, année, code[a] et âge	Number - Nombre			Rate - Taux		
	Both sexes Les deux sexes	Male Masculin	Female Féminin	Both sexes Les deux sexes	Male Masculin	Female Féminin
ASIA - ASIE						
Kazakhstan[13]						
2013 (C)						
10 months - 10 mois	42	21	21	0.1	♦0.1	♦0.1
11 months - 11 mois	41	26	15	0.1	♦0.1	♦0.1
Kuwait - Koweït						
2013 (C)						
Total	453	246	207	7.6	8.1	7.2
Less than 1 day - Moins de 1 jour	102	52	50	1.7	1.7	1.7
1 - 6 days - 1 - 6 jours	89	52	37	1.5	1.7	1.3
7 - 27 days - 7 - 27 jours	96	56	40	1.6	1.8	1.4
7 - 13 days - 7 - 13 jours	49	28	21	0.8	♦0.9	♦0.7
14 - 20 days - 14 - 20 jours	28	16	12	♦0.5	♦0.5	♦0.4
21 - 27 days - 21 - 27 jours	19	12	7	♦0.3	♦0.4	♦0.2
28 days - 11 months - 28 jours - 11 mois	166	86	80	2.8	2.8	2.8
28 days - less than 2 months - 28 jours - moins de 2 mois	61	32	29	1.0	1.0	♦1.0
2 months - 2 mois	23	15	8	♦0.4	♦0.5	♦0.3
3 months - 3 mois	22	9	13	♦0.4	♦0.3	♦0.5
4 months - 4 mois	14	8	6	♦0.2	♦0.3	♦0.2
5 months - 5 mois	9	3	6	♦0.2	♦0.1	♦0.2
6 months - 6 mois	9	4	5	♦0.2	♦0.1	♦0.2
7 months - 7 mois	6	3	3	♦0.1	♦0.1	♦0.1
8 months - 8 mois	4	3	1	♦0.1	♦0.1	-
9 months - 9 mois	6	3	3	♦0.1	♦0.1	♦0.1
10 months - 10 mois	7	3	4	♦0.1	♦0.1	♦0.1
11 months - 11 mois	5	3	2	♦0.1	♦0.1	♦0.1
Kyrgyzstan - Kirghizstan						
2013 (C)						
Total	3 093	1 743	1 350	19.9	21.8	17.9
Less than 1 day - Moins de 1 jour	902	512	390	5.8	6.4	5.2
1 - 6 days - 1 - 6 jours	1 128	659	469	7.3	8.2	6.2
7 - 27 days - 7 - 27 jours	286	151	135	1.8	1.9	1.8
7 - 13 days - 7 - 13 jours	171	95	76	1.1	1.2	1.0
14 - 20 days - 14 - 20 jours	61	32	29	0.4	0.4	♦0.4
21 - 27 days - 21 - 27 jours	54	24	30	0.3	♦0.3	0.4
28 days - 11 months - 28 jours - 11 mois	777	421	356	5.0	5.3	4.7
28 days - less than 2 months - 28 jours - moins de 2 mois	145	84	61	0.9	1.1	0.8
2 months - 2 mois	88	55	33	0.6	0.7	0.4
3 months - 3 mois	89	48	41	0.6	0.6	0.5
4 months - 4 mois	89	41	48	0.6	0.5	0.6
5 months - 5 mois	58	29	29	0.4	♦0.4	♦0.4
6 months - 6 mois	65	38	27	0.4	0.5	♦0.4
7 months - 7 mois	61	35	26	0.4	0.4	♦0.3
8 months - 8 mois	48	24	24	0.3	♦0.3	♦0.3
9 months - 9 mois	52	29	23	0.3	♦0.4	♦0.3
10 months - 10 mois	42	17	25	0.3	♦0.2	♦0.3
11 months - 11 mois	40	21	19	0.3	♦0.3	♦0.3
Maldives						
2013 (C)						
Total	46	29	17	...	...	...
Less than 1 day - Moins de 1 jour	12	7	5	...	...	...
1 - 6 days - 1 - 6 jours	10	7	3	...	...	...
7 - 27 days - 7 - 27 jours	7	4	3	...	...	...
7 - 13 days - 7 - 13 jours	5	3	2	...	...	...
14 - 20 days - 14 - 20 jours	2	1	1	...	...	...
21 - 27 days - 21 - 27 jours	-	-	-	...	...	...
28 days - 11 months - 28 jours - 11 mois	17	11	6	...	...	...
28 days - less than 2 months - 28 jours - moins de 2 mois	5	3	2	...	...	...
2 months - 2 mois	2	1	1	...	...	...
3 months - 3 mois	2	1	1	...	...	...
4 months - 4 mois	4	4	-	...	...	...
5 months - 5 mois	-	-	-	...	...	...
6 months - 6 mois	-	-	-	...	...	...
7 months - 7 mois	1	1	-	...	...	...
8 months - 8 mois	-	-	-	...	...	...
9 months - 9 mois	1	-	1	...	...	...
10 months - 10 mois	1	-	1	...	...	...
11 months - 11 mois	1	1	-	...	...	...

16. Infant deaths and infant mortality rates by age and sex: latest available year, 2005 - 2014
Décès d'enfants de moins d'un an et taux de mortalité infantile selon l'âge et le sexe : dernière année disponible, 2005 - 2014 (continued - suite)

Continent, country or area, year, code[a] and age / Continent, pays ou zone, année, code[a] et âge	Number - Nombre			Rate - Taux		
	Both sexes Les deux sexes	Male Masculin	Female Féminin	Both sexes Les deux sexes	Male Masculin	Female Féminin
ASIA - ASIE						
Myanmar						
2013* (+U)						
Total	11 516	6 379	5 137	...	...	...
Less than 1 day - Moins de 1 jour	281	159	122	...	...	...
1 - 6 days - 1 - 6 jours	4 616	2 603	2 013	...	...	...
7 - 27 days - 7 - 27 jours	1 333	753	580	...	...	...
7 - 13 days - 7 - 13 jours	753	435	318	...	...	...
14 - 20 days - 14 - 20 jours	337	202	135	...	...	...
21 - 27 days - 21 - 27 jours	244	117	127	...	...	...
28 days - 11 months - 28 jours - 11 mois	5 285	2 864	2 422	...	...	...
28 days - less than 2 months - 28 jours - moins de 2 mois	1 123	638	486	...	...	...
2 months - 2 mois	1 053	615	438	...	...	...
3 months - 3 mois	735	395	341	...	...	...
4 months - 4 mois	456	229	227	...	...	...
5 months - 5 mois	387	198	189	...	...	...
6 months - 6 mois	362	207	155	...	...	...
7 months - 7 mois	304	153	151	...	...	...
8 months - 8 mois	268	134	134	...	...	...
9 months - 9 mois	221	110	111	...	...	...
10 months - 10 mois	194	100	93	...	...	...
11 months - 11 mois	182	85	97	...	...	...
Oman[18]						
2011 (U)						
Total	598	316[19]	269[19]	...	...	...
Less than 1 day - Moins de 1 jour	100	50[19]	47[19]	...	...	...
1 - 6 days - 1 - 6 jours	118	57	61	...	...	...
7 - 27 days - 7 - 27 jours	75	34	41	...	...	...
7 - 13 days - 7 - 13 jours	36	16	20	...	...	...
14 - 20 days - 14 - 20 jours	23	10	13	...	...	...
21 - 27 days - 21 - 27 jours	16	8	8	...	...	...
28 days - 11 months - 28 jours - 11 mois	174	95	79	...	...	...
28 days - less than 2 months - 28 jours - moins de 2 mois	54	26	28	...	...	...
2 months - 2 mois	24	16	8	...	...	...
3 months - 3 mois	22	10	12	...	...	...
4 months - 4 mois	12	10	2	...	...	...
5 months - 5 mois	16	10	6	...	...	...
6 months - 6 mois	13	6	7	...	...	...
7 months - 7 mois	3	2	1	...	...	...
8 months - 8 mois	10	4	6	...	...	...
9 months - 9 mois	3	1	2	...	...	...
10 months - 10 mois	9	4	5	...	...	...
11 months - 11 mois	8	6	2	...	...	...
Unknown - Inconnu	131	81[19]	40[19]	...	...	...
Pakistan[20]						
2007 (I)						
Total	288 191	167 402	120 789	75.2	83.5	66.2
Less than 1 day - Moins de 1 jour	11 990	8 027	3 963	3.1	4.0	2.2
1 - 6 days - 1 - 6 jours	115 664	74 312	41 352	30.2	37.0	22.7
7 - 27 days - 7 - 27 jours	39 726	23 382	16 344	10.4	11.7	9.0
7 - 13 days - 7 - 13 jours	21 846	13 191	8 655	5.7	6.6	4.7
14 - 20 days - 14 - 20 jours	16 376	9 475	6 901	4.3	4.7	3.8
21 - 27 days - 21 - 27 jours	1 504	716	788	0.4	0.4	0.4
28 days - 11 months - 28 jours - 11 mois	120 811	61 681	59 130	31.5	30.8	32.4
28 days - less than 2 months - 28 jours - moins de 2 mois	23 563	9 553	14 010	6.2	4.8	7.7
2 months - 2 mois	10 666	7 662	3 004	2.8	3.8	1.6
3 months - 3 mois	16 938	9 692	7 246	4.4	4.8	4.0
4 months - 4 mois	10 577	4 135	6 442	2.8	2.1	3.5
5 months - 5 mois	14 148	8 863	5 285	3.7	4.4	2.9
6 months - 6 mois	17 012	6 641	10 371	4.4	3.3	5.7
7 months - 7 mois	8 480	4 209	4 271	2.2	2.1	2.3
8 months - 8 mois	6 221	5 116	1 105	1.6	2.6	0.6
9 months - 9 mois	7 602	3 819	3 783	2.0	1.9	2.1
10 months - 10 mois	3 546	1 291	2 255	0.9	0.6	1.2
11 months - 11 mois	2 058	700	1 358	0.5	0.3	0.7
Philippines						
2012 (C)						
Total	22 254	12 987	9 267	12.4	13.9	10.8
Less than 1 day - Moins de 1 jour	3 499	1 981	1 518	2.0	2.1	1.8

16. Infant deaths and infant mortality rates by age and sex: latest available year, 2005 - 2014
Décès d'enfants de moins d'un an et taux de mortalité infantile selon l'âge et le sexe : dernière année disponible, 2005 - 2014 (continued - suite)

Continent, country or area, year, code[a] and age / Continent, pays ou zone, année, code[a] et âge	Number - Nombre			Rate - Taux		
	Both sexes Les deux sexes	Male Masculin	Female Féminin	Both sexes Les deux sexes	Male Masculin	Female Féminin
ASIA - ASIE						
Philippines						
2012 (C)						
1 - 6 days - 1 - 6 jours	5 998	3 705	2 293	3.4	4.0	2.7
7 - 27 days - 7 - 27 jours	3 262	1 859	1 403	1.8	2.0	1.6
7 - 13 days - 7 - 13 jours	1 689	983	706	0.9	1.1	0.8
14 - 20 days - 14 - 20 jours	816	460	356	0.5	0.5	0.4
21 - 27 days - 21 - 27 jours	757	416	341	0.4	0.4	0.4
28 days - 11 months - 28 jours - 11 mois	9 495	5 442	4 053	5.3	5.8	4.7
28 days - less than 2 months - 28 jours - moins de 2 mois	2 242	1 347	895	1.3	1.4	1.0
2 months - 2 mois	1 267	711	556	0.7	0.8	0.6
3 months - 3 mois	974	553	421	0.5	0.6	0.5
4 months - 4 mois	832	461	371	0.5	0.5	0.4
5 months - 5 mois	749	422	327	0.4	0.5	0.4
6 months - 6 mois	753	419	334	0.4	0.4	0.4
7 months - 7 mois	684	415	269	0.4	0.4	0.3
8 months - 8 mois	619	356	263	0.3	0.4	0.3
9 months - 9 mois	511	288	223	0.3	0.3	0.3
10 months - 10 mois	428	236	192	0.2	0.3	0.2
11 months - 11 mois	436	234	202	0.2	0.3	0.2
Qatar						
2013 (C)						
Total	157	97	60	6.6	8.0	5.2
Less than 1 day - Moins de 1 jour	-	-	-	-	-	-
1 - 6 days - 1 - 6 jours	72	49	23	3.0	4.0	♦2.0
7 - 27 days - 7 - 27 jours	23	16	7	♦1.0	♦1.3	♦0.6
7 - 13 days - 7 - 13 jours	14	9	5	♦0.6	♦0.7	♦0.4
14 - 20 days - 14 - 20 jours	5	3	2	♦0.2	♦0.2	♦0.2
21 - 27 days - 21 - 27 jours	4	4	-	♦0.2	♦0.3	-
28 days - 11 months - 28 jours - 11 mois	62	32	30	2.6	2.6	2.6
28 days - less than 2 months - 28 jours - moins de 2 mois	11	7	4	♦0.5	♦0.6	♦0.3
2 months - 2 mois	16	8	8	♦0.7	♦0.7	♦0.7
3 months - 3 mois	10	5	5	♦0.4	♦0.4	♦0.4
4 months - 4 mois	7	4	3	♦0.3	♦0.3	♦0.3
5 months - 5 mois	4	3	1	♦0.2	♦0.2	♦0.1
6 months - 6 mois	3	1	2	♦0.1	♦0.1	♦0.2
7 months - 7 mois	4	3	1	♦0.2	♦0.2	♦0.1
8 months - 8 mois	1	-	1	-	-	♦0.1
9 months - 9 mois	3	1	2	♦0.1	♦0.1	♦0.2
10 months - 10 mois	1	-	1	-	-	♦0.1
11 months - 11 mois	2	-	2	♦0.1	-	♦0.2
Republic of Korea - République de Corée[21]						
2013 (C)						
Total	1 305	698	607	3.0	3.1	2.9
Less than 1 day - Moins de 1 jour	177	99	78	0.4	0.4	0.4
1 - 6 days - 1 - 6 jours	321	173	148	0.7	0.8	0.7
7 - 27 days - 7 - 27 jours	254	133	121	0.6	0.6	0.6
7 - 13 days - 7 - 13 jours	118	64	54	0.3	0.3	0.3
14 - 20 days - 14 - 20 jours	89	47	42	0.2	0.2	0.2
21 - 27 days - 21 - 27 jours	47	22	25	0.1	♦0.1	♦0.1
28 days - 11 months - 28 jours - 11 mois	553	293	260	1.3	1.3	1.2
28 days - less than 2 months - 28 jours - moins de 2 mois	164	87	77	0.4	0.4	0.4
2 months - 2 mois	87	39	48	0.2	0.2	0.2
3 months - 3 mois	75	34	41	0.2	0.2	0.2
4 months - 4 mois	62	37	25	0.1	0.2	♦0.1
5 months - 5 mois	47	27	20	0.1	♦0.1	♦0.1
6 months - 6 mois	28	21	7	♦0.1	♦0.1	-
7 months - 7 mois	19	11	8	-	-	-
8 months - 8 mois	29	10	19	♦0.1	-	♦0.1
9 months - 9 mois	17	11	6	-	-	-
10 months - 10 mois	14	8	6	-	-	-
11 months - 11 mois	11	8	3	-	-	-
Singapore - Singapour						
2014 (+C)						
Total	83	42[4]	40[4]	...	...	...
Less than 1 day - Moins de 1 jour	14	9	5	...	...	...
1 - 6 days - 1 - 6 jours	23	12[4]	10[4]	...	...	...
7 - 27 days - 7 - 27 jours	13	2	11	...	...	...
7 - 13 days - 7 - 13 jours	10	1	9	...	...	...

16. Infant deaths and infant mortality rates by age and sex: latest available year, 2005 - 2014
Décès d'enfants de moins d'un an et taux de mortalité infantile selon l'âge et le sexe : dernière année disponible, 2005 - 2014 (continued - suite)

Continent, country or area, year, code[a] and age Continent, pays ou zone, année, code[a] et âge	Number - Nombre			Rate - Taux		
	Both sexes Les deux sexes	Male Masculin	Female Féminin	Both sexes Les deux sexes	Male Masculin	Female Féminin

ASIA - ASIE

Singapore - Singapour
2014 (+C)

14 - 20 days - 14 - 20 jours	3	1	2	...	...	...
21 - 27 days - 21 - 27 jours	-	-	-	...	...	...
28 days - 11 months - 28 jours - 11 mois	33	19	14	...	...	...
28 days - less than 2 months - 28 jours - moins de 2 mois	8	5	3	...	...	...
2 months - 2 mois	7	5	2	...	...	...
3 months - 3 mois	7	4	3	...	...	...
4 months - 4 mois	4	2	2	...	...	...
5 months - 5 mois	1	-	1	...	...	...
6 months - 6 mois	2	-	2	...	...	...
7 months - 7 mois	1	-	1	...	...	...
8 months - 8 mois	3	3	-	...	...	...
9 months - 9 mois	-	-	-	...	...	...
10 months - 10 mois	-	-	-	...	...	...
11 months - 11 mois	-	-	-	...	...	...

State of Palestine - État de Palestine
2007 (U)

Total	794	420	374	...	...	...
Less than 1 day - Moins de 1 jour	42	24	18	...	...	...
1 - 6 days - 1 - 6 jours	183	113	70	...	...	...
7 - 27 days - 7 - 27 jours	156	79	77	...	...	...
7 - 13 days - 7 - 13 jours	79	44	35	...	...	...
14 - 20 days - 14 - 20 jours	47	19	28	...	...	...
21 - 27 days - 21 - 27 jours	30	16	14	...	...	...
28 days - 11 months - 28 jours - 11 mois	413	204	209	...	...	...
28 days - less than 2 months - 28 jours - moins de 2 mois	111	64	47	...	...	...
2 months - 2 mois	56	25	31	...	...	...
3 months - 3 mois	50	28	22	...	...	...
4 months - 4 mois	32	14	18	...	...	...
5 months - 5 mois	40	20	20	...	...	...
6 months - 6 mois	28	17	11	...	...	...
7 months - 7 mois	19	8	11	...	...	...
8 months - 8 mois	19	10	9	...	...	...
9 months - 9 mois	22	8	14	...	...	...
10 months - 10 mois	21	5	16	...	...	...
11 months - 11 mois	15	5	10	...	...	...

Tajikistan - Tadjikistan[13]
2008 (U)

Total	2 480	1 478	1 002	...	...	...
Less than 1 day - Moins de 1 jour	420	255	165	...	...	...
1 - 6 days - 1 - 6 jours	699	443	256	...	...	...
7 - 27 days - 7 - 27 jours	248	140	108	...	...	...
7 - 13 days - 7 - 13 jours	145	87	58	...	...	...
14 - 20 days - 14 - 20 jours	63	33	30	...	...	...
21 - 27 days - 21 - 27 jours	40	20	20	...	...	...
28 days - 11 months - 28 jours - 11 mois	1 113	640	473	...	...	...
28 days - less than 2 months - 28 jours - moins de 2 mois	180	103	77	...	...	...
2 months - 2 mois	155	92	63	...	...	...
3 months - 3 mois	138	77	61	...	...	...
4 months - 4 mois	111	71	40	...	...	...
5 months - 5 mois	106	56	50	...	...	...
6 months - 6 mois	106	62	44	...	...	...
7 months - 7 mois	75	43	32	...	...	...
8 months - 8 mois	79	49	30	...	...	...
9 months - 9 mois	56	23	33	...	...	...
10 months - 10 mois	56	39	17	...	...	...
11 months - 11 mois	51	25	26	...	...	...

Thailand - Thaïlande
2011 (+U)

Total	5 275	2 964	2 311	...	...	...
Less than 1 day - Moins de 1 jour	587	326	261	...	...	...
1 - 6 days - 1 - 6 jours	1 612	931	681	...	...	...
7 - 27 days - 7 - 27 jours	987	534	453	...	...	...
7 - 13 days - 7 - 13 jours	527	285	242	...	...	...
14 - 20 days - 14 - 20 jours	276	149	127	...	...	...
21 - 27 days - 21 - 27 jours	184	100	84	...	...	...

16. Infant deaths and infant mortality rates by age and sex: latest available year, 2005 - 2014
Décès d'enfants de moins d'un an et taux de mortalité infantile selon l'âge et le sexe : dernière année disponible, 2005 - 2014 (continued - suite)

Continent, country or area, year, code[a] and age / Continent, pays ou zone, année, code[a] et âge	Number - Nombre			Rate - Taux		
	Both sexes Les deux sexes	Male Masculin	Female Féminin	Both sexes Les deux sexes	Male Masculin	Female Féminin
ASIA - ASIE						
Thailand - Thaïlande						
2011 (+U)						
28 days - 11 months - 28 jours - 11 mois	2 089	1 173	916	...	...	...
28 days - less than 2 months - 28 jours - moins de 2 mois	556	329	227	...	...	...
2 months - 2 mois	360	203	157	...	...	...
3 months - 3 mois	249	152	97	...	...	...
4 months - 4 mois	193	98	95	...	...	...
5 months - 5 mois	160	91	69	...	...	...
6 months - 6 mois	141	74	67	...	...	...
7 months - 7 mois	103	55	48	...	...	...
8 months - 8 mois	106	51	55	...	...	...
9 months - 9 mois	87	41	46	...	...	...
10 months - 10 mois	77	45	32	...	...	...
11 months - 11 mois	57	34	23	...	...	...
Turkey - Turquie						
2013 (C)						
Total	13 900	7 532	6 368	10.8	11.4	10.2
Less than 1 day - Moins de 1 jour	1 920	1 004	916	1.5	1.5	1.5
1 - 6 days - 1 - 6 jours	4 248	2 444	1 804	3.3	3.7	2.9
7 - 27 days - 7 - 27 jours	2 693	1 469	1 224	2.1	2.2	2.0
7 - 13 days - 7 - 13 jours	1 414	787	627	1.1	1.2	1.0
14 - 20 days - 14 - 20 jours	736	402	334	0.6	0.6	0.5
21 - 27 days - 21 - 27 jours	543	280	263	0.4	0.4	0.4
28 days - 11 months - 28 jours - 11 mois	5 039	2 615	2 424	3.9	4.0	3.9
28 days - less than 2 months - 28 jours - moins de 2 mois	1 459	790	669	1.1	1.2	1.1
2 months - 2 mois	779	421	358	0.6	0.6	0.6
3 months - 3 mois	580	302	278	0.5	0.5	0.4
4 months - 4 mois	482	250	232	0.4	0.4	0.4
5 months - 5 mois	379	186	193	0.3	0.3	0.3
6 months - 6 mois	301	157	144	0.2	0.2	0.2
7 months - 7 mois	278	133	145	0.2	0.2	0.2
8 months - 8 mois	230	108	122	0.2	0.2	0.2
9 months - 9 mois	196	98	98	0.2	0.1	0.2
10 months - 10 mois	183	83	100	0.1	0.1	0.2
11 months - 11 mois	172	87	85	0.1	0.1	0.1
EUROPE						
Åland Islands - Îles d'Åland						
2013 (C)						
Total	-	-	-	...	...	...
Albania - Albanie						
2013 (C)						
Total	282	171	111	7.9	9.2	6.5
Less than 1 day - Moins de 1 jour	100	56	44	2.8	3.0	2.6
1 - 6 days - 1 - 6 jours	59	36	23	1.7	1.9	♦1.3
7 - 27 days - 7 - 27 jours	40	26	14	1.1	♦1.4	♦0.8
7 - 13 days - 7 - 13 jours	25	15	10	♦0.7	♦0.8	♦0.6
14 - 20 days - 14 - 20 jours	11	7	4	♦0.3	♦0.4	♦0.2
21 - 27 days - 21 - 27 jours	4	4	-	♦0.1	♦0.2	-
28 days - 11 months - 28 jours - 11 mois	83	53	30	2.3	2.8	1.8
28 days - less than 2 months - 28 jours - moins de 2 mois	29	22	7	♦0.8	♦1.2	♦0.4
2 months - 2 mois	15	8	7	♦0.4	♦0.4	♦0.4
3 months - 3 mois	8	4	4	♦0.2	♦0.2	♦0.2
4 months - 4 mois	6	1	5	♦0.2	♦0.1	♦0.3
5 months - 5 mois	5	4	1	♦0.1	♦0.2	♦0.1
6 months - 6 mois	5	5	-	♦0.1	♦0.3	-
7 months - 7 mois	2	2	-	♦0.1	♦0.1	-
8 months - 8 mois	5	3	2	♦0.1	♦0.2	♦0.1
9 months - 9 mois	4	1	3	♦0.1	♦0.1	♦0.2
10 months - 10 mois	4	3	1	♦0.1	♦0.2	♦0.1
11 months - 11 mois	-	-	-	-	-	-
Andorra - Andorre						
2009 (C)						
Total	1	-	1	...	...	...
Less than 1 day - Moins de 1 jour	-	-	-	...	...	...
1 - 6 days - 1 - 6 jours	1	-	1	...	...	...

16. Infant deaths and infant mortality rates by age and sex: latest available year, 2005 - 2014
Décès d'enfants de moins d'un an et taux de mortalité infantile selon l'âge et le sexe : dernière année disponible, 2005 - 2014 (continued - suite)

Continent, country or area, year, code[a] and age / Continent, pays ou zone, année, code[a] et âge	Number - Nombre			Rate - Taux		
	Both sexes Les deux sexes	Male Masculin	Female Féminin	Both sexes Les deux sexes	Male Masculin	Female Féminin
EUROPE						
Andorra - Andorre						
2009 (C)						
7 - 27 days - 7 - 27 jours	-	-	-	...	...	...
28 days - 11 months - 28 jours - 11 mois...........................	-	-	-	...	...	...
Austria - Autriche						
2013 (C)						
Total........................	245	144	101	3.1	3.5	2.6
Less than 1 day - Moins de 1 jour	111	66	45	1.4	1.6	1.2
1 - 6 days - 1 - 6 jours	43	30	13	0.5	0.7	♦0.3
7 - 27 days - 7 - 27 jours	29	17	12	♦0.4	♦0.4	♦0.3
7 - 13 days - 7 - 13 jours	14	9	5	♦0.2	♦0.2	♦0.1
14 - 20 days - 14 - 20 jours	10	6	4	♦0.1	♦0.1	♦0.1
21 - 27 days - 21 - 27 jours	5	2	3	♦0.1	-	♦0.1
28 days - 11 months - 28 jours - 11 mois........................	62	31	31	0.8	0.8	0.8
28 days - less than 2 months - 28 jours - moins de 2 mois	24	13	11	♦0.3	♦0.3	♦0.3
2 months - 2 mois........................	5	3	2	♦0.1	♦0.1	♦0.1
3 months - 3 mois........................	7	4	3	♦0.1	♦0.1	♦0.1
4 months - 4 mois........................	6	3	3	♦0.1	♦0.1	♦0.1
5 months - 5 mois........................	2	2	-	-	-	-
6 months - 6 mois........................	3	1	2	-	-	♦0.1
7 months - 7 mois........................	6	-	6	♦0.1	-	♦0.2
8 months - 8 mois........................	2	1	1	-	-	-
9 months - 9 mois........................	4	2	2	♦0.1	-	♦0.1
10 months - 10 mois........................	2	1	1	-	-	-
11 months - 11 mois	1	1	-	-	-	-
Belarus - Bélarus						
2013 (C)						
Total........................	407	238	169	3.4	3.9	3.0
Less than 1 day - Moins de 1 jour	44	23	21	0.4	♦0.4	♦0.4
1 - 6 days - 1 - 6 jours	70	38	32	0.6	0.6	0.6
7 - 27 days - 7 - 27 jours	84	49	35	0.7	0.8	0.6
7 - 13 days - 7 - 13 jours	44	29	15	0.4	♦0.5	♦0.3
14 - 20 days - 14 - 20 jours	22	12	10	♦0.2	♦0.2	♦0.2
21 - 27 days - 21 - 27 jours	18	8	10	♦0.2	♦0.1	♦0.2
28 days - 11 months - 28 jours - 11 mois........................	209	128	81	1.8	2.1	1.4
28 days - less than 2 months - 28 jours - moins de 2 mois	63	37	26	0.5	0.6	♦0.5
2 months - 2 mois........................	33	19	14	0.3	♦0.3	♦0.2
3 months - 3 mois........................	18	12	6	♦0.2	♦0.2	♦0.1
4 months - 4 mois........................	17	13	4	♦0.1	♦0.2	♦0.1
5 months - 5 mois........................	24	15	9	♦0.2	♦0.2	♦0.2
6 months - 6 mois........................	14	8	6	♦0.1	♦0.1	♦0.1
7 months - 7 mois........................	10	5	5	♦0.1	♦0.1	♦0.1
8 months - 8 mois........................	10	7	3	♦0.1	♦0.1	♦0.1
9 months - 9 mois........................	8	4	4	♦0.1	♦0.1	♦0.1
10 months - 10 mois........................	8	5	3	♦0.1	♦0.1	♦0.1
11 months - 11 mois	4	3	1	-	-	-
Belgium - Belgique[22]						
2010 (C)						
Total........................	465	276	189	3.6	4.1	3.0
Less than 1 day - Moins de 1 jour	123	70	53	0.9	1.1	0.8
1 - 6 days - 1 - 6 jours	101	64	37	0.8	1.0	0.6
7 - 27 days - 7 - 27 jours	68	43	25	0.5	0.6	♦0.4
7 - 13 days - 7 - 13 jours	39	27	12	0.3	♦0.4	♦0.2
14 - 20 days - 14 - 20 jours	16	10	6	♦0.1	♦0.2	♦0.1
21 - 27 days - 21 - 27 jours	13	6	7	♦0.1	♦0.1	♦0.1
28 days - 11 months - 28 jours - 11 mois........................	173	99	74	1.3	1.5	1.2
28 days - less than 2 months - 28 jours - moins de 2 mois	37	25	12	0.3	♦0.4	♦0.2
2 months - 2 mois........................	19	13	6	♦0.1	♦0.2	♦0.1
3 months - 3 mois........................	27	14	13	♦0.2	♦0.2	♦0.2
4 months - 4 mois........................	13	5	8	♦0.1	♦0.1	♦0.1
5 months - 5 mois........................	24	16	8	♦0.2	♦0.2	♦0.1
6 months - 6 mois........................	7	3	4	♦0.1	-	♦0.1
7 months - 7 mois........................	9	6	3	♦0.1	♦0.1	-
8 months - 8 mois........................	15	9	6	♦0.1	♦0.1	♦0.1
9 months - 9 mois........................	7	3	4	♦0.1	-	♦0.1
10 months - 10 mois........................	13	5	8	♦0.1	♦0.1	♦0.1
11 months - 11 mois	2	-	2	-	-	-

16. Infant deaths and infant mortality rates by age and sex: latest available year, 2005 - 2014
Décès d'enfants de moins d'un an et taux de mortalité infantile selon l'âge et le sexe : dernière année disponible, 2005 - 2014 (continued - suite)

Continent, country or area, year, codeᵃ and age / Continent, pays ou zone, année, codeᵃ et âge	Number - Nombre			Rate - Taux		
	Both sexes Les deux sexes	Male Masculin	Female Féminin	Both sexes Les deux sexes	Male Masculin	Female Féminin
EUROPE						
Bosnia and Herzegovina - Bosnie-Herzégovine						
2010 (C)						
Total	216	125	91	6.4	7.2	5.6
Less than 1 day - Moins de 1 jour	74	43	31	2.2	2.5	1.9
1 - 6 days - 1 - 6 jours	89	56	33	2.7	3.2	2.0
7 - 27 days - 7 - 27 jours	19	13	6	♦0.6	♦0.8	♦0.4
7 - 13 days - 7 - 13 jours	10	6	4	♦0.3	♦0.3	♦0.2
14 - 20 days - 14 - 20 jours	6	6	-	♦0.2	♦0.3	-
21 - 27 days - 21 - 27 jours	3	1	2	♦0.1	♦0.1	♦0.1
28 days - 11 months - 28 jours - 11 mois	34	13	21	1.0	♦0.8	♦1.3
28 days - less than 2 months - 28 jours - moins de 2 mois	5	2	3	♦0.1	♦0.1	♦0.2
2 months - 2 mois	10	6	4	♦0.3	♦0.3	♦0.2
3 months - 3 mois	1	-	1	-	-	♦0.1
4 months - 4 mois	5	2	3	♦0.1	♦0.1	♦0.2
5 months - 5 mois	3	1	2	♦0.1	♦0.1	♦0.1
6 months - 6 mois	3	1	2	♦0.1	♦0.1	♦0.1
7 months - 7 mois	-	-	-	-	-	-
8 months - 8 mois	1	-	1	-	-	♦0.1
9 months - 9 mois	4	-	4	♦0.1	-	♦0.2
10 months - 10 mois	1	1	-	-	♦0.1	-
11 months - 11 mois	1	-	1	-	-	♦0.1
Bulgaria - Bulgarie						
2013 (C)						
Total	489	283	206	7.3	8.3	6.3
Less than 1 day - Moins de 1 jour	96	59	37	1.4	1.7	1.1
1 - 6 days - 1 - 6 jours	111	65	46	1.7	1.9	1.4
7 - 27 days - 7 - 27 jours	75	42	33	1.1	1.2	1.0
28 days - 11 months - 28 jours - 11 mois	207	117	90	3.1	3.4	2.8
Croatia - Croatie						
2013 (C)						
Total	162	93	69	4.1	4.5	3.6
Less than 1 day - Moins de 1 jour	52	30	22	1.3	1.4	♦1.1
1 - 6 days - 1 - 6 jours	40	21	19	1.0	♦1.0	♦1.0
7 - 27 days - 7 - 27 jours	35	19	16	0.9	♦0.9	♦0.8
7 - 13 days - 7 - 13 jours	21	10	11	♦0.5	♦0.5	♦0.6
14 - 20 days - 14 - 20 jours	11	7	4	♦0.3	♦0.3	♦0.2
21 - 27 days - 21 - 27 jours	3	2	1	♦0.1	♦0.1	♦0.1
28 days - 11 months - 28 jours - 11 mois	35	23	12	0.9	♦1.1	♦0.6
28 days - less than 2 months - 28 jours - moins de 2 mois	9	5	4	♦0.2	♦0.2	♦0.2
2 months - 2 mois	5	3	2	♦0.1	♦0.1	♦0.1
3 months - 3 mois	6	3	3	♦0.2	♦0.1	♦0.2
4 months - 4 mois	-	-	-	-	-	-
5 months - 5 mois	2	1	1	♦0.1	-	♦0.1
6 months - 6 mois	4	3	1	♦0.1	♦0.1	♦0.1
7 months - 7 mois	2	2	-	♦0.1	♦0.1	-
8 months - 8 mois	3	2	1	♦0.1	♦0.1	♦0.1
9 months - 9 mois	-	-	-	-	-	-
10 months - 10 mois	1	1	-	-	-	-
11 months - 11 mois	3	3	-	♦0.1	♦0.1	-
Czech Republic - République tchèque						
2013 (C)						
Total	265	158	107	2.5	2.9	2.1
Less than 1 day - Moins de 1 jour	38	20	18	0.4	♦0.4	♦0.3
1 - 6 days - 1 - 6 jours	67	41	26	0.6	0.7	♦0.5
7 - 27 days - 7 - 27 jours	46	27	19	0.4	♦0.5	♦0.4
7 - 13 days - 7 - 13 jours	28	17	11	♦0.3	♦0.3	♦0.2
14 - 20 days - 14 - 20 jours	13	8	5	♦0.1	♦0.1	♦0.1
21 - 27 days - 21 - 27 jours	5	2	3	-	-	♦0.1
28 days - 11 months - 28 jours - 11 mois	114	70	44	1.1	1.3	0.8
28 days - less than 2 months - 28 jours - moins de 2 mois	36	22	14	0.3	♦0.4	♦0.3
2 months - 2 mois	20	13	7	♦0.2	♦0.2	♦0.1
3 months - 3 mois	15	10	5	♦0.1	♦0.2	♦0.1
4 months - 4 mois	7	5	2	♦0.1	♦0.1	-
5 months - 5 mois	13	7	6	♦0.1	♦0.1	♦0.1
6 months - 6 mois	3	3	-	-	♦0.1	-
7 months - 7 mois	8	3	5	♦0.1	♦0.1	♦0.1
8 months - 8 mois	3	2	1	-	-	-
9 months - 9 mois	3	3	-	-	♦0.1	-

16. Infant deaths and infant mortality rates by age and sex: latest available year, 2005 - 2014

Décès d'enfants de moins d'un an et taux de mortalité infantile selon l'âge et le sexe : dernière année disponible, 2005 - 2014 (continued - suite)

Continent, country or area, year, code[a] and age / Continent, pays ou zone, année, code[a] et âge	Number - Nombre			Rate - Taux		
	Both sexes Les deux sexes	Male Masculin	Female Féminin	Both sexes Les deux sexes	Male Masculin	Female Féminin
EUROPE						
Czech Republic - République tchèque						
2013 (C)						
10 months - 10 mois	3	2	1	-	-	-
11 months - 11 mois	3	-	3	-	-	♦0.1
Denmark - Danemark[23]						
2013 (C)						
Total	194	95	99	3.5	3.3	3.6
Less than 1 day - Moins de 1 jour	83	42	41	1.5	1.5	1.5
1 - 6 days - 1 - 6 jours	49	24	25	0.9	♦0.8	♦0.9
7 - 27 days - 7 - 27 jours	21	11	10	♦0.4	♦0.4	♦0.4
7 - 13 days - 7 - 13 jours	13	7	6	♦0.2	♦0.2	♦0.2
14 - 20 days - 14 - 20 jours	7	3	4	♦0.1	♦0.1	♦0.1
21 - 27 days - 21 - 27 jours	1	1	-	-	-	-
28 days - 11 months - 28 jours - 11 mois	41	18	23	0.7	♦0.6	♦0.8
28 days - less than 2 months - 28 jours - moins de 2 mois	12	5	7	♦0.2	♦0.2	♦0.3
2 months - 2 mois	7	4	3	♦0.1	♦0.1	♦0.1
3 months - 3 mois	3	2	1	♦0.1	♦0.1	-
4 months - 4 mois	5	2	3	♦0.1	♦0.1	♦0.1
5 months - 5 mois	5	2	3	♦0.1	♦0.1	♦0.1
6 months - 6 mois	-	-	-	-	-	-
7 months - 7 mois	-	-	-	-	-	-
8 months - 8 mois	2	1	1	-	-	-
9 months - 9 mois	3	1	2	♦0.1	-	♦0.1
10 months - 10 mois	2	-	2	-	-	♦0.1
11 months - 11 mois	2	1	1	-	-	-
Estonia - Estonie						
2013 (C)						
Total	28	13	15	...	...	...
Less than 1 day - Moins de 1 jour	7	1	6	...	...	...
1 - 6 days - 1 - 6 jours	3	3	-	...	...	...
7 - 27 days - 7 - 27 jours	6	2	4	...	...	...
7 - 13 days - 7 - 13 jours	4	1	3	...	...	...
14 - 20 days - 14 - 20 jours	2	1	1	...	...	...
21 - 27 days - 21 - 27 jours	-	-	-	...	...	...
28 days - 11 months - 28 jours - 11 mois	12	7	5	...	...	...
28 days - less than 2 months - 28 jours - moins de 2 mois	4	-	4	...	...	...
2 months - 2 mois	4	3	1	...	...	...
3 months - 3 mois	1	1	-	...	...	...
4 months - 4 mois	1	1	-	...	...	...
5 months - 5 mois	-	-	-	...	...	...
6 months - 6 mois	-	-	-	...	...	...
7 months - 7 mois	1	1	-	...	...	...
8 months - 8 mois	-	-	-	...	...	...
9 months - 9 mois	-	-	-	...	...	...
10 months - 10 mois	1	1	-	...	...	...
11 months - 11 mois	-	-	-	...	...	...
Finland - Finlande[24]						
2013 (C)						
Total	102	58	44	1.8	1.9	1.6
Less than 1 day - Moins de 1 jour	28	17	11	♦0.5	♦0.6	♦0.4
1 - 6 days - 1 - 6 jours	24	10	14	♦0.4	♦0.3	♦0.5
7 - 27 days - 7 - 27 jours	12	9	3	♦0.2	♦0.3	♦0.1
28 days - 11 months - 28 jours - 11 mois	38	22	16	0.7	♦0.7	♦0.6
France[25]						
2013 (C)						
Total	2 710	1 512	1 198	3.5	3.8	3.1
Less than 1 day - Moins de 1 jour	663	370	293	0.8	0.9	0.8
1 - 6 days - 1 - 6 jours	635	354	281	0.8	0.9	0.7
7 - 27 days - 7 - 27 jours	586	314	272	0.7	0.8	0.7
7 - 13 days - 7 - 13 jours	302	163	139	0.4	0.4	0.4
14 - 20 days - 14 - 20 jours	167	100	67	0.2	0.2	0.2
21 - 27 days - 21 - 27 jours	117	51	66	0.1	0.1	0.2
28 days - 11 months - 28 jours - 11 mois	826	474	352	1.1	1.2	0.9
28 days - less than 2 months - 28 jours - moins de 2 mois	245	138	107	0.3	0.3	0.3
2 months - 2 mois	129	79	50	0.2	0.2	0.1
3 months - 3 mois	90	44	46	0.1	0.1	0.1
4 months - 4 mois	90	49	41	0.1	0.1	0.1
5 months - 5 mois	76	44	32	0.1	0.1	0.1

Continent, country or area, year, code[a] and age / Continent, pays ou zone, année, code[a] et âge	Number - Nombre			Rate - Taux		
	Both sexes Les deux sexes	Male Masculin	Female Féminin	Both sexes Les deux sexes	Male Masculin	Female Féminin
EUROPE						
France[25]						
2013 (C)						
6 months - 6 mois	41	26	15	0.1	♦0.1	-
7 months - 7 mois	37	23	14	-	♦0.1	-
8 months - 8 mois	40	24	16	0.1	♦0.1	-
9 months - 9 mois	29	15	14	-	-	-
10 months - 10 mois	23	17	6	-	-	-
11 months - 11 mois	26	15	11	-	-	-
Germany - Allemagne						
2013 (C)						
Total	2 250	1 268	982	3.3	3.6	3.0
Less than 1 day - Moins de 1 jour	753	421	332	1.1	1.2	1.0
1 - 6 days - 1 - 6 jours	420	229	191	0.6	0.7	0.6
7 - 27 days - 7 - 27 jours	355	204	151	0.5	0.6	0.5
7 - 13 days - 7 - 13 jours	178	106	72	0.3	0.3	0.2
14 - 20 days - 14 - 20 jours	107	56	51	0.2	0.2	0.2
21 - 27 days - 21 - 27 jours	70	42	28	0.1	0.1	♦0.1
28 days - 11 months - 28 jours - 11 mois	722	414	308	1.1	1.2	0.9
28 days - less than 2 months - 28 jours - moins de 2 mois	192	107	85	0.3	0.3	0.3
2 months - 2 mois	112	65	47	0.2	0.2	0.1
3 months - 3 mois	90	57	33	0.1	0.2	0.1
4 months - 4 mois	92	55	37	0.1	0.2	0.1
5 months - 5 mois	52	32	20	0.1	0.1	♦0.1
6 months - 6 mois	48	25	23	0.1	♦0.1	♦0.1
7 months - 7 mois	45	24	21	0.1	♦0.1	♦0.1
8 months - 8 mois	24	11	13	-	-	-
9 months - 9 mois	23	12	11	-	-	-
10 months - 10 mois	21	13	8	-	-	-
11 months - 11 mois	23	13	10	-	-	-
Gibraltar						
2006 (+C)						
Total	1	1	-	...	...	...
Less than 7 days - Moins de 7 jours	-	-	-	...	...	...
7 - 27 days - 7 - 27 jours	-	-	-	...	...	...
28 days - 11 months - 28 jours - 11 mois	1	1	-	...	...	...
28 days - 2 months - 28 jours - 2 mois	-	-	-	...	...	...
3 months - 3 mois	1	1	-	...	...	...
4 - 11 months - 4 - 11 mois	-	-	-	...	...	...
Greece - Grèce						
2013 (C)						
Total	347	200	147	3.7	4.1	3.2
Less than 1 day - Moins de 1 jour	77	44	33	0.8	0.9	0.7
1 - 6 days - 1 - 6 jours	95	56	39	1.0	1.2	0.9
7 - 27 days - 7 - 27 jours	77	46	31	0.8	0.9	0.7
28 days - 11 months - 28 jours - 11 mois	98	54	44	1.0	1.1	1.0
Hungary - Hongrie[26]						
2013 (C)						
Total	448	265	183	5.0	5.8	4.2
Less than 1 day - Moins de 1 jour	26	12	14	♦0.3	♦0.3	♦0.3
1 - 6 days - 1 - 6 jours	106	58	48	1.2	1.3	1.1
7 - 27 days - 7 - 27 jours	94	62	32	1.0	1.3	0.7
7 - 13 days - 7 - 13 jours	49	33	16	0.5	0.7	♦0.4
14 - 20 days - 14 - 20 jours	34	22	12	0.4	♦0.5	♦0.3
21 - 27 days - 21 - 27 jours	11	7	4	♦0.1	♦0.2	♦0.1
28 days - 11 months - 28 jours - 11 mois	209	126	83	2.3	2.7	1.9
28 days - less than 2 months - 28 jours - moins de 2 mois	81	53	28	0.9	1.2	♦0.6
2 months - 2 mois	29	22	7	♦0.3	♦0.5	♦0.2
3 months - 3 mois	16	9	7	♦0.2	♦0.2	♦0.2
4 months - 4 mois	20	9	11	♦0.2	♦0.2	♦0.3
5 months - 5 mois	16	10	6	♦0.2	♦0.2	♦0.1
6 months - 6 mois	13	10	3	♦0.1	♦0.2	♦0.1
7 months - 7 mois	9	5	4	♦0.1	♦0.1	♦0.1
8 months - 8 mois	9	-	9	♦0.1	-	♦0.2
9 months - 9 mois	8	4	4	♦0.1	♦0.1	♦0.1
10 months - 10 mois	5	2	3	♦0.1	-	♦0.1
11 months - 11 mois	3	2	1	-	-	-

16. Infant deaths and infant mortality rates by age and sex: latest available year, 2005 - 2014
Décès d'enfants de moins d'un an et taux de mortalité infantile selon l'âge et le sexe : dernière année disponible, 2005 - 2014 (continued - suite)

Continent, country or area, year, code[a] and age / Continent, pays ou zone, année, code[a] et âge	Number - Nombre			Rate - Taux		
	Both sexes Les deux sexes	Male Masculin	Female Féminin	Both sexes Les deux sexes	Male Masculin	Female Féminin
EUROPE						
Iceland - Islande						
2013 (C)						
Total	8	2	6	...	...	...
Less than 1 day - Moins de 1 jour	2	1	1	...	...	...
1 - 6 days - 1 - 6 jours	1	-	1	...	...	...
7 - 27 days - 7 - 27 jours	3	1	2	...	...	...
7 - 13 days - 7 - 13 jours	1	-	1	...	...	...
14 - 20 days - 14 - 20 jours	1	-	1	...	...	...
21 - 27 days - 21 - 27 jours	1	1	-	...	...	...
28 days - 11 months - 28 jours - 11 mois	2	-	2	...	...	...
28 days - less than 2 months - 28 jours - moins de 2 mois	1	-	1	...	...	...
2 months - 2 mois	-	-	-	...	...	...
3 months - 3 mois	-	-	-	...	...	...
4 months - 4 mois	-	-	-	...	...	...
5 months - 5 mois	1	-	1	...	...	...
6 months - 6 mois	-	-	-	...	...	...
7 months - 7 mois	-	-	-	...	...	...
8 months - 8 mois	-	-	-	...	...	...
9 months - 9 mois	-	-	-	...	...	...
10 months - 10 mois	-	-	-	...	...	...
11 months - 11 mois	-	-	-	...	...	...
Ireland - Irlande						
2011 (+C)						
Total	262	150	112	3.5	4.0	3.1
Less than 1 day - Moins de 1 jour	88	43	45	1.2	1.1	1.2
1 - 6 days - 1 - 6 jours	59	38	21	0.8	1.0	♦0.6
7 - 27 days - 7 - 27 jours	41	30	11	0.6	0.8	♦0.3
7 - 13 days - 7 - 13 jours	18	13	5	♦0.2	♦0.3	♦0.1
14 - 20 days - 14 - 20 jours	17	13	4	♦0.2	♦0.3	♦0.1
21 - 27 days - 21 - 27 jours	6	4	2	♦0.1	♦0.1	♦0.1
28 days - 11 months - 28 jours - 11 mois	74	39	35	1.0	1.0	1.0
28 days - less than 2 months - 28 jours - moins de 2 mois	20	12	8	♦0.3	♦0.3	♦0.2
2 months - 2 mois	17	7	10	♦0.2	♦0.2	♦0.3
3 months - 3 mois	11	4	7	♦0.1	♦0.1	♦0.2
4 months - 4 mois	5	5	-	♦0.1	♦0.1	-
5 months - 5 mois	6	3	3	♦0.1	♦0.1	♦0.1
6 months - 6 mois	3	1	2	-	-	♦0.1
7 months - 7 mois	2	1	1	-	-	-
8 months - 8 mois	1	-	1	-		-
9 months - 9 mois	4	3	1	♦0.1	♦0.1	-
10 months - 10 mois	4	2	2	♦0.1	♦0.1	♦0.1
11 months - 11 mois	1	1	-	-	-	-
Italy - Italie						
2013 (C)						
Total	1 493	864	629	2.9	3.3	2.5
Less than 1 day - Moins de 1 jour	268	153	115	0.5	0.6	0.5
1 - 6 days - 1 - 6 jours	447	279	168	0.9	1.1	0.7
7 - 27 days - 7 - 27 jours	311	175	136	0.6	0.7	0.5
7 - 13 days - 7 - 13 jours	151	87	64	0.3	0.3	0.3
14 - 20 days - 14 - 20 jours	92	47	45	0.2	0.2	0.2
21 - 27 days - 21 - 27 jours	68	41	27	0.1	0.2	♦0.1
28 days - 11 months - 28 jours - 11 mois	467	257	210	0.9	1.0	0.8
28 days - less than 2 months - 28 jours - moins de 2 mois	149	90	59	0.3	0.3	0.2
2 months - 2 mois	69	31	38	0.1	0.1	0.2
3 months - 3 mois	50	20	30	0.1	♦0.1	0.1
4 months - 4 mois	44	26	18	0.1	♦0.1	♦0.1
5 months - 5 mois	35	21	14	0.1	♦0.1	♦0.1
6 months - 6 mois	33	21	12	0.1	♦0.1	-
7 months - 7 mois	27	10	17	♦0.1	-	♦0.1
8 months - 8 mois	20	16	4	-	♦0.1	-
9 months - 9 mois	18	11	7	-	-	-
10 months - 10 mois	13	6	7	-	-	-
11 months - 11 mois	9	5	4	-	-	-
Latvia - Lettonie						
2013 (C)						
Total	91	51	40	...	...	...
Less than 1 day - Moins de 1 jour	18	9	9	...	...	...
1 - 6 days - 1 - 6 jours	19	10	9	...	...	...

Continent, country or area, year, codeª and age / Continent, pays ou zone, année, codeª et âge	Number - Nombre			Rate - Taux		
	Both sexes Les deux sexes	Male Masculin	Female Féminin	Both sexes Les deux sexes	Male Masculin	Female Féminin
EUROPE						
Latvia - Lettonie						
2013 (C)						
7 - 27 days - 7 - 27 jours	15	9	6	...	...	...
7 - 13 days - 7 - 13 jours	8	6	2	...	...	...
14 - 20 days - 14 - 20 jours	7	3	4	...	...	...
21 - 27 days - 21 - 27 jours	-	-	-	...	...	...
28 days - 11 months - 28 jours - 11 mois	39	23	16	...	...	...
28 days - less than 2 months - 28 jours - moins de 2 mois	13	5	8	...	...	...
2 months - 2 mois	6	4	2	...	...	...
3 months - 3 mois	5	3	2	...	...	...
4 months - 4 mois	1	1	-	...	...	...
5 months - 5 mois	7	7	-	...	...	...
6 months - 6 mois	-	-	-	...	...	...
7 months - 7 mois	1	-	1	...	...	...
8 months - 8 mois	1	1	-	...	...	...
9 months - 9 mois	5	2	3	...	...	...
10 months - 10 mois	-	-	-	...	...	...
11 months - 11 mois	-	-	-	...	...	...
Liechtenstein						
2013 (C)						
Total	2	-	2	...	...	...
Less than 1 day - Moins de 1 jour	-	-	-	...	...	...
1 - 6 days - 1 - 6 jours	1	-	1	...	...	...
7 - 27 days - 7 - 27 jours	-	-	-	...	...	...
28 days - 11 months - 28 jours - 11 mois	1	-	1	...	...	...
Lithuania - Lituanie						
2013 (C)						
Total	110	66	44	3.7	4.3	3.0
Less than 1 day - Moins de 1 jour	28	19	9	♦0.9	♦1.2	♦0.6
1 - 6 days - 1 - 6 jours	17	11	6	♦0.6	♦0.7	♦0.4
7 - 27 days - 7 - 27 jours	19	11	8	♦0.6	♦0.7	♦0.5
7 - 13 days - 7 - 13 jours	8	6	2	♦0.3	♦0.4	♦0.1
14 - 20 days - 14 - 20 jours	7	4	3	♦0.2	♦0.3	♦0.2
21 - 27 days - 21 - 27 jours	4	1	3	♦0.1	♦0.1	♦0.2
28 days - 11 months - 28 jours - 11 mois	46	25	21	1.5	♦1.6	♦1.4
28 days - less than 2 months - 28 jours - moins de 2 mois	16	7	9	♦0.5	♦0.5	♦0.6
2 months - 2 mois	8	3	5	♦0.3	♦0.2	♦0.3
3 months - 3 mois	5	2	3	♦0.2	♦0.1	♦0.2
4 months - 4 mois	3	3	-	♦0.1	♦0.2	-
5 months - 5 mois	2	2	-	♦0.1	♦0.1	-
6 months - 6 mois	3	1	2	♦0.1	♦0.1	♦0.1
7 months - 7 mois	4	4	-	♦0.1	♦0.3	-
8 months - 8 mois	1	-	1	-	-	♦0.1
9 months - 9 mois	2	1	1	♦0.1	♦0.1	♦0.1
10 months - 10 mois	1	1	-	-	♦0.1	-
11 months - 11 mois	1	1	-	-	♦0.1	-
Luxembourg						
2013 (C)						
Total	24	13	11	...	...	...
Less than 1 day - Moins de 1 jour	17	12	5	...	...	...
1 - 6 days - 1 - 6 jours	-	-	-	...	...	...
7 - 27 days - 7 - 27 jours	2	1	1	...	...	...
7 - 13 days - 7 - 13 jours	-	-	-	...	...	...
14 - 20 days - 14 - 20 jours	-	-	-	...	...	...
21 - 27 days - 21 - 27 jours	3	1	2	...	...	...
28 days - 11 months - 28 jours - 11 mois	5	-	5	...	...	...
Malta - Malte						
2013 (C)						
Total	27	14	13	...	...	...
Less than 1 day - Moins de 1 jour	10	7	3	...	...	...
1 - 6 days - 1 - 6 jours	4	2	2	...	...	...
7 - 27 days - 7 - 27 jours	4	1	3	...	...	...
7 - 13 days - 7 - 13 jours	2	1	1	...	...	...
14 - 20 days - 14 - 20 jours	2	-	2	...	...	...
21 - 27 days - 21 - 27 jours	-	-	-	...	...	...
28 days - 11 months - 28 jours - 11 mois	9	4	5	...	...	...
28 days - less than 2 months - 28 jours - moins de 2 mois	3	2	1	...	...	...
2 months - 2 mois	2	1	1	...	...	...

16. Infant deaths and infant mortality rates by age and sex: latest available year, 2005 - 2014
Décès d'enfants de moins d'un an et taux de mortalité infantile selon l'âge et le sexe : dernière année disponible, 2005 - 2014 (continued - suite)

Continent, country or area, year, code[a] and age / Continent, pays ou zone, année, code[a] et âge	Number - Nombre			Rate - Taux		
	Both sexes Les deux sexes	Male Masculin	Female Féminin	Both sexes Les deux sexes	Male Masculin	Female Féminin
EUROPE						
Malta - Malte						
2013 (C)						
3 months - 3 mois	1	-	1	...	...	...
4 months - 4 mois	-	-	-	...	...	...
5 months - 5 mois	2	1	1	...	...	...
6 months - 6 mois	-	-	-	...	...	...
7 months - 7 mois	-	-	-	...	...	...
8 months - 8 mois	-	-	-	...	...	...
9 months - 9 mois	1	-	1	...	...	...
10 months - 10 mois	-	-	-	...	...	...
11 months - 11 mois	-	-	-	...	...	...
Montenegro - Monténégro						
2013 (C)						
Total	33	21	12	...	...	...
Less than 1 day - Moins de 1 jour	1	1	-	...	...	...
1 - 6 days - 1 - 6 jours	20	16	4	...	...	...
7 - 27 days - 7 - 27 jours	5	1	4	...	...	...
28 days - 11 months - 28 jours - 11 mois	7	3	4	...	...	...
Netherlands - Pays-Bas[27]						
2009 (C)						
Total	711	...	...	3.8	...	...
Less than 1 day - Moins de 1 jour	240	...	...	1.3	...	...
1 - 6 days - 1 - 6 jours	166	...	...	0.9	...	...
7 - 27 days - 7 - 27 jours	122	...	...	0.7	...	...
7 - 13 days - 7 - 13 jours	73	...	...	0.4	...	...
14 - 20 days - 14 - 20 jours	41	...	...	0.2	...	...
21 - 27 days - 21 - 27 jours	8	...	...	-	...	...
28 days - 11 months - 28 jours - 11 mois	183	...	...	1.0	...	...
28 days - less than 2 months - 28 jours - moins de 2 mois	59	...	...	0.3	...	...
2 months - 2 mois	25	...	...	♦0.1	...	...
3 months - 3 mois	20	...	...	♦0.1	...	...
4 months - 4 mois	15	...	...	♦0.1	...	...
5 months - 5 mois	13	...	...	♦0.1	...	...
6 months - 6 mois	15	...	...	♦0.1	...	...
7 months - 7 mois	12	...	...	♦0.1	...	...
8 months - 8 mois	9	...	...	-	...	...
9 months - 9 mois	4	...	...	-	...	...
10 months - 10 mois	8	...	...	-	...	...
11 months - 11 mois	3	...	...	-	...	...
Norway - Norvège[28]						
2013 (C)						
Total	140	65	75	2.4	2.2	2.6
Less than 1 day - Moins de 1 jour	32	15	17	0.5	♦0.5	♦0.6
1 - 6 days - 1 - 6 jours	37	16	21	0.6	♦0.5	♦0.7
7 - 27 days - 7 - 27 jours	29	15	14	♦0.5	♦0.5	♦0.5
Poland - Pologne						
2013 (C)						
Total	1 684	937	747	4.6	4.9	4.2
Less than 1 day - Moins de 1 jour	519	287	232	1.4	1.5	1.3
1 - 6 days - 1 - 6 jours	327	197	130	0.9	1.0	0.7
7 - 27 days - 7 - 27 jours	318	167	151	0.9	0.9	0.8
28 days - 11 months - 28 jours - 11 mois	520	286	234	1.4	1.5	1.3
Portugal[8]						
2013 (C)						
Total	244	146	98	2.9	3.5	2.4
Less than 1 day - Moins de 1 jour	50	28	22	0.6	♦0.7	♦0.5
1 - 6 days - 1 - 6 jours	53	37	16	0.6	0.9	♦0.4
7 - 27 days - 7 - 27 jours	58	36	22	0.7	0.9	♦0.5
7 - 13 days - 7 - 13 jours	36	26	10	0.4	♦0.6	♦0.2
14 - 20 days - 14 - 20 jours	15	6	9	♦0.2	♦0.1	♦0.2
21 - 27 days - 21 - 27 jours	7	4	3	♦0.1	♦0.1	♦0.1
28 days - 11 months - 28 jours - 11 mois	83	45	38	1.0	1.1	0.9
28 days - less than 2 months - 28 jours - moins de 2 mois	26	16	10	♦0.3	♦0.4	♦0.2
2 months - 2 mois	18	12	6	♦0.2	♦0.3	♦0.1
3 months - 3 mois	9	4	5	♦0.1	♦0.1	♦0.1
4 months - 4 mois	7	4	3	♦0.1	♦0.1	♦0.1
5 months - 5 mois	7	3	4	♦0.1	♦0.1	♦0.1
6 months - 6 mois	3	-	3	-	-	♦0.1

Continent, country or area, year, code[a] and age Continent, pays ou zone, année, code[a] et âge	Number - Nombre			Rate - Taux		
	Both sexes Les deux sexes	Male Masculin	Female Féminin	Both sexes Les deux sexes	Male Masculin	Female Féminin
EUROPE						
Portugal[8]						
2013 (C)						
7 months - 7 mois	2	-	2	-	-	-
8 months - 8 mois	2	1	1	-	-	-
9 months - 9 mois	4	1	3	-	-	♦0.1
10 months - 10 mois	3	2	1	-	-	-
11 months - 11 mois	2	2	-	-	-	-
Republic of Moldova - République de Moldova[29]						
2013 (C)						
Total	359	181	178	9.5	9.3	9.6
Less than 1 day - Moins de 1 jour	88	48	40	2.3	2.5	2.2
1 - 6 days - 1 - 6 jours	81	43	38	2.1	2.2	2.1
7 - 27 days - 7 - 27 jours	60	30	30	1.6	1.5	1.6
28 days - 11 months - 28 jours - 11 mois	124	55	69	3.3	2.8	3.7
28 days - less than 2 months - 28 jours - moins de 2 mois	124	55	69	3.3	2.8	3.7
Unknown - Inconnu	6	5	1	♦0.2	♦0.3	♦0.1
Romania - Roumanie						
2013 (C)						
Total	1 677	944	733	9.2	10.0	8.3
Less than 1 day - Moins de 1 jour	186	105	81	1.0	1.1	0.9
1 - 6 days - 1 - 6 jours	515	301	214	2.8	3.2	2.4
7 - 27 days - 7 - 27 jours	278	149	129	1.5	1.6	1.5
7 - 13 days - 7 - 13 jours	139	74	65	0.8	0.8	0.7
14 - 20 days - 14 - 20 jours	83	41	42	0.5	0.4	0.5
21 - 27 days - 21 - 27 jours	56	34	22	0.3	0.4	♦0.2
28 days - 11 months - 28 jours - 11 mois	698	389	309	3.8	4.1	3.5
28 days - less than 2 months - 28 jours - moins de 2 mois	219	120	99	1.2	1.3	1.1
2 months - 2 mois	107	59	48	0.6	0.6	0.5
3 months - 3 mois	82	52	30	0.4	0.6	0.3
4 months - 4 mois	71	40	31	0.4	0.4	0.4
5 months - 5 mois	62	35	27	0.3	0.4	♦0.3
6 months - 6 mois	52	32	20	0.3	0.3	♦0.2
7 months - 7 mois	32	15	17	0.2	♦0.2	♦0.2
8 months - 8 mois	23	13	10	♦0.1	♦0.1	♦0.1
9 months - 9 mois	19	10	9	♦0.1	♦0.1	♦0.1
10 months - 10 mois	16	7	9	♦0.1	♦0.1	♦0.1
11 months - 11 mois	15	6	9	♦0.1	♦0.1	♦0.1
Russian Federation - Fédération de Russie[13]						
2012 (C)						
Total	16 306	9 219	7 087	8.6	9.4	7.7
Less than 1 day - Moins de 1 jour	1 897	1 009	888	1.0	1.0	1.0
1 - 6 days - 1 - 6 jours	5 072	2 961	2 111	2.7	3.0	2.3
7 - 27 days - 7 - 27 jours	3 438	1 958	1 480	1.8	2.0	1.6
7 - 13 days - 7 - 13 jours	1 798	1 020	778	0.9	1.0	0.8
14 - 20 days - 14 - 20 jours	952	560	392	0.5	0.6	0.4
21 - 27 days - 21 - 27 jours	688	378	310	0.4	0.4	0.3
28 days - 11 months - 28 jours - 11 mois	5 898	3 290	2 608	3.1	3.4	2.8
28 days - less than 2 months - 28 jours - moins de 2 mois	2 063	1 166	897	1.1	1.2	1.0
2 months - 2 mois	942	525	417	0.5	0.5	0.5
3 months - 3 mois	691	372	319	0.4	0.4	0.3
4 months - 4 mois	562	333	229	0.3	0.3	0.2
5 months - 5 mois	417	221	196	0.2	0.2	0.2
6 months - 6 mois	334	184	150	0.2	0.2	0.2
7 months - 7 mois	252	139	113	0.1	0.1	0.1
8 months - 8 mois	219	127	92	0.1	0.1	0.1
9 months - 9 mois	172	86	86	0.1	0.1	0.1
10 months - 10 mois	134	74	60	0.1	0.1	0.1
11 months - 11 mois	112	63	49	0.1	0.1	0.1
Unknown - Inconnu	1	1	-	-	-	-
Serbia - Serbie[30]						
2013 (+C)						
Total	413	246	167	6.3	7.3	5.2
Less than 1 day - Moins de 1 jour	133	88	45	2.0	2.6	1.4
1 - 6 days - 1 - 6 jours	125	73	52	1.9	2.2	1.6
7 - 27 days - 7 - 27 jours	55	24	31	0.8	♦0.7	1.0
7 - 13 days - 7 - 13 jours	22	10	12	♦0.3	♦0.3	♦0.4
14 - 20 days - 14 - 20 jours	18	7	11	♦0.3	♦0.2	♦0.3
21 - 27 days - 21 - 27 jours	15	7	8	♦0.2	♦0.2	♦0.3

16. Infant deaths and infant mortality rates by age and sex: latest available year, 2005 - 2014
Décès d'enfants de moins d'un an et taux de mortalité infantile selon l'âge et le sexe : dernière année disponible, 2005 - 2014 (continued - suite)

Continent, country or area, year, code[a] and age / Continent, pays ou zone, année, code[a] et âge	Number - Nombre			Rate - Taux		
	Both sexes Les deux sexes	Male Masculin	Female Féminin	Both sexes Les deux sexes	Male Masculin	Female Féminin
EUROPE						
Serbia - Serbie[30]						
2013 (+C)						
28 days - 11 months - 28 jours - 11 mois	100	61	39	1.5	1.8	1.2
28 days - less than 2 months - 28 jours - moins de 2 mois	34	21	13	0.5	♦0.6	♦0.4
2 months - 2 mois	18	11	7	♦0.3	♦0.3	♦0.2
3 months - 3 mois	12	6	6	♦0.2	♦0.2	♦0.2
4 months - 4 mois	6	3	3	♦0.1	♦0.1	♦0.1
5 months - 5 mois	10	8	2	♦0.2	♦0.2	♦0.1
6 months - 6 mois	8	6	2	♦0.1	♦0.2	♦0.1
7 months - 7 mois	4	3	1	♦0.1	♦0.1	-
8 months - 8 mois	4	1	3	♦0.1	-	♦0.1
9 months - 9 mois	1	1	-	-	-	-
10 months - 10 mois	1	1	-	-	-	-
11 months - 11 mois	2	-	2	-	-	♦0.1
Slovakia - Slovaquie						
2013 (C)						
Total	301	158	143	5.5	5.6	5.3
Less than 1 day - Moins de 1 jour	55	26	29	1.0	♦0.9	♦1.1
1 - 6 days - 1 - 6 jours	54	30	24	1.0	1.1	♦0.9
7 - 27 days - 7 - 27 jours	69	44	25	1.3	1.6	♦0.9
7 - 13 days - 7 - 13 jours	42	25	17	0.8	♦0.9	♦0.6
14 - 20 days - 14 - 20 jours	13	7	6	♦0.2	♦0.2	♦0.2
21 - 27 days - 21 - 27 jours	14	12	2	♦0.3	♦0.4	♦0.1
28 days - 11 months - 28 jours - 11 mois	123	58	65	2.2	2.1	2.4
28 days - less than 2 months - 28 jours - moins de 2 mois	44	19	25	0.8	♦0.7	♦0.9
2 months - 2 mois	15	6	9	♦0.3	♦0.2	♦0.3
3 months - 3 mois	11	2	9	♦0.2	♦0.1	♦0.3
4 months - 4 mois	12	5	7	♦0.2	♦0.2	♦0.3
5 months - 5 mois	8	5	3	♦0.1	♦0.2	♦0.1
6 months - 6 mois	10	8	2	♦0.2	♦0.3	♦0.1
7 months - 7 mois	7	3	4	♦0.1	♦0.1	♦0.1
8 months - 8 mois	7	4	3	♦0.1	♦0.1	♦0.1
9 months - 9 mois	1	-	1	-	-	-
10 months - 10 mois	3	3	-	♦0.1	♦0.1	-
11 months - 11 mois	5	3	2	♦0.1	♦0.1	♦0.1
Slovenia - Slovénie						
2013 (C)						
Total	62	32	30	...	...	...
Less than 1 day - Moins de 1 jour	22	11	11	...	...	...
1 - 6 days - 1 - 6 jours	7	4	3	...	...	...
7 - 27 days - 7 - 27 jours	10	8	2	...	...	...
7 - 13 days - 7 - 13 jours	3	3	-	...	...	...
14 - 20 days - 14 - 20 jours	5	4	1	...	...	...
21 - 27 days - 21 - 27 jours	2	1	1	...	...	...
28 days - 11 months - 28 jours - 11 mois	23	9	14	...	...	...
28 days - less than 2 months - 28 jours - moins de 2 mois	7	4	3	...	...	...
2 months - 2 mois	3	-	3	...	...	...
3 months - 3 mois	3	1	2	...	...	...
4 months - 4 mois	3	1	2	...	...	...
5 months - 5 mois	3	2	1	...	...	...
6 months - 6 mois	2	-	2	...	...	...
7 months - 7 mois	-	-	-	...	...	...
8 months - 8 mois	1	-	1	...	...	...
9 months - 9 mois	-	-	-	...	...	...
10 months - 10 mois	1	1	-	...	...	...
11 months - 11 mois	-	-	-	...	...	...
Spain - Espagne						
2013 (C)						
Total	1 149	627	522	2.7	2.9	2.5
Less than 1 day - Moins de 1 jour	292	148	144	0.7	0.7	0.7
1 - 6 days - 1 - 6 jours	261	149	112	0.6	0.7	0.5
7 - 27 days - 7 - 27 jours	248	136	112	0.6	0.6	0.5
7 - 13 days - 7 - 13 jours	139	74	65	0.3	0.3	0.3
14 - 20 days - 14 - 20 jours	68	41	27	0.2	0.2	♦0.1
21 - 27 days - 21 - 27 jours	41	21	20	0.1	♦0.1	♦0.1
28 days - 11 months - 28 jours - 11 mois	348	194	154	0.8	0.9	0.7
28 days - less than 2 months - 28 jours - moins de 2 mois	109	69	40	0.3	0.3	0.2
2 months - 2 mois	53	25	28	0.1	♦0.1	♦0.1

16. Infant deaths and infant mortality rates by age and sex: latest available year, 2005 - 2014
Décès d'enfants de moins d'un an et taux de mortalité infantile selon l'âge et le sexe : dernière année disponible, 2005 - 2014 (continued - suite)

Continent, country or area, year, code[a] and age / Continent, pays ou zone, année, code[a] et âge	Number - Nombre			Rate - Taux		
	Both sexes Les deux sexes	Male Masculin	Female Féminin	Both sexes Les deux sexes	Male Masculin	Female Féminin
EUROPE						
Spain - Espagne						
2013 (C)						
3 months - 3 mois	35	19	16	0.1	♦0.1	♦0.1
4 months - 4 mois	22	13	9	♦0.1	♦0.1	-
5 months - 5 mois	21	11	10	-	♦0.1	-
6 months - 6 mois	28	11	17	♦0.1	♦0.1	♦0.1
7 months - 7 mois	28	18	10	♦0.1	♦0.1	-
8 months - 8 mois	17	9	8	-	-	-
9 months - 9 mois	11	7	4	-	-	-
10 months - 10 mois	12	7	5	-	-	-
11 months - 11 mois	12	5	7	-	-	-
Sweden - Suède						
2013 (C)						
Total	306	168	138	2.7	2.9	2.5
Less than 1 day - Moins de 1 jour	84	50	34	0.7	0.9	0.6
1 - 6 days - 1 - 6 jours	71	38	33	0.6	0.6	0.6
7 - 27 days - 7 - 27 jours	39	20	19	0.3	♦0.3	♦0.3
28 days - 11 months - 28 jours - 11 mois	112	60	52	1.0	1.0	0.9
Switzerland - Suisse						
2012 (C)						
Total	296	156	140	3.6	3.7	3.5
Less than 1 day - Moins de 1 jour	158	85	73	1.9	2.0	1.8
1 - 6 days - 1 - 6 jours	49	22	27	0.6	♦0.5	♦0.7
7 - 27 days - 7 - 27 jours	32	19	13	0.4	♦0.4	♦0.3
7 - 13 days - 7 - 13 jours	19	13	6	♦0.2	♦0.3	♦0.2
14 - 20 days - 14 - 20 jours	10	5	5	♦0.1	♦0.1	♦0.1
21 - 27 days - 21 - 27 jours	3	1	2	-	-	♦0.1
28 days - 11 months - 28 jours - 11 mois	57	30	27	0.7	0.7	♦0.7
28 days - less than 2 months - 28 jours - moins de 2 mois	14	4	10	♦0.2	♦0.1	♦0.3
2 months - 2 mois	5	3	2	♦0.1	♦0.1	♦0.1
3 months - 3 mois	8	3	5	♦0.1	♦0.1	♦0.1
4 months - 4 mois	8	5	3	♦0.1	♦0.1	♦0.1
5 months - 5 mois	8	8	-	♦0.1	♦0.2	-
6 months - 6 mois	1	1	-	-	-	-
7 months - 7 mois	1	1	-	-	-	-
8 months - 8 mois	4	2	2	-	-	♦0.1
9 months - 9 mois	4	2	2	-	-	♦0.1
10 months - 10 mois	3	-	3	-	-	♦0.1
11 months - 11 mois	1	1	-	-	-	-
TFYR of Macedonia - L'ex-R. y. de Macédoine						
2013 (C)						
Total	237	129	108	10.2	10.7	9.8
Less than 1 day - Moins de 1 jour	60	29	31	2.6	♦2.4	2.8
1 - 6 days - 1 - 6 jours	79	51	28	3.4	4.2	♦2.5
7 - 27 days - 7 - 27 jours	40	19	21	1.7	♦1.6	♦1.9
28 days - 11 months - 28 jours - 11 mois	58	30	28	2.5	2.5	♦2.5
Ukraine[31]						
2013 (+C)						
Total	4 030	2 309	1 721	8.0	8.9	7.1
Less than 1 day - Moins de 1 jour	592	342	250	1.2	1.3	1.0
1 - 6 days - 1 - 6 jours	1 024	598	426	2.0	2.3	1.7
7 - 27 days - 7 - 27 jours	815	463	352	1.6	1.8	1.4
7 - 13 days - 7 - 13 jours	421	251	170	0.8	1.0	0.7
14 - 20 days - 14 - 20 jours	210	110	100	0.4	0.4	0.4
21 - 27 days - 21 - 27 jours	184	102	82	0.4	0.4	0.3
28 days - 11 months - 28 jours - 11 mois	1 599	906	693	3.2	3.5	2.8
28 days - less than 2 months - 28 jours - moins de 2 mois	530	301	229	1.1	1.2	0.9
2 months - 2 mois	271	165	106	0.5	0.6	0.4
3 months - 3 mois	193	103	90	0.4	0.4	0.4
4 months - 4 mois	139	77	62	0.3	0.3	0.3
5 months - 5 mois	114	75	39	0.2	0.3	0.2
6 months - 6 mois	81	44	37	0.2	0.2	0.2
7 months - 7 mois	64	36	28	0.1	0.1	♦0.1
8 months - 8 mois	71	39	32	0.1	0.2	0.1
9 months - 9 mois	45	20	25	0.1	♦0.1	♦0.1
10 months - 10 mois	47	23	24	0.1	♦0.1	♦0.1
11 months - 11 mois	44	23	21	0.1	♦0.1	♦0.1

16. Infant deaths and infant mortality rates by age and sex: latest available year, 2005 - 2014
Décès d'enfants de moins d'un an et taux de mortalité infantile selon l'âge et le sexe : dernière année disponible, 2005 - 2014 (continued - suite)

Continent, country or area, year, code[a] and age Continent, pays ou zone, année, code[a] et âge	Number - Nombre			Rate - Taux		
	Both sexes Les deux sexes	Male Masculin	Female Féminin	Both sexes Les deux sexes	Male Masculin	Female Féminin
EUROPE						
United Kingdom of Great Britain and Northern Ireland - Royaume-Uni de Grande-Bretagne et d'Irlande du Nord[32] 2012 (+C)						
Total	3 347	1 912	1 435	4.1	4.6	3.6
Less than 1 day - Moins de 1 jour	1 083	627	456	1.3	1.5	1.2
1 - 6 days - 1 - 6 jours	693	399	294	0.9	1.0	0.7
7 - 27 days - 7 - 27 jours	542	297	245	0.7	0.7	0.6
7 - 13 days - 7 - 13 jours	274	153	121	0.3	0.4	0.3
14 - 20 days - 14 - 20 jours	154	75	79	0.2	0.2	0.2
21 - 27 days - 21 - 27 jours	114	69	45	0.1	0.2	0.1
28 days - 11 months - 28 jours - 11 mois	1 029	589	440	1.3	1.4	1.1
28 days - less than 2 months - 28 jours - moins de 2 mois	348	202	146	0.4	0.5	0.4
2 months - 2 mois	170	90	80	0.2	0.2	0.2
3 months - 3 mois	115	67	48	0.1	0.2	0.1
4 months - 4 mois	87	58	29	0.1	0.1	♦0.1
5 months - 5 mois	48	34	14	0.1	0.1	-
6 months - 6 mois	68	37	31	0.1	0.1	0.1
7 months - 7 mois	45	22	23	0.1	♦0.1	♦0.1
8 months - 8 mois	45	26	19	0.1	♦0.1	-
9 months - 9 mois	26	10	16	-	-	-
10 months - 10 mois	45	18	27	0.1	-	♦0.1
11 months - 11 mois	32	25	7	-	♦0.1	-
OCEANIA - OCÉANIE						
Australia - Australie 2013 (+C)						
Total	1 094	589	505	3.6	3.7	3.4
Less than 1 day - Moins de 1 jour	482	249	233	1.6	1.6	1.6
1 - 6 days - 1 - 6 jours	146	81	65	0.5	0.5	0.4
7 - 27 days - 7 - 27 jours	135	71	64	0.4	0.4	0.4
7 - 13 days - 7 - 13 jours	63	34	29	0.2	0.2	♦0.2
14 - 20 days - 14 - 20 jours	42	21	21	0.1	♦0.1	♦0.1
21 - 27 days - 21 - 27 jours	30	16	14	0.1	♦0.1	♦0.1
28 days - 11 months - 28 jours - 11 mois	331	188	143	1.1	1.2	1.0
28 days - less than 2 months - 28 jours - moins de 2 mois	102	58	44	0.3	0.4	0.3
2 months - 2 mois	65	35	30	0.2	0.2	0.2
3 months - 3 mois	41	25	16	0.1	♦0.2	♦0.1
4 months - 4 mois	30	18	12	0.1	♦0.1	♦0.1
5 months - 5 mois	19	9	10	♦0.1	♦0.1	♦0.1
6 months - 6 mois	12	8	4	-	♦0.1	-
7 months - 7 mois	17	13	4	♦0.1	♦0.1	-
8 months - 8 mois	14	9	5	-	♦0.1	-
9 months - 9 mois	9	3	6	-	-	-
10 months - 10 mois	11	6	5	-	-	-
11 months - 11 mois	11	4	7	-	-	-
French Polynesia - Polynésie française 2008 (C)						
Total	23	...	...	...	...	...
Less than 7 days - Moins de 7 jours	14	...	...	...	...	...
7 - 27 days - 7 - 27 jours	-	...	...	...	...	...
28 days - 11 months - 28 jours - 11 mois	9	...	...	...	...	...
New Caledonia - Nouvelle-Calédonie 2007 (C)						
Total	25	15	10	...	...	...
Less than 1 day - Moins de 1 jour	-	-	-	...	...	...
1 - 6 days - 1 - 6 jours	11	9	2	...	...	...
7 - 27 days - 7 - 27 jours	6	2	4	...	...	...
7 - 13 days - 7 - 13 jours	6	2	4	...	...	...
14 - 20 days - 14 - 20 jours	-	-	-	...	...	...
21 - 27 days - 21 - 27 jours	-	-	-	...	...	...
28 days - 11 months - 28 jours - 11 mois	8	4	4	...	...	...
28 days - less than 2 months - 28 jours - moins de 2 mois	-	-	-	...	...	...
2 months - 2 mois	-	-	-	...	...	...
3 months - 3 mois	-	2	-	...	...	...
4 months - 4 mois	-	-	-	...	...	...
5 months - 5 mois	-	-	-	...	...	...

16. Infant deaths and infant mortality rates by age and sex: latest available year, 2005 - 2014
Décès d'enfants de moins d'un an et taux de mortalité infantile selon l'âge et le sexe : dernière année disponible, 2005 - 2014 (continued - suite)

Continent, country or area, year, code[a] and age / Continent, pays ou zone, année, code[a] et âge	Number - Nombre			Rate - Taux		
	Both sexes Les deux sexes	Male Masculin	Female Féminin	Both sexes Les deux sexes	Male Masculin	Female Féminin
OCEANIA - OCÉANIE						
New Caledonia - Nouvelle-Calédonie						
2007 (C)						
6 months - 6 mois	2	2	-	...	...	...
7 months - 7 mois	-	-	-	...	...	...
8 months - 8 mois	-	-	-	...	...	...
9 months - 9 mois	-	-	-	...	...	...
10 months - 10 mois	-	-	-	...	...	...
11 months - 11 mois	4	-	4	...	...	...
New Zealand - Nouvelle-Zélande[8]						
2014 (+C)						
Total	326	181	145	5.7	6.1	5.2
Less than 1 day - Moins de 1 jour	149	75	74	2.6	2.5	2.7
1 - 6 days - 1 - 6 jours	57	33	24	1.0	1.1	♦0.9
7 - 27 days - 7 - 27 jours	29	18	11	♦0.5	♦0.6	♦0.4
7 - 13 days - 7 - 13 jours	11	7	4	♦0.2	♦0.2	♦0.1
14 - 20 days - 14 - 20 jours	11	7	4	♦0.2	♦0.2	♦0.1
21 - 27 days - 21 - 27 jours	7	4	3	♦0.1	♦0.1	♦0.1
28 days - 11 months - 28 jours - 11 mois	91	55	36	1.6	1.9	1.3
28 days - less than 2 months - 28 jours - moins de 2 mois	24	14	10	♦0.4	♦0.5	♦0.4
2 months - 2 mois	19	12	7	♦0.3	♦0.4	♦0.3
3 months - 3 mois	11	8	3	♦0.2	♦0.3	♦0.1
4 months - 4 mois	9	6	3	♦0.2	♦0.2	♦0.1
5 months - 5 mois	6	3	3	♦0.1	♦0.1	♦0.1
6 months - 6 mois	2	1	1	-	-	-
7 months - 7 mois	7	4	3	♦0.1	♦0.1	♦0.1
8 months - 8 mois	6	4	2	♦0.1	♦0.1	♦0.1
9 months - 9 mois	2	1	1	-	-	-
10 months - 10 mois	3	2	1	♦0.1	♦0.1	-
11 months - 11 mois	2	-	2	-	-	♦0.1

FOOTNOTES - NOTES

Italics: data from civil registers which are incomplete or of unknown completeness. - Italiques : données incomplètes ou dont le degré d'exactitude n'est pas connu, provenant des registres de l'état civil.

♦ Rates based on 30 or fewer infant deaths. - Taux basés sur 30 décès d'enfants ou moins.

* Provisional. - Données provisoires.

[a] 'Code' indicates the source of data, as follows:
  C - Civil registration, estimated over 90% complete
  U - Civil registration, estimated less than 90% complete
  | - Other source, estimated reliable
  + - Data tabulated by date of registration rather than occurence
  ... - Information not available

Le 'Code' indique la source des données, comme suit :
  C - Registres de l'état civil considérés complets à 90 p. 100 au moins
  U - Registres de l'état civil qui ne sont pas considérés complets à 90 p. 100 au moins
  | - Autre source, considérée pas douteuses
  + - Données exploitées selon la date de l'enregistrement et non la date de l'événement
  ... - Information pas disponible

[1] Excludes the islands of St. Brandon and Agalega. - Non compris les îles St. Brandon et Agalega.
[2] Excluding live-born infants who died before their birth was registered. - Non compris les enfants nés vivants décédés avant l'enregistrement de leur naissance.
[3] Unrevised data. - Les données n'ont pas été révisées.
[4] Data for male and female categories may exclude infant deaths of unknown sex. - Les données pour les catégories hommes et femmes peuvent exclure décès d'enfant de sexe inconnu.

[5] Including Canadian residents temporarily in the United States, but excluding United States residents temporarily in Canada. - Y compris les résidents canadiens se trouvant temporairement aux Etats-Unis, mais ne comprenant pas les résidents des Etats-Unis se trouvant temporairement au Canada.
[6] Excluding infant deaths to mothers living abroad. - Exception faite des décès d'enfants en bas âge survenus lorsque la mère résidait à l'étranger.
[7] Data refer to urban areas only. - Données ne concernant que les zones urbaines.
[8] Data refer to resident population only. - Pour la population résidante seulement.
[9] Including deaths abroad and deaths of unknown residence of mother. - Y compris décès à l'étranger et décès de nourrissons nés de mères dont le lieu de résidence n'est pas connu.
[10] Excludes nomadic Indian tribes. - Non compris les tribus d'Indiens nomades.
[11] Data refer to infants 30 days - 12 months old. - Les données se réfèrent aux nouveaux-nés âgées de 30 jours à 12 mois.
[12] Source: Reports of the Ministry of Health. - Source : Rapports du Ministère de la Santé.
[13] Excluding infants born alive of less than 28 weeks' gestation, of less than 1 000 grams in weight and 35 centimeters in length, who die within seven days of birth. - Non compris les enfants nés vivants après moins de 28 semaines de gestations, pesant moins de 1 000 grammes, mesurant moins de 35 centimètres et décédés dans les sept jours qui ont suivi leur naissance.
[14] Source: Births and Deaths Registration Office. - Source: Le bureau des << Births and Deaths Registration >>.
[15] Data refer to government controlled areas. - Les données se rapportent aux zones contrôlées par le Gouvernement.
[16] Includes data for East Jerusalem and Israeli residents in certain other territories under occupation by Israeli military forces since June 1967. Including deaths abroad of Israeli residents who were out of the country for less than a year. - Y compris les données pour Jérusalem-Est et les résidents israéliens dans certains autres territoires occupés depuis 1967 par les forces armées israéliennes. Y compris les décès à l'étranger de résidents israéliens qui ont quitté le pays depuis moins d'un an.
[17] Data refer to Japanese nationals in Japan only. - Les données se raportent aux nationaux japonais au Japon seulement.

[18] Data from Births and Deaths Notification System (Ministry of Health and all health care providers). Data for all population, citizens and foreigners. - Les données proviennent du système de notification des naissances et des décès (Ministère de la santé et tous prestataires de soins de santé). Les données portent sur la population entière, les citoyens et les étrangers.

[19] Excluding unknown sex. - Non compris le sexe inconnu.

[20] Excluding data for the Pakistan-held part of Jammu and Kashmir, the final status of which has not yet been determined. Based on the results of the Pakistan Demographic Survey. - Non compris les données concernant la partie du Jammu et Cachemire occupée par le Pakistan dont le statut définitif n'a pas été déterminé. Données extraites de l'enquête démographique effectuée par le Pakistan.

[21] Excluding alien armed forces, civilian aliens employed by armed forces, and foreign diplomatic personnel and their dependants. - Non compris les militaires étrangers, les civils étrangers employés par les forces armées ni le personnel diplomatique étranger et les membres de leur famille les accompagnant.

[22] Including armed forces stationed outside the country, but excluding alien armed forces stationed in the area. - Y compris les militaires nationaux hors du pays, mais non compris les militaires étrangers en garnison sur le territoire.

[23] Excluding Faeroe Islands and Greenland shown separately, if available. - Non compris les Îles Féroé et le Groenland, qui font l'objet de rubriques distinctes, si disponible.

[24] Excluding Åland Islands. - Non compris les Îles d'Åland.

[25] Including armed forces stationed outside the country. - Y compris les militaires hors du pays.

[26] Starting from 2013 data refer only to infant deaths among usual residents regardless whether it occurred in the country or abroad. - A partir de 2013, les données se rapportent seulement aux décès d'enfants de moins d'un an parmi les résidents habituels, survenus dans le pays ou hors du pays.

[27] Including residents outside the country if listed in a Netherlands population register. - Englobe les résidents se trouvant à l'étranger à condition qu'ils soient inscrits sur le registre de population des Pays-Bas.

[28] Including residents temporarily outside the country. - Y compris les résidents se trouvant temporairement hors du pays.

[29] Excluding Transnistria and the municipality of Bender. - Les données ne tiennent pas compte de l'information sur la Transnistria et la municipalité de Bender.

[30] Excludes data for Kosovo and Metohia. - Sans les données pour le Kosovo et Metohie.

[31] Data includes deaths resulting from births with weight 500g and more (if weight is unknown - with length 25 centimeters and more, or with gestation during 22 weeks or more). - Y compris les décès de nouveau-nés de 500 grammes ou plus (si le poids est inconnu – de 25 centimètres de long ou plus, ou après une grossesse de 22 semaines ou plus).

[32] Excluding Channel Islands (Guernsey and Jersey) and Isle of Man, shown separately, if available. - Non compris les îles Anglo-Normandes (Guernesey et Jersey) et l'île de Man, qui font l'objet de rubriques distinctes, si disponible.

Table 17 - *Demographic Yearbook 2014*

Table 17 presents maternal deaths and maternal mortality ratios for as many years available between 2003 and 2012.

Description of variables: Maternal deaths are defined for the purposes of the Demographic Yearbook as those caused by deliveries and complications of pregnancy, childbirth and the puerperium, within 42 days of termination of pregnancy. They are usually defined as deaths coded "38-41" for ICD-9 Basic Tabulation List or as deaths coded "A34", "O00-O95", "O98-O99" for ICD-10, respectively. However, data for ICD-10 shown in this table include deaths due to "O96" and "O97" which refer to deaths from any obstetric cause occurring more than 42 days but less than one year after delivery and death from sequelae of direct obstetric causes occurring one year or more after delivery.

For further information on the definition of maternal mortality from the tenth revisions of the *International Statistical Classification of Diseases and Related Health Problems*[1], see also section 4.3 of the Technical Notes.

Statistics on maternal death presented in this table are provided by the World Health Organisation. They are limited to countries or areas that meet the criterion that cause-of-death statistics are either classified by or convertible to the ninth or tenth revisions mentioned above. Data that are classified by the tenth revision are set in bold in the table.

Ratios computation: Maternal mortality ratios are the annual number of maternal deaths per 100 000 live births (table 9) in the same year. These ratios have been calculated by the Statistics Division of the United Nations Department of Economic and Social Affairs. If maternal mortality data are considered incomplete, or if live birth data for the year are not available, no ratio has been calculated. Ratios based on 30 or fewer maternal deaths are identified by the symbol "♦".

Reliability of data: Countries and areas that have incomplete (less than 90 per cent completeness) or of unknown completeness of cause of deaths data coverage are considered to provide unreliable data, which are set in *italics* rather than in roman type. Ratios on these data are not computed. Information on completeness is normally provided by the World Health Organisation. When this is not the case, information on completeness is set to coincide with that of table 18. The reliability of data for the completeness of cause of death provided by the World Health Organisation[2] may differ from the reliability of data for the total number of reported deaths. Therefore, there are cases when the quality code in table 18 does not correspond with the typeface used in this table.

Territorial composition as set in Section 2.2 of "Technical Notes on the Statistical Tables", including or excluding certain population of a country refers only to the denominator.

Limitations: Statistics on maternal deaths are subject to the same qualifications that have been set forth for vital statistics in general and death statistics in particular as discussed in section 4 of the Technical Notes. The reliability of the data, an indication of which is described above, is an important factor in considering the limitations. In addition, maternal-death statistics are subject to all the qualifications relating to cause-of-death statistics. These have been set forth in section 4 of the Technical Notes.

Maternal mortality ratios are subject to the limitations of the data on live births with which they have been calculated. These have been set forth in the technical notes for table 9. Specific information pertaining to individual countries or areas is given in the footnotes to table 9.

The calculation of the maternal mortality ratios based on the total number of live births approximates the risk of dying from complications of pregnancy, childbirth or puerperium. Ideally this rate should be based on the number of women exposed to the risk of pregnancy, in other words, the number of women conceiving. Since it is impossible to know how many women have conceived, the total number of live births is used in calculating this rate.

Earlier data: Maternal deaths and maternal mortality ratios have been shown in previous issues of the *Demographic Yearbook*. For information on specific years covered, the reader should consult the Index.

It should however be noted that in issues prior to 1975, maternal mortality rates were calculated using the female population rather than live births for the denominators. Therefore, maternal mortality ratios published since 1975 are not comparable to the earlier maternal death rates.

NOTES

[1] *International Statistical Classification of Diseases and Related Health Problems*, Tenth Revision, Volume 2, World Health Organization, Geneva, 1992. The publication is available online at: http://www.who.int/classifications/icd/en/
[2] For more information on specific method used for countries, see "Mathers CD, Bernard C, Iburg KM, Inoue M, Ma Fat D, Shibuya K et al. *Global burden of disease in 2002: data sources, methods and results*. Geneva, World Health Organization, 2003 (GPE Discussion Paper No. 54).

Tableau 17 – *Annuaire démographique 2014*

Le tableau 17 présente des statistiques et des taux de mortalité liée à la maternité pour les années disponibles entre 2003 et 2012.

Description des variables : aux fins de *l'Annuaire démographique*, les décès liés à la maternité sont ceux entraînés par l'accouchement ou les complications de la grossesse, de l'accouchement et des suites de couches dans un délai de 42 jours après la terminaison de la grossesse. Ils sont généralement associés aux codes 38 à 41 dans le cas de la liste de base pour la mise en tableaux de la CIM-9 et aux codes A34, O00 à O95 et O98 et O99 dans le cas de la CIM-10. Les statistiques associées à des codes correspondant à la CIM-10 englobent des décès de type O96 et O97, qui désignent les décès liés à des causes obstétriques se produisant après 42 jours mais moins d'un an après l'accouchement et les décès entraînés par les séquelles de complications obstétriques directes qui se produisent un an ou plus après l'accouchement.

Pour plus de précisions concernant les définitions de la mortalité liée à la maternité dans la dixième révision de la *Classification statistique internationale des maladies et des problèmes de santé connexes*[1], se reporter également à la section 4.3 des Notes techniques.

Les statistiques de mortalité liée à la maternité présentées dans le tableau 17 émanent de l'Organisation mondiale de la santé. Elles ne se rapportent qu'aux pays ou zones qui répondent aux critères selon lesquels les statistiques relatives à la cause des décès sont conformes à la liste de la neuvième ou de la dixième révision de la CIM ou peuvent être aisément comparées aux catégories de cette liste. Les données conformes à la dixième révision sont indiquées en gras dans le tableau.

Calcul des taux : les taux de mortalité maternelle représentent le nombre annuel de décès dus à la maternité pour 100 000 naissances vivantes (données du tableau 9) de la même année. Ces taux ont été calculés par la Division de statistique du Département des affaires économiques et sociales de l'Organisation des Nations Unies. Si les données des décès dus à la maternité sont incomplètes ou si les naissances vivantes pour l'année ne sont pas disponibles, les taux ne sont pas calculés. Les taux fondés sur 30 décès liés à la maternité ou moins sont signalés par le signe "♦".

Fiabilité des données : les statistiques relatives aux pays et aux zones pour lesquels la couverture des données concernant les causes de décès est incomplète (mois de 90 pour cent) ou dont le degré de complétude n'est pas connue sont jugés douteuses et apparaissent en *italique* et non en caractères romains. Les taux correspondant ne sont pas calculés. L'information sur la complétude est normalement fournie par l'Organisation Mondiale de la Santé. Si ce n'est pas le cas, l'information sur la complétude est reprise de tableau 18. La fiabilité des données relatives aux causes de décès fournie par l'Organisation Mondiale de la Santé[2] peut différer de la fiabilité des données relatives au nombre de décès enregistrés. En conséquence, il peut apparaitre de différences entre les codes de fiabilité du tableau 18 et du présent tableau.

La composition territoriale est définie dans la Section 2.2 des "Notes Techniques sur les tableaux statistiques". L'inclusion ou l'exclusion de certaines populations d'un pays ne concerne que le dénominateur.

Insuffisance des données : les statistiques de la mortalité liée à la maternité appellent toutes les réserves qui ont été formulées à propos des statistiques de l'état civil en général et des statistiques relatives à la mortalité en particulier (voir la section 4 des Notes techniques). La fiabilité des données, au sujet de laquelle des indications ont été fournies plus haut, est un facteur important. En outre, les statistiques de la mortalité liée à la maternité appellent les mêmes réserves que celles exposées à la section 4 des Notes techniques en ce qui concerne les statistiques des causes de décès.

Les taux de mortalité maternelle appellent également toutes les réserves formulées à propos des statistiques des naissances vivantes qui ont servi à leur calcul (voir à ce sujet les notes techniques relatives au tableau 9). Des précisions sur certains pays ou zones sont données dans les notes se rapportant au tableau 9.

En prenant le nombre total des naissances vivantes comme base pour le calcul des taux de mortalité maternelle, on obtient une mesure approximative de la probabilité de décès dus aux complications de la grossesse, de l'accouchement et des suites de couches. Idéalement, ces taux devraient être calculés sur la base du nombre de femmes exposées aux risques liés à la grossesse, c'est-à-dire sur la base du nombre de femmes qui conçoivent. Étant donné qu'il est impossible de connaître le nombre de femmes ayant conçu, c'est le nombre total de naissances vivantes que l'on utilise pour calculer ces taux.

Données publiées antérieurement : des statistiques concernant les décès liés à la maternité (nombre de décès et taux) ont déjà été présentées dans des éditions antérieures de *l'Annuaire démographique*. Pour plus de précisions concernant les années pour lesquelles ces données ont été publiées, se reporter à l'index.

Il faut souligner que, avant 1975, les taux de mortalité maternelle étaient calculés sur la base de la population féminine et non sur celle du nombre de naissances vivantes. Ils ne sont donc pas comparables à ceux qui figurent dans les éditions de l'*Annuaire démographique* parues après 1975.

NOTES

[1] *Classification statistique internationale des maladies et des problèmes de santé connexes*, dixième révision, volume 2. Genève, Organisation mondiale de la santé, 1992.
[2] Pour plus d'information sur les méthodes spécifiques utilisées pour les pays, voir "Mathers CD, Bernard C, Iburg KM, Inoue M, Ma Fat D, Shibuya K et al. *Global burden of disease in 2002: data sources, methods and results*. Geneva, World Health Organization, 2003 (GPE Discussion Paper No. 54).

Continent and country or area / Continent et pays ou zone	Co-de[a]	2003	2004	2005	2006	2007	2008	2009	2010	2011	2012
AFRICA - AFRIQUE											
Egypt - Égypte											
Number - Nombre	C	...	...	...	604	567	449	579	519	550	...
Rate - Taux	C	...	...	...	32.6	29.1	21.9	26.1	23.0	22.5	...
Mauritius - Maurice											
Number - Nombre	+C	4	3	4	3	6	6	10	4	5	9
Rate - Taux	+C	♦20.7	♦15.6	♦21.3	♦17.0	♦35.2	♦36.6	♦65.2	♦26.7	♦34.0	♦62.1
Mayotte											
Number - Nombre	C	...	...	...	...	...	...	...	...	-	...
Morocco - Maroc											
Number - Nombre	U	...	...	...	...	...	74	...	...	98	...
Reunion - Réunion											
Number - Nombre	...	3	4	4	5	...	2	1	1	5	
Seychelles											
Number - Nombre	+C	1	-	1	-	-	1	1	...	...	-
Rate - Taux	+C	♦66.8	-	♦65.1	-	-	♦64.7	♦63.3	...	...	-
South Africa - Afrique du Sud											
Number - Nombre	U	898	1 158	1 249	1 388	1 762	1 808	1 880	1 658	...	...
AMERICA, NORTH - AMÉRIQUE DU NORD											
Anguilla											
Number - Nombre	...	-	-	-	-	...	1	-	1	-	-
Antigua and Barbuda - Antigua-et-Barbuda											
Number - Nombre	+U	-	-	-	-	1	-	-	...	...	...
Aruba											
Number - Nombre	...	...	1	...	-	-	-	-	-	2	-
Bahamas											
Number - Nombre	...	...	2[1]	4[2]	...	...	3[1]	7[1]	5[1]	...	...
Rate - Taux	...	...	...	♦72.1	...	...	...	...	...	...	...
Barbados - Barbade											
Number - Nombre	C	...	...	...	1	...	2	-	-	2	...
Rate - Taux	C	...	...	...	♦29.3	...	...	...	...	...	...
Belize											
Number - Nombre	...	...	3[1]	10[2]	3[2]	2[2]	2[2]	4[2]	4[2]	...	...
Rate - Taux	...	...	...	♦119.1	...	...	...	...	...	...	...
Bermuda - Bermudes											
Number - Nombre	...	...	-	-	1	-	-	-	-	...	...
British Virgin Islands - Îles Vierges britanniques											
Number - Nombre	...	-	...	...	...	...	...	-	-	...	...
Canada											
Number - Nombre	C	23	20	...	28	24	34	29	24	18	...
Rate - Taux	C	♦6.9	♦5.9	...	♦7.9	♦6.5	9.0	♦7.6	♦6.4	♦4.8	...
Cayman Islands - Îles Caïmanes											
Number - Nombre	...	...	-	...	...	...	-	-	-	...	...
Costa Rica											
Number - Nombre	...	24[1]	25[1]	24[1]	24[1]	10[1]	20[1]	10[2]	14[2]	17[2]	22[2]
Rate - Taux	...	...	...	...	...	...	...	♦13.3	♦19.7	♦23.1	♦30.0
Cuba											
Number - Nombre	C	62	56	66	62	42	57	66	61	61	...
Rate - Taux	C	45.3	44.0	54.7	55.7	37.3	46.5	50.8	47.8	45.8	...
Dominica - Dominique											
Number - Nombre	+C	-	-	-	-	-	1	-	2	-	...
Rate - Taux	+C	-	-	-	-	-	♦103.7	-	♦214.4	...	...
Dominican Republic - République dominicaine											
Number - Nombre	U	58	85	...	...	...	...	56	37	...	...
El Salvador											
Number - Nombre	+U	27	22	23	21	17	18	14	19	16	...
Grenada - Grenade											
Number - Nombre	...	...	-[1]	-[1]	-[1]	-[1]	-[2]	-[2]	-[2]	-[2]	2[2]
Guadeloupe											
Number - Nombre	...	4	3	1	2	...	2	1	1	-	...
Guatemala											
Number - Nombre	U	293	296	354	298	310	328	346	355	315	356

17. Maternal deaths and maternal mortality ratios: 2003 - 2012
Mortalité liée à la maternité, nombre de décès et taux : 2003 - 2012 (continued - suite)

Continent and country or area / Continent et pays ou zone	Code[a]	2003	2004	2005	2006	2007	2008	2009	2010	2011	2012
AMERICA, NORTH - AMÉRIQUE DU NORD											
Haiti - Haïti											
Number - Nombre	...	124	...	...	...	...	...	...	...	...	...
Martinique											
Number - Nombre	...	2	1	-	1	...	1	2	-	2	...
Mexico - Mexique											
Number - Nombre	+C	1 332	1 266	1 269	1 188	1 122	1 135	1 230	1 000	1 027	1 036
Rate - Taux	+C	61.5	58.7	59.3	55.2	51.3	50.6	54.6	46.1	45.4	47.3
Montserrat											
Number - Nombre	...	-	-		-		-		-	-	...
Nicaragua											
Number - Nombre	+U	88	108	93	93	...	69	78	80	71	...
Panama											
Number - Nombre	...	34[3]	23[3]	...	36[3]	40[4]	41[4]	29[4]	41[4]	59[4]	...
Rate - Taux	...	...	...	...	...	59.4	59.6	♦42.4	60.3	80.5	...
Puerto Rico - Porto Rico											
Number - Nombre	...	8	...	5	...		6	10	6	...	
Saint Kitts and Nevis - Saint-Kitts-et-Nevis											
Number - Nombre	+U	2	-	-	1	-	1	-	-	1	...
Saint Lucia - Sainte-Lucie											
Number - Nombre	C	...	...	...	...	...	1	...	3	1	1
Saint Pierre and Miquelon - Saint Pierre-et-Miquelon											
Number - Nombre	...	...	...	-	-		-			...	...
Saint Vincent and the Grenadines - Saint-Vincent-et-les Grenadines											
Number - Nombre	...	-[4]	1[4]	...	-	-	2[4]	-[4]	2[4]	1[4]	-[4]
Rate - Taux	...	-	♦55.4	...	...	...	♦105.2	-	♦112.1	♦58.0	-
Trinidad and Tobago - Trinité-et-Tobago											
Number - Nombre	U	...	...	...	12	...	11	...	...	...	...
Turks and Caicos Islands - Îles Turques et Caïques											
Number - Nombre	...	1	1	-	...		-	1	...	...	...
United States of America - États-Unis d'Amérique											
Number - Nombre	C	545	697	760	756	766	795	962	825	...	...
Rate - Taux	C	13.3	17.0	18.4	17.7	17.7	18.7	23.3	20.6	...	...
United States Virgin Islands - Îles Vierges américaines											
Number - Nombre	...	-	...	-	...		...	-	-	...	...
AMERICA, SOUTH - AMÉRIQUE DU SUD											
Argentina - Argentine											
Number - Nombre	+C	321	313	290	341	332	319	422	331	318	280
Rate - Taux	+C	46.0	42.5	40.7	49.0	47.4	42.8	56.6	43.8	42.0	37.9
Brazil - Brésil											
Number - Nombre	...	1 597[1]	1 672[1]	1 661[1]	1 634[1]	1 613[1]	1 641[2]	1 884[2]	1 665[2]	1 680[2]	...
Rate - Taux	...	...	...	...	...	...	58.8	68.4	60.3	59.5	...
Chile - Chili											
Number - Nombre	C	33	42	48	47	42	36	43	46	46	...
Rate - Taux	C	14.1	18.2	20.8	20.3	17.5	14.6	17.0	18.4	18.6	...
Colombia - Colombie											
Number - Nombre	...	...	546[1]	504[1]	519[2]	503[2]	433[2]	496[2]	474[2]	459[2]	...
Rate - Taux	...	...	...	...	72.6	70.9	60.5	70.9	72.4	69.0	...
Ecuador - Équateur											
Number - Nombre	U	139	129	143	135	176	162	208	202	239	202
French Guiana - Guyane française											
Number - Nombre	...	1	1	1	1	...	4	1	3	-	...
Guyana											
Number - Nombre	U	21	19	24	20	...	16	9	20	...	...

17. Maternal deaths and maternal mortality ratios: 2003 - 2012
Mortalité liée à la maternité, nombre de décès et taux : 2003 - 2012 (continued - suite)

Continent and country or area Continent et pays ou zone	Code[a]	2003	2004	2005	2006	2007	2008	2009	2010	2011	2012
AMERICA, SOUTH - AMÉRIQUE DU SUD											
Paraguay											
Number - Nombre	+U	150	154	135	123	...	117	128	100	94	...
Peru - Pérou											
Number - Nombre	+U	...	...	...	...	155	192	163	137	...	...
Suriname											
Number - Nombre	...	...	...	7[1]	4[1]	...	...	9[2]	11[2]	...	...	...
Rate - Taux	...	...	...	...	...	...	...	♦89.1	♦112.3	...	...	...
Uruguay											
Number - Nombre	C	...	9	...	...	...	6	11	2	...	...
Rate - Taux	C	...	♦18.0	...	...	...	♦12.7	♦23.3	♦4.2	...	...
Venezuela (Bolivarian Republic of) - Venezuela (République bolivarienne du)											
Number - Nombre	C	321	318	351	356	332	377	434	...	...	...
Rate - Taux	C	57.8	49.9	52.7	55.1	54.0	64.8	73.1	...	...	...
ASIA - ASIE											
Armenia - Arménie											
Number - Nombre	U	8	...	...	10	...	16	12	4	6	5
Azerbaijan - Azerbaïdjan											
Number - Nombre	U	21	34	...	...	30	...	...	...	...	...
Bahrain - Bahreïn											
Number - Nombre	C	...	...	...	-	3	3	3	...	...	...
Rate - Taux	C	...	...	...	-	♦18.7	♦17.6	♦16.8	...	...	...
Brunei Darussalam - Brunéi Darussalam											
Number - Nombre	+C	...	...	...	...	1	-	1	1	-	...
Rate - Taux	+C	...	...	...	...	♦15.8	-	♦15.1	♦15.6	-	...
China, Hong Kong SAR - Chine, Hong Kong RAS											
Number - Nombre	...	2	2	2	1	1	2	2	1	1	...
Cyprus - Chypre											
Number - Nombre	U	...	-	2	1	-	1	-	1	-	...
Georgia - Géorgie											
Number - Nombre	...	...	...	...	11[2]	2[2]	...	32[2]	13[1]	...	14[1]
Rate - Taux	...	...	...	...	♦23.0	♦4.1	...	50.5	...	...	...
Iraq											
Number - Nombre	U	...	...	...	...	...	62	...	...	...	...
Israel - Israël											
Number - Nombre	C	3	6	4	11	7	8	5	7	2	...
Rate - Taux	C	♦2.1	♦4.1	♦2.8	♦7.4	♦4.6	♦5.1	♦3.1	♦4.2	♦1.2	...
Japan - Japon											
Number - Nombre	C	74	56	66	63	39	41	61	49	43	...
Rate - Taux	C	6.6	5.0	6.2	5.8	3.6	3.8	5.7	4.6	4.1	...
Jordan - Jordanie											
Number - Nombre	U	...	...	...	...	...	25	26	...	...	...
Kazakhstan											
Number - Nombre	...	67[1]	63[1]	81[1]	100[1]	107[1]	86[2]	94[2]	65[2]	...	41[2]
Rate - Taux	...	...	...	...	...	...	24.1	26.4	17.7	...	10.8
Kuwait - Koweït											
Number - Nombre	C	...	...	...	1	-	5	7	3	6	...
Rate - Taux	C	...	...	...	♦1.9	-	♦9.2	♦12.4	♦5.2	♦10.3	...
Kyrgyzstan - Kirghizstan											
Number - Nombre	...	52[1]	56[1]	66[1]	67[1]	64[1]	70[2]	86[2]	75[2]	...	...
Rate - Taux	...	...	...	...	...	...	55.0	63.5	51.3	...	...
Malaysia - Malaisie											
Number - Nombre	U	...	...	...	128	...	133	...	...	...	...
Maldives											
Number - Nombre	...	-[3]	2[3]	1[3]	...	2[4]	4[3]	...	7[3]	4[3]	...
Rate - Taux	...	...	...	...	...	♦30.4	...	...	...	...	...
Oman											
Number - Nombre	U	...	...	...	...	...	...	3	6	...	...
Philippines											
Number - Nombre	C	...	...	...	...	...	1 731	...	...	...	...
Rate - Taux	C	...	...	...	...	...	97.0	...	...	...	...

17. Maternal deaths and maternal mortality ratios: 2003 - 2012
Mortalité liée à la maternité, nombre de décès et taux : 2003 - 2012 (continued - suite)

Continent and country or area / Continent et pays ou zone	Code[a]	2003	2004	2005	2006	2007	2008	2009	2010	2011	2012
ASIA - ASIE											
Qatar											
Number - Nombre	...	...	...	...	...	1[2]	5[2]	2[2]	4[1]	2[1]	1[1]	...
Rate - Taux	...	...	...	...	...	♦7.1	♦31.9	♦11.6	♦21.8	...	...	...
Republic of Korea - République de Corée											
Number - Nombre	C	58	59	53	54	...	39	48	75	85	56
Rate - Taux	C	11.8	12.5	12.2	12.0	...	8.4	10.8	16.0	18.0	11.6
Saudi Arabia - Arabie saoudite											
Number - Nombre	U	...	...	...	...	...	...	54	...	...	...
Singapore - Singapour											
Number - Nombre	+U	2	1	4	3	...	2	-	1	2	...
Sri Lanka											
Number - Nombre	+U	...	...	...	53	...	...	...	...	...	...
Tajikistan - Tadjikistan											
Number - Nombre	U	36	37	28	...	...	...	...	...	...	...
Thailand - Thaïlande											
Number - Nombre	+U	...	...	...	92	...	...	...	...	...	...
Turkey - Turquie											
Number - Nombre	+U	...	...	...	...	...	...	37	46	58	...
United Arab Emirates - Émirats arabes unis											
Number - Nombre	+U	...	...	...	...	...	1	2	4	...	...
Uzbekistan - Ouzbékistan											
Number - Nombre	U	151	156	145	...	...	...	...	...	...	...
EUROPE											
Albania - Albanie											
Number - Nombre	U	1	1	...	...	...	...	...	...	...	...
Austria - Autriche											
Number - Nombre	C	2	3	3	2	3	2	2	1	2	1
Rate - Taux	C	♦2.6	♦3.8	♦3.8	♦2.6	♦3.9	♦2.6	♦2.6	♦1.3	♦2.6	♦1.3
Belarus - Bélarus											
Number - Nombre	C	18	...	...	...	7	3	1	...	...	...
Rate - Taux	C	♦20.3	...	...	...	♦6.8	♦2.8	♦0.9	...	...	...
Belgium - Belgique											
Number - Nombre	C	...	1	...	9	...	7	6	8	...	...
Rate - Taux	C	...	♦0.9	...	♦7.3	...	♦5.5	♦4.7	♦6.1	...	...
Bosnia and Herzegovina - Bosnie-Herzégovine											
Number - Nombre	U	...	...	...	...	...	...	...	...	2	...
Bulgaria - Bulgarie											
Number - Nombre	C	4	7	8	5	8	5	4	6	2	3
Rate - Taux	C	♦5.9	♦10.0	♦11.3	♦6.8	♦10.6	♦6.4	♦4.9	♦7.9	♦2.8	♦4.3
Croatia - Croatie											
Number - Nombre	C	3	3	3	4	6	3	6	4	4	3
Rate - Taux	C	♦7.6	♦7.4	♦7.1	♦9.7	♦14.3	♦6.9	♦13.5	♦9.2	♦9.7	♦7.2
Czech Republic - République tchèque											
Number - Nombre	C	4	5	3	9	3	7	3	3	2	6
Rate - Taux	C	♦4.3	♦5.1	♦2.9	♦8.5	♦2.6	♦5.9	♦2.5	♦2.6	♦1.8	♦5.5
Denmark - Danemark											
Number - Nombre	C	...	-	-	5	...	4	4	-	2	-
Rate - Taux	C	...	-	-	♦7.7	...	♦6.2	♦6.4	-	♦3.4	-
Estonia - Estonie											
Number - Nombre	C	4	4	2	1	-	-	-	1	1	1
Rate - Taux	C	♦30.7	♦28.6	♦13.9	♦6.7	-	-	-	♦6.3	♦6.8	♦7.1
Finland - Finlande											
Number - Nombre	C	2	7	3	4	1	5	1	3	-	2
Rate - Taux	C	♦3.5	♦12.1	♦5.2	♦6.8	♦1.7	♦8.4	♦1.7	♦4.9	-	♦3.4
France											
Number - Nombre	C	56	53	41	59	60	52	75	68	45	...
Rate - Taux	C	7.4	6.9	5.3	7.4	7.6	6.5	9.5	8.5	5.7	...
Germany - Allemagne											
Number - Nombre	C	30	37	28	41	28	36	35	35	32	31
Rate - Taux	C	♦4.2	5.2	♦4.1	6.1	♦4.1	5.3	5.3	5.2	4.8	4.6

Continent and country or area / Continent et pays ou zone	Co-de[a]	2003	2004	2005	2006	2007	2008	2009	2010	2011	2012
EUROPE											
Greece - Grèce											
Number - Nombre	C	2	3	-	3	2	-	4	6	4	...
Rate - Taux	C	♦1.9	♦2.8	-	♦2.7	♦1.8	-	♦3.4	♦5.2	♦3.8	...
Hungary - Hongrie											
Number - Nombre	C	7	4	5	8	8	17	18	14	9	9
Rate - Taux	C	♦7.4	♦4.2	♦5.1	♦8.0	♦8.2	♦17.1	♦18.7	♦15.5	♦10.2	♦10.0
Iceland - Islande											
Number - Nombre	C	-	-	-	-	-	-	-	...	...	...
Ireland - Irlande											
Number - Nombre	+C	-	1	2	-	1	3	3	3	...	...
Rate - Taux	+C	-	♦1.6	♦3.3	-	♦1.4	♦4.0	♦4.0	♦4.0	...	...
Italy - Italie											
Number - Nombre	C	28	...	...	11	13	13	19	16	...	...
Rate - Taux	C	♦5.1	...	...	♦2.0	♦2.3	♦2.3	♦3.3	♦2.8	...	...
Latvia - Lettonie											
Number - Nombre	+C	3	2	1	2	6	2	7	4	-	4
Rate - Taux	+C	♦14.2	♦9.7	♦4.6	♦8.7	♦25.0	♦8.2	♦31.8	♦20.2	-	♦20.1
Lithuania - Lituanie											
Number - Nombre	+C	1	5	4	-	2	3	-	2	2	3
Rate - Taux	+C	♦3.3	♦16.8	♦13.6	-	♦6.7	♦9.5	-	♦6.5	♦6.6	♦9.8
Luxembourg											
Number - Nombre	+C	-	1	1	-	1	1	-	1	-	1
Rate - Taux	+C	-	♦18.3	♦18.6	-	♦18.3	♦17.9	-	♦17.0	-	♦16.6
Malta - Malte											
Number - Nombre	+C	-	-	-	-	-	1	-	-	-	...
Rate - Taux	+C	-	-	-	-	-	♦24.9	-	-	-	...
Montenegro - Monténégro											
Number - Nombre	C	...	...	...	-	1	-	-	...	...	...
Rate - Taux	C	...	...	...	-	♦12.8	-	-	...	...	...
Netherlands - Pays-Bas											
Number - Nombre	+C	8	10	16	15	9	8	9	4	3	6
Rate - Taux	+C	♦4.0	♦5.2	♦8.5	♦8.1	♦5.0	♦4.3	♦4.9	♦2.2	♦1.7	♦3.4
Norway - Norvège											
Number - Nombre	+C	7	-	2	5	4	3	1	3	3	-
Rate - Taux	+C	♦12.4	-	♦3.5	♦8.5	♦6.8	♦5.0	♦1.6	♦4.9	♦5.0	-
Poland - Pologne											
Number - Nombre	C	14	17	11	11	11	19	8	9	9	4
Rate - Taux	C	♦4.0	♦4.8	♦3.0	♦2.9	♦2.8	♦4.6	♦1.9	♦2.2	♦2.3	♦1.0
Portugal											
Number - Nombre	+C	8	...	...	...	5	4	7	8	5	4
Rate - Taux	+C	♦7.1	...	...	...	♦4.9	♦3.8	♦7.0	♦7.9	♦5.2	♦4.5
Republic of Moldova - République de Moldova											
Number - Nombre	...	8[3]	9[3]	8[3]	6[4]	7[4]	17[4]	7[4]	18[4]	6[4]	12[4]
Rate - Taux	...	...	...	...	♦16.0	♦18.4	♦43.6	♦17.2	♦44.5	♦15.3	♦30.4
Romania - Roumanie											
Number - Nombre	+C	65	52	37	34	33	30	47	51	50	23
Rate - Taux	+C	30.6	24.0	16.7	15.5	15.4	♦13.5	21.1	24.0	25.5	♦11.4
Russian Federation - Fédération de Russie											
Number - Nombre	+C	463[5]	352	370	352	356	359	388	298	...	...
Rate - Taux	+C	31.3	23.4	25.4	23.8	22.1	20.9	22.0	16.7	...	...
San Marino - Saint-Marin											
Number - Nombre	+U	...	...	-	...	...	...	...	...	...	...
Serbia - Serbie											
Number - Nombre	...	...	2[3]	10[3]	9[3]	-[3]	4[3]	6[3]	12[4]	7[4]	10[4]
Rate - Taux	...	...	...	...	...	...	...	...	♦17.6	♦10.7	♦14.9
Slovakia - Slovaquie											
Number - Nombre	C	2	3	2	3	-	2	6	-	...	...
Rate - Taux	C	♦3.9	♦5.6	♦3.7	♦5.6	-	♦3.5	♦9.8	-	...	...
Slovenia - Slovénie											
Number - Nombre	C	-	2	1	3	3	2	1	-	...	...
Rate - Taux	C	-	♦11.1	♦5.5	♦15.8	♦15.1	♦9.2	♦4.6	-	...	...
Spain - Espagne											
Number - Nombre	C	20	21	18	14	13	24	17	20	14	10
Rate - Taux	C	♦4.5	♦4.6	♦3.9	♦2.9	♦2.6	♦4.6	♦3.4	♦4.1	♦3.0	♦2.2
Sweden - Suède											
Number - Nombre	C	2	2	6	5	2	6	6	3	1	5
Rate - Taux	C	♦2.0	♦2.0	♦5.9	♦4.7	♦1.9	♦5.5	♦5.4	♦2.6	♦0.9	♦4.4

Continent and country or area / Continent et pays ou zone	Code[a]	2003	2004	2005	2006	2007	2008	2009	2010	2011	2012
EUROPE											
Switzerland - Suisse											
Number - Nombre	C	**4**	**4**	**4**	**6**	**1**	**8**	**3**	**3**	...	...
Rate - Taux	C	♦**5.6**	♦**5.5**	♦**5.5**	♦**8.2**	♦**1.3**	♦**10.4**	♦**3.8**	♦**3.7**	...	...
TFYR of Macedonia - L'ex-R. y. de Macédoine											
Number - Nombre	...	**1**[2]	...	...	**1**	-	-	**1**	**2**	...	...
Rate - Taux	...	♦**3.7**	...	...	...	...	...	...	...	...	...
Ukraine											
Number - Nombre	+C	71	56	75	70	...	79	129	116	85	66
Rate - Taux	+C	17.4	13.1	17.6	15.2	...	15.5	25.2	23.3	16.9	12.7
United Kingdom of Great Britain and Northern Ireland - Royaume-Uni de Grande-Bretagne et d'Irlande du Nord											
Number - Nombre	+C	53	55	51	50	56	49	74	40	...	...
Rate - Taux	+C	7.6	7.7	7.1	6.7	7.3	6.2	9.4	5.0	...	...
OCEANIA - OCÉANIE											
Australia - Australie											
Number - Nombre	C	**8**	**12**	...	**9**	...	**6**	**9**	**12**	**12**	...
Rate - Taux	C	♦**3.2**	♦**4.7**	...	♦**3.3**	...	♦**2.0**	♦**3.0**	♦**4.0**	♦**4.0**	...
Fiji - Fidji											
Number - Nombre	+C	...	...	...	...	...	...	**5**	...	**4**	...
Rate - Taux	+C	...	...	...	...	...	...	♦**27.5**	...	...	...
New Zealand - Nouvelle-Zélande											
Number - Nombre	+C	**4**	**4**	**6**	**9**	**13**	**7**	**11**	**6**	...	...
Rate - Taux	+C	♦**7.1**	♦**6.9**	♦**10.4**	♦**15.2**	♦**20.3**	♦**10.9**	♦**17.6**	♦**9.4**	...	...

FOOTNOTES - NOTES

Data in bold refer to maternal deaths based on ICD-10 Classification, otherwise data refer to maternal deaths based on ICD-9 Classification. - Les données en typographie gras se rapportent aux décès maternelles basées sur la classification CIM-10, autrement les données se rapportent aux décès maternelles basées sur la classification CIM-9.

Italics: data from civil registers which are incomplete or of unknown completeness. - Italiques : données incomplètes ou dont le degré d'exactitude n'est pas connu, provenant des registres de l'état civil.

* Provisional. - Données provisoires.

♦ Rates based on 30 or fewer deaths. - Taux basés sur 30 décès ou moins.

a 'Code' indicates the source of data, as follows:
C - Civil registration, estimated over 90% complete
U - Civil registration, estimated less than 90% complete
| - Other source, estimated reliable
+ - Data tabulated by date of registration rather than occurence
... - Information not available

Le 'Code' indique la source des données, comme suit :
C - Registres de l'état civil considérés complèts à 90 p. 100 au moins
U - Registres de l'état civil qui ne sont pas considérés complèts à 90 p. 100 au moins
| - Autre source, considérée pas douteuses
+ - Données exploitées selon la date de l'enregistrement et non la date de l'événement
... - Information pas disponible

1 The code is U. - Le code est U.
2 The code is C. - Le code est C.
3 The code is +U. - Le code est +U.
4 The code is +C. - Le code est +C.

5 For 2003 and before, data on cause of death do not include the Chechnya region. Therefore, rates must be used with caution as they are based on the total population, which is assumed to include all regions. - Pour 2003 et avant, les données sur les causes de décès ne comprennent par la région de Chechnya. Par conséquent, les taux doivent être utilisés avec précaution car ils sont basés sur la population totale, qui est supposée inclure toutes les régions.

Table 18 - *Demographic Yearbook 2014*

Table 18 presents deaths and crude death rates by urban/rural residence for as many years as possible between 2010 and 2014.

Description of variables: Death is defined as the permanent disappearance of all evidence of life at any time after live birth has taken place (post-natal cessation of vital functions without capability of resuscitation).

Statistics on the number of deaths are obtained from civil registers unless otherwise noted. For those countries or areas where civil registration statistics on deaths are considered reliable (estimated completeness of 90 per cent or more), the death rates shown have been calculated on the basis of registered deaths.

The urban/rural classification of deaths is that provided by each country or area; it is presumed to be based on the national census definitions of urban population that have been set forth at the end of the technical notes for table 6.

For certain countries, there is a discrepancy between the total number of deaths shown in this table and those shown in subsequent tables for the same year. Usually this discrepancy arises because the total number of deaths occurring in a given year is revised although the remaining tabulations are not.

Rate computation: Crude death rates are the annual number of deaths per 1 000 mid-year population.

Rates by urban/rural residence are the annual number of deaths, in the appropriate urban or rural category, per 1 000 corresponding mid-year population. These rates are calculated by the Statistics Division of the United Nations based on the appropriate reference population (for example: total population, nationals only etc.) if known and available. If the reference population is not known or unavailable the total population is used to calculate the rates. Therefore, if the population that is used to calculate the rates is different from the correct reference population, the rates presented might under- or overstate the true situation in a country or area.

Rates presented in this table are limited to those countries or areas with a minimum number of 30 deaths in a given year.

Reliability of data: Each country or area has been asked to indicate the estimated completeness of the deaths recorded in its civil register. These national assessments are indicated by the quality codes "C", "U" and "|" that appear in the first column of this table. "C" indicates that the data are estimated to be virtually complete, that is, representing at least 90 per cent of the deaths occurring each year, while "U" indicates that data are estimated to be incomplete that is, representing less than 90 per cent of the deaths occurring each year. The code "|" indicates that the source of data is different than civil registration and is explained by a footnote. The code "..." indicates that no information was provided regarding completeness or no assessment has been done in the country.

Data from civil registers that are reported as incomplete or of unknown completeness (code "U" or "...") are considered unreliable. They appear in italics in this table; rates based on these data are not computed.

Limitations: Statistics on deaths are subject to the same qualifications as have been set forth for vital statistics in general and death statistics in particular as discussed in section 4 of the Introduction.

The reliability of the data, an indication of which is described above, is an important factor in considering the limitations. In addition, some deaths are tabulated by date of registration and not by date of occurrence; these have been indicated with a plus sign "+". Whenever the lag between the date of occurrence and date of registration is prolonged and, therefore, a large proportion of the death registrations are delayed, death statistics for any given year may be seriously affected. However, delays in the registration of deaths are less common and shorter than in the registration of live births.

International comparability in mortality statistics may also be affected by the exclusion of deaths of infants who were born alive but died before the registration of the birth or within the first 24 hours of life. Statistics of this type are footnoted.

In addition, it should be noted that rates are affected also by the quality and limitations of the population estimates that are used in their computation. The problems of under-enumeration or over-enumeration and, to some extent, the differences in definition of total population have been discussed in section 3 of the Introduction dealing with population data in general, and specific information pertaining to individual countries or areas is given in the footnotes to table 3.

It should be emphasized that crude death rates -- like other crude rates, such as of birth, marriage and divorce -- may be seriously affected by the age-sex structure of the populations to which they relate. Nevertheless, they do provide a simple measure of the level and changes in mortality.

The comparability of data by urban/rural residence is affected by the national definitions of urban and rural used in tabulating these data. It is assumed, in the absence of specific information to the contrary, that the definitions of urban and rural used in connection with the national population census were also used in the compilation of the vital statistics for each country or area. However, it cannot be excluded that, for a given country or area, different definitions of urban and rural are used for the vital statistics data and the population census data respectively. When known, the definitions of urban used in national population censuses are presented at the end of the technical notes for table 6. As discussed in detail in the technical notes for table 6, these definitions vary considerably from one country or area to another.

Earlier data: Deaths and crude death rates have been shown in each issue of the Demographic Yearbook. For information on specific years covered, the reader should consult the Index.

Tableau 18 – *Annuaire démographique 2014*

Le tableau 18 présente le nombre des décès et les taux bruts de mortalité selon le lieu de résidence (zone urbaine ou rurale) pour le plus grand nombre d'années possible entre 2010 et 2014.

Description des variables : Le décès est défini comme la disparition permanente de tout signe de vie à un moment quelconque postérieur à la naissance vivante (cessation des fonctions vitales après la naissance sans possibilité de réanimation).

Sauf indication contraire, les statistiques relatives au nombre de décès sont établies sur la base des registres d'état civil. Pour les pays ou zones où les données concernant l'enregistrement des décès par les services de l'état civil sont jugées sûres (complétude estimée à 90 p. 100 ou plus), les taux de mortalité ont été calculés d'après les décès enregistrés.

La répartition des décès entre zones urbaines et zones rurales est celle qui a été communiquée par chaque pays ou zone ; on part du principe qu'elle repose sur les définitions de la population urbaine utilisées pour les recensements nationaux, qui sont reproduites à la fin des notes techniques du tableau 6.

Pour quelques pays il y a une discordance entre le nombre total des décès présenté dans ce tableau et ceux présentés après pour la même année. Habituellement ces différences apparaissent lorsque le nombre total des décès pour une certaine année a été révisé alors que les autres tabulations ne l'ont pas été.

Calcul des taux : Les taux bruts de mortalité représentent le nombre annuel de décès pour 1 000 habitants en milieu d'année.

Les taux selon le lieu de résidence (zone urbaine ou rurale) représentent le nombre annuel de décès, classés selon la catégorie urbaine ou rurale appropriée, pour 1 000 habitants en milieu d'année. Ces taux sont calculés par la division de statistique des Nations Unies sur la base de la population de référence adéquate (par exemple : population totale, nationaux seulement, etc.) si connue et disponible. Si la population de référence n'est pas connue ou n'est pas disponible, la population totale est utilisée pour calculer les taux. Par conséquent, si la population utilisée pour calculer les taux est différente de la population de référence adéquate, les taux présentés sont susceptibles de sous ou sur estimer la situation réelle d'un pays ou d'un territoire.

Les taux présentés dans ce tableau se rapportent seulement aux pays ou zones où l'on a enregistré un nombre minimal de 30 décès au cours d'une année donnée.

Fiabilité des données : Il a été demandé à chaque pays ou zone d'indiquer le degré estimatif de complétude des données sur les décès d'enfants de moins d'un an figurant dans ses registres d'état civil. Ces évaluations nationales sont signalées par les codes de qualité "C", "U" et "|" qui apparaissent dans la deuxième colonne du tableau.

La lettre "C" indique que les données sont jugées à peu près complètes, c'est-à-dire qu'elles représentent au moins 90 p. 100 des décès survenus chaque année ; la lettre "U" signifie que les données sont jugées incomplètes, c'est-à-dire qu'elles représentent moins de 90 p.100 des décès survenus chaque année. Le symbole "|" indique que la source des données n'est pas un registre de l'état civil ; le symbole, dans ce cas, est accompagné par une note explicative. Le code "..." dénote qu'aucun renseignement n'a été communiqué quant à la complétude des données.

Les données provenant des registres de l'état civil qui sont déclarées incomplètes ou dont le degré de complétude n'est pas connu (code "U" ou "...") sont jugées douteuses. Elles apparaissent en italique dans le présent tableau et les taux correspondants n'ont pas été calculés.

Insuffisance des données : Les statistiques relatives à la mortalité appellent les mêmes réserves que celles qui ont été formulées à propos des statistiques de l'état civil en général et des statistiques relatives aux décès en particulier (voir la section 4 des Notes techniques).

La fiabilité des données, au sujet de laquelle des indications ont été fournies plus haut, est un facteur important. Il faut également tenir compte du fait que, dans certains cas, les décès sont classés par date d'enregistrement et non par date d'occurrence ; ces cas ont été signalés par le signe "+". Chaque fois que le décalage entre le décès et son enregistrement est grand et qu'une forte proportion des décès fait l'objet d'un enregistrement tardif, les statistiques relatives aux décès survenus pendant l'année peuvent être considérablement faussées.

En règle générale, toutefois, les décès sont enregistrés beaucoup plus rapidement que les naissances vivantes, et les retards prolongés sont rares.

Un autre facteur qui nuit à la comparabilité internationale est la pratique qui consiste à ne pas inclure dans les statistiques de la mortalité les enfants nés vivants mais décédés avant l'enregistrement de leur naissance ou dans les 24 heures qui ont suivi la naissance. Quand pareil facteur a joué, cela a été signalé en note à la fin du tableau.

Il convient de noter par ailleurs que l'exactitude des taux dépend également de la qualité et des limitations des estimations de la population qui sont utilisées pour leur calcul. Le problème des erreurs par excès ou par défaut commises lors du dénombrement et, dans une certaine mesure, le problème de l'hétérogénéité des définitions de la population totale ont été examinés à la section 3 de l'Introduction, relative à la population en général ; des indications concernant certains pays ou zones sont données en note à la fin du tableau 3.

Il faut souligner que les taux bruts de mortalité, de même que les taux bruts de natalité, de nuptialité et de divortialité, peuvent varier très sensiblement selon la composition par âge et par sexe de la population à laquelle ils se rapportent. Ils offrent néanmoins un moyen simple de mesurer le niveau et l'évolution de la mortalité.

La comparabilité des données selon le lieu de résidence (zone urbaine ou rurale) peut être limitée par les définitions nationales des termes « urbain » et « rural » utilisées pour le classement de ces données. En l'absence d'indications contraires, on a supposé que les mêmes définitions avaient servi pour le recensement national de la population et pour l'établissement des statistiques de l'état civil pour chaque pays ou zone. Toutefois, il n'est pas exclu que, pour une zone ou un pays donné, des définitions différentes aient été retenues. Les définitions du terme « urbain » utilisées pour les recensements nationaux de population ont été présentées à la fin du tableau 6 lorsqu'elles étaient connues. Comme on l'a précisé dans les notes techniques relatives au tableau 6, ces définitions varient considérablement d'un pays ou d'une zone à l'autre.

Données publiées antérieurement : les différentes éditions de l'*Annuaire démographique* contiennent des statistiques des décès et des taux bruts de mortalité. Pour plus de précisions concernant les années pour lesquelles ces données ont été publiées, se reporter à l'index.

18. Deaths and crude death rates, by urban/rural residence: 2010 - 2014
Décès et taux bruts de mortalité, selon la résidence, urbaine/rurale : 2010 - 2014

Continent, country or area, and urban/rural residence — Continent, pays ou zone et résidence, urbaine/rurale	Code[a]	Number - Nombre					Rate - Taux				
		2010	2011	2012	2013	2014	2010	2011	2012	2013	2014
AFRICA - AFRIQUE											
Algeria - Algérie[1]											
Total	U	157 193	161 862	169 815	168 136	173 781	...	...	...	...	...
Benin - Bénin[2]											
Total	I	78 248	78 670	79 116	...	...	8.9	8.7	8.4	...	...
Botswana[3]											
Total	U	...	...	12 270	...	...	...	...	...	...	...
Cabo Verde											
Total	C	2 917	...	...	...	...	5.6	...	...	...	...
Djibouti											
Total	U	1 051	1 011	...	...	...	...	...	...	...	...
Egypt - Égypte											
Total	C	483 385	493 086	529 512	511 183	...	6.1	6.1	6.4	6.0	...
Urban - Urbaine	C	226 304	228 368	251 809	285 611	...	6.7	6.6	7.1	7.9	...
Rural - Rurale	C	257 081	264 718	277 703	225 572	...	5.7	5.8	5.9	4.7	...
Ghana[4]											
Total	I	163 534	...	...	...	...	6.6	...	...	...	...
Urban - Urbaine	I	68 322	...	...	...	...	5.4	...	...	...	...
Rural - Rurale	I	95 212	...	...	...	...	7.9	...	...	...	...
Kenya											
Total	U	185 100	182 652	187 811	194 332	198 611	...	...	...	...	...
Lesotho											
Total	+U	7 864	5 314	7 751	...	...	...	...	...	...	...
Mauritius - Maurice[5]											
Total	+C	9 131	9 170	9 343	9 440	9 682	7.1	7.3	7.4	7.5	7.7
Urban - Urbaine	+C	4 251	4 182	4 117	4 189	4 203	8.0	8.2	8.1	8.1	8.1
Rural - Rurale	+C	4 880	4 988	5 226	5 251	5 479	6.5	6.7	7.0	7.1	7.4
Namibia - Namibie[6]											
Total	I	...	22 668	...	...	...	...	10.7	...	...	...
Urban - Urbaine	I	...	7 858	...	...	...	...	8.7	...	...	...
Rural - Rurale	I	...	14 810	...	...	...	...	12.2	...	...	...
Niger											
Total	+U	1 023	6 761	...	...	...	...	...	...	...	...
Reunion - Réunion											
Total	C	4 221	...	...	...	...	5.1	...	...	...	...
Rwanda											
Total	U	141 256	140 519	139 499	...	...	...	...	...	...	...
Saint Helena ex. dep. - Sainte-Hélène sans dép.											
Total	C	53	49	62	55	61	12.5	11.5	15.0	13.1	13.8
Sao Tome and Principe - Sao Tomé-et-Principe[7]											
Total	I	...	...	1 287	...	...	...	...	6.9	...	...
Senegal - Sénégal[8]											
Total	I	132 218	134 450	135 468	136 460	...	10.6	10.5	10.3	10.1	...
Seychelles											
Total	+C	664	691	651	717	725	7.4	7.9	7.4	8.0	7.9
Sierra Leone											
Total	...	10 847	13 674	12 767	...	...	...	...	...	...	...
Urban - Urbaine	...	5 441	2 967	4 948	...	...	...	...	...	...	...
Rural - Rurale	...	5 406	10 707	7 819	...	...	...	...	...	...	...
South Africa - Afrique du Sud											
Total	U	578 953	580 460	575 546	565 310	551 389	...	...	...	...	...
Tunisia - Tunisie											
Total	U	60 438	63 258	62 224	60 386	...	...	...	...	...	...
United Republic of Tanzania - République Unie de Tanzanie											
Total	...	573 213	565 099	555 975	...	...	...	...	...	...	...
Zambia - Zambie[9]											
Total	I	164 385	...	...	...	...	13.1	...	...	...	...
Urban - Urbaine	I	62 665	...	...	...	...	12.5	...	...	...	...
Rural - Rurale	I	101 720	...	...	...	...	13.6	...	...	...	...

18. Deaths and crude death rates, by urban/rural residence: 2010 - 2014
Décès et taux bruts de mortalité, selon la résidence, urbaine/rurale : 2010 - 2014 (continued - suite)

Continent, country or area, and urban/rural residence Continent, pays ou zone et résidence, urbaine/rurale	Co-de[a]	Number - Nombre					Rate - Taux				
		2010	2011	2012	2013	2014	2010	2011	2012	2013	2014

AMERICA, NORTH - AMÉRIQUE DU NORD

Anguilla[10]											
Total	+C	66	55	38	72	...	4.0	4.1	2.8	5.3	...
Antigua and Barbuda - Antigua-et-Barbuda											
Total	+C	491	...	...	...	...	5.4	...	...	...	...
Aruba											
Total	C	619	633	595	560	643	6.1	6.2	5.7	5.3	6.0
Bahamas											
Total	+C	2 023	2 117	1 995	*2 062	...	6.0	5.9	5.5	*5.6	...
Bermuda - Bermudes[11]											
Total	C	475	429	422	471	...	7.4	6.8	6.8	7.6	...
Canada[12]											
Total	C	244 968	243 651	252 309	256 982	*268 056	7.2	7.1	7.3	7.3	*7.5
Cayman Islands - Îles Caïmanes											
Total	C	152	176	*172	*170	153	2.8	3.2	*3.0	*3.0	2.6
Costa Rica											
Total	C	19 077	18 801	19 200	19 647	*20 553	4.2	4.1	4.1	4.2	*4.3
Urban - Urbaine	C	9 887	9 642	9 665	9 891	*14 481	3.0	2.9	2.9	2.9	*4.2
Rural - Rurale	C	9 190	9 159	9 535	9 756	*6 072	7.4	7.3	7.5	7.6	*4.7
Cuba											
Total	C	91 065	87 044	89 372	92 273	96 312	8.2	7.8	8.0	8.2	8.6
Urban - Urbaine	C	76 091	...	75 354	78 107	...	9.0	...	8.9	9.1	...
Rural - Rurale	C	14 974	...	14 018	14 166	...	5.4	...	5.2	5.5	...
Curaçao											
Total	C	1 246	1 276	1 246	1 250	1 370	8.4	8.5	8.2	8.1	8.8
Dominica - Dominique											
Total	+C	588	...	...	...	...	...	...	...	...	...
Dominican Republic - République dominicaine											
Total	U	*35 735*	*35 301*	*35 392*	*34 375*	...	...	...	...	...	...
Urban - Urbaine[13]	U	*27 017*	*26 781*	*27 255*	*26 977*	...	...	...	...	...	...
Rural - Rurale[13]	U	*7 436*	*7 763*	*7 678*	*6 796*	...	...	...	...	...	...
El Salvador											
Total	C	32 586	33 211	32 148	...	...	5.3	5.3	5.1	...	...
Urban - Urbaine	C	23 684	23 621	22 153	...	...	6.0	5.9	5.4	...	...
Rural - Rurale	C	8 902	9 590	9 995	...	...	4.0	4.4	4.6	...	...
Greenland - Groenland											
Total	C	504	476	459	444	461	8.9	8.4	8.1	7.9	8.2
Urban - Urbaine	C	415	407	389	379	388	8.7	8.5	8.1	7.9	8.0
Rural - Rurale	C	89	69	70	65	73	10.0	8.0	8.2	7.9	9.1
Grenada - Grenade											
Total	+C	828	803	856	...	...	7.9	7.5	8.0	...	...
Guadeloupe[14]											
Total	C	2 963	2 835	2 873	2 951	...	7.3	7.0	7.1	7.3	...
Guatemala											
Total	C	72 748	72 354	71 980	...	...	5.1	4.9	4.8	...	...
Urban - Urbaine[13]	C	39 331	37 781	...	...	...	...	...	...	...	...
Rural - Rurale[13]	C	32 219	33 137	...	...	...	...	...	...	...	...
Honduras											
Total	+U	*36 812*	*37 211*	...	...	...	...	...	...	...	...
Jamaica - Jamaïque[15]											
Total	U	*21 503*	*16 926*	*16 998*	*15 427*	...	...	...	...	...	...
Martinique[14]											
Total	C	2 844	...	...	...	...	7.2	...	...	...	...
Mexico - Mexique[16]											
Total	+C	590 886	589 646	601 259	610 730	...	5.2	5.1	5.1	5.2	...
Urban - Urbaine[13]	+C	446 324	444 372	455 905	460 898	...	5.4	5.3	5.4	5.4	...
Rural - Rurale[13]	+C	134 637	133 517	133 577	139 093	...	4.3	4.2	4.1	4.3	...
Montserrat											
Total	+C	40	55	44	45	32	8.0	11.2	8.9	9.1	6.4
Nicaragua											
Total	+U	*19 944*	...	...	...	...	...	...	...	...	...
Panama											
Total	U	*16 542*	*16 367*	*17 350*	*17 767*	*16 913*	...	...	...	...	...
Urban - Urbaine	U	*10 864*	*11 027*	*11 712*	*12 546*	...	...	...	...	...	...
Rural - Rurale	U	*5 678*	*5 340*	*5 638*	*5 221*	...	...	...	...	...	...

18. Deaths and crude death rates, by urban/rural residence: 2010 - 2014
Décès et taux bruts de mortalité, selon la résidence, urbaine/rurale : 2010 - 2014 (continued - suite)

Continent, country or area, and urban/rural residence — Continent, pays ou zone et résidence, urbaine/rurale	Code[a]	Number - Nombre					Rate - Taux				
		2010	2011	2012	2013	2014	2010	2011	2012	2013	2014

AMERICA, NORTH - AMÉRIQUE DU NORD

Puerto Rico - Porto Rico											
Total	C	29 526	30 146	30 053	29 368	30 224	7.9	8.2	8.2	8.1	8.5
Saint Vincent and the Grenadines - Saint-Vincent-et-les Grenadines											
Total	+C	827	882	858	...	...	7.5	8.0	7.8	...	...
Sint Maarten (Dutch part) - Saint-Martin (partie néerlandaise)[17]											
Total	+C	160	173	180	171	...	4.5	5.2	5.2	4.7	...
United States of America - États-Unis d'Amérique											
Total	C	2 468 435	2 515 458	2 543 279	2 596 993	...	8.0	8.1	8.1	8.2	...

AMERICA, SOUTH - AMÉRIQUE DU SUD

Argentina - Argentine											
Total	C	318 602	319 059	319 539	326 197	...	7.8	7.7	7.7	7.7	...
Bolivia (Plurinational State of) - Bolivie (État plurinational de)[18]											
Total	I	...	...	127 050	...	...	...	...	12.3	...	...
Urban - Urbaine	I	...	...	83 506	...	...	...	...	12.0	...	...
Rural - Rurale	I	...	...	43 544	...	...	...	...	12.9	...	...
Brazil - Brésil[19]											
Total	U	1 117 675	1 148 165	1 157 214	1 180 796	...	...	...	...	...	...
Chile - Chili											
Total	C	97 930	94 985	98 711	*99 770	...	5.7	5.5	5.7	*5.7	...
Urban - Urbaine	C	82 966	81 552	85 352	...	...	5.6	5.4	5.6	...	...
Rural - Rurale	C	14 964	13 433	13 359	...	...	6.7	6.0	5.9	...	...
Colombia - Colombie											
Total	U	200 524	195 823	199 756	...	...	...	...	...	...	...
Urban - Urbaine[13]	U	157 143	156 717	158 814	...	...	...	...	...	...	...
Rural - Rurale[13]	U	36 577	36 161	38 056	...	...	...	...	...	...	...
Ecuador - Équateur[20]											
Total	U	61 681	62 304	63 511	63 104	...	...	...	...	...	...
Urban - Urbaine	U	46 324	47 235	50 635	49 912	...	...	...	...	...	...
Rural - Rurale	U	15 357	15 069	12 859	13 192	...	...	...	...	...	...
French Guiana - Guyane française[14]											
Total	C	773	...	...	...	...	3.4	...	...	...	...
Guyana											
Total	+C	4 651	4 527	...	...	...	6.2	6.0	...	...	...
Paraguay											
Total	+U	...	...	22 807	...	...	...	...	...	...	...
Peru - Pérou[21]											
Total	+U	99 334	96 852	97 989	94 394	...	...	...	...	...	...
Suriname											
Total	C	3 484	3 441	3 687	3 557	...	6.6	6.4	6.8	6.5	...
Urban - Urbaine	C	2 379	2 401	2 566	2 371	...	...	...	7.1	...	...
Rural - Rurale	C	1 105	1 040	1 121	1 186	...	...	...	6.1	...	...
Uruguay											
Total	C	33 157	32 807	33 354	32 795	...	9.8	9.6	9.7	9.5	...
Venezuela (Bolivarian Republic of) - Venezuela (République bolivarienne du)											
Total	C	130 597	136 803	142 988	147 901	...	4.6	4.7	4.9	5.0	...

ASIA - ASIE

Armenia - Arménie[22]											
Total	C	27 921	27 963	*27 514	*27 196	*27 872	8.6	8.6	*8.7	*9.0	...

18. Deaths and crude death rates, by urban/rural residence: 2010 - 2014
Décès et taux bruts de mortalité, selon la résidence, urbaine/rurale : 2010 - 2014 (continued - suite)

Continent, country or area, and urban/rural residence / Continent, pays ou zone et résidence, urbaine/rurale	Co-de[a]	Number - Nombre					Rate - Taux				
		2010	2011	2012	2013	2014	2010	2011	2012	2013	2014
ASIA - ASIE											
Azerbaijan - Azerbaïdjan[22]											
Total	+C	53 580	53 762	55 017	54 383	...	5.9	5.9	5.9	5.8	...
Urban - Urbaine	+C	28 369	28 567	29 577	28 863	...	5.9	5.9	6.0	5.8	...
Rural - Rurale	+C	25 211	25 195	25 440	25 520	...	5.9	5.8	5.8	5.8	...
Bahrain - Bahreïn											
Total	C	2 401	2 528	2 613	2 588	...	2.0	2.1	2.2	2.1	...
Bangladesh											
Total	U	842 095	828 000	826 000	...	...	...	...	...	...	...
Urban - Urbaine	U	187 470	176 000	189 000	...	...	...	...	...	...	...
Rural - Rurale	U	654 625	652 000	637 000	...	...	...	...	...	...	...
Brunei Darussalam - Brunéi Darussalam											
Total	+C	...	1 235	1 216	1 398	...	...	3.1	...	...	...
China - Chine[23]											
Total	I	9 510 000	9 600 000	9 660 000	9 720 000	9 770 000	7.1	7.1	7.2	7.2	7.2
China, Hong Kong SAR - Chine, Hong Kong RAS											
Total	C	42 194	42 346	43 917	43 397	*45 100	6.0	6.0	6.1	6.0	*6.2
China, Macao SAR - Chine, Macao RAS											
Total	C	1 774	1 845	1 841	1 920	1 939	3.3	3.4	3.2	3.2	3.1
Cyprus - Chypre[24]											
Total	C	5 103	5 504	5 665	5 141[25]	...	6.2	6.5	6.6	6.0	...
Georgia - Géorgie[22]											
Total	C	47 864	49 818	49 348	48 553	...	10.7	11.1	11.0	...	...
Urban - Urbaine	C	24 866	25 771	...	...	...	10.5	10.8	...	...	...
Rural - Rurale	C	22 998	24 047	...	...	...	11.0	11.4	...	...	...
India - Inde[26]											
Total	I	...	...	...	...	...	7.2	7.1	7.0	7.0	...
Urban - Urbaine	I	...	...	...	...	...	5.8	5.7	5.6	5.6	...
Rural - Rurale	I	...	...	...	...	...	7.7	7.6	7.6	7.5	...
Iran (Islamic Republic of) - Iran (République islamique d')[27]											
Total	C	441 042	383 504	367 539	372 279	...	5.9	5.1	4.8	4.8	...
Urban - Urbaine[13]	C	280 912	278 141	281 367	285 117	...	5.5	5.2	5.2	5.1	...
Rural - Rurale[13]	C	142 997	98 343	86 093	87 063	...	6.2	4.6	4.0	4.1	...
Iraq											
Total	U	...	...	...	*189 118	...	...	...	...	...	...
Israel - Israël[28]											
Total	C	39 613	40 889	42 100	41 643	42 085	5.2	5.3	5.3	5.2	5.1
Urban - Urbaine[13]	C	37 190	38 435	39 563	39 149	39 560	5.3	5.4	5.5	5.3	...
Rural - Rurale[13]	C	2 417	2 449	2 529	2 489	2 515	3.8	3.7	3.7	3.6	...
Japan - Japon[29]											
Total	C	1 197 012	1 253 066	1 256 359	1 268 436	...	9.3	9.8	9.8	10.0	...
Urban - Urbaine[13]	C	1 054 725	1 103 338	1 112 495	1 124 417	...	...	...	...	...	...
Rural - Rurale[13]	C	140 473	147 235	142 359	142 556	...	...	...	...	...	...
Jordan - Jordanie[30]											
Total	U	21 550	21 730	22 785	23 898	...	...	...	...	...	...
Kazakhstan[22]											
Total	C	146 370	144 944	142 880	135 950	...	9.0	8.8	8.5	8.0	...
Urban - Urbaine	C	84 177	83 551	82 943	78 581	...	9.5	9.2	9.0	8.4	...
Rural - Rurale	C	62 193	61 393	59 937	57 369	...	8.4	8.2	7.9	7.5	...
Kuwait - Koweït											
Total	C	5 448	5 339	5 950	5 909	...	1.9	1.7	1.8	1.7	...
Kyrgyzstan - Kirghizstan											
Total	C	36 174	35 941	36 186	34 880	*35 564	7.0	6.8	6.8	6.1	*6.1
Urban - Urbaine	C	13 328	13 098	13 098	12 507	...	7.3	7.1	7.1	6.5	...
Rural - Rurale	C	22 846	22 843	23 088	22 373	...	6.8	6.7	6.6	5.9	...
Lebanon - Liban											
Total	C	22 926	26 070	23 452	24 013	27 020	...	6.9	...	...	...
Malaysia - Malaisie											
Total	C	130 978	135 463	*136 836	...	...	4.6	4.7	*4.6	...	...
Maldives											
Total	C	1 105	1 137	1 135	1 120	...	3.5	3.5	3.4	3.3	...
Urban - Urbaine	C	458[31]	468[31]	564[31]	513	...	...	...	...	...	...
Rural - Rurale	C	611[31]	615[31]	555[31]	607	...	...	...	...	...	...

18. Deaths and crude death rates, by urban/rural residence: 2010 - 2014
Décès et taux bruts de mortalité, selon la résidence, urbaine/rurale : 2010 - 2014 (continued - suite)

Continent, country or area, and urban/rural residence / Continent, pays ou zone et résidence, urbaine/rurale	Code[a]	Number - Nombre					Rate - Taux				
		2010	2011	2012	2013	2014	2010	2011	2012	2013	2014
ASIA - ASIE											
Mongolia - Mongolie											
Total	+C	18 293	19 155	17 761	17 247	16 521	6.7	6.9	6.3	5.9	5.6
Urban - Urbaine	+C	11 580	12 462	13 444	11 182	11 406	6.4	6.7	7.0	5.7	5.7
Rural - Rurale	+C	6 713	6 693	4 317	6 065	5 115	7.1	7.2	4.7	6.5	5.3
Myanmar											
Total	+U	*346 205*	*342 420*	*250 874*	*257 216*	...	...	...	...	...	...
Urban - Urbaine	+U	*95 672*	*93 500*	*114 766*	*119 823*	...	...	...	...	...	...
Rural - Rurale	+U	*250 533*	*248 920*	*136 108*	*137 393*	...	...	...	...	...	...
Nepal - Népal[32]											
Total	|	...	129 978	...	...	...	...	4.5	...	...	...
Urban - Urbaine	|	...	21 844	...	...	...	...	...	...	...	...
Rural - Rurale	|	...	108 134	...	...	...	...	...	...	...	...
Oman[33]											
Total	U	*7 414*	*7 667*	*7 884*	*7 669*		...	...	...	...	...
Philippines											
Total	C	488 265	498 486	514 745	...	...	5.2	5.3	5.3	...	...
Qatar											
Total	C	1 970	1 949	2 031	2 133	*2 366	1.1	1.1	1.1	1.1	*1.1
Republic of Korea - République de Corée[34]											
Total	C	255 405	257 396	267 221	266 257	...	5.1	5.1	5.3	5.3	...
Urban - Urbaine[13]	C	172 779	174 968	181 379	182 888	...	4.3	4.3	4.4	4.4	...
Rural - Rurale[13]	C	82 590	82 416	85 840	83 360	...	8.7	8.7	9.1	9.0	...
Saudi Arabia - Arabie saoudite[35]											
Total	...	*100 073*	*102 066*	*104 195*	*106 521*		...	...	...	...	...
Singapore - Singapour											
Total	+C	17 610	18 027	18 481	18 938	19 393	4.7	4.8	4.8	4.9	5.0
Sri Lanka											
Total	+C	*128 603	*123 261	*122 063	*127 124	...	*6.2	*5.9	*6.0	*6.2	...
State of Palestine - État de Palestine[36]											
Total	U	*10 764*	*11 333*	*11 676*	*11 013*		...	...	...	...	...
Syrian Arab Republic - République arabe syrienne[37]											
Total	+U	*91 981*	...	...	...	...	...	...	...	...	...
Tajikistan - Tadjikistan[22]											
Total	U	*31 937*	*32 909*	*32 828*	*31 706*		...	...	...	...	...
Urban - Urbaine	U	*9 723*	*9 876*	*9 846*	*10 091*		...	...	...	...	...
Rural - Rurale	U	*22 214*	*23 033*	*22 982*	*21 615*		...	...	...	...	...
Thailand - Thaïlande											
Total	+U	*411 331*	*414 670*	*415 141*	*426 065*	435 624	...	...	...	...	...
Turkey - Turquie											
Total	C	366 187	375 923	376 000	372 094	*390 121	5.0	5.1	5.0	4.9	*5.1
United Arab Emirates - Émirats arabes unis[38]											
Total	...	*7 414*	*7 350*	...	...	...	...	...	...	...	...
Uzbekistan - Ouzbékistan[22]											
Total	C	138 411	143 253	145 988	145 672	...	4.9	4.9	4.9	4.9	...
Yemen - Yémen											
Total	U	*28 494*	*23 662*	*28 596*	*35 066*[39]	...	...	...	...	...	...
EUROPE											
Åland Islands - Îles d'Åland											
Total	C	233	277	323	269	*246	8.4	9.8	11.4	9.4	*8.5
Urban - Urbaine	C	92	120	124	115	*102	8.2	10.7	11.0	10.1	*8.9
Rural - Rurale	C	141	157	199	154	*144	8.4	9.3	11.6	8.9	*8.3
Albania - Albanie											
Total	C	20 107	20 012	20 870	20 442	...	6.9	6.9	7.2	7.1	...
Andorra - Andorre											
Total	C	239	275	303	...	...	2.8	3.5	3.9	...	...
Austria - Autriche											
Total	C	77 199[40]	76 479[40]	79 436[40]	79 526[40]	*77 667	9.2	9.1	9.4	9.4	*9.1

Continent, country or area, and urban/rural residence / Continent, pays ou zone et résidence, urbaine/rurale	Code[a]	Number - Nombre					Rate - Taux				
		2010	2011	2012	2013	2014	2010	2011	2012	2013	2014
EUROPE											
Belarus - Bélarus											
Total	C	137 132	135 090	126 531	125 326	...	14.4	14.3	13.4	13.2	...
Urban - Urbaine	C	78 840	78 947	75 234	75 275	...	11.1	11.0	10.5	10.4	...
Rural - Rurale	C	58 292	56 143	51 297	50 051	...	24.4	24.2	22.6	22.6	...
Belgium - Belgique											
Total	C	105 152[41]	104 292[41]	109 076[41]	109 334[41]	*104 755	9.7	9.4	9.8	9.8	*9.3
Urban - Urbaine[41]	C	103 605	102 762	107 536	...	...	9.6	9.4	...	...	...
Rural - Rurale[41]	C	1 547	1 530	1 540	...	...	9.9	9.6	...	...	...
Bosnia and Herzegovina - Bosnie-Herzégovine											
Total	C	35 118	35 522	35 692	35 837	34 824	9.1	9.2	9.3	9.3	9.1
Bulgaria - Bulgarie											
Total	C	110 165	108 258	109 281	104 345	*108 952	14.6	14.7	15.0	14.4	*15.0
Urban - Urbaine	C	65 759	65 182	66 333	...	...	12.2	12.2	12.5	...	...
Rural - Rurale	C	44 406	43 076	42 948	...	...	20.7	21.4	21.6	...	...
Croatia - Croatie											
Total	C	52 096	51 019	51 710	50 386	*50 839	12.1	11.9	12.1	11.8	*12.0
Urban - Urbaine	C	26 508	25 774	26 313	25 464	...	...	...	...	...	...
Rural - Rurale	C	25 588	25 245	25 397	24 922	...	...	...	...	...	...
Czech Republic - République tchèque											
Total	C	106 844	106 848	108 189	109 160	*105 665	10.2	10.2	10.3	10.4	*10.0
Urban - Urbaine	C	78 001	78 209	79 297	79 923	...	...	...	...	10.4	...
Rural - Rurale	C	28 843	28 639	28 892	29 237	...	...	...	...	10.3	...
Denmark - Danemark[42]											
Total	C	54 368	52 516	52 325	52 470		9.8	9.4	9.4	9.4	
Estonia - Estonie											
Total	C	15 790	15 244	15 450	15 244	...	11.9	11.5	11.7	11.6	...
Urban - Urbaine	C	10 784[13]	10 428	10 632	10 044	...	11.9	11.5	11.8	11.2	...
Rural - Rurale	C	5 004[13]	4 816	4 818	5 200	...	11.7	11.3	11.5	12.4	...
Faeroe Islands - Îles Féroé											
Total	C	348	371	406	364	...	7.2	7.6	8.4	7.6	...
Urban - Urbaine	C	97	140	135	119	...	5.4	7.8	7.5	6.6	...
Rural - Rurale	C	251	231	271	245	...	8.2	7.6	8.9	8.1	...
Finland - Finlande											
Total	C	50 654[43]	50 308[43]	51 384[43]	51 472	51 595	9.5	9.4	9.5	9.5	9.5
Urban - Urbaine[43]	C	30 844	30 835	31 745	...	...	8.5	8.4	8.6	...	...
Rural - Rurale[43]	C	19 810	19 473	19 639	...	...	11.7	11.5	11.6	...	...
France[44]											
Total	C	540 469	534 795	559 227	558 408	*542 800	8.6	8.5	8.8	8.8	*8.5
Urban - Urbaine[45]	C	408 348	404 706	422 986	422 803	...	...	...	...	...	...
Rural - Rurale[45]	C	130 094	128 444	134 423	133 734	...	...	...	...	...	...
Germany - Allemagne											
Total	C	858 768	852 328	869 582	893 825	*868 373	10.5	10.6	10.8	11.1	*10.8
Gibraltar[46]											
Total	+C	231	241	264	230	...	7.3	7.5	8.1	7.0	...
Greece - Grèce											
Total	C	109 084	111 099	116 668	111 794	*113 877	9.8	10.0	10.5	10.1	*10.4
Urban - Urbaine	C	60 992	62 095	64 919	...	...	...	...	...	...	...
Rural - Rurale	C	48 092	49 004	51 749	...	...	...	...	...	...	...
Guernsey - Guernesey											
Total	C	497	535	547	556	526	8.0	8.5	8.7	8.9	8.4
Hungary - Hongrie											
Total	C	130 456	128 795	129 440	126 677	*121 489	13.0	12.9	13.0	12.8	*12.3
Urban - Urbaine[47]	C	86 304	85 721	86 137	85 164	...	12.4	12.3	12.5	...	...
Rural - Rurale[47]	C	43 570	42 498	42 752	41 383	...	14.3	14.0	14.0	...	...
Iceland - Islande											
Total	C	2 020	1 986[48]	1 955	2 154	...	6.4	6.2	6.1	6.7	...
Urban - Urbaine	C	1 869	1 958[48]	1 815	1 980	...	6.3	6.2	6.0	6.5	...
Rural - Rurale	C	151	28[48]	140	174	...	7.3	...	6.8	8.4	...
Ireland - Irlande											
Total[49]	C	27 961	28 456	29 186	...	...	6.1	6.2	6.4	...	...
Total	+C	...	...	...	30 018	29 095	...	...	...	6.5	6.3
Isle of Man - Île de Man											
Total	+C	809	816	799	792	787	9.8	9.7	9.4	9.2	9.1
Italy - Italie											
Total	C	587 488	593 402	612 883	600 744	...	9.9	10.0	10.3	10.0	...

18. Deaths and crude death rates, by urban/rural residence: 2010 - 2014
Décès et taux bruts de mortalité, selon la résidence, urbaine/rurale : 2010 - 2014 (continued - suite)

Continent, country or area, and urban/rural residence / Continent, pays ou zone et résidence, urbaine/rurale	Code[a]	Number - Nombre					Rate - Taux				
		2010	2011	2012	2013	2014	2010	2011	2012	2013	2014
EUROPE											
Jersey											
Total	+C	801	727	774	717	...	8.3	7.4	7.9	...	...
Latvia - Lettonie											
Total	C	30 040	28 540	29 025	28 691	*28 438	14.3	13.9	14.3	14.3	*14.2
Urban - Urbaine	C	19 557	18 483	18 950	18 764	...	13.7	13.3	13.8	13.8	...
Rural - Rurale	C	10 483	10 057	10 075	9 927	...	15.5	15.1	15.3	15.3	...
Liechtenstein											
Total	C	238	248	224	246	...	6.6	6.8	6.1	6.7	...
Lithuania - Lituanie											
Total	C	42 120	41 037	40 938	41 511	*40 210	13.6	13.6	13.7	14.0	*13.7
Urban - Urbaine	C	25 114	24 822	25 030	25 403	...	12.1	12.3	12.5	12.8	...
Rural - Rurale	C	17 006	16 215	15 908	16 108	...	16.5	16.1	16.1	16.5	...
Luxembourg											
Total	C	3 760	3 819	3 876	3 822	...	7.4	7.4	7.3	7.0	...
Malta - Malte											
Total	C	3 010	3 267	3 418	3 236	...	7.3	7.8	8.1	7.6	...
Monaco[50]											
Total	C	535	499	429	567[51]	524[51]	15.0	13.8	11.9	15.3	...
Montenegro - Monténégro											
Total	C	5 633	5 847	5 922	5 917	6 014	9.1	9.4	9.5	9.5	9.7
Netherlands - Pays-Bas[52]											
Total	C	136 058	135 741	140 813	141 245	...	8.2	8.1	8.4	8.4	...
Urban - Urbaine	C	90 257	...	...	...	...	8.1	...	...	...	...
Rural - Rurale	C	45 801	...	...	...	...	8.3	...	...	...	...
Norway - Norvège[53]											
Total	C	41 499	41 393	41 992	41 131	*40 435	8.5	8.4	8.4	8.1	*7.9
Poland - Pologne											
Total	C	378 478	375 501	384 788	387 312	...	9.8	9.7	10.0	10.1	...
Urban - Urbaine	C	227 452	225 524	233 015	...	...	9.7	9.6	10.0	...	...
Rural - Rurale	C	151 026	149 977	151 773	...	...	10.0	9.9	10.0	...	...
Portugal[16]											
Total	C	105 954	102 848	107 612	106 543	*104 782	10.0	9.7	10.2	10.2	*10.0
Republic of Moldova - République de Moldova[54]											
Total	C	43 631	39 249	39 560	38 060	*39 489	12.2	11.0	11.1	10.7	*11.1
Urban - Urbaine	C	13 413	12 541	12 792	...	...	9.1	8.5	8.6	...	...
Rural - Rurale	C	30 218	26 708	26 768	...	...	14.5	12.9	12.9	...	...
Romania - Roumanie											
Total	C	259 723	251 439	255 539	246 967	...	12.8	12.5	12.7	12.4	...
Urban - Urbaine	C	117 632	114 648	117 661	114 091	...	10.8	10.5	10.9	10.6	...
Rural - Rurale	C	142 091	136 791	137 878	132 876	...	15.2	14.8	14.9	14.4	...
Russian Federation - Fédération de Russie[22]											
Total	C	2 028 516	1 925 720	1 906 335	*1 878 269	*1 913 613	14.2	13.5	13.3	*13.1	...
Urban - Urbaine	C	1 421 734	1 356 696	1 353 635	...	...	13.5	12.8	12.8	...	...
Rural - Rurale	C	606 782	569 024	552 700	...	...	16.1	15.2	14.8	...	...
San Marino - Saint-Marin											
Total	+C	222	222	237	247	...	6.7	6.6	7.1	7.4	...
Serbia - Serbie[55]											
Total	+C	103 211	102 935	102 400	100 300	*102 197	14.2	14.2	14.2	14.0	*14.3
Urban - Urbaine	+C	53 822	54 128	53 878	53 169	...	12.6	12.6	12.6	12.4	...
Rural - Rurale	+C	49 389	48 807	48 522	47 131	...	16.4	16.5	16.6	16.3	...
Slovakia - Slovaquie											
Total	C	53 445	53 594	52 437	52 089	...	9.9	9.9	9.7	9.6	...
Urban - Urbaine	C	26 549	26 576	26 106	26 482	...	...	9.0	8.9	9.0	...
Rural - Rurale	C	26 896	27 018	26 331	25 607	...	...	11.0	10.7	10.3	...
Slovenia - Slovénie											
Total	C	18 609	18 699	19 257	19 334	*18 886	9.1	9.1	9.4	9.4	*9.2
Urban - Urbaine	C	9 675	9 717	10 108	9 268	...	9.4	9.5	9.9	8.8	...
Rural - Rurale	C	8 934	8 982	9 149	10 066	...	8.7	8.7	8.9	10.0	...
Spain - Espagne											
Total	C	380 234	386 017	401 122	388 600	...	8.2	8.3	8.6	8.3	...
Sweden - Suède											
Total	C	90 487	89 938	91 938	90 402	*88 781	9.6	9.5	9.7	9.4	*9.1

18. Deaths and crude death rates, by urban/rural residence: 2010 - 2014
Décès et taux bruts de mortalité, selon la résidence, urbaine/rurale : 2010 - 2014 (continued - suite)

Continent, country or area, and urban/rural residence / Continent, pays ou zone et résidence, urbaine/rurale	Co-de[a]	Number - Nombre					Rate - Taux				
		2010	2011	2012	2013	2014	2010	2011	2012	2013	2014
EUROPE											
Switzerland - Suisse											
Total	C	62 649	62 091	64 173	64 961	*62 800	8.0	7.8	8.0	8.0	*7.7
Urban - Urbaine	C	45 923	45 451	47 017	...	...	...	7.8	8.0	...	...
Rural - Rurale	C	16 726	16 640	17 156	...	...	...	8.0	8.2	...	...
TFYR of Macedonia - L'ex-R. y. de Macédoine											
Total	C	19 113	19 465	20 134	19 208	*19 682	9.3	9.5	9.8	9.3	*9.5
Urban - Urbaine	C	11 442	11 478	12 082	...	...	...	...	...	...	...
Rural - Rurale	C	7 671	7 987	8 052	...	...	...	...	...	...	...
Ukraine[56]											
Total	+C	698 235	664 588	663 139	662 368	...	15.2	14.5	14.5	14.6	...
Urban - Urbaine	+C	431 130	411 025	411 787	412 553	...	13.7	13.1	13.1	...	...
Rural - Rurale	+C	267 105	253 563	251 352	249 815	...	18.6	17.7	17.7	...	...
United Kingdom of Great Britain and Northern Ireland - Royaume-Uni de Grande-Bretagne et d'Irlande du Nord[57]											
Total	+C	561 666	552 232	569 024	574 945	...	8.9	8.7	8.9	9.0	...
OCEANIA - OCÉANIE											
American Samoa - Samoas américaines											
Total	C	247	283	...	...	...	3.7	...	...	...	...
Australia - Australie											
Total	+C	143 473	146 932	147 098	147 678	...	6.5	6.6	6.5	6.4	...
Urban - Urbaine[58]	+C	85 367	87 054	87 315	87 835	...	4.5	4.6	4.5	4.4	...
Rural - Rurale[58]	+C	57 339	59 350	59 143	59 265	...	17.5	18.0	17.8	17.7	...
Cook Islands - Îles Cook[59]											
Total	+C	92	72	104	115	*113	3.9	3.7	5.3	6.2	*6.1
Fiji - Fidji											
Total	+C	...	...	6 724	...	...	...	...	7.8	...	...
French Polynesia - Polynésie française											
Total	C	1 261	1 242	1 359	...	...	4.7	4.6	5.1	...	...
Guam[60]											
Total	C	872	842	894	904	952	5.5	5.3	5.6	5.6	5.9
Kiribati											
Total	U	599	494	...	...	...	...	...	...	...	...
Nauru											
Total	C	69	75	...	...	...	...	7.4	...	...	...
New Caledonia - Nouvelle-Calédonie											
Total	C	1 191	1 320	1 322	...	...	4.8	5.2	5.1	...	...
New Zealand - Nouvelle-Zélande[16]											
Total	+C	28 438	30 082	30 099	29 568	31 063	6.5	6.9	6.8	6.7	6.9
Urban - Urbaine[13]	+C	25 475	27 138	27 050	26 525	27 931	6.8	7.2	7.1	6.9	7.2
Rural - Rurale[13]	+C	2 915	2 920	3 029	3 020	3 099	4.8	4.7	4.9	4.8	5.0
Niue - Nioué[61]											
Total	C	15	9	...	...	...	...	...	...	...	...
Norfolk Island - Île Norfolk[62]											
Total	+C	16	18	20	11	13	...	...	...	...	...
Palau - Palaos											
Total	C	168	173	164	192	...	8.1	8.3	7.8	...	...
Samoa[63]											
Total	+U	127	591	...	...	...	...	...	...	...	...

FOOTNOTES - NOTES

Italics: data from civil registers which are incomplete or of unknown completeness. - Italiques : données incomplètes ou dont le degré d'exactitude n'est pas connu, provenant des registres de l'état civil.

* Provisional. - Données provisoires.

[a] 'Code' indicates the source of data, as follows:
C - Civil registration, estimated over 90% complete
U - Civil registration, estimated less than 90% complete
| - Other source, estimated reliable

+ - Data tabulated by date of registration rather than occurence
... - Information not available

Le 'Code' indique la source des données, comme suit :
C - Registres de l'état civil considérés complets à 90 p. 100 au moins
U - Registres de l'état civil qui ne sont pas considérés complets à 90 p. 100 au moins
| - Autre source, considérée pas douteuses
+ - Données exploitées selon la date de l'enregistrement et non la date de l'événement
... - Information pas disponible

[1] Excluding live-born infants who died before their birth was registered. Data refer to Algerian population only. - Non compris les enfants nés vivants décédés avant l'enregistrement de leur naissance. Les données ne concernent que la population algérienne.
[2] Data are projections presented in Annuaire Statistique 2010. - Les données sont des projections présentées dans l'Annuaire Statistique 2010.
[3] Source: Vital Statistics Report 2012. - Source: Vital Statistics Report 2012.
[4] Data refer to the 12 months preceding the census in September. - Les données se rapportent aux 12 mois précédant le recensement de septembre.
[5] Excludes the islands of St. Brandon and Agalega. - Non compris les îles St. Brandon et Agalega.
[6] Data refer to the 12 months preceding the census in August. - Les données se rapportent aux 12 mois précédant le recensement d'août.
[7] Data refer to the 12 months preceding the census in May. - Les données se rapportent aux 12 mois précédant le recensement de mai.
[8] Based on estimates and projections from 'Agence Nationale de la Statistique et de la Démographie'. - Données fondées sur des estimations et des projections provenant de l'Agence Nationale de la Statistique et de la Démographie.
[9] Data refer to the 12 months preceding the census in October. - Les données se rapportent aux 12 mois précédant le recensement de octobre.
[10] Excluding visitors. - Ne comprend pas les visiteurs.
[11] Excluding non-residents and foreign service personnel and their dependants. - À l'exclusion des non-résidents et du personnel diplomatique et de leurs charges de famille.
[12] Data refer to the twelve months from 1 July of the current year to 30 June of the following year. Including Canadian residents temporarily in the United States, but excluding United States residents temporarily in Canada. - Les données font référence aux douze mois de 1 juillet de l'année actuelle à 30 juin de l'année suivante. Y compris les résidents canadiens se trouvant temporairement aux Etats-Unis, mais ne comprenant pas les résidents des Etats-Unis se trouvant temporairement au Canada.
[13] The total number may include 'Unknown residence', but the categories urban and rural do not. - Le nombre total peut inclure les personnes dont la résidence n'est pas connue, à l'inverse des catégories de population urbaine et rurale.
[14] Excluding live-born infants who died before their birth was registered. - Non compris les enfants nés vivants décédés avant l'enregistrement de leur naissance.
[15] Data have been adjusted for undercoverage of infant deaths and sudden and violent deaths. - Ajusté pour la sous-estimation de la mortalité infantile, du nombre de morts soudaines et de morts violentes.
[16] Data refer to resident population only. - Pour la population résidante seulement.
[17] Source: Population Registry and STAT/CBS estimates. - Source: Estimations du registre de la population/STAT/CBS.
[18] Data refer to the 12 months preceding the census in November. - Données se rapportant aux 12 mois précédant le recensement de novembre.
[19] Including deaths abroad and deaths of unknown place of residence. - Y compris décès à l'étranger et décès dont le lieu de résidence n'est pas connu.
[20] Excludes nomadic Indian tribes. - Non compris les tribus d'Indiens nomades.
[21] Source: Reports of the Ministry of Health. - Source : Rapports du Ministère de la Santé.
[22] Excluding infants born alive of less than 28 weeks' gestation, of less than 1 000 grams in weight and 35 centimeters in length, who die within seven days of birth. - Non compris les enfants nés vivants après moins de 28 semaines de gestation, pesant moins de 1 000 grammes, mesurant moins de 35 centimètres et décédés dans les sept jours qui ont suivi leur naissance.
[23] For statistical purposes, the data for China do not include those for the Hong Kong Special Administrative Region (Hong Kong SAR), Macao Special Administrative Region (Macao SAR) and Taiwan province of China. Data have been estimated on the basis of the annual National Sample Survey on Population Changes. - Pour la présentation des statistiques, les données pour la Chine ne comprennent pas la Région Administrative Spéciale de Hong Kong (Hong Kong RAS), la Région Administrative Spéciale de Macao (Macao RAS) et Taïwan province de Chine. Les données ont été estimées sur la base de l'enquête annuelle "National Sample Survey on Population Changes".

[24] Data refer to government controlled areas. - Les données se rapportent aux zones contrôlées par le Gouvernement.
[25] Data refer to deaths of residents only. - Les données renvoient aux décès de résidents uniquement.
[26] Rates were obtained by the Sample Registration System of India, which is a large demographic survey. Includes data for the Indian-held part of Jammu and Kashmir, the final status of which has not yet been determined. - Les taux ont été obtenus par le Système de l'enregistrement par échantillon de l'Inde qui est une large enquête démographique. Y compris les données pour la partie du Jammu et du Cachemire occupée par l'Inde dont le statut définitif n'a pas encore été déterminé.
[27] Data refer to the Iranian Year which begins on 21 March and ends on 20 March of the following year. - Les données concernent l'année iranienne, qui commence le 21 mars et se termine le 20 mars de l'année suivante.
[28] Includes data for East Jerusalem and Israeli residents in certain other territories under occupation by Israeli military forces since June 1967. Including deaths abroad of Israeli residents who were out of the country for less than a year. - Y compris les données pour Jérusalem-Est et les résidents israéliens dans certains autres territoires occupés depuis 1967 par les forces armées israéliennes. Y compris les décès à l'étranger de résidents israéliens qui ont quitté le pays depuis moins d'un an.
[29] Data refer to Japanese nationals in Japan only. - Les données se raportent aux nationaux japonais au Japon seulement.
[30] Excluding data for Jordanian territory under occupation since June 1967 by Israeli military forces. Excluding foreigners, including registered Palestinian refugees. - Non compris les données pour le territoire jordanien occupé depuis juin 1967 par les forces armées israéliennes. Non compris les étrangers, mais y compris les réfugiés de Palestine enregistrés.
[31] Excluding deaths occurred abroad. - Hormis les décès à l'étranger.
[32] Data refer to the 12 months preceding the census in June. - Les données se rapportent aux 12 mois précédant le recensement de juin.
[33] Data for all population, citizens and foreigners. Data from Births and Deaths Notification System (Ministry of Health and all health care providers). - Les données portent sur la population entière, les citoyens et les étrangers. Les données proviennent du système de notification des naissances et des décès (Ministère de la santé et tous prestataires de soins de santé).
[34] Excluding alien armed forces, civilian aliens employed by armed forces, and foreign diplomatic personnel and their dependants. - Non compris les militaires étrangers, les civils étrangers employés par les forces armées ni le personnel diplomatique étranger et les membres de leur famille les accompagnant.
[35] Projections based on the final results of the 2004 Population and Housing Census. - Projections basées sur les résultats définitifs du recensement de la population et de l'habitat de 2004.
[36] Source: Palestinian Central Bureau of Statistics, Population Register, updated version 05/01/2015. - Source: Bureau central de statistique palestinien, registre de la population, version actualisée jusqu'au 05/01/2015.
[37] Excluding nomad population and Palestinian refugees. Excluding live-born infants who died before their birth was registered. - Non compris la population nomade et les réfugiés de Palestine. Non compris les enfants nés vivants décédés avant l'enregistrement de leur naissance.
[38] The registration of births and deaths is conducted by the Ministry of Health. An estimate of completeness is not provided. - L'enregistrement des naissances et des décès est mené par le Ministère de la Santé. Le degré estimatif de complétude n'est pas fourni.
[39] Including Non-Yemeni deaths. - Y compris les décès non-yéménites.
[40] Including deaths of nationals abroad. - Y compris les décès des nationaux survenus à l'étranger.
[41] Including armed forces stationed outside the country, but excluding alien armed forces stationed in the area. - Y compris les militaires nationaux hors du pays, mais non compris les militaires étrangers en garnison sur le territoire.
[42] Excluding Faeroe Islands and Greenland shown separately, if available. - Non compris les Iles Féroé et le Groenland, qui font l'objet de rubriques distinctes, si disponible.
[43] Excluding Åland Islands. - Non compris les Îles d'Åland.
[44] Including armed forces stationed outside the country. - Y compris les militaires nationaux hors du pays.
[45] The data for urban and rural exclude the nationals outside the country. - Les données relatives à la population urbaine et rurale n'englobent pas les nationaux se trouvant à l'étranger.
[46] Excluding armed forces. - Non compris les militaires en garnison.
[47] The urban and rural categories do not include the data of foreigners, persons of unknown residence and the homeless, whereas the total category includes them. - Les chiffres portant sur la population urbaine et rurale n' incluent pas les données relatives aux étrangers, aux personnes dont la résidence n'est pas connue et aux personnes sans domicile fixe, à l'inverse, le total les inclut.

⁴⁸ Definition of localities was revised in 2011 causing a break with the previous series. - La rupture par rapport aux séries précédentes s'explique par le fait que la définition des localités a été révisée depuis 2011.

⁴⁹ Data refer to events registered within one year of occurrence. - Les données portent sur des événements enregistrés dans l'année pendant laquelle ils sont survenus.

⁵⁰ Including residents outside the country. - Y compris les résidents hors du pays.

⁵¹ Including still births. - Les données comprennent les mortinaissances.

⁵² Including residents outside the country if listed in a Netherlands population register. - Englobe les résidents se trouvant à l'étranger à condition qu'ils soient inscrits sur le registre de population des Pays-Bas.

⁵³ Including residents temporarily outside the country. - Y compris les résidents se trouvant temporairement hors du pays.

⁵⁴ Excluding Transnistria and the municipality of Bender. - Les données ne tiennent pas compte de l'information sur la Transnistria et la municipalité de Bender.

⁵⁵ Excludes data for Kosovo and Metohia. - Sans les données pour le Kosovo et Metohie.

⁵⁶ Data includes deaths resulting from births with weight 500g and more (if weight is unknown - with length 25 centimeters and more, or with gestation during 22 weeks or more). - Y compris les décès de nouveau-nés de 500 grammes ou plus (si le poids est inconnu – de 25 centimètres de long ou plus, ou après une grossesse de 22 semaines ou plus).

⁵⁷ Excluding Channel Islands (Guernsey and Jersey) and Isle of Man, shown separately, if available. - Non compris les îles Anglo-Normandes (Guernesey et Jersey) et l'île de Man, qui font l'objet de rubriques distinctes, si disponible.

⁵⁸ Urban refers to Greater Capital City Statistical Areas, and rural refers to other areas within the state or territory. - Urbain renvoie aux zones statistiques de la capitale métropolitaine, et rural aux autres zones de l'État ou territoire.

⁵⁹ Excluding Niue, shown separately, which is part of Cook Islands, but because of remoteness is administered separately. - Non compris Nioué, qui fait l'objet d'une rubrique distincte et qui fait partie des îles Cook, mais qui, en raison de son éloignement, est administrée séparément.

⁶⁰ Including United States military personnel, their dependants and contract employees. - Y compris les militaires des Etats-Unis, les membres de leur famille les accompagnant et les agents contractuels des Etats-Unis.

⁶¹ Includes deaths occurred in New Zealand but buried in Niue and deaths occurred in Niue but buried elsewhere. - Y compris les personnes décédées en Nouvelle-Zélande qui sont enterrées à Nioué et les personnes décédées à Nioué qui sont enterrées ailleurs.

⁶² Data cover the period from 1 July of the previous year to 30 June of the present year. - Pour la période allant du 1er juillet de l'année précédente au 30 juin de l'année en cours.

⁶³ The coverage of registration is estimated at 70 per cent. - Le degré de complétude de l'enregistrement est évalué à 70 pour cent.

Table 19 - *Demographic Yearbook 2014*

Table 19 presents deaths by age and sex and age-specific death rates by sex for the latest available year between 2005 and 2014.

Description of variables: Age is defined as age at last birthday, that is, the difference between the date of birth and the date of the occurrence of the event, expressed in completed solar years. The age classification used in this table is the following: under 1 year, 1-4 years, 5-year age groups through 95-99 years, and 100 years or over.

Rate computation: Age-specific death rates by sex are the annual number of deaths in each age-sex group per 1 000 population in the same age-sex group. These rates are calculated by the Statistics Division of the United Nations.

Deaths at unknown age and the population of unknown age are excluded from age-specific rate calculations but are part of the death rate for all ages combined.

Death rates for infants under one year of age in this table differ from the infant mortality rates shown elsewhere, because the latter are computed per 1 000 live births rather than per 1 000 population.

The population used in computing the rates is the estimated or the enumerated population by age and sex reported to United Nations Statistics Division. First priority is given to an estimate and second priority to census returns of the year to which the deaths refer.

Rates presented in this table have been limited to those for countries or areas having at least a total of 100 deaths in a given year. Moreover, rates specific for individual sub-categories that are based on 30 or fewer deaths are identified by the symbol "♦".

Reliability of data: Data from civil registers of deaths that are reported as incomplete (less than 90 per cent completeness) or of unknown completeness are considered unreliable and are set in italics rather than in roman type. Table 18 and the technical notes for that table provide more detailed information on the completeness of death registration. For more information about the quality of vital statistics data in general and the information available on the basis of the completeness estimates in particular, see section 4.2 of the Introduction.

Rates are not computed if data from civil registers of deaths are reported as incomplete (less than 90 per cent completeness) or of unknown completeness, and therefore deemed unreliable.

Limitations: Statistics on deaths by age and sex are subject to the same qualifications as are set forth for vital statistics in general and death statistics in particular as discussed in section 4 of the Introduction.

The reliability of the data is an important factor in considering the limitations. In addition, some deaths are tabulated by date of registration and not by date of occurrence; these have been indicated by a plus sign "+". Whenever the lag between the date of occurrence and date of registration is prolonged and, therefore, a large proportion of the death registrations are delayed, death statistics for any given year may be seriously affected. However, delays in the registration of deaths are less common and shorter than in the registration of live births.

International comparability in mortality statistics may also be affected by the exclusion of deaths of infants who were born alive but died before the registration of the birth or within the first 24 hours of life. Statistics of this type are footnoted.

Because these statistics are classified according to age, they are subject to the limitations with respect to accuracy of age reporting similar to those already discussed in connection with section 3.1.3 of the Introduction. The factors influencing the accuracy of reporting may be somewhat dissimilar in vital statistics (because of the differences in the method of taking a census and registering a death) but, in general, the same errors can be observed.

The absence of data in the unknown age group does not necessarily indicate completely accurate reporting and tabulation of the age item. It is often an indication that the unknowns have been eliminated by assigning ages to them before tabulation, or by proportionate distribution after tabulation.

International comparability of statistics on deaths by age is also affected by the use of different methods to determine age at death. If age is obtained from an item that simply requests age at death in completed years or is derived from information on year of birth and death rather than from information on complete date (day, month and year) of birth and death, the number of deaths classified in the under-one-year age group will tend to be reduced and the number of deaths in the next age group will tend to be somewhat increased. A similar bias may affect other age groups but its impact is usually negligible. Information on this factor is given in the footnotes when known.

Limitations of rates: Rates shown in this table are subject to the same limitations that affect the corresponding data and are set forth in the technical notes for table 18. These include differences in the completeness of registration, the treatment of infants who were born alive but died before the registration of their birth or within the first 24 hours of life, the method used to determine age at death and the quality of the reported information relating to age at death. In addition, some rates are based on deaths tabulated by date of registration and not by date of occurrence; these have been indicated with a plus sign "+".

The problem of obtaining precise correspondence between deaths (numerator) and population (denominator) as regards the inclusion or exclusion of armed forces, refugees, displaced persons and other special groups is particularly difficult where age-specific death rates are concerned. Even when deaths and population do correspond conceptually, comparability of the rates may be affected by abnormal conditions such as absence from the country or area of large numbers of young men in the military forces or working abroad as temporary workers. Death rates may appear high in the younger ages, simply because a large section of the able-bodied members of the age group, whose death rates under normal conditions might be less than the average for persons of their age, is not included. Therefore, care should be exercised in using these rates for comparative purposes.

Also, in a number of cases the rates shown here for all ages combined differ from crude death rates shown elsewhere, because in this table they are computed on the population for which an appropriate age-sex distribution was available, while the crude death rates shown elsewhere may utilize a different total population. The population by age and sex might refer to a census date within the year rather than to the mid-point, or it might be more or less inclusive as regards ethnic groups, armed forces and so forth. In a few instances, the difference is attributable to the fact that the rates in this table were computed on the mean population whereas the corresponding rates in other tables were computed on an estimate for 1 July.

Earlier data: Age-specific deaths and death rates by sex have been shown for the latest available year in each issue of the Yearbook since the 1955 issue. For information on specific years covered, the reader should consult the Historical Index.

Tableau 19 – *Annuaire démographique 2014*

Le tableau 19 présente les données disponibles les plus récentes, entre 2005 et 2014, sur les décès et les taux de mortalité selon l'âge et le sexe.

Description des variables : L'âge considéré est l'âge au dernier anniversaire, c'est-à-dire la différence entre la date de naissance et la date du décès, exprimée en années solaires révolues. La classification par âge est la suivante : moins d'un an, 1 à 4 ans, groupes quinquennaux jusqu'à 95-99 ans et 100 ans et plus.

Calcul des taux : les taux de mortalité selon l'âge et le sexe représentent le nombre annuel de décès survenus pour chaque sexe et chaque groupe d'âge pour 1 000 personnes du même groupe. Ces taux ont été calculés par la Division de statistique de l'ONU.

On n'a pas tenu compte des décès à un âge inconnu ni de la population d'âge inconnu, sauf dans les taux de mortalité pour tous les âges combinés.

Il convient de noter que, dans ce tableau, les taux de mortalité des groupes de moins d'un an sont différents des taux de mortalité infantile qui figurent dans d'autres tableaux, ces derniers ayant été établis pour 1 000 naissances vivantes et non pour 1 000 habitants.

Les chiffres de population utilisés pour le calcul des taux proviennent de dénombrements ou de répartitions estimatives de la population selon l'âge et le sexe. On a utilisé de préférence les estimations de la population; à défaut, on s'est contenté des données censitaires se rapportant à l'année des décès.

Les taux présentés dans ce tableau ne se rapportent qu'aux pays ou zones où l'on a enregistré un total d'au moins 100 décès pendant l'année. Les taux relatifs à des sous-catégories, qui sont fondés sur 30 décès ou moins, sont signalés par le signe "♦".

Fiabilité des données : Les données sur les décès issues des registres d'état civil qui sont déclarées incomplètes (degré d'exhaustivité inférieur à 90 p.100) ou dont le degré d'exhaustivité n'est pas connu sont jugées douteuses et apparaissent en italique et non en caractères romains. Le tableau 18 et les notes techniques s'y rapportant présentent des renseignements plus détaillés sur le degré d'exhaustivité de l'enregistrement des décès. Pour plus de précisions sur la qualité des statistiques de l'état civil en général et le degré de complétude en particulier, voir la section 4.2 de l'Introduction.

On a choisi de ne pas faire figurer dans le tableau 19 des taux calculés à partir de données sur les décès issues de registres d'état civil qui sont déclarées incomplètes (degré d'exhaustivité inférieur à 90 p. 100) ou dont le degré d'exhaustivité n'est pas connu.

Insuffisance des données : Les statistiques des décès selon l'âge et le sexe appellent les mêmes réserves que les statistiques de l'état civil en général et les statistiques relatives à la mortalité en particulier (voir la section 4 de l'Introduction).

La fiabilité des données est un facteur important. Il faut également tenir compte du fait que, dans certains cas, les données relatives aux décès sont classées par date d'enregistrement et non par date d'occurrence ; ces cas ont été signalés par le signe "+". Chaque fois que le décalage entre le décès et son enregistrement est grand et qu'une forte proportion des décès fait l'objet d'un enregistrement tardif, les statistiques des décès de l'année peuvent être considérablement faussées. En règle générale, toutefois, les décès sont enregistrés beaucoup plus rapidement que les naissances vivantes, et les retards prolongés sont rares.

Un autre facteur qui nuit à la comparabilité internationale est la pratique de certains pays ou zones qui consiste à ne pas inclure dans les statistiques des décès les enfants nés vivants mais décédés avant l'enregistrement de leur naissance ou dans les 24 heures qui ont suivi la naissance, pratique qui conduit à sous-évaluer le nombre de décès à moins d'un an. Quand pareil facteur a joué, cela a été signalé en note à la fin du tableau.

Étant donné que les statistiques relatives à la mortalité sont classées selon l'âge, elles appellent les mêmes réserves concernant l'exactitude des déclarations d'âge que celles qui ont été formulées à la section 3.1.3 des Introduction. Dans le cas des données d'état civil, les facteurs qui interviennent à cet égard sont parfois un peu différents, du fait que le recensement et l'enregistrement des décès se font par des méthodes différentes, mais, d'une manière générale, les erreurs observées sont les mêmes.

Si aucun nombre ne figure dans la rangée réservée aux âges inconnus, cela ne signifie pas nécessairement que les déclarations d'âge et le classement par âge sont tout à fait exacts. C'est souvent une indication que l'on a attribué un âge aux personnes d'âge inconnu avant l'exploitation des données ou qu'elles ont été réparties proportionnellement entre les différents groupes après cette opération.

Le manque d'uniformité des méthodes suivies pour obtenir l'âge au moment du décès nuit également à la comparabilité internationale des données. Si l'âge est connu, soit d'après la réponse à une simple question sur l'âge du décès en années révolues, soit d'après l'année de la naissance et l'année du décès, et non d'après des renseignements concernant la date exacte (jour, mois et année) de la naissance et du décès, le nombre de décès classés dans la catégorie « moins d'un an » sera entaché d'une erreur par défaut et le chiffre figurant dans la catégorie suivante d'une erreur par excès.

Les données pour les autres groupes d'âge pourront être entachées d'une distorsion analogue, mais les répercussions seront généralement négligeables. Les imperfections, lorsqu'elles étaient connues, ont été signalées en note à la fin du tableau.

Insuffisance des taux : les taux présentés dans le tableau 19 appellent les mêmes réserves que celles formulées à propos des fréquences correspondantes (voir à ce sujet les notes techniques se rapportant au tableau 18). Leurs imperfections tiennent notamment aux différences d'exhaustivité de l'enregistrement, au classement des enfants nés vivants mais décédés avant l'enregistrement de leur naissance ou dans les 24 heures qui ont suivi la naissance, à la méthode utilisée pour obtenir l'âge au moment du décès, et à la qualité des déclarations concernant l'âge au moment du décès. En outre, dans certains cas, les données relatives aux décès sont classées par date d'enregistrement et non par date de l'événement ; ces cas ont été signalés par le signe "+".

S'agissant des taux de mortalité par âge, il est particulièrement difficile d'établir une correspondance exacte entre les décès (numérateur) et la population (dénominateur) du fait de l'inclusion ou de l'exclusion des militaires, des réfugiés, des personnes déplacées et d'autres groupes spéciaux. Il convient d'ajouter que, même lorsque population et décès correspondent, la comparabilité des taux peut être compromise par des conditions anormales telles que l'absence du pays ou de la zone d'un grand nombre de jeunes gens qui sont sous les drapeaux ou qui travaillent à l'étranger comme travailleurs temporaires. Il arrive ainsi que les taux de mortalité paraissent élevés parmi les groupes les plus jeunes simplement parce que l'on en a exclu un grand nombre d'individus en bonne santé pour lesquels le taux de mortalité pourrait être, dans des conditions normales, inférieur à la moyenne observée pour les personnes du même âge. Par conséquent, il importe d'être prudent quand on les utilise ces taux de mortalité dans des comparaisons.

De même, les taux indiqués pour tous les âges combinés diffèrent dans plusieurs cas des taux bruts de mortalité qui figurent dans d'autres tableaux, parce qu'ils se rapportent à une population pour laquelle on disposait d'une répartition par âge et par sexe appropriée, tandis que les taux bruts de mortalité indiqués ailleurs peuvent avoir été calculés sur la base d'un chiffre de population totale différent. Ainsi, il est possible que les chiffres de population par âge et par sexe proviennent d'un recensement effectué dans le courant de l'année et non au milieu de l'année, et qu'ils se différencient des autres chiffres de population en excluant ou en incluant certains groupes ethniques, les militaires, etc. Quelquefois, la différence tient à ce que les taux du tableau 19 ont été calculés sur la base de la population moyenne, alors que les taux correspondants des autres tableaux reposent sur une estimation au 1er juillet.

Données publiées antérieurement : Les éditions de l'*Annuaire démographique* parues depuis 1955 présentent les statistiques les plus récentes dont on disposait à l'époque sur les décès selon l'âge et le sexe et sur les taux de mortalité selon l'âge et le sexe. Pour plus de précisions concernant les années pour lesquelles ces données ont été publiées, se reporter à l'index historique.

19. Deaths by age and sex and age-specific death rates by sex: latest available year, 2005 - 2014
Décès et taux de mortalité selon l'âge et le sexe : dernière année disponible, 2005 - 2014

Continent, country or area, date, code[a] and age (in years) / Continent, pays ou zone, date, code[a] et âge (en années)	Number - Nombre			Rate - Taux		
	Both sexes Les deux sexes	Male Masculin	Female Féminin	Both sexes Les deux sexes	Male Masculin	Female Féminin
AFRICA - AFRIQUE						
Algeria - Algérie[1]						
2014 (U)						
Total	173 781	90 012	83 768	...	...	...
0	22 282	12 176	10 106	...	...	...
1 - 4	3 204	1 674	1 530	...	...	...
5 - 9	1 621	878	743	...	...	...
10 - 14	1 177	667	510	...	...	...
15 - 19	1 718	1 028	690	...	...	...
20 - 24	2 663	1 773	891	...	...	...
25 - 29	3 069	1 932	1 137	...	...	...
30 - 34	3 371	1 996	1 376	...	...	...
35 - 39	3 762	2 074	1 688	...	...	...
40 - 44	4 331	2 256	2 075	...	...	...
45 - 49	5 277	2 726	2 551	...	...	...
50 - 54	6 538	3 606	2 932	...	...	...
55 - 59	7 628	4 281	3 347	...	...	...
60 - 64	10 181	5 768	4 412	...	...	...
65 - 69	10 034	5 504	4 530	...	...	...
70 - 74	13 913	7 508	6 404	...	...	...
75 - 79	18 417	9 211	9 206	...	...	...
80 - 84	21 715	10 480	11 235	...	...	...
85 +	32 879	14 474	18 406	...	...	...
Botswana[2]						
2012 (U)						
Total	12 270	6 352	5 918	...	...	...
0	33	13	20	...	...	...
1 - 4	225	124	101	...	...	...
5 - 9	89	46	43	...	...	...
10 - 14	67	36	31	...	...	...
15 - 19	138	76	62	...	...	...
20 - 24	327	163	164	...	...	...
25 - 29	600	276	324	...	...	...
30 - 34	870	416	454	...	...	...
35 - 39	953	507	446	...	...	...
40 - 44	795	442	353	...	...	...
45 - 49	736	387	349	...	...	...
50 - 54	706	427	279	...	...	...
55 - 59	661	392	269	...	...	...
60 - 64	637	385	252	...	...	...
65 - 69	615	361	254	...	...	...
70 - 74	696	399	297	...	...	...
75 - 79	707	376	331	...	...	...
80 - 84	831	390	441	...	...	...
85 +	1 537	570	967	...	...	...
Unknown - Inconnu	1 047	566	481	..	..	..
Congo[3]						
2009 (+U)						
Total	7 554	...	...	...	...	...
0 - 4	2 150	...	...	...	...	...
5 - 14	2 905	...	...	...	...	...
15 - 59	292	...	...	...	...	...
60 +	2 207	...	...	...	...	...
Egypt - Égypte						
2013 (C)						
Total	511 183	284 212	226 971	6.0	6.6	5.5
0	38 753	20 791	17 962	...	...	...
1 - 4	11 379	6 229	5 150	1.5	1.6	1.4
5 - 9	4 610	2 769	1 841	0.5	0.6	0.4
10 - 14	4 351	2 803	1 548	0.6	0.7	0.4
15 - 19	7 008	5 133	1 875	0.9	1.3	0.5
20 - 24	8 042	5 853	2 189	0.9	1.3	0.5
25 - 29	8 640	5 924	2 716	1.0	1.4	0.7
30 - 34	8 522	5 586	2 936	1.3	1.6	0.9
35 - 39	9 134	5 786	3 348	1.7	2.2	1.3
40 - 44	11 516	7 328	4 188	2.5	3.2	1.8
45 - 49	20 204	13 119	7 085	4.8	6.1	3.4
50 - 54	33 330	21 655	11 675	9.0	11.6	6.3

19. Deaths by age and sex and age-specific death rates by sex: latest available year, 2005 - 2014
Décès et taux de mortalité selon l'âge et le sexe : dernière année disponible, 2005 - 2014 (continued - suite)

Continent, country or area, date, code[a] and age (in years) Continent, pays ou zone, date, code[a] et âge (en annèes)	Number - Nombre			Rate - Taux		
	Both sexes Les deux sexes	Male Masculin	Female Féminin	Both sexes Les deux sexes	Male Masculin	Female Féminin

AFRICA - AFRIQUE

Egypt - Égypte
2013 (C)

55 - 59	45 099	28 711	16 388	14.7	18.7	10.8
60 - 64	56 319	33 854	22 465	24.7	29.8	19.6
65 - 69	54 246	30 162	24 084	34.0	38.2	29.8
70 - 74	52 817	27 426	25 391	50.5	53.2	47.8
75 - 79	51 372	25 119	26 253	85.5	85.3	85.6
80 +	85 841	35 964	49 877	175.9	148.7	202.7
80 - 84	44 191	19 848	24 343	...	...	...
85 +	41 650	16 116	25 534	...	...	...

Ghana[4]
2010 (|)

Total	163 534	84 214	79 320	6.6	7.0	6.3
0	28 068	15 807	12 261	38.4	42.7	34.0
1 - 4	17 868	9 424	8 444	6.7	6.9	6.4
5 - 9	6 275	3 437	2 838	2.0	2.2	1.8
10 - 14	3 641	1 587	2 054	1.2	1.1	1.4
15 - 19	4 399	1 752	2 647	1.7	1.3	2.0
20 - 24	5 467	2 117	3 350	2.4	1.9	2.7
25 - 29	6 325	2 516	3 809	3.1	2.7	3.4
30 - 34	8 218	3 397	4 821	4.9	4.3	5.4
35 - 39	8 215	3 579	4 636	5.8	5.3	6.2
40 - 44	8 855	4 141	4 714	7.5	7.2	7.7
45 - 49	7 573	3 715	3 858	8.1	8.2	8.0
50 - 54	8 577	4 376	4 201	10.3	11.1	9.6
55 - 59	5 656	3 564	2 092	10.8	13.8	7.9
60 - 64	7 159	4 418	2 741	15.0	19.5	11.0
65 - 69	5 670	3 360	2 310	19.3	24.7	14.7
70 - 74	8 443	5 096	3 347	24.0	34.1	16.6
75 - 79	6 197	3 599	2 598	30.1	40.4	22.2
80 - 84	6 543	3 346	3 197	41.1	53.7	33.1
85 - 89	4 436	2 166	2 270	53.4	65.8	45.3
90 - 94	3 650	1 797	1 853	71.5	94.6	57.8
95 +	2 299	1 020	1 279	99.3	116.6	88.9

Kenya[5]
2011 (U)

Total	174 487	96 026	78 461	...	...	...
0	23 167	12 119	11 048	...	...	...
1 - 4	12 129	6 530	5 599	...	...	...
5 - 14	9 145	4 949	4 196	...	...	...
15 - 24	11 961	5 931	6 030	...	...	...
25 - 34	21 054	11 329	9 725	...	...	...
35 - 44	21 605	12 382	9 223	...	...	...
45 - 54	18 606	11 124	7 482	...	...	...
55 - 74	29 686	17 525	12 161	...	...	...
75 +	27 134	14 137	12 997	...	...	...

Lesotho
2010 (+U)

Total	7 864	4 154	3 710	...	...	...
0 - 4	271	147	124	...	...	...
5 - 9	69	34	35	...	...	...
10 - 14	67	43	24	...	...	...
15 - 19	112	50	62	...	...	...
20 - 24	237	106	131	...	...	...
25 - 29	477	199	278	...	...	...
30 - 34	727	347	380	...	...	...
35 - 39	732	383	349	...	...	...
40 - 44	675	376	299	...	...	...
45 - 49	583	337	246	...	...	...
50 - 54	627	406	221	...	...	...
55 - 59	550	363	187	...	...	...
60 - 64	484	302	182	...	...	...
65 - 69	388	234	154	...	...	...
70 - 74	502	256	246	...	...	...
75 - 79	481	227	254	...	...	...
80 - 84	384	153	231	...	...	...

19. Deaths by age and sex and age-specific death rates by sex: latest available year, 2005 - 2014
Décès et taux de mortalité selon l'âge et le sexe : dernière année disponible, 2005 - 2014 (continued - suite)

Continent, country or area, date, code[a] and age (in years) / Continent, pays ou zone, date, code[a] et âge (en années)	Number - Nombre			Rate - Taux		
	Both sexes Les deux sexes	Male Masculin	Female Féminin	Both sexes Les deux sexes	Male Masculin	Female Féminin
AFRICA - AFRIQUE						
Lesotho						
2010 (+U)						
85 +	441	158	283	...	...	...
Unknown - Inconnu	57	33	24	..	..	..
Malawi[6]						
2008 (|)						
Total	135 865	70 991	64 874	10.0	10.6	9.4
0 - 4	56 721	29 832	26 889	20.9	21.9	20.0
0	30 508	16 606	13 902	50.9	54.9	46.9
1 - 4	26 213	13 226	12 987	12.4	12.5	12.4
5 - 9	6 413	3 350	3 063	2.8	2.9	2.7
10 - 14	5 333	3 071	2 262	3.5	4.1	2.9
15 - 19	4 266	1 863	2 403	3.1	2.7	3.4
20 - 24	7 188	3 038	4 150	6.1	5.1	7.0
25 - 29	7 903	3 405	4 498	7.6	6.8	8.3
30 - 34	9 042	4 280	4 762	9.7	10.4	9.2
35 - 39	7 200	3 813	3 387	9.7	10.3	9.0
40 - 44	6 004	3 410	2 594	10.8	12.2	9.4
45 - 49	4 275	2 436	1 839	9.7	11.3	8.2
50 - 54	3 414	2 092	1 322	10.7	13.3	8.2
55 +	18 106	10 401	7 705	34.1	40.9	27.9
55 - 59	2 447	1 523	924	...	...	...
60 - 64	2 978	1 827	1 151	...	...	...
65 - 69	2 314	1 372	942	...	...	...
70 - 74	2 871	1 665	1 206	...	...	...
75 - 79	2 149	1 254	895	...	...	...
80 - 84	2 151	1 138	1 013	...	...	...
85 +	3 196	1 622	1 574	...	...	...
Mali[7]						
2009 (|)						
Total	62 371	34 387	27 984	4.3	4.8	3.8
0 - 4	29 336	16 098	13 238	11.2	12.1	10.2
5 - 9	3 486	1 933	1 553	1.5	1.6	1.3
10 - 14	1 598	914	684	0.9	1.0	0.8
15 - 19	1 638	777	861	1.1	1.1	1.1
20 - 24	1 570	712	858	1.4	1.3	1.4
25 - 29	1 618	752	866	1.6	1.7	1.6
30 - 34	1 729	839	890	2.1	2.2	2.1
35 - 39	1 604	798	806	2.5	2.5	2.5
40 - 44	1 547	858	689	2.8	3.2	2.5
45 - 49	1 462	890	572	3.3	3.9	2.6
50 - 54	1 527	884	643	4.0	4.7	3.3
55 - 59	1 544	954	590	5.5	6.4	4.4
60 - 64	1 960	1 201	759	7.8	9.4	6.1
65 - 69	1 958	1 152	806	11.8	13.0	10.5
70 - 74	2 093	1 198	895	15.7	17.8	13.5
75 - 79	1 891	1 113	778	24.5	27.2	21.5
80 +	3 372	1 836	1 536	39.4	43.7	35.2
Unknown - Inconnu	2 438	1 478	960	..	..	..
Mauritius - Maurice[8]						
2014 (+C)						
Total	9 682	5 329	4 353	7.7	8.5	6.8
0	194	96	98	14.3	14.0	14.7
1 - 4	20	11	9	♦0.3	♦0.4	♦0.3
5 - 9	15	10	5	♦0.2	♦0.2	♦0.1
10 - 14	26	16	10	♦0.3	♦0.3	♦0.2
15 - 19	46	30	16	0.5	♦0.6	♦0.3
20 - 24	80	56	24	0.8	1.1	♦0.5
25 - 29	107	76	31	1.2	1.7	0.7
30 - 34	164	111	53	1.7	2.2	1.1
35 - 39	214	162	52	2.2	3.3	1.1
40 - 44	271	176	95	3.2	4.1	2.3
45 - 49	464	309	155	5.0	6.6	3.3
50 - 54	628	427	201	6.8	9.3	4.3
55 - 59	794	515	279	10.0	13.3	6.9
60 - 64	1 018	640	378	15.2	20.0	10.8
65 - 69	1 046	604	442	24.1	30.8	18.6

19. Deaths by age and sex and age-specific death rates by sex: latest available year, 2005 - 2014
Décès et taux de mortalité selon l'âge et le sexe : dernière année disponible, 2005 - 2014 (continued - suite)

Continent, country or area, date, code[a] and age (in years) / Continent, pays ou zone, date, code[a] et âge (en années)	Number - Nombre			Rate - Taux		
	Both sexes Les deux sexes	Male Masculin	Female Féminin	Both sexes Les deux sexes	Male Masculin	Female Féminin
AFRICA - AFRIQUE						
Mauritius - Maurice[8]						
2014 (+C)						
70 - 74	964	548	416	34.9	46.0	26.5
75 - 79	1 069	552	517	54.2	68.9	44.1
80 - 84	971	439	532	83.0	101.1	72.3
85 +	1 591	551	1 040	160.7	176.8	153.3
85 - 89	904	357	547	...	...	...
90 - 94	495	150	345	...	...	...
95 - 99	151	37	114	...	...	...
100 +	41	7	34	...	...	...
Morocco - Maroc						
2007 (U)						
Total	105 222	66 522	38 700	...	...	...
0	5 140	2 823	2 317	...	...	...
1 - 4	2 320	1 266	1 054	...	...	...
5 - 9	1 075	591	484	...	...	...
10 - 14	859	533	326	...	...	...
15 - 19	1 575	1 024	551	...	...	...
20 - 24	2 204	1 442	762	...	...	...
25 - 29	2 503	1 570	933	...	...	...
30 - 34	2 705	1 660	1 045	...	...	...
35 - 39	2 948	1 767	1 181	...	...	...
40 - 44	3 400	2 052	1 348	...	...	...
45 - 49	4 547	2 766	1 781	...	...	...
50 - 54	5 616	3 672	1 944	...	...	...
55 - 59	6 132	4 046	2 086	...	...	...
60 - 64	7 193	4 626	2 567	...	...	...
65 - 69	10 331	6 494	3 837	...	...	...
70 - 74	12 441	7 990	4 451	...	...	...
75 - 79	13 183	8 491	4 692	...	...	...
80 +	20 051	13 159	6 892	...	...	...
Unknown - Inconnu	999	550	449	..	..	..
Namibia - Namibie[9]						
2011 (I)						
Total	22 668	12 491	10 177	10.7	12.2	9.3
0	2 685	1 411	1 274	41.9	44.1	39.6
1 - 4	1 346	719	627	6.1	6.5	5.7
5 - 9	447	255	192	1.9	2.1	1.6
10 - 14	384	212	172	1.6	1.7	1.4
15 - 19	577	298	279	2.4	2.5	2.3
20 - 24	918	537	381	4.3	5.1	3.5
25 - 29	1 233	645	588	7.0	7.4	6.5
30 - 34	1 591	890	701	10.7	12.1	9.2
35 - 39	1 487	873	614	11.9	14.3	9.6
40 - 44	1 323	807	516	13.5	17.2	10.1
45 - 49	1 140	698	442	14.2	18.6	10.3
50 - 54	917	535	382	14.9	19.5	11.2
55 - 59	891	562	329	18.6	26.1	12.5
60 - 64	994	584	410	24.4	31.7	18.3
65 - 69	766	424	342	24.6	32.3	19.0
70 - 74	739	424	315	30.7	41.3	22.8
75 - 79	682	382	300	39.5	54.5	29.3
80 - 84	792	402	390	55.3	76.2	43.1
85 - 89	638	282	356	68.6	90.2	57.6
90 - 94	549	234	315	80.6	98.4	71.1
95 +	1 003	403	600	178.7	228.6	155.8
Unknown - Inconnu	1 566	914	652	..	..	..
Niger						
2011 (+U)						
Total	6 761	...	...	...	...	...
0	236	...	...	...	...	...
1 - 4	329	...	...	...	...	...
5 - 9	120	...	...	...	...	...
10 - 14	81	...	...	...	...	...
15 - 19	147	...	...	...	...	...
20 - 24	242	...	...	...	...	...
25 - 29	319	...	...	...	...	...

Continent, country or area, date, codea and age (in years) Continent, pays ou zone, date, codea et âge (en années)	Number - Nombre			Rate - Taux		
	Both sexes Les deux sexes	Male Masculin	Female Féminin	Both sexes Les deux sexes	Male Masculin	Female Féminin
AFRICA - AFRIQUE						
Niger						
2011 (+U)						
30 - 34	378	...	...	...	...	...
35 - 39	414	...	...	...	...	...
40 - 44	470	...	...	...	...	...
45 - 49	485	...	...	...	...	...
50 - 54	495	...	...	...	...	...
55 - 59	443	...	...	...	...	...
60 - 64	541	...	...	...	...	...
65 - 69	443	...	...	...	...	...
70 - 74	517	...	...	...	...	...
75 - 79	347	...	...	...	...	...
80 - 84	298	...	...	...	...	...
85 - 89	112	...	...	...	...	...
90 - 94	90	...	...	...	...	...
95 - 99	26	...	...	...	...	...
100 +	53	...	...	...	...	...
Unknown - Inconnu	175	...	...	..	..	..
Republic of South Sudan - République de Soudan du Sud[10]						
2008 (|)						
Total	165 898	88 797	77 101	20.1	20.7	19.4
0	29 217	12 384	16 833	126.4	101.6	154.1
1 - 4	55 674	29 144	26 530	51.9	51.4	52.5
5 - 9	22 571	12 351	10 220	17.4	17.9	16.8
10 - 14	12 487	6 785	5 702	11.8	11.9	11.7
15 - 19	11 665	6 297	5 368	13.1	13.6	12.6
20 - 24	9 256	5 556	3 700	12.5	15.4	9.8
25 - 29	6 022	4 063	1 959	8.6	12.1	5.4
30 - 34	4 496	2 634	1 862	8.4	10.2	6.7
35 - 39	3 046	2 237	809	6.4	9.4	3.4
40 - 44	2 627	1 605	1 022	7.7	9.3	6.1
45 - 49	1 656	993	663	6.0	6.6	5.3
50 - 54	1 513	977	536	7.7	9.3	5.8
55 - 59	946	618	328	7.8	9.1	6.1
60 - 64	1 094	668	426	9.5	10.4	8.3
65 - 69	908	528	380	12.4	12.7	12.0
70 - 74	1 036	766	270	17.5	22.0	11.0
75 - 79	487	415	72	16.8	23.8	6.3
80 - 84	493	277	216	20.1	19.4	21.2
85 - 89	355	229	126	32.3	34.0	29.6
90 - 94	177	110	67	24.0	24.6	23.2
95 +	172	160	12	25.1	41.7	♦4.0
Reunion - Réunion						
2007 (C)						
Total	4 045	2 247	1 798	5.1	5.9	4.4
0 - 4	114	58	56	1.7	1.7	1.7
0	99	49	50	...	...	...
1 - 4	15	9	6	...	...	...
5 - 9	6	6	-	♦0.1	♦0.2	-
10 - 14	10	7	3	♦0.1	♦0.2	♦0.1
15 - 19	32	25	7	0.5	♦0.7	♦0.2
20 - 24	44	35	9	0.8	1.3	♦0.3
25 - 29	39	27	12	0.8	♦1.1	♦0.4
30 - 34	55	37	18	1.0	1.4	♦0.6
35 - 39	97	68	29	1.5	2.3	♦0.9
40 - 44	158	106	52	2.4	3.3	1.5
45 - 49	211	150	61	4.0	5.9	2.3
50 - 54	236	183	53	5.1	8.2	2.2
55 - 59	266	188	78	7.5	10.7	4.4
60 - 64	287	176	111	10.8	14.1	7.9
65 - 69	375	246	129	17.4	24.8	11.1
70 - 74	427	250	177	25.9	34.7	19.1
75 - 79	448	231	217	39.5	50.3	32.2
80 - 84	496	222	274	65.3	78.9	57.3
85 - 89	393	149	244	106.6	140.6	92.9
90 - 94	233	66	167	166.1	182.8	160.3

19. Deaths by age and sex and age-specific death rates by sex: latest available year, 2005 - 2014
Décès et taux de mortalité selon l'âge et le sexe : dernière année disponible, 2005 - 2014 (continued - suite)

Continent, country or area, date, code[a] and age (in years) Continent, pays ou zone, date, code[a] et âge (en années)	Number - Nombre			Rate - Taux		
	Both sexes Les deux sexes	Male Masculin	Female Féminin	Both sexes Les deux sexes	Male Masculin	Female Féminin
AFRICA - AFRIQUE						
Reunion - Réunion						
2007 (C)						
95 + ...	118	17	101	308.9	♦369.6	300.6
95 - 99	96	15	81	...	...	...
100 + ...	22	2	20	...	...	...
Saint Helena ex. dep. - Sainte-Hélène sans dép.						
2014 (C)						
Total..............	61	36	25	...	...	...
0	1	-	1	...	...	...
1 - 4	-	-	-	...	...	...
5 - 9	-	-	-	...	...	...
10 - 14	-	-	-	...	...	...
15 - 19	-	-	-	...	...	...
20 - 24	-	-	-	...	...	...
25 - 29	1	1	-	...	...	...
30 - 34	-	-	-	...	...	...
35 - 39	-	-	-	...	...	...
40 - 44	-	-	-	...	...	...
45 - 49	1	1	-	...	...	...
50 - 54	-	-	-	...	...	...
55 - 59	4	2	2	...	...	...
60 - 64	7	5	2	...	...	...
65 - 69	7	5	2	...	...	...
70 - 74	9	6	3	...	...	...
75 - 79	7	6	1	...	...	...
80 - 84	7	4	3	...	...	...
85 - 89	8	4	4	...	...	...
90 - 94	4	1	3	...	...	...
95 - 99	5	1	4	...	...	...
100 + ...	-	-	-	...	...	...
Sao Tome and Principe - Sao Tomé-et-Principe[11]						
2012 (I)						
Total..............	1 287	735	552	7.2	8.3	6.1
0	132	82	50	...	...	...
1 - 4	69	41	29	...	...	...
5 - 9	18	5	13	♦0.7	♦0.4	♦1.0
10 - 14	29	20	10	♦1.4	♦1.9	♦0.9
15 - 19	29	23	6	♦1.6	♦2.5	♦0.7
20 - 24	54	36	18	3.4	4.5	♦2.3
25 - 29	39	26	13	2.6	♦3.5	♦1.7
30 - 34	41	31	10	3.3	5.0	♦1.6
35 - 39	61	41	20	6.3	8.4	♦4.1
40 - 44	51	34	17	6.5	8.6	♦4.4
45 - 49	49	24	25	7.8	♦7.9	♦7.7
50 - 54	77	44	33	14.4	16.9	12.0
55 - 59	52	21	31	13.6	♦11.6	15.4
60 - 64	86	59	27	32.3	44.1	♦20.4
65 - 69	60	33	27	31.2	35.9	♦26.8
70 - 74	102	60	42	54.3	70.6	40.9
75 - 79	103	51	52	73.0	83.7	64.8
80 + ...	234	104	130	170.1	198.1	152.8
Seychelles						
2014 (+C)						
Total..............	725	425	300	7.9	9.4	6.5
0	17	12	5	♦11.2	♦15.3	♦6.8
1 - 4	5	3	2	♦0.8	♦1.0	♦0.7
5 - 9	-	-	-	-	-	-
10 - 14	2	1	1	♦0.3	♦0.3	♦0.3
15 - 19	5	5	-	♦0.9	♦1.7	-
20 - 24	12	7	5	♦1.9	♦2.1	♦1.6
25 - 29	15	8	7	♦2.1	♦2.1	♦2.1
30 - 34	15	12	3	♦1.9	♦3.0	♦0.7
35 - 39	22	13	9	♦3.1	♦3.8	♦2.4
40 - 44	28	22	6	♦3.7	♦5.5	♦1.7
45 - 49	40	29	11	6.1	♦9.5	♦3.1
50 - 54	47	34	13	6.5	9.7	♦3.5
55 - 59	58	42	16	11.9	16.8	♦6.8

Continent, country or area, date, code[a] and age (in years) Continent, pays ou zone, date, code[a] et âge (en années)	Number - Nombre			Rate - Taux		
	Both sexes Les deux sexes	Male Masculin	Female Féminin	Both sexes Les deux sexes	Male Masculin	Female Féminin
AFRICA - AFRIQUE						
Seychelles						
2014 (+C)						
60 - 64	58	38	20	16.2	22.1	♦10.8
65 - 69	55	40	15	22.0	33.1	♦11.6
70 - 74	61	32	29	33.7	39.4	♦29.0
75 - 79	75	45	30	55.3	91.3	♦34.8
80 - 84	71	35	36	73.0	118.2	53.3
85 - 89	70	28	42	143.7	♦225.8	115.7
90 - 94	44	14	30	240.4	♦341.5	♦211.3
95 - 99	19	3	16	♦380.0	♦600.0	♦355.6
100 +	6	2	4	♦750.0	♦2000.0	♦571.4
South Africa - Afrique du Sud[5]						
2011 (U)						
Total	505 803	260 569[12]	243 237[12]	...	...	...
0	27 981	14 583[12]	12 914[12]	...	...	...
1 - 4	9 927	5 218[12]	4 663[12]	...	...	...
5 - 9	4 290	2 299[12]	1 984[12]	...	...	...
10 - 14	3 847	2 065[12]	1 777[12]	...	...	...
15 - 19	7 577	4 055[12]	3 497[12]	...	...	...
20 - 24	17 283	8 434[12]	8 769[12]	...	...	...
25 - 29	30 679	14 686[12]	15 851[12]	...	...	...
30 - 34	36 895	19 259[12]	17 502[12]	...	...	...
35 - 39	39 355	22 069[12]	17 182[12]	...	...	...
40 - 44	35 913	20 566[12]	15 251[12]	...	...	...
45 - 49	35 356	20 609[12]	14 687[12]	...	...	...
50 - 54	34 949	20 762[12]	14 120[12]	...	...	...
55 - 59	34 119	20 043[12]	14 029[12]	...	...	...
60 - 64	34 849	20 082[12]	14 710[12]	...	...	...
65 - 69	30 815	16 727[12]	14 064[12]	...	...	...
70 - 74	32 870	16 263[12]	16 586[12]	...	...	...
75 - 79	27 817	11 542[12]	16 257[12]	...	...	...
80 - 84	26 361	9 834[12]	16 513[12]	...	...	...
85 - 89	16 928	5 895[12]	11 020[12]	...	...	...
90 - 94	11 378	3 286[12]	8 089[12]	...	...	...
95 - 99	3 335	836[12]	2 495[12]	...	...	...
100 +	878	203	675	...	...	...
Unknown - Inconnu	2 401	1 253[12]	602[12]	..	..	..
Swaziland[11]						
2007 (I)						
Total	18 367	8 738	9 629	21.8	21.5	22.0
0 - 4	4 843	2 131	2 712	44.1	38.9	49.4
0	3 613	1 555	2 058	...	...	...
1 - 4	1 230	576	654	...	...	...
5 - 9	408	198	210	3.6	3.5	3.8
10 - 14	302	165	137	2.7	3.0	2.4
15 - 19	431	174	257	4.3	3.5	5.1
20 - 24	1 145	353	792	13.0	8.3	17.6
25 - 29	1 773	707	1 066	25.2	20.9	29.2
30 - 34	1 792	839	953	34.3	32.8	35.7
35 - 39	1 586	828	758	36.3	40.0	32.9
40 - 44	1 145	652	493	33.7	44.0	25.7
45 - 49	865	502	363	29.6	39.3	22.1
50 - 54	752	453	299	32.9	43.5	24.0
55 - 59	557	364	193	30.8	43.7	19.8
60 - 64	618	342	276	37.0	51.0	27.6
65 - 69	436	238	198	32.9	43.1	25.6
70 - 74	392	214	178	48.0	66.7	35.9
75 - 79	283	158	125	45.4	68.0	31.9
80 +	612	261	351	95.3	122.1	82.0
Unknown - Inconnu	427	159	268	..	..	..
Zambia - Zambie[13]						
2010 (I)						
Total	164 385	87 693	76 692	12.6	13.6	11.6
0	35 103	18 953	16 150	79.7	86.1	73.2
1 - 4	28 943	15 297	13 646	16.0	17.0	15.0
5 - 9	8 405	4 519	3 886	4.4	4.7	4.0

19. Deaths by age and sex and age-specific death rates by sex: latest available year, 2005 - 2014
Décès et taux de mortalité selon l'âge et le sexe : dernière année disponible, 2005 - 2014 (continued - suite)

Continent, country or area, date, code[a] and age (in years) Continent, pays ou zone, date, code[a] et âge (en annèes)	Number - Nombre			Rate - Taux		
	Both sexes Les deux sexes	Male Masculin	Female Féminin	Both sexes Les deux sexes	Male Masculin	Female Féminin
AFRICA - AFRIQUE						
Zambia - Zambie[13]						
2010 (|)						
10 - 14	4 836	2 550	2 286	2.7	2.9	2.6
15 - 19	5 856	2 821	3 035	3.8	3.8	3.9
20 - 24	7 967	3 746	4 221	6.7	6.8	6.6
25 - 29	10 471	5 112	5 359	9.9	10.3	9.6
30 - 34	11 305	5 986	5 319	13.5	14.1	12.8
35 - 39	9 972	5 698	4 274	14.6	16.0	13.1
40 - 44	7 336	4 334	3 002	15.5	17.3	13.5
45 - 49	6 021	3 603	2 418	16.0	19.1	12.9
50 - 54	4 770	2 687	2 083	16.7	19.4	14.3
55 - 59	3 546	2 056	1 490	18.3	21.3	15.3
60 - 64	3 929	2 146	1 783	23.3	27.4	19.8
65 - 69	3 363	1 732	1 631	27.4	30.5	24.7
70 - 74	4 084	2 138	1 946	43.8	48.7	39.4
75 +	8 478	4 315	4 163	65.1	67.1	63.2
AMERICA, NORTH - AMÉRIQUE DU NORD						
Anguilla[14]						
2013 (+C)						
Total	72	43	29	...	...	...
0	3	2	1	...	...	...
1 - 4	-	-	-	...	...	...
5 - 9	-	-	-	...	...	...
10 - 14	-	-	-	...	...	...
15 - 19	2	2	-	...	...	...
20 - 24	1	1	-	...	...	...
25 - 29	2	2	-	...	...	...
30 - 34	-	-	-	...	...	...
35 - 39	2	1	1	...	...	...
40 - 44	-	-	-	...	...	...
45 - 49	1	1	-	...	...	...
50 - 54	5	3	2	...	...	...
55 - 59	5	3	2	...	...	...
60 - 64	3	3	-	...	...	...
65 - 69	7	3	4	...	...	...
70 - 74	4	3	1	...	...	...
75 - 79	9	5	4	...	...	...
80 - 84	8	5	3	...	...	...
85 +	20	9	11	...	...	...
Aruba						
2014 (C)						
Total	643	334	309	6.0	6.5	5.4
0	5	4	1	♦3.6	♦5.7	♦1.5
1 - 4	3	2	1	♦0.6	♦0.8	♦0.4
5 - 9	-	-	-	-	-	-
10 - 14	2	-	2	♦0.3	-	♦0.6
15 - 19	4	2	2	♦0.5	♦0.5	♦0.5
20 - 24	4	3	1	♦0.6	♦0.9	♦0.3
25 - 29	5	3	2	♦0.8	♦1.0	♦0.7
30 - 34	7	6	1	♦1.1	♦2.0	♦0.3
35 - 39	5	2	3	♦0.7	♦0.6	♦0.8
40 - 44	8	5	3	♦1.0	♦1.3	♦0.7
45 - 49	9	8	1	♦1.0	♦2.0	♦0.2
50 - 54	31	18	13	3.3	♦4.1	♦2.6
55 - 59	43	30	13	5.4	♦8.2	♦3.0
60 - 64	58	34	24	9.1	11.5	♦7.1
65 - 69	70	43	27	15.1	21.0	♦10.5
70 - 74	73	46	27	22.5	31.9	♦15.0
75 - 79	106	49	57	44.8	51.3	40.3
80 - 84	95	55	40	65.6	98.8	44.8
85 - 89	65	26	39	100.4	♦116.3	92.1
90 - 94	42	6	36	178.3	♦87.3	215.8
95 +	22	4	18	♦249.8	♦226.8	♦255.6

Continent, country or area, date, code[a] and age (in years) / Continent, pays ou zone, date, code[a] et âge (en années)	Number - Nombre			Rate - Taux		
	Both sexes Les deux sexes	Male Masculin	Female Féminin	Both sexes Les deux sexes	Male Masculin	Female Féminin
AMERICA, NORTH - AMÉRIQUE DU NORD						
Bahamas						
2012 (+C)						
Total	1 995	1 094	901	5.5	6.2	4.9
0	57	26	31	8.6	♦7.6	9.7
1 - 4	18	10	8	♦0.7	♦0.8	♦0.7
5 - 9	9	5	4	♦0.3	♦0.3	♦0.3
10 - 14	8	6	2	♦0.3	♦0.4	♦0.1
15 - 19	27	17	10	♦0.9	♦1.1	♦0.6
20 - 24	57	42	15	1.9	2.9	♦1.0
25 - 29	49	42	7	1.8	3.2	♦0.5
30 - 34	72	52	20	2.8	4.1	♦1.5
35 - 39	84	47	37	3.1	3.5	2.6
40 - 44	100	58	42	3.6	4.4	2.9
45 - 49	130	72	58	4.9	5.6	4.2
50 - 54	159	84	75	6.8	7.5	6.2
55 - 59	147	94	53	8.5	11.4	5.9
60 - 64	149	83	66	12.2	14.5	10.2
65 - 69	147	87	60	16.1	21.0	12.1
70 - 74	183	96	87	27.6	32.9	23.5
75 - 79	176	93	83	43.0	54.4	34.9
80 - 84	170	81	89	98.0	154.6	74.0
85 - 89	116	61	55	143.7	279.8	91.5
90 +	137	38	99	259.0	351.9	222.0
90 - 94	90	30	60	...	...	...
95 - 99	36	6	30	...	...	...
100 +	11	2	9	...	...	...
Barbados - Barbade						
2007 (+C)						
Total	2 195	1 143	1 052	...	...	...
0	31	18	13	...	...	...
1 - 4	8	5	3	...	...	...
5 - 9	5	3	2	...	...	...
10 - 14	8	6	2	...	...	...
15 - 19	17	13	4	...	...	...
20 - 24	10	4	6	...	...	...
25 - 29	15	14	1	...	...	...
30 - 34	30	16	14	...	...	...
35 - 39	38	23	15	...	...	...
40 - 44	45	26	19	...	...	...
45 - 49	58	28	30	...	...	...
50 - 54	76	46	30	...	...	...
55 - 59	90	54	36	...	...	...
60 - 64	113	63	50	...	...	...
65 - 69	142	83	59	...	...	...
70 - 74	182	105	77	...	...	...
75 - 79	309	160	149	...	...	...
80 - 84	281	152	129	...	...	...
85 - 89	339	139	200	...	...	...
90 - 94	199	59	140	...	...	...
95 +	97	30	67	...	...	...
Unknown - Inconnu	102	96	6	..	..	..
Bermuda - Bermudes[15]						
2013 (C)						
Total	471	251	220	7.6	8.5	6.8
0	1	1	-	♦1.6	♦3.2	-
1 - 4	2	1	1	♦0.7	♦0.7	♦0.7
5 - 9	1	1	-	♦0.3	♦0.6	-
10 - 14	-	-	-	-	-	-
15 - 19	1	1	-	♦0.3	♦0.7	-
20 - 24	4	4	-	♦1.3	♦2.8	-
25 - 29	3	3	-	♦0.9	♦1.9	-
30 - 34	6	5	1	♦1.4	♦2.4	♦0.5
35 - 39	3	2	1	♦0.7	♦0.9	♦0.5
40 - 44	11	8	3	♦2.3	♦3.3	♦1.2
45 - 49	10	9	1	♦1.9	♦3.4	♦0.4
50 - 54	21	13	8	♦3.8	♦5.0	♦2.8
55 - 59	25	20	5	♦5.1	♦8.8	♦1.9

19. Deaths by age and sex and age-specific death rates by sex: latest available year, 2005 - 2014
Décès et taux de mortalité selon l'âge et le sexe : dernière année disponible, 2005 - 2014 (continued - suite)

Continent, country or area, date, code[a] and age (in years) Continent, pays ou zone, date, code[a] et âge (en années)	Number - Nombre			Rate - Taux		
	Both sexes Les deux sexes	Male Masculin	Female Féminin	Both sexes Les deux sexes	Male Masculin	Female Féminin

AMERICA, NORTH - AMÉRIQUE DU NORD

Bermuda - Bermudes[15]
2013 (C)

60 - 64	32	22	10	8.2	♦12.0	♦4.9
65 - 69	33	15	18	10.2	♦10.1	♦10.4
70 - 74	39	21	18	16.6	♦19.9	♦13.9
75 - 79	60	30	30	32.8	♦38.1	♦28.7
80 - 84	70	34	36	54.9	69.4	45.8
85 +	149	61	88	156.2	216.3	131.0
85 - 89	76	37	39	...	...	...
90 - 94	48	19	29	...	...	...
95 - 99	20	5	15	...	...	...
100 +	5	-	5	...	...	...

Canada[16]
2008 (C)

Total	238 617	120 426	118 191	7.2	7.3	7.0
0	1 911	1 057	854	5.3	5.7	4.8
1 - 4	265	153	112	0.2	0.2	0.2
5 - 9	201	117	84	0.1	0.1	0.1
10 - 14	246	160	86	0.1	0.2	0.1
15 - 19	894	607	287	0.4	0.5	0.3
20 - 24	1 264	935	329	0.6	0.8	0.3
25 - 29	1 282	878	404	0.6	0.8	0.4
30 - 34	1 376	911	465	0.6	0.8	0.4
35 - 39	2 064	1 290	774	0.9	1.1	0.7
40 - 44	3 392	2 063	1 329	1.3	1.6	1.0
45 - 49	5 803	3 453	2 350	2.1	2.5	1.7
50 - 54	8 635	5 300	3 335	3.4	4.2	2.6
55 - 59	11 334	6 904	4 430	5.3	6.5	4.1
60 - 64	14 606	8 946	5 660	8.1	10.1	6.2
65 - 69	17 282	10 349	6 933	12.8	15.9	10.0
70 - 74	22 194	13 006	9 188	20.9	26.1	16.3
75 - 79	30 733	17 061	13 672	34.0	42.2	27.4
80 - 84	38 476	19 414	19 062	57.7	72.4	47.8
85 - 89	38 943	16 289	22 654	99.3	120.8	88.0
90 - 94	25 509	8 717	16 792	170.3	207.4	155.8
95 - 99	10 191	2 465	7 726	262.3	284.7	255.9
100 +	2 011	347	1 664	364.8	326.4	373.9
Unknown - Inconnu	5	4	1	..	..	..

Cayman Islands - Îles Caïmanes
2014 (C)

Total	153	80	73	2.6	2.8	2.4
0	2	1	1	...	...	...
1 - 4	1	-	1	...	...	...
5 - 9	1	-	1	...	...	...
10 - 14	-	-	-	...	...	...
15 - 19	1	1	-	...	...	...
20 - 24	4	3	1	...	...	...
25 - 29	2	2	-	...	...	...
30 - 34	2	1	1	...	...	...
35 - 39	2	1	1	...	...	...
40 - 44	4	4	-	...	...	...
45 - 49	6	1	5	...	...	...
50 - 54	9	7	2	...	...	...
55 - 59	10	7	3	...	...	...
60 - 64	7	5	2	...	...	...
65 +	102	47	55	26.9	26.6	27.1

Costa Rica
2014* (C)

Total	20 553	11 658	8 895	4.3	5.0	3.6
1 - 4	607	300	307	...	...	...
5 - 9	166	87	79	0.5	0.5	0.5
10 - 14	88	52	36	0.2	0.3	0.2
15 - 19	213	144	69	0.5	0.6	0.3
20 - 24	352	264	88	0.8	1.2	0.4
25 - 29	434	312	122	1.1	1.5	0.6
30 - 34	384	278	106	1.1	1.6	0.6
35 - 39	439	309	130	1.4	2.0	0.8

19. Deaths by age and sex and age-specific death rates by sex: latest available year, 2005 - 2014
Décès et taux de mortalité selon l'âge et le sexe : dernière année disponible, 2005 - 2014 (continued - suite)

Continent, country or area, date, code[a] and age (in years) Continent, pays ou zone, date, code[a] et âge (en années)	Number - Nombre			Rate - Taux		
	Both sexes Les deux sexes	Male Masculin	Female Féminin	Both sexes Les deux sexes	Male Masculin	Female Féminin
AMERICA, NORTH - AMÉRIQUE DU NORD						
Costa Rica						
2014* (C)						
40 - 44	517	349	168	1.7	2.4	1.0
45 - 49	745	472	273	2.5	3.3	1.8
50 - 54	981	631	350	3.1	4.5	2.0
55 - 59	1 198	765	433	4.6	6.2	3.1
60 - 64	1 419	879	540	7.3	9.8	5.1
65 - 69	1 579	954	625	10.5	14.4	7.5
70 - 74	1 818	1 061	757	18.5	23.9	14.0
75 - 79	2 214	1 250	964	26.6	34.0	20.7
80 - 84	2 499	1 323	1 176	41.4	50.7	34.3
85 +	4 730	2 151	2 579	...	...	...
Unknown - Inconnu	170	77	93	..	..	..
Cuba						
2013 (C)						
Total	92 273	49 706	42 567	8.2	8.9	7.6
0	525	291	234	4.2	4.5	3.9
1 - 4	196	125	71	0.4	0.5	0.3
5 - 9	100	64	36	0.2	0.2	0.1
10 - 14	151	90	61	0.2	0.3	0.2
15 - 19	283	181	102	0.4	0.5	0.3
20 - 24	434	283	151	0.5	0.7	0.4
25 - 29	538	366	172	0.7	0.9	0.5
30 - 34	569	389	180	0.9	1.2	0.6
35 - 39	963	651	312	1.2	1.6	0.8
40 - 44	1 792	1 139	653	1.8	2.3	1.3
45 - 49	2 984	1 863	1 121	2.9	3.6	2.1
50 - 54	3 954	2 403	1 551	4.9	6.1	3.7
55 - 59	4 739	2 896	1 843	7.6	9.6	5.7
60 - 64	6 819	4 025	2 794	11.9	14.4	9.4
65 - 69	8 881	5 132	3 749	18.1	21.9	14.7
70 - 74	10 563	6 143	4 420	27.2	33.0	21.8
75 - 79	11 683	6 271	5 412	43.5	50.0	37.8
80 - 84	12 741	6 693	6 048	70.5	81.6	61.2
85 +	24 339	10 682	13 657	146.1	153.2	141.0
85 - 89	11 692	5 455	6 237	...	...	...
90 - 94	7 824	3 361	4 463	...	...	...
95 - 99	3 731	1 467	2 264	...	...	...
100 +	1 092	399	693	...	...	...
Unknown - Inconnu	19	19	-	..	..	..
Curaçao						
2014 (C)						
Total	1 370	727	643	8.8	10.2	7.6
0	24	8	16	♦12.3	♦8.1	♦16.6
1 - 4	1	1	-	♦0.1	♦0.2	-
5 - 9	1	1	-	♦0.1	♦0.2	-
10 - 14	1	1	-	♦0.1	♦0.2	-
15 - 19	5	5	-	♦0.5	♦0.9	-
20 - 24	8	7	1	♦0.9	♦1.6	♦0.2
25 - 29	4	4	-	♦0.5	♦1.0	-
30 - 34	8	6	2	♦0.9	♦1.6	♦0.4
35 - 39	17	12	5	♦1.9	♦3.1	♦1.0
40 - 44	23	10	13	♦2.1	♦2.0	♦2.1
45 - 49	34	19	15	2.8	♦3.6	♦2.3
50 - 54	59	32	27	4.6	5.7	♦3.7
55 - 59	87	60	27	7.7	12.2	♦4.3
60 - 64	107	67	40	10.8	15.4	7.2
65 - 69	135	88	47	16.4	24.2	10.2
70 - 74	165	103	62	28.2	41.6	18.4
75 - 79	173	90	83	39.1	48.3	32.4
80 - 84	191	88	103	68.8	79.1	61.9
85 - 89	163	73	90	113.4	146.9	95.6
90 - 94	113	41	72	178.5	222.2	160.5
95 - 99	43	10	33	203.8	♦227.3	197.6
100 +	8	1	7	♦202.5	♦111.1	♦229.5

19. Deaths by age and sex and age-specific death rates by sex: latest available year, 2005 - 2014
Décès et taux de mortalité selon l'âge et le sexe : dernière année disponible, 2005 - 2014 (continued - suite)

Continent, country or area, date, code[a] and age (in years) / Continent, pays ou zone, date, code[a] et âge (en annèes)	Number - Nombre			Rate - Taux		
	Both sexes Les deux sexes	Male Masculin	Female Féminin	Both sexes Les deux sexes	Male Masculin	Female Féminin
AMERICA, NORTH - AMÉRIQUE DU NORD						
Dominica - Dominique						
2006 (+C)						
Total	536	285	251	7.5	7.9	7.2
0 - 4	14	12	2	♦2.2	♦3.7	♦0.7
0	13	11	2	...	...	...
1 - 4	1	1	-	...	...	...
5 - 9	1	1	-	♦0.1	♦0.3	-
10 - 14	2	2	-	♦0.3	♦0.6	-
15 - 19	8	7	1	♦1.2	♦2.0	♦0.3
20 - 24	9	6	3	♦2.0	♦2.5	♦1.4
25 - 29	5	3	2	♦1.0	♦1.2	♦0.8
30 - 34	9	5	4	♦1.6	♦1.7	♦1.4
35 - 39	8	6	2	♦1.5	♦2.1	♦0.8
40 - 44	8	5	3	♦1.8	♦2.1	♦1.5
45 - 49	23	7	16	♦6.5	♦3.6	♦9.9
50 - 54	17	9	8	♦6.0	♦6.1	♦5.9
55 - 59	19	11	8	♦7.9	♦9.1	♦6.8
60 - 64	19	13	6	♦8.4	♦12.7	♦4.9
65 - 69	34	16	18	14.6	♦14.7	♦14.6
70 - 74	57	26	31	30.9	♦29.9	31.9
75 - 79	76	39	37	57.1	65.4	50.3
80 - 84	68	38	30	75.5	107.3	♦54.8
85 +	152	73	79	184.2	253.5	147.1
Unknown - Inconnu	7	6	1	..	..	..
Dominican Republic - République dominicaine						
2013 (U)						
Total	34 375	21 071	13 304	...	...	...
0	643	438	205	...	...	...
1 - 4	196	125	71	...	...	...
5 - 9	146	92	54	...	...	...
10 - 14	190	126	64	...	...	...
15 - 19	500	373	127	...	...	...
20 - 24	886	716	170	...	...	...
25 - 29	871	631	240	...	...	...
30 - 34	996	696	300	...	...	...
35 - 39	993	653	340	...	...	...
40 - 44	1 300	860	440	...	...	...
45 - 49	1 532	980	552	...	...	...
50 - 54	1 973	1 363	610	...	...	...
55 - 59	2 139	1 404	735	...	...	...
60 - 64	2 517	1 605	912	...	...	...
65 - 69	2 760	1 721	1 039	...	...	...
70 - 74	3 129	1 953	1 176	...	...	...
75 - 79	3 613	2 050	1 563	...	...	...
80 - 84	3 776	2 087	1 689	...	...	...
85 - 89	2 676	1 388	1 288	...	...	...
90 - 94	1 779	890	889	...	...	...
95 - 99	1 161	548	613	...	...	...
Unknown - Inconnu	599	372	227	..	..	..
El Salvador						
2012 (C)						
Total	32 148	17 862	14 286	...	...	...
0	795	446	349	...	...	...
1 - 4	214	122	92	...	...	...
5 - 9	114	68	46	...	...	...
10 - 14	248	145	103	...	...	...
15 - 19	788	605	183	...	...	...
20 - 24	874	685	189	...	...	...
25 - 29	900	718	182	...	...	...
30 - 34	1 078	858	220	...	...	...
35 - 39	1 107	838	269	...	...	...
40 - 44	1 174	810	364	...	...	...
45 - 49	1 283	811	472	...	...	...
50 - 54	1 529	898	631	...	...	...
55 - 59	1 757	1 012	745	...	...	...
60 - 64	2 116	1 196	920	...	...	...
65 - 69	2 260	1 163	1 097	...	...	...

Continent, country or area, date, code[a] and age (in years) Continent, pays ou zone, date, code[a] et âge (en années)	Number - Nombre			Rate - Taux		
	Both sexes Les deux sexes	Male Masculin	Female Féminin	Both sexes Les deux sexes	Male Masculin	Female Féminin
AMERICA, NORTH - AMÉRIQUE DU NORD						
El Salvador						
2012 (C)						
70 - 74	2 810	1 485	1 325	...	...	...
75 - 79	3 206	1 585	1 621	...	...	...
80 - 84	3 552	1 668	1 884	...	...	...
85 +	6 285	2 703	3 582	...	...	...
Unknown - Inconnu	58	46	12	..	..	..
Greenland - Groenland						
2014 (C)						
Total	461	240	221	8.2	8.1	8.3
0	6	3	3	...	...	...
1 - 4	1	1	-	♦0.3	♦0.6	-
5 - 9	1	-	1	♦0.3	-	♦0.5
10 - 14	2	-	2	♦0.5	-	♦1.0
15 - 19	8	6	2	♦1.9	♦2.9	♦1.0
20 - 24	15	8	7	♦3.3	♦3.4	♦3.1
25 - 29	10	8	2	♦2.3	♦3.7	♦0.9
30 - 34	5	3	2	♦1.3	♦1.5	♦1.0
35 - 39	7	4	3	♦2.2	♦2.3	♦2.1
40 - 44	10	8	2	♦3.0	♦4.3	♦1.3
45 - 49	23	13	10	♦4.4	♦4.6	♦4.2
50 - 54	20	12	8	♦4.1	♦4.4	♦3.6
55 - 59	37	25	12	9.9	♦11.8	♦7.4
60 - 64	50	31	19	18.9	20.6	♦16.6
65 - 69	49	24	25	27.7	♦22.9	♦34.9
70 - 74	68	38	30	51.8	54.5	♦48.8
75 - 79	61	31	30	93.4	100.3	♦87.2
80 - 84	57	19	38	151.6	♦127.5	167.4
85 - 89	26	5	21	♦209.7	♦111.1	♦265.8
90 - 94	4	1	3	♦210.5	♦125.0	♦272.7
95 +	1	-	1	...	...	...
Guatemala						
2011 (C)						
Total	72 354	41 295	31 059	...	...	...
0	7 413	4 202	3 211	...	...	...
1 - 4	2 552	1 313	1 239	...	...	...
5 - 9	705	387	318	...	...	...
10 - 14	907	502	405	...	...	...
15 - 19	2 281	1 581	700	...	...	...
20 - 24	2 738	2 111	627	...	...	...
25 - 29	2 864	2 167	697	...	...	...
30 - 34	2 819	2 051	768	...	...	...
35 - 39	2 680	1 855	825	...	...	...
40 - 44	2 659	1 778	881	...	...	...
45 - 49	2 920	1 832	1 088	...	...	...
50 - 54	3 400	1 928	1 472	...	...	...
55 - 59	3 786	1 999	1 787	...	...	...
60 - 64	4 096	2 157	1 939	...	...	...
65 - 69	4 250	2 199	2 051	...	...	...
70 - 74	4 824	2 499	2 325	...	...	...
75 - 79	5 709	2 944	2 765	...	...	...
80 - 84	6 215	3 110	3 105	...	...	...
85 - 89	4 931	2 418	2 513	...	...	...
90 - 94	2 716	1 267	1 449	...	...	...
95 - 99	793	315	478	...	...	...
100 +	148	49	99	...	...	...
Unknown - Inconnu	948	631	317	..	..	..
Jamaica - Jamaïque[17]						
2011 (I)						
Total	21 001	10 061[12]	8 618[12]	7.8	7.6	6.3
0 - 4	361	187[12]	163[12]	1.6	1.7	1.5
5 - 9	118	53[12]	61[12]	0.5	0.4	0.5
10 - 14	128	74	54	0.5	0.5	0.4
15 - 19	382	288[12]	90[12]	1.5	2.3	0.7
20 - 24	521	423[12]	92[12]	2.5	4.2	0.9
25 - 29	515	367[12]	136[12]	2.4	3.6	1.2
30 - 34	451	304[12]	134[12]	2.0	2.9	1.1

19. Deaths by age and sex and age-specific death rates by sex: latest available year, 2005 - 2014
Décès et taux de mortalité selon l'âge et le sexe : dernière année disponible, 2005 - 2014 (continued - suite)

Continent, country or area, date, code[a] and age (in years) Continent, pays ou zone, date, code[a] et âge (en annèes)	Number - Nombre			Rate - Taux		
	Both sexes Les deux sexes	Male Masculin	Female Féminin	Both sexes Les deux sexes	Male Masculin	Female Féminin

AMERICA, NORTH - AMÉRIQUE DU NORD

Jamaica - Jamaïque[17]
2011 (|)

35 - 39	557	319[12]	224[12]	2.4	3.0	1.8
40 - 44	609	329[12]	268[12]	3.1	3.3	2.7
45 - 49	631	324[12]	299[12]	4.7	4.8	4.4
50 - 54	749	418[12]	320[12]	6.4	6.8	5.7
55 - 59	702	367[12]	319[12]	8.1	8.1	7.8
60 - 64	1 003	501[12]	482[12]	14.6	14.9	13.7
65 - 69	1 031	554[12]	448[12]	15.7	17.5	13.2
70 - 74	1 343	700[12]	610[12]	22.4	24.6	19.3
75 +	9 932	4 853	4 918	94.6	115.9	77.9
75 - 79	1 567	805[12]	722[12]	...	...	...
80 - 84	1 721	876[12]	806[12]	...	...	...
85 - 89	3 057	1 259	1 798	...	...	...
90 +	3 505	1 913	1 592	...	...	...
Unknown - Inconnu	1 968	-	-	..	..	...

Martinique[18]
2007 (C)

Total	2 830	1 439	1 391	7.1	7.7	6.5
0 - 4	51	31	20	2.0	2.4	♦1.6
0	47	28	19	...	...	...
1 - 4	4	3	1	...	...	...
5 - 9	4	3	1	♦0.1	♦0.2	♦0.1
10 - 14	7	5	2	♦0.2	♦0.3	♦0.1
15 - 19	16	12	4	♦0.5	♦0.8	♦0.3
20 - 24	26	22	4	♦1.1	♦1.9	♦0.3
25 - 29	19	13	6	♦1.0	♦1.5	♦0.6
30 - 34	35	22	13	1.4	♦2.1	♦0.9
35 - 39	36	22	14	1.2	♦1.6	♦0.8
40 - 44	53	31	22	1.6	2.0	♦1.2
45 - 49	64	46	18	2.0	3.2	♦1.1
50 - 54	107	68	39	4.1	5.6	2.8
55 - 59	97	57	40	4.3	5.5	3.2
60 - 64	146	91	55	7.8	10.3	5.5
65 - 69	226	135	91	14.2	18.7	10.4
70 - 74	305	173	132	21.3	27.2	16.6
75 - 79	382	200	182	35.8	44.2	29.6
80 - 84	443	217	226	59.2	76.6	48.6
85 - 89	388	168	220	92.5	122.1	78.1
90 - 94	269	91	178	137.9	159.6	128.9
95 +	156	32	124	212.8	196.3	217.5

Mexico - Mexique[19]
2013 (+C)

Total	610 730	341 276[12]	269 003[12]	...	...	...
0	27 760	15 524[12]	12 137[12]	...	...	...
1 - 4	5 366	3 000[12]	2 364[12]	...	...	...
5 - 9	2 592	1 480[12]	1 111[12]	...	...	...
10 - 14	3 200	1 932[12]	1 268[12]	...	...	...
15 - 19	8 507	6 058[12]	2 447[12]	...	...	...
20 - 24	12 573	9 627[12]	2 945[12]	...	...	...
25 - 29	13 280	10 214[12]	3 061[12]	...	...	...
30 - 34	14 649	10 973[12]	3 665[12]	...	...	...
35 - 39	17 409	12 611[12]	4 787[12]	...	...	...
40 - 44	20 379	13 885[12]	6 488[12]	...	...	...
45 - 49	25 281	16 132[12]	9 139[12]	...	...	...
50 - 54	31 963	19 428[12]	12 528[12]	...	...	...
55 - 59	38 629	22 677[12]	15 949[12]	...	...	...
60 - 64	44 115	24 911[12]	19 197[12]	...	...	...
65 - 69	50 094	27 842[12]	22 243[12]	...	...	...
70 - 74	56 116	30 256[12]	25 855[12]	...	...	...
75 - 79	63 150	32 922[12]	30 221[12]	...	...	...
80 - 84	65 171	32 008[12]	33 159[12]	...	...	...
85 - 89	54 710	25 337[12]	29 368[12]	...	...	...
90 - 94	35 072	15 193[12]	19 878[12]	...	...	...
95 - 99	13 157	5 129[12]	8 016[12]	...	...	...

19. Deaths by age and sex and age-specific death rates by sex: latest available year, 2005 - 2014
Décès et taux de mortalité selon l'âge et le sexe : dernière année disponible, 2005 - 2014 (continued - suite)

Continent, country or area, date, code[a] and age (in years) / Continent, pays ou zone, date, code[a] et âge (en années)	Number - Nombre			Rate - Taux		
	Both sexes Les deux sexes	Male Masculin	Female Féminin	Both sexes Les deux sexes	Male Masculin	Female Féminin
AMERICA, NORTH - AMÉRIQUE DU NORD						
Mexico - Mexique[19]						
2013 (+C)						
100 +	4 344	1 555[12]	2 789[12]	...	...	...
Unknown - Inconnu	3 213	2 582[12]	388[12]	..	..	..
Montserrat						
2013 (+C)						
Total	45	21	24	...	...	...
0	-	-	-	...	...	...
1 - 4	-	-	-	...	...	...
5 - 9	-	-	-	...	...	...
10 - 14	-	-	-	...	...	...
15 - 19	-	-	-	...	...	...
20 - 24	-	-	-	...	...	...
25 - 29	-	-	-	...	...	...
30 - 34	-	-	-	...	...	...
35 - 39	1	-	1	...	...	...
40 - 44	-	-	-	...	...	...
45 - 49	1	-	1	...	...	...
50 - 54	-	-	-	...	...	...
55 - 59	2	1	1	...	...	...
60 - 64	2	2	-	...	...	...
65 - 69	2	1	1	...	...	...
70 - 74	4	2	2	...	...	...
75 - 79	5	3	2	...	...	...
80 - 84	5	2	3	...	...	...
85 - 89	10	3	7	...	...	...
90 - 94	13	7	6	...	...	...
95 - 99	-	-	-	...	...	...
100 +	-	-	-	...	...	...
Nicaragua						
2010 (+U)						
Total	19 944	11 416	8 528	...	...	...
0	1 891	1 077	814	...	...	...
1 - 4	252	155	97	...	...	...
5 - 9	155	86	69	...	...	...
10 - 14	182	95	87	...	...	...
15 - 19	458	313	145	...	...	...
20 - 24	564	428	136	...	...	...
25 - 29	672	514	158	...	...	...
30 - 34	615	458	157	...	...	...
35 - 39	697	491	206	...	...	...
40 - 44	758	495	263	...	...	...
45 - 49	843	540	303	...	...	...
50 - 54	997	594	403	...	...	...
55 - 59	1 166	693	473	...	...	...
60 - 64	1 258	704	554	...	...	...
65 - 69	1 385	787	598	...	...	...
70 - 74	1 584	863	721	...	...	...
75 - 79	1 740	931	809	...	...	...
80 +	4 727	2 192	2 535	...	...	...
Panama						
2013 (U)						
Total	17 767	10 248	7 519	...	...	...
0	1 106	627	479	...	...	...
1 - 4	304	163	141	...	...	...
5 - 9	110	55	55	...	...	...
10 - 14	111	65	46	...	...	...
15 - 19	324	243	81	...	...	...
20 - 24	396	311	85	...	...	...
25 - 29	375	272	103	...	...	...
30 - 34	424	302	122	...	...	...
35 - 39	444	298	146	...	...	...
40 - 44	527	348	179	...	...	...
45 - 49	589	363	226	...	...	...
50 - 54	770	475	295	...	...	...
55 - 59	895	537	358	...	...	...
60 - 64	1 033	678	355	...	...	...

Continent, country or area, date, code[a] and age (in years) Continent, pays ou zone, date, code[a] et âge (en années)	Number - Nombre			Rate - Taux		
	Both sexes Les deux sexes	Male Masculin	Female Féminin	Both sexes Les deux sexes	Male Masculin	Female Féminin
AMERICA, NORTH - AMÉRIQUE DU NORD						
Panama						
2013 (U)						
65 - 69	1 296	766	530	...	...	...
70 - 74	1 439	846	593	...	...	...
75 - 79	1 769	994	775	...	...	...
80 - 84	1 863	1 007	856	...	...	...
85 - 89	1 728	868	860	...	...	...
90 - 94	1 327	628	699	...	...	...
95 - 99	650	259	391	...	...	...
100 +	165	61	104	...	...	...
Unknown - Inconnu	122	82	40	..	..	..
Puerto Rico - Porto Rico						
2014 (C)						
Total	30 224	16 327	13 897	...	...	...
0	242	144	98	...	...	...
1 - 4	28	13	15	...	...	...
5 - 9	15	8	7	...	...	...
10 - 14	19	15	4	...	...	...
15 - 19	131	105	26	...	...	...
20 - 24	322	282	40	...	...	...
25 - 29	299	242	57	...	...	...
30 - 34	310	235	75	...	...	...
35 - 39	372	251	121	...	...	...
40 - 44	478	322	156	...	...	...
45 - 49	719	446	273	...	...	...
50 - 54	1 042	648	394	...	...	...
55 - 59	1 467	966	501	...	...	...
60 - 64	2 022	1 286	736	...	...	...
65 - 69	2 801	1 749	1 052	...	...	...
70 - 74	3 166	1 837	1 329	...	...	...
75 - 79	3 679	1 960	1 719	...	...	...
80 - 84	4 144	2 109	2 035	...	...	...
85 - 89	4 177	1 857	2 320	...	...	...
90 - 94	3 067	1 204	1 863	...	...	...
95 - 99	1 288	485	803	...	...	...
100 +	403	134	269	...	...	...
Unknown - Inconnu	33	29	4	..	..	..
Saint Lucia - Sainte-Lucie						
2005* (C)						
Total	1 107	625	482	6.7	7.8	5.7
0 - 4	53	30	23	3.9	♦4.4	♦3.3
0	46	28	18	...	...	...
1 - 4	7	2	5	...	...	...
5 - 9	2	1	1	♦0.1	♦0.1	♦0.1
10 - 14	7	4	3	♦0.4	♦0.5	♦0.3
15 - 19	14	12	2	♦0.8	♦1.4	♦0.2
20 - 24	19	15	4	♦1.2	♦1.9	♦0.5
25 - 29	24	18	6	♦1.8	♦2.7	♦0.9
30 - 34	33	21	12	2.6	♦3.5	♦1.9
35 - 39	25	19	6	♦2.1	♦3.3	♦1.0
40 - 44	40	30	10	3.6	♦5.6	♦1.8
45 - 49	38	28	10	4.4	♦6.5	♦2.3
50 - 54	49	25	24	7.6	♦7.6	♦7.5
55 - 59	42	23	19	8.4	♦9.6	♦7.3
60 - 64	82	52	30	20.1	27.5	♦13.7
65 - 69	103	63	40	28.8	37.5	21.1
70 - 74	88	52	36	29.2	36.6	22.6
75 - 79	114	72	42	58.7	79.4	40.5
80 +	361	154	207	127.0	129.4	125.3
80 - 84	154	70	84	...	...	...
85 +	207	84	123	...	...	...
Unknown - Inconnu	13	6	7	..	..	..
Saint Vincent and the Grenadines -						
Saint-Vincent-et-les Grenadines						
2012 (+C)						
Total	858	474	384	...	...	...
0	26	15	11	...	...	...

19. Deaths by age and sex and age-specific death rates by sex: latest available year, 2005 - 2014
Décès et taux de mortalité selon l'âge et le sexe : dernière année disponible, 2005 - 2014 (continued - suite)

Continent, country or area, date, code[a] and age (in years) / Continent, pays ou zone, date, code[a] et âge (en années)	Number - Nombre			Rate - Taux		
	Both sexes Les deux sexes	Male Masculin	Female Féminin	Both sexes Les deux sexes	Male Masculin	Female Féminin
AMERICA, NORTH - AMÉRIQUE DU NORD						
Saint Vincent and the Grenadines - Saint-Vincent-et-les Grenadines						
2012 (+C)						
1 - 4	3	3	-	...	...	...
5 - 9	2	2	-	...	...	...
10 - 14	5	3	2	...	...	...
15 - 19	6	3	3	...	...	...
20 - 24	9	7	2	...	...	...
25 - 29	14	10	4	...	...	...
30 - 34	14	10	4	...	...	...
35 - 39	25	15	10	...	...	...
40 - 44	34	17	17	...	...	...
45 - 49	45	26	19	...	...	...
50 - 54	62	45	17	...	...	...
55 - 59	50	34	16	...	...	...
60 - 64	51	37	14	...	...	...
65 - 69	73	42	31	...	...	...
70 - 74	63	36	27	...	...	...
75 - 79	105	55	50	...	...	...
80 - 84	103	40	63	...	...	...
85 +	167	73	94	...	...	...
Unknown - Inconnu	1	1	-	..	..	..
Trinidad and Tobago - Trinité-et-Tobago						
2005 (C)						
Total	9 885	5 702	4 183	...	...	...
0	266	149	117	...	...	...
1 - 4	39	23	16	...	...	...
5 - 9	20	13	7	...	...	...
10 - 14	31	14	17	...	...	...
15 - 19	136	94	42	...	...	...
20 - 24	234	185	49	...	...	...
25 - 29	246	182	64	...	...	...
30 - 34	252	170	82	...	...	...
35 - 39	258	161	97	...	...	...
40 - 44	434	284	150	...	...	...
45 - 49	479	306	173	...	...	...
50 - 54	540	345	195	...	...	...
55 - 59	712	452	260	...	...	...
60 - 64	812	482	330	...	...	...
65 - 69	949	568	381	...	...	...
70 - 74	927	515	412	...	...	...
75 - 79	1 057	572	485	...	...	...
80 - 84	1 043	552	491	...	...	...
85 +	1 445	631	814	...	...	...
Unknown - Inconnu	5	4	1	..	..	..
Turks and Caicos Islands - Îles Turques et Caïques						
2005 (C)						
Total	53	32	21	...	...	...
0	1	1	-	...	...	...
1 - 4	-	-	-	...	...	...
5 - 9	-	-	-	...	...	...
10 - 14	1	1	-	...	...	...
15 - 19	1	1	-	...	...	...
20 - 24	-	-	-	...	...	...
25 - 29	2	2	-	...	...	...
30 - 34	8	5	3	...	...	...
35 - 39	3	2	1	...	...	...
40 - 44	3	1	2	...	...	...
45 - 49	1	1	-	...	...	...
50 - 54	2	-	2	...	...	...
55 - 59	2	2	-	...	...	...
60 - 64	2	2	-	...	...	...
65 - 69	-	-	-	...	...	...
70 - 74	3	3	-	...	...	...
75 - 79	6	1	5	...	...	...
80 - 84	5	3	2	...	...	...

19. Deaths by age and sex and age-specific death rates by sex: latest available year, 2005 - 2014
Décès et taux de mortalité selon l'âge et le sexe : dernière année disponible, 2005 - 2014 (continued - suite)

Continent, country or area, date, code[a] and age (in years) Continent, pays ou zone, date, code[a] et âge (en années)	Number - Nombre			Rate - Taux		
	Both sexes Les deux sexes	Male Masculin	Female Féminin	Both sexes Les deux sexes	Male Masculin	Female Féminin
AMERICA, NORTH - AMÉRIQUE DU NORD						
Turks and Caicos Islands - Îles Turques et Caïques						
2005 (C)						
85 +	11	5	6	...	...	...
Unknown - Inconnu	2	2	-	..	..	..
United States of America - États-Unis d'Amérique						
2013 (C)						
Total	2 596 993	1 306 034	1 290 959	...	...	...
0	23 440	13 119	10 321	...	...	...
1 - 4	4 068	2 323	1 745	...	...	...
5 - 9	2 427	1 383	1 044	...	...	...
10 - 14	2 913	1 694	1 219	...	...	...
15 - 19	9 480	6 759	2 721	...	...	...
20 - 24	19 006	14 105	4 901	...	...	...
25 - 29	21 056	15 023	6 033	...	...	...
30 - 34	24 407	16 439	7 968	...	...	...
35 - 39	27 821	17 544	10 277	...	...	...
40 - 44	41 752	25 528	16 224	...	...	...
45 - 49	66 833	40 531	26 302	...	...	...
50 - 54	110 891	67 466	43 425	...	...	...
55 - 59	152 981	93 996	58 985	...	...	...
60 - 64	185 146	112 329	72 817	...	...	...
65 - 69	214 509	124 324	90 185	...	...	...
70 - 74	239 920	133 574	106 346	...	...	...
75 - 79	277 314	146 166	131 148	...	...	...
80 - 84	347 699	169 174	178 525	...	...	...
85 +	825 198	304 462	520 736	...	...	...
Unknown - Inconnu	132	95	37	..	..	..
United States Virgin Islands - Îles Vierges américaines						
2007 (C)						
Total	727	424	303	6.6	8.1	5.2
0 - 4	14	8	6	♦1.9	♦2.1	♦1.6
0	12	6	6	...	...	...
1 - 4	2	2	-	...	...	...
5 - 9	-	-	-	-	-	-
10 - 14	2	1	1	♦0.2	♦0.2	♦0.2
15 - 19	9	8	1	♦1.1	♦2.0	♦0.2
20 - 24	16	15	1	♦2.3	♦4.7	♦0.3
25 - 29	20	14	6	♦3.7	♦5.7	♦2.1
30 - 34	16	10	6	♦2.6	♦3.7	♦1.8
35 - 39	16	13	3	♦2.2	♦3.9	♦0.7
40 - 44	33	21	12	4.1	♦5.6	♦2.8
45 - 49	26	13	13	♦3.2	♦3.3	♦3.1
50 - 54	50	34	16	6.6	9.6	♦3.9
55 - 59	51	29	22	6.8	♦8.1	♦5.6
60 - 64	79	55	24	10.7	15.3	♦6.3
65 - 69	50	36	14	10.1	14.8	♦5.5
70 - 74	68	43	25	18.8	26.6	♦12.5
75 +	273	120	153	59.0	63.7	55.7
Unknown - Inconnu	4	4	-	..	..	..
AMERICA, SOUTH - AMÉRIQUE DU SUD						
Argentina - Argentine						
2013 (C)						
Total	326 197	169 109[12]	156 688[12]	7.8	8.3	7.4
0	8 174	4 565[12]	3 599[12]	11.8	13.0	10.6
1 - 4	1 357	754[12]	598[12]	0.5	0.5	0.4
5 - 9	702	418[12]	284[12]	0.2	0.2	0.2
10 - 14	902	521[12]	379[12]	0.3	0.3	0.2
15 - 19	2 964	2 155[12]	803[12]	0.9	1.2	0.5
20 - 24	3 733	2 854[12]	870[12]	1.1	1.6	0.5
25 - 29	3 441	2 469[12]	964[12]	1.0	1.5	0.6
30 - 34	3 834	2 582[12]	1 247[12]	1.2	1.6	0.8
35 - 39	4 468	2 897[12]	1 570[12]	1.5	1.9	1.0
40 - 44	5 621	3 485[12]	2 131[12]	2.2	2.8	1.7

Continent, country or area, date, code[a] and age (in years) / Continent, pays ou zone, date, code[a] et âge (en années)	Number - Nombre			Rate - Taux		
	Both sexes Les deux sexes	Male Masculin	Female Féminin	Both sexes Les deux sexes	Male Masculin	Female Féminin

AMERICA, SOUTH - AMÉRIQUE DU SUD

Argentina - Argentine
2013 (C)

45 - 49	7 732	4 838[12]	2 889[12]	3.4	4.3	2.5
50 - 54	11 442	7 217[12]	4 215[12]	5.4	7.0	3.8
55 - 59	16 755	10 556[12]	6 189[12]	8.5	11.4	6.0
60 - 64	23 448	14 861[12]	8 567[12]	13.5	18.3	9.2
65 - 69	28 861	17 905[12]	10 934[12]	20.2	27.7	14.0
70 - 74	33 182	19 582[12]	13 579[12]	29.5	40.4	21.1
75 - 79	38 538	20 845[12]	17 675[12]	44.6	61.2	33.7
80 +	130 340	50 245	80 004	127.2	150.8	115.7
80 - 84	47 155	22 079[12]	25 046[12]	...	...	...
85 +	83 185	28 166[12]	54 958[12]	...	...	...
Unknown - Inconnu	703	360[12]	191[12]	..	..	..

Bolivia (Plurinational State of) - Bolivie (État plurinational de)[20]
2012 (I)

Total	127 050	59 027	68 023	12.6	11.8	13.5
0	5 363	2 406	2 957	26.6	23.4	29.9
1 - 4	6 695	3 085	3 610	7.5	6.8	8.3
5 - 9	2 531	1 183	1 348	2.5	2.3	2.8
10 - 14	1 961	827	1 134	1.8	1.5	2.1
15 - 19	3 699	1 460	2 239	3.3	2.6	4.1
20 - 24	4 767	1 618	3 149	4.9	3.3	6.5
25 - 29	4 089	1 393	2 696	5.0	3.4	6.6
30 - 34	4 323	1 556	2 767	5.7	4.2	7.3
35 - 39	4 670	1 868	2 802	7.4	6.0	8.7
40 - 44	4 597	1 849	2 748	8.4	6.8	10.0
45 - 49	5 769	2 483	3 286	12.5	10.9	14.0
50 - 54	6 298	2 849	3 449	15.6	14.3	16.9
55 - 59	6 851	2 946	3 905	21.1	18.5	23.7
60 - 64	9 105	4 256	4 849	32.5	31.7	33.3
65 - 69	9 801	4 792	5 009	47.9	48.8	47.1
70 - 74	9 701	4 649	5 052	63.6	64.7	62.7
75 - 79	9 798	4 756	5 042	98.7	105.7	92.9
80 - 84	11 190	5 952	5 238	138.0	172.7	112.3
85 - 89	8 493	4 674	3 819	224.0	294.3	173.3
90 - 94	3 927	2 332	1 595	267.8	388.9	184.0
95 +	3 422	2 093	1 329	415.6	633.3	269.6

Brazil - Brésil
2013 (U)

Total	1 180 796[21]	670 986[12]	509 526[12]	...	...	...
0	31 944[21]	17 827[12]	14 082[12]	...	...	...
1 - 4	6 012[21]	3 297[12]	2 713[12]	...	...	...
5 - 9	3 613[21]	2 116[12]	1 497[12]	...	...	...
10 - 14	5 111[21]	3 180[12]	1 930[12]	...	...	...
15 - 19	20 167[21]	16 203[12]	3 964[12]	...	...	...
20 - 24	25 976[21]	21 464[12]	4 510[12]	...	...	...
25 - 29	27 017[21]	21 258[12]	5 757[12]	...	...	...
30 - 34	29 960[21]	22 026[12]	7 932[12]	...	...	...
35 - 39	32 469[21]	22 776[12]	9 691[12]	...	...	...
40 - 44	39 374[21]	26 291[12]	13 081[12]	...	...	...
45 - 49	52 241[21]	33 655[12]	18 585[12]	...	...	...
50 - 54	65 978[21]	42 228[12]	23 750[12]	...	...	...
55 - 59	80 875[21]	50 457[12]	30 418[12]	...	...	...
60 - 64	91 566[21]	55 788[12]	35 777[12]	...	...	...
65 - 69	101 618[21]	59 610[12]	42 005[12]	...	...	...
70 - 74	114 358[21]	64 677[12]	49 679[12]	...	...	...
75 - 79	124 680[21]	65 671[12]	59 006[12]	...	...	...
80 - 84	126 302[21]	60 334[12]	65 966[12]	...	...	...
85 - 89	104 692[21]	45 082[12]	59 609[12]	...	...	...
90 - 94	60 265[21]	23 175[12]	37 090[12]	...	...	...
95 - 99	25 351[21]	8 678[12]	16 664[12]	...	...	...
100 +	7 026[21]	2 087[12]	4 937[12]	...	...	...
Unknown - Inconnu	4 201[21]	3 106[12]	883[12]	..	..	..

Continent, country or area, date, code[a] and age (in years) Continent, pays ou zone, date, code[a] et âge (en annèes)	Number - Nombre			Rate - Taux		
	Both sexes Les deux sexes	Male Masculin	Female Féminin	Both sexes Les deux sexes	Male Masculin	Female Féminin
AMERICA, SOUTH - AMÉRIQUE DU SUD						
Chile - Chili						
2012 (C)						
Total	98 711	51 814	46 897	5.7	6.0	5.3
0	1 812	978	834	7.2	7.6	6.7
1 - 4	296	162	134	0.3	0.3	0.3
5 - 9	177	100	77	0.1	0.2	0.1
10 - 14	217	132	85	0.2	0.2	0.1
15 - 19	620	435	185	0.4	0.6	0.3
20 - 24	894	674	220	0.6	0.9	0.3
25 - 29	955	723	232	0.7	1.0	0.3
30 - 34	1 139	811	328	0.9	1.3	0.5
35 - 39	1 434	1 009	425	1.2	1.7	0.7
40 - 44	2 081	1 365	716	1.7	2.2	1.2
45 - 49	3 035	2 000	1 035	2.5	3.3	1.7
50 - 54	4 231	2 736	1 495	3.7	4.9	2.6
55 - 59	5 394	3 360	2 034	5.9	7.5	4.3
60 - 64	6 495	3 875	2 620	9.0	11.2	6.9
65 - 69	8 820	5 298	3 522	15.3	19.8	11.4
70 - 74	10 367	5 921	4 446	24.2	30.9	18.7
75 - 79	12 133	6 542	5 591	39.1	50.3	31.0
80 +	38 611	15 693	22 918	111.8	124.6	104.4
80 - 84	14 772	7 154	7 618	...	...	...
85 - 89	12 237	5 044	7 193	...	...	...
90 - 94	7 714	2 595	5 119	...	...	...
95 - 99	3 194	766	2 428	...	...	...
100 +	694	134	560	...	...	...
Colombia - Colombie						
2012 (U)						
Total	199 756	113 055[12]	86 654[12]	...	...	...
0	8 220	4 608[12]	3 602[12]	...	...	...
1 - 4	1 603	876[12]	726[12]	...	...	...
5 - 9	905	515[12]	390[12]	...	...	...
10 - 14	1 221	690[12]	530[12]	...	...	...
15 - 19	4 327	3 412[12]	912[12]	...	...	...
20 - 24	6 066	4 989[12]	1 075[12]	...	...	...
25 - 29	5 983	4 786[12]	1 197[12]	...	...	...
30 - 34	5 567	4 230[12]	1 333[12]	...	...	...
35 - 39	5 116	3 558[12]	1 556[12]	...	...	...
40 - 44	5 691	3 739[12]	1 952[12]	...	...	...
45 - 49	6 833	4 189[12]	2 643[12]	...	...	...
50 - 54	8 513	5 057[12]	3 455[12]	...	...	...
55 - 59	10 978	6 498[12]	4 480[12]	...	...	...
60 - 64	12 713	7 405[12]	5 305[12]	...	...	...
65 - 69	14 487	8 301[12]	6 186[12]	...	...	...
70 - 74	18 881	10 525[12]	8 356[12]	...	...	...
75 - 79	22 220	11 658[12]	10 561[12]	...	...	...
80 - 84	24 021	12 139[12]	11 882[12]	...	...	...
85 - 89	19 318	8 763[12]	10 555[12]	...	...	...
90 - 94	11 467	4 791[12]	6 676[12]	...	...	...
95 - 99	4 271	1 649[12]	2 622[12]	...	...	...
100 +	935	336[12]	599[12]	...	...	...
Unknown - Inconnu	420	341[12]	61[12]	..	..	..
Ecuador - Équateur[22]						
2013 (U)						
Total	63 104	34 911 (U)	28 193	...	...	...
0	2 928	1 612	1 316	...	...	...
1 - 4	1 004	556	448	...	...	...
5 - 9	463	266	197	...	...	...
10 - 14	577	320	257	...	...	...
15 - 19	1 208	799	409	...	...	...
20 - 24	1 626	1 250	376	...	...	...
25 - 29	1 690	1 270	420	...	...	...
30 - 34	1 737	1 251	486	...	...	...
35 - 39	1 659	1 104	555	...	...	...
40 - 44	1 743	1 097	646	...	...	...
45 - 49	2 107	1 272	835	...	...	...

19. Deaths by age and sex and age-specific death rates by sex: latest available year, 2005 - 2014
Décès et taux de mortalité selon l'âge et le sexe : dernière année disponible, 2005 - 2014 (continued - suite)

Continent, country or area, date, code[a] and age (in years) / Continent, pays ou zone, date, code[a] et âge (en années)	Number - Nombre			Rate - Taux		
	Both sexes Les deux sexes	Male Masculin	Female Féminin	Both sexes Les deux sexes	Male Masculin	Female Féminin
AMERICA, SOUTH - AMÉRIQUE DU SUD						
Ecuador - Équateur[22]						
2013 (U)						
50 - 54	2 600	1 491	1 109	...	...	...
55 - 59	3 261	1 880	1 381	...	...	...
60 - 64	3 776	2 205	1 571	...	...	...
65 - 69	4 431	2 460	1 971	...	...	...
70 - 74	5 091	2 835	2 256	...	...	...
75 - 79	6 238	3 373	2 865	...	...	...
80 - 84	6 978	3 582	3 396	...	...	...
85 - 89	6 611	3 208	3 403	...	...	...
90 - 94	4 589	2 001	2 588	...	...	...
95 - 99	2 182	838	1 344	...	...	...
100 +	555	211	344	...	...	...
Unknown - Inconnu	50	30	20	..	...	..
French Guiana - Guyane française[18]						
2007 (C)						
Total	690	405	285	3.2	3.8	2.6
0 - 4	95	50	45	3.5	3.6	3.3
0	77	39	38	...	...	...
1 - 4	18	11	7	...	...	...
5 - 9	9	4	5	♦0.3	♦0.3	♦0.4
10 - 14	8	5	3	♦0.3	♦0.4	♦0.3
15 - 19	13	10	3	♦0.7	♦1.0	♦0.3
20 - 24	14	12	2	♦0.9	♦1.6	♦0.2
25 - 29	16	11	5	♦1.1	♦1.6	♦0.6
30 - 34	23	15	8	♦1.4	♦2.0	♦0.9
35 - 39	28	21	7	♦1.8	♦2.8	♦0.8
40 - 44	41	24	17	2.9	♦3.5	♦2.4
45 - 49	48	35	13	4.1	5.9	♦2.3
50 - 54	26	16	10	♦2.7	♦3.3	♦2.1
55 - 59	32	24	8	4.6	♦6.5	♦2.4
60 - 64	33	25	8	7.4	♦10.5	♦3.8
65 - 69	48	24	24	17.0	♦16.5	♦17.5
70 - 74	46	29	17	21.8	♦28.3	♦15.7
75 - 79	62	32	30	46.6	53.9	♦40.8
80 - 84	57	26	31	60.7	♦66.5	56.6
85 - 89	50	27	23	84.0	♦112.0	♦65.0
90 - 94	28	12	16	♦129.0	♦176.5	♦107.4
95 +	13	3	10	♦123.8	♦111.1	♦128.2
95 - 99	10	3	7	...	...	...
100 +	3	-	3	...	...	...
Paraguay						
2012 (+U)						
Total	22 807	12 911[12]	9 888[12]	...	...	...
0	465	256[12]	207[12]	...	...	...
1 - 4	156	83[12]	73[12]	...	...	...
5 - 9	114	60[12]	54[12]	...	...	...
10 - 14	144	85[12]	59[12]	...	...	...
15 - 19	457	334[12]	123[12]	...	...	...
20 - 24	564	430[12]	134[12]	...	...	...
25 - 29	490	366[12]	124[12]	...	...	...
30 - 34	528	349[12]	179[12]	...	...	...
35 - 39	535	341[12]	194[12]	...	...	...
40 - 44	633	403[12]	230[12]	...	...	...
45 - 49	926	570[12]	356[12]	...	...	...
50 - 54	1 251	789[12]	462[12]	...	...	...
55 - 59	1 501	936[12]	565[12]	...	...	...
60 - 64	1 738	1 111[12]	627[12]	...	...	...
65 - 69	1 944	1 132[12]	811[12]	...	...	...
70 - 74	2 288	1 300[12]	987[12]	...	...	...
75 - 79	2 317	1 286[12]	1 031[12]	...	...	...
80 - 84	2 654	1 327[12]	1 325[12]	...	...	...
85 +	4 081	1 742[12]	2 338[12]	...	...	...
Unknown - Inconnu	21	11[12]	9[12]	..	..	...

Continent, country or area, date, code[a] and age (in years) Continent, pays ou zone, date, code[a] et âge (en années)	Number - Nombre			Rate - Taux		
	Both sexes Les deux sexes	Male Masculin	Female Féminin	Both sexes Les deux sexes	Male Masculin	Female Féminin
AMERICA, SOUTH - AMÉRIQUE DU SUD						
Peru - Pérou[23]						
2013 (+U)						
Total	94 394	50 519	43 875	...	...	...
0	4 390	2 434	1 956	...	...	...
1 - 4	1 206	683	523	...	...	...
5 - 9	645	347	298	...	...	...
10 - 14	670	347	323	...	...	...
15 - 19	1 310	832	478	...	...	...
20 - 24	1 730	1 183	547	...	...	...
25 - 29	1 898	1 284	614	...	...	...
30 - 34	1 988	1 363	625	...	...	...
35 - 39	2 365	1 482	883	...	...	...
40 - 44	2 620	1 552	1 068	...	...	...
45 - 49	3 154	1 817	1 337	...	...	...
50 - 54	4 146	2 335	1 811	...	...	...
55 - 59	4 647	2 588	2 059	...	...	...
60 - 64	5 639	3 043	2 596	...	...	...
65 - 69	6 907	3 758	3 149	...	...	...
70 - 74	8 354	4 508	3 846	...	...	...
75 - 79	10 309	5 610	4 699	...	...	...
80 - 84	11 815	6 003	5 812	...	...	...
85 - 89	10 444	5 133	5 311	...	...	...
90 - 94	6 755	2 945	3 810	...	...	...
95 - 99	2 667	1 031	1 636	...	...	...
100 +	735	241	494	...	...	...
Suriname						
2013 (C)						
Total	3 557	2 036	1 521	6.5	7.4	5.5
0	168	95	73	...	...	...
1 - 4	35	17	18	0.9	♦0.8	♦0.9
5 - 9	16	8	8	♦0.3	♦0.3	♦0.3
10 - 14	20	15	5	♦0.4	♦0.6	♦0.2
15 - 19	53	31	22	1.1	1.3	♦0.9
20 - 24	72	53	19	1.6	2.3	♦0.8
25 - 29	81	45	36	1.9	2.1	1.7
30 - 34	95	61	34	2.3	3.0	1.7
35 - 39	114	75	39	2.9	3.9	2.0
40 - 44	150	100	50	4.0	5.4	2.7
45 - 49	180	126	54	5.3	7.4	3.2
50 - 54	243	161	82	8.2	11.0	5.5
55 - 59	237	142	95	9.5	11.6	7.4
60 - 64	249	159	90	12.9	17.2	8.9
65 - 69	330	188	142	22.3	27.1	18.0
70 - 74	347	191	156	31.9	38.3	26.4
75 - 79	390	205	185	52.5	62.1	44.7
80 +	777	364	413	103.8	118.1	93.8
80 - 84	365	195	170	...	...	...
85 - 89	224	100	124	...	...	...
90 - 94	124	50	74	...	...	...
95 - 99	53	15	38	...	...	...
100 +	11	4	7	...	...	...
Uruguay						
2013 (C)						
Total	32 795	16 631[12]	16 150[12]	...	...	...
0	431	239[12]	192[12]	...	...	...
1 - 4	65	37[12]	28[12]	...	...	...
5 - 9	45	16[12]	29[12]	...	...	...
10 - 14	68	39[12]	29[12]	...	...	...
15 - 19	237	180[12]	57[12]	...	...	...
20 - 24	255	200[12]	55[12]	...	...	...
25 - 29	268	199[12]	69[12]	...	...	...
30 - 34	285	204[12]	81[12]	...	...	...
35 - 39	354	227[12]	127[12]	...	...	...
40 - 44	475	301[12]	174[12]	...	...	...
45 - 49	644	391[12]	253[12]	...	...	...
50 - 54	1 020	683[12]	337[12]	...	...	...

Continent, country or area, date, code[a] and age (in years) / Continent, pays ou zone, date, code[a] et âge (en années)	Number - Nombre			Rate - Taux		
	Both sexes Les deux sexes	Male Masculin	Female Féminin	Both sexes Les deux sexes	Male Masculin	Female Féminin
AMERICA, SOUTH - AMÉRIQUE DU SUD						
Uruguay						
2013 (C)						
55 - 59	1 533	966[12]	567[12]	...	...	...
60 - 64	2 002	1 288[12]	714[12]	...	...	...
65 - 69	2 596	1 648[12]	948[12]	...	...	...
70 - 74	3 374	2 021[12]	1 352[12]	...	...	...
75 - 79	4 130	2 255[12]	1 875[12]	...	...	...
80 - 84	5 403	2 482[12]	2 919[12]	...	...	...
85 - 89	4 906	1 859[12]	3 041[12]	...	...	...
90 - 94	3 159	974[12]	2 184[12]	...	...	...
95 +	1 341	285[12]	1 056[12]	...	...	...
Unknown - Inconnu	204	137[12]	63[12]	..	..	..
Venezuela (Bolivarian Republic of) - Venezuela (République bolivarienne du)						
2013 (C)						
Total	147 901	90 389	57 512	4.9	6.0	3.8
0	7 630	4 402	3 228	...	...	...
1 - 4	1 196	660	536	...	...	...
5 - 9	705	407	298	0.2	0.3	0.2
10 - 14	888	544	344	0.3	0.4	0.3
15 - 19	4 692	3 976	716	1.7	2.9	0.5
20 - 24	7 173	6 319	854	2.7	4.6	0.6
25 - 29	5 922	4 980	942	2.3	3.9	0.7
30 - 34	5 078	3 966	1 112	2.2	3.4	1.0
35 - 39	4 821	3 467	1 354	2.3	3.4	1.3
40 - 44	4 795	3 218	1 577	2.6	3.5	1.7
45 - 49	5 930	3 775	2 155	3.4	4.4	2.5
50 - 54	7 981	5 139	2 842	5.3	6.9	3.7
55 - 59	9 781	6 151	3 630	7.9	10.2	5.8
60 - 64	11 253	7 096	4 157	11.3	14.6	8.1
65 - 69	11 454	6 958	4 496	15.4	19.5	11.6
70 - 74	12 139	7 109	5 030	23.7	29.8	18.4
75 - 79	12 988	7 147	5 841	37.2	45.5	30.4
80 +	33 475	15 075	18 400	112.8	117.9	109.0
80 - 84	13 352	6 716	6 636	...	...	...
85 - 89	10 686	4 812	5 874	...	...	...
90 - 94	6 324	2 431	3 893	...	...	...
95 - 99	2 399	882	1 517	...	...	...
100 +	714	234	480	...	...	...
ASIA - ASIE						
Armenia - Arménie[24]						
2009 (C)						
Total	27 560	14 253	13 307	8.5	9.1	8.0
0 - 4	528	299	229	2.7	2.9	2.5
0	454	258	196	10.7	11.4	9.9
1 - 4	74	41	33	0.5	0.5	0.5
5 - 9	40	18	22	0.2	♦0.2	♦0.3
10 - 14	40	31	9	0.2	0.3	♦0.1
15 - 19	145	106	39	0.5	0.7	0.3
20 - 24	152	107	45	0.5	0.7	0.3
25 - 29	211	155	56	0.7	1.1	0.4
30 - 34	243	183	60	1.0	1.6	0.5
35 - 39	320	223	97	1.6	2.3	0.9
40 - 44	547	404	143	2.6	4.1	1.3
45 - 49	1 044	728	316	4.0	5.8	2.3
50 - 54	1 431	980	451	6.2	9.0	3.7
55 - 59	1 715	1 142	573	10.1	14.8	6.2
60 - 64	1 539	962	577	15.5	22.1	10.3
65 - 69	2 522	1 477	1 045	27.0	37.7	19.3
70 - 74	4 463	2 419	2 044	40.9	54.4	31.5
75 - 79	5 211	2 484	2 727	68.1	81.3	59.3
80 - 84	4 781	1 854	2 927	110.6	129.6	101.2
85 +	2 628	681	1 947	262.4	271.6	259.3
85 - 89	1 702	454	1 248	...	...	...

19. Deaths by age and sex and age-specific death rates by sex: latest available year, 2005 - 2014
Décès et taux de mortalité selon l'âge et le sexe : dernière année disponible, 2005 - 2014 (continued - suite)

Continent, country or area, date, code[a] and age (in years) Continent, pays ou zone, date, code[a] et âge (en annèes)	Number - Nombre			Rate - Taux		
	Both sexes Les deux sexes	Male Masculin	Female Féminin	Both sexes Les deux sexes	Male Masculin	Female Féminin
ASIA - ASIE						
Armenia - Arménie[24]						
2009 (C)						
90 - 94	637	141	496	...	...	...
95 - 99	212	52	160	...	...	...
100 +	77	34	43	...	...	...
Azerbaijan - Azerbaïdjan[24]						
2013 (+C)						
Total	54 383	29 096	25 287	5.8	6.2	5.3
0 - 4	2 234	1 247	987	2.7	2.8	2.6
0	1 862	1 028	834	10.7	11.0	10.4
1 - 4	372	219	153	0.6	0.6	0.5
5 - 9	194	121	73	0.3	0.4	0.2
10 - 14	187	108	79	0.3	0.3	0.3
15 - 19	373	239	134	0.5	0.6	0.4
20 - 24	619	429	190	0.7	0.9	0.4
25 - 29	669	476	193	0.7	1.1	0.4
30 - 34	731	520	211	0.9	1.3	0.5
35 - 39	900	639	261	1.4	2.0	0.8
40 - 44	1 373	972	401	2.2	3.2	1.2
45 - 49	2 299	1 591	708	3.5	5.1	2.0
50 - 54	3 700	2 524	1 176	5.6	8.0	3.4
55 - 59	4 180	2 806	1 374	8.9	12.6	5.6
60 - 64	4 477	2 811	1 666	15.1	20.5	10.5
65 - 69	3 245	1 847	1 398	21.6	27.8	16.7
70 - 74	6 296	3 273	3 023	41.9	51.5	34.8
75 - 79	9 479	4 420	5 059	67.1	76.6	60.6
80 - 84	7 667	3 295	4 372	107.7	113.7	103.7
85 - 89	3 783	1 353	2 430	154.7	152.7	155.9
90 - 94	1 244	303	941	184.1	150.1	198.6
95 - 99	407	70	337	309.5	223.6	336.3
100 +	326	52	274	432.9	1793.1	378.5
Bahrain - Bahreïn						
2013 (C)						
Total	2 588	1 549[12]	1 020[12]	2.1	2.0	2.2
0	141	71[12]	51[12]	7.2	7.1	5.3
1 - 4	30	14	16	♦0.4	♦0.4	♦0.5
5 - 9	17	10	7	♦0.2	♦0.2	♦0.2
10 - 14	12	5	7	♦0.2	♦0.1	♦0.2
15 - 19	34	30	4	0.5	♦0.8	♦0.1
20 - 24	65	49	16	0.6	0.8	♦0.4
25 - 29	75	54	21	0.4	0.4	♦0.4
30 - 34	115	91	24	0.7	0.7	♦0.5
35 - 39	104	78	26	0.8	0.9	♦0.6
40 - 44	117	89	28	1.1	1.2	♦0.8
45 - 49	136	86	50	1.6	1.6	1.7
50 - 54	182	116	66	2.9	3.0	2.8
55 - 59	219	152	67	5.2	5.7	4.3
60 - 64	206	136	70	9.5	10.2	8.4
65 - 69	187	94	93	16.9	15.9	18.1
70 - 74	222	113	109	28.5	28.8	28.1
75 - 79	257	120	137	50.8	51.8	49.9
80 - 84	214	121	93	74.5	89.8	61.1
85 +	252	117	135	109.9	110.2	109.7
85 - 89	142	63	79	...	...	...
90 - 94	68	39	29	...	...	...
95 - 99	28	9	19	...	...	...
100 +	14	6	8	...	...	...
Unknown - Inconnu	3	3	-	..	..	..
Bhutan - Bhoutan[11]						
2005 (I)						
Total	4 498	2 390	2 108	7.1	7.2	7.0
0	503	270	233	40.8	44.3	37.5
1 - 4	269	143	126	5.4	5.6	5.1
5 - 9	139	85	54	2.0	2.4	1.5
10 - 14	88	46	42	1.1	1.2	1.1
15 - 19	126	65	61	1.7	1.7	1.6
20 - 24	123	65	58	1.7	1.6	1.9

19. Deaths by age and sex and age-specific death rates by sex: latest available year, 2005 - 2014
Décès et taux de mortalité selon l'âge et le sexe : dernière année disponible, 2005 - 2014 (continued - suite)

Continent, country or area, date, code[a] and age (in years) Continent, pays ou zone, date, code[a] et âge (en années)	Number - Nombre			Rate - Taux		
	Both sexes Les deux sexes	Male Masculin	Female Féminin	Both sexes Les deux sexes	Male Masculin	Female Féminin
ASIA - ASIE						
Bhutan - Bhoutan[11]						
2005 (I)						
25 - 29	133	74	59	2.3	2.4	2.3
30 - 34	145	79	66	3.4	3.4	3.4
35 - 39	182	107	75	4.7	5.1	4.3
40 - 44	174	95	79	5.8	5.9	5.7
45 - 49	250	129	121	9.0	8.7	9.5
50 - 54	204	113	91	9.3	9.6	8.9
55 - 59	239	126	113	14.6	14.4	14.8
60 - 64	291	145	146	20.0	19.2	20.8
65 - 69	331	163	168	29.1	27.2	31.3
70 - 74	368	188	180	42.1	41.8	42.4
75 +	933	497	436	96.8	102.7	90.8
Brunei Darussalam - Brunéi Darussalam						
2008 (+C)						
Total	1 091	636	455	...	...	...
0	45	24	21	...	...	...
1 - 4	16	11	5	...	...	...
5 - 9	6	2	4	...	...	...
10 - 14	5	1	4	...	...	...
15 - 19	13	7	6	...	...	...
20 - 24	20	13	7	...	...	...
25 - 29	25	22	3	...	...	...
30 - 34	29	19	10	...	...	...
35 - 39	38	23	15	...	...	...
40 - 44	45	32	13	...	...	...
45 - 49	73	43	30	...	...	...
50 - 54	69	47	22	...	...	...
55 - 59	73	38	35	...	...	...
60 - 64	63	36	27	...	...	...
65 - 69	105	59	46	...	...	...
70 - 74	103	51	52	...	...	...
75 - 79	131	76	55	...	...	...
80 - 84	105	52	53	...	...	...
85 - 89	65	45	20	...	...	...
90 - 94	33	16	17	...	...	...
95 - 99	24	14	10	...	...	...
100 +	5	5	-	...	...	...
China - Chine[25]						
2010 (I)						
Total	7 421 990	4 293 783	3 128 207	5.6	6.3	4.8
0	60 217	32 026	28 191	4.4	4.3	4.5
1 - 4	39 591	23 119	16 472	0.6	0.7	0.6
5 - 9	21 183	13 621	7 562	0.3	0.4	0.2
10 - 14	23 088	15 243	7 845	0.3	0.4	0.2
15 - 19	40 469	28 088	12 381	0.4	0.5	0.3
20 - 24	62 552	43 738	18 814	0.5	0.7	0.3
25 - 29	60 661	42 497	18 164	0.6	0.8	0.4
30 - 34	79 960	55 804	24 156	0.8	1.1	0.5
35 - 39	140 531	98 382	42 149	1.2	1.6	0.7
40 - 44	216 353	149 111	67 242	1.7	2.3	1.1
45 - 49	262 531	179 446	83 085	2.5	3.3	1.6
50 - 54	337 397	226 888	110 509	4.3	5.6	2.9
55 - 59	494 339	324 817	169 522	6.1	7.9	4.2
60 - 64	586 160	377 069	209 091	10.0	12.6	7.3
65 - 69	695 662	435 007	260 655	16.9	21.0	12.8
70 - 74	999 653	599 394	400 259	30.3	36.5	24.2
75 - 79	1 162 694	657 140	505 554	48.7	58.3	40.2
80 - 84	1 081 704	553 704	528 000	80.9	93.6	70.8
85 - 89	686 462	306 678	379 784	121.9	139.4	110.7
90 - 94	279 569	104 048	175 521	177.1	196.0	167.6
95 - 99	74 729	23 292	51 437	202.0	197.9	203.9
100 +	16 485	4 671	11 814	458.8	527.7	436.2
China, Hong Kong SAR - Chine, Hong Kong RAS						
2013 (C)						
Total	43 397	24 138[12]	19 255[12]	6.0	7.2	5.0
0	100	65	35	...	...	...

19. Deaths by age and sex and age-specific death rates by sex: latest available year, 2005 - 2014
Décès et taux de mortalité selon l'âge et le sexe : dernière année disponible, 2005 - 2014 (continued - suite)

Continent, country or area, date, code[a] and age (in years) / Continent, pays ou zone, date, code[a] et âge (en annèes)	Number - Nombre			Rate - Taux		
	Both sexes Les deux sexes	Male Masculin	Female Féminin	Both sexes Les deux sexes	Male Masculin	Female Féminin
ASIA - ASIE						
China, Hong Kong SAR - Chine, Hong Kong RAS						
2013 (C)						
1 - 4	40	19	21	...	...	...
5 - 9	30	17	13	♦0.1	♦0.1	♦0.1
10 - 14	28	17	11	♦0.1	♦0.1	♦0.1
15 - 19	61	35	26	0.2	0.2	♦0.1
20 - 24	106	69	37	0.2	0.3	0.2
25 - 29	162	96	66	0.3	0.4	0.2
30 - 34	254	153	101	0.4	0.7	0.3
35 - 39	353	216	137	0.6	0.9	0.4
40 - 44	527	285	242	0.9	1.2	0.7
45 - 49	930	551	379	1.5	2.0	1.1
50 - 54	1 550	961	589	2.4	3.1	1.7
55 - 59	2 254	1 461	793	4.0	5.2	2.8
60 - 64	2 708	1 841	867	6.1	8.4	3.9
65 - 69	2 726	1 876	850	9.2	12.6	5.8
70 - 74	3 553	2 466	1 087	16.7	22.5	10.5
75 - 79	5 642	3 621	2 021	26.8	36.0	18.4
80 - 84	7 503	4 265	3 238	47.5	61.4	36.6
85 +	14 846	6 111	8 735	102.7	128.9	89.9
Unknown - Inconnu	24	13[12]	7[12]	..	..	..
China, Macao SAR - Chine, Macao RAS						
2014 (C)						
Total	1 939	1 086	853	3.1	3.6	2.7
0	15	7	8	♦2.3	♦2.1	♦2.6
1 - 14	3	1	2	-	-	♦0.1
15 - 39	66	43	23	0.3	0.3	♦0.2
40 - 64	567	378	189	2.3	3.3	1.5
65 - 79	467	300	167	12.3	15.4	9.0
80 +	821	357	464	68.4	87.1	58.7
Cyprus - Chypre[26]						
2013 (C)						
Total	5 141	2 798	2 343	6.0	6.7	5.3
0 - 4	15	12	3	♦0.3	♦0.5	♦0.1
0	15	12	3	♦1.6	♦2.6	♦0.7
1 - 4	-	-	-	-	-	-
5 - 9	4	2	2	♦0.1	♦0.1	♦0.1
10 - 14	9	7	2	♦0.2	♦0.3	♦0.1
15 - 19	14	11	3	♦0.3	♦0.4	♦0.1
20 - 24	25	20	5	♦0.4	♦0.6	♦0.2
25 - 29	24	18	6	♦0.3	♦0.5	♦0.2
30 - 34	27	19	8	♦0.4	♦0.6	♦0.2
35 - 39	35	24	11	0.6	♦0.8	♦0.3
40 - 44	61	45	16	1.0	1.6	♦0.5
45 - 49	68	45	23	1.2	1.7	♦0.8
50 - 54	113	79	34	2.0	2.8	1.1
55 - 59	188	128	60	3.7	5.1	2.3
60 - 64	279	188	91	5.9	8.1	3.8
65 - 69	428	272	156	10.9	14.3	7.6
70 - 74	503	318	185	16.5	22.0	11.5
75 - 79	719	413	306	31.2	39.5	24.4
80 - 84	902	468	434	59.0	73.0	48.9
85 - 89	956	422	534	120.2	134.0	111.1
90 - 94	510	202	308	181.4	183.0	180.4
95 +	261	105	156	432.1	462.6	413.8
95 - 99	219	95	124	...	...	...
100 +	42	10	32	...	...	...
Democratic People's Republic of Korea - République populaire démocratique de Corée[13]						
2008 (I)						
Total	216 616	112 827	103 789	9.0	9.6	8.4
0	6 686	3 593	3 093	19.6	20.6	18.5
1 - 4	2 552	1 372	1 180	1.9	2.0	1.8
5 - 9	1 680	960	720	0.9	1.0	0.8
10 - 14	1 614	869	745	0.8	0.8	0.8
15 - 19	2 426	1 348	1 078	1.2	1.3	1.1
20 - 24	3 171	1 922	1 249	1.7	2.0	1.4

19. Deaths by age and sex and age-specific death rates by sex: latest available year, 2005 - 2014
Décès et taux de mortalité selon l'âge et le sexe : dernière année disponible, 2005 - 2014 (continued - suite)

Continent, country or area, date, code[a] and age (in years) Continent, pays ou zone, date, code[a] et âge (en années)	Number - Nombre			Rate - Taux		
	Both sexes Les deux sexes	Male Masculin	Female Féminin	Both sexes Les deux sexes	Male Masculin	Female Féminin
ASIA - ASIE						
Democratic People's Republic of Korea - République populaire démocratique de Corée[13]						
2008 (I)						
25 - 29	3 528	2 160	1 368	2.0	2.4	1.6
30 - 34	3 907	2 424	1 483	2.3	2.8	1.8
35 - 39	5 792	3 655	2 137	2.6	3.3	1.9
40 - 44	6 312	3 907	2 405	3.1	3.9	2.4
45 - 49	6 468	3 915	2 553	4.1	5.1	3.2
50 - 54	7 630	4 715	2 915	5.8	7.4	4.3
55 - 59	11 295	7 113	4 182	12.5	16.8	8.7
60 - 64	26 360	16 815	9 545	24.9	35.3	16.4
65 - 69	34 068	22 281	11 787	37.3	58.7	22.1
70 - 74	34 093	18 886	15 207	51.5	82.7	35.0
75 - 79	28 690	10 991	17 699	85.5	138.7	69.1
80 +	30 344	5 901	24 443	163.8	238.8	152.3
Georgia - Géorgie[24]						
2013 (C)						
Total	48 553	24 869	23 684	...	...	...
0 - 4	755	436	319	...	...	...
0	640	379	261	...	...	...
1 - 4	115	57	58	...	...	...
5 - 9	65	42	23	...	...	...
10 - 14	60	44	16	...	...	...
15 - 19	121	92	29	...	...	...
20 - 24	235	191	44	...	...	...
25 - 29	284	211	73	...	...	...
30 - 34	421	321	100	...	...	...
35 - 39	560	433	127	...	...	...
40 - 44	855	647	208	...	...	...
45 - 49	1 396	1 040	356	...	...	...
50 - 54	2 179	1 572	607	...	...	...
55 - 59	2 877	2 060	817	...	...	...
60 - 64	3 429	2 292	1 137	...	...	...
65 - 69	3 232	1 972	1 260	...	...	...
70 - 74	6 003	3 217	2 786	...	...	...
75 - 79	8 531	4 009	4 522	...	...	...
80 - 84	8 502	3 583	4 919	...	...	...
85 - 89	6 161	2 005	4 156	...	...	...
90 - 94	2 029	457	1 572	...	...	...
95 - 99	508	81	427	...	...	...
100 +	167	23	144	...	...	...
Unknown - Inconnu	183	141	42	..	..	..
Iran (Islamic Republic of) - Iran (République islamique d')[27]						
2013 (+C)						
Total	346 936	197 974	148 962	...	...	...
0	8 015	4 466	3 549	...	...	...
1 - 4	3 825	2 081	1 744	...	...	...
5 - 9	2 271	1 261	1 010	...	...	...
10 - 14	2 050	1 196	854	...	...	...
15 - 19	4 664	3 251	1 413	...	...	...
20 - 24	7 543	5 423	2 120	...	...	...
25 - 29	9 393	6 255	3 138	...	...	...
30 - 34	8 884	6 162	2 722	...	...	...
35 - 39	7 850	5 495	2 355	...	...	...
40 - 44	9 026	6 210	2 816	...	...	...
45 - 49	10 639	7 123	3 516	...	...	...
50 - 54	14 615	9 646	4 969	...	...	...
55 - 59	18 414	11 813	6 601	...	...	...
60 - 64	20 875	12 357	8 518	...	...	...
65 - 69	23 159	13 023	10 136	...	...	...
70 - 74	27 875	15 299	12 576	...	...	...
75 - 79	43 148	23 850	19 298	...	...	...
80 - 84	46 542	24 067	22 475	...	...	...
85 +	58 165	29 005	29 160	...	...	...
Unknown - Inconnu	19 983	9 991	9 992	..	..	..

19. Deaths by age and sex and age-specific death rates by sex: latest available year, 2005 - 2014
Décès et taux de mortalité selon l'âge et le sexe : dernière année disponible, 2005 - 2014 (continued - suite)

Continent, country or area, date, code[a] and age (in years) Continent, pays ou zone, date, code[a] et âge (en annèes)	Number - Nombre			Rate - Taux		
	Both sexes Les deux sexes	Male Masculin	Female Féminin	Both sexes Les deux sexes	Male Masculin	Female Féminin
ASIA - ASIE						
Israel - Israël[28]						
2014 (C)						
Total	42 085	20 979	21 106	...	...	...
0	529	287	242	...	...	...
1 - 4	139	78	61	...	...	...
5 - 9	73	39	34	...	...	...
10 - 14	73	45	28	...	...	...
15 - 19	167	126	41	...	...	...
20 - 24	239	187	52	...	...	...
25 - 29	202	142	60	...	...	...
30 - 34	253	169	84	...	...	...
35 - 39	351	208	143	...	...	...
40 - 44	473	296	177	...	...	...
45 - 49	649	394	255	...	...	...
50 - 54	1 052	651	401	...	...	...
55 - 59	1 587	980	607	...	...	...
60 - 64	2 409	1 506	903	...	...	...
65 - 69	2 992	1 802	1 190	...	...	...
70 - 74	3 267	1 895	1 372	...	...	...
75 - 79	5 194	2 736	2 458	...	...	...
80 - 84	6 731	3 224	3 507	...	...	...
85 - 89	7 613	3 123	4 490	...	...	...
90 - 94	5 866	2 272	3 594	...	...	...
95 - 99	1 722	637	1 085	...	...	...
100 +	504	182	322	...	...	...
Japan - Japon[29]						
2013 (C)						
Total	1 268 436	658 684	609 752	10.0	10.6	9.3
0	2 185	1 193	992	...	...	...
1 - 4	773	425	348	...	...	...
5 - 9	453	269	184	0.1	0.1	0.1
10 - 14	467	284	183	0.1	0.1	0.1
15 - 19	1 268	876	392	0.2	0.3	0.1
20 - 24	2 423	1 726	697	0.4	0.5	0.2
25 - 29	2 894	2 010	884	0.4	0.6	0.3
30 - 34	3 909	2 533	1 376	0.5	0.7	0.4
35 - 39	6 436	4 161	2 275	0.7	0.9	0.5
40 - 44	10 124	6 515	3 609	1.1	1.3	0.8
45 - 49	14 053	9 045	5 008	1.7	2.2	1.2
50 - 54	20 581	13 509	7 072	2.7	3.5	1.8
55 - 59	31 365	21 243	10 122	4.0	5.5	2.6
60 - 64	62 932	43 625	19 307	6.4	9.1	3.9
65 - 69	82 495	57 081	25 414	9.6	13.8	5.7
70 - 74	111 419	74 813	36 606	14.9	21.5	9.2
75 - 79	161 275	101 777	59 498	25.6	36.7	16.8
80 - 84	224 159	127 275	96 884	47.2	67.7	33.8
85 +	528 697	189 897	338 800	117.9	145.9	106.4
85 - 89	244 044	112 565	131 479	...	...	...
90 - 94	177 392	54 875	122 517	...	...	...
95 - 99	85 282	19 208	66 074	...	...	...
100 +	21 979	3 249	18 730	...	...	...
Unknown - Inconnu	528	427	101	..	..	..
Kazakhstan[24]						
2013 (C)						
Total	135 950	74 804	61 146	8.0	9.2	7.0
0	4 367	2 502	1 865	11.6	13.0	10.2
1 - 4	1 071	630	441	0.8	0.9	0.6
5 - 9	433	246	187	0.3	0.3	0.3
10 - 14	376	224	152	0.3	0.4	0.3
15 - 19	921	614	307	0.7	0.9	0.5
20 - 24	1 933	1 421	512	1.2	1.8	0.6
25 - 29	2 751	2 032	719	1.8	2.7	0.9
30 - 34	3 589	2 700	889	2.8	4.2	1.4
35 - 39	4 563	3 386	1 177	3.9	5.9	1.9
40 - 44	5 332	3 887	1 445	4.8	7.3	2.5
45 - 49	6 571	4 686	1 885	6.2	9.3	3.4
50 - 54	9 554	6 743	2 811	9.2	14.0	5.1

19. Deaths by age and sex and age-specific death rates by sex: latest available year, 2005 - 2014
Décès et taux de mortalité selon l'âge et le sexe : dernière année disponible, 2005 - 2014 (continued - suite)

Continent, country or area, date, code[a] and age (in years) / Continent, pays ou zone, date, code[a] et âge (en années)	Number - Nombre			Rate - Taux		
	Both sexes Les deux sexes	Male Masculin	Female Féminin	Both sexes Les deux sexes	Male Masculin	Female Féminin
ASIA - ASIE						
Kazakhstan[24]						
2013 (C)						
55 - 59	10 873	7 312	3 561	13.9	20.9	8.2
60 - 64	12 617	8 045	4 572	20.9	31.8	13.0
65 - 69	9 335	5 601	3 734	30.2	45.1	20.3
70 - 74	15 744	8 170	7 574	41.7	59.9	31.4
75 - 79	17 012	7 901	9 111	72.5	97.9	59.2
80 - 84	13 622	4 908	8 714	108.4	133.5	98.0
85 - 89	10 636	2 823	7 813	187.2	201.9	182.4
90 - 94	3 382	676	2 706	276.8	240.0	287.8
95 - 99	848	141	707	357.1	216.6	410.1
100 +	274	41	233	290.3	139.0	359.0
Unknown - Inconnu	146	115	31	..	..	..
Kuwait - Koweït						
2013 (C)						
Total	5 909	3 753	2 156	1.7	2.0	1.4
0	440	236	204	...	...	...
1 - 4	92	52	40	...	...	...
5 - 9	59	38	21	0.2	0.3	♦0.2
10 - 14	48	29	19	0.2	♦0.3	♦0.2
15 - 19	92	77	15	0.5	0.7	♦0.2
20 - 24	119	98	21	0.4	0.7	♦0.1
25 - 29	186	143	43	0.4	0.6	0.2
30 - 34	197	154	43	0.4	0.6	0.2
35 - 39	241	192	49	0.6	0.9	0.3
40 - 44	292	227	65	0.9	1.2	0.5
45 - 49	347	282	65	1.5	2.1	0.7
50 - 54	442	339	103	3.0	3.7	1.8
55 - 59	399	301	98	4.5	5.5	2.9
60 - 64	421	261	160	8.6	9.4	7.6
65 - 69	446	250	196	16.5	17.7	15.1
70 - 74	494	270	224	28.5	29.8	27.1
75 - 79	515	246	269	54.3	52.2	56.4
80 +	705	341	364	87.1	85.6	88.6
80 - 84	325	145	180	...	...	...
85 - 89	226	116	110	...	...	...
90 - 94	95	48	47	...	...	...
95 +	59	32	27	...	...	...
Unknown - Inconnu	374	217	157	..	..	..
Kyrgyzstan - Kirghizstan						
2013 (C)						
Total	34 880	19 714	15 166	...	...	...
0	3 093	1 743	1 350	...	...	...
1 - 4	512	303	209	...	...	...
5 - 9	165	89	76	...	...	...
10 - 14	185	106	79	...	...	...
15 - 19	343	229	114	...	...	...
20 - 24	545	375	170	...	...	...
25 - 29	721	523	198	...	...	...
30 - 34	862	620	242	...	...	...
35 - 39	1 197	870	327	...	...	...
40 - 44	1 433	1 013	420	...	...	...
45 - 49	1 840	1 320	520	...	...	...
50 - 54	2 598	1 801	797	...	...	...
55 - 59	2 639	1 728	911	...	...	...
60 - 64	2 756	1 734	1 022	...	...	...
65 - 69	1 829	1 061	768	...	...	...
70 - 74	3 114	1 704	1 410	...	...	...
75 - 79	3 730	1 804	1 926	...	...	...
80 - 84	3 710	1 581	2 129	...	...	...
85 - 89	2 449	847	1 602	...	...	...
90 - 94	810	203	607	...	...	...
95 - 99	217	39	178	...	...	...
100 +	120	10	110	...	...	...
Unknown - Inconnu	12	11	1	..	..	..

19. Deaths by age and sex and age-specific death rates by sex: latest available year, 2005 - 2014
Décès et taux de mortalité selon l'âge et le sexe : dernière année disponible, 2005 - 2014 (continued - suite)

Continent, country or area, date, code[a] and age (in years) / Continent, pays ou zone, date, code[a] et âge (en années)	Number - Nombre			Rate - Taux		
	Both sexes Les deux sexes	Male Masculin	Female Féminin	Both sexes Les deux sexes	Male Masculin	Female Féminin
ASIA - ASIE						
Malaysia - Malaisie						
2012* (C)						
Total	136 836	78 813	58 023	4.7	5.2	4.1
0	3 204	1 837	1 367	6.3	7.0	5.5
1 - 4	720	381	339	0.4	0.4	0.3
5 - 9	583	326	257	0.2	0.2	0.2
10 - 14	767	489	278	0.3	0.4	0.2
15 - 19	2 019	1 583	436	0.7	1.1	0.3
20 - 24	2 210	1 682	528	0.8	1.1	0.4
25 - 29	2 253	1 637	616	0.8	1.1	0.4
30 - 34	2 729	1 974	755	1.1	1.5	0.7
35 - 39	3 390	2 407	983	1.7	2.3	1.0
40 - 44	4 481	3 072	1 409	2.4	3.3	1.6
45 - 49	6 367	4 164	2 203	3.8	4.8	2.7
50 - 54	9 159	5 972	3 187	6.3	7.9	4.5
55 - 59	10 987	7 046	3 941	9.4	11.8	6.9
60 - 64	12 980	8 096	4 884	14.5	17.9	11.0
65 - 69	14 050	8 564	5 486	23.2	28.3	18.1
70 - 74	16 151	9 299	6 852	38.3	45.0	31.9
75 - 79	16 474	8 508	7 966	62.1	67.8	57.0
80 - 84	13 807	6 162	7 645	95.4	96.5	94.5
85 - 89	8 792	3 556	5 236	121.3	116.6	124.7
90 - 94	4 209	1 517	2 692	120.0	102.4	132.9
95 +	1 504	541	963	...	...	...
Maldives						
2013 (C)						
Total	1 120	649	471	3.3	3.8	2.8
0	46	29	17	6.6	◆8.2	◆4.9
1 - 4	21	11	10	◆0.8	◆0.8	◆0.8
5 - 9	4	3	1	◆0.1	◆0.2	◆0.1
10 - 14	9	4	5	◆0.3	◆0.3	◆0.4
15 - 19	16	8	8	◆0.5	◆0.4	◆0.5
20 - 24	20	14	6	◆0.5	◆0.7	◆0.3
25 - 29	20	13	7	◆0.5	◆0.7	◆0.4
30 - 34	20	12	8	◆0.7	◆0.9	◆0.5
35 - 39	17	9	8	◆0.8	◆0.8	◆0.7
40 - 44	16	10	6	◆0.8	◆1.1	◆0.6
45 - 49	26	17	9	◆1.5	◆2.1	◆1.0
50 - 54	40	29	11	2.7	◆3.9	◆1.5
55 - 59	62	37	25	6.3	7.2	◆5.2
60 - 64	62	38	24	10.3	12.2	◆8.3
65 - 69	73	45	28	14.5	17.7	◆11.2
70 - 74	198	111	87	41.5	45.7	37.2
75 - 79	195	104	91	53.9	52.8	55.2
80 +	275	155	120	100.1	91.6	113.9
80 - 84	151	85	66	...	...	...
85 - 89	92	53	39	...	...	...
90 - 94	28	15	13	...	...	...
95 - 99	4	2	2	...	...	...
100 +	-	-	-	...	...	...
Mongolia - Mongolie						
2014 (+C)						
Total	16 521	9 953	6 568	5.6	6.9	4.3
0	1 251	723	528	17.3	19.5	14.9
1 - 4	304	154	150	1.2	1.2	1.2
5 - 9	115	75	40	0.4	0.6	0.3
10 - 14	120	79	41	0.5	0.7	0.4
15 - 19	200	128	72	0.8	1.0	0.6
20 - 24	311	221	90	1.1	1.5	0.6
25 - 29	440	331	109	1.5	2.2	0.7
30 - 34	511	400	111	2.0	3.2	0.8
35 - 39	734	534	200	3.1	4.7	1.7
40 - 44	960	687	273	4.7	7.0	2.6
45 - 49	1 273	926	347	7.2	11.0	3.7
50 - 54	1 597	1 067	530	10.7	15.2	6.7
55 - 59	1 598	1 064	534	15.6	22.7	9.6
60 - 64	1 408	905	503	22.4	32.5	14.4

Continent, country or area, date, code[a] and age (in years)	Number - Nombre			Rate - Taux		
Continent, pays ou zone, date, code[a] et âge (en années)	Both sexes Les deux sexes	Male Masculin	Female Féminin	Both sexes Les deux sexes	Male Masculin	Female Féminin
ASIA - ASIE						
Mongolia - Mongolie						
2014 (+C)						
65 - 69	1 212	697	515	29.3	39.1	21.9
70 - 74	1 330	703	627	39.0	46.7	32.9
75 - 79	1 174	550	624	58.1	65.6	52.7
80 - 84	972	388	584	78.3	87.2	73.4
85 - 89	579	214	365	125.5	139.5	118.5
90 - 94	301	74	227	159.3	146.5	163.9
95 - 99	99	27	72	256.1	♦325.3	237.2
100 +	32	6	26	329.9	♦387.1	♦319.0
Myanmar						
2013* (+U)						
Total	257 216	150 333	106 883	...	...	...
0	11 516	6 731	4 785	...	...	...
1 - 4	1 769	1 034	735	...	...	...
5 - 9	2 551	1 461	1 091	...	...	...
10 - 14	2 381	1 349	1 032	...	...	...
15 - 19	3 682	2 265	1 417	...	...	...
20 - 24	5 165	3 234	1 932	...	...	...
25 - 29	7 598	5 005	2 593	...	...	...
30 - 34	11 104	8 080	3 024	...	...	...
35 - 39	13 265	9 705	3 560	...	...	...
40 - 44	14 970	10 930	4 040	...	...	...
45 - 49	16 302	11 500	4 802	...	...	...
50 - 54	17 336	11 588	5 748	...	...	...
55 - 59	18 524	11 646	6 878	...	...	...
60 - 64	19 656	11 551	8 106	...	...	...
65 - 69	20 421	11 614	8 807	...	...	...
70 - 74	22 822	11 881	10 941	...	...	...
75 - 79	24 684	12 391	12 293	...	...	...
80 - 84	21 216	9 514	11 702	...	...	...
85 +	22 253	8 856	13 397	...	...	...
Oman[30]						
2013 (U)						
Total	7 669	5 048	2 621	...	...	...
0	772	436	336	...	...	...
1 - 4	163	97	66	...	...	...
5 - 9	69	45	24	...	...	...
10 - 14	72	55	17	...	...	...
15 - 19	158	123	35	...	...	...
20 - 24	301	251	50	...	...	...
25 - 29	375	309	66	...	...	...
30 - 34	324	264	60	...	...	...
35 - 39	254	202	52	...	...	...
40 - 44	281	229	52	...	...	...
45 - 49	333	253	80	...	...	...
50 - 54	426	309	117	...	...	...
55 - 59	479	329	150	...	...	...
60 - 64	513	317	196	...	...	...
65 +	3 149	1 829	1 320	...	...	...
Pakistan[31]						
2007 (I)						
Total	1 019 533	598 820	420 713	6.8	7.8	5.8
0 - 4	365 729	205 840	159 889	18.7	21.0	16.4
5 - 9	33 029	16 652	16 376	1.5	1.4	1.5
10 - 14	20 510	6 871	13 640	1.0	0.6	1.4
15 - 19	27 417	16 500	10 917	1.6	1.8	1.3
20 - 24	20 192	11 195	8 997	1.5	1.6	1.3
25 - 29	23 990	13 101	10 888	2.2	2.5	2.0
30 - 34	11 624	8 007	3 617	1.4	2.0	0.8
35 - 39	24 880	11 482	13 398	3.0	2.8	3.2
40 - 44	30 926	18 802	12 124	4.6	5.4	3.7
45 - 49	27 537	17 884	9 652	4.4	5.5	3.2
50 - 54	43 405	30 870	12 535	9.5	12.7	5.8
55 - 59	51 031	35 120	15 911	14.4	18.8	9.5
60 - 64	68 531	41 470	27 061	23.4	25.3	20.9
65 - 69	58 286	35 664	22 621	28.6	32.2	24.3

19. Deaths by age and sex and age-specific death rates by sex: latest available year, 2005 - 2014
Décès et taux de mortalité selon l'âge et le sexe : dernière année disponible, 2005 - 2014 (continued - suite)

Continent, country or area, date, code[a] and age (in years) Continent, pays ou zone, date, code[a] et âge (en annèes)	Number - Nombre			Rate - Taux		
	Both sexes Les deux sexes	Male Masculin	Female Féminin	Both sexes Les deux sexes	Male Masculin	Female Féminin
ASIA - ASIE						
Pakistan[31]						
2007 (I)						
70 - 74	82 325	49 296	33 029	56.2	57.5	54.4
75 - 79	37 357	24 072	13 285	57.1	67.2	44.9
80 - 84	34 079	21 720	12 359	79.6	86.6	69.6
85 +	58 685	34 274	24 411	165.7	168.9	161.4
Philippines						
2012 (C)						
Total	514 745	296 614	218 131	5.3	6.1	4.6
0	22 254	12 987	9 267	...	...	...
1 - 4	9 237	4 982	4 255	...	...	...
5 - 9	5 098	2 858	2 240	0.5	0.5	0.4
10 - 14	4 766	2 787	1 979	0.5	0.5	0.4
15 - 19	7 857	5 136	2 721	0.8	1.0	0.6
20 - 24	10 867	7 392	3 475	1.2	1.6	0.8
25 - 29	11 719	8 089	3 630	1.5	2.1	0.9
30 - 34	14 337	9 686	4 651	2.0	2.7	1.3
35 - 39	16 698	11 071	5 627	2.7	3.5	1.8
40 - 44	21 593	14 201	7 392	3.8	4.9	2.7
45 - 49	27 180	17 829	9 351	5.5	7.1	3.8
50 - 54	33 824	22 165	11 659	8.1	10.6	5.6
55 - 59	41 049	26 860	14 189	12.6	16.6	8.6
60 - 64	45 908	29 589	16 319	18.8	25.3	12.9
65 - 69	46 028	28 381	17 647	27.3	36.8	19.3
70 - 74	50 099	28 671	21 428	42.2	56.0	31.7
75 - 79	51 356	26 347	25 009	66.5	84.6	54.3
80 +	94 815	37 551	57 264	133.5	148.2	125.4
80 - 84	42 231	18 923	23 308	...	...	...
85 - 89	30 132	11 242	18 890	...	...	...
90 - 94	16 006	5 458	10 548	...	...	...
95 +	6 446	1 928	4 518	...	...	...
Unknown - Inconnu	60	32	28	..	..	..
Qatar						
2013 (C)						
Total	2 133	1 604	529	1.1	1.1	1.0
0	157	97	60	7.0	8.7	5.3
1 - 4	27	18	9	♦0.3	♦0.4	♦0.2
5 - 9	18	12	6	♦0.2	♦0.2	♦0.1
10 - 14	20	15	5	♦0.2	♦0.4	♦0.1
15 - 19	51	45	6	0.7	1.0	♦0.2
20 - 24	115	109	6	0.5	0.6	♦0.2
25 - 29	137	120	17	0.4	0.4	♦0.2
30 - 34	167	146	21	0.5	0.6	♦0.3
35 - 39	139	128	11	0.6	0.7	♦0.2
40 - 44	147	136	11	0.8	0.9	♦0.3
45 - 49	159	134	25	1.3	1.4	♦0.9
50 - 54	172	136	36	2.1	2.1	2.0
55 - 59	152	125	27	3.0	3.2	♦2.5
60 - 64	130	88	42	5.9	5.4	7.4
65 - 69	98	52	46	9.9	7.8	14.1
70 - 74	134	66	68	24.9	20.5	31.5
75 - 79	135	70	65	37.8	32.3	46.2
80 +	174	106	68	45.9	52.3	38.5
80 - 84	93	55	38	...	...	...
85 - 89	44	31	13	...	...	...
90 - 94	19	13	6	...	...	...
95 +	18	7	11	...	...	...
Unknown - Inconnu	1	1	-	..	..	..
Republic of Korea - République de Corée[32]						
2013 (C)						
Total	266 257	146 599	119 658	5.3	5.8	4.8
0	1 305	698	607	2.9	3.0	2.8
1 - 4	342	192	150	0.2	0.2	0.2
5 - 9	253	160	93	0.1	0.1	0.1
10 - 14	272	176	96	0.1	0.1	0.1
15 - 19	812	557	255	0.2	0.3	0.2
20 - 24	1 217	831	386	0.4	0.5	0.2

19. Deaths by age and sex and age-specific death rates by sex: latest available year, 2005 - 2014
Décès et taux de mortalité selon l'âge et le sexe : dernière année disponible, 2005 - 2014 (continued - suite)

Continent, country or area, date, code[a] and age (in years) Continent, pays ou zone, date, code[a] et âge (en années)	Number - Nombre			Rate - Taux		
	Both sexes Les deux sexes	Male Masculin	Female Féminin	Both sexes Les deux sexes	Male Masculin	Female Féminin
ASIA - ASIE						
Republic of Korea - République de Corée[32]						
2013 (C)						
25 - 29	1 565	1 019	546	0.5	0.6	0.3
30 - 34	2 670	1 706	964	0.7	0.8	0.5
35 - 39	3 603	2 377	1 226	0.9	1.2	0.6
40 - 44	6 274	4 337	1 937	1.4	1.9	0.9
45 - 49	8 996	6 496	2 500	2.2	3.1	1.2
50 - 54	14 105	10 355	3 750	3.3	4.9	1.8
55 - 59	15 649	11 713	3 936	4.5	6.8	2.3
60 - 64	16 230	11 833	4 397	6.7	10.0	3.5
65 - 69	19 466	13 496	5 970	10.1	14.8	5.8
70 - 74	32 904	21 203	11 701	19.1	28.1	12.1
75 - 79	41 226	23 281	17 945	32.8	46.2	23.8
80 - 84	40 839	18 116	22 723	54.4	72.7	45.3
85 - 89	32 877	11 535	21 342	98.4	125.6	88.2
90 - 94	19 021	5 257	13 764	168.1	206.5	157.0
95 - 99	5 552	1 090	4 462	254.0	291.5	246.2
100 +	1 043	161	882	384.0	438.7	375.5
Unknown - Inconnu	36	10	26	..	..	..
Saudi Arabia - Arabie saoudite[33]						
2005 (...)						
Total	92 486	54 253	38 233	...	...	...
0 - 4	12 889	6 692	6 197	...	...	...
5 - 9	977	524	453	...	...	...
10 - 14	977	566	411	...	...	...
15 - 19	1 350	791	559	...	...	...
20 - 24	1 695	998	697	...	...	...
25 - 29	2 248	1 371	877	...	...	...
30 - 34	2 750	1 681	1 069	...	...	...
35 - 39	3 309	2 131	1 178	...	...	...
40 - 44	3 997	2 698	1 299	...	...	...
45 - 49	4 754	3 266	1 488	...	...	...
50 - 54	5 285	3 629	1 656	...	...	...
55 - 59	5 538	3 658	1 880	...	...	...
60 - 64	6 116	3 756	2 360	...	...	...
65 - 69	6 924	3 985	2 939	...	...	...
70 - 74	8 082	4 448	3 634	...	...	...
75 - 79	8 176	4 484	3 692	...	...	...
80 +	17 419	9 575	7 844	...	...	...
Singapore - Singapour						
2014 (+C)						
Total	19 393	10 534[12]	8 858[12]	5.0	5.5	4.5
0	83	42[12]	40[12]	...	...	...
1 - 4	21	14	7	...	...	...
5 - 9	14	8	6	♦0.1	♦0.1	♦0.1
10 - 14	18	10	8	♦0.1	♦0.1	♦0.1
15 - 19	68	47	21	0.3	0.4	♦0.2
20 - 24	123	97	26	0.5	0.7	♦0.2
25 - 29	139	103	36	0.5	0.8	0.3
30 - 34	172	120	52	0.6	0.9	0.3
35 - 39	218	152	66	0.7	1.0	0.4
40 - 44	366	247	119	1.2	1.6	0.7
45 - 49	512	308	204	1.7	2.0	1.3
50 - 54	835	511	324	2.6	3.2	2.1
55 - 59	1 358	874	484	4.7	6.1	3.4
60 - 64	1 580	1 029	551	6.8	8.9	4.7
65 - 69	1 816	1 150	666	11.3	14.7	8.0
70 - 74	2 075	1 259	816	19.4	25.5	14.2
75 - 79	2 596	1 444	1 152	34.0	42.8	27.1
80 - 84	2 793	1 408	1 385	57.7	72.1	47.9
85 +	4 606	1 711	2 895	118.5	132.3	111.6
85 - 89	2 365	1 035	1 330	...	...	...
90 - 94	1 471	478	993	...	...	...
95 - 99	600	156	444	...	...	...
100 +	170	42	128	...	...	...
Unknown - Inconnu	-	-	-	..	..	..

19. Deaths by age and sex and age-specific death rates by sex: latest available year, 2005 - 2014
Décès et taux de mortalité selon l'âge et le sexe : dernière année disponible, 2005 - 2014 (continued - suite)

Continent, country or area, date, code[a] and age (in years) / Continent, pays ou zone, date, code[a] et âge (en annèes)	Number - Nombre			Rate - Taux		
	Both sexes Les deux sexes	Male Masculin	Female Féminin	Both sexes Les deux sexes	Male Masculin	Female Féminin
ASIA - ASIE						
Sri Lanka[34]						
2008 (+C)						
Total	123 814	73 690	50 124	6.1	7.4	4.9
0 - 4	4 132	2 303	1 829	2.4	2.7	2.2
0	3 362	1 888	1 474	...	...	...
1 - 4	770	415	355	...	...	...
5 - 9	473	257	216	0.3	0.3	0.2
10 - 14	527	303	224	0.3	0.3	0.2
15 - 19	1 312	879	433	0.7	0.9	0.4
20 - 24	2 043	1 569	474	1.1	1.7	0.5
25 - 29	2 199	1 666	533	1.4	2.1	0.7
30 - 34	2 112	1 560	552	1.4	2.1	0.7
35 - 39	2 515	1 859	656	1.7	2.5	0.9
40 - 44	3 540	2 670	870	2.5	3.9	1.2
45 - 49	5 149	3 809	1 340	4.2	6.4	2.1
50 - 54	6 879	4 999	1 880	6.2	9.3	3.3
55 - 59	8 597	6 052	2 545	10.8	16.0	6.1
60 - 64	10 087	6 740	3 347	16.9	23.3	10.9
65 - 69	11 431	7 044	4 387	24.0	32.0	17.1
70 - 74	14 912	8 437	6 475	41.0	49.6	33.4
75 - 79	14 766	7 803	6 963	63.4	70.9	56.6
80 +	33 101	15 707	17 394	163.1	174.5	153.9
80 - 84	15 413	7 616	7 797	...	...	...
85 - 89	10 467	4 915	5 552	...	...	...
90 - 94	4 842	2 216	2 626	...	...	...
95 - 99	1 842	773	1 069	...	...	...
100 +	537	187	350	...	...	...
Unknown - Inconnu	39	33	6	..	...	...
State of Palestine - État de Palestine[35]						
2013 (U)						
Total	11 013	5 917	5 096	...	...	...
0	827	474	353	...	...	...
1 - 4	310	157	153	...	...	...
5 - 9	129	71	58	...	...	...
10 - 14	114	67	47	...	...	...
15 - 19	192	132	60	...	...	...
20 - 24	204	156	48	...	...	...
25 - 29	157	105	52	...	...	...
30 - 34	171	119	52	...	...	...
35 - 39	192	113	79	...	...	...
40 - 44	229	136	93	...	...	...
45 - 49	376	256	120	...	...	...
50 - 54	510	318	192	...	...	...
55 - 59	694	433	261	...	...	...
60 - 64	825	495	330	...	...	...
65 - 69	1 052	584	468	...	...	...
70 - 74	1 088	525	563	...	...	...
75 - 79	1 286	615	671	...	...	...
80 - 84	1 230	530	700	...	...	...
85 - 89	828	382	446	...	...	...
90 - 94	379	155	224	...	...	...
95 - 99	155	66	89	...	...	...
100 +	65	28	37	...	...	...
Tajikistan - Tadjikistan[24]						
2013 (U)						
Total	31 706	17 685	14 021	...	...	...
0	3 622	2 121	1 501	...	...	...
1 - 4	668	367	301	...	...	...
5 - 9	213	131	82	...	...	...
10 - 14	190	105	85	...	...	...
15 - 19	351	216	135	...	...	...
20 - 24	565	343	222	...	...	...
25 - 29	670	417	253	...	...	...
30 - 34	689	425	264	...	...	...
35 - 39	813	528	285	...	...	...
40 - 44	909	572	337	...	...	...
45 - 49	1 202	730	472	...	...	...

19. Deaths by age and sex and age-specific death rates by sex: latest available year, 2005 - 2014
Décès et taux de mortalité selon l'âge et le sexe : dernière année disponible, 2005 - 2014 (continued - suite)

Continent, country or area, date, code[a] and age (in years) / Continent, pays ou zone, date, code[a] et âge (en années)	Number - Nombre			Rate - Taux		
	Both sexes Les deux sexes	Male Masculin	Female Féminin	Both sexes Les deux sexes	Male Masculin	Female Féminin
ASIA - ASIE						
Tajikistan - Tadjikistan[24]						
2013 (U)						
50 - 54	1 761	1 019	742	...	...	...
55 - 59	1 990	1 189	801	...	...	...
60 - 64	2 413	1 302	1 111	...	...	...
65 - 69	1 934	1 126	808	...	...	...
70 - 74	3 350	1 935	1 415	...	...	...
75 - 79	3 956	2 125	1 831	...	...	...
80 - 84	3 465	1 766	1 699	...	...	...
85 - 89	1 894	915	979	...	...	...
90 - 94	694	245	449	...	...	...
95 - 99	177	52	125	...	...	...
100 +	94	14	80	...	...	...
Unknown - Inconnu	86	42	44	..	..	..
Thailand - Thaïlande						
2011 (+U)						
Total	414 670	235 189	179 481	...	...	...
0	5 275	2 964	2 311	...	...	...
1 - 4	7 182	4 102	3 080	...	...	...
5 - 9	1 616	978	638	...	...	...
10 - 14	2 060	1 317	743	...	...	...
15 - 19	5 140	3 896	1 244	...	...	...
20 - 24	5 659	4 383	1 276	...	...	...
25 - 29	7 307	5 531	1 776	...	...	...
30 - 34	10 659	7 862	2 797	...	...	...
35 - 39	13 981	10 135	3 846	...	...	...
40 - 44	18 346	12 894	5 452	...	...	...
45 - 49	23 390	16 016	7 374	...	...	...
50 - 54	27 255	18 201	9 054	...	...	...
55 - 59	29 801	19 075	10 726	...	...	...
60 - 64	33 121	20 047	13 074	...	...	...
65 - 69	34 744	20 202	14 542	...	...	...
70 +	189 134	87 586	101 548	...	...	...
Turkey - Turquie						
2013 (C)						
Total	372 094	205 028	167 066	4.9	5.3	4.4
0	13 900	7 532	6 368	11.3	11.9	10.7
1 - 4	3 285	1 755	1 530	0.7	0.7	0.6
5 - 9	1 844	980	864	0.3	0.3	0.3
10 - 14	1 720	1 064	656	0.3	0.3	0.2
15 - 19	3 053	2 183	870	0.5	0.7	0.3
20 - 24	3 016	2 183	833	0.5	0.7	0.3
25 - 29	3 225	2 259	966	0.5	0.7	0.3
30 - 34	3 777	2 488	1 289	0.6	0.8	0.4
35 - 39	4 690	3 022	1 668	0.8	1.0	0.6
40 - 44	6 750	4 400	2 350	1.3	1.6	0.9
45 - 49	10 388	7 013	3 375	2.2	2.9	1.4
50 - 54	15 535	10 641	4 894	3.7	5.0	2.3
55 - 59	21 987	15 321	6 666	6.2	8.7	3.7
60 - 64	27 829	18 833	8 996	10.1	14.0	6.4
65 - 69	33 017	20 810	12 207	16.1	21.9	11.1
70 - 74	42 782	24 799	17 983	28.4	36.7	21.6
75 - 79	50 976	27 446	23 530	47.3	59.5	38.2
80 - 84	62 248	29 696	32 552	75.9	88.4	67.2
85 - 89	42 897	16 792	26 105	125.6	149.0	114.0
90 +	19 172	5 808	13 364	193.6	224.0	182.9
90 - 94	14 369	4 730	9 639	...	...	...
95 - 99	3 736	911	2 825	...	...	...
100 +	1 067	167	900	...	...	...
Unknown - Inconnu	3	3	-	..	..	..

19. Deaths by age and sex and age-specific death rates by sex: latest available year, 2005 - 2014
Décès et taux de mortalité selon l'âge et le sexe : dernière année disponible, 2005 - 2014 (continued - suite)

Continent, country or area, date, code[a] and age (in years) Continent, pays ou zone, date, code[a] et âge (en années)	Number - Nombre			Rate - Taux		
	Both sexes Les deux sexes	Male Masculin	Female Féminin	Both sexes Les deux sexes	Male Masculin	Female Féminin
EUROPE						
Åland Islands - Îles d'Åland						
2013 (C)						
Total	269	145	124	9.4	10.2	8.7
0	-	-	-	-	-	-
1 - 4	-	-	-	-	-	-
5 - 9	-	-	-	-	-	-
10 - 14	-	-	-	-	-	-
15 - 19	2	1	1	♦1.2	♦1.2	♦1.2
20 - 24	-	-	-	-	-	-
25 - 29	-	-	-	-	-	-
30 - 34	-	-	-	-	-	-
35 - 39	1	1	-	♦0.6	♦1.1	-
40 - 44	1	1	-	♦0.5	♦1.1	-
45 - 49	3	3	-	♦1.4	♦2.9	-
50 - 54	4	4	-	♦2.1	♦4.2	-
55 - 59	7	6	1	♦3.5	♦6.3	♦1.0
60 - 64	11	8	3	♦5.4	♦8.2	♦2.9
65 - 69	27	16	11	♦14.1	♦16.4	♦11.7
70 - 74	34	31	3	26.6	46.7	♦4.9
75 - 79	32	17	15	33.4	♦38.9	♦28.8
80 - 84	33	18	15	47.7	♦58.8	♦38.9
85 - 89	52	21	31	100.9	♦116.3	92.5
90 - 94	40	12	28	196.6	♦216.2	♦189.2
95 - 99	19	6	13	♦417.6	♦600.0	♦366.2
100 +	3	-	3	♦666.7	-	♦1000.0
Albania - Albanie						
2013 (C)						
Total	20 442	10 990	9 452	7.1	7.5	6.6
0	282	171	111	8.0	9.3	6.5
1 - 4	70	38	32	0.5	0.5	0.5
5 - 9	42	23	19	0.2	♦0.3	♦0.2
10 - 14	57	32	25	0.3	0.3	♦0.2
15 - 19	156	95	61	0.6	0.7	0.5
20 - 24	164	121	43	0.7	1.0	0.4
25 - 29	143	96	47	0.7	0.9	0.5
30 - 34	165	116	49	0.9	1.3	0.5
35 - 39	185	127	58	1.1	1.5	0.6
40 - 44	290	192	98	1.5	2.1	1.0
45 - 49	450	298	152	2.3	3.1	1.5
50 - 54	705	462	243	3.4	4.4	2.3
55 - 59	954	632	322	5.2	6.9	3.5
60 - 64	1 163	775	388	8.2	10.9	5.5
65 - 69	1 448	962	486	13.5	17.7	9.2
70 - 74	2 622	1 534	1 088	25.5	30.8	20.5
75 - 79	3 426	1 948	1 478	47.9	55.3	40.7
80 - 84	3 582	1 788	1 794	93.8	105.3	84.5
85 +	4 538	1 580	2 958	196.1	197.7	195.2
85 - 89	2 519	943	1 576	...	...	...
90 - 94	1 456	510	946	...	...	...
95 - 99	433	102	331	...	...	...
100 +	130	25	105	...	...	...
Andorra - Andorre						
2012 (C)						
Total	303	168	135	3.9	4.3	3.6
0 - 4	4	3	1	♦1.1	♦1.6	♦0.5
0	4	3	1	♦6.9	♦10.4	♦3.4
1 - 4	-	-	-	-	-	-
5 - 9	1	-	1	♦0.2	-	♦0.5
10 - 14	-	-	-	-	-	-
15 - 19	1	-	1	♦0.3	-	♦0.6
20 - 24	1	1	-	♦0.3	♦0.5	-
25 - 29	2	-	2	♦0.4	-	♦0.8
30 - 34	2	2	-	♦0.3	♦0.6	-
35 - 39	3	2	1	♦0.4	♦0.5	♦0.3
40 - 44	6	4	2	♦0.8	♦1.1	♦0.6
45 - 49	10	8	2	♦1.4	♦2.2	♦0.6
50 - 54	7	5	2	♦1.2	♦1.6	♦0.7

19. Deaths by age and sex and age-specific death rates by sex: latest available year, 2005 - 2014
Décès et taux de mortalité selon l'âge et le sexe : dernière année disponible, 2005 - 2014 (continued - suite)

Continent, country or area, date, code[a] and age (in years) / Continent, pays ou zone, date, code[a] et âge (en années)	Number - Nombre			Rate - Taux		
	Both sexes Les deux sexes	Male Masculin	Female Féminin	Both sexes Les deux sexes	Male Masculin	Female Féminin
EUROPE						
Andorra - Andorre						
2012 (C)						
55 - 59	14	10	4	♦3.0	♦4.1	♦1.8
60 - 64	20	12	8	♦5.4	♦6.1	♦4.6
65 - 69	26	17	9	♦8.9	♦11.0	♦6.6
70 - 74	31	23	8	15.4	♦23.6	♦7.7
75 - 79	34	24	10	19.9	♦28.6	♦11.4
80 - 84	35	17	18	23.7	♦25.6	♦22.1
85 - 89	51	23	28	54.9	♦59.2	♦51.9
90 - 94	37	12	25	82.6	♦66.7	♦93.3
95 - 99	14	5	9	♦80.7	♦71.9	♦86.5
100 +	4	-	4	♦56.3	-	♦112.7
Austria - Autriche[36]						
2013 (C)						
Total	79 526	37 958	41 568	9.4	9.2	9.6
0	245	144	101	3.1	3.6	2.7
1 - 4	54	33	21	0.2	0.2	♦0.1
5 - 9	36	18	18	0.1	♦0.1	♦0.1
10 - 14	47	29	18	0.1	♦0.1	♦0.1
15 - 19	124	87	37	0.3	0.4	0.2
20 - 24	219	160	59	0.4	0.6	0.2
25 - 29	230	172	58	0.4	0.6	0.2
30 - 34	272	182	90	0.5	0.7	0.3
35 - 39	393	265	128	0.7	1.0	0.5
40 - 44	677	422	255	1.0	1.3	0.8
45 - 49	1 413	933	480	2.0	2.6	1.4
50 - 54	2 177	1 448	729	3.3	4.4	2.2
55 - 59	2 910	1 935	975	5.4	7.3	3.6
60 - 64	4 121	2 656	1 465	8.7	11.7	6.0
65 - 69	5 543	3 534	2 009	13.4	18.2	9.2
70 - 74	8 308	5 028	3 280	19.2	25.4	14.0
75 - 79	8 422	4 727	3 695	32.3	42.4	24.8
80 - 84	13 217	6 503	6 714	60.4	76.9	50.1
85 - 89	16 023	5 816	10 207	114.2	138.2	103.8
90 - 94	11 621	3 157	8 464	215.5	249.9	205.0
95 - 99	2 821	603	2 218	347.3	386.3	338.0
100 +	653	106	547	504.2	504.8	504.1
Belarus - Bélarus						
2013 (C)						
Total	125 326	63 012	62 314	13.2	14.3	12.3
0	407	238	169	3.5	4.0	3.0
1 - 4	127	73	54	0.3	0.3	0.3
5 - 9	88	61	27	0.2	0.3	♦0.1
10 - 14	73	41	32	0.2	0.2	0.1
15 - 19	236	170	66	0.5	0.7	0.3
20 - 24	635	488	147	0.9	1.3	0.4
25 - 29	1 017	801	216	1.3	2.0	0.6
30 - 34	1 506	1 168	338	2.1	3.3	1.0
35 - 39	2 144	1 639	505	3.2	5.0	1.5
40 - 44	2 786	2 112	674	4.3	6.7	2.0
45 - 49	4 016	2 973	1 043	5.9	9.2	2.9
50 - 54	6 745	5 022	1 723	8.7	13.9	4.1
55 - 59	9 213	6 522	2 691	13.8	22.0	7.3
60 - 64	11 081	7 803	3 278	20.0	33.5	10.2
65 - 69	8 928	5 643	3 285	28.1	45.5	17.0
70 - 74	13 526	7 335	6 191	37.4	60.0	25.9
75 - 79	18 689	8 223	10 466	63.4	92.8	50.8
80 - 84	20 571	7 100	13 471	98.3	130.8	86.9
85 - 89	16 132	4 148	11 984	166.3	204.2	156.3
90 - 94	5 891	1 174	4 717	264.3	291.0	258.4
95 - 99	1 198	205	993	363.5	410.0	355.2
100 +	317	73	244	586.0	879.5	532.8
Belgium - Belgique[37]						
2013 (C)						
Total	109 334	53 908	55 426	9.8	9.8	9.8
0	436	248	188	3.4	3.8	3.0
1 - 4	111	63	48	0.2	0.2	0.2

19. Deaths by age and sex and age-specific death rates by sex: latest available year, 2005 - 2014
Décès et taux de mortalité selon l'âge et le sexe : dernière année disponible, 2005 - 2014 (continued - suite)

Continent, country or area, date, code[a] and age (in years) Continent, pays ou zone, date, code[a] et âge (en années)	Number - Nombre			Rate - Taux		
	Both sexes Les deux sexes	Male Masculin	Female Féminin	Both sexes Les deux sexes	Male Masculin	Female Féminin

EUROPE

Belgium - Belgique[37]
2013 (C)

5 - 9	57	31	26	0.1	0.1	♦0.1
10 - 14	48	30	18	0.1	♦0.1	♦0.1
15 - 19	166	108	58	0.3	0.3	0.2
20 - 24	302	225	77	0.4	0.6	0.2
25 - 29	384	271	113	0.5	0.8	0.3
30 - 34	416	288	128	0.6	0.8	0.3
35 - 39	666	406	260	0.9	1.1	0.7
40 - 44	1 063	675	388	1.4	1.7	1.0
45 - 49	1 775	1 085	690	2.2	2.6	1.7
50 - 54	2 908	1 785	1 123	3.6	4.4	2.8
55 - 59	4 359	2 703	1 656	6.0	7.5	4.5
60 - 64	5 897	3 783	2 114	9.0	11.8	6.4
65 - 69	7 621	4 836	2 785	13.7	18.1	9.7
70 - 74	8 865	5 454	3 411	20.9	28.0	14.9
75 - 79	13 411	7 707	5 704	34.1	45.1	25.6
80 - 84	19 640	9 688	9 952	61.7	78.6	51.0
85 - 89	22 071	8 982	13 089	118.5	146.6	104.7
90 - 94	14 537	4 606	9 931	210.8	250.5	196.4
95 - 99	3 698	812	2 886	320.9	378.2	307.8
100 +	903	122	781	492.9	562.2	483.6

Bosnia and Herzegovina - Bosnie-Herzégovine
2010 (C)

Total	35 118	17 900	17 218	9.1	9.5	8.8
0 - 4	252	143	109	1.5	1.7	1.3
0	216	125	91	6.5	7.3	5.6
1 - 4	36	18	18	0.3	♦0.3	♦0.3
5 - 9	28	19	9	♦0.1	♦0.2	♦0.1
10 - 14	27	14	13	♦0.1	♦0.1	♦0.1
15 - 19	84	58	26	0.3	0.4	♦0.2
20 - 24	120	92	28	0.4	0.6	♦0.2
25 - 29	165	130	35	0.6	1.0	0.3
30 - 34	160	109	51	0.7	0.9	0.4
35 - 39	254	180	74	1.0	1.5	0.6
40 - 44	432	265	167	1.5	1.9	1.2
45 - 49	844	553	291	2.7	3.7	1.9
50 - 54	1 465	980	485	5.5	7.2	3.7
55 - 59	2 141	1 429	712	9.2	13.6	5.6
60 - 64	2 610	1 647	963	14.3	19.1	10.0
65 - 69	3 390	2 032	1 358	16.8	22.6	12.1
70 - 74	6 045	3 199	2 846	32.8	38.8	27.9
75 - 79	6 948	3 344	3 604	57.7	66.1	51.6
80 - 84	6 006	2 440	3 566	125.3	124.5	125.9
85 +	4 119	1 254	2 865	164.3	175.6	159.9
85 - 89	3 105	966	2 139	...	...	...
90 - 94	737	210	527	...	...	...
95 - 99	245	69	176	...	...	...
100 +	32	9	23	...	...	...
Unknown - Inconnu	28	12	16	..	..	..

Bulgaria - Bulgarie
2013 (C)

Total	104 345	54 827	49 518	14.3	15.5	13.2
0	489	283	206	7.4	8.3	6.5
1 - 4	115	70	45	0.4	0.5	0.3
5 - 9	66	39	27	0.2	0.2	♦0.2
10 - 14	66	41	25	0.2	0.3	♦0.2
15 - 19	139	96	43	0.4	0.6	0.3
20 - 24	304	231	73	0.7	1.0	0.3
25 - 29	335	238	97	0.7	0.9	0.4
30 - 34	510	368	142	1.0	1.4	0.6
35 - 39	781	528	253	1.4	1.8	0.9
40 - 44	1 338	893	445	2.5	3.3	1.7
45 - 49	2 072	1 475	597	4.4	6.1	2.6
50 - 54	3 501	2 466	1 035	7.0	9.8	4.1
55 - 59	5 601	3 949	1 652	10.8	15.8	6.2
60 - 64	8 078	5 669	2 409	15.4	23.5	8.5

19. Deaths by age and sex and age-specific death rates by sex: latest available year, 2005 - 2014
Décès et taux de mortalité selon l'âge et le sexe : dernière année disponible, 2005 - 2014 (continued - suite)

Continent, country or area, date, code[a] and age (in years) Continent, pays ou zone, date, code[a] et âge (en années)	Number - Nombre			Rate - Taux		
	Both sexes Les deux sexes	Male Masculin	Female Féminin	Both sexes Les deux sexes	Male Masculin	Female Féminin
EUROPE						
Bulgaria - Bulgarie						
2013 (C)						
65 - 69	10 409	6 779	3 630	23.4	34.6	14.5
70 - 74	11 563	6 742	4 821	33.8	47.5	24.1
75 - 79	16 670	8 363	8 307	56.5	72.2	46.3
80 - 84	19 365	8 266	11 099	98.7	112.9	90.3
85 - 89	15 634	5 919	9 715	172.1	189.2	163.2
90 - 94	6 334	2 133	4 201	273.8	287.0	267.6
95 - 99	837	233	604	397.4	374.0	407.3
100 +	138	46	92	423.3	410.7	429.9
Croatia - Croatie						
2013 (C)						
Total	50 386	24 988	25 398	11.8	12.2	11.5
0	162	93	69	4.0	4.4	3.6
1 - 4	45	28	17	0.3	♦0.3	♦0.2
5 - 9	17	8	9	♦0.1	♦0.1	♦0.1
10 - 14	21	16	5	♦0.1	♦0.1	-
15 - 19	85	63	22	0.3	0.5	♦0.2
20 - 24	120	92	28	0.5	0.7	♦0.2
25 - 29	154	111	43	0.6	0.8	0.3
30 - 34	200	148	52	0.7	1.0	0.4
35 - 39	280	177	103	1.0	1.2	0.7
40 - 44	413	273	140	1.5	2.0	1.0
45 - 49	851	591	260	2.8	4.0	1.7
50 - 54	1 505	1 040	465	4.8	6.8	2.9
55 - 59	2 432	1 704	728	7.7	11.0	4.5
60 - 64	3 522	2 488	1 034	12.4	18.4	7.0
65 - 69	3 590	2 360	1 230	17.1	25.3	10.6
70 - 74	5 801	3 454	2 347	28.3	40.0	19.8
75 - 79	8 755	4 453	4 302	49.2	65.0	39.4
80 - 84	10 177	4 237	5 940	86.7	107.2	76.3
85 +	12 256	3 652	8 604	180.0	201.2	172.3
85 - 89	7 875	2 511	5 364	...	...	...
90 - 94	3 713	990	2 723	...	...	...
95 - 99	544	124	420	...	...	...
100 +	124	27	97	...	...	...
Czech Republic - République tchèque						
2013 (C)						
Total	109 160	55 098	54 062	10.4	10.7	10.1
0	265	158	107	2.4	2.8	2.0
1 - 4	66	39	27	0.1	0.2	♦0.1
5 - 9	51	29	22	0.1	♦0.1	♦0.1
10 - 14	37	26	11	0.1	♦0.1	-
15 - 19	185	138	47	0.4	0.5	0.2
20 - 24	334	257	77	0.5	0.8	0.2
25 - 29	394	286	108	0.6	0.8	0.3
30 - 34	522	388	134	0.6	0.9	0.3
35 - 39	839	590	249	0.9	1.2	0.5
40 - 44	1 141	790	351	1.5	2.1	1.0
45 - 49	1 876	1 301	575	2.6	3.6	1.7
50 - 54	2 730	1 817	913	4.3	5.7	2.9
55 - 59	5 288	3 618	1 670	7.2	10.1	4.5
60 - 64	8 832	5 928	2 904	12.0	16.9	7.6
65 - 69	12 124	7 734	4 390	19.1	26.6	12.7
70 - 74	12 070	7 160	4 910	28.5	39.2	20.4
75 - 79	13 657	7 208	6 449	45.2	60.5	35.3
80 - 84	18 978	8 175	10 803	79.7	97.5	70.1
85 - 89	18 400	6 417	11 983	145.9	172.3	134.9
90 - 94	9 442	2 621	6 821	255.6	288.0	245.0
95 - 99	1 588	356	1 232	361.2	393.8	352.7
100 +	341	62	279	466.5	413.3	480.2
Denmark - Danemark[38]						
2013 (C)						
Total	52 470	26 111	26 359	9.4	9.4	9.3
0	194	95	99	3.4	3.2	3.5
1 - 4	43	29	14	0.2	♦0.2	♦0.1
5 - 9	20	8	12	♦0.1	-	♦0.1

19. Deaths by age and sex and age-specific death rates by sex: latest available year, 2005 - 2014
Décès et taux de mortalité selon l'âge et le sexe : dernière année disponible, 2005 - 2014 (continued - suite)

Continent, country or area, date, code[a] and age (in years) Continent, pays ou zone, date, code[a] et âge (en annèes)	Number - Nombre			Rate - Taux		
	Both sexes Les deux sexes	Male Masculin	Female Féminin	Both sexes Les deux sexes	Male Masculin	Female Féminin
EUROPE						
Denmark - Danemark[38]						
2013 (C)						
10 - 14	23	16	7	♦0.1	♦0.1	-
15 - 19	79	55	24	0.2	0.3	♦0.1
20 - 24	95	62	33	0.3	0.3	0.2
25 - 29	112	73	39	0.3	0.4	0.2
30 - 34	147	97	50	0.5	0.6	0.3
35 - 39	263	174	89	0.7	0.9	0.5
40 - 44	464	290	174	1.2	1.5	0.9
45 - 49	853	557	296	2.0	2.6	1.4
50 - 54	1 397	878	519	3.7	4.6	2.8
55 - 59	2 180	1 333	847	6.2	7.5	4.8
60 - 64	3 169	1 947	1 222	9.3	11.6	7.1
65 - 69	4 920	3 001	1 919	13.8	17.2	10.6
70 - 74	5 478	3 190	2 288	22.1	26.9	17.6
75 - 79	6 684	3 602	3 082	37.7	44.8	31.9
80 - 84	8 270	4 185	4 085	70.0	85.2	59.1
85 - 89	8 669	3 730	4 939	117.4	143.7	103.2
90 - 94	6 465	2 101	4 364	200.2	234.7	187.0
95 - 99	2 455	596	1 859	325.9	397.9	308.1
100 +	490	92	398	504.1	601.3	486.0
Estonia - Estonie						
2013 (C)						
Total	15 244	7 232	8 012	11.5	11.7	11.4
0	28	13	15	♦2.0	♦1.8	♦2.2
1 - 4	17	6	11	♦0.3	♦0.2	♦0.4
5 - 9	12	7	5	♦0.2	♦0.2	♦0.1
10 - 14	9	3	6	♦0.1	♦0.1	♦0.2
15 - 19	24	16	8	♦0.4	♦0.5	♦0.3
20 - 24	60	51	9	0.7	1.1	♦0.2
25 - 29	81	58	23	0.8	1.2	♦0.5
30 - 34	138	110	28	1.5	2.4	♦0.6
35 - 39	151	113	38	1.7	2.4	0.9
40 - 44	205	154	51	2.2	3.3	1.1
45 - 49	284	209	75	3.3	5.0	1.7
50 - 54	524	360	164	5.6	8.1	3.4
55 - 59	777	526	251	8.8	13.1	5.2
60 - 64	1 162	812	350	14.1	23.1	7.4
65 - 69	1 172	780	392	19.4	32.0	10.9
70 - 74	1 751	1 012	739	27.1	43.1	17.9
75 - 79	2 185	1 057	1 128	43.4	65.6	33.0
80 - 84	2 624	1 023	1 601	70.6	100.3	59.4
85 - 89	2 465	631	1 834	128.8	152.7	122.2
90 - 94	1 201	238	963	226.0	261.5	218.6
95 - 99	304	46	258	325.5	362.2	319.7
100 +	70	7	63	489.5	♦583.3	480.9
Faeroe Islands - Îles Féroé						
2013 (C)						
Total	364	206	158	7.6	8.3	6.8
0	-	-	-	-	-	-
1 - 4	-	-	-	-	-	-
5 - 9	-	-	-	-	-	-
10 - 14	-	-	-	-	-	-
15 - 19	-	-	-	-	-	-
20 - 24	2	1	1	♦0.7	♦0.6	♦0.8
25 - 29	2	2	-	♦0.9	♦1.5	-
30 - 34	-	-	-	-	-	-
35 - 39	4	4	-	♦1.3	♦2.4	-
40 - 44	3	2	1	♦0.9	♦1.2	♦0.7
45 - 49	4	2	2	♦1.1	♦1.1	♦1.2
50 - 54	8	5	3	♦2.5	♦3.1	♦1.9
55 - 59	12	9	3	♦4.1	♦5.9	♦2.1
60 - 64	25	17	8	♦8.7	♦11.4	♦5.7
65 - 69	26	15	11	♦10.8	♦11.6	♦9.9
70 - 74	36	22	14	19.9	♦23.8	♦15.9
75 - 79	40	32	8	30.2	48.3	♦12.1
80 - 84	59	35	24	54.4	76.1	♦38.4

19. Deaths by age and sex and age-specific death rates by sex: latest available year, 2005 - 2014
Décès et taux de mortalité selon l'âge et le sexe : dernière année disponible, 2005 - 2014 (continued - suite)

Continent, country or area, date, code[a] and age (in years) Continent, pays ou zone, date, code[a] et âge (en années)	Number - Nombre			Rate - Taux		
	Both sexes Les deux sexes	Male Masculin	Female Féminin	Both sexes Les deux sexes	Male Masculin	Female Féminin
EUROPE						
Faeroe Islands - Îles Féroé						
2013 (C)						
85 - 89	65	32	33	99.4	144.1	76.4
90 - 94	50	23	27	176.7	♦258.4	♦139.2
95 +	28	5	23	♦359.0	♦250.0	♦396.6
Finland - Finlande						
2013 (C)						
Total	51 472	25 631	25 841	9.5	9.6	9.4
0	102	58	44	1.7	1.9	1.5
1 - 4	35	16	19	0.1	♦0.1	♦0.2
5 - 9	18	13	5	♦0.1	♦0.1	-
10 - 14	27	14	13	♦0.1	♦0.1	♦0.1
15 - 19	95	58	37	0.3	0.4	0.2
20 - 24	185	138	47	0.5	0.8	0.3
25 - 29	222	173	49	0.7	1.0	0.3
30 - 34	283	216	67	0.8	1.2	0.4
35 - 39	318	236	82	1.0	1.4	0.5
40 - 44	455	310	145	1.4	1.9	0.9
45 - 49	856	580	276	2.3	3.1	1.5
50 - 54	1 242	836	406	3.3	4.5	2.2
55 - 59	2 173	1 486	687	5.8	8.0	3.6
60 - 64	3 357	2 267	1 090	8.8	12.1	5.6
65 - 69	4 426	2 953	1 473	12.9	18.0	8.3
70 - 74	4 549	2 842	1 707	19.5	26.7	13.4
75 - 79	6 145	3 480	2 665	32.9	43.7	24.9
80 - 84	8 468	4 089	4 379	58.9	76.1	48.6
85 - 89	9 547	3 618	5 929	110.9	136.8	99.5
90 - 94	6 406	1 759	4 647	198.6	236.9	187.1
95 - 99	2 167	438	1 729	331.3	376.9	321.4
100 +	396	51	345	563.3	576.3	561.4
France[39]						
2012 (C)						
Total	559 227	281 468	277 759	8.8	9.1	8.5
0 - 4	3 174	1 788	1 386	0.8	0.9	0.7
0	2 643	1 479	1 164	3.4	3.8	3.1
1 - 4	531	309	222	0.2	0.2	0.1
5 - 9	298	162	136	0.1	0.1	0.1
10 - 14	365	199	166	0.1	0.1	0.1
15 - 19	1 032	729	303	0.3	0.4	0.2
20 - 24	1 751	1 301	450	0.5	0.7	0.2
25 - 29	2 003	1 468	535	0.5	0.8	0.3
30 - 34	2 485	1 753	732	0.6	0.9	0.4
35 - 39	3 724	2 489	1 235	0.9	1.2	0.6
40 - 44	6 509	4 355	2 154	1.5	2.0	1.0
45 - 49	10 827	7 067	3 760	2.5	3.3	1.7
50 - 54	16 881	11 249	5 632	4.0	5.4	2.6
55 - 59	24 454	16 710	7 744	6.0	8.5	3.7
60 - 64	33 129	22 684	10 445	8.2	11.7	5.0
65 - 69	33 793	22 651	11 142	11.2	15.7	7.0
70 - 74	38 076	24 317	13 759	16.4	23.0	10.9
75 - 79	59 955	34 915	25 040	27.2	37.4	19.8
80 - 84	90 672	46 166	44 506	49.7	66.1	39.6
85 - 89	111 079	46 643	64 436	94.4	121.3	81.3
90 - 94	79 942	26 749	53 193	167.7	206.8	153.2
95 - 99	29 993	6 755	23 238	306.8	362.7	293.7
100 +	9 085	1 318	7 767	466.5	474.1	465.3
Germany - Allemagne						
2013 (C)						
Total	893 825	429 645	464 180	11.1	10.9	11.3
0	2 250	1 268	982	3.3	3.6	3.0
1 - 4	434	245	189	0.2	0.2	0.1
5 - 9	307	177	130	0.1	0.1	0.1
10 - 14	302	155	147	0.1	0.1	0.1
15 - 19	985	653	332	0.2	0.3	0.2
20 - 24	1 536	1 078	458	0.3	0.4	0.2
25 - 29	1 950	1 361	589	0.4	0.5	0.2
30 - 34	2 589	1 739	850	0.5	0.7	0.3

19. Deaths by age and sex and age-specific death rates by sex: latest available year, 2005 - 2014
Décès et taux de mortalité selon l'âge et le sexe : dernière année disponible, 2005 - 2014 (continued - suite)

Continent, country or area, date, code[a] and age (in years) Continent, pays ou zone, date, code[a] et âge (en années)	Number - Nombre			Rate - Taux		
	Both sexes Les deux sexes	Male Masculin	Female Féminin	Both sexes Les deux sexes	Male Masculin	Female Féminin

EUROPE

Germany - Allemagne
2013 (C)

35 - 39	3 458	2 230	1 228	0.7	1.0	0.5
40 - 44	6 809	4 334	2 475	1.2	1.5	0.9
45 - 49	14 540	9 394	5 146	2.1	2.7	1.5
50 - 54	24 391	15 819	8 572	3.7	4.8	2.6
55 - 59	33 800	22 113	11 687	6.0	7.9	4.1
60 - 64	46 093	29 835	16 258	9.2	12.2	6.3
65 - 69	54 132	34 278	19 854	13.8	18.2	9.7
70 - 74	97 538	60 160	37 378	20.6	27.3	14.7
75 - 79	129 693	73 251	56 442	34.5	44.5	26.7
80 - 84	153 586	74 824	78 762	66.4	82.8	55.9
85 - 89	167 418	60 479	106 939	120.6	141.9	111.2
90 - 94	115 791	29 749	86 042	213.3	243.2	204.6
95 - 99	28 802	5 437	23 365	356.1	394.8	348.1
100 +	7 421	1 066	6 355	479.1	496.3	476.3

Greece - Grèce
2013 (C)

Total	111 794	57 630	54 164	10.1	10.6	9.6
0	346	200	146	3.5	3.9	3.0
1 - 4	58	27	31	0.1	♦0.1	0.1
5 - 9	53	30	23	0.1	♦0.1	♦0.1
10 - 14	58	33	25	0.1	0.1	♦0.1
15 - 19	128	92	36	0.2	0.3	0.1
20 - 24	263	200	63	0.4	0.6	0.2
25 - 29	304	239	65	0.4	0.7	0.2
30 - 34	507	366	141	0.6	0.9	0.4
35 - 39	635	434	201	0.8	1.0	0.5
40 - 44	1 026	673	353	1.2	1.6	0.8
45 - 49	1 719	1 183	536	2.2	3.0	1.3
50 - 54	2 586	1 738	848	3.5	4.8	2.2
55 - 59	3 819	2 614	1 205	5.6	7.9	3.4
60 - 64	5 069	3 545	1 524	7.9	11.7	4.6
65 - 69	7 098	4 770	2 328	12.2	17.3	7.6
70 - 74	9 105	5 681	3 424	17.6	23.9	12.3
75 - 79	16 133	9 028	7 105	32.4	41.4	25.4
80 - 84	23 299	11 252	12 047	63.9	72.6	57.4
85 - 89	22 640	9 540	13 100	121.7	132.0	115.1
90 - 94	12 002	4 455	7 547	201.2	200.7	201.6
95 - 99	4 019	1 299	2 720	260.0	254.4	262.8
100 +	927	231	696	241.6	188.0	266.9

Hungary - Hongrie
2013 (C)

Total	126 677	61 820	64 857	12.8	13.1	12.5
0	448	265	183	5.0	5.8	4.2
1 - 4	68	39	29	0.2	0.2	♦0.2
5 - 9	40	22	18	0.1	♦0.1	♦0.1
10 - 14	61	33	28	0.1	0.1	♦0.1
15 - 19	160	109	51	0.3	0.4	0.2
20 - 24	240	166	74	0.4	0.5	0.2
25 - 29	308	223	85	0.5	0.7	0.3
30 - 34	440	293	147	0.6	0.8	0.4
35 - 39	949	653	296	1.1	1.5	0.7
40 - 44	1 434	968	466	2.0	2.7	1.3
45 - 49	2 716	1 834	882	4.3	5.8	2.7
50 - 54	4 739	3 237	1 502	7.7	10.9	4.7
55 - 59	9 038	6 050	2 988	11.9	17.1	7.4
60 - 64	11 310	7 329	3 981	16.9	24.3	10.8
65 - 69	12 114	7 443	4 671	22.6	32.4	15.2
70 - 74	14 112	7 802	6 310	31.9	45.0	23.5
75 - 79	17 259	8 162	9 097	52.4	71.4	42.4
80 - 84	20 925	8 264	12 661	88.4	110.1	78.4
85 - 89	18 389	5 777	12 612	150.0	173.8	141.2
90 - 94	9 723	2 669	7 054	225.6	254.3	216.3
95 - 99	1 820	405	1 415	346.2	328.6	351.6
100 +	384	77	307	301.5	174.2	369.2

19. Deaths by age and sex and age-specific death rates by sex: latest available year, 2005 - 2014
Décès et taux de mortalité selon l'âge et le sexe : dernière année disponible, 2005 - 2014 (continued - suite)

Continent, country or area, date, code[a] and age (in years) / Continent, pays ou zone, date, code[a] et âge (en années)	Number - Nombre			Rate - Taux		
	Both sexes Les deux sexes	Male Masculin	Female Féminin	Both sexes Les deux sexes	Male Masculin	Female Féminin
EUROPE						
Iceland - Islande						
2013 (C)						
Total	2 154	1 091	1 063	6.7	6.7	6.6
0	8	2	6	♦1.8	♦0.9	♦2.7
1 - 4	3	1	2	♦0.2	♦0.1	♦0.2
5 - 9	2	1	1	♦0.1	♦0.1	♦0.1
10 - 14	2	2	-	♦0.1	♦0.2	-
15 - 19	4	2	2	♦0.2	♦0.2	♦0.2
20 - 24	11	8	3	♦0.4	♦0.6	♦0.3
25 - 29	8	6	2	♦0.4	♦0.5	♦0.2
30 - 34	19	17	2	♦0.8	♦1.4	♦0.2
35 - 39	13	8	5	♦0.6	♦0.7	♦0.5
40 - 44	20	12	8	♦1.0	♦1.1	♦0.8
45 - 49	34	20	14	1.6	♦1.9	♦1.3
50 - 54	52	30	22	2.4	♦2.8	♦2.0
55 - 59	71	46	25	3.6	4.6	♦2.5
60 - 64	103	53	50	6.1	6.2	6.0
65 - 69	156	94	62	11.5	13.7	9.3
70 - 74	178	96	82	18.7	21.0	16.6
75 - 79	247	133	114	32.6	37.5	28.2
80 - 84	386	210	176	61.6	75.4	50.6
85 - 89	459	212	247	124.1	145.0	110.5
90 - 94	252	108	144	174.9	223.4	150.5
95 - 99	98	26	72	339.1	♦309.5	351.2
100 +	28	4	24	♦727.3	♦666.7	♦738.5
Ireland - Irlande						
2013 (+C)						
Total	30 018	15 211	14 807	6.5	6.7	6.4
0	228	119	109	3.2	3.2	3.1
1 - 4	47	24	23	0.2	♦0.2	♦0.2
5 - 9	31	15	16	0.1	♦0.1	♦0.1
10 - 14	27	18	9	♦0.1	♦0.1	♦0.1
15 - 19	74	54	20	0.3	0.4	♦0.1
20 - 24	141	103	38	0.5	0.8	0.3
25 - 29	171	136	35	0.5	0.9	0.2
30 - 34	240	165	75	0.6	0.9	0.4
35 - 39	261	183	78	0.7	1.0	0.4
40 - 44	373	248	125	1.1	1.5	0.7
45 - 49	595	373	222	1.9	2.4	1.4
50 - 54	903	537	366	3.2	3.8	2.6
55 - 59	1 220	745	475	4.9	6.0	3.8
60 - 64	1 727	1 052	675	7.8	9.5	6.0
65 - 69	2 321	1 427	894	12.4	15.3	9.5
70 - 74	2 865	1 728	1 137	21.0	26.0	16.2
75 - 79	3 809	2 125	1 684	36.4	44.1	29.8
80 - 84	4 923	2 517	2 406	68.4	83.0	57.7
85 +	10 062	3 642	6 420	163.0	184.4	152.9
Italy - Italie						
2013 (C)						
Total	600 744	290 354	310 390	10.0	9.9	10.0
0	1 493	864	629	2.9	3.3	2.5
1 - 4	322	191	131	0.1	0.2	0.1
5 - 9	207	132	75	0.1	0.1	0.1
10 - 14	241	144	97	0.1	0.1	0.1
15 - 19	610	433	177	0.2	0.3	0.1
20 - 24	959	695	264	0.3	0.4	0.2
25 - 29	1 149	836	313	0.4	0.5	0.2
30 - 34	1 560	1 058	502	0.4	0.6	0.3
35 - 39	2 659	1 687	972	0.6	0.8	0.4
40 - 44	4 555	2 815	1 740	0.9	1.2	0.7
45 - 49	7 767	4 776	2 991	1.6	2.0	1.2
50 - 54	11 343	6 993	4 350	2.6	3.3	1.9
55 - 59	15 924	9 998	5 926	4.1	5.3	3.0
60 - 64	24 067	15 251	8 816	6.6	8.7	4.7
65 - 69	35 060	22 288	12 772	10.4	13.9	7.3
70 - 74	52 089	31 989	20 100	17.0	22.8	12.2
75 - 79	76 831	43 975	32 856	29.6	38.9	22.4

19. Deaths by age and sex and age-specific death rates by sex: latest available year, 2005 - 2014
Décès et taux de mortalité selon l'âge et le sexe : dernière année disponible, 2005 - 2014 (continued - suite)

Continent, country or area, date, code[a] and age (in years) Continent, pays ou zone, date, code[a] et âge (en années)	Number - Nombre			Rate - Taux		
	Both sexes Les deux sexes	Male Masculin	Female Féminin	Both sexes Les deux sexes	Male Masculin	Female Féminin
EUROPE						
Italy - Italie						
2013 (C)						
80 - 84	110 882	55 991	54 891	55.7	71.8	45.3
85 - 89	127 394	52 784	74 610	104.4	130.6	91.4
90 - 94	89 084	29 002	60 082	180.8	217.0	167.4
95 - 99	29 018	7 046	21 972	301.1	342.7	289.8
100 +	7 520	1 406	6 114	438.8	488.9	428.7
Latvia - Lettonie						
2013 (C)						
Total	28 691	13 518	15 173	14.3	14.7	13.9
0	74	40	34	3.7	3.9	3.5
1 - 4	41	26	15	0.5	♦0.6	♦0.4
5 - 9	19	15	4	♦0.2	♦0.3	♦0.1
10 - 14	19	11	8	♦0.2	♦0.2	♦0.2
15 - 19	31	24	7	0.3	♦0.5	♦0.2
20 - 24	80	57	23	0.6	0.8	♦0.3
25 - 29	145	108	37	1.0	1.4	0.5
30 - 34	248	181	67	1.9	2.7	1.0
35 - 39	321	243	78	2.4	3.7	1.2
40 - 44	521	363	158	3.7	5.3	2.2
45 - 49	758	536	222	5.5	8.1	3.1
50 - 54	1 225	886	339	8.1	12.6	4.2
55 - 59	1 631	1 151	480	11.9	18.7	6.3
60 - 64	2 047	1 361	686	16.7	26.5	9.6
65 - 69	2 323	1 466	857	23.6	38.3	14.2
70 - 74	3 443	1 890	1 553	32.5	50.8	22.6
75 - 79	4 125	1 896	2 229	50.8	74.9	39.8
80 - 84	4 641	1 694	2 947	82.6	111.7	71.9
85 - 89	4 291	1 061	3 230	145.6	177.7	137.4
90 - 94	2 093	378	1 715	261.4	278.1	258.0
95 - 99	499	104	395	428.3	514.9	410.2
100 +	110	22	88	662.7	♦1157.9	598.6
Unknown - Inconnu	6	5	1	..	..	..
Liechtenstein						
2013 (C)						
Total	246	123	123	6.7	6.7	6.6
0	-	-	-	-	-	-
1 - 4	-	-	-	-	-	-
5 - 9	-	-	-	-	-	-
10 - 14	-	-	-	-	-	-
15 - 19	1	1	-	♦0.5	♦0.9	-
20 - 24	-	-	-	-	-	-
25 - 29	-	-	-	-	-	-
30 - 34	1	-	1	♦0.4	-	♦0.9
35 - 39	1	-	1	♦0.4	-	♦0.8
40 - 44	6	3	3	♦2.0	♦2.0	♦2.0
45 - 49	6	6	-	♦1.9	♦3.9	-
50 - 54	6	4	2	♦2.0	♦2.7	♦1.3
55 - 59	10	6	4	♦3.8	♦4.5	♦3.0
60 - 64	16	11	5	♦6.9	♦9.5	♦4.3
65 - 69	23	11	12	♦11.6	♦11.0	♦12.1
70 - 74	29	15	14	♦19.8	♦21.4	♦18.4
75 - 79	21	10	11	♦21.9	♦24.3	♦20.1
80 - 84	34	17	17	54.8	♦68.8	♦45.6
85 - 89	40	14	26	102.3	♦123.9	♦93.5
90 - 94	39	18	21	245.3	♦418.6	♦181.0
95 - 99	9	6	3	♦360.0	♦600.0	♦200.0
100 +	2	1	1	♦400.0	♦500.0	♦333.3
Lithuania - Lituanie						
2012 (C)						
Total	40 938	20 691	20 247	13.7	15.0	12.6
0 - 4	141	82	59	0.9	1.1	0.8
0	118	68	50	3.9	4.4	3.4
1 - 4	23	14	9	♦0.2	♦0.2	♦0.2
5 - 9	26	13	13	♦0.2	♦0.2	♦0.2
10 - 14	28	21	7	♦0.2	♦0.3	♦0.1
15 - 19	115	87	28	0.6	0.9	♦0.3

536

19. Deaths by age and sex and age-specific death rates by sex: latest available year, 2005 - 2014
Décès et taux de mortalité selon l'âge et le sexe : dernière année disponible, 2005 - 2014 (continued - suite)

Continent, country or area, date, code[a] and age (in years) Continent, pays ou zone, date, code[a] et âge (en annèes)	Number - Nombre			Rate - Taux		
	Both sexes Les deux sexes	Male Masculin	Female Féminin	Both sexes Les deux sexes	Male Masculin	Female Féminin
EUROPE						
Lithuania - Lituanie						
2012 (C)						
20 - 24	212	180	32	1.0	1.6	0.3
25 - 29	263	220	43	1.4	2.2	0.5
30 - 34	391	326	65	2.2	3.7	0.7
35 - 39	581	433	148	3.0	4.6	1.5
40 - 44	871	648	223	4.1	6.3	2.0
45 - 49	1 330	959	371	6.0	9.1	3.2
50 - 54	2 098	1 521	577	8.8	13.7	4.5
55 - 59	2 349	1 672	677	12.4	19.7	6.5
60 - 64	2 970	2 100	870	17.5	29.3	8.9
65 - 69	3 316	2 153	1 163	23.7	39.4	13.7
70 - 74	4 458	2 567	1 891	31.1	49.3	20.7
75 - 79	5 686	2 775	2 911	47.7	71.4	36.3
80 - 84	6 835	2 613	4 222	80.3	105.1	70.1
85 - 89	5 839	1 544	4 295	139.9	162.2	133.3
90 - 94	2 559	586	1 973	229.1	257.1	221.9
95 - 99	710	143	567	348.9	322.8	356.2
100 +	160	48	112	418.3	484.8	395.1
Luxembourg						
2013 (C)						
Total	3 822	1 864	1 958	7.1	6.9	7.3
0	23	13	10	♦3.8	♦4.2	♦3.4
1 - 4	3	2	1	♦0.1	♦0.2	♦0.1
5 - 9	2	2	-	♦0.1	♦0.1	-
10 - 14	3	2	1	♦0.1	♦0.1	♦0.1
15 - 19	8	4	4	♦0.2	♦0.2	♦0.3
20 - 24	13	11	2	♦0.4	♦0.6	♦0.1
25 - 29	14	7	7	♦0.4	♦0.4	♦0.4
30 - 34	28	13	15	♦0.7	♦0.6	♦0.7
35 - 39	23	13	10	♦0.6	♦0.6	♦0.5
40 - 44	40	24	16	0.9	♦1.1	♦0.8
45 - 49	87	43	44	2.0	1.9	2.1
50 - 54	144	96	48	3.7	4.8	2.5
55 - 59	170	113	57	5.2	6.8	3.5
60 - 64	227	152	75	8.4	11.1	5.6
65 - 69	254	152	102	11.8	14.3	9.4
70 - 74	336	204	132	18.8	24.8	13.6
75 - 79	458	250	208	31.3	38.9	25.3
80 - 84	696	366	330	58.3	76.2	46.2
85 - 89	723	273	450	112.8	140.2	100.9
90 - 94	422	106	316	194.0	193.8	194.1
95 - 99	126	16	110	276.9	♦213.3	289.5
100 +	20	1	19	♦312.5	♦62.5	♦395.8
Malta - Malte						
2013 (C)						
Total	3 236	1 636	1 600	7.6	7.7	7.5
0	27	14	13	♦6.6	♦6.5	♦6.6
1 - 4	2	1	1	♦0.1	♦0.1	♦0.1
5 - 9	-	-	-	-	-	-
10 - 14	1	1	-	-	♦0.1	-
15 - 19	5	3	2	♦0.2	♦0.2	♦0.2
20 - 24	15	10	5	♦0.5	♦0.6	♦0.3
25 - 29	7	6	1	♦0.2	♦0.4	♦0.1
30 - 34	10	7	3	♦0.3	♦0.4	♦0.2
35 - 39	17	15	2	♦0.6	♦1.0	♦0.1
40 - 44	22	14	8	♦0.8	♦1.0	♦0.6
45 - 49	42	28	14	1.6	♦2.2	♦1.1
50 - 54	70	44	26	2.3	2.9	♦1.7
55 - 59	117	76	41	3.9	5.0	2.8
60 - 64	205	136	69	7.0	9.3	4.7
65 - 69	307	202	105	10.8	14.7	7.1
70 - 74	285	173	112	18.3	24.1	13.3
75 - 79	486	249	237	34.7	41.3	29.8
80 - 84	585	280	305	64.2	82.4	53.3
85 - 89	563	220	343	114.9	127.7	107.9
90 - 94	363	125	238	214.7	244.6	201.7

Continent, country or area, date, code[a] and age (in years) / Continent, pays ou zone, date, code[a] et âge (en années)	Number - Nombre			Rate - Taux		
	Both sexes Les deux sexes	Male Masculin	Female Féminin	Both sexes Les deux sexes	Male Masculin	Female Féminin
EUROPE						
Malta - Malte						
2013 (C)						
95 - 99	95	28	67	301.6	♦383.6	276.9
100 +	12	4	8	♦250.0	♦266.7	♦242.4
Montenegro - Monténégro						
2013 (C)						
Total	5 917	3 080	2 837	9.5	10.0	9.0
0	33	21	12	4.4	♦5.4	♦3.4
1 - 4	5	1	4	♦0.2	♦0.1	♦0.3
5 - 9	3	3	-	♦0.1	♦0.2	-
10 - 14	5	2	3	♦0.1	♦0.1	♦0.2
15 - 19	16	8	8	♦0.4	♦0.4	♦0.4
20 - 24	24	19	5	♦0.6	♦0.9	♦0.2
25 - 29	30	21	9	♦0.7	♦0.9	♦0.4
30 - 34	27	20	7	♦0.6	♦0.9	♦0.3
35 - 39	46	29	17	1.1	♦1.4	♦0.8
40 - 44	72	47	25	1.8	2.3	♦1.2
45 - 49	137	80	57	3.3	3.8	2.7
50 - 54	225	156	69	5.2	7.2	3.2
55 - 59	350	240	110	8.3	11.4	5.2
60 - 64	494	317	177	13.6	18.6	9.3
65 - 69	487	304	183	20.8	29.0	14.1
70 - 74	847	456	391	34.9	43.4	28.4
75 - 79	1 067	521	546	58.2	68.5	50.8
80 - 84	996	457	539	95.6	108.0	87.2
85 - 89	725	279	446	169.9	174.5	167.2
90 - 94	258	78	180	216.6	205.3	221.9
95 - 99	48	13	35	280.7	♦250.0	294.1
100 +	22	8	14	♦354.8	♦381.0	♦341.5
Netherlands - Pays-Bas[40]						
2013 (C)						
Total	141 245	68 360	72 885	8.4	8.2	8.6
0	645	353	292	3.7	3.9	3.4
1 - 4	93	53	40	0.1	0.1	0.1
5 - 9	70	43	27	0.1	0.1	♦0.1
10 - 14	88	48	40	0.1	0.1	0.1
15 - 19	216	137	79	0.2	0.3	0.2
20 - 24	294	194	100	0.3	0.4	0.2
25 - 29	381	266	115	0.4	0.5	0.2
30 - 34	396	236	160	0.4	0.5	0.3
35 - 39	649	385	264	0.6	0.7	0.5
40 - 44	1 262	743	519	1.0	1.2	0.8
45 - 49	2 187	1 184	1 003	1.7	1.8	1.6
50 - 54	3 728	2 131	1 597	3.0	3.4	2.6
55 - 59	5 558	3 252	2 306	5.0	5.8	4.1
60 - 64	8 180	4 736	3 444	7.8	9.0	6.6
65 - 69	11 839	7 171	4 668	12.6	15.4	9.8
70 - 74	13 265	8 054	5 211	19.9	25.2	15.0
75 - 79	17 582	10 023	7 559	34.3	43.7	26.7
80 - 84	24 019	12 007	12 012	63.6	80.2	52.6
85 - 89	25 564	10 333	15 231	116.9	143.6	103.7
90 - 94	18 146	5 592	12 554	209.9	250.3	195.8
95 - 99	6 077	1 264	4 813	341.7	389.5	331.1
100 +	1 006	155	851	519.1	596.2	507.2
Norway - Norvège[41]						
2013 (C)						
Total	41 131	19 893	21 238	8.1	7.8	8.4
0	140	65	75	2.3	2.1	2.6
1 - 4	31	15	16	0.1	♦0.1	♦0.1
5 - 9	20	10	10	♦0.1	♦0.1	♦0.1
10 - 14	16	10	6	♦0.1	♦0.1	-
15 - 19	86	56	30	0.3	0.3	♦0.2
20 - 24	142	104	38	0.4	0.6	0.2
25 - 29	160	124	36	0.5	0.7	0.2
30 - 34	183	132	51	0.5	0.8	0.3
35 - 39	252	166	86	0.7	0.9	0.5
40 - 44	393	248	145	1.0	1.3	0.8

19. Deaths by age and sex and age-specific death rates by sex: latest available year, 2005 - 2014
Décès et taux de mortalité selon l'âge et le sexe : dernière année disponible, 2005 - 2014 (continued - suite)

Continent, country or area, date, code[a] and age (in years) Continent, pays ou zone, date, code[a] et âge (en années)	Number - Nombre			Rate - Taux		
	Both sexes Les deux sexes	Male Masculin	Female Féminin	Both sexes Les deux sexes	Male Masculin	Female Féminin
EUROPE						
Norway - Norvège[41]						
2013 (C)						
45 - 49	571	353	218	1.6	1.9	1.2
50 - 54	890	528	362	2.7	3.1	2.3
55 - 59	1 436	900	536	4.6	5.7	3.5
60 - 64	2 033	1 244	789	7.1	8.6	5.6
65 - 69	3 172	1 932	1 240	11.8	14.4	9.2
70 - 74	3 312	1 960	1 352	18.5	22.9	14.5
75 - 79	4 364	2 447	1 917	32.9	41.1	26.3
80 - 84	6 508	3 415	3 093	60.7	77.3	49.0
85 - 89	8 099	3 442	4 657	112.2	134.5	99.9
90 - 94	6 538	2 111	4 427	194.1	226.1	181.8
95 - 99	2 399	558	1 841	331.3	369.3	321.3
100 +	386	73	313	466.5	485.0	462.3
Poland - Pologne						
2013 (C)						
Total	387 312	201 696	185 616	10.1	10.9	9.4
0	1 684	937	747	4.6	4.9	4.2
1 - 4	306	167	139	0.2	0.2	0.2
5 - 9	179	106	73	0.1	0.1	0.1
10 - 14	282	161	121	0.2	0.2	0.1
15 - 19	987	731	256	0.5	0.7	0.2
20 - 24	1 626	1 342	284	0.6	1.0	0.2
25 - 29	2 062	1 657	405	0.7	1.1	0.3
30 - 34	2 768	2 178	590	0.9	1.4	0.4
35 - 39	3 987	3 058	929	1.4	2.1	0.6
40 - 44	5 629	4 267	1 362	2.3	3.4	1.1
45 - 49	8 642	6 332	2 310	3.7	5.4	2.0
50 - 54	16 491	11 870	4 621	6.2	9.1	3.4
55 - 59	28 306	19 733	8 573	9.7	14.0	5.6
60 - 64	36 965	24 822	12 143	14.3	20.7	8.8
65 - 69	33 861	21 836	12 025	19.9	29.1	12.7
70 - 74	36 068	21 225	14 843	28.4	41.1	19.8
75 - 79	50 372	26 238	24 134	44.0	61.7	33.5
80 - 84	63 589	27 076	36 513	74.2	95.3	63.8
85 - 89	56 596	18 460	38 136	127.8	151.9	118.7
90 - 94	28 897	7 797	21 100	210.3	237.3	201.9
95 - 99	6 610	1 434	5 176	318.4	338.5	313.3
100 +	1 405	269	1 136	340.1	328.6	342.9
Portugal[42]						
2013 (C)						
Total	106 543	54 170	52 373	10.2	10.9	9.6
0	244	146	98	2.8	3.3	2.3
1 - 4	73	46	27	0.2	0.2	♦0.1
5 - 9	45	23	22	0.1	♦0.1	♦0.1
10 - 14	58	34	24	0.1	0.1	♦0.1
15 - 19	121	79	42	0.2	0.3	0.2
20 - 24	212	156	56	0.4	0.5	0.2
25 - 29	265	192	73	0.4	0.6	0.2
30 - 34	393	275	118	0.6	0.8	0.3
35 - 39	752	503	249	0.9	1.3	0.6
40 - 44	1 211	840	371	1.5	2.2	0.9
45 - 49	1 997	1 364	633	2.6	3.7	1.6
50 - 54	2 960	2 094	866	4.0	5.9	2.2
55 - 59	3 842	2 735	1 107	5.6	8.4	3.1
60 - 64	5 212	3 570	1 642	8.1	11.8	4.8
65 - 69	6 665	4 345	2 320	11.7	16.9	7.5
70 - 74	9 051	5 558	3 493	18.9	26.4	13.0
75 - 79	14 514	8 062	6 452	33.3	44.6	25.3
80 - 84	20 058	9 929	10 129	62.8	81.3	51.3
85 - 89	21 007	8 618	12 389	122.9	152.3	108.3
90 - 94	12 819	4 357	8 462	211.4	247.0	196.8
95 - 99	4 250	1 106	3 144	298.6	290.1	301.8
100 +	794	138	656	264.5	167.6	301.2

19. Deaths by age and sex and age-specific death rates by sex: latest available year, 2005 - 2014
Décès et taux de mortalité selon l'âge et le sexe : dernière année disponible, 2005 - 2014 (continued - suite)

Continent, country or area, date, code[a] and age (in years) / Continent, pays ou zone, date, code[a] et âge (en années)	Number - Nombre			Rate - Taux		
	Both sexes Les deux sexes	Male Masculin	Female Féminin	Both sexes Les deux sexes	Male Masculin	Female Féminin
EUROPE						
Republic of Moldova - République de Moldova[43]						
2012 (C)						
Total	39 560	20 774	18 786	11.1	12.1	10.2
0 - 4	484	252	232	2.5	2.5	2.5
0	404	203	201	10.4	10.1	10.7
1 - 4	80	49	31	0.5	0.6	0.4
5 - 9	46	29	17	0.2	♦0.3	♦0.2
10 - 14	64	37	27	0.3	0.4	♦0.3
15 - 19	183	140	43	0.7	1.1	0.3
20 - 24	246	190	56	0.7	1.1	0.3
25 - 29	324	244	80	0.9	1.4	0.5
30 - 34	467	348	119	1.6	2.4	0.8
35 - 39	733	524	209	2.9	4.2	1.6
40 - 44	970	712	258	4.3	6.5	2.2
45 - 49	1 670	1 237	433	7.0	11.0	3.5
50 - 54	2 779	1 939	840	10.1	15.2	5.7
55 - 59	3 521	2 308	1 213	15.0	21.7	9.4
60 - 64	4 194	2 598	1 596	23.0	32.6	15.6
65 - 69	3 249	1 815	1 434	30.7	40.5	23.5
70 - 74	5 351	2 625	2 726	53.2	68.8	43.7
75 - 79	5 726	2 499	3 227	79.0	96.7	69.2
80 - 84	5 308	2 046	3 262	111.5	128.8	102.9
85 - 89	3 038	889	2 149	148.9	150.2	148.4
90 - 94	1 033	306	727	190.0	191.6	189.3
95 - 99	151	31	120	129.8	78.5	156.3
100 +	23	5	18	♦53.6	♦33.8	♦63.8
Romania - Roumanie						
2013 (C)						
Total	246 967	128 901	118 066	12.4	13.2	11.5
0	1 677	944	733	9.3	10.2	8.4
1 - 4	300	187	113	0.4	0.5	0.3
5 - 9	195	116	79	0.2	0.2	0.2
10 - 14	227	145	82	0.2	0.3	0.2
15 - 19	473	311	162	0.4	0.6	0.3
20 - 24	802	594	208	0.7	0.9	0.4
25 - 29	945	693	252	0.7	1.0	0.4
30 - 34	1 241	858	383	0.9	1.2	0.6
35 - 39	2 192	1 564	628	1.4	1.9	0.8
40 - 44	3 782	2 677	1 105	2.4	3.3	1.4
45 - 49	5 428	3 885	1 543	4.1	5.8	2.4
50 - 54	8 846	6 245	2 601	7.3	10.4	4.3
55 - 59	15 680	11 023	4 657	10.9	16.0	6.2
60 - 64	20 332	13 668	6 664	15.4	22.5	9.4
65 - 69	20 378	12 833	7 545	21.9	31.2	14.6
70 - 74	28 111	15 884	12 227	33.7	46.1	25.0
75 - 79	40 132	19 744	20 388	54.4	69.2	45.1
80 - 84	44 484	19 101	25 383	92.2	107.6	83.3
85 - 89	34 465	12 924	21 541	153.6	167.6	146.2
90 - 94	14 539	4 692	9 847	234.1	244.8	229.3
95 - 99	2 221	659	1 562	337.8	346.8	334.1
100 +	517	154	363	438.5	424.2	444.9
Russian Federation - Fédération de Russie[24]						
2011 (C)						
Total	1 925 720	997 494	928 226	13.5	15.1	12.1
0 - 4	16 465	9 472	6 993	2.1	2.3	1.8
0	13 168	7 572	5 596	8.0	9.0	7.0
1 - 4	3 297	1 900	1 397	0.5	0.6	0.5
5 - 9	1 972	1 160	812	0.3	0.3	0.2
10 - 14	2 006	1 249	757	0.3	0.4	0.2
15 - 19	6 656	4 634	2 022	0.8	1.1	0.5
20 - 24	18 666	14 374	4 292	1.5	2.3	0.7
25 - 29	32 160	24 684	7 476	2.7	4.1	1.3
30 - 34	45 451	34 852	10 599	4.1	6.4	1.9
35 - 39	50 630	38 270	12 360	5.0	7.7	2.4
40 - 44	55 007	40 708	14 299	6.0	9.1	3.0
45 - 49	81 813	60 225	21 588	7.7	12.0	3.8
50 - 54	124 961	89 971	34 990	10.9	17.1	5.6

19. Deaths by age and sex and age-specific death rates by sex: latest available year, 2005 - 2014
Décès et taux de mortalité selon l'âge et le sexe : dernière année disponible, 2005 - 2014 (continued - suite)

Continent, country or area, date, code[a] and age (in years) / Continent, pays ou zone, date, code[a] et âge (en années)	Number - Nombre			Rate - Taux		
	Both sexes Les deux sexes	Male Masculin	Female Féminin	Both sexes Les deux sexes	Male Masculin	Female Féminin
EUROPE						
Russian Federation - Fédération de Russie[24]						
2011 (C)						
55 - 59	156 587	108 205	48 382	15.6	24.9	8.5
60 - 64	177 990	118 728	59 262	22.7	36.6	12.9
65 - 69	111 156	66 246	44 910	27.8	44.4	17.9
70 - 74	263 633	136 875	126 758	40.8	62.8	29.6
75 - 79	232 616	99 250	133 366	65.5	92.9	53.7
80 - 84	290 314	94 614	195 700	101.1	129.8	91.4
85 - 89	172 178	35 533	136 645	166.8	187.8	162.0
90 - 94	56 714	9 585	47 129	244.6	241.3	245.3
95 - 99	18 647	2 652	15 995	320.7	294.4	325.5
100 +	2 562	320	2 242	352.6	232.1	380.8
Unknown - Inconnu	7 536	5 887	1 649	..	..	..
San Marino - Saint-Marin						
2012 (+C)						
Total	237	110	127	7.1	6.8	7.4
0 - 4	-	-	-	-	-	-
0	-	-	-	-	-	-
1 - 4	-	-	-	-	-	-
5 - 9	-	-	-	-	-	-
10 - 14	-	-	-	-	-	-
15 - 19	-	-	-	-	-	-
20 - 24	-	-	-	-	-	-
25 - 29	-	-	-	-	-	-
30 - 34	-	-	-	-	-	-
35 - 39	1	1	-	♦0.4	♦0.7	-
40 - 44	4	1	3	♦1.3	♦0.7	♦1.9
45 - 49	1	-	1	♦0.3	-	♦0.6
50 - 54	5	5	-	♦1.9	♦3.9	-
55 - 59	7	4	3	♦3.3	♦3.9	♦2.7
60 - 64	10	4	6	♦5.2	♦4.3	♦6.0
65 - 69	10	6	4	♦5.9	♦7.4	♦4.6
70 - 74	17	9	8	♦12.6	♦13.7	♦11.6
75 - 79	34	20	14	30.1	♦37.8	♦23.3
80 - 84	44	24	20	49.4	♦67.9	♦37.2
85 - 89	50	19	31	91.1	♦93.4	89.7
90 - 94	34	12	22	140.8	♦169.0	♦129.0
95 - 99	17	3	14	♦274.2	♦285.7	♦271.8
100 +	2	1	1	♦400.0	...	♦200.0
Unknown - Inconnu	1	1	-	..	..	..
Serbia - Serbie[44]						
2013 (+C)						
Total	100 300	50 910	49 390	14.0	14.6	13.4
0	413	246	167	6.3	7.3	5.2
1 - 4	53	25	28	0.2	♦0.2	♦0.2
5 - 9	38	18	20	0.1	♦0.1	♦0.1
10 - 14	54	35	19	0.2	0.2	♦0.1
15 - 19	129	90	39	0.3	0.4	0.2
20 - 24	193	148	45	0.5	0.7	0.2
25 - 29	289	201	88	0.6	0.8	0.4
30 - 34	462	322	140	0.9	1.3	0.6
35 - 39	580	393	187	1.2	1.5	0.8
40 - 44	900	595	305	1.9	2.5	1.3
45 - 49	1 686	1 094	592	3.6	4.7	2.5
50 - 54	3 124	2 048	1 076	6.1	8.2	4.1
55 - 59	5 653	3 744	1 909	10.1	13.8	6.6
60 - 64	8 540	5 579	2 961	15.4	21.2	10.1
65 - 69	8 381	5 150	3 231	22.3	30.1	15.8
70 - 74	12 059	6 633	5 426	36.3	45.9	28.9
75 - 79	18 565	9 100	9 465	63.7	75.9	55.2
80 - 84	20 633	8 854	11 779	111.6	124.1	103.8
85 - 89	13 321	4 873	8 448	182.0	189.5	178.0
90 - 94	4 674	1 598	3 076	272.0	289.3	263.8
95 - 99	449	133	316	323.0	286.0	341.6
100 +	104	31	73	395.4	360.5	412.4

Continent, country or area, date, code[a] and age (in years) Continent, pays ou zone, date, code[a] et âge (en années)	Number - Nombre			Rate - Taux		
	Both sexes Les deux sexes	Male Masculin	Female Féminin	Both sexes Les deux sexes	Male Masculin	Female Féminin
EUROPE						
Slovakia - Slovaquie						
2013 (C)						
Total	52 089	26 866	25 223	9.6	10.2	9.1
0	301	158	143	5.4	5.5	5.3
1 - 4	62	35	27	0.3	0.3	♦0.2
5 - 9	44	23	21	0.2	♦0.2	♦0.2
10 - 14	45	28	17	0.2	♦0.2	♦0.1
15 - 19	107	72	35	0.3	0.5	0.2
20 - 24	192	144	48	0.5	0.7	0.3
25 - 29	250	199	51	0.6	0.9	0.2
30 - 34	330	241	89	0.7	1.0	0.4
35 - 39	538	372	166	1.2	1.6	0.8
40 - 44	703	479	224	1.9	2.5	1.2
45 - 49	1 271	894	377	3.5	4.9	2.1
50 - 54	2 153	1 548	605	5.8	8.4	3.2
55 - 59	3 539	2 490	1 049	9.1	13.3	5.2
60 - 64	4 880	3 388	1 492	14.3	21.3	8.1
65 - 69	4 816	3 048	1 768	20.0	29.3	12.9
70 - 74	5 664	3 343	2 321	30.8	45.9	20.9
75 - 79	6 732	3 330	3 402	50.2	69.3	39.5
80 - 84	8 795	3 438	5 357	90.7	110.8	81.3
85 - 89	7 213	2 441	4 772	149.9	179.9	138.1
90 - 94	3 774	1 044	2 730	241.7	253.3	237.5
95 - 99	566	131	435	290.9	240.1	310.6
100 +	114	20	94	233.8	♦126.2	285.7
Slovenia - Slovénie						
2013 (C)						
Total	19 334	9 555	9 779	9.4	9.4	9.4
0	62	32	30	2.9	2.9	♦2.9
1 - 4	11	8	3	♦0.1	♦0.2	♦0.1
5 - 9	7	4	3	♦0.1	♦0.1	♦0.1
10 - 14	10	5	5	♦0.1	♦0.1	♦0.1
15 - 19	25	18	7	♦0.3	♦0.4	♦0.1
20 - 24	58	46	12	0.5	0.8	♦0.2
25 - 29	69	55	14	0.5	0.8	♦0.2
30 - 34	85	63	22	0.5	0.8	♦0.3
35 - 39	140	97	43	0.9	1.2	0.6
40 - 44	190	133	57	1.3	1.8	0.8
45 - 49	322	213	109	2.1	2.7	1.4
50 - 54	555	396	159	3.6	5.1	2.1
55 - 59	1 010	698	312	6.6	9.0	4.2
60 - 64	1 352	937	415	9.9	13.7	6.0
65 - 69	1 378	954	424	14.1	20.7	8.2
70 - 74	1 901	1 186	715	21.0	29.5	14.2
75 - 79	2 650	1 455	1 195	36.2	49.5	27.2
80 - 84	3 693	1 659	2 034	67.5	89.5	56.2
85 - 89	3 375	1 038	2 337	116.7	138.9	109.0
90 - 94	1 930	470	1 460	204.8	235.7	196.4
95 - 99	401	72	329	336.7	393.4	326.4
100 +	110	16	94	486.7	♦432.4	497.4
Spain - Espagne						
2013 (C)						
Total	388 600	198 553	190 047	8.3	8.7	8.0
0	1 149	627	522	2.7	2.8	2.5
1 - 4	281	147	134	0.1	0.1	0.1
5 - 9	212	114	98	0.1	0.1	0.1
10 - 14	185	102	83	0.1	0.1	0.1
15 - 19	366	245	121	0.2	0.2	0.1
20 - 24	580	415	165	0.2	0.3	0.1
25 - 29	824	573	251	0.3	0.4	0.2
30 - 34	1 344	932	412	0.4	0.5	0.2
35 - 39	2 334	1 453	881	0.6	0.7	0.4
40 - 44	3 821	2 489	1 332	1.0	1.3	0.7
45 - 49	6 795	4 491	2 304	1.8	2.4	1.3
50 - 54	10 178	6 798	3 380	3.1	4.1	2.0
55 - 59	13 246	9 091	4 155	4.7	6.5	2.9
60 - 64	17 375	12 183	5 192	7.0	10.0	4.0

19. Deaths by age and sex and age-specific death rates by sex: latest available year, 2005 - 2014
Décès et taux de mortalité selon l'âge et le sexe : dernière année disponible, 2005 - 2014 (continued - suite)

Continent, country or area, date, code[a] and age (in years) / Continent, pays ou zone, date, code[a] et âge (en années)	Number - Nombre			Rate - Taux		
	Both sexes Les deux sexes	Male Masculin	Female Féminin	Both sexes Les deux sexes	Male Masculin	Female Féminin
EUROPE						
Spain - Espagne						
2013 (C)						
65 - 69	23 406	16 120	7 286	10.2	14.8	6.0
70 - 74	28 036	18 443	9 593	15.9	22.7	10.1
75 - 79	47 692	28 552	19 140	28.3	39.1	20.0
80 - 84	71 966	37 394	34 572	52.0	67.7	41.5
85 - 89	79 443	34 100	45 343	98.4	121.6	86.1
90 - 94	55 359	18 514	36 845	172.4	198.1	161.8
95 - 99	19 879	4 935	14 944	269.5	289.6	263.5
100 +	4 129	835	3 294	317.9	297.0	323.6
Sweden - Suède						
2013 (C)						
Total	90 402	43 660	46 742	9.4	9.1	9.7
0	306	168	138	2.7	2.9	2.5
1 - 4	52	28	24	0.1	◆0.1	◆0.1
5 - 9	35	17	18	0.1	◆0.1	◆0.1
10 - 14	41	29	12	0.1	◆0.1	-
15 - 19	133	91	42	0.2	0.3	0.2
20 - 24	291	209	82	0.4	0.6	0.3
25 - 29	337	240	97	0.5	0.8	0.3
30 - 34	309	223	86	0.5	0.7	0.3
35 - 39	400	259	141	0.7	0.8	0.5
40 - 44	566	337	229	0.9	1.0	0.7
45 - 49	1 012	605	407	1.5	1.8	1.2
50 - 54	1 555	943	612	2.6	3.1	2.1
55 - 59	2 355	1 378	977	4.1	4.8	3.4
60 - 64	3 978	2 441	1 537	6.9	8.5	5.3
65 - 69	6 736	4 000	2 736	11.2	13.5	9.0
70 - 74	7 883	4 657	3 226	18.1	22.0	14.4
75 - 79	10 117	5 645	4 472	31.9	38.8	26.1
80 - 84	14 665	7 384	7 281	60.1	72.6	51.2
85 - 89	18 153	7 981	10 172	112.1	134.7	99.1
90 - 94	15 185	5 496	9 689	203.9	241.8	187.3
95 - 99	5 385	1 373	4 012	340.8	377.8	329.8
100 +	908	156	752	488.8	543.6	478.8
Switzerland - Suisse						
2013 (C)						
Total	64 961	31 257	33 704	8.0	7.8	8.2
0	320	183	137	4.0	4.4	3.5
1 - 4	45	29	16	0.1	◆0.2	◆0.1
5 - 9	29	17	12	◆0.1	◆0.1	◆0.1
10 - 14	30	16	14	◆0.1	◆0.1	◆0.1
15 - 19	111	77	34	0.3	0.3	0.2
20 - 24	148	109	39	0.3	0.4	0.2
25 - 29	189	144	45	0.4	0.5	0.2
30 - 34	225	153	72	0.4	0.5	0.3
35 - 39	317	188	129	0.6	0.7	0.5
40 - 44	569	365	204	0.9	1.2	0.7
45 - 49	986	624	362	1.5	1.8	1.1
50 - 54	1 493	937	556	2.4	3.0	1.8
55 - 59	2 153	1 368	785	4.1	5.2	3.0
60 - 64	2 962	1 867	1 095	6.5	8.3	4.7
65 - 69	4 209	2 613	1 596	9.9	12.7	7.3
70 - 74	5 297	3 202	2 095	15.9	20.6	11.7
75 - 79	7 089	3 994	3 095	26.9	34.6	20.9
80 - 84	10 783	5 452	5 331	53.1	67.8	43.5
85 - 89	13 148	5 337	7 811	104.2	124.4	93.8
90 - 94	10 501	3 507	6 994	198.3	232.5	184.7
95 - 99	3 681	946	2 735	330.8	380.0	316.6
100 +	676	129	547	465.6	500.0	458.1
TFYR of Macedonia - L'ex-R. y. de Macédoine						
2013 (C)						
Total	19 208	10 136	9 072	9.3	9.8	8.8
0	237	129	108	10.2	10.7	9.7
1 - 4	24	11	13	◆0.3	◆0.2	◆0.3
5 - 9	17	11	6	◆0.2	◆0.2	◆0.1
10 - 14	14	6	8	◆0.1	◆0.1	◆0.1

19. Deaths by age and sex and age-specific death rates by sex: latest available year, 2005 - 2014
Décès et taux de mortalité selon l'âge et le sexe : dernière année disponible, 2005 - 2014 (continued - suite)

Continent, country or area, date, code[a] and age (in years) Continent, pays ou zone, date, code[a] et âge (en annèes)	Number - Nombre			Rate - Taux		
	Both sexes Les deux sexes	Male Masculin	Female Féminin	Both sexes Les deux sexes	Male Masculin	Female Féminin
EUROPE						
TFYR of Macedonia - L'ex-R. y. de Macédoine						
2013 (C)						
15 - 19	45	28	17	0.3	♦0.4	♦0.3
20 - 24	67	43	24	0.4	0.5	♦0.3
25 - 29	105	70	35	0.6	0.8	0.4
30 - 34	103	64	39	0.6	0.8	0.5
35 - 39	135	77	58	0.9	1.0	0.8
40 - 44	228	162	66	1.6	2.2	0.9
45 - 49	422	277	145	2.9	3.7	2.0
50 - 54	692	460	232	4.9	6.4	3.3
55 - 59	1 158	783	375	8.6	11.6	5.6
60 - 64	1 590	1 031	559	13.6	18.4	9.2
65 - 69	1 780	1 030	750	20.9	26.0	16.4
70 - 74	2 544	1 390	1 154	36.5	44.1	30.3
75 - 79	3 524	1 745	1 779	65.4	74.5	58.4
80 - 84	3 454	1 522	1 932	118.4	128.3	111.7
85 - 89	2 164	922	1 242	209.8	226.1	199.1
90 - 94	803	336	467	331.0	407.0	291.8
95 - 99	86	34	52	...	...	...
100 +	16	5	11	...	...	...
Ukraine[45]						
2012 (+C)						
Total	663 139	325 584	337 555	14.6	15.5	13.8
0 - 4	5 234	2 993	2 241	2.1	2.3	1.9
0	4 371	2 496	1 875	8.6	9.5	7.6
1 - 4	863	497	366	0.4	0.5	0.4
5 - 9	512	289	223	0.2	0.3	0.2
10 - 14	489	297	192	0.3	0.3	0.2
15 - 19	1 405	993	412	0.6	0.8	0.3
20 - 24	3 620	2 782	838	1.1	1.6	0.5
25 - 29	6 444	4 882	1 562	1.7	2.5	0.8
30 - 34	9 780	7 394	2 386	2.8	4.3	1.4
35 - 39	12 687	9 372	3 315	3.9	5.8	2.0
40 - 44	15 444	11 175	4 269	5.0	7.5	2.7
45 - 49	21 300	15 561	5 739	6.8	10.5	3.4
50 - 54	33 200	23 772	9 428	9.5	14.9	4.9
55 - 59	42 620	29 353	13 267	13.8	21.9	7.6
60 - 64	55 172	36 184	18 988	20.1	31.9	11.8
65 - 69	46 174	27 387	18 787	28.2	44.2	18.5
70 - 74	98 138	50 599	47 539	43.2	64.3	32.0
75 - 79	91 773	40 470	51 303	65.4	87.9	54.4
80 - 84	107 983	37 136	70 847	108.0	131.8	98.7
85 - 89	78 126	18 777	59 349	163.9	173.1	161.2
90 - 94	25 931	4 889	21 042	238.6	209.1	246.7
95 - 99	5 879	973	4 906	357.5	278.9	378.7
100 +	641	93	548	167.7	101.3	188.6
Unknown - Inconnu	587	213	374	..	..	..
United Kingdom of Great Britain and Northern Ireland - Royaume-Uni de Grande-Bretagne et d'Irlande du Nord[46]						
2013 (+C)						
Total	574 945	278 262	296 683	9.0	8.8	9.1
0	3 030	1 724	1 306	3.8	4.2	3.3
1 - 4	541	291	250	0.2	0.2	0.2
5 - 9	290	161	129	0.1	0.1	0.1
10 - 14	326	183	143	0.1	0.1	0.1
15 - 19	918	629	289	0.2	0.3	0.2
20 - 24	1 466	1 030	436	0.3	0.5	0.2
25 - 29	1 956	1 338	618	0.4	0.6	0.3
30 - 34	2 752	1 779	973	0.6	0.8	0.4
35 - 39	3 778	2 431	1 347	0.9	1.2	0.7
40 - 44	6 364	3 974	2 390	1.4	1.8	1.1
45 - 49	9 657	5 893	3 764	2.1	2.6	1.6
50 - 54	13 669	8 092	5 577	3.1	3.8	2.5
55 - 59	18 883	11 199	7 684	5.0	6.0	4.0
60 - 64	28 205	16 892	11 313	7.9	9.7	6.2
65 - 69	42 206	24 860	17 346	12.2	14.7	9.7

19. Deaths by age and sex and age-specific death rates by sex: latest available year, 2005 - 2014
Décès et taux de mortalité selon l'âge et le sexe : dernière année disponible, 2005 - 2014 (continued - suite)

Continent, country or area, date, code[a] and age (in years) / Continent, pays ou zone, date, code[a] et âge (en années)	Number - Nombre			Rate - Taux		
	Both sexes Les deux sexes	Male Masculin	Female Féminin	Both sexes Les deux sexes	Male Masculin	Female Féminin
EUROPE						
United Kingdom of Great Britain and Northern Ireland - Royaume-Uni de Grande-Bretagne et d'Irlande du Nord[46]						
2013 (+C)						
70 - 74	51 979	29 960	22 019	20.4	24.9	16.4
75 - 79	72 349	39 543	32 806	34.6	41.5	28.8
80 - 84	96 765	48 185	48 580	62.4	74.0	54.0
85 - 89	104 450	44 741	59 709	111.5	129.7	101.0
90 - 94	81 336	27 615	53 721	191.3	217.4	180.2
95 - 99	27 903	6 753	21 150	301.1	329.1	293.1
100 +	6 122	989	5 133	441.5	481.3	434.6
OCEANIA - OCÉANIE						
American Samoa - Samoas américaines						
2006 (C)						
Total	267	156	111	...	...	...
0	17	9	8	...	...	...
1 - 4	7	3	4	...	...	...
5 - 9	1	1	-	...	...	...
10 - 14	5	2	3	...	...	...
15 - 19	3	-	3	...	...	...
20 - 24	5	4	1	...	...	...
25 - 29	4	3	1	...	...	...
30 - 34	5	5	-	...	...	...
35 - 39	10	6	4	...	...	...
40 - 44	9	4	5	...	...	...
45 - 49	19	10	9	...	...	...
50 - 54	18	11	7	...	...	...
55 - 59	21	13	8	...	...	...
60 - 64	23	15	8	...	...	...
65 - 69	27	18	9	...	...	...
70 - 74	31	22	9	...	...	...
75 - 79	28	19	9	...	...	...
80 - 84	13	6	7	...	...	...
85 +	21	5	16	...	...	...
2011 (C)						
Total	283	...	...	...	...	...
0	9	...	...	...	...	...
1 - 4	4	...	...	...	...	...
5 - 9	-	...	...	...	...	...
10 - 14	1	...	...	...	...	...
15 - 19	5	...	...	...	...	...
20 - 24	-	...	...	...	...	...
25 - 29	7	...	...	...	...	...
30 - 34	8	...	...	...	...	...
35 - 39	8	...	...	...	...	...
40 - 44	12	...	...	...	...	...
45 - 49	21	...	...	...	...	...
50 - 54	22	...	...	...	...	...
55 - 59	34	...	...	...	...	...
60 - 64	32	...	...	...	...	...
65 - 69	32	...	...	...	...	...
70 - 74	32	...	...	...	...	...
75 - 79	21	...	...	...	...	...
80 - 84	13	...	...	...	...	...
85 +	22	...	...	...	...	...
Australia - Australie						
2013 (+C)						
Total	147 678	75 782	71 896	6.4	6.6	6.2
0	1 094	589	505	...	...	...
1 - 4	216	120	96	0.2	0.2	0.2
5 - 9	136	77	59	0.1	0.1	0.1
10 - 14	136	81	55	0.1	0.1	0.1
15 - 19	463	310	153	0.3	0.4	0.2
20 - 24	676	478	198	0.4	0.6	0.2

19. Deaths by age and sex and age-specific death rates by sex: latest available year, 2005 - 2014
Décès et taux de mortalité selon l'âge et le sexe : dernière année disponible, 2005 - 2014 (continued - suite)

Continent, country or area, date, code[a] and age (in years) / Continent, pays ou zone, date, code[a] et âge (en annèes)	Number - Nombre			Rate - Taux		
	Both sexes Les deux sexes	Male Masculin	Female Féminin	Both sexes Les deux sexes	Male Masculin	Female Féminin

OCEANIA - OCÉANIE

Australia - Australie
2013 (+C)

25 - 29	801	575	226	0.5	0.7	0.3
30 - 34	986	653	333	0.6	0.8	0.4
35 - 39	1 276	824	452	0.8	1.1	0.6
40 - 44	1 954	1 209	745	1.2	1.5	0.9
45 - 49	2 810	1 734	1 076	1.8	2.3	1.4
50 - 54	4 102	2 514	1 588	2.6	3.3	2.0
55 - 59	5 586	3 425	2 161	4.0	5.0	3.1
60 - 64	7 609	4 656	2 953	6.1	7.6	4.7
65 - 69	10 574	6 681	3 893	9.8	12.4	7.1
70 - 74	12 455	7 666	4 789	15.9	20.0	12.0
75 - 79	16 336	9 520	6 816	27.7	34.4	21.8
80 - 84	23 214	12 292	10 922	52.1	63.4	43.3
85 - 89	27 934	12 689	15 245	96.9	114.7	85.8
90 - 94	20 364	7 421	12 943	168.4	192.4	157.1
95 - 99	7 554	2 003	5 551	283.1	306.7	275.5
100 +	1 384	254	1 130	368.7	323.2	380.7
Unknown - Inconnu	18	11	7	..	..	..

Cook Islands - Îles Cook[47]
2009 (+C)

Total	67	37	30	...	...	...
0	2	1	1	...	...	...
1 - 4	1	1	-	...	...	...
5 - 9	-	-	-	...	...	...
10 - 14	-	-	-	...	...	...
15 - 19	3	2	1	...	...	...
20 - 24	3	3	-	...	...	...
25 - 29	1	1	-	...	...	...
30 - 34	2	1	1	...	...	...
35 - 39	4	3	1	...	...	...
40 - 44	-	-	-	...	...	...
45 - 49	2	1	1	...	...	...
50 - 54	3	1	2	...	...	...
55 - 59	1	1	-	...	...	...
60 - 64	6	3	3	...	...	...
65 - 69	8	4	4	...	...	...
70 - 74	9	1	8	...	...	...
75 - 79	8	5	3	...	...	...
80 +	14	9	5	...	...	...

Fiji - Fidji
2008 (+C)

Total	6 471	3 519	2 952	7.7	8.2	7.2
0	319	180	139	18.9	20.4	17.3
1 - 4	128	70	58	1.9	2.0	1.8
5 - 9	45	29	16	0.6	◆0.7	◆0.4
10 - 14	42	25	17	0.5	◆0.6	◆0.4
15 - 19	70	34	36	0.9	0.8	0.9
20 - 24	104	64	40	1.3	1.6	1.0
25 - 29	124	65	59	1.7	1.7	1.6
30 - 34	120	61	59	1.9	1.8	1.9
35 - 39	183	114	69	3.2	3.9	2.5
40 - 44	296	168	128	5.3	5.9	4.7
45 - 49	446	279	167	8.8	10.7	6.7
50 - 54	549	344	205	13.2	16.3	10.0
55 - 59	663	381	282	20.5	23.3	17.6
60 - 64	737	409	328	29.9	33.5	26.3
65 - 69	718	385	333	40.4	44.8	36.3
70 - 74	621	303	318	57.2	59.1	55.5
75 +	1 306	608	698	103.5	108.7	99.3
75 - 79	564	290	274	...	...	...
80 - 84	360	156	204	...	...	...
85 - 89	246	113	133	...	...	...
90 - 94	71	27	44	...	...	...
95 +	65	22	43	...	...	...

19. Deaths by age and sex and age-specific death rates by sex: latest available year, 2005 - 2014
Décès et taux de mortalité selon l'âge et le sexe : dernière année disponible, 2005 - 2014 (continued - suite)

Continent, country or area, date, code[a] and age (in years) / Continent, pays ou zone, date, code[a] et âge (en années)	Number - Nombre			Rate - Taux		
	Both sexes Les deux sexes	Male Masculin	Female Féminin	Both sexes Les deux sexes	Male Masculin	Female Féminin
OCEANIA - OCÉANIE						
Kiribati						
2011 (U)						
Total	481	279	202	...	...	...
0 - 4	132	75	57	...	...	...
5 - 19	14	10	4	...	...	...
20 - 29	34	24	10	...	...	...
30 - 39	28	15	13	...	...	...
40 - 49	60	37	23	...	...	...
50 - 59	74	42	32	...	...	...
60 - 69	54	34	20	...	...	...
70 +	85	42	43	...	...	...
Marshall Islands - Îles Marshall						
2006 (+U)						
Total	318	171	147	...	...	...
0	27	17	10	...	...	...
1 - 4	13	7	6	...	...	...
5 - 9	4	3	1	...	...	...
10 - 14	1	1	-	...	...	...
15 - 19	11	7	4	...	...	...
20 - 24	8	4	4	...	...	...
25 - 29	6	5	1	...	...	...
30 - 34	10	4	6	...	...	...
35 - 39	15	10	5	...	...	...
40 - 44	20	10	10	...	...	...
45 - 49	16	11	5	...	...	...
50 - 54	26	11	15	...	...	...
55 - 59	38	26	12	...	...	...
60 - 64	21	9	12	...	...	...
65 +	102	46	56	...	...	...
Nauru						
2011 (C)						
Total	75	41	34	...	...	...
0	10	5	5	...	...	...
1 - 4	1	1	-	...	...	...
5 - 9	-	-	-	...	...	...
10 - 14	1	1	-	...	...	...
15 - 19	-	-	-	...	...	...
20 - 24	2	2	-	...	...	...
25 - 29	5	1	4	...	...	...
30 - 34	4	1	3	...	...	...
35 - 39	2	1	1	...	...	...
40 - 44	2	2	-	...	...	...
45 - 49	6	3	3	...	...	...
50 - 54	15	7	8	...	...	...
55 - 59	9	7	2	...	...	...
60 - 64	6	2	4	...	...	...
65 - 69	4	2	2	...	...	...
70 +	8	6	2	...	...	...
New Caledonia - Nouvelle-Calédonie						
2010 (C)						
Total	1 191	701	490	4.8	5.5	4.0
0 - 4	22	10	12	♦1.1	♦1.0	♦1.3
0	19	9	10	...	...	...
1 - 4	3	1	2	...	...	...
5 - 9	9	8	1	♦0.5	♦0.8	♦0.1
10 - 14	1	1	-	-	♦0.1	-
15 - 19	14	11	3	♦0.6	♦1.0	♦0.3
20 - 24	23	17	6	♦1.2	♦1.7	♦0.6
25 - 29	32	23	9	1.7	♦2.5	♦1.0
30 - 34	20	14	6	♦1.1	♦1.5	♦0.6
35 - 39	42	32	10	2.1	3.1	♦1.0
40 - 44	34	25	9	1.8	♦2.6	♦1.0
45 - 49	46	33	13	2.8	3.9	♦1.6
50 - 54	77	46	31	5.6	6.6	4.6
55 - 59	68	49	19	6.0	8.5	♦3.4
60 - 64	114	86	28	11.6	16.6	♦6.0
65 - 69	114	74	40	15.9	20.3	11.4

19. Deaths by age and sex and age-specific death rates by sex: latest available year, 2005 - 2014
Décès et taux de mortalité selon l'âge et le sexe : dernière année disponible, 2005 - 2014 (continued - suite)

Continent, country or area, date, code[a] and age (in years) / Continent, pays ou zone, date, code[a] et âge (en années)	Number - Nombre			Rate - Taux		
	Both sexes Les deux sexes	Male Masculin	Female Féminin	Both sexes Les deux sexes	Male Masculin	Female Féminin
OCEANIA - OCÉANIE						
New Caledonia - Nouvelle-Calédonie						
2010 (C)						
70 - 74	130	79	51	23.6	29.9	17.8
75 - 79	131	67	64	36.6	39.4	34.1
80 +	314	126	188	80.9	81.4	80.6
80 - 84	132	60	72	...	...	...
85 - 89	97	43	54	...	...	...
90 - 94	52	17	35	...	...	...
95 +	33	6	27	...	...	...
New Zealand - Nouvelle-Zélande[19]						
2014 (+C)						
Total	31 063	15 655	15 408	6.9	7.1	6.7
0	326	181	145	5.5	6.0	5.1
1 - 4	54	30	24	0.2	♦0.2	♦0.2
5 - 9	37	27	10	0.1	♦0.2	♦0.1
10 - 14	28	15	13	♦0.1	♦0.1	♦0.1
15 - 19	122	89	33	0.4	0.6	0.2
20 - 24	158	118	40	0.5	0.7	0.3
25 - 29	151	101	50	0.5	0.7	0.3
30 - 34	165	111	54	0.6	0.8	0.4
35 - 39	227	150	77	0.8	1.2	0.5
40 - 44	387	219	168	1.2	1.5	1.0
45 - 49	584	343	241	1.9	2.3	1.5
50 - 54	975	563	412	3.1	3.7	2.5
55 - 59	1 255	705	550	4.5	5.2	3.8
60 - 64	1 667	951	716	6.8	8.0	5.7
65 - 69	2 308	1 392	916	10.7	13.2	8.3
70 - 74	2 846	1 657	1 189	17.8	21.4	14.3
75 - 79	3 595	1 985	1 610	31.7	37.5	26.6
80 - 84	4 866	2 509	2 357	58.8	68.7	51.0
85 +	11 312	4 509	6 803	145.6	158.4	138.2
85 - 89	5 498	2 541	2 957	...	...	...
90 - 94	4 102	1 507	2 595	...	...	...
95 - 99	1 464	413	1 051	...	...	...
100 +	248	48	200	...	...	...
Niue - Nioué[48]						
2009 (C)						
Total	12	6	6	...	...	...
0	-	-	-	...	...	...
1 - 4	-	-	-	...	...	...
5 - 9	-	-	-	...	...	...
10 - 14	-	-	-	...	...	...
15 - 19	-	-	-	...	...	...
20 - 24	-	-	-	...	...	...
25 - 29	-	-	-	...	...	...
30 - 34	-	-	-	...	...	...
35 - 39	-	-	-	...	...	...
40 - 44	-	-	-	...	...	...
45 - 49	-	-	-	...	...	...
50 - 54	-	-	-	...	...	...
55 - 59	2	2	-	...	...	...
60 - 64	-	-	-	...	...	...
65 - 69	-	-	-	...	...	...
70 - 74	1	-	1	...	...	...
75 - 79	1	1	-	...	...	...
80 +	8	3	5	...	...	...
Northern Mariana Islands - Îles Mariannes septentrionales						
2005 (U)						
Total	188	107	81	...	...	...
0	5	1	4	...	...	...
1 - 4	4	3	1	...	...	...
5 - 9	-	-	-	...	...	...
10 - 14	3	2	1	...	...	...
15 - 19	1	-	1	...	...	...
20 - 24	3	2	1	...	...	...
25 - 29	10	3	7	...	...	...

19. Deaths by age and sex and age-specific death rates by sex: latest available year, 2005 - 2014
Décès et taux de mortalité selon l'âge et le sexe : dernière année disponible, 2005 - 2014 (continued - suite)

Continent, country or area, date, code[a] and age (in years) / Continent, pays ou zone, date, code[a] et âge (en années)	Number - Nombre			Rate - Taux		
	Both sexes Les deux sexes	Male Masculin	Female Féminin	Both sexes Les deux sexes	Male Masculin	Female Féminin

OCEANIA - OCÉANIE

Northern Mariana Islands - Îles Mariannes septentrionales
2005 (U)

30 - 34	11	9	2	...	...	...
35 - 39	7	4	3	...	...	...
40 - 44	11	6	5	...	...	...
45 - 49	7	6	1	...	...	...
50 - 54	17	13	4	...	...	...
55 - 59	19	11	8	...	...	...
60 - 64	20	9	11	...	...	...
65 - 69	20	14	6	...	...	...
70 - 74	20	11	9	...	...	...
75 - 79	13	6	7	...	...	...
80 - 84	8	5	3	...	...	...
85 - 89	5	1	4	...	...	...
90 - 94	2	-	2	...	...	...
95 - 99	2	1	1	...	...	...
100 +	-	-	-	...	...	...

Palau - Palaos
2005 (C)

Total	134	...	...	6.7	...	...
0	5	...	...	♦18.5	...	...
1 - 4	1	...	...	♦0.9	...	...
5 - 9	-	...	...	-	...	...
10 - 14	-	...	...	-	...	...
15 - 19	2	...	...	♦1.4	...	...
20 - 24	1	...	...	♦0.8	...	...
25 - 29	5	...	...	♦3.2	...	...
30 - 34	4	...	...	♦2.2	...	...
35 - 39	6	...	...	♦3.1	...	...
40 - 44	9	...	...	♦4.8	...	...
45 - 49	13	...	...	♦8.5	...	...
50 - 54	14	...	...	♦11.8	...	...
55 - 59	9	...	...	♦12.3	...	...
60 - 64	10	...	...	♦19.8	...	...
65 - 69	8	...	...	♦21.4	...	...
70 - 74	11	...	...	♦42.8	...	...
75 +	36	...	...	71.1	...	...

Pitcairn
2007 (C)

Total	1	...	...	...	...	...
0	-	...	...	...	...	...
1 - 4	-	...	...	...	...	...
5 - 9	-	...	...	...	...	...
10 - 14	-	...	...	...	...	...
15 - 19	-	...	...	...	...	...
20 - 24	-	...	...	...	...	...
25 - 29	-	...	...	...	...	...
30 - 34	-	...	...	...	...	...
35 - 39	-	...	...	...	...	...
40 - 44	-	...	...	...	...	...
45 - 49	-	...	...	...	...	...
50 - 54	-	...	...	...	...	...
55 - 59	-	...	...	...	...	...
60 - 64	-	...	...	...	...	...
65 - 69	-	...	...	...	...	...
70 - 74	-	...	...	...	...	...
75 - 79	1	...	...	...	...	...
80 - 84	-	...	...	...	...	...
85 - 89	-	...	...	...	...	...
90 +	-	...	...	...	...	...

Samoa[20]
2011 (|)

Total	812	427	385	4.3	4.4	4.2
0 - 4	92	58	34	3.4	4.2	2.6
0	78	51	27	...	...	...
1 - 4	14	7	7	...	...	...

19. Deaths by age and sex and age-specific death rates by sex: latest available year, 2005 - 2014
Décès et taux de mortalité selon l'âge et le sexe : dernière année disponible, 2005 - 2014 (continued - suite)

Continent, country or area, date, code[a] and age (in years) Continent, pays ou zone, date, code[a] et âge (en annèes)	Number - Nombre			Rate - Taux		
	Both sexes Les deux sexes	Male Masculin	Female Féminin	Both sexes Les deux sexes	Male Masculin	Female Féminin
OCEANIA - OCÉANIE						
Samoa[20]						
2011 (|)						
5 - 9	4	1	3	♦0.2	♦0.1	♦0.3
10 - 14	2	-	2	♦0.1	-	♦0.2
15 - 19	10	7	3	♦0.5	♦0.7	♦0.3
20 - 24	12	5	7	♦0.8	♦0.6	♦1.0
25 - 29	10	8	2	♦0.8	♦1.2	♦0.3
30 - 34	6	4	2	♦0.5	♦0.7	♦0.4
35 - 39	20	8	12	♦1.8	♦1.4	♦2.3
40 - 44	19	12	7	♦1.8	♦2.1	♦1.4
45 - 49	38	20	18	4.3	♦4.4	♦4.2
50 - 54	48	28	20	6.3	♦7.1	♦5.5
55 - 59	49	22	27	8.3	♦7.3	♦9.3
60 - 64	69	37	32	17.3	18.5	16.2
65 - 69	76	36	40	22.5	22.4	22.6
70 - 74	101	59	42	39.5	49.7	30.7
75 +	250	120	130	74.5	92.2	63.4
75 - 79	80	45	35	...	...	...
80 - 84	84	37	47	...	...	...
85 - 89	62	30	32	...	...	...
90 - 94	17	6	11	...	...	...
95 - 99	7	2	5	...	...	...
100 +	-	-	-	...	...	...
Unknown - Inconnu	6	2	4	..	..	..
Tonga[49]						
2006 (|)						
Total	709	402	307	6.9	7.6	6.1
0 - 4	61	38	24	5.1	6.2	♦4.1
0	53	32	21	...	...	...
1 - 4	8	6	3	...	...	...
5 - 9	10	5	4	♦0.9	♦0.8	♦0.7
10 - 14	7	4	4	♦0.6	♦0.6	♦0.7
15 - 19	12	8	3	♦1.1	♦1.3	♦0.6
20 - 24	11	9	2	♦1.0	♦1.6	♦0.4
25 - 29	7	5	2	♦0.9	♦1.2	♦0.5
30 - 34	12	9	4	♦2.1	♦3.2	♦1.4
35 - 39	12	7	5	♦2.1	♦2.4	♦1.8
40 - 44	19	11	8	♦3.8	♦4.4	♦3.2
45 - 49	29	18	11	♦6.8	♦8.8	♦4.9
50 - 54	29	16	13	♦7.7	♦8.9	♦6.5
55 - 59	37	23	15	11.8	♦15.6	♦9.0
60 - 64	53	33	20	18.5	23.9	♦13.5
65 - 69	49	28	21	20.2	♦22.5	♦17.7
70 - 74	70	38	32	37.5	39.7	35.2
75 +	288	149	139	135.1	141.2	129.2
75 - 79	95	54	41	...	...	...
80 +	193	95	98	...	...	...
Tuvalu						
2005 (U)						
Total	59	33	26	...	...	...
0	6	5	1	...	...	...
1 - 4	2	1	1	...	...	...
5 - 9	-	-	-	...	...	...
10 - 14	-	-	-	...	...	...
15 - 19	-	-	-	...	...	...
20 - 24	1	1	-	...	...	...
25 - 29	-	-	-	...	...	...
30 - 34	1	1	-	...	...	...
35 - 39	2	2	-	...	...	...
40 - 44	2	2	-	...	...	...
45 - 49	3	3	-	...	...	...
50 - 54	6	3	3	...	...	...
55 - 59	4	3	1	...	...	...
60 - 64	7	2	5	...	...	...
65 - 69	6	2	4	...	...	...
70 - 74	1	-	1	...	...	...
75 - 79	8	4	4	...	...	...

19. Deaths by age and sex and age-specific death rates by sex: latest available year, 2005 - 2014
Décès et taux de mortalité selon l'âge et le sexe : dernière année disponible, 2005 - 2014 (continued - suite)

Continent, country or area, date, code[a] and age (in years) / Continent, pays ou zone, date, code[a] et âge (en années)	Number - Nombre			Rate - Taux		
	Both sexes Les deux sexes	Male Masculin	Female Féminin	Both sexes Les deux sexes	Male Masculin	Female Féminin
OCEANIA - OCÉANIE						
Tuvalu						
2005 (U)						
80 - 84	*8*	*3*	*5*	...	...	...
85 + ...	*2*	*1*	*1*	...	...	...
Wallis and Futuna Islands - Îles Wallis et Futuna						
2008 (C)						
Total...........................	90	51	39	...	...	...
0 - 4	1	1	-	...	...	...
5 - 9	-	-	-	...	...	...
10 - 14	1	1	-	...	...	...
15 - 19	2	1	1	...	...	...
20 - 24	4	3	1	...	...	...
25 - 29	4	4	-	...	...	...
30 - 34	3	3	-	...	...	...
35 - 39	2	1	1	...	...	...
40 - 44	-	-	-	...	...	...
45 - 49	2	1	1	...	...	...
50 - 54	2	1	1	...	...	...
55 - 59	4	2	2	...	...	...
60 - 64	5	4	1	...	...	...
65 - 69	12	8	4	...	...	...
70 - 74	15	9	6	...	...	...
75 - 79	13	4	9	...	...	...
80 - 84	11	4	7	...	...	...
85 - 89	5	3	2	...	...	...
90 - 94	4	1	3	...	...	...
95 - 99	-	-	-	...	...	...
100 + ...	-	-	-	...	...	...

FOOTNOTES - NOTES

♦ Rates based on 30 or fewer deaths. - Taux basés sur 30 décès ou moins.

Italics: estimates which are less reliable. - Italiques : estimations moins sûres.

* Provisional. - Données provisoires.

[a] 'Code' indicates the source of data, as follows:
 C - Civil registration, estimated over 90% complete
 U - Civil registration, estimated less than 90% complete
 | - Other source, estimated reliable
 + - Data tabulated by date of registration rather than occurence
 ... - Information not available

Le 'Code' indique la source des données, comme suit :
 C - Registres de l'état civil considérés complets à 90 p. 100 au moins
 U - Registres de l'état civil qui ne sont pas considérés complets à 90 p. 100 au moins
 | - Autre source, considérée pas douteuses
 + - Données exploitées selon la date de l'enregistrement et non la date de l'événement
 ... - Information pas disponible

[1] Excluding live-born infants who died before their birth was registered. Data refer to Algerian population only. - Non compris les enfants nés vivants décédés avant l'enregistrement de leur naissance. Les données ne concernent que la population algérienne.
[2] Source: Vital Statistics Report 2012. - Source: Vital Statistics Report 2012.
[3] Data from civil registration centres of Brazzaville, Dolisie, Nkayi, Mossendijo and Ouesso communes. - Données issues des centres d'enregistrement des faits d'état-civil des communes de Brazzaville, Dolisie, Nkayi, Mossendijo et Ouesso.
[4] Data refer to the 12 months preceding the census in September. - Les données se rapportent aux 12 mois précédant le recensement de septembre.
[5] Unrevised data. - Les données n'ont pas été révisées.

[6] Data refer to the 12 months preceding the census in June. - Les données se raportent aux 12 mois précédant le recensement de juin.
[7] Data refer to the 12 months preceding the census in April. - Les données se rapportent aux douze mois précédant le recensement d'avril.
[8] Excludes the islands of St. Brandon and Agalega. - Non compris les îles St. Brandon et Agalega.
[9] Data refer to the 12 months preceding the census in August. - Les données se rapportent aux 12 mois précédant le recensement d'août.
[10] Data refer to the 12 months preceding the census in April. The figures in this table are derived from survey data. They are representative only of private households, internally displaced persons, refugees and nomads, and do not include cattle camps, institutional households, homeless people or overnight travelers. - Les données se rapportent aux douze mois précédant le recensement d'avril. Les chiffres de ce tableau proviennent de données d'enquête. Ils représentent exclusivement les ménages privés et les déplacés, réfugiés et nomades; ils ne comprennent ni les personnes se trouvant dans des camps pastoraux et des établissements collectifs, ni les sans-abri, ni les voyageurs.
[11] Data refer to the 12 months preceding the census in May. - Les données se rapportent aux 12 mois précédant le recensement de mai.
[12] Figures for male and female may not add up to the total, since they do not include the category "Unknown". - La somme des chiffres indiqués pour les sexes masculin et féminin peut n'être pas égale au total parce qu'elle n'inclut pas la catégorie " inconnue ".
[13] Data refer to the 12 months preceding the census in October. - Les données se rapportent aux 12 mois précédant le recensement de octobre.
[14] Excluding visitors. - Ne comprend pas les visiteurs.
[15] Excluding non-residents and foreign service personnel and their dependants. - À l'exclusion des non-résidents et du personnel diplomatique et de leurs charges de famille.
[16] Including Canadian residents temporarily in the United States, but excluding United States residents temporarily in Canada. - Y compris les résidents canadiens se trouvant temporairement aux Etats-Unis, mais ne comprenant pas les résidents des Etats-Unis se trouvant temporairement au Canada.
[17] Data refer to population in private households. Data refer to period from 1 January 2010 to 3 April 2011. - Les données portent sur la population des

ménages privés. Les données concernent la période du 1 janvier 2010 au 3 avril 2011.

[18] Excluding live-born infants who died before their birth was registered. - Non compris les enfants nés vivants décédés avant l'enregistrement de leur naissance.

[19] Data refer to resident population only. - Pour la population résidante seulement.

[20] Data refer to the 12 months preceding the census in November. - Données se rapportant aux 12 mois précédant le recensement de novembre.

[21] Including deaths abroad and deaths of unknown place of residence. - Y compris décès à l'étranger et décès dont le lieu de résidence n'est pas connu.

[22] Excludes nomadic Indian tribes. - Non compris les tribus d'Indiens nomades.

[23] Source: Reports of the Ministry of Health. - Source : Rapports du Ministère de la Santé.

[24] Excluding infants born alive of less than 28 weeks' gestation, of less than 1 000 grams in weight and 35 centimeters in length, who die within seven days of birth. - Non compris les enfants nés vivants après moins de 28 semaines de gestations, pesant moins de 1 000 grammes, mesurant moins de 35 centimètres et décédés dans les sept jours qui ont suivi leur naissance.

[25] For statistical purposes, the data for China do not include those for the Hong Kong Special Administrative Region (Hong Kong SAR), Macao Special Administrative Region (Macao SAR) and Taiwan province of China. Data refer to the 12 months preceding the census in November. - Pour la présentation des statistiques, les données pour la Chine ne comprennent pas la Région Administrative Spéciale de Hong Kong (Hong Kong RAS), la Région Administrative Spéciale de Macao (Macao RAS) et Taïwan province de Chine. Données se rapportant aux 12 mois précédant le recensement de novembre.

[26] Data refer to government controlled areas. Data refer to deaths of residents only. - Les données se rapportent aux zones contrôlées par le Gouvernement. Les données renvoient aux décès de résidents uniquement.

[27] Data refer to the Iranian Year which begins on 21 March and ends on 20 March of the following year. - Les données concernent l'année iranienne, qui commence le 21 mars et se termine le 20 mars de l'année suivante.

[28] Includes data for East Jerusalem and Israeli residents in certain other territories under occupation by Israeli military forces since June 1967. Including deaths abroad of Israeli residents who were out of the country for less than a year. - Y compris les données pour Jérusalem-Est et les résidents israéliens dans certains autres territoires occupés depuis 1967 par les forces armées israéliennes. Y compris les décès à l'étranger de résidents israéliens qui ont quitté le pays depuis moins d'un an.

[29] Data refer to Japanese nationals in Japan only. - Les données se raportent aux nationaux japonais au Japon seulement.

[30] Data from Births and Deaths Notification System (Ministry of Health and all health care providers). Data for all population, citizens and foreigners. - Les données proviennent du système de notification des naissances et des décès (Ministère de la santé et tous prestataires de soins de santé). Les données portent sur la population entière, les citoyens et les étrangers.

[31] Excluding data for the Pakistan-held part of Jammu and Kashmir, the final status of which has not yet been determined. Based on the results of the Pakistan Demographic Survey. - Non compris les données concernant la partie du Jammu et Cachemire occupée par le Pakistan dont le statut définitif n'a pas été déterminé. Données extraites de l'enquête démographique effectuée par le Pakistan.

[32] Excluding alien armed forces, civilian aliens employed by armed forces, and foreign diplomatic personnel and their dependants. - Non compris les militaires étrangers, les civils étrangers employés par les forces armées ni le personnel diplomatique étranger et les membres de leur famille les accompagnant.

[33] The registration of births and deaths is conducted by the Ministry of Health. An estimate of completeness is not provided. - L'enregistrement des naissances et des décès est mené par le Ministère de la Santé. Le degré estimatif de complétude n'est pas fourni.

[34] Excluding data from Mulative and Killnochchi districts. - À l'exclusion des données des districts de Mulative et Killnochchi.

[35] Source: Palestinian Central Bureau of Statistics, Population Register, updated version 05/01/2015. - Source: Bureau central de statistique palestinien, registre de la population, version actualisée jusqu'au 05/01/2015.

[36] Including deaths of nationals abroad. - Y compris les décès des nationaux survenus à l'étranger.

[37] Including armed forces stationed outside the country, but excluding alien armed forces stationed in the area. - Y compris les militaires nationaux hors du pays, mais non compris les militaires étrangers en garnison sur le territoire.

[38] Excluding Faeroe Islands and Greenland shown separately, if available. - Non compris les Iles Féroé et le Groenland, qui font l'objet de rubriques distinctes, si disponible.

[39] Including armed forces stationed outside the country. - Y compris les militaires nationaux hors du pays.

[40] Including residents outside the country if listed in a Netherlands population register. - Englobe les résidents se trouvant à l'étranger à condition qu'ils soient inscrits sur le registre de population des Pays-Bas.

[41] Including residents temporarily outside the country. - Y compris les résidents se trouvant temporairement hors du pays.

[42] Data refer to usually resident population. - Les données concernent la population habituellement résidente.

[43] Excluding Transnistria and the municipality of Bender. - Les données ne tiennent pas compte de l'information sur la Transnistria et la municipalité de Bender.

[44] Excludes data for Kosovo and Metohia. - Sans les données pour le Kosovo et Metohie.

[45] Data includes deaths resulting from births with weight 500g and more (if weight is unknown - with length 25 centimeters and more, or with gestation during 22 weeks or more). - Y compris les décès de nouveau-nés de 500 grammes ou plus (si le poids est inconnu – de 25 centimètres de long ou plus, ou après une grossesse de 22 semaines ou plus).

[46] Excluding Channel Islands (Guernsey and Jersey) and Isle of Man, shown separately, if available. - Non compris les îles Anglo-Normandes (Guernesey et Jersey) et l'île de Man, qui font l'objet de rubriques distinctes, si disponible.

[47] Excluding Niue, shown separately, which is part of Cook Islands, but because of remoteness is administered separately. Unrevised data. - Non compris Nioué, qui fait l'objet d'une rubrique distincte et qui fait partie des îles Cook, mais qui, en raison de son éloignement, est administrée séparément. Les données n'ont pas été révisées.

[48] Includes deaths occurred in New Zealand but buried in Niue and deaths occurred in Niue but buried elsewhere. - Y compris les personnes décédées en Nouvelle-Zélande qui sont enterrées à Nioué et les personnes décédées à Nioué qui sont enterrées ailleurs.

[49] Estimate based on results of the Population Census. - Estimation fondeé sur les résultats du recensement de la population.

Table 20 - *Demographic Yearbook 2014*

Table 20 presents the life tables' probabilities of dying in the five year interval following specified ages ($_5q_x$), for each sex, for the latest available year between 2002 and 2014. The probabilities are multiplied by a thousand, that is, the values presented in the table are 1000*$_5q_x$.

Male and female probabilities of dying are shown separately for selected ages beginning at birth and proceeding at every fifth age thereafter up to age 100.

The values presented in the table are derived by the United Nations Statistics Division from the official complete life tables reported by the countries or areas.

Data are shown with one decimal regardless of the number of digits provided in the original computation.

The life table is a statistical device for summarizing the mortality experience of a population, from which the probability of dying, survivorship and expectation of life can be calculated. It is based on the assumption that the theoretical cohort is subject, throughout its existence, to the age-specific mortality rates observed at a particular time. Thus, levels of mortality prevailing at the time a life table is constructed are assumed to remain unchanged into the future until all members of the cohort have died.

Reliability of data: The values shown in this table are derived from official complete life tables. It is assumed that, if necessary, the basic data (population and deaths classified by age and sex) have been adjusted for deficiencies before their use in constructing the complete life tables.

Limitations: The life tables' probabilities of dying are subject to the same qualifications as have been set forth for population statistics in general and death statistics in particular, as discussed in sections 3 and 4, respectively, of the Technical Notes. They must be interpreted strictly using the underlying assumption that surviving cohorts are subjected to the same age-specific mortality rates of the period to which the life table refers.

Earlier data: The life tables' probabilities of dying at specified ages, for each sex, have been shown in previous issues of the *Demographic Yearbook*. For information on specific years covered, the reader should consult the Historical Index.

Tableau 20 – *Annuaire démographique 2014*

Le tableau 20 donne les probabilités de décès dans l'intervalle de cinq ans que suit l'âge spécifié ($_5q_x$), pour chaque sexe, pour la dernière année disponible entre 2002 et 2014. Les probabilités sont multipliées par mille, c'est-à-dire que les valeurs indiquées dans le tableau sont égales à $1000 {}^* {}_5q_x$.

Les probabilités de décès sont indiquées séparément pour les hommes et les femmes pour différents âges, depuis la naissance puis tous les cinq ans jusqu'à 100 ans.

Les chiffres indiqués dans ce tableau ont été calculés par la Division de statistique de l'Organisation des Nations Unies à partir des tables de mortalité complètes communiquées par les pays ou zones.

Les données sont arrondies à la première décimale, indépendamment du nombre de décimales qui figurent dans le calcul initial.

La table de mortalité est un moyen statistique que s'utilise pour donner un aperçu complet de la mortalité d'une population incluant les probabilités de décès et l'espérance de vie à chaque âge. Les tables de mortalité reposent sur l'hypothèse que chaque cohorte théoriquement distinguée connaît, pendant toute son existence, les taux de mortalité par âge observé à un moment donné. Les taux de mortalité correspondant à l'époque à laquelle sont calculées les tables de mortalité sont ainsi censés demeurer inchangées dans l'avenir jusqu'au décès de tous les membres de la cohorte.

Fiabilité des donnés : Les chiffres indiqués dans ce tableau ont été calculés à partir des tables officielles de mortalité complètes. En ce qui concerne les chiffres extraits de tables officielles de mortalité, on part du principe que les données de base (effectif de la population et nombre de décès selon l'âge et le sexe) ont été ajustées, en tant que de besoin, avant de servir à l'établissement de la table de mortalité.

Insuffisance des données : Les probabilités de décès appellent les mêmes réserves que celles qui ont été formulées à propos des statistiques de la population en général et des statistiques de mortalité en particulier (voir les sections 3 et 4 des Notes techniques). Lorsque l'on interprète les données, il ne faut jamais perdre de vue que, par hypothèse, les cohortes de survivants sont soumises, pour chaque âge, aux conditions de mortalité de la période visée par la table de mortalité.

Données publiées antérieurement : Les probabilités de décès pour chaque sexe figuraient déjà dans des éditions antérieures de *l'Annuaire démographique*. Pour plus de précisions concernant les années pour lesquelles ces données ont été publiées, se reporter à l'index historique.

20. Probability of dying in the five year interval following specified age (5qx), by sex, latest available year: 2002 - 2014
Probabilité de décès dans l'intervalle de cinq ans qui suit un âge donné (5qx), par sexe, dernière année disponible : 2002 - 2014

Continent, country or area and date / Continent, pays ou zone et date	Age (in years) - Age (en années)																				
	0	5	10	15	20	25	30	35	40	45	50	55	60	65	70	75	80	85	90	95	100
AFRICA - AFRIQUE																					
Republic of South Sudan - République de Soudan du Sud 2010																					
Male - Hommes	130.6	14.1	10.8	18.5	25.6	27.0	28.8	33.1	40.1	51.8	70.0	98.7	143.7	213.2	316.6	457.7	624.2	785.1	907.0	...	...
Female - Femmes	111.9	13.7	10.7	18.4	25.9	27.8	30.2	35.2	43.3	56.8	78.0	111.6	164.6	245.8	362.8	513.5	678.3	826.7	931.7	...	...
Zimbabwe 2001 - 2002																					
Male - Hommes	116.9	18.0	12.8	12.2	30.6	70.9	129.9	193.2	193.5	186.2	175.7	177.3	167.1	186.5	197.2	270.7	297.7	432.4	545.1	...	...
Female - Femmes	100.5	15.2	10.8	15.2	46.7	97.4	141.4	159.8	125.9	122.9	101.0	99.6	100.9	122.5	128.8	161.1	223.5	304.5	438.0	...	...
AMERICA, NORTH - AMÉRIQUE DU NORD																					
Canada 2000 - 2002																					
Male - Hommes	6.9	0.5	1.3	3.6	4.2	4.2	4.9	6.0	9.8	14.2	23.1	35.7	58.9	93.6	147.5	232.0	356.1	522.1	699.2	832.4	...
Female - Femmes	5.5	0.4	0.7	1.5	1.7	1.7	2.3	3.6	5.5	8.8	13.9	22.4	35.1	55.7	88.8	145.8	244.8	402.2	576.2	750.4	...
Costa Rica 2014																					
Male - Hommes	10.0	0.9	1.3	3.7	6.1	7.0	7.9	9.2	11.8	16.6	23.7	35.0	53.3	83.5	127.6	199.2	295.9	423.7	586.4	758.5	*1000
Female - Femmes	8.3	0.6	0.9	1.5	2.0	2.0	2.7	3.8	5.5	8.4	13.0	20.9	33.2	53.9	85.6	140.8	234.8	368.0	535.1	720.9	*1000
Cuba 2011 - 2013																					
Male - Hommes	6.0	1.0	1.3	2.4	3.5	4.5	5.7	7.3	10.5	17.5	29.3	44.9	67.2	100.5	148.8	223.2	334.7	477.3	602.9	645.4	*1000
Female - Femmes	5.6	0.9	0.9	1.4	1.9	2.4	3.0	4.1	6.5	11.0	18.7	29.3	44.6	67.0	104.8	168.7	270.2	421.1	577.7	655.4	*1000
Curaçao 2011 - 2014																					
Male - Hommes	8.8	0.5	0.7	2.3	7.6	9.6	11.0	11.2	10.2	15.1	29.7	52.8	70.7	116.4	164.2	229.7	347.7	492.8	709.7	743.4	*1000
Female - Femmes	13.1	0.0	0.2	1.4	1.7	2.8	4.4	4.0	8.5	8.1	16.5	21.6	37.3	58.5	90.1	151.3	265.9	389.9	547.6	782.0	*1000
Greenland - Groenland 2009 - 2013																					
Male - Hommes	15.4	0.5	2.8	15.7	22.9	16.2	14.3	13.6	18.4	25.9	35.9	72.3	87.1	167.8	303.9	470.3	648.6	758.8	...	...	...
Female - Femmes	7.0	0.5	2.7	10.3	8.0	2.5	6.9	10.8	9.1	20.1	26.0	50.6	83.8	147.4	209.0	326.2	565.3	731.9	970.6	...	...
Guadeloupe 2002																					
Male - Hommes	8.7	1.1	2.1	4.6	9.3	11.1	10.0	12.7	14.6	24.3	31.1	45.3	68.9	95.0	141.6	219.3	290.6	421.7	994.4	*1000	...
Female - Femmes	6.0	0.3	0.3	1.2	2.9	1.4	4.3	5.8	8.0	8.1	10.9	22.1	39.9	55.5	87.1	112.0	212.4	331.5	984.3	*1000	...
Jamaica - Jamaïque 2006																					
Male - Hommes	31.7	2.8	2.5	4.5	6.5	6.5	7.0	9.4	14.5	23.2	37.5	60.5	96.9	153.2	236.8	353.8	502.7	667.6	817.2	921.8	*1000
Female - Femmes	18.0	1.3	1.1	1.7	2.6	3.4	4.3	5.9	8.7	13.9	22.8	38.0	63.2	104.5	169.8	268.2	405.3	574.1	747.0	883.6	*1000
Martinique 2007																					
Male - Hommes	11.6	1.0	1.1	4.2	8.8	7.5	8.8	8.5	10.4	13.5	26.7	28.9	42.2	87.6	122.7	202.9	325.3	532.7	663.7	834.4	*1000
Female - Femmes	7.8	0.4	0.7	0.6	2.1	2.9	4.6	4.1	4.8	5.3	11.3	14.8	28.6	45.6	76.8	135.3	216.7	362.2	508.4	810.4	*1000
Mexico - Mexique 2005																					
Male - Hommes	21.6	1.7	2.2	4.3	7.4	9.9	12.0	15.1	20.3	28.7	41.3	59.9	86.6	124.3	176.5	246.8	337.7	448.7	574.2	702.2	*1000
Female - Femmes	17.4	1.3	1.2	1.8	2.4	3.1	4.3	6.4	9.9	15.4	23.9	37.2	57.5	88.4	134.4	201.1	293.6	414.1	557.1	705.8	*1000
Panama[1] 2013																					
Male - Hommes	22.4	2.0	2.5	7.3	13.2	14.8	13.6	13.1	14.9	19.8	28.4	41.7	61.8	91.3	133.9	193.8	275.2	380.5	507.1	644.6	*1000
Female - Femmes	17.0	1.3	1.5	2.5	3.5	4.5	5.5	6.8	8.7	11.8	16.8	25.1	38.5	59.9	93.6	145.5	222.6	330.8	470.7	629.9	*1000
United States of America - États-Unis d'Amérique 2013																					
Male - Hommes	7.6	0.7	0.8	3.1	6.0	6.8	7.7	8.9	12.2	19.1	30.0	44.8	63.0	86.9	130.4	200.0	313.4	479.8	673.0	832.0	*1000
Female - Femmes	6.3	0.5	0.6	1.3	2.2	2.8	3.8	5.2	7.7	12.2	18.7	26.7	38.0	57.6	90.5	146.5	240.5	393.6	587.8	771.5	*1000

555

20. Probability of dying in the five year interval following specified age (5qx), by sex, latest available year: 2002 - 2014
Probabilité de décès dans l'intervalle de cinq ans qui suit un âge donné (5qx), par sexe, dernière année disponible : 2002 - 2014 (continued - suite)

Continent, country or area and date / Continent, pays ou zone et date	Age (in years) - Age (en années)																				
	0	5	10	15	20	25	30	35	40	45	50	55	60	65	70	75	80	85	90	95	100

AMERICA, SOUTH - AMÉRIQUE DU SUD

Argentina - Argentine
2008 - 2010
Male - Hommes	15.8	1.3	1.8	5.3	7.5	7.9	8.1	10.0	14.5	22.1	37.3	59.5	89.5	133.8	194.0	289.6	431.2	568.1	692.6	804.3	*1000
Female - Femmes	13.0	1.0	1.2	2.2	2.6	3.1	4.0	5.7	8.4	13.2	20.4	31.0	45.5	68.2	105.9	175.1	309.8	460.7	614.6	762.3	*1000

Bolivia (Plurinational State of) - Bolivie (État plurinational de)[2]
2014 - 2015
Male - Hommes	72.6	9.8	5.9	10.2	14.9	16.0	17.7	21.5	25.0	32.5	40.6	57.5	82.5	113.0	157.9	228.3	314.9	454.6	603.8	787.0	*1000
Female - Femmes	63.0	8.3	5.0	6.4	7.5	8.3	10.2	13.4	17.2	23.6	31.9	44.5	67.0	93.9	126.2	180.7	266.2	362.7	460.1	652.9	*1000

Brazil - Brésil[1]
2012
Male - Hommes	19.7	1.6	2.0	8.8	13.4	13.6	14.5	16.8	21.7	30.1	43.1	60.4	83.5	120.3	176.5	256.9	*1000	...	...	...	...
Female - Femmes	16.4	1.2	1.3	2.4	3.0	3.8	5.1	6.9	10.2	15.7	23.0	33.6	49.5	76.1	118.4	182.6	*1000	...	...	...	...

Chile - Chili
2012
Male - Hommes	9.2	0.7	1.0	3.1	4.4	5.1	6.4	8.2	10.9	16.0	24.0	36.6	54.0	93.9	143.5	226.6	383.4	549.4	655.9	*1000	...
Female - Femmes	7.9	0.8	0.7	1.4	1.6	1.6	2.6	3.4	5.7	8.2	12.8	21.3	34.1	55.3	89.4	143.6	262.1	415.4	620.3	*1000	...

Ecuador - Équateur[3]
2010 - 2015
Male - Hommes	24.8	1.0	1.1	3.1	5.1	7.9	12.0	12.2	13.7	19.7	29.3	45.2	69.0	106.1	167.6	253.8	384.8	555.6	723.5	853.4	*1000
Female - Femmes	21.1	1.1	1.0	1.6	1.9	2.1	2.8	3.9	5.9	9.3	13.9	21.8	34.7	59.3	104.9	193.8	333.1	522.2	701.5	847.3	*1000

French Guiana - Guyane française
2007
Male - Hommes	16.3	1.5	2.1	4.9	7.7	8.1	10.0	14.0	17.2	29.4	16.0	32.3	52.4	79.5	135.5	261.3	306.7	474.0	733.7	...	...
Female - Femmes	15.1	1.9	1.3	1.4	1.2	3.0	4.6	4.2	11.9	11.0	10.4	11.6	26.7	85.4	77.4	203.8	253.1	321.1	434.3	...	...

Uruguay
2004
Male - Hommes	20.0	1.3	1.3	3.5	5.8	6.8	7.2	9.0	12.8	21.2	36.4	62.2	95.4	145.2	204.6	305.7	430.5	610.5	776.7	862.5	*1000
Female - Femmes	15.5	1.0	1.1	1.6	1.9	2.7	3.8	5.2	7.9	12.5	19.4	30.5	41.2	63.4	97.2	177.7	292.9	472.0	654.3	820.5	*1000

ASIA - ASIE

Armenia - Arménie
2006 - 2007
Male - Hommes	15.3	1.1	1.1	2.9	3.9	4.9	7.3	11.4	20.4	28.6	45.0	68.2	112.2	173.3	246.9	350.8	495.4	691.9	870.7	975.9	...
Female - Femmes	11.9	1.0	0.9	0.9	1.6	1.8	2.7	4.4	7.8	11.3	18.4	29.4	52.7	95.7	158.1	254.3	413.9	670.0	851.3	957.0	...

Azerbaijan - Azerbaïdjan
2013
Male - Hommes	13.5	1.8	1.6	2.9	4.6	5.3	6.7	10.1	15.7	24.9	39.2	62.3	98.4	134.0	223.2	325.1	533.1	630.5	532.8	706.7	...
Female - Femmes	12.4	1.2	1.3	1.8	2.1	2.1	2.7	4.0	6.0	10.1	17.1	28.5	51.8	84.3	154.6	268.6	439.6	616.2	686.1	823.8	...

China, Hong Kong SAR - Chine, Hong Kong RAS
2013
Male - Hommes	3.0	0.7	0.6	0.8	1.5	2.2	3.3	4.5	6.1	9.8	15.4	25.8	40.4	63.3	104.8	168.3	270.8	411.0	583.5	762.6	*1000
Female - Femmes	2.0	0.5	0.4	0.6	0.8	1.1	1.5	2.1	3.5	5.5	8.7	13.6	19.2	29.4	49.3	89.8	170.5	294.5	465.0	661.9	*1000

China, Macao SAR - Chine, Macao RAS
2002 - 2005
Male - Hommes	7.2	0.6	0.4	1.7	3.9	5.4	6.2	7.6	9.0	13.6	17.8	25.8	43.1	72.1	128.9	239.9	369.5	574.4	841.2	991.4	*1000
Female - Femmes	5.2	0.4	0.2	0.9	1.5	1.9	2.3	3.8	4.7	5.9	7.4	10.9	19.3	33.3	70.4	186.2	317.0	485.2	717.3	923.7	*1000

Israel - Israël[4]
2009 - 2013
Male - Hommes	4.6	0.6	0.7	1.7	2.6	3.0	3.4	4.3	6.3	10.3	17.4	29.0	46.6	72.4	111.7	177.3	290.4	462.0	618.4	767.4	*1000
Female - Femmes	4.0	0.5	0.4	0.7	0.9	1.1	1.6	2.4	3.8	6.2	10.1	16.2	26.1	42.9	73.1	130.5	238.5	413.3	602.9	782.0	*1000

Japan - Japon
2010
Male - Hommes	3.4	0.5	0.6	1.3	3.0	3.3	3.7	5.0	7.6	12.0	19.1	30.4	47.3	70.0	108.1	183.7	306.5	473.8	658.4	820.7	...
Female - Femmes	2.9	0.4	0.4	0.8	1.3	1.5	2.0	2.8	4.2	6.4	9.6	13.6	19.9	29.1	48.0	86.8	161.1	302.6	506.4	721.5	...

20. Probability of dying in the five year interval following specified age (5qx), by sex, latest available year: 2002 - 2014
Probabilité de décès dans l'intervalle de cinq ans qui suit un âge donné (5qx), par sexe, dernière année disponible : 2002 - 2014 (continued - suite)

Continent, country or area and date / Continent, pays ou zone et date	0	5	10	15	20	25	30	35	40	45	50	55	60	65	70	75	80	85	90	95	100

ASIA - ASIE

Kazakhstan
2012
Male - Hommes	18.1	2.1	2.1	4.9	9.5	15.0	22.5	30.6	37.5	49.5	72.7	107.0	157.3	204.8	286.8	397.7	531.1	638.2	732.6	812.3	...
Female - Femmes	14.5	1.6	1.2	2.4	3.3	4.9	7.4	10.3	13.8	18.6	28.5	43.8	68.1	99.5	161.7	268.0	427.7	602.1	790.3	887.7	...

Kyrgyzstan - Kirghizstan
2013
| Male - Hommes | 25.2 | 1.5 | 2.1 | 4.1 | 6.3 | 9.8 | 14.8 | 24.5 | 30.9 | 44.2 | 64.1 | 87.2 | 130.2 | 171.3 | 268.4 | 362.6 | 619.1 | 807.1 | 915.5 | 923.6 | *1000 |
| Female - Femmes | 20.4 | 1.4 | 1.6 | 2.1 | 2.9 | 3.7 | 5.9 | 9.2 | 12.4 | 16.4 | 26.0 | 40.1 | 62.8 | 95.8 | 161.5 | 258.1 | 450.3 | 660.7 | 808.2 | 882.3 | *1000 |

Qatar
2006
| Male - Hommes | 10.2 | 0.8 | 1.8 | 9.4 | 8.9 | 6.5 | 5.6 | 6.6 | 7.1 | 9.0 | 16.1 | 22.1 | 42.2 | 88.0 | 167.5 | 248.6 | 376.7 | *1000 | ... | ... | ... |
| Female - Femmes | 9.0 | 1.3 | 0.9 | 2.2 | 1.4 | 2.4 | 1.2 | 1.8 | 3.8 | 6.7 | 9.8 | 22.1 | 76.0 | 120.2 | 253.6 | 354.1 | 348.3 | *1000 | ... | ... | ... |

Republic of Korea - République de Corée
2013
| Male - Hommes | 3.9 | 0.6 | 0.6 | 1.5 | 2.4 | 3.1 | 4.2 | 5.8 | 9.3 | 14.9 | 23.0 | 33.1 | 47.8 | 71.8 | 124.3 | 209.7 | 338.2 | 503.0 | 667.3 | 800.7 | *1000 |
| Female - Femmes | 3.5 | 0.4 | 0.4 | 0.8 | 1.2 | 1.8 | 2.4 | 3.1 | 4.3 | 6.0 | 8.4 | 11.3 | 17.4 | 28.9 | 56.3 | 110.0 | 214.0 | 371.4 | 558.5 | 731.7 | *1000 |

Singapore - Singapour[5]
2014
| Male - Hommes | 2.5 | 0.3 | 0.5 | 1.3 | 1.9 | 1.8 | 2.6 | 3.5 | 6.0 | 9.6 | 16.5 | 28.1 | 42.4 | 68.5 | 119.5 | 189.0 | 290.5 | 425.3 | 592.2 | 766.9 | *1000 |
| Female - Femmes | 2.6 | 0.2 | 0.4 | 0.7 | 0.7 | 0.8 | 1.3 | 1.9 | 3.4 | 5.9 | 9.9 | 15.4 | 23.8 | 38.1 | 69.4 | 123.1 | 209.9 | 337.8 | 506.7 | 694.3 | *1000 |

Turkey - Turquie
2013
| Male - Hommes | 16.5 | 1.7 | 1.9 | 3.7 | 4.2 | 3.8 | 4.3 | 6.3 | 10.1 | 16.6 | 27.5 | 45.4 | 74.7 | 121.4 | 193.6 | 299.4 | 441.8 | 610.3 | 775.1 | 899.4 | *1000 |
| Female - Femmes | 14.8 | 1.6 | 1.3 | 1.4 | 1.5 | 1.9 | 2.4 | 3.3 | 4.9 | 7.8 | 12.8 | 21.7 | 37.6 | 65.6 | 113.6 | 193.2 | 316.5 | 486.7 | 682.0 | 851.8 | *1000 |

EUROPE

Austria - Autriche
2013
| Male - Hommes | 4.3 | 0.4 | 0.7 | 1.8 | 2.9 | 3.1 | 3.2 | 4.8 | 6.5 | 12.9 | 21.7 | 35.6 | 56.8 | 86.6 | 117.9 | 191.9 | 324.0 | 506.5 | 722.3 | 882.0 | ... |
| Female - Femmes | 3.2 | 0.5 | 0.4 | 0.8 | 1.1 | 1.0 | 1.6 | 2.3 | 3.9 | 6.8 | 11.0 | 17.5 | 29.5 | 44.9 | 66.6 | 117.0 | 224.6 | 416.8 | 647.8 | 850.0 | ... |

Belarus - Bélarus
2013
| Male - Hommes | 5.2 | 1.0 | 1.0 | 3.0 | 6.9 | 10.1 | 16.1 | 24.5 | 33.7 | 45.7 | 67.1 | 104.2 | 150.7 | 198.0 | 271.8 | 375.2 | 497.3 | 630.3 | 760.6 | 870.5 | ... |
| Female - Femmes | 4.0 | 0.8 | 0.7 | 1.3 | 2.2 | 2.8 | 4.8 | 7.2 | 10.2 | 14.4 | 21.5 | 33.9 | 50.5 | 77.8 | 127.7 | 224.5 | 364.5 | 545.3 | 741.0 | 899.6 | ... |

Belgium - Belgique
2006
| Male - Hommes | 4.4 | 0.6 | 0.7 | 2.6 | 4.6 | 4.4 | 5.6 | 7.1 | 10.7 | 17.3 | 27.2 | 42.4 | 65.1 | 93.3 | 149.7 | 248.7 | 387.2 | 570.9 | 751.3 | 886.0 | ... |
| Female - Femmes | 3.9 | 0.5 | 0.6 | 1.3 | 1.1 | 1.8 | 2.4 | 3.8 | 5.8 | 10.2 | 16.3 | 22.5 | 33.8 | 48.2 | 79.3 | 149.1 | 270.8 | 466.0 | 663.7 | 835.2 | ... |

Bulgaria - Bulgarie
2010 - 2012
| Male - Hommes | 11.9 | 1.0 | 1.6 | 3.1 | 4.8 | 5.6 | 7.1 | 9.7 | 17.2 | 30.5 | 51.7 | 80.4 | 116.1 | 155.2 | 225.0 | 325.9 | 472.1 | 632.4 | 764.1 | 886.4 | ... |
| Female - Femmes | 9.1 | 1.0 | 1.0 | 1.8 | 1.8 | 2.1 | 3.1 | 5.5 | 8.7 | 13.7 | 21.2 | 31.4 | 47.2 | 72.7 | 127.0 | 231.4 | 395.0 | 597.0 | 738.0 | 891.0 | ... |

Czech Republic - République tchèque
2013
| Male - Hommes | 3.6 | 0.5 | 0.6 | 2.4 | 3.9 | 3.9 | 4.7 | 6.0 | 10.1 | 17.8 | 28.5 | 49.4 | 81.6 | 124.4 | 175.7 | 263.4 | 388.0 | 550.8 | 731.8 | 886.6 | ... |
| Female - Femmes | 2.5 | 0.4 | 0.2 | 1.0 | 1.2 | 1.5 | 1.7 | 2.8 | 4.8 | 8.4 | 14.2 | 22.4 | 37.8 | 60.6 | 95.8 | 164.2 | 295.9 | 494.3 | 741.0 | 932.7 | ... |

Denmark - Danemark[6]
2012 - 2013
| Male - Hommes | 4.1 | 0.3 | 0.4 | 1.3 | 2.1 | 2.3 | 3.0 | 4.5 | 8.1 | 13.1 | 23.2 | 38.3 | 56.6 | 86.5 | 128.4 | 213.6 | 357.9 | 537.0 | 722.8 | 887.8 | ... |
| Female - Femmes | 4.3 | 0.2 | 0.2 | 0.8 | 0.9 | 1.2 | 1.7 | 2.2 | 4.5 | 7.4 | 14.4 | 25.0 | 36.3 | 53.9 | 90.0 | 157.9 | 267.4 | 414.3 | 625.6 | 822.5 | ... |

Estonia - Estonie
2013
| Male - Hommes | 2.7 | 0.8 | 0.6 | 2.5 | 5.4 | 6.1 | 11.4 | 11.6 | 17.0 | 24.8 | 40.7 | 64.2 | 107.3 | 145.3 | 198.4 | 284.7 | 397.1 | 537.7 | 740.5 | 815.4 | ... |
| Female - Femmes | 3.8 | 0.8 | 0.9 | 1.4 | 1.0 | 2.4 | 3.2 | 4.4 | 5.7 | 8.7 | 16.0 | 25.8 | 37.6 | 52.0 | 89.0 | 152.1 | 264.5 | 467.5 | 663.2 | 819.6 | ... |

Finland - Finlande[7]
2012
| Male - Hommes | 3.1 | 0.4 | 0.5 | 2.3 | 4.2 | 4.8 | 5.3 | 6.9 | 10.4 | 16.4 | 24.1 | 38.4 | 58.8 | 87.6 | 127.4 | 200.8 | 338.8 | 522.6 | 720.2 | 875.8 | ... |
| Female - Femmes | 3.0 | 0.6 | 0.3 | 1.3 | 1.8 | 2.0 | 2.0 | 3.0 | 4.3 | 7.0 | 11.8 | 18.6 | 28.0 | 42.9 | 67.6 | 116.2 | 226.2 | 410.8 | 635.5 | 827.8 | ... |

20. Probability of dying in the five year interval following specified age (5qx), by sex, latest available year: 2002 - 2014
Probabilité de décès dans l'intervalle de cinq ans qui suit un âge donné (5qx), par sexe, dernière année disponible : 2002 - 2014 (continued - suite)

Continent, country or area and date / Continent, pays ou zone et date	0	5	10	15	20	25	30	35	40	45	50	55	60	65	70	75	80	85	90	95	100
EUROPE																					
France[8]																					
2010 - 2012																					
Male - Hommes	4.5	0.4	0.5	2.0	3.5	4.1	4.7	6.6	10.3	16.7	27.9	41.9	56.6	76.8	110.2	175.2	290.7	467.5	669.9	844.0	...
Female - Femmes	3.7	0.4	0.4	0.9	1.2	1.4	1.9	3.1	5.1	8.6	13.2	18.4	24.8	35.2	53.4	94.6	181.6	340.0	560.7	771.4	...
Germany - Allemagne																					
2009 - 2011																					
Male - Hommes	4.7	0.5	0.5	1.7	2.7	3.0	3.6	4.9	7.9	14.3	25.2	39.8	58.9	86.4	131.1	216.1	344.3	519.4	704.8	848.0	...
Female - Femmes	3.8	0.4	0.4	0.9	1.1	1.3	1.7	2.6	4.5	8.1	13.5	20.3	31.1	45.0	71.7	134.3	250.2	441.8	654.2	814.0	...
Greece - Grèce																					
2012																					
Male - Hommes	3.9	0.5	0.6	2.1	3.6	3.9	4.8	5.9	8.8	14.5	24.3	39.6	58.2	82.7	123.0	205.5	342.8	494.8	639.6	788.6	...
Female - Femmes	3.3	0.5	0.4	0.8	1.0	1.3	1.8	2.6	4.3	7.3	11.2	16.5	24.4	38.9	70.2	145.6	289.3	453.7	606.1	764.5	...
Hungary - Hongrie																					
2013																					
Male - Hommes	6.7	0.5	0.7	1.8	2.7	3.1	4.2	7.0	13.7	28.4	52.5	82.5	113.9	150.3	207.6	303.4	430.2	635.1	867.1	986.5	...
Female - Femmes	4.9	0.4	0.6	1.0	1.2	1.4	2.0	3.5	6.8	13.6	23.2	36.0	52.1	73.7	111.8	194.5	327.9	558.1	836.2	984.4	...
Iceland - Islande																					
2012 - 2013																					
Male - Hommes	1.5	0.4	0.5	0.8	2.6	3.1	6.6	4.1	6.8	8.4	13.4	23.4	34.7	65.8	87.2	158.6	310.5	493.6	704.1	791.8	...
Female - Femmes	2.5	0.2	0.5	0.4	1.1	1.1	0.9	2.1	5.1	4.3	8.6	13.4	30.8	49.9	72.1	125.7	236.4	406.8	588.0	834.8	...
Ireland - Irlande																					
2005 - 2007																					
Male - Hommes	4.9	0.6	0.8	3.6	5.4	4.7	5.1	5.7	8.6	13.3	21.1	33.3	54.5	88.7	148.8	247.0	395.4	567.3	730.3	919.0	...
Female - Femmes	4.5	0.4	0.7	1.6	1.5	1.6	2.0	3.0	5.2	9.2	13.6	21.3	33.8	53.6	90.1	153.4	284.4	460.3	643.4	800.7	...
Italy - Italie																					
2013																					
Male - Hommes	4.0	0.4	0.6	1.6	2.4	2.7	3.1	4.1	6.1	10.0	16.4	26.9	44.0	68.8	111.7	181.8	313.1	500.0	679.1	864.3	...
Female - Femmes	3.3	0.4	0.4	0.7	0.9	1.0	1.5	2.2	3.7	6.1	9.8	14.8	23.7	36.1	60.6	108.0	209.3	381.1	583.0	810.8	...
Latvia - Lettonie																					
2006																					
Male - Hommes	10.5	1.4	1.6	3.0	6.2	11.3	18.6	28.3	40.6	56.3	76.6	104.3	143.2	199.8	282.1	397.7	547.0	712.6	...	...	...
Female - Femmes	12.7	1.3	1.2	1.5	2.2	3.2	4.8	7.3	11.2	17.3	26.7	41.0	63.0	96.1	145.1	215.5	312.2	436.5	...	...	...
Lithuania - Lituanie																					
2013																					
Male - Hommes	5.1	0.4	1.0	4.4	8.2	11.3	15.7	23.3	32.4	47.5	65.1	92.0	131.0	176.6	219.8	292.4	423.0	588.7	783.2	882.1	*1000
Female - Femmes	3.9	1.2	0.5	1.9	1.5	3.1	4.0	6.0	10.2	15.3	21.7	31.2	46.2	66.4	97.6	165.3	307.8	501.4	699.2	845.7	*1000
Luxembourg																					
2011 - 2013																					
Male - Hommes	2.5	0.3	0.3	2.0	2.6	2.8	3.1	3.7	5.6	10.6	21.7	35.6	53.0	79.5	121.0	180.7	329.3	527.5	689.5	*1000	...
Female - Femmes	1.6	0.1	0.4	1.4	0.7	1.6	1.8	2.9	3.3	8.1	13.1	18.1	30.2	45.7	68.7	119.0	223.0	411.4	653.3	*1000	...
Malta - Malte																					
2012																					
Male - Hommes	5.6	0.5	0.4	0.4	2.3	2.2	5.4	4.8	6.1	12.6	14.8	26.8	46.3	77.4	112.0	220.3	378.6	640.6	887.5	975.9	*1000
Female - Femmes	6.0	0.6	0.9	0.8	0.0	2.0	2.7	1.8	5.6	4.5	11.8	13.5	27.6	41.3	67.7	130.5	273.1	474.9	737.6	853.6	*1000
Netherlands - Pays-Bas																					
2009																					
Male - Hommes	4.8	0.5	0.6	1.4	2.3	2.4	3.0	4.1	6.6	10.7	18.7	30.3	49.9	79.1	132.1	225.2	363.5	539.8	738.0	...	...
Female - Femmes	4.1	0.4	0.5	0.8	1.0	1.3	1.7	2.9	5.0	8.9	15.0	21.5	32.5	47.8	76.4	136.1	249.6	428.5	644.7	...	...
Norway - Norvège																					
2012																					
Male - Hommes	3.3	0.4	0.6	1.5	3.2	3.3	4.2	4.9	6.0	9.5	17.2	26.3	45.2	70.3	111.2	192.3	335.0	513.3	727.7	859.1	...
Female - Femmes	2.7	0.4	0.6	0.8	1.0	1.2	1.4	2.4	3.9	6.7	10.6	17.1	28.2	46.4	75.5	127.0	232.7	402.3	640.0	837.9	...
Poland - Pologne																					
2012																					
Male - Hommes	5.9	0.6	0.7	3.1	5.0	5.6	6.9	10.8	17.5	28.8	46.4	70.1	100.4	137.3	189.2	271.9	388.8	529.1	679.2	814.9	...
Female - Femmes	4.8	0.4	0.6	1.1	1.1	1.3	2.0	3.3	5.8	10.5	17.9	28.2	42.6	61.6	93.6	160.8	278.6	436.3	614.7	781.5	...
Portugal																					
2011 - 2013																					
Male - Hommes	4.3	0.5	0.7	1.6	2.9	3.2	4.4	7.0	11.5	19.0	29.5	41.2	55.0	82.7	126.8	206.6	361.9	650.0	867.4	971.8	...
Female - Femmes	3.6	0.5	0.5	0.8	1.1	1.2	1.9	3.0	5.1	7.9	11.0	16.1	23.7	37.4	65.2	123.3	252.3	524.9	791.0	948.7	...
Republic of Moldova - République de Moldova																					
2012																					
Male - Hommes	12.2	1.4	2.0	4.4	5.6	7.1	11.3	19.8	30.9	50.0	71.2	102.2	157.9	176.7	292.1	388.4	503.1	558.6	*1000	...	...
Female - Femmes	12.1	1.1	1.2	1.6	1.8	2.4	3.6	8.1	10.6	16.1	26.8	44.1	78.0	103.1	191.4	289.0	418.9	550.8	*1000	...	...

20. Probability of dying in the five year interval following specified age (5qx), by sex, latest available year: 2002 - 2014
Probabilité de décès dans l'intervalle de cinq ans qui suit un âge donné (5qx), par sexe, dernière année disponible : 2002 - 2014 (continued - suite)

Continent, country or area and date / Continent, pays ou zone et date	0	5	10	15	20	25	30	35	40	45	50	55	60	65	70	75	80	85	90	95	100
EUROPE																					
Romania - Roumanie 2011 - 2013																					
Male - Hommes	11.8	1.2	1.6	3.1	4.5	4.1	5.8	9.7	16.4	30.4	51.9	78.8	109.2	149.2	213.3	307.0	438.0	596.7	744.7	863.6	...
Female - Femmes	9.6	0.8	0.9	1.4	1.7	1.6	2.6	4.1	6.8	12.0	20.3	30.7	47.2	73.0	122.4	215.1	366.0	549.6	724.2	861.4	...
Russian Federation - Fédération de Russie 2012																					
Male - Hommes	11.6	1.7	1.8	5.4	11.6	19.0	30.3	36.8	42.1	56.4	77.9	110.6	155.6	193.8	273.2	361.6	481.9	577.2	694.9	771.0	*1000
Female - Femmes	9.5	1.1	1.2	2.5	3.4	5.6	9.0	11.6	14.3	18.9	26.2	39.5	57.7	84.1	137.1	230.5	372.9	543.1	716.4	825.0	*1000
San Marino - Saint-Marin 2013																					
Male - Hommes	2.4	0.6	1.2	2.7	2.7	2.3	0.9	2.6	5.2	3.0	10.8	28.9	31.0	53.1	81.0	167.4	300.6	458.9	674.0	923.3	...
Female - Femmes	1.3	0.0	0.7	1.5	0.7	0.0	0.8	0.7	4.4	4.9	8.3	11.7	16.6	30.5	56.9	81.0	171.2	350.3	539.6	820.0	
Serbia - Serbie[9] 2010 - 2012																					
Male - Hommes	8.1	0.5	0.9	2.4	3.7	4.7	6.4	8.2	13.3	25.5	44.0	69.0	101.6	145.8	216.4	334.2	492.1	676.0	856.4	973.0	...
Female - Femmes	6.5	0.6	0.9	1.1	1.5	2.0	2.6	4.3	7.4	12.8	21.1	33.3	50.4	82.2	147.2	265.6	432.9	632.3	840.3	975.2	...
Slovakia - Slovaquie 2013																					
Male - Hommes	6.7	0.8	1.0	2.3	3.6	4.6	5.2	8.0	12.4	24.1	41.3	65.0	101.8	138.2	208.0	299.4	427.7	587.3	756.6	896.4	...
Female - Femmes	6.2	0.8	0.7	1.1	1.2	1.3	2.1	3.7	6.0	10.5	16.1	25.6	40.3	62.8	100.6	180.8	343.0	585.1	849.2	983.5	...
Slovenia - Slovénie 2013																					
Male - Hommes	3.6	0.4	0.5	1.8	3.8	3.8	3.9	6.0	8.7	13.3	25.2	44.2	66.9	100.3	138.5	221.8	369.9	521.1	711.7	858.0	...
Female - Femmes	3.2	0.3	0.6	0.7	1.1	1.1	1.5	2.9	4.0	7.1	10.6	20.6	29.9	40.5	68.9	127.8	250.5	433.8	648.8	803.5	...
Spain - Espagne 2013																					
Male - Hommes	3.4	0.4	0.4	1.1	1.7	2.0	2.6	3.5	6.3	12.1	20.5	32.2	49.0	71.3	108.6	177.3	291.9	464.9	641.1	770.1	*1000
Female - Femmes	3.0	0.4	0.4	0.6	0.7	0.9	1.2	2.2	3.5	6.3	10.1	14.4	20.0	29.9	50.0	94.8	190.0	357.1	569.6	739.3	*1000
Sweden - Suède 2012																					
Male - Hommes	3.5	0.4	0.5	1.4	3.2	3.6	3.2	3.8	5.4	9.2	15.2	25.0	40.8	65.6	109.3	186.3	322.6	519.0	727.6	886.1	...
Female - Femmes	2.7	0.3	0.5	0.9	1.1	1.1	1.6	2.8	3.4	6.4	11.0	16.2	26.3	45.6	71.4	126.8	229.8	416.2	644.1	827.2	...
Switzerland - Suisse 2012																					
Male - Hommes	4.4	0.2	0.4	1.8	2.2	2.1	2.7	3.8	5.7	9.1	15.4	25.9	41.8	64.2	99.4	165.2	288.6	488.4	713.5	869.7	...
Female - Femmes	3.9	0.3	0.2	0.5	0.9	0.9	1.4	2.1	3.2	5.6	10.0	16.1	23.7	35.5	57.6	104.1	201.1	380.8	627.6	833.4	...
TFYR of Macedonia - L'ex-R. y. de Macédoine 2011																					
Male - Hommes	9.9	0.8	1.0	2.0	2.5	2.9	3.6	6.5	10.3	20.4	35.3	57.5	89.0	138.0	209.4	334.4	526.7	713.5	830.7	...	...
Female - Femmes	8.8	0.4	0.6	1.1	0.8	1.4	2.1	3.5	6.3	11.1	18.4	30.6	48.4	84.5	155.5	275.7	468.1	674.9	751.2	...	...
Ukraine 2013																					
Male - Hommes	10.5	1.1	1.4	4.0	7.2	12.0	20.3	29.3	36.5	50.9	72.3	101.9	151.5	197.4	267.0	363.8	483.5	578.1	671.9	756.8	...
Female - Femmes	8.2	0.7	1.0	1.7	2.5	4.0	6.6	10.0	13.1	17.6	24.1	37.0	57.7	87.7	143.3	244.9	390.8	557.8	731.5	877.1	...
United Kingdom of Great Britain and Northern Ireland - Royaume-Uni de Grande-Bretagne et d'Irlande du Nord[10] 2012																					
Male - Hommes	5.3	0.5	0.6	1.6	2.5	3.1	4.1	5.8	8.7	12.5	18.6	29.9	46.9	73.2	120.2	192.2	316.4	492.9	672.1	843.0	...
Female - Femmes	4.2	0.4	0.4	0.8	1.1	1.5	2.2	3.2	5.2	8.2	13.0	20.6	31.2	48.8	81.1	137.4	243.5	406.5	604.7	791.1	...
OCEANIA - OCÉANIE																					
Australia - Australie 2011 - 2013																					
Male - Hommes	5.0	0.5	0.5	2.1	3.1	3.6	4.3	5.6	7.7	11.3	17.2	26.1	40.1	62.7	100.6	170.4	288.1	464.7	663.3	821.5	...
Female - Femmes	4.0	0.4	0.5	1.2	1.3	1.4	2.1	3.0	4.7	7.1	10.6	16.0	24.2	37.4	62.9	108.9	202.1	370.3	586.4	777.7	...

20. Probability of dying in the five year interval following specified age (5qx), by sex, latest available year: 2002 - 2014
Probabilité de décès dans l'intervalle de cinq ans qui suit un âge donné (5qx), par sexe, dernière année disponible : 2002 - 2014 (continued - suite)

Continent, country or area and date / Continent, pays ou zone et date	Age (in years) - Age (en années)																				
	0	5	10	15	20	25	30	35	40	45	50	55	60	65	70	75	80	85	90	95	100
OCEANIA - OCÉANIE																					
New Zealand - Nouvelle-Zélande 2010 - 2012																					
Male - Hommes	6.1	0.5	0.8	3.4	4.6	3.5	4.0	5.7	8.1	11.8	18.0	27.1	41.8	67.1	109.4	179.5	298.0	478.1	665.0	835.4	...
Female - Femmes	4.9	0.3	0.6	1.6	1.9	1.9	2.5	3.6	5.4	8.6	12.4	17.8	28.7	46.7	73.7	123.9	222.0	394.3	608.0	811.8	...

FOOTNOTES - NOTES

* Open-ended group (e.g. 80 years or over). - Groupe d'âge ouvert (par exemple, 80 ans ou plus).

[1] Excluding Indian jungle population. - Non compris les Indiens de la jungle.

[2] Data refer to the 12 months from 30 June 2014 to 30 June 2015. - Les données font référence aux douze mois de 30 juin 2014 à 30 juin 2015.

[3] Data refer to projections based on the 2010 Population Census. Excludes nomadic Indian tribes. - Les données se réfèrent aux projections basées sur le recensement de la population de 2010. Non compris les tribus d'Indiens nomades.

[4] Includes data for East Jerusalem and Israeli residents in certain other territories under occupation by Israeli military forces since June 1967. - Y compris les données pour Jérusalem-Est et les résidents israéliens dans certains autres territoires occupés depuis 1967 par les forces armées israéliennes.

[5] Provisional data. Data refer to resident population which comprises Singapore citizens and permanent residents. - Données provisoires. Les données se rapportent à la population résidente composé des citoyens de Singapour et des résidents permanents.

[6] Excluding Faeroe Islands and Greenland shown separately, if available. - Non compris les Iles Féroé et le Groenland, qui font l'objet de rubriques distinctes, si disponible.

[7] Excluding Åland Islands. - Non compris les Îles d'Åland.

[8] Provisional data. - Données provisoires.

[9] Excludes data for Kosovo and Metohia. - Sans les données pour le Kosovo et Metohie.

[10] Excluding Channel Islands (Guernsey and Jersey) and Isle of Man, shown separately, if available. - Non compris les îles Anglo-Normandes (Guernesey et Jersey) et l'île de Man, qui font l'objet de rubriques distinctes, si disponible.

Table 21 - *Demographic Yearbook 2014*

Table 21 presents life expectancy at specified ages for each sex, for the latest available year between 1995 and 2014.

Description of variables: Life expectancy at age x, e_x, is defined as the average number of years of life remaining to persons who have reached age *x* if they continue to be subject to the mortality conditions of the period indicated in the life table.

Male and female life expectancy values are shown separately at selected ages beginning at birth and proceeding at every fifth age thereafter up to age 100.

The table shows life expectancy derived from a complete or abridged life table as reported by the country or area.

Data are shown with one decimal regardless of the number of digits provided in the original computation.

The life table is a statistical device for summarizing the mortality experience of a population, from which the probability of dying, survivorship and life expectancy can be calculated. It is based on the assumption that the theoretical cohort is subject, throughout its existence, to the age-specific mortality rates observed at a particular time. Thus, levels of mortality prevailing at the time a life table is constructed are assumed to remain unchanged into the future until all members of the cohort have died.

Reliability of data: The values shown in this table come from official life tables. It is assumed that, if necessary, the basic data (population and deaths classified by age and sex) have been adjusted for deficiencies before their use in constructing the life tables.

Limitations: Life expectancy values are subject to the same qualifications as have been set forth for population statistics in general and death statistics in particular, as discussed in sections 3 and 4, respectively, of the Technical Notes. They must be interpreted strictly using the underlying assumption that surviving cohorts are subjected to the same age-specific mortality rates of the period to which the life table refers.

Earlier data: Life expectancy values at specified ages for each sex have been shown in previous issues of the *Demographic Yearbook*. For information on specific years covered, the reader should consult the Historical Index.

Tableau 21 – *Annuaire démographique 2014*

Le tableau 21 présente les espérances de vie à des âges déterminés, pour chaque sexe, pour la dernière année disponible entre 1995 et 2014.

Description des variables : L'espérance de vie à l'âge x, e_x, se définit comme le nombre moyen d'années restant à vivre aux hommes et aux femmes qui ont atteint l'âge x, à supposer qu'ils continuent de connaître les mêmes conditions de mortalité observées pendant la période sur laquelle porte la table de mortalité.

Les chiffres sont présentés séparément pour chaque sexe à partir de la naissance et puis tous les cinq ans jusqu'à 100 ans.

Dans le tableau figurent les espérances de vie calculées selon les tables de mortalité complètes ou abrégées communiquées par les pays et les zones.

Les données sont arrondies à la première décimale, indépendamment du nombre de décimales qui figurent dans le calcul initial.

La table de mortalité est un moyen statistique que s'utilise pour donner un aperçu complet de la mortalité d'une population incluant les probabilités de décès et l'espérance de vie à chaque âge. Les tables de mortalité reposent sur l'hypothèse que chaque cohorte théoriquement distinguée connaît, pendant toute son existence, les taux de mortalité par âge observé à un moment donné. Les taux de mortalité correspondant à l'époque à laquelle sont calculées les tables de mortalité sont ainsi censés demeurer inchangées dans l'avenir jusqu'au décès de tous les membres de la cohorte.

Fiabilité des donnés : Les chiffres figurant dans ce tableau proviennent de tables officielles de mortalité. En ce qui concerne les chiffres extraits de tables officielles de mortalité, on part du principe que les données de base (effectif de la population et nombre de décès selon l'âge et le sexe) ont été ajustées, en tant que de besoin, avant de servir à l'établissement de la table de mortalité.

Insuffisance des données : les espérances de vie appellent les mêmes réserves que celles qui ont été formulées à propos des statistiques de la population en général et des statistiques de mortalité en particulier (voir les sections 3 et 4 des Notes techniques). Lorsque l'on interprète les données, il ne faut jamais perdre de vue que, par hypothèse, les cohortes de survivants sont soumises, pour chaque âge, aux conditions de mortalité de la période visée par la table de mortalité.

Données publiées antérieurement : les espérances de vie à des âges déterminés pour chaque sexe figuraient déjà dans des éditions antérieures de *l'Annuaire démographique*. Pour plus de précisions concernant les années pour lesquelles ces données ont été publiées, se reporter à l'index historique.

21. Life expectancy at specified ages for each sex: latest available year, 1995 - 2014
Espérance de vie à un âge donné pour chaque sexe : dernière année disponible, 1995 - 2014

Continent, country or area and date / Continent, pays ou zone et date	Age (in years) - Age (en années)																				
	0	5	10	15	20	25	30	35	40	45	50	55	60	65	70	75	80	85	90	95	100
AFRICA - AFRIQUE																					
Algeria - Algérie[1]																					
2014																					
Male - Hommes	76.6	73.7	68.9	64.0	59.2	54.5	49.8	45.0	40.3	35.7	31.1	26.7	22.5	18.6	14.8	11.6	8.7	6.5	...	...	...
Female - Femmes	77.8	74.7	69.8	64.9	60.1	55.2	50.4	45.6	40.8	36.2	31.6	27.1	22.7	18.5	14.6	10.9	7.8	5.2	...	...	...
Benin - Bénin[2]																					
2002																					
Male - Hommes	57.2	63.4	59.1	54.7	50.2	45.9	41.8	37.8	33.8	30.0	26.2	22.7	19.4	16.2	13.2	10.6	8.1	5.5	3.8	...	...
Female - Femmes	61.3	65.4	61.2	56.7	52.3	48.1	43.9	39.9	36.0	32.1	28.3	24.6	21.2	18.0	14.2	10.8	7.7	4.8	2.9	...	...
Botswana[3]																					
2006																					
Male - Hommes	54.0	57.6	54.0	49.7	45.6	41.8	37.9	34.0	30.0	26.2	22.4	19.9	15.4	12.3	9.4	7.0	4.8	...	...	...	...
Female - Femmes	66.0	65.7	61.4	56.8	52.3	47.8	43.4	39.1	34.7	30.4	26.2	22.1	18.2	14.5	11.2	8.3	5.8	...	...	...	...
Burkina Faso[4]																					
2006																					
Male - Hommes	55.8	60.0	55.9	51.3	46.9	42.8	38.6	34.5	30.5	26.6	22.8	19.3	16.0	12.9	10.3	8.1	6.2	4.8	...	...	...
Female - Femmes	57.5	61.6	57.6	53.1	48.6	44.4	40.2	36.1	32.0	28.0	24.1	20.3	16.8	13.5	10.7	8.4	6.4	4.9	...	...	...
Burundi																					
2008																					
Male - Hommes	46.0	49.7	46.5	42.5	39.0	35.8	32.4	28.9	25.4	21.9	18.6	15.3	12.3	9.5	7.2	5.2	3.8	...	...	...	...
Female - Femmes	51.8	55.4	52.1	47.9	44.0	40.3	36.7	33.0	29.2	25.4	21.5	17.8	14.2	11.0	8.3	6.0	4.4	...	...	...	...
Côte d'Ivoire																					
2006																					
Male - Hommes	49.6	...	...	...	...	...	...	...	...	...	...	...	...	...	...	...	...	...	...	...	...
Female - Femmes	53.0	...	...	...	...	...	...	...	...	...	...	...	...	...	...	...	...	...	...	...	...
Djibouti																					
1998																					
Male - Hommes	49.0	...	...	...	...	...	...	...	...	...	...	...	...	...	...	...	...	...	...	...	...
Female - Femmes	52.0	...	...	...	...	...	...	...	...	...	...	...	...	...	...	...	...	...	...	...	...
Egypt - Égypte																					
2011																					
Male - Hommes	68.6	65.5	60.6	55.7	50.9	46.1	41.4	36.6	31.9	27.3	23.1	19.2	15.7	12.2	9.1	6.4	3.4	...	...	...	...
Female - Femmes	71.4	68.1	63.2	58.2	53.3	48.4	43.5	38.7	33.9	29.1	24.5	20.1	16.1	12.3	8.8	5.7	2.4	...	...	...	...
Ghana																					
2005																					
Male - Hommes	58.3	...	...	...	...	...	...	...	...	...	...	...	...	...	...	...	...	...	...	...	...
Female - Femmes	62.0	...	...	...	...	...	...	...	...	...	...	...	...	...	...	...	...	...	...	...	...
Guinea-Bissau - Guinée-Bissau																					
2008 - 2009																					
Male - Hommes	49.2	49.8	45.3	41.0	36.8	32.8	29.3	26.2	23.3	20.7	18.0	15.5	13.1	11.2	9.4	8.0	6.8	...	...	...	...
Female - Femmes	51.2	50.1	45.7	41.5	37.8	34.4	31.3	28.4	25.6	22.9	20.0	17.4	14.9	12.8	10.6	8.8	7.1	...	...	...	...
Kenya																					
1989 - 1999																					
Male - Hommes	52.9	54.8	51.1	46.6	42.3	38.3	34.5	31.0	27.7	24.4	21.0	17.7	14.5	11.6	8.9	6.7	5.0	3.8	3.1	2.5	...
Female - Femmes	60.4	63.0	59.0	54.3	49.9	45.9	42.2	38.6	34.8	30.9	27.0	23.1	19.3	15.6	12.2	9.2	6.7	4.8	3.6	2.5	...
2009																					
Male - Hommes	58.0	...	...	...	...	...	...	...	...	...	...	...	...	...	...	...	...	...	...	...	...
Female - Femmes	61.0	...	...	...	...	...	...	...	...	...	...	...	...	...	...	...	...	...	...	...	...
Lesotho																					
2006[5]																					
Male - Hommes	39.8	40.4	36.0	31.5	27.2	23.6	20.9	19.2	18.2	17.3	16.4	14.9	13.2	11.3	9.4	7.4	5.3	2.9	...	...	...
Female - Femmes	42.9	42.7	38.4	33.8	29.6	26.3	24.2	23.2	22.8	22.3	21.5	20.2	18.6	16.7	14.5	12.1	9.6	7.4	...	...	...
2011																					
Male - Hommes	39.4	...	...	...	...	...	...	...	...	...	...	...	...	...	...	...	...	...	...	...	...
Female - Femmes	45.3	...	...	...	...	...	...	...	...	...	...	...	...	...	...	...	...	...	...	...	...
Malawi																					
1992 - 1997																					
Male - Hommes	43.5	52.1	49.5	45.7	41.9	38.4	34.8	31.2	27.6	24.0	20.6	17.3	14.1	11.2	8.6	6.3	4.4	...	...	...	...
Female - Femmes	46.8	54.5	52.0	48.2	44.4	40.6	36.9	33.2	29.6	25.9	22.2	18.6	15.1	11.9	9.2	6.8	4.6	...	...	...	...
2008																					
Male - Hommes	47.4	...	...	...	...	...	...	...	...	...	...	...	...	...	...	...	...	...	...	...	...
Female - Femmes	50.6	...	...	...	...	...	...	...	...	...	...	...	...	...	...	...	...	...	...	...	...
Mauritius - Maurice[6]																					
2012 - 2014																					
Male - Hommes	71.0	67.1	62.1	57.2	52.4	47.7	43.1	38.6	34.2	29.8	25.7	21.8	18.2	14.9	11.9	9.4	7.2	5.7	...	...	...
Female - Femmes	77.6	73.6	68.7	63.7	58.8	54.0	49.2	44.4	39.6	35.0	30.5	26.2	22.0	18.1	14.6	11.5	8.7	6.5	...	...	...

21. Life expectancy at specified ages for each sex: latest available year, 1995 - 2014
Espérance de vie à un âge donné pour chaque sexe : dernière année disponible, 1995 - 2014 (continued - suite)

Continent, country or area and date / Continent, pays ou zone et date	0	5	10	15	20	25	30	35	40	45	50	55	60	65	70	75	80	85	90	95	100
AFRICA - AFRIQUE																					
Morocco - Maroc																					
2013																					
Male - Hommes	72.4	...	...	...	...	...	...	...	...	...	...	...	...	...	...	...	...	...	...	...	...
Female - Femmes	75.1	...	...	...	...	...	...	...	...	...	...	...	...	...	...	...	...	...	...	...	...
Mozambique																					
2014																					
Male - Hommes	50.2	54.0	50.0	45.6	41.6	37.7	33.9	30.1	26.5	22.9	19.6	16.4	13.5	10.9	8.7	6.8	5.0	...	...	...	...
Female - Femmes	55.4	59.0	54.8	50.3	46.1	42.1	38.1	34.1	30.2	26.3	22.5	19.0	15.7	12.7	10.0	7.7	5.8	...	...	...	...
Namibia - Namibie																					
2011																					
Male - Hommes	53.3	52.4	48.0	43.4	39.0	35.1	31.5	28.6	25.8	23.2	20.6	17.7	15.1	12.6	9.8	7.4	5.6	...	...	...	...
Female - Femmes	60.5	59.6	55.1	50.5	46.1	42.0	38.4	35.2	32.0	28.7	25.2	21.6	17.9	14.5	11.3	8.6	6.5	...	...	...	...
Republic of South Sudan - République de Soudan du Sud																					
2010																					
Male - Hommes	54.4	57.4	53.2	48.8	44.6	40.7	36.8	32.8	28.9	25.0	21.2	17.6	14.2	11.2	8.5	6.3	4.5	3.2	2.2	1.5	...
Female - Femmes	54.5	56.2	51.9	47.5	43.3	39.4	35.4	31.5	27.5	23.7	19.9	16.4	13.1	10.2	7.7	5.6	4.1	2.9	2.0	1.4	...
Reunion - Réunion																					
2009																					
Male - Hommes	74.9	...	...	...	...	...	...	...	...	...	...	...	20.3	...	...	...	...	...	...	...	...
Female - Femmes	82.7	...	...	...	...	...	...	...	...	...	...	...	25.6	...	...	...	...	...	...	...	...
Rwanda																					
2002																					
Male - Hommes	48.4	58.4	54.4	49.9	45.6	41.6	37.5	33.5	29.4	25.4	21.6	17.9	14.5	11.4	8.6	6.3	4.6	...	...	...	...
Female - Femmes	53.8	63.1	58.8	54.3	49.9	45.7	41.4	37.2	32.9	28.7	24.5	20.4	16.5	12.9	9.8	7.1	5.1	...	...	...	...
2009																					
Male - Hommes	49.4	...	...	...	...	...	...	...	...	...	...	...	...	...	...	...	...	...	...	...	...
Female - Femmes	53.3	...	...	...	...	...	...	...	...	...	...	...	...	...	...	...	...	...	...	...	...
Saint Helena ex. dep. - Sainte-Hélène sans dép.																					
2003 - 2012																					
Male - Hommes	72.0	68.1	63.4	...	53.9	...	44.2	...	35.5	...	27.1	...	19.3	...	12.5	...	7.2	...	...	...	...
Female - Femmes	79.7	75.3	70.3	...	60.3	...	51.0	...	41.8	...	32.0	...	23.0	...	15.5	...	8.6	...	...	...	...
Sao Tome and Principe - Sao Tomé-et-Principe																					
2011 - 2012																					
Male - Hommes	62.1	59.5	54.6	50.1	45.8	41.6	37.5	33.4	29.6	25.8	22.1	18.4	15.2	12.0	9.8	7.4	5.0	...	...	...	...
Female - Femmes	68.7	65.9	61.2	56.5	51.8	47.1	42.5	38.0	33.5	29.3	25.3	21.7	18.2	14.9	11.8	9.0	6.6	...	...	...	...
Senegal - Sénégal[7]																					
2011																					
Male - Hommes	56.9	...	...	...	...	...	...	...	...	...	...	...	...	...	...	...	...	...	...	...	...
Female - Femmes	59.8	...	...	...	...	...	...	...	...	...	...	...	...	...	...	...	...	...	...	...	...
Seychelles																					
2007																					
Male - Hommes	68.9	65.0	60.2	55.3	50.5	45.9	41.6	37.0	32.7	28.7	24.4	20.9	17.1	14.1	11.0	9.0	7.4	...	...	...	...
Female - Femmes	77.7	73.3	68.5	63.5	58.5	53.7	48.9	44.3	39.5	35.3	31.0	26.4	22.2	18.5	15.1	12.1	9.2	...	...	...	...
2014																					
Male - Hommes	68.4	...	...	...	...	...	...	...	...	...	...	...	...	...	...	...	...	...	...	...	...
Female - Femmes	78.3	...	...	...	...	...	...	...	...	...	...	...	...	...	...	...	...	...	...	...	...
Sierra Leone																					
2004																					
Male - Hommes	47.5	...	...	...	...	...	...	...	...	...	...	...	...	...	...	...	...	...	...	...	...
Female - Femmes	49.4	...	...	...	...	...	...	...	...	...	...	...	...	...	...	...	...	...	...	...	...
South Africa - Afrique du Sud																					
2009																					
Male - Hommes	53.5	...	...	...	...	...	...	...	...	...	...	...	...	...	...	...	...	...	...	...	...
Female - Femmes	57.2	...	...	...	...	...	...	...	...	...	...	...	...	...	...	...	...	...	...	...	...
Swaziland																					
2007																					
Male - Hommes	42.2	44.9	40.5	36.0	31.5	27.5	24.9	23.3	22.1	20.9	19.1	17.4	15.4	13.6	10.9	8.9	...	...	...	...	...
Female - Femmes	43.1	48.2	43.9	39.3	35.0	32.3	30.9	30.3	29.5	27.6	25.1	22.7	19.5	16.8	13.5	10.5	...	...	...	...	...

Continent, country or area and date / Continent, pays ou zone et date	Age (in years) - Age (en années)																				
	0	5	10	15	20	25	30	35	40	45	50	55	60	65	70	75	80	85	90	95	100
AFRICA - AFRIQUE																					
Tunisia - Tunisie																					
1995																					
Male - Hommes	69.6	67.5	62.7	57.9	53.1	48.4	43.8	39.2	34.6	30.1	25.8	21.6	17.7	14.1	10.8	7.9	5.2	3.5	...	...	...
Female - Femmes	73.1	70.7	65.9	61.0	56.2	51.3	46.5	41.7	37.0	32.4	27.8	23.3	19.1	15.0	11.3	7.8	4.8	2.9	...	...	...
2011																					
Male - Hommes	72.9	...	...	...	...	...	...	...	...	...	...	...	...	...	...	...	...	...	...	...	...
Female - Femmes	76.9	...	...	...	...	...	...	...	...	...	...	...	...	...	...	...	...	...	...	...	...
Uganda - Ouganda[8]																					
2002																					
Male - Hommes	48.8	53.0	49.2	44.8	40.5	36.6	33.6	31.0	28.4	25.8	23.2	20.4	17.2	14.4	11.6	9.2	6.7	4.1	...	...	...
Female - Femmes	52.0	56.0	52.1	47.6	43.3	39.6	36.7	34.2	31.5	28.6	25.6	22.3	18.9	15.7	12.6	9.9	7.0	4.2	...	...	...
Zimbabwe																					
2001 - 2002																					
Male - Hommes	45.8	44.2	40.0	35.4	30.9	26.8	23.8	22.1	21.8	21.3	20.4	19.2	17.7	15.7	13.7	11.4	9.5	7.5	6.2	5.2	...
Female - Femmes	50.3	48.6	44.2	39.7	35.3	32.1	30.4	30.1	30.2	29.0	27.6	25.3	22.9	20.2	17.6	14.8	12.2	9.9	8.1	7.3	...
AMERICA, NORTH - AMÉRIQUE DU NORD																					
Anguilla																					
2000 - 2002																					
Male - Hommes	76.5	72.1	67.1	62.1	57.3	53.1	48.4	43.7	39.4	34.7	30.2	25.4	21.1	16.5	12.7	10.0	8.0	6.9	...	...	...
Female - Femmes	81.1	76.4	71.4	66.4	61.4	57.1	52.7	47.7	42.7	38.3	33.5	28.7	24.0	19.4	15.3	10.8	8.3	7.6	...	...	...
Antigua and Barbuda - Antigua-et-Barbuda																					
2010																					
Male - Hommes	74.0	...	...	...	...	...	...	...	...	...	...	...	...	...	...	...	...	...	...	...	...
Female - Femmes	79.7	...	...	...	...	...	...	...	...	...	...	...	...	...	...	...	...	...	...	...	...
Aruba																					
2010 - 2011																					
Male - Hommes	73.9	69.4	64.4	59.5	54.6	50.0	45.4	40.8	36.3	31.7	27.3	23.1	19.1	15.3	12.3	9.4	7.3	5.0	3.5	2.7	...
Female - Femmes	79.8	76.2	71.2	66.2	61.3	56.4	51.5	46.6	42.0	37.3	32.6	27.9	23.8	19.7	16.0	12.5	9.5	6.8	5.0	3.8	...
Bahamas																					
1999 - 2001																					
Male - Hommes	69.9	...	...	...	...	...	...	...	...	...	...	...	...	...	...	...	...	...	...	...	...
Female - Femmes	76.4	...	...	...	...	...	...	...	...	...	...	...	...	...	...	...	...	...	...	...	...
Bermuda - Bermudes																					
2014																					
Male - Hommes	77.1	72.4	67.4	62.5	57.7	53.2	48.7	44.1	39.5	34.9	30.4	25.9	21.7	17.7	14.1	10.7	7.7	5.0	...	...	...
Female - Femmes	84.7	79.9	74.9	69.9	64.9	59.9	55.0	50.1	45.2	40.4	35.6	30.9	26.4	22.0	17.9	13.8	10.5	7.5	...	...	...
British Virgin Islands - Îles Vierges britanniques																					
2004																					
Male - Hommes	69.9	...	...	...	...	...	...	...	...	...	...	...	...	...	...	...	...	...	...	...	...
Female - Femmes	78.5	...	...	...	...	...	...	...	...	...	...	...	...	...	...	...	...	...	...	...	...
Canada																					
2006 - 2008																					
Male - Hommes	78.5	74.0	69.1	64.1	59.3	54.5	49.7	44.9	40.2	35.5	30.9	26.5	22.3	18.3	14.7	11.4	8.5	6.2	4.5	...	...
Female - Femmes	83.2	78.6	73.6	68.7	63.8	58.9	53.9	49.1	44.2	39.4	34.7	30.2	25.7	21.5	17.4	13.7	10.4	7.5	5.4	...	...
Cayman Islands - Îles Caïmanes[9]																					
2006																					
Male - Hommes	76.3	72.1	67.1	62.1	57.7	53.3	48.9	44.0	39.3	34.5	29.8	25.3	20.8	17.1	13.6	10.2	8.2	6.4	3.3	5.3	2.5
Female - Femmes	83.8	79.8	74.8	69.8	65.1	60.1	55.2	50.2	45.3	40.4	35.7	30.9	26.1	21.9	17.5	13.9	10.4	6.9	7.0	3.1	2.5
Costa Rica																					
2014																					
Male - Hommes	77.2	73.0	68.1	63.1	58.4	53.7	49.1	44.4	39.8	35.3	30.8	26.5	22.4	18.5	14.9	11.7	9.0	6.7	4.8	3.3	2.1
Female - Femmes	82.3	77.9	73.0	68.1	63.2	58.3	53.4	48.5	43.7	38.9	34.2	29.6	25.2	21.0	17.0	13.4	10.1	7.4	5.3	3.6	2.3
Cuba																					
2011 - 2013																					
Male - Hommes	76.5	72.0	67.0	62.1	57.3	52.5	47.7	42.9	38.2	33.6	29.2	25.0	21.0	17.3	14.0	11.0	8.4	6.3	4.9	3.8	2.0
Female - Femmes	80.4	75.9	71.0	66.0	61.1	56.2	51.4	46.5	41.7	36.9	32.3	27.9	23.6	19.6	15.8	12.4	9.4	6.9	5.1	3.8	2.1

Continent, country or area and date / Continent, pays ou zone et date	0	5	10	15	20	25	30	35	40	45	50	55	60	65	70	75	80	85	90	95	100
AMERICA, NORTH - AMÉRIQUE DU NORD																					
Curaçao																					
2011 - 2014																					
Male - Hommes	74.8	70.4	65.4	60.5	55.6	51.0	46.5	42.0	37.4	32.8	28.3	24.0	20.2	16.6	13.4	10.6	8.0	5.8	4.2	4.1	5.4
Female - Femmes	81.0	77.0	72.0	67.0	62.1	57.2	52.4	47.6	42.8	38.1	33.4	28.9	24.5	20.4	16.5	12.8	9.6	7.2	5.2	3.6	2.9
Dominica - Dominique																					
2008																					
Male - Hommes	73.8	...	...	...	...	...	...	...	...	...	...	...	...	...	...	...	...	...	...	...	...
Female - Femmes	78.2	...	...	...	...	...	...	...	...	...	...	...	...	...	...	...	...	...	...	...	...
Dominican Republic - République dominicaine																					
2010 - 2015																					
Male - Hommes	70.0	67.5	62.6	57.7	53.0	48.7	44.3	40.0	35.6	31.3	27.2	23.3	19.6	16.2	13.2	10.5	...	...	...	...	...
Female - Femmes	74.8	71.8	66.9	62.0	57.1	52.4	47.7	43.1	38.5	34.1	29.7	25.5	21.6	17.9	14.6	11.7	...	...	...	...	...
El Salvador[10]																					
2000 - 2005																					
Male - Hommes	65.4	62.6	57.8	52.9	48.7	45.0	41.5	37.8	34.1	30.4	26.8	23.3	20.0	16.7	13.8	11.1	9.0	...	...	...	...
Female - Femmes	74.9	72.0	67.1	62.3	57.5	52.9	48.2	43.6	39.0	34.6	30.3	26.1	22.1	18.4	15.0	12.0	9.6	...	...	...	...
Greenland - Groenland																					
2009 - 2013																					
Male - Hommes	68.5	64.8	59.9	55.1	50.7	46.9	42.6	38.2	33.7	29.2	24.9	20.6	16.8	13.1	9.9	7.4	5.7	4.4	3.1	4.0	...
Female - Femmes	73.7	69.4	64.4	59.5	55.0	50.5	45.7	40.9	36.3	31.6	27.1	22.7	18.7	15.1	11.9	9.0	6.6	5.0	3.7	3.2	...
Guadeloupe																					
2002																					
Male - Hommes	74.6	70.2	65.3	60.5	55.7	51.2	46.8	42.2	37.7	33.2	29.0	24.8	20.9	17.3	13.8	10.6	7.9	5.1	2.0	0.5	...
Female - Femmes	81.5	77.0	72.1	67.1	62.1	57.3	52.4	47.6	42.9	38.2	33.5	28.8	24.4	20.3	16.4	12.7	9.0	5.7	2.3	0.5	...
Guatemala																					
1995 - 2000																					
Male - Hommes	61.4	60.6	56.0	51.2	46.8	42.7	38.8	34.9	31.2	27.4	23.7	20.1	16.8	13.6	10.7	8.2	6.1	...	...	...	...
Female - Femmes	67.2	66.2	62.6	56.9	52.3	47.7	43.3	38.9	34.6	30.4	26.3	22.3	18.6	15.2	12.0	9.2	6.9	...	...	...	...
Jamaica - Jamaïque																					
2006																					
Male - Hommes	69.7	67.0	62.2	57.3	52.6	47.9	43.2	38.5	33.8	29.3	24.9	20.8	16.9	13.5	10.4	7.8	5.8	4.1	2.9	2.1	1.5
Female - Femmes	75.2	71.6	66.7	61.7	56.8	52.0	47.1	42.3	37.6	32.9	28.3	23.9	19.7	15.9	12.4	9.4	6.9	5.0	3.5	2.4	1.7
Martinique																					
2007																					
Male - Hommes	76.5	72.4	67.5	62.6	57.8	53.3	48.7	44.1	39.5	34.9	30.3	26.1	21.8	17.6	14.1	10.7	7.7	5.2	3.7	1.8	...
Female - Femmes	82.9	78.5	73.6	68.6	63.7	58.8	54.0	49.2	44.4	39.6	34.8	30.1	25.6	21.2	17.1	13.4	10.0	7.1	4.6	1.9	...
Mexico - Mexique																					
2008																					
Male - Hommes	72.8	69.2	64.3	59.4	54.7	50.0	45.5	40.9	36.5	32.1	27.9	23.9	20.2	16.8	13.7	11.0	8.7	6.6	4.9	3.5	2.6
Female - Femmes	77.5	73.8	68.9	63.9	59.0	54.2	49.3	44.5	39.7	35.1	30.6	26.2	22.1	18.3	14.8	11.7	9.0	6.8	4.9	3.5	2.6
2014																					
Male - Hommes	72.1	...	...	...	...	...	...	...	...	...	...	...	...	...	...	...	...	...	...	...	...
Female - Femmes	77.6	...	...	...	...	...	...	...	...	...	...	...	...	...	...	...	...	...	...	...	...
Nicaragua																					
2005 - 2010																					
Male - Hommes	63.4	47.9	44.2	40.5	36.5	32.5	28.6	24.9	21.3	17.7	14.6	11.6	9.0	6.5	...	...	...	...	...	...	...
Female - Femmes	68.9	52.1	47.6	43.0	38.5	34.1	29.8	25.7	21.9	18.1	14.9	11.8	9.3	6.9	...	...	...	...	...	...	...
Panama[11]																					
2013																					
Male - Hommes	74.4	71.1	66.2	61.4	56.8	52.5	48.3	43.9	39.4	35.0	30.7	26.5	22.5	18.8	15.4	12.4	9.8	7.6	5.7	4.1	2.5
Female - Femmes	80.5	76.9	72.0	67.1	62.2	57.5	52.7	48.0	43.3	38.6	34.1	29.6	25.3	21.2	17.4	13.9	10.8	8.2	6.0	4.2	2.5
Puerto Rico - Porto Rico																					
2008 - 2010																					
Male - Hommes	74.9	70.6	65.6	60.7	56.0	51.7	47.4	43.0	38.5	34.1	29.9	25.9	22.0	18.4	15.0	11.9	9.1	7.0	...	...	...
Female - Femmes	82.6	78.2	73.2	68.3	63.3	58.5	53.6	48.8	44.0	39.4	34.8	30.3	25.9	21.7	17.8	14.1	10.9	8.4	...	...	...
Saint Kitts and Nevis - Saint-Kitts-et-Nevis																					
1998																					
Male - Hommes	68.2	65.0	60.1	55.3	50.5	45.8	41.1	36.5	32.7	28.5	24.3	20.6	16.6	13.3	11.0	9.1	6.6	4.7	3.4	2.2	0.4
Female - Femmes	70.7	67.5	62.5	57.6	52.7	48.0	43.4	38.8	34.4	29.8	25.4	21.3	17.6	14.3	11.3	8.9	6.3	4.6	3.3	2.2	0.4

21. Life expectancy at specified ages for each sex: latest available year, 1995 - 2014
Espérance de vie à un âge donné pour chaque sexe : dernière année disponible, 1995 - 2014 (continued - suite)

Continent, country or area and date / Continent, pays ou zone et date	Age (in years) - Age (en années)																				
	0	5	10	15	20	25	30	35	40	45	50	55	60	65	70	75	80	85	90	95	100
AMERICA, NORTH - AMÉRIQUE DU NORD																					
Saint Lucia - Sainte-Lucie 2005																					
Male - Hommes	69.9	66.4	61.5	56.6	52.0	47.4	43.1	38.6	34.3	30.1	25.9	21.7	17.9	14.7	11.8	9.0	7.2	5.2	...	...	...
Female - Femmes	75.7	72.2	67.3	62.4	57.5	52.6	47.8	43.2	38.4	33.8	29.2	25.0	20.8	17.2	13.8	10.4	7.7	4.8	...	...	...
Saint Vincent and the Grenadines - Saint-Vincent-et-les Grenadines 2001																					
Male - Hommes	66.9	63.9	59.2	54.3	49.6	45.1	40.7	36.5	32.3	28.2	24.1	19.9	16.2	12.8	9.7	7.3	4.3	4.1	...	...	...
Female - Femmes	72.9	69.3	64.5	59.5	54.7	49.8	45.2	40.7	36.1	31.7	27.3	23.0	19.0	14.6	10.8	7.3	4.1	3.6	...	...	...
Sint Maarten (Dutch part) - Saint-Martin (partie néerlandaise) 2011 - 2012																					
Male - Hommes	69.2	65.5	60.6	55.7	51.0	46.9	42.5	38.2	33.9	29.5	25.3	21.2	17.6	13.8	10.4	7.4	5.2	4.0	...	...	...
Female - Femmes	77.1	72.3	67.4	62.6	57.8	52.8	48.0	43.1	38.2	33.5	28.6	24.0	19.4	14.9	11.5	8.1	5.0	1.8	...	...	...
Trinidad and Tobago - Trinité-et-Tobago 2000																					
Male - Hommes	68.3	65.2	60.3	55.5	50.7	46.1	41.7	37.3	33.1	29.0	24.9	21.2	17.9	14.7	12.0	9.7	7.8	...	...	...	...
Female - Femmes	73.7	70.2	65.3	60.4	55.6	50.9	46.2	41.7	37.1	32.7	28.4	24.4	20.7	17.4	14.4	11.7	9.6	...	...	...	...
Turks and Caicos Islands - Îles Turques et Caïques 2001																					
Male - Hommes	79.0	75.3	70.3	65.3	60.3	55.8	50.8	46.0	41.2	37.1	33.0	28.4	24.3	20.8	17.5	12.5	7.5	4.1	...	...	...
Female - Femmes	77.4	72.5	67.5	62.5	57.5	52.9	48.2	43.4	38.6	33.8	29.6	25.0	20.0	17.0	13.2	11.7	10.3	8.8	...	...	...
United States of America - États-Unis d'Amérique 2013																					
Male - Hommes	76.4	72.0	67.1	62.1	57.3	52.6	48.0	43.3	38.7	34.1	29.7	25.6	21.7	17.9	14.4	11.2	8.3	5.9	4.1	2.8	2.0
Female - Femmes	81.2	76.7	71.7	66.8	61.8	57.0	52.1	47.3	42.6	37.9	33.3	28.9	24.6	20.5	16.6	12.9	9.7	7.0	4.8	3.3	2.3
AMERICA, SOUTH - AMÉRIQUE DU SUD																					
Argentina - Argentine 2008 - 2010																					
Male - Hommes	72.1	68.2	63.3	58.4	53.7	49.1	44.5	39.8	35.2	30.7	26.3	22.2	18.5	15.0	11.9	9.2	6.9	5.2	4.0	3.1	2.6
Female - Femmes	78.8	74.8	69.9	65.0	60.1	55.3	50.5	45.6	40.9	36.2	31.7	27.3	23.1	19.0	15.2	11.7	8.6	6.3	4.7	3.5	2.9
Bolivia (Plurinational State of) - Bolivie (État plurinational de)[12] 2014 - 2015																					
Male - Hommes	66.4	66.6	62.2	57.5	53.1	48.9	44.6	40.4	36.2	32.1	28.1	24.2	20.5	17.1	13.9	11.0	8.6	6.3	4.6	3.2	2.8
Female - Femmes	71.4	71.1	66.7	62.1	57.4	52.8	48.3	43.7	39.3	34.9	30.7	26.7	22.8	19.2	15.9	12.9	10.1	7.9	6.0	4.1	1.1
Brazil - Brésil[11] 2012																					
Male - Hommes	71.0	67.4	62.5	57.6	53.1	48.8	44.4	40.0	35.7	31.4	27.3	23.4	19.8	16.3	13.2	10.5	8.2	...	...	...	...
Female - Femmes	78.3	74.6	69.7	64.8	59.9	55.1	50.3	45.5	40.8	36.2	31.7	27.4	23.3	19.4	15.7	12.5	9.7	...	...	...	...
2013																					
Male - Hommes	71.3	...	...	...	...	...	...	...	...	...	...	...	...	...	...	...	...	...	...	...	...
Female - Femmes	78.5	...	...	...	...	...	...	...	...	...	...	...	...	...	...	...	...	...	...	...	...
Chile - Chili 2012																					
Male - Hommes	76.2	71.9	66.9	62.0	57.2	52.4	47.7	43.0	38.3	33.7	29.2	24.9	20.7	16.7	13.2	9.9	7.1	4.9	3.0	4.5	...
Female - Femmes	81.3	77.0	72.0	67.1	62.2	57.3	52.4	47.5	42.6	37.9	33.2	28.6	24.1	19.9	15.9	12.2	8.8	6.0	3.4	3.7	...
Colombia - Colombie 2010 - 2015																					
Male - Hommes	72.1	68.9	64.0	59.1	54.5	50.1	45.7	41.3	36.8	32.3	27.9	23.7	19.7	16.0	12.7	9.8	7.4	...	...	...	...
Female - Femmes	78.5	74.9	70.0	65.1	60.2	55.4	50.6	45.8	41.0	36.3	31.7	27.2	22.9	18.8	15.0	11.6	8.7	...	...	...	...

Continent, country or area and date / Continent, pays ou zone et date	Age (in years) - Age (en années)																				
	0	5	10	15	20	25	30	35	40	45	50	55	60	65	70	75	80	85	90	95	100
AMERICA, SOUTH - AMÉRIQUE DU SUD																					
Ecuador - Équateur[13]																					
2010 - 2015																					
Male - Hommes	73.2	70.0	65.1	60.2	55.3	50.6	46.0	41.5	37.0	32.5	28.1	23.9	19.9	16.1	12.7	9.8	7.2	5.2	3.6	2.4	0.5
Female - Femmes	78.8	75.5	70.6	65.6	60.7	55.8	51.0	46.1	41.3	36.5	31.8	27.2	22.8	18.5	14.5	10.9	7.8	5.5	3.8	2.5	0.5
French Guiana - Guyane française																					
2007																					
Male - Hommes	75.1	71.3	66.4	61.5	56.8	52.2	47.7	43.1	38.7	34.3	30.3	25.7	21.5	17.5	13.8	10.5	8.2	5.7	3.6	2.1	...
Female - Femmes	80.8	77.0	72.1	67.2	62.3	57.4	52.6	47.8	43.0	38.5	33.9	29.2	24.5	19.9	16.6	12.7	10.2	7.8	5.1	2.2	...
Paraguay																					
1990 - 1995																					
Male - Hommes	66.3	65.5	60.8	56.0	51.3	46.7	42.1	37.5	32.9	28.5	24.2	20.2	16.5	13.2	10.2	7.7	5.6	...	...	...	...
Female - Femmes	70.8	69.3	64.5	59.7	54.9	50.1	45.4	40.7	36.0	31.5	27.0	22.8	18.7	14.9	11.5	8.5	6.3	...	...	...	...
2005 - 2010																					
Male - Hommes	69.7	...	...	...	...	...	...	...	...	...	...	...	...	...	...	...	...	...	...	...	...
Female - Femmes	73.9	...	...	...	...	...	...	...	...	...	...	...	...	...	...	...	...	...	...	...	...
Peru - Pérou[11]																					
2010 - 2015																					
Male - Hommes	71.5	69.0	64.3	59.4	54.7	50.0	45.5	40.9	36.4	32.0	27.7	23.6	19.8	16.2	13.0	10.1	7.7	...	...	...	...
Female - Femmes	76.8	73.8	69.0	64.1	59.3	54.5	49.7	45.0	40.3	35.7	31.2	26.9	22.7	18.7	15.0	11.7	8.8	...	...	...	...
Suriname																					
2011 - 2013																					
Male - Hommes	69.3	65.7	60.8	55.9	51.3	46.8	42.3	37.9	33.7	29.5	25.5	21.7	18.1	14.8	11.8	9.1	6.5	4.7	...	...	...
Female - Femmes	75.1	71.6	66.6	61.8	57.0	52.3	47.7	43.1	38.4	33.9	29.5	25.2	21.1	17.0	13.3	9.9	6.9	4.7	...	...	...
Uruguay																					
2010																					
Male - Hommes	72.8	68.5	63.6	58.7	54.0	49.4	44.8	40.2	35.6	31.0	26.6	22.4	18.6	15.1	12.0	9.3	7.0	5.2	4.0	...	...
Female - Femmes	80.0	75.6	70.7	65.8	60.9	56.1	51.2	46.4	41.6	36.9	32.3	27.9	23.6	19.5	15.6	12.0	8.9	6.4	4.5	...	...
Venezuela (Bolivarian Republic of) - Venezuela (République bolivarienne du)																					
1995 - 2000																					
Male - Hommes	68.6	66.6	61.8	56.9	52.3	47.8	43.3	38.8	34.3	29.9	25.6	21.6	17.9	14.5	11.4	8.6	5.9	...	...	...	...
Female - Femmes	74.5	72.1	67.2	62.3	57.5	52.6	47.8	43.1	38.4	33.7	29.2	24.9	20.8	16.9	13.3	9.9	6.9	...	...	...	...
2007																					
Male - Hommes	70.7	...	...	...	...	...	...	...	...	...	...	...	...	...	...	...	...	...	...	...	...
Female - Femmes	76.6	...	...	...	...	...	...	...	...	...	...	...	...	...	...	...	...	...	...	...	...
ASIA - ASIE																					
Afghanistan																					
2004																					
Male - Hommes	45.0	...	...	...	...	...	...	...	...	...	...	...	...	...	...	...	...	...	...	...	...
Female - Femmes	44.0	...	...	...	...	...	...	...	...	...	...	...	...	...	...	...	...	...	...	...	...
Armenia - Arménie																					
2006 - 2007																					
Male - Hommes	70.2	66.3	61.4	56.4	51.6	46.8	42.0	37.3	32.7	28.3	24.1	20.1	16.4	13.1	10.3	7.8	5.7	3.9	2.6	1.6	0.7
Female - Femmes	76.6	72.5	67.6	62.7	57.7	52.8	47.9	43.0	38.2	33.5	28.8	24.3	20.0	15.9	12.4	9.2	6.4	4.1	2.7	1.8	0.7
Azerbaijan - Azerbaïdjan																					
2013																					
Male - Hommes	71.6	67.6	62.7	57.8	53.0	48.2	43.4	38.7	34.1	29.6	25.3	21.2	17.4	14.1	10.8	8.2	5.9	5.0	5.1	3.3	0.5
Female - Femmes	76.8	72.8	67.9	63.0	58.1	53.2	48.3	43.4	38.6	33.8	29.1	24.6	20.2	16.2	12.4	9.2	6.6	4.8	3.7	2.6	0.8
Bahrain - Bahreïn																					
2001																					
Male - Hommes	73.2	69.3	64.4	59.5	54.7	49.9	45.2	40.4	35.6	30.9	26.4	22.0	17.8	14.1	11.3	9.5	...	...	...	...	...
Female - Femmes	76.2	72.0	67.1	62.1	57.2	52.3	47.4	42.5	37.7	32.9	28.2	23.7	19.6	15.9	12.9	10.9	...	...	...	...	...
2010 - 2015																					
Male - Hommes	75.8	...	...	...	...	...	...	...	...	...	...	...	...	...	...	...	...	...	...	...	...
Female - Femmes	77.4	...	...	...	...	...	...	...	...	...	...	...	...	...	...	...	...	...	...	...	...

21. Life expectancy at specified ages for each sex: latest available year, 1995 - 2014
Espérance de vie à un âge donné pour chaque sexe : dernière année disponible, 1995 - 2014 (continued - suite)

Continent, country or area and date / Continent, pays ou zone et date	Age (in years) - Age (en années)																				
	0	5	10	15	20	25	30	35	40	45	50	55	60	65	70	75	80	85	90	95	100

ASIA - ASIE

Bangladesh
2011
| Male - Hommes | 67.9 | 65.5 | 60.8 | 56.1 | 51.3 | 46.5 | 41.8 | 37.1 | 32.6 | 28.2 | 24.1 | 20.2 | 16.6 | 13.2 | 10.0 | 6.7 | 4.4 | ... | ... | ... | ... |
| Female - Femmes | 70.3 | 67.8 | 63.1 | 58.3 | 53.6 | 48.8 | 44.0 | 39.3 | 34.7 | 30.1 | 25.6 | 21.4 | 17.4 | 13.8 | 10.3 | 6.7 | 5.6 | ... | ... | ... | ... |

2013
| Male - Hommes | 68.8 | ... | ... | ... | ... | ... | ... | ... | ... | ... | ... | ... | ... | ... | ... | ... | ... | ... | ... | ... | ... |
| Female - Femmes | 71.4 | ... | ... | ... | ... | ... | ... | ... | ... | ... | ... | ... | ... | ... | ... | ... | ... | ... | ... | ... | ... |

Bhutan - Bhoutan
2005
| Male - Hommes | 65.7 | ... | ... | ... | ... | ... | ... | ... | ... | ... | ... | ... | ... | ... | ... | ... | ... | ... | ... | ... | ... |
| Female - Femmes | 66.9 | ... | ... | ... | ... | ... | ... | ... | ... | ... | ... | ... | ... | ... | ... | ... | ... | ... | ... | ... | ... |

Brunei Darussalam - Brunéi Darussalam
2008
| Male - Hommes | 76.6 | ... | ... | ... | ... | ... | ... | ... | ... | ... | ... | ... | ... | ... | ... | ... | ... | ... | ... | ... | ... |
| Female - Femmes | 79.8 | ... | ... | ... | ... | ... | ... | ... | ... | ... | ... | ... | ... | ... | ... | ... | ... | ... | ... | ... | ... |

China - Chine[14]
2010
| Male - Hommes | 66.8 | ... | ... | ... | ... | ... | ... | ... | ... | ... | ... | ... | ... | ... | ... | ... | ... | ... | ... | ... | ... |
| Female - Femmes | 70.5 | ... | ... | ... | ... | ... | ... | ... | ... | ... | ... | ... | ... | ... | ... | ... | ... | ... | ... | ... | ... |

China, Hong Kong SAR - Chine, Hong Kong RAS
2013
| Male - Hommes | 81.1 | 76.3 | 71.4 | 66.4 | 61.5 | 56.6 | 51.7 | 46.9 | 42.1 | 37.3 | 32.6 | 28.1 | 23.8 | 19.7 | 15.8 | 12.4 | 9.3 | 6.8 | 4.9 | 3.4 | 2.3 |
| Female - Femmes | 86.7 | 81.9 | 76.9 | 72.0 | 67.0 | 62.1 | 57.1 | 52.2 | 47.3 | 42.5 | 37.7 | 33.0 | 28.4 | 23.9 | 19.6 | 15.5 | 11.7 | 8.6 | 6.1 | 4.2 | 2.8 |

China, Macao SAR - Chine, Macao RAS
2011 - 2014
| Male - Hommes | 79.6 | 74.9 | 70.0 | 65.0 | 60.1 | 55.3 | 50.5 | 45.7 | 41.0 | 36.4 | 31.9 | 27.4 | 23.2 | 19.1 | 15.2 | 12.0 | 9.1 | 7.0 | ... | ... | ... |
| Female - Femmes | 86.0 | 81.2 | 76.2 | 71.3 | 66.4 | 61.5 | 56.5 | 51.7 | 46.8 | 42.0 | 37.2 | 32.6 | 28.1 | 23.6 | 19.3 | 15.3 | 12.0 | 9.4 | ... | ... | ... |

Cyprus - Chypre[15]
2013
| Male - Hommes | 80.0 | 75.1 | 70.2 | 65.3 | 60.4 | 55.5 | 50.7 | 45.8 | 41.0 | 36.3 | 31.6 | 27.0 | 22.6 | 18.5 | 14.7 | 11.2 | 8.2 | 5.9 | ... | ... | ... |
| Female - Femmes | 84.8 | 79.8 | 74.9 | 69.9 | 64.9 | 60.0 | 55.0 | 50.1 | 45.2 | 40.3 | 35.4 | 30.6 | 25.9 | 21.4 | 17.2 | 13.1 | 9.5 | 6.6 | ... | ... | ... |

Democratic People's Republic of Korea - République populaire démocratique de Corée
2008
| Male - Hommes | 65.6 | ... | ... | ... | ... | ... | ... | ... | ... | ... | ... | ... | ... | ... | ... | ... | ... | ... | ... | ... | ... |
| Female - Femmes | 72.7 | ... | ... | ... | ... | ... | ... | ... | ... | ... | ... | ... | ... | ... | ... | ... | ... | ... | ... | ... | ... |

Georgia - Géorgie
2010
| Male - Hommes | 70.2 | 66.3 | 61.3 | 56.4 | 51.6 | 46.9 | 42.2 | 37.6 | 33.0 | 28.7 | 24.7 | 20.9 | 17.4 | 14.2 | 11.5 | 9.2 | 7.5 | 6.5 | ... | ... | ... |
| Female - Femmes | 78.6 | 74.5 | 69.6 | 64.6 | 59.7 | 54.8 | 49.9 | 45.0 | 40.2 | 35.5 | 30.8 | 26.3 | 22.0 | 18.0 | 14.3 | 11.1 | 8.8 | 7.5 | ... | ... | ... |

India - Inde[16]
2002 - 2006
| Male - Hommes | 62.6 | 63.8 | 59.3 | 54.6 | 49.9 | 45.4 | 40.9 | 36.5 | 32.2 | 28.0 | 24.0 | 20.2 | 16.7 | 13.6 | 10.9 | ... | ... | ... | ... | ... | ... |
| Female - Femmes | 64.2 | 67.4 | 62.9 | 58.2 | 53.7 | 49.2 | 44.8 | 40.2 | 35.7 | 31.3 | 26.9 | 22.7 | 18.9 | 15.4 | 12.4 | ... | ... | ... | ... | ... | ... |

Indonesia - Indonésie
2012
| Male - Hommes | 67.7 | ... | ... | ... | ... | ... | ... | ... | ... | ... | ... | ... | ... | ... | ... | ... | ... | ... | ... | ... | ... |
| Female - Femmes | 71.7 | ... | ... | ... | ... | ... | ... | ... | ... | ... | ... | ... | ... | ... | ... | ... | ... | ... | ... | ... | ... |

Iran (Islamic Republic of) - Iran (République islamique d')
1996
| Male - Hommes | 66.1 | 64.6 | 59.9 | 55.1 | 50.5 | 46.0 | 41.4 | 36.8 | 32.3 | 27.9 | 23.7 | 19.8 | 16.2 | 12.9 | 10.1 | 7.7 | 5.7 | 4.2 | 3.1 | ... | ... |
| Female - Femmes | 68.4 | 66.8 | 62.1 | 57.3 | 52.7 | 48.0 | 43.5 | 39.0 | 34.5 | 30.1 | 25.8 | 21.7 | 17.8 | 14.3 | 11.1 | 8.4 | 6.2 | 4.5 | 3.2 | ... | ... |

2011
| Male - Hommes | 71.5 | ... | ... | ... | ... | ... | ... | ... | ... | ... | ... | ... | ... | ... | ... | ... | ... | ... | ... | ... | ... |
| Female - Femmes | 74.0 | ... | ... | ... | ... | ... | ... | ... | ... | ... | ... | ... | ... | ... | ... | ... | ... | ... | ... | ... | ... |

21. Life expectancy at specified ages for each sex: latest available year, 1995 - 2014
Espérance de vie à un âge donné pour chaque sexe : dernière année disponible, 1995 - 2014 (continued - suite)

Continent, country or area and date / Continent, pays ou zone et date	Age (in years) - Age (en années)																				
	0	5	10	15	20	25	30	35	40	45	50	55	60	65	70	75	80	85	90	95	100
ASIA - ASIE																					
Iraq																					
1997																					
Male - Hommes	58.0	...	...	...	...	...	...	...	...	...	...	...	...	...	...	...	...	...	...	...	...
Female - Femmes	59.0	...	...	...	...	...	...	...	...	...	...	...	...	...	...	...	...	...	...	...	...
Israel - Israël[17]																					
2009 - 2013																					
Male - Hommes	79.9	75.3	70.3	65.3	60.5	55.6	50.8	45.9	41.1	36.4	31.7	27.2	23.0	18.9	15.2	11.8	8.8	6.3	4.6	3.3	2.5
Female - Femmes	83.5	78.9	73.9	68.9	64.0	59.0	54.1	49.2	44.3	39.5	34.7	30.0	25.5	21.1	16.9	13.0	9.6	6.7	4.7	3.2	2.3
Japan - Japon[18]																					
2013																					
Male - Hommes	80.2	75.5	70.5	65.5	60.6	55.8	50.9	46.1	41.3	36.6	31.9	27.4	23.1	19.1	15.3	11.7	8.6	6.1	4.3	2.9	2.0
Female - Femmes	86.6	81.8	76.9	71.9	66.9	62.0	57.1	52.2	47.3	42.5	37.7	33.1	28.5	24.0	19.6	15.4	11.5	8.2	5.5	3.7	2.4
Jordan - Jordanie[19]																					
2012																					
Male - Hommes	72.7	69.1	64.2	59.3	54.4	49.6	44.8	40.0	35.2	30.5	26.0	21.7	17.8	14.2	10.9	8.2	6.0	...	...	...	...
Female - Femmes	76.7	73.1	68.1	63.2	58.2	53.3	48.4	43.6	38.7	33.9	29.3	24.7	20.3	16.2	12.4	9.2	6.8	...	...	...	...
Kazakhstan																					
2012																					
Male - Hommes	64.8	61.0	56.1	51.3	46.5	41.9	37.5	33.3	29.3	25.3	21.5	18.0	14.8	12.1	9.6	7.4	5.7	4.5	3.7	2.9	2.0
Female - Femmes	74.3	70.4	65.5	60.6	55.7	50.9	46.2	41.5	36.9	32.4	27.9	23.7	19.6	15.9	12.3	9.2	6.6	4.7	3.2	2.4	1.8
Kuwait - Koweït																					
1990 - 1995																					
Male - Hommes	73.3	...	...	...	...	...	...	...	...	...	...	...	...	...	...	...	...	...	...	...	...
Female - Femmes	77.2	...	...	...	...	...	...	...	...	...	...	...	...	...	...	...	...	...	...	...	...
Kyrgyzstan - Kirghizstan																					
2013																					
Male - Hommes	66.3	63.1	58.1	53.3	48.5	43.8	39.2	34.7	30.5	26.4	22.5	18.9	15.4	12.4	9.4	7.0	4.5	3.1	2.1	2.0	1.9
Female - Femmes	74.3	70.8	65.9	61.0	56.1	51.3	46.5	41.7	37.1	32.5	28.0	23.7	19.6	15.7	12.1	9.0	6.2	4.3	3.0	2.4	1.7
Lao People's Democratic Republic - République démocratique populaire lao[20]																					
2005																					
Male - Hommes	59.0	...	...	...	...	...	...	...	...	...	...	...	...	...	...	...	...	...	...	...	...
Female - Femmes	63.0	...	...	...	...	...	...	...	...	...	...	...	...	...	...	...	...	...	...	...	...
Malaysia - Malaisie																					
2010																					
Male - Hommes	71.9	67.6	62.7	57.8	53.1	48.4	43.6	39.0	34.5	30.0	25.7	21.6	17.9	14.3	11.2	8.5	6.0	...	...	...	...
Female - Femmes	76.6	72.2	67.2	62.3	57.4	52.5	47.6	42.8	38.0	33.3	28.7	24.3	20.1	16.1	12.5	9.3	6.7	...	...	...	...
Maldives																					
2009																					
Male - Hommes	72.5	68.7	63.8	59.0	54.1	49.2	44.4	39.5	34.7	29.9	25.2	20.6	16.3	12.3	8.8	6.1	...	...	...	...	...
Female - Femmes	74.2	70.2	65.3	60.4	55.5	50.6	45.6	40.8	35.8	31.0	26.3	21.6	17.1	12.9	9.1	6.0	...	...	...	...	...
2011																					
Male - Hommes	72.8	...	...	...	...	...	...	...	...	...	...	...	...	...	...	...	...	...	...	...	...
Female - Femmes	74.8	...	...	...	...	...	...	...	...	...	...	...	...	...	...	...	...	...	...	...	...
Mongolia - Mongolie																					
1998 - 2007																					
Male - Hommes	63.1	61.3	56.5	51.6	46.9	42.3	38.0	33.7	29.7	25.9	22.4	19.2	16.1	13.7	12.0	...	...	...	...	...	...
Female - Femmes	70.2	68.9	64.0	59.1	54.2	49.5	44.8	40.2	35.7	31.3	27.2	23.3	19.7	16.7	14.3	...	...	...	...	...	...
2014																					
Male - Hommes	65.9	...	...	...	...	...	...	...	...	...	...	...	...	...	...	...	...	...	...	...	...
Female - Femmes	75.5	...	...	...	...	...	...	...	...	...	...	...	...	...	...	...	...	...	...	...	...
Myanmar[21]																					
2011																					
Male - Hommes	65.9	67.4	62.5	57.6	52.8	48.1	43.7	39.5	35.4	31.4	27.6	23.9	20.3	16.5	13.6	11.4	9.7	8.9	...	...	...
Female - Femmes	70.9	74.8	69.9	65.0	60.2	55.4	50.7	46.1	41.5	37.0	32.5	28.2	23.9	19.8	16.5	13.7	11.9	10.3	...	...	...
Nepal - Népal																					
2011																					
Male - Hommes	65.4	...	...	...	...	...	...	...	...	...	...	...	...	...	...	...	...	...	...	...	...
Female - Femmes	67.9	...	...	...	...	...	...	...	...	...	...	...	...	...	...	...	...	...	...	...	...
Oman																					
2013																					
Male - Hommes	74.8	70.9	66.0	61.1	56.4	51.8	47.1	42.4	37.6	33.0	28.5	24.3	20.4	16.9	13.6	10.4	...	...	...	...	...
Female - Femmes	78.5	74.3	69.4	64.4	59.5	54.6	49.7	44.8	39.9	35.1	30.5	25.9	21.6	17.5	13.8	10.2	...	...	...	...	...

21. Life expectancy at specified ages for each sex: latest available year, 1995 - 2014
Espérance de vie à un âge donné pour chaque sexe : dernière année disponible, 1995 - 2014 (continued - suite)

Continent, country or area and date / Continent, pays ou zone et date	Age (in years) - Age (en années)																				
	0	5	10	15	20	25	30	35	40	45	50	55	60	65	70	75	80	85	90	95	100

ASIA - ASIE

Pakistan[22]
2007
| Male - Hommes | 63.6 | 65.3 | 60.7 | 55.9 | 51.3 | 46.7 | 42.2 | 37.7 | 33.3 | 29.0 | 25.0 | 21.3 | 18.1 | 15.2 | 12.7 | 10.8 | 9.2 | 7.3 | ... | ... | ... |
| Female - Femmes | 67.6 | 68.6 | 64.1 | 59.5 | 54.9 | 50.3 | 45.7 | 41.1 | 36.5 | 32.1 | 27.7 | 23.5 | 19.6 | 16.2 | 13.4 | 10.9 | 8.6 | 6.1 | ... | ... | ... |

Qatar
2008
| Male - Hommes | 77.9 | 73.7 | 68.8 | 63.9 | 59.1 | 54.3 | 49.4 | 44.6 | 39.8 | 35.0 | 30.3 | 25.6 | 21.2 | 17.0 | 13.3 | 9.9 | 7.1 | ... | ... | ... | ... |
| Female - Femmes | 78.1 | 73.9 | 68.9 | 64.0 | 59.1 | 54.1 | 49.2 | 44.3 | 39.3 | 34.5 | 29.6 | 24.9 | 20.5 | 16.6 | 13.2 | 10.0 | 7.8 | ... | ... | ... | ... |

2011
| Male - Hommes | 76.5 | ... | ... | ... | ... | ... | ... | ... | ... | ... | ... | ... | ... | ... | ... | ... | ... | ... | ... | ... | ... |
| Female - Femmes | 81.0 | ... | ... | ... | ... | ... | ... | ... | ... | ... | ... | ... | ... | ... | ... | ... | ... | ... | ... | ... | ... |

Republic of Korea - République de Corée
2013
| Male - Hommes | 78.5 | 73.8 | 68.9 | 63.9 | 59.0 | 54.1 | 49.3 | 44.5 | 39.7 | 35.1 | 30.6 | 26.2 | 22.0 | 18.0 | 14.2 | 10.8 | 8.0 | 5.8 | 4.2 | 3.1 | 2.4 |
| Female - Femmes | 85.1 | 80.4 | 75.4 | 70.4 | 65.5 | 60.5 | 55.6 | 50.8 | 45.9 | 41.1 | 36.3 | 31.6 | 27.0 | 22.4 | 18.0 | 13.9 | 10.3 | 7.3 | 5.1 | 3.6 | 2.7 |

Saudi Arabia - Arabie saoudite[23]
2012
| Male - Hommes | 72.8 | ... | ... | ... | ... | ... | ... | ... | ... | ... | ... | ... | ... | ... | ... | ... | ... | ... | ... | ... | ... |
| Female - Femmes | 75.2 | ... | ... | ... | ... | ... | ... | ... | ... | ... | ... | ... | ... | ... | ... | ... | ... | ... | ... | ... | ... |

Singapore - Singapour[24]
2014
| Male - Hommes | 80.5 | 75.7 | 70.7 | 65.7 | 60.8 | 55.9 | 51.0 | 46.1 | 41.3 | 36.5 | 31.9 | 27.4 | 23.1 | 19.0 | 15.2 | 11.9 | 9.0 | 6.7 | 4.8 | 3.3 | 2.2 |
| Female - Femmes | 84.9 | 80.2 | 75.2 | 70.2 | 65.2 | 60.3 | 55.3 | 50.4 | 45.5 | 40.6 | 35.9 | 31.2 | 26.6 | 22.2 | 18.0 | 14.1 | 10.7 | 7.9 | 5.6 | 3.9 | 2.6 |

State of Palestine - État de Palestine
2001
| Male - Hommes | 70.5 | 67.5 | 62.7 | 57.8 | 53.1 | 48.4 | 43.6 | 38.9 | 34.2 | 29.6 | 25.2 | 21.1 | 17.2 | 13.8 | 10.7 | 8.1 | 6.1 | ... | ... | ... | ... |
| Female - Femmes | 73.6 | 70.3 | 65.5 | 60.5 | 55.7 | 50.9 | 46.1 | 41.3 | 36.6 | 32.0 | 27.5 | 23.2 | 19.0 | 15.2 | 11.7 | 8.8 | 6.4 | ... | ... | ... | ... |

2014
| Male - Hommes | 71.8 | ... | ... | ... | ... | ... | ... | ... | ... | ... | ... | ... | ... | ... | ... | ... | ... | ... | ... | ... | ... |
| Female - Femmes | 74.7 | ... | ... | ... | ... | ... | ... | ... | ... | ... | ... | ... | ... | ... | ... | ... | ... | ... | ... | ... | ... |

Tajikistan - Tadjikistan
2008
| Male - Hommes | 69.7 | 67.9 | 63.0 | 58.1 | 53.3 | 48.5 | 43.7 | 39.1 | 34.6 | 30.1 | 25.7 | 21.6 | 17.9 | 14.7 | 12.2 | 10.4 | 9.2 | ... | ... | ... | ... |
| Female - Femmes | 74.8 | 72.5 | 67.6 | 62.7 | 57.8 | 52.9 | 48.1 | 43.4 | 38.6 | 33.9 | 29.4 | 25.0 | 21.0 | 17.5 | 14.7 | 12.5 | 11.1 | ... | ... | ... | ... |

2011
| Male - Hommes | 70.9 | ... | ... | ... | ... | ... | ... | ... | ... | ... | ... | ... | ... | ... | ... | ... | ... | ... | ... | ... | ... |
| Female - Femmes | 74.1 | ... | ... | ... | ... | ... | ... | ... | ... | ... | ... | ... | ... | ... | ... | ... | ... | ... | ... | ... | ... |

Thailand - Thaïlande
2005 - 2006
| Male - Hommes | 69.9 | ... | ... | ... | ... | ... | ... | ... | ... | ... | ... | ... | ... | ... | ... | ... | ... | ... | ... | ... | ... |
| Female - Femmes | 77.6 | ... | ... | ... | ... | ... | ... | ... | ... | ... | ... | ... | ... | ... | ... | ... | ... | ... | ... | ... | ... |

Turkey - Turquie
2013
| Male - Hommes | 73.7 | 69.9 | 65.0 | 60.1 | 55.3 | 50.6 | 45.8 | 40.9 | 36.2 | 31.5 | 27.0 | 22.7 | 18.7 | 14.9 | 11.6 | 8.8 | 6.5 | 4.6 | 3.3 | 2.3 | 1.6 |
| Female - Femmes | 79.4 | 75.6 | 70.7 | 65.8 | 60.9 | 56.0 | 51.1 | 46.2 | 41.4 | 36.6 | 31.8 | 27.2 | 22.7 | 18.5 | 14.6 | 11.2 | 8.2 | 5.8 | 4.0 | 2.7 | 1.8 |

United Arab Emirates - Émirats arabes unis
2006
| Male - Hommes | 76.7 | 72.5 | 67.6 | 62.7 | 57.9 | 53.1 | 48.3 | 43.5 | 38.7 | 33.9 | 29.3 | 24.8 | 20.7 | 16.9 | 13.8 | 11.3 | 10.2 | ... | ... | ... | ... |
| Female - Femmes | 78.8 | 74.5 | 69.5 | 64.6 | 59.7 | 54.8 | 49.8 | 44.9 | 40.0 | 35.2 | 30.4 | 25.8 | 21.6 | 18.0 | 15.4 | 14.0 | 14.5 | ... | ... | ... | ... |

Viet Nam
2014
| Male - Hommes | 70.6 | 67.7 | 62.9 | 58.1 | 53.3 | 48.6 | 43.9 | 39.1 | 34.5 | 30.0 | 25.8 | 21.8 | 18.2 | 15.0 | 12.3 | 10.0 | 8.3 | ... | ... | ... | ... |
| Female - Femmes | 76.0 | 72.2 | 67.2 | 62.3 | 57.4 | 52.5 | 47.7 | 42.9 | 38.1 | 33.5 | 29.0 | 24.6 | 20.6 | 16.8 | 13.6 | 11.0 | 8.9 | ... | ... | ... | ... |

Yemen - Yémen
2004
| Male - Hommes | 60.2 | ... | ... | ... | ... | ... | ... | ... | ... | ... | ... | ... | ... | ... | ... | ... | ... | ... | ... | ... | ... |
| Female - Femmes | 62.0 | ... | ... | ... | ... | ... | ... | ... | ... | ... | ... | ... | ... | ... | ... | ... | ... | ... | ... | ... | ... |

Continent, country or area and date / Continent, pays ou zone et date	\multicolumn{21}{c}{Age (in years) - Age (en années)}
	0	5	10	15	20	25	30	35	40	45	50	55	60	65	70	75	80	85	90	95	100

EUROPE

Åland Islands - Îles d'Åland
2013

	0	5	10	15	20	25	30	35	40	45	50	55	60	65	70	75	80	85	90	95	100
Male - Hommes	78.9	73.9	68.9	63.9	59.3	54.3	49.3	44.3	39.5	34.7	30.1	25.7	21.4	17.2	13.5	11.5	8.5	5.7	3.5	1.6	1.0
Female - Femmes	85.8	80.8	75.8	70.8	66.3	61.3	56.3	51.3	46.3	41.3	36.3	31.3	26.4	21.7	17.9	13.3	10.0	6.6	4.2	2.6	1.0
Albania - Albanie **2013**																					
Male - Hommes	76.0	71.9	66.9	62.0	57.3	52.5	47.7	43.0	38.3	33.7	29.2	24.8	20.6	16.6	12.9	9.6	6.9	5.0	...	...	...
Female - Femmes	80.3	75.9	71.0	66.1	61.3	56.4	51.5	46.6	41.8	37.0	32.2	27.6	23.0	18.6	14.3	10.6	7.4	5.1	...	...	...
Austria - Autriche **2013**																					
Male - Hommes	78.5	73.8	68.8	63.9	59.0	54.1	49.3	44.4	39.7	34.9	30.3	25.9	21.8	17.9	14.4	11.0	7.9	5.5	3.7	2.4	...
Female - Femmes	83.6	78.8	73.9	68.9	63.9	59.0	54.1	49.2	44.3	39.4	34.7	30.0	25.5	21.2	17.1	13.1	9.5	6.5	4.2	2.8	...
Belarus - Bélarus **2013**																					
Male - Hommes	67.3	62.6	57.7	52.7	47.9	43.2	38.6	34.2	30.0	25.9	22.0	18.4	15.3	12.5	10.0	7.8	6.0	4.5	3.4	2.5	1.8
Female - Femmes	77.9	73.2	68.2	63.3	58.3	53.5	48.6	43.8	39.1	34.5	30.0	25.6	21.4	17.4	13.6	10.2	7.4	5.2	3.5	2.3	1.4
Belgium - Belgique **2006**																					
Male - Hommes	77.0	71.4	66.5	61.5	56.7	51.9	47.1	42.4	37.7	33.1	28.6	24.3	20.3	16.5	12.9	9.7	7.1	5.0	3.4	2.5	...
Female - Femmes	82.7	77.0	72.1	67.1	62.2	57.3	52.4	47.5	42.6	37.9	33.2	28.7	24.3	20.1	16.0	12.1	8.8	6.1	4.1	2.8	...
Bosnia and Herzegovina - Bosnie-Herzégovine **2003**																					
Male - Hommes	71.3	...	...	...	...	...	...	...	...	...	...	...	...	...	...	...	...	...	...	...	...
Female - Femmes	76.7	...	...	...	...	...	...	...	...	...	...	...	...	...	...	...	...	...	...	...	...
Bulgaria - Bulgarie **2010 - 2012**																					
Male - Hommes	70.6	66.5	61.5	56.6	51.8	47.0	42.3	37.6	32.9	28.4	24.2	20.4	17.0	13.9	10.9	8.4	6.2	4.5	3.3	2.5	0.5
Female - Femmes	77.5	73.2	68.3	63.4	58.5	53.6	48.7	43.8	39.1	34.4	29.8	25.4	21.2	17.1	13.2	9.7	6.9	4.7	3.2	2.2	0.5
Czech Republic - République tchèque **2013**																					
Male - Hommes	75.2	70.5	65.5	60.6	55.7	50.9	46.1	41.3	36.5	31.9	27.4	23.1	19.2	15.7	12.5	9.7	7.2	5.2	3.6	2.4	1.6
Female - Femmes	81.1	76.3	71.4	66.4	61.4	56.5	51.6	46.7	41.8	37.0	32.3	27.7	23.3	19.1	15.1	11.5	8.2	5.5	3.5	2.1	1.2
Denmark - Danemark[25] **2012 - 2013**																					
Male - Hommes	78.0	73.3	68.3	63.4	58.4	53.6	48.7	43.8	39.0	34.3	29.7	25.4	21.3	17.4	13.8	10.4	7.5	5.3	3.6	2.4	...
Female - Femmes	81.9	77.3	72.3	67.3	62.4	57.4	52.5	47.6	42.7	37.9	33.1	28.6	24.2	20.1	16.1	12.4	9.2	6.6	4.4	2.9	...
Estonia - Estonie **2013**																					
Male - Hommes	72.7	67.9	62.9	58.0	53.1	48.4	43.7	39.1	34.6	30.1	25.8	21.8	18.1	15.0	12.1	9.4	7.2	5.3	3.6	2.7	1.8
Female - Femmes	81.3	76.6	71.7	66.7	61.8	56.9	52.0	47.2	42.4	37.6	32.9	28.4	24.1	19.9	15.8	12.1	8.8	6.1	4.2	3.0	2.0
Faeroe Islands - Îles Féroé **2008**																					
Male - Hommes	76.8	72.5	67.7	62.7	57.9	53.0	48.1	43.3	38.5	33.9	29.3	24.8	20.8	17.0	13.4	10.1	7.6	6.0	4.6	3.2	...
Female - Femmes	82.3	77.8	72.8	67.8	62.9	57.9	53.0	48.1	43.2	38.2	33.4	28.7	24.3	20.0	15.9	12.5	9.2	6.6	4.4	3.3	...
Finland - Finlande[26] **2012**																					
Male - Hommes	77.5	72.7	67.8	62.8	57.9	53.2	48.4	43.7	38.9	34.3	29.9	25.5	21.4	17.6	14.1	10.7	7.8	5.4	3.7	2.5	1.6
Female - Femmes	83.4	78.7	73.7	68.7	63.8	58.9	54.0	49.1	44.3	39.5	34.7	30.1	25.6	21.3	17.1	13.2	9.5	6.5	4.3	2.8	1.7
France[27] **2010 - 2012**																					
Male - Hommes	78.3	73.7	68.7	63.7	58.9	54.1	49.3	44.5	39.8	35.2	30.7	26.5	22.6	18.8	15.1	11.7	8.6	6.0	4.1	2.8	...
Female - Femmes	84.8	80.2	75.2	70.2	65.3	60.4	55.4	50.5	45.7	40.9	36.2	31.7	27.2	22.9	18.6	14.5	10.7	7.5	5.0	3.3	...
Germany - Allemagne **2009 - 2011**																					
Male - Hommes	77.7	73.1	68.1	63.1	58.3	53.4	48.6	43.7	38.9	34.2	29.7	25.4	21.3	17.5	13.9	10.6	7.8	5.5	3.8	2.7	2.0
Female - Femmes	82.7	78.0	73.1	68.1	63.2	58.2	53.3	48.4	43.5	38.7	34.0	29.4	25.0	20.7	16.5	12.6	9.1	6.3	4.3	3.0	2.1
Gibraltar **2001**																					
Male - Hommes	78.5	73.5	68.5	63.5	58.5	53.5	...	43.5	...	33.9	...	25.8	...	17.9	...	11.3	...	...	...	...	...
Female - Femmes	83.3	79.5	75.0	70.0	65.0	60.0	...	50.3	...	40.3	...	30.3	...	20.6	...	13.7	...	...	...	...	...

21. Life expectancy at specified ages for each sex: latest available year, 1995 - 2014
Espérance de vie à un âge donné pour chaque sexe : dernière année disponible, 1995 - 2014 (continued - suite)

Continent, country or area and date / Continent, pays ou zone et date	Age (in years) - Age (en années)																				
	0	5	10	15	20	25	30	35	40	45	50	55	60	65	70	75	80	85	90	95	100
EUROPE																					
Greece - Grèce																					
2012																					
Male - Hommes	77.9	73.2	68.3	63.3	58.4	53.6	48.8	44.1	39.3	34.6	30.1	25.8	21.7	17.9	14.3	10.9	8.1	5.9	4.4	3.2	2.2
Female - Femmes	83.0	78.2	73.3	68.3	63.4	58.4	53.5	48.6	43.7	38.9	34.1	29.5	25.0	20.5	16.2	12.2	8.9	6.4	4.7	3.3	2.3
Hungary - Hongrie																					
2013																					
Male - Hommes	72.0	67.5	62.5	57.6	52.7	47.8	42.9	38.1	33.4	28.8	24.6	20.8	17.4	14.3	11.4	8.7	6.4	4.3	2.6	1.5	0.6
Female - Femmes	78.7	74.1	69.2	64.2	59.3	54.3	49.4	44.5	39.6	34.9	30.3	26.0	21.9	17.9	14.1	10.6	7.5	4.9	2.9	1.5	0.6
Iceland - Islande																					
2012 - 2013																					
Male - Hommes	80.8	75.9	70.9	66.0	61.0	56.2	51.3	46.7	41.8	37.1	32.4	27.8	23.4	19.1	15.3	11.5	8.2	5.7	3.9	2.8	1.5
Female - Femmes	83.7	78.9	73.9	68.9	64.0	59.0	54.1	49.2	44.3	39.5	34.6	29.9	25.3	21.0	16.9	13.0	9.5	6.7	4.5	2.6	1.5
Ireland - Irlande																					
2005 - 2007																					
Male - Hommes	76.8	72.2	67.2	62.3	57.5	52.8	48.0	43.3	38.5	33.8	29.2	24.8	20.6	16.6	13.0	9.8	7.1	5.1	3.6	2.6	1.9
Female - Femmes	81.6	76.9	72.0	67.0	62.1	57.2	52.3	47.4	42.5	37.7	33.1	28.5	24.0	19.8	15.8	12.1	8.8	6.2	4.3	3.1	2.1
Isle of Man - Île de Man																					
1996																					
Male - Hommes	73.6	68.6	63.6	58.6	53.6	49.1	44.6	40.2	35.8	31.2	26.7	22.4	18.4	15.1	12.0	9.3	7.5	5.2	4.7	3.2	0.5
Female - Femmes	79.9	75.1	70.1	65.1	60.1	55.1	50.1	45.1	40.2	35.4	30.7	26.2	22.0	18.3	14.5	11.3	8.6	5.9	3.7	2.0	1.5
Italy - Italie																					
2013																					
Male - Hommes	79.8	75.1	70.2	65.2	60.3	55.4	50.6	45.7	40.9	36.1	31.5	27.0	22.6	18.6	14.7	11.3	8.2	5.7	3.9	2.6	1.7
Female - Femmes	84.6	79.9	74.9	70.0	65.0	60.1	55.1	50.2	45.3	40.5	35.7	31.0	26.4	22.0	17.7	13.7	10.0	7.0	4.7	3.0	1.9
Latvia - Lettonie																					
2013																					
Male - Hommes	69.5	64.9	60.0	55.1	50.2	45.4	40.7	36.2	31.9	27.6	23.7	20.1	16.8	13.8	11.2	8.7	6.5	4.7	3.2	1.9	...
Female - Femmes	79.0	74.4	69.4	64.5	59.5	54.6	49.7	45.0	40.2	35.6	31.2	26.8	22.5	18.5	14.7	11.1	8.0	5.4	3.5	2.4	...
Lithuania - Lituanie																					
2013																					
Male - Hommes	68.5	63.9	58.9	54.0	49.2	44.6	40.0	35.6	31.4	27.4	23.6	20.1	16.9	14.0	11.5	9.0	6.7	4.8	3.3	2.5	2.1
Female - Femmes	79.4	74.7	69.8	64.8	59.9	55.0	50.2	45.4	40.6	36.0	31.5	27.2	23.0	19.0	15.1	11.5	8.2	5.7	3.9	2.7	2.0
Luxembourg																					
2011 - 2013																					
Male - Hommes	79.9	75.1	70.1	65.1	60.2	55.4	50.5	45.7	40.8	36.0	31.4	27.0	22.9	18.9	15.3	11.9	8.7	6.2	4.3	1.9	...
Female - Femmes	84.3	79.4	74.5	69.5	64.6	59.6	54.7	49.8	44.9	40.1	35.4	30.8	26.3	22.0	17.9	13.9	10.3	7.2	4.8	2.5	...
Malta - Malte																					
2013																					
Male - Hommes	79.6	75.2	70.2	65.2	60.3	55.4	50.5	45.7	40.9	36.1	31.4	26.9	22.5	18.4	14.6	11.2	8.2	6.2	...	...	...
Female - Femmes	84.0	79.6	74.6	69.6	64.7	59.8	54.8	49.9	44.9	40.0	35.2	30.5	25.9	21.5	17.1	13.1	9.8	7.1	...	...	...
Netherlands - Pays-Bas																					
2009																					
Male - Hommes	78.5	73.8	68.8	63.9	59.0	54.1	49.2	44.4	39.5	34.8	30.1	25.6	21.4	17.3	13.6	10.3	7.5	5.3	3.6	2.6	...
Female - Femmes	82.7	77.8	72.8	67.9	62.9	58.0	53.1	48.2	43.3	38.5	33.8	29.3	24.9	20.6	16.5	12.7	9.2	6.4	4.3	2.9	...
2011																					
Male - Hommes	79.2	...	...	...	...	...	...	...	...	...	...	...	...	...	...	...	...	...	...	...	...
Female - Femmes	82.8	...	...	...	...	...	...	...	...	...	...	...	...	...	...	...	...	...	...	...	...
Norway - Norvège																					
2012																					
Male - Hommes	79.4	74.7	69.7	64.8	59.8	55.0	50.2	45.4	40.6	35.8	31.2	26.7	22.3	18.2	14.4	10.9	7.8	5.5	3.7	2.6	2.3
Female - Femmes	83.4	78.6	73.7	68.7	63.8	58.8	53.9	49.0	44.1	39.2	34.5	29.8	25.3	21.0	16.9	13.0	9.5	6.6	4.3	2.8	1.9
Poland - Pologne																					
2012																					
Male - Hommes	72.7	68.1	63.2	58.2	53.4	48.7	43.9	39.2	34.6	30.2	26.0	22.1	18.6	15.4	12.4	9.7	7.4	5.5	4.1	3.0	2.2
Female - Femmes	81.0	76.4	71.4	66.5	61.5	56.6	51.7	46.8	41.9	37.1	32.5	28.0	23.8	19.7	15.8	12.2	9.0	6.5	4.6	3.2	2.3
Portugal																					
2011 - 2013																					
Male - Hommes	76.9	72.2	67.3	62.3	57.4	52.6	47.7	42.9	38.2	33.6	29.2	25.0	21.0	17.1	13.4	9.9	6.8	4.2	2.6	1.6	1.1
Female - Femmes	82.8	78.1	73.1	68.2	63.2	58.3	53.3	48.4	43.6	38.8	34.1	29.4	24.9	20.4	16.1	12.0	8.3	5.2	3.2	1.9	1.2
Republic of Moldova - République de Moldova[28]																					
2012																					
Male - Hommes	67.2	63.1	58.1	53.3	48.5	43.7	39.0	34.5	30.1	26.0	22.2	18.7	15.5	13.0	10.2	8.4	7.1	6.9	7.8	...	...
Female - Femmes	75.0	70.9	66.0	61.0	56.1	51.2	46.4	41.5	36.8	32.2	27.7	23.4	19.3	15.7	12.2	9.5	7.4	5.9	5.3	...	...

21. Life expectancy at specified ages for each sex: latest available year, 1995 - 2014
Espérance de vie à un âge donné pour chaque sexe : dernière année disponible, 1995 - 2014 (continued - suite)

Continent, country or area and date / Continent, pays ou zone et date	Age (in years) - Age (en années)																				
	0	5	10	15	20	25	30	35	40	45	50	55	60	65	70	75	80	85	90	95	100
EUROPE																					
Romania - Roumanie 2011 - 2013																					
Male - Hommes	71.2	67.1	62.2	57.3	52.4	47.6	42.8	38.1	33.4	28.9	24.7	21.0	17.5	14.4	11.4	8.8	6.6	4.8	3.5	2.6	1.9
Female - Femmes	78.3	74.0	69.1	64.1	59.2	54.3	49.4	44.5	39.7	35.0	30.4	25.9	21.7	17.6	13.8	10.3	7.4	5.2	3.7	2.6	1.9
Russian Federation - Fédération de Russie 2012																					
Male - Hommes	64.6	60.3	55.4	50.5	45.8	41.3	37.0	33.1	29.3	25.4	21.8	18.4	15.4	12.8	10.2	8.1	6.4	5.1	4.0	3.0	1.4
Female - Femmes	75.9	71.6	66.7	61.7	56.9	52.1	47.3	42.8	38.2	33.7	29.3	25.1	21.0	17.1	13.4	10.2	7.4	5.3	3.8	2.8	1.8
San Marino - Saint-Marin 2013																					
Male - Hommes	81.7	76.9	72.0	67.0	62.2	57.4	52.5	47.6	42.7	37.9	33.0	28.3	24.1	19.7	15.7	11.8	8.6	6.1	4.1	2.3	...
Female - Femmes	86.4	81.5	76.5	71.5	66.6	61.6	56.6	51.7	46.7	41.9	37.1	32.4	27.7	23.2	18.8	14.8	10.8	7.4	5.0	2.7	...
Serbia - Serbie[29] 2013																					
Male - Hommes	72.5	68.0	63.1	58.1	53.3	48.4	43.6	38.9	34.2	29.6	25.2	21.2	17.5	14.2	11.1	8.3	6.1	4.3	...	...	...
Female - Femmes	77.7	73.1	68.2	63.2	58.3	53.4	48.4	43.6	38.7	34.0	29.4	24.9	20.7	16.6	12.8	9.4	6.6	4.5	...	...	...
Slovakia - Slovaquie 2013																					
Male - Hommes	72.9	68.4	63.4	58.5	53.6	48.8	44.0	39.2	34.5	29.9	25.6	21.6	17.9	14.6	11.6	8.9	6.7	4.8	3.4	2.2	0.8
Female - Femmes	79.6	75.1	70.2	65.2	60.3	55.3	50.4	45.5	40.7	35.9	31.3	26.7	22.4	18.2	14.2	10.5	7.2	4.7	2.8	1.5	0.6
Slovenia - Slovénie 2013																					
Male - Hommes	77.0	72.3	67.3	62.3	57.4	52.6	47.8	43.0	38.2	33.6	29.0	24.7	20.7	17.0	13.6	10.3	7.5	5.4	3.7	2.5	2.0
Female - Femmes	83.2	78.4	73.5	68.5	63.5	58.6	53.7	48.7	43.9	39.1	34.3	29.6	25.2	20.9	16.7	12.7	9.2	6.4	4.3	3.0	2.1
Spain - Espagne 2013																					
Male - Hommes	80.0	75.2	70.3	65.3	60.4	55.5	50.6	45.7	40.8	36.1	31.5	27.1	22.9	19.0	15.2	11.7	8.7	6.2	4.5	3.5	3.4
Female - Femmes	85.6	80.9	75.9	70.9	66.0	61.0	56.0	51.1	46.2	41.4	36.6	32.0	27.4	22.9	18.5	14.4	10.6	7.4	5.1	3.7	3.1
Sweden - Suède 2012																					
Male - Hommes	79.9	75.1	70.2	65.2	60.3	55.5	50.7	45.8	41.0	36.2	31.5	27.0	22.6	18.4	14.5	11.0	7.9	5.4	3.6	2.4	1.6
Female - Femmes	83.5	78.8	73.8	68.8	63.9	59.0	54.0	49.1	44.2	39.4	34.6	30.0	25.4	21.0	16.9	13.0	9.5	6.5	4.3	2.9	1.9
Switzerland - Suisse 2012																					
Male - Hommes	80.5	75.8	70.9	65.9	61.0	56.1	51.2	46.4	41.5	36.8	32.1	27.5	23.2	19.1	15.2	11.6	8.4	5.7	3.8	2.5	1.7
Female - Femmes	84.7	80.0	75.0	70.0	65.1	60.1	55.2	50.3	45.4	40.5	35.7	31.0	26.5	22.1	17.8	13.7	10.0	6.8	4.4	2.9	2.0
TFYR of Macedonia - L'ex-R. y. de Macédoine 2011																					
Male - Hommes	73.0	68.7	63.8	58.8	53.9	49.1	44.2	39.3	34.6	29.9	25.5	21.3	17.4	13.9	10.7	7.8	5.5	3.8	2.8	2.4	...
Female - Femmes	77.0	72.7	67.8	62.8	57.9	52.9	48.0	43.1	38.2	33.4	28.8	24.3	20.0	15.8	12.1	8.8	6.1	4.3	3.4	2.9	...
Ukraine 2013																					
Male - Hommes	66.3	62.0	57.1	52.2	47.4	42.7	38.2	33.9	29.9	25.9	22.2	18.7	15.5	12.8	10.3	8.2	6.4	5.2	4.2	3.3	2.2
Female - Femmes	76.2	71.8	66.9	62.0	57.1	52.2	47.4	42.7	38.1	33.6	29.1	24.8	20.6	16.7	13.1	9.8	7.2	5.1	3.6	2.5	1.6
United Kingdom of Great Britain and Northern Ireland - Royaume-Uni de Grande-Bretagne et d'Irlande du Nord[30] 2012																					
Male - Hommes	79.0	74.4	69.4	64.5	59.6	54.7	49.9	45.1	40.3	35.6	31.1	26.6	22.3	18.3	14.5	11.2	8.2	5.8	4.0	2.8	2.2
Female - Femmes	82.7	78.0	73.1	68.1	63.1	58.2	53.3	48.4	43.5	38.7	34.0	29.5	25.0	20.7	16.7	12.9	9.5	6.7	4.6	3.2	2.3
OCEANIA - OCÉANIE																					
American Samoa - Samoas américaines 2006																					
Male - Hommes	68.5	...	...	...	...	...	...	...	...	...	...	...	...	...	...	...	...	...	...	...	...
Female - Femmes	76.2	...	...	...	...	...	...	...	...	...	...	...	...	...	...	...	...	...	...	...	...

Continent, country or area and date / Continent, pays ou zone et date	Age (in years) - Age (en années)																				
	0	5	10	15	20	25	30	35	40	45	50	55	60	65	70	75	80	85	90	95	100
OCEANIA - OCÉANIE																					
Australia - Australie																					
2011 - 2013																					
Male - Hommes	80.1	75.5	70.5	65.5	60.7	55.8	51.0	46.2	41.5	36.8	32.2	27.7	23.4	19.2	15.3	11.8	8.6	6.1	4.2	2.9	2.3
Female - Femmes	84.3	79.7	74.7	69.7	64.8	59.9	55.0	50.1	45.2	40.4	35.7	31.1	26.5	22.1	17.9	13.9	10.2	7.2	4.8	3.3	2.5
Cook Islands - Îles Cook[31]																					
2006																					
Male - Hommes	69.5	66.0	61.3	56.5	52.0	47.4	42.8	38.1	33.6	29.1	24.8	20.9	17.5	14.3	11.4	9.0	7.3	...	...	...	...
Female - Femmes	76.2	72.4	67.4	62.4	57.4	52.7	48.0	43.2	38.4	33.6	29.1	24.7	20.4	16.4	12.6	9.5	6.9				
Fiji - Fidji																					
1996																					
Male - Hommes	64.5	...	...	...	...	42.4	...	...	...	...	...	...	...	10.7	...	...	...	...	...	...	...
Female - Femmes	68.7	...	...	...	...	46.4	...	...	...	...	...	...	...	13.0	...	...	...	...	...	...	...
2007																					
Male - Hommes	65.3	...	...	...	...	...	...	...	...	...	...	...	...	...	...	...	...	...	...	...	...
Female - Femmes	69.6	...	...	...	...	...	...	...	...	...	...	...	...	...	...	...	...	...	...	...	...
French Polynesia - Polynésie française																					
2010																					
Male - Hommes	73.2	69.1	64.1	59.3	54.6	50.0	45.3	40.6	35.8	31.2	26.8	22.7	19.0	15.4	12.4	9.9	7.2	5.1	...	...	...
Female - Femmes	78.3	74.2	69.3	64.3	59.4	54.4	49.6	44.8	40.0	35.3	30.6	26.3	22.1	17.8	14.3	11.1	7.8	5.2	...	...	...
2012																					
Male - Hommes	73.3	...	...	...	...	...	...	...	...	...	...	...	...	...	...	...	...	...	...	...	...
Female - Femmes	78.2	...	...	...	...	...	...	...	...	...	...	...	...	...	...	...	...	...	...	...	...
Guam																					
2014																					
Male - Hommes	75.8	...	...	...	...	...	...	...	...	...	...	...	...	...	...	...	...	...	...	...	...
Female - Femmes	82.1	...	...	...	...	...	...	...	...	...	...	...	...	...	...	...	...	...	...	...	...
Kiribati																					
2005																					
Male - Hommes	58.9	58.2	53.6	48.9	44.4	40.0	35.6	31.3	27.1	23.1	19.4	16.0	13.0	10.4	8.3	6.6	5.3	4.2	...	...	...
Female - Femmes	63.1	62.6	57.9	53.1	48.6	44.1	39.7	35.4	31.2	27.1	23.2	19.5	16.1	13.1	10.4	8.1	6.2	4.7	...	...	...
Marshall Islands - Îles Marshall																					
2004																					
Male - Hommes	67.0	...	...	...	...	...	...	...	...	...	...	...	...	...	...	...	...	...	...	...	...
Female - Femmes	70.6	...	...	...	...	...	...	...	...	...	...	...	...	...	...	...	...	...	...	...	...
Micronesia (Federated States of) - Micronésie (États fédérés de)																					
2000																					
Male - Hommes	66.5	...	...	...	...	...	...	...	...	...	...	...	...	...	...	...	...	...	...	...	...
Female - Femmes	67.5	...	...	...	...	...	...	...	...	...	...	...	...	...	...	...	...	...	...	...	...
Nauru																					
2006																					
Male - Hommes	55.2	...	...	...	...	...	...	...	...	...	...	...	...	...	...	...	...	...	...	...	...
Female - Femmes	57.1	...	...	...	...	...	...	...	...	...	...	...	...	...	...	...	...	...	...	...	...
New Caledonia - Nouvelle-Calédonie																					
2010																					
Male - Hommes	74.4	69.8	65.0	60.0	55.3	50.8	46.3	41.7	37.3	32.8	28.4	24.3	20.3	17.0	13.9	11.0	8.3	6.1	4.7	5.0	...
Female - Femmes	80.7	76.2	71.2	66.2	61.3	56.5	51.8	46.9	42.1	37.3	32.6	28.4	23.9	19.6	15.6	12.0	9.0	6.6	4.7	3.1	...
New Zealand - Nouvelle-Zélande																					
2012 - 2014																					
Male - Hommes	79.6	75.1	70.1	65.2	60.4	55.6	50.8	46.0	41.2	36.5	32.0	27.5	23.2	19.0	15.1	11.6	8.5	6.0	...	...	...
Female - Femmes	83.3	78.7	73.7	68.8	63.9	59.0	54.0	49.2	44.3	39.5	34.8	30.2	25.7	21.4	17.2	13.3	9.9	6.9	...	...	...
Niue - Nioué																					
2006																					
Male - Hommes	67.0	...	...	...	...	...	...	...	...	...	...	...	...	...	...	...	...	...	...	...	...
Female - Femmes	76.0	...	...	...	...	...	...	...	...	...	...	...	...	...	...	...	...	...	...	...	...

Continent, country or area and date / Continent, pays ou zone et date	Age (in years) - Age (en années)																				
	0	5	10	15	20	25	30	35	40	45	50	55	60	65	70	75	80	85	90	95	100
OCEANIA - OCÉANIE																					
Northern Mariana Islands - Îles Mariannes septentrionales																					
2009																					
Male - Hommes	74.5	...	...	...	...	...	...	...	...	...	...	...	...	...	...	...	...	...	...	...	...
Female - Femmes	79.9	...	...	...	...	...	...	...	...	...	...	...	...	...	...	...	...	...	...	...	...
Palau - Palaos																					
2005																					
Male - Hommes	66.3	...	...	...	...	...	...	...	...	...	...	...	...	...	...	...	...	...	...	...	...
Female - Femmes	72.1	...	...	...	...	...	...	...	...	...	...	...	...	...	...	...	...	...	...	...	...
Papua New Guinea - Papouasie-Nouvelle-Guinée																					
2000																					
Male - Hommes	53.7	54.1	50.2	45.7	41.6	37.7	33.7	29.8	25.9	22.1	18.5	15.0	11.9	9.2	6.9	5.0	3.6	2.6	1.7	0.6	...
Female - Femmes	54.8	54.7	50.8	46.3	42.1	38.1	34.1	30.1	26.2	22.3	18.6	15.2	12.0	9.2	6.8	5.0	3.6	2.5	1.6	0.6	...
Samoa																					
2006																					
Male - Hommes	71.5	...	...	...	...	...	...	...	...	...	...	...	...	...	...	...	...	...	...	...	...
Female - Femmes	74.2	...	...	...	...	...	...	...	...	...	...	...	...	...	...	...	...	...	...	...	...
Solomon Islands - Îles Salomon																					
1999																					
Male - Hommes	60.6	...	...	...	...	...	...	...	...	...	...	...	...	...	...	...	...	...	...	...	...
Female - Femmes	61.6	...	...	...	...	...	...	...	...	...	...	...	...	...	...	...	...	...	...	...	...
Tonga																					
2006																					
Male - Hommes	67.3	64.1	59.3	54.5	49.9	45.4	40.7	36.2	31.6	27.2	23.4	19.4	15.9	13.0	9.4	6.3	4.0	...	...	...	...
Female - Femmes	73.0	69.3	64.6	59.8	55.0	50.1	45.2	40.4	35.7	31.3	27.1	23.0	19.0	15.3	11.6	8.6	6.1	...	...	...	...
Tuvalu																					
1997 - 2002																					
Male - Hommes	61.7	59.5	54.8	50.0	45.2	40.6	35.9	32.1	28.0	24.1	20.0	17.1	13.7	10.8	9.0	6.9	5.4	...	...	...	...
Female - Femmes	65.1	62.6	57.7	53.7	50.0	45.3	40.9	36.6	32.2	28.1	23.8	20.3	16.9	13.2	10.6	7.9	6.4	...	...	...	...
Vanuatu																					
1999																					
Male - Hommes	65.6	...	...	...	...	...	...	...	...	...	...	...	...	...	...	...	...	...	...	...	...
Female - Femmes	69.0	...	...	...	...	...	...	...	...	...	...	...	...	...	...	...	...	...	...	...	...
Wallis and Futuna Islands - Îles Wallis et Futuna																					
2003																					
Male - Hommes	73.1	...	...	...	...	...	...	...	...	...	...	...	...	...	...	...	...	...	...	...	...
Female - Femmes	75.5	...	...	...	...	...	...	...	...	...	...	...	...	...	...	...	...	...	...	...	...

FOOTNOTES - NOTES

[1] Data refer to Algerian population only. - Les données ne concernent que la population algérienne.

[2] Based on the results of the Population Census. - D'après les résultats du recensement de la population.

[3] Based on the results of the Botswana Demographic Survey. - Données extraites de l'enquête démographique effectuée par le Botswana.

[4] Based on the results of the 2006 Population and Housing Census. - Données fondées sur les résultats du recensement de la population et de l'habitat de 2006.

[5] Data refer to the 12 months preceding the census in April. - Les données se rapportent aux douze mois précédant le recensement d'avril.

[6] Excludes the islands of St. Brandon and Agalega. - Non compris les îles St. Brandon et Agalega.

[7] Data refer to national projections. - Les données se réfèrent aux projections nationales.

[8] Based on underlying data of the 2002 Population Census. - Données fondées sur le recensement de la population de 2002.

[9] Data are based on a small number of deaths. - Les données sont basées sur un nombre limité de décès.

[10] Data refer to projections based on the 1992 Population Census. - Les données se réfèrent aux projections basées sur le recensement de la population de 1992.

[11] Excluding Indian jungle population. - Non compris les Indiens de la jungle.

[12] Data refer to the 12 months from 30 June 2014 to 30 June 2015. - Les données font référence aux douze mois de 30 juin 2014 à 30 juin 2015.

[13] Data refer to projections based on the 2010 Population Census. Excludes nomadic Indian tribes. - Les données se réfèrent aux projections basées sur le recensement de la population de 2010. Non compris les tribus d'Indiens nomades.

[14] For statistical purposes, the data for China do not include those for the Hong Kong Special Administrative Region (Hong Kong SAR), Macao Special Administrative Region (Macao SAR) and Taiwan province of China. - Pour la présentation des statistiques, les données pour la Chine ne comprennent pas la Région Administrative Spéciale de Hong Kong (Hong Kong RAS), la Région Administrative Spéciale de Macao (Macao RAS) et Taïwan province de Chine.

[15] Data refer to government controlled areas. - Les données se rapportent aux zones contrôlées par le Gouvernement.

[16] Includes data for the Indian-held part of Jammu and Kashmir, the final status of which has not yet been determined. - Y compris les données pour la partie du

Jammu et du Cachemire occupée par l'Inde dont le statut définitif n'a pas encore été déterminé.

[17] Includes data for East Jerusalem and Israeli residents in certain other territories under occupation by Israeli military forces since June 1967. - Y compris les données pour Jérusalem-Est et les résidents israéliens dans certains autres territoires occupés depuis 1967 par les forces armées israéliennes.

[18] Data refer to Japanese nationals in Japan only. - Les données se raportent aux nationaux japonais au Japon seulement.

[19] Excluding data for Jordanian territory under occupation since June 1967 by Israeli military forces. Excluding foreigners, including registered Palestinian refugees. - Non compris les données pour le territoire jordanien occupé depuis juin 1967 par les forces armées israéliennes. Non compris les étrangers, mais y compris les réfugiés de Palestine enregistrés.

[20] Based on the results of the 2005 Population and Housing Census. - Données fondées sur les résultats du recensement de la population et de l'habitat de 2005.

[21] Data refer to urban areas only. - Données ne concernant que les zones urbaines.

[22] Excluding data for the Pakistan-held part of Jammu and Kashmir, the final status of which has not yet been determined. Based on the results of the Pakistan Demographic Survey. - Non compris les données concernant la partie du Jammu et Cachemire occupée par le Pakistan dont le statut définitif n'a pas été déterminé. Données extraites de l'enquête démographique effectuée par le Pakistan.

[23] Projections based on the final results of the 2004 Population and Housing Census. - Projections basées sur les résultats définitifs du recensement de la population et de l'habitat de 2004.

[24] Data refer to resident population which comprises Singapore citizens and permanent residents. Provisional data. - Les données se rapportent à la population résidente composé des citoyens de Singapour et des résidents permanents. Données provisoires.

[25] Excluding Faeroe Islands and Greenland shown separately, if available. - Non compris les Iles Féroé et le Groenland, qui font l'objet de rubriques distinctes, si disponible.

[26] Excluding Åland Islands. - Non compris les Îles d'Åland.

[27] Provisional data. - Données provisoires.

[28] Excluding Transnistria and the municipality of Bender. - Les données ne tiennent pas compte de l'information sur la Transnistria et la municipalité de Bender.

[29] Excludes data for Kosovo and Metohia. - Sans les données pour le Kosovo et Metohie.

[30] Excluding Channel Islands (Guernsey and Jersey) and Isle of Man, shown separately, if available. - Non compris les îles Anglo-Normandes (Guernesey et Jersey) et l'île de Man, qui font l'objet de rubriques distinctes, si disponible.

[31] Excluding Niue, shown separately, which is part of Cook Islands, but because of remoteness is administered separately. - Non compris Nioué, qui fait l'objet d'une rubrique distincte et qui fait partie des îles Cook, mais qui, en raison de son éloignement, est administrée séparément.

Table 22 - *Demographic Yearbook 2014*

Table 22 presents the number of marriages and crude marriage rates by urban/rural residence for every year with available data between 2010 and 2014.

Description of variables: Marriage is defined as the act, ceremony or process by which the legal relationship of spouses is constituted. The legality of the union may be established by civil, religious or other means as recognized by the laws of each country[1].

Marriage statistics in this table, therefore, include both first marriages and remarriages after divorce, widowhood or annulment. They do not, unless otherwise noted, include resumption of marriage ties after legal separation. These statistics refer to the number of marriages performed, and not to the number of persons marrying.

Statistics shown are obtained from civil registers of marriage. Exceptions, such as data from church registers, are identified in footnotes.

The urban/rural classification of marriages is that provided by each country or area; it is presumed to be based on the national census definitions of urban population which have been set forth at the end of the notes for table 6.

For certain countries, there is a discrepancy between the total number of marriages shown in this table and those shown in subsequent tables for the same year. Usually this discrepancy arises because the total number of marriages occurring in a given year is revised although the remaining tabulations are not.

Rate computation: Crude marriage rates are the annual number of marriages per 1 000 mid-year population. Rates by urban/rural residence are the annual number of marriages, in the appropriate urban or rural category, per 1 000 corresponding mid-year population. Rates presented in this table have been limited to those for countries or areas having at least a total of 30 marriages in a given year. These rates are calculated by the Statistics Division of the United Nations based on the appropriate reference population (for example: total population, nationals only, etc.) if known and available. If the reference population is not known or unavailable the total population is used to calculate the rates. Therefore, if the population that is used to calculate the rates is different from the correct reference population, the rates presented might under- or overstate the true situation in a country or area.

Reliability of data: Each country or area has been asked to indicate the estimated completeness of the number of marriages recorded in its civil register. These national assessments are indicated by the quality codes "C" and "U" that appear in the first column of this table.

"C" indicates that the data are estimated to be virtually complete, that is, representing at least 90 per cent of the marriages occurring each year, while "U" indicates that data are estimated to be incomplete, that is representing less than 90 per cent of the marriages occurring each year. The code "..." indicates that no information was provided regarding completeness.

Data from civil registers which are reported as incomplete or of unknown completeness (coded "U" or "...") are considered unreliable. They appear in italics in this table; rates are not computed for these data.

These quality codes apply only to data from civil registers. For more information about the quality of vital statistics data in general, see section 4.2 of the Technical Notes.

Limitations: Statistics on marriages are subject to the same qualifications that have been set forth for vital statistics in general and marriage statistics in particular as discussed in section 4 of the Technical Notes.

The fact that marriage is a legal event, unlike birth and death that are biological events, has implications for international comparability of data. Marriage has been defined, for statistical purposes, in terms of the laws of individual countries or areas. These laws vary throughout the world. In addition, comparability is further limited because some countries or areas compile statistics only for civil marriages although religious marriages may also be legally recognized; in other countries or areas, the only available records are church registers and, therefore, the statistics may not reflect marriages that are civil marriages only.

Because in many countries or areas marriage is a civil legal contract which, to establish its legality, must be celebrated before a civil officer, it follows that for these countries or areas registration would tend to be almost automatic at the time of, or immediately following, the marriage ceremony. This factor should be kept in mind when considering the reliability of data, described above. For this reason the practice of tabulating data by date of registration does not generally pose serious problems of comparability as it does in the case of birth and death statistics.

As indicators of family formation, the statistics on the number of marriages presented in this table are bound to be deficient to the extent that they do not include either customary unions, which are not registered even though they are considered legal and binding under customary law, or consensual unions (also known as extra-legal or de facto unions). In general, lower marriage rates over a period of years are an indication of higher incidence of customary or consensual unions.

In addition, rates are affected also by the quality and limitations of the population estimates that are used in their computation. The problems of under-enumeration or over-enumeration and, to some extent, the differences in definition of total population have been discussed in section 3 of the Technical Notes dealing with population data in general, and specific information pertaining to individual countries or areas is given in the footnotes to table 3.

Strict correspondence between the numerator of the rate and the denominator is not always obtained; for example, marriages among civilian and military segments of the population may be related to civilian population. The effect of this may be to increase the rates, but, in most cases, this effect is negligible.

It should be emphasized that crude marriage rates like crude birth, death and divorce rates, may be seriously affected by the age-sex-marital structure of the population to which they relate. Crude marriage rates do, however, provide a simple measure of the level and changes in marriage.

The comparability of data by urban/rural residence is affected by the national definitions of urban and rural used in tabulating these data. It is assumed, in the absence of specific information to the contrary, that the definitions of urban and rural used in connection with the national population census were also used in the compilation of the vital statistics for each country or area. However, it cannot be excluded that, for a given country or area, different definitions of urban and rural are used for the vital statistics data and the population census data respectively. When known, the definitions of urban in national population censuses are presented at the end of the technical notes for table 6. As discussed in detail in the notes, these definitions vary considerably from one country or area to another.

In addition to problems of comparability, marriage rates classified by urban/rural residence are also subject to certain special types of bias. If, when calculating marriage rates, different definitions of urban are used in connection with the vital events and the population data, and if this results in a net difference between the numerator and denominator of the rate in the population at risk, then the marriage rates would be biased. Urban/rural differentials in marriage rates may also be affected by whether the vital events have been tabulated in terms of place of occurrence or place of usual residence. This problem is discussed in more detail in section 4.1.4.1 of the Technical Notes.

Earlier data: Marriages and crude marriage rates have been shown in each issue of the *Demographic Yearbook*. For more information on specific topics, and years for which data are reported, readers should consult the Historical Index.

NOTES

[1] *Principles and Recommendations for a Vital Statistics System Revision 3,* Sales No. E.13.XVII.10, United Nations, New York, 2014.

Tableau 22 – *Annuaire démographique 2014*

Le tableau 22 présente des données sur les mariages et les taux bruts de nuptialité selon le lieu de résidence (zone urbaine ou rurale) pour les années où l'information est disponible entre 2010 et 2014.

Description des variables : le mariage désigne l'acte, la cérémonie ou la procédure qui établit un rapport légal entre les époux. L'union peut être rendue légale par une procédure civile ou religieuse, ou par toute autre procédure, conformément à la législation du pays[1].

Les statistiques de la nuptialité présentées dans ce tableau comprennent donc les premiers mariages et les remariages faisant suite à un divorce, un veuvage ou une annulation. Toutefois, sauf indication contraire, elles ne comprennent pas les unions reconstituées après une séparation légale. Ces statistiques se rapportent au nombre de mariages célébrés, non au nombre de personnes qui se marient.

Les statistiques présentées reposent sur l'enregistrement des mariages par les services de l'état civil. Les exceptions (données provenant des registres des églises, par exemple) font l'objet d'une note à la fin du tableau.

La classification des mariages selon le lieu de résidence (zone urbaine ou rurale) est celle qui a été communiquée par chaque pays ou zone ; on part du principe qu'elle repose sur les définitions de la population urbaine utilisées pour les recensements nationaux telles qu'elles sont reproduites à la fin des notes se rapportant au tableau 6.

Pour quelques pays il y a une discordance entre le nombre total de mariages présenté dans ce tableau et ceux présentés après pour la même année. Habituellement ces différences apparaissent lorsque le nombre total des mariages pour une certaine année a été révisé alors que les autres tabulations ne l'ont pas été.

Calcul des taux : les taux bruts de nuptialité représentent le nombre annuel de mariages pour 1 000 habitants au milieu de l'année. Les taux selon le lieu de résidence (zone urbaine ou rurale) représentent le nombre annuel de mariages, classés selon la catégorie urbaine ou rurale appropriée, pour 1 000 habitants au milieu de l'année. Les taux de ce tableau ne se rapportent qu'aux pays ou zones où l'on a enregistré un total d'au moins 30 mariages pendant une année donnée. Ces taux sont calculés par la division de statistique des Nations Unies sur la base de la population de référence adéquate (par exemple : population totale, nationaux seulement, etc.) si connue et disponible. Si la population de référence n'est pas connue ou n'est pas disponible, la population totale est utilisée pour calculer les taux. Par conséquent, si la population utilisée pour calculer les taux est différente de la population de référence adéquate, les taux présentés sont susceptibles de sous ou sur estimer la situation réelle d'un pays ou d'un territoire.

Fiabilité des données : il a été demandé à chaque pays ou zone d'indiquer le degré estimatif de complétude des données sur les mariages figurant dans ses registres d'état civil. Ces évaluations nationales sont signalées par les codes de qualité "C" et "U" qui apparaissent dans la deuxième colonne du tableau.

La lettre "C" indique que les données sont jugées à peu près complètes, c'est-à-dire qu'elles représentent au moins 90 p. 100 des mariages survenus chaque année ; la lettre "U" signale que les données sont jugées incomplètes, c'est-à-dire qu'elles représentent moins de 90 p. 100 des mariages survenus chaque année. Le code "..." indique qu'aucun renseignement n'a été communiqué quant à la complétude des données.

Les données issues des registres de l'état civil qui sont déclarées incomplètes ou dont le degré de complétude n'est pas connu (code "U" ou "...") sont jugées douteuses. Elles apparaissent en italique dans le tableau et les taux correspondants n'ont pas été calculés.

Les codes de qualité ne s'appliquent qu'aux données provenant des registres de l'état civil. Pour plus de précisions sur la qualité des données reposant sur les statistiques de l'état civil en général, voir la section 4.2 des Notes techniques.

Insuffisance des données : les statistiques relatives aux mariages appellent les mêmes réserves que celles qui ont été formulées à propos des statistiques de l'état civil en général et des statistiques concernant la nuptialité en particulier (voir la section 4 des Notes techniques).

Le fait que le mariage soit un acte juridique, à la différence de la naissance et du décès, qui sont des faits biologiques, a des répercussions sur la comparabilité internationale des données. Aux fins de la statistique, le mariage est défini par la législation de chaque pays ou zone. Cette législation varie d'un pays à l'autre. La comparabilité est limitée en outre du fait que certains pays ou zones ne réunissent des statistiques que pour les mariages civils, bien que les mariages religieux y soient également reconnus par la loi ; dans d'autres, les seuls relevés disponibles sont les registres des églises et, en conséquence, les statistiques peuvent ne pas rendre compte des mariages exclusivement civils.

Étant donné que, dans de nombreux pays ou zones, le mariage est un contrat juridique civil qui, pour être légal, doit être conclu devant un officier d'état civil, il s'ensuit que dans ces pays ou zones l'enregistrement se fait à peu près systématiquement au moment de la cérémonie ou immédiatement après. Il faut tenir compte de cet élément lorsque l'on évalue la fiabilité des données, dont il est question plus haut. C'est pourquoi la pratique consistant à exploiter les données selon la date de l'enregistrement ne pose généralement pas les graves problèmes de comparabilité auxquels on se heurte dans le cas des statistiques concernant les naissances et les décès.

Les statistiques relatives au nombre des mariages présentées dans ce tableau donnent une idée forcément trompeuse de la formation des familles, dans la mesure où elles ne tiennent compte ni des mariages coutumiers, qui ne sont pas enregistrés bien qu'ils soient considérés comme légaux et créateurs d'obligations en vertu du droit coutumier, ni des unions consensuelles (appelées également unions non légalisées ou unions de fait). En général, une diminution du taux de nuptialité pendant un certain nombre d'années indique une augmentation des mariages coutumiers ou des unions consensuelles.

L'exactitude des taux dépend également de la qualité et des insuffisances des estimations de population qui sont utilisées pour leur calcul. Le problème des erreurs par excès ou par défaut commises lors du dénombrement et, dans une certaine mesure, le problème de l'hétérogénéité des définitions de la population totale ont été examinés à la section 3 des Notes techniques relative à la population en général ; des indications concernant les différents pays ou zones sont données en note à la fin du tableau 3.

Il n'a pas toujours été possible d'obtenir une correspondance rigoureuse entre le numérateur et le dénominateur pour le calcul des taux. Par exemple, les mariages parmi la population civile et les militaires sont parfois rapportés à la population civile. Cela peut avoir pour effet d'accroître les taux, mais, dans la plupart des cas, il est probable que la différence sera négligeable.

Il faut souligner que les taux bruts de nuptialité, de même que les taux bruts de natalité, de mortalité et de divortialité, peuvent varier sensiblement selon la structure par âge et par sexe de la population à laquelle ils se rapportent. Les taux bruts de nuptialité offrent néanmoins un moyen simple de mesurer la fréquence et l'évolution des mariages.

La comparabilité des données selon le lieu de résidence (zone urbaine ou rurale) peut être limitée par les définitions nationales des termes « urbain » et « rural » utilisées pour le classement de ces données. En l'absence d'indications contraires, on a supposé que les mêmes définitions avaient servi pour le recensement national de la population et pour l'établissement des statistiques de l'état civil pour chaque pays ou zone. Toutefois, il n'est pas exclu que, pour une zone ou un pays donné, des définitions différentes aient été retenues. Les définitions du terme « urbain » utilisées pour les recensements nationaux de population ont été présentées à la fin des notes techniques du tableau 6 lorsqu'elles étaient connues. Comme on l'a précisé dans les notes techniques relatives au tableau 6, ces définitions varient considérablement d'un pays ou d'une zone à l'autre.

Outre les problèmes de comparabilité, les taux de nuptialité classés selon le lieu de résidence (zone urbaine ou rurale) sont également sujets à des distorsions particulières. Si l'on utilise des définitions différentes du terme « urbain » pour classer les faits d'état civil et les données relatives à la population lors du calcul des taux et qu'il en résulte une différence nette entre le numérateur et le dénominateur pour le taux de la population exposée au risque, les taux de nuptialité s'en trouveront faussés. La différence entre ces taux pour les zones urbaines et rurales pourra aussi être faussée selon que les faits d'état civil auront été classés d'après le lieu où ils se sont produits ou d'après le lieu de résidence habituel. Ce problème est examiné plus en détail à la section 4.1.4.1 des Notes techniques.

Données publiées antérieurement : les différentes éditions de *l'Annuaire démographique* regroupent des données sur le nombre des mariages. Pour plus de précisions concernant les années et les sujets pour lesquels des données ont été publiées, se reporter à l'index historique.

NOTE

[1] *Principes et recommandations pour un système de statistique de l'état civil, troisième révision,* numéro de vente : E.13.XVII.10, publication des Nations Unies, New York, 2014.

22. Marriages and crude marriage rates, by urban/rural residence: 2010 - 2014
Mariages et taux bruts de nuptialité, selon la résidence, urbaine/rurale : 2010 - 2014

Continent, country or area, and urban/rural residence / Continent, pays ou zone et résidence, urbaine/rurale	Code[a]	Number - Nombre					Rate - Taux				
		2010	2011	2012	2013	2014	2010	2011	2012	2013	2014
AFRICA - AFRIQUE											
Algeria - Algérie[1]											
Total	...	344 819	369 031	371 280	387 947	386 422	...	...	...	...	...
Botswana											
Total	+U	4 416	4 601	5 214	...	...	...	...	...	...	...
Cabo Verde											
Total	+C	1 167	1 158	...	...	...	2.3	2.2	...	...	...
Egypt - Égypte[2]											
Total	+C	864 857	897 969	922 425	909 350	...	11.0	11.2	11.2	10.7	...
Urban - Urbaine	+C	354 223	353 048	416 060	371 995	...	10.5	10.2	11.8	10.3	...
Rural - Rurale	+C	510 634	544 921	506 365	537 355	...	11.4	11.8	10.7	11.1	...
Lesotho											
Total	+U	8 342	3 188	...	...	...	...	...	...	...	...
Mauritius - Maurice[3]											
Total	+C	10 555	10 499	10 382	9 575	9 959	8.2	8.4	8.3	7.6	7.9
Urban - Urbaine	+C	3 174	3 195	3 096	2 902	3 216	5.9	6.3	6.1	5.6	6.2
Rural - Rurale	+C	7 381	7 304	7 286	6 673	6 743	9.9	9.8	9.8	9.0	9.1
Niger											
Total	+U	1 640	6 750	...	...	...	...	...	...	...	...
Saint Helena ex. dep. - Sainte-Hélène sans dép.											
Total	C	8	15	12	8	7	...	...	...	...	...
Seychelles[4]											
Total	+C	1 440	1 525	1 748	1 708	1 655	16.0	17.4	19.8	19.0	18.1
South Africa - Afrique du Sud											
Total	...	170 826	167 264	...	...	...	...	...	...	...	...
Tunisia - Tunisie											
Total	...	87 081	91 590	...	...	...	...	...	...	...	...
AMERICA, NORTH - AMÉRIQUE DU NORD											
Anguilla[5]											
Total	C	62	47	56	42	...	3.8	3.5	4.2	3.1	...
Aruba											
Total	C	633	550	574	523	617	6.2	5.3	5.5	4.9	5.7
Bahamas											
Total	+C	1 939	1 916	1 941	...	...	5.8	5.4	5.4	...	...
Total[6]	+U	...	...	...	*3 617	...	...	...	...	...	...
Bermuda - Bermudes											
Total	C	619	555	601	471	...	9.7	8.8	9.6	7.6	...
Cayman Islands - Îles Caïmanes											
Total	+C	530[7]	533[7]	473[7]	527[7]	452	9.7	9.6	8.3	9.4	7.8
Costa Rica[8]											
Total	C	23 955	25 013	26 112	25 725	*25 909	5.3	5.4	5.6	5.5	*5.4
Urban - Urbaine	C	12 564	13 127	13 567	12 229	*17 905	3.8	3.9	4.0	3.6	*5.2
Rural - Rurale	C	11 391	11 886	12 545	13 496	*8 004	9.2	9.5	9.9	10.5	*6.1
Cuba[9]											
Total	C	58 490	59 676	55 759	61 449	...	5.2	5.3	5.0	5.5	...
Urban - Urbaine	C	54 300	54 847	49 837	56 462	...	6.5	6.5	5.9	6.6	...
Rural - Rurale	C	4 190	4 829	5 922	4 987	...	1.5	1.7	2.2	1.9	...
Curaçao											
Total	C	874	859	741	665	...	5.9	5.7	4.9	4.3	...
Dominican Republic - République dominicaine											
Total	+C	43 797	44 253	43 307	45 163	...	4.6	4.6	4.5	4.6	...
El Salvador[10]											
Total	...	30 279	31 220	29 267	...	...	...	...	...	...	...
Urban - Urbaine	...	10 905	11 702	7 757	...	...	...	...	...	...	...
Rural - Rurale	...	19 374	19 518	21 510	...	...	...	...	...	...	...
Guadeloupe											
Total	C	1 402	1 259	1 291	1 136	...	3.5	3.1	3.2	2.8	...
Guatemala											
Total	C	73 124	78 285	84 253	...	...	5.1	5.3	5.6	...	...
Jamaica - Jamaïque											
Total	+C	20 910	20 685	20 175	...	...	7.7	7.7	7.5	...	...

Continent, country or area, and urban/rural residence / Continent, pays ou zone et résidence, urbaine/rurale	Code[a]	Number - Nombre					Rate - Taux				
		2010	2011	2012	2013	2014	2010	2011	2012	2013	2014
AMERICA, NORTH - AMÉRIQUE DU NORD											
Martinique											
Total	C	1 279	...	...	...	...	3.2	...	...	...	...
Mexico - Mexique											
Total	+C	567 943	570 152	584 498	582 077	...	5.0	4.9	5.0	4.9	...
Urban - Urbaine[11]	+C	421 265	416 784	429 923	417 507	...	5.1	5.0	5.1	4.9	...
Rural - Rurale[11]	+C	118 146	121 836	120 184	114 568	...	3.7	3.8	3.7	3.5	...
Montserrat											
Total	+...	17	19	16	18	...	...	...	...	...	...
Panama[8]											
Total	C	12 981	15 135[12]	14 201	13 213	...	3.5	4.1	3.7	3.4	...
Urban - Urbaine	C	9 753	11 625[12]	10 995	10 535	...	4.1	4.7	4.4	4.1	...
Rural - Rurale	C	3 228	3 510[12]	3 206	2 678	...	2.5	2.8	2.5	2.1	...
Puerto Rico - Porto Rico											
Total	C	17 790	18 001	17 948	17 010	16 668	4.8	4.9	4.9	4.7	4.7
Sint Maarten (Dutch part) - Saint-Martin (partie néerlandaise)											
Total	+C	266	187	166	230	...	7.5	5.6	4.8	6.3	...
United States of America - États-Unis d'Amérique											
Total	C	2 096 000	2 118 000	...	...	...	6.8	6.8	...	...	...
AMERICA, SOUTH - AMÉRIQUE DU SUD											
Argentina - Argentine											
Total	C	123 208	128 797	131 922	123 810	...	3.0	3.1	3.2	2.9	...
Bolivia (Plurinational State of) - Bolivie (État plurinational de)											
Total	U	37 686	25 531	34 542		...	...	...	...	...	...
Brazil - Brésil											
Total	+U	977 620	1 026 736	1 041 440	1 052 477[13]	...	...	...	...	...	...
Chile - Chili											
Total	+C	60 362	64 768	63 736	...	...	3.5	3.8	3.7	...	...
Urban - Urbaine[14]	+C	54 747	59 619	58 606	...	...	3.7	4.0	3.9	...	...
Rural - Rurale[14]	+C	5 615	5 149	5 130	...	...	2.5	2.3	2.3	...	...
Ecuador - Équateur[15]											
Total	U	74 800	73 579	57 753	53 986	...	...	...	...	...	...
Urban - Urbaine	U	...	...	...	44 721	...	...	...	...	...	...
Rural - Rurale	U	...	...	...	9 265	...	...	...	...	...	...
French Guiana - Guyane française											
Total	C	581	...	...	...	...	2.5	...	...	...	...
Guyana[16]											
Total	C	4 239	4 846	5 128	4 667	4 679	5.6	6.5	6.8	6.2	...
Paraguay											
Total	U	...	...	20 967	...	...	...	...	...	...	...
Peru - Pérou[17]											
Total	+C	82 043	97 693	107 380	89 763	...	2.8	3.3	3.6	2.9	...
Suriname											
Total	C	2 264	2 337	2 204	2 190	...	4.3	4.3	4.1	4.0	...
Uruguay											
Total	C	10 629	9 604	9 631	...	...	3.1	2.8	2.8	...	...
Venezuela (Bolivarian Republic of) - Venezuela (République bolivarienne du)											
Total	C	94 977	103 004	102 077	99 065	...	3.3	3.6	3.5	3.3	...
ASIA - ASIE											
Armenia - Arménie											
Total	+C	16 904	19 706	...	...	...	5.2	6.0	...	...	...

22. Marriages and crude marriage rates, by urban/rural residence: 2010 - 2014
Mariages et taux bruts de nuptialité, selon la résidence, urbaine/rurale : 2010 - 2014 (continued - suite)

Continent, country or area, and urban/rural residence / Continent, pays ou zone et résidence, urbaine/rurale	Code[a]	Number - Nombre					Rate - Taux				
		2010	2011	2012	2013	2014	2010	2011	2012	2013	2014
ASIA - ASIE											
Azerbaijan - Azerbaïdjan											
Total	+C	79 172	88 145	79 065	86 852	...	8.7	9.6	8.5	9.2	...
Urban - Urbaine	+C	41 592	45 494	42 293	46 324	...	8.7	9.4	8.6	9.2	...
Rural - Rurale	+C	37 580	42 651	36 772	40 528	...	8.8	9.9	8.4	9.2	...
Bahrain - Bahreïn											
Total	...	4 960	6 769	7 559	7 463	7 673	...	...	...	...	...
Bangladesh											
Total	...	1 885 109	2 066 820	2 027 350	...	...	...	...	...	...	...
Urban - Urbaine	...	416 761	443 040	446 516	...	...	...	...	...	...	...
Rural - Rurale	...	1 468 348	1 623 780	1 580 834	...	...	...	...	...	...	...
Brunei Darussalam - Brunéi Darussalam											
Total	...	...	2 726	2 671	2 741	...	...	...	...	...	...
China - Chine[18]											
Total	+C	12 410 000	12 471 000	12 971 000	...		9.3	9.3	9.6	...	...
China, Hong Kong SAR - Chine, Hong Kong RAS											
Total	C	52 558	58 369	60 459	55 274	...	7.5	8.3	8.5	7.7	...
China, Macao SAR - Chine, Macao RAS											
Total	+C	3 103	3 545	3 783	4 153	4 085	5.8	6.5	6.7	7.0	6.6
Cyprus - Chypre[19]											
Total	C	6 081	6 210	5 806	5 493	...	7.3	7.3	6.7	6.4	...
Georgia - Géorgie											
Total	C	34 675	30 863	30 412	34 693	...	7.8	6.9	6.8	...	...
Urban - Urbaine[14]	C	18 563	17 625	...	...	...	7.9	7.4	...	...	...
Rural - Rurale[14]	C	16 112	13 238	...	...	...	7.7	6.3	...	...	...
Indonesia - Indonésie											
Total	U	2 207 224	2 319 821	...	...	...	...	...	...	...	...
Iran (Islamic Republic of) - Iran (République islamique d')[20]											
Total	+C	891 627	874 792	829 968	774 513	...	12.0	11.6	10.9	10.1	...
Urban - Urbaine	+C	622 397	...	...	...	...	12.1	...	...	...	...
Rural - Rurale	+C	269 230	...	...	...	...	11.7	...	...	...	...
Israel - Israël[21]											
Total	C	47 855	51 271	50 474	...	...	6.3	6.6	6.4	...	...
Urban - Urbaine[22]	C	43 035	46 034	45 371	...	...	6.2	6.5	6.3	...	...
Rural - Rurale[22]	C	3 736	4 034	3 900	...	...	5.9	6.2	5.8	...	...
Japan - Japon[23]											
Total	+C	700 214	661 895	668 869	660 613	...	5.5	5.2	5.2	5.2	...
Urban - Urbaine[14]	+C	647 127	613 035	620 373	613 648	...	...	...	...	...	...
Rural - Rurale[14]	+C	53 087	48 860	48 496	46 965	...	...	...	...	...	...
Jordan - Jordanie[24]											
Total	+C	62 107	64 665	70 621	70 965	...	10.2	10.3	11.1	10.9	...
Kazakhstan											
Total	C	146 443	160 494	164 681	168 447	...	9.0	9.7	9.8	9.9	...
Urban - Urbaine	C	88 084	97 321	102 889	107 494	...	9.9	10.8	11.2	11.5	...
Rural - Rurale	C	58 359	63 173	61 792	60 953	...	7.9	8.4	8.1	7.9	...
Kuwait - Koweït											
Total	C	13 993	19 860	14 320	15 118	...	4.8	6.4	4.4	4.4	...
Kyrgyzstan - Kirghizstan											
Total	C	50 362	56 509	55 176	53 578	...	9.7	10.7	10.3	9.4	...
Urban - Urbaine	C	15 198	15 930	16 622	17 329	...	8.3	8.6	9.0	9.0	...
Rural - Rurale	C	35 164	40 579	38 554	36 249	...	10.5	11.9	11.0	9.5	...
Lebanon - Liban											
Total	C	41 758	42 500	38 691	38 737	41 049	...	11.2	...	...	...
Mongolia - Mongolie											
Total	+C	9 349	11 869	12 822	15 785	17 332	3.4	4.3	4.5	5.4	5.8
Urban - Urbaine	+C	6 272	8 245	8 718	10 613	12 075	3.5	4.4	4.6	5.4	6.1
Rural - Rurale	+C	3 077	3 624	4 104	5 172	5 257	3.3	3.9	4.4	5.5	5.4
Oman[25]											
Total	+U	20 820	26 540	29 840	...	...	...	...	...	...	...
Philippines											
Total	U	482 480	476 408	482 399	...	...	...	...	...	...	...
Qatar											
Total	C	2 977	3 293	3 532	3 619	...	1.7	1.9	1.9	1.8	...

22. Marriages and crude marriage rates, by urban/rural residence: 2010 - 2014
Mariages et taux bruts de nuptialité, selon la résidence, urbaine/rurale : 2010 - 2014 (continued - suite)

Continent, country or area, and urban/rural residence / Continent, pays ou zone et résidence, urbaine/rurale	Code[a]	Number - Nombre					Rate - Taux				
		2010	2011	2012	2013	2014	2010	2011	2012	2013	2014
ASIA - ASIE											
Republic of Korea - République de Corée[26]											
Total	+C	326 104	329 087	327 073	322 807	...	6.5	6.6	6.5	6.4	...
Urban - Urbaine[22]	+C	261 077	266 713	266 463	263 992	...	6.5	6.6	6.5	6.4	...
Rural - Rurale[22]	+C	56 502	54 441	52 829	50 906	...	6.0	5.8	5.6	5.5	...
Singapore - Singapour[27]											
Total	+C	24 363	27 258	27 936	26 254	28 407	6.5	7.2	7.3	6.8	7.3
Sri Lanka											
Total	+U	*200 985	*200 314	*198 710	*180 760	...	...	...	...	...	...
State of Palestine - État de Palestine											
Total	C	37 228	36 284	40 292	42 698	...	9.2	8.7	9.4	9.7	...
Syrian Arab Republic - République arabe syrienne[28]											
Total	+U	227 808	...	...	...	...	...	...	...	...	...
Tajikistan - Tadjikistan											
Total	+C	100 759	94 730	97 653	96 989	...	13.4	12.3	12.4	12.0	...
Urban - Urbaine	+C	25 624	25 068	25 115	25 306	...	12.8	12.3	12.0	11.8	...
Rural - Rurale	+C	75 135	69 662	72 538	71 683	...	13.6	12.3	12.5	12.1	...
Turkey - Turquie[29]											
Total	C	582 715	592 775	603 751	600 138	...	8.0	8.0	8.0	7.9	...
Uzbekistan - Ouzbékistan											
Total	C	292 300	287 800	299 000	304 900	...	10.4	9.9	10.1	10.2	...
EUROPE											
Åland Islands - Îles d'Åland											
Total	C	143	113	141	118	*114	5.1	4.0	5.0	4.1	*4.0
Urban - Urbaine	C	50	44	59	46	*53	4.5	3.9	5.2	4.0	*4.6
Rural - Rurale	C	93	69	82	72	*61	5.6	4.1	4.8	4.2	*3.5
Albania - Albanie											
Total	C	25 428	25 556	22 891	23 820	...	8.7	8.8	7.9	8.2	...
Andorra - Andorre											
Total	C	287	283	288	...	...	3.4	3.6	3.7	...	...
Austria - Autriche[30]											
Total	C	37 545	36 426	38 592	36 140	...	4.5	4.3	4.6	4.3	...
Belarus - Bélarus											
Total	C	76 978	86 785	76 245	87 127	...	8.1	9.2	8.1	9.2	...
Urban - Urbaine	C	63 813	71 795	62 828	71 702	...	9.0	10.0	8.7	9.9	...
Rural - Rurale	C	13 165	14 990	13 417	15 425	...	5.5	6.4	5.9	7.0	...
Belgium - Belgique[31]											
Total	C	42 159	41 001	*40 500	...	...	3.9	3.7	*3.6	...	...
Urban - Urbaine	C	41 582	40 455	...	...	...	3.9	3.7	...	...	...
Rural - Rurale	C	577	546	...	...	...	3.7	3.4	...	...	...
Bosnia and Herzegovina - Bosnie-Herzégovine											
Total	C	19 541	19 156	18 980	18 387	18 409	5.1	5.0	4.9	4.8	4.8
Bulgaria - Bulgarie[32]											
Total	C	24 286	21 448	21 167	21 943	...	3.2	2.9	2.9	3.0	...
Urban - Urbaine	C	19 262	16 704	16 357	...	...	3.6	3.1	3.1	...	...
Rural - Rurale	C	5 024	4 744	4 810	...	...	2.3	2.4	2.4	...	...
Croatia - Croatie											
Total	C	21 294	20 211	20 323	19 169	...	5.0	4.7	4.8	4.5	...
Urban - Urbaine	C	11 964	11 333	11 386	10 691	...	...	...	...	...	...
Rural - Rurale	C	9 330	8 878	8 937	8 478	...	...	...	...	...	...
Czech Republic - République tchèque											
Total	C	46 746	45 137	45 206	43 499	...	4.5	4.3	4.3	4.1	...
Urban - Urbaine	C	35 007	33 601	33 403	31 976	...	...	...	...	4.2	...
Rural - Rurale	C	11 739	11 536	11 803	11 523	...	...	...	...	4.1	...
Denmark - Danemark[33]											
Total	C	30 949	27 198	28 503	27 503	...	5.6	4.9	5.1	4.9	...
Estonia - Estonie											
Total	C	5 066	5 499	5 888	5 630	...	3.8	4.1	4.5	4.3	...
Urban - Urbaine[34]	C	3 515	3 837	4 000	3 963	...	3.9	4.2	4.4	4.4	...
Rural - Rurale[34]	C	1 352	1 396	1 594	1 368	...	3.2	3.3	3.8	3.3	...

22. Marriages and crude marriage rates, by urban/rural residence: 2010 - 2014
Mariages et taux bruts de nuptialité, selon la résidence, urbaine/rurale : 2010 - 2014 (continued - suite)

Continent, country or area, and urban/rural residence / Continent, pays ou zone et résidence, urbaine/rurale	Co-de[a]	Number - Nombre					Rate - Taux				
		2010	2011	2012	2013	2014	2010	2011	2012	2013	2014
EUROPE											
Faeroe Islands - Îles Féroé											
Total	C	232	206	237	259	...	4.8	4.2	4.9	5.4	...
Finland - Finlande											
Total	C	29 809[35]	28 295[35]	28 737[35]	25 119	...	5.6	5.3	5.3	4.6	...
Urban - Urbaine[35]	C	22 403	21 331	21 459	...	...	6.2	5.8	5.8	...	...
Rural - Rurale[35]	C	7 406	6 964	7 278	...	...	4.4	4.1	4.3	...	...
France[36]											
Total	C	245 334	231 100	239 840	225 784	...	3.9	3.7	3.8	3.5	...
Urban - Urbaine[37]	C	190 401	178 548	186 141	175 735	...	...	...	...	...	...
Rural - Rurale[37]	C	51 644	50 308	51 425	47 878	...	...	...	...	...	...
Germany - Allemagne											
Total	C	382 047	377 816	387 423	373 655	...	4.7	4.7	4.8	4.6	...
Gibraltar[38]											
Total	+C	198	176	204	195	...	6.3	5.5	6.3	6.0	...
Greece - Grèce											
Total	C	56 338	55 099	49 705	51 256	...	5.1	5.0	4.5	4.6	...
Urban - Urbaine	C	39 903	39 624	35 464	...	...	...	...	...	...	...
Rural - Rurale	C	16 435	15 475	14 241	...	...	...	...	...	...	...
Guernsey - Guernesey											
Total	C	334	340	325	...	...	5.3	5.4	5.2	...	...
Hungary - Hongrie[9]											
Total	C	35 520	35 812	36 161	36 986	...	3.6	3.6	3.6	3.7	...
Urban - Urbaine[39]	C	26 288	26 793	26 678	27 189	...	3.8	3.9	3.9	...	...
Rural - Rurale[39]	C	8 775	8 607	9 117	9 424	...	2.9	2.8	3.0	...	...
Iceland - Islande											
Total	C	1 547	1 456[40]	...	...	...	4.9	4.6	...	...	...
Urban - Urbaine[40]	C	...	1 432	...	...	...	...	4.6	...	...	...
Rural - Rurale[40]	C	...	24	...	...	...	...	...	...	...	...
Ireland - Irlande											
Total	+C	20 594	19 855	20 713	20 680	22 045	4.5	4.3	4.5	4.5	4.8
Italy - Italie											
Total	C	217 700	204 830	207 138	194 057	...	3.7	3.4	3.5	3.2	...
Jersey											
Total	+C	546	515	557	...	...	5.6	5.3	5.7	...	...
Latvia - Lettonie[8]											
Total	C	9 290	10 760	11 244	11 436	...	4.4	5.2	5.5	5.7	...
Urban - Urbaine	C	6 516	...	...	...	...	4.6	...	...	...	...
Rural - Rurale	C	2 774	...	...	...	...	4.1	...	...	...	...
Liechtenstein[8]											
Total	C	186	163	185	...	...	5.2	4.5	5.0	...	...
Lithuania - Lituanie											
Total	C	18 688	19 221	20 660	20 469	...	6.0	6.3	6.9	6.9	...
Urban - Urbaine	C	13 110	13 546	14 432	14 166	...	6.3	6.7	7.2	7.1	...
Rural - Rurale	C	5 578	5 675	6 228	6 303	...	5.4	5.6	6.3	6.5	...
Luxembourg[38]											
Total	C	1 749	1 714	1 782	1 722	...	3.5	3.3	3.4	3.2	...
Malta - Malte											
Total	C	2 596	2 562	2 823	2 578	...	6.3	6.2	6.7	6.1	...
Montenegro - Monténégro											
Total	C	3 675	3 528	3 305	3 847	...	6.0	5.7	5.3	6.2	...
Netherlands - Pays-Bas[41]											
Total	C	75 399	71 572	70 315	64 549	...	4.5	4.3	4.2	3.8	...
Norway - Norvège[13]											
Total	C	23 577	23 135	24 346	23 916	...	4.8	4.7	4.9	4.7	...
Poland - Pologne											
Total	C	228 337	206 471	203 850	180 396	...	5.9	5.4	5.3	4.7	...
Urban - Urbaine	C	137 218	122 737	119 401	...	...	5.9	5.2	5.1	...	...
Rural - Rurale	C	91 119	83 734	84 449	...	...	6.0	5.5	5.6	...	...
Portugal											
Total	C	39 993	36 035	34 423	31 998	...	3.8	3.4	3.3	3.1	...
Republic of Moldova - République de Moldova											
Total	C	26 483	25 900	24 262	24 449	...	7.4	7.3	6.8	6.9	...
Urban - Urbaine	C	13 242	13 191	12 287	...	...	9.0	8.9	8.3	...	...
Rural - Rurale	C	13 241	12 709	11 975	...	...	6.4	6.1	5.8	...	...

Continent, country or area, and urban/rural residence / Continent, pays ou zone et résidence, urbaine/rurale	Code[a]	Number - Nombre					Rate - Taux				
		2010	2011	2012	2013	2014	2010	2011	2012	2013	2014
EUROPE											
Romania - Roumanie											
Total	C	115 778	105 599	107 760	107 507	...	5.7	5.2	5.4	5.4	...
Urban - Urbaine	C	74 787	67 962	68 821	68 985	...	6.8	6.2	6.4	6.4	...
Rural - Rurale	C	40 991	37 637	38 939	38 522	...	4.4	4.1	4.2	4.2	...
Russian Federation - Fédération de Russie											
Total	C	1 215 066	1 316 011[42]	1 213 598[42]	...	...	8.5	9.2	8.5	...	...
Urban - Urbaine[42]	C	...	978 039	911 015	...	...	...	9.3	8.6	...	...
Rural - Rurale[42]	C	...	337 972	302 583	...	...	...	9.0	8.1	...	...
San Marino - Saint-Marin[43]											
Total	C	213	205	203	221		6.4	6.1	6.1	6.6	
Serbia - Serbie[44]											
Total	+C	35 815	35 808	34 639	36 209	...	4.9	4.9	4.8	5.1	...
Urban - Urbaine	+C	23 633	23 564	22 622	23 573	...	5.5	5.5	5.3	5.5	...
Rural - Rurale	+C	12 182	12 244	12 017	12 636	...	4.1	4.2	4.1	4.4	...
Slovakia - Slovaquie[8]											
Total	C	25 415	25 621	26 006	25 491	...	4.7	4.7	4.8	4.7	...
Urban - Urbaine	C	14 528	14 608	14 950	14 491	...	...	5.0	5.1	4.9	...
Rural - Rurale	C	10 887	11 013	11 056	11 000	...	...	4.5	4.5	4.4	...
Slovenia - Slovénie[45]											
Total	C	6 528	6 671	7 057	6 254	...	3.2	3.3	3.4	3.0	...
Urban - Urbaine	C	3 274	3 430	3 622	3 295	...	3.2	3.4	3.5	3.1	...
Rural - Rurale	C	3 254	3 241	3 435	2 959	...	3.2	3.2	3.3	2.9	...
Spain - Espagne											
Total	C	165 641	158 220	163 173	154 470	...	3.6	3.4	3.5	3.3	...
Sweden - Suède[13]											
Total	C	50 028	47 564	50 616	51 554	...	5.3	5.0	5.3	5.4	...
Switzerland - Suisse[46]											
Total	C	43 257	42 083	42 654	39 794	...	5.5	5.3	5.3	4.9	...
Urban - Urbaine	C	33 328	32 279	32 589	...	...	...	5.5	5.5	...	...
Rural - Rurale	C	9 929	9 804	10 065	...	...	...	4.7	4.8	...	...
TFYR of Macedonia - L'ex-R. y. de Macédoine											
Total	C	14 155	*14 797	13 991	13 982	...	6.9	*7.2	6.8	6.8	...
Urban - Urbaine	C	7 750	...	...	...	...	...	...	...	...	...
Rural - Rurale	C	6 405	...	...	...	...	...	...	...	...	...
Ukraine											
Total	+C	305 933	355 880	278 276	304 232	...	6.7	7.8	6.1	6.7	...
Urban - Urbaine	+C	231 680	270 245	211 819	235 108	...	7.4	8.6	6.8	...	...
Rural - Rurale	+C	74 253	85 635	66 457	69 124	...	5.2	6.0	4.7	...	...
United Kingdom of Great Britain and Northern Ireland - Royaume-Uni de Grande-Bretagne et d'Irlande du Nord[47]											
Total	C	280 444	285 391	...	...	...	4.5	4.5	...	...	...
OCEANIA - OCÉANIE											
American Samoa - Samoas américaines											
Total	C	227	191	...	...	...	3.4	...	...	...	...
Australia - Australie											
Total	+C	121 176	121 752	123 244	118 962	...	5.5	5.4	5.4	5.1	...
Cook Islands - Îles Cook[48]											
Total	+C	846	918	894	843	...	35.7	47.6	45.8	45.3	...
French Polynesia - Polynésie française											
Total	C	1 331	1 431	1 699	...	...	5.0	5.3	6.3	...	...
Guam											
Total	C	1 484	1 579	1 658	1 462	1 463	9.3	9.9	10.4	9.1	9.1
New Caledonia - Nouvelle-Calédonie											
Total	C	908	880	880	...	...	3.6	3.5	3.4	...	...

22. Marriages and crude marriage rates, by urban/rural residence: 2010 - 2014
Mariages et taux bruts de nuptialité, selon la résidence, urbaine/rurale : 2010 - 2014 (continued - suite)

Continent, country or area, and urban/rural residence / Continent, pays ou zone et résidence, urbaine/rurale	Co-de[a]	Number - Nombre					Rate - Taux				
		2010	2011	2012	2013	2014	2010	2011	2012	2013	2014
OCEANIA - OCÉANIE											
New Zealand - Nouvelle-Zélande[8]											
Total....................	+C	20 940	20 231	20 521	19 237[13]	...	4.8	4.6	4.7	4.3	...
Norfolk Island - Île Norfolk[49]											
Total....................	+C	26	34	31	19	15	...	14.8	...	...	...
Samoa											
Total....................	U	*1 052*	*953*	...	...	...	...	...	...	...	...

FOOTNOTES - NOTES

Italics: data from civil registers which are incomplete or of unknown completeness. - Italiques : données incomplètes ou dont le degré d'exactitude n'est pas connu, provenant des registres de l'état civil.

* Provisional. - Données provisoires.

[a] 'Code' indicates the source of data, as follows:
C - Civil registration, estimated over 90% complete
U - Civil registration, estimated less than 90% complete
| - Other source, estimated reliable
+ - Data tabulated by date of registration rather than occurence
... - Information not available

Le 'Code' indique la source des données, comme suit :
C - Registres de l'état civil considérés complèts à 90 p. 100 au moins
U - Registres de l'état civil qui ne sont pas considérés complèts à 90 p. 100 au moins
| - Autre source, considérée pas douteuses
+ - Données exploitées selon la date de l'enregistrement et non la date de l'événement
... - Information pas disponible

[1] Data refer to Algerian population only. - Les données ne concernent que la population algérienne.
[2] Including marriages resumed after 'revocable divorce' (among Moslem population), which approximates legal separation. - Y compris les unions reconstituées après un 'divorce révocable' (parmi la population musulmane), qui est à peu près l'équivalent d'une séparation légale.
[3] Excludes the islands of St. Brandon and Agalega. - Non compris les îles St. Brandon et Agalega.
[4] Including visitors. - Y compris les visiteurs.
[5] Excluding visitors. - Ne comprend pas les visiteurs.
[6] Including non-residents. - Y compris les non-résidents.
[7] Either bride or groom or both are residents. - Le marié, la mariée ou les deux sont résidents.
[8] Data refer to marriages registered at the place of residence of the groom. - Correspond aux mariages enregistrés dans le lieu de résidence du marié.
[9] Marriages registered by residence of bride. - Les mariages sont enregistrés selon le lieu de résidence de la mariée.
[10] Including marriages where bride/groom are non-residents. - Y compris les mariages pour lesquels le marié et la mariée sont des non-résidents.
[11] The difference between 'Total' and the sum of urban and rural is due to the unknown place of residence of bride/wife. Urban and rural distribution refers to the usual residence of the bride/wife. - La différence entre le « Total » et la somme des chiffres urbains et ruraux s'explique par le fait que le lieu de résidence de la mariée ou de la femme n'est pas toujours connu. La répartition entre résidence urbaine et résidence rurale fait référence au lieu de résidence habituel de la mariée ou de la femme.
[12] The increase in marriages is due to the project "Legally united families", coordinated by the Ministry of the Presidency. - L'augmentation des mariages est une conséquence du projet <<Familles légalement unies >> organisé par le ministère de la présidence.
[13] Includes same sex marriages. - Y compris les mariages entre personnes du même sexe.

[14] Urban and rural distribution refers to the usual residence of the groom/husband. - La répartition entre résidence urbaine et résidence rurale fait référence au lieu de résidence habituel du marié ou du mari.
[15] Excludes nomadic Indian tribes. - Non compris les tribus d'Indiens nomades.
[16] Excluding Amerindians. - Non compris les Amérindiens.
[17] Data are compiled from the National Registers of Identification and Civil Status (RENIEC). - Les données sont rédigées à partir des Registres Nationaux d'Identification et d'État Civil (RENIEC).
[18] For statistical purposes, the data for China do not include those for the Hong Kong Special Administrative Region (Hong Kong SAR), Macao Special Administrative Region (Macao SAR) and Taiwan province of China. - Pour la présentation des statistiques, les données pour la Chine ne comprennent pas la Région Administrative Spéciale de Hong Kong (Hong Kong RAS), la Région Administrative Spéciale de Macao (Macao RAS) et Taïwan province de Chine.
[19] Data refer to government controlled areas. Data refer to marriages of residents only. - Les données se rapportent aux zones contrôlées par le Gouvernement. Les données ne portent que sur les mariages de résidents.
[20] Data refer to the Iranian Year which begins on 21 March and ends on 20 March of the following year. - Les données concernent l'année iranienne, qui commence le 21 mars et se termine le 20 mars de l'année suivante.
[21] Includes data for East Jerusalem and Israeli residents in certain other territories under occupation by Israeli military forces since June 1967. - Y compris les données pour Jérusalem-Est et les résidents israéliens dans certains autres territoires occupés depuis 1967 par les forces armées israéliennes.
[22] The total number may include 'Unknown residence', but the categories urban and rural do not. Urban and rural distribution refers to the usual residence of the groom/husband. - Le nombre total peut inclure les personnes dont la résidence n'est pas connue, à l'inverse des catégories de population urbaine et rurale. La répartition entre résidence urbaine et résidence rurale fait référence au lieu de résidence habituel du marié ou du mari.
[23] Data refer to Japanese nationals in Japan only. - Les données se raportent aux nationaux japonais au Japon seulement.
[24] Excluding data for Jordanian territory under occupation since June 1967 by Israeli military forces. Excluding foreigners, including registered Palestinian refugees. - Non compris les données pour le territoire jordanien occupé depuis juin 1967 par les forces armées israéliennes. Non compris les étrangers, mais y compris les réfugiés de Palestine enregistrés.
[25] Data refer to registered events only. - Les données ne concernent que les événements enregistrés.
[26] Excluding alien armed forces, civilian aliens employed by armed forces, and foreign diplomatic personnel and their dependants. - Non compris les militaires étrangers, les civils étrangers employés par les forces armées ni le personnel diplomatique étranger et les membres de leur famille les accompagnant.
[27] Excluding marriages previously officiated outside Singapore or under religious and customary rites. - Ne comprend pas les mariages prononcés ailleurs qu'à Singapour ni les mariages religieux ou coutumiers.
[28] Excluding nomad population. - Non compris les nomades.
[29] Data from MERNIS (Central Population Administrative System). - Données de MERNIS (Système central de données démographiques).
[30] Excluding aliens temporarily in the area. - Non compris les étrangers se trouvant temporairement dans le territoire.
[31] Including armed forces stationed outside the country and alien armed forces in the area, if the marriage is performed by local authority. - Y compris les militaires nationaux hors du pays et les militaires étrangers en garnison sur le territoire, si le mariage a été célébré par l'autorité locale.
[32] Including nationals outside the country, but excluding foreigners in the country. - Y compris les nationaux à l'étranger, mais non compris les étrangers sur le territoire.

[33] Excluding Faeroe Islands and Greenland shown separately, if available. - Non compris les Iles Féroé et le Groenland, qui font l'objet de rubriques distinctes, si disponible.

[34] Urban and rural distribution of marriages and divorces is displayed by place of residence of groom/husband. The difference between 'Total' and the sum of urban and rural is due to the unknown place of residence of grooms/husbands and to grooms/husbands living outside the country. - La répartition des mariages et des divorces entre zones urbaines et zones rurales est fondée sur le lieu de résidence du marié ou du mari. La différence entre le « Total » et la somme des chiffres urbains et ruraux s'explique par le fait que la résidence du marié ou du mari n'est pas toujours connue ou est située à l'étranger.

[35] Only marriages in which the bride was resident in Finland. Excluding Åland Islands. - Ne porte que sur les mariages pour lesquels la mariée réside en Finlande. Non compris les Îles d'Åland.

[36] Including armed forces stationed outside the country. - Y compris les militaires nationaux hors du pays.

[37] The data for urban and rural exclude the nationals outside the country. - Les données relatives à la population urbaine et rurale n'englobent pas les nationaux se trouvant à l'étranger.

[38] Data refer to marriages where one or both partners are residents. - Les données portent sur les mariages pour lesquels l'un des deux partenaires ou les deux sont résidents.

[39] The urban and rural categories do not include the data of foreigners, persons of unknown residence and the homeless, whereas the total category includes them. - Les chiffres portant sur la population urbaine et rurale n' incluent pas les données relatives aux étrangers, aux personnes dont la résidence n'est pas connue et aux personnes sans domicile fixe, à l'inverse, le total les inclut.

[40] Definition of localities was revised in 2011 causing a break with the previous series. Data for residence abroad are excluded. Data refer to common residence after marriage. - La rupture par rapport aux séries précédentes s'explique par le fait que la définition des localités a été révisée depuis 2011. Les données relatives aux résidents à l'étranger sont exclues. Données se rapportant à la résidence commune après le mariage.

[41] Marriages of couples of which at least one partner is recorded in a Dutch municipal register, irrespective of the country where the marriage was performed. Includes same sex marriages. Including residents outside the country if listed in a Netherlands population register. - Correspond aux mariages pour lesquels au moins l'un des partenaires est inscrit sur un registre municipal néerlandais, quel que soit le pays dans lequel le mariage est célébré. Y compris les mariages entre personnes du même sexe. Englobe les résidents se trouvant à l'étranger à condition qu'ils soient inscrits sur le registre de population des Pays-Bas.

[42] Data refer to population 15 years of age or more. - Les données concernent la population âgée de 15 ans ou plus.

[43] Includes civil and religious marriages as well as not specified. - Englobe les mariages civils et religieux et ceux pour lesquels rien n'a été indiqué.

[44] Excludes data for Kosovo and Metohia. - Sans les données pour le Kosovo et Metohie.

[45] Data refer to residence of groom or bride before marriage. - Données relatives au lieu de résidence du marié ou de la mariée avant le mariage.

[46] Data based on the residence of groom if he has permanent address in the country, otherwise, based on the residence of bride. If neither partner is a permanent resident, the marriage is not included in the official statistics. - Les données sont fondées sur la résidence du marié si celui-ci a une adresse permanente dans le pays, sinon elles sont fondées sur la résidence de la mariée. Si aucun des deux partenaires n'est un résident permanent, le mariage n'apparaît pas dans les statistiques officielles.

[47] Excluding Channel Islands (Guernsey and Jersey) and Isle of Man, shown separately, if available. - Non compris les îles Anglo-Normandes (Guernesey et Jersey) et l'île de Man, qui font l'objet de rubriques distinctes, si disponible.

[48] Excluding Niue, shown separately, which is part of Cook Islands, but because of remoteness is administered separately. - Non compris Nioué, qui fait l'objet d'une rubrique distincte et qui fait partie des îles Cook, mais qui, en raison de son éloignement, est administrée séparément.

[49] Data cover the period from 1 July of the previous year to 30 June of the present year. - Pour la période allant du 1er juillet de l'année précédente au 30 juin de l'année en cours.

Table 23 - *Demographic Yearbook 2014*

Table 23 presents the marriages cross-classified by age of groom and age of bride for the latest available year between 2005 and 2014.

Description of variables: Marriage is defined as the act, ceremony or process by which the legal relationship of spouses is constituted. The legality of the union may be established by civil, religious or other means as recognized by the laws of each country[1].

Marriage statistics in this table, therefore, include both first marriages and remarriages after divorce, widowhood or annulment. They do not, unless otherwise noted, include resumption of marriage ties after legal separation. These statistics refer to the number of marriages performed, and not to the number of persons marrying.

Age is defined as age at last birthday, that is, the difference between the date of birth and the date of the occurrence of the event, expressed in completed solar years. The age classification used for brides in this table is the following: under 15 years, 5-year age groups through 90-94, and 95 years and over, depending on the availability of data. Age classification for grooms is restricted to: under 15 years, 5-year age groups from 15 to 59, and 60 years and over.

In an effort to provide interpretation of these statistics, countries or areas providing data on marriages by age of groom and bride have been requested to specify "the minimum legal age at which marriage can take place with and without parental consent". This information is presented in the table 23-1 below.

Reliability of data: Data from civil registers of marriages that are reported as incomplete (less than 90 per cent completeness) or of unknown completeness are considered unreliable and are set in *italics* rather than in roman type. Table 22 and the technical notes for that table provide more detailed information on the completeness of marriage registration. For more information about the quality of vital statistics data in general, see Section 4.2 of the Technical Notes.

Limitations: Statistics on marriages by age of groom and age of bride are subject to the same qualifications as have been set forth for vital statistics in general and marriage statistics in particular as discussed in Section 4 of the Technical Notes.

The fact that marriage is a legal event, unlike birth and death that are biological events, has implications for international comparability of data. Marriage has been defined, for statistical purposes, in terms of the laws of individual countries or areas. These laws vary throughout the world. In addition, comparability is further limited because some countries or areas compile statistics only for civil marriages although religious marriages may also be legally recognized; in other countries or areas, the only available records are church registers and, therefore, the statistics may not reflect marriages that are civil marriages only.

Because in many countries or areas marriage is a civil legal contract which, to establish its legality, must be celebrated before a civil officer, it follows that for these countries or areas registration would tend to be almost automatic at the time of, or immediately following, the marriage ceremony. This factor should be kept in mind when considering the reliability of data, described above.

Because these statistics are classified according to age, they are subject to the limitations with respect to accuracy of age reporting similar to those already discussed in connection with Section 3.1.3 of the Technical Notes. It is probable that biases are less pronounced in marriage statistics, because information is obtained from the persons concerned and since marriage is a legal act, the participants are likely to give correct information. However, in some countries or areas, there appears to be a concentration of marriages at the legal minimum age for marriage and at the age at which valid marriage may be contracted without parental consent, indicating perhaps an overstatement in some cases to comply with the law.

Aside from the possibility of age misreporting, it should be noted that marriage patterns at younger ages, that is, for ages up to 24 years, are influenced to a large extent by laws regarding the minimum age for marriage.

Factors that may influence age reporting, particularly at older ages include an inclination to understate the age of the bride in order that it may be equal to or less than that of the groom.

The absence of data in the unknown age group does not necessarily indicate completely accurate reporting and tabulation of the age item. It is sometimes an indication that the unknowns have been eliminated by assigning ages to them before tabulation, or by proportionate distribution after tabulation.

Another age-reporting factor that must be kept in mind in using these data is the variation that may result from calculating age at marriage from year of birth rather than from day, month and year of birth. Information on this factor is given in footnotes when known.

Earlier data: Marriages by age of groom and age of bride have been shown for the latest available year in most issues of the *Demographic Yearbook*. Data cross-classified by age of groom and bride have been presented in previous issues featuring marriage and divorce statistics. For information on the specific topics and the years covered, readers should consult the Historical Index.

23-1 Minimum legal age at which marriage can take place

Country or area	With parental consent		Without parental consent	
	Groom	Bride	Groom	Bride
Africa				
Botswana	18	18	21	21
Burkina Faso[2]	18	15	20	17
Burundi[4]			21	18
Egypt	18	16	21	21
Ghana			18	18
Liberia	16	16	21	18
Libya[3]	18	18		
Malawi[4]			18	18
Mauritius	16	16	18	18
Morocco[4]			18	18
Namibia	18	18	21	21
Saint Helena ex. Dep.	16	16	21	21
Senegal	Under 18	Under 18	18	18
Seychelles	16	16	18	18
Sierra Leone[4]			18	18
South Africa	18	15	21	21
Swaziland	18	18	21	21
Uganda[4, 5]			18	18
Zimbabwe	16	16	18	18
America, North				
Anguilla	16	16	18	18
Aruba	18	16	18	18
Bermuda	16	16	18	18
Canada[6]	16	16	18	18
Cayman Islands	16	16	18	18
Costa Rica	15	15	18	18
Cuba	16	14	18	16
Curaçao			18	18
Dominican Republic	16	15	18	18

Country or area	With parental consent		Without parental consent	
	Groom	Bride	Groom	Bride
El Salvador	15	14	18	18
Greenland[4]			18	18
Jamaica	16	16	18	18
Mexico[7]	16	14	18	18
Montserrat[8]	16	16	18	18
Panama	16	14	18	18
Puerto Rico	18	16	21	21
Trinidad and Tobago[9]	Under 18	Under 18	18	18
America, South				
Brazil	16	16	18	18
Chile	16	16	18	18
Colombia	14	14	18	18
Ecuador	12	12	18	18
Suriname	17	15	21	21
Uruguay	16	16	18	18
Venezuela (Bolivarian Republic of)	14	12	18	18
Asia				
Armenia			18	17
Azerbaijan	18	17		
Bahrain			15	
Cambodia			18	18
China, Hong Kong SAR	16	16	21	21
China, Macao SAR	16	16	18	18
Cyprus	16	16	18	18
Georgia	16	16	18	18
Indonesia			19	16
Iran	18	15		
Israel[4]			17	17
Japan	18	16	20	20
Kazakhstan	16	16	18	17
Kyrgyzstan	16	16	18	18
Malaysia[10]	18	16 and 18	18 and 21	16 and 21
Nepal	18	18	20	20
Oman[4]			18	18
Philippines	18	18	21	21
Republic of Korea	18	18	20	20
Singapore[11]	Under 21	Under 21	21	21
State of Palestine[12]		14.5	15.5	
Tajikistan	17	17	18	18
Turkey	16	16	18	18

Country or area	With parental consent		Without parental consent	
	Groom	*Bride*	*Groom*	*Bride*
Uzbekistan			17	17
Europe				
Åland Islands[16]			18	18
Albania			18	18
Austria[13]	16	16	18	18
Belarus[14]			18	18
Belgium			18	18
Bosnia and Herzegovina			18	18
Bulgaria	16	16	18	18
Croatia	16	16	18	18
Czech Republic[15]	16	16	18	18
Denmark	15	15	18	18
Estonia	15	15	18	18
Faeroe Islands			18	18
Finland[16]			18	18
France[4]			18	18
Germany[17]	16	16	18	18
Gibraltar	16	16	18	18
Greece[18]			18	18
Hungary	16	16	18	18
Iceland	No limit	No limit	18	18
Ireland[4,19]			18	18
Isle of Man	16	16	18	18
Italy	16	16	18	18
Jersey	16	16	18	18
Latvia	16	16	18	18
Liechtenstein[13]			18	18
Lithuania[20]	15	15	18	18
Luxembourg			18	18
Malta			16	16
Montenegro	16	16	18	18
Netherlands	16	16	18	18
Norway	16	16	18	18
Poland[21]			18	18
Portugal	16	16	18	18
Republic of Moldova			18	16
Romania	16	16	18	18
Russian Federation	16	16	18	18
Serbia[22]	16	16	18	18

Country or area	With parental consent		Without parental consent	
	Groom	*Bride*	*Groom*	*Bride*
Slovakia			16	16
Slovenia	15	15	18	18
Spain	14	14	18	18
Sweden[23]			18	18
Switzerland	16	16	18	18
TFYR of Macedonia	16	16	18	18
Ukraine[13]	16	16	18	18
United Kingdom of Great Britain and Northern Ireland	16	16	18	18
Oceania				
Australia	16	16	18	18
Cook Islands	16	16	21	21
Guam[24]	Under 18	Under 18	18	18
New Caledonia			18	18
New Zealand	16	16	18	18

NOTES

[1] *Principles and Recommendations for a Vital Statistics System Revision 3,* Sales No. E.13.XVII.10, United Nations, New York, 2014.

[2] In addition, an age waiver may be granted by a civil court for a serious reason from 15 years for women and 18 years for men.

[3] According to the Islamic law, marriage requires parental consent. Consent of the bride herself, as well as the guardian's consent are fundamental in the marriage contract. Young men usually choose the consent of the parents. Minimum age at marriage is usually 18 years. According to the law, marriage is not restricted to individuals over the age of 18 years.

[4] The minimum legal age at which marriage can take place is the same respectively for bride and groom with or without parental consent.

[5] As reported by Uganda Bureau of Statistics, marriages with or without parental consent may occur much earlier than 18 years of age.

[6] Marriage is under provincial and territory legislations. Without parental consent, the minimum legal age at which marriage can take place is 18 years of age in all provinces and territories in Canada except in British Columbia, Newfoundland and Labrador, Nova Scotia, Nunavut, and Yukon where the minimum legal age is 19 years. With parental consent, the minimum legal age is 16 years in all provinces except in Northwest Territories, Nunavut, and Yukon. With parental consent, in Northwest Territories, and Yukon the minimum legal age is 15 years whereas in Nunavut, the minimum legal age is 18 years.

[7] Each of the 31 Federal States and the Federal District has its own civil code for marriage. Exceptions to ages given in the table are as follows: without parental consent, the minimum legal age at which marriage can take place in Baja California and Tlaxcala is 16 years for males and 14 years for females whereas in Baja California Sur, it is 16 years for females. With parental consent, the minimum legal age for marriage is 16 years for both males and females in Aguascalientes, Campeche, Chiapas, Distrito Federal, Guerrero, Jalisco, Morelos, Puebla, Quintana Roo, Querétaro, San Luis Potosí, and Sonora. With parental consent, the minimum legal age for marriage is under 18 years for both males and females in Coahuila, Hidalgo, and Zacatecas. The Minimum legal age for marriage remains the same respectively for bride and groom with or without parental consent in Baja California, Baja California Sur and Tlaxcala.

[8] Consent can be given by a guardian or a person who has custody of the child wishing to marry. Also the Governor has discretion to permit persons as young as 15 years and 1 day old to marry, if he thinks that getting married is in the best interest of the persons who are intending to marry and the persons in this instance must have also received the necessary consent.

[9] With parental consent, age for marriage is 14 years for males and 12 years for females in a civil marriage; 16 years for males and 12 years for females in a Muslim marriage; 18 years for males and 14 years for females in a Hindu marriage; and 18 years for males and 16 for females in Orisa marriage.

[10] Without parental consent, it is 21 years of age for non-Muslim males and 18 years of age for Muslim males whereas it is 21 years of age for non-Muslim females and 16 years of age for Muslim females. For marriage with parental consent, it is 18 years of age for males whereas it is 18 years of age for non-Muslim females and 16 years of age for Muslim females.

[11] Specified minimum legal marriage age refers to marriages contracted under the Women's Charter. For Muslim marriages under the Administration of Muslim Law Act, no marriage shall be solemnised when either party is below the age of 18 years. Notwithstanding that, Muslim women below the age of 18 years who have attained the age of puberty may be married under the Administration of the Muslim Law Act.

[12] The legal marriage age for females is 14 years, 6 months and 22 days. There must be parental consent (father or brother if the father is dead). The legal marriage age for males is 15 years, 6 months and 21 days. Parental consent is not required.

[13] Persons less than 18 years old need a decision of the court.

[14] In compliance with the Marriage and Family Code of the Republic of Belarus, in the exclusive cases related to pregnancy, childbirth, and in case of acquiring by a juvenile of a full legal capacity under lawful age, the civil registration offices are in a position to reduce the marriage age of espousing persons, but not more than by 3 years. The marriage age is to be reduced by an application of espousing persons; the parental consent is not required.

[15] If it is in accordance with the social purpose of marriage, only the court may, for important reasons, allow the marriage of a minor over 16 years.

[16] Persons less than 18 years old need the permission of the Ministry of Justice.

[17] Marriage at 16-17 years of age requires that the other spouse be an adult already betrothed (18 years) and an exemption from the requirement of majority by a competent family court.

[18] Under some conditions (e.g. pregnancy) the marriage can take place without age restrictions.

[19] An exemption on the minimum age can be granted by court order if granting of such an exemption is in the best interests of the parties to the intended marriage and good reasons for the application can be demonstrated.

[20] In addition to parental consent, persons less than 18 years old need judicial approval. In case of pregnancy, marriage can be allowed below 15 years of age.

[21] Females can marry at the age of 16 or 17 years with parental and court consent.

[22] A marriage cannot be entered into by a minor. The court may exceptionally and for important reasons approve of entrance into marriage by a minor older than sixteen years. Without this approval, the marriage is invalid and the court shall declare the invalidity even without a petition.

[23] With parental consent, no limit but authorities must approve; without parental consent, 18 years of age for Swedish citizens.

[24] Under 18, both a court order and parent or legal guardian consent are needed.

Tableau 23 – *Annuaire démographique 2014*

Le tableau 23 présente des statistiques concernant les mariages classés selon l'âge de l'époux et selon l'âge de l'épouse pour les années où les données sont disponibles entre 2005 et 2014.

Description des variables : le mariage désigne l'acte, la cérémonie ou la procédure qui établit un rapport légal entre les époux. L'union peut être rendue légale par une procédure civile ou religieuse, ou par toute autre procédure, conformément à la législation du pays[1].

Les statistiques de la nuptialité présentées dans ce tableau comprennent donc les premiers mariages et les remariages faisant suite à un divorce, un veuvage ou une annulation. Toutefois, sauf indication contraire, elles ne comprennent pas les unions reconstituées après une séparation légale. Ces statistiques se rapportent au nombre de mariages célébrés, non au nombre de personnes qui se marient.

L'âge désigne l'âge au dernier anniversaire, c'est-à-dire la différence entre la date de naissance et la date de l'événement, exprimée en années solaires révolues. Le classement par âge pour l'épouse utilisé dans ce tableau comprend les groupes suivants : moins de 15 ans, groupes quinquennaux jusqu'à 90-94 ans, et 95 ans et plus, selon la disponibilité des données. Le classement par âge pour l'époux est : moins de 15 ans, groupes quinquennal de 15 jusqu' à 59 ans et 60 ans et plus.

Dans un effort de fournir l'interprétation de ces statistiques, les pays ou les zones fournissant des données sur les mariages par l'âge de l'épouse et de par l'âge de l'époux ont été demandés d'indiquer "l'âge légal minimum avec auquel le mariage peut avoir lieu avec et sans consentement parental". Cette information est présentée dans le tableau 23-1 ci-dessous.

Fiabilité des données : les données sur les mariages issues des registres de l'état civil qui sont déclarées incomplètes (degré de complétude inférieur à 90 p. 100) ou dont le degré de complétude n'est pas connu sont jugées douteuses et apparaissent en italique et non en caractères romains. Le tableau 22 et les notes techniques s'y rapportant présentent des renseignements plus détaillés sur le degré de complétude de l'enregistrement des mariages. Pour plus de précisions sur la qualité des données reposant sur les statistiques de l'état civil en général, voir la section 4.2 des notes techniques.

Insuffisance des données : les statistiques des mariages selon l'âge de l'époux et selon l'âge de l'épouse appellent les mêmes réserves que celles formulées à propos des statistiques de l'état civil en général et des statistiques de la nuptialité en particulier (voir la section 4 des Notes techniques).

Le fait que le mariage soit un acte juridique, à la différence de la naissance et du décès, qui sont des faits biologiques, a des répercussions sur la comparabilité internationale des données. Aux fins de la statistique, le mariage est défini par la législation de chaque pays ou zone. Cette législation varie d'un pays à l'autre. La comparabilité est limitée en outre du fait que certains pays et zones ne réunissent des statistiques que pour les mariages civils, bien que les mariages religieux y soient également reconnus par la loi ; dans d'autres, les seuls relevés disponibles sont les registres des églises et, en conséquence, les statistiques peuvent ne pas rendre compte des mariages exclusivement civils.

Le mariage étant, dans de nombreux pays ou zones, un contrat juridique civil qui, pour être légal, doit être conclu devant un officier d'état civil, il s'ensuit que, dans ces pays ou zones, l'enregistrement se fait à peu près systématiquement au moment de la cérémonie ou immédiatement après. Il faut tenir compte de cet élément lorsque l'on évalue la fiabilité des données, dont il est question plus haut.

Étant donné que ces statistiques sont classées selon l'âge, elles appellent les mêmes réserves concernant l'exactitude des déclarations d'âge que celles dont il a déjà été question à la section 3.1.3 des Notes techniques. Il est probable que les statistiques de la nuptialité sont moins faussées par ce genre d'erreur, car les renseignements sont donnés par les intéressés eux-mêmes, et, comme le mariage est un acte juridique, il y a toutes chances que leurs déclarations soient exactes. Toutefois, dans certains pays ou zones, il semble y avoir une concentration de mariages à l'âge minimal légal de nubilité ainsi qu'à l'âge auquel le mariage peut être valablement contracté sans le consentement des parents, ce qui peut indiquer que certains déclarants se vieillissent pour se conformer à la loi.

Outre la possibilité d'erreurs dans les déclarations d'âge, il convient de noter que la législation fixant l'âge minimal de nubilité influe notablement sur les caractéristiques de la nuptialité pour les premiers âges, c'est-à-dire jusqu'à 24 ans.

Parmi les facteurs pouvant exercer une influence sur les déclarations d'âge, en particulier celles qui sont faites par des personnes plus âgées, il faut citer la tendance à diminuer l'âge de l'épouse de façon qu'il soit égal ou inférieur à celui de l'époux.

Si aucun nombre ne figure dans la rangée réservée aux âges inconnus, cela ne signifie pas nécessairement que les déclarations d'âge et l'exploitation des données par âge aient été tout à fait exactes. C'est parfois une indication que l'on a attribué un âge aux personnes d'âge inconnu avant l'exploitation des données ou qu'elles ont été réparties proportionnellement entre les différents groupes après cette opération.

Il importe de ne pas oublier non plus, lorsque l'on utilisera ces données, que l'on calcule parfois l'âge des conjoints au moment du mariage sur la base de l'année de naissance seulement et non d'après la date exacte (jour, mois et année) de naissance. Des renseignements à ce sujet sont donnés en note chaque fois que possible.

Donnés publiées antérieurement : on trouve dans la plupart des éditions de l'*Annuaire démographique* des statistiques concernant les mariages selon l'âge de l'époux et selon l'âge de l'épouse qui ont été établies à partir des données les plus récentes dont on disposait à l'époque. Des données croisant l'âge des époux ont été présentées dans des éditions antérieurs, plus particulièrement consacrées aux statistiques de la nuptialité et de la divortialité. Pour plus de précisions concernant les années et les sujets pour lesquels des données ont été publiées, se reporter à l'index historique.

23-1 L'âge légal minimum avec auquel le mariage peut avoir lieu

Pays ou zone	Avec consentement parental		Sans consentement parental	
	Epoux	Epouse	Epoux	Epouse
Afrique				
Afrique du Sud	18	15	21	21
Botswana	18	18	21	21
Burkina Faso[2]	18	15	20	17
Burundi[4]			21	18
Egypte	18	16	21	21
Ghana			18	18
Libéria	16	16	21	18
Libye[3]	18	18		
Malawi[4]			18	18
Maurice	16	16	18	18
Maroc[4]			18	18
Namibie	18	18	21	21
Ouganda[4, 5]			18	18
Sainte-Hélène sans dép.	16	16	21	21
Sénégal	moins de 18	moins de 18	18	18
Seychelles	16	16	18	18
Sierra Leone[4]			18	18
Swaziland	18	18	21	21
Zimbabwe	16	16	18	18
Amérique du Nord				
Anguilla	16	16	18	18
Aruba	18	16	18	18
Bermudes	16	16	18	18

Pays ou zone	Avec consentement parental		Sans consentement parental	
	Epoux	Epouse	Epoux	Epouse
Canada[6]	16	16	18	18
Costa Rica	15	15	18	18
Cuba	16	14	18	16
Curaçao			18	18
El Salvador	15	14	18	18
Groenland[4]			18	18
Îles Caïmanes	16	16	18	18
Jamaïque	16	16	18	18
Mexique[7]	16	14	18	18
Montserrat[8]	16	16	18	18
Panama	16	14	18	18
Porto Rico	18	16	21	21
République dominicaine	16	15	18	18
Trinité-et-Tobago[9]	moins de 18	moins de 18	18	18
Amérique du Sud				
Brésil	16	16	18	18
Chili	16	16	18	18
Colombie	14	14	18	18
Equateur	12	12	18	18
Suriname	17	15	21	21
Uruguay	16	16	18	18
Venezuela (République bolivarienne du)	14	12	18	18
Asie				
Arménie			18	17
Azerbaïdjan	18	17		
Bahreïn			15	
Cambodge			18	18
Chine, Hong Kong RAS	16	16	21	21
Chine, Macao RAS	16	16	18	18
Chypre	16	16	18	18
État de Palestine[10]		14.5	15.5	
Géorgie	16	16	18	18
Indonésie			19	16
Iran (République islamique d')	18	15		
Israël[4]			17	17
Japon	18	16	20	20
Kazakhstan	16	16	18	17
Kirghizistan	16	16	18	18

Pays ou zone	Avec consentement parental		Sans consentement parental	
	Epoux	Epouse	Epoux	Epouse
Malaisie[11]	18	16 et 18	18 et 21	16 et 21
Népal	18	18	20	20
Oman[4]			18	18
Ouzbékistan			17	17
Philippines	18	18	21	21
République de Corée	18	18	20	20
Singapour[12]	moins de 21	moins de 21	21	21
Tadjikistan	17	17	18	18
Turquie	16	16	18	18
Europe				
Albanie			18	18
Allemagne[13]	16	16	18	18
Autriche[14]	16	16	18	18
Bélarus[15]			18	18
Belgique			18	18
Bosnie-Herzégovine			18	18
Bulgarie	16	16	18	18
Croatie	16	16	18	18
Danemark	15	15	18	18
Espagne	14	14	18	18
Estonie	15	15	18	18
Fédération de Russie	16	16	18	18
Finlande[16]			18	18
France[4]			18	18
Gibraltar	16	16	18	18
Grèce[17]			18	18
Hongrie	16	16	18	18
Île de Man	16	16	18	18
Îles d'Åland			18	18
Îles Féroé			18	18
Irlande[4, 18]			18	18
Islande[4]			18	18
Italie	16	16	18	18
Jersey	16	16	18	18
L'ex-R. y. de Macédoine	16	16	18	18
Lettonie	16	16	18	18
Liechtenstein[144]			18	18

Pays ou zone	Avec consentement parental		Sans consentement parental	
	Epoux	Epouse	Epoux	Epouse
Lituanie[19]	15	15	18	18
Luxembourg			18	18
Malte			16	16
Monténégro	16	16	18	18
Norvège	16	16	18	18
Pays-Bas	16	16	18	18
Pologne[20]			18	18
Portugal	16	16	18	18
République de Moldova			18	16
République tchèque	16	16	18	18
Roumanie	16	16	18	18
Royaume-Uni de Grande-Bretagne et d'Irlande du Nord	16	16	18	18
Serbie[21]	16	16	18	18
Slovaque			16	16
Slovénie	15	15	18	18
Suede[22]			18	18
Suisse	16	16	18	18
Ukraine	16	16	18	18
Océanie				
Australie	16	16	18	18
Guam	Moins de 18	Moins de 18	18	18
Îles Cook	16	16	21	21
Nouvelle-Calédonie			18	18
Nouvelle-Zélande	16	16	18	18

NOTES

[1] *Principes et recommandations pour un système de statistique de l'état civil, troisième révision,* numéro de vente : E.13.XVII.10, publication des Nations Unies, New York, 2014.

[2] De plus, une dispense d'âge peut être accordée par un tribunal civil pour motif grave à partir de 15 ans pour les femmes et de 18 ans pour les hommes.

[3] Conformément à la loi islamique, le mariage requiert le consentement parental. Le consentement de la mariée, elle-même ainsi que le consentement du tuteur sont fondamentaux dans le contrat de mariage. Les jeunes hommes choisissent habituellement le consentement des parents. L'âge minimum du mariage est généralement 18 ans. Conformément à la loi, le mariage n'est pas limité aux individus âgés de plus de 18 ans.

[4] L'âge minimum légal du mariage est le même respectivement pour le marié et la mariée, avec ou sans le consentement parental.

[5] Tel que le signale l' "Uganda Bureau of Statistics", les mariages avec ou sans le consentement parental peuvent se produire beaucoup plus tôt que 18 ans.

[6] Le mariage est en vertu des législations provinciales et territoriales. Sans le consentement des parents, l'âge minimum légal du mariage est de 18 ans dans toutes les provinces et territoires du Canada sauf en Colombie-Britannique, Terre-Neuve-et-Labrador, la Nouvelle-

Écosse, du Nunavut et du Yukon, où l'âge minimum légal est de 19 ans. Avec le consentement des parents, l'âge minimum légal est de 16 ans dans toutes les provinces sauf dans les Territoires du Nord-Ouest, Nunavut et Yukon. Avec le consentement des parents, dans les Territoires du Nord-Ouest et le Yukon l'âge minimum légal est de 15 ans alors que dans le Nunavut, l'âge minimum légal est de 18 ans.

[7] Chacun des 31 Etats fédéraux et du District fédéral a son propre code civil pour le mariage. Les exceptions aux âges figurant sur le tableau sont les suivantes : sans le consentement des parents, l'âge minimum légal du mariage en Basse-Californie et au Tlaxcala est de 16 ans pour les hommes et 14 ans pour les femmes alors que dans la Basse-Californie du Sud, il est de 16 ans pour les femmesfemelles. Avec le consentement des parents, l'âge minimum légal du mariage est de 16 ans pour les hommes et les femmes les femelles à Aguascalientes, Campeche, Chiapas, Distrito Federal, Guerrero, Jalisco, Morelos, Puebla, Quintana Roo, Querétaro, San Luis Potosí et Sonora. Avec le consentement des parents, l'âge minimum légal du mariage est en-dessous de 18 ans pour les hommes et femmes à Coahuila, Hidalgo, et Zacatecas. L'âge minimum légal du mariage reste le même, respectivement pour les mariés avec ou sans le consentement parental en Basse-Californie, Basse Californie du Sud et Tlaxcala.

[8] Le consentement peut être donné par un tuteur ou une personne qui a la garde de l'enfant qui souhaitent se marier. En outre, le gouverneur a la faculté de permettre aux personnes âgés d'au moins 15 ans et 1 jour de se marier, s'il pense que le mariage est dans le meilleur intérêt des personnes qui ont l'intention de s'unir et que les personnes concernées aient également reçu le consentement nécessaire.

[9] Avec l'âge du le consentement parental, l'âge minimum du mariage pour se marier est de 14 ans pour les hommes et de 12 ans pour les femmes pour un mariage civil ; de 16 ans pour les hommes et de 12 ans pour les femmes pour un mariage musulman ; de 18 ans pour les hommes et de 14 ans pour les femmes pour un mariage hindou, et de18 ans pour les hommes et de 16 pour les femmes pour un mariage orisa.

[10] L'âge légal du mariage pour les femmes est de 14 ans, 6 mois et 22 jours. Le consentement parental (du père ou du frère si le père est mort) est requis. L'âge légal du mariage pour les hommes est de 15 ans, 6 mois et 21 jours. Le consentement parental n'est pas nécessaire.

[11] Sans le consentement parental, il est de 21 ans pour les hommes non-musulmans et de 18 ans pour les hommes musulmans alors qu'il est de 21 ans pour les femmes non-musulmanes et il est de 16 ans pour les femmes musulmanes. Pour le mariage avec le consentement parental, il est de 18 ans pour les hommes alors qu'il est de 18 ans pour les femmes non-musulmanes et il est de 16 ans pour les femmes musulmanes

[12] L'âge minimum légal du mariage spécifié correspond à des mariages contractés en vertu de la Charte des femmes. Pour les mariages musulmans sous l'administration de la « Loi sur le Droit Musulman », aucun mariage ne doit être célébré lorsque l'une des parties est en dessous de l'âge de 18 ans. Néanmoins, les femmes musulmanes en dessous de l'âge de 18 ans qui ont atteint l'âge de la puberté peuvent être mariées dans le cadre de l'administration de la « Loi sur le Droit Musulman ».

[13] Le mariage à 16-17 ans exige que l'autre conjoint soit un adulte déjà fiancée (18 ans) ainsi qu'une exemption de l'obligation de la majorité par un juge aux affaires familiales.

[14] Les personnes âgées de moins de 18 ans doivent obtenir l'autorisation de la justice.

[15] En conformité avec le Code du mariage et la famille de la République du Bélarus, dans les cas exclusifs liés à la maternité, l'accouchement et en cas d'acquisition par un mineur d'une pleine capacité juridique en vertu de l'âge légal, les bureaux d'état civil sont en mesure de de réduire l'âge du mariage des personnes souhaitant se marier, de 3 ans au plus. L'âge du mariage est abaissé suite à une demande des personnes se mariant, le consentement parental n'est pas nécessaire.

[16] Les personnes âgées de moins de 18 ans doivent obtenir l'autorisation du ministère de la justice.

[17] Dans certaines conditions (par exemple la grossesse), le mariage peut avoir lieu sans restriction d'âge.

[18] Une exemption sur l'âge minimum peut être accordée par ordonnance du tribunal si l'octroi d'une telle exemption est dans le meilleur intérêt des parties ayant l'intention de se marier et si la demande est appuyée par de bonnes raisons.

[19] En plus du consentement parental, les personnes de moins de 18 ans doivent obtenir l'autorisation du tribunall'approbation judiciaire. En cas de grossesse, le mariage peut être autorisé en dessous de 15 ans.

[20] Les femmes peuvent se marier à l'âge de 16 ou 17 ans avec l'autorisation des parents et du tribunal de la cour.

[21] Un mariage ne peut être conclu par un mineur. Le tribunal peut, exceptionnellement et pour des raisons importantes approuver l'entrée en mariage par un mineur de plus de seize ans. Sans cet accord, le mariage est invalide et le tribunal est en mesure de prononcer sa nullité, même sans une demande explicite.

[22] Avec le consentement des parents, aucune limite mais les autorités doivent approuver. Sans le consentement parental, l'âge minimum légal du mariage est de 18 ans pour les citoyens suédois.

23. Marriages by age of groom and by age of bride: latest available year, 2005 - 2014
Mariages selon l'âge de l'époux et selon l'âge de l'épouse : dernière année disponible, 2005 - 2014

Continent, country or area, year, code[a] and age of bride / Continent, pays ou zone, date, code[a] et âge de l'épouse	Total	0-14	15-19	20-24	25-29	30-34	35-39	40-44	45-49	50-54	55-59	60+	Unknown Inconnu
				Age of groom - - âge de l'époux									
AFRICA - AFRIQUE													
Botswana													
2010 (+U)													
Total	4 416	-	-	42	598	1 194	1 005	610	392	243	160	172	...
0 - 14	-	-	-	-	-	-	-	-	-	-	-	-	...
15 - 19	6	-	-	2	1	3	-	-	-	-	-	-	...
20 - 24	361	-	-	29	155	107	41	19	6	4	-	-	...
25 - 29	1 511	-	-	8	353	622	331	131	42	17	2	5	...
30 - 34	1 209	-	-	2	67	397	428	172	88	38	12	5	...
35 - 39	593	-	-	1	15	46	173	186	105	38	22	7	...
40 - 44	335	-	-	-	3	10	28	75	97	67	32	23	...
45 - 49	206	-	-	-	3	4	3	20	47	56	41	32	...
50 - 54	109	-	-	-	1	4	-	5	6	18	39	36	...
55 - 59	45	-	-	-	-	1	1	-	1	5	9	28	...
60 - 64	24	-	-	-	-	-	-	1	-	-	3	20	...
65 +	17	-	-	-	-	-	-	1	-	-	-	16	...
Egypt - Égypte[1]													
2013 (+C)													
Total	909 350	...	11 883[j]	185 423	399 988	171 437	55 078	26 900	18 941	13 918	9 668	14 179	1 935
18 - 19	221 772	...	6 801[j]	76 163	107 223	26 642	3 510	670	338	193	99	125	8
20 - 24	372 716	...	3 902[j]	92 928	194 131	64 160	11 723	2 851	1 447	716	411	415	32
25 - 29	184 740	...	821[j]	13 362	85 403	54 289	17 493	6 233	3 214	1 854	979	1 069	23
30 - 34	64 519	...	195[j]	1 953	9 739	21 058	13 917	7 439	4 368	2 614	1 482	1 743	11
35 - 39	29 776	...	59[j]	485	1 990	3 686	6 294	6 078	4 341	2 859	1 864	2 117	3
40 - 44	15 300	...	26[j]	198	608	949	1 412	2 637	2 961	2 588	1 661	2 258	2
45 - 49	9 457	...	30[j]	137	377	340	492	686	1 724	1 849	1 541	2 279	2
50 - 54	5 037	...	16[j]	74	187	146	154	214	406	1 011	1 070	1 757	2
55 - 59	2 123	...	8[j]	19	103	55	46	51	98	176	416	1 151	-
60 - 64	1 054	...	5[j]	15	54	42	14	17	35	45	100	727	-
65 - 69	430	...	9[j]	21	32	13	5	5	3	8	26	308	-
70 - 74	144	...	1[j]	4	9	7	3	3	1	2	2	112	-
75 +	188	...	1[j]	22	49	13	3	5	1	-	7	87	-
Unknown - Inconnu	2 094	...	9[j]	42	83	37	12	11	4	3	10	31	1 852
Lesotho													
2011 (+U)													
Total	3 162	-	10	265	980	764	458	268	183	109	66	59	-
0 - 14	-	-	-	-	-	-	-	-	-	-	-	-	-
15 - 19	144	-	8	69	55	10	1	-	-	1	-	-	-
20 - 24	924	-	2	178	524	159	48	5	4	1	2	1	-
25 - 29	979	-	-	16	360	397	122	44	18	14	4	4	-
30 - 34	574	-	-	1	37	184	196	77	45	21	7	6	-
35 - 39	299	-	-	-	3	12	85	109	56	19	10	5	-
40 - 44	122	-	-	1	-	2	4	32	44	22	11	6	-
45 - 49	60	-	-	-	-	-	2	1	16	19	14	8	-
50 - 54	32	-	-	-	-	-	-	-	-	11	13	8	-
55 - 59	16	-	-	-	1	-	-	-	-	1	5	9	-
60 - 64	8	-	-	-	-	-	-	-	-	-	-	8	-
65 - 69	2	-	-	-	-	-	-	-	-	-	-	2	-
70 - 74	2	-	-	-	-	-	-	-	-	-	-	2	-
75 +	-	-	-	-	-	-	-	-	-	-	-	-	-
Unknown - Inconnu	-	-	-	-	-	-	-	-	-	-	-	-	-
Mauritius - Maurice[2]													
2014 (+C)													
Total	9 959	...	98	1 105	2 799	2 488	1 377	728	502	394	245	220	3
15 - 19	707	...	72	327	208	76	19	2	-	1	-	2	-
20 - 24	2 521	...	21	604	1 143	592	127	21	7	2	3	1	-
25 - 29	2 871	...	3	134	1 197	1 034	375	75	31	10	5	5	2
30 - 34	1 648	...	1	31	200	609	494	213	69	17	10	4	-
35 - 39	879	...	-	5	38	138	288	220	117	46	16	11	-
40 - 44	470	...	1	2	9	27	49	132	128	87	28	7	-
45 - 49	401	...	-	2	3	11	17	49	106	136	51	26	-
50 - 54	269	...	-	-	1	1	6	14	35	75	82	55	-
55 - 59	112	...	-	-	-	-	2	2	5	14	42	47	-
60 +	80	...	-	-	-	-	-	-	4	6	8	62	-
Unknown - Inconnu	1	...	-	-	-	-	-	-	-	-	-	-	1

Continent, country or area, year, code[a] and age of bride / Continent, pays ou zone, date, code[a] et âge de l'épouse	Age of groom - - âge de l'époux												
	Total	0-14	15-19	20-24	25-29	30-34	35-39	40-44	45-49	50-54	55-59	60+	Unknown Inconnu
AFRICA - AFRIQUE													
Reunion - Réunion													
2008 (C)													
Total	3 149	-	15	338	787	681	514	306	185	150	62	111	-
0 - 14	1	-	1	-	-	-	-	-	-	-	-	-	-
15 - 19	91	-	8	45	26	7	2	2	1	-	-	-	-
20 - 24	679	-	4	235	296	99	28	13	3	-	1	-	-
25 - 29	858	-	2	42	391	264	117	30	7	4	1	-	-
30 - 34	584	-	-	12	52	232	185	56	29	10	4	4	-
35 - 39	384	-	-	3	16	55	134	106	38	25	4	3	-
40 - 44	234	-	-	-	4	16	34	77	49	28	13	13	-
45 - 49	144	-	-	1	1	7	11	18	34	40	18	14	-
50 - 54	94	-	-	-	1	1	3	4	19	30	12	24	-
55 - 59	39	-	-	-	-	-	-	-	3	10	7	19	-
60 - 64	16	-	-	-	-	-	-	-	2	2	1	11	-
65 - 69	16	-	-	-	-	-	-	-	-	1	1	14	-
70 - 74	7	-	-	-	-	-	-	-	-	-	-	7	-
75 +	2	-	-	-	-	-	-	-	-	-	-	2	-
Saint Helena ex. dep. - Sainte-Hélène sans dép.													
2012 (C)													
Total	12	-	-	-	1	3	-	2	5	-	-	1	...
0 - 14	-	-	-	-	-	-	-	-	-	-	-	-	...
15 - 19	-	-	-	-	-	-	-	-	-	-	-	-	...
20 - 24	-	-	-	-	-	-	-	-	-	-	-	-	...
25 - 29	2	-	-	-	1	1	-	-	-	-	-	-	...
30 - 34	2	-	-	-	-	1	-	1	-	-	-	-	...
35 - 39	3	-	-	-	-	1	-	-	2	-	-	-	...
40 - 44	2	-	-	-	-	-	-	1	1	-	-	-	...
45 - 49	1	-	-	-	-	-	-	-	1	-	-	-	...
50 - 54	1	-	-	-	-	-	-	-	1	-	-	-	...
55 - 59	1	-	-	-	-	-	-	-	-	-	-	1	...
60 - 64	-	-	-	-	-	-	-	-	-	-	-	-	...
65 - 69	-	-	-	-	-	-	-	-	-	-	-	-	...
70 - 74	-	-	-	-	-	-	-	-	-	-	-	-	...
75 +	-	-	-	-	-	-	-	-	-	-	-	-	...
Seychelles[3]													
2014 (+C)													
Total	1 655	...	2	62	284	458	320	202	158	92	43	34	...
15 - 19	15	...	1	6	4	1	2	1	-	-	-	-	...
20 - 24	119	...	1	30	41	27	11	4	3	-	1	1	...
25 - 29	465	...	-	14	185	170	69	14	9	3	-	1	...
30 - 34	471	...	-	6	40	207	119	61	25	12	-	1	...
35 - 39	247	...	-	4	10	38	87	56	35	13	2	2	...
40 - 44	152	...	-	1	4	10	26	40	43	17	9	2	...
45 - 49	108	...	-	1	-	4	4	20	32	26	18	3	...
50 - 54	44	...	-	-	-	-	1	3	9	15	6	10	...
55 - 59	25	...	-	-	-	1	1	2	2	5	6	8	...
60 - 64	7	...	-	-	-	-	-	1	-	1	1	4	...
65 - 69	-	...	-	-	-	-	-	-	-	-	-	-	...
70 - 74	-	...	-	-	-	-	-	-	-	-	-	-	...
75 +	2	...	-	-	-	-	-	-	-	-	-	2	...
South Africa - Afrique du Sud													
2011 (...)													
Total	167 264	2	189	8 719	36 903	38 827	30 474	19 424	13 105	7 955	5 028	6 638	...
0 - 14	4	-	-	2	-	2	-	-	-	-	-	-	...
15 - 19	2 199	-	96	1 002	703	256	90	33	8	4	4	3	...
20 - 24	25 542	-	72	5 690	12 489	4 977	1 589	431	172	67	36	19	...
25 - 29	50 977	-	13	1 598	19 588	18 847	7 485	2 245	786	246	105	64	...
30 - 34	35 124	-	2	308	3 266	11 855	12 206	4 737	1 764	620	210	156	...
35 - 39	22 456	-	4	84	637	2 266	7 236	6 955	3 296	1 209	479	290	...
40 - 44	13 030	-	1	26	167	456	1 449	3 799	3 943	1 859	783	547	...
45 - 49	8 221	-	-	6	44	129	310	940	2 365	2 270	1 203	954	...
50 - 54	4 674	-	-	3	7	25	88	228	586	1 294	1 293	1 150	...
55 - 59	2 480	-	-	-	2	9	16	44	140	285	692	1 292	...
60 - 64	1 340	1	-	-	-	3	4	8	31	81	177	1 035	...
65 - 69	653	-	1	-	-	1	-	3	13	12	36	587	...

23. Marriages by age of groom and by age of bride: latest available year, 2005 - 2014
Mariages selon l'âge de l'époux et selon l'âge de l'épouse : dernière année disponible, 2005 - 2014 (continued - suite)

Continent, country or area, year, code[a] and age of bride / Continent, pays ou zone, date, code[a] et âge de l'épouse	Total	Age of groom - - âge de l'époux											
		0-14	15-19	20-24	25-29	30-34	35-39	40-44	45-49	50-54	55-59	60+	Unknown Inconnu
AFRICA - AFRIQUE													
South Africa - Afrique du Sud													
2011													
70 - 74	322	-	-	-	-	-	-	1	1	6	8	306	...
75 +	242	1	-	-	-	1	1	-	-	2	2	235	...
Tunisia - Tunisie													
2011 (...)													
Total	91 590	...	228[f]	5 724	24 725	30 919	15 770	5 904	2 881	4 652[s]	...	...	787
0 - 19	6 504	...	...	...	...	...	...	...	...	...	...	...	...
20 - 24	24 862	...	...	...	...	...	...	...	...	...	...	...	...
25 - 29	31 959	...	...	...	...	...	...	...	...	...	...	...	...
30 - 34	15 109	...	...	...	...	...	...	...	...	...	...	...	...
35 - 39	6 123	...	...	...	...	...	...	...	...	...	...	...	...
40 - 44	3 104	...	...	...	...	...	...	...	...	...	...	...	...
45 - 49	1 744	...	...	...	...	...	...	...	...	...	...	...	...
50 +	1 267	...	...	...	...	...	...	...	...	...	...	...	...
Unknown - Inconnu	918	...	...	...	...	...	...	...	...	...	...	...	...
AMERICA, NORTH - AMÉRIQUE DU NORD													
Anguilla[4]													
2013 (C)													
Total	42	4	9	9	4	4	4	1	-	1	...	...	6
0 - 14	5	2	2	-	-	-	1	-	-	-	...	...	-
15 - 19	12	1	5	3	3	-	-	-	-	-	...	...	-
20 - 24	9	-	1	5	1	1	1	-	-	-	...	...	-
25 - 29	5	1	1	1	-	2	-	-	-	-	...	...	-
30 - 34	3	-	-	-	-	-	2	1	-	-	...	...	-
35 - 39	2	-	-	-	-	1	-	-	-	1	...	...	-
40 - 44	-	-	-	-	-	-	-	-	-	-	...	...	-
45 - 49	-	-	-	-	-	-	-	-	-	-	...	...	-
50 - 54	-	-	-	-	-	-	-	-	-	-	...	...	-
Unknown - Inconnu	6	-	-	-	-	-	-	-	-	-	...	...	6
Aruba													
2014 (C)													
Total	617	-	5	45	121	111	77	78	55	47	46	32	-
0 - 14	-	-	-	-	-	-	-	-	-	-	-	-	-
15 - 19	11	-	2	5	1	2	-	1	-	-	-	-	-
20 - 24	85	-	2	22	35	17	5	2	2	-	-	-	-
25 - 29	159	-	1	16	54	45	19	18	6	-	-	-	-
30 - 34	88	-	-	2	16	24	19	13	8	2	1	3	-
35 - 39	74	-	-	-	7	16	19	13	9	5	4	1	-
40 - 44	68	-	-	-	2	5	8	19	11	14	6	3	-
45 - 49	57	-	-	-	1	2	3	5	11	12	15	8	-
50 - 54	41	-	-	-	1	-	2	5	5	10	11	7	-
55 - 59	18	-	-	-	1	-	-	1	2	1	7	6	-
60 - 64	7	-	-	-	-	-	2	1	-	1	2	1	-
65 - 69	4	-	-	-	-	-	-	-	1	1	-	2	-
70 - 74	-	-	-	-	-	-	-	-	-	-	-	-	-
75 +	2	-	-	-	-	-	-	-	-	1	-	1	-
Unknown - Inconnu	3	-	-	-	3	-	-	-	-	-	-	-	-
Bahamas													
2012 (+C)													
Total	1 941	-	7	198	424	393	339	190	157	102	127	4	...
0 - 14	65	-	3	26	20	7	7	2	-	-	-	-	...
15 - 19	326	-	1	108	112	65	26	6	3	2	3	-	...
20 - 24	500	-	2	31	198	134	81	28	18	5	3	-	...
25 - 29	347	-	1	21	64	104	79	41	25	7	5	-	...
30 - 34	280	-	-	8	19	47	95	50	32	18	11	-	...
35 - 39	187	-	-	4	8	28	32	38	39	20	16	2	...
40 - 44	115	-	-	-	2	4	15	18	27	29	20	-	...
45 - 49	65	-	-	-	1	4	2	6	11	16	24	1	...
50 - 54	51	-	-	-	-	-	2	1	-	5	43	-	...
55 - 59	5	-	-	-	-	-	-	-	2	-	2	1	...
60 - 64	-	-	-	-	-	-	-	-	-	-	-	-	...

Continent, country or area, year, code[a] and age of bride / Continent, pays ou zone, date, code[a] et âge de l'épouse	Age of groom - - âge de l'époux												
	Total	0-14	15-19	20-24	25-29	30-34	35-39	40-44	45-49	50-54	55-59	60+	Unknown Inconnu

AMERICA, NORTH - AMÉRIQUE DU NORD

Bermuda - Bermudes
2013 (C)

	Total	0-14	15-19	20-24	25-29	30-34	35-39	40-44	45-49	50-54	55-59	60+	Unknown Inconnu
Total	471	-	-	17	71	117	82	65	41	35	22	21	...
0 - 14	-	-	-	-	-	-	-	-	-	-	-	-	...
15 - 19	1	-	-	1	-	-	-	-	-	-	-	-	...
20 - 24	30	-	-	10	11	6	3	-	-	-	-	-	...
25 - 29	101	-	-	4	44	37	9	4	1	1	1	-	...
30 - 34	113	-	-	1	11	50	32	16	-	1	2	-	...
35 - 39	74	-	-	-	4	15	26	17	7	4	1	-	...
40 - 44	49	-	-	-	-	4	9	18	9	6	2	1	...
45 - 49	40	-	-	1	1	3	1	10	13	6	3	2	...
50 - 54	33	-	-	-	-	1	1	-	9	12	4	6	...
55 - 59	18	-	-	-	-	1	1	-	2	4	7	3	...
60 - 64	8	-	-	-	-	-	-	-	-	1	2	5	...
65 - 69	3	-	-	-	-	-	-	-	-	-	-	3	...
70 - 74	-	-	-	-	-	-	-	-	-	-	-	-	...
75 +	1	-	-	-	-	-	-	-	-	-	-	1	...

Costa Rica[5]
2014* (C)

	Total	0-14	15-19	20-24	25-29	30-34	35-39	40-44	45-49	50-54	55-59	60+	Unknown Inconnu
Total	25 909	-	397	3 658	6 805	5 519	3 253	1 914	1 327	1 009	705	1 138	184
0 - 14	1	-	-	1	-	-	-	-	-	-	-	-	-
15 - 19	1 661	-	226	808	425	112	49	22	4	3	5	3	4
20 - 24	5 635	-	120	1 921	2 268	821	285	103	62	27	12	9	7
25 - 29	7 131	-	38	663	2 897	2 152	802	299	147	66	29	23	15
30 - 34	4 735	-	8	171	882	1 720	1 096	474	186	99	47	43	9
35 - 39	2 355	-	1	58	213	486	646	439	238	148	63	60	3
40 - 44	1 458	-	3	20	62	130	226	351	281	189	104	87	5
45 - 49	1 094	-	1	7	28	56	88	140	258	226	140	149	1
50 - 54	710	-	-	1	8	20	33	51	93	156	144	203	1
55 - 59	419	-	-	-	-	3	12	21	31	65	109	177	1
60 - 64	246	-	-	-	1	-	2	6	17	17	39	164	-
65 - 69	124	-	-	-	-	-	-	1	2	5	9	107	-
70 - 74	69	-	-	-	-	1	2	2	-	2	-	62	-
75 +	53	-	-	-	1	1	-	-	1	-	2	48	-
Unknown - Inconnu	218	-	-	8	20	17	12	5	7	6	2	3	138

Cuba[6]
2013 (C)

	Total	0-14	15-19	20-24	25-29	30-34	35-39	40-44	45-49	50-54	55-59	60+	Unknown Inconnu
Total	61 449	1	903	7 368	10 835	7 759	7 386	7 660	6 640	4 363	2 691	5 841	2
0 - 14	61	-	21	22	10	4	4	-	-	-	-	-	-
15 - 19	4 036	-	520	1 980	992	271	126	55	42	22	6	22	-
20 - 24	11 305	1	259	3 449	4 013	1 662	872	500	252	131	54	112	-
25 - 29	11 094	-	64	1 255	3 643	2 562	1 609	1 044	493	193	74	157	-
30 - 34	6 911	-	17	307	1 106	1 657	1 557	1 150	603	255	111	147	1
35 - 39	6 597	-	10	153	518	815	1 548	1 693	1 024	479	140	217	-
40 - 44	6 759	-	4	106	269	453	993	1 722	1 715	799	311	386	1
45 - 49	5 892	-	6	52	156	192	469	979	1 580	1 196	577	685	-
50 - 54	3 863	-	1	26	68	91	136	363	652	864	706	956	-
55 - 59	2 091	-	1	9	28	19	39	105	184	283	464	959	-
60 - 64	1 405	-	-	5	18	12	17	34	52	98	172	997	-
65 - 69	830	-	-	2	6	9	11	8	25	31	45	693	-
70 - 74	392	-	-	2	1	8	4	5	13	10	23	326	-
75 +	212	-	-	-	7	4	1	1	5	2	8	184	-
Unknown - Inconnu	1	-	-	-	-	-	-	1	-	-	-	-	-

Curaçao
2010 (C)

	Total	0-14	15-19	20-24	25-29	30-34	35-39	40-44	45-49	50-54	55-59	60+	Unknown Inconnu
Total	874	-	3	70	127	137	117	106	103	76	69	58	8
0 - 14	-	-	-	-	-	-	-	-	-	-	-	-	-
15 - 19	15	-	1	7	6	1	-	-	-	-	-	-	-
20 - 24	101	-	2	36	29	18	9	4	2	1	-	-	-
25 - 29	196	-	-	18	69	57	22	15	11	2	2	-	-
30 - 34	147	-	-	6	15	42	32	21	18	8	3	2	-
35 - 39	135	-	-	1	5	14	31	30	27	15	8	4	-
40 - 44	79	-	-	2	2	2	12	16	19	13	9	4	-
45 - 49	86	-	-	-	-	2	9	15	15	19	15	11	-
50 - 54	55	-	-	-	1	1	1	4	8	11	19	10	-
55 - 59	33	-	-	-	-	-	-	1	3	4	11	14	-

606

23. Marriages by age of groom and by age of bride: latest available year, 2005 - 2014
Mariages selon l'âge de l'époux et selon l'âge de l'épouse : dernière année disponible, 2005 - 2014 (continued - suite)

Continent, country or area, year, code[a] and age of bride / Continent, pays ou zone, date, code[a] et âge de l'épouse	Total	0-14	15-19	20-24	25-29	30-34	35-39	40-44	45-49	50-54	55-59	60+	Unknown Inconnu
AMERICA, NORTH - AMÉRIQUE DU NORD													
Curaçao													
2010													
60 - 64	9	-	-	-	-	-	1	-	-	3	-	5	-
65 - 69	4	-	-	-	-	-	-	-	-	-	1	3	-
70 - 74	6	-	-	-	-	-	-	-	-	-	1	5	-
75 +	-	-	-	-	-	-	-	-	-	-	-	-	-
Unknown - Inconnu	8	-	-	-	-	-	-	-	-	-	-	-	8
Dominican Republic - République dominicaine													
2013 (+C)													
Total	45 163	2	390	5 601	9 033	7 977	5 730	4 889	3 797	2 724	1 947	2 781	292
0 - 14	18	-	1	8	3	3	2	-	1	-	-	-	-
15 - 19	2 202	1	136	1 071	557	225	92	38	35	16	17	14	-
20 - 24	9 655	-	165	2 975	3 395	1 608	614	362	247	126	87	71	5
25 - 29	9 647	-	39	923	3 305	2 717	1 149	665	359	243	129	115	3
30 - 34	7 403	-	24	353	1 018	2 091	1 711	981	562	314	178	169	2
35 - 39	5 172	-	10	142	390	724	1 264	1 188	681	329	205	238	1
40 - 44	3 940	1	4	63	178	337	491	967	843	502	271	283	-
45 - 49	2 867	-	3	36	100	158	223	423	647	596	334	345	2
50 - 54	1 839	-	2	12	38	61	102	164	246	402	385	427	-
55 - 59	1 043	-	-	3	17	23	40	68	96	127	227	442	-
60 - 64	555	-	2	3	6	4	18	14	40	41	73	353	1
65 - 69	251	-	2	2	3	-	6	6	16	11	23	182	-
70 - 74	118	-	-	3	3	2	3	2	8	4	7	86	-
75 +	69	-	-	2	-	5	5	3	4	4	4	42	-
Unknown - Inconnu	384	-	2	5	20	19	10	8	12	9	7	14	278
El Salvador[7]													
2012 (...)													
Total	29 267	-	1 098	6 586	6 762	5 101	3 026	2 078	1 528	989	671	1 294	134
0 - 14	37	-	10	16	6	3	2	-	-	-	-	-	-
15 - 19	3 670	-	544	1 856	787	250	113	53	25	12	5	9	16
20 - 24	8 329	-	414	3 407	2 652	1 113	374	176	90	37	12	19	35
25 - 29	6 227	-	80	933	2 304	1 713	647	264	153	70	27	23	13
30 - 34	4 049	-	16	230	704	1 360	902	414	223	82	47	53	18
35 - 39	2 433	-	14	69	179	436	654	509	272	134	74	84	8
40 - 44	1 604	-	4	25	58	118	208	410	348	175	107	149	2
45 - 49	1 144	-	2	6	18	54	80	174	290	234	125	157	4
50 - 54	633	-	-	3	6	15	16	43	84	162	140	164	-
55 - 59	403	-	1	1	1	6	5	10	23	61	89	206	-
60 - 64	242	-	1	-	1	2	2	10	10	12	26	177	1
65 +	279	-	2	1	-	2	3	3	3	7	13	245	-
Unknown - Inconnu	217	-	10	39	46	29	20	12	7	3	6	8	37
Guatemala													
2011 (C)													
Total	78 286	17	9 779	27 197	18 081	9 430	4 619	2 550	1 635	1 375	1 126	2 362	115
0 - 14	1 122	4	513	458	109	31	5	1	1	-	-	-	-
15 - 19	22 191	12	6 733	11 231	3 124	788	191	52	27	9	6	6	12
20 - 24	25 037	1	2 199	12 176	7 600	2 137	592	162	69	39	16	25	21
25 - 29	13 633	-	267	2 705	5 632	3 393	1 009	338	135	61	39	42	12
30 - 34	6 599	-	46	494	1 284	2 336	1 504	497	192	115	64	63	4
35 - 39	3 263	-	11	83	240	588	933	780	283	165	77	96	7
40 - 44	1 869	-	2	19	49	112	266	504	401	255	116	144	1
45 - 49	1 436	-	1	8	17	31	78	156	373	379	184	205	4
50 - 54	1 094	-	-	1	6	8	26	41	107	260	335	306	4
55 - 59	760	-	-	-	1	-	8	13	32	70	225	410	1
60 - 64	511	-	-	2	-	-	1	2	8	15	44	438	1
65 - 69	332	-	1	-	1	1	-	2	2	3	14	308	-
70 - 74	183	-	-	-	-	-	-	-	-	2	2	178	1
75 +	139	-	-	-	-	-	-	-	-	1	1	137	-
Unknown - Inconnu	117	-	6	20	18	5	6	2	5	1	3	4	47
Jamaica - Jamaïque													
2006 (+C)													
Total	23 181	-	70	2 153	5 477	4 987	3 749	2 672	1 676	1 032	568	797	-
0 - 14	-	-	-	-	-	-	-	-	-	-	-	-	-
15 - 19	368	-	31	168	89	35	23	11	6	1	1	3	-
20 - 24	3 726	-	22	1 251	1 579	531	195	86	31	19	4	8	-

23. Marriages by age of groom and by age of bride: latest available year, 2005 - 2014
Mariages selon l'âge de l'époux et selon l'âge de l'épouse : dernière année disponible, 2005 - 2014 (continued - suite)

Continent, country or area, year, code[a] and age of bride / Continent, pays ou zone, date, code[a] et âge de l'épouse	Total	Age of groom - - âge de l'époux											Unknown Inconnu
		0-14	15-19	20-24	25-29	30-34	35-39	40-44	45-49	50-54	55-59	60+	

AMERICA, NORTH - AMÉRIQUE DU NORD

Jamaica - Jamaïque
2006

25 - 29	6 263	-	11	501	2 670	1 870	742	277	108	43	15	26	-
30 - 34	4 635	-	4	136	715	1 660	1 242	525	199	86	41	27	-
35 - 39	3 194	-	1	62	266	571	940	765	360	123	55	51	-
40 - 44	2 190	-	1	18	105	221	402	635	440	202	102	64	-
45 - 49	1 452	-	-	15	35	75	147	273	364	292	133	118	-
50 - 54	708	-	-	1	15	18	39	63	122	200	105	145	-
55 - 59	327	-	-	1	-	5	17	24	28	45	71	136	-
60 - 64	179	-	-	-	2	1	1	10	15	15	27	108	-
65 - 69	84	-	-	-	1	-	-	2	1	4	10	66	-
70 - 74	35	-	-	-	-	-	-	1	2	1	3	28	-
75 +	20	-	-	-	-	-	1	-	-	1	1	17	-

Martinique
2007 (C)

Total	1 341	-	19	128	297	284	185	155	117	63	32	61	-
0 - 14	-	-	-	-	-	-	-	-	-	-	-	-	-
15 - 19	55	-	11	35	8	1	-	-	-	-	-	-	-
20 - 24	217	-	4	63	108	25	13	4	-	-	-	-	-
25 - 29	273	-	3	20	123	99	16	7	1	4	-	-	-
30 - 34	243	-	1	4	38	97	65	24	11	2	1	-	-
35 - 39	173	-	-	4	12	42	54	49	9	3	-	-	-
40 - 44	146	-	-	1	3	11	26	47	45	10	3	-	-
45 - 49	84	-	-	1	3	6	6	19	29	14	5	1	-
50 - 54	53	-	-	-	2	3	3	3	15	11	10	6	-
55 - 59	31	-	-	-	-	-	1	-	7	12	3	8	-
60 - 64	24	-	-	-	-	-	-	1	-	4	8	11	-
65 - 69	12	-	-	-	-	-	1	-	-	2	-	9	-
70 - 74	16	-	-	-	-	-	-	1	-	1	2	12	-
75 +	14	-	-	-	-	-	-	-	-	-	-	14	-

Mexico - Mexique
2013 (+C)

Total	582 077	50	46 678	164 530	152 613	89 921	46 829	26 314	15 843	11 336	8 476	19 487	1 187
0 - 14	1 470	14	773	516	118	34	5	4	3	2	-	1	-
15 - 19	110 631	23	34 510	55 850	14 777	3 752	1 076	360	126	47	27	83	19
20 - 24	176 774	7	10 050	86 471	56 559	16 122	4 690	1 431	536	239	105	564	191
25 - 29	134 146	3	1 064	17 760	64 918	34 570	10 328	3 341	1 123	552	257	230	272
30 - 34	66 903	3	158	2 915	12 777	27 005	14 646	5 462	2 043	1 000	401	493	251
35 - 39	34 953	-	61	667	2 553	6 379	11 616	7 346	3 151	1 492	789	899	155
40 - 44	20 193	-	18	153	589	1 456	3 244	5 870	4 112	2 144	1 172	1 435	124
45 - 49	13 128	-	5	55	142	373	860	1 734	3 379	2 800	1 679	2 101	85
50 - 54	9 144	-	2	18	37	94	221	524	969	2 205	2 016	3 058	47
55 - 59	5 974	-	2	5	14	37	64	152	279	605	1 432	3 384	22
60 - 64	3 565	-	-	2	7	4	20	42	73	160	425	2 832	9
65 - 69	1 986	-	-	3	1	3	6	13	20	47	112	1 781	7
70 - 74	1 011	-	-	3	2	1	2	5	3	15	31	949	4
75 +	2 199	-	35	112	119	91	51	30	26	28	30	1 677	1
Unknown - Inconnu	1 187	-	18	148	286	239	174	134	92	51	23	22	-

Montserrat
2013 (+...)

Total	18	-	-	1	3	1	5	2	5	1	-	-	...
0 - 14	-	-	-	-	-	-	-	-	-	-	-	-	...
15 - 19	-	-	-	-	-	-	-	-	-	-	-	-	...
20 - 24	3	-	-	1	1	1	-	-	-	-	-	-	...
25 - 29	3	-	-	-	1	-	2	-	-	-	-	-	...
30 - 34	2	-	-	-	-	-	-	-	2	-	-	-	...
35 - 39	3	-	-	-	1	-	1	-	1	-	-	-	...
40 - 44	5	-	-	-	-	-	-	2	1	1	1	-	...
45 - 49	1	-	-	-	-	-	-	-	1	-	-	-	...
50 - 54	1	-	-	-	-	-	-	-	-	1	-	-	...
55 - 59	-	-	-	-	-	-	-	-	-	-	-	-	...
60 - 64	-	-	-	-	-	-	-	-	-	-	-	-	...
65 - 69	-	-	-	-	-	-	-	-	-	-	-	-	...
70 - 74	-	-	-	-	-	-	-	-	-	-	-	-	...
75 +	-	-	-	-	-	-	-	-	-	-	-	-	...

23. Marriages by age of groom and by age of bride: latest available year, 2005 - 2014
Mariages selon l'âge de l'époux et selon l'âge de l'épouse : dernière année disponible, 2005 - 2014 (continued - suite)

Continent, country or area, year, code[a] and age of bride / Continent, pays ou zone, date, code[a] et âge de l'épouse	Total	0-14	15-19	20-24	25-29	30-34	35-39	40-44	45-49	50-54	55-59	60+	Unknown Inconnu
AMERICA, NORTH - AMÉRIQUE DU NORD													
Panama[5]													
2013 (C)													
Total	13 213	-	151	1 639	2 890	2 528	1 656	2 026[n]	...	976[o]	...	928	419
0 - 14	9	-	3	4	-	-	-	1[n]	...	-[o]	...	-	1
15 - 19	569	-	83	275	118	45	12	9[n]	...	3[o]	...	-	24
20 - 24	2 528	-	48	888	960	367	131	61[n]	...	9[o]	...	7	57
25 - 29	3 141	-	7	316	1 268	892	353	195[n]	...	36[o]	...	15	59
30 - 34	2 228	-	2	74	338	802	486	376[n]	...	61[o]	...	35	54
35 - 39	1 416	-	2	22	96	235	411	470[n]	...	98[o]	...	43	39
40 - 49	1 727	-	1	9	29	118	207	734[n]	...	409[o]	...	179	41
50 - 59	758	-	-	1	4	-	10	109[n]	...	290[o]	...	327	17
60 - 69	276	-	-	-	-	-	1	4[n]	...	37[o]	...	232	2
70 +	84	-	-	-	-	-	-	-[n]	...	3[o]	...	81	-
Unknown - Inconnu	477	-	5	50	77	69	45	67[n]	...	30[o]	...	9	125
Puerto Rico - Porto Rico													
2014 (C)													
Total	16 668	-	278	2 577	3 622	2 876	1 995	1 448	1 102	910	637	1 217	6
0 - 14	2	-	-	2	-	-	-	-	-	-	-	-	-
15 - 19	808	-	194	471	101	24	13	1	4	-	-	-	-
20 - 24	3 328	-	75	1 616	1 150	334	104	27	12	6	4	-	-
25 - 29	3 783	-	4	390	1 777	1 032	365	143	43	14	8	7	-
30 - 34	2 664	-	4	78	447	1 011	654	291	107	42	15	15	-
35 - 39	1 843	-	-	14	113	352	574	406	222	102	44	16	-
40 - 44	1 307	-	1	4	29	87	204	387	285	181	70	59	-
45 - 49	1 020	-	-	1	4	29	64	137	273	238	147	127	-
50 - 54	753	-	-	1	1	3	12	47	112	210	152	215	-
55 - 59	466	-	-	-	-	2	3	8	31	84	126	212	-
60 - 64	336	-	-	-	-	2	2	1	11	23	48	249	-
65 - 69	205	-	-	-	-	-	-	-	2	6	19	178	-
70 - 74	87	-	-	-	-	-	-	-	-	2	4	81	-
75 +	60	-	-	-	-	-	-	-	-	2	-	58	-
Unknown - Inconnu	6	-	-	-	-	-	-	-	-	-	-	-	6
Saint Vincent and the Grenadines - Saint-Vincent-et-les Grenadines													
2009 (+C)													
Total	573	...	...	...	...	...	...	...	...	...	...	...	...
0 - 14	-	...	...	...	...	...	...	...	...	...	...	...	...
15 - 19	3	...	...	...	...	...	...	...	...	...	...	...	...
20 - 24	48	...	...	...	...	...	...	...	...	...	...	...	...
25 - 29	134	...	...	...	...	...	...	...	...	...	...	...	...
30 - 34	120	...	...	...	...	...	...	...	...	...	...	...	...
35 - 39	84	...	...	...	...	...	...	...	...	...	...	...	...
40 - 44	59	...	...	...	...	...	...	...	...	...	...	...	...
45 - 49	48	...	...	...	...	...	...	...	...	...	...	...	...
50 - 54	28	...	...	...	...	...	...	...	...	...	...	...	...
55 - 59	16	...	...	...	...	...	...	...	...	...	...	...	...
60 - 64	15	...	...	...	...	...	...	...	...	...	...	...	...
65 +	8	...	...	...	...	...	...	...	...	...	...	...	...
Unknown - Inconnu	10	...	...	...	...	...	...	...	...	...	...	...	...
Trinidad and Tobago - Trinité-et-Tobago													
2005 (C)													
Total	8 144	-	122	1 350	2 247	1 591	927	703	458	297	180	269	-
0 - 14	3	-	1	-	1	1	-	-	-	-	-	-	-
15 - 19	623	-	72	300	178	50	14	7	1	-	-	1	-
20 - 24	2 285	-	39	794	907	355	120	43	16	7	2	2	-
25 - 29	2 127	-	9	197	911	629	234	89	36	12	7	3	-
30 - 34	1 177	-	-	38	186	376	288	179	62	21	11	16	-
35 - 39	716	-	-	15	45	125	189	187	90	36	16	13	-
40 - 44	503	-	1	4	15	45	61	130	131	58	32	26	-
45 - 49	330	-	-	-	2	8	10	49	90	80	39	52	-
50 - 54	188	-	-	2	1	2	6	10	24	59	44	40	-
55 - 59	92	-	-	-	-	-	1	6	5	19	15	46	-

23. Marriages by age of groom and by age of bride: latest available year, 2005 - 2014
Mariages selon l'âge de l'époux et selon l'âge de l'épouse : dernière année disponible, 2005 - 2014 (continued - suite)

Continent, country or area, year, code[a] and age of bride / Continent, pays ou zone, date, code[a] et âge de l'épouse	Total	Age of groom - - âge de l'époux											Unknown Inconnu
		0-14	15-19	20-24	25-29	30-34	35-39	40-44	45-49	50-54	55-59	60+	
AMERICA, NORTH - AMÉRIQUE DU NORD													
Trinidad and Tobago - Trinité-et-Tobago													
2005													
60 - 64	56	-	-	-	-	-	3	3	2	5	10	33	-
65 +	43	-	-	-	-	-	1	-	1	-	4	37	-
Unknown - Inconnu	1	-	-	-	1	-	-	-	-	-	-	-	-
Turks and Caicos Islands - Îles Turques et Caïques													
2005 (C)													
Total	489	-	-	19	88	149	95	69	34	20	6	8	1
0 - 14	-	-	-	-	-	-	-	-	-	-	-	-	-
15 - 19	3	-	-	1	1	1	-	-	-	-	-	-	-
20 - 24	40	-	-	12	18	8	1	1	-	-	-	-	-
25 - 29	120	-	-	4	45	48	14	5	2	1	-	1	-
30 - 34	142	-	-	2	19	69	31	13	5	3	-	-	-
35 - 39	103	-	-	-	5	18	37	28	9	5	1	-	-
40 - 44	37	-	-	-	-	1	9	15	7	2	1	2	-
45 - 49	31	-	-	-	-	4	3	5	7	7	4	1	-
50 - 54	8	-	-	-	-	-	-	2	2	2	-	2	-
55 - 59	3	-	-	-	-	-	-	-	1	-	-	2	-
60 - 64	1	-	-	-	-	-	-	-	1	-	-	-	-
65 +	-	-	-	-	-	-	-	-	-	-	-	-	-
Unknown - Inconnu	1	-	-	-	-	-	-	-	-	-	-	-	1
2008 (C)													
Total	486	...	-	20	110	114	94	63	51	17	10	7	-
15 - 19	2	...	...	...	...	...	...	...	...	...	...	...	...
20 - 24	47	...	...	...	...	...	...	...	...	...	...	...	...
25 - 29	134	...	...	...	...	...	...	...	...	...	...	...	...
30 - 34	127	...	...	...	...	...	...	...	...	...	...	...	...
35 - 39	94	...	...	...	...	...	...	...	...	...	...	...	...
40 - 44	37	...	...	...	...	...	...	...	...	...	...	...	...
45 - 49	26	...	...	...	...	...	...	...	...	...	...	...	...
50 - 54	12	...	...	...	...	...	...	...	...	...	...	...	...
55 - 59	6	...	...	...	...	...	...	...	...	...	...	...	...
60 - 64	-	...	...	...	...	...	...	...	...	...	...	...	...
65 +	1	...	...	...	...	...	...	...	...	...	...	...	...
Unknown - Inconnu	-	...	...	...	...	...	...	...	...	...	...	...	...
AMERICA, SOUTH - AMÉRIQUE DU SUD													
Bolivia (Plurinational State of) - Bolivie (État plurinational de)													
2012 (U)													
Total	34 542	...	...	...	...	...	...	...	...	...	1 864[t]	...	11
15 - 24	11 851	...	...	...	...	...	...	...	...	...	...	...	...
25 - 34	16 113	...	...	...	...	...	...	...	...	...	...	...	...
35 - 44	3 944	...	...	...	...	...	...	...	...	...	...	...	...
45 - 54	1 335	...	...	...	...	...	...	...	...	...	...	...	...
55 +	1 247	...	...	...	...	...	...	...	...	...	...	...	...
Unknown - Inconnu	52	...	...	...	...	...	...	...	...	...	...	...	...
Brazil - Brésil													
2013 (+U)													
Total	1048777	55	31 476	201 413	273 029	210 536	117 899	72 208	49 415	33 207	22 523	36 677	339
0 - 14	319	10	96	125	58	22	4	3	-	1	-	-	-
15 - 19	126 699	17	20 682	66 081	28 055	8 234	2 360	734	297	114	61	60	4
20 - 24	247 428	18	8 123	92 735	95 030	35 179	10 440	3 525	1 382	566	211	206	13
25 - 29	252 640	4	1 733	29 965	102 915	76 824	25 774	8 970	3 616	1 572	678	578	11
30 - 34	175 867	5	552	8 934	34 489	62 771	39 176	16 568	7 296	3 328	1 504	1 231	13
35 - 39	95 548	1	188	2 413	8 911	19 152	25 574	19 347	10 255	4 927	2 443	2 330	7
40 - 44	58 318	-	61	758	2 418	5 642	9 518	13 921	11 982	6 689	3 632	3 692	5
45 - 49	39 775	-	25	256	788	1 887	3 466	6 069	9 025	7 806	4 793	5 658	2
50 - 54	24 639	-	6	66	220	572	1 107	2 133	3 746	5 256	4 884	6 647	2
55 - 59	13 507	-	3	36	70	143	301	610	1 271	1 939	2 852	6 281	1
60 - 64	7 164	-	1	9	26	59	111	217	349	668	977	4 746	1

23. Marriages by age of groom and by age of bride: latest available year, 2005 - 2014
Mariages selon l'âge de l'époux et selon l'âge de l'épouse : dernière année disponible, 2005 - 2014 (continued - suite)

Continent, country or area, year, code[a] and age of bride / Continent, pays ou zone, date, code[a] et âge de l'épouse	Total	Age of groom - - âge de l'époux											
		0-14	15-19	20-24	25-29	30-34	35-39	40-44	45-49	50-54	55-59	60+	Unknown Inconnu
AMERICA, SOUTH - AMÉRIQUE DU SUD													
Brazil - Brésil													
2013													
65 - 69	3 598	-	2	12	13	17	35	61	123	214	333	2 786	2
70 - 74	1 721	-	-	3	5	7	8	18	45	89	110	1 436	-
75 +	1 190	-	-	5	9	12	14	27	23	35	43	1 020	2
Unknown - Inconnu	364	-	4	15	22	15	11	5	5	3	2	6	276
Chile - Chili													
2012 (+C)													
Total	63 736	...	673	8 245	16 431	14 022	8 079	4 645	3 438	2 593	1 979	3 631	...
15 - 19	2 374	...	384	1 305	484	142	46	8	2	3	-	-	...
20 - 24	12 098	...	237	4 927	4 849	1 465	437	130	32	12	5	4	...
25 - 29	18 087	...	35	1 615	8 461	5 575	1 642	487	171	62	22	17	...
30 - 34	12 004	...	10	293	2 124	5 196	2 799	955	378	158	53	38	...
35 - 39	6 392	...	3	79	398	1 222	2 165	1 358	663	286	139	79	...
40 - 44	4 013	...	2	18	87	300	685	1 048	902	503	252	216	...
45 - 49	3 101	...	1	5	20	83	232	451	781	680	426	422	...
50 - 54	2 313	...	-	2	5	30	59	164	338	533	486	696	...
55 - 59	1 571	...	-	-	2	4	11	34	127	225	386	782	...
60 - 64	873	...	1	1	-	2	3	6	30	96	149	585	...
65 - 69	500	...	-	-	1	2	-	4	11	25	44	413	...
70 - 74	259	...	-	-	-	-	-	-	2	7	13	237	...
75 +	151	...	-	-	-	1	-	-	1	3	4	142	...
Ecuador - Équateur[8]													
2013 (U)													
Total	53 986	35	3 779	14 590	14 903	9 016	4 339	2 314	1 484	1 014	810	1 500	202
0 - 14	393	5	164	157	42	17	5	1	-	1	-	-	1
15 - 19	9 263	16	2 559	4 688	1 420	387	114	32	19	8	5	-	15
20 - 24	16 575	4	871	7 584	5 749	1 706	435	135	39	20	3	10	19
25 - 29	13 039	8	119	1 727	6 023	3 567	1 053	315	134	45	24	10	14
30 - 34	6 429	1	21	295	1 270	2 491	1 425	527	211	79	67	30	12
35 - 39	3 027	-	13	55	250	613	881	604	301	159	78	71	2
40 - 44	1 758	-	-	24	54	150	294	468	361	193	103	110	1
45 - 49	1 136	1	3	3	15	33	76	152	289	257	150	150	7
50 - 54	777	-	3	1	4	14	23	44	89	169	199	229	2
55 - 59	498	-	3	2	-	3	6	14	24	51	122	271	2
60 - 64	310	-	3	-	2	2	2	4	11	19	36	231	-
65 - 69	206	-	2	1	1	2	-	4	1	7	10	178	-
70 - 74	113	-	1	4	4	-	-	-	-	2	3	99	-
75 +	157	-	4	11	13	5	5	2	2	1	6	107	1
Unknown - Inconnu	305	-	13	38	56	26	20	12	3	3	4	4	126
French Guiana - Guyane française													
2007 (C)													
Total	667	...	5	48	123	150	108	79	47	48	26	33	-
15 - 19	30	...	-	10	13	4	-	1	1	-	1	-	-
20 - 24	93	...	3	22	33	15	8	7	-	1	2	2	-
25 - 29	151	...	1	5	51	57	17	7	5	2	6	-	-
30 - 34	135	...	1	8	16	41	35	18	7	7	2	-	-
35 - 39	98	...	-	3	6	20	27	20	11	2	6	3	-
40 - 44	62	...	-	-	4	7	10	15	10	9	2	5	-
45 - 49	55	...	-	-	-	3	5	9	10	16	4	8	-
50 - 54	23	...	-	-	-	2	4	2	3	6	2	4	-
55 - 59	13	...	-	-	-	1	2	-	-	3	1	6	-
60 - 64	2	...	-	-	-	-	-	-	-	1	-	1	-
65 - 69	4	...	-	-	-	-	-	-	-	1	-	3	-
70 - 74	1	...	-	-	-	-	-	-	-	-	-	1	-
75 - 79	-	...	-	-	-	-	-	-	-	-	-	-	-
80 - 84	-	...	-	-	-	-	-	-	-	-	-	-	-
85 +	-	...	-	-	-	-	-	-	-	-	-	-	-
Paraguay													
2008 (U)													
Total	18 832	-	583	5 084	6 143	3 229	1 516	826	516	337	212	376	10
0 - 14	9	-	2	4	3	-	-	-	-	-	-	-	-
15 - 19	3 668	-	391	1 879	999	276	77	27	11	4	2	2	-
20 - 24	5 912	-	158	2 340	2 336	736	207	79	26	19	5	6	-
25 - 29	4 722	-	21	691	2 194	1 219	367	112	60	31	13	14	-

23. Marriages by age of groom and by age of bride: latest available year, 2005 - 2014
Mariages selon l'âge de l'époux et selon l'âge de l'épouse : dernière année disponible, 2005 - 2014 (continued - suite)

Continent, country or area, year, code[a] and age of bride / Continent, pays ou zone, date, code[a] et âge de l'épouse	Total	0-14	15-19	20-24	25-29	30-34	35-39	40-44	45-49	50-54	55-59	60+	Unknown Inconnu
AMERICA, SOUTH - AMÉRIQUE DU SUD													
Paraguay													
2008													
30 - 34	2 075	-	6	112	460	729	404	222	83	33	13	12	1
35 - 39	1 009	-	4	28	102	182	317	195	89	45	21	25	1
40 - 44	560	-	1	16	30	52	95	118	128	60	36	24	-
45 - 49	345	-	-	6	13	17	30	49	79	74	36	41	-
50 - 54	205	-	-	1	2	8	12	18	25	40	46	53	-
55 - 59	135	-	-	2	2	4	2	2	10	18	27	68	-
60 - 64	69	-	-	1	-	2	3	2	2	10	7	42	-
65 - 69	41	-	-	-	-	1	1	-	1	2	3	32	1
70 - 74	32	-	-	-	-	-	1	1	2	1	2	25	-
75 +	33	-	-	-	-	-	-	-	-	-	1	32	-
Unknown - Inconnu	17	-	-	4	2	3	-	1	-	-	-	-	7
Peru - Pérou[9,10]													
2010 (+C)													
Total	25 907	-	239	2 913	6 562	6 610	3 921	2 227	1 224	2 211[s]	...	...	...
0 - 14	6	-	5	-	-	-	-	1	-	-[s]	...	...	...
15 - 19	939	-	136	491	191	74	31	9	3	4[s]	...	...	...
20 - 24	4 805	-	82	1 694	1 880	766	254	86	21	22[s]	...	...	...
25 - 29	7 793	-	11	529	3 342	2 576	894	264	86	91[s]	...	...	...
30 - 34	5 669	-	4	134	900	2 445	1 346	538	180	122[s]	...	...	...
35 - 39	2 976	-	-	34	168	551	1 051	685	286	201[s]	...	...	...
40 - 44	1 520	-	-	9	39	116	248	459	328	321[s]	...	...	...
45 - 49	864	-	-	1	9	27	65	127	234	401[s]	...	...	...
50 +	1 335	-	1	21	33	55	32	58	86	1 049[s]	...	...	...
Venezuela (Bolivarian Republic of) - Venezuela (République bolivarienne du)													
2013 (C)													
Total	99 065	341	10 139	25 151	25 848	15 793	8 804	5 400	3 394	2 008	1 087	1 100	...
0 - 14	40	1	13	11	7	4	2	1	-	-	-	1	...
15 - 19	2 900	90	1 816	724	161	50	24	10	8	3	5	9	...
20 - 24	19 664	146	5 269	10 234	2 931	741	211	70	29	11	8	14	...
25 - 29	26 700	55	2 049	9 272	11 297	2 911	784	207	63	31	11	20	...
30 - 34	19 461	31	651	3 250	7 299	5 868	1 643	499	134	44	17	25	...
35 - 39	11 218	13	200	1 012	2 558	3 422	2 636	898	323	108	20	28	...
40 - 44	7 146	1	76	393	988	1 603	1 793	1 490	553	168	53	28	...
45 - 49	4 646	2	28	145	364	682	978	1 078	883	340	89	57	...
50 - 54	2 956	-	15	55	126	298	396	657	694	484	160	71	...
55 - 59	1 850	1	10	25	63	114	193	273	390	398	250	133	...
60 +	2 484	1	12	30	54	100	144	217	317	421	474	714	...
ASIA - ASIE													
Armenia - Arménie													
2009 (+C)													
Total	18 773	...	153	4 608	7 796	3 482	1 313	560	325	208	132	196	-
15 - 19	2 010	...	122	928	825	124	11	-	-	-	-	-	-
20 - 24	9 521	...	28	3 366	4 655	1 278	170	19	2	3	-	-	-
25 - 29	4 516	...	2	282	2 151	1 474	478	95	27	7	-	-	-
30 - 34	1 467	...	-	26	130	539	455	215	76	17	9	-	-
35 - 39	528	...	-	4	20	47	165	154	92	32	10	4	-
40 - 44	238	...	-	2	8	13	22	52	72	42	16	11	-
45 - 49	161	...	1	-	2	4	6	14	39	53	20	22	-
50 - 54	153	...	-	-	4	3	4	8	8	45	47	34	-
55 - 59	101	...	-	-	-	-	1	2	4	5	25	64	-
60 +	78	...	-	-	1	-	1	1	5	4	5	61	-
Azerbaijan - Azerbaïdjan													
2013 (+C)													
15 - 19	20 791	...	437	9 759	8 643	1 763	162	17	6	1	-	3	...
15 +	86 852	...	712	26 208	34 344	13 402	5 464	2 920	1 522	967	550	763	...
20 - 24	38 318	...	242	14 391	17 418	5 100	943	185	28	9	-	2	...
25 - 29	15 285	...	26	1 769	7 099	4 153	1 588	490	115	34	9	2	...
30 - 34	6 147	...	3	226	988	1 902	1 673	914	312	96	27	6	...

Continent, country or area, year, code[a] and age of bride / Continent, pays ou zone, date, code[a] et âge de l'épouse	Total	0-14	15-19	20-24	25-29	30-34	35-39	40-44	45-49	50-54	55-59	60+	Unknown Inconnu
ASIA - ASIE													
Azerbaijan - Azerbaïdjan													
2013													
35 - 39	2 914	...	2	40	139	384	830	766	445	200	63	45	...
40 - 44	1 562	...	1	11	36	72	216	414	359	249	124	80	...
45 - 49	916	...	-	4	6	19	41	106	200	236	144	160	...
50 - 54	523	...	-	1	2	7	8	23	45	122	122	193	...
55 - 59	225	...	1	1	5	-	2	5	10	17	52	132	...
60 +	171	...	-	6	8	2	1	-	2	3	9	140	...
Bahrain - Bahreïn													
2014 (...)													
Total	7 673	...	175	2 221	3 024	1 052	447	266	173	301[s]	...	...	14
0 - 14	27	...	6	14	5	2	-	-	-	-[s]	...	...	-
15 - 19	1 425	...	116	799	444	42	10	3	2	6[s]	...	...	3
20 - 24	2 817	...	23	1 057	1 380	270	50	19	6	12[s]	...	...	-
25 - 29	1 396	...	3	87	690	412	109	45	24	26[s]	...	...	-
30 - 34	569	...	1	20	83	189	142	68	29	37[s]	...	...	-
35 - 39	299	...	1	3	23	43	76	66	41	46[s]	...	...	-
40 - 44	162	...	-	1	7	6	19	27	40	62[s]	...	...	-
45 - 49	74	...	-	1	2	5	2	11	13	40[s]	...	...	-
50 +	50	...	-	-	-	-	3	6	6	35[s]	...	...	-
Unknown - Inconnu	854	...	25	239	390	83	36	21	12	37[s]	...	...	11
Brunei Darussalam - Brunéi Darussalam													
2008 (...)													
Total	2 391	-	68	527	870	534	177	73	53	40	23	26	-
0 - 14	6	...	...	...	...	...	...	...	...	...	...	...	...
15 - 19	205	...	...	...	...	...	...	...	...	...	...	...	...
20 - 24	701	...	...	...	...	...	...	...	...	...	...	...	...
25 - 29	954	...	...	...	...	...	...	...	...	...	...	...	...
30 - 34	403	...	...	...	...	...	...	...	...	...	...	...	...
35 - 39	66	...	...	...	...	...	...	...	...	...	...	...	...
40 - 44	37	...	...	...	...	...	...	...	...	...	...	...	...
45 - 49	15	...	...	...	...	...	...	...	...	...	...	...	...
50 - 54	3	...	...	...	...	...	...	...	...	...	...	...	...
55 - 59	1	...	...	...	...	...	...	...	...	...	...	...	...
60 - 64	-	...	...	...	...	...	...	...	...	...	...	...	...
65 - 69	-	...	...	...	...	...	...	...	...	...	...	...	...
70 - 74	-	...	...	...	...	...	...	...	...	...	...	...	...
75 +	-	...	...	...	...	...	...	...	...	...	...	...	...
Unknown - Inconnu	-	...	...	...	...	...	...	...	...	...	...	...	...
China, Hong Kong SAR - Chine, Hong Kong RAS													
2013 (C)													
Total	55 274	...	176	3 652	12 798	14 719	8 180	5 110	3 581	2 815	1 836	2 407	...
15 - 19	650	...	94	324	135	55	23	9	5	4	-	1	...
20 - 24	7 273	...	71	2 415	2 647	1 180	489	227	117	76	33	18	...
25 - 29	18 048	...	8	718	8 039	5 790	1 788	857	425	233	125	65	...
30 - 34	14 388	...	3	127	1 623	6 505	3 233	1 287	720	474	248	168	...
35 - 39	6 661	...	-	41	252	929	1 988	1 351	836	581	351	332	...
40 - 44	4 088	...	-	18	70	183	510	989	778	621	424	495	...
45 - 49	2 175	...	-	9	22	50	108	295	500	473	283	435	...
50 - 54	1 153	...	-	-	4	19	31	75	146	275	235	368	...
55 - 59	482	...	-	-	6	6	8	15	44	65	112	226	...
60 - 64	170	...	-	-	-	2	2	1	8	10	17	130	...
65 - 69	88	...	-	-	-	-	-	1	1	2	7	77	...
70 - 74	47	...	-	-	-	-	-	2	1	1	-	43	...
75 +	51	...	-	-	-	-	-	1	-	-	1	49	...
China, Macao SAR - Chine, Macao RAS													
2009 (+C)													
Total	3 035	-	18	608	1 023	697	286	157	98	68	39	41	-
0 - 14	-	-	-	-	-	-	-	-	-	-	-	-	-
15 - 19	66	-	5	40	17	3	1	-	-	-	-	-	-
20 - 24	993	-	12	445	353	125	36	14	5	3	-	-	-
25 - 29	1 166	-	1	109	575	313	94	42	13	11	7	1	-
30 - 34	444	-	-	10	62	212	83	33	25	12	5	2	-

Continent, country or area, year, code[a] and age of bride / Continent, pays ou zone, date, code[a] et âge de l'épouse	Age of groom - - âge de l'époux												
	Total	0-14	15-19	20-24	25-29	30-34	35-39	40-44	45-49	50-54	55-59	60+	Unknown Inconnu
ASIA - ASIE													
China, Macao SAR - Chine, Macao RAS													
2009													
35 - 39	195	-	-	4	9	30	62	41	26	8	8	7	-
40 - 44	72	-	-	-	5	8	9	17	12	9	6	6	-
45 - 49	58	-	-	-	1	4	1	7	16	14	8	7	-
50 - 54	20	-	-	-	1	2	-	3	1	9	2	2	-
55 - 59	11	-	-	-	-	-	-	-	-	1	2	8	-
60 - 64	4	-	-	-	-	-	-	-	-	1	1	2	-
65 - 69	1	-	-	-	-	-	-	-	-	-	-	1	-
70 +	5	-	-	-	-	-	-	-	-	-	-	5	-
2014 (+C)													
Total	4 085	...	...	525[g]	...	...	...	...	417[r]	...	...	...	...
0 - 24	1 031	...	...	...	...	...	...	...	...	...	...	...	...
25 - 34	2 489	...	...	...	...	...	...	...	...	...	...	...	...
35 - 44	368	...	...	...	...	...	...	...	...	...	...	...	...
45 +	197	...	...	...	...	...	...	...	...	...	...	...	...
Cyprus - Chypre[11,12]													
2013 (C)													
Total	5 493	-	22	437	1 854	1 711	597	322	187	127	69	132	35
0 - 14	-	-	-	-	-	-	-	-	-	-	-	-	-
15 - 19	80	-	7	41	18	10	2	-	2	-	-	-	-
20 - 24	805	-	8	237	395	130	22	9	4	-	-	-	-
25 - 29	2 298	-	5	111	1 161	785	147	44	26	12	3	4	-
30 - 34	1 290	-	2	23	215	639	241	102	31	23	5	8	1
35 - 39	521	-	-	19	48	117	134	102	57	23	11	10	-
40 - 44	214	-	-	6	10	23	38	44	29	31	15	18	-
45 - 49	129	-	-	-	5	6	8	16	30	22	13	29	-
50 - 54	64	-	-	-	2	-	3	4	6	13	14	22	-
55 - 59	30	-	-	-	-	-	1	1	2	2	6	18	-
60 +	27	-	-	-	-	-	1	-	-	1	2	23	-
Unknown - Inconnu	35	-	-	-	-	1	-	-	-	-	-	-	34
Georgia - Géorgie													
2011 (C)													
Total	30 863	...	1 013[h]	7 972	8 522	5 705	3 513	1 915	1 047	534	285	353	4
16 - 19	4 554	...	...	...	...	...	...	...	...	...	...	...	...
20 - 24	10 875	...	...	...	...	...	...	...	...	...	...	...	...
25 - 29	7 155	...	...	...	...	...	...	...	...	...	...	...	...
30 - 34	4 052	...	...	...	...	...	...	...	...	...	...	...	...
35 - 39	2 053	...	...	...	...	...	...	...	...	...	...	...	...
40 - 44	1 040	...	...	...	...	...	...	...	...	...	...	...	...
45 - 49	567	...	...	...	...	...	...	...	...	...	...	...	...
50 - 54	280	...	...	...	...	...	...	...	...	...	...	...	...
55 - 59	145	...	...	...	...	...	...	...	...	...	...	...	...
60 +	142	...	...	...	...	...	...	...	...	...	...	...	...
Unknown - Inconnu	-	...	...	...	...	...	...	...	...	...	...	...	...
Iran (Islamic Republic of) - Iran (République islamique d')[13]													
2013 (+C)													
Total	774 513	313	36 155	276 392	284 624	103 873	30 799	14 090	7 795	5 618	4 456	10 298	100
0 - 14	41 437	128	6 842	24 984	8 499	760	132	58	16	10	-	5	3
15 - 19	234 974	135	22 578	129 780	71 685	9 263	1 057	266	95	60	22	31	2
20 - 24	252 586	38	5 551	99 107	114 731	27 891	3 761	884	286	135	91	107	4
25 - 29	148 912	5	931	19 088	74 423	40 506	9 375	2 783	922	399	206	272	2
30 - 34	56 347	4	214	2 811	13 021	20 644	10 694	4 645	2 032	981	580	720	1
35 - 39	20 576	-	27	519	1 877	4 004	4 536	3 559	2 337	1 413	926	1 377	1
40 - 44	9 376	-	8	80	314	658	1 049	1 501	1 422	1 342	1 077	1 924	1
45 - 49	4 397	1	1	15	52	117	154	328	519	810	680	1 720	-
50 - 54	2 725	-	2	4	13	20	26	54	140	362	563	1 541	-
55 - 59	1 481	-	1	2	4	5	6	11	23	82	228	1 118	1
60 - 64	807	-	-	-	2	1	6	1	2	15	64	716	-
65 - 69	408	-	-	-	-	1	2	-	1	5	14	385	-
70 - 74	227	-	-	-	1	1	-	-	-	-	4	221	-
75 +	170	-	-	1	1	1	1	-	-	3	1	161	1
Unknown - Inconnu	90	2	-	1	1	1	-	-	-	1	-	-	84

23. Marriages by age of groom and by age of bride: latest available year, 2005 - 2014
Mariages selon l'âge de l'époux et selon l'âge de l'épouse : dernière année disponible, 2005 - 2014 (continued - suite)

Continent, country or area, year, code[a] and age of bride / Continent, pays ou zone, date, code[a] et âge de l'épouse	Total	0-14	15-19	20-24	25-29	30-34	35-39	40-44	45-49	50-54	55-59	60+	Unknown Inconnu
ASIA - ASIE													
Israel - Israël[14]													
2012 (C)													
Total	50 474	...	1 804	11 900	18 481	10 188	3 519	1 401	696	447	325	541	1 172
15 - 19	6 901	...	1 292	3 498	1 498	260	39	6	-	-	-	-	308
20 - 24	17 575	...	461	7 642	6 903	1 792	279	43	15	3	2	-	435
25 - 29	15 873	...	5	492	8 978	4 929	990	203	48	14	3	1	210
30 - 34	5 548	...	-	39	802	2 706	1 325	395	110	40	14	10	107
35 - 39	1 955	...	1	5	76	335	700	452	185	90	23	20	68
40 - 44	652	...	-	2	9	27	83	195	166	88	34	27	21
45 - 49	402	...	-	-	1	3	6	37	102	106	77	60	10
50 - 54	260	...	-	-	-	-	3	3	25	62	81	79	7
55 - 59	171	...	-	-	-	-	-	-	4	7	49	107	4
60 - 64	133	...	-	-	-	-	-	1	1	2	16	111	2
65 - 69	62	...	-	-	-	-	-	-	-	-	1	61	-
70 - 74	19	...	-	-	-	-	-	-	-	-	-	19	-
75 +	14	...	-	-	-	-	-	-	-	-	-	14	-
Unknown - Inconnu	909	...	45	222	214	136	94	66	40	35	25	32	-
Japan - Japon[15]													
2013 (+C)													
Total	544 976	-	5 423	56 550	176 765	134 947	82 911	43 648	19 283	9 966	6 036	9 446	1
0 - 14	-	-	-	-	-	-	-	-	-	-	-	-	-
15 - 19	10 737	-	4 126	4 377	1 271	555	234	87	42	20	10	15	-
20 - 24	84 180	-	1 164	38 200	28 263	10 332	3 944	1 414	437	230	108	88	-
25 - 29	204 408	-	98	11 200	118 933	50 879	16 271	4 813	1 338	475	226	175	-
30 - 34	126 760	-	24	2 144	23 184	58 066	29 308	9 774	2 719	881	375	285	-
35 - 39	67 077	-	6	517	4 289	12 643	26 777	15 326	5 008	1 527	591	393	-
40 - 44	27 097	-	3	96	718	2 126	5 286	9 798	5 424	2 139	848	659	-
45 - 49	11 087	-	2	16	88	287	918	1 995	3 455	2 341	1 107	878	-
50 - 54	5 744	-	-	-	19	51	146	355	687	1 878	1 372	1 236	-
55 - 59	3 177	-	-	-	-	7	21	67	137	372	1 060	1 513	-
60 - 64	2 271	-	-	-	-	1	5	16	31	82	264	1 872	-
65 - 69	1 341	-	-	-	-	-	1	3	5	19	61	1 252	-
70 - 74	687	-	-	-	-	-	-	-	-	1	11	674	1
75 +	410	-	-	-	-	-	-	-	-	1	3	406	-
Unknown - Inconnu	-	-	-	-	-	-	-	-	-	-	-	-	-
Jordan - Jordanie													
2010[16] (+C)													
Total	62 107	...	16 151	25 559	12 760	4 002	1 795	1 151	437	252[s]	...	...	-
18 - 19	1 262	...	1 017	191	40	11	1	2	-	-[s]	...	...	-
20 - 24	14 272	...	6 768	6 453	835	139	42	20	7	8[s]	...	...	-
25 - 29	25 434	...	6 276	12 608	5 720	633	120	45	16	16[s]	...	...	-
30 - 34	11 523	...	1 603	4 782	3 679	1 153	197	70	25	14[s]	...	...	-
35 - 39	4 064	...	299	1 043	1 434	819	350	92	19	8[s]	...	...	-
40 - 44	2 365	...	99	321	681	647	358	217	35	7[s]	...	...	-
45 - 49	1 139	...	35	81	220	283	249	196	57	18[s]	...	...	-
50 - 54	639	...	14	37	73	152	169	121	53	20[s]	...	...	-
55 - 59	425	...	12	18	35	80	95	107	56	22[s]	...	...	-
60 - 64	318	...	11	7	21	40	66	97	39	37[s]	...	...	-
65 +	666	...	17	18	22	45	148	184	130	102[s]	...	...	-
Kazakhstan													
2013 (C)													
Total	168 447	101[d]	3 612[j]	57 563	60 803	22 537	10 618	5 553	3 077	2 126	1 229	1 228	...
0 - 17	1 392	38[d]	367[j]	789	174	19	3	1	-	1	-	-	...
18 - 19	19 707	49[d]	2 280[j]	12 409	4 319	555	73	17	3	1	1	-	...
20 - 24	79 862	11[d]	889[j]	39 230	33 107	5 486	899	178	36	14	9	3	...
25 - 29	37 703	2[d]	63[j]	4 541	19 985	9 429	2 705	668	220	64	21	5	...
30 - 34	14 237	-[d]	12[j]	481	2 642	5 502	3 632	1 345	408	145	48	22	...
35 - 39	7 447	-[d]	1[j]	85	460	1 273	2 563	1 834	776	308	98	49	...
40 - 44	3 675	1[d]	-[j]	21	85	225	598	1 178	826	471	177	93	...
45 - 49	1 932	-[d]	-[j]	3	24	42	114	256	594	523	234	142	...
50 - 54	1 249	-[d]	-[j]	2	4	4	26	60	173	448	303	229	...
55 - 59	674	-[d]	-[j]	-	2	1	5	14	30	119	266	237	...
60 +	568	-[d]	-[j]	1	1	1	-	2	11	32	72	448	...
Unknown - Inconnu	1	-[d]	-[j]	1	-	-	-	-	-	-	-	-	...

23. Marriages by age of groom and by age of bride: latest available year, 2005 - 2014
Mariages selon l'âge de l'époux et selon l'âge de l'épouse : dernière année disponible, 2005 - 2014 (continued - suite)

Continent, pays ou zone, date, code[a] et âge de l'épouse	Total	0-14	15-19	20-24	25-29	30-34	35-39	40-44	45-49	50-54	55-59	60+	Unknown Inconnu
ASIA - ASIE													
Kuwait - Koweït													
2013 (C)													
Total	15 118	-	322	4 357	5 256	2 452	1 116	680	935[r]	...	...	...	...
0 - 14	-	-	-	-	-	-	-	-	.[r]	...	...	...	...
15 - 19	2 697	-	250	1 626	692	98	16	6	9[r]	...	...	...	...
20 - 24	5 788	-	63	2 376	2 593	588	106	33	29[r]	...	...	...	...
25 - 29	3 515	-	7	300	1 624	1 024	347	116	97[r]	...	...	...	...
30 - 34	1 614	-	-	35	258	549	372	226	174[r]	...	...	...	...
35 - 39	789	-	1	15	61	136	186	167	223[r]	...	...	...	...
40 - 44	385	-	1	3	20	34	64	93	170[r]	...	...	...	...
45 +	330	-	-	2	8	23	25	39	233[r]	...	...	...	...
Kyrgyzstan - Kirghizstan													
2013 (C)													
Total	53 578	-	864	18 918	20 365	6 526	2 961	1 732	921	574	308	409	...
0 - 14	-	-	-	-	-	-	-	-	-	-	-	-	...
15 - 19	11 100	-	692	6 927	3 208	244	20	6	-	1	-	2	...
20 - 24	25 806	-	153	11 201	12 070	2 048	282	36	11	5	-	-	...
25 - 29	9 397	-	15	723	4 651	2 829	869	231	61	14	2	2	...
30 - 34	3 481	-	2	61	374	1 213	1 104	514	151	51	8	3	...
35 - 39	1 766	-	1	5	49	150	556	604	251	90	30	30	...
40 - 44	941	-	1	1	10	35	114	286	264	125	57	48	...
45 - 49	520	-	-	-	2	5	8	46	154	149	85	71	...
50 - 54	309	-	-	-	1	1	8	6	23	114	77	79	...
55 - 59	153	-	-	-	-	1	-	2	4	23	40	83	...
60 - 64	60	-	-	-	-	-	-	1	2	1	8	48	...
65 - 69	18	-	-	-	-	-	-	-	-	-	1	17	...
70 - 74	13	-	-	-	-	-	-	-	-	1	-	12	...
75 +	14	-	-	-	-	-	-	-	-	-	-	14	...
Mongolia - Mongolie													
2009 (+C)													
Total	34 071	...	1 742[j]	15 582	10 852	4 219	1 057	369	147	103[s]	...	...	-
18 - 19	3 283	...	...	...	...	...	...	...	...	...	...	...	...
20 - 24	17 343	...	...	...	...	...	...	...	...	...	...	...	...
25 - 29	8 841	...	...	...	...	...	...	...	...	...	...	...	...
30 - 34	3 187	...	...	...	...	...	...	...	...	...	...	...	...
35 - 39	1 003	...	...	...	...	...	...	...	...	...	...	...	...
40 - 44	274	...	...	...	...	...	...	...	...	...	...	...	...
45 - 49	95	...	...	...	...	...	...	...	...	...	...	...	...
50 +	45	...	...	...	...	...	...	...	...	...	...	...	...
Philippines[17]													
2012 (U)													
Total	481 220	...	11 724[f]	125 421	165 012	95 129	38 959	18 618	10 174	16 134[s]	...	...	49
0 - 19	54 119	...	6 911[f]	30 475	11 873	3 078	986	439	174	183[s]	...	...	-
20 - 24	172 166	...	4 366[f]	75 724	63 575	19 346	5 190	1 988	871	1 100[s]	...	...	6
25 - 29	142 799	...	358[f]	16 079	72 293	38 139	9 964	3 062	1 333	1 571[s]	...	...	-
30 - 34	63 892	...	67[f]	2 417	14 130	27 443	12 354	4 175	1 622	1 680[s]	...	...	4
35 - 39	23 778	...	10[f]	476	2 380	5 378	7 666	4 399	1 771	1 698[s]	...	...	-
40 - 44	11 309	...	2[f]	154	523	1 264	1 996	3 193	2 080	2 096[s]	...	...	1
45 - 49	6 189	...	4[f]	42	141	329	583	1 010	1 668	2 410[s]	...	...	2
50 +	6 912	...	5[f]	47	92	149	219	351	653	5 394[s]	...	...	2
Unknown - Inconnu	56	...	1[f]	7	5	3	1	1	2	2[s]	...	...	34
Qatar													
2012 (C)													
Total	3 532	...	71	963	1 214	678	256	145	104	55	21	25	...
0 - 19	687	...	57	390	199	33	8	-	-	-	-	-	...
20 - 24	1 359	...	12	506	597	192	32	8	9	2	1	-	...
25 - 29	798	...	1	51	336	275	81	29	11	8	5	1	...
30 - 34	371	...	1	11	58	129	73	53	33	9	3	1	...
35 - 39	181	...	-	3	19	31	44	29	32	13	5	5	...
40 - 44	72	...	-	1	4	12	9	16	11	11	4	4	...
45 - 49	40	...	-	1	1	3	6	8	5	7	3	6	...
50 - 54	19	...	-	-	-	2	3	2	3	5	-	6	...
55 - 59	3	...	-	-	-	2	-	-	-	-	-	1	...
60 +	2	...	-	-	-	1	-	-	-	-	-	1	...

Continent, country or area, year, code[a] and age of bride / Continent, pays ou zone, date, code[a] et âge de l'épouse	Total	0-14	15-19	20-24	25-29	30-34	35-39	40-44	45-49	50-54	55-59	60+	Unknown Inconnu
ASIA - ASIE													
2013 (C)													
Total	3 619	...	70[f]	983	1 325	593	270	152	120	62	20	24	...
0 - 19	582	...	...	...	...	...	...	...	...	...	...	...	...
20 - 24	1 412	...	...	...	...	...	...	...	...	...	...	...	...
25 - 29	877	...	...	...	...	...	...	...	...	...	...	...	...
30 - 34	369	...	...	...	...	...	...	...	...	...	...	...	...
35 - 39	206	...	...	...	...	...	...	...	...	...	...	...	...
40 - 44	112	...	...	...	...	...	...	...	...	...	...	...	...
45 - 49	41	...	...	...	...	...	...	...	...	...	...	...	...
50 - 54	17	...	...	...	...	...	...	...	...	...	...	...	...
55 - 59	3	...	...	...	...	...	...	...	...	...	...	...	...
60 +	-	...	...	...	...	...	...	...	...	...	...	...	...
Republic of Korea - République de Corée[18]													
2013 (+C)													
Total	322 807	-	946	9 405	78 492	132 526	48 492	21 978	11 744	8 806	5 357	5 061	-
0 - 14	15	-	8	3	1	3	-	-	-	-	-	-	-
15 - 19	4 422	-	673	891	566	557	879	723	118	12	-	3	-
20 - 24	27 723	-	233	6 247	10 910	6 071	2 096	1 546	494	104	17	5	-
25 - 29	124 486	-	21	1 890	54 801	58 024	7 232	1 655	616	178	59	10	-
30 - 34	102 351	-	8	302	11 400	62 826	22 834	3 713	858	273	106	31	-
35 - 39	27 304	-	3	58	707	4 420	12 862	6 951	1 579	495	159	70	-
40 - 44	13 960	-	-	11	90	529	2 147	5 640	3 471	1 447	439	186	-
45 - 49	9 495	-	-	2	12	78	372	1 439	3 343	2 926	983	340	-
50 - 54	7 169	-	-	1	4	14	61	280	1 064	2 727	2 113	905	-
55 - 59	3 570	-	-	-	1	4	7	26	173	561	1 289	1 509	-
60 - 64	1 298	-	-	-	-	-	2	5	25	76	163	1 027	-
65 - 69	587	-	-	-	-	-	-	-	3	7	23	554	-
70 - 74	304	-	-	-	-	-	-	-	-	-	5	299	-
75 +	123	-	-	-	-	-	-	-	-	-	1	122	-
Unknown - Inconnu	-	-	-	-	-	-	-	-	-	-	-	-	-
Singapore - Singapour[19]													
2014 (+C)													
Total	28 407	-	70	1 625	9 834	8 444	3 697	2 053	1 090	764	456	374	-
0 - 14	-	-	-	-	-	-	-	-	-	-	-	-	-
15 - 19	286	-	44	134	54	20	19	5	3	4	3	-	-
20 - 24	4 042	-	23	1 019	1 910	643	227	116	54	39	7	4	-
25 - 29	12 820	-	1	389	6 783	4 084	932	383	153	50	30	15	-
30 - 34	6 704	-	2	55	917	3 175	1 496	594	238	143	56	28	-
35 - 39	2 390	-	-	22	134	402	821	543	230	128	72	38	-
40 - 44	1 127	-	-	3	27	91	155	298	228	160	106	59	-
45 - 49	566	-	-	3	6	19	36	96	132	139	76	59	-
50 - 54	287	-	-	-	3	8	9	17	43	78	64	65	-
55 - 59	117	-	-	-	-	2	1	1	5	22	36	50	-
60 +	68	-	-	-	-	-	1	-	4	1	6	56	-
Unknown - Inconnu	-	-	-	-	-	-	-	-	-	-	-	-	...
Sri Lanka													
2007 (+U)													
Total	196 236	-	4 874	50 475	77 223	37 758	13 636	5 693	3 065	1 585	988	939	-
0 - 14	20	-	7	7	5	1	-	-	-	-	-	-	-
15 - 19	35 127	-	3 814	19 794	10 010	1 301	168	27	6	3	1	3	-
20 - 24	73 649	-	899	26 759	35 730	8 980	1 043	174	44	12	4	4	-
25 - 29	55 088	-	135	3 335	29 096	18 013	3 732	560	160	29	16	12	-
30 - 34	17 764	-	15	432	1 881	8 373	5 319	1 316	310	74	29	15	-
35 - 39	7 468	-	3	123	400	864	2 930	2 070	815	185	47	31	-
40 - 44	3 529	-	-	10	74	184	350	1 307	1 008	389	157	50	-
45 - 49	1 852	-	-	8	14	31	74	194	600	536	278	117	-
50 - 54	958	-	1	5	8	8	18	39	98	299	294	188	-
55 - 59	471	-	-	1	5	2	2	6	17	43	138	257	-
60 - 64	193	-	-	1	-	1	-	-	6	13	21	151	-
65 - 69	71	-	-	-	-	-	-	-	1	1	1	68	-
70 - 74	31	-	-	-	-	-	-	-	-	1	2	28	-
75 +	15	-	-	-	-	-	-	-	-	-	-	15	-

Continent, country or area, year, code[a] and age of bride / Continent, pays ou zone, date, code[a] et âge de l'épouse	Total	0-14	15-19	20-24	25-29	30-34	35-39	40-44	45-49	50-54	55-59	60+	Unknown Inconnu
ASIA - ASIE													
State of Palestine - État de Palestine													
2013 (C)													
Total	42 698	...	2 912	17 337	14 342	4 271	1 396	748	541	399	286	466	...
12 - 14	634	...	175	356	95	8	-	-	-	-	-	-	...
15 - 19	18 425	...	2 434	10 021	5 016	811	100	22	11	7	1	2	...
20 - 24	16 951	...	279	6 579	7 358	2 074	440	113	62	25	14	7	...
25 - 29	4 001	...	21	337	1 683	1 005	460	261	119	64	28	23	...
30 - 34	1 437	...	1	41	160	305	280	206	175	109	79	81	...
35 - 39	684	...	2	3	23	52	90	92	105	107	91	119	...
40 - 44	342	...	-	-	5	16	22	42	44	54	41	118	...
45 - 49	148	...	-	-	2	-	3	11	19	23	21	69	...
50 - 54	52	...	-	-	-	-	1	1	4	8	6	32	...
55 - 59	19	...	-	-	-	-	-	-	2	2	5	10	...
60 - 64	2	...	-	-	-	-	-	-	-	-	-	2	...
65 +	3	...	-	-	-	-	-	-	-	-	-	3	...
Tajikistan - Tadjikistan													
2013 (+C)													
Total	96 989	-	3 379	50 138	26 671	7 858	4 254	2 469	991	531	282	307	109
0 - 14	-	-	-	-	-	-	-	-	-	-	-	-	-
15 - 19	41 960	-	3 167	29 446	8 852	464	3	-	1	-	-	-	27
20 - 24	35 320	-	210	20 076	12 820	1 864	281	42	1	-	-	-	26
25 - 29	10 982	-	-	558	4 797	3 824	1 310	338	93	39	2	-	21
30 - 34	4 883	-	-	-	165	1 634	1 860	784	243	124	54	14	5
35 - 39	2 502	-	-	-	-	50	789	1 032	327	147	75	78	4
40 - 44	842	-	-	-	-	-	3	269	276	141	70	82	1
45 - 49	237	-	-	-	-	-	-	-	47	72	51	67	-
50 - 54	85	-	-	-	-	-	-	-	-	8	30	47	-
55 - 59	10	-	-	-	-	-	-	-	-	-	-	10	-
60 - 64	6	-	-	-	-	-	-	-	1	-	-	5	-
65 - 69	3	-	-	-	-	-	-	-	-	-	-	3	-
70 - 74	1	-	-	-	-	-	-	-	-	-	-	1	-
75 +	-	-	-	-	-	-	-	-	-	-	-	-	-
Unknown - Inconnu	158	-	2	58	37	22	8	4	2	-	-	-	25
Turkey - Turquie[20]													
2013 (C)													
Total	600 138	...	13 546[f]	155 555	241 462	103 064	35 982	16 537	10 291	6 915	5 005	8 421	3 360
0 - 19	123 120	...	9 834[f]	58 992	44 360	8 309	958	163	35	12	9	5	443
20 - 24	213 019	...	3 111[f]	77 919	100 343	25 956	3 846	682	202	64	23	21	852
25 - 29	145 037	...	374[f]	14 356	79 318	38 281	8 903	1 988	656	197	80	67	817
30 - 34	53 463	...	68[f]	1 824	11 146	21 705	11 531	4 040	1 564	567	260	165	593
35 - 39	22 989	...	19[f]	330	1 663	4 545	6 868	4 865	2 403	1 051	482	416	347
40 - 44	11 632	...	2[f]	54	282	750	1 579	2 825	2 716	1 592	842	829	161
45 - 49	6 804	...	1[f]	16	47	146	269	610	1 560	1 723	1 093	1 263	76
50 - 54	3 962	...	-[f]	1	12	22	46	118	314	910	1 110	1 388	41
55 - 59	2 371	...	-[f]	-	1	2	12	22	53	194	625	1 445	17
60 - 64	1 326	...	-[f]	-	-	1	4	-	13	28	126	1 149	5
65 - 69	625	...	-[f]	-	-	-	-	-	3	2	17	598	5
70 - 74	272	...	-[f]	-	-	-	-	-	-	1	2	266	3
75 +	154	...	-[f]	-	-	-	-	1	1	-	-	152	-
Unknown - Inconnu	15 364	...	137[f]	2 063	4 290	3 347	1 966	1 223	771	574	336	657	-
EUROPE													
Åland Islands - Îles d'Åland													
2013 (C)													
Total	118	-	1	5	15	31	18	9	16	11	7	5	...
0 - 14	-	-	-	-	-	-	-	-	-	-	-	-	...
15 - 19	-	-	-	-	-	-	-	-	-	-	-	-	...
20 - 24	9	-	1	4	3	1	-	-	-	-	-	-	...
25 - 29	30	-	-	1	9	13	3	1	2	1	-	-	...
30 - 34	24	-	-	-	3	14	5	1	1	-	-	-	...
35 - 39	17	-	-	-	-	2	7	4	3	1	-	-	...
40 - 44	10	-	-	-	-	1	2	3	1	2	1	-	...

23. Marriages by age of groom and by age of bride: latest available year, 2005 - 2014
Mariages selon l'âge de l'époux et selon l'âge de l'épouse : dernière année disponible, 2005 - 2014 (continued - suite)

Continent, country or area, year, code[a] and age of bride / Continent, pays ou zone, date, code[a] et âge de l'épouse	Total	0-14	15-19	20-24	25-29	30-34	35-39	40-44	45-49	50-54	55-59	60+	Unknown Inconnu
EUROPE													
Åland Islands - Îles d'Åland													
2013													
45 - 49	14	-	-	-	-	-	1	-	7	3	3	-	...
50 - 54	6	-	-	-	-	-	-	-	2	2	2	-	...
55 - 59	4	-	-	-	-	-	-	-	-	2	1	1	...
60 - 64	-	-	-	-	-	-	-	-	-	-	-	-	...
65 - 69	2	-	-	-	-	-	-	-	-	-	-	2	...
70 - 74	1	-	-	-	-	-	-	-	-	-	-	1	...
75 +	1	-	-	-	-	-	-	-	-	-	-	1	...
Albania - Albanie													
2013 (C)													
Total	23 820	...	154[f]	4 209	10 364	5 730	1 906	749	315	193	99	101	...
0 - 19	5 635	...	107[f]	1 842	2 922	693	65	5	1	-	-	-	...
20 - 24	10 054	...	42[f]	2 123	5 023	2 395	416	48	4	3	-	-	...
25 - 29	5 277	...	3[f]	205	2 191	1 955	733	148	33	8	1	-	...
30 - 34	1 710	...	2[f]	27	192	607	491	277	84	23	3	4	...
35 - 39	644	...	-[f]	9	30	65	168	199	101	40	26	6	...
40 - 44	251	...	-[f]	2	4	11	26	58	64	54	22	10	...
45 - 49	126	...	-[f]	-	2	3	7	11	22	43	18	20	...
50 - 54	63	...	-[f]	-	-	1	-	2	5	18	17	20	...
55 - 59	38	...	-[f]	-	-	-	-	1	1	4	9	23	...
60 - 64	12	...	-[f]	1	-	-	-	-	-	-	3	8	...
65 - 69	6	...	-[f]	-	-	-	-	-	-	-	-	6	...
70 - 74	4	...	-[f]	-	-	-	-	-	-	-	-	4	...
75 +	-	...	-[f]	-	-	-	-	-	-	-	-	-	...
Austria - Autriche[21]													
2013 (C)													
Total	36 140	-	166	2 648	7 180	8 897	5 657	3 801	2 815	2 049	1 355	1 572	...
0 - 14	-	-	-	-	-	-	-	-	-	-	-	-	...
15 - 19	680	-	93	408	139	31	7	2	-	-	-	-	...
20 - 24	4 764	-	60	1 694	2 026	679	186	60	35	14	3	7	...
25 - 29	9 572	-	12	417	3 919	3 680	1 033	313	129	43	18	8	...
30 - 34	8 223	-	-	92	882	3 640	2 333	813	301	100	37	25	...
35 - 39	4 459	-	-	24	146	667	1 551	1 235	515	208	63	50	...
40 - 44	3 004	-	1	9	43	151	413	917	788	406	171	105	...
45 - 49	2 330	-	-	3	15	35	101	332	714	595	316	219	...
50 - 54	1 666	-	-	1	6	7	27	111	270	497	432	315	...
55 - 59	824	-	-	-	3	5	3	15	45	149	230	374	...
60 - 64	357	-	-	-	1	-	2	2	11	26	60	255	...
65 - 69	179	-	-	-	-	1	1	1	5	8	20	143	...
70 - 74	62	-	-	-	-	-	-	-	2	2	2	56	...
75 +	20	-	-	-	-	1	-	-	-	1	3	15	...
Belarus - Bélarus													
2013 (C)													
Total	87 127	89[d]	1 659[j]	24 508	28 498	12 840	6 927	4 253	2 979	2 434	1 507	1 433	...
0 - 17	961	45[d]	283[j]	495	118	13	5	2	-	-	-	-	...
18 - 19	5 554	31[d]	692[j]	3 446	1 177	155	37	10	2	3	1	-	...
20 - 24	33 436	11[d]	565[j]	16 490	13 191	2 487	516	115	38	17	6	-	...
25 - 29	22 354	2[d]	102[j]	3 418	11 072	5 353	1 627	531	157	57	26	9	...
30 - 34	10 147	-[d]	13[j]	534	2 336	3 417	2 304	960	390	146	33	14	...
35 - 39	5 405	-[d]	3[j]	106	490	1 068	1 644	1 175	576	239	68	36	...
40 - 44	3 346	-[d]	1[j]	12	95	264	587	1 003	803	369	155	57	...
45 - 49	2 146	-[d]	-[j]	5	13	63	151	315	650	618	224	107	...
50 - 54	1 825	-[d]	-[j]	2	5	18	47	116	278	696	469	194	...
55 - 59	1 057	-[d]	-[j]	-	1	1	8	20	72	238	385	332	...
60 +	896	-[d]	-[j]	-	-	1	1	6	13	51	140	684	...
Belgium - Belgique[22,23]													
2010 (C)													
Total	42 159	-	100	3 343	11 662	8 743	5 567	4 016	3 093	2 416	1 527	1 692	...
0 - 14	-	-	-	-	-	-	-	-	-	-	-	-	...
15 - 19	672	-	46	363	197	43	11	6	3	2	-	1	...
20 - 24	6 935	-	43	2 186	3 442	886	206	107	34	16	11	4	...
25 - 29	13 021	-	8	632	6 768	3 925	1 089	343	170	55	21	10	...
30 - 34	7 218	-	1	109	966	2 934	1 971	738	311	117	41	30	...
35 - 39	4 622	-	1	28	182	684	1 531	1 229	580	243	85	59	...

Continent, country or area, year, code[a] and age of bride / Continent, pays ou zone, date, code[a] et âge de l'épouse	Total	0-14	15-19	20-24	25-29	30-34	35-39	40-44	45-49	50-54	55-59	60+	Unknown Inconnu
EUROPE													
Belgium - Belgique[22,23]													
2010													
40 - 44	3 335	-	1	15	68	175	511	1 056	799	456	145	109	...
45 - 49	2 707	-	-	5	29	68	185	387	779	679	336	239	...
50 - 54	1 895	-	-	2	6	15	45	122	307	620	462	316	...
55 - 59	1 006	-	-	2	3	13	12	18	80	182	320	376	...
60 - 64	428	-	-	-	-	-	3	9	25	33	82	276	...
65 - 69	174	-	-	1	-	-	1	1	3	10	17	141	...
70 - 74	83	-	-	-	-	-	-	-	2	3	4	74	...
75 +	63	-	-	-	1	-	2	-	-	-	3	57	...
Bosnia and Herzegovina - Bosnie-Herzégovine													
2012 (C)													
Total	18 235	-	147	3 617	6 959	3 922	1 571	739	438	259	185	398	-
0 - 14	-	-	-	-	-	-	-	-	-	-	-	-	-
15 - 19	1 885	-	91	1 028	606	122	27	6	2	1	-	2	-
20 - 24	6 191	-	48	2 130	2 958	844	160	36	7	5	2	1	-
25 - 29	5 764	-	8	403	2 936	1 833	431	113	26	10	2	2	-
30 - 34	2 228	-	-	42	405	941	581	172	66	14	2	5	-
35 - 39	871	-	-	10	35	150	292	240	92	34	14	4	-
40 - 44	437	-	-	1	9	20	56	117	122	60	19	33	-
45 - 49	349	-	-	2	6	6	13	41	85	76	52	68	-
50 - 54	237	-	-	-	2	4	6	10	30	39	52	94	-
55 - 59	136	-	-	-	-	-	2	3	6	17	34	74	-
60 - 64	78	-	-	-	-	2	1	1	-	1	7	66	-
65 - 69	27	-	-	-	-	-	-	-	1	2	1	23	-
70 - 74	18	-	-	-	-	-	-	-	1	-	-	17	-
75 +	9	-	-	-	-	-	-	-	-	-	-	9	-
Unknown - Inconnu	5	-	-	1	2	-	2	-	-	-	-	-	-
Bulgaria - Bulgarie[24]													
2012 (C)													
Total	21 167	-	202	2 957	7 343	5 173	2 571	1 169	559	419	281	493	...
0 - 14	-	-	-	-	-	-	-	-	-	-	-	-	...
15 - 19	1 357	-	157	788	316	78	12	1	3	2	-	-	...
20 - 24	6 045	-	37	1 751	2 953	1 034	220	29	10	6	2	3	...
25 - 29	7 196	-	7	355	3 546	2 357	724	140	38	17	6	6	...
30 - 34	3 199	-	1	45	440	1 362	913	294	84	37	14	9	...
35 - 39	1 582	-	-	13	72	286	548	420	147	64	18	14	...
40 - 44	702	-	-	4	8	38	115	218	166	87	43	23	...
45 - 49	390	-	-	1	3	15	31	57	83	91	65	44	...
50 - 54	270	-	-	-	4	2	6	9	23	83	75	68	...
55 - 59	177	-	-	-	1	1	2	1	3	28	43	98	...
60 - 64	130	-	-	-	-	-	-	-	2	4	13	111	...
65 - 69	73	-	-	-	-	-	-	-	-	-	2	71	...
70 - 74	31	-	-	-	-	-	-	-	-	-	-	31	...
75 +	15	-	-	-	-	-	-	-	-	-	-	15	...
Croatia - Croatie													
2013 (C)													
Total	19 169	-	113	2 294	6 787	5 286	2 234	920	505	324	224	480	2
0 - 14	-	-	-	-	-	-	-	-	-	-	-	-	-
15 - 19	764	-	75	438	190	49	6	1	4	1	-	-	-
20 - 24	4 479	-	35	1 351	2 171	722	141	40	14	3	-	2	-
25 - 29	7 350	-	2	433	3 639	2 467	629	120	39	11	6	3	1
30 - 34	3 760	-	1	60	676	1 719	931	253	76	25	13	6	-
35 - 39	1 277	-	-	9	97	287	401	274	130	52	17	10	-
40 - 44	536	-	-	2	11	39	101	167	122	52	23	19	-
45 - 49	328	-	-	-	1	3	17	47	83	80	37	60	-
50 - 54	272	-	-	1	-	-	6	14	22	70	68	91	-
55 - 59	195	-	-	-	-	-	1	1	11	19	41	122	-
60 - 64	106	-	-	-	-	-	-	2	2	8	14	80	-
65 - 69	53	-	-	-	-	-	-	1	-	2	3	47	-
70 - 74	31	-	-	-	-	-	-	-	-	2	-	29	-
75 +	13	-	-	-	-	-	-	-	-	-	2	11	-
Unknown - Inconnu	5	-	-	-	2	-	1	-	-	1	-	-	1

620

23. Marriages by age of groom and by age of bride: latest available year, 2005 - 2014
Mariages selon l'âge de l'époux et selon l'âge de l'épouse : dernière année disponible, 2005 - 2014 (continued - suite)

Continent, country or area, year, code[a] and age of bride / Continent, pays ou zone, date, code[a] et âge de l'épouse	Total	0-14	15-19	20-24	25-29	30-34	35-39	40-44	45-49	50-54	55-59	60+	Unknown Inconnu

Age of groom - - âge de l'époux

EUROPE

Czech Republic - République tchèque
2013 (C)

	Total	0-14	15-19	20-24	25-29	30-34	35-39	40-44	45-49	50-54	55-59	60+	Unknown
Total	43 499	-	91	2 577	11 449	12 414	7 372	3 394	2 208	1 380	1 081	1 533	...
0 - 14	-	-	-	-	-	-	-	-	-	-	-	-	...
15 - 19	431	-	41	214	102	53	14	4	1	1	1	-	...
20 - 24	6 046	-	35	1 543	2 714	1 187	404	112	29	10	7	5	...
25 - 29	15 697	-	6	625	6 906	5 635	1 878	441	134	41	23	8	...
30 - 34	9 903	-	4	136	1 385	4 380	2 740	815	290	93	34	26	...
35 - 39	4 897	-	4	47	261	939	1 763	1 049	498	194	82	60	...
40 - 44	2 334	-	1	9	60	164	427	679	574	242	99	79	...
45 - 49	1 608	-	-	3	15	47	110	210	460	392	231	140	...
50 - 54	1 084	-	-	-	5	9	33	61	161	281	268	266	...
55 - 59	763	-	-	-	1	-	3	20	46	97	235	361	...
60 - 64	411	-	-	-	-	-	-	2	11	23	83	292	...
65 - 69	231	-	-	-	-	-	-	1	3	6	15	206	...
70 - 74	67	-	-	-	-	-	-	-	1	-	3	63	...
75 +	27	-	-	-	-	-	-	-	-	-	-	27	...

Denmark - Danemark[25]
2013 (C)

	Total	0-14	15-19	20-24	25-29	30-34	35-39	40-44	45-49	50-54	55-59	60+	Unknown
Total	27 503	-	43	1 217	5 460	6 120	4 464	2 794	2 365	1 694	1 178	1 594	574
0 - 14	-	-	-	-	-	-	-	-	-	-	-	-	-
15 - 19	181	-	23	85	40	10	-	2	1	-	-	-	20
20 - 24	2 585	-	11	797	1 118	353	107	44	15	5	3	1	131
25 - 29	7 170	-	2	231	3 384	2 361	664	206	90	43	14	11	164
30 - 34	5 640	-	1	40	621	2 605	1 578	462	153	58	16	15	91
35 - 39	3 548	-	-	5	103	454	1 476	902	377	110	47	23	51
40 - 44	2 191	-	-	3	25	88	334	739	605	243	73	49	32
45 - 49	1 913	-	-	5	9	17	94	239	699	506	198	97	49
50 - 54	1 370	-	-	-	-	2	15	55	242	485	350	199	22
55 - 59	817	-	-	1	-	-	-	9	50	115	300	331	11
60 - 64	476	-	-	-	-	1	-	2	9	30	73	359	2
65 - 69	298	-	-	-	-	-	-	-	2	10	34	251	1
70 - 74	105	-	-	-	-	-	-	-	2	2	5	96	-
75 +	91	-	-	-	-	-	-	-	-	-	2	89	-
Unknown - Inconnu	1 118	-	6	50	160	229	196	134	120	87	63	73	-

Estonia - Estonie
2013 (C)

	Total	0-14	15-19	20-24	25-29	30-34	35-39	40-44	45-49	50-54	55-59	60+	Unknown
Total	5 630	-	32	575	1 568	1 241	793	567	326	239	135	154	...
0 - 14	-	-	-	-	-	-	-	-	-	-	-	-	...
15 - 19	137	-	17	77	30	10	1	2	-	-	-	-	...
20 - 24	1 106	-	11	369	521	149	38	11	4	1	1	1	...
25 - 29	1 647	-	2	106	797	509	154	52	17	7	2	1	...
30 - 34	1 107	-	2	17	171	426	294	128	47	15	5	2	...
35 - 39	671	-	-	5	35	120	230	173	69	30	4	5	...
40 - 44	379	-	-	1	11	14	64	134	91	48	13	3	...
45 - 49	235	-	-	-	3	9	10	45	64	69	19	16	...
50 - 54	165	-	-	-	-	3	2	18	20	54	49	19	...
55 - 59	96	-	-	-	-	-	-	3	9	12	31	41	...
60 - 64	54	-	-	-	-	1	-	1	5	3	10	34	...
65 - 69	17	-	-	-	-	-	-	-	-	-	1	16	...
70 - 74	11	-	-	-	-	-	-	-	-	-	-	11	...
75 +	5	-	-	-	-	-	-	-	-	-	-	5	...

Finland - Finlande[26],[27]
2012 (C)

	Total	0-14	15-19	20-24	25-29	30-34	35-39	40-44	45-49	50-54	55-59	60+	Unknown
Total	28 737	-	251	2 523	6 946	6 455	3 818	2 545	2 599	1 424	1 026	1 150	...
0 - 14	-	-	-	-	-	-	-	-	-	-	-	-	...
15 - 19	630	-	173	344	76	25	8	3	1	-	-	-	...
20 - 24	3 937	-	63	1 621	1 693	413	92	36	10	6	3	-	...
25 - 29	8 252	-	11	426	4 149	2 731	646	185	71	21	9	3	...
30 - 34	5 565	-	2	78	796	2 594	1 457	411	171	42	11	3	...
35 - 39	3 167	-	-	30	149	524	1 177	784	332	124	30	17	...
40 - 44	2 150	-	1	11	43	119	293	694	679	194	97	19	...
45 - 49	2 399	-	1	11	22	28	123	341	1 032	492	233	116	...
50 - 54	1 130	-	-	2	12	14	20	63	225	385	287	122	...
55 - 59	753	-	-	-	4	7	2	21	57	124	248	290	...

23. Marriages by age of groom and by age of bride: latest available year, 2005 - 2014
Mariages selon l'âge de l'époux et selon l'âge de l'épouse : dernière année disponible, 2005 - 2014 (continued - suite)

Continent, country or area, year, code[a] and age of bride / Continent, pays ou zone, date, code[a] et âge de l'épouse	Total	\multicolumn{12}{c}{Age of groom - - âge de l'époux}
		0-14	15-19	20-24	25-29	30-34	35-39	40-44	45-49	50-54	55-59	60+	Unknown Inconnu
EUROPE													
Finland - Finlande[26,27]													
2012													
60 - 64	443	-	-	-	2	-	-	7	14	32	96	292	...
65 - 69	195	-	-	-	-	-	-	-	5	3	10	177	...
70 - 74	75	-	-	-	-	-	-	-	2	1	2	70	...
75 +	41	-	-	-	-	-	-	-	-	-	-	41	...
France[28]													
2013 (C)													
Total	225 784	1	194	11 133	53 123	54 149	33 020	23 560	15 978	13 118	9 313	12 195	...
0 - 14	19	-	1	5	7	5	-	-	1	-	-	-	...
15 - 19	1 689	1	76	802	575	165	47	17	2	2	-	2	...
20 - 24	24 229	-	101	7 513	12 083	3 339	761	249	101	47	19	16	...
25 - 29	63 815	-	8	2 231	33 389	20 848	4 985	1 476	537	197	98	46	...
30 - 34	49 068	-	4	389	5 522	23 871	12 656	4 289	1 404	588	187	158	...
35 - 39	27 659	-	2	116	978	4 327	10 414	7 322	2 624	1 160	448	268	...
40 - 44	20 367	-	2	53	330	1 059	3 130	7 294	4 715	2 287	914	583	...
45 - 49	13 983	-	-	13	128	355	706	2 074	4 329	3 603	1 637	1 138	...
50 - 54	11 364	-	-	7	74	132	220	649	1 707	3 678	2 823	2 074	...
55 - 59	6 775	-	-	2	25	34	70	145	400	1 176	2 212	2 711	...
60 - 64	3 966	-	-	2	8	10	25	37	114	293	758	2 719	...
65 - 69	1 794	-	-	-	3	2	3	6	39	68	184	1 489	...
70 - 74	630	-	-	-	-	-	-	2	3	17	27	581	...
75 +	426	-	-	-	1	2	3	-	2	2	6	410	...
Germany - Allemagne													
2013 (C)													
Total	373 655	-	722	21 879	80 265	91 663	52 795	36 271	31 363	24 752	15 714	18 231	...
0 - 14	-	-	-	-	-	-	-	-	-	-	-	-	...
15 - 19	3 812	-	369	2 198	916	210	58	21	16	15	6	3	...
20 - 24	44 956	-	287	14 382	21 272	6 452	1 572	565	254	96	50	26	...
25 - 29	105 295	-	44	4 231	46 645	39 148	10 305	3 132	1 182	383	149	76	...
30 - 34	84 450	-	17	779	9 521	38 312	22 878	8 502	3 013	958	301	169	...
35 - 39	40 528	-	4	171	1 425	6 101	14 002	10 988	5 103	1 807	584	343	...
40 - 44	26 704	-	1	80	316	1 026	2 877	8 425	8 033	3 868	1 307	771	...
45 - 49	26 772	-	-	24	105	298	812	3 356	9 134	7 808	3 331	1 904	...
50 - 54	21 023	-	-	9	47	76	215	1 023	3 634	7 306	5 265	3 448	...
55 - 59	10 772	-	-	5	12	24	57	196	786	1 933	3 495	4 264	...
60 - 64	5 370	-	-	-	6	11	11	46	166	475	966	3 689	...
65 - 69	2 160	-	-	-	-	2	3	11	31	80	208	1 825	...
70 - 74	1 228	-	-	-	-	1	1	5	9	16	41	1 155	...
75 +	585	-	-	-	-	2	4	1	2	7	11	558	...
Greece - Grèce													
2012 (C)													
Total	49 705	29	925	5 997	17 024	15 157	5 964	2 255	1 074	690	348	242	-
0 - 14	1	-	1	-	-	-	-	-	-	-	-	-	-
15 - 19	204	23	143	31	6	1	-	-	-	-	-	-	-
20 - 24	2 224	5	368	1 183	485	139	29	7	4	3	1	-	-
25 - 29	11 260	-	276	2 628	6 287	1 728	257	57	20	5	1	1	-
30 - 34	17 344	1	99	1 543	7 064	7 233	1 207	148	28	15	5	1	-
35 - 39	9 705	-	29	458	2 382	4 155	2 152	429	73	22	4	1	-
40 - 44	4 285	-	8	117	549	1 347	1 363	693	157	40	10	1	-
45 - 49	1 964	-	1	21	157	366	596	456	264	81	15	7	-
50 - 54	1 075	-	-	10	54	121	204	251	239	147	34	15	-
55 - 59	667	-	-	3	24	49	91	131	135	144	71	19	-
60 - 64	433	-	-	2	12	12	41	47	91	107	81	40	-
65 - 69	247	-	-	1	3	5	15	21	33	67	53	49	-
70 - 74	149	-	-	-	-	1	8	9	18	36	35	42	-
75 +	147	-	-	-	1	-	1	6	12	23	38	66	-
Hungary - Hongrie[6]													
2013 (C)													
Total	36 986	-	219	2 075	8 478	10 534	7 121	3 252	1 658	1 065	1 026	1 558	-
0 - 14	-	-	-	-	-	-	-	-	-	-	-	-	-
15 - 19	739	-	162	328	144	57	27	10	6	2	2	1	-
20 - 24	4 708	-	47	1 136	2 056	977	365	82	27	10	2	6	-
25 - 29	11 950	-	8	434	4 812	4 536	1 606	397	96	26	20	15	-
30 - 34	8 691	-	-	113	1 120	3 734	2 603	776	218	60	40	27	-
35 - 39	5 002	-	2	54	280	1 002	1 962	1 043	401	136	73	49	-

23. Marriages by age of groom and by age of bride: latest available year, 2005 - 2014
Mariages selon l'âge de l'époux et selon l'âge de l'épouse : dernière année disponible, 2005 - 2014 (continued - suite)

Continent, country or area, year, code[a] and age of bride / Continent, pays ou zone, date, code[a] et âge de l'épouse	Total	Age of groom - - âge de l'époux											Unknown Inconnu
		0-14	15-19	20-24	25-29	30-34	35-39	40-44	45-49	50-54	55-59	60+	
EUROPE													
Hungary - Hongrie[6]													
2013													
40 - 44	2 191	-	-	7	55	181	453	678	420	196	123	78	-
45 - 49	1 289	-	-	3	10	39	86	204	336	312	169	130	-
50 - 54	853	-	-	-	1	8	12	49	108	215	238	222	-
55 - 59	743	-	-	-	-	-	4	12	35	61	245	386	-
60 - 64	503	-	-	-	-	-	3	1	9	38	81	371	-
65 - 69	194	-	-	-	-	-	-	-	2	8	23	161	-
70 - 74	88	-	-	-	-	-	-	-	-	1	8	79	-
75 +	35	-	-	-	-	-	-	-	-	-	2	33	-
Unknown - Inconnu	-	-	-	-	-	-	-	-	-	-	-	-	-
Iceland - Islande[29,30]													
2011 (C)													
Total	1 458	-	3	77	302	334	272	161	111	74	64	55	5
0 - 14	-	-	-	-	-	-	-	-	-	-	-	-	-
15 - 19	6	-	-	2	4	-	-	-	-	-	-	-	-
20 - 24	152	-	3	52	69	21	1	3	1	1	-	-	1
25 - 29	371	-	-	19	173	115	44	9	5	3	1	1	1
30 - 34	350	-	-	3	43	157	104	25	9	3	4	1	1
35 - 39	243	-	-	1	7	33	101	62	22	9	6	1	1
40 - 44	113	-	-	-	3	6	14	44	28	11	3	4	-
45 - 49	94	-	-	-	1	-	6	15	36	24	7	4	1
50 - 54	68	-	-	-	-	1	1	2	9	18	25	12	-
55 - 59	30	-	-	-	-	-	1	-	1	4	15	9	-
60 - 64	18	-	-	-	-	-	-	1	-	1	2	14	-
65 - 69	7	-	-	-	-	-	-	-	-	-	1	6	-
70 - 74	2	-	-	-	-	-	-	-	-	-	-	2	-
75 +	1	-	-	-	-	-	-	-	-	-	-	1	-
Unknown - Inconnu	3	-	-	-	2	1	-	-	-	-	-	-	-
Ireland - Irlande													
2012 (+C)													
Total	20 713	...	102	516	4 523	8 245	3 896	1 585	766	452	258	370	...
15 - 19	237	...	80	91	43	17	5	-	-	-	1	-	...
20 - 24	968	...	22	258	457	168	40	13	7	3	-	-	...
25 - 29	6 485	...	-	136	2 944	2 670	578	110	33	10	-	4	...
30 - 34	8 016	...	-	25	930	4 640	1 858	419	102	28	11	3	...
35 - 39	2 827	...	-	5	120	673	1 149	588	200	67	15	10	...
40 - 44	995	...	-	1	20	54	228	331	198	99	40	24	...
45 - 49	542	...	-	-	8	18	29	97	157	120	71	42	...
50 - 54	340	...	-	-	-	3	6	21	53	97	81	79	...
55 - 59	168	...	-	-	1	2	2	4	12	25	33	89	...
60 - 64	89	...	-	-	-	-	1	2	2	3	6	75	...
65 - 69	26	...	-	-	-	-	-	-	1	-	-	25	...
70 - 74	17	...	-	-	-	-	-	-	-	1	-	16	...
75 +	3	...	-	-	-	-	-	-	-	-	-	3	...
Isle of Man - Île de Man													
2005 (C)													
Total	404	-	6	42	72	87	63	51	26	22	17	18	-
0 - 14	-	...	...	...	...	...	...	...	...	...	...	...	...
15 - 19	5	...	...	...	...	...	...	...	...	...	...	...	...
20 - 24	65	...	...	...	...	...	...	...	...	...	...	...	...
25 - 29	98	...	...	...	...	...	...	...	...	...	...	...	...
30 - 34	79	...	...	...	...	...	...	...	...	...	...	...	...
35 - 39	61	...	...	...	...	...	...	...	...	...	...	...	...
40 - 44	40	...	...	...	...	...	...	...	...	...	...	...	...
45 - 49	26	...	...	...	...	...	...	...	...	...	...	...	...
50 - 54	16	...	...	...	...	...	...	...	...	...	...	...	...
55 - 59	5	...	...	...	...	...	...	...	...	...	...	...	...
60 - 64	7	...	...	...	...	...	...	...	...	...	...	...	...
65 - 69	1	...	...	...	...	...	...	...	...	...	...	...	...
70 - 74	-	...	...	...	...	...	...	...	...	...	...	...	...
75 - 79	1	...	...	...	...	...	...	...	...	...	...	...	...
Italy - Italie													
2013 (C)													
Total	194 057	...	290	7 396	38 296	58 739	38 800	20 381	11 342	6 860	4 539	7 414	...
15 - 19	1 916	...	136	1 092	491	140	40	11	3	2	1	-	...

Continent, country or area, year, code[a] and age of bride / Continent, pays ou zone, date, code[a] et âge de l'épouse	Total	0-14	15-19	20-24	25-29	30-34	35-39	40-44	45-49	50-54	55-59	60+	Unknown Inconnu
EUROPE													
Italy - Italie													
2013													
20 - 24	19 411	...	114	4 499	9 484	3 866	1 007	303	88	22	14	14	...
25 - 29	58 028	...	23	1 407	22 145	24 454	7 441	1 812	465	155	64	62	...
30 - 34	53 349	...	8	284	5 130	24 827	16 141	4 843	1 401	411	182	122	...
35 - 39	27 926	...	3	72	807	4 521	11 065	7 058	2 698	1 018	387	297	...
40 - 44	14 463	...	3	20	135	707	2 509	4 745	3 433	1 563	781	567	...
45 - 49	8 376	...	1	10	67	154	486	1 269	2 377	1 913	1 053	1 046	...
50 - 54	5 060	...	1	8	25	41	82	284	704	1 291	1 079	1 545	...
55 - 59	2 970	...	1	2	10	19	20	50	155	385	724	1 604	...
60 - 64	1 449	...	-	-	1	8	5	4	17	78	203	1 133	...
65 - 69	630	...	-	1	1	-	1	-	1	16	38	572	...
70 - 74	265	...	-	1	-	1	1	1	-	3	8	250	...
75 +	214	...	-	-	-	1	2	1	-	3	5	202	...
Latvia - Lettonie[5]													
2013 (C)													
Total	11 436	-	47	1 161	3 488	2 488	1 412	981	592	479	316	472	...
0 - 14	-	-	-	-	-	-	-	-	-	-	-	-	-
15 - 19	218	-	31	116	50	14	5	1	1	-	-	-	-
20 - 24	2 163	-	12	723	1 062	274	61	21	6	1	2	1	-
25 - 29	3 811	-	4	264	1 935	1 125	326	110	30	12	5	-	-
30 - 34	1 912	-	-	37	340	797	444	170	72	31	12	9	-
35 - 39	1 190	-	-	18	73	202	398	301	106	58	26	8	-
40 - 44	736	-	-	2	25	57	115	242	166	76	28	25	-
45 - 49	511	-	-	-	3	14	51	98	136	130	48	31	-
50 - 54	382	-	-	-	-	4	10	28	61	121	94	64	-
55 - 59	224	-	-	-	-	-	2	8	11	38	69	96	-
60 - 64	120	-	-	-	-	-	-	1	2	6	24	87	-
65 - 69	82	-	-	-	-	-	-	-	1	4	5	72	-
70 - 74	54	-	-	-	-	1	-	1	-	1	1	50	-
75 +	33	-	-	1	-	-	-	-	-	1	2	29	-
Unknown - Inconnu	-	-	-	-	-	-	-	-	-	-	-	-	-
Liechtenstein[5]													
2012 (C)													
Total	185	-	-	8	30	59	33	19	20	10	2	4	...
Lithuania - Lituanie													
2013 (C)													
Total	20 469	-	126	2 859	7 781	4 282	2 099	1 219	769	560	332	442	-
0 - 14	1	-	-	-	1	-	-	-	-	-	-	-	-
15 - 19	618	-	81	351	142	34	9	1	-	-	-	-	-
20 - 24	5 353	-	40	1 901	2 709	548	104	37	14	-	-	-	-
25 - 29	7 572	-	4	506	4 240	2 042	543	151	58	23	5	-	-
30 - 34	3 024	-	1	85	558	1 272	710	256	87	37	12	6	-
35 - 39	1 553	-	-	12	102	305	525	348	163	65	25	8	-
40 - 44	927	-	-	1	23	61	164	290	202	103	56	27	-
45 - 49	569	-	-	-	6	18	28	106	156	135	69	51	-
50 - 54	431	-	-	3	-	1	13	24	73	147	96	74	-
55 - 59	198	-	-	-	-	1	2	5	13	41	55	81	-
60 - 64	101	-	-	-	-	-	-	1	3	7	11	79	-
65 - 69	60	-	-	-	-	-	1	-	-	2	3	54	-
70 - 74	48	-	-	-	-	-	-	-	-	-	-	48	-
75 +	14	-	-	-	-	-	-	-	-	-	-	14	-
Unknown - Inconnu	-	-	-	-	-	-	-	-	-	-	-	-	-
Luxembourg[31]													
2013 (C)													
Total	1 722	-	2	99	387	446	261	175	116	111	66	56	3
0 - 14	-	-	-	-	-	-	-	-	-	-	-	-	-
15 - 19	24	-	-	13	7	4	-	-	-	-	-	-	-
20 - 24	191	-	1	53	103	21	8	3	2	-	-	-	-
25 - 29	504	-	1	23	200	181	64	23	2	7	1	1	1
30 - 34	438	-	-	3	62	190	105	46	17	8	4	2	1
35 - 39	213	-	-	2	10	44	57	53	26	13	5	3	-
40 - 44	130	-	-	2	5	4	22	33	29	20	11	3	1
45 - 49	104	-	-	2	-	-	3	14	34	30	13	8	-
50 - 54	64	-	-	1	-	2	2	1	4	24	20	10	-
55 - 59	37	-	-	-	-	-	-	1	1	9	9	17	-

23. Marriages by age of groom and by age of bride: latest available year, 2005 - 2014
Mariages selon l'âge de l'époux et selon l'âge de l'épouse : dernière année disponible, 2005 - 2014 (continued - suite)

Continent, country or area, year, code[a] and age of bride / Continent, pays ou zone, date, code[a] et âge de l'épouse	Age of groom - - âge de l'époux												
	Total	0-14	15-19	20-24	25-29	30-34	35-39	40-44	45-49	50-54	55-59	60+	Unknown Inconnu
EUROPE													
Luxembourg[31]													
2013													
60 - 64	11	-	-	-	-	-	-	1	-	-	3	7	-
65 - 69	3	-	-	-	-	-	-	-	-	-	-	3	-
70 - 74	1	-	-	-	-	-	-	-	-	-	-	1	-
75 +	1	-	-	-	-	-	-	-	-	-	-	1	-
Unknown - Inconnu	1	-	-	-	-	-	-	-	1	-	-	-	-
Malta - Malte													
2013 (C)													
Total	2 578	-	1	126	874	728	336	167	116	84	65	73	8
0 - 14	-	-	-	-	-	-	-	-	-	-	-	-	-
15 - 19	14	-	1	10	2	-	1	-	-	-	-	-	-
20 - 24	361	-	-	68	204	66	17	5	1	-	-	-	-
25 - 29	1 009	-	-	37	542	330	75	19	4	1	1	-	-
30 - 34	598	-	-	7	113	265	143	46	10	8	2	3	1
35 - 39	234	-	-	2	10	53	82	41	24	12	8	2	-
40 - 44	131	-	-	1	3	10	15	40	30	15	10	7	-
45 - 49	90	-	-	-	-	3	-	11	33	24	11	8	-
50 - 54	73	-	-	-	-	1	3	4	10	20	19	16	-
55 - 59	28	-	-	-	-	-	-	1	2	2	11	12	-
60 - 64	21	-	-	-	-	-	-	-	2	2	2	15	-
65 - 69	6	-	-	-	-	-	-	-	-	-	-	6	-
70 - 74	4	-	-	-	-	-	-	-	-	-	1	3	-
75 +	1	-	-	-	-	-	-	-	-	-	-	1	-
Unknown - Inconnu	8	-	-	1	-	-	-	-	-	-	-	-	7
Montenegro - Monténégro													
2009 (C)													
Total	3 829	...	26	619	1 371	876	425	232	131	66	31	52	-
0 - 14	-	...	-	-	-	-	-	-	-	-	-	-	...
15 - 19	376	...	15	172	131	41	11	4	1	-	-	1	-
20 - 24	1 268	...	9	358	600	217	53	22	6	2	1	-	-
25 - 29	1 243	...	1	75	549	406	151	47	12	1	1	-	-
30 - 34	517	...	-	8	81	176	135	79	33	5	-	-	-
35 - 39	203	...	-	3	8	32	60	47	33	16	2	2	-
40 - 44	96	...	-	2	1	2	15	25	31	10	7	3	-
45 - 49	55	...	1	1	-	1	-	7	12	15	7	11	-
50 - 54	34	...	-	-	1	1	-	1	1	15	6	9	-
55 - 59	22	...	-	-	-	-	-	-	2	1	5	14	-
60 - 64	8	...	-	-	-	-	-	-	-	1	2	5	-
65 - 69	7	...	-	-	-	-	-	-	-	-	-	7	-
70 - 74	-	...	-	-	-	-	-	-	-	-	-	-	-
75 +	-	...	-	-	-	-	-	-	-	-	-	-	-
Netherlands - Pays-Bas													
2009[32,33,34] (C)													
Total	72 119	...	85	4 976	16 276	17 802	11 712	7 321	4 939	3 443	2 300	3 265	-
0 - 14	-	-	-	-	-	-	-	-	-	-	-	-	...
15 - 19	687	...	47	385	178	49	17	8	3	-	-	-	-
20 - 24	11 006	...	32	3 710	5 283	1 374	408	120	56	14	5	4	-
25 - 29	20 820	...	4	735	8 958	7 932	2 233	615	211	87	26	19	-
30 - 34	15 428	...	2	108	1 548	6 998	4 516	1 456	522	162	66	50	-
35 - 39	8 770	...	-	24	239	1 136	3 385	2 481	947	347	118	93	-
40 - 44	5 477	...	-	10	47	232	843	1 888	1 455	646	211	145	-
45 - 49	3 879	...	-	3	13	54	239	575	1 193	1 035	482	285	-
50 - 54	2 754	...	-	1	7	19	57	136	436	884	707	507	-
55 - 59	1 553	...	-	-	-	6	10	35	83	213	501	705	-
60 - 64	962	...	-	-	2	2	3	5	26	42	146	736	-
65 - 69	489	...	-	-	1	-	-	2	7	12	32	435	-
70 - 74	170	...	-	-	-	-	1	-	-	1	3	165	-
75 +	124	...	-	-	-	-	-	-	-	-	3	121	-
Norway - Norvège													
2012 (C)													
Total	24 077	-	38	1 503	5 000	5 362	3 852	2 786	1 989	1 440	1 018	1 089	...
0 - 14	-	-	-	-	-	-	-	-	-	-	-	-	...
15 - 19	352	-	19	164	105	35	14	10	3	1	-	1	...
20 - 24	3 246	-	15	1 069	1 372	457	164	79	51	21	7	11	...
25 - 29	6 632	-	3	226	2 933	2 215	721	289	140	61	25	19	...

23. Marriages by age of groom and by age of bride: latest available year, 2005 - 2014
Mariages selon l'âge de l'époux et selon l'âge de l'épouse : dernière année disponible, 2005 - 2014 (continued - suite)

Continent, pays ou zone, date, code[a] et âge de l'épouse	Total	0-14	15-19	20-24	25-29	30-34	35-39	40-44	45-49	50-54	55-59	60+	Unknown Inconnu
EUROPE													
Norway - Norvège													
2012													
30 - 34	5 312	-	-	29	486	2 197	1 503	614	245	129	64	45	...
35 - 39	3 099	-	1	13	82	386	1 128	840	352	154	79	64	...
40 - 44	2 083	-	-	1	19	55	259	718	553	270	128	80	...
45 - 49	1 463	-	-	1	2	10	51	180	477	416	201	125	...
50 - 54	981	-	-	-	1	4	9	48	137	301	291	190	...
55 - 59	505	-	-	-	-	1	2	6	24	74	177	221	...
60 - 64	231	-	-	-	-	1	1	2	5	13	37	172	...
65 - 69	129	-	-	-	-	-	-	-	2	-	8	119	...
70 - 74	28	-	-	-	-	-	-	-	-	-	1	27	...
75 +	15	-	-	-	-	-	-	-	-	-	-	15	...
Unknown - Inconnu	1	-	-	-	-	1	-	-	-	-	-	-	...
Poland - Pologne													
2012 (C)													
Total	203 850	-	911	35 828	89 905	41 502	15 386	6 593	3 804	3 013	2 515	4 393	-
0 - 14	-	-	-	-	-	-	-	-	-	-	-	-	-
15 - 19	6 351	-	560	4 117	1 382	232	50	5	3	1	1	-	-
20 - 24	66 827	-	321	25 910	33 537	5 899	884	188	58	22	5	3	-
25 - 29	79 944	-	22	5 237	48 694	20 706	4 055	868	230	63	51	18	-
30 - 34	26 609	-	6	457	5 500	12 168	5 912	1 621	551	260	84	50	-
35 - 39	9 907	-	1	91	655	2 098	3 539	2 081	844	353	172	73	-
40 - 44	4 354	-	1	13	112	316	722	1 299	944	560	245	142	-
45 - 49	2 837	-	-	2	14	69	163	350	773	708	437	321	-
50 - 54	2 586	-	-	1	9	11	45	135	274	695	697	719	-
55 - 59	2 024	-	-	-	1	3	9	37	86	253	607	1 028	-
60 - 64	1 246	-	-	-	-	-	5	4	28	71	166	972	-
65 - 69	650	-	-	-	1	-	-	4	7	19	30	589	-
70 - 74	324	-	-	-	-	-	-	-	2	6	13	303	-
75 +	191	-	-	-	-	-	2	1	4	2	7	175	-
Unknown - Inconnu	-	-	-	-	-	-	-	-	-	-	-	-	-
Portugal[35]													
2013 (C)													
Total	31 998	-	115	2 713	8 768	8 611	4 705	2 365	1 515	1 074	749	1 383	-
0 - 14	-	-	-	-	-	-	-	-	-	-	-	-	-
15 - 19	554	-	60	318	128	28	14	3	3	-	-	-	-
20 - 24	4 557	-	43	1 642	2 012	622	156	53	16	8	1	4	-
25 - 29	10 065	-	10	573	4 986	3 370	833	179	74	23	6	11	-
30 - 34	7 682	-	-	142	1 348	3 556	1 796	522	185	66	38	29	-
35 - 39	3 807	-	1	28	227	818	1 335	796	349	142	60	51	-
40 - 44	2 006	-	1	8	46	169	421	535	422	208	111	85	-
45 - 49	1 269	-	-	1	13	33	104	204	312	288	152	162	-
50 - 54	888	-	-	-	4	10	37	56	110	237	205	229	-
55 - 59	538	-	-	-	3	4	8	15	35	76	127	270	-
60 - 64	351	-	-	1	1	1	-	2	6	18	39	283	-
65 - 69	139	-	-	-	-	-	1	-	2	5	5	126	-
70 - 74	78	-	-	-	-	-	-	-	-	2	2	74	-
75 +	64	-	-	-	-	-	-	-	1	1	3	59	-
Unknown - Inconnu	-	-	-	-	-	-	-	-	-	-	-	-	-
Republic of Moldova - République de Moldova[36]													
2012 (C)													
Total	18 565	-	308	7 229	7 959	2 219	583	143	61	37	12	13	1
0 - 14	-	-	-	-	-	-	-	-	-	-	-	-	-
15 - 19	2 706	-	189	1 743	675	83	11	3	1	1	-	-	-
20 - 24	10 091	-	108	4 720	4 452	710	92	5	2	-	2	-	-
25 - 29	4 470	-	9	714	2 535	975	188	39	7	2	-	1	-
30 - 34	938	-	1	41	274	384	191	33	9	4	1	-	-
35 - 39	241	-	-	8	19	64	79	44	17	9	-	1	-
40 - 44	66	-	-	3	4	1	20	17	15	5	1	-	-
45 - 49	25	-	1	-	-	1	1	1	9	10	1	1	-
50 - 54	11	-	-	-	-	-	1	1	1	2	3	3	-
55 - 59	10	-	-	-	-	-	-	-	-	3	3	4	-
60 - 64	5	-	-	-	-	1	-	-	-	1	1	2	-
65 - 69	-	-	-	-	-	-	-	-	-	-	-	-	-
70 - 74	1	-	-	-	-	-	-	-	-	-	1	-	-

23. Marriages by age of groom and by age of bride: latest available year, 2005 - 2014
Mariages selon l'âge de l'époux et selon l'âge de l'épouse : dernière année disponible, 2005 - 2014 (continued - suite)

Continent, country or area, year, code[a] and age of bride / Continent, pays ou zone, date, code[a] et âge de l'épouse	Total	Age of groom - - âge de l'époux											Unknown Inconnu
		0-14	15-19	20-24	25-29	30-34	35-39	40-44	45-49	50-54	55-59	60+	
EUROPE													
Republic of Moldova - République de Moldova[36]													
2012													
75 +	-	-	-	-	-	-	-	-	-	-	-	-	-
Unknown - Inconnu	1	-	-	-	-	-	-	-	-	-	-	-	1
Romania - Roumanie													
2013 (C)													
Total	107 507	-	452	14 620	41 012	25 640	12 103	5 547	3 035	1 868	1 417	1 813	-
0 - 14	-	-	-	-	-	-	-	-	-	-	-	-	-
15 - 19	6 720	-	285	3 251	2 418	586	144	28	3	5	-	-	-
20 - 24	32 733	-	139	8 908	16 989	5 222	1 156	227	60	17	6	9	-
25 - 29	36 272	-	21	2 153	18 447	11 359	3 238	743	196	75	28	12	-
30 - 34	15 243	-	5	246	2 595	6 576	3 969	1 270	387	106	55	34	-
35 - 39	7 526	-	2	52	472	1 562	2 641	1 661	685	248	130	73	-
40 - 44	3 903	-	-	6	68	272	763	1 146	896	422	191	139	-
45 - 49	2 231	-	-	2	19	52	156	371	607	527	293	204	-
50 - 54	1 252	-	-	-	2	11	29	82	151	318	354	305	-
55 - 59	858	-	-	2	2	-	5	11	41	101	283	413	-
60 - 64	472	-	-	-	-	-	2	5	6	39	62	358	-
65 - 69	171	-	-	-	-	-	-	2	3	6	10	150	-
70 - 74	78	-	-	-	-	-	-	-	-	4	4	70	-
75 +	48	-	-	-	-	-	-	1	-	-	1	46	-
Unknown - Inconnu	-	-	-	-	-	-	-	-	-	-	-	-	-
Russian Federation - Fédération de Russie													
2012[37] (C)													
Total	1213598	...	15 848	312 104	402 995	191 131	105 357	63 778	43 196	34 745	21 315	23 078	51
15 - 19	81 342	...	9 599	50 495	18 055	2 523	468	130	38	20	7	6	1
20 - 24	425 562	...	5 186	200 558	173 664	35 196	7 918	2 062	620	221	80	54	3
25 - 29	337 474	...	802	50 809	166 737	80 206	26 188	8 444	2 758	1 022	326	182	-
30 - 34	154 765	...	189	8 034	34 743	52 674	34 829	15 241	5 645	2 339	749	318	4
35 - 39	83 803	...	50	1 683	7 769	15 610	25 204	18 450	9 030	4 074	1 366	564	3
40 - 44	45 822	...	17	377	1 571	3 745	7 817	13 055	10 391	5 807	2 044	996	2
45 - 49	31 345	...	1	94	327	880	2 159	4 456	9 684	8 528	3 435	1 778	3
50 - 54	25 096	...	1	37	89	230	606	1 487	3 793	9 098	6 198	3 553	4
55 - 59	14 880	...	1	7	22	46	121	360	985	2 837	5 299	5 202	-
60 +	13 481	...	2	8	16	20	47	91	252	798	1 811	10 424	12
Unknown - Inconnu	28	...	-	2	2	1	-	2	-	1	-	1	19
San Marino - Saint-Marin[38]													
2011 (C)													
Total	205	-	-	8	40	55	28	18	13	6	5	10	22
0 - 14	-	-	-	-	-	-	-	-	-	-	-	-	-
15 - 19	1	-	-	-	-	-	-	-	-	-	-	-	1
20 - 24	6	-	-	-	5	1	-	-	-	-	-	-	-
25 - 29	49	-	-	2	20	14	1	2	2	-	-	-	8
30 - 34	42	-	-	-	5	16	9	1	2	2	-	-	7
35 - 39	22	-	-	-	-	2	9	5	1	-	1	1	3
40 - 44	12	-	-	-	-	1	1	4	3	1	-	-	2
45 - 49	8	-	-	-	-	-	1	-	1	1	3	2	-
50 - 54	5	-	-	-	-	-	-	1	-	2	-	1	1
55 - 59	1	-	-	-	-	-	-	-	-	-	-	1	-
60 - 64	1	-	-	-	-	-	-	-	-	-	-	1	-
65 - 69	-	-	-	-	-	-	-	-	-	-	-	-	-
70 - 74	1	-	-	-	-	-	-	-	-	-	-	1	-
75 +	-	-	-	-	-	-	-	-	-	-	-	-	-
Unknown - Inconnu	57	-	-	6	10	21	7	5	4	-	1	3	-
Serbia - Serbie[39]													
2013 (+C)													
Total	36 209	-	299	4 185	11 726	9 919	4 463	1 902	1 104	753	624	1 149	85
0 - 14	-	-	-	-	-	-	-	-	-	-	-	-	-
15 - 19	2 017	-	195	1 011	591	170	35	12	2	1	-	-	-
20 - 24	8 659	-	89	2 400	4 114	1 597	330	73	23	9	7	6	11
25 - 29	12 357	-	12	631	5 821	4 384	1 146	233	72	17	12	11	18
30 - 34	6 724	-	1	83	983	3 170	1 733	469	175	52	21	17	20
35 - 39	2 676	-	-	17	125	482	955	620	297	100	54	23	3
40 - 44	1 295	-	1	12	35	68	182	368	303	168	75	79	4

Continent, country or area, year, code[a] and age of bride / Continent, pays ou zone, date, code[a] et âge de l'épouse	Total	0-14	15-19	20-24	25-29	30-34	35-39	40-44	45-49	50-54	55-59	60+	Unknown Inconnu
EUROPE													
Serbia - Serbie[39]													
2013													
45 - 49	755	-	-	6	5	7	43	76	150	199	127	139	3
50 - 54	660	-	-	1	2	4	14	23	55	151	172	235	3
55 - 59	387	-	-	1	1	1	5	6	12	32	113	215	1
60 - 64	300	-	-	1	2	1	-	5	4	12	32	243	-
65 - 69	125	-	-	1	-	2	1	3	2	3	3	110	-
70 - 74	58	-	-	-	-	-	-	-	2	1	4	51	-
75 +	29	-	1	1	2	-	3	1	2	-	4	15	-
Unknown - Inconnu	167	-	-	20	45	33	16	13	5	8	-	5	22
Slovakia - Slovaquie[5]													
2013 (C)													
Total	25 491	-	431	2 429	8 124	7 417	3 512	1 388	733	504	381	572	...
0 - 14	-	-	-	-	-	-	-	-	-	-	-	-	...
15 - 19	1 063	-	340	526	145	31	15	4	1	1	-	-	...
20 - 24	4 807	-	80	1 380	2 252	839	194	35	16	5	4	2	...
25 - 29	10 039	-	9	423	4 757	3 540	998	198	61	35	9	9	...
30 - 34	5 327	-	2	75	786	2 471	1 346	403	142	59	28	15	...
35 - 39	2 169	-	-	21	150	459	760	450	166	87	49	27	...
40 - 44	784	-	-	2	19	60	155	216	177	83	41	31	...
45 - 49	472	-	-	1	10	13	37	63	121	115	62	50	...
50 - 54	308	-	-	1	3	4	4	16	31	87	89	73	...
55 - 59	259	-	-	-	2	-	2	2	14	23	73	143	...
60 - 64	163	-	-	-	-	-	1	1	4	7	24	126	...
65 - 69	61	-	-	-	-	-	-	-	-	2	2	57	...
70 - 74	29	-	-	-	-	-	-	-	-	-	-	29	...
75 +	10	-	-	-	-	-	-	-	-	-	-	10	...
Slovenia - Slovénie[40]													
2013 (C)													
Total	6 254	-	25	447	1 748	1 844	1 027	452	265	166	102	178	-
0 - 14	-	-	-	-	-	-	-	-	-	-	-	-	-
15 - 19	107	-	13	58	30	5	-	-	1	-	-	-	-
20 - 24	890	-	8	256	442	153	22	6	2	1	-	-	-
25 - 29	2 248	-	4	100	1 064	778	230	44	16	6	3	3	-
30 - 34	1 541	-	-	23	172	739	437	111	40	7	4	8	-
35 - 39	715	-	-	7	33	141	272	158	66	19	13	6	-
40 - 44	302	-	-	3	6	23	53	97	69	32	11	8	-
45 - 49	172	-	-	-	1	2	10	27	47	51	17	17	-
50 - 54	119	-	-	-	-	1	3	6	17	37	25	30	-
55 - 59	74	-	-	-	-	2	-	2	6	10	16	38	-
60 - 64	50	-	-	-	-	-	-	1	1	2	10	36	-
65 - 69	19	-	-	-	-	-	-	-	-	1	2	16	-
70 - 74	8	-	-	-	-	-	-	-	-	-	1	7	-
75 +	9	-	-	-	-	-	-	-	-	-	-	9	-
Unknown - Inconnu	-	-	-	-	-	-	-	-	-	-	-	-	-
Spain - Espagne													
2013 (C)													
Total	151 433	-	191	3 603	25 108	48 666	33 715	16 470	8 845	5 526	3 753	5 556	-
0 - 14	1	-	-	1	-	-	-	-	-	-	-	-	-
15 - 19	861	-	69	388	245	112	32	9	3	1	1	1	-
20 - 24	8 194	-	72	1 834	3 712	1 721	553	150	87	33	13	19	-
25 - 29	37 970	-	28	947	15 421	15 994	4 023	1 009	325	123	50	50	-
30 - 34	47 991	-	15	319	4 619	24 677	13 577	3 240	915	330	169	130	-
35 - 39	27 302	-	5	72	794	5 059	12 127	6 026	1 954	724	320	221	-
40 - 44	13 081	-	2	26	190	802	2 694	4 508	2 639	1 200	544	476	-
45 - 49	7 317	-	-	12	75	194	547	1 187	2 093	1 563	821	825	-
50 - 54	4 463	-	-	4	36	73	123	276	658	1 166	1 018	1 109	-
55 - 59	2 341	-	-	-	11	19	27	47	136	309	607	1 185	-
60 - 64	1 158	-	-	-	4	13	9	11	31	60	184	846	-
65 - 69	452	-	-	-	1	2	3	5	3	11	20	407	-
70 - 74	175	-	-	-	-	-	-	-	-	5	3	167	-
75 +	127	-	-	-	-	-	-	2	1	1	3	120	-
Unknown - Inconnu	-	-	-	-	-	-	-	-	-	-	-	-	-

23. Marriages by age of groom and by age of bride: latest available year, 2005 - 2014
Mariages selon l'âge de l'époux et selon l'âge de l'épouse : dernière année disponible, 2005 - 2014 (continued - suite)

Continent, country or area, year, code[a] and age of bride / Continent, pays ou zone, date, code[a] et âge de l'épouse	Total	0-14	15-19	20-24	25-29	30-34	35-39	40-44	45-49	50-54	55-59	60+	Unknown Inconnu
EUROPE													
Sweden - Suède													
2012 (C)													
Total	50 044	-	69	1 803	7 703	10 419	8 284	5 587	4 328	2 880	2 142	2 688	4 141
0 - 14	-	-	-	-	-	-	-	-	-	-	-	-	-
15 - 19	668	-	33	130	81	26	7	1	1	-	-	1	388
20 - 24	4 680	-	27	1 194	1 729	551	164	63	30	7	4	2	909
25 - 29	11 233	-	5	378	4 640	3 898	1 046	288	123	41	15	12	787
30 - 34	10 932	-	2	71	1 004	4 783	3 106	858	319	104	37	30	618
35 - 39	7 543	-	1	12	183	930	3 005	1 924	666	218	81	54	469
40 - 44	5 154	-	1	10	43	175	732	1 768	1 317	434	192	87	395
45 - 49	3 922	-	-	5	19	42	178	525	1 383	905	407	180	278
50 - 54	2 665	-	-	2	2	7	36	127	395	863	690	383	160
55 - 59	1 595	-	-	1	2	6	5	28	75	242	526	647	63
60 - 64	934	-	-	-	-	1	5	4	16	58	150	657	43
65 - 69	468	-	-	-	-	-	-	1	2	8	36	396	25
70 - 74	160	-	-	-	-	-	-	-	-	-	4	153	3
75 +	90	-	-	-	-	-	-	-	1	-	-	86	3
Switzerland - Suisse[41]													
2012 (C)													
Total	42 654	-	86	2 861	8 945	11 731	7 299	4 307	2 738	1 916	1 213	1 558	-
0 - 14	-	-	-	-	-	-	-	-	-	-	-	-	-
15 - 19	592	-	38	320	176	37	11	3	5	-	1	1	-
20 - 24	5 487	-	37	1 854	2 392	761	223	119	60	18	15	8	-
25 - 29	11 830	-	5	511	4 628	4 489	1 360	496	186	94	39	22	-
30 - 34	11 514	-	5	98	1 339	5 203	3 111	1 038	427	170	76	47	-
35 - 39	5 655	-	-	41	250	968	1 973	1 393	593	255	99	83	-
40 - 44	2 936	-	-	22	98	176	435	869	692	348	159	137	-
45 - 49	2 004	-	1	10	33	52	123	258	504	524	274	225	-
50 - 54	1 365	-	-	2	19	30	49	88	213	351	313	300	-
55 - 59	702	-	-	3	7	10	11	33	45	115	174	304	-
60 - 64	313	-	-	-	1	4	3	4	8	28	47	218	-
65 - 69	146	-	-	-	2	-	-	4	3	8	8	121	-
70 - 74	71	-	-	-	-	1	-	2	2	4	5	57	-
75 +	39	-	-	-	-	-	-	-	-	1	3	35	-
Unknown - Inconnu	-	-	-	-	-	-	-	-	-	-	-	-	-
TFYR of Macedonia - L'ex-R. y. de Macédoine													
2012 (C)													
Total	13 991	-	268	3 264	5 246	3 025	1 039	479	287	158	87	138	...
0 - 14	-	-	-	-	-	-	-	-	-	-	-	-	...
15 - 19	1 727	-	208	1 024	405	74	11	3	-	2	-	-	...
20 - 24	4 972	-	58	1 953	2 238	605	94	15	4	2	2	1	...
25 - 29	4 413	-	2	261	2 313	1 467	284	64	18	3	-	1	...
30 - 34	1 618	-	-	18	257	770	377	132	36	18	4	6	...
35 - 39	578	-	-	3	27	87	219	143	73	14	6	6	...
40 - 44	309	-	-	1	4	17	46	96	82	33	14	16	...
45 - 49	178	-	-	1	-	1	7	20	54	47	19	29	...
50 - 54	112	-	-	1	-	3	1	4	16	31	21	35	...
55 - 59	42	-	-	-	-	-	-	1	1	4	19	17	...
60 - 64	24	-	-	-	-	-	-	-	3	3	1	17	...
65 - 69	6	-	-	-	1	-	-	-	-	-	-	5	...
70 - 74	5	-	-	-	-	-	-	1	-	1	-	3	...
75 +	7	-	-	2	1	1	-	-	-	-	1	2	...
Ukraine													
2013 (+C)													
Total	304 232	-	5 638	82 689	101 854	47 671	24 031	14 047	9 174	7 491	4 907	6 730	-
0 - 14	-	-	-	-	-	-	-	-	-	-	-	-	-
15 - 19	29 768	-	3 569	17 949	6 954	1 094	151	33	14	2	1	1	-
20 - 24	115 048	-	1 792	52 456	47 373	10 539	2 148	479	149	69	20	23	-
25 - 29	78 596	-	207	10 455	38 179	20 214	6 593	1 969	627	238	79	35	-
30 - 34	33 936	-	52	1 452	7 460	11 676	7 831	3 448	1 237	520	176	84	-
35 - 39	17 460	-	9	280	1 534	3 220	5 127	3 905	1 977	929	314	165	-
40 - 44	10 066	-	6	55	267	729	1 602	2 875	2 283	1 398	556	295	-
45 - 49	6 781	-	3	33	67	140	441	989	1 864	1 902	834	508	-
50 - 54	5 469	-	-	4	13	44	107	273	784	1 810	1 422	1 012	-
55 - 59	3 332	-	-	2	3	13	26	60	198	481	1 119	1 430	-

23. Marriages by age of groom and by age of bride: latest available year, 2005 - 2014
Mariages selon l'âge de l'époux et selon l'âge de l'épouse : dernière année disponible, 2005 - 2014 (continued - suite)

Continent, pays ou zone, date, code[a] et âge de l'épouse	Total	0-14	15-19	20-24	25-29	30-34	35-39	40-44	45-49	50-54	55-59	60+	Unknown Inconnu

Age of groom - - âge de l'époux

EUROPE

Ukraine
2013

	Total	0-14	15-19	20-24	25-29	30-34	35-39	40-44	45-49	50-54	55-59	60+	Unknown Inconnu
60 +	3 776	-	-	3	4	2	5	16	41	142	386	3 177	-
Unknown - Inconnu	-	-	-	-	-	-	-	-	-	-	-	-	-

United Kingdom of Great Britain and Northern Ireland - Royaume-Uni de Grande-Bretagne et d'Irlande du Nord[42]
2010 (C)

	Total	0-14	15-19	20-24	25-29	30-34	35-39	40-44	45-49	50-54	55-59	60+	Unknown Inconnu
Total	280 444	-	953	21 358	71 229	66 208	41 473	27 517	19 583	12 562	8 140	11 421	-
0 - 14	-	-	-	-	-	-	-	-	-	-	-	-	-
15 - 19	3 052	-	582	1 556	612	176	70	35	9	5	5	2	-
20 - 24	38 975	-	292	13 649	17 116	5 325	1 667	566	239	66	26	29	-
25 - 29	85 307	-	57	4 743	41 761	26 417	8 245	2 632	933	311	119	89	-
30 - 34	59 525	-	13	952	9 172	26 368	14 655	5 457	1 967	604	204	133	-
35 - 39	33 497	-	5	314	1 907	5 998	11 699	8 013	3 658	1 250	376	277	-
40 - 44	21 842	-	4	97	454	1 405	3 719	7 062	5 289	2 421	871	520	-
45 - 49	16 193	-	-	31	147	405	1 112	2 792	5 151	3 647	1 693	1 215	-
50 - 54	10 119	-	-	10	48	83	247	772	1 767	3 015	2 327	1 850	-
55 - 59	5 562	-	-	5	7	23	43	138	447	918	1 734	2 247	-
60 - 64	3 484	-	-	1	4	7	12	38	99	262	623	2 438	-
65 - 69	1 641	-	-	-	1	1	3	10	19	52	130	1 425	-
70 - 74	746	-	-	-	-	-	-	2	3	7	27	707	-
75 +	501	-	-	-	-	-	1	-	2	4	5	489	-
Unknown - Inconnu	-	-	-	-	-	-	-	-	-	-	-	-	-

OCEANIA - OCÉANIE

Australia - Australie[43]
2013 (+C)

	Total	0-14	15-19	20-24	25-29	30-34	35-39	40-44	45-49	50-54	55-59	60+	Unknown Inconnu
Total	118 962	-	372	12 748	35 991	28 189	14 569	8 926	5 772	4 822	3 178	4 395	...
0 - 14	-	-	-	-	-	-	-	-	-	-	-	-	...
15 - 19	1 808	-	200	949	486	122	24	10	7	8	-	-	...
20 - 24	20 447	-	121	8 558	8 767	2 057	539	192	106	54	22	31	...
25 - 29	41 308	-	45	2 624	21 637	12 185	3 095	987	376	170	99	88	...
30 - 34	24 955	-	4	442	4 187	11 342	5 764	1 996	637	345	127	110	...
35 - 39	11 072	-	3	125	647	1 987	3 777	2 488	1 085	522	277	163	...
40 - 44	7 020	-	-	27	176	351	1 030	2 291	1 599	869	403	274	...
45 - 49	4 799	-	-	19	66	103	257	715	1 360	1 249	577	452	...
50 - 54	3 449	-	-	3	17	29	60	201	485	1 129	827	698	...
55 - 59	2 051	-	-	-	5	8	8	34	96	372	588	939	...
60 - 64	1 083	-	-	-	-	5	13	7	17	85	190	765	...
65 - 69	580	-	-	-	3	-	-	5	3	16	55	498	...
70 - 74	208	-	-	-	-	-	-	-	-	3	13	190	...
75 +	182	-	-	-	-	-	-	-	-	-	-	182	...

Fiji - Fidji
2008 (+C)

	Total	0-14	15-19	20-24	25-29	30-34	35-39	40-44	45-49	50-54	55-59	60+	Unknown Inconnu
Total	8 180	...	99	1 960	2 932	1 346	741	454	296	158	95	99	-
15 - 19	1 050	...	...	...	...	...	...	...	...	...	...	...	...
20 - 24	3 049	...	...	...	...	...	...	...	...	...	...	...	...
25 - 29	2 024	...	...	...	...	...	...	...	...	...	...	...	...
30 - 34	903	...	...	...	...	...	...	...	...	...	...	...	...
35 - 39	493	...	...	...	...	...	...	...	...	...	...	...	...
40 - 44	310	...	...	...	...	...	...	...	...	...	...	...	...
45 - 49	200	...	...	...	...	...	...	...	...	...	...	...	...
50 - 54	83	...	...	...	...	...	...	...	...	...	...	...	...
55 - 59	44	...	...	...	...	...	...	...	...	...	...	...	...
60 - 64	14	...	...	...	...	...	...	...	...	...	...	...	...
65 +	10	...	...	...	...	...	...	...	...	...	...	...	...
Unknown - Inconnu	-	...	...	...	...	...	...	...	...	...	...	...	...

23. Marriages by age of groom and by age of bride: latest available year, 2005 - 2014
Mariages selon l'âge de l'époux et selon l'âge de l'épouse : dernière année disponible, 2005 - 2014 (continued - suite)

Continent, country or area, year, code[a] and age of bride / Continent, pays ou zone, date, code[a] et âge de l'épouse	Total	0-14	15-19	20-24	25-29	30-34	35-39	40-44	45-49	50-54	55-59	60+	Unknown Inconnu
OCEANIA - OCÉANIE													
New Caledonia - Nouvelle-Calédonie 2010 (C)													
Total	908	...	2[f]	62	149	200	171	169[n]	...	90[o]	...	65	-
0 - 19	13	...	1[f]	6	2	2	1	1[n]	...	-[o]	...	-	-
20 - 24	118	...	-[f]	36	51	18	10	2[n]	...	1[o]	...	-	-
25 - 29	194	...	1[f]	16	77	63	20	13[n]	...	3[o]	...	1	-
30 - 34	205	...	-[f]	4	14	94	62	27[n]	...	4[o]	...	-	-
35 - 39	139	...	-[f]	-	3	19	55	52[n]	...	7[o]	...	3	-
40 - 49	150	...	-[f]	-	2	4	22	65[n]	...	41[o]	...	16	-
50 - 59	59	...	-[f]	-	-	-	1	9[n]	...	30[o]	...	19	-
60 +	30	...	-[f]	-	-	-	-	-[n]	...	4[o]	...	26	-
New Zealand - Nouvelle-Zélande[5,34] 2013 (+C)													
Total	19 237	-	82	1 730	4 713	4 418	2 481	1 665	1 224	1 101	730	1 093	...
0 - 14	-	-	-	-	-	-	-	-	-	-	-	-	...
15 - 19	446	-	82	272	66	18	4	2	2	-	-	-	...
20 - 24	3 692	-	-	1 458	1 731	347	93	39	15	4	4	1	...
25 - 29	5 902	-	-	-	2 916	2 264	490	152	52	15	9	4	...
30 - 34	3 556	-	-	-	-	1 789	1 199	388	105	41	24	10	...
35 - 39	1 777	-	-	-	-	-	695	642	276	108	36	20	...
40 - 44	1 303	-	-	-	-	-	-	442	480	250	84	47	...
45 - 49	983	-	-	-	-	-	-	-	294	427	165	97	...
50 - 54	682	-	-	-	-	-	-	-	-	256	265	161	...
55 - 59	430	-	-	-	-	-	-	-	-	-	143	287	...
60 - 64	228	-	-	-	-	-	-	-	-	-	-	228	...
65 - 69	132	-	-	-	-	-	-	-	-	-	-	132	...
70 - 74	62	-	-	-	-	-	-	-	-	-	-	62	...
75 +	44	-	-	-	-	-	-	-	-	-	-	44	...
Niue - Nioué 2009 (C)													
Total	12	...	-	2	3	4	-	1	1	-	1	-	-
15 - 19	-	...	...	...	...	...	...	...	...	...	...	...	...
20 - 24	-	...	...	...	...	...	...	...	...	...	...	...	...
25 - 29	3	...	...	...	...	...	...	...	...	...	...	...	...
30 - 34	4	...	...	...	...	...	...	...	...	...	...	...	...
35 - 39	3	...	...	...	...	...	...	...	...	...	...	...	...
40 - 44	-	...	...	...	...	...	...	...	...	...	...	...	...
45 - 49	1	...	...	...	...	...	...	...	...	...	...	...	...
50 - 54	1	...	...	...	...	...	...	...	...	...	...	...	...
55 - 59	-	...	...	...	...	...	...	...	...	...	...	...	...
60 - 64	-	...	...	...	...	...	...	...	...	...	...	...	...
65 +	-	...	...	...	...	...	...	...	...	...	...	...	...
Wallis and Futuna Islands - Îles Wallis et Futuna 2008 (C)													
Total	53	-	1	14	23	8	3	2	-	2	-	-	-
0 - 14	-	...	...	...	...	...	...	...	...	...	...	...	...
15 - 19	9	...	...	...	...	...	...	...	...	...	...	...	...
20 - 24	18	...	...	...	...	...	...	...	...	...	...	...	...
25 - 29	12	...	...	...	...	...	...	...	...	...	...	...	...
30 - 34	7	...	...	...	...	...	...	...	...	...	...	...	...
35 - 39	5	...	...	...	...	...	...	...	...	...	...	...	...
40 - 44	-	...	...	...	...	...	...	...	...	...	...	...	...
45 - 49	1	...	...	...	...	...	...	...	...	...	...	...	...
50 - 54	-	...	...	...	...	...	...	...	...	...	...	...	...
55 - 59	-	...	...	...	...	...	...	...	...	...	...	...	...
60 - 64	1	...	...	...	...	...	...	...	...	...	...	...	...
65 - 69	-	...	...	...	...	...	...	...	...	...	...	...	...
70 - 74	-	...	...	...	...	...	...	...	...	...	...	...	...
75 +	-	...	...	...	...	...	...	...	...	...	...	...	...

FOOTNOTES - NOTES

Italics: data from civil registers which are incomplete or of unknown completeness. - Italiques : données incomplètes ou dont le degré d'exactitude n'est pas connu, provenant des registres de l'état civil.

* Provisional. - Données provisoires.

a   'Code' indicates the source of data, as follows:
C - Civil registration, estimated over 90% complete
U - Civil registration, estimated less than 90% complete
| - Other source, estimated reliable
+ - Data tabulated by date of registration rather than occurence
... - Information not available

Le 'Code' indique la source des données, comme suit :
C - Registres de l'état civil considérés complèts à 90 p. 100 au moins
U - Registres de l'état civil qui ne sont pas considérés complèts à 90 p. 100 au moins
| - Autre source, considérée pas douteuses
+ - Données exploitées selon la date de l'enregistrement et non la date de l'événement
... - Information pas disponible

b   Refers to 0-15 years of age. - Données se raportent au groupe d'âges 0-15.
c   Refers to 0-16 years of age. - Données se raportent au groupe d'âges 0-16.
d   Refers to 0-17 years of age. - Données se raportent au groupe d'âges 0-17.
e   Refers to 0-18 years of age. - Données se raportent au groupe d'âges 0-18.
f   Refers to 0-19 years of age. - Données se raportent au groupe d'âges 0-19.
g   Refers to 0-24 years of age. - Données se raportent au groupe d'âges 0-24.
h   Refers to 16-19 years of age. - Données se raportent au groupe d'âges 16-19.
i   Refers to 17-19 years of age. - Données se raportent au groupe d'âges 17-19.
j   Refers to 18-19 years of age. - Données se raportent au groupe d'âges 18-19.
k   Refers to 19-24 years of age. - Données se raportent au groupe d'âges 19-24.
l   Refers to 20-29 years of age. - Données se raportent au groupe d'âges 20-29.
m   Refers to 30-39 years of age. - Données se raportent au groupe d'âges 30-39.
n   Refers to 40-49 years of age. - Données se raportent au groupe d'âges 40-49.
o   Refers to 50-59 years of age. - Données se raportent au groupe d'âges 50-59.
p   Refers to 35+ years of age. - Données se raportent au groupe d'âges 35+.
q   Refers to 40+ years of age. - Données se raportent au groupe d'âges 40+.
r   Refers to 45+ years of age. - Données se raportent au groupe d'âges 45+.
s   Refers to 50+ years of age. - Données se raportent au groupe d'âges 50+.
t   Refers to 55+ years of age. - Données se raportent au groupe d'âges 55+.

1   Including marriages resumed after 'revocable divorce' (among Moslem population), which approximates legal separation. - Y compris les unions reconstituées après un 'divorce révocable' (parmi la population musulmane), qui est à peu près l'équivalent d'une séparation légale.

2   Excludes the islands of St. Brandon and Agalega. - Non compris les îles St. Brandon et Agalega.

3   Including visitors. - Y compris les visiteurs.

4   Excluding visitors. - Ne comprend pas les visiteurs.

5   Data refer to marriages registered at the place of residence of the groom. - Correspond aux mariages enregistrés dans le lieu de résidence du marié.

6   Marriages registered by residence of bride. - Les mariages sont enregistrés selon le lieu de résidence de la mariée.

7   Including marriages where bride/groom are non-residents. - Y compris les mariages pour lesquels le marié et la mariée sont des non-résidents.

8   Excludes nomadic Indian tribes. - Non compris les tribus d'Indiens nomades.

9   Data are compiled from the National Registers of Identification and Civil Status (RENIEC). - Les données sont rédigées à partir des Registres Nationaux d'Identification et d'État Civil (RENIEC).

10   Data refers to metropolitan Lima and Callao. - Les données font référence à la région métropolitaine de Lima et Callao.

11   Data refer to marriages of residents only. - Les données ne portent que sur les mariages de résidents.

12   Data refer to government controlled areas. - Les données se rapportent aux zones contrôlées par le Gouvernement.

13   Data refer to the Iranian Year which begins on 21 March and ends on 20 March of the following year. - Les données concernent l'année iranienne, qui commence le 21 mars et se termine le 20 mars de l'année suivante.

14   Includes data for East Jerusalem and Israeli residents in certain other territories under occupation by Israeli military forces since June 1967. - Y compris les données pour Jérusalem-Est et les résidents israéliens dans certains autres territoires occupés depuis 1967 par les forces armées israéliennes.

15   Data refer to Japanese nationals in Japan only; and to grooms and brides married for the first time whose marriages occurred and were registered in the same year. - Les données se raportent aux nationaux japonais au Japon seulement; et aux époux et épouses mariés pour la première fois, dont le mariage a été célébré et enregistré la même année.

16   Excluding data for Jordanian territory under occupation since June 1967 by Israeli military forces. Excluding foreigners, including registered Palestinian refugees. - Non compris les données pour le territoire jordanien occupé depuis juin 1967 par les forces armées israéliennes. Non compris les étrangers, mais y compris les réfugiés de Palestine enregistrés.

17   Excluding marriages by groom and bride that are under "Married" status. - Sauf mariages entre personnes qui ont le statut de « marié(e) ».

18   Excluding alien armed forces, civilian aliens employed by armed forces, and foreign diplomatic personnel and their dependants. - Non compris les militaires étrangers, les civils étrangers employés par les forces armées ni le personnel diplomatique étranger et les membres de leur famille les accompagnant.

19   Excluding marriages previously officiated outside Singapore or under religious and customary rites. - Ne comprend pas les mariages prononcés ailleurs qu'à Singapour ni les mariages religieux ou coutumiers.

20   Data from MERNIS (Central Population Administrative System). - Données de MERNIS (Système central de données démographiques).

21   Excluding aliens temporarily in the area. - Non compris les étrangers se trouvant temporairement dans le territoire.

22   Since 2003, marriage between persons of the same sex is authorized in Belgium, but the sex of spouses is not revealed. In this table, husband is used for first spouse, whereas wife is used for second spouse. - Depuis 2003, le mariage entre personnes de même sexe est autorisé en Belgique, mais le sexe des conjoints n'est pas indiqué. Dans ce tableau, la mention "époux" est utilisée pour le premier conjoint et la mention "épouse" pour le second conjoint.

23   Including armed forces stationed outside the country and alien armed forces in the area, if the marriage is performed by local authority. - Y compris les militaires nationaux hors du pays et les militaires étrangers en garnison sur le territoire, si le mariage a été célébré par l'autorité locale.

24   Including nationals outside the country, but excluding foreigners in the country. - Y compris les nationaux à l'étranger, mais non compris les étrangers sur le territoire.

25   Excluding Faeroe Islands and Greenland shown separately, if available. - Non compris les Îles Féroé et le Groenland, qui font l'objet de rubriques distinctes, si disponible.

26   Excluding Åland Islands. - Non compris les Îles d'Åland.

27   Only marriages in which the bride was resident in Finland. - Ne porte que sur les mariages pour lesquels la mariée réside en Finlande.

28   Including armed forces stationed outside the country. - Y compris les militaires nationaux hors du pays.

29   Data for residence abroad are excluded. - Les données relatives aux résidents à l'étranger sont exclues.

30   Data refer to common residence after marriage. - Données se rapportant à la résidence commune après le mariage.

31   Data refer to marriages where one or both partners are residents. - Les données portent sur les mariages pour lesquels l'un des deux partenaires ou les deux sont résidents.

32   Marriages of couples of which at least one partner is recorded in a Dutch municipal register, irrespective of the country where the marriage was performed. - Correspond aux mariages pour lesquels au moins l'un des partenaires est inscrit sur un registre municipal néerlandais, quel que soit le pays dans lequel le mariage est célébré.

33   Including residents outside the country if listed in a Netherlands population register. - Englobe les résidents se trouvant à l'étranger à condition qu'ils soient inscrits sur le registre de population des Pays-Bas.

34   Includes same sex marriages. - Y compris les mariages entre personnes du même sexe.

35   Groom refers to the man for opposite sex marriages, and to spouse 1 as specified in the Civil Register for same sex marriages. Bride refers to the woman for opposite sex marriages, and to spouse 2 as specified in the Civil Register for same sex marriages. - Marié se réfère à l'homme en cas de mariage entre personnes de sexe différent et à l'époux 1 inscrit sur le Registre d'état civil en cas de mariage entre personnes du même sexe. Mariée se réfère à la femme en cas de mariage entre personnes de sexe différent et à l'époux 2 inscrit sur le Registre d'état civil en cas de mariage entre personnes du même sexe.

36   Data refer to first marriages only. - Données se rapportent aux premiers mariages seulement.

37   Data refer to population 15 years of age or more. - Les données concernent la population âgée de 15 ans ou plus.

38   Includes civil and religious marriages as well as not specified. - Englobe les mariages civils et religieux et ceux pour lesquels rien n'a été indiqué.

39   Excludes data for Kosovo and Metohia. - Sans les données pour le Kosovo et Metohie.

⁴⁰ Data refer to residence of groom or bride before marriage. - Données relatives au lieu de résidence du marié ou de la mariée avant le mariage.

⁴¹ Data based on the residence of groom if he has permanent address in the country, otherwise, based on the residence of bride. If neither partner is a permanent resident, the marriage is not included in the official statistics. - Les données sont fondées sur la résidence du marié si celui-ci a une adresse permanente dans le pays, sinon elles sont fondées sur la résidence de la mariée. Si aucun des deux partenaires n'est un résident permanent, le mariage n'apparaît pas dans les statistiques officielles.

⁴² Excluding Channel Islands (Guernsey and Jersey) and Isle of Man, shown separately, if available. - Non compris les îles Anglo-Normandes (Guernesey et Jersey) et l'île de Man, qui font l'objet de rubriques distinctes, si disponible.

⁴³ Data for certain cells suppressed by national statistical office for confidentiality reasons. - Les données pour certaines cases ont été supprimées par le bureau national de statistiques pour des raisons de confidentialité.

Table 24 - *Demographic Yearbook 2014*

Table 24 presents the number of divorces and crude divorce rates for as many years as possible between 2010 and 2014.

Description of variables: Divorce is defined as a final legal dissolution of a marriage, that is, the separation of husband and wife which confers on the parties the right to remarriage under civil, religious and/or other provisions, according to the laws of each country[1].

Unless otherwise noted, divorce statistics exclude legal separations that do not allow remarriage. These statistics refer to the number of divorces granted, and not to the number of persons divorcing.

Divorce statistics are obtained from court records and/or civil registers according to national practice. The actual compilation of these statistics may be the responsibility of the civil registrar, the national statistical office or other government offices.

The urban/rural classification of divorces is that provided by each country or area; it is presumed to be based on the national census definitions of urban population, which have been set forth at the end of the technical notes for table 6.

Rate computation: Crude divorce rates by urban/rural residence are the annual number of divorces per 1 000 mid-year population. Rates presented in this table have been limited to those countries or areas having at least a total of 30 divorces in a given year. These rates are calculated by the Statistics Division of the United Nations based on the appropriate reference population (for example: total population, nationals only etc.) if known and available. If the reference population is not known or unavailable the total population is used to calculate the rates. Therefore, if the population that is used to calculate the rates is different from the correct reference population, the rates presented might under- or overstate the true situation in a country or area.

Reliability of data: Each country or area has been asked to indicate the estimated completeness of the divorces recorded in its civil register. These national assessments are indicated by the quality codes "C" and "U" that appear in the first column of this table.

"C" indicates that the data are estimated to be virtually complete, that is, representing at least 90 per cent of the divorces that occur each year, while "U" indicates that data are estimated to be incomplete, that is, representing less than 90 per cent of the divorces occurring each year. The code "..." indicates that no information was provided regarding completeness.

Data from civil registers that are reported as incomplete or of unknown completeness (coded "U" or "...") are considered unreliable. They appear in *italics* in this table and the rates were not computed on data so coded. These quality codes apply only to data from civil registers. For more information about the quality of vital statistics data in general, see section 4.2 of the Technical Notes.

Limitations: Statistics on divorces are subject to the same qualifications as have been set forth for vital statistics in general and divorce statistics in particular as discussed in section 4 of the Technical Notes.

Divorce, like marriage, is a legal event, and this has implications for international comparability of data. Divorce has been defined, for statistical purposes, in terms of the laws of individual countries or areas. The laws pertaining to divorce vary considerably from one country or area to another. This variation in the legal provision for divorce also affects the incidence of divorce, which is relatively low in countries or areas where divorce decrees are difficult to obtain.

Since divorces are granted by courts and statistics on divorce refer to the actual divorce decree, effective as of the date of the decree, marked year-to-year fluctuations may reflect court delays and clearances rather than trends in the incidence of divorce. The comparability of divorce statistics may also be affected by tabulation procedures. In some countries or areas annulments and/or legal separations may be included. This practice is more common for countries or areas in which the number of divorces is small. Information on this practice is given in the footnotes when known.

The registration of a divorce in many countries or areas is the responsibility solely of the court or the authority which granted it. Since the registration recording such cases is part of the records of the court proceedings, divorces are likely to be registered soon after the decree is granted. For this reason the practice of tabulating data by date of registration does not generally pose serious problems of comparability as it does in the case of birth and death statistics.

As noted briefly above, the incidence of divorce is affected by the relative ease or difficulty of obtaining a divorce according to the laws of individual countries or areas. The incidence of divorce is also affected by the ability of individuals to meet financial and other costs of the court procedures. Connected with this aspect is the influence of certain religious faiths on the incidence of divorce. For all these reasons, divorce statistics are not strictly comparable as measures of family dissolution by legal means. Furthermore, family dissolution by other than legal means, such as separation, is not measured in statistics for divorce.

For certain countries or areas there is or was no legal provision for divorce in the sense used here, and therefore no data for these countries or areas appear in this table.

In addition, it should be noted that rates are affected also by the quality and limitations of the population estimates that are used in their computation. The problems of under-enumeration or over-enumeration, and to some extent, the differences in definition of total population, have been discussed in section 3 of the Technical Notes dealing with population data in general, and specific information pertaining to individual countries or areas is given in the footnotes to table 3.

As will be seen from the footnotes, strict correspondence between the numerator of the rate and the denominator is not always obtained; for example, divorces among civilian plus military segments of the population may be related to civilian population only. The effect of this may be to increase the rates but, in most cases, the effect is negligible.

As mentioned above, data for some countries or areas may include annulments and/or legal separations. This practice affects the comparability of the crude divorce rates. For example, inclusion of annulments in the numerator of the rates produces a negligible effect on the rates, but inclusion of legal separations may have a measurable effect on the level.

It should be emphasized that crude divorce rates like crude birth, death and marriage rates may be seriously affected by age-sex structure of the populations to which they relate. Like crude marriage rates, they are also affected by the existing distribution of the population by marital status. Nevertheless, crude divorce rates provide a simple measure of the level and changes in divorces.

The comparability of data by urban/rural residence is affected by the national definitions of urban and rural used in tabulating these data. It is assumed, in the absence of specific information to the contrary, that the definitions of urban and rural used in connection with the national population census were also used in the compilation of the vital statistics for each country or area. However, it cannot be excluded that, for a given country or area, different definitions of urban and rural are used for the vital statistics data and the population census data respectively. When known, the definitions of urban in national population censuses are presented at the end of the technical notes for table 6. As discussed in detail in the notes, these definitions vary considerably from one country or area to another.

In addition to problems of comparability, divorce rates classified by urban/rural residence are also subject to certain special types of bias. If, when calculating divorce rates, different definitions of urban are used in connection with the vital events and the population data, and if this results in a net difference between the numerator and denominator of the rate in the population at risk, then the divorce rates would be biased. Urban/rural differentials in divorce rates may also be affected by whether the vital events have been tabulated in terms of place of occurrence or place of usual residence. This problem is discussed in more detail in section 4.1.4.1 of the Technical Notes.

Earlier data: Divorces have been shown in previous issues of the Demographic Yearbook. The earliest data, which were for 1935, appeared in the 1951 issue. For more information on specific topics and years for which data are reported, readers should consult the Historical Index.

NOTES

[1] For definition, please see section 4.1.1 of the Technical Notes.

Tableau 24 – *Annuaire démographique 2014*

Le tableau 24 présente des statistiques concernant les divorces et les taux bruts de divortialité, pour le plus grand nombre d'années possible entre 2010 et 2014.

Description des variables : le divorce est la dissolution légale et définitive des liens du mariage, c'est-à-dire la séparation de l'époux et de l'épouse qui confère aux parties le droit de se remarier civilement ou religieusement, ou selon toute autre procédure, conformément à la législation du pays[1].

Sauf indication contraire, les statistiques de la divortialité n'englobent pas les séparations légales qui excluent un remariage. Ces statistiques se rapportent aux jugements de divorce prononcés, non aux personnes divorcées.

Les statistiques de la divortialité proviennent, selon la pratique suivie par chaque pays, des actes des tribunaux et/ou des registres de l'état civil. L'officier d'état civil, les services nationaux de statistique ou d'autres services gouvernementaux peuvent être chargés d'établir ces statistiques.

La classification des divorces selon le lieu de résidence (zone urbaine ou rurale) est celle qui a été communiquée par chaque pays ou zone ; on part du principe qu'elle repose sur les définitions de la population urbaine utilisées pour les recensements nationaux, qui sont reproduites à la fin des notes techniques du tableau 6.

Calcul des taux : les taux bruts de divortialité selon le lieu de résidence (zone urbaine ou rurale) représentent le nombre annuel de divorces enregistrés pour 1 000 habitants au milieu de l'année. Les taux de ce tableau ne se rapportent qu'aux pays ou zones où l'on a enregistré un total d'au moins 30 divorces pendant une année donnée. Ces taux sont calculés par la division de statistique des Nations Unies sur la base de la population de référence adéquate (par exemple : population totale, nationaux seulement, etc.) si connue et disponible. Si la population de référence n'est pas connue ou n'est pas disponible, la population totale est utilisée pour calculer les taux. Par conséquent, si la population utilisée pour calculer les taux est différente de la population de référence adéquate, les taux présentés sont susceptibles de sous ou sur estimer la situation réelle d'un pays ou d'un territoire.

Fiabilité des données : il a été demandé à chaque pays ou zone d'indiquer le degré estimatif de complétude des données sur les divorces figurant dans ses registres d'état civil. Ces évaluations nationales sont désignées par les codes de qualité "C" et "U" qui apparaissent dans la deuxième colonne du tableau.

La lettre "C" indique que les données sont jugées à peu près complètes, c'est-à-dire qu'elles représentent au moins 90 p. 100 des divorces survenus chaque année ; la lettre "U" signale que les données sont jugées incomplètes, c'est-à-dire qu'elles représentent moins de 90 p. 100 des divorces survenus chaque année. Le code "..." indique qu'aucun renseignement n'a été communiqué quant à la complétude des données.

Les données issues des registres de l'état civil qui sont déclarées incomplètes ou dont le degré de complétude n'est pas connu (code "U" ou "...") sont jugées douteuses. Elles apparaissent en italique dans le tableau et les taux correspondants n'ont pas été calculés. Les codes de qualité ne s'appliquent qu'aux données extraites des registres de l'état civil. Pour plus de précisions sur la qualité des données reposant sur les statistiques de l'état civil en général, voir la section 4.2 des notes techniques.

Insuffisance des données : les statistiques des divorces appellent les mêmes réserves que celles formulées à propos des statistiques de l'état civil en général et des statistiques de divortialité en particulier (voir la section 4 des notes techniques).

Le divorce est, comme le mariage, un acte juridique, et ce fait influe sur la comparabilité internationale des données. Aux fins de la statistique, le divorce est défini par la législation de chaque pays ou zone. La législation sur le divorce varie considérablement d'un pays ou d'une zone à l'autre, ce qui influe aussi sur la fréquence des divorces, laquelle est relativement faible dans les pays ou zones où le jugement de divorce est difficile à obtenir.

Du fait que les divorces sont prononcés par les tribunaux et que les statistiques de la divortialité se rapportent aux jugements de divorce proprement dits, qui prennent effet à la date où ces jugements sont rendus, il se peut que des fluctuations annuelles accusées traduisent le rythme plus ou moins rapide auquel les affaires sont jugées plutôt que l'évolution de la fréquence des divorces. Les méthodes d'exploitation des données peuvent aussi influer sur la comparabilité des statistiques de la divortialité. Dans certains pays ou zones, ces statistiques peuvent comprendre les annulations et/ou les séparations légales. C'est notamment le cas dans les pays ou zones où les divorces sont peu nombreux. Lorsqu'ils sont connus, des renseignements à ce propos sont donnés en note à la fin du tableau.

Étant donné que dans de nombreux pays ou zones, le tribunal ou l'autorité qui a prononcé le divorce est seul habilité à enregistrer cet acte, et, comme l'acte d'enregistrement figure alors sur les registres du tribunal, l'enregistrement suit généralement de peu le jugement. C'est pourquoi la pratique consistant à exploiter les données selon la date de l'enregistrement ne pose généralement pas les graves problèmes de comparabilité auxquels on se heurte dans le cas des statistiques des naissances et des décès.

Comme on l'a brièvement mentionné ci-dessus, la fréquence des divorces est fonction notamment de la facilité relative avec laquelle la législation de chaque pays ou zone permet d'obtenir le divorce. Elle dépend également de la capacité des intéressés à supporter les frais de procédure. Il faut aussi citer l'influence de certaines religions sur la fréquence des divorces. Pour toutes ces raisons, les statistiques de divortialité ne sont pas rigoureusement comparables et ne permettent pas de mesurer exactement la fréquence des dissolutions légales des mariages. De plus, elles ne rendent pas compte des cas de dissolution extrajudiciaire du mariage, comme la séparation.

Dans certains pays ou zones, il n'existe ou il n'existait pas de législation sur le divorce selon l'acception retenue aux fins de ce tableau, si bien que l'on ne dispose pas de données les concernant.

De surcroît, il convient de noter que l'exactitude des taux dépend également de la qualité et des insuffisances des estimations de population qui sont utilisées pour leur calcul. Le problème des erreurs par excès ou par défaut commises lors du dénombrement et, dans une certaine mesure, le problème de l'hétérogénéité des définitions de la population totale ont été examinés à la section 3 des notes techniques, relative à la population en général ; des explications concernant les différents pays ou zones sont données en note à la fin du tableau 3.

Comme on le verra dans les notes, il n'a pas toujours été possible d'obtenir une correspondance rigoureuse entre le numérateur et le dénominateur pour le calcul des taux. Par exemple, les divorces parmi la population civile et les militaires sont parfois rapportés à la population civile seulement. Cela peut avoir pour effet d'accroître les taux, mais, dans la plupart des cas, il est probable que la différence sera négligeable.

Comme indiqué plus haut, les données concernant certains pays ou zones peuvent comprendre les annulations et/ou les séparations légales. Cette pratique influe sur la comparabilité des taux bruts de divortialité. Par exemple, l'inclusion des annulations dans le numérateur a une influence négligeable, mais l'inclusion des séparations légales peut avoir un effet appréciable.

Il faut souligner que les taux bruts de divortialité, de même que les taux bruts de natalité, de mortalité et de nuptialité, peuvent varier sensiblement selon la structure par âge et par sexe. Comme les taux bruts de nuptialité, ils peuvent également varier en raison de la répartition de la population selon l'état matrimonial. Les taux bruts de divortialité offrent néanmoins un moyen simple de mesurer la fréquence et l'évolution des divorces.

La comparabilité des données selon le lieu de résidence (zone urbaine ou rurale) peut être limitée par les définitions nationales des termes « urbain » et « rural » utilisées pour la mise en tableaux de ces données. En l'absence d'indications contraires, on a supposé que les mêmes définitions avaient servi pour le recensement national de la population et pour l'établissement des statistiques de l'état civil pour chaque pays ou zone. Toutefois, il n'est pas exclu que, pour une zone ou un pays donné, des définitions différentes aient été retenues. Les définitions du terme « urbain » utilisées pour les recensements nationaux de population ont été présentées à la fin des notes techniques du tableau 6 lorsqu'elles étaient connues. Comme on l'a précisé dans les notes techniques relatives au tableau 6, ces définitions varient considérablement d'un pays ou d'une zone à l'autre.

Outre les problèmes de comparabilité, les taux de divortialité classés selon le lieu de résidence (zone urbaine ou rurale) sont également sujets à des distorsions particulières. Si l'on utilise des définitions différentes du terme « urbain » pour classer les faits d'état civil et les données relatives à la population lors du calcul des taux et qu'il en résulte une différence nette entre le numérateur et le dénominateur pour le taux de la population exposée au risque, les taux de divortialité s'en trouveront faussés. La différence entre ces taux pour les zones urbaines et rurales pourra aussi être faussée selon que les faits d'état civil auront été classés d'après le lieu de l'événement ou d'après le lieu de résidence habituel. Ce problème est examiné plus en détail à la section 4.1.4.1 des notes techniques.

Données publiées antérieurement : des statistiques concernant les divorces ont déjà été présentées dans des éditions antérieures de l'*Annuaire démographique*. Les plus anciennes, qui portaient sur 1935, ont été publiées dans l'édition de 1951. Pour plus de précisions concernant les années et les sujets pour lesquels des données ont été publiées, se reporter à l'index historique.

NOTE

[1] Pour la définition, voir la section 4.1.1 des Notes techniques.

24. Divorces and crude divorce rates by urban/rural residence: 2010 - 2014
Divorces et taux bruts de divortialité selon la résidence, urbaine/rurale : 2010 - 2014

Continent, country or area, and urban/rural residence / Continent, pays ou zone et résidence, urbaine/rurale	Code[a]	Number - Nombre					Rate - Taux				
		2010	2011	2012	2013	2014	2010	2011	2012	2013	2014
AFRICA - AFRIQUE											
Egypt - Égypte[1]											
Total	+C	149 376	151 933	155 261	162 583	...	1.9	1.9	1.9	1.9	...
Urban - Urbaine	+C	85 686	87 091	91 789	91 040	...	2.5	2.5	2.6	2.5	...
Rural - Rurale	+C	63 690	64 842	63 472	71 543	...	1.4	1.4	1.3	1.5	...
Lesotho											
Total	+U	127	143	142	...	...	...	...	...	...	...
Mauritius - Maurice[2]											
Total	+C	1 837	1 788	2 003	1 584	2 262	1.4	1.4	1.6	1.3	1.8
Mozambique											
Total	+U	869	...	...	...	...	...	...	...	...	...
Saint Helena ex. dep. - Sainte-Hélène sans dép.											
Total	C	...	1	5	7	4	...	...	...	...	...
Seychelles											
Total	+C	156	165	158	193	158	1.7	1.9	1.8	2.1	1.7
South Africa - Afrique du Sud											
Total	...	22 936	20 980	...	...	...	...	...	...	...	...
Tunisia - Tunisie											
Total	...	12 871	12 651	...	...	...	...	...	...	...	...
AMERICA, NORTH - AMÉRIQUE DU NORD											
Aruba											
Total	C	457	470	464	477	468	4.5	4.6	4.4	4.5	4.3
Bahamas											
Total	+C	399	...	...	...	...	1.2	...	...	...	...
Bermuda - Bermudes											
Total	C	210	177	145	165	104	3.3	2.8	2.3	2.7	1.7
Costa Rica											
Total	C	11 556	...	11 593	13 349	*10 864	2.5	...	2.5	2.8	*2.3
Cuba											
Total	C	32 318	29 712	32 005	32 848	...	2.9	2.7	2.9	2.9	...
Urban - Urbaine	C	30 181	27 654	30 028	30 819	...	3.6	3.3	3.5	3.6	...
Rural - Rurale	C	2 137	2 058	1 977	2 029	...	0.8	0.7	0.7	0.8	...
Curaçao											
Total	C	393	396	386	366	...	2.6	2.6	2.5	2.4	...
Dominican Republic - République dominicaine											
Total	+C	17 674	17 927	17 820	18 882	...	1.9	1.9	1.8	1.9	...
El Salvador											
Total	...	6 103	6 053	6 674[4]	...	...	...	...	...	...	...
Urban - Urbaine	...	3 003[3]	3 022[3]	6 463[4]	...	...	...	...	...	...	...
Rural - Rurale	...	3 100[3]	3 031[3]	211[4]	...	...	...	...	...	...	...
Guadeloupe											
Total	C	690	860	902	806	...	1.7	2.1	2.2	2.0	...
Guatemala											
Total	C	3 645	4 344	5 157	...	...	0.3	0.3	0.3	...	...
Jamaica - Jamaïque											
Total	+C	2 371	1 960	2 409	...	...	0.9	0.7	0.9	...	...
Mexico - Mexique											
Total	+C	86 042	91 285	99 509	108 727	...	0.8	0.8	0.9	0.9	...
Urban - Urbaine[5]	+C	77 951	82 623	89 927	97 087	...	0.9	1.0	1.1	1.1	...
Rural - Rurale[5]	+C	3 733	4 122	4 723	5 305	...	0.1	0.1	0.1	0.2	...
Panama											
Total	C	3 583	3 848	4 132	4 083	...	1.0	1.0	1.1	1.1	...
Urban - Urbaine	C	3 078	3 300	3 514	3 453	...	1.3	1.3	1.4	1.3	...
Rural - Rurale	C	505	548	618	630	...	0.4	0.4	0.5	0.5	...
Puerto Rico - Porto Rico											
Total	C	13 913	13 349	14 325	12 908	11 776	3.7	3.6	3.9	3.6	3.3
Sint Maarten (Dutch part) - Saint-Martin (partie néerlandaise)											
Total	+C	80	95	...	99	...	2.3	2.8	...	2.7	...

24. Divorces and crude divorce rates by urban/rural residence: 2010 - 2014
Divorces et taux bruts de divortialité selon la résidence, urbaine/rurale : 2010 - 2014 (continued - suite)

Continent, country or area, and urban/rural residence / Continent, pays ou zone et résidence, urbaine/rurale	Co-de[a]	Number - Nombre					Rate - Taux				
		2010	2011	2012	2013	2014	2010	2011	2012	2013	2014
AMERICA, NORTH - AMÉRIQUE DU NORD											
United States of America - États-Unis d'Amérique[6]											
Total	C	872 000	877 000	...	...	...	2.8	2.8	...	...	...
AMERICA, SOUTH - AMÉRIQUE DU SUD											
Brazil - Brésil											
Total	...	239 070	347 583	341 600	324 921		...	...	...	...	...	...
Chile - Chili											
Total	C	1 558	...	...	...	...	0.1	...	...	...	...
Ecuador - Équateur[7]											
Total	U	18 231	21 466	20 299	21 122		...	...	...	...	...	...
Urban - Urbaine	U	...	...	...	19 458		...	...	...	...	...
Rural - Rurale	U	...	...	...	1 664		...	...	...	...	...
Peru - Pérou											
Total	+C	9 016[8]	5 625[9]	13 126[9]	14 103[9]	...	0.3	0.2	0.4	0.5	
Suriname[10]											
Total	C	622	488	528	602	...	1.2	0.9	1.0	1.1	...
Venezuela (Bolivarian Republic of) - Venezuela (République bolivarienne du)											
Total	...	25 871	28 653	30 660	31 355		...	...	...	...	...	...
ASIA - ASIE											
Armenia - Arménie											
Total	+C	10 425	3 188	...	...	...	3.2	1.0	...	...	...
Azerbaijan - Azerbaïdjan											
Total	+C	9 061	10 747	11 087	11 730	...	1.0	1.2	1.2	1.2	...
Urban - Urbaine	+C	6 753	7 931	8 212	8 451	...	1.4	1.6	1.7	1.7	...
Rural - Rurale	+C	2 308	2 816	2 875	3 279	...	0.5	0.7	0.7	0.7	...
Bahrain - Bahreïn											
Total	...	1 569	1 408	1 649	1 824	1 795	...	...	...	...	...
Bangladesh											
Total	...	120 395	124 110	125 787	...	...	...	...	...	...	...
Urban - Urbaine	...	26 587	29 250	31 483	...	...	...	...	...	...	...
Rural - Rurale	...	93 808	94 860	94 304	...	...	...	...	...	...	...
Brunei Darussalam - Brunéi Darussalam											
Total	...	...	475	570	502	...	...	...	...	...	...
China - Chine[11]											
Total	+C	2 680 000	2 111 000	2 388 000		...	2.0	1.6	1.8	...	...
China, Hong Kong SAR - Chine, Hong Kong RAS											
Total	...	18 167	19 597	21 125	22 271	20 019	...	...	...	...	...
China, Macao SAR - Chine, Macao RAS											
Total	+C	889	998	1 147	1 172	1 308	1.7	1.8	2.0	2.0	2.1
Cyprus - Chypre[12]											
Total	C	1 929	1 934	2 036	1 857	...	2.3	2.3	2.4	2.2	...
Urban - Urbaine[13]	C	1 471	1 518	1 597	1 444	...	...	...	...	...	...
Rural - Rurale[13]	C	396	354	363	333	...	...	...	...	...	...
Georgia - Géorgie											
Total	C	4 726	5 850	7 136	8 089	...	1.1	1.3	1.6	...	...
Urban - Urbaine	C	3 636	4 384	...	...	...	1.5	1.8	...	...	...
Rural - Rurale	C	1 090	1 466	...	...	...	0.5	0.7	...	...	...
Indonesia - Indonésie											
Total	U	285 184	276 791	...	...	...	...	...	...	...	...

24. Divorces and crude divorce rates by urban/rural residence: 2010 - 2014
Divorces et taux bruts de divortialité selon la résidence, urbaine/rurale : 2010 - 2014 (continued - suite)

Continent, country or area, and urban/rural residence / Continent, pays ou zone et résidence, urbaine/rurale	Code[a]	Number - Nombre					Rate - Taux				
		2010	2011	2012	2013	2014	2010	2011	2012	2013	2014
ASIA - ASIE											
Iran (Islamic Republic of) - Iran (République islamique d')[14]											
Total	+C	137 200	142 841	150 324	155 369	...	1.8	1.9	2.0	2.0	...
Urban - Urbaine	+C	116 643	...	...	...	...	2.3	...	...	...	...
Rural - Rurale	+C	20 557	...	...	...	...	0.9	...	...	...	...
Israel - Israël[15]											
Total	C	13 042	13 460	13 685	...	...	1.7	1.7	1.7	...	...
Urban - Urbaine[13]	C	11 906	12 244	12 451	...	...	1.7	1.7	1.7	...	...
Rural - Rurale[13]	C	871	932	955	...	...	1.4	1.4	1.4	...	...
Japan - Japon[16]											
Total	+C	251 378	235 719	235 406	231 383	...	2.0	1.8	1.8	1.8	...
Urban - Urbaine	+C	230 064	216 337	216 322	212 844	...	...	...	...	...	...
Rural - Rurale	+C	21 314	19 382	19 084	18 539	...	...	...	...	...	...
Jordan - Jordanie[17]											
Total	+C	15 707	16 086	17 696	18 976	...	2.6	2.6	2.8	2.9	...
Kazakhstan											
Total	C	41 617	44 862	48 513	51 482	...	2.5	2.7	2.9	3.0	...
Urban - Urbaine	C	31 054	33 792	36 232	38 365	...	3.5	3.7	3.9	4.1	...
Rural - Rurale	C	10 563	11 070	12 281	13 117	...	1.4	1.5	1.6	1.7	...
Kuwait - Koweït											
Total	C	5 965	6 254	6 672	6 904	...	2.0	2.0	2.0	2.0	...
Kyrgyzstan - Kirghizstan											
Total	C	8 155	8 705	8 698	9 052	...	1.6	1.7	1.6	1.6	...
Urban - Urbaine	C	4 459	4 497	4 609	5 255	...	2.4	2.4	2.5	2.7	...
Rural - Rurale	C	3 696	4 208	4 089	3 797	...	1.1	1.2	1.2	1.0	...
Lebanon - Liban											
Total	+C	5 897	6 879	6 498	6 644	7 206	...	1.8	...	...	...
Mongolia - Mongolie											
Total	+C	3 054	3 222	2 467	3 522	3 750	1.1	1.2	0.9	1.2	1.3
Urban - Urbaine	+C	2 619	2 760	2 096	2 978	3 333	1.5	1.5	1.1	1.5	1.7
Rural - Rurale	+C	435	462	371	544	417	0.5	0.5	0.4	0.6	0.4
Oman[18]											
Total	+U	*2 736*	*3 805*	*3 570*	...	...	...	...	...	...	...
Qatar											
Total	C	1 172	1 108	1 420	1 325	...	0.7	0.6	0.8	0.7	...
Republic of Korea - République de Corée[19]											
Total	+C	116 858	114 284	114 316	115 292	...	2.3	2.3	2.3	2.3	...
Urban - Urbaine[20]	+C	90 708	88 273	88 785	89 793	...	2.2	2.2	2.2	2.2	...
Rural - Rurale[20]	+C	22 333	22 398	22 213	22 218	...	2.4	2.4	2.3	2.4	...
Singapore - Singapour											
Total	+C	6 969	7 234	6 893	7 133	6 861	1.8	1.9	1.8	1.9	1.8
State of Palestine - État de Palestine											
Total	C	6 150	6 155	6 574	7 114	...	1.5	1.5	1.5	1.6	...
Syrian Arab Republic - République arabe syrienne[21]											
Total	+U	*28 202*	...	...	...	...	...	...	...	...	...
Tajikistan - Tadjikistan											
Total	+C	6 019	6 762	7 417	7 920	...	0.8	0.9	0.9	1.0	...
Urban - Urbaine	+C	3 181	2 811	2 973	3 264	...	1.6	1.4	1.4	1.5	...
Rural - Rurale	+C	2 838	3 951	4 444	4 656	...	0.5	0.7	0.8	0.8	...
Turkey - Turquie[22]											
Total	C	118 568	120 117	123 325	125 305	...	1.6	1.6	1.6	1.6	...
Uzbekistan - Ouzbékistan											
Total	C	17 800	18 600	17 900	24 000	...	0.6	0.6	0.6	0.8	...
EUROPE											
Åland Islands - Îles d'Åland											
Total	C	52	53	63	54	*51	1.9	1.9	2.2	1.9	*1.8
Urban - Urbaine	C	25	26	34	29	*21	...	...	3.0	...	...
Rural - Rurale	C	27	27	29	25	*30	...	...	...	...	*1.7
Albania - Albanie											
Total	C	3 478	3 642	3 561	3 747	...	1.2	1.3	1.2	1.3	...

24. Divorces and crude divorce rates by urban/rural residence: 2010 - 2014
Divorces et taux bruts de divortialité selon la résidence, urbaine/rurale : 2010 - 2014 (continued - suite)

Continent, country or area, and urban/rural residence / Continent, pays ou zone et résidence, urbaine/rurale	Code[a]	Number - Nombre					Rate - Taux				
		2010	2011	2012	2013	2014	2010	2011	2012	2013	2014
EUROPE											
Austria - Autriche[23]											
Total	C	17 442	17 295	17 006	15 958	...	2.1	2.1	2.0	1.9	...
Belarus - Bélarus											
Total	C	36 655	38 584	39 034	36 105	...	3.9	4.1	4.1	3.8	...
Urban - Urbaine	C	31 603	33 105	33 197	31 239	...	4.5	4.6	4.6	4.3	...
Rural - Rurale	C	5 052	5 479	5 837	4 866	...	2.1	2.4	2.6	2.2	...
Belgium - Belgique[24]											
Total	C	28 903	27 522	*27 400	...	...	2.7	2.5	*2.5	...	...
Urban - Urbaine	C	28 616	27 216	...	...	...	2.7	2.5	...	...	...
Rural - Rurale	C	287	306	...	...	...	1.8	1.9	...	...	...
Bosnia and Herzegovina - Bosnie-Herzégovine											
Total	C	1 676	2 309	2 294	1 608	1 655	0.4	0.6	0.6	0.4	0.4
Bulgaria - Bulgarie[25]											
Total	C	11 012	10 581	11 947	10 908	...	1.5	1.4	1.6	1.5	...
Urban - Urbaine	C	9 254	8 849	9 861	...	...	1.7	1.7	1.9	...	...
Rural - Rurale	C	1 758	1 732	2 086	...	...	0.8	0.9	1.0	...	...
Croatia - Croatie											
Total	C	5 058	5 662	5 659	5 992	...	1.2	1.3	1.3	1.4	...
Urban - Urbaine	C	3 514	3 955	3 894	4 105	...	...	...	...	...	...
Rural - Rurale	C	1 544	1 707	1 765	1 887	...	...	...	...	...	...
Czech Republic - République tchèque											
Total	C	30 783	28 113	26 402	27 895	...	2.9	2.7	2.5	2.7	...
Urban - Urbaine	C	23 497	22 170	20 753	21 882	...	...	...	...	2.8	...
Rural - Rurale	C	7 286	5 943	5 649	6 013	...	...	...	...	2.1	...
Denmark - Danemark[26]											
Total	C	14 460	14 484	15 709	18 875	...	2.6	2.6	2.8	3.4	...
Estonia - Estonie											
Total	C	2 989	3 099	3 142	3 343	...	2.2	2.3	2.4	2.5	...
Urban - Urbaine[27]	C	2 106	2 169	2 168	2 275	...	2.3	2.4	2.4	2.5	...
Rural - Rurale[27]	C	812	848	892	888	...	1.9	2.0	2.1	2.1	...
Faeroe Islands - Îles Féroé											
Total	C	92	87	78	77	...	1.9	1.8	1.6	1.6	...
Finland - Finlande[10]											
Total	C	13 567[28]	13 416[28]	12 977[28]	13 766	...	2.5	2.5	2.4	2.5	...
Urban - Urbaine[28]	C	10 187	10 041	9 625	...	...	2.8	2.7	2.6	...	...
Rural - Rurale[28]	C	3 380	3 375	3 352	...	...	2.0	2.0	2.0	...	...
France											
Total	C	130 810	129 802	125 217	121 849	...	2.1	2.1	2.0	1.9	...
Germany - Allemagne											
Total	C	187 027	187 640	179 147	169 833	...	2.3	2.3	2.2	2.1	...
Gibraltar											
Total	+C	72	93	91	84	...	2.3	2.9	2.8	2.6	...
Greece - Grèce											
Total	C	13 275	...	...	...	...	1.2	...	...	...	...
Hungary - Hongrie[10]											
Total	C	23 873	23 335	21 830	20 209	...	2.4	2.3	2.2	2.0	...
Urban - Urbaine[29]	C	17 643	17 132	16 164	15 044	...	2.5	2.5	2.4	...	...
Rural - Rurale[29]	C	6 043	5 998	5 457	4 928	...	2.0	2.0	1.8	...	...
Iceland - Islande[30]											
Total	C	571	516	...	...	...	1.8	1.6	...	...	...
Urban - Urbaine[31]	C	533	504	...	...	...	1.8	1.6	...	...	...
Rural - Rurale[31]	C	30	4	...	...	...	1.5	...	...	...	...
Ireland - Irlande											
Total	+C	3 113	2 819	2 892	...	2 629	0.7	0.6	0.6	...	0.6
Italy - Italie											
Total	C	54 160	53 806	51 319	...	...	0.9	0.9	0.9	...	...
Latvia - Lettonie											
Total	C	4 930	8 302	7 311	7 031	...	2.4	4.0	3.6	3.5	...
Liechtenstein[32]											
Total	C	87	91	*87	...	...	2.4	2.5	*2.4	...	...
Lithuania - Lituanie											
Total	C	10 006	10 341	10 399	9 974	...	3.2	3.4	3.5	3.4	...
Urban - Urbaine	C	6 836	7 128	7 359	6 924	...	3.3	3.5	3.7	3.5	...
Rural - Rurale	C	3 170	3 213	3 040	3 050	...	3.1	3.2	3.1	3.1	...

24. Divorces and crude divorce rates by urban/rural residence: 2010 - 2014
Divorces et taux bruts de divortialité selon la résidence, urbaine/rurale : 2010 - 2014 (continued - suite)

Continent, country or area, and urban/rural residence — Continent, pays ou zone et résidence, urbaine/rurale	Code[a]	Number - Nombre					Rate - Taux				
		2010	2011	2012	2013	2014	2010	2011	2012	2013	2014
EUROPE											
Luxembourg											
Total	C	1 083	1 218	1 074	1 163	...	2.1	2.3	2.0	2.1	...
Malta - Malte											
Total	C	...	42	441	338	...	...	0.1	1.1	0.8	...
Montenegro - Monténégro											
Total	C	520	471	515	499	...	0.8	0.8	0.8	0.8	...
Netherlands - Pays-Bas[33]											
Total	C	33 723	33 755	34 721	33 636	...	2.0	2.0	2.1	2.0	...
Norway - Norvège[34]											
Total	C	10 228	10 207	9 929	10 212	...	2.1	2.1	2.0	2.0	...
Poland - Pologne											
Total	C	61 300	64 594	64 432	66 132	...	1.6	1.7	1.7	1.7	...
Urban - Urbaine[35]	C	47 394	49 186	48 552	...	...	2.0	2.1	2.1	...	...
Rural - Rurale[35]	C	13 423	14 855	15 336	...	...	0.9	1.0	1.0	...	...
Portugal[36]											
Total	C	27 556	26 751	25 380	22 525	...	2.6	2.5	2.4	2.2	...
Republic of Moldova - République de Moldova											
Total	C	11 504	11 120	10 637	...	...	3.2	3.1	3.0	...	...
Urban - Urbaine	C	10 174	8 647	7 765	...	...	6.9	5.8	5.2	...	...
Rural - Rurale	C	1 330	2 473	2 872	...	...	0.6	1.2	1.4	...	...
Romania - Roumanie											
Total	C	32 632	35 780	31 324	28 507	...	1.6	1.8	1.6	1.4	...
Urban - Urbaine	C	22 144	25 152	21 790	19 594	...	2.0	2.3	2.0	1.8	...
Rural - Rurale	C	10 488	10 628	9 534	8 913	...	1.1	1.1	1.0	1.0	...
Russian Federation - Fédération de Russie											
Total	C	639 321	669 376	644 101	...	...	4.5	4.7	4.5	...	...
Urban - Urbaine	C	...	523 697	502 494	...	...	...	5.0	4.7	...	...
Rural - Rurale	C	...	145 679	141 607	...	...	...	3.9	3.8	...	...
San Marino - Saint-Marin											
Total	+C	61	82	49	54	...	1.8	2.5	1.5	1.6	...
Serbia - Serbie[37]											
Total	+C	6 644	8 251	7 372	8 170	...	0.9	1.1	1.0	1.1	...
Urban - Urbaine	+C	4 901	6 192	5 410	5 761	...	1.1	1.4	1.3	1.3	...
Rural - Rurale	+C	1 743	2 059	1 962	2 409	...	0.6	0.7	0.7	0.8	...
Slovakia - Slovaquie											
Total	C	12 015	11 102	10 948	10 946	...	2.2	2.1	2.0	2.0	...
Urban - Urbaine	C	7 772	7 053	6 804	6 840	...	...	2.4	2.3	2.3	...
Rural - Rurale	C	4 243	4 049	4 144	4 106	...	...	1.6	1.7	1.7	...
Slovenia - Slovénie											
Total	C	2 430	2 298	2 509	2 351	...	1.2	1.1	1.2	1.1	...
Urban - Urbaine	C	1 416	1 308	1 422	1 307	...	1.4	1.3	1.4	1.2	...
Rural - Rurale	C	1 014	990	1 087	1 044	...	1.0	1.0	1.1	1.0	...
Spain - Espagne											
Total	C	102 690	103 290	104 262	95 427	...	2.2	2.2	2.2	2.0	...
Sweden - Suède[34]											
Total	C	23 593	23 389	23 422	26 933	...	2.5	2.5	2.5	2.8	...
Switzerland - Suisse											
Total	C	22 081	17 566	17 550	17 119	...	2.8	2.2	2.2	2.1	...
Urban - Urbaine[38]	C	17 095	13 603	13 457	...	...	...	2.3	2.3	...	...
Rural - Rurale[38]	C	4 986	3 963	4 093	...	...	...	1.9	1.9	...	...
TFYR of Macedonia - L'ex-R. y. de Macédoine											
Total	C	1 720	1 753	1 926	2 045	...	0.8	0.9	0.9	1.0	...
Urban - Urbaine	C	1 116	...	...	...	...	...	...	...	...	...
Rural - Rurale	C	604	...	...	...	...	...	...	...	...	...
Ukraine[39]											
Total	+C	126 068	182 490	168 508	164 939	...	2.7	4.0	3.7	3.6	...
Urban - Urbaine	+C	98 568	...	...	...	...	3.1	...	...	...	...
Rural - Rurale	+C	27 500	...	...	...	...	1.9	...	...	...	...
United Kingdom of Great Britain and Northern Ireland - Royaume-Uni de Grande-Bretagne et d'Irlande du Nord[40]											
Total	C	132 338	129 764	130 469	...	...	2.1	2.1	2.0	...	...

24. Divorces and crude divorce rates by urban/rural residence: 2010 - 2014
Divorces et taux bruts de divortialité selon la résidence, urbaine/rurale : 2010 - 2014 (continued - suite)

Continent, country or area, and urban/rural residence / Continent, pays ou zone et résidence, urbaine/rurale	Code[a]	Number - Nombre					Rate - Taux				
		2010	2011	2012	2013	2014	2010	2011	2012	2013	2014
OCEANIA - OCÉANIE											
Australia - Australie											
Total	C	50 240	48 935	49 917	47 638	...	2.3	2.2	2.2	2.1	...
Guam											
Total	C	849	878	869	742	749	5.3	5.5	5.4	4.6	4.7
New Caledonia - Nouvelle-Calédonie[41]											
Total	C	*305	...	...	...	...	*1.2	...	...	...	...
New Zealand - Nouvelle-Zélande											
Total	+C	8 874	8 551	8 785	8 279	...	2.0	2.0	2.0	1.9	...

FOOTNOTES - NOTES

Italics: data from civil registers which are incomplete or of unknown completeness. - Italiques : données incomplètes ou dont le degré d'exactitude n'est pas connu, provenant des registres de l'état civil.

* Provisional. - Données provisoires.

[a] 'Code' indicates the source of data, as follows:
C - Civil registration, estimated over 90% complete
U - Civil registration, estimated less than 90% complete
| - Other source, estimated reliable
+ - Data tabulated by date of registration rather than occurence
... - Information not available

Le 'Code' indique la source des données, comme suit :
C - Registres de l'état civil considérés complèts à 90 p. 100 au moins
U - Registres de l'état civil qui ne sont pas considérés complèts à 90 p. 100 au moins
| - Autre source, considérée pas douteuses
+ - Données exploitées selon la date de l'enregistrement et non la date de l'événement
... - Information pas disponible

[1] Including 'revocable divorces' (among Muslim population), which approximate legal separations. - Y compris les 'divorces révocables' (parmi la population musulmane), qui sont plus au moins l'équivalent des séparations légales.
[2] Excludes the islands of St. Brandon and Agalega. - Non compris les îles St. Brandon et Agalega.
[3] Urban and rural distribution refers to the usual residence of the bride/wife. Unrevised data. - La répartition entre résidence urbaine et résidence rurale fait référence au lieu de résidence habituel de la mariée ou de la femme. Les données n'ont pas été révisées.
[4] Data refer to the usual residence of the wife and excludes divorces granted in the country of wives living abroad. - Données relatives à la résidence habituelle de l'épouse, sauf cas de divorces prononcés dans les pays d'épouses vivant à l'étranger.
[5] Urban and rural distribution refers to the usual residence of the bride/wife. The difference between 'Total' and the sum of urban and rural is due to the unknown place of residence of bride/wife. - La répartition entre résidence urbaine et résidence rurale fait référence au lieu de résidence habituel de la mariée ou de la femme. La différence entre le « Total » et la somme des chiffres urbains et ruraux s'explique par le fait que le lieu de résidence de la mariée ou de la femme n'est pas toujours connu.
[6] Excluding data for California, Georgia, Hawaii, Indiana, Louisiana, and Minnesota. - Non compris les données pour la Californie, la Géorgie, Hawaii, l'Indiana, la Louisiane et le Minnesota.
[7] Excludes nomadic Indian tribes. - Non compris les tribus d'Indiens nomades.
[8] Source: The National Registry of Municipalities (RENAMU). - Source : Le Registre National des Municipalités (RENAMU).
[9] Data are compiled from the National Registers of Identification and Civil Status (RENIEC). - Les données sont rédigées à partir des Registres Nationaux d'Identification et d'État Civil (RENIEC).
[10] Including annulments. - Y compris les annulations.

[11] Including annulments. For statistical purposes, the data for China do not include those for the Hong Kong Special Administrative Region (Hong Kong SAR), Macao Special Administrative Region (Macao SAR) and Taiwan province of China. - Y compris les annulations. Pour la présentation des statistiques, les données pour la Chine ne comprennent pas la Région Administrative Spéciale de Hong Kong (Hong Kong RAS), la Région Administrative Spéciale de Macao (Macao RAS) et Taïwan province de Chine.
[12] Data refer to government controlled areas. - Les données se rapportent aux zones contrôlées par le Gouvernement.
[13] The total number may include 'Unknown residence', but the categories urban and rural do not. The urban and rural residence is recorded according to the place of usual residence of husband. - Le nombre total peut inclure les personnes dont la résidence n'est pas connue, à l'inverse des catégories de population urbaine et rurale. Le lieu de résidence (zone urbaine ou zone rurale) correspond au lieu de résidence habituel du mari.
[14] Data refer to the Iranian Year which begins on 21 March and ends on 20 March of the following year. - Les données concernent l'année iranienne, qui commence le 21 mars et se termine le 20 mars de l'année suivante.
[15] Includes data for East Jerusalem and Israeli residents in certain other territories under occupation by Israeli military forces since June 1967. - Y compris les données pour Jérusalem-Est et les résidents israéliens dans certains autres territoires occupés depuis 1967 par les forces armées israéliennes.
[16] Data refer to Japanese nationals in Japan only. - Les données se raportent aux nationaux japonais au Japon seulement.
[17] Excluding data for Jordanian territory under occupation since June 1967 by Israeli military forces. Excluding foreigners, including registered Palestinian refugees. - Non compris les données pour le territoire jordanien occupé depuis juin 1967 par les forces armées israéliennes. Non compris les étrangers, mais y compris les réfugiés de Palestine enregistrés.
[18] Data refer to registered events only. - Les données ne concernent que les événements enregistrés.
[19] Excluding alien armed forces, civilian aliens employed by armed forces, and foreign diplomatic personnel and their dependants. - Non compris les militaires étrangers, les civils étrangers employés par les forces armées ni le personnel diplomatique étranger et les membres de leur famille les accompagnant.
[20] The total number may include 'Unknown residence', but the categories urban and rural do not. Urban and rural distribution refers to the usual residence of the groom/husband. - Le nombre total peut inclure les personnes dont la résidence n'est pas connue, à l'inverse des catégories de population urbaine et rurale. La répartition entre résidence urbaine et résidence rurale fait référence au lieu de résidence habituel du marié ou du mari.
[21] Excluding nomad population. - Non compris les nomades.
[22] Data from MERNIS (Central Population Administrative System). - Données de MERNIS (Système central de données démographiques).
[23] Excluding aliens temporarily in the area. - Non compris les étrangers se trouvant temporairement dans le territoire.
[24] Including divorces among armed forces stationed outside the country and alien armed forces in the area. - Y compris les divorces de militaires nationaux hors du pays et les militaires étrangers en garnison sur le territoire.
[25] Including annulments. Including nationals outside the country, but excluding foreigners in the country. - Y compris les annulations. Y compris les nationaux à l'étranger, mais non compris les étrangers sur le territoire.
[26] Excluding Faeroe Islands and Greenland shown separately, if available. - Non compris les Iles Féroé et le Groenland, qui font l'objet de rubriques distinctes, si disponible.

²⁷ Urban and rural distribution of marriages and divorces is displayed by place of residence of groom/husband. The difference between 'Total' and the sum of urban and rural is due to the unknown place of residence of grooms/husbands and to grooms/husbands living outside the country. - La répartition des mariages et des divorces entre zones urbaines et zones rurales est fondée sur le lieu de résidence du marié ou du mari. La différence entre le « Total » et la somme des chiffres urbains et ruraux s'explique par le fait que la résidence du marié ou du mari n'est pas toujours connue ou est située à l'étranger.

²⁸ Excluding Åland Islands. - Non compris les Îles d'Åland.

²⁹ The urban and rural categories do not include the data of foreigners, persons of unknown residence and the homeless, whereas the total category includes them. - Les chiffres portant sur la population urbaine et rurale n'incluent pas les données relatives aux étrangers, aux personnes dont la résidence n'est pas connue et aux personnes sans domicile fixe, à l'inverse, le total les inclut.

³⁰ Data refer to common residence before divorce. - Données se rapportant à la résidence commune avant le divorce.

³¹ Total includes residence abroad, but the categories urban and rural do not. - Le total compris résidence à l'étranger, à l'inverse des catégories de population urbaine et rurale.

³² Excluding annulments. Data refer to marriages registered at the place of residence of the groom. - Ne comprend pas les annulations. Correspond aux mariages enregistrés dans le lieu de résidence du marié.

³³ Based on the general office for civil registration. Including same sex divorces. - Données provenant des services généraux d'état civil. Y compris les divorces entre conjoints du même sexe.

³⁴ Including same sex divorces. - Y compris les divorces entre conjoints du même sexe.

³⁵ Data for urban and rural exclude divorces if both persons live abroad. - Les données pour les zones urbaines et rurales excluent le divorce si les deux personnes vivent à l'étranger.

³⁶ Data refer to resident spouses only. - Les données concernent uniquement les conjoints résidents.

³⁷ Excludes data for Kosovo and Metohia. - Sans les données pour le Kosovo et Metohie.

³⁸ Urban/rural distribution is based on updated classification on December 31 2008. - La répartition entre zone urbaine et zone rurale est fondée sur la classification mise à jour le 31 décembre 2008.

³⁹ Data are given according to the state of civil registration (under the Law of Ukraine "On state registration of acts of civil status" from 1 July 2010). - Les données sont fournies selon l'état de l'état civil (en vertu de la loi ukrainienne du 1er juillet 2010 sur l'enregistrement des actes de l'état civil).

⁴⁰ Excluding Channel Islands (Guernsey and Jersey) and Isle of Man, shown separately, if available. - Non compris les îles Anglo-Normandes (Guernesey et Jersey) et l'île de Man, qui font l'objet de rubriques distinctes, si disponible.

⁴¹ Based on place of residence at marriage, not at divorce. - Les divorces sont comptés en fonction du lieu de résidence au mariage, pas au divorce.

Table 25 - *Demographic Yearbook 2014*

Table 25 presents the number of divorces according to the duration of marriage and the percentage distribution for the latest available year between 2005 and 2014.

Description of variables: Divorces are the final legal dissolutions of a marriage, which confer on the parties the right to remarry as defined by the laws of each country or area. Unless otherwise noted, divorce statistics exclude legal separations which do not allow remarriage. These statistics refer to the number of divorces granted, and not to the number of persons divorcing.

Duration of marriage is defined as the interval of time between the day, month and year of marriage and the day, month and year of divorce in completed years. This definition refers to the "legal" duration rather than the "effective" duration, it having been calculated until the day, month and year of the actual divorce decree rather than until the separation date or the date when the couple ceased to live as man and wife.

The duration of marriage classification used in this table to the extent possible, is the following: under one year, single years of duration through 9 years, 10-14 years, 15-19 years, 20 years and over and duration unknown, when appropriate.

Reliability of data: Data from civil registers of divorces which are reported as incomplete (less than 90 per cent completeness) or of unknown completeness are considered unreliable and are set in italics rather than in roman type. For more information about the quality of vital statistics data in general, see section 4.2 of the Technical Notes.

Limitations: Statistics on divorces by duration of marriage are subject to the same qualifications which have been set forth for vital statistics in general and divorce statistics in particular as discussed in Section 4 of the Technical Notes.

Earlier data: Divorces by duration by marriage, cross-classified by age of husband and by age of wife have been shown previously in issues of the Demographic Yearbook featuring marriage and divorce. For information on years covered, readers should consult the Historical Index.

Tableau 25 – *Annuaire démographique 2014*

Le tableau 25 indique le nombre de divorces selon la durée du mariage et la répartition des pourcentages, pour la dernière année disponible entre 2005 et 2014.

Description des variables : le divorce est la dissolution définitive des liens du mariage qui confère aux parties le droit de se remarier, telle qu'elle est définie par la législation de chaque pays ou zone. Sauf indication contraire, les statistiques de la divortialité n'englobent pas les séparations légales qui excluent le remariage. Ces statistiques se rapportent aux jugements de divorce prononcés, non aux personnes divorcées.

La durée du mariage correspond à l'intervalle du temps qui s'est écoulé entre la date exacte (jour, mois et année) du mariage et la date exacte (jour, mois et année) du divorce exprimé en années révolues. Cette définition est celle de la durée "légale" du mariage et non de sa durée "effective", puisque la durée est calculée jusqu'à la date (jour, mois et année) du jugement de divorce et non jusqu'à la date de la séparation ou la date à laquelle le couple a cessé de vivre comme mari et femme.

Le classement selon la durée du mariage utilisé dans ce tableau dans la mesure du possible comprend les catégories suivantes : moins d'un an, une catégorie par an jusqu'à 9 ans inclus, 10-14 ans, 15-19 ans, 20 ans et plus et, le cas échéant, une catégorie pour la durée du mariage inconnue.

Fiabilité des données : les données sur les divorces provenant des registres de l'état civil qui sont déclarées incomplètes (degré de complétude inférieur à 90 pour cent) ou dont le degré de complétude n'est pas connu, sont jugées douteuses et apparaissent en italique et non en caractères romains. Pour plus de précisions sur la qualité des données reposant sur les statistiques de l'état civil en général, voir la section 4.2 des Notes techniques.

Insuffisance des données : les statistiques des divorces selon la durée du mariage, appellent toutes les réserves qui ont été formulées à propos des statistiques de l'état civil en general et des statistiques des divorces en particulier (voir les explications figurant à la section 4 des Notes techniques).

Données publiées antérieurement : les statistiques des divorces selon la durée du mariage, classées selon l'âge de l'époux, d'une part, et selon l'âge de l'épouse, d'autre part, ont été présentées dans des éditions antérieures de l'Annuaire démographique qui avaient comme sujet spécial la nuptialité et la divortialité. Pour plus de précisions concernant les années pour lesquelles ces données ont été publiées, on se reportera à l'index historique.

25. Divorces and percentage distribution by duration of marriage, latest available year: 2005 - 2014
Divorces et répartition des pourcentages selon la durée du mariage, dernière année disponible: 2005 - 2014

Continent, country or area, year, code and duration of marriage (in years) Continent, pays ou zone, année, code et durée du mariage (en années)	Number of divorces Nombre de divorces	Per cent Pour cent
AFRICA - AFRIQUE		
Egypt - Égypte[1]		
2013 (+C)		
Total	162 583	100.0
Less than 1 - Moins de 1	26 190	16.1
1	18 130	11.2
2	11 937	7.3
3	8 878	5.5
4	7 434	4.6
5	6 531	4.0
6	5 203	3.2
7	4 497	2.8
8	3 649	2.2
9	3 299	2.0
10 - 14	11 370	7.0
15 - 19	6 143	3.8
20 +	10 316	6.3
Not stated - Inconnu	39 006	24.0
Lesotho		
2012 (+U)		
Total	142	100.0
Less than 1 - Moins de 1	-	0.0
1	5	3.5
2	9	6.3
3	11	7.7
4	7	4.9
5	12	8.5
6	12	8.5
7	10	7.0
8	6	4.2
9	13	9.2
10 - 14	23	16.2
15 - 19	14	9.9
20 +	20	14.1
Mauritius - Maurice[2]		
2014 (+C)		
Total	2 262	100.0
Less than 1 - Moins de 1	7	0.3
1	49	2.2
2	95	4.2
3	147	6.5
4	99	4.4
5	125	5.5
6	167	7.4
7	138	6.1
8	136	6.0
9	125	5.5
10 - 14	457	20.2
15 - 19	310	13.7
20 +	407	18.0
Seychelles		
2014 (+C)		
Total	158	100.0
Less than 1 - Moins de 1	2	1.3
1	6	3.8
2	5	3.2
3	7	4.4
4	9	5.7
5	8	5.1
6	6	3.8
7	10	6.3
8	11	7.0
9	7	4.4
10 - 14	41	25.9
15 - 19	21	13.3
20 +	25	15.8

Continent, country or area, year, code and duration of marriage (in years) Continent, pays ou zone, année, code et durée du mariage (en années)	Number of divorces Nombre de divorces	Per cent Pour cent
AFRICA - AFRIQUE		
South Africa - Afrique du Sud		
2011 (...)		
Total	20 980	100.0
Less than 1 - Moins de 1	102	0.5
1	650	3.1
2	1 059	5.0
3	1 322	6.3
4	1 356	6.5
5	1 206	5.7
6	1 164	5.5
7	1 120	5.3
8	1 145	5.5
9	900	4.3
10 - 14	3 782	18.0
15 - 19	2 738	13.1
20 +	3 512	16.7
Not stated - Inconnu	924	4.4
AMERICA, NORTH - AMÉRIQUE DU NORD		
Aruba		
2014 (C)		
Total	468	100.0
Less than 1 - Moins de 1	-	0.0
1	10	2.1
2	19	4.1
3	30	6.4
4	22	4.7
5	30	6.4
6	27	5.8
7	23	4.9
8	21	4.5
9	24	5.1
10 - 14	124	26.5
15 - 19	61	13.0
20 +	77	16.5
Bermuda - Bermudes		
2014 (C)		
Total	104	100.0
Less than 1 - Moins de 1	-	0.0
1	6	5.8
2	1	1.0
3	3	2.9
4	3	2.9
5	7	6.7
6	8	7.7
7	1	1.0
8	5	4.8
9	5	4.8
10 - 14	23	22.1
15 - 19	23	22.1
20 +	19	18.3
Cuba		
2013 (C)		
Total	32 848	100.0
Less than 1 - Moins de 1	2 242	6.8
1	2 882	8.8
2	2 651	8.1
3	2 476	7.5
4	2 035	6.2
5	1 743	5.3
6	1 443	4.4
7	1 194	3.6
8	897	2.7
9	992	3.0
10 - 14	3 835	11.7

Continent, country or area, year, code and duration of marriage (in years) Continent, pays ou zone, année, code et durée du mariage (en années)	Number of divorces Nombre de divorces	Per cent Pour cent

AMERICA, NORTH - AMÉRIQUE DU NORD

Cuba
2013 (C)
15 - 19	4 252	12.9
20 +	6 189	18.8
Not stated - Inconnu	17	0.1

Dominican Republic - République dominicaine
2013 (+C)
Total	18 882	100.0
Less than 1 - Moins de 1	15	0.1
1	176	0.9
2	291	1.5
3	377	2.0
4	349	1.8
5	382	2.0
6	351	1.9
7	348	1.8
8	251	1.3
9	229	1.2
10 - 14	868	4.6
15 - 19	601	3.2
20 +	696	3.7
Not stated - Inconnu	13 948	73.9

El Salvador
2012 (...)
Total	7 138	100.0
Less than 1 - Moins de 1	77	1.1
1	161	2.3
2	239	3.3
3	271	3.8
4	320	4.5
5	302	4.2
6	296	4.1
7	293	4.1
8	300	4.2
9	311	4.4
10 - 14	1 508	21.1
15 - 19	1 138	15.9
20 +	1 705	23.9
Not stated - Inconnu	217	3.0

Jamaica - Jamaïque[3]
2007 (+C)
Total	1 140	100.0
Less than 1 - Moins de 1	-	0.0
1	1	0.1
2	3	0.3
3	22	1.9
4	42	3.7
5	53	4.6
6	62	5.4
7	89	7.8
8	96	8.4
9	75	6.6
10 - 14	294	25.8
15 - 19	160	14.0
20 +	242	21.2

Mexico - Mexique[4]
2013 (+C)
Total	108 727	100.0
Less than 1 - Moins de 1	150	0.1
1	5 139	4.7
2	5 260	4.8
3	5 111	4.7
4	5 344	4.9
5	5 410	5.0
6	4 929	4.5
7	4 763	4.4

AMERICA, NORTH - AMÉRIQUE DU NORD

Mexico - Mexique[4]
2013 (+C)
8	4 453	4.1
9	4 115	3.8
10 - 14	19 442	17.9
15 - 19	15 056	13.8
20 +	28 987	26.7
Not stated - Inconnu	568	0.5

Panama
2013 (C)
Total	4 083	100.0
Less than 5 - Moins de 5	719	17.6
5 - 9	960	23.5
10 - 14	673	16.5
15 - 19	526	12.9
20 +	1 205	29.5

Trinidad and Tobago - Trinité-et-Tobago
2005 (C)
Total	2 785	100.0
Less than 1 - Moins de 1	-	0.0
1	40	1.4
2	77	2.8
3	80	2.9
4	92	3.3
5	142	5.1
6	149	5.4
7	120	4.3
8	144	5.2
9	111	4.0
10 - 14	572	20.5
15 - 19	417	15.0
20 +	838	30.1
Not stated - Inconnu	3	0.1

Turks and Caicos Islands - Îles Turques et Caïques
2005 (C)
Total	24	100.0
Less than 1 - Moins de 1	-	0.0
1	-	0.0
2	-	0.0
3	-	0.0
4	2	8.3
5	3	12.5
6	3	12.5
7	2	8.3
8	4	16.7
9	1	4.2
10 - 14	5	20.8
15 - 19	2	8.3
20 +	2	8.3

AMERICA, SOUTH - AMÉRIQUE DU SUD

Brazil - Brésil
2013 (...)
Total	324 921	100.0
Less than 1 - Moins de 1	8 580	2.6
1	14 630	4.5
2	15 909	4.9
3	15 914	4.9
4	15 922	4.9
5	15 781	4.9
6	14 600	4.5
7	13 684	4.2
8	12 335	3.8
9	11 255	3.5

25. Divorces and percentage distribution by duration of marriage, latest available year: 2005 - 2014
Divorces et répartition des pourcentages selon la durée du mariage, dernière année disponible: 2005 - 2014 (continued - suite)

Continent, country or area, year, code and duration of marriage (in years) Continent, pays ou zone, année, code et durée du mariage (en années)	Number of divorces Nombre de divorces	Per cent Pour cent	Continent, country or area, year, code and duration of marriage (in years) Continent, pays ou zone, année, code et durée du mariage (en années)	Number of divorces Nombre de divorces	Per cent Pour cent
AMERICA, SOUTH - AMÉRIQUE DU SUD			**ASIA - ASIE**		
Brazil - Brésil			Armenia - Arménie		
2013 (...)			2009 (+C)		
10 - 14	44 752	13.8	Total	2 829	100.0
15 - 19	35 597	11.0	Less than 1 - Moins de 1	92	3.3
20 +	104 521	32.2	1	161	5.7
Not stated - Inconnu	1 441	0.4	2	148	5.2
Chile - Chili			3	126	4.5
2010 (C)			4	117	4.1
Total	1 558	100.0	5 - 9	445	15.7
Less than 1 - Moins de 1	11	0.7	10 - 14	426	15.1
1	17	1.1	15 - 19	514	18.2
2	36	2.3	20 +	800	28.3
3	35	2.2	Azerbaijan - Azerbaïdjan		
4	36	2.3	2013 (+C)		
5	32	2.1	Total	11 730	100.0
6	28	1.8	Less than 1 - Moins de 1	316	2.7
7	39	2.5	1	803	6.8
8	38	2.4	2	978	8.3
9	47	3.0	3	935	8.0
10 - 14	270	17.3	4	885	7.5
15 - 19	211	13.5	5	863	7.4
20 +	610	39.2	6	810	6.9
Not stated - Inconnu	148	9.5	7	742	6.3
Ecuador - Équateur[5]			8	595	5.1
2013 (U)			9	518	4.4
Total	21 122	100.0	10 - 14	1 423	12.1
Less than 1 - Moins de 1	142	0.7	15 - 19	957	8.2
1	407	1.9	20 +	1 905	16.2
2	723	3.4	Bahrain - Bahreïn		
3	876	4.1	2014 (...)		
4	1 059	5.0	Total	1 795	100.0
5	1 085	5.1	Less than 1 - Moins de 1	492	27.4
6	1 003	4.7	1 - 2	368	20.5
7	956	4.5	3 - 4	164	9.1
8	807	3.8	5 - 6	126	7.0
9	787	3.7	7 - 9	126	7.0
10 - 14	3 842	18.2	10 - 14	169	9.4
15 - 19	2 983	14.1	15 - 19	94	5.2
20 +	6 452	30.5	20 +	145	8.1
Suriname[6]			Not stated - Inconnu	111	6.2
2013 (C)			Brunei Darussalam - Brunéi Darussalam		
Total	602	100.0	2008 (...)		
Less than 1 - Moins de 1	-	0.0	Total	534	100.0
1 - 3	119	19.8	Less than 1 - Moins de 1	7	1.3
4 - 6	109	18.1	1	18	3.4
7 - 9	76	12.6	2	30	5.6
10 - 12	71	11.8	3	35	6.6
13 - 15	65	10.8	4	43	8.1
16 - 18	45	7.5	5	53	9.9
19 - 21	24	4.0	6	32	6.0
22 - 24	24	4.0	7	43	8.1
25 - 27	25	4.2	8	32	6.0
28 - 30	14	2.3	9	30	5.6
31 - 33	9	1.5	10 - 14	92	17.2
34 - 36	8	1.3	15 - 19	52	9.7
37+	13	2.2	20 +	67	12.5
Venezuela (Bolivarian Republic of) - Venezuela (République bolivarienne du)			China, Macao SAR - Chine, Macao RAS		
2013 (...)			2014 (+C)		
Total	31 355	100.0	Total	1 308	100.0
Less than 1 - Moins de 1	62	0.2	Less than 5 - Moins de 5	238	18.2
1 - 4	2 347	7.5	5 - 9	499	38.1
5 - 9	8 123	25.9	10 - 14	168	12.8
10 - 14	6 391	20.4	15 +	403	30.8
15 - 19	5 537	17.7	Cyprus - Chypre[7]		
20 +	8 777	28.0	2009 (C)		
Not stated - Inconnu	118	0.4	Total	1 738	100.0
			Less than 1 - Moins de 1	66	3.8
			1	142	8.2

25. Divorces and percentage distribution by duration of marriage, latest available year: 2005 - 2014
Divorces et répartition des pourcentages selon la durée du mariage, dernière année disponible: 2005 - 2014 (continued - suite)

Continent, country or area, year, code and duration of marriage (in years) Continent, pays ou zone, année, code et durée du mariage (en années)	Number of divorces Nombre de divorces	Per cent Pour cent
ASIA - ASIE		
Cyprus - Chypre[7]		
2009 (C)		
2	107	6.2
3	127	7.3
4	120	6.9
5	106	6.1
6	108	6.2
7	84	4.8
8	80	4.6
9	60	3.5
10 - 14	267	15.4
15 - 19	167	9.6
20 + ...	304	17.5
Georgia - Géorgie		
2013 (C)		
Total..	8 089	100.0
Less than 1 - Moins de 1	544	6.7
1	412	5.1
2	468	5.8
3	483	6.0
4	491	6.1
5	427	5.3
6	423	5.2
7	312	3.9
8	271	3.4
9	211	2.6
10 - 14	1 019	12.6
15 - 19	1 119	13.8
20 + ...	1 898	23.5
Not stated - Inconnu	11	0.1
Iran (Islamic Republic of) - Iran (République islamique d')[8]		
2011 (+C)		
Total..	142 841	100.0
Less than 1 - Moins de 1	19 730	13.8
1	17 091	12.0
2	13 761	9.6
3	11 763	8.2
4	9 339	6.5
5	8 140	5.7
6	7 292	5.1
7	6 068	4.2
8	5 480	3.8
9	4 726	3.3
10 - 14	16 231	11.4
15 - 19	9 344	6.5
20 + ...	13 643	9.6
Not stated - Inconnu	233	0.2
Israel - Israël[9]		
2012 (C)		
Total..	13 685	100.0
Less than 1 - Moins de 1	819	6.0
1	875	6.4
2	803	5.9
3	685	5.0
4	663	4.8
5	617	4.5
6	533	3.9
7	474	3.5
8	461	3.4
9	391	2.9
10 - 14	1 690	12.3
15 - 19	1 285	9.4
20 + ...	2 114	15.4
Not stated - Inconnu	2 275	16.6
ASIA - ASIE		
Japan - Japon[10]		
2013 (+C)		
Total..	231 383	100.0
Less than 1 - Moins de 1	14 333	6.2
1	16 374	7.1
2	15 423	6.7
3	14 533	6.3
4	13 371	5.8
5 - 9	48 422	20.9
10 - 14	32 554	14.1
15 - 19	23 660	10.2
20 + ...	38 032	16.4
Not stated - Inconnu	14 681	6.3
Kazakhstan		
2013 (C)		
Total..	51 482	100.0
Less than 1 - Moins de 1	3 237	6.3
1	4 200	8.2
2	4 383	8.5
3	3 965	7.7
4	3 613	7.0
5 - 9	13 813	26.8
10 - 14	5 994	11.6
15 - 19	4 442	8.6
20 + ...	7 834	15.2
Not stated - Inconnu	1	0.0
Kuwait - Koweït		
2011 (C)		
Total..	6 254	100.0
Less than 1 - Moins de 1	1 403	22.4
1	809	12.9
2	581	9.3
3	434	6.9
4	389	6.2
5 - 9	1 241	19.8
10 - 14	547	8.7
15 - 19	348	5.6
20 + ...	499	8.0
Not stated - Inconnu	3	0.0
Kyrgyzstan - Kirghizstan		
2013 (C)		
Total..	9 052	100.0
Less than 1 - Moins de 1	578	6.4
1	560	6.2
2	692	7.6
3	608	6.7
4	587	6.5
5	592	6.5
6	521	5.8
7	461	5.1
8	397	4.4
9	325	3.6
10 - 14	1 206	13.3
15 - 19	872	9.6
20 + ...	1 653	18.3
Mongolia - Mongolie		
2010 (+C)		
Total..	3 054	100.0
Less than 1 - Moins de 1	101	3.3
1 - 3	576	18.9
4 - 6	601	19.7
7 - 9	395	12.9
10 + ...	1 381	45.2
Qatar		
2012 (C)		
Total..	1 420	100.0
Less than 1 - Moins de 1	438[11]	30.8

25. Divorces and percentage distribution by duration of marriage, latest available year: 2005 - 2014
Divorces et répartition des pourcentages selon la durée du mariage, dernière année disponible: 2005 - 2014 (continued - suite)

Continent, country or area, year, code and duration of marriage (in years) / Continent, pays ou zone, année, code et durée du mariage (en années)	Number of divorces / Nombre de divorces	Per cent / Pour cent	Continent, country or area, year, code and duration of marriage (in years) / Continent, pays ou zone, année, code et durée du mariage (en années)	Number of divorces / Nombre de divorces	Per cent / Pour cent
ASIA - ASIE			**ASIA - ASIE**		
Qatar			Turkey - Turquie[13]		
2012 (C)			2013 (C)		
1	156	11.0	Total	125 305	100.0
2	129	9.1	Less than 1 - Moins de 1	4 385	3.5
3	96	6.8	1	12 455	9.9
4	74	5.2	2	9 815	7.8
5 - 9	212	14.9	3	8 421	6.7
10 - 14	145	10.2	4	7 907	6.3
15 - 19	73	5.1	5	7 496	6.0
20 +	82	5.8	6	6 845	5.5
Not stated - Inconnu	15	1.1	7	6 018	4.8
Republic of Korea - République de Corée[12]			8	5 267	4.2
2013 (+C)			9	4 690	3.7
Total	115 292	100.0	10 - 14	18 404	14.7
Less than 1 - Moins de 1	5 275	4.6	15 - 19	14 158	11.3
1	5 993	5.2	20 +	19 190	15.3
2	5 713	5.0	Not stated - Inconnu	254	0.2
3	5 510	4.8			
4	4 808	4.2	**EUROPE**		
5	4 989	4.3			
6	4 827	4.2	Austria - Autriche[14]		
7	4 372	3.8	2012 (C)		
8	3 871	3.4	Total	17 006	100.0
9	3 474	3.0	Less than 1 - Moins de 1	282	1.7
10 - 14	16 851	14.6	1	818	4.8
15 - 19	17 176	14.9	2	982	5.8
20 +	32 433	28.1	3	959	5.6
Singapore - Singapour			4	912	5.4
2014 (+C)			5	892	5.2
Total	6 861	100.0	6	954	5.6
Less than 5 - Moins de 5	1 286	18.7	7	919	5.4
5 - 9	2 023	29.5	8	825	4.9
10 - 14	1 271	18.5	9	594	3.5
15 - 19	848	12.4	10 - 14	2 643	15.5
20 +	1 433	20.9	15 - 19	2 272	13.4
State of Palestine - État de Palestine			20 +	3 954	23.3
2013 (C)			Belarus - Bélarus		
Total	7 114	100.0	2012 (C)		
Less than 1 - Moins de 1	3 191	44.9	Total	39 034	100.0
1	1 085	15.3	Less than 1 - Moins de 1	1 211	3.1
2	528	7.4	1	2 931	7.5
3	389	5.5	2	3 061	7.8
4	243	3.4	3	3 148	8.1
5	202	2.8	4	3 177	8.1
6	156	2.2	5 - 9	9 818	25.2
7	132	1.9	10 - 14	5 932	15.2
8	111	1.6	15 - 19	3 811	9.8
9	120	1.7	20 +	5 945	15.2
10 - 14	399	5.6	Belgium - Belgique[15]		
15 - 19	196	2.8	2010 (C)		
20 +	362	5.1	Total	28 903	100.0
Tajikistan - Tadjikistan			Less than 1 - Moins de 1	61	0.2
2013 (+C)			1	721	2.5
Total	7 920	100.0	2	1 394	4.8
Less than 1 - Moins de 1	1 001	12.6	3	1 683	5.8
1	757	9.6	4	1 689	5.8
2	810	10.2	5	1 543	5.3
3	789	10.0	6	1 432	5.0
4	763	9.6	7	1 241	4.3
5	652	8.2	8	1 168	4.0
6	359	4.5	9	1 132	3.9
7	262	3.3	10 - 14	4 757	16.5
8	231	2.9	15 - 19	4 028	13.9
9	155	2.0	20 +	8 054	27.9
10 - 14	514	6.5			
15 - 19	459	5.8			
20 +	812	10.3			
Not stated - Inconnu	356	4.5			

25. Divorces and percentage distribution by duration of marriage, latest available year: 2005 - 2014
Divorces et répartition des pourcentages selon la durée du mariage, dernière année disponible: 2005 - 2014 (continued - suite)

Continent, country or area, year, code and duration of marriage (in years) Continent, pays ou zone, année, code et durée du mariage (en années)	Number of divorces Nombre de divorces	Per cent Pour cent	Continent, country or area, year, code and duration of marriage (in years) Continent, pays ou zone, année, code et durée du mariage (en années)	Number of divorces Nombre de divorces	Per cent Pour cent
EUROPE			EUROPE		
Bosnia and Herzegovina - Bosnie-Herzégovine			Denmark - Danemark[17]		
2010 (C)			2013 (C)		
Total	1 676	100.0	Total	18 875	100.0
Less than 1 - Moins de 1	100	6.0	Less than 1 - Moins de 1	263	1.4
1	139	8.3	1	675	3.6
2	121	7.2	2	909	4.8
3	133	7.9	3	1 074	5.7
4	131	7.8	4	1 194	6.3
5	94	5.6	5	1 221	6.5
6	71	4.2	6	1 138	6.0
7	72	4.3	7	1 104	5.8
8	64	3.8	8	964	5.1
9	46	2.7	9	918	4.9
10 - 14	244	14.6	10 - 14	3 627	19.2
15 - 19	139	8.3	15 - 19	2 513	13.3
20 +	322	19.2	20 +	3 137	16.6
Bulgaria - Bulgarie[16]			Not stated - Inconnu	138	0.7
2013 (C)			Estonia - Estonie		
Total	10 908	100.0	2013 (C)		
Less than 1 - Moins de 1	128	1.2	Total	3 343	100.0
1	310	2.8	Less than 1 - Moins de 1	81	2.4
2	383	3.5	1	173	5.2
3	467	4.3	2	175	5.2
4	514	4.7	3	194	5.8
5	499	4.6	4	218	6.5
6	513	4.7	5	197	5.9
7	508	4.7	6	196	5.9
8	423	3.9	7	171	5.1
9	408	3.7	8	151	4.5
10 - 14	1 783	16.3	9	135	4.0
15 - 19	1 594	14.6	10 - 14	463	13.8
20 +	3 378	31.0	15 - 19	270	8.1
Croatia - Croatie			20 +	919	27.5
2013 (C)			Finland - Finlande[6]		
Total	5 992	100.0	2013 (C)		
Less than 1 - Moins de 1	80	1.3	Total	13 766	100.0
1	168	2.8	Less than 1 - Moins de 1	148	1.1
2	257	4.3	1	761	5.5
3	288	4.8	2	1 044	7.6
4	301	5.0	3	949	6.9
5	296	4.9	4	952	6.9
6	289	4.8	5	856	6.2
7	285	4.8	6	766	5.6
8	240	4.0	7	707	5.1
9	246	4.1	8	647	4.7
10 - 14	1 075	17.9	9	571	4.1
15 - 19	837	14.0	10 - 14	2 157	15.7
20 +	1 630	27.2	15 - 19	1 521	11.0
Czech Republic - République tchèque			20 +	2 682	19.5
2013 (C)			Not stated - Inconnu	5	0.0
Total	27 895	100.0	France		
Less than 1 - Moins de 1	217	0.8	2011 (C)		
1	877	3.1	Total	129 802	100.0
2	1 109	4.0	Less than 1 - Moins de 1	158	0.1
3	1 235	4.4	1	1 468	1.1
4	1 367	4.9	2	3 489	2.7
5	1 438	5.2	3	5 045	3.9
6	1 352	4.8	4	6 173	4.8
7	1 190	4.3	5	6 788	5.2
8	1 102	4.0	6	6 914	5.3
9	957	3.4	7	6 488	5.0
10 - 14	4 642	16.6	8	6 088	4.7
15 - 19	3 832	13.7	9	5 573	4.3
20 +	8 210	29.4	10 - 14	25 093	19.3
Not stated - Inconnu	367	1.3	15 - 19	17 840	13.7
			20	3 299	2.5
			21	3 124	2.4

25. Divorces and percentage distribution by duration of marriage, latest available year: 2005 - 2014
Divorces et répartition des pourcentages selon la durée du mariage, dernière année disponible: 2005 - 2014 (continued - suite)

Continent, country or area, year, code and duration of marriage (in years) Continent, pays ou zone, année, code et durée du mariage (en années)	Number of divorces Nombre de divorces	Per cent Pour cent	Continent, country or area, year, code and duration of marriage (in years) Continent, pays ou zone, année, code et durée du mariage (en années)	Number of divorces Nombre de divorces	Per cent Pour cent
EUROPE			EUROPE		
France			Iceland - Islande[18]		
2011 (C)			2011 (C)		
22	2 849	2.2	4	36	7.0
23	2 599	2.0	5	38	7.4
24	2 383	1.8	6	28	5.4
25	2 188	1.7	7	20	3.9
26	2 069	1.6	8	33	6.4
27	1 949	1.5	9	16	3.1
28	1 917	1.5	10 - 14	101	19.6
29	1 874	1.4	15 - 19	63	12.2
30	6 633	5.1	20 +	100	19.4
35 +	7 801	6.0	Italy - Italie		
Germany - Allemagne			2010 (C)		
2012 (C)			Total	54 160	100.0
Total	179 147	100.0	Less than 1 - Moins de 1	2	0.0
Less than 1 - Moins de 1	26	0.0	1	8	0.0
1	1 151	0.6	2	7	0.0
2	5 794	3.2	3	45	0.1
3	7 366	4.1	4	526	1.0
4	7 080	4.0	5	1 370	2.5
5	8 979	5.0	6	1 913	3.5
6	9 686	5.4	7	2 332	4.3
7	9 366	5.2	8	2 537	4.7
8	9 121	5.1	9	2 645	4.9
9	8 290	4.6	10 - 14	11 610	21.4
10 - 14	34 352	19.2	15 - 19	10 621	19.6
15 - 19	26 609	14.9	20 +	20 544	37.9
20 +	51 327	28.7	Latvia - Lettonie		
Greece - Grèce			2012 (C)		
2010 (C)			Total	7 311	100.0
Total	13 275	100.0	Less than 1 - Moins de 1	66	0.9
Less than 1 - Moins de 1	1	0.0	1	157	2.1
1	59	0.4	2	268	3.7
2	508	3.8	3	323	4.4
3	774	5.8	4	462	6.3
4	665	5.0	5	624	8.5
5	696	5.2	6	489	6.7
6	624	4.7	7	404	5.5
7	676	5.1	8	310	4.2
8	568	4.3	9	267	3.7
9	550	4.1	10 - 14	931	12.7
10 - 14	2 326	17.5	15 - 19	795	10.9
15 - 19	1 970	14.8	20 +	2 215	30.3
20 +	3 588	27.0	Liechtenstein		
Hungary - Hongrie[6]			2012* (C)		
2013 (C)			Total	87	100.0
Total	20 209	100.0	Less than 1 - Moins de 1	-	0.0
Less than 1 - Moins de 1	205	1.0	1	7	8.0
1	588	2.9	2	4	4.6
2	854	4.2	3	2	2.3
3	845	4.2	4	4	4.6
4	958	4.7	5	9	10.3
5	953	4.7	6	7	8.0
6	963	4.8	7	7	8.0
7	935	4.6	8	5	5.7
8	872	4.3	9	3	3.4
9	855	4.2	10 - 14	10	11.5
10 - 14	3 563	17.6	15 - 19	14	16.1
15 - 19	2 966	14.7	20 +	15	17.2
20 +	5 652	28.0	Lithuania - Lituanie		
Iceland - Islande[18]			2012 (C)		
2011 (C)			Total	10 399	100.0
Total	516	100.0	Less than 1 - Moins de 1	138	1.3
Less than 1 - Moins de 1	6	1.2	1	418	4.0
1	16	3.1	2	552	5.3
2	20	3.9	3	629	6.0
3	37	7.2	4	670	6.4
			5	620	6.0

Continent, country or area, year, code and duration of marriage (in years) / Continent, pays ou zone, année, code et durée du mariage (en années)	Number of divorces / Nombre de divorces	Per cent / Pour cent
EUROPE		
Lithuania - Lituanie		
2012 (C)		
6	565	5.4
7	421	4.0
8	356	3.4
9	320	3.1
10 - 14	1 337	12.9
15 - 19	1 274	12.3
20 +	3 099	29.8
Luxembourg		
2013 (C)		
Total	1 163	100.0
Less than 1 - Moins de 1	-	0.0
1	10	0.9
2	28	2.4
3	48	4.1
4	77	6.6
5	54	4.6
6	51	4.4
7	59	5.1
8	75	6.4
9	52	4.5
10 - 14	239	20.6
15 - 19	170	14.6
20 +	300	25.8
Malta - Malte		
2011 (C)		
Total	42	100.0
Less than 1 - Moins de 1	-	0.0
1	-	0.0
2	-	0.0
3	-	0.0
4	-	0.0
5	-	0.0
6	1	2.4
7	1	2.4
8	-	0.0
9	-	0.0
10 - 14	15	35.7
15 - 19	4	9.5
20 +	21	50.0
Montenegro - Monténégro		
2013 (C)		
Total	499	100.0
Less than 1 - Moins de 1	21	4.2
1	29	5.8
2	29	5.8
3	38	7.6
4	36	7.2
5	31	6.2
6	25	5.0
7	27	5.4
8	21	4.2
9	16	3.2
10 - 14	85	17.0
15 - 19	49	9.8
20 +	92	18.4
Netherlands - Pays-Bas[19]		
2013 (C)		
Total	33 636	100.0
Less than 1 - Moins de 1	345	1.0
1	1 161	3.5
2	1 506	4.5
3	1 700	5.1
4	1 701	5.1
5	1 698	5.0
6	1 545	4.6
7	1 384	4.1
EUROPE		
Netherlands - Pays-Bas[19]		
2013 (C)		
8	1 351	4.0
9	1 327	3.9
10 - 14	6 198	18.4
15 - 19	4 706	14.0
20 +	9 014	26.8
Norway - Norvège		
2013 (C)		
Total	10 212	100.0
Less than 1 - Moins de 1	11	0.1
1	163	1.6
2	428	4.2
3	526	5.2
4	598	5.9
5	645	6.3
6	571	5.6
7	545	5.3
8	518	5.1
9	437	4.3
10 - 14	1 955	19.1
15 - 19	1 309	12.8
20 +	2 244	22.0
Not stated - Inconnu	262	2.6
Poland - Pologne		
2013 (C)		
Total	66 132	100.0
Less than 1 - Moins de 1	440	0.7
1	1 993	3.0
2	3 142	4.8
3	3 874	5.9
4	4 201	6.4
5	3 935	6.0
6	3 395	5.1
7	2 863	4.3
8	2 504	3.8
9	2 334	3.5
10 - 14	10 530	15.9
15 - 19	8 434	12.8
20 +	18 487	28.0
Portugal[20]		
2013 (C)		
Total	22 525	100.0
Less than 1 - Moins de 1	388	1.7
1	595	2.6
2	746	3.3
3	741	3.3
4	873	3.9
5	977	4.3
6	960	4.3
7	840	3.7
8	835	3.7
9	777	3.4
10 - 14	4 116	18.3
15 - 19	3 428	15.2
20 +	7 249	32.2
Republic of Moldova - République de Moldova		
2012 (C)		
Total	10 637	100.0
Less than 1 - Moins de 1	307	2.9
1	632	5.9
2	763	7.2
3	766	7.2
4	799	7.5
5	708	6.7
6	636	6.0

Continent, country or area, year, code and duration of marriage (in years) / Continent, pays ou zone, année, code et durée du mariage (en années)	Number of divorces / Nombre de divorces	Per cent / Pour cent
EUROPE		
Republic of Moldova - République de Moldova		
2012 (C)		
7	499	4.7
8	412	3.9
9	372	3.5
10 - 14	1 335	12.6
15 - 19	1 219	11.5
20 +	2 189	20.6
Romania - Roumanie		
2013 (C)		
Total	28 507	100.0
Less than 1 - Moins de 1	634	2.2
1	1 224	4.3
2	1 472	5.2
3	1 584	5.6
4	1 744	6.1
5	1 782	6.3
6	1 808	6.3
7	1 428	5.0
8	1 259	4.4
9	1 197	4.2
10 - 14	4 690	16.5
15 - 19	3 556	12.5
20 +	6 129	21.5
Russian Federation - Fédération de Russie		
2011 (C)		
Total	669 376	100.0
Less than 1 - Moins de 1	33 567	5.0
1	50 768	7.6
2	58 099	8.7
3	57 871	8.6
4	50 042	7.5
5 - 9	165 467	24.7
10 - 14	82 645	12.3
15 - 19	60 911	9.1
20 +	109 624	16.4
Not stated - Inconnu	382	0.1
San Marino - Saint-Marin		
2012 (+C)		
Total	49	100.0
Less than 1 - Moins de 1	-	0.0
1	-	0.0
2	-	0.0
3	1	2.0
4	1	2.0
5	2	4.1
6	2	4.1
7	4	8.2
8	4	8.2
9	1	2.0
10 - 14	8	16.3
15 - 19	5	10.2
20 +	21	42.9
Serbia - Serbie[21]		
2013 (+C)		
Total	8 170	100.0
Less than 1 - Moins de 1	276	3.4
1	401	4.9
2	451	5.5
3	422	5.2
4	388	4.7
5	368	4.5
6	390	4.8
7	379	4.6
8	345	4.2
9	320	3.9
10 - 14	1 394	17.1
EUROPE		
Serbia - Serbie[21]		
2013 (+C)		
15 - 19	1 061	13.0
20 +	1 975	24.2
Slovakia - Slovaquie		
2013 (C)		
Total	10 946	100.0
Less than 1 - Moins de 1	63	0.6
1	263	2.4
2	373	3.4
3	422	3.9
4	498	4.5
5	485	4.4
6	435	4.0
7	417	3.8
8	416	3.8
9	435	4.0
10 - 14	1 835	16.8
15 - 19	1 720	15.7
20 +	3 584	32.7
Slovenia - Slovénie		
2013 (C)		
Total	2 351	100.0
Less than 1 - Moins de 1	28	1.2
1	82	3.5
2	88	3.7
3	108	4.6
4	96	4.1
5	111	4.7
6	94	4.0
7	91	3.9
8	82	3.5
9	73	3.1
10 - 14	369	15.7
15 - 19	290	12.3
20 +	839	35.7
Spain - Espagne		
2013 (C)		
Total	95 427	100.0
Less than 1 - Moins de 1	897	0.9
1	2 419	2.5
2	3 308	3.5
3	4 531	4.7
4	4 889	5.1
5	5 061	5.3
6	4 878	5.1
7	4 278	4.5
8	4 049	4.2
9	3 840	4.0
10 - 14	16 373	17.2
15 - 19	12 974	13.6
20 +	27 930	29.3
Sweden - Suède[22]		
2013 (C)		
Total	26 933	100.0
Less than 1 - Moins de 1	585	2.2
1	1 591	5.9
2	2 067	7.7
3	2 571	9.5
4	2 505	9.3
5	1 819	6.8
6	1 554	5.8
7	1 342	5.0
8	1 153	4.3
9	977	3.6
10 - 14	3 695	13.7

Continent, country or area, year, code and duration of marriage (in years) Continent, pays ou zone, année, code et durée du mariage (en années)	Number of divorces Nombre de divorces	Per cent Pour cent
EUROPE		
Sweden - Suède[22]		
2013 (C)		
15 - 19	2 389	8.9
20 +	4 685	17.4
Switzerland - Suisse		
2013 (C)		
Total	17 119	100.0
Less than 1 - Moins de 1	141	0.8
1	349	2.0
2	567	3.3
3	682	4.0
4	730	4.3
5	941	5.5
6	1 066	6.2
7	944	5.5
8	854	5.0
9	749	4.4
10 - 14	3 079	18.0
15 - 19	2 248	13.1
20 +	4 769	27.9
TFYR of Macedonia - L'ex-R. y. de Macédoine		
2013 (C)		
Total	2 045	100.0
Less than 1 - Moins de 1	99	4.8
1	172	8.4
2	120	5.9
3	144	7.0
4	112	5.5
5	101	4.9
6	114	5.6
7	79	3.9
8	80	3.9
9	65	3.2
10 - 14	296	14.5
15 - 19	254	12.4
20 +	409	20.0
Ukraine[23]		
2012 (+C)		
Total	49 807	100.0
Less than 1 - Moins de 1	3 738	7.5
1	4 609	9.3
2	3 723	7.5
3	3 217	6.5
4	3 257	6.5
5 - 9	9 458	19.0
10 - 14	4 826	9.7
15 - 19	4 219	8.5
20 +	12 760	25.6
United Kingdom of Great Britain and Northern Ireland - Royaume-Uni de Grande-Bretagne et d'Irlande du Nord[24]		
2011 (C)		
Total	129 764	100.0
Less than 1 - Moins de 1	38	0.0
1	1 863	1.4
2	4 348	3.4
3	6 343	4.9
4	7 180	5.5
5	7 245	5.6
6	7 670	5.9
7	7 771	6.0
8	6 910	5.3
9	5 989	4.6
10 - 14	24 231	18.7
15 - 19	17 386	13.4
20 +	32 790	25.3

Continent, country or area, year, code and duration of marriage (in years) Continent, pays ou zone, année, code et durée du mariage (en années)	Number of divorces Nombre de divorces	Per cent Pour cent
OCEANIA - OCÉANIE		
Australia - Australie		
2013 (C)		
Total	47 638	100.0
Less than 1 - Moins de 1	-	0.0
1	609	1.3
2	2 203	4.6
3	2 709	5.7
4	3 247	6.8
5	2 942	6.2
6	2 516	5.3
7	2 304	4.8
8	2 061	4.3
9	1 838	3.9
10 - 14	7 811	16.4
15 - 19	6 120	12.8
20 +	13 271	27.9
Not stated - Inconnu	7	0.0
New Caledonia - Nouvelle-Calédonie[25]		
2005 (C)		
Total	341	100.0
Less than 1 - Moins de 1	1	0.3
1	6	1.8
2	6	1.8
3	12	3.5
4	16	4.7
5	17	5.0
6	23	6.7
7	21	6.2
8	18	5.3
9	27	7.9
10 - 14	66	19.4
15 - 19	53	15.5
20 +	75	22.0
New Zealand - Nouvelle-Zélande		
2013 (+C)		
Total	8 279	100.0
Less than 1 - Moins de 1	187	2.3
1	-	0.0
2	-	0.0
3	348	4.2
4	360	4.3
5	423	5.1
6	406	4.9
7	405	4.9
8	381	4.6
9	342	4.1
10 - 14	1 538	18.6
15 - 19	1 257	15.2
20 +	2 632	31.8
Northern Mariana Islands - Îles Mariannes septentrionales[26]		
2007 (U)		
Total	160	100.0
Less than 1 - Moins de 1	2	1.3
1	3	1.9
2	5	3.1
3	9	5.6
4	4	2.5
5	14	8.8
6	11	6.9
7	9	5.6
8	6	3.8
9	8	5.0
10 - 14	34	21.3
15 - 19	20	12.5
20 +	35	21.9

25. Divorces and percentage distribution by duration of marriage, latest available year: 2005 - 2014
Divorces et répartition des pourcentages selon la durée du mariage, dernière année disponible: 2005 - 2014 (continued - suite)

Continent, country or area, year, code and duration of marriage (in years) Continent, pays ou zone, année, code et durée du mariage (en années)	Number of divorces Nombre de divorces	Per cent Pour cent	Continent, country or area, year, code and duration of marriage (in years) Continent, pays ou zone, année, code et durée du mariage (en années)	Number of divorces Nombre de divorces	Per cent Pour cent
OCEANIA - OCÉANIE			OCEANIA - OCÉANIE		
Samoa			Samoa		
2009 (U)			2009 (U)		
Total	48	100.0	7	3	6.3
Less than 1 - Moins de 1	-	0.0	8	2	4.2
1	-	0.0	9	2	4.2
2	-	0.0	10 - 14	4	8.3
3	2	4.2	15 - 19	10	20.8
4	-	0.0	20 +	7	14.6
5	1	2.1	Not stated - Inconnu	15	31.3
6	2	4.2			

FOOTNOTES - NOTES

Italics: estimates which are less reliable. - Italiques: estimations moins sûres.

* Provisional. - Données provisoires.

'Code' indicates the source of data, as follows:
C - Civil registration, estimated over 90% complete
U - Civil registration, estimated less than 90% complete
| - Other source, estimated reliable
+ - Data tabulated by date of registration rather than occurence.
... - Information not available

Le 'Code' indique la source des données, comme suit:
C - Registres de l'état civil considérés complets à 90 p. 100 au moins.
U - Registres de l'état civil qui ne sont pas considérés complets à 90 p. 100 au moins.
| - Autre source, considérée pas douteuses.
+ - Données exploitées selon la date de l'enregistrement et non la date de l'événement.
... - Information non disponible.

[1] Including 'revocable divorces' (among Muslim population), which approximate legal separations. - Y compris les 'divorces révocables' (parmi la population musulmane), qui sont plus au moins l'équivalent des séparations légales.
[2] Excludes the islands of St. Brandon and Agalega. - Non compris les îles St. Brandon et Agalega.
[3] Because of rounding, totals are not in all cases the sum of the respective components. - Les chiffres étant arrondis, les totaux ne correspondent pas toujours rigoureusement à la somme des composants respectifs.
[4] Duration of marriage is defined as the time from the day of celebration of the marriage till the day of filing of the divorce. - La durée du mariage est définie comme la période s'écoulant depuis le jour de la célébration de l'union jusqu'à la date de la demande de divorce.
[5] Excludes nomadic Indian tribes. - Non compris les tribus d'Indiens nomades.
[6] Including annulments. - Y compris les annulations.
[7] Data refer to government controlled areas. - Les données se rapportent aux zones contrôlées par le Gouvernement.
[8] Data refer to the Iranian Year which begins on 21 March and ends on 20 March of the following year. - Les données concernent l'année iranienne, qui commence le 21 mars et se termine le 20 mars de l'année suivante.
[9] Includes data for East Jerusalem and Israeli residents in certain other territories under occupation by Israeli military forces since June 1967. - Y compris les données pour Jérusalem-Est et les résidents israéliens dans certains autres territoires occupés depuis 1967 par les forces armées israéliennes.
[10] Data refer to Japanese nationals in Japan only. - Les données se raportent aux nationaux japonais au Japon seulement.
[11] Data include 308 cases of before consummation. - Dont 308 cas avant consommation du mariage.
[12] Excluding alien armed forces, civilian aliens employed by armed forces, and foreign diplomatic personnel and their dependants. - Non compris les militaires étrangers, les civils étrangers employés par les forces armées ni le personnel diplomatique étranger et les membres de leur famille les accompagnant.
[13] Data from MERNIS (Central Population Administrative System). - Données de MERNIS (Système central de données démographiques).
[14] Excluding aliens temporarily in the area. - Non compris les étrangers se trouvant temporairement dans le territoire.
[15] Including armed forces stationed outside the country, but excluding alien armed forces stationed in the area. - Y compris les militaires nationaux hors du pays, mais non compris les militaires étrangers en garnison sur le territoire.
[16] Including annulments. Including nationals outside the country, but excluding foreigners in the country. - Y compris les annulations. Y compris les nationaux à l'étranger, mais non compris les étrangers sur le territoire.
[17] Excluding Faeroe Islands and Greenland shown separately, if available. - Non compris les îles Féroé et le Groenland, qui font l'objet de rubriques distinctes, si disponible.
[18] Data refer to common residence before divorce. - Données se rapportant à la résidence commune avant le divorce.
[19] Based on the general office for civil registration. Including same sex divorces. - Données provenant des services généraux d'état civil. Y compris les divorces entre conjoints du même sexe.
[20] Data refer to resident spouses only. - Les données concernent uniquement les conjoints résidents.
[21] Excludes data for Kosovo and Metohia. - Sans les données pour le Kosovo et Metohie.
[22] Including same sex divorces. - Y compris les divorces entre conjoints du même sexe.
[23] Unrevised data. - Les données n'ont pas été révisées.
[24] Excluding Channel Islands (Guernsey and Jersey) and Isle of Man, shown separately, if available. - Non compris les îles Anglo-Normandes (Guernesey et Jersey) et l'île de Man, qui font l'objet de rubriques distinctes, si disponible.
[25] Based on place of residence at marriage, not at divorce. - Les divorces sont comptés en fonction du lieu de résidence au mariage, pas au divorce.
[26] Data refer to the islands of Saipan, Tinian and Rota only. - Les données se réfèrent uniquement aux îles de Saipan, Tinian et Rota.

Continent and country or area Continent et pays ou zone	Population estimates (in thousands) - Estimations de population (en milliers)									
	2005	2006	2007	2008	2009	2010	2011	2012	2013	2014

AFRICA - AFRIQUE

Algeria - Algérie	33 268	33 749	34 262	34 811	35 402	36 036	36 717	37 439	38 186	38 934
Angola	17 913	18 541	19 184	19 842	20 520	21 220	21 942	22 686	23 448	24 228
Benin - Bénin	8 182	8 444	8 708	8 974	9 241	9 510	9 779	10 050	10 322	10 598
Botswana	1 864	1 896	1 930	1 968	2 007	2 048	2 090	2 133	2 177	2 220
Burkina Faso	13 422	13 834	14 264	14 709	15 166	15 632	16 107	16 591	17 085	17 589
Burundi	7 934	8 218	8 515	8 822	9 138	9 461	9 790	10 125	10 466	10 817
Cabo Verde	474	478	481	484	487	490	495	501	507	514
Cameroon - Cameroun	18 127	18 597	19 078	19 570	20 075	20 591	21 119	21 659	22 211	22 773
Central African Republic - République centrafricaine	4 056	4 127	4 202	4 280	4 361	4 445	4 531	4 620	4 711	4 804
Chad - Tchad	10 068	10 424	10 780	11 140	11 511	11 896	12 299	12 715	13 146	13 587
Comoros - Comores	619	634	649	665	682	699	716	734	752	770
Congo	3 503	3 605	3 716	3 833	3 951	4 066	4 177	4 286	4 394	4 505
Côte d'Ivoire	18 133	18 486	18 862	19 262	19 685	20 132	20 604	21 103	21 622	22 157
Democratic Republic of the Congo - République démocratique du Congo	56 090	57 927	59 835	61 809	63 845	65 939	68 087	70 291	72 553	74 877
Djibouti	778	789	799	810	820	831	842	853	865	876
Egypt - Égypte	74 942	76 274	77 605	78 976	80 442	82 041	83 788	85 661	87 614	89 580
Equatorial Guinea - Guinée équatoriale	626	646	666	686	707	729	751	774	797	821
Eritrea - Érythrée	4 191	4 304	4 406	4 501	4 594	4 690	4 790	4 892	4 999	5 110
Ethiopia - Éthiopie	76 608	78 736	80 892	83 080	85 302	87 562	89 859	92 191	94 558	96 959
Gabon	1 378	1 409	1 441	1 474	1 507	1 542	1 577	1 613	1 650	1 688
Gambia - Gambie	1 441	1 488	1 536	1 587	1 639	1 693	1 749	1 807	1 867	1 928
Ghana	21 390	21 952	22 528	23 116	23 713	24 318	24 929	25 545	26 164	26 787
Guinea - Guinée	9 669	9 898	10 153	10 427	10 716	11 012	11 316	11 629	11 949	12 276
Guinea-Bissau - Guinée-Bissau	1 463	1 495	1 527	1 561	1 597	1 634	1 674	1 715	1 757	1 801
Kenya	35 349	36 286	37 251	38 244	39 270	40 328	41 420	42 543	43 693	44 864
Lesotho	1 926	1 940	1 956	1 972	1 990	2 011	2 033	2 057	2 083	2 109
Liberia - Libéria	3 270	3 385	3 522	3 673	3 821	3 958	4 080	4 190	4 294	4 397
Libya - Libye	5 802	5 907	6 018	6 123	6 209	6 266	6 289	6 283	6 266	6 259
Madagascar	18 290	18 826	19 371	19 927	20 496	21 080	21 679	22 294	22 925	23 572
Malawi	12 748	13 112	13 498	13 905	14 329	14 770	15 227	15 700	16 190	16 695
Mali	12 881	13 310	13 759	14 223	14 695	15 167	15 639	16 112	16 592	17 086
Mauritania - Mauritanie	3 154	3 242	3 328	3 415	3 502	3 591	3 683	3 777	3 873	3 970
Mauritius - Maurice[1]	1 222	1 228	1 233	1 238	1 243	1 248	1 253	1 258	1 264	1 269
Mayotte	178	184	190	196	203	209	215	221	227	234
Morocco - Maroc	30 385	30 691	31 011	31 351	31 715	32 108	32 532	32 984	33 453	33 921
Mozambique	21 127	21 738	22 360	22 995	23 648	24 321	25 017	25 733	26 467	27 216
Namibia - Namibie	2 027	2 054	2 083	2 116	2 152	2 194	2 240	2 292	2 347	2 403
Niger	13 485	13 996	14 528	15 085	15 672	16 292	16 946	17 636	18 359	19 114
Nigeria - Nigéria	139 611	143 318	147 153	151 116	155 207	159 425	163 771	168 240	172 817	177 476
Republic of South Sudan - République de Soudan du Sud	8 100	8 446	8 815	9 209	9 623	10 056	10 510	10 981	11 454	11 911
Reunion - Réunion	792	801	809	817	824	831	837	843	849	855
Rwanda	9 008	9 231	9 481	9 750	10 025	10 294	10 556	10 817	11 078	11 342
Sao Tome and Principe - Sao Tomé-et-Principe	153	157	160	164	167	171	175	178	182	186
Senegal - Sénégal	11 269	11 578	11 897	12 230	12 582	12 957	13 357	13 780	14 221	14 673
Seychelles	89	90	91	92	92	93	94	95	95	96
Sierra Leone	5 071	5 243	5 391	5 522	5 647	5 776	5 909	6 043	6 179	6 316
Somalia - Somalie	8 467	8 687	8 909	9 133	9 357	9 582	9 807	10 034	10 268	10 518
South Africa - Afrique du Sud	48 353	49 028	49 694	50 349	50 992	51 622	52 237	52 837	53 417	53 969
Sudan - Soudan	31 990	32 809	33 638	34 470	35 297	36 115	36 918	37 712	38 515	39 350
Swaziland	1 105	1 118	1 135	1 154	1 174	1 193	1 212	1 232	1 251	1 269
Togo	5 578	5 732	5 890	6 053	6 220	6 391	6 566	6 746	6 929	7 115
Tunisia - Tunisie	10 102	10 196	10 299	10 408	10 522	10 639	10 759	10 881	11 006	11 130
Uganda - Ouganda	28 042	29 001	29 992	31 014	32 067	33 149	34 260	35 401	36 573	37 783
United Republic of Tanzania - République Unie de Tanzanie	39 066	40 261	41 522	42 845	44 222	45 649	47 123	48 646	50 213	51 823
Western Sahara - Sahara occidental	428	449	467	483	498	512	525	538	550	561
Zambia - Zambie	12 044	12 382	12 739	13 115	13 508	13 917	14 344	14 787	15 246	15 721
Zimbabwe	12 984	13 128	13 298	13 495	13 721	13 974	14 256	14 565	14 898	15 246

AMERICA, NORTH - AMÉRIQUE DU NORD

Anguilla	13	13	13	13	14	14	14	14	14	14
Antigua and Barbuda - Antigua-et-Barbuda	83	83	84	85	86	87	88	89	90	91
Aruba	100	101	101	101	101	102	102	102	103	103
Bahamas	329	336	342	349	355	361	367	372	378	383
Barbados - Barbade	274	275	276	277	278	280	281	282	283	283

Continent and country or area / Continent et pays ou zone	Population estimates (in thousands) - Estimations de population (en milliers)									
	2005	2006	2007	2008	2009	2010	2011	2012	2013	2014
AMERICA, NORTH - AMÉRIQUE DU NORD										
Belize	283	291	298	306	314	322	329	337	344	352
Bermuda - Bermudes	65	65	65	65	64	64	64	63	63	62
Bonaire, Saba and Sint Eustatius - Bonaire, Saba et Saint-Eustache	14	15	17	18	20	21	22	23	24	24
British Virgin Islands - Îles Vierges britanniques	23	24	25	26	26	27	28	29	29	30
Canada	32 256	32 611	32 982	33 363	33 747	34 126	34 500	34 868	35 231	35 588
Cayman Islands - Îles Caïmanes	49	50	51	53	54	56	57	58	58	59
Costa Rica	4 248	4 309	4 369	4 430	4 488	4 545	4 600	4 654	4 706	4 758
Cuba	11 261	11 275	11 284	11 290	11 297	11 308	11 324	11 343	11 363	11 379
Curaçao	129	132	136	140	144	148	150	153	154	156
Dominica - Dominique	71	71	71	71	71	71	71	72	72	72
Dominican Republic - République dominicaine	9 238	9 371	9 504	9 636	9 768	9 898	10 027	10 155	10 281	10 406
El Salvador	5 947	5 968	5 986	6 004	6 021	6 038	6 055	6 072	6 090	6 108
Greenland - Groenland	57	57	57	57	57	57	56	56	56	56
Grenada - Grenade	103	103	104	104	104	105	105	105	106	106
Guadeloupe[2]	451	453	454	455	456	457	459	461	464	466
Guatemala	13 184	13 490	13 798	14 107	14 418	14 732	15 049	15 369	15 691	16 015
Haiti - Haïti	9 263	9 409	9 557	9 705	9 853	10 000	10 145	10 289	10 431	10 572
Honduras	6 880	7 007	7 134	7 259	7 383	7 504	7 621	7 736	7 849	7 962
Jamaica - Jamaïque	2 678	2 691	2 705	2 717	2 730	2 741	2 752	2 763	2 773	2 783
Martinique	397	397	397	396	395	395	395	395	396	396
Mexico - Mexique	109 748	111 383	113 139	114 973	116 816	118 618	120 365	122 071	123 740	125 386
Montserrat	5	5	5	5	5	5	5	5	5	5
Nicaragua	5 379	5 450	5 522	5 595	5 667	5 738	5 808	5 877	5 946	6 014
Panama	3 319	3 379	3 438	3 499	3 559	3 621	3 682	3 744	3 806	3 868
Puerto Rico - Porto Rico	3 761	3 750	3 739	3 728	3 718	3 710	3 702	3 696	3 691	3 687
Saint Kitts and Nevis - Saint-Kitts-et-Nevis	49	50	50	51	52	52	53	54	54	55
Saint Lucia - Sainte-Lucie	165	168	170	173	175	177	179	181	182	184
Saint Pierre and Miquelon - Saint Pierre-et-Miquelon	6	6	6	6	6	6	6	6	6	6
Saint Vincent and the Grenadines - Saint-Vincent-et-les Grenadines	109	109	109	109	109	109	109	109	109	109
Sint Maarten (Dutch part) - Saint-Martin (partie néerlandaise)	33	33	32	32	33	33	34	35	36	38
Trinidad and Tobago - Trinité-et-Tobago	1 297	1 303	1 309	1 315	1 322	1 328	1 335	1 342	1 348	1 354
Turks and Caicos Islands - Îles Turques et Caïques	26	28	29	29	30	31	32	32	33	34
United States of America - États-Unis d'Amérique	296 140	298 861	301 656	304 473	307 232	309 876	312 390	314 799	317 136	319 449
United States Virgin Islands - Îles Vierges américaines	108	107	107	107	107	106	106	106	106	106
AMERICA, SOUTH - AMÉRIQUE DU SUD										
Argentina - Argentine	39 145	39 559	39 970	40 382	40 799	41 223	41 656	42 095	42 538	42 980
Bolivia (Plurinational State of) - Bolivie (État plurinational de)	9 125	9 283	9 441	9 600	9 759	9 918	10 078	10 239	10 400	10 562
Brazil - Brésil	188 479	190 698	192 785	194 770	196 701	198 614	200 518	202 402	204 259	206 078
Chile - Chili	16 097	16 280	16 463	16 646	16 830	17 015	17 201	17 388	17 576	17 763
Colombia - Colombie	43 286	43 836	44 375	44 902	45 416	45 918	46 406	46 881	47 342	47 791
Ecuador - Équateur	13 735	13 967	14 205	14 448	14 691	14 935	15 177	15 419	15 661	15 903
Falkland Islands (Malvinas) - Îles Falkland (Malvinas)	3	3	3	3	3	3	3	3	3	3
French Guiana - Guyane française	203	210	216	222	228	234	240	247	254	261
Guyana	742	744	746	748	751	753	756	758	761	764
Paraguay	5 795	5 883	5 966	6 047	6 128	6 210	6 294	6 379	6 466	6 553
Peru - Pérou	27 610	27 950	28 293	28 642	29 002	29 374	29 760	30 159	30 565	30 973
Suriname	492	496	501	507	513	518	523	529	533	538
Uruguay	3 326	3 331	3 340	3 351	3 363	3 374	3 386	3 397	3 408	3 420
Venezuela (Bolivarian Republic of) - Venezuela (République bolivarienne du)	26 769	27 221	27 671	28 117	28 559	28 996	29 428	29 854	30 276	30 694
ASIA - ASIE										
Afghanistan	24 400	25 184	25 878	26 529	27 207	27 962	28 809	29 727	30 683	31 628
Armenia - Arménie	3 015	3 002	2 988	2 975	2 966	2 963	2 968	2 978	2 992	3 006
Azerbaijan - Azerbaïdjan[3]	8 563	8 662	8 763	8 869	8 980	9 100	9 228	9 361	9 497	9 630
Bahrain - Bahreïn	867	941	1 027	1 116	1 197	1 261	1 306	1 334	1 349	1 362
Bangladesh	142 930	144 839	146 593	148 252	149 906	151 617	153 406	155 257	157 157	159 078
Bhutan - Bhoutan	651	667	681	695	708	720	732	744	755	765
Brunei Darussalam - Brunéi Darussalam	362	368	374	381	387	393	399	406	411	417

Continent and country or area / Continent et pays ou zone	Population estimates (in thousands) - Estimations de population (en milliers)									
	2005	2006	2007	2008	2009	2010	2011	2012	2013	2014

ASIA - ASIE

	2005	2006	2007	2008	2009	2010	2011	2012	2013	2014
Cambodia - Cambodge	13 320	13 525	13 729	13 934	14 144	14 364	14 593	14 832	15 079	15 328
China - Chine[4]	1 305 601	1 312 601	1 319 625	1 326 691	1 333 807	1 340 969	1 348 174	1 355 387	1 362 514	1 369 436
China, Hong Kong SAR - Chine, Hong Kong RAS	6 842	6 856	6 879	6 910	6 949	6 994	7 044	7 102	7 164	7 227
China, Macao SAR - Chine, Macao RAS	468	480	493	507	521	535	547	558	568	578
Cyprus - Chypre[5]	1 033	1 048	1 063	1 077	1 090	1 104	1 117	1 129	1 142	1 154
Democratic People's Republic of Korea - République populaire démocratique de Corée	23 813	23 970	24 112	24 244	24 372	24 501	24 631	24 763	24 896	25 027
Georgia - Géorgie[6]	4 475	4 429	4 386	4 343	4 299	4 250	4 196	4 139	4 083	4 035
India - Inde	1 144 326	1 162 088	1 179 686	1 197 070	1 214 182	1 230 985	1 247 446	1 263 590	1 279 499	1 295 292
Indonesia - Indonésie	226 255	229 264	232 297	235 361	238 465	241 613	244 808	248 038	251 268	254 455
Iran (Islamic Republic of) - Iran (République islamique d')...	70 122	70 923	71 721	72 531	73 371	74 253	75 184	76 157	77 152	78 144
Iraq	27 018	27 717	28 424	29 163	29 971	30 868	31 868	32 958	34 107	35 273
Israel - Israël	6 604	6 755	6 921	7 094	7 263	7 420	7 563	7 695	7 818	7 939
Japan - Japon	126 979	127 137	127 250	127 318	127 341	127 320	127 253	127 140	126 985	126 795
Jordan - Jordanie	5 333	5 530	5 759	6 010	6 267	6 518	6 760	6 994	7 215	7 416
Kazakhstan	15 452	15 603	15 755	15 916	16 098	16 311	16 554	16 821	17 100	17 372
Kuwait - Koweït	2 264	2 389	2 539	2 705	2 881	3 059	3 239	3 420	3 594	3 753
Kyrgyzstan - Kirghizstan	5 115	5 167	5 229	5 301	5 380	5 465	5 554	5 648	5 746	5 844
Lao People's Democratic Republic - République démocratique populaire lao	5 745	5 839	5 940	6 045	6 153	6 261	6 367	6 473	6 580	6 689
Lebanon - Liban	3 987	4 057	4 085	4 109	4 182	4 337	4 592	4 924	5 287	5 612
Malaysia - Malaisie[7]	25 796	26 263	26 731	27 197	27 661	28 120	28 573	29 022	29 465	29 902
Maldives	305	310	316	321	327	333	339	345	351	357
Mongolia - Mongolie	2 526	2 558	2 593	2 630	2 670	2 713	2 759	2 808	2 859	2 910
Myanmar	49 985	50 356	50 699	51 030	51 370	51 733	52 125	52 544	52 984	53 437
Nepal - Népal	25 507	25 794	26 064	26 325	26 593	26 876	27 179	27 501	27 835	28 175
Oman	2 507	2 553	2 594	2 652	2 762	2 944	3 210	3 545	3 907	4 236
Pakistan	153 356	156 524	159 768	163 097	166 521	170 044	173 670	177 392	181 193	185 044
Philippines	86 141	87 593	88 966	90 297	91 642	93 039	94 501	96 017	97 572	99 139
Qatar	837	988	1 179	1 389	1 591	1 766	1 905	2 016	2 101	2 172
Republic of Korea - République de Corée	47 606	47 902	48 205	48 510	48 807	49 090	49 357	49 608	49 847	50 074
Saudi Arabia - Arabie saoudite	24 745	25 420	26 084	26 743	27 409	28 091	28 788	29 496	30 201	30 887
Singapore - Singapour	4 496	4 615	4 733	4 850	4 965	5 079	5 191	5 300	5 405	5 507
Sri Lanka	19 526	19 672	19 814	19 950	20 079	20 201	20 316	20 422	20 522	20 619
State of Palestine - État de Palestine	3 579	3 663	3 755	3 855	3 960	4 069	4 181	4 298	4 418	4 542
Syrian Arab Republic - République arabe syrienne	18 133	18 728	19 426	20 097	20 567	20 721	20 501	19 979	19 323	18 772
Tajikistan - Tadjikistan	6 806	6 950	7 099	7 254	7 415	7 582	7 754	7 931	8 112	8 296
Thailand - Thaïlande	65 864	66 174	66 354	66 453	66 548	66 692	66 903	67 164	67 451	67 726
Timor-Leste	989	1 008	1 021	1 031	1 042	1 057	1 078	1 102	1 129	1 157
Turkey - Turquie	67 861	68 705	69 515	70 344	71 261	72 310	73 517	74 849	76 224	77 524
Turkmenistan - Turkménistan	4 748	4 802	4 858	4 918	4 979	5 042	5 107	5 173	5 240	5 307
United Arab Emirates - Émirats arabes unis	4 482	5 171	6 010	6 900	7 705	8 329	8 735	8 953	9 040	9 086
Uzbekistan - Ouzbékistan	25 922	26 243	26 587	26 953	27 338	27 740	28 158	28 592	29 033	29 470
Viet Nam	84 204	84 980	85 771	86 589	87 449	88 358	89 322	90 336	91 379	92 423
Yemen - Yémen	20 504	21 094	21 701	22 323	22 954	23 592	24 235	24 883	25 533	26 184

EUROPE

	2005	2006	2007	2008	2009	2010	2011	2012	2013	2014
Albania - Albanie	3 082	3 051	3 011	2 968	2 930	2 902	2 886	2 881	2 883	2 890
Andorra - Andorre	81	83	85	86	85	84	82	79	76	73
Austria - Autriche	8 235	8 269	8 301	8 331	8 361	8 392	8 424	8 455	8 487	8 517
Belarus - Bélarus	9 641	9 594	9 556	9 526	9 505	9 492	9 488	9 491	9 497	9 500
Belgium - Belgique	10 561	10 632	10 705	10 779	10 854	10 930	11 005	11 080	11 153	11 226
Bosnia and Herzegovina - Bosnie-Herzégovine	3 833	3 839	3 840	3 840	3 838	3 835	3 832	3 828	3 824	3 818
Bulgaria - Bulgarie	7 683	7 625	7 568	7 514	7 460	7 407	7 355	7 304	7 253	7 201
Croatia - Croatie	4 378	4 369	4 357	4 344	4 330	4 316	4 302	4 287	4 271	4 256
Czech Republic - République tchèque	10 231	10 271	10 330	10 398	10 460	10 507	10 534	10 545	10 545	10 543
Denmark - Danemark	5 418	5 441	5 467	5 495	5 524	5 551	5 577	5 601	5 624	5 647
Estonia - Estonie	1 356	1 349	1 344	1 340	1 336	1 332	1 328	1 324	1 320	1 316
Faeroe Islands - Îles Féroé	48	49	49	49	49	49	48	48	48	48
Finland - Finlande[8]	5 246	5 267	5 289	5 314	5 340	5 368	5 396	5 425	5 453	5 480
France	61 242	61 610	61 966	62 310	62 641	62 961	63 268	63 562	63 845	64 121
Germany - Allemagne	81 247	81 056	80 855	80 666	80 520	80 435	80 425	80 478	80 566	80 646
Gibraltar	29	29	30	30	30	31	31	31	32	32
Greece - Grèce	11 070	11 098	11 131	11 162	11 179	11 178	11 153	11 110	11 055	11 001
Holy See - Saint-Siège	1	1	1	1	1	1	1	1	1	1
Hungary - Hongrie	10 096	10 078	10 064	10 051	10 035	10 015	9 989	9 958	9 925	9 890

Annex I: Mid-year population, United Nations estimates: 2005 - 2014
Annexe I : Population au milieu de l'année, estimations des Nations Unies : 2005 - 2014 (continued - suite)

Continent and country or area / Continent et pays ou zone	Population estimates (in thousands) - Estimations de population (en milliers)									
	2005	2006	2007	2008	2009	2010	2011	2012	2013	2014
EUROPE										
Iceland - Islande	297	301	305	310	314	318	321	323	325	327
Ireland - Irlande	4 204	4 294	4 389	4 480	4 559	4 617	4 653	4 668	4 671	4 675
Isle of Man - Île de Man	80	81	82	83	84	84	85	86	86	87
Italy - Italie	58 657	58 918	59 139	59 319	59 467	59 588	59 679	59 738	59 771	59 789
Latvia - Lettonie	2 228	2 199	2 171	2 144	2 117	2 091	2 064	2 037	2 012	1 989
Liechtenstein	35	35	35	36	36	36	37	37	37	37
Lithuania - Lituanie	3 343	3 306	3 264	3 220	3 172	3 123	3 071	3 016	2 964	2 917
Luxembourg	458	466	475	485	496	508	520	532	545	557
Malta - Malte	397	400	403	406	409	412	414	416	417	418
Monaco	34	34	35	36	36	37	37	37	38	38
Montenegro - Monténégro	616	617	619	620	621	622	623	624	625	625
Netherlands - Pays-Bas	16 332	16 401	16 463	16 520	16 575	16 632	16 690	16 749	16 809	16 868
Norway - Norvège[9]	4 624	4 667	4 717	4 772	4 830	4 891	4 954	5 018	5 083	5 148
Poland - Pologne	38 464	38 479	38 500	38 526	38 551	38 575	38 594	38 609	38 619	38 620
Portugal	10 480	10 517	10 551	10 577	10 590	10 585	10 559	10 515	10 460	10 402
Republic of Moldova - République de Moldova[10]	4 158	4 145	4 128	4 111	4 096	4 084	4 078	4 075	4 074	4 072
Romania - Roumanie	21 408	21 206	20 980	20 742	20 510	20 299	20 112	19 945	19 794	19 652
Russian Federation - Fédération de Russie	143 623	143 338	143 180	143 123	143 127	143 158	143 211	143 288	143 367	143 429
San Marino - Saint-Marin	29	30	30	30	30	31	31	31	31	32
Serbia - Serbie[11]	9 187	9 155	9 130	9 110	9 087	9 059	9 024	8 983	8 938	8 893
Slovakia - Slovaquie	5 385	5 388	5 392	5 397	5 402	5 407	5 411	5 415	5 419	5 423
Slovenia - Slovénie	1 997	2 006	2 017	2 031	2 043	2 052	2 059	2 063	2 065	2 066
Spain - Espagne[12]	43 855	44 538	45 210	45 817	46 295	46 601	46 708	46 637	46 455	46 260
Sweden - Suède	9 030	9 087	9 153	9 226	9 303	9 382	9 462	9 543	9 624	9 703
Switzerland - Suisse	7 409	7 480	7 560	7 647	7 737	7 831	7 926	8 023	8 119	8 211
TFYR of Macedonia - L'ex-R. y. de Macédoine	2 043	2 047	2 051	2 055	2 059	2 062	2 066	2 069	2 073	2 076
Ukraine[13]	46 795	46 503	46 249	46 028	45 831	45 647	45 478	45 320	45 165	45 002
United Kingdom of Great Britain and Northern Ireland - Royaume-Uni de Grande-Bretagne et d'Irlande du Nord	60 210	60 649	61 152	61 690	62 221	62 717	63 165	63 574	63 956	64 331
OCEANIA - OCÉANIE										
American Samoa - Samoas américaines	59	59	58	57	56	56	55	55	55	55
Australia - Australie[14]	20 274	20 606	20 976	21 370	21 771	22 163	22 542	22 911	23 270	23 622
Cook Islands - Îles Cook	19	20	20	20	20	20	20	21	21	21
Fiji - Fidji	822	827	835	843	852	860	867	874	880	886
French Polynesia - Polynésie française	255	258	260	263	265	268	271	274	277	280
Guam	158	158	158	158	159	159	161	163	165	168
Kiribati	92	94	96	98	101	103	105	107	109	110
Marshall Islands - Îles Marshall	52	52	52	52	52	52	53	53	53	53
Micronesia (Federated States of) - Micronésie (États fédérés de)	106	106	105	104	104	104	103	104	104	104
Nauru	10	10	10	10	10	10	10	10	10	10
New Caledonia - Nouvelle-Calédonie	229	232	236	239	243	246	250	253	256	260
New Zealand - Nouvelle-Zélande	4 135	4 188	4 238	4 285	4 329	4 369	4 404	4 436	4 465	4 495
Niue - Nioué	2	2	2	2	2	2	2	2	2	2
Northern Mariana Islands - Îles Mariannes septentrionales	64	62	60	57	55	54	53	53	54	55
Palau - Palaos	20	20	20	20	20	20	21	21	21	21
Papua New Guinea - Papouasie-Nouvelle-Guinée	6 087	6 236	6 387	6 540	6 694	6 848	7 001	7 155	7 309	7 464
Samoa	180	181	182	183	185	186	187	189	190	192
Solomon Islands - Îles Salomon	469	481	492	503	515	526	538	549	561	572
Tokelau - Tokélaou	1	1	1	1	1	1	1	1	1	1
Tonga	101	102	102	103	103	104	104	105	105	106
Tuvalu	10	10	10	10	10	10	10	10	10	10
Vanuatu	209	215	220	225	231	236	242	247	253	259
Wallis and Futuna Islands - Îles Wallis et Futuna	14	14	14	14	14	14	13	13	13	13

SOURCE

United Nations, Department of Economic and Social Affairs, Population Division (2015). 2015 Revision of World Population Prospects - Organisation des Nations Unies, Département des affaires économiques et sociales, Division de la population (2015). Perspectives de la population mondiale : La révision de 2015

FOOTNOTES - NOTES

[1] Including Agalega, Rodrigues and Saint Brandon. - Y compris Agalega, Rodrigues et Saint Brandon.

[2] Including Saint-Barthélemy and Saint-Martin (French part). - Y compris Saint-Barthélemy et Saint-Martin (partie française).

[3] Including Nagorno-Karabakh. - Y compris le Haut-Karabakh.

[4] For statistical purposes, the data for China do not include Hong Kong and Macao Special Administrative Regions (SAR) of China. - A des fins statistiques, les données pour la Chine ne comprennent pas les Régions Administratives Spéciales (SAR) de Hong Kong et Macao.

[5] Refers to the whole country. - Les données se rapportent au pays en entier.

[6] Including Abkhazia and South Ossetia. - Y compris l'Abkhazie et l'Ossétie du Sud.

[7] Including Sabah and Sarawak. - Y compris le Sabah et le Sarawak.

[8] Including Åland Islands. - Y compris les îles Åland.

[9] Including Svalbard and Jan Mayen Islands. - Y compris Svalbard et l'île Jan Mayen.

[10] Including Transnistria. - Y compris la Transnistrie.

[11] Including Kosovo. - Y compris le Kosovo.

[12] Including Canary Islands, Ceuta and Melilla. - Y compris les îles Canaries, Ceuta et Melilla.

[13] Including Crimea. - Y compris la Crimée.

[14] Including Christmas Island, Cocos (Keeling) Islands and Norfolk Island. - Y compris les îles Christmas, Cocos (Keeling) et Norfolk.

Continent and country or area Continent et pays ou zone	Crude birth rate - Taux bruts de natalité	Crude death rate - Taux bruts de mortalité	Infant mortality rate - Décès d'enfants de moins d'un an	Life expectancy at birth - Espérance de vie à la naissance		Total fertility rate - Indice synthétique de fécondité	Natural increase - Accroissement naturel
				Male - Masculin	Female - Féminin		
AFRICA - AFRIQUE							
Algeria - Algérie...	25.1	5.1	30.3	72.1	76.8	2.93	19.9
Angola	46.2	14.2	96.2	50.2	53.2	6.20	32.0
Benin - Bénin	36.6	9.6	68.7	57.8	60.6	4.89	27.1
Botswana	25.6	7.5	32.5	61.8	66.5	2.90	18.1
Burkina Faso	40.8	10.0	66.5	56.7	59.3	5.65	30.8
Burundi	44.2	11.7	77.9	54.2	58.0	6.08	32.5
Cabo Verde	21.8	5.5	20.1	71.1	74.7	2.37	16.3
Cameroon - Cameroun	37.5	11.9	73.5	53.7	56.0	4.82	25.6
Central African Republic - République centrafricaine............	34.3	15.2	93.5	47.8	51.3	4.41	19.1
Chad - Tchad	45.9	14.5	95.8	50.1	52.2	6.31	31.5
Comoros - Comores	34.6	7.7	58.1	61.2	64.5	4.60	26.8
Congo	37.3	9.0	50.6	60.0	62.9	4.95	28.3
Côte d'Ivoire	37.4	13.9	73.4	50.2	51.9	5.10	23.5
Democratic Republic of the Congo - République démocratique du Congo	42.6	10.7	73.2	56.7	59.5	6.15	31.9
Djibouti	25.7	8.7	55.3	60.0	63.2	3.30	17.0
Egypt - Égypte	28.5	6.2	18.9	68.7	73.1	3.38	22.3
Equatorial Guinea - Guinée équatoriale	35.5	11.0	70.1	55.9	58.6	4.97	24.5
Eritrea - Érythrée	35.0	6.9	46.5	60.9	65.2	4.40	28.2
Ethiopia - Éthiopie	33.2	7.8	50.0	61.3	65.0	4.59	25.4
Gabon	30.8	9.0	43.2	63.2	64.1	4.00	21.8
Gambia - Gambie	42.8	9.0	47.1	58.5	61.2	5.78	33.8
Ghana	33.5	9.2	51.1	60.1	62.0	4.25	24.3
Guinea - Guinée	37.6	10.4	59.2	57.6	58.5	5.14	27.2
Guinea-Bissau - Guinée-Bissau	37.7	12.4	91.9	53.0	56.5	4.95	25.3
Kenya	35.4	8.7	52.5	59.1	62.2	4.44	26.7
Lesotho..	28.9	14.9	60.1	49.2	49.6	3.26	13.9
Liberia - Libéria	35.7	9.0	61.2	59.3	61.2	4.83	26.7
Libya - Libye	21.7	5.3	24.3	68.8	74.4	2.53	16.4
Madagascar...	34.8	6.9	36.8	63.0	66.0	4.50	27.9
Malawi	39.6	8.6	60.1	59.9	62.0	5.25	31.0
Mali	44.4	11.0	84.0	57.4	57.0	6.35	33.4
Mauritania - Mauritanie	34.0	8.1	67.3	61.3	64.3	4.69	25.9
Mauritius - Maurice[1]	11.4	7.3	12.0	70.7	77.7	1.50	4.0
Mayotte..	31.7	2.5	4.2	76.0	82.9	4.10	29.2
Morocco - Maroc	21.3	5.7	26.3	72.6	74.6	2.56	15.5
Mozambique...	40.0	11.8	64.4	52.9	56.2	5.45	28.2
Namibia - Namibie	30.2	7.3	33.5	61.6	67.0	3.60	22.9
Niger	49.8	9.6	59.8	59.9	61.6	7.63	40.2
Nigeria - Nigéria	40.3	13.3	76.3	52.0	52.6	5.74	27.0
Republic of South Sudan - République de Soudan du Sud ...	37.3	12.0	77.7	54.1	56.0	5.15	25.3
Reunion - Réunion	15.7	5.5	4.2	76.0	82.9	2.24	10.2
Rwanda	32.9	7.5	49.2	59.7	66.3	4.05	25.4
Sao Tome and Principe - Sao Tomé-et-Principe	34.9	7.1	43.5	64.2	68.2	4.67	27.8
Senegal - Sénégal	38.9	6.6	44.3	63.9	67.6	5.18	32.4
Seychelles..	18.0	7.6	10.2	68.7	77.9	2.33	10.4
Sierra Leone	36.9	14.1	94.4	49.7	50.7	4.79	22.8
Somalia - Somalie	43.9	12.4	79.5	53.3	56.5	6.61	31.5
South Africa - Afrique du Sud	21.0	12.5	38.3	54.9	59.1	2.40	8.6
Sudan - Soudan	33.7	7.9	53.3	61.6	64.6	4.46	25.8
Swaziland	30.2	14.1	64.6	49.7	48.5	3.36	16.1
Togo...	36.3	9.3	50.2	58.3	59.7	4.69	27.0
Tunisia - Tunisie	18.4	6.6	18.7	72.3	77.0	2.16	11.8
Uganda - Ouganda	43.7	10.2	61.2	55.7	58.8	5.91	33.4
United Republic of Tanzania - République Unie de Tanzanie	39.7	7.3	37.0	62.6	65.6	5.24	32.4
Western Sahara - Sahara occidental	19.1	5.6	37.2	65.9	69.8	2.20	13.5
Zambia - Zambie	40.6	9.7	55.4	57.2	60.3	5.45	30.9
Zimbabwe...	36.1	11.1	48.4	53.6	56.0	4.02	25.0
AMERICA, NORTH - AMÉRIQUE DU NORD							
Antigua and Barbuda - Antigua-et-Barbuda	16.5	6.2	9.1	73.3	78.2	2.10	10.4
Aruba	10.3	8.3	14.8	72.9	77.8	1.68	2.0
Bahamas..	15.4	6.0	9.1	72.0	78.1	1.89	9.4
Barbados - Barbade	12.2	10.5	9.6	72.9	77.7	1.79	1.8
Belize...	23.3	5.6	14.3	67.2	72.7	2.64	17.7

Continent and country or area Continent et pays ou zone	Crude birth rate - Taux bruts de natalité	Crude death rate - Taux bruts de mortalité	Infant mortality rate - Décès d'enfants de moins d'un an	Life expectancy at birth - Espérance de vie à la naissance		Total fertility rate - Indice synthétique de fécondité	Natural increase - Accroissement naturel
				Male - Masculin	Female - Féminin		
AMERICA, NORTH - AMÉRIQUE DU NORD							
Canada	10.9	7.3	4.7	79.7	83.8	1.61	3.6
Costa Rica	15.1	4.7	9.3	76.7	81.7	1.85	10.4
Cuba	10.5	7.7	5.5	77.1	81.3	1.63	2.8
Curaçao	13.3	8.2	10.3	74.5	80.7	2.10	5.1
Dominican Republic - République dominicaine	21.4	6.0	25.1	70.2	76.5	2.53	15.3
El Salvador	17.5	6.7	17.0	67.9	77.1	1.97	10.8
Grenada - Grenade	19.4	7.2	9.6	70.8	75.6	2.18	12.1
Guadeloupe[2]	13.7	7.1	5.8	76.8	84.0	2.17	6.6
Guatemala	27.7	5.4	22.6	67.9	75.0	3.30	22.3
Haiti - Haïti	25.5	8.9	47.0	60.2	64.4	3.13	16.6
Honduras	21.7	5.0	27.8	70.4	75.4	2.47	16.7
Jamaica - Jamaïque	17.6	6.8	15.0	73.1	77.9	2.08	10.8
Martinique	11.7	8.0	6.4	77.8	84.4	1.95	3.8
Mexico - Mexique	19.3	4.8	18.8	74.0	78.9	2.29	14.5
Nicaragua	21.0	4.8	20.0	71.4	77.5	2.32	16.2
Panama	19.8	5.0	15.2	74.3	80.5	2.48	14.9
Puerto Rico - Porto Rico	12.1	7.9	6.3	75.2	83.2	1.64	4.2
Saint Lucia - Sainte-Lucie	15.5	7.2	10.9	72.2	77.6	1.92	8.3
Saint Vincent and the Grenadines - Saint-Vincent-et-les Grenadines	16.4	7.0	16.5	70.7	74.9	2.01	9.4
Trinidad and Tobago - Trinité-et-Tobago	14.7	9.2	24.8	66.9	73.8	1.80	5.5
United States of America - États-Unis d'Amérique	12.6	8.2	6.0	76.5	81.3	1.89	4.4
United States Virgin Islands - Îles Vierges américaines	14.1	7.4	9.4	77.2	82.9	2.30	6.6
AMERICA, SOUTH - AMÉRIQUE DU SUD							
Argentina - Argentine	17.8	7.6	13.7	72.2	79.8	2.35	10.2
Bolivia (Plurinational State of) - Bolivie (État plurinational de)	24.4	7.6	42.9	65.3	70.2	3.04	16.8
Brazil - Brésil	15.1	6.1	20.3	70.3	77.9	1.82	9.1
Chile - Chili	13.5	5.1	7.2	78.1	84.1	1.78	8.4
Colombia - Colombie	16.2	5.8	17.9	70.2	77.4	1.93	10.4
Ecuador - Équateur	21.2	5.2	21.1	72.8	78.4	2.59	16.1
French Guiana - Guyane française	26.1	3.2	9.5	75.8	82.6	3.48	22.9
Guyana	18.8	8.0	33.2	64.0	68.6	2.60	10.8
Paraguay	21.7	5.6	28.8	70.7	74.9	2.60	16.1
Peru - Pérou	20.4	5.6	18.6	71.5	76.8	2.50	14.8
Suriname	18.6	7.3	17.4	67.8	74.2	2.40	11.2
Uruguay	14.4	9.3	12.7	73.3	80.4	2.04	5.1
Venezuela (Bolivarian Republic of) - Venezuela (République bolivarienne du)	20.0	5.5	13.8	69.9	78.2	2.41	14.5
ASIA - ASIE							
Afghanistan	35.6	8.6	71.1	58.7	61.1	5.14	27.1
Armenia - Arménie	13.3	9.0	13.2	70.7	78.4	1.55	4.3
Azerbaijan - Azerbaïdjan[3]	21.2	7.0	39.6	67.5	73.8	2.30	14.2
Bahrain - Bahreïn	15.4	2.3	6.9	75.6	77.4	2.10	13.0
Bangladesh	20.4	5.5	33.1	69.9	72.3	2.23	14.8
Bhutan - Bhoutan	18.2	6.3	30.5	68.6	69.1	2.10	11.9
Brunei Darussalam - Brunéi Darussalam	16.6	3.0	4.2	76.6	80.4	1.90	13.6
Cambodia - Cambodge	24.5	6.3	29.9	65.5	69.6	2.70	18.2
China - Chine[4]	12.4	7.0	11.6	74.0	77.0	1.55	5.4
China, Hong Kong SAR - Chine, Hong Kong RAS	10.1	6.0	1.8	80.9	86.6	1.20	4.0
China, Macao SAR - Chine, Macao RAS	11.2	4.8	4.1	78.1	82.5	1.19	6.4
Cyprus - Chypre[5]	11.5	6.8	4.2	77.7	82.2	1.46	4.7
Democratic People's Republic of Korea - République populaire démocratique de Corée	14.4	9.2	22.0	66.3	73.3	2.00	5.3
Georgia - Géorgie[6]	13.7	11.5	13.7	70.9	78.1	1.81	2.2
India - Inde	20.4	7.4	41.4	66.1	68.9	2.48	13.0
Indonesia - Indonésie	20.5	7.2	25.0	66.6	70.7	2.50	13.3
Iran (Islamic Republic of) - Iran (République islamique d')	18.1	4.7	14.8	74.0	76.2	1.75	13.4
Iraq	35.1	5.3	32.1	67.0	71.4	4.64	29.8
Israel - Israël	21.5	5.3	3.5	80.2	83.8	3.05	16.1
Japan - Japon	8.3	10.0	2.2	80.0	86.5	1.40	-1.7

Annex II: Vital statistics summary, United Nations estimates: 2010-2015
Annexe II: Aperçu des statistiques de l'état civil, estimations des Nations Unies : 2010-2015 (continued - suite)

Continent and country or area Continent et pays ou zone	Crude birth rate - Taux bruts de natalité	Crude death rate - Taux bruts de mortalité	Infant mortality rate - Décès d'enfants de moins d'un an	Life expectancy at birth - Espérance de vie à la naissance		Total fertility rate - Indice synthétique de fécondité	Natural increase - Accroissement naturel
				Male - Masculin	Female - Féminin		
ASIA - ASIE							
Jordan - Jordanie	27.9	3.9	17.1	72.2	75.5	3.51	24.0
Kazakhstan	22.5	8.9	14.1	64.3	73.9	2.64	13.6
Kuwait - Koweït	20.7	2.5	8.6	73.3	75.6	2.15	18.1
Kyrgyzstan - Kirghizstan......................	27.1	6.4	19.6	66.4	74.3	3.12	20.7
Lao People's Democratic Republic - République démocratique populaire lao	27.2	7.0	46.8	64.1	66.8	3.10	20.2
Lebanon - Liban	15.0	4.6	9.3	77.1	80.9	1.72	10.3
Malaysia - Malaisie[7]	16.9	4.8	6.8	72.2	76.9	1.97	12.1
Maldives	21.7	3.8	9.0	75.4	77.4	2.18	17.9
Mongolia - Mongolie	24.6	6.2	25.8	64.8	73.3	2.68	18.4
Myanmar	18.2	8.3	46.5	63.6	67.7	2.25	10.0
Nepal - Népal	21.0	6.5	32.4	67.6	70.5	2.32	14.5
Oman	20.8	2.7	7.3	74.7	78.9	2.88	18.1
Pakistan	29.8	7.5	69.8	65.0	66.8	3.72	22.2
Philippines	24.0	6.7	23.2	64.7	71.6	3.04	17.3
Qatar	12.1	1.5	6.5	77.1	79.7	2.08	10.6
Republic of Korea - République de Corée...	9.2	5.5	2.9	78.0	84.6	1.26	3.6
Saudi Arabia - Arabie saoudite.............	20.8	3.4	15.3	72.8	75.5	2.85	17.4
Singapore - Singapour	9.3	4.5	1.8	79.6	85.6	1.23	4.8
Sri Lanka	16.4	6.7	8.2	71.2	78.0	2.11	9.8
State of Palestine - État de Palestine....	33.1	3.6	20.6	70.7	74.7	4.28	29.5
Syrian Arab Republic - République arabe syrienne	24.1	5.6	17.9	64.0	76.3	3.03	18.5
Tajikistan - Tadjikistan........................	31.0	5.7	39.9	65.9	72.8	3.55	25.3
Thailand - Thaïlande	11.2	7.7	11.2	70.8	77.6	1.54	3.5
Timor-Leste	38.7	7.0	43.9	66.1	69.5	5.91	31.7
Turkey - Turquie	17.3	5.7	12.6	71.5	78.1	2.10	11.5
Turkmenistan - Turkménistan	21.5	7.8	46.7	61.3	69.7	2.34	13.7
United Arab Emirates - Émirats arabes unis	11.2	1.5	6.2	76.0	78.2	1.82	9.7
Uzbekistan - Ouzbékistan	23.3	7.0	44.0	64.9	71.6	2.48	16.3
Viet Nam	17.4	5.8	19.3	70.7	80.3	1.96	11.6
Yemen - Yémen..................................	33.2	7.1	53.6	62.2	64.9	4.35	26.1
EUROPE							
Albania - Albanie	13.1	7.2	14.4	75.0	80.2	1.78	6.0
Austria - Autriche...............................	9.5	9.4	3.1	78.5	83.6	1.47	0.1
Belarus - Bélarus...............................	11.7	14.2	4.0	65.3	77.0	1.58	-2.5
Belgium - Belgique	11.6	9.8	3.3	78.0	83.0	1.82	1.8
Bosnia and Herzegovina - Bosnie-Herzégovine..........	9.1	10.3	7.6	73.7	78.8	1.28	-1.2
Bulgaria - Bulgarie	9.4	15.1	9.0	70.6	77.6	1.52	-5.7
Croatia - Croatie................................	9.8	12.4	3.9	73.6	80.4	1.52	-2.6
Czech Republic - République tchèque....	10.2	10.1	2.5	75.4	81.3	1.45	0.1
Denmark - Danemark	10.4	9.7	3.5	78.0	81.9	1.73	0.8
Estonia - Estonie	10.7	11.9	3.2	71.6	81.1	1.59	-1.2
Finland - Finlande[8]	10.7	9.6	2.3	77.6	83.4	1.75	1.0
France	12.4	8.9	3.3	78.8	84.9	2.00	3.5
Germany - Allemagne	8.3	10.8	3.1	78.2	83.1	1.39	-2.5
Greece - Grèce..................................	8.9	10.5	2.8	77.6	83.6	1.34	-1.6
Hungary - Hongrie	9.3	13.2	4.6	71.2	78.5	1.34	-3.8
Iceland - Islande................................	13.6	6.3	2.0	80.7	83.8	1.96	7.3
Ireland - Irlande.................................	15.4	6.4	2.9	78.4	82.7	2.01	9.1
Italy - Italie	8.6	9.7	2.3	80.3	85.2	1.43	-1.1
Latvia - Lettonie	10.0	14.5	6.5	68.9	78.7	1.48	-4.6
Lithuania - Lituanie	10.2	15.2	3.8	67.4	78.8	1.57	-5.0
Luxembourg	11.3	7.4	1.6	78.9	83.7	1.57	3.9
Malta - Malte.....................................	8.9	8.8	4.8	78.6	82.0	1.44	0.2
Montenegro - Monténégro	11.9	9.9	4.4	73.8	78.2	1.71	2.0
Netherlands - Pays-Bas	10.6	8.4	3.5	79.4	83.1	1.75	2.2
Norway - Norvège[9]	11.7	8.4	2.5	79.2	83.4	1.80	3.3
Poland - Pologne................................	10.4	9.8	4.6	73.1	81.1	1.37	0.6
Portugal	8.5	10.3	3.3	77.4	83.5	1.28	-1.8
Republic of Moldova - République de Moldova[10]	10.9	11.2	10.9	67.2	75.4	1.27	-0.3
Romania - Roumanie	9.4	12.9	9.6	70.9	78.1	1.48	-3.5
Russian Federation - Fédération de Russie..................	12.7	13.9	8.2	64.2	75.6	1.66	-1.1
Serbia - Serbie[11]	10.2	12.7	9.8	71.8	77.5	1.56	-2.4
Slovakia - Slovaquie...........................	10.5	9.8	4.9	72.2	79.7	1.37	0.7

Continent and country or area Continent et pays ou zone	Crude birth rate - Taux bruts de natalité	Crude death rate - Taux bruts de mortalité	Infant mortality rate - Décès d'enfants de moins d'un an	Life expectancy at birth - Espérance de vie à la naissance		Total fertility rate - Indice synthétique de fécondité	Natural increase - Accroissement naturel
				Male - Masculin	Female - Féminin		
EUROPE							
Slovenia - Slovénie..	10.5	9.4	2.9	76.9	83.1	1.58	1.0
Spain - Espagne[12]...	9.3	8.8	3.0	79.4	85.1	1.32	0.5
Sweden - Suède..	12.0	9.4	2.8	80.1	83.7	1.92	2.6
Switzerland - Suisse...	10.2	8.1	3.7	80.4	84.7	1.52	2.1
TFYR of Macedonia - L'ex-R. y. de Macédoine..............	11.3	9.2	10.1	72.9	77.5	1.51	2.0
Ukraine[13]..	10.8	15.3	9.2	65.7	75.7	1.49	-4.5
United Kingdom of Great Britain and Northern Ireland - Royaume-Uni de Grande-Bretagne et d'Irlande du Nord	12.6	9.2	4.2	78.5	82.4	1.92	3.5
OCEANIA - OCÉANIE							
Australia - Australie[14]...	13.5	6.7	4.0	79.9	84.3	1.92	6.8
Fiji - Fidji..	20.7	6.8	16.0	66.9	72.9	2.61	13.9
French Polynesia - Polynésie française	16.5	5.5	6.9	74.0	78.6	2.07	11.0
Guam...	17.5	4.8	9.7	76.1	81.5	2.42	12.7
Kiribati	29.2	7.1	46.7	62.6	68.9	3.79	22.1
Micronesia (Federated States of) - Micronésie (États fédérés de)	23.6	6.2	32.7	68.0	69.9	3.33	17.4
New Caledonia - Nouvelle-Calédonie	15.7	6.9	13.1	73.6	79.3	2.13	8.7
New Zealand - Nouvelle-Zélande.................................	13.7	6.8	4.3	79.7	83.4	2.05	6.8
Papua New Guinea - Papouasie-Nouvelle-Guinée..............	29.1	7.7	47.6	60.3	64.5	3.84	21.3
Samoa..	26.4	5.4	19.7	70.0	76.4	4.16	21.0
Solomon Islands - Îles Salomon.................................	30.9	5.9	38.0	66.2	69.0	4.06	25.0
Tonga...	25.7	6.1	20.4	69.7	75.6	3.79	19.6
Vanuatu	26.9	4.8	23.9	69.6	73.6	3.41	22.2

SOURCE

United Nations, Department of Economic and Social Affairs, Population Division (2015). 2015 Revision of World Population Prospects - Organisation des Nations Unies, Département des affaires économiques et sociales, Division de la population (2015). Perspectives de la population mondiale : La révision de 2015

FOOTNOTES - NOTES

[1] Including Agalega, Rodrigues and Saint Brandon. - Y compris Agalega, Rodrigues et Saint Brandon.
[2] Including Saint-Barthélemy and Saint-Martin (French part). - Y compris Saint-Barthélemy et Saint-Martin (partie française).
[3] Including Nagorno-Karabakh. - Y compris le Haut-Karabakh.
[4] For statistical purposes, the data for China do not include Hong Kong and Macao Special Administrative Regions (SAR) of China. - A des fins statistiques, les données pour la Chine ne comprennent pas les Régions Administratives Spéciales (SAR) de Hong Kong et Macao.
[5] Refers to the whole country. - Les données se rapportent au pays en entier.
[6] Including Abkhazia and South Ossetia. - Y compris l'Abkhazie et l'Ossétie du Sud.
[7] Including Sabah and Sarawak. - Y compris le Sabah et le Sarawak.
[8] Including Åland Islands. - Y compris les îles Åland.
[9] Including Svalbard and Jan Mayen Islands. - Y compris Svalbard et l'île Jan Mayen.
[10] Including Transnistria. - Y compris la Transnistrie.
[11] Including Kosovo. - Y compris le Kosovo.
[12] Including Canary Islands, Ceuta and Melilla. - Y compris les îles Canaries, Ceuta et Melilla.
[13] Including Crimea. - Y compris la Crimée.
[14] Including Christmas Island, Cocos (Keeling) Islands and Norfolk Island. - Y compris les îles Christmas, Cocos (Keeling) et Norfolk.

Subject-matter	Year of issue	Time coverage	Subject-matter	Year of issue	Time coverage
A			**Annulments**	1958	1948-57
				1968	1958-67
Abortions, Legal.....................	1971	Latest		1976	1966-75
	1972	1964-72			
	1973	1965-73	**Annulment rates**	1958	1948-57
	1974	1965-74		1968	1958-67
	1975	1965-74		1976	1966-75
	1976	1966-75			
	1977	1967-76			
	1978	1968-77	**B**		
	1979	1969-78	**Bibliography**	1948	1930-48
	1980	1971-79		1949/50	1930-50
	1981	1972-80		1951-1952	1930-51[i]
	1982	1973-81		1953	1900-53
	1983	1974-82		1954	1900-54[i]
	1984	1975-83		1955	1900-55[i]
	1985	1976-84			
	1986	1977-85	**Births**	1948	1932-47
	1987	1978-86		1949/50	1934-49
	1988	1979-87		1951	1935-50
	1989	1980-88		1952	1936-51
	1990	1981-89		1953	1950-52
	1991	1982-90		1954	1938-53
	1992	1983-91		1955	1946-54
	1993	1984-92		1956	1947-55
	1994	1985-93		1957	1948-56
	1995	1986-94		1958	1948-57
	1996	1987-95		1959	1949-58
	1997	1988-96		1960	1950-59
	1998	1989-97		1961	1952-61
	1999	1990-98		1962	1953-62
	2000	1991-99		1963	1954-63
	2001	1993-01		1964	1960-64
	2002	1993-02		1965	1946-65
	2003	1994-03		1966	1957-66
	2004	1995-04		1967	1963-67
	2005	1996-05		1968	1964-68
	2006	1997-06		1969	1950-69
	2007	1998-07		1970	1966-70
	2008	1999-08		1971	1967-71
	2009-2010	2001-10		1972	1968-72
	2011	2002-11		1973	1969-73
	2012	2003-12		1974	1970-74
	2013	2004-13		1975	1956-75
	2014	2005-14		1976	1972-76
				1977	1973-77
				1978	1974-78
- by age of mother and number of previous live births of mother	1971-1975	Latest		1978HS[ii]	1948-78
	1977-1981	Latest		1979	1975-79
	1983-2014	Latest		1980	1976-80
				1981	1962-81
				1982	1978-82
				1983	1979-83
Ageing (see: Population)				1984	1980-84

Subject-matter	Year of issue	Time coverage	Subject-matter	Year of issue	Time coverage
	1985	1981-85		1966-1968	Latest
	1986	1967-86		1969	1963-68
	1987	1983-87		1970-1974	Latest
	1988	1984-88		1975	1966-74
	1989	1985-89		1976-1978	Latest
	1990	1986-90		1978HS[ii]	1948-77
	1991	1987-91		1979-1980	Latest
	1992	1983-92		1981	1972-80
	1993	1989-93		1982-1985	Latest
	1994	1990-94		1986	1977-85
	1995	1991-95		1987-1991	Latest
	1996	1992-96		1992	1983-92
	1997	1993-97		1993-1997	Latest
	1997HS[iii]	1948-97		1997HS[iii] [3]	1948-96
	1998	1994-98		1998-99	Latest
	1999	1995-99		1999CD[iv]	1990-98
	1999CD[iv]	1980-99		2000-2014	Latest
	2000	1996-00			
	2001	1997-01	- by age of mother and birth order	1949/50	1936-47
	2002	1998-02		1954	Latest
	2003	1999-03		1959	1949-58
	2004	2000-04		1965	1955-64
	2005	2001-05		1969	1963-68
	2006	2002-06		1975	1966-74
	2007	2003-07		1981	1972-80
	2008	2004-08		1986	1977-85
	2009-2010	2006-10		1999CD[iv]	1990-98
	2011	2007-11			
	2012	2008-12	- by age of mother and sex of child	1965-1968	Latest
	2013	2009-13		1969	1963-68
	2014	2010-14		1970-1974	Latest
- by age of father	1949/50	1942-49		1975	1966-74
	1954	1936-53		1976-1978	Latest
	1959	1949-58		1978HS[ii]	1948-77
	1965	1955-64		1979-1980	Latest
	1969	1963-68		1981	1972-80
	1975	1966-74		1982-1985	Latest
	1981	1972-80		1986	1977-85
	1999CD[iv]	1990-98		1987-1991	Latest
	2007-2014	Latest		1992	1983-92
				1993-1997	Latest
- by age of mother	1948	1936-47		1997HS[iii]	1948-96
	1949/50	1936-49		1998-99	Latest
	1954	1936-53		1999CD[iv]	1990-98
	1955-1956	Latest			
	1958	Latest			
	1959	1949-58			
	1960-1964	Latest			
	1965	1955-64			

Subject-matter	Year of issue	Time coverage	Subject-matter	Year of issue	Time coverage
	1956	1947-55		1999	1995-99
	1957	1948-56		1999CD[iv]	1985-99
	1958	1948-57		2000	1996-00
	1959	1920-54[v]		2001	1997-01
		1953-58		2002	1998-02
	1960	1950-59		2003	1999-03
	1961	1945-59[v]		2004	2000-04
		1952-61		2005	2001-05
	1962	1945-54[v]		2006	2002-06
		1952-62		2007	2003-07
	1963	1945-59[v]		2008	2004-08
		1954-63		2009-2010	2006-10
	1964	1960-64		2011	2007-11
	1965	1920-64[v]		2012	2008-12
		1950-65		2013	2009-13
	1966	1950-64[v]		2014	2010-14
		1957-66	- by age of father	1949/50	1942-49
	1967	1963-67		1954	1936-53
	1968	1964-68		1959	1949-58
	1969	1925-69[v]		1965	1955-64
		1954-69		1969	1963-68
	1970	1966-70		1975	1966-74
	1971	1967-71		1981	1972-80
	1972	1968-72		1986	1977-85
	1973	1969-73		1999CD[iv]	1990-98
	1974	1970-74		2007-2014	Latest
	1975	1956-75			
	1976	1972-76	- by age of mother	1948	1936-47
	1977	1973-77		1949/50	1936-49
	1978	1974-78		1951	1936-50
	1978HS[ii]	1948-78		1952	1936-50
	1979	1975-79		1953	1936-52
	1980	1976-80		1954	1936-53
	1981	1962-81		1955-1956	Latest
	1982	1978-82		1959	1949-58
	1983	1979-83		1965	1955-64
	1984	1980-84		1969	1963-68
	1985	1981-85		1975	1966-74
	1986	1967-86		1976-1978	Latest
	1987	1983-87		1978HS[ii]	1948-77
	1988	1984-88		1979-1980	Latest
	1989	1985-89		1981	1972-80
	1990	1986-90		1982-1985	Latest
	1991	1987-91		1986	1977-85
	1992	1983-92		1987-1991	Latest
	1993	1989-93		1992	1983-92
	1994	1990-94		1993-1997	Latest
	1995	1991-95		1997HS[iii]	1948-96
	1996	1992-96		1998-1999	Latest
	1997	1993-97			
	1997HS[iii]	1948-97			
	1998	1994-98			

Subject-matter	Year of issue	Time coverage	Subject-matter	Year of issue	Time coverage
	1999CD[iv]	1990-98		1982	1978-82
	2000-2014	Latest		1983	1979-83
				1984	1980-84
- by age of mother and birth order	1954	1948 and 1951		1985	1981-85
				1986	1967-86
	1959	1949-58		1987	1983-87
	1965	1955-64		1988	1984-88
	1969	1963-68		1989	1985-89
	1975	1966-74		1990	1986-90
	1981	1972-80		1991	1987-91
	1986	1977-85		1992	1983-92
	1999CD[iv]	1990-98		1993	1989-93
				1994	1990-94
- by age of mother and urban/rural residence (see: by urban/rural residence, below)				1995	1991-95
				1996	1992-96
				1997	1993-97
				1998	1994-98
				1999	1995-99
- by birth order	1951	1936-49		1999CD[iv]	1985-99
	1952	1936-50		2000	1996-00
	1953	1936-52		2001	1997-01
	1954	1936-53		2002	1998-02
	1955	Latest		2003	1999-03
	1959	1949-58		2004	2000-04
	1965	1955-64		2005	2001-05
	1969	1963-68		2006	2002-06
	1975	1966-74		2007	2003-07
	1981	1972-80		2008	2004-08
	1986	1977-85		2009-2010	2006-10
	1999CD[iv]	1990-98		2011	2007-11
				2012	2008-12
- by urban/rural residence	1965	Latest		2013	2009-13
	1967	Latest		2014	2010-14
	1968	1964-68	- by urban/rural residence and age of mother		
	1969	1964-68		1965	Latest
	1970	1966-70		1969	Latest
	1971	1967-71		1975	1966-74
	1972	1968-72		1976-1980	Latest
	1973	1969-73		1981	1972-80
	1974	1970-74		1982-1985	Latest
	1975	1956-75		1986	1977-85
	1976	1972-76		1987-1991	Latest
	1977	1973-77		1992	1983-92
	1978	1974-78		1993-1997	Latest
	1979	1975-79		1997HS[iii]	1948-96
	1980	1976-80		1998-1999	Latest
	1981	1962-81		1999CD[iv]	1990-98
				2000-2006	Latest

Index
Historical index
(See notes at end of index)

Subject-matter	Year of issue	Time coverage	Subject-matter	Year of issue	Time coverage
				1963	1955-63
C				1965	1955-65
Child-woman ratios	1949/50	1900-50		1968	1955-67
	1954	1900-52		1969	Latest
	1955	1945-54		1978HS[ii]	1948-77
	1959	1935-59		1997HS[iii]	1948-96
	1963	1955-63	- living, by age of mother and urban/rural residence		
	1965	1945-65			
	1969	Latest			
	1975	1966-74		1971	1962-71
	1978HS[ii]	1948-77		1973	1965-73
	1981	1962-80		1975	1965-74
	1986	1967-85		1981	1972-80
	1997HS[iii]	1948-96		1986	1977-85
	1999CD[iv]	1980-99		1997HS[iii]	1948-96
- by urban/rural residence	1965	Latest	**Cities (see: Population)**		
	1969	Latest	**D**		
Children			**Deaths**	1948	1932-47
- ever born, by age of mother	1949/50	Latest		1949/50	1934-49
	1954	1930-53		1951	1935-50
	1955	1945-54		1952	1936-51
	1959	1949-58		1953	1950-52
	1963	1955-63		1954	1946-53
	1965	1955-65		1955	1946-54
	1969	Latest		1956	1947-55
	1978HS[ii]	1948-77		1957	1940-56
	1997HS[iii]	1948-96		1958	1948-57
- ever born, by age of mother and urban/rural residence				1959	1949-58
				1960	1950-59
	1971	1962-71		1961	1952-61
	1973	1965-73		1962	1953-62
	1975	1965-74		1963	1954-63
	1981	1972-80		1964	1960-64
	1986	1977-85		1966	1947-66
	1997HS[iii]	1948-96		1967	1963-67
- involved in divorces	1958	1949-57		1968	1964-68
	1968	1958-67		1969	1965-69
	1976	1966-75		1970	1966-70
	1982	1972-81		1971	1967-71
	1990	1980-89		1972	1968-72
- living, by age of mother	1949/50	Latest		1973	1969-73
	1954	1930-53		1974	1965-74
	1955	1945-54		1975	1971-75
	1959	1949-58		1976	1972-76
				1977	1973-77
				1978	1974-78
				1978HS[ii]	1948-78
				1979	1975-79
				1980	1971-80
				1981	1977-81
				1982	1978-82
				1983	1979-83

Subject-matter	Year of issue	Time coverage	Subject-matter	Year of issue	Time coverage
	1984	1980-84	- by age and sex and urban/rural residence		
	1985	1976-85		1967-1973	Latest
	1986	1982-86		1974	1965-73
	1987	1983-87		1975-1979	Latest
	1988	1984-88		1980	1971-79
	1989	1985-89		1981-1984	Latest
	1990	1986-90		1985	1976-84
	1991	1987-91		1986-1991	Latest
	1992	1983-92		1992	1983-92
	1993	1989-93		1993-1995	Latest
	1994	1990-94		1996	1987-95
	1995	1991-95		1997	Latest
	1996	1987-96		1997HS[iii]	1948-96
	1997	1993-97		1998-2006	Latest
	1997HS[iii]	1948-97			
	1998	1994-98	- by cause	1951	1947-50
	1999	1995-99		1952	1947-51[vi]
	2000	1996-00		1953	Latest
	2001	1997-01		1954	1945-53
	2002	1998-02		1955-1956	Latest
	2003	1999-03		1957	1952-56
	2004	2000-04		1958-1960	Latest
	2005	2001-05		1961	1955-60
	2006	2002-06		1962-1965	Latest
	2007	2003-07		1966	1960-65
	2008	2004-08		1967-1973	Latest
	2009-2010	2006-10		1974	1965-73
	2011	2007-11		1975-1979	Latest
	2012	2008-12		1980	1971-79
	2013	2009-13		1981-1984	Latest
	2014	2010-14		1985	1976-84
- by age and sex	1948	1936-47		1986-1991	Latest
	1951	1936-50		1991PA[vii]	1960-90
	1955-1956	Latest		1992-1995	Latest
	1957	1948-56		1996	1987-95
	1958-1960	Latest		1997-2000	Latest
	1961	1955-60		2002	1995-02
	1962-1965	Latest		2004	1995-04
	1966	1961-65		2006	2002-06
	1967-1973	Latest		2008	2004-08
	1974	1965-73		2011	2006-10
	1975-1979	Latest		2013	2008-12
	1978HS[ii]	1948-77			
	1980	1971-79	- by cause, age and sex	1951	Latest
	1981-1984	Latest		1952	Latest
	1985	1976-84		1957	Latest
	1986-1991	Latest		1961	Latest
	1992	1983-92		1967	Latest
	1993-1995	Latest		1974	Latest
	1996	1987-95		1980	Latest
	1997	Latest		1985	Latest
	1997HS[iii]	1948-96		1991PA[vii]	1960-90
	1998-2014	Latest		1996	Latest

Subject-matter	Year of issue	Time coverage	Subject-matter	Year of issue	Time coverage
	1954	1920-39[v]		2000	1996-00
		1946-53		2001	1997-01
	1955	1920-34[v]		2002	1998-02
		1946-54		2003	1999-03
	1956	1947-55		2004	2000-04
	1957	1930-56		2005	2001-05
	1958	1948-57		2006	2002-06
	1959	1949-58		2007	2003-07
	1960	1950-59		2008	2004-08
	1961	1945-59[v]		2009-2010	2006-10
		1952-61		2011	2007-11
	1962	1945-54[v]		2012	2008-12
		1952-62		2013	2009-13
	1963	1945-59[v]		2014	2010-14
		1954-63			
	1964	1960-64	- by age and sex	1948	1935-47
	1965	1961-65		1949/50	1936-49
	1966	1920-64[v]		1951	1936-50
		1951-66		1952	1936-51
	1967	1963-67		1953	1940-52
	1968	1964-68		1954	1946-53
	1969	1965-69		1955-1956	Latest
	1970	1966-70		1957	1948-56
	1971	1967-71		1961	1952-60
	1972	1968-72		1966	1950-65
	1973	1969-73		1972	Latest
	1974	1965-74		1974	1965-73
	1975	1971-75		1975-1979	Latest
	1976	1972-76		1978HS[ii]	1948-77
	1977	1973-77		1980	1971-79
	1978	1974-78		1981-1984	Latest
	1978HS[ii]	1948-78		1985	1976-84
	1979	1975-79		1986-1991	Latest
	1980	1971-80		1991PA[vii]	1950-1990
	1981	1977-81		1992	1983-1992
	1982	1978-82		1993-1995	Latest
	1983	1979-83		1996	1987-95
	1984	1980-84		1997	Latest
	1985	1976-85		1997HS[iii]	1948-96
	1986	1982-86		1998-2014	Latest
	1987	1983-87			
	1988	1984-88	- by age and sex and urban/rural		
	1989	1985-89	residence	1967	Latest
	1990	1986-90		1972	Latest
	1991	1987-91		1974	1965-73
	1992	1983-92		1975-1979	Latest
	1993	1989-93		1980	1971-79
	1994	1990-94		1981-1984	Latest
	1995	1991-95		1985	1976-84
	1996	1987-96		1986-1991	Latest
	1997	1993-97		1991PA[vii]	1950-1990
	1997HS[iii]	1948-97		1992	1983-1992
	1998	1994-98		1993-1995	Latest
	1999	1995-99		1996	1987-95

Subject-matter	Year of issue	Time coverage	Subject-matter	Year of issue	Time coverage
	1997	Latest	- by occupation,		
	1997HS[iii]	1948-96	age and sex	1957	Latest
	1998-2006	Latest			
			- by occupation and		
- by cause	1951	1947-49	age, males	1961	Latest
	1952	1947-51[vi]		1967	Latest
	1953	1947-52	- by urban/rural		
	1954	1945-53	residence	1967	Latest
	1955-1956	Latest		1968	1964-68
	1957	1952-56		1969	1965-69
	1958-1960	Latest		1970	1966-70
	1961	1955-60		1971	1967-71
	1962-1965	Latest		1972	1968-72
	1966	1960-65		1973	1969-73
	1967-1973	Latest		1974	1965-74
	1974	1965-73		1975	1971-75
	1975-1979	Latest		1976	1972-76
	1980	1971-79		1977	1973-77
	1981-1984	Latest		1978	1974-78
	1985	1976-84		1979	1975-79
	1986-1991	Latest		1980	1971-80
	1991PA[vii]	1960-90		1981	1977-81
	1992-1995	Latest		1982	1978-82
	1996	1987-95		1983	1979-83
	1997-2000	Latest		1984	1980-84
	2002	1995-02		1985	1976-85
	2004	1995-04		1986	1982-86
	2006	2002-06		1987	1983-87
	2008	2004-08		1988	1984-88
	2011	2006-10		1989	1985-89
	2013	2008-12		1990	1986-90
				1991	1987-91
- by cause, age	1957	Latest		1992	1983-92
and sex				1993	1989-93
	1961	Latest		1994	1990-94
	1991PA[vii]	1960-90		1995	1991-95
				1996	1987-96
- by cause and sex	1967	Latest		1997	1993-97
	1974	Latest		1998	1994-98
	1980	Latest		1999	1995-99
	1985	Latest		1987	1983-87
	1996	Latest		1988	1984-88
	2006	2002-06		1989	1985-89
	2008	2004-08		1990	1986-90
	2011	2006-10		1991	1987-91
	2013	2008-12		1992	1983-92
				1993	1989-93
- by marital status,				1994	1990-94
age and sex	1961	Latest		1995	1991-95
	1967	Latest		1996	1987-96
	1974	Latest		1997	1993-97
	1980	Latest		1998	1994-98
	1985	Latest		1999	1995-99
	1996	Latest		2000	1996-00
	2003	Latest			

Subject-matter	Year of issue	Time coverage	Subject-matter	Year of issue	Time coverage
	2007	2007		1964	1960-64
	2008	2008		1965	1961-65
	2009-2010	2010		1966	1962-66
	2011	2011		1967	1963-67
	2012	2012		1968	1949-68
	2013	2013		1969	1965-69
	2014	2014		1970	1966-70
				1971	1967-71
- of regions	1949/50	1920-49		1972	1968-72
	1952-1999	Latest		1973	1969-73
	2000	2000		1974	1970-74
	2001	2001		1975	1971-75
	2002	2002		1976	1957-76
	2003	2003		1977	1973-77
	2004	2004		1978	1974-78
	2005	2005		1979	1975-79
	2006	2006		1980	1976-80
	2007	2007		1981	1977-81
	2008	2008		1982	1963-82
	2009-2010	2010		1983	1979-83
	2011	2011		1984	1980-84
	2012	2012		1985	1981-85
	2013	2013		1986	1982-86
	2014	2014		1987	1983-87
				1988	1984-88
- of the world	1949/50	1920-49		1989	1985-89
	1952-1999	Latest		1990	1971-90
	2000	2000		1991	1987-91
	2001	2001		1992	1988-92
	2002	2002		1993	1989-93
	2003	2003		1994	1990-94
	2004	2004		1995	1991-95
	2005	2005		1996	1992-96
	2006	2006		1997	1993-97
	2007	2007		1998	1994-98
	2008	2008		1999	1995-99
	2009-2010	2010		2000	1996-00
	2011	2011		2001	1997-01
	2012	2012		2002	1998-02
	2013	2013		2003	1999-03
	2014	2014		2004	2000-04
				2005	2001-05
Disability (see: Population)				2006	2002-06
				2007	2003-07
Divorces.................................	1951	1935-50		2008	2004-08
	1952	1936-51		2009-2010	2006-10
	1953	1950-52		2011	2007-11
	1954	1946-53		2012	2008-12
	1955	1946-54		2013	2009-13
	1956	1947-55		2014	2010-14
	1957	1948-56			
	1958	1940-57	- by age of husband		
	1959	1949-58		1968	1958-67
	1960	1950-59		1976	1966-75
	1961	1952-61		1982	1972-81
	1962	1953-62			
	1963	1954-63			

Subject-matter	Year of issue	Time coverage	Subject-matter	Year of issue	Time coverage
	1987	1975-86	- by duration of marriage	2007	Latest
	1990	1980-89		2009-2010	Latest
- by age of wife	1968	1958-67		2012	Latest
	1976	1966-75		2014	Latest
	1982	1972-81	- by number of children involved	2007	Latest
	1987	1975-86			
	1990	1980-89			
- by age of wife classified by age of husband			Divorce rates............................	1952	1935-51
				1953	1936-52
	1958	1946-57		1954	1946-53
	1968	Latest		1955	1946-54
	1976	Latest		1956	1947-55
	1982	Latest		1957	1948-56
	1982	Latest		1958	1930-57
	1990	Latest		1959	1949-58
- by duration of marriage	1958	1948-57		1960	1950-59
	1968	1958-67		1961	1952-61
	1976	1966-75		1962	1953-62
	1982	1972-81		1963	1954-63
	1990	1980-89		1964	1960-64
	2007	Latest		1965	1961-65
	2009-2010	Latest		1966	1962-66
	2012	Latest		1967	1963-67
	2014	Latest		1968	1920-64[v]
					1953-68
- by duration of marriage and age of husband, wife				1969	1965-69
				1970	1966-70
	1958	1946-57		1971	1967-71
	1968	Latest		1972	1968-72
	1976	Latest		1973	1969-73
	1982	Latest		1974	1970-74
	1990	Latest		1975	1971-75
- by number of children involved	1958	1948-57		1976	1957-76
	1968	1958-67		1977	1973-77
	1976	1966-75		1978	1974-78
	1982	1972-81		1979	1975-79
	1990	1980-89		1980	1976-80
	2007	Latest		1969	1965-69
- by urban/rural residence				1970	1966-70
	2002	1998-02		1971	1967-71
	2003	1999-03		1972	1968-72
	2004	2000-04		1973	1969-73
	2005	2001-05		1974	1970-74
	2006	2002-06		1975	1971-75
	2007	2003-07		1976	1957-76
	2008	2004-08		1977	1973-77
	2009-2010	2006-10		1978	1974-78
	2011	2007-11		1979	1975-79
	2012	2008-12		1980	1976-80
	2013	2009-13		1969	1965-69
	2014	2010-14		1970	1966-70
Divorce, percentage distribution				1971	1967-71
				1972	1968-72

Subject-matter	Year of issue	Time coverage	Subject-matter	Year of issue	Time coverage
	1973	1969-73	- for married couples		
	1974	1970-74		1953	1935-52
	1975	1971-75		1954	1935-53
	1976	1957-76		1958	1935-56
	1977	1973-77		1968	1935-67
	1978	1974-78		1976	1966-75
	1979	1975-79		1978HS[ii]	1948-77
	1980	1976-80		1982	1972-81
	1981	1977-81		1990	1980-89
	1982	1963-82	- by urban/rural residence		
	1983	1979-83		2002	1998-02
	1984	1980-84		2003	1999-03
	1985	1981-85		2004	2000-04
	1986	1982-86		2005	2001-05
	1987	1983-87		2006	2002-06
	1988	1984-88		2007	2003-07
	1989	1985-89		2008	2004-08
	1990	1971-90		2009-2010	2006-10
	1991	1987-91		2011	2007-11
	1992	1988-92		2012	2008-12
	1993	1989-93		2013	2009-13
	1994	1990-94		2014	2010-14
	1995	1991-95			
	1996	1992-96	**E**		
	1997	1993-97			
	1998	1994-98	**Economically active population (see: Population)**		
	1999	1995-99			
	2000	1996-00			
	2001	1997-01	**Economically inactive population (see: Population)**		
	2002	1998-02			
	2003	1999-03			
	2004	2000-04	**Emigrants (see: Migration)**		
	2005	2001-05			
	2006	2002-06	**Ethnic composition (see: Population)**		
	2007	2003-07			
	2008	2004-08			
	2009-2010	2006-10	**Expectation of life (see: Life tables)**		
	2011	2007-11			
	2012	2008-12			
	2013	2009-13	**F**		
	2014	2010-14	**Fertility rates**		
- by age of husband			- general	1948	1936-47
	1968	Latest		1949/50	1936-49
	1976	Latest		1951	1936-50
	1982	Latest		1952	1936-50
	1987	1975-86		1953	1936-52
	1990	Latest		1954	1936-53
				1955-1956	Latest
- by age of wife	1968	Latest		1959	1949-58
	1976	Latest		1960-1964	Latest
	1982	Latest		1965	1955-64
	1987	1975-86		1966-1974	Latest
	1990	Latest		1975	1966-74

Subject-matter	Year of issue	Time coverage	Subject-matter	Year of issue	Time coverage
	1985	1975-84		1966	1956-65
	1986	1977-85		1967-1968	Latest
	1987	1982-86		1969	1963-68
	1988	1983-87		1974	1965-73
	1989	1984-88		1975	1966-74
	1990	1985-89		1980	1971-79
	1991	1986-90		1981	1972-80
	1992	1987-91		1985	1976-84
	1993	1988-92		1986	1977-85
	1994	1989-93		1996	1987-95
	1995	1990-94			
	1996	1987-95	- by sex	1961	1952-60
	1997	1992-96		1965	5 Latest
	1998	1993-97		1969	1963-68
	1999	1994-98		1975	1966-74
	1999CD[iv]	1990-98		1981	1972-80
	2000	1995-99		1986	1977-85
	2001	1997-01			
	2002	1998-02	- by urban/rural residence		
	2003	1999-03		1971	1966-70
	2004	2000-04		1972	1967-71
	2005	2001-05		1973	1968-72
	2006	2002-06		1974	1965-73
	2007	2003-07		1975	1966-74
	2008	2004-08		1976	1971-75
	2009-2010	2006-10		1977	1972-76
	2011	2007-11		1978	1973-77
	2012	2008-12		1979	1974-78
	2013	2009-13		1980	1971-79
	2014	2010-14		1981	1972-80
				1982	1977-81
- by age of mother	1954	1936-53		1983	1978-82
	1959	1949-58		1984	1979-83
	1965	1955-64		1985	1975-84
	1969	1963-68		1986	1977-85
	1975	1966-74		1987	1982-86
	1981	1972-80		1988	1983-87
	1986	1977-85		1989	1984-88
- by age of mother and birth order	1954	Latest		1990	1985-89
	1959	1949-58		1991	1986-90
	1965	3-Latest		1992	1987-91
	1969	1963-68		1993	1988-92
	1975	1966-74		1994	1989-93
	1981	1972-80		1995	1990-94
	1986	1977-85		1996	1987-95
- by period of gestation				1997	1992-96
	1957	1950-56		1998	1993-97
	1959	1949-58		1999	1994-98
	1961	1952-60		1999CD[iv]	1990-98
	1965	5-Latest		2000	1995-99
				2001	1997-01

Subject-matter	Year of issue	Time coverage	Subject-matter	Year of issue	Time coverage
	1988	1983-87	gestation		
	1989	1984-88		1959	1949-58
	1990	1985-89		1961	1952-60
	1991	1986-90		1965	5-Latest
	1992	1987-91		1966	1956-65
	1993	1988-92		1967-1968	Latest
	1994	1989-93		1969	1963-68
	1995	1990-94		1974	1965-73
	1996	1987-95		1975	1966-74
	1997	1992-96		1980	1971-79
	1998	1993-97		1981	1972-80
	1999	1994-98		1985	1976-84
	1999CD[iv]	1990-98		1986	1977-85
	2000	1995-99	- by urban/rural residence		
	2001	1997-01		1971	1966-70
	2002	1998-02		1972	1967-71
	2003	1999-03		1973	1968-72
	2004	2000-04		1974	1965-73
	2005	2001-05		1975	1966-74
	2006	2002-06		1976	1971-75
	2007	2003-07		1977	1972-76
	2008	2004-08		1978	1973-77
	2009-2010	2006-10		1979	1974-78
	2011	2007-11		1980	1971-79
	2012	2008-12		1981	1972-80
	2013	2009-13		1982	1977-81
	2014	2010-14		1983	1978-82
				1984	1979-83
- by age of mother	1954	1936-53		1985	1975-84
	1959	1949-58		1986	1977-85
	1965	1955-64		1987	1982-86
	1969	1963-68		1988	1983-87
	1975	1966-74		1989	1984-88
	1981	1972-80		1990	1985-89
	1986	1977-85		1991	1986-90
	1996	1987-95		1992	1987-91
	1999CD[iv]	1990-98		1993	1988-92
				1994	1989-93
- by age of mother and birth order				1995	1990-94
	1954	Latest		1996	1987-95
	1959	1949-58		1997	1992-96
	1965	3-Latest		1998	1993-97
	1969	1963-68		1999	1994-98
	1975	1966-74		1999CD[iv]	1990-98
	1981	1972-80		2000	1995-99
	1986	1977-85		2001	1997-01
	1999CD[iv]	1990-98		2002	1998-02
				2003	1999-03
- by period of	1957	1950-56		2004	2000-04
				2005	2001-05
				2006	2002-06

Index
Historical index
(See notes at end of index)

Subject-matter	Year of issue	Time coverage	Subject-matter	Year of issue	Time coverage
	1974	1965-74		1986-1991	Latest
	1975	1971-75		1992	1983-92
	1976	1972-76		1993-1995	Latest
	1977	1973-77		1996	1987-95
	1978	1974-78		1997-2004	Latest
	1978HS[ii]	1948-78		2005	1996-05
	1979	1975-79		2006-2014	Latest
	1980	1971-80			
	1981	1977-81			
	1982	1978-82	- by age and sex and urban/rural residence		
	1983	1979-83		1967-1973	Latest
	1984	1980-84		1974	1965-73
	1985	1976-85		1975-1979	Latest
	1986	1982-86		1980	1971-79
	1987	1983-87		1981-1984	Latest
	1988	1984-88		1985	1976-84
	1989	1985-89		1986-1991	Latest
	1990	1986-90		1992	1983-92
	1991	1987-91		1993-1995	Latest
	1992	1983-92		1996	1987-95
	1993	1989-93		1997-1999	Latest
	1994	1990-94			
	1995	1991-95	- by month	1967	1962-66
	1996	1987-96		1974	1965-73
	1997	1993-97		1980	1971-79
	1997HS[iii]	1948-97		1985	1976-84
	1998	1994-98	- by urban/rural residence		
	1999	1995-99		1967	Latest
	2000	1996-00		1968	1964-68
	2001	1997-01		1969	1965-69
	2002	1998-02		1970	1966-70
	2003	1999-03		1971	1967-71
	2004	2000-04		1972	1968-72
	2005	2001-05		1973	1969-73
	2006	2002-06		1974	1965-74
	2007	2003-07		1975	1971-75
	2008	2004-08		1976	1972-76
	2009-2010	2006-10		1977	1973-77
	2011	2007-11		1978	1974-78
	2012	2008-12		1979	1975-79
	2013	2009-13		1980	1971-80
	2014	2010-14		1981	1977-81
- by age and sex	1948	1936-47		1982	1978-82
	1951	1936-49		1983	1979-83
	1957	1948-56		1984	1980-84
	1961	1952-60		1985	1976-85
	1962-1965	Latest		1986	1982-86
	1966	1956-65		1987	1983-87
	1967-1973	Latest		1988	1984-88
	1974	1965-73		1989	1985-89
	1975-1979	Latest		1990	1986-90
	1980	1971-79		1991	1987-91
	1981-1984	Latest		1992	1983-92
	1985	1976-84		1993	1989-93

690

Subject-matter	Year of issue	Time coverage	Subject-matter	Year of issue	Time coverage
	1969	1965-69		1982	1972-81
	1970	1966-70		1983-1986	Latest
	1971	1967-71		1987	1975-86
	1972	1968-72		1988-1989	Latest
	1973	1969-73		1990	1980-1989
	1974	1970-74		1991-1997	Latest
	1975	1971-75		1998	1993-97
	1976	1957-76		1999	1994-98
	1977	1973-77		2000	1995-99
	1978	1974-78		2001	1997-01
	1979	1975-79		2002	1998-02
	1980	1976-80		2003	1999-03
	1981	1977-81		2004	2000-04
	1982	1963-82		2005	2001-05
	1983	1979-83		2006-2014	Latest
	1984	1980-84			
	1985	1981-85	- by age of bride classified by age of groom		
	1986	1982-86			
	1987	1983-87		1958	1948-57
	1988	1984-88		1968	Latest
	1989	1985-89		1976	Latest
	1990	1971-90		1982	Latest
	1991	1987-91		1990	Latest
	1992	1988-92		2006-2014	Latest
	1993	1989-93			
	1994	1990-94	- by age of bride and previous marital status		
	1995	1991-95			
	1996	1992-96		1958	1948-57
	1997	1993-97		1968	Latest
	1998	1994-98		1976	Latest
	1999	1995-99		1982	Latest
	2000	1996-00		1990	Latest
	2001	1997-01	- by age of groom	1948	1936-47
	2002	1998-02		1949/50	1936-49
	2003	1999-03		1958	1948-57
	2004	2000-04		1959-1967	Latest
	2005	2001-05		1968	1958-67
	2006	2002-06		1969-1975	Latest
	2007	2003-07		1976	1966-75
	2008	2004-08		1977-1981	Latest
	2009-2010	2006-10		1982	1972-81
	2011	2007-11		1983-1986	Latest
	2012	2008-12		1987	1975-86
	2013	2009-13		1988-1989	Latest
	2014	2010-14		1990	1980-1989
				1990-1997	Latest
- by age of bride	1948	1936-47		1998	1993-97
	1949/50	1936-49		1999	1994-98
	1958	1948-57		2000	1995-99
	1959-1967	Latest		2001	1997-01
	1968	1958-67		2002	1998-02
	1969-1975	Latest		2003	1999-03
	1976	1966-75		2004	2000-04
	1977-1981	Latest		2005	2001-05

Subject-matter	Year of issue	Time coverage	Subject-matter	Year of issue	Time coverage
		1934-51		2002	1998-02
	1953	1920-39[v]		2003	1999-03
		1940-52		2004	2000-04
	1954	1920-39[v]		2005	2001-05
		1946-53		2006	2002-06
	1955	1920-34[v]		2007	2003-07
		1946-54		2008	2004-08
	1956	1947-55		2009-2010	2006-10
	1957	1948-56		2011	2007-11
	1958	1930-57		2012	2008-12
	1959	1949-58		2013	2009-13
	1960	1950-59		2014	2010-14
	1961	1952-61			
	1962	1953-62	- by age and sex	1948	1936-46
	1963	1954-63		1949/50	1936-49
	1964	1960-64		1953	1936-51
	1965	1956-65		1954	1936-52
	1966	1962-66		1958	1935-56
	1967	1963-67		1968	1955-67
	1968	1920-64[v]		1976	1966-75
		1953-68		1982	1972-81
	1969	1965-69		1987	1975-86
	1970	1966-70		1990	1980-89
	1971	1967-71	- by sex among marriageable population		
	1972	1968-72		1958	1935-56
	1973	1969-73		1968	1935-67
	1974	1970-74		1976	1966-75
	1975	1971-75		1982	1972-81
	1976	1957-76		1990	1980-89
	1977	1973-77	- by urban/rural residence		
	1978	1974-78		1968	Latest
	1979	1975-79		1969	1965-69
	1980	1976-80		1970	1966-70
	1981	1977-81		1971	1967-71
	1982	1963-82		1972	1968-72
	1983	1979-83		1973	1969-73
	1984	1980-84		1974	1970-74
	1985	1981-85		1975	1971-75
	1986	1982-86		1976	1957-76
	1987	1983-87		1977	1973-77
	1988	1984-88		1978	1974-78
	1989	1985-89		1979	1975-79
	1990	1971-90		1980	1976-80
	1991	1987-91		1981	1977-81
	1992	1988-92		1982	1963-82
	1993	1989-93		1983	1979-83
	1994	1990-94		1984	1980-84
	1995	1991-95		1985	1981-85
	1996	1992-96		1986	1982-86
	1997	1993-97		1987	1983-87
	1998	1994-98		1988	1984-88
	1999	1995-99		1989	1985-89
	2000	1996-00		1990	1971-90
	2001	1997-01		1991	1987-91

Subject-matter	Year of issue	Time coverage	Subject-matter	Year of issue	Time coverage
	1952	1949-51		1999	1996-99
	1954	1950-53		2000	1995-00
	1957	1953-56		2001	1997-01
	1959	1955-58		2002	1998-02
	1962	1958-61		2003	1999-03
	1966	1960-65		2004	2000-04
	1970	1962-69		2005	2001-05
	1977	1967-76		2006	2002-06
	1989	1975-88		2007	2003-07
by country or area of last residence				2008	2004-08
	1948	1945-47		2009-2010	2006-10
	1949/50	1945-48		2011	2007-11
	1951	1948-50		2012	2008-12
	1952	1949-51		2013	2009-13
	1954	1950-53		2014	2010-14
	1957	1953-56			
	1959	1956-58	**Neo-natal mortality**		
	1977	1958-76	- by sex	1948	1936-47
	1989	1975-88		1951	1936-50
	1948	1945-47		1957	1948-56
	1949/50	1945-48		1961	1952-60
- refugees, by country or area of destination:				1963-1965	Latest
				1966	1961-65
				1967	1962-66
repatriated by the International Refugee Organization	1952	1947-51		2000-2014	Latest
			- by sex and urban/rural residence	1968-1973	Latest
				1974	1965-73
resettled by the International Refugee Organization	1952	1947-51		1975-1979	Latest
				1980	1971-79
				1981-1984	Latest
				1985	1976-84
Mortality [see: Death(s), Death rates, infant deaths, infant mortality rates, Foetal death(s), Foetal death ratios, Life tables, Maternal deaths, Maternal mortality rates, Neonatal deaths, Neo-natal mortality rates, Perinatal mortality, Post-neo-natal deaths, Post-neo-natal mortality rates]				1986-1991	Latest
				1992	1983-92
				1993-1995	Latest
				1996	1987-95
				1997	Latest
				1997HS[iii]	1948-96
				1998-1999	Latest
			Neo-natal mortality rates		
			- by sex	1948	1936-47
N				1951	1936-50
				1957	1948-56
				1961	1952-60
Natality (see: Births and Birth rates)				1966	1956-65
				1967	1962-66
				2000-2014	Latest
Natural increase rate..............	1958-1978	Latest	- by sex and urban/rural residence		
	1978HS[ii]	1948-78		1971-1973	Latest
	1979-1997	Latest		1974	1965-73
	1998	1995-98			

Subject-matter	Year of issue	Time coverage	Subject-matter	Year of issue	Time coverage
and age			- by literacy, age and sex and urban/rural residence		
	1983	1974-83		1973	1965-73[vi]
	1989	Latest		1979	1970-79[vi]
- by ethnic composition and sex				1983	1974-83
	1956	1945-55		1988	1980-88[vi]
	1963	1955-63		1993	1985-93
	1964	1955-64[vi]	- by localities of:		
	1971	1962-71	100000+ inhabitants	1948	Latest
	1973	1965-73[vi]		1952	Latest
	1979	1970-79[vi]		1955	1945-54
	1983	1974-83		1960	1920-61
	1988	1980-88[vi]		1962	1955-62
	1993	1985-93		1963	1955-63[vi]
- by households, number and size (see also: Households)				1970	1950-70
	1955	1945-54		1971	1962-71
	1962	1955-62		1973	1965-73[vi]
	1963	1955-63[vi]		1979	1970-79[vi]
	1968	Latest		1983	1974-83
	1971	1962-71		1988	1980-88[vi]
	1973	1965-73[vi]		1993	1985-93
	1976	Latest	20000+ inhabitants	1948	Latest
	1982	Latest		1952	Latest
	1987	1975-86		1955	1945-54
	1990	1980-89		1960	1920-61
	1995	1985-95		1962	1955-62
- by language and sex				1963	1955-63[vi]
	1956	1945-55		1970	1950-70
	1963	1955-63		1971	1962-71
	1964	1955-64[vi]		1973	1965-73[vi]
	1971	1962-71		1979	1970-79[vi]
	1973	1965-73[vi]		1983	1974-83
	1979	1970-79[vi]		1988	1980-88[vi]
	1983	1974-83		1993	1985-93
	1988	1980-88[vi]	- by locality size-classes and sex		
	1993	1985-93		1948	Latest
- by level of education, age and sex				1952	Latest
	1956	1945-55		1955	1945-54
	1963	1955-63		1962	1955-62
	1964	1955-64[vi]		1963	1955-63[vi]
	1971	1962-71		1971	1962-71
	1973	1965-73[vi]		1973	1965-73[vi]
	1979	1970-79[vi]		1979	1970-79[vi]
	1983	1974-83		1983	1974-83
	1988	1980-88[vi]		1988	1980-88[vi]
	1993	1985-93		1993	1985-93
- by literacy, age and sex (see also: illiteracy, below)			- by major civil divisions		
	1948	Latest		1952	Latest
	1955	1945-54		1955	1945-54
	1963	1955-63		1962	1955-62
	1964	1955-64[vi]		1963	1955-63[vi]
	1971	1962-71		1971	1962-71

Subject-matter	Year of issue	Time coverage	Subject-matter	Year of issue	Time coverage
				1972	1962-72
- civil division (see: by major civil divisions, above)			by industry, status and sex and urban/rural residence		
				1973	1965-73[vi]
- density (see: Density)				1979	1970-79[vi]
				1984	1974-84
- Disabled	1991PA[vii]	Latest		1988	1980-88[vi]
- economically active:				1994	1985-94
by age and sex	1945	1945-54	by living arrangements, age, sex and urban/rural residence		
	1956	1945-55			
	1964	1955-64		1987	1975-86
	1972	1962-72		1995	1985-95
by age and sex and urban/rural residence			by occupation, age and sex		
	1973	1965-73[vi]		1956	1945-55
	1979	1970-79[vi]		1964	1955-64
	1984	1974-84		1972	1962-72
	1988	1980-88[vi]	by occupation, age and sex and urban/rural residence		
	1994	1985-94			
by age and sex, per cent	1949/50	1930-48			
	1954	Latest		1973	1965-73[vi]
	1955	1945-54		1979	1970-79[vi]
	1956	1945-55		1984	1974-84
	1964	1955-64		1988	1980-88[vi]
	1972	1962-72		1994	1985-94
by age and sex, per cent and urban/rural residence			by occupation, status and sex		
	1973	1965-73[vi]		1956	1945-55
	1979	1970-79[vi]		1964	1955-64
	1984	1974-84		1972	1962-72
	1988	1980-88[vi]	by occupation, status and sex and urban/rural residence		
	1994	1985-94			
by industry, age and sex	1956	1945-55			
	1964	1955-64		1973	1965-73[vi]
	1972	1962-72		1979	1970-7vi[vi]
by industry, age, sex and urban/rural residence				1984	1974-84
				1988	1980-88[vi]
	1973	1965-74[vi]		1994	1985-94
	1979	1970-79[vi]			
	1984	1974-84	by sex	1948	Latest
	1988	1980-88[vi]		1949/50	1926-48
	1994	1985-94		1955	1945-54
by industry, status and sex				1956	1945-55
				1960	1920-60
	1948	Latest		1963	1955-63
	1949/50	Latest		1964	1955-64
	1955	1945-54		1970	1950-70
	1964	1955-64			

Index
Historical index
(See notes at end of index)

Subject-matter	Year of issue	Time coverage
	1961	1950-60
	1962	1950-61
	1963	1958-62
		1960-62
	1964	1958-63
		1960-63
	1965	1958-64
		1960-64
	1966	1958-66
		1960-66
	1967	1960-67
		1963-67
	1968	1960-68
		1963-68
	1969	1960-69
		1963-69
	1970	1963-70
		1965-70
	1971	1963-71
		1965-71
	1972	1963-72
		1965-72
	1973	1965-73
		1970-73
	1974	1965-74
		1970-74
	1975	1965-75
		1970-75
	1976	1965-76
		1970-76
	1977	1965-77
		1970-77
	1978-1979	1970-75
	1980-1983	1975-80
	1984-1986	1980-85
	1987-1992	1985-90
	1993-1997	1990-95
	1998-2000	1995-00
	2001-2005	2000-05
	2006-2010	2005-10
	2011-2014	2010-15
- Homeless by age and sex	1991PA[vii]	Latest
- illiteracy rates by sex	1948	Latest
	1955	1945-54
	1960	1920-60
	1963	1955-63[vi]
	1964	1955-64[vi]
	1970	1950-70

Subject-matter	Year of issue	Time coverage
- illiteracy rates by sex and urban/rural residence		
	1973	1965-73
	1979	1970-79[vi]
	1983	1974-83
	1988	1980-88[vi]
	1993	1985-93
- illiterate, by sex	1948	Latest
	1955	1945-54
	1960	1920-60
	1963	1955-63
	1964	1955-64
	1970	1950-70
- illiterate, by sex and age	1948	Latest
	1955	1945-54
	1963	1955-63
	1964	1955-64[vi]
	1970	1950-70
- illiterate, by sex and age and urban/rural residence		
	1973	1965-73
	1979	1970-79[vi]
	1983	1974-83
	1988	1980-88[vi]
	1993	1985-93
- illiterate, by sex and urban/rural residence		
	1973	1965-73
	1979	1970-79[vi]
	1983	1974-83
	1988	1980-88[vi]
	1993	1985-93
- in collective living quarters and homeless	1991PA[vii]	Latest
- in households (see: by household type, above, also: Households)		
- in localities (see: by localities and by locality size-classes, above)		
- increase rates (see: growth rates, above)		
- literacy rates: by sex (see also: illiteracy rates, above)	1955	1945-54

Subject-matter	Year of issue	Time coverage	Subject-matter	Year of issue	Time coverage
	1954	1920-54		2006	1997-06
	1955	1920-55		2007	1998-07
	1956	1920-56		2008	1999-08
	1957	1940-57		2009-2010	2001-10
	1958	1939-58		2011	2002-11
	1959	1940-59		2012	2003-12
	1960	1920-60		2013	2004-13
	1961	1941-61		2014	2005-14
	1962	1942-62			
	1963	1943-63	- of major regions	1949/50	1920-49
	1964	1955-64		1951	1950
	1965	1946-65		1952	1920-51
	1966	1947-66		1953	1920-52
	1967	1958-67		1954	1920-53
	1968	1959-68		1955	1920-54
	1969	1960-69		1956	1920-55
	1970	1950-70		1957	1920-56
	1971	1962-71		1958	1920-57
	1972	1963-72		1959	1920-58
	1973	1964-73		1960	1920-59
	1974	1965-74		1961	1920-60
	1975	1966-75		1962	1920-61
	1976	1967-76		1963	1930-62
	1977	1968-77		1964	1930-63
	1978	1969-78		1965	1930-65
	1978HS[ii]	1948-78		1966	1930-66
	1979	1970-79		1967	1930-67
	1980	1971-80		1968	1930-68
	1981	1972-81		1969	1930-69
	1982	1973-82		1970	1950-70
	1983	1974-83		1971	1950-71
	1984	1975-84		1972	1950-72
	1985	1976-85		1973	1950-73
	1986	1977-86		1974	1950-74
	1987	1978-87		1975	1950-75
	1988	1979-88		1976	1950-76
	1989	1980-89		1977	1950-77
	1990	1981-90		1978	1950-78
	1991	1982-91		1979	1950-79
	1992	1983-92		1980	1950-80
	1993	1984-93		1981	1950-81
	1994	1985-94		1982	1950-82
	1995	1986-95		1983	1950-83
	1996	1987-96		1984	1950-84
	1997	1988-97		1985	1950-85
	1997HS[iii]	1948-97		1986	1950-86
	1998	1989-98		1987	1950-87
	1999	1990-99		1988	1950-88
	2000	1991-00		1989	1950-89
	2001	1992-01		1990	1950-90
	2002	1993-02		1991	1950-91
	2003	1994-03		1992	1950-92
	2004	1995-04		1993	1950-93
	2005	1996-05		1994	1950-94

Index
Historical index
(See notes at end of index)

Subject-matter	Year of issue	Time coverage	Subject-matter	Year of issue	Time coverage
	1979	1970-79		1984	1975-84
	1980	1971-80		1985	1976-85
	1981	1972-81		1986	1977-86
	1982	1973-82		1987	1978-87
	1983	1974-83		1988	1979-88
	1984	1975-84		1989	1980-89
	1985	1976-85		1990	1981-90
	1986	1977-86		1991	1982-91
	1987	1978-87		1992	1983-92
	1988	1979-88		1993	1984-93
	1989	1980-89		1994	1985-94
	1990	1981-90		1995	1986-95
	1991	1982-91		1996	1987-96
	1992	1983-92		1997	1988-97
	1993	1984-93		1998	1989-98
	1994	1985-94		1999	1990-99
	1995	1986-95		2000	1991-00
	1996	1987-96		2001	1992-01
	1997	1988-97		2002	1993-02
	1998	1989-98		2003	1994-03
	1999	1990-99		2004	1995-04
	2000	1991-00		2005	1996-05
	2001	1992-01		2006	1997-06
	2002	1993-02		2007	1998-07
	2003	1994-03		2008	1999-08
	2004	1995-04		2009-2010	2001-10
	2005	1996-05		2011	2002-11
	2006	1997-06		2012	2003-12
	2007	1998-07		2013	2004-13
	2008	1999-08		2014	2005-14
	2009-2010	2001-10			
	2011	2002-11			
	2012	2003-12	by single years of age and sex	1971	1962-71
	2013	2004-13		1973	1965-73[vi]
	2014	2005-14		1979	1970-79[vi]
				1983	1974-83
percent	1948	Latest		1993	1985-93
	1952	1900-51	female: by number of children born alive and age	1971	1962-71
	1955	1945-54		1973	1965-73[vi]
	1960	1920-60		1975	1965-74
	1962	1955-62		1978HS[ii]	1948-77
	1970	1950-70		1981	1972-80
	1971	1962-71		1986	1977-85
	1973	1965-73		1997HS[iii]	1948-96
	1974	1966-74	female: by number of children living and age	1971	1962-71
	1975	1967-75		1973	1965-73[vi]
	1976	1967-76		1975	1965-74
	1977	1968-77		1978HS[ii]	1948-77
	1978	1969-78			
	1979	1970-79			
	1980	1971-80			
	1981	1972-81			
	1982	1973-82			
	1983	1974-83			

Subject-matter	Year of issue	Time coverage	Subject-matter	Year of issue	Time coverage
	1981	1972-80		1985	1976-84
	1986	1977-85		1986-1991	Latest
	1997HS[iii]	1948-96		1992	1983-92
				1993-1995	Latest
Post-neo-natal deaths:				1996	1987-95
- by sex	1948	1936-47		1997	Latest
	1951	1936-50		1997HS[ii]	1948-96
	1957	1948-56		1998-2014	Latest
	1961	1952-60			
	1963-1965	Latest	- by urban/rural residence	1971-1973	Latest
	1966	1961-65		1974	1965-73
	1967	1962-66		1975-1979	Latest
	1968-1973	Latest		1980	1971-79
	1974	1965-73		1981-1984	Latest
	1975-1979	Latest		1985	1976-84
	1980	1971-79		1986-1991	Latest
	1981-1984	Latest		1992	1983-92
	1985	1976-84		1993-1995	Latest
	1986-1991	Latest		1996	1987-95
	1992	1983-92		1997	Latest
	1993-1995	Latest		1997HS[ii]	1948-96
	1996	1987-95		1998-1999	Latest
	1997	Latest			
	1997HS[ii]	1948-96			
	1998-2014	Latest			
- by urban/rural residence	1971-1973	Latest			
	1974	1965-73			
	1975-1979	Latest			
	1980	1971-79			
	1981-1984	Latest			
	1985	1976-84			
	1986-1991	Latest			
	1992	1983-92			
	1993-1995	Latest			
	1996	1987-95			
	1997	Latest			
	1997 HS[ii]	1948-96			
	1998-1999	Latest			

R

Rates (see under following subject-matter headings: Annulments, Births, Deaths, Divorces, Fertility, Illiteracy, Infant Mortality, Intercensal, Life Tables, Literacy Marriages, Maternal mortality, Natural increase, Neo-natal mortality, Population growth, Post-neo-natal mortality, Reproduction)

Ratios (see under following subject matter headings: Births, Child-woman, Fertility, Foetal deaths, Perinatal mortality)

Subject-matter	Year of issue	Time coverage
Post-neo-natal mortality rates:		
- by sex	1948	1936-47
	1951	1936-50
	1957	1948-56
	1961	1952-60
	1966	1956-65
	1967	1962-66
	1968-1973	Latest
	1974	1965-73
	1975-1979	Latest
	1980	1971-79
	1981-1984	Latest

Refugees, by country or area of destination:

Subject-matter	Year of issue	Time coverage
- repatriated by the International Refugee Organization	1952	1947-51
- resettled by the International Refugee Organization	1952	1947-51

Religion and sex (see: Population)

Subject-matter	Year of issue	Time coverage	Subject-matter	Year of issue	Time coverage
Reproduction rates, gross and net..........	1948	1920-47	**Surface area**		
	1949/50	1900-48	- of continents	1949/50 -	
	1954	1920-53		1999	Latest
	1965	1930-64		2000	2000
	1969	1963-68		2001	2001
	1975	1966-74		2002	2002
	1978HS[ii]	1948-77		2003	2003
	1981	1962-80		2004	2004
	1986	1967-85		2005	2005
	1997HS[iii]	1948-96		2006	2006
	1999CD[iv]	1980-99		2007	2007
				2008	2008
Rural/urban births [see: Birth(s)]				2009-2010	2010
				2011	2011
				2012	2012
Rural/urban population (see: Population: urban/rural residence)				2013	2013
				2014	2014
			- of countries or areas	1948-2014	Latest
S					
			- of macro-regions	1964-1999	Latest
Sex (see appropriate subject entry, e.g., Births, Death rates, Migration, Population, etc.)				2000	2000
				2001	2001
				2002	2002
				2003	2003
Size of (living) family:				2004	2004
- female population by age (see also: Children)	1949/50	Latest		2005	2005
	1954	1930-53		2006	2006
	1955	1945-54		2007	2007
	1959	1949-58		2008	2008
	1963	1955-63		2009-2010	2010
	1965	1955-65		2011	2011
	1968	1955-67		2012	2012
	1969	Latest		2013	2013
	1971	1962-71		2014	2014
	1973	1965-73[vi]	- of regions	1952-1999	Latest
	1975	1965-74		2000	2000
	1978HS[ii]	1948-77		2001	2001
	1981	1972-80		2002	2002
	1986	1977-85		2003	2003
	1997HS[iii]	1948-96		2004	2004
				2005	2005
Special text (see separate listing in Appendix to this Index)				2006	2006
				2007	2007
				2008	2008
				2009-2010	2010
Special topic (see: Topic of each Demographic Yearbook)				2011	2011
				2012	2012
				2013	2013
				2014	2014
Still birth(s) [see: Foetal death(s), late)]			- of the world	1949/50 -	
				1999	Latest

Subject-matter	Year of issue	Time coverage	Subject-matter	Year of issue	Time coverage
	1965	1955-65	characteristics		
	1969	Latest		1962	1955-62
	1971	1962-71		1971	1962-71
	1973	1965-73[vi]		1973	1965-73[vi]
	1975	1965-75		1979	1970-79[vi]
	1981	1972-81		1983	1974-83
	1986	1977-86		1988	1980-88[vi]
	1992	1983-92		1993	1985-93
Geographic characteristics	1952	1900-51	-Population trends	1960	1920-60
	1955	1945-54		1970	1950-70
	1962	1955-62			
	1964	1955-64[vi]			
	1971	1962-71			
	1973	1965-73[vi]			
	1979	1970-79[vi]			
	1983	1974-83			
	1988	1980-88[vi]			
	1993	1985-93			
Household characteristics	1955	1945-54			
	1962	1955-62			
	1963	1955-63[vi]			
	1971	1962-71			
	1973	1965-73[vi]			
	1976	1966-75			
	1983	1974-83			
	1987	1975-86			
	1995	1985-95			
	2013	1995-2013			
Personal	1955	1945-54			

U

Urban/rural births
(see: Births)

Urban/rural deaths
(see: Deaths)

Urban/rural infant deaths
(see: Infant deaths)

Urban/rural population
(see: Population:
urban/rural residence)

**Urban/rural population
by average size of
households** (see:
Households)

APPENDIX

Special text of each Demographic Yearbook:

Divorce:

'Uses of Marriage and Divorce Statistics', 1958.

Marriage:

'Uses of Marriage and Divorce Statistics', 1958.

Households:

'Concepts and definitions of households, householder and institutional population', 1987.

Migration:

'Statistics of International Migration', 1977.

Mortality:

'Recent Mortality Trends', 1951.
'Development of Statistics of Causes of Death', 1951.
'Factors in Declining Mortality', 1957.
'Notes on Methods of Evaluating the Reliability of Conventional Mortality Statistics', 1961.
'Recent Trends of Mortality', 1966.
'Mortality Trends among Elderly Persons', 1991PA[vii].

Natality:

'Graphic Presentation of Trends in Fertility', 1959.
'Recent Trends in Birth Rates', 1965.
'Recent Changes in World Fertility', 1969.

Population

'World Population Trends, 1920-1949', 1949/50.
'Urban Trends and Characteristics', 1952.
'Background to the1950 Censuses of Population', 1955.
'The World Demographic Situation', 1956.
'How Well Do We Know the Present Size and Trend of the World's Population?', 1960.
'Notes on Availability of National Population Census Data and Methods of Estimating their Reliability', 1962.
'Availability and Adequacy of Selected Data Obtained from Population Censuses Taken 1955-1963', 1963.
'Availability of Selected Population Census Statistics: 1955-1964', 1964.
'Statistical Concepts and Definitions of Urban and Rural Population', 1967.
'Statistical Concepts and Definitions of Household', 1968.
'How Well Do We Know the Present Size and Trend of the World's Population?', 1970.
'United Nations Recommendations on Topics to be Investigated in a Population Census
Compared with Country Practice in National Censuses taken 1965-1971', 1971.
'Statistical Definitions of Urban Population and their Use in Applied Demography', 1972.
'Dates of National Population and Housing Census carried out during the decade1965-1974', 1974.
'Dates of National Population and/or Housing Censuses taken or anticipated during the decade 1975-1984', 1979.
'Dates of National Population and/or Housing Censuses taken during the decade1965-1974 and taken or anticipated during the decade 1975-1984', 1983.
'Dates of National Population and/or Housing Censuses taken during the decade1975-1984 and taken or anticipated during the decade 1985-1994', 1988 and 1993.
'Statistics Concerning the Economically Active Population: An Overview', 1984.

'Disability', 1991PA[vii].
'Population Ageing', 1991PA[vii].
'Special Needs for the Study of Population Ageing and Elderly Persons', 1991PA[vii].

General Notes

This cumulative index covers the contents of each of the 65 issues of the Demographic Yearbook. 'Year of issue' stands for the particular issue in which the indicated subject-matter appears. Unless otherwise specified, 'Time coverage' designates the years for which annual statistics are shown in the Demographic Yearbook referred to in 'Year of issue' column. 'Latest' or '2-Latest' indicates that data are for latest available year(s) only.

---

[i] Only titles not available for preceding bibliography.

[ii] Historical Supplement to the 30th DYB published in a separate volume in year 1979.

[iii] Historical Supplement to the 49th DYB published in a separate volume (CD-ROM) in year 2000.

[iv] Supplement to the 51st DYB focusing on natality published in a separate volume (CD-ROM) in year 2002.

[v] Five-year average rates.

[vi] Only data not available for preceding issue.

[vii] Population ageing published in separate volume.

Index
Index historique (suite)
(Voir notes à la fin de l'index)

Index
Index historique (suite)
(Voir notes à la fin de l'index)

Index
Index historique (suite)
(Voir notes à la fin de l'index)

Sujet	Année de l'édition	Période considérée	Sujet	Année de l'édition	Période considérée
résidence (urbaine/rurale)				2011	2006-10
	1974	1965-73		2013	2008-12
	1975-1979	Dernière			
	1980	1971-79	-selon la résidence		
	1981-1984	Dernière	(urbaine/rurale)	1967	Dernière
	1985	1976-84		1968	1964-68
	1986-1991	Dernière		1969	1965-69
	1992	1983-92		1970	1966-70
	1993-1995	Dernière		1971	1967-71
	1996	1987-95		1972	1968-72
	1997	Dernière		1973	1969-73
	1997SR [ii]	1948-96		1974	1965-74
	1998-2006	Dernière		1975	1971-75
				1976	1972-76
-selon la cause	1951	1947-50		1977	1973-77
	1952	1947-51 [iii]		1978	1974-78
	1953	Dernière		1979	1975-79
	1954	1945-53		1980	1971-80
	1955-1956	Dernière		1981	1977-81
	1957	1952-56		1982	1978-82
	1958-1960	Dernière		1983	1979-83
	1961	1955-60		1984	1980-84
	1962-1965	Dernière		1985	1976-85
	1966	1960-65		1986	1982-86
	1967-1973	Dernière		1987	1983-87
	1974	1965-73		1988	1984-88
	1975-1979	Dernière		1989	1985-89
	1980	1971-79		1990	1986-90
	1981-1984	Dernière		1991	1987-91
	1985	1976-84		1992	1983-92
	1986-1995	Dernière		1993	1989-93
	1996	1987-95		1994	1990-94
	1997-2000	Dernière		1995	1991-95
	2002	1995-02		1996	1987-96
	2004	1995-04		1997	1993-97
	2006	2002-06		1998	1994-98
	2008	2004-08		1999	1995-99
	2011	2006-10		2001	1997-01
	2013	2008-12		2002	1998-02
				2003	1999-03
-selon la cause, l'âge et le sexe	1951	Dernière		2004	2000-04
	1952	Dernière [iii]		2005	2001-05
	1957	Dernière		2006	2002-06
	1961	Dernière		2007	2003-07
	1967	Dernière		2008	2004-08
	1974	Dernière		2009-2010	2006-10
	1980	Dernière		2011	2007-11
	1985	Dernière		2012	2008-12
	1991 VP [v]	1960-90		2013	2009-13
	1996	Dernière		2014	2010-14
-selon la cause, l'âge et le sexe et la résidence (urbaine/rurale)	1967	Dernière	-selon l'état matrimonial, l'âge et le sexe	1958	Dernière
				1961	Dernière
-selon la cause et le sexe	1967	Dernière		1967	Dernière
	1974	Dernière		1974	Dernière
	1980	Dernière		1980	Dernière
	1985	Dernière		1985	Dernière
	1991VP [v]	1960-90		1991 VP [v]	1950-90
	1996	Dernière		1996	Dernière
	2006	2002-06		2003	Dernière
	2008	2004-08			

Index
Index historique (suite)
(Voir notes à la fin de l'index)

Index
Index historique (suite)
(Voir notes à la fin de l'index)

Index
Index historique (suite)
(Voir notes à la fin de l'index)

Sujet	Année de l'édition	Période considérée	Sujet	Année de l'édition	Période considérée
	2003	Dernière		2004	2004
-selon la profession, l'âge et le sexe	1957	Dernière		2005	2005
				2006	2006
				2007	2007
-selon la profession et l'âge (sexe masculin)	1961	Dernière		2008	2008
	1967	Dernière		2009-2010	2010
				2011	2011
-selon la résidence (urbaine/rurale)	1967	Dernière		2012	2012
	1968	1964-68		2013	2013
	1969	1965-69		2014	2014
	1970	1966-70	-des grandes régions (continentales)	1964-1999	Dernière
	1971	1967-71		2000	2000
	1972	1968-72		2001	2001
	1973	1969-73		2002	2002
	1974	1965-74		2003	2003
	1975	1971-75		2004	2004
	1976	1972-76		2005	2005
	1977	1973-77		2006	2006
	1978	1974-78		2007	2007
	1979	1975-79		2008	2008
	1980	1971-80		2009-2010	2010
	1981	1977-81		2011	2011
	1982	1978-82		2012	2012
	1983	1979-83		2013	2013
	1984	1980-84		2014	2014
	1985	1976-85			
	1986	1982-86			
	1987	1983-87	-des pays ou zones	1948-1999	Dernière
	1988	1984-88		2000	2000
	1989	1985-89		2001	2001
	1990	1986-90		2002	2002
	1991	1987-91		2003	2003
	1992	1983-92		2004	2004
	1993	1989-93		2005	2005
	1994	1990-94		2006	2006
	1995	1991-95		2007	2007
	1996	1987-96		2008	2008
	1997	1993-97		2009-2010	2010
	1998	1994-98		2011	2011
	1999	1995-99		2012	2012
	2000	1996-00		2013	2013
	2001	1997-01		2014	2014
	2002	1998-02			
	2003	1999-03	-des régions	1949/50	1920-49
	2004	2000-04		1952-1999	Dernière
	2005	2001-05		2000	2000
	2006	2002-06		2001	2001
	2007	2003-07		2002	2002
	2008	2004-08		2003	2003
	2009-2010	2006-10		2004	2004
	2011	2007-11		2005	2005
	2012	2008-12		2006	2006
	2013	2009-13		2007	2007
	2014	2010-14		2008	2008
				2009-2010	2010
Densité de population:				2011	2011
-des continents	1949/50	1920-49		2012	2012
	1951-1999	Dernière		2013	2013
	2001	2001		2014	2014
	2002	2002			
	2003	2003	-du monde	1949/50	1920-49

Index
Index historique (suite)
(Voir notes à la fin de l'index)

Index
Index historique (suite)
(Voir notes à la fin de l'index)

Index
Index historique (suite)
(Voir notes à la fin de l'index)

Sujet	Année de l'édition	Période considérée	Sujet	Année de l'édition	Période considérée
-pour la population mariée	1953	1935-52		1978SR [i]	1948-77
	1954	1935-53		1981	1972-80
	1958	1935-56		1986	1977-85
	1968	1935-67		1997SR [ii]	1948-96
	1976	1966-75	-vivants, selon l'âge de la mère		
	1978SR [i]	1948-77		1940/50	Dernière
	1982	1972-81		1954	1930-53
	1990	1980-89		1955	1945-54
				1959	1949-58
-selon l'âge de l'épouse	1968	Dernière		1963	1955-63
	1976	Dernière		1965	1955-65
	1982	Dernière		1968	1955-67
	1987	1975-86		1969	Dernière
	1990	Dernière		1971	1962-71
				1973	1965-73 [iii]
-selon l'âge de l'époux	1968	Dernière		1975	1965-74
	1976	Dernière		1978SR [i]	1948-77
	1982	Dernière		1981	1972-80
	1987	1975-86		1986	1977-85
	1990	Dernière		1997SR [ii]	1948-96
-selon la résidence (urbaine/rurale)	2002	1998-02	**Espérance de vie** (voir: Mortalité, tables de)		
	2003	1999-03			
	2004	2000-04	**Etat matrimonial** (voir la rubrique appropriée par sujet, p.ex., Décès, Population, etc.)		
	2005	2001-05			
	2006	2002-06			
	2007	2003-07			
	2008	2004-08	**F**		
	2009-2010	2006-10	**Fécondité, indice synthétique de**	1987-1997	Dernière
	2011	2007-11		1997SR [ii]	1948-96
	2012	2008-12		1998	1995-98
	2013	2009-13		1999	1996-99
	2014	2010-14		1999CD [vii]	1980-99
Durée du mariage (voir: Divorces)				2000	1995-00
				2001	1997-01
E				2002	1998-02
				2003	1999-03
				2004	2000-04
				2005	2001-05
Emigrants (voir: Migration internationale)				2006	2002-06
				2007	2003-07
Enfants, nombre:				2008	2004-08
-dont il est tenu compte dans les divorces	1958	1948-57		2009-2010	2006-10
	1968	1958-67		2011	2007-11
	1976	1966-75		2012	2008-12
	1982	1972-81		2013	2009-13
	1990	1980-89		2014	2010-14
-mis au monde, selon l'âge de la mère	1949/50	Dernière	**Fécondité proportionnelle**.........	1949/50	1900-50
	1954	1930-53		1954	1900-52
	1955	1945-54		1955	1945-54
	1959	1949-58		1959	1935-59
	1963	1955-63		1963	1955-63
	1965	1955-65		1965	1955-65
	1969	Dernière		1969	Dernière
	1971	1962-71		1975	1966-74
	1973	1965-73 [iii]		1978SR [i]	1948-77
	1975	1965-74		1981	1962-80
				1986	1967-85

Index
Index historique (suite)
(Voir notes à la fin de l'index)

Index
Index historique (suite)
(Voir notes à la fin de l'index)

Index
Index historique (suite)
(Voir notes à la fin de l'index)

Index
Index historique (suite)
(Voir notes à la fin de l'index)

Index
Index historique (suite)
(Voir notes à la fin de l'index)

Index
Index historique (suite)
(Voir notes à la fin de l'index)

Index
Index historique (suite)
(Voir notes à la fin de l'index)

Sujet	Année de l'édition	Période considérée	Sujet	Année de l'édition	Période considérée
	1967	1963-67		1986-1991	Dernière
	1968	1964-68		1992	1983-92
	1969	1965-69		1993-1995	Dernière
	1970	1966-70		1996	1987-95
	1971	1967-71		1997-2004	Dernière
	1972	1968-72		2005	1996-05
	1973	1969-73		2006-2014	Dernière
	1974	1965-74			
	1975	1971-75	-selon l'âge et le sexe et la résidence (urbaine/rurale)	1968-1973	Dernière
	1976	1972-76		1974	1965-73
	1977	1973-77		1975-1979	Dernière
	1978	1974-78		1980	1971-79
	1978SR [i]	1948-78		1981-1984	Dernière
	1979	1975-79		1985	1976-84
	1980	1971-80		1986-1991	Dernière
	1981	1977-81		1992	1983-92
	1982	1978-82		1993-1995	Dernière
	1983	1979-83		1996	1987-95
	1984	1980-84		1997-1999	Dernière
	1985	1976-85			
	1986	1982-86	-selon la résidence (urbaine/rurale)	1967	Dernière
	1987	1983-87		1968	1964-68
	1988	1984-88		1969	1965-69
	1989	1985-89		1970	1966-70
	1990	1986-90		1971	1967-71
	1991	1987-91		1972	1968-72
	1992	1983-92		1973	1969-73
	1993	1989-93		1974	1965-74
	1994	1990-94		1975	1971-75
	1995	1991-95		1976	1972-76
	1996	1987-96		1977	1973-77
	1997	1993-97		1978	1974-78
	1997SR [ii]	1948-97		1979	1975-79
	1998	1994-98		1980	1971-80
	1999	1995-99		1981	1977-81
	2000	1996-00		1982	1978-82
	2001	1997-01		1983	1979-83
	2002	1998-02		1984	1980-84
	2003	1999-03		1985	1976-85
	2004	2000-04		1986	1982-86
	2005	2001-05		1987	1983-87
	2006	2002-06		1988	1984-88
	2007	2003-07		1989	1985-89
	2008	2004-08		1990	1986-90
	2009-2010	2006-10		1991	1987-91
	2011	2007-11		1992	1983-92
	2012	2008-12		1993	1989-93
	2013	2009-13		1994	1990-94
	2014	2010-14		1995	1991-95
				1996	1987-96
-selon l'âge et le sexe	1948	1936-47		1997	1993-97
	1951	1936-49		1998	1994-98
	1957	1948-56		1999	1995-99
	1961	1952-60		2000	1996-00
	1962-1965	Dernière		2001	1997-01
	1966	1956-65		2002	1998-02
	1967-1973	Dernière		2003	1999-03
	1974	1965-73		2004	2000-04
	1975-1979	Dernière		2005	2001-05
	1980	1971-79		2006	2002-06
	1981-1984	Dernière		2007	2003-07
	1985	1976-84			

Index
Index historique (suite)
(Voir notes à la fin de l'index)

Sujet	Année de l'édition	Période considérée	Sujet	Année de l'édition	Période considérée
	2008	2004-08		1990	1986-90
	2009-2010	2006-10		1991	1987-91
	2011	2007-11		1992	1983-92
	2012	2008-12		1993	1989-93
	2013	2009-13		1994	1990-94
	2014	2010-14		1995	1991-95
				1996	1987-96
-selon le mois	1967	1962-66		1997	1993-97
	1974	1965-73		1997SR [ii]	1948-97
	1980	1971-79		1998	1994-98
	1985	1976-84		1999	1995-99
				2000	1996-00
Mortalité infantile, taux de	1948	1932-47		2001	1997-01
	1949/50	1932-49		2002	1998-02
	1951	1930-50		2003	1999-03
	1952	1920-34 [vi]		2004	2000-04
		1934-51		2005	2001-05
	1953	1920-39 [vi]		2006	2002-06
		1940-52		2007	2003-07
	1954	1920-39 [vi]		2008	2004-08
		1946-53		2009-2010	2006-10
	1955	1920-34 [vi]		2011	2007-11
		1946-54		2012	2008-12
	1956	1947-55		2013	2009-13
	1957	1948-56		2014	2010-14
	1958	1948-57			
	1959	1949-58	-selon l'âge et le sexe	1948	1936-47
	1960	1950-59		1951	1936-49
	1961	1945-59 [vi]		1957	1948-56
		1952-61		1961	1952-60
	1962	1945-59 [vi]		1966	1956-65
		1952-62		1967	1962-66
	1963	1945-59 [vi]		1971-1973	Dernière
		1954-63		1974	1965-73
	1964	1960-64		1975-1979	Dernière
	1965	1961-65		1980	1971-79
	1966	1920-64 [vi]		1981-1984	Dernière
		1951-66		1985	1976-84
	1967	1963-67		1986-1991	Dernière
	1968	1964-68		1992	1983-92
	1969	1965-69		1993-1995	Dernière
	1970	1966-70		1996	1987-95
	1971	1967-71		1997-2014	Dernière
	1972	1968-72			
	1973	1969-73	-selon l'âge et le sexe et la résidence (urbaine/rurale)	1971-1973	Dernière
	1974	1965-74		1974	1965-73
	1975	1971-75		1975-1979	Dernière
	1976	1972-76		1980	1971-79
	1977	1973-77		1981-1984	Dernière
	1978	1974-78		1985	1976-84
	1978SR [i]	1948-78		1986-1991	Dernière
	1979	1975-79		1992	1983-92
	1980	1971-80		1993-1995	Dernière
	1981	1977-81		1996	1987-95
	1982	1978-82		1997-1999	Dernière
	1983	1979-83			
	1984	1980-84	-selon la résidence (urbaine/rurale)		
	1985	1976-85		1967	Dernière
	1986	1982-86		1968	1964-68
	1987	1983-87		1969	1965-69
	1988	1984-88		1970	1966-70
	1989	1985-89		1971	1967-71

Index
Index historique (suite)
(Voir notes à la fin de l'index)

Index
Index historique (suite)
(Voir notes à la fin de l'index)

Index
Index historique (suite)
(Voir notes à la fin de l'index)

Index
Index historique (suite)
(Voir notes à la fin de l'index)

Index
Index historique (suite)
(Voir notes à la fin de l'index)

Index
Index historique (suite)
(Voir notes à la fin de l'index)

Sujet	Année de l'édition	Période considérée	Sujet	Année de l'édition	Période considérée
	1960	1950-59		1975	1966-74
	1961	1952-61		1981	1972-80
	1962	1953-62		1986	1977-85
	1963	1954-63		1999CD [vii]	1990-98
	1964	1960-64			
	1965	1946-65	-légitimes	1948	1936-47
	1966	1957-66		1949/50	1936-49
	1967	1963-67		1954	1936-53
	1968	1964-68		1959	1949-58
	1969	1950-69		1965	1955-64
	1970	1966-70		1969	1963-68
	1971	1967-71		1975	1966-74
	1972	1968-72		1981	1972-80
	1973	1969-73		1986	1977-85
	1974	1970-74		1999CD [vii]	1990-98
	1975	1956-75	-légitimes selon l'âge de la mère		
	1976	1972-76		1954	1936-53
	1977	1973-77		1959	1949-58
	1978	1974-78		1965	1955-64
	1978SR [i]	1948-78		1969	1963-68
	1979	1975-79		1975	1966-74
	1980	1976-80		1981	1972-80
	1981	1962-81		1986	1977-85
	1982	1978-82	-légitimes selon l'âge du père		
	1983	1979-83		1959	1949-58
	1984	1980-84		1965	1955-64
	1985	1981-85		1969	1963-68
	1986	1967-86		1975	1966-74
	1987	1983-87		1981	1972-80
	1988	1984-88		1986	1977-85
	1989	1985-89	-légitimes selon la durée du mariage		
	1990	1986-90		1948	1936-47
	1991	1987-91		1949/50	1936-49
	1992	1983-92		1954	1936-53
	1993	1989-93		1959	1949-58
	1994	1990-94		1965	1955-64
	1995	1991-95		1969	1963-68
	1996	1992-96		1975	1966-74
	1997	1993-97		1981	1972-80
	1997SR [ii]	1948-97		1986	1977-85
	1998	1994-98		1999CD [vii]	1990-98
	1999	1995-99	-selon l'âge de la mère	1948	1936-47
	1999CD [vii]	1980-99		1949/50	1936-49
	2000	1996-00		1954	1936-53
	2001	1997-01		1955-1956	Dernière
	2002	1998-02		1958	Dernière
	2003	1999-03		1959	1949-58
	2004	2000-04		1960-1964	Dernière
	2005	2001-05		1965	1955-64
	2006	2002-06		1966-1968	Dernière
	2007	2003-07		1969	1963-68
	2008	2004-08		1970-1974	Dernière
	2009-2010	2006-10		1975	1966-74
	2011	2007-11		1976-1978	Dernière
	2012	2008-12		1978SR [i]	1948-77
	2013	2009-13		1979-1980	Dernière
	2014	2010-14		1981	1972-80
				1982-1985	Dernière
-illégitimes (voir également: légitimes)				1986	1977-85
	1959	1949-58		1987-1991	Dernière
	1965	1955-64		1992	1983-92
	1969	1963-68		1993-1997	Dernière

Index
Index historique (suite)
(Voir notes à la fin de l'index)

Sujet	Année de l'édition	Période considérée	Sujet	Année de l'édition	Période considérée
	1997SR [ii]	1948-96'	-selon la profession du père	1965	Dernière
	1998-1999	Dernière		1969	Dernière
	1999CD [vii]	1990-98			
	2000-2014	Dernière	-selon la résidence (urbaine/rurale)		
				1965	Dernière
-selon l'âge de la mère et le rang de naissance				1967	Dernière
	1949/50	1936-47		1968	1964-68
	1954	Dernière		1969	1964-68
	1959	1949-58		1970	1966-70
	1965	1955-64		1971	1967-71
	1969	1963-68		1972	1968-72
	1975	1966-74'		1973	1969-73
	1981	1972-80		1974	1970-74
	1986	1977-85		1975	1956-75
	1999CD [vii]	1990-98		1976	1972-76
				1977	1973-77
-selon l'âge de la mère et la résidence (urbaine/rurale) (voir: selon la résidence (urbaine/rurale), ci-dessous)				1978	1974-78
				1979	1975-79
				1980	1976-80
				1981	1962-81
-selon l'âge de la mère et le sexe				1982	1978-82
	1965-1968	Dernière		1983	1979-83
	1969	1963-68		1984	1980-84
	1970-1974	Dernière		1985	1981-85
	1975	1966-74		1986	1967-86
	1976-1978	Dernière		1987	1983-87
	1978SR [i]	1948-77		1988	1984-88
	1979-1980	Dernière		1989	1985-89
	1981	1972-80		1990	1986-90
	1982-1985	Dernière		1991	1987-91
	1986	1977-85		1992	1983-92
	1987-1991	Dernière		1993	1989-93
	1992	1983-92		1994	1990-94
	1993-1997	Dernière		1995	1991-95
	1997SR [ii]	1948-96		1996	1992-96
	1998-1999	Dernière		1997	1993-97
	1999CD [vii]	1990-98		1998	1994-98
	2000-2014	Dernière		1999	1995-99
				1999CD [vii]	1980-99
-selon l'âge du père	1949/50	1942-49		2000	1996-00
	1954	1936-53		2001	1997-01
	1959	1949-58		2002	1998-02
	1965	1955-64		2003	1999-03
	1969	1963-68		2004	2000-04
	1975	1966-74		2005	2001-05
	1981	1972-80		2006	2002-06
	1986	1977-85		2007	2003-07
	1999CD [vii]	1990-98		2008	2004-08
	2007-2014	Dernière		2009-2010	2006-10
				2011	2007-11
-selon la durée de gestation	1975	Dernière		2012	2008-12
	1981	1972-80		2013	2009-13
	1986	1977-85		2014	2010-14
	1999CD [vii]	1990-98			
			-selon la résidence (urbaine/rurale) et l'âge de la mère		
-selon la durée du mariage (voir: légitimes selon la durée du mariage)				1965	Dernière
				1969-1974	Dernière
				1975	1966-74
				1976-1980	Dernière
-selon le mois	2002	1980-02		1981	1972-80
				1982-1985	Dernière
				1986	1977-85

Index
Index historique (suite)
(Voir notes à la fin de l'index)

Index
Index historique (suite)
(Voir notes à la fin de l'index)

Sujet	Année de l'édition	Période considérée	Sujet	Année de l'édition	Période considérée
	1984	1980-84		1987-1992	1985-90
	1985	1981-85		1993-1997	1990-95
	1986	1967-86		1998-2000	1995-00
	1987	1983-87		2001-2005	2000-05
	1988	1984-88		2006-2010	2005-10
	1989	1985-89		2011-2014	2010-15
	1990	1986-90			
	1991	1987-91	pour le monde	1949/50	1947
	1992	1983-92		1956-1977	Dernière
	1993	1989-93		1978-1979	1970-75
	1994	1990-94		1980-1983	1975-80
	1995	1991-95		1984-1986	1980-85
	1996	1992-96		1987-1992	1985-90
	1997	1993-97		1993-1997	1990-95
	1997SR [ii]	1948-97		1998-2000	1995-00
	1998	1994-98		2001-2005	2000-05
	1999	1995-99		2006-2010	2005-10
	1999CD [vii]	1985-99		2011-2014	2010-15
	2000	1996-00			
	2001	1997-01	-illégitimes (voir également légitimes)	1959	1949-58
	2002	1998-02	-légitimes	1954	1936-53
	2003	1999-03		1959	1949-58
	2004	2000-04		1965	Dernière
	2005	2001-05		1969	Dernière
	2006	2002-06		1975	Dernière
	2007	2003-07		1981	Dernière
	2008	2004-08		1986	Dernière
	2009-2010	2006-10	-légitimes selon l'âge de la mère	1954	1936-53
	2011	2007-11		1959	1949-58
	2012	2008-12		1965	Dernière
	2013	2009-13		1969	Dernière
	2014	2010-14		1975	Dernière
				1981	Dernière
-estimatifs:				1986	Dernière
pour les continents	1949/50	1947	-légitimes selon l'âge du père	1959	1949-58
	1956-1977	Dernière		1965	Dernière
	1978-1979	1970-75		1969	Dernière
	1980-1986	1975-80		1975	Dernière
	1987-1992	1985-90		1981	Dernière
	1993-1997	1990-95		1986	Dernière
	1998-2000	1995-00	-légitimes selon la durée du mariage	1959	1950-57
	2001-2005	2000-05		1965	Dernière
	2006-2010	2005-10		1969	Dernière
	2011-2014	2010-15		1975	Dernière
pour les grandes régions	1964-1977	Dernière	-selon l'âge de la mère	1948	1936-47
	1978-1979	1970-75		1949/50	1936-49
	1980-1983	1975-80		1951	1936-50
	1984-1986	1980-85		1952	1936-50
	1987-1992	1985-90		1953	1936-52
	1993-1997	1990-95		1954	1936-53
	1998-2000	1995-00		1955-1956	Dernière
	2001-2005	2000-05		1959	1949-58
	2006-2010	2005-10		1965	1955-64
	2011-2014	2010-15		1969	1963-68
				1975	1966-74
pour les régions	1949/50	1947		1976-1978	Dernière
	1956-1977	Dernière		1978SR [i]	1948-77
	1978-1979	1970-75			
	1980-1983	1975-80			
	1984-1986	1980-85			

Index
Index historique (suite)
(Voir notes à la fin de l'index)

Index
Index historique (suite)
(Voir notes à la fin de l'index)

Sujet	Année de l'édition	Période considérée	Sujet	Année de l'édition	Période considérée
Nuptialité, taux de	1948	1932-47		1978	1974-78
	1949/50	1932-49		1979	1975-79
	1951	1930-50		1980	1976-80
	1952	1920-34 [vi]		1981	1977-81
		1934-51		1982	1963-82
	1953	1920-39 [vi]		1983	1979-83
		1940-52		1984	1980-84
	1954	1920-39 [vi]		1985	1981-85
		1946-53		1986	1982-86
	1955	1920-34 [vi]		1987	1983-87
		1946-54		1988	1984-88
	1956	1947-55		1989	1985-89
	1957	1948-56		1990	1971-90
	1958	1930-57		1991	1987-91
	1959	1949-58		1992	1988-92
	1960	1950-59		1993	1989-93
	1961	1952-61		1994	1990-94
	1962	1953-62		1995	1991-95
	1963	1954-63		1996	1992-96
	1964	1960-64		1997	1993-97
	1965	1956-65		1998	1994-98
	1966	1962-66		1999	1995-99
	1967	1963-67		2000	1996-00
	1968	1920-646		2001	1997-01
		1953-68		2002	1998-02
	1969	1965-69		2003	1999-03
	1970	1966-70		2004	2000-04
	1971	1967-71		2005	2001-05
	1972	1968-72		2006	2002-06
	1973	1969-73		2007	2003-07
	1974	1970-74		2008	2004-08
	1975	1971-75		2009-2010	2006-10
	1976	1957-76		2011	2007-11
	1977	1973-77		2012	2008-12
	1978	1974-78		2013	2009-13
	1979	1975-79		2014	2010-14
	1980	1976-80			
	1981	1977-81	-selon l'âge et le sexe	1948	1936-46
	1982	1963-82		1949/50	1936-49
	1983	1979-83		1953	1936-51
	1984	1980-84		1954	1936-52
	1985	1981-85		1958	1935-56
	1986	1982-86		1968	1955-67
	1987	1983-87		1976	1966-75
	1988	1984-88		1982	1972-81
	1989	1985-89		1987	1975-86
	1990	1971-90		1990	1980-89
	1991	1987-91			
	1992	1988-92	-selon la résidence (urbaine/rurale)	1968	Dernière
	1993	1989-93		1969	1965-69
	1994	1990-94		1970	1966-70
	1995	1991-95		1971	1967-71
	1996	1992-96		1972	1968-72
	1997	1993-97		1973	1969-73
	1998	1994-98		1974	1970-74
	1999	1995-99		1975	1971-75
	1972	1968-72		1976	1957-76
	1973	1969-73		1977	1973-77
	1974	1970-74		1978	1974-78
	1975	1971-75		1979	1975-79
	1976	1957-76		1980	1976-80
	1977	1973-77		1981	1977-81

Index
Index historique (suite)
(Voir notes à la fin de l'index)

Index
Index historique (suite)
(Voir notes à la fin de l'index)

Index
Index historique (suite)
(Voir notes à la fin de l'index)

Index
Index historique (suite)
(Voir notes à la fin de l'index)

Index
Index historique (suite)
(Voir notes à la fin de l'index)

Index
Index historique (suite)
(Voir notes à la fin de l'index)

Index
Index historique (suite)
(Voir notes à la fin de l'index)

Index
Index historique (suite)
(Voir notes à la fin de l'index)

Index
Index historique (suite)
(Voir notes à la fin de l'index)

Sujet	Année de l'édition	Période considérée	Sujet	Année de l'édition	Période considérée
	1983	1974-83		1971	1962-71
	1989	1980-88		1972	Dernière
-selon la nationalité				1973	1965-73
juridique et le sexe	1956	1945-55		1974-1997	Dernière
	1963	1955-63		1997SR [ii]	1948-97
	1964	1955-64 [iii]		1998-2004	Dernière
	1971	1962-71		2005	1996-05
	1973	1965-73 [iii]		2006	1997-06
-selon la nationalité				2007	1998-07
juridique et le sexe et l'âge	1977	Dernière		2008	1999-08
	1983	1974-83		2009-2010	2001-10
	1989	1980-88		2011	2002-11
-selon les principales				2012	2003-12
divisions administratives				2013	2004-13
(voir: des principales				2014	2005-14
divisions administratives, ci-			-urbaine/rurale (résidence)	1968	1964-68
dessus)				1969	1965-69
-selon la religion et le sexe	1956	1945-55		1970	1950-70
	1963	1955-63		1971	1962-71
	1964	1955-64 [iii]		1972	1968-72
	1971	1962-71		1973	1965-73
	1973	1965-73 [iii]		1974	1966-74
	1979	1970-79 [iii]		1975	1967-75
	1983	1974-83		1976	1967-76
	1988	1980-88 [iii]		1977	1968-77
	1993	1985-93		1978	1969-78
-selon la résidence				1979	1970-79
(urbaine/rurale) (voir:				1980	1971-80
urbaine/rurale (résidence),				1981	1972-81
ci-dessous)				1982	1973-82
-selon le sexe:				1983	1974-83
dénombrée	1948-1952	Dernière		1984	1975-84
	1953	1950-52		1985	1976-85
	1954-1959	Dernière		1986	1977-86
	1960	1900-61		1987	1978-87
	1961	Dernière		1988	1979-88
	1962	1900-62		1989	1980-89
	1963	1955-63		1990	1981-90
	1964	1955-64		1991	1982-91
	1965-1969	Dernière		1992	1983-92
	1970	1950-70		1993	1984-93
	1971	1962-71		1994	1985-94
	1972	Dernière		1995	1986-95
	1973	1965-73		1996	1987-96
	1974-1978	Dernière		1997	1988-97
	1978SR [i]	1948-78		1998	1989-98
	1979-1982	Dernière		1999	1990-99
	1983	1974-83		2000	1991-00
	1984-1991	Dernière		2001	1992-01
	1991 VP [v]	1950-90		2002	1993-02
	1992-1997	Dernière		2003	1994-03
	1997SR [ii]	1948-97		2004	1995-04
	1998-2014	Dernière		2005	1996-05
estimée	1948-			2006	1997-06
	1949/50	1945 et		2007	1998-07
		Dernière		2008	1999-08
	1951-1954	Dernière [iii]		2009-2010	2001-10
	1955-1959	Dernière		2011	2002-11
	1960	1940-60		2012	2003-12
	1961-1969	Dernière		2013	2004-13
	1970	1950-70		2014	2005-14

Index
Index historique (suite)
(Voir notes à la fin de l'index)

Index
Index historique (suite)
(Voir notes à la fin de l'index)

Sujet	Année de l'édition	Période considérée	Sujet	Année de l'édition	Période considérée
	1962	1955-62		1979	1970-79
	1963	1955-63		1980	1971-80
	1964	1955-64 [iii]		1981	1972-81
	1967	Dernière		1982	1973-82
	1970	1950-70		1983	1974-83
	1971	1962-71		1984	1975-84
	1972	Dernière		1985	1976-85
	1973	1965-73		1986	1977-86
	1974	1966-74		1987	1978-87
	1975	1967-75		1988	1979-88
	1976	1967-76		1989	1980-89
	1977	1968-77		1990	1981-90
	1978	1969-78		1991	1982-91
	1979	1970-79		1992	1983-92
	1980	1971-80		1993	1984-93
	1981	1972-81		1994	1985-94
	1982	1973-82		1995	1986-95
	1983	1974-83		1996	1987-96
	1984	1975-84		1997	1988-97
	1985	1976-85		1998	1989-98
	1986	1977-86		1999	1990-99
	1987	1978-87		2000	1991-00
	1988	1979-88		2001	1992-01
	1989	1980-89		2002	1993-02
	1990	1981-90		2003	1994-03
	1991	1982-91		2004	1995-04
	1992	1983-92		2005	1996-05
	1993	1984-93		2006	1997-06
	1994	1985-94		2007	1998-07
	1995	1986-95		2008	1999-08
	1996	1987-96		2009-2010	2001-10
	1997	1988-97		2011	2002-11
	1998	1989-98		2012	2003-12
	1999	1990-99		2013	2004-13
	2000	1991-00		2014	2005-14
	2001	1992-01			
	2002	1993-02	-Vieillissement indicateurs divers	1991 VP [v]	1950-90
	2003	1994-03	-Villes (voir: des villes, ci-dessus)		
	2004	1995-04			
	2005	1996-05			
	2006	1997-06			
	2007	1998-07			
	2008	1999-08			
	2009-2010	2001-10			
	2011	2002-11			
	2012	2003-12			
	2013	2004-13			
	2014	2005-14			
pourcentage	1948	Dernière			
	1952	1900-51			
	1955	1945-54			
	1960	1920-60			
	1962	1955-62			
	1970	1950-70			
	1971	1962-71			
	1973	1965-73			
	1974	1966-74			
	1975	1967-75			
	1976	1967-76			
	1977	1968-77			
	1978	1969-78			

R

Rapports (voir: Fécondité proportionnelle; Mortalité fœtale (tardive), rapports de; Mortalité périnatale, rapports de; Natalité proportionnelle; Rapports enfants-femmes)

Rapports enfants-femmes	1949/50	1900-50
	1954	1900-52
	1955	1945-54
	1959	1935-59
	1963	1955-63
	1965	1945-65
	1969	Dernière
	1975	1966-74
	1978SR [i]	1948-77
	1981	1962-80
	1986	1967-85

Index
Index historique (suite)
(Voir notes à la fin de l'index)

Index
Index historique (suite)
(Voir notes à la fin de l'index)

Index
Index historique (suite)
(Voir notes à la fin de l'index)

Sujet	Année de l'édition	Période considérée
Taux (voir: Accroissement intercensitaire de la population; Accroissement naturel; Alphabétisme; Analphabétisme; Annulation; Divortialité; Fécondité Intercensitaire; Mortalité Infantile, Mortalité maternelle; Mortalité néonatale; Mortalité post-néonatale; Mortalité, tables de; Mortalité; Natalité; Nuptialité; Reproduction; taux bruts et nets de)		
Taux bruts de reproduction (voir: Reproduction)		
Taux nets de reproduction (voir: Reproduction)		
Texte spécial (voir liste détaillée dans l'Appendice de cet index)		

Urbaine/rurale (décès) (voir:

Sujet	Année de l'édition	Période considérée
Décès)		
Urbaine/rurale (ménages: dimension moyenne des) (voir: Ménages)		
Urbaine/rurale (mortalité infantile) (voir: Mortalité infantile)		
Urbaine/rurale(naissances) (voir: Naissances)		
Urbaine/rurale(population) (voir: Population selon la résidence (urbaine/rurale))		

Vieillissement (voir: Population)

Villes (voir: Population)

Index
Index historique (suite)
(Voir notes à la fin de l'index)

APPENDICE

Texte spécial de chaque Annuaire démographique

Divorce:

"Application des statistiques de la nuptialité et de la divortialité", 1958.

Mariage:

"Application des statistiques de la nuptialité et de la divortialité", 1958.

Ménages:

"Concepts et définitions des ménages, du chef de ménage et de la population des collectivités", 1987.

Migration:

"'Statistiques des migrations internationales",1977.

Mortalité:

"Tendances récentes de la mortalité", 1951.
"Développement des statistiques des causes de décès",1951.
"Les facteurs du fléchissement de la mortalité",1957.
"Notes sur les méthodes d'évaluation de la fiabilité des statistiques classiques de la mortalité",1961.
"Mortalité: Tendances récentes",1966.
"Tendances de la mortalité chez les personnes âgées",1991VP [v].

Natalité:

"Présentation graphiques des tendances de la fécondité",1959.

"Taux de natalité: Tendances récentes",1965.

Population: ..

"Tendances démo-graphiques mondiales,1920-1949",1949/50.
"Mouvements d'urbanisation et ses caractéristiques",1952.
"Les recensements de population de 1950",1955.
"Situation démographique mondiale",1956.
"Ce que nous savons de l'état et de l'évolution de la population mondiale",1960.
"Notes sur les statistiques disponibles des recensements nationaux de population et méthodes d'évaluation de leur exactitude",1962.
"Disponibilité et qualité de certaines données statistiques fondées sur les recensements de population effectués entre 1955 et 1963",1963.
"Disponibilité de certaines statistiques fondées sur les recensements de population: 1955-1964",1964.

"Définitions et concepts statistiques de la population urbaine et de la population rurale",1967.
"Application des statistiques de la nuptialité et de la divortialité",1958.
"Ce que nous savons de l'état et de l'évolution de la population mondiale",1970.
"Recommandations de l'Organisation des Nations Unies quant aux sujets sur lesquels doit porter un recensement de population, en regard de la pratique adoptée par les différents pays dans les recensements nationaux effectués de 1965 à 1971",1971.
"Les définitions statistiques de la population urbaine et leurs usages en démographie appliquée",1972.

"Evolution récente de la fécondité dans le monde",1969.
"Dates des recensements nationaux de la population et de l'habitation effectués au cours de la décennie

Index
Index historique (suite)
(Voir notes à la fin de l'index)

1965-1974", 1974.

"Dates des recensements nationaux de la population et de l'habitation effectués ou prévus, au cours de la décennie 1975-1984",1979.

"Dates des recensements nationaux de la population et/ou de l'habitation effectués au cours de la décennie 1965-1974 et effectués ou prévus au cours de la décennie1975-1984",1983.

"Définitions et concepts statistiques du ménage",1968.

"Dates des recensements nationaux de la population et/ou de l'habitation effectués au cours de la décennie 1975-1984 et effectués ou prévus au cours de la décennie1985-1994", 1988, 1993.

"Statistiques concernant la population active: un aperçu",1984.

"'Etude du vieillissement et de la situation des personnes âgées: Besoins particuliers",1991VP [v].

"Les incapacités", 1991VP [v].

"Le vieillissement", 1991VP [v].

Notes générales

Cet index alphabétique donne la liste des sujets traités dans chacune de 65 éditions de l'Annuaire démographique. La colonne "Année de l'édition" indique l'édition spécifique dans laquelle le sujet a été traité. Sauf indication contraire, la colonne "Période considérée" désigne les années pour lesquelles les statistiques annuelles apparaissant dans l'Annuaire démographique sont indiquées sous la colonne "Année de l'édition". La rubrique "Dernière" ou " 2-Dernières" indique que les données représentent la ou les dernières années disponibles seulement.

[i] Le Supplément rétrospectif du 30ème Annuaire Démographique fait.l'objet d'un tirage spécial publié en 1979.

[ii] Le Supplément rétrospectif du 49ème Annuaire Démographique fait l'objet d'un tirage spécial (CD-ROM) publié en 2000

[iii] Données non disponibles dans l'édition précédente seulement.

[iv] Titres non disponibles dans la bibliographie précédente seulement.

[v] Taux moyens pour 5 ans.

[vi] Vieillissement de la population.

[vii] Le Supplément du 51 Annuaire Démographique, ayant comme suject la natalité, fait l'objet d'un tirage spécial (CD-ROM) publié en 2002.